THE OXFORD DICTIONARY OF THE JEWISH RELIGION

THE OXFORD DICTIONARY OF THE JEWISH RELIGION

EDITORS IN CHIEF

R. J. Zwi Werblowsky   Geoffrey Wigoder

NEW YORK • OXFORD
OXFORD UNIVERSITY PRESS
1997

OXFORD UNIVERSITY PRESS

Oxford New York
Athens Auckland Bangkok Bogotá Bombay Buenos Aires
Calcutta Cape Town Dar es Salaam Delhi Florence Hong Kong
Istanbul Karachi Kuala Lumpur Madras Madrid Melbourne
Mexico City Nairobi Paris Singapore Taipei Tokyo Toronto

and associated companies in
Berlin Ibadan

Published by Oxford University Press, Inc.,
198 Madison Avenue, New York, New York 10016

Oxford is a registered trademark of Oxford University Press

Library of Congress Cataloging-in-Publication Data

The Oxford dictionary of the Jewish religion / R. J. Zwi Werblowsky,
Geoffrey Wigoder, editors in chief.
p. cm.
Includes bibliographical references.
ISBN 0-19-508605-8
1. Judaism—Dictionaries. I. Werblowsky, R. J. Zwi (Raphael
Jehudah Zwi), 1924– . II. Wigoder, Geoffrey, 1992– .
BM50.094 1997
296′.03—dc21 96-45517 CIP

EDITORIAL AND PRODUCTION STAFF

DEVELOPMENT EDITORS: Marion Osmun, Jeffrey Edelstein
DATABASE DESIGNER: Catherine Guldner

PROJECT EDITOR: Scott Lenz

EDITORIAL ASSISTANTS: Sarah Schwarz, Susan McMichaels
COPYEDITORS: Judith Sandman, Eric Schwartz, Carl Rosen
PROOFREADERS: Ellen Thorn, Martha Goldstein
MANUSCRIPT PREPARATION: Leonid Petlakh,
Emily Milner, Judith Hancock
BIBLIOGRAPHIC RESEARCHERS: Stephen Goranson, Shmuel Moss,
Marlene Schiffman, Rebecca Malamud, Shulamith Berger
MANUFACTURING CONTROLLER: Eric Schwartz
BOOK DESIGNER: Joan Greenfield

ADMINISTRATIVE ASSISTANTS (JERUSALEM): Meira Hod,
Ruth Pepperman, Georgette Corcos, David Brown

Printing (last digit): 9 8 7 6 5 4 3 2 1

Printed in the United States of America
on acid-free paper

PREFACE

The Oxford Dictionary of the Jewish Religion, envisioned as a companion volume to *The Oxford Dictionary of the Christian Church,* is designed to be a scholarly, accessible reference to the whole of Jewish religion. The more than three-millennium history of the Jewish people and Jewish religious thought has undoubtedly made a unique contribution to Western civilization and thus warrants the special attention that this volume gives to the subject.

CONCEPT

As editors in chief, we have carefully chosen the term *Jewish religion* rather than *Judaism* for the title of this work. Though the two terms are often used interchangeably, *Judaism* implies a more secular focus and a broad sociocultural approach to the subject; the scope of this dictionary is the Jewish "religion" per se. Despite the absence of consensus on the nature of religion and the lack of a widely accepted definition of the term, writers, editors, and readers seem to share a general, though at times vague, notion of what is meant by it: a combination of attitudes, beliefs (often systematized by theology), and practices ranging from prayer and/or meditation to prescribed codes of conduct (frequently codified in law books) that shape individual lives as well as social structures.

The decision to call this work a dictionary of the "Jewish religion" is not without its problems. There are many dictionaries and encyclopedias of religion(s), varying in size, content, and orientation. Both the word *religion* and its semantic spectrum are part of the history of Western culture, shaped as it is by Christianity. The term has percolated, for better or worse, from the West to other cultural traditions and (in translation) to other languages. Although there is general agreement that because of its Western origins the use of *religion* preempts discourse on many issues that are conceived differently in various cultures, the term is, nevertheless, widely established. The use of the word therefore must take into account cultural specificities.

The Hebrew language originally had no equivalent to *religion*. *Torah* (teaching), the accumulated corpus of divine scriptural revelation—especially in the Pentateuch—and oral revelation, with its divinely sanctioned modes of interpretation, perhaps comes closest to it. (When a word for religion became necessary, a loan word derived from Persian, *dat,* came into use.) *Torah* (as well as its analogues in other traditions) is so all-encompassing in both its individual and social aspects that some authors have preferred to define it as a "way of life" rather than a "religion."

Any work on the Jewish religion, because of its all-encompassing character, must incorporate subjects that would be considered irrelevant or even extraneous in dictionaries of some other religions. The most striking example is the field of law (Heb. *halakhah*), with its roots in biblical legislation, later developed and refined throughout the ages as administered by rabbinic courts. The teachers of Jewish religion were legal scholars rather than theologians; hence, also the *prima facie* unexpected inclusion in the present work of entries on such topics as insurance, barter, and alimony. At the same time, systematic theology, which only arrived some twenty centuries after the time of Moses, has to be fully represented.

Another specific character of the Jewish religion, "chosenness," requires mention, especially in a world in which religions are generally thought of as universal. Nonuniversal religions practiced in antiquity or tribal societies tend to be considered obsolete. But the Jewish religion, alongside its universalistic elements, sees itself essentially as the religion of one particular people or nation, bound to God by a special covenantal relationship that also implies a special bond to a particular land, Erets Yisra'el.

Almost all religions have a concept and doctrine of the religious community (e.g., church, *ummah*, *saṅgha*), but in this case, the community that perceives itself as the bearer of the divine charge and promise is a historical, concrete, and nonmetaphorical "people of God." This gives the Jewish religion an ethnonational quality that is not found in most current religious systems; this quality is reflected in this dictionary.

For most of its history, especially after the destruction of the Second Temple in 70 CE, the Jewish religion was basically monolithic. Two centuries ago, the Emancipation brought in its wake Reform Judaism, subsequently supplemented by Conservative Judaism and Reconstructionism. Historical differences and contemporary pluralism mean that on many issues there is no single voice. Though limitations of scope make it impossible to provide exhaustive coverage in this dictionary, every attempt has been made—with the assistance of special consultants—to state all views and varying practices, including recent developments. However, since many views and practices are still evolving, they do not lend themselves to the definitive treatment that can be given, for example, to rabbinics or medieval philosophy. As editors in chief, we have made every effort to achieve balance and to present content that is descriptive and informative and in which ideology is reported but does not affect the subject matter.

DEVELOPMENT

One of the results of the Holocaust tragedy was the destruction of the great centers of Jewish scholarship in Europe. Fortunately, two other centers were in the process of emerging—in Israel and the United States—and these have taken over unquestioned leadership in the field. Most of our contributors were drawn from these two centers, and this bipolarity was assisted coincidentally by the fact that we are from Jerusalem while the Oxford University Press administrative team was working out of New York.

In 1966 we served as editors for the single-volume *Encyclopedia of the Jewish Religion*, published by Massada Press in Jerusalem but allowed to go out of print within four or five years. In 1992 Itzhak J. Carmin Karpman, a New York publishers' agent who had an interest in the work, approached Oxford University Press with a proposal to reprint it for an American audience. Claude Conyers, editorial director of scholarly reference works at Oxford, responded immediately and enthusiastically with the suggestion that the work be used instead as a basis for a new, updated, and considerably expanded work, provided the original editors could be engaged. His was the vision of an *Oxford Dictionary of the Jewish Religion*, and he has since played a central role in the development of the concept and its execution.

Much has changed since the publication of our earlier work, and consequently this volume is very different from its predecessor. Developments in scholarship and practice as well as the much larger compass of the dictionary meant that more than half the entries had to be newly commissioned. Although we found some of the articles to be basically adequate, all have been thoroughly rewritten. Because the earlier work contained no bibliographies, the entire bibliographical apparatus, seen as a crucial element in this dictionary, has been newly added. All the new entries are signed by their contributors' names, while those derived from the former volume, as well as new entries written by the two of us, are unsigned.

The work has been conceived to present, in a single volume, as much information as possible about the Jewish religion; the additional tool of the bibliographies opens each topic to further research. Thus, it is directed to both the scholar and the layperson seeking a reference book that is concise but not abbreviated, authoritative but not overly technical, in which they can follow the entire variegated kaleidoscope of subjects embraced under the term *Jewish religion*.

This is not the first single-volume work on the Jewish religion, but it has set itself especially high scholarly standards. This is reflected in the incorporation of bibliographies; in bibliographical information contained in the body of the entries (notably dates and places of the *editio princeps*); and in the liberal use of Hebrew terminology, following trends in recent Jewish scholarship. Thus the festivals, fast days, and prayers are named in transliterated Hebrew. English forms are used as entry terms when they easily reflect a Hebrew term ("Sick, Visiting the" instead of *Biqqur Ḥolim*), but Hebrew terms are used when the English form is almost meaningless when encountered out of context (e.g., *Kil'ayim* rather than "Mixed Species"). In each such case, the English equivalent is given as a blind entry, from which the reader unfamiliar with Hebrew terminology is directed to the article.

Because this work is not a general Jewish encyclopedia, but a dictionary focused on Jewish religion, our criteria for choosing subjects of entries were fairly clear. There is no entry summarizing the general history of the Jews, for example, and entries on such important historical topics as the Holocaust and the State of Israel confine themselves to religious angles. As in any reference book, however, subjectivity in the selection of entries eventually must emerge. Although concensus reigns on the selection of subjects of most major entries, when it comes to determining which individuals are to be included—be they biblical figures, rabbinic authors, or modern scholars—a dividing line has to be drawn. Inevitably, disagreements arise as to whether certain figures lie above or below that line. In this case, on the basis of our experience with reference works, we drew up an initial list of proposed subjects of entries and of people we judged to have made a contribution specifically to the Jewish religion, independent of people famous in Jewish history for other reasons. This list was then organized into categories and sent for approval to our advisory editors, a panel of distinguished scholars in various fields, for their review, emendment, and approval. The advisory editors also worked with us in suggesting contributors for entries.

Considerable leeway was left to the contributors. They were given general guidelines but within these parameters were free to write their entries as they saw fit. Thanks to the judicious selection of contributors, virtually all presented an objective assessment of their subjects and avoided imposing their own theories or viewpoints. Every effort has been made to ensure that all sides are represented in cases of differences of opinion between various trends and in conflicting scholarly theories. All entries were reviewed by one or both of us and on occasions submitted to the advisory editors for additional input.

EDITORIAL PRACTICES

Entries are in alphabetical order, arranged strictly letter by letter. In a work of this nature, the treatment of each entry is necessarily concise; however, extensive cross-referencing provides a guide to complementary entries containing additional relevant information. Cross-references are indicated in two ways: by the use of an asterisk before a word, directing the reader to the entry beginning with that word, and by "see" cross-references, both in the body of an entry and at its conclusion. Bibliographies also direct the reader to further sources of information.

Exact references are provided to biblical and rabbinical sources. The main source for biblical quotations is the Jewish Publication Society of America's Tanakh (Philadelphia, 1985), but contributors have been allowed to use other translations of their choice. References to the Talmud Yerushalmi are preceded by Y.; to the Tosefta', by T. References to the Mishnah and the Talmud Bavli are unmarked.

Transliteration from the Hebrew poses problems for all works of Jewish scholarship. The sixteen-volume *Encyclopaedia Judaica* (1971) uses no less than three systems! We adopted one that generally allows for transliteration back into Hebrew—including the differentiation between *h* for *he* and *ḥ* for *ḥet* and the use of ' for *alef* and ʿ for *ʿayin*. However, to avoid the use of diacritics as much as possible, no differentiation is made between *sin* and *samekh* or *tet* and *taf*. Letters with a Dagesh Forte are doubled except in the case of letters transliterated by two English letters (viz. *ts* for *tsadiq* and *sh* for *shin*). Transliterations of Hebrew words are based on spellings in Avraham Even-Shoshan's *Ha-Millon ha-Ḥadash* (7 vols., Jerusalem, 1979). The system of transliteration is found on page xiii.

Exceptions to our transliteration system have been made for personal and place names from biblical and apocryphal literature. These names are used in the familiar forms found in the Revised Standard Version of the Bible. Hebrew and Yiddish personal names from later periods are transliterated (e.g., Shelomoh, not Solomon) unless the person in question wrote his name in Latin characters. For surnames, we have used the Library of Congress Name Authorities on CD-ROM (CDMARC Names; published and distributed by the U.S. Library of Congress). On occasion, this system follows different rules of transliteration from those of the dictionary, leading in some instances to orthographies different from those otherwise used in this volume. Despite the discrepancy, we felt it advisable to conform to an accepted authority so as to facilitate the search for persons whose names would be spelled in alternative forms in other works as well as to ease research in reference libraries and on-line catalogs. In most cases in which the orthographic discrepancy is significant, the spelling according to our transliteration system has been included as a blind entry referring the reader to the form in which it appears in the dictionary. Entry terms begin with the elements *ben* and *ibn* only when they constitute a commonly used part of a surname, such as *Ibn Ezra*.

The bibliographies, found at the end of each article, give priority to recent English-language research but also incorporate classic studies and important works in other languages, mainly Hebrew. The spellings of author's names and book titles were determined by the form used in the sources consulted. Although we made no restrictions on the publication dates of books cited in the bibliographies, only journal articles published since 1980 are included.

ACKNOWLEDGMENTS

The entire work was processed at the New York offices of Oxford University Press under the expert and devoted coordination of Scott Lenz. We are deeply grateful to Claude Conyers, Scott Lenz, Catherine Guldner, Sarah Schwarz, and the rest of the staff at Oxford University Press for their contributions in bringing this work to fruition. We also express our appreciation of the initiative of Itzhak Karpman, who unfortunately did not live to see its completion. We owe much to our advisory editors, Joseph Dan, Edward Fram, Martha Himmelfarb, Lawrence A. Hoffman, Shalom Paul, Aviezer Ravitsky, Robert M. Seltzer, Shmuel Shilo, and Daniel Sperber, and to our consultants, Elliot N. Dorff, Arthur Green, and Kerry M. Olitzky. Three of our advisers, Robert M. Seltzer, Shalom Paul, and Edward Fram, provided steady support and special assistance, for which we are particularly grateful.

R. J. Zwi Werblowsky
Geoffrey Wigoder
Jerusalem
Kislev 5697–December 1996

ABBREVIATIONS

abbr. abbreviation
Akk. Akkadian
Ala. Alabama
Am. *Amos*
annot. annotator; annotated
approx. approximately
Arab. Arabic
'Arakh. *'Arakhin*
Aram. Aramic
Ariz. Arizona
Ark. Arkansas
Assyr. Assyrian
'A. Z. *'Avodah Zarah*
Bab. Babylonian
Bar. *Baruch*
B. B. *Bava' Batra'*
BCE before the Common Era
Beits. *Beitsah*
Bekh. *Bekhorot*
Ber. *Berakhot*
Bib. Heb. Biblical Hebrew
Bik. *Bikkurim*
B. M. *Bava' Metsi'a'*
B. Q. *Bava' Qamma'*
c. *circa*, approximately
Calif. California
CE of the Common Era
Chr. *Chronicles*
Col. *Colossians*
comp(s). compiler(s)
Conn. Connecticut
Cor. *Corinthians*
corr. corrected
D.C. District of Columbia
Del. Delaware
Dem. *Dema'i*
Dn. *Daniel*
Dt. *Deuteronomy*
Dt. Rab. *Deuteronomy Rabbah*
Eccl. *Ecclesiastes*
Eccl. Rab. *Ecclesiastes Rabbah*
ed(s). editor(s); edition
'Eduy. *'Eduyyot*
e.g. *exempli gratia*, for example
Eng. English; England
enl. enlarged
Eph. *Ephesians*
'Eruv. *'Eruvin*
esp. especially
Est. *Esther*
Est. Rab. *Esther Rabbah*
et al. *et alii*, and others
etc. *et cetera*, and so forth
et seq. *et sequentes*, and the following
Ex. *Exodus*
Ex. Rab. *Exodus Rabbah*
Ez. *Ezekial*
Ezr. *Ezra*
fl. flourished
Fla. Florida
Ga. Georgia
Gal. *Galatians*
Ger. German
Git. *Gittin*
Gn. *Genesis*
Gn. Rab. *Genesis Rabbah*
Gr. Greek
Ḥag. *Ḥagigah*
Ḥal. *Ḥallah*
Hb. *Habakkuk*
Heb. Hebrew
Heb. *Hebrews*
Hg. *Haggai*
Hor. *Horayot*
Hos. *Hosea*
Ḥul. Ḥullin
ibid. *ibidem*, in the same place (as the one immediately preceding)
i.e. *id est*, that is
Ill. Illinois
Ind. Indiana
Is. *Isaiah*
Jas. *James*
Jb. *Job*
Jer. *Jeremiah*
Jgs. *Judges*
Jl. *Joel*
Jn. *John*
Jon. *Jonah*
Jos. *Joshua*
Kans. Kansas
Kel. *Kelim*
Ker. *Keritot*
Ket. *Ketubbot*
Kgs. *Kings*
Kil. *Kil'ayim*
KJV King James Version
Ky. Kentucky
La. Louisiana
Lam. *Lamentations*
Lam. Rab. *Lamentations Rabbah*
Lat. Latin
lit. literally
Lk. *Luke*
loc. cit. *loco citato*, in the place cited
Lv. *Leviticus*
Lv. Rab. *Leviticus Rabbah*
M.A. Master of Arts
Ma'as. *Ma'asrot*
Ma'as. Sh. *Ma'aser Sheni*
Mak. *Makkot*
Makh. *Makhshirin*
Mal. *Malachi*
Mc. *Maccabees*
Md. Maryland
Meg. *Megillah*
Me'il. *Me'ilah*
Men. *Menaḥot*
Mi. *Micah*
Mich. Michigan
Mid. *Middot*
Minn. Minnesota
Miq. *Miqva'ot*
Miss. Mississippi
Mk. *Mark*
Mo. Missouri
Mod. Heb. Modern Hebrew
Mo'ed Q. *Mo'ed Qatan*
Mont. Montana
MS *manuscriptum*, manuscript (pl., MSS)
MT Masoretic Text
Mt. *Matthew*
n(n). note(s)
Na. *Nahum*
Naz. *Nazir*
N.C. North Carolina
n.d. no date

N. Dak. North Dakota
Nebr. Nebraska
Ned. *Nedarim*
Neg. *Nega'im*
Neh. *Nehemiah*
Nev. Nevada
N.H. New Hampshire
Nid. *Niddah*
N.J. New Jersey
Nm. *Numbers*
N. Mex. New Mexico
Nm. Rab. *Numbers Rabbah*
no. number
n.p. no place
n.s. new series
N.Y. New York
Ob. *Obadiah*
Ohal. *Ohalot*
Okla. Oklahoma
op. cit. *opere citato*, in the work cited
Oreg. Oregon
'Orl. *'Orlah*
p(p). page(s)
Pa. Pennsylvania
Par. *Parah*
Pes. *Pesaḥim*
Ph.D. Philosophiae Doctor, Doctor of Philosophy
Phil. *Philippians*
Phlm. *Philemon*
pl. plural
Prv. *Proverbs*
Ps. *Psalms*
pt(s). part(s)
Pt. *Peter*
pub. published
Qid. *Qiddushin*
Qin. *Qinnim*
r. reigned; ruled
R. Rabbi
repr. reprinted
Resp. *Responsa*
rev. revised
R. ha-Sh. *Ro'sh ha-Shanah*
R.I. Rhode Island
Rom. *Romans*
Ru. *Ruth*
Ru. Rab. *Ruth Rabbah*
Rus. Russian
Rv. *Revelation*
San. *Sanhedrin*
S.C. South Carolina
S. Dak. South Dakota
sec(s). section(s)
ser. series
Sg. *Song of Songs*
Sg. Rab. *Song of Songs Rabbah*
Shab. *Shabbat*
Sheq. *Sheqalim*
Shev. *Shevu'ot*
sing. singular
Sm. *Samuel*
Sot. *Sotah*
Span. Spanish
Suk. *Sukkah*
s.v. *sub verbo*, under the word (pl., s.v.v.)
T. Tosefta'
Ta'an. *Ta'anit*
Tam. *Tamid*
Tem. *Temurah*
Tenn. Tennessee
Ter. *Terumot*
Tev. Y. *Tevul Yom*
Tex. Texas
Thes. *Thessalonians*
Ti. *Titus*
Tm. *Timothy*
Toh. *Tohorot*
trans. translator(s); translation
Turk. Turkish
Ug. Ugaritic
updat. updated
'Uqts. *'Uqtsin*
U.S. United States
v(v). verse(s)
Va. Virginia
viz. *videlicet*, namely
vol(s). volume(s)
Vt. Vermont
Wash. Washington
Wis. Wisconsin
W. Va. West Virginia
Wyo. Wyoming
Y. Talmud Yerushalmi
Yad. *Yadayim*
Yev. *Yevamot*
Yi. Yiddish
Zav. *Zavim*
Zec. *Zechariah*
Zep. *Zephaniah*
Zev. *Zevaḥim*

HEBREW TRANSLITERATION TABLE

Hebrew Name	*Character*	*English Transliteration*
alef	א	’ (word-initial alef is not noted)
beit, veit	ב ב	b, v
gimel	ג	g
dalet	ד	d
heh	ה	h
vav	ו	v
zayin	ז	z
ḥet	ח	ḥ
tet	ט	t
yud	י	y
kaf, khaf	כ כ	k, kh
lamed	ל	l
mem	מ	m
nun	נ	n
samekh	ס	s
‘ayin	ע	‘
pei, fei	פ פ	p, f
tsadiq	צ	ts
quf	ק	q
raish	ר	r
shin	שׁ	sh
sin	שׂ	s
taf	ת	t

Note: All consonants that have a Dagesh Forte are transliterated by a double letter (except for *shin* and *tsadiq*).
All vowels (below) are shown in relation to the letter *mem* (מ).

Vowels:	
מָ	a
מַ	a
מֲ	a
מֶ	e
מֵ	e
מֱ	e
מִ	i
מִי	i
מֹ	o
מוֹ	o
מֻ	u
מוּ	u
מֵי	either ei as in *sifrei* or ai as in *gabba’i*
מְ	Sheva na only is transliterated by e.

CONTRIBUTORS

S. Zalman Abramov, *Chairman of the Board of Overseers, Hebrew Union College, Jerusalem; Chair of Weizmann Memorial Foundation; and Former Deputy Speaker of the Knesset*

Daniel Abrams, *Independent Scholar, Beersheba*

Shmuel Ahituv, *Professor of Bible and Ancient Near Eastern Studies, Ben-Gurion University of the Negev*

Tamar Alexander, *Professor of Hebrew Literature, Ben-Gurion University of the Negev*

Marc D. Angel, *Rabbi of the Congregation Shearith Israel, The Spanish and Portuguese Synagogue, New York City*

Yaakov Ariel, *Assistant Professor of Religious Studies, The University of North Carolina at Chapel Hill*

Gershon Bacon, *Senior Lecturer in Jewish History, Bar-Ilan University*

Steven Ballaban, *Assistant Principal for Judaic Studies, Yavneh Day School, Cincinnati*

Shalom Bar-Asher, *Professor, Lifshitz Religious College for Teachers, Jerusalem*

Benjamin Beit-Hallahmi, *Professor, Department of Psychology, University of Haifa*

David Berger, *Professor of History, Brooklyn College and the Graduate School, The City University of New York*

David Biale, *Koret Professor of Jewish History, The Graduate Theological Union, Berkeley*

Judith Bleich, *Professor of Judaic Studies, Touro College, New York City*

Gerald J. Blidstein, *M. M. Hubert Professor of Talmudic Law, Ben-Gurion University of the Negev*

Gideon Bohak, *Assistant Professor, Classical Studies, University of Michigan, and Fellow, Michigan Society of Fellows*

Ross Brann, *Professor and Chair of Near Eastern Studies, Cornell University*

Marc Bregman, *Associate Professor of Rabbinic Literature, Hebrew Union College-Jewish Institute of Religion, Jerusalem*

Athalya Brenner, *Professor of the Feminism and Christianity Chair, Catholic University of Nijmegen*

Gary M. Bretton-Granatoor, *Senior Rabbi, Stephen Wise Free Synagogue, New York City*

Robert Brody, *Associate Professor of Talmud, The Hebrew University of Jerusalem*

Herbert Bronstein, *Lecturer in Religion, Lake Forest College, and Resident Scholar, North Shore Congregation Israel, Glencoe, Illinois*

Michael L. Brown, *Adjunct Professor of Old Testament and Jewish Studies, Regent University of Divinity, Virginia Beach, Virginia*

Michael Broyde, *Senior Lecturer in Law, Emory University School of Law*

Elisheva Carlebach, *Associate Professor of Jewish History, Queens College, The City University of New York*

Simeon B. Chavel, *Ph.D. Candidate, Bible Department, The Hebrew University of Jerusalem*

Robert Chazan, *Scheuer Professor of Hebrew and Judaic Studies, New York University*

Esther Glickler Chazon, *Assistant Professor of Jewish Studies and Associate Director of the Orion Center for the Study of the Dead Sea Scrolls and Associated Literature, The Hebrew University of Jerusalem*

Michael Chernick, *Chair, Rabbinics Department, Hebrew Union College-Jewish Institute of Religion, New York, and Deutsch Professor of Jewish Jurisprudence and Social Justice, Hebrew Union College-Jewish Institute of Religion, Brookdale Center, New York*

Chaim Cohen, *Associate Professor of Biblical Hebrew and Ancient Semitic Languages, Departments of Hebrew Language and Bible, Ben-Gurion University of the Negev*

Jeremy Cohen, *Associate Professor of Jewish History, Tel Aviv University, and Melton Professor of Jewish History, Ohio State University*

Lavinia Cohn-Sherbok, *Honorary Research Fellow, University of Kent*

Sidnie White Crawford, *Associate Professor of Religious Studies, Albright College, Reading, Pennsylvania*

Joseph Dan, *Gershom Scholem Professor of Kabbalah, The Hebrew University of Jerusalem*

Abraham David, *Senior Researcher at the Jewish National and University Library, The Hebrew University of Jerusalem*

Aaron Demsky, *Associate Professor of Jewish History, Bar-Ilan University*

Elliot Nelson Dorff, *Rector and Professor of Philosophy, University of Judaism, Los Angeles*

A. Stanley Dreyfus, *Lecturer on Commentaries, Hebrew Union College-Jewish Institute of Religion, Rabbinic School, New York*

Dennis M. Dreyfus, *Lecturer in History, Hunter College, The City University of New York*

Marsha Bryan Edelman, *Associate Professor of Music, Gratz College, Philadelphia*

Rachel Elior, *Professor of Jewish Mysticism, Department of Jewish Studies, The Hebrew University of Jerusalem*

Shifra Epstein, *Assistant Professor of Hebrew Language and Folklore, Emory University*

Leon A. Feldman, *Professor of Hebraic Studies, Emeritus, Rutgers - The State University of New Jersey*

Adam S. Ferziger, *Instructor, Department of Jewish History, Bar-Ilan University*

Aryei Fishman, *Associate Professor, Department of Sociology and Anthropology, Bar-Ilan University*

Talya Fishman, *Associate Professor of History, Rice University*

Nili Sacher Fox, *Department of Asian and Middle Eastern Studies, University of Pennsylvania*

Edward Fram, *Norbert Blechner Lecturer in Eastern European Jewish Culture, Ben-Gurion University of the Negev*

Richard A. Freund, *Ralph Wardle Professor of the Humanities and Chair, Department of Philosophy and Religion, University of Nebraska at Omaha*

Shamma Friedman, *Professor of Talmud, Jewish Theological Seminary of America, Jerusalem, and Bar-Ilan University; and Founding Director, The Society for the Interpretation of the Talmud*

Yaakov Gartner, *Senior Lecturer of Rabbinical Literature, Bar-Ilan University*

Rela Mintz Geffen, *Professor of Sociology, Gratz College, Philadelphia*

Jane S. Gerber, *Professor of Jewish History, Graduate School, The City University of New York*

David A. Glatt-Gilad, *Lecturer in Bible, Ben-Gurion University of the Negev*

Gabriel M. Goldstein, *Curator, Yeshiva University Museum, New York City*

Isaac B. Gottlieb, *Senior Lecturer, Department of Bible, Bar-Ilan University*

Arthur Green, *Phillip W. Lown Professor of Jewish Thought, Brandeis University*

Blu Greenberg, *Author and Lecturer, Riverdale, New York*

Ben Tzion Greenberger, *Rabbi, Congregation Mitzpe Nevo, Maale Adumim, Israel; Registrar of Non Profit Societies, Ministry of Interior, State of Israel*

Mayer I. Gruber, *Associate Professor of Bible, Department of Bible, Ben-Gurion University of the Negev*

Jeffrey S. Gurock, *Libby M. Klaperman Professor of Jewish History, Yeshiva University*

Jay M. Harris, *Harry Austryn Wolfson Professor of Jewish Studies, Harvard University*

Christine E. Hayes, *Assistant Professor of Classical Judaica, Yale University*

Joel Hecker, *Assistant Professor, Reconstructionist Rabbinical College, Wyncote, Pennsylvania*

Samuel C. Heilman, *Professor of Sociology and Holder of the Harold Proshansky Chair in Jewish Studies, The City University of New York*

Arthur Hertzberg, *Professor Emeritus of Religion, Dartmouth College, and Brounfman Visiting Professor of the Humanities, New York University*

Shmuel Himelstein, *Rabbi and Independent Scholar, Jerusalem*

Martha Himmelfarb, *Professor of Religion, Princeton University*

Richard G. Hirsch, *Rabbi; Executive Director, World Union for Progressive Judaism, Jerusalem*

Marc Hirshman, *Senior Lecturer in Jewish Education, Melton Centre, The Hebrew University of Jerusalem*

Lawrence A. Hoffman, *Professor of Liturgy, Hebrew Union College-Jewish Institute of Religion, New York*

Gershon David Hundert, *Professor of History and Jewish Studies, McGill University*

Victor Hurowitz, *Associate Professor of Bible and Ancient Near Eastern Studies, Ben-Gurion University of the Negev*

Judith Brin Ingber, *Independent Scholar, St. Louis Park, Minnesota, and Co-Director of Dance and Music Troupe Voices of Sepharad*

Benjamin Ish-Shalom, *Associate Professor of Jewish Philosophy and Rector of Beit Morasha of Jerusalem-Center for Advanced Jewish Studies*

Ze'ev Kainan, *Educational Director, The Bible Lands Museum, Jerusalem*

Ephraim Kanarfogel, *Professor of Jewish History, Yeshiva University*

Lawrence J. Kaplan, *Associate Professor of Rabbinics and Jewish Philosophy, McGill University*

Steven Kaplan, *Associate Professor of Comparative Religion and African Studies, The Hebrew University of Jerusalem*

Dovid Katz, *Director of Research, Oxford Institute for Yiddish Studies, and Research Fellow, St. Antony's College*

Yael Levine Katz, *Independent Scholar, Jerusalem, Ph.D. from the Talmud Department, Bar-Ilan University*

Menachem Kellner, *Wolfson Professor of Jewish Thought, University of Haifa*

Peter Knobel, *Rabbi of Beth Emet the Free Synagogue, Evanston, Illinois*

Miles Krassen, *Assistant Professor of Judaic and Near Eastern Studies and Religion, Oberlin College*

Benny Kraut, *Professor of Jewish History and Head, Judaic Studies Program, University of Cincinnati*

Leonard Kravitz, *Professor of Midrash and Homiletics, Hebrew Union College-Jewish Institute of Religion, New York*

Daniel J. Lasker, *Norbert Blechner Professor of Jewish Values, Ben-Gurion University of the Negev*

Peter Lenhardt, *Independent Scholar, Jerusalem*

Shalom Lilker, *Independent Scholar, Kfar Hamaccabi, Israel*

Timothy H. Lim, *Lecturer in Dead Sea Scrolls and Christian Origins, Department of Hebrew, University of Edinburgh*

Paul Mandel, *Department of Hebrew Literature, The Hebrew University of Jerusalem*

Lea Mazor, *Bible Department, The Hebrew University of Jerusalem*

Paul Mendes-Flohr, *Professor of Modern Jewish Thought, The Hebrew University of Jerusalem*

Jacob Meskin, *Lecturer, Department of Religion, Princeton University*

Chaim Milikowsky, *Professor of Talmud, Bar-Ilan University*

Adam Mintz, *Rabbi, Lincoln Square Synagogue, New York City, and Doctoral Candidate in Jewish History, Skirball Department of Hebrew and Judaic Studies, New York University*

Sharon Liberman Mintz, *Curator of Jewish Art, Library of the Jewish Theological Seminary*

Samuel Morell, *Associate Professor of Hebrew, State University of New York at Binghamton*

Francisco Moreno Carvalho, *Independent Scholar, Jerusalem*

Leib Moscovitz, *Lecturer in Talmud, Bar-Ilan University*

David N. Myers, *Associate Professor of Jewish History, University of California at Los Angeles*

Joan Nathan, *Independent Scholar, Washington, District of Columbia*

Aryeh Newman, *Senior Lecturer, Emeritus, The Hebrew University of Jerusalem*

Louis E. Newman, *Associate Professor of Religion and Director, Program in Judaic Studies, Carleton College, Northfield, Minnesota*

Kerry M. Olitzky, *Director, School of Education and Graduate Studies Program, and National Director for Research and Educational Development, Hebrew Union College-Jewish Institute of Religion, New York*

Mordechai Pachter, *Associate Professor of Jewish Thought, The University of Haifa*

Herbert H. Paper, *Professor of Linguistics and Near Eastern Languages, Hebrew Union College-Jewish Institute of Religion, Cincinnati*

Shalom Paul, *Professor and Chair of the Bible Department, The Hebrew University of Jerusalem*

Chaim Pearl, *Rabbi Emeritus, Conservative Synagogue Adath Israel, Riverdale, New York*

Shlomo H. Pick, *Senior Rabbi Lecturer of Jewish Studies, Ludwig and Erica Jesselson Institute for Advanced Torah Studies, Bar-Ilan University*

Didier Y. Reiss, *Ph.D. Candidate, History Department, University of California at Los Angeles*

Gary A. Rendsburg, *Professor of Near Eastern Studies, Cornell University*

Gerhart M. Riegner, *Honorary Vice-President, World Jewish Congress and Honorary President, International Council of Christians and Jews*

Ira Robinson, *Professor of Judaic Studies and Chair of the Department of Religion, Concordia University, Montreal*

Gavriel D. Rosenfeld, *Lecturer, History Department, University of California at Los Angeles*

Tamar Ross, *Senior Lecturer in Jewish Thought, Bar-Ilan University and Midreshet Lindenbaum, Jerusalem*

Adam Rubin, *Ph.D. Candidate, History Department, University of California at Los Angeles*

Bracha Sack, *Associate Professor of Jewish Thought, Department of History, Ben-Gurion University of the Negev*

Marc Saperstein, *Goldstein Professor of Jewish History and Thought, Washington University, St. Louis*

Jacob J. Schacter, *Senior Rabbi, The Jewish Center, New York City; Editor,* The Torah u-Madda Journal; *and Adjunct Assistant Professor of Jewish Studies, Stern College, New York City*

Lawrence H. Schiffman, *New York University*

Elijah J. Schochet, *Professor of Rabbinical Literature, University of Judaism, Los Angeles*

Baruch J. Schwartz, *Lecturer in Bible, Tel Aviv University*

Fern Seckbach, *Independent Scholar, Efrat, Israel*

Robert M. Seltzer, *Professor of History and Director of the Jewish Social Studies Program, Hunter College and the Graduate School of The City University of New York*

William Shaffir, *Professor of Sociology, McMaster University, Hamilton, Ontario*

Marc Shapiro, *Weinberg Professor of Judaic Studies, University of Scranton*

Michael Shashar, *Independent Scholar, Jerusalem*

Eugene R. Sheppard, *Ph.D. Candidate, History Department, University of California at Los Angeles*

Byron L. Sherwin, *Vice-President and Professor of Jewish Philosophy and Mysticism, Spertus Institute of Jewish Studies, Chicago*

Eliav Shochetman, *Professor, The Faculty of Law, The Hebrew University of Jerusalem*

Michael A. Signer, *Abrams Professor of Jewish Thought and Culture, University of Notre Dame*

Lou H. Silberman, *Hillel Professor of Jewish Literature and Thought, Emeritus, Vanderbilt University, and Adjunct Professor, Judaic Studies, University of Arizona*

Daniel Sinclair, *Principal, Jews' College, London*

Gabriel A. Sivan, *Independent Scholar, Executive Council Member, World Jewish Bible Center, Jerusalem*

David E. Sklare, *Senior Researcher, Center for the Study of Judeo-Arabic Culture, Ben-Zvi Institute of Jerusalem*

Norman Solomon, *Fellow in Modern Jewish Thought, Oxford Centre for Hebrew and Jewish Studies, and Lecturer in Theology, University of Oxford*

Haym Soloveitchik, *University Professor, Revel Graduate School, Yeshiva University*

Daniel Sperber, *Milan Roven Professor for Talmudic Studies, Bar-Ilan University*

Jacob J. Staub, *Academic Dean, Reconstructionist Rabbinical College, Wyncote, Pennsylvania*

Marvin A. Sweeney, *Professor of Hebrew Bible, School of Theology at Claremont, and Professor of Religion, The Claremont Graduate School*

Joseph Tabory, *Professor of Talmud, Bar-Ilan University*

Sol Tanenzapf, *Associate Professor of Humanities, York University, Toronto*

Adam Teller, *Junior Lecturer in Jewish History, University of Haifa*

Jeffrey H. Tigay, *Ellis Professor of Hebrew and Semitic Languages and Literatures, University of Pennsylvania*

Emanuel Tov, *Professor, Department of Bible, The Hebrew University of Jerusalem*

Ellen M. Umansky, *Carl and Dorothy Bennett Professor of Judaic Studies, Fairfield University, Fairfield, Connecticut*

Mervin F. Verbit, *Professor of Sociology, Brooklyn College, The City University of New York*

Mark Verman, *Visiting Associate Professor of Religion, Gustavus Adolphus College, Saint Peter, Minnesota*

Avraham Walfish, *Rabbi; Lecturer in Judaic Studies and Jewish Education, Herzog College and Bar-Ilan University*

Mark Washofsky, *Associate Professor of Rabbinics, Hebrew Union College-Jewish Institute of Religion, Cincinnati*

Shalva Weil, *Senior Researcher, NCJW Research Institute for Innovation in Education, The Hebrew University of Jerusalem*

Chava Weissler, *Associate Professor of Religion Studies and Philip and Muriel Berman Chair of Jewish Civilization, Lehigh University*

Michael James Williams, *Lecturer in Old Testament, Calvin Theological Seminary, Grand Rapids*

Sherwin T. Wine, *Rabbi; Co-Chair and Co-Dean, International Institute for Secular Humanistic Judaism, Farmington Hills, Michigan*

Jeffrey R. Woolf, *Lecturer in Talmud, Bar-Ilan University*

Nissim Yosha, *The Institute of Jewish Studies, The Hebrew University of Jerusalem*

THE OXFORD DICTIONARY OF THE JEWISH RELIGION

A

AARON (Heb. Aharon), first *high priest; great-grandson of Levi; elder brother of *Moses and his spokesman before Pharaoh. While articles of law are normally introduced in the Torah by the formula, "the Lord spoke unto Moses, saying . . . ," in *Leviticus* 10.8, Aaron is the exclusive vehicle for the revelation of God-given instructions. Numerous passages—some assigned by Bible critics to the Yahvist source (*Ex.* 6.13, 7.8, 9.8), and some assigned to the Priestly source (e.g., *Ex.* 12.1; *Lv.* 11.1, 13.1, 14.33, 15.1)—depict Moses and Aaron as partners in the mediation of God's revealed instructions: "And the Lord spoke to Moses and Aaron, saying . . . ." Aaron was responsible for making the *golden calf and summoning the Israelites to worship it as the deity who brought them out of Egypt (*Ex.* 32). Refusing to take responsibility for his actions, he claimed that the calf was not his doing but rather, "I threw it [the gold] into the fire, and this calf emerged [of itself miraculously]" (*Ex.* 32.24). The Lord was angry enough with Aaron to have destroyed him (*Dt.* 9.20), but Aaron was spared by virtue of Moses' prayer on his behalf. According to *Numbers* 12.2, Miriam and Aaron challenged Moses' privileged status with the rhetorical question, "Has the Lord spoken only through Moses; has he not spoken also through us?" The Lord responded to this question by explaining that because the communication between him and Moses represented a unique level of intimacy, Aaron and Miriam should both be careful not to speak against Moses (*Nm.* 12.8). Aaron and his descendants were selected to serve as priests; together with his sons, he was duly anointed by Moses upon the completion of the Tabernacle. Aaron officiated in the Holy of Holies for almost forty years until his death in the wilderness. Other descendants of the tribe of Levi were appointed to perform various services in the Tabernacle (and later in the Temple), but to Aaron and his descendants (see AARONIDES)—the *kohanim* (priests)—was reserved the direct and immediate contact with the sanctuary and altar. This was their inheritance; they received no inheritance of land in Canaan (*Nm.* 18.20). Aaron is frequently mentioned as a symbol of the priesthood in general, and in rabbinic literature his name was a byword for piety and the pursuit of peace (cf. *Avot* 1.12). The rabbis also extolled the bond of brotherly love between Moses and Aaron.

• Henry Bamberger, "Aaron: Changing Perceptions," *Judaism* 42.2 (1993): 199–213. Manfred Görg, "Aaron von einem Titel zu Name?" *Biblische Zeitschrift* 32 (1986): 11–17. Marsha White, "The Elohistic Description of Aaron," in *Studies in the Pentateuch*, edited by J. A. Emerton, Supplements to Vetus Testamentum, vol. 41 (Leiden, 1990), pp. 149–159. Aelred Cody, *A History of the Old Testament Priesthood*, Analecta Biblica, no. 35 (Rome, 1969). Jacob Milgrom, *Leviticus 1–16*, The Anchor Bible, vol. 3 (New York, 1991), s.v., "Aaron."

—MAYER I. GRUBER

AARONIDES, priests descended from *Aaron, brother of Moses and Miriam. They are referred to in Hebrew as "sons of Aaron" (*Lv.* 3.8, 21.1; *Nm.* 10.8; *Jos.* 21.4; *Neh.* 12.47; *1 Chr.* 24.1). According to *1 Chronicles* 6.34, 23.13, and 24.19, and *2 Chronicles* 26.16–21, members of this family of priests received the exclusive prerogatives of burning incense, ministering, and blessing.

—MAYER I. GRUBER

ABARBANEL. See ABRAVANEL FAMILY.

ABBA' (Aram.; אַבָּא; father; corresponding to the Hebrew *av*), honorary title conferred on some of the tanna'im and amora'im (for example, Abba' Guryon and Abba' Sha'ul). According to Maimonides, it was synonymous with *rabbi*. The title passed into Christian usage to denote high ecclesiastical office, as in medieval Latin, *abbas*; Italian, *abbate*; German, *abt*; French, *abbé*; and English, *abbot*.

• Myron B. Lerner, "Le-Ḥeqer ha-Qinuyim veha-To'arim," *Teudah* 4 (1986): 93–113.

ABBA' (3d–4th cent.), Babylonian and Palestinian amora'. He studied in Babylonia with R. Huna' and R. Yehudah bar Yeḥezqe'l, and in Erets Yisra'el (where he eventually settled, in spite of R. Yehudah's objections; *Ber.* 24b) with R. Abbahu in Caesarea and with Reish Laqish and R. El'azar ben Pedat in Tiberias. After R. El'azar's death, he was both a colleague and student of R. 'Ammi and R. Assi, the new Tiberias academy heads. He was a wealthy silk trader (*B. Q.* 117b), able to support lavish preparations for the Sabbath (*Shab.* 119a). He frequently traveled between Erets Yisra'el and Babylonia, where he was called "our teacher in Erets Yisra'el" (*San.* 17b). In this capacity, he served as a conduit of the traditions developed in the schools of the two countries, although when eulogizing R. Huna', he claimed that the *shekhinah* would have rested on him had he not resided in Babylonia (*Mo'ed Q.* 25a). He is frequently cited in both *halakhah* and *aggadah* in the Talmuds and *midrashim* and was known for his generous and sensitive spirit (cf. *Ket.* 67b; *Qid.* 59a; *Yoma'* 87a).

• Wilhelm Bacher, *Die Agada der palästinensischen Amoräer* (1892–1899; Hildesheim, 1965). Mordecai Margaliot, ed., *Entsiqlopediyyah le-Ḥakhmei ha-Talmud veha-Ge'onim*, revised and updated by Yehuda Eisenberg (Tel Aviv, 1995).

—MICHAEL L. BROWN

ABBA' ARIKHA'. See RAV.

ABBAHU (died 309), Palestinian amora'; one of the main disciples of R. Yoḥanan and head of the rabbinical academy at Caesarea. A distinguished preacher, he was noted for his modesty and humanity; his better-known sayings include, "Where a repentant sinner stands, even a completely righteous man may not stand" (*Ber.* 34a) and "The world exists through the man who effaces himself" (*Ḥul.* 89a). Fluent in Greek (4. *Yev.* 4.2), handsome (*B. M.* 84a), and wealthy (*Shab.* 119a, in Rashi), he enjoyed high respect among the Roman representatives, which added to his stature among his colleagues (Y., *Meg.* 3.2). Abbahu sharply opposed sectarians and Christians, and his scriptural expositions were often directed to polemical ends. He decreed that the Samaritans should be regarded as gentiles. Abbahu probably headed the group of rabbis of Caesarea credited with redacting the juridical section of the Talmud Yerushalmi. Legend has it that when he died the columns of Caesarea wept; scholars have related this to a historical event recorded by the church fathers in 309.

• Wilhelm Bacher, *Die Agada der palästinensischen Amoräer* (Strassburg, 1892–1899). Lee I. Levine, "R. Abbahu of Caesarea," in *Christianity, Judaism and Other Greco-Roman Cults*, edited by Jacob Neusner (Leiden, 1975), vol. 4, pp. 56–76. Saul Lieberman, *Greek in Jewish Palestine* (New York, 1942). —DANIEL SPERBER

ABBA' MARI BEN MOSHEH HA-YARḤI (13th–14th cent.), Provençal scholar. He was instrumental in getting R. Shelomoh ben Avraham *Adret (Rashba') to issue in Barcelona a ban on the study of philosophy for students younger than twenty-five years of age and then influenced many communities in southern France to accept the ban. In Montpellier, where he was residing at the time (1305), opposition and counterbans were issued against him and his faction. The controversy came to an abrupt end with the expulsion of the Jews from Languedoc in 1306. In his *Minḥat Qena'ot* (Pressburg, 1838), he collected the various letters and pamphlets concerning this affair, a eulogy for Menaḥem *Me'iri, and his essay "Sefer ha-Yareaḥ," in which he accepted some of Maimonides' principles of faith: the existence, unity, and incorporeality of God; creation of the world by God; and God's special providence. Abba' Mari corresponded with Adret, and a number of his *responsa* have been published in *She'elot Teshuvot ha-Rashba'* (Rome, c.1480); he also wrote religious poetry. See also MAIMONIDEAN CONTROVERSY.

• Yitzhak Baer, *A History of the Jews in Christian Spain*, vol. 1 (Philadelphia, 1961), pp. 289ff. Henrich Gross, *Gallia judaica: Dictionnaire géographique de la France d'après les sources rabbiniques* (Paris, 1897; repr. Amsterdam, 1969, with a supplement by Simon Schwarzfuchs). Joseph Sarachek, *Faith and Reason: The Conflict over the Rationalism of Maimonides* (New York, 1970). —SHLOMO H. PICK

ABBA' SHA'UL (2d cent. CE), Palestinian tanna'. The Talmud singles him out, with evident exaggeration, as the tallest man in his (and thereby each succeeding) generation (*Nid*. 24b–25a). He described himself as a gravedigger (*Nid*. 24b), although the Talmud refers to an Abba' Sha'ul who was the baker for the household of R. *Yehudah ha-Nasi' (*Pes*. 34a). A colleague of R. *Yehudah bar Il'ai and R. *Me'ir, R. Abba' Sha'ul often employed both his own terminology and different versions of tannaitic sources from that of his contemporaries (cf. *Git*. 5.4), prompting some scholars to speak of a "mishnah of Abba' Sha'ul." He transmitted traditions on the services and utensils of the Second Temple (e.g. *Pes*. 57a–b), on the development of the fetus (Y., *Nid*. 3.3, 50d), and on burial customs (e.g., *Nid*. 61a), and he excluded from the world to come any Jew who pronounced the Tetragrammaton (*San*. 10.1; see GOD, NAMES OF). He taught that men should emulate the gracious character of God (*Shab*. 133b to Ex. 15.2) and that prayer from a prepared heart was efficacious (*Ber*. 31a to *Ps*. 10.17).

• Wilhelm Bacher, *Die Agada der Tannaiten* (1903; Berlin, 1965–1966). Israel Konovitz, comp., *Ma'arakhot Tanna'im: Osef Shalem shel Mishnatam u-Ma'amreihem ba-Sifrut ha-Talmudit veha-Midrashit* (Jerusalem, 1967–1969). Israel Lewy, *Über einige Fragmente aus der Mischna des Abba Shaul* (Berlin, 1876). —MICHAEL L. BROWN

ABBAYEI (c.278–338), Babylonian amora'; his real name was Naḥmani. An orphan, Abbayei was raised by his uncle *Rabbah bar Naḥmani. A poor man, Abbayei emphasized the importance of physical labor, and in order to be free to study and teach during the day, he cultivated his small landholding at night. Later in life, however, he appears to have grown richer and acquired many properties (*Ḥul*. 105a), which he leased out to tenant farmers (*Ket*. 60a), who employed many workers (*Ber*. 45b). In his early childhood and youth he studied with his colleague *Rava' in *Pumbedita under Rabbah and R. *Yosef ben Ḥiyya', and in later life—when Abbayei was head of the academy at Pumbedita and Rava' at Maḥoza'—they argued over many points of law (with six exceptions, the decisions of Rava' were accepted as the norm). Their wide-ranging legal discussions became a byword for acumen and keen argument and are regarded as among the finest examples of Talmudic dialectics. Abbayei was among the first to distinguish between the literal (**peshat*) and exegetical (**derash*) interpretation of biblical text. He had the deepest regard for the amora'im in Palestine, saying that "one of them is worth two of us" (*Ket*. 75a). He studied the Palestinian legal tradition (*San*. 44b), and Palestinian colleagues who came to Babylonia were permitted to follow their own customs, even when those customs were more lenient than those of Babylonia (*Pes*. 51a). His famous dicta included: "The whole [point] of the Torah is to propagate peace" (*Git*. 59a); "There is no real poverty except in knowledge" (*Ned*. 41a); "And thou shalt love the Lord thy God [*Dt*. 6.5]—[means] that you shall cause the name of Heaven to be loved" (*Yoma'* 86a).

On his death the Pumbedita academy was closed, and Rava' was recognized as head of all the Babylonian Talmudic academies.

• Aaron Hyman, *Toledot Tanna'im ve-'Amora'im*, 3 vols. (London, 1910). Wilhelm Bacher, *Die Agada der babylonischen Amoräer* (Strassburg, 1878), pp. 107–113. —DANIEL SPERBER

ABBREVIATIONS (Heb. *ra'shei tevot* [beginnings of words]). Contractions of single words or groups of words have been used in Hebrew since at least the second century BCE, when they appeared on Maccabean coins. The Talmud as well as all subsequent rabbinic writings make extensive use of a system of word abbreviations: dots, strokes, or double strokes over the first, second, or third letter of a word indicate that the remaining letters of the word are eliminated; also common is the practice of substituting a stroke for the last one of two letters of a word (especially for plurals). Where the initials of several words are contracted to form a single element, the abbreviation is indicated by one or two strokes over the line between the last two letters. The habit of abbreviating groups of words to one word (such as UNESCO and similar formations in modern English usage) is very old in Hebrew, in which such abbreviations for certain books (e.g., Tanakh for Bible from Torah, Nevi'im, Ketuvim [Torah, Prophets, Hagiographa], the three components of the Jewish Bible; or Shas from *shishah sedarim*, the six orders that make up the Mishnah and by extension the Talmud), names (Rashi for R. Shelomoh Yitsḥaqi; Rambam for R. Mosheh ben Maimon), concepts (Taryag, the Hebrew numerological equivalent of the number 613, for the total number of commandments in the Torah), and titles (*admor* for *adonenu, morenu ve-rebbenu* [our master, our teacher, our rabbi], the title generally accorded to a Hasidic rabbi) became words in their own right. Abbreviations were often used as mnemonic devices, one of the best known being the *acrostic quoted in the Pesaḥ Haggadah for the Hebrew names of the Ten Plagues (*detsakh, ʿadash, be'aḥav*). Abbreviations were, and are, commonly used by pious Jews in writing or printing God's name, or words whose last letters form God's name (e.g., words ending with the Hebrew letters *yud* and *heh*, which together spell out the word Yah, one of God's names). Such abbreviations are commonly used in writing God's name on any paper or document that might ultimately be thrown away, as opposed to religious works, which are customarily buried after they are no longer usable. Even religious works often do not contain the Tetragrammaton, the holiest, four-letter, name of God; instead, the word is abbreviated by two *yuds*. Another abbreviation, found in certain old religious works, is the merging of two Hebrew letters into a single letter symbol. The most common occurrence of this was a combined letter representing the *alef-lamed* combination, a construct that appears in many Hebrew words, the two-letter combination itself forming one of God's names. On occasion, authors employed numerous abbreviations in their works to cut down the number of pages—and hence the cost—of publication of their works. Various family names are derived from abbreviations; for example, Katz (*kohen tsedeq* [righteous priest]) and Segal (*segan leviyyah* [Levitical aide]). Abbreviations also played a role in rabbinic and mystical exegesis (see NOTARIQON); for example, for the purposes of *gimatriyyah*, and especially in magic.

• Shemuel Ashkenazi and Dov Yarden, *Otsar Rashei Tevot* (Jerusalem, 1965). Aaron Demsky and Meir Bar-Ilan, "Writing in Ancient Israel and Early Judaism," in *Mikra: Text, Translation, Reading and Interpretation of the Hebrew Bible in Ancient Judaism and Early Christianity*, edited by M. J. Mulder (Assen and Philadelphia, 1988), pp. 29–30.

—SHMUEL HIMELSTEIN

ABDUCTION. See KIDNAPPING.

ABEL. See CAIN AND ABEL.

ABIATHAR (Heb. Evyatar), priest of the family of *Eli and son of Ahimelech. Chief priest at the sanctuary of Nob, Abiathar was the sole survivor of Saul's massacre of the priests of that city for the assistance they had afforded David on his flight from Saul. Abiathar thereupon joined David's party, accompanying him on his wanderings and serving him as keeper of the priestly *ephod. He was appointed chief priest when David ascended the throne and was one of the king's closest advisers. Because of his support for the succession of Adonijah rather than Solomon to the kingship upon the death of King David, he was banished by Solomon to his native Anathoth, was deprived of the privilege of acting as high priest, and was replaced by Zadok (*1 Kgs*. 2.26–35). Solomon, however, showed Abiathar mercy for two reasons: his faithful service during the reign of David; and his having suffered along with David while he was being persecuted by Saul. According to the narrative in *1 Kings* 2.27, Solomon's removal of Abiathar from the priesthood was meant to fulfill the anonymous prophecy in *1 Samuel* 2.27–36 that the corrupt priests of the house of Eli would be replaced by "a faithful priest who will continually walk before my king." It is widely surmised that Jeremiah's origin "from among the priests who were at Anathoth" (*Jer*. 1.1) indicates that he was a descendant of Abiathar.

• John Bright, *A History of Israel*, 3d ed. (Philadelphia, 1981). Yehezkel Kaufmann, *The Religion of Israel*, abridged and translated by Moshe Greenberg (Chicago, 1960), p. 420. Roland de Vaux, *Ancient Israel*, 2 vols. (New York, 1965).

—MAYER I. GRUBER

ABIB. See AVIV.

ABI-ḤASIRA, YAʿAQOV (1807–1880), Moroccan rabbinical authority, born in Tafilalet. Although he wrote chiefly about the *halakhah*, the Bible, and ethics, he was revered by his contemporaries and later generations as "the famous saint, the divine kabbalist, the wonder-worker, the holy candle." His descendants collected the legends woven around him in a work entitled *Maʿaseh Nissim* (Jerusalem, 1968), which belongs to the genre of hagiographic accounts of the lives of Yitsḥaq *Luria or Yisra'el ben Eliʿezer *Baʿal Shem Tov. Abi-Ḥasira established a *yeshivah* in his home that attracted many students, particularly from among the poor, and to support them, he traveled around the region to collect funds. He was also involved in communal affairs, represented the Jews before the authorities, and participated in disputations with Muslim clerics. His teachings combined kabbalistic thought and social conservatism, but his influence was less through his writings than his pious and ascetic way of life. He longed to settle in Erets Yisra'el but died in Damanhūr, near Alexandria, on his way there. Most of his works were published in Jerusalem.

• Dan Manor, *Qabbalah u-Musar be-Maroqo: Darko shel R. Yaʿaqov Aviḥatsira* (Jerusalem, 1982).

—SHALOM BAR-ASHER

ABIMELECH, the name of two biblical figures.

Abimelech, king of Gerar, is mentioned in *Genesis* 20 and 21 in relation to Abraham and in *Genesis* 26 in relation to Isaac. In *Genesis* 20 and 26 Abimelech is reported as taking Sarah and Rebekah, respectively, into his palace after their husbands, Abraham and Isaac, respectively, present their wives as their sisters in order to save their own lives. In both instances the scheme is uncovered before Abimelech actually cohabits with them. Since he was completely innocent and unaware of the subterfuge, he is righteously indignant and escapes punishment. These two narratives are variants on a single tradition. In *Genesis* 21.25, and in *Genesis* 26.15–16 and 26.18–21, Abimelech is involved in a dispute with Abraham and Isaac, respectively, over wells. In both cases he is accompanied by his military commander, Phicol (*Gn.* 21.22, 32, 26.26), and both stories conclude with treaties between him and the patriarchs (*Gn.* 21.27–32, 26.28–31). These stories also represent two versions of a single tradition.

Abimelech, son of Gideon (*Jgs.* 8.31), though not reckoned among the judges, became the ruler of Shechem for three years, when, with the aid of "worthless and reckless men," he murdered all, save one (Jotham), of the seventy sons of *Gideon, thereby eliminating all possible contenders. Later on there arose a dispute between Abimelech and the "lords of Shechem" (his original supporters), who conspired with Gaal, son of Ebed, and his army to depose him. Abimelech and his men attacked Gaal, drove him from the city, and went on to slaughter the inhabitants of Shechem, destroying the city and sowing it with salt. In the course of a subsequent battle, Abimelech was mortally wounded by a millstone thrown down upon him from a tower by a woman. So as not to suffer the ignominy of being slain by a woman, he commanded his armorbearer to kill him (*Jgs.* 9.54).

• E. F. Campbell, Jr., "Shechem in the Amarna Archive," in *Shechem: The Biography of a Biblical City*, edited by G. Ernest Wright (New York, 1965), pp. 191–207. E. F. Campbell, Jr., "Two Amarna Notes: The Shechem City-State and Amarna Administrative Terminology," in *Magnalia Dei: The Mighty Acts of God: Essays on the Bible and Archaeology in Memory of G. Ernest Wright*, edited by Frank Moore Cross et al. (Garden City, N.Y., 1976), pp. 39–54. Richard S. Hess, *Amarna Personal Names* (Winona Lake, Ind., 1993), pp. 18–19. Victor H. Matthews and Baruch Halpern, "Abimelech," *Anchor Bible Dictionary*, vol. 1 (New York, 1992), pp. 20–22. Geoffrey Wigoder and Shalom M. Paul et al., eds., "Abimelech," *Illustrated Dictionary and Concordance of the Bible* (New York, 1986), pp. 19–20.

—SHALOM PAUL

ABITUR, YOSEF BEN YITSḤAQ IBN (c.940–1024), Spanish rabbinic authority and liturgical poet; also known as Ibn Shatanash. He studied with *Mosheh ben Ḥanokh in Cordova. When Abitur's hopes of heading the Cordova Yeshivah were frustrated by his opponents, he moved east in 987 and settled in Egypt, living mostly in Fostat. He was highly respected and corresponded with the Babylonian ge'onim Sherira' ben Ḥanina' and Ha'i. Abitur wrote *responsa* noted for their moderate innovativeness. Abitur's extensive sacred poetry (three hundred of his *piyyutim* have been preserved) was in the Spanish tradition. He also wrote secular poetry, including poems both of friendship and of condemnation of his opponents. Some of his poems have been printed, but most are to be found still scattered in hundreds of manuscripts.

• Israel Davidson, *Otsar ha-Shirah veha-Piyyut: Mi-Zeman Ḥatimat Kitvei ha-Qodesh ad Re'shit Tequfat ha-Haskalah*, 4 vols. (New York, 1970).

—SHALOM BAR-ASHER

ABLUTION, washing or cleansing the body, generally for a religious purpose. Jewish law deals with both total and partial ablution. The biblical statement "he shall bathe his flesh in water" (*Lv.* 15.16) refers to total immersion of the body in a ritual bath (**miqveh*) or flowing river water. Before immersion, the body must already be scrupulously clean so that nothing can interpose between flesh and water; even finger- and toenails are pared to ensure that no dirt remains beneath them. Immersion (*tevilah*) is a religious act specifically undertaken to achieve the ritual purity (see IMPURITY) required for participation in certain religious ceremonies. Thus, not only did the high priest immerse himself before conducting the service on Yom Kippur, but each priest who participated in the Temple service was also required to undergo immersion besides washing his hands and feet at the Laver (*Ex.* 30.18–21). The Torah also requires full immersion for women after their menstrual flow and for men after a sexual emission (*Lv.* 15.16–33). The Mishnah attributes to Ezra a decree that each male should immerse himself before reciting the morning prayer or studying. Matutinal immersion was practiced by the *Hemerobaptists and by ascetics, mystics, and Ḥasidim of later times (see BAPTISM). There are two kinds of partial ablution: the washing of the hands and feet as prescribed by the Bible for priests ministering in the Temple (in the synagogue, *kohanim* about to recite the Birkat ha-Kohanim have their hands washed by Levites in the congregation); and the washing of hands (*netilat yadayim*) prescribed by the rabbis for various occasions (e.g., before partaking of bread, after leaving a bathroom, on waking from sleep, and on leaving a cemetery [*Shulḥan ʿArukh, Oraḥ Ḥayyim* 4.18]). In these cases, the hands are regarded as having contracted a limited form of impurity that does not apply to the entire body; hence, it is sufficient to clean them alone. The rabbis paid particular attention to the washing of hands: R. ʿAqiva' used the little water allowed him during his imprisonment by the Romans for washing rather than drinking (*ʿEruv.* 21b); and the sage Eliʿezer ben Ḥanokh was excommunicated for doubting the need to wash one's hands (*ʿEduy.* 65a). In modern Orthodox and Conservative practice, the only mandatory bodily immersion is that of the menstruating woman (*niddah*), the woman who has recently given birth, and the proselyte (see PROSELYTE). Pious custom among some Orthodox requires immersion by males prior to the onset of festivals. Bodily immersion is also used for the process of conversion by men and women. Some non-Orthodox women follow the traditional practice of immersion after the menstrual cycle; non-Orthodox men, for spiritual purification.

• Aryeh Kaplan, *Waters of Eden: An Exploration of the Concept of Mikvah–Renewal and Rebirth* (New York, 1984). Jacob Neusner, *A History of the Mishnaic Law of Purities* (Leiden, 1977), pt. 22.

ABOAB, ʿIMMANU'EL (c.1555–1628), author. Born in Portugal to Marrano parents, he escaped in his youth to Italy where he lived openly as a Jew. He moved to various cities and spent his latter years in Erets Yisra'el; he died in Jerusalem. His Spanish *Nomologia o discursos legales* (Amsterdam, 1629), directed to Marranos, endeavors to prove the veracity of the oral law.

• Cecil Roth, *The History of the Jews in Venice* (Philadelphia, 1930), pp. 68, 207, 315.

ABOAB, YITSḤAQ (14th–15th cent.), Talmudic scholar, probably Spanish. His homiletic classic, *Menorat ha-Ma'or* (Constantinople, 1541), collected ethical rabbinic teachings and arranged them according to subject matter. The work achieved widespread popularity; was translated into Yiddish, Spanish, Judeo-Spanish, and German; and contributed to the dissemination of rabbinic ethics among medieval Jews.

• Yaacov Y. Rainman, ed. and trans., *Menoras Hamaor: The Weekday Festivals, Rosh Chodesh, Chanukah, Purim*, an annotated, translated excerpt from Yitsḥaq Aboab's *Menorat ha-Ma'or* (Lakewood, N.J., 1986).

ABOAB DA FONSECA, YITSḤAQ (1605–1693), rabbi. At the age of twenty-one, he was appointed *ḥakham* in Amsterdam. In 1642 he journeyed to Brazil with Amsterdam Jews of Portuguese origin and officiated at Recife as the first rabbi; he was the first Jewish author in the Western Hemisphere. After the Portuguese reconquest of Brazil in 1654, he returned to Amsterdam, where he headed a rabbinical academy. He was a member of the rabbinical tribunal that excommunicated Baruch *Spinoza. Aboab da Fonseca's works include a Spanish translation of and commentary on the Pentateuch (Amsterdam, 1688).

• Alexander Marx, *Studies in Jewish History and Booklore* (New York, 1944), pp. 209–211. Gershom Gerhard Scholem, *Sabbatai Ṣevi: The Mystical Messiah, 1626–1676*, translated by R. J. Zwi Werblowsky (Princeton, 1973). Arnold Wiznitzer, *Jews in Colonial Brazil* (New York, 1960).

ABOMINATION, a term used to call attention to an action or type of behavior, only occasionally an object (e.g., a graven image in *Dt*. 7.26; a forbidden food in *Dt*. 14.3) and never a person, considered repulsive by either God or man. *Deuteronomy* outlaws practices that are "abhorrent to the Lord" and accuses the Canaanite peoples of being guilty of them all (*Dt*. 12.31). Among these are child sacrifice (*Dt*. 12.31), recourse to magic and divination (*Dt*. 18.12), the bringing of a harlot's hire or the price of a dog in payment of a vow (*Dt*. 23.19), and the use of false weights and measures (*Dt*. 25.16). Paganism is intrinsically abhorrent (*Dt*. 7.25–26), and its practitioners are called "nations of abominations" (*Ezr*. 9.14). Israel's abominations, that is, the foreign gods she repeatedly worships, enrage God (*Dt*. 32.16); the prophet Ezekiel attributes God's decision to bring about the destruction of Jerusalem to Israel's contamination of the pure and exclusive worship of the Lord (*Ez*. 5.9, 11, 6.9, 8.6–13). Sexual crimes are referred to as abominations in *Leviticus* 18.6–30. It is said that Erets Yisra'el itself will "vomit out" any nation—Canaanite or Israelite—guilty of such practices, and that the individual practitioner is doomed to divine punishment.

• William W. Hallo, "Biblical Abominations and Sumerian Taboos," *Jewish Quarterly Review* 76 (1985): 21–40. Delbert R. Hillers, "Analyzing the Abominable: Our Understanding of Canaanite Religion," *Jewish Quarterly Review* 75 (1985): 253–269. Harry A. Hoffner, "Incest, Sodomy and Bestiality in the Ancient Near East," in *Orient and Occident: Essays Presented to Cyrus H. Gordon on the Occasion of his Sixty-fifth Birthday*, Alter Orient und Altes Testament, Bd. 22 (Kevelaer and Neukirchen-Vluyn, 1973), pp. 81–90. Jacob Klein and Yitsḥaq Tsarfati, "'To'evah ve-To'avot be-Sifrut ha-Mesopotamit uva-Miqra'," *Beer Sheva* 3 (1988): 131–148. W. H. Picket, "The Meaning and Function of 'T'B/TO 'Evah' in the Hebrew Bible," Ph.D dissertation, Hebrew Union College, 1985. Moshe Weinfeld, *Deuteronomy and the Deuteronomic School* (Winona Lake, Ind., 1992), pp. 266–269. —BARUCH J. SCHWARTZ

ABORTION. The killing of a fetus does not carry the death penalty in Jewish law, since a fetus is only considered a person in criminal cases once its major part has emerged from its mother's body. This is derived from the Bible, which provides that the penalty for assaulting a pregnant woman and causing her to miscarry is financial compensation to her husband. The biblical rule governing homicide, that is, "a life for a life," only applies if the woman also dies as a result of the assault (*Ex*. 21.22–23). The Mishnah permits the killing of a fetus, even during childbirth, in order to save the mother's life (*Ohal*. 7.6). There is, however, a clear distinction between not providing a criminal sanction for feticide and permitting it outright; hence, many rabbinic authorities maintain that nontherapeutic abortion is indeed forbidden by rabbinic law. The scope of therapeutic abortion is not a narrowly defined one, and there are many ongoing debates in this area of *halakhah*. Maimonides seemed to confine therapeutic abortion to cases in which the fetus poses a direct and immediate threat to the physical and mental health of the mother. Abortions of pregnancies resulting from rape or which would result in the mother's loss of sight or hearing have also been considered justified in Jewish law. Opinions are divided regarding the abortion of the fetus of a mother who contracted rubella during pregnancy and in relation to severe disorders that may be detected by genetic analysis during the early part of pregnancy; for example, Tay-Sachs disease and Down's syndrome. With regard to the abortion of defective fetuses, the lenient school permits abortion until the seventh month. The issues of fetal reduction in artificial reproductive procedures and of the use of fetal tissue for research and therapeutic purposes have generally been treated in a permissive fashion in Jewish law. In general, Reform Judaism supports choice in the area of abortion.

• J. David Bleich, "Abortion in Halakhic Literature," in *Jewish Bioethics*, edited by Fred Rosner and J. David Bleich (New York, 1979), pp. 134–177. David M. Feldman, *Marital Relations, Birth Control and Abortion in Jewish Law* (New York, 1974), pp. 251–294. Walter Jacob and Moshe Zemer, eds., *The Fetus and Fertility: Essays and Responsa* (Pittsburgh, 1995). Immanuel Jakobovits, *Jewish Medical Ethics* (New York, 1959), pp. 170–191. Isaac Klein, "Abortion and Jewish Tradition," in *Contemporary Jewish Ethics*, edited by Menachem Marc Kellner (New York, 1978), pp. 270–278. Daniel B. Sinclair, "The Legal Basis for the Prohibition in Abortion in Jewish Law," *Israel Law Review* 15:1 (1980): 109–130. —DANIEL SINCLAIR

ABRABANEL. See ABRAVANEL FAMILY.

ABRAHAM (Heb. Avraham), father and founder of the Hebrew people; the first of the *patriarchs. The story of Abraham's life as recorded in *Genesis* 11.27–25.18 is a combination of several traditions. Scholars are divided as to the time in which Abraham lived, dating him anywhere between 2000 and 1400, but most place him in the eighteenth century BCE. According to biblical tradition, though Abraham's ancestors (including his father, Terah) worshiped many gods (see *Jos*. 24.2), he was the first to worship only one and is considered the founder of the monotheist tradition and the first Hebrew (or Israelite or Jew). More accurately, however, Abraham's own religion can be labeled monolatry (the worship of one deity, without denying the existence of other gods), which only later evolved into monotheism (the belief in one deity).

The biblical account begins with God speaking to Abraham (first called Abram [*Gn*. 11.27–17.5], then a dialectal variant, Abraham, interpreted in *Gn*. 17.5 as "Father of a multitude of nations") and commanding him to leave his native Mesopotamia, where he was born in the vicinity of Ur of the Chaldees, and to go to the land of Canaan (*Gn*. 12). Abraham, at the age of seventy-five, and his wife *Sarah (Sarai) immigrated to Canaan and there lived in various cities, notably Hebron. God promised Abraham offspring who would develop into a great nation and possession of the land of Canaan (the "promised land"). The ensuing narrative revolves around the fulfillment of this promise. His son *Ishmael was born to a secondary wife, *Hagar, and at Sarah's insistence they were driven away. Sarah miraculously gave birth to a son in old age, Isaac (*Gn*. 21), who was to be the heir of the covenantal promise. A dramatic crisis, endangering this promise, occurred when God commanded Abraham to sacrifice Isaac (the *ʿ*aqedah*; *Gn*. 22). Abraham passed this supreme test of his faith in God by his readiness to obey, but God prevented the consummation of the sacrifice. The *covenant established between God and Abraham (*Gn*. 15) forms the basis of biblical religion: God will be the God of Abraham and his descendants, and Abraham and his descendants will be the people of God. The binding symbol of the covenant is *circumcision. The story of the ʿ*aqedah* is followed by the account of Sarah's death (including Abraham's purchase of the cave of *Machpelah in Hebron for a burial site; *Gn*. 23) and the procurement of a bride, *Rebekah, for Isaac (*Gn*. 24). The Bible notes that, in addition to Hagar and Sarah, Abraham had a third wife, Keturah, whom he married after Sarah's death, and through her six additional children were born (*Gn*. 25.1–6). When Abraham died, his sons Isaac and Ishmael buried him next to Sarah in the cave of Machpelah (*Gn*. 25.7–10).

The Midrash tells many stories about Abraham, for example, his smashing of Terah's idols while still a youth and his institution of morning prayers. He is the symbol of *hospitality (*Gn*. 18) and the first of the guests welcomed in the *Ushpizin ceremony in the *sukkah* during Sukkot. Abraham plays an important role in Islam, since Muslims view Abraham as the founder of their religion as well, with descent passing from Abraham through Ishmael to later historical Arabs, and the Qur'an includes many stories of Abraham derived from both biblical and Midrashic sources.

• Benjamin Mazar, ed., *Patriarchs*, The World History of the Jewish People, 1st series, vol. 2 (Tel Aviv, 1970). Alan R. Millard and Donald J. Wiseman, eds., *Essays on the Patriarchal Narratives* (Leicester, Eng., 1980). Gerhard von Rad, *Genesis: A Commentary*, rev. ed. by John Bowden (London, 1985). Nahum M. Sarna, *Genesis*, The JPS Torah Commentary (Philadelphia, 1989). Nahum M. Sarna, *Understanding Genesis* (New York, 1970). Roland de Vaux, *The Early History of Israel* (Philadelphia, 1978).

—GARY A. RENDSBURG

ABRAHAM, APOCALYPSE OF. See APOCALYPSE OF ABRAHAM.

ABRAHAM, TESTAMENT OF. See TESTAMENT OF ABRAHAM.

ABRAHAMITES. See JUDAIZING SECTS.

ABRAMSKY, YEḤEZQEʾL (1886–1976), rabbi and scholar. He was born in Lithuania and studied at the *yeshivot* of Tels, Mir, and Slobodka. He was also a student of R. Ḥayyim Soloveichik of Brisk and of R. Ḥayyim ʿOzer Grodzenski of Vilna. After World War I, Abramsky became rabbi of Slutsk and later of Smolensk. In 1928 he was permitted by the Soviet authorities to publish a journal (which he edited with S. Y. Zevin), *Yagdil Torah*, on halakhic issues. However, in 1930 he was sentenced to hard labor for his efforts to strengthen Judaism in the Soviet Union. Released in 1932 after international appeals for clemency, he immigrated to London, where he worked to strengthen traditional Jewish life in England, becoming rabbi of the Maḥzike ha-Das synagogue and *dayyan* (judge) of the London *beit din* (rabbinic court). In 1951 he retired and moved to Jerusalem. In Israel, he was appointed a member of Agudat Israel's Moʿetset Gedolei ha-Torah (rabbinic leadership council) and became a significant and influential figure in Israeli Orthodox circles. He was also president of the Vaʿad ha-Yeshivot (Council of Yeshivot).

Abramsky wrote extensively on Talmudic and halakhic subjects; most of his books bear the title *Ḥazon Yeḥezqeʾl*. His most prominent work is a commentary on Toseftaʾ (*Toseftaʾ Ḥazon Yeḥezqeʾl*, 19 vols. [1925–1967]). He also wrote *Qovets Maʾamarim Dinei Mammonot* (1979) and *Peninei Rabbenu Yeḥezqeʾl le-Sheqidat ha-Torah ule-Yirʾah* (1983).

• Yosef Buḳsboim, ed., *Sefer ha-Ziqqaron: Li-Khevodo ule- Zikhro shel Yeḥezqel Avramsqi* (Jerusalem, 1977–1978).

—IRA ROBINSON

ABRAVANEL FAMILY, influential Spanish, Portuguese, and Italian scholars.

Yitsḥaq Abravanel (1437–1508), Bible commentator, philosopher, statesman, and communal leader. He succeeded his father as treasurer to King Alfonso V of Portugal. Because he was believed to be involved in a plot against King João II, Yitsḥaq was sentenced to death *in absentia* but managed to flee to Castile. In 1492, however, although an influential minister at the court of Ferdinand and Isabella of Spain, he failed to dissuade them from executing the expulsion of Spanish Jewry. He himself fled to Naples and then to Venice, where his talents as financial adviser to the monarch soon brought him into the forefront of public activity.

His literary productions cover many subjects in the realm of biblical exegesis, philosophy, and theology. Abravanel's political experience is much in evidence in his diffuse biblical commentary dealing with the entire Bible (except the Hagiographa). For example, in his commentary on *1 Samuel* 8 (the institutions of monarchy) he praises the constitution of Venice as the best form of government. He compared the social institutions of biblical times with those of his own day, which he was in a unique position to observe through his long diplomatic experience. While drawing heavily on his forerunners, he did so with a keen critical sense and occasionally accepted the opinions of Christian scholars when they did not conflict with the Jewish faith.

Compared to the classical medieval exegesis, his treatment of the Bible is copious and discursive yet lucid and popular. Instead of commenting on individual verses, he divided the Pentateuch into thematic sections, prefacing each by a number of varied queries, the answers to which constituted the bulk of his commentary. Often sermonic in character, the commentary is largely philosophical and eschews philological or kabbalistic explanations of the text. Nevertheless, though rejecting philosophical allegory, Abravanel held that the Bible contained an esoteric as well as a literal meaning. A rationalist by training as well as by inclination, his position remained strictly traditional, and though much absorbed in philosophy, he maintained that it must take second place to religion. He also opposed the tendency to sum up the totality of Judaism in a given set of dogmatic principles and held that all elements of the Torah equally shared divine authority and significance. His original view of messianism is expressed, for example, in his commentary on the *Book of Daniel*, in which he also attacks Christian scholars for manipulating the biblical text in order to suit their own particular views. In some of his commentaries, he affirms belief in the coming Messiah, who he thought would appear in the year 1503 and whose advent would be preceded by the resurrection of the dead; the tribulations associated with the expulsion from Spain were thus regarded as the period of trial before the coming of the Messiah.

Abravanel's philosophy is neither original nor free from internal contradictions. His main purpose was to liberate Jewish philosophy—especially that of Maimonides—from those elements that detract from complete faith. Thus, one of his disciples reports that after expounding the views of Maimonides in a lecture, he concluded, "Thus the opinion of our master, Mosheh son of Maimon, but not that of our master, Mosheh son of Amram" (i.e., the biblical Moses). He argued that it was through prophecy that God communicated his truth to humanity, and he attacked any naturalistic explanation of biblical phenomenon. He differed from Maimonides in his conception of the source of prophecy, which he held lay not in the active intellect but in God himself. Abravanel believed that Israel is the recipient of special divine providence, whereas other nations receive providence only indirectly through the working of natural law. Yitsḥaq's works, which include commentaries on *Avot*, the Pesaḥ Haggadah, and Maimonides' *Guide of the Perplexed*, were eagerly read by the Spanish exiles, and their forecast of an imminent messianic era helped pave the way for the initial success of David *Re'uveni and Shelomoh *Molkho. Yitsḥaq's philosophical speculations, however—the last link in the chain of medieval Jewish philosophy—exercised little future influence, partly because of the growing counterattraction of kabbalistic thought. His biblical commentaries were not studied long by Jews, but in Latin translations they influenced Christian scholars from the sixteenth through the eighteenth century.

His writings included commentaries on the Pentateuch (Venice, 1579) and the Prophets (Pesaro, 1511–1512 and 1520); the messianic work *Maʿeyenei ha-Yeshuʿah* (Ferrara, 1551); and the philosophical works *ʿAteret Zeqenim* (Sabionetta, 1557) and *Ro'sh Amanah* (Constantinople, 1508).

Yehudah Abravanel (c.1460–1521), Italian philosopher, poet, and physician; son of Yitsḥaq Abravanel; also known as Leone Ebreo or Leo Hebraeus. Yehudah Abravanel's infant son was forcibly baptized in Portugal; he laments this event in his poem "Telunah ʿal Zeman." A practicing physician in Naples, Yehudah also published four poems in memory of his father. His Latin work *De coeli harmonia* has not survived, and his reputation rests on his posthumously published *Dialoghi d'amore*, one of the first philosophical works written in Italian.

Modeled on the Platonic dialogue, *Dialoghi d'amore* examines the nature of spiritual and intellectual love, which is regarded by Abravanel as the principle dominating all existence and reaching its apotheosis in the love of God (*amore intellectivo di Dio*). This love, according to Abravanel, permeates the entire universe, and through it all creatures attain their perfection. God is identified with love; hence, the soul reaches God by loving him. The mutual love that exists between God and the universe creates a powerful circle of love, turning on every section of the cosmos from the highest celestial sphere to the lowest earthly stone. The goal of individual love lies in the joy of the lover in union with the beloved, who embodies all that is good and beautiful. Ultimate love involves the same union of God the creator with his creation. From this central theory derives a wealth of reflections on religion, metaphysics, mysticism, ethics, esthetics, logic, psychology, cosmology, mythology, astrology, and astronomy. Abravanel's humanist thought is influenced both by the Neoplatonist philosophy cultivated in the fifteenth-century Platonic academy of Florence and by the works of Maimonides and Ibn Gabirol. This typically Renaissance work exerted a considerable influence on sixteenth-century European thought and lyric poetry (e.g., Michelangelo, Tasso, Camoëns, Montaigne, Bruno, Spinoza) and was followed by a large number of imitative treatises, although by the end of the sixteenth century it was virtually forgotten. It was not widely known in Jewish circles. *Dialoghi d'amore* was first published in Rome in 1535 and within twenty years had at least five editions. The book was twice translated into Spanish and three times into French. A facsimile, *Leone Ebreo*, edited by C. Gebhardt (with introduction and bibliography), appeared in *Bibliotheca Spinozana* (vol. 3 [Heidelberg, 1929]) and in an English translation, *Leo Hebraeus*, by F. Friedeberg-Seeley and J. H. Barnes (1937).

• **Yitsḥaq Abravanel**: Yitzhak Baer, *A History of the Jews in Christian Spain*, translated by Louis Schoffmann et al., vol. 2 (Philadelphia, 1961–1966). Menahem Marc Kellner, *Principles of Faith* (London and Toronto, 1982). Jacob Samuel Minkin, *Abrabanel and the Expulsion of the Jews from Spain* (New York, 1938). Benzion Netanyahu, *Don Isaac Abravanel* (Philadelphia, 1968). Joseph Sarachek, *Don Isaac Abravanel* (New York, 1938). Ephraim Shmueli, *Don Yitsḥaq Abarbanel ve-Gerush Sefarad* (n.p., 1963). Colette Sirat, *A History of Jewish Philosophy in the Middle Ages* (Cambridge, 1985), pp. 393–397. J. B. Trends and Herbert M. J. Loewe, eds., *Isaac Abravanel: Six Lectures* (Cambridge, 1937). **Yehudah Abravanel**: Julius Guttman, *Philosophies of Judaism* (New York, 1964), pp. 259–263. Cecil Roth, *The Jews in the Renaissance* (Philadelphia, 1959), pp. 128–136. Colette Sirat, *A History of Jewish Philosophy in the Middle Ages* (Cambridge, 1985), pp. 407–409.

ABROGATION OF LAWS. The abrogation of Torah law (biblical commandments) by the sages falls into three distinctly different categories: temporary abrogation, permanent abrogation, and incidental abrogation. Each of these three broad categories can be understood separately.

Temporary Abrogation. Jewish law recognizes the authority of the sages of every generation to suspend Torah laws on a case-by-case basis when the continued enforcement will be profoundly deleterious to the needs of the Jewish people. As Maimonides states (*Hilkhot Mamrim* 2.4) "just as a doctor may amputate a hand or a foot to save the patient's life, so too, a *beit din* may decree, in proper circumstances, a temporary violation of the *mitsvot* to preserve all of them." However, these suspensions—derived from the conduct of Elijah on Mount Carmel, which violated Jewish law (*1 Kgs.* 18. 19–26)—may not be of any significant duration. One, and perhaps the only, exception to the temporary nature of the abrogation, is in the area of criminal law, where the Talmud notes that local courts have the authority to punish criminals if the court feels that without such punishment society might deteriorate into lawlessness. The court-ordered killing of a person in a situation where Jewish law would not normally sanction this person's death is considered a temporary suspension of the prohibition to kill.

Permanent Abrogation. Jewish law recognized the right of the Talmudic sages, whose ordination was considered part of the unbroken chain from Moses, to suspend permanently the fulfillment of any given commandment when such suspension could be done through inactivity rather than activity. Thus, the Talmudic sages decreed that one may not blow the shofar on Ro'sh ha-Shanah when it falls on the Sabbath, and that one may not use a *lulav* on the first day of Sukkot when that date falls on the Sabbath. Both of these decrees were permanent even though the effect of these Talmudic rulings was to abrogate the fulfillment of the biblical directive. A minority of later scholars limits this authority to cases where the Bible did not explicitly permit the activity that the sages sought to curtail. Although *Rava' and *Ḥisda' dispute as to whether the sages have the authority to prevent the fulfillment of a biblical obligation even through affirmative action (*Yev.* 89a–b), the normative decision is that the active permanent abrogation of Jewish law is a power not granted even to the Talmudic sages.

Incidental Abrogation. The sages developed a number of incidental techniques that had the effect of increasing the number of cases where they could abrogate the effect of an action, including a *mitsvah*. Since the Talmudic sages had the authority to make ownerless a person's property (*hefqer beit din hefqer*), they also had the authority to reverse the effect of those actions done by a person that are predicated on their ownership of particular items. Thus, *Sheqalim* 1.2 tells that the illicit hybrid plants grown by violators of Jewish law were declared ownerless so as to punish those who violate Jewish law, and later authorities applied this principle to justify a variety of communal decrees.

Finally, and quite separately, there were a limited number of cases where, out of mercy to *ʿagunot* (see ʿAGUNAH), the sages of Talmudic times appear to have abrogated a number of the classical rules relating to the ending of marriages. There remains to this day a dispute among the decisors concerning the exact rationale for these decrees and whether they really involved the abrogation of any Torah commandment.

• Menachem Elon, *Jewish Law: History, Sources, Principles*, 4 vols. (Philadelphia, 1994), pp. 509–519. Aaron Kirschenbaum, *Equity in Jewish Law* (Hoboken, N.J., 1991), pp. 179–209. —MICHAEL BROYDE

ABSALOM (Heb. Avshalom), the third of the six sons born to King *David during the seven years he was enthroned at Hebron, capital of Judah. Absalom's mother was Maacah, daughter of King Talmai of Geshur (*1 Chr.* 3.1–4). The statement in *2 Samuel* 14.27 that "Absalom had three sons and a daughter whose name was Tamar; she was a beautiful woman" is a notable exception to the general rule that biblical genealogies name only the husbands and sons, while the wives and daughters are nameless. Perhaps this later Tamar was named for Absalom's beautiful sister (*2 Sm.* 13.10ff.), who was raped by Amnon, their paternal half brother. Absalom, in turn, avenged her violation by having Amnon executed while the latter was drunk (*2 Sm.* 13.28–29), after which Absalom took refuge in the palace of his maternal grandfather for three years (*2 Sm.* 13.37). At the end of that time, Joab sent the wise woman of Tekoa to convince David to allow Absalom to return unharmed to Jerusalem. The king agreed but refused to meet him face to face for another two years. Later, Absalom organized a populist rebellion against David (*2 Sm.* 15), and Absalom had to flee Jerusalem and take refuge at Mahanaim. In the course of the civil war that ensued, Absalom was caught in a terebinth (*2 Sam.* 18.9) by his long hair (see *1 Sm.* 14.25–26). Defying David's orders to spare his beloved son, his general Joab drove three darts into Absalom's chest and then had his arms-bearers beat Absalom to death. In response to King David's inconsolable grief at the loss of his son, "the victory that day was turned into mourning for all the troops," who "stole into town that day like troops ashamed after running away in battle" (*2 Sm.* 19.3–4).

• James Stokes Ackerman, "Knowing Good and Evil: A Literary Analysis of the Court History in 2 Samuel 9–20 and 1 Kings 1–2," *Journal of Biblical Literature* 109 (1990): 41–61. Charles Conroy, *Absalom, Absalom*, Analecta Biblica, no. 81 (Rome, 1978). J. P. Fokkelman, *Narrative Art and Poetry in the Books of Samuel*, vol. 1 (Assen, 1981), pp. 99–266.

—MAYER I. GRUBER

ABSOLUTION FROM VOWS. See VOWS AND OATHS.

ABSTINENCE. See ASCETICISM.

ABUDARHAM, DAVID BEN YOSEF (14th cent.), Spanish author of a commentary on the liturgy, the encyclopedic *Sefer Abudarham*. The book draws on a vast range of sources (the Talmud, the ge'onim, and later commentators), many of which are otherwise unknown. Abudarham fully expounded the prayer book, *piyyutim*, and the Haggadah, described divergences in local customs, explained the calendar, and elucidated rabbinical regulations governing prayer and benedictions. *Sefer Abudarham* was first published in Lisbon in 1490 and frequently reprinted. A scholarly edition by S. A. Wertheimer appeared in Jerusalem in 1959 and 1963.

• Yitzhak Baer, *A History of the Jews in Christian Spain*, vol. 1 (Philadelphia, 1961–1966), p. 214. Stefan C. Reif, *Judaism and Hebrew Prayer* (Cambridge, 1993), p. 204.

ABUḤATSEIRA', YAʿAQOV. See ABI-ḤASIRA, YAʿAQOV.

ABU ʿISSA AL-ISFAHANI (8th cent.), founder of the first Jewish sect to emerge under Islam. His original name was Yitsḥaq ben Yaʿaqov, but he became known in Hebrew as ʿOvadyah (Servant of the Lord). The Iranian plateau was fertile ground for Islamic as well as Jewish sectarianism in the eighth century. Abu ʿIssa did not claim to be the Messiah but rather the last of five messengers (Abraham, Moses, Jesus, Muḥammad) who were forerunners of the Messiah. Many Persian Jews accepted his claim, and some ten thousand joined him in rebellion against the Abbasid rulers during the turbulent first half of the eighth century. After several years, the revolt was put down, and Abu ʿIssa was killed in the fighting. His followers invested him with supernatural powers and believed that he had not been killed but was hidden and would soon reappear to lead them to Erets Yisra'el. His followers, particularly Yudghan and Mushka, adhered to distinctive practices (e.g., seven daily prayers instead of three, a prohibition against divorce, a ban on the consumption of meat and wine), which combined aspects of Judaism with asceticism. Since the Isawites (or Isunians), as Abu ʿIssa's followers were known, did not diverge from normative Judaism in their observance of holidays or in the basic teachings and practices of Judaism, rabbinical authorities permitted marriage with them. The Isawites continued on the margins of an ever stronger rabbinic community, nurtured by Muslim mystical movements and expectations of the return of their leader. A handful of Isawites still existed in Damascus in the tenth century.

• Zvi Ankori, *Karaites in Byzantium: The Formative Years, 970–1100* (New York, 1959), introduction. Salo W. Baron, "Messianism and Sectarian Trends," in *A Social and Religious History of the Jews*, vol. 5 (New York, 1957), pp. 138–208. —JANE S. GERBER

ABULAFIA, AVRAHAM BEN SHEMUʿEL (13th cent.), Spanish mystic. Moved by what he called "the spirit of prophecy," Abulafia went to Rome to convert Pope Nicholas III to Judaism and was saved from being burned at the stake only by the pope's sudden death. His predictions of the imminent end of the world led to the charge of messianic pretension, for which he was persecuted by the rabbis, notably Shelomoh ben Avraham *Adret. Abulafia founded a new school of mysticism that taught methods of inducing states of illumination and mystical ecstasy through contemplation of the letters of the Hebrew *alphabet. Since these letters were the constituent elements of God's name, the path to the highest stage of illumination lay in meditation upon these coded divine names, by means of the science of letter combination (*ḥokhmat ha-tseruf*). Abulafia emphasized ecstatic experience rather than theosophical doctrines; hence, he called his method "The Path of the Names," in contrast to the path of the *sefirot*. Abulafia regarded his system as a continuation of the teaching of Maimonides, whom he admired as a kabbalist and on whose *Guide of the Perplexed* he wrote a commentary. Since Maimonides equated the highest stage of spiritual contemplation with prophecy, Abulafia also named his system "Prophetic [ecstatic] Kabbalah." Although Abulafia's work was not widely known and little of it appeared in print, his teaching greatly influenced later kabbalistic practice, especially in sixteenth-century Safed.

• Moshe Idel, *Language, Torah, and Hermeneutics in Abraham Abulafia* (Albany, N.Y., 1989). Moshe Idel, *The Mystical Experience in Abraham Abulafia* (Albany, N.Y., 1988). Moshe Idel, *Studies in Ecstatic Kabbalah* (Albany, N.Y., 1988).

ABULAFIA FAMILY, a family of Castilian Talmudists.

Me'ir ben Todros ha-Levi Abulafia (c.1170–1244), Castilian Talmudist who lived most of his life in Toledo, playing a significant role in the organizational life of his community and of Spanish Jewry as a whole. He was the first European scholar to attack Moses *Maimonides for his theory of resurrection (which Abulafia believed would be corporeal) and other doctrines, thus precipitating the bitter thirty-year *Maimonidean Controversy. Abulafia was regarded as the leading contemporary Castilian rabbinic authority, and many scholars, including Nahmanides, submitted their halakhic queries for his decision. Abulafia's main work is the Aramaic *Peratei Peratim*, which consisted of *novellae* on most of the Talmud; only the sections on *Bava' Batra'* (Salonika, 1790) and *Sanhedrin* (Salonika, 1798) have survived. Writing at great length, Abulafia carefully analyzed all possible applications of the law; he explained difficult words by reference to Arabic. He also studied *Masorah, on which he wrote *Masoret Seyag la-Torah* (Florence, 1750), and wrote poems that throw an interesting light on his period.

Todros ben Yosef Abulafia (c.1220–1298), Spanish kabbalist and chief rabbi of Castile; nephew of Me'ir ben Todros ha-Levi Abulafia. Though he was close to the court, the asceticism that he practiced as well as preached was in sharp contrast to the general licentiousness of contemporary Jewish courtiers. He denounced the laxity of the Jews of Castile and demanded high standards of morality and religious observance. Abulafia's mystical teachings stressed the gnostic elements of Kabbalah. His *Otsar ha-Kavod* (1879), a mystical commentary on Talmudic legends, is a difficult work replete with esoteric references.

• Bernard Septimus, *Hispano-Jewish Culture in Transition: The Career and Controversies of Ramah* (Cambridge, Mass., 1982).

ACADEMIES, seats of higher rabbinic learning in Talmudic times until the end of the geonic period. The Hebrew term for an academy was **yeshivah* (sitting), derived from the fixed seating arrangements for the rabbis and their pupils. The Aramaic equivalent, *metivta'*, was used in Babylonia. The first academies were in Palestine (Erets Yisra'el) and Babylonia.

Institutions for the study of both the written and oral law were held by the ancient rabbis to be so essential a feature of Jewish life that they could not conceive of a time when academies did not exist. The **aggadah* is replete with stories of the *patriarchs—especially Jacob—studying at the famous academy of Shem and Eber (cf. *Gn. Rab*. 68.11). The idealization of the academy is such that R. *Ḥama' bar Ḥanina' states, "Academies never ceased to exist in the history of our forefathers" (*Yoma'* 28b). According to rabbinic tradition, the chief exponents of the law were carried away into the Babylonian exile together with King Jehoiachin (*Git*. 88a). The main point of this assertion is to support the claim of the Babylonian academies that they preserved the authentic sacred tradition, since they did not suffer the trauma of the destruction of the Second Temple and the oppression and decline experienced by the Palestinian academies. In any case, Babylonia became a great center of Jewish learning; so much so that *Hillel, who moved from Babylonia to Palestine, is generally thought to have taken with him the rich heritage of Babylonian scholarship. There are references to an academy on the Temple mount in Jerusalem, during the Second Temple period (*Suk*. 53a; T., *San*. 7.1).

After the destruction of the Second Temple in 70 CE, the academy no less than the local synagogue replaced it as the center of Jewish religion and Jewish nationhood. The basic character of rabbinic Judaism was forged in the academy set up at *Yavneh, but there soon grew up other centers of Jewish learning. These centers usually constituted major courts of law (*battei din*) as well as places of study. Several outstanding pupils of R. *Yoḥanan ben Zakk'ai established academies at Lydda, Peqi'in, Sikhnin, Bene Beraq, and elsewhere in Palestine. But it was at Yavneh that the great work of establishing the definite form of prayer, of determining the biblical canon, and of codifying the oral law was begun.

The period of the *Bar Kokhba' Revolt (131–135) was one of great crisis for the Palestinian academies, and many scholars left for Babylonia, Rome, and elsewhere. After the rebellion, Jewish learning in Palestine was able to recover only in Galilee, where the official academies of the patriarchs were set up, first at Usha', then Sepphoris, *Beit She'arim, and *Tiberias. It was here, under the leadership of R. *Shim'on ben Gamli'el and R. *Yehudah ha-Nasi', that the *Mishnah underwent its final redaction and was put into written form.

The completion of Mishnah and *Tosefta' brought an end to the period of the tanna'im (see TANNA'). Henceforth, the work of the academies was to interpret the Mishnah and its parallel literature. This began the period of the amora'im (see AMORA'), which lasted in Palestine until the completion of the *Talmud Yerushalmi, in the academy of Tiberias at the end of the fourth century. Apart from Tiberias, the academy of R. *Abbahu in Caesarea contributed much to the Talmud Yerushalmi, and there were other centers at Sepphoris and Lydda. In the early fifth century, as a result of Byzantine oppression, the academies of Palestine began to decline, and many scholars left for Babylonia. Not until the Arab conquest in the seventh century were they to recover in any measure, but it was already too late to overtake the firmly established hegemony of the Babylonian schools.

The history of academies in Babylonia before the period of the Bar Kokhba' Revolt can only be conjectured. Definite historical information becomes available only with the Bar Kokhba' period. The students of R. *'Aqiva' fled abroad—R. *Yosei ben Ḥalafta' to Cappadocia, R. *Me'ir to Asia Minor, R. *El'azar ben Shammu'a and R. *Yoḥanan ha-Sandelar to Nisibis, and R. Nehemiah to Babylonia. The students of R. Yishma'el, R. Yonatan and R. Josiah went to Hutsal. They either established their own temporary schools or joined the few already existing ones. Of the latter, the most famous were those of Yehudah ben Bathyra, in existence before the destruction of the Second Temple, and of Ḥananyah, nephew of R. Yehoshu'a, at Nehar Pekod, established around the end of the first century. Ḥananyah had attempted to usurp the leadership of the Palestinian academies after the Bar Kokhba' Revolt by assuming their prerogatives of establishing the dates for the festivals, intercalating the years, and so forth. Only after a struggle did the students of R. 'Aqiva', who reassembled in Usha' in Palestine after the end of the persecutions, succeed in forcing Ḥananyah to relinquish this usurped authority. The students of R. Yishma'e'l, however, did not return to Palestine. Remaining in Hutsal-Nehardea in Babylonia, and at Nisibis, they provided a strong stimulus to Babylonian study. During the patriarchate of R. Yehudah ha-Nasi' in Palestine, Abba' bar Abba' was spiritual head of the Babylonian community in Nehardea. There were frequent exchanges in questions of *halakhah* between him and the scholars of Palestine. His son Shemu'el inherited this leadership and was the recognized head of the first generation of amora'im in Babylonia. Shemu'el's distinguished colleague R. Abba' Arikha', known as *Rav, returned from Palestine and established the great academy at *Sura in south Babylonia. At this time, the number of students at the academies was at its maximum. In addition to the twelve hundred regular students at the academy of Rav (*Ket*. 106a), who probably received most of their material support from the resources of the academy, there assembled twice a year in the months of Adar and Elul (see KALLAH MONTHS) students from all parts of Babylonia to hear lectures on the particular tractate assigned each half year for home study. The institution of the *kallah* months was also taken over by the academy at *Pumbedita, which had replaced the one at *Nehardea, destroyed in 259. The Pumbedita academy was removed by *Rava' to his native Maḥoza, where it was augmented by many pupils fleeing Roman persecution in Palestine. His successor *Naḥman ben Yitsḥaq returned to Pumbedita, while his contemporary *Papa' located his academy at Naresh, near Sura. During this period, the editing of the Talmud Bavli, according to the varying traditions of Pumbedita and Naresh, may be seriously considered to have begun. The close of the Talmud marks the end of the amoraic period. The savora'im (see SAVORA') continued the work of the academy, but probably limited themselves to adding explanatory notes to the Talmud and to publishing it. With the Arab conquest, the geonic period, marked by a revival of the academy of Pumbedita and Sura, was inaugurated.

As to the structure of the academy, it was headed by a **ro'sh yeshivah*, or (in Aramaic) *resh metivta'* (head of the academy), who would sit and expound to his audience through a **meturgeman* (interpreter), who was also called an amora' (*Ber.* 27b). Since not all of the students would immediately grasp what had been said, leading disciples would repeat and explain the lesson (*B. Q.* 117a). The students would then repeat the lesson orally (*'Eruv.* 54b). These leading disciples were sometimes called *reshei kallah* (leaders of the rows), possibly because they sat in the front row of the academy. The students were arranged according to knowledge and seniority, the more advanced students in the front rows and the junior ones in the back rows. Different academies had different numbers of rows. Palestinian academies appear to have had three semicircular rows, patterning themselves on the Sanhedrin, while sources tell of Babylonian academies with seven or even twenty-four rows. The *ro'sh yeshivah* was generally appointed by the sages of the academy, and on occasion, several candidates would compete for the position; the ability to make an irrefutable statement appears to have been the criterion for election (*Hor.* 14a). Ultimately, the aim of the academies was to produce scholars who were conversant in all fields of oral law and who could derive from existing *halakhah* laws applicable to new situations (*Ḥul.* 9a). In most cases, they specialized in law, but there also appear to have been academies where the emphasis was on *aggadah*.

The nature of rabbinic instruction in Babylonia during the period of the amora'im, and in particular the existence of organized rabbinic academies at this time, are the subject of much scholarly controversy. Information on these questions comes primarily from two types of sources: hints and assertions within the Talmud Bavli, and statements in geonic literature, especially in the Epistle of *Sherira' Ga'on. The reliability of these sources has, in recent years, been questioned on various grounds; in particular, some have argued that the ge'onim projected back to the amoraic period institutions with which they were familiar themselves, which had actually originated only in this later period.

During most of the geonic period, there were two leading academies: those of Sura and Pumbedita; both of these relocated to Baghdad at about the end of the ninth century but retained their names. At times, one or the other academy was temporarily split into two, when its scholars were unable to agree on the appointment of a ga'on; the academy of Sura was closed throughout most of the second half of the tenth century. A third academy was officially headed by the *exilarch; it had close ties with the academy of Sura, and it appears that when geonic sources refer to "the two academies," it is these two institutions to which they are referring.

In striking contrast to the situation during the Talmudic period, the geonic academies were well-organized institutions dominated by a small number of scholarly families. Although it was almost unheard of for a son to succeed his father as ga'on (the only exception being that of *Ha'i Ga'on, at the end of the period), many ge'onim were the sons, grandsons or other relatives of previous ge'onim. The ge'onim were generally appointed at an advanced age and served for only a few years each, presumably until they died or became unable to fulfill their duties. The selection of a ga'on was apparently left in most cases to the scholars of the academy, but the exilarch sometimes took an active role in this process, even bringing scholars from one academy to head the other in certain cases.

Each academy had a number of leading officials, beginning with the ga'on at its head and his second-in-command, the *av beit din*, or *dayyana' be-bava'*. Below these were seven scholars, each of whom was known as an *alluf* or *resh kallah*, and who were considered responsible for ten scholars apiece among the inner core of seventy, which was viewed as a continuation of the ancient *Sanhedrin. These scholars were expected to be in constant attendance at the academy and were supported by stipends, while larger numbers of students and scholars joined the academy on a temporary and less formal basis, especially in the *kallah* months. The scribe of the academy, who conducted its correspondence, was an important figure; this position was sometimes a stepping-stone to the gaonate itself.

The academies had two main sources of income: donations, which were often sent together with questions addressed to the ga'on; and taxes imposed on the Jewish communities of particular territories, which were considered to be subject to their authority. In these territories the academies exercised very considerable power, including the appointment of judges and other local officials. Elsewhere their authority was based on a voluntary relationship, founded on the widespread recognition of their preeminence as interpreters of the Talmud and its application to practical life. This found expression in the custom of addressing queries on Talmudic and legal matters to the academies; the answers (**responsa*) were dictated by the ga'on, on behalf of and with the participation of other leading members of the academy. These *responsa* are the characteristic literary vehicle of the period, and they had a major impact on later rabbinic literature.

The curriculum of the academies was based on the Talmud Bavli, although not all of its tractates were studied regularly. Normally two tractates were studied in any given year, one in each "semester," which consisted of five months during which most of the students studied a selected tractate at their homes, followed by a *kallah* month during which they gathered at the academy for communal review, discussion, and examinations. The Talmud was transmitted primarily by oral recitation, although use was sometimes made of written texts as well. In addition to the canonical Talmudic text, there were extra-Talmudic halakhic traditions which were transmitted orally in fixed formulations in the circles of the academies; these constitute one of the sources of works produced in the early geonic period: **She'iltot*, **Halakhot Pesuqot*, and **Halakhot Gedolot*.

From about the middle of the fourth century until the ninth whatever rabbinic academies may have operated in Palestine have left almost no direct traces in the available sources. This period was less of a wilderness than it once appeared, as information is now available on intellectual and literary activity on an impressive scale in various fields, but there is almost no evidence concerning an institutional site for these activities. There are some indications that Tiberias, which had been the home of the leading Palestinian academy in the amoraic period, continued to play a central role in the ninth century, although the sources do not speak unequivocally of a functioning academy.

Relatively abundant documentation concerning a central Palestinian academy becomes available only in the tenth and eleventh centuries, thanks to the material preserved in the Cairo *Genizah, which includes hundreds of documentary items bearing on that academy in this period. When viewed from the perspective of approximately contemporaneous Babylonian institutions, the Palestinian academy may be said to have combined the functions of the two leading Babylonian academies (Sura and Pumbedita) with those of the exilarchate. The head of the Palestinian academy was recognized by the Muslim authorities as the official representative of the Jewish community in the area known as the *reshut*, comprising Palestine, Lebanon, Syria, and Egypt, in temporal as well as in religious matters. In the surviving documents relating to this institution, it is the political and administrative dimensions of the academy that figure most prominently. Intellectual discussions of the sort that predominate in the writings of the Babylonian ge'onim are few and far between, although some scholars have suggested that the Genizah finds may present a misleading picture in this respect. In general, the intellectual culture of Palestine in this period presents a different picture from that of Babylonia: while the intellectual elite of Babylonia traditionally concentrated almost exclusively on the study of the Talmud and its practical application in matters of *halakhah*, literary creativity in Palestine was much more varied, encompassing such fields as **midrash*, **piyyut*, and Masoretic and related studies, in addition to halakhic and Talmudic literature.

In its internal organization, the Palestinian academy, even more than the comparable Babylonian institutions, was dominated by a small number of families (two of which were of priestly origin); it was not unusual for several members of the same immediate family to hold leading positions, simultaneously, or for a son to inherit his father's place at the head of the academy. The Palestinian academy shared with its Babylonian counterparts the titles of the two highest-ranking officials: ga'on and *av beit din*. The next five scholars in the academic hierarchy received numerical titles: The Third (in the academy), The Fourth, and so on. Another important title, with which religious or communal leaders from outside the academy were dignified, was *ḥaver* (comparable to the Babylonian titles of *alluf* and *resh kallah*).

The granting of honorary titles to outsiders was one aspect of a complex web of relationships that linked the academy with a far-flung Diaspora, including not only the *reshut*, which was officially subject to the Palestinian center, but also other territories (such as Sicily and parts of Italy) that had been included in the Byzantine empire. The heads of the academy were consulted on communal as well as legal issues and appointed religious functionaries for the communities of the *reshut*. In contrast, the academy was largely dependent on the financial support and political connections of Jewish communities outside Palestine. The most important of these was the community of Egypt.

The history of the Palestinian academy is marked by a series of struggles between factions and contenders for leadership, both within the academy itself and in the larger Jewish community; this can be interpreted in large part as reflecting the rise and decline of competing Jewish centers. The rise of the Jewish communities of the Maghreb brought into prominence families of North Africa, and they contended for the leadership of the Palestinian academy from about the 980s, producing many of its ge'onim in the eleventh century. In the course of this century, there was increasing competition from the Egyptian center, which came to a head during the tenure of *Evyatar ben Eliyyahu ha-Kohen. As a result of political and economic vicissitudes, the academy, which had operated for hundreds of years in Jerusalem and other Palestinian cities (notably Ramleh), had to move to Tyre and thence to Damascus, a step that seriously weakened its remaining claim to legitimate authority and strengthened the relative position of other contenders. By the early twelfth century the academy had moved to Fustat, where it was absorbed into the Egyptian Jewish community.

• Shraga Abramson, *Ba-Merqazim uva-Tefutsot bi-Tequfat ha-Ge'onim* (Jerusalem, 1965). Shraga Abramson, *ʿInyanot be-Sifrut ha-Ge'onim* (Jerusalem, 1974). Simḥa Assaf, *Tequfat ha-Ge'onim ve-Sifrutah* (Jerusalem, 1967). Menahem Ben-Sasson, "Shivrei Iggerot meha-Genizah: Le-Toledot Ḥiddush ha-Qesharim shel Yeshivot Bavel ʿim ha-Maʿarav," *Tarbiz* 56.2 (1987): 171–209. Robert Brody, "Sifrut ha-Ge'onim veha-Teqst ha-Talmudi," *Meḥqerei Talmud* 1 (1990): 237–303. Mark R. Cohen, "Administrative Relations between Palestinian and Egyptian Jewry during the Fatimid Period," in *Egypt and Palestine: A Millennium of Association, 868–1948*, edited by Amnon Cohen and Gabriel Baer (Jerusalem and New York, 1984), pp. 113–135. Isaiah Gafni, *Yehudei Bavel bi-Tequfat ha-Talmud* (Jerusalem, 1990). Moshe Gil, "The Babylonian Yeshivot and the Maghrib in the Early Middle Ages," *Proceedings of the American Academy for Jewish Research* 57 (1991): 69–120. Moshe Gil, *Erets Yisra'el bi-Tequfat ha-Muslamit ha-Ri'shonah, 634–1099* (Tel Aviv, 1983). Moshe Gil, *A History of Palestine, 634–1099*, translated from the Hebrew by Ethel Broido (New York, 1992). Louis Ginzberg, *Geonica* (1909; Jerusalem, 1986). David Mordecai Goodblatt, *Rabbinic Instruction in Sasanian Babylonia* (Leiden, 1975). Abraham Grossman, "Yeshivat Erets Yisra'el: Yetsiratah ha-Ruḥanit veha-Ziqah Eleiha," in *Sefer Yerushalayim: Ha-Tequfah ha-Muslamit ha-Ri'shonah, 638–1099*, edited by Joshua Prawer (Jerusalem, 1987), pp. 179–214. Benjamin Manasseh Lewin, ed., *Iggeret Rav Sherira' Ga'on* (1921; Jerusalem, 1982). Jacob Mann, *The Jews in Egypt and in Palestine under the Fatimid Caliphs*

(1920–1922; New York, 1970). Jacob Mann, *Texts and Studies in Jewish History and Literature* (Cincinnati, 1931–1935). Mordecai Margulies, comp., *Hilkhot Erets Yisra'el min ha-Genizah* (Jerusalem, 1973). Adolf Neubauer, *Mediaeval Jewish Chronicles and Chronological Notes* (1887–1895; Jerusalem, 1967). Jacob Neusner, *A History of the Jews in Babylonia*, Brown Judaic Studies, no. 62 (Chico, Calif., 1984). Samuel Abraham Poznanski, *ʿInyanim Shonim ha-Nogʿim li-Tequfat ha-Ge'onim* (Warsaw, 1909).

—DANIEL SPERBER AND ROBERT BRODY

ACADEMY ON HIGH (Heb. *yeshivah shel maʿlah*), heavenly academy. In what is possibly its oldest attestation, *Sifrei* on *Numbers* 92, the Hebrew term refers to the tribunal that is the heavenly counterpart of the earthly *Sanhedrin. Such an understanding of *yeshivah shel maʿlah* is reflected also in the formula permitting sinners to join in the *Kol Nidrei service, introduced into the Ashkenazi ritual by R. *Me'ir ben Barukh of Rothenburg in the thirteenth century, and in the prayer for adding a new name to a person who is critically ill. A heavenly court of law composed of angels is referred to in the Talmud Yerushalmi as *beit din shel maʿlah*. The scholar David M. Goodblatt has demonstrated that in most amoraic sources, *yeshivah* generally means law court rather than academy. Since, however, the earthly *beit din* or Sanhedrin in tannaitic and amoraic sources not only combined executive, legislative, and judicial functions but also performed the functions of a faculty of law (*San*. 4.3–4), *yeshivah shel maʿlah* and its Aramaic equivalent *metivta' di-rqiʿa* (heavenly *metivta'*) frequently refer to a heavenly college of rabbinic studies, admission to which is rewarded to the souls of those who on earth were teachers, scholars, or persons who provided financial support to Torah scholars (*Pes*. 53b; *B. M.* 85b–86a). Origen's (185–253 CE) notion of a heavenly academy lends support to the latter view of the *yeshivah shel maʿlah*, which is reflected also in the Zohar and cognate literature. Kabbalistic sources distinguish between the *metivta' di-rqiʿa*, presided over by *Metatron, and the Academy on High, presided over by God. According to these sources the heavenly academy is subdivided into academic departments, such as the Academy of Moses, the Academy of Aaron, and the Academy of Love. In the Zoharic scheme only the souls of males are admitted to these departments, while women assemble on the eves of Sabbaths and festivals for classes in the knowledge of God taught by Miriam (Zohar, "Shelaḥ Lekhah," p. 163a).

• Henry A. Fischel, "Story and History: Observations on Greco-Roman Rhetoric and Pharisaism," in *American Oriental Society, Middle West Branch, Semi-Centennial Volume*, edited by Denis Sinor (Bloomington, 1969), pp. 80–81. David M. Goodblatt, *Rabbinic Instruction in Sasanian Babylonia*, Studies in Judaism in Late Antiquity, vol. 9 (Leiden, 1975), pp. 68, 85. Gershom Gerhard Scholem, "The Sources of the Legend of Rabbi Gaddiel the Babe in Kabbalistic Literature," in *Le-ʿAgnon Shai*, 2d ed., edited by Dov Sadan and Efraim Elimelech Urbach (Jerusalem, 1966), pp. 290–305.

—MAYER I. GRUBER

ACCENTS, signs employed in the biblical text to mark the cantillation for the public reading of the Torah, *haftarah*, and Five Scrolls; in Hebrew, *taʿamei ha-miqra'*, ([signs indicating] the sense of the reading) or *neginot* ([signs of] the melodies); in popular (Yiddish) terminology, **trop* signs. Like the vowel signs (see ALPHABET, HEBREW; MASORAH; VOCALIZATION), accents were introduced by the Masoretes in the eighth and ninth centuries CE. However, they were not an innovation; their purpose was to represent graphically, and to fix permanently, a tradition that had existed orally for many centuries, references to which are found throughout Talmudic literature. The accents exist in three different systems: Babylonian, Palestinian, and Tiberian; less developed systems exist among the Samaritans. The Tiberian system is the most elaborate and, as in all matters of Masorah, became authoritative; it has been used exclusively since the early medieval period. The accent signs are found in all printed Bibles, and in manuscripts they are placed both above and below the letters of the text, alongside the vowel signs. Torah scrolls, however, have neither vowel nor accent signs; the reader is required to learn the correct pronunciation and cantillation in advance of the public reading in the synagogue.

The cantillation of the Bible according to the masoretic accents is primarily a system of correctly dividing the text into its constituent parts, so that the content, as understood by the tradition, is accurately transmitted. Each sign represents a fixed melody that the listener comes to recognize as pausal or connective. Thus, every verse of the Bible, whatever its content, has the same musical theme; the variations are a result of length, sentence structure, and internal division.

The Tiberian system has two sets of signs, one for the strictly poetic books (*Psalms*, *Proverbs*, and the poetic portions of *Job*), and one for the remaining prose books. The prose-book accents are still used in the public chanting in the synagogue, and precise musical values for each sign are preserved by Jewish communities throughout the world. In the elaborate Ashkenazi tradition, different musical modes exist for Torah, *haftarah*, *Esther*, *Lamentations*, festival scrolls, and High Holy Day readings, even though all of these belong to the same prose-book system of accent signs. The musical traditions of the poetic books have fallen into disuse.

Each set of accents consists of disjunctives and conjunctives, referred to figuratively as masters and servants. The disjunctives, which include the verse-end mark (*sof pasuq* or *silluq*), indicate the divisions. They are traditionally known by terms such as emperors, kings, dukes, and counts. They occur according to a precise binary system of continuous dichotomy. Each verse is divided into two parts wherever its content best allows. The two parts may be of unequal length: the system is not quantitative but literary. Each of the two parts is, if long enough, subdivided, in turn, into two; and so on, until there remain no word groups long enough to subdivide. The concluding word of each division is marked with a disjunctive accent, in descending hierarchical order. The sections obtained by the first dichotomy conclude with the two emperors, *etnaḥta'* and *sof pasuq*, respectively; each of the emperors, if the section it concludes subdivides again, shares its domain with one or more kings; each king shares its section with one or more dukes; and so on. The remaining words, which mark no divisions, are given conjunctive accents; these, too, occur in precise order, each master having his own fixed servants. Thus, every word has a musical notation, with the exception of hyphenated words, which make up a single musical unit. The disjunctives mark both verse division and musical intonation, while the conjunctives are of musical importance only. None of the accent signs is equivalent to any of the modern punctuation marks (period, comma, semicolon, etc.); each one varies in syntactical significance from one verse to the next.

The accents serve another purpose as well. They are intoned on the syllable that receives the stress, thus preserving correct pronunciation and meaning. For historical reasons, however, some of the signs are not actually written (or printed) on the stressed consonant, and the reader must employ other rules to determine which syllable is to receive the musical accentuation. The rabbis of the Talmud, as well as many of the traditional commentators, attach significance to the verse division as represented by the accents, although only in recent times has the system begun to be understood in all its fine detail. Avraham ibn Ezra admonished the student to pay no heed to any interpretation that is not in accord with the accents, and as a general rule this warning was observed. Yet Ibn Ezra himself, as well as most other commentators, both ancient and modern, occasionally explained the text in a manner contrary to the accent signs.

• Mordechai Breuer, *Ta'amei ha-Miqra'* (Jerusalem, 1982). Miles B. Cohen, *The System of Accentuation in the Hebrew Bible* (Minneapolis, 1969). S. Kogut, *Ha-Miqra' ben Te'amim le-Farshanut* (Jerusalem, 1994). William Wickes, *Two Treatises on the Accentuation of the Old Testament* (Oxford, 1881, 1887; repr. New York, 1970). Israel Yeivin, *Introduction to the Tiberian Masorah* (Missoula, Mont., 1980), pp. 157–274.

—BARUCH J. SCHWARTZ

ACCULTURATION. See ASSIMILATION.

ACHAN, member of the tribe of Judah during the period of Joshua's conquest of Canaan (also called Achar in *1 Chronicles* 2.7). After the men of Ai unexpectedly routed the Israelites on the battlefield (*Jos.* 7.2–5), God informed Joshua that an Israelite had stolen from the *ḥerem* (the proscribed spoil) from the conquest of Jericho and that he, the Lord, would not return to be with Israel until they had purged from their midst the perpetrator of this sin (*Jos.* 7.10–15). Lots were then cast, and Achan finally confessed to having stolen "a fine Shinar mantle, two hundred shekels of silver, and a wedge of gold weighing fifty shekels" (*Jos.* 7.16–21). He and his entire immediate family were then taken together with the forbidden booty to a valley, where they were burned and stoned by all Israel (*Jos.* 7.22–25). God's anger was then appeased, but the resulting huge mound of stones used in Achan's stoning remained as a landmark for this place, which was named the Valley of Achor (*Jos.* 7.26). The story is a powerful example of the doctrine of communal retribution—an individual commits a sin and all Israel is punished—and offers an etiological explanation for the name of the Valley of Achor.

• Robert G. Boling, *Joshua*, The Anchor Bible (Garden City, N.Y., 1982), pp. 216–230. Moshe Garsiel, *Biblical Names: A Literary Study of Midrashic Derivations and Puns* (Ramat Gan, 1991), pp. 20, 142. Leonard J. Greenspoon, "Achan," in *Anchor Bible Dictionary*, vol. 1 (New York, 1992), p. 54. Carolyn J. Pressler, "Achor," in *Anchor Bible Dictionary*, vol. 1 (New York, 1992), p. 56.

—CHAIM COHEN

ACOSTA, URIEL (1585–1640), religious skeptic born in Portugal of *Marrano parents. His study of the Hebrew Bible led him to doubt Christianity; to live openly as a Jew, he escaped with his family to Amsterdam, where he discovered, however, that the Judaism to which he had converted was different from the idea he had formed of it during his studies. Finding many of the rituals unbearable and recognizing only his literal understanding of the Hebrew Bible as Jewish, he attacked orally and in print (*Examen dos tradiçoens phariseas conferidas con a ley escrita* [1624]) both the general rabbinic tradition and the particular doctrines of immortality and resurrection. The communal authorities found his attacks intolerable not only as heresy but also as endangering the Jews' recently legitimized status in Dutch society. As a result he was excommunicated from Judaism. Poverty and isolation forced him to recant (1633), but he soon repeated his attacks on rabbinic Judaism, called himself a deist who followed a natural law, and was again put under ban. In 1640 he recanted once more but was required to subject himself to flogging (the usual penitential precondition for the lifting of the ban) and public penance. Having undergone the ordeal, he wrote a short autobiography (English translation in L. Schwartz, *Memories of My People* [1963], pp. 84–94) and then committed suicide. His tragic fate and abortive spiritual odyssey have inspired several novels and dramas by modern Jewish authors.

• Yoshuah Barjitzchak, *Uriel da Costa* (The Hague, 1962). Josef Kastein, *Uriel da Costa* (Vienna, 1935). Jean Pierre Osier, *D'Uriel da Costa à Spinoza* (Paris, 1983).

ACQUISITION. The methods of acquiring property, known in Hebrew as *qinyan*, lie at the heart of both proprietary and contractual rights in Jewish civil law. A formal *qinyan* is necessary in order to effect the transfer of ownership of both movable and immovable property. Among the methods of acquiring movable property is lifting (*hagbahah*) or pulling (*meshikhah*) the object that is being acquired. Pulling is used when very heavy objects or livestock are involved (*B. M.* 8b; *B. B.* 86a). Grasping an object (*mesirah*) is a valid form of *qinyan* when it is done at the behest of the transferor (*B. B.* 75b). These methods are derived from the concept of "acquisition through one's courtyard" (*qinyan ḥatser*), according to which any object that comes into a person's possession and control is legally acquired by that individual. The same rule applies to property within a radius of four cubits around a person, provided that the person is capable of exercising control over the object in question (*B. M.* 11a). Buried treasure, therefore, belongs to the finder, since the owner of the courtyard does not know of its existence and does not, therefore, have any control over it (*B. M.* 25b). Immovable property is acquired by an act of ownership (*ḥazaqah*), such as fencing a field, locking a house, or making improvements to the property (*B. B.* 42a; Maimonides, *Hilkhot Mekhirah* 1.8). There are other methods that do not effect the legal transfer of property but simply indicate the intention of the parties to conclude a transaction. These methods include acquisition by money; deed (*shetar*); barter (*ḥalifin*); the symbolic exchange of property (*qinyan sudar*); the acquisition of movables incidental to land (*qinyan agav qarqa'*); and a handshake and the transfer of a key.

In principle, Jewish law does not recognize a simple parol contract; hence, contractual obligations can only be created using the same method by which ownership rights in property are acquired, namely, *qinyan*. The transition from the classical forms of tangible *qinyan* to more abstract methods probably reflects the need to solve the problem of the legal, as opposed to the ethical (*B. M.* 49a), non recognition of purely oral undertakings in Jewish law.

• J. David Bleich, *Contemporary Halakhic Problems* (New York, 1989), pp. 332–334, 360–361. Menachem Elon, *Jewish Law: History, Sources, Principles* (Philadelphia, 1994), pp. 580–584. Menachem Elon, *The Principles of Jewish Law* (Jerusalem, 1975), pp. 205–210. Isaac Herzog, *The Main Institutions of Jewish Law*, vol. 1 (London, 1965), pp. 137–200.

–DANIEL SINCLAIR

ACRONYMS. Though there may be a few isolated and dubious instances of acronyms in the Bible (for example, the use of the Hebrew letter *yud* to represent the name of God), acronyms were commonly employed in Talmudic literature as an exegetical tool in expounding the *aggadah*, although they are referred to by name only once in the Mishnah, in *Shabbat* 12.5. The use of acronyms is the thirtieth of Eli'ezer ben Yosei ha-Galili's thirty-two hermeneutic rules. In *Genesis* 41.43, when the people cry out the word *avrekh* before Joseph, it is interpreted as "*av* be-ḥokhmah *rakh* be-shanim" (father in wisdom [though] tender in years; *Sifrei* on *Dt.* 1). Acronyms are used extensively as a tool in the interpretation of dreams (*Ber.* 57a) and analogously in Hellenistic writings. They also appear frequently in kabbalistic literature. From the medieval period on, acronyms commonly were used to indicate personal names, such as *Rashi* for *R*abbi *Sh*elomoh ben *Yi*tsḥaq and *Rambam* for *R*abbi *M*osheh *b*en *M*aimon. They are now employed in Modern Hebrew, from slang to technical and scientific terms. See also NOTARIQON.

• Shmuel Ashkenazi and Dov Jarden, *Otsar Rashei Tevot* (Jerusalem, 1966). Isaac Avineri, *Yad ha-Lashon* (Tel Aviv, 1964), pp. 108–109, 383–385. Saul Lieberman, *Hellenism in Jewish Palestine*, 2d ed. (New York, 1962), pp. 68–75. Naphtali H. Tur-Sinai, *Peshuto shel Miqra'*, 2d ed. (Jerusalem, 1967), p. 262.

–SHALOM PAUL

ACROSTICS, literary devices, employed especially in verse. Alphabetic acrostics are found in the Bible (e.g., *Ps.* 34; *Ps.* 119; *Prv.* 31.10–31; *Lam.* 1–4). Acrostics appeared frequently in Hebrew literature from the Byzantine period on, especially in the liturgy (e.g., Ein Ke'loheinu, An'im Zemirot, the *seliḥot* prayers), where this device facilitated the memorization of prayers and the organization of *piyyutim* (particularly important before the invention of the printing press). From the sixth century on, acrostics were often based on the author's name (e.g., Lekhah Dodi) or, less frequently, on a biblical quotation. Some translations, especially of the alphabetic confessional litanies in the modern liberal prayer books, replicate an acrostic construction in English.

• Ismar Elbogen, *Jewish Liturgy: A Comprehensive History*, translated by Raymond P. Scheindlin (Philadelphia, 1993). Joseph Heinemann, *Prayer in the Talmud*, Studia Judaica, Bd. 9 (Berlin and New York, 1977), pp. 139–150, 240–243. Saul Lieberman, *Hellenism in Jewish Palestine*, 2d ed. (New York, 1962), pp. 78–82. Moritz Steinschneider, *Jewish Literature from the Eighth to the Eighteenth Century*, 2d ed. (New York, 1965), pp. 149–151.

–PETER LENHARDT

ACTS OF ALEXANDRIAN MARTYRS, a group of disparate texts, written between the first and the early third century CE, and known solely from papyri fragments found in Egypt. The texts usually take the form of a protocol of a conversation that supposedly took place between an Alexandrian patriot and a hostile Roman emperor, a conversation that often ends with the former's execution. In addition to their strong anti-Roman tendencies, some of these texts also display distinctly anti-Jewish sentiments. One text contains a description, from an Alexandrian point of view, of a dispute between a Jewish embassy, headed by *Agrippa I, and an Alexandrian embassy in front of Emperor Claudius I (41–54), a dispute also described from the Jewish point of view by *Philo. In another text an Alexandrian leader accuses Trajan of having a council "full of impious Jews." While the historicity of some of the incidents described in these texts is less than certain and the claims voiced by their protagonists can never be taken at face value, *Acts* supplies important data on the Jews' life in Roman Alexandria, and especially on the anti-Jewish feelings common in at least some Greco-Egyptian circles in that city.

• Herbert A. Musurillo, *The Acts of the Pagan Martyrs* (Oxford, 1954; repr. Salem, N.H., 1988). Victor (Avigdor) Tcherikover and Alexander Fuks, *Corpus Papyrorum Iudaicarum*, vol. 2 (Cambridge, Mass., 1960), nos. 154–159, pp. 55–107.

–GIDEON BOHAK

ADADI, AVRAHAM (1800–1874), North African rabbinical authority born in Tripoli, Libya, where he helped devise a comprehensive system of popular education for the young. To support this, he and the other rabbinical authorities issued the *gabella taqqanah*, an ordinance requiring all Jews in the community to contribute 3/1,000th of their income. He moved to Erets Yisra'el and was one of the rabbis sent abroad as an emissary by the Jews of Safed to collect money from the Jews of Egypt, Iraq, Persia, Damascus, and Morocco. A member of the Safed *beit din* from 1838 to 1874, Adadi was a noted Talmudist, expert not only in the text but also in the historical differences between the tanna'im and amora'im. He also wrote on the customs of the Jews of Tripoli. His responsa, *Va-Yiqra' Avraham* (Leghorn, 1864), used the works of two noted scholars—Yehudah *Ayash of Algiers and Ḥayyim Yosef David *Azulai—who also investigated local customs. He paid special attention to questions of divorce, although his *Ha-Shomer Emet* (printed with *Va-Yiqra' Avraham* [Livorno, 1848; repr. Brooklyn, N.Y., 1992]) was largely devoted to the writing of Torah scrolls. *Ha-Shomer Emet* also contains an autobiography of Adadi on pages 5–10.

• Nahum Slouschz, *Massa'i be-'Erets Luv*, vol. 1 (Tel Aviv, 1937), pp. 24ff. Abraham Ya'ari, *Sheluḥei Erets Yisra'el* (Jerusalem, 1977), pp. 675ff.

–SHALOM BAR-ASHER

ADAM (אָדָם; human), biblical designation of the first human in *Genesis* 1–5, *1 Chronicles* 1.1, and possibly *Job* 28; progenitor of the human species; also a collective reference to humankind (*Gn.* 1.27) and to each and every person individually (e.g., *Lv.* 1.2). In Hebrew, the term never appears in the plural; the word *people*, both male and female, is frequently expressed by *benei adam* (the sons of Adam; e.g., *Ps*. 36.8). In *Genesis* 6, *benot ha-adam* (the daughters of the human) designates women. In Phoenician, on the other hand, the masculine plural *adamim* (men) is contrasted with *ashot* (woman).

Adam's origin is related in two distinct biblical accounts. *Genesis* 1.26–30 is a brief narrative. Both male and female humans were created in the divine image by God on the sixth day of Creation; they were to multiply and rule over all life. The biblical account in *Genesis* 2–3 is more comprehensive. God fashioned man out of earth, breathed into his nostrils the breath of life, and charged him with tending and keeping the garden of *Eden. *Eve, Adam's helpmeet, was created from his rib. Succumbing to temptation, they ate of Eden's forbidden *tree of knowledge of good and evil, for which they were expelled and punished. Critical scholarship recognizes here the narratives of two different authors, possibly two ancient Israelite epic tales. The narratives are projected from two different points of view. The first portrays humanity against the background of universal creation, while the second evaluates the universe from the viewpoint of man. Both, however, are alike in presenting humans as Godlike, and both are purely monotheistic in conception. There are certain affinities with Mesopotamian and Egyptian tales, but the biblical story is unique in the grandeur of its ethical concept.

In *Leviticus* and other Pentateuchal texts assigned by the documentary hypothesis to the Priestly source and holiness codes, the term *adam* is frequently used to refer to a person of either sex in regard to obligations that apply equally to men and women (*Lv*. 24.17; *Nm*. 5.6).

Some readers interpret the statement that woman was created from the rib of Adam (*Gn*. 2.22) as a suggestion that womankind is subordinate or was an afterthought in the scheme of creation. S. N. Kramer, however, sees in the assertion that the woman who is called Eve (Ḥavvah [She Who Makes Live]) was created from the rib of Adam a reflection of the pun found in the Sumerian myth of Enki and Ninhursag. The goddess created for the healing of Enki's rib is Nintu, which means "lady of the rib" and "lady who makes life." Rashi follows various *midrashim* in construing the Hebrew *tselaʿ* in *Genesis* 2.22 not as *rib* but as *side* and sees in the apparent contradiction between *Genesis* 1.27, in which *adam* is created "male and female," and *Genesis* 2, in which woman is created from the side of Adam, reference to humankind having been created in two phases. In the first phase, man and woman were joined together like Siamese twins; while in the second phase, they were separated into two sides. This accounts for the urge of persons of both sexes to form lifelong attachments with members of the opposite sex, thereby reuniting with their missing sides (*Gn*. 2.24).

Elaborations of the Adam story are found in the postbiblical Apocrypha and pseudepigrapha. Patristic writings stress Adam's fall and original sin. Talmudic treatment, some of it also reflected in the Qur'an, discusses God's purpose in creating man and also man's relations to the heavenly hosts as well as to lower forms of creation. Kabbalists maintained that Adam received a revelation from God, the secrets of which were preserved by the mystics, and thus they speak of a mystical Adam, the *Adam Qadmon.

• Phyllis A. Bird, "'Male and Female He Created Them': Gen. 1:27b in the Context of the Priestly Account of Creation," *Harvard Theological Review* 74 (1981): 129–159. Albert van den Branden, "La Creation de l'homme et de la femme d'après le document Jahviste," *Bibbia e Oriente* 32 (1990): 193–208. Hans Goedicke, "Adam's Rib," in *Biblical and Related Studies Presented to Samuel Iwry*, edited by Ann Kort and Scott Morschauser (Winona Lake, Ind., 1985), pp. 73–76. Mayer I. Gruber, *The Motherhood of God and Other Studies*, South Florida Studies in the History of Judaism, no. 57 (Atlanta, 1992). Arvid Schou Kapelrud, "You Shall Surely Not Die," in *History and Traditions of Early Israel: Studies Presented to Eduard Nielsen*, edited by André Lemaire and Benedikt Otzen, Supplements to Vetus Testamentum, vol. 50 (Leiden, 1993), pp. 50–61. Samuel Noah Kramer, *History Begins at Sumer* (Garden City, N.Y., 1959). Fritz Maass, "Adham," in *Theological Dictionary of the Old Testament*, vol. 1 (Grand Rapids, 1974), pp. 75–87. Paul Morris and Deborah F. Sawyer, eds., *A Walk in the Garden* (Sheffield, Eng., 1992). Phyllis Trible, *God and the Rhetoric of Sexuality* (Philadelphia, 1978).

—MAYER I. GRUBER

ADAM AND EVE, BOOK OF. See BOOK OF ADAM AND EVE.

ADAM QADMON (אָדָם קַדְמוֹן; Primordial Man), kabbalistic symbol of the world of the *sefirot*, wherein the divine macrocosm is pictured in the image of the human microcosm, just as the material form of man, the creature, is held to reflect the spiritual form of existence of God, the creator. The notion of a mystical Primordial Man seems to reflect earlier, gnostic types of speculation. The term *adam qadmon* is found in the *tiqqunim* of the Zohar, whereas the Zohar itself uses the term *adam dele-ʿela'* (celestial man). According to Yitsḥaq *Luria, who developed this symbol in an original way, Adam Qadmon is the first configuration of the divine light flowing from God, the *Ein Sof, into the primordial space made possible by **tsimtsum* (i.e., the withdrawing of the creator within himself). Adam Qadmon is thus the highest form of the manifestation of the divinity after the process of *tsimtsum*. The *sefirot* come into existence as divine lights breaking out from the eyes, ears, nose, and mouth of Adam Qadmon. The Lurianic doctrine of **tiqqun* is based upon the analogy between the biblical Adam, on the anthropological plane, and Adam Qadmon, on the ontological plane. Thus man before his fall is a kind of cosmic being reflecting the divine totality as symbolized in Adam Qadmon.

• Gershom Gerhard Scholem, *Major Trends in Jewish Mysticism* (New York, 1995). Gershom Gerhard Scholem, *On the Kabbalah and Its Symbolism* (New York, 1972).

ADAR (אֲדָר), name of Assyrian–Babylonian origin for the twelfth month of the religious year, sixth of the civil year. Its zodiacal sign is Pisces. The feast of *Purim, which falls on 14 Adar (and Shushan Purim, which falls on 15 Adar), imparts a festive character to the entire month: "When Adar enters, joy increases" (*Taʿan*. 29a). The Second Temple was dedicated on 3 Adar (*Ezr*. 6.14–16). According to rabbinical tradition, 7 Adar is the anniversary of both the birth and the death of Moses (*Meg*. 13b) and was a date for rejoicing—or alternatively fasting—among various Jewish communities (the fast day was observed in 17th-cent. Turkey, Italy, and northern Europe, and the custom spread to Hasidic circles). Nine

Adar was said to be the date of the split between the school of Hillel and the school of Shamm'ai and was decreed a fast day. Thirteen Adar was called Nicanor Day to mark the anniversary of *Judah the Maccabee's defeat of Syrian general Nicanor in 161 BCE; originally it was observed as a festival but later became the Fast of Esther (see TAʿANIT ESTER). Sixteen Adar was designated a feast day; according to tradition, Nehemiah recommenced the rebuilding of the walls of Jerusalem on that day. Twenty Adar, the date of *Ḥoni ha-Meʿaggel's miraculous invocation of rain, was observed at one time as a feast day. In leap years, Adar Sheni (second month of Adar, also called Ve-Adar) is inserted after the month of Adar (which in this case is called Adar Ri'shon, first month of Adar; see CALENDAR). During such years, most observances (including *bar* and *bat mitsvah*) normally held in Adar are moved to Adar Sheni. When a death occurs in Adar in an ordinary year, the **yortsayt* is observed in the first month of Adar even in a leap year. Adar Sheni is intercalated seven times in a nineteen-year lunar cycle in order to bring the Hebrew calendar into line with the general solar calendar. Adar is twenty-nine days in length in an ordinary year, thirty days in a leap year. Adar Sheni always has twenty-nine days.

• Nathan Bushwick, *Understanding the Jewish Calendar* (New York, 1989). George Zinberg, *Jewish Calendar Mystery Dispelled* (New York, 1963). —CHAIM PEARL

ADAR, SEVENTH OF. See ZAYIN BA-'ADAR.

ADASS JESHURUN. See ADASS JISROEL.

ADASS JISROEL (Congregation of Israel) or Adass Jeshurun, names chosen by strictly Orthodox German congregations that left Reform-dominated communities to become independent separatist congregations (*Austrittsgemeinden*). Samson Raphael *Hirsch took the lead in Frankfurt, renaming his congregation Adass Jeschurun (1851), and this example was followed in Cologne (1867). New York City's Kahal Adath Jeshurun (the "Breuer Shul," in Manhattan's Washington Heights neighborhood) is a direct successor. Most of these breakaway synagogues preferred the name Adass Jisroel or Adass Jeshurun as an expression of their concept of "authentic [Torah-true] Judaism." They were established in Berlin (1869), Vienna (1897), London (1911), Königsberg (1913), and other Jewish centers, but they represented only a small segment of the Neo-Orthodox movement (see NEO-ORTHODOXY).

• Alexander Carlebach, *Adass Yeshurun of Cologne* (Belfast, 1964). Hermann Schwab, *The History of Orthodox Jewry in Germany*, translated by Irene R. Birnbaum (London, 1950). Max Mordechai Sinasohn, ed., *Adas Jisroel Berlin* (Jerusalem, 1966). —GABRIEL A. SIVAN

ADDA' BAR AHAVAH (3d cent.), Babylonian amora', to be distinguished from the fourth century Babylonian amora' of the same name (cf. *B. B.* 22a–b). He was reputedly born on the day of the death of R. Yehudah ha-Nasi' (*Qid.* 72a–b), and it was claimed that his son was born circumcised (*Shab.* 135a). His piety and his miraculous powers (e.g., Y., *Taʿan.* 3.11, 67a) were legendary; it was even believed that his very presence could prevent calamity (cf. *Taʿan.* 20b). He was a student of Rav at Sura (Y., *Shab.* 1.2, 3a) and was known there especially for his halakhic rulings. The *Baraiyta' de-Rav Adda'*, a work on intercalation (cited as late as the 14th cent., but now lost), is attributed to him. He believed his longevity to be the fruit of his lifelong godly habits, which included religious zeal, discipline, respect, kindness, social grace, and self-control (Y., *Taʿan.* 3.13, 67a).

• Wilhelm Bacher, *Die Agada der babylonischen Amoräer* (1913; Hildesheim, 1967). Aaron Hyman, *Toledot Tanna'im ve-'Amora'im* (1910; Jerusalem, 1987). —MICHAEL L. BROWN

ADDIR BI-MELUKHAH (אַדִּיר בִּמְלוּכָה; Mighty in Kingship), eight-stanza, alphabetical acrostic hymn listing divine epithets and based on a legend in *Genesis Rabbah* 6.2. It was introduced by Ashkenazim into the Pesaḥ Haggadah in the Middle Ages. Addir bi-Melukhah was probably written in France or Germany, although the date is obscure. It is also known from its refrain as Ki Lo Na'eh (For to Him, Praise Is Due). See also ADDIR HU'.

• Menahem Kasher, *Haggadah Shelemah*, 3d ed. (Jerusalem, 1967).

ADDIR HU' (אַדִּיר הוּא; Mighty Is He), alphabetic acrostic hymn containing a prayer for the speedy rebuilding of the Temple. In the Avignon rite it was recited on all festivals; it was adopted into the Haggadah of Pesaḥ in fifteenth-century Germany. Originally Addir Hu' was sung only on the second Seder night and *Addir bi-Melukhah on the first, but since the eighteenth century both hymns have been sung on both nights, especially in the Ashkenazi tradition.

• Ernst Daniel Goldschmidt, *Haggadah shel Pesaḥ* (Jerusalem, 1960), p. 97. Abraham Zebi Idelsohn, *Jewish Music: Its Historical Development* (New York, 1992). —PETER LENHARDT

ADDITIONAL SERVICE. See MUSAF.

ADDITIONAL SOUL. See NESHAMAH YETERAH.

ADEL. See ODEL.

ADENI, SHELOMOH (1567–1626), commentator on the *Mishnah. He was born in Sanaa, Yemen, but as a young child went with his family to Safed in Erets Yisra'el. Subsequently he and his family moved to Jerusalem. He studied Kabbalah with R. Ḥayyim *Vital and *halakhah* with R. Betsal'el Ashkenazi. In 1592 Adeni settled in Hebron, where he earned his livelihood teaching children. He is best known for his commentary on the Mishnah, *Melekhet Shelomoh* (Vilna, 1905), to which he brings an extensive knowledge of both Talmuds, the Midrash, and later rabbinical authorities. Especially important was his determination of the Mishnah text based on old manuscripts preserved in Erets Yisra'el. He began his work on the Mishnah when he was twenty-two and continued until his death. He also wrote sacred poetry.

• Yehuda Ratzabi, "R. Shelomoh Adeni ve-Ḥibburo *Melekhet Shelomoh*," *Sinai* 106 (1990): 243–254. —SHALOM BAR-ASHER

ADIABENE, a small kingdom in northern Mesopotamia (roughly the region of the Little Zab and Great Zab rivers in present-day Iraq), whose ruler Izates, along with his mother, Helena, and his brother, Monobaz, converted to Judaism in approximately 45 CE. Their conversion and subsequent attachment to the Jewish people are described in great detail by Josephus (*Antiquities of the Jews* 20.2–4) and are also mentioned several times in rabbinic literature (e.g., *Naz*. 3.6; T., *Suk*. 1.1; *Gn. Rab*. 46.11). According to Josephus, Helena and Izates learned from itinerant Jews how to worship God in the Jewish manner, and Izates even underwent circumcision, in spite of his mother's fear that his subjects would object to their king's involvement in foreign rites. Helena subsequently went to Jerusalem, where her generosity and royal wealth helped alleviate a severe famine and earned her the gratitude of the Jewish masses (cf. T., *Pe'ah* 4.18). Following Izates' death, Helena returned to Adiabene. When she, too, died, Monobaz, Izates' successor to the throne, sent Izates' and Helena's bones to be buried in a royal sepulcher she had prepared in Jerusalem, known today as the Tomb of Kings, north of the Old City of Jerusalem. —GIDEON BOHAK

'ADLAYADA' (Aram.; עַדְלָיָדַע), Purim carnival. This name is derived from the rabbinic remark that on Purim a man should revel until he does not know (*'ad de-la' yada'*) to distinguish between "blessed be Mordecai" and "cursed be Haman" (*Meg*. 7.2). The name is given to Purim-carnival processions held in Israel.

• Daniel Alder, "Drinking on Purim: When to Say When," *Judaism* 40.1 (Winter 1991): 6–15. Toby Blum-Dobkin, "The Landsberg Carnival: Purim in a Displaced Persons Center," in *Purim, the Face and the Mask: Essays and Catalogue of an Exhibition* (New York, 1979), pp. 52–58. Cedric Ginsberg, "Purim: The Festival of Fun," *Jewish Affairs* 48.1 (1992): 49–54.

ADLER, FELIX (1851–1933), social, educational, and religious reformer. Adler was born in Alzey, Germany, and immigrated to the United States at age six, when his father, R. Samuel Adler, accepted the pulpit of New York's prestigious Reform Temple Emanu-El. Having graduated from Columbia University in 1870, Adler returned to Germany to study at the Universities of Berlin and Heidelberg from 1870 to 1873. Under the impact of historicism, evolution, Bible criticism, and Neo-Kantianism, he broke intellectually with theism and Judaism. He formulated a belief in moral law independent of a personal deity, which he insisted had to find expression in activist social reform.

Following a brief tenure at Cornell University from 1873 to 1876, Adler established the New York Society for Ethical Culture in 1876. Under his leadership and fired by his commitment to applied social ethics, the society pioneered such ventures as a free kindergarten, a free district nursing program, a workingman's lyceum, and a workingman's school (the Ethical Culture School). Adler served as a mentor for mostly non-Jewish leaders, who established other societies across the country, resulting in a national and ultimately international Ethical Cultural movement, dedicated to alleviating the problems of industrialization and urbanization.

Perceived as a renegade by the Jewish establishment in the early decades, Adler was admired by many Jews. He chaired the National Child Labor Committee from 1904 to 1921, founded the *International Journal of Ethics* in 1920, and was appointed professor of political and social ethics at Columbia University in 1902. However, Alder's departure from Judaism rankled, even as he spoke out forcefully against antisemitism. In particular, his opposition to Jewish nationalism led to tensions with Zionists.

His main works are *Creed and Deed* (New York, 1877), *The Religion of Duty* (New York, 1905), *An Ethical Philosophy of Life* (New York, 1918), and *The Reconstruction of the Spiritual Ideal* (New York, 1918).

• Horace L. Friess, *Felix Adler and Ethical Culture: Memories and Studies* (New York, 1981). Robert S. Guttchen, *Felix Adler* (New York, 1974). Benny Kraut, *From Reform Judaism to Ethical Culture: The Religious Evolution of Felix Adler* (Cincinnati, 1979). David S. Muzzey, *Ethics as a Religion*, 2d ed. (New York, 1967). Howard B. Radest, *Toward Common Ground: The Story of the Ethical Societies in the United States* (New York, 1969). —BENNY KRAUT

ADLER, NATAN (1741–1800), German rabbi and kabbalist. A recognized scholar at the age of twenty, he founded a *yeshivah* in his native Frankfurt am Main, which attracted many pupils. While engaged in several branches of Torah studies, his particular leaning was toward Kabbalah. He and a group of his followers conducted prayer services in his home using a different rite (the prayer book of Yitsḥaq Luria, recited in a Sephardi pronunciation) from that accepted in German communities. This aroused the anger of the community heads, and in 1782 a ban was placed on the *minyan* and sanctions were placed on Adler. After spending three years in Boskovice, Moravia (1782–1785), he returned to Frankfurt, reopened his *yeshivah*, and restarted his *minyan*, which led to a renewal of the ban, but this was lifted during his last fatal illness. He never published any works, but the notes he wrote in the margins of his Mishnah volumes were later published as *Mishnat Rabbi Natan* (Frankfurt am Main, 1862). The Ḥatam Sofer (see SOFER FAMILY) was his pupil.

• Josef Unna, "Nathan Hacohen Adler (1741–1800)," in *Guardians of Our Heritage (1724–1953)*, edited by Leo Jung (New York, 1958), pp. 165–

ADLER FAMILY, a family of British rabbis.

Nathan Marcus Adler (1803–1890) became chief rabbi of the British empire in 1845. He was born and officiated in Hanover until moving to England. Thanks to his firm leadership, nationwide pastoral tours, and enlightened Orthodoxy, Anglo-Jewry remained traditional in outlook. He established Jews' College for the training of ministers (1855) and helped plan London's United Synagogue (1870).

Hermann Adler (1839–1911), who succeeded his father, Nathan, as chief rabbi in 1891, also came from Hanover and possessed a German doctorate. He enhanced the prestige of the chief rabbinate, which he regarded as parallel to the authority of the leadership of the Christian churches. More amenable to change than his father, he copied the clothing style of the Anglican clergy for himself and for the Anglo-Jewish ministry and sanctioned choirs composed of both men and women. He denounced political Zionism and often clashed with Orthodox immigrant leaders.

• Marcus Nathan Adler, *The Adler Family* (London, 1909). Geoffrey Alderman, *Modern British Jewry* (Oxford, 1992). Eugene C. Black, *The Social Politics of Anglo-Jewry, 1880–1920* (Oxford, 1988). I. Finestein, *Jewish Society in Victorian England* (London, 1993). Lloyd P. Gartner, *The Jewish Immigrant in England 1870–1914*, 2d. ed. (London, 1973), pp. 114–116, 209–210. Salmond S. Levin, ed., *A Century of Anglo-Jewish Life 1870–1970* (London, 1971), pp. 13–19, and *passim*. V. D. Lipman, *A History of the Jews in Britain since 1858* (New York, 1990), pp. 23–25, 51–54, 89ff., 120–122, 247. —GABRIEL A. SIVAN

ADMOR. See TSADDIQ.

ADOLESCENCE. See ADULT.

ADONAI. See GOD, NAMES OF.

ADONAI ADONAI EL RAḤUM VE-ḤANUN. See THIRTEEN ATTRIBUTES.

ADONAI BE-QOL SHOFAR (יְיָ בְּקוֹל שׁוֹפָר; The Lord [Ascends] Amid the Blasts of the Shofar); *pizmon* (*piyyut with a refrain) chanted in the Sephardi Ro'sh ha-Shanah liturgy after the Torah and *haftarah* readings and before the sounding of the shofar, when the holiday falls on a weekday. Each of the four stanzas begins with the latter half of *Psalms* 49.6 and ends with the opening half of the verse. The *piyyut* implores God to sound the shofar of redemption soon. In the Yemenite version, an acrostic suggests that the poet's name is Yaʿaqov.

• Israel Davidson, *Otsar ha-Shirah veha-Piyyut: Mi-Zeman Ḥatimat Kitvei ha-Qodesh ad Re'shit Tequfat ha-Haskalah* (New York, 1970), vol. 1, p. 38, n. 782. David de Sola Pool, ed. and trans., *Prayers for the New Year: According to the Custom of the Spanish and Portuguese Jews* (New York, 1948), pp. 223f. —A. STANLEY DREYFUS

ADON ʿOLAM (אֲדוֹן עוֹלָם; Eternal Lord), dogmatic hymn of unknown authorship probably dating from the geonic period (although it has also been ascribed to Shelomoh *ibn Gabirol). It extols in poetic form the unity, timelessness, and providence of God, in whom it also expresses faith and trust. Adon ʿOlam is generally recited at the beginning of the Shaḥarit service in the Ashkenazi rite and in many rites at the conclusion of the Musaf service. In some rites it is sung after the Maʿariv service on Sabbaths and festivals. Many Jews recite Adon ʿOlam before falling asleep (which may have been the original intention of its author), and it is also customary to say it on a deathbed. In Morocco, it was recited while the bride was led under the bridal canopy.

• Ismar Elbogen, *Jewish Liturgy: A Comprehensive History*, translated by Raymond P. Scheindlin (Philadelphia, 1993). Abraham Idelsohn, *Jewish Liturgy and Its Development* (New York, 1932).

ADOPTION. The creation of a parent and child relationship solely by virtue of a legal act is unknown to Jewish law. The *halakhah* recognizes only natural familial bonds for the purposes of establishing personal status. It is, however, a *mitsvah* to bring up an *orphan in one's home, and there is no objection to adoptive parents and adopted children referring to each other as if they were members of a natural family unit (*2 Sm.* 21.8; *San.* 19b). An adoptive father does not fulfill the halakhic obligation to procreate, and an adoptive mother is still liable to undergo *ḥalitsah* in the case of her husband's death. If an adoptive parent dies intestate, then the adopted children have no claim to the estate under Jewish law. A secular form of adoption exists in Israeli law under the Adoption of Children Law of 1960, but its scope is limited to matters outside the realm of personal status.

• Michael Gold, "Adoption: A New Problem for Jewish Law," *Judaism* 36 (1987): 443–450. Raphael Patai, *Sex and Family in the Bible and the Middle East* (Garden City, N.Y., 1959). —DANIEL SINCLAIR

ADOSHEM. See GOD, NAMES OF.

ʿADOT HA-MIZRAḤ (עֲדוֹת הַמִּזְרָח; communities of the East), also known as Oriental Jews. The term denotes Jews from Asia and Africa, numbering approximately one million, nearly all of whom went to Israel after 1948. They comprised ancient, deeply rooted Jewish communities whose origins date back to remote antiquity, in some cases to the first dispersion of Jews in 597 BCE. The largest of these communities was the Jewish community of Morocco, numbering approximately 285,000 before its departure. In Israel, they are often included, inaccurately, under the classification "Sephardi" and for religious purposes are under the competence of the Sephardi chief rabbi. However, they constitute a third grouping; they are neither Sephardi nor Ashkenazi, having had no Spanish or central European experience in their history but having for the most part remained in the Middle East and Muslim lands.

The Jews from Muslim lands shared a basically religious outlook toward life. Their expression of Judaism was traditional and familial. They did not experience the movements of Haskalah and reform that led to the emergence of denominationalism among Jews in Europe and America. As Middle Eastern Jews settled in new urban and rural settlements in Israel, their family loyalties, settlement patterns, occupational distribution, and ethnic residential concentration shaped the persistence of ethnic-group identification. Their ethnic origin also tended to correlate with social inequality in Israel.

The term *ʿAdot ha-Mizraḥ* is frequently regarded as a pejorative term by those it is intended to describe. Technically, Jews from Middle Eastern countries are not "Oriental," nor are they necessarily "Eastern." The term arose in the 1950s as social workers and anthropologists sought to integrate immigrants from Islamic countries into Israeli society. The working assumption of these communal workers was that the traditional cultures of the "Eastern" Jews should be discarded. In many cases, the ancient mores that the immigrants had treasured were reluctantly relinquished.

During the 1970s, a new sense of ethnic pride and the revival and legitimatization of minority cultures globally led to a new appreciation of the "communities" and their diverse heritages in Israel. The customs, stories, and folkways of the communities from Muslim lands were collected and integrated into the Israeli school curriculum. At the same time, Jews from the Near East became a social and political force to reckon with, and the term *ʿAdot ha-Mizraḥ*, or simply "the ʿAdot," lost some of its negative connotations. Constituting the majority of the Jewish population of Israel, their interests could no longer be ignored. Such indigenous customs as the veneration of "saintly" rabbis and the visitation of their gravesites reemerged. Ancient popular festivals, such as the *Mimunah of the Moroccan Jews, the Rus-el-Begh of the Kurdish Jews, and the Zaharani of the Persian Jews, were revived. While Jews from Muslim lands are quite similar to Jews from Christian countries in most respects, they exhibit distinctive food habits, musical traditions, and some expressions of popular religious culture, reflective of the general Jewish pattern of appropriating and adapting the customs and traditions of the dominant culture of the environment in which they live for long periods of time. Fundamental similarities between Jews of Muslim lands and Jews of Europe outweigh the differences among the communities.

• Hayyim Cohen and Zvi Yehuda, eds., *Asian and African Jews in the Middle East 1860–1971: An Annotated Bibliography* (Jerusalem, 1976). Shmuel N. Eisenstadt, *The Absorption of Immigrants* (Glencoe, Ill., 1955). Sammy Smooha, *Israel: Pluralism and Conflict* (Berkeley, 1978). Nissim Yosha, "The Heritage of Oriental Jewrey in Israeli Education and Culture," *Encyclopaedia Judaica Yearbook* (Jerusalem, 1985) pp. 106–18.

–JANE S. GERBER

ADRET, SHELOMOH BEN AVRAHAM (c.1235–1310), Spanish rabbinical authority; known by the acronym Rashba'. For over forty years he was a rabbi in Barcelona and was regarded as the outstanding spiritual leader of Spanish Jewry of his time. His thousands of halakhic *responsa* are outstanding for their clear exposition; they also contain valuable historical and cultural information. He deals with all facets of religious, family, and civil law, and his decisions laid the foundation for *Yaʿaqov ben Asher's *Arbaʿah Turim* and Yosef Karo's *Shulḥan ʿArukh*. Adret wrote *novellae* on the Talmud, only a section of which (on 15 tractates) has been published, combining the erudite traditions of French and Spanish rabbinical scholarship. In the *novellae* Adret keenly analyzes selected portions of the Talmud, reconciling apparent contradictions. His other works include a commentary on rabbinical legends and writings on home rituals and the laws of the Sabbath and festivals. Adret studied philosophy and defended Maimonides in the revived Maimonidean Controversy; he opposed both rationalistic allegory and excessive mysticism. He did not object to scientific or philosophical pursuits but opposed concentrating on these fields to the detriment of Torah study. While refusing to ban secular studies outright, he forbade them to students under the age of twenty-five. Adret also engaged in polemics and replied to the Dominican Raymond Martini's *Pugio fidei* with a work setting out to prove the eternity of the Torah and the importance of the practical commandments.

• Aviezer Burnstein, *The Rashba* (Jerusalem, 1979). Isidore Epstein, *The Responsa of Rabbi Solomon ben Adreth of Barcelona, 1235–1310, as a Source of the History of Spain* (New York, 1968).

ADULT. Nowhere in the Bible is there any clear indication of the age at which a minor attains majority. The only relevant statements are that an able-bodied male was liable for military service from the age of twenty (*Nm*. 1.3) and that the Levite entered into the service of the sanctuary at the age of twenty-five (*Nm*. 8.24) or thirty (*Nm*. 4.3). Rabbinic law, however, established the appearance of the first signs of puberty as the onset of majority, generally the age of twelve years and one day in the case of females, and thirteen years and one day in the case of males (*Nid*. 52a). Upon attaining the age of twelve years and a day, a female ceased to be a minor and entered the category of *naʿarah* (girl), in which she remained for six months until she became fully adult. The attainment of such majority did not, however, come automatically to a boy or girl with age. The ages were selected as the normal period during which the first signs of puberty (two pubic hairs called *simanim* [signs]) appear. Where no such signs are evident, minority could extend to the age of twenty, and in some cases even thirty-five. Naturally, maternity or childbearing would establish adulthood in a female even in the absence of other signs. A person who attains his majority is responsible for all religious and ritual matters. In the Mishnah, thirteen is described as the age "for the fulfillment of commandments" (*Avot* 5.23), although persons under twenty were not held liable for those sins punishable "at the hands of heaven" (*Shab*. 89b). The desirability of a *ḥazzan* having a beard established the minimum age for a regular officiant at eighteen or twenty. In Israel, the age of consent for marriage is seventeen, but permission to marry earlier may be given by a secular court. See also BAR MITSVAH; BAT MITSVAH.

• Joseph M. Baumgarten, "4Q502, Marriage or Golden Age Ritual?" *Journal of Jewish Studies* 34 (1983): 125–135. Joseph Fleishman, "The Age of Legal Maturity in Biblical Law," *Journal of the Ancient Near Eastern Society* 21 (1992): 35–48.

ADULTERY (Heb. *ni'uf*). The prohibition on adultery is contained in the Ten Commandments (*Ex*. 20.13; *Dt*. 5.17). It, together with incest, is one of the three cardinal offenses (the other two being idolatry and bloodshed) that may not be perpetrated even if the alternative is death (*San*. 74a). Under biblical law, adultery was a capital crime and both the adulterer and the adulteress were to be executed (*Lv*. 20.10). It was not a criminal offense for a married man to have sexual relations with an unmarried woman since polygamy was permitted in Jewish law.

In the light of the generally secret nature of adultery, the Bible provides that a husband who suspected his wife of this offense could force her to undergo the ordeal of the "waters of bitterness" (*Nm*. 5.12–31). If the suspected wife (**sotah*) were guilty, she would suffer in those organs of the body with which she had sinned (*Sot*.

1.7). This *ordeal of jealousy was abolished at the time of the Mishnah (*Sot*. 9.9).

Adultery by a husband, however, became grounds for divorce (*Shulḥan ʿArukh, Even ha-ʿEzer* 154.1). No marriage is permitted between an adulteress and her lover (*Sot*. 25a). The husband of an adulterous woman must divorce her, and any product of the forbidden union is a **mamzer*.

• David Amram, *The Jewish Law of Divorce* (London, 1897), pp. 93–97. Louis Epstein, *Sex Laws and Customs in Judaism* (New York, 1948), pp. 194–215. Ephraim Neufeld, *Ancient Hebrew Marriage Laws* (London, 1944), pp. 163–175. Emanuel Rackman, "The Case of the Sotah in Jewish Law: Ordeal or Psychodrama?" *National Jewish Law Review* 3 (1988): 49–64.

—DANIEL SINCLAIR

AFENDOPOLO, KALEV (c.1464–1525), *Karaite scholar and poet. He was probably born in Adrianople and lived most of his life in the village of Kramariya on the outskirts of Constantinople, where he served as head of the Karaite community. He also spent some years in Belgorod-Dnestrovski. He studied Karaite law under his brother-in-law, Eliyyahu ben Mosheh *Bashyazi, while the Rabbanite scholar Mordekhai Comtino taught him mathematics, geometry, astronomy, and Greco-Arabic philosophical literature. Afendopolo was thoroughly familiar with and influenced by the philosophical works of Moses Maimonides, whom he refers to as "the divine sage." Even though he had close friendships with a number of Rabbanite scholars, he retained a traditional Karaite ideology.

Afendopolo wrote at least twenty-four different works in the areas of religious law, philosophy, mathematics, and belles-lettres, as well as numerous liturgical poems, most of which are still in manuscript or have been lost. In his books, he tended to collect citations of earlier scholars, but he frequently then interpreted these in an original fashion.

His major works of religious law include an incompleted supplement to Eliyyahu Bashyazi's *Adderet Eliyyahu; Iggeret ha-Maspeqqet*, on the laws of slaughtering and forbidden foods; and *Patshegen Ketav ha-Dat*, concerning the weekly Torah readings, *haftarot*, and blessings. His major works in philosophy are *ʿAsarah Ma'marot* (sermons; extracts of this work were printed in the book *Dod Mordekhai*) and indices to Aharon ben Eliyyahu's *ʿEts Ḥayyim* and Yehudah ben Eliyyahu Hadassi's *Eshkol ha-Kofer*. Major scientific works include *Mikhlol Yofi*, on astronomical calendrical calculations, and a commentary on Nicomachean arithmetic. Afendopolo's poetic works include *Avner ben Ner*, an ethical work in the form of biblical rhymed prose, and *Gan ha-Melekh*, aphorisms and riddles.

• Jacob Mann, *Texts and Studies in Jewish History and Literature*, vol. 2 (Cincinnati, 1935), s.v. index. Samuel Poznanski in *Otsar Yisra'el*, edited by Judah D. Eisenstein (Jerusalem, 1951), vol. 2, pp. 172–174. Leon Weinberger, *Shirat ha-Qodesh la-Rabbaniyyim ve-Qara'im be-Derom Mizraḥ Eiropah* (Cincinnati, 1991), pp. 613–668, with an English introduction.

—DAVID E. SKLARE

AFIQOMAN (אֲפִיקוֹמָן), name given to the piece taken from the middle of the three unleavened breads on the Seder table on Pesaḥ eve and eaten at the conclusion of the meal by all present. The paschal meal in the Temple ended with the tasting of the paschal lamb, and the *afiqoman* symbolizes this custom. The tradition is for the celebrant to hide half of the middle piece of *matsah* before reciting the *Haggadah of Pesaḥ; this is meant to arouse the curiosity of the younger participants, and the custom has developed, especially in Ashkenazi communities, for children to remove the *afiqoman*, hide it elsewhere, and refuse to reveal its whereabouts until it has been "ransomed" by the promise of a gift. In Eastern communities it became a custom to keep a piece of the *afiqoman* during the ensuing year as a charm against the so-called *evil eye.

The origin of the word (first found in the Mishnah) is disputed, and various etymologies have been suggested.

• Edward Halper, "A Note on the Afikoman," *Response* 15.1 (1986): 23–27. Reuven Kashany, "Ha-'Afiqoman be-Masoret ha-ʿAmmamit shel ʿAdot Yisra'el," *Ba-Maʿarakhah* 232 (1980): 15, 31. Menaḥem Kasher, *Haggadah Shelemah*, (Jerusalem, 1966–1967), pp. 171–176. Saul Lieberman, *Ha-Yerushalmi ki-Feshuto* (Jerusalem, 1934), pp. 521–522.

AFTERLIFE. The biblical conception of what occurs after the death of the body appears to be that the individual's vital principle descends to the *she'ol*, a Hades-like underworld, where it leads a kind of shadow existence. "The dead praise not the Lord, neither any that go down into silence" (*Ps*. 115.17). When *Saul, in his anguished last night, sought to communicate with the deceased *Samuel, the necromancer at En-dor brought Samuel up from the underworld, not down from heaven (*1 Sam*. 28). Later, various new concepts developed in response to intellectual influences from Persia and Greece. Whereas there is no differentiation between the righteous and the wicked in the *she'ol*, the problem of theodicy (see GOOD AND EVIL), and of *reward and punishment after death, gained in importance during the Second Temple period. One possible solution to the problem of individual eschatology was to posit the existence of a spiritual *soul that, as the core of the human personality, survived, and possibly also preceded, its connection with a body. This view was indebted to Greek influences, both Platonic and Neoplatonic. The idea that a future afterlife involved a bodily *resurrection was espoused by the *Pharisees (and also held by *Jesus), in contrast to the *Sadducees, who opposed that idea as a nonscriptural innovation. This was one of the few Pharisaic dogmas deemed important enough to be explicitly affirmed in the daily liturgy; it is the subject of the third benediction of the *ʿAmidah. The various positions were reconciled in the proposition that individual souls were provisionally judged after death, going first temporarily to hell, to expiate their sins, and then to heaven ("paradise"). From this discarnate state they will ultimately be called to the resurrection and final judgment. This solution is expressed in the daily morning prayer: "O my God, the soul which you have given me is pure. You did breathe it into me . . . and you will take it from me [at death] but will restore it to me hereafter [at the resurrection]."

The soul to which the prayer refers is considered to be

immortal, though created. Most of these beliefs began to crystallize in the period of persecutions immediately preceding the Maccabean Revolt (see DANIEL) and, subsequently, became an accepted part of the tradition, though different authors maintained different emphases. For some, the belief in the afterlife of a spiritual soul implied an otherworldly orientation: "This world is like a vestibule to the world to come. Prepare yourself in the vestibule so that you may enter the banquet hall" (*Avot* 4.21; see ʿOLAM HA-ZEH AND ʿOLAM HA-BAʾ). Compared to this view, the belief in a bodily resurrection appeared to be grossly material. As a philosopher, *Maimonides found difficulties with this dogma and had to defend himself against the accusation of denying it; it is, however, included in his *Thirteen Principles of Faith. The kabbalists developed a theory of *gilgul* (transmigration), rejected by non-kabbalistic orthodoxy. Enlightenment and post-enlightenment rationalism, and in their wake modern *Reform Judaism, held the belief in an immortal soul to be rationally defensible or even necessary, unlike the "primitive" and materialist notion of a bodily resurrection. Many modern thinkers have re-interpreted the concept of immortality metaphorically. Hermann *Cohen, for example, has written of "the historical living on of the individual in the historical continuity of the people" (*Religion of Reason* [1971], p. 301).

• George W. Buchanan, *Revelation and Redemption: Jewish Documents from the Fall of Jerusalem to the Death of Naḥmanides* (Dillsboro, Ind., 1978), pp. 525–569. Robert Goldenberg, "Bound up in the Bond of Life: Death and Afterlife in Jewish Tradition," in *Death and Afterlife: Perspectives of World Religions*, edited by Hiroshi Obayashi (New York, 1992). Martha Himmelfarb, *Tours of Hell: An Apocalyptic Form in Jewish and Christian Literature* (Philadelphia, 1983). Saul Lieberman, "On Sins and Their Punishments," in *Texts and Studies* (New York, 1974). Saul Lieberman, "Some Aspects of After Life in Early Rabbinic Literature," in *Harry Austryn Wolfson Jubilee Volume*, vol. 2 (Jerusalem, 1965). George W. E. Nickelsburg, *Resurrection, Immortality, and Eternal Life in Intertestamental Judaism*, Harvard Theological Studies 26 (Cambridge, Mass., 1972). Simcha P. Raphael, *Jewish Views of the Afterlife* (Northvale, N.J., 1994). Klaas Spronk, *Beatific Afterlife in Ancient Israel and in the Ancient Near East* (Neukirchen-Vluyn, 1986). Nicholas J. Tromp, *Primitive Conceptions of Death and the Nether World in the Old Testament* (Rome, 1969).

AFTERNOON SERVICE. See MINḤAH.

AGED. The Bible uses various terms to describe the condition of being old. The most frequently used term is *zaqen* (old or aging), which is applied to Abraham (*Gn.* 24.1), and thereafter to Isaac, Jacob, and various other biblical figures. Sometimes the word is immediately followed by the phrase, "advanced in years." Other terms employed in the Bible include *sevaʿ yamim* (sated in days; *Gn.* 35.29), *sevaʿ* (hoary head; *Lv.* 19.32), *maleʾ yamim* (full of days; *Jer.* 6.11), and *ziqnah* (old age; *Is.* 46.4). The two most frequent terms used are *sevaʿ* and *ziqnah*, the former denoting greater age than the latter. The different levels of old age are enumerated in *Avot* 5.21: "at the age of sixty"—*ziqnah* (old age); "at the age of seventy"—*sevaʿ* (hoary head); "at the age of eighty"—*gevurah* (strength). The Bible specifies in *Genesis* 6.3 that man's "days will be a hundred twenty years" but decreases that number in *Psalms* 90.10, "the days of our lives are seventy years, and if with exceeding strength, eighty years." An outstanding biblical depiction of old age appears in *Ecclesiastes* 12.1–7; its pessimism is echoed in *Psalms* 71.9, "Do not cast me off in the time of old age." Both the Bible and the Talmud refer to the frailty brought about by advancing age. *Ecclesiastes* 12.1 says, "Remember now your Creator in the days of your youth, while the evil days come not, nor the years draw nigh, when you shall say, I have no pleasure in them." The psalmist pleads, "Cast me not off in the time of old age; forsake me not when my strength fails" (*Ps.* 71.9). Age takes its toll upon one's mental faculties, as explained in *Avot* 4.25: "One who studies Torah as a child, to what may he be compared? To ink written upon new paper. And one who studies when he is old, to what may he be compared? To ink on a palimpsest." Both the Bible and rabbinic literature lay great store by respect for the aged; for example, "You shall rise up before the hoary head, and honor the face of the old man" (*Lv.* 19.32). Various other verses echo the importance of respecting the aged; thus, "The beauty of old men is the gray head" (*Prv.* 20.29) and "Do not despise your mother when she is old" (*Prv.* 23.22). The Talmud relates (*Bik.* 11b) that whenever R. Me'ir saw an old man, even if the man were an ignoramus, he would rise as a sign of respect, exclaiming, "the very fact that he has grown old is a sign that he has acquired merit." The sages interpreted *zaqen* as an acronym for the words *zeh qanah ḥokhmah*, one who has acquired wisdom, thus expanding the requirement of extending honor to include even young sages.

While the Talmud does not state any objective criteria for old age, there are various subjective criteria. For example, a priest in the Temple and a ritual slaughterer are considered to be old when their hands tremble. A woman is considered old if when addressed as "mother" she no longer takes umbrage (*Shulḥan ʿArukh, Yoreh Deʿah*, 189.29). There are derogatory references to the aged (e.g., an old man is compared to a monkey [*Eccl. Rab.* 1.2] or when it is said, "there is no taste in the aged" [*Shab.* 89b]) and a few Talmudic statements that praise old age.

Care for the aged has always been considered one of the primary obligations of the Jewish community, and it has been defined in ethical and halakhic works. Rabbi Naḥman of Bratslav wrote, "Gauge a country's prosperity by its treatment of the aged" (*Sefer ha-Middot* 66). From the eighteenth century on, a *moshav zeqenim* (old age home) was established in many places.

• Shimon Bergman and Jack Habib, *Aging in the Jewish World: Continuity and Change* (Jerusalem, 1992). Sanford Finkel and Rhona Finkel, "Judaism and Mental Health in the Later Years," *Journal of Aging and Judaism* 5.3 (1991): 191–204. Steven Carr Reuben, "Old Age: Appearance and Reality," *Journal of Psychology and Judaism* 16.3 (1992): 137–191. Michael A. Signer, "Honor the Hoary Head: The Aged in the Medieval European Jewish Community," in *Aging and the Aged in Medieval Europe*, edited by Michael M. Sheehan (Toronto, 1990), pp. 39–48. Moshe Weinfeld, "The Phases of Human Life in Mesopotamian and Jewish Sources," in *Priests, Prophets and Scribes: Essays on the Formation and Heritage of Second Temple Judaism In Honour of Joseph Blenkinsopp*, edited by Eugene Ulrich et al. (Sheffield, Eng., 1992), pp. 182–189.

AGENT (Heb. *shaliaḥ*), a person appointed to act as another's representative in matters of Jewish law or ritual, for example, one who acts as a proxy in cases of betrothal or divorce, or a *sheliaḥ tsibbur, one who leads the congregation in prayer. "A person's agent is regarded as the person himself" (*Ned.* 72b; *Qid.* 41b), therefore any act committed by a duly appointed agent is regarded as having been committed by the principal, who bears full responsibility for it (while the agent bears no liability). The agent must be of the same legal status and standing as his principal. The appointment of a minor, an imbecile, or a deaf-mute as an agent is invalid, as is any appointment by them (*B. Q.* 6.4). The death of the principal automatically voids the agency. An agent is regarded as acting in his principal's interest and not to his detriment; in any dispute as to whether the agent has exceeded the terms of his agency, this consideration is taken into account. The law of agency applies only to legal acts: "One cannot be an agent for a transgression" (*Qid.* 42b). A person committing a crime as the agent of a principal is held responsible for his act.

• Israel Herbert Levinthal, *The Jewish Law of Agency, with Special Reference to the Roman and Common Law* (New York, 1923).

AGGADAH (אַגָּדָה), the nonlegal contents of the *Talmud and *Midrash, including—often by way of biblical exegesis—ethical and moral teaching, theological speculation, legends, folklore, gnomic sayings, prayers, historical information, praise of Israel and Erets Yisra'el, interpretation of dreams, and expressions of messianic faith and longing. Many theories have been advanced as to the origin of the name *aggadah*. Some derive it from the Hebrew *huggad* (things that are said or spoken, in contrast to biblical stories, which are written); some take it from the rabbinic expression used in expounding scripture, *maggid ha-katuv*, "scripture states." Still others connect it with the scriptural verse *ve-higgadeta le-vinekha*, "and you shall tell to your son" (*Ex.* 13.8), which implies the relating of something other than the Law and its ordinances. The Mishnah contains relatively little *aggadah*, and that usually appears at the end of treatises or after individual sections within the treatise as a kind of epilogue to the completed study of a unified segment of legal subject matter. However, about a third of the Talmud Yerushalmi and approximately a fourth of the Talmud Bavli is comprised of *aggadah*. Here, too, it is frequently introduced to mark off one section of legal study from another.

The *aggadah* serves not only as a kind of relief from strenuous, concentrated halakhic discourse, but also to keep the ethical ideals of the Torah ever fresh and meaningful, complementing the **halakhah* but lacking its binding character. It elaborates and develops the stories of scripture so as to draw from them the maximum of moral instruction. Unlike *halakhah*, *aggadah* need not derive from an ancient recognized source but may be the free individual creation of every generation. The *aggadah* is rich in literary forms, including parable, metaphor, personification, satire, and poetry. It plays with homonymous roots, it computes the numerical value of letters to gain new information, it substitutes letters to reveal new nuances of meaning in scripture, and it even interprets individual letters of particular words as the abbreviation of a series of words. The Hebrew Bible is more often a source of the *aggadah* than the *halakhah* is, for *aggadah* concerns itself as much with the Prophets and the Hagiographa as it does with the Pentateuch. Like *halakhah*, *aggadah* developed rules (*middot*; see HERMENEUTICS) for the exposition of scripture, though the number of its rules is greater than that for *halakhah* (e.g., the thirty-two rules ascribed to *Eli'ezer ben Yosei ha-Galili), and the application of its rules is much freer. Some of these hermeneutic rules have been found to resemble the ancient methods for the interpretation of dreams and oracles, and similarities have been pointed out between the dream interpretation of the rabbis and the *Onirocriticus* of Artemidorus. Whereas only a few rules could be admitted for the elaboration and elucidation of *halakhah*, almost every currently established literary device could be used in *aggadah*. Although *aggadah* has no systematic philosophy, it deals in its own way with basic theological and moral problems. Many non-Jewish concepts found their way into *aggadah*, and almost all the schools of Greek thought left traces there.

There were ancient traditions of *aggadah*, just as there were of *halakhah*, and they are usually introduced by a phrase such as *masoret aggadah*, "it is an aggadic tradition." Thus, the *midrash Shoḥer Tov* to *Psalms* 18.32 related the aggadic tradition that Judah killed Esau after the death of Isaac. *Tanḥuma'* (58.17) mentions a "tradition" that Jerusalem will only be rebuilt after the ingathering of the Diaspora. Collections or "books" of *aggadah* seem to be very old. The Talmud Yerushalmi (*Kil.* 32b) notes an aggadic book on *Psalms* that was known at the time of R. Yehudah. A Talmudic passage (*San.* 57b) suggests the existence of a collection of *aggadah* on *Genesis*. R. Yoḥanan (Y., *Hor.* 48b) stated that he knew all the *aggadah* except for that to *Proverbs* and *Ecclesiastes*. That these collections were actually committed to writing is implied by a report to the effect that R. Yoḥanan and Reish Laqish read from such a book on the Sabbath (*Tem.* 14b) or by such statements as "one who reads *aggadah* from a book will not quickly forget it" (Y., *Ber.* 9). As a natural extension of the Aramaic exposition of the Torah reading in the synagogue, *aggadah* was also the source of the sermon, which it finally dominated to the exclusion of *halakhah*. Even in the academies, students would ask their teachers for instruction in *aggadah* when the latter were too tired to teach *halakhah*.

The first book of edited *aggadah* does not antedate the fourth century CE. Besides appearing in sections of the Mishnah, Tosefta', and Talmudic literature, many aggadic statements are included in the so-called halakhic *midrashim* (see MIDRASHIC LITERATURE) as well. The bulk of the *aggadah*, however, is contained in works compiled in the post-Talmudic era, the most prominent being those Midrashic compilations included in the *Midrash Rabbah and *Tanḥuma'-Yelammedenu collections and in such nonexegetical aggadic works as (*Avot de-Rabbi Natan*, **Pirqei de-Rabbi Eli'ezer*, and *Tanna' de-*

Vei Eliyyahu [see SEDER ELIYYAHU]). Numerous other collections and single aggadic works exist, some extant only in manuscripts. In the Middle Ages many anthologies of *aggadah* were composed; among these are the **Yalqut Shim'oni* (Germany, 13th cent.) and the **Midrash ha-Gadol* (Yemen, c.13th cent.). The aggadic sections of the Talmud were collected in the sixteenth century in the *'Ein Ya'aqov* of Ya'aqov ben Shelomoh ibn Ḥaviv (see IBN ḤAVIV FAMILY). Modern scientific study of *aggadah* began with Leopold *Zunz. There have been several modern collections, notably that of Louis *Ginzberg, who, in his *Legends of the Jews* (1909–1928), arranged the *aggadah* according to the chronological order of the scriptures. The *Sefer ha-Aggadah* (1910) of Ḥayyim Naḥman Bialik and Yehoshu'a Ḥana Rawnitzki brought the *aggadah* to a broad public (English translation, in W. G. Braude, *The Book of Legends* [New York, 1992]). See also HOMILETICS.

• Renee Bloch, "Midrash," in *Approaches to Ancient Judaism*, edited by William S. Green, (Missoula, Mont., 1978). Joseph M. Davis, "Literary Studies of Aggadic Narrative—A Bibliography," *Judaic and Christian Interpretations of Texts: Contents and Contexts*, edited by Jacob Neusner, (Lanham, Md., 1987), pp. 185–218. Jonah Frankel, *Darkhei ha-'Aggadah veha-Midrash* (Ramat Gan, 1991). I. Frankel, *Peshat in Talmudic and Midrashic Literature* (Toronto, 1956). Louis Ginzberg, *The Legends of the Jews*, 7 vols. (Philadelphia, 1909–1938). Yitzhak Heinemann, *Darkhei ha-'Aggadah* (Jerusalem, 1954). J. L. Kugel and R. A. Greer, *Early Biblical Interpretation* (Philadelphia, 1986). Saul Lieberman, *Greek in Jewish Palestine* (New York, 1942). Efraim Elimelech Urbach, *Hazal, Pirke Emunot ve-De'ot* (n.p., 1969). Leopold Zunz, *Ha-Derashot be-Yisra'el ve-Hishtalshelutan ha-Historit*, translated from the second German edition of 1892, with corrections and supplements by Chanoch Albeck (Jerusalem, 1954). • Menachem Mendel Kasher and Jacob Ber Mandelbaum, eds. and trans., *Sarei ha-'Elef*, rev. and corr. ed. (Jerusalem, 1978).

—MARC BREGMAN

AGGADAT BE-RE'SHIT, a late Midrashic work (probably 9th or 10th cent.), with affinities to *Tanḥuma'-Yelammedenu literature. It contains one unique particularity: each of the twenty-eight homilies consists of three parts. The first part comments on the first verse of a portion of *Genesis*, following the order of the biblical book according to the *triennial cycle of Bible reading (an early Palestinian custom) as it was practiced in the author's locale. The second part comments on a verse stemming from one of the Prophetic books and is related to the Prophetic synagogal reading for that Sabbath. At the end of each homily comes a Midrashic exposition of a verse or verses from *Psalms*, possibly indicating that this biblical book was recited regularly in the synagogue in the locale of the author. Solomon Buber, the most recent editor of *Aggadat Be-Re'shit* (Kraków, 1903), asserts that the large amount of material common to this text and the recension of *Midrash Tanḥuma'* (which he also edited) originated in the latter; this has not been proven.

—CHAIM MILIKOWSKY

AGGADAT ESTER, a Midrashic compilation on the *Book of Esther*, published for the first time by Solomon Buber (Kraków, 1897) on the basis of two Yemenite manuscripts, with additions, notes, and corrections by Yehudah Behak (Vilna, 1925; repr. 1964, 1982). Ḥanokh Albeck's contention that *Aggadat Ester* is the Yemenite Midrashic anthology **Midrash ha-Gadol* (13th–14th cent.) to the *Book of Esther* has been disputed by Menaḥem Kasher.

AGGADAT MASHIAḤ a short (approx. 5 pgs.) exposition of the events that will lead up to the final messianic era with its resurrection of the dead and ingathering of the exiles. These events are framed by the prophetic word of Balaam (*Nm*. 24.17–19), and *Aggadat Mashiaḥ* was therefore included by R. Toviyyah ben Eli'ezer in his biblical commentary *Leqaḥ Tov* (the only source for the text). Especially noteworthy is the clear demarcation of the two Messiahs, the Messiah, Son of Joseph, from Galilee, who will defeat Israel's enemies but who will then himself be killed, and the Messiah, Son of David, the messianic king who will reign forever. The author seems to allude to some sort of mass apostasy, reflected in his attack on those Jews who "have bad thoughts about God" and those who "go from Israel to join the Nations of the World." Yehudah ibn Shemu'el, the most recent editor of this text (*Midreshei Ge'ullah* [Jerusalem, 1954], pp. 101–106), claimed that the work is dependent upon the messianic narrative *Book of Zerubbabel*, but this is incorrect. Their points of contact derive from earlier traditions, and stylistically, *Aggadat Mashiaḥ* seems to be earlier.

—CHAIM MILIKOWSKY

AGLA' (אַגְלָ״א), magic word said to be composed of the initials of the phrase *Attah gibbor le-'olam Adonai*, "You are mighty forever, O Lord," which appears in the 'Amidah prayer. During the Middle Ages, German Christians also used the phrase as a talisman against fire and inscribed it—together with a cross—on wooden bowls; they interpreted the letters as initials of the German phrase *Allmächtiger Gott, Lösche Aus*, "Almighty God, extinguish the conflagration."

• Louis Finkelstein, "The Development of the 'Amidah," in *Contributions to the Scientific Study of Jewish Liturgy*, edited by Jakob Josef Petuchowski (New York, 1970), pp. 91–133. Kaufmann Kohler, "The Origin and Composition of the Eighteen Benedictions with a Translation of Corresponding Essene Prayers in the Apostolic Constitutions," in *Contributions to the Scientific Study of Jewish Liturgy*, edited by Jakob Joseph Petuchowski (New York, 1970), pp. 52–90.

AGNOSTICISM. As originally formulated in the nineteenth century by T. H. Huxley, agnosticism designated an attitude of suspended judgment, particularly in religious matters. In this sense, it was incompatible with religious tradition, which considered the existence of God as well as certain other beliefs as absolutely certain and beyond any doubt or even necessity of proof. The problem of evil and suffering might lead to anguish about God's justice (as in the *Book of Job*) but not usually to doubts regarding his existence and power. Agnostic tendencies, denying the possibility of metaphysical knowledge, did exist in pre-modern (ancient Greek as well as medieval) philosophy but were criticized by others, such as *Sa'adyah ben Yosef Ga'on. The view, espoused by many philosophers, theologians, and mystics, that the divine was beyond human comprehension, should not be confused with agnosticism. Thus, Moses *Maimonides taught that humans can "comprehend only the fact that He exists, but not His essence" (*Guide of the Perplexed* 1.58). This theology was then extended to all that is beyond human earthly experience, as when Maimonides asserts that "we can obtain no knowledge of the essence of the heavens" (loc. cit.). The insistence on the limitations of the human mind ("If I knew Him, I would be He," wrote Sa'adyah) often functioned as a wise methodological reservation, inducing people to concentrate on intellectually manageable problems.

• Martin E. Marty, *Varieties of Unbelief* (Garden City, N.Y., 1966). John Lancaster Spalding, *Religion, Agnosticism, and Education* (Chicago, 1902). Gordon Stein, *The Encyclopedia of Unbelief* (Buffalo, N.Y., 1985). James Ward, *Naturalism and Agnosticism*, 4th ed. (New York, 1971).

AGRARIAN LAWS. The economy envisaged by the laws of the Torah was purely agricultural. The children of the covenant were entering a land of milk and honey, blessed by the *seven species (*Dt*. 8.8). The Holy Land was to be divided according to tribal areas, except for the tribe of Levi, and each family within the tribe was to receive its portion. Alienation of this ancestral land could be only temporary. Every seventh year was a sabbatical year (see SHEMITTAH; *Ex*. 23.10–11; *Lv*. 25.1ff.), when, in addition to the cancellation of debts, all major agricultural work was prohibited. In Temple times the fiftieth year was the jubilee (see YOVEL; *Lv*. 25), when all land had to be returned to its original owners. As a result, the price of land was reckoned according to the number of crops it would produce until the jubilee year.

To such an extent was agriculture regarded as the essential occupation of the Jews in biblical times that the term *Canaanite* was synonymous with *trader* (*Zec*. 14.21; *Hos*. 12.8). Many of the Israelite feasts, particularly the Shalosh Regalim, have an agricultural basis. *Pesaḥ was a herdsman's and farmer's festival; *Shavu'ot was the festival of the new grains; *Sukkot was the gathering in of the fall harvest. The common element of these festive occasions was thanksgiving to God for his blessings.

According to the rabbis, most of the agricultural and animal husbandry laws are applicable only in Erets Yisra'el, but many were applied by the rabbis outside the land. Some apply only to the Temple period, others to all time. Inside Erets Yisra'el, there were gradations of status, depending on whether the land was within the historic boundaries established and thus sanctified by the first and second conquests (those of Joshua and those in postexilic times, respectively).

In the first order of the Mishnah, called *Zera'im (Seeds), the details of the various agrarian laws are dealt with exhaustively. The underlying assumption of the laws is that Erets Yisra'el belongs to God (*Lv*. 25.23) and is therefore holy ground. The agricultural laws are regarded as "commandments dependent on the land [of Israel]." By observing certain restrictions and separating parts of the harvests as an offering or for gifts to priests, Levites, and the poor, the owner of the soil becomes conscious of his status as a mere steward, who acts in behalf of the true owner.

The agrarian laws fall into a number of categories. **Kil'ayim* is the prohibition against mixing two or more kinds of seed in one field or against grafting different kinds of fruit trees (*Lv*. 19.19; *Dt*. 22.9). **Pe'ah* refers to the corner of the harvested field to be left for the poor (*Lv*. 19.9–10, 23.22; *Dt*. 24.19–22), *leqet* to gleanings that fall and must be left for the poor (*Lv*. 19.9–10), and *shikhḥah* to sheaves that have been overlooked and must also be left for the poor (see LEQET, SHIKHḤAH, AND PE'AH). *Terumah* and **ma'asrot* are the heave offering and tithes, respectively (*Nm*. 18.8ff.; *Dt*. 14.22–27, 26.12–15). The *terumah* is given to a priest and the first tithe to a Levite, who in turn separates a tithe of the tithe for the priest. A second tithe must be consumed by the owner and his family in Jerusalem; however, every third year this is donated to the poor (today *terumah* may not be eaten by the priest because of ritual uncleanness; the second tithe is always redeemed, while the first must be separated and given to a Levite—an arrangement is generally made by which he agrees to sell it back to the owner in return for a small consideration). **Ḥallah* is a portion of dough to be given to the priest (*Nm*. 15.17–21). **'Orlah* is the prohibition against eating or making use of the fruit of a newly planted tree during the first three years of its growth, while *reva'i* refers to the obligation to redeem the fruit of the fourth year of the vineyard (*Lv*. 19.23–25). Finally, *bikkurim* are the *first fruits of the seven species (*Ex*. 23.19; *Dt*. 26.1ff.) that are offered to the priest in the Temple.

With the modern resettlement of Jews in Erets Yisra'el and their reinvolvement with agricultural pursuits, many of the laws that had become academic have taken on a practical application. While laws such as first fruits applied only in Temple times, laws such as tithes, heave offerings, *'orlah*, the sabbatical and jubilee years, and the law of the firstborn of animals are regarded as applicable today. Apart from *'orlah*, however, it is tacitly conceded that modern economic conditions do not permit the literal application of these laws. Advantage is taken of legal loopholes to fulfill the spirit of these laws without necessarily applying the letter. This is particularly true concerning the sabbatical year. Agricultural settlements act in accordance with the far-reaching concessions worked out by Chief Rabbi Avraham Yitsḥaq Kook (see KOOK FAMILY), including the possibility of selling land to non-Jews during the sabbatical year, thereby creating a legal fiction through which land could be cultivated. Agricultural products sold to the public in Israel are certified to the effect that "tithes and heave offerings have been duly taken" and the religious sector is careful to pay attention to the observance of the relevant agricultural laws.

• Alan J. Avery-Peck, *Mishnah's Division of Agriculture* (Chico, Calif., 1985). Isidor Grunfeld, "Kilayim—Diverse Kinds," in *The Jewish Dietary Laws* (London, 1972), vol. 2, pp. 45–55. Isidor Grunfeld, *Shemittah and Yobel* (London, 1972). Dovid Marchant, *Understanding Shmittoh; Halachos of Shmittoh* (Jerusalem and New York, 1993).

AGRIPPA I (c.11 BCE–44 CE), king of Judea, 41–c.44. The grandson of Herod the Great, Agrippa was probably born in Judea but was raised and educated in Rome, in circles closely connected with the imperial court. In 37 his friend the emperor Caligula (37–41) appointed him king of the former Herodian territories in the Golan and in southern Syria. In 39 the Galilee and Transjordan areas and in 41 the whole of Judea were added to his kingdom. Agrippa is noted both for his involvement in the imperial court on behalf of his fellow Jews and for his persecution of the early Christian movement. He seems to have been very popular among his Jewish subjects, was sympathetic to the Pharisees, and is favorably mentioned in Talmudic sources.

• Emil Schürer, *The History of the Jewish People in the Age of Jesus Christ, 175 B.C.–A.D. 135*, new English edition revised and edited by Geza Vermes and Fergus Millar, vol. 1 (Edinburgh, 1973), pp. 442–454. Daniel R. Schwartz, *Agrippa I: The Last King of Judaea*, Texte und Studien zum Antiken Judentum 23 (Tübingen, 1990). —GIDEON BOHAK

AGUDAS HA-RABONIM. See UNION OF ORTHODOX RABBIS OF THE UNITED STATES AND CANADA.

AGUDAT ISRAEL, also known as the Agudah, a world organization of strictly Orthodox Jewry; political party in interwar Europe and in modern Israel. Established in order to defend the traditional Jewish way of life and to counter the influence of competing religious or secular ideologies, especially Zionism, Agudat Israel nevertheless adopted a series of ideological and organizational innovations. The very act of organizing an Orthodox political party, a concession to the sociopolitical exigencies of the time, was an innovation that more extreme Orthodox elements rejected on principle. The initiative for the formation of Agudat Israel came from the separatist Orthodox communities of Germany, which hoped to enlist the support of the great rabbinical figures and the Orthodox masses of eastern Europe in the fight against Zionism and Reform Judaism. Its founding conference was held in Kattowitz (Katowice), Upper Silesia, in 1912. The conference laid the ground work for the process of forming the international apparatus of the organization and for the founding of national branches of the movement. Depending on local political conditions, the branches took the form of either lobbying groups (e.g., in England, the United States) or of actual political parties (in Poland, Latvia, and, later, in Israel). The two supreme bodies of Agudat Israel are its Council of Torah Sages (Moʿetset Gedolei ha-Torah), the rabbinical body that reviews and supervises all major decisions of the movement, and the Great Assembly (Kenesiyyah Gedolah), the periodic world gathering of Agudah representatives from various countries. The interwar period, punctuated by the first three Great Assemblies (1923, 1929, 1937), witnessed the consolidation and expansion of the Agudah's work on the national and international levels. In Poland, its politicians were elected to parliament and municipal councils, and gained control of major communities. They achieved government recognition for their network of Jewish schools and sponsored the innovative *Beth Jacob schools for women. On the international level, Agudat Israel endeavored to provide an independent Orthodox voice on all major Jewish issues, whether it be calendar reform or the proposed partition of Palestine. The Holocaust destroyed the major centers of Agudat Israel in Europe; since then, Israel and the United States have become the primary centers of activity. Despite its reservations about Zionism as a secular ideology, the Agudah made its peace with the newly founded State of Israel and has become an integral part of Israeli politics, even joining government coalitions. In the realm of doctrine, the Agudah developed the concept of "Daʿat Torah," which invested the rabbinic sages with almost infallible insight and authority to rule on political, economic, and social matters, as well as strictly religious issues.

• Gershon Bacon, "Agudath Israel in Poland, 1916–1939: An Orthodox Jewish Response to the Challenges of Modernity," Ph.D. dissertation, Columbia University, 1979. Gershon Bacon, *The Politics of Tradition* (Jerusalem, 1996). Joseph Friedenson, "A Concise History of Agudath Israel," in *Yaʿakov Rosenheim Memorial Anthology* (New York, 1968). Gary S. Schiff, *Tradition and Politics: The Religious Parties of Israel* (Detroit, 1977). —GERSHON BACON

ʿAGUNAH (עֲגוּנָה), a term that first occurs in *Ruth* 1.13, refers to a married woman who is legally barred from marrying another man as a result of either insufficient evidence of her husband's death or his refusal or inability to give her a *divorce (in Jewish law, only a man can initiate a divorce). Talmudic law contains a number of provisions designed to alleviate the evidentiary burden of proving her husband's death, for example, the acceptance of the testimony of one witness only and reliance upon hearsay evidence. Women, slaves, handmaidens and relatives are also eligible to testify in *ʿagunah* cases (*Yev*. 6.17, 93b; *Shulḥan ʿArukh, Even ha-ʿEzer* 17.3, 56). The circumstances under which the husband is alleged to have died are taken into account and if, for example, he disappeared in a body of water with clearly visible physical boundaries, then his death will be presumed, provided that there was a witness who waited sufficiently long at the scene of the disappearance in order to establish that the husband did not come to the surface and survive (*Yev*. 120a–121b; *Shulḥan ʿArukh, Even ha-ʿEzer* 17.32). Stringency is to be avoided in *ʿagunah* cases, and finding ways of permitting *ʿagunot* to remarry is regarded as a *mitsvah (Resp. Ro'sh* no. 51; *Shulḥan ʿArukh, Even ha-ʿEzer* 17.21). If an *ʿagunah* does remarry and her first husband reappears on the scene, then she must be divorced by both men, and the children from the second marriage are regarded as *mamzerim*. The Talmud refers to a practice in the time of David of soldiers giving their wives conditional divorces, which would take effect only if they did not return from battle within a set period of time (*Ket*. 9b). This practice, which was intended to prevent the proliferation of *ʿagunot*, has been followed by some rabbinical authorities in recent times. The problem of the recalcitrant husband who will not give his wife a *get* (bill of divorce) has become a pressing one in the modern era due to the advent of civil divorce and its availability to Jews. The recent Orthodox approach to this problem is to devise a prenuptial agreement in which the husband commits himself to appearing before a *beit din* for the purpose of giving a *get*. This agreement may be enforced by communal and/or legal sanctions aimed at depriving him of certain benefits and advantages of both a religious and a civil nature. The Conservative movement adopted this approach in 1969 and also uses the halakhic institution of conditional marriage, both of which must be instituted at the time of marriage. If all else fails, the Conservative movement will annul the marriage, using the Talmud's empowerment of rabbis to do so (*hafqaʿat qiddushin*). The Reform movement has rejected the concept of *ʿagunah* entirely, on the principle of equality; civil divorce generally suffices.

• J. David Bleich, "Modern-Day *Agunot*: A Proposed Remedy," *Jewish Law Annual* 4 (1981): 167–187. M. Chiger, "Ruminations Over the *Agunah* Problem," *Jewish Law Annual* 4 (1981): 207–225. Elliot N. Dorff and Arthur Rosett, *A Living Tree: The Roots and Growth of Jewish Law* (Albany, 1988), pp. 523–545. David Novak, "The Agunah, or the Case of the Unco-operative Husband," in *Law and Theology in Judaism* (New York, 1974), pp. 31–54. Mark Washofsky, "The Recalcitrant Husband: The Problem of a Definition," *Jewish Law Annual* 4 (1981): 144–166.

–DANIEL SINCLAIR

AHAB (Heb. Aḥʾav), seventh king of Israel and son of Omri; reigned over Samaria for twenty-two years (c.874–853). The verdict of the *Book of Kings* concerning his reign is exceptionally harsh (1 *Kgs*. 16.30, 33; 21.25–26; cf. *Mi*. 6.13), probably because he did not oppose (and perhaps even on occasion actively participated in) his wife *Jezebel's patronization of the Canaanite Baal cult (1 *Kgs*. 16.31; 2 *Kgs*. 21.3; see Baal Worship). Intended to highlight the theologically negative aspects of his rule, the Bible records his mostly hostile encounters with prophets: Elijah's prophecy of a drought and the subsequent contest of faith on Mount Carmel (*1Kgs*. 17.1, 18.1–46); his hostile meeting with Elijah (*1 Kgs*. 18.16–19); encounters with an anonymous prophet on three occasions (*1 Kgs*. 20.13–14, 22, 28) and with another anonymous prophet who castigated him for sparing Ben-hadad, thus violating the laws of *ḥerem* (*1 Kgs*. 20.35–43); and the murder of Naboth and the appropriation of his vineyard (*1 Kgs*. 21.1–29. Elijah's hostile encounter with Ahab on this occasion includes the famous accusation "Thus said the Lord: 'Would you murder and also take possession?'" [*1 Kgs*. 21.17–29; cf. *1 Kgs*. 22.38; *2 Kgs*. 9.25–26, 30–37]).

The selective recording of the events of Ahab's reign in the biblical account for obviously tendentious theological and didactic reasons is supplemented by ancient Near Eastern sources. These afford glimpses of one of the most important Israelite reigns during the First Temple period, when Moab was a vassal of Israel. In only three isolated verses does the Bible even mention the relationship between Israel and Moab during the reign of Ahab. The *Second Book of Kings* 1.1 and 3.5, when taken together, imply that King Mesha of Moab rebelled against Israel, its sovereign, upon the death of Ahab. The *Second Book of Kings* 3.4 just as clearly implies that prior to the rebellion, Moab had been paying an enormous tribute to Israel. In fact, Israel's conquest of Moab during Omri's reign and the subsequent period of vassalrage, which ended only upon the death of Ahab, is clearly described in the Moabite Mesha Stela as a period when the chief Moabite god Chemosh "was angry with his land."

Ahab was one of the leaders of the southern Syrian coalition against the Assyrian king Shalmaneser III at the battle of Qarqar (853 BCE). Israel contributed two thousand war chariots to the united coalition forces, more than any of the other allies. Although Assyrian annals claimed a massive victory for Shalmaneser, the fact that Shalmaneser's records indicate that he fought this same coalition four more times, in 849, 848, 845, and 841, clearly demonstrates that it was only after the last of these campaigns (long after Ahab's death) that the western states were finally subjugated.

• John C. L. Gibson, *Textbook of Syrian Semitic Inscriptions*, vol. 1 (Oxford, 1971), pp. 71–83. William W. Hallo, "From Qarqar to Carchemish: Assyria and Israel in the Light of New Discoveries," in *Biblical Archaeologist Reader*, vol. 2, edited by David N. Freedman and Edward F. Campbell (Garden City, N.Y., 1962), pp. 156–161. T. C. Mitchell, "Israel and Judah until the Revolt of Jehu," in *The Cambridge Ancient History*, 2d ed., edited by John Boardman et al. (Cambridge, 1982), vol. 3, pt. 2, pp. 466–479. Wayne T. Pitard, *Ancient Damascus: A Historical Study of the Syrian City-State from Earliest Times until Its Fall to the Assyrians in 732* BCE (Winona Lake, Ind., 1987), pp. 114–132. James B. Pritchard, ed., *Ancient Near Eastern Texts Relating to the Old Testament*, 3d ed. (Princeton, 1969), pp. 178–179. W. Thiel, "Ahab," in *Anchor Bible Dictionary*, edited by David N. Freedman et al. (New York, 1992), pp. 100–104.

–CHAIM COHEN

AḤAD HA-ʿAM (1856–1927), pen name of Asher Ginzberg, meaning "one of the people"; writer and Zionist philosopher. Born of a Hasidic family in the Ukraine, Ginzberg achieved the reputation of a brilliant young Talmudist before studying modern philosophy, which he understood as irrevocably undermining religious faith. In 1884 he moved to Odessa, where he came into close contact with the Ḥovevei Zion movement and began in 1889 to write the occasional essays that made him one of the most prominent figures in modern Hebrew literature. In the debate over the future of the early Zionist movement and Jewish culture, Aḥad ha-ʿAm called for more intense educational efforts to strengthen Jewish national consciousness. Rejecting calls for the radical transformation of Jewish values, he advocated pursuit of Jewish continuity in secular terms, praising absolute justice as an essential Jewish value.

After 1897 Aḥad ha-ʿAm criticized Theodor Herzl's political Zionism for what he felt were its unrealistic and inauthentic Jewish aims, holding that Zionism was a means for protecting the Jewish people from demoralization and assimilation rather than a response to the failure of Jews to achieve political and social integration in the Diaspora. Drawing on nineteenth-century evolutionary views, Aḥad ha-ʿAm conceived of the Jewish people as a national ego, endowed with a collective will to survive and possessing a distinctive cultural–spiritual personality that had emerged through the ancient struggles between priesthood and prophecy and later in the practical ethos of the Pharisees. Renewed Jewish settlements in Erets Yisraʾel would serve as a spiritual center that would nurture new Hebraic cultural forms, strengthening and enriching Jewish loyalties in the Diaspora and counteracting the corrosive individualism of modern society.

Aḥad ha-ʿAm's influence was considerable among spiritual or cultural Zionists, including Martin Buber and Gershom Scholem, even when they rejected his philosophical views.

In 1907 Aḥad ha-ʿAm moved to London and in 1922

settled in Tel Aviv, where he completed the editing of his collected essays and several volumes of letters.

• Aḥad ha-ʿAm, *Essays, Letters, Memoirs*, edited and translated by Leon Simon (Oxford, 1946). Shlomo Avineri, "Aḥad ha-ʿAm: The Spiritual Dimensions of the Jewish State," in *The Making of Modern Zionism: Intellectual Origins of the Jewish State* (New York, 1981), pp. 112–124. Jacques Kornberg, ed., *At the Crossroads: Essays on Aḥad ha-ʿAm* (Albany, 1983). Nathan Rotenstreich, *ʿAl Aḥad ha-ʿAm* (Jerusalem, 1956). Leon Simon, *Aḥad ha-ʿAm, Asher Ginzberg: A Biography* (Philadelphia, 1960). Steven J. Zipperstein, *Elusive Prophet: Aḥad ha-ʿAm and the Origins of Zionism* (Berkeley, 1993). —ROBERT M. SELTZER

AḤA' OF SHABḤA (c.680–750), Babylonian rabbi, also known as Aḥa'i, who taught for many years at the academy of *Pumbedita. He was the editor (or, less probably, the author) of *She'iltot*, a collection of homiletic questions. (An early example of this genre is found in Talmud tractate *Shabbat* 30a–b.)

The collection associated with Aḥa' contains approximately 170 homilies arranged according to the weekly Pentateuchal readings. Some of these homilies, as well as homilies belonging to this genre though not included in the collection of Aḥa', were incorporated into other works, especially **Halakhot Gedolot*. Topics were chosen to appeal to a relatively broad audience. Each homily, after an introductory section, propounds a question that is finally resolved following an intermediate section in which rabbinic material relating to the general topic is quoted. The primary significance of the work for modern scholars lies in its attestation of an early version of the Talmud Bavli. The *editio princeps* was published in Venice in 1566. A critical edition was published by S. K. Mirsky (5 vols. [1959–1977]).

• Samuel K. Mirsky, ed., *She'iltot de-Rav Aḥai Ga'on* (Jerusalem, 1982). Shraga Abramson, *ʿInyanot be-Sifrut ha-Ge'onim* (Jerusalem, 1974). Robert Brody, *Le-Toledot Nusaḥ ha-She'iltot* (Jerusalem, 1991). Robert Brody, "Sifrut ha-Ge'onim ve- ha-Teqst ha-Talmudi," *Meḥqerei Talmud* 1 (1990): 237–303. —ROBERT BRODY

AḤARIT HA-YAMIM. See ESCHATOLOGY.

AHARON BEN ELIYYAHU (c.1328–1369), *Karaite scholar born in Nicomedia and active in Constantinople. He was frequently referred to as Aharon the Younger to distinguish him from *Aharon ben Yosef ha-Rofe', the Elder. Aharon the Younger sought to provide an authoritative basis for Karaite religious life with his trilogy of Karaite lore: *ʿEts Ḥayyim*, completed in 1346, on theology (edited by Franz Delitzsch [Leipzig, 1841]); *Gan ʿEden*, completed in 1354, on Karaite law (1864; Ramleh, 1972); and *Keter Torah*, completed in 1362, a commentary on the Pentateuch (1866; Ramleh, 1972). In his works, Aharon demonstrates a wide and deep acquaintance with Karaite and Rabbanite learning, as well as with Arabic philosophical literature. He also composed a number of religious poems, some of which were included in the Karaite liturgy.

Aharon's *ʿEts Ḥayyim* was the last Karaite attempt to provide a rational basis for religious beliefs and was meant to be the Karaite counterpart to Maimonides' *Guide of the Perplexed.* Unlike Maimonides, Aharon did not seek to create a new synthesis of religion with Aristotelian philosophy but instead reformulated the Mutazili thought of his Karaite predecessors. While he was openly critical of the Maimonidean approach, his book manifests a much greater appreciation and understanding of Avraham ibn Ezra and Maimonides than do the commentaries of his predecessor Aharon ben Yosef ha-Rofe'. In contrast, *ʿEts Ḥayyim* reveals a more independent, resistant attitude toward the Andalusian Rabbanites than do the works of such fifteenth-century Karaites as Eliyyahu Bashyazi or Kalev Afendopolo. *ʿEts Ḥayyim* was popular among later Karaites, and a commentary was written on it by Simḥah Lutski.

In his *Gan ʿEden*, Aharon retains a strict interpretation of Karaite law, although he does not accept the restrictive consanguine theory of forbidden marriage. This work was the last major codification of Karaite practice before the fifteenth-century reforms of the Bashyazi family. In his biblical commentary, Aharon adopted the general Karaite preference for literal interpretation but shows the influence of the Spanish Rabbanite commentators and grammarians, inserting metaphorical comments where appropriate.

• Zvi Ankori, *Karaites in Byzantium: The Formative Years, 970–1100* (New York, 1959). Daniel Frank, "The Religious Philosophy of the Karaite Aaron ben Elijah: The Problem of Divine Justice," Ph.D. dissertation, Harvard University, 1991. Isaac Husik, *A History of Mediaeval Jewish Philosophy* (New York, 1916), pp. 362–387. —DAVID E. SKLARE

AHARON BEN ME'IR (10th cent.), Palestinian *ga'on. He is known primarily for his role in the calendrical controversy of 921 and 922, which pitted Palestinian leaders against Babylonian leaders. As the official head of Palestinian Jewry, he issued a proclamation concerning the fixing of the Jewish *calendar for the years 921 through 924. The Babylonian authorities, who followed a different interpretation of certain calendrical rules, arrived at different dates and called on the Jewish world at large to disregard his proclamation and follow the Babylonian version of the calendar. A bitter exchange followed, and the Jewish world was deeply divided. Eventually, the Babylonian version prevailed. In addition to providing the opportunity for *Saʿadyah ben Yosef Ga'on to distinguish himself in the Babylonian cause, contributing to his advancement in Babylonian academic circles, this controversy marked the last stand of the Palestinian authorities against the encroachment of Babylonian influence in legal matters.

• Ḥayyim Yeḥi'el Bornstein, *Maḥloqet Rav Saʿadyah Ga'on u-Ven Me'ir* (Warsaw, 1904). Moshe Gil, *A History of Palestine, 634–1099*, translated from the Hebrew by Ethel Broido (New York, 1992). Henry Malter, *Saadia Gaon* (1921; Hildesheim, 1978). —ROBERT BRODY

AHARON BEN MOSHEH BEN ASHER. See BEN ASHER FAMILY.

AHARON BEN MOSHEH HA-LEVI OF STAROSIELCE (1766–1828), Hasidic master. In his lifetime, Aharon ha-Levi was recognized as the most prominent adherent and original exponent of the teachings of R. *Shneur Zalman of Lyady within the *Ḥabad Hasidic movement. The tempestuous dispute that erupted after the death of Shneur Zalman resulted in both the dynastic succession of his son, Dov Ber Schneersohn, to the leadership of the evolving Ḥabad movement and to a significant ideological schism directed by Aharon. The second generation of Ḥabad was torn by the conflict arising from Aharon's attempts to disseminate extensive and systematic explanations of the writings of Shneur Zalman concerning the secrets of divine worship among the uninitiated, as well as his definitive interpretation of Ḥabad divine worship. Further, Aharon formulated a dialectic worldview that denied an independent existence to all reality, since all things, in his contention, possessed true actuality only within the divine entity. This position engendered a mystical divine worship based in total self-abnegation and denial resulting in mystical union with God. His works include *Shaʿarei ha-ʿAvodah* (Shklov, 1821), *Shaʿarei ha-Yiḥud veha-'Emunah* (Shklov, 1820), and *ʿAvodat ha-Levi* (Lwów, 1866).

• Rachel Elior, *The Paradoxical Ascent to God: The Kabbalistic Theosophy of Habad Hasidism* (Albany, 1993). Rachel Elior, *Torat ha-'Elohut ba-Dor ha-Sheni shel Ḥasidut Ḥabad* (Jerusalem, 1982). Louis Jacobs, *Seeker of Unity: The Life and Works of Aaron of Starosseljie* (London, 1966; New York, 1967). Naftali Loewenthal, *Communicating the Infinite: The Emergence of the Habad School* (Chicago, 1990). —RACHEL ELIOR

AHARON BEN SHEMU'EL, legendary miracle worker from Baghdad who revealed esoteric teachings, magic, and "secrets of prayers" to the Jewish communities in southern Italy. Two sources describe his deeds: the eleventh-century chronicle *Megillat Aḥimaʿats*, which includes a detailed description of his voyage to Italy and several tales of his miraculous activities there; and the genealogy of the *Kalonimos family, written by *Elʿazar ben Yehudah of Worms in his commentary on the prayers (MS Paris, 772, etc.). According to this second source, Aharon revealed the secrets of the prayers to the forefathers of the Kalonimids, who settled in the Rhineland in the ninth century. According to *Megillat Aḥimaʿats*, Aharon was the son of the Babylonian ga'on and was banished from his home because he used magic to make a lion perform menial work. He reportedly revived a dead child, recognized a dead person who tried to serve as a leader of the prayers in the synagogue, and performed several other miracles. It is possible that there is a historical basis to these legends, but they are insufficient to establish the exact date and circumstances of Aharon's life.

• Joseph Dan, "The Emergence of Jewish Mysticism in Medieval Europe," in *Mystics of the Book*, edited by E. Herrera (New York, 1992). Sara Zfasman, *The Jewish Tale in the Middle Ages: Between Ashkenaz and Sepharad* (Jerusalem, 1993). —JOSEPH DAN

AHARON BEN YAʿAQOV HA-KOHEN OF LUNEL (13th–14th cent.), Provençal scholar and codifier. Despite his appellation, he was probably from Narbonne. Exiled from southern France in 1306, he migrated to Majorca. He was the author of the *Orḥot Ḥayyim* (pt. 1, Florence, 1750; pt. 2, Berlin, 1902), a compendium of Jewish law and custom based on Provençal, German, French, and Spanish works, which he revised upon arriving on Majorca to include some local customs. The anonymous *Kol Bo* (1490) is considered by some scholars to be an abbreviated version of *Orḥot Ḥayyim*, but others view *Kol Bo* as a first draft. In addition to Jewish law, copies of *Orḥot Ḥayyim* in manuscript form also include chapters on faith, philosophy, the natural sciences, the Messiah, reward and punishment, the intercalation of the calendar, and formulas for documents.

• Heinrich Gross, *Gallia judaica: Dictionnaire géographique de la France d'après les sources rabbiniques*, with a supplement by Simon Schwarzfuchs (Paris, 1897; repr. Amsterdam, 1969). Moshe Schlesinger, ed., *Sefer Orḥot Ḥayyim*, pt. 2 (New York, 1959). —SHLOMO H. PICK

AHARON BEN YOSEF HA-KOHEN SARGADO, ga'on of *Pumbedita from 943 to 960. Surprisingly, he was not a scion of one of the families traditionally associated with the academy, but a prosperous merchant. Although he was a bitter enemy of *Saʿadyah ben Yosef Ga'on, Aharon's literary activity shows unmistakable signs of Saʿadyah's influence. In addition to the traditional writing of *responsa*, few of which have survived, Aharon wrote a commentary, in Arabic, as yet unpublished, on the second half of the *Book of Deuteronomy*, which was popular until at least the twelfth century.

• Benjamin Manasseh Lewin, ed., *Iggeret Rav Sherira' Ga'on* (1921; Jerusalem, 1982). Henry Malter, *Saadia Gaon* (1921; Hildesheim, 1978). Jacob Mann, *The Jews in Egypt and in Palestine under the Fatimid Caliphs* (1920–1922; New York, 1970). Adolf Neubauer, *Mediaeval Jewish Chronicles and Chronological Notes* (1887–1895; Jerusalem, 1967). —ROBERT BRODY

AHARON BEN YOSEF HA-LEVI (13th–14th cent.), Talmudic scholar and commentator also known as Harah. He was born in Barcelona and was a student of Moses *Nahmanides.

Very few of Aharon ben Yosef ha-Levi's works have survived. Best-known are his commentaries on Talmudic tractates *Ketubbot* and *Beitsah*; his commentary on two tractates of Yitsḥaq Alfasi's code, *Berakhot* and *Taʿanit*; and his critique of R. Shelomoh ben Avraham Adret's *Torat ha-Bayit*, on Jewish home and family ritual law. This critique, *Bedeq ha-Bayit*, appears in standard editions of *Torat ha-Bayit*. Though Aharon ben Yosef ha-Levi has also been credited with the authorship of *Sefer ha-Mitsvot*, a popular work on the 613 commandments, this view is unsubstantiated.

• Ḥayyim Yosef David Azulai, *Shem ha-Gedolim he-Ḥadash*, 2 vols. (Jerusalem, 1979). —MICHAEL CHERNICK

AHARON BEN YOSEF HA-ROFE' (c.1250–1320), *Karaite scholar and exegete, known as the Elder to distinguish him from *Aharon ben Eliyyahu, the Younger, who lived about a century later. The sole fact known about Aharon the Elder's life is that in 1279 he was living in Solkhat, Crimea, where he disputed the calendar with the Rabbanites. He also probably lived in Constantinople. His major work is *Sefer ha-Mivḥar* (Yevpatoriya 1835), a commentary on the Pentateuch completed in 1293. He takes a literal approach, although his work includes a significant amount of theological content and an occasional aggadic interpretation, usually taken from *Rashi. He demonstrates a deep and appreciative knowledge of rabbinic literature and quotes frequently from both Karaite and Rabbanite predecessors, in particular, Avraham ibn Ezra. Aharon the Elder's theological approach is based on Kalam, although the influence of

Maimonidean Aristotelianism can also be discerned; he thus represents the beginning of a change in Karaite religious thought. *Sefer ha-Mivḥar* was widely used by later Karaites, and seven supercommentaries were written on it. Aharon also wrote commentaries on the Former Prophets and on *Isaiah* 1–59 (published as *Mivḥar Yesharim* [Yevpatoriya, 1836]), *Psalms* 1–71, and *Job* (which has not survived). In addition, he wrote an unfinished Hebrew grammar, *Kelil Yofi* (Constantinople, 1581; Yevpatoriya, 1847), which shows the influence of Yonah ibn Yanaḥ. Aharon set the Karaite liturgy and introduced a number of Spanish Rabbanite *piyyutim* into it. His redaction became accepted as the final version of the Karaite prayer service, and some of his own liturgical poems were included in the Karaite prayer book.

• Zvi Ankori, *Karaites in Byzantium: The Formative Years, 970–1100* (New York, 1959). Daniel Lasker, "Aaron ben Joseph and the Transformation of Karaite Thought," in *Torah and Wisdom: Essays in Honor of Arthur Hyman*, edited by Ruth Link-Salinger (New York, 1992), pp. 121–128. Jacob Mann, *Texts and Studies in Jewish History and Literature*, vol. 2 (Cincinnati, 1935). —DAVID E. SKLARE

AHARON BEREKHYAH BEN MOSHEH OF MODENA (17th cent.), Italian kabbalist; best known as a compiler of liturgical manuals. His most widely known and frequently reprinted work is *Maʿavar Yabboq* (Venice, 1626), which deals with deathbed conduct and confessions and the laws governing burial and mourning.

• Mark R. Cohen et al., eds., *The Autobiography of a Seventeenth-Century Venetian Rabbi: Leon Modena's Life of Judah* (Princeton, 1988).

AHARON HA-LEVI OF BARCELONA (13th–14th cent.), Spanish Talmudist. He is the author of *Sefer ha-Ḥinnukh*, in which the 613 *commandments are enumerated in the order in which they appear in the Pentateuch and are expounded according to rabbinic tradition. The book was translated into Latin and French.

AḤARONIM (אַחֲרוֹנִים; later ones), in rabbinic literature, a term referring to contemporary scholars or those of recent generations. The dividing line between the **ri'shonim* (early ones) and the *aḥaronim* is not clearly demarcated. Beginning in the first half of the fifteenth century, *aḥaronim* was most often used in Ashkenazi circles to refer to rabbinic scholars who lived after the mid-fourteenth century, when the Black Death and attacks against German Jews decimated Jewish communities. According to other views, the *aḥaronim* came after Yosef *Karo, who wrote the *Shulḥan ʿArukh*. Generally, authorities of this period, which stretches to the present day, defer to the opinions of scholars of earlier periods, whom they view as superior to themselves but not necessarily to one another.

• Israel Jacob Yuval, "Ri'shonim ve-'Aḥaronim, Antiki et Moderni," *Zion* 57.4 (1992): 369–394, with English summary. —EDWARD FRAM

AHASUERUS (Heb. Aḥasheverosh). [*This entry discusses the biblical Persian king; for a discussion of the legendary wanderer, see* WANDERING JEW.] King of Persia mentioned in the *Book of *Esther* and believed by modern scholars to correspond to King Xerxes I (r. 486–465), Ahasuerus is pictured as very weak and capricious, easily influenced by his advisors and by the queen. He is the only figure mentioned in *Esther* who is referred to elsewhere in the Bible, appearing in *Daniel* 9.1 (where he is referred to mistakenly as the father of Darius rather than his son) and *Ezra* 4.6. There is also some discussion of Ahasuerus in the *aggadah*, where some positive things are said about him, including the assertion that he was one of the few kings in history who was able to rule over the entire earth (*Meg*. 11a; *Targum Sheni* to *Est* 1.2).

Scholars are now convinced that the name *Ahasuerus*, in its Biblical Hebrew form, is the equivalent of the Persian *Xshavarsha*, which is used to refer to King Xerxes I, the fourth king of the Achaemenian dynasty founded by Cyrus the Great. This corresponds to the Akkadian name *Hish'arshu* (and *Ahshiwarshu*) and the official Aramaic name *Ḥeshirush*. These names have long been known from fifth-century BCE Aramaic papyri and from trilingual inscriptions in Persian, Akkadian, and Elamite. A variant form of the spelling with an initial *aleph* is now attested in an Aramaic papyrus fragment from Elephantine dating to 484 BCE.

• Rainer Degen et al., *Neue Ephermeris für semitische Epigraphik*, vol. 3 (Wiesbaden, 1978), pp. 29–31, no. 4. Alan R. Millard, "In Praise of Ancient Scribes," *Biblical Archaeologist* 45 (1982): 151. Carey A. Moore, *Esther*, The Anchor Bible (Garden City, N.Y., 1971), pp. xxxv–xli, 3–4. E. M. Yamauchi, "Ahasuerus," in *The Anchor Bible Dictionary*, edited by David N. Freedman et al., vol. 1 (New York, 1992), p. 105. —SHALOM PAUL

AHAVAH RABBAH AND AHAVAT ʿOLAM (אַהֲבָה רַבָּה; אַהֲבַת עוֹלָם; Great Love and Everlasting Love), two variations of the second blessing before the *Shemaʿ mentioned in the Talmud (*Ber*. 11b). In the Ashkenazi rite, Ahavah Rabbah is recited in the morning, while Ahavat ʿOlam is recited in the evening. In all other rites Ahavat ʿOlam is used both in the morning and evening services. The central theme of this blessing is the giving of the Torah as an act of love by God to Israel. Another element is the prayer for the ability to study the Torah and fulfill all its teachings. The Sephardi rite emphasizes divine love and deeds of redemption.

• Ismar Elbogen, *Jewish Liturgy*, translated by Raymond P. Scheindlin (Philadelphia, 1993), pp. 12–20, 168–169. Ezra Fleischer, *Ha-Yotsrot be-Hithavutam be-Hitpathutam* (Jerusalem, 1984), *passim*. Lawrence A. Hoffman, *The Canonization of the Synagogue Service* (Notre Dame, Ind., 1979), pp. 30–39. —PETER LENHARDT

AHAVAT YISRA'EL. See LOVE.

AḤA'Y OF SHABḤA. See AḤA' OF SHABḤA.

AḤER. See ELISHA' BEN AVUYAH.

AHIJAH THE SHILONITE (10th cent. BCE), a prophet from the premonarchic cultic center of *Shiloh. In his prophecies Ahijah encouraged the revolt against King *Solomon and the subsequent division of Solomon's empire by the Ephraimite Jeroboam ben Nebat. Ahijah met Jeroboam on the highway between Jerusalem and Shechem and tore his outer garment into twelve pieces, giving ten of them to Jeroboam to represent symbolically the ten tribes that God gave to Jeroboam, with the other two to remain with Solomon. Because of God's later dissatisfaction with Jeroboam, the then blind Ahijah prophesied to a disguised wife of Jeroboam the demise of his dynasty (*1 Kgs*. 11.29–40, 14.1–18). Rabbinic tradition designated Ahijah as one of the seven righteous men whose combined lifespans cover the history of the world. The others are *Adam, Methusaleh, Shem, *Jacob, Amram, and *Elijah. In Hasidic legend Ahijah figures as the mystical teacher of Yisra'el ben Eliʿezer *Baʿal Shem Tov.

• Israel Finkelstein, *Shiloh: The Archaeology of a Biblical Site* (Tel Aviv, 1993), *passim*. Robert R. Wilson, *Prophecy and Society in Ancient Israel* (Philadelphia, 1980). —AARON DEMSKY

AḤIQAR, BOOK OF. See BOOK OF AḤIQAR.

AHITHOPHEL (Heb. Aḥitofel), adviser to *David, noted for his wisdom ("The counsel of Ahithophel was as if a man inquired of the word of God" [*2 Sm*. 16.23]). Ahithophel later went over to the rebellious *Absalom, but his advice, which might have meant success for the rebellion, was rejected in favor of the counterproposal made by Hushai the Archite (acting on the command of David). Seeing that his counsel went unheeded, Ahithophel committed suicide. In later Jewish tradition, Ahithophel became the archetype of an evil, provocative, overproud adviser (the rabbis say he is denied a share in the world to come), while in medieval literature he is depicted as a Mephistophelian figure to whom is ascribed a *Book of Lots* dealing with the divination of future events. According to a Midrashic legend, Ahithophel was the grandfather of Bath-sheba and teacher of Socrates.

• Randall C. Bailey, *David in Love and War: The Pursuit of Power in 1 Samuel 10–12*, Journal for the Study of the Old Testament, Supplement Series 75 (Sheffield, Eng., 1989).

AḤOT QETANNAH (אָחוֹת קְטַנָּה; Little Sister), a *pizmon* (a **piyyut* with a refrain) for the eve of Ro'sh ha-Shanah in the Sephardi and Yemenite liturgies and incorporated into some Ashkenazi liturgies under the influence of the mystics. The initial letters of the eight stanzas spell out the author's name, Avraham Ḥazzan (Ghirondi, born in Salonika, 1533). *Aḥot qetannah*, the opening words, are taken from *Song of Songs* 8.8. According to the Midrash, Israel, the Little Sister, seeks reconciliation with her Divine Lover. The poet describes the suffering Israel has endured during the past year, concluding each stanza with the refrain, "Let the year end with its curses." The final stanza, in anticipation of a better future, ends, "Let the new year begin with its blessings!"

• Abraham Z. Idelsohn, *Jewish Liturgy and Its Development* (New York, 1967), p. 215. —A. STANLEY DREYFUS

ʿAKKUM (עַכּוּ״ם; abbr. for Heb. worshipers of stars and constellations), idol worshipers. The term reflects an era when astrology was evidently particularly widespread, and much pagan worship was centered around the stars and planets. *ʿAkkum* was often used in rabbinic literature to refer to an idolater or heathen as opposed to a Christian (*nokhri* or *goy* [gentile]). However, Christian polemicists alleged that the term was an abbreviation for "worshipers of Christ and Muḥammad" or "worshipers of Christ and Mary."

• J. S. Bloch, *Israel and the Nations* (Berlin and Vienna, 1927), pp. 65–75, 85–86.

AKNIN, YOSEF BEN YEHUDAH IBN. See IBN AKNIN, YOSEF BEN YEHUDAH.

ALAMI, SHELOMOH (c.1370–1420), Spanish ethical writer who experienced the Spanish persecutions of 1391 and later moved to Portugal, where in 1415 he wrote *Iggeret ha-Musar*. In the book, also known as the *Iggeret ha-Tokhaḥah veha-'Emunah*, he suggests that the troubles of his people were caused by their own evil deeds. He condemns the learned as being either preoccupied with subtle Talmudic problems or with vainly trying to reconcile Jewish learning with fashionable philosophy; the rich had become too interested in luxury and had discarded their Judaism, while the ordinary people had not always been honest in their dealings with the gentiles. He also contrasts the style of Christian religious and liturgical behavior with the lack of decorum and carelessness of the Jews. The earliest of the eighteen editions of *Iggeret ha-Musar* appeared in Constantinople in 1510; and the latest, edited by A. N. Habermann, in Jerusalem in 1946.

• Yitzhak Baer, *A History of the Jews in Christian Spain*, translated by Louis Schoffmann et al., vol. 2 (Philadelphia, 1966).

ALASHKAR, MOSHEH (1466–1547), rabbinic scholar. Born in Spain, Alashkar was among the Jews expelled in 1492. After staying for a time in Tunis and in Patras, Greece, he reached Cairo, where he was appointed *dayyan*. In his later years he went to Jerusalem, where he remained in contact on halakhic matters with various Diaspora communities, such as Italy and Greece. He was in particularly close contact with the scholars of Crete. Alashkar is especially known for his *responsa* to distinguished contemporaries (Venice, 1554), and he had halakhic disputes with Yaʿaqov *Berab, the leading authority in Safed, among others. He also wrote on Kabbalah and was the author of *piyyutim*; one of them was included in the Sephardi **baqqashot* (publ. in Y. Zarki, *Yefeh Nof* [Sabionetta, 1573]).

• Heimann Michael, *Or ha-Ḥayyim* (Jerusalem, 1965), pp. 529–530.

ALASHKAR, YOSEF (15th cent.), North African rabbinic scholar; son of Mosheh (1417–1468), a distinguished physician and kabbalist, and author of a work in verse on the laws of ritual slaughter. Although Yosef wrote many works, little is known of his life other than that he studied in Tlemcen. His multifaceted writings include a lengthy commentary on *Avot*; a work on the laws of ritual slaughter; an ethical book, *Refu'at ha-Nefesh; Porat Yosef* on the Masorah; and a work on Yaʿaqov ben Asher's *Arbaʿah Turim (Oraḥ Ḥayyim)*. These remain in manuscript. His first and most important book was *Sefer Tsofnat Paʿneaḥ* (edited by Moshe

Idel [Jerusalem, 1991]), in which he drew connections between subjects in the Bible and oral law with astronomical, philosophical, and kabbalistic themes. After his death, his tomb became a place of pilgrimage for Jews in Algeria.

• Yaakov S. Shpigel, ed., *Ma'asekhet Avot: 'Im Perush Mirkevet ha-Mishneh* (Lod, 1993), includes bibliography. —SHALOM BAR-ASHER

ALBALAG, YITSḤAQ (13th cent.), philosopher and translator who lived in northern Spain or southern France; a follower of Aristotelianism as interpreted by Averroës. In 1292 Albalag translated al-Ghazali's *Maqasid al-falasifah* into Hebrew and added his own comments where he disagreed with the author's views. His prologue, which he called *Sefer Tiqqun ha-De'ot* (edited by Georges Vajda [Jerusalem, 1973]), includes an explanation of the creation as related in *Genesis*. Contrary to Maimonides, Albalag held that it is possible to prove the eternity of the world philosophically. Albalag was responsible for disseminating the ideas of Averroës among Jewish thinkers and was one of the chief Jewish exponents of the "double truth" theory, according to which there is no compromise between the conflicting truths of theology and philosophy. Each establishes its rules in its own manner, and a thesis may be true and false at the same time—philosophically true and theologically false, or vice versa.

• Georges Vajda, *Isaac Albalag: Averroiste juif, traducteur et annotateur d'Al-Ghazali* (Paris, 1969), includes bibliography. —FRANCISCO MORENO CARVALHO

ALBECK FAMILY, scholars of rabbinics.

Shalom Albeck (1858–1920). Born and educated in Warsaw, Albeck was a prolific scholar who undertook a biographical lexicon of rabbinic figures (*Mishpeḥot Soferim*, pt. 1 [1903]). He became involved in a protracted scholarly controversy when he expressed doubt about the textual authenticity of B. H. Auerbach's edition of *Avraham ben Yitsḥaq of Narbonne's *Sefer ha-'Eshkol* (Halberstadt, 1861), accusing the editor of forgery. Albeck finally issued his own critical edition (Berlin, 1910) which, upon his death, was continued by his son, Ḥanokh.

Ḥanokh Albeck (1890–1972). Born in Łowicz, Poland, he studied at both the Israelitisch-Theologische Lehranstalt in Vienna and the University of Vienna. In 1920 he began work as a research scholar at the Akademie für die Wissenschaft des Judentums in Berlin. He also served for a decade as professor of Talmud at the Berlin Hochschule für die Wissenschaft des Judentums before moving to Jerusalem and joining the faculty of the Hebrew University, where he taught from 1936 to 1956. He concluded in his *Untersuchungen über die Redaktion der Mishna* (Berlin, 1923) that the compilers of the Talmud did not edit but only collected scattered older material. In his *Untersuchungen über die halakhischen Midraschim* (Berlin, 1927), he stated that variant types of halakhic *midrashim* were the result of divergent redactions. Albeck published a critical edition of the Mishnah (1952–1959), edited the Hebrew translation of Leopold *Zunz's *Gottesdienstliche Vorträge* (Jerusalem, 1947), and completed the edition of *Genesis Rabbah* started by Julius Theodor.

• A. M. Habermann in *Ishim u-Demuyyot be-Ḥokhmat Yisra'el be-'Eiropah ha-Mizraḥit*, edited by Samuel K. Mirsky (New York, 1959), pp. 319–323. *Sefer ha-Yovel le-Rabbi Ḥanokh Albeq* (Jerusalem, 1963), includes bibliography 1912–1963. —DIDIER Y. REISS

ALBO, YOSEF (c.1380–1444), Spanish philosopher; pupil of Ḥasda'i ben Avraham *Crescas. In 1213 and 1214 Albo was one of the chief Jewish spokesmen in the Disputation of *Tortosa, imposed on the Jews by the church authorities. Following the disputation, widespread conversion occurred among Spanish Jews, and Albo wrote his *Sefer ha-'Iqqarim* to stem this tendency and strengthen those whose faith was wavering. This book was the final major statement of medieval Jewish *philosophy and, though undoubtedly affected by the atmosphere of Christian attacks on Judaism, represents a positive attempt to determine the roots of Jewish religion. Albo considers first the question of salvation and finds his answer in the proper conception of law. His preoccupation with law and his relegation of belief in the coming of the Messiah to the level of a secondary, rather than a primary, principle may well be his response to the Christian emphasis on faith and messianism. He focused on the delineation of the three kinds of law that guide humanity. Conventional and natural law suffice to care for earthly needs, such as peace and economic security. Only divine or revealed law can assure salvation. By setting forth three basic principles—belief in the existence of God, revelation, and retribution—under which he subsumed what he called the *shorashim* (secondary or derivative roots or principles), Albo intended to enable people to distinguish between true and pseudodivine laws. There are eight *shorashim*; four of them are connected to the first principle, the existence of God, and they are God's unity, his incorporeity, his independence of time, and his perfection. To the second principle, divine revelation, are connected three other *shorashim*: divine knowledge, prophecy, and the authenticity of Moses' mission. The final *shoresh*, connected to the third principle, retribution, is divine providence. From the *shorashim* he derives six "branches," which are not fundamentals to faith: creation *ex nihilo*, Moses as the greatest prophet, the eternal validity of the Torah, the potential for perfection by observing even a simple commandment, resurrection of the dead, and the advent of the Messiah. In typical medieval fashion, Albo tried to advance arguments for divine law based on human reason and experience, but in the last analysis he had to rest his case on revelation and belief in the reality of miracles. Albo's book was a great success in the Jewish world. The first edition appeared in Soncino in 1485. Another edition, under the title *Ohel Ya'aqov*, with a commentary by Ya'aqov ben Shemu'el Bunem of Brześć, appeared in Freiburg in 1584. An edition with an extensive commentary, called *'Ets Shatul*, by Gedalyah ben Shelomoh Lipschitz appeared in Venice in 1618. Some Christian theologians, including Hugo Grotius and Richard Simon, held *Sefer ha-'Iqqarim* in high esteem. A five-volume critical edition with English translation and annotations was published by Isaac Husik (Philadelphia, 1929–1930).

• Warren Z. Harvey, "Albo's Discussion of Time," *Jewish Quarterly Review* 70 (1980): 210–238. Isaac Husik, *A History of Medieval Jewish Philosophy* (Philadelphia, 1940), pp. 406–427. Aron Tanzer, *Die Religionsphilosophie Joseph Albo's nach seinem Werke "Ikkarim"* (Frankfurt am Main, 1896). –FRANCISCO MORENO CARVALHO

ALCALAY, ISAAC (1882–1978), rabbi. Born in Sofia, he received his rabbinical training and doctorate in Vienna and became rabbi of the Sephardi community of Belgrade in 1910. He was appointed chief rabbi of Yugoslavia in 1923 and a senator of the Yugoslav parliament in 1932. After fleeing the German occupation in 1941, he arrived in the United States. He was chief rabbi of the Central Sephardic Jewish Community of America from 1943 to 1968.

• Joseph M. Papo, *Sephardim in Twentieth-Century America* (San Jose, Calif., 1987), pp. 330–333. –MARC D. ANGEL

ALCHEMY, the branch of chemistry dedicated to the transformation of base metals into gold. The precepts of alchemy had some impact on Jewish scientists, philosophers, and mystics during the Middle Ages and early modern times. Several favorable references to it are to be found in the works of Jewish philosopher–scientists in the twelfth and thirteenth centuries, but there is no indication that any of them dedicated a specific study to the subject, or performed experiments guided by the principles of this field. Alchemy remained a relatively marginal subject in Jewish intellectual discourse, and some scholars expressed opposition to it. It had more impact on Jewish *magic, and several medieval and early modern magical texts make use of alchemical (often combined with astrological) signs and concepts. For example, it is evident from the writings of Avraham ibn Ezra that he was aware of the principles of alchemy and viewed them as part of the body of scientific knowledge, but there is no indication that he placed particular emphasis on them (as opposed to *astrology, which plays an important role in his work).

Alchemy had a greater impact on the medieval *Kabbalah. Its symbols were included in comprehensive kabbalistic systems, which presented all aspects of celestial existence as united in one chain of *emanation of divine powers. The terminology and techniques of the alchemists intrigued Jewish mystics, who interpreted the processes described as analogous to hidden processes of the divine world, and as reflecting the characteristics of divine powers. This is especially evident in the more magical aspects of kabbalistic speculations, where often astrological symbols are combined (as is often the case in non-Jewish alchemical treatises as well). The most influential use of alchemical concepts is found in the *Zohar. Several sections of the Zohar, and of the Hebrew kabbalistic works of Mosheh de León, use alchemical processes and terminology as components of the homiletical interpretation of biblical verses in a kabbalistic manner. R. Yoḥanan Aliman, a kabbalist who wrote at the end of the fifteenth century, included alchemy among his many interests in sciences and magical procedures. The Safed kabbalist R. Ḥayyim Vital wrote an alchemical treatise and indicated his interest in this topic in other ways as well.

One of the more important aspects of the impact of alchemy on Jewish thought was its relationship to biblical hermeneutics. Many biblical figures, verses, and events were interpreted as embodying or reflecting alchemical principles, and difficult passages in scriptures were understood as representing truths pointed out by alchemical theory. In this way, the Bible was used to legitimize the "craft," as well as to demonstrate its antiquity. There were several alchemists who contributed meaningfully to the development of medieval and early modern alchemical literature who were Jews or Jewish converts to Christianity, but they did not write in Hebrew, so their works were not integrated into Jewish scientific tradition. Alchemical tradition includes legends about prominent Jewish figures in the history of this science, from Elijah the Prophet to Maria Hebraica, who was reputed to have lived in the first century in Egypt and to have discovered important alchemical techniques. Such legends, coupled with the attribution of alchemical knowledge to biblical figures, created an image of a major Jewish element in the history of alchemy. Yet within Jewish culture itself its impact remained marginal.

• Raphael Patai, *The Jewish Alchemists: A History and Source Book* (Princeton, 1991). Raphael Patai, "Maria the Jewess: Founding Mother of Alchemy," *Ambix: The Journal of the Society for the History of Alchemy and Chemistry* 29 (1982): 177–197. Gershom Gerhard Scholem, *Alchemie und Kabbala* (Frankfurt am Main, 1994). –JOSEPH DAN

ALCIMUS, high priest in Jerusalem from c.162 to 159 BCE. Following the restoration of the sacrificial cult by *Judah the Maccabee in 164 BCE, the post of high priest seems to have remained vacant for about two years, until the Seleucid king Demetrius I nominated Alcimus. His nomination was approved by the scribes and the *Hasideans but not by Judah. Once in office, Alcimus alienated the Hasideans by murdering sixty of their adherents. This deed as well as his opposition to Judah and his destruction of the walls of the inner court of the Temple were condemned in the extant Jewish sources.

• Martin Hengel, *Judaism and Hellenism*, translated by John Bowden, 2 vols. (Philadelphia, 1974). Emil Schürer, *The History of the Jewish People in the Age of Jesus Christ, 175 B.C.–A.D. 135*, new English version revised and edited by Geza Vermes and Fergus Millar, vol. 1 (Edinburgh, 1973) pp. 168–170. Victor Tcherikover, *Hellenistic Civilization and the Jews*, translated by S. Applebaum (Philadelphia, 1966), pp. 228–231. –GIDEON BOHAK

ALDABI, ME'IR (c.1310–1360), Spanish mystical philosopher. A grandson of *Asher ben Yeḥi'el, Aldabi was the author of *Shevilei Emunah*, an encyclopedic treatise on the existence and nature of God, creation, the geography of the earth, human physiology and psychology, rules for health, the nature of the soul, Jewish law, human destiny, and the final redemption of Israel. The work is divided into ten paths, or sections, and seems to have been based largely on the ideas of Gershon ben Shelomoh of Arles, Moses *Nahmanides, Yosef ben Yaʿaqov ibn *Zaddik, *Hillel ben Shemu'el, Moses *Maimonides, Shelomoh ben Avraham *Adret, and *Baḥya ben Yosef ibn Paquda'. Aldabi, who settled in Jerusalem, was well-versed in both Talmud and kabbalistic literature and seems to have had some knowledge of Arabic. He believed that the ideas of the Greek philosophers were ultimately derived from Hebrew sources, and his aim seems to have been to compile all of knowledge into one volume. The work, first published in Riva di Trento (1518), was popular and went through several editions.

• George Sarton, *Introduction to the History of Science*, vol. 3, *Science and Learning in the Fourteenth Century* (Baltimore, 1927–1948), s.v. index. Isaac Hirsch Weiss, *Dor Dor ve-Dorshav*, vol. 5 (Vienna, 1871–1891), pp. 117, 141, 214.

ʿALEINU (עָלֵינוּ; It Is Our Duty to Praise), prayer proclaiming divine sovereignty over the world; though probably composed earlier, it is attributed by tradition to the school of Rav, from the third century, as an introduction to the *Malkhuyyot section of the *Ro'sh ha-Shanah Musaf service. From the fourteenth century on, it began to be used as the concluding prayer for all services in all rites. The prayer was also the object of slanderous accusations. The phrase "for they prostrate themselves to vanity and emptiness and pray to a god who cannot save them" was interpreted by the Christian authorities as a specific attack upon Christianity and was censored by them. It was later deleted from many printed editions of the Ashkenazi ritual in order to prevent libels and persecutions. The Sephardim, who recite only the first paragraph of the prayer at the end of their daily prayer, and who lived mainly in Islamic countries, still retain it. Most Ashkenazi Orthodox congregations in Israel have reinstituted this phrase, whereas some of the progressive editions of the prayer book continue to omit it. The prayer, a confident and triumphant proclamation of God's universal kingship in a pagan world, was invested during medieval times with special solemnity and awe and became particularly associated with martyrdom. The martyrs of Blois, in 1171, are said to have been heard singing the ʿAleinu from the burning pyre.

• Ismar Elbogen, *Jewish Liturgy: A Comprehensive History* (Philadelphia, 1993), pp. 71–72. Joseph Heinemann, *Prayer in the Talmud: Forms and Patterns* (Berlin, 1977), pp. 269–275. Lawrence A. Hoffman, *Gates of Understanding* (New York, 1984), vol. 2, pp. 42–46. Jakob J. Petuchowski, *Prayerbook Reform in Europe: The Liturgy of European Liberal and Reform Judaism* (New York, 1968), pp. 298–306. Stefan C. Reif, *Judaism and Hebrew Prayer: New Perspectives on Jewish Liturgical History* (Cambridge, 1993), pp. 208–209. —PETER LENHARDT

ALEKSANDER ZISKIND BEN MOSHEH OF GRODNO (c.1740–1794), Lithuanian kabbalist and author of ethical works. He frequently cites his teacher Aryeh Leib of Königsberg in his *Qarnei Or*, a commentary on the *Zohar. A student of Lurianic Kabbalah, his most noted work is the *Yesod ve-Shoresh ha-ʿAvodah*, a kabbalistic ethical interpretation of various biblical commandments. It was first published in 1794, and has been frequently reprinted since then (corrected edition, Jerusalem, 1959), often with his lengthy ethical will.

• Simeon A. Friedenstein, *ʿIr Gibborim* (Vilna, 1880), pp. 62–63. —STEVEN BALLABAN

ALEXANDRIAN MARTYRS, ACTS OF. See ACTS OF ALEXANDRIAN MARTYRS.

ALFANDARI, SHELOMOH ELIʿEZER BEN YAʿAQOV (1826–1930), rabbinical scholar. Born in Constantinople, he was head of a *yeshivah* by the age of twenty-five. When he was thirty, he was a member of the city's religious council, and he obtained the annulment of an order conscripting Jews into the Turkish army. He was **ḥakham bashi* of Damascus from 1899 to 1903 and of Safed from 1903 to 1918. He was influenced by practical Kabbalah. His scholarship was widely respected, and his *responsa* and rulings were accepted.

• David Z. Lanyado, *Li-Qedoshim asher ba-'Arets*, 2d ed. (Jerusalem, 1980), pp. 5–6, 61, 76. Moshe Z. Neriah, *Liqqutei ha-Rei'yah* (Jerusalem, 1995), pp. 149–165. —SHALOM BAR-ASHER

ALFASI, DAVID (10th cent.), *Karaite lexicographer and commentator. He was born in Fez, Morocco, and lived for a number of years in Jerusalem, where he wrote his *Kitab Jamiʿ al-Alfaz*, a Judeo-Arabic lexicon of the Bible. This dictionary was an important step forward in the development of Hebrew philology. Alfasi had a fine sense for language and pointed out many parallels between biblical Hebrew, Mishnaic Hebrew, Aramaic, and Arabic. He made use of the ancient Aramaic Bible translations by Onkelos and Yonatan ben ʿUzzi'el, as well as the more contemporary commentary of Saʿadyah Ga'on. Levi ben Yefet compiled a short version of the lexicon, which was used by ʿAli ben Yisra'el and ʿAli ibn Suleyman when composing their dictionaries. Alfasi also wrote commentaries on *Psalms* and the *Song of Songs*, which do not seem to have survived.

• Solomon L. Skoss, *Hebrew–Arabic Dictionary of the Bible, Known as Kitab Jami al-Alfaz, of David ben Abraham*, 2 vols. (New Haven, 1936; New York, 1981), introduction. Aharon Maman, "The Lexical Element in David Alfasi's Dictionary Definitions," in *Genizah Research After Ninety Years*, edited by Joshua Blau and Stefan C. Reif (Cambridge, 1992), pp. 119–125. —DAVID E. SKLARE

ALFASI, YITSḤAQ (1013–1103), Talmudic authority and codifier; known as Rif. Born in Algeria, he studied with R. Ḥanan'el ben Ḥushi'el in Kairouan and settled in Fez (hence the name Alfasi, i.e., of Fez), where he lived until the age of seventy-five. He was then forced to flee to Spain, where he headed the community of Lucena. Alfasi was an important link in the process of transferring the center of Talmudic studies from east to west. The last of the Babylonian ge'onim, R. Ha'i, died when Alfasi was twenty-five, and by way of the North African academies, Spain began to emerge as the new focus of Talmudic learning. Alfasi was the first major rabbinical authority to teach in Spain. Hundreds of his *responsa* have been preserved, most of them originally written in Arabic and addressed to communities in Spain and North Africa. His *Sefer ha-Halakhot* (Constantinople, 1509) is one of the basic works of Jewish legal codification. Its objectives were to extract legal subject matter from the Talmud and determine halakhic rulings, and to present a digest of the Talmud that would facilitate and popularize its study. His brief explanations, inserted into the original Talmud text, brilliantly clarify difficult and obscure points. Writing at the conclusion of the geonic period, Alfasi was able to present an authoritative summation of geonic thought and legislation while concentrating on the actual Talmud text, which, by that time, was often neglected. *Sefer ha-Halakhot* influenced many scholars and codifiers, constituting a primary source for Moses *Maimonides. It was also, in turn, the subject of numerous other works, both critical and supportive, and during the following centuries in western Europe, particularly in Spain, rabbinical study was based not on the Talmud but on Alfasi's work. See CODIFICATION OF LAW.

• Charles Ber Chavel, *Perush Eḥad mi-Gedolei ha-Ri'shonim le-Hilkhot ha-Rif* (New York, 1960). Shamma Friedman, ed., *Halakhot Rabbati of R. Isaac Alfasi* (Jerusalem, 1974), a facsimilie edition, with an English introduction and bibliography. Schaul Schaffer, *Ha-Rif u-Mishnato* (Jerusalem, 1966).

ALGAZI FAMILY, family of rabbis and community leaders active from the sixteenth through the nineteenth century in Turkey, Crete, Erets Yisra'el, and Egypt.

Nissim Shelomoh ben Avraham Algazi (1610–1683), rabbi born in Bursa, Turkey. In 1635 he moved to Jerusalem, but in approximately 1646 he settled in Smyrna, where he established a *beit midrash*. He spent his last years, from 1670 on, back in Jerusalem. His writings include commentaries on the Talmud and *aggadah* and four volumes of homilies.

Yisra'el Ya'aqov ben Yom Tov Algazi (1680–1756), grandson of Nissim Shelomoh; rabbi and kabbalist. By 1737, he had left his native Smyrna, lived in Safed, and settled in Jerusalem. He revitalized the spiritual life of the Jerusalem community, establishing *yeshivot* and leading the influential Beit El and Ahavat Shalom, circles of kabbalists. He produced works on many halakhic subjects, a work on Talmudic methodology, and a homiletic commentary on the Torah; it has been surmised that he was also the author of the anonymous *Ḥemdat Yamim*. Revered by Sephardi Jewry, he was appointed chief rabbi of Jerusalem (*ri'shon le-Tsiyyon*) shortly before his death. The circles of mystics to which he belonged believed in the possibility of a return from the dead, and there is a document defining the goals of his circle dated from a year after his death and bearing his signature.

Yom Tov ben Yisra'el Ya'aqov Algazi (1727–1802), son of Yisra'el Ya'aqov and outstanding halakhist and kabbalist. A friend of Ḥayyim Yosef David Azulai, Algazi was appointed chief rabbi of Jerusalem in 1776. Among his works are sermons and *responsa*, a commentary on a halakhic text of Nahmanides, which he discovered in Italy, and a study of the laws of divorce, *Get Mequshar* (1767).

• Meir Benayahu, *Rabbi Ḥayyim Yosef David Azulai* (Jerusalem, 1959), pp. 351ff. (on Yisra'el Ya'aqov), pp. 353–354 (on Yom Tov). Gershom Gerhard Scholem, *Sabbatai Ṣevi: The Mystical Messiah, 1626–1676* (Princeton, 1973).

'AL HA-NISSIM (עַל הַנִּסִּים; [We Thank You] for the Miracles), addition inserted into the *'Amidah and *Birkat ha-Mazon on the festivals of *Purim and *Ḥanukkah. After the initial formula, a brief account of the events commemorated on the festival is recited. The version that has become accepted is first known from the prayer book of R. *'Amram bar Sheshna' (9th cent.), though different rites exhibit minor textual variants. The Conservative prayer book contains a version to be recited on Yom ha-'Atsma'ut.

• Ismar Elbogen, *Jewish Liturgy: A Comprehensive History*, translated by Raymond P. Scheindlin (Philadelphia, 1993). Macy Nulman, *The Encyclopedia of Jewish Prayer* (Northvale, N.J., 1993).

'AL ḤET' (עַל חֵטְא; For the Sin), a litany of confession, also known as Viddui Rabbah, recited in the Minḥah service preceding Yom Kippur and in every service on Yom Kippur except the concluding service, when it is replaced by *Attah Noten Yad. The congregation first recites these confessions silently and then repeats them aloud, together with the reader, as part of the confession connected to the Yom Kippur 'Amidah since tannaitic times. The list of sins is in alphabetical order (the Sephardi version includes one sin for each letter, the Ashkenazi, two). Shorter versions exist from the geonic period, as do expanded versions from the Middle Ages. The 'Al Ḥet' is recited in the first person plural, as a corporate and not an individual act, and enumerates sins in the domain of human relations and acts of diminishing the image of God, begging God's forgiveness.

• Meir Tsevi Gruzman, *'Al Ḥet' u-Teshuvah* (Tel Aviv, 1986).

—PETER LENHARDT

ALIEN. See STRANGER.

ALIMAN, YOḤANAN (c.1435–1504), author of a philosophical commentary on the *Song of Songs*; also known as Allemano. Born in Constantinople, he later immigrated to Italy. His most famous pupil was the Christian Hebraist and kabbalist Pico della Mirandola. *Ḥesheq Shelomoh* (Leghorn, 1790), the title of his commentary on the *Song of Songs*, is the longest of four books he is known to have written and the only one which has been printed (this, only in part). It reveals a thorough knowledge of Greek and Arabic philosophy. In the introduction to the work he seeks to demonstrate that King Solomon had a command of all fields of human inquiry. Aliman's other works are *'Einei ha-'Edah*, a commentary on the Pentateuch; *Ḥayyei 'Olam*, on how to achieve union with God; and *Sefer Liqqutim*, a collection of *novellae*, wise sayings, and aphorisms, some from works no longer extant.

• Umberto Cassuto, *Gli Ebrei a Firenze* (Firenze, 1918). Cecil Roth, *The Jews in the Renaissance* (Philadelphia, 1959), pp. 118–121.

—STEVEN BALLABAN

ALIMONY. There is no provision in Jewish law for the maintenance of a divorced wife by her husband (*Shulḥan 'Arukh, Even ha-'Ezer* 82.6). A divorced woman does, however, receive a lump sum, consisting of the **ke-tubbah*, an additional increment known as the *tosefet ketubbah*, and her dowry (*nedunyah*). This lump sum is intended to provide a divorced woman with all the financial support she requires. Even if she has forfeited her *ketubbah* as a result of misconduct during marriage, she is entitled to receive back her dowry (*Shulḥan 'Arukh, Even ha-'Ezer* 115.5). A husband who lives with his wife and does not ensure that she has a proper *ketubbah* is condemned by the Talmud in the strongest of terms (*Ket*. 54b). Notwithstanding the fact that divorce terminates a husband's obligation to maintain his wife, it is a *mitsvah* to support a divorced spouse in preference to the poor at large (Isserles, *Even ha-ʿEzer* 119.8).

• Louis Epstein, *The Jewish Marriage Contract* (New York, 1927). Yehoshua Liebermann, "The Economics of *Kethubah* Valuation," *History of Political Economy* 15 (1983): 519–528. —DANIEL SINCLAIR

ʿALIYYAH (עֲלִיָּה; ascent, going up), a word applied to three different kinds of ascent.

Ascent to Heaven. The only explicit reference in the Bible to a miraculous ascent to heaven is that of the prophet Elijah (*2 Kgs*. 2.1–13). The Midrash (*Gn. Rab.* 25.1) denies that Enoch ascended to heaven, against the views of the sectarians (*minim*), who so interpreted *Genesis* 5.24, but apocalyptic literature regarded both Enoch and Moses (the latter on the basis of his ascent of Mount Sinai) as having made the ascent to heaven and returned to earth; they are both the subjects of apocalypses bearing their names and centering on their ascension. Other figures who ascended to heaven according to apocalyptic and rabbinic literature include Isaiah, Baruch, Ezra, and even post-biblical rabbis such as Yishmaʿeʾl ben Elishaʿ. In some instances the ascent is described as a journey to a permanent paradise; in others it is a temporary mystical ascent followed by a return to earth.

Ascent to Erets Yisra'el. The geographical elevation of Erets Yisra'el, relative to low-lying Egypt, is the basis of the concept of going down from Israel to Egypt (*Gn.* 12.10) and going up from Egypt to Israel (*Gn.* 13.1). From this, *ʿaliyyah* was applied to journeys from any country to Israel, whether for *pilgrimage on the occasion of the *Shalosh Regalim or for permanent settlement. Biblical law requires every male Israelite to make the *ʿaliyyat regel* (festival pilgrimage) and visit the Temple three times a year (*Ex.* 23.14). After the destruction of the Second Temple, such pilgrimages were made as voluntary acts of piety. With the *exile, the rabbis of the Talmudic period and subsequent ages went to great lengths to emphasize the importance of permanent settlement in Israel, apart from the duty of pilgrimage: "One should rather dwell in Israel even among a non-Jewish majority than outside Israel even in the midst of a Jewish majority" (T., *ʿA. Z.* 4.3); "He who dwells in the land of Israel is regarded as having God ever with him, but he who dwells outside Israel is as one who has no God" (*ʿA. Z.* 4.5). Both statements stem from the aggadic discussion of the Mishnaic law that states that a man can force his family to follow him to settle in Israel, and if the wife refuses to do so, she loses her marriage settlement in case of divorce (*Ket.* 110b). Maimonides ruled that the refusal of a husband or wife to accompany his or her spouse to Erets Yisra'el constitutes grounds for divorce (*Hilkhot Ishut* 13). Faced with the problem of a sizable migration from Babylon to Israel, third-century Babylonian amora' R. Yehudah came out strongly against *ʿaliyyah* to Erets Yisra'el, going so far as to declare it a biblical transgression (*Ket.* 110b). Similarly during the twelfth and thirteenth centuries, when *ʿaliyyah* from England, France, and Germany was assuming considerable proportions as a result of the increasing insecurity of the Jews in those countries, tosafist R. Ḥayyim Kohen ruled that the religious duty to settle in the Holy Land no longer applied, since it was too difficult to observe all the additional commandments applicable there and the penalty for transgressing them was severe. Another reason *ʿaliyyah* was discouraged was because of the danger of travel. Rabbi Me'ir ben Baruch of Rothenburg (13th cent.) took a middle position and in a *responsum* sanctioned *ʿaliyyah* to Israel only if one's economic livelihood was assured there. Talmudic precept and later expositions of religious law kept alive the ideal of permanent settlement in Erets Yisra'el, exemplified by distinguished rabbis, Talmudists, kabbalists, and pietists (e.g., Nahmanides in 1266, ʿOvadyah Bertinoro in 1488, Yosef Karo and his followers in the 16th cent., Yeshaʿyahu Horowitz in 1621, Yehudah Ḥasid ha-Levi and his 1,500 followers in 1700, Menaḥem Mendel of Vitebsk and 300 Ḥasidim in 1777). Dwelling in Erets Yisra'el was of profound mystical significance for the kabbalists, who cited the authority of the *Zohar. This tradition continued among the Ḥasidim of eastern Europe. There was also a steady *ʿaliyyah* from North Africa. With the growth of modern Zionism and the establishment of the State of Israel in 1948, religious factors and motivations have continued to play an important part in the mass *ʿaliyyah* of Jews from all parts of the world. Some of those immigrating to Israel, especially from Muslim lands (e.g., Yemen), were motivated by traditional messianism, and religious Jews saw the mass immigration as the fulfillment of the biblically prophesied ingathering of the *exiles. Classical nineteenth-century *Reform Judaism expunged references for a return to Zion from its ideology and liturgy, but this was revised in the mid-twentieth century. Some Orthodox Jews reject modern Zionism as an erroneous human attempt to force *redemption (see ZIONISM).

Ascent to the Reading of the Law. When the Torah is read in the synagogue (see QERI'AT HA-TORAH), individuals are called up to the reading. This honor is known as an *ʿaliyyah*. In ancient times although one went down to conduct the prayers (the reading desk was recessed in the floor), the Torah scroll was read from an elevated platform (cf. *Neh.* 8.4); hence the use of the word *ʿaliyyah*. Only males over the age of thirteen are called up to the Torah in Orthodox congregations; women are now called up in non-Orthodox synagogues. The first *ʿaliyyah* is reserved for a *kohen* (see PRIESTHOOD), the second for a Levite. The third *ʿaliyyah* and the sixth are regarded as the most prestigious. Until the thirteenth century the person called up to the Torah read the portion himself; for those unable to do so, a reader was appointed. By the fourteenth century, a reader was appointed to recite the portion for all, so as not to put the ignorant to shame, and the person called up only recited the relevant blessings. Today a boy celebrating his *bar mitsvah* and a girl her *bat mitsvah* often read the portion to which they are called. In most rites persons are called up by their first name and patronymic. Often in non-Orthodox synagogues, people are called by the names of both parents.

• Martha Himmelfarb, *Ascent to Heaven in Jewish and Christian Apocalypses* (New York, 1993). Ephraim Kanarfogel, "The ʿAliyah of 'Three Hundred Rabbis' in 1211: Tosafist Attitudes toward Settling in the Land of Israel," *Jewish Quarterly Review* 76 (1986): 191–215. Mark Verman, "Aliyah and Yeridah: The Journeys of the Besht and R. Nachman to Israel," in *Approaches to Judaism in Medieval Times*, vol. 3, edited by David Blumenthal (Atlanta, 1988), pp. 159–171. Zvi Yehuda, "The Place of Aliyah in Moroccan Jewry's Conception of Zionism," *Studies in Zionism* 6 (1985): 199–210.

ʿALIYYAH LA-REGEL. See PILGRIMAGE.

ʿALIYYAH LA-TORAH. See ʿALIYYAH.

ALKABEZ, SHELOMOH (1505–c.1576), kabbalist and poet; immigrated to Erets Yisra'el from Salonika. He was among the founders of the sixteenth-century kabbalistic community of *Safed. Alkabez was the student of R. Mosheh Albildah and R. Yosef *Taitazak in Salonika; his student and brother-in-law was R. Mosheh *Cordovero. Before leaving Salonika in 1534, he delivered a sermon in which he explained that his impending trip was based upon a theory of national redemption. On his way to Erets Yisra'el he stayed in Nikopol and Adrianople. From Nikopol, where he celebrated Shavuʿot with R. Yosef Karo, Alkabez sent a letter to Salonika in which he described the revelation of a **maggid* to Karo and encouraged his readers to immigrate to Erets Yisra'el. On his way he also wrote a letter to Karo concerning kabbalistic matters (published at the end of his *Berit ha-Levi*).

Alkabez wrote several works, but only a few of them have survived. Two important works that concern his doctrine of the divinity are still in manuscript. His major works available in print are *Menot ha-Levi* (Venice, 1585), a commentary to the *Book of Esther*, which he presented as a wedding gift to his wife's family (1529); *Ayyelet Ahavim* (Venice, 1512), a commentary to the *Song of Songs*; *Berit ha-Levi* (Lemberg, 1863), a commentary to the Passover Haggadah; and *Shoresh Yishai* (Constantinople, 1561 or 1566), a commentary to *Ruth*, which he composed in Safed. Alkabez's thought influenced Cordovero and many other later kabbalists. In *Ayyelet Ahavim*, Alkabez included a biographical love story describing the kabbalist's intimate relationship with the Torah, his love of the study of Torah, the difficulties he encounters, his ideals, and his accomplishments. In *Berit ha-Levi*, he stresses the importance of the Zoharic corpus and attacks those who mock it. In his published prayers, he lyricizes the anguish of the exile from Spain and the desolate state of Erets Yisra'el. Alkabez's most celebrated prayer, the poem *Lekhah Dodi, has been incorporated into the Friday evening service.

• Simon G. Bernstein, *R. Shelomoh Alkabets: der shafer fun der Yiddisher "Marselieze"* (New York, 1958). Mordechai Pachter, *Mi-Tsefunot Tsefat* (Jerusalem, 1994). Bracha Sack, "The Mystical Theology of Solomon Alkabez," Ph.D. dissertation, Brandeis University, 1977.

—BRACHA SACK AND DANIEL ABRAMS

ALKALAI, YEHUDAH SHELOMOH ḤAI (1798–1878), forerunner of modern *Zionism and Sephardi rabbi of Zemun, near Belgrade. He was one of a small group of mid-nineteenth-century Orthodox rabbis who maintained that Jews had to take the initiative to settle in Erets Yisra'el for their own security and not await messianic auspices for the return to Zion. At first his ideas remained within traditional rabbinic yearnings for Zion and kabbalistic calculations focusing on 1840 (5600 in the Jewish calendar) as the messianic year. However, his growing awareness of contemporary historical developments led him to reinterpret the religious texts as calling on the Jewish people to resettle their ancestral homeland by natural means as a necessary prelude to the supernatural redemption. In a series of books and pamphlets and visits to the main capitals of Europe he outlined a program that anticipated the main ingredients of modern Zionism. He proposed the establishment of a representative assembly of Jewish religious and secular leaders, the adoption of Hebrew as the unifying national language, productivization of the settlers, diversification of the economy, and revival of the biblical tithe, whereby every Jew would contribute a tenth of his or her income toward the rebuilding of Zion. He failed at first to achieve any substantial support, encountering opposition from Jewish assimilationists who wished to integrate into the countries of their adoption and from pietists who regarded human intervention in the messianic consummation as blasphemy. In the 1860s and 1870s, during which period he emigrated to Erets Yisra'el (1874), he found his ideas shared by a small but growing number of individuals and groups that had become involved in the practical efforts to settle the land.

• Marc Angel, *Voices in Exile* (New York, 1991). Arthur Hertzberg, *The Zionist Idea* (New York, 1959). Jacob Katz, "The Forerunners of Zionism and The Jewish National Movement," in *Jewish Emancipation and Self-Emancipation*, (Philadelphia, 1986), pp. 89–115. Jacob Katz, "Meshiḥiyyut u-Le'umiyyut be-Mishnato shel ha-Rav Yehudah Alqala'i," in *Le'umiyyut Yehudit* (Jerusalem, 1979), pp. 264–284. Itzak Raphael, *Kitvei ha-Rav Yehudah Alqala'i* (n.p., 1974).

—ARYEH NEWMAN

ALLEGORY. As a mode of interpretation of the Bible, allegory was a central and crucial step in the development of Jewish thought. The first significant allegorist in Jewish literature was Philo, who continued a tradition that reached back at least to Aristobulus of Paneas, of whose work only sparse quotations survive. Philo's extensive writings and commentaries present an allegorical reading of the Bible that uncovers its inner message of the ascent of the soul to higher, spiritual spheres. He nevertheless also upholds the literal meaning and validity of the commandments: "It is true that circumcision does indeed portray the excision of pleasure . . . but let us not on this account repeal the law laid down for circumcising."

Philo has been viewed as the inaugurator of scriptural philosophy, which was to remain the hallmark of Jewish philosophy until Spinoza. The problematic nature of allegorical interpretation is seen in the brief passage quoted above. How far can one go in attributing another, albeit deeper, meaning to scripture without invalidating the commandments of the Torah? As philosophy reentered the mainstream of rabbinic Judaism with Saʿadyah Ga'on, the legitimacy of the allegorical approach lay at the heart of numerous controversies in the Middle Ages. In the fourteenth century, Abba' Mari castigated the followers of Maimonides, who presumed to turn Abraham and Sarah into symbols of form and matter. Against the philosophers, the kabbalists held that "the prayers and rituals of the Torah had to be preserved as symbols of the transcendence that erupts into our world, not as allegories of ideas inherent in the world . . ." (Gershom Scholem, *Origins of the Kabbalah*).

Talmudic and Midrashic literature are replete with interpretations of scripture that are symbolical rather than allegorical. Thus according to *Genesis Rabbah* 70.8, Jacob's well symbolizes Zion, the Sanhedrin, or even the synagogue. Moses' raised hands, water, and the tree of life all signify the Torah (*Mekhilta' de-Rabbi Yishmaʿeʾl* on "Be-Shallaḥ"). The wicked are designated by the sun and the sea in the opening chapter of *Ecclesiastes*. This method of interpretation differs, however, from the sustained allegorical development by Philo, if only because the anthological nature of rabbinic literature does not permit extensive and systematic treatment. Rabbi Yishmaʿe'l ben Elishaʿ, who held that "the Torah was speaking in the language of man," and his school would naturally have been more receptive to the allegorical method. The amoraic *aggadah* abounds in the type of exegesis cited above.

The connection between allegory and apologetics has been a subject of scholarly debate. It is obvious that allegory could serve as an effective tool for those interested in preserving a sacred text while altering its meaning at one and the same time. The implicit possibility of the annulment of the text accounts for some of the vehement opposition to allegorical interpretation.

• Daniel Boyarin, *Intertextuality and the Reading of the Midrash* (Bloomington, Ind., 1990). Isaak Heinemann, *Altjudische Allegoristik* (Breslau, 1936). Gershom Gerhard Scholem, *Origins of the Kabbalah*, edited by R. J. Zwi Werblowsky, translated from the German by Allan Arkush (Philadelphia, 1987). David Winston, "Philo and the Contemplative Life," in *Jewish Spirituality*, edited by Arthur Green (New York, 1986), vol. 1, pp. 198–231.

—MARC HIRSHMAN

ALLEMANNO, YOḤANAN. See ALIMAN, YOḤANAN.

ALMEMAR. See BIMAH.

ALMOSNINO FAMILY, a family of Spanish origin prominent in various Mediterranean communities, notably Salonika.

Mosheh ben Barukh Almosnino (c.1515–1580), rabbi, scholar, and homilist. He served various congregations in Salonika and worked to unite the many Jewish communities, though with little success. His book of homilies, *Ma'amats Koaḥ* (Venice, 1588), is an important source for his philosophy. Of special interest is the section on the nature of life, which reflects his general spiritual outlook. He questions the extent to which the laws of justice, in *halakhah* and in ethics, apply for all times and in all circumstances. Thus the refusal to look at a married woman who is drowning he dismisses as foolish pietism and says that *halakhah* must be applied with common sense and wisdom. Insistence on performing even the greatest *mitsvah* at the cost of endangering life contradicts the basic law of preserving life. The laws of justice must be made to fit specific situations and cannot be viewed as ideal abstractions. Almosnino was the author of various compositions, including a commentary on *Avot*, a commentary on the Five Scrolls, a book of ethics (in Ladino), and *responsa*.

Yosef ben Yitsḥaq Almosnino (1642–1689), a descendant of Mosheh ben Barukh; rabbinical authority and kabbalist. Born in Salonika, Yosef served as rabbi in Belgrade. He was a supporter of Shabbateanism. Many of his works were lost in a fire.

• Charles J. Abeles, "Moses Almosnino, His Ethical and Other Writings: A Study of the Life and Works of a Prominent Sixteenth Century Salonikan Rabbi," Ph.D. dissertation, Dropsie College, 1957. Michael Molho, "Dos obras maestras en ladino de Moises Almosnino," in *Estudios y ensayos sobre topicos judios* (Buenos Aires, 1958). S. Rosenberg, "'Al Derekh ha-Rov," in *Shenaton ha-Mishpat ha-ʿIvri* 14–15 (1988–1989): 189–216.

—SHALOM BAR-ASHER

AL-MUKAMMIS, DAVID. See MUKAMMIS, DAVID IBN MARWAN.

AL-NAKAWA, YISRA'EL BEN YOSEF (died 1391), Spanish scholar; martyred in his native Toledo. He belonged to an important Jewish family from Spain that subsequently immigrated to northern Africa and Turkey. He wrote the ethical work *Menorat ha-Ma'or*, which was probably the basis for the better-known work of the same name by Yitsḥaq *Aboab. The book deals with practical aspects of religious life and incorporates a wealth of maxims gathered from Talmudic *aggadah*, later rabbinic sources, and the Zohar. It has twenty chapters and begins with an acrostic poem based on the author's name. Each chapter also begins with an acrostic poem based on the name Yisra'el. The book was printed in 1578, and an abridgment was published in 1593 in Kraków under the title *Menorat Zahav Kullah*. A new edition, based on the single surviving manuscript of the work that is in Oxford, was published by Hyman Enelow (4 vols. [New York, 1929–1932]). A number of *piyyutim* written by Al-Nakawa have survived.

• N. Ben-Menaḥem, Introduction to *Menorat ha-Ma'or*, by Isaac Aboab (Jerusalem, 1954).

—FRANCISCO MORENO CARVALHO

ALPHABET, HEBREW. The Hebrew alphabet is an offshoot of the Canaanite alphabet, the first purely alphabetical script. In the course of its history, Hebrew employed two distinct forms of this alphabet. The first was the ancient Hebrew alphabet, used until the Babylonian exile. Even after the exile, this script appeared on practically all Jewish coins, throughout some Dead Sea manuscripts, and in other Dead Sea manuscripts for the writing of divine names only. In general use, the ancient Hebrew alphabet was replaced by an eastern Aramaic script, itself derived from the Canaanite alphabet; only the Samaritans retained the ancient Hebrew alphabet. In the first two centuries CE, the Aramaic alphabet (*ketav ashuri*) developed into the specifically Jewish square script (*ketav merubbaʿ*; see SCRIPT, HEBREW). At various times cursive forms developed locally (e.g., *Rashi script). Jews used the Hebrew alphabet extensively in writing such vernacular languages as Aramaic, Arabic, Persian, Turkish, Berber, Spanish, Provençal, Italian, medieval and modern German, Judeo-Spanish, and Yiddish. Until modern times religious Jews avoided using gentile scripts, which were said to trouble the spiritual purity of the eyes.

The order of the Hebrew alphabet was apparently fixed from the start and was employed as a literary device in alphabetic acrostical psalms. It was the Greeks who first conceived of using the letters of the alphabet as numerical signs (the Israelites used special number symbols). The method was adopted in the first centuries CE by Jews and is still extensively employed. It gave rise to **gimatriyyah*, in which the numerical values of the letters of a word are added together and compared with those of other words for exegetical, homiletic, and mystical uses. The method of inserting the letters in Torah scrolls is minutely regulated by *halakhah* and custom; of special interest are the **tagin* (crowns) placed over seven of the letters. The religious significance of the Hebrew alphabet is mainly bound up with the writing of divine names. While the Tetragrammaton must not be written at all under ordinary circumstances, and when written by a Torah scribe, only after proper ritual purification, all other names, substitutes, and abbreviations for the divine name are also holy and must not be defiled or destroyed.

At first, vowels were not indicated. In the course of time, certain letters (*y*, *v*, *'*, *h*) also came to serve as vowel indicators. This use was gradually extended to cases where there was already a vowel, so that *y* came to mark *i* and *e* and *v* to mark *u* and *o*. This system of *matres lectionis* is only partly, and rather inconsistently, used in standard Hebrew Bibles. The occurrence of defective and full spellings is regulated by tradition, and failure to observe it can invalidate a Torah scroll or a divorce document. In the seventh through the ninth century, various systems arose—one of which subsequently came into general use—for indicating vowels by the addition of signs above, below, and (rarely) inside the letters. This complement to the Hebrew alphabet did not, however, become an integral part of it. Vowel signs (*nequdot*) do not appear in Torah scrolls; they are not used in documents, nor do they appear in most books for practical use (see VOCALIZATION).

Today the way in which the Bible text is vocalized is held to be of absolute authority in Orthodox circles. Other students of the Bible are willing to accept, for exegetical purposes, alternative vocalizations of the same consonantal skeleton, which are possible with many Hebrew words.

Most of the basic concepts of the alphabet used by Jewish mystics were established in the Midrash. The statement (*Avot* 5.1) that the universe was created by ten divine utterances postulates that language is first and foremost a divine tool of creation rather than a human means of communication. The Talmud attributes to Bezalel ben Uri, the builder of the Tabernacle in the desert (*Ber.* 55a), the "knowledge of the letters by which the heaven and earth were created," which he used in order to create God's earthly abode in harmony with the celestial one. The Midrash (*Gn. Rab.* 1.1) states that God "was consulting the Torah and creating the world," implying that the linguistic entity preceded the material and spiritual components of the universe, serving as a blueprint of the divine endeavor.

Language, which for the Midrash is the Hebrew language, is thus conceived as an aspect of divine wisdom. It is, therefore, as infinite as its source and cannot be pinned down to a specific layer of meaning that will exhaust its message. Every verse includes within it an infinite number of meanings and divine messages, which serve humanity for eternity. Every generation and every scholar can and should find in it new messages (all of which were revealed to Moses on Mount Sinai). Judaism in late antiquity did not hesitate, therefore, to present several, or even dozens, of different interpretations of every verse. To claim that one interpretation was the true one would amount to limiting divine wisdom.

The meaning of language, and especially that of the alphabet, was changed in a revolutionary manner. If God created the universe by the utterance of several verses, the power of creation could not be just the literal meaning of *yehi or*, "Let there be light." It could, in the same way, be in the sound of these words, in the number of letters, in the numerical value of these letters, in the shapes of these letters, or any other aspect of the semiotic message. When vocalization marks and musical signs (*te'amim*) were added to the Hebrew biblical verses, their shapes and names became aspects of that semiotic message; the same is true of the crowns that adorn the Hebrew letters. The order of the letters in a verse can be changed in order to reveal new layers of meaning, as can *acronyms, enabling the hermeneutic interpreter to use dozens of methods to change every word into every other.

These concepts developed gradually in late antiquity, increasing in importance. By the seventh century there were treatises dedicated completely to such interpretations, like the **Alphabet of Rabbi 'Aqiva'*, which is completely based on the interpretation of the shapes of the letters of the Hebrew alphabet. The use of *gimatriyyah*, **notariqon*, and *temurah* (interchange of letters) became increasingly frequent at the beginning of the Middle Ages. The medieval mystics inherited these methods, at least in their essential forms, as a part of their tradition, and developed them in a radical manner.

Earlier mystics, authors of Heikhalot and Merkavah literature, were relatively uninterested in language mysticism. The main source of medieval speculations on this subject was the **Sefer Yetsirah*.

Language mysticism became central to the circles of mystics who emerged in Europe in the second half of the twelfth century. The earliest work of the Kabbalah, **Sefer ha-Bahir*, includes numerous sections dedicated to the interpretation of the shapes of the letters, their vocalization marks, and their musical signs (though *gimatriyyah* plays only a small role). A significant part of *Sefer ha-Bahir* can be read as a commentary on the alphabet. Other schools, especially the *'Iyyun circle (the main text of which is *Sefer ha-'Iyyun*), identify mystical speculation with the method of letter combinations contained in the *Sefer Yetsirah*. Many early mystics wrote commentaries on the *Sefer Yetsirah*, in which the letters and language are conceived as keys to universal and divine mysteries.

One of the most radical expressions of the medieval concept of the alphabet is a work by R. *Elʿazar ben Yehudah of Worms, *Sefer ha-Ḥokhmah*. It presents seventy-three gates of wisdom, which are the different methods by which each of the verses of the Bible can and should be interpreted. This work is one of the strongest expressions of the belief in the infinity of semiotic messages contained in every sacred text. Many medieval kabbalists developed similar systems. The most influential expression of this attitude to language can be found in the works of Avraham ben Shemu'el *Abulafia.

Two central Hebrew mystical works of the fourteenth century deal almost exclusively with the concept of language as a key to divine mysteries. One is *Baddei ha-'Aron* by R. Shem Tov ibn Ga'on (the work was written in Jerusalem and Safed between 1315 and 1325), and the other is *Sefer ha-Temunah*, an anonymous work of this period. In *Baddei ha-'Aron* the author analyzed the central aspects of language and related them directly to the various realms within the divine world. *Sefer ha-Temunah* is based on the images of the letters, which are regarded as the images of God himself.

Not all kabbalists attached the same importance to the alphabet and to linguistic speculation. These played a minor role among the kabbalists in Provence, in the Gerona circle, and even in the Zohar itself. An important section of the Zohar discusses the shapes of the letters, yet more often than not these elements are marginal. Even the use of the numerical value of words and verses is secondary in the Zohar to other methods of homiletical interpretation. Later kabbalists also differ in their attitude to these methods.

• Joseph Dan, "The Language of Creation and its Grammar, Tradition and Translation," *Tradition und Translation: Festschrift für Carsten Colpe*, edited by C. Elsas (Berlin, 1994), pp. 42–63. Robert M. Haralick, *The Inner Meaning of the Hebrew Letters* (Northvale, N.J., 1995). Moshe Idel, "Reification of Language in Jewish Mysticism," in *Mysticism and Language*, edited by Steven Katz (New York, 1992), pp. 11–25. Elias Lipiner, *Ḥazon ha-'Otiyyot: Torat ha-'Ideot shel ha-'Alefbet ha-ʿIvri* (Jerusalem, 1989). Joseph Naveh, *Origins of the Alphabet*, rev. ed. (Herzlia, 1994). Colette Sirat, *La Lettre hebraique et sa signification*, bound with *Micrography as Art*, by Leila Avrin (Paris and Jerusalem, 1981). Ada Yardeni, *Sefer ha-Ketav ha-ʿIvri: Toledot, Yesodot, Signonot, ʿItsuv* (Jerusalem, 1991).

–JOSEPH DAN

ALPHABET OF BEN SIRA, Hebrew work of the geonic period, preserved in several different recensions. It recounts in a highly parodical manner some frivolous episodes loosely woven around the figure of Ben Sira, who is said to have been born to Jeremiah's daughter, impregnated by her own father's semen. Some of the episodes incorporate alphabetically arranged aphorisms, which Ben Sira supposedly composed and which gave the work its name, while others include his responses to King Nebuchadnezzar's questions on such varied subjects as the reason why farts were created, the causes of animosity between cats and dogs, and the sexual habits of ravens.

• Norman Bronznick, "The Alphabet of Ben Sira," in *Rabbinic Fantasies*, edited by David Stern and Mark Mirsky (Philadelphia, 1990), pp. 167–202. Eli Yassif, *Sippurei Ben Sira' bi-Yemei ha-Beinayyim* (Jerusalem, 1984).

–GIDEON BOHAK

ALPHABET OF RABBI ʿAQIVA', one of several Midrashic works on the letters of the Hebrew *alphabet, attributed to R. ʿAqiva' but probably composed between the seventh and the ninth century CE. Largely mystical and eschatological in content, this work seems related to Merkavah literature and *Shiʿur Qomah* speculation. Different versions of the *Alphabet of Rabbi ʿAqiva'* have survived, several of which were published by Solomon Aaron and Abraham Joseph Wertheimer (*Battei Midrashot*, vol. 2 [Jerusalem, 1968], pp. 333–418).

• Hermann Leberecht Strack and Günter Stemberger, *Introduction to the Talmud and Midrash*, rev. and updat. ed., translated by Markus Bockmuehl (Minneapolis, 1992).

–MARC BREGMAN

ALQABETS, SHELOMOH. See ALKABEZ, SHELOMOH.

ALROY, DAVID (12th cent.), pseudo-*Messiah. He succeeded his father, Shelomoh, as leader of a messianic movement in Kurdistan with a widespread Jewish following. His true name was Menaḥem ben Shelomoh. His adopted name was designed to bolster his messianic claims, since the provenance of a Messiah from the lineage of King David forms an integral part of the Jewish messianic tradition. Alroy's dramatic career was noted by the twelfth-century Jewish traveler Benjamin of Tudela, in a derogatory Muslim account by Samau'al al-Magribi, and in a novel *The Wondrous Tale of Alroy* (1839) by Benjamin Disraeli. Alroy launched a campaign to reach the Holy Land from Mosul in Iraq. He dispatched emissaries to Baghdad to alert the Jews to prepare for their miraculous return to Erets Yisra'el. When they awaited deliverance on their rooftops in vain, the official Jewish leadership grew alarmed and pronounced their opposition to the movement. Muslim authorities also opposed Alroy. He was assassinated around 1160, but his charismatic personality guaranteed the survival of a mystique surrounding his memory, particularly in Iran. A group of his followers (Menaḥemites) in Azerbaijan continued to believe in his Messiahship after his death.

• Salo W. Baron, *A Social and Religious History of the Jews* (New York, 1957), vol. 5, pp. 202–205. George W. Buchanan, ed. and trans., *Revelation and Redemption: Jewish Documents from the Fall of Jerusalem to the Death of Naḥmanides* (Dillsboro, Ind., 1978).

–JANE S. GERBER

ALSHEKH, MOSHEH (c.1507–1600), rabbinical scholar and Bible exegete. Born in Adrianople, Turkey, in 1498 to parents who had fled Spain in 1492, he studied in Salonika under Yosef *Taitazak and Yosef *Karo, later settling in Safed, where he served as *dayyan* in Karo's court. His *responsa* were published by his son Ḥayyim in Vienna in 1605 and heavily influenced the glosses of *Shabbetai ben Me'ir ha-Kohen on the **Shulḥan ʿArukh*. Apart from his *responsa*, Alshekh is best known for his voluminous homiletic commentaries on the Bible that were greatly influenced by Yitsḥaq Abravanel (see ABRAVANEL FAMILY). Four of these commentaries were published during the author's lifetime: *Ḥavatselet ha-Sharon* on *Daniel* (Constantinople, 1563), *Shoshanat ha-ʿAmaqim* on *Song of Songs* (Venice, 1591), *Rav Peninim* on *Proverbs* (Venice, 1592), and *Torat Mosheh* on *Genesis* (Constantinople, 1593). Eight more of Alshekh's Bible commentaries were published after his death by his son. His commentaries tend to the allegorical as a compromise between the rationalist and esoteric approaches to textual commentary. Alshekh was one of the first commentators to popularize the idea of four levels of interpretation associated with the acronym *pardes.

• Giovanni Bernardo de Rossi, *Dizionerio Storico degli autori ebrei e delle loro opere*, 2 vols. (Bologna, 1978; repr. of the 1802 ed.). Yom Tov Porges, ed., *She'elot u-Teshuvot Maharam Alshekh* (Safed, 1975). Shimon Shalem, *Rabbi Moses Alshekh* (Jerusalem, 1966).

—MAYER I. GRUBER

ALTAR, structure upon which *sacrifices were offered to the deity. The Hebrew term *mizbeaḥ* is derived from *z v ḥ* (slaughter). Altars in the Bible are divided into two types: temporary or private altars erected on specific occasions and for specific purposes, and temple altars. To the former class belong Noah's altar (*Gn*. 8.20) and the altars built by Abraham, Isaac, and Jacob (*Gn*. 12.7, 26.25, 33.20) as they traversed the land of Canaan, worshiping God as they went. In this category, too, are the altars erected by Moses following the victory over Amalek (*Ex*. 17.15) and at Mount Sinai when the covenant ceremony, including the sacrificial meal, was performed (*Ex*. 20.21–23). Such altars occasionally achieved some renown and were recalled by later generations; an example is the altar built by Joshua on Mount Ebal, upon which he inscribed a copy of the teaching of Moses (*Jos*. 8.30–32, as commanded in *Dt*. 27. 1–8). At other times altars would be put to their designated use and thereafter be forgotten. Such was the case, for instance, with the altar erected by Elijah on Mount Carmel in order to compete with the priests of Baal and demonstrate the lordship of God. According to the law in *Exodus* 20.21–23, altars were to be made of earth; stone altars were permitted provided that the stones not be hewn, since this would necessitate the use of the sword, an instrument of war. The sanctity of the altar occasionally made it a haven for manslayers, who would seize the four "horns" of the altar and escape arrest; biblical law stipulates, however, that the intentional killer not be allowed this form of *asylum (*Ex*. 21.14; *1 Kgs*. 1.50–53, 2.28–34).

Temple altars were designed to be permanent fixtures, and the sacrificial worship performed in a temple would be of an institutionalized and routine character. Furthermore, although individuals might occasionally sacrifice upon private, local altars scattered about the countryside, certain individual offerings, such as firstlings, offerings in fulfillment of vows, tithes, and the pilgrimage festival offerings had to be made on temple altars.

Local altars, subsequently called *high places, were prohibited by biblical (Deuteronomic) law, and once the Tabernacle was built, private field altars were outlawed (*Lv*. 17.3–7). According to the *Book of Deuteronomy* and the historical literature associated with it, the central sacrificial altar of the Temple was the sole legitimate place of worship (*Dt*. 12.5–14) from the moment the Temple was erected.

In addition to the sacrificial altars that existed at each of the minor Israelite temples, the sacrificial altar of the Tabernacle in the wilderness (described in *Ex*. 27.1–8; see also 29.38–46) and that of Solomon's Temple (*1 Kgs*. 8.64; *2 Kgs*. 16.14; *Ez*. 9.2) are the most important of the temple altars in the Bible. The former was designed to be portable; it was made of wood overlaid with bronze, measured 5 × 5 × 3 cubits, and was located in the Tabernacle courtyard. The latter stood in the Temple court in Jerusalem. It too was of bronze and according to *2 Chronicles* 4.1 was many times the size of the former.

Both the Tabernacle and Solomon's Temple in Jerusalem had another altar as well; the inner altar, used for offering incense (*Ex*. 30.1–10; *1 Kgs*. 7.48). It was of greater sanctity than the sacrificial altar: it was of gold, not bronze; it stood inside the Temple, not in the court; access to it was restricted to the high priest; and it was employed as part of the daily inner ritual of the divine abode. Incense was offered upon it in the morning and evening.

Upon their return from the Babylonian exile, the Jews erected an altar before rebuilding the Temple, indicating that the restoration of regular sacrificial worship took precedence over the Temple itself.

In Second Temple times, the sacrificial altar was the focus of great rejoicing on the annual celebration of Sukkot. The sacrificial legislation of the Bible presumes that both altars—the inner and the outer—along with the Ark are contaminated by the wrongdoings and impurities of Israel. They therefore need to be purged regularly so that the divine presence, believed to abide in the Temple, does not depart. Thus, in addition to their primary function in the offering of sacrifices and incense, they figure prominently in all rituals of atonement (i.e., purification of the sacred precincts). The crucial role of the altar in securing atonement was recognized by rabbinic tradition as well, and after the destruction of the Second Temple, this role was replaced by charity. The table on which meals were taken in the Jewish home was considered a substitute for the altar (*Ber*. 55a; T., *Sot*. 15.11–13) and many customs derived from this identification. The detailed description of the altar found in the Bible served as the basis for allegorical and mystical elaboration in later aggadic and kabbalistic literature.

• Menahem Haran, *Temples and Temple-Service in Ancient Israel* (Winona Lake, Ind., 1985). Jacob Milgrom, *Leviticus 1–16*, The Anchor Bible, vol. 3 (New York, 1991).

—BARUCH J. SCHWARTZ

ALTER FAMILY. See GER.

AL TIQREI (אַל תִּקְרֵי; do not read), Midrashic device by which biblical phrases are reinterpreted by slight changes, such as revocalization. The object was not to change the meaning of a phrase but to add extra meaning. For example, the end of the Talmudic tractate *Berakhot* (64a) quotes the verse "And all your children shall be taught of the Lord, and great shall be the peace of your children" (*Is*. 54.13) and states "Read not [*al tiqrei*] 'your children' (*banayikh*) but 'your builders' (*bonayikh*), namely the sages."

AMALEKITES, ancient nomadic people living in the Sinai desert and the southern portions of the land of Canaan. According to the biblical account (*Gn*. 36.9–12), they were of Edomite stock. At Rephidim, the children of Israel, on their way from Egypt to Mount Sinai, were treacherously attacked by the Amalekites, whom they repelled after a battle of varying fortunes. Thereafter the Amalekites were regarded as Israel's inveterate foes, whose annihilation became a sacred obligation (*Ex.* 17.8–16; *Dt.* 25.17–19). This is recalled liturgically on the Sabbath preceding Purim (see SABBATHS, SPECIAL). Saul's failure to fulfill the commandment of total annihilation (*1 Sm.* 15) led to the annulment of the rights of his descendants to succeed to the throne of Israel. The Amalekites suffered defeat at the hands of David (*2 Sm.* 8.12) and were finally wiped out during the reign of King Hezekiah of Judah (8th cent. BCE; *1 Chr.* 4.43). Rabbinic literature dwells on Amalek's role as Israel's permanent archenemy. *Haman is said to be descended from the Amalekites, his cognomen "Agagi" taken to indicate his descent from Agag, king of Amalek (*1 Sm.* 15.8). Whenever the Jews failed to abide by the covenant, the Amalekites are said to have prevailed over them. Only after the final destruction of the Amalekites will God and his throne be complete.

• Felix-Marie Abel, *Géographie de la Palestine* (Paris, 1933). Samuel R. Driver, *A Critical and Exegetical Commentary on Deuteronomy*, The International Critical Commentary, 3d. ed., vol. 5 (Edinburgh, 1902), pp. 286–88. Louis Ginzberg, *Legends of the Jews* (Philadelphia, 1946).

–DAVID A. GLATT-GILAD

AMEN (אָמֵן; "So be it"), expression occurring fourteen times in the Bible and signifying assent to an oath (e.g., *Dt.* 27.15), agreement or corroboration (e.g., *1 Kgs.* 1.36), or blessing and praise of God (*Ps.* 41.14). The term was also used as a public response after the prayers and blessings of the priests and Levites (cf. *Neh.* 8.6; *1 Chr.* 16.36; *Ps.* 106.48), although in the Temple it was part of a larger formula (*Ps.* 72.18–19). In synagogue practice, *amen* is the response to every benediction, and in Sephardi synagogues, the *amen* response is also interjected at many other parts of the service. According to the rabbis, it is obligatory to say *amen* on hearing a blessing, and the person who says it is regarded as if he had recited the blessing himself, just as a person who says *amen* after an oath is regarded as having sworn the oath himself (*Shev.* 29a). *Amen* is rarely said by the person who himself makes the benediction. The rabbis suggested homiletically that the word is derived from the initials of the phrase *El melekh ne'eman*, "God, faithful king" (*San.* 111a). The term passed into Christian and to some extent Islamic usage.

• Haim Gevaryahu, "Amen and Hallelujah: Their Development as Liturgical Responses," *Dor le-Dor* 13.2 (1984–1985): 93–97. H. W. Hogg, "'Amen': Notes on Its Significance and Use in Biblical and Post-Biblical Times," *Jewish Quarterly Review*, o.s. 9 (1897): 1–23. Klaus Seybold, "Zur Vorgeschichte der liturgischen Formel 'Amen,'" *Theologische Zeitschrift* 48.1 (1992): 109–117.

ʿAM HA-'ARETS (עַם הָאָרֶץ; people of the land), a term that in biblical usage referred to natives of a land (whether Israelite or non-Israelite) or (in the plural) to foreign populations. In postexilic biblical texts (*Ezra* and *Nehemiah*), the term was applied to the inhabitants of Palestine who were hostile to the returning exiles and lax in faith and observance. During the tannaitic period, *ʿam ha-'arets* was applied to one who disregarded that which was considered essential to religious piety; thus, shifts in the definition of religious piety led to changing characterizations of an *ʿam ha-'arets*. Prior to the destruction of the Second Temple, *ʿam ha-'arets* generally referred to a person neglectful in the observance of positive commandments, particularly the laws of tithes and ritual purity. Groups, the members of which were called *ḥaverim*, were formed by those who wished to set themselves apart from the *ʿamei ha-'arets* in order to guard against consumption of untithed produce or contraction of ritual impurity.

A second meaning of *ʿam ha-'arets*—namely, an ignoramus—came to the fore after the destruction of the Temple. Today the term *ʿam ha-'arets* connotes one who lacks knowledge of Jewish ritual and tradition.

• Gedalia Alon, *The Jews in Their Land in the Talmudic Age*, translated by Gershon Levi, vol. 2 (Jerusalem, 1984), pp. 506–514, 677–680. Adolf Büchler, *Der Galiläische ʿAm ha-ares des zweitern Jahrhunderts* (Vienna, 1906). Louis Finkelstein, *The Pharisees*, 3d ed. (Philadelphia, 1966), vol. 2, pp.754–761. Aharon Oppenheimer, *The ʿAm Ha-aretz: A Study in the Social History of the Jewish People in the Hellenistic–Roman Period* (Leiden, 1977). Ephraim Elimelech Urbach, "ʿAm ha-Aretz," in *Proceedings of the First World Congress of Jewish Studies* (Jerusalem, 1952), pp. 362–366.

–CHRISTINE E. HAYES

ʿAMIDAH (עֲמִידָה; Standing), the main statutory prayer in Jewish public and private worship since the destruction of the Second Temple; it is recited standing. According to the rabbis, all of the prescribed synagogue services that were seen as replacements for former obligatory services in the Temple (Shaḥarit, Minḥah, Maʿariv on weekdays, together with Musaf on Shabbat and festivals and Neʿilah on Yom Kippur; *Ber.* 26b) incorporate the ʿAmidah in one of its forms as their central feature. Rabbinic literature referred to the ʿAmidah as the Shemonah ʿEsreh (Eighteen), based on the original number of weekday benedictions it contained, although today, with additions from the Babylonian rite, it contains nineteen benedictions. The ʿAmidah, as the (obligatory) prayer par excellence, was also referred to simply as Tefillah or, in Aramaic, as Tseluta' (both words meaning *prayer*). Even if the exact wording was subject to change until modern times, the sages shaped the ʿAmidah as the institutionalized "standing" before God, which enables individuals and congregations to express praise and pleas before God. The ʿAmidah is said silently by the private worshiper and, in the morning and afternoon congregational services (in the presence of a *minyan*), repeated aloud by the reader. The opening of the ʿAmidah consists of three blessings; these are followed by twelve or thirteen blessings on weekdays and one on holidays; the ʿAmidah closes with three final blessings. Certain changes are made according to the Jewish calendar, including variations for the seasons and additions for the ʿAseret Yemei Teshuvah and for public fasts.

The ʿAmidah opens with *Avot (Fathers), praising the God of the patriarchs (in Reform tradition, the matriarchs as well) and their descendants. The Avot is followed by the Gevurot (Almighty), an address to God who creates eternal life and resurrects the dead. The Qedushat ha-Shem (The Holiness of the Name) follows. It is an equation of God's holiness with his name, represented by the Tetragrammaton, which was revealed to Israel and in whose holiness worshipers share by repeating the divine name in its substitute forms in every rabbinic benediction. The opening sentence is replaced by the *Qedushah, in differing forms, as the climax of holiness in the congregational service, in the reader's repetition of the ʿAmidah.

The first of the intermediary benedictions for weekdays is Daʿat (Knowledge), which addresses God as the one who enables people to distinguish, to understand, and to know. In the evening ʿAmidah for the conclusion of Sabbaths and festivals, the *Havdalah blessing is added; it refers to the need for knowledge to distinguish between the different kinds of times in the Jewish calendar. Next is Teshuvah (*Repentance), a request for God to bring the worshiper back to him; Seliḥah (Forgiveness), a prayer for forgiveness for sins and transgressions; *Ge'ullah (Redemption), a prayer for redemption from suffering; Refu'ah (Healing), a request for the healing of the sick of the people of Israel, which may include a private prayer specifying a particular individual; and Birkat ha-Shanim (Blessing of Years), a blessing for the seasons (thus a request for crops) and for the material prosperity of the individual and the congregation. The next section deals with subjects of public and/or national interest. Qibbuts Galuyyot (Ingathering of the *Exiles) deals with the return of the exiles to Erets Yisra'el as one of the conditions of national existence. Hashavat ha-Mishpat (Restoration of Righteous Jurisdiction) asks for a return to divine law and life according to God's rulings. *Birkat ha-Minim (Blessing of the Heretics) concerns humbling the heretics and other destructive elements in the life of a congregation (early rites included mention of the Notserim, asking God to mark a border between rabbinic and Jewish-Christian communities). ʿAl ha-Tsaddiqim (For the Pious) asks for the reward of pious contributions to public life. Binyan Yerushalayim (Building Jerusalem) is a plea for the restoration of the divine presence in the Temple and of the kingdom of the House of David by the rebuilding of Jerusalem. Mashiaḥ ben David (Messiah, Son of David) is a prayer for the restoration of the Davidic dynasty and the coming of the Messiah. This benediction, attested in the first millennium of rabbinic prayer only in the Babylonian rite, which stresses the subject of the preceding benediction, raises the number of benedictions to nineteen. In nineteenth-century Reform Judaism both benedictions were reformulated. Shomeʿa Tefillah (Hear Our Prayers), a plea concluding the intermediary section, expresses the confidence that God is the one who hears prayer. The single intermediate blessing on Sabbaths and festivals (Qedushat ha-Yom) refers to the particular nature of the day in question. The Ro'sh ha-Shanah Musaf contains three intermediate blessings.

Every ʿAmidah concludes with three benedictions, the first of which is the *ʿAvodah (Worship). This prayer for the return of God's presence to the place of the Temple to restore biblical forms of worship was altered or omitted in Reform Judaism. An insertion for Ro'sh Ḥodesh and Ḥol ha-Moʿed, *Yaʿaleh ve-Yavo', connects the remembrance of the merits of the ancestors with a plea for mercy. Hoda'ah (Thanksgiving) is a benediction of thanksgiving for God's mercies, with special insertions for Purim and Ḥanukkah, *ʿAl ha-Nissim. Shalom (Peace) is a prayer for peace alluding to the *Birkat ha-Kohanim (*Nm.* 6.24–26), which may be recited in public prayer by the descendants of the priestly families on special occasions or read by the reader before the repetition of this benediction resembling the Temple service. Even though the ʿAmidah is called "the petitionary prayer," its benedictions express confidence in redemption. Although the ʿAmidah is obligatory for the individual, the first person plural is used throughout, making the ʿAmidah the prayer of all Israel; private petitions may be inserted, usually at its end.

• Ismar Elbogen, *Jewish Liturgy: A Comprehensive History*, translated by Raymond P. Scheindlin (Philadelphia, 1993), pp. 24–54. Joseph Heinemann, *Prayer in the Talmud: Forms and Patterns*, Studia Judaica 9 (Berlin and New York, 1977). Joseph H. Hertz, ed., *The Authorised Daily Prayer Book of the United Hebrew Congregation of the British Empire* (London, 1943), vol. 1, pp. 130–160. Reuven Kimelman, "The Daily ʿAmidah and the Rhetoric of Redemption," *Jewish Quarterly Review* 79 (1988–1989): 165–197. *Literature of the Synagogue*, edited with introduction and notes by Joseph Heinemann with Jakob J. Petuchowski (New York, 1975), pp. 29–79. Jakob J. Petuchowski, ed., *Contributions to the Scientific Study of Jewish Liturgy* (New York, 1970), pp. 1–177, 373–458. Jakob J. Petuchowski, *Prayerbook Reform in Europe: The Liturgy of European Liberal and Reform Judaism* (New York, 1968), pp. 214–239. Emil Schürer, *The History of the Jewish People in the Age of Jesus Christ, 175 B.C.–A.D. 135*, translated and edited by Geza Vermes et al. (Edinburgh, 1979), vol. 2, pp. 454–463.

—PETER LENHARDT

AMITTAI, synagogal poets from Oria, in southern Italy.

Amittai (c.800 CE) is credited with the composition of a number of poems in the style of early Palestinian *piyyutim*, some of which were adopted into the Italian and German rites.

Amittai ben Shefatyah (late 9th cent. CE), grandson of Amittai and believed to be the author of most of the forty *piyyutim* that are connected with the Amittai name, was one of the major *payyetanim* of the early Italian-Ashkenazi school of Hebrew liturgical poetry. His penitential prayer Adonai, Adonai, El Raḥum ve-Ḥannun has been incorporated into the Neʿilah service for Yom Kippur. He also wrote dirges lamenting the anti-Jewish outbreaks in his time (in particular the compulsory conversions enforced under Byzantine emperor Basil I), and several of his poems poignantly express the Jewish longing for Zion.

• T. Carmi, ed., *The Penguin Book of Hebrew Verse* (New York, 1981), pp. 91, 235–240. Y. David, ed., *Shirei Amittai* (Jerusalem, 1975). Ezra Fleischer, *Yotsrot be-Hithavutam ve-Hitpatḥuttam* (Jerusalem, 1984), index s.v. Amittai. Benjamin Klar, ed., *Megillat Aḥimaʿats*, 2nd ed. (Jerusalem 1973; 1974 printing), pp. 12, 95–96. Cecil Roth, *The History of the Jews of Italy* (Philadelphia, 1946), pp. 50–53. Jefim Schirmann, "The Beginning of Hebrew Poetry in Italy," in *The World History of the Jewish People*, vol. 2, *The Dark Ages*, edited by Cecil Roth (Tel Aviv, 1966), pp. 250, 252–256.

—PETER LENHARDT

ʿAMMI BAR NATAN (fl. 279 CE), amora' and disciple of R. *Yoḥanan bar Nappaḥa' who headed the *Tiberias academy after Yoḥanan's death in 279. With his colleague R. *Assi, ʿAmmi regularly toured Palestine to encourage religious study. ʿAmmi was responsible for the Jewish judiciary and strove to ensure that religious judges (*dayyanim*) be chosen on their merit and not—as had been the tendency—for their wealth. A righteous man who cared for the needy (*Shab*. 10a) and looked after the interests of proselytes (Y., *Ḥag*. 1.7), ʿAmmi traveled to Palmyra to intercede with Queen Zenobia on behalf of a certain Jew held there as captive (Y., *Ter*. 8). Among his famous dicta were: "One should not trouble the community too much" (*Taʿan*. 14b) and "There is no death without sin, no suffering without iniquity" (*Shab*. 55a).

• Wilhelm Bacher, *Die Agada der palästinensischen Amoräer* (Strassburg, 1892–1899). Zacharias Frankel, *Mevo' ha-Yerushalmi* (1870; Jerusalem, 1967). Isaak Halevy, *Dorot ha-Ri'shonim* vol. 2 (1923; Jerusalem, 1979). Aaron Hyman, *Toledot Tanna'im ve-'Amora'im* (1910; Jerusalem, 1987).

—DANIEL SPERBER

AMMON AND MOAB, two neighboring countries of ancient Israel, to the east of the Jordan River and the Dead Sea, in what is today the kingdom of Jordan. (The capital of Ammon was situated in present-day Amman.) Biblical tradition recognizes a close relationship between Israel and these two nations, as they are traced back to the incestuous union of Lot, Abraham's nephew, and his two daughters (*Gn*. 19.30–38). The cultures of Israel, Ammon, and Moab shared much in common. For example, the Ammonite, Moabite, and Hebrew languages are dialects of the Canaanite language and were mutually intelligible. Ammon (whose chief deity was Milcom) and Moab (whose patron deity was Chemosh) developed as independent kingdoms in Transjordan sometime in the Early Iron Age (c.13th/12th cent. BCE) and often were at odds with the various tribes of Israel. The earliest Ammonite king recorded in the Bible is Nahash, who besieged the Israelite town Jabesh-gilead and was subsequently defeated by Saul (*1 Sm*. 11), who also defeated Moab (*1 Sm*. 14.47–48). Soon after Israel became a monarchy, David conquered these two countries and incorporated them into his kingdom. Probably after Solomon's death, Ammon and Moab became independent once more. Later, Omri, king of Israel, subjugated Moab, but within a few decades Moab declared its independence. This event is detailed in an important epigraphic remain, the Mesha Stele (or Moabite Stone, today in the Louvre), written by the Moabite king Mesha (*2 Kgs*. 3) around 850 BCE. Both Ammon and Moab became Assyrian vassals during the time of Tiglath-pileser III (7th cent. BCE). Because of the tensions that dominated the histories of Israel and its two neighbors, the *Book of Deuteronomy* legislates that "No Ammonite or Moabite shall be admitted into the congregation of the Lord" (*Dt*. 23.4). This is interpreted to mean that an Israelite woman cannot marry a man from these two countries. However, it appears that an Ammonite or Moabite woman could become an Israelite, since Ruth was a Moabite who adopted the religion of her mother-in-law Naomi (*Ru*. 1), married Boaz, and eventually became the great-grandmother of David. In post-biblical times, the Talmud relaxed the attitude toward Ammonites and Moabites, and R. Yehoshuʿa ben Ḥananyah permitted the conversion of their males on the grounds that the original people could no longer be distinguished; even priests were permitted to marry the daughter of such a convert (*Yev*. 77a).

• John Andrew Dearman, ed., *Studies in the Mesha Inscription and Moab* (Atlanta, 1989). Donald J. Wiseman, ed., *Peoples of Old Testament Times* (Oxford, 1973). A. van Zyl, *The Moabites* (Leiden, 1960).

—GARY A. RENDSBURG

AMNON OF MAINZ. See U-NETANNEH TOQEF.

AMORA' (Aram.; אָמוֹרָא; speaker, interpreter), name given to a rabbinic teacher in both Palestine and Babylonia during the Talmudic period. In the early amoraic period (c.220–260) there is often little distinction between the tannaitic (see TANNA') and amoraic methods. As the amoraic period continued, however, the amora'im began to regard the Mishnah and other tannaitic sources as the authoritative basis for their own rulings. Support from a tannaitic source strengthened the opinion of an amora'; an objection weakened it and forced the amora' to cite a tannaitic tradition of equal or greater authority or to reinterpret the tannaitic source of the objection. Furthermore, as the amora'im progressed, their traditions preserved more discussions of issues rather than short dictums expressing a norm.

The basic methods of Palestinian and Babylonian amora'im were similar. Nevertheless, Palestinian amora'im tended to interpret the Mishnah and other tannaitic sources closer to their plain meaning than the Babylonian amora'im. This was a result of their proximity to the world in which the tannaitic tradition had grown. For the Babylonians, much of the tannaitic tradition was imported from Palestine and grafted onto a different social, economic, and religious reality. Therefore, the Babylonian amora'im sometimes interpreted their tannaitic sources less in accord with their simple meaning.

The Babylonian amoraic period extended across seven generations, to approximately 530 CE, while the Palestinian amoraic period ended in approximately 450 CE. This explains, to some degree, the larger scope of Babylonian Talmudic law and lore. It may also explain why the redaction of the Talmud Bavli seems more polished than the less accessible formulation of the Talmud Yerushalmi. This, however, is subject to considerable current academic debate (see Jacob Neusner's *The Formation of the Babylonian Talmud*).

Among the best-known Babylonian amora'im are Rav and Shemu'el (1st generation); R. Yehudah and R. Huna' (2d generation); Rabbah, R. Yosef, R. Naḥman, R. Ḥisda', and R. Sheshet (3d generation); Rava' and Abbayei (4th generation); R. Papa' and Ravina' (5th generation); R. Ashi (6th generation); and Mar bar R. Ashi (7th generation). The best-known Palestinian amora'im are R. Ḥiyya', R. Hoshaʿyah, and R. Yehoshuʿa ben Levi (1st generation); R. Yoḥanan and R. Shimʿon ben Laqish (2d generation); R. Abbahu, R. Elʿazar ben Pedat, R. ʿAmmi, R. Assi, and R. Zeʿira' (3d generation); R. Yonah and R. Yosei bar Abin (4th generation); and R. Mana' and Yosei bar Abin II (5th generation).

Palestinian amora'im are distinguished in title from Babylonian amora'im. The former are called "Rabbi," indicating complete judiciary competence in all matters of law, whereas those in Babylonia are called "Rav." Babylonian rabbinic authorities did not possess the right to judge cases involving fines. The two groups kept in contact through the frequent visits of scholars specially appointed to bring the teachings of Erets Yisra'el to Babylonia and vice versa; some rabbis moved from one rabbinic center to the other. There is even some evidence of occasional hostility between amora'im in Erets Yisra'el and Babylonian newcomers. Nevertheless, both Talmuds reflect considerable interaction between Babylonia and Erets Yisra'el.

The great centers of amoraic instruction in Erets Yisra'el were in Tiberias, Sepphoris, and Caesarea; in Babylonia, in Nehardea, Sura, Pumbedita, and Maḥoza. The total number of amora'im mentioned in the sources exceeds three thousand.

• Wilhelm Bacher, *Die Agada der babylonischen Amoräer* (Strassburg, 1878). Wilhelm Bacher, *Die Agada der palastinensischen Amoräer*, 3 vols. (Strassburg, 1892–1899). Moshe Beer, *The Babylonian Amoraim* (Tel Aviv, 1974). Zekharyah Frankel, *Mevo' ha-Yerushalmi* (Breslau, 1870; Berolini, 1923, 1966). Aaron Hyman, *Toledot Tanna'im ve-'Amora'im*, 3 vols. (London, 1910). Mordekhai Margoliot, *Encyclopedia of Talmudic and Geonic Literature being a Biographical Dictionary of the Tanaim, Amoraim and Geonim* (Tel Aviv, 1961). Jacob Neusner, *History of the Jews in Babylonia*, 5 vols. (Leiden, 1966–1970).

—MICHAEL CHERNICK

AMORITES, early Semitic inhabitants of Palestine. The name refers to a particular people (e.g., *Gn.* 15.19–21; *Jos.* 10.5; *Jgs.* 3.5) that was annihilated or assimilated by the Israelites or, collectively, to the group (e.g., *Dt.* 1.27; *2 Sam.* 21.2; *Am.* 2.9–10) of Canaanite nations that were indigenous to the land of Canaan before the Israelite conquest. The word is derived from the Akkadian *amurru* (western), which, beginning with the Old Akkadian period, specifically is used to designate uncivilized "westerners" (i.e., non-Mesopotamian barbarians from the west, unacquainted with such amenities as permanent housing, eating cooked meat, agriculture, or municipal government). In approximately 2000 BCE, the Amorites invaded Babylonia, at first contributing to the fall of the Ur III dynasty and later on establishing their own bases of power in such places as Mari and finally the first dynasty of Babylon (see BABYLONIA; HAMMURABI). The vassal kingdom of Amurru in Syria in the fourteenth century BCE contributed some eighteen of the Amarna Letters (EA 60–62, 156–161, 371). Much effort has been exerted by scholars to reconstruct Amorite as an independent dialect within the Northwest Semitic languages (i.e., exclusive of the Canaanite and Aramaic subgroups). The data are based almost exclusively on proper names, and there is no possibility of contextual corroboration.

In Talmudic times, the Amorites were regarded as the prototypes of the early Canaanite population and were viewed as the chief bearers of a false faith. Evil customs and superstitions were known as "the ways of the Amorites" (*Shab.* 67a), and the rabbis applied the name Amorites to all idolaters.

• Giorgio Buccellati, *The Amorites of the Ur III Period* (Naples, 1966). Ignace J. Gelb, *Computer-Aided Analysis of Amorite*, Assyriological Studies 21 (Chicago, 1980). Alfred Haldar, *Who Were the Amorites?* (Leiden, 1971). Herbert B. Huffmon, *Amorite Personal Names in the Mari Texts* (Baltimore, 1965). Shlomo Izre'el, *Amurru Akkadian: A Linguistic Study* (Atlanta, 1991). Alan R. Millard, "Amorites," in the *New Bible Dictionary*, edited by J. D. Douglas and N. Hillyer, 2d ed. (Downer's Grove, Ill., 1982), pp. 31–32.

—CHAIM COHEN

AMOS (8th cent. BCE), the earliest of the literary prophets. He lived in the period before the Assyrian invasions that destroyed the northern kingdom of Israel. Born in the Judean town of Tekoa, south of Bethlehem, Amos prophesied during the reigns of Uzziah, king of Judah, and Jeroboam II, king of Israel (1.1). Amos was a pastoralist and an agriculturalist who experienced five visions from God, which prompted him to announce the downfall of the northern kingdom of Israel and the death of its king. Speaking at Bethel, the royal sanctuary of the northern kingdom, he defended his prophetic calling, dissociating himself from the professional prophets and soothsayers until he was evicted by the high priest Amaziah (7.10–19). The prophet shocked his audience by proclaiming the impending doom of the then flourishing nation. His message emphasized the moral decay of the northern kingdom, especially its mistreatment of the poor, hungry, and landless. Amos was a master of rhetoric and ironic reversal. Thus, his oracles against the foreign nations, designed to gain the approval of his listeners, culminate in a condemnation of the northern kingdom of Israel (chaps. 1–2). He reversed the popular conception of the "Day of the Lord" by portraying it as a day of darkness and judgment rather than of light and bliss (5.18–20). Amos maintained that of all nations, Israel was the most vulnerable to divine retribution because of its status as a "chosen people" (3.2), which had been widely understood as conferring unconditional benefits and security (cf. 2.9–11, 9.7–10). Amos also proclaimed the important new principles of the primacy of morality over the cult and the decisive role of social morality in determining national destiny (5.21–27). He foretold destruction, but his prophecy ends with a description of Israel's future restoration under a Davidic monarch (9.11–15). According to the Talmud (*Mak.* 24a), all 613 commandments of the Bible were summed up in Amos's single dictum "Seek me and live!" (5.4).

The *Book of Amos* is the third book of the Minor Prophets. It contains four major sections. The first contains the prophet's condemnations of a series of foreign nations as well as of Judah and Israel (chaps. 1–2). The series is designed to win the assent of the audience by condemning Israel's enemies and then to shock the listeners by culminating with a condemnation of Israel itself. The second section (chaps. 3–4) identifies God as the one who brings about Israel's punishment. Here Amos condemns the upper-class women of Samaria and levels a sharp castigation at the cult. The third section (chaps. 5–6) exhorts the audience to seek the Lord and live (this is the only ray of hope that the prophet sees until the end of the book), while describing further the judgment that will come upon the people if they do not. The final section (chaps. 7–9) provides the legitimation for the prophet's message by describing five visions in which he perceived God's commission to speak as a prophet. The book ends with the announcement of the future restoration of the "fallen booth of David" (9.11) along with blessings of bounty and security for Israel. The presence of a superscription in *Amos* 1.1 and a narrative concerning the prophet's eviction from the sanctuary at Bethel in 7.10–17 indicates that someone other than the prophet assembled the book in its present form, perhaps during the reign of King Josiah of Judah who destroyed the sanctuary at Bethel.

• Francis I. Andersen and David Noel Freedman, *Amos*, The Anchor Bible, vol. 26A (New York, 1989). A. Graeme Auld, *Amos*, Guides to Biblical Scholarship: Old Testament Guides (Sheffield, Eng., 1986). William Rainey Harper, *A Critical and Exegetical Commentary on Amos and Hosea*, International Critical Commentary (New York, 1905). Yehezkel Kaufmann, *The Religion of Israel*, translated by Moshe Greenberg (Chicago, 1960). James Luther Mays, *Amos: A Commentary*, The Old Testament Library (Philadelphia, 1969). Shalom M. Paul, *Amos*, Hermeneia—A Critical and Historical Commentary on the Bible (Minneapolis, 1991). Meir Weiss, *Sefer ʿAmos*, 2 vols. (Jerusalem, 1992), in Hebrew.

—MARVIN A. SWEENEY

ʿAMRAM BAR SHESHNAʾ (9th cent.), gaʾon; head of a breakaway faction of the *Sura academy and later, perhaps, of the mother institution. A number of his *responsa* have been preserved, but he is best known for his prayer book, the *Seder Rav ʿAmram*, which he edited in response to the request of a scholar in Barcelona. This, the earliest known comprehensive Jewish prayer book, contained both liturgical texts and halakhic instructions and was extremely influential in medieval Europe. Its popularity led scholars and copyists to expand the text by inserting passages (many of them based on geonic *responsa*) dealing with related topics and to revise it in accordance with liturgical customs current in their own communities, as a result of which it is frequently impossible to establish the original text with any degree of certainty. *Seder Rav ʿAmram* has been edited by Daniel Goldschmidt (1971) with an English translation by D. Hedegard (weekday prayers, 1951) and T. Kronholn (Sabbath prayers, 1974).

• Robert Brody, "Rav ʿAmram bar Sheshnaʾ: Gaʾon Sura?" *Tarbiz* 56.3 (1987): 327–345.

—ROBERT BRODY

AMULETS (Heb. *qemiʿim*), objects worn as charms against evil (sickness, bad luck, the "*evil eye," etc.). An amulet usually contains Bible verses that refer to protection against harm, such as "I will put none of the diseases upon you, which I have put upon the Egyptians, for I am the Lord your healer" (*Ex.* 15.26), or combinations of letters and symbols, names of angels, and so on. The Toseftaʾ (T., *Shab.* 5.9) speaks of an "effective amulet" (*qameʿa mumḥeh*) as one that has healed three times, "whether it be an amulet of writing or an amulet of herb roots" (Rashi explains the word *qameʿa* [*Shab.* 61a] as anything that can be tied into a knot). The Mishnah, too, indirectly recognizes the practice of wearing amulets when it rules that "an amulet which has not yet proven its effectiveness" may not be worn in the street on the Sabbath (*Shab.* 6.2). Amulets were very common throughout the ancient Near East and many have been uncovered in archeological excavations. The earlier magical traditions that formed the basis for the wearing of amulets subsequently merged with certain kabbalistic notions, for example, the mystical nature of the name of God and, hence, the efficacy of its representation by various combinations of letters. These gave rise to the so-called "practical Kabbalah," as distinct from the doctrinal and theosophical "speculative" Kabbalah. Some medieval authorities (e.g., Maimonides) opposed the use of amulets, dismissing them as superstitious folly. In the later Middle Ages, amulets were written by rabbis with a reputation for kabbalistic competence (see EYBESCHUETZ, YONATAN) or by "holy name" specialists (*baʿalei shem*; the founder of Hasidism, Yisraʾel ben Eliʿezer *Baʿal Shem Tov was originally such a writer of amulets). Amulets may be written on parchment or made of silver or other metals. They may contain letters, words, or symbolic elements (magic squares, triangles, the five fingers of the hand) and are an important expression of folk art. The use of amulets is still prevalent in Israel and among Oriental and Hasidic Jews. Not all amulets are worn; some are hung on the walls of a birth chamber, in a car, or placed wherever real or imagined danger lurks. Amulets written by contemporary holy men are prized. Miniature books, such as *Psalms*, are also considered amulets, and are popular among soldiers in the Israeli army.

• Henry Abramowitch and Shifra Epstein, "Driving Amulets in Jerusalem," *The Mankind Quarterly* 29 (1988): 161–164. Eli Davis and David F. Frankel, *The Hebrew Amulet: Biblical-Medical-General* (Jerusalem, 1995). Gedalyah Nigal, *Magic, Mysticism and Hasidism: The Supernatural in Jewish Thought* (Northvale, N.J., 1994), pp. 123–124. Joshua Trachtenberg, *Jewish Magic and Superstition: A Study in Folk Religion* (New York, 1974), pp. 132–152.

—SHIFRA EPSTEIN

ANAGRAMS, literary device by which the letters of a word or sentence are transposed to form a new word or sentence. Examples are found in the Bible and were often used in Talmudic and Midrashic literature as a basis for aggadic interpretations of biblical texts. Influenced by Midrashic and Arabic literature, the anagram became a favorite device of medieval Hebrew poets and was also frequently used in Kabbalah (and in *amulets).

• Matityahu Glazerson, *Letters of Fire: Mystical Insights into the Hebrew Language* (Jerusalem, 1991).

ʿANAN BEN DAVID (8th cent.), founder of the Ananite sect in Babylonia; considered by the *Karaites to be their founder. Details of ʿAnan's life are obscure. The tenth-century Karaite Qirqisani reports that ʿAnan was "the first to bring to light a great deal of the truth about the scriptural ordinances. He was learned in the lore of the Rabbanites." Traditions reported in twelfth-century sources relate that ʿAnan was descended from the Davidic line and was to be appointed exilarch (head of the Jewish community in Babylonia). However, because of his heretical tendencies, his younger brother was selected. Thereupon, ʿAnan gathered around himself a group of sectarians and set himself up as an alternative exilarch. This led to his arrest on the order of the caliph and a narrow escape from a death sentence as a rebel. While this story is probably more fable than fact, ʿAnan does appear to have been a scholarly Rabbanite of aristocratic descent, who for reasons of his own consolidated around himself a non-normative group of Jews. A variety of non-rabbinic Jewish traditions were alive in sectarian movements active in this period on the eastern fringes of the caliphate. When ʿAnan appeared, he brought some of these traditions closer to the center of Jewish culture and gave them a new focus and legitimacy. A combination of historical sources indicates that he founded his sect between 762 and 767.

The Ananites seem to have remained a small group loyal to the traditions to which ʿAnan gave literary expression in his *Sefer ha-Mitsvot*. They continued to exist as a separate group until the eleventh century, when their remnants were absorbed by the Karaites. Even though the later Karaites frequently disagreed with the rulings in *Sefer ha-Mitsvot*, they considered ʿAnan to be the originator of their sect, and his descendants were respected and honored as *nesi'im*, descendants of the royal, Davidic line.

Sefer ha-Mitsvot, written in Aramaic, reflects rabbinic methods of legal exegesis of the biblical text, but it formulates a strict and ascetic religious practice that stresses the mourning and sorrow that should be maintained in light of the destruction of the Temple. ʿAnan introduced changes in the method of determination and intercalation of the calendar, prohibited having any fire burn on the Sabbath (even if lit previously), established a seventy-day fast, and greatly extended the degrees of forbidden relationships. His rulings for the synagogue and its prayer rites are modeled on the priestly service in the Temple. ʿAnan also wrote another legal work called *Fadhlaka*, and Qirqisani reports that he wrote a work on transmigration of souls. Scholars have found some similarities between ʿAnan's teachings and Sadducean and Qumran traditions. Significant fragments of *Sefer ha-Mitsvot* have survived and have been published by A. Harkavy, *Studien und Mitteilungen* 8 (1903); Solomon Schechter, *Documents of Jewish Sectaries* 2 (1910); J. N. Epstein, *Tarbiz* 7 (1935/1936): 283–290; and J. Mann, *Journal of Jewish Lore and Philosophy* 1 (1919): 329–353.

• Haggai Ben-Shammai in *Religionsgesprache im Mittelalter: 25th Wolfenbutteler Symposions* (Wiesbaden, 1993), pp. 11–26. Haggai Ben-Shammai in *Studies in Muslim–Jewish Relations* 1 (1993): 19–29. Leon Nemoy, *Karaite Anthology* (New Haven, 1952), pp. 3–20, 395, and s.v. index. Leon Nemoy in *Semitic Studies in Memory of Immanuel Löw*, edited by Sandor Scheiber (Budapest, 1947), pp. 239–248. Naphtali Wieder, *The Judean Scrolls and Karaism* (London, 1962).

—DAVID E. SKLARE

ANATOLI, YAʿAQOV BEN ABBA' MARI (13th cent.), homilist, translator, and physician. He started his career in France but had settled in Naples by 1231. There he was a close associate of Michael Scot, a favorite of Emperor Frederick II. Anatoli himself was the emperor's physician. His best-known work was *Malmad ha-Talmidim* (Lyck, 1866), a collection of sermons on the weekly Torah readings. He attacked ascetic practices, notably excessive fasting and mortification of the body, and fanaticism and superstition, associating them with elements in Christianity. Most of his sermons were directed against religious laxity and the mechanical performance of the commandments. In his translation of Aristotle's *Organon*, he urges Jews to master logic in order to be able to respond to Christian polemics.

• Jeremy Cohen, *The Friars and the Jews: The Evolution of Medieval Anti-Judaism* (Ithaca, N.Y., 1982), pp. 229–236. Marc Saperstein, "Christians and Christianity in the Sermons of Jacob Anatoli," *Jewish History* 6 (1992): 225–242. Marc Saperstein, ed., *Jewish Preaching, 1200–1800* (New Haven, 1989), pp. 15–16, 111–123. Isadore Twersky, "Joseph ibn Kaspi, Portrait of a Medieval Jewish Intellectual," in *Studies in Medieval Jewish History and Literature* (Cambridge, Mass., and London, 1979), pp. 231–257.

—SHALOM BAR-ASHER

ANAV FAMILY, family of scholars in Italy. The family claimed to be descended from aristocratic families brought by Titus to Rome after the destruction of the Temple in Jerusalem in 70 CE.

Binyamin ben Avraham Anav (13th cent.), scholar in Rome; brother of Tsidqiyahu. Besides a wide knowledge of *halakhah*, he was involved in philosophical speculation, mathematics, and astronomy. He wrote liturgical poems, many of which were incorporated into the Roman rite, the "Maḥzor Roma'."

Tsidqiyahu ben Avraham Anav (13th cent.), rabbi in Rome; brother of Binyamin. He studied under famous scholars in Italy and outside. His halakhic work *Shibbolei ha-Leqet* deals with the sources and underlying reasons for ritual observances. It also deals with the rules of benedictions, prayers, Sabbath, Ro'sh Ḥodesh, Ḥanukkah, Purim, and feasts and fasts. He discusses laws of mourning, circumcision, fringes (*tsitsit*), phylacteries (*tefillin*), as well as ritual slaughtering and the consumption of ritually clean animals and forbidden foods. It was published by S. Buber in 1886 and in a critical edition by S. Mirsky in 1966.

Yehudah ben Binyamin Anav (c.1215–after 1280), rabbi in Rome, cousin of Binyamin and Tsidqiyahu. He was the teacher of Tsidqiyahu. He wrote commentaries on the *halakhot* of Alfasi, on Mishnah *Sheqalim*, and a summary of the laws of *sheḥitah* and *terefah*.

Yeḥi'el ben Yequti'el Anav (13th cent.), author and copyist in Rome, nephew of Yehudah ben Binyamin. He published an important ethical treatise *Maʿalot ha-Middot*, a description of good attributes and their opposite, with the aim of encouraging his contemporaries to act ethically and to warn them against bad influences. His sources were not only the Bible and rabbinic literature but also philosophical works and Christian moral writings. He composed an elegy on the destruction of a Roman synagogue by fire in 1284. He was also a copyist of Hebrew manuscripts, the most important of which (known as MS Leiden) contains a large section of the Talmud Yerushalmi.

• Ḥayyim Yosef David Azulai, *Shem ha-Gedolim* (Jerusalem, 1991). Abraham Berliner, *Geschichte der Juden in Rom von der altesten Zeit bis zur Gegenwart* (Frankfurt a. M., 1893). Simon Bernfeld, *Sefer ha-Demaʿot* (Berlin, 1924). Israel Davidson, *Otsar ha-Shirah veha-Piyyut*, 4 vols. (New York, 1970). Moritz Güdemann, *Geschichte des Erziehungswesens und der Cultur der Juden in Frankreich und Deutschland* (Vienna, 1880). Hermann Vogelstein and Paul Rieger, *Geschichte der Juden in Rom*, 2 vols. (Berlin, 1895–1896).

—LEON A. FELDMAN

ANDEROGINOS (אַנְדְּרוֹגִינוֹס; hermaphrodite), in Jewish law the term for an animal or human with both male and female characteristics and organs. This is to be distinguished from the *tumtum*, a person with dual sexual characteristics whose sex cannot be determined. The legal status of the *anderoginos* is the subject of some dispute. The majority opinion is that it is regarded as both a questionable male and a questionable female. This means that in certain areas of Jewish law the *anderoginos* is treated as a male, and in other areas as a female. According to the majority opinion, an androgynous individual is permitted to marry but is not obligated to have children (T., *Bik*. 2).

• *Entsiqlopedyah Talmudit* (Jerusalem, 1947–), vol. 2, pp. 55–60.

–MARC SHAPIRO

'ANENU (עֲנֵנוּ; Answer Us), prayer inserted on fast days in the Ge'ullah (seventh blessing) by the reader and in the Shema' Kolenu blessing (Birkat Tefillah, the seventeenth blessing) by the congregation in the repetition of the *'Amidah at the Shaḥarit and Minḥah services. 'Anenu beseeches God to "answer in time of trouble." The earliest formulation may be in the Talmud Yerushalmi (*Ber*. 4.3), but the existing versions contain a number of divergences, that of the Ashkenazi rite being closest to the Yerushalmi version.

• Ismar Elbogen, *Jewish Liturgy: A Comprehensive History*, translated by Raymond P. Scheindlin (Philadelphia, 1993). Macy Nulman, *The Encyclopedia of Jewish Prayer* (Northvale, N.J., 1993).

ANGEL OF DEATH, the angel who takes the human soul from the body. While the Bible refers to "destroying angels" (*2 Sm*. 24.16; *Is*. 37.36), the concept of the angel of death only developed in the post-biblical period. According to the third-century Palestinian amora' R. *Shim'on ben Laqish (*B. B*. 16a), the "accuser," Satan, and the evil inclination that tempts and leads to sin are one and the same, for the wages of sin are death. Both Satan and the angel of death are often referred to as the angel *Samael, the head of the realm of evil. According to the Talmud, Israel accepted the Torah so that the angel of death would have no hold on them (*'A. Z*. 5a), that is to say the "Torah of Life" is the antidote to death. Many customs and superstitions developed from the belief in an angel of death. Beginning in the thirteenth century, for example, it became customary in some places to pour out all water found in the room at the time of a person's death. This practice probably originated in the belief that the angel of death pierced his victim with a sword dipped in poison, some of which may have dripped into the water found in the room at the moment of death. In eastern Europe a glass of water and a towel were placed next to the bed of a person about to die so that the angel of death could wash the poison from his sword and then wipe it dry.

• Bernard J. Bamberger, *Fallen Angels* (Philadelphia, 1952). David E. Fass, "How the Angels Do Serve," *Judaism* 40.3 (1991): 281–289. Theodor H. Gaster, *The Holy and the Profane: Evolution of Jewish Folkways* (New York, 1955), pp. 242–247. Dov Noy, "Das Meidel un der Royber," *Haifa Yahrbuch für Literatur und Kunst* 5 (1969): 177–224. Joshua Trachtenberg, *Jewish Magic and Superstition: A Study in Folk Religion* (New York, 1939). Ḥaim Schwarzbaum, *Shorashim ve-Nofim*, edited by Eli Yassif (Beersheva, 1993), pp. 56–73.

–MAYER I. GRUBER

ANGELS. Conceived of as supernatural, celestial beings, angels play a role in Jewish thought and literature from earliest biblical times, yet angelology has never become a major systematized branch of Jewish theology. Various names are applied to angelic beings in scripture. Like the Greek word *angelos*, from which *angel* is derived, the Hebrew word *mal'akh* signifies primarily a messenger or agent; it is as God's messenger that the *mal'akh* becomes an angel. Other designations for spiritual entities are: *benei Elohim* or *benei Elim* (sons of God; *Gn*. 6.4; *Ps*. 29.1, respectively); *qedoshim* (holy ones; *Ps*. 89.6, 89.8); *'ir* (watcher, envoy; *Dn*. 4.10, 4.14); and sometimes simply *ish* (man; *Gn*. 18.2, 32.25). More distinctive appellations are reserved for the supernatural creatures connected with the divine throne or chariot: *seraphim (*Is*. 6.2); *keruvim* (cherubim; *Ez*. 10.3; cf. *Gn*. 3.24); *ḥayyot* (living creatures; *Ez*. 1.5); **ofannim* (wheels; *Ez*. 1.15ff.). Notwithstanding the variety of generic names by which angels are called and the use of descriptive expressions indicative of their mission, such as "the angel which has redeemed" (*Gn*. 48.16), "the angel that destroyed" (*2 Sm*. 24.16), and so on, it is significant that with the exception of certain postexilic references, these heavenly spirits are depicted in the Bible as lacking individuality, personal names, and hierarchical rank. In the course of their duties, they assume many forms, the shape varying with their task. Most often, especially in the earlier narratives, they appear as human beings, but irrespective of their commission, they remain completely obedient to the divine will. Even *Satan, the adversary, is none other than the Lord's official prosecutor and is subservient to his authority. The concept of rebellious angels belongs to post-biblical Jewish literature.

Angelic functions are numerous and as a rule beneficent. Thus, they come to the aid of Hagar, apprise Abraham that a son will be born to him, guard the Israelites against the pursuing Egyptians, protect them during their wanderings in the wilderness, and interpret the visions of Zechariah and Daniel. At other times angels (to be distinguished from the *demons of a later epoch) are given punitive missions—to destroy Sodom and Gomorrah (*Gn*. 19), punish the citizens of Jerusalem (*Ez*. 9), and smite the camp of Assyria (*2 Kgs*. 19.35). In heaven the angels surround God's throne and form his council and court (*1 Kgs*. 22.19ff.). They also constitute the celestial choir that has sung unceasing praise to the Creator since the beginning of time (*Jb*. 38.7). Inconsistencies discernible in the portrayal of angelic activities (e.g., the "sons of God" marrying the daughters of men, *Gn*. 6.2ff.) appear to be due to the fact that varied strands of thought and belief combine to form the fabric of biblical angelology. In some instances, forces deified by heathen people were reduced to the status of angels and thus brought under the control of the one God. During other periods it was felt that the very transcendental character of God postulated the presence of beings to mediate between him and the world. In many passages the angel merely personifies a divine attribute or embodies God's will in history or is an objectivization of the prophet's vision. It is noteworthy, however, that in large parts of the Bible angels are conspicuously absent. It is conjectured that the prophetic and priestly circles, as well as the so-called Deuteronomic school, were opposed to the doctrine of angels inasmuch as it derogated from the absolute divinity of the one God.

The Babylonian exile had a marked effect on Jewish angelology, as attested to in the statement, "The names of the angels were brought by the Jews from Babylonia" (Y., *R. ha-Sh.* 1.2). The angels became individualized, were given specific names, and were graded, like Babylonian spirits, into different ranks. Ezekiel speaks of seven angels, six of whom wrought destruction, while the seventh acted as a scribe. Zechariah saw "a man riding upon a red horse," who was chief of those who "walk to and fro through the earth" (*Zec.* 1.8–19). The new conception of the deity was so transcendental that it was no longer God but "the angel that talked with me" who instructed the prophet (*Zec.* 1.9, 14). In the Bible, this process reaches its climax in the *Book of Daniel*. Here the angels are classified; two high-ranking angels have individual names (*Michael and Gabriel); and national guardian angels (*sarim*) are introduced for the first time (*Dn.* 8.16, 10.20–21).

The evolution of angelology advanced still further in post-biblical apocalyptic literature, especially in *1*, *2*, and *3 Enoch*, *Jubilees*, the *Testaments of the Twelve Patriarchs*, and the Sibylline Oracles. The world of angels now becomes so bizarre and chaotic as to leave an impression of unbridled imagination. Essentially, the angels serve as the media of revelation and the instruments by which God governs the world. Their numbers are astronomical; their varieties almost endless. All the elements and phenomena of nature are given tutelary spirits. Certain angelic categories are of special interest. Frequent reference is made to the angel of peace. The seven (or four) archangels are usually deemed to be the highest angelic echelon (*1 En.* 20.1–8). They may be identifiable with the "watchers" of Daniel, the "angels of the presence" (see *Is.* 63.9), and the "ministering angels" of rabbinic ideology. Mystic lore devoted special attention to the divine chariot (*Ez.* 1–3) attended by the host of heavenly angels. At the other end of the scale, the fallen angels, who for their sins were cast from heaven to the nether world (see *Gn.* 6.4; *Is.* 14.12–15), are given prominence in the apocalyptic works but find no place in rabbinic literature. It is they who begot the demons and are seducers of women. They were subjugated by the archangels but not annihilated. This polarization of the angel world into good and evil spirits is a major feature of angelology to which it appears the Essenes made a considerable contribution. The Sadducees, on the other hand, seem to have been strenuously opposed to it.

A highly developed angelology is also found in the Talmud, Midrash, and the Palestinian Targum. Under Magian and Zoroastrian influence, the angelic hosts proliferated, but in rabbinic Judaism, the evil spirits, even the *mal'akhei ḥabbalah* (angels of destruction), remained under the surpeme control of the one God. There are many aggadic sayings on the subject of angels: they are made of fire, or of fire and water divinely harmonized; some are transitory and live only to sing a single hymn of praise to the Creator, others are eternal, a few are of cosmic proportions. It was a moot point whether the permanent angels were formed on the second, fourth, or fifth day of Creation. They certainly were not created on the first day, lest it be thought that they were God's partners in the creative process. They are called *elyonim* (higher beings) to distinguish them from the *taḥtonim* (lower beings), the denizens of the earth. They have no will of their own but loyally carry out the divine commands. Mostly they seek the good for pious men and the well-being of Israel in particular. Wherever no personal agent is mentioned in the Bible, the *aggadah* tends to fill the vacuum with angels. Thus, they are given an important role in the creation of man, the sacrifice of Isaac, and the story of Esther. There are seventy or seventy-two guardian angels of the nations (cf. Septuagint, *Dt.* 32.8). They constitute the divine council and the court. Individual Israelites also have guardian angels. A Jew is given one angel with the fulfillment of each commandment, and two accompany each Jew constantly. On Sabbath eve, a good and evil angel accompany each worshiper as he returns from the synagogue. In the sanctuary on high, the *mal'akhei ha-sharet* (ministering angels) perform the priestly functions, with Michael acting as a kind of high priest. There are seven heavens, each in the charge of an archangel. Of special eminence is the *mal'akh ha-panim* (angel of the presence), also called Amshapands and identified with Enoch. There are numerous allusions to angels of destruction. The most terrible of the destroying angels is the *mal'akh ha-mavet* (the angel of death), who waits at the bedside of the sick. At the tip of his sword hangs a lethal drop of venom. Originally the angel of death, like other angels, personified a function of the divine will, but gradually he acquired a definitely demonic individuality. He is linked and at times identified with *Satan (who tempts and accuses), the evil inclination, and *Samael, the prince of demons.

All the great Jewish philosophers except Philo adopted a rationalistic view of angels. Ibn Daud, Maimonides, and Levi ben Gershom identified them with the pure intellects who governed the planetary bodies. Saʿadyah Ga'on and Yehudah ha-Levi regarded them as manifestations of prophetic visions created for a specific mission; Yehudah ha-Levi, however, considered the angels of the "higher world" as eternal. In the Kabbalah, both speculative and practical angelology assumes its most extravagant forms. Distinctions were made between male and female angels (Zohar 1.11, 9b). While the Talmud (Y., *Ber.* 9:13) depicts the angels as servants of God and prohibits supplicating them for help, ancient mystical texts (Heikhalot, Zohar, and later kabbalistic literature) attributed to them the most extraordinary powers; despite the disapproval of many rabbinic authorities, appeals were made to them in the form of *amulets, incantations, and even through interpolations in the liturgy. Kabbalistic angelology remained, nevertheless, essentially monotheistic. Most rabbinic texts agree that man, in spite of his bodily materiality, ranks above the angels.

References to angels are still preserved in the traditional liturgy. They occur *inter alia* in the preface to the Qedushah, the *seliḥot*, and in the Shofarot passages. The ministering angels and the angels of peace are addressed in the hymn Shalom ʿAleikhem, recited in the Ashkenazi rite after the evening service on Friday night. Generally speaking, contemporary Judaism regards allusions to angels in scripture and in the liturgy as of poetic and symbolic significance rather than of doctrinal import or factual significance. Reform Judaism has tended to remove liturgical references to angels.

• Gustav Davidson, *A Dictionary of Angels* (New York, 1967). Concepcion Gonzalo Rubio, *La Angelologia en la literatura rabínica y Sefardi*, Biblioteca Nueva Sefarad, vol. 2 (Barcelona, 1977). Alexander Kohut, *Über die jüdische Angelologie und Daemonologie in ihrer Abhängigkeit vom Parsismus*, Abhandlugen für die Kunde des Morgenlandes, Bd. 4, nr. 3 (Leipzig, 1866; repr. Nendeln, Liechtenstein, 1966). Michael Mach, *Entwicklungsstadien des jüdischen Engelglaubens in vorrabbinischer Zeit*, Texte und Studien zum antiken Judentum, 34 (Tübingen, 1992). Reuben Margaliot, *Malakhei ʿElyon* (Jerusalem, 1987). Morris B. Margolies, *A Gathering of Angels* (New York, 1994). Saul M. Olyan, *A Thousand Thousands Served Him: Exegesis and the Naming of Angels in Ancient Judaism*, Texte und Studien zum antiken Judentum, 36 (Tübingen, 1993). Alexander Rofé, *Ha-'Emunah be-Mal'akhim ba-Miqra'* (Jerusalem, 1979). Peter Schäfer, *Rivalität zwischen Engeln und Menschen*, Studia Judaica, Bd. 5 (Berlin, 1975). Gertrud Schiller, *Die boten Gottes* (Kassel, 1951). Moïse Schwab, *Vocabulaire de l'angélologie* (Paris, 1897; repr. Milan, 1989). Joshua Trachtenberg, *Jewish Magic and Superstition* (Cleveland, 1961), pp. 69–77, 97–103.

ANI MA'AMIN. See THIRTEEN PRINCIPLES OF FAITH.

ANIMALS, TREATMENT OF. Jewish law prohibits the infliction of unnecessary pain on animals, referred to in Hebrew as the prohibition of *tsaʿar baʿalei ḥayyim*. One of the *Noahic laws is the ban on eating a limb taken from a living animal (*Gn*. 9.4). The Bible is replete with detailed references to the obligation to be kind to animals and not overwork them (*Lv*. 22.27–28; *Dt*. 22.4, 22.6), saying that God "delivers" man and beast alike (*Ps*. 36.7). Rabbinic law directed that one must feed one's animals before feeding one's self, which recalls the special trait that marked Rebekah as Isaac's future wife (*Gn*. 24.14). The Talmud (*B. M*. 32a–b) discusses whether the prohibition against inflicting pain on animals is of biblical or rabbinic origin. Most Talmudic and post-Talmudic authorities agree that the prohibition is of biblical origin (*Shulḥan ʿArukh, Oraḥ Ḥayyim* 305.19). The rabbis ruled that many Sabbath laws could be infringed to rescue an animal from death or pain (*Shab*. 128b). However, this does not prevent the necessary killing of animals for either the health or safety of humans. Indeed, the *Shulḥan ʿArukh* (*Even ha-ʿEzer* 5:14) avers that the prohibition of *tsaʿar baʿalei ḥayyim* is inapplicable in the case of significant human need. Thus, Galician rabbi Jacob Reischer, writing in *Shevut Yaʿaqov* 3.71 during the dawn of medical experimentation in the early 1700s, states that one may test medicines on animals to determine their efficacy on people. There are, however, a number of modern authorities who rule that such conduct is impious and should not be carried out by honorable individuals. A similar approach can be found in the writings of R. Mosheh Feinstein (*Shulḥan ʿArukh, Ḥoshen Mishpat* 2.47), who notes that pious people do not even directly kill insects that bother them.

• J. David Bleich, "Judaism and Animal Experimentation," *Tradition* 22.1 (Spring 1986): 1–36. Noah Cohen, *Tsaʿar Baʿalei Ḥayyim: The Prevention of Cruelty to Animals*, 2d ed. (Jerusalem, 1976). Joseph Hurewitz, *The Care of Animals in Jewish Life and Lore* (New York, 1926). Fred Rosner, "Judaism and Human Experimentation," in *Jewish Bioethics*, edited by Fred Rosner and J. David Bleich (New York, 1979), pp. 387–397

—MICHAEL BROYDE

ANIMAL SACRIFICES. See SACRIFICES.

ANʿIM ZEMIROT. See SHIR HA-KAVOD.

ANINUT (אֲנִינוּת), interval between death and burial of a close relative. During this period the mourner is called *onen*. The *onen* is absolved from observing all Torah precepts, including praying and putting on *tefillin*, and is expected to concentrate on preparation for the funeral. He is forbidden to eat meat or drink wine. Should a Sabbath intervene during this period, the *onen* must observe the Sabbath precepts as usual. See also MOURNING.

• Aaron Felder, *Yesodei Smochos: Mourning and Remembrance in Halachah and Jewish Tradition* (New York, 1992). Maurice Lamm, *The Jewish Way in Death and Mourning* (New York, 1972). Aaron Levine, *To Comfort the Bereaved: A Guide for Mourners and Those Who Visit Them* (Northvale, N.J., 1994).

ANNA' BE-KOAḤ (אָנָּא בְּכֹחַ; We Beg You! with the Strength [of Your Right Hand's Greatness]), a supplication for divine protection and for the acceptance of the community's prayers, ascribed to the first-century teacher Neḥunya' ben ha-Qanah, but probably composed by a medieval mystic. According to the kabbalists, the initial letters of the forty-two words of the prayer represent the forty-two-lettered name of God, as set out in *Qiddushin* 71a. In some prayer books Anna' be-Koaḥ is incorporated into the daily morning service and into the Sabbath eve service before Lekhah Dodi. In other liturgies that avoid mysticism, the prayer was either eliminated or else printed in a smaller typeface as a reluctant accommodation. It has not been included in non-Orthodox liturgies.

• Abraham E. Millgram, *Jewish Worship* (Philadelphia, 1971), pp. 498f. Nosson Scherman, ed., *Siddur Kol Yaacov: The Complete ArtScroll Siddur* (Brooklyn, N.Y., 1987), p. 315.

—A. STANLEY DREYFUS

ANOINTING, the application of *oil to a person or object, expressed in Hebrew by the verb *mashaḥ* (from which the term *messiah is derived) and in later times by the verb *sakh*. In ancient times, everyday anointing of the body was done for medical, cosmetic, and hygienic reasons (the last two being prohibited on fasts and during mourning, as they are forms of physical pleasure [*Yoma'* 8.1]), and the anointing of certain foodstuffs had culinary importance. In religious usage, anointing signifies consecration. Moses was commanded to see to the preparation of sacred anointing oil, composed of pure olive oil mixed with the most expensive fragrant spices: myrrh, cinnamon, aromatic cane, and cassia (*Ex*. 29.21, 30.22–25, 40.9–14). This oil was to be applied to each and every sacred person, conveying to them a quality of contagious holiness: "whatever touches them shall become consecrated" (*Ex*. 30.29). The effect of physical contact between such anointed objects and profane objects was said to be deadly.

The sacred oil was also to be used to anoint *Aaron and his sons as well, along with their sacred vestments, thus consecrating them and their descendants for all time to the *priesthood. Although the investiture of the priests included elaborate sacrificial rituals, the anointing and donning of *priestly vestments most clearly indicated sacred status (*Ex.* 29.36, etc.). Thus, the day of the high priest's investiture is referred to as the day of "the anointed priests" (*Nm.* 3.3). For the high priest alone, the anointing oil was not merely applied but poured on his head (*Lv.* 8.12). Rabbinic literature regularly calls the high priest "the anointed priest" and refers to the priest appointed to address the armed forces before going out to battle (*Dt.* 20.2) as "the priest anointed for war" (e.g., *Sot.* 8.1). The anointing ceremonies were carried out after the Tabernacle was erected (*Lv.* 8.10–12, 30; *Nm.* 7.1).

From the time of Saul on, religious anointing was used in the Israelite monarchy. The anointing of the king by a prophet was an indication that he had been chosen by God, that is, consecrated to his task as earthly legate of the divine king. Saul and David were anointed privately by Samuel (*1 Sm.* 9.1, 10.1, 12–13, 16.3), as was Jehu by the agent of Elisha (*2 Kgs.* 9). Public anointings, while they may have been carried out with or without divine sanction, were nonetheless religious acts. The public anointing of David at Hebron (*2 Sm.* 5.3, 17) confirmed the earlier anointing by Samuel, whereas the anointing of Solomon by Zadok the priest (*1 Kgs.* 1.39) and of Joash and Jehoaichim (*2 Kgs.* 11.12 and 23.20) seems to have been a response to rival claims to the throne or to opposition parties. Sensing the extraordinary nature of these cases, the rabbis of the Talmud interpreted that as a rule kings are anointed only at the inauguration of a new dynasty.

The possibility that King Hazael of Aram may have been anointed by an Israelite prophet at God's command (Elijah, according to *1 Kgs.* 19.15–16; or perhaps Elisha, as in *2 Kgs.* 9) suggests the idea that God, as universal king, appoints the rulers of all nations. In *Isaiah* 45.1, Cyrus, king of Persia, who permitted the return of the Jews to their ancient land, is called the anointed of God.

The Israelite king, believed to be chosen by God, is called "the Lord's anointed" (*mashiaḥ* [*1 Sm.* 2.10, 24.7, 11, 26.16; *2 Sm.* 1.14, 16, 19.22, 22.51, 23.1, and frequently in the *Psalms*]). It was the hope for eventual reestablishment of Israel's ancient sovereignty and of the Davidic monarchy that embodied it that led to the use of the term *mashiaḥ* to denote the future king (Messiah) of Israel. This term lent itself to Israel's hopes for its future restoration in general (messianism). Anointing played no role in Jewish ritual after the destruction of the Second Temple. The Talmudic rabbis conveyed many traditions concerning anointing, notably in *Horayot* 11b–12a.

• Gary A. Anderson, *A Time to Mourn, a Time to Dance: The Expression of Grief and Joy in Israelite Religion* (University Park, Pa., 1991), pp. 45–49. Menahem Haran, *Temples and Temple-Service in Ancient Israel* (Oxford, 1978), pp. 175–188. Jacob Milgrom, *Leviticus 1–16: A New Translation with Introduction and Commentary*, The Anchor Bible, vol. 3 (New York, 1991), pp. 553–555.

—BARUCH J. SCHWARTZ

ANTHROPOMORPHISM, the attribution to God of human qualities, such as human form (anthropomorphism proper, e.g., God's figure, hands, eyes, etc.) and human emotions (anthropopathism, e.g., God loves, is angry, etc.). Anthropomorphism, which is taken for granted in many primitive and pagan religions, becomes an issue when the concept of a spiritual and transcendent God, especially as elaborated by philosophy, conflicts with apparent anthropomorphism in authoritative texts (e.g., the Bible, rabbinic *aggadah*, etc.). Nineteenth-century scholars claimed to have discovered evidence of a gradual evolution from an anthropomorphic to a more spiritual conception of God in the biblical texts, but this is now held to be an oversimplification. Biblical writers do not hesitate to resort to anthropomorphism (God walks in the garden of Eden, passes over the houses of the children of Israel, dwells in Zion, is moved by love or feelings of revenge, etc.), but they frequently use qualifying language. Many of the definite anthropomorphisms are obviously not meant to be taken literally but are the language of imagery. The *Targums (Onkelos in particular) as well as the Hellenistic philosophers (*Philo) rendered this anthropomorphistic imagery by qualifying circumlocutions or interpreted it allegorically, so as to avoid all danger of misunderstanding. Rabbinic usage, too, did not shy away from anthropomorphism, and it was attacked by the *Karaites and others for its alleged primitive crudity. The great medieval Jewish philosophers, Moses *Maimonides in particular, undertook to interpret all objectionable anthropomorphisms; namely, to translate them into abstract, conceptual language (see God, Attributes of). The mystics and kabbalists evolved new—to some, shocking—anthropomorphisms, as well as theories and concepts to deal with them. Ultimately the issue is one of enabling human beings to speak validly both of a god (in theology) and to a god (in prayer) who is utterly transcendent. The choice seems to be between saying nothing at all (the "mystic silence") and daring to speak of him in human terms; that is, in the only language men possess to indicate that he is actively meaningful in human life (as a creator, father, king, lover, redeemer). The conviction of God's spirituality and transcendence as it finally developed in Judaism was so radical and deep that even the most daring anthropomorphism could be used without risk or danger.

• Meir Bar-Ilan, "The Hand of God: A Chapter in Rabbinic Anthropomorphism," *Rashi 1040–1990: Hommage à Ephraïm E. Urbach*, edited by Gabrielle Sed-Rajna (Paris, 1993), pp. 321–335. Moses Gaster, *Studies and Texts in Folklore, Magic, Medieval Romance, Hebrew Apocrypha, and Samaritan Archeology*, vol. 2 (New York, 1971), pp. 1130–1153. Carmel McCarthy, "The Treatment of Biblical Anthropomorphisms in Pentateuchal Targums," in *Back to the Sources: Biblical and Near Eastern Studies in Honour of Dermot Ryan*, edited by Kevin J. Cathcart and John F. Healy (Dublin, Ireland, 1989), pp. 45–66. J. Samuel Preus, "Anthropomorphism and Spinoza's Innovations," *Religion* 25 (1995): 1–8. Gershom Gerhard Scholem, *Jewish Gnosticism, Merkabah Mysticism and Talmudic Tradition* (New York, 1960), pp. 36–42, 118–126. David Stern, "*Imitatio Hominis*: Anthropomorphism and the Character(s) of God in Rabbinic Literature," *Prooftexts* 12.2 (1992): 151–174. Elliot Wolfson, "Images of God's Feet: Some Observations on the Divine Body in Judaism," in *People of the Body: Jews and Judaism from an Embodied Per-*

spective, edited by Howard Eilberg-Schwartz (Albany, 1993), pp. 143–181.

ANTIBI FAMILY, family of rabbis in Aleppo, Egypt, and Erets Yisra'el.

Yitsḥaq ben Shabbetai Antibi (died 1804) of Aleppo, was the author of *Ohel Yitsḥaq*, a collection of sermons; *Beit Av* (Leghorn, 1849), on Maimonides and Yosef Karo; and *responsa* (in Yehudah Qatsin's *Maḥaneh Yehudah* [Leghorn, 1803]).

Ya'aqov Antibi (died 1846), born in Aleppo, was rabbi in Damascus for forty years and the author of *Abbir Ya'aqov*, a collection of *novellae*. His religious poems were included in the Damascus *baqqashot* (see BAQQASHAH).

Avraham ben Yitsḥaq Antibi (1765–1858), son of Yitsḥaq ben Shabbetai, was a scholar of great learning and a strong community leader, who issued *taqqanot* to enforce his rulings. He is the author of *Yoshev Ohalim* (Leghorn, 1825), a collection of sermons; *Penei ha-Bayit* (Leghorn, 1843), a commentary on Shelomoh Adret's *Torat ha-Bayit* and on the *Shulḥan 'Arukh*; the popular ethical work *Ḥokhmah u-Musar* (Leghorn, 1850; Jerusalem, 1961; edited by J. Avadi Shayev [Jerusalem, 1980]), which incorporated *Ḥuqqei Nashim*, on matrimonial law, and *Penei Ohel Mo'ed* (Jerusalem, 1959), a collection of homiletical discourses for the Sabbath, in which he speculated on the date of redemption. His most important work is *Mor va-'Ahalot* (Leghorn, 1843), a collection of *responsa*, which sheds much light on the life of the Jews of Syria in his time.

• David Z. Lanyado, *Li-Qedoshim asher ba-'Arets* (Jerusalem, 1980).

–SHALOM BAR-ASHER

ANTIGONUS OF SOKHO (c.200 BCE), sage; disciple of *Shim'on ha-Tsaddiq. The sole aphorism preserved in his name is the statement in *Avot* 1.3: "Be not like servants who serve their master in the hope of receiving a reward, but be like those servants who serve their masters with no expectation of receiving a reward; and let the fear of heaven be upon you." His two pupils, Zadko and Boethus, are reported to have misinterpreted this as a repudiation of the belief in retribution in the world to come (*Avot de-Rabbi Natan* 5.2). From these two pupils emerged the deviant sects of the *Zadokites and the *Boethusians.

• Raymond Harari, "Rabbinic Perceptions of the Boethusians," Ph.D. dissertation, New York University, 1995.

–DANIEL SPERBER

ANTINOMIANISM, theoretical negation and actual transgression of traditional law on various grounds. Tendencies and movements denying the validity of the received ritual and moral norms or, at least, encouraging their neglect, have appeared in different periods and for various reasons. In Hellenistic Egypt, and again in the Middle Ages, the interpretation of the Torah by means of *allegory led to the substitution of allegorical and symbolic meanings for the literal meaning and thus at times tended to undermine the strict observance of the law. The abolition of the Law by Jesus, and its fulfillment through the "New Covenant," is a central feature of Paul's theology, for example.

The Talmudic sages were concerned with the possibility of antinomian trends and regarded even Solomon's transgressions as antinomian in nature. According to the Talmud Yerushalmi (*San* 2.6), Solomon believed that since he knew the reasons for the law, he could ensure that his transgressions would not negatively affect him. God's reply is a complete rejection of antinomianism: "Solomon and a thousand like him will be annihilated before a single letter of the Torah will be abolished." Another Talmudic passage (*Yoma'* 67b) polemicizes against those who would make light of certain ritual laws because of their lack of evident reasons and insists that it is those laws especially which Satan "urges one to transgress," but since God has ordained them, humans have no right to question them.

Concerns about antinomianism are common in medieval Jewish literature. All who ventured into the field of *ta'amei ha-mitsvot* (suggesting reasons for the commandments [see COMMANDMENTS, REASONS FOR]) had to confront this issue. Some scholars, including Maimonides, thought that without a rational basis, people would reject the law (agnostic antinomianism), whereas others believed that by offering reasons, obedience to the law would be undermined (philosophical antinomianism).

Mystical and messianic movements were often suspected of antinomian tendencies. While none can be ascribed to the classical Kabbalah, extreme antinomianism made its appearance in both the theology and the practice of Shabbateanism (see SHABBETAI TSEVI) and Frankism (see FRANK, YA'AQOV). Their followers were able to draw support from assorted statements in rabbinic and kabbalistic literature, which speak of abolishment of the *mitsvot* in messianic days. Slightly altering the wording of one of the traditional liturgical formulas, the Shabbateans blessed God who "permits that which is forbidden." Reform Judaism has also had an antinomian aspect, in that many of its leading thinkers claimed that the ritual law was a hindrance to true spirituality and should be discarded in modern times.

• William D. Davies, *The Torah in the Messianic Age and/or the Age to Come* (Philadelphia, 1952). Jacob Katz, *Ha-Halakhah ba-Meitsar* (Jerusalem, 1992), pp. 261–278. Gershom Gerhard Scholem, *Major Trends in Jewish Mysticism* (New York, 1974). Gershom Gerhard Scholem, *The Messianic Idea in Judaism: And Other Essays on Jewish Spirituality* (New York, 1971). Isadore Twersky, *Introduction to the Code of Maimonides*, Yale Judaica Series 22 (New Haven, 1980), pp. 391–397.

–MARC SHAPIRO

ANTIOCHUS, SCROLL OF. See SCROLL OF ANTIOCHUS.

ANTIOCHUS IV EPIPHANES (r. 175–164), Seleucid king of Syria, described in contemporary sources as eccentric and unpredictable, a ruthless despot who could also be extremely pious and generous. Soon after ascending to the throne, he intervened in Jewish religious life in Jerusalem, where he deposed the pious high priest Onias III and appointed Onias's brother, the Hellenizer Jason, in his stead. Some three years later he deposed Jason and appointed another Hellenizer, Menelaus. In

169 and perhaps again in 168, Antiochus plundered Jerusalem and the Temple. In 167 he ordered the desecration of the Temple and the abolition of Torah observances. Circumcision, Sabbath observance, or the possession of a Torah scroll were made punishable by death, the walls of Jerusalem were razed to the ground, and foreigners were settled in a newly built citadel in the city's midst. Antiochus's motivation in attempting to extirpate the Jewish religion as well as the extent of the Jewish Hellenizers' involvement are matters of much scholarly debate, and the available sources do not allow any clear-cut answers. Antiochus had not anticipated the ensuing armed revolt led by the *Hasmoneans and their supporters, which led Antiochus's son and successor, Antiochus V Eupator, to rescind his father's anti-Jewish decrees in 162 and to restore to the Jews the right to live according to their own laws.

• Elias J. Bickerman, *The God of the Maccabees: Studies on the Meaning and Origin of the Maccabean Revolt*, Studies in Judaism in Late Antiquity, vol. 32, translated by Horst R. Moehring (Leiden, 1979). Erich S. Gruen, "Hellenism and Persecution: Antiochus IV and the Jews," in *Hellenistic History and Culture*, edited by Peter Green (Berkeley, 1993), pp. 238–274. Otto Mørkholm, *Antiochus IV of Syria* (Copenhagen, 1966). Victor Tcherikover, *Hellenistic Civilization and the Jews*, translated by S. Applebaum (Philadelphia, 1966).

—GIDEON BOHAK

ANTISEMITISM, hatred of and hostility to the Jews. The term was coined in 1879 by the German anti-Jewish writer Wilhelm Marr, but it has entered general usage to apply to all manifestations of hatred of the Jewish people throughout the ages, and as such it has a long history. It even precedes the enmity of the Christian church toward the Jews for their alleged crime of deicide and their refusal to accept Jesus. Indeed, the expression of animosity toward the Jews is found as early as the statement of Haman: "There is a certain people scattered abroad and dispersed among the people in all the provinces of the kingdom, and their laws are diverse from all people, neither keep they the king's laws, therefore it is not for the king's profit to suffer them" (*Est*. 3.8). That verse contains many traditional aspects of antisemitism, including the discomfort with the dispersion of the Jews; the suspicions aroused by their customs, giving rise to "the dislike of the like for the unlike"; the accusation that they are an alien element potentially harmful to the state (cf. *Ex*. 1.10) and that, in any case, they are disloyal to it; and the belief in their dispensability as a useless element.

Much of the early hatred of the Jews was based on the Jewish rejection of paganism. The Jewish refusal to worship images led to a series of clashes with the Hellenistic and Roman authorities and to the antagonism to Jews expressed, for example, in the works of certain classical authors. Other peoples accepted the existence of the gods of other nations; only the Jews refused absolutely to acknowledge such existence or to send tribute. Moreover, Jewish religious practices (e.g., marriage customs, dietary laws) cut them off from social intercourse with their neighbors. The necessity for Jews to live in close proximity to one another (for the proper observance of the Sabbath, in order to be close to a synagogue, and so forth) as well as their inability to perform certain communal or national obligations (e.g., military service) for religious reasons also emphasized their apartness. Pagan (Hellenistic) antisemitism was rife in the first century BCE and the first century CE, particularly in Alexandria, and was probably accentuated by Jewish proselytizing activities and the concomitant Jewish denigration of the practices of other religions. However, it was in the Christian world that antisemitism assumed the most tragic proportions. Although *Christianity denied all other religions, it found itself in a particularly hostile position with regard to the "mother religion" from which it claimed its descent but which had rejected it. The spread and ultimate political success of Christianity led to the emergence of the doctrine that the Jews were hated by God, who had rejected them for their sinfulness and obstinacy. Jews were gradually forced out of every sphere of political influence and deprived of civil and political rights. The Christian church's attempts to erect barriers between Jew and non-Jew were translated into legislation affecting all aspects of Jewish life. Conversion to Judaism became an offense punishable by death, and a movement for the destruction of synagogues and forced conversion (see CONVERSION, FORCED) of the Jews was strong from the fifth century on. Exclusion of Jews from economic life was the next objective, and in the later Middle Ages expulsions were frequent. Hatred of the Jews was fed by liturgical and other (e.g., dramatic) commemorations of the crucifixion of Jesus, which were liable to erupt with particular violence at the Easter season, the occasion for organized attacks on the Jews. Religious antisemitism reached its first climax in the period of the Crusades, and the Fourth Lateran Council (1215) passed a series of anti-Jewish measures. In this atmosphere many anti-Jewish libels—notably the *blood libel—received universal credence throughout the Christian world. The ultimately religious nature of Christian antisemitism was demonstrated by the fact that baptism automatically removed all disabilities from a Jew. In fact, discrimination and persecution had the avowed purpose of producing conversion, and there is no record of church discrimination against converted Jews earlier than the sixteenth century, when such discrimination occurred in Spain. The doctrine of the medieval church that by their crime of deicide and their refusal to accept the divinity of Jesus the Jews had become the "spawn of the devil" and the enemies of God was largely responsible for the concept that Jews, as a group, were inherently wicked and depraved and had to be treated accordingly. In the Muslim world, antisemitic developments were far less overt, except in periods of religious extremism. There was little specific antisemitism, and Jews were treated (or ill-treated) like other infidels.

The end of the Middle Ages did not bring any major changes in antisemitism. The Counter-Reformation in the Catholic world renewed and increased anti-Jewish legislation and enforced the introduction of the ghetto system. Protestants in general followed the medieval pattern, and Luther advocated an extreme anti-Jewish policy, but it was in Protestant countries that anti-

Jewish barriers were first removed. In the nineteenth century, the religious foundations of Christian Europe were weakened and with them religious prejudices, except in czarist Russia, which followed the Eastern rite of Christianity, and wherever the Catholic church continued to press an antisemitic policy.

In the nineteenth century "scientific" antisemitism gradually took the place of religious antisemitism. The Jews were said to represent a distinct Semitic ethnic group inferior to the Nordic or Aryan people among whom they lived. Hence, their integration and assimilation into their environment, even if possible, would corrupt society and bring about the decline of prevailing standards. Modern antisemitism was thus built on racial, not religious, foundations, and the adoption of the prevailing faith no longer provided an escape route for persecuted Jews. Modern racial antisemitism reached its tragic apogee with the rise of Hitler and his infamous Final Solution of the Jewish problem. Responsible contemporary church leaders, realizing the dangers of antisemitism as well as the common ground of people of all faiths, have condemned antisemitism and are making efforts to spread attitudes of tolerance and understanding, and Pope John Paul II has castigated antisemitism as a sin. Antisemitism continues to be prevalent in many places, largely with a socioeconomic motivation, but a residue of religious causation continues in the Christian world, and in Islamic lands it has been fanned by anti-Zionism.

• Shmuel Almog, *Antisemitism through the Ages*, translated from Hebrew by Nathan Reisner (Oxford, 1988). David Berger, ed., *History and Hate: The Dimensions of Anti-Semitism* (Philadelphia, 1986). Susan Sarah Cohen, *Antisemitism: An Annotated Bibliography* (New York and London, 1987–1994). Malcolm Hay, *The Roots of Christian Anti-Semitism* (New York, 1981). Arthur Hertzberg, *Antisemitism and Jewish Uniqueness: Ancient and Contemporary*, The B. G. Rudolph Lectures in Judaic Studies (Syracuse, 1975). Jacob Katz, *From Prejudice to Destruction: Antisemitism, 1700–1933* (Cambridge, Mass., 1980). Gavin I. Langmuir, *History, Religion and Anitsemitism* (Berkeley, 1990). Gavin I. Langmuir, *Toward a Definition of Antisemitism* (Berkeley, 1990). Bernard Lewis, *Semites and Anti-Semites: An Inquiry into Conflict and Prejudice* (London, 1986). H. A. Oberman, *The Roots of Anti-Semitism in the Age of Renaissance and Reformation* (Philadelphia, 1984). Bruce F. Pauley, "Bibliographical Essay: Recent Publications and Primary Sources on Austrian Antisemitism in the Nineteenth and Twentieth Centuries," *Leo Baeck Year Book* 38 (1993): 409–423. Lèon Poliakov, *The History of Anti-Semitism* (London, 1974–). Jehuda Reinharz, *Living with Antisemitism: Modern Jewish Responses* (Hanover, N.H., 1987). Jean-Paul Sartre, *Anti-Semite and Jew* (New York, 1948). Herbert A. Strauss, ed., *A Bibliography of Antisemitism: The Library of the Zentrum für Antisemitismusforschung at the Technical University of Berlin*, 3 vols., compiled by Lydia Bressem and Antje Gerlach (Munich, New York, London, Paris, 1989).

ANUSIM. See MARRANOS.

APIQOROS (אֶפִּיקוֹרוֹס; heretic), form used in rabbinic literature of the name of the Greek philosopher Epicurus (4th cent. BCE). His teaching that pleasure (but only if philosophically and properly understood) was the highest good and that the soul perished with the body caused his name to become synonymous with unbelief in Jewish parlance. The Talmud therefore applied the name to all heretics, and the term was eventually used to refer to all unbelievers and skeptics. The Mishnah (*Avot* 2.19) urged the believer to learn "how to answer the Epicurean," that is, the unbeliever. Maimonides classified as *apiqorsim* those who disbelieve in prophecy in general, those who deny the prophecy of Moses, and those who do not believe that God knows an individual's thoughts. They were regarded as completely wicked and without any lot in the future world. The **Shulḥan ʿArukh*, which defines an *apiqoros* as one who rejects the divine origin of the Torah as well as prophecy, deems that person worthy of death. Since medieval times, the term has also been applied in popular parlance to Jews who are lax in traditional observance. See also HERESY.

• Henry A. Fischel, ed., *Essays in Greco-Roman and Related Talmudic Literature* (New York, 1977). Howard Jones, *The Epicurean Tradition* (London, 1989).

APOCALYPSE, a text that recounts divine revelations to human beings on such topics as the end of the world and the Day of Judgment, the fate of souls after death, the divine throne and the angelic hosts that surround it, and astronomical and cosmological phenomena. Although the terms *apocalypse* and *apocalyptic* are associated with the end of the world, the Greek word from which the English derives means *uncovering* or *revelation*, without regard to the content of the revelation. In some apocalypses, eschatology is the dominant concern, while in others it plays a smaller role.

The first apocalypses date from the third century BCE. The Jews of Erets Yisra'el and Egypt continued to compose apocalypses through the rest of the Second Temple period, and several apocalypses were written in response to the destruction of the Second Temple (70 CE). About a dozen Jewish apocalypses have survived. While the biblical prophets prophesied in their own names, the apocalypses were attributed by their authors to heroes of the past; for example, Ezra, the hero of the apocalypse *4 Ezra*, was an important leader of the Persian period, while Enoch, the hero of a number of apocalypses, was the mysterious patriarch who "walked with God and was not" (*Gn*. 5.21–24). With the exception of the biblical *Book of Daniel*, the apocalypses survived because they were transmitted by Christians. Apocalypses written in Hebrew or Aramaic were translated first into Greek and later into other languages used by Christians; even apocalypses originally written in Greek sometimes survived in translation. Early Christians also composed apocalypses of their own, including the *Book of Revelation* in the New Testament. Both Jews and Christians continued to write apocalypses through the Middle Ages.

While prophetic literature consists primarily of the words the prophets hear the Lord speak, the apocalypses place their revelations in the context of narratives. The revelation itself is conveyed either through symbolic visions or a journey to places inaccessible to human beings, usually the heavens. Both of these modes of revelation represent developments of forms found in prophetic literature. Only a few instances of symbolic visions appear in earlier prophets, but they play a central role in the prophecies of Zechariah, who was active at the time of the building of the Second Temple (520–515).

The prominence of visions that require angelic interpretation in *Zechariah* and the apocalypses reflects the growing importance of interpretation in biblical religion in the Second Temple period. The journey or ascent in the apocalypses is a development of a form that first appears in Ezekiel's vision of the new temple (*Ez.* 40–48), in which the prophet is taken on a guided tour of this structure by an angel. On the whole, symbolic visions are associated with accounts of Israel's history culminating in predictions about the end of the world, while the tour offers readers a glimpse of the heavenly realm, the fate of souls after death, or the secrets of nature. *Daniel, 4 Ezra*, and *2 Baruch* are examples of apocalypses with symbolic visions, while the "Book of the Watchers" (*1 En.* 1–36), *2 Enoch*, and *3 Baruch* are among the apocalypses involving journeys or ascents. The categories are not mutually exclusive; the *Apocalypse of Abraham* involves an ascent to heaven that concludes with a symbolic vision.

The eschatology of the apocalypses is more deterministic than that of prophetic literature. While the prophets hope to persuade their listeners to repent and thus avert catastrophe, the apocalypses view the coming judgment as the inevitable conclusion of a plan formulated long ago. The goal of pious behavior is not to head off disaster but to secure a place among the righteous at the last judgment. This new attitude is usually presumed to derive from feelings of powerlessness caused by the loss of political independence in the period of the Second Temple. The attribution of the apocalypses to ancient heroes emphasizes that the course of history is predetermined. In addition, the ancient hero can prophesy accurately about events that have already occurred, thus lending authority to the genuinely predictive elements of the apocalypses.

Speculation in the apocalypses about the angelic inhabitants of the heavens and especially the divine throne, which is deeply indebted to the *Book of Ezekiel*, is part of a larger phenomenon in the literature of the Second Temple period. Scholars have usually viewed the growth of angelology as reflecting a feeling of alienation and distance from God, but the filling of the heavens with angels can also be understood as an effort to bridge the distance between humanity and the divine.

The reward and punishment of souls after death, an important concern of several apocalypses, is a theme that emerges only in the Second Temple period. The desire to provide recompense for those who did not receive their just deserts in this life seems to have intensified during the Maccabean Revolt (166–164), when pious Jews suffered precisely for their piety.

Several apocalypses show an interest in cosmological phenomena, including the sun and the moon, winds, rain, and so on. This interest can be understood in the context of the created world as an expression of God's greatness, which is found in biblical *wisdom literature.

• George W. Buchanan, *Revelation and Redemption: Jewish Documents of Deliverance from the Fall of Jerusalem to the Death of Nahmanides* (Dillsboro, Ind., 1978), pp. 337–450. James H. Charlesworth, ed., *The Old Testament Pseudepigrapha*, vol. 1, *Apocalyptic Literature and Testaments* (Garden City, N.Y., 1983). John J. Collins, *The Apocalyptic Imagination: An Introduction to the Jewish Matrix of Christianity* (New York, 1984). Paul D. Hanson, ed., *Visionaries and Their Apocalypses*, Issues in Religion and Theology 4 (Philadelphia and London, 1983). Martha Himmelfarb, *Ascent to Heaven in Jewish and Christian Apocalypses* (New York and Oxford, 1993). Martha Himmelfarb, "The Apocalyptic Vision," in *The Oxford Study Bible*, edited by M. J. Suggs, K. D. Sakenfeld, and J. R. Mueller (New York, 1992), pp. 181–189. George W. E. Nickelsburg, *Jewish Literature between the Bible and the Mishnah* (Philadephia, 1981). Christopher Rowland, *The Open Heaven: A Study of Apocalyptic in Judaism and Early Christianity* (New York, 1982). H.F.D. Sparks, ed., *The Apocryphal Old Testament* (Oxford, 1984). Michael E. Stone, "Apocalyptic Literature," in *Jewish Writings of the Second Temple Period*, edited by M. E. Stone, Compendia Rerum Iudaicarum ad Novum Testamentum 2.2 (Philadelphia, 1984), pp. 383–441.

—MARTHA HIMMELFARB

APOCALYPSE OF ABRAHAM, pseudepigraphous work extant only in a Slavonic version. Written originally in Hebrew or (less likely) Aramaic, it is the work of a Jewish author, although in its present form it contains at least one Christian interpolation. As it alludes to the destruction of the Temple, it must have been written after 70 CE, most likely toward the end of the first century or the beginning of the second. The contents fall into two distinct sections, the first of which recounts Abraham's conversion from the idolatry of his father Terah to the worship of the one true God. The second section contains Abraham's apocalyptic journey through the heavens, during which he is shown the whole of human history, from Adam and Eve to the destruction of the Temple, followed by the final judgment, the arrival of the Messiah, the ingathering of the exiles, and the restoration of the Temple.

• Martha Himmelfarb, *Ascent to Heaven in Jewish and Christian Apocalypses* (New York and Oxford, 1993), pp. 61–66, 136–138. Ryszard Rubinkiewicz, "Apocalypse of Abraham," in *The Old Testament Pseudepigrapha*, edited by James H. Charlesworth, vol. 1 (Garden City, N.Y., 1983), pp. 681–705.

—GIDEON BOHAK

APOCRYPHA AND PSEUDEPIGRAPHA, a body of literature, primarily of Jewish authorship, from the Second Temple period and the years following. Although the works included in the two groupings have much in common with each other, the categories themselves have quite different histories. The works classed as the Apocrypha are the fifteen books or portions of books that appear in the Old Testament of the Vulgate, Jerome's Latin translation of the Christian Bible, but not in the Hebrew Bible. The fifteen books are *1 Esdras, 2 Esdras, Tobit, Judith, Additions to Esther, Wisdom of Solomon, Ben Sira, 1 Baruch, Letter of Jeremiah, Prayer of Azariah and the Song of the Three Young Men, Susanna, Bel and the Dragon, Prayer of Manasseh, 1 Maccabees*, and *2 Maccabees*.

Jerome translated the Old Testament from the Hebrew, but the apocryphal books formed part of the Old Latin translation that preceded Jerome's. Jerome included these works in his translation but noted that they were not found in the Hebrew. Until the sixteenth century and the rise of Protestantism, the works were treated as part of the Old Testament by the Western church. Because the books did not form part of the Hebrew Bible, Protestants placed the books in a separate, inferior, category; the term *apocrypha* means "hidden" in Greek. The Catholic church, in response, affirmed the canonicity of all of these texts except for the *Prayer of Manasseh* and *1* and *2 Esdras*, which were relegated to an appendix printed after the New Testament. The remaining twelve books it classed as deuterocanonical, that is, admitted to the canon later than the other books of the Bible but canonical nonetheless.

With the exception of *2 Esdras*, the books of the Apocrypha formed part of the Greek Bible used by the Jews of Egypt in the centuries immediately before and after the turn of the era. Thus the question arises as to why they were not included in the Hebrew Bible. Some, such as the *Wisdom of Solomon* and *2 Maccabees*, were excluded because they were composed in Greek. Some of those with Hebrew or Aramaic originals were deemed too late for inclusion either on the basis of the author (Ben Sira) or the events described (*1 Maccabees*). The absence of other works, such as *Tobit* and *Judith*, has no obvious explanation.

The Apocrypha, then, is a fixed group of works, established in the course of debates between Christians. In contrast, the pseudepigrapha (falsely attributed writings) category is a scholarly invention. The texts treated under this heading are extremely diverse. The classic collection of R. H. Charles, *Apocrypha and Pseudepigrapha of the Old Testament* (1913), includes seventeen pseudepigraphous works. H.F.D. Sparks's *Apocryphal Old Testament* (1984), a revision of the Charles volume, includes sixteen texts that did not appear in Charles, while it omits six of the texts Charles included. The two-volume collection of J. H. Charlesworth (1983, 1985) is even more expansive, with over sixty titles. These collections share a core of texts including the apocalypses *1 Enoch*, *2 Enoch*, *2 Baruch*, and *3 Baruch*, as well as *Jubilees* and the *Testaments of the Twelve Patriarchs*. These texts have in common the claim to be the work of heroes of the biblical past. Other texts frequently classed as pseudepigraphous, such as *Joseph and Asenath* and the *Life of Adam and Eve*, recount stories about these heroes without making claims about authorship. In the coming decades, texts from the *Dead Sea Scrolls, undeniably of early Jewish provenance, might well be considered as part of the pseudepigrapha. The Dead Sea Scrolls have already yielded important evidence for the Hebrew and Aramaic originals of some of the pseudepigrapha previously known only in translation.

• R. H. Charles, ed., *Apocrypha and Pseudepigrapha of the Old Testament*, 2 vols. (Oxford, 1913). James H. Charlesworth, ed., *The Old Testament Pseudepigrapha*, 2 vols. (Garden City, N.Y., 1983, 1985). James H. Charlesworth, *The Pseudepigrapha and Modern Research, with a Supplement*, Septuagint and Cognate Studies 7 (Chico, Calif., 1981). Robert A. Kraft, "The Pseudepigrapha in Christianity," in *Tracing the Threads: Studies in the Vitality of the Jewish Pseudepigrapha*, edited by John C. Reeves, Early Judaism and Its Literature 6 (Atlanta, 1994), pp. 55–86. Bruce M. Metzger, *An Introduction to the Apocrypha* (New York, 1957). Bruce M. Metzger, ed., *The New Oxford Annotated Apocrypha, Expanded Edition* (New York, 1991). George W. E. Nickelsburg, *Jewish Literature between the Bible and the Mishnah* (Philadelphia, 1981). E. Schürer, *The History of the Jewish People in the Age of Jesus Christ*, revised and edited by G. Vermes et al. (Edinburgh, 1983–1987) vol. 3, pp. 177–341, 470–808. H. F. D. Sparks, ed., *The Apocryphal Old Testament* (Oxford, 1984).

—MARTHA HIMMELFARB

APOLOGETICS, the defense of a position in the face of critical challenge. The apologetic defense of Judaism and the Jewish people is generally considered to have originated in Hellenistic Alexandria. Beginning in the mid-second century BCE, and continuing for several centuries, such works as the *Sibylline Oracles and the **Wisdom of Solomon* attempted to portray the superiority of Jewish ethics and practice over the allegedly immoral views and behavior of the pagan world. *Philo's work was also meant to demonstrate that Judaism contained in the most perfect form all the intellectual and moral achievements and ideals of Hellenistic philosophy and piety. As against its usual pejorative connotation, apologetics must be considered a natural form of reaction to criticism, whether from hostile or objective sources or from self-questioning. On occasion Jewish apologetics has exaggerated its case, but for the most part it has been a record of restatement of Jewish concepts in the light of anti-Jewish attack and contempt or genuine cultural difference. Frequently its purpose was not so much to convince others as to heighten Jewish morale. Jewish apologetics reflected the various environments in which the Jews have felt the need of responding. Thus, *Josephus Flavius, in his *Against Apion*, was reacting to the antisemitic calumnies then current in Alexandria. In presenting his account of Jewish history he also essayed a summary statement of the religious and moral values of normative Judaism: "The laws given us are disposed after the best manner for the advancement of piety, for mutual communion with one another, for a general love of mankind, also for justice, for sustaining labors with fortitude, and for a contempt for death." Later Jewish apologetics reasserted Judaism against Greek philosophy, Christianity, Islam (*Yehudah ha-Levi's *Kuzari* dealt with all three), and, in the modern period, against scientific positivism and defended Jews against various forms of prejudice and antisemitism. Apologists have not only defended Judaism but also made valuable and permanent contributions to Jewish thought and tradition. Thus, the intellectual achievement of *Maimonides literally transformed Judaism. His demonstration of the compatibility of Judaism with Aristotelian philosophy gave new content and meaning to many traditional concepts, such as prophecy, the hereafter, and many others. By applying philosophical methods of reasoning, he further spiritualized the Jewish conception of God. Jewish apologetics is less "apologetic" than the term indicates. Occasionally, and with great courage, Jews have gone on the attack. Thus, the Muslims were charged at various times with moral laxity and Islam with distorting the Bible. Yosef Kimḥi (12th cent.; see KIMḤI FAMILY) began the practice of countering Christian attacks by circulating Jewish replies that often contained vigorous criticism of Christian morality and theology. Moses *Mendelssohn's *Jerusalem* (1783) was a milestone in Jewish apologetics, marking the opening of the Jewish struggle for *emancipation. Apologetics in the nineteenth and twentieth centuries had to defend Judaism against the *blood libel and recrudescent antisemitism generally. As a reflection of the spiritual level both of general society and of the Jewish people, Jewish apologetics continues to be developed as Jews wish to defend, interpret, or reconstruct their cultural theory and way of life in interaction with their environment. See also POLEMICS.

• David Berger, *The Jewish–Christian Debate in the High Middle Ages* (Philadelphia, 1979). Judah David Eisenstein, *Ozar Wikuhim: A Collection of Polemics and Disputations* (New York, 1928). Moriz Friedlander, *Geschichte der juedischen Apologetik* (Zurich, 1903). Oliver Shaw Rankin, *Jewish Religious Polemic of Early and Later Centuries: A Study of Documents Here Rendered into English* (Edinburgh, 1956). Moritz Steinschneider, *Polemische und apologetische Literatur in arabischer Sprache zwischen Muslimen, Christen und Juden, nebst Anhangen verwandten Inhalts* (Leipzig, 1877).

APOSTASY, the abandonment of one's faith and practice for another religion. The first large-scale apostasy from Judaism seems to have occurred during the events preceding the Maccabean Revolt from 166 to 164 and involved mainly the upper strata of Jewish society in Jerusalem who had abandoned traditional practice for the Hellenistic way of life. That the abandonment of Jewish practice by early Judeo-Christians was regarded as apostasy can be seen in Irenaeus's interpretation of *Acts* 21.21 (*Adversus haereses* 1.262): James, the leader of those Judeo-Christians, and his followers, the *Ebionites, "repudiated the apostle Paul, maintaining that he was an apostate from the Law." The most famous apostate mentioned by name in the Talmud is *Elisha' ben Avuyah, a contemporary of R. 'Aqiva' and teacher of R. Me'ir and one of the most distinguished rabbis of his era. After his apostasy, the rabbis referred to him merely as Aḥer (Another One). As a bitterly persecuted minority religion, Judaism inevitably regarded apostasy as a despicable act of desertion, treason, and weakness. Hatred of apostasy grew as many apostates, either to still their consciences or to demonstrate their zeal in their newly adopted faith, took a prominent part in anti-Jewish *polemics and denunciations. Among the most notorious were the leaders on the Christian side of the three famous medieval *disputations: Nicholas Donin in Paris (1240), Pablo Christiani in Barcelona (1263), and Jerónimo de Santa Fé (Joshua ha-Lorki) in the Disputation of Tortosa (1413–1414). Another medieval apostate who did untold harm to his former coreligionists was Shelomoh ha-Levi, rabbi of Burgos, who converted to Christianity after the pogroms of 1391. As Pablo de Santa Maria, bishop of Burgos, he became a member of the triumvirate forming the Regency Council during the minority of King Juan II. His harsh decrees against the Jews, aimed at humbling their pride and breaking their spirit, succeeded in bringing about a wave of conversions. Another famous apostate, Johannes *Pfefferkorn advocated the confiscation of the Talmud in sixteenth-century Germany. Special understanding was extended by the rabbis to forced apostates who in many cases continued as secret Jews (Heb. *anusim*; see CONVERSION, FORCED; MARRANOS). Apostasy to Islam was not infrequent, but these apostates initiated little of the anti-Jewish activity that was so often undertaken by their Christian counterparts. The status of apostates in religious law was frequently discussed in rabbinic literature; for example, whether a penitent apostate required a ceremony of readmission to Judaism or whether the wife of an apostate required a valid divorce or his sister-in-law *ḥalitsah*. The apostate (Heb. *meshummad* or *mumar), although a sinner, is still regarded essentially as a Jew; however, that person loses certain rights and privileges of an Israelite and is disqualified from giving testimony or performing ritual slaughter. The Talmud classifies apostates in various categories; for example, "an apostate as regards one commandment only" (that is, one who regularly violates a particular precept) and "an apostate as regards the whole Torah." Another distinction is made between the *mumar le-hakh'is*, who violates a precept in a spirit of rebellion and denies its divine authority, and the *mumar le-te'avon*, who violates the precept because he is not strong enough to withstand temptation. Many of the Talmudic laws regarding the treatment of the various categories of *mumar* have fallen into disuse. It became a custom for families to observe mourning for members who apostasized. In the past two centuries, the process of *emancipation has led to widespread *assimilation in the framework of which many Jews converted to Christianity. Fringe groups that call themselves *Jewish Christians are classified by Jews as apostates.

• Haim Beinart, "The Conversos in Spain and Portugal in the 16th to 18th Centuries," in *Moreshet Sepharad: The Sephardi Legacy* (Jerusalem, 1992), vol. 2, pp. 43–67. Haim Beinart, "The Great Conversion and the Converso Problem," in *Moreshet Sepharad: The Sephardi Legacy* (Jerusalem, 1992), vol. 1, pp. 346–382. Natalie Isser, *Antisemitism During the French Second Empire* (New York, 1991). Yaacov Lev, "Persecutions and Conversion to Islam in Eleventh-Century Egypt," *The Medieval Levant: Studies in Memory of Eliyahu Ashtor*, edited by B. Z. Kedar and A. L. Udovitch (Haifa, 1988), pp. 73–91. Arthur Darby Nock, *Conversion: The Old and the New in Religion from Alexander the Great to Augustine of Hippo* (London and New York, 1933). Ben Zion Shereshevsky, "Apostasy," in *Principles of Jewish Law*, edited by Menachem Elon (Jerusalem, 1975), pp. 377–399. Stanley M. Wagner, "The Meshumad and Mumar in Talmudic Literature," in *The Jacob Dolnitzky Memorial Volume: Studies in Jewish Law, Philosophy, Literature and Language* (Skokie, Ill., 1982), pp. 198–227. Solomon Zeitlin, "Mumar and Meshumad," in *Studies in the Early History of Judaism*, vol. 3 (New York, 1975), pp. 246–248. Samuel L. Zitron, *Meshumodim* (Warsaw, 1923), in Yiddish.

APOTROPOS. See GUARDIAN.

APPROBATION (Heb. *haskamah*), official authorization prefixed to a book. With the introduction of printing, it became customary to preface Hebrew books with an approbatory note by one or more recognized rabbinic authorities. This was originally instituted as a voluntary measure by Jewish authorities to avoid unnecessary friction with the church. A decision by a rabbinical conference at Ferrara in 1554 stated that every Hebrew book required the *haskamah* of a committee composed of three rabbis and a representative of the community before it was printed. Later, the *haskamah* was used as an instrument to ensure that no Hebrew book contained material that could be regarded as heretical. The *haskamah*, which was in the interest of both author and publisher, fulfilled a double purpose: it served as an imprimatur, assuring the reader that there was nothing heretical or otherwise objectionable in a book; and it also contained a prohibition (sometimes phrased in the form of a *ḥerem) forbidding others to reprint the book within a specified number of years, assuring the book's copyright. See also CENSORSHIP.

APTA, AVRAHAM YEHOSHUʿA HESCHEL. See AVRAHAM YEHOSHUʿA HESCHEL.

APTOWITZER, VICTOR (1871–1942), scholar of rabbinics. Born in Ternopol, Galicia, Aptowitzer studied both at the University of Vienna and at the Israelitisch-Theologische Lehranstalt in that city. From 1909 until he migrated to Jerusalem in 1938, he taught rabbinics in the latter institution. Aptowitzer's monumental work, *Das Schriftwort in der rabbinischen Literatur* (4 vols. [Vienna, 1906–1915]), investigated variant readings of the biblical text contained in the Talmud and the Midrash. He also edited the tosafist Eliʿezer ben Yo'el's *Sefer Ra'abiyyah* (2 vols. [Berlin, 1913–1935]), furnishing it with an introduction (1938).

• *Sefer Zikkaron le-Vet ha-Midrash le-Rabbanim be-Vinah* (Jerusalem, 1946), pp. 46ff. —DIDIER Y. REISS

ʿAQAVYAH BEN MAHALAL'EL (1st cent. BCE), sage of the late Second Temple period. Several of his halakhic sayings are quoted in tannaitic literature. He differed from the majority of contemporary scholars on a number of issues connected with the laws of purity. His fellow scholars said they would elect him to the position of **av beit din* if he would change his views, but he resolutely refused to do so, saying: "Better that I be called a fool all my days, than that I be wicked before the Lord for a single hour and that men may say he withdrew his opinion for the sake of gaining power" (*ʿEduy*. 5.6). As a result, according to some opinions, he was excommunicated. However, he instructed his son to accept the views of the majority: "I heard my view from the majority, and my fellows heard it from the majority. I stood steadfast to my view as did they. However, you heard this view from an individual [i.e., ʿAqavyah]. Best to reject the minority opinion and accept that of the majority" (*ʿEduy*. 5.7). His best-known saying is "Consider three things, and you will not come within the power of sin . . . know from where you come—from a putrefying drop; to where you go—to a place of dust, worms, and maggots; and before whom you will have to give an account—before the Holy One Blessed be He" (*Avot* 3.1). ʿAqavyah provided answers to these questions of a moral nature to teach humility and the fear of heaven.

• Gedalia Alon, *Meḥqarim be-Toledot Yisra'el* (Tel Aviv, 1967), pp. 115–120. Saul Lieberman, *Tosefta ki-Feshutah*, vol. 5 (New York, 1962), pp. 1292–1294. —DANIEL SPERBER

AQDAMUT MILLIN (Aram.; אַקְדָּמוּת מִלִּין; Introduction), *piyyut* recited in Ashkenazi synagogues on the morning of *Shavuʿot (where two days are observed, it is said on the first) immediately prior to the reading of the Torah; in some rites, it is read after the first verse of the portion of the Law. Possibly originally intended as an introduction to the Aramaic translation of the Decalogue, which was recited in the synagogue on this festival, Aqdamut Millin was composed by R. Me'ir ben Yitsḥaq Nahoraʿi of Worms (11th cent.). The poem contains a doxology and the reply of Israel to its persecutors, describing the ultimate bliss assured for Israel and the punishment foreseen for hostile nations. It is a ninety-line acrostic based on a double alphabet and the author's name. One of its two traditional melodies has become a central feature of the Ashkenazi service on Shavuʿot.

• *Akdamus: With a New Translation and Commentary Anthologized from the Traditional Rabbinic Literature*, trans. and compiled by Avrohom Yaakov Salamon (New York, 1978). Ismar Elbogen, *Jewish Liturgy: A Comprehensive History*, translated by Raymond P. Scheindlin (Philadelphia, 1993).

ʿAQEDAH (עֲקֵדָה; binding), the story of the binding of *Isaac (*Gn*. 22). After Ishmael, *Abraham's elder son, had been sent away, leaving Isaac as heir to the blessing of his father, Abraham was commanded by God to take Isaac to a mountain in the land of Moriah and there to offer him as a sacrifice. Abraham unquestioningly obeyed. As he was about to slaughter Isaac, his hand was stayed by an angel, who informed him that he was being tested. A ram caught by its horns in a nearby thicket was offered in place of Isaac. The angel then informed Abraham that he would be blessed because he was prepared in complete trust to sacrifice his "only son."

The story provided the basis for the development of a wide spectrum of interpretations, which offer a variety of theological understandings, and became a vehicle for confronting the tragic experiences of the Jewish community over the centuries. On its own terms, the story establishes the selfless nature of Abraham's devotion to God. This association with the readiness for martyrdom apparently gave rise to the Midrashic account that Isaac was actually slain and burnt and then returned to life when his ashes were touched by the dew of resurrection. This version also found expression in the prayer of the individual who sounds the *shofar on Ro'sh ha-Shanah: "Gaze upon the ashes of Isaac our father, heaped upon the altar, and deal with your people, Israel, according to the attribute of mercy." In the Sephardi rite, a poetic version of the *ʿaqedah* is sung before the sounding of the shofar.

The story of the *ʿaqedah* is read in the synagogue on the second day of Ro'sh ha-Shanah. Midrashic interpretations of the sacrifice provide the basis for a number of *piyyutim* that deal with the forgiveness of sin. Some of these poems reflect the tragedies that occurred in the Rhineland toward the end of the eleventh century. Rabbi Efrayim ben Yaʿaqov of Bonn wrote: "Recall to our credit the many *ʿaqedahs* / The saints, men and women, slain for your sake. / Remember the righteous martyrs of Judah, / Those that were bound of Jacob." In many rites, the *ʿaqedah* chapter (*Gn*. 22) is recited as part of the daily morning prayer.

The sounding of the shofar on Ro'sh ha-Shanah is connected in several prayers with the ram offered in Isaac's stead. Rabbi Abbahu explained the sound of the shofar: "The Holy One, blessed be He, said 'Sound the ram's horn before me that I may remember in your favor the binding of Isaac the son of Abraham, and I will account it to you as though you had bound yourselves before me' " (*R. ha-Sh*. 16a).

The early church fathers believed that the story of the *'aqedah* symbolically prefigured the death of Jesus (see *Rom.* 8.32). There is a reference to the story in the Qur'an (*Sura* 37.100–109), but most Muslim theologians connect it with Ishmael rather than Isaac.

• Erich Auerbach, *Mimesis: The Representation of Reality in Western Literature* (Garden City, N.Y., 1957), pp. 1–20. Emil L. Fackenheim, *Quest for Past and Future* (Bloomington, Ind., 1968), pp. 52–65. Joseph Fitzmyer, *Romans*, The Anchor Bible (Garden City, N.Y., 1993), pp. 531–532. W. Gunther Plaut, ed., *The Torah: A Modern Commentary* (New York, 1981), pp. 149–154. Nahum M. Sarna, ed., *Genesis*, The JPS Torah Commentary (Philadelphia, 1989), Excursus 17, "The Meaning of the Akedah," pp. 150–154; Excursus 18, "The Akedah in Jewish Tradition," pp. 392–394. Shalom Spiegel, *The Last Trial: On the Legends and Lore of the Command to Offer Isaac as a Sacrifice: The Akedah* (New York, 1969). Ephraim A. Speiser, *Genesis*, The Anchor Bible (Garden City, N.Y., 1964), pp. 161–166.

—LOU H. SILBERMAN

'AQIVA' BEN YOSEF (c.40–135), tanna' who laid the foundation for the exposition and organization of the oral law as later codified in the *Mishnah. About two hundred and seventy halakhic statements and over one hundred aggadic sayings are preserved in his name; an additional two hundred traditions about 'Aqiva', cited by other sages, also appear in the Talmud and Midrash.

'Aqiva' was probably born in western Judea. He learned methods of scriptural interpretation (*midrash*) from Naḥum of Gimzo and studied with R. Eli'ezer Hurqanos (who initiated him into mysticism) in Lydda and with R. Yehoshu'a ben Ḥananyah in Peqi'in (Judea). His own school (*beit midrash*) was located in Bene Beraq.

Far removed from the world of learning as a youth, he is described as a shepherd, but he was motivated to study Torah by contemplating the world around him and by his wife Raḥel, daughter of the rich Kalba' Savu'a'. Several traditions relate how 'Aqiva' left his wife for twelve or thirteen years to study with the aforementioned teachers, returning with thousands of students, to whom he publicly expressed his gratitude for his wife's support and encouragement, saying, "Much hardship has she endured with me for the sake of the Torah" (*Avot de-Rabbi Natan* 6).

'Aqiva' flourished as a scholar and teacher at the end of the first century CE. He traveled with Gamli'el II to Rome and was sent by the patriarch to Babylonia. Following Gamli'el's death, 'Aqiva' played a crucial role in scholarly and public life. Traditions speak of his large number of pupils (300; 12,000; 24,000, according to different sources), including all of the outstanding authorities of the next generation. He enthusiastically supported the Bar Kokhba' Revolt, the only sage on record to have done so, calling Shim'on *bar Kokhba' "the king Messiah" (for which he was criticized by his fellow rabbis; Y., *Ta'an.* 4.7–8).

'Aqiva' emphasized love for God and for one's fellow man, declaring the commandment to "Love your neighbor as yourself" (*Lv.* 19.18) to be the great principle of the Torah. Like all of the sages, 'Aqiva' understood the *Song of Songs* to be an allegory for the love relationship between Israel and God (ensuring its incorporation into the biblical canon) but went even further in his praise of the book ("all Scripture is holy, but the Song of Songs is the Holy of Holies" [*Yad.* 3.5]), evidently considering the *Song of Songs* to be a mystical text; this may have influenced his views on marital love: "When husband and wife are worthy, the divine presence [*shekhinah*] abides with them" (*Sot.*17a).

His role in *halakhah* was central. Many sources stress that the arrangement of *halakhot* in the Mishnah follows his own. Rabbi Yoḥanan ruled that any anonymous opinion in a *mishnah* is the majority opinion and attributed anonymous opinions to his teacher, R. 'Aqiva' (*San.* 86a). 'Aqiva' 's rulings, or those of his students, are found throughout the Mishnah and even more so in the *baraiytot* of both Talmuds. He based halakhic teachings on his interpretations of the Bible and derived laws from apparently superfluous words in the text, considering not only the content but also the language to be divine (see HERMENEUTICS), unlike his colleague R. Yishma'e'l ben Elisha', for whom a stylistic repetition was not a source of *halakhah*. The methods of interpretation of R. 'Aqiva' were possibly related to his mystical beliefs about the nature of the Torah.

No single event in the lives of the sages received as much attention in the sources as the martyrdom of 'Aqiva' during the Hadrianic persecutions, which inspired the concept of *qiddush ha-Shem*, the willingness to lay down one's life to sanctify God's name. Hadrian had forbidden the study of the Torah, but 'Aqiva' continued to teach; even while imprisoned in Caesarea, he continued to issue halakhic rulings. He was flayed to death when he was approximately ninety years old and was buried in Antipatris. The account of his martyrdom has been incorporated into the liturgy of Yom Kippur and Tish'ah be-'Av, in the dirge of the *Ten Martyrs.

• Gedalia Alon, *The Jews in Their Land in the Talmudic Age*, vol. 2 (Jerusalem, 1984). *The Book of Legends, Sefer ha-Aggadah: Legends from the Talmud and Midrash*, edited by Ḥayyim N. Bialik and Y. H. Rawnitzky, translated by W. G. Braude (New York, 1992), pp. 232–242. Louis Finkelstein, *Akiba: Scholar, Saint and Martyr* (New York, 1936). Judah Goldin, "The Period of the Talmud (135 BCE–1035 CE)," in *The Jews: Their History, Culture, and Religion*, edited by Louis Finkelstein, vol. 1 (New York, 1960), pp. 115–215. Judah Goldin, "Towards a Profile of the Tanna, Aqiba ben Joseph," in *Studies in Midrash and Related Literature*, edited by B. L. Eichler and J. H. Tigay (Philadelphia, 1988), pp. 299–323. Israel Konowitz, *Rabbi Akiva: Osef Shalem shel Divrei Rabbi Akiva ba-Sifrut ha-Talmudit veha-Midrashit* (Jerusalem, 1965). Marcus Lehmann, *Akiba*, adapted from the German by Joseph Leftwich (New York, 1961). Charles Primus, *Aqiva's Contribution to the Law of Zera'im* (Leiden, 1977). Shemu'el Safrai, *R. 'Aqiva' ben Yosef* (Jerusalem, 1971).

—ISAAC B. GOTTLIEB

AQUILA (2d cent. CE), proselyte who translated the Hebrew Bible into Greek while revising an earlier Greek translation, namely, that of *Theodotion. Theodotion's version was extremely literal and included numerous syntactical errors. It was influenced by Palestinian rabbinical exegesis, in particular the principles of interpretation of R. *'Aqiva' ben Yosef. The translation was meant to meet the demand for a version more in accord with the spirit of Judaism than the *Septuagint, since the latter translation had become the basis for the Holy Writ and beliefs of the Christian community. Aquila strove to avoid renderings that had become part of the Christian vocabulary. His version was widely used by Jews in Greek-speaking countries, and it is quoted in the

Talmud. Aquila's version was also transmitted as part of Origen's Hexapla, but on the whole, very little of his translation has been preserved. The Talmud identified Aquila with Onkelos (see TARGUM).

• Dominique Barthélemy, *Les Devanciers d'Aquila*, Supplements to Vetus Testamentum, vol. 10 (Leiden, 1963). Kyösti Hyvärinen, *Die Übersetzung von Aquila*, Coniectanea Biblica, Old Testament Series, vol. 10 (Lund, 1977). A. E. Silverstone, *Aquila and Onkelos*, Semitic Languages Series, no. 1; Publications of the University of Manchester, no. 194 (Manchester, 1931; Israel, 1970).

'ARAKHIN (עֲרָכִין; Values or Worths), tractate in the Mishnah order Qodashim, consisting of nine chapters, with related material to be found in the Tosefta' and the Talmud Bavli. *'Arakhin* deals with the laws of vows to the Temple concerning persons or land (*Lv*. 27). Persons may not themselves be consecrated, but their monetary worth may be pledged to the Sanctuary, and the tractate outlines different methods of evaluating the monetary worth of a person. The consecration of land or immovable properties in Erets Yisra'el is subject to various restrictions outlined in *'Arakhin*, designed primarily to safeguard the special bond between a person and his home or ancestral inheritance. The text of the Talmud Bavli tractate was translated into English by Leo Jung in the Soncino Talmud. See also ESTIMATES.

• Chanoch Albeck, ed., *Shishah Sidrei Mishnah, Seder Qodashim* (Jerusalem, 1956). Philip Blackman, ed. and trans., *Mishnayot*, vol. 5, *Order Qodashim* (Gateshead, 1973). Pinhas Kehati, ed., *Mishnah: A New Translation with a Commentary, Seder Qodashim*, vol. 2, *Bekhorot, 'Arakhin* (Jerusalem, 1995). Hermann Leberecht Strack, *Introduction to the Talmud and Midrash* (1931; Minneapolis, 1992). Abraham Weiss, "Le-Ḥeqer ha-Sifruti shel ha-Mishnah," *Hebrew Union College Annual* 16 (1941): 3–9 (Hebrew section).

—AVRAHAM WALFISH

ARAMA, YITSḤAQ (c.1420–1494), Spanish rabbi. He was among the Jews expelled from Spain in 1492, and he died in Naples or Salonika. Influenced by Christian example, he adopted the practice of delivering philosophical sermons, and his discourses on the weekly Torah readings and the Five Scrolls form the basis for his best-known work, *'Aqedat Yitsḥaq*. The work has 105 chapters, each divided into two parts: in the first, he examines a philosophical idea in the light of biblical and rabbinical texts; the second part is a biblical commentary in which the difficulties and questions from the text are resolved with the help of the philosophical approach expounded in the first part. Arama believed that God could suspend the laws of nature and perform miracles. The natural world is ruled by the laws of nature, but humans, created in the image of God, also have power over nature. Although Arama had a philosophical bent, he put religious truth before philosophical truth. He believed in various methods of Bible interpretation but stressed that the plain meaning was primary. He postulated three basic Jewish tenets, namely, belief in Creation, in the Torah, and in reward and punishment in a future world. His book was extremely popular and was imitated by subsequent philosophic preachers. It was first printed in Salonika in 1582; a condensed English translation by E. Munk appeared in Jerusalem in 1986. Arama wrote commentaries on *Proverbs* and on the Five Scrolls, as well as a polemic on the relationship between religion and philosophy.

• Marvin Fox, "R. Isaac Arama's Philosophical Exegesis of the Golden Calf Episode," in *Minhah le-Nahum: Biblical and Other Studies Presented to Nahum Sarna* (Sheffield, Eng., 1993), pp. 87–102. Sarah Heller Wilensky, *R. Yitsḥaq 'Aramah u-Mishnato* (Jerusalem, 1956).

—FRANCISCO MORENO CARVALHO

ARAMAIC, North Semitic language closely related to Hebrew. Its written use is documented in Syria from the ninth century BCE; it appears slightly later in Babylonia, where it seems gradually to have ousted the Babylonian-Assyrian language from everyday speech. Under the Achaemenids, Aramaic became the administrative language of the western half of the Persian empire (Imperial Aramaic), and as such appears in the documents of the Jewish military colony at Elephantine (see YEB) in Egypt (6th cent. BCE). In all probability the use of Aramaic in portions of the biblical books of *Ezra* and *Daniel* also represents this Imperial Aramaic, although Biblical Aramaic is somewhat modernized in spelling and grammar. The use of Aramaic as a trade language (lingua franca) and as the everyday language of mixed populations spread widely. In Second Temple Palestine, Aramaic replaced Hebrew as the language of everyday speech. It was probably brought back from Babylonia by the returning exiles. The original Canaanite script of early Hebrew was changed to the more widespread Aramaic (square) script. Documents of the period could be written in either language, sometimes even a mixture; the Jewish marriage document, the **ketubbah*, then formulated, is still written in Aramaic. The vernacular of Palestine was probably Aramaic. The Aramaic translations of the Bible (see TARGUM) may have been for the benefit of those who did not understand Hebrew or may have been viewed as a commentary on the Bible, containing additional material and read in Aramaic to distinguish it from the original text, which was always read first. In some places local Aramaic dialects developed into literary languages, the most important being Syriac. Among Jews, a number of such literary dialects evolved at various places and times: early Judean Aramaic, preserved in inscriptions and in some texts of the Dead Sea Scrolls; the Aramaic of the Targums, which differs from one to the other; the Galilean dialect of the Talmud Yerushalmi; Samaritan Aramaic; the Aramaic of the Talmud Bavli; the later Babylonian Aramaic of the ge'onim; the Aramaic of the Zohar; and the modern spoken Aramaic of the Kurdish Jews of northern Iraq, particularly the Zakho dialect, which was used in religious works. As a language of religious importance, Aramaic has been considered only slightly inferior to Hebrew. Although, according to the rabbis, "the ministering angels do not understand Aramaic" (*Shab*. 12b), Aramaic penetrated into, for example, the *Qaddish, the *Kol Nidrei, and the Haggadah of Pesaḥ (Ha' Laḥma' 'Anya'). The Aramaic Targum Onkelos to the Torah acquired a sanctity almost equal to that of the original, expressed in the halakhic obligation to read the weekly portion in private "twice in Hebrew, once in the Targum." When, in the tenth century, the community of Fez abolished the recitation of the Targum, the scholar Yehudah ibn Quraish wrote a treatise pointing out the importance of this reading. Under the influence of the Zohar, Aramaic became the principal language of Jewish mysticism. The Lurianic movement and Hasidism introduced further Aramaic prayers into the liturgy. Above all, the position of Aramaic was assured by its use in both the Talmud Bavli and the Talmud Yerushalmi.

• Abraham Ben-Jacob, *'Ivrit ve-'Aramit bi-Leshon Yehudei Bavel* (Jerusalem, 1985). Klaus Beyer, *The Aramaic Language* (Göttingen, 1986). Edward Y. Kutscher, *Hebrew and Aramaic Studies* (Jerusalem, 1977). James M. Lindenberger, *Ancient Aramaic and Hebrew Letters*, Writings from the Ancient World, no. 4 (Atlanta, 1994). Michael Sokoloff, ed., *Arameans, Aramaic, and the Aramaic Literary Tradition*, Bar-Ilan Studies in Near Eastern Languages and Cultures (Ramat Gan, 1983).

ARAMEANS, group of *Aramaic-speaking Semitic tribes who settled in the Fertile Crescent, particularly in the Syrian region, in the last two centuries of the second millennium BCE. They established a number of kingdoms north of Israel, among them, Aram-Zobah (defeated by King David), and Aram-Damascus (often called simply Aram), the principal Aramic state during the ninth and eighth centuries BCE. The Arameans adopted the Phoenician alphabet and carried it throughout the Near East and, via the Persians, to India; their scribes in the service of the kings of Assyria made Aramaic the international language of diplomacy and commerce.

When Sargon II of Assyria (721–705) successfully put down the revolt led by Jehobad of Hamath, the Arameans ceased to exist as a nation. From that time on the designation Aramean, as applied, for example, to Jews in fifth-century BCE Elephantine (see YEB), referred to persons whose spoken language was Aramaic.

Apart from spreading their language to the extent that it became the international tongue of western Asia even before the Persian period, the Syrian Arameans exercised comparatively little cultural influence on the surrounding peoples; this applied equally to their religion, though exceptions can be found; for example, in the introduction of the Damascus cult in Jerusalem by Ahaz (*2 Kgs*. 16ff.; *2 Chr*. 28.3) and in the Elephantine papyri. The Arameans worshiped both their own traditional gods and those of the areas in which they settled (e.g., Phoenician, Hittite, and Assyrian deities); the chief god of the Syrian Arameans was Hadad. Although the Israelites and Arameans were bitter enemies from the time of David and many conflicts between them are recorded in *Kings*, they were regarded as a single family in patriarchal times; Aram was the homeland of Abraham, to which his family looked for their wives (cf. *Dt*. 26.5). At one time it appears that the Israelite religion exercised a certain influence in Aram (see the story of Naaman in *2 Kgs*. 5 and the names of certain Aramean rulers, for example, Jehobad).

• André Dupont-Sommer, *Les Araméens* (Paris, 1949). Jonas C. Greenfield, "Aspects of Aramean Religion," in *Ancient Israelite Religion: Essays in Honor of Frank Moore Cross*, edited by P. D. Miller, P. D. Hanson, and S. D. McBride (Philadelphia, 1987), pp. 67–78. A. Malamat, "The Arameans," in *Peoples of Old Testament Times*, edited by D. J. Wiseman (Oxford, 1973), pp. 134–155. A. R. Millard, "Assyrians and Arameans," *Iraq* 45 (1983): 101–108. Roger Timothy O'Callaghan, *Aram Naharaim* (Rome, 1948). Wayne T. Pitard, *Ancient Damascus* (Winona Lake, Ind., 1987). Hélène S. Sader, *Les États araméens de Syrie depuis leur fondation jusqu'à leur transformations en provinces assyriennes*, Beiruter Texte und Studien 36 (Wiesbaden, 1987).

—MAYER I. GRUBER

ARBA'AH MINIM. See FOUR SPECIES.

ARBA'AH TURIM. See SHULḤAN 'ARUKH; YA'AQOV BEN ASHER.

ARBA' AMMOT (אַרְבַּע אַמּוֹת; four cubits), one of the classical measures of distance. An *ammah* is a halakhic measure of distance of between eighteen and twenty-four inches, the distance between the elbow and fingers of an average-size person. Four *ammot* are thus between seventy-two and ninety-six inches. The measure of four *ammot* is the applicable distance of control over one's property, place, and courtyard. Thus, the area around a person within a radius of four *ammot* has the same legal status as his property, assuming he has physical dominion over it. The Talmud Bavli states that one acquires control over items within four *ammot* even without express intent to acquire possession, whereas the Talmud Yerushalmi requires an express declaration of ownership in order to acquire possession of property within this distance.

• "Arba Ammot," in *Entsiqlopedyah Talmudit* (Jerusalem, 1947–), vol. 2, pp. 153–156. Menachem Elon, *Jewish Law: History, Sources, Principles*, 4 vols. (Philadelphia, 1994). Dennis Wald, "Rabbinic Real Estate Law," rabbinic thesis, Hebrew Union College, 1978.

—MICHAEL BROYDE

ARBA' KANFOT. See TSITSIT.

ARBA' KOSOT. See FOUR CUPS.

ARBA' PARASHIYYOT. See SABBATHS, SPECIAL.

ARBITRATION (Heb. *borerut*), the determining of a dispute between parties by a mediator chosen or agreed to by them. The Talmud discusses whether in civil disputes the application of the strict letter of the law (the method said to be favored by Moses) is preferable to an attempt to reach a compromise between disputing parties (said to be favored by Aaron). Both views are argued with considerable vigor; in the end, however, R. Yosei's view, that "it is forbidden to effect a compromise, and whosoever does so is a sinner," is rejected in favor of the view that "to effect a compromise is praiseworthy" (*San*. 6b). The law of arbitration is a consequence of this ruling (*Shulḥan 'Arukh, Ḥoshen Mishpat* 12.2). Arbitration takes place either before a duly constituted *beit din*, with the litigants given the right to demand the disqualification of any of the rabbis, or through what is called *zabla' ve-zabla'* (a phrase made up of the initial letters of the sentence, "One chooses [an arbitrator] to represent him, and the other does likewise"), whereby each litigant chooses an arbitrator, and these two arbitrators agree on a third arbitrator, independent of the wishes of the litigants. The decision of the arbitrators is final. In most western *battei din*, rabbis rule on disputes in accordance with the arbitration laws of their respective countries, so that their decisions are enforceable in the civil court.

In the State of Israel, a law of arbitration based in part upon Jewish law was adopted in 1968.

• Shillem Warhaftig, *Dinei 'Avodah ba-Mishpat he-'Avar* (Tel Aviv, 1969).

ARCHISYNAGOGOS (Gr.; head of the synagogue), title of the honorary official who supervised the religious aspects of synagogue affairs; used frequently in Hellenistic and Roman Jewish communities during the last centuries BCE until about 300 CE (the Talmud Bavli translates the title as **parnas*). The *archisynagogos* was the spiritual head of the community and was considered inferior only to the **talmid ḥakham* in Jewish learning. The *archisynagogos* was responsible for regulating services, selecting the **ba'al qeri'ah*, **ba'al tefillah*, and those who would preach. The *archisynagogos* may have been responsible for constructing the synagogue building. He represented the community in its dealings with the secular authorities. He was not necessarily a person of great learning, but his office demanded an extensive acquaintance with ritual and liturgical practice. It is possible that once elected he served until retirement or death. The title might even have been hereditary, passed down from father to son. It is also found as a title of honor applied to women and even children.

• Bernadette J. Brooten, *Women Leaders in the Ancient Synagogue: Inscriptional Evidence and Background Issues* (Chico, Calif., 1982). Ross S. Kraemer, "A New Inscription from Malta and the Question of Women Elders in the Diaspora Jewish Communities," *Harvard Theological Review* 78 (1985): 431–438. Samuel Krauss, *Synagogale Altertümer* (Berlin, 1922). Baruch Lifshitz, *Donateurs et fondateurs dans les synagogues juives* (Paris, 1967).

—SHMUEL HIMELSTEIN

ARI. See LURIA, YITSḤAQ.

ARISTEAS, LETTER OF. See LETTER OF ARISTEAS.

ARISTOBULUS OF PANEAS (2d cent. BCE), philosopher who lived in Egypt probably during the reign of Ptolemy VI (180–145) and of whose works only fragments survive. From these fragments, Aristobulus emerges as an exegete eager to expound on the wisdom of the Torah and present it to Jewish and non-Jewish readers. He explained, for example, that seemingly anthropomorphic biblical expressions (e.g., "the hand of God") should not be taken literally but interpreted allegorically (*hand* actually means power), since God has no physical form. While Aristobulus borrowed his ideas and his interpretive techniques from various Greek philosophers, he insisted that the Greek writers themselves, including Homer, Hesiod, Pythagoras, Socrates, and Plato, had been familiar with the Bible (which they consulted in Greek translations supposedly prepared long before the *Septuagint) and borrowed many of its precepts.

• Adela Yarbro Collins, "Aristobulus," in *Old Testament Pseudepigrapha*, edited by James H. Charlesworth (Garden City, N.Y., 1985), vol. 2, pp. 831–842. Nikolaus Walter, *Der Thoraausleger Aristobulos*, Texte und Untersuchungen zur Geschichte der altchristlichen Literatur 86 (Berlin, 1964), the most detailed discussion of Aristobulus's work.

—GIDEON BOHAK

ARISTOTELIANISM, a philosophy that entered Jewish circles during the ninth and tenth centuries, largely through Arabic translations; later medieval Jewish philosophers also benefited from Hebrew translations of Arabic editions. Although the available versions were somewhat abbreviated, they preserved Aristotle's basic intent. Jewish reaction to Aristotle was, therefore, based on accurate understanding. Aristotle's influence on Jewish theology and philosophy first became predominant in the work of Avraham *ibn Daud in the twelfth century and reached its fruition and classic statement in the work of Moses *Maimonides, to whom Aristotle had "reached the highest degree of intellectual perfection open to man," except for prophetic inspiration.

The effects of Aristotelianism on Jewish thought were profound and lasting. Aristotle's philosophy gave new scope and discipline to the reasoning capacities of the mind, and the medieval Jewish philosophers were quick to apply it to the basic notions of religion (revelation, faith versus knowledge, immortality, etc.). On the one hand, Aristotelianism offered the possibility of a purer, less primitively anthropomorphic conception of God; on the other hand, it was admitted, even by Maimonides, to harbor dangers. Jewish rationalism wholeheartedly adopted Aristotle's views on the incorporeality, pure actuality, and eternity of God, but it had to reject his theory of the eternity of the universe and of God as the unmoved mover. God the creator could not be considered coeval with the universe, and God as an active force was not the philosopher's passive and unmoved mover. Since Aristotle's teachings could not be held to disprove the biblical view of God's creativity, it was maintained that Judaism was intellectually justified in retaining its ancient position of believing in *creatio ex nihilo*.

Aristotle's influence proved effective in changing both the general mood of Jewish philosophy and some of its particulars. Jewish philosophers now went to great pains to prove what in its own terms required no proof, namely, revelation. In so important an issue as individual providence, Maimonides supports Aristotelian views as against Jewish tradition, in holding that divine providence operates on behalf of the human species rather than the individual. Maimonides explains miracles by building them into the original divine order of things. Through Maimonides, Aristotelianism exerted a continuing influence on Jewish thought until the seventeenth century.

• Paul B. Fenton, "The Arabic and Hebrew Versions of the Theology of Aristotle," in *Pseudo-Aristotle in the Middle Ages: The Theology and Other Texts*, edited by Jill Kraye, W. F. Ryan and C. B. Schmitt, Warburg Institute Surveys and Texts, vol. 11 (London, 1986), pp. 241–264. Daniel H. Frank, "Humility as a Virtue: A Maimonidean Critique of Aristotle's Ethics," in *Moses Maimonides and His Time*, edited by Eric L. Ormsby (Washington, D.C., 1989), pp. 89–99. Joel L. Kramer, "Maimonides on Aristotle and Scientific Method," in *Moses Maimonides and His Time*, edited by Eric L. Ormsby (Washington, D.C., 1989), pp. 53–88. Jonathan W. Malino, "Aristotle on Eternity: Does Maimonides Have a Reply?" in *Maimonides and Philosophy*, edited by Shlomo Pines and Yirmiyahu Yovel (Dordrecht and Boston, 1986), pp. 53–64. C.F.J. Martin, "Maimonides and Aristotelian Moral Philosophy," in *Sobre la vida y obra de Maimonides*, edited by Jesus Pelaez del Rosal (Cordova, 1991), pp. 349–357. Ephraim Navon, "Plato Versus Aristotle: Hermann Cohen's Interpretation of Maimonides," *Il Cannocchiale: Rivista de studi filosofici* 1–2 (1991): 29–43. Bezalel Safran, "Maimonides and Aristotle on Ethical Theory," *Alei Shefer* (Ramat Gan, 1990), pp. 133–161. Colette Sirat, *A History of Jewish Philosophy in the Middle Ages* (Cambridge, 1985), pp. 141–155. Leon D. Stitskin, *Judaism as a Philosophy: The Philosophy of Abraham bar Hiyya, 1065–1143* (Brooklyn, N.Y., 1960).

ARK, SYNAGOGUE. See ARON HA-QODESH.

ARK OF NOAH. God commanded *Noah (*Gn.* 6.14–16) to build an enormous three-storied ark of gopher wood coated with bitumen. By inhabiting the ark, Noah, his family, and specimens of all animal life were saved from the *Flood. A parallel Babylonian legend refers to an ark of considerably larger proportions built by Utnapishtim in order to escape the evil design of the gods. The main difference between the craft in the Mesopotamian epics and the ark in the biblical narrative is that the latter is rudderless and floats on the waters without the aid of a helmsman (who is brought aboard in the Mesopotamian narrative), since God is the protector of Noah and his family. Rabbinic literature (e.g., *San.* 108b) adds more details to the biblical description of the ark and elaborates on the moral concern of the story. The ark is said to have been built from cedars planted a hundred twenty years before the flood in order to grant humanity an ample opportunity for repentance.

• Lloyd R. Bailey, "Noah's Ark," *The Anchor Bible Dictionary*, vol. 4 (New York, 1992), p. 1131. Umberto Cassuto, *A Commentary on the Book of Genesis*, pt. 2, *From Noah to Abraham* (Jerusalem, 1964), pp. 59–61. Chaim Cohen and J. Blau, "Tavah," in *ʿOlam ha-Tanakh: Be-Re'shit* (Tel Aviv, 1982), p. 58. Brian Lewis, *The Sargon Legend: A Study of the Akkadian Text and the Tale of the Hero Who Was Exposed at Birth* (Cambridge, Mass., 1980), p. 46.

ARK OF THE COVENANT (Heb. *aron* [chest] *ha-berit*, short form of *aron ha-berit YHVH* [Ark of the Covenant of the LORD], also called *aron ha-ʿedut* [Ark of the Testimony], *aron YHVH* [Ark of the LORD], and *aron ha-Elohim* [Ark of God]), essentially a portable chest; the most sacred object in biblical religion, the primary purpose of which was to represent the presence of God (*Ex.* 25.10–22, 37.1–9). Though rabbinic interpretation and medieval commentaries tended to unite the separate biblical traditions of the Ark into a single account, three distinct schools of thought can be detected.

According to the Priestly tradition, the Ark was built of acacia wood and measured 2.5 × 2.5 × 1.5 cubits. It was overlaid inside and out with pure gold, and its top was surrounded by a gold rim. Two carrying poles were inserted into gold rings on the sides of the Ark and were never to be removed. The *ʿedut* (testimony) received from God (*Ex.* 25.21, 40.20; *Lv.* 16.13) was placed in the Ark. The *ʿedut* is never precisely described, though in *Exodus* 31.18, 32.15, and 34.29 it seems to be associated with the tablets of the Law. In any case, it must have been some piece of physical evidence of Moses' meeting with God, and it lent its name to the Tabernacle as a whole ("the Tabernacle of the *ʿedut*"; *Ex.* 38.21; *Nm.* 1.50). An inseparable part of the Ark was its elaborate lid, the solid gold *kapporet* (etymology unclear: some translate simply "cover"; others, "mercy seat"). This consisted of two golden cherubim with outspread wings, upon which the divine Majesty was said to be enthroned. The Ark was permanently kept shrouded in the darkness of the inaccessible inner sanctum; view and touch were prohibited and presumed fatal. Even for transport from place to place, extreme precautions were taken in order to prevent unauthorized approach to, or sight of, the Ark (*Nm.* 4.1–20). Both as a sort of divine footstool and throne (see, e.g., *Jer* 3.16–17; *1 Chr.* 28.2) and as a receptacle for the "relic" of God's revelation, the Ark has its counterparts in ancient Near Eastern tradition; for instance, it is thought that treaty documents were occasionally deposited at the feet of the image of the deity. A third role, however, seems to be exclusively biblical: the Ark served as the meeting place between God and Moses, the divine voice emanating from between the wings of the cherubim and dictating all of the commands of the Law (*Ex.* 25.22; *Lv.* 1.1; *Nm.* 7.89; see GIVING OF THE TORAH).

The non-Priestly, "epic" tradition pictures the Ark more as a divine palladium, upon which the warrior God "rides" seated upon his cherubim (*1 Sm.* 4.4). No mention is made of a Tabernacle or of anything placed in the Ark; the Ark was carried in the open, in full view of the Israelites but at a distance ahead of the camp, on their march through the wilderness (*Nm.* 10.33–36) and in their battles of conquest (*Nm.* 14.44; *Jos.* 6). It was believed to be extremely powerful (*Ps.* 132.8): as long as it remained positioned in the Jordan River, the waters ceased their flow (*Jos.* 3–4); when it was captured by the Philistines, Israel was defeated in battle, but the Philistines suffered a dire plague until they returned the Ark to the Israelite camp (1 *Sm.* 4–6); and when touched or gazed upon by unauthorized persons, it struck them dead (*1 Sm.* 6.19; *2 Sm.* 6.6–8). This view, too, is paralleled in ancient Near Eastern texts. The Ark was housed in a series of temporary tents; eventually King David had it brought to Jerusalem (*2 Sm.* 6), where it was later installed in the innermost sanctum of the Solomonic Temple (*2 Sm.* 7; *1 Kgs.* 6.19, 8.1–11).

Deuteronomy relates that Moses constructed a simple wooden ark, for the sole purpose of housing the tablets of the Law. He assigned to the Levites the sacred task of carrying the Ark (*Dt.* 10.1–8); later, at the end of Moses' lifetime, the Torah book he wrote was also deposited in the Ark, alongside the tablets, entrusted to the safekeeping of the Levites (*Dt.* 31.9, 25–26). *Deuteronomy* thus anticipates the role of the Holy Ark (**aron ha-qodesh*) in later Judaism, though the term "Holy Ark" appears in the Bible only once, at the end of *Chronicles* (*2 Chr.* 35.3). The Ark ultimately disappeared; there was no Ark in the Second Temple.

• Yehoshua Gitay, "Reflections of the Poetics of the Samuel Narrative: The Question of the Ark Narrative," *Catholic Biblical Quarterly* 54 (1992): 221–230. Leon Ritmeyer, "The Ark of the Covenant: Where it Stood in Solomon's Temple," *Biblical Archaeology Review* 22.1 (Jan.–Feb. 1996): 46–55, 70–72. C. L. Seow, "Ark Processions in the Politics of Monarchy," Ph.D. dissertation, Harvard University, 1984. Karel van der Toorn and C. Houtman, "David and the Ark," *Journal of Biblical Literature* 113 (1994): 209–231.

—BARUCH J. SCHWARTZ

ARMILOS, eschatological figure who appears in geonic literature. The origin of the name, of which there are many variants, is obscure. It may be a corruption of Romulus, the mythical founder of Rome, or of Ahriman, the Persian god of evil, who wages incessant war against Ahura Mazda, the spirit of good. Saʿadyah Ga'on, in his summary of eschatological traditions (*Emunot ve-Deʿot* 8.6), describes Armilos as the king of Edom (Christian Rome), who at the end of days will slay the Messiah, Son of Joseph, conquer Jerusalem, and cruelly persecute the Jewish people until his final defeat by the Messiah, Son of David. A similar account is given by Ha'i Ga'on, who regards the war with Armilos as preceding that with Gog and Magog. Other sources (*Midrash va-Yosha'*, *Nistarot de-Rabbi Shimʿon ben Yoḥai*) refer to Armilos as the successor to Gog and Magog. Armilos is depicted as a monstrosity: his head is bald, his forehead leprous; one of his eyes is large, the other small; he is deaf in the right ear; his right arm is maimed; his left hand is two-and-a-half-ells long. In some late pseudepigraphs, Armilos is said to be the horrendous offspring of evil men, or Satan. Armilos claims to be the Messiah, or even God, and is accepted as such by the sons of Esau but is rejected by the Jews. In the ensuing struggle, the Ephraimite Messiah and a million Jews are slain, but Armilos is vanquished by God or the Davidic Messiah. In addition to Ezekiel's Gog and Magog, and the Persian Ahura Mazda and Ahriman, the composite Armilos legend appears to have been influenced by the Christian Christ and Antichrist and certain pagan myths.

• George W. Buchanan, ed. and trans., *Revelation and Redemption: Jewish Documents of Deliverance from the Fall of Jerusalem to the Death of Nachmanides* (Dillsboro, Ind., 1978). Samson H. Levey, *The Messiah: An Aramaic Interpretation: The Messianic Exegesis of the Targum* (Cincinnati, 1974).

ARON HA-QODESH (אֲרוֹן הַקֹּדֶשׁ; among Sephardim called Heikhal [pronounced *Ekhal* in some Spanish and Portuguese communities]). Originally the term *aron* referred to the *Ark of the Covenant in the Tabernacle, and thereafter in the Temple, in which the two tablets of the Law were kept (*Ex.* 25.10ff., 37.1ff.). Over the course of time, it came to be used for the shrine or closet—often in a specially built recess—in which the Torah scrolls are kept in the *synagogue. There was often a niche on either side of the ark for prayer books. In Talmudic times, the ark was referred to as *tevah* (chest; *Taʿan* 2.1) and was portable, carried (sometimes wheeled) into the synagogue only when needed for the service. It is the custom in the west to build the ark into (or leave it free-standing in front of) the wall facing east, in the direction of Jerusalem. In Israel the ark is placed in the direction of the Temple mount. Hence the ark is the synagogue's most important architectural feature and is usually beautifully designed and ornamented. In Ashkenazi and some other synagogues, a curtain (*parokhet*; *Ex.* 27.21) is hung before the ark. In front of it is a raised platform reached by steps (see BIMAH). The platform was used by priests when pronouncing Birkat ha-Kohanim, while solemn oaths were sworn before the sacred ark. In modern times, originally in Reform temples, the platform was enlarged to incorporate the reader's desk and a lectern, an arrangement that eventually was employed also by Conservative and many Orthodox congregations. In Classical Reform temples, the ark was not necessarily in or along the wall facing Jerusalem. The eternal lamp (*ner tamid*) is placed above the ark. The tablets of the Law are a popular decoration of the ark and the *parokhet*. The opening of the synagogue ark (see PETIḤAH) for the purpose of taking out or returning the Torah scrolls on the occasion of public reading is conducted in solemn ceremony, with the congregation rising to its feet. The ark is regarded by Jewish law to be the holiest part of the synagogue, to the extent that one may not sell an ark even to build a synagogue (*Meg*. 3.1)—such an action would be considered a "decline in holiness" (Rashi on *Meg*. 26a). The ark plays a central role in prayer, in addition to its use as the receptacle for the Torah scrolls. Thus it is customary to open the ark for the recitation of several of the more important prayers, with the congregation rising to its feet. In some ancient and North African and eastern synagogues, multiple arks (two or three or even more) are placed next to each other along the eastern wall.

• David Cassuto, "A Venetian Parokhet and Its Design Origins," *Jewish Art* 14 (1988): 35–43. Gil Hüttenmeister, "Aron ha-Qodesh ve-Hitpateḥut Batei ha-Keneset ha-ʿAtiqim," *World Congress of Jewish Studies* 8 (Jerusalem, 1982): 1–5. –SHMUEL HIMELSTEIN

ARRABY MOOR, official title of the chief rabbi of Portugal, dating back to at least the thirteenth century. In addition to his religious duties, the *arraby moor* was charged with overseeing all communal funds and the funds of orphans that had been entrusted to guardians. He was also responsible for the conduct of all Jewish leaders—both laymen and rabbis. To prevent him from assuming too much power, he was not permitted to appoint rabbis without the approval of the community involved or to waive the payment of any taxes or levies. The last *arraby moor*, Simon Maimi, was tortured to death in 1497, in an attempt to force him along with all other Portuguese Jews to convert. The position of *arraby moor* was largely analogous to that of the **rab de la corte* in Spain.

• Salo Baron, *The Jewish Community: Its History and Structure to the American Revolution* (Philadelphia, 1942), vol. 1, p. 285; vol. 3, p. 65. Cecil Roth, *A History of the Marranos* (Philadelphia, 1959), p. 60. Simon Schwarzfuchs, *A Concise History of the Rabbinate* (Oxford and Cambridge, Mass., 1993), pp. 44–48. –SHMUEL HIMELSTEIN

ART. The earliest written records of Judaism's attitude toward art are to be found in the Bible. The passages concerning the building of the Tabernacle (*Ex*. 31.1–6, 35.30–36.2) emphasize the importance of its esthetic component. Its chief architect, Bezalel, is endowed with divine wisdom and inspiration that enables him to fulfill God's mandate. This positive approach toward art is moderated by other biblical statements that suggest that the creation of certain images may constitute a form of idolatry. The most significant texts to deal with this theme are: the second commandment (*Ex*. 20.4), which decrees "You shall not make for yourself a sculptured image or any likeness of what is in the heavens above, or on the earth below, or in the waters under the earth" and (*Ex*. 20.20) "With Me, therefore, you shall not make any gods of silver, nor shall you make for yourselves any gods of gold."

The conflicting biblical attitudes toward art are reflected in the divergent views expressed by the rabbis regarding various forms of art throughout the centuries. Because the second commandment's statement concerning the creation of graven images is immediately followed by the statement "You shall not bow down to them nor serve them," the rabbis interpreted the second commandment as an injunction against art made for the purpose of idolatry. Despite a popular misconception, based on the second commandment, that denied the existence of art among the Jewish people, art produced and owned for decorative purposes was never comprehensively prohibited by rabbinical authorities. Early rabbinic discussions concerning the permissibility of images centered on the text of *Exodus* 20.20. In interpreting this passage, the rabbis prohibited the depiction of angels, dragons, the sun, moon and stars, as well as the four figures of the divine chariot from the prophet's vision (*Ez*. 1). These images were singled out because they were considered to be the attendants of God and because the viewer might be tempted to worship them (*ʿA. Z.* 42b–43b). Under certain circumstances, however, these forbidden images were permitted. The Talmud relates that for educational purposes, R. Gamli'el was permitted to use diagrams with illustrations of the moon (*R. ha-Sh*. 24a–24b). This Talmudic passage also includes a discussion concerning the depiction of the human face, which was prohibited because man was created in the image of God. Although the sources do not deal explicitly with the prohibition against the representation of God in material form, it appears to have been understood that the depiction of the deity was strictly forbidden (most probably based on *Dt*. 4.15–19).

The rabbis further distinguished between two-dimensional and three-dimensional art. With the exception of representations of the "attendants" of God, creating two-dimensional images on paintings, tapestries and illuminated manuscripts was deemed permissible. Three-dimensional images, however, such as signet rings and sculpture, elicited more controversy because of the idea that a three-dimensional art object appears lifelike and may cause the viewer to venerate it in a manner bordering on idolatry. *Maimonides ruled that all sculpture is permitted, except for the attendants of God and the human figure (*Mishneh Torah, Sefer Maddaʿ, ʿAvodah Zarah* 3.10). This was the position of many other prominent rabbis, including *Yaʿaqov ben Asher, who systematically laid out these prohibitions in his legal code (*Arbaʿah Turim, Yoreh Deʿah* 141). He added the further clarification that it is only a fully sculpted human figure, comprising both head and torso, that is prohibited.

The rabbinic approach to synagogue decoration varied dramatically at different times and in different places. Beginning in the first century, *synagogues in Erets Yisra'el and throughout the Diaspora were often elaborately decorated. The walls of the synagogue of Dura-Europos, in Syria (3d cent. CE), were adorned with an extensive cycle of biblical illustrations. Additionally, many synagogues, built from the fourth through the sixth centuries, contain mosaic floors filled with both Jewish and Greco-Roman elements, including images of biblical personalities, mythological figures and zodiacal illustrations. An indirect rabbinic stamp of approval for this practice can be found in a *genizah* fragment published by J. N. Epstein (*Tarbiz* 3 [1931]). This text, of a previously unknown passage from the Talmud Yerushalmi (*ʿA. Z.* 42c–d) states that "in the days of Rav Yoḥanan [3d cent.] they began to paint on walls and he did not prevent them" and "in the days of Rav Abun [4th cent.] they began to make designs on mosaics and he did not prevent them."

Other rabbis were less tolerant. In the twelfth century, Elyaqim ben Yosef of Mainz insisted that the stained glass windows be removed from a synagogue in Cologne because they contained two-dimensional images of lions and serpents (*Mordekhai, ʿAvodah Zarah* 840). Rabbi Yosef Karo, quoting R. Me'ir of Padua, expressed concern that it may appear as though Jews were bowing down to the images which decorated the synagogue. He consequently suggested that all sculptured images which directly faced the worshipers be eliminated (*Avqat Rokhel* 63, 65). With regard to tapestries, he ruled that a curtain hung before a Torah ark may contain images, even human, provided that the image was not heavily embroidered and thus remained only two-dimensional (*Avqat Rokhel* 66). Rabbi Mosheh Trani, his colleague, decreed that it was improper for a Torah ark to be decorated with two carved lions (*She'elot u-Teshuvot* 30). Even the rabbinic authorities, who technically permitted two-dimensional art, expressed concern that the decorative images may distract the attention of the worshiper from his prayers. Maimonides recommended that if an individual is standing in prayer before a decorated wall or tapestry, he should avert his eyes so as not to disturb his concentration (*Teshuvot ha-Rambam* 215 [Jerusalem, 1958–1961]). Similarly, R. Yitsḥaq ben Mosheh of Vienna recalled seeing in his youth, images of trees and birds covering the walls of the synagogue of Meissen. He believed that such decoration ought to be forbidden as the pictures detracted from concentration on prayers (*Or Zaruʿa, ʿAvodah Zarah* 43b). Medieval rabbinic authorities voiced comparable concerns regarding illuminated Hebrew manuscripts. Although R. Me'ir of Rothenburg did not directly prohibit the practice of illustrating Hebrew manuscripts, he strongly discouraged the decoration of prayer books because he believed that the worshiper would be unable to concentrate properly on his prayers (T., *Yoma'* 54a). Nevertheless, many of the extant medieval Hebrew prayer books are replete with decorative and figurative images.

An examination of a variety of art objects produced and owned by Jews reveals that the actual practice of the Jews may have been at variance with rabbinic consensus (see CEREMONIAL OBJECTS; TORAH ORNAMENTS). In the seventeenth century, R. Avraham di Boton of Salonika was questioned concerning the growing phenomenon of decorated *ketubbot* (marriage contracts). He stated that even though these documents may contain images of the bride and groom, as well as depictions of the sun and the moon, they need not be destroyed (*Leḥem Rav* 15). This view was reiterated in the eighteenth century by R. Yitsḥaq Lampronti, the chief rabbi of Ferrara. Recent rabbinical rulings by R. Mosheh *Feinstein in his work *Iggerot Mosheh* (*Yoreh Deʿah* II 55) and by R. Avraham Yitsḥaq Kook (see KOOK FAMILY) in his work *Iggerot ha-Re'ayah* (vol. 1, 10) demonstrate the continuing attention given to the issue of art and images on the part of Orthodox rabbis. The prevailing tendency today is toward a liberal interpretation of the laws regarding painting and sculpture.

Despite the ambivalence expressed by rabbinic authorities throughout history, art has played a critical role in enhancing the Jewish religious experience. Jews expressed themselves through a variety of art forms, including synagogue architecture and decoration, ceremonial objects, manuscript illumination, paintings, and funerary art. The diversity of art objects extant indicates that Jews have consistently adopted and adapted the artistic elements of the dominant culture in which they lived. Moreover, the prevailing artistic attitudes of the host country frequently played an important role in defining the concurrent Jewish approach to art. In Islamic regions where depiction of the human figure was frowned upon, or even prohibited outright, Jews conformed to popular custom and avoided the use of figures as well. In European countries, however, where no such stricture was imposed, Jews often created figural art.

The Temple and its implements have served as a source of imagery for many works of Jewish art in subsequent centuries. The only known artifact extant from the First Temple is a miniature carved ivory pomegranate with an inscription dedicating it to the house of the Lord. Coins minted by Jews during the First Jewish Revolt (66–70) contain a representation of the façade of the Temple on the obverse side; on the reverse, a *lulav* and *etrog* are depicted. Other early artifacts of Jewish art consist primarily of funerary art. Gold-glass discovered in Roman catacombs of the third and fourth centuries was decorated with Jewish symbols such as the Menorah, the Ark, and various Temple implements. Additional examples of Jewish funerary art include ossuaries and sarcophagi that were embellished with floral motifs and symbolic religious elements. The earliest extant decorated Hebrew manuscripts were produced in the late tenth and early eleventh centuries. These works, written in Egypt, contain elaborately ornamented pages, but no figural art, an influence of the surrounding Islamic culture. Beginning with the thirteenth century, almost all decorated Hebrew manuscripts were produced in western Europe, especially in Germany, France, Italy and on the Iberian Peninsula. These books, comprising Bibles, liturgical works, legal codes, and philosophical, literary and medical texts, constitute the largest body of Jewish artistic expression from the Middle Ages. Many of these books contain figural imagery, in keeping with the artistic norms of the European countries in which they were produced. Ceremonial objects, including Sabbath lamps, Ḥanukkah lamps, circumcision tools, Purim and Pesaḥ objects, ceremonial cups, and Torah ornaments were created by Jews or commissioned from contemporary artists. Paintings of rabbinic figures are extant from the seventeenth century and were widely disseminated in the eighteenth and nineteenth centuries. The nineteenth century also ushered in a popular demand by middle-class Jews for genre paintings depicting Jewish festivals, ceremonies, and smaller details of daily Jewish life. In the contemporary period, Jews have continued to integrate art into all aspects of their religious life, and artists have incorporated modern techniques and styles into the ceremonial objects currently being produced.

• Robert Gordis and Moshe Davidowitz, eds., *Art in Judaism: Studies in the Jewish Artistic Experience* (New York, 1975). Grace Cohen Grossman, *Jewish Art* (New York, 1995). Joseph Gutmann, *Hebrew Manuscript Painting* (New York, 1978). Yael Israeli and Miriam Tadmor, eds., *Treasures of the Holy Land: Ancient Art from the Israel Museum* (New York, 1986). *Jewish Art* (1974–), formerly known as the *Journal of Jewish Art*. Avram Kampf, *Chagall to Kitaj: Jewish Experience in Twentieth Century Art* (New York, 1990). Carol Herselle Krinsky, *Synagogues of Europe* (New York and Cambridge, Mass., 1985). Lee I. Levine, ed., *Ancient Synagogues Revealed* (Jerusalem, 1982). Leo Ary Mayer, *Bibliography of Jewish Art* (Jerusalem, 1967). Bezalel Narkiss, *Hebrew Illuminated Manuscripts* (Jerusalem, 1969). Cecil Roth, *Jewish Art: An Illustrated History* (Tel Aviv, 1961). Shalom Sabar, *Ketubbah: Jewish Marriage Contracts of the Hebrew Union College Skirball Museum and Klau Library* (Philadelphia, 1990). Gabrielle Sed-Rajna, *L'Art juif* (Paris, 1995). Rachel Wischnitzer, *The Architecture of the European Synagogue* (Philadelphia, 1964). Rachel Wischnitzer, *Synagogue Architecture in the United States: History and Interpretation* (Philadelphia, 1955).

—SHARON LIBERMAN MINTZ

ARTAPANUS (2d cent. BCE), Jewish writer from Egypt about whom very little is known and of whose work, *On the Jews*, only a few abridged fragments survive. These fragments deal with the Egyptian phases in the lives of Abraham, Joseph, and especially Moses and are of a highly legendary character. Artapanus's main aim seems to have been to stress the Jews' contribution to Egyptian culture: Abraham taught the Egyptian king astrology; Joseph embarked on extensive agrarian reforms; and Moses invented boats and weapons, taught the Greek mystic poet Orpheus, conquered Ethiopia, taught the natives to circumcise themselves, and, most surprising, taught the Egyptians how to worship their sacred animals. Subsequently Moses led the Jews across the Red Sea and out of Egypt. Artapanus's work, which is unique in its mixture of Jewish, Egyptian, and Greek elements, may have been known in an abridged form to *Josephus Flavius.

• John J. Collins, "Artapanus," in James H. Charlesworth, ed., *Old Testament Pseudepigrapha* (Garden City, N.Y., 1985), vol. 2, pp. 889–903. Carl R. Holladay, *Fragments from Hellenistic Jewish Authors*, vol. 1 (Chico, Calif., 1983), pp. 189–243.

—GIDEON BOHAK

ARTICLES OF FAITH. See CREED; THIRTEEN PRINCIPLES OF FAITH.

ARTIFICIAL INSEMINATION. See ARTIFICIAL REPRODUCTION TECHNIQUES.

ARTIFICIAL REPRODUCTION TECHNIQUES. The first reference to artificial insemination in Judaism appears in the Talmud, in a passage dealing with the permissibility of a marriage between a high priest and a pregnant virgin (*Ḥag.* 15a). The Talmud attributes the virgin's pregnant condition to bathing in water into which a man's semen had previously been ejaculated. Apparently the marriage is permitted, and the conclusion is that artificial insemination by a donor (AID) does not constitute adultery or any other form of prohibited sexual relationship, since it does not involve active sexual intercourse. According to the majority of modern authorities, therefore, a child who is the product of AID is not a *mamzer. Nevertheless the practice is generally frowned upon, because of its wider implications, that is, the possibility of incest between the AID child and the sperm donor's offspring. Another implication of AID is that the child follows the lineage of the donor, and not that of the mother's husband. The AID son of a *kohen* will not therefore be a *kohen*, nor will his mother be exempt from the law of the levirate marriage in the event of her husband's death. The preservation of secrecy regarding an AID individual's conception is clearly incompatible with the requirements of Jewish law, and this fact accounts for a large part of the rabbinic opposition to the practice. Even so, based on a rabbinic ruling of Elliot N. Dorff, the Conservative Movement has permitted donor insemination on condition that either the identity of the donor be made known to the couple and child or, short of that, that enough information about his genetic makeup and character be made known to them as possible. This condition is not only imposed in an effort to avoid the possibility of incurring the genetic diseases or defects that come with consanguineous unions; it is also intended for the psychological benefits of giving the child information about his or her genetic roots and a better understanding of some of his or her interests and talents. Moreover, the Conservative ruling requires the couple to undergo counseling to deal with the psychological issues that arise from the asymmetry of their genetic relationship to the child: the spouse who did not contribute biologically to the creation of the child may experience jealousy and feelings of alienation from the other spouse or from the child, and so counseling is necessary. According to the Conservative ruling, though, neither of these issues is sufficient to prohibit donor insemination or egg donation. Orthodox decisors permit artificial insemination by the husband, although some authorities only permit it as a last resort. According to one authority, the *mitsvah* to "be fruitful and multiply" is not fulfilled except by means of sexual intercourse, but most maintain that it is. Surrogacy is the subject of debate among contemporary halakhic authorities, since, in addition to problems such as the possibility of incest, the issue of establishing maternity also arises where the fertilized egg is placed into the womb of a surrogate mother during gestation. Some authorities adopt the view that the method by which the child came into the world is irrelevant to the fulfillment of the *mitsvah* of procreation, and a prohibition on in vitro fertilization would prevent the husband from carrying out a religious obligation and threaten the continuation of the marriage. In general, Reform Judaism allows for artificial reproduction techniques. Fetal reduction is permitted according to Jewish law. See also SURROGACY.

• J. David Bleich, "In Vitro Fertilization: Questions of Maternal Identity and Conversion," *Tradition* 25.4 (1991): 82–102. Michael J. Broyde, "The Establishment of Maternity and Paternity in Jewish and American Law," *National Jewish Law Review* 3 (1988): 117–158. Alfred S. Cohen, "Artificial Insemination," *Journal of Halacha and Contemporary Society* 13 (1987): 43–59. Elliot Dorff, "Artificial Insemination, Egg Donation, and Adoption," *Conservative Judaism* (Fall 1996). Richard V. Grazi, ed., *Be Fruitful and Multiply: Fertility Therapy and the Jewish Tradition*, with an introduction by Immanuel Jakobovits (Jerusalem, 1994). Walter Jacob and Moshe Zemer, eds., *The Fetus and Fertility: Essays and Responsa* (Pittsburgh, 1995). Fred Rosner, "Artificial Insemination in Jewish Law," in *Jewish Bioethics*, edited by Fred Rosner and J. David Bleich (New York, 1979), pp. 105–118. Elie Spitz, "'Through Her I Too Shall Bear a Child': Birth Surrogates in Jewish Law," *Journal of Religious Ethics* 24.1 (Spring 1996): 65–98.

—DANIEL SINCLAIR

ʿARVIT. See MAʿARIV.

ARYEH LEIB BEN ASHER GUNZBERG. See GUNZBERG, ARYEH LEIB BEN ASHER.

ARYEH LEIB OF SHPOLA (1725–1811), popular leader of Ukrainian Hasidism. A man of relatively little education, he served as beadle in Zlotopolye, a small town in Podolia. In his later years he attracted a significant following as a saint and wonderworker. During his youth, he had once met Yisraʾel ben Eliʿezer *Baʿal Shem Tov and had reportedly received his blessing. From Zlotopolye he moved to nearby Shpola and became known as the Shpolar Zayde (Grandfather of Shpola). When *Naḥman of Bratslav moved to Zlotopolye in 1800, he came into direct conflict with the Shpolar Zayde, and fierce verbal battles ensued between the two leaders. It is possible that Naḥman chose Zlotopolye precisely to show his opposition to the popular "tsaddiqism" that the Shpolar Zayde represented. The conflict died down after Naḥman moved to Bratslav in 1802. Aryeh Leib of Shpola typified the simple Hasidic holy man, more highly reputed for miracles than for learning, a well-known figure especially within the Ukrainian heartland of Hasidism.

• Arthur Green, *Tormented Master: A Life of Rabbi Nahman of Bratslav* (New York, 1979). Yehudah Rosenberg, *Tifʾeret Maharal* (New York, 1912), essentially a work of fiction, but see pp. 100ff.

—ARTHUR GREEN

ASAPHITES, temple guild of singers and musicians headed by Asaph, the son of Berechiah, a Levite, who, together with his relatives Heman, son of Joel, and Ethan, son of Kushaiah, was put in charge of providing both instrumental and vocal music to accompany the procession of the Ark of the Covenant from the house of Obed-edom to Jerusalem (*1 Chr.* 15.17–24). According to *1 Chronicles* 15.19 and 16.5, Asaph was among the cymbal players, while according to *1 Chronicles* 16.7, King David put Asaph in charge of the music, both vocal and instrumental, that accompanied the daily sacrificial worship "before the Ark of the Covenant." The *First Book of Chronicles* 25.2 mentions the sons of Asaph, or Asaphites, who were members of the guild. The authorship of Psalms 50 and 73 through 83 is attributed to the members of this guild. In *Ezra* 2.41 (*Neh.* 7.44) temple singers and Asaphites are synonymous.

• Harry Peter Nasuti, *Tradition, History, and the Psalms of Asaph*, Dissertation Series (Society of Biblical Literature), no. 88 (Atlanta, 1989). Nahum M. Sarna, *Songs of the Heart* (New York, 1993).

—MAYER I. GRUBER

ʿASARAH BE-TEVET (עֲשָׂרָה בְּטֵבֵת), the tenth day of the Hebrew month of Tevet and one of four minor fasts relating to the destruction of the Temple. In *Zechariah* 8.19 it is referred to as "the fast of the tenth [month]," counting Nisan as the first month. Historically, the fast of Tevet commemorates the beginning of the Babylonian siege of Jerusalem in 586 BCE, which led to the capture of the city and the destruction of the First Temple (*2 Kgs.* 25.1; *Jer.* 52.4; *Ez.* 24.2). Like other minor fasts (except *Tish'ah be-'Av), the fast of Tevet begins at sunrise on the morning of the day itself. *Seliḥot* are read during the morning services. The appointed Torah readings for the day are *Exodus* 32.11–14 and *Exodus* 34.1–10 in the morning and afternoon, and in the Ashkenazi tradition *Isaiah* 55.6–8 is the **haftarah* in the afternoon service. The fast of Tevet is the only fast that may be observed on a Friday, because of the reference in *Ezekiel* 24.2 to "this self-same day," which stresses the precise date of the enemy siege.

In recent years, the Israeli chief rabbinate declared 'Asarah be-Tevet as "World Qaddish Day," a day on which *Qaddish and memorial prayers are to be recited for the victims of the Holocaust whose dates of death are unknown.

• J. D. Eisenstein, *Otsar Dinim u-Minhagim* (Tel Aviv, 1975). Eliyahu Ki Tov, *The Book of Our Heritage* (Jerusalem, 1968), pp. 325–334. Chaim Pearl, *A Guide to the Minor Festivals and Fasts* (London, 1963), pp. 53–56. Judah Rosenthal, "The Four Commemorative Fast Days," *The Seventy-Fifth Anniversary Volume of the Jewish Quarterly Review* (Philadelphia, 1967), pp. 446–459.

—CHAIM PEARL

ASCENSION OF ISAIAH, apocryphal work of composite origin, extant only in an Ethiopic version, although Greek, Latin, and Slavonic fragments have also been found. In its present form, the book is the work of a Christian author, but it is based in part on earlier Jewish material. Its first half (chaps. 1–5) describes how Isaiah was executed by King Manasseh, who had the prophet sawed in half with a wooden saw. The description includes a detailed account of Isaiah's prophecy, in which he foretold future events, including the arrival of Jesus. While the prophecy is, at least in part, a Christian interpolation, the story of Isaiah's martyrdom is also echoed in the Talmud, and there is little doubt concerning the work's Jewish origin. It probably was written in Hebrew, sometime between the second century BCE and the first century CE. The second part of the *Ascension of Isaiah* (chaps. 6–11), describing Isaiah's vision, is entirely Christian in origin.

• Martha Himmelfarb, *Ascent to Heaven in Jewish and Christian Apocalypses* (New York, 1993), pp. 55–59. Michael A. Knibb, "Martyrdom and Ascension of Isaiah," *The Old Testament Pseudepigrapha*, edited by James H. Charlesworth, vol. 2 (Garden City, N.Y., 1985), pp. 143–176.

—GIDEON BOHAK

ASCETICISM, the term is derived from a Greek word, meaning "exercise" or "training," used in connection with athletics. Philosophers then applied the word to moral and spiritual training, and from there it passed into religious usage, signifying the practice of religious austerities to expiate past sins or to achieve spiritual perfection. The dominant tendency in Judaism does not encourage asceticism, since the body is not considered as inherently evil. The pleasures of this world should not be suppressed but enjoyed in moderation and with gratitude to God. The only ascetic practice formally prescribed is fasting. The *flogging that pious persons undergo on the eve of Yom Kippur is not so much ascetic flagellation as a symbolic expiation of transgressions for which the law prescribes the punishment of stripes; moreover, the ceremony is not general but is left to personal piety. According to one rabbinic dictum, man will be accountable at his judgment for permissible pleasures deliberately rejected (Y., *Kid.* 4.12). A similar view is expressed by R. El'azar ha-Qappar, who explains the sin-offering of the *Nazirite (*Nm.* 6.11) as an expiation of his guilt in "denying himself the use of wine which the Torah permits," adding that "if a man who only denies himself wine is termed a sinner, how much more so is this true of one who is an ascetic in all things" (*Naz.* 19a). One of the main forms of asceticism, *celibacy, is ruled out by the first precept, "Be fruitful and multiply" (*Gn.* 1.28), and celibates are traditionally barred from certain religious functions. When under the crushing blow of the destruction of the Temple, "large numbers in Israel adopted ascetic practices, binding themselves neither to eat meat nor to drink wine," R. Yehoshu'a ben Ḥananyah opposed them vigorously (*B. B.* 60b). Ascetic tendencies nevertheless existed at all periods and often dominated Jewish piety, especially in certain sectarian circles. The ascetic practices adopted by the *Essenes and related sects in the Second Temple period went far beyond the discipline of holiness enjoined by the Pharisees. *Karaite asceticism was exemplified by the *Avelei Tsiyyon. Medieval moralist and mystical literature bears witness to the increasing importance of the ascetic ideal. The subject is discussed at some length in *Ḥovot ha-Levavot* by *Baḥya ben Yosef ibn Paquda'. Asceticism, he holds, is necessary for the purpose of controlling man's passions and purifying his soul from earthly dross. Only an ascetic can achieve that solitude and abandonment to God that leads to the ultimate purpose of the religious life, the perfect love of God. Baḥya agrees that Nazirites and saints are a minority, a kind of spiritual counterpoise to the majority who tend to lose themselves to the world, and he concludes that the form of asceticism most in keeping with the precepts of the Torah consists in leading a life of moderation while participating in the world with all its struggles and temptations. Moses *Maimonides' teaching of the Golden Mean (*Ḥilkhot De'ot* 2) is strongly influenced by Aristotelian ethics, and his doctrine of moderation is far less severely ascetic than the widely read penitential tracts of *Yonah ben Avraham Gerondi, for example. Mystic circles have always practiced ascetic disciplines, and the preparations of the Merkavah mystics involved strict fasts and other practices. It was mainly the *Kabbalah, particularly in the sixteenth and seventeenth centuries, that developed traditional asceticism into a system of mortification in which penitential and mystical motives combined. Much of the ascetic tradition survived also in *Hasidism, in spite of the original Hasidic teaching that communion with God was to be attained not through mortification but through *joy. Modern Jewish writers, in keeping with the tendency of the age, generally emphasize the affirmation of *life in Judaism and treat asceticism as an alien or at least marginal phenomenon.

• Steven D. Fraade, "Ascetical Aspects of Ancient Judaism," in *Jewish Spirituality: From the Bible to the Middle Ages*, edited by Arthur Green (New York, 1986), pp. 253–288. Howard Kreisel, "Asceticism in the Thought of R. Bahya Ibn Paquda," *Da'at* 21 (1988): 5–22. James A. Montgomery, "Ascetic Strains in Early Judaism," *Journal of Biblical Literature* 51 (1932): 184–213. Georges Vajda, *La Theologie ascetique de Bahya ibn Paquda* (Paris, 1947). Vincent L. Wimbush, ed., *Ascetic Behavior in Greco-Roman Antiquity: A Sourcebook* (Minneapolis, 1990). Vincent L. Wimbush and Richard Valantasis, eds., *Asceticism* (New York, 1995), includes extensive bibliography.

ʿASEH (עֲשֵׂה; do!), a positive commandment; normally the term refers to a positive biblical commandment as opposed to a positive rabbinic commandment. Most positive commandments entail an action, such as praying, waving a *lulav*, or repaying debts; however, there are a number of positive commandments the primary purpose of which is to prevent an activity. These commandments are referred to as *issurei ʿaseh*. Other positive commandments merely correct violations of negative commandments, such as the obligation to return what one has stolen. There is no sacrificial penitence explicitly mentioned in the Bible for the nonfulfillment of a positive commandment, although some assert that an *ʿolah* sacrifice is brought in such a case. There are 248 positive commandments among the 613 *mitsvot* in the Pentateuch according to calculations performed in the Middle Ages. See also COMMANDMENTS, 613; LO' TAʿASEH; MITSVAH.

• Charles B. Chavel, trans., *The Commandments: Sefer ha-Mitzvoth of Maimonides*, 2 vols. (London, 1976). Menachem Elon, *Jewish Law: History, Sources, Principles*, 4 vols. (Philadelphia, 1994).
—MICHAEL BROYDE

ʿASERET HA-DIBBEROT. See TEN COMMANDMENTS.

ʿASERET YEMEI TESHUVAH (עֲשֶׂרֶת יְמֵי תְּשׁוּבָה; Ten Days of Repentance), penitential period commencing with *Ro'sh ha-Shanah and concluding with *Yom Kippur. According to the Mishnah (*R. ha-Sh*. 1.2), 1 Tishrei (New Year) is the Day of Judgment. The Talmud, however, explains (*R. ha-Sh*. 16b) that on Ro'sh ha-Shanah final judgment is passed only on the "perfectly righteous" and the "utterly wicked"; judgment of all others is suspended until Yom Kippur on the tenth of the month. As a result, the entire ten-day period became one of penitence, in anticipation of that final judgment. Only slight changes are made in the liturgy for the days between the two festivals. The reading of **seliḥot* continues during these days. Prayers for life are inserted in the ʿAmidah; the wording of the third and eighth benedictions is changed to emphasize the concept of the sovereignty of God; and the ʿAmidah is followed by the recitation of *Avinu Malkenu. The ten days constitute a period of solemnity though not of mourning; fasting, where it is practiced, has a purely penitential character. It became customary prior to Yom Kippur to visit cemeteries, to make contributions to charity, and, among some penitents, to undergo a symbolic flagellation. The Sabbath during these days between Ro'sh ha-Shanah and Yom Kippur is called Shabbat Shuvah (see SABBATHS, SPECIAL).

• Shmuel Y. Agnon, ed., *Days of Awe: Being a Treasury of Traditions, Legends, and Learned Commentaries Concerning Rosh ha-Shanah, Yom Kippur, and the Days Between* (New York, 1965).

ASHAMNU (אָשַׁמְנוּ; We Have Trespassed), an ancient litany of *confession listing twenty-four sins in alphabetical order; also referred to as Viddui Zuta' (the Small Confession). The alphabetic arrangement dates from geonic times, tracing back to amoraic formulations of confession. It is now said in all synagogue services on Yom Kippur and is part of almost all public confessions. The worshiper beats his or her breast upon reciting each sin as an expression of contrition.

• Ismar Elbogen, *Jewish Liturgy: A Comprehensive History*, translated by Raymond P. Scheindlin (Philadelphia, 1993). —PETER LENHARDT

ASHER, the eighth of Jacob's children and his second by Zilpah, Leah's maidservant (*Gn*. 30.12–13). The official territorial allotment of the tribe of Asher was along the plain of Acre, extending into present-day Lebanon (*Jos*. 19.24–31), an area which was said to be rich in bread (*Gn*. 49.20) and oil (*Dt*. 33.24). From the references to Asher in the inscriptions of the Egyptian kings Seti I and Ramses II (14th–13th cents.) it would appear that Asher was one of the earliest settled tribes in Canaan. Yet, over the course of time, the Asherites did not maintain a firm hold in the north, and major Asherite clans amalgamated with the central hill-country tribes of Benjamin and Ephraim. This phenomenon is highlighted primarily by the genealogy list in *1 Chronicles* 7.30–40, in which the eponyms Serah, Malchiel, Shelesh, and Shual all correspond to known locations in Ephraimite or Benjaminite territory.

• Yohanan Aharoni, *The Land of the Bible: A Historical Geography*, 2d rev. ed., translated and edited by A. F. Rainey (London, 1979), pp. 235, 257–58, 315. Aaron Demsky, "Ha-Gene'ologiyah shel Benei Asher," *Eretz-Israel* 24 (1993): 68–73. Shmuel Yeivin, *The Israelite Conquest of Canaan* (Istanbul, 1971). —DAVID A. GLATT-GILAD

ASHERAH, name of Canaanite mother goddess, the consort of El. In a popular fertility cult she appears as the female counterpart of Baal. Many clay female figurines found throughout the Levant are assumed to represent Asherah. In the Bible the term *asherah* generally refers to a wooden pole or tree planted as a cultic installation beside altars and steles (*matsevot*) at shrines (*bamot*). The injunction to destroy the *asherot* is explicit in *Deuteronomy* (7.5, 12.3) and *Exodus* (34.13) and was carried out by certain reforming kings (i.e., Asa, Hezekiah, and Josiah). Opinion is divided on the extent and nature of Asherah worship in Israel. Her cult was especially active during the reigns of Ahab (*1 Kgs*. 16.32–33) and Manasseh (*2 Kgs*. 21.7). A number of inscriptions from Kuntillet Ajrud in northern Sinai mention "Yahweh and his Asherah," referring either to a consort or a cultic object.

• Walter A. Meier, *ʾAšerah: Extrabiblical Evidence*, Harvard Semitic Monographs, no. 37 (Atlanta, 1986). Saul M. Olyan, *Asherah and the Cult of Yahweh in Israel*, Monograph Series (Society of Biblical Literature), no. 34 (Atlanta, 1988). Richard J. Pettey, *Asherah: Goddess of Israel*, American University Studies, Series VII, Theology and Religion, vol. 74 (New York, 1990). —NILI SACHER FOX

ASHER BEN DAVID (13th cent.), kabbalist and the nephew of R. Yitsḥaq ben Avraham ha-Nahor, leader of the early kabbalistic school in southern France at the beginning of the thirteenth century. According to an epistle of R. Yitsḥaq, Asher was sent by his uncle to Gerona in Catalonia to join and direct the kabbalists in that center. Rabbi Yitsḥaq was critical of them for publishing their teachings, and Asher was probably sent to prevent them from doing that. He was one of the first kabbalists to include ethical teachings in his writings, a practice that became dominant in the Gerona school. He wrote a treatise on the *thirteen attributes, *Perush Shelosh-ʿEsreh ha-Middot*, which includes both kabbalistic and ethical teachings, and several other works of a similar character.

• Joseph Dan and R. Elior, eds., *Qabbalat R. Asher ben David* (Jerusalem, 1979). Gershom Gerhard Scholem, *Origins of the Kabbalah* (Princeton, 1986), pp. 252–253, 401–403, 431–433. —JOSEPH DAN

ASHER BEN MESHULLAM OF LUNEL (12th cent.), southern French rabbinical scholar, known as the Ro'sh of Lunel. He devoted himself to continual study, fasted, refrained from eating meat, and was not concerned with worldly matters. Nonetheless, he was praised for his positive attitude toward science by Yehudah ibn Tibbon, who copied an ethical work for him. Some of Asher's *responsa* and decisions have been preserved in the writings of later rabbis, and he wrote a treatise on the laws of excommunication and an essay on the laws of the festivals. His *Sefer ha-Mattanot* was apparently part of a comprehensive work dealing with the entirety of Jewish civil law.

• Simha Assaf, *Mi-Sifrut ha-Ge'onim*, includes sections of *Sefer ha-Mattanot* (Jerusalem, 1933), pp. 1–31. Heinrich Gross, *Gallia judaica: Dictionnaire géographique de la France d'après les sources rabbiniques*, with a supplement by Simon Schwarzfuchs (Paris, 1897; repr. Amsterdam, 1969). Isadore Twersky, *Rabad of Posquières: A Twelfth-Century Talmudist* (Philadelphia, 1980). —SHLOMO H. PICK

ASHER BEN SHA'UL OF LUNEL (12th–13th cent.), French rabbinic scholar. Asher, younger brother of kabbalist Yaʿaqov Nazir, should not be confused with Asher ben Meshullam of Lunel. Asher ben Sha'ul is the author of *Sefer ha-Minhagot*, of which only a part has been published from an incomplete manuscript. The second book of its kind written in Europe, and an invaluable aid to migrating populations, it cataloged the local customs of Narbonne and Lunel, tracing their sources to the Talmud and Midrash, to the writings of the ge'onim, and to French and Spanish rabbinic authorities.

• Simha Assaf, *Sifran shel Ri'shonim* (Jerusalem, 1935), pp. 121–182. Binyamin Ze'ev Benedikt, *Merkaz ha-Torah be-Provans* (Jerusalem, 1985). Heinrich Gross, *Gallia judaica: Dictionnaire géographique de la France d'après les sources rabbiniques*, with a supplement by Simon Schwarzfuchs (Paris, 1897; repr. Amsterdam, 1969). —SHLOMO H. PICK

ASHER BEN YEḤI'EL (c.1250–1327), codifier; also known as Ro'sh and Asheri. The leading pupil of R. *Me'ir ben Barukh of Rothenburg, he was regarded as the spiritual leader of German Jewry after R. Me'ir's death; but when conditions in Germany grew too difficult, he left the country and from 1305 headed the rabbinical academy in Toledo, Spain. His authority was recognized by Jews of all communities, and his *responsa* (of which over 1,000 have been published) constitute a rich source of the halakhic development and Jewish history of the thirteenth and fourteenth centuries. His simple and logical glosses on the Talmud were collected and printed in all subsequent editions of the Talmud. His legal decisions were noted for their intellectual independence and rigor; he ruled that a *dayyan* must give decisions on the basis of the Talmud alone, while later authorities could be quoted only as additional support. He bitterly opposed any attempt to give secular subjects precedence over religious ones and prohibited secular studies to students under the age of twenty-five. In his teachings, Asher combined the acumen of the Ashkenazi tosafists with the logic and orderliness of the Spanish scholars. His chief halakhic work, the compendium *Pisqei ha-Ro'sh*, covers all halakhic practices of his time and was the basis for all subsequent codes, including the authoritative *Arbaʿah Turim* of his son *Yaʿaqov ben Asher.

• Daniel Richter, *Die Responsen des Rabbi Ascher ben Jechiel (Rosch)* (Zurich, 1992).

ASHI (c.352–427), Babylonian amora' regarded as the spiritual head of the Babylonian community and for fifty-two years head of the *Sura academy, which he reestablished at Mata Meḥasya. His great achievement was the redaction of the *Talmud Bavli on the basis of the amoraic discussions of the Mishnah. He is credited with having produced two versions of this redaction (*B. B.* 157b), which according to tradition appeared thirty years apart. The amoraic traditions Ashi received were fixed and edited but lacked any order or arrangement; he clarified and sifted the various versions to determine their final form with the assistance of the circle of scholars that he established in Mata Meḥasya. Further additions—including Ashi's views—and changes were introduced before the compilation was definitively concluded, but the form underwent no material modification. Hence, according to *Bava' Metsiʿa'* 86a, "Rav Ashi and Ravina end[ed] the [period of] decision [*hora'ah*]," which is generally understood to mean that subsequent authorities are duty-bound to follow their legal rulings. Ashi himself owned numerous estates (*Git.* 49a; *Moʿed Q.* 12b; *Ned.* 62b) and lived in luxury (*Ber.* 31b). His wealth, status, and the positive political and economic situation of the Jews under Yesdegard II permitted Ashi to devote his life to his formidable project. He did this in a spirit of humbleness (*San.* 7b) and devotion to his studies as well as his students (*B. B.* 3b). There is ongoing scholarly discussion as to the extent of his editorial activity and which stratum of the Talmudic text is the result of his redaction and which of subsequent generations of amora'im and the later savora'im.

• Gershom Bader, *The Encyclopedia of Talmudic Sages*, translated from the Yiddish by Solomon Katz (Northvale, N.J., and London, 1988). Aaron Hyman, *Toledot Tanna'im ve-'Amora'im* (1910; Jerusalem, 1987). Mordecai Margaliot, ed., *Entsiqlopediyyah le-Ḥakhmei ha-Talmud veha-Ge'onim* (Jerusalem, 1946). —DANIEL SPERBER

ASHKAVAH (אַשְׁכָּבָה; Laying to Rest), Sephardi term for the prayer for the dead, also called Hashkavah, corresponding to the Ashkenazi *Yizkor. It is said on the Sabbath, festivals, and Mondays and Thursdays (see SHENI VA-ḤAMISHI) by an individual, not as part of the congregational liturgy, after he has been called to the reading of the Torah. It is also recited after burial and on anniversaries of death (both at the cemetery and in the synagogue), where it corresponds to the Ashkenazi

*El Male' Raḥamim. Different texts are recited for men and for women.

• Macy Nulman, *The Encyclopedia of Jewish Prayer: Ashkenazic and Sephardic Rites* (Northvale, N.J., 1993).

ASHKENAZI, BETSAL'EL (1520–1591), rabbi and Talmudic scholar in Cairo and Jerusalem; one of the outstanding authorities of the sixteenth century. Born to an Ashkenazi family in Erets Yisra'el, he studied in Jerusalem and in Cairo under *David ben Shelomoh ibn Avi Zimra, whom he succeeded as chief rabbi of Cairo. In Cairo Ashkenazi founded a *yeshivah* that numbered Yitsḥaq *Luria among its pupils. As chief rabbi Ashkenazi became embroiled in a conflict with the *nagid* (head of the Egyptian Jewish community), as a result of which the office of *nagid* was abolished. In 1588 he went to Jerusalem where he was appointed chief rabbi. He traveled widely as an emissary, and under his influence Purim was fixed as a day for sending contributions to Jews in the Holy Land.

His best-known work is *Shittah Mequbbetset* (also called *Asefet Zeqenim*; sections of which have been published, but not the entire work), a compilation of comments on the Talmud by Ashkenazi and Sephardi scholars from the end of the geonic period onward, which has preserved much early material otherwise unknown. Both this work and his introduction to Talmudic study, *Kelalei ha-Talmud* (published by A. Marx in *Festschrift David Hoffman* [Berlin, 1914]), exhibit the characteristics of Ashkenazi, as distinct from Sephardi, Talmudic scholarship: compilations, notes, comments, and critical rather than unified, methodical expositions. Ashkenazi also studied and copied old manuscripts, publishing glosses on the Talmud and early commentators and often throwing light on correct textual readings. His *responsa* (Venice, 1595) reflect his social and judicial activities as chief rabbi. The first two *responsa* deal with the laws of tithes and *terumot* and reflect the rabbinical preoccupation with agricultural laws at that time in Erets Yisra'el.

• Sh. Z. Havlin, "Intellectual Creativity," in *Toledot Yehudei Mitsrayim ba-Tequfah ha-'Otomanit (1517–1914)*, edited by Jacob M. Landau (Jerusalem, 1988), pp. 249–266. —SHALOM BAR-ASHER

ASHKENAZI, ELI'EZER BEN ELIYYAHU (1513–1586), rabbinic scholar, legal decisor, and exegete. After studying with R. Yosef Taitazak in Salonika, he went to Egypt, where he served as a rabbi and judge from 1539 to 1561. He then lived in Famagusta, Cyprus, for fifteen years, served as rabbi in Cremona, traveled subsequently to Venice, and ultimately settled in Poland, where he served several communities, including Kraków. He published a commentary to the *Book of Esther* (*Yosef Leqaḥ*; Verona, 1576) and *Ma'aseh Adonai* (Venice, 1583), which seeks to find the morals of the stories in the Pentateuch. Ashkenazi brought expressions of Sephardi rationalism to Europe. Italian scholars, such as Eliyyahu of Pesaro and 'Azaryah ben Mosheh dei Rossi, noted his competence in languages and the sciences in addition to his Talmudic erudition, and his legal opinions were sought in Poland.

• Isaac Barzilay, *Yoseph Shlomo Delmedigo, Yashar of Candia* (Leiden, 1974), pp. 233–234, n.s. Haim H. Ben-Sasson, *Hagut ve-Hanhagah* (Jerusalem, 1959), pp. 13–16, 34–36, 169. Jacob Elbaum, *Petiḥut ve-Histagrut* (Jerusalem, 1990), pp. 165–169, and index. —EPHRAIM KANARFOGEL

ASHKENAZI, TSEVI HIRSCH (1660–1718), rabbi and Talmudic scholar; known as Ḥakham Tsevi. Born in Moravia, he pursued his Talmudic studies in Salonika, where he came under the influence of Sephardi teachers and their methods. He served as *ḥakham* in Sarajevo, founded a study group in Altona, and was rabbi in Hamburg and Wandsbek from 1707 through 1709. In 1710 he was appointed chief rabbi of the Ashkenazi community of Amsterdam but became embroiled in quarrels with lay leaders of his own as well as the Sephardi community and was forced to leave in 1714. He died in Lwów shortly after being appointed rabbi there.

His collected *responsa* touch upon some of the most celebrated and controversial cases to confront the European rabbinate; for example, the nature of a *golem and whether it can be counted in a *minyan*, David *Nieto's "pantheist" sermon, questions pertaining to the differences between Ashkenazi and Sephardi custom, and the regulation of Jewish communal organizations.

When the Shabbatean theologian Neḥemyah Ḥayon arrived in Amsterdam, Ashkenazi, together with Mosheh Ḥagiz (see ḤAGIZ FAMILY), conducted a campaign against him that involved rabbis all over Europe and the East. Ya'aqov *Emden, Ashkenazi's son, continued his father's anti-Shabbateanism. Ashkenazi's *responsa* are to be found in *Responsa Ḥakham Tsevi* (1712); *Divrei Meshullam* (1783); and *Decision del Zevi Asqunazi, con su Bet Din* . . . (1705; English translation in Leon Roth's "David Nieto and the Orthodoxy of Spinozism," *Chronicon Spinozanum* 1[1921]: 278–282).

• Morris Lichtenstein, "Zevi Ashkenazi or Chacham Zevi," rabbinic thesis, Hebrew Union College, 1916. H. A. Tikotski, ed., *Sefer She'elot u-Teshuvot ha-Niqra' Ḥakham Tsevi* (Jerusalem, 1995), includes bibliography and index. —ELISHEVA CARLEBACH

ASHKENAZI, YEHUDAH (18th cent.), *dayyan* in Tiktin, Lithuania; son of Shim'on Ashkenazi, a scribe in Frankfurt am Main. Yehudah Ashkenazi is best known as the author of *Ba'er Heitev*, a commentary on the **Shulḥan 'Arukh*. First published along with the Amsterdam edition of the *Shulḥan 'Arukh* in 1742, *Ba'er Heitev* is a digest of the major commentators to the *Shulḥan 'Arukh* who preceded Ashkenazi, along with the explanations, *novellae*, and rulings of other halakhists. Modern printed editions of the *Shulḥan 'Arukh* carry sections from Ashkenazi's *Ba'er Heitev* or *Oraḥ Ḥayyim* and *Even ha-'Ezer*. The commentary by the same name and similar format to *Yoreh De'ah* and *Ḥoshen Mishpat* is the work of R. Zekharyah Mendel ben Aryeh Leib.

• Simon Chones, *Toledot ha-Poseqim* (New York, 1945), p. 92. Menachem Elon, *Jewish Law: History, Sources, Principles* (Philadelphia, 1994), p. 1437. —MARK WASHOFSKY

ASHKENAZI, YOSEF (1525–1572), rabbi in Europe and Erets Yisra'el and critical commentator on the *Mishnah, whose glosses are noted in such works as Shelomoh Adeni's *Melekhet Shelomoh* and Ḥayyim Yosef

David Azulai's *Birkei Yosef*. His devotion to Mishnah study earned him the title Tanna' of Safed, and he is said to have studied Mishnah with R. Yitsḥaq Luria, the eminent kabbalist of that community. Ashkenazi was a kabbalist and a fierce opponent of the rationalistic, philosophical tradition represented by Maimonides and others.

• Ḥayyim Azulai, *Shem ha-Gedolim* (Vilna, 1852), vol. 1, no. 112.

—MARK WASHOFSKY

ASHKENAZIM. The name *Ashkenaz* is first mentioned in the genealogical table of the descendants of Noah (*Gn*. 10.3) as that of the eldest son of Gomer the son of Japheth. Although the Targum and the Midrash, probably on grounds of assonance, identify the third son, Togarmah, with Germany, in the geonic period (which began in the 9th cent.) the name *Ashkenaz* became identified with Germany (as Sefarad in *Ob*. 1.20 was identified with Spain). In tenth-century Christian Europe, Jewish communal and social life as well as Jewish scholarship developed in the three Rhineland communities of Speyer, Worms, and Mayence. From there, they spread westward to France through Rashi and his descendants and eastward to Germany and Bohemia, establishing a unity of custom, ritual, and law differing from the parallel tradition developing in what was then Muslim Europe—Spain. As a result, the word *Ashkenaz*, from having a purely geographical connotation, became applied to a religious and cultural tradition of those who followed the custom that had its origin among German Jews. With the drift of German Jews over the eastern borders of their country into the Slavonic lands in the sixteenth century and the adoption by the Jews in those countries of the traditions (and language; see YIDDISH) of the German Jews, the word *Ashkenazi* received an even wider connotation. The distinctions are not fundamental—all liturgies have much in common—but there are differences in wording or prayers and in the additional prayers (*piyyutim*, etc.) introduced. The Ashkenazi pronunciation of *Hebrew differs from the Sephardi, and their musical traditions also diverge. The deviations in practices are so considerable that Ashkenazim could not accept Yosef *Karo's codification, the **Shulḥan ʿArukh*, based on Sephardi custom, until it was supplemented by Mosheh *Isserles's *Mappah*. Although in the purely liturgical sphere there is a difference between the Ashkenazi ritual and the Polish variation, the word is generally applied to all Jews of European origin and customs—that is, to all Jews of the western tradition (apart from comparatively small groups of Jews of Spanish and Portuguese origin and tradition)—in the same way as the name Sephardi is generally applied to all Jews of eastern countries who follow the parallel Spanish tradition. Thus the Jewish communities of the United States, England, and the countries of the British Commonwealth are mainly Ashkenazi because of the largely Polish derivation of these communities. These two main divisions of world Jewry have persisted to the present. The Ashkenazi tradition was of intense devotion to *study, expressed most visibly in their *yeshivot*, and in the rigid observance of *halakhah*. However, with the advent of emancipation, the non-Orthodox movements emerged in Ashkenazi milieus. In parts of the western world, such as Latin America and France, the differences between Ashkenazim and Sephardim are still a factor in Jewish communal life, although these are lessening, partly as a consequence of intermarriage between the two communities. Many new prayer books, especially non-Orthodox, freely choose from both traditions.

Despite the efforts to weld the Jews of the State of Israel into an entity, the division into Ashkenazim and Sephardim remains marked in certain spheres. Israeli legislation provides for both an Ashkenazi and a Sephardi chief rabbi, and this is carried down to the rabbinates in the towns of Israel. Liturgical differences remain, although in the Israeli army a unified version of the prayers has been worked out. Before World War II, 90 percent of world Jewry was Ashkenazi, but as a result of the Holocaust and low Ashkenazi birthrates, this has dropped to under 80 percent. The population of Israel is almost equally divided between Ashkenazim and non-Ashkenazim.

• Israel M. Ta-Shema, *Early Franco-German Ritual and Custom* (Jerusalem, 1992). H. J. Zimmels, *Ashkenazim and Sephardim: Their Relations, Differences, and Problems as Reflected in the Rabbinical Responsa* (London, 1958).

ASHREI (אַשְׁרֵי; Happy Are They), the alphabetic Psalm 145, read daily in the Shaḥarit and Minḥah services, prefixed by two verses that begin with the word *ashrei* (hence, the reading is commonly called by that name) and ending with *Psalms* 115.18. The Talmud quotes the saying of R. Eliʿezer ben Hurqanos: "Whoever recites the 145th Psalm thrice daily is assured of entering the world to come" (*Ber*. 4b); the addition of the two introductory verses with the threefold repetition of the word *ashrei* may be connected with this. The line from the first introductory verse, "Happy are they who dwell in your house," may explain the ancient pious custom of spending an hour in the synagogue prior to the service. While each verse of Psalm 145 begins with a successive letter of the alphabet, the verse beginning with the letter *nun* is missing. However, the Septuagint, the Syriac translation of the psalm, and a text of the psalm found in the *Dead Sea Scrolls include such a verse. Ashrei incorporates congregational responses indicating its liturgical use in the Second Temple. The prayer is sometimes read responsively by the reader and congregation.

• David Kimhi, *The Commentary of Rabbi David Kimhi on Psalms CXX–CL*, edited and translated by Joshua Baker and Ernest W. Nicholson (Cambridge, 1973). Nahum M. Sarna, *Songs of the Heart* (New York,

ASIDEANS. See HASIDEANS.

ASMAKHTA' (Aram.; אַסְמַכְתָּא; support), Talmudic term used in two unrelated contexts, in oral law and in civil law.

In Oral Law. An *asmakhta'* is a scriptural verse cited in support of an oral law but not meant to imply that that particular oral law actually derives from a scriptural verse. An *asmakhta'* merely indicates some tie, however slight, between rabbinic legislation and scripture, thus demonstrating that rabbinic law was foreseen and alluded to in the Bible.

In Civil Law. An *asmakhta'* is an undertaking that is legally flawed because of the lack of serious, deliberate intent (*gemirat da'at*) on the part of the promisor. Such flawed stipulations are those that are considered unreasonable and are connected with conditions of a contract. Thus, one who agrees to pay an exorbitant fine if he does not fulfill a specific condition of a contract is not bound by his stipulation, since he is considered to have promised without really intending to pay the exorbitant fine.

• Menachem Elon, *Jewish Law: History, Sources, Principles*, 4 vols. (Philadelphia, 1994). Michael Guttmann, *Asmakhta' (Breslau, 1924). Berachyahu Lifshitz, Asmakhta': Ḥiyuv ve-Qinyan ba-Mishpat ha-'Ivri* (Jerusalem, 1988).

ASMODEUS (Heb. Ashmeda'i), name of an evil spirit. He is first mentioned in the *Book of *Tobit* as the king of the demons, who fell in love with Sarah, daughter of Raguel, and slew all those who wished to marry her until Tobit, instructed by the angel Raphael (Asmodeus's chief antagonist), rendered him harmless and married her. A long account of Ashmeda'i appears in the Talmud (*Git*. 68a–b), relating how Solomon succeeded in capturing him and forcing him into service for the building of the Temple. Later aggadic legend depicts Asmodeus as a merry trickster rather than an evil demon, while according to some sources his influence is actually beneficent and is directed to guarding the moral order of the universe. The name Asmodeus seems to be derived from the Persian *aesma daeva*, the Zoroastrian "spirit of anger."

• Bernard Jacob Bamberger, *Fallen Angels* (Philadelphia, 1952). Gustav Davidson, *A Dictionary of Angels: Including the Fallen Angels* (New York, 1967). —JOSEPH DAN

ASSAF, SIMḤAH (1889–1953), rabbinic scholar and Jewish historian. Assaf was born in Lubań, Belorussia, studied at the *yeshivah* in Tels, and was ordained in 1910. From 1914 to 1919 he taught at a modern *yeshivah* in Odessa, which he headed from 1915 to 1919. He then spent two years traveling and studying in Paris and Germany before moving to Jerusalem in 1921 as an instructor in Talmud at the Mizrachi Teachers' Seminary. When the Hebrew University of Jerusalem opened in 1925, Assaf was appointed lecturer on the geonic period; he became a full professor in 1936. He was active in administrative matters at the Hebrew University, serving as chairman of the Institute of Jewish Studies, as dean of humanities, and from 1948 to 1950 as rector. He also played an important role in public affairs after the establishment of the State of Israel, serving as a justice on the Supreme Court.

Assaf published several important critical editions of manuscripts and *responsa* of the geonic period, but his most important work is *Meqorot le-Toledot ha-Ḥinnukh be-Yisra'el* (1525–1943), a four-volume anthology of sources relating to Jewish education, exploring social and cultural history.

• Umberto Cassuto, ed., *Sefer Assaf* (Jerusalem, 1952–1953). *Le-Zikhro shel Simḥah Assaf* (Jerusalem, 1953). —ADAM RUBIN

ASSAULT. The act of inflicting physical harm on another is punishable in Jewish law by lashes and violates the biblical prohibition found in *Deuteronomy* 25.3. The victim may also be entitled to compensation. Since Jewish law does not normally authorize two punishments for the same illicit act, the Talmud (*Mak*. 4b) derives from both hermeneutic rules and rules of logic that compensation is to be paid and lashes forgone. In reality, lashes were only administered in assault cases in which no monetary damages were due. In addition, Talmudic sages decreed in specific cases that additional fines were to be paid by one who commits assault.

By the Middle Ages, numerous *taqqanot* governed the different types of damages assessable in cases of assault. Although the Talmud appears to deny any post-Talmud *beit din* the authority to punish physically one who commits assault, such punishments were frequently meted out by medieval decisors under their exigency jurisdictional authority. For example, Yehudah ben Asher ordered the hands cut off of an assailant who assaulted a judge on a rabbinical court (*Zirḥon Yehudah* 58).

In order to be liable for monetary damages in the case of assault, no criminal intent need be demonstrated, although there is a dispute among the classical decisors as to whether one is liable for damage caused to another when there was no negligence at all.

Included in a special category of people who were exempt from paying damages caused by their assault were licensed doctors, a father or teacher disciplining a child, and a court officer in the course of his duties. So, too, one who consented to be assaulted waived his financial claim against his assailant.

• Haim H. Cohn, "Assault," in *Principles of Jewish Law*, edited by Menachem Elon (Jerusalem, 1975), pp. 480–482. "Adam ha-Mazziq," in *Entsiqlopedyah Talmudit* (Jerusalem, 1947–), vol. 1, pp. 218–226. Stephen M. Passamaneck, "R. Judah Ben Asher on Capital Penalties," *Jewish Law Association Studies* 7 (1994): 153–172. —MICHAEL BROYDE

ASSEMBLY, GREAT. See KENESET HA-GEDOLAH.

ASSEMBLY OF JEWISH NOTABLES, gathering in Paris, from 26 July 1806 through 6 April 1807, of one hundred and eleven Jewish lay leaders and rabbis summoned by Napoléon Bonaparte "to revive among Jews the civil morality weakened during their long debasement." Believing that the emperor had their best interests at heart, leaders of French Jewry had earlier submitted a blueprint for the establishment of *rabbinical seminaries and other communal improvements. Before the assembly, however, Napoléon attacked the Jews as "a nation within a nation" that must be reformed through exceptional laws aimed at curbing their "evil practices" and transforming them into loyal "French citizens of the Mosaic faith." With much pomp and circumstance, he therefore convened an "Assembly of the Israelites of France and the Kingdom of Italy" to give these deputies the appearance of willing collaborators.

The opening session, deliberately held on a Sabbath to

test the assembly's religious character, produced two opposing camps—one "philosophic" and largely composed of Jews of Portuguese origin, the other "rabbinic" (Orthodox) and made up of Jews from Alsace-Lorraine, Avignon, and Italy. Abraham Furtado, the freethinking Bordeaux deputy, was elected president and secretly was told how Napoléon wished twelve questions (posed by the imperial commissioners) to be answered. During the months that followed, however, it was Joseph David Sinzheim, Strasbourg's erudite chief rabbi, who formulated authoritative replies on the Talmudic basis of **dina' de-malkhuta' dina'* (the law of the land must be upheld when there is no clash with *halakhah*). The patriotism of French Jews was accordingly reemphasized, though they were forced to surrender their juridical autonomy; no religious sanction was given to mixed marriages. Once Napoléon became aware that the assembly's resolutions needed a supreme religious authority to make them operative, thus impelling Jews to "look upon France as their Jerusalem," he devised the mustering of a French Sanhedrin (see SANHEDRIN, FRENCH).

• Robert Anchel, *Napoléon et les juifs* (Paris, 1928), includes comprehensive bibliography. Barukh Mevorakh, ed., *Napolei'on u-Tequfato* (Jerusalem, 1968). Simon Schwarzfuchs, *Napoleon, the Jews and the Sanhedrin* (London, 1979), pp. 45–87. Zosa Szajkowski, "Judaica-Napoleonica," *Studies in Bibliography and Booklore* 2 (1956): 107–152, republished in *Jews and the French Revolutions of 1789, 1830 and 1848* (New York, 1970), pp. 971–1016. Diogene Tama, *Procès verbal des séances de l'Assemblé des Députés français professant la religion Israélite* (Paris, 1806), translated by F. D. Kirwan in *Transactions of the Parisian Sanhedrin* (London, 1807).

—GABRIEL A. SIVAN

ASSI (3d cent.), Babylonian amora' from the town of Hutsal, near Nehardea. His authority was widely recognized throughout Babylonia, and a number of his ordinances are quoted in the Talmud. He appears to have headed his own academy, called Sidra' de-Assi (Y., *Beits.* 1.7). He was a contemporary of *Rav and often differed from him; many of their controversies having been recorded. He died shortly after Rav, that is, after 248 (*Nid.* 36b).

—DANIEL SPERBER

ASSI (3d–4th cent.), Palestinian amora' who, together with his colleague R. *ʿAmmi bar Natan, were known to the Babylonian rabbis of the time as "the Palestinian judges." He was of Babylonian origin and studied in his youth during the lifetime of Shemu'el (died 254). He must have reached Palestine in the middle of the third century, since he studied under R. Ḥanina' and R. Yehoshuʿa ben Levi, who probably died in the 250s. However, his main mentor was Yoḥanan (died 278), and after his death, with R. ʿAmmi, he became the leading figure in the Tiberian rabbinate. He was a pious and charitable man, who had a special relationship with proselytes (Y., *Ḥag.* 1.7).

—DANIEL SPERBER

ASSIMILATION. The Talmud relates that during the captivity in Egypt the large majority of ancient Hebrews assimilated into Egyptian society; only a minority left Egypt for the desert and for their ultimate destination, the Promised Land. On the other hand, so long as Jewish independence prevailed, in the days of both the First and Second Temples, the Jewish majority assimilated many minorities into the Jewish people and the Jewish religion. The biblical *Book of Ruth* even makes the heroine of the story, who chose to follow her former mother-in-law to the land of the Jews from her native Moab, into the great-grandmother of King David.

The Hellenizers, whom the Maccabees defeated in Judea in the second century BCE, preferred Hellenistic culture and pagan religion to the ways and faith of their own people. Much more often, however, assimilation does not result from choice but is caused by force. For many centuries Jews were a persecuted minority, especially in Europe, and their religion was said to be the "synagogue of Satan." Conventional accounts of Jewish history in the Middle Ages are full of admiration for those who resisted conversion; many became martyrs rather than abjure their faith. In fact, even taking into account the murder of thousands by the Crusaders and other persecutors, the Jewish community in Europe was reduced to no more than ten or twenty thousand in the twelfth century because so many Jews chose to abandon this dangerous identity. This choice was always available in the Middle Ages: it was safe to convert to the majority religion and become part of the majority culture; remaining a Jew represented danger and the inevitability of persecution. No adequate study exists of the numbers of Jews who, generation after generation, fell away, but the proportion was significant.

The nature of assimilation changed in the seventeenth century. The purpose of the state was redefined in Holland and, soon, in the rest of western Europe. Government no longer existed to promote the true faith; it aimed to increase the wealth of the state. Therefore, Jews who brought money with them, or who were likely to increase economic activity, were allowed into major port cities and other economic centers. These Jews were soon mixing socially with non-Jews of their economic station. Through conversion and intermarriage, a number of great Jewish fortunes became the source of the wealth of titled families all over Europe. In the eighteenth century, the most modern ideologies made assimilation a virtue. The Enlightenment offered a vision of a regenerated society, free of ancient prejudices, in which everyone could participate as an equal. Jews were being asked to enter this brave new world by giving up their religion and identity. The enlighteners were as critical of Christianity as they were of Judaism, but the situation for Jews was different. Even after Jews and Christians would have abandoned their religion for a new society governed by reason, Frenchmen and Germans would still be living within their own culture. Jews would enter this new society only by leaving their minority culture behind.

In the nineteenth century, belonging to the organized Jewish community was no longer compulsory; it had become a voluntary act. *Reform Judaism proposed the near total abandonment of Jewish ethnic culture. Antisemitism, however, did not disappear in the new age; it became more virulent as the nineteenth century wore on. Some Jews turned to Zionism to normalize the Jews by reestablishing their own state. Even as they differed in their prescriptions for dealing with the threat of antisemitism, Reform Jews and Zionists agreed that the central problem of the Jews was their safety and their economic and political equality, not the preservation of their own culture. The majority of Jews, even so, clung to their inherited culture. Religion remained a stronger force among the Jewish masses, especially in eastern Europe, than any of the modern ideologies.

In the turbulent twentieth century, a third of world Jewry moved to new homes in the era of mass migration, a third were murdered by the Nazis and their collaborators during World War II, and the Jewish population of the new State of Israel grew from six hundred thousand to four million. At the end of this century, the clashing forces of assimilation and Jewish continuity remain powerful and intense.

• Sidney Goldstein, "Profile of American Jewry: Insights from the 1990 National Jewish Population Survey," *American Jewish Year Book* (New York, 1992), pp. 76–173. Arthur Hertzberg, *The Jews in America: Four Centuries of an Uneasy Encounter* (New York, 1989). Barry A. Kosmin et al., *Highlights of the CJF 1990 National Jewish Population Survey*, Council of Jewish Federations (New York, 1991). Peter Y. Medding, Gary A. Tobin, Sylvia Barack Fishman, and Mordechai Rimor, "Jewish Identity in Conversionary and Mixed Marriages," *American Jewish Year Book* (New York, 1992), pp. 3–75. Usiel O. Schmelz and Sergio DellaPergola, *Basic Trends in American Jewish Demography*, Jewish Sociology Papers (New York, 1988).

—ARTHUR HERTZBERG

ASSUMPTION OF MOSES, pseudepigraphous work known also as *The Testament of Moses* and extant, in mutilated form, in one Latin manuscript. The Latin text is a translation from a lost Greek version, but it is unclear whether Greek was the original language or a translation from a lost Hebrew or Aramaic original. As the work refers to Herod and his children, it probably was written in the early first century CE, and Erets Yisra'el is its most likely place of origin. It describes Moses' farewell words to Joshua, including a description of Israel's future history from the entry into Erets Yisra'el to the Roman period, the final judgment, and the salvation of Israel. This historical description is followed by Moses' attempt to encourage Joshua, who is terrified of the task entrusted to him.

• George W. E. Nickelsburg, ed. *Studies on the Testament of Moses*, Septuagint and Cognate Studies 4 (Cambridge, Mass., 1973). John Priest, "The Testament of Moses," in *The Old Testament Pseudepigrapha*, edited by James H. Charlesworth, vol. 1 (Garden City, N.Y., 1983), pp. 919–934. Johannes Tromp, *The Assumption of Moses: A Critical Edition with Commentary*, Studia in Veteris Testamenti Pseudepigrapha 10 (Leiden and New York, 1993).

—GIDEON BOHAK

ASSYRIA, an ancient region in Mesopotamia. It first appears in the historical record in the middle of the third millennium BCE in the form of a few autonomous city-states, chief among them Aššur and Nineveh (cf. *Gn.* 10.11–12), both located on the upper-middle Tigris (cf. *Gn.* 2.14). Both of these cities were part of the Old Akkadian empire of Sargon of Agade (c.2334–2279). While this foreign domination of Aššur continued under the Sumerian Third Dynasty of Ur (c.2112–2004), a turning point occurred at the end of that period when Aššur regained its independence and embarked upon a new age of political stability and economic prosperity marked especially by intensive commercialization. This period came to an end as a result of the Amorite invasion, when Aššur was conquered and an Amorite kingdom was established in all of Assyria (see AMORITES). This kingdom did not endure long, and most of its important territories and finally Aššur itself were eventually conquered by *Hammurabi of Babylon (1792–1750; see BABYLONIA). Sometime after the death of Hammurabi, Aššur and the other cities of Assyria regained their independence but came under the heavy influence of Hurrian expansionism; the major Assyrian site bearing witness to Hurrian influence is the city of Nuzi, which has yielded more than thirty-five hundred cuneiform documents. The period of the "dark ages" in Assyrian history continued for almost four centuries. The "awakening" of Assyria as a political and military power under Aššur-uballit I (1363–1328) and his successors was the prelude to the establishment of the Neo-Assyrian empire (911–609), the largest and most powerful empire the ancient Near East had yet seen. It is almost exclusively with reference to this empire that references to Assyria appear in the Bible. From the time of Shalmaneser III (858–824), the Hebrew people fought frequently against the Assyrians, and it was the armies of Assyria under Shalmaneser V and Sargon II that brought to an end the kingdom of Israel and deported many of its inhabitants. The prophets characterized the succeeding Assyrian invasions as divine scourges. Isaiah saw Assyria as the rod of divine ire destined to rule the earth but be broken by Israel (*Is.* 10.5ff.). His intuition was fulfilled in the sudden arrest of Assyrian progress before the gates of Jerusalem (701 BCE), and the subsequent Assyrian withdrawal probably assisted the prophet in impressing on the people his monotheistic message. Isaiah, Micah, and Zephaniah all looked on Assyria as the final enemy prior to the establishment of divine rule on earth.

• J. Bottero and D. O. Edzard in *The Near East: The Early Civilizations*, edited by Elena Cassin (New York, 1967), pp. 129–130, 145–147, 165–168, 194–198, 201–205. C. J. Gadd, J. M. Munn-Rankin, and D. J. Wiseman in *Cambridge Ancient History*, 3d. ed., edited by I.E.S. Edwards et al., vol. 2, pt. 2 (Cambridge, 1975), pp. 21–48, 274–306, 443–481. A. K. Grayson in *Cambridge Ancient History*, 2d ed., edited by John Boardman et al., vol. 3, pt. 1 (Cambridge, 1982), pp. 238–281. A. K. Grayson and J. Oates in *Cambridge Ancient History*, 2d ed., edited by John Boardman et al., vol. 3, pt. 2 (Cambridge, 1991), pp. 71–61, 194–228, 162–193. A. K. Grayson, "History and Culture of Assyria," in *The Anchor Bible Dictionary*, vol. 4 (New York, 1992), pp. 732–755. William W. Hallo and William K. Simpson, *The Ancient Near East: A History* (New York, 1971), pp. 27–183. J. R. Kupper in *Cambridge Ancient History*, 3d ed., edited by I.E.S. Edwards et al., vol. 2, pt. 1 (Cambridge, 1973), pp. 1–8. Jorgen Laessoe, *People of Ancient Assyria: Their Inscriptions and Correspondence* (London, 1963). M.E.L. Mallowan and H. Lewy in *Cambridge Ancient History*, 3d ed., edited by I.E.S. Edwards, et al., vol. 1, pt. 2 (Cambridge, 1971), pp. 298–304, 707–770. A. Leo Oppenheim and Erica Reiner, *Ancient Mesopotamia*, 2d ed. (Chicago, 1977), pp. 163–170 and *passim*. H.W.F. Saggs, *The Might that Was Assyria* (New York, 1984). Wolfram von Soden, *The Ancient Orient: An Introduction to the Study of the Ancient Near East* (Grand Rapids, 1994), pp. 49–59.

—CHAIM COHEN

ASSYRIAN EXILE, the mass deportation of Israelites from the northern kingdom of Israel to Assyria. An Assyrian policy of deportation of captive peoples is first attested in the ninth century, but only in the mid-eighth century, under Tiglath-pileser III, was there a two-way exchange of populations designed to prevent rebellion of conquered nations. The first recorded exile of Israelites from their land took place in 732 BCE after Pekah, king of the northern kingdom of Israel, joined the Arameans in rebellion against Assyria. Tiglath-pileser conquered the bulk of the kingdom of Israel, including Galilee and Gilead (*2 Kgs*. 15.29). Archaeological evidence of destruction is widespread at northern sites, such as Hazor and Megiddo, while Assyrian inscriptions list exiled captives. The territory of northern Israel was reduced to the territory of Samaria and its environs on Mount Ephraim. A few years later, Israel's last king, Hoshea, joined the Egyptians in an anti-Assyrian alliance. In response, Tiglath-pileser's son, Shalmaneser V, in 722 besieged Samaria and by 721 had conquered it (*2 Kgs*. 17.6). The Israelites from that region were exiled by his successor, Sargon II, in 720. Sargon's annals record 27,290 exiles. They were resettled on Assyrian lands, while captives of other nations were settled in Samaria (see SAMARITANS). A number of Assyrian documents contain biblical names probably belonging to exiles. The striking growth of Jerusalem at that time indicates that many belonging to the so-called ten lost tribes fled into Judah before the deportations. Others may have returned from Babylonia with the Judeans in 538 BCE. The theological evaluation of the Deuteronomist presents the Assyrian exile as punishment for the nation's idolatrous practices. Most of the exiles presumably assimilated into the peoples among whom they were settled, but legends of the survival of the lost tribes have continued to the present (see TRIBES OF ISRAEL).

• Gosta W. Ahlstrom, *The History of Ancient Palestine* (Minneapolis, 1993). Bob Becking, *The Fall of Samaria: An Historical and Archaeological Study*, Studies in the History of the Ancient Near East, vol. 2 (Leiden, 1992). John Bright, *A History of Israel*, 3d ed. (Philadelphia, 1981). Mordechai Cogan and Hayim Tadmor, *II Kings: A New Translation*, The Anchor Bible (Garden City, N.Y., 1988). John Gray, *I and II Kings: A Commentary*, 2d rev. ed. (Philadelphia, 1976). James Bennett Pritchard, ed., *Ancient Near Eastern Texts Relating to the Old Testament*, 3d ed. (Princeton, 1969).

—NILI SACHER FOX

ASTROLOGY, study that assumes and professes to interpret the influence of heavenly bodies on human affairs. According to the Talmud, R. Ḥanina' said, "The planet of a person decides whether he shall be wise or wealthy, and Israel has its planet." Rabbi Yoḥanan said, "Israel has no planet; as it is written [*Jer*. 10.2]: 'Thus says the Lord, Learn not the way of the heathens, and be not dismayed at the signs of the heaven, for the heathens are dismayed by them' " (*Shab*.156a). The opponents of astrological belief (R.Yoḥanan, R. Yehudah, Rav) confine themselves to denying this influence on Israel but do not deny its efficacy for others. The Midrash (*Gn. Rab*. 44.14) interprets *Genesis*.15.5 as meaning, "And he took him outside the scope of astrology," and has God say to Abraham, "You are a prophet and not an astrologer." There is ample evidence, however, that the more rational view was not accepted, despite the definite element of *determinism and absence of free will inherent in this belief. The sages held that by observance of the Torah the Jew could change the destiny decreed by the constellations.

Belief in astrology has been widespread throughout the ages, not only among the common people. References to it as both valid and reliable abound in rabbinical literature, and it was accepted without question by medieval authorities. In fact, it was held that, unlike animals, every human being is born under the influence of a particular planet (*Shab*. 53b, 146a). Rava' stated explicitly that "Length of life, children, and sustenance depend not on merit but on one's planet" (*Mo'ed Q*. 28a), and "lucky" days and periods are often taken into account. Among the outstanding medieval thinkers who endorsed astrology were Sa'adyah ben Yosef Ga'on, Shelomoh ibn Gabirol, Avraham bar Ḥayya' (who was criticized by Yehudah ben Barzillai al-Bargeloni for relying "on a Chaldean custom"), Avraham ibn Ezra, Nahmanides, as well as the kabbalists. The only medieval authority roundly condemning belief in astrology was *Maimonides, who included it in his code among such prohibited superstitions as witchcraft, sorcery, and soothsaying. Maimonides concluded his chapter on superstitions with one of his few statements in the *Mishneh Torah* in which he allowed his own views to prevail over the statements of the Talmud: "These and similar things are all lies and deceit . . . It is not fitting for Israel to be attracted by these follies or to believe that they have any efficacy. Whosoever believes that they are possible, though the Torah has forbidden their practice, is but a fool" (*Ḥilkhot 'Akkum* 11.16). The universal Jewish phrase of congratulation, *mazzal tov* (good luck; literally, a good constellation), is a relic of the belief in astrology. See also ZODIAC.

• Jacques Halbronn, *Le monde juif et l'astrologie* (Milano, 1985). Lester J. Ness, "Astrology and Judaism in Late Antiquity," Ph.D. dissertation, Miami University, 1990. Joshua Trachtenberg, *Jewish Magic and Superstition: A Study in Folk Religion* (New York, 1974).

ASTRONOMY, like all sciences in ancient and medieval times, was studied for its religious implications, but for the Jews there was never any question of star worship; the stars as part of the heavenly host are themselves conceived as worshiping God. The stars also influenced terrestrial events (see ASTROLOGY). The Bible contains no reference to the science of astronomy, but many references show a knowledge of astronomy. The apocryphal *Book of Enoch* devotes several chapters to movements of heavenly bodies and to determining the relative length of nights and days. The necessity for the accurate fixation of the *calendar for purposes of determining the dates of the festivals made the authorities of the Mishnaic period adept in astronomy. Their main expertise was in determining which months were to be regarded as *plene* (full months of thirty days) and which as having only twenty-nine days. A full month was called "a month big with foetus" (*'ubbar*), and since the prerogative of fixing the new moon was jealously guarded by the Sanhedrin, the general name for astronomical calculations was *sod ha-'ibbur* (the secret of intercalation). Notable astronomers in Talmudic times included R. Yehoshu'a ben Ḥananyah, whose statement that a certain star "rises once in seventy years" has been taken to refer to Halley's comet, fifteen hundred years before its "official" discovery (*Hor*. 10a), and Shemu'el, who claimed that "the paths of heaven are as clear to me as the paths of [my native] Nehardea" but nevertheless pleaded ignorance of the incidence of comets (*Ber.* 58b). The Talmudic sages regarded a knowledge of astronomy as highly desirable for the study of Torah and even saw it as a religious duty for the wise (based on *Ps.*19.1–2; cf. *Shab.* 75a). In the Middle Ages, the Jews, especially in Spain, were among the outstanding astronomers. See also COSMOLOGY.

• Selig Brodetsky, *Astronomy in the Babylonian Talmud* (Brooklyn, N.Y., 1979). Bernard Goldstein, *Theory and Observation in Ancient and Medieval Astronomy* (London, 1985).

ASUFI (אֲסוּפִי), Talmudic term for a child found abandoned in a public place. The mystery surrounding the child's origin casts doubt on its lineage and it is, therefore, considered a "doubtful *mamzer*" with the result that he or she can marry neither a Jew nor another *mamzer* (*Kid.* 74a). The stigma of *mamzerut*, however, only applies to an *asufi* if there is no hint of parental care in the circumstances of the child's abandonment. Circumcision or abandonment in a safe public place, such as a synagogue, are evidence of such care, and the child is then treated as a regular Jew of untainted lineage (*Kid.* 73b; Maimonides, *Laws of Forbidden Intercourse* 15.31; *Shulḥan ʿArukh, Even ha-ʿEzer* 4.31).

• *Entsiqlopedyah Talmudit* (Jerusalem, 1947–), vol. 2, pp. 71–74. Judah D. Eisenstein, ed., *Otsar Yisra'el* (Jerusalem, 1951), vol. 2, p. 145.
—DANIEL SINCLAIR

ASYLUM. Biblical law grants the right of asylum to one who has committed accidental manslaughter. Almost immediately following the biblical command "You shall not murder" (*Ex.* 20.13) is the law "Whoever fatally strikes a person shall be put to death" (*Ex.* 21.12). This is followed by the double provision regulating asylum: "If, however, he did not do it by design . . . I will assign you a place to which he can flee, but if anyone schemes against his fellow, killing him deliberately, you must remove him from my altar" (*Ex.* 21.13–14). Biblical law thus recognizes two immutable principles: one who commits involuntary homicide is provided by God himself with a place of refuge; but the deliberate murderer cannot take refuge anywhere, not even at the altar in the Temple. This is distinct from the widespread view in the ancient world that altars grant those who touch them immunity from harm by conveying sanctity (see Adonijah's successful attempt in *1 Kgs.* 1.50–51 and Joab's unsuccessful one in *1 Kgs.* 2.28–34)—an idea that Torah law rejects.

All shedding of human blood must be expiated by the shedding of the blood of the killer, otherwise the spilled blood will leave an indelible stain on the land (*Gn.* 9.6; *Nm.* 35.33–34), endangering its inhabitants. This postulate stems from the theological premise that since man is created in God's image, the killing of a human being is tantamount to the murder of God. Yet there are times when this form of expiation is impossible or unthinkable (for example, when the killer is unknown [*Dt.* 21.1–9]; or when the killing takes place in war [*Nm.* 31]). Even in the case of an accidental killing, the victim's closest relatives, his *blood avengers, may attempt to realize their right to exact vengeance. Biblical law therefore provides an escape for the killer; he may take refuge in a designated asylum city (*ʿir miqlat*). So long as he remains there, the blood avenger may not harm him; if he leaves, the blood avenger may kill him with impunity.

In order to guarantee that the right of asylum would be enjoyed only by those entitled to it, the law stipulates that only after the court has determined that the killing was accidental may the killer reside securely in the city of refuge. Furthermore, a deliberate murderer may not seek refuge, even in exchange for payment of a fine.

However, some death, even a symbolic one, is necessary to atone for the blood of the innocent victim. For this reason the law of *Numbers* 35 requires that the killer be confined to the asylum city until the death of the incumbent high priest. As the ritual representative of all Israel, his death formally atones for all unexpiated killing that has taken place during his tenure, after which the homicide may leave the city of refuge.

The land was divided into three equal parts, with one asylum city assigned to each district (*Dt.* 19.3). Ultimately, six cities were set aside for refuge, three on each side of the Jordan (*Nm.* 35.13–15; *Dt.* 4.41–43, 19.1–10). The Talmud Bavli interprets *Numbers* 35.6 to mean that all forty-eight Levitical cities were to be considered cities of refuge. The subject is treated in Talmud tractate **Makkot*. There is no evidence of asylum after the First Temple period.

• Moshe Greenberg, "Some Postulates of Biblical Criminal Law," in *Sefer ha-Yovel li-Yeḥezk'el Kaufmann*, edited by Menahem Haran (Jerusalem, 1960), pp. 5–28. Jacob Milgrom, *Numbers*, The JPS Torah Commentary (Philadelphia, 1990), pp. 504–511. Jacob Milgrom, "Sancta Contagion and Altar/City Asylum," Supplements to Vetus Testamentum, vol. 32 (1981): 278–310. Moshe Weinfeld, *Deuteronomy and the Deuteronomic School* (Oxford, 1976), pp. 236–237.
—BARUCH J. SCHWARTZ

ATHALIAH (Heb. ʿAtalyah; r. 842–836 BCE), queen of Judah. She was the disputed daughter of Omri, king of Israel, or Ahab (*2 Kgs.* 8.18), and she was the wife of Jehoram, king of Judah, and mother of his son and successor Ahaziah (*2 Kgs.* 8.26; *2 Chr.* 22.2). According to *2 Kings* 11 (cf. *2 Chr.* 22–24), after her son was killed by Jehu, she killed all the candidates for succession but one, Ahaziah's infant son, Joash, and reigned for six years. She was responsible for introducing Baal worship during the reign of both her husband and son. A priestly coup in her seventh regnal year, led by Jehoiada and carried out in the Jerusalem Temple, enthroned Joash. Athaliah rushed to the Temple to try and stop the ceremony but was removed and killed.

• Tomoo Ishida, *The Royal Dynasties in Ancient Israel*, Beihefte zur Zeitschrift für die altestamentliche Wissenschaft, vol. 142 (Berlin, 1970), pp. 159–161. Cecile Kahn-Kanner, "ʿAtalyah ve-Tadmitah ha-Miqra'it," master's thesis, Tel Aviv University, 1982, with English summary.
—ATHALYA BRENNER

ATḤALTA' DI-GE'ULLAH (Aram.; אַתְחַלְתָּא דִּגְאֻלָּה; beginning of the redemption), Talmudic term (*Meg.* 17b) synonymous with the concepts of the ingathering of the *exiles and the restoration of the Jewish people to its land. Rabbinic sources compare Israel's future redemption to dawn breaking slowly on the horizon, then spreading its radiance far and wide (Y., *Ber.* 1.1; *Sg. Rab.* 6.16). This idea inspired Religious Zionist thinkers, such as Avraham Yitsḥaq Kook (see KOOK FAMILY), who spoke of the Balfour Declaration (1917) and Jewish settlement in Erets Yisra'el in terms of *atḥalta' di-ge'ullah*. A kindred expression, "the dawn of our redemption," has been used in the *Tefillah le-Shalom ha-Medinah.

• Tsevi Yaron, *Mishnato shel ha-Rav Kuk* (Jerusalem, 1974), pp. 270–274, 311. —GABRIEL A. SIVAN

ATONEMENT, a doctrine resting on the belief that there exists a relationship between individuals and God according to which God looks favorably on people and desires their well-being. That relationship is disturbed when humans fail to act in accordance with the will of God. God does not, however, desire the perdition of people for upsetting that relationship: "As I live, says the Lord, I have no pleasure in the death of the wicked but that the wicked turn from his way and live. Turn you, turn you from your evil ways" (*Ez.* 33.11). Thus God desires the restoration of the desirable norm through the forgiveness of sin. Forgiveness depends on people's expiation of their sin, and it is that expiation that constitutes atonement. Atonement can be effected in a number of ways. It can be achieved through the payment of compensation for wrong committed, through suffering, or through the performance of certain rituals, but all of these presuppose accompanying *repentance and the rectification of one's way of life. The Hebrew word for atonement (*kapparah*) is derived from a legal term signifying "ransom" or "compensation" (paid, for example, by the owner of an ox that has gored a man [*Ex.* 21.30]) and from there passed into ritual and theological use. The Talmud insists that sacrifices were accepted as atonement only for those sins committed in ignorance or unwittingly, but that for those committed deliberately, no sacrifice could avail. Thus, an element of repentance was introduced into the sacrificial rite, which was an act of contrition. Among the common people, however, a tendency developed to regard the sacrifice in itself as a propitiatory offering that would avert divine wrath for a sin committed deliberately, and sacrificing could serve as an atonement for all sins. The prophets inveighed sharply against this belief, stressing instead the moral aspects in such passages as "Shall I come before him with burnt offerings, with calves a year old? He has showed you, O man, what is good, and what does the Lord require of you, but to do justly, and love mercy and walk humbly with your God" (*Mi.* 6.6–8) or the statement of Hosea, "Instead of bulls we will pay [the offering of] our lips" (*Hos.* 14.3). With the destruction of the Temple and the automatic abolition of the sacrificial system, these and similar verses formed the basis of the doctrine of the existence of alternatives to the sacrificial system. These alternative means of atonement can be effected through suffering, repentance, prayer, and good works. In the first category come the statements that "sufferings wipe out transgressions" (Y., *San.* 10) and "death wipes out transgressions" (*Shev.* 8b), though "death expiates together with repentance" (*Yoma'* 8.8). Repentance, which must always include verbal *confession (*viddui*), is the broad highway to atonement, and rabbinical literature is replete with references to the efficacy of repentance; the effectiveness of *Yom Kippur depends on sincere repentance, and a preparatory ten-day period is assigned to suitable preparation (see 'ASERET YEMEI TESHUVAH). This applies, however, only to sins committed against God; atonement for a wrong against a fellow human involves the seeking of forgiveness and appropriate restitution (*Yoma'* 8.9). Virtually every aspect of "good works" is mentioned as a means of atonement, for instance, "now that there are no sacrifices, a man's table acts as an atonement" (*Ber.* 58a); "acts of kindness bring atonement" (*R. ha-Sh.* 18a); "Charity brings atonement" (*B. B.* 9a); and "good works avert the evil decree" (*Ta'an.* 16a). Repentance must at all times be accompanied by change of conduct, and sincerity is a basic component of atonement. Generally speaking, the doctrine of vicarious atonement plays very little role in Judaism, although suggestions of it are not entirely absent, as in the statement, "the death of the righteous atones [for the world]" (*Lv. Rab.* 20.7).

• Adolf Büchler, *Studies in Sin and Atonement in Rabbinic Literature of the First Century* (New York, 1967). Naftali Hoffner, *Our Faith and Strength* (Spring Valley, N.Y., 1994). Chaim Nussbaum, *The Essence of Teshuvah: A Path to Repentance* (Northvale, N.J., 1993). Nosson Scherman, Hersh Goldwurm, and Avie Gold, eds., *Yom Kippur: Its Significance, Laws, and Prayers* (Brooklyn, N.Y., 1989).

ATONEMENT, DAY OF. See YOM KIPPUR.

'ATSERET. See SHAVU'OT.

ATSILUT (אֲצִילוּת; emanation), term used by rationalists, esoterics, and mystics as a Hebrew translation of the philosophical (essentially Neoplatonic) concept of *emanation. The term is already found in the poetry of Shelomoh ibn Gabirol and Yehudah ha-Levi, and it appears throughout Yehudah ibn Tibbon's (see IBN TIBBON FAMILY) translations into Hebrew of philosophical works in the second half of the twelfth century. Rabbi Avraham ibn Ezra (followed by some Ashkenazi Ḥasidim) used the root *d v q* rather than *a ts l* to convey the same concept. *Atsilut* appears in the late-twelfth-century *Baraiyta'de-Yosef ben 'Uzzi'el* and other treatises of the Unique Cherub circle, as well as in the works of the early kabbalists (but not in *Sefer ha-Bahir*).

The Hebrew term, when used by the kabbalists, is an example of the transformation of a philosophical term into a mystical symbol, which expresses the interrelationship between higher and lower divine powers. Among rationalists, the term denotes the actual process of evolvement of one spiritual realm from another. A treatise entitled *Atsilut*, of unknown authorship and date, reflects the older, pre-fourteenth century Kabbalah.

• Gershom Gerhard Scholem, *Origins of the Kabbalah* (Princeton, 1987), pp. 281–298, 422–426, 446–452. Isaiah Tishby, ed., *The Wisdom of the Zohar* (Oxford, 1989), vol. 1, pp. 230–370. —JOSEPH DAN

ATTAH EḤAD (אַתָּה אֶחָד; You Are One), prayer of geonic origin that introduces the intermediate benediction in the Sabbath afternoon *ʿAmidah. While emphasizing the threefold uniqueness of God the Creator, his people Israel, and the holy day of rest, Attah Eḥad also underlines the spiritual reward that Sabbath-observant Jews will have in the afterlife. It is based on a Midrashic interpretation of *1 Chronicles* 17.21 (see *tosafot* to *Ḥag.* 3b). The sentence relating that the patriarchs enjoyed and rested on the Sabbath derives from a Talmudic tradition (*Yoma'* 28b; *Gn. Rab.* 11. 7–9).

• Ismar Elbogen, *Jewish Liturgy: A Comprehensive History*, translated by Raymond P. Scheindlin (Philadelphia, 1993). Macy Nulman, *The Encyclopedia of Jewish Prayer* (Northvale, N.J., 1993).

—GABRIEL A. SIVAN

ATTAH HAR'ETA LA-DAʿAT (אַתָּה הָרְאֵתָ לָדַעַת; "It has been clearly shown to you [that the Lord, he is God . . . "]), phrase introducing the biblical verses chanted responsively before all Torah scrolls are removed from the synagogue ark and carried in processions (*haqqafot) on the eve and morning of *Simḥat Torah. These verses, first recited by the cantor (or other worshipers in turn), are then repeated by the entire congregation. Ashkenazim chant them to a melody recalling the cantillation used for the *Esther* scroll on *Purim. A shorter sequence is read when Torah scrolls are taken from the ark on Sabbaths and other holy days. In the Sephardi, ʿAdot ha-Mizraḥ, and Hasidic rites, this shorter sequence also begins with Attah Har'eta (*Dt.* 4.35); in the Ashkenazi rite it opens with Ein Kamokhah (*Ps.* 86.8).

• Ismar Elbogen, *Jewish Liturgy: A Comprehensive History*, translated by Raymond P. Scheindlin (Philadelphia, 1993). Macy Nulman, *The Encyclopedia of Jewish Prayer* (Northvale, N.J., 1993). —GABRIEL A. SIVAN

ATTAH NOTEN YAD (אַתָּה נוֹתֵן יָד), a prayer in the confession (*viddui*) for the *Neʿilah service of Yom Kippur, beginning, "You stretch forth your hand to sinners, and your right hand is extended to receive transgressors." This is followed by the prayer, Attah Hivdalta (You Have Set Apart). Both poems share a common theme: God always stands ready to forgive sinners if they repent in sincerity and turn away from violence and oppression. To that end, he has established Yom Kippur, because it is not his will to destroy evil-doers, but to pardon them once they return to him. These prayers, mentioned in *Yoma'* 87b, are found in all traditional and modern prayer books.

• Max Arzt, *Justice and Mercy: Commentary on the Liturgy of the New Year and the Day of Atonement* (New York, 1963), pp. 278ff. Ismar Elbogen, *Jewish Liturgy: A Comprehensive History*, translated by Raymond P. Scheindlin (Philadelphia, 1993), p. 127. —A. STANLEY DREYFUS

ATTAR FAMILY, a family of rabbis in Morocco.

Ḥayyim ibn Mosheh ibn Attar (1696–1743), rabbi and kabbalist. He was born in Salé, Morocco, to a family of Spanish origin. He settled in the important center of Meknes, where he became a kabbalist. Catastrophic events, including anti-Jewish decrees and a famine, awakened in him a determination to go to Erets Yisra'el. En route, in 1739, he was delayed in Leghorn, where he stayed to establish a large *yeshivah*. In 1741 he left Italy for Acre and eventually settled in Jerusalem, where he founded the Midrash Keneset Yisra'el, whose students were noted for their piety and asceticism, which included devotion to prayer and to making pilgrimages to the graves of famous rabbis. His *yeshivah* had an advanced and an elementary department, and ʿAttar headed the former. He died only a year after reaching Jerusalem, but the *yeshivah* continued until 1866.

His *Ri'shon le-Tsiyyon* (Constantinople, 1750) was based on his educational method, which concentrated on the study of the **poseqim*, particularly Maimonides. *Or ha-Ḥayyim* (Venice, 1742) is a commentary on the Pentateuch that was especially popular in Poland, where it was influential in Hasidic circles. Attar held that tradition should be accepted uncritically. *Peri To'ar* (Amsterdam, 1742) is his commentary on the *Shulḥan ʿArukh, Yoreh Deʿah*.

Yehudah ben Yaʿaqov ibn Attar (1655–1733), grandson of Ḥayyim ibn Mosheh ibn Attar; Moroccan rabbinical authority. He was born in Fez and earned his livelihood as a craftsman. In his early thirties he was already recognized throughout northern Morocco as an outstanding rabbi. After a short period in Meknes (1701–1704), he returned to Fez and became *av beit din* (head of the rabbinic court). One of his distinguished disciples, Yaʿaqov *ibn Zur, described him as the greatest rabbi in the Arab world and praised him as an innovator in *halakhah*, particularly expert in the laws of ritual slaughter, and a fine preacher (*darshan*). In collaboration with Yaʿaqov ibn Zur, Yehudah ibn Attar issued ordinances designed to protect the lower social classes. His published works include a collection of *responsa* called *Beit Yehudah* (Jerusalem, 1989), *Minḥat Yehudah* (Meknes, 1940), and *Meqor Ḥayyim* (Jerusalem, 1898), a compendium of the customs of the Fez community in matters of ritual slaughter.

• **Ḥayyim ibn Mosheh ibn Attar**: Shalom Bar-Asher, "The Jews of North Africa and the Land of Israel," in *The Land of Israel: Jewish Perspectives*, edited by Lawrence A. Hoffman (Notre Dame, Ind., 1986). Benjamin Klar, ed., *Rabbi Ḥayyim ibn ʿAttar: ʿAliyyato le-'Erets Yisra'el* (Jerusalem, 1951). Reuben Margaliot, *Toledot Rabbenu Ḥayyim ibn ʿAttar . . .* (Jerusalem, 1988). **Yehudah ben Yaʿaqov ibn Attar:** Shalom Bar-Asher, *Sefer ha-Taqqanot* (Jerusalem, 1990), pp. 259–317. Georges Vajda, ed., *Recueil de textes historiques judeo-marocains* (Paris, 1951), pp. 75–96.

—SHALOM BAR-ASHER

AUFRUFEN (Yi. *oyfrufn*; to be called up [to the Torah reading]), among Yiddish- and German-speaking Ashkenazi Jews, the calling up to the reading of the Torah of a groom on the Sabbath preceding his wedding. This festive occasion is often followed by a collation tendered by the groom's parents. In some Ashkenazi communities, the *Aufrufen* is held two weeks before the wedding, while in Eastern communities, the groom is called to the reading of the Torah on the Sabbath after his marriage.

• Maurice Lamm, *The Jewish Way in Love and Marriage* (San Francisco, 1980), pp. 189–190. —SHMUEL HIMELSTEIN

AUSTRITTSGEMEINDE (Ger.; secession community), German Neo-Orthodox community. In Germany in the second half of the nineteenth century, for tax purposes and other reasons, members of each religion had to belong to that religion's communal structure. Because the majority of German Jews of that era had adopted Reform Judaism, those Jews who still remained Orthodox felt themselves increasingly alienated from the local structure but were prevented by law from leaving it—unless they declared themselves as being "without religion." Finally in 1876, despite opposition of the Reform Jews in Germany, the Prussian parliament passed its *Austrittsgesetz* (secession law), which specified that "a Jew is permitted to leave his local congregation, for religious reasons, without leaving Judaism." This paved the way for a separate Orthodox communal structure, the *Austrittsgemeinde*, which at first consisted of the Adass Jeshurun congregation of Frankfurt, led by R. Samson Raphael *Hirsch, and a number of small congregations in other locations. Although Hirsch led those who had left the organized community, not all Orthodox rabbis followed his lead. Indeed, the majority of Orthodox Jews remained within the general community structure, after receiving assurances that the community would guarantee them the independence to meet their religious needs. As Jews who belonged to the *Austrittsgemeinde* fled the German antisemitism of the 1930s, they established synagogues in different places, notably in New York and in Johannesburg, that bore the name Adass Jeshurun and that propagated the religious ideology of Samson Raphael Hirsch.

• Robert Liberles, "Between Community and Separation: The Resurgence of Orthodoxy in Frankfurt, 1838–1877," Ph.D. dissertation, Jewish Theological Seminary of America, 1979. —SHMUEL HIMELSTEIN

AUTO-DA-FÉ. See INQUISITION.

AUTONOMY, a form of self-government in which Jews, even though not living in their own sovereign land, were granted the right to control much of their own lives in the religious, judicial, and social spheres. The autonomy that Jews enjoyed at various times during the two thousand years of exile was almost always a group autonomy—individuals who belonged to the group were allowed certain specified rights—as opposed to territorial autonomy, in which those living in a certain territory have rights within that particular area. In most cases, whatever autonomy Jews enjoyed was the result of a grant by the governing authorities, which could be withdrawn at any moment. As early as the Greek and Roman eras, Jews in cities with large Jewish populations, such as Alexandria, enjoyed a considerable degree of freedom in shaping their lives. Later, in the Middle Ages, Jews were frequently granted various rights of self-rule by the reigning monarch or ecclesiastic, often after having made a direct contribution to the ruler's coffers or having provided some other benefit or service to him or his government. Jews generally enjoyed the right to determine for themselves those matters that affected them internally but were restricted in those areas that impinged on their contacts with others, such as trade or litigation with non-Jews. Certain actions that might be construed as "insulting" to the Christian religion were often forbidden. Thus there were regions where Jews were prohibited from leaving their homes during Christian religious processions or on certain Christian holy days.

In Islamic lands, Jews as well as Christians were considered "Peoples of the Book" and enjoyed a similar autonomy. A noteworthy example was Babylonia, where the head of the Jewish community (the exilarch) held a position of high honor in the general society, and the ga'on, the head of the academy, was recognized by the Sassanian rulers and subsequently by the caliphate.

Historically, Jewish life has been regulated by various autonomous bodies. Rabbinic courts of law were empowered to adjudicate in cases in which both litigants were Jews and to force their decision upon the litigants, using if necessary the threat of social and religious ostracism to ensure compliance. Jewish communal authorities had the right to assess each Jew his share of the communal tax burden and then force him to pay. The most powerful autonomous body until the *Emancipation was the *qehillah*, the local community council, which by means of **taqqanot* (enactments) filled an ongoing legislative function within each community.

A change occurred with emancipation, when Jews were granted the rights and duties of all other citizens. Those Jewish communal organizations that now exist in the Diaspora are voluntary autonomous associations. See also COMMUNITY.

• Daniel H. Frank, ed., *Autonomy and Judaism* (Albany, 1992). Moshe Sokol, ed., *Rabbinic Authority and Personal Autonomy* (Northvale, N.J., 1992).

AUTOPSIES. The dissection of a corpse counters various biblical prohibitions (*Ḥul.* 11b; *B. B.* 154a) and is only permitted for the sake of saving human life or if civil law requires it to resolve a legal matter. The leading rabbinic *responsum* in this area is by R. Yeḥezqe'l Landau, who was prepared to permit a post-mortem examination on the victim of a bladder disease if the results would be immediately beneficial for another patient suffering from the same illness. Since the chances of such a direct and immediate benefit were very remote, Landau did not allow the autopsy in this particular case. According to R. Yaʿaqov Ettlinger, it is permissible to carry out a post-mortem if the deceased had freely consented to such a procedure during his lifetime. Modern authorities permit autopsies for the purpose of establishing the cause of death and in the case of hereditary diseases. Corneal grafts are also permitted. Rabbi Mosheh Feinstein allowed post-mortem needle biopsies of various organs, since such procedures do not constitute desecration of a corpse. It is also permissible to remove samples of blood through a needle puncture and to carry out a post-mortem peritoneoscopy. The trend among modern halakhists is to relax the strict prohibition on post-mortems that are not immediately therapeutic in nature but are nevertheless reasonably likely to be instrumental in the saving of human life. All body parts used in a post-mortem must, wherever possible, be returned to the family for burial. In the State of Israel, since the passage of the Anatomy and Physiology Act in

1953, autopsies have been the subject of intensive parliamentary and public debate. This law gives fairly wide powers to physicians to order an autopsy, but in practice the wishes of the family are taken into account when an autopsy is under consideration. In general, Reform Judaism permits autopsies.

• Isaac Klein, *Responsa and Halakhic Studies* (New York, 1975), pp. 34–42. *The Mount Sinai Hospital and Medical Center Symposia on Medicine and Halacha (Jewish Law)*, vol. 2, pt. 2, *Halacha and Autopsy* (Chicago, 1970–). Fred Rosner, "Autopsy in Jewish Law and the Israeli Autopsy Controversy," in *Jewish Bioethics*, edited by Fred Rosner and J. David Bleich (New York, 1979), pp. 331–348. —DANIEL SINCLAIR

AV (אָב), fifth month of the Jewish religious year, eleventh of the civil year. The rabbis said "When Av comes in, gladness must be diminished" (*Ta'an.* 4.6), and the month is also called Menaḥem (Comforter). "Av" either is a reference to the divine father (*av*) comforting his people after the destruction of the Temple, which took place in that month, or to the name of the Messiah, who, tradition says, will be born on 9 Av. Av always has thirty days, and its zodiacal sign is Leo; the name of the month is not mentioned in the Bible and is derived from the Akkadian language.

One Av is the date observed as the anniversary of the death of Aaron. The first nine days of Av (see BEIN HA-METSARIM) are a sorrowful period culminating with 9 Av, *Tish'ah be-'Av, a fast day commemorating, among other Jewish calamities, the destruction of both Temples. The Sabbath before 9 Av was at one time known as the Sabbath of Punishment and later as the Sabbath of Vision (Shabbat Ḥazon, from the opening word of the prophetic portion from the *Book of Isaiah*). It became customary during these nine days not to eat meat or drink wine (except on the Sabbath) or perform marriages; however, festivities—such as a circumcision feast—are observed as usual during this period. Fifteen Av was a day of rejoicing in the Second Temple period (see TU BE-'AV).

• Nathan Bushwick, *Understanding the Jewish Calendar* (New York, 1989). George Zinberg, *Jewish Calendar Mystery Dispelled* (New York, 1963). —CHAIM PEARL

AVADDON (אֲבַדּוֹן; place of destruction), a poetic synonym for the nether world. Etymologically, *avaddon* is derived from the verb meaning "to be destroyed," together with the appended nominal suffix meaning "place of." *Avaddon* occurs only six times in the Bible, in *Psalms* (88.12), *Proverbs* (15.11, 27.21), and *Job* (26.6, 28.22, 31.12). Just as the other terms for the nether world are personified (e.g., *Is.* 5.14, 28.15, 18; *Hb.* 2.5), *avaddon* is similarly personified as insatiable (*Prv.* 27.21; cf. *Is.* 5.14 and *Hb.* 2.5), bearing witness (*Jb.* 28.22; cf. *Ps.* 44.2), and even naked (*Jb.* 26.6; cf. *Prv.* 15.11 and *Jb.* 24.7).

• H. G. Grether, "Abaddon," in *The Anchor Bible Dictionary*, vol. 1 (New York, 1992), p. 6. M. Hutter, "Abaddon," in *Dictionary of Deities and Demons in the Bible* (Leiden, 1995), pp. 1–2. N. J. Tromp, *Primitive Conceptions of Death and the Netherworld in the Old Testament* (Rome, 1969), pp. 80–81. —CHAIM COHEN

'AVADIM, minor tractate, consisting of three chapters, compiled (probably in Palestine) during the period of the ge'onim, dealing with the laws of *slavery. Laws regarding slaves follow the halakhic division of slaves into three categories: Hebrew manservants, Hebrew maidservants, and "Canaanite" (i.e., gentile) slaves. Laws discussed include the forms of acquisition and manumission of slaves as well as the mutual obligations of slave and master. The tension between the slave as chattel and as personality governs many of the laws in this tractate.

• Michael Higger, ed. and trans., *Seven Minor Treatises* (1930; Jerusalem, 1971). —AVRAHAM WALFISH

'AVADIM HAYINU (עֲבָדִים הָיִינוּ; "we were slaves"), the first words of the answer to the four questions (**mah nishtannah*) in the *Pesaḥ *Seder (see HAGGADAH OF PESAḤ). As prescribed in Mishnah *Pesaḥim* 10.4, the response to the questions must "begin with humiliation and conclude with glory." According to Shemu'el (3d cent. CE), the first requirement is fulfilled by the clause *'Avadim hayinu*, "We were slaves to Pharaoh in Egypt," and the second requirement by the remainder of the sentence, "and the Lord our God brought us out . . . ," a happy culmination to the degradation of servitude (*Pes.* 116a). The passage concludes with the reminder that God's liberation affected not only the Hebrew slaves in Egypt but also their descendants to the very present and that, therefore, it is proper to look upon Pesaḥ not as a single episode in Jewish history but, instead, as a symbol of God's repeated deliverance of his people.

• Nahum N. Glatzer, ed., *The Passover Haggadah*, based on the commentaries of E. D. Goldschmidt (New York, 1969), p. 23. Abraham Z. Idelsohn, *Jewish Liturgy and Its Development* (New York, 1967), p. 180. —A. STANLEY DREYFUS

AVAQ RIBBIT. See MONEYLENDING.

AV BEIT DIN. See BEIT DIN.

AVELEI TSIYYON (אֲבֵלֵי צִיּוֹן; Mourners for Zion [based on *Is.* 61.3]), groups of Jews who, after the destruction of the Second Temple, observed daily mourning customs and ascetic practices and devoted much time to praying for the redemption of Zion. The Talmud (*B.B.* 60b) refers to the custom of ascetics who abstained from meat and wine as a sign of mourning. After the Arab conquest of Jerusalem in the seventh century CE, Jews were allowed to settle again in Jerusalem, which encouraged a revival of messianic feelings and of the Avelei Tsiyyon. The group in Jerusalem lived in great poverty and was dependent on donations from Diaspora communities. Groups of Avelei Tsiyyon also existed in Germany, Italy, Yemen, and other eastern countries. Most of the *Karaites who established an important community in Jerusalem in the tenth and eleventh centuries adopted the group's customs and developed special mourning practices and liturgies. Karaite leaders, such as Daniyye'l ben Mosheh al-*Qumisi and *Sahl ben Matsliaḥ, wrote to the Karaites in the Diaspora encouraging them to come to Jerusalem in order to live as ascetics and pray for the redemption. Almost all traces of the Avelei Tsiyyon in Palestine were lost after the conquest of Palestine by the Seljuks in 1071 and the Crusaders in 1099, although the twelfth-century traveler

Benjamin of Tudela reports that he heard of similar groups in Yemen and Germany.

• Salo W. Baron, *A Social and Religious History of the Jews*, vol. 5 (New York, 1957), pp. 185, s.v. index. M. Zucker in *Sefer ha-Yovel . . . Ḥ. Albeck* (Jerusalem, 1963), pp. 378–401. H. Ben-Shammai in *Keneset ʿEzra': Sifrut ve-Ḥayyim be-Veit ha-Keneset: Asupat Maʿamarim Mugeshet le-ʿEzra' Fleisher* (Jerusalem, 1994), pp. 191–234. —DAVID E. SKLARE

AVELUT. See MOURNING.

AVENGER OF BLOOD. See BLOOD AVENGER.

ʿAVERAH. See SIN.

AV HA-RAḤAMIM (אַב הָרַחֲמִים; Merciful Father), martyrs' memorial dirge; probably composed after the Crusader massacres between 1096 and 1099. It is found only in the Ashkenazi rite. The prayer, whose author is unknown, was originally said twice a year (on the Sabbaths before Shavuʿot and before Tishʿah be-'Av), but it later became customary to recite it every Sabbath (with certain exceptions, varying in different communities). It calls on God to avenge the Jews who have been murdered, thus expressing the frustration of a powerless community in the face of disaster. A short prayer with the same opening is recited in certain Orthodox synagogues before the reading of the Torah.

• Israel Davidson, *Thesaurus of Medieval Jewish Poetry*, vol. 1 (New York, 1970), p. 40. Ismar Elbogen, *Jewish Liturgy: A Comprehensive History*, translated by Raymond P. Scheindlin (Philadelphia and New York, 1993), p. 162. Mary Nulman, *The Encyclopedia of Jewish Prayer* (Northvale, N.J., 1993) pp. 54–55. Eric Werner, "Traces of Jewish Hagiolatry," *Hebrew Union College Annual* 51 (1980): 39–60.

AVI AVI (אָבִי אָבִי; My Father, My Father), a Sephardi **qinah* recited on 9 *Av, the occasion commemorating the destruction of the First Temple in 586 BCE and the Second Temple in 70 CE. The poem has a refrain, *Bore', ʿad annah . . . ?*, "Creator, how long . . . ?" The author, an otherwise unknown Binyamin, portrays Zion as a dove trapped by a snare, sitting desolate, and crying out for relief from suffering.

• Israel Davidson, *Otsar ha-Shirah veha-Piyyut: Mi-Zeman Ḥatimat Kitvei ha-Qodesh ʿad Re'shit Tequfat ha-Haskalah* (New York, 1970), vol. 2, p. 13, no. 275. —A. STANLEY DREYFUS

AVINU MALKENU (אָבִינוּ מַלְכֵּנוּ; Our Father, Our King), litany of supplication recited during the *ʿAseret Yemei Teshuvah (except on Sabbath and the afternoon service prior to Yom Kippur) and on fast days (except Tishʿah be-'Av); each line begins with the words *avinu malkenu*. The Talmud (*Taʿan.* 25b) relates that the basic formula was recited by R. ʿAqiva' on the occasion of a drought. Avinu Malkenu created a new pattern of petitional prayer by connecting the most intimate and the most formal epithets applying to God (father, king in the opening formula) and *confession of sins (in the opening and concluding line) with the confession of faith and the plea for divine grace. This basic pattern was later elaborated on, and by geonic times the prayer contained some twenty-nine verses (and later, in the Ashkenazi rite, forty-four). In Reform usage, the prayer is recited only on Ro'sh ha-Shanah and Yom Kippur and sometimes modified in translation and even in the Hebrew to avoid the biblical and rabbinic description of God as father and king in the light of feminist criticism.

• Ismar Elbogen, *Jewish Liturgy: A Comprehensive History*, translated by Raymond P. Scheindlin (Philadelphia, 1993). Joseph Heinemann, *Prayer in the Talmud*, Studia Judaica, Bd. 9 (Berlin and New York, 1977), pp. 150–151, 189–190. Lawrence A. Hoffman, ed., *Gates of Understanding*, vol. 2 (New York, 1984), pp. 23–25. —PETER LENHARDT

AVINU SHE-BA-SHAMAYIM (אָבִינוּ שֶׁבַּשָּׁמַיִם; "Our Father, who is in heaven"), a phrase that occurs only once in the traditional *siddur* (*prayer book) as the beginning of an invocation: in the last paragraph of the Morning Benedictions (see BIRKHOT HA-SHAḤAR). The old liturgists may have avoided this usage because it is the beginning of the Lord's Prayer (*Mt.* 6.9) that Jesus taught to his disciples. Occasionally occurring in the *siddur* is the formula, "May it be the will of our Father who is in heaven . . . ." Liturgical variants of *Avinu she-ba-shamayim* are *Elohenu she-ba-shamayim*, "Our God who is in heaven," and, in Aramaic, *Maran di-vi-shemaya'*, "Our Master who is in heaven." Much more common is the invocation **Avinu malkenu*, "Our Father, our King." The Yiddish equivalent has been much used in Hasidic prayers and petitions.

• Claude G. Montefiore, *Rabbinic Literature and Gospel Teachings* (London, 1930), pp. 125ff. —A. STANLEY DREYFUS

AVIV (אָבִיב), Abib in English Bible translations (cf. *Dt.* 16.1), is the first month of the year according to biblical nomenclature, corresponding to the Hebrew month of *Nisan. The word probably originally referred to the season of the ripening of the corn and was later applied to the spring season in general. —CHAIM PEARL

ʿAVODAH (עֲבוֹדָה), the sacred service; usually applied to the service performed by the priests in the *Temple and, more specifically, to the service conducted by the *high priest on *Yom Kippur. This is described in *Leviticus* 16.2–34, and a liturgical and poetic version is included in the *Musaf service for Yom Kippur. The basis for this version is passages from *Yoma'* (which gives a lengthy description of the ʿAvodah, elaborated in both Talmuds) together with appropriate *piyyutim* (called ʿAvodah; see PIYYUT), which vary between the Ashkenazi, Sephardi, and other rites. The Reform liturgy confines its ʿAvodah section to the high priest's confession.

The ʿAvodah on Yom Kippur was the most important religious function of the high priest and the most awesome moment of the Temple ritual. It was the sole occasion that he entered the Holy of Holies, where he sought atonement three times, first for himself, then for the priestly family, and finally for the entire people of Israel. It was also the only time that he uttered the Tetragrammaton, the ineffable name of God (YHVH). The ʿAvodah as the Temple sacrifice generally led to several rabbinic statements that indicate its centrality until the Temple fell and made sacrifice impossible. The rabbis said that the world stands on three things: Torah, ʿAvodah, and kindness (*Avot* 1.2). With the destruction of the Second Temple, it was laid down that "prayer is *ʿavodah*" (*Pirqei de-Rabbi Eliʿezer*, 16). The Talmudic phrase

"What is *ʿavodah* in the heart? It is prayer" (*Taʿan.* 2a) led to the common appellation of prayer as "*ʿavodah* in the heart."

• Max Arzt, *Justice and Mercy: A Commentary on the Liturgy of the New Year and the Day of Atonement* (New York, 1963). I. Brodie and J. Rabbinowitz, eds., *Studies in Jewish History: The Adolph Büchler Memorial Volume* (London, New York, 1956), pp. 24–63. Adolf Büchler, "Zur Geschichte des Tempelkultus in Jerusalem," in *Festschrift zu Daniel Chwolson* (Berlin, 1899), pp. 1–41. Menahem Haran, *Temples and Temple-Service in Ancient Israel* (Winona Lake, Ind., 1985). Lawrence A. Hoffman, *Beyond the Text: A Holistic Approach to Liturgy* (Bloomington, Ind., 1987), pp. 102–148. Yom-tov Lewinsky, *Entsiqlopedyah Havai u-Masoret ba-Yahadut*, vol. 2 (Tel Aviv, 1975), pp. 523–524. Zvi Malachi, "Seder ʿAvodat Yom ha-Kippurim: Meqorotav ve-Toledotav shel ha-Sug ha-Piyyuti," in *Be-No'am Si'aḥ: Peraqim mi-Toledot Sifrutenu* (Lod, 1983), pp. 76–103. Solomon Zeitlin, *Studies in the Early History of Judaism* (New York, 1973), pp. 143–175.
—CHAIM PEARL

ʿAVODAH ZARAH (עֲבוֹדָה זָרָה; Idolatrous Worship), tractate in Mishnah order Neziqin, consisting of five chapters, with related material in the Tosefta' and in both Talmuds. It deals with laws concerning the prohibition against idolatry and the attitude to be adopted toward objects and people associated with idolatrous practices. Founded upon biblical strictures, the tractate seeks to apply these principles to the reality of life under pagan Roman domination. The Mishnah extends its discussion of idolatry to include the broader issue of demarcating the permissible boundaries of Jewish intercourse with pagans in the commercial and cultural spheres. Certain forms of social intercourse—intermarriage, for example—were strictly prohibited.

Other laws in this tractate delineate objects and places that are to be regarded as idolatrous as well as the prohibitions that attach to them. Special attention is devoted to the subject of wine belonging to or touched by a pagan, due to the special significance of wine in worship and in social contacts. An edition of the manuscript in the library of the Jewish Theological Seminary of America was published by S. Abramson in 1957. The Talmud Bavli tractate was translated into English by A. Mishcon and A. Cohen in the Soncino Talmud (1935).

• Chanoch Albeck, ed., *Shishah Sidrei Mishnah, Seder Neziqin* 2d ed., (Jerusalem, 1956). Philip Blackman, ed. and trans., *Mishnayot*, vol. 4, *Order Neziqin* (Gateshead, 1973). Pinhas Kehati, ed., *Mishnah: A New Translation with a Commentary, Seder Neziqin*, vol. 2, *Bava' Batra', Sanhedrin* (Jerusalem, 1988). Saul Lieberman, *Hellenism in Jewish Palestine* (1950; New York, 1994). Hermann Leberecht Strack, *Introduction to the Talmud and Midrash* (1931; Minneapolis, 1992).
—AVRAHAM WALFISH

AVOT (אָבוֹת; Fathers), name of a prayer and of a Mishnaic tractate.

Prayer. *Avot* is the first blessing in the ʿAmidah, so called because of its reference to "the God of Abraham, the God of Isaac, and the God of Jacob"; the eulogy of "God of our fathers"; and its concluding reference to God as the "shield of Abraham." The prayer invokes the merits of the ancestors (see ZEKHUT AVOT). According to rabbinic legend, the blessing was instituted by Abraham when escaping from Ur. In certain contemporary non-Orthodox liturgies, references are added to the *matriarchs.

• Ismar Elbogen, *Jewish Liturgy: A Comprehensive History*, translated by Raymond P. Scheindlin (Philadelphia, 1993). Avrohom Chaim Feuer, *Shemoneh Esrei: The Amidah/The Eighteen Blessings* (Brooklyn, N.Y., 1990).

Tractate. The tractate *Avot*, in Mishnah order Neziqin, is also known as *Pirqei Avot*. It contains five chapters, to which was added, probably in geonic times, a sixth chapter, "Pereq Qinyan Torah," containing teachings in praise of Torah study. There is no parallel Tosefta'; however, the minor tractate **Avot de-Rabbi Natan* serves as a kind of Tosefta' to *Avot*. It has no *gemara'* in either Talmud, but there exists a nineteenth-century collection of related Talmudic material known as *Masseḥet Avot ʿim Talmud Bavli ve-Yerushalmi*. The name *Avot* is thought to derive from a title commonly accorded to leading sages, whose aphorisms, containing ethical and spiritual wisdom, are collected in the tractate. Alternatively, the title *Avot* may be understood to mean fundamental principles (cf. *Shab.* 1.1; *B. Q.* 1.1).

Avot is the sole Mishnaic tractate devoid of halakhic content; nor does it contain aggadic narrative. It may have been placed in Neziqin as a juxtaposition to the discussion of judiciary matters, legal character, and the ethical teachings of the judges and spiritual leaders of the community. *Bava' Qamma'* 30a suggests that scrupulous observance of *neziqin* (monetary laws) and of the precepts of *Avot* are pathways to piety.

The major themes of *Avot* include the centrality of Torah study and its relation to observance of commandments, freedom of choice, divine providence, divine and human justice, reward and punishment, the world to come, and the nature of a pious personality. The first two chapters present the chain of transmission of the oral law from Moses to the Men of the *Keneset ha-Gedolah and include rabbinic teachings and aphorisms in chronological order, listing eminent teachers, among whom the patriarchal descendants of Hillel and R. Yoḥanan ben Zakk'ai and his disciples are prominently featured. This structure serves to emphasize the close connection between legal and ethical authority in rabbinic thinking. In the following two chapters, the chronological structure is abandoned and the maxims of the rabbis are arranged according to thematic, associative, and mnemonic principles characteristic of the Mishnah as a whole. The bulk of the fifth chapter comprises statements based on numerical teachings, opening with ten sayings by means of which the world was created and concluding with four types of rabbinic students.

A mark of *Avot*'s popularity and influence is its inclusion in the liturgical recitations of many communities and in many editions of the traditional prayer book. As a result, *Avot* has been reproduced and reprinted more often than any other Talmudic work and has been translated into many languages. English translations are to be found in prayer books and standard translations of the Mishnah.

• Judah Goldin, *The Living Talmud* (New York, 1957). R. Travers Herford, Pirkē Arboth (New York, 1925).
—AVRAHAM WALFISH

AVOT DE-RABBI NATAN, a minor tractate that serves as a companion volume to tractate *Avot*. Similar in form to the Tosefta', it relates to much of the material in *Avot* and largely follows the same order as *Avot*. *Avot de-Rabbi Natan* is traditionally ascribed to the second-century tanna' R. Natan ha-Bavli, even though he preceded R. Yehudah ha-Nasi', redactor of the Mishnah. This discrepancy as well as the appearance in *Avot de-Rabbi Natan* of many later sages and a good deal of clearly later material may be explained by assuming that the material in *Avot de-Rabbi Natan* underwent numerous redactions and that the earliest redaction of it corresponded to a pre-Mishnaic redaction of tractate *Avot*. This may further account for the existence of *Avot de-Rabbi Natan* in two versions, A and B, first published together in a scientific edition by Solomon Schechter in 1887.

In addition to the maxims and teachings of the sages, which complement the material found in *Avot*, *Avot de-Rabbi Natan* also contains a great deal of Midrashic material, including lengthy digressions on such topics as the creation of Adam and Eve, Adam and Eve and the serpent, and the deaths of Moses and Aaron. There are many biographical anecdotes about the sages, some of which provide important insights into their thinking. Prominent issues discussed in *Avot de-Rabbi Natan* include the dispute between Beit Hillel and Beit Shamm'ai about whether Torah study should be the province of the elite or broadly based; the Sadducean denial of the world to come; the character and teachings of Elisha' ben Avuyah; the siege of Jerusalem; and the religious performances that filled the spiritual gap left by the destruction of the Temple. English translations of *Avot de-Rabbi Natan* have been done by Judah Goldin (*The Fathers According to Rabbi Nathan* [version A; New Haven, 1955]) and Anthony J. Saldarini (*The Fathers According to Rabbi Nathan* [version B; Leiden, 1975]).

An English translation of the tractate also appears in *The Minor Tractates of the Talmud* (Soncino edition, 1966).

• Louis Finkelstein, *Mavo' le-Massekhtot Avot ve-'Avot de-Rabbi Natan* (New York, 1950).

—AVRAHAM WALFISH

AVOT MELA'KHOT (אָבוֹת מְלָאכוֹת), the thirty-nine chief categories of work or creative activity forbidden on the *Sabbath. These general categories have been divided into many different subcategories, which are called *toladot* (progeny, i.e., secondary prohibitions). The importance of determining whether a particular prohibited activity is an *av* (father, i.e., primary prohibition) or a *toladah* is limited to the forms of sacrificial penitence required during Temple times and whether multiple violations require multiple acts of penitence or a single act of penitence.

According to R. Ḥanina' bar Ḥama', the *avot mela'khot* are "based on the work done to create the Tabernacle. Rabbi Yonatan ben Eli'ezer in the name of Rabbi Shim'on ben Yosei ben Laqunya' states that the thirty-nine categories are based on the number of times that the word *mela'khah* [and its cognates] appears in the Bible" (*Shab.* 49b). Yet other origins for the number thirty-nine can also be found. The thirty-nine prohibited categories are: plowing, sowing, reaping, gathering sheaves, threshing, winnowing, separating, grinding, sifting, kneading, baking, shearing, bleaching, combing, dyeing, spinning, making a warp, making a thread, weaving threads, splitting threads, knotting, untying a knot, sewing, tearing, trapping, slaughtering, skinning, tanning, ruling lines, scraping hides, cutting to size, writing, erasing, building, destroying, finishing a job, lighting fire, extinguishing a fire, and carrying.

• "Avot Mela'khot," in *Entsiqlopedyah Talmudit* (Jerusalem, 1947–), vol. 1, pp. 44–47. Mordecai ben Avraham Banet, *Magen Avot: 'Al ha-Lamed-Tet Avot Melakhot* (Jerusalem, 1967).

—MICHAEL BROYDE

AVOT NEZIQIN. See TORTS.

AVRAHAM ABELE OF GOMBIN. See GOMBINER, AVRAHAM ABELE.

AVRAHAM BAR ḤAYYA' (died c.1136), philosopher and polymath in Spain. He lived in Barcelona, but little is known about his life apart from his having occupied a leading position in the Jewish, and perhaps in the general, community. He wrote in Hebrew on astronomy and astrology, mathematics, geography, optics, and music. As a translator from Arabic to Latin he collaborated with the Christian scholar Plato of Tivoli, who introduced the Ptolemaic system to the western world. His philosophical works were the first to be written in Hebrew, and Avraham bar Ḥayya' had to coin much of the terminology. His choice of a type of Mishnaic Hebrew was highly influential in the development of the language.

His two main philosophical works are *Megillat ha-Megalleh* (edited by A. Poznanski [1921]), an eschatological work written to determine the end of time (concluding that the Messiah would appear some time between 1136 and 1448, the latter year being the date for the resurrection of the dead), and *Hegyon ha-Nefesh ha-'Atsuvah* (edited by G. Wigoder [1971]), dealing with ethical and philosophical problems supported by proofs adduced from homiletic exegesis of the Bible. The main topics of the latter are creation, repentance, good and evil, and the saintly life. Two of the book's four sections are based on expositions of the prophetical portions read on Yom Kippur.

Unlike many other medieval philosophers, Avraham bar Ḥayya' does not seek proofs for the existence of God, which he assumes, as he does creation *ex nihilo*. His work to reconcile Jewish cosmogony and other non-Jewish philosophies has usually been classified as Neoplatonic (notably his theory of emanations and doctrine of light) with an element of Aristotelianism (L. D. Stitskin, however [in *Judaism as a Philosophy*], claims that he was the first Jewish Aristotelian, notably in his theories of form and matter and of potentiality and actuality). The scientific work of Avraham bar Ḥayya' is frequently quoted by Christian scholars, although it was his philosophic and eschatological writings that influenced Jewish thinkers throughout the Middle Ages. Moreover, he was a source for kabbalistic writers, including the author of the *Sefer ha-Bahir*, and members of the *Ḥasidei Ashkenaz.

• Isaac Husik, *History of Medieval Jewish Philosophy* (New York, 1941), pp. 114–124. Leon D. Stitskin, *Judaism as a Philosophy: The Philosophy of Abraham bar Ḥayya, 1065–1143* (Brooklyn, N.Y., 1960). Geoffrey Wigoder's Introduction to *The Meditation of the Sad Soul*, by Abraham bar Ḥayya (New York, 1969).

AVRAHAM BEN ʿAZRI'EL (13th cent.), Bohemian Talmudist; a student of the Ḥasidei Ashkenaz. His *Arugat ha-Bosem*, written c.1234, includes extensive comments on Sabbath and festival *piyyutim* and on penitential prayers. The work demonstrates the author's extensive learning in all branches of rabbinic literature; however, because of its prolixity, it was virtually forgotten until its discovery by Abraham *Berliner in 1874. Its importance was then recognized as a source for the teachings of the ri'shonim.

• Efraim Elimelekh Urbach, *Arugat ha-Bosem* (Jerusalem, 1939).

AVRAHAM BEN DAVID OF POSQUIÈRES (c.1120–1198), southern French Talmudist, also known as Rabad III. Menaḥem *Me'iri referred to him as "the greatest of commentators." His explications of the Talmud and conceptual formulations revealed originality of his keen powers of analytical thinking. Although only two complete original commentaries have been recently published from manuscripts, many of his other commentaries can be reconstructed by means of extensive quotations in later medieval works. He was particularly expert at composing topical essays in which he analyzed pertinent halakhic texts and formulated final halakhic decisions. These include essays on the four species for Sukkot (*Hilkhot Lulav*); his code on tractate *Yadayim*, *Perush Yadayim*; his *Ḥibbur Harsha'ot*; *Issur Mashehu* (which deals with the dietary laws [published in part in *Sifron shel Ri'shonim*, edited by S. Asaf (Jerusalem, 1935)]); and *Baʿalei Nefesh* (Venice, 1602; Jerusalem, 1964, which includes *Hilkhot Lulav*, *Ḥibbur Harsha'ot* and *Perush Yadayim*). *Baʿalei Nefesh* deals for the most part with family purity, and the last chapter suggests the means by which a man could attain self-control and purity of heart in sexual matters. Avraham also wrote a comprehensive commentary to the *Midreshei Halakhah*, but only his commentary to the *Sifra'* on *Leviticus* is extant (Constantinople, 1523; Vienna, 1862). Likewise he penned scholarly commentaries to the Mishnaic tractates of *ʿEduyyot* and *Qinnim* (which appear in standard editions of Talmud). He is also known for his critical notes (*hassagot*) on the works of Yitsḥaq Alfasi, Zeraḥyah ha-Levi, and Maimonides. His critique of the venerable codifier Alfasi was deferential but objective. However, his strictures of Zeraḥyah were acrimonious, reflecting a lifelong literary quarrel between them. Avraham accused Zeraḥyah of plagiarism, undue reliance upon northern French commentaries, and ineptness. Avraham's review, written at the end of his life, of Maimonides' *Mishneh Torah* reflects a critical attitude toward philosophy. Avraham was influential in the dissemination of Kabbalah in southern France, and one or two kabbalistic works have been attributed to him. His son and grandsons were involved in kabbalistic studies, and they claimed to have been his disciples in this field. Dozens of *responsa* by Avraham (Y. Kafaḥ, ed. [Jerusalem, 1964]) demonstrate his role as community leader in southern France. He was constantly asked to adjudicate legal problems, and his decisions were regarded as authoritative. He ran his own rabbinical academy in Posquières.

• Heinrich Gross, *Gallia judaica: Dictionnaire géographique de la France d'après les sources rabbiniques* (Paris, 1897; repr. Amsterdam, 1969, with a supplement by Simon Schwarzfuchs). Daniel Jeremy Silver, *Maimonidean Criticism and the Maimonidean Controversy 1180–1240* (Leiden, 1965). Haym Soloveitchik, "History of Halakhah–Methodological Issues: A Review Essay of Isadore Twersky's 'Rabad of Posquières,'" *Jewish History* 5.1 (Spring 1991): 75–124. Haym Soloveitchik, "Rabad of Posquières: A Programmatic Essay," in *Studies in the History of Jewish Society in the Middle Ages and the Modern Period*, edited by Imanu'el Etkes and Yosef Salmon (Jerusalem, 1980), pp. 7–40. Israel M. Ta-Shema, *Rabbi Zeraḥiah ha-Levi–Baʿal ha-Ma'or u-Venei Ḥugo: Le-Toldot ha-Safrut ha-Rabanit be-Provans* (Jerusalem, 1992). Isadore Twersky, *Rabad of Posquières: A Twelfth-Century Talmudist* (Philadelphia, 1980).

—SHLOMO H. PICK

AVRAHAM BEN DOV BER OF MEZHIRECH (c.1741–1776), Hasidic rabbi; son of *Dov Ber of Mezhirech, the second central leader of the Hasidic movement. Growing up in the circle of his father's disciples, Avraham was known as the study partner of R. *Shneur Zalman of Lyady. Legend has it that he was a master of secret lore, perhaps learned from his father, which he imparted to Shneur Zalman, who in turn was his teacher when it came to the revealed Torah. Avraham heightened the ascetic tendencies of his father, turning away from the rejection of asceticism that characterized Yisra'el ben Eliʿezer *Baʿal Shem Tov's approach to life. He was an inner-directed and otherworldly person. Thus, he did not leave disciples or lead a community, despite a great attachment to the ideal of the *tsaddiq*, as is evident in his surviving writings. His early death was considered a great tragedy among the disciples of his father. His teachings were collected in *Ḥesed le-'Avraham* (Chernovtsy, 1851).

• *Entsiqlopedyah la-Ḥasidut*, vol. 2 (Jerusalem, 1986), p. 32. Samuel A. Horodezky, *Ha-Ḥasidut veha-Ḥasidim*, 4 vols. (Tel Aviv, 1953), vol. 2, pp. 47–56.

—ARTHUR GREEN

AVRAHAM BEN ELIʿEZER HA-LEVI (1460–1528), kabbalist in Spain before the expulsion of 1492, who after that time wandered in many communities of Italy, Greece, Turkey, and Egypt, finally settling in Jerusalem in 1514. In his many treatises, he described the transformation of the *Kabbalah, during and immediately after the period of the expulsion, into an intense messianic and apocalyptic system of thought. His writings are dedicated to the elucidation of the date of the redemption, expounding biblical and kabbalistic sources. He wrote commentaries on *Daniel*; on the "Ḥeleq" chapter in the Talmud (*San.* 10), which has strong eschatological elements; and on the apocalyptic "prophecy of the child," which was famous at the end of the fifteenth century. In his *Iggeret Sod ha-Ge'ullah*, written in Jerusalem in 1521, he presented his proof that the *Messiah would come in the following decade and called for repentance in preparation. Most of his writings were not printed, but sections of his treatises have been published by Gershom Gerhard Scholem.

• Ira Robinson, "Abraham ben Eliezer Halevi: Kabbalist and Messianic Visionary of the Early Sixteenth Century," Ph.D. dissertation, Harvard University, 1980.

—JOSEPH DAN

AVRAHAM BEN ELIYYAHU OF VILNA (1750–1808), scholar; son of R. *Eliyyahu ben Shelomoh Zalman of Vilna (the Vilna Ga'on), the greatest Talmudist of his time. In addition to publishing a few of his father's works, in which he incorporated some of his father's oral teachings, Avraham was a significant scholar in his own right. His major field of interest was Midrashic literature. In this area he published *Rav Pe'alim* (1894), a commentary on over one hundred different *midrashim*. He also published an edition of *Midrash Aggadat be-Re'shit* (Vilna, 1802), commentaries on the *Book of Psalms* and Targum Onkelos, and *Gevulot Erets* (Berlin, 1821), a work devoted to geography. Following in his father's footsteps, he was well acquainted with secular learning.

• Samuel Joseph Fün, *Qiryah Ne'emanah* (Jerusalem, 1968). Judah Leib Maimon, ed., *Sefer ha-Gera'* (Jerusalem, 1953). —MARC SHAPIRO

AVRAHAM BEN MOSHEH BEN MAIMON (1186–1237), religious philosopher; temporal and spiritual head of the Jewish community in Egypt, succeeding his father, Moses *Maimonides. Like his father, with whom he studied philosophy and medicine, he was a physician to the royal court. He was responsible for many enactments, one of which, prohibiting the issuing of a ban of excommunication by a single rabbi, became generally accepted. He was the author of rabbinic *responsa* (edited by A. Freimann [Jerusalem, 1938]); a commentary on the Torah (only the commentary on *Genesis* and *Exodus* has been preserved, edited by Ernest Wiesenberg [London, 1959]); philosophical writings defending his father's thought, notably *Milḥamot Adonai* (edited by Re'uven M. Margaliot [Jerusalem, 1953]) on the subject of God's incorporeity; and *Kitab al-Abidin* (only partly preserved, Eng. translation by Samuel Rosenblatt, *The High Ways to Perfection of Abraham Maimonides*, 2 vols. [New York, 1927]), an encyclopedic work on religion, ethics, and philosophy. This last, divided into four books, is a commentary on the saying of R. *Shim'on ha-Tsaddiq: "The world rests on three things: Torah, the worship of God, and charity" (*Avot* 1.2). It is informed by deep mystical piety, and it reflects, as do some of his practices, the influence of Sufism. This led him to modify some of the philosophical and ethical ideas of his father, although in general he followed his father's rationalism. Avraham expounds the "highways to perfection" taught by revelation, which lead humans to communion with God; these include asceticism, mastery of the passions, and concentration of all one's thoughts upon God.

• S. D. Goitein, "Abraham Maimonides and his Pietist Circle," in *Jewish Medieval and Renaissance Studies*, edited by Alexander Altmann (Cambridge, Mass., 1967), pp. 145-164. Julius Guttmann, *Philosophies of Judaism* (New York, 1964), pp. 192–195. Re'uven Margaliot, *Toledot Rabbenu Avraham Maimoni ben ha-Rambam* (Lvov, 1930). —FRANCISCO MORENO CARVALHO

AVRAHAM BEN NATAN OF LUNEL (c.1155–c.1215), Provençal Talmudic scholar. A kinsman of Yitsḥaq Abba' Mari of Marseilles, Avraham studied under Avraham ben David of Posquières and with the scholars of Lunel, then traveled north to study under the noted tosafist R. Yitsḥaq of Dampierre, and finally settled in Toledo, Spain, where he became a member of the rabbinical court. During his extensive travels in Provence and northern France, Germany, England, and Spain, he observed local customs, particularly those dealing with synagogue and prayer ritual, and recorded them in a work entitled *Minhag 'Olam* (popularly known as *Sefer ha-Minhag*; originally published in Constantinople in 1519 and republished in Berlin in 1855 [edited by A. N. Goldberg]). The book, the first of its kind in Europe, explains the origin and development of various customs according to rabbinic sources and became a handbook for migrant Jews in unfamiliar locales. Avraham also wrote a commentary to the tractate *Kallah Rabbati*, a brief code on dietary laws and the laws of ritual slaughter, and some *responsa*.

• For a critical edition of *Minhag 'Olam* with an extensive introduction, see Yizhak Raphael, *Sefer ha-Manhig* (Jerusalem, 1978). Isidore Twersky, *Rabad of Posquieres* (Cambridge, Mass., 1962), pp. 240–244. —SHLOMO H. PICK

AVRAHAM BEN YITSḤAQ OF NARBONNE (c.1090–1159), southern French Talmudist. Head of the Narbonne academy and rabbinical court, he was known as R. Avraham Av Beit Din (Ravi Abad, also known as Rabad II). He was the author of *Sefer ha-Eshkol* (edited by Shalom and Ḥanokh Albeck [1935–1958]), an abbreviated version of *Yehudah ben Barzillai al-Bargeloni's *Sefer ha-'Ittim* and the first major work of codification to appear in southern France. This volume influenced subsequent halakhic literature. A collection of Avraham's *responsa* has been published (edited by Y. Kafaḥ [Jerusalem, 1962]), in which his role as community leader is reflected. He was constantly called upon to adjudicate disputes and legal problems and to explain difficult passages of the Talmud. He also wrote a commentary to the Talmud, but only part of one tractate is extant.

• Heinrich Gross, *Gallia judaica: Dictionnaire géographique de la France d'après les sources rabbiniques*, with a supplement by Simon Schwarzfuchs (Paris, 1897; repr. Amsterdam, 1969). Binyamin Ze'ev Benedikt, *Merkaz ha-Torah be-Provans*, (Jerusalem, 1985). Israel M. Ta-Shema, *Rabbi Zeraḥiah ha-Levi–Ba'al ha-Ma'or u-Venei Ḥugo: Le-Toldot ha-Safrut ha-Rabbanit be-Provans* (Jerusalem, 1992). Isadore Twersky, *Rabad of Posquières: A Twelfth–Century Talmudist* (Philadelphia, 1980). —SHLOMO H. PICK

AVRAHAM BEN YOSHIYYA'HU YERUSHALMI (c.1685–1734), *Karaite scholar and author. He lived in Chufut-Kale, Crimea, although he reports that he wandered elsewhere, and evidently supported himself by teaching children and serving as a cantor. According to common Karaite practice, his father was given the cognomen Yerushalmi after making a pilgrimage to Jerusalem. Avraham's son and grandson, Shemu'el and Binyamin Aga, respectively, were communal leaders of the Crimean Karaites and served as minters and treasury agents to the Tatar khans. Most of Avraham's theological treatise *Emunah Omen*, completed in 1712 (published in 1846), is devoted to an exploration of the differences between the Karaite and Rabbanite conception of the fundamentals of law, concluding that the disagreement is actually small. He demonstrates an exceptionally broad and respectful acquaintance with Talmudic and medieval Rabbanite literature, although he opposed the study of secular sciences. His other works include *Sha'ol Sha'al*, on the laws of ritual slaughter; a short sermon; and two liturgical poems found in Karaite prayer books.

• Abraham Geiger, *Nachgelassene Schriften*, 5 vols. (Berlin, 1875–1878), vol. 2, pp. 351–357. Jacob Mann, *Texts and Studies in Jewish History and Literature*, vol. 2 (Cincinnati, 1935), pp. 318, 1277–1278. Samuel Poznanski, *The Karaite Literary Opponents of Saadiah Gaon* (London, 1908), no. 47. —DAVID E. SKLARE

AVRAHAM GERSHON OF KUTÓW (died 1761), rabbi and kabbalist. He was a member of the rabbinic court and probably of the pietistic **kloyz* circle in Brody during the 1740s. In 1747 he settled in the Holy Land, living first in Hebron and then from 1753 in Jerusalem, where he was a member of the mostly Sephardi Beit El kabbalistic conventicle. His sister Ḥannah was the wife of Yisra'el ben Eli'ezer *Ba'al Shem Tov, and R. Gershon Kitover, as Avraham Gershon was also known, figures prominently in the legends collected in **Shivḥei ha-Besht*. A letter from the Ba'al Shem Tov to R. Gershon is one of the most important sources about the religious life of the founder of Hasidism.

• Yaakov S. Gepner, *Or Ki Tov* (Jerusalem, 1968). Abraham Joshua Heschel, *The Circle of the Ba'al Shem Tov* (1949; repr. Chicago, 1985), pp. 44–112. —ARTHUR GREEN

AVRAHAM HA-LEVI (1640–1717), rabbinical scholar born in Cairo, who became the halakhic authority of Egyptian Jewry in his time, a period known as *dor de'ah* (generation of knowledge). Egypt was famous for its sages, and Avraham, as head of the rabbinic court (*av beit din*), was respected throughout the Middle East and as far away as Morocco and Italy. He was considered, along with *David ben Shelomoh ibn Avi Zimra (Radbaz) and Ya'aqov Castro (Mahariqash), as one of the three pillars of Egyptian learning. He was cited by the leading Ashkenazi and Sephardi authorities. His *responsa* were published after his death by Moshe Tawil in *Ginnat Veradim* (Constantinople, 1716–1717); Pinḥas 'Ovadyah has edited a modern edition (Jerusalem, 1991). Avraham was especially noted for his expertise on divorce, fighting, and, among other things, those who tried to escape the rabbinical authorities by recourse to Muslim *shariah*. His *Ya'ir Nativ* on divorce customs is printed as part of *Ginnat Veradim*.

• Shelomoh Z. Havlin, *Rabbi Avraham ha-Levi* (Jerusalem, 1983), in Hebrew with an English summary. —SHALOM BAR-ASHER

AVRAHAM YEHOSHU'A HESCHEL (died 1825), Hasidic master and author; known as the Apter Rebbe. One of the most powerful Hasidic leaders of his generation, he was a disciple of Elimelekh of Lyzhansk and Yeḥi'el Mikha'el of Zloczów. Avraham began his career as a rabbi of Kolbuszowa but became famous as the rabbi of Opatów (Apta). He also spent a number of years as rabbi of Jassy. The last part of his life was spent in Medzhibozh (Podolia), where Hasidism's founder, the Ba'al Shem Tov, had his center. Here Avraham achieved his greatest renown, opposing the Haskalah, mediating Hasidic disputes, and raising funds for the Hasidic community in Erets Yisra'el. He was at heart a mystic, and typical of the school of the Maggid of Mezhirech, his sermons were often delivered in ecstatic states of inspiration. Like other Hasidic masters, he claimed knowledge of previous lives and would regale his followers with reminiscences of events from the biblical and early rabbinic periods. He explained that the reason for his many incarnations was to perfect the attribute of love. Collections of his homilies were printed posthumously. The most famous of these is *Ohev Yisra'el* (Lover of Israel), named after the epithet that he requested for his tombstone.

• Leon J. Berle, *Rabbi Avraham Yehoshu'a Heshil, ha-Rav me-'Apta* (Jerusalem, 1984). Martin Buber, *Tales of the Ḥasidim* (New York, 1947). Rivka Schatz Uffenheimer, *Hasidism as Mysticism* (Princeton, 1993). —MILES KRASSEN

AVREKH (אַבְרֵךְ; young man), originally a term applied to Joseph by the Egyptians (*Gn.* 41.43), which the Midrash (*Gn. Rab.* 90.3) homiletically interpreted as "*av* [an elder] in wisdom and *rakh* [young] in years." The term is now used for a married *yeshivah* student who has not yet entered the labor market and is still studying in a **kolel*. —SHMUEL HIMELSTEIN

AVTALYON (1st cent. BCE), colleague of *Shema'yah. Together they constituted the fourth of the **zugot* (pairs) in the chain of transmission outlined in *Pirqei *Avot*, where they are said to have received the tradition from *Yehudah ben Tabb'ai and *Shim'on ben Shetaḥ. While Shema'yah was the *nasi'*, Avtalyon was the *av beit din* of the supreme rabbinic court. Both are said to have been descendants of proselytes (*Git.* 57b; *San.* 96b). Some scholars identify Avtalyon with the Pollio mentioned by Josephus as being one of the Pharisaic leaders during the time of *Herod (*Antiquities of the Jews* 15.1–4, 370). According to a variant reading in *Antiquities of the Jews* (14.172), it was Avtalyon, and not Sameas (Shema'yah?) who was the "upright man and for this reason superior to fear," who denounced Hyrcanus and his colleagues in the *Sanhedrin for their cowardice in refusing to judge Herod. Some hold that his exhortation, "Scholars be careful with your words, lest you incur the penalty of exile and be banished to a place of evil waters (i.e., heretical teachings), and the disciples who follow you into exile are likely to drink of them and die" (*Avot* 1.11), reflects contemporary conditions and refers to the punishments meted out by the regime. The allusion may also refer to Avtalyon's teacher, who fled to Alexandria during the reign of Alexander Yannai, as well as to the Herodian persecutions of his own time.

• Gershom Bader, *The Encyclopedia of Talmudic Sages* (Northvale, N.J., 1988). R. Travers Herford, ed., *Pirke Avot: The Ethics of the Fathers* (New York, 1969). —DANIEL SPERBER

AVTINAS, family whose duty it was to mix the *incense in the Temple (*Sheq.* 5.1). Originally the family was denounced for refusing to teach the manufacturing of incense to others (*Yoma'* 3.11). The sages sent to Alexandria for skilled perfumers; however, they were unable to make the column of smoke from the incense rise in a vertical shaft, as had the Avtinas family. The sages then agreed to double their remuneration (*Yoma'* 38a). A later generation explained that the reason they had refused to divulge their secret formula was that they believed the Temple would soon be destroyed, and they feared that their incense would be used for idolatry.

• Judah Nadich, ed., *Legends of the Rabbis*, 2 vols. (Northvale, N.J., 1994).
—DANIEL SPERBER

AYASH, YEHUDAH (1700–1759), Algerian rabbinical authority. Born in Almahdia, he was taken by his father, himself a noted rabbi, to Algiers, where he studied with Rabbi Rafa'el Tseror. Upon Tseror's death in 1728, Ayash succeeded him as *av beit din* of Algiers. Ayash was an influential figure by virtue of his daily expositions in any place where Torah was studied, and on Sabbaths masses crowded the central synagogue to hear his sermons. He cooperated closely with the Jewish leader Rafa'el Ya'aqov Bus'ara', who helped him publish his first book, *Leḥem Yehudah* (Leghorn, vol. 1, 1745; vol. 2, 1758), devoted to comments on Maimonides. Following a dispute with community leaders, Ayash left for Leghorn, where he taught from 1756 to 1758, and continued to Erets Yisra'el. In Algiers he had published a *responsum* in his halakhic work *Beit Yehudah* (Leghorn, 1746) to the effect that if there is a conflict between *'aliyyah* to Erets Yisra'el and the obligation to honor one's parents, the former takes precedence. He settled in Jerusalem, where he headed the Keneset Yisra'el Yeshivah founded by Ḥayyim ben Mosheh *Attar. Ayash's sons Ya'aqov Mosheh, Yehuda, and Avraham were distinguished rabbis, while his three grandsons served as emissaries of the Jerusalem community.

• Shalom Bar-Asher, "Shetai Te'udot be-Hora'at ha-Temurot be-'Aliyyah mi-Tsefon Afrikah," *Bat Qol* 1 (1991): 71–82. Yehuda Messing, "Rabbi Yehudah 'Ayy'ash Gedolei Rabbanei Maroqqo ve-Algeria," in *Ve-Hayu Einekha Ro'ot et Morekha* (Jerusalem, 1981), pp. 83–95.
—SHALOM BAR-ASHER

'AYIN HA-RA'. See Evil Eye.

AYLLON, SHELOMOH BEN YA'AQOV (c.1660–1728), Sephardi rabbi. It is not certain whether he was born in Safed or Salonika. While in Leghorn, Italy, on behalf of the community of Safed, he maintained theological contacts with the Shabbatean rabbis Binyamin ha-Kohen and Avraham Rovigo. In 1689 he was nominated *ḥakham* of the Spanish-Portuguese community of London, a position he quit after ten years in office owing to personal disputes within the community. In 1700 he was elected *ḥakham* of the senior community of Amsterdam and head of the Ets Ḥayyim rabbinical school, where he served for twenty-eight years, admired by all community members. However, a bitter controversy took place between Ayllon and the *ḥakham* Tsevi Hirsch *Ashkenazi. Ayllon publicly supported Neḥemyah *Ḥayon, who was suspected, rightly as is now known, of Shabbateanism, while Ashkenazi criticized Ḥayon's writings and issued a ban against him. The controversy developed beyond theology into an Ashkenazi-Sephardi dispute, at the end of which Tsevi Hirch Ashkenazi was compelled to leave Amsterdam. Ayllon's halakhic and kabbalistic writings are still in manuscript, but the latter shows that the accusation of being a clandestine Shabbatean believer was well-founded. In his tract he closely follows the teachings of *Natan of Gaza regarding the two primordial lights, *or she-yesh bo maḥashavah* (the intelligent light) and *or she-'ein bo maḥashavah* (the nonintelligent light), and the role of the Messiah in harmonizing them, as well as the Messiah's apotheosis.

• Moses Gaster, *History of the Ancient Synagogue of the Spanish and Portuguese Jews* (London, 1901), pp. 22–30. Jacob S. Da Silva Rosa, *Geschiedenis der Portugeesche Joden te Amsterdam, 1593–1925* (Amsterdam, 1925), pp. 111–112.
—NISSIM YOSHA

'AZARAH (עֲזָרָה), a late Hebrew term designating the surrounding rim of the altar (*Ez.* 43.14, 43.17, 43.20, 45.19) as well as the courtyard of the Temple (*2 Chr.* 4.9, 6.13). There were three courtyards in the Second Temple: the women's courtyard (*'*ezrat nashim*), from which fifteen steps led up to the courtyard of the Israelites, which led in to the priest's courtyard. According to a tradition preserved in the Talmud Yerushalmi (Y., *Ta'an.* 4.2; cf. *Sifrei* on *Deuteronomy* 356), three Torah scrolls, bearing variant readings, were found in the Temple courtyard. The sages thereupon "confirmed the [reading found in] two [of the three scrolls] and abrogated the other." Underlying this tradition was the custom of depositing an official copy of the Torah in the Temple courtyard so that copyists could correct their versions on the basis of this canonical version. The same idea is reflected in the legend found in **Avot de-Rabbi Natan* 19.19 and elsewhere, according to which Moses prepared thirteen copies of the Torah, one for each tribe of Israel and a thirteenth copy that was placed in the Ark of the Covenant. This last copy was, like the later scroll of the *'azarah*, the official version against which all copies were to be compared.

• Saul Lieberman, *Hellenism in Jewish Palestine* (New York, 1950). Shemaryahu Talmon, "Three Scrolls They Found in the Temple Court," in *Sefer Segal: M. H. Segal Festschrift*, edited by Jehoshua M. Grintz and Jacob Liver (Jerusalem, 1964), pp. 25–37. Emanuel Tov, *Textual Criticism of the Hebrew Bible* (Minneapolis, 1992).
—MAYER I. GRUBER

AZAZEL, name mentioned in *Leviticus* 16 in connection with the ritual of Yom Kippur. The high priest would cast lots over two he-goats, designating one "for the Lord" and the other "for Azazel," and confess over the latter all the iniquities of the children of Israel. Thereafter this goat was sent away "by the hand of an appointed man into the wilderness." In Talmudic times the goat was thrown from the top of a precipice near Jerusalem, and if the tuft of scarlet wool fastened to it turned white (cf. *Is.* 1.18), this was taken as a sign of God's forgiveness. The meaning of the word *azazel* is variously explained: "the place of sending away [the goat]" (Septuagint); "scapegoat" (Vulgate); or "rugged mountain" (Talmud). The ritual is generally taken to symbolize the complete removal of the people's transgressions. The concept of *azazel* may have a pre-Israelite origin connected with the worship of *se'irim*—goatlike demons (cf. *Lv.* 17.7). In Judaism, it became the symbol of casting out of sinfulness from Israel's borders (cf. *Lv.* 14.1–7; *Zec.* 5.5–11). In apocalyptic and late aggadic as well as kabbalistic literature, Azazel is conceived of as a fallen angel and even as a prototype of *Satan. The term *azazel* (only *Lv*. 16.8, 10, 26) has also been understood as the personal name or epithet of a demythologized demon, popularly identified with the Canaanite god of death, Mot (in Ugaritic, *Mt*). However, its use in the Hebrew Bible is limited to priestly sanctioned participation (together with and on behalf of the God of Israel, cf. especially *Lv*. 16.7–8) in the annual Yom Kippur purgation ritual.

• Baruch Levine, *Leviticus*, The JPS Torah Commentary (Philadelphia, 1989), pp. 102, 250–253. Oswald Loretz, *Leberschau, Sündenbock, Asasel in Ugarit and Israel* (Altenberge, 1985), pp. 50–57. Jacob Milgrom, *Leviticus 1–16*, The Anchor Bible (New York, 1991), pp. 1020–1021. Hayim Tawil, "'Azazel the Prince of the Steppe: A Comparative Study," *Zeitschrift für die alttestamentliche Wissenschaft* 92 (1980): 43–59. K. van der Toorn et al., eds., "Azazel," in *Dictionary of Deities and Demons in the Bible* (Leiden, 1995). D. P. Wright, "Azazel," in *The Anchor Bible Dictionary*, vol. 1 (New York, 1992), pp. 536–537. —CHAIM COHEN

AZHAROT (אַזְהָרוֹת; exhortations), liturgical poems dealing with the enumeration and explanation of the 613 commandments (the numerical value of the word *azharot* in Hebrew is 613). These poems were called *azharot* after the initial word of an early composition of this nature dating from the geonic period. They were recited in the Shavu'ot liturgy, especially among the Sephardim, before Musaf but were transferred to Minḥah. *Azharot* were written by early *payyetanim* and by many famous medieval rabbis and poets including Sa'adyah Ga'on and Shelomoh ibn Gabirol (whose *azharot* were widely used among the Sephardim and Yemenites); however, these compositions also aroused opposition, such as that expressed by Avraham ibn Ezra, who compared a person who recites *azharot* to one who enumerates a list of herbs without any appreciation of their remedial properties.

• Ismar Elbogen, *Jewish Liturgy: A Comprehensive History*, translated by Raymond P. Scheindlin (Philadelphia and New York, 1993), pp. 174, 256. Ezra Fleischer, *Shirat ha-Qodesh ha-'Ivrit bi-Yemei ha-Beinayim* (Jerusalem, 1975).

AZIKRI, EL'AZAR BEN MOSHEH (1533–1600), kabbalist, commentator, preacher, and poet; an outstanding representative of Safed's spirituality in the sixteenth century. A disciple of R. Yosef Sagis and R. Mosheh *Cordovero, he was ordained by R. Ya'aqov *Berab in 1596. As the spiritual leader of two groups (*ḥavurot*) of mystics and ascetics in Safed, Ḥaverim Maqshivim and Sukkat Shalom, he wrote for them a kabbalistic ethical manual named *Millei de-Shemayya'* (Tel Aviv, 1991). This work is based on Azikri's own ecstatic religious experiences, which he recorded in his diary. This diary, written in a terse, enigmatic manner, was published in its entirety as *Mitsfunot Tsefat* (edited by M. Pachter [Jerusalem, 1994]). It reflects the inner world of an ecstatic kabbalist, dedicating himself to the path of ascent in the degrees of ecstatic contemplation, self-purification, and communion (*devequt*) with God. In 1588 Azikri wrote his manual *Ḥaredim* (Venice, 1601), which had an influence on Hasidism. Its most influential section, *Divrei Kibbushin*, is a compilation of chapters from *Millei de-Shemayya'*. Azikri's commentaries on some tractates of the Talmud Bavli as well as his many homiletic commentaries on the Pentateuch remain in manuscript form. His commentaries on *Berakhot* and *Beitsah* of the Talmud Yerushalmi were printed (Zhitomir, 1860; New York, 1967). His love poems (*piyyutim*) to God were included in almost all the editions of *Ḥaredim*. The most popular of these poems, *Yedid Nefesh*, is printed in the prayer books of almost all the Jewish communities in the world; in many of them, it opens the Friday evening *Qabbalat Shabbat service. There is an English translation by Nina Davis in *Jewish Quarterly Review* 9 (1896/1897): 290. See also KABBALAH; MYSTICISM.

• Salo W. Baron et al., eds., *Sefer Yovel le-Yitsḥaq Baer* (Jerusalem, 1960), p. 262. Israel Frantsos, introduction to *Talmud Yerushalmi, Massekhet Beitsah*, with a commentary by El'azar ben Mosheh Azkiri (New York, 1967). —MORDECHAI PACHTER

'AZRI'EL OF GERONA (13th cent.), one of the leading kabbalists in Catalonia. His mystical works are based on the teachings of R. Yitsḥaq Saggi Nahor and the *Sefer ha-Bahir*, combined with contemporary philosophical, mainly Neoplatonic terminology. His *Perush ha-'Aggadot* (Jerusalem, 1985) united ancient traditions with contemporary thought, offering a systematic amalgamation of the new kabbalistic symbolism with ancient Talmudic legends. His works influenced other Catalonian kabbalists, including Moses *Nahmanides, and Spanish Kabbalah as a whole.

• Moshe Idel, *Kabbalah: New Perspectives* (New Haven, 1988). Gershom Scholem, *Kabbalah* (New York, 1974), pp. 391–393. Yeshayahu Tishbi, *Peirush ha-'Aggadot le-Rabbi 'Azri'el* (Jerusalem, 1945). —JOSEPH DAN

AZ ROV NISSIM (אָז רוֹב נִסִּים; Then You [Performed] Many Miracles), a *piyyut* by Yann'ai (6th cent. CE), incorporated into the *Haggadah for the first evening of *Pesaḥ and also recited in congregations following the German rite on Shabbat ha-Gadol (the Sabbath preceding Pesaḥ) and the first day of Pesaḥ. Az Rov Nissim is an alphabetical acrostic with the refrain after each three-line stanza, "And it came to pass at midnight." The poet cites twelve instances of God's intervention at night on Pesaḥ to deliver his people. The final strophes look forward to Israel's final deliverance, which is also to take place at midnight. Many modern editors of the Haggadah have eliminated the poem because of its recondite allusions. It was given a free translation in verse form for the Reform *Union Haggadah* of 1923.

• Nahum N. Glatzer, ed., *The Passover Haggadah*, based on the commentaries of E. D. Goldschmidt (New York, 1969), pp. 86ff. —A. STANLEY DREYFUS

AZULAI, AVRAHAM (c.1570–1643), scholar, rabbi, and kabbalist. Born in Fez, he received a rabbinical education and studied medieval philosophy in its Aristotelian form. Under the influence of Mosheh Cordovero's *Pardes Rimmonim*, he chose Kabbalah as his special interest. Although acquainted with Lurianic Kabbalah, Azulai in the main adopted Cordovero's system. At an early age Azulai went to Erets Yisra'el and, after wandering between Hebron, Jerusalem, and Gaza, settled in Hebron, where he studied Cordovero's books and Lurianic manuscripts. There he wrote *Or ha-Levanah*, corrections to the text of the Zohar, as well as his *magnum opus, Or ha-Ḥammah*, a full commentary on the Zohar based on Cordovero's writings, to which he added *Or ha-Ganuz*, his own *novellae* on the Zohar, and *Zoharei Ḥammah*, based on Mosheh bar Mordekhai Galante's commentary on the Zohar. Two of Azulai's works, *Ḥesed le-'Avraham* (Amsterdam, 1685), a systematic analysis of Kabbalah, and *Baʿalei Berit Avram*, a commentary on the Bible (Jerusalem, 1982), exhibit a strong philosophical influence in their terminology and conceptual usage.

• Yisrael Maimaran, *Ḥofesh ha-Beḥirah be-Haguto shel R. Avraham Azulai* (Jerusalem, 1993). Ronit Meroz, "Sefer 'Or ha-Ganuz' le-Rabbi Avraham Azulai," *Kiryat Sefer* 60 (1985): 310–324. Bracha Sack, "Li-Meqorotav shel Sefer 'Ḥesed le-'Avraham' le-Rabbi Avraham Azulai," *Kiryat Sefer* 56 (1981): 164–175. Bracha Sack, "The Influence of Cordovero on Seventeenth-Century Jewish Thought," in *Jewish Thought in the Seventeenth Century*, edited by Isadore Twersky and B. Septimus (Cambridge, Mass., 1987), pp. 365–376. Gershom Gerhard Scholem, *Kitvei ha-Yad ha-ʿIvriyim*, vol. 1, *Qabbalah* (Jerusalem, 1930), p. 144. Y. Tishby, "Yaḥaso shel Rabbi Avraham Azulai le-Qabbalat Ramak ule-Qabbalat Ha-'Ari," *Sefunot* 16 (1980): 191–203.

—NISSIM YOSHA

AZULAI, ḤAYYIM YOSEF DAVID (1724–1806), rabbinical scholar, kabbalist, and bibliographer; known by the acronym Ḥida'. Born in Jerusalem, he was sixteen years old when he wrote his first book, precursor to his *Shem ha-Gedolim* (1774, 1786), a vast guide to twenty-two hundred books and thirteen hundred rabbis. He traveled extensively as an emissary on behalf of the Jewish community in Erets Yisra'el. He was the first Jewish scholar to study the manuscripts of Italy and France. Azulai served as rabbi in Jerusalem, Hebron, Cairo, and, from 1778, in Leghorn. His literary diary, *Maʿagal Tov* (edited by A. Freimann [1921–1934]), is an invaluable account of his travels, experiences, and ideas. He was the author of over eighty books on *halakhah* and ethics and was a noted kabbalist, composing prayers that became part of *Tefillat ha-Ḥodesh*, a Sephardi prayer book in use since the mid-eighteenth century.

• Meir Benayahu, *Rabbi Ḥayyim Yosef David Azulai* (Jerusalem, 1959). Meir Benayahu, ed., *Sefer ha-Ḥida'* (Jerusalem, 1959).

—SHALOM BAR-ASHER

B

BAʿAL HA-TURIM. See Yaʿaqov ben Asher.

BAʿAL NES (בַּעַל נֵס; miracle master), a holy man or saint. A *baʿal nes* may be a simple man or one who is acknowledged by the religious authorities, such as the *tsaddiq*, rabbi, or *ḥakham*. The *baʿal nes* is recognized by his capacity to perform miracles through prayer or because miracles happen to him (*Nid*. 31a). Many important religious figures are said to have had this capacity, including Maimonides, R. Yehudah ben Shemu'el he-Ḥasid, Yitsḥaq Luria, the Baʿal Shem Tov, the Lubavitcher Rebbe, and Baba Sali, head of the Abi-Ḥasira dynasty, revered by Moroccan Jews. A story is told about R. Me'ir (2d cent.), who was called a *baʿal nes* after miraculously rescuing his sister-in-law from prison. The prison guard who helped R. Me'ir was to be executed for his complicity, but a moment before his execution he cried out "God of Rabbi Me'ir, deliver me" and was miraculously spared (*ʿA. Z.* 18b). It became customary for a person in trouble to repeat forty times the phrase "God of Rabbi Me'ir, deliver me," a folk tradition that is still practiced today in certain circles.

The title *baʿal nes* was attributed to another R. Me'ir who lived in Tiberias during the thirteenth century (see Me'ir Baʿal ha-Nes).

• Hippolyte Delehaye, *The Legends of the Saints* (New York, 1962). Louis Jacobs, *Holy Living: Saints and Saintliness in Judaism* (Northvale, N.J., 1990). —TAMAR ALEXANDER

BAʿAL QERI'AH (בַּעַל קְרִיאָה; master of reading; reader), Ashkenazi description of the person who reads the Torah in the synagogue (see Qeri'at ha-Torah). Originally, each person who was called up would read his own portion if he were capable of doing so, and a *baʿal qeri'ah* would read the portion only for those unable to read it themselves. Later, in order to avoid embarrassing those incapable of reading their own portion, a single *baʿal qeri'ah* was instituted for all readings. Among Yemenites, it is still usual for individuals to read the portion for which they are called up. The Sephardi term for *baʿal qeri'ah* is *qore'*.

• Ismar Elbogen, *Jewish Liturgy: A Comprehensive History*, translated by Raymond P. Scheindlin (Philadelphia, New York, and Jerusalem, 1993), pp. 138–141. Macy Nulman, *The Concise Encyclopedia of Jewish Music* (New York, 1975), pp. 19. —SHMUEL HIMELSTEIN

BAʿAL SHEM (בַּעַל שֵׁם; master of the [divine] name), a medieval term, first found in Hasidic literature (*Sefer ha-Shem*, MS, British Library 737; MS, St. Petersburg 82), describing a magician who is the "master of the holy name," by which means he performs supernatural acts. A *baʿal Shem* is characterized by his knowledge of secret, potent divine and angelic names, which enable him to force the celestial powers to perform his wishes. The term *baʿal Shem* is associated with people who were reputed to possess esoteric knowledge and hence were in demand as scribes of amulets and masters of popular medicine and magic (overcoming demons and spirits, discovering thieves, etc.). One of the most popular books of magical and medical formulas, *Mifalot Elohim*, is attributed to R. Yo'el Baʿal Shem. Another (legendary?) figure is that of R. Adam Baʿal Shem, who is described in *Shivḥei ha-Besht* as the teacher of the *Baʿal Shem Tov, founder of the modern Hasidic movement. The Baʿal Shem Tov, himself, was a wandering healer and scribe of amulets (the appelation Baʿal Shem Tov [master of the good name] is a common one, and was not given to R. Yisra'el ben Eliʿezer in order to distinguish him from other magicians, as suggested by several of his biographers; it denotes the use of good names rather than those of the powers of evil).

• Gershom Gerhard Scholem, *Kabbalah* (Jerusalem, 1974), pp. 310–311. —JOSEPH DAN

BAʿAL SHEM TOV, YISRA'EL BEN ELIʿEZER (c.1700–1760), founder of *Hasidism; known by the acronym Besht. Little is known of his life, and few reliable biographical documents exist. According to legend, he was orphaned while a child and spent a great deal of his time in solitude and meditation in the woods and fields around his home in Podolia. For some years, he was assistant to a teacher and acted as sexton of the *beit midrash*. Until his *hitgallut*, an important concept in Hasidism signifying the revelation of one's true spiritual worth and message, he studied assiduously, acquiring wide knowledge of both the revealed law and secret lore, but concealed his knowledge, affecting the personality of a simple, unlettered Jew. He traveled in Podolia, Volhynia, and Galicia, where, by virtue of his prayers and *amulets, he achieved a reputation as a healer and a comforter to those in need; hence, the appellation *Baʿal Shem (or Baʿal Shem Tov [Master of the Good Name], abbreviated to Besht). The charms that he prepared contained only his own and his mother's name—Yisra'el son of Sarah—unlike the more traditional forms that always contained one of the holy names of God. Many legends grew around his personality and life, often described as a miraculous chain of events: that Elijah the prophet foretold his birth; that his soul was a spark from that of the Messiah; and that he was taught both exoteric and secret Torah by Elijah himself and by Ahijah the Shilonite, Elijah's teacher. In approximately 1740, the Baʿal Shem Tov settled in Medzhibozh, where he established a *beit midrash* that attracted many adherents. They came seeking his spiritual guidance in the worship of God, in order to receive his blessing, and to beseech his prayer and intercession for their spiritual and physical welfare. While drawing upon the kabbalistic doctrines of Yosef *Karo and Yitsḥaq *Luria, he invested them with new meaning and thus created an original and distinctive type of mysticism. The Baʿal Shem Tov did not commit his teachings to writing; they were handed down orally and preserved in numerous sayings recorded by his followers. His sayings imparted joy and warmth and warned against sadness and mortification that "stultify the heart." Even the most simple may serve the omnipresent God through inner joy. Many stories are found in Hasidic folklore describing the Baʿal Shem Tov and the great leaders of Hasidism at prayer. True prayer is pictured as a state that freed the personality from the trammels of the body and allowed the soul to cleave to God. When the Baʿal Shem Tov prayed, it was said that his entire body would tremble, that those present would be seized with shivering, and that the building would shake. The emphasis on *intent (*kavvanah*), which formed one of the major points of controversy (see MITNAGGEDIM) concerning the movement, was a further tenet of the Baʿal Shem Tov. *Kavvanah*, he said, is the "soul of the deed." The Baʿal Shem Tov argued that all things in the world are imbued with divine vitality and that this is the foundation of existence. The assumption of the omnipresence of God in all things and in all dimensions of existence becomes a criterion for reevaluating the whole of human experience. The Baʿal Shem Tov's *beit midrash* in Medzhibozh and the shrine erected over his grave became centers of pilgrimage. The writings of R. *Yaʿaqov Yosef ha-Kohen of Polonnoye, one of the Baʿal Shem Tov's students, include many of his sayings; another student, R. *Dov Ber of Mezhirech, succeeded the Baʿal Shem Tov as the leader of Hasidism.

• Simon Dubnow, *Toledot ha-Ḥasidut* (Tel Aviv, 1966). Rachel Elior, *Israel Baʿal Shem Tov: Between Magic and Mysticism* (Jerusalem, 1996). Immanuel Etkes, "Hasidism as a Movement: The First Stage," in *Hasidism, Continuity or Innovation?*, edited by Bezalel Safran (Cambridge, Mass., 1988). Abraham Joshua Heschel, *The Circle of the Baʿal Shem Tov: Studies in Hasidism* (Chicago, 1985). Moshe Rosman, *Founder of Hasidism: A Quest for the Historical Baʿal Shem Tov* (Berkeley, 1996). Moshe Rosman, "Miedzyboz and Rabbi Yisraʾel Baʿal Shem Tov," *Zion* 52 (1987): 177–189. Gershom Gerhard Scholem, "Demuto ha-Historit shel ha-Besht," in *Devarim be-Go*, edited by Avraham Shapira (Tel Aviv, 1975), pp. 287–324.

—RACHEL ELIOR

BAʿAL TEFILLAH (בַּעַל תְּפִילָּה; master of prayer), Ashkenazi term designating the person who leads the prayers in the presence of a *minyan*; also known as the *sheliaḥ tsibbur*. In ancient times, the *baʿal tefillah* would recite certain prayers on behalf of those congregants who did not know the texts; they would listen as the *baʿal tefillah* recited the prayers aloud and fulfill their ritual obligations by making appropriate responses (*amen*, *barukh hu' u-varukh shemo*, etc.). The advent of printed books did not eliminate this function, since some worshipers are still unfamiliar with the service. Today the *baʿal tefillah* may also serve as a kind of assistant *cantor, typically presiding at weekday services in a style less musically ornate than that of the *ḥazzan*.

• Ismar Elbogen, *Jewish Liturgy: A Comprehensive History*, translated by Raymond P. Scheindlin (Philadelphia, New York, and Jerusalem, 1993), pp. 372–374.

—MARSHA BRYAN EDELMAN

BAʿAL TEQIʿAH (בַּעַל תְּקִיעָה; master of the shofar blowing), Ashkenazi designation for the person who blows the *shofar on *Roʾsh ha-Shanah on behalf of the congregants, in fulfillment of the commandment "In the seventh month, on the first day of the month . . . it will be a day of blowing the shofar for you" (*Nm.* 29.1). The *baʿal teqiʿah* (among Sephardim, simply called *toqeʿa*) also blows the shofar at the end of *Yom Kippur and, in the Sephardi rite, on Hoshaʿnaʾ Rabbah. Traditionally, any male congregant may blow the shofar, but preference was given to a pious man. It is customary among Ashkenazim for the *baʿal teqiʿah* to wear a *kitel*. Before blowing the shofar, he recites special blessings for the occasion.

• Macy Nulman, *The Concise Encyclopedia of Jewish Music* (New York, 1975), pp. 21–22.

—SHMUEL HIMELSTEIN

BAʿAL TESHUVAH (בַּעַל תְּשׁוּבָה), a person who repents of non-observance of any of the *mitsvot* (see REPENTANCE). Such an individual is highly praised by the rabbis and must not be reminded of past misdeeds (*Yoma'* 86b). Traditionally, a *baʿal teshuvah* (or *ḥozer biteshuvah*) was expected to express repentance by confession, fast and prayer, expressions of contrition, and resolutions not to repeat the sin(s). Rabbi Abbahu said that "in a place where the *baʿal teshuvah* stands not even the completely righteous has a place" (*Ber.* 34b). In recent decades, the term has been applied to Jews who move from a non-observant to an observant lifestyle. Since the 1970s, the phenomenon of non-religious Jews becoming strictly Orthodox has been called the Baʿal Teshuvah movement. Many of these individuals study in special Baʿal Teshuvah *yeshivot* in Israel and the United States.

• Janet O'Dea Aviad, *Return to Judaism: Religious Renewal in Israel* (Chicago, 1983). Murray Herbert Danziger, *Returning to Tradition: The Contemporary Revival of Orthodox Judaism* (New Haven, 1989). Lynn Davidman, *Tradition in a Rootless World: Women Turn to Orthodox Judaism* (Berkeley, 1991).

BAAL WORSHIP, worship of Canaanite fertility and weather god. Baal (lord, master), also known as Hadad, is the son of El (head of the Canaanite pantheon) and the most prominent Canaanite deity, who resides on the coastal mountain Saphon. In Ugaritic texts from Ras Shamra, Baal is the mighty storm god who defeats the sea god, Yamm, and the dragon monster, Lotan. In an encounter with the god of the underworld, Mot, Baal dies, but his sister and consort, Anath, succeeds in bringing him back to life. This myth of the dying and rising god parallels nature's cycles of sterility and fertility. Baal's cult animal is the bull, and he is sometimes pictured in reliefs with a thunderbolt as spear and a mace. The name Baal is sometimes a part of a place name (e.g., Baal-hazor, Baal-hamon), which could indicate Baal's importance as a local deity. Baal worship frequently threatened the Israelites' pure worship of their God. Even before entering Canaan, Israel is said to have sinned by sacrificing to and participating in rites for Baal-peor (*Nm.* 25.1–9). According to the *Book of Judges*, the Israelites repeatedly forsook the Lord for Baal and *Asherah (*Jgs.* 2.13, 3.7). Prophets such as Hosea and Jeremiah often condemned the people for their allegiance to Baal. The threat of Baalism reached its height in the days of King Ahab and Jezebel. Elijah attempted to solve the problem by challenging the priests of Baal on Mount Carmel (*1 Kgs.* 18). A number of years later, King Jehu of Israel destroyed the Baal sanctuary in Samaria, along with Baal's priests and followers (*2 Kgs.* 10). When Judah was ruled by Queen Athaliah, there was a Baal shrine in Jerusalem (*2 Kgs.* 11.18). The Judean reformer kings Hezekiah and Josiah sought to eliminate Baalism. Since only a few biblical names belonging to Israelites contain a Baal theophoric element, and personal names on inscriptions and seals from the period of the divided monarchy are overwhelmingly Yahvistic, it seems that Baal worship was not as widespread in Israel as previously believed and that it rarely supplanted Yahvism. Some of Baal's attributes, however, were transferred to the God of Israel: Psalm 29 depicts Yahveh with many of the characteristics of the Canaanite storm god, and Baal's victory over the sea re-echoes in the triumphs of Israel's God (cf. *Ps.* 74.13–14; *Jb.* 7.12).

• William Foxwell Albright, *Yahweh and the Gods of Canaan* (Garden City, N.Y., 1968). Frank Moore Cross, *Canaanite Myth and Hebrew Epic* (Cambridge, Mass., 1973). John Gray, *The Legacy of Canaan: The Ras Shamra Texts and Their Relevance to the Old Testament*, 2d rev. ed., Supplements to Vetus Testamentum, vol. 5 (Leiden, 1965). Yehezkel Kaufmann, *The Religion of Israel: From Its Beginning to the Babylonian Exile*, translated by Moshe Greenberg (Chicago, 1960). Jeffrey H. Tigay, *You Shall Have No Other Gods: Israelite Religion in the Light of Hebrew Inscriptions*, Harvard Semitic Studies, no. 31 (Atlanta, 1986).

—NILI SACHER FOX

BABEL, TOWER OF. See TOWER OF BABEL.

BABYLONIA. The originally insignificant city-state of Babylon, located on the Euphrates, was elevated by *Hammurabi (r.1792–1750) and his dynasty (the first dynasty of Babylon) to the capital city and cultural metropolis of southern Mesopotamia. Eventually, all of southern Mesopotamia came to be known as Babylonia, while northern Mesopotamia was called *Assyria. The other major period of Babylonian supremacy was the Neo-Babylonian (or Chaldean) empire first established by Nabopolassar (r.625–605), which endured until the conquest of Babylon by *Cyrus II of Persia in 539 BCE, after which Babylon never regained independence. It appears that the original form of the name of the city-state was Babilla, one of the very old place names in Mesopotamian sources that originated neither in Sumerian nor Akkadian, the two main languages of Mesopotamian documents, but rather was derived from one of the languages spoken by the indigenous residents of Mesopotamia before the Sumerian arrival at the dawn of the historical period (the end of the fourth millennium BCE). The ancient Hebrews derived the Hebrew designation *Bavel* from the Hebrew verb *b l l* (mix together, confuse; in *Gn.* 11.7, 9 God confused the languages of the builders of the Tower of Babel). In the Bible, Babylon and its environs are also called Shinar (*Gn.* 10.10, 11.2, 14.1, 9; *Jos.* 7.21; *Is.* 11.11; *Zec.* 5.11; *Dn.* 1.2), a designation that also occurs in Egyptian and Akkadian documents as early as the fifteenth century BCE. Though its origin is still uncertain, some scholars think that it is a transliteration of one of the Sumerian terms for that region. The name Babel appears in the Bible in several contexts: as part of the prehistory of Israel described in *Genesis* 1–12, in the table of nations, referring here to Babel, Erech, Accad, and Calneh as the mainstays of Nimrod's kingdom (*Gn.* 10.10); in the etiological story of the founding of the city of Babylon based on the building of a ziggurat there (*Gn.* 11.1–9); in the story of the Chaldean ruler Merodach-baladan, who sent envoys to Hezekiah to enlist the aid of Judah, apparently in an attempt to rebel against Assyria, after which the prophet Isaiah warned that Babylon would eventually sack Jerusalem and carry off as plunder all the treasures that Hezekiah had displayed before the Babylonians (*2 Kgs.* 20.12–19; *Is.* 39.1–8); in the story of the capture of Judah (597 BCE) and the destruction of the First Temple (587–586 BCE) by Nebuchadnezzar II (605–562), son of the founder of the Neo-Babylonian empire, who exiled the Judeans en masse to Babylon (*2 Kgs.* 24–25; *Jer.* 39–41, 52; *2 Chr.* 36); and in the account of the capture of Babylon by Cyrus II of Persia (539 BCE) and the end of the Babylonian exile, when the last Babylonian king, Nabonidus (556–539), turned the majority of the people against him by attempting a religious revolution and replacing the patron deity and longtime chief god of Babylon, Marduk, with the moon god Sin as the head of the pantheon. Babylon lost its independence forever in a somewhat ignominious fashion, when Cyrus entered the city as the "legitimate" ruler "appointed" by Marduk, encountered no significant resistance, and proceeded to restore Marduk to his "rightful" place at the head of the Babylonian pantheon. Only the prophets of Israel must have been truly dismayed, for they had prophesied total destruction for Babylon as punishment from God (e.g., *Is.* 46; *Jer.* 50–51). Nevertheless, the final historical irony occurred one year later, in 538 BCE, when the very event that had one year earlier resulted in Babylon's extinction as an independent state now gave rise to the edict of Cyrus (*Ez.* 1.1–4, 6.1–5; *2 Chr.* 36.22–23), allowing the Judeans to return to Zion, rebuild their Holy Temple, and restore their national identity, which the Babylonians had attempted to extinguish.

Only some of the exiles elected to return to Judah; the others remained in Babylonia (they made pilgrimages to Jerusalem), where a number of towns were completely populated by Jews. Under Parthian rule, they enjoyed extensive self-government and were headed by an *exilarch. Following the decline of Palestinian Jewry resulting from the Bar Kokhba' Revolt (c.132–135), rabbinic *academies were established in Babylonia. Initially these acknowledged the authority of the Palestinians, but as the latter declined, the Babylonian academies became the focus of Jewish learning and culture. The supreme expression was the *Talmud Bavli, which henceforth became the basis of study and decision-making throughout the Jewish world. The Babylonian academies remained the center of authority especially after the abolition of the Palestinian patriarchate in 425. During the period of the ge'onim (see GA'ON), all communities and rabbis turned to Babylonia for guidance and decisions on their religious problems (see RESPONSA). This hegemony lasted until the time of *Ha'i Ga'on, after which Babylonia was superseded by centers in the west.

• Albert K. Grayson, *Assyrian and Babylonian Chronicles* (Locust Valley, N.Y., 1975). Richard S. Hess and David T. Tsumura, *I Studied Inscriptions from Before the Flood: Ancient Near Eastern Literary and Linguistic Approaches to Genesis 1–11* (Winona Lake, Ind., 1994), especially articles by Lambert, Millard, Miller, Wiseman, Gelb, Speiser, and Sasson. Jacob Neusner, *A History of The Jews in Babylonia* (Leiden, 1969). A. L. Oppenheim and Erica Reiner, *Ancient Mesopotamia*, rev. ed. (Chicago, 1977). H. W. F. Saggs, *The Greatness That Was Babylon* (New York, 1962). Donald J. Wiseman, *Chronicles of Chaldaean Kings, 626–556* BC (London, 1956). Donald J. Wiseman, *Nebuchadrezzar and Babylon* (Oxford, 1985).

—CHAIM COHEN

BABYLONIAN EXILE, the period from 16 March 597 BCE, when significant numbers of Judahites were forcibly deported to Babylonia, until the edict of Cyrus in April 538, which allowed the Jews to return from Babylonia to Jerusalem for the purpose of rebuilding the Temple destroyed by the forces of the Babylonian king Nebuchadnezzar in August c.587. In 603 King Jehoiakim of Judah became Nebuchadnezzar's vassal. In 601, however, Jehoiakim rebelled (*2 Kgs*. 24.1), and in 598 Nebuchadnezzar's armies set out for Judah to put down the rebellion. A group of Judahites who sought to placate the Babylonians assassinated Jehoiakim and enthroned his son Jehoiachin in his place. Three months later Jerusalem surrendered, and Jehoiachin and most of the nobility and officialdom along with ten thousand able-bodied males were exiled to Babylonia (*2 Kgs*. 24.12–16). Among the exiles was the prophet *Ezekiel. Nebuchadnezzar installed Jehoiachin's uncle Zedekiah as king of Judah. Nevertheless biblical texts (*Ez*. 1; *Jer*. 27ff.), epigraphs from both Judah and Babylonia, and Nebuchadnezzar himself continued to regard Jehoiachin as the legitimate king of Judah. Between 595 and 594, civil unrest in Babylonia inspired the Judahites and other nations to renounce their loyalty to the Babylonian ruler. Although the prophets Jeremiah in Judah and Ezekiel in Babylonia sought to discourage the Jews from rebelling, in 589 King Zedekiah revolted, and Nebuchadnezzar responded by laying siege to Jerusalem, which he conquered in July 587. Zedekiah was captured and forced to witness the execution of his sons before he himself was blinded and carried away in chains to Babylon. A month later, on 7 Av (observed as a fast by Karaite Jews to this day; Rabbanite Jews fast instead on 9 Av), Nebuzaradan, the Babylonian king's chief official, burnt Solomon's Temple, destroyed the walls of Jerusalem, and carried away another 832 Jews into exile. The Babylonians then appointed Gedaliah as governor of Judah; however, he was assassinated by Judean nationalists (*2 Kgs*. 25); in putting down this final Judean rebellion Nebuzaradan exiled another 740 Jews (582). The majority of Judahites remained in the land of Judah, and their everyday life was not appreciably affected by the political events. The small number of exiles enumerated in *2 Kings* and *Jeremiah* explains the small number of returnees enumerated in *Ezra* 2 (*Neh*. 7). With the destruction of the Temple and the Babylonian exile, which were believed to have been divine retribution for the nation's sins, the historical books of the Bible come to an end. Information concerning the lives of the exiles in Babylonia is sparse, but several facts are available. Most of the deportees lived in small communities (*Ez*. 3.15) headed by their own elders (*Ez*. 8.1, 14.1, 20.1), were encouraged to marry (*Jer*. 29.6), and owned their own houses (*Jer*. 29.5). It was probably during this period that the institution of the *synagogue emerged. The exiles, it is thought, came together to pray for the return to Zion and the rebuilding of the Temple and sought words of comfort from the prophets (Ezekiel, Deutero-Isaiah). The rabbis stated that during this period the square Hebrew script was adopted and the months of the year were given Babylonian names. Although Cyrus allowed the exiles to return, many chose to remain in Babylonia.

• Peter R. Ackroyd, *Exile and Restoration* (Philadelphia, 1968). Elias Bickerman, "The Babylonian Captivity," in *The Cambridge History of Judaism*, vol. 1, *Introduction; The Persian Period*, edited by W. D. Davies and L. Finkelstein (Cambridge, 1984), pp. 342–358. Ormond Edwards, "The Year of Jerusalem's Destruction: 2 Addaru 597 B.C. Reinterpreted," *Zeitschrift für die altestamentliche Wissenschaft* 104 (1992): 101–106. Michael Heltzer, "A Recently Published Babylonian Tablet and the Province of Judah after 516 B.C.E.," *Transeuphratene* 5 (1992): 57–61. Peter Kingsley, "Ezekiel by the Grand Canal: Between Jewish and Babylonian Tradition," *Journal of the Royal Asiatic Society*, 3d ser., vol. 2 (1992): 339–346. Ralph W. Klein, *Israel in Exile* (Philadelphia, 1979).

—MAYER I. GRUBER

BABYLONIAN TALMUD. See TALMUD.

BACHARACH, NAFTALI (17th cent.), one of the most important kabbalists before the eruption of the Shabbatean movement; author of the influential work *Emeq ha-Melekh* (1648). Bacharach was born in Frankfurt and lived there most of his life, but he also visited Poland for several years and claimed to have visited Safed, where he said he received traditions from the school of Yitsḥaq Luria; this claim, however, seems to be unfounded. He also claimed to be the original source of the traditions concerning Luria presented in the writings of Yosef Shelomoh *Del-Medigo, but the truth seems to be that, on the contrary, it was he who made use of the Italian scholar's writings. *Emeq ha-Melekh* is a systematic presentation of Lurianic Kabbalah, emphasizing its radical aspects and dwelling in detail on the powers of evil in the created and heavenly realms. The author presents the writings of R. Ḥayyim Vital as his main source, but actually he based his system on the writings of R. Yisra'el Sarug, who developed an original version of the Lurianic teachings. *Emeq ha-Melekh* greatly influenced Shabbatean authors in the seventeenth century and, later, Hasidic and Mitnaggedic writers in the nineteenth century. But there was also severe criticism leveled against Bacharach, and his loyalty to the teachings of Luria was questioned. Among his critics were Mosheh Ḥagiz and Yeshayahu Bassan in the eighteenth century.

• Gershom Gerhard Scholem, *Kabbalah* (Jerusalem, 1974), pp. 394–395.

—JOSEPH DAN

BACHARACH, YA'IR ḤAYYIM (1638–1702), German Talmudist and rabbi. An independent thinker, who often disagreed with earlier rabbinic authorities, Bacharach—who was well-versed in secular studies—declared in one of his *responsa* (*Ḥavvat Ya'ir*, no. 9), "the chief of the Greek philosophers has written; Socrates is my friend, Plato is my friend, but the truth is my most beloved friend." Bacharach was strongly opposed to the use of elaborate *pilpul* to harmonize halakhic difficulties. He was an avid student of Kabbalah. Greatly interested, also, in the Shabbatean movement, he collected manuscripts concerning *Shabbetai Tsevi.

Bacharach wrote *'Ets Ḥayyim*, a comprehensive three-part compendium of Jewish thought, and a collection of 238 *responsa* entitled *Ḥavvat Ya'ir* (Frankfort, 1699). The title is a double entendre: in Hebrew, "the tents of Ya'ir" (*Nm.* 32.41); in German, "The Ya'ir of Ḥavvah," a tribute to his grandmother Ḥavvah. Most of Bacharach's other works remain in manuscript.

For the last three years of Bacharach's life, he served as the rabbi of Worms, a position previously held by both his father and grandfather.

• A. Marx, "Some Notes on the Life of R. Ya'ir Ḥayyim Bacharach," in *Essays in Honour of the Very Rev. Dr. J. H. Hertz* (London, 1944), pp. 307–311. —ELIJAH J. SCHOCHET

BACHELORHOOD. See CELIBACY.

BACHER, WILHELM (1850–1913), scholar born in Liptó-Szent-Miklós, Hungary. Ordained as a rabbi at the Breslau Rabbinical Seminary in 1876, Bacher was named professor at the Landesrabbinerschule in Budapest in 1877, where he remained for the rest of his life. Bacher was a versatile scholar and wrote over six hundred articles on a wide range of subjects, including biblical exegesis, Hebrew philology, and Judeo-Persian literature. He is best known for his pioneering six volumes on the **aggadah*, *Die Agada der babylonischen Amoräer* (1878), as well as for *Die Agada der Tannaiten* (2 vols. [1884–1890]), and *Die Agada der palästinensischen Amoräer* (3 vols. [1892–1899]). These volumes corrected, reorganized, and put into chronological order hundreds of aggadic sources.

• Lajos Blau, *Bacher Vilmos elete es Mukodese* (Budapest, 1910), pp. 40–81. Moshe Carmilly, ed., *The Rabbinical Seminary of Budapest, 1877–1977* (New York, 1986), pp. 151–161, 255–264. —GAVRIEL D. ROSENFELD

BADḤAN (בַּדְחָן), in Ashkenazi communities, a folk poet and singer in charge of wedding ceremonies and other religious feasts and celebrations. Entertaining at weddings is considered a commendable religious deed (a *mitsvah*) worthy of reward in the next world (*Ta'an.* 22a). The art of the *badḥan* lies in his spontaneous improvisation of new songs and rhymed prose (*derashah*) for each celebration. He may deliver Talmudic-styled parodies, invite the celebrants to dance while deciphering their names by means of the technique of *gimatriyyah* (the numerical value of the Hebrew letters), or create witty word plays about people's looks or character.

In recent generations, the performative range of the *badḥan* has become more theatrical; he may even appear in different costumes for his various roles. In spite of the strong objection from rabbis and other religious community leaders, who consider the *badḥan*'s form of entertainment mocking and reckless, the custom has deep roots in Ashkenazi folklore and, although it has declined in the twentieth century, continues to the present.

• Zvi Friedhaber, "Mitzvah Dances at Jewish Weddings," in *Peraqim be-Ḥeqer Minhagei Ḥatunnah*, edited by Issachar Ben-Ami and Dov Noy (Jerusalem, 1974), pp. 69–73. Yom-Tow Lewinsky, "Righteous Women," in *Sefer Zambrov* (Tel Aviv, 1963), discusses a well-known female *badḥan*, Malke of Zambrów. —TAMAR ALEXANDER

BAECK, LEO (1873–1956), German Reform rabbi, scholar, theologian, and communal leader. Baeck was one of the towering figures of twentieth-century German–Jewish life. Beginning his rabbinate in Oppeln (1897–1907), he moved to Dusseldorf (1907–1912) and then to Berlin in 1912, where he remained until 1942. Influenced by Hermann Cohen and responding to Adolf von Harnack's *The Essence of Christianity*, Baeck presented, in *The Essence of Judaism* (German, 1905; English, 1936) and in subsequent works, such as *The Pharisees* (1947) and *Judaism and Christianity* (1958), a contrast between "classic religion," committed to moral action, and "romantic religion," committed to emotion. In classic religion (Judaism), one becomes free through the commandments; in romantic religion (Christianity), through grace. In *This People Israel* (New York, 1964), part of which was written in the concentration camp of Theresienstadt but which was completed a few days before his death, Baeck presented his vision of the religious role of the Jewish people, at the core of which lay morality. The key to Judaism is its polarity between "mystery" (the manifestation of the divine in humans) and commandments (the demands of ethical monotheism). The head of the liberal rabbinate in Germany from 1923, Baeck became the head of all German Jewry in 1933, after the Nazi decrees destroyed the legal status of German Jewry. Though he had a number of opportunities to escape from Germany, he remained at his post until he was deported in 1942 to the Theresienstadt concentration camp. After the war, he settled in London. In the 1950s he became a visiting professor at the Hebrew Union College in Cincinnati.

• Henry W. Brann, "Leo Baeck," in *Great Jewish Thinkers of the Twentieth Century*, edited by Simon Noveck (Washington, 1963), pp. 133–158. Albert Friedlander, *Leo Baeck, Teacher of Theresienstadt* (London, 1973). Walter Homolka, *Jewish Identity in Modern Times: Leo Baeck and German Protestantism* (Providence, 1995). Paul Morris, "The Essence of Leo Baeck," *European Judaism* 21.2 (1988): 34–41. W. Gunther Plaut, "The Man Who Saved My Life," *CCAR Journal* 41.3 (Summer 1994): 21–24. Eliezer Schweid, "Prophetic Mysticism," in *Ḥashivah me-Ḥadash: Peritsot ba-Maḥashavah ha-Yehudit ha-Datit veha-Le'ummit ba-Me'ah ha-'Esrim* (Jerusalem, 1991). —LEONARD KRAVITZ

BAER, YITZHAK (1888–1980), scholar of medieval history. Born in Halberstadt, Germany, Baer received his doctorate from Freiburg University in 1912. His greatest scholarly contribution lies in the field of Spanish–Jewish history, particularly during the Christian period. He undertook an exhaustive review of royal archives and Jewish communal records in Spain. This work resulted in his publication of two volumes of primary sources, *Die Juden im christlichen Spanien* (1929, 1936). Following his immigration to Palestine and appointment as professor of Jewish history at the Hebrew University of Jerusalem, Baer published a third volume on Spain, *Toledot ha-Yehudim bi-Sefarad ha-Notsrit* (Jerusalem, 1945; published in English as *The History of the Jews in Christian Spain* [Philadelphia, 1992]), a monumental narrative account of Jewish life in Christian Spain. His book *Galut* (Germany, 1936; New York, 1947) presented a highly schematic and lugubrious portrait of Jewish history in the Diaspora. Written in the early years of the Nazi reign in Germany, it underscored Baer's own Zionist inclinations, according to which Jewish life in Erets Yisra'el was superior to life outside it. Toward the end of his career, Baer embarked on a new field of historical research, the study of the Second Temple period. A Festschrift published in his honor in Jerusalem in 1961 includes a bibliography of his writings up to 1959.

• Benjamin R. Gampel's introduction to Y. Baer, *A History of the Jews in Christian Spain* (Philadelphia, 1992). David N. Myers, *Re-Inventing the Jewish Past* (New York, 1995). E. Shmueli, "The Jerusalem School of Jewish History," *Proceedings of the American Academy for Jewish Research* 53 (1986): 147–178. —DAVID N. MYERS

BAḤ. See SIRKES, YO'EL BEN SHEMU'EL.

BAHIR, SEFER HA-. See SEFER HA-BAHIR.

BAḤUR (בָּחוּר; chosen one), in the Bible, refers to a picked soldier (*1 Sm.* 26.2) or a person in the prime of his youth and vigor (cf. *Eccl.* 11.9, 12.1). Since the word was often juxtaposed with *betulah* (virgin; *Dt.* 32.5; *Is.* 62.5; *Lam.* 1.16), it was regarded in later Hebrew as the equivalent of an unmarried man (*Ket.* 7a). Its use is now largely confined to this meaning, as the general title given both to a bachelor and particularly to an (unmarried) *yeshivah student (Yi. *bokher*).

BAḤUR, ELIYYAHU. See LEVITA, ELIYYAHU.

BAḤYA, PSEUDO- (11th–12th cent.), anonymous author of *Kitab Ma'ani al-Nafs*. Although the work was ascribed to *Baḥya ben Yosef ibn Paquda', this ascription is now generally rejected since *Kitab Ma'ani al-Nafs* is completely Neoplatonist in its orientation, whereas Baḥya' follows both Neoplatonism and the Kalam. Its author argues that the soul is a spiritual being, independent of the body. He divides the universe into ten emanations; namely, the active intellect or wisdom (*shekhinah*), the universal soul, nature, matter, the celestial sphere, stars, fire, air, water, and earth. Human beings are formed from all ten emanations, but the human soul is most nearly related to the universal soul and the active intellect. In its descent to the human body, it must pass through all the emanations, all of which leave traces of their influence—accounting for the differences in the human temperament. These impurities must be removed if the soul is to be reunited once more with its spiritual source. Nothing is known of the author, and his work was little known by later philosophers. The original Arabic was edited by Ignaz Goldziher and published in 1907 in Berlin; Isaac Broydé published a Hebrew translation (*Torot ha-Nefesh*) in 1896 in Paris.

• Julius Guttman, *Philosophies of Judaism* (New York, 1964), pp. 124–127. Isaac Husik, *History of Mediaeval Jewish Philosophy* (New York, 1932), pp. 106–113.

BAḤYA BEN ASHER (died 1320), Bible commentator. Born in Saragossa, Spain, he served as judge (*dayyan*) in the rabbinical court and preacher (*darshan*) in that city. A disciple of Shelomoh ben Avraham Adret, Baḥya was among the first writers to quote the Zohar. Although he refers to the Zohar as "The Midrash of Rabbi Shim'on bar Yoḥ'ai," he generally distinguishes it from rabbinic literature. Baḥya's most important work was his commentary on the Torah, which has been reprinted in more than twenty editions since 1492 and in eleven supercommentaries known in full, from fragments, or from quotations. This commentary heavily influenced the **Tse'enah u-Re'enah*. Baḥya employs a fourfold method of interpretation associated with the acronym **pardes*. These four levels of interpretation are *peshat*, contextual interpretation; *derekh ha-Midrash*, insights from the Midrash; *derekh ha-sekhel*, insights from philosophy; and *derekh ha-Kabbalah*, insights from the esoteric lore of the Jewish mystics. Baḥya's other works are a commentary on *Avot*; *Kad ha-Qemaḥ* (Constantinople, 1515), a collection of sixty sermons concerning the essentials of Jewish religious practice; and *Shulḥan shel Arba'* (Mantua, 1514), a work in four chapters, the first three of which explain the *halakhot* pertaining to meals eaten in this world, while the fourth discusses the banquet of the righteous in the world to come. Baḥya's works are especially important because of their numerous references to the kabbalistic works of Nahmanides' generation, while his Bible commentary helps to explain the meaning of mystical elements in Nahmanides' Bible commentary.

• Bela Bernstein, *Die Schrifterklärung des Bachja b. Ascher ibn Chalawa und ihre Quellen* (Berlin, 1891). Charles B. Chavel, *Kitvei Rabbenu Baḥya'* (Jerusalem, 1969). Efraim Gottlieb, *The Kabbalah in the Writings of R. Baḥya' ben Asher Ibn Ḥalawa'* (Jerusalem, 1970). Herbert Millen, "Bahya Ben Asher: The Exegetical and Ethical Components of His Writing," D.H.L. thesis, Yeshiva University, 1974. —MAYER I. GRUBER

BAḤYA BEN YOSEF IBN PAQUDA' (11th cent.), philosopher and moralist; author of *Ḥovot ha-Levavot* (Duties of the Heart), one of the most popular works of spiritual and ethical guidance in Judaism. Little is known of Baḥya's life, except that he lived in Muslim Spain and was a judge in a rabbinic court. It was perhaps in this capacity that he became sensitive to the dangers of emphasizing outward punctiliousness in the observance of law (the duties of the limbs) to the neglect of the inward, spiritual duties of the heart. The work of Baḥya is modeled on Muslim mystical literature, which conducts the reader through the various stages of the inner life toward spiritual perfection and loving communion with God. His proof of God's essential attributes—his existence, unity, and eternity—as well as his proofs of creation are largely derived from *Kalam. Despite his indebtedness to Muslim mysticism and Arabic Neoplatonism, *Ḥovot ha-Levavot* is a classic of Jewish piety. In his understanding of human nature and the path to perfection, Baḥya follows the Platonic tradition. The soul, of celestial origin, is placed by divine decree within the body, in whose service it is in danger of forgetting its supernatural calling. The growth of the soul is aided by the inspiration of reason (both a faculty residing in humans and a supernatural entity) and by the revealed Torah. The obligations imposed by the latter correspond to the blessings God has showered on humanity, especially on the Jew as a member of the chosen people; they also specify the general duties suggested by simple reason, and in particular the duty of gratitude toward the benefactor. The marvelous microcosmic nature of human beings serves a double purpose: that of leading people to God through the contemplation of creation, since God can be known in no other way; and that of inculcating the duty of gratitude toward the benefactor. One must fulfill all duties to God without wavering. Trust in God rests on two principles: God knows what is good for humanity better than does humanity itself; and while people are free with respect to their intentions and decisions, the realization of their acts is solely determined by the divine will. A strong spiritual life demands agreement between one's conscience and one's performance. Ascetic discipline leads to the uppermost rung of spirituality, which is the love of God. Baḥya eschews the more extreme forms of asceticism (for example, seclusion from society) but advocates a middle path: the true ascetic is one who is always with God while at the same time performing his duties within society. Belief in the afterlife is an important aspect of his system. Baḥya's work, written in Judeo-Arabic, has been translated into many languages, and *Ḥovot ha-Levavot* was one of the most frequently printed guides to Jewish spiritual life. It was translated into Hebrew by Yehudah ibn Tibbon in 1160 and was one of the first Hebrew books to be printed (Naples, 1489). It was translated into English by Moses Hyamson (1965) and Menahem Mansoor (1973). Baḥya also wrote a number of *piyyutim*.

• Michael Fishbane, "Action and Non-Action in Jewish Spirituality," *Judaism* 33 (1984): 318–329. Lenn E. Goodman, "Bahya on the Antimony of Free Will and Predestination," *Journal of the History of Ideas* 44 (1983): 115–130. Georges Vajda, *La Theólogie ascétique de Bahya Ibn Paquda*, Cahiers de la Société Asiatique 7 (Paris, 1947).

BAILMENT. See SHOMERIM.

BAIS YAʿAQOV. See BETH JACOB SCHOOLS .

BALAAM (Heb. Bilʿam), son of Beor; a pagan seer from Pethor in northern Mesopotamia. According to the biblical account (*Nm.* 22–24), Balak, king of Moab, asked Balaam to curse the Israelites when they approached his country on their way from the wilderness to Canaan. Instead, Balaam uttered blessings under divine inspiration. Balaam is described both as a typical pagan soothsayer and as a genuine prophet of God. Talmudic tradition regards him as one of the prophets God raised among the nations, equal to Moses in prophetic power, but at the same time utterly wicked—on Balaam's advice the Midianites enticed Israel to immorality and idolatry of Baal-peor. The story of Balaam's ass is much debated between literalistic and allegoristic commentators; Maimonides, for example, held that Balaam dreamed that his ass spoke. The story is an example of early Israelite satire that demonstrates the power of God over that of a pagan seer, who sees (and speaks) only what God permits. The words of Balaam, "How goodly are your tents, O Jacob, and your dwelling places, O Israel" (*Nm.* 24.5), are the first words uttered each morning upon entering the synagogue. Balaam's statement, "A star shall come forth from Jacob and a scepter shall rise out of Israel" (*Nm.* 24.17), was widely interpreted as a messianic prediction; it was applied to Shimʿon bar Kokhbaʾ (Shimʿon, son of the star), who led the second revolt against Rome (132–135).

• *The Balaam Text from Deir ʿAlla Re-evalutated: Proceedings of the International Symposium held at Leiden, 21–24 August 1989*, edited by J. Hoftijzer and G. van der Kooij (Leiden and New York, 1991). Judith Reesa Baskin, *Pharaoh's Counsellors: Job, Jethro, and Balaam in Rabbinic and Patristic Tradition*, Brown Judaic Studies, no. 47 (Chico, Calif., 1983). John T. Greene, *Balaam and his Interpreters: A Hermeneutical History of the Balaam Traditions*, Brown Judaic Studies, no. 244 (Atlanta, 1992). Jo Ann Hackett, *The Balaam Text from Deīr ʿAllā*, Harvard Semitic Monographs, no. 31 (Chico, Calif., 1984). Jo Ann Hackett, "Some Observations on the Balaam Tradition at Deir ʿAlla," *Biblical Archaeologist* 49 (1986): 216–222. Michael S. Moore, *The Balaam Traditions*, Dissertation Series (Society of Biblical Literature), no. 113 (Atlanta, 1990). Alexander Rofé, *"Sefer Bilʿam": Be-Midbar 22.2–24.25*, ʿIyyunim ba-Miqraʾ uvi-Tequfato 6 (Jerusalem, 1979). —MARVIN A. SWEENEY

BAL TASHḤIT (בַּל תַּשְׁחִית; do not destroy), biblical prohibition against destroying fruit trees, even when laying siege to a city (*Dt.* 20.19–20), extended by the Talmud to cover all senseless destruction or waste (*Shab.* 129a; *B. Q.* 91b). The rabbis permitted destruction if there was an ultimately constructive objective (e.g., cutting trees for building or in order to let other trees grow).

BAMAH. See HIGH PLACE.

BAMBERGER, SELIGMANN BAER (1807–1878), Bavarian rabbi and Orthodox leader in Germany. At an assembly of Jewish representatives convened by the Bavarian government in 1836, it was his firm stand that led to the Reform party's unexpected defeat. As district rabbi of Würzburg from 1840, Bamberger headed the *yeshivah* there and founded a seminary that trained hundreds of Jewish teachers. The "Würzburger Rav" (as he became known) spoke for a popular, countrified Orthodoxy and was one of the last great German Talmudists. His works comprised *responsa* and practical *halakhah*, but together with his son (Shimʿon Simḥah), he also annotated Yitsḥaq ibn Ghayyat's *Halakhot Kelulot* (*Shaʿarei Simḥah* [1861–1862]). During the 1870s, Bamberger opposed the secession of autonomous Orthodox communities (as advocated by Samson Raphael *Hirsch), maintaining that Orthodox Jewry should present a united front and insist upon its rights within the framework of the general community. His collected *responsa* appeared in *Yad ha-Levi* (Jerusalem, 1965).

• Shaul Esh, *The Bamberger Family; The Descendants of Rabbi Seligmann Bär Bamberger* (Jerusalem, 1964). Leo Jung, ed., *Jewish Leaders, 1750–1940* (New York, 1953), pp. 181–195. Hermann Schwab, *The History of Orthodox Jewry in Germany*, translated by Irene R. Birnbaum (London, 1950), pp. 73–81. —GABRIEL A. SIVAN

BA-MEH MADLIQIN (בַּמֶּה מַדְלִיקִין; "With what may one light [the Sabbath lamp]?"), the opening words of the second chapter of the Mishnah tractate *Shabbat*, recited during the Sabbath eve service—in some rites before the main part of the service, in others after the ʿAmidah. It states which wicks and oils may (and may not) be used in the Sabbath lamp. The reading was originally introduced in geonic times, possibly as an anti-Karaite polemic. Ba-Meh Madliqin is not recited when the Sabbath coincides with or immediately follows a holiday.

BA-MIDBAR. See NUMBERS, BOOK OF.

BA-MIDBAR RABBAH. See NUMBERS RABBAH.

BAN. See EXCOMMUNICATION.

BANET, MORDEKHAI (1753–1829), Moravian rabbi who served in Nikolsburg and Ludenburg, eventually rising to the position of district rabbi of Moravia. The head of a large and renowned *yeshivah* in Nikolsburg, his publications include *Bi'ur Mordekhai* (2 vols. [Vienna, 1805, 1813]), *novellae* on *Sefer Mordekhai* by R. *Mordekhai ben Hillel; *Parashat Mordekhai* (Szeged, 1889), a collection of *responsa*; and *Maḥashevet Mordekhai* (Mukachevo, 1908), homiletical insights on the Torah. Banet was a staunch opponent of the nascent religious reform movement in Europe. His *responsum* condemning the reformist Hamburg Temple prayer book is included in *Eleh Divrei ha-Berit* (Hamburg, 1819), a collection of such writings by leading traditionalists. He was also a leading critic of Sha'ul ben Tsevi Hirsch *Berlin's book *Besamim Ro'sh* (Berlin, 1793), which purported to contain previously unknown *responsa* of the eminent medieval halakhist R. Asher ben Yeḥi'el. Banet deduced that the work, in which R. Asher took positions remarkably similar to those enunciated by champions of the Enlightenment, was a forgery.

• Rubin Faerber, *Pe'er Mordekhai* (Tel Aviv, 1951).

—MARK WASHOFSKY

BANISHMENT, expulsion from one's normal residence. Biblical law legislates banishment only in the case of accidental slayers who find *asylum from blood vengeance in the cities of refuge; the rabbis, however, insisted that this banishment was no mere protective asylum, but had also an atoning function. Banishment from the land is the major punishment that God visits on his people (see EXILE), as it was a punishment in the cases of Adam and Cain. In the Second Temple period, banishment was occasionally decreed as a punishment in criminal cases. Banishment is not recognized in Jewish law as a normal form of punishment, though medieval courts resorted to it in order to rid the community of heretical individuals (see EXCOMMUNICATION). In some periods mystics would take up voluntary exile (*galut*) or wanderings (*gerushim*) to promote mystical atonement.

BAPTISM, ritual purification by total immersion in water (*tevilah*). During the Second Temple period, baptism was practiced by many pietist groups and sects (see ESSENES; JOHN THE BAPTIST). It was required of converts to Judaism and became the distinctive conversion rite of the Christian church (*Mk.* 1.9; *Acts* 2.38–41, 8.38, 19.3–5). The practice of total immersion has largely given way in Christianity to a ceremonial sprinkling of water. See also ABLUTION; HEMEROBAPTISTS; MIQVEH.

• Harold Henry Rowley, *From Moses to Qumran* (London and New York, 1963), pp. 211–235. Lawrence H. Schiffman, *Who Was a Jew? Rabbinic and Halakhic Perspectives on the Jewish Christian Schism* (Hoboken, N.J., 1985), pp. 25–36.

BAPTISM, FORCED. See CONVERSION, FORCED.

BAQQASHAH (בַּקָּשָׁה; entreaty, supplication), name given to two types of *piyyutim* (see PIYYUT). The first consists of works written in prose or rhymed verse (by authors such as *Sa'adyah ben Yosef Ga'on, *Baḥya ben Yosef ibn Paquda', and Shelomoh *ibn Gabirol) with philosophical or theological content, mainly for private meditation. The second type is a shorter composition in the style of Spanish liturgical poetry with a strict rhyming pattern (for example, Yitsḥaq ben Levi ibn Mar Sha'ul's Elohei 'al Tedineni and El'azar ben Mosheh *Azikri's later *Yedid Nefesh). Baqqashot is also the name given to a service of *piyyutim* printed at the commencement of Sephardi prayer books from the seventeenth century on and recited or sung by congregants before the Sabbath Shaḥarit service. In Syria (Aleppo and Damascus) and Morocco, and in related congregations in twentieth-century Erets Yisra'el, the singing of *baqqashot* developed into a more independent liturgical activity.

• Abraham De Sola et al., eds., *The Form of Prayers: According to the Custom of the Spanish and Portuguese Jews* (Philadelphia, 1926), pp. 90–91. Ismar Elbogen, *Jewish Liturgy: A Comprehensive History*, translated by Raymond P. Scheindlin (Philadelphia, 1993), p. 250.

—PETER LENHARDT

BARAIYTA' (Aram.; בָּרַיְתָא), a term referring to a tannaitic pericope appearing in the Talmud, which means "[a tannaitic statement] external [to the Mishnah]." It is used for Midrashic tannaitic material or, more frequently, for halakhic tannaitic material. *Baraiytot* are often parallel to pericopes of existing tannaitic works, such as the Tosefta'. Such *baraiytot* are rarely identical in wording to their parallels. Divergencies, rather than deriving from an independent source, usually resulted from editorial reworking (to achieve harmonization with the Mishnah, for example), especially in the Talmud Bavli. The Talmud Yerushalmi sometimes abbreviates *baraiytot*. Some *baraiytot* in the Talmud Bavli that have no parallels elsewhere may be post-tannaitic creations. The Talmud commonly accords tannaitic statements found in *baraiytot* equal authority to those in the Mishnah and often rules according to *baraiytot* against the Mishnah. Originally there was no special word to designate *baraiytot*; the Talmud Yerushalmi refers both to the Mishnah and to *baraiytot* with the word *matnita'*. Fourth-generation Babylonian amora'im increasingly introduced the term *baraiyta'*, paralleling a growing tendency to award the Mishnah canonic status. The term was extended to the various tannaitic works themselves: the Tosefta' and the Midrash, for instance, were referred to as *baraiytot*, in contrast to the Mishnah.

• Chanoch Albeck, *Meḥqarim bi-Varaiyta' ve-Tosephta' ve-Yaḥasan le-Talmud*, 4th ed. (Jerusalem 1969). Chanoch Albeck, *Mavo' la-Talmudim* (Tel Aviv, 1987). Jacob Nahum Epstein, *Mevo'ot le-Sifrut ha-Tanna'im* (Jerusalem, 1957). Michael Higger, ed., *Otsar ha-Baraiytot* (New York, 1938–1948).

—SHAMMA FRIEDMAN

BARAIYTA' DE-MELE'KHET HA-MISHKAN, an ancient work, containing tannaitic material, apparently compiled, like other *baraiytot*, after the redaction of the Mishnah. It describes the manner in which the Tabernacle was constructed. It is occasionally cited in the Talmud and by early post-Talmudic authorities. It was first published in Venice in 1608, and a critical edition was published by Meir Friedmann in 1908.

—AVRAHAM WALFISH

BARAIYTA' DE-NIDDAH, an ancient work containing aggadic and halakhic material relating to the laws of the menstrual woman (*Lv.* 15.19–33). It contains many stringent rulings, tending to follow the opinion of Beit Shamm'ai rather than that of Beit Hillel. Leading scholars believe that many of the book's rulings, although at variance with accepted Talmudic law, are rooted in ancient Palestinian rabbinic sources. It was first mentioned by Nahmanides and was published by C. M. Horowitz in 1890.

—AVRAHAM WALFISH

BARAIYTA' OF THIRTY-TWO RULES, an ancient work presenting thirty-two hermeneutic principles utilized in the aggadic interpretation of scripture, ascribed by tradition to R. Yosei ben El'azar the Galilean, a second-century tanna'. Some scholars, on the basis of linguistic proof and the existence in the work of later material, date the work to the period of the later ge'onim. Others differentiate between the original layer of the work, dating to the tannaitic period, containing only the rules themselves, and later layers, which added examples and applications of the rules. Some of the rules, such as *gimatriyyah* (calculating the numerical value of a word) and *notariqon* (interpretation of a word as an acrostic or breaking a word into two), while going far beyond normal exegetical understanding, were nonetheless common modes of interpreting literary texts, as well as dreams, during the time of the rabbis.

• Hyman Gerson Enelow, ed., *Mishnat Rabbi Eli'ezer o Midrash Sheloshim u-Shetaim Middot* (New York, 1933). Menachem Mendel Kasher and Jacob Ber Mandelbaum, eds. and trans., *Sarei ha-'Elef*, rev. and corr. ed. (Jerusalem, 1978), vol. 1, pp. 38–39.

—AVRAHAM WALFISH

BARCELONA, DISPUTATION OF, Jewish–Christian public *disputation held in 1263. In the latter part of the thirteenth century, a Jewish convert to Christianity named Friar Paul Christian developed a fresh approach to *polemics, mining the Talmud and Midrash for statements demonstrating the truth of Christianity, just as the Hebrew Bible itself had been mined.

In Barcelona, Moses *Nahmanides, the most distinguished rabbi on the Iberian Peninsula, found himself face to face with Paul Christian in a public disputation initiated by Dominican friars and sponsored and attended by King James I of Aragon himself. The items on the agenda were not new; they included the propositions that the Messiah had already come, that he was both human and divine, that he suffered and was killed for the sins of mankind, and that the ceremonial law ended with his coming. What was novel was the claim that these propositions could be proved through a combination of biblical and Talmudic evidence.

Nahmanides attempted to abort the argument by maintaining that since the rabbis lived after the time of Jesus and manifestly refrained from embracing Christianity, the argument for a Christological Talmud was absurd. When the disputation proceeded anyway, he maintained that the Midrash, or the nonlegal corpus of the rabbis, was not doctrinally binding and that no argument based upon this material had the power to compel Jewish assent. Paul was not silenced; the debate went on to address a host of detailed issues and culminated in a public exchange between the two protagonists at Sabbath services in a Barcelona synagogue.

A Latin account of the disputation awards victory to Paul. Controversy surrounds the authenticity of the vigorous anti-Christian pronouncements that Nahmanides reports in his Hebrew narrative of the disputation. At the end of the Hebrew narrative, it is stated that the king informed Nahmanides in a private conversation that he had never seen someone who was in error defend his position so impressively. While there is no doubt that Jewish and Christian observers perceived the outcome differently, there can be little question that Nahmanides' performance succeeded in preserving Jewish morale in the face of a new attack, which subsequent Christians were to develop into a deadly assault on late medieval Jewry. Nahmanides, under church threats, was forced to leave Spain and moved to Erets Yisra'el.

• Robert Chazan, *Barcelona and Beyond* (Berkeley, 1992). Hyam Maccoby, ed., *Judaism on Trial* (Rutherford, N.J., 1982). Nahmanides, *Writings and Discourses*, edited and translated by Charles Ber Chavel (New York, 1978), vol. 2, pp. 656–696.

—DAVID BERGER

BAREHEADEDNESS. See COVERING OF THE HEAD.

BAREKHU (בָּרְכוּ), first word of *Barekhu et Adonai ha-mevorakh*, "Bless the Lord who is [to be] blessed," which has become the customary synagogue formula of invitation to prayer. It is based on the phrase "Bless the Lord," which occurs frequently in the Bible (e.g., *Ps.* 135.19; *Neh.* 9.5). This formula (cf. *Ber.* 50a) serves as the opening of both the morning and evening prayers in the synagogue (those sections of the morning prayer now preceding Barekhu did not originally form part of the obligatory synagogue prayers) and also constitutes the introduction to the public reading from the Torah. While the reader chants Barekhu, the congregation reads silently a prayer beginning *Yitbarakh* (of which different versions exist in the various rites); when the reader concludes the invitation, the congregation responds aloud: "Blessed is the Lord who is [to be] blessed for ever and ever." *Genizah* fragments have shown that the Barekhu formula was not used among Palestinian Jews. It became customary for the reader in the invocation and the congregants in the response to bow at the word *barekhu/barukh*. Eastern-Sephardi and Hasidic Jews repeat Barekhu before 'Aleinu at the end of Shaḥarit and Ma'ariv. Barekhu was used for the Zimmun (the invitation to *Birkat ha-Mazon) but was later replaced by the Nevarekh (let us bless) formula, which is used today.

• Ismar Elbogen, *Jewish Liturgy: A Comprehensive History*, translated by Raymond P. Scheindlin (Philadelphia, 1993). Macy Nulman, *The Encyclopedia of Jewish Prayer* (Northvale, N.J., 1993).

BAR KOKHBA', SHIM'ON (died 135 CE), leader of the second Jewish revolt against Rome. His real name, known from his military dispatches found in the Judean desert caves, was Bar Kosiba'. He was given the sobriquet Bar Kokhba', Son of the Star, an allusion to *Numbers* 24.17, widely taken to refer to the *Messiah, by those who saw in him the messianic redeemer.

The revolt started in 132 CE and was the result of still simmering Jewish opposition to Roman rule on both practical and nationalistic grounds. The immediate cause may have been the prohibition of circumcision or the increased messianic fervor resulting from the possibility that the Temple might be rebuilt. Initially the Jews were successful, and Bar Kokhba' set up an entire government and may even have restored sacrifice in Jerusalem under his high priest, El'azar. With the arrival of greater Roman forces, the country was gradually retaken.

Bar Kokhba' was a stern commander who concerned himself with numerous minor details. The texts recently discovered in the Judean desert indicate his concern for observance of the Sabbath and Jewish holidays. The rabbis debated his messianic status, but it is clear that many of his followers and even R. *'Aqiva' ben Yosef saw him as the Messiah. His success in freeing Jerusalem certainly contributed to this impression, and his use of the title *nasi'* (prince) may have been designed to encourage this perception.

Bar Kokhba' was killed at Betar in 135 CE, in what was doubtless the last great battle of the revolt. By this time the Romans had reconquered most of Judea, and the only remaining resistance must have been in the Judean desert. Historical sources on the revolt are scanty. Some have linked the holiday of *Lag ba-'Omer to the Bar Kokhba' period.

• Richard S. Marks, *The Image of Bar Kokhba in Traditional Jewish Literature: False Messiah and National Hero* (University Park, Pa., 1994). Lawrence H. Schiffman, *From Text to Tradition, A History of Second Temple and Rabbinic Judaism* (Hoboken, N.J., 1991), pp. 171–174. Emil Schürer, *The History of the Jewish People in the Age of Jesus Christ*, revised and edited by Geza Vermes, F. Millar, and M. Black, vol. 1 (Edinburgh, 1973), pp. 514–557. E. Mary Smallwood, *The Jews under Roman Rule: From Pompey to Diocletian: A Study in Political Relations*, Studies in Judaism in Late Antiquity 20 (Leiden, 1981), pp. 428–466. Yigael Yadin, *Bar-Kokhba: The Rediscovery of the Legendary Hero of the Second Jewish Revolt against Rome* (New York, 1971).

—LAWRENCE H. SCHIFFMAN

BAR MITSVAH (בַּר מִצְוָה; son of [the] commandment), an adult male Jew obligated to perform the commandments; hence, the ceremony at which a thirteen-year-old boy becomes an adult member of the community for ceremonial purposes (including that of making up a *minyan*). Although one of the most widely observed of all Jewish rites, it is devoid of ancient authority or sanction. The term itself in its present-day connotation is unknown in the Talmud, though it is found as a general term applying to an adult male (*B. M.* 96a). The Talmud merely states that a male child reaches his religious majority on attaining puberty, which as a general but not an exclusive rule is set at the age of thirteen years and a day (*Kid.* 16b). From this age on, he is regarded as a responsible person, liable for the results of his own actions, and it is for this reason that Rabbi El'azar enjoins that when a child reaches this age the father should recite the blessing *Barukh she-Petarani ("Blessed is he who has freed me from the responsibility for this child" [*Gn. Rab.* 63.14]). The performance of all the duties of a Jew are now incumbent on the youth (*Avot* 5.21). Since about the fourteenth century the term *bar mitsvah* has been used only to refer to a boy on the attainment of his religious majority. An elaborate ceremony has developed, generally divided into the religious ceremony in the synagogue and the subsequent social celebration. The synagogue ceremony normally takes place among Ashkenazim on the first Sabbath after the actual thirteenth Hebrew birthdate, though it can be held on any weekday when scripture reading takes place. A characteristically visible expression of the *bar mitsvah* in observant circles is that the boy begins to put on *tefillin* daily. In some communities of Baghdadi provenance, the first putting on of phylacteries on the day following the ceremony is made the occasion of a separate ceremony. In medieval Europe, community statutes strictly regulated and limited the extent of the festivities and gifts and provided for similar celebrations for poor boys at the community's expense. Today, the celebration and presents are often on a lavish scale. In the synagogue the *bar mitsvah* boy is called to the reading of a portion of the Law, usually the last portion, the **maftir* (in some cases the boy reads the entire weekly portion) and also reads the **haftarah*. In some communities, the boy reads a special prayer for the occasion. The custom for the boy to be specially addressed in synagogue has become widespread only recently. It became the custom for the boy to deliver a learned discourse (*derashah*). He also receives gifts from family and friends. Rabbinic justification for the social celebration has been found in a Midrashic interpretation of *Genesis* 21.8, "And Abraham made a great feast on the day that Isaac was weaned," to the effect that it refers not to his weaning from his mother but from the "evil inclination" (*Gn. Rab.* 53.14), that is, on his attaining religious majority. The banquet thereby qualifies as a Se'udat Mitsvah, that is, a feast celebrating the fulfillment of a religious commandment. Among some eastern Sephardi communities the boy begins to don *tefillin* at age twelve or twelve and a half, and some even hold the *bar mitsvah* ceremony at this earlier age. The boy delivers his discourse when first putting on *tefillin*, and it is therefore known as *derush li-tefillin* (*tefillin* discourse). Another eastern Sephardi custom that has become common in Israel and in North America among Ashkenazi congregations as well as Sephardi ones is for members of the congregation to throw candies at the boy when he has finished his Torah reading. In recent years many *bar mitsvah* boys from Israel and abroad hold the ceremony in front of the *Western Wall. In many kibbutzim an annual ceremony is held for all boys and girls who have reached the age of *bar* and **bat mitsvah*. At one point, Reform Judaism introduced *confirmation as a replacement for *bar mitsvah*, but now it is usually a supplementary ceremony held two or three years later. In the United States a *bar mitsvah* ceremony is sometimes held in non-Orthodox congregations for adult men who did not have a *bar mitsvah* observance at the usual age.

• Nachman Cohen, *Bar, Bat Mitzvah and Beyond* (Yonkers, N.Y., 1988). Azriel Louis Eisenberg, *The Bar Mitzvah Treasury* (New York, 1952). Yaakov Salomon and Yonah Weinrib, *Bar Mitzvah, Its Observance and Significance* (Brooklyn, N.Y., 1991).

BAR QAPPARA' (3d cent. CE), Palestinian scholar (also known as Elaʿzar) and a disciple of *Yehudah ha-Nasi', who made an independent collection of legal traditions (*B. B.* 154b). The Talmud quotes some of his sayings, epigrams, fables, and riddles—many in a poetic style, to which he was probably referring when he said (based on *Gn.* 9.27), "The words of Torah should be couched in the tongue of Japheth in the tent of Shem." Although he was interested in scientific inquiry (*Shab.* 75a), he counseled against going beyond the accepted parameters of research ("further than the ends of the heavens" [*Gn. Rab.* 1.10]). He is considered by some scholars to have been the chief editor of the **Sifrei Zuta'*.

• Gershom Bader, *The Encyclopedia of Talmudic Sages*, translated from the Yiddish by Solomon Katz (Northvale, N.J., and London, 1988). Aaron Hyman, *Toledot Tanna'im ve-'Amora'im* (1910; Jerusalem, 1987). Saul Lieberman, *Sifrei Zuta': Midrashah shel Lod; Talmudah shel Qeisarin* (New York, 1968). Mordecai Margaliot, ed., *Entsiqlopediyyah le-Ḥakhmei ha-Talmud veha-Ge'onim* (Jerusalem, 1946). —DANIEL SPERBER

BARRENNESS. The first and most basic of the divine commandments is procreation (*Gn.* 1.28). In general, the Bible presents infertility as a punishment and a curse (*Lv.* 20.20–21; *2 Sm.* 6.23), for example, when a desperate Rachel cries out to her husband, Jacob, that she would rather be dead than childless (*Gn.* 30.1). Three matriarchs, Sarah, Rebekah, and Rachel, suffered from barrenness and only conceived after much prayer and supplication. The Talmud suggests that their condition was a means of provoking them to pray, and the prayer of such righteous individuals is of inestimable spiritual value (*B. B.* 16a). The most dramatic biblical example of the nexus between prayer and infertility is the story of Hannah (*1 Sm.* 1). The prophet Isaiah comforts the childless, explaining that in God's eyes, the infertile who obey the commandments will have "a monument and a name better than sons and daughters" (*Is.* 56.1–6). Jewish law contains various provisions for divorce on grounds of infertility, and in Talmudic law a man should divorce his wife if she has been barren for ten years (*Yev.* 6.6; 64a); however, in practice, divorce in such situations is not mandatory. Rabbinic literature contains many references to the notion that supporting or teaching a child is tantamount to fulfilling the *mitsvah* of procreation (*San.* 19b). Barrenness and its cure were the subject of folklore and superstition.

• Richard V. Grazi, ed., *Be Fruitful and Multiply: Fertility Therapy and the Jewish Tradition* (Jerusalem, 1994). Fred Rosner, *Medicine in the Bible and the Talmud*, The Library of Jewish Law and Ethics, vol. 5 (New York, 1995), pp. 127–131. Shmuel Shilo, "Impotence as a Ground for Divorce," *Jewish Law Annual* 4 (1981): 127–143. —DANIEL SINCLAIR

BARTER (Heb. *ḥalifin*), a mode of acquisition consummated by the exchange of items of property (movable or immovable, animate or inanimate, sale or gift). When one party takes possession of an object, the second party automatically and irrevocably acquires an object in exchange, wherever it is located, although no additional act of acquisition has been performed. Because the parties desire to exchange specific items, it is not required that the objects be of equal value, and the laws against fraud are inapplicable. Ultimately, the convenience of this mode of transfer resulted in the development of the *qinyan sudar* (symbolic barter). As opposed to real barter, which involves the exchange of the actual items being acquired, symbolic barter does not require that the object bartered constitute the actual consideration for the object acquired. In the most common variant, a kerchief (*sudar*) is symbolically and temporarily given by the vendee to the vendor (as a *mattanah al menat le-haḥzir*, "a conditional gift that will be returned by the donee"); upon the vendor's acquiring the *sudar*, the actual object of the transaction is automatically acquired by the vendee. The validity of this symbolic mode of acquisition found scriptural support in *Ruth* 4.7: "Now this was the custom in former time in Israel concerning redeeming and concerning exchanging, to confirm all things: a man drew off his shoe and gave it to his neighbor."

• Shalom Albeck, *Dinei ha-Mammonot ba-Talmud* (Tel Aviv, 1976), pp. 153–168. Menachem Elon, ed., *The Principles of Jewish Law* (Jerusalem, 1975), pp. 197, 233. Isaac Herzog, *The Main Institutions of Jewish Law*, 2d ed., 2 vols. (London, 1965), vol. 1, pp. 179–182. —BEN TZION GREENBERGER

BARUCH, BOOKS OF, a number of works purporting to have been written by *Baruch ben Neriah, disciple and amanuensis of the prophet Jeremiah.

The apocryphal *1 Baruch*, preserved in Greek, is a composite work of two sections. The first is a letter of Baruch, which he reads to Jehoiachin and the exiles in Babylonia; this moves them to confess their sins and send money offerings to the Temple. The second section contains two poems: the first admonishes Israel to return to God and to seek wisdom; the second recounts the plight of the nation and promises future deliverance. It is not clear whether the two sections were originally written by the same author and whether they were written in Greek or translated from a lost Hebrew or Aramaic original. Dating each of the sections is equally difficult; the book as a whole may tentatively be dated from the first century BCE or CE.

The Syriac *Apocalypse of Baruch* was probably written in Hebrew after the destruction of the Second Temple in 70 CE but is extant only in Syriac and Arabic translations. A small papyrus fragment of its Greek version was found in Egypt. In the work, Baruch narrates how he witnessed the destruction of Jerusalem by the Chaldeans and describes the visions that he subsequently saw. The visions stress such themes as the future destruction of the gentiles, the coming of the Messiah, and the deliverance of Israel and are often couched in a highly symbolic idiom.

The Greek *Apocalypse of Baruch*, probably written in Greek toward the end of the first century CE, is extant both in Greek and in a Slavonic version and contains, in its current form, several Christian interpolations. It describes Baruch's journey through the five heavens, during which he sees the glorification of the righteous and the punishments meted out to the unrighteous as well as some cosmic phenomena, such as the marvelous phoenix bird.

The Rest of the Words of Baruch or *The Rest of the Words of Jeremiah* (*4 Baruch*), probably written originally in Hebrew or Aramaic, is preserved in Greek, Ethiopic, Armenian, and Slavonic and contains some Christian sections. Apparently written at the end of the first century CE or the beginning of the second, it recounts how Baruch remained in Jerusalem while Jeremiah accompanied the exiles to Babylon but returned at their head sixty- six years later.

• **On 1 Baruch:** Carey A. Moore, *Daniel, Esther and Jeremiah: The Additions*, The Anchor Bible, vol. 44 (Garden City, N.Y., 1977), pp. 255–316. **On 2 Baruch:** Albertus Frederik Johannes Klijn, "2 (Syriac Apocalypse of) Baruch," in *The Old Testament Pseudepigrapha*, edited by James H. Charlesworth, vol. 1 (Garden City, N.Y., 1983), pp. 615–652. **On 3 Baruch:** Harry E. Gaylord, "3 (Greek Apocalypse of) Baruch," in *The Old Testament Pseudepigrapha*, edited by James H. Charlesworth, vol. 1 (Garden City, N.Y., 1983), pp. 653–679. **On 4 Baruch:** Stephen Edward Robinson, "4 Baruch," in *The Old Testament Pseudepigrapha*, edited by James H. Charlesworth, vol. 2 (Garden City, N.Y., 1985), pp. 413–425.

—GIDEON BOHAK

BARUCH BEN NERIAH, trusted scribe and friend of *Jeremiah. He was responsible for publicizing the contents of a scroll containing Jeremiah's prophecies (*Jer*. 36.1–10). After King Jehoiakim had this scroll burned, Baruch recopied its contents along with additional material (*Jer*. 36.27–32). Many scholars attribute the biographical material in *Jeremiah* to Baruch. The recent discovery of a seal impression mentioning Baruch's name and profession seems to confirm his status as a professional scribe. Baruch's reputation inspired several pseudepigraphous works bearing his name (see BARUCH, BOOKS OF).

• James Muilenberg, "Baruch the Scribe," in *Proclamation and Presence: Old Testament Essays in Honour of Gwynne Henton Davies*, edited by John I. Durham and J. R. Porter (London, 1970), pp. 215–238.

—DAVID A. GLATT-GILAD

BARUKH (בָּרוּךְ; blessed, praised [with regard to God the two words are identical in meaning]), the opening word of the standard formula of *benediction that is one of the basic forms of Jewish prayer. The Talmud attributes many of the benedictions beginning with the formula "Blessed are you, O Lord our God, king of the universe" to the Men of the *Keneset ha-Gedolah, but this is questioned by scholars.

BARUKH ADONAI LE-ʿOLAM (בָּרוּךְ יְיָ לְעוֹלָם; Praised Be the Lord Forever), a compilation of biblical verses, recited in the weekday evening service between *Hashkivenu (the second benediction after the *Shemaʿ) and the *ʿAmidah. This passage, written in the geonic period, may have been added to the service as a surrogate for the nineteen benedictions of the ʿAmidah, which is not repeated aloud in the evening service, since the name of God is mentioned nineteen times in the passage. Barukh Adonai le-ʿOlam invokes God's protection for the night and prays for final redemption. The passage is included in the Conservative liturgy.

• Ismar Elbogen, *Jewish Liturgy: A Comprehensive History*, translated by Raymond P. Scheindlin (Philadelphia, 1993), pp. 87ff. Abraham E. Millgram, *Jewish Worship* (Philadelphia, 1971), pp. 159ff.

—A. STANLEY DREYFUS

BARUKH DAYYAN EMET (בָּרוּךְ דַּיַּן אֱמֶת; "Blessed be the true judge"), benediction pronounced on hearing bad tidings (*Ber*. 9.2), since a Jew is meant to praise God both in joy and in sorrow. The formula is generally recited on hearing the report of a death; close relatives say the full liturgical formula ("Blessed are you, O Lord our God, king of the universe, the true judge"). It is also said on seeing ruined synagogues or holy sites.

BARUKH HA-SHEM (בָּרוּךְ הַשֵּׁם; "Blessed be the name [of God]"), expression, equivalent to the English "Thank God," used on hearing good tidings or in everyday speech as an utterance of well-being. It occurs in *Psalms* 68.20 (*Barukh Adonai*), and sometimes the complete phrase is used—*Barukh ha-Shem* [used for Adonai] *yom yom*, "Blessed is the Lord day by day."

BARUKH HU' U-VARUKH SHEMO (בָּרוּךְ הוּא וּבָרוּךְ שְׁמוֹ; "Blessed be he, and blessed be his name"), response by the congregation to the mention of the divine name in the first half of a benediction ("Blessed are you, O Lord"; see BENEDICTIONS), the response to the second half being *amen*. If the listener intends to be included in the recitation of the benediction (for example, in the Qiddush or Havdalah), the response is omitted.

• Naftali Wieder, in *Studies in Rabbinic Literature, Bible, and Jewish History*, edited by E. Z. Malamed et al. (Ramat Gan, 1982), pp. 277–290.

BARUKH OF MEDZHIBOZH (c.1756–1810), Hasidic master, the second son of Yisraʾel ben Eliʿezer *Baʿal Shem Tov's daughter Odel. He was educated under the supervision of R. Pinḥas ben Avraham *Shapiro of Korets. After 1777, when R. *Menaḥem Mendel of Vitebsk departed for Erets Yisraʾel, bringing to an end his partial hegemony over the disciples of the Maggid of Mezhirech (see DOV BER OF MEZHIRECH), Barukh began to act as a Hasidic leader. First in Tulchin and later in Medzhibozh, he established an impressive court, hoping that all Ḥasidim would turn to him as heir to the Baʿal Shem Tov and guardian of his burial place. Barukh initiated the dynastic pattern of Hasidic succession as well as the idea of establishing a Hasidic court. He was also the first Hasidic master to be recognized by the Russian government as a major Jewish power. Other masters spurned his claim to leadership, however, and there ensued a series of public conflicts with *Levi Yitsḥaq of Berdichev, *Shneur Zalman of Lyady, and Barukh's own nephew, *Naḥman of Bratslav. The Hasidism represented by Barukh was noted more for its growing numerical and political strength and claims of leadership than for profundity or originality of thought. A volume of Barukh's collected teachings and sayings, *Butsina' di-Nehora'*, was published in Lwów in 1880.

• *Entsiqlopedyah la-Ḥasidut*, vol. 2 (Jersualem, 1986), pp. 374–377. Arthur Green, *Tormented Master: A Life of Rabbi Nahman of Bratslav* (New York, 1979). A Shisha-Halevi in *'Alei Sefer* 8 (1980): 155–157.

—ARTHUR GREEN

BARUKH SHE-'AMAR (בָּרוּךְ שֶׁאָמַר; "Blessed be he who spoke"), opening words of the *Pesuqei de-Zimra' (Ashkenazi term) or Zemirot (Sephardi term). According to the prayer book of R. 'Amram bar Sheshna', these words recited by the *ḥazzan* signaled the commencement of public morning worship.

• Ismar Elbogen, *Jewish Liturgy: A Comprehensive History*, translated by Raymond P. Scheindlin (Philadelphia, New York, and Jerusalem, 1993), pp. 72–74. Macy Nulman, *The Encyclopedia of Jewish Prayer* (London, 1993), pp. 89–91. Macy Nulman, *The Concise Encyclopedia of Jewish Music* (New York, 1975), pp. 26–27.

BARUKH SHEM KEVOD MALKHUTO LE-'OLAM VA-'ED (בָּרוּךְ שֵׁם כְּבוֹד מַלְכוּתוֹ לְעוֹלָם וָעֶד; "Blessed be the name of the glory of his kingdom for ever and ever"), response recited after the first verse of the *Shema'; originally it was recited by worshipers in the Temple when the high priest uttered the Tetragrammaton on Yom Kippur (*Yoma'* 6.2). In the Orthodox tradition it is said in an undertone to distinguish it from the rest of the Shema', which is a biblical quotation. Only on Yom Kippur is this phrase recited aloud, recalling the tradition of the Temple service. As an expression of the awareness of the holiness of the divine name, it uses a circumlocution ("the name of the glory of his kingdom"). The phrase is recited after utterance of the Tetragrammaton (YHVH and its correlatives), particularly in instances where there is doubt concerning the recitation of a blessing, such as the benediction for putting on the **tefillin* of the head, or a mystical prayer such as *Anna' ba-Koaḥ without the requisite *kavvanah* (see INTENT). A Talmudic legend (*Pes.* 56b) relates that when Jacob was dying he asked his sons if they indeed believed in the one God: their response was to state the Shema', whereupon Jacob responded *barukh shem kevod malkhuto le-'olam va-'ed*.

• Joseph Heinemann, *Prayer in the Talmud* (Berlin and New York, 1977). Elie Munk, *The World of Prayer*, 2 vols. (New York, 1954–1963).

—PETER LENHARDT

BARUKH SHE-PETARANI (בָּרוּךְ שֶׁפְּטָרַנִי; Blessed Be He Who Has Freed Me [from the Responsibility for This Child]), name of the blessing (quoted in *Gn. Rab.* 63.14) recited by the father of a boy celebrating his **bar mitsvah*. The child now assumes responsibility for his actions as a member of the religious community. In the Reform service, Barukh she-Petarani is replaced by the *She-Heḥeyanu benediction, while in many Conservative congregations the *Mi she-Berakh blessing often takes its place.

• Yaakov Salomon, *Bar Mitzvah, Its Observance and Significance: A Compendium* (Brooklyn, N.Y., 1991).

BAR YOḤ'AI. See SHIM'ON BAR YOḤ'AI.

BASHYAZI, ELIYYAHU BEN MOSHEH (c.1420–1490), *Karaite scholar and theologian. He was a member of a family of legal scholars known for its liberal tendencies. His grandfather, Menaḥem, allowed the kindling of Sabbath candles, a reform of Karaite custom that met with opposition. Eliyyahu was born in Adrianople and moved with his family to Constantinople in 1455. He soon became the religious leader of the community and his authority came to be accepted by the Karaite communities of Turkey, Crimea, Poland, and Lithuania. He was an advocate of the rapprochement with Rabbanism taking place at that time and made use of rabbinic sources. His great code of Karaite law, *Adderet Eliyyahu* (Constantinople, 1530–1531; Yevpatoriya, 1835; Odessa, 1870; Ramleh, 1966), was quickly accepted as binding and remains the final authoritative Karaite code to this day. In this work, he provided the liberal rulings of his grandfather and father, Mosheh, with a theoretical basis grounded in earlier Karaite literature. It also contains a philosophical presentation of the ten Karaite principles of faith. In addition, Eliyyahu wrote three polemical works (*Iggeret ha-Yerushah* [directed against the Rabbanites], *Iggeret ha-Tsom*, and *Iggeret Gid ha-Nasheh* [both responding to his Karaite opponents]); a work on astronomical instruments and calculations (*Keli ha-Neḥoshet*); as well as several religious hymns that entered the Karaite prayer book. Some of his correspondence with the Lithuanian Karaites has survived.

• Zvi Ankori, "Beit Bashyazi ve-Taqqanotav," introduction to *Adderet Eliyyahu*, by Eliyyahu ben Mosheh Bashyazi (Ramleh, 1966). Daniel Lasker, in *Meḥqerei Yerushalayim be-Maḥashevet Yisra'el* 3 (1983/1984): 405–425. Leon Nemoy, *Karaite Anthology* (New Haven, 1952), pp. 236–270.

—DAVID E. SKLARE

BASIR, YOSEF BEN AVRAHAM (c.980–c.1040), *Karaite author and theologian. Because of his blindness, Yosef was known by the euphemistic cognomen, "the Seer" (Basir, ha-Ro'eh in Hebrew). He came from Basra, Iraq, and traveled to Jerusalem to join its flourishing community of Karaite scholars and ascetics, studying there with Yusuf ibn Nuḥ. He soon achieved a position of religious and intellectual leadership, illustrated by the fact that he was one of the few Karaites who wrote *responsa* on both theological and legal topics. Among his pupils were Yeshu'a ben Yehudah, who became a leading authority in his own right, and Toviyyah ben Mosheh of Constantinople, who translated a number of Basir's works into Hebrew.

Basir wrote (actually dictated) at least eighteen works in theology, legal theory, religious law, and polemics, in addition to his *responsa*. His major theological work is *Kitab al-Muḥtawi* (translated as *Sefer ha-Ne'imot*). He later wrote a shorter version entitled *Kitab al-Tamyiz* (also known as *al-Mansuri*, translated as *Maḥkhimat Peti*). In these works, he shows himself to be a student of the Basran school of Mu'tazili Kalam and was particularly influenced by his older Muslim contemporary Abu al-Ḥasan 'Abd al-Jabbar. In these works, Basir sought to define the rational basis of ethics and religious knowledge. His most important work of law is *Kitab al-*

Istibsar, divided into at least ten sections, some of which were translated into Hebrew. He was one of the first to oppose the "catenary" theory of forbidden marriage that made life difficult for Karaites. Basir's theological concerns also find expression in his legal works. He wrote polemical works against Islam, the Samaritans, and the Rabbanites. The last included his polemic against his older contemporary Shemu'el ben Ḥofni Ga'on, whom he had met in Baghdad. Basir was familiar with rabbinic literature and discussed the problematics of rabbinic tradition in a number of his works. His only work to have been published is *Kitab al-Muḥtawi* (as *Al-Kitab al-Muḥtawi de Yusuf al-Basir*, edited by Georges Vajda and David R. Blumenthal [Leiden, 1985]). All others (where they have survived) remain in manuscript fragments, mostly in the British Library and Firkovitch collections in Saint Petersburg. Later Karaites considered Basir to be one of their important authorities.

• Jacob Mann, *Texts and Studies in Jewish History and Literature* vol. 2 (Cincinnati, 1935). Samuel Poznanski, *Karaite Literary Opponents of Sa'adyah Ga'on* (London, 1908), no. 16. David Sklare in *The Jews of Medieval Islam: Community, Society, Identity*, edited by Daniel Frank (Leiden, 1995).

—DAVID E. SKLARE

BASOLA, MOSHEH (died 1560), rabbinic figure in sixteenth-century Italy; scion of a French family. Basola held rabbinic posts in various Italian cities: Fano, Pesaro, and Ancona, where he settled prior to 1540. In 1522, he journeyed to Erets Yisra'el. The written record of his impressions of the Jewish communities of Jerusalem and other locations in Erets Yisra'el is an important historical document. Basola took an active role in the halakhic debates of his generation. In 1560 he moved to Safed, where he died. His extant works include legal decisions, which were cited by contemporary scholars; various writings, including *Masa'ot Erets Yisra'el* (edited by Itzhak Ben-Zvi [Jerusalem, 1939]); and homilies.

• Ruth Lamdan, "The Boycott of Ancona: Viewing the Other Side of the Coin," in *Mi-Lisbon le-Saloniki ve-Kushta*, edited by Zvi Ankori (Tel Aviv, 1988), pp. 135–154. Ruth Lamdan, "Shenei Qetavim Mi-shel R. Mosheh Basola," *Michael* 8 (1985): 171–193.

—ABRAHAM DAVID

BASTARD. See ILLEGITIMACY; MAMZER.

BATHING. See ABLUTION; MIQVEH.

BATLANIM (בַּטְלָנִים), idle persons, men of leisure. In a religious context, the reference is to *'asarah batlanim*, ten men who are able to devote their time to the needs of the community; for example, ensuring that there will always be a prayer quorum (*minyan*) for each of the daily prayers. The Mishnah defines a town as a place that has at least ten *batlanim*, while a place with fewer than ten is considered a village. According to *Rashi (on *Meg.* 3b, 5a; *B. Q.* 82a), the *'asarah batlanim* are community employees paid for their work, but R. Nissim disputes this. In modern usage the term has a pejorative connotation.

• Menahem M. Kasher, "'Asarah Batlanim," in *Torah Shelemah*, vol. 15 (New York, 1953), pp. 136ff. Joseph Tabory, "Shetei He'arot be-Ḥovat Qeri'at ha-Megillah," *Meḥqerei Ḥag* 3 (1992): 73–81.

—SHMUEL HIMELSTEIN

BAT MITSVAH (בַּת מִצְוָה; daughter of [the] commandment), an adult female Jew obligated to perform the commandments; hence, the ceremony on the occasion of a girl's reaching her majority (twelve years and a day in Jewish law but sometimes postponed to the age of thirteen, which is the age for boys to have the comparable ceremony, the **bar mitsvah*), when she is regarded as assuming responsibility for her actions. The concept of a (nonsynagogal) ceremony for girls was introduced by the Neo-Orthodox nineteenth-century German rabbi Ya'aqov *Ettlinger and was accepted in other European communities and also in certain Muslim countries. As part of a synagogue service, the *bat mitsvah* was introduced in the 1920s in the United States by the founder of the Reconstructionist movement, Mordecai M. *Kaplan, with his own daughter. It has become a regular feature in Reform, Conservative, and Reconstructionist synagogues, where the girl may read from the Torah and address the congregation. It has recently begun to appear in some Orthodox (but not ultra-Orthodox) circles as well, although the main observance there is usually not within a synagogue service but at home or in the synagogue hall. Occasionally, a *bat mitsvah* ceremony is held for a group of girls at the same time. In the United States a *bat mitsvah* ceremony is sometimes held in non-Orthodox congregations for adult women who did not have a *bat mitsvah* observance at the usual age. The Reform movement has developed an appropriate service (in the *Gates of Prayer*), and the Conservative prayer book (*Sim Shalom*) has special prayers and readings.

• Ben Zion Bokser, "Shabbat Morning Bat Mitsvah," in *Proceedings of the Committee on Jewish Law and Standards, 1980–1985* (New York, 1988), pp. 41–42. Nachman Cohen, *Bar, Bat Mitzvah and Beyond* (Yonkers, N.Y., 1988). Susan Grossman and Rivka Haut, eds., *Daughters of the King: Women and the Synagogue: A Survey of History, Halakhah, and Contemporary Realities* (Philadelphia, 1992). Yaakov Salomon and Yonah Weinrib, *Bar Mitzvah, Its Observance and Significance* (Brooklyn, N.Y., 1991).

BAT QOL (בַּת קוֹל; daughter of a voice, i.e., echo), a term in rabbinic literature that denotes a heavenly voice announcing divine reactions to certain events and, at times, even approval of halakhic decisions. The *bat qol* could be heard by individuals or by groups of people and thus differs from *prophecy, in which the divine communication is received by a person already in a special relationship with God. The *bat qol*, like other forms of heavenly pronouncement, was not necessarily accepted as authoritative in halakhic matters, since the rabbis held that the Torah "is not in heaven" (*Dt.* 30.12) and that legal decisions had to be arrived at by the established hermeneutic and discursive methods (*B. M.* 59b).

—DANIEL SPERBER

BAVA' BATRA' (Aram.; בָּבָא בָּתְרָא; Last Gate), third tractate of the Mishnah order Neziqin, and last of the *Bavot* (gates) tractates (see BAVA' QAMMA'), consisting of ten chapters, with related material in the Tosefta' and both Talmuds. *Bava' Batra'* deals with rights and obligations vis-à-vis one's neighbors and community, and with laws concerning purchases, inheritances, and written contracts. The legal issues that arise include the right to privacy, the protection and beautification of the environment, municipal taxation, honest business practices, wills, and liens on property. Study of the subjects treated in *Bavot* was regarded by the rabbis as requiring great moral insight as well as legal acumen, as indicated in the citation from R. Yishmaʿe'l ben Elishaʿ that concludes *Bava' Batra'*: "One who wishes to grow wise should occupy himself with the laws of financial matters, for there is no subject in the Torah greater than they, inasmuch as they are like a flowing fountain."

The tractate was translated into English by Isidore Epstein in the Soncino Talmud (1935).

• Chanoch Albeck, ed., *Shishah Sidrei Mishnah, Seder Neziqin*, 2d ed. (Jerusalem, 1956). Philip Blackman, ed. and trans., *Mishnayot*, vol. 4, *Order Neziqin* (Gateshead, 1973). David Daube, "The Civil Law of the Mishnah: The Arrangement of the Three Gates," in *Collected Works of David Daube*, edited by Calum M. Carmichael (Berkeley, 1992), vol. 1, pp. 257–304. Pinhas Kehati, ed., *Mishnah: A New Translation with a Commentary, Seder Neziqin*, vol. 2, *Bava' Batra', Sanhedrin* (Jerusalem, 1988). Hermann Leberecht Strack, *Introduction to the Talmud and Midrash* (1931; Minneapolis, 1992). —AVRAHAM WALFISH

BAVA' METSIʿA' (Aram.; בָּבָא מְצִיעָא; Middle Gate), second tractate of the Mishnah order Neziqin, and middle of the three *Bavot* (gates) tractates (see BAVA' QAMMA'), consisting of ten chapters, with related material in the Tosefta' and both Talmuds. *Bava' Metsiʿa'* deals with laws relating to found property, bailments, purchases, usury, hiring, and renting. In most of these areas, biblical law is interpreted and expanded in order to render it applicable to contemporary situations. Thus, to the biblical command to return lost items, the Mishnah adds categories of found items that need not be returned; and methods for determining the identity of the owner, caring for the item while waiting to return it, compensating a person for time and expenses incurred while caring for and returning the item, and resolving conflicts of values involved in certain cases of returning found items. The Mishnah's extreme concern for the welfare of the underprivileged is evidenced by the laws in *Bava' Metsiʿa'* regarding the right of a laborer to eat at his employer's expense, the obligation of an employer not to delay even slightly the payment of wages, and limitations on the right of a lender to take property of the borrower as security for a loan.

An English translation by S. Daiches and H. F. Freedman is in the Soncino Talmud (1935).

• Chanoch Albeck, ed., *Shishah Sidrei Mishnah, Seder Neziqin*, 2d ed., (Jerusalem, 1956). Philip Blackman, ed. and trans., *Mishnayot*, vol. 4, *Order Neziqin* (Gateshead, 1973). David Daube, "The Civil Law of the Mishnah: The Arrangement of the Three Gates," in *Collected Works of David Daube*, edited by Calum M. Carmichael (Berkeley, 1992), vol. 1, pp. 257–304. Pinhas Kehati, ed., *Mishnah: A New Translation with a Commentary, Seder Neziqin*, vol. 1, *Bava' Qamma', Bava' Metsiʿa'* (Jerusalem, 1987). Hayim Lapin, "Early Rabbinic Civil Law and the Literature of the Second Temple Period," *Jewish Studies Quarterly* 2 (1995): 149–183. Hermann Leberecht Strack, *Introduction to the Talmud and Midrash* (1931; Minneapolis, 1992). —AVRAHAM WALFISH

BAVA' QAMMA' (Aram.; בָּבָא קַמָּא; First Gate), first tractate of the Mishnah order Neziqin and first of the *Bavot* (gates) tractates, consisting of ten chapters. Because of its great length (thirty chapters), the tractate *Neziqin* was divided into three "gates" (*Bava' Qamma'*, **Bava' Metsiʿa'*, and **Bava' Batra'*), or sections, of ten chapters each.

Bava' Qamma' discusses laws of torts: property damage, physical injury, and theft. The Mishnah conceptualizes and expands the biblical law of property damage, for example, treating damage caused by domestic animals (*Ex.* 21.35–36, 22.4), pits (*Ex.* 21.33–34), or fire (*Ex.* 22.5) as archetypes (*avot*) for the owner's responsibility for damage caused by improperly guarded things or animals. Special laws govern the obligation to make restitution for the damage caused and the conditions of payment. The Mishnah discusses four archetypes of property damage (*B. Q.* 1.1), followed by a separate discussion of theft and bodily injury; however, the Tosefta' (*B. Q.* 9.1) treats theft and bodily injury as part of an extended framework of thirteen archetypes.

Bava' Qamma' divides the laws of *theft into two categories: theft by force (*gezelah*), which requires return of the stolen item or—if the item is not extant or has undergone significant change—its monetary equivalent (only when accompanied by a false oath does *gezelah* mandate a further penalty); and burglary (*genevah*), which incurs a penalty of double payment or—regarding theft of an ox or a sheep—a quadruple or quintuple payment.

Bodily injury is unique among the torts discussed in *Bava' Qamma'*, requiring payment for indirect injuries, including pain, healing costs, loss of workdays, and compensation for shame. The Mishnah also requires the perpetrator of the tort to request forgiveness, in addition to the payment of restitution, and condemns refusal by the injured party to grant forgiveness.

An English translation by E. W. Kirzner appears in the Soncino Talmud (1935).

• Chanoch Albeck, ed., *Shishah Sidrei Mishnah, Seder Neziqin* 2d ed. (Jerusalem, 1956). Philip Blackman, ed. and trans., *Mishnayot*, vol. 4, *Order Neziqin* (Gateshead, 1973). David Daube, "The Civil Law of the Mishnah: The Arrangement of the Three Gates," in *Collected Works of David Daube*, edited by Calum M. Carmichael (Berkeley, 1992), vol. 1, pp. 257–304. Pinhas Kehati, ed., *Mishnah: A New Translation with a Commentary, Seder Neziqin*, vol. 1, *Bava' Qamma', Bava' Metsiʿa'* (Jerusalem, 1987). Hermann Leberecht Strack, *Introduction to the Talmud and Midrash* (1931; Minneapolis, 1992). —AVRAHAM WALFISH

BAVLI. See TALMUD.

BEADLE. See SHAMMASH.

BEARDS. Among the ancient Hebrews (like other peoples of their time), the beard was considered a symbol of manhood and was carefully tended, trimmed (in later periods especially in honor of Sabbaths and festivals), and anointed. Its removal—except as a sign of mourning (*Jb.* 1.20)—was a disgrace (cf. *2 Sm.* 10.4–5), though shaving was obligatory in certain purification ceremonies (cf. *Lv.* 14.9). The key biblical injunction is in *Leviticus* (19.27, 21.5), "You shall not destroy the sidegrowth of your beard." Although probably originally a prohibition against imitating pagan worshipers, it was interpreted by the rabbis as a prohibition against shaving. They specifically forbade the removal of sideburns and hair on certain places on the cheek and chin. Some

Orthodox Jews today do not cut their sideburns (see PE'OT). However, interpretations of the ban on "destroying" the hair left the possibility of shaving the hair without technically infringing this prohibition (for example, by depilatory or electric razor, seen as not "destroying" the hair). The kabbalists, especially of the school of Yitsḥaq *Luria, ascribed mystic significance to the beard and would not even trim it, some even keeping a bag around their beard to collect hairs that might fall out. Ḥasidim also attached great importance to the beard.

Shaving and haircuts are forbidden on Sabbaths and festivals, when they are considered work, and when a person is in mourning or during periods of mourning (such as the *'Omer period and the three weeks before *Tish'ah be-'Av).

• Moshe Wiener, *Hadrat Panim* (North Woodmere, N.Y., 1978).

BEDERSI, YEDA'YAH BEN AVRAHAM (c.1270–1340), southern French philosopher, poet, scientist, and possibly physician, also known as Yeda'yah ha-Penini. He may have originated in Béziers (hence Bedersi). He lived in Perpignan and Montpellier. His poetical compositions include the *Baqqashat ha-Memim*, a one-thousand-word prayer, each word beginning with the letter *mem*; possibly a similar work, each word beginning with the letter *alef*; and *Ohev Nashim* (Berlin, 1884). His most popular work is *Sefer Beḥinat 'Olam* (Mantua, 1476; English trans. London, 1806), on the futility of this world and its pursuits and the superiority of the intellectual life.

He also wrote a number of commentaries on Jewish and non-Jewish works including commentaries on various *midrashim* and *Pirqei Avot*; Avicenna's *Canon of Medicine*; and Averroës's commentary on Aristotle's *Physics*. He wrote a summary of Aristotle's *On the Soul; Ketav ha-Da'at*, a paraphrase of al-Farabi's *Treatise on the Intellect; Ma'amar be-Hafkhei ha-Mahalakh*, which deals with Averroës's commentary on Aristotle's *De Caelo* and in which he attacks another, unnamed scholar, and *Ketav ha-Hit'atsemut*, a refutation of that scholar's response; and *Ma'amar ha-Dan ba-Tsurot ha-Peratiyyot o-Ishiyyot*, on personal and individual forms. Yeda'yah supported the study of philosophy and wrote a rebuttal, *Iggeret ha-Hitnatselut* (Venice, 1545), to Shelomoh ben Avraham Adret's prohibition against it. He is possibly the author of *Avvat Nafesh*, a supercommentary on Avraham ibn Ezra, although the attribution has been disputed.

• Abraham S. Halkin, "Yedaiah Bedershi's Apology," in *Jewish Medieval and Renaissance Studies*, edited by Alexander Altmann (Cambridge, Mass., 1967), pp. 165–184. Shlomo Pines, "Individual Forms in the Thought of Yedaya Bedersi," in *Harry Austryn Wolfson Jubilee Volume* (Jerusalem, 1965), pp. 187–201. Ernest Renan, *Les Écrivains juifs français du XIVe siècle* (Paris, 1893), pp. 13–56. Mark Saperstein, "Selected Passages from Yedaiah Bedersi's Commentary on the Midrashim," in *Studies in Medieval Jewish History and Literature*, edited by Isadore Twersky, vol. 2 (Cambridge, Mass., 1984), pp. 423–440. Jefim Schirmann, *Ha-Shirah ha-'Ivrit bi-Sefarad uve-Provans* (Jerusalem, 1960), vol. 2, pp. 489–498, 696. Colette Sirat, *A History of Jewish Philosophy in the Middle Ages* (Cambridge, 1990), pp. 274–277. —STEVEN BALLABAN

BEDIQAH (בְּדִיקָה; examination), a halakhic term denoting various kinds of inspection or examination in connection with ritual and legal questions, more particularly with regard to the ritual slaughtering of animals for food. *Bediqah* is made of the knife before slaughtering to make sure it is absolutely sharp; the windpipe and esophagus of a slaughtered animal to ascertain whether they have been properly cut; and the inner organs, particularly the lungs of a slaughtered animal, to ascertain whether it suffered from any serious disease. Examination of witnesses in court is called *bediqat ha-'edim*. The search for leaven on the day before Pesaḥ is called **be-diqat ḥamets*.

BEDIQAT ḤAMETS (בְּדִיקַת חָמֵץ; search for leaven). The biblical injunction "even the first day shall ye put away leaven out of your houses" (*Ex.* 12.15) was interpreted by the rabbis as referring to the day preceding Pesaḥ, namely, 14 Nisan. To make sure that "there be no leaven found in your houses" (*Ex.* 12.19), the rabbis instituted a ceremonial search for leavened substances (*Pes.* 1.1, 7b–8a). *Bediqat ḥamets* takes place after dark on the eve of 14 Nisan (when the first day of Pesaḥ falls on a Sunday, the search for leaven is conducted on the preceding Thursday evening), when all nooks and crannies are examined by candlelight and the leaven swept out by a feather. As a formal religious ceremony, *bediqat ḥamets* is preceded by a benediction ("Blessed are you . . . who has commanded us concerning the destruction of leaven"). If leaven is found, it is burned on the next morning (*bi'ur ḥamets*). Since *bediqat ḥamets* has become a highly formalized ritual, it is customary with some to hide small pieces of bread (according to the Lurianic kabbalists, ten in number) to make sure that the search will not be in vain. After the search, an Aramaic formula is recited, renouncing ownership of any leaven that may have escaped detection.

• Philip Goodman, ed., *The Passover Anthology* (Philadelphia, 1993). Macy Nulman, *The Encyclopedia of Jewish Prayer* (Northvale, N.J., 1993), p. 16.

BE-'EZRAT HA-SHEM (בְּעֶזְרַת הַשֵּׁם; "With the help of the Name [of God]"), expression of pious hope used since the Middle Ages; often written in initials (see ABBREVIATIONS) at the head of letters or used in speech in a way similar to the English "God willing." The Aramaic equivalent *be-siyya'tta' di-shemayya'*, "with the help of (God in) heaven," is also sometimes used.

• M. Hallamish, "Meqomah shel ha-Qabbalah ba-Minhag," in Daniel Sperber, *Minhag Yisra'el*, vol. 3 (Jerusalem, 1994).

BEGGING. The paucity of references to beggars in biblical times may be attributed to the extensive regulations to provide for the poor (see POVERTY). These included reversion of property to the original owner in the sabbatical year, the cancellation of debts in the jubilee year, and agricultural regulations (such as the laws of gleanings; see LEQET, SHIKHḤAH, AND PE'AH). There is no biblical Hebrew word for begging, and possible references are oblique (cf. "I have not seen the righteous forsaken nor his seed seeking bread" [*Ps.* 37.25]).

Beggars are mentioned in the New Testament (e.g., *Mk.* 10.46; *Acts* 3.2), and they were a recognized feature of society in Mishnaic and Talmudic times. The rabbis condemn beggars who fake disabilities or even mutilate themselves in order to win sympathy (*Pe'ah* 8, 9). Rabbi El'azar expresses gratitude to scoundrels who beg under false pretenses as this gives a rationale for not donating to every single mendicant (*Ket.* 68a).

In the medieval Jewish community, relief for the poor was so well organized that beggars were not a common phenomenon. *Rashi states expressly that in view of the extent of communal support there is no need to give to a beggar who goes from door to door; some communities outlawed beggars. The phenomenon, however, became widespread after periods of great tragedy led to communal impoverishment, during the Crusades, for example, and after the Chmielnicki massacres in eastern Europe from 1648 to 1649. After the latter, the *shnorrer* or *beytler* (Yi.; beggar) became a familiar figure. The communities provided facilities for itinerant beggars to sleep and gave them modest sums to reach the next town. They were invited to weddings, where a special table was set aside for them. Beggars would gather at the approach to a cemetery, stretching out their hands and repeating "Charity saves from death" (*Prv.* 10.2). Rabbinic tradition, though insisting on the duty of charity, discourages begging and considers the honest earning of a living, including menial labor, as a religious obligation.

• Israel Abrahams, *Jewish Life in the Middle Ages* (London, 1932), pp. 331ff. Salo Baron, *The Jewish Community: Its History and Structure to the American Revolution* (Philadelphia, 1942), vol. 1, pp. 131, 363; vol. 2, pp. 321–325. Bernard Septimus, "Kings, Angels or Beggars: Tax Law Spirituality in a Hispano-Jewish Responsum," *Studies in Medieval Jewish History and Literature*, 2 (1984): 309–335. Efraim Elimelech Urbach, "Megamot Datiyyot ve-Hevratiyot be-Torat ha-Tsedakah shel Ḥazal," *Me'olamam shel Ḥakhamim* (Jerusalem, 1988), pp. 97–124.

BEHEADING. See CAPITAL PUNISHMENT.

BEHEMOTH, an animal described in *Job* 40.15–24 and in pseudepigraphous and rabbinic lore. Behemoth, like *Leviathan (cf. *Jb.* 40.25–32), was a legendary animal. In the messianic age there will be a fight between Behemoth and Leviathan. The righteous will be spectators at the fight and afterwards will feast on the flesh of the animals at the messianic banquet (*Pirqei de-Rabbi Eli'ezer* 2). In modern biblical scholarship, attempts have been made to identify the two creatures with the hippopotamus (Behemoth) and crocodile (Leviathan). Both of these creatures, however, should be thought of as demythologized supernatural sea-monsters, who were conceived of as having been created by God in primordial times, but who later rebelled against him. Allusions to this rebellion occur in *Isaiah* 27.1, 51.9–10, *Psalms* 74.13–14, and especially in *Job* 3.8, 7.12, 9.13, 26.12–13. There are clear parallels in Ugaritic mythology where such terms as *ltn* (leviathan), *ym* (sea), *tnn* (dragon), and *btn brḥ/qltn* (elusive/twisting sea serpent) all occur as names and epithets of the divine protagonists.

• Chaim Cohen, *Biblical Hapax Legomena in the Light of Akkadian and Ugaritic* (Missoula, Mont., 1978), pp. 50–51, 97–100. Chaim Cohen in *Sefer Prof. H.M.Y. Gevaryahu*, edited by Ben-Tsiyyon Lurya et al., vol. 2 (Jerusalem, 1989), pp. 74–81. A. Cooper and M. H. Pope in *Ras Shamra Parallels: The Texts from Ugarit and the Hebrew Bible*, vol. 3 (Rome, 1981), pp. 369–383, 388–391, 424–428, 441–444. Robert Gordis, *The Book of Job* (New York, 1978), pp. 569–572. Marvin H. Pope, *Job*, The Anchor Bible, 3d ed. (Garden City, N.Y., 1967), pp. 556–559. Mary K. Wakeman, *God's Battle with the Monster: A Study in Biblical Imagery* (Leiden, 1973), pp. 113–177.

—CHAIM COHEN

BEIN HA-METSARIM (בֵּין הַמְּצָרִים; between the straits; cf. *Lam.* 1.3), a period of three weeks of mourning lasting from 17 Tammuz to 9 Av; it consists of two parts; one of lesser intensity, from 17 Tammuz to 1 Av; and one of greater intensity, from 1 to 9 Av, known as the Nine Days. Bein ha-Metsarim corresponds to the day on which Nebuchadnezzar breached the walls of Jerusalem (on *Shiv'ah 'Asar be-Tammuz) through the day on which the First Temple was destroyed (see TISH'AH BE-'AV). For the entire mourning period, observant Jews do not celebrate festive occasions, and no marriages are performed. On the three Sabbaths during the three weeks, the prophetical readings in the synagogue consist of prophecies of doom (*Jer.* 1, 2, and *Is.* 1); in some rites, these are chanted to a special melody, and the three *haftarot* are known as *talata' de-pur'anuta'* (the Three [Sabbaths] of Suffering). The Sabbath before 9 Av is known as Shabbat Ḥazon (see SABBATHS, SPECIAL). During the nine-day period, the eating of meat and the drinking of wine is proscribed among Ashkenazim and various other communities, except on the Sabbath. Most non-Ashkenazim generally observe the more intensive period of mourning only during the week of Tish'ah be-'Av, although there are variations among different communities.

• Ismar Elbogen, *Jewish Liturgy: A Comprehensive History*, translated by Raymond P. Scheindlin (Philadelphia, 1993). Yosef Y. Grossman, *Mourning over Churban* (New York, 1987).

BEIT DIN (בֵּית דִּין; house of judgment), a court of law guided by the principles of recognized **halakhah* in dealing with matters of civil, criminal, or religious law. The command to appoint judges and establish courts of law is mentioned in *Deuteronomy* 16.18. During the Temple and Mishnaic periods, there were three types of *battei din*. The lowest, which was found in almost all towns, consisted of three judges who had authority to adjudicate civil cases. The judges received their authorization from the heads of the academies or from the patriarch. A higher court consisted of twenty-three judges and was empowered to judge criminal cases. This court was sometimes called the small Sanhedrin. Any town of 120 inhabitants had the right to appoint such a court. The highest type of court was the Great Beit Din or the *Sanhedrin. It consisted of seventy or seventy-one members, who, during the Temple period, sat in the Chamber of the Hewn Stone in the precinct of the Temple and were the source of final authority for the interpretation of law and the establishment of new legislation. The Sanhedrin also appointed the judges of the lower courts. After the destruction of the Temple, the Sanhedrin sat at Yavneh and was recognized as the central authority for all Jews. Its two leaders were the **nasi'* (president) and the *av beit din* (head of the court). Because of the gradual decline in the status and condition of Palestinian Jewry, it steadily lost authority and eventually disappeared. Since membership depended upon an unbroken chain of *ordination, it became impossible to reconstitute such a court when ordination ceased, sometime in the sixth century. Yet Jewish centers continued almost everywhere to have courts, usually presided over by the leading rabbinic scholar of the vicinity. In many places these had almost complete *autonomy. In Spain, Jewish courts, delegated by the king, were even granted criminal jurisdiction. Among the courts of later Jewish history, the most famous perhaps was that of the Council of the Four Lands, which, up to 1764, served as a court of final appeal for Polish Jewry. When Jewish autonomy broke down after *Emancipation, the authority of Jewish courts for the most part became limited to ritual questions. In the State of Israel today, the rabbinical courts enjoy official recognition in all matters of personal status. This is a continuation of the situation under the British Mandate, when Jewish courts were recognized as having the same authority as Muslem religious courts in the areas of marriage and divorce.

In post-Talmudic times the function of a *beit din* is completely different from the articulated purpose of the Great Beit Din (Sanhedrin) in pre-Talmudic times. The term *beit din* in post-Talmudic times commonly denotes the system of courts developed to apply the rules of law found in *halakhah*. Unlike pre-Talmudic times, in which the *beit din* was the source of nearly all advances in Jewish law, in post-Talmudic times a *beit din* decides what the law is as it is applied in any particular case; however, the role of decisors has moved from the *beit din* to the *poseq* (see POSEQIM), the individual who decides in cases where there is no adversarial proceeding.

So, too, the pronouncements of one *beit din* do not create binding *halakhah* for other *battei din*, unless, as is the case of the official rabbinical courts in Israel, there is an agreed structure for an appeal based on a decree (**taqqanah*) of a rabbinical authority. Even within Israel, many *battei din* do not participate in the official rabbinical court system and are not part of its appellate process. So, too, while in pre-Emancipation Europe there were many communal *battei din*, there was no hierarchical appellate structure.

Av beit din is the term used to denote the **dayyan* (judge) who procedurally conducts the *beit din* and functions as its leader.

• Isaac Herzog, "The Administration of Justice in Ancient Israel," in *Judaism: Law and Ethics* (London, 1974), pp. 107–143. Mark F. Lewis, "The First Court: The Bet Din in Today's American Judicial System," *The Jewish Lawyer* 9 (Spring 1993): 15–22. Asher Maoz, "Enforcement of Religious Courts' Judgements under Israeli Law," *Journal of Church and State* 33 (Summer 1991): 473–494. David Menahem Shohet, *The Jewish Court in the Middle Ages* (New York, 1931). —MICHAEL BROYDE

BEIT HA-MIQDASH. See TEMPLE.

BEIT ḤAYYIM (בֵּית חַיִּים; house of the living), euphemism for *cemetery.

BEIT HILLEL AND BEIT SHAMM'AI, the two most important schools of Pharisaic rabbinic sages. The Houses of *Hillel and *Shamm'ai were named for the great teachers who flourished in the last half of the first century BCE and the early first century CE. After some period in which Beit Shamm'ai prevailed, Beit Hillel emerged as dominant when the sages assembled at Yavneh after the fall of Jerusalem in 70 CE.

Virtually no contemporary sources are available regarding the relationship between the schools before the destruction of the Temple. Almost all information comes from later rabbinic traditions, which tended to embellish and expand the traditions they had received. Later rabbinic accounts claim that despite their differences of opinion the houses generally respected each other and were even connected through ties of marriage. Yet the more than three hundred controversies attributed to these schools in Talmudic literature indicate that there must have been a protracted struggle between them, until in the early second century the views of Beit Hillel were finally accepted as authoritative. Its views were for the most part normative in later Mishnaic and Talmudic Judaism, although the views of Shamm'ai were accepted in a few cases.

Various attempts have been made to explain the differences between these schools in a general way. Most common is the claim that Beit Shamm'ai represented the wealthier classes, while Beit Hillel was poorer. Hence, the rulings of Beit Hillel are assumed to have been more favorable to those of less means. It has also been suggested that the differences between the two schools resulted from the personalities of their founders, but this approach is based on a falsely negative picture of Shamm'ai, itself based on some selectively applied Talmudic passages. Others have suggested that these schools were guided by differing hermeneutical approaches for interpreting the Bible, including their conception of legal and religious issues and the role of intention in Jewish law. Finally, some believe the school of Shamm'ai preserves older Sadducean law. No one theory, however, succeeds in explaining the manifold differences of opinion between Beit Hillel and Beit Shamm'ai on all kinds of detailed matters of Jewish law. Rather, the differences are to be attributed to a complex set of factors, some arising from the internal dynamics of Pharisaic rabbinic law and some from the historical context in which the schools functioned.

• Louis Ginzberg, "The Significance of the Halakhah for Jewish History," in *On Jewish Law and Lore* (New York, 1977), pp. 77–124. Alexander Guttmann, *Rabbinic Judaism in the Making: A Chapter in the History of the Halakhah from Ezra to Judah I* (Detroit, 1970), pp. 59–124. Jacob Neusner, *From Politics to Piety: The Emergence of Pharisaic Judaism* (New York, 1973), pp. 97–103. Jacob Neusner, *The Rabbinic Traditions about the Pharisees before 70*, vol. 2, *The Houses* (Leiden, 1971). —LAWRENCE H. SCHIFFMAN

BEIT KENESET. See SYNAGOGUE.

BEIT MIDRASH (בֵּית מִדְרָשׁ; house of study), a place for the study of religious Jewish texts, primarily the Mishnah, Talmud, codes, and *responsa*. The term first occurs in *Ecclesiasticus* 51.50. At the fixed times for communal prayer, those in the *beit midrash* halt their studies and recite the prayers. In the Talmudic period, the term *beit midrash* was almost synonymous with that of **yeshivah* (academy). The first *beit midrash* is said to have been founded by *Shemaʿyah and *Avtalyon. The rabbis ruled that the sanctity of the *beit midrash* was greater than that of the synagogue, because a synagogue was used only for prayer, whereas the *beit midrash* served for both prayer and study of the Torah. The Talmudic rabbis preferred to pray in the *beit midrash* rather than adjourn to the synagogue (*Ber.* 8a). In medieval times, the *beit midrash* was usually located in the same building as the synagogue, or close by, and was maintained by the community. In Germany, the *beit midrash* was termed the *Klaus* (from the Lat. *claustrum* [cloister]), and in eastern Europe, *kloiz*, while in Muslim countries it was called simply *midrash*. Senior students would spend most of their day either in individual study or under the guidance of a *ro'sh yeshivah* (head of the academy). The *beit midrash* was also a place for general popular study, and almost all who went to the synagogue for prayer would also spend some time before or after in the *beit midrash*. It also served as a communal library of rabbinic literature. Jewish legend refers to the antiquity of the institution by ascribing its beginnings to the *beit midrash* established after the Flood by Noah's son Shem (father of the Semites) and his son Eber where Jacob is said to have studied for fourteen years after fleeing from Esau. Midrashic terminology (*Gn. Rab.* 63.10) suggests that boys under thirteen years of age study in the *beit sefer* (house of the book), while those thirteen and above study in the *beit midrash*. It was customary in Talmudic times to recite a special prayer upon entering the *beit midrash*. The Talmud preserves many such prayers, including one by R. Neḥunya' ben ha-Qanah, who, upon entering, prayed to be saved from errors of understanding or interpreting the *halakhah*, and who, upon leaving, would give thanks to heaven for having cast his lot "among those who dwell in the House of Study" (*Ber.* 28b). Study was pursued both day and night, as well as on the Sabbath and holidays. Students who spent their time in the *beit midrash* were permitted to eat and sleep there (actions forbidden in the synagogue). The *halakhah* permits the selling of a synagogue to build a *beit midrash*, since by doing so one is attaining a higher degree of holiness. According to the *aggadah*, God, too, has his own *beit midrash*, and, R. Yehoshu'a ben Levi says, "One who enters the synagogues and *battei midrash* in this world will be admitted into the synagogues and *battei midrash* in the world to come" (*Dt. Rab.* 7.1). Nowadays, *beit midrash* is used primarily in reference to the central study hall of *yeshivot*, although certain small synagogues are also referred to as *battei midrash*.

• Steven Fine et al., *Sacred Realm: The Emergence of the Synagogue in the Ancient World* (New York, 1996). Z. Ilan, "The Synagogue and Beth Midrash of Meroth," in *Ancient Synagogues in Israel*, edited by Rachel Hachlili, BAR International Series 499 (Oxford, 1989). Dan Urman, *Ancient Synagogues: Historical Analysis and Archaeological Discovery*, 2 vols. (Leiden, 1995). Dan Urman, "House of Assembly and the House of Study: Are They One and the Same?" *Journal of Jewish Studies* 44 (1993): 236–257.

—SHMUEL HIMELSTEIN

BEIT 'OLAM (בֵּית עוֹלָם; everlasting house), euphemism for *cemetery.

BEITSAH (בֵּיצָה; Egg), tractate in the Mishnah order Mo'ed, consisting of five chapters, with related material in the Tosefta' and both Talmuds. The popular title *Beitsah* derives from its first word, whereas the original title, *Yom Tov* (Festival), reflects the general content of the tractate, which deals with prohibited and permitted labor on festivals. Following the biblical rule that preparation of food—prohibited on the Sabbath—is permitted on festivals (*Ex.* 12.16), the tractate outlines the laws pertaining to preparation of food on festivals. Both the preparation of food and the sacrificial service in the Temple served as grounds for some of the earliest (*Ḥag.* 2.2) and most contentious (*Ḥag.* 2.11) controversies in Mishnaic *halakhah*. This is reflected in the first two chapters of *Beitsah*, which focus on a series of controversies between *Beit Hillel and Beit Shamm'ai.

An English translation by M. Ginsberg appears in the Soncino Talmud (1938).

• Chanoch Albeck, ed., *Shishah Sidrei Mishnah, Seder Mo'ed* (Jerusalem, 1952). Philip Blackman, ed. and trans., *Mishnayot*, vol. 2, *Order Mo'ed* (Gateshead, 1973). Pinhas Kehati, ed., *Mishnah: A New Translation with a Commentary, Seder Mo'ed*, vol. 4, *Yoma', Sukkah, Beitsah, Ro'sh ha-Shanah* (Jerusalem, 1990). Hermann Leberecht Strack, *Introduction to the Talmud and Midrash* (1931; Minneapolis, 1992).

—AVRAHAM WALFISH

BEIT SHAMM'AI. See BEIT HILLEL AND BEIT SHAMM'AI.

BEIT SHE'ARIM, Jewish city at the end of the Second Temple period and the first centuries following the destruction of the Temple; located about one-and-a-half miles south of the present Qiryat Tivon near Haifa. It attained special importance in 170, when *Yehudah ha-Nasi' transferred his academy there, thus making it the seat of the *Sanhedrin. Beit She'arim became a famous burial place for Jews both inside and outside Palestine; Yehudah ha-Nasi' and other members of his family were buried there. Since 1936, many catacombs and tombs, as well as the remains of a synagogue, have been unearthed at Beit She'arim. The inscriptions on the doors, lintels, and walls above the tombs are in Hebrew, Aramaic, Greek, and Palmyrene.

• Manfred Görg, "Besara–Beit She'arim," *Biblische Notizen* 52 (1990): 7–10. Shemu'el Safrai, "Beit She'arim be-Sifrut ha-Talmudit," in *Be-Yemei ha-Bayit uve-Yemei ha-Mishnah* (Jerusalem, 1994). Ze'ev Weiss, "Social Aspects of Burial in Beit She'arim: Archeological Finds and Talmudic Sources," in *The Galilee in Late Anitquity*, edited by Lee I. Levine (New York, 1992).

BEKHOR. See FIRSTBORN.

BEKHOROT (בְּכוֹרוֹת; Firstborn), tractate in the Mishnah order Qodashim, consisting of nine chapters, with related material in the Tosefta' and Talmud Bavli, dealing with laws concerning the *firstborn of men and animals (*Ex.* 13.2, 13.12ff.; *Nm.* 18.15ff.), as well as the tithing (see TITHES) of animals (*Lv.* 27.31–33). The firstborn is consecrated to God, either by offering it as a sacrifice (an unblemished calf, lamb, or kid), by presenting it as a gift to the priest (an unblemished calf, lamb, or kid), or by redeeming it from the priest (human firstborn or donkey). The Mishnah distinguishes between a father's firstborn son, who inherits a double portion, (*Dt.* 21.17) and a mother's firstborn son; her status determines his consecration to God (*Bekh.* 8).

• Chanoch Albeck, ed., *Shishah Sidrei Mishnah, Seder Qodashim* (Jerusalem, 1956). Philip Blackman, ed. and trans., *Mishnayot*, vol. 5, *Order Qodashim* (Gateshead, 1973). Pinhas Kehati, ed., *Mishnah: A New Trans-*

lation with a Commentary, Seder Qodashim, vol. 2, *Bekhorot, ʿArakhin* (Jerusalem, 1995). Hermann Leberecht Strack, *Introduction to the Talmud and Midrash* (1931; Minneapolis, 1992). —AVRAHAM WALFISH

BEKHOR SHOR, YOSEF BEN YITSḤAQ. See YOSEF BEN YITSḤAQ BEKHOR SHOR.

BEL AND THE DRAGON. See DANIEL, ADDITIONS TO BOOK OF.

BELIAL, biblical term used to designate wickedness and subversive or wicked individuals. The etymology of the word is unclear. Some say it is derived from a combination of the Hebrew *beli* (without) plus the root *yaʿal* (profit, be of worth) so that it means "worthlessness." Others suggest that it is derived from the root *balaʿ* (swallow), in reference to mythological descriptions of the underworld that "swallows" the living. According to rabbinic tradition, the word is derived from a combination of *beli* (without) and *ʿol* (yoke) in reference to those who throw off the yoke of God (*San.* 111b). In pseudepigraphous literature, the term appears in Greek as either Belial or Beliar and serves as a proper name for Satan, as it does in the New Testament, *2 Corinthians* 6.15. In Qumran literature, Belial leads the forces of darkness against the forces of light.

• Theodore J. Lewis, "Belial," in *The Anchor Bible Dictionary*, edited by David Noel Freedman et al., vol. 1 (New York, 1992), pp. 654–656. Benedikt Otzen, "Beliyyaʿal," in *Theological Dictionary of the Old Testament*, edited by Johannes Botterweck and Helmer Ringgren; translated by John T. Willis, vol. 2 (Grand Rapids, 1975), pp. 131–136. —MARVIN A. SWEENEY

BELIEF. See CREED; THIRTEEN PRINCIPLES OF FAITH.

BELLS. The description of the gold pomegranate-shaped bells sewn around the hem of the high priest's robe, so that he would be heard when he entered and left the Holy of Holies, is the sole biblical reference to bells (*Ex.* 28.33–35). By rabbinic tradition, seventy-two bells were sewn around the high priest's hem. Torah-scroll decorations, such as silver breastplates or *rimmonim* (pomegranates), which are mounted on the (often pomegranate-shaped) wooden staves on which the Torah scroll is wound, often had little bells as part of their decoration, probably inspired by the high priest's robe.

• Cornelis Houtman, "On the Pomegranates and the Golden Bells of the High Priest's Mantle," *Vetus Testamentum* 40 (1990): 223–229. Macy Nulman, *The Concise Encyclopedia of Jewish Music* (New York, 1975), pp. 30–31. —SHMUEL HIMELSTEIN

BELSHAZZAR, the last king of the Babylonian empire according to *Daniel* 5. He is the subject of the famous "handwriting on the wall" episode, in which, as he was feasting, an inscription appeared on the wall that Daniel interpreted as referring to Belshazzar's impending downfall at the hands of the Persians and Medes. Daniel states that Belshazzar was deserving of this fate because of his effrontery toward God in worshiping idols while drinking from vessels looted from the Temple at the time of its destruction. In Babylonian sources Belshazzar is known as the son of Nabonidus, the last king of the Babylonian empire (556–539). The biblical account, which identifies Belshazzar as the son of Nebuchadnezzar (*Dn.* 5.2), may represent a process of historical telescoping between the figures of the famous Nebuchadnezzar and the enigmatic Nabonidus, since Belshazzar was the prince regent during the ten years that Nabonidus absented himself from Babylon and went to live in Teima in the Arabian Desert.

• Paul-Alain Beaulieu, *The Reign of Nabonidus, King of Babylon 556–539 B.C.*, Yale Near Eastern Researches 10 (New Haven, 1989). R. P. Dougherty, *Nabonidus and Belshazzar*, Yale Oriental Series, Researches vol. 15 (New Haven, 1929). Harold L. Ginsberg, *Studies in Daniel* (New York, 1948), pp. 25–26. James A. Montgomery, *A Critical and Exegetical Commentary on the Book of Daniel*, The International Critical Commentary, vol. 24 (Edinburgh, 1927), pp. 66–72. —DAVID A. GLATT-GILAD

BELZ, a town in eastern Galicia, seat of a significant Hasidic dynasty founded by R. Shalom Roqeaḥ (1779–1855). He viewed the Haskalah (Enlightenment) as a severe danger to traditional Judaism and was succeeded by his son Yehoshuʿa (1825–1894), who, in an attempt to counteract the pace of Jewish assimilation, formed the Maḥzike ha-Das (Upholders of the Faith) organization. Yehoshuʿa was succeeded by Yissakhar Dov (1854–1927), who strongly opposed Zionism. Rabbi Aharon Roqeaḥ (1880–1957), his son, was persecuted by the Nazis and eventually settled in Israel. He was succeeded by R. Yissakhar Dov Roqeaḥ (born 1948), his brother's son, who established the dynasty's headquarters in Jerusalem. Initially opposed to any form of Zionism, Belz Ḥasidim have traditionally supported the Agudat Israel party. Outside of Erets Yisra'el, there are Belz communities in Montréal, New York, London, Antwerp, and Zurich.

• Janet Belcove-Shalin, ed., *New World Hasidim: Ethnographic Studies of Hasidic Jews in North America* (New York, 1995). Tzvi Rabinowicz, *Hasidism: The Movement and Its Masters* (Northvale, N.J., 1988). —WILLIAM SHAFFIR

BE-MOTSA'EI MENUḤAH (בְּמוֹצָאֵי מְנוּחָה; At the Going Out of [the Day of] Rest), an alphabetical acrostic (though lacking the letter *samekh*) *seliḥah* (see SELIḤOT) chanted in the Ashkenazi rite on the Saturday night before Ro'sh ha-Shanah. This *seliḥah*, possibly composed by a medieval poet named Shemu'el, has eight stanzas with the refrain, "O hear our song and our prayer." It is found in Orthodox and non-Orthodox liturgies. A similarly named *piyyut*, Be-Motsa'ei Yom Menuḥah, by Yaʿaqov of Lunel is recited following **havdalah* in many Western and Eastern communities. It contains a prayer that the prophet Elijah will come and bring redemption.

• Abraham Rosenfeld, trans. and annot., *The Authorised Selichot for the Whole Year*, 3d ed. (London, 1962), pp. 13f. —A. STANLEY DREYFUS

BENAMOZEGH, ELIYYAHU (1822–1900), Italian theologian. He was born in Leghorn to a family that had emigrated from Morocco. He served as rabbi of Leghorn and taught in that city's rabbinical school. His major work, *Em la-Miqra'* (1862–1865), was received in the rabbinical world with hostility and was publicly burned by the rabbis of Aleppo and Damascus. Unlike his scholarly contemporaries, such as Heinrich Graetz and Shemu'el David Luzzatto, Benamozegh had a positive attitude toward *Kabbalah; he demanded it receive a special status like the Bible and the Talmud. He regarded Judaism as the crown of humankind and stressed that Judaism must take the lead in maintaining the universalistic belief in monotheism. By identifying foreign elements that had penetrated Jewish tradition, he felt he was following rabbinic precedent. He examined the customs and traditions of ancient peoples, combining studies of linguistics, criticism, archaeology, history, and anthropology with a deep knowledge of the Bible, Midrash, and Kabbalah. The suppression of *Em la-Miqra'* and its sequel, *Em la-Masoret*, on Talmudic and kabbalistic traditions, by the sages of Jerusalem and other rabbis prevented his works from reaching Jews in Near Eastern and North African lands. The rabbinical decisions aimed at preventing criticism and modernization were backed by the Ottoman authorities. Benamozegh, who was called the Plato of Italian Jewry, produced many other studies in Hebrew, French, and Italian. He was highly regarded by non-Jews, including Giuseppe Mazzini, and his *Israël et l'humanité* (1914), on the universal aspects of Judaism, achieved a wide readership.

• Alessandro Guetta, "Un Kabbaliste à l'heure du progrès: Le Cas d'Elie Benamozegh," *Revue de l'historie des religions* 208 (1991): 415–436. Yaron Harel, "The Edict to Destroy Em la-Miqra', Aleppo 1865," *Hebrew Union College Annual* 64 (1993): 26–36, in Hebrew.

—SHALOM BAR-ASHER

BEN ASHER FAMILY, a family of masoretic scholars.

Mosheh ben Asher (9th cent.), fourth in the line of Tiberian Masoretes descended from Asher the Elder and father of the last, Aharon ben Mosheh ben Asher. The family may have had Karaite sympathies. Mosheh is author of the oldest extant Hebrew Bible codex of the Former and Latter Prophets, copied in Tiberias in 897. Decorated with Islamic-style artwork, the manuscript is in the Karaite synagogue in Cairo. In only one-third of the cases do Mosheh's vocalization and cantillation agree with those of his son whose method is the basis of the modern Masoretic Text. More than half of the readings accord with Mosheh ben David ben Naftali, the other great Tiberian Masorete. Song of the Vine, a poem comparing Israel to a vine producing the prophets, is probably also the work of Mosheh.

Aharon ben Mosheh ben Asher (10th cent.), Palestinian Hebrew grammarian, son of Mosheh; one of the last representatives of the Tiberian school of Masoretes, in which his family had figured prominently. He produced a carefully edited biblical text by finalizing a system of vowel points and *accents that were added to the consonantal base of the Masoretic Text (see BIBLE TEXT). In due course, Ben Asher's system prevailed over other systems of *vocalization and became the basis for most manuscripts and subsequently all Bible editions. The Aleppo Codex, considered a model codex by Maimonides, and the Codex Leningrad B19A are the most faithful representatives of the Ben Asher system.

• **Mosheh ben Asher:** Shnayer Z. Leiman, *The Canon and Masorah of the Hebrew Bible* (New York, 1974). Fred N. Reiner, "Masoretes and Rabbis: A Comparison of Biblical Interpretations," rabbinic dissertation, Hebrew Union College, 1973. **Aharon ben Mosheh ben Asher:** Aron Dotan, *Ben Asher's Creed: A Study of the History of the Controversy*, Masoretic Studies, no. 3 (Missoula, Mont., 1977). Moshe H. Goshen-Gottstein, "The Rise of the Tiberian Bible Text," in *Biblical and Other Studies*, edited by Alexander Altmann, Texts and Studies, vol. 1 (Cambridge, Mass., 1963), pp. 79–122. William Wickes, *A Treatise on the Accentuation of the Twenty-one So-called Prose Books of the Old Testament, with a Facsimile of a Page of the Codex Assigned to Ben-Asher in Aleppo* (Oxford, 1887).

—DENNIS M. DREYFUS

BENATTAR, ḤAYYIM. See ATTAR FAMILY.

BENATTAR, YEHUDAH. See ATTAR FAMILY.

BEN ʿAZZAI, SHIMʿON. See SHIMʿON BEN ʿAZZAI.

BENÇAO, a Sephardi term corresponding to the Ashkenazi **bentshn* and denoting blessing in general, both words being derived from later forms of the Latin *benedicere*. *Bençao* denotes the particular form of prayer known as "benediction" and the *Birkat ha-Mazon. The word has been corrupted into *besam*.

BENEDICTIONS (Heb. *berakhot*), a liturgical term denoting prayer, or praise of God, that is formulated in a special style. The term is technically applied only to a prayer that contains in its opening or concluding sentence, or in both, the words *Barukh attah Adonai*, "Blessed are you, O Lord"; if appearing at the beginning of the prayer, the formula continues with the words *Eloheinu melekh ha-ʿolam*, "our God, king of the universe." After this unvarying formula comes the specific praise, appropriate to each particular prayer. Of all the various formulas of praise, the benediction was eventually chosen to serve exclusively in any obligatory prayer. It is modeled on a biblical pattern (*Ps*. 119.12), although it underwent some modification. Benediction formulas are found frequently in the Dead Sea Scrolls, but are used interchangably with others (not all contain the word *you*, and they refer to God by various names and epithets). By the third century CE, all the statutory forms of the benediction had been fixed: a benediction had to contain the word *you*; the Tetragrammaton (pronounced Adonai) had to be used (and no other epithets of God); when used as an opening formula it had to contain mention of God's kingship. Although invariably commencing with a direct address to God, the benediction continues, with very few exceptions, by referring to God in the third person; on the other hand, any section of the obligatory part of the liturgy, which does not open with the benediction formula (such as all the intermediary benedictions of the *ʿAmidah), invariably uses the second person in addressing God. The exclusive use of the benediction style for obligatory prayers was apparently intended to provide a distinguishing mark by which normative standard prayers are differentiated from individual and private ones. Hence the Talmud lays down that "unnecessary" use of the benediction (*berakhah le-vatalah*), including its use in nonobligatory prayer, is prohibited and regarded as a transgression of *Exodus* 20.7: "You shall not take the name of the Lord your God in vain." Since, however, no objection is raised to the use of the divine name in private prayer as such, but only to its use in the benediction formula, it is clear that the intention was to reserve the latter exclusively for statutory prayers. Hence the presence or absence of this formula at the beginning or end of any part of the liturgy can serve to determine if the prayer in question forms part of the obligatory service. At times individuals would use the benediction to conclude their private prayers, but this practice was forbidden by later authorities. The benediction is used both in synagogue and in private or domestic prayers as long as they are obligatory, for example, the *Qiddush.

Three forms of benediction are used: the short form, which opens with the benediction formula; the long form, which often (but not always) opens and concludes with it; and "a benediction following upon a preceding one," in which the benediction formula serves as conclusion. The first type is frequently used for a short benediction, such as that spoken before partaking of any food; the third is used extensively in the longer portions of the obligatory daily prayers, such as the ʿAmidah, the benedictions of the *Shemaʿ, and *Birkat ha-Mazon, all of which consist of a series of benedictions, of which only the first belongs to the long form, while all the subsequent ones no longer open but only conclude with the formula.

Benedictions can be divided according to their contents and liturgical function. Apart from the series of benedictions that constitute the main portions of all obligatory daily prayers, there are many, mostly of the short form, recited for certain occasions. Benedictions of enjoyment are recited before partaking of any food or drink. For each of the more important categories of food or drink, especially bread, cake, wine, fruit, or vegetables, a special benediction is used, for instance, "Blessed are you . . . who brings forth bread from the earth,"or ". . . who creates the fruit of the vine"; while for any other type of food or drink (meat, eggs, fish, sweets, etc.), there is one uniform benediction, ". . . by whose word all things came into being." (Several additional special formulas were known in the old Palestinian rite but have fallen into disuse.) Various benedictions to be recited before enjoying the smell of flowers, spices, and so on belong to this category. Apart from Birkat ha-Mazon, two benedictions are to be recited after the enjoyment of food or drink: the longer one (a condensation of Birkat ha-Mazon into one benediction of the long form) to be used after wine, cake, and those kinds of fruit mentioned in *Deuteronomy* 8.8; and the shorter one to be used after all other types of food or drink.

Benedictions are also recited before performing a **mitsvah*; for example, putting on **tefillin*, kindling the Sabbath lights, or sounding the *shofar. All benedictions recited over a *mitsvah* open with "Blessed are you . . . who has sanctified us by his commandments and commanded us . . ."; after this follow two or three words indicating which commandment is about to be performed. These benedictions are to be recited before the *mitsvah* is observed, with only a few exceptions (e.g., the benediction on the occasion of the ritual washing of one's hands, spoken after the ablution). In selected cases, if a commandment is performed for the first time or for the first time in any particular year, the additional benediction "Blessed . . . who has kept us alive . . . and made us reach this time" is recited.

Various benedictions of praise or thanksgiving are to be recited on seeing lightning, the ocean, a king, or a great scholar or on hearing either good or bad news. With this group might also be counted the "blessings of the morning" (now usually recited in the synagogue before *Shaḥarit proper), including "Blessed . . . who restores souls to dead bodies"; ". . . who opens the eyes of the blind"; ". . . who clothes the naked"; and ". . . who supplies my every want."

Individual benedictions or arrangements of several benedictions are to be recited on special liturgical occasions, such as Qiddush, *Havdalah, *Shevaʿ Berakhot, and seeing the new moon.

Occasionally the term *berakhah* is used in the liturgy in a nontechnical sense concerning a blessing or prayer that does not contain the *barukh* formula, as in the *Birkat ha-Kohanim and the *Birkat ha-Ḥodesh. According to R. Me'ir, a man should utter at least one hundred benedictions every day. The fact that at various times throughout the day the Jew is obliged to recite a blessing and so turn his thoughts to God is one of the most characteristic features of the discipline of sanctification. Everyday actions, such as getting up and dressing in the morning, eating or drinking, the observance of natural phenomena, or the receiving of glad or sad news, all provide occasion for praising God and thus take on religious significance. Through the benediction a physical action becomes an act of worship. In the case of *mitsvot*, the preceding benedictions serve the purpose of preparing the mind of the worshiper to perform the *mitsvah* not as mere routine but joyfully and as a conscious act of observance. Since the occasions for benedictions arise throughout the day—at home as well as at work—they help to overcome the cleavage between the holy and the profane in life and are designed to make one's entire life a continuous service to God. Traditionally the benedictions were attributed to the Men of the *Keneset ha-Gedolah. See also BLESSING AND CURSING.

• Elias J. Bickerman, "Bènèdiction et prière," in *Studies in Jewish and Christian History*, vol. 2 (Leiden, 1980), pp. 313–323. B. Bokser, "Blessings and Misvot, the History of the Halakhah, and the Beginnings of the Gemara," in *Jewish Law in Our Time*, edited by Ruth Hyman (New York, 1982), pp. 3–17. Ismar Elbogen, *Jewish Liturgy: A Comprehensive History*, translated by Raymond P. Scheindlin (Philadelphia, 1993), pp. 5–6. Joseph Heinemann, *Prayer in the Talmud: Forms and Patterns* (Berlin, 1977). Lawrence A. Hoffman, "Blessings and Their Translation in Current Jewish Liturgies," *Worship* 60.2 (1986): 134–161. Bilha Nitzan, "Benedictions and Instructions for the Eschatological Community," *Revue de Qumran* 16 (1993): 77–90. Margarete Schlüter, "Zum Formular der Beracha," *Frankfurter judaistische Beiträge* 11 (1983): 47–56. Saul P. Wachs, "Some Reflections on Two Genres of Berakhah," *Journal of Synagogue Music* 22.1–2 (1992): 24–39.

BENEI BETEIRA', prominent family of scholars (1st cent. BCE–1st cent. CE) that, according to tradition, renounced the leading position it had held after the deaths of *Shemaʿyah and *Avtalyon in favor of *Hillel, whose appointment as president of the Sanhedrin it promoted. Several members of the family are mentioned in the Talmud. Some scholars conjecture that the family was named after the city of Bathyra in northern Transjordan, and others have linked them with the famous warlike family of Zamaris, which settled in Bathyra and became a major ally of Herod; however, these identifications are unlikely.

• Israel Ben-Shalom, *The School of Shammai and the Zealots' Struggle against Rome* (Jerusalem, 1973), pp. 62–75. —DANIEL SPERBER

BENE ISRAEL, Indian Jews originally from the villages of the Konkan region of what is now the state of Maharashtra, who settled in Bombay and other cities in India in the nineteenth and twentieth centuries.

According to their tradition, the ancestors of the Bene Israel originated in Israel but were shipwrecked off the Konkan coast in the year 175 BCE or earlier. They lost all of their holy books and only remembered the Shema' prayer. In the course of time, they adopted a number of Hindu customs. They were discovered by David Rahabi, a Jew from Cochin, possibly in the eighteenth century. The Bene Israel observed the Sabbath and refrained from work on that day; they were circumcised; they ate only kosher food and observed many, but not all, of the Jewish festivals. They had no synagogues, observed Ro'sh ha-Shanah for only one day, and did not know of Ḥanukkah. The first Bene Israel synagogue, the Gate of Mercy, was established by a Bene Israel officer in the British Indian army, Samuel Divekar, in Bombay in 1796. From then on, the community was assisted in its religious revival and adaptation to normative Judaism by Cochin Jews from the Malabar coast, Christian missionaries who arrived in the Konkan in 1810, and Baghdadi Jews who settled in Bombay (and Calcutta) from this period on.

Gradually, the Bene Israel left the Konkan villages, and their traditional occupation of oil pressing, and began to move to Bombay, Pune, Ahmedabad, Delhi, and Karachi, as well as Aden Protectorate. Numbering six thousand individuals in the 1830s, the community had expanded to over twenty thousand by 1948. After the British withdrew from India in 1947 and the State of Israel was established in 1948, the Bene Israel began immigrating to Israel. Today, an estimated forty thousand people of Bene Israel descent live in Israel; five thousand remain in India.

The Bene Israel were not recognized by Israel's chief rabbinate as full Jews when they first came to live in Israel because of doubts concerning their origin. Between 1962 and 1964 they organized a series of strikes demanding full recognition, and in 1964 the chief rabbinate withdrew its halakhic objections and declared the Bene Israel "full Jews in every respect."

In India, the Bene Israel strictly observed endogamy, marrying only members of their own community. In Israel, the Bene Israel still generally marry within their ethnic community, although some marry Jews of other origins.

• Benjamin J. Israel, *The Bene Israel of India: Some Studies* (Bombay, 1984). Benjamin J. Israel, *Religious Evolution among the Bene Israel of India since 1750* (Bombay, 1963). Haeem Samuel Kehimkar, *The History of the Bene Israel of India* (Tel Aviv, 1937). Rebecca Reuben, *The Bene Israel of Bombay* (Cambridge, 1913). Joan Roland, *Jews in British India: Identity in a Colonial Era* (Hanover, N.H., 1989). Schifra Strizower, *The Children of Israel: The Bene Israel of Bombay* (Oxford, 1971). Shalva Weil, "The Influence of Caste Ideology in Israel," in *Cultural Transition: The Case of Immigrant Youth*, edited by Meir Gotesman (Jerusalem, 1988), pp. 150–161. —SHALVA WEIL

BENJAMIN (Heb. Binyamin), the youngest of Jacob's twelve sons by his favorite wife, Rachel, who died in childbirth. His mother had called him Ben-oni (Son of My Suffering), but his father renamed him Benjamin (Son of the Right Hand). His name may hint at the fact that the domain of the tribe of Benjamin was located to the right side, that is, to the south of the territory of the tribe of Joseph, Benjamin's older and only full brother (*Gn.* 35.18). The Samaritan Pentateuch interprets the name Benjamin as Son of the Days, that is, old age. Benjamin plays a special role in the Joseph stories, testing the brothers' loyalty to each other and their remorse for their jealousy and for selling Joseph into slavery.

The small tribal territory of Benjamin lay between the border cities of Bethel to the north and Jerusalem to the south. It was the first area conquered by Joshua after crossing the Jordan, and it included the famous sites of Jericho, Gilgal, Ai, and Gibeon (*Jos.* 4–10). During the early period of the Judges, the Benjaminite judge, Ehud ben Gera, freed the Israelites from the domination of Eglon, king of Moab (*Jgs.* 3.12–30). The Benjaminites were skilled in the use of weapons and developed an ambidextrous fighting technique (*Jgs.* 3.4, 20.16). Because of their barbaric behavior toward an itinerant Levite and his concubine, the Benjaminites were attacked by a coalition of the rest of the tribes during the priesthood of Phineas ben Eleazar. The war centered on the main city of Gibeah, which was treated as an *'ir ha-niddaḥat* (condemned city; *Dt.* 13.13–19). The conflict ended in the near-annihilation of the tribe. Its survival was made possible because the remaining six hundred men were allowed to marry women taken from Shiloh and Jabesh-gilead (*Jgs.* 19–21).

Under the Benjaminite King *Saul, Gibeah (by this time, known as Gibeath Saul) became the first capital of the Israelite monarchy. The central cultic site of Saul's reign was the great *bamah* (high place) located at Gibeon (el-Jib), where the descendants of Eleazar ben Aaron served; the other priestly line of Ithamar ben Aaron, which had previously served at Shiloh, now resided in Nob. Realizing the importance of the territory of Benjamin in protecting the northern flank of his new capital of Jerusalem, David assiduously severed all of its northern ties and suppressed any resurgent Saulite allegiances. The success of this policy is seen in the incorporation of Benjamin into the Judean kingdom after Solomon's death (c.930 BCE).

After the destruction of the First Temple and the demise of the kingdom of Judah in 586 BCE, the territory of Benjamin took on new importance when the Babylonians appointed Gedaliah as governor and established his capital at Mizpah. In the Second Temple period, tribal affiliations gave way to national identity, as can be seen when the Benjaminite Mordecai is referred to as "the Jew" (*Est.* 2.5). Nevertheless, later Jews, such as Paul (*Rom.* 11.1; *Phil.* 3.5), preserved an awareness of their Benjaminite ancestry.

• Yohanan Aharoni, *The Land of the Bible: A Historical Geography*, 2d ed. (Philadelphia, 1979), *passim*. Burton MacDonald, "The Biblical Tribe of Benjamin: Its Origins and Its History during the Period of the Judges of Israel," Ph.D. dissertation, Catholic University of America, 1974. Klaus-Dietrich Schunck, *Benjamin: Untersuchungen zur Entstehung und Geschichte eines israelitischen Stammes*, Beiheft zur Zeitschrift für die alttestamentliche Wissenschaft 86 (Berlin, 1963). —AARON DEMSKY

BEN ME'IR, AHARON. See AHARON BEN ME'IR.

BEN NAFTALI, MOSHEH BEN DAVID (10th cent.), Hebrew grammarian and masoretic scholar (see MASORAH), one of the last representatives of the Tiberian school of Masoretes. No information is known about his life. The Ben Naftali system differed slightly from the Ben Asher (see BEN ASHER FAMILY) system. The differences between the two systems have been recorded in Misha'el ben ʿUzzi'el's *Kitab al-Khulaf*. It is not clear which manuscripts best represent the Ben Naftali text.

• Moshe H. Goshen-Gottstein, "The Rise of the Tiberian Bible Text," in *Biblical and Other Studies*, edited by Alexander Altmann, Texts and Studies, vol. 1 (Cambridge, Mass., 1963), pp. 79–122.

BEN SHIMʿON, RAFA'EL (1848–1928), rabbinical authority in Egypt; chief rabbi of Cairo from 1891. He faced the problems of modernity with understanding and leniency, and while affirming the role of the rabbis in maintaining tradition, he taught that they must also face a world of change. The role of the rabbis in Egypt at this time was of particular significance, apart from them there was little Jewish scholarship. Ben Shimʿon was particularly active in finding legal ways to circumvent the problem of deserted wives (*ʿagunot*), which was particularly pressing in view of the number of young brides left behind by their husbands who had migrated from Egypt. His works include *Nehar Mitsrayim* (1908), on the practices of the Jews of Egypt. He lived his last years in Palestine.

• Tsevi Zohar, *Masoret u-Temurah: Hitmoddedut Ḥakhmei Yisra'el be-Mitsrayim uve-Suryah ʿim Etgerei ha-Modernizatsyah, 1880–1920* (Jerusalem, 1993). —SHALOM BAR-ASHER

BEN SIRA, ALPHABET OF. See ALPHABET OF BEN SIRA.

BEN SIRA, WISDOM OF. See WISDOM OF BEN SIRA.

BEN SORER U-MOREH (בֵּן סוֹרֵר וּמוֹרֶה; rebellious son), according to the Bible, "a defiant and rebellious son" who "refuses to listen to his parents' voice," and "a glutton and a drunkard." He is to be brought before the elders of the city and stoned to death (*Dt*. 21.18–21). The Talmud hedges this biblical provision with a number of reservations and declares that "there never has been, nor will there ever be, an execution of a rebellious son." According to this view, the law was originally propounded for educational and deterrent purposes only (*San*. 71a). These reservations include limiting the period in which the law of the rebellious son could be applied, to the three months following his thirteenth birthday; fixing huge minimal quantities of food and drink, which had to be consumed before the sentence could be passed; and requiring that the voices of both parents possess identical physical properties (*San*. 69a–70b). According to R. Yonatan, however, the law of the rebellious son was put into practice and he states that he had sat on the grave of such a son (*San*. 71a). The rabbinic justification of the execution of the rebellious son is the principle that "he is judged in accordance with his likely end," that is, his bad habits will eventually lead to serious criminal acts, and it is preferable that he die innocent rather than guilty (*San*. 82a). In light of other ancient Near Eastern codes, it is arguable that the biblical law was designed to limit the power of the *pater familias* by extending the crime to breaches of the authority of the mother, as well as that of the father.

• Gerald Blidstein, *Honor Thy Father and Mother* (New York, 1975), pp. 12, 17, 173n.2. Menachem Elon, *Jewish Law: History, Sources, Principles* (Philadelphia, 1994), pp. 365–366. —DANIEL SINCLAIR

BENTSHN (Yi.; בענטשן), term derived from Latin *benedicere* (to bless) by way of the Old French; applied more particularly to the blessing of children by their parents, *Birkat ha-Mazon, the recitation of the *Birkat ha-Gomel, and lighting the Sabbath candles. It corresponds to the Sephardi term **bençao*.

BENTSUR, YAʿAQOV. See IBN ZUR, YAʿAQOV.

BENVENISTE FAMILY, family of Sephardi scholars, especially in the Ottoman empire.

Ḥayyim ben Yisra'el Benveniste (1603–1673), lived and officiated in his native Constantinople, in Tirya, and in Smyrna, where in 1662 he became chief rabbi. This was a period of the arrival in Smyrna of groups from various places, and Benveniste, with a highly regarded knowledge of the halakhic literature of his predecessors and contemporaries, mediated their disputes and helped to unify the community leadership. He was respectful of the varied *minhagim* of the communities scattered throughout the Ottoman empire, though he was very strict in his rulings concerning ritual slaughter and dietary laws. An outstanding codifier, he wrote an eight-volume work based on Karo's *Shulḥan ʿArukh* in which he collects the views of later authorities and adds some earlier ones whom Karo had omitted (Leghorn, 1658; Constantinople, 1716). Many of his *responsa* are to be found in *Ba'ei Ḥayyei* (Salonika, 1788–1791). He also wrote *Sefer Pesaḥ Meʿubbin* (Venice, 1692) on the laws of Pesaḥ and *novellae* to tractate *Sanhedrin*.

Yehoshuʿa Refa'el Benveniste (1595–1666), rabbinical authority and poet in Turkey; brother of R. Ḥayyim Benveniste. He served in Constantinople and Bursa but was sought out for his rulings by people from all parts of the Ottoman empire, even by the Karaites. He commented on the Talmud Yerushalmi but ruled that when the two Talmuds differed, the Talmud Bavli should be given precedence. His commentary, *Sedeh Yehoshuʿa* has been frequently republished, most recently in Jerusalem in 1972. Almost unique for the rabbis in his region of the time, he had a broad secular education—in medicine and linguistics. He was also a poet, writing religious poems, poems of friendship, and didactic verse.

His *responsa* were published in Jerusalem in 1982 under the title *Sha'ar Yehoshu'a*.

• J. Barnai, in *Pe'amim* 48 (1991): 66–84. Leah Bornstein-Makoretski, "The Jewish Community in Istanbul in the Mid-Seventeenth Century: Its Sephardi and Romaniote Personalities and Sages," *Michael* 9 (1985): 27–54, in Hebrew. Baruch ha-Levi Epstein, *Meqor Barukh* (New York, 1954). H. Inalcik, "Istanbul," in *The Encyclopedia of Islam* (Leiden, 1978), vol. 4, pp. 241–248. Yosef Tobi, in *Dappim le-Meḥqar be-Sifrut* (1988): 19–34. J. R. Hacker, "Jewish Autonomy in the Ottoman Empire: Its Scope and Limits," in *Temurot ba-Historyah ha-Yehudit ha-Ḥadashah*, edited by S. Alrnog (Jerusalem, 1987), pp. 349–388. —SHALOM BAR-ASHER

BEN ZOMA', SHIM'ON. See SHIM'ON BEN ZOMA'.

BEQUESTS. See INHERITANCE.

BERAB, YA'AQOV (c.1474–1546), Talmudist. Born in Spain, Berab became rabbi of Fez in Morocco at the age of eighteen. From there he moved to Egypt, where he headed a major rabbinic academy that counted Yosef *Karo among its students, and finally settled in Safed. He was considered one of the foremost rabbinic authorities of his age, and in 1538 he initiated the abortive attempt to renew rabbinic ordination (**semikhah*, which had lapsed in the amoraic period) as a first step toward reestablishing the *Sanhedrin, reuniting the Jewish people under one spiritual authority, and hastening the advent of redemption. He himself was the first *samukh* (ordained rabbi) named by the rabbis of Safed and in turn gave *semikhah* to a number of others, including Yosef Karo. The scheme was opposed by R. Levi ibn Ḥaviv of Jerusalem and by others and after an acrimonious controversy ultimately failed. Shortly after this abortive initiative, Berab had to flee from Safed, probably because of problems with the Turkish authorities.

• Jacob Katz, "The Dispute Between Jacob Berab and Levi ibn Habib over Renewing Ordination," in *Studies in Jewish History*, Binah, vol. 1, edited by Joseph Dan (New York, 1989), pp. 119–141.

BERAḤ DODI (בְּרַח דּוֹדִי; "Make haste my beloved"), the opening words of three liturgical compositions recited in the Ashkenazi rite before the Shaḥarit 'Amidah on the first and second days and the intermediate Sabbath of Pesaḥ. The words come from the *Song of Songs* (8.14), which is read in the synagogue on Pesaḥ. All three compositions, by tenth-century authors, are based on the traditional interpretation of the *Song of Songs* as an allegory of the love between God and Israel.

• Dovid Landesman, trans. and annot., *The Commentary of Rav Naftali Tzvi Yehuda Berlin to Shir ha-Shirim* (Kefar Ḥasidim, Israel, 1993), p. 282.

BERAKHAH. See BENEDICTIONS.

BERAKHAH AḤARONAH (בְּרָכָה אַחֲרוֹנָה; Last Blessing [in contradistinction to the "first blessing" said before partaking of any food]), the shorter form of *Birkat ha-Mazon said after partaking of food other than bread prepared from the five primary grains, wine, and food specified in *Deuteronomy* 8.8 as characteristic of Israel. The Berakhah Aḥaronah briefly summarizes the ordinary Birkat ha-Mazon. After partaking of food that requires neither the full grace nor the Berakhah Aḥaronah, an even shorter blessing is recited (Bore' Nefashot).

• Ismar Elbogen, *Jewish Liturgy: A Comprehensive History*, translated by Raymond P. Scheindlin (Philadelphia, New York, and Jerusalem, 1993), pp. 48. Macy Nulman, *The Encyclopedia of Jewish Prayer* (London, 1993), pp. 96–97. Ephraim Yehudah Wiesenberg, "The Shorter Forms of Grace after Meals and of the Amidah," *Niv Hamidrashia* 18–19 (1984): 69–84.

BERAKHAH LE-VATTALAH (בְּרָכָה לְבַטָּלָה), a blessing made in vain. According to a simple understanding of the words of the Talmud (*Ber.* 33a), such a blessing violates the biblical prohibition found in *Exodus* 20.7. This is the ruling of Maimonides and many other authorities. However, most decisors of Jewish law accept that one who recites an unneeded blessing violates only a rabbinic commandment and not a biblical commandment. The biblical prohibition limits the use of the divine name outside of prayer or ritual. These rules are codified in the *Shulḥan 'Arukh, Oraḥ Ḥayyim* 215(4).

• "Berakhah She'ennah Tseriḥah," *Entsiqlopedyah Talmudit* (Jerusalem, 1947–) vol. 4, pp. 280–285. —MICHAEL BROYDE

BERAKHAH ME'EIN SHALOSH (בְּרָכָה מֵעֵין שָׁלוֹשׁ; the Blessing Summarizing the Three [First Blessings of the Birkat ha-Mazon]), an abbreviated form of the *Birkat ha-Mazon. The giving of thanks after a meal is enjoined in *Deuteronomy* 8.10. When the repast includes bread, the full four blessings of the Birkat ha-Mazon are to be recited. Three of these blessings are considered biblical in origin; the last is rabbinical. An abbreviated version, to be recited over food prepared from the five species of grain (wheat, barley, rye, oats, spelt) or the fruits of Erets Yisra'el (grapes, figs, olives, dates, pomegranates), is designated Berakhah Me'ein Shalosh. Several other abbreviated forms of the Birkat ha-Mazon were composed for the benefit of children, as well as for adults under time constraints. One that is still widely used was published by R. Naftali ben David Zekharyah Mendel in 1603. In modern times, shortened versions of the Birkat ha-Mazon have been prepared by the editors of Conservative, Reconstructionist, and Reform prayer books.

• Isaac Klein, *A Guide to Jewish Religious Practice* (New York, 1979), pp. 44f. —A. STANLEY DREYFUS

BERAKHOT (בְּרָכוֹת; Benedictions), tractate in the Mishnah order Zera'im, consisting of nine chapters, with related material in the Tosefta' and both Talmuds. *Berakhot* outlines the daily liturgical requirements of rabbinic Judaism, in which a central role is played by prayers with a fixed formal structure known as *benedictions. These prayers address praise, thanksgiving, or supplication to God, opening and sometimes concluding with the formula: "Blessed are you, O Lord." Talmudic law strictly regulates when benedictions are to be pronounced and what form of benediction is appropriate for each occasion. The benedictions of tractate *Berakhot* encompass normal daily activities, from awakening to retiring, with particular emphasis on benedictions before and after eating.

The tractate opens with a discussion of the laws regarding the twice-daily recitation of the *Shema', in which a Jew reaffirms his belief in one God and his commitment to the divine word and commandments, and continues with the laws governing the daily prayer service. Following a discussion of the benedictions over food and other laws associated with meals, the tractate concludes with benedictions to be recited over special experiences and occasions.

Tractate *Berakhot* is the first tractate in standard arrangements of the Mishnah. Its portrayal of the central role played by Judaism's theological tenets in a Jew's daily life serves as an appropriate opening to the Mishnah corpus. The tractate, while focusing on halakhic practice subsequent to the destruction of the Temple, opens and closes with allusions to the Temple, reflecting the centrality of the Temple service within Jewish consciousness even after its destruction.

The tractate was translated into English by Maurice Simon in the Soncino Talmud (1948).

• Chanoch Albeck, ed., *Shishah Sidrei Mishnah, Seder Zera'im* (Jerusalem, 1957). Philip Blackman, ed. and trans., *Mishnayot*, vol. 1, *Order Zera'im* (Gateshead, 1973). Jacob David Herzog, ed. and trans., *Mishnah* (Jerusalem, 1945). Max Kadushin, *Worship and Ethics* (Evanston, Ill., 1964). Pinhas Kehati, ed., *Mishnah: A New Translation with a Commentary, Seder Zera'im*, vol. 1, *Berakhot, Pe'ah* (Jerusalem, 1989). Hermann Leberecht Strack, *Introduction to the Talmud and Midrash* (1931; Minneapolis, 1992). Angelo Vivian, "Il trattato mishnico Berakhot e la sua concettualizzazione," in *Journal biblische und judaistische Studien: Festschrift für Paolo Sacchi*, edited by Angelo Vivian (Frankfurt am Main, 1990), pp. 383–534.
—AVRAHAM WALFISH

BERDUGO, RAFA'EL (1747–1822), rabbinical authority in Meknes, Morocco. He belonged to a distinguished rabbinical family that had played a leading role in Meknes for many generations. During his lifetime, however, Meknes lost much of its importance as a major Jewish center. Berdugo, influenced by the decline of the secular community leaders, determined that the *beit din* should be the central communal authority. His *responsa* and *novellae*, notably *Mishpatim Yesharim* (2 vols. [Kraków, 1891]), reflect his struggles with the community leadership and emphasize the independent and moral role of the *dayyanim*. Berdugo's writings on the Bible and Midrash displayed great expertise, and he used them to strengthen his social teachings. He opposed hereditary communal positions and insisted on their being determined by public choice. He was a popular figure and did not let his great learning distance him from the masses. His signaled the emergence of a new type of leadership in North African Jewry.

• Shalom Bar-Asher, "Ma'avaq Battei ha-Din ba-Yeḥidim uva-'Arka'ut ha-Shilton ha-Muslami," *Shilton ve-Hanhagah* (Jerusalem, 1995): 179–205. Elisha Nachmani, "R. Refa'el Berdugo u-Ferushav la-Torah," master's thesis, Bar Ilan University, 1988, with English introduction.
—SHALOM BAR-ASHER

BEREIRAH (בְּרֵירָה; choosing, selection), a legal term designating a situation the facts of which or the legal implications of which become definitely known only at some future time. The question is whether there can be retroactive recognition of such. The Talmud distinguishes between the kinds of *bereirah* in which the present condition of doubt is due to the person, although the situation itself has certainty, and the kind in which the situation itself is doubtful. The first category of *bereirah*, personal doubt, is again divided into two categories: one in which the definite outcome depends upon the individual himself, and one in which it depends upon the will or action of others. Classic rabbinic law allows for the use of this type of analysis when the prohibition or obligation is only rabbinic in nature (*yesh bereirah mi-de-rabbanan*) and prohibits the use of this analytical tool when a biblical obligation is at stake (*ein bereirah min ha-Torah*).

• "Bereirah," in *Entsiqlopedyah Talmudit* (Jerusalem, 1947), vol. 4, pp. 215–246.

BE-RE'SHIT. See GENESIS, BOOK OF.

BE-RE'SHIT RABBAH. See GENESIS RABBAH.

BE-RE'SHIT RABBATI. See GENESIS RABBATI.

BERGMAN, SAMUEL HUGO (1883–1975), Israeli philosopher and educator. A native of Prague, he was influenced by the teachings of *Aḥad ha-'Am and Martin *Buber and regarded the cultural renaissance sponsored by Zionism not only as leading to the formation of a secular Jewish culture but also as fostering the renewal of Jewish religiosity and religious observance. His theological position was inspired by Buber and Franz *Rosenzweig. He felt that the Jewish return to Erets Yisra'el and to physical labor would lead to the restoration of "cosmic unity." In 1920 he settled in Jerusalem, where he became the first director of the Jewish National and University Library. His writings include *Faith and Reason: An Introduction to Modern Jewish Thought* (New York, 1963), and *The Quality of Faith: Essays on Judaism and Morality* (Jerusalem, 1970).

• William Kluback, *Courageous Universality: The Work of Schmuel Hugo Bergman* (Atlanta, 1992).
—PAUL MENDES-FLOHR

BERIT. See CIRCUMCISION; COVENANT.

BERKOVITS, ELIEZER (1908–1992), Orthodox rabbi and theologian. Born in Transylvania, Berkovits served as a rabbi in Berlin, Leeds (England), and Sydney (Australia) before moving to the United States. Between 1950 and 1958 he served as a rabbi in Boston and then taught at the Hebrew Theological College in Chicago. He lived his last years in Jerusalem. His earlier books were devoted to theological aspects of Judaism, but his later works were devoted to the theology of the Holocaust, notably his *Faith after the Holocaust* (1973). There he writes that Auschwitz is unique in the magnitude of its horror but not in the problem it presents to faith. Jewish thinkers have consistently affirmed that human beings have free will and that they can use this freedom to perpetrate violence and oppression. It is the "hiding of the face of God" (*hester panim*) that makes human freedom of will possible and preserves human autonomy and dignity before the overwhelming power of God. The very survival of the Jewish people after the suffering of Auschwitz, however, is evidence of God's elusive presence in history; the establishment of the State of Israel saved the Jews from extinction through hopelessness.

Berkovits strongly opposed the Jewish–Christian dialogue movement. He held that the age of Christian militancy was over and that the world was post-Christian. The new interest of Christians in freedom of religion was because of their interest in freedom for Christians. He writes of the moral bankruptcy of Christian civilization and of the spiritual bankruptcy of Christianity, citing the extermination of six million Jews—one and a half million of them children—in the very heart of Christian Europe. He called the New Testament the most dangerous antisemitic tract in history, which has poisoned the hearts of millions (see HOLOCAUST THEOLOGY). Eliezer Berkovitz also wrote *Towards Historic Judaism* (1943), *Major Themes in Modern Philosophies of Judaism* (1975), *Not in Heaven: The Nature and Function of Halakha* (1983), and *Jewish Women in Time and Torah* (1990).

• Reuven P. Bulka, "Different Paths, Common Thrust: The Shoalogy of Berkovits and Frankl," *Tradition* 19 (Winter 1981): 322–339. Charles Raffel, "Eliezer Berkovits," in *Interpreters of Judaism in the Late Twentieth Century*, edited by Steven T. Katz (Washington, 1993), pp. 1–15.

—SOL TANENZAPF

BERLIN, NAFTALI TSEVI YEHUDAH (1816–1893), head of the Volozhin Yeshivah from 1854–1892; known by the acronym ha-Netsiv. The early years of his life were spent in almost hermitic study, during which he acquired an extraordinary mastery of rabbinic literature. In Volozhin, he went through the Talmud Bavli from beginning to end with his students. His written work displays a keen interest in relatively neglected rabbinic texts, showing their importance to an understanding of rabbinic tradition. He was also active in the early Zionist movement, Ḥibbat Tsiyyon. His work includes commentaries on *Sifrei* (*Emeq ha-Netsiv*, 3 vols. [Jerusalem, 1959–1961]) and the Torah (*Haʿameq Davar* [Vilna, 1879–1880]); two commentaries on the *Song of Songs* (Warsaw, 1886); a commentary on the *She'iltot* (Vilna, 1861–1867), the first post-Talmudic rabbinic work; commentaries on various tractates of the Talmud Bavli and Talmud Yerushalmi; *responsa* (a selection published in 2 vols. [Warsaw, 1892]); a commentary on the *Mekhilta'*; notes on the *Sifra'*; and various ephemerae, including correspondence pertaining to the early Zionist movement and an essay explaining the causes of modern antisemitism, stimulated by the outbreak of pogroms in Russia in 1881.

• Baruch ha-Levi Epstein, *My Uncle the Netsiv: Rabbi Naftali Zvi Yehudah Berlin* (Brooklyn, N.Y., 1988). Dovid Landesman, trans. and annot., *Rinah shel Torah: The Commentary of Rav Naftali Tzvi Yehudah Berlin to Shir ha-Shirim* (Kefar Ḥasidim, Israel, 1993).

—JAY M. HARRIS

BERLIN, SHA'UL BEN TSEVI HIRSCH (1740–1794), German rabbi and Haskalah sympathizer. Son of the chief rabbi of Berlin, Hirschel Levin, he was ordained rabbi at the age of twenty by several distinguished authorities. In 1768 he became *av beit din* in Frankfurt an der Oder, but by 1782, disillusioned with the rabbinate, he had settled in Berlin. There he defended the *maskil* Naftali Herz Wessely in the face of widespread rabbinic opposition and covertly criticized the rabbinic culture of his day. Berlin's reputation rests on several provocative compositions. His anonymous pamphlet criticizing Ḥayyim Yosef David Azulai's *Birkei Yosef* prompted Azulai's response in *Maḥazik Berakhah*. Berlin's pseudonymous *Ketav Yosher* (published posthumously, Berlin, 1794) satirized the rabbinic approach to pedagogy and blamed its obscurantist curriculum for inculcating superstitious beliefs and practices. The anonymous *Mitspeh Yequti'eli* (1789) attacked *Torat Yequti'el, novellae* on *Yoreh Deʿah* composed by R. Refa'el ha-Kohen, rabbi of Altona, Hamburg, and Wandsbek (a relative and a political rival), and charged its author with tolerating corruption. Berlin's father defended his son in the ensuing controversy. Berlin published the pseudonymous *Besamim Ro'sh* (Berlin, 1793), a collection of 392 previously unknown *responsa* attributed to R. Asher ben Yeḥi'el (and medieval contemporaries), to which he added his own gloss, *Kassa' de-Ḥarsena'*. This text, written in a highly elusive style, has had two lives. Viewed by some (even in Berlin's lifetime) as a critique and caricature of halakhic literature, sections of the *yeshivah* world continue to regard *Besamim Ro'sh* as an authoritative work. Shortly before his death Berlin went to London to become the rabbi of the Ashkenazi community but died before he could assume the appointment.

• David S. Edelstein, *Seder Halakhah* (Monroe, 1990). Moshe Pelli, "Saul Berlin," in *The Age of Haskalah: Studies in Hebrew Literature of the Enlightenment in Germany* (Leiden, 1979).

—TALYA FISHMAN

BERLIN, YESHAʿYAHU BEN YEHUDAH LOEB (1725–1799), scholar and rabbi, also known as Isaiah Pick. Berlin was elected to a rabbinical post only late in his life, in 1783 in Breslau. He is best known as a prolific composer of glosses to classical rabbinic works. He annotated and glossed Aḥa' Ga'on's *She'iltot*, Natan ben Yeḥi'el of Rome's *ʿArukh*, Targum Onkelos, Alfasi, Maimonides' *Mishneh Torah*, and others. His best-known contribution is his composition of *Masoret ha-Shas*, now printed in every edition of the Talmud, in which he cites parallel passages and emends and compares texts. He was also renowned for his amicable dealings with figures from a variety of religious and political positions.

• Yequti'el Aryeh Kamelhar, *Dor De'ah* (Piotrkow, 1935; repr. Jerusalem, 1969).

—JOEL HECKER

BERLINER, ABRAHAM (1833–1915), literary historian and bibliographer. Born in Poznań, Berliner served as a local teacher until joining the staff of the Berlin Rabbinical Seminary in 1873 as teacher and librarian. He searched the libraries of Europe for Jewish manuscripts and books and furthered the publication of old Jewish literature by reviving, in 1885, the Mekize Nirdamim society, which published medieval works in all branches of study. Berliner published the first critical edition of Rashi's commentary on the Torah (1866) as well as a modern edition of Targum Onkelos (1884). He wrote extensively on Italian Jewry as well as bibliographical works. After briefly publishing the *Magazin für jüdische Geschichte und Literature* (1874–1875), Berliner joined David Tsevi *Hoffmann in coediting its successor journal, the *Magazin für die Wissenschaft des Judentums*, with the Hebrew supplement *Otsar Tov* (1875–1893).

• Aron Freimann and Meier Hildesheimer, eds., *Birkat Avraham: Festschrift zum Siebzigsten Geburstage A. Berliner* (Berlin, 1903), includes bibliography until 1903. —DIDIER Y. REISS

BERLIN RABBINICAL SEMINARY, seminary for the training of Orthodox rabbis, founded in Berlin in 1873 by Ezriel *Hildesheimer (it was often referred to as Hildesheimer's Seminary; its formal name was Rabbiner Seminar für das orthodoxe Judentum) in the spirit of *Neo-Orthodoxy, combining *Torah ʿim derekh erets* (religious studies with secular knowledge). The seminary faced opposition both from the ultra-Orthodox and from the Reform (students had to promise not to officiate in synagogues that used organs). The seminary was headed successively by Hildesheimer, David Tsevi *Hoffmann, Joseph Wohlgemuth, and Yeḥi'el *Weinberg and had a faculty of distinguished scholars. Its graduates served modern Orthodox congregations in Europe and the United States. After the Nazis came to power, an attempt to transfer the seminary to Palestine was vetoed by the ultra-Orthodox in Palestine; the seminary was closed in 1938.

BERNAYS, ISAAC (1792–1849), chief rabbi of Hamburg from 1821 and precursor of *Neo-Orthodoxy. Born in Mainz, he studied at Abraham Bing's *yeshivah* in Würzburg, also attending the university there. Bernays's combination of traditionalism with youthfulness and his academic background induced the Hamburg community to elect him their chief rabbi after the controversy between 1818 and 1820 over the establishment of a Reform temple. Bernays adopted the Sephardi title of *ḥakham* (sage) to distinguish his authority from that of Reform leaders. The first Orthodox rabbi to deliver weekly sermons in German, he also donned clerical attire, made synagogue worship and life-cycle events more decorous, and modernized the Hamburg *talmud Torah*, educating pupils about good citizenship as well as religious observance. After a period of relative tranquillity, the Temple Association's building of a new edifice and issue of a revised prayer book (1841) provoked Bernays, whose hostile declaration was supported by Yaʿaqov *Ettlinger of Altona, an even more zealous opponent of Reform. Bernays's ideas (e.g., Israel's "universal mission") greatly influenced Samson Raphael *Hirsch.

• Helga Krohn, *Die Juden in Hamburg 1800–1850* (Frankfurt am Main, 1967). Michael A. Meyer, *Response to Modernity: A History of the Reform Movement in Judaism* (New York, 1988), pp. 60–61, 114–117. Stephen M. Poppel, "The Politics of Religious Leadership: The Rabbinate in Nineteenth-Century Hamburg," *Leo Baeck Institute Year Book* 28 (1983): 439–470. —GABRIEL A. SIVAN

BERTINORO, ʿOVADYAH (c.1450–1509), *Mishnah commentator, also known as ʿOvadyah Yare of Bertinoro. Born in the Italian town of Bertinoro, ʿOvadyah was educated in northern Italy and was a student of Yosef *Colon. In 1486 he traveled to Erets Yisra'el, a journey that took him some sixteen months and that led him through many Eastern communities. The series of letters he wrote describing his journey is an invaluable source for reconstructing late fifteenth-century Jewish life in the Mediterranean basin. Bertinoro settled in Jerusalem, where he revitalized the Jewish community and was recognized as the leading halakhic authority of Erets Yisra'el and Egypt.

He is best known for his lucid commentary on the entire Mishnah, in which he provides the upshot of the Talmudic discussion in light of the medieval authorities, especially *Rashi and *Maimonides. His work made it possible to study the Mishnah independently of the Talmud, while also indicating the normative *halakhah*. It quickly became the standard Mishnah commentary and from its first appearance (Venice, 1558–1559) was printed in almost all subsequent editions of the Mishnah. A Latin translation was made for the benefit of Christian Hebraists. Bertinoro also wrote *piyyutim*, *responsa*, and commentaries on the *Sefer Mitsvot Gadol* of *Mosheh ben Yaʿaqov of Coucy and the *Mishneh Torah* of Maimonides. Bertinoro is reputed to have written a supercommentary on Rashi's Torah commentary that has not survived. The ascription to Bertinoro of the work *ʿOmer Naqa'* is erroneous.

• Chanoch Albeck, *Mavo' la-Mishnah* (Jerusalem, 1959), pp. 249–252. M. Artom and A. David, in *Jews in Italy: Studies Dedicated to the Memory of U. Cassuto*, edited by Haim Beinart (Jerusalem, 1988), pp. 24–108. R. Bonfil in *Pe'amim* 37 (1988):42–54. Avraham David, *ʿAliyyah ve-Hityashvut be-'Erets Yisra'el ba-Me'ah ha-16* (Jerusalem, 1993). E. Horowitz, *Pe'amim* 37 (1988): 31–40. Israel Lerner, *Rabbenu ʿOvadyah mi-Bartenurah* (Jerusalem, 1988). E. Shohatman, *Pe'amim* 37 (1988): 3–23. A. Toaff, *Pe'amim* 37 (1988): 24–30. Abraham Ya'ari, *Zikhronot Erets Yisra'el* (Ramat Gan, 1974). —JEFFREY R. WOOLF

BERURYAH (2d cent. CE), wife of R. *Me'ir and daughter of R. *Ḥanina' ben Teradyon, renowned for both her scholarship and her piety. The Talmud tells stories of her exemplary wisdom and kindness and quotes many of her halakhic and aggadic sayings. Her father was burned to death for teaching Torah, her mother executed, her sister forced into a brothel (*ʿA. Z.* 17b–18a), and her brother killed by bandits (minor tractate *Semaḥot* 12). Beruryah bore all these tragedies with fortitude and without complaint. When both her sons died suddenly on a Sabbath, she concealed the fact from her husband until the end of the Sabbath so as not to cause him to grieve on the holy day. When R. Me'ir burst into tears, she reminded him of *Job* 1.21, "The Lord has given, and the Lord has taken away." She is the only woman recorded in Talmudic literature as having participated in halakhic discussions with the rabbis, and on two occasions her legal opinion was accepted as authoritative. Beruryah figures as the heroine in many literary works.

• Aaron Hyman, *Toledot Tanna'im ve-'Amora'im*, 3 vols. (London, 1910), pp. 294–295. —DANIEL SPERBER

BESAMIM. See SPICES.

BESHT. See BAʿAL SHEM TOV, YISRA'EL BEN ELIʿEZER.

BE-SIMAN TOV. See GREETINGS AND CONGRATULATIONS.

BETA ISRAEL (House of Israel), the term by which Ethiopian Jews refer to themselves. Between 1977 and 1993, almost forty-five thousand Ethiopian Jews were brought to Israel. There is no Beta Israel community in Ethiopia today.

The Beta Israel were frequently depicted as an ancient Jewish group, descendants of the tribe of Dan. According to this view, their religious system was a form of pre-Talmudic Judaism that dated back to the First Temple period. According to the most recent studies, however, they are an ethnic group that emerged in Ethiopia during the past five hundred years. Their religion is best understood as a form of non-Talmudic Judaism that has no direct connection to any ancient Jewish group. Rather, its numerous Jewish elements are derived either from biblical commandments or from the strongly Bible-centered practices of the Ethiopian Orthodox church, such as the circumcision of male children on the eighth day after birth, the use of Geez (ancient Ethiopic) as a sacred language, and their religious hierarchy.

Prior to the late nineteenth century, the Beta Israel were not familiar with other Jewish communities or forms of Judaism. They did not know the Talmud or rabbinic literature, had no working knowledge of Hebrew, did not have synagogues, rabbis, *bar* or *bat mitsvah*, *tefillin*, or *mezuzot*, nor did they celebrate Ḥanukkah, Simḥat Torah, or Purim.

Prior to the twentieth century, the Beta Israel were led by celibate monks. More recently a priest, known as a **qes* or *kahen*, headed the religious leadership, performing services, including animal sacrifices, and guiding community members. The *dabtara* (a cantor and scribe) was responsible for the liturgy and the preparation of manuscripts.

The most important work in the Beta Israel canon was the Orit (Torah or Bible), in Geez. They also had approximately twenty apocryphal works not found among other Jewish groups. The most important of these were *Te'ezaza Sanbat*, *Mota Muse*, *Gadla Abraham*, and *Arde'et*. Beta Israel prayers, usually in Geez, but also in Agawinnya, a Cushitic language, were also preserved both orally and in manuscript form.

The Beta Israel ritual cycle consisted of weekly, monthly, and annual festivals. The most important holiday was the Sabbath (Sanbat), which was strictly observed. Every seventh Sabbath (Yesanbat Sanbat) was commemorated with special prayers. Mondays and Thursdays were fast days. Monthly holidays included the celebration of the new moon, fasts on the tenth and twenty-ninth day of every month, and the festival of St. Mikael (Michael) on the twelfth. Annual holidays based on the Bible included Berhana Saraga (The Light Has Appeared), which was celebrated on the first day of the seventh month; Astasreyo, a fast day, on the tenth day of the same month; and Fasika (Passover) from the fifteenth to the twenty-second of the first month. Ma'rar (Harvest) was commemorated twice: once as dictated in the Bible seven weeks after Passover and again on the twelfth day of the ninth month (seven weeks after Ba'ala Masallat [Festival of Booths]), to coincide with the Ethiopian harvest. Seged, a distinctive Beta Israel pilgrimage holiday, was commemorated seven weeks after Astasreyo.

The Beta Israel cosmology focussed upon Egzi'abher, god creator of the world. There was also widespread belief in other spiritual beings, including angels and zar spirits, which possess their victims.

The Beta Israel religion has developed and evolved over the past five hundred years. During the twentieth century, it has been strongly influenced by external Jewish practices, and many distinctive traditions, such as sacrifice, monasticism, and the commemoration of the new moon, have been abandoned. Such normative Jewish customs as the use of Hebrew, a cycle of weekly Torah readings, and Purim and Ḥanukkah celebrations have been added. In the past, Beta Israel were known as Falashas. This name has pejorative connotations and is no longer used.

• Steven H. Kaplan, "'Falasha' Religion: Ancient Judaism or Evolving Ethiopian Tradition?" *Jewish Quarterly Review* 79.1 (1988): 49–65. Steven H. Kaplan, *Les Falashas* (Turnhout, 1990). Wolf Leslau, *Coutumes et croyances des Falachas* (Paris, 1957). Wolf Leslau, *Falasha Anthology* (New Haven, 1951; repr. New York, 1963, 1969). Kay Kaufman Shelemay, *Music, Ritual, and Falasha History* (East Lansing, Mich., 1986). Shalvah Vail, *Emunot u-Minhagim Datiyyim shel Yehudei Etiyopiyah be-Yisra'el* (Jerusalem, 1989).

—STEVEN KAPLAN

BETHEL, a Northwest Semitic god first attested in the treaty between Esarhaddon, king of Assyria, and his vassal, King Ba'al of Tyre (675 BCE). "If you violate this treaty," King Ba'al is warned, "may Bethel and Anath-bethel hand you over to a people-eating lion." In the Aramaic papyri from Yeb dating to the fifth century BCE, it occurs as the first element in names of deities as well as in the personal name Bethel-sarezer in *Zechariah* 7.2. Bethel appears as a divine name in *Jeremiah* 48.13 and may also occur in *Hosea* 12.5. —MAYER I. GRUBER

BETHEL (Heb. Beit El), city frequently cited in Hebrew Scriptures (mentioned sixty-four times), generally identified with Tell Beitin, approximately nineteen kilometers north of Jerusalem. The original name of the city was Luz, which *Jacob renamed Bethel (House of God), in commemoration of his vision of angels ascending and descending a ladder between heaven and earth (*Gn*. 28). According to another tradition (*Gn*. 35.1–15), Jacob named the town Bethel upon his return from Haran. With the division of the kingdom, King Jeroboam I of Israel made Bethel a major cultic site, for which he set up a golden calf (*1 Kgs*. 12.29–33). It was at the shrine of Bethel that *Amos preached and came into conflict with Amaziah the priest (*Am*. 7.10–17). Amos's declaration, "Bethel shall be turned into nought" (*Am*. 5.5), inspired Hosea to refer to Bethel by the dysphemism Beth-aven (House of Nought; *Hos*. 4.15, 10.5). As part of his extensive religious reform inspired by the book of *Deuteronomy*, King Josiah (622 BCE) dismantled the altar of Bethel and contaminated it so that Bethel could no longer rival the one legitimate holy city of Jerusalem (*2 Kgs*. 23.15).

• Nadav Na'aman, "Bethel and Beth Aven," *Zion* 50 (1985): 15–25, in Hebrew, summary in English. —MAYER I. GRUBER

BETH JACOB SCHOOLS (House of Jacob), school system for ultra-Orthodox girls founded by Sarah *Schenirer in Kraków in 1917. Until that time, such girls had not received formal educations. The network of schools was expanded under the auspices of *Agudat Israel, and teachers' seminaries were also opened. There were some two hundred schools in the Beth Jacob movement in eastern Europe before World War II. These were closed under the Nazis, but after the war, affiliated schools opened in western countries, particularly in Israel, where there are over one hundred Beth Jacob schools.

• Zevi Scharfstein, ed., *Ha-Ḥinnukh veha-Tarbut ha-'Ivrit be-'Eiropah bein Shetei Milḥamot ha-'Olam* (New York, 1957).

BETHLEHEM (Heb. Beit Leḥem), a town located nine kilometers south of Jerusalem. Its importance in Jewish tradition stems from it being the place of origin of King *David and the place where David was anointed (*1 Sm.* 16.1–13). Consequently, it came to be regarded as the birthplace of the future descendant of David who would rule all of Israel (*Mi.* 5.1). Micah's prophecy is the source of the messianic hope associated with the city. Just north of the city is the traditional site of *Rachel's tomb. For the last two thousand years, this site has been the destination of pilgrims, especially Jewish women, who have found strength in the story of Rachel's life and her role as an intercessor (*Jer.* 31.15–16).

• Aaron Demsky, "The Clans of Ephrath: Their Territory and History," *Tel Aviv* 13.14 (1986–1987): 46–59. Samuel H. Dresner, *Rachel* (Minneapolis, 1994). L. H. Vincent and F. M. Abel, *Bethléem: Le Santuarie de la Nativité* (Paris, 1914). P. W. Walker, *Holy City, Holy Places: Christian Attitudes to Jerusalem and the Holy Land in the Fourth Century* (Oxford, 1990). —AARON DEMSKY

BETROTHAL (Heb. *shiddukhin*), an agreement to marry at some future date. *Shiddukhin* (also *erusin* or *qiddushin*) is a legal term, in contrast to the current, popular terms of *betrothal* or *engagement*. In Talmudic times, marriage without preliminary betrothal was frowned upon in Jewish practice; the prescribed punishment was flogging (*Qid.* 12b). Betrothal is accompanied by a festive celebration but does not create any conjugal relationship; both parties are free to retract their promise of marriage without having compromised their marital eligibility. Because of the time lag between the betrothal and the wedding (*ḥatunnah*), the Talmud (*Qid.* 50b) discusses the question of whether gifts received by the bride (*kallah*) from the groom (*ḥatan*) are an indication that formal *qiddushin* has taken place; if so, the woman would require a divorce if the wedding were canceled. Jewish law left the matter to local custom, and ultimately, when *qiddushin* and *nissu'in* were combined into a single ceremony, the giving of gifts was no longer considered a potential problem. The aggrieved party in a cancellation of betrothal can claim reimbursement for loss suffered and demand compensation for humiliation. Suit for breach of promise is justified if the other side retracted any of the agreed terms or if, in the meantime, some grave disqualification developed or came to light. The bridegroom, however, is urged on ethical grounds not to break off the betrothal because of monetary disappointment. A document called *tena'im* is drawn up with the terms of *shiddukhin* and includes the time, place, and size of the wedding, as well as any other obligations such as the dowry or other financial matters. It also specifies the penalties payable by a defaulting party. The nonfulfillment of the *tena'im* does not release the aggrieved party after the marriage has occurred from his (or her) duties toward the spouse; the remedy is to sue for ordinary breach of contract. Today, formal *shiddukhin* with *tena'im* is not generally observed outside of Orthodox Judaism.

Betrothal, as part of the marriage ceremony, requires an act of *qinyan* (*acquisition) of the bride by the groom. In accepting something of value from the groom and giving her consent, the new relationship is effected. While anything of value might be used, a ring has become the most common object. While the transaction requires the bride's consent, in the traditional ceremony she is the passive recipient. In Reform, Conservative, and Reconstructionist ceremonies, there is a mutual *qinyan*. The bride and groom each give and receive rings and recite the marriage formula: "With this ring be thou consecrated to me as my wife [husband] according to the law of Moses and the faith of Israel." Once *qiddushin* has taken place, the couple requires a *get* (Jewish *divorce) to dissolve the relationship.

• Anita Diamant, *The New Jewish Wedding* (New York, 1985). Zeev Falk, *Jewish Matrimonial Law in the Middle Ages* (London, 1966). Rela M. Geffen, ed., *Celebration and Renewal: Rites of Passage in Judaism* (Philadelphia, 1993). Hyman E. Goldin, *Hamadrich: The Rabbi's Guide* (New York, 1956). Isaac Klein, *A Guide to Jewish Religious Practice* (New York, 1979). Maurice Lamm, *The Jewish Way in Love and Marriage* (San Francisco, 1980). —PETER KNOBEL

BEZALEL BEN URI (Heb. Betsal'el), chief craftsman of the desert Tabernacle and its appurtenances. He is described as one whom God has singled out by name and endowed with artistic skill and ability (*Ex.* 31.1–11, 35.30–35). Bezalel's Judahite origins are traced in *1 Chronicles* 2.18–20, in which Bezalel appears as the sixth generation from Judah through the line of Perez.

• Umberto Cassuto, *A Commentary on the Book of Exodus*, translated from the Hebrew by Israel Abrahams (Jerusalem, 1967), pp. 401–403. A. Leo Oppenheim, "Assyriological Gleanings IV: The Shadow of the King," *Bulletin of the American Schools of Oriental Research* 107 (October 1947): 7–11. —DAVID A. GLATT-GILAD

BIBAGO, AVRAHAM (c.1425–1489), Spanish philosopher, homilist, and physician; also known as Bilbaz, Bibas, or Vivas. Born in Saragossa, he was conversant with Islamic and Christian philosophy in their original languages, as well as Jewish sources. He used his knowledge of Christianity to defend Judaism in religious disputations held at the court of John II of Aragon as well as in his writings. His significant works include *Derekh Emunah* (Constantinople, 1521; facsimile ed. Jerusalem, 1970), completed near the end of his life and the best known of his writings, intended, in part, to demonstrate the superiority of Judaism in the achievement of human happiness; *Zeh Yenaḥemenu* (Salonika, 1522), a sermon on the creation of the world; and a treatise advancing the argument for the creation of the world against the opinion of Aristotle and others who held that the world has existed through eternity. Bibago's minor works include *Ma'amar ʿal Ribbui ha-Tsurot*, on the plurality of forms; and commentaries on Averroës's *Middle Commentaries* (completed in Huesca in 1446) and *Metaphysics*. The introduction to the latter was edited by M. Steinschneider in 1883. Other minor treatises and correspondences also survive.

• Allan Lazaroff, *The Theology of Abraham Bibago: A Defense of the Divine Will, Knowledge, and Providence in Fifteenth-Century Spanish-Jewish Philosophy* (University, Ala., 1981). Colette Sirat, *A History of Jewish Philosophy in the Middle Ages* (Cambridge and New York, 1990), pp. 384–389, 452.

—STEVEN BALLABAN

BIBLE, Judaism's corpus of sacred writings, a collection of literary works produced by the Israelite people in ancient times and passed down to the present. From the outset, it was believed that these works were written by divine inspiration, the result of direct revelation and of prophecy in its various forms. The Jewish religion is based upon them, virtually all of Jewish law and thought are derived from them, and it is mostly from them that the origins and early history of Jewish civilization and of the Hebrew language are known. Judaism's view of itself as a religion based upon a permanently fixed body of sacred literature has earned for the Jewish people the epithet "People of the Book."

Names and Divisions. The word *bible* is derived from the Greek *ta biblia*, a translation of the Hebrew term *ha-sefarim* (the books). This term, which first appears in the Bible itself (*Dn.* 9.2), attests to the fact that by late biblical times, the idea of a corpus of sacred books was already accepted. In rabbinic times the same idea was expressed by the term *ha-ketubbim* (the writings). The Latin phrase *Biblia sacra* is a translation of yet another original Hebrew expression, *kitvei ha-qodesh* (sacred writings, holy scriptures). All these terms are in the plural, and are thus more accurate than the English *Bible*, which gives the mistaken impression that the Bible is a single book.

The rabbinic term for the biblical literature, *miqra'* (that which is read [aloud]), expresses another essential feature—that the biblical books were not only written down but also passed on orally, read aloud in the synagogue and study house. Precise knowledge of the text of the Bible was the hallmark of literacy in Jewish civilization, providing the entire Jewish world with a common religious, linguistic, and literary frame of reference.

The Bible consists of thirty-one separate books: the *Torah or Pentateuch (consisting of the five books of Moses [*Genesis, Exodus, Leviticus, Numbers*, and *Deuteronomy*; see ḤUMMASH]), *Joshua, Judges, Samuel, Kings, Isaiah, Jeremiah, Ezekiel, Hosea, Joel, Amos, Obadiah, Jonah, Micah, Nahum, Habakkuk, Zephaniah, Haggai, Zechariah, Malachi, Psalms, Proverbs, Job, Song of Songs, Ruth, Lamentations, Ecclesiastes, Esther, Daniel, Ezra-Nehemiah*, and *Chronicles*. Jewish tradition, however, following the number of actual parchment *scrolls used in ancient times to contain these thirty-one books, arrives at a smaller number, twenty-four: the five sections of the Torah are counted as five separate books, since in ancient times each one was written on its own scroll, while the twelve minor prophetic books (*Hosea* through *Malachi*) were all combined on a single scroll and are therefore counted as one book (the Twelve). The division of *Samuel, Kings*, and *Chronicles* into *1* and *2 Samuel, 1* and *2 Kings*, and *1* and *2 Chronicles*, respectively, as well as the division of *Ezra-Nehemiah* into two books, developed when the Bible was translated into Greek. Modern Bibles, therefore, appear to contain thirty-nine books, though in reality they contain the same thirty-one.

Christianity, since it claims to be a fulfillment of the Jewish scriptures, accepts the sanctity and normative nature of the books of the Hebrew Bible. Christians, however, attach equal, if not greater, sanctity to their own sacred writings, which, they hold, supersede the Jewish scriptures. Christians thus use the term *Bible* or *Holy Bible* to refer to the Hebrew Bible together with the Christian scriptures, called by Christians the Old and New Testaments (see OLD TESTAMENT; NEW TESTAMENT).

Rabbinic tradition customarily divides the Bible into three sections. The first, the Torah, has the greatest authority and is believed to be of the greatest antiquity. The second section is the Prophets, including the historical books of *Joshua, Judges, Samuel*, and *Kings*, as well as all of the prophetic books (see PROPHETS, BOOKS OF THE; FORMER PROPHETS; LATTER PROPHETS). The final section is the Writings, (*Hagiographa), which refers to all of the remaining books, including *Psalms*, the *wisdom literature, the Five Scrolls (see ḤAMESH MEGILLOT), and so forth. Since medieval times, Jews have referred to the Hebrew Bible as Tanakh, an acronym to denote these three groups (*t* for Torah, *n* for Nevi'im [Prophets], and *k* for Ketuvim [Writings]).

Another arrangement of the biblical books, apparently current in the ancient Jewish community of Alexandria, is preserved in the *Septuagint, the Greek translation of the Bible. In this three-part division, the historical books are grouped together (*Genesis* through *Kings* with *Ruth* added after *Judges*, followed by *Chronicles, Ezra, Nehemiah*, and *Esther*); the poetic books follow (*Job, Psalms, Proverbs, Ecclesiastes*, and *Song of Songs*); and the prophetic books (here including *Daniel*) conclude the canon. This generic grouping fails to keep the Torah in a class by itself and identifies prophecy as the climax of the Bible. These two features may account for the acceptance of this division in the Christian world, since Christianity abrogated Torah law and saw its own gospel as the fulfillment of Old Testament messianic prophecies.

Canon. The body of sacred literature constituting the Bible is called the *canon* (Gr.; measuring rod, model, standard). No record exists, however, of a particular time and place at which the biblical canon was established, and no single authoritative institution ever existed in Jewish history that would have had the power to establish the canon. Rather, the canonization of the Bible was a natural, gradual process, by which those writings popularly believed to be of great antiquity and divinely inspired were accorded sacred status. The Talmudic rabbis occasionally refer to the difference between sacred writings and works to which no sanctity was attributed; for instance, in connection with the ritual cleansing of the hands. Sacred writings were held to "defile" the hands (probably a rabbinic reinterpretation of the ancient idea that sacred objects convey "contagious" sanctity), whereas nonsacred books were not. The criterion for determining to which category certain books belonged was always the same: sacred books were believed to be written *be-ruaḥ ha-qodesh* (by the holy spirit) that is, divinely inspired. Rabbinic sources refer to controversy concerning the *Song of Songs, Ecclesiastes*, and *Esther*; all three were ultimately accorded sacred status. The rabbis considered withdrawing two other books, *Ezekiel* and *Proverbs*, from circulation because some of the material they contain is halakhically or ideologically problematic (*Shab*. 13b, 30b; *Ḥag*. 13a), but the essential sanctity of the books was never questioned. Many books excluded from the Hebrew canon survived in the Septuagint and hence in the Catholic Bible; other books are spuriously attributed to biblical figures but are evidently of much later origin. They are known, respectively, as the *Apocrypha and pseudepigrapha. It would appear that the rabbis had a definite idea of when divine inspiration ceased and all authority passed to the sages, namely, with the coming of Alexander the Great in the late fourth century BCE. Books that they believed to have been written prior to this date, including all works that they sincerely believed dated from First Temple times or earlier, qualified for sacred status; books that were held to be later than this did not.

Contents. Historically speaking, the Bible is the written record of Israel's religious civilization for the first thousand years of its existence. It includes a continuous historical narrative covering the period beginning with the Torah and ending with *Kings*, complemented by the parallel account in *Chronicles*. This largest component of the biblical collection provides the history of Israel throughout its formative period. Israel's origins are traced within the history of mankind, following which we are told of the initial, temporary sojourn of Israel's ancestors in Canaan; the birth of the Israelite people; its enslavement in Egypt; its miraculous redemption from bondage (see EXODUS); the establishment of its covenant with God, and of its legal, social, and religious institutions, in preparation for national life (see GIVING OF THE TORAH); and its journey to the land of its forefathers. The historical narrative tells of Israel's successful campaign to conquer Canaan; of its early tribal federation and military exploits under the leadership of local charismatic chieftains (judges); and of the eventual unification of the Israelite tribes under a centralized monarchy. The beginning of the monarchic period under David and Solomon is presented as the epitome of Israel's history, whereas the schism of the united Israelite kingdom marks the start of its demise. Several centuries of uninterrupted rule of Davidic kings in the south (Judah), paralleled by centuries of instability in the north (Israel), end in catastrophe for both kingdoms: the Assyrians destroy the northern kingdom and exile its inhabitants, and Babylonia finally overruns the south and deports its population. These events, covering roughly the years from 1800 to 600 BCE, constitute the greater part of biblical history; what follows in *Ezra* and *Nehemiah* is but a sequel, in which the beginnings of the "return to Zion" of some Babylonian exiles and the earliest stages of their attempt to reestablish a religious and national center in Judah are recounted. Biblical history is told from a completely religious point of view. Israel is presented as a nation chosen by the one *God to enter into a unique relationship called a *covenant: having fulfilled the unconditional promise to the patriarchs to turn them into a great nation and provide them with the land of Canaan, God promises to bestow upon them the blessings of nature, prosperity, military might, and peace, in return for absolute fidelity, that is, to worship him alone, in accord with the dictates of his law, to shun all pagan religious practices, and to keep all his commands in the civil, social, moral, cultic, and personal spheres. The biblical books present Israel's successes and misfortunes, including its ultimate decline and fall, as a direct function of the extent of its compliance with the divine will. Every event in the life of Israel as a people, its leaders as embodiments of the whole nation, and each individual, is understood to be the result of divine favor or displeasure, contingent upon the moral and religious behavior of human beings. The primary aim of the biblical historians was to demonstrate that God controls historical events. Time and again they note that for additional facts and figures other works (which have not survived) should be consulted; this indicates that history, per se, was not their aim, but rather a selective telling of events for the purpose of instilling beliefs and teachings.

The books of *Ruth, Esther*, and *Daniel*, though not included in either of the continuous historical accounts, provide novel-like narratives of other events believed to have occurred at various points in Israelite history.

Israel's laws, held to be divinely revealed, constitute the terms of the covenant. The laws cover every area of behavior: murder and homicide, theft and fraud, damages and slavery, marriage and divorce, sexual and family relations, land tenure and agriculture, ritual purity and defilement, permitted and prohibited foods, sacrifice and the maintenance of the place of worship, the priests and the Levites, Sabbaths and festivals, tithes and alms, the outlawing of idolatry and pagan practices, ceremonies of commemoration, labor laws, and the judicial process, to name some of the major categories. They are contained in four law codes found at various points in the books of *Exodus, Leviticus, Numbers*, and *Deuteronomy*.

Interspersed throughout the narrative in *Samuel, Kings*, and *Chronicles* are the stories of the lives and careers of most of Israel's prophets, along with occasional brief records of their words. A select few of these "messengers of God," who have given their names to the books of *Isaiah* through *Malachi* (with the exception of *Jonah*), are known as the "literary prophets." In the books bearing their names, elaborate, polished versions of their oracles and speeches are recorded at length (see PROPHECY).

The religious poetry of Israel, primarily contained in the *Book of Psalms* but occasionally included in other books and poetic prayers, of thanksgiving, praise, petition, penitence, victory, defeat, joy, lamentation, historical contemplation, and so forth, provides the record of a rich lyric tradition imbued with Israel's religious beliefs, experience, and longings.

Wisdom literature, found in the books of *Proverbs, Job*, and *Ecclesiastes*, as well as in occasional psalms and narratives, is designed to provide practical wisdom and guidance. These profound works of contemplation and theological reflection are aimed at confronting man's existential condition in light of Israel's monotheistic teachings. In a class by itself is the love poetry contained in the *Song of Songs*.

Literary Form. The biblical books exhibit a wide variety of literary genres and styles. Narratives are generally in prose, though they contain highly poetic features. The stories include self-contained accounts of single events—legendary or chronological, symbolic or realistic, liturgical or mythological—as well as lengthy, systematic, historiographic treatments. Prophetic oration employs every type of rhetoric: poetry and prose, exhortation, harangue, encouragement, historical sermon, parable, words of consolation, to name but a few. Religious poetry includes every type of prayer, from the most fragmentary blessings and curses to the most elaborate hymns. Wisdom literature employs folk sayings and tales, disputations and meditations. The legal literature includes case law, commands and prohibitions ("thou shalt" and "thou shalt not"), and priestly instructions, all occurring both in isolation and in lengthy series, the types often mixed and intertwined. The wealth of literary forms attests to the advanced stage of civilization at which biblical Israel had arrived; the endless ways in which the various forms are modified, combined, and enhanced show that Israelite literary creativity was anything but conservative. Many of these literary styles—some of the legal pronouncements and wisdom sayings, and a great deal of the poetry—have their counterparts, indeed their origins, in the literatures of the other peoples of the ancient Near East and indicate the many ways in which Israel employed this rich, common cultural heritage for its own religious purposes. Others, the narrative prose and historiography in particular, seem to have been developed by Israelite writers and constitute a major component of Israel's original contribution to the forms of literary creativity.

Language. The Bible is written almost entirely in Hebrew, the language of ancient Israel. In fact, the biblical literature is the primary source for knowledge of the Hebrew language in ancient times. The only exceptions are brief Aramaic passages occurring in *Genesis* 31.47 and *Jeremiah* 10.11, and the Aramaic sections of *Daniel* (2.4–7.28) and *Ezra* (4.8–6.18 and 7.12–26). Scholars have suggested that a few additional portions, though they are in Hebrew, were actually translated from Aramaic originals. In the Hebrew of the Bible a historical development can be clearly observed. Archaic linguistic forms, which had probably fallen into disuse by biblical times, are displayed in biblical poetry, especially of the early period. Classical biblical prose of the First Temple period can be distinguished from the Hebrew of Second Temple times, providing a sound basis for determining the date of authorship of many of the biblical works. Among the features of late Biblical Hebrew are certain Aramaic influences, looser syntactical structure, and unique vocabulary. Biblical poetry, like the poetry of Canaan, is not characterized by rhyme or meter but by parallelism, the convention by which each poetic line is composed of two complementary parts, syntactically parallel and often synonymous.

Dating and Authorship. The rabbis of the Talmud (*B. B.* 14b–15a), proceeding from the assumption that detailed historical knowledge must have its source in divine revelation, attributed each of the historical books to the prophetic figure nearest in time to the events related; the Torah, as well as *Job*, was held to have been written by Moses; *Joshua* by Joshua; *Judges, Ruth*, and the opening chapters of *Samuel* by Samuel; the remainder of *Samuel* by Gad and Nathan; and *Kings* by Jeremiah, who was also credited with writing his own book. Remarkably, Ezra, rather than a prophet, was held to be the author of his own book and *Chronicles*, perhaps because, in the Talmudic view, these later historical works were not as obviously divine. Based on the fact that a number of psalms bear the caption "to [or of] David" and that the book of *Samuel* speaks of David's musical talent and calls him (according to one interpretation of the phrase) "the sweet singer of Israel" (*2 Sm.* 23.1), the entire *Book of Psalms* was held to have been written by David, though he is said to have incorporated the writings of ten earlier figures, including Abraham, Moses, and the sons of Korah. Following an obscure passage in *Proverbs* 25.1 attributing literary activity of some sort to "the men of King Hezekiah of Judah," the rabbis assigned a number of books to "Hezekiah and his colleagues": *Isaiah* (since he prophesied during Hezekiah's reign), *Proverbs*, the *Song of Songs*, and *Ecclesiastes*. The remaining books (*Ezekiel*, the twelve minor prophetic books, *Daniel*, and *Esther*) were supposed to have been written by an undefined body called "the Men of the Great Assembly," sometimes taken to mean Haggai, Zechariah, and Malachi. In many cases, it is clear that the rabbis were speaking only of the final collection and editing of the material; the actual authors were the prophets themselves.

Modern scholarship, recognizing that the Talmudic tradition is dogmatic rather than factual, endeavors to address the question of authorship of the biblical books on objective, textual grounds. The biblical books, as many other ancient works, contain no direct indication of who composed them. Statements made by the narrator, such as "Moses wrote this teaching" (*Dt.* 31.9) and "Mordecai wrote down these things" (*Est.* 9.20), are not colophons; they merely inform the reader that a character in the story wrote something down, but they do not claim to refer to the work as a whole. Only a few books appear to be the works of the individuals for whom they are named; generally, assigning the authorship to a particular individual is mere guesswork. However, content, language, intent, and historical horizon enable scholars to posit the approximate time period in which a book, or a portion of a book, was probably composed. On these grounds, the Torah, told from the vantage point of a narrator located on the western side of the Jordan and addressed to an audience of Israelites living after the establishment of the monarchy, most likely was composed in the middle of the First Temple period (though some scholars place it later). The historical work of *Joshua, Judges, Samuel,* and *Kings* aims at explaining the destruction of the Temple and the exile of the two kingdoms and must be dated to the end of the period, that is, to the time of the Babylonian exile.

Bible Criticism. Critical Bible scholarship has made important strides based on the recognition that many of the books, rather than being literary unities, appear to have been written by multiple authors during distinct time periods. Literary discrepancies, such as duplication, contradiction, discontinuity, and stylistic variation, are proof of early and late material within the same book. It has become evident that many of the biblical works actually took shape gradually, over a period of time, and the stages of literary development often correspond with stages in the religious history of Israel.

Nowhere has this investigation been more intense than in the critical study of the Torah. Disentanglement of the narrative strands, combined with the recognition that the four law codes are completely independent of each other, led to the widely acclaimed theory, the documentary hypothesis, that the Torah is an amalgamation of four separate, originally complete, and independent documents, each containing its own account of Israel's early history and its own version of the divine law. Study of the four separate documents, or sources, thus obtained has enabled scholars to characterize them and to assign them to historical periods. The documents, since their authors are unknown, are designated as follows. The Yahvist or Yahvistic source, J, is so called because it credits the patriarchs with the knowledge of God's personal name YHVH (scholars surmise it was pronounced Yahveh), while the other sources do not; the J source includes only a brief law code (the covenant made in *Ex.* 34.10–26) and regularly speaks of God in overtly human form. The J source is held to be the oldest document (9th or 8th cent. BCE), though some scholars disagree. The Elohist or Elohistic source, E, which claims that the name of God, Elohim, was first revealed to Moses at the burning bush (*Ex.* 3), includes the Decalogue (see TEN COMMANDMENTS) and the law code of *Exodus* 21–24 (see COVENANT, BOOK OF THE). The E source is assigned to the eighth century and is associated with the rise of prophecy. The Deuteronomic source, D, comprises most of the *Book of Deuteronomy* and is believed originally to have stood alone. It includes the Deuteronomic law code (*Dt.* 12–26) and the orations of Moses delivered along with it. Its pervasive demand for the centralization of all sacrificial worship at a single shrine is unique in the Torah, and scholars associate it with the cultic reform undertaken by King Josiah of Judah, supposing D to be the Law book found by Josiah's men in the Temple (*2 Kgs.* 22–23). The books of *Joshua, Judges, Samuel,* and *Kings* appear to have been edited in light of the D source's theology; they are referred to as the Deuteronomistic history, and their author is called the Deuteronomist. Some scholars believe that the D source itself was originally part of this work. The Priestly document or code, P, is the largest and most distinctive source; it is clearly the host document into which the others have been inserted, but it is probably not the most ancient. Bible scholars are divided on whether it is earlier or later than the D source and whether or not it can be assigned to First Temple times. The P source is distinguished by its detailed attention to matters of Temple worship and the priesthood, and by its highly developed legal system and theology. Classical Bible criticism (Higher Criticism) posited a linear, historical relationship between the sources of the Torah, reconstructing Israel's religious history on this basis. Today there is great diversity of opinion regarding the documentary hypothesis, with no common consensus having been reached among scholars. Traditional Judaism, on the other hand, developed its own ways of dealing with the literary discrepancies and historical questions that have led scholars to these critical hypotheses (see BIBLE EXEGESIS; MIDRASH). Textual criticism, which developed in recent centuries, holds that as a result of human error, mistakes occurred in copying the text before it was standardized; scholars have made many suggestions for emending the text, often based on comparisons of early translations.

Unity in Diversity. The diversity of form, content, authorship, and date does not obscure the essential unity of the biblical collection. The cultural milieu, the ancient Near East, of which Israel was an integral part, is evident everywhere. The historical horizon—the rise and fall of the independent Israelite kingdom in its own national territory, the land of Canaan—is all-pervasive, even in those books that deal with events before the Israelites' appearance on the scene and after their destruction and exile. The Bible is the literary expression of ancient Israel's religious world. The biblical books are not just any poetry, law, narrative, or history, but rather the literature that places God, his demands of Israel, and his involvement in Israel's affairs in the center. The central position occupied by God in the biblical books is the primary factor that gave rise to the notion that God was indeed their source.

The Text and Its Transmission. The biblical books were first written in the ancient Hebrew script, which was replaced in Second Temple times by the script used today. Early Hebrew employed vowel letters (*yud, heh, vav*) only minimally; later Hebrew used them much more generously, and the biblical text that eventually became standard reflects a sort of compromise. Though there may have been an original or first edition of each biblical book, the copies that circulated in ancient times were not uniform, as may be seen from the earliest witnesses to the biblical text such as the *Dead Sea Scrolls, the *Samaritan Pentateuch, and the Septuagint. The desire to achieve a single, standard text arose in rabbinic times, partially in response to the method of *midrash*, in which laws and teachings were derived from particular textual details, thus requiring that all Jews have identical texts of the Bible. The transmission of the Bible from generation to generation was the task of skilled copyists but was paralleled by the oral transmission carried out by expert public readers in the synagogue. The eventual need to combine these two traditions and to give graphic representation to the vowels and melody (see ACCENTS) that had been transmitted orally and never written down gave rise to the *Masorah and the work of the Masoretes. The earliest biblical texts were in scroll form; in medieval times there arose manuscript masoretic Bibles containing vowels and musical accents. Full uniformity in the biblical text became much more feasible after the rise of printing.

• Richard Elliott Friedman, *Who Wrote the Bible?* (New York, 1987). Shamma Friedman, "The Holy Scriptures Defile the Hands: The Transformation of a Biblical Concept in Rabbinic Theology," in *Minhah le-Nahum: Biblical and Other Studies Presented to Nahum M. Sarna in Honour of his 70th Birthday*, edited by Marc Brettler and Michael Fishbane, Journal for the Study of the Old Testament, Supplement Series 154 (Sheffield, Eng., 1993), pp. 117–132. *The JPS Torah Commentary*, 5 vols. (Philadelphia, 1989–1991). Yehezkel Kaufmann, *The Religion of Israel: From Its Beginnings to the Babylonian Exile*, edited and translated by Moshe Greenberg (Chicago, 1960), pp. 153–211. Douglas A. Knight and Gene M. Tucker, *The Hebrew Bible and its Modern Interpreters* (Philadelphia and Chico, Calif., 1985). Shayner Z. Leiman, *The Canonization of Hebrew Scripture* (1976; repr. New Haven, 1991). Gabriel Sivan, *The Bible and Civilization* (New York, 1973). J. Alberto Soggin, *Introduction to the Old Testament: From Its Origins to the Closing of the Alexandrian Canon*, 3d ed. (Louisville, Ky., 1989). Emanuel Tov, *Textual Criticism of the Hebrew Bible* (Minneapolis and Assen/Maastricht, 1992).

–BARUCH J. SCHWARTZ

BIBLE, LOST BOOKS OF THE. The canonical books of the Bible represent only a remnant of early Hebrew literature, and scripture itself mentions a number of sourcebooks that have not survived. These sources fall into a number of different categories: poetic works that recounted the battles of ancient Israel, for example, the *Book of the Wars of the Lord* (*Nm.* 21.14) and the *Book of Jashar* (*Jos.* 10.13; *2 Sm.* 1.18); annalistic works that contained the details of the Israelite–Judean kings' wars and building projects, such as *Acts of King Solomon* (*1 Kgs.* 11.41), *Chronicles of the Kings of Israel* (*1 Kgs.* 14.19, etc.), and *Chronicles of the Kings of Judah* (*1 Kgs.* 14.29, etc.; these latter works were probably similar in format to the annals of the ancient Mesopotamian kings and important source material for the author of the biblical book of **Kings*); and prophetic works that concentrated on the careers of their protagonists, for instance, *Words of Samuel the Seer*, *Words of Nathan the Prophet*, *Words of Gad the Seer* (*1 Chr.* 29.29), *Visions of Jedo the Seer* (*2 Chr.* 9.29), and *Words of Shemaiah the Prophet and Iddo the Seer* (*2 Chr.* 12.15). The various prophetic works are mentioned exclusively in **Chronicles*, which occasionally blurs the boundaries between these prophetic collections and the annalistic genre (cf. *2 Chr.* 20.34, 32.32). It is therefore possible that the chronicler views the prophets themselves as responsible for the official historiography of the monarchic period, a notion which also finds expression in the chronicler's unique citation of the *Midrash of the Book of Kings* (*2 Chr.* 24.27).

• Otto Eissfeldt, *The Old Testament : An Introduction*, translated from the 3d German ed. by P. R. Ackroyd (New York, 1965), pp. 132–134. Sara Japhet, *I and II Chronicles: A Commentary*, The Old Testament Library (Louisville, Ky., 1993). James A. Montgomery, *A Critical and Exegetical Commentary on the Books of Kings*, edited by Henry Snyder Gehman, The International Critical Commentary on the Holy Scriptures of the Old and New Testaments, vol. 9 (Edinburgh, 1976), pp. 30–38.

–DAVID A. GLATT-GILAD

BIBLE CANON. See BIBLE.

BIBLE COMMENTATORS. See BIBLE EXEGESIS.

BIBLE EXEGESIS, the interpretation and exposition of the biblical text, in order to apply it practically or as a form of study in its own right. The earliest exegesis can be found in the Bible itself. Later biblical books contain examples of implicit reinterpretations of the earlier books, especially of the *Torah (Pentateuch). This "intra-biblical" exegesis is generally not aimed at simple elucidation; there was little need for this since the language and concepts of the earlier works were still clear enough. At most, a word or phrase that had gone into disuse would be used to enlarge creatively on an earlier theme, provide a reconciliation of conflicting texts, ascribe later norms to earlier periods, or re-apply ancient law to contemporary conditions. Such exegesis is the forerunner of rabbinic **midrash*.

Since all Jewish religious culture perceives itself as being derived from the Bible, Judaism as a whole can be seen as the exegesis of scripture in the widest sense. However, the Torah's legal prescriptions are laconic and pertain to their ancient context. As time passed, they needed to be expanded, elaborated upon, and applied to changed conditions. Further, the Bible contains different traditions and is frequently ambiguous; opposing laws and teachings needed to be harmonized. By Second Temple times, the historical and social conditions of the Bible had ceased to exist, and the intellectual and theological climate had changed dramatically. The world of biblical belief had to be brought into line with later thought, and the value and relevance of the biblical laws had to be redefined. Rabbinic teaching that addressed these needs is known as *midrash* (from the Hebrew verb *darash*, meaning "to investigate, inquire"). *Midrash* originated as a popular enterprise of the spiritual leadership, and was generally conducted orally. Evidence that the public reading of the Torah was accompanied in the Second Temple period by simultaneous exposition is found as early as *Nehemiah* 8.8 and throughout rabbinic literature. The rich literary record of Midrashic exegesis comprises a major portion of the *Talmud, and much of it is preserved in the Midrashic collections. Characteristic of the Midrashic method is the assumption—which stems from the belief in the divine authorship of the Torah—that no word or phrase, not even verbal repetition of the same law or teaching, is devoid of its own unique significance, and that every verse, every work, even every letter, can have a multiplicity of meanings. The underlying postulate that divine speech was fundamentally different from human speech enabled the Talmudic sages to divorce words and phrases from context and to disregard the rules of grammar and syntax—thus the words of the Bible became a virtually inexhaustible source of law and edification.

Midrashic exegesis is traditionally divided into *midrash halakhah* and *midrash aggadah*. The former aims at deriving and elucidating legal norms. It draws upon the biblical text, primarily the legal portions of the Torah, proceeding on the principle that every legal statement has specific practical implications. The latter elaborates primarily upon narrative, prophecy, and psalm. It explores plots, characters, and messages, and endeavors to explain inconsistencies, motivations, and obscurities and to supply continuity and causality where the biblical text is silent. Above all, it seeks to provide edifying and inspiring moral teaching, not only where it is implicit in the text, but also on the strength of its own amplification of the text. In time, the rabbis of the Talmudic period formulated lists of hermeneutical rules by which Midrashic interpretations were generated: *Hillel listed seven and R. Yishmaʿeʾl enumerated thirteen for *midrash halakhah*. Later authorities defined thirty-two rules for *midrash aggadah*.

Midrashic exegesis seems to have been the primary orientation of biblical study throughout the Talmudic period. Thereafter, though active Midrashic interpretation of scripture declined and eventually ceased, study of the Bible through the eyes of rabbinic *midrash* remained paramount. This is due to the centrality, in Jewish life, of Talmud study, in which the Midrash plays a central role, and to the definitive role played by *midrash* in the formation of normative *halakhah*. While some Jewish thinkers throughout the ages have viewed rabbinic *midrash* as the true intent of scripture, embedded therein by its divine author in order to be discovered by its inspired interpreters, most authorities, as well as modern scholars, agree that the Midrash is a human creation, artfully devised for the purpose of grounding the teachings of the sages in the sacred writings.

To the extent that the sectarians of the Qumran community accepted the authority of the Bible, their doctrines and practices were also the outcome of a unique form of biblical exegesis. The development of mystical trends in Judaism was also supported by a form of biblical exegesis, in which esoteric doctrines were sought in the supposed hidden meanings of certain biblical texts (see KABBALAH). In particular the biblical account of Creation (*Gn.* 1; see MAʿASEH BE-REʾSHIT) and the first chapter of *Ezekiel* (see MAʿASEH MERKAVAH) provided the basis for mystical exegesis. Of special importance in the history of biblical exegesis was *Philo, whose allegorical method of exposition (see ALLEGORY) was designed in order to interpret the Bible in terms of Hellenistic thought.

Translation can also be a form of exegesis (see BIBLE TRANSLATIONS). The need to translate the biblical books into the vernacular (Aramaic, and eventually Greek; see SEPTUAGINT) arose with the decline of Hebrew as a spoken language. Some of these translations (see TARGUM) included Midrashic elements, while others were quite literal. The translations found in the Aramaic *targumim* were the starting point for later exegetes.

While there are occasional hints that the Talmudic rabbis were aware of the existence of a simpler level of meaning than that of *midrash*—that is, *peshuto shel miqraʾ*, or the syntactic, contextual sense of the biblical passage—there is no evidence that they sought to expound this, or that they accorded it any preferential status. The statements that "the Torah speaks in human language" and "the biblical text cannot escape its contextual meaning" were not in rabbinic times exegetical principles of a general nature. A turning point came with the rise of Karaism in the eighth century. The *Karaites rejected the *oral law (i.e., rabbinic tradition and authority). Spurred by the rise of linguistic studies in the Arabic-speaking world, they argued their claims on grammatical and etymological grounds. The Rabbanites moved to meet the challenge with exegesis that could withstand linguistic criticism. The great defender of the rabbinic tradition against Karaism was *Saʿadyah ben Yosef Gaʾon, a pioneer in the field of philology and lexicography. The explanatory notes that he composed to accompany his Arabic translation of the Bible ushered in a new epoch of Bible exegesis, that of the running commentary. Henceforth the task of the exegete was defined as that of providing a full exposition of the biblical text, to be studied along with it, aimed at explicating the contextual meaning of scripture on solid grammatical grounds. *Shemuʾel ben Ḥofni Gaʾon followed Saʿadyah to some extent, but the Jewish scholars of Muslim Spain were his true intellectual heirs. Their contributions to biblical exegesis remain significant to this day. The foundations were laid chiefly by Menaḥem ben Saruk and Dunash ben Labrat (10th cent.), and developed by Yehudah Hayyuj and Yonah ibn Janaḥ (both c.1000). The greatest representative of the golden age of the Spanish school of exegesis was Avraham *ibn Ezra, who, having left Spain, produced commentaries on almost all of the biblical books while wandering throughout Christian Europe. These have remained the definitive word on the method of philological exegesis, clearly laying out the features distinguishing it from rabbinic *midrash*.

The rise of biblical exegesis in northern Europe, while it occurred at approximately the same time, seems to have been spurred by other causes. The popularity of the Talmud Bavli in early Ashkenaz produced a form of study devoted to elucidating the internal logic and continuity of the text. The biblical commentaries of *Rashi, the best-known of the medieval exegetes, exemplifies the application of this method to the study of the Bible as well. In his commentary on the Torah, the adherence to the internal logic of the text is fused with the attempt to encapsulate the normative halakhic *midrash* on the legal portions of the Torah and to summarize whatever aggadic *midrash* can be incorporated with ease into the nonlegal sections. This commentary became immensely popular throughout the Jewish world and is a mainstay of Jewish knowledge to the present.

With the rise of Jewish–Christian polemic over the interpretation of the Bible in medieval Europe, the exegetical tradition, in both its Spanish and northern French forms, was compelled to relinquish the arbitrariness of the Midrashic approach in order to combat the similarly arbitrary interpretations of Christian exegetes. Together with a certain amount of already extant interest in the Hebrew language in twelfth-century France, which grew with the rise of rationalism, and the eventual arrival of some of the works of the Spanish grammarians, this led to the development of the school of philological commentary, or **peshat*, in northern Europe. This is best represented in the commentaries of Rashi's grandson R. *Shemu'el ben Me'ir, R. Yosef *Kara, R. *Yosef ben Yitsḥaq Bekhor Shor, R. *Eliʿezer of Beaugency, and R. Ḥizqiyahu bar Manoaḥ Ḥizkuni.

The philosophical works of *Maimonides, which contain much explicit and implicit biblical exegesis, had an enormous effect on biblical commentators from the thirteenth century on. His influence can be detected in the writings of the most renowned of the Provençal exegetes, R. David Kimḥi, whose commentaries combine Spanish philology and philosophy with French literary sensitivity, as well as providing a selection of rabbinic *midrash* in deference to its popularity. The influence of Maimonides can also be felt in the work of *Nahmanides, whose commentary on the Torah remains true to Spanish rationalism but has room both for the Midrash and for extensive allusion to the "hidden wisdom" of the Kabbalah. Mystical teachings culminated in the *Zohar, the great classic of Spanish Kabbalah, which appeared at the end of the thirteenth century and is essentially a kabbalistic *midrash* on the Torah. The end of the Spanish period is marked by the discursive commentaries of Yitsḥaq Abravanel, which appeared on the eve of the Italian Renaissance. Other notable post-classical biblical exegetes are R. Yeshaʿyahu of Trani, R. Asher ben Yaʿaqov, R. *Levi ben Gershom, and R. ʿOvadyah ben Yaʿaqov *Sforno.

The modern period in Jewish Bible exegesis is signaled by the appearance of the German translations, accompanied by Hebrew commentaries, edited by Moses *Mendelssohn. From this point onward, Jewish biblical exegesis is influenced in varying degrees by historical-critical scholarship. Modern sensibilities are perceptible, though barely, in the commentaries of J. Z. Mecklenburg, Naftali Tsevi Yehudah *Berlin, and Me'ir Leibush *Malbim, and are echoed, in the form of penetrating analyses of traditional commentators, in the writings of Nehama Leibowitz. Among the more prominent attempts at refuting Bible criticism are those of Samson Raphael *Hirsch and David Tsevi *Hoffmann. Leading Jewish biblical commentators began gradually to incorporate the critical method and its findings, while at the same time retaining the best insights of the Talmudic sages and the traditional exegetes. This trend began with Shemu'el David *Luzzatto and A. B. Ehrlich, continued with Umberto *Cassuto, and culminated in the thoroughly critical twentieth-century commentaries of Yehezkel *Kaufmann and M. Z. Segal, and, more recently, those of Moshe Greenberg, Sara Japhet, Baruch A. Levine, Jacob Milgrom, Shalom Paul, Nahum M. Sarna, Moshe Weinfeld, M. Weiss, and Y. Zakovitch.

• Michael Fishbane, *Garments of Torah: Essays in Biblical Hermeneutics* (Bloomington, Ind., 1989). Michael Fishbane, *Biblical Interpretation in Ancient Israel* (Oxford, 1985). Steven Fraade, *From Tradition to Commentary: Torah and its Interpretation in the Midrash Sifre to Deuteronomy* (Albany, 1991). Benjamin Gelles, *Peshat and Derash in the Exegesis of Rashi* (Leiden, 1981). E. Greenstein, "Medieval Bible Commentaries," in *Back to the Sources*, edited by Barry W. Holtz (New York, 1984), pp. 213–259. David Weiss Halivni, *Peshat and Derash: Plain and Applied Meaning in Rabbinic Exegesis* (New York, 1991). David Weiss Halivni, *Midrash, Mishnah and Gemara: The Jewish Predilection for Justified Law* (Cambridge, Mass., 1986). Menahem Haran, *Biblical Research in Hebrew* (Jerusalem, 1970). Jay M. Harris, *How Do We Know This? Midrash and the Fragmentation of Modern Judaism*. (Albany, 1995). Louis Jacobs, comp., *Jewish Biblical Exegesis* (New York, 1973). Sarah Kamin, "Rashi's Exegetical Categorization with Respect to the Distinction between Peshat and Derash," in *Immanuel* 11 (1980): 16–32. Jon Levenson, *Sinai and Zion: An Entry into the Jewish Bible* (Minneapolis, 1985). Jacob Neusner, *The Oral Torah: The Sacred Books in Judaism* (Atlanta, 1991). Peter Ochs, ed., *The Return to Scripture in Judaism and Christianity: Essays in Post-critical Scriptural Interpretation* (New York, 1993). E.I.J. Rosenthal, "The Study of the Bible in Medieval Judaism," in *The Cambridge History of the Bible*, vol. 2 (Cambridge, 1969), pp. 252–279. Nahum Sarna, *Understanding Genesis* (New York, 1966). Nahum Sarna, "Hebrew and Bible Studies in Medieval Spain," in *The Sephardi Heritage*, edited by R. David Barnett, vol. 1 (London, 1971), pp. 323–368. Michael A. Signer, "How the Bible Has Been Interpreted in Jewish Tradition" in *The New Interpreter's Bible*, edited by L. Keck et al. (Nashville, 1994), vol. 1, pp. 65–82. Uriel Simon, *Four Approaches to the Book of Psalms* (Albany, N.Y., 1991). David Sperling, ed., *Students of the Covenant: A History of Jewish Biblical Scholarship in North America* (Atlanta, 1992). Geza Vermes, "Bible and Midrash: Early Old Testament Exegesis," in *The Cambridge History of the Bible*, vol. 1 (Cambridge, 1970), pp. 199–231.

—BARUCH J. SCHWARTZ

BIBLE READINGS IN THE SYNAGOGUE. See HAFTARAH; QERI'AT HA-TORAH.

BIBLE TEXT, the exact wording of the Bible, in Hebrew and translation, in various forms (ancient scrolls, medieval manuscripts, and modern editions), of which the Masoretic Text (see MASORAH), handed down for centuries as the central text of Judaism, is the best known. The largest number of manuscripts of the Hebrew Bible, especially from the Middle Ages, represent the Masoretic Text, while precursors of that text, almost identical to the medieval copies, have been found among the *Dead Sea Scrolls. Among these scrolls, found in various places in the Judean Desert, are other versions of the Bible text, dating from the third century BCE through the second century CE. These are the earliest extant evidence of the biblical text. Also important is the *Samaritan Pentateuch, which in its present form is a sectarian reworking of an earlier biblical text. But the layer of revision is thin, so that the presectarian text, which happens to agree with several texts from among the Dead Sea Scrolls, provides important textual information. Other evidence of the biblical text is found in the *Bible translations made in antiquity into Greek, Aramaic, Syriac, Latin, and other languages. Although the Hebrew text from which the translations have been made is reconstructed with great difficulty, the reconstruction is worthwhile, because the Hebrew text underlying these translations at times is different from the Masoretic Text.

The various representatives of the biblical text differ from each other in minor as well as more significant details. Minor differences pertain to such matters as spelling (orthography) and small grammatical elements, such as pronouns, the connective *vav*, verbal forms, and conjunctions. Larger differences pertain to the omission or addition of single words, complete sentences, or, in rare cases, complete sections. For example, in *Jeremiah* the *Septuagint as well as two Qumran manuscripts (4QJer[b,d]) are much shorter than the Masoretic Text. One of the scrolls of the *Book of Samuel* from Qumran (4QSam[a]) lacks several sections of the Masoretic Text, while it adds others.

No single source is considered to reflect the best or the original text of the Bible. In fact, it is not clear whether there existed an original text of the Bible; the opinions of scholars diverge on this matter. Even though in traditional Judaism and Christianity the Masoretic Text is said to reflect the central text of the Bible, many scholars do not consider it to contain such an original text. Guided by contextual arguments, they try to determine in each individual instance which of the transmitted readings contains the contextually best version.

At all stages of its transmission, the biblical text was considered holy, but in early times the concept of holiness did not prevent scribes from changing the text, adding or omitting details. Before the Masoretic Text started to be handed down with great precision, it, too, was subject to the changing approaches of the early *soferim* (see SOFER). As a result, all the texts of the Bible, including the Masoretic Text, show evidence of earlier scribal activity, including scribal errors that are part and parcel of the scribal transmission of any text. The different types of scribal errors (omissions, additions, changes, interchanges of similar letters, glosses) are now recognizable through a comparison of the early texts of the Bible. The later rabbis ascribed divine inspiration to every Masoretic letter, and a single mistake renders a Torah scroll invalid and unusable. See also BIBLE.

• James Barr, *The Variable Spellings of the Hebrew Bible*, The Schweich Lectures of the British Academy (Oxford, 1989). Dominique Barthélemy et al., *Preliminary and Interim Report on the Hebrew Old Testament Text Project*, vols. 1–5, 2d ed. (New York, 1979–1980). Frank Moore Cross, *The Ancient Library of Qumran and Modern Biblical Studies*, rev. ed. (Garden City, N.Y., 1961). Frank Moore Cross and Shemaryahu Talmon, eds., *Qumran and the History of the Biblical Text* (Cambridge, Mass., and London, 1976). Ferdinand Deist, *Witness to the Old Testament* (Pretoria, 1988). Christian D. Ginsburg, *Introduction to the Massoretico-Critical Edition of the Hebrew Bible* (London, 1897; repr. New York, 1966). P. Kyle McCarter, *Textual Criticism: Recovering the Text of the Hebrew Bible*, Guides to Biblical Scholarship, Old Testament Series (Philadelphia, 1986). M. J. Mulder, ed., *Mikra, Text, Translation, Reading and Interpretation of the Hebrew Bible in Ancient Judaism and Early Christianity*, Compendia Rerum Iudaicarum ad Novum Testamentum, section two, vol. 1 (Assen and Minneapolis, 1988). Alexander Sperber, *A Historical Grammar of Biblical Hebrew* (Leiden, 1966). Shemaryahu Talmon, "The Old Testament Text," in *The Cambridge History of the Bible*, edited by R. P. Ackroyd and C. F. Evans, vol. 1 (Cambridge, 1970), pp. 159–199. Emanuel Tov, "Hebrew Biblical Manuscripts from the Judaean Desert: Their Contribution to Textual Criticism," *Journal of Jewish Studies* 39 (1988): 5–37. Emanuel Tov, *The Text-Critical Use of the Septuagint in Biblical Research*, Jerusalem Biblical Studies 3 (Jerusalem, 1981). Emanuel Tov, *Textual Criticism of the Hebrew Bible* (Minneapolis and Assen/Maastricht, 1992). Israel Yeivin, *Introduction to the Tiberian Masorah*, translated and edited by E. J. Revell, Society of Biblical Literature, Masoretic Studies 5 (Missoula, Mont., 1980).

—EMANUEL TOV

BIBLE TRANSLATIONS. The primary purpose of translating the Hebrew Bible in antiquity as well as in modern times was and is to meet the religious needs of Jews and Christians in worship and in study. Through translation, the Bible, which has been rendered into more than a thousand tongues, exerted a formative influence on many languages and cultures and enriched them with its ideas, idioms, and phrases reflecting the content of the Bible as well as the Hebrew language, in the latter case through a literal translation of the Hebrew (for example, the phrase "to find grace [favor] in the eyes of," which appears in the King James Version and is a direct translation of the Hebrew, is now part and parcel of the English language). Translations that did not aim at a literal representation of the Hebrew Bible incorporated differing quantities of exegesis at all levels. Some ancient translations reflect so much contextual exegesis that the individual words of the Hebrew text can no longer be identified. In these cases one speaks of an ancient *midrash* or a paraphrase retelling of the biblical text. Because of their exegetical layers, most ancient translations are of great importance for understanding the interpretation of the Bible in antiquity. A further reason for the importance of the ancient versions is that they date to an early period when the Hebrew text was not yet fixed. Hence, some of the translations reflect an original that differs in major or minor details from the Masoretic Text (see MASORAH). The earliest translations were oral, both in Aramaic and Greek; eventually they developed into the *Targum and the *Septuagint. The Jewish community of Palestine, which spoke Aramaic, and the Greek-speaking community of Alexandria needed Aramaic and Greek translations to follow the synagogue reading. Of the Pentateuchal Targums, that of Onkelos is the oldest and adheres most closely to the original; the various Palestinian Targums (Yerushalmi or Pseudo-Jonathan; the so-called fragmentary Targum; manuscript Vatican Neophyti 1) contain much aggadic material. The Targum to the Former and Latter Prophets is traditionally ascribed to *Yonatan ben ʿUzzi'el. The extant remains of a Palestinian Targum to the Prophets are fragmentary. The Targums to the Hagiographa, except for *Psalms*, are diffuse and of a Midrashic nature. The Targum to *Proverbs* resembles the Syriac *Peshitta' and is apparently of Christian origin. Though the Targums originated at an early period when Hebrew was first superseded by Aramaic, they received their final form in the fourth or fifth century CE. The oldest written translation is the ancient Greek (*koine*) version called the Septuagint (Seventy, or LXX). The Septuagint is invaluable for the textual study of the Bible since the Hebrew original underlying it differed considerably from the Masoretic recension. The rendering of the earlier biblical books is fairly literal; that of the later books is more paraphrastic. In the second century CE, three further Greek translations were made. *Aquila's is excessively literal and accords with the method of exegesis of R. ʿAqivaʾ; the rendering of *Symmachus is free and polished; *Theodotion's, combining elegance with fidelity, is mainly a revision of the Septuagint based on the Hebrew. These minor Greek versions are preserved in commentaries of the church fathers, who extracted them from Origen's Hexapla. The Syriac version, called Peshittaʾ (the Simple [translation]), was redacted in the second century. The Old Latin version or Itala (3d cent.) is a translation of the Septuagint; but the Vulgate (the Common [translation]), composed by Jerome (4th cent.) is a graceful Latin rendering of the Hebrew and became the standard Bible of the Catholic church. Later translations include Saʿadyah Gaʾon's in Arabic (Tafsir), tenth century; Moses Arragel's in Spanish, 1432; Martin Luther's in German, 1523 to 1532; the English Authorized Version, 1611, and the Revised Version, 1885; the German translation by Franz Rosenzweig and Martin Buber, 1925 to 1938; and the English translation of the Jewish Publication Society of America, 1917, and its new rendering of the Pentateuch, 1962, and of the whole Bible, 1988.

• James Barr, *Comparative Philology and the Text of the Old Testament* (Oxford, 1968; Winona Lake, Ind., 1987), pp. 238–272. Sebastian P. Brock, "Bibelübersetzungen, I," *Theologische Realenzyklopädie*, vol. 6 (Berlin and New York, 1980), pp. 161ff. S. R. Driver, *Notes on the Hebrew Text and the Topography of the Books of Samuel, with an Introduction on Hebrew Palaeography and the Ancient Versions*, 2d ed. (Oxford, 1913), pp. xxxiii–xxxix. Moshe H. Goshen-Gottstein, "Theory and Practice of Textual Criticism—The Text-Critical Use of the Septuagint," *Textus* 3 (1963): 130–158. M. J. Mulder, ed., *Mikra: Text, Translation, Reading and Interpretation of the Hebrew Bible in Ancient Judaism and Early Christianity*, Compendia Rerum Iudaicarum ad Novum Testamentum, section two, vol. 1 (Assen/Maastricht and Philadelphia, 1988). B. J. Roberts, *The Old Testament and Versions—The Hebrew Text in Transmission and the History of the Ancient Versions* (Cardiff, 1951). Emanuel Tov, *Textual Criticism of the Hebrew Bible* (Minneapolis and Assen/Maastricht, 1992). Ernst Würthwein, *The Text of the Old Testament: An Introduction to the Biblia Hebraica*, rev. ed. (Grand Rapids and Leiden, 1995).

BIGAMY. See POLYGAMY.

BIKKURIM (בִּכּוּרִים; First Fruits), last tractate of Mishnah order Zeraʿim, consisting of three chapters, with related material in the Toseftaʾ and in the Talmud Yerushalmi. The tractate deals with the laws concerning the offering of *first fruits (*Ex*. 23.19; *Dt*. 26.1–11), which served as a thanksgiving to God for his giving Erets Yisraʾel to the Jews. The presentation of the first fruits to the priest was accompanied by the recital of a passage of thanksgiving (*Dt*. 26.5–10). First fruits were limited to the *seven species (*Dt*. 8.8) representing the bounty of the land; they were brought only by the owner of the land on which they grew, and only persons eligible to inherit a portion of the land could recite the thanksgiving passage. According to one rabbinic opinion (*Bik*. 1.10), *bikkurim* could not be brought from Transjordan. *Bikkurim* were designated while still growing in the field.

The Mishnah describes the public ceremony that marked the bringing of *bikkurim* in Second Temple times, stressing the democratic nature of the ceremony in which rich and poor alike participate and in which "even King Agrippa" (*Bik*. 3.4) hoisted his basket onto his shoulders to honor God.

The Mishnah tractate was translated into English in Herbert Danby's *The Mishnah* (Oxford, 1933).

• Chanoch Albeck, ed., *Shishah Sidrei Mishnah, Seder Zeraʿim* (Jerusalem, 1957). Philip Blackman, ed. and trans., *Mishnayot*, vol. 1, *Order Zeraʿim* (Gateshead, 1973). Pinhas Kehati, ed., *Mishnah: A New Translation with a Commentary, Seder Zeraʿim*, vol. 3, *Maʿaser Sheni, Ḥallah, ʿOrlah, Bikkurim* (Jerusalem, 1994). Hermann Leberecht Strack, *Introduction to the Talmud and Midrash* (1931; Minneapolis, 1992).

–AVRAHAM WALFISH

BILL OF DIVORCE. See DIVORCE.

BIMAH (בִּימָה; platform, pulpit), a raised platform in the center of the *synagogue on which is situated the desk for reading the Torah scroll. A platform for reading the Torah is mentioned in *Nehemiah* 8.4, and there was one in the famous synagogue of Alexandria (*Suk*. 51b). In medieval times, the *bimah* became a dominant feature in the synagogue, and designers were constantly faced with the problem of creating a balance between the two foci: the ark (see ARON HA-QODESH) and the *bimah*. During this period, the platform was the center of attention, and because the hall was a place of assembly for nonreligious functions as well, the site of the platform determined the design. In central and eastern Europe, the *bimah* was often integrated with the central support columns. In Spain, and later in Italy, the platform was placed at the western end of the synagogue. In Sephardi synagogues, the cantor prays from the *bimah*, whereas in Conservative, Reform, and many Orthodox rites, the cantor stands before the ark. Some rabbinical authorities (for example, Moses *Maimonides [*Yad, Hilkhot Tefillah* 11.3]) hold that the *bimah* must be in the center of the building, but Yosef *Karo and most modern rabbis do not regard this as essential. Polish synagogues paid particular attention to the platform, which became an integral architectural element thanks to the introduction of the four central pillars between which the *bimah* was placed. In eastern Europe it was frequently enclosed by wrought iron. In modern times—initially under Reform influence—it has often been combined with the ark platform. Among Sephardim the platform is called *tevah* (chest). The word *bimah*, which appears in the Talmud, is derived from the Greek for a speaker's tribune. Another term frequently used for the platform, *almemar*, is derived from the Arabic *al-minbar* (chair, pulpit).

• Ismar Elbogen, *Jewish Liturgy: A Comprehensive History*, translated by Raymond P. Scheindlin (Philadelphia, New York, and London, 1993), pp. 361. S. D. Goitein, "Anbul—Bimah shel Beit ha-Kenesset," *Ha-Yishuv be-Erets Yisraʾel be-Reʾshit ha-Islam uvi-Tequfat ha-Tsalbanim le-ʿOr Kitvei ha-Genizah* (Jerusalem, 1980), pp. 219–255.

–SHMUEL HIMELSTEIN

BINDING OF ISAAC. See ʿAQEDAH.

BINYAMIN BEN MOSHEH NAHAWENDI (9th cent.), *Karaite scholar. He lived sixty or seventy years after *ʿAnan ben David and is considered one of the founders of the Karaite sect; indeed, the earliest use of the term *Karaites* appears in the colophon of his *Sefer*

Dinim. He probably lived in Persia or Iraq. Yaqub Qirqisani relates that Binyamin was "learned in the lore of the Rabbanites and strong in Scripture, and served for many years as a judge." Binyamin took an independent approach in legal decision making and was open to adopting Rabbanite rulings that seemed reasonable, even if they had no scriptural support. He was the first Karaite to write in Hebrew; most of those who came after him in the tenth and eleventh centuries wrote in Arabic. He wrote two books on law: *Sefer Mitsvot*, on ceremonial law, known only from quotations; and *Sefer Dinim*, on civil and criminal law, published under the title *Masat Binyamin* (1835; Ramleh, 1978). He also composed commentaries on a number of biblical books that were well regarded by Avraham ibn Ezra. Fragments of Binyamin's commentaries on *Genesis, Isaiah*, and *Daniel* have been identified, while his commentary on the *Song of Songs* is mentioned by Yefet ben ʿAli (in his commentary to *Isaiah*), and his commentary to *Ecclesiastes* is mentioned by Salmon ben Yeruḥim at the beginning of his own commentary to *Ecclesiastes*, and in which he criticizes Binyamin's tendency toward allegorical interpretations. Binyamin also may have commented on the books of *Judges* and *Samuel*. He was the first Karaite to deal with theological matters, although his view that the world was not created by God but by an intermediate angel was rejected by later Karaites.

• Jacob Mann, *Texts and Studies in Jewish History and Literature*, vol. 2 (Cincinnati, 1935), pp. 11–12, 17. Leon Nemoy, *Karaite Anthology* (New Haven, 1952), pp. 21–29. —DAVID E. SKLARE

BIQQUR ḤOLIM. See SICK, VISITING THE.

BIRKAT HA-GOMEL (בִּרְכַּת הַגּוֹמֵל), benediction of thanksgiving uttered after deliverance from danger. Based on Psalm 107, the Talmud (*Ber*. 54b) rules that a special blessing of thanksgiving is to be said after a desert crossing, after a sea voyage, on being freed from incarceration, or on recovery from a serious illness. It is recited in the synagogue on being called to the reading of the Torah. The blessing thus prescribed is called the Birkat ha-Gomel from its formula, "Blessed are you O Lord . . . who bestows favors [*gomel*] on those unworthy of them." Since the psalm explicitly mentions thanksgiving "in the assembly of the people" after each of those deliverances, the blessing must be recited publicly, and the congregation must respond, "He who has bestowed good upon you, may he bestow further good upon you." In many congregations the Birkat ha-Gomel is recited by women at their first attendance in the synagogue after giving birth.

• J. David Bleich, "*Birkat Ha-Gomel* and *Tefillat Ha-Derekh* for Air Travelers," *Tradition* 23.3 (1988): 109–115. Moshe Weinfeld, "The Comparison of a Passage from the Samas Hymn (lines 65–78) with Psalm 107," in *28th Rencontre Assyriologique Internationale in Vienna, July 6–9, 1981, Beiheft of Archiv für Orientforschung* (Horn, Austria, 1982), pp. 275–279.

BIRKAT HA-ḤAMMAH (בִּרְכַּת הַחַמָּה; Blessing of the Sun), one of the rarest ceremonies, held every twenty-eight years, when the *sun enters a new cycle (and traditionally stands at the same position as at its creation). The ceremony is held after morning prayers on the first Wednesday in the month of Nisan. The order of service comprises appropriate scriptural verses (*Ps*. 84.12, 72.5, 75.2; *Mal*. 3.20), Psalm 148, the blessing of God "who fashions the works of creation," and Talmudic passages. A prayer quorum is not essential, but a large number of participants is desirable. The ceremony was last held on 8 April 1953 (the central observance in Israel took place on Mount Zion in Jerusalem) and on 18 March 1981 (at the Western Wall). The ceremony will next take place on 8 April 2009.

• S. Gandz, *Studies in Hebrew Astronomy and Mathematics* (New York, 1970), pp. 150–168. Macy Nulman, *The Encyclopedia of Jewish Prayer* (Northvale, N.J., and London, 1993), pp. 100–101.

BIRKAT HA-ḤODESH (בִּרְכַּת הַחֹדֶשׁ; Blessing of the New Moon), public announcement of the day(s) of the forthcoming *Ro'sh Ḥodesh (first of the month) made in the synagogue on the preceding Sabbath, after the reading of the Torah (see QERI'AT HA-TORAH). The rite, introduced in geonic times, derives from the ancient custom of Qiddush ha-Ḥodesh, by which the official date of the beginning of the new month was determined by the Sanhedrin (minor tractate *Soferim* 19.9). It was introduced by the Rabbanites, who had adopted the fixed *calendar of *Hillel II and could therefore announce the date in advance, to counter the *Karaites, who continued the ancient custom of requiring personal observation of the new moon before determining the date of Ro'sh Ḥodesh. Birkat ha-Ḥodesh is accompanied by various prayers; the opening passage, Yehi Ratson (found since the eighteenth century only in the Ashkenazi rite), is an adaptation of a private prayer of the third-century amora' Rav (*Ber*. 16b). Though not part of the obligatory prayers, Birkat ha-Ḥodesh is invested with great solemnity and chanted to a moving tune. Sephardi and Oriental rites contain other introductory prayers for the ingathering of exiles and on behalf of the rabbis, also based on prayers mentioned in the Talmud. Birkat ha-Ḥodesh is not recited before the new moon of Tishrei (Ro'sh ha-Shanah), when it is assumed everyone knows the date. The Sabbath of the announcement is known as Shabbat Mevarekhin (Sabbath for the Blessing). In recent times, women's rituals have developed around the lunar cycle, especially with reference to the ancient custom of a women's holiday at the time of the new moon. In connection with this tradition, women often make this Sabbath into a special event.

• Ismar Elbogen, *Jewish Liturgy: A Comprehensive History*, translated by Raymond P. Scheindlin (Philadelphia, New York, and Jerusalem, 1993), pp. 103–104.

BIRKAT HA-KOHANIM (בִּרְכַּת הַכֹּהֲנִים; Blessing of the Priests), benediction prescribed in *Numbers* 6.22–27 to be said in the Temple by the priestly descendants of Aaron (see PRIESTHOOD) after the daily sacrifice. The Birkat ha-Kohanim was subsequently introduced into the repetition of the ʿAmidah in the *Shaḥarit and *Musaf services. It is recited by *kohanim* (Jews of priestly descent) in the Diaspora during Musaf among Ashkenazim and during Shaḥarit among Sephardim on festivals (except on a Sabbath) and on Yom Kippur; the reader recites it on all other occasions. The Spanish-Portuguese congregation in Amsterdam is unique in that the priests chant the blessing during the Shaḥarit service every Sabbath; the custom was introduced in honor of *Shabbetai Tsevi and was not abolished even after the debacle of the messianic movement. In Israel the priests recite it on weekdays; on the Sabbath, the new moon, and festivals; on Yom kippur (including during the Ne'ilah service); and on Tish'ah be-'Av. After removing their shoes and having their hands washed by *Levites, the *kohanim* ascend the *dukhan* (the platform before the ark; hence the Ashkenazi expression *dukhenen*—to recite the Birkat ha-Kohanim), and with arms raised to shoulder height, fingers outstretched, palms facing outward, thumbs touching (with the first two fingers of each hand separated from the last two fingers), and heads covered with prayer shawls (see TALLIT), they recite the benediction in unison (" . . . who has sanctified us with the sanctity of Aaron, and has commanded us to bless your people Israel in love") and then repeat the blessing word for word after the reader. The Birkat ha-Kohanim is explained by the rabbis as: "The Lord bless you"—with wealth; "and keep you"—accepting your prayers; "make his face to shine upon you"—with knowledge and understanding; "the Lord lift up his countenance upon you"—accepting your prayers, "and give you peace"—at all times and with all people. The ceremony has been abolished in some Conservative congregations. Reform Judaism did away with priestly prerogatives, although the Birkat ha-Kohanim itself is often recited by the rabbis as a closing benediction.

• Ismar Elbogen, *Jewish Liturgy: A Comprehensive History*, translated by Raymond P. Scheindlin (Philadelphia, 1993), pp. 63–66. S. S. Feldman, "The Blessing of the Kohenites," in *The Psychodynamics of American Jewish Life*, edited by N. Kiell (New York, 1967), pp. 403–430.

BIRKAT HA-LEVANAH. See QIDDUSH LEVANAH.

BIRKAT HA-MAZON (בִּרְכַּת הַמָּזוֹן), grace said after meals. The obligation to recite Birkat ha-Mazon is inferred from the verse "And you shall eat, and be satisfied, and bless the Lord your God for the good land he has given you" (*Dt.* 8.10). The halakhic requirement concerning the complete Birkat ha-Mazon applies only to a meal that includes bread. The Birkat ha-Mazon consists of three benedictions: the Birkat ha-Zan, thanksgiving to God for the food he has provided; the Birkat ha-'Arets, thanksgiving for the gift of Erets Yisra'el; and Boneh Yerushalayim, a petition for the rebuilding of Jerusalem. These three blessings formed the core of the Birkat ha-Mazon, but the rabbis added a fourth (Ha-Tov veha-Meitiv) after the destruction of the Second Temple. In later times, prayers were added for the welfare of the host, for an honorable livelihood, and so on. The verses commencing *ha-raḥaman* (the all-merciful) are a late addition, and their number varies according to different rites: Maimonides lists three; Yemenite Jews, four; *Maḥazor Vitry*, twelve; the Sephardim, eighteen; the Roman rite, twenty-two; and modern Ashkenazi custom, nine. Special prayers were included for the Sabbath, festivals, Purim, Ḥanukkah, and Ro'sh Ḥodesh. Under certain conditions, an abbreviated form of the Birkat ha-Mazon is recited. Grace must be said at the place where the meal has been eaten. The Zimmun is the invitatory formula that is recited before the Birkat ha-Mazon when three or more adults have eaten together (*mezumman*). Traditionally those counted are male, although according to the Talmud three or more women who have eaten together should also recite Zimmun (*Ber.* 45b). Later rabbinic authorities were divided as to whether a woman could be counted together with the men. The great majority of non-Orthodox count participants of either sex, while Sephardim permit a boy over six who understands what he is saying to be counted. One person summons the others to the blessing and the others respond (*Ber.* 7.1–5, 49b–50a). The custom and formula are ancient and according to the Talmud were as old as *Shim'on ben Shetaḥ (Y., *Ber.* 7.2). On weekdays, the Birkat ha-Mazon is preceded in some rites by Psalm 137; and on Sabbaths, by Psalm 126. At circumcisions and wedding feasts, poetic interpolations are customary. There is also a special form for recitation in the house of mourners. If certain kinds of fruits or cake or wine only are consumed, a shortened version, consisting of one benediction that contains all the main motifs, is used; after all other kinds of food, a still shorter version is recited. Recitation of the Birkat ha-Mazon is obligatory where food at least the size of an olive has been eaten. A brief version is often used by Reform Jews. In certain Sephardi communities an additional hymn is sometimes added (Bendigamos among western Sephardim; Ya Kominos among Ladino-speaking Jews). See also BENÇAO; BENTSHN.

• Ismar Elbogen, *Jewish Liturgy: A Comprehensive History*, translated by Raymond P. Scheindlin (Philadelphia and New York, 1993), pp. 48, 103, 141. Louis Finkelstein, "The Birkat ha-Mazon," in *Pharisaism in the Making: Selected Essays* (New York, 1972). Macy Nulman, *The Encyclopedia of Jewish Prayer* (Northvale, N.J., 1993), pp. 107–109. Elliot Salo Schoenberg, "A Note on Birkat Hamazon," *Conservative Judaism* 37.4 (1984): 86–89. Moshe Weinfeld, "Grace After Meals in Qumran," *Journal of Biblical Literature* 111 (1992): 427–440.

BIRKAT HA-MINIM (בִּרְכַּת הַמִּינִים), the benediction (actually a curse) concerning **minim* (heretics). It constitutes the twelfth of the benedictions of the *'Amidah* and was composed from earlier sources by *Shemu'el ha-Qatan (c.100 CE) at the request of *Gamli'el II (*Ber.* 28b) who instituted it as a statutory prayer. The text has undergone many changes and revisions, and the original wording cannot be reconstructed with certainty. *Genizah* texts of the benediction include a reference to *ntsrm*, commonly identified as Jewish-Christians. The present opening *vela-malshinim* (and for the informers) is a late substitution, but was particularly pertinent to the circumstances faced by the medieval Jewish community. Due to various historical circumstances, including church censorship, changes were introduced in its wording. The prayer has been modified or omitted in certain Reform prayer books.

• R. Travers Herford, *Christianity in Talmud and Midrash* (London, 1903). Reuven Kimelman, "*Birkat ha-Minim* and the Lack of Evidence for an Anti-Christian Jewish Prayer in Late Antiquity," in *Jewish and Christian Self-Definition*, vol. 2, *Aspects of Judaism in the Graeco-Roman Period*, edited by E. P. Sanders et al. (Philadelphia, 1981), pp. 391–403.

BIRKAT HA-MOTSI' (בִּרְכַּת הַמּוֹצִיא; the Bringing Out Blessing), benediction said before a meal that reads, "Blessed . . . who brings forth bread from the earth" (see BENEDICTIONS). *Bread is taken as standing for the meal in general, and therefore the Birkat ha-Motsi' is the standard blessing; however, the grace before a meal may vary acording to the types of food about to be consumed. According to tradition, the custom was introduced by the Men of the *Keneset ha-Gedolah. The main grace of thanksgiving is said after the meal (see BIRKAT HA-MAZON).

BIRKAT HA-SHIR (בִּרְכַּת הַשִּׁיר; Blessing of the Song), a prayer also known as Nishmat Kol Ḥai from its initial words. It concludes the *Pesuqei de-Zimra', preceding the *Shemaʿ and its blessings, in the morning service for Sabbaths, festivals, and the High Holy Days and is recited at the *Pesaḥ *Seder following the *Hallel. According to the Talmud, part of it is excerpted from an ancient prayer for rain (*Ber.* 59b). Written in poetic hyperbole, Birkat ha-Shir sings of the desire of every living creature to praise God for his mercies and acts of deliverance, even though human speech is utterly inadequate to the task of declaring the glory and beneficence of the creator. This prayer is found in all traditional and modern prayer books. A curious medieval legend found in France and Germany assigns its authorship to the apostle Peter, a claim that is disputed in *Maḥazor Vitry* (c.1100).

• Philip Birnbaum, ed. and trans., *Ha-Siddur ha-Shalem: Daily Prayer Book* (New York, 1949), pp. 331f. Ismar Elbogen, *Jewish Liturgy: A Comprehensive History*, translated by Raymond P. Scheindlin (Philadelphia, 1993), pp. 96, 105, 195, 412. —A. STANLEY DREYFUS

BIRKAT HA-TORAH (בִּרְכַּת הַתּוֹרָה; blessing of the Torah), the Talmudic name for the second benediction preceding the recitation of the Shemaʿ (see AHAVAH RABBAH AND AHAVAT ʿOLAM) and the common name for the blessing recited before studying the Torah and also before and after being called to the public reading of the Torah. Because the study of the Torah is considered a foremost religious duty, it has to be preceded by the recitation of an appropriate benediction. Various formulas are quoted in the Talmud in the name of different teachers; some of them appear in the opening of the morning service, which includes, in addition to prayers, Torah study in the form of quotations from the Mishnah. Blessings are also recited by individuals called to the reading of the Torah (the original version has been traditionally ascribed to Ezra on the basis of *Neh.* 8.4–6), the opening benediction being "Blessed are you who has chosen us from the nations and given us your Torah," and concluding with "Blessed . . . who has given us the Torah of truth and has planted everlasting life in our midst." An additional formula blessing God for giving the Torah is found in the concluding benediction after the reading of the **haftarah* on Sabbaths and holidays.

• Ismar Elbogen, *Jewish Liturgy: A Comprehensive History*, translated by Raymond P. Scheindlin (Philadelphia, 1993), pp. 140–141. —PETER LENHARDT

BIRKHOT HA-NEHENIN (בִּרְכוֹת הַנֶּהֱנִין; blessings for things enjoyed), blessings recited over things providing pleasure, such as food or drink. The rabbis taught that enjoyment of the gifts of God should always be accompanied by the benediction of thanksgiving. The most important blessings, instituted by the rabbis, are recited before and after food or drink, with specific benedictions for bread, any other confectionery, wine, drinks other than wine, fruit, and vegetables. Reciting the blessing over bread before a meal that contains bread is sufficient to cover all other foods eaten during the meal, except wine and fruit (which are important in themselves). Also in the category of *birkhot ha-nehenin* are benedictions to be recited before enjoying the aroma of fragrant flowers or spices. See also BENEDICTIONS.

• Baruch Bokser, "Ma'al and Blessings over Food," *Journal of Biblical Literature* 100 (1981): 557–574. Joseph Heinemann, *Prayer in the Talmud: Forms and Practices* (Berlin, 1977). —CHAIM PEARL

BIRKHOT HA-SHAḤAR (בִּרְכוֹת הַשַּׁחַר; Morning Benedictions), a series of blessings recited originally in Talmudic times upon wakening, each individual benediction suiting the particular occasion or action. The Talmud records fifteen such blessings. Immediately upon stirring from sleep Elohai Neshamah ("O my God, the soul which you gave me") was said; while upon hearing the cock crow, rising, dressing, washing the hands, and so on, the appropriate blessings were pronounced, concluding with a prayer for guidance through the Torah and salvation from sin (*Ber.* 60b). The ge'onim later transferred the Birkhot ha-Shaḥar to the commencement of the synagogue service. Prayers for deliverance from arrogant men and mishaps (*Ber.* 16b), exhortations to fear God privately and publicly, remembrances of man's insignificance before God, and assertions of God's covenant with the patriarchs were added. The three negative Birkhot ha-Shaḥar ("who has not made me a heathen, a slave, a woman," cf. *Men.* 43b), the content of which is partly modeled on similar Greek prayers, have been reformulated in some modern rites. (Already in the thirteenth century, the liturgical authority Abudarham added a blessing for women thanking God for "having created me according to his will," and a recently discovered medieval Provençal manuscript also provides an alternative text.) In non-Orthodox prayer books, these blessings have been recorded in positive, egalitarian terms (cf. thanking God "who made me a Jew," "who made me free" in the Conservative formulation).

• Ismar Elbogen, *Jewish Liturgy: A Comprehensive History*, translated by Raymond P. Scheindlin (Philadelphia, 1993). Joseph Heinemann, *Prayer in the Talmud: Forms and Patterns* (Berlin, 1977).

BIRTH. Though the Bible associates birth with pain from the very beginning of human history (*Gn.* 3.16), Jewish authorities have never regarded the suffering of this curse as a mandatory obligation, and they sanctioned the use of analgesics to mitigate it just as they favored a man's efforts to overcome the parallel curse of hardship in tilling the soil (*Gn.* 17–19) through the use of agricultural machinery. The Bible regards childbearing as a blessing (*Gn.* 16.1–4, 30.22–24; *1 Sm.* 1.4–20). Although it is the wife who bears the children, the primary obligation to procreate is the husband's. According to biblical law, a mother was considered ritually impure for thirty-three days after the birth of a male child and for sixty-six days after the birth of a female; at the conclusion of this period she offered a sacrifice of purification (*Lv.* 12.1–8). In a reference to a Caesarean section, the Mishnah denies the rights of the first-born both to a first child "extracted through the wall (of the abdomen)" and to further children (*Bekh.* 8.2). A woman in confinement enjoys religious concessions in Jewish law. For the first three days she is deemed in mortal danger, and Sabbath and other laws may be disregarded for her needs, as would be the practice for any other gravely ill patient; from then until the seventh day, religious laws may be violated for her if she so requests, and from that point until the thirtieth day, she is regarded as a patient who is not in danger, though fires may still be made for her on the Sabbath to protect her from the cold. From the fifteenth century on, it became a custom among European Jews for the mother to pay a special visit to the synagogue upon recovering from birth, and an appropriate prayer was composed for the occasion. There are many folkloristic beliefs and customs associated with birth, some of them censured in rabbinic writings for their superstitious nature. Traditional Jewish law does not allow fathers to be present during childbirth.

Out of a desire for greater participation in Jewish life, many Jewish mothers have introduced or renewed ceremonies and celebrations marking the birth of children, particularly those welcoming daughters, such as *simḥat bat* or *zeved ha-bat*. In non-Orthodox synagogues, mothers, or both parents, take part in a ceremonial naming of a daughter.

• Anita Diamant, *The Jewish Baby Book* (New York, 1988). Theodor H. Gaster, *The Holy and the Profane: Evolution of Jewish Folkways* (New York, 1980). Menahem Hacohen, *Sefer Ḥayyei Adam* (Jerusalem, 1990). Immanuel Jakobovits, *Jewish Medical Ethics* (New York, 1959). David Novak, "Be Fruitful and Multiply," in *Celebration and Renewal*, edited by Rela M. Geffen (Philadelphia, 1993). Hayim Shoys, *The Lifetime of a Jew Throughout the Ages of Jewish History* (New York, 1950). Susan Weidman Schneider, *Jewish and Female: Choices and Changes in Our Lives Today* (New York, 1984), pp. 120–130, 225–229.

BIRTH CONTROL. Procreation is the first scriptural commandment (*Gn.* 1.28), and a prohibition against the destruction of male seed is traceable to the biblical account of Onan, who "spilled his seed on the ground" while having intercourse with his wife (*Gn.* 38.9–10). Onan was "put to death by the Lord," and many commentators attribute this punishment to his spilling of the seed during intercourse. References to the evils of the destruction of male seed are found in the Talmud (*Nid.* 13a), Midrash (*Gn. Rab.* 23.24), and Zohar (*Va-Yeshev* 188a; *Va-Yeḥi* 219b), but the precise definition of the prohibition and its scope is the subject of debate among classical halakhists. In light of the fact that the focus of both the positive commandment to procreate and the prohibition against seed destruction is on the male, female contraception is considered preferable to any method used by the male. Indeed, a "cup of sterility" for the purpose of inducing permanent female infertility is mentioned in the Talmud (*Yev.* 65b), and its use is permitted in cases where there is a history of painful births and where the woman's husband has already fulfilled the commandment to procreate. The Talmud also discusses short-term contraception and permits it in the cases of minors, pregnant women, and nursing mothers (*Yev.* 12b). The principle underlying this complex discussion is that the prevention of danger to life and health constitutes a valid halakhic justification for the use of birth control. The situations to which modern authorities have extended this principle include unduly frequent birth, temporary physical weakness, excessive fatigue, constant miscarriage, and serious concern for the birth of genetically defective children. Some authorities permit the use of birth control when there is a serious educational problem in relation to existing children of the family, but in principle, the use of birth control for economic reasons is forbidden under Jewish law. In all cases in which contraception is permitted, the method employed should comply, as much as possible, with halakhic criteria, such as use by the female and indirect means of preventing conception rather than direct destruction of the semen. In general, the birth control pill is the preferred method of contraception, provided that its use does not endanger the woman and due account is taken of the possibility of menstrual bleeding between cycles. The Conservative rabbinate, in its Rabbinic Letter on Intimate Relations, affirms the permissibility of using birth control devices along the lines and for the reasons enumerated above, but it also says that couples should think seriously of having three or four children in light of the serious demographic problems Jews are facing today as a result of the destruction of a third of the world's Jewish population during the Holocaust, a continuing birth rate among Jews below replacement level, and the hemorrhaging of Jewish ranks through assimilation and intermarriage. In general, Reform Judaism supports birth control.

• Elliot N. Dorff, *"This is My Lover, This is My Friend": A Rabbinic Letter on Intimate Relations* (New York, 1996). Getsel Ellinson, *Tikhnun ha-Mishpahah u-Meniat Herayon* (Tel Aviv, 1976–1977). David M. Feldman, *Birth Control in Jewish Law: Marital Relations, Contraception, and Abortion as Set Forth in the Classic Texts of Jewish Law*, 3d ed. with epilogue (New York, 1995). Immanuel Jakobovits, *Jewish Medical Ethics* (New York, 1959), pp. 167–169. Immanuel Jakobovits, *Population Explosion: The Jewish Attitude to Birth Control* (London, 1969). Fred Rosner, "Contraception in Jewish Law" in *Jewish Bioethics*, edited by Fred Rosner and J. David Bleich (New York, 1979), pp. 86–96. —DANIEL SINCLAIR

BIRTHDAYS. No observances or celebrations are traditionally connected in Jewish custom with the anniversary of a person's birth. The only birthdays taken note of—because of their religious implications—are the thirteenth in the case of a boy (**bar mitsvah*) and the twelfth for a girl (**bat mitsvah*). In modern times, both in the Diaspora and Israel, birthdays are regularly celebrated, but without religious significance, although special birthdays (e.g., the seventieth, the eightieth) may be marked by being called to read the Torah in the synagogue. In some cases the sixtieth birthday is specially marked, because reaching it is evidence that one is not guilty of a sin, the punishment for which is early (i.e., before 60) death.

• Jules Harlow, ed., *Likkutei Tefillah: A Rabbi's Manual* (New York, 1965), pp. 51–55. Yitzhak D. Gilat, "Thirteen Years-Old: The Age of Commandments?" in *Studies in the Development of the Halakha* (Ramat Gan, 1992), pp. 19–31.

BIRTHRIGHT, rights inherent in the status of being the *firstborn. Birthright is mentioned in the Bible in connection with its sale by Esau to Jacob for "a mess of pottage" (*Gn.* 25.31–34). Jewish tradition ascribes particular significance to this sale, seeing in it the discarding of the spiritual heritage of Abraham by Esau, who by virtue of his birth was entitled to be its inheritor. According to Jewish tradition, before the institution of the hereditary priesthood, the firstborn of each family was automatically designated as the spiritual leader of the home (Rashi on *Gn.* 25.31). In the Bible, the hereditary "spiritual" birthright is in several instances transferred from the firstborn (Ishmael to Isaac; Esau to Jacob; Manasseh to Ephraim); this is understood to illustrate the fact that entrance into the spiritual heritage (as opposed to the material inheritance, which cannot legally be bypassed) is ultimately dependent upon merit. Maimonides codifies this principle when he states that although all hereditary offices pass to the firstborn, this is only so when the firstborn is fit to assume the responsibilities of office (*Hilkhot Melakhim* 1.7). See also BEKHOROT; INHERITANCE.

• Reuben Ahroni, "Why Did Esau Spurn the Birthright: A Study in Biblical Interpretation," *Judaism* 29 (1980): 322–331.

BISHOP OF THE JEWS (Lat. *episcopus judaeorum*), title of unclear significance given by the medieval Christian authorities to Jewish community heads or rabbis. In the twelfth and the thirteenth centuries, the term was applied in England to a *kohen*.

• Salo Baron, *The Jewish Community: Its History and Structure to the American Revolution*, vol. 1 (Philadelphia, 1942), p. 297. A. Hildesheimer, "Bishof ha-Yehudim," *Sinai* 105 (1990): 142–165. Henry Gerald Richardson, *The English Jewry under Angevin Kings* (London, 1960), p. 121. Simon Schwarzfuchs, *A Concise History of the Rabbinate* (Oxford and Cambridge, 1993), p. 39.

BITTAḤON (בִּטָּחוֹן; trust), a noun derived from the root *b ṭ ḥ* (trust in, rely on), which occurs in the Bible, especially in *Psalms*. It most frequently refers to faith in God, his providence, and his saving presence. In later usage the noun came to mean steadfast trust in God, and in many contexts it is indistinguishable from *emunah* (faith). Many medieval writers and moralists titled their tracts on the pious life *The Book of Emunah and Bittaḥon*. The modern Hebrew noun also means safety and security.

• Efraim E. Urbach, *The Sages: Their Concepts and Beliefs*, 2 vols. (Jerusalem, 1975), vol. 1, pp. 32–36. R. J. Zwi Werblowsky, "Faith, Hope and Trust: A Study in the Concept of Bittahon," in *Papers of the Institute of Jewish Studies, London*, edited by J. G. Weiss (Jerusalem, 1964), vol. 1, pp. 95–139.

BITTER HERBS. See MAROR.

BITTUL HA-TAMID. See ʿIKKUV HA-TEFILLAH.

BIʿUR ḤAMETS (בִּעוּר חָמֵץ; destruction of leaven), the act of destroying, preferably by fire, any leaven (see ḤAMETS) in one's possession on the morning of 14 Nisan (one day before Pesaḥ), in accordance with the rabbinic interpretation of *Exodus* 12.15, "even the first day shall you put away leaven out of your houses." To make sure that "no leaven shall be seen with you" (*Dt.* 16.4) during the Pesaḥ festival, leaven should, on the eve of the festival, be either burned (*biʿur*) or disowned (*bittul*). Traditionally, both methods are followed; after the burning, an Aramaic formula is recited by which ownership of any leaven that may have escaped detection is formally renounced. See also BEDIQAT ḤAMETS.

• Philip Goodman, ed., *The Passover Anthology* (Philadelphia, 1961).

BLASER, YITSḤAQ BEN MOSHEH SHELOMOH (1837–1907), Lithuanian rabbi and leading figure in the *Musar movement founded by Yisra'el *Salanter. After several years in Saint Petersburg, Blaser became head of the *kolel* (advanced *yeshivah*) in Kovno and helped establish various Musar educational institutions in Lithuania, including the influential *yeshivah* of *Slobodka. Blaser's ethical teachings, published in *Or Yisra'el* in 1900, were widely studied in Musar circles. He emphasized that knowledge alone did not enable an individual to achieve a state of intense religiosity ("fear of the Lord"). Instead, one should contemplate one's finitude, sinfulness, and repeated failure in obeying God. Blaser also published several works on *halakhah* and many articles. In 1904 Blaser settled in Jerusalem, where he died.

• Dov Katz, *Tenuʿat ha-Musar* (Tel Aviv, 1954). Chaim Zaichyk, *Ha-Me'orot ha-Gedolim* (New York, 1962), pp. 109–129.

BLASPHEMY, the reviling of God, that is, of his holy name, punishable according to the Bible by stoning (*Lv.* 24.15–16). The Talmud restricts capital punishment to blasphemy of the Tetragrammaton: when using any other of the divine names or attributes, the blasphemer is subject only to corporal punishment (*San.* 56a). Blasphemy is prohibited by one of the seven *Noahic laws, but the prohibition does not extend (as in other religions) to the reviling of sacred institutions or customs. In order to avoid repetition of the blasphemy during a trial, a special procedure, involving a substitution for the actual blasphemous phrase, is adopted in presenting the evidence. However, the court cannot pronounce the blasphemer guilty without having heard the exact words allegedly spoken by the accused. Therefore, upon the conclusion of the evidence, the court is cleared and one of the witnesses repeats the exact words used. On hearing the blasphemous words, the members of the court rend their garments as a sign of grief and pass sentence. Josephus records that the body of a person executed for blasphemy was exposed unburied until sunset (*Antiquities of the Jews* 4.202), the ignominy proclaiming the reprehensible and heinous nature of the crime. Despite the gravity of the offense, the blasphemer who does penance may become reconciled with God. After Jewish courts no longer had authority to inflict the death sentence, blasphemy was usually punished by excommunication.

• Haim Cohn, "Capital Punishment," in *Principles of Jewish Law*, edited by Menachem Elon (Jerusalem, 1975), p. 529. Leonard W. Levy, *Blasphemy: Verbal Offense Against the Sacred, from Moses to Salman Rushdie* (New York, 1993).

BLEMISHES (Heb. *mumim*), physical defects that disqualify a priest from performing his office in the Temple (*Lv*. 21.17–21) and an animal for use as a sacrifice (*Lv*. 22.20–25). In addition to physical blemishes, the priest is disqualified from service if he was born in unlawful wedlock, is in mourning, is in a state of drunkenness, is disheveled, is practicing idolatry, has committed a homicide, has lost his voice (*Ḥul*. 24a), or is too young (*Nm*. 4.43). Nonphysical blemishes may also occur in the case of animals; for example, an animal is disqualified from use as a sacrifice if it has served as an object of worship. The reason for disqualification by blemish is stated by the prophet Malachi (*Mal*. 1.8): a gift that is unacceptable to an exalted personality is surely so when the presentation is to God. The sages went into great detail in enumerating blemishes in animals (*Bekh*. 6) and priests (*Bekh*. 7), and Maimonides listed fifty types of blemishes disqualifying animals and ninety types of blemishes disqualifying priests (*Hilkhot Bi'at ha-Miqdash*, chs. 7 and 8). Blemishes on a bride or groom that could not have been known by the other party prior to the marriage or that render intercourse between the parties unbearable are valid reasons to vitiate the marriage bond. Moral blemishes are treated at length in numerous rabbinic passages, typical of which is the statement that "he who finds fault in others is influenced by the blemish in himself" (*Qid*. 70b).

• Jacob Milgrom, *Studies in Cultic Theology and Terminology* (Leiden, 1983).

BLESSING AFTER DELIVERANCE FROM DANGER. See Birkat ha-Gomel.

BLESSING AND CURSING. In Hebrew, the word *barakh*, commonly translated "bless," is used in the standard invocation to prayer (*barekhu et Adonai*, "Bless ye the Lord") and in benedictions for giving thanks and praise to God, not only for his benefits but even for such misfortunes as one is called upon to suffer. "In exactly the same way as a blessing is uttered for boons, so is one uttered for misfortunes" (*Ber*. 54a). The common belief is that not only can God bring good fortune (blessing) or misfortune (curse) upon a person but that this power is also invested—albeit indirectly—in humans, who can invoke God's blessing or curse on others. The strength of this belief is illustrated by the competition of Jacob and Esau for the blessing of their father, Isaac (*Gn*. 27). Prior to his death Jacob blessed his children (*Gn*. 49); and Moses, the children of Israel (*Dt*. 33). Balaam, the heathen prophet, was forced by a power greater than himself to turn his intended curses into blessings (*Nm*. 23–24). The power of blessing and cursing is held to be very great; thus David on his deathbed urges his son Solomon to execute Shimei ben Gera because "he cursed me with a grievous curse" (*1 Kgs*. 2.8), while the Talmud states, "The curse of a sage—even when undeserved—comes to pass" (*Ber*. 56a) and "Regard not lightly the blessing of an ordinary person" (*Ber*. 7a). On occasion, in rabbinic literature the verb *barukh* (bless) means to curse. Jewish folklore attributes great power to the curse, which was believed to hold power even over the dead. Specifically forbidden by the Bible is the cursing of God, parents, or the deaf; the penalty in the first two instances is death. While the rabbis prohibit cursing, it is allowed in certain instances, such as cursing the wicked (*Men*. 64b).

• Herbert Chanan Brichto, *The Problem of "Curse" in the Hebrew Bible*, Journal of Biblical Literature, Monograph Series, vol. 13 (Philadelphia, 1963). Christopher Wright Mitchell, *The Meaning of Brk "To Bless" in the Old Testament*, Society of Biblical Literature (Dissertation Series) no. 95 (Atlanta, 1987). Joshua Trachtenberg, *Jewish Magic and Superstition* (New York, 1961). Claus Westermann, *Blessings: In the Bible and the Life of the Church* (Philadelphia, 1978).

BLESSING OF CHILDREN (Heb. *birkat banim*). Although the importance attached to parental blessing is evident in many biblical passages (e.g., *Gn*. 27, 49), the custom of blessing the children on the eve of the Sabbath (and in some rites also on festivals) is a much later innovation, probably originating in the Middle Ages. The customary formula consists of the phrase "[May] God make you as Ephraim and Manasseh" (cf. *Gn*. 48.20) for boys, and "[May] God make you as Sarah, Rebekah, Rachel, and Leah" (cf. *Ru*. 4.11) for girls, followed by the *Birkat ha-Kohanim (*Nm*. 6.24–26). The parent places both hands on the head of the child while pronouncing the blessing, which is given to adult children as well. In the Sephardi rite, a child is blessed after the father or child has performed a religious function in the synagogue (e.g., *'aliyyah*). Special formulae of the blessing exist for particular occasions, for example, the eve of Yom Kippur. —Chaim Pearl

BLESSING OVER LIGHTS. See Kindling of Lights.

BLESSINGS. See Benedictions.

BLESSINGS OVER TORAH. See Birkat ha-Torah.

BLINDNESS. A number of biblical figures, including Isaac, Jacob, and Eli, are reported to have lost their sight in their old age, while it is specifically stated that Moses at the age of a hundred twenty retained his sight (*Dt*. 34.7). God is said on occasion to have used blindness as a punishment; the term is often used metaphorically with various pejorative implications. In ancient times, the blind, like other disabled, were regarded as outcasts. Biblical law specifically forbids taking advantage of a person who is blind or in any other way physically disabled (*Lv*. 19.14; *Dt*. 27.18). Blindness was a ritual defect disqualifying a priest from performing any function at the altar (*Lv*. 21.17–23); blind animals were disqualified as sacrifices (*Lv*. 22.21–22).

The rabbis, in order not to stigmatize the blind, used

various euphemisms to refer to them, such as *me'or 'einayim* (bright of eyes) or *saggi nahor* (much light). They sought to dispel popular prejudices, insisting that the blind were fully normal and that any restrictions were due solely to their physical disability. They discussed which of the commandments had to be observed by the blind and from which commandments the blind were exempt. Rabbi Yehudah ha-Nasi' was prepared to exempt the blind from all commandments; others exempted them only from positive commandments. Rabbi Yosef ben Ḥiyya' and R. Sheshet, who were both blind, felt that the blind should observe all commandments (*Pes.* 116b). Most authorities, however, were more pragmatic in their approach and decided based on the nature of the particular *mitsvah*. For example, the Talmud says that a blind person is exempt from turning to Jerusalem in prayer if he has no way of determining the direction but rather should turn his heart toward God (*Ber.* 29a). The blind had to bless the new moon and the Ḥanukkah lights but not the Havdalah light. A totally blind man was not allowed to serve as judge (*Shulḥan 'Arukh, Ḥoshen Mishpat* 7.2), although this ruling was not accepted by some authorities. In modern times, the question of the permissibility of cornea transplants to save or restore sight has been decided positively by almost all rabbinic authorities.

BLOOD (Heb. *dam*), regarded in the Bible as the vital element of all living things, as is made clear from such verses as "the blood is life" (*Lv.* 17.11; *Dt.* 12.23–24). This is also the reason why Noah and his descendants were forbidden to consume the blood of animal flesh (*Gn.* 9.4); the consumption of blood was regarded as equivalent to eating the living animal. The prohibition against consuming blood is repeated several times in the Bible and is the basis of the detailed laws elaborated in the Talmud concerning the ritual preparation of *meat. Even after an animal or bird belonging to a permitted species (*Lv.* 11.2–8; *Dt.* 14.4–6, 11) has been slaughtered in accordance with ritual regulations, the blood is still forbidden. Whereas the meat of sacrificial animals was partly burned and partly eaten, the blood was poured away at the base of the altar. It is blood that unites families and tribes, and the obligation to avenge a murder falls on the kin (the *blood avenger). The Talmud, however, limits the prohibition to blood in the arteries, which is removed by ritual slaughter or by cutting the veins, and to blood which has emerged on the surface of the meat. Blood within the meat itself is permitted, but the surface blood must be removed by "kashering" (soaking the meat in water, salting, and rinsing) or by grilling the meat. Liver is regarded as containing so much blood that only grilling on an open fire is permitted. The blood of fish does not come under this prohibition, but so great was the abhorrence of blood by the rabbis that they extended the original prohibitions (for example, by forbidding the eating of bread stained from the blood of one's own gums—see DIETARY LAWS). Menstrual blood is considered especially unclean, and the biblical regulations concerning it are further extended by the Talmud (see MENSTRUATION).

• John Bowman, "Metaphorically Eating and Drinking the Body and Blood," *Abr-Nahrian* 22 (1984): 1–6. Stephen A. Geller, "Blood Cult: Toward a Literary Theology of the Priestly Work of the Pentateuch," *Prooftexts* 12 (1992): 97–124. Allen S. Maller, "The Bridegroom of Blood," *Jewish Bible Quarterly* 21 (1993): 10–44. Baruch J. Schwartz, "The Prohibitions Concerning the 'Eating' of Blood in Leviticus 17," in *Priesthood and Cult in Ancient Israel*, edited by Gary A. Andersen and Saul M. Olyan (Sheffield, Eng., 1991), pp. 34–66. Marc Vervenne, "The Blood is the Life and the Life is the Blood: Blood as Symbol of Life and Death in Biblical Tradition," in *Ritual and Sacrifice in the Near East*, edited by J. Quaegebeur (Leuven, 1993), pp. 451–470.

BLOOD AVENGER, the term used in biblical law to denote the next of kin of a homicide victim. In the biblical view, the shedding of innocent human blood cannot go unexpiated: "Whoever sheds the blood of man, by man shall his blood be shed, for in his image did God make man" (*Gn.* 9.6). The blood of the victim is portrayed as "crying out from the ground" (*Gn.* 4.10) for redemption. It was assumed that the victim's nearest kin would be most interested in avenging the blood of the slain person, an expression of the tribal and familial solidarity characteristic of biblical times.

The Torah refers explicitly to the blood avenger in the context of accidental homicide, establishing the principle that a person found guilty of involuntary manslaughter may escape the blood avenger by taking refuge in an *asylum city (*Nm.* 35.12, 35.24–25). It may have been that, at an early stage, in cases of deliberate murder the next of kin was entitled to see to the execution of the killer. Joab, for instance, kills Abner to avenge the killing of his brother Asahel (*2 Sm.* 3.26–27). There are even cases of blood vengeance for crimes other than murder: Absalom kills his brother Amnon for raping his sister Tamar (*2 Sm.* 13.23–29). Eventually, however, the trial and execution of criminal murderers was deemed the responsibility of the court. Only in cases of accidental killing did the blood avenger have the right to exact vengeance—and only if the killer failed to take refuge in an asylum city (*Nm.* 35.19, 35.26–27). God is often referred to as Israel's blood avenger, punishing her enemies (*Dt.* 32.43; *Ps.* 79.10).

The subject of blood avengers is discussed by the sages in tractate **Makkot*. They discuss whether blood vengeance is a right or a sacred duty, who is required to act as an avenger, and other related topics. It is uncertain whether the rules formulated by the Talmud relate to any particular historical reality.

• Moshe Greenberg, "More Reflections on Biblical Law," in *Studies in Bible*, edited by Sara Japhet, Scripta Hierosolymitana 31 (Jerusalem, 1986), pp. 1–17. Jacob Milgrom, *Numbers*, The JPS Torah Commentary (Philadelphia, 1990), pp. 291–296, 504–511. Dale Patrick, *Old Testament Law* (Atlanta, 1985).

—BARUCH J. SCHWARTZ

BLOOD LIBEL, the accusation—frequently leveled in the Middle Ages, during the nineteenth century, and propagated again during the Nazi period—that Jews use the blood of a Christian for their religious rites, particularly in the preparation of unleavened bread for Pesaḥ. The ritual murder libel dates from pre-Christian times; Apion charged the Jews with annually fattening a Greek for sacrifice in the Temple (Josephus, *Against Apion* 2.8.95), while the Romans made the same charge against the early Christians. The first well-known medieval accusation occurred in England in 1144, the alleged victim being William of Norwich. The libel subsequently spread throughout Europe and was expanded to include the theme that Jews torture Christian children in a reenactment of the Passion of Jesus. Another famous child martyr was Little St. Hugh of Lincoln, who was found dead in 1255 and who is the subject of the Prioress's Tale in Chaucer's *Canterbury Tales*. (Lincoln Cathedral now has an inscription asking forgiveness for the sin of murderous slanders of libel.) The accusation frequently served as a pretext for anti-Jewish outrages and has been a major factor in Christian *antisemitism. Among the most notorious blood libels in the nineteenth and twentieth centuries were the Damascus Affair of 1840, the Tiszaeslar accusation of 1882, and the accusation against Mendel Beilis in Russia in 1912. During the Hitler persecution the allegation was constantly repeated by Julius Streicher in his obscene antisemitic publication *Der Stürmer*. The allegation, which has been repeatedly proved as completely baseless, was formally and repeatedly denounced by rulers and popes, but they were unable to eradicate the folk belief. Since Vatican II (1962–1965), the Catholic church has moved to eliminate the last practices of praying to victims of alleged ritual murders (for example, at Trent in Italy and Rinn in Austria).

• Jacob Barnai, "Blood Libels in the Fifteenth to Nineteenth Centuries," in *Antisemitism Through the Ages*, edited by Shmuel Almog (Oxford, 1988), pp. 189–194. Alan Dundes, "The Ritual Murder or Blood Libel Legend: A Study of Anti-Semitic Victimization through Projective Inversion," *Temenos* 25 (1989): 7–32. Alan Dundes, ed., "A Selected Bibliography: Suggestions for Further Reading on the Blood Libel Legend," in *The Blood Libel Legend* (Madison, Wis., 1991), pp. 379–381. Paul Oskar Kristeller, "The Alleged Murder of Simon of Trent (1475) and Its Literary Repercussion: A Bibliographical Study," *Proceedings of the American Academy for Jewish Research* 59 (1993): 103–135. Cecil Roth, *The Ritual Murder Libel and the Jew* (London, 1935). Maurice Samuel, *Blood Accusation* (London, 1966). M. Schultz, "The Blood Libel: A Motif in the History of Childhood," *Journal of Psychohistory* 14 (1986): 1–24.

BOAZ. See Jachin and Boaz.

BOBOV, Hasidic dynasty, named after a town (Bobowa) in western Galicia, established by R. Shelomoh Halberstam (1847–1906) and deriving from the Zanz Hasidic dynasty. After the Holocaust, R. Shelomoh's grandson, R. Solomon Halberstam, found refuge in the United States. The sect's headquarters are in Boro Park in Brooklyn, New York. Bobov has several centers in Israel including a small town near Bat Yam. It also maintains branches in London, Antwerp, Toronto, and Montréal. The dynasty is renowned for its musical creativity.

• Janet Belcove-Shalin, ed., *New World Hasidim: Ethnographic Studies of Hasidic Jews in America* (Albany, 1995). Tzvi Rabinowicz, *Hasidism: The Movement and Its Masters* (Northvale, N.J., 1988).

—William Shaffir

BODEQ (בּוֹדֵק; examiner), term applied to the official who inspects a ritually slaughtered animal for its ritual fitness for consumption (see Bediqah). The inspection is usually carried out by the slaughterer himself, and a licensed ritual slaughterer is generally called *shoḥet u-vodeq* (slaughterer and examiner). See also Shoḥet.

—Shmuel Himelstein

BODY. The juxtaposition of body and *soul as representing the physical and spiritual, or evil and good, in man is nowhere evident in the Hebrew scriptures. Indeed, there are no specific terms for body and soul in biblical Hebrew. Man's creation is described as "the breath of life" breathed into the nostrils of man who was "formed of the dust of the ground" (*Gn*. 2.7). The notion that "the dust returneth to the earth as it was, and the spirit returneth unto God who gave it" (*Eccl*. 12.7) is a later development. At any rate, no distinction between body and soul is made during life. Ancient Hebrew does, however, make the distinction (still preserved in the New Testament) between flesh (*basar*) and spirit (*ruaḥ*). In rabbinic writings, the body was sometimes regarded as the seat of passion and the cause of sin; yet both body and soul were held jointly accountable for deeds committed. The human body is deemed as the possession of God; man, as its custodian, is responsible for protecting it from mutilation, and Maimonides includes in his religious code a detailed regimen of diet, exercise, and other rules to ensure the health of the body (*Yad, Hilkhot De'ot* 4). In death, too, the body is inviolable; hence, the insistence on its speedy interment (cf. *Dt*. 12.23) and the Orthodox opposition to *cremation, *autopsies and dissections, embalming, or any other violation of its integrity. The belief in the physical *resurrection, as well as in the incorporeality of God, is incorporated in the *Thirteen Principles of Faith listed by Maimonides.

• Lawrence Fine, "Purifying the Body in the Name of the Soul," in *People of the Body: Jews and Judaism from an Embodied Perspective*, edited by Howard Eilberg-Schwartz (Albany, 1992), pp. 117–142. Samuel Kottek, "Maimonides on the Treatment of Body and Soul," *Israeli Academic Center in Cairo: Bulletin* 12 (1989): 24–28. Nissan Rubin, "The Sages' Conception of the Body and Soul," in *Essays in the Social Scientific Study of Judaism and Jewish Society*, edited by Simcha Fishbane (Montréal, 1990), pp. 47–103. Byron L. Sherwin, "The Human Body: A Window to the Divine," in *Toward a Jewish Theology: Methods, Problems and Possibilities* (New York, 1991), pp. 149–158. Gordon Tucker, "Body and Soul in Jewish Tradition," *Proceedings of the Rabbinical Assembly of America* 45 (1985): 141–156. Eli Yassif, "The Body Never Lies: The Body in Medieval Jewish Folk Narratives," in *People of the Body: Jews and Judaism from an Embodied Perspective*, edited by Howard Eilberg-Schwartz (Albany, 1992), pp. 203–221.

BOETHUSIANS, members of a religious-political party active in the century preceding the destruction of the Second Temple in 70 CE and existing for some time after that event. They were associated with the high priesthood and were close to, though not identical with, the *Sadducees. The rabbis considered them primarily a religious sect, founded by Boethus, a heretical disciple of the Mishnaic authority *Antigonus of Sokho. Other scholars connect the Boethusians with Shim'on ben Boethus, high priest in King Herod's time; the family is thought to have belonged to the Benei Ḥezir, known from inscriptions up to the second century CE. The Talmud describes the Boethusians contemptuously and characterizes them as arrogant and selfish.

• Raymond Hariri, "Rabbinic Perceptions of the Boethusians," Ph.D. dissertation, New York University, 1995. —DANIEL SPERBER

BONAFOUX, DANI'EL (c.1645–c.1715), *ḥazzan* (see CANTOR) and Shabbatean believer with prophetic pretensions. Born in Salonika, he settled in Smyrna. He was a follower of Avraham Miguel Cardoso, who often mentioned him in his letters, and he led Cardoso's supporters in Smyrna. In 1680 Bonafoux returned to Salonika but did not join the Shabbatean group that converted to Islam in 1683. Like his master Cardoso, he strongly opposed antinomic acts (except the "Messiah's" personal apostasy) as well as the doctrine of the apotheosis of the "Messiah." Nevertheless, after returning to Smyrna he continued to have visionary experiences and was expelled in 1702. In 1710 he was in Egypt and upon returning to Smyrna claimed to have received a letter from the ten lost tribes praising the "Messiah," Shabbetai Tsevi. —NISSIM YOSHA

BOOK OF ADAM AND EVE, pseudepigraphous work extant in Greek, Latin, Slavonic, Armenian, and Georgian, as well as several Coptic fragments. These versions differ greatly from each other, and the work's textual history is far from clear. Its original language may have been Greek, but neither Hebrew nor Aramaic can be ruled out. Its date and place of composition are unknown, but a Jewish origin is probable in spite of several Christian interpolations. It recounts events in the life of Adam and Eve following their expulsion from paradise, including their encounters with Satan, the birth of their children, Adam's tour of heaven, his failed attempt to avoid death, Adam and Eve's recollections of their expulsion from the garden of Eden, and their deathbed instructions to their children. The work ends with Adam and Eve's death and burial.

• Marshall D. Johnson, "Life of Adam and Eve," in *The Old Testament Pseudepigrapha*, edited by James H. Charlesworth, vol. 2 (Garden City, N.Y., 1985), pp. 249–295. Michael E. Stone, *A History of the Literature of Adam and Eve*, Early Judaism and Its Literature, no. 3 (Atlanta, Ga., 1992). —GIDEON BOHAK

BOOK OF AḤIQAR, a court legend extant in widely divergent recensions in numerous languages, including Aramaic, Greek, Syriac, Arabic, Ethiopian, Armenian, Slavonic, and Romanian. It probably was not written by Jews, but it was known both to the Jewish community of Elephantine (see YEB)—in its Aramaic recension—in the fifth century BCE and to the author of the *Book of *Tobit*, which states that the hero of the work belonged to the lost ten tribes (cf. esp. *Tb*. 14.10). The story itself recounts how Aḥiqar, the seal bearer of the Assyrian kings, is falsely accused of treason by his adopted son, Nadan. Aḥiqar is sent to his death, but the executioner spares his life. Subsequently the king regrets having sentenced his wise counselor to death, and Aḥiqar is summoned back to the royal court, where he again renders many useful services. An extensive part of the story is devoted to Aḥiqar's wise proverbs and ethical sayings, in the familiar style of the *wisdom literature, with which he tries to educate his adopted son.

• J. Rendel Harris, F. C. Conybeare, and Agnes Smith Lewis, *The Story of Aḥiḳar from the Aramaic, Syriac, Arabic, Armenian, Ethiopic, Old Turkish, Greek and Slavonic Versions*, 2d ed., rev. and corr. (Cambridge, 1913). James M. Lindenberger, "Ahiqar," in *The Old Testament Pseudepigrapha*, edited by James H. Charlesworth, vol. 2 (Garden City, N.Y., 1985), pp. 479–507. James M. Lindenberger, *The Aramaic Proverbs of Ahiqar* (Baltimore and London, 1983). Emil Schürer, *The History of the Jewish People in the Age of Jesus Christ, 175 B.C.–A.D. 135*, a new English version revised and edited by Geza Vermes, Fergus Millar, and Martin Goodman, vol. 3, pt. 1 (Edinburgh, 1986). —GIDEON BOHAK

BOOK OF CREATION. See SEFER YETSIRAH.

BOOK OF JASHAR, name of a lost work of ancient Hebrew poetry mentioned in the Bible (*Jos*. 10.13; *2 Sm*. 1.18) containing two short pieces of biblical poetry (*Jos*. 10.12–13; *2 Sm*. 1.19–27). Since the references to the *Book of Jashar* in both *Joshua* and *Samuel* are in the context of military heroics (Joshua's battle at Gibeon and the noble deaths of Saul and Jonathan on the battlefield at Gilboa), the lost book is presumed to have been a collection of epic material detailing the battles of the early Israelites. An anonymous author in the Middle Ages, probably in eleventh-century Spain, borrowed the title for his compilation of popular *midrashim*, but there is no connection between this ethical work and the lost ancient work. See also BIBLE, LOST BOOKS OF THE.

• Eduard Nielsen, *Oral Tradition* (London, 1954). —GARY A. RENDSBURG

BOOK OF LIFE. The metaphorical concept of the Book of Life is biblical (cf. *Ex*. 32.32; *Mal*. 3.16; *Ps*. 69.29); to be omitted or "blotted out" from the book meant death. This idea was subsequently connected with the notion of an annual balancing of each person's deeds by the heavenly bodies on the days of judgment—Ro'sh ha-Shanah and Yom Kippur. If an individual's balance is positive, he will be inscribed in the Book of Life on Ro'sh ha-Shanah; the entry will be sealed on Yom Kippur (*R. ha-Sh*. 16b). Various additions containing references to the Book of Life are inserted in the ʿAmidah during the *ʿAseret Yemei Teshuvah. The traditional New Year's wish, "may you be inscribed and sealed for a good year," refers to the same idea. The Book of Life inspired two of the best-known sayings in *Pirqei Avot*: "Know what is above you: a seeing eye, a hearing ear, and all your deeds are written in a book" (2.1); and "The ledger is open and the hand records . . ." (3.20).

• S. Y. Agnon et al., eds., *Days of Awe: A Treasury of Jewish Wisdom for Reflection, Repentance, and Renewal on the High Holy Days* (New York, 1995). Jean Leclercq, "Pour l'histoire de la symbolique du Livre de Vie," in *Kecharitomene*, edited by C. Augrain and T. Koehler (Paris, 1990), pp. 595–602. Shalom Paul, "Heavenly Tablets and the Book of Life," in *The Gaster Festshrift*, edited by David Marcus (New York, 1974).

BOOK OF THE CHRONICLES OF THE KINGS OF JUDAH AND ISRAEL. See BIBLE, LOST BOOKS OF THE.

BOOK OF THE WARS OF THE LORD, name of a lost work of ancient Hebrew poetry mentioned only once in the Bible (*Nm*. 21.14). Two verses in the Torah (*Nm*. 21.14–15) are said to derive from an earlier source called the *Book of the Wars of the Lord*. These poetic lines are extremely difficult to interpret, though they clearly deal with the Israelites marching through the territory of Moab. Probably this book was an anthology of ancient poetry recalling God's triumphs on behalf of the people of Israel. The medieval commentator Moses Nahmanides suggested that the short victory poem in *Numbers* 21.27–30 is also derived from the *Book of the Wars of the Lord* or a similar source. See also BIBLE, LOST BOOKS OF THE.

• Eduard Nielsen, *Oral Tradition* (London, 1954).
–GARY A. RENDSBURG

BOOK OF ZERUBBABEL, a Hebrew apocalypse, originally written by a Byzantine Jew in the seventh century CE and preserved in several different recensions. It consists of the apocalyptic visions of *Zerubbabel, the governor of Judah during the Persian period, in which one Jewish *Messiah, Son of Joseph, will be killed by his archenemy Armilus, but a second Messiah, Son of David, will prevail, a new Temple will be built, and the whole of Israel will be gathered into Jerusalem.

• Martha Himmelfarb, "Sefer Zerubbabel," in *Rabbinic Fantasies: Imaginative Narratives from Classical Hebrew Literature*, edited by David Stern and Mark Jay Mirsky (Philadelphia and New York, 1990), pp. 67–90. Robert L. Wilken, "The Restoration of Israel in Biblical Prophecy: Christian and Jewish Responses in the Early Byzantine Period," in *"To See Ourselves as Others See Us": Christians, Jews, "Others" in Late Antiquity*, edited by Jacob Neusner and Ernest S. Frerichs (Chico, Calif., 1985), pp. 443–471.
–GIDEON BOHAK

BOOKS, BURNING OF. Jewish law forbids the burning of books that contain the divine name, even if they have become disused or are secular or heretical. Such books are put away to molder (*Shab*. 116a; see GENIZAH). Despite this, R. *Tarfon, in his vigorous denunciation of the "books of the sectarians" (probably in this context Judeo-Christians), declared that should such books come to his notice, he would unhesitatingly burn them, even if they should contain the mention of the divine name. Thus the ceremonial burning of books became a symbol of arch heresy. Such a fate was actually meted out to the philosophical works of Maimonides during the fierce controversy that erupted over the doctrines espoused in them, and they were publicly burned in southern France in 1233 (see MAIMONIDEAN CONTROVERSY). In this century the ceremonial burning of Mordecai Menahem *Kaplan's Reconstructionist prayer book by extreme Orthodox elements in New York City was an unusual modern example. On the other hand, Jewish books have often been consigned to the flames by non-Jewish authorities, notably the twenty-four cartloads of the Talmud burned in Paris in 1242, the burning of Jewish books in Rome in 1332 and 1553 (see TALMUD, BURNING OF THE), and the Nazi burning of books by Jewish authors in 1933.

• Uriel Simon, "Yishaki: A Spanish Biblical Commentator Whose 'Book Should Be Burned,'" in *Minḥah le-Nahum, Biblical and Other Studies Presented to Nahum M. Sarna in Honour of His 70th Birthday*, edited by M. Brettler and M. Fishbane, Journal for the Study of the Old Testament, Supplement Series 154 (Sheffield, Eng., 1993), pp. 300–317. Guy Stern, *Nazi Book Burning and the American Response* (Detroit, 1991).

BOOKS, PROHIBITED. The Mishnah lists those who "have no share in the world to come" (*San*. 10.1), among whom, R. ʿAqiva' adds, is "he that reads the *external books*" (probably a reference to noncanonical books; see APOCRYPHA AND PSEUDEPIGRAPHA). Rabbinic literature seems, therefore, to prohibit the reading of certain books. The only book that can be positively identified as banned in the Talmudic discussion in *Sanhedrin* 100b is the *Wisdom of Ben Sira*, although the Talmud itself quotes from it extensively on various occasions. There is, therefore, reason to believe that the prohibition is only against public and not private reading of such books. Another case of rabbinical prohibition concerned the book of "Hamiros" (sometimes identified with Homer), mentioned as a forbidden book in the Talmud Yerushalmi, *Sanhedrin* 10.28. This work, however, is regarded by R. ʿAqiva' as permitted, "as though one were reading an epistle."

There is no equivalent in Judaism to the *Index expurgatorius* of the Roman Catholic church, although certain heretical books are popularly referred to as *treif pasul* (Yiddish vernacular, "unfit and invalid"). In the Middle Ages, fierce controversy raged around rabbinical attempts to ban philosophical works, especially those of Maimonides, at least to readers under the age of twenty-five (see MAIMONIDEAN CONTROVERSY). See also CENSORSHIP.

• S. A. Hirsch, "Johann Reuchlin, the Father of the Study of Hebrew among Christians," in *A Book of Essays* (London, 1905). S. Z. Leiman, *The Canonization of Hebrew Scripture: The Talmudic and Midrashic Evidence*, 2d ed. (New Haven, 1991). Daniel J. Silver, *Maimonidean Criticism and the Maimonidean Controversy: 1180–1240* (Leiden, 1965).

BOOTH. See SUKKAH.

BOOTHS, FESTIVAL OF. See SUKKOT.

BORROWING. See LOANS.

BOTON FAMILY, family of rabbis from Salonika.

Avraham ben Mosheh di Boton (died 1588), author of *Leḥem Mishneh* (Venice, 1609; it has been frequently republished), a commentary on Maimonides' *Mishneh Torah*. His *responsa* were published in *Leḥem Rav* (Smyrna, 1660).

Me'ir ben Avraham di Boton (1575–1649), son of Avraham ben Mosheh; rabbi in Gallipoli. Few of his *responsa* have survived.

Yaʿaqov ben Avraham di Boton (died 1687), grandson of Avraham ben Mosheh. His *responsa* contain information on the economic situation in Salonika; they were published in *ʿEdut be-Yaʿaqov* (Salonika, 1720).

• Y. Barnai, in *Toledot ha-Yehudim be-'Artsot ha-'Islam*, edited by Joseph Tobi et al. (Jerusalem, 1981), pp. 88–95.
–SHALOM BAR-ASHER

BRAZEN SEA, an immense, molten-bronze water receptacle that stood in the courtyard of Solomon's Temple (*1 Kgs*. 7.23–26; *2 Chr*. 4.2–5). It is said to have been ten cubits in diameter, five cubits deep, and thirty cubits in circumference. It was supported by twelve bronze oxen and featured elaborate floral ornamentation. According to *Exodus* 30.17–21, priests were required to wash their hands and feet before entering the sacred precincts to perform their cultic duties; the Brazen Sea in the Temple was the successor to the much simpler laver in the Tabernacle. Still, its size indicates that it may also have been symbolic. In ancient Near Eastern tradition, the Temple was often thought of as a microcosm or cosmic center; the Brazen Sea would thus represent the actual waters of the seas. The Brazen Sea is reported to have been lowered to floor level by Ahaz (*2 Kgs.* 16.17) and later smashed and carried off to Babylon (*2 Kgs.* 25.13). The magnificent Brazen Sea of Solomonic times was replaced by a *kiyyor* (laver), a private immersion chamber for the priest, and a functioning outer **miqveh* in the Second Temple.

• Michael Avi-Yonah, "Beit ha-Miqdash ha-Sheni," in *Sefer Yerushalayim*, edited by Michael Avi-Yonah, vol. 1 (Jerusalem and Tel Aviv, 1956), pp. 392–418.

—BARUCH J. SCHWARTZ

BRAZEN SERPENT. See NEHUSHTAN.

BREACH OF TRUST. The only biblical laws relating to breach of trust refer to a bailee, one who holds property in trust (see SHOMERIM). As in the case of a guardian who must, if suspect, take an oath to the effect that "he has not put his hand to his neighbor's goods" (*Ex.* 22.10), others, such as a partner at the dissolution of joint interests who is suspected of wrongdoing by another partner or a middleman suspected by a principal party, are obligated to take the same oath. An exception is the testamentary guardian, who cannot be compelled to swear on mere suspicion but must, however, render full account. If a bailee falsely denies possession of the bailment and his deceit is proved, he is rendered untrustworthy and consequently debarred from taking an oath or acting as a witness.

• Emanuel B. Quint, *A Restatement of Rabbinic Civil Law*, vols. 1–2 (Northvale, N.J., 1990–1991). Yisroel Reisman, *The Laws of Ribbis: The Laws of Interest and Their Application to Everyday Life and Business* (Brooklyn, N.Y., 1995).

BREAD (Heb. *leḥem*). The Semitic word from which *leḥem* is derived originally referred to the main element of a meal. In Hebrew civilization this came to mean bread; namely, a baked dough prepared from one of the five species of grain (wheat, barley, rye, oats, and spelt). The blessing over bread ("Blessed are you . . . who brings forth bread from the earth"; see BIRKAT HA-MOTSI') is considered adequate for the whole meal, and no separate *benedictions have to be recited over individual foods. Hands should be ritually washed before partaking of bread, and the full *Birkat ha-Mazon is recited only when bread has been eaten. A portion of the dough (**ḥallah*) when baking bread was formerly given to the priests, and twelve loaves of bread were kept on a golden table in the inner sanctuary of the Temple (see SHOWBREAD). During the festival of *Pesaḥ, the eating of regular leavened bread is forbidden, and only unleavened bread (**matsah*) is permitted. The *manna was welcomed as "bread from heaven" (*Ex.* 16.4), and on the Sabbath two loaves are placed on the table in remembrance of the double portion of manna gathered in the wilderness on Sabbath eves. According to the Talmud (*Ber.* 50b), bread must be handled with respect and not thrown from one person to another. Some considered bread sprinkled with salt as the food of the poor (*Ber.* 2b), while others regarded the combination as efficacious in repelling evil spirits.

• Roy Gane, "Bread of the Presence" and "Creator-in-Residence," *Vetus Testamentum* 42.2 (1992): 179–203. Erwin Goodenough, *Jewish Symbols in the Greco-Roman Period*, Bollingen Series 37, vols. 5–6 (New York, 1956). Samuel Krauss, *Talmudische Archaeologie*, vol. 1 (Hildesheim, 1966), pp. 99–105.

BREAKING OF THE VESSELS (Heb. *shevirat ha-kelim*), the fracturing of the vessels or channels into which the powerful divine light was pouring during the process of creation. This primordial catastrophe occupies a central position in the creation myth formulated by R. Yitsḥaq *Luria, though most of his disciples, especially R. Ḥayyim Vital (see VITAL FAMILY), almost completely concealed it because of the audacity of its theological implications. The doctrine is nevertheless disclosed in the writings of R. Yosef ibn Tabul. Occurring before the universe came into existence, this catastrophe affected the **sefirot*, which constitute the divine pleroma. Luria used and transformed concepts developed by earlier kabbalists, including Mosheh ben Yaʿaqov *Cordovero, the leading kabbalist in Safed before him, in describing this breaking of the vessels and the consequent falling and scattering of sparks of the divine light. Lurianic myth describes every subsequent crisis, such as the sin of Adam or the golden calf, as a repetition of the primordial *shevirah*.

• Gershom Gerhard Scholem, *Major Trends in Jewish Mysticism* (New York, 1995), chap. 7. Isaiah Tishby, *Torat ha-Raʿ veha-Qellipah be-Kabbalat ha-'Ari* (Jerusalem, 1942).

—JOSEPH DAN

BREASTPLATE. See EPHOD.

BREATH. See SOUL.

BRESLAU RABBINICAL SEMINARY, institution in Breslau for the training of rabbis; the first modern seminary in central Europe, known as the Jüdische-Theologische Seminar, it was founded with a bequest from a local philanthropist, Jonas Fränkel, who wished it to be headed by Abraham *Geiger (who conceived the project). However, Geiger was judged too liberal by Fränkel's executors, who appointed Zacharias *Frankel as president of the institution that opened in 1854 with a number of noted scholars (including Heinrich *Graetz) on its faculty. Initially, the seminary included departments for rabbinic students, teacher training, and high school students; however, the latter two departments were closed in 1867 and 1887, respectively. Teacher training was resumed in the 1920s. The seminary promulgated the teaching of "positive, historical Judaism," which meant that while its instruction was basically Orthodox, the critical study of sources was permitted. Its rabbis served congregations (some of them Reform) in Europe and the United States. On Kristallnacht, 9 November 1938, the seminary and most of its impressive library were destroyed; teaching ceased early in 1939.

BREUER FAMILY, leaders of German Orthodoxy in the late nineteenth and early twentieth centuries.

Salomon Breuer (1850–1926), leader of the separatists in German *Neo-Orthodoxy. Born in Nitra, Slovakia, he received both a traditional education at the *yeshivah* in Pressburg and a university education before assuming the rabbinate of Pápa, Hungary. From 1888, when he succeeded his father-in-law, Samson Raphael *Hirsch, as rabbi of the Frankfurt *Austrittsgemeinde, Breuer displayed unrelenting hostility toward communal Orthodox and Zionist endeavors and was a cofounder of the *Agudat Israel movement. He also established an important Lithuanian-style *yeshivah* in Frankfurt.

Isaac Breuer (1883–1946), son of Salomon Breuer, a practicing lawyer, and one of the *Agudat Israel's leading spokesmen and ideologists from 1912. Breuer, however, gradually modified his anti-Zionist sentiments after the Balfour Declaration of 1917 and after his departure from Nazi Germany in 1936. As head of the breakaway Poʿalei Agudat Yisra'el (Ultra-Orthodox Labor) movement in British-ruled Palestine, he criticized traditional Agudist attitudes and spoke for the establishment of an independent Jewish state in which all parties would endeavor to cooperate under the rule of the Torah. His major works include *Messiasspuren* (1918), and *Das jüdische Nationalheim* (1925).

• **Salomon Breuer**: Solomon Ehrmann, "Salomon Breuer," in *Guardians of Our Heritage*, edited by Leo Jung (New York, 1958), pp. 619–646. Isidor Grunfeld, *Three Generations: The Influence of Samson Raphael Hirsch on Jewish Life and Thought* (London, 1958). Hermann Schwab, *The History of Orthodox Jewry in Germany* (London, 1950), pp. 120–122 and *passim*. **Isaac Breuer**: Rivka Horwitz, ed., *Yitsḥaq Broyer: ʿIyyunim be-Mishnato* (Ramat Gan, 1988). Alan Mittleman, *Between Kant and Kabbalah: An Introduction to Isaac Breuer's Philosophy of Judaism*, SUNY Series in Judaica (Albany, N.Y., 1990). —GABRIEL A. SIVAN

BRIBERY (Heb. *shoḥad*), the conveyance of a gift in order to influence judgment; prohibited in *Exodus* 23.8 and *Deuteronomy* 16.19. Whereas culpability extends to the person who offers the bribe and to the person who accepts it, the Bible directs its remarks primarily to judges. The rabbis considered all forms of gift taking by a judge as impairing his impartiality, even if the bribe was offered with a view to condemning the guilty or vindicating the innocent (*Ket*. 105a). The slightest courtesy or favor received often provided grounds for the self-disqualification of the judge. Bribery is mentioned as one of the twelve crimes that evoke the curse of heaven (*Dt*. 27.25). The strictness of the laws concerning bribery led in very early times, when a judge received no fixed stipend, to the practice of his receiving an equal fee from both parties. In order, however, to ensure the freedom and integrity of the judicial authority, it gradually became the custom for communities to pay a judge's stipend from communal funds.

• Emanuel B. Quint, *A Restatement of Rabbinic Civil Law*, vol. 1 (Northvale, N.J., 1990).

BRIDEGROOMS OF THE TORAH. See Ḥatan Torah and Ḥatan Be-Re'shit.

BRIDES AND BRIDEGROOMS. See Betrothal.

BRODA FAMILY, family of rabbis that traces its descent from R. *Yehudah Liva' ben Betsal'el, the Maharal of Prague.

Avraham ben Sha'ul Broda (died 1717), of Metz and Frankfurt am Main, among other cities; he was born in Bohemia. Rabbi Yonatan *Eybeschuetz was his student. Broda's several volumes of Talmudic *novellae* include *Eshel Avraham* (Frankfurt am Main, 1747) on tractates *Pesaḥim, Bava' Batra'*, and *Ḥullin*.

Ḥayyim Broda (died 1823), great-great-grandson of Avraham. He is the author of *Torah Or ve-Derekh Ḥayyim* (Grodno, 1823) on the laws of ritual slaughter, written to defend the *Shulḥan ʿArukh* against the attacks on it made by *Shabbetai ben Me'ir ha-Kohen in *Gevurot Anashim*.

• Azriel Meir Broda, *Mishpaḥat Broda* (Warsaw, 1938). —MARK WASHOFSKY

BROKERAGE, the function of an intermediary in any legal transaction. In Jewish law, the broker is considered an *agent, but since he is paid for his services, he is liable for loss, theft, or any personal negligence, as is the paid bailee. In disputes concerning the broker's activities, he may clear himself by oath if there are no witnesses and he insists that he was authorized to accept the terms realized. The marriage broker (**shaddekhan*), who acts as a go-between in arranging marriages, is also classed as a broker and is legally entitled to remuneration.

• Yisroel Reisman, *The Laws of Ribbis: The Laws of Interest and Their Application to Everyday Life and Business* (Brooklyn, N.Y., 1995).

BRUNA, YISRA'EL (c.1400–1480), rabbinic scholar, communal leader, and legal authority. He studied with R. Yisra'el Isserlein and with R. Yaʿaqov Weil. Many issues concerning the prerogatives and parameters of the nascent professional rabbinate in Ashkenaz surfaced during his career. In his first post in his native Brno, he had to endure the competition of a later arrival. When he went to Regensburg, where he opened a *yeshivah*, he was vigorously attacked by another academy head. With the death of this rival, he was acknowledged as the leader of the community, and with the deaths of Isserlein and Weil, he was recognized as the leading halakhic authority in Germany.

Bruna was imprisoned by the authorities on at least two occasions: in 1456, to spur the collection of a coronation tax imposed by Frederick III; and in 1474, as the result of a spurious blood libel charge brought by an apostate. Frederick III, among others, was instrumental in securing his release. A collection of Bruna's *responsa* has survived (Salonika, 1788).

• Yedidya Dinari, *Ḥakhamei Ashkenaz be-Shelhei Yemei ha-Beinayim* (Jerusalem, 1984), pp. 457–458. Israel Yuval, *Ḥakhamim be-Doram: Manhigut ha-Ruḥanit shel Yehudei Germanyah be-Shelhei Yemei ha-Beinayim* (Jerusalem, 1989). —EPHRAIM KANARFOGEL

BUBER, MARTIN (1878–1965), religious philosopher. Born in Vienna, but raised in Lemberg, the capital of the Austrian crownland of Galicia, he received a traditional Jewish education in conjunction with secular studies. Although he had abandoned religious observance already in his teens, he maintained an active interest in the classical texts of Judaism, especially scripture, and in Hasidism. He became a renowned interpreter of both of these expressions, as he put it, of Israel's dialogue with God. He took from Hasidism the concept of personal piety as the essence of Judaism, but selectively rejected those aspects which he felt had no place in true religiosity. His presentation of Hasidism in a series of works recounting Hasidic anecdotes and parables (including *The Legend of the Baal Shem* [1955]; *The Tales of Rabbi Nachman* [1956]; and *Tales of the Hasidim*, 2 vols. [1947–1948]), and his adaptation of its ideas to Western thought (see NEO-HASIDISM) brought this east European movement to the Western world. Buber joined the Zionist movement soon after it was founded by Theodor Herzl, with whom he worked closely. They eventually parted ways when Buber endorsed the view that the movement's primary task was not attainment of Jewish political power but rather the promotion of Jewish cultural renewal. Henceforth, he found himself in a minority position on most issues facing the movement (e.g., the Arab question), to which he remained loyal until his death in Jerusalem, where he settled in 1938.

Buber's religious thought gained its most mature expression in *I and Thou* (*Ich und Du*, 1923; Eng. *I and Thou* [New York, 1970]). At the heart of his teachings is the concept of dialogue, which posits that God, the "Eternal Thou," addresses the individual through the varied experiences of life (from the seemingly ephemeral and trivial to the grand and momentous). These demand from the individual a dialogical response, or a confirmation of the Thou, the unique presence of the other who stands before one. In responding to the other as Thou, the self, or I, in turn, finds his or her own presence confirmed in turn. As a response to the continuously renewing presence and address of the other, dialogue must be born ever anew. The I–Thou response thus requires spontaneity and cannot be determined by fixed expressions, gestures and formulations. It also follows that God's address, refracted or revealed as it is through the other, is also spontaneous. Accordingly, authentic divine service to God is grounded in spontaneous responses to God who continuously turns to one in the eternal flux of life. The conclusion Buber drew was that formal prayer and ritual were not the preeminent expressions of religious devotion. This view, he acknowledged, placed him in an anomalous position within Jewish religious thought. Yet, he insisted, as a community of faith Judaism is ultimately distinguished by its witness to the dialogical principle, which informs its central myths and sacred texts. As a Zionist, he held that Jewish religious life in the Diaspora had been falsely constricted to the synagogue and the home, and had thus lost hold of dialogue as the founding moment of Judaism. By restoring to the Jews the sociological conditions of a full communal life, Zionism would allow for the possibility that the Jews' public life, guided once again by the principle of dialogue, would become a realm of relation to divinity. The reappropriation of the public sphere as the "dialogical" responsibility of the community of faith, Buber taught, is in consonance with the supreme injunction of the prophets, and thus constitutes the renewal of what he called Hebrew, or biblical, humanism. Buber also applied the concept of dialogue to the Jewish–Christian relationship, holding that both Judaism and Christianity were authentic paths to God. Together with Franz Rosenzweig, he pioneered the major shift in focus in the Jewish–Christian relationship that developed after World War II. Also with Rosenzweig he translated the Bible into German, a version which sought to capture the meanings and rhythms of the original Hebrew. Among Buber's other books were *The Kingship of God* (1967), *Moses* (1946), *The Knowledge of Man* (1965), and *Israel and the World* (1963).

• Margot Cohen and Rafael Buber, eds., *Martin Buber: A Bibliography of His Writings, 1897–1978* (Jerusalem, Munich, and New York, 1980). Maurice Friedman, *Martin Buber's Life and Work*, 3 vols. (New York, 1981–1988). Paul Arthur Schilpp and Maurice Friedman, eds., *The Philosophy of Martin Buber*, The Library of Living Philosophers (La Salle, Ill., 1967), critical essays on various aspects of Buber's thought, containing an appendix of "Replies of My Critics" by Buber. Pamela Vermes, *Buber* (London, 1988).

—PAUL MENDES-FLOHR

BÜCHLER, ADOLF (1867–1939), historian and theologian. Born in Hungary, he graduated from the Budapest Rabbinical Seminary in 1891 and became professor of Talmud and history at the Israelitisch-Theologische Lehranstalt in Vienna in 1893. From 1906 until his death, he was principal of Jews' College in London. Büchler wrote widely on such topics as Bible, Talmud, Midrash, and archaeology. He is best known for his work on the Second Temple period. Especially noteworthy was his study *Das Synedrion in Jerusalem und das grosse Beth-din in der Quaderkammer des jerusalemischen Tempels* (1902), which analyzed the existence of an institution responsible for overseeing Jewish religious life—ha-Beit Din ha-Gadol—distinct from the Sanhedrin.

• I. Brodie and J. Rabbinowitz, eds., *Studies in Jewish History: The Adolf Büchler Memorial Volume* (London, 1956).

—GAVRIEL D. ROSENFELD

BUDAPEST RABBINICAL SEMINARY, a school for the training of rabbis that opened in 1877. In 1864 the Hungarian authorities had asked three rabbis to draw up plans for such a seminary, but the Orthodox rabbis of Hungary—who fought all innovations and reforms—opposed the proposal, which was supported by the Neologists and Status Quo Ante elements. However, an Orthodox petition to the emperor in 1877 to postpone the opening of the seminary was turned down, and the seminary commenced its activities under its rector R. Moses Bloch. Shortly after the seminary opened, Emperor Francis Joseph I visited, and in 1917 the school was renamed the Francis Joseph National Rabbinical Seminary (later the National Rabbinical Seminary). Many distinguished scholars have served on its faculty, including rectors Wilhelm Bacher and Ludwig Blau. Like the *Breslau Rabbinical Seminary, instruction at the Budapest seminary was Orthodox, but the critical study of sources was permitted. Classes were suspended in October 1944, and the Hungarian Nazis occupied the building. Much of the three-hundred-thousand-volume library was destroyed. Teaching resumed in March 1945, and the seminary's postwar rectors have been David Samuel Löwinger, Alexander Schreiber, and Joseph Schweitzer. Since World War II, the Budapest Rabbinical Seminary has been the only rabbinical seminary in eastern Europe.

• Moshe Carmilly, ed., *The Rabbinical Seminary of Budapest, 1877–1977* (New York, 1986).

BULAN. See KHAZARS.

BURGLARY (Heb. *maḥteret*). According to the Bible, a thief found breaking into a home may be killed by the owner (*Ex.* 22.1). It is assumed (*San.* 62a) that the burglar, knowing that every man will do his utmost to defend his property, is prepared to kill if necessary. The owner may therefore anticipate the burglar and act first in self-defense. The Bible adds (*Ex.* 22.2), "If the sun be risen upon him there shall be bloodguilt for him," which is understood to mean that should it be clear that the thief has not come with the intention to kill but is nevertheless killed, the killer is guilty of a capital crime. See also ROBBERY; THEFT.

• Emanuel B. Quint, *A Restatement of Rabbinic Civil Law*, vol. 1 (Northvale, N.J., 1990).

BURIAL. The only method of disposing of the dead, according to traditional Jewish law, is by placing the body of the deceased in the earth or in a sepulcher. *Cremation is therefore prohibited, but it is permitted by Reform Judaism. This practice of burying the dead is based on *Deuteronomy* 21.23, which enjoins the decent disposal of the body of the publicly hanged criminal by burial on the selfsame day. Because even a convicted felon must receive an honorable burial, it follows that to be denied burial is the greatest humiliation that can be inflicted upon the deceased. The reverence attached to burial is an outstanding feature of Jewish practice. Respect for the dead is the guiding principle of Jewish funeral and burial practices. The task of ensuring a proper burial is regarded as one of the greatest acts of benevolence, and the prohibition against deriving any benefit from the dead has resulted in the custom of responsibility for burial being assumed by the communal organization known as the **ḥevrah qaddisha'* (holy society). In North America, it is common for the burial society to work in cooperation with a commercial funeral home. According to Jewish law, burial must take place as soon as possible. Funeral (*levayah*) and burial do not take place on the Sabbath or festivals because of the prohibitions against work. However, because of the honor of the deceased, burial may take place on the second day of a festival. The body is ritually washed (**tohorah*) and wrapped in a simple shroud (the practice of *tohorah* is not generally observed by Reform Jews). In Western countries, as in biblical times (*Gn.* 50.26), a coffin generally is used; however, in Eastern countries and the State of Israel, a coffin is dispensed with. Burial customs vary from country to country, but in general they are characterized by the utmost simplicity. The body is borne to the grave on a bier and interred with a brief *funeral service. Exhumation is forbidden except for reinterment in a family grave or in Erets Yisra'el. Jews of priestly descent (*kohanim*) are forbidden to contaminate themselves by contact with the dead or by too close proximity (4 cubits, approximately 6 feet) to a grave, except when they are mourners, that is, the deceased is a parent, sibling, spouse, or child. *Kohanim* are therefore usually buried at the end of a row or in the front row to enable their relatives who are *kohanim* to visit the grave. Attendance at a funeral is regarded as an act of particular piety and part of the fulfillment of the commandment to comfort the mourners. At the conclusion of burial, those present form two rows, and the mourners pass between them and are offered condolence with the words *Ha-Maqom yenaḥem etḥem betokh she'ar avelei Tsiyyon vi-Yerushalayim*, "May God comfort you among the mourners of Zion and Jerusalem." It is from this moment that official *mourning commences. See also SHIVʿAH.

• Hayyim Halevy Donin, *To Be A Jew: A Guide to Jewish Observance in Contemporary Life* (New York, 1972). Hyman Goldin, *Hamadrikh: The Rabbi's Guide* (New York, 1956). Jules Harlow, ed., *Liqqutei Tefillah: A Rabbi's Manual* (New York, 1965). Isaac Klein, *A Guide for Jewish Religious Practice* (New York, 1992). Peter Knobel, "Rites of Passage," in *Judaism: A People and Its History*, edited by Robert Seltzer (New York, 1989). Maurice Lamm, *The Jewish Way in Death and Mourning* (New York, 1969). Simeon Maslin, ed., *Gates of Mitzvah: Shaarei Mitzvah, a Guide to the Jewish Life Cycle* (New York, 1979). David Polish, ed. *Maglei Tsedeq: A Rabbi's Manual*, with notes by W. Gunther Plaut (New York, 1988). Tzvi Rabinowicz, *A Guide to Life: Jewish Laws and Customs of Mourning* (London, 1964).

—PETER KNOBEL

BURIAL SOCIETY. See ḤEVRAH QADDISHA'.

BURNING BUSH, the thorn bush, possibly a wild acacia shrub, from which God spoke to Moses in the wilderness and called him to his prophetic mission (*Ex.* 3.1–10). The divine appearance was in the form of a flame of fire, but though "the bush burned with fire . . . the bush was not consumed." The burning bush has often been interpreted, in homiletics and in art, as a symbol of Israel.

• Nahum M. Sarna, *Exploring Exodus* (New York, 1986), pp. 39–42.

—SHALOM PAUL

BURNT OFFERING (Heb. *ʿolah*), one type of animal *sacrifices in ancient times. The distinguishing feature of the *ʿolah* is that all of the animal's flesh is consumed on the altar; no part (other than the hide) is left for the consumption or use of the priest or the worshiper (*Lv.* 1). This is expressed in its name, *ʿolah* (that which goes up [in smoke]), and its alternative name *kalil* (entire); its traditional English name is holocaust. It is the most profound expression of the worshiper's desire to present a gift to God, in recognition, reverence, homage, thanks, or for expiation. Its versatility can be seen in the fact that the Bible does not specify when an individual might choose to sacrifice a voluntary burnt offering. It was required, however, in the consecration of the priests (*Ex.* 29.15), the purification of the leper (*Lv.* 15.15, 30), the purification following childbirth (*Lv.* 12.6–8), and by the Nazirite at the conclusion of his vow (*Nm.* 6.11ff.). The rabbis also held that it was required in order to atone for failure to observe performative commands. Three types of burnt offerings were acceptable: a bull from the herd, a sheep or a goat from the flock, or a fowl. In the public sacrificial system, the *tamid* (daily morning and evening sacrifices; see PERPETUAL OFFERING) and the *musaf* (additional sacrifices on Sabbaths, Ro'sh Ḥodesh, and festivals) were all burnt offerings (*Ex.* 29.38–42; *Nm.* 28–29) from the herd or flock.

• George Buchanan Gray, *Sacrifice in the Old Testament: Its Theory and Practice* (New York, 1971), pp. 1–20. Baruch A. Levine, *In the Presence of the Lord* (Leiden, 1974). Baruch A. Levine, *Leviticus: The Traditional Hebrew Text* (Philadelphia, 1989), pp. 4–9. Jacob Milgrom, *Leviticus 1–16*, The Anchor Bible, vol. 3 (Garden City, N.Y., 1991), pp. 146–177.

—BARUCH J. SCHWARTZ

BUZAGLO, SHALOM (c.1700–1780), rabbi and kabbalist. He was born in Marrakesh and brought up in southern Morocco, which was then a kabbalistic center. He fled persecution by the sultan and settled in London, where he wrote his major kabbalistic works *Hadrat Melekh* and *Miqdash Melekh*, a commentary on the Zohar (Amsterdam and London, 1750–1755). He strove to reconcile Mosheh ben Ya'aqov Cordovero's kabbalistic system with doctrines of the Lurianic school, as did many contemporary kabbalists. In addition to his literary activities, Buzaglo served as a judge on the Ashkenazi rabbinical court (*beit din*) of London.

• Joseph BenNaim, *Sefer Malkhei Rabbanan* (Jerusalem, 1931). Gershom Gerhard Scholem, *Bibliographia Kabbalistica* (Berlin, 1933), pp. 188–191.

—NISSIM YOSHA

BYZANTINE RITE, the prayer rite of the Jews of the eastern Roman empire, akin in some respects to the Italian rite. The Byzantine rite contains many special poems (*piyyutim*, *seliḥot*, etc.) added to the regular prayers. It was contained in the *Maḥazor Romaniyyah*, which was printed a number of times in the sixteenth and seventeenth centuries but was eventually superseded in Turkey and the Balkans by the Sephardi rite. Since the eighteenth century the Byzantine rite has survived only in Corfu and Kaffa in the Crimea.

• S. Bernstein, "Ha-Maḥzor ke-Minhag Kappa, Toldotav ve-Hitpatḥuto," in *Sefer ha-Yovel li-Khevod Shmuel Kalman Mirsky* (New York, 1957), pp. 451–538. Daniel Goldschmidt, "'Al Maḥazor Romaniyyah u-Minhago" and "Maḥzorim ke-Minhag Kehillot Yavan," in *Meḥqerei Tefillah u-Fiyyut* (Jerusalem, 1978), pp. 122–152, 217–288.

C

CABALA. See KABBALAH.

CAIN AND ABEL (Heb. Qayin and Hevel), oldest sons of *Adam and *Eve, born after the banishment from the garden of Eden. Cain was a tiller of the soil, and Abel, the younger of the two, was a shepherd. When each made an offering to the Lord—Abel from the firstlings of the flock and Cain from the fruits of the soil—only that of Abel was accepted. Cain, in frustration and jealousy, then killed his brother, for which he was doubly cursed: the ground would no longer yield to him its produce, and he was condemned to be a ceaseless wanderer on earth. God, however, provided him with a bodily mark that would serve to protect him against all future murderers. He eventually settled in the land of Nod, married, and had a child, Enoch (*Gn.* 4). According to rabbinic legend, he was accidentally killed by his descendant Lamech (*Tanḥuma' Be-Re'shit*, Vienna ed., 6b).

• Umberto Cassuto, *A Commentary on the Book of Genesis*, vol. 1, *From Adam to Noah* (Jerusalem, 1989), pp. 178–248. Nahum M. Sarna, *Understanding Genesis* (New York, 1966), pp. 28–32. Claus Westermann, *Genesis 1–11*, translated by John J. Scullion (Minneapolis, 1984), pp. 279–320.
—SHALOM PAUL

CALEB (Heb. Kalev), one of the twelve spies sent by Moses to scout out the land of Canaan prior to the Israelite invasion (*Nm.* 13.1–20). Only Caleb, the representative of the tribe of Judah, and Joshua, from the tribe of Ephraim, favored the immediate conquest, whereas the other ten spies demurred. As a result, the Israelites refused to engage in the attack and were condemned not to enter Israel but to wander for forty years in the wilderness. From that generation, only Caleb, Joshua, and those Israelites who were under the age of twenty finally entered the Promised Land (*Nm.* 14). As a reward for his faithfulness, Caleb was granted by Joshua the city of Hebron (*Jos.* 14.6–14), and Caleb dispossessed the giants who lived there (*Jos.* 15.13–14). He promised his daughter Achsah in marriage to whomever would capture the city of Debir, a feat accomplished by Othniel, son of Kenaz (*Jos.* 15.17; *Jgs.* 1.12–13).

• Jacob Milgrom, *Numbers*, The JPS Torah Commentary (Philadelphia, 1990), pp. 391–392.
—SHALOM PAUL

CALENDAR. The Jewish calendar, though complicated, is so accurate that, unlike the Julian and Gregorian calendars, it has never had to be adjusted.

The Lunisolar Calendar. Until *Hillel II instituted a permanent calendar based on astronomical calculations (in 358), the fixing of *Ro'sh Ḥodesh (the new moon) was determined by observation and the evidence of witnesses. Earlier, the practice of adding a second day to festivals (except for Yom Kippur) was introduced for communities lying at a distance from Erets Yisra'el, because they would not know in time on precisely which of two days the appearance of the new moon had been officially confirmed by the authorities in Jerusalem, and this could lead to confusion regarding the exact date of a festival occuring during that month. The length of the lunar month was established by the rabbis as twenty-nine days, twelve hours, and 793 parts (thousandths). Ignoring the fraction, twelve lunar months in this system comprise 354 days. Since the solar year consists of 365 days (again ignoring the fractions), it was therefore necessary to make provision for a discrepancy of eleven days per year. This was achieved by intercalating seven leap months (Adar II) over the course of a nineteen-year cycle. The third, sixth, eighth, eleventh, fourteenth, seventeenth, and nineteenth years are designated leap years and contain thirteen months (the year 5749 [=1988–1989], for instance, began such a cycle). Adjustments are made to provide for the fractions, and a completely recurrent cycle occurs every 371 years. With regard to the lunar months, the twelve extra hours accumulated over each month are provided for by making some months "defective," that is twenty-nine days long, and others "full," consisting of thirty days. Ideally Nisan, Sivan, Av, Tishrei, Kislev, and Shevat have thirty days, and Iyyar, Tammuz, Elul, Ḥeshvan, Tevet, and Adar have twenty-nine (that is, a strict alternation of full and defective months). However, because of necessary adjustments, this regular alternation is not strictly followed, though no year may have less than five or more than seven "full" months. In a leap year, Adar I has thirty days and Adar II has twenty-nine. In the case of a "full" month, both the thirtieth day of that month and the first of the next are celebrated as Ro'sh Ḥodesh, since the second half of the thirtieth day actually belongs to the new moon. In the case of *Ro'sh ha-Shanah, the only festival of the Jewish calendar to occur on the first of the month, it proved impracticable to rely on the observation of the new moon of Tishrei, as the information would have arrived too late to notify all the various communities of the advent of the New Year. Therefore both the first day of Tishrei and the thirtieth day of the previous month, Elul, were regarded as the New Year; of all the biblical festivals, Ro'sh ha-Shanah alone is observed for two days, even in Erets Yisra'el. (There was, however, a period during the Middle Ages when Ro'sh ha-Shanah was observed for one day only in Erets Yisra'el). Elul is always defective, with the result that the two days of Ro'sh ha-Shanah (1 and 2 Tishrei) are traditionally regarded as "one long day." The accepted names of the months are of Babylonian origin. Before the Babylonian exile, they had other names or were merely identified by their numerical order. The first month was Nisan, but the religious year began in Tishrei. The rabbis were greatly concerned with establishing the precise moment between twilight and complete darkness, when one day ends and the next begins, in order to determine the commencement, and more particularly the conclusion, of Sabbaths and festivals. Nightfall was designated as that moment when three stars of the second magnitude become visible, estimated as the moment when the sun is seven degrees below the horizon. The Jewish calendar is reckoned from the date of Creation, which, on the basis of other biblical dates, is placed at 3760 BCE. To calculate Jewish dates one first deducts 1240 from the Common Era date and then adds 5000 (for dates falling between Ro'sh ha-Shanah and 31 December, one adds another year); thus 2000 CE corresponds to the Jewish year 5760–5761. Various sectarian groups had calendars that differed from that determined by the rabbis. These included the Samaritans, the Sadducees, and the Dead Sea sect. These calendars created friction when festivals were observed on different dates. See also DAY AND NIGHT; entries for individual months.

• Nathan Bushwick, *Understanding the Jewish Calendar* (New York, 1989). George Zinberg, *Jewish Calendar Mystery Dispelled* (New York, 1963).

–CHAIM PEARL

Sectarian Calendars. Jewish sectarian groups have calculated months and holidays by non-normative systems. Two non-canonical books of the late Second Temple period, *Enoch* and *Jubilees*, refer to a 364-day solar calendar. The year comprises twelve months of thirty days each, two solstice days and two equinox days. There are indications that the Dead Sea sect adopted this calendar. Intercalations in a six-year cycle may have been used to keep the calendar synchronous with the 365-¼-day solar year. According to the Bible, the *'omer* is to be offered on the "morrow of the Sabbath." For the normative calendar, this is interpreted as the second day of Pesaḥ. Those who advocate the solar calendar take the "morrow of the Sabbath" to mean Sunday, as do the Boethusians and Samaritans. The Samaritan calendar fixes the first day of the month by the conjunction of the moon with the sun, not by the new moon. Months are numbered rather than named. Leap years occur seven times in nineteen years, but months are not intercalated at set intervals. Jews of the Diaspora did not always comply with calendrical rulings. In Syrian Antioch from 328–342, Pesaḥ was celebrated in March, with no regard to rabbinical dicta. Nor did sects in Erets Yisra'el always follow the standard calendar without variation. In the eighth century, the Karaites, following Muslim practice, returned to direct observation of the new moon. Eleven centuries later, after much controversy, it was decided, at least among Crimean Karaites, that mathematical calculation, like for the Rabbanite calendar, would supplement observation. Although the Beta Israel consider *Enoch* and *Jubilees* sacred, their calendar is lunisolar with a leap year every fourth year.

• Zvi Ankori, *Karaites in Byzantium: The Formative Years, 970–1100* (New York, 1959). Joseph M. Baumgarten, *Studies in Qumran Law*, Studies in Judaism in Late Antiquity 24 (Leiden, 1977). Sylvia Powels, *Der Kalender der Samaritaner* (Berlin, 1977).

–DENNIS M. DREYFUS

CALF, GOLDEN. See GOLDEN CALF.

CALUMNY. See SLANDER.

CAMPANTON, YITSḤAQ (1360–1463), Spanish rabbi. He was head of a *yeshivah* in Zamora in western Spain and was known as the ga'on of Castile. His only surviving work, *Darkhei ha-Talmud*, lays out a method for the study of the Talmud that was very influential. It was used by Ya'aqov *Berab in his *yeshivah* in Safed.

• H. Z. Dimitrovski in *Sefunot* 7 (1962/3): 83–96.

CANAAN, LAND OF. The name *Kinakhnum* (Canaanites) appears for the first time in an Akkadian document from the archives of the the kingdom of Mari (19th–18th cent. BCE). The Canaanites are frequently mentioned in Akkadian, Ugaritic, and Egyptian documents from the fifteenth through the thirteenth century BCE, when the name Canaan was applied to the land west of the Euphrates up to the Mediterranean. This definition is supported by a proposed etymology of the name Canaan from the West Semitic root *k n '* (bow down). Thus, Canaan is the land where the sun bows down, that is, sets in the evening, or the West Land.

A more precise definition for Canaan is suggested by other documents, beginning with the fourteenth century BCE. A letter from a Babylonian king to the pharaoh, found in the archives of the Egyptian foreign office at Tell al-'Amarna, states: "Canaan is your land and its kings are your servants." From here it appears that the name Canaan was applied to the Egyptian realm in Asia, which expanded or shrank according to political developments in the ancient Near East.

According to *Numbers* 34.1–12, the borders of Canaan stretched from Wadi el-'Arish to Mount Hor to Hama to the area northeast of Damascus on the fringes of the Syrian Desert. This description, however, most likely reflects the Egyptian province of Canaan of the thirteenth century BCE.

In the Bible, the name Canaan became a designation for Erets Yisra'el, and its non-Israelite population (except for the Philistines) were generally called Canaanites. At times, the Bible differentiated between the Canaanites, who inhabited the coastal plain and the valleys, and the Amorites, who inhabited the highland (cf. *Nm.* 13. 29). In the tenth century BCE, the era of the united monarchy of Israel, the names Canaan and Canaanites were confined to the Phoenicians, who lived on the coast of the Mediterranean, stretching from Mount Carmel northward. Since the Phoenicians were occupied in international commerce, the word *Canaanite* became synonymous with *merchant* (cf. *Is.* 23.8: "Who was it that planned this for crown-wearing Tyre, whose merchants are nobles, whose traders [lit. Canaanites] the world honored?"). From here, too, was derived the word *kin'ah*, meaning merchandise (*Jer.* 10.17).

The Phoenicians themselves never used the names Canaan or Canaanites, since the political fragmentation of Phoenicia prevented the emergence of a national identity; these names were used only by foreigners. A rare exception is a bilingual coin from Laodicea on the northern Syrian coast that states in Phoenician: "Laodicea which is in Canaan." The Punic inhabitants of North Africa in the fourth century CE, aware of their heritage, still called themselves Chananai, that is, Canaanites. The Bible equates Canaanite cultic practices with idolatry and immorality and warns the people, on pain of dire punishment, against "walking in their ways" and intermarrying with them. After the Israelites settled in the land of Canaan and adapted to a sedentary agricultural way of life with its concomitant fertility and Baal cults, these prohibitions were often ignored, and it was only after a long struggle, waged mainly by the prophets, that the Israelite religious culture prevailed.

• William Foxwell Albright, "The Role of the Canaanites in the History of Civilization," in *The Bible and the Ancient Near East: Essays in Honor of William Foxwell Albright*, edited by George Ernest Wright (Garden City, N.Y., 1965), pp. 438–487. John Gray, *The Canaanites* (New York, 1964). Donald B. Harden, *The Phoenicians*, Ancient Peoples and Places, vol. 26 (New York, 1962). Benjamin Mazar, "Canaan and the Canaanites," in *Biblical Israel: State and People*, edited by Shmuel Ahituv (Jerusalem, 1992), pp. 16–21. Alan Ralph Millard, "The Canaanites," in *Peoples of Old Testament Times*, edited by Donald John Wiseman (Oxford, 1973), pp. 29–52. Roland de Vaux, *The Early History of Israel*, 2 vols. translated by David Smith (London, 1978), pp. 125–152.

–SHMUEL AHITUV

CANAANITES, name given by the Bible to the original inhabitants of the land of Canaan prior to the Israelite conquest under *Joshua. In biblical tradition, the Canaanites are believed to have descended from Canaan, youngest son of Ham, one of the three sons of Noah (*Gn*. 9.14, 10.6). They include several peoples or tribes, but always numbered among them were the Canaanites proper, Hittites, Amorites, Perizzites, Jebusites, and Hivites. Sometimes Girgashites are listed; occasionally other tribes, such as Sidonites, Hamathites, Refaim, and Kenites are named as well. Noah cursed Canaan for the depravity of Ham his father (*Gn*. 9.24–25), destining him to be subjugated by Shem—thereby foretelling the eventual displacement of the Canaanites by the Israelites (descended from Shem), consistently justified by the Bible as the inevitable outcome of the sexual licentiousness practiced by the Canaanites (*Gn*. 15.16, 18.4–9, 19.31–38, 20.1–12; esp. *Lv*. 18.24–30, 20.22–24). Though the Bible may have exaggerated the extent, Canaanite sexual practices were, in fact, less strictly controlled than Israelite sexual practices.

While the patriarchs lived as nomadic sojourners among the Canaanites, at the time of the *Exodus from Egypt, the Israelites were told that under God's leadership and with his assistance they would succeed in effortlessly taking over the Canaanites' land (*Ex*. 3.8, 3.17, 23.20–33), so long as they refrained from any contact with Canaanite gods, eradicated all traces of their forms of worship (*Ex*. 23.24–25), shunned all sexual and marital intermingling with them (*Ex*. 34.11–16), and avoided the temptation to grant them reprieve from the divine edict of expulsion (*Ex*. 23.27–33; *Dt*. 7.2). The aversion to intermarrying with the Canaanites is alluded to in the stories of the patriarchs (*Gn*. 24.3, 28.6).

Elsewhere God charges the Israelites themselves with the task of dispossessing the Canaanites (*Nm*. 33.50–56), threatening dire consequences if they fail to do so, and in *Deuteronomy* it is made clear that the conquest is to be a war of annihilation of the local peoples (*Dt*. 7.1–26, 20.16–18). *Deuteronomy* 12.29–31, as well as certain prophetic books (e.g., *Hos*. 1–3), expresses a particular abhorrence for Canaanite religious practices; Canaanite paganism, in which the gods El and Baal and the goddess Asherah figured prominently, is held by many scholars to have been a fertility cult, in which sexual practices were central, though recently this assumption has been questioned.

• Stephen A. Geller, "The Sack of Shechem: The Use of Typology in Biblical Covenant Religion," *Prooftexts* 10 (1990): 1–15. Delbert R. Hillers, "Analyzing the Abominable: Our Understanding of Canaanite Religion," *Jewish Quarterly Review* 75 (1985): 253–269. Harry A. Hoffner, "Incest, Sodomy and Bestiality in the Ancient Near East," in *Orient and Occident: Essays Presented to Cyrus H. Gordon*, Alter Orient und Altes Testament, Bd. 22 (Kevelaer, Ger., 1973), pp. 81–90. Niels Peter Lemche, *The Canaanites and Their Land: The Tradition of the Canaanites*, Journal for the Study of the Old Testament, Supplement Series 110 (Sheffield, Eng., 1991). Baruch J. Schwartz, "Selected Chapters of the Holiness Code," Ph.D. dissertation, Hebrew University, 1987, pp. 76–77, 103–108.

–BARUCH J. SCHWARTZ

CANDELABRUM. See MENORAH.

CANDLES. In Jewish tradition the lighting of candles (formerly oil lamps) is characteristic of occasions both of joy and sorrow. As a symbol of joy it is an essential feature of the festive board on Sabbaths and holidays. The custom of lighting candles was instituted by the *Pharisees during the time of the Second Temple. The lighting of two Sabbath candles (because of the two versions of the Decalogue that speak of "remembering" and "observing" the Sabbath day), together with the recitation of the appropriate blessing, is the prerogative of the mistress of the household (*Shab*. 2.6–7). A Talmudic legend relates that the angels who accompany a man from the synagogue on the Sabbath eve bless his home as soon as they see the lighted candles. Among Ashkenazim, a special braided candle is lit in the *Havdalah service at the end of the Sabbath. The kindling of lights is the core of the *Ḥanukkah festival, while a lighted candle is used on Pesaḥ eve in the search for **ḥamets* (leaven). In some communities the parents of the bride and groom hold lighted candles at the marriage ceremony. The verse "the spirit of man is the candle of the Lord" (*Prv*. 20.27) is considered the origin of the use of candles in *mourning rites. Candles are kindled and placed at the head of the deceased; they are also lit during the week of mourning, on the anniversary of the death, and on the eve of Yom Kippur. The candles may not be made of tallow, which is a nonkosher fat. See also LIGHT; MEMORIAL LIGHT; MENORAH.

• B. M. Levin, "Le-Toledot Ner Shabbat," in *Essays and Studies in Memory of Linda A. Miller* (New York, 1938), pp. 55–68. Israel Ta-Shema, "Ner shel Kavod," in *Minhag Ashkenaz ha-Kadmon* (Jerusalem, 1992), pp. 135–145. Chava Weissler, "Woman as High Priest: A Kabbalistic Prayer in Yiddish for Lighting Sabbath Candles," *Jewish History* 5.1 (Spring 1991): 1–26.

CANON (from Gr. *kanōn* [measuring rod, standard]), term that originally designated standards of excellence; it eventually came to refer to the authoritative body of Holy Scriptures. See also BIBLE. –BARUCH J. SCHWARTZ

CANOPY. See ḤUPPAH.

CANTICLES. See SONG OF SONGS, BOOK OF.

CANTILLATION. See ACCENTS; CANTORIAL MUSIC.

CANTOR (Heb. *ḥazzan*). The ritual of the Temple service was presided over by a priest (*kohen*) and Levitical choir(s). The notion of a single individual leading communal worship is related to the evolution of the synagogue after the destruction of the Temple. The earliest references (in the Talmud Yerushalmi) to a prayer leader use the term **sheliaḥ tsibbur* (representative of the community). At first, there was no need for a professional rendering of the liturgy; the congregation could be led by any knowledgeable member. The term *ḥazzan* originally denoted a community official carrying out a variety of nonmusical functions. The necessity for special expertise arose in the geonic period because of the decline of Hebrew and the incorporation into the service of *piyyutim*, many of which were expected to be extemporaneously improvised by the cantor. An exclusive caste of *ḥazzanim* emerged as the position was handed down from father to son.

The cantor's status varied with the times. The qualifications for office were many (cf. *Ta'an.* 16a): the *ḥazzan* had to be of mature age, preferably married and with children, well versed in scripture and liturgy, and a respected and religiously observant member of the community with a pleasant voice and appearance. In many communities it was customary to limit the cantor's salary, so that his prayers on behalf of the congregation, particularly those for physical and economic sustenance, would be especially fervent. In the course of time, emphasis was laid almost exclusively on vocal quality, and complaints were frequently leveled by rabbis against the shortcomings of those cantors whose fervor was of a histrionic rather than a religious nature.

The first use of the term *cantor* came in conjunction with the synagogue reforms of the nineteenth century. Using the model of J. S. Bach, the famed eighteenth-century *Kantor* of Leipzig, German synagogues eliminated traditional synagogue *nussaḥ* and expected their cantors to function more as choral directors and composers than as soloists. Salomon *Sulzer of Vienna was the first to combine classical Western musical training with a strong grounding in synagogue music. He and those who followed him endeavored to raise the artistic standards of synagogue music and of the cantorate. Formal schools to train cantors were established in Germany and have also existed in the United States since 1948.

Some congregations have restricted or even eliminated the musical role of the cantor in favor of greater congregational participation. This is especially common among smaller congregations, who continue to depend upon the *sheliaḥ tsibbur* for their routine musical needs. Just as frequently, though, the modern cantor, like the *ḥazzan* of old, serves a variety of synagogue and community functions. He, or in recent years she (except among Orthodox congregations), performs pastoral and educational as well as musical roles.

• Irene Heskes, ed., *The Cantorial Art* (New York, 1966). Abraham Z. Idelsohn, *Jewish Music in Its Historical Development* (New York, 1929; repr. 1967; 1992). Mark Slobin, *Chosen Voices: The Story of the American Cantorate* (Urbana, Ill., 1989).

—MARSHA BRYAN EDELMAN

CANTORIAL MUSIC (Heb. *ḥazzanut*) today refers to the body of music used in the ritual recitation of liturgical texts by a specially trained precentor (*ḥazzan*; see CANTOR). Its roots go back to the music of the ancient Temple, where Levitical choirs chanted antiphonal and responsorial songs. The first use of the term (in Hebrew) was a pejorative ninth-century reference to the practice of adding elaborately sung religious poetry (*piyyutim*) to the worship service. The rendering of these liturgical poems became increasingly popular during the Middle Ages, requiring the talents of an expert soloist; as the expectation grew that the singer himself would extemporaneously compose new *piyyutim*, the task became reserved for a specially trained cadre of performers, *ḥazzanim*. Some *piyyutim* had specific melodies composed for them (or compiled from other sources, including older *piyyutim* whose texts had fallen out of favor), but it also fell to the *ḥazzan* to chant other sections of the service utilizing a system of **nussaḥ*. The *ḥazzan* rendered a text, ordinarily combining fixed series of musical motives with passages freely improvised within the parameters of a particular scale. In this era, long before published prayer books, cantorial music helped worshipers and *ḥazzanim* alike recall the proper texts, and the chanting of liturgical passages according to their accepted melodies became obligatory. A variety of these musical traditions evolved among separate Ashkenazi, Sephardi, and 'Adot ha-Mizraḥ communities, all containing specific themes that help to identify the section of the service being chanted and even the specific occasion on which the prayers are being offered. In the Sephardi and 'Adot ha-Mizraḥ communities, quasi-liturgical hymns associated with holiday and life-cycle celebrations were also included in the body of traditional cantorial music and were generally sung in a similar (if somewhat more elaborate) manner. Notwithstanding the level of musical interest generated by these complex systems, cantorial music always took its cues from the text, which remained of primary importance.

Since the nineteenth century, some Ashkenazi communities, influenced by the Western culture surrounding them, have rejected the limiting assumptions associated with traditional cantorial music in favor of freer assimilation of external musical practices. In particular, operatic conventions gave birth to the hazzanic recitative and a golden age of *ḥazzanut*, during which talented cantor–composers chanted their new brand of cantorial music both in the synagogue and on the concert stage, sometimes accompanied by a *choir. On the other hand, Reform synagogues replaced the Eastern-based idea of *nussaḥ* with German hymn tunes sung in four-part harmony to *organ accompaniment. As the synagogue service has adapted to the needs of contemporary worshipers, congregational melodies, in some cases adhering to the traditional *nussaḥ*, while in other cases ignoring it entirely, have again changed the face of cantorial music. See also MUSIC.

• Abraham Z. Idelsohn, *Jewish Music in Its Historical Development* (New York, 1929; repr. 1967, 1992). Eric Werner, *A Voice Still Heard: The Sacred Songs of the Ashkenazic Jews* (University Park, Pa., 1976). Max Wohl-

berg, "The Hazzanic Recitative," *Musica Judaica* 10.1 (1987–1988): 40–51.
—MARSHA BRYAN EDELMAN

CAPITAL PUNISHMENT. Although biblical law specifies the death penalty for various types of crime, this form of punishment was rarely carried out. Rabbinic interpretation of biblical law made it almost impossible to sentence a person to death: two witnesses to the crime were required to come forward, and the perpetrator had to be given specific warning about the gravity of the act and the punishment it carried prior to his actually committing the crime. Thus the death penalty came in time to be no more than an indication of the seriousness of a sin. Indeed, a court that over a period of seventy years condemned a single person to death was considered by some rabbis of the Talmud to be a "bloodthirsty" court (*Mak*. 1.10). The offenses for which biblical law ordered the death penalty were murder; adultery, incest, and certain other sexual sins; blasphemy; idolatry; desecration of the Sabbath; witchcraft; kidnaping; and striking or dishonoring one's parents. Bodies of those executed were publicly exhibited until nightfall (*Dt*. 21.22–23). Capital cases could be tried only by a *beit din* of at least twenty-three judges. Methods of execution were stoning, burning, slaying with a sword, and strangulation, depending upon the crime. Strangulation was the method of execution in all cases where the manner of capital punishment was not specifically described in the Bible (*San*. 52b, 89a). Hanging was not permitted as a method of execution, and the reference to hanging in *Deuteronomy* 21.22 is interpreted as meaning exposure after death, to be imposed in the case of idolaters and blasphemers. Stoning in biblical times consisted of the people throwing stones at the convicted person until death resulted (cf. *Lv*. 24.23), but according to later rabbinic interpretation, stoning should take the form of throwing the guilty person from an elevation. The rabbinic definition of burning (forcing a hot wick, later taken to mean molten metal [*San*. 7.2] down the throat of the condemned individual) also differs from what is ordinarily meant by the term, though the Sadducees disagreed with the Pharisees about this question. There is no record of the application of this method of execution. Long before the destruction of the Temple, Roman authorities denied the Sanhedrin the right to impose capital punishment on sinners. Rare cases of capital punishment decreed by Jewish courts, usually against informers, are mentioned, however, in the literature of the Middle Ages. In the State of Israel, capital punishment has been abolished except for the crimes of genocide and wartime treason (and has only been applied in the case of Adolf Eichmann).

• Herman Schulz, *Das Todesrecht im Alten Testament*, Beiheft zur Zeitschrift fur die Altestamentliche Wissenschaft, vol. 114 (Berlin, 1969).

CAPTIVES. The Bible makes no provision for the treatment of captives taken by Israelites, with the exception of the laws concerning the marriage of an Israelite and a captive woman (*Dt*. 21.10–14). The Talmud and other Jewish sources did, however, concern themselves with the very real problems facing Jews in captivity. The rabbis regarded captivity in foreign lands as worse than death or famine (*B. B*. 8b). Consequently the ransoming of captives was regarded as the most sacred duty a Jew could fulfill, taking precedence over all other forms of benevolence or charity (see RANSOM). One was permitted to use money originally collected for another cause in order to provide the necessary funds, and even a Torah scroll could be sold to raise money to ransom captives (*tosafot* on *B. B*. 8b). A woman taken into captivity by foreign soldiers took precedence over a man when it came to ransom, but she was, upon her release, barred from marrying into the priesthood; if she was the wife of a priest, she had to be divorced. The extreme lengths to which Jewish communities were willing to go in order to redeem their brethren forced up the ransom price of Jewish captives, and as a measure of self-protection, an enactment was promulgated forbidding the ransoming of a captive at a price higher than the normal value, except under exceptional circumstances (*Git*. 45a). Among the notable captives in Jewish history is *Mosheh ben Ḥanokh (10th cent.), who was taken by a Moorish pirate in the Mediterranean. Ransomed by the Cordova community, he later laid the foundations for the study of the Talmud in Spain. When R. *Me'ir ben Barukh of Rothenburg (13th cent.) was imprisoned by Emperor Rudolf I and held for ransom in Alsace, he refused to allow his community to provide the necessary funds for his release, lest it encourage the authorities to blackmail other communities by imprisoning and holding their rabbis for ransom.

• Ya'akov Blidstein, "The Redemption of Captives in Halakhic Tradition: Problems and Policy," in *Organizing Rescue: National Jewish Solidarity in the Modern Period*, edited by S. Troen et al. (London, 1992), pp. 20–30. Menachem Elon, *Jewish Law: History, Sources, Principles*, 4 vols. (Philadelphia, 1994).

CARCASS (Heb. *nevelah*), the body of an animal that died other than by valid *ritual slaughter (*sheḥitah*) or as prey of a wild beast. A carcass may not be eaten but is to be given to a resident alien or sold to a non-Jew (*Dt*. 15.21; *Pes*. 21b). One who touches or eats a piece of carcass contracts ritual impurity (*Lv*. 11.39–40). These laws apply both to animals that are normally permitted as food and to those that are forbidden. A limb torn from a living animal (**eiver min ha-ḥai*) is also considered a carcass.

CARDOSO FAMILY, a family of Spanish *conversos*.

Isaac Cardoso (1604–1683), physician and scholar. He was born in Portugal to a *converso* family that moved to Spain in order to ameliorate its living conditions. Cardoso was raised in Spain, educated at the universities of Salamanca and Valladolid, and for almost five decades lived as a nominal Christian. After a brilliant academic career at Valladolid, he moved to Madrid, where he gained access to its social and intellectual life and published several literary and scientific books. He eventually rose to court physician. In 1648, at the height of his fame, he suddenly left Spain for Italy together with his much younger brother, Avraham Miguel, probably out of fear of the Inquisition. Cardoso first settled in Venice as a professing Jew, where he wrote and published *Philosophia libera* (1673), his *magnum opus*. Later, he settled in Verona as physician of the ghetto. Like most of the former *conversos* he adopted the messianic enthusiasm of the Shabbatean movement. However, after *Shabbetai Tsevi converted to Islam, Isaac strongly disagreed with his brother, who fervently continued to support the movement and severed their relations. Cardoso defended Jews and Judaism in his famous work *Las excelencias y calumnias de los Hebreos* (Amsterdam, 1679), in which he refuted accusations against the Jews found in classical and contemporary literature, praising their merits and their contributions to the countries in which they resided.

Avraham Miguel Cardoso (1626–1706), Shabbatean leader; brother of Isaac. Born in Rio Secco, Spain, he studied theology and perhaps also medicine in a Spanish university. He escaped in 1648 to Venice, Italy, where he openly professed his Judaism. After several years in Leghorn and Cairo, he settled in Tripoli as the bey's physician. In 1655 he became a fervent follower of Shabbetai Tsevi, persisting in his belief even after the "Messiah's" apostasy. Cardoso became an active propagandist of the messianic movement, traveling between Italy, Tunis, Constantinople, Smyrna, Gallipoli, Adrianople, Chios, Crete, and Rodosto. In 1703 he tried to settle in Safed but was prevented from doing so by the spiritual leaders in the Holy Land. He was excommunicated in almost all of the communities in which he stayed and was eventually expelled from them. Finally, he reached Alexandria, where he was killed by his nephew during a family quarrel.

Although Cardoso headed a small Shabbatean sect, he was recognized and venerated by the believers as one of the three major leaders beside the "Messiah" and Natan of Gaza. He vehemently opposed the apostates, except Shabbetai Tsevi, and railed against the attempts to apotheosize the "Messiah" and against the antinomian trends within the movement. He also attacked the Christian Trinity, regarding it as a distortion of the true secret of divinity. Toward the end of his days, Cardoso referred to himself as "Messiah ben Joseph," claiming his role was to reveal to the "Messiah ben David" (Shabbetai Tsevi) the secret of divinity, which had been forgotten during the course of the long *galut* (exile), the knowledge of which is a precondition for the redemption to come. For this purpose, Cardoso wrote more than sixty *derushim* (tractates), which were disseminated in many communities. His distinction between the "First Cause," accepted by all people in every age as the supreme divinity, and the God of Israel, who emanated from the "First Cause," does not indicate, according to Cardoso, any ontological dichotomy between them but rather the limited ability of the human intellect to apprehend the supreme phase of the divine. In fact, it is the God of Israel, the internal soul of the divinity, who is to be worshiped. His views reflect his Neoplatonic education, and his support of the metaphoric interpretative school of Lurianic Kabbalah was also inspired by his academic education.

• **Isaac Cardoso:** Yosef Hayim Yerushalmi, *From Spanish Court to Italian Ghetto* (New York, 1971). **Avraham Miguel Cardoso:** Y. I. Liebes, "Miguel Cardoso meḥabro shel sefer Raza' de-Mehemanuta' ha-Meyuḥas le-Shabbetai Tsevi," *Kiryat Sefer* 55 (1980): 603–613. Gershom Gerhard Scholem, "Ḥadashot li-Yedi'at Abraham Cardoso," in *Abhandlungen zur Erinnerung an Hirsch Perez Chajes* (Vienna, 1933), pp. 324–350. Nissim Yosha, "Ha-Reqa' ha-Filosofi le-Te'olog Shabbetai: Qavvim le-Havanat Torat ha-'Elohut shel Abraham Miguel Cardoso," in *Galut Aḥar Golah*, edited by Aaron Mirksy, Avraham Grossman, and Yosef Kaplan (Jerusalem, 1988), pp. 541–572.

—NISSIM YOSHA

CARO, YOSEF. See KARO, YOSEF.

CASPI, YOSEF BEN ABBA' MARI (1279–1340), southern French commentator and philosopher. Caspi wrote a commentary on Maimonides' *Guide of the Perplexed*; commentaries on the Bible, stressing literal interpretations of the text; and books on Hebrew grammar. Some of his philosophical conclusions (such as arguing for the eternity of the universe) and his naturalistic explanations of biblical miracles were condemned as heretical by many rabbinical authorities. In a testament to his son, Caspi gives a program of studies for the young that reflects his intellectual universe. Alongside traditional Jewish learning, such as Bible and Talmud, his curriculum includes arithmetic, geometry, astronomy, ethics (especially the Mishnaic tractate *Avot* with Maimonides' commentaries), logic, theology, Aristotle's *Metaphysics*, and the *Guide* of Maimonides.

• Isaiah Dimant, "Exegesis, Philosophy and Language in the Writing of Joseph ibn Caspi," Ph.D. dissertation, University of California at Los Angeles, 1979. Basil Herring, *Joseph ibn Kaspi's Gevia Kesef: A Study in Medieval Jewish Philosophic Bible Commentary* (New York, 1982).

—FRANCISCO MORENO CARVALHO

CASSUTO, UMBERTO (1883–1951), Italian-born Israeli Bible scholar. An ordained rabbi, Cassuto devoted the earlier part of his career to research on Italian-Jewish history. From 1939 until his death, he taught Bible at the Hebrew University of Jerusalem. He was one of the early pioneers in Ugaritic studies, demonstrating the many links and contrasts between ancient Canaanite and biblical literature. Cassuto was particularly interested in the composition of the *Book of Genesis*. According to the documentary hypothesis, *Genesis* was a clumsy composite of three distinctive written sources; Cassuto, on the other hand, highlighted the literary artistry that drew together an epic substratum along with various oral traditions into a unified whole. Two of Cassuto's major works are *Biblical and Oriental Studies*, translated from the Hebrew and Italian by I. Abrahams (Jerusalem, 1973 and 1975); and *A Commentary on the Book of Genesis*, translated from the Hebrew by I. Abrahams (Jerusalem, 1961 and 1964).

• Haim Beinart, ed., *Jews in Italy: Studies Dedicated to the Memory of U. Cassuto on the 100th Anniversary of His Birth* (Jerusalem, 1988), includes bibliography.

—DAVID A. GLATT-GILAD

CASTRATION. The Hebrews were one of the few nations of antiquity to enact a religious prohibition against the emasculation of men and even animals. Originally the biblical interdict only stipulated the exclusion of castrated animals from serving as sacrifices on the altar (*Lv.* 22.24) and of him "that is crushed or maimed in his privy parts" from entering "into the assembly of the Lord," that is, from marrying within the Jewish congregation (*Dt.* 23.2; *Shab.* 110b–111a). In the Talmud and codes, the prohibition is extended to include any impairment of the male reproductive organs in domestic animals, beasts, or birds, as well as in man, in addition to the castration of a person who is already impotent (*Shab.* 110b). It is suggested that this is a universal prohibition included in the Noahic laws (*San.* 56b).

The problems that this raised for animal husbandry are discussed in halakhic literature (see STERILIZATION).

• Mark M. Dvorzetsky, *Europah on Kindler* (Tel Aviv, 1961), on Nazis and castration. Schneir Levin, "Jacob's Limp," *Judaism* 44 (Summer 1995): 325–327.

CASUISTRY. See PILPUL.

CATACOMBS, subterranean burial vaults. This method of *burial is thought to have originated in Jewish Palestine, and detailed descriptions of it are given in the Talmud. It was usual for bodies to be placed in sarcophagi and then after a year for the bones to be put in smaller ossuaries that were inserted in vaults in the catacombs. Six specifically Jewish catacombs have been discovered in Rome (where the system was adopted by Christians), and they contain such characteristic Jewish symbols as the seven-branched candelabrum, the *lulav*, and the *etrog*; the inscriptions are in Greek and Latin, with some in Hebrew. Examples of this method of burial can be seen in the Herodian family sepulcher and the graves of the Sanhedrin in Jerusalem, as well as in the extensive array of second-, third-, and fourth-century sepulchers at *Beit She'arim used by Jews from all parts of the Middle East.

• Harry J. Leon, *The Jews of Ancient Rome* (Philadelphia, 1960). Leonard V. Rutgers, *The Jews of Late Ancient Rome: Evidence of Cultural Interaction in the Roman Diaspora* (Leiden, 1995).

CATECHISM, a compendium of instruction, mostly in the form of questions and answers, designed for children and uneducated persons. It was especially favored as a means of instruction for prospective proselytes. The earliest known example of a catechism is contained in the *Didache*, a Christian manual of instruction for converts dating probably from the second century; that catechism was originally a Jewish manual of instruction later adapted for Christian use. As a rule, Jewish religious instruction focused on the study of the basic texts—Bible, Mishnah, and Talmud—and the use of catechismal literature was discouraged. *Leqaḥ Tov*, by Avraham Jagel of Venice (1587), one of the first catechisms introduced into Jewish literature, went through a number of editions, but the author's hope for its use as a textbook in schools was never fulfilled. Since the Emancipation, scores of such manuals have been published and were particularly favored by Reform Judaism in the nineteenth century. Question-and-answer handbooks setting forth rules of circumcision and ritual slaughter (*sheḥitah*) have been common.

• E. Schreiber, in *Jewish Encyclopedia* (1903), vol. 3, pp. 621–624.

CATHOLIC CHURCH. See ROMAN CATHOLIC CHURCH.

CELIBACY. The idea that a person ought not to marry is entirely foreign to Judaism. The opening phrase in the major code of matrimonial law leaves no doubt as to the obligation to marry and raise children: "Every man is obliged to marry in order to fulfil the duty of procreation, and whoever is not engaged in propagating the race is accounted as if he shed blood, diminishing the divine image and causing his presence to depart from Israel" (*Shulḥan 'Arukh, Even ha-'Ezer* 1.1). Only one exception to this rule is recognized by the Talmud, and that is the case of an individual such as Ben 'Azzai whose "soul was bound up with the Torah and is constantly occupied with it" (Maimonides, *Laws of Marriage* 15.3). Not only is matrimony regarded as the ideal state of existence, but an unmarried person is debarred from high religious and judicial office. Both high priests and judges in capital cases must be married, and single men are, in principle, unfit to act as synagogue readers (*Yoma'* 1.1; *San.* 36b; *Shulḥan 'Arukh, Oraḥ Ḥayyim* 53.9). No Jewish moralist has ever encouraged celibacy, and in this respect, there is a marked difference between Jewish values and those of Christianity.

• David Feldman, *Marital Relations, Birth Control, and Abortion in Jewish Law* (New York, 1974), pp. 21–45. Eliezer Berkovits, *Crisis and Faith* (New York, 1976), pp. 48–81. Eugene Borowitz, "Reading the Jewish Tradition on Marital Sexuality," *Journal of Reform Judaism* 29 (1982): 1–15.

—DANIEL SINCLAIR

CEMETERY. Even the smallest of Jewish communities had their own cemetery or at least a designated section of a non-Jewish cemetery set aside for the *burial of the dead. It is the community's responsibility to see that there is a proper burial place for the indigent or for unclaimed bodies (*meit mitsvah*). Various names for a cemetery are used in the Bible and in Jewish tradition, such as "the house of graves" (*Neh.* 11.3), "the house of eternity," and the euphemistic "house of the living" (based on *Jb.* 30.23). Since dead bodies and graves are a source of ritual impurity, the cemetery is usually situated beyond town limits. The cemetery is also invested with a certain sanctity, and any activity therein that might tend to show disregard for the dead, such as eating or drinking, is forbidden. Out of respect for the dead, individuals should not walk on graves, except where it is impossible to get from one grave to another. A new cemetery is dedicated with a special service. While it is the practice to bury only Jews in a Jewish cemetery, cemeteries owned by Reform congregations permit the non-Jewish spouse of a member to be buried in the family plot. It is the usual practice to bury husband and wife next to each other. Frequently, a cemetery contains buildings for the performance of burial rites (see TOHORAH). In some cases, graves were allotted in strict rotation, conforming to the notion of death as the great leveler; however, priests are usually interred in plots accessible to relatives, and a group of graves can be obtained to serve as family plots. In North America, it is the almost universal custom for individuals and families to purchase specific plots in advance. In some cemeteries, special sections are set aside for people to be honored. Suicides as well as apostates and individuals of evil repute are buried outside the line of graves, near the cemetery wall. According to Jewish law, however, this discriminatory practice does not apply in the case of a suicide of unsound mind. Since that is the usual verdict today, the regulation is largely disregarded. It is customary to visit a grave on the anniversary of death, on fast days, during the month of Elul, and on the eve of Yom Kippur, but the rabbis warned against visiting cemeteries too often and suggested that visits should not be made more than once every thirty days. See also CATACOMBS.

• Hyman Goldin, *Hamadrikh: The Rabbi's Guide* (New York, 1956). Jules Harlow, ed., *Liqqutei Tefillah: A Rabbi's Manual* (New York, 1965). Isaac Klein, *A Guide to Jewish Religious Practice* (New York, 1992). Maurice Lamm, *The Jewish Way in Death and Mourning* (New York, 1969). David Polish, ed., *Maglei Tsedeq: A Rabbi's Manual*, with notes by W. Gunther Plaut (New York, 1988). Tzvi Rabinowicz, *A Guide to Life: Jewish Laws and Customs of Mourning* (London, 1964).

—PETER KNOBEL

CENSORSHIP of Hebrew books for the purpose of removing words or passages considered offensive to *Christianity was undertaken from time to time during the Middle Ages on the instructions of government or church authority, and the practice continued until the end of the czarist regime. The earliest example followed the Disputation of *Barcelona when Jews in Aragon were ordered to expunge all passages from Hebrew books regarded as objectionable. At its most extreme, Christian censorship of Jewish books resulted in the burning of all copies of the Talmud and other works (see BOOKS, BURNING OF; TALMUD, BURNING OF THE). More generally it consisted of orders to replace such words as **goy* (gentile) with *Samaritan* or *idolater* (to show that the reference was not to Christians) or to delete complete passages. For example, whole passages that referred to Christianity (as well as Islam) as a relative advance—although based on error—toward the acknowledgment by the entire world of the sovereignty of God were extensively expurgated from the last chapter of Maimonides' *Mishneh Torah*. The papal bull of 1554, allowing Jews to possess only those books that were not considered blasphemous, signaled the systematic censorship of Jewish books in Italy; as a result of this censorship, which was often undertaken by Jewish apostates, all passages regarded as hostile or contradictory to Christian doctrines were blacked out. In 1595 the Catholic church instituted the *Index expurgatorius* of Hebrew books. Censors blacked out passages in thousands of Hebrew books, while many Hebrew classics were placed on the general *Index* of banned books. In the nineteenth century, government censorship in eastern Europe was applied to Hebrew and Yiddish literature, and Hasidic works in particular were destroyed.

Rabbinic law prohibits the Jew from reading heretical or immoral books (cf. *San.* 100b). To ensure that a book contained no objectionable material, the custom arose of fixing *approbations by eminent rabbis to printed works; this prevented the expression of heterodox views. In 1554, Italian rabbis established a system of self-censorship aimed at anticipating church censorship, an example that was followed in other countries. One case of self-censorship was the deletion by Ashkenazi Jews of a sentence from the *ʿAleinu prayer in the face of (unjustified) allegations that the passage in question was meant as a disparagement of Jesus. Books were banned because they were considered erotic or because they contained legal decisions regarded as incorrect. Censorship was also a tool in ideological struggles, for example, between Ḥasidim and Mitnaggedim, or in the Orthodox fight against Reform. Another form of self-censorship was practiced by some philosophical and kabbalistic authors, who feared that their at times audacious doctrines might be misunderstood or even lead to heresy.

• Charles Berlin, *Hebrew Printing and Bibliography* (New York, 1976), pp. 199–241. Abraham Berliner, *Censur und Confiscation Hebraischer Bücher im Kirchenstaate* (Frankfurt, 1891). Arlen Blyum, "Hebrew Publications and the Soviet Censor in the 1920's," *East European Jewish Affairs* 23 (1993): 91–99. Moshe Carmilly, *Censorship and Freedom of Expression in Jewish History* (New York, 1977). Moshe Carmilly, "Jewish Writers Confronted by Censorship in the Habsburg Empire and Romania in the 18th–19th Centuries," *Studia Judaica* 2 (1993): 18–35. Ismar Elbogen, *Jewish Liturgy: A Comprehensive History*, translated by Raymond P. Scheindlin (Philadelphia, New York, and Jerusalem, 1993), pp. 284–285. William Popper, *The Censorship of Hebrew Books* (New York, 1899; repr. 1968). M. T. Walton and P. J. Walton, "In Defense of the Church Militant: The Censorship of the Rashi Commentary in the Magna Biblia Rabbinica," *Sixteenth Century Journal* 21 (1990): 385–400.

CENSUS. Possible census records from the ancient Near East are related to taxes, military conscription, and land apportionment. The Bible reports instances in which the entire population of Israel was enumerated (*2 Sm.* 24; *1 Chr.* 21); instances in which all males of military age were enumerated (*Nm.* 1–4, 26); and several cases in which armed forces were counted before battle (*Jos.* 8.10–12; *1 Sm.* 11.8, 13.15, 15.4, 17.5, 18.1; *1 Kgs.* 20.15, 20.26–27; *2 Kgs.* 3.6; *2 Chr.* 25.5).

The first census of Israelites, taken at the foot of Mount Sinai, was held in the second year after the Exodus (*Nm.* 1.1–2). The second census, taken in the Plains of Moab, was carried out in the fortieth year. Since entry into Canaan was to have occurred immediately after departing from Sinai, both censuses served the dual purpose of preparing the camp for the wars of conquest as well as enumerating the population for dividing up the land. Because the numbers of Israelites recorded in these censuses seem so large, modern scholars have proposed nonliteral interpretations, such as translating the word *elef* as military unit rather than one thousand. These explanations seem unlikely.

Jewish authorities hold that biblical censuses were carried out by indirect counting. Each person would give a half-shekel in silver; the total weight of all silver collected would be multiplied by two, and the resulting number would be equal to the total population. This was to avoid direct enumeration of the people and prevent disasters, which, it was feared, might occur as a result (*Ex.* 30.11–16). However, it is more likely that the desert censuses were conducted by registering the names of individuals and then counting the names, a method that would also have avoided a direct count of the people.

The taking of a census was regarded as a source of bad luck. David incurred divine wrath and a plague when counting the Israelites (*2 Sm.* 24.1; *1 Chr.* 21, 27.24). Traditional authorities attribute this to the fact that David's census was not authorized and served no purpose other than royal conceit. To prevent plagues from occurring when censuses were carried out, a poll tax was levied to ransom the lives of the enumerees. A fear of censuses may be rooted in ancient beliefs that numbering implied limiting or control (cf. *Hos.* 2.1). It has also been suggested that since censuses were associated with military activity, and that many of the people counted in a military muster would not return from battle alive, the very act of counting people induced fear. Certain Jews are still reluctant to be counted in censuses, and until recently some Orthodox Jews in Israel would not participate in censuses. When gathering the ten men needed for a **minyan*, it is customary to count not with numbers but according to a verse with ten words, such as *Psalms* 28.9, or, popularly, by the fiction of counting negatives, as in "not one, not two. . . . "

• Avigdor (Victor) Hurowitz, "How Were the Israelites Counted?: Numbers 1:2 and the Like in Light of a New Ostracon from Tel 'Ira," *Beer-Sheva* 3 (1989): 53–62. A. Mandansky, "On Biblical Censuses," *Journal of Official Statistics* 2 (1986): 561–569. Ernest Neufeld, "The Sins of the Census," *Judaism* 43 (1994): 196–204.

–VICTOR HUROWITZ

CENTRAL CONFERENCE OF AMERICAN RABBIS (CCAR), organization of Reform rabbis in the United States and Canada, with members in other parts of the world. Founded in 1889 by Isaac Mayer *Wise, by 1994 it had a membership of over a thousand six hundred rabbis, with a constantly growing proportion of women. The CCAR publishes prayer books for Reform congregations (*Gates of Prayer* for Sabbaths and weekdays, and *Gates of Repentance* for the High Holy Days) and has produced hymnals, Pesaḥ Haggadahs, and a rabbi's manual. In the early part of the twentieth century, the conference adopted a critical attitude toward Jewish nationalism, despite the fervent pro-Zionist position of such prominent members as Stephen S. *Wise and Abba Hillel Silver. This course was sharply reversed in the 1930s when the conference adopted a pro-Zionist stand, at the same time returning to Hebrew in the service and promoting a more positive attitude toward ritual in the synagogue and in family life. The CCAR has always upheld the separation of church and state in America and also in the State of Israel. The conference publishes an annual *Yearbook* (of which over one hundred volumes have appeared and have been cumulatively indexed). Conference headquarters are in New York City. See also UNION OF AMERICAN HEBREW CONGREGATIONS.

CEREAL OFFERING. See MEAL OFFERING.

CEREMONIAL OBJECTS. Many types of appurtenances have been crafted for use in ritual ceremonies. Some are essential to the ritual; others are used to beautify the religious practice. The precept of *hiddur mitsvah* (beautification of the commandment), requiring the performance of religious commandments in a beautiful way (*Shab.* 133b), is based on the verse "this is my Lord and I will beautify him" (*Ex.* 15.2). Decorated instruments (knives, shields, medicine bottles) are often used by the *mohel* performing ritual circumcisions. At the Pidyon ha-Ben ceremony, the infant is placed on a tray; silver examples of such trays frequently depict the *'aqedah*. Decorated ceremonial objects associated with weddings include the *ḥuppah* (canopy) under which the ceremony takes place, special cups (often interlocking), rings, and ornamented *ketubbot* (marriage contracts). Water vessels, combs, and nail-cleaning implements for use in ritually cleansing a corpse are often ornamented with inscriptions or imagery related to death. Many objects are associated with Sabbath meals, including Qiddush cups and various objects related to the *ḥallah* (plates, knives, covers). Special lamps or candlesticks are used for kindling the Sabbath lights; the star-shaped hanging lamp known as a *Judenstern* was popular. Plates, cups, candleholders, and spice containers are used in the Havdalah ceremony, which concludes the Sabbath. In Ashkenazi communities, tower-shaped spice containers, echoing central European architecture, are very common, as are fruit- and flower-shaped containers. Inscribed, decorated shofars were used in some communities on Ro'sh ha-Shanah. Decorative containers, frequently of silver, are used to store the *etrog* on Sukkot. Ḥanukkah lamps are essential to the celebration of the holiday. There are two basic types of Ḥanukkah *menorot*: eight-branched lamps resembling the seven-branched Menorah of the Tabernacle and Temple; and bench-type lamps, with eight lights arranged along a slightly elevated horizontal surface, frequently with a decorative backplate. *Esther* scrolls, read on Purim, are often ornamented with decorative borders or illustrations, or are housed in ornamental cases. Also associated with Purim are decorative noisemakers and plates for sending gifts (*mishloaḥ manot*). Decorative vessels are often used for the foods of the Pesaḥ Seder: wine cups and decanters; *matsah* covers or bags; and plates (often three-tiered) or containers to hold the ceremonial foods. Ceremonial cups (for Sabbath or festival Qiddush, circumcision, weddings, Elijah, etc.) are sometimes modeled after sumptuous, contemporary wine vessels. In Islamic countries, where the consumption of alcohol was prohibited, Jewish ceremonial cups were often modeled after Western examples. Ceremonial objects often stylistically resemble secular artifacts crafted of the same material or having a parallel function in the same locale and period, and often incorporate local decorative motifs and approaches. Objects originally crafted for secular use were frequently adapted for ceremonial purposes. See also ART; SYNAGOGUE; TORAH ORNAMENTS.

• Chaya Benjamin, "The Sephardic Journey: 500 Years of Jewish Ceremonial Objects," in *The Sephardic Journey, 1492–1992* (New York, 1992), exhibition catalogue. Joseph Gutmann, *Jewish Ceremonial Art* (New York, 1968). Stephen Kayser, ed., *Jewish Ceremonial Art: A Guide to the Appreciation of the Art Objects Used in Synagogue and Home*, 2d ed. (Philadelphia, 1959). Barbara Kirschenblatt-Gimblett, *Fabric of Jewish Life: Textiles from the Jewish Museum Collection* (New York, 1977). Mordecai Narkiss, *Menorat ha-Ḥanukkah* (Jerusalem, 1939). Cecil Roth, ed., *Jewish Art: An Illustrated History* (London, 1961). Isaiah Shachar, *Jewish Tradition in Art: The Feuchtwanger Collection of Judaica*, translated and edited by R. Grafman (Jerusalem, 1981). Jay Weinstein, *A Collector's Guide to Judaica* (New York, 1985).

–GABRIEL M. GOLDSTEIN

CHAJES, TSEVI HIRSCH (1805–1855), Galician rabbi and author. He was appointed rabbi of the prestigious community of Zólkiew in 1828, where he came under the influence of Naḥman Krochmal, head of the community at that time, and other moderate Maskilim. In his writings and in his public activities, Chajes took a unique and often lonely stance, identifying neither with the Maskilim nor the Ḥasidim. Although he agreed with many of the demands of the Maskilim for changes in Jewish life (for example, he supported calls for Jews to engage in agriculture and presented himself for examinations in secular knowledge, the only traditional rabbi to do so), Chajes remained a staunch defender of tradition. His relations with Hasidic leaders and the Hasidic masses were mixed. Leading rabbis differed with his critical approach to traditional texts, while Maskilim found his approach too moderate and apologetic. A move to the rabbinate of Kalisz in 1852 brought Chajes no respite. He encountered severe opposition from local Ḥasidim and the suspicion of Russian officialdom. His works include *Torat Nevi'im* (1836), on the eternity of Torah and the principles of the written and oral Torah; *Iggeret Biqoret* (1853), studies on the Targum and Midrash and their history; *Mevo' ha-Talmud* (1845), an introduction to the Talmud outlining the history of the oral law (translated into English as *Student's Guide through the Talmud* [London, 1952; New York, 1960]); and *Darkhei ha-Hora'ah* (1842), on the principles for deciding matters of Jewish law. His collected works were published in two volumes (*Kol Sifrei Maharat Chajes* [Jerusalem, 1958]).

• Israel David Bet-Halevi, *Rabbi Tsevi Hirsh Ḥayes* (Tel Aviv, 1956). Meir Hershkovitz, *Maharats Ḥayot: Toledot Rabbi Tsevi Hirsh Ḥayot u-Mishnato* (Jerusalem, 1972). —GERSHON BACON

CHANGE OF NAME. See NAMES.

CHAPLAINS. The appointment of chaplains in the military is a comparatively recent innovation, although the "priest anointed for war"—a Talmudic term for the priest referred to in *Deuteronomy* 20.2—could possibly be regarded as a prototype. The first Jewish military chaplains in the United States were appointed in 1862 during the Civil War. The National Jewish Welfare Board's chaplains' committee first organized the chaplaincy in the United States during World War I. It published special prayer books and other publications for Jews in the armed forces. During World War II, there were 311 Jewish chaplains in the U.S. military. The first Jewish chaplain to the British Army was officially appointed in 1892. Jewish chaplains have also served in other countries, including France, Italy, and Germany. With the establishment of the State of Israel, a chief rabbi was appointed to the Israeli army with the rank of *aluf-mishneh* (lieutenant colonel). A chaplain is attached to each brigade and a chaplain-sergeant to each battalion. The Israeli chaplaincy has published a unified prayer book for use by all Israeli soldiers. Rabbis may also serve as chaplains in hospitals and nursing homes.

• Louis Barish, ed., *Rabbis in Uniform: The Story of the American Jewish Military Chaplain* (New York, 1962). Bertram W. Korn, *Centennial of the Jewish Chaplaincy in the United States, 1862–1962* (New York, 1963). I. Slomovitz, "The Fighting Rabbis: A History of Jewish Military Chaplains, 1860–1945," Ph.D. dissertation, Loyola University, Chicago, 1995.

CHARIOT MYSTICISM. See MA'ASEH MERKAVAH.

CHARITY. The Hebrew word *tsedaqah*, which in the Bible refers to any kind of righteous conduct, is limited in the Talmud to one aspect of *righteousness, namely, the giving of alms or assistance to the poor through material gifts. For all other acts of benevolence or kindness the phrase **gemilut ḥesed* (or *ḥasadim*) is employed, and the distinction between the two types is defined by the following passage: "In three respects *gemilut ḥasadim* is superior to *tsedaqah*. *Tsedaqah* can be performed only with one's material possessions, *gemilut ḥasadim* both in kind and in personal service. *Tsedaqah* can be given only to the poor, *gemilut ḥasadim* to both rich and poor. *Tsedaqah* can be performed only for the living, *gemilut ḥasadim* for the living and the dead" (*Suk.* 49b). Although *gemilut ḥasadim* has "no fixed measure" and is one of the three pillars upon which the world stands (*Avot* 1.2), the rabbis nevertheless extol the virtue of *tsedaqah*, in the simple sense of almsgiving, as one of the greatest of good deeds. Together with prayer and atonement, it can avert an evil fate divinely decreed for the coming year on Ro'sh ha-Shanah. The practice of *tsedaqah* is enjoined throughout the Bible: "You shall open your hand wide to your brother, to the poor and the needy in your land" (*Dt.* 15.11); "He that has pity on the poor lends to the Lord" (*Ps.* 19.17); and the righteous man is one who is "father to the poor" (*Jb.* 29.15). Provision for those in want has at all times been regarded as a sacred duty. The very use of the word *tsedaqah*, which is derived from the Hebrew word for justice, shows that the relief of poverty is a matter of duty—an assessment upon the rich for the benefit of the poor—and not voluntary philanthropy. It is for this reason that the rendering of *tsedaqah* as charity—which implies an act of pure and unrequited benevolence—is incorrect. The duty of *tsedaqah* will never end as long as "the poor shall not cease out of the land" (*Dt.* 15.11), and the prophet enjoins us to "deal your bread to the hungry, and that you bring the poor that are cast out to your house. When you see the naked man cover him, that you do not hide yourself from your own flesh" (*Is.* 58.7). The rabbis lay great stress upon the spirit in which *tsedaqah* is given, rather than upon the act of giving or the amount involved. Referring to *Deuteronomy* 15.11, they demand not only that "you shall surely give to him" but that "your heart shall not be grieved when you give to him"; the reward for *tsedaqah* is directly related to the measure of kindness in it. Hillel, in giving *tsedaqah*, took into consideration the standard of living to which the recipient had been accustomed before falling upon evil days, and even provided one unfortunate with a horse and servant (*Ket.* 67b). *Tsedaqah* should represent at least a tenth of one's income (see TITHES) but should not exceed 20 percent, lest the giver lapse into penury (*Ket.* 50a). Under no circumstances is a male recipient to be put to shame by having the alms given to him in public, while giving alms to a female secretly is frowned upon by some authorities, lest suspicion be cast on her character (*Ḥag.* 5a). The highest form of almsgiving is when the donor and recipient are ignorant of each other's identity. Maimonides (*Hilkhot Mattenot 'Aniyyim* 10.7–18) enumerated eight degrees of *tsedaqah*, ranging from the highest level, rehabilitative *tsedaqah*, to the lowest, *tsedaqah* given with feelings of resentment. Customary forms of *tsedaqah* have included **hakhnasat kallah* (aiding a couple about to be married to obtain the necessary items for setting up a household); **me'ot ḥittim* (supplying the poor with their Pesaḥ needs); the *ransom of captives; and provision for education, soup kitchens, temporary lodgings for poor travelers, hospital services, old-age homes for the needy, and free burial for the indigent.

• Boris David Bogen, *Jewish Philanthropy* (New York, 1917). Lewis J. Prockter, "Alms and the Man: The Merits of Charity," *Journal of Northwest Semitic Languages* 17 (1991): 69–80. Alexander Scheiber, "'Iggerot Kabtsanim min ha-Genizah," in *Hagut 'Ivrit be-'Eiropa*, edited by Menahem Zohary and Aryeh Tartakover (Jerusalem, 1969), pp. 266–275. Paul Spiegel, ed., *Zedaka: Judische Sozialarbeit im Wandel der Zeit: 75 Jahre Zentralwohlfartsstelle der Juden in Deutschland 1917–1992* (Frankfurt am Main, 1992). Efraim Elimelech Urbach, "Megamot Datiyyot ve-Ḥevratiyyot be-Torat ha-Tsedaqah shel Ḥazal," in *Me'Olamam shel Khaḥamim* (Jerusalem, 1988), pp. 97–124. Moshe Weinfeld, "Justice and Righteousness" and "Mishpat u-Tzedakah: The Expression and Its Meaning," in *Justice and Righteousness: Biblical Themes and Their Influence*, edited by Henning Graf Reventlow and Yair Hoffman (Sheffield, Eng., 1992), pp. 228–246. —SHMUEL HIMELSTEIN

CHAZARS. See KHAZARS.

CHERUBIM (Heb. *keruvim*), celestial beings, depicted as winged creatures with both human and animal characteristics. Placed east of Eden after Adam's sin, to prevent further access to the tree of life (*Gn*. 3.24), the cherubim were assigned primarily, according to the Bible, to serve as the seat, or throne, of the *kevod* YHVH, the divine majesty (or presence; see SHEKHINAH). They fulfill this task in two ways: first, by spiriting him from place to place throughout the universe (God is described as riding upon a cherub as he glides through the heavens [*2 Sm*. 22.11; *Ps*. 18.11]; thus, the cherubim symbolize his omnipresence); and second, by bearing him aloft on a throne in his heavenly palace (God is depicted as a king "who sits upon the cherubim" [*Is*. 37.16; *Ps*. 80.2, 99.1]).

The cover of the *Ark of the Covenant, earthly symbol of God's presence, consisted of two golden cherubim with outspread wings, upon which the divine majesty was said to be enthroned in his earthly abode and upon which he was carried (*Ex*. 25.18ff.; *1 Sm*. 4.4; *2 Sm*. 6.2); the cherub motif was also woven into the fabric of the Tabernacle curtains and veil (*Ex*. 26). Likewise, in the inner sanctum of Solomon's Temple, two enormous, self-standing cherubim stood with their wings outstretched over the Ark (*1 Kgs*. 6.23ff.). These earthly cherubim are to be understood as substitutes for the real, heavenly ones, since sculptural representations of the deity were shunned by the Israelite religion. The most explicit description of these heavenly beings is found in Ezekiel's vision of the four-faced cherubim of the divine chariot (see MA'ASEH MERKAVAH). In the prophet's vision, their appearance (*Ez*. 1) and gradual exit from the Temple (*Ez*. 10–11) signify the departure of God from his dwelling, the destruction of the Temple, and the exile of the people. Their promised return (*Ez*. 43) signifies Israel's eventual ingathering and the rebuilding of the Temple. Some aspects of the cherub motif are common to other ancient Near Eastern peoples; the name itself may be related to the Akkadian *kuribu*, a protective spirit with specific nonhuman features.

The cherubim also figure prominently in mystical literature and are identified with God's invisible glory, an emanation of the great fire of the divine presence, and as the model used by God in the creation of man.

• Moshe Greenberg, *Ezekiel 1–20*, The Anchor Bible (Garden City, N.Y., 1983), pp. 51–59, 195–206. Menahem Haran, *Temples and Temple-Service in Ancient Israel* (Oxford, 1979), pp. 246–275. —BARUCH J. SCHWARTZ

CHIEF RABBINATE, an office of preeminence. Since the cessation of the Sanhedrin, there has been no basis in Jewish law for the institution of a chief rabbinate, since in theory every rabbi who has the necessary qualifications possesses spiritual authority equal to that of every other rabbi. Nevertheless, throughout the Common Era it has become the practice in various countries to appoint one rabbi as the spiritual or representative head of the community, to whose authority all other rabbis in his jurisdiction are subject. Three factors contributed to the institution of such an office: the appointment of one man by the civil authorities in order to establish a channel of communication between the government and the Jewish community (see CROWN RABBI); the voluntary acceptance by the Jewish community and its rabbis of one outstanding figure as chief rabbi; and an appointment made by the Jewish community on its own initiative as a necessary consequence of its internal communal organization. In the first category belong the appointments by the kings of Aragon and Castile of district chief rabbis during the Middle Ages, the appointment by the kings of England of archpresbyters, and the appointment by the German emperors of chief rabbis who, in addition to their rabbinic duties, were responsible for the collection of taxes imposed upon the community. Among the titles in use since the Middle Ages for the rabbi filling such a position are **rab de la corte* (Castile), **arraby moor* (Portugal), **Landesrabbiner* (Germany) and **ḥakham bashi* (Turkey). The chief rabbis of France in the years from 1807 to 1906, whose appointments were made by state-controlled consistories first established by Napoléon, belong in a similar category. Examples of chief rabbis in the second category, those chosen for their outstanding merits by the Jewish community, are such medieval figures as R. Shelomoh ben Avraham *Adret (Rashba') of Barcelona, known as El Rab d'España, and R. *Me'ir ben Barukh of Rothenburg (who also belongs to the first category). The chief rabbinate of the British Commonwealth is the most extensive and best-organized example of the third category and has its parallels on a lesser scale in various European countries and in South Africa. In the United States and in Canada the institution is unknown, although there were aborted attempts to institute a chief rabbinate in the United States at the turn of the century. In 1920, the British mandatory authorities in Palestine passed an ordinance instituting a chief rabbinate, an institution that was taken over by the State of Israel. The chief rabbinate in Israel is headed by two chief rabbis, one Ashkenazi and one Sephardi, as had been the case under the mandatory ordinance. While each such chief rabbi in Israel has the title of *rav ra'shi* (chief rabbi), the Sephardi chief rabbi also has the title of *ri'shon le-Tsiy-*

yon, a title in use since the sixteenth century, and probably much earlier. According to one tradition, when Mosheh ben Yehonatan Galante (1620–1689; see GALANTE FAMILY) was appointed spiritual head of the Jerusalem community, he modestly refused to assume the title of Ra'vad (an acronym for *rav, av beit din*, "rabbi, head of the rabbinic court"), hitherto held by the chief rabbi, but agreed to the title of *ri'shon le-Tsiyyon* (cf. *Is.* 41.27) on the principle of first among equals. The Sephardi community decided that in the future all chief rabbis of Jerusalem would be known by the appellation *ri'shon le-Tsiyyon*. The authority of the Turkish chief rabbi of Constantinople extended to Erets Yisra'el during the period from the death of Galante until 1842, when a new *ri'shon le-Tsiyyon* was elected, confirmed by the Turkish authorities, and granted official status, equal to that of the Christian patriarchs, with jurisdiction over the entire province. Today, on formal occasions, as a sign of his office, the *ri'shon le-Tsiyyon* appears in an elaborately embroidered gown and ornate round hat.

In Israel, the office of chief rabbi is elective, and those elected serve for a single ten-year term and are not eligible for reelection. In addition to the national chief rabbis, each large city in Israel has two chief rabbis, one Ashkenazi and one Sephardi, while smaller towns will often have a single chief rabbi. All questions of personal status in Israel are governed solely by rabbinic laws. That and the governmental nature of the appointment invests the Israeli chief rabbinate with great practical authority, aside from its natural prestige in the Orthodox Jewish world.

• Geoffrey Alderman, "The British Chief Rabbinate: A Most Peculiar Practice," *European Judaism* 23.2 (1990): 45–58. Geoffrey Alderman, "Power, Authority and Status in British Jewry: The Chief Rabbinate and Shechita," in *Outsiders and Outcasts: Essays in Honour of William J. Fishman*, edited by Geoffrey Alderman (London, 1993), pp. 12–31. Arnold Enker, "A Central Rabbinic Authority: Costs and Trade-Offs," in *Israel as a Religious Reality*, edited by Chaim I. Waxman (Northvale, N.J., 1994), pp. 105–117. Aharon Lichtenstein, "The Israel Chief Rabbinate: A Current Halakhic Perspective," *Tradition* 26.4 (1992): 26–38. Simon Schwarzfuchs, *A Concise History of the Rabbinate* (Oxford and Cambridge, 1993).

—SHMUEL HIMELSTEIN

CHILDREN. Barrenness and childlessness are regarded in Judaism as the greatest of misfortunes. The cry of Abraham, "O Lord God, what will you give me, seeing I go childless" (*Gn.* 15.2), and Rachel's lament, "Give me children, else I die" (*Gn.* 30.1), are echoed by the Talmudic statement that includes "him who is childless" (*Ned.* 64b) among the four categories of living men who are considered as dead. A male is regarded as a child until attaining the age of thirteen and a day; a female twelve and a day. Children are free of all legal and religious obligations and are not punishable for misdeeds, although they are expected to begin accustoming themselves to Jewish practices as they approach their majority. The Jewish attitude toward children is one of unbounded love, combined with a solid sense of sober responsibility. This love is expressed in the rhetorical question "Is it possible for a father to hate his son?" (*San.* 105a) and the statement "a man can be envious of anyone except his own son and his disciple" (*San.* 105a). The father–child relationship is a symbol for the relationship between God and Israel, thus the passage in the Ro'sh ha-Shanah liturgy "If you regard us as your children, have mercy on us as a father to his child." Parents discharge their responsibility toward their children by teaching them the precepts of Judaism. A child who follows the path of the Torah not only ensures the continuity of Judaism but also confers salvation upon the souls of his parents after death: the *Qaddish, insofar as it became a prayer for mourners, derives from this idea. According to the Talmud, one of the three categories of people who will inherit the world to come is those "who bring up their children in the way of the Torah" (*Pes.* 113a), and "he who has a son who toils in the Torah is regarded as not having died" (*Gn. Rab.* 49). A father is enjoined never to favor one child over another (*Shab.* 10b); the bondage of the Israelites in Egypt is traced back to the favoritism shown by Jacob to Joseph. Similarly, a father should never fail to fulfill the promises he has made to his children, lest he lead them to tell untruths (*Suk.* 46b). The ideal child is one who attends a school of religious study (*Shab.* 119b) and to whom the rabbis apply the verse "touch not my anointed" (*1 Chr.* 16.20), in contrast to the "child brought up in captivity among the heathens." A striking exception to the otherwise universally accepted doctrine of a child's lack of responsibility and consequent freedom from punishment is noted in the law of the rebellious son (see BEN SORER U-MOREH). The rabbis believed the responsibility for a child's rebelliousness rested ultimately on the shoulders of the parents (*San.* 71–72). See also FATHER; MOTHER.

• Gerald J. Blidstein, *Honor Thy Father and Mother: Filial Responsibility in Jewish Law and Ethics* (New York, 1976). Shaye J. D. Cohen, ed., *The Jewish Family in Antiquity* (Atlanta, 1993). Louis M. Epstein, *The Jewish Marriage Contract: A Study in the Status of the Woman in Jewish Law* (New York, 1927). Fran G. Marcus, *Rituals of Childhood: Jewish Acculturation in Medieval Europe* (New Haven, 1996). David J. Wolpe, *Teaching Your Children about God: A Modern Jewish Approach* (New York, 1993).

CHILDREN'S PRAYERS AND SERVICES. Parents are encouraged to familiarize their children from a very early age with basic prayers. The most widely taught in this connection are *Modeh Ani and the *Shema'. Some modern prayer books (such as the *Authorised Daily Prayer Book*, edited by S. Singer, the standard British prayer book) include brief morning and night prayers for young children.

Organized children's Sabbath and festival services were introduced by Reform Judaism in nineteenth-century Germany. The custom was adopted by Conservative and some Orthodox congregations. The tendency is for much or all of the services to be conducted by the children themselves. The services usually consist of an abbreviated version of the regular prayers and are often conducted in the vernacular. Special prayer books have been published for children's services.

Certain Sephardi congregations encourage boys who have not yet reached *bar mitsvah* age to recite a certain sentence in the morning service or even read the *haftarah*, while in Ashkenazi synagogues it has become common for a young boy (or girl in non-Orthodox congregations) to lead the reading of the An'im Zemirot prayer (see SHIR HA-KAVOD). Children's services are virtually unknown in Israel.

• B. Gottschalk, *Der juedische Jugendgottesdienst nach Theorie und Praxis* (Berlin, 1915). Rina Rosenberg, "The Development of the Concept of Prayer in Jewish-Israeli Children and Adolescents," *Studies in Jewish Education* 5 (1990): 91–129. —CHAIM PEARL

CHIROMANCY. The belief in reading an individual's character from the lines on his palms and forehead seems to have been prevalent in Judaism in antiquity. The earliest detailed description of chiromancy occurs among the treatises of Heikhalot and Merkavah literature, the mysticism of the Talmudic period. The key treatise, *Hakkarat Panim ve-Sidrei Sirtutin*, has been published and analyzed by Gershom Scholem; some other texts were published later. These served as a basis for the detailed elaboration of chiromancy that was included in the Zohar, the most influential text of Jewish mysticism. Several sections are dedicated to this subject (vol. 2, 70a–77a), as is an independent treatise that is part of the Zohar, *Raza' de-Razin*. Numerous kabbalists included such material in their works. This practice reflects the belief that an individual's character and fate are imprinted on his body before birth, and that life is actually the unraveling of these potentialities, which can be recognized by an expert.

• Gershom Gerhard Scholem, "Hakkarat Panim ve-Sidrei Sirtutin," in *Sefer Assaf*, edited by Umberto Cassuto (Jerusalem, 1953), pp. 459–495. Gershom Gerhard Scholem, *Kabbalah* (Jerusalem, 1974), pp. 317–319. —JOSEPH DAN

CHOICE. See FREE WILL.

CHOIR. Asaph, Heman, and Jeduthun, of the tribe of Levi, were appointed by King David to lead choral singing accompanying the placement of the Ark of the Covenant in Jerusalem; they and their families also presided over ceremonies at the dedication of the Temple. Choral singing (by all-male choirs) of antiphonal and responsorial songs played an important role in regular worship in the First and Second Temples but was banned when the Temple was destroyed in 70 CE. In 1605 R. Leone *Modena issued a *responsum* permitting choral music for the purpose of glorifying God. Salamone *Rossi of Mantua reintroduced choral singing to the synagogue with the publication (1622–1623) of thirty-three settings of psalms and other liturgical texts, but the regular addition of choral music to the synagogue service came to an end with the Austrian conquest of Mantua between 1628 and 1630. Sephardi communities seemed more accepting of choral music for various festive occasions; Jewish and non-Jewish composers wrote choral–orchestral works for the dedications of Italian synagogues in Venice and Ferrara, as well as choral hymns for congregations in Amsterdam. However, the regular inclusion of choral singing in the synagogue began with the German reforms of the nineteenth century. The practice began in Reform congregations to have "mixed choirs" (men and women) and also non-Jewish choristers. Salomon *Sulzer was the first composer to set to music for cantor and choir the entire annual liturgy. His student, Louis *Lewandowski, who was not a cantor but the first full-time synagogue choral conductor, published a similar work with organ accompaniment. Russian composers like David Nowakowsky and Zavel Zilberts contributed to the traditional *chorshul* (choral synagogue) with works for all-male choruses. For a time choral singing threatened to inhibit the participation of lay congregants, but since the 1950s, North American composers writing choral music for Reform and Conservative congregations have increasingly produced singable melodies and refrains that encourage all worshipers to participate. See also CANTORIAL MUSIC.

• Abraham Z. Idelsohn, *Jewish Music in Its Historical Development* (New York, 1929; repr. 1967, 1992). —MARSHA BRYAN EDELMAN

CHOLENT. See TSHOLNT.

CHORIN, AHARON BEN KALMAN (1766–1844), pioneer advocate of *Reform Judaism in Hungary. Born in Moravia, he graduated from the *yeshivah* of Yeḥezqe'l Landau in Prague and then served as rabbi of Arad, Transylvania, from 1789. Imbued with the spirit of Jewish Enlightenment, Chorin took a highly independent line in his *responsa* and sermons, declaring sturgeon to be kosher and condemning practices (e.g., *kapparot* and the use of amulets) that he regarded as superstitious. However, it was the publication of *'Emeq ha-Shaveh* (Prague, 1803), which heralded a series of controversial works reinterpreting the oral law, that first angered the traditional rabbinate. After justifying the Berlin and Hamburg Reform temple innovations (1818), Chorin supported and often anticipated radical Reform measures: bareheaded worship, an abbreviated mourning period (*shiv'ah*), abolition of the Kol Nidrei prayer on Yom Kippur eve, the deletion of Jewish national elements from the liturgy, the granting of permission to play the organ in the synagogue and to travel and write on the Sabbath, and even mixed marriages. Chorin's opponents dubbed him Aḥer, an acronym of his name recalling the apostate *Elisha' ben Avuyah.

• Leopold Löw, *Aron Chorin: Eine biographische Skizze* (Szeged, 1863); reprinted in Löw's collected works: *Gesammelte Schriften*, 5 vols. (Szeged, 1889–1890), vol. 2, pp. 251–420. —GABRIEL A. SIVAN

CHOSEN PEOPLE. The belief that the Jewish people have been chosen by God above all other peoples (also called election) is frequently mentioned in the Bible and occupies a prominent place in Jewish liturgy. *Deuteronomy* 14.2 states, "For you are a holy people unto the Lord your God, and the Lord has chosen you to be a peculiar people unto himself, above all the nations that are upon the face of the earth." The blessing recited by a person called to the reading of the Torah is "Blessed are you . . . who has chosen us out of all peoples and given us the Torah"; and the specific festival portion of the 'Amidah begins "You have chosen us from all peoples; you have loved us and taken pleasure in us, and have exalted us over all tongues." The doctrine of a chosen people is therefore central in Jewish theology, but there are differences of opinion as to its precise meaning.

Interpretations vary from a narrow concept of superiority to attempts at ethical and even universalist formulations. The frequent biblical emphasis on the election of Israel led to the idea, also found in later rabbinic literature, that there was a moral or even racial excellence inherent in the Jewish people as such, and references to the superiority of those who are "of the seed of Abraham our Father" (e.g., *Beits.* 32b) abound. Inevitably the doctrine of election also led to an ethnocentric view of world history. The notion of a chosen people is also related to that of a "holy nation" (e.g., *Ex.* 19.5–6: "Now therefore if you will obey my commandments and keep my covenant, then you shall be a peculiar people unto me above all people"), and election is accounted for as an act of divine love and faithfulness to the divine promise (*Dt.* 7.6–9). In spite of their severe castigation of Israel's failings, the prophets generally assumed the permanence of Israel's election under the *covenant. If election meant heavier responsibility and stricter standards rather than greater privileges (*Am.* 3.2), then Israel was proved to be God's chosen people also in exile and punishment (*Jeremiah, Ezekiel*). Although Deutero-Isaiah had proclaimed that God's dealings with Israel would make the latter a source of light to all the nations, the idea was not systematically developed, and Jewish commentators did not as a rule interpret the Suffering Servant of *Isaiah* 53 as a figure of Israel suffering for the sake of mankind. The emphasis on Israel's continued election became stronger when rival religions (e.g., the claim of the Roman Catholic church to be the true Israel) or historical circumstances (e.g., oppression and persecution) contradicted Israel's claim to be the chosen people. The treatment that medieval Jewry received at the hands of its neighbors was not such as to encourage universalist tendencies. Medieval philosophers paid relatively little attention to the doctrine of the chosen people (it is not mentioned in Maimonides' Thirteen Principles of Faith), the major exception being Yehudah ha-Levi, for whom Israel was a superior race. The unique historic and cosmic status of Israel was a fundamental tenet of the Kabbalah (echoed in Hasidism and in the teachings of Yehudah Liva' ben Betsal'el and Avraham Yitsḥaq Kook), but rationalism, modernism, and emancipation made the notion of a chosen people increasingly problematical. Abraham Geiger still held that the Jewish people possessed a unique gift for religion, and he and other Reform thinkers tended to regard the dispersion as part of Israel's mission to serve as God's instrument in disseminating its specific insight of the relationship between the human and the divine. This attitude has been modified subsequently, and some groups (Reform, Reconstructionist) have repudiated the traditional doctrine of a chosen people and have deleted all references to it from the prayer book. The sociohistorical and spiritual rather than racial character of the traditional concept of the chosen people is clearly brought out by rabbinic law, which accords to the convert all the rights and privileges of the born Jew. This attitude, the earliest expression of which is found in the biblical *Book of Ruth*, was succinctly formulated by Maimonides: "Whosoever adopts Judaism and confesses the unity of God as is prescribed in the Torah is counted among the disciples of Abraham our father. These men are Abraham's household." This principle strictly applied in halakhic procedure—a convert discards his (or her) patronymic and becomes "the son [or daughter] of Abraham our father."

• Henri Altan, "Chosen People" in *Contemporary Jewish Religious Thought*, edited by Arthur A. Cohen and Paul R. Mendes-Flohr (New York, 1987), pp. 55–59. Arnold M. Eisen, *The Chosen People in America* (Bloomington, Ind., 1983), chap. 1.

CHRISTIANITY, a religion that grew out of Judaism and at first existed as a Jewish sect. The founder and early adherents were all Jews (see JEWISH CHRISTIANS) and much light has been thrown on their teachings by comparing them with both rabbinic doctrines and those contained in the *Dead Sea Scrolls. Christianity adopted not only the Hebrew Bible but much of its traditional interpretation as well, in addition to many elements from Jewish liturgy. *Jesus preached the imminent advent of the kingdom of heaven, but in spite of his anti-Pharisaic criticisms he was in many ways closer to the Pharisees than to their opponents, the Sadducees. He did not intend to abolish the traditional law (cf. *Mt.* 5.17), and his supplication prayer, known as the Lord's Prayer, bears a striking resemblance to the traditional Short Prayer (*Tefillah Qetsarah). After the Crucifixion, his followers regarded themselves as Jews who were committed to a belief in the messiahship of Jesus and his early return. It was *Paul who developed Christianity in a way that prepared for a complete break with the parent religion.

Drawing on doctrines current in sectarian circles, Paul developed a theology that laid the foundation for gentile Christianity: Jesus' death had redeemed sinful man from his state of sin; the Law had been fulfilled and superseded (i.e., abolished), and salvation was now attainable through baptism and faith in the Messiah. With the growth of gentile Christianity, the original Jewish Christians (*Ebionites, also called *minim* [sectarians, heretics]) became a minority of "heretics," even inside the church. With the introduction of a solemn curse on *minim* into the ʿAmidah prayer, the Jewish community finalized its breach with Christianity. However, Christianity could never regard Judaism as just another religion. The Roman Catholic church insisted that its roots were sunk deep in the history of Israel, that the events recounted in the *New Testament were the fulfillment of the promises made in the Hebrew Bible (now called the *Old Testament), that its founder was the Messiah and son of David expected by Jewish tradition, that it was the heir of God's covenant with Israel—in short, that it was the "true Israel" (*verus Israel*).

Early church practices and liturgy strongly influenced by Judaism included the Eucharist, the prominent role of the *Psalms* in prayer, and the concept of the Sabbath day and of the institution of the church (which derived from the synagogue). Christian theology was deeply indebted to typology according to which the Hebrew Bible was to be read as a preparation for Christianity. This position inevitably led to a complicated and ambivalent attitude toward Israel in which affirmation and utter rejection, acceptance and hatred, were intertwined. In order to come into its own, the church had to picture Israel as dispossessed, rejected, or even cursed. This competitive situation, aggravated by Israel's stubborn refusal throughout the centuries to be in any way impressed by the religious claims of Christianity, has provided the basis for the tragic history of Christian *antisemitism.

The development and growth of Christian antisemitism can be traced through the books of the New Testament and beyond those to the writings of the church fathers and later authors. The destruction of the Temple and the disastrous failure of the first and second (Bar Kokhba') rebellions were taken as proof that Israel's historic role had come to an end, whereas Christianity continued to spread until it finally became the official religion of the Roman empire. (From the Jewish point of view, Rome, with all its evil associations [Edom], was henceforth identified with Christianity.) Although Judaism was tolerated and given a status of its own in medieval Europe, Jews were subjected to humiliation, persecution, and frequent violence. The official theory claimed that Jews should be allowed to live, albeit in abject degradation, as a terrible warning to all those who would reject the Christian savior. Toward the later Middle Ages, Christian antisemitism became more violent. The *Crusades, with their wholesale massacres of Jewish communities, the repeated accusations of ritual murder (see Blood Libel) and desecration of the Host, expulsions, forced conversions (see Conversion, Forced), and the activities of the *Inquisition brought Jewish suffering at the hands of Christianity to an unprecedented high. Antisemitic stereotypes became deeply ingrained throughout the Christian world, with the Jews branded as "Christ killers." Theological *disputations that at one time had been conducted in a spirit of relative fairness were increasingly forced on the Jews in order to embarrass them. All the more extensive was the development of polemical literature (see Apologetics; Polemics)—both on a high philosophical plane and on a crudely derogatory (e.g., **Toledot Yeshu*) level.

In spite of the conflicts, there were mutual influences between the two religions, in the sense both of adopting and rejecting certain ideas and practices; for example, *Maimonides exercised considerable influence on Albertus Magnus, Thomas Aquinas, and Meister Eckhart, whereas Jewish theological doctrines were often formulated with polemical intent against Christian teachings. Christian influence is noticeable in such Jewish customs as **yortsayt* and prayers for the dead. The church dissociated its Easter date from that of Pesaḥ to avoid celebrating on the Jewish festival; conversely, Jewish customs were discontinued because they were also practiced by Christians, for example, kneeling at prayer (see also Ḥuqqat ha-Goyyim). These mutual influences, however, had little affect on the general moral climate.

Luther's hostile attitude to Judaism was the same as that prevalent in the earlier Middle Ages, and the Counter-Reformation in the Roman Catholic church served to revive and enforce even more severe anti-Jewish legislation (the yellow badge, the *ghetto system). Some English Puritans seemed ready to adopt a different attitude toward the Jews, but, generally speaking, it is only in recent times that Christian churches and theologians, largely under the shock of Hitler's persecution, began to press for a radical revision of the Christian approach to Judaism. It was realized that traditional church teaching had created antisemitic prejudices that contributed to the atmosphere in which the Holocaust became possible. The Roman Catholic church in the 1965 *Nostra aetate* document of the Second Vatican Council repudiated the teaching that Jews of all times were to be held responsible for the death of Jesus and subsequently insisted on the continuing validity of God's covenant with the Jewish people. Most Protestant churches have also revised their attitude toward the Jews, with all Christians condemning antisemitism. Western churches are beginning to stress the Jewish roots of Christianity. On the Jewish side, theological evaluation of Christianity varied with the times and individual thinkers. It was generally admitted that Christianity, like Islam, was different from paganism, and as a monotheistic faith could be considered as one of the ways by which Providence gradually led the gentiles toward true religion. It was never doubted, however, that Christianity was essentially a false religion, and according to some authorities (e.g., Maimonides) it could not even be regarded as a genuinely monotheistic faith. Some modern thinkers (particularly Franz *Rosenzweig) have assigned an especially important role to Christianity and describe its relationship to Judaism as a complementary one. See also Church Fathers; Interfaith Relations; Protestantism; Roman Catholic Church.

• James H. Charlesworth, ed., *Jews and Christians: Exploring the Past, Present and Future* (New York, 1990). Eugene J. Fisher and Leon Klenicki, eds., *In Our Time: The Flowering of the Jewish–Catholic Dialogue* (New York, 1990). Walter Jacob, *Christianity through Jewish Eyes* (New York, 1974).

CHRONICLES, BOOK OF (Heb. *Divrei ha-Yamim*), the last book in the *Hagiographa section of the Hebrew Bible, which describes the history of the kingdom of Judah up to the Babylonian exile. In the *Septuagint, *Chronicles* is included among the historical books and placed between *Kings* and *Ezra*. Originally one work, by the sixteenth century it had entered printed Hebrew Bibles as *1 Chronicles* and *2 Chronicles*, following the precedents of the Greek translation and the Vulgate. On the basis of its style, language, and genealogical information, *Chronicles* can be dated to the end of the Persian period or the beginning of the Hellenistic period, the fourth century BCE. *Chronicles* contains genealogies, beginning with Adam, including the twelve sons of Jacob and the tribal composition of Israel, and ending with the lists of inhabitants of Jerusalem at the time of the return from the Babylonian exile (*1 Chr.* 1–9); a description of the reign of David (with the omission of David's more reprehensible acts, such as the Bath-sheba affair, which are incorporated in the parallel *Book of Samuel*), along with details concerning David's war-related activities, the organization of the priesthood and the people, and his preparations for building the Temple (*1 Chr.* 10–29); a description of the reign of Solomon with emphasis on the building and dedication of the Temple (*2 Chr.* 1–9); and the subsequent history of Judah, with a sympathetic and apologetic emphasis on the kingdom of Judah and the actions of its kings, in which almost all references to the northern kingdom of Israel (*2 Chr.* 10–36) are deliberately omitted. The house of David as a centralizing force in the development of the nation and the significance of the Temple and Temple cult are the overall focuses of the work, which also stresses the role of the Zadokite priesthood and the Levites. Although the contents of *Chronicles* resemble other sections of the Bible (especially *Samuel* and *Kings*), salient ideological concepts in *Chronicles* set it apart from the earlier books. The greater role given to the popular voice in public life indicates the evolving belief that the king must answer to the people (*1 Chr.* 13.1). The concept of reward and punishment based solely on the deeds or misdeeds of each generation (in contrast to the *Book of Kings*, in which punishment is cumulative from one generation to the next) seems to reflect the teachings of the exilic prophet *Ezekiel. The presentation of Israelite history in *Chronicles* was designed to address the concerns and aspirations of the Jewish community in the fifth and fourth centuries BCE.

• Sara Japhet, *1 and 2 Chronicles: A Commentary*, The Old Testament Library (London, 1993). Sara Japhet, *The Ideology of the Book of Chronicles and Its Place in Biblical Thought*, translated from the Hebrew by Anna Barber (Frankfurt am Main and New York, 1989). Yehezkel Kaufmann, *History of the Religion of Israel*, vol. 4, *From the Babylonian Captivity to the End of Prophecy*, translated from the Hebrew by C. W. Efroymson (New York, Jerusalem, and Dallas, 1977), pp. 533–563. Julius Wellhausen, *Prolegomena to the History of Israel*, translated from the German by J. S. Black and A. Menzies (Edinburgh, 1885), pp. 171–227. Hugh G. M. Williamson, *1 and 2 Chronicles*, The New Century Bible Commentary (Grand Rapids, and London, 1982).

—DAVID A. GLATT-GILAD

CHRONOLOGY. See CALENDAR.

CHUETAS, name given to the *crypto-Jews or *Marranos of the Balearic Islands. Crypto-Judaism arose in Spain as a result of the massive anti-Jewish violence and forced conversions that began in 1391. The number of crypto-Jews swelled due to intensive missionary activities by Friar Vincent Ferrer in Majorca in 1415 and a pogrom in 1435, which marked the end of officially tolerated Judaism on the island. Both the word *marrano* and the word *chueta* probably mean pig, an indication of the contempt in which crypto-Jews were held by the Christian population even after their adoption of Christianity. Despite their forced conversion, the Chuetas were confined to ghettos and subject to persecutions by the Inquisition.

For approximately two centuries after their conversion, some Chuetas attempted to continue the practice of Judaism secretly; gradually their Judaism diverged markedly from normative Judaism. Occasionally the Inquisition would institute autos-da-fé of Chuetas. Inquisitorial trials and punishments between 1679 and 1691 resulted in the virtual eradication of Judaizing practices on the island. The descendants of the victims lived on as Chuetas, Christians known to be of Jewish descent, retaining only faint traces of Judaism in their way of life. Mass attempts to leave the island in the 1680s were unsuccessful.

In 1782 the Chuetas were permitted to leave their ghetto and reside on any part of the island. Their further mistreatment was declared a punishable offense by royal decree. Today, many are still concentrated in the Calle de las Plateria in Palma as silversmiths and the owners of jewelry stores. Many also specialize as musicians, doctors, and dentists on the island. Although they are completely assimilated, their Jewish origins are known, and they retain a sense of Jewishness from their past. They are still subjected to negative stereotyping. Brief Chueta attempts to return to Judaism after the creation of the State of Israel in 1948 failed.

• Baruch Braunstein, *The Chuetas of Marjorca: Conversos and the Inquisition of Majorca* (New York, 1936). Kenneth Moore, *Those of the Street: The Catholic–Jews of Mallorca* (Notre Dame, 1976). Angela S. Selke, *The Conversos of Majorca: Life and Death in a Crypto-Jewish Community in XVII Century Spain* (Jerusalem, 1986). —JANE S. GERBER

CHURCH. See CHRISTIANITY; PROTESTANTISM; ROMAN CATHOLIC CHURCH.

CHURCH FATHERS, principal theologians and leaders of Christianity from the end of the apostolic period (early 2d cent.) until the early Middle Ages. Anti-Judaic teachings, traditionally known as Adversus Iudaeos literature, figured prominently in patristic preaching and writing and found a permanent niche at the heart of Christian theology. Owing to the Jewish origins of Christianity and its claim to represent the sole legitimate fulfillment of the biblical covenant, the church fathers were obliged to defend their faith against charges of heresy and innovation, on the one hand, and to demonstrate the error of Judaism, despite its long history, on the other hand.

Three stages can be distinguished in the development of patristic Adversus Iudaeos literature. The ante-Nicene, pre-Constantinian fathers (e.g., the author of the *Epistle of Barnabas*, Justin Martyr, Melito of Sardis, Tertullian, and Cyprian) manifest the insecurities of a church still deemed illegal and persecuted by the emperors of Rome, and disadvantaged in its effort to discredit the more ancient practices of the Jews. Subsequent Eastern fathers (e.g., Eusebius, John Chrysostom, Ephraem Syrus, and Aphraates) proceed from a position of greater strength but are still forced to confront large, vibrant Jewish communities. The post-Nicene Latin fathers (e.g., Ambrose of Milan, Augustine, and Isidore of Seville) are generally more theoretical, evidencing less genuine interaction with thriving Jewish communities and aiming principally at establishing the integrity of Christianity in matters bearing little upon the Jews.

In spite of their hostile attitude toward Judaism, some

of the church fathers drew on the techniques and substance of rabbinic Bible commentary and *aggadah*; patristic literature has therefore proven valuable in the study of *midrash* and comparative exegesis. See also ANTISEMITISM; ROMAN CATHOLIC CHURCH.

• B. Blumenkranz, *Die Judenpredigt Augustins* (Basle, 1946). Marc Hirshman, *Mikra and Midrash: A Comparison of Rabbinics and Patristics* (Tel Aviv, 1992). R. G. Jenkins, "The Biblical Text of the Commentaries of Eusebius and Jerome on Isaiah," *Abr-Nahrain* 22 (1984): 64–78. N.R.M. de Lange, *Origen and the Jews* (Cambridge, 1976). E. P. Sanders et al., eds., *Jewish and Christian Self-Definition*, 3 vols. (Philadelphia, 1980–1982). Marcel Simon, *Verus Israel: A Study in the Relations between Christians and Jews in the Roman Empire (135–425)*, translated by H. McKeating (Oxford, 1986). R. L. Wilken, *Judaism and the Early Christian Mind* (New Haven, 1971). A. L. Williams, *Adversus Judaeos: A Bird's-Eye View of Jewish Apologetic until the Renaissance* (Cambridge, 1935).

–JEREMY COHEN

CIRCUMCISION (Heb. *milah*), removal of the foreskin in an operation performed on all male Jewish children on the eighth day after birth and also upon male converts to Judaism. Circumcision was enjoined by God upon Abraham and his descendants (*Gn.* 17.10–12) and has always been regarded as the supreme obligatory sign of loyalty and adherence to Judaism. As the sign of the *covenant (*berit*) "sealed in the flesh," circumcision came to be known as *berit milah* or the "covenant of our father Abraham." The presence of the foreskin was regarded as a blemish, and perfection was to be attained by its removal (cf. *Ned.* 31b). The generation born in the wilderness, however, was not circumcised, an omission repaired by Joshua (*Jos.* 5.2–9). Many Hellenistic Jews, particularly those who participated in athletics at the gymnasium, had an operation performed to conceal the fact of their circumcision (*1 Mc.* 1.15). Similar action was taken during the Hadrianic persecution, in which period a prohibition against circumcision was issued. It was probably in order to prevent the possibility of obliterating the traces of circumcision that the rabbis added to the requirement of cutting the foreskin that of *peri'ah* (laying bare the glans). To this was added a third requirement, *metsitsah* (sucking of the blood). This was originally done by the *mohel* (circumciser) applying his lips to the penis and drawing off the blood by sucking. For hygienic reasons, a glass tube with a wad of cotton wool inserted in the middle is now generally employed, or the blood is simply drawn off by the use of some absorbent material. Unless medical reasons interpose, the circumcision must take place on the eighth day after birth, even if that day falls on a Sabbath or Yom Kippur. If circumcision has been postponed for medical reasons, the ceremony may not take place on a Sabbath or major festival. The only exception permitted to the otherwise universal requirement of circumcision is if two previous children of the family have died as a result of the operation; that is, in cases of hereditary hemophilia. The duty of circumcising the child is the responsibility of the father. In his absence or in case of his failure to do so, the religious authorities are bound to see that it is performed. The occasion of a circumcision is regarded as a festive event for the whole community and takes place, where possible, in the presence of a *minyan*. If one of the participants (the father, godfather, or *mohel*) is in synagogue on that day, all penitential and supplicatory prayers are omitted. A sentence in the prayer of Elijah (*1 Kgs.* 19.10), "for the children of Israel have forsaken your covenant," was understood by the rabbis to mean that the Israelites had abandoned the rite of circumcision, which is always referred to (on the basis of *Gn.* 17.9) as the *berit* (covenant). Elijah is regarded as the patron of circumcision, and it is said that his spirit is present at all circumcisions. This is the origin of the chair of Elijah (see ELIJAH, CHAIR OF), now an integral part of the ceremony. In eastern communities, and in Hasidic groups, where the ceremony takes place in the synagogue, such a chair is a permanent feature of synagogue appurtenances. Among Ashkenazim, it is customary to appoint a couple as *kvatter* (godparents). The godmother carries the child from his mother's room to the room in which the ceremony will take place and gives him to the child's father, who, in turn, hands him to the *mohel*. The *mohel* places the child upon the chair of Elijah and proclaims, "this is the chair of Elijah, may he be remembered for good." He then lifts up the child, places him upon a cushion in the lap of the godfather (**sandaq*), and, in this position, after the *mohel* recites the appropriate blessings, the operation is performed. The father also recites a blessing to God "who has sanctified us by his commandments and commanded us to enter our sons into the covenant of Abraham." According to some authorities, the father also says the *She-Heḥeyanu blessing. The *mohel* then recites a prayer dating from geonic times, in the course of which a name is bestowed on the child. The circumcision ceremony is normally followed by a Se'udat Mitsvah, a meal of religious character. Special hymns are sung, and blessings for the parents, the *sandaq*, the child, and the *mohel*, as well as for the advent of the Messiah and the righteous priest, are inserted in the Birkat ha-Mazon. Nineteenth-century Reform Jews were opposed to circumcision, but now it is usually performed, although often by a doctor rather than a *mohel*. Circumcision is enjoined upon male proselytes (and slaves) as an essential condition of their acceptance into the Jewish faith. Circumcision was widespread in many ancient cultures. Some of these also practiced female circumcision, which was never allowed in Judaism.

• Berit Mila Board of Reform Judaism, *Berit Mila in the Reform Context* (New York, 1990). Anita Diamant, *The New Jewish Baby Book: Names, Ceremonies, and Customs* (Woodstock, Vt., 1994). Lawrence A. Hoffman, *Covenant of Blood: Circumcision and Gender in Rabbinic Judaism* (Chicago, 1996). Paysach J. Krohn, *Bris Milah: Circumcision, the Covenant of Abraham: A Compendium* (Brooklyn, N.Y., 1985).

CIRCUMSTANTIAL EVIDENCE. See EVIDENCE.

CITIES OF REFUGE. See ASYLUM.

CITRON. See ETROG.

CITY OF DAVID. See JERUSALEM.

CIVIL COURTS. Jewish law contains a prohibition against recourse to non-Jewish courts of justice. The prohibition originally derived from the fear of being inveigled into a recognition of idolatry (*'A. Z.* 13a). Certain exceptions were made; for example, for the witnessing of documents, except in the case of writs of divorce or manumission (*Git.* 90b). In the second century, however, R. Tarfon issued a blanket prohibition against Jews having any recourse to non-Jewish courts, even if their dispensation of justice was identical with that of the Jewish courts. He quoted *Exodus* 21.1 in support of his decision (*Git.* 88b).

In their desire and anxiety to maintain the autonomy of Jewish communities in the Diaspora, medieval Jewish authorities insisted that Jews bring their disputes only before their own courts and harshly condemned those having recourse to civil courts even by mutual agreement. The only generally recognized exception permitted by the *Shulḥan 'Arukh* (*Ḥoshen Mishpat* 26.1) was if the defendant failed to appear before the Jewish court (*beit din*) after three successive summonses, in which case the *beit din* issued permission to the plaintiff to apply to the civil authorities.

The scope of the prohibition against litigating in civil courts has been subject to a considerable amount of controversy since the abandonment of Jewish judicial autonomy. A number of different approaches have been suggested. Some say that using Jewish courts, even if not run according to Jewish law, is not inconsistent with the prohibition against civil courts. Others recommend arbitration panels that are not actually part of any legal system. Yet others rule that administrative law courts are not prohibited. Some nineteenth-century authorities suggested that *arbitration, whether by Jews or gentiles, was permitted.

Equally problematic was the relationship between public and private law. The prohibition against litigating in secular courts is not applicable when the cause of action lies primarily with the secular government. As the relationship between public and private secular law grows more complex, the proper role of the prohibition against litigating in secular courts becomes more unclear.

Finally, the status of the secular courts in the State of Israel is in dispute. Some are inclined to rule that secular courts in Israel are like the Talmudic "courts of Syria" that were not completely prohibited by Jewish law. Yet others see no distinction between Israeli courts and the civil courts of other countries.

• Menachem Elon, *Jewish Law: History, Sources, Principles* (Philadelphia, 1994), pp. 24–34, 1914–1917. Michael Broyde, *The Pursuit of Justice: Jewish Perspectives on Practicing Law* (New York, 1996), pp. 13–24. Arnold N. Enker, "Aspects of Interaction between the Torah Law, the King's Law, and the Noahide Law in Jewish Criminal Law," *Cardozo Law Review* 12 (1991): 1137–1156. Shmuel Shilo, "Equity as a Bridge between Jewish and Secular Law," *Cardozo Law Review* 12 (1991): 737–751.

—MICHAEL BROYDE

CIVIL LAW. Jewish civil law may be defined as that area of divinely authorized law that deals with matters other than criminal and ritual. Civil law occupies a modest place in the Bible itself, but as it developed during the Talmudic period and later, it came to constitute the main part of Jewish law. The civil law of the Bible reflects the life of a predominantly agricultural community, and there is little material dealing with commerce. With the development of commerce from the Second Temple period onward, and the necessity of paying taxes to foreign rulers, the area of commercial law expanded greatly, as is reflected in the Mishnah and in the Talmud. The laws of contracts, expressed or implied, were studied in detail. The development of civil law continued during the geonic period and later in *responsa* and codes. The basic orders of the Mishnah concerned with civil law are Nashim and Neziqin (though these sections also deal with other matters). The former treats the laws of marriage and divorce, property rights of husbands and wives, and the rights and obligations of slaves. The nature of civil courts, legal procedure, the administration of oaths, as well as most laws dealing with money matters, land, inheritance, pledges, loans and interest, torts, and bailments are found in Neziqin, particularly in the first three tractates of this order: *Bava' Qamma', Bava' Metsi'a'*, and *Bava' Batra'*. Rabbinic sources distinguish between rules applicable in ritual law (*issur'a*) and rules applicable in civil law (*mamon'a*). The principle of equity (for example, in application of the biblical commandment "and you shall do that which is right and good") was often enforced in order to mitigate any special severity that might arise from the strict application of the law in certain cases. Whereas no non-Jewish authority could change or influence ceremonial law, in matters of civil law, the law of the land would be considered valid (*dina' de-malkhuta' dina'*) by rabbinic legislators for certain purposes. Nevertheless, Jews were always urged to bring litigation to rabbinic courts and not to the *civil courts. In many parts of the Diaspora, rabbinic courts were given full jurisdiction by the government; elsewhere their status was that of a court of arbitration. In the State of Israel, litigants can choose to go to rabbinic instead of secular courts in civil suits.

In modern Israel, the field of civil law has been greatly transformed by the reinvigorated study of those areas of Jewish law that correspond to modern civil law in the rubric of *mishpat 'Ivri*, as Jewish civil law is now called. It is hoped that *mishpat 'Ivri* will address the many modern problems of commerce and life by incorporating Jewish law into modern Israeli civil law (for example, in the areas of civil procedure or the return of lost property). This has met, however, with considerable opposition from both religious and secular segments of the community.

• Arnold J. Cohen, *An Introduction to Jewish Civil Law* (Jerusalem and New York, 1991). Menachem Elon, *Jewish Law: History, Sources, Principles*, translated by Bernard Auerbach and Melvin J. Sykes (Philadelphia, 1994), pp. 46–75, 1575–1619.

—MICHAEL BROYDE

CIVIL RIGHTS. See EMANCIPATION.

CLEAN AND UNCLEAN ANIMALS. Animals whose flesh may be eaten according to Jewish *dietary laws are considered clean; those whose flesh is not permitted are considered unclean. Clean and unclean animals are first mentioned in the Bible in the story of Noah, who took into the ark seven pairs of every clean animal but only two pairs of unclean animals. *Leviticus* 11.1–47 and *Deuteronomy* 14.3–25 list clean and unclean animals together with the principles by which they are classified. Clean quadrupeds are those that both chew their cuds and have cloven hooves. Pigs, which are unclean, have cloven hooves but do not chew their cuds. True fish are those having both fins and scales. These are clean, while, for example, eels and shellfish are excluded. No general principles are given to determine the cleanness of fowl, but about twenty unclean fowl are listed. In general, it may be said that the specific list of unclean fowl in the Bible consists of birds of prey only, thus implying the permissible character of those not birds of prey. All reptiles and insects are prohibited, with the exception of four types of locusts mentioned by name and which the biblical list specifies as having "knees above their legs to jump with upon the ground."

CLEANLINESS. Personal cleanliness and hygiene are stressed in the Bible (*Dt.* 23.10–15), in rabbinic literature, and in all Jewish law codes. Cleanliness is not to be confused with the concept and practices of **tohorah* (ritual purity), but immersion in the ritual bath (**miqveh*), which is the major means of obtaining ritual cleanness, requires prior cleaning and washing of the body (see IMPURITY). In certain instances, such as *ablution of the hands before partaking of bread or engaging in prayer, ritual and hygienic motives are intertwined. Halakhic insistence on ritual immersion at regular intervals (for example, in the case of the menstruous woman and the frequent voluntary immersion of males), although motivated by considerations of ritual purity, gave rise to a high level of personal hygiene among Jews. In fact, so important does Judaism consider personal cleanliness that the obligatory abstention from washing on Yom Kippur is taken to be an "affliction" (*Yoma'* 8). The rabbis taught that daily washing honored God (*Shab.* 50b). Personal hygiene is considered by the rabbis to extend also to modesty, decency, and cleanliness of dress, an attitude voiced in an extreme fashion by the statement "A scholar upon whose garment a speck of dirt is found is worthy of death" (*Shab.* 114a). A person with a soiled or torn garment may not lead prayers (*Meg.* 4.6). During the Middle Ages, Jews prided themselves on their clean habits and neatness of dress. Maimonides considered the achievement of cleanliness in dress and body to be among the general objectives of the Bible, adding that an outer appearance of cleanliness and propriety should reflect inner purity of heart. The *Shulḥan ʿArukh* (*Oraḥ Ḥayyim* 4.18, 158–165) lists occasions when hands should be washed: upon arising each morning, after urination and defecation, after taking off one's shoes or touching any part of the body customarily covered, after visiting a cemetery, after undressing, before and after meals, after marital relations, and after coming into contact with lice.

• Averell S. Darling, "The Levitical Code: Hygiene or Holiness," in *Medicine and the Bible*, edited by Bernard Palmer (Exeter, 1986), pp. 85–99. Samuel S. Kottek, "General Hygiene in the Works of Flavius Josephus," *Koroth* 9.3–4 (1986): 316–344. Samuel Krauss, *Talmudische Archaeologie*, vol. 1 (Hildesheim, 1966), pp. 209–233.

CODIFICATION OF LAW. Since at least the first century of the common era, Jewish observance has been predicated upon the rabbinic interpretation of the Bible as expressed in the *oral law. By the second century, the oral law was being formulated in various academies in Erets Yisra'el in a brief, prescriptive form that marked the beginning of the creation of legal collections. Approximately at the end of the second century, a number of these collections were edited by R. *Yehudah ha-Nasi' into what became known as the *Mishnah. In terms of its presentation, the Mishnah was detached from its biblical foundations. Organized topically, the work gave few biblical sources for its rulings, though it did cite numerous variant opinions. However, the detailed discussion of the Mishnah by the amora'im in both *Talmuds only increased the possibilities for uncertainty. Abandoning the style, form, and mission of the Mishnah, the amora'im rarely came to clear conclusions.

Emerging from the Talmudic period without a clear code of law, contemporary rabbis had to decide numerous questions of practice. Many decisions from the savoraic and early geonic periods were ultimately collected by *Yehuda'i ben Naḥman Ga'on (fl. 8th cent.) and recorded by his students in the **Halakhot Pesuqot*. More than simply a collection of precedents, the monograph attempted to come to practical legal conclusions on numerous matters that remained unclear in the Talmud Bavli. Generally following Talmudic organization, the work seems to have been directed at those familiar with the Talmudic but not expert enough in it to come to practical conclusions independently. The compilation served as a source for many legal summaries and popularizations, most notably the **Halakhot Qetsuvot* (9th cent., perhaps Italy) and the **Halakhot Gedolot* attributed to Shimʿon Qayyara'.

With the rise of Talmudic learning in North Africa and Spain around the year 1000, further attempts at codification were made, the most important among them being Yitsḥaq *Alfasi's eleventh-century *Halakhot*. Independent of the ge'onim, yet generally agreeing with their legal conclusions, the work presented its author's views. Set in the language and form of the Talmud, the work eliminated most of the Talmudic discussion, presenting only the relevant legal conclusions and the occasional original exposition meant to justify specific rulings. Most significantly, Alfasi added rules for determining the law when the Talmudic discussion led to no clear conclusion. While Alfasi primarily relied on the Talmud Bavli, he made use of the Talmud Yerushalmi for those matters on which the Talmud Bavli did not reach a decision or was silent.

Undoubtedly one of the most original works of codification was Moses *Maimonides' *Mishneh Torah*, written in Egypt in the second half of the twelfth century. Maimonides, who frequently disagreed with the legal views of the ge'onim, noted that he was writing the code because the conditions of his time had made study ever more difficult, resulting in a decline in knowledge. To ease accessibility to the law, Maimonides abandoned Mishnaic organization and divided his work topically into fourteen books. The code, written in Mishnaic Hebrew, again to ease its use, rarely attempted to justify legal conclusions or divulged sources for rulings. Unlike all other codes, the *Mishneh Torah* dealt with every aspect of Jewish law, irrespective of whether it could currently be observed (e.g., laws of sacrifice, monarchy).

Codification continued in Spain and Provence, where authorities like Yitsḥaq ibn Ghiyyat, *Yehudah ben Barzillai al-Bargeloni of Barcelona, *Avraham ben Yitsḥaq of Narbonne, and *Yitsḥaq ben Abba' Mari of Marseilles, relied heavily upon the geonic tradition in compiling their collections. Provence only began to emerge as an independent center of legal thought with *Avraham ben David of Posquières (12th cent.), who was unencumbered by geonic perceptions of Talmudic sources. Yet the emerging Provençal school was quickly eclipsed by the legal methodology of the tosafists.

Nothing could have been further removed from the apodictic approach of Maimonides' code than the halakhic activities of the tosafists in northern France and Germany during the twelfth and thirteenth centuries. Unaware of Maimonides' efforts, the tosafists returned to the Talmudic sources, where their dialectics produced myriad new halakhic possibilities. The relatively simple, definitive codes that had previously characterized halakhic codification in Franco-Germany, works such as the *Roqeaḥ* of *El'azar ben Yehudah of Worms, could not stand in the face of the massive textual and halakhic alternatives that had been raised. Subsequently works, such as the thirteenth-century *Or Zaru'a* of *Yitsḥaq ben Mosheh, demanded keen intellect and independence of thought to decide the law in an age of so many legal possibilities.

One of Yitsḥaq ben Mosheh's students, *Me'ir ben Barukh of Rothenburg, had great influence on subsequent developments in halakhic codification. Although not a codifier himself, he was viewed as a master of *halakhah* and his behavior and teachings were assiduously noted by his students, who often based their practical decisions upon them. Two halakhic works by his disciples became standard texts: *Mordekhai ben Hillel's *Sefer Mordekhai* and *Asher ben Yeḥi'el's *Hilkhot ha-Ro'sh*. The latter gained particularly wide currency as its author, forced to flee persecutions in Germany, became the leading halakhic figure in early fourteenth-century Spain and often incorporated both Ashkenazi and Sephardi traditions in his work.

The tosafist methodology became ensconced in Spanish-Jewish jurisprudence in the thirteenth century through its use by Moses *Nahmanides. His student Shelomoh ben Avraham *Adret attempted a work of codification in which he paid great attention to halakhic development from the Talmudic period. The work, however, is incomplete. A second student of Nahmanides, Shemu'el ben Yitsḥaq ha-Sardi, composed *Sefer ha-Terumot*, a code of civil law that also attempted to show the progression of legal thought.

By the mid-fourteenth century, there was little consensus on practical legal matters. As Asher ben Yeḥi'el's son, *Ya'aqov ben Asher, wrote, "there is no law that does not have difference of opinions." To remove such doubt, Ya'aqov composed a new legal code, the *Arba'ah Turim*, which eschewed all previous manners of organization, being divided into four books that discussed, respectively, blessings, festivals, and fast days; laws of kashrut, menstrual purity, mourning, and other rituals; matrimonial law; and civil and criminal law. After reviewing a number of opinions on each matter, Ya'aqov presented his own rulings, often giving great weight to his father's decisions. The work remained a preeminent code until the early seventeenth century.

Even after the completion of the *Arba'ah Turim*, legal compendiums continued to be written. The trend toward briefer presentations continued with the appearance of Yosef *Karo's **Shulḥan'Arukh* in Venice in 1564 and 1565. Following the organization of the *Arba'ah Turim* and generally basing himself on a consensus of opinion among Alfasi, Maimonides, and Asher ben Yeḥi'el, Karo presented the law in the briefest of terms, although he had laid the foundations for his decisions in a separate commentary on the *Arba'ah Turim*, entitled *Beit Yosef*.

Due to Karo's use of consensus, the *Shulḥan 'Arukh* had a distinctly Sephardi emphasis. It became acceptable in the Ashkenazi world only when glossed by Mosheh *Isserles of Kraków, who added both Ashkenazi customs and recent Ashkenazi rulings to the work (1570–1571). Like previous attempts at codification, the *Shulḥan 'Arukh* was initially opposed by many who believed that the law could not be reduced to simple rules. However, by the seventeenth century, there had appeared supercommentaries to various sections of the *Shulḥan 'Arukh*, such as those by Yehoshu'a *Falk, *Shabbetai ben Me'ir ha-Kohen, and *David ben Shemu'el ha-Levi, effectively ensuring that work's position as the point of departure for subsequent discussion.

Halakhic works continued to be produced in subsequent centuries, most comprising *responsa* and commentaries on the *Shulḥan 'Arukh*. This prompted various attempts to incorporate recent legal thought into codes organized along the lines of the *Shulḥan 'Arukh*. A popular example of this genre was Avraham *Danzig's *Ḥayyei Adam* (1810) and *Ḥokhmat Adam* (1814–1815) on matters of ritual, while the *Shulḥan 'Arukh* of *Shneur Zalman of Lyady was a more scholarly undertaking in this direction. Yeḥi'el Mikhal *Epstein's *'Arukh ha-Shulḥan* (1884–1917) was unusual in its scope, dealing with all aspects of contemporary law as well as with many matters not in current use (e.g., Sanhedrin). It also attempted to return to a fuller presentation of the law. *Yisra'el Me'ir ha-Kohen's *Mishnah Berurah* (1892–1898), which has attained a high reputation in many modern circles, is a commentary on the first section of *Shulḥan ʿArukh* that attempts to provide background to the rulings of *Shulḥan ʿArukh* while incorporating recent developments in halakhic thought and practice. Yaʿaqov Ḥayyim Sofer produced a similar work reflecting developments in the Sephardi community, entitled *Kaf ha-Ḥayyim* (1905–1957). That work also represents a concerted effort to incorporate the kabbalistic practices of Yitsḥaq Luria into normative halakhic practice.

In the last decades of the twentieth century, numerous legal digests have appeared, almost exclusively in the area of ritual law (e.g., Sabbath), and with a tendency toward stringency. Such works have been published in Modern Hebrew, English, and other languages to facilitate a broader familiarization with practical rules. Non-Orthodox (Conservative, Reform, and Reconstructionist) views of *halakhah* have yet to be detailed in a recognized code.

• Menachem Elon, *Jewish Law: History, Sources, Principles*, 4 vols. (Philadelphia, 1994). Nahum Rakover, ed., *Maimonides as Codifier of Jewish Law* (Jerusalem, 1987). Nahum Rakover, *The Multi-Language Bibliography of Jewish Law* (Jerusalem, 1990), p. 308. Haym Soloveitchik, "Rabad of Posquières: A Programmatic Essay," in *Peraqim be-Toledot ha-Ḥevrah ha-Yehudit bi-Yemei ha-Beinayim uva-'et ha-Ḥadash: Muqdashim li-Profesor Yaʿaqov Kats*, edited by E. Etkes and Yosef Salmon (Jerusalem, 1980), pp. 7–40. Isadore Twersky, *Introduction to The Code of Maimonides (Mishneh Torah)*, Yale Judaica Series 22 (New Haven, 1980). Isadore Twersky, "The Shulḥan ʿArukh: Enduring Code of Jewish Law," repr. in *Studies in Jewish Law and Philosophy* (New York, 1982), pp. 130–147. Efraim E. Urbach, *The Halakhah: Its Sources and Development*, (Ramat Gan, 1986). Phyllis Weisbard and David Schonberg, eds., *Jewish Law: Bibliography of Sources and Scholarship in English* (Littleton, Colo., 1989), pp. 57–62.

—EDWARD FRAM

COFFIN. The practice in the ancient Middle East was to bury bodies in wood, stone, or clay coffins decorated with designs and inscriptions. However, the only biblical reference to a coffin is in the case of Joseph (*Gn.* 50.26), and use of coffins by Jews dates only from the late Second Temple period. In some places it was customary to remove the bottom of the coffin in accordance with the verse "You are dust and to dust you shall return" (*Gn.* 3.19). It was strictly forbidden to plunder or derive benefit from a coffin. Maimonides ruled that coffins should be made of wood and be without ornamentation so as to emphasize the equality of all. No metal nails may be used, and the cover must be made of a single flat board. French pietists made the coffin of a scholar from the wood of the table at which he had studied. The use of coffins became widespread in the Diaspora, although many communities, including the kabbalists, did not use them. In recent centuries, the use of coffins has become common practice in order to conform to the requirements of secular law. In the State of Israel, *burials are generally made on a bier, without a coffin. An exception is made for leaders of the state and for fallen soldiers.

• Elizabeth Bloch-Smith, *Judahite Burial Practices and Beliefs about the Dead* (Sheffield, Eng., 1992). Maurice Lamm, *The Jewish Way in Death and Mourning* (New York, 1969). Byron R. McCane, "Jews, Christians, and Burial in Roman Palestine," Ph.D. dissertation, Duke University, 1992.

COHEN. See PRIESTHOOD; for last name, see also KOHEN.

COHEN, HERMANN (1842–1916), German philosopher and founder of the Marburg school of neo-Kantianism. Prominently associated with Reform Judaism, Cohen sought to demonstrate the fundamental compatibility of the Reform conception of Jewish faith with Kant's ethical idealism. Interpreting the latter's teachings in a novel fashion, he understood ethics as summoning society to the task of forging the future in accordance with rationally determined moral principles of justice and peace. This understanding of ethics, he held, was anticipated by biblical monotheism, especially as interpreted by the prophets who envisioned a messianic future—which would witness the manifestation of God's oneness in the moral unity of humanity—as paradoxically a divine promise, whose realization was a human, moral responsibility. In his last years—after his retirement from his professorial position in Marburg in 1912 and his move to Berlin—he emended his views by introducing the notion of "sin"—or the individual's anguished realization of his or her own moral failings. This consciousness of one's sin, Cohen contended, bears the danger that the sinful individual will despair of his or her own moral worth, and abandon all subsequent moral effort. The self-estrangement brought about by the feeling of one's sinfulness requires, in Cohen's judgment, the concept of a forbearing God who by the act of forgiveness serves to reintegrate the individual into an ethically committed humanity. The atonement for sin is not effected by God's grace, but by the individual who, in acknowledging God's forgiveness, in effect rededicates him or herself to the moral task incumbent upon rational humanity. Religion is thus preeminently a series of acts of atonement, in the form of rites and prayers expressing remorse and repentance, focused on a merciful, forgiving God. The reconciliation between God and the individual thus achieved, in turn, requires that God be conceived not as an idea but as a being who relates to the finite, ever-changing world of becoming, of which the human being is a part. Despite the fundamental ontological distinction separating them, being and becoming—God and the individual—are interrelated through what Cohen called "correlation." God and the individual are in correlation when an individual cognizant of God's mercy—a solicitous, forgiving love—rededicates him or herself to emulating these divine qualities. Cohen spoke of correlation as a shared holiness in which God and the individual are "coworkers in the work of creation." Cohen set forth these views most forcefully in his posthumously published work, *Religion der Vernunft aus den Quellen des Judentums* (1919; English translation by Simon Kaplan, *Religion of Reason Out of the Sources of Judaism* [New York, 1972]), in which he expounded his new conception of religion through a selective exegesis of the sources of classical Judaism in the Bible, Midrash, and liturgy. These traditional expressions of Jewish piety, Cohen argues, exemplify the most refined conception of religion. A selection of his Jewish writings, translated by Eva Jospe, appeared under the title *Reason and Hope* (New York, 1971).

• Samuel H. Bergman, *Faith and Reason: An Introduction to Modern Jewish Thought* (Washington, 1961), pp. 22–47. Emil L. Fackenheim, *Hermann Cohen: After Fifty Years*, The Leo Baeck Memorial Lecture 12 (New York, 1969). Helmut Holzhey, *Cohen und Natorp*, 2 vols. (Basel, 1986). Jacob Klatzkin, *Herman Kohen: Shitato be-Musar u-Mishnato be-Yahadut* (Berlin, 1923). —PAUL MENDES-FLOHR

COHEN DE HERRERA, AVRAHAM (c.1562–1635), kabbalist. Born to a *converso* family, probably in Italy, he was captured by Lord Essex while in Cadiz, Spain, in the commercial service of Sultan al-Mansur of Morocco, and taken to London as a Spanish prisoner. He was freed before 1600 after a long diplomatic exchange between the sultan and Queen Elizabeth. Back in Italy, he met Yisra'el *Sarug, who taught him Lurianic Kabbalah. After a short stay in Hamburg, Cohen de Herrera moved, in 1619, to Amsterdam, where he continued his commercial activities and spiritual assignments, such as heading a rabbinical committee to approve Yosef Shelomoh *Del-Medigo's *Elim*.

Cohen de Herrera wrote *Casa de la divinidad*, *Puerto del cielo* as well as the *Epitome y compendio de la logica* in Spanish in order to familiarize his fellow ex-*conversos* with Lurianic Kabbalah. The first two writings were translated into Hebrew by his disciple Yitsḥaq *Aboab da Fonseca and published in 1655, twenty years after Cohen de Herrera's death.

Cohen de Herrera, like Spinoza, integrated many elements of Renaissance philosophy into his work and was recognized by his followers (Yitsḥaq Aboab da Fonseca, Avraham Miguel Cardoso, Yosef Ergas, David Nieto, and Barukh of Kosov) as the father of the metaphoric interpretative school of Lurianic Kabbalah, where the **tsimtsum* (contraction) is a nonrealistic metaphor.

• Alexander Altmann, "Lurianic Kabbala in a Platonic Key: Abraham Cohen Herrera's *Puerta del Cielo*," *Hebrew Union College Annual* 53 (1982): 317–355. Guiseppa Saccaro Battisti, "Herrera and Spinoza on Divine Attributes," *Italia* 4.1 (1985): 21–58. Guiseppa Saccaro Battisti, "La cultura filosofica del rinascimento italiano nella '*Puerta del cielo*' di Abraham Cohen Herrera," *Italia Judaica* 2 (1986): 296–334. Kenneth Krabbenhoft, "The Mystic in Tradition: Abraham Cohen Herrera and Platonic Theology," Ph.D. dissertation, New York University, 1982. Gershom Gerhard Scholem, *Avraham Kohen Hirirah* (Jerusalem, 1978). Nissim Yosha, *Mitos u-Metaforah: Ha-Parshanut ha-Filosofit shel R. Avraham Kohen Hirirah le-Qabbalat ha-Ari* (Jerusalem, 1994). —NISSIM YOSHA

COLLEGIO RABBINICO ITALIANO, the first modern rabbinical seminary, founded in 1829 in Padua. Its most outstanding teacher was Shemu'el David *Luzzatto. The school closed in 1871 and reopened on a smaller scale in Rome in 1887. In 1899 the seminary moved to Florence under the leadership of Shemu'el Hirsch Margulies, and back to Rome in 1939. Closed by the Fascists, it reopened in 1955. A Sephardi branch was opened on the island of Rhodes in 1928 and closed in 1939.

COLON, YOSEF (c.1420–1480) Italian halakhist, also known as Mahariq. Colon was raised in Chambray, the capital of Savoy. Educated primarily by his father, he early distinguished himself in the rabbinic culture of Savoy. In the early 1450s, he moved to Piedmont and later lived in the vicinity of Venice, Mantua, and Pavia.

Colon was, along with Yisra'el ben Petaḥyah Isserlein, the outstanding Ashkenazi authority of the age. His opinion was solicited by scholars throughout Italy and Germany, and his *responsa* had a decisive influence not only upon Italian Jewry but on all subsequent halakhic developments. Editions of his *responsa* (Venice, 1519 et al.) achieved wide distribution. His opinions were cited extensively by later authorities and exerted critical influence upon Yosef Karo and Mosheh Isserles.

Colon's *responsa* are distinguished by his encyclopedic knowledge and methodical analysis of sources. He attempts to identify the basic principles underlying his sources and to elucidate the conceptual framework within which he gives rulings. The *Mishneh Torah* of Maimonides enjoys a preeminent place in his writings.

Colon's *responsa* are marked by great deference to authorities of the past. Hesitating to decide among them, he resorted to methods of legal determination that removed or minimized this necessity. He maintained great independence from his contemporaries, however, and became embroiled in a number of controversies with prominent rabbinic authorities, such as Yisra'el Bruna and Mosheh Capsali, **ḥakham bashi* of the Ottoman empire.

• Jakob Freimann, ed., in *Leket Yosher*, by Joseph ben Moses, vol. 2 (Berlin, 1903), XXXIII, no. 61. Abraham Fuchs, "Historical Material in the Responsa of Rabbi Israel Bruna," D. H. L. dissertation, Yeshiva University, 1974. Moritz Gudemann, *Ha-Torah vehe-Ḥayyim bi-Yemei ha-Beinayim, be-Tsarfat ve-'Ashkenaz*, translated by Abraham Friedberg, (Tel Aviv, 1968), pp. 186–190. Samuel A. Horodezky, in *Le-Qorot ha-Rabbanut* (Warsaw, 1914), pp. 45–55. Renata Segre, *The Jews in Piedmont*, vol. 1 (Tel Aviv, 1986), p. 284, n. 617. Shlomo Simonsohn, *The History of the Jews in the Duchy of Mantua* (Jerusalem, 1977), pp. 704–705. Shlomo Simonsohn, *The Jews in the Duchy of Milan*, vol. 2 (Jerusalem, 1982), p. 749, n. 1826. Isaac H. Weiss, *Dor Dor ve-Dorshav*, vol. 5 (Berlin, 1924), pp. 269–273. Jeffrey Woolf, "The Life and Responsa of Rabbi Joseph Colon ben Solomon Trabotto, Maharik," Ph.D. dissertation, Harvard University, 1991. —JEFFREY R. WOOLF

COLUMBUS PLATFORM, document outlining the "Guiding Principles of *Reform Judaism" adopted by the *Central Conference of American Rabbis at a convention held in Columbus, Ohio, in 1937. The platform superseded the *Pittsburgh platform adopted in 1885, which had served as the basic document of American Reform Judaism. The Columbus platform consisted of three sections—Judaism and Its Foundations, Ethics, and Religious Practice—and differed on many essential points from its predecessor. For example, it defined Judaism as "a way of life," not exclusively as a religion, and emphasized customs, symbols, and ceremonies, the cultivation of distinctive forms of religious art and music, and the use of Hebrew in worship and instruction. One of the most striking changes came in the modification of the previous hostile attitude toward Zionism and Erets Yisra'el. It accepted the principle of Jewish peoplehood and stated that it was "the obligation of all Jewry to aid in the upbuilding of the Jewish homeland by making it not only a haven of refuge for the oppressed but also a center of Jewish cultural and spiritual life." The platform also rejected the charge of dual loyalties by saying that while Jews assume the full duties and responsibilities of citizenship in all lands where they live, this did not contradict their obligation to help in the rebuilding of Palestine. It concluded by linking the restoration of Palestine with the establishment of the Kingdom of God.

• David Polish, *Renew Our Days: The Zionist Issue in Reform Judaism* (Jerusalem, 1976), pp. 199–203.

COMMANDMENT. See MITSVAH.

COMMANDMENTS, REASONS FOR (Heb. *ta'amei ha-mitsvot*). It has long been debated whether the positive and negative biblical commandments (613 in number according to rabbinic tradition; see COMMANDMENTS, 613) had reasons beyond the arbitrary will of the divine legislator, and, more specifically, reasons that made sense to human understanding. The precept to wear fringes on the garment is explained in the Pentateuch (*Nm.* 15.39) "that ye may look upon it and remember all the commandments." The subject was discussed in Talmudic and Midrashic literature. The purification ritual with the ashes of a *red heifer (*Nm.* 19) was usually cited as an example of a rationally inexplicable law. The problem was compounded by the rationalist tendencies of medieval philosophy. *Sa'adyah ben Yosef Ga'on distinguished between legal and moral rules that human reason would have formulated even without scripture and those that depended wholly on revelation. Moses *Maimonides held that all divinely given commandments were rational; the distinction was between those whose reason we could understand and those who were as yet beyond our limited comprehension. The overriding purpose of all *mitsvot*, from the dietary and ceremonial laws to theological doctrines (e.g., the prohibition of idolatrous practices), was to provide a physical, social, moral, and intellectual regime that would lead individuals to the highest spiritual perfection. This view was shared, with minor differences in emphasis, by most thinkers and expounded in works such as the *Sefer ha-Ḥinnukh* ascribed to R. Aharon ha-Levi of Barcelona (c.1300). The kabbalists interpreted the commandments very differently. The Torah being essentially a manifestation of the Godhead, that is, of the ten **sefirot*, the system of *mitsvot* corresponds to this sefirotic realm, and every commandment is thus correlated to some point in it and has as its purpose the promotion of the inner divine union, namely (in Lurianic terminology) the "raising of the sparks." The earliest kabbalistic writings are devoted to expounding this mystical significance of the commandments. On the exoteric level, observance is understood as the way to serve God, as an aid in our struggle against the evil inclination (see YETSER HA-RA' AND YETSER HA-TOV), and as a gift of God to enhance life, gain merit, and become worthy of the world to come (see 'OLAM HA-ZEH AND 'OLAM HA-BA').

With the exception of Samson Raphael *Hirsch, who treated the subject in a manner similar to that of Maimonides and gave a reason for each specific *mitsvah*, most writers in the modern period write about the *mitsvot* in more general terms. Thinkers such as Moses *Mendelssohn, Shemu'el David *Luzzatto, Mordecai Menahem *Kaplan, Eliezer *Berkovits, Abraham Joshua *Heschel, and Louis Jacobs write within an ongoing tradition. Nevertheless, the nature of the question has changed significantly in modern times. Instead of asking, "What reasons did God have for commanding us to keep the *mitsvot?*" modern authors ask, "What reasons do I have for keeping the *mitsvot?*"

• Isaak Heinemann, *Ta'amei ha-Mitsvot be-Sifrut Yisra'el* (Jerusalem, 1958). Samson Raphael Hirsch, *Horeb: A Philosophy of Jewish Laws and Observances*, translated by Isidor Grunfeld (New York, 1994). Menachem Recanati, *Ta'amei ha-Mitsvot* (London, 1962).

COMMANDMENTS, 613 (Heb. *taryag mitsvot*). According to a tradition recorded in the Talmud Bavli (*Mak.* 23b), the number of commandments in the Torah is 613. They are divided into 248 positive and 365 negative commandments, said to correspond to the 248 bones of the body and the 365 days of the solar year (also to the 365 muscles of the human body). Although it is physically impossible for any one person to fulfill all of the commandments, it is nevertheless customary to refer to a particularly righteous person as one who fulfills all *taryag mitsvot* (see Rash ion *Gn.* 32.5). The 613 commandments are binding only on Jews; gentiles are obligated to the seven commandments of the *Noahic laws.

The antiquity of the tradition of 613 commandments is the subject of dispute. Although there are tannaitic passages that reflect this tradition, Efraim Elimelech Urbach has argued that the concept of 613 commandments is amoraic and that any such statements in the tannaitic literature are later interpolations. The veracity of the concept of 613 commandments has also been questioned, in particular by the medieval moralist Baḥya ben Yosef ibn Paquda' and the biblical commentators Avraham ibn Ezra and Nahmanides. According to Ibn Paquda', the 613 commandments only refer to "duties of the limbs" but do not take into account "duties of the heart."

Because no count of the Pentateuchal laws yields precisely the number 613, various rules were formulated defining the principles according to which the biblical injunctions and prohibitions should be counted. A number of medieval scholars produced divergent lists of the 613 commandments. The first of these lists is found in **Halakhot Gedolot*, a halakhic work dating from the geonic period. Later enumerations of the commandments are to be found in works by such renowned scholars as Sa'adyah ben Yosef Ga'on and Ḥefets ben Yatsliaḥ.

The most famous enumeration of the 613 commandments is Moses Maimonides' *Sefer ha-Mitsvot*. This work, originally written in Arabic, divides the commandments into positive and negative. In his introduction, Maimonides sets down fourteen rules that explain his method. These rules became the starting point for all later discussions of theories of enumeration. Both Maimonides' introduction, as well as his detailed enumeration, were subject to great dispute, and the critical strictures of Nahmanides stand out in this regard. In the 1980's the Lubavitch movement, as part of its emphasis on the writings of Maimonides, appealed to all Jewish women to study one commandment a day from *Sefer ha-Mitsvot*.

Among the post-Maimonidean works that record and comment on the 613 commandments, noteworthy is the thirteenth-century anonymous **Sefer ha-Ḥinnukh*. Written in Spain, this work is structured around the various Torah portions rather than the positive and negative commandments. Other important works dating from the thirteenth century are *Sefer Mitsvot Gadol*, by the French Talmudist Mosheh ben Yaʿaqov of Coucy, and *Sefer Mitsvot Qatan*, by Yitsḥaq ben Yosef of Corbeil. In addition to the prose works based on the 613 commandments, there is also a poetic genre known as **azharot* (warnings; the numerical value of the Hebrew word is 613). The best known of the *azharot* is a poem by Shelomoh ibn Gabirol that is included in the Sephardi liturgy.

• Gersion Appel, *A Philosophy of Mizvot* (New York, 1975). Charles B. Chavel, trans., *The Commandments: Sefer ha-Mizvoth of Maimonides*, 2 vols. (London, 1967). Abraham Chill, *The Mitzvot* (Jerusalem, 1974). Ismar Elbogen, *Ha-Tefillah be-Yisra'el* (Tel Aviv, 1972). S. Greenberg, "The Multiplication of the Mitzvot," in *Mordechai M. Kaplan: Jubilee Volume*, edited by Moshe Davis (New York, 1953), pp. 381–397. Yehiel M. Guttmann, *"Beḥinat ha-Mizvot" and "Beḥinat Kiyyum ha-Mizvot": A Survey of the Systems Employed by the Sages for the Enumeration of the Mizvot* (Breslau, 1931). Abraham H. Rabinowitz, *Taryag: A Study of the Origin and Historical Development . . . of the Tradition . . .* (Jerusalem, 1967). Efraim E. Urbach, *The Sages: Their Concepts and Beliefs*, 2 vols. (Jerusalem, 1979). Leopold Zunz, *Die Synagogale Poesie des Mittelalters* (Frankfurt, 1920).

—MARC SHAPIRO

COMMANDMENTS, TEN. See TEN COMMANDMENTS.

COMMENTARIES. See BIBLE EXEGESIS; TALMUD.

COMMUNITY, a term used to render a variety of Hebrew expressions (such as *qehillah*, *ʿedah*, *qahal*, *tsibbur*, *kelal*), each with specific legal, social, and ethical connotations. The widest and at the same time most fundamental concept of the Jewish community is that of a "people" or "nation." Within this general framework, the large community has organized itself into many types of individual communities in its unceasing endeavor to survive under changing conditions. Loose tribal associations gave way in the period of the First Temple to a growing centralization of wealth and power, which did not, however, affect the largely autonomous life of the small towns. With agriculture dominating trade and industry, Erets Yisra'el's towns—with populations seldom above one thousand—were economically and in a great measure politically self-sufficient. The tradition of local autonomy (for example, the "*elders at the gate of the city" and the assemblies for purposes of worship) was to a great extent responsible for the later ability of the Jews to survive in exile. The disintegrating effects of the destruction of the First Temple and deportation were countered by a new form of religious and national association, centered around the *synagogue. It appears that the Babylonian exiles in the sixth century BCE gathered on Sabbaths for a service of prayer and for encouragement from their spiritual leader. But the synagogue was not merely a new type of center for worship; the congregation also marked a new form of local association, which, with variations, has served as the nucleus of Jewish community organization in the Diaspora down to the present day. These local congregations, which fulfilled secular as well as religious functions, depended for whatever unity they were able to achieve upon the authority of the spiritual and lay leadership that guided them—elders, priests, prophets, teachers, and rabbis. Spiritual leadership often transcended national territories, as evidenced by the authority wielded by the Erets Yisra'el patriarchs over the Diaspora Jewish communities throughout the widespread Roman empire and the authority of the Babylonian academies over North African and Spanish Jewry. Religious authority and communal solidarity were so strong that when the Roman government deprived the Jewish courts of justice of their authority by converting them into courts of arbitration (398 CE), or after the suppression of the Erets Yisra'el patriarchate (425 CE), there was still no weakening of internal Jewish community organization. In the Talmudic era, Jews lived in "villages," "cities," or "walled towns," and fell into three categories—"full residents," who had lived in the area for more than twelve months; "half-residents," who had lived there between thirty days and a year; and "transients," who had lived in the area for less than thirty days. At first these Jewish communities were governed by councils consisting of three or seven members, although later there were cases of councils consisting of twelve members. These councils were in charge of communal institutions, raising taxes and disbursing the monies raised, and even regulating prices and wages. They also appointed individuals to supervise the raising and distribution of charitable funds. For centuries congregations and the network of welfare and mutual aid activities that they fostered have served as cohesive agents in Jewish communities throughout the world. Such an organizational form was particularly effective in the small towns that made up the Jewish world of the medieval and early modern periods. The leaders of different communities sometimes met together in *councils and synods, thereby evolving patterns of organization transcending the local community. The Jewish community thus played a key role in safeguarding the Jewish people and their values. It was a corporate body responsible for every aspect of Jewish life. The local community provided the requisite instruments for dealing with both the outside world and the basic structure of inner life. The fact that Jews lived in their own quarter, either forcibly (see GHETTO) or voluntarily, facilitated the existence of an essentially closed society, which had only limited contact with the non-Jewish population. The community—called in Hebrew "the holy community" (*qehillah qedoshah* or *qahal qadosh*)—combined its mundane tasks with a sense of divine mission, based on the Torah and *halakhah*. Intellectual ability, based on mastery of the Jewish law, helped to determine the community leadership, which was shared with the affluent. The community assembly was a main instrument of policy making. The obligations of mutual help were accepted by all members of the community, in accordance with the Talmudic dictum that "All Israelites are responsible for each other" (*Shev*. 39a). This involved the establishment in every community of a network of religious, educational, social, and philanthropic institutions. The community maintained the synagogue, the school, and the cemetery, while "societies" looked after the sick and aged, buried the dead, ransomed Jews in captivity, dowered poor brides, and cared for the needy, orphans, and widows. The hub of community life was the synagogue, which served many functions—place of prayer, house of study for children and adults, seat of the law court, place of community assembly, and social center.

The nature of the Jewish community changed with emancipation. Under Napoléon (see SANHEDRIN, FRENCH) Jews lost their traditional autonomy and were recognized as citizens like all others, though sharing, as individuals, a particular religion. This trend spread throughout Europe (and was always the case in the United States): membership in the community was no longer compulsory but voluntary. Jews had to decide whether or not to contribute to community funds. Jewish courts of law were relevant only for those who chose to have recourse to them. General schooling was provided by the state, and only education in Jewish matters remained the responsibility of the community or the synagogue. State social-security and health schemes provided services for which Jews had previously depended on the community. New priorities emerged, including support for the State of Israel and Jews in distress in other countries, community relations and interfaith activities, public relations, and support for Jewish education, including higher education. In the United States an umbrella federation of constituent associations has become an important expression of Jewish communal organization.

The modern trend toward the concentration of Jewish populations in and around large cities and the heterogeneity of thought and behavior characteristic of modern democratic societies have largely destroyed the unified and homogeneous character of the traditional local community. New community organizations on a national level are of different kinds. Freedom of association in a democratic society, the phenomenon of antisemitism, and the establishment of the State of Israel brought new challenges and problems. In both the sociology and theology of Judaism the precise nature of the Jewish community continues to be a major issue, about which opinions range from traditional conceptions originating in rabbinic theology of the Community of Israel (Keneset Yisra'el) as a mystical body whose transcendent character is merely reflected in the earthly, historical people to sociological definitions of the community in terms of its identifying racial, cultural, or social traits. See also AUTONOMY; TAQQANOT HA-QAHAL.

• Everett E. Gendlet, "Community," in *Contemporary Jewish Religious Thought*, edited by Arthur A. Cohen and Paul Mendes-Flohr (New York, 1987). Mordecai Kaplan, *Judaism as a Civilization* (New York, 1935). Mark Zborowski and Elizabeth Herzog, *Life Is with People: The Culture of the Shtetl* (New York, 1962).

COMMUNITY REGULATIONS. See TAQQANAH.

COMPASSION (Heb. *raḥamim*). The Hebrew word for compassion is etymologically related to *reḥem* (womb), and compassion is regarded as the quintessential feeling of a mother for her child (cf. *Is*. 49.15, "Can a woman forget her sucking child, that she should not have compassion on the son of her womb?"). It is considered an outstanding virtue. The Talmud states that "Whosoever shows compassion to God's creatures is surely of the seed of Abraham," and conversely, "he who fails to show compassion is certainly not of such descent" (*Beits*. 32b; cf. *Yev*. 79a). The Jewish people are referred to by the rabbis as the "compassionate children of compassionate sires" (based on *Qid*. 4a). The Torah repeatedly enjoins compassion for the powerless and defenseless, such as widows, orphans, and strangers. Mercy is a divine attribute, and God is often referred to as *ha-raḥaman* (the compassionate one) or as *av ha-raḥamim* (father of compassion); thus, showing compassion is one of the main examples of the *imitation of God. A synonym for both God and the Torah is the frequently used Talmudic word *raḥamana'*. The Talmud relates that when the Egyptians, who had been so cruel to the Israelites, were drowned in the Red Sea, the angels sought to sing songs of praise to God. God, though, forbade them to do so, exclaiming, "My creatures are drowning in the sea, and you would rejoice!" (*Meg*. 10b). Since "God's compassion is extended to all his creatures" (*Ps*. 145.9), compassion should likewise extend beyond the human race to the lowliest of God's creatures (*Gn. Rab*. 33.3), and cruelty to animals is considered a biblical prohibition (see ANIMALS, TREATMENT OF). On the other hand, misplaced compassion often leads to cruelty and crime; the rabbis cite Saul's compassion in his battle against the Amalekites as a case in point (cf. *1 Sm*. 15.9, 22.17–19). Compassion must not interfere with the proper exercise of justice, though the law sometimes takes compassion into account in the passing of judgments (cf. *Ket*. 9.2).

• Ruth Adler, "Compassion for Living Things: A Theme in Jewish Literature and Folklore," in *Ninth World Congress of Jewish Studies*, Division D, vol. 2 (Jerusalem, 1986), pp. 67–72. Dianne Bergant, "Compassion in the Bible," in *Compassionate Ministry*, edited by Gary Sapp (Birmingham, Ala., 1993), pp. 9–34. Samuel S. Dresner, "Rachel and Leah: Sibling Tragedy or the Triumph of Piety and Compassion?" *Bible Review* 6.2 (1990): 22–27, 40–42. Eva Fogelman, "Rescuers of Jews During the Holocaust: A Model for a Caring Community," *Tikkun* 9 (March–April 1994): 61–64. Leo Jung, "The Supreme Triad," in *Justice, Justice Thou Shalt Pursue*, edited by Ronald Sobel (New York, 1975).

—SHMUEL HIMELSTEIN

COMPROMISE (Heb. *pesharah*), a term for the court-directed process by which disputes are settled. Unlike other legal systems, Jewish law permitted direct judicial participation in the settlement process and created rules governing the parameters of a court-mandated compromise. Indeed, the classical codes recount that a *beit din* offered litigants either law (*din*) or compromise (*pesharah*). There is a dispute between various authorities as to how compromise differs from *din*; R. ʿAqiva' Eger (19th cent.) stated that a settlement achieved through compromise may deviate from the award that one would receive according to law by no more than a third. Others disagree and grant greater latitude to court-ordered compromise. In modern times nearly all *beit din* proceedings are done through the rubric of compromise rather than law.

• Dov Bressler, "Arbitration and the Courts in Jewish Law," *Journal of Halacha and Contemporary Society* 9 (1985): 105–126. Michael Broyde, *The Pursuit of Justice: Jewish Perspectives on Practicing Law* (New York, 1996). Eliʿezer Valdenberg, *Sefer She'elot u-Teshuvot: Tsits Eliʿezer* (Jerusalem, 1960), vol. 11, p. 93. —MICHAEL BROYDE

COMPULSION. See DURESS.

COMTAT VENAISSON, name of a former province of southeast France, now the Département of Vaucluse, in which were located four historic Jewish communities: Avignon, Carpentras, Cavaillon, and L'Isle-sur-la Sorgue. Avignon was founded in the second or third century CE; the others are apparently not older than the twelfth century. The Jews of the area spoke their own language, Judeo-Provençal, and had their own liturgical traditions. Among the latter was the replacement of Sim Shalom (the final benediction of the *ʿAmidah in the morning service) by Shalom Rav, which does not occur at all in the Sephardi liturgy and which in the Ashkenazi liturgy is read only in the afternoon and evening services. Other unique features of the ritual were the omission of the ʿAleinu prayer at the conclusion of each service, and the substitution for the regular Birkat ha-Shir on the Sabbath during the Christian Holy Week with a prayer entitled Nishmat de-Yom Hesger which commemorates an old prohibition against Jews leaving their homes during that period.

• Emile Camau, *Les Juifs en Provence* (Paris, 1928). Armand Lunel, *Juifs, du Languedoc, de la Provence, et des États français du pape* (Paris, 1975). René Moulinas, *Les Juifs du pape en France: Les communautés d'Avignon et du Comtat Venaissin aux 17e et 18e siècles* (Paris, 1981). Herbert S. Pick, "Minhag Provans," master's thesis, Bar Ilan University, 1977. —A. STANLEY DREYFUS

CONCUBINAGE, cohabitation of a woman with one particular man but without either *qiddushin* or a *ketubbah* (*San*. 21a). Medieval authorities disagreed over the question of whether the taking of a concubine is prohibited or permitted. Some authorities permit it, provided that the concubine observes the rules of *niddah*. The majority prohibit concubinage, although there is a dispute as to the nature of the prohibition (Otsar ha-Poseqim, *Even ha-ʿEzer* 26.3–8). In more recent times, the prohibition is almost unanimous and it is generally agreed that "no woman is permitted to any man except through *qiddushin, ḥuppah, shevaʿ berakhot* and *ketubbah*" (*Resp. Radbaz* 4, no. 225). Concubinage carries none of the rights associated with marriage, although some authorities do require a "*get* out of stringency." Children born to a concubine do, however, acquire rights of both a personal status and a pecuniary nature (*Resp. Rashba'* 4, no. 314). A "common law wife" under Israeli law is in a position similar to that of a concubine in terms of personal status.

• Judah D. Eisenstein, ed., *Otsar Yisra'el* (Jerusalem, 1951), vol. 8, pp. 229–230. —DANIEL SINCLAIR

CONDITIONS (Heb. *tena'im*). Jewish law allows the imposition of conditions on many different types of transactions. For example, conditions can be imposed on financial transactions (e.g., *Shulḥan ʿArukh, Ḥoshen Mishpat* 307) or ritual actions (e.g., *Shulḥan ʿArukh, Oraḥ Ḥayyim* 273.1). Unlike other legal systems, Jewish law allowed one to impose both prospective and retrospective conditions on a marriage or divorce (e.g., *Shulḥan ʿArukh, Even ha-ʿEzer* 38). As a general rule, when a condition is imposed on a transaction and is not fulfilled, the underlying activity is retroactively void: if a woman is conditionally divorced but the condition is not fulfilled, she does not have the status of a divorcee in Jewish law (*Shulḥan ʿArukh, Even ha-ʿEzer* 6.1).

Jewish law recognizes implicit, as well as explicit, conditions. Thus, one who enters into a labor contract when no conditions of employment are specified does so in accordance with the customary conditions imposed on all such agreements in the locale in which that person resides. Indeed, a condition can be conditionally imposed by merely announcing that one's actions are predicated on a future event, even if that event is not explicitly stated as a condition (*Shulḥan ʿArukh, Ḥoshen Mishpat* 207.1–4).

The Talmud (*Ket*. 74a; *Yev*. 106a) states, however, that conditions may not be imposed on a *ḥalitsah* (see LEVIRATE MARRIAGE) ceremony. *Tosafot* on *Ketubbot* 74a states that *ḥalitsah* is different from marriage and divorce in that *ḥalitsah* cannot be done through an agent, and there can be no conditions imposed on anything that cannot be done through an agent. Nahmanides, commenting on *Bava' Batra'* 126, notes a different limitation on the right to impose conditions. He says that conditions can be made that affect only the people in the transaction and not others. Mosheh Feinstein (*Iggerot Mosheh, Yoreh Deʿah* 2.124) notes the possibility of conditional conversions. The *Shulḥan ʿArukh* discusses the precise legal formulation needed to validly make a condition in *Even ha-ʿEzer* 39–40 and *Ḥoshen Mishpat* 307.

• Boaz Cohen, "Conditions in Jewish and Roman Law," in *Harry Austryn Wolfson Jubilee Volume*, edited by the American Academy for Jewish Research (Jerusalem, 1965), pp. 203–232. Zvi Ehrman, "Conditions," in *Principles of Jewish Law*, edited by Menachem Elon (Jerusalem, 1974), pp. 174–177. —MICHAEL BROYDE

CONFESSION, a term with distinct meanings in Jewish litergy and in Jewish law.

In Litergy. Confession is the admission and acknowledgment of guilt or wrongdoing that might otherwise remain undisclosed. Confession (*viddui*) is a means of expiation and atonement for such wrongdoing and is one of the three essential elements of true *repentance (the other two being regret for the action committed and a resolve not to repeat it). Thus the sin offering in the Temple was accompanied by confession, and, relying on further biblical traditions (e.g. *2 Sm*. 12), the rabbis held that there could be no remission of sin without confession. Confession is made directly to God (and by no means through an intermediary) and may be said individually, in one's private prayers, or collectively, institutionalized in public congregational confession, such as during *Yom Kippur. The wording of the liturgical confession is based upon that given by the high priest in the Temple following the ordinance (*Lv.* 16.21) "Aaron shall . . . confess . . . all the iniquities and transgressions of the Israelites," and although there was originally no fixed wording for the confession, traditional formulas emerged and were incorporated into the liturgy. Various formulas for private confessions are also suggested in rabbinic literature; for example: " 'How shall a man make [private] confession on the eve of the Day of Atonement?' He should say 'I confess for all the wrongs that I have committed. I have taken the path of evil and all I did I will not do alike. May it be your will, O Lord my God, to pardon me for all my iniquities, forgive me all my transgressions, and grant me atonement for all my sins'" (*Lv. Rab.* 3.3). Public confessions appear in the liturgies for penitential and fast days (for example the last lines of *Avinu Malkenu), as well as for every Monday and Thursday (see SHENI VA-ḤAMISHI), containing, in contrast to their congregational setting, detailed enumerations of sins. Private confession is said by some at night before retiring and also by a bridegroom and bride before their wedding. Since confession in general is recognized as having the power to effect atonement for sins, confession on one's deathbed is a matter of great importance and is recommended in the Talmud (*Shab.* 32a), which cites the precedent of *Achan (*Jos.* 7.19). A traditional formula, which incorporates the Mishnaic petition "May my death be an atonement for all the sins . . . of which I have been guilty toward you" (*San.* 6.2), evolved and is recorded by Nahmanides. The custom of confession regularly to a trusted friend or master was practiced in some mystic circles, particularly in some of the sixteenth century kabbalistic brotherhoods, but did not gain wider currency.

• Ismar Elbogen, *Jewish Liturgy: A Comprehensive History*, translated by Raymond P. Scheindlin (Philadelphia, 1993), pp. 125–126, 178–183. Moshe Greenberg, *Biblical Prose Prayer: As a Window to the Popular Religion of Ancient Israel*, The Taubman Lectures in Jewish Studies, 6 (Berkeley, 1983), pp. 19–37. Elie Munk, *The World of Prayer*, vol. 2 (New York, 1963), pp. 239–250. Solomon Schechter, *Studies in Judaism*, vol. 3 (Philadelphia, 1908), p. 358. —PETER LENHARDT

In Law. Confession denotes two different legal concepts. The first is confession of judgment in a civil matter, which Jewish law rules to be a valid acknowledgment of debt. Unlike other forms of testimony that can be impeached on the basis of countertestimony, a confession of judgment in a civil matter is irrefutable evidence of the validity of the debt; such a confession of judgment is the equivalent of one hundred witnesses and is unimpeachable. This is so even if the confession of judgment is clearly untrue, unless the presence of the debt diminishes the rights of other creditors.

The second form of confession is confession of guilt in a criminal or ritual matter. In this case, a contrary rule is adopted, which maintains that confessions of guilt are categorically inadmissible to prove legal guilt and that one may not confess to a violation of law that would label one an evildoer. Thus, one who confesses to a murder may not be punished based on the confession, and the confession is inadmissible in a *beit din*. (Jewish law does, however, recognize the validity of a Noahic court that uses confessions to determine guilt.) In a case where a person confesses to a violation of law that has both civil and criminal consequences, the civil consequences are applied and the criminal consequences are not. Thus, a woman who confesses to adultery would forfeit the *ketubbah* upon divorce but would not be punished as an adulteress and need not be divorced, as is the law in cases of provable adultery.

• Arnold Enker, "Self Incrimination," in *Jewish Law and Current Legal Problems*, edited by Nahum Rakover (Jerusalem, 1984), pp. 169–174. Phillip Segal, "Reflections on Ethical Elements of Judaic Halakhah," *Duquesne Law Review* 23 (1985): 863–903. Shalom M. Valakh, *Be'urei ha-Viddui* (Bene Beraq, 1989). —MICHAEL BROYDE

CONFIRMATION, a religious innovation introduced in 1810 in Kassel, Germany, as a Reform alternative, for young men and women, to the *bar mitsvah*. As a rite of passage at age sixteen, it was felt to be more in keeping with the times, as it was closer to adulthood. It also ensured that young people would continue to study for several years after the age of twelve or thirteen. There was never a fixed formula for the ceremony, though the group ceremony often takes place on Shavu'ot to symbolize the commitment of a new generation to the Sinai covenant. Today it is practiced in the Reform and Reconstructionist movements, and, in a more limited way, in the Conservative movement as an additional life-cycle event. During the first half of the twentieth century, in the Conservative movement, confirmation enabled adolescent girls to participate in a public, religious, rite-of-passage ceremony.

• Isaac Klein, *A Guide to Jewish Religious Practice* (New York, 1979), pp. 152–153. Melvin L. and Shoshana R. Silberman, "From Bar/Bat Mitzvah Through the Teen Years: Challenges to Parent and Community," in *Celebration and Renewal: Rites of Passage in Judaism*, edited by Rela Mintz Geffen (Philadelphia, 1993). —RELA MINTZ GEFFEN

CONFISCATION. The Talmud (*Yev.* 89b; *Mak.* 16a) rules that Jewish courts may expropriate property and impose fines other than those mentioned in the Bible (e.g., *Ex.* 21.32). The source of this power is referred to as *hefqer beit din hefqer*, which loosely translates as "court ordered abandonment of property is validly abandoned." It is generally understood that this power can be exercised not only by rabbinic authorities but also by the government of the community (*Shulḥan 'Arukh, Ḥoshen Mishpat* 2.1). Included in the power to divest one of ownership was the power to assign ownership to another. However, this power was significantly limited when used by the government; the government is obligated to pay just compensation for items that it confiscates from individuals other than as a form of punishment (*Mishneh Torah, Ḥilkhot Melakhim* 3.8), and any items taken from an individual without compensation are considered stolen.

The power of *hefqer beit din* is significant not only in terms of the punishment of criminals or the orderly operation of public laws, but as a source of legislative power in law. Many of the laws enacted by Talmudic sages that shifted property rights from one person to another were justified through the power of *hefqer beit din*;

for example, the rule that minors could sell property. The power of expropriation significantly enhanced the sages' authority over areas of law other than financial law. For example, the power of expropriation provided the source to annul improper marriages (*Yev.* 110a) and other regulations in the field of family law. Any change in legal rule that caused a financial loss to one party, or any change in status predicated on receiving financial consideration, could be effected by the operation of *hefqer beit din*.

• Haim H. Cohn, "Expropriation," in *Principles of Jewish Law*, edited by Menachem Elon (Jerusalem, 1975), pp. 448–450. Menachem Elon, *Jewish Law: History, Sources, Principles* (Philadelphia, 1994), pp. 507–515. "Hefker Beit Din," *Entsiqlopedyah Talmudit* (Jerusalem, 1947–), vol. 10, pp. 95–110.

—MICHAEL BROYDE

CONFLICT OF OPINION (Heb. *maḥloqet ha-poseqim*). The process by which a conflict of opinion is resolved is one of the unique features of post-Talmudic law. There is frequently more than one answer to any particular question of law, each of which is a fully legitimate expression of law consistent with the Talmudic data and yet not so analytically persuasive as to disprove other possible explanations. In addition, Jewish law developed certain procedural rules for functionally resolving disputes in cases where no substantive resolution is actually possible.

In the Second Temple era, disputes of law were ultimately resolved by the *Sanhedrin, which was the final authority on Jewish law. One who defied this body was liable to the death penalty under the laws of **zaqen mamre'*. However, when this body ceased functioning, Jewish law was essentially decentralized. Since that time, individual decisors and communities have been charged with making decisions consistent with the substantive rules of law found in the Talmud and later codes.

Since conflicting answers to any particular question of Jewish law could be provided by different decisors, later authorities would evaluate the analytic soundness of each of these possible answers and discard those that were considered inconsistent with the Talmudic data. Frequently it would not be possible to determine with certainty which opinion among decisors was the one most consistent with the Talmudic data, which is the primary method of determining correctness. In those apparently unresolvable disputes, later authorities used other principles (such as following the majority of decisors; being strict in the case of a biblical prohibition and lenient in the case of a rabbinic one; following the lenient rule in the laws of mourning; or following the case-specific rules of double doubt). Beneath these principles were a considerable number of other rules designed to resolve still unresolvable disputes. Included in this category were such concepts as custom, economic necessity, and time of need.

Some decisors engrossed themselves in the Talmudic discourse to resolve disputes. Other decisors were more inclined to use the other principles in cases where the favored method did not produce clear results.

• Eliezer Ehrenpreis, "Safeq and Sefeq Sefaqa': Their Relationship to Scientific Observation," *Gesher* 8 (1981): 90–108. Menachem Elon, *Jewish Law: History, Sources, Principles*, 4 vols. (Philadelphia, 1994).

—MICHAEL BROYDE

CONGRATULATIONS. See GREETINGS AND CONGRATULATIONS.

CONGREGATION. See COMMUNITY; SYNAGOGUE.

CONSECRATION. See DEDICATION; HOLINESS.

CONSENT. See APPROBATION.

CONSERVATIVE JUDAISM, a religious movement that developed primarily in the United States in the twentieth century, inspired by the nineteenth-century Historical school of Judaism in Europe (see HISTORICAL MOVEMENT). The Enlightenment ideology that brought full citizenship to the Jews of western Europe and the United States in the late eighteenth and nineteenth centuries simultaneously engendered considerable intermarriage and assimilation. The Historical movement, led by Zacharias *Frankel (1801–1875), sought to stem that tide by applying new, historical methods to the study of the Jewish tradition within the context of traditional Jewish practices and a commitment to Jewish nationhood, Erets Yisra'el, and the Hebrew language. It sought, in other words, to conserve tradition in the modern setting, hence, the name of the movement, Conservative Judaism.

Jewish law and thought have changed over time. The tradition remained coherent, however, because those calling it their own saw their ideas and practices as deeply rooted in the concepts and acts of their forebears. The Historical view thus puts great emphasis on Judaism as practiced by the Jewish people from generation to generation. Solomon *Schechter called attention to this in his concept of catholic Israel (*kelal Yisra'el*), according to which it is Judaism as practiced by the people committed to it that ultimately has authority. This emphasis on Jewish peoplehood, while influenced by Jewish secularists like Aḥad ha-ʿAm, was, in the hands of the progenitors of the Conservative movement, distinctly religious in character: Jewish law and thought were important not only because they were the heritage of the Jewish people, but because they represented the ways in which Jews conceive of and worship God.

This prepared the groundwork for the ideological and legal developments of the twentieth century. Since the Conservative movement saw Judaism as a dynamic, developing tradition practiced by a people, it hesitated, in contrast to the Reform movement, which, in 1885 and 1937, issued platform statements, to draw sharp ideological lines. In the judgment of its mid-twentieth-century exponents, like Robert Gordis, Simon Greenberg, Mordecai Menahem *Kaplan, and Mordecai Waxman, and their successors, such as Elliot N. Dorff and Neil Gillman, that would not only be counterproductive but untrue to the historical realities of tradition. They each wrote books on what they conceived Conservative Judaism to be. Though these writings expressed the views and ideas of their individual authors, they also enabled the movement to maintain a sense of identity while not proscribing other variations. Even with the creation of a Commission on the Philosophy of the Conservative Movement, the document it produced in 1988, *Emet ve-'Emunah: Statement of Principles of Conservative Judaism,* was a consensus document that set out the broad parameters of Conservative Jewish belief and practice but left much room for inclusion of affiliates of varying ideologies. Common to all Conservative ideologies has been a strong emphasis on the Jewish people and their culture and home in Erets Yisra'el; an affirmation of the indispensably religious character of Jewish identity, albeit with wide variations as to how Jewish religious commitments are interpreted; an assertion of the binding, but developing character of Jewish law; a dedication to the study of Jewish sources in both traditional and new, historical ways; and a strong commitment to both Jewish tradition and modernity and to the need to integrate, rather than bifurcate, the two.

There has not emerged a similar, movement-sponsored code of Jewish practice. The closest approximation, Isaac Klein's *A Guide to Jewish Religious Practice* (1979), is a respected but also only an individual articulation. The communal decisions of the Conservative movement on matters of Jewish practice are made by its Committee on Law and Standards. That body has produced a rich corpus of rabbinic *responsa*, but only some of them have been published to date, and they, in any case, do not even pretend to be a full-fledged code guiding every aspect of Jewish practice. With regard to many issues of Jewish law, Conservative Jewish practice has been determined by communal custom, leaving no need for such a code, and where there is no agreement, the differences among synagogues are viewed as a healthy sign of wrestling with tradition and applying it to regional circumstances.

There have, however, been movement-sponsored prayer books. One of the first genuine voices of the Conservative movement was the *Sabbath and Festival Prayer Book,* edited by Morris Silverman and published first in 1946 by a joint Prayer Book Commission of the movement's rabbinic and congregational bodies, which contained the traditional liturgy in its usual, Hebrew form, but included several notable changes. Three of the opening morning blessings were rephrased from the negative to the positive—specifically, from "who has not made me a gentile" to "who has made me an Israelite"; from "who has not made me a slave" to "who has made me a free person"; and from "who has not made me a woman" to "who has made me in his image." Another important change occurred in the Musaf service, where the traditional prayer for the restoration of the sacrificial services in the Temple was changed to the past tense so that those sacrifices are remembered as a stimulus for the worshiper's own form of devotion to God, prayer. This effectively articulated that the Conservative movement did not look forward to the rebuilding of the Temple and the restoration of its sacrificial cult. These changes have been maintained and amplified in the *Weekday Prayer Book* (1961) and in the full prayer book, *Siddur Sim Shalom* (1985).

Conservative Judaism construes Jewish law as binding, but changes can be made through its rabbinic leaders, especially through its Committee on Jewish Law and Standards. Most of the Conservative movement's rabbinic decisions have simply applied Jewish law to new circumstances, but Conservative Judaism has instituted important changes in the role of *women in Jewish life. Mixed seating during worship has characterized Conservative synagogues from their earliest days in America; the first *bat mitsvah,* that of Mordecai Kaplan's daughter, took place in 1922; women were allowed to read the Torah and recite the blessings over it according to a 1954 ruling; a clause was introduced into the Conservative marriage document (*ketubbah*) to alleviate the inequality embedded in traditional Jewish divorce law; women could be counted for a prayer quorum according to a 1973 ruling; women were admitted to rabbinical school beginning in 1984; and many Conservative synagogues are now fully egalitarian, men and women playing equal roles in worship and in the other aspects of synagogue leadership.

The schools of higher Jewish learning of the Conservative movement are the *Jewish Theological Seminary of America in New York; the *University of Judaism in Los Angeles; the *Seminario Rabínico Latinoamericano in Buenos Aires; and the Beit Midrash in Jerusalem (in Israel the Conservative movement is referred to as the Masorti movement). Conservative rabbis, cantors, and teachers are organized, respectively, through the Rabbinical Assembly, the Cantors' Assembly, the Educators' Assembly. The Solomon Schechter Day School Association is affiliated with the Conservative movement, as are other youth and camping programs. The synagogue arm of the Conservative movement is the *United Synagogue of Conservative Judaism and the *World Council of Synagogues.

There have been two breakaways from the Conservative movement. The left wing began *Reconstructionism, while the Conservative decision to allow women into rabbinical school led the right wing to form its own organization, the Union for Traditional Conservative Judaism. In 1990 the latter dropped its affiliation with the Conservative movement and changed its name to the Union for Traditional Judaism. This group subsequently opened a rabbinical school and established its own board of halakhic inquiry.

• Nina Beth Cardin and David Wolf Silverman, eds., *The Seminary at 100: Reflections on the Jewish Theological Seminary and the Conservative Movement* (New York, 1987). *Conservative Judaism*, a journal published quarterly since 1945 by the Jewish Theological Seminary of America and the Rabbinical Assembly. Moshe Davis, *The Emergence of Conservative Judaism* (Philadelphia, 1963). Elliot N. Dorff, *Conservative Judaism: Our Ancestors to Our Descendants* (New York, 1977). Elliot N. Dorff, "The Ideology of Conservative Judaism: Sklare After Thirty Years," *American Jewish History* 74.2 (December 1984): 102–117. Neil Gillman, *Conser-*

vative Judaism: The New Century (West Orange, N.J., 1993). Robert Gordis, *Understanding Conservative Judaism* (New York, 1978). Pamela S. Nadell, *Conservative Judaism in America: A Bibliographical Dictionary and Sourcebook* (New York, 1988). Seymour Siegel, ed., *Conservative Judaism and Jewish Law* (New York, 1977). Seymour Siegel and Elliot Gertel, eds., *God in the Teachings of Conservative Judaism* (New York, 1985). Marshall Sklare, *Conservative Judaism: An American Religious Movement* (Glencoe, Ill., 1955). Mordecai Waxman, ed., *Tradition and Change: The Development of the Conservative Movement* (New York, 1958).

–ELLIOT NELSON DORFF

CONSISTOIRE, governing body of a Jewish communal district. The institution was established by the Napoleonic decree of 1808 following the outcome of the French *Sanhedrin, which provided for the creation of consistories of both clerical and lay participants throughout France with a central *consistoire* in Paris under three grand rabbis and two laymen. This replaced the previous rabbinical and communal structure. It was later responsible for the maintenance of the rabbinical seminary (founded in 1830) and the chief rabbinate (established in 1844). Algeria had a *consistoire* from 1845. The system still prevails in France, Belgium, and Luxembourg.

CONSOLATION. See MOURNING.

CONTEMPT OF COURT. There is no crime in Jewish law called contempt of court, as is found in common law. Rather the idea of contempt of court posits a general obligation to obey the rulings of a *beit din*. This manifests itself in different ways. Defiance of an order of a *beit din* can lead to excommunication. More frequently, however, court-authorized social pressure is applied to individuals who refuse to abide by a decision of the *beit din*. This is repeatedly referred to in the law codes (*Shulḥan ʿArukh, Yoreh Deʿah* 334.43; *Ḥoshen Mishpat* 1.5, 1.6, 2.1, 8.5, 11.1, 11.5, 16.3, 18.3, 100.3). Even in cases where a court cannot issue an order directing a person to perform or not to perform a particular act, but in which the *beit din* merely states that this particular conduct is a *mitsvah*, it is a form of contempt of court to decline to listen to the words of the sages, which can be addressed through social punishment. This was probably first used in the context of a husband who refused to participate in a Jewish divorce, in a case where Jewish law does not mandate that a divorce be given. Nonetheless, a *beit din* may inform the husband that a divorce is a *mitsvah* and authorize social sanctions if he does not participate in the Jewish divorce. This is given the formal name *harḥaqot de-Rabbenu Tam*, the separations ordered by R. *Yaʿaqov ben Me'ir Tam, creator of this form of social pressure.

• Menachem Elon, *Jewish Law: History, Sources, Principles*, 4 vols. (Philadelphia, 1994). ʿOvadyah Yosef, *Yabi'a Omer* (Jerusalem, 1953–), vol. 7, p. 23 (*Even ha-ʿEzer*).

–MICHAEL BROYDE

CONTRACEPTION. See BIRTH CONTROL.

CONTRACT. See DEED.

CONTRACTION. See TSIMTSUM.

CONTROVERSIES. The existence or emergence of deviating views or movements (schismatic, heretical, or sectarian) inevitably produced controversies in which one group attacked the other's position and defended its own. Controversies often crystallized in literary works and were thus responsible for an important part of theological literature. The Bible, for instance, contains many polemics against paganism. The breach with the *Samaritans resulted in a long, drawn-out struggle, the religious core of which was the question of whether Judaism was based on the Torah alone or on the entire Bible, as well as on the Samaritan claims regarding Mount *Gerizim. In the Second Temple period, the Hellenizers (see HELLENISM), profoundly influenced by Greek thought, engaged in controversy with representatives of traditional Jewish thought. The same period saw intensive controversy among the sects, especially between the *Sadducees and *Pharisees. The Pharisees, with their broader interpretation of the Torah, disagreed with the narrow Sadducean tradition. Sectarian controversies involving the *Essenes and others are probably reflected in the *Dead Sea Scrolls, while controversies with *Jewish Christians are preserved in rabbinic literature. The legal controversies between the schools of Hillel and Shamm'ai (see BEIT HILLEL AND BEIT SHAMM'AI) were over matters of interpretation rather than fundamentals of faith. The disputes with the *Karaites, forcefully led by *Saʿadyah ben Yosef Ga'on, were over the acceptance or nonacceptance of rabbinic law; the Karaites dubbed their opponents Rabbanites. The rationalist and philosophical views of Moses *Maimonides brought about the *Maimonidean Controversy, in which his opponents banned his works. Various kabbalistic manifestations were sharply criticized by the mainstream rabbis. The messianic movement led by *Shabbetai Tsevi evoked bitter controversy, of which the Frankist (see FRANK, YAʿAQOV) and the Emden–Eybeschuetz (see EMDEN, YAʿAQOV; EYBESCHUETZ, YONATAN) controversies were two offshoots. The rise of *Hasidism in the second half of the eighteenth century led to violent disputes in eastern Europe between the Ḥasidim and their opponents, the *Mitnaggedim. *Emancipation engendered a religious pluralism that led to bitter controversies between the Orthodox and non-Orthodox. The disputes between Orthodoxy and Reform, which were initially directed against such individuals as Abraham *Geiger, acquired an ideological tone after the first Reform council at Brunswick in 1844; they have continued with varying degrees of intensity ever since. The nineteenth century saw an intense controversy surrounding the *Haskalah. The advent of modern *Zionism led to violent disagreements between advocates of a return to Zion and their opponents, including the Reform movement, assimilationists, and some Orthodox Jews.

In the twentieth century, internal divisions, such as those within Orthodoxy or the Conservative movement, or those between religious and secular Jews, have led to the diversification of controversies, as has the creation of the State of Israel. See also MINIM; POLEMICS. For controversies with non-Jews, see DISPUTATIONS.

• Raphael Jospe and Stanley M. Wagner, eds., *Great Schisms in Jewish History* (Denver and New York, 1981). Reuben Kaufman, *Great Sects and Schisms in Judaism* (New York, 1967). Menachem Mor, ed., *Jewish Sects, Religious Movements, and Political Parties*, Studies in Jewish Civilization 3 (Omaha, 1992). Jacob Neusner, ed., *Controversies in the Study of Judaic Religion and Theology*, Origins of Judaism 4 (New York, 1990). J. Julius Scott, *Customs and Controversies: Intertestamental Backgrounds of the New Testament* (Grand Rapids, 1995).

CONVERSION, FORCED. The forced conversion of the Idumeans (Edomites) to Judaism by John Hyrcanus (135–105) is the only such recorded case of forced conversions to Judaism. On the other hand, Jews have been the victims of forced conversions throughout their history. Rabbis have issued special enactments to provide for Jews who were unable to observe their religion openly, the first case of which occurred in the period immediately preceding the Maccabean Revolt in 168 BCE. Forced conversions to Christianity as a result of mob violence occurred in the Roman empire from the fourth through the sixth century, and it later became state policy in Visigothic Spain and elsewhere. During the *Crusades, a number of Jewish communities, especially in the Rhineland, were given the alternative of baptism or death; in most cases they chose the latter alternative. When, after the persecutions, those who had adopted the dominant faith to save their lives applied to return to the Jewish fold, all rabbinical authorities, including *Gershom ben Yehudah and *Rashi, insisted that they be treated with the utmost tact and consideration, and any mention of their previous lapse was forbidden. If, after their forced conversion (see APOSTASY), they had made efforts to practice Judaism secretly, they were not to be regarded as apostates. Even Moses *Maimonides, who ruled in his *Mishneh Torah* that a Jew should accept death rather than abandon a single commandment under compulsion, agreed that apostasy under threat of death was not to be punished. The Almohade persecution in Spain and North Africa in 1148 produced a wave of forced conversions. *Maimon ben Yosef, in his *Iggeret ha-Shemad*, encouraged the forced converts to "hang on by their fingertips." Maimonides permitted the outward assumption of Islam to save one's life, since the Muslims, unlike the Christians, required only a formal declaration of adherence to their faith and did not insist on the abandonment of Jewish practices. Forced conversions under Muslim pressure also produced the Daggatun—a Moroccan Berber tribe, traditionally of Jewish origin; and the *Jedid al-Islam, in nineteenth-century Persia. The most extensive forced conversion in Jewish history occurred in Spain following the widespread anti-Jewish excesses that began in Seville in 1391. These converts were called *Marranos (Heb. *anusim* [forced ones]). A considerable number of Jews remained loyal to the faith despite strong pressures and peril. It was they who were expelled from Spain in 1492. A number of them proceeded to Portugal where they were forcibly converted in 1496; in subsequent centuries, many Portuguese Marranos maintained, in secret, a number of modified Jewish practices (see CRYPTO-JEWS). Problems in Jewish law arose as to the Jewishness of the descendants of forced converts and Marranos who were unable to return to Judaism; it was decided that such a person, upon returning to Judaism, was not required to undergo the obligatory ceremony for proselytes.

• Martin Goodman, *Mission and Conversion: Proselytizing in the Religious History of the Roman Empire* (Oxford, 1994). Benzion Netanyahu, *The Origins of the Inquisition in Fifteenth-Century Spain* (New York, 1995). Dan Ross, *Acts of Faith: A Journey to the Fringes of Jewish Identity* (New York, 1984).

CONVERSION FROM JUDAISM. See APOSTASY.

CONVERSION TO JUDAISM. See PROSELYTE.

CONVERSOS. See MARRANOS.

COPPER SCROLL, one of the *Dead Sea Scrolls, the only Qumran text to be inscribed on metal. Strictly speaking, it is not a "scroll" but a copper plaque. It was discovered in Cave 3 in 1952, having become badly oxidized and brittle. In order to unroll it, the *Copper Scroll* had to be segmented into long strips. Written in Hebrew (with Greek ciphers), it describes in a factual manner some sixty-four hiding places of treasures, scrolls, and a second copy of the *Copper Scroll*. Controversy has arisen over the interpretation of the document, and unsuccessful treasure hunting has been conducted. Some believe that the sheer size of the treasures described in the *Copper Scroll* are more imaginary than real; they do not believe the scroll was produced by the Qumran community. Others argue that the dry realism of the *Copper Scroll*'s language is evidence of its documental nature and consider it part of the Qumran-Essene library. A third group believes that the *Copper Scroll* describes not the hidden possessions of the Qumran community but the treasures and archive of the Second Temple.

• John Marco Allegro, *The Treasure of the Copper Scroll* (Garden City, N.Y., 1960). Maurice Baillet, J. T. Milik, and Roland de Vaux, *Les 'Petites Grottes' de Qumrân*, Discoveries in the Judean Desert, vol. 3 (Oxford, 1962), pp 201–302. Norman Golb, "The Problem of the Origin and Identification of the Dead Sea Scrolls," *Proceedings of the American Philosophical Society* 124 (1980): 68–82. Judah K. Lefkovits, "The Copper Scroll-3Q15: A New Reading, Translation and Commentary," Ph.D. dissertation, New York University, 1993. Bargil Pixner, "Unravelling the Copper Scroll Code: A Study on the Topography of 3Q15," *Revue de Qumran* 11.43 (1983): 323–365.

—TIMOTHY H. LIM

COPPER SERPENT. See NEHUSHTAN.

CORDOVERO, MOSHEH BEN YA'AQOV (1522–1570), kabbalist. He studied with R. Yosef *Karo and R. Shelomoh *Alkabez, who was his brother-in-law. R. Yitsḥaq *Luria considered himself a student of Cordovero. Cordovero's family apparently came from Cordoba and may have lived for a time in Portugal. Cordovero served as the head of the Portuguese *yeshivah* in Safed.

His first major work was *Pardes Rimmonim* (Kraków, 1592), which he completed at the age of twenty-six. This treats such central kabbalistic subjects as the nature of the divine, theodicy, the cosmos, the human being, and the worship of God. Many themes are found repeatedly in his works. One is the parable of fire and spheres, which is explicated in his *magnum opus, Or Yaqar* (Jerusalem, 1962– , 23 vols. to date [Part of *Or Yaqar* is named *Shiʿur Qomah*, which is his introduction to his *Commentary to the Iddrot* and was issued separately in Warsaw in 1883]). Prior to the emanation of the **sefirot*, there existed the *Ein Sof, the transcendent aspect of the divine. In order to emanate the *sefirot*, which are the revealed aspect of the divine, the Ein Sof retracted within itself (**tsimtsum*) and made space for their presence. The *sefirot* were then emanated, each one in the form of a sphere encased within a sphere. The divine essence, symbolized by fire, was then able to penetrate these spheres, which functioned as vessels. This fire was, however, less potent than the fire that surrounded the spheres. Another example of Cordovero's mythic system can be found in his *Elimah* (Lemberg, 1881), in which he describes the nature of God's pleasure. The beneficence and joy of the Ein Sof is not complete until the *sefirot*, which emanated from him, return to him. The Jewish people are expected ultimately, by virtue of learning the Torah and fulfilling the commandments, to return with the *sefirost* to the Ein Sof and participate in the divine joy that marks their reunification.

Cordovero's three major works are *Pardes Rimmonim*, *Or Yaqar*, and *Elimah*. *Or Yaqar* is a running commentary to the complete Zoharic corpus, the Pentateuch, and the *Book of Creation*. Cordovero's prayer book, *Tefillah le-Mosheh* (Przemyśl, 1892), which contains his *Perush Tefillot Ro'sh ha-Shanah* and his *Perush Seder ʿAvodat Yom ha-Kippurim*), contains his commentary to the prayers. A significant section of *Elimah* remains in manuscript. This work contains discussions concerning the nature of the divine and the cosmos as well as evil, humankind, and the Torah. Cordovero also composed *Tomer Devorah* (1589), which serves as an appendix to *Elimah* and is a practical guide of ethics based on the divine attributes. (There is an English translation of *Tomer Devorah* by Louis Jacobs [London, 1960]). Cordovero also composed two other works. In *Or Neʿerav* (Venice, 1587) he expounds the importance of the study of Kabbalah. In *Sefer Gerushin* (Venice, 1601), he documents his mystical activities, in the year 1548, near the graves of the righteous, not far from Safed.

Cordovero poses philosophical questions, but his ensuing discussions reveal his mythic tendencies. His daily rituals were based on theurgic and magical practices that involved bringing down the divine efflux. Cordovero sought to identify with his spiritual models, who were largely based on Zoharic figures. This intention was infused with strong messianic feeling. He held that it was the mystic's duty to intervene in the cosmic order so that he could hasten the redemption. The imitation of the ways of the Zoharic figures characterizes his works no less than those of Yitsḥaq Luria. Each one contains the themes of the affinity between souls and the central importance of intention in prayer (see INTENT). Cordovero studied all the various kabbalistic systems that preceded him. He was influenced by the theosophical–theurgical Kabbalah, particularly that of the Zohar, and also adopted the ecstatic Kabbalah of Avraham ben Shemu'el *Abulafia. He wrote *Torat ha-Qabbalah* (edited by Samuel Horodetzky [Berlin, 1924]). Cordovero's thought greatly influenced both later kabbalistic thought and Hasidism.

• Yosef Ben Shlomo, *Torat ha-'Elohut shel R. Mosheh Cordovero* (Jerusalem, 1965). Bracha Sack, *Be-Shaʿarei ha-Qabbalah shel Rabbi Mosheh Cordovero* (Beersheba, 1995).

—BRACHA SACK AND DANIEL ABRAMS

CORNERS. See LEQET, SHIKHḤAH, AND PE'AH; PE'AH.

CORPORAL PUNISHMENT. See FLOGGING.

CORPSE, a dead human body. In biblical times all who came into contact with a corpse were rendered ritually unclean, as was the building where the corpse was situated together with all inhabitants and any uncovered vessels inside. Purification was effected by sprinkling all contaminated persons and objects on the third day after defilement with water containing ashes of the *red heifer, with an additional sprinkling on the seventh day, together with the immersion of the person defiled and his clothes (*Nm*. 19.14–22). These regulations are expanded in the Mishnah tractate **Ohalot*. *Burial of a corpse was a religious obligation (*Lv*. 21); only the high priest and Nazirites were absolutely forbidden to come into contact with a corpse. In rabbinic law the prohibition against contact with a corpse applied to all members of priestly families; hence, *kohanim* cannot remain under the same roof with a corpse, attend burials, or visit the cemetery. In all cases where contact was permitted, subsequent washing of the hands was made obligatory. Care of the corpse is regarded as a particularly meritorious *mitsvah* and is organized by the **ḥevrah qaddisha'*. Between death and burial the corpse is not to be left alone. Before the funeral the corpse is washed (see TOHORAH). The Orthodox conception of "reverence for the dead body" requires that burial take place within twenty-four hours of death whenever possible.

• Avraham M. Avidan, *Darkhei Ḥesed* (Jerusalem, 1978).

COSMOLOGY. The connotations of the words *heaven*, *earth*, and *created* have been a constant subject of inquiry and speculation. Traditional Jewish teaching (the rabbis, Philo, and most medieval philosophers) insisted that creation was made from nothing (*ex nihilo*), but some thinkers, claiming the support of the biblical account itself, held that the universe was fashioned from preexistent, formless matter and interpreted the biblical passages accordingly. By the time of the early rabbis, no systematic doctrine concerning the act of creation had developed. The subject, known as *Maʿaseh Be-Re'shit, was considered an esoteric discipline restricted to initiates only because of the dangers—in particular of dualist and gnostic heresies—that it harbored for the average mind. Nevertheless, much cosmogonic and cosmological speculation is contained in Talmudic and Midrashic *aggadah*. It is prominent in such writings as the **Pirqei de-Rabbi Eliʿezer*, *Midrash Qonen*, and other subsequent influences on the *Kabbalah, a system in which man, namely the Jew, is held to occupy a central position in the cosmos. This anthropocentric tendency reached its acme in the teachings of Yitsḥaq ben Shelomoh *Luria regarding the "breaking of the vessels" and the cosmic *tiqqun*. Whereas kabbalistic cosmogony and cosmology were greatly influenced by the Neoplatonic tradition, most medieval philosophers followed the Aristotelian system. *Maimonides summarized his cosmological views in his code (*Hilkhot Yesodei ha-Torah*) and thereby codified the Ptolemaic system, according to which the earth, surrounded by concentric, incorporeal, and "intelligent" spheres, was held to be the center of the universe. Throughout ancient and medieval times, cosmogony was closely allied to theology in general and mysticism in particular, especially since religious language always used cosmic terminology: things divine are "heavenly" as contrasted with things material and earthly; the spirit soars to "higher spheres" (hence, the influence of cosmology on mystical experience); and so on. Modern *science rendered a completely literal acceptance of the traditional imagery, and of biblical cosmography in particular, a virtual impossibility. There are still literalists and fundamentalists in Orthodox circles, but the general tendency is to agree that the biblical account of Creation is to be read for its moral and religious message rather than for its scientific meaning. See also CREATION.

• Isaac Husik, *A History of Mediaeval Jewish Philosophy* (New York, 1974). Robert K. McIver, "Cosmology as a Key to the Thought-World of Philo of Alexandria," *Andrews University Seminary Studies* 26 (1988): 267–279.

COSTUME. Information on clothing customs in biblical times suffers from a paucity of illustrative material as well as uncertainty concerning the meaning of clothing terms. The only biblical injunctions in the matter of dress are the prohibition against the wearing of *shaʿatnez* (cloth woven of wool and linen; *Lv*. 19.19; see KIL'AYIM), the commandment to place fringes upon the four corners of one's garments (*Nm*. 15.37–41; see TALLIT; TSITSIT), and the prohibition against the "abomination" of wearing the dress or accouterments of the opposite sex (*Dt*. 22.5), though the commentators largely limit this prohibition to men wearing such dress for lewd purposes. Almost all the clothing terms in the Mishnah, Talmud, and Midrash derive from Greek or Latin. During the Talmudic period, the duty of adopting distinctive Jewish garb was raised to the level of a biblical commandment, based upon an interpretation of *Leviticus* 18.3, "Neither shall ye walk in their ordinances." According to the Midrash, one of the four factors contributing to the redemption of the children of Israel from Egypt was that "they did not change their [distinctively Jewish] garments [for prevailing Egyptian fashions]" (*Lv. Rab*. 32.5). The law against Jews wearing the garments of gentiles makes it clear that the prohibition is confined, in the words of Yosef Karo, to "garments peculiarly distinctive of the gentiles," or, as Mosheh *Isserles puts it, "to such garments that suggest brazenness or have an idolatrous connection." Nonetheless, the custom developed for Jews to wear a unique costume as a demonstration of their Jewish identity.

During the late Middle Ages, Polish Jews adopted the then obsolete dress of the Polish noblemen, the fur-trimmed hat (*shtreiml*) and the long caftan (*kapota* or *tazliq*; a long outer garment reaching to the ankles), to which the Ḥasidim added, for religious reasons, a girdle (Yi. *gartel*) around the waist (to distinguish, when praying, the "pure" upper part of the body from the "impure" lower and also to symbolize the commandment to "gird one's loins" in God's service). For mystical reasons, Hasidic garments buttoned from right to left. This garb is still worn by Ḥasidim and in certain ultra-Orthodox Jewish circles and has been invested with a quasi-sanctity.

Married Jewish women typically wore head coverings, and from a certain period, men did as well (see COVERING OF THE HEAD; WIGS). Change of garments was obligatory, where possible, on Sabbaths and festivals (*Shab*. 113a), and scholars were also supposed to wear distinctive clothing (*Ber*. 43b; *Shab*. 113a).

The Jewish badge ordained by the Fourth Lateran Council (1215) in order to prevent social mixing between Jews and Christians inspired later authorities to insist that Jews wear some distinguishing article of apparel (such as a badge or hat). In the Middle Ages, Jewish authorities in western Europe issued a series of *sumptuary laws designed to help Jews resist Christian fashions and to avoid the arousal of envy by Christians for Jewish ostentation. See also KITEL.

• Thérèse Metzger and Mendel Metzger, *Jewish Life in the Middle Ages* (Fribourg, 1982), pp. 111–150. Herman Pollack, *Jewish Folkways in Germanic Lands (1648–1806): Studies in the Aspects of Daily Life* (Cambridge, Mass., 1971), pp. 85–95. Alfred Rubens, *A History of Jewish Costume* (London, 1973), includes bibliography. Yedida K. Stillman, "Costume in the Middle East," *Middle East Association Bulletin* 26.1 (1992): 13–38. Yedida K. Stillman, "Jewish Costume and Textile Studies: The State of the Art," *Jewish Folklore and Ethnology Review* 10.2 (1988): 5–9. Aaron Verthaim, *Law and Custom in Hasidism* (Hoboken, N.J., 1992).

COUNCILS AND SYNODS, gatherings of rabbis, sometimes convened by the rulers of countries in which Jews lived, sometimes in conjunction with laymen, for the purpose of safeguarding the Jewish religion, regulating the inner life of the Jewish community and its relationship with the outer world, or framing extralegal communal enactments that would thereafter be binding upon all those represented. Antecedents may be discerned in the Great Assembly (*Keneset ha-Gedolah) and in rabbinical meetings after the destruction of the Second Temple, such as that at *Yavneh (c.90 CE), where the biblical canon was determined, or Usha' (c.138; see USHA', SYNOD OF), where halakhic rules were laid out. One provision adopted by the latter (see *Ket*. 49b–50a) required parents to care for their children as long as they were minors, and if parents deeded their property to their children during their lifetimes, the children were required to maintain the parents out of the estate. Councils and synods as distinctive aspects of Jewish self-government developed in the Jewish communities of the Rhineland and northern France at the beginning of the second millennium CE. The first synod in medieval Jewish history was convened (c.1150) by the brothers *Shemu'el ben Me'ir and *Yaʿaqov ben Me'ir Tam, grandsons of Rashi, and was followed by a second synod in 1160. Two of the resulting enactments were the prohibition against having recourse to gentile courts of law and an amendment to R. *Gershom ben Yehudah's prohibition against polygamy, which permitted a man to take a second wife if a hundred rabbis from three different provinces testified that his first wife was insane and, hence, incapable of accepting a divorce. An indication of the spirit of the times was a decision by this synod to forbid the purchase of a crucifix or any Christian ritual object by a Jew, lest Jews be falsely accused later of defiling the objects involved and thereby endanger the community. An important topic at many synods was that of finding ways to ease the lot of the *ʿ*agunah*—a woman whose husband was missing or who refused to give his wife a divorce, thus making it impossible for her to remarry. Two important synods were held in Mainz in 1220 and 1223 under the leadership of the most distinguished rabbis of the day, *Elʿazar ben Yehudah of Worms and *Eliʿezer ben Yo'el ha-Levi of Bonn. The enactments passed there became generally accepted by Ashkenazi Jewry. Gradually these synods extended the scope of their activities to include every phase of the religious, economic, social, and family life of the Jews. In Spain the available evidence shows that councils and synods were convened by the rulers to review financial and civil matters within the Jewish community. In 1552, Middle Eastern rabbis convened a synod in Jerusalem to determine the sabbatical year. The most important and long-lived synod in Jewish history was the Polish Council of the Four Lands, which consisted of thirty delegates—both rabbinical and lay—and met twice yearly at the fairs of Lublin and Jarosław. This council embraced every possible aspect of Jewish activity. In the religious sphere, for instance, it safeguarded strict observance of the law and bitterly fought the followers of *Shabbetai Tsevi and the Frankists (see FRANK, YAʿAQOV). It lasted for some two centuries beginning in 1550. Synods in Saint Petersburg were convened on several occasions during the nineteenth century by the Russian government, the last in 1879 to satisfy governmental interest in Jewish marriage and divorce laws. One of the most famous of modern synods was the Grand Sanhedrin (see SANHEDRIN, FRENCH) convoked by Napoléon Bonaparte in 1807, at which Jews recognized the authority of civil law and set up a central Jewish communal administration in France. A notable synod took place in Kraków in 1903; all the rabbis present (about 50) took a public oath that the *blood libel was absolutely false and that neither the Talmud nor any other rabbinic book contains any mention of the ritual use of blood, which would be contrary to Jewish law. Except for the synod convened by Napoléon, all the synods until the mid-nineteenth century were intent on strengthening the observance of *halakhah*. That was not the case with the conferences covered by the modern Reform movement, such as the *rabbinical conferences at Brunswick in 1844, Frankfurt in 1845, and Breslau (Wrocław) in 1846. It was at the Frankfurt conference that Zacharias *Frankel parted company with those of the Reform movement and became one of the founders of the Historical school (later Conservative Judaism). One of the most decisive meetings in the history of Reform took place in 1885 in Pittsburgh, Pennsylvania, and produced the *Pittsburgh platform, which guided the movement for several decades. The Central Conference of Reform Rabbis met in 1937 in Columbus, Ohio, and reversed the opposition to Jewish nationalism expressed in the 1885 platform (see COLUMBUS PLATFORM). Each convention of the *Central Conference of American Rabbis (Reform), the *Rabbinical Assembly (Conservative), and the *Rabbinical Council of America (Orthodox) takes stands on problems in contemporary Jewish life, and the same is true for the periodic conventions of the European Orthodox chief rabbis.

• Simon Dubnow, *Pinkas ha-Medinah* (Berlin, 1925). Hyman G. Enelow, "The Jewish Synod: A Study of the History of an Institution," thesis, Hebrew Union College, 1902. Louis Finkelstein, *Jewish Self-Government in the Middle Ages* (New York, 1964). Louis Lewin, *Die Landessynode der grosspolnischen Judenschaft* (Frankfurt, 1926).

COUNTING OF ʿOMER. See ʿOMER.

COURTS. See BEIT DIN; SANHEDRIN.

COVENANT (Heb. *berit*), an agreement by which two contracting parties enter into a special kind of relationship (e.g., of solidarity, friendship, obedience, etc.). The biblical concept of covenant has its roots in ancient Near Eastern models but thoroughly transforms them. A covenant could be made between man and his fellow or between man and God and was usually confirmed by some kind of ritual symbolizing the union of the partners. Such bonds between men are illustrated by the biblical accounts of the covenant between Jacob and Laban (*Gn.* 31.44) and that between the king and the people during the reign of Zedekiah (*Jer.* 34). In the former, God is invoked as a witness of the sanctity of the covenant (*Gn.* 31.53); the latter solemnly provided for the release of all Hebrew slaves, and its subsequent breach by the slave owners was also regarded as a breach of the basic covenant between God and the people of Israel (*Jer.* 34.14–16). The account in *Jeremiah* (34.18–19) also describes the ceremonial part of the covenant, which consisted of the two parties passing between the two halves of a calf (cf. the Hebrew idiom *karat berit* [cutting a covenant]; *Gn.* 15). The covenant that God made with Abraham and subsequently confirmed to Isaac and Jacob is fundamental to the theological understanding of the development of Judaism. The original covenant with the patriarchs was renewed, this time with the whole people, at Sinai (*Ex.* 24), where the people accepted the obligations of the law ("the two tablets of the covenant"; cf. *Ex.* 31.18, 32.15ff.). The covenant was renewed again by Ezra (*Neh.* 8). God's eternal fidelity to his covenant, in spite of Israel's backsliding, is a major theme in *aggadah* and liturgy (cf. also *Lv.* 26.42–45). The new covenant mentioned by the prophets (e.g., *Jer.* 31.30–33) is understood as spiritual renewal, written on their hearts, and not as a new covenant replacing the old. Outward signs serve to testify to the permanent validity of a covenant, notably *circumcision—*berit milah*, the covenant par excellence—for the covenant of Abraham and the Sabbath (*Ex.* 31.16–17). Other, more specific, covenants conferred the priesthood on the house of Aaron (*Nm.* 25.12–13) and kingship on the house of David (*Ps.* 132). A covenant involving mankind as a whole, and indeed the entire natural order, was made with Noah (*Gn.* 9.12–15); according to *Jeremiah* (33.19–21, 25–26) the specific covenants with Israel and David are everlasting. The traditional idea of a covenant between God and his people is presupposed by the prophets and forms the background of their preaching. The prophetic curses are also to be understood in the light of traditional maledictions attached to treaties, imposed upon whoever breaks the terms of the pact.

• "Covenant Davidic," in *Interpreter's Dictionary of the Bible*, edited by Keith Crim, sup. vol. (Nashville, 1976). Arnold M. Eisen, "Covenant" in *Contemporary Jewish Religious Thought*, edited by Arthur A. Cohen and Paul R. Mendes-Flohr (New York, 1987), pp. 107–112.

COVENANT, BOOK OF THE (Heb. *Sefer ha-Berit*) as used in the Torah (*Ex.* 24.7), the written listing of "all the words of the Lord and all the statutes," spoken by God to Moses on Mount Sinai (*Ex.* 20.19–23, 33; see GIVING OF THE TORAH) and written down by Moses upon his descent from the mountain. Moses read this document aloud to the people, who, in a covenant ceremony featuring the blood of sacrificial offerings, unanimously reaffirmed their solemn promise to abide by all the commandments contained in the "book" (*Ex.* 24.3–8).

Modern biblical scholars use the term to refer to the law code in *Exodus* 21–23, incorporated in the Elohist (E) source. Similarly, the term "Minor Book of the Covenant" refers to the shorter law code, also designated by the Torah as a covenant, in *Exodus* 34.10–26, assigned by scholars to the Yahvist (J) source.

The term has also been used for the document found in the Temple when renovations were undertaken by King *Josiah of Judah in 622 BCE (*2 Kgs.* 23.2, 21; *2 Chr.* 34.30), as a result of which a major cultic reform was conducted. This document is referred to both as a *Sefer ha-Berit* and as a *Sefer ha-Torah* (Book of Instruction [or Law]); thus, it is traditionally believed to have been a long lost copy of the entire Torah that had been neglected during the previous reigns. Biblical scholars believe it to have been the book of **Deuteronomy*. See also BIBLE.

• Brevard S. Childs, *The Book of Exodus* (Philadelphia, 1974), pp. 440–496. Mordechai Cogan and Hayim Tadmor, *II Kings*, The Anchor Bible (Garden City, N.Y., 1988), pp. 277–304. Shalom M. Paul, *Studies in the Book of the Covenant in the Light of Cuneiform*, Supplements to Vetus Testamentum, vol. 18 (Leiden, 1970).

–BARUCH J. SCHWARTZ

COVENANT OF ABRAHAM. See CIRCUMCISION.

COVERING OF THE HEAD (Heb. *kissui ro'sh*). There is little basis in ancient Jewish law for the custom of going about with the head covered, or even for covering the head during prayer and other religious exercises. It is an outstanding example of custom (see MINHAG) assuming the force of law. The most explicit reference to it in the Talmud is the statement of R. Huna' ben Yehoshu'a that he would never walk four cubits bareheaded, since "the Divine Presence is above my head" (*Qid.* 31a). Thus, covering the head became a sign of reverence and awe and an acknowledgment of the omnipresence of God. The Bible prescribes that the high priest wear a miter (*Ex.* 28), but otherwise bareheadedness (*gillui ro'sh*) was the prevailing custom. The Babylonian custom was to cover the head, especially during prayer, as a mark of piety, and with the ascendency of Babylonian influence (including the Talmud Bavli), the importance of covering the head grew. The growth of Islam subsequently strengthened the concept of keeping the head covered during prayer. Yitsḥaq Alfasi (*Qid.* [Vienna ed.] 217b) and Maimonides (*Yad, Hilkhot De'ot* 6, *Hilkhot Tefillah* 5.5) both followed the Babylonian tradition and prohibited uncovered heads. Yet it took a long time for this custom to gain universal acceptance. As late as the thirteenth century, R. Yitsḥaq ben Mosheh of Vienna expressed his disapproval of boys going up to read the Torah bareheaded: "The custom of our rabbis in France of reciting blessings with uncovered head does not meet with my approval" (*Or Zaru'a* 11.43). Shclomoh Luria (16th cent.) wrote in a *responsum* (No. 72): "I do not know of any prohibition against pronouncing blessings with uncovered head . . . were it not for the fact that I am not accustomed to differ from the ancient teachers, I would be inclined to be lenient and utter blessings, or even recite the Shema', with uncovered head . . . the prohibition against uncovering the head even when not at prayer astonishes me; I do not know its source." Rabbi Eliyyahu ben Shelomoh Zalman of Vilna (the Vilna Ga'on) agreed with him that the prohibition was based on custom only. However, the seventeenth-century rabbi David ha-Levi of Ostrog found religious prescription in his interpretation of the Talmudic view of *Leviticus* 18.3, "we shall not walk in their ordinances" (*ḥuqqat ha-goyyim*); that is, Jews should cover their heads at prayer because Christians do not. The wearing of a skullcap (Heb. *kippah*; Yi. *yarmulke*), found among Ashkenazim from the early eighteenth century, became a universal custom among Orthodox Jews. The prevalent custom among strictly Orthodox Jews is to keep their heads covered at all times during their waking hours, and all traditionalist Jews cover their heads when praying. When the *Reform movement emerged in nineteenth-century Germany, the covering of the head, even at prayer, was one of the customs it tended to abandon. *Neo-Orthodoxy, seeking to combine tradition with life in a non-Jewish society, gave limited permission for Jews to go bareheaded when among non-Jews, setting a precedent for *Conservative Judaism, which made covering the head obligatory only at prayer and study. In the course of time, different attitudes emerged among the Reform: certain temples in the United States even forbade covering the head, although Hungarian *Neology (Hungarian brand of Reform Judaism) retained the practice at worship. More recently, there has been a growing tendency among Reform Jews to pray with covered heads, and a number of younger Conservative and Orthodox rabbis and laypeople wear head coverings throughout the day. This is, in some measure, the result of the influence of Israeli religious Jews who follow that practice. For married women, the obligation to cover the head goes back to ancient times (see *Is*. 3.17; *B. Q*. 8.6) and a wife's public bareheadedness was grounds for divorce (*Ket*. 7.6). In modern times, Orthodox married women cover their heads with a *wig or head scarf when in public. In Hasidic communities, women cut off all their hair before marriage and thereafter wear a head scarf (Yi. *tikhel*). In Yemen, unmarried women, too, covered their hair. Traditionally, men covered their heads to show respect for the presence of God; women did so as a sign of feminine modesty. Many feminists, therefore, in all modern movements of Judaism, while refusing to wear a head covering for the sake of modesty, have encouraged the use of a covering, particularly during prayer, as a similar gesture of respect for God. The practice within Conservative congregations regarding head covering for women is now in flux and varies considerably.

• Michael J. Broyde, Lilli Krakowski, and Marc Shapiro, "Further on Women's Hair Covering: An Exchange," *Judaism* 40 (1991): 79–94. Marc Shapiro, "Another Example of 'Minhag America,'" *Judaism* 39 (1990): 145–154.

COVETOUSNESS, the wrongful desire to possess what belongs by right to another. The tenth commandment (*Ex*. 20.17), which forbids covetousness, is the only commandment in the Decalogue trangressable by thought rather than action, and rabbinic teaching takes it for granted that man can conquer his sinful desires. The later books of the Bible (especially *Prv*.) outspokenly condemn covetousness as a major sin undermining society and moral relationships (cf. *Mi*. 1.1–2). God abhors the covetous man (*Ps*. 10.3); the rabbis regard the violation of the tenth commandment as a violation of the entire Decalogue (*Pes*. 107a). They also say that the covetous man will eventually lose whatever is his (*Sot*. 9a). On the other hand, spiritual covetousness, which takes the form of a desire to emulate others in spiritual matters, is regarded as praiseworthy on the grounds that "the envy of scholars increases wisdom" (*B. B*. 21a).

• Adriana Destro, *The Law of Jealousy: Anthropology of Sotah*, Brown Judaic Studies, no. 181 (Atlanta, 1989). Yo'el ben Aharon Shvarts, *Sefer Middat ha-Qin'ah* (Jerusalem, 1991–1992). –SHMUEL HIMELSTEIN

CREATION. The question of how the cosmos and its workings (in biblical language, "heaven and earth and all their array," *Gn*. 2.1) came into existence has preoccupied all cultures and given rise to a large number of "creation myths." The first chapter of the Bible introduces God—who later reveals himself also as ruler of the universe, lawgiver, judge, redeemer, loving father, lord of history, and the source of providence—the Creator. The universe and human beings are not divine but are created. The *Sabbath, observance of which was specifically incumbent on Israel as a sign of God's *covenant with them, is the weekly commemoration of this original act. The account in *Genesis* does not use philosophical terminology and has lent itself to various interpretations, but it came to be taken as an assertion of creation out of nothing (*creatio ex nihilo*): "God said . . . and there was . . . ," rather than the giving of form to some primordial, eternal, and preexistent matter. The latter view, argued in terms of Greek philosophical tradition in either Platonic or Aristotelian versions, was rejected by most, though not all, medieval theologians, who argued (e.g., Moses *Maimonides) that although the orthodox position was as incapable of proof as its alternative and had to be accepted on the authority of Scripture, it was nevertheless rationally defensible. Some medieval thinkers also suggested a distinction between the biblical verbs *bara'* (creation out of nothing) and *yatsar* (creation out of something). Belief in one Creator–God ruled out dualism, pantheism, and emanationism, although the last came to the fore again in connection with the kabbalistic doctrine of emanations (**sefirot*). See also COSMOLOGY.

• Bernard W. Anderson, ed., *Creation in the Old Testament* (Philadelphia, 1984). Julius Guttmann, *Philosophies of Judaism*, translated by David W. Silverman (New York, 1973). Isaac Husik, *A History of Mediaeval Jewish Philosophy* (New York, 1958). Jacob J. Staub, *The Creation of the World according to Gersonides* (Chicago, 1982). Norbert Samuelson, *The First Seven Days: A Philosophical Commentary on the Creation of Genesis* (Atlanta, 1992). Colette Sirat, *A History of Jewish Philosophy in the Middle Ages* (Cambridge, 1990).

CREATION, BOOK OF. See SEFER YETSIRAH.

CREDIT. See DEBTS; LOANS.

CREED, an authoritative and binding summary of the articles of faith and the fundamental doctrines of a religious community, usually set out in the form of dogmatic statements or questions and answers (*catechism). Whereas the process of the formulation and adoption of such creeds has been a major feature of the history of Christianity, it has played almost no role in the spiritual development of Judaism. The absence of a supreme ecclesiastical body authorized to formulate a catechism is not the sole reason for the virtual absence of creeds in Judaism. It was often felt that the very idea of such formulation ran counter to certain fundamental tendencies in Jewish theology, which is concerned not only with beliefs but very largely with commandments, of which R. Yehudah ha-Nasi' said, "Be as heedful of a light precept as of a grave one for you know not the grant of reward for each precept" (*Avot* 2.1). In the view of the ancient rabbis, faithful and devout observance of the commandments (with its implicit faith) was more important than faith in the sense of formal and credal assent to theological statements; hence, the Midrash could put into the mouth of God the wish: "Would that they abandoned me, but observed my commandments—since the light thereof will turn them again to me" (*Lam. Rab*. introd.). Man is judged by his actions and not by the creed he professes. The nearest approach to a creed in Judaism is to be seen in certain rabbinic statements emphasizing religious fundamentals or defining the actions or beliefs by which a person forfeits his share in the **'olam ha-ba'* or qualifies as an apostate (see APOSTASY). Rabbi Siml'ai (*Mak*. 23b–24a) declared the eleven injunctions of Psalm 15, the six of *Isaiah* 33.16, the three of *Micah* 6.8, and *Habakkuk* 2.4 ("The righteous shall live by his faith") to be the quintessence of the 613 precepts (see COMMANDMENTS, 613), although R. ʿAqiva' stated that the commandment "You shall love your neighbor as yourself" (*Lv.* 19.18) was the "great principle of the Torah" (*Sifra' Qedoshim* 4). All these statements, however, cannot be said to constitute a creed. *Philo (1st cent. CE) was the first philosopher to formulate something like a creed, but his five principles (the existence and rulership of God, the unity of God, the creation of the world, the unity of creation, and divine providence) left little mark on the subsequent history of Jewish theology. Of the various attempts made by the medieval philosophers to formulate a creed, the most successful and enduring is Maimonides' statement of the *Thirteen Principles of Faith, but despite its popularity (the well-known hymn *Yigdal is a poetic version) it has never been formally regarded as binding, and several thinkers objected to it on various grounds. The philosopher Ḥasda'i Crescas reduced the principles to six (divine omniscience and omnipotence, providence, prophecy, human freedom, and the purpose of Torah [spirituality and felicity] and of man [to love God]). Yosef *Albo in his *ʿIqqarim* opposes Maimonides and maintains that there are only three basic dogmas: the existence of God, divine revelation, and retribution. No doubt there always was a body of beliefs or even dogmas held by Jews—not necessarily identical at all times and in all groups—but these beliefs were generally implicit in law and practice, expressed in liturgy and prayer (e.g., the confession of the unity of God in the *Shemaʿ, or of the resurrection of the dead in the ʿAmidah), or expounded in moral and homiletical literature, rather than formally defined in credal statements. In the nineteenth century, creeds came to play a greater role in Judaism. The *Reform movement, partly in imitation of the Christian churches, partly in order to clarify and justify its own deviation from traditional rabbinic Judaism, tried to state its beliefs in declarations or "platforms" (cf., e.g., the *Pittsburgh platform) that partook of a credal, but not necessarily dogmatic, nature. Creeds were also embedded in catechisms that were particularly popular in the nineteenth century. See also DOGMA.

• Louis Jacobs, *A Jewish Theology* (London, 1973). Louis Jacobs, *Principles of the Jewish Faith* (London, 1964). Menahem Kellner, "Heresy and the Nature of Faith in Medieval Jewish Philosophy," *Jewish Quarterly Review* 77 (1987): 299–318.

CREMATION, disposal of the dead by burning. Interment of the dead in the ground or burial in a cave or mausoleum has been Jewish practice throughout history. Rabbinic ruling, based on *Deuteronomy* 21.33 and codified by Maimonides (*Sefer ha-Mitsvot* 231, 53b) and in the *Shulḥan ʿArukh* (*Yoreh Deʿah* 362), regards interment as a positive command.

Various biblical references to burnings at the burial of some kings (*Jer.* 34.5; *2 Chr.* 16.14, 21.19) probably relate to the burning of incense as a mark of respect. The case of the people of Jabesh-gilead who burned the mutilated bodies of King Saul and his sons (*1 Sm.* 31.9–13; *2 Sm.* 2.5) was unique, and cremations are not reported in any other biblical narratives.

Halakhic authorities prohibited cremation. Capital punishment by burning, mentioned in biblical law, was interpreted as the pouring of molten lead down the criminal's throat (*San.* 7.2; Y., *San* 7.24b). One argument against cremation is that it is a rejection of the concept of *kevod ha-met* (respect due to the deceased); to commit the body to destruction by fire is tantamount to the deliberate burning of something that was once sacred. Cremation was also held to imply a rejection of the belief in physical *resurrection.

In spite of the general prohibition against cremation, the Orthodox United Synagogue in London, as well as some leading rabbis in western Europe, have permitted it as long as the ashes, after a normal funeral service, are buried in a coffin. The Conservative Rabbinical Assembly law committee in the United States permits its rabbis to officiate at a service in a funeral home before a body is taken to a crematorium. The Reform movement permits the practice, though it is discouraged in some communities, and its rabbis may officiate at the service and the burial of ashes in cemeteries.

• Isaac Klein, *A Guide to Jewish Religious Practice* (New York, 1979), pp. 275–276. Tzvi Rabinowicz, *A Guide to Life: Jewish Laws and Customs of Mourning* (London, 1964).

—CHAIM PEARL

CRESCAS, ḤASDA'I BEN AVRAHAM (c.1340–1410), Spanish philosopher. He was born and taught in Barcelona, where he was a leader of the community and later *crown rabbi of Aragon. In his later years he lived in Saragossa. His main work, *Or Adonai*, is a closely reasoned critique of Aristotle and the Aristotelian rationalist tradition in Jewish thought, as represented in particular by Maimonides. Crescas propounded an innate Jewish teaching, based on logic as well as Jewish sources, to replace what he saw as an alien philosophy. Steering a middle course between philosophic rationalism on the one hand, and a growing Spanish tendency toward mysticism on the other, Crescas rejected the traditional proofs for the existence of God and insisted that certainty in this matter rested solely on the authority of the Bible. He criticized Maimonides' formulation of thirteen principles of faith and proposed his own list of basic principles. Fundamental is the existence of God, which implies his unity, incorporeity, and uniqueness. Then come six essential dogmas: God's omniscience; his providence; his omnipotence; prophecy (the prophet being elected for love of God); human freedom; the purpose of the Torah and of human kind (to love God). There are also obligatory beliefs, denial of which constitutes heresy: creation *ex nihilo*; immortality of the soul; reward and punishment; resurrection of the righteous; eternity of the Torah; superiority of Moses over other prophets; the Urim and Thummim oracle that enabled the high priest to foresee the future; and the coming of the Messiah. According to Crescas, love of God rather than specific beliefs regarding the nature of creation or an intellectual understanding of the divine was the main concern of religion. His criticism of the twenty-five principles of Aristotelian physics as presented by Maimonides at the beginning of the second book of his *Guide of the Perplexed* implied a conception of the world in which infinity is a reality and the eternity of the world should, therefore, not be a problem for a believer. Crescas also criticized Maimonides for his failure to quote sources, cite the opinions of others, and offer halakhic solutions for new situations in his *Mishneh Torah*. Maimonides' halakhic work was, in the eyes of Crescas, limited and rigid like the Aristotelian universe. *Or Adonai* was written in Hebrew and completed in 1410. It was first printed in Ferrara in 1555 and was translated into English in 1929 by Harry A. Wolfson as *Crescas' Critique of Aristotle*. Crescas, who lost a son in the anti-Jewish riots of 1391, also wrote a critique of the Christian religion to win back Jewish apostates. Written in Catalan, it has survived only in a Hebrew translation by Yosef Shem Tov made in 1451 called *Bittul ʿIqqari ha-Notserim* (*The Refutation of the Christian Principles*, translated by Daniel J. Lasker [Albany, 1992]). *A Sermon for Passover*, with philosophic considerations about God and the human free will, has been published from two manuscripts (*Derashat ha-Pesaḥ le-Rabbi Ḥasda'i Kreskas . . .* , edited by Aviezer Ravitzky [Jerusalem, 1989]). Crescas's theological work was continued and popularized by his disciple Yosef *Albo, and his writings influenced Spinoza.

• Warren Zev Harvey, "Crescas versus Maimonides on Knowledge and Pleasure," in *A Straight Path: Studies in Medieval Philosophy and Culture: Essays in Honor of Arthur Hyman*, edited by Ruth Link-Salinger Hyman (Washington D.C., 1988), pp. 113–123. Warren Zev Harvey, "The Philosopher and Politics: Gersonides and Crescas," in *Scholars and Scholarship: The Interaction between Judaism and Other Cultures*, edited by Leo Landman (New York, 1990), pp. 53–65. Shlomo Pines, *Scholasticism after Thomas Aquinas and the Teachings of Hasdai Crescas and his Predecessors*, Israel Academy of Sciences and Humanities Proceedings, vol. 1, no. 10 (Jerusalem, 1967). Aviezer Ravitzky, *Derashat ha-Pesaḥ le Rabbi Ḥasda'i Crescas u-Meḥqarim be-Mishnato ha-Filosofit* (Jerusalem, 1988). Tamar M. Rudavsky, "The Theory of Time in Maimonides and Crescas," *Maimonidean Studies* 1 (1990): 143–162. Meyer Waxman, *The Philosophy of Don Hasdai Crescas* (New York, 1920). Harry Austryn Wolfson, Introduction to *Crescas' Critique of Aristotle* (Cambridge, Mass., 1929), also contains a bibliography.

—FRANCISCO MORENO CARVALHO

CRIMINAL LAW. See PENAL LAW.

CRIMINAL PROCEDURE. Jewish criminal law and criminal court procedure are dealt with in Mishnah tractate **Sanhedrin* (particularly chaps. 3 and 4), which emphasizes the differences in the treatment of civil and criminal cases. Whereas the former may be tried in a court of three judges, the latter requires a court of at least twenty-three. In criminal cases, the judges must consider first the arguments for acquittal before turning to any charges made against the accused. A majority of one is required for acquittal, but a majority of two is needed for condemnation. There can be no retrial once a defendant has been acquitted of a criminal charge, whereas there can be any number of retrials if there is a guilty verdict. Any witness may be heard for the defense of the accused, but there are serious limitations to accepting witnesses for the prosecution. A guilty verdict cannot be declared on the day of the completion of the trial, but no delay is necessary before a verdict of innocence. Judges in criminal cases must be priests or Levites, of especially pure lineage. Witnesses in criminal cases are given a severe warning to tell nothing but the truth and are cross-examined in a most painstaking manner. A court that perseveres in its cross-examination is considered especially praiseworthy. At least two witnesses are required to secure condemnation and almost any contradiction renders their testimony invalid. Hearsay or circumstantial evidence is not tolerated in the court. Even where guilt was certain, many courts hesitated to pronounce a death sentence and would search for an argument to free the accused; rabbinic law exhibits an aversion to capital punishment. Some rabbis are quoted as saying that a court that pronounced a death sentence even once in seventy years was a "bloody court." In periods of national emergency and the like, men were put to death for such crimes as informing, but this was not usually a court procedure.

Many modern scholars maintain that the medieval decisors of Jewish law developed a system of criminal law and criminal procedure predicated on the system of justice called the king's law (*din melekh*) or on the intrinsic power of a Jewish court to punish violators of Jewish law, and that these procedural rules were used by Jewish courts to punish violations even when a violation could not be proven to the satisfaction of the requirements of Talmudic laws. These scholars maintain that the intent of the rules of Talmudic law was to punish only flagrant, intentional violations of law and that the normative rules of criminal procedure were governed by the king's law or similar concepts.

• Arnold N. Enker, "Aspects of Interaction between the Torah Law, the King's Law, and the Noahide Law in Jewish Criminal Law," *Cardozo Law Review* 12 (1991): 1137–1156. Aaron Kirschenbaum, *Self-Incrimination in Jewish Law* (New York, 1970). Irene Merker Rosenberg and Yale L. Rosenberg, "In the Beginning: The Talmudic Rule against Self-Incrimination," *New York University Law Review* 63 (1988): 955–1050.

—MICHAEL BROYDE

CRITICISM, BIBLICAL. See BIBLE.

CROWN OF ROYALTY. See KETER.

CROWN OF THE LAW. See KETER.

CROWN RABBI, rabbi appointed by the secular authorities as the official representative of the Jewish community to the government. From 1394 to 1401, for instance, Yosef Orabuena, physician to the king of Navarre, was appointed as *rabi mayor de los Judeos del reyna*, "chief rabbi of the Jews of the kingdom," and in 1432 Avraham Benveniste convoked a synod in Valladolid in his capacity as **rab de la corte* (court rabbi). Such appointments were not necessarily made on the basis of the piety or scholarship of the nominee, and for this and other reasons the appointments were looked at somewhat askance by the Jewish community. This dissociation was most pronounced in czarist Russia, where the crown rabbis (**kazyonny ravvin*) were regarded as mere government puppets, whose authority was completely ignored in all but purely official matters, while the real spiritual authority was vested in the *dukhovner* (Orthodox rabbis) who were the real heads of the community. See also CHIEF RABBINATE.

• Simon Schwarzfuchs, *A Concise History of the Rabbinate* (Oxford and Cambridge, 1993), pp. 38–49. —SHMUEL HIMELSTEIN

CRUSADES, the holy wars proclaimed by the papacy and western Christianity in western Europe at the end of the eleventh century with the avowed purpose of wresting the Holy Sepulcher from the hands of the Muslims. The Crusades marked a turning point in the history of the Jews of Christian Europe. From the prime objective of defeating the "infidels" in the Holy Land, Christians turned in an outburst of hate against the Jewish "infidels" in their midst. As early as 1094, Godfrey of Bouillon declared that he would avenge the blood of Jesus on the Jews, leaving none alive. The First Crusade of 1096 brought with it the virtual extermination of such ancient Jewish communities as Speyer, Worms, and Mainz. The tragedy is commemorated to the present day in the Ashkenazi rite in a Sabbath prayer (*Av ha-Raḥamim) for "the holy congregations who laid down their lives for the sanctification of the Divine Name" and in the dirge Arzei Levanon found in the liturgy for 9 Av. The concept of *martyrdom became a supreme value in Ashkenazi Jewry, and the choice of death over conversion was compared with the sacrifice of Isaac (see ʿAQEDAH). When the Crusaders finally reached Palestine and stormed Jerusalem in 1099, they drove all Jews there into a synagogue and burned them alive. The pattern of anti-Jewish massacres, following resolute refusal on the part of the Jews to accept conversion to Christianity, was repeated throughout Europe during subsequent Crusades, although in the Second Crusade they were protected by Bernard of Clairvaux, who equated killing a Jew with killing Jesus and forbade attacks on Jews. The Crusades increased Jewish–Christian tensions and were the prelude to a period of intensive Christian antisemitism (blood libels, allegations of Host desecration, expulsions, etc.).

• Robert Chazan, "The Impact of the Crusades upon Medieval Jewry," *The Solomon Goldman Lectures* 4 (1985): 135–148. Gerson D. Cohen, "The Hebrew Crusade Chronicles and the Ashkenazic Tradition," in *Minha le-Nahum: Biblical and Other Studies Presented to Nahum M. Sarna*, edited by Marc Brettler and Michael Fishbane (Sheffield, Eng., 1993), pp. 36–53. John Gilchrist, "The Perception of Jews in the Canon Law in the Period of the First Two Crusades," *Jewish History* 3.1 (1988): 9–24. Vladimir P. Goss, ed., *The Meeting of Two Worlds: Cultural Exchange between East and West during the Period of the Crusades* (Kalamazoo, 1986). Joshua Prawer, *The World of the Crusaders* (Jerusalem, 1972). Sylvia Schein, "The Jewish Settlement in Palestine in the Crusader Period," in *The Jewish Settlement in Palestine, 634–1881*, edited by Alex Carmel, P. Schaefer and Y. Ben-Artzi (Wiesbaden, 1990), pp. 22–39.

CRYPTO-JEWS, Jews who, as a result of coercion—usually the threat of death—outwardly adopt the dominant faith yet clandestinely continue to maintain Jewish practices. Such groups existed after the Christian Visigoths imposed forced conversion in Spain in the seventh century and the Almohads imposed Islam in North Africa and Spain in the twelfth century. From the late thirteenth century to the sixteenth century, baptized Jews, known as *neofiti* (neophytes), continued to observe Jewish practices in southern Italy, with their center in Trani, and were persecuted by the Catholic church. *Marranos (and *Chuetas in Majorca) are the best-known examples. The crypto-Judaism of the *Dönmeh (those who continued to follow *Shabbetai Tsevi even after his adoption of Islam) belongs to a different category. Their outward acceptance of Islam was a voluntary act undertaken to follow the example of their master. In 1838, the Jews of Mashhad (Persia) were the victims of an outburst of mob violence and were faced with the alternatives of death or the adoption of Islam. Those who could not escape outwardly took the Islamic faith but maintained their Jewish practices and religious exercises with extreme devotion, eventually returning to Judaism (see JEDID AL-ISLAM). See also CONVERSION, FORCED.

• Haim Hillel Ben-Sasson, "The Generation of the Spanish Exiles Considers Its Fate," *Binah* 1 (1989): 83–98. Frances Hernandez, "The Secret Jews of the Southwest," *American Jewish Archives* 44.1 (1992): 411–454. Yosef Kaplan, "From Apostasy to Return to Judaism: The Portuguese Jews in Amsterdam," *Binah* 1 (1989): 99–117. Moshe Lazar, "Scorched Parchments and Tortured Memories: The Jewishness of the Anussim (Crypto-Jews)," in *Cultural Encounters: The Impact of the Inquisition in Spain and the New World*, edited by Mary Elizabeth Perry and Anne J. Cruz (Berkeley, 1991), pp. 176–206. Cecil Roth, *A History of the Marranos* (New York, 1959). Angela S. Selke, *The Conversos of Majorca* (Jerusalem, 1986).

CULI, YAʿAQOV (c.1685–1732), rabbi and author of the first parts of the Judeo-Spanish encyclopedic Bible commentary *Meʿam Loʿez*. Born in Erets Yisra'el, Culi was the grandson of R. Mosheh ibn Ḥabib of Jerusalem, and in 1714 he moved to Constantinople, where he married the daughter of R. Yehudah Rosanes, head of the city's *beit din*, and was appointed *dayyan*. *Meʿam Loʿez* was intended for the "Sephardi nation," which had reached its height in the late seventeenth and early eighteenth centuries in its western European and Mediterranean communities. Culi published the first volume of *Meʿam Loʿez*, on *Genesis*, in 1730 and was working on the next volume, on *Exodus*, when he died. However, he left manuscripts allowing other scholars to continue his work. The volumes on the Pentateuch were concluded in 1782; volumes on many of the later books of the Bible followed.

The commentary draws its sources from the traditional branches of Jewish learning: Talmudic studies expressed in Bible commentaries, halakhic literature, and *responsa*; *midrash* and *aggadah*; and kabbalistic literature, notably the Zohar. There is also a rich vein of legends, proverbs, and anecdotes. The work is completely free of Shabbatean traits, although the influence of Shabbetai Tsevi was still strong in parts of Turkey. It is possible that Culi's objective was to bring back Jews from heretical influences to the traditional sources by making these available in the language they understood—Judeo-Spanish. Culi carefully distinguishes the various sources before producing his synthesis, and his method was continued by his successors, from Yitsḥaq Magriso to Yitsḥaq Peraḥyah, who completed the commentary. Despite the fact that the work was only concluded at the end of the nineteenth century, it forms a consistent unit, especially the commentary on the Pentateuch. At the same time, some of the later writers made their own mark, such as Rafa'el Ḥiyya' Pontremoli, who wrote the commentary on *Esther*, in which he noted the Purim customs of the Jews of Izmir and Jerusalem. *Me'am Lo'ez* is written in a popular style and is regarded as a masterpiece of Judeo-Spanish literature. It has profoundly influenced Ladino-speaking Jews and was reprinted many times.

• L. Landau, "Khuli's Attitude towards Shabbateanism," *Pe'amim* 15 (1982): 58–66. Michael Molho, *Le-Me'am Lo'ez* (Salonika, 1945).

—SHALOM BAR-ASHER

CURSING. See BLESSING AND CURSING.

CURTAIN, ARK. See PAROKHET.

CUSTODIAN. See GUARDIAN.

CUSTOM. See MINHAG.

CYRUS, (Heb. Koresh), Persian King Cyrus II (r. 550–530), founder of the Achaemenian dynasty and the Persian empire. His major contribution to Jewish history was the conquest of Babylon in 539 BCE, setting the stage for the Edict of Cyrus in 538 BCE, which allowed the Judean exiles to return to Jerusalem and rebuild the Second Temple (*Ezr.* 1.1–4; 6.1–5; *2 Chr.* 36.22–23). Cyrus's actions ended the period of the Babylonian exile and ushered in the return to Zion and the beginning of the Second Temple period. Accordingly, Cyrus was the only non-Israelite in the Hebrew Bible to be theologically labeled the *mashiaḥ* (anointed one) of God, whom God had specifically chosen to carry out his mission on behalf of his people Israel (*Isa.* 44.24–45.8). In the Cyrus Cylinder (*ANET*[3], 315–316), on the other hand, the priests of Marduk wrote that deposed chief god Marduk had specifically chosen Cyrus to conquer Babylon in order to restore him to the head of the Babylonian pantheon.

• James B. Pritchard, ed., *Ancient Near Eastern Texts Relating to the Old Testament*, 3d ed. (Princeton, 1969), pp. 315–316. Haim Tadmor, "The Historical Background to the Edict of Cyrus," in *'Oz le-David: Qovets Meḥqarim be-Tanakh Mugash le-David ben Guryon bi-Mele'ot lo Shivim ve-Sheva' Shanim* (Jerusalem, 1964), pp. 450–473, in Hebrew. T. Cuyler Young, Jr., "Cyrus," in *The Anchor Bible Dictionary*, vol. 1 (New York, 1992), pp. 1231–1232.

—CHAIM COHEN

D

DA COSTA, URIEL. See Acosta, Uriel.

DAF YOMI (דַּף יוֹמִי; daily page [i.e., of the Talmud]), a program whereby individuals throughout the world study the same single Talmudic folio page (i.e., two sides) each day, thereby ensuring that participants in the program complete the entire Talmud in approximately seven and a half years. The *daf yomi* was first proposed by R. Me'ir *Shapira' at the 1923 congress of the Agudat Israel movement as a way to enable Jews who studied the Talmud regularly to have a common Talmudic topic to discuss when they met. The *daf yomi* has become an established part of the Orthodox life, with hundreds of classes being offered daily throughout the world. Those involved in the program who are traveling often attend classes in whichever city they happen to be. In recent years the *daf yomi* has been distributed in the form of cassette tapes, with each daily tape running approximately an hour. There are also cities where the *daf yomi* is available by telephone twenty-four hours a day (except for Sabbaths and festivals) from a prerecorded tape.

• Yehoshu'a Boimel, *A Blaze in the Darkening Gloom: The Life of Rav Meir Shapiro* (Spring Valley, N.Y., 1994). —SHMUEL HIMELSTEIN

DAMAGES. See Torts.

DAMASCUS DOCUMENT, one of the texts of the *Qumran community. It is also known as the *Zadokite Document* or *Covenant of Damascus*, and copies of it were found both in the Qumran caves (see Dead Sea Scrolls) and the Cairo *Genizah. There are two medieval copies (MSS A and B) from the storeroom of the Ezra Synagogue in Cairo and ten exemplars (5Q12, 6Q15, 4Q266–273) from the Qumran caves. Reconstruction of the document from the original manuscripts and fragments shows that the original may be roughly divided into five sections: an introduction, admonitions, various laws on purity and sacrifices, rules regulating entrance into and life in the community, and a conclusion. The medieval recension of the *Damascus Document* appears to be shorter than the Qumran version, leaving out the introduction and conclusion as well as various laws and communal rules from the third section. Where the medieval manuscripts and Qumran fragments overlap, however, the differences are minor.

The *Damascus Document*, at least according to the longer Qumran version, has been characterized as primarily a legal text with an introductory admonition. It shares with the **Rule of the Community* and **Temple Scroll* manuscripts distinctive legal teachings (e.g., on polygamy, incest, and oils), although some have been adapted for life in outlying communities. The admonitions section of the *Damascus Document* is important for the study of the origins of the Qumran community, since it appears to recount the gathering of a faithful remnant under the leadership of a Teacher of Righteousness. The work relates that members of the sect left the land of Judah to sojourn in the land of Damascus, hence, its name, but scholarly opinions differ as to whether the reference to Damascus is to be taken literally.

• Joseph M. Baumgarten, "The Cave 4 Versions of the Qumran Penal Code," *Journal of Jewish Studies* 43.2 (1992): 268–276. Magen Broshi, ed., *The Damascus Document Reconsidered* (Jerusalem, 1992). Philip R. Davies, *The Damascus Document: An Interpretation of the "Damascus Document,"* (Sheffield, Eng., 1983). Louis Ginzberg, *An Unknown Jewish Sect* (New York, 1976). —TIMOTHY H. LIM

DAN, the fifth of Jacob's children and the first born to his maidservant Bilhah (*Gn*. 30.5–6). Originally Dan was assigned a territorial allotment northwest of Judah in the coastal plain. However when this area proved too restrictive due to combined Amorite and Philistine pressure, the tribe relocated to the far north of Israel at the foot of Mount Hermon (*Jos*. 19.40–48). This transitional period in the history of the tribe is reflected in the Samson stories (*Jgs*. 13–16) as well as in the account of the tribe's conquest of Laish, which they renamed Dan (*Jgs*. 18). This site achieved notoriety in biblical tradition as a major cultic center of the northern kingdom of Israel, in which the golden calf, erected by Jeroboam I, was worshiped (*1 Kgs*. 12.28–30). Excavations at modern Tel Dan have uncovered remains of what may have been Jeroboam's sanctuary as well as extensive fortifications.

• Avraham Biran and Joseph Naveh, "An Aramaic Stele Fragment from Tel Dan," *Israel Exploration Journal* 43 (1993): 81–98. Avraham Biran, "Tell Dan: Five Years Later," *Biblical Archaeologist* 43 (1980): 168–182. H. M. Nieman, *Die Daniten* (Göttingen, 1985). —DAVID A. GLATT-GILAD

DANCE. The Bible illustrates examples of dance among the Israelites: Miriam led the women in dance after crossing the Red Sea (*Ex*. 15.20–21); the people danced around the golden calf (*Ex*. 32.19); and David's ecstatic solo in front of the Ark on its arrival in Jerusalem (*2 Sm*. 6.14–16) epitomized individual joy.

Dance was used on the *Shalosh Regalim, the pilgrim festivals to Jerusalem. It was featured at the *Simḥat Beit ha-Sho'evah (*Suk*. 53a), and dancing with burning torches is described in *Sukkah* 5.4. Later, on Simḥat Torah, it became customary to dance with the scrolls of the Torah in the synagogue. In Second Temple times, young girls danced in the vineyards on *Tu be-'Av, when the young men selected their brides. The Talmud refers to dance, and *responsa* literature contains many examples of dance practice in Diaspora communities.

The Talmud commands all wedding guests to dance to ensure the joy of the bride and groom (*Ket*. 17a). In medieval Germany, the *Tanzhaus* or community dance house was built because of the need for the whole community to dance at weddings; the rabbi sometimes functioned as the dance leader. Later the **badḥan* or jokester led the *mitsvah tanzes*, a genre of wedding dances developed especially in the Hasidic communities. Yemenite wedding dances include special dances for the bride at the henna ceremonies. Although both Sephardi and Ashkenazi communities developed different repertoires for men and women—the rabbis forbade mixed dancing—the Sephardim permitted dance during the Sabbath while the Ashkenazim did not. Dance played a major role among males in Hasidic worship, which stressed the aspect of joy.

As Jews reestablished life in Erets Yisra'el in the twentieth century, the *ḥalutsim* (pioneers), especially on the kibbutzim, re-created ancient agricultural festivals (first fruits, *'omer*, etc.) incorporating dance. Immigrants from Muslim lands brought with them the various dance traditions that had developed in their own communities.

• Doug Adams and Judith Rock, "Biblical Criteria in Dance: Modern Dance as Prophetic Form," in *Dance as Religious Studies*, edited by D. Adams and D. Apostlos-Cappandona (New York, 1990), pp. 80–91. Ruth Eshel, *Li-Reqod 'im ha-Ḥalom* (Tel Aviv, 1991). Zvi Friedhaber, *Ha-Maḥol be-'Am Yisra'el* (Tel Aviv, 1985). Zvi Friedhaber, "Jewish Dance Traditions Through the Ages," *Israel Dance*, pt. 1, 3 (March 1994): 57–58; pt. 2, 4 (October 1994): 116–117. Gurit Kadman, *'Am Roqed* (Tel Aviv, 1968). Kay Troxell, ed., *Resources in Sacred Dance: Annotated Bibliography from Jewish Traditions* (Peterborough, N.H., 1991).

—JUDITH BRIN INGBER

DANGER. Two biblical verses—"Only take heed to yourself and keep your soul diligently" and "take good heed to your souls" (*Dt*. 4.9, 4.15, respectively)—were interpreted by the rabbis as a positive biblical commandment enjoining the duty of personal safety and the consequent avoidance of danger to life. The Talmud prohibits, among a long list of other things, entering a ruined building (*Ber*. 3a), drinking contaminated water (*Pes*. 112a), and not taking dietary precautions (*Ḥul*. 9b). In addition, the Talmud rules that "a man should never court danger in the hope that he will be miraculously delivered" (*Shab*. 32a). A corollary to this injunction to preserve one's own life is the doctrine of *piqquaḥ nefesh*, the sacred duty to go to any lengths to save the life of another human being. This duty is a major principle of law, taking precedence over and annulling all other prescriptions of Judaism with the exception of the three cardinal sins of idolatry, sexual immorality, and the shedding of innocent blood (*Ket*. 19a). In particular, all the laws of the Sabbath or even Yom Kippur can be overridden in the face of this duty (*Ber*. 61b; *Yoma'* 8.7). When the saving of life is involved, there must be no hesitation or delay, nor may the duty be delegated to another person, but "even the greatest in Israel" must perform it (T., *Shab*. 16). All illnesses are regarded as endangering life, so that the laws of *piqquaḥ nefesh* also operate in the case of sickness, and the instructions of a physician must be followed. A person who persists in fasting on Yom Kippur in defiance of a doctor's orders is regarded as having profaned that holy day by refusing to eat.

• Weston W. Fields, "The Motif 'Night as Danger' Associated with Three Biblical Destruction Narratives," in *Shaarei Talmon: Studies in the Bible, Qumran, and Ancient Near East Presented to Shemaryahu Talmon*, edited by M. Fishbane et al. (Winona Lake, Ind., 1992), pp. 17–32.

DANIEL (Heb. Daniyye'l), hero of the *Book of Daniel*, which is found in the third section of the Bible, the Hagiographa, between the *Book of Esther* and the *Book of Ezra*. He is portrayed as an exilic prophet and may be modeled on the Daniel famous for his righteousness, along with Noah and Job, who is mentioned in *Ezekiel* 14.14, 20 and 28.3. The Ugaritic epic of Aqhat mentions a righteous king named Daniel, who supplicates the gods and functions as a judge, championing the cause of widows and orphans.

The *Book of Daniel*, composed both in Hebrew (chaps. 1–2.4, 8–12) and Aramaic (chaps. 2.5–7.28), is divided into two sections reflecting two different literary genres. The first section, which consists of chapters 1 through 6, is a collection of independent, first-person tales about Daniel and his three companions, given the Babylonian names of Shadrach, Meshach, and Abed-nego, who, after being deported to Babylonia, rose to prominence in the courts of Nebuchadnezzar, Belshazzar, and Darius the Mede. Chapters 7 through 12 are a collection of third-person, pseudonymous, apocalyptic tales of symbolic visions interpreted by an angelic figure, which take place in the courts of Belshazzar, Darius the Mede, and Cyrus. According to tradition, the entire book was written by Daniel during the Babylonian exile.

The first section, dated by scholars to the Hellenistic period, approximately the mid-fourth century BCE, commences with the account of Daniel and his three friends training for the king's service, while strictly adhering to the observance of the dietary laws. In chapter 2, Daniel interprets Nebuchadnezzar's dream about a colossal statue as symbolizing the rise of four successive pagan kingdoms—Babylonia, Media, Persia, and Greece—and their ultimate collapse, crushed by a stone representing the deity. Chapter 3 relates the miracle of the blazing furnace into which Daniel's three compatriots are hurled after they refuse to obey Nebuchadnezzar's order to worship a golden idol and from which they emerge unscathed. Nebuchadnezzar's dream of a hewn tree and his being turned into a wild animal is interpreted by Daniel in chapter 4 as foreshadowing the king's temporary punishment of insanity for the sin of hubris and his eventual restoration. Chapter 5 recounts the feast of Belshazzar and Daniel's interpretation of the mystical handwriting on the wall as referring to the ultimate division of the pagan kingdom. Chapter 6 tells the miracle of the lions' den, into which Daniel is tossed when fellow ministers report to Darius the Mede that Daniel had continued his three-times-a-day prayer vigil, even after the king prohibited all prayers except those to himself. Daniel emerges from the den uninjured, while his detractors, who were similarly punished, were devoured instantaneously. All of these stories offer a paradigm for Jews living in the Diaspora, showing that a person can maintain complete fidelity to his religion against the religious demands of pagan rulers.

Section two, chapters 7 through 12, dated to the Maccabean period, reflects the persecutions of Antiochus IV Epiphanes from 168 to 164 clothed in symbolic language. Chapter 7, recounting the emergence of four beasts from the sea, is interpreted by an angel to refer to the rise of four successive kingdoms, the fourth that of the Seleucids, whose last king, Antiochus, would institute an oppressive reign of three and a half years, only to be completely annihilated by the rise of a fifth and final kingdom, that of the God of Israel. That deity is depicted here (7.9) anthropomorphically as an old man with white hair called the "Ancient of Days." In chapter 8, a two-horned ram (Media and Persia) is engaged in combat with a he-goat (Greece), who, after breaking the former's horns, has his own horns broken into four, representing the kingdom of Alexander the Great and later Greek kingdoms, eventually leading to the growth of a "small horn" (Antiochus IV). Daniel is informed by the angel Gabriel, in chapter 9, that Jeremiah's prophecy of the seventy years of the destruction of Jerusalem (*Jer.* 15.11–12, 29.10) is to be understood as seventy weeks of years, that is 490 years, at the end of which Antiochus will defile the Temple by placing within it an "appalling abomination"—the statue of Zeus—that will eventually be destroyed (9.27). Chapters 10 through 12 present a historical panorama from Cyrus to Antiochus IV (539–164), calculating the end of world history and the final resurrection of the wholly righteous (12.2–3). This formed the basis for mystic and apocalyptic calculations of the end of days and the advent of the Messiah. Section two is characterized by *ex eventu* prophecies (prophecies recounting events that have already occurred); it depicts supernatural forces active in the universe, with each nation having its own angelic champion (Israel is protected by Michael); it relates the concept of predetermination in history; and it contains a message of hope to the Jews during the difficult period of persecution. Several fragments of eight manuscripts of the *Book of Daniel* have been discovered at Qumran, dating from the late second century BCE to the early first century CE.

• John Joseph Collins, *The Apocalyptic Vision of the Book of Daniel*, Harvard Semitic Monographs, no. 16 (Missoula, Mont., 1977). John Joseph Collins, *Daniel: A Commentary on the Book of Daniel*, edited by Frank Moore Cross, Hermeneia—A Critical and Historical Commentary on the Bible (Minneapolis, 1993). Harold Louis Ginsberg, *Studies in Daniel* (New York, 1948). Louis F. Hartman and Alexander A. Di Lella, *The Book of Daniel*, The Anchor Bible, vol. 23 (Garden City, N.Y., 1978). André Lacocque, *The Book of Daniel*, translated by David Pallauer (Atlanta, 1979).

—SHALOM PAUL

DANIEL, ADDITIONS TO BOOK OF, three extended passages found in the Greek translation of the *Book of *Daniel* but not in the text preserved in the Hebrew Bible. These textual units did not belong in the original *Book of Daniel*, as can be seen from their contents and their intrusion in the flow of the narrative, but it is less clear whether they were translated from Hebrew or Aramaic or originally composed in Greek. Dating the additions is equally difficult, especially since it is possible that they circulated independently before being appended to the Danielic corpus. The first of the three additions, *The Song of the Three Children*, builds on the events of *Daniel* 3.8–30, where Hananiah, Mishael, and Azariah are thrown into the fiery furnace. The addition includes Azariah's prayer, in which he blesses God, admits the nation's sins, and asks God not to abandon his servants. The Lord's angel subsequently descends into the furnace and protects the three young men from the flames. Seeing this, they sing a hymn of thanksgiving, blessing the Lord and exalting his powers. The second of the three additions, *Susanna and the Elders*, tells the story of Susanna, a married Jewish woman who is falsely accused of idolatry by two Jewish elders whose sexual advances she had rejected. On the basis of their testimony she is tried and sentenced to death. As she is about to be executed, Daniel appears on the scene, and by cross-examining the two elders demonstrates the falsity of their testimony. Susanna is freed, and the two elders are summarily executed. The third of the three additions, *Bel and the Dragon* (or *Snake*), consists of two short stories recounting Daniel's schemes against the Babylonian idols. In one story, Daniel proves that the enormous quantities of food supposedly consumed by the Babylonian god Bel actually are stolen every night by his priests. The priests are put to death and Bel's idol and temple are destroyed. In the other story, Daniel feeds a snake, whom the Babylonians worship, with a mixture of pitch, fat, and hair, causing the creature's death. The angry Babylonians throw Daniel into the lions' den, but the prophet Habakkuk sustains him there until his eventual release. English translations are to be found in standard editions of the Apocrypha.

• Carey A. Moore, *Daniel, Esther and Jeremiah: The Additions*, The Anchor Bible, vol. 44 (Garden City, N.Y., 1977), pp. 23–149. Emil Schürer, *The History of the Jewish People in the Age of Jesus Christ, 175 B.C.–A.D. 135*, new English version revised and edited by Geza Vermes and Fergus Millar, vol. 3.2 (Edinburgh, 1973), pp. 722–730. Lawrence M. Wills, *The Jew in the Court of the Foreign King: Ancient Jewish Court Legends*, Harvard Dissertations in Religion, no. 26 (Minneapolis, 1990).

—GIDEON BOHAK

DANIYYE'L BEN MOSHEH AL-QUMISI. See QUMISI, DANIYYE'L BEN MOSHEH AL-.

DANZIG, AVRAHAM BEN YEḤI'EL MIKHAL (1748–1820), rabbi, scholar, and legal interpreter. Named for the city of his birth, Danzig served as **dayyan* (judge) in Vilna from 1794 to 1812. He is best known for his two systematically ordered codifications of the **Shulḥan ʿArukh*. His *Ḥayyei Adam* (Vilna, 1810), on the laws of daily practice, and his *Ḥokhmat Adam* (Vilna, 1812), on the dietary laws, presented the regulations and rationales contained in the *Oraḥ Ḥayyim* and *Yoreh Deʿah* sections of the *Shulḥan ʿArukh* in a clear, orderly, and helpful manner.

• Simon M. Chones, *Toledot ha-Poseqim* (Warsaw, 1910).

—JACOB MESKIN

DARI, MOSHEH (12th–13th cent.), the greatest medieval *Karaite poet. His poetry shows that he was heavily influenced by the Spanish school of Hebrew poetry, that of Shelomoh ibn Gabirol, Yehudah ha-Levi, and Avraham ibn Ezra. Dari's parents emigrated from Spain to the city of Darʿa in Morocco, and Mosheh was born in Alexandria, Egypt, and also lived in Damascus and Jerusalem; he was a physician by profession. He composed more than 550 poems, both liturgical and secular. Only a selection from his two-part *diwan* (collection of poetry), which was written in Egypt, has been published (I. Davidson, *Horeb* 3 [1936]: 28–42). A *maqama* on personages from Alexandria (I. Davidson, *Maddaʿei ha-Yahadut* 2 [1926–1927]: 297–308) has been attributed to

Dari as a work of his youth, although this has been questioned.

• Leon Nemoy, *Karaite Anthology* (New Haven, 1952), pp. 133–146. Simhah Pinsker, *Liqqutei Qadmoniyot* (Vienna, 1860), pp. 46–105, 113–121. Giuliano Tamani, "La Tradizione del *canzionere* di Moshe Dari," *Henoch* 6 (1984): 205–224.

–DAVID E. SKLARE

DARKHEI SHALOM (דַּרְכֵי שָׁלוֹם; ways of peace), the rubric of *darkhei shalom* is one of the principles underlying the legislative activity of the rabbis. The major goal of legislation based upon this principle is the prevention of disputes and the promotion of public peace and tranquility. Mishnaic examples of such legislative activity that have remained in force despite the fact that no such obligations or rights exist under regular Talmudic law are the enactment that non-Jews must always be greeted and the provision that property rights may be held in relation to the contents of animal traps and fish nets (*Git*. 5.8–9). The Talmud develops ownership rights in relation to bees, doves, geese, and fowl on the basis of this principle (*B. Q*. 114b). A similar rubric, *mi-shum eivah* (to prevent enmity), was also propounded by the rabbis and provides the basis for a number of important laws with respect to legal relations between husband and wife, parents and children, and Jews and non-Jews (*Ket*. 47a, 58b; *ʿA. Z*. 26a).

• Zebi Hirsch Chajes, *The Student's Guide Through the Talmud* (London, 1952), pp. 70–71. Aaron Kirschenbaum, *Equity in Jewish Law*, vol. 2, *Beyond Equity: Halakhic Aspirationism in Jewish Civil Law* (New York, 1991), pp. 153–158.

–DANIEL SINCLAIR

DARSHAN (דַּרְשָׁן; expounder), beginning in the Talmudic period, the term for a preacher or homilist. The word comes from the same Hebrew root as *Midrash, and the *darshan* was seen as the quintessential creator of Midrashic material, particularly of a homiletical or aggadic nature. The *darshan* preached the *derashah* (sermon or homily) in the synagogue on Sabbaths and holidays; the *derashah* was related to the Torah or *haftarah* readings for those days. The preacher usually was seated, possibly on a special chair or throne. The *meturgeman* or amora' standing alongside sometimes translated the *darshan*'s homily from Hebrew into Aramaic and delivered it with musical intonation. These features of Talmudic preaching emphasized the respected role the *darshan* played in ancient synagogue life. However, *darshanim* did not hesitate to engage in active repartee with their audiences, answering questions posed by members of the congregation. Though most of the *darshanim* whose comments make up much of rabbinic literature were ordained rabbis, some local preachers criticized the official rabbinic establishment (see *Gn. Rab*. 80.1). *Darshanim* continue to preach, with some exceptions, in many parts of the Jewish world. See also MAGGID.

• Marc Bregman, "The Darshan: Preacher and Teacher of Talmudic Times," *The Melton Journal* 14 (1982). Joseph Heinemann and Jakob Josef Petuchowski, eds., *Literature of the Synagogue* (New York, 1975).

DAVID (reigned c.1010–970), second king of Israel; youngest son of Jesse of the tribe of Judah. Born in Bethlehem, where he herded his father's sheep, he is described as "skilled in music, a man of valor and a warrior, sensible in speech and handsome in appearance, and the Lord is with him" (*1 Sm*. 16.18). Having despaired of the reign of *Saul, the prophet *Samuel was sent on a clandestine mission to anoint David as king (*1 Sm*. 1–13). The biblical account of the early relationship between David and Saul is confused and contradictory. According to *1 Samuel* 16, Saul suffered from depression and melancholia, and David, "the sweet singer of Israel" (*2 Sm*. 23.1), was brought to court in order to raise the king's spirit through his musical abilities. According to *1 Samuel* 17, it was David's victory over the Philistine warrior Goliath that drew the king's attention to him. The relationship between the two began to deteriorate with the public acclaim accorded to David's military prowess (*1 Sm*. 18.6–9ff.). Following an unsuccessful attempt on his life by Saul, whose daughter Michal he had married, David fled to the Judean wilderness, where he gathered around himself an army of four hundred followers and became an ally of the Philistines (*1 Sm*. 18–30). He subsequently spared Saul's life on two occasions (*1 Sm*. 24, 26). After Saul's death in the battle of Gilboa, David—at the age of thirty—was crowned king. He won victories over external enemies, including the Philistines, and proceeded to conquer *Jerusalem, which he made the capital of his kingdom. After this success David brought the *Ark of the Covenant to Jerusalem, an act that highlighted the cultic significance of the city. He was subsequently assured by the prophet Nathan of an enduring dynasty (*2 Sm*. 7). In 1994 a monument written in Aramaic relating the victory of a king of Aram over Israel was discovered at Dan in northern Israel and contains the first extra-biblical reference to the "house [dynasty] of David." David's desire to build the Temple was thwarted by Nathan, who informed David, in God's name, that only David's son would merit this distinction. According to the *Book of *Chronicles*, which presents a highly positive view of David's life by omitting almost all of the negative episodes, the rationale for David's unsuitability to build the Temple was that he was a man of war who had shed too much blood (*1 Chr*. 22.8). Nevertheless, according to this account David formulated the plans for the building of the Temple and also organized the priests, Levites, musicians, and gatekeepers connected with it.

David's wars occupy an important place in the biblical account. The united monarchy that he established expanded greatly, encompassing large portions of Transjordan, Greater Syria up to the Euphrates River, and Philistia along the Mediterranean coast, and was unmatched in the history of ancient Israel. Nevertheless David's military successes did not ensure him either a tranquil court life or universal domestic allegiance. The rivalry among his sons and the traditional conflict of interest between Judah and the northern tribes fueled the far-reaching, if ultimately unsuccessful, revolts of his son Absalom and Sheba, son of Bichri. Even David's commission of Solomon as his successor came about in the shadow of intrigues and betrayals. The biblical account of David's life story (*1 Sm*. 16ff.; *2 Sm*.; *1 Kgs*. 1–

2; *1 Chr.* 10ff.) faithfully portrays his complex character—as statesman, warrior, poet, friend, and lover, in times of good and ill fortune (notably in his adultery with Bath-sheba and the murder of her husband), sinning and repentant. Tradition ascribes to David the composition of many psalms (see PSALMS, BOOK OF). In later generations his exemplary qualities became the ideal of Israelite kingship, and God's covenant with David was considered as firm and eternal as his covenant with Israel (see *Jer.* 33.19–26 and the many references in the liturgy); hence, it is said that the future king and restorer of Israel's fortunes will be a scion of the house of David (*Is.* 9.5–6, 11.10; see MESSIAH). The copious aggadic treatment of David is, in the main, highly laudatory; it has also found its way into the Qur'an. Christianity regards David as an ancestor of *Jesus. The degree to which David's personality fired the popular imagination is expressed in the adage, "David king of Israel lives forever" (*R. ha-Sh.* 25a). The traditional site of his tomb in Jerusalem has become the object of pilgrimages (see DAVID, TOMB OF).

• Yohanan Aharoni, *The Land of the Bible: A Historical Geography*, 2d rev. and enl. ed., translated from the Hebrew and edited by A. F. Rainey (London, 1979), pp. 291–305. J. P. Fokkelman, *Narrative Art and Poetry in the Books of Samuel*, vol. 1, *King David*; vol. 2, *The Crossing Fates* (Assen, 1981 and 1985). David M. Gunn, *The Story of King David: Genre and Interpretation*, Journal for the Study of the Old Testament, Supplement Series 6 (Sheffield, Eng., 1978). T. Ishida, ed., *Studies in the Period of David and Solomon and Other Essays: Papers Read at the International Symposium for Biblical Studies, Tokyo, 5–7 December, 1979* (Tokyo, 1982). P. Kyle McCarter, *1 Samuel* and *2 Samuel*, The Anchor Bible, vols. 8 and 9 (Garden City, N.Y., 1980 and 1984). Abraham Rosner, *David's Leben und Charakter nach Talmud und Midrasch* (Oldenburg, Ger., 1908). Leonhard Rost, *The Succession to the Throne of David*, translated from the German by M. D. Rutter and D. M. Gunn (Sheffield, Eng., 1982). J. Alberto Soggin, "The Davidic-Solomonic Kingdom," in *Israelite and Judaean History*, edited by John H. Hayes and J. Maxwell Miller, The Old Testament Library (London, 1977), pp. 332–363.

—DAVID A. GLATT-GILAD

DAVID, CITY OF. See JERUSALEM.

DAVID, DYNASTY OF. In *2 Samuel* 7.11–16, in response to his plan to build God a house (i.e., a temple), *David is told that, on the contrary, God will build David a house, that is, a hereditary, dynastic monarchy. David's incredulity (*2 Sm.* 7.19) and his earnest prayer that this promise be fulfilled (*2 Sm.* 7.25–29) indicate just how extraordinary this promise—the Davidic covenant (*2 Sm.* 23.5; *Ps.* 89.4, 35)—was in biblical thought. Sometimes it is presented as an unconditional grant, in which God resolves that even if some of the Davidic rulers sin against him, he will chasten them but never reject them (*2 Sm.* 7.14–15; *Ps.* 89.29–38); elsewhere, it is thought to be contingent upon David's descendants' loyalty to God's commands (*1 Kgs.* 2.4, 8.25, 9.3–7; *Ps.* 132.11–12). David's son *Solomon ruled a united Israel after him. After the schism, the southern kingdom of Judah alone continued to be ruled by David's descendants, twenty in number, the last of whom was Zedekiah (see KINGS, BOOK OF). With the destruction of the First Temple, the Davidic monarchy ended. The prophecies of Ezekiel foresaw the restoration of the ancient dynasty, and some of the earliest leaders of the return to Zion (Zerubbabel and perhaps Sheshbazzar) were scions of the Davidic house. When hopes for reinstating the Davidic line failed to materialize, however, the belief in the eternity of the Davidic dynasty led to the messianic hope characteristic of Second Temple times and of later Judaism, according to which a Davidic king will arise at some future time and restore Israel's fortunes as of old (see MESSIAH).

• Kenneth Pomykala, *The Davidic Dynasty Tradition in Early Judaism: Its History and Significance for Messianism* (Atlanta, 1995).

—BARUCH J. SCHWARTZ

DAVID, SHIELD OF. See MAGEN DAVID.

DAVID, TOMB OF. The Bible relates that David was buried "in the city of David" (*1 Kgs.* 2.10). There are a number of references to the tombs of the house of David, but these were apparently destroyed or obliterated after the Bar Kokhba' Revolt (c.132–135). The site was probably southeast of present-day Jerusalem (near the village of Silwan). Popular tradition refused to accept the disappearance of David's tomb, and various sites (especially in Bethlehem) came to be venerated. The present localization of the tomb at a site to the south of old Jerusalem on what is (erroneously) called Mount Zion dates back a thousand years. For centuries the Arab custodians forbade Jews access to the tomb, but after the establishment of the State of Israel in 1948, it became a center of Jewish pilgrimage, especially since Jews could no longer visit the Western Wall, which remained in the Jordanian section of Jerusalem. After the Six-Day War in 1967, when Israel captured the Old City of Jerusalem, the Tomb of David became a secondary site of pilgrimage. Visits to the Tomb of David are customarily made, particularly by the Sephardim of Jerusalem, on Shavu'ot, the traditional date of King David's death.

• Ora Limor, "The Origins of a Tradition: King David's Tomb on Mount Zion," *Tradition* 44 (1988): 454–462. J. Pinkerfeld, "David's Tomb: Notes on the History of the Building," in *L. M. Rabinowitz Fund for the Exploration of Ancient Synagogues Bulletin*, vol. 3, edited by S. Levy et al. (Jerusalem, 1960). Hershel Shanks, "Is This King David's Tomb?" *Biblical Archaeology Review* 21 (January–February 1995): 62–67.

DAVID BEN SHELOMOH IBN AVI ZIMRA (1479–1573), rabbinical authority and kabbalist, known by the acronym Ridbaz. Scion of a distinguished family in the Spanish town of Zamora, he was among the refugees of the expulsion of 1492 and at age thirteen arrived in Safed in Erets Yisra'el. He then lived in Jerusalem until moving to Egypt in 1513. After a short stay in Alexandria, he settled in Cairo, where he became head of Egyptian Jewry, giving authority to the new *battei din*, thereby strengthening the autonomy of dozens of communities. As their religious leader, he issued a number of ordinances (*taqqanot*). His reputation was widespread, and he wrote *responsa* to queries from many lands.

David was a spokesman for rabbinical Judaism in disputations with Muslim and with Karaite scholars. He returned to Erets Yisra'el in, or about, 1553, spending the last twenty years of his life in Jerusalem and Safed, where he served as *dayyan*.

His expertise was in *halakhah* and Kabbalah. He approached textual study critically, comparing different manuscripts to reach the most accurate reading. His halakhic decisions tended to be stringent, although he chided those who "heap restrictions on restrictions." He wrote about the methodology of the Talmud and laid down rules for Talmudic interpretation in the event of conflict among later authorities. Although a kabbalist, he gave preference to the Talmud where this clashed with mystical thinking.

Over twenty-four hundred of his *responsa* were published in *Teshuvot ha-Ridbaz* (7 vols. [Warsaw, 1882]), and others have been discovered. They throw much light on Jewish religious, communal, social, and economic life in his time, particularly in the eastern Mediterranean countries. He wrote many works on *halakhah*, including *Yeqar Tiferet*, which is a partial commentary on Maimonides' *Mishneh Torah* (Smyrna, 1757), and on Kabbalah.

• Israel M. Goldman, *The Life and Times of Rabbi David ibn Abi Zimra* (New York, 1970), includes bibliography of published works and manuscripts. Abraham Gross, "The Expulsion and the Search for the Ten Tribes," *Judaism* 41 (1992): 130–147. Hirsch J. Zimmels, *Rabbi David Ibn Abi Simra (RDbS): Ein Beitrag zur Kulturgeschichte der Juden in der Turkei im 16. Jahrhundert auf Grund seiner Gutachten* (Breslau, 1932).

—SHALOM BAR-ASHER

DAVID BEN SHEMU'EL HA-LEVI (1586–1667), Polish halakhist and rabbi; known as Taz, an acronym of the title of his best-known work. A student of his father-in-law, Yo'el ben Shemu'el Sirkes, David established a study house in Kraków before becoming rabbi in Poznań in 1620 and Ostrog in 1641, where he succeeded Sirkes. During the Chmielnicki uprising, David fled Poland, composing two penitentiary prayers commemorating his miraculous escape (published in *Yalqut Menaḥem* by Menaḥem Mendel Biber in 1903). In 1654 he returned to a rabbinic post in Lwów, where he died. An outstanding figure, he took part in the meetings of the Polish-Jewish autonomous body, the Council of the Four Lands. His major work, *Turei Zahav*, is a commentary on the **Shulḥan ʿArukh* and the *Arbaʿah Turim*. Although his stated aim was to harmonize the various halakhic rulings that had appeared, the work is not merely a legal code but also a discussion and commentary on the sources of the works. He used **pilpul* as a hermeneutic tool and tended to leniency on issues involving social and economic hardship. After the publication of the first volume of *Turei Zahav*, on *Yoreh Deʿah* (Lublin, 1646), he engaged in a dispute with *Shabbetai ben Me'ir ha-Kohen, whose parallel commentary was issued in the same year. David's other, less authoritative, volumes of *Turei Zahav* were published posthumously (Hamburg, 1692; Zólkiew, 1754; Berlin, 1766). Despite his somewhat critical approach to the *Shulḥan ʿArukh*, his work became one of the two standard commentaries printed together with it. He also wrote *Divrei David* (Dyhernfurth, 1689), a supercommentary on Rashi's commentary on the Pentateuch.

• Benzion Katz, *Rabbanut, Ḥasidut, Haskalah* (Tel Aviv, 1956–1958), pp. 105–107. Elijah Schochet, *"Taz": Rabbi David Halevi* (New York, 1979), includes bibliographical references.

—ADAM TELLER

DAY AND NIGHT. The Hebrew word *yom* (day) can refer both to the period of daylight (as opposed to nighttime) and to the entire span of twenty-four hours. The twenty-four hour day is reckoned from evening to evening. In Jewish law, part of a day is often taken as a full day, for example, in counting the days of mourning or in calculating the eighth day after birth for circumcision. Many commandments may be fulfilled only during the daytime. A Talmudic hour constitutes one-twelfth of the period of daylight and therefore varies with the seasons. The period from sunset until the "rising of the morning star" constitutes the night (Heb. *laylah*). There is, however, some doubt as to the exact incidence of the two outer limits. In discussing the advent of night the rabbis differ as to whether its hour is to be reckoned from sunset or from the appearance of the stars; for this reason the Sabbath and festivals are regarded as beginning with sunset, or "when the sun is at the top of the trees," but they conclude with the appearance of three stars of medium magnitude on the following night. Similarly the end of night is reckoned either when one can distinguish between blue and white or between blue and green (*Ber.* 1.2). The night is divided into three (*Ber.* 3a) or four (*Ber.* 3b) watches. In Jewish law certain activities cannot be undertaken at night, such as the beginning of court sessions, the signing of documents, or the passing of a capital verdict. The obligatory night reading of the Shemaʿ can be carried out at any time before dawn, but the rabbis taught that it should be read before midnight, that is before the middle of the hours of darkness, depending on the season. See also ʿEREV; MORNING; TWILIGHT.

• Mordehai Meishor, "Yom, Yomam, Yemama," *Leshonenu le-ʿAm* 37 (1986): 203–212. David Pahmer, "The International Dateline and Related Issues," *Journal of Halacha and Contemporary Society* 21 (1991): 60–83. Meir Ydit, "The Counting of 'Day' and 'Night,'" *Conservative Judaism* 35.1 (1981): 25–29.

—CHAIM PEARL

DAY OF ATONEMENT. See YOM KIPPUR.

DAY OF JUDGMENT. See YOM HA-DIN.

DAY OF THE LORD, originally, the day on which the Lord would reveal himself to the nations in all his power and might to destroy the enemies of Israel in punishment for their sins against his people. Some scholars have suggested that the concept grew out of the Day of War, when the Lord manifests himself as a "man of war" (*Ex.* 15.3) "mighty in battle" (*Ps.* 24.8). The idea occurs repeatedly in prophetic literature (*Isaiah*, *Joel*, *Amos*, *Obadiah*, *Zephaniah*, and *Malachi*). During the period of the Babylonian exile, Day of the Lord prophecies were directed against specific peoples (Babylonia, *Is.* 13.6–13; Egypt, *Is.* 46.2–12) and included promises of salvation for Israel (*Is.* 61.2–3; *Ez.* 34.12). See also YOM HA-DIN.

• Christopher Rowland, *The Open Heaven: A Study of Apocalyptic in Judaism and Early Christianity* (London, 1982). Shemaryahu Talmon, *Eschatology and History in Biblical Judaism* (Jerusalem, 1986).

DAYS OF AWE. See YAMIM NORA'IM.

DAYYAN (דַּיָּן; judge), title given to the judge of a rabbinic court. According to the Talmud, the *Sanhedrin of the Chamber of Hewn Stone (*lishkat ha-gazit*), which met in the Temple, consisted of seventy-one judges; lower courts of twenty-three judges were to be found on the Temple mount and in every community containing a Jewish population of at least a hundred twenty adult males. In smaller communities, the courts had only three judges. This system did not parallel the modern system of appellate courts; each court was of different jurisdiction. Monetary matters could be heard by courts of three, but capital cases, among others, only by courts of twenty-three. Certain matters were the sole prerogative of the Sanhedrin of seventy-one. Since *ordination could be conferred only in Erets Yisra'el, the jurisdiction of judges in the Diaspora was restricted (e.g., even in civil cases, they could not impose fines). With the lapse of ordination, judges were considered *sheliḥim* (representatives of properly ordained *dayyanim*). Over the course of time the function of judge was combined with that of rabbi (see RABBI AND RABBINATE), and in medieval times, in many countries, rabbinic courts enjoyed considerable autonomy. A single judge was deemed competent to try a case if he was recognized as an outstanding scholar (*mumḥeh*) or if the parties agreed to accept his decision; otherwise cases were heard by more than one judge—usually three. In exceptional cases a judge could reach his decision by exercising his judgment rather than by applying the letter of the law. In addition to scholarship, a judge also had to possess certain moral qualities: a good name, humility, fear of God, detestation of money, love of truth, and love of his fellow man. According to the Talmud, familiarity with languages and secular subjects as well as an impressive physical appearance were also desirable qualities of a judge. Once appointed, a judge was to be held in high esteem, and the Bible (*Ex.* 22.27) prohibits his disparagement. Those disqualified from acting as witnesses (see WITNESS) were also disqualified from serving as judges. Presently, even in the State of Israel, most cases of law are heard in the general courts, and only cases regarding issues of personal status are heard by rabbinic judges. See also BEIT DIN.

• Adolf Büchler, *Ha-Sanhedrin* (Jerusalem, 1974). Hugo Mantel, *Studies in the History of the Sanhedrin* (Cambridge, Mass., 1965). Emanuel B. Quint, *Jewish Jurisprudence: Its Sources and Modern Applications* (Chur, Switzerland, 1980).

DAYYENU (דַּיֵּנוּ; It Would Suffice Us), thanksgiving litany, recited during the Pesaḥ *Seder service, with the repeated refrain *dayyenu*. It is of unknown authorship but possibly dates to the ninth century CE (it first appears in the *siddur* of *Saʿadyah ben Yosef Ga'on). It lists the accumulation of divine favors for which Israel is grateful to God.

• Ernst Daniel Goldschmidt, *Haggadah shel Pesaḥ* . . . (Jerusalem, 1960), pp. 48–51. Menahem M. Kasher, *Haggadah Shelemah* (Jerusalem, 1967), pp. 55–58. Menahem M. Kasher, ed., *Israel Passover Haggadah* (New York, 1950).

DEAD, PRAYERS FOR THE. See EL MALE' RAḤAMIM; QADDISH; YIZKOR.

DEAD SEA SCROLLS, a collection of fragmentary remains of almost 850 ancient Jewish documents. The first seven scrolls were discovered in a cave at the shore of the Dead Sea in 1947. Between 1952 and 1956 an additional ten caves yielded scrolls and scroll fragments. These documents were painstakingly assembled by 1960, but for a variety of reasons most of the documents remained unpublished for several decades. By the 1990s, scholarly editions and translations of the remaining texts were rapidly being published, and the entire corpus was available for study.

It is generally believed that these scrolls were gathered by a sect (see QUMRAN COMMUNITY) that occupied the ruins known as Khirbat *Qumran from some time after 150 BCE until 68 CE, when this site, adjacent to the caves where the scrolls were found, was destroyed by the Romans during the Great Revolt of the Jews against Rome. The composition of the texts included in the scrolls ranges over a very long period, beginning with the earliest books of the Hebrew Bible. The nonbiblical works were composed between the third century BCE and the turn of the era. The preserved manuscripts date from the third century BCE through the early first century CE, although the vast majority of the scrolls were copied in the first two centuries BCE. This dating, originally arrived at by paleographical and archaeological study of the ruins, has been confirmed by sophisticated carbon-14 dating. This means that most of the works preserved in this ancient library were not composed by the sectarians who inhabited the building complex at Qumran. It also means that the texts are pre-Christian and for this reason have no direct references to Jesus or John the Baptist.

From the earliest stages of Qumran research, it has been determined that the scrolls, the caves, and the ruins were related. This is because the caves preserve a unique pottery assemblage, including a type of jar specific to Qumran in which some of the scrolls were found. The only exception is an exemplar from nearby Jericho, which was the nearest commercial center to Qumran.

The archaeological excavation of the ruins, carried out between 1951 and 1956, determined that the site was occupied during a number of periods. Initially, Qumran served as a border outpost in the period of the divided monarchy, and some remains of an Iron Age cistern and some walls testify to this period. The core of the building complex seems to have been in use by 150 BCE, and shortly afterward the period of sectarian occupation seems to have begun. This period featured a large communal dining hall and a great number of ritual baths and Jewish burials. Some interruption of the occupation may have occurred as a result of the earthquake that hit Judea in 31 BCE, but otherwise the buildings continued to be used until their destruction at the hands of the Romans.

Since the remains at the site indicate appropriate facilities for a Jewish religious group (loosely termed a sect), and since the documents include previously unknown compositions by such a group, it has been concluded that the sect occupied the building complex at Qumran, gathered the scrolls of the Bible as well as works by their own and other authors, and hid them in the caves where they were found two millennia later.

The scrolls can be divided roughly into three separate categories. Approximately one third of the material represents books of the Hebrew Bible. Parts of all of the books of the Hebrew Bible are found except for *Esther*. While some scholars believe that *Esther* was not part of the biblical canon at Qumran, others see its absence from among the biblical fragments as mere coincidence. A second group of scrolls is made up of apocryphal or pseudepigraphous texts, that is, Jewish texts from Second Temple times that in some way relate to the Bible and that were part of the general literary heritage of the Jewish people at this time. In certain cases, these books were previously known in Greek, Ethiopic, or other languages, and the Qumran manuscripts preserved the text in the original language. In other instances these are previously unknown works. The third type of texts is that of the sectarian compositions, works composed and transmitted within the group. These texts are the most important for the discussion of the identification of the sect. However, the collection as a whole must be studied to illumine the history of Judaism during this period, later developments in Judaism, and the rise of Christianity.

In 1910 two fragmentary medieval manuscripts of a previously unknown work recovered from the Cairo *Genizah appeared in England. These manuscripts were later determined to be part of the Dead Sea Scrolls, when ten partial copies of the same text were found in the Qumran caves. The publication of this text in effect began the debate over the identity of what would become known as the Dead Sea sect even before the discovery of scrolls in the Judean desert in 1947. Various theories identified members of the sect as Pharisees, Sadducees, Essenes, Christians, Zealots, and Karaites. Some scholars argued that these were the documents of a previously unknown group.

After the discovery of the Qumran scrolls in 1947, most scholars identified the sect with the *Essenes, a group mentioned by Josephus, Philo, and other ancient writers. This is the prevailing view among scholars, even though the precise meaning of the word *Essene* is uncertain, and it does not occur in the Dead Sea Scrolls. Recently, some have concluded that the Jewish legal tradition of the sect stems from that of the *Sadducees, which has led to modifications of the Essene theory, namely that the Essenes grew out of a group of Sadducees who split from their brethren in the aftermath of the Maccabean Revolt (166–164). Others have called for a redefinition of the term *Essene* to designate a type of sectarian group but not necessarily one particular sect.

The scrolls have done much to shed light upon the Hebrew Bible in the first two centuries BCE. They provide early evidence for the concept of a three-part biblical canon—Torah, Prophets, and Writings—as found in the rabbinic tradition. While all the books that are part of the accepted canon were also considered holy by the sectarians (with the possible exception of *Esther*), it is possible that they also included *Jubilees* and a version of the Testament of Levi in their Bible.

Within the books there is also evidence of textual variation. Indeed, the sectarians tolerated multiple texts of the same book, in a way that later Jews would have found unacceptable. A few biblical fragments show evidence of the Hebrew text that was translated into Greek as the *Septuagint. Other fragments show evidence of the text that formed the basis for the Samaritan Pentateuch. The vast majority of texts are either of the Proto-Masoretic variety, pointing toward the fixed texts of the Talmudic period, or of a mixed type that often included the linguistic forms known from the compositions of the Qumran group. Yet by the time of the Masada and Bar Kokhba' texts, from the first centuries CE, the proto-Masoretic text had become standard. No New Testament texts have been found at Qumran.

The scrolls attest to the rich variety of approaches that existed to Jewish law and theology in the second and first centuries BCE. In addition, they have also made clear the extent to which messianic speculation was practically the norm in many Jewish groups at this time. They have indirectly thrown light on the early history of rabbinic tradition, since they preach so extensively against the approach of the *Pharisees, the forerunners of the rabbis. Much of what is known as the rabbinic tradition in the Mishnah was already the norm among the Pharisees in this period, a conclusion that has confirmed the historical value of both Josephus and later rabbinic accounts.

The scrolls also help scholars to understand better the origins of Christianity. Much of what was interpreted as foreign influence is understood to stem from Jewish roots. It is now more clearly understood how Jesus differed from the Jewish groups of his time. Yet no direct links can be shown between Jesus and the scrolls; in fact, many substantial differences exist between his teachings and those of the Qumran sect.

The Dead Sea Scrolls have opened up a new chapter in the study of Judaism. The investigation of these documents is really only at its beginning, and many more important conclusions are still anticipated.

• John J. Collins, *The Scepter and the Star: The Messiahs of the Dead Sea Scrolls and Other Ancient Literature* (New York, 1995). Frank Moore Cross, *The Ancient Library of Qumran and Modern Biblical Studies*, 3d ed. (Sheffield, Eng., 1995). Florentino García Martínez, *The Dead Sea Scrolls Translated: The Qumran Texts in English* (Leiden, 1994). Florentino García Martínez and Julio Trebolle Barrera, *The People of the Dead Sea Scrolls: Their Writings, Beliefs and Practices* (Leiden, 1995). Lawrence H. Schiffman, *The Eschatological Community of the Dead Sea Scrolls: A Study of the Rule of the Congregation*, Society for Biblical Literature Monographs 38 (Atlanta, 1989). Lawrence H. Schiffman, *The Halakhah at Qumran* (Leiden, 1975). Lawrence H. Schiffman, *Reclaiming the Dead Sea Scrolls* (Philadelphia, 1994). Lawrence H. Schiffman, *Sectarian Law in the Dead Sea Scrolls: Courts, Testimony, and the Penal Code*, Brown Judaic Studies 33 (Chico, Calif., 1983). Eugene Ulrich and James VanderKam, eds., *The Community of the Renewed Covenant: The Notre Dame Symposium on the Dead Sea Scrolls* (Notre Dame, 1994). James C. VanderKam, *The Dead Sea Scrolls Today* (Grand Rapids, 1994). Roland de Vaux, *Archaeology and the Dead Sea Scrolls* (London, 1973). Geza Vermes, *The Dead Sea Scrolls: Qumran in Perspective*, 3d ed. (London, 1994). Yigael Yadin, *The Temple Scroll: The Hidden Law of the Dead Sea Sect* (New York, 1985).

–LAWRENCE H. SCHIFFMAN

DEAD SEA SECT. See QUMRAN COMMUNITY.

DEAF, RETARDED, AND MINORS, a group of persons deprived of legal rights in Jewish law because they are regarded as lacking understanding and responsibility. "Deaf" refers to the deaf-mute and excludes such categories as a person who is mute but who can hear or a person who once possessed the powers of speech and hearing. According to the Talmud, the deaf, retarded, and minors cannot claim property by virtue of undisturbed possession, their business transactions are invalid, and they are barred as witnesses. They are exempt from punishment if they cause injury to others, but if they themselves are injured, the person responsible is liable. Talmudic law allows the marriage of a deaf-mute, and specifies that the marriage can be contracted by signs.

• Tzvi Marx, *Halakha and Handicap: Jewish Law and Ethics on Disability* (Jerusalem and Amsterdam, 1992).

DEATH occurs with the cessation of respiration and heartbeat. Brain death is accepted by all Reform, Conservative, and Reconstructionist decisors but only by some Orthodox decisors. The rabbis stressed the natural aspect of death and tried to minimize the dread with which it is anticipated. Since the human body belongs to God as creator and the time of death is therefore determined by God, death must not be precipitated (see SUICIDE). It is forbidden by Jewish law to do anything to hasten death. Not only is *euthanasia strictly forbidden, but anyone who performs the slightest action that may inadvertently hasten death is regarded as having shed innocent blood. However, the issues are complex and have been a major topic of discussion among rabbis throughout the centuries. New medical technologies have raised questions about the treatment of the dying (see MEDICAL ETHICS).

The Bible contains almost no information about life after death. There is an implicit belief that the spirit survives death, but there is no mention of a doctrine of divine retribution. Under some circumstances, the deceased could be contacted; for example, the deceased prophet Samuel is conjured by the witch of En-dor at the request of King Saul (*1 Sm.* 28.7ff.). The spirit of a dead person descends to Sheol, where it continues in some kind of shadowy existence. However, the lack of a fully developed belief in life after death did not diminish respect for the body, and a proper *burial was required. Belief in a connection between the living and the dead led to *necromancy, which was prohibited (*Dt.* 18.10). The Bible emphasizes that the fate of the body is "from dust to dust" (*Gn.* 3.19; *Ps.* 104.29ff.). However, the *Book of Daniel* (12.2) mentions the *resurrection of the righteous.

A more clearly defined doctrine of the nature of the soul and of its relationship with the divine after death emerged in the post-biblical period. By the time of the Talmud, the concept of an *afterlife had become highly developed and had a number of components. Souls continued after death and received either *reward or punishment based on the person's conduct during life (divine retribution). The righteous were assigned to the garden of *Eden to receive their reward, and the wicked were assigned to *Geihinnom to receive their punishment, which was generally not supposed to last more than twelve months. The Pharisees developed the doctrine of bodily *resurrection, which was one of the major doctrinal disputes between the Pharisees and Sadducees. The controversial nature of the concept of resurrection can be seen from the discussions in the Talmud (*San.* 10). In the Middle Ages, Maimonides included resurrection and divine reward and punishment in his *Thirteen Principles of Faith.

In rabbinic thought, death came to the world through sin, either through the sin of Adam or through one's own personal sin. Though the rabbis list a number of individuals who died without sin (*Shab.* 55b), a prevalent idea in Judaism is that death constitutes a punishment for sinfulness. This view is supported by the doctrine that "there is not a righteous person on earth who does good and does not sin" (*Eccl.* 7.20). Thus, "Even Moses and Aaron died through their sin, as it is said, 'Because you believed not in me' . . . . Hence had you believed in me, your time would not have come to depart" (*Shab.* 55a). As a result of this doctrine, the rabbis go to great lengths to explain the death of children. The barrier between life and death is regarded as complete and impenetrable, though the view is expressed that the corpse remains sensate until the grave is covered over or until it disintegrates (*Shab.* 152a). Death brings with it a purging of sin (*Shab.* 8b) and acts as a kind of atonement (*Sifrei* on *Nm.*, "Shelaḥ" 112). A person should not be allowed to die alone, and relatives and friends should remain with the dying person to the end. As soon as a person dies, the eyes are reverently closed; those present say the *Tsidduq ha-Din and formally rend their garments. Common practices (*Shulḥan ʿArukh, Yoreh Deʿah* 339.5), probably of superstitious origin, include covering mirrors and pouring out standing water in the home of the deceased.

Reform Judaism, in the Pittsburgh platform of 1885, explicitly rejected resurrection and the concept of the garden of Eden and Geihinnom as places of, respectively, reward and punishment. Reform Judaism emphasized, immortality of the soul and naturalistic immortality, that is, the continuation of a person's influence on the world even after death.

• Hayyim Halevy Donin, *To Be A Jew* (New York, 1991). Hyman Goldin, *Hamadrikh: The Rabbi's Guide* (New York, 1956). Jules Harlow, ed., *Liqqutei Tefillah: A Rabbi's Manual* (New York, 1965), Louis Jacobs, *A Jewish Theology* (New York, 1974). Isaac Klein, *A Guide to Jewish Religious Practice* (New York, 1992). Peter Knobel, "Rites of Passage," in *Judaism: A People and Its History*, edited by Robert Seltzer (New York, 1989). Maurice Lamm, *The Jewish Way in Death and Mourning* (New York, 1969). George Nickelsburg, *Resurrection, Immortality, and Eternal Life in Intertestamental Judaism* (Cambridge, Mass., 1972). David Polish, ed., *Maglei Tsedek: A Rabbi's Manual*, with notes by W. Gunther Plaut (New York, 1988). Emile Puech, *La Croyance des Esséniens en la vie future: Immortalité, résurrection, vie éternelle? Histoire d'une croyance dans le judaïsme ancien* (Paris, 1993). Tzvi Rabinowicz, *A Guide to Life: Jewish Laws and Customs of Mourning* (London, 1964). —PETER KNOBEL

DEBORAH (Heb. Devorah; 12th cent. BCE), prophet, judge, poet, and military leader in the period of the Judges. Two stories relate her great achievements: a prose account (*Jgs.* 4) and a victory poem attributed to her (*Jgs.* 5). According to the prose narrative, she was a local judge in Ephraim who had an oracle and summoned Barak with a plan to deliver the Israelites from the Canaanite king Jabin of Hazor. Barak agreed to fight only if she went with him; whereupon she predicted that a woman would decide the fate of the battle (*Jgs.* 4.9).

After the battle by the Kishon River between the soldiers of the tribes of Zebulun and Naphtali, and Sisera, the Canaanite, the latter fled, only to be killed by Jael, thus fulfilling Deborah's prediction. The poem differs in details as to the exact place of battle, the participating tribes, and the extent of God's supernatural intervention. It is constructed around female figures: Deborah, "a mother in Israel"; Jael; and Sisera's mother.

• Yaira Amit, *Sefer Shofetim: Omanut ha-ʿArikhah* (Jerusalem, 1992), pp. 185–205. Mieke Bal, *Murder and Difference: Gender, Genre, and Scholarship on Sisera's Death* (Bloomington, Ind., 1988). L. L. Bronner, "Valorized or Vilified? The Women of Judges in Midrashic Sources," in *A Feminist Companion to the Book of Judges*, edited by Athalya Brenner (Sheffield, Eng., 1993), pp. 78–86. —ATHALYA BRENNER

DEBTS. The Bible insists that a creditor refrain from embarrassing his debtor or acting in an exacting manner toward him (*Ex.* 22.24). Debts were dissolved every seventh year (see PEROZBOL; SHEMITTAH). All Israelites who had been sold into slavery to pay off debts were released or redeemed in the jubilee year (see YOVEL). A debtor's goods could not be seized in the event of his failure to meet his obligations, though at a later period this ruling had to be modified. According to post-biblical legislation, a loan (or a sale on credit) is presumed to fall due in thirty days in the absence of any special terms. When a date for payment has been set, neither the creditor nor his executors may demand payment prior to the date originally agreed upon. After repayment, acquittance is to be made by a formally attested receipt (*shover*). Since the geonic period, a creditor could insist, at or after the time of contract, that the debtor repay the loan only in the presence of witnesses. Upon partial repayment the creditor may insist upon receiving a new bond for the remainder or he may offer a *shover* for the part paid. For an orally incurred debt (where no bond exists) the debtor is entitled to a *shover* on payment. Transference of a debt from the creditor to a third party, to whom the creditor is himself indebted, is considered valid if the transference takes place in the presence of all three parties. When a loan is contracted without formal bond, the real estate of the borrower is not subject to seizure by the creditor in the event of failure to repay the loan. Usury is condemned in the Bible; Jewish law is equally condemnatory of charging interest, although historical circumstances necessitated certain modifications in this respect. See also LOANS; MONEYLENDING.

• Gregory Chirichigno, *Debt-slavery in Israel and the Ancient Near East* (Sheffield, Eng., 1993).

DECALOGUE. See TEN COMMANDMENTS.

DECREES. See TAQQANAH.

DEDICATION (Heb. *ḥanukkah*), ceremony whereby a building is dedicated to a sacred purpose, or a plot of land is dedicated to be used for a *cemetery. There is explicit reference in the Bible to the formal dedication of the three biblical sanctuaries: the Sanctuary in the wilderness (*Nm.* 7), the Temple of Solomon (*1 Kgs.* 8; *2 Chr.* 5–6, as well as *Ps.* 30—the Psalm of Dedication), and the Second Temple (of the altar, *Ezr.* 3.9–12; and of the Temple, *Ezr.* 6.16–18). In the post-biblical period, the rededication of the Temple by *Judah the Maccabee three years after its desecration by the Syrians led to the institution of the eight-day festival of *Ḥanukkah (*1 Mc.* 4). Ceremonies for the dedication of other sacred buildings are of comparatively late origin. It is possible that homes were dedicated in biblical times (*Dt.* 20.5), but if so, the custom lapsed. Until recently Ashkenazim merely affixed the **mezuzah* and uttered the appropriate blessing, although an order of domestic service for the dedication of a home was evolved among Sephardim. In the nineteenth century, the British chief rabbinate composed a prayer for *ḥanukkat ha-bayit* (dedication of the house), which includes Psalms 30 and 15, those verses of Psalm 119 that acrostically spell the word *berakhah* (blessing), and special words of dedication. The occasion is accompanied by a feast for those attending—when dedicating a house in Erets Yisra'el, the feast is obligatory because a **mitsvah* is being fulfilled; elsewhere it is optional. There is no standard or statutory service for the consecration of a synagogue, but it usually includes Psalm 30 and seven circuits of the synagogue with scrolls of the Torah. There is also an order of service for the dedication of a cemetery, including the recitation of penitential prayers at the morning service on the day of dedication. Members of the burial society (**ḥevrah qaddisha'*) fast on the day of the dedication. A medieval custom, sanctioned by R. *Yehudah ben Shemu'el he-Ḥasid but no longer practiced, was to kill a cock (the word *gever* in Hebrew means both "cock" and "man") and bury it as the first funeral in the newly dedicated cemetery.

• Yochanan Zweig, "The Dedication of the Tabernacle," *Tradition* 25.1 (1989): 11–16.

DEDICATION, FEAST OF. See ḤANUKKAH.

DEED, a legal document. In the Bible, the word *sefer* indicates a legal document (*Dt.* 24.1–3); in rabbinic literature, *shetar*. The term *get*, originally also used by the rabbis for any legal document, came gradually to refer only to a bill of *divorce. In Jewish law, every legal document consists of two parts: the *tofes*, a general formula standardized for different types of documents; and the *toref*, an open portion containing the specific terms and nature of the individual contract, the names of the parties, date, time, and so on. While for all normal transactions ready-made documents may be used, in the case of a bill of divorce the document must be specially prepared. A formally attested document enjoys a presumption of validity; however, if this presumption is called into question, a court may rule on the authenticity (*qiyyum* or *henpeq*) of the document. A document may serve in a dual capacity: it may act as the validating instrument (see ACQUISITION) in the purchase of land; or as proof that ownership was transferred by means of some other acquisition. In the case of a bill of divorce, the actual transfer of the document from husband to wife (in front of witnesses) effects the divorce. The act of betrothal may be performed in like manner. While documents may be entered as valid evidence, witnesses may not testify in writing.

• Menachem Elon, *Jewish Law: History, Sources, Principles*, 4 vols. (Philadelphia, 1994).

DEGREES, SONG OF (Heb. Shir ha-Maʿalot), the superscription on Psalm 120 through Psalm 134. The title may refer to the custom of reciting the psalms while traveling up to Jerusalem or while ascending the Temple steps. It is customary among Ashkenazim to recite these psalms after the Minḥah service on the Sabbaths between Sukkot and Pesaḥ and on Tu bi-Shevat. One of these psalms (126) is sung before Birkat ha-Mazon on Sabbaths and festivals as a reminder of Zion. This custom, based on passages from the Zohar, is late and first appears in print in the seventeenth century.

• Cuthbert C. Keet, *A Liturgical Study of the Psalter: A Consideration of Some Liturgical and Ceremonial Aspects of Jewish Worship Exhibited in the Book of Psalms* (London, 1928). —SHALOM PAUL

DEISM, in contrast to theism, is the view that God exists as the cause of the universe but does not actively influence its operation. The universe created by the God of deistic thought has been compared to a clock that, once constructed and wound, functions independently of its maker. Deism reached its classical form in the eighteenth century. Traditional theism, both biblical and rabbinic, although also using much philosophical terminology, such as God as the "First Cause," is opposed to deism, since theism assumes God's constant *providence and solicitude for his creation (and individual creatures), his power to intervene in the course of nature and history (*miracles, *revelation), and his moral judgment of human actions. Mystical thinkers (e.g., the kabbalists), far from attributing independent existence to the universe, held that it would return to utter nothingness and nonbeing if God's sustaining presence were withdrawn even for a moment. Deism was a major influence on the eighteenth-century Enlightenment and was popular among its thinkers as "Natural Religion," that is, religion without revelation. Deism, therefore, in spite of its plea for tolerance, exhibited contempt for Jewish (meaning biblical) superstitions, such as belief in revelation, miracles, and the like. The Jews were thus, by definition, regarded as an "illiterate, barbarous, and ridiculous people," and deism must therefore be counted among the influences in modern *antisemitism.

• Arthur Hertzberg, *The French Enlightenment and the Jews* (New York, 1968). Moshe Pelli, "The Impact of Deism on the Hebrew Literature of the Enlightenment in Germany," in *The Age of Haskalah: Studies in Hebrew Literature of the Enlightenment in Germany* (Leiden, 1979). Lèon Poliakov, *The History of Anti-Semitism* (London, 1974).

DEITY. See God.

DELLA REINA, YOSEF (15th cent.), kabbalist and hero of a legend about an attempt to end the power of Satan and bring about the messianic redemption by magical means. Della Reina belonged to a school of kabbalists in Spain that developed new concepts concerning the powers of evil and redemption. Rabbi Avraham ben Eliʿezer ha-Levi, a kabbalist who emigrated to Jerusalem at the beginning of the sixteenth century, recorded in his *Iggeret Sod ha-Ge'ullah* the earliest version of a story describing R. Yosef della Reina's attempt to overcome Samael and Amon of No; he failed when he was seduced into burning incense before them. This story was known in Safed, and both Mosheh ben Yaʿaqov *Cordovero and Ḥayyim Vital (see Vital Family) refer to it. An elaborate novel based on this story was written by Shelomoh Navarro of Jerusalem, who pretended it was based on an ancient manuscript, in the mid-seventeenth century. Navarro converted to Christianity in 1664; however, his version became the standard, copied and printed many times. A Shabbatean version of this story, in Yiddish, was preserved by R. Leib ben ʿOzer of Amsterdam. Dozens of literary adaptations, in prose, poetry, and drama, abound in modern Hebrew literature.

• Gershom Gerhard Scholem, "Concerning the Story of Rabbi Yosef Dela Reina," in *Studies in Jewish Religious and Intellectual History Presented to Alexander Altmann*, edited by Siegfried Stein and R. Loewe (London, 1979), pp. 101–108. Z. Shazar, "The Story of Rabbi Yosef Dela Reina in the Sabatian Tradition," in *Eder ha-Yekar: S. A. Horodetzky Festschrift* (Jerusalem, 1947), pp. 97–118. —JOSEPH DAN

DEL-MEDIGO, ELIYYAHU (c.1460–1497), philosopher and physician. Born in Crete, he lived in Padua, where he gave lectures on philosophy; his best-known Christian disciple was Pico della Mirandola. Del-Medigo was greatly influenced by Averroës and translated some of his works via Hebrew into Latin. Besides his translations, Del-Medigo also wrote in Hebrew and Latin about Averroës's commentaries on Aristotle and other philosophical subjects. Del-Medigo's *Beḥinat ha-Dat* seeks to reconcile philosophy and religion, holding that each has its own domain and that they do not therefore conflict. Should philosophy and revelation seem to contradict each other, philosophy must defer. In particular, the philosopher must not tamper with the basic doctrines of divine existence, revelation, and retribution. Del-Medigo attacked the kabbalists and denied that the Zohar was written by R. Shimʿon bar Yoḥ'ai.

• Kalman Bland, "Elijah del Medigo's Averroist Response to the Kabbalahs of Fifteenth-Century Jewry and Pico della Mirandola," *Journal of Jewish Thought and Philosophy* 1.1 (1991): 23–53. Aryeh Motzkin, "Elia Del Medigo, Averroes, and Averroism" *Italia* 6.1–2 (1987): 7–19. —FRANCISCO MORENO CARVALHO

DEL-MEDIGO, YOSEF SHELOMOH (1591–1655), rabbi, philosopher, and scholar; known by the acronym Yashar (Yosef Shelomoh Rofe' [doctor]) of Candia. Born in Crete to a famous scholarly family, he received a Jewish and classical education. He studied astronomy and mathematics under Galileo, as well as medicine and philosophy at the University of Padua and Jewish studies with the help of Leone Modena from Venice. Del-Medigo wandered through Egypt, Turkey, Poland, and Lithuania, where he participated in scientific dialogues with Muslim, Christian, and Karaite scholars. In Vilna he served as private physician of Prince Radziwill. Later, Del-Medigo reached Hamburg, where he served as rabbi and preacher. In 1629 he arrived in Amsterdam, where *Manasseh ben Israel published Del-Medigo's book

Elim, an answer to queries addressed to him by the Karaite scholar Zeraḥ ben Natan of Troki. This close dialogue with a Karaite rabbi caused concern among the leaders of the community, who appointed a rabbinical committee to examine the contents of the book. In the same year Del-Medigo's disciple Shemu'el Ashkenazi published in Basel Del-Megido's *Ta'alumot Ḥokhmah*, followed in 1631 by *Novelot Ḥokhmah*. Del-Medigo moved to Frankfurt am Main, where he served for many years as the community's physician. Toward the end of his life he spent several years in Prague, where he died. Del-Megido was famous for his equivocal attitude toward Kabbalah. Some scholars concluded that his defense of it in *Matsref la-Ḥokhmah* (Odessa, 1864) was not genuine.

• Isaac Barzilay, *Yoseph Shlomo Delmedigo, Yashar of Candia: His Life, Works, and Times* (Leiden, 1974). Cecil Roth, *A Life of Menasseh ben Israel: Rabbi, Printer, and Diplomat* (Philadelphia, 1945), pp. 132–134.

—NISSIM YOSHA

DEMA'I (דְּמַאי; perhaps), name of a certain kind of agricultural produce and of a Mishnaic tractate.

Agricultural Produce. *Dema'i*, a term probably derived from the Aramaic word *dema'*, is used to denote doubtfully tithed agricultural produce. The Talmud cites a decree to the effect that any person buying produce from an ignorant person (*'am ha-'arets*) was required to separate the *tithes specified under biblical law (*Sot.* 47b–48a). This rule applied only to tithes, not to the priestly dues (*terumah*). The reasons for this distinction are that the eating of produce from which *terumah* has not been separated is a capital offense (*San.* 83a) and the amount of produce that must be taken in order to fulfill the biblical requirement of taking *terumah* is much smaller than that required for tithes (*Ḥul.* 137b). The ignorant would, therefore, separate *terumah* but could not be relied upon to make a similar effort with respect to tithes.

• Judah D. Eisenstein, *Otsar Yisra'el* (Jerusalem, 1951), vol. 4, pp. 55–56. Hermann Strack, *Introduction to the Talmud and Midrash* (Minneapolis, 1992)

—DANIEL SINCLAIR

Tractate. The tractate *Dema'i*, in Mishnah order Zera'im, consists of seven chapters, with related material in the Tosefta' and in the Talmud Yerushalmi. The tractate deals with the laws regarding produce purchased from an *'am ha-'arets*, a common person whose commitment to the laws of tithing is suspect. In order to permit the use of such produce, the purchaser is required to separate from it certain tithes and to treat them with the appropriate sanctity.

Individuals who undertook meticulously to observe the laws of tithing were regarded as reliable, and produce purchased from them was not considered *dema'i*. The laws of *dema'i* effectively divided Jewish society into groups of suspect *'amei ha-'arets* and *ḥaverim* (initiates), whose piety might prevent them from eating at the table of an *'am ha-'arets*. Tractate *Dema'i* introduced halakhic mechanisms that enable an initiate to be a guest at an *'am ha-'arets*'s table without relaxing his standards of piety.

An English translation of the tractate is in Herbert Danby's *The Mishnah* (Oxford, 1933).

• Chanoch Albeck, ed., *Shishah Sidrei Mishnah, Seder Zera'im* (Jerusalem, 1957). Philip Blackman, ed. and trans., *Mishnayot*, vol. 1, *Order Zera'im* (Gateshead, 1973). Jacob David Herzog, ed. and trans., *Mishnah* (Jerusalem, 1945). Pinhas Kehati, ed., *Mishnah: A New Translation with a Commentary, Seder Zera'im*, vol. 2, *Dema'i, Kil'ayim, Shevi'it* (Jerusalem, 1992). Hermann Leberecht Strack, *Introduction to the Talmud and Midrash* (1931; Minneapolis, 1992).

—AVRAHAM WALFISH

DEMOCRACY, form of government in which sovereignty resides in the people. Although many of the values and moral principles underlying democracy are affirmed by (and often derived from) the Bible, the way of life envisaged for the Israelites in the Bible cannot properly be termed a democracy. The Bible greatly influenced the development of democratic ideas in seventeenth-century England and eighteenth-century America, and the organization of the ancient Israelite tribes might also have been a kind of primitive democracy. Nevertheless, a system that provides for both a hereditary monarchy and a hereditary priestly caste cannot be so termed, even though kings often ruled by popular consent (Saul, David, Simon the Hasmonean). *Deuteronomy* 17.14–20 and other scriptural passages envisage a limited constitutional monarchy, but the basic conception is essentially theocratic (see THEOCRACY).

The rabbis of the Second Temple period further developed the nomocratic principle (rule of the divinely revealed law). They recognized no political or spiritual prerogatives of the priesthood (except in matters of religious precedence) and rejected prophetic authority, since prophecy in this view had come to an end with *Malachi. Within the body of sages qualified to interpret the law, decisions were arrived at by the process of counting and deciding (i.e., by majority vote); failure to submit to the majority decision rendered a scholar a rebellious elder (*zaqen mamre'*).

In principle the *synagogue and Jewish *community were highly democratic, but in practice there was a tendency to oligarchy, with power in the hands of the wealthy and the rabbinical hierarchy. It has been suggested that it is not so much the political theory underlying biblical and rabbinic law that has turned Jews into champions of democracy as the social and moral values implicit in traditional Jewish teaching.

• Naomi Ben-Asher, *Democracy's Hebrew Roots*, 2d ed. (New York, 1953). Zeev W. Falk, "Democracy," in *Law and Religion* (Jerusalem, 1981), pp. 43–57. Immanuel Jakobovits, "Judaism and Democracy," in *Journal of a Rabbi* (New York, 1966), pp. 105–110. Abraham Isaac Katsh, *The Biblical Heritage of American Democracy* (New York, 1977).

DEMONS. Belief in demons or evil spirits has played a relatively unimportant role in doctrinal Judaism, though it was prominent in folk tradition. Jewish theology, as reflected in biblical and rabbinic literature, did not deny the existence of supernatural beings capable of causing harm, but the absolute sovereignty and omnipotence attributed to God (*Dt.* 4.35) reduced the importance of such demonic forces. Apocalyptic literature exhibits dualistic influences, originating in Persian teaching (Ormizd and Ahriman). The Essenes seem to have cultivated an esoteric lore regarding evil spirits and to have practiced exorcism. Demonology plays a major role in the work of medieval kabbalists. In rabbinic Judaism, demonology belongs primarily to the realm of *aggadah* and folklore, and rarely impinges on the *halakhah*. In the Bible, all cosmic agencies, both beneficent and malign, are controlled by God's will. Forces of destruction are his messengers of punishment (e.g., *Ex*. 12.33), and even *Satan is only his servant (*Jb*. 1.2). But the survival of earlier animistic beliefs is attested to by the references to *se'irim* (*Lv*. 17.7, "satyrs"; Arab. *jinn*) or *shedim* (*Dt*. 32.17, "demons" or "devils") and the like. At times, scripture derisively applies demonic terminology to the pagan deities (*Dt*. 32.17). In rabbinic times, under Babylonian and Persian influence, demonology—like angelology (see ANGELS)—assumed considerable importance in aggadic thought and general Jewish folklore. Many of the demons became individualized and were given specific names, often of foreign origin. The chief generic names are *shedim*, *mazziqim* (injurers), *ruḥot* (spirits), and *mal'akhei ḥabbalah* (angels of destruction). These demons are invisible and their numbers legion. Like angels, they possess wings, can fly from one end of the world to the other, and know the future; like human beings, they eat and drink, procreate, and die (*Ḥag*. 16a). They live in ruins and desolate places and are most active at night. As a rule they are malevolent and the cause of various diseases; in Geihinnom they torture the wicked. But some are friendly and useful to man; these were employed, for example, in the construction of the Tabernacle and Temple. Their king is *Asmodeus (*Git*. 68a–b), *Samael, or *Azazel. Agrat bat Maḥalat is the queen of demons, as is Lilith, who slays newborn infants, but Satan rules over them all. The only true defense against demonic injury is the observance of commandments, though special prayers were also prescribed and *amulets worn. It is said that demons were created at twilight on the eve of the Sabbath (*Pes*. 54b) or that they are descended from "fallen angels" (cf. *Gn*. 6.1–4). In pseudepigraphous literature, the guardian angels of gentile nations, as well as Satan himself, are also depicted as fallen angels. Medieval Jewish philosophers, with the exception of Avraham ibn Ezra and Maimonides, accepted belief in demons. The kabbalists called the demonic realm **sitra' aḥra'* (the other side) and also developed the concept of *qelippah* (shell of evil), which wages an incessant war against the element of "holiness"; they also contributed to the increasing popularization of amulets. Later Jewish folklore referred to *letsim* (mischievous imps) and also absorbed many non-Jewish superstitions.

• Bernard Jacob Bamberger, *Fallen Angels* (Philadelphia, 1952). *Dictionary of Deities and Demons in the Bible*, edited by Karel van der Toorn et al. (Leiden, 1995). Leo Jung, *Fallen Angels in Jewish, Christian, and Mohammedan Literature* (1926; repr. New York, 1974). Joshua Trachtenberg, *Jewish Magic and Superstition: A Study in Folk Religion* (New York, 1984).

DENUNCIATION (Heb. *mesirah*), the act of informing on Jews or the Jewish community to non-Jewish authorities. The insecurity of the Jews in Talmudic and medieval times, and their urgent need for solidarity in a hostile world, made denunciation the most heinous crime in the Jewish community and the informer (*malshin* or *moser*; *delator*) its most despicable character. Every step against him, even taking his life, was permitted in order to safeguard the interests of the community. When the imprecation against "sectarians" in the *'Amidah became obsolete (as sectarians were no longer a danger), the wording was changed so as to include all kinds of informers and slanderers (*Ber*. 28b). The Talmud says that all informers will go down to Geihinnom for eternal punishment (*R. ha-Sh*. 17a). If their life is in danger, nothing should be done to save them (*'A. Z*. 26b). In medieval times, many steps were taken against them. In France, R. Tam convened a gathering of scholars to take measures against informers. In Rhineland synagogues, they were cursed every Sabbath. In Spain, R. Asher ben Yeḥi'el of Toledo referred to the carrying out of death sentences against informers (*Resp*. VIII 1.8).

Maimonides stated that in the Maghreb (west Morocco) it was a "normal occurrence" for informers to be handed over to the non-Jewish authorities for punishment. In his code he laid down that it is lawful to put informers to death (*Hilkhot Ḥovel u-Mazziq*). The usual action taken against such offenders was their excommunication (*ḥerem*), though sometimes they were subjected to mutilation.

• Menachem Elon, *Jewish Law: History, Sources, Principles*, 4 vols. (Philadelphia, 1994).

DERASH (דְּרָשׁ; exposition), a word derived from the verb *d r sh*, meaning to search out the sense of or to seek to understand the sacred text (see *Dt*. 13.15, 17.4, 9). Ezra declared that he has directed his mind to do this (*Ezr*. 7.10). Elsewhere in the scriptures, the word means occupation with divine commandments and the texts in which they are embedded. In the tannaitic period (1st–2d cent.), the term refers more specifically to the interpretation of individual passages (**midrash*). *Derash*, homiletical exposition, is often contrasted with *peshat*, the literal meaning (see PARDES). In addition, it refers to the public interpretation of the scriptures (also *derashah*); the expounder was known as a **darshan*.

• Wilhelm Bacher, *Die exegetische Terminologie der jüdischen Traditionsliteratur* (Leipzig, 1905), vol. 1, pp. 25–27, 103–105; vol. 2, pp. 41–43. Hermann L. Strack, *Introduction to the Talmud and Midrash* (Philadelphia, 1931), p. 6.

—LOU H. SILBERMAN

DERASHAH. See HOMILETICS.

DEREKH ERETS (דֶּרֶךְ אֶרֶץ; "way of the land"), phrase used with varying connotations in rabbinic literature. In *Avot* 2.2 and 6.6 it means the worldly occupation or trade by which one earns one's livelihood, while in *Numbers Rabbah* 31.23 it means normal procedure. Most commonly, however, the phrase connotes etiquette or correct conduct, implying proper behavior and politeness. It is the subject of two post-Talmudic treatises, *Derekh Erets Rabbah* and *Derekh Erets Zuta'* (see DEREKH ERETS RABBAH AND ZUTA'). The rabbis ascribed such correct behavior to worthy biblical figures, and even to the Almighty himself, and often use the phrase "the Torah thus teaches us *derekh erets*" (e.g., "The Torah thus teaches us *derekh erets* that a man should first build his house, then plant his vineyard, and only then take a wife," *Sot.* 44a; "The Torah teaches us *derekh erets* that a man should always inquire after the welfare of his host," *B. M.* 87a; "The Holy One, blessed be he, thus teaches us *derekh erets* that a man should refrain from using a fruit-bearing tree to build his house," *Ex. Rab.* 35.2). The laws of *derekh erets* cover all aspects of human life, including the relationship between spouses, family members, and friends; ways of dressing and eating; modes of address; procedure in visiting superiors; and use of language. Thus, one should not rejoice among people who weep or weep among those who rejoice (*Derekh Erets Rabbah* 7.7); ask the price of an item when one has no intention of buying it, for this falsely raises the hopes of the seller (*Derekh Erets Rabbah* 8.6); or, when a guest, offer the host's small children food without first obtaining permission to do so from the parents (*Derekh Erets Rabbah* 9.3). The rabbinic dictum "*Derekh erets* precedes Torah" inspired the motto of *Neo-Orthodoxy as expounded by Samson Raphael *Hirsch, "Torah together with *derekh erets*," in which *derekh erets* refers to the general culture.

• Michael Higger, The Treatises *Derek Erez* (New York, 1935). Daniel Sperber, *Derech Erez Zuta: Chapters Five to Eight* (Ramat Gan, 1990).

—SHMUEL HIMELSTEIN

DEREKH ERETS RABBAH AND ZUTA', two minor tractates appended to standard editions of the Talmud Bavli at the conclusion of tractate *ʿAvodah Zarah*. Both works appear to be collections of tannaitic and amoraic material compiled during the post-Talmudic period. They contain both ethical maxims and norms of etiquette. Many of the rules of conduct are illustrated with stories drawn from the lives of the early rabbis. They were edited and translated into English by Michael Higger (1935). An independent composition, entitled **Pereq ha-Shalom*, which extols the value of peace, is appended to standard editions of *Derekh Erets Zuta'*.

• Michael Higger, ed. and trans., *The Treatises Derek Erez* (New York, 1935). Marcus van Loopik, *The Ways of the Sages and the Way of the World: The Minor Tractates of the Babylonian Talmud; Derekh Erets Rabbah, Derekh Erets Zuta', Pereq ha-Shalom* (Tübingen, 1991). Daniel Sperber, *A Commentary on Derech Erez Zuta* (Jerusalem, 1990). Daniel Sperber, *Great Is Peace: Perek ha-Shalom from the Talmudic Tractate Derekh Eretz Zuta* (Jerusalem, 1979).

—AVRAHAM WALFISH

DESECRATION (Heb. *ḥillul*), a violation of the sacred or hallowed character of an object; a diversion of purpose from the sacred to the profane. Most such transgressions in Jewish law relate to the Temple ritual (e.g., the use of Temple objects for nonsacred purposes) or to the comportment of the priests (e.g., the ban that prohibits a high priest from marrying an unsuitable wife or a deformed priest from participating in the Temple service). Since God commands Israel to be a holy people, any act of desecration is also a desecration of God's holy name (*Lv.* 21.6; *Ez.* 22.26). Both idolatry and social immorality were held to be particularly reprehensible. The punishment for desecration is generally excommunication from the people of Israel (*karet*) or the death penalty (to be administered by divine intervention). See also ḤILLUL HA-SHEM; ḤILLUL SHABBAT; SACRILEGE.

• Shear Y. Cohen, "Between Love and Rebuke," *Tradition* 28 (Winter, 1994): 4–10, on action against public Sabbath desecration in Israel. John R. Price, "The Desecration and Restoration of the Temple as an Eschatalogical Motif in the Tanach, Jewish Apocalyptic Literature, and the New Testament," Ph.D. dissertation, University of Texas at Austin, 1993.

—SHALOM PAUL

DESECRATION OF THE NAME. See ḤILLUL HA-SHEM.

DESECRATION OF THE SABBATH. See ḤILLUL SHABBAT.

DESTRUCTION OF PROPERTY. See BAL TASHḤIT.

DETERMINISM, the view that whatever happens is determined in advance, either by causal necessity or by God's knowledge or decree; the latter category is known as *predestination. Although determinism is accepted in one form or another by many religious philosophies, Judaism has tended to consider *free will and the exercise of free choice as a precondition for the religious and moral life. Moral indeterminacy seems to be assumed both by the Bible, which bids man to choose between *good and evil, and by the rabbis, who hold that the decision for following the good inclination rather than the evil (see YETSER HA-RAʿ AND YETSER HA-TOV) rests with every individual. Determinism is discussed by most philosophers in connection with the problem of free will. That the doctrine of free will is compatible with the theory of God's foreknowledge is asserted by Maimonides (*Mishneh Torah, Hilkhot Teshuvah* 5), who also emphatically rejects the doctrine of predestination. Modern Jewish philosophers discuss determinism mainly in the light of scientific concepts of causality; the same problem was discussed under the heading of *astrology by medieval thinkers, whose theories of stellar determination correspond to those of natural causality found in later periods. See also PROVIDENCE.

• Hubert Dethier, "Some Remarks on the Political Philosophy of Maimonides and al-Farabi with Regard to Their Conception of Astral Determinism and in the Light of German Idealism," in *Sobre la vida y obra de Maimonides: I Congreso Internacional (Cordova, 1985)*, edited by Jesus Pelaez del Rosal (Cordova, 1991), pp. 95–115. Morris M. Faierstein, "The Deterministic Theology of Rabbi Mordecai Joseph Leiner of Izbica," *Proceedings of the Rabbinical Assembly* 51 (1990): 186–196. Seymour W. Feldman, "A Debate Concerning Determinism in Late Medieval Jewish Philosophy," *Proceedings of the American Academy for Jewish Research* 51 (1984): 15–54. Jerome I. Gellman, "Freedom and Determinism in Maimonides' Philosophy," in *Moses Maimonides and His Time*, edited by Eric L. Ormsby (Washington, D.C., 1989), pp. 139–150. Lenn Evan Goodman, "Determinism and Freedom in Spinoza, Maimonides, and Aristotle: A Retrospective Study," in *Responsibility, Character and the Emotions. New Essays in Moral Psychology*, edited by Ferdinand Schoeman (Cambridge, Mass., 1987), pp. 107–164.

DEUTERO-ISAIAH. See ISAIAH.

DEUTERONOMIC SOURCE (D), in the view of critical biblical scholarship, one of the originally separate documents from which the Torah was composed, consisting of most of the *Book of *Deuteronomy*. The law code found in *Deuteronomy* 12–26 is regarded by Bible scholars as being distinct from other law codes in the Torah. Scholars also refer to the final redactor of *Joshua*, *Judges*, *Samuel*, and *Kings* (the Former Prophets) as the

Deuteronomist, because the editorial framework of these books reflects the historical and theological viewpoint of *Deuteronomy*. See BIBLE.

• E. W. Nicholson, *Deuteronomy and Tradition* (Philadelphia, 1967). Moshe Weinfeld, *Deuteronomy and the Deuteronomic School* (Oxford, 1983). —BARUCH J. SCHWARTZ

DEUTERONOMY, BOOK OF (Heb. *Devarim* [Words]; from the book's first distinctive word), the fifth and last book of the Torah, containing *Moses' farewell address to the children of Israel, his final blessing and "song," and an account of his death. The Jewish rabbis called it *Mishneh Torah* (repetition of the Torah; hence, its Greek name *Deuteronomion*, "second," from which the English form derives) based on *Deuteronomy* 17.18. Moses reminds the people of their frequent disobedience and lack of faith in God, and he exhorts them to fidelity. He stresses the blessings and happiness that result from obedience and the curses that follow transgression; future sins of the people, he prophesies, will be severely punished, but eventually God will usher in an era of happiness and glory. According to Jewish tradition, Moses spoke the contents of *Deuteronomy* during the thirty-seven days preceding his demise and wept when uttering the last verses, dictated to him by God, describing his death (although the Talmud gives another version in which the last verses were written by Joshua, *B. B.* 15a). The book recapitulates the main religious principles and legislation, including the *Ten Commandments, contained in the previous books but also adds new laws, most of which have a humanistic dimension. An important feature of the book is its emphasis on the unification of all cultic activity in a central sanctuary. All other worship is absolutely banned. The book insists on the uniqueness of God and his choice of Israel, from which derive the practical obligations owed him by the Israelites, such as the absolute rejection of idolatry. There also appears a more abstract conception of God, who no longer is said to dwell personally in the Temple—only his "Name" resides there (*Dt.* 12.11). The Ark, moreover, which formerly was conceived to be the footstool of God, is now interpreted to be merely the place where the tablets of the covenant are lodged. Modern scholars, who maintain that the Pentateuch is composed of several documents, regard the *Book of Deuteronomy* as an independent source (referred to as "D," see BIBLE), the dating of which has been widely disputed, ranging from premonarchic to postexilic. It is generally understood that *Deuteronomy* is the "book of law" found by the high priest Hilkiah in the Temple in 621 BCE during the reign of King *Josiah of Judah; the priest's discovery provided the impetus for the king's religious reform in Judah (*2 Kgs.* 22–23). Another feature that ties *Deuteronomy* to the age of Josiah is the strong linguistic and structural resemblance that the book exhibits with vassal treaties of Neo-Assyrian kings in the seventh century BCE. Phrases such as "to love . . . with all your heart" (*Dt.* 6.5, 11.13, 30.6) and "to obey the voice of" (*Dt.* 15.5, 28.1, 30.20), which in the political context of Assyrian treaties signified the relationship of absolute loyalty of the vassal to the king, take on a theological dimension in *Deuteronomy* by defining the treaty-covenantal relationship as pertaining to God and his people. The entire structure of the book also follows the tripartite pattern of treaties known throughout the ancient Near East: introduction (chaps. 1–11), legal corpus (chaps. 12–26), and blessings and curses (chaps. 27–30). *Deuteronomy* exerted a profound influence on biblical literature commonly assigned to the seventh century BCE and onward, such as the Former Prophets corpus and the *Book of Jeremiah*. Most scholars regard these latter works as having been shaped by the Deuteronomic school.

• Samuel Rolles Driver, *A Critical and Exegetical Commentary on Deuteronomy*, 3d ed., The International Critical Commentary, vol. 5 (Edinburgh, 1902). Ernest W. Nicholson, *Deuteronomy and Tradition* (Philadelphia, 1967). Moshe Weinfeld, *Deuteronomy and the Deuteronomic School* (Oxford, 1972). —DAVID A. GLATT-GILAD

DEUTERONOMY RABBAH, Midrashic work on the *Book of *Deuteronomy* incorporated into the medieval anthology *Midrash Rabbah. It is not a commentary on every verse of *Deuteronomy*, but a collection of homilies, where each section begins with a *halakhah*. *Deuteronomy Rabbah* survives in at least two different versions, both of which belong to the *Tanḥuma'-Yelammedenu.

Deuteronomy Rabbah, as found in the printed editions of Midrash Rabbah, MS Parma De Rossi 1240 and fragments, circulated primarily in France and Germany; it contains twenty-seven literary homilies on the triennial-cycle weekly lections of *Deuteronomy*. The version published by Saul Lieberman (Jerusalem, 1974) is found in most manuscripts of Midrash Rabbah and contains alternate or additional Midrashic material (the extent of which varies in different manuscripts) of the Tanḥuma'-Yelammedenu type that circulated primarily in Spain and North Africa. An English translation by J. Rabbinowitz appeared in the Soncino edition of Midrash Rabbah (London, 1939; repr. 1961).

• Saul Lieberman, ed., *Midrash Devarim Rabbah* 3d ed. (Jerusalem, 1974). Hermann Leberecht Strack, *Introduction to the Talmud and Midrash* (1931; Minneapolis, 1992). Leopold Zunz, *Ha-Derashot be-Yisra'el ve-Hishtalshelutan ha-Historit*, edited by Chanoch Albeck (1892; Jerusalem, 1974). —MARC BREGMAN

DEVARIM. See DEUTERONOMY, BOOK OF.

DEVARIM RABBAH. See DEUTERONOMY RABBAH.

DEVEQUT (דְּבֵקוּת; cleaving, devotion), term used in the specific sense of loving attachment to God (cf. *Dt.* 11.22). Commenting on *Deuteronomy* 13.5, the Talmud (*Sot.* 14a) asks, "Is it possible to cleave unto God? Is it not said 'The Lord your God is a devouring fire?' " and explains that *devequt* means imitating God's attributes of mercy and kindness (see IMITATION OF GOD). Halakhic codifiers (e.g., *Mosheh ben Ya'aqov of Coucy and Moses *Maimonides) included *devequt* among the positive commandments. Medieval philosophers and mystics used the term to mean communion with God, which they considered to be the ultimate goal of religious life and spiritual endeavor. Some scholars, however, maintain that the traditional conception of the transcendence of God precludes the total and complete "mystical union" with God that many other religious systems speak about. Under kabbalistic influence and later under the influence of Hasidism, meditative as well as ecstatic *devequt* became generally accepted ideals. *Devequt* involves the practice of devotion (*kavvanah*; see INTENT), by which man removes the barriers between himself and God and establishes spiritual communion by "divesting himself of his material being" (*hitpashtut ha-gashmiyyut*).

• Gershom Gerhard Scholem, "Devekuth, or Communion with God," in *The Messianic Idea in Judaism and Other Essays on Jewish Spirituality* (New York, 1971).

DEVIL. See DEMONS; SATAN.

DEVIR. See TEMPLE.

DEVOTION. See INTENT.

DEVOTIONAL LITERATURE, religious literature not found in sacred texts (the Bible, Talmud, prayer book) and designed primarily to increase piety and devotion, rather than the knowledge of theological or ritual matters. It may be found at the margins of rabbinical literature (*Derekh Erets Rabbah, Derekh Erets Zuta', Seder Eliyyahu*), in the medieval exempla literature, and at the margins of almost every area of Jewish literary activity (*halakhah*, philosophy, ethical writings, mysticism, and confession). Devotional literature represented an effort by the learned circles to reach a broader audience; it also represented a response to the ideal of learned Judaism by circles that stressed piety and devotion, such as the medieval Ḥasidei Ashkenaz. In a wider sense, devotional literature includes such liturgical (see LITURGY) compilations as the *ma'amadot* (selections of scriptural and Talmudic passages for daily reading) and additional nonliturgical prayers and hymns (such as *Adon 'Olam and *baqqashot* [see *BAQQASHAH]) to be said in private devotion, many of which have made their way into the more comprehensive prayer books. A special aspect of devotional literature is the use of the vernacular, as in the case of the *teḥinnot* (supplications), biblical and Midrashic stories retold in Yiddish, often specifically for women (see TḤINNUS; TSE'ENAH U-RE'ENAH), or in Ladino (*Me'am Lo'ez*) and bilingual editions.

• Moses Gaster, *The Exempla of the Rabbis*, 2d ed. (New York, 1968). Arthur Green, ed., *Jewish Spirituality: From the Bible through the Middle Ages*, World Spirituality 13 (New York, 1986). Arthur Green, ed., *Jewish Spirituality: From the the Sixteenth-Century Revival to the Present*, World Spirituality 4 (New York, 1987). Judah ben Samuel, *Medieval Jewish Mysticism: The Book of the Pious*, translated by Sholom Alchanan Singer (Northbrook, Ill., 1971). Marcus van Loopik, *The Ways of the Sages and the Way of the World: The Minor Tractates of the Babylonian Talmud: Derekh Erets Rabbah, Derekh Eretz Zuta', Pereq ha-Shalom* (Tübingen, 1991).

—PETER LENHARDT

DEW, PRAYER FOR. See TEFILLAT TAL.

DHIMMI. Jews, Christians, and Zoroastrians living under Islam were known as *ahl ad-dhimma* (people of the covenant) or *dhimmis* and were subject to special discriminatory regulations under Islamic law. Since they possessed a book of revelation (*ahl el-kitab*), they were permitted to remain in Muslim lands, in contrast to pagans who were killed or forcibly converted. *Dhimmis* were required to pay discriminatory poll taxes (*djizya*) and land taxes (*haradj*) and had to wear distinguishing clothing. They were not permitted to ride horses or to build new synagogues and churches, and they were required to show special deference to Muslims. In exchange for their subordination, *dhimmis* were granted religious autonomy and a wide measure of economic freedom. The legal category of *dhimmi* was onerous, combining features of humiliation and discrimination with low-level toleration.

• Jane Gerber, "Anti-Semitism and the Muslim World," in *History and Hate: The Dimensions of Anti-Semitism*, edited by David Berger (Philadelphia, 1986). Bat Ye'or, *The Dhimmi: Jews and Christians under Islam*, translated by David Maisel et al. (Rutherford, N.J., 1985).

—JANE S. GERBER

DIALECTICS. See PILPUL.

DIASPORA. See EXILE.

DIBBUQ. See DYBBUK.

DIENA, 'AZRI'EL BEN SHELOMOH (died 1536), Italian rabbinic authority and scion of a French family that had settled in Piedmont. In his youth he taught in Reggio and moved to Pavia no later than 1514. For a few years he resided in Viadana, in the Mantua region. By 1526 he was rabbi of Sabbioneta, where he remained for the rest of his life. He corresponded on halakhic subjects with other leading authorities. His works include approximately three hundred *responsa*, which have been published in two volumes (1977–1979). They shed valuable light on all aspects of Italian Jewry in his day and also reflect his personality. In a letter to Avraham ha-Kohen of Bologna (1530), Diena condemned David *Re'uveni, an adventurer who aroused messianic hopes in the early sixteenth century and was greatly honored in many Italian communities. However, he wrote favorably of the false messiah Shelomoh *Molkho.

• Yacov Boksenboim, ed., *She'elot u-Teshuvot Rabbi 'Azri'el Shelomoh Dayenah*, 2 vols. (Tel Aviv, 1977–1979). Robert Bonfil, *Rabbis and Jewish Communities in Renaissance Italy*, translated by Jonathan Chipman (Oxford and New York, 1990).

—ABRAHAM DAVID

DIETARY LAWS. Jewish dietary laws apply only to animal foods, with the exception of *'*orlah* (forbidden fruit; i.e., the prohibition against eating the fruit of a tree during the first three years after planting [*Lv*. 19.23]; after the destruction of the Temple, the fruit of the fourth year was also forbidden), **ḥadash* (new corn; i.e., the ban on eating bread made from a fresh crop of corn until the second day of Pesaḥ [*Lv*. 23.14]), **tevel* (untithed produce; i.e., the ban on eating produce until the tithe has been set aside, applicable only in Erets Yisra'el), **kil'ayim* (diverse kinds; i.e., the prohibition against sowing diverse kinds of seed together, also applicable only in Erets Yisra'el [*Dt*. 22.9]); and *nesekh* (wine of libation; i.e., the prohibition against wine that had been used, or was suspected of having been prepared, for idolatrous libation, later extended to include any wine prepared or even touched by a non-Jew). Otherwise all fruits and vegetables are permitted.

Quadrupeds permitted for consumption are enumerated in *Deuteronomy* 14.4–5 (see CLEAN AND UNCLEAN ANIMALS). *Leviticus* 11.3 specifies that "Whatsoever parts the hoof and is wholly cloven-footed and chews the cud, that may you eat." Both conditions are necessary (*Lv*. 4–7). Only fish that have both fins and scales are permitted (*Lv*. 11. 9–12). Fish that have scales in their natural habitat but shed them before or upon being taken from the water are permitted. A number of birds are forbidden (*Lv*. 11.13), but no general characteristics are given in the Bible to distinguish between permitted and forbidden fowl (distinguishing signs are mentioned by the Mishnah [*Ḥul*. 3] and by the Talmud [*Ḥul*. 65b]). Since uncertainty exists as to the exact identification of the fowl listed as forbidden in the Bible, only those birds traditionally known as "clean" are used for food. Eggs of unclean birds are forbidden. Winged animals that creep on the ground may not be eaten. Exceptions are listed in *Leviticus* 11.20–22. All kinds of worms, mites, snails, and the like are forbidden (*Lv*. 41).

Flesh may not be torn from a living animal (**eivar min ha-ḥai*; *Gn*. 9.4; *San*. 59b), and all animals and birds, but not fish, require *ritual slaughter (*sheḥitah*), which alone renders the animal lawfully fit for consumption. A flaw in the performance of or arising from ritual slaughter renders the animal *nevelah* (carrion) and unfit for food. The term **terefah* originally designated the *meat of animals maimed or torn by wild beasts but gradually became the term used to designate all food, especially meat, that is forbidden, for whatever reason, by law. In particular, an animal found to be suffering from one or more of the defects or diseases listed in the Mishnah (*Ḥul*. 3) is called *terefah*. Maimonides lists seventy such cases under eight main headings: *derusah*, an animal that has been mauled by wild animals or birds; *nequvah*, an animal with a pierced or perforated membrane or organ; *ḥaserah*, an animal defective from birth; *netulah*, an animal missing a limb, organ, or part; *qerʿah*, a torn animal; *nefulah*, an animal that has fallen, so that internal injury is suspected; *pesuqah*, a split animal; and *shevurah*, a broken animal.

Part of the abdominal fat (**ḥelev*) of the ox, sheep, and goat is forbidden (*Lv*. 7.23), as is the sciatic nerve (**gid ha-nasheh*; cf. *Gn*. 32.33). Permitted fat is called *shuman*.

The blood of fish is permitted; that of beasts and birds is forbidden (*Lv*. 17.12–14); hence, all meat must be made kosher or rendered fit for cooking by a process called *meliḥah*, which consists of both soaking (for half an hour) and covering with salt (for one hour) and then rinsing the salt off before the dish may be prepared for food.

Blood specks render eggs unfit for consumption. The products of non-kosher cattle, beasts, birds, or fish (e.g., asses' milk, or caviar prepared from sturgeon roe) are also forbidden. Honey is an exception to this rule; the rabbis assumed that the bee merely sucks out and then discharges the nectar of a flower, and that the honey, therefore, does not contain any part of the bee itself.

Any mixture of meat and *milk is strictly forbidden; separate sets of utensils must be provided for both the preparation and serving of meat and milk dishes. Fish is not considered meat in this respect. Dairy foods may not be eaten for some time after the consumption of meat, and the same applies to meat after cheese; custom varies as to the length of time (one hour, three hours, six hours) that should elapse (*Shulḥan ʿArukh*, *Yoreh Deʿah* 89 and gloss). Utensils that have been used in the preparation or serving of nonkosher foods or for a mixture of meat and milk foods may not be used subsequently for kosher foods (see KASHER). On the basis of the threefold repetition of the prohibition against seething a kid in its mother's milk (*Ex*. 23.19, 34.26; *Dt*. 16.21), it is forbidden to cook, eat, or benefit from a mixture of meat and dairy foods. Food that is **parev* may be eaten with either milk or meat.

Medieval thinkers, in an attempt to rationalize the dietary laws, said that while much remains to be discovered, enough is known to warrant the conviction that their observance produces beneficial effects upon the human body (a view expressed by Maimonides, *Guide of the Perplexed* 3.48). This apologetic attempt to explain the dietary laws has been criticized for missing their basic intent. Thus the Midrash states, "Let not a man say 'I do not like the flesh of swine'; on the contrary, he should say, 'I like it, but what can I do, seeing that the Torah has forbidden it to me?' " (*Sifra'* on *Lv*. 20.26). This suggests that the rabbis regarded divine legislation as a sufficient reason, especially as it called upon the human capacities for discipline, obedience, and mastery of oneself (*Gn. Rab*. 44.1). In the Bible, observance of the dietary laws is a way of sanctifying God (*Lv*. 11.44–45), that is, of marking the people Israel off from all other peoples as specially devoted to God. The dietary laws thus serve both to identify the Israelite nation and to symbolize their devotion to God. Some Jewish thinkers (Philo, Maimonides), influenced by Greek thought, interpret the sanctification as resting in the acquisition of self-control and the habit of mastering the appetites—"They accustom us to restrain the growth of desire, the indulgence in seeking that which is pleasant, and the disposition to consider the pleasure of eating and drinking the end of man's existence" (*Guide of the Perplexed* 3.25). Modern scholarship suggests explanations of the biblical dietary laws in terms of anthropological theory.

The nineteenth-century German Reform leader Abraham *Geiger held that the dietary laws were anachronistic relics and that if they were not to be observed in their entirety should be totally abolished. In 1885 a conference of U.S. Reform rabbis in Pittsburgh affirmed that "all laws regulating diet are apt to obstruct modern spiritual elevation," and the American Reform leader Isaac Mayer *Wise expressed regret at the emphasis placed on these laws by Orthodox Judaism. Modern Reform theory and practice has changed these attitudes considerably, so that now, according to the last official platform statement of the Reform movement (the 1976 Centennial Perspective), each Reform Jew has a duty to learn about these and other religious practices and to integrate them in daily life, each in his or her own way.

For the Conservative movement, the dietary laws are binding, but they are interpreted and applied somewhat differently from at least some forms of Orthodox practice. Swordfish, for example, is accepted as kosher by Conservative, but not Orthodox, rabbinic rulings, and Conservative Jews are more likely than Orthodox Jews to find it acceptable within the requirements of Jewish law to eat dairy and *parev* foods in non-kosher restaurants.

• Mary Douglas, *Purity and Danger* (London, 1984), for an anthropological perspective. Samuel H. Dresner, *The Jewish Dietary Laws*, rev. and exp. ed. (New York, 1982). Isidor Grunfeld, *The Jewish Dietary Laws*, 2 vols. (London, 1982). Walter Houston, *Purity and Monotheism: Clean and Unclean Animals in Biblical Law* (Sheffield, Eng., 1993). Simeon Maslin, *Gates of Mitzvah* (New York, 1979), pp. 130–132. Jacob Milgrom, *Leviticus 1–16*, The Anchor Bible, vol. 3 (New York, 1991), pp. 643–742. Arthur Waskow, *Down-to-Earth Judaism: Food, Money, Sex and the Rest of Life* (New York, 1995), pp. 15–143.

DIMI OF NEHARDEA (4th cent.), Babylonian amora'. According to *Iggeret Rav Sherira' Ga'on*, Dimi headed the Pumbedita academy from 385 until his death in 388. In contrast to Rava', Dimi was known to prefer a careful teacher who covered less ground than a careless teacher who moved rapidly, since a mistake once learned stayed implanted in the mind (*B. B.* 21a–b). This precision may be reflected in the fact that he sometimes passed on teachings in language that differed from the standard sources (e.g., *R. ha-Sh.* 20a). His best known aggadic statement is that hospitality is greater than early attendance at the house of study (*Shab.* 127a).

• Chanoch Albeck, *Mavo' la-Talmudim* (Tel Aviv, 1987). Aaron Hyman, *Toledot Tanna'im ve-'Amora'im* (1910; Jerusalem, 1987).

—MICHAEL L. BROWN

DIN (דִּין; judgment), a religious law or lawsuit; a legal decision or verdict. Rabbi Shimʿon ben Gamli'el declared that *din* was one of the three elements by which the world is preserved, the others being truth and peace (*Avot* 1.18), and, in fact the three are identical: if *din* has been achieved, so have truth and peace (Y., *Taʿan.* 4). A law court is a home for judgment (**beit din*), and a judgment has to be impartial, with no favoritism (*Yev.* 91a). In theological terminology, *din* signifies the divine attribute of severe judgment and destructive punishment; it is held in check by divine mercy (*ḥesed*) or compassion (*raḥamim*). In Kabbalah, Din is an alternative name for Gevurah as the fifth of the **sefirot*.

• Menachem Elon, *Jewish Law: History, Sources, Principles*, 4 vols. (Philadelphia, 1994).

DINA' DE-MALKHUTA' DINA' (Aram.; דִּינָא דְמַלְכוּתָא דִּינָא; the law of the government is law), legal principle meaning that the law of the land in which a Jew resides is binding and must be obeyed (*Ned.* 28a; *Git.* 10b). The only exceptions to this precept are laws that contradict the fundamentals of Jewish law, such as robbery and violence or issues of personal status. The rule of *dina' de-malkhuta' dina'* was first articulated by the amora' Shemu'el in regard to the Jews living under Sassanid rule in Babylonia.

• Leo Landman, *Jewish Law in the Diaspora: Confrontation and Accommodation* (Philadelphia, 1968).

DINEI SHAMAYIM (דִּינֵי שָׁמַיִם; courts of heaven), term used to denote cases in which a Jewish court will not compel payment or authorize punishment for a particular activity, though some payment or punishment is appropriate; the court will, however, decree that until the defendant pays the appropriate amount owed, the Divine will not forgive the wrong done. Indeed, there were some authorities who ruled that nonpayment of the amount owed was a form of theft. Others aver that one who declines to pay is called an evildoer and may not testify in a law court. Modern scholars have used this concept to argue that judges have an obligation to tell defendants not only what their legal obligations are but also what the morally proper conduct is in any given case.

On rare occasion, the term *dinei shamayim* is used to refer to divine punishment for sin, such as the Flood (*Gn.* 6) or the destruction of Sodom and Gomorrah (*Gn.* 18).

• "Dinei Shamayim," in *Entsiqlopedyah Talmudit* (Jerusalem, 1947–), vol. 7, pp. 382–396. Menachem Elon, *Jewish Law: History, Sources, Principles* (Philadelphia, 1994), pp. 161–164.

—MICHAEL BROYDE

DIN TORAH (דִּין תּוֹרָה), a legal hearing conducted in compliance with halakhic regulations. According to Jewish law, disputes had to be brought for adjudication before a **beit din* and not before a secular (non-Jewish) court. In the modern world, however, only the more religiously observant Jews go to rabbinic courts. In Israel all matters of personal status are adjudicated by religious courts.

DISINTERMENT. See Burial.

DISPENSATION (Heb. *hetter*), action by a competent halakhic authority to relax certain laws in order to alleviate hardship. Such power can only be exercised in the case of laws of rabbinic origin, or in connection with matters whose origin is in custom (**minhag*), but not in matters affecting biblical law. Thus the dispensation given by the Israeli chief rabbinate to allow land to be worked under certain conditions during the sabbatical year is contingent on the premise that the prohibition regarding the sabbatical year is now based only on rabbinic ordinance. The Ashkenazi dispensation of one hundred rabbis, granted to one who may not ordinarily by law divorce his insane wife in order to remarry, rests on the fact that polygamy is permitted by the Torah, while monogamy is a rabbinic innovation. A *hetter hora'ah* is a dispensation to serve in a rabbinical position (see Ordination). *Hetter ʿisqa'* (business dispensation) was a formula by which it was permitted to take interest. See also Loans; Moneylending.

• J. David Bleich, "Hetter Iska: Student Loans, Margin Accounts, Purchase Money Mortgages, Etc.," *Tradition* 26 (Fall 1991): 76–79.

DISPUTATIONS, public controversies between representatives of opposing faiths. An early example is the disputation between the Jews and the Samaritans mentioned by Josephus (*Antiquities of the Jews* 13.3.4.74–75); another is that recorded in the Mishnah (*ʿA. Z.* 4.7) between philosophers in Rome and Jewish elders. There are several references in the Talmud to discussions between rabbis and Romans (and other pagans), but the circumstances in which they were held are not specified. Early Christian literature reports many disputations with Jews, all of them concluding with the Jewish protagonists' acceptance of Christianity; references to such disputations are to be found in Talmudic literature. Throughout the Middle Ages, Jews on occasion discussed with their Muslim and Christian neighbors the issues that separated their faiths. Although such discussions were viewed as dangerous and generally discouraged by the religious leadership of all three groups, the constant contacts of daily life made such exchanges inescapable.

During the twelfth century, western Christendom became increasingly concerned with convincing others of the truth of the Christian faith. New lines of argumentation were developed, and, with the support of political authorities, missionizing sermons were forced upon Jews and Muslims. An important variant of the forced sermon was the forced disputation. The first was the Disputation of *Paris in 1240, in which the challenger was Nicholas Donin, a Jewish apostate, and his opponent, R. Yeḥi'el ben Yosef of Paris. As a result of this debate, twenty-four cartloads of copies of the Talmud were consigned to the flames in 1242.

The Disputation of *Barcelona of 1263 signified a major landmark in the history of forced disputations. Conceived by the Dominicans as an opportunity to test the new missionizing strategies of the apostate Friar Paul Christian, the confrontation between the friar and one of the greatest of the medieval rabbis, Moses Nahmanides of Gerona, was conducted publicly in Barcelona, under the patronage of King James I. Friar Paul Christian argued that rabbinic texts revealed the rabbis recognition of the truths of Christianity. In the disputation itself, Nahmanides was limited to rebutting the friar's reading of these rabbinic texts, although in his own report of the proceedings he portrays himself as leading an attack against fundamental elements of Christian belief and behavior.

Over the next few centuries, forced disputations were a recurring and problematic aspect of Jewish existence. The longest was the Disputation of *Tortosa (1413–1415), in which the apostate Hieronymus de Sancta Fide (whose Hebrew name was Yehoshuʿa ha-Lorki) faced twenty-two of the most distinguished rabbis of the time. The disputation lasted for over sixty-three sessions and was organized with all the trappings of a public entertainment.

Maimonides banned Jewish–Muslim disputations. More unusual were the disputations of 1757 and 1759—organized at the instigation of Christian ecclesiastical authorities—between rabbinic spokesmen and Frankists (see Frank, Yaʿaqov). See also Polemics.

• David Berger, *The Jewish-Christian Debate in the High Middle Ages* (Philadelphia, 1979), pp. 3–37. Judah D. Eisenstein, *Otsar Vikkuḥim* (New York, 1928). Antonio Pacios, *La Disputa de Tortosa* (Madrid, 1957). James William Parkes, *Conflict of the Church and Synagogue* (London, 1934). Oliver Shaw Rankin, *Jewish Religious Polemic of Early and Later Centuries: A Study of Documents Here Rendered into English* (Edinburgh, 1956). Siegfried Stein, *Jewish-Christian Disputations in Thirteenth Century Narbonne* (London, 1969). A. L. Williams, *Adversus Judaeos: A Bird's-Eye View of Jewish Apologetic until the Renaissance* (Cambridge, 1935).

DISSECTION. See Autopsies.

DIVINATION. See Oracles.

DIVINE ATTRIBUTES. See God, Attributes of.

DIVINE NAMES. See God, Names of.

DIVINE PUNISHMENT. The Bible invokes divine punishment for two types of offenses. The first consists of crimes for which eyewitnesses are not usually available, such as sexual offenses (*Lv*. 20.17–18, 18–29) and the nonobservance of Pesaḥ (*Ex*. 12.15) and Yom Kippur (*Lv*. 23.29–30). The second includes offenses of a religious or sacerdotal nature, such as the failure to circumcise (*Gn*. 17.14) or to bring certain sacrifices (*Nm*. 9.13). In many instances the term **karet* (cutting off) is used to designate divine punishment (*Lv*. 20. 2–5), and it would appear from the Bible that offenses punishable by *karet* are of a more serious nature than those merely involving death at the hands of heaven. In the Talmud, *karet* is understood as premature death before the age of fifty or death without leaving any issue (*Moʿed Q*. 28a). The Talmud also reads divine punishment into the fate of every undetected murderer who comes to a grim end (*Mak*. 10b). It is arguable that the Talmudic doctrine marks a transition from divine penalties per se, to the invocation of heavenly sanctions solely against those who manage to evade the hands of the human court. Indeed, under Talmudic law, divine capital punishment is absolved by the administration of a lashing (*Mak*. 13a–b). The concept of *din shamayim* (heavenly judgment) is found in the Talmud as a means of encouraging individuals to pay compensation for damage for which they are responsible, even though they are not under any strict legal obligation to pay such compensation.

• Adolf Büchler, *Studies in Sin and Atonement in the Rabbinic Literature of the First Century* (London, 1928). H. Cohn, "Divine Punishment," in *The Principles of Jewish Law*, edited by Menachem Elon (Jerusalem, 1974), pp. 522–524. Aaron Kirschenbaum, *Equity in Jewish Law* (New York, 1991), pp. 137–177.

—DANIEL SINCLAIR

DIVINE SERVICE. See Prayer; Prayer Book.

DIVORCE. The Bible allows for a man to divorce his wife if he has found something "obnoxious" or "unclean" (left undefined) about her, in which case he writes her a bill of divorcement, hands it to her, and sends her away (*Dt*. 24.1–4). From this, it was concluded that the right of divorce rests solely with the husband and that the act requires a written document (*Git*. 20a). A man could not divorce his wife if he falsely accused her of not being a virgin at the time of marriage (*Dt*. 22.19) or if he had previously raped her (*Dt*. 22.28–29). Divorce is denounced by Malachi (2.14–16).

In the post-biblical period, a marriage is dissolved by a ceremony in which the husband gives his wife a bill of divorce (*get*) in the presence of a competent rabbinical court. The court does not dissolve the marriage, but merely supervises the complicated procedure, making sure that it is in accord with religious law. An official of the court then makes a record of the divorce and gives a certificate of the record to both parties. A court has jurisdiction, however, to make a declaration on the validity or nullity of a supposed marriage, in which case its decree is final. By the strict letter of the law, divorce is an arbitrary right to be exercised by the husband whenever he might feel so inclined. From very early times, however, the marriage contract (see KETUBBAH) contained stipulations protecting the wife from the husband's capricious misuse of this power. Since the time of R. *Gershom ben Yehudah (11th cent.), divorcing a wife against her will has been absolutely prohibited among Ashkenazi Jews, and in many Sephardi communities as well (*Shulḥan Arukh, Even ha-ʿEzer*, 119.6). As it stands now, all that is required for divorce is the mutual consent of husband and wife. The divorce document (nearly all in Aramaic) is written by a scribe according to strict rules. There are specific grounds in Jewish law that entitle one of the parties to compel the other spouse to agree to a divorce. Among the main grounds are refusal of cohabitation, apostasy, loathsome chronic disease rendering marital relations impossible, moral dissoluteness, grossly insulting behavior, ill-treatment, well-founded suspicion of adultery committed by the wife, and impotency of the husband. In such instances the party seeking the divorce may apply to a rabbinical court, which acts as an investigating body, to decide what degree of pressure may be exerted to prevail on the recalcitrant party to "agree" to a divorce. Although a husband's agreement that is obtained by coercion renders the *get* void, this is not the case when compulsion is ordered by a rabbinical court. Even then, however, a declaration of acquiescence on the part of the husband is essential. Since, in principle, Jewish law permits *polygamy, if a wife obstinately refuses to accept a divorce that her husband is entitled to give, the husband can be granted permission to remarry without the dissolution of his former marriage. However, the remarriage of a Jewish woman without a *get* entails the most serious consequences for herself: her second marriage is considered an act of *adultery, and the children of that union are regarded as mamzerim (see MAMZER). Rabbis therefore make every effort to secure a *get* for the woman. Where the divorce was not dictated or justified by circumstances, it is considered to be a virtuous deed for a man to remarry his divorced wife. Remarriage with the first husband is, however, precluded if the wife has meantime married another man or if the husband is a priest. A divorcée (like a widow) may not remarry until ninety-one days have elapsed in order that the paternity of a child with whom she may be pregnant might not be in doubt. The marriage of an adulterous wife and her consort after divorce has been obtained is forbidden. A husband cannot divorce his wife if she is insane. If the wife is deemed to be incurably insane, however, the signatures of one hundred rabbis are required to give the husband permission to marry a second time; this rule is an exception to the 900-year-old Ashkenazi enactment forbidding polygamous marriages. In any case, the sick wife must be provided for. At the time of divorce, the rabbinical court deals with monetary settlements and the custody of children. Maintenance to be paid after divorce (see ALIMONY) is unknown in Jewish law, which sees divorce as "complete severance." In deciding which one of the divorced parties is to vacate the joint dwelling, rabbis are guided by the maxim that the reestablishment of a homestead is more difficult for a man than for a woman. Other considerations, however, may reverse this rule. In countries where a *get* has no legal effect, rabbis will not arrange for a Jewish divorce before a civil divorce is granted. On the other hand, civil divorce is not recognized by rabbinical law unless it is supplemented by a *get*. Under certain conditions divorce is obligatory, but where it is optional everything possible is done to discourage its hasty exercise. The Talmud quotes a saying: "The altar sheds tears for him who divorces his first wife" (*San*. 22a). Indeed, the causeless divorce of a first wife, even if valid, is deemed to be an act contrary to the will of the Almighty. Yet where continued life together is absolutely impossible, it is recognized that no impediment should hinder the release by divorce.

The fact that, in traditional Judaism, only the husband can initiate divorce, creates many problems today. Each branch of Judaism is attempting to redress the issue. The Reform movement dispenses with the need for a *get*, accepting a civil divorce as sufficient. The Conservative movement has amended the *ketubbah* with a paragraph accepting the authority of the Conservative *beit din* to deal with recalcitrant spouses in case of divorce. The Orthodox have not been successful at implementing any widely recognized prenuptial agreement, although there have been attempts. In the State of Israel there is no civil divorce and all divorce is by the religious authorities. In particular cases, obdurate husbands, who have refused to give a *get* when so instructed by the rabbinic court, have been handed over to the secular authorities and imprisoned until they relent. See also ʿAGUNAH; DOWRY; GITTIN; WOMEN.

• David W. Amram, *The Jewish Law of Divorce According to Jewish Law and Talmud* (New York, 1968). Reuven P. Bulka, *Jewish Divorce Ethics* (Ogdensburg, N.Y., 1992). Ze'ev Falk, *Jewish Matrimonial Law in the Middle Ages* (London, 1966), pp. 113–143. Jacob Fried, ed., *Jews and Divorce* (New York, 1968). Irwin Haut, " 'The Altar Weeps': Divorce in Jewish Law," in *Celebration and Renewal*, edited by Rela M. Geffen (Philadelphia, 1993). Irwin Haut, *Divorce in Jewish Life and Law* (New York, 1983), with bibliography. Moses Mielziner, *Jewish Law of Marriage and Divorce in Ancient and Modern Times* (1884; repr. Littleton, Colo., 1987). Shlomo Riskin, "The Moredet. A Study of the Rebellious Wife and Her Status in Initiating a Divorce in Jewish Law," Ph.D. dissertation, New York University, 1982. Shlomo Riskin, *Women and Jewish Divorce* (Hoboken, N.J., 1989).

DOCUMENTARY HYPOTHESIS. See BIBLE.

DOGMA, authoritative formulation of the tenets of a faith. In Judaism, the tendency has been to stress religious practices rather than theological beliefs and articles of faith. Various Jewish thinkers, however, mainly as a reaction to contact with other religions and philosophies, felt the need to formulate the basic principles of Judaism. Influenced by Islam, the Karaites composed articles of faith, and under a similar impetus, Jewish medieval thinkers endeavored to codify Jewish doctrines of faith (see MAIMONIDES, MOSES; THIRTEEN PRINCIPLES OF FAITH). In his work *Jerusalem*, Moses Mendelssohn reasserted that Judaism (as opposed to Christianity) had no dogma, the acceptance of which is a necessary prerequisite for salvation. Some thinkers have suggested that Judaism does have dogmas, in the form of certain common assumptions of faith, but no doctrinal system. See also CREED.

• William D. Davies, ed., *Torah and Dogma* (Cambridge, Mass., 1968). Menachem M. Kellner, *Dogma in Medieval Jewish Thought: From Maimonides to Abravanel* (Oxford, 1986).

DOMAIN (Heb. *reshut*), ownership of and control over the use of land. The rabbis distinguish between public and private domain in three instances. First, regarding Sabbath observance, they list four types of domain: private domain (*reshut ha-yaḥid*), where carrying is permitted on the Sabbath; public domain (*reshut ha-rabbim*), such as streets and squares, where carrying is forbidden; semi-private domain (*karmelit*), for example, fields, the sea, and booths in a street, where carrying is forbidden; and semi-public domain (*meqom petur*), for example, a trench. Second, in cases of ritual uncleanness, a private domain is where there are less than three individuals; with three or more, it becomes public. Finally, in cases of claims for damages, a public domain is any place or road to which there is public access; any person who causes injury there is himself liable to pay compensation.

• Menachem Elon, *Jewish Law: History, Sources, Principles*, 4 vols. (Philadelphia, 1994).

DÖNMEH (Turk.; converts or apostates), crypto-Jewish sect in Turkey, originating with followers of *Shabbetai Tsevi. The Jews called them *minim* (sectarians), and they called themselves *ma'aminim* (believers [in Shabbetai Tsevi]). Following Shabbetai's conversion to Islam in 1666, many of his most fervent followers continued to believe in his Messiahship, and some even converted to Islam themselves. While openly Muslim, in secret they maintained many Jewish practices, blending them with Shabbatean additions and much antinomian behavior. They soon split into at least three groups, differing in customs and ideas and rarely intermarrying with Jews, Muslims, or sectarians from rival groups. They adhered to their own version of the Ten Commandments but were noted for their licentious practices. Dönmeh activism included extensive proselytizing in central Europe and especially in Poland. Their main population centers were in Constantinople, İzmir, and particularly Salonika, where they maintained close relations with Muslim mystics of the Bektaşi order. They also had close relations with leaders of the Young Turk revolution in 1908; the Young Turk finance minister, David Bey, was of Dönmeh origin. The different Dönmeh groups of Salonika shared one cemetery. Recent research has revealed that they preserved a substantial core of Judaic practices and maintained contacts with believers in Shabbetai Tsevi who had not converted to Islam. They continued to speak Judeo-Spanish into the latter part of the nineteenth century and retained their Hebrew and Sephardi names with their Turkish names. Most Dönmeh moved from Salonika to Constantinople in 1924 with the Turkish and Greek population exchanges resulting from the establishment of the Turkish Republic. Although their numbers subsequently dwindled, they are reported to continue to celebrate festivals connected with the life of Shabbetai Tsevi and to possess their own mosque in İstanbul.

• Itzhak Ben-Zvi, *The Exiled and the Redeemed*, translated by Isaac A. Abbady (Philadelphia, 1957), pp. 131–153. Gershom Gerhard Scholem, *The Messianic Idea in Judaism and Other Essays on Jewish Spirituality* (New York, 1971), pp. 142–166. Stanford J. Shaw, *The Jews of the Ottoman Empire and the Turkish Republic* (New York, 1991).

–JANE S. GERBER

DONNOLO, SHABBETAI (913–c.982) Italian physician. Donnolo, who was born in Oria in southern Italy, is the first known Jewish medical author in Europe. In his *Sefer Ḥakhmoni* (1880), a commentary on **Sefer Yetsirah*, he discusses astrology and seeks to show that human beings are created not in the image of God but as microcosms of the universe. In the preface, Donnolo describes how he was ransomed from the Saracens as a child and later studied medicine. This commentary was quoted by many Jewish thinkers, including Rashi. Donnolo is chiefly remembered for his *Sefer ha-Mirqaḥot* (Jerusalem, 1950), one of the earliest Hebrew treatises on medical matters. It includes instructions for making over one hundred remedies, all derived from vegetable sources. Although he claimed to have studied Arabian, Indian, and Babylonian medicine, all of his drugs seem to be of Greek or Latin origin. He also wrote *Sefer ha-Mazzalot*, of which very little survives, and *Pizmon*, a ritual poem. Parts of his lost commentary on the *Baraiyta' de-Shemu'el* are quoted by Pseudo-Sa'adyah in his commentary on *Sefer Yetsirah*. Donnolo's theological ideas influenced the *Ḥasidei Ashkenaz, and he is seen as a forerunner of the School of Salerno, the earliest scientific school in Christian Europe.

• David Castelli, *Il commento di Shabbetai Donnolo sul libro vella creazione* (Firenze, 1880). Harry Friedenwald, *Jews and Medicine* (Baltimore, 1944), pp. 148–152, 171–172, 223–224. Sussman Muntner, *Rabbi Shabbetai Donnolo* (Jerusalem, 1949). Elliot R. Wolfson. "The Theosophy of

Shabbetai Donnolo," in *The Frank Talmage Memorial Volume II*, edited by Barry Walfish (Haifa, 1992), pp. 281–316.

—LAVINIA COHN-SHERBOK

DOSA' BEN HARKINAS (1st–2d cent.), Palestinian tanna'. He lived during the days of the Second Temple and into the beginning of the second century (cf. *Neg.* 1.4). He was the respected senior of R. Yehoshu'a ben Ḥananyah, R. El'azar ben 'Azaryah, and R. 'Aqiva', in whose presence he once supported his position by invoking a tradition that he traced back to Haggai the prophet (*Yev.* 16a). His counsel to R. Yehoshu'a to submit to the calendrical judgment of R. Gamli'el, even though Dosa' believed it to be incorrect, is based on his watershed principle that calling into question the decisions of the ruling court (*beit din*) of the day would necessitate calling into question the rulings of every court dating back to Moses. Each rabbinical court must be regarded as if it were that of Moses himself (*R. ha-Sh.* 24b–25a, with reference to *Ex.* 24.9). The best-known dictum of Dosa' is "Morning sleep, midday wine, talking with children, and sitting in the assemblies of the ignorant remove a man from this world" (*Avot* 3.10). His halakhic rulings, found both in the Mishnah and *baraiytot* (e.g., *Suk.* 52a–b; *'Eduy.* 3.1–6), tended toward leniency and were consistently in harmony with Beit Hillel.

• Aaron Hyman, *Toledot Tanna'im ve-'Amora'im* (1910; Jerusalem, 1987). Israel Konovitz, comp., *Ma'arakhot Tanna'im: Osef Shalem shel Mishnatam u-Ma'amareihem ba-Sifrut ha-Talmudit veha-Midrashit* (Jerusalem, 1967–1969), vol. 2, pp. 9–16.

—MICHAEL L. BROWN

DOST'AI BEN YANN'AI (2d cent.), Palestinian tanna'. A contemporary of R. Yehudah ha-Nasi', he transmitted the traditions of R. Me'ir (his primary teacher), R. Yosei ben Ḥalafta', and R. El'azar ben Shammu'a. He is primarily known for his aggadic teachings. He taught that a person who deliberately forgets his studies is considered as though he had committed a capital offense (*Avot* 3.10).

• Wilhelm Bacher, *Die Agada der Tannaiten* (1903; Berlin, 1965–1966). Israel Konovitz, comp., *Ma'arakhot Tanna'im: Osef Shalem shel Mishnatam u-Ma'amareihem ba-Sifrut ha-Talmudit veha-Midrashit* (Jerusalem, 1967–1969).

—MICHAEL L. BROWN

DOUBT (Heb. *safeq*). In instances in Jewish law where either the law is undecided or the facts are uncertain, a state of doubt exists. The *halakhah* has evolved a detailed code of procedure and criteria by means of which each instance is to be resolved. Cases concerning biblical law are to be decided in conformity with the stricter view of the deciding rabbis, while those involving laws of rabbinic origin are to be resolved according to the more lenient opinion of the rabbis (*Ḥul.* 9b). There are two exceptions to this rule. In questionable monetary cases, even those involving biblical law, the more lenient view is acted upon, since one cannot dispossess a property holder without valid proof; cases that may pose a danger to life are to be resolved in whichever manner will best obviate the suspected danger. The more lenient ruling adopted in connection with rabbinic law rests upon the assumption that the sages issued decrees only in cases of certainty. In cases involving remote doubt or improbablility, the more lenient view is adopted, even in deciding matters of biblical law.

• Menachem Elon, *Jewish Law: History, Sources, Principles*, 4 vols. (Philadelphia, 1994).

DOV BER OF MEZHIRECH (c.1704–1772), Hasidic master, known as the Maggid (preacher) of Mezhirech. In his youth, he studied rabbinic literature with Ya'aqov Yehoshu'a Falk. In addition to his Talmudic studies, he became an expert in the kabbalistic teachings of Yitsḥaq Luria. A life of extreme and protracted asceticism left him an invalid. This, according to Hasidic accounts, led him to the founder of Hasidism, Yisra'el ben Eli'ezer Ba'al Shem Tov, who was renowned as a healer. According to tradition, they met only twice, but that was sufficient for the Maggid to become a proponent of Hasidism. Some time after the death of his master, Dov Ber emerged as the most powerful of the Hasidic leaders. By 1766 he had established an influential school to which many of those who would succeed in establishing Hasidism as a popular movement in the Ukraine, Lithuania, Galicia, and Poland were attracted. Despite his weak health and contemplative nature, Dov Ber was an inspired and charismatic figure. An eyewitness account of a Shabbat at the Maggid's court appears in the autobiography of Solomon Maimon, the philosopher. The proselytizing efforts and ecstatic behavior of Dov Ber's students provoked organized opposition, for the most part limited to areas under the influence of the Vilna Ga'on. In 1772 the first of a series of bans against the Ḥasidim was enacted. Shortly thereafter, possibly weakened by this conflict, Dov Ber died. Among his most prominent disciples were Menaḥem Mendel of Vitebsk, Aharon of Karlin, Levi Yitsḥaq of Berdichev, Elimelekh of Lyzhansk, and Shneur Zalman of Lyady. Utilizing the terminology of the Lurianic Kabbalah, Dov Ber charted a unique course that is both mystical and magical. At root, only God is real, and worship consists primarily of *devequt*, binding one's consciousness to God. Although he adopted the Lurianic cosmology, Dov Ber developed an interpretation that emphasized ecstatic and psychological elements. He specifically rejected Luria's complex system of *kavvanah* in favor of a more single-minded immersion in the divine presence. Prayer is a process of contemplative ascent, in the course of which a person must discard all sense of personal existence. At its apex, one reaches the state of *'ayin* (i.e., nothingness). Paradoxically, a person only becomes truly human when this union with the divine occurs. Such a person not only achieves a kind of personal salvation but becomes the agency for magically bringing down *shefa'* (divine abundance) to the material world. This became the basis for the model of the **tsaddiq*. Dov Ber's teachings were recorded by Levi Yitsḥaq of Berdichev and published posthumously in *Maggid Devarav le-Ya'aqov*, compiled by his student Shelomoh of Lutsk (edited by Rivka Schatz Uffenheimer [Jerusalem, 1990]).

• Martin Buber, *Tales of the Hasidim* (New York, 1947). Miles Krassen, " 'Devequt' and Faith in Zaddiqim: The Religious Tracts of Meshullam Feibush Heller of Zbarazh," Ph.D. dissertation, University of Pennsylvania, 1990. Jacob I. Schochet, *The Great Maggid: The Life and Teachings of Rabbi Dov Ber of Mezhirech* (Brooklyn, N.Y., 1989). Rivka Schatz Uffenheimer, *Hasidism as Mysticism* (Princeton, 1993). Joseph Weiss, *Studies in Eastern European Jewish Mysticism* (London, 1985).

—MILES KRASSEN

DOWRY(Heb. *nedunyah*), property brought by a bride to her husband in the form of either movable or immovable goods. In biblical times, it was the bridegroom who paid a sum of money (*mohar* [bride's price]) to the bride's father (as is still the custom in the Arab world). ʿAdot ha-Mizraḥ who immigrated to Israel followed this practice, which has now all but disappeared. The bridal dowry is, however, also found in the Bible (e.g., *Gn*. 24.59–61; *Jgs*. 1.15; *1 Kgs*. 9.16), and by the Talmudic period, the tradition of a dowry had become universal and the *mohar* unknown. According to Jewish custom, a bride should be dowered by her father (or his estate) in proportion to his means. In cases in which a father is not able to provide a dowry for his daughter, it is the community's obligation to do so. A man has no proprietary rights over his wife's property, acquired either before or after her marriage, but is granted as much of its income as he expends on the upkeep of the household. This grant is explained historically as being in consideration of his obligation to ransom his wife, a not uncommon need in ancient days. The donor of a gift to a wife may deny the husband the benefit of its income. Even a "rebellious" wife (one who does not fulfill her marital obligations) must be returned her dowry in the event of divorce. A wife may deliver to her husband by agreement the control and administration of all or part of her property, which must be fully restored to her, together with an additional amount (usually 50 percent), upon dissolution of the marriage. Such property and its assessed value are recorded in the marriage contract (**ketubbah*). By law, the husband is responsible for its deterioration and fall in market value but may claim any rise in its value. A husband may not dispose of his wife's immovable property without her acquiescence. The practice of providing a dowry has largely disappeared among North American Jews, except in the most traditionalistic circles.

• Louis Epstein, *The Jewish Marriage Contract* (1927; repr. New York, 1972). Maurice Lamm, *The Jewish Way in Love and Marriage* (San Francisco, 1980).

—PETER KNOBEL

DOXOLOGY (from Gr.; expression of praise, or, proclaiming the glory [of God]), a technical term in Christian liturgy that is likewise applicable to certain formulas of praise, and the prescribed responses to them, in the Jewish liturgy. Early doxologies and their responses are found at the conclusion of each of the five books of **Psalms* (cf. *Ps*. 72.19, 106.48). The chief doxologies in the Jewish liturgy, each with its response, are the *Barekhu, the *Shemaʿ, the *Qedushah, and the *Qaddish. Common to all these is an emphasis upon the infinitude of God. Also, in a broader sense, the liturgy is arranged in accordance with a principle enunciated by R. Simla'i (3rd cent. CE): "One should always praise the Holy One, blessed be He, and [only] thereafter pray [for personal needs]." On that basis, the *Pesuqei de-Zimra' (chiefly from *Psalms*) precede the *ʿAmidah in the morning service.

• Eric Werner, *The Sacred Bridge* (New York, 1959), pp. 273–312.

—A. STANLEY DREYFUS

DRACHMAN, BERNARD (1861–1945), Orthodox rabbi in the United States. He was born in New York and brought up in Jersey City, New Jersey. While studying in Germany, he identified with Orthodoxy and was ordained at the *Breslau Rabbinical Seminary. Back in the United States, he refused to serve in any congregation that ritually deviated from traditional Judaism. He was rabbi of several New York City synagogues—Beth Israel Bikkur Cholim (1887–1889); Zichron Ephraim of Yorkville, a congregation of central European Jews (1889–1909); and English-speaking rabbi at Harlem's Ohel Zedek (1909–1922), which attracted newly acculturated, traditional eastern European Jews. From its founding in 1887 until 1908, Drachman taught at the *Jewish Theological Seminary of America, where he trained rabbis to protect American Orthodoxy among the religiously disaffected youngsters of New York City's Lower East Side.

From 1900 on, as a Seminary professor and a founder of the *Union of Orthodox Jewish Congregations of America, he was intimately involved with the Jewish Endeavor Society, downtown New York City's Orthodox youth synagogue movement. In 1916 he began a twenty-year career as a professor of pedagogy at the Rabbi Isaac Elchanan Theological Seminary, as that school, under Bernard Revel, began emerging as American Orthodoxy's flagship institution. He wrote *The Unfailing Light: Memoirs of an American Rabbi* (New York, 1948) and translated *The Nineteen Letters of Ben Uziel: Being a Spiritual Presentation of the Principles of Judaism by Samson Raphael Hirsch* (New York, 1899).

• Moshe Davis, *The Emergence of Conservative Judaism: The Historical School in Nineteenth Century America* (Philadelphia, 1965). Jeffrey S. Gurock, "From Exception to Role Model: Bernard Drachman and the Evolution of Jewish Religious Life in America, 1880–1920," *American Jewish History* (June 1987): 456–484. Jeffrey S. Gurock, "Resisters and Accommodators: Varieties of Orthodox Rabbis in America, 1886–1983," *American Jewish Archives* (November 1983): 120–125.

—JEFFREY S. GUROCK

DREAMS, regarded in the Bible, as in many cultures, as one of the channels through which God reveals his will and intentions, and both Jewish and non-Jewish individuals can be recipients of such communications (for example, Joseph in *Gn*. 37, Daniel in *Dn*. 2.19, Laban in *Gn*. 31.29, Pharaoh in *Gn*. 41, or Balaam in *Nm*. 22.20). With the exception of Joseph and Daniel (both of whom interpreted dreams in foreign courts), dream interpretation by Jews is absent from the Bible. *Numbers* 12.6–7 considers prophetic experiences to be dreamlike visions, with the notable exception of the face-to-face encounter between God and Moses. Jeremiah, however, contrasts the "word of God" given to true prophets with the dream revelations claimed by false prophets (*Jer*. 23).

Dreams came to be regarded as a means by which the divine and supernatural worlds come into contact with human beings. Following certain biblical examples, dreams were later regarded as means of revealing the future. One of the longest sustained passages devoted to a single subject in all the aggadic sections of the Talmud is that dealing with dreams and their interpretations (*Ber.* 55a–57b). The treatment ranges from profound psychological insight into the nature of dreams to folklore and superstition. For example, the Talmud writes: "Just as there is no chaff without straw so there cannot be a dream without nonsense" (see also *Git.* 52a); "Part of a dream may be fulfilled but not the whole"; and "A man sees in dreams only what is suggested by his thoughts." According to the Talmud, some dream omens can have more than one possible interpretation. For example, the meaning assigned to dreaming that one is naked depends upon the locale of the dream: if the dream is set in Babylon, it is a sign of freedom from sin; if it is set in Erets Yisra'el, it is a sign of the absence of good deeds. These and many similar statements in Talmudic literature further strengthened popular belief in the significance of dreams, and it became customary to fast after a bad dream (*ta'anit ḥalom*), even on the Sabbath, although later authorities tried to limit permission to fast on the Sabbath to specific dreams (*Shulḥan 'Arukh, Oraḥ Ḥayyim*, 288). A Talmudic formula (*Ber.* 55b) for the fulfillment of a good dream or the changing of a bad dream to a good one, to be uttered during the *Birkat ha-Kohanim in the synagogue, is still found in some prayer books. It was to enable the recitation of this prayer that a pause was inserted between each of the three verses in the Birkat ha-Kohanim.

Maimonides says that dreams are a product of the imagination (*Guide of the Perplexed* 236–238). However, medieval Hebrew literature abounds with references to the significance of dreams. In twelfth- and thirteenth-century Germany, halakhists even referred to legal decisions revealed to them in dreams. Mystics practiced "dream questions," that is, asking a question before going to sleep and interpreting the night's dreams as an answer to that question. Magical manuals include detailed instructions concerning this practice. In the sixteenth-century, R. Shelomoh Almoli of Constantinople wrote *Pitron Ḥalomot*, which in its Yiddish translation was widely circulated in eastern Europe.

**Sefer Ḥasidim* includes many stories of dreams that came true or that involved visitations from the dead. It even tells the story of two men who made a pact with each other that the one who died first would appear to the other in a dream and relate to him secrets from the other world. Rabbi Ḥayyim Vital, in sixteenth-century Safed, related in his diary many dreams that expressed his messianic pretensions; he included both his own dreams and dreams that others had dreamed about him. Other kabbalistic works, from the Zohar to the *Sefer ha-Qanah*, include examples of this literary genre. Several of the dreams of R. Naḥman of Bratslav are preserved in *Ḥayyei Moharan*, a work by R. Natan of Nemirov, his disciple. Jewish rationalistic philosophers debated the relationship between dreams and prophecy and admitted the existence of an element of imagination in both. This phenomenon was addressed by several rabbis, most notably R. Manasseh ben Israel in his *Nishmat Ḥayyim*.

• Isaac Afik, "Tefisat ha-Ḥalom etsel Ḥazal," Ph.D. dissertation, Bar Ilan University, 1990. Shaul Bar, "Dreams in the Bible," Ph.D. dissertation, New York University, 1987. Joseph Dan, *Sippur ha-'Ivri be-Yemei ha-Benayim* (Jerusalem, 1974). Robert Karl Gnuse, *The Dream Theophany of Samuel: Its Structure in Relation to Ancient Near Eastern Dreams and Its Theological Significance* (Lanham, Md., 1984). Monford Harris, *Studies in Jewish Dream Interpretation* (Northvale, N.J., 1994). Adolf Lowinger, *Der Traum in der jüdischen Literatur* (Leipzig, 1908).

—JOSEPH DAN

DRESS. See COSTUME.

DRINK OFFERING. See LIBATION.

DRUNKENNESS. The prophets and later biblical books and the Apocrypha contain warnings against intoxication, which is described as the source of many misfortunes (e.g., *Is.* 28.1; *Prv.* 23.19–21, 31.4–5). It is indicative of the almost complete absence of drunkenness as a serious social and moral problem among Jews that the Talmud contains few legal references to the subject, such as that a person under the influence of alcohol is legally responsible for his actions unless he has attained the state of oblivion attributed to Lot (cf. *Gn.* 19.3; *'Eruv.* 65a). Next to Lot, Noah (*Gn.* 9.22ff.) serves as a biblical example of the objectionableness of intoxication. A drunken person is forbidden to conduct a service (*Ber.* 31a), and the death of the two sons of Aaron (*Lv.* 10.1–4) is attributed by the rabbis to the fact that they entered the sanctuary in a state of intoxication (*Lv.* 9). The lighter side of drunkenness is illustrated by the permission, if not the duty, to become so intoxicated on the holiday of *Purim as to be unable to distinguish between "Blessed be Mordecai" and "Cursed be Haman" (*Meg.* 21a), but rabbinic authors are at pains to point out that this injunction should not be taken too seriously. See also WINE.

• David Novak, "Alcohol and Drug Abuse in the Perspective of Jewish Tradition," *Judaism* 33 (1984): 221–232. Gerard Weindling, "Alcohol and Drunkenness in the Bible and the Talmud," *Koroth* 9.1–2 (1985): 230–241.

DUALISM, the doctrine—metaphysical or moral—that holds that all being can be reduced to or derives from two ultimate and contrasting principles.

The ancient religion of Persia (Zoroastrianism) saw history as a cosmic struggle between the power of light and goodness and that of darkness and evil. A slightly different form of dualism was assumed by *gnosticism, which distinguished between a lower, evil deity, responsible for the creation of this world, and a higher, more transcendent good deity. The source of these doctrines is man's experience of the radical opposition between *good and evil. The prophets, however, insisted that God alone was the source of both light and darkness, good and evil (*Is.* 45.7), and the Talmudic literature frequently condemns all forms of gnostic dualism (*shetei reshuyyot* [two powers]) as heresy. Dualistic tendencies manifested themselves more than once in Jewish religious history (e.g., in such apocryphal books as **Jubilees* and the *Testaments of the Twelve Patriarchs*, in the *Dead Sea Scrolls, and in the medieval kabbalistic doctrine of evil [notably, the **sitra' aḥra'*, "the other side of God"]), but they were kept in check by a basic and uncompromising *monotheism (see DEMONS; SATAN).

A philosophical dualism, stemming from Greece (Plato) and opposing spirit to matter, exerted considerable influence on Jewish thinking and morals, both in the Hellenistic period (cf. *Philo) and later, particularly in the Middle Ages. The logical consequence of this was contempt of the body, matter, and "this world" and a thoroughgoing *asceticism that, however, was partly inhibited by the rabbinic tradition that considered the physical universe and its enjoyment as essentially good, provided they are hallowed in the service of God. Modern writers tend to emphasize the biblical affirmation of the blessed life on this earth as a more adequate form of spirituality than one that negates matter (see BODY; SEX; SIN).

By positing a radical distinction between the absolute being of God the Creator, and the contingent, created being of all other things, the Bible and subsequent Jewish tradition affirmed another kind of dualism. Although created being derives from its creator, the two still cannot be identified, as is done by the doctrines known as *pantheism or monism.

• Godfrey Rolles Driver, *The Judaean Scrolls* (Oxford, 1965), pp. 550–562. Julius Guttmann, *Philosophies of Judaism* (New York, 1964), index. Alan F. Segal, *Two Powers in Heaven: Early Rabbinic Reports about Christianity and Gnosticism* (Leiden, 1977). Yeshayahu Tishby, *Mishnat ha-Zohar*, vol. 1 (Jerusalem, 1949), pp. 285–343. Geo Widengren, *Apocalyptique iranienne et dualisme qoumranien* (Paris, 1995).

DUBNOW, SIMON (1860–1941), historian. Born in Belorussia, Dubnow revolted against his family's traditional Judaism and entered a Russian government school after his *bar mitsvah*. Drawn to the Enlightenment but unable to gain admission to a university, he began writing for the Russian–Jewish press. Under the influence of the work of Heinrich *Graetz, Dubnow came to see the study of Jewish history as his calling and the most suitable form of self-knowledge for secular Jews who could not subscribe to formal religion. In Odessa in the 1890s, he propounded "autonomism," calling for the recognition of Jewish communal autonomy and minority cultural rights in the Diaspora, especially in a multinational Russian state. In Saint Petersburg, after 1905, he developed his sociological interpretation of Jewish history, emphasizing the adaptation of Jewish communal institutions to varied social conditions and formulating a sequence of hegemonies of outstanding Jewish Diaspora centers in different periods of Jewish history. Dubnow trained a generation of young Jewish historians, especially in the history of the Jews of eastern Europe, and laid stress upon the Yiddish language.

Among Dubnow's writings are *Letters on Old and New Judaism* (1907), the *History of the Jews of Russia and Poland* (1916–1920), a ten-volume *World History of the Jewish People* (first published in German translation, 1925–1929; later published in Hebrew, the Russian original, Yiddish, and English), the *History of Hasidism* (rev., 1930–1932), and a three-volume autobiography, *Book of Life* (1934–1940).

After leaving the Soviet Union in 1922 because of his opposition to Communism, Dubnow settled in Berlin until 1934. When the Nazis came to power in Germany, he moved to Riga, where he was murdered in the Holocaust.

• Sophie Dubnov-Erlich, *The Life and Work of S. M. Dubnov*, translated by Judith Vowles, edited by Jeffrey Shandler, with an introductory essay by Jonathan Frankel (Bloomington, Ind., 1991). Simon Rawidowicz, ed., *Sefer Shim'on Dubnov: Ma'amarim, Iggerot* (London, Jerusalem, and Waltham, Mass., 1954), with bibliography. Aaron Steinberg, ed., *Simon Dubnov: L'homme et son ouvre* (Paris, 1963), with bibliography.

—ROBERT M. SELTZER

DUEREN, YITSḤAQ BEN ME'IR (died c.1300), German rabbinical authority. Little is known of his life. His best-known work, *Sha'arei Dura'*, also known as *Issur ve-Hetter* (Kraków, 1534), deals with the laws of forbidden foods and especially the laws of salting; its second part is about the laws of menstruation. It is written clearly and succinctly and is based mainly on the ruling of Ashkenazi authorities. It was frequently used by Yosef Karo and Mosheh Isserles. Leading authorities wrote commentaries on the work that were frequently reprinted.

• Israel Elfenbein, ed., *Minhagim Yeshenim mi-Dura'* (New York, 1948).

DUKHAN. See BIRKAT HA-KOHANIM.

DUNASH IBN TAMIM (c.890–960), also known as Adonim and Abu Sahl; North African physician, philosopher, and scholar. Dunash was a student of Yitsḥaq *Israeli, and he served as a court physician in Kairouan. He was the author of an astronomical work, at least one medical text, and a commentary on *Genesis* 1, all of which are now lost. He is also mentioned by Mosheh *ibn Ezra as the author of a book comparing the Hebrew, Syriac, and Arabic languages, especially in their word origins.

In his commentary on the **Sefer Yetsirah* (edited by M. Grossberg [1902]), composed in the years 955 and 956 and influenced by the Neoplatonic teaching of Yitsḥaq Israeli, Dunash writes that he intended at a future date to show that Arabic was derived from Hebrew. It is for this commentary that he is chiefly remembered; it was written in Arabic, but for centuries it only survived in Hebrew translation, and fragments of the original have been found in the Cairo Genizah. The commentary posited a regulated hierarchical universe formed by a transcendent, spiritual Creator. It was in circulation until the fifteenth century but by then had ceased to be influential. Dunash was also quoted by Muslim writers, but the possibility suggested by them that he converted to Islam is now discounted.

• Alexander Altmann and Samuel Miklos Stern, eds., *Isaac Israeli* (Westport, Conn., 1958), index. Menaḥem ben Sason, "Mishpaḥah bi-Tequfat Shinuyim: 'Iyyun ba-Mifgash ha-Halakhah veha-Historiyah bi-Tsefon Afriqah 'im 'Edut Ḥadashah al Dunash ibn Tamim," *Sefunot* 5.2 (1991): 51–69.

DURAN, PROFIAT (c.1345–1414), also known as Efod (Hebrew acronym of "I, Profiat Duran"); Spanish grammarian, philosopher, and apologist. Duran was born in Perpignan but later lived in Catalonia. After the persecutions of 1391, he seems to have been forcibly converted to Christianity and for a number of years, under the name of Honoratus de Bonafide, served as astrologer to King Juan I of Aragon. He is chiefly remembered for his two polemical works against Christianity. In his *Iggeret ʿal Tehi ka-'Avotekha* (Constantinople, 1570) he showed in a witty style the inconsistencies between Christian doctrines and the findings of Aristotelian philosophy. The work takes the form of a letter to David Bont Bonjorn, who was a convinced Jewish convert to Christianity. Initially, it was misunderstood by its Christian readers, who called it *Alteca Boteca* and thought it was meant literally, not ironically. Subsequently, when its real import was grasped, it was publicly condemned and burned. Later, Yosef ibn Shem Tov wrote a commentary on it. Duran's other polemical work, composed with the encouragement of Ḥasda'i ben Avraham *Crescas, was *Sefer Kelimat ha-Goyyim*. In this he analyzed such Christian doctrines as the divinity of Jesus, the Trinity, the Incarnation, the Virgin Birth, and original sin, with the object of showing how they were incompatible with the teachings of the New Testament. He also pointed out errors in the Vulgate and argued that they were the result of St. Jerome having been helped by a less than knowledgeable Jew, resulting in misquotation of the Hebrew Bible by Jerome and other church fathers. Duran also wrote a commentary on Maimonides' *Guide of the Perplexed*, notes on Averroes's commentary on the *Almagest*, a commentary on parts of Avraham *ibn Ezra's commentary on the Pentateuch, various astronomical treatises, a criticism of Yosef ibn Naḥamias's *Or ʿOlam*, a letter of condolence to R. Avraham ben Yitsḥaq ha-Levi that contains many of his philosophical ideas, and a history of the persecution of the Jews from the time of the Second Temple, which is now lost. In addition, he produced a grammatical work, the *Maʿaseh Efod*, which describes how Hebrew was pronounced by the Spanish community in the fourteenth century. In the introduction, he affirmed his belief in the perfection of the Torah and argued that the preservation of Torah was the reason for Jewish existence. At the same time he maintained that neither philosophical nor kabbalistic speculation were incompatible with the study of Torah. Duran's works were used by later Jewish apologists such as Yosef ibn Shem Tov and Shem Tov ibn Shaprut. *Iggeret ʿal Tehi ka-'Avotekha* and *Sefer Kelimat ha-Goyyim* were published by J. D. Eisenstein in his *Otsar Vikkuḥim* (1928).

• Yitzhak Baer, *A History of the Jews in Christian Spain*, 2 vols. (Philadelphia, 1961–1966).

–LAVINIA COHN-SHERBOK

DURAN FAMILY, a family of rabbis and scholars.

Shimʿon ben Tsemaḥ Duran (1361–1444), rabbinic authority and religious philosopher known by the acronym Rashbats. He studied in his native Majorca and in Aragon. In addition to his religious education, he studied medicine and practiced in Majorca. After losing all of his belongings in the 1391 anti-Jewish outbreak, he moved to Algiers, where he served as a member of the *beit din* of *Yitsḥaq ben Sheshet Perfet (whom he succeeded as chief rabbi of Algiers in 1408). Because this was a full-time occupation, he had to break precedent and accept a salary, and he wrote *responsa* permitting sages to receive payment from community funds. His ordinances (*taqqanot*) on matrimonial matters retained their validity among North African Jewry for centuries. As a halakhist, he opposed stringency that had no Talmudic backing and stressed the use of logic in reaching legal decisions.

He was strongly influenced by Maimonides but did not accept certain of his philosophical views. He rejected Maimonides' opinion that the divine attributes were all negative and asserted that they were positive and identical with the essence of God. He held that humans receive a special soul from God (*neshamah*), which is responsible for their rationality, and this soul has the potentiality of immortality, depending upon the bearer's righteousness. He followed Maimonides' theory of prophecy but laid greater stress on the component of God's grace. He reduced the number of fundamental principles to three: the existence of God, the divine origin of the Torah through revelation, and the doctrine of reward and punishment (a formulation adopted by Yosef *Albo).

Duran was an enthusiastic follower of the Kabbalah, which he often quoted in his writings. He was also an outstanding polemicist. In his writings against the *Karaites, he stressed the oral law as the key to understanding the written law. He was familiar with Christian writings, holding that they had to be studied in order to be refuted. In his anti-Christian polemics, he argued that Jesus and his disciples observed the commandments and that his crucifixion was not the result of neglect of the Torah but because of messianic claims. In disputes with Muslims, he sought to prove the human origin of the Qur'an.

Duran's major work, *Magen Avot* (Leghorn, 1785; Vienna, 1864), covers subjects other than philosophy and relates to many areas of science. His writings include over nine hundred collected *responsa* (*Teshuvot Shimʿon ben Tsemaḥ*, usually known by the acronym *Tashbetz* [Amsterdam, 1738–1741; Lwów, 1891]) and branch out beyond legal matters to such fields as mathematics, astronomy, and Hebrew grammar. Duran also wrote *piyyutim*, in addition to commentaries on earlier poems.

Shelomoh ben Shimʿon Duran (c.1400–1467), known by the acronym Rashbash; rabbi in Algiers and son of Shimʿon ben Tsemaḥ Duran. He studied with his father; his education extended beyond Jewish subjects to medicine, the natural sciences, and philosophy. A member of his father's *beit din*, he succeeded him after his death as rabbi of Algiers. Like his father, he was for many generations regarded as an outstanding authority by the Jews of North Africa. His main works are his *responsa*, published in *Teshuvot ha-Rashbash* (Leghorn, 1742), which deal not only with halakhic issues but also with matters of faith and philosophy, and *Tiqqun Soferim* (Leghorn, 1744) on contract law. Duran also wrote the polemical *Milḥemet Mitsvah* (in J. D. Eisenstein, *Otsar Vikkuḥim* [1928], pp. 134ff.) to refute the attacks of the apostate Yehoshuʿa Lorki on the Talmud.

Tsemaḥ ben Shelomoh Duran (15th cent.), rabbinical scholar in Algiers; second son of Shelomoh ben Shimʿon Duran. He was *dayyan* in Algiers, together with his two brothers Aharon and Shimʿon, and was well-versed in medicine, philosophy, and Kabbalah, toward which his attitude was positive. He laid down important rulings concerning Marranos, whom he regarded as halakhically Jewish. Some of his *responsa* are quoted by Yosef Karo, while one hundred fifty of his *responsa* were printed together with those of his brother Shimʿon in *Yakhin u-Voʿaz* (Leghorn, 1782).

• **Shimʿon ben Tsemaḥ Duran:** "The Principles of Judaism according to Rabbi Simon ben Zemah Duran," Ph.D. dissertation, Yeshivah University, 1970. Isidore Epstein, *Studies in the Communal Life of the Jews of Spain as Reflected in the Responsa of Rabbi Solomon ben Adreth and Rabbi Simon ben Zemach Duran* (New York, 1968). **Shelomoh ben Shimʿon Duran:** Shalom Bar-Asher, "Basic Trends in the History of the Jews of the Maghreb and the Rise of the Center in Algiers, 1391–1492," *Peʿamim* 31 (1987): 22–39, in Hebrew. Abraham M. Hershman, *Rabbi Isaac ben Sheshet Perfet and His Times* (New York, 1973). Abraham Shusterman, "A Study in Fifteenth-Century Spanish–Jewish Polemics: As Reflected in the Writings of the Duran Family," rabbinic thesis, Hebrew Union College, 1930.

—SHALOM BAR-ASHER

DURESS (Heb. *ones*), forcing a person to speak or perform an act, or to abstain from acting or speaking, against the person's will. According to the Talmud, individuals are responsible for their actions only if they are initiated and performed of their own free will (*B. Q.* 28b). This principle is derived from *Deuteronomy* 22.25–28, according to which a betrothed virgin who has been raped is freed from all penalty, since she acted under compulsion (*Ned.* 27a). While various types of duress are recognized by *halakhah*, compulsion as grounds for extenuating circumstances refers only to physical violence or a threat to the life of the person concerned (following the phrase in *Lv.* 18.5, "he shall live by them [the commandments]," that is, not die by them [*Ket.* 33b]). Compulsion to commit one of the three cardinal sins—idolatry, murder, or an adulterous or incestuous act (*San.* 74a)—is to be resisted even at the cost of one's life. However, a person who violates one of these three precepts under duress remains unpunished by human courts (Yitsḥaq ben Sheshet Perfet, *Resp.* 4, 11, 387). A divorce granted under duress is invalid, and a woman who is forced to agree to wedlock is considered unmarried by law. Oaths or vows taken under duress are also invalid and carry neither obligation nor penalty. Similarly, a gift bestowed under duress may be rescinded (Shemu'el ben Me'ir on *B. B.* 47b), but a sale or purchase concluded under similar circumstances remains valid (*Shulḥan ʿArukh, Ḥoshen Mishpat* 205.1). Saving one's life by means of another's property is permitted, but compensation must be made to the owner of the property; likewise, an injury caused under duress to one's fellow must still be compensated (*B. Q.* 27a).

• Eliahu C. Benzimra, "Necessity and Duress in Jewish Criminal Law: A Monograph on the Law of *Ones*," Dr. of Law thesis, Hebrew University of Jerusalem, 1979. Arnold N. Enker, *Duress and Necessity in the Criminal Law* (Ramat Gan, 1977), in Hebrew and English.

DUSTAN (Dositheans), *Samaritan sect. Details are obscure; however, there are accounts of such a sect from the fourth century BCE and from the fourth century CE. The sect is mentioned in Samaritan sources, as well as by the church fathers and Muslim writers. Descriptions of the earlier sect mention various ways in which it diverged from the main Samaritan group, including differences in calendar, liturgy, and ritual law. The later Dustan sect had variations in the biblical text and in the calendar, and they observed all festivals on Sabbaths. The original sect may have continued to exist for a considerable time, and further sects may have derived from it.

• Stanley J. Isser, *The Dositheans: A Samaritan Sect in Late Antiquity*, Studies in Judaism in Late Antiquity 17 (Leiden, 1976).

DUTY (Heb. *ḥovah*), an obligation or due, payable by man to God or to his fellow man. The rabbinic idiom for fulfilling one's duty, *"yots'ei yedei ḥovato,"* literally means emerging from the hold of one's obligation. *Ḥovah* is distinct from **mitsvah*, which can also signify a commendable, but not necessarily obligatory, action (*reshut*); for example, each of the three daily prayer services is a *mitsvah*, but whereas the morning and afternoon services are obligatory, the evening service is *reshut*. The rabbis insist that the commandments are to be observed as a duty and not in order to be rewarded (*Avot* 1.3). The *Ḥovot ha-Levavot* by *Baḥya ben Yosef ibn Paquda' distinguishes between the duties of the spiritual life and the ceremonial and practical obligations, the "duties of the limbs." The rabbis considered the performance of positively commanded actions, which expressed the desire to obey God's will, morally superior to voluntary good deeds.

Medieval philosophers maintained that duties of a moral nature, as distinct from ritual commandments, were independent of divine revelation since human reason and conscience would have formulated them. The philosopher Immanuel Kant asserted that true ethics must be "autonomous." A system of duties imposed by an "outside," that is heteronomous, source (e.g., God as in the case of Judaism) was of necessity inferior. This issue played an important role in the thinking of Hermann *Cohen and Franz *Rosenzweig, among others (see COMMANDMENTS, REASONS FOR).

• David Daube, "Duty and Beauty," in *Collected Works of David Daube*, edited by Calum M. Carmichael (Berkeley, 1992), pp. 449–454.

DYBBUK, the disembodied spirit of a dead person that finds no rest on account of sins committed during life. A dybbuk seeks a haven in the body of a living person, talking through the mouth of the host and acting as an evil influence. Possession by a dybbuk is often taken as a sign of hidden sin on the part of the person possessed. The dybbuk can be exorcised by a religious rite.

The use of the term *dybbuk* is not attested before the seventeenth century, when belief in dybbuks became widespread, especially in eastern Europe and in Hasidic folklore, and found expression in popular legends and literature. The growing popularity of the belief is connected with that of *gilgul* (the *transmigration of souls), or, to be more precise, of *'ibbur* (the "impregnation" of a living person or soul by another spirit), and is largely due to the doctrines developed by the disciples of Yitsḥaq Luria.

• Gedalyah Nigal, *Magic, Mysticism and Hasidism: The Supernatural in Jewish Thought* (Northvale, N.J., 1994), pp. 67–112.

—SHIFRA EPSTEIN

E

EARTH. See COSMOLOGY; CREATION.

EAST. See MIZRAḤ.

EBIONITES, designation applied to members of a Judeo-Christian movement within the early church. Their name probably derives from the Hebrew *evyon* (poor), a word that gradually assumed a theological connotation and was used by the eschatological groups to describe themselves: though they appeared poor, oppressed, and lowly (*evyonim*), they thought themselves destined to "inherit the kingdom of God" (see *Mt.* 5.3 and numerous references to *evyonim* in the *Dead Sea Scrolls). Knowledge of the Ebionites is derived solely from the polemical tracts of their orthodox Christian opponents, whose accounts are far from objective. From these narratives, it seems that the Ebionites were strict in their adherence to Jewish law and insisted that all devout Christians were bound by it. They observed the Sabbath and held their agapes (love feasts) on Sundays. While some of them accepted the divinity of Jesus, they refused to ascribe to him any kind of transcendental nature. Other Ebionites completely rejected Jesus' divinity but held that he was the *Messiah, chosen by God at the time of his baptism. The Ebionites were firm in their rejection of Paul and his teachings, which they regarded as heretical.

• Albertus Frederik Johannes Klijn and G. J. Reinink, *Patristic Evidence for Jewish-Christian Sects*, Supplements to Novum Testamentum 36 (Leiden, 1973).

–GIDEON BOHAK

ECCLESIASTES, BOOK OF, one of the Five Scrolls (see ḤAMESH MEGILLOT) in the Hagiographa. It belongs to the genre of *wisdom literature and deals with universal philosophical questions rather than with Israel's covenant and history. The speaker, called Qohelet (which is the Hebrew name of the book and has been erroneously translated as Preacher), presents himself as having amassed great wisdom and wealth, in order to determine what, of anything, is of lasting value and how, if at all, God interacts with human beings. The book consists of his ruminations and findings: that all is controlled by God through a predetermined, unchangeable plan ("nothing new under the sun," *Eccl.* 1.9; "to every thing there is a season," *Eccl.* 3.1); that God torments humans by planting in their hearts the desire to comprehend this plan but preventing them from ever doing so; that human misery is caused by this, along with the refusal to remember the past; that the only true happiness is the enjoyment of one's earthly wealth; that this is indeed God's gift, but it is dispensed arbitrarily and is not necessarily a reward for virtue, thus, the moral governance of the world is crooked and cannot be rectified; and that the same final end—death—awaits all: righteous and wicked, the wise and the fool, human and animal. Acknowledging the impenetrable boundary between human beings and a totally omnipotent and unknowable God leads Qohelet to conclude that, since no other form of satisfaction exists, one ought to make the best of this earthly life, enjoying whatever blessings God has seen fit to grant. The end of the book enjoins humans to fear God and keep his commands, this submissive, subservient obedience to God without expectation of reward being the "whole of man" (*Eccl.* 12.13), the entire purpose of his existence. Since the speaker styles himself as "son of David, king in Jerusalem" (1.1, 12, 16, 2.9) and as the wisest man ever to live, it is most likely that the author wished to identify him with King *Solomon (*1 Kgs.* 3.5–28, 5.9–14, 10.1–13). Rabbinic tradition, while accepting this view (suggesting that Solomon arrived at his cynical views in his old age), attributes the actual writing of the book to King Hezekiah and his associates (*B. B.* 15a). Biblical scholars detect late elements in the book, including Greek influences, and tend to date it to the Hellenistic period. In Midrashic exegesis, Qohelet's apparent hedonism and his absolute denial of divine justice and of the afterlife were somewhat attenuated, bringing the book more into line with normative Jewish ideas. Still, some sages did not count it among the sacred scriptures (see BIBLE); others accepted its sanctity but advocated removing it from circulation, in light of its questionable theology (*'Eduy.* 5.3; *Yad.* 3.5; *Lv. Rab.* 28). Qohelet's closing call for obedience to the commands of God (*Eccl.* 12.13) saved the book from oblivion: heterodox ideas are not shunned in Judaism as long as loyalty to the commandments is not affected. *Ecclesiastes* is read in Ashkenazi synagogues on the Sabbath of Sukkot (if there is no intermediate Sabbath, it is read on Shemini 'Atseret).

• James L. Crenshaw, *Ecclesiastes: A Commentary*, Old Testament Library (London, 1988). Michael V. Fox, *Qohelet and His Contradictions*, Journal for the Study of the Old Testament, Supplement Series 71 (Sheffield, Eng., 1989). Harold L. Ginsberg, *Studies in Koheleth* (New York, 1950). Robert Gordis, *Koheleth: The Man and His World* (New York, 1968). Charles F. Whitley, *Koheleth: His Language and Thought*, Beiheft zur Zeitschrift für die alttestamentliche Wissenschaft 148 (Berlin, 1979).

–BARUCH J. SCHWARTZ

ECCLESIASTES RABBAH, *midrash* written in Erets Yisra'el on the *Book of *Ecclesiastes*. *Midrash* or *Haggadat Qohelet*, as it was called in the Middle Ages, and more rarely *Midrash Ḥazita'* (see SONG OF SONGS RABBAH), covers almost every verse of *Ecclesiastes*. It is divided, in the manuscripts, into three uneven sections (which correspond today to chapters 1–6, 7–9.6, 9.7–12.14). The work draws heavily on earlier aggadic compositions, such as *Genesis Rabbah* and *Leviticus Rabbah*, and Julius Theodor reckoned that about one-fifth of *Ecclesiastes Rabbah* is made up of proems from these earlier works. This highlights the anthological nature of the composition, which is a very rich compendium of Erets Yisra'el aggadic traditions arranged under the headings of verses of *Ecclesiastes*. It contains the most extensive collection, for its period, of stories on Christian–Jewish relations (*Eccl. Rab.* 1.8). Louis Ginzberg showed that Jerome, in the late fourth century, made use of Hebrew traditions appearing in this *midrash*, but in its present form, it was redacted probably around the beginning of the seventh century CE. Though written in Rabbinic Hebrew and Galilean Aramaic, many scholars see traces of influence of the Talmud Bavli on *Ecclesiastes Rabbah*. This *midrash* circulated in the Middle Ages in an abbreviated version, later called *Ecclesiastes Zuta'* (edited by Solomon Buber). It was first published in Pesaro in 1519. An English translation by Avraham Cohen appeared in the Soncino Midrash (1939).

• Louis Ginzberg, "Die Haggada bei den Kirchenvätern," in *Abhandlungen zur Erinnerung an Hirsch Perez Chajes* edited by V. Aptowitzer and A. Z. Schwarz (Vienna, 1933), pp. 22–50. Marc G. Hirshman, "The Greek Fathers and the Aggada on Ecclesiastes," *Hebrew Union College Annual* 59 (1988): 137–165. Marc G. Hirshman, "Midrash Qohelet Rabbah," Ph.D. dissertation, Jewish Theological Seminary of America, 1982. Johannes Wachten, *Midrasch-Analyse: Strukturen im Midrasch Qohelet Rabba* (Hildesheim, 1978). Leopold Zunz, *Ha-Derashot be-Yisra'el ve-Hishtalshelutan ha-Historit*, edited by Chanoch Albeck (1892; Jerusalem, 1974).

—MARC HIRSHMAN

ECCLESIASTICUS. See WISDOM OF BEN SIRA.

ÉCOLE RABBINIQUE DE FRANCE. See SÉMINAIRE ISRAÉLITE DE FRANCE.

ECSTASY. See HITLAHAVUT.

EDELS, SHEMU'EL ELI'EZER (1555–1631), Polish Talmudist; known by the acronym Maharsha' (from Morenu ha-Rav Shemu'el Adels). He studied in and headed a *yeshivah* in Posen (Poznań) for several decades, supported by his wealthy mother-in-law, Edel, by whose name he came to be known, and later served as head of the *yeshivot* of Lublin and Ostróg.

An innovator in the area of Talmudic study, Edels developed a style of learning centered on *novellae* (**ḥiddushim*), the discovery of which was often inspired by Edels's analyses of perplexing discussions found in the writings of the tosafists. Ironically, Edels's terse writing style occasionally left his readers uncertain of his own "solutions" and prompted them to develop their own *novellae*.

Edels likewise subjected aggadic portions of the Talmud to rigorous rational investigation and permitted himself periodically to draw upon his knowledge of philosophy for their explication. He exhibited critical textual analysis skills, pointing out on occasion erroneous interpolations in the texts of Rashi and the tosafists.

Edels was revered by his contemporaries and ensuing generations, and the study of his *Ḥiddushei Halakhot* (found in standard editions of the Talmud), became a requirement for Talmudic students.

• Samuel A. Horodezky, *Le-Qorot ha-Rabbanut* (Warsaw, 1911), pp. 183–190.

—ELIJAH J. SCHOCHET

EDEN, GARDEN OF. The expression "garden of Eden" is occasionally replaced by the parallel phrases "the garden of YHVH" (*Gn.* 13.10; *Is.* 51.3) and "the garden of Elohim" (*Ez.* 28.13, 31.8–9). According to the biblical tale, God planted a garden in Eden (*Gn.* 2.8–3.24) and charged *Adam with tending it. It was watered by a river that parted into four streams: Pishon, Gihon, Tigris, and Euphrates. Here *Eve induced Adam to eat with her the fruit of the *tree of knowledge of good and evil, though this was forbidden by God. Thus they gained a new insight into life but at the same time forfeited God's trust. Humans were ejected from the garden lest they also partake of the *tree of life and thereby secure immortality. The way to the garden was henceforth barred by the flaming sword of the angelic guardians. Another version of the story is found in *Ezekiel* 28.13–20. Several theories have been advanced as to the supposed site of the garden, though none is conclusive. The meaning of Eden is also debated. In the past, the favored derivation was from the Assyrian *edinnu*, derived from Sumerian, meaning "plain" or "steppe." Today, however, its etymology has been clarified in the light of a ninth-century BCE Akkadian–Aramaic bilingual inscription discovered in 1979 at Tel Fekheriyeh (near the Syrian–Turkish border). In this source, the root appears in the Aramaic version meaning "to be fruitful, plentiful," or "to be well-watered" (see also *Gn.* 18.2; *Ps.* 36.9). This etymology corresponds to the depiction of the garden of Eden as a luxuriously watered and fruitful place (*Gn.* 2.8–10), which became a major symbol in the Hebrew Bible of fertile and well-irrigated land (*Gn.* 13.10; *Jl.* 2.3; *Ez.* 36.35). This is also ultimately the connection between the Greek usage of the term **paradise* to translate *(gan) Eden* in the Septuagint (e.g., *Gn.* 2.8) and the parallel usage of the Biblical Hebrew term *pardes* (well-watered grove, orchard; *Eccl.* 2.5–6). The parallel to the garden of Eden in the Sumerian creation myth is Dilmun, where sickness and death were unknown and which became the abode of the immortals. In the Sumerian and Babylonian myths, however, the story is governed by the contest of rival forces, whereas the biblical account is wholly subservient to a moral design. The Christian doctrines of the fall and original sin are based on interpretations of the biblical Eden story that are unknown in ancient Jewish exegesis, and it was only in medieval kabbalistic literature that doctrines like those of original sin and a primal fall were developed. Rabbinic texts distinguish between two gardens of Eden: an earthly garden and a heavenly one, the latter being the abode of bliss (paradise), reserved for the souls of the righteous. See also HEAVEN.

• Elias J. Bickerman, *Four Strange Books of the Bible* (New York, 1967), p. 141. Louis Ginzberg, *Legends of the Jews* (Philadelphia, 1938–46), s.v. index. Jonas C. Greenfield, "Notes on the Akkadian–Aramaic Bilingual Statue from Tell Fekherye," in *Orientalia J. Duchesne-Guillemin Emerito Oblata*, Acta Iranica 23 (Leiden, 1984), pp. 219–224. Jonas C. Greenfield and Aaron Shaffer in *Iraq* 46 (1983): 109–116. E. Y. Kutscher, *Millim ve-Toldotehen* (Jerusalem, 1965), pp. 22–23. A. R. Millard, "The Etymology of Eden," *Vetus Testamentum* 34 (1984): 103–106. A. R. Millard and P. Bordreuil, "A Statue from Syria with Assyrian and Aramaic Inscriptions," *Biblical Archaeologist* 45.3 (1982): 135–141. Howard N. Wallace, "Eden, Garden of," in *The Anchor Bible Dictionary*, vol. 2 (New York, 1992), pp. 281–283.

—CHAIM COHEN

EDUCATION. The duty to instruct the people in God's commandments (cf. "you shall teach them diligently to your children," *Dt.* 6.7) is often emphasized in the Bible. At first, education was a matter of parental precept and example, supported by tradition and oral teachings. Literacy seems to have been widespread in ancient Israel (cf. *Jgs.* 8.14), and toward the end of the First Temple period, there is evidence of formal religious instruction by the Levites (cf. *2 Chr.* 7.7ff.). The institution by Ezra of regular public readings of the Torah on Mondays and Thursdays—the days when farmers came to market—as well as the emergence of a nonpriestly class of scribes and scholars gave new impetus to education. The liturgical reading of the Torah was accompanied by exposition and instruction. *Shimʿon ben Shetaḥ (1st cent. BCE) decreed that all youths aged sixteen or seventeen years were to receive a formal education, but teachers were only appointed in Jerusalem (Y., *Ket.* 50b). In the next century, the high priest, Yehoshuʿa ben Gamla' (died c.69 CE), instituted elementary education for boys from the age of six and the appointment of teachers everywhere (*B. B.* 21a). The Mishnah (*Avot* 5.23) specifies the ages for the beginning of instruction: at age five a child is to begin studying the Torah, at age ten the Mishnah, and at age fifteen the *gemara'*. The Talmudic period saw the formulation of educational standards that remained in place until the onset of the modern period. Mild corporal punishment was permitted. According to the Talmud, the ideal number of pupils in a class was twenty-five; a teacher with between forty and forty-nine students was entitled to have an assistant, whose salary, like his, had to be paid by the local community. Should the number of students exceed fifty, a second teacher would have to be engaged (*B. B.* 21a). **Talmud Torah* (study of Torah) was considered the most laudable of activities, and scholarship was a religious ideal. Higher rabbinic education was given in the **beit midrash*, which was usually nearby the synagogue. In Babylonia, nonprofessional scholars would leave their farms or trade for the semiannual study month (**kallah*). These retreats were geared to laymen rather than to scholars of the Talmudic *academies. Elementary education took place in a *beit sefer* (school)—known later as a **ḥeder* (room; in many cases such education was offered in a room of the teacher's home)—which was often maintained by the community. A father is required to teach his son Torah as well as a trade. *Talmud Torah* was restricted to boys, and the rabbis were critical of formal education for girls. Women were expected to learn only those laws relevant to them, and this within the confines of the home. Nevertheless, there were women, both in the Talmudic and in the medieval periods, whose scholarship was acknowledged by the rabbis. The tendency to restrict the curriculum to Jewish learning, and more particularly to Talmudic studies, became even more marked in the medieval and post-Reformation ghetto. During the Middle Ages, rabbis in many towns established their own **yeshivah* or school for religious, especially Talmudic, studies. Sixteenth- and seventeenth-century *yeshivot* in eastern Europe were outstanding. In the nineteenth century, proposals by *Haskalah writers and others to reform the educational system—with the establishment of the *ḥeder metuqqan* (improved or modernized *ḥeder*)—aroused violent Orthodox opposition. On the other hand, *Neo-Orthodoxy in central Europe promoted a combination of secular and Torah studies. With the entry of Jews into modern society and the spread of universal education, the place of the Jewish school was taken, in Western countries, almost entirely by the general school, and Jewish education was limited to afternoon or Sunday "Hebrew school" classes organized by local synagogues. In recent decades, a tendency toward a more markedly Jewish education has asserted itself, partly through religious, partly through Zionist inspiration. In Israel there are three school systems—a general system, a general religious system, and the Ḥinnukh ʿAtsm'ai system run by the *Ḥaredim. Nowadays, many a religious day school in the Diaspora calls itself a *talmud Torah* or *yeshivah*, and alongside the old-style *yeshivot*, institutions have developed combining the traditional Talmudic curriculum with a standard elementary and/or secondary education. Modern social and cultural trends have affected not only the methods, contents, and aims of these schools but also their underlying philosophies of education. One of the greatest changes in this regard is in the Jewish education now offered to girls and women in all frameworks including the Orthodox (although among the Orthodox, coeducation is not the general rule). A major change among more Orthodox males is that many now remain in special *yeshivot* (see KOLEL) for years after marriage. There has been a significant growth in the *yeshivah* student population throughout the world, especially in Israel and in the United States. Since World War II, there has been a great growth in the percentage of students attending Jewish day schools, and schools now exist among all the religious streams—Orthodox, Conservative, and Reform. Also on the rise, especially in the United States, are Jewish-studies faculties in universities.

• Glenda Abramson and Tudor Parfitt, eds., *Jewish Education and Learning: Published in Honor of Dr. David Patterson on the Occasion of His Seventieth Birthday* (Chur, Switzerland, 1994). Judith R. Baskin, "Some Parallels in the Education of Medieval Jewish and Christian Women," *Jewish History* 5.1 (Spring, 1991): 41–52. Moshe Davis ed., *Teaching Jewish Civilization* (New York, 1995). Isidore Fishman, *The History of Jewish Education in Central Europe from the End of the 16th Century to the End of the 18th Century* (London, 1944). Paul E. Kretzmann, *Education Among the Jews from the Earliest Times to the End of the Talmudic Period, 500 A.D.* (Boston, 1922). Nathan Morris, *Toledot ha-Ḥinnukh Shel ʿAm Yisra'el*, 3 vols. (Tel Aviv, 1960–1964).

—SHMUEL HIMELSTEIN

ʿEDUYYOT (עֵדֻיּוֹת; Testimonies), tractate in Mishnah order Neziqin, consisting of eight chapters, with related material in Tosefta'. It is one of the earliest tractates in the Mishnah, compiled in Yavneh not long after the destruction of the Second Temple, and reflects the profound changes within halakhic institutions that followed that event. Unlike other tractates in the Mishnah, *ʿEduyyot* has no unifying subject matter. It consists largely of testimonies of Yavnean sages regarding earlier halakhic traditions. Much of *ʿEduyyot* is preoccupied with the issue of halakhic controversy, primarily the highly divisive controversies between Beit Hillel and Beit Shamm'ai. *ʿEduyyot* establishes important principles of determining halakhic authority, balancing the idea of majority rule against the Mishnaic practice of preserving minority opinions as legitimate halakhic options that may be followed under certain circumstances.

An English translation of the Mishnah tractate is in Herbert Danby's *The Mishnah* (Oxford, 1933).

• Chanoch Albeck, ed., *Shishah Sidrei Mishnah, Seder Neziqin*, 2d ed. (Jerusalem, 1956). Philip Blackman, ed. and trans., *Mishnayot*, vol. 4, *Order Neziqin* (Gateshead, 1973). Pinhas Kehati, ed., *Mishnah: A New Translation with a Commentary, Seder Neziqin*, vol. 3, *Makkot, Shevu'ot, 'Eduyyot* (Jerusalem, 1988). Hermann Leberecht Strack, *Introduction to the Talmud and Midrash* (1931; Minneapolis, 1992).

—AVRAHAM WALFISH

EFRAYIM MOSHEH ḤAYYIM OF SUDYLKOW. See MOSHEH ḤAYYIM EFRAYIM OF SUDYLKOW.

EFRAYIM SHELOMOH BEN AHARON OF LUNTSHITS (died 1619), known as ʿOlelot Efrayim from his work of that name; Polish preacher and rabbi. Born in Łęczyca, he studied under Shelomoh Luria in Lublin. Efrayim Shelomoh's outspoken preaching led to his flight to Jarosław, where he lived in penury. His homiletic skill was recognized by the Jewish autonomous body, the Council of the Four Lands, before which he preached, and was rewarded by its financial support. He became head of a *yeshivah* in Lemberg (Lwów) and in 1604 rabbi of Prague, where he died. He published six works: *ʿIr Gibborim* (Basle, 1580), *ʿOlelot Efrayim* (Lublin, 1590), *Oraḥ le-Ḥayyim* (Lublin, 1595), *Keli Yaqar* (Lublin, 1602), *Siftei Daʿat* (Prague, 1610–1611), and *ʿAmudei Shesh* (Prague, 1618). His writing is characterized by colorful use of language, extensive knowledge of Jewish texts, and incisive social criticism. He saw himself as interpreting the moral message of the sources he used, and he was strongly opposed to the use of *pilpul* as a hermeneutic tool, appreciating the mystical sense of Torah and *halakhah*. He approved the study of mathematics and astronomy as aids to understanding classical Jewish texts. He criticized the rabbinate, particularly for allowing the purchase of positions and appointments based on family connections (*yiḥus*). He also bitterly attacked wealth, which he saw as a corrupting influence, and the wealthy—arguing that the choice of leaders should be based on moral criteria, not on possessions or mental ability alone.

• Jacob Elbaum, *Petiḥut ve-Histagrut: Ha-Yetsirah ha-Ruḥanit–ha-Sifrutit be-Polin uve-'Artsot Ashkenaz be-Shilhe ha-Me'ah ha-Shesh-ʿEsreh* (Jerusalem, 1990), *passim*, with extensive bibliography. —ADAM TELLER

EGER, ʿAQIVAʾ (1761–1837), German rabbinic authority. Born in Eisenstadt, Eger, at age twelve, went to Breslau to study under his uncle, R. Binyamin Wolf Eger. ʿAqivaʾ was married at sixteen to the daughter of Yitsḥaq Margolis of Lissa, where he studied for ten more years. Although averse to the rabbinate as a profession, financial difficulties in 1791 forced ʿAqivaʾ to accept a position in the Brandenburg region. He remained there until 1815, when, after a protracted struggle between traditionalist and modernizing forces regarding his appointment, he became rabbi of the city of Poznań, the prominent community with which his name was thereafter associated.

Eger's tenure in Poznań was marked by constant battles with reformist elements on the communal board. Nonetheless, he spoke out openly in favor of political emancipation and enjoyed the respect of the highest government officials. His decrees during the 1831 cholera epidemic helped to limit its spread and merited him a royal letter from Frederick William III.

Eger's modesty and humanity were the subjects of popular legends, and his hundreds of *responsa* (1834; pt. 2, 1839) attest to his revered position among the leading contemporary Torah authorities. Among his most noted works are: *Gilyon ha-Shas* (1830–1834), notes on the Talmud Bavli printed next to the text of the Vilna edition; *Haggahot* (1859), glosses printed on the pages of the standard *Shulḥan ʿArukh*; and *Ḥiddushim* (1858), Talmudic *novellae*.

• Judith Bleich, "Rabbi Akiva Eger and the Nascent Reform Movement," *Proceedings of the Ninth World Congress of Jewish Studies* B3 (1986): 1–8. Jacob H. Sinason, *The Gaon of Posen: A Portrait of Rabbi Akiva Guens-Eger* (London, 1989). Leopold Wreschner, *Rabbi Akiba Eger: Ein volkstumliche Biographie* (Frankfurt am Main, 1913).

—ADAM S. FERZIGER

ʿEGLAH ʿARUFAH (עֶגְלָה עֲרוּפָה; decapitated calf), a heifer whose neck was broken as a ritual atonement for an unsolved murder. According to *Deuteronomy* 21.1–9, if a corpse was discovered in a field and the identity of the murderer could not be ascertained, the elders of the town closest to the body were commanded to take a heifer "that has never been worked, that has never pulled in a yoke" and break its neck "in an overflowing valley that is not plowed or sown." They then had to recite a formula proclaiming their innocence, while the priests added a prayer for the forgiveness of the people. The *ʿeglah ʿarufah* ritual was performed in order to atone for the community, which shared indirect responsibility for the shedding of innocent blood. Some commentators view the use of an unworked heifer as symbolic of a life that has been snuffed out prematurely. The laws of the *ʿeglah ʿarufah* are developed in the Mishnah (*Sot*. 9.1–9) and Talmud Bavli (*Sot*. 44b–47b). According to the Mishnah (*Sot*. 9.9), the custom was discontinued early in the first century CE, after the occurrence of murders grew in frequency.

• Samuel R. Driver, *A Critical and Exegetical Commentary on Deuteronomy*, 3d ed., The International Critical Commentary, vol. 5. (Edinburgh, 1902), pp. 241–244. Dale Patrick, *Old Testament Law* (Atlanta, 1985).

—DAVID A. GLATT-GILAD

EḤAD MI YODEʿA (אֶחָד מִי יוֹדֵעַ; Who Knows One?), a song of medieval origin and unknown authorship sung in Ashkenazi rites at the end of the Pesaḥ *Seder service. It is made up of thirteen riddles (possibly because the numerical value of the Hebrew word *eḥad* [one] is thirteen) and was inserted especially to maintain the interest of children participating in the service. It was originally composed as a song for festivals in general; from the fourteenth century it was reserved for the Seder.

• Ernst Daniel Goldschmidt, *Haggadah shel Pesaḥ* . . . (Jerusalem, 1960), p. 98.

EHUD, son of Gera, a Benjamite, one of the minor judges. He saved the Israelites from Eglon, king of Moab, by a clever stratagem. He fashioned a double-edged dagger, which he concealed inside his garments. Upon gaining admittance to the king's presence on the pretext of bearing a secret message from God, Ehud thrust the dagger into the king's belly. He escaped before the incident was discovered and went on to lead the Israelites to victory over the Moabites (*Jgs.* 3).

• Robert G. Boling, *Judges*, The Anchor Bible 6A (Garden City, N.Y., 1975), pp. 84–88. Louis Feldman, "Josephus's Portrait of Ehud," in *Pursuing the Text: Studies in Honor of Ben Zion Wacholder*, edited by J. Reeves et al. (Sheffield, Eng., 1994), pp. 177–201. J. Alberto Soggin, *Judges: A Commentary*, translated by John Bowden, The Old Testament Library (London, 1981), pp. 48–56. —SHALOM PAUL

EIGHTEEN BENEDICTIONS. See ʿAMIDAH.

EIKHAH. See LAMENTATIONS, BOOK OF.

EIKHAH RABBAH. See LAMENTATIONS RABBAH.

ʿEIN HA-RAʿ. See EVIL EYE.

EINHORN, DAVID (1809–1879), Reform rabbi. Born in Germany, Einhorn held rabbinical positions in Germany and then in Budapest, until the authorities closed his synagogue under pressure from the Orthodox after he had served there only two months. He moved to the United States in 1855 and officiated in Baltimore (1855–1861, leaving because of his opposition to slavery), Philadelphia (1861–1866), and New York (1866–1879). Einhorn was the spokesman of radical Reform in the United States, denying the continued authority of the Talmud and introducing Sunday services at which worship was conducted with uncovered head to the accompaniment of organ music. A brilliant preacher (in German—his last sermon was a plea for the retention of German in Reform congregations) and a considerable rabbinical scholar, he taught that the ceremonial laws of Moses were only symbolic, that biblical miracles were allegories, and that Judaism should maintain only that which is rational. The ritual elements of Judaism hindered the rational comprehension of revelation. In the messianic age, Einhorn argued, Israel's unique insight would be universalized, and Jews would no longer have—or require—a separate identity.

His prayer book, *ʿOlat Tamid* (1856), was composed mostly in German (the text reads from left to right), with a small number of prayers in Hebrew. It omitted prayers for the revival of sacrifice, the return to Zion, and the resurrection of the dead. The English version (prepared by his son-in-law Emil Hirsch) formed the basis of the *Union Prayer Book*.

Einhorn engaged in fierce disputes with Isaac Mayer *Wise, whom he regarded as too moderate and too willing to compromise for the sake of unity. In 1869 he (and Samuel Adler) challenged Wise by calling a conference in Philadelphia. Delegates at this conference passed resolutions advocating radical Reform in theology, liturgy, and practice (one resolution called for the bride to be an equal partner in the marriage ceremony).

Einhorn's collected sermons, edited by his son-in-law Kauffman Kohler, appeared in the *David Einhorn Memorial Volume* (New York, 1911).

• Gershon Greenberg, "Mendelssohn in America: David Einhorn's Radical Reform Judaism," *Leo Baeck Institute Yearbook* 27 (1982): 281–294. Sefton D. Temkin, *Isaac Mayer Wise* (Oxford and New York, 1992).

EIN KE'LOHEINU (אֵין כֵּאלֹהֵינוּ; There Is None Like Our God), hymn of praise, recited in the Sephardi rite at the end of the Shaḥarit service, extolling the uniqueness of God; among Ashkenazim it is said only on Sabbaths and festivals at the conclusion of the Musaf service. It is of early origin and is found in the prayer book of R. *ʿAmram bar Sheshna' and the *Maḥazor Vitry* (see SIMḤAH BEN SHEMU'EL OF VITRY). In old sources, the order of the first lines was reversed, but it was changed to form the acrostic "Amen, blessed be you." The conclusion in the Ashkenazi version constitutes an introduction to the following *Pittum ha-Qetoret reading.

• Ismar Elbogen, *Jewish Liturgy: A Comprehensive History*, translated by Raymond P. Scheindlin (Philadelphia, 1993), pp. 71, 90, 95, 99.

EIN SOF (אֵין סוֹף; No End), kabbalistic term indicating the supreme divinity, the Godhead, the source of all divine and earthly existence. It may have originated with Hebrew descriptions of the Aristotelian concept of the primal cause. Several kabbalistic systems, including the Zohar, equate it with the first and highest *sefirah* (divine emanation), the *keter* (supreme crown), while others opposed this identification and insisted that the Ein Sof was beyond the *sefirot*. Some kabbalistic texts described the Ein Sof as the ultimate source of divine will or divine thought. According to most kabbalistic systems, the Ein Sof is beyond the reach even of mystical contemplation, but some kabbalists, including R. Yitsḥaq ben Shemu'el of Acre at the beginning of the fourteenth century, described the possibility of spiritual union with it.

• Gershom Gerhard Scholem, *Kabbalah* (Jerusalem and New York, 1974), pp. 87–96. Gershom Gerhard Scholem, *Origins of the Kabbalah* (Princeton, 1987), pp. 130–131, 265–289, 276–277, 431–444. Isaiah Tishby, *The Wisdom of the Zohar*, vol. 1 (Oxford, 1989). —JOSEPH DAN

EIN YAʿAQOV. See IBN ḤAVIV FAMILY .

EISENSTADT, ME'IR (died 1744), rabbinic scholar; known as Maharam Esh. He was born in Poland and served as rabbi in Szydlowiec, Worms, Prossnitz, and Eisenstadt, where he remained for twenty-six years as community rabbi and headed a noted *yeshivah*. One of his students was R. Yonatan *Eybeschuetz, who lived in Eisenstadt's home following the death of his parents. Eisenstadt's literary fame rests largely upon his *Panim Me'irot* (Amsterdam, 1715), a collection of halakhic *responsa* and *novellae* on the Talmudic tractates *Beitsah, Gittin, Qiddushin, Bava' Qamma'*, and *Zevaḥim*.

• Zsigmond Schwartz, *Shem Ha-Gedolim li-Gedolei Hungaryyah* (New York, 1958), pp. 153–154. —MARK WASHOFSKY

EIVAR MIN HA-ḤAI (אֵיבָר מִן הַחַי; a limb from the living), the prohibition, derived from *Deuteronomy* 12.23, against eating a limb or organ torn from a living animal, beast, or bird. This prohibition is one of the seven *Noahic laws (*San.* 56a), derived from the verse "only flesh with the life thereof . . . shall you not eat" (*Gn.* 9.4) enjoined upon Noah. The rabbis ruled that although one may derive benefit from a limb taken from a living animal, such as by feeding it to another animal, it is forbidden to sell the limb or even give it to a non-Jew, since the Noahic laws are binding upon gentiles as well as upon Jews. The rule does not apply to fish, which do not require ritual slaughter.

• Isidor Grunfeld, *The Jewish Dietary Laws*, 2 vols. (London, 1982). I. M. Levinger, *Mazon Kasher min ha-Ḥai* (Jerusalem, 1980).

EL; EL ʿELYON. See God, Names of.

EL ADON (אֵל אָדוֹן; God, the Lord [of All Works]), alphabetical hymn recited in the *Yotser benedictions preceding the *Shemaʿ on Sabbath mornings. Composed by mystics of the geonic era, it replaces the briefer twenty-two-word (El Barukh Gedol Deʿah) poem read on weekdays. Using imagery drawn from Psalm 19 and the vision of Ezekiel, El Adon praises the beneficent harmony of God's creation. —GABRIEL A. SIVAN

ELʿAZAR BEN ʿARAKH (1st cent.), Palestinian tanna'. He was the favorite student of R. Yoḥanan ben Zakk'ai, who said "If all the sages of Israel, including R. Eliʿezer ben Hurqanos, were on one side of the scale, and R. Elʿazar ben ʿArakh was on the other side, he would outweigh them all" (because of his originality and creativity, like "a surging spring"; *Avot* 2.8). According to another tradition, reflecting his interest in mystical studies, when Elʿazar began to expound on *maʿaseh merkavah*, fire fell from heaven, the trees burst into song, an angel cried out from the fire, and R. Yoḥanan praised God and extolled his student: ". . . for you expound well and carry out precepts well. Happy are you, Abraham our father, that Elʿazar ben ʿArakh descended from you" (*Ḥag*. 14b). Upon R. Yoḥanan's death, rather than join his teacher's other disciples in Yavneh, he followed his wife's advice and remained in luxurious Emmaus, after which his influence was diminished (according to some traditions, he forgot all his learning, then had it restored; *Shab*. 147b; *Eccl. Rab*. 7.7, sec. 2). He taught: "Be constant in Torah study, know what to reply to an *apiqoros*, and know before whom you labor, for your employer is faithful and will pay you your wages for your work" (*Avot* 2.14).

• Wilhelm Bacher, *Die Agada der Tannaiten* (1903; Berlin, 1965–1966). Israel Konovitz, comp., *Maʿarakhot Tanna'im: Osef Shalem shel Mishnatam u-Ma'amreihem ba-Sifrut ha-Talmudit veha-Midrashit* (Jerusalem, 1967–1969). Jacob Neusner, *Development of a Legend: Studies on the Traditions Concerning Yohanan ben Zakkai* (Leiden, 1970). —MICHAEL L. BROWN

ELʿAZAR BEN ʿAZARYAH (1st–2d cent.), tanna'. He came from a wealthy aristocratic family. While still in his teens, he succeeded R. Gamli'el, when the latter was temporarily deposed from the presidency of the *Yavneh academy. After Gamli'el's reinstatement, Elʿazar continued to play a central role in the communal and religious life of his time and traveled to Rome with Gamli'el for meetings with the Roman authorities and the Jewish community. Elʿazar was an outstanding preacher and aggadist and is credited with some of the basic maxims of the Talmud, for example, "Saving a life takes precedence over the Sabbath" (*Shab*. 132a); "The Day of Atonement does not atone for sins against one's fellow man until the person sinned against has been appeased" (*Yoma'*, end); "Without Torah there can be no virtuous behavior, without virtuous behavior there can be no Torah" (i.e., the one is worthless without the other, *Avot* 3.21); and "The Bible is written in human language"(*Qid*. 17b, in defense of the literal interpretation of scripture). He was also responsible for the hermeneutical principle (see Hermeneutics) according to which a biblical verse can be interpreted in the light of the preceding or following verse.

• Tzvee Zahavy, *The Traditions of Eleazar Ben Azariah*, Brown Judaic Studies 2 (Missoula, Mont., 1977). —DANIEL SPERBER

ELʿAZAR BEN PEDAT (4th cent.), Babylonian and Palestinian amora'; usually referred to simply as Elʿazar. Of priestly lineage, he was born in Babylonia and received instruction from Shemu'el and Rav before settling in Erets Yisra'el, where he was ordained. He was taught by R. Hoshaʿyah Rabbah in Caesarea and by R. Ḥanina' bar Ḥama' in Sepphoris (see Y., *Ter*. 8.5, 45c; in *Meg*. 15a, R. Elʿazar transmits the famous dictum of R. Ḥanina' that he who states a saying in the name of its originator brings redemption to the world). He also studied with R. Yoḥanan bar Nappaḥa', succeeding him as head of the Tiberias academy in 279 but dying that same year (according to *Iggeret Rav Sherira' Ga'on*). In the Talmud Yerushalmi, he often passes on traditions in the name of Ḥiyya' ben Abba', with whom he worked harmoniously (Y., *B. M*. 10.4, 12c). It was said that his absorption in Torah study was such that he would become oblivious to material matters ("he sat in the lower market of Sepphoris, while his garment lay in the upper market of Sepphoris," *ʿEruv*. 54b). His repute as a Torah scholar was equally acclaimed: according to R. Yoḥanan (*Yev*. 72b) he once seemed "like Moses expounding from the mouth of the Almighty," and in his old age he was known as "the Master of the Land of Yisra'el" (*Yoma'* 9b).

He is mentioned thousands of times in the Talmud and *midrashim*, and the Talmudic phrase "they sent from there" (*San*. 17b) is used with specific reference to his teachings being brought to Babylonia. Through his brilliant and encyclopedic scholarship, he was one of the formative sages in the development of the oral law. He also laid down principles for resolving halakhic disputes in the tannaitic sources (as passed on, in particular, by R. Yehudah ha-Nasi'; cf. *Yev*. 42b). Some of his teachings and aggadic comments have taken on almost proverbial significance in Judaism: the practice of charity is greater than all sacrifices, but acts of kindness are greater than charity (*Suk*. 49b); a man without a wife is not a man (*Yev*. 63a; cf. *Git*. 90b, where it is stated that the altar weeps over the man who divorces his first wife); and, a person should continue to hold out hope for mercy, even when a sharp sword lays on his neck (*Ber*. 10a).

Both his poverty and generosity were fabled (*Taʿan*. 25a; Y., *B. M*. 2.3, 8c). At times he could barely afford to eat (in spite of earning his living by testing coins; *B. Q*. 100a), which led to weakness and health problems (*Ber*. 16b). But he refused to accept gifts from the *nasi'*, citing *Proverbs* 15.27, "he who hates gifts shall live" (see *Meg*. 28a), and stressed to all the members of his household the necessity of practicing hospitality without earthly reward (Y., *Pe'ah* 8.6, 21a).

• Wilhelm Bacher, *Die Agada der palästinensischen Amoräer* (1892–1899; Hildesheim, 1965). Gershom Bader, *The Encyclopedia of Talmudic Sages*, translated from the Yiddish by Solomon Katz (Northvale, N.J. and London, 1988). Jacob Nahum Epstein, *Mavo' le-Nusaḥ ha-Mishnah*, 2d ed. (Tel Aviv, 1964). Isaak Halevy, *Dorot ha-Ri'shonim* vol. 2 (1923; Jerusalem, 1979). Aaron Hyman, *Toledot Tanna'im ve-'Amora'im* (1910; Jerusalem, 1987). —MICHAEL L. BROWN

ELʿAZAR BEN SHAMMUʿA (2d cent.), Palestinian tanna'. Tradition relates that after the twelve thousand pairs of disciples of R. ʿAqiva' had died (purportedly because of their lack of respect for one another), ʿAqiva' elevated five last disciples, of whom R. Elʿazar, a priest (*Sot.* 39a) born in Alexandria, was the most prominent (*Yev.* 62b; *Gn. Rab.* 61.3), comparable in learning to his teacher (cf. *ʿEruv.* 53a). After the Bar Kokhba' Revolt, he and the other disciples were ordained by R. Yehudah ben Bava', in violation of the Roman ban (*San.* 14a). Elʿazar fled for safety until the Hadrianic persecutions waned, then returned to Galilee to establish his academy (Y., *Ḥag.* 3.1, 78d). He was one of the teachers of R. Yehudah ha-Nasi' (*Men.* 18a), who reported that the students in R. Elʿazar's academy had to sit cramped six to one cubit (*ʿEruv.* 53a). Later, R. Yehudah included some of his rulings in the Mishnah (e.g., *Git.* 9.4; however, there is constant confusion in the sources between R. Elʿazar and R. Eliʿezer ben Hurqanos). Called the happiest of the sages by Rav (*Ket.* 40a), he lived (according to a later tradition) to be 105, the result of scrupulous piety toward God and man (*Meg.* 27b), dying as one of the fabled *Ten Martyrs, commended by a divine voice for his lifelong purity (*San.* 14a; *Midrash Elleh Ezkerah*).

Once Elʿazar and R. Yoḥanan ha-Sandelar decided to go to Nisibis, Babylonia, to study with R. Yehudah ben Batyra', but when they reached Sidon, they tearfully recalled Erets Yisra'el and returned home exclaiming "Dwelling in Erets Yisra'el is equivalent to keeping all the commandments of the Torah" (*Sifrei* on *Dt.* 80).

Elʿazar taught that only he who studied Midrash, *halakhot*, and *aggadot* was a fully rounded scholar. He emphasized the importance of teachers and students treating one another with respect and honor (*Avot* 4.12, in clear contrast to the poor behavior of the previous disciples of R. ʿAqiva').

• Wilhelm Bacher, *Die Agada der Tannaiten* (1903; Berlin, 1965–1966). Aaron Hyman, *Toledot Tanna'im ve-'Amora'im* (1910; Jerusalem, 1987). Israel Konovitz, comp., *Maʿarakhot Tanna'im: Osef Shalem shel Mishnatam u-Ma'amreihem ba-Sifrut ha-Talmudit veha-Midrashit* (Jerusalem, 1967–1969). Jacob Neusner, *A History of the Jews in Babylonia* (Leiden, 1969). —MICHAEL L. BROWN

ELʿAZAR BEN SHIMʿON (2d cent.), Palestinian tanna'. Together with his father, R. *Shimʿon bar Yoḥ'ai (*Suk.* 45b), he is the subject of extensive aggadic material, including their fabled thirteen years of hiding from the Romans in a cave (cf. *Shab.* 33b; *B. M.* 85a) and their alleged authorship of the *Zohar. Elʿazar was pressured into working for the Roman government, helping to apprehend Jewish thieves, in spite of the disapproval of his colleagues (*B. M.* 83b). However, his stature was such that upon his death his widow refused to marry R. Yehuda ha-Nasi' (with whom Elʿazar had frequent halakhic disputes), claiming that Yehudah was not her late husband's equal (*B. M.* 84b). Elʿazar is cited directly in the Mishnah only three times (e.g., *Beits.* 4.5, although several anonymous *mishnayot* were later attributed to him; cf. *Ḥul.* 30a) but is mentioned often in *baraiytot* in the Tosefta' and Talmuds. The comment in his eulogy that he was a liturgical poet (*Lv. Rab.* 30.1) led some to identify him incorrectly with R. Elʿazar Kallir.

• Wilhelm Bacher, *Die Agada der Tannaiten* (1903; Berlin, 1965–1966). Israel Konovitz, comp., *Maʿarakhot Tanna'im: Osef Shalem shel Mishnatam u-Ma'amreihem ba-Sifrut ha-Talmudit veha-Midrashit* (Jerusalem, 1967–1969). —MICHAEL L. BROWN

ELʿAZAR BEN TSADOQ (1st–2d cent.), Palestinian tanna'. Of priestly lineage, he was the son of R. Tsadoq, a noted tanna' of the late Second Temple period (cf. *Git.* 55b–57a). He transmitted traditions and personal recollections (e.g., *Ḥul.* 90b; *Suk.* 41b) related to Second Temple services and customs, also recounting some of the horrible sufferings that took place at the time of the Temple's destruction (*Lam. Rab.* 1.47; T., *Ket.* 5.10). He was among the sages who subsequently convened at Yavneh, dealing especially with calendrical matters and working closely with R. Gamli'el (e.g., *Pes.* 37a). He eventually disseminated the Yavneh traditions among the sages who convened at Usha'. For his teaching on suffering, reward and punishment, and the afterlife, see *Qiddushin* 40b to *Job* 8.7 and *Proverbs* 14.12; for his adage on good deeds, see *Nedarim* 62a. His grandson, also Elʿazar ben Tsadoq, was a tanna' of the late second century.

• Wilhelm Bacher, *Die Agada der Tannaiten* (1903; Berlin, 1965–1966). Aaron Hyman, *Toledot Tanna'im ve-'Amora'im* (1910; Jerusalem, 1987). Israel Konovitz, comp., *Maʿarakhot Tanna'im: Osef Shalem shel Mishnatam u-Ma'amreihem ba-Sifrut ha-Talmudit veha-Midrashit* (Jerusalem, 1967–1969). —MICHAEL L. BROWN

ELʿAZAR BEN YEHUDAH OF WORMS (c.1165–1230), the most well-known writer of esoteric theology and ethics of the Kalonimos school of Ashkenazi Hasidism (see ḤASIDEI ASHKENAZ), which flourished in the Rhineland in the twelfth and thirteenth centuries. His teacher was R. *Yehudah ben Shemu'el he-Ḥasid, the leader of that school. Elʿazar's best-known work is the halakhic code *Roqeaḥ* (Fano, 1505), a word that is numerically identical to Elʿazar. To this work he added an extensive ethical introduction, which deals with the norms of piety (*ḥasidut*) and repentance. He wrote an extensive commentary on the prayers, which survived in three manuscript editions, each probably representing an original version of this work that was reedited by the author. This work is based in part on Yehudah ben Shemu'el he-Ḥasid's commentary, which is lost; Elʿazar's is the first commentary on the prayers that has survived. When Yehudah died in 1217, Elʿazar began to commit to writing the esoteric traditions of the Kalonimos school in a series of books. Five of these are collected in his *Sodei Razayya'* (edited by I. Kamelhar [1936]): *Sod Maʿaseh be-Re'shit*, *Sod ha-Merkavah*, *Sefer ha-Shem*, *Ḥokhmat ha-Nefesh* (Lwów, 1876) and the commentary on **Sefer Yetsirah* (Przemyśl, 1883). The basis of his thought is the utter spirituality and transcendent uniqueness of God, from whose concealed essence there emanates the visible glory that links the infinite divine with finite creation. He also wrote commentaries on biblical books and on *piyyutim*. In his *Sefer ha-Ḥokhmah*, written in 1217, he presented his methodological concepts, the system of seventy-three gates of wisdom according to which divine truth is organized. Repentance plays a major role in his teaching. His wife and daughters were massacred by Crusaders before his eyes, and he dedicated a poem to their memory. His disciples included *Yitsḥaq ben Mosheh of Vienna and *Avraham ben ʿAzri'el.

• Joseph Dan, "The Emergence of Jewish Mysticism in Medieval Europe," in *Mystics of the Book*, edited by Robert A. Herrera (New York, 1993). Yisrael Kamelhar, *Rabbenu El'azar mi-Germaizah ha-"Roqeah": Qorot Hayav u-Meoratav* (Tel Aviv, 1974). Ivan G. Marcus, *Piety and Society: The Jewish Pietists of Medieval Germany* (Leiden, 1979). Gershom Gerhard Scholem, *Major Trends in Jewish Mysticism* (New York, 1961), pp. 80–120. —JOSEPH DAN

ELʿAZAR BEN YOSEI (2d cent.), Palestinian tanna', to be distinguished from Elʿazar ben Yosei, the fourth-century Palestinian amora'. Often quoted with praise by his father, Yosei ben Ḥalafta' (e.g., *Pes.* 117a), he is cited directly in the Tosefta', though not in the Mishnah; however, many anonymous *mishnayot* are to be attributed to him (e.g., *Kel.* 11.3). The Talmud counts him among the Yavneh sages and relates that he journeyed to Rome with R. Shimʿon ben Yoḥai to appeal to Caesar to rescind his decree forbidding circumcision and Sabbath observance (*Shab.* 33b). He emphasized the efficacious power of Israel's charity and kindness (*B. B.* 10a).

• Wilhelm Bacher, *Die Agada der Tannaiten* (1903; Berlin, 1965–1966). Israel Konovitz, comp., *Ma'arakhot Tanna'im: Osef Shalem shel Mishnatam u-Ma'amreihem ba-Sifrut ha-Talmudit veha-Midrashit* (Jerusalem, 1967–1969). —MICHAEL L. BROWN

ELʿAZAR HA-QALLIR. See KALLIR, ELʿAZAR.

ELʿAZAR HA-QAPPAR (2d cent.), Palestinian tanna', probably to be distinguished from Bar Qappara', apparently his son. He is quoted in the Mishnah, *baraiytot*, and Talmuds and was a member of the academy of R. Yehudah ha-Nasi' (T., *Ohal.* 18.18). He taught that envy, lust, and ambition take a man out of the world (*Avot* 4.21) and described in detail the fearful reality of the final judgment (*Avot* 4.22). Other preserved teachings concern the sin of denying oneself the pleasures of life (*Taʿan.* 11a, to *Nm.* 6.11), Second Temple customs relating to Yom Kippur (*Yoma'* 67a), poverty (*Shab.* 151b), and the importance of national unity and the greatness of peace (*Sifrei* on *Nm.* 42). The epithet Ha-Qappar may be derived from the town of Qefira' in the Golan, where an inscription was discovered in 1969 bearing his name (or that of his son); the Syriac *qufra'* (asphalt dealer); or the Hebrew *qapparis* (caper blossom), indicating that he may have worked with spices or drugs related to the plant.

• Wilhelm Bacher, *Die Agada der Tannaiten* (1903; Berlin, 1965–1966). Dan Urman, "Eliʿezer ha-Qappar u-Var Qappara': Ha-'Umnam Av u-Veno?" *Be'er Shevʿa* 2 (1985): 7–25. —MICHAEL L. BROWN

ELʿAZAR ROQEAḤ. See ELʿAZAR BEN YEHUDAH OF WORMS.

ELBOGEN, ISMAR (1874–1943), scholar and teacher. Born in Poznań, Elbogen was one of the most important intellectual and institutional forces in early twentieth-century Jewish scholarship in Germany. He studied in Breslau, both at the local university and at the Breslau Rabbinical Seminary. He was appointed *Dozent* at the liberal Hochschule für die Wissenschaft des Judentums in 1902, where he remained for over thirty-five years. Elbogen's most significant research lay in the area of Jewish liturgy, in which he produced a major study entitled *Der jüdische Gottesdienst in seiner geschichtlichen Entwicklung* (1913), which surveyed the history of Jewish synagogal prayer. Elbogen also published widely in the field of Jewish history, including a volume on Jewish history in Germany and a supplementary volume to Heinrich *Graetz's history of the Jews (*A Century of Jewish Life* [1944]). Elbogen immigrated to the United States in 1938, where he served as editor for a large and diverse array of journals and encyclopedias in German, English, and Hebrew.

• Regi Elbogen, *Ismar Elbogen, 1874–1943: A Biography* (New York, 1946); repr. from *Historica Judaica* 8:1 (April 1946): 69–94. —DAVID N. MYERS

ELDAD AND MEDAD, two Israelites who were among the seventy elders who started prophesying in the wilderness when the spirit of God rested upon them. Joshua insisted on silencing them, but Moses reacted with the words, "Would that all the Lord's people were prophets" (*Nm.* 11.29).

• Jacob Milgrom, *Numbers*, The JPS Torah Commentary (Philadelphia, 1990), pp. 89–91, 380–384. —SHALOM PAUL

ELDAD HA-DANI (9th cent.), traveler of uncertain origin who claimed to come from the lost tribe of Dan. He announced the existence of an independent Jewish kingdom in Ethiopia comprised of remnants of the tribes of Naphtali, Gad, Asher, and Dan. His warring kingdom lived across the *Sambatyon from the "sons of Moses." This mythical river was believed to be a mighty torrent of stones all week that rested on the Sabbath. Eldad gave vivid descriptions of the customs of his community to the Jews of Kairouan. His announcement of Jewish sovereignty stirred the imagination of Mediterranean Jewry who eagerly hoped to learn of the lost ten tribes and their traditions regarding the advent of the Messiah. His divergent rituals regarding *sheḥitah* puzzled his North African Jewish audience, who wrote to Tsemaḥ Ga'on, the leading scholar in Baghdad, regarding his identity and that of the Jews he represented. The ga'on reassured his interlocutors in Kairouan that, although Eldad's customs were indeed at variance with the norm, they need not be considered heretical. Diversity of practice was commonplace in the Diaspora. Eldad also presented his audiences with a number of unknown Hebrew designations of a zoological and botanical nature.

Eldad's account was extremely popular among medieval Jews and was first printed in Mantua in 1480. Some medieval authorities such as Me'ir ben Barukh of Rothenburg and Avraham ibn Ezra regarded him as an impostor. Some scholars assert that Eldad's account influenced Christian legends of Prester John. Some modern scholars, however, postulate on linguistic grounds and internal evidence that Eldad originated among the Jews of Ethiopia.

• Elkan N. Adler, ed. and trans., *Jewish Travellers* (New York, 1930). Salo W. Baron, *A Social and Religious History of the Jews*, vol. 6 (New York, 1958). Haim Z. Hirschberg, *History of the Jews in North Africa*, edited and translated by Eliezer Bashan and Robert Attal, vol. 1 (Leiden, 1974). –JANE S. GERBER

ELDERS (Heb. *zeqenim*), in ancient times, the authoritative body ruling the people or state. The first such group to be appointed was during the time of Moses (*Nm.* 11.16–17), but similar bodies are reported to have existed earlier, both among the Jews in Egypt (*Ex.* 3.16, 12.21) and at Sinai, where seventy elders were privileged to accompany Moses up the mountain (*Ex.* 24.1). On several subsequent occasions (e.g., *1 Kgs.* 21.8–14, the narrative of Naboth's vineyard) the elders are mentioned as a representative and an advisory, though never a legislative, body. The Mishnah (*Avot* 1.1) reports that the elders constituted a link in the chain of tradition between Joshua and the prophets. Reference to the elders is found in the *Book of Ezra* (10.8), and it is possible that they were the basis for the *Keneset ha-Gedolah. Many scholars maintain that the elders participated in administering affairs of state until the Hasmonean period and that their functions were eventually incorporated into those of the Sanhedrin. The elders doubtless included men noted for their sagacity and learning, not necessarily for their great age. See also GEROUSIA.

• Roland de Vaux, *Ancient Israel*, translated by John McHugh (New York, 1961), pp. 138, 152–153. –SHALOM PAUL

ELECTION OF ISRAEL. See CHOSEN PEOPLE.

ELEGY. See QINAH.

ELEPHANTINE. See YEB.

ELI, high priest at Shiloh and judge in Israel before and during the days of *Samuel's youth (*1 Sm.* 1–4). When Eli was a priest at the sanctuary in Shiloh, he did not recognize Hannah's praying and rebuked her for assumed drunkenness (*1 Sm.* 1.9–18). Similarly, when the young Samuel heard God calling to him in the sanctuary, Eli did not recognize the divine communication until the third call (*1 Sm.* 3). His sons Hophni and Phinehas are portrayed as wicked priests who had no regard for God, abused "the offering of the Lord" (cf. *1 Sm.* 2.29), and "lay with the women who served at the entrance of the tent of meeting" (*1 Sm.* 2.22). For these reasons, the house of Eli was condemned by an unnamed "man of God" (*1 Sm.* 2.27), who stated that God would choose a "faithful priest" whose descendants would replace the line of Eli (*1 Sm.* 2.29–35). Eli died upon hearing that the Philistines had killed his sons and captured the Ark of the Covenant, which his sons had carried into battle as a talisman to ensure Israel's victory (*1 Sm.* 4).

• J. P. Fokkelman, *Narrative Art and Poetry in the Books of Samuel*, vol. 4, *Vow and Desire, 1 Sam. 1–12*, Studia Semitica Neerlandica 31 (Assen/Maastricht, 1993). Moshe Garsiel, *The First Book of Samuel: A Literary Study of Comparative Structures, Analogies, and Parallels* (Ramat Gan, 1985). P. Kyle McCarter, *1 Samuel*, The Anchor Bible, vol. 8 (Garden City, N.Y., 1980). Robert Polzin, *Samuel and the Deuteronomist*, pt. 2, *1 Samuel* (San Francisco, 1989). –MARVIN A. SWEENEY

ELIʿEZER BEN HURQANOS (1st–2d cent.), *tanna', pupil of *Yoḥanan ben Zakk'ai (whom he helped to smuggle out of Jerusalem during the Roman siege), and teacher of R. *ʿAqiva' ben Yosef; he was also known as Eliʿezer the Great. After the destruction of the Temple, Eliʿezer ben Hurqanos headed the academy of Lydda and was a leading member of the Sanhedrin. He was one of the central figures in the critical transitional period following the destruction of the Second Temple. As depicted in the sources, he possessed a phenomenal memory and accumulated and retained ancient traditions of the Second Temple period that were in opposition to the new tendencies of the *Yavneh academy. His many halakhic opinions tended to be stringent, based as they were on the teachings of the school of Shamm'ai (see BEIT HILLEL AND BEIT SHAMM'AI). His protracted struggle with the *nasi'* (patriarch) and other members of the Sanhedrin and his refusal to accept the majority ruling culminated in his excommunication and ostracism from the academy (*B. M.* 59b).

• Yitzhak D. Gilat, *R. Eliezer ben Hyrcanus: A Scholar Outcast* (Ramat Gan, 1984). Jacob Neusner, *Eliezer ben Hyrcanus: The Tradition and the Man* (Leiden, 1973). –DANIEL SPERBER

ELIʿEZER BEN NATAN OF MAINZ (c.1090–1170), rabbinic scholar, tosafist, and legal authority; known by the acronym Raban. He studied in Mainz in the period just after the First Crusade (on which he wrote a booklet). In 1150, together with R. Yaʿaqov ben Me'ir Tam and R. Shemu'el ben Me'ir, he promulgated the so-called Troyes ordinances, **taqqanot* in various fields of Jewish law.

Rabbi Eliʿezer's major work, called *Sefer Raban* or *Even ha-ʿEzer* (Prague, 1610), contains halakhic rulings and *responsa* following the order of the Talmudic tractates. It includes much information about the scholars and practices of France, Germany, and Babylonia. Another work attributed to Raban, *Tsafnat Paʿneaḥ*, has not survived, although it appears to have been related to *Sefer Raban*. Rabbi Eliʿezer commented extensively on *piyyutim* and other aspects of the liturgy. Subsequent Ashkenazi commentators on the prayers often added their remarks to the commentary of Raban. *Sefer Raban* was published with a commentary by Solomon Z. Ehrenreich in 1926).

• Victor Aptowitzer, *Mavo' le-Sefer Rabiyah* (Jerusalem, 1938), pp. 49–57. Efraim E. Urbach, *Baʿalei ha-Tosafot* (Jerusalem, 1980), vol. 1, pp. 173–184. –EPHRAIM KANARFOGEL

ELIʿEZER BEN YO'EL HA-LEVI OF BONN (c.1140–1225), rabbinic scholar, tosafist, and legal authority; known by the acronym Rabiah or Ravyah. He was the grandson of R. *Eliʿezer ben Natan of Mainz, the leading halakhist of twelfth-century Germany. His father, R. Yo'el ha-Levi of Bonn, was venerated by tosafists in both Germany and northern France. Eliʿezer traveled throughout Germany, studying with such masters as Rabbi Eliʿezer of Metz, R. Yehudah ben Shemu'el he-Ḥasid, and R. Yehudah ben Kalonimos of Speyer. He established his academy in Bonn and moved to Cologne toward the end of his life.

The bulk of his major work of Jewish law, known as *Sefer Rabiyah* (vols. 1–3 [1933–1935]) or *Avi ha-ʿEzri*, was published by Victor Aptowitzer in three volumes, along with an introductory volume containing biographical descriptions of Eliʿezer and his family, teachers, and students (vol. 4 was edited by M. H. Fischel [1965]; additional volumes have been published by David Dablitsky [1976–1989]). This work is a collection of legal decisions, *responsa, tosafot*, and other extracts arranged according to the order of the tractates of the Talmud. Eliʿezer also wrote a separate work on the orders of Nashim and Neziqin entitled *Avi'asaf*, which was cited in Ashkenazi rabbinic works of the thirteenth and fourteenth centuries but is no longer extant. The beginning of Eliʿezer's treatise, entitled *Seder Bayit Sheni*, has survived.

He refused compensation for teaching Torah and turned down formal rabbinic office. He was a leading proponent of the Ashkenazi practice of adhering to the view of the majority in matters of communal government, defending this position against challenges from rabbinic scholars of northern France.

• Efraim E. Urbach, *Baʿalei ha-Tosafot* (Jerusalem, 1980), vol. 1, pp. 378–388 and index. —EPHRAIM KANARFOGEL

ELIʿEZER BEN YOSEI HA-GALILI (2d cent.), tanna'; pupil of R. *ʿAqiva' ben Yosef, he was one of those who established the academy at *Yavneh (*Ber.* 63b) and then in Usha'. A noted aggadist, he is credited with having laid down thirty-two hermeneutical rules for the interpretation of the *aggadah* (see HERMENEUTICS). These were preserved in a special *baraiyta'*, which is printed in some Talmud editions after the tractate *Berakhot*. It was also discovered in a manuscript entitled *The Mishnah of Rabbi Eliʿezer*, to which was appended another longer *midrash* attributed to him, but probably of a much later date, also known as *Midrash Aggur*. He is only mentioned once in the Mishnah (*Sot.* 5.3) but frequently in *baraiytot*. His halakhic dicta are few, and most of his extant statements are of an aggadic nature.

• Gershom Bader, *The Encyclopedia of Talmudic Sages*, translated from the Yiddish by Solomon Katz (Northvale, N.J., and London, 1988). Hyman Gerson Enelow, ed., *Mishnat Rabbi Eliʿezer o Midrash Sheloshim u-Shetayim Middot* (New York, 1933). Aaron Hyman, *Toledot Tanna'im ve-'Amora'im* (1910; Jerusalem, 1987). Menachem Mendel Kasher and Jacob Ber Mandelbaum, eds. and trans., *Sarei ha-'Elef*, rev. and corr. ed. (Jerusalem, 1978), vol. 1, pp. 38–39. Mordecai Margaliot, ed., *Entsiqlopediyyah le-Ḥakhmei ha-Talmud veha-Ge'onim* (Jerusalem, 1946). —DANIEL SPERBER

ELIʿEZER OF BEAUGENCY (12th cent.), biblical exegete. Eliʿezer was part of the northern French school of biblical exegesis. These scholars, beginning with *Rashi, focused their efforts on explaining the Bible according to the plain meaning of the text (see PESHAT). Three commentaries by Eliʿezer of Beaugency have been preserved: *Isaiah* (published by Nutt [1879]), *Ezekiel*, and the *Twelve Minor Prophets* (published by Poznanski [1907–1913]). From citations in these commentaries, scholars believe that Eliʿezer probably also wrote commentaries on the Pentateuch, *Jeremiah, Psalms, Ecclesiastes*, and *Daniel*. Eliʿezer's commentaries are distinguished by clarity of style. He placed particular emphasis on the historical allusions in the prophetic books, and although he admired the work of his predecessors, he did not hesitate to disagree with them. Eliʿezer's commentaries provide a window into the broader cultural life of northern French Jews. He frequently provided glosses, in Old French, on Hebrew words (see LAʿAZ). He also knew Latin, and he cites the Vulgate in his commentaries in order to refute Christological interpretations of the prophetic literature. His commentaries focus on the themes of martyrdom and exile, in an effort to provide spiritual sustenance to Jews of his generation, who had endured the Crusades and other, less-violent, forms of Christian evangelization.

• Samuel Poznanski, *Perush ʿal Yeḥezqel u-Terei ʿAsar* (Warsaw, 1913), see introduction. —MICHAEL A. SIGNER

ELIʿEZER OF TOUQUES (died c.1290), rabbinic scholar and tosafist. He studied with R. Yitsḥaq ben Mosheh of Vienna and was the teacher of R. Ḥayyim Palti'el. He was considered by his contemporaries to be on a par with R. Me'ir ben Barukh of Rothenburg, the leading German scholar of the late thirteenth century.

Rabbi Eliʿezer was one of the last editors of *tosafot*. His *tosafot* were based primarily on earlier ones by R. Shimshon ben Avraham of Sens and R. Yehudah ben Yitsḥaq. The disciples of R. Me'ir of Rothenburg used R. Eliʿezer's *tosafot* extensively, which hastened their acceptance. The printed *tosafot* to the tractates of *Shabbat, Pesaḥim, Ketubbot, Gittin, Bava' Qamma', Bava' Metsiʿa', Bava' Batra', Shevuʿot*, and *Ḥullin* were edited by R. Eliʿezer, making him the most important editor of the standard *tosafot* texts. It is unclear whether R. Eliʿezer hailed from the village of Touques (in Normandy) or whether he arrived there from Germany, where several members of his family lived.

• Efraim E. Urbach, *Baʿalei ha-Tosafot* (Jerusalem, 1980), vol. 2, pp. 581–585 and index. —EPHRAIM KANARFOGEL

ELIJAH (Heb. Eliyyahu; 9th cent. BCE), prophet in the northern kingdom of Israel who appears in the narratives of *1 Kings* (18–19; 21) and *2 Kings* (1–2) during the reigns of kings Ahab, Ahaziah, and Jehoram. It is generally believed that Elijah came from Gilead in Transjordan, based on his identification as the "Tishbite" in biblical tradition. The Hebrew text in *1 Kings* 17.1 refers to him as a "sojourner in Gilead," but it does not identify Tishbe as a place name. The Septuagint, on the other hand, refers to "Tishbe in Gilead" in *1 Kings* 17.1. Elijah is portrayed as a miracle worker who feeds the widow of Zarephath and restores life to her dead son as a means to legitimate his prophetic calling. His Transjordanian origins could account for his opposition to the religious and political policies of the Omride monarch Ahab and his Tyrian-born wife Jezebel, who promoted the worship of the god Melqart. Elijah fought the Arameans' efforts to bring the country into a closer relationship with the Phoenicians. Elijah called for the exclusive worship of God. Together with his successor, *Elisha, he helped to bring about the overthrow of the Omride dynasty. Elijah is best known for his contest on Mount Carmel against the four hundred fifty prophets of Baal (see BAAL WORSHIP) and the four hundred prophets of *Asherah (*1 Kings* 18). Both Elijah and the pagan prophets prepared altars and called upon their respective deities to light the sacrificial fires in order to demonstrate their divine powers. Although the prophets of Baal spent half a day in pleading, frenzied dancing, and self-immolation, they received no response. After pouring water over his altar, Elijah called upon God, who sent a fire that consumed the entire altar. When Jezebel sought to kill Elijah for executing the prophets of Baal, Elijah fled to Mount Horeb (Mount *Sinai) where he lodged in a cave (*1 Kgs*. 19). Like Moses in *Exodus* 33, Elijah experienced a divine revelation, which included wind, earthquake, and fire. God did not appear to Elijah in any of these phenomena but only in the form of a "still small voice" (*1 Kgs*. 19.12); he commanded him to anoint Hazael as king of Aram and Jehu as the new king of Israel (tasks eventually fulfilled by Elisha), and to appoint Elisha as his prophetic successor, in order to prepare for the overthrow of the Omride dynasty. Elijah is also known for his condemnation of Ahab for his role in the murder of Naboth the Jezreelite (*1 Kgs*. 21). When Ahab was frustrated in his attempts to buy Naboth's vineyard, Jezebel had Naboth executed on trumped-up charges of treason so that Ahab could then take possession of the vineyard without cost. Like Moses, Elijah's death was not witnessed by human beings. Instead, he was carried off by a chariot and horses of fire to heaven in a whirlwind before the eyes of his successor Elisha (*2 Kgs*. 2). Some thought Jesus to be Elijah (e.g., *Mt*. 16.14; *Mk*. 6.15), but Jesus denied this and attributed the role to John the Baptist (e.g., *Mt*. 11.14; *Mk*. 9.17ff.).

The prophecy in *Malachi* 3.23, in which Elijah appears as the precursor of the *Messiah who will "turn the hearts of the fathers to the children and the hearts of the children unto their fathers," combined with the fact that he did not die, succeeded in producing the image of the ever present prophet, wandering incognito over the earth, sometimes in the garb of a nomad, to aid in moments of distress and danger, appearing to scholars and mystics to teach them hidden truths, and acting as a celestial messenger. In folklore Elijah also appears in synagogues as a tenth man to make up the prayer quorum (*minyan*). The word *teiqu* in the Talmud is considered (popularly, but doubtfully) an acronym for the sentence meaning that the answer will eventually be given by Elijah. From the belief that he taught Talmudic sages emerged the **Seder Eliyyahu*, supposedly communicated to R. ʿAnan, the basis of the Midrashic compilation known as *Tanna' de-Vei Eliyyahu*. Identified with the "angel of the covenant" in *Malachi* 3.1, where the word for covenant, *berit*, suggested the *berit milah*, the *circumcision, Elijah came especially to be associated with the circumcision ceremony and was thought to be present at every such occasion as guardian and witness (see ELIJAH, CHAIR OF). He is also associated with the Pesaḥ *Seder: the custom of a fifth cup of wine, known as the "cup of Elijah," has given rise to the popular belief in his invisible presence. (In fact, there was a dispute in the Talmud about whether to drink four or five cups at the Seder, and the fifth cup is placed there *teiqu*—to await Elijah's decision.) In hopes of his arrival, the front door is opened in the course of the evening to welcome him. The prominence of Elijah in the *Havdalah liturgy ushering out the Sabbath (including the popular hymn Eliyyahu ha-Navi') is also connected with his traditional role as harbinger of the Messiah.

• John Gray, *I and II Kings*, 3d ed., fully rev., The Old Testament Library (London, 1977, 1985 printing). Alan J. Hauser and Russell Gregory, *From Carmel to Horeb: Elijah in Crisis*, Journal for the Study of the Old Testament, Supplement Series, no. 85; Bible and Literature Series, no. 19 (Sheffield, Eng., 1990). Burke O. Long, *1 Kings*, The Forms of the Old Testament Literature, vol. 9 (Grand Rapids, 1984). Burke O. Long, *2 Kings*, The Forms of the Old Testament Literature, vol. 10 (Grand Rapids, 1991). Eliezer Margoliyot, *Eliyyahu ha-Navi' be-Sifrut Yisra'el* (Jerusalem, 1960). Alexander Rofé, *The Prophetical Stories* (Jerusalem, 1988). Aharon Wiener, *The Prophet Elijah in the Development of Judaism* (Boston, 1978).

—MARVIN A. SWEENEY

ELIJAH, BOOKS OF. Two different works are known as the *Apocalypse of Elijah*. In spite of their many differences, the two works share some traits and may both have been based on an earlier Jewish text(s). Moreover, there are other Elijah traditions in Jewish and in Christian literature, some of which may ultimately have derived from the same postulated text(s).

The Coptic *Apocalypse of Elijah* is a Christian work, originally written in Greek but extant only in a Coptic translation. It was composed in Egypt in the second half of the third century CE. It is a composite work, which includes an exhortation to prayer and fasting, a brief overview of historical events, and a description of the last days, the coming of the Antichrist, and the cosmic upheavals that will precede the final judgment.

The Hebrew *Apocalypse of Elijah* is a Jewish work, written in Hebrew and generally dated in the geonic period (6th–10th cent.). It purports to record the revelations made to Elijah on Mount Carmel by the archangel Michael and contains descriptions of Elijah's heavenly journey and of future events, such as the advent of the Antichrist, the eschatological upheavals, and the salvation of the righteous.

• George Wesley Buchanan, *Revelation and Redemption: Jewish Documents of Deliverance from the Fall of Jerusalem to the Death of Naḥmanides* (Dillsboro, Ind., 1978), pp. 426–441. David Frankfurter, *Elijah in Upper Egypt: The Apocalypse of Elijah and Early Egyptian Christianity* (Minneapolis, 1993). Michael E. Stone and John Strugnell, coll. and trans., *The Books of Elijah, Parts 1–2*, Texts and Translations, no. 18; Pseudepigrapha, no. 8 (Missoula, Mont., 1979). Orval S. Wintermute, "Apocalypse of Elijah," in *The Old Testament Pseudepigrapha*, edited by James H. Charlesworth, vol. 1 (Garden City, N.Y., 1983), pp. 721–753.

—GIDEON BOHAK

ELIJAH, CHAIR OF (Heb. *kise' shel Eliyyahu*), a special chair placed for *Elijah the prophet at every *circumcision ceremony. When the baby boy is brought into the room for the circumcision, he is, in some customs, first placed on Elijah's chair as the **mohel* says "This is the chair of Elijah the prophet, of blessed memory"; in other customs (such as the Moroccan) the **sandaq* sits in the chair during the ceremony. One reason given for the symbolic presence of Elijah at the circumcision ceremony (Zohar on *Gn.* 93a) is that Elijah, the personification of uncompromising zeal, complained to God that the children of Israel had "forsaken your covenant" (*1 Kgs.* 19.10). God therefore decreed that he should be present at every circumcision in order to testify that the people are in fact faithful to the covenant (Zohar on *Gn.* 17.10; *Pirqei de-Rabbi Eliʿezer*, end of 29; *Shulḥan ʿArukh, Yoreh Deʿah* 265.11). Based on *Malachi* 3.1, Elijah is mentioned in rabbinic sources as "the angel of the covenant" (and circumcision is the sign of the covenant). In Sephardi communities, Elijah's chair is a permanent item of the synagogue furniture. This may derive from the time when all circumcisions were held in the synagogue.

• Yosef David Weisberg, *Otzar Habrith: Encyclopedia of Brith Milah* (Jerusalem, 1985), pp. 126–129. —CHAIM PEARL

ELIJAH, CUP OF. See ELIJAH.

ELIMELEKH OF LYZHANSK (1717–1787), Hasidic master and author. A disciple of Dov Ber of Mezhirech, he became the most influential Hasidic leader in Galicia after his teacher's death in 1772. He was one of the first to develop a Hasidic court. As the **tsaddiq*, he was supported primarily by contributions that accompanied requests for his prayers. By nature, he was extremely ascetic. In his youth, he wandered around the pale of settlement with his brother *Zusya of Hanipoli, symbolically identifying with the exile of the *shekhinah*. His many disciples were instrumental in spreading and establishing Hasidism in Poland. Among them were Yaʿaqov Yitsḥaq, ha-Ḥozeh mi-Lublin; Menaḥem Mendel ben Yosef of Rymanów; and Avraham Yehoshuʿa Heschel. In his work *No'am Elimelekh* (edited by Gedalyah Nigal [Jerusalem, 1978]), he was one of the first to grapple with the paradoxes involved in the theory of the *tsaddiq*. The *tsaddiq* must be a figure who can combine the spiritual aspiration of being entirely immersed in God with a compassionate concern for the material well-being of his followers. Essential to the *tsaddiq*'s path were periodic falls. By deliberately descending, even through the commission of light transgressions, the *tsaddiq* could achieve even greater heights and uplift his community with him.

• Martin Buber, *Tales of the Hasidim* (New York, 1947). Louis Jacobs, *Jewish Mystical Testimonies* (New York, 1978), pp. 196–216. Rivka Schatz Uffenheimer, *Hasidism as Mysticism* (Princeton, 1993).

—MILES KRASSEN

ELISHA (9th cent. BCE), prophet in the northern kingdom of Israel; son of Shaphat from Abel-meholah, Gilead. Elisha prophesied during the reigns of Jehoram, Jehu, Jehoahaz, and Jehoash. Elisha was designated as the prophetic successor to *Elijah, who threw his mantle upon Elisha (*1 Kgs.* 19.19–21) while he was plowing his fields. The primary narratives concerning Elisha's career appear in *2 Kings* 2–13. Much more than is the case with Elijah, Elisha's prophetic status is legitimated by a series of legendary stories that portray him as a miracle worker and powerful "man of God." He parted the waters of the Jordan (*2 Kgs.* 2.14); called on a bear to kill the boys who taunted him for his baldness (2.19–25); filled a widow's jar with oil to save her from debt (4.1–7); brought the Shunammite woman's dead son back to life (4.8–37); cured the leprosy of Naaman, the general of the Aramean forces (5.1–19); brought leprosy upon Gehazi for his dishonesty (5.20–27); caused an iron ax head to float (6.1–7); and blinded an Aramean raiding party (6.8–23). Apparently, these stories were originally preserved among the "sons of the prophets," that is, the prophetic guild of which Elisha was the leader. His most important role was initiating the revolt of Jehu against the royal house of Omri, in which *Jezebel, the Phoenician-born wife of Ahab, was executed. Following the instructions of his late master, Elijah, Elisha anointed Hazael to take control of the Aramean throne and anointed Jehu as the next king of Israel, thereby paving the way for the overthrow of the Omride dynasty and the purge of Baal worship (*2 Kgs.* 8.7–15, 9.1–37).

• John Gray, *I and II Kings: A Commentary*, 2d ed. (London, 1970). Burke O. Long, *2 Kings*, The Forms of Old Testament Literature, vol. 10 (Grand Rapids, 1991). Rick D. Moore, *God Saves: Lessons from the Elisha Stories*, Journal for the Study of the Old Testament, Supplement Series 95 (Sheffield, Eng., 1990). Alexander Rofé, *The Prophetical Stories: The Narratives About the Prophets in the Hebrew Bible, Their Literary Types and History* (Jerusalem, 1988). —MARVIN A. SWEENEY

ELISHAʿ BEN AVUYAH (2d. cent.), tanna'; teacher of R. *Me'ir. His doctrines stress the virtue of ethical behavior, without which mere legal observance is valueless. Deeply affected by the failure of the Bar Kokhba' Revolt (which he might have opposed) and influenced by mysticism, he came to reject rabbinic Judaism (especially the theory of reward and punishment and the resurrection of the dead) and apparently accepted one of the then widespread branches of heretical gnostic thought. The Talmud (which, in view of his defection, never calls him by name, but refers to him as Aḥer [another]) mentions his absorption in sectarian literature and Hellenistic song (*Ḥag.* 15b); it also relates that he endeavored to influence students to abandon their Talmudic studies. The rabbis found it difficult to understand how such a great sage could have left the fold and suggested a variety of explanations, some of which serve to mitigate his personal responsibility for his actions (e.g., *Qid.* 39b). Rabbi Me'ir was the only one of his disciples who continued a personal relationship with him, begging him to repent even in his final hour. Me'ir continued to learn from him, and this was later explained in the following manner: R. Me'ir found a pomegranate; he ate its flesh, and threw away its peel (*Ḥag.* 15b).

• Gershom Gerhard Scholem, *Jewish Gnosticism, Merkabah Mysticism and Talmudic Tradition*, 2d. ed. (New York, 1965). Milton Steinberg, *As a Driven Leaf* (New York, 1939), a novel. —DANIEL SPERBER

ELI TSIYYON (אֱלִי צִיּוֹן; Lament, O Zion), alphabetical hymn of medieval origin describing the misery accompanying the destruction of the Second Temple. It is sung in Ashkenazi rites on Tishʿah be-'Av after the reading of *qinot* (dirges); the congregation stands for what is the climax of the service. The traditional melody, the origin of which is debated by musicologists, has influenced the chanting of other prayers recited during the three weeks of mourning (see BEIN HA-METSARIM) culminating in Tishʿah be-'Av.

• Adele Berlin, ed. and trans., *Biblical Poetry Through Medieval Jewish Eyes* (Bloomington, Ind., 1991).

ELIYYAHU BEN SHELOMOH ZALMAN OF VILNA (1720–1797), Lithuanian Talmudist, halakhist, kabbalist, and biblical commentator, popularly known as the Vilna Ga'on or Ha-Gra', an acronym for Ha-Ga'on Rabbenu Eliyyahu, whose erudition established him as one of Judaism's greatest post-medieval scholars. A precocious child and virtually self-taught, he reputedly knew the Torah at age three and a half, had delivered a learned discourse in the Vilna synagogue at six and a half, and had mastered Talmudic literature by age nine.

The Vilna Ga'on contributed to every aspect of traditional Jewish scholarship in over seventy works, including commentaries to scripture and the Mishnah, commentaries and glosses to the Talmuds Bavli and Yerushalmi as well as the *Shulḥan ʿArukh*, commentaries on tannaitic Midrashic works, as well as over thirty commentaries on kabbalistic texts. He was also the author of a Hebrew grammar book and composed treatises on astronomy, geometry, and geography, encouraging his disciples to master the sciences. However, he fiercely opposed the study of philosophy.

He applied sophisticated philological expertise in analyzing texts, subjecting them to both internal and external criticism, proposing emendations to establish correct readings, and determining proper understanding of the text unclouded by fanciful pilpulistic expositions. His commentary on the *Shulḥan ʿArukh* sought to clarify the nature of halakhic disputes and trace all legislation to its primary source, the Talmud. He advocated a disciplined progression in studies, recommending that students possess a thorough knowledge of the rules of grammar and familiarity with all of scripture before commencing the study of the oral law.

The Vilna Ga'on's ascetic lifestyle and passionate devotion to scholarship caused him to shun socializing. He slept only two hours out of each twenty-four-hour period. He occupied no public position and had no community responsibilities other than to study and teach a small circle of disciples.

The emergence of the Hasidic movement prompted him to enter the public sphere. He leveled several bans of excommunication against Ḥasidim between 1772 and 1796 for alleged halakhic and theological infractions. Perceiving Shabbatean influences in the new movement and disturbed by monastic and quasi-pantheistic elements in the writings of his Hasidic adversary, *Shneur Zalman of Lyady, the Vilna Ga'on apparently feared that Hasidism could dethrone Torah study from its preeminent position by extolling moralistic literature over Talmudic texts and religious ecstasy over sober study, and by revering the Hasidic **tsaddiq* for his charismatic powers rather than his Torah scholarship.

Although the Vilna Ga'on stood as the preeminent kabbalistic scholar of his era and, according to his disciples, received nightly revelations from heaven, his attitude toward such visions was characterized by reticence. He did not welcome "intrusions from heaven" but preferred the mental exertion of study and rational analysis in order to arrive at the truth.

He was a fiercely independent scholar who did not hesitate to dispute the authorities of earlier generations if he deemed their interpretations to be in error. His disciple Ḥayyim ben Yitsḥaq *Volozhiner testified, "I was warned by the Ga'on not to submit, even to the decisions of our rabbis, the authors of the *Shulḥan ʿArukh*, when it came to matters of halakhah" (*Ḥut ha-Meshullash* no. 9).

The Vilna Ga'on's major published works are *Commentary to the Pentateuch* (Dubrovno, 1804), *Commentary to Shulḥan ʿArukh* (1803–1885, found in standard editions of the *Shulḥan ʿArukh*), *Commentary to Mekhilta'* (1844), *Commentary to Sifra'* (1911), *Commentary to Sifrei* (1866), *Commentary to Sifra' de-Tseniʿuta'* (Vilna, 1820), *Commentary to Zohar* (Vilna, 1820), *Commentary to Proverbs* (Petaḥ Tikvah, 1985), and *Glosses to the Talmud* (found in standard editions of the Talmud).

• Elijah Meir Bloch, ed., *Ru'aḥ Eliyyahu* (Brooklyn, N.Y., 1954). Jacob Israel Dienstag, *Rabbenu Eliyyahu mi-Vilna: Reshimah Bibliografit* (New York, 1949). Louis Ginzberg, "The Gaon, Rabbi Elijah Wilna," in *Students, Scholars and Saints* (Philadelphia, 1928). Samuel Jakob Jazkan, *Rabbenu Eliyyahu mi-Vilna* (Warsaw, 1900), includes bibliography. Betsal'el Landoi, *Ha-Ga'on he- Ḥasid mi-Vilna* (Jerusalem, 1967); English version, *The Gaon of Vilna*, adapted by Yonason Rosenblum (Brooklyn, N.Y., 1994). Joshua Heschel Levin, *Sefer ʿAliyyot Eliyyahu* (Vilna, 1855; repr. Jerusalem, 1989). Yehudah Leib Maimon, *Toledot ha-Gra'* (Jerusalem, 1970). Elijah Schochet, *The Hasidic Movement and the Ga'on of Vilna* (Northvale, N.J., 1994). Mordecai Wilensky, *Ḥasidim u-Mitnaggedim*, 2 vols. (Jerusalem, 1970). —ELIJAH J. SCHOCHET

ELLEH EZKERAH (אֵלֶּה אֶזְכְּרָה; "These things I remember"), opening words of an elegy written as an alphabetic acrostic for the *Ten Martyrs that, in the Ashkenazi rite, is read during the repetition of the Musaf service on *Yom Kippur and, in the Sephardi and ʿAdot ha-Mizraḥ rites, on the fast of *Tishʿah be-'Av. Ostensibly a poetic version of the *Midrash Elleh Ezkerah*, describing Hadrian's campaign against the Jews in the second century CE, this dirge reflects the contemporary massacre of innocents during the First Crusade (1096–1099) and the poet's own attempt to justify bewildering calamities: "Hatred pursues us; through all the years / Ignorance like a monster has devoured our martyrs. . . ."

• Max Arzt, *Justice and Mercy: Commentary on the Liturgy of the New Year and the Day of Atonement* (New York, 1963), pp. 253–257. —GABRIEL A. SIVAN

ELLU DEVARIM SHE-'EIN LAHEM SHIʿUR (אֵלּוּ דְּבָרִים שֶׁאֵין לָהֶם שִׁעוּר; "These are the things without measure"), the opening words of a composite paragraph in the Morning Benedictions (Birkhot ha-Shaḥar) with which the daily liturgy begins; the passages cited are Mishnah *Pe'ah* 1.1 and *Shabbat* 127a. "Things without measure" refers to activities prescribed by the law. A minimum level of compliance with these things is sometimes fixed, but the maximum is to be determined by the generosity of the individual. Among these are the portion of the harvest left behind for the poor (*pe'ah*), according to *Leviticus* 23.22; the practice of benevolence, including personal service as well as charity for the needy; and the study of the Torah, which may be pursued both day and night, according to *Joshua* 1.8. Next are enumerated various activities that both promote the welfare of society and provide a reward in the future world for the one who does them. These include providing a dowry for a bride, visiting the sick, and burying the dead. A thoughtful reading of this passage is considered a partial fulfillment of the duty to study the law. Ellu Devarim she-'Ein Lahem Shi'ur is found in all traditional and modern prayer books.

• Israel Abrahams, *A Companion to the Authorized Daily Prayer Book* (New York, 1966), pp. 11–15. Philip Birnbaum, ed., *Daily Prayer Book* (New York, 1949), pp. 15f. —A. STANLEY DREYFUS

EL MALE' RAḤAMIM (אֵל מָלֵא רַחֲמִים; God, Full of Compassion), prayer for the repose of the souls of the dead (*hazkarat neshamot*). This prayer is recited when a person observing a **yortsayt* is called to the reading of the Torah to pray for the soul of the deceased relative. In many Orthodox synagogues, the mourner makes a donation to charity, and this is mentioned in the prayer. Its current form is late, probably dating from the time of the Chmielnicki pogroms (1648–1649), though the custom of praying for the repose of the dead dates back to earlier times. In many Ashkenazi communities, the prayer is also recited after a burial, on the thirtieth day after a death, at tombstone consecrations, and after the recitation of the *Yizkor prayer on the Shalosh Regalim and on Yom Kippur. It corresponds to the Sephardi *Ashkavah prayer. The text is shortened in Reform services. A special version has been composed for victims of the Holocaust. El Male' Raḥamim is usually chanted to a solemn melody.

• Ismar Elbogen, *Jewish Liturgy: A Comprehensive History* , translated by Raymond P. Scheindlin (Philadelphia, New York, and Jerusalem, 1993), p. 162. Eric L. Friedland, "The Atonement Memorial Service in the American Mahzor," *Hebrew Union College Annual* 55 (1984): 243–282. Macy Nulman, *The Encyclopedia of Jewish Prayer* (London, 1993), pp. 64–65. Eric Werner, "Traces of Jewish Hagiolatry," *Hebrew Union College Annual* 51 (1980): 39–60.

EL MELEKH NE'EMAN (אֵל מֶלֶךְ נֶאֱמָן; "God, faithful king"), a phrase interposed in the Babylonian and Ashkenazi rites (but not the Sephardi and Ḥabad) between the *Ahavah Rabbah benediction and the recitation of the *Shema'; its initial letters form the word **amen*. The phrase may have been introduced in order to preface the Shema' with the basic idea of divine kingship, which does not occur in the Shema' itself. Some authors explain that the words *El melekh ne'eman* are added to the Shema' based on the Midrashic view that there must be 248 words in it (*Tanḥuma' [Buber] Leviticus* 37b–38a with note 25), to correspond to the 248 parts that, according to the rabbis, made up the human body. It is recited only when the Shema' is said in private prayer. (In public prayer, the first three words of the third paragraph of the Shema' are repeated to bring the number of words up to 248.) The old Palestinian rite, instead of *El melekh ne'eman*, has benedictions proclaiming God's kingship and unity that are recited before performing a ritual commandment.

• Ismar Elbogen, *Jewish Liturgy: A Comprehensive History*, translated by Raymond P. Scheindlin (Philadelphia, 1993), p. 20. Joseph Heinemann, *Prayer in the Talmud* (Berlin, 1977), p. 161. —PETER LENHARDT

EL NORA' 'ALILAH (אֵל נוֹרָא עֲלִילָה; God, Whose Deeds Are Awesome), a *seliḥah* (see SELIḤOT) in the *Ne'ilah service for Yom Kippur, by Mosheh ibn Ezra. Each of the seven stanzas concludes with a reference to the "closing of the gates," an allusion to the practice of closing the portals of the Jerusalem Temple at nightfall. The poet prays that by that moment, which marks the end of Yom Kippur, the community's repentance may be complete and acceptable to God. This *seliḥah*, originally recited only in the Sephardi rite, has been incorporated into a number of Ashkenazi prayer books, and likewise into the Conservative, Reconstructionist, and Reform liturgies.

• Lawrence A. Hoffman, ed., *Gates of Understanding: Shaare Binah*, vol. 2, *Appreciating the Days of Awe*, with notes by Chaim Stern and A. Stanley Dreyfus (New York, 1984), pp. 152, 227. Abraham Z. Idelsohn, *Jewish Liturgy and Its Development* (New York, 1967), pp. 247, 294. —A. STANLEY DREYFUS

ELOHIM. See GOD, NAMES OF.

ELOHIST SOURCE (E), one of the originally separate documents from which the Torah was composed in the view of critical biblical scholarship. It was so-called because it refers to God as Elohim. See also BIBLE.

—BARUCH J. SCHWARTZ

ELUL (אֱלוּל), sixth month in the religious calendar; twelfth and last in the civil. It has twenty-nine days and its zodiac sign is Virgo. The name is Babylonian in origin and first occurs in *Nehemiah* 6.15. During Temple times, messengers would travel from Jerusalem to the Diaspora to announce the date of the new moon of Elul so that the following new moon, *Ro'sh ha-Shanah (the month of Tishrei), could be accurately determined. Elul is a month of repentance and preparation for Yom Kippur. In the Ashkenazi rite the *shofar is sounded throughout the month of Elul after the Shaḥarit service (except on Sabbaths and the eve of the New Year) in order to inspire a mood of penitence. Sephardi Jews call Elul the month of mercy and recite **seliḥot* nightly throughout the month; Ashkenazim start their recitation of *seliḥot* on the Saturday evening preceding the New Year (unless the New Year falls on Monday or Tuesday, in which case the recitation of *seliḥot* is commenced a week earlier).

• Nathan Bushwick, *Understanding the Jewish Calendar* (New York, 1989). Ellen Robbins, "Studies in the Prehistory of the Jewish Calendar," Ph.D. thesis, New York University, 1989. George Zinberg, *Jewish Calendar Mystery Dispelled* (New York, 1963). —CHAIM PEARL

EMANATION, the process by which entities (personal or impersonal) proceed directly from a higher to a lower entity. Unlike the act of *creation, which is defined as an act of will of a personal Creator, emanation is often conceived as an impersonal and almost natural process, like the emanation of rays from the sun. Doctrines of emanation generally suppose a higher degree of affinity, or even a substantial identity, between the various forms of being—they may be higher or lower, spiritual or material, but ultimately all derive from a single source—whereas the doctrine of creation implies an essential discontinuity between the Creator and all other beings. Doctrines of emanation are prominent in *gnosticism, *Neoplatonism, and various mystical systems. Since medieval philosophy was heavily influenced by both Neoplatonic and Aristotelian doctrines, different theories were held by different thinkers regarding the emanation of lower levels of being (e.g., the sublunar universe) from higher ones (e.g., the celestial spheres). These views, however, referred to the created universe, contradicting Greek philosophical, especially Neoplatonic, traditions. Religious Orthodoxy insisted that the universe as such was "created out of nothing" (see also COSMOLOGY). The chief works of Jewish mysticism, namely kabbalistic literature, combined gnostic and Neoplatonic elements, developing an esoteric doctrine of emanation (**atsilut*) as an inner-divine process describing the complex structure of the one deity—reminiscent in some ways of the Christian Trinity. The kabbalistic doctrine of emanation is concerned with the procession of the "divine worlds" rather than with the origin of the cosmos as a whole, and it describes the fullness of the manifest Godhead (**sefirot*) as it emerges from the hidden depths of *Ein Sof. The symbolic and speculative elucidation of the nature and character of this process is one of the main themes of theoretical kabbalistic literature (e.g., in the *Zohar and in the works of Mosheh ben Yaʿaqov *Cordovero). Whether emanation is restricted to the sphere of the divine or whether it also extends to the lower worlds is a matter of controversy among kabbalistic schools.

• David B. Burrell, "Creation or Emanation: Two Paradigms of Reason," in *God and Creation*, edited by D. Burrell and B. McGinn (Notre Dame, 1990), pp. 27–37. William Dunphy, "Maimonides' Not-So-Secret Position on Creation," in *Moses Maimonides and His Time*, edited by E. Ormsby (Washington, D.C., 1989), pp. 151–172. Elliot K. Ginsburg, "The Image of the Divine and Person in Zoharic Kabbalah," in *In Search of the Divine*, edited by Larry Shinn (New York, 1987), pp. 61–94. Lenn E. Goodman, ed., *Neoplatonism and Jewish Thought* (Albany, 1992).

EMANCIPATION. From late antiquity and throughout the Middle Ages until the American and French Revolutions at the end of the eighteenth century, Jews lived everywhere under special laws. To be sure, in medieval Europe the legal and political system identified everyone as a member of a specific group, caste, or profession, with laws applicable to each. Nonetheless, the Jews were different, because the very existence of their religion betokened their denial of the dominant religion, Christianity. They were limited by laws that forbade them the right to employment in most trades or the right to own land, and they could live only where they could buy or wangle special permission. Therefore, in the eighteenth century, when the demand for equality for all began to move toward the center of politics, Jews had a special, intense need to be released from their legal ghetto.

The source of the willingness at the beginning of the modern era by some in western Europe to grant the Jews equality was twofold. Some statesmen had begun to welcome Jews in the seventeenth century in the name of mercantilism; that is, because they wanted rich Jews who would bring advantage to the state. In the eighteenth century, the Enlightenment taught that man could be reformed through improved social conditions. It followed that Jews could be taken from the ghetto and refashioned to fit into the larger society through equality and education. These notions combined to create the first document in which Jews were given full equality, the Constitution of the United States, which was adopted in 1789. In the English colonies in North America, every hand and every artisan on the frontier was necessary, regardless of his religion. The authors of the Constitution were also, for the most part, men of the Enlightenment who believed in human perfectibility. Emancipation happened in the United States as a matter of course. In France, the "Jewish question" had been debated in books and pamphlets for several decades before the French Revolution because the Jewish community was so large, numbering some forty thousand members. The ten thousand, somewhat assimilated Sephardim (Jews who had crossed the Pyrenees to escape the Inquisition) were quickly granted equality by special decree in January 1790, but the debate about the thirty thousand, Yiddish-speaking, and totally unassimilated Jews who lived in eastern France continued to the very last day of the National Assembly. The new state simply could not refuse to grant Jews equality after it had already made hangmen, actors, and vagabonds into equal citizens. The persistent motif was that individual Jews would be given equality provided they were assimilated. Twenty years later, Napoléon even tried to get the Jews to agree that every third marriage would be to a non-Jew and that the central Jewish organization would be responsible for military recruitment and for the "good conduct" of the community (see ASSEMBLY OF JEWISH NOTABLES; CONSISTOIRE; SANHEDRIN, FRENCH). He failed to prevail, but the shadow of this pressure remained.

For the Jews themselves, Emancipation raised fundamental questions about how they were to conceive and organize their inner life. In Holland, where the revolutionary armies of France made possible the creation of the Batavian Republic in the 1790s, there was an open debate. Jewish conservatives preferred to forgo all the rights of citizenship because they wanted only broader economic rights and the preservation of their own self-governing Jewish community. The liberals, who wanted to become Batavian citizens of the Jewish faith, won the internal battle. In less overt terms, this battle was repeated in much of Europe. The old believers everywhere preferred a gentler version of their existing life, but the Jewish bourgeoisie and the increasingly Westernized intelligentsia invariably prevailed. The internal battle was, however, secondary to the rising tide of opinion in western and central Europe that discrimination was against the law of progress and that the modern state could not function if it continued to impose medieval laws of exclusion on the Jewish minority. Until the end of the Napoleonic empire, Jews were equal in law in every territory that his armies had conquered. When the French empire came to an end at the battle of Waterloo in 1815, Emancipation was reversed everywhere except in France itself.

However, during the nineteenth century, Emancipation was finally achieved throughout central and western Europe. Eastern Europe had to await the fall of the tsar in 1917 before Jews in Russia and the Russian empire (including Poland) were emancipated and received civil rights. In the Muslim world, European colonial powers spread Emancipation to some countries, but in more distant parts, such as Yemen, the Jews were only emancipated when they moved to the State of Israel, which itself represented a new achievement: the appearance of a Jewish nation among the nations of the world.

The struggle for Emancipation had been closely connected to the struggle for religious freedom and the separation between church and state. As long as Christianity was regarded as the state religion or the state as a Christian state, it followed that those who did not profess the faith were denied the privileges of full citizenship and civil rights. Thus, for example, the struggle for the admission of a Jew to the British Parliament centered on the abolition of the oath that every member had to take "on the true faith of a Christian." In many European countries, Judaism was recognized as an official faith to the extent that the government levied taxes on all professing Jews for the upkeep of Jewish religious and communal institutions. Already under Napoléon Emancipation involved relinquishment by the Jews of internal legal jurisdiction over their members; the role of the rabbi was restricted to religious matters.

Emancipation led to far-reaching changes in Jewish social and religious life. The Jews now had to face the challenge of living in two worlds. With the disappearance of external forces that had unified the community, secularization and *assimilation set in and many Jews converted to Christianity, more of them out of the desire to join the majority society than out of religious conviction. *Reform Judaism was founded on the one hand to provide an alternative for those Jews who found traditional Judaism incompatible with modernity and on the other in the conviction that Emancipation and liberalism heralded a messianic age. The Talmudic rule **dina' de-malkhuta' dina'* was comprehensively reinterpreted by the reformers, and laws maintaining Jewish exclusiveness were jettisoned. Even Orthodoxy was influenced by the Emancipation, and *Neo-Orthodoxy was based on the principle that strict Orthodoxy was compatible with complete social participation in the cultural and civic spheres of national life. With Emancipation and consequent acculturation the nature of *Jewish identity changed radically, and the comparatively monolithic Jewish historical identity now gave way to a variety of forms of identification. See JEW, WHO IS A?, CONTROVERSY; PLURALISM, RELIGIOUS.

• Shmuel Ettinger, "The Modern Period," in *A History of the Jewish People*, edited by Haim H. Ben-Sasson (Cambridge, Mass., 1976) pp. 727–1096. Arthur Hertzberg, *The French Enlightenment and the Jews* (New York, 1968). Jacob Katz, *Out of the Ghetto: The Social Background of Jewish Emancipation* (Cambridge, Mass., 1973). Michael A. Meyer, *The Origins of the Modern Jew: Jewish Idenity and European Culture in Germany, 1749–1824* (Detroit, 1967). —ARTHUR HERTZBERG

EMDEN, YA'AQOV (1697–1776), rabbinic scholar and authority; known as Yavets, an acronym of Ya'aqov ben Tsevi. Born in Altona, where he lived most of his life, Emden was greatly influenced by the Torah studies and anti-Shabbatean polemical activities of his father Tsevi Hirsch *Ashkenazi. Emden was a preeminent scholar who produced an extensive literary *oeuvre* covering virtually all aspects of Jewish intellectual creativity including commentaries on the Bible (lost), the Mishnah (including a separate volume on *Avot*), the Talmud (in manuscript), the *siddur*, and the *Shulḥan 'Arukh*; almost four hundred *responsa*; a major ethical tract; a book on grammar; several sermons; and an autobiography called *Megillat Sefer* (1896). He played a major role in the eighteenth-century battle against Shabbateanism. In the last two and a half decades of his life, he became obsessed with exposing any vestiges of that generally subterranean movement, motivated perhaps in part by the presence of Shabbateanism within his own immediate family. In 1751 he accused R. Yonatan *Eybeschuetz, recently elected chief rabbi of the neighboring communities of Hamburg, Altona, and Wandsbek and one of the leading rabbinic figures of his generation, of being a clandestine follower of *Shabbetai Tsevi. This extremely serious charge, effectively one of heresy, gave rise to an intense, bitter, and repercussive controversy. Local secular authorities and the Danish monarch were drawn by both sides into the conflict, as were leading rabbis from across the Jewish world. Emden also called into question the antiquity and sanctity of the *Zohar, and in his polemics, he was also contemptuous of Maimonides' *Guide of the Perplexed*. Emden lived long enough to witness the emergence of the *Haskalah. Unlike some of his more traditional colleagues, he shared some of the openness to secular culture found in that movement headed by his acquaintance Moses *Mendelssohn. At the same time, Emden rejected its fundamental assumptions and vehemently opposed its effect on his contemporaries. Though he held no office, he was able to disseminate his writings widely using his personal printing press.

• Yehudah Liebes, "Meshiḥiyyuto shel R. Ya'aqov Emden ve-Yaḥaso le-Shabbeta'ut," *Tarbiz* 49 (1979–1980): 122–165. Moshe Perlmutter, *R. Yehonatan Eybeschutz ve-Yaḥaso el ha-Shabbeta'ut* (Jerusalem, 1947). Jacob J. Schacter, "Rabbi Jacob Emden: Life and Major Works," Ph.D. dissertation, Harvard University, 1988. Azriel Schochat, *'Im Ḥilufei Tequfot* (Jerusalem, 1960). Avraham H. Wagenaar, *Toledot Yavets* (Amsterdam, 1868; repr. Lublin, 1880). —JACOB J. SCHACTER

EMET VE-'EMUNAH AND EMET VE-YATSIV (אֱמֶת וֶאֱמוּנָה; אֱמֶת וְיַצִּיב; True and Trustworthy; True and Firm), openings of the *Ge'ullah blessing to be said after reciting the three paragraphs of the *Shema' in the evening and morning service respectively. The Talmud Bavli states that whoever does not recite Emet ve-Yatsiv in the morning and Emet ve-'Emunah in the evening has not fulfilled his obligations (*Ber.* 12a). The evening formulation differs from the morning one in accord with the biblical phrase "to proclaim . . . your faithfulness each night" (*Ps.* 92.2). The prayer professes the eternal truth of divine revelation and faith in the unity of God.

• Ismar Elbogen, *Jewish Liturgy:A Comprehensive History*, translated by Raymond P. Scheindlin (Philadelphia, 1993), pp. 21–22, 86–87.
–PETER LENHARDT

EMISSARY. See SHALIAḤ.

EMUNAH. See FAITH.

END OF DAYS. See ESCHATOLOGY.

ENGAGEMENT. See BETROTHAL.

ENLIGHTENMENT. See HASKALAH.

ENOCH (Heb. Ḥanokh), the name of two biblical figures. The earlier Enoch (for whom the first city was named; *Gn.* 4.17–18) was the eldest son of Cain and father of Irad.

The next known Enoch was the son of Jared and father of Methuselah. Enoch lived "three hundred sixty and five years, and . . . he walked with God and he was not, for God took him" (*Gn.* 5.21–24). This enigmatic statement describing his death was interpreted in later literature as symbolizing his miraculous ascension alive to heaven, where he enjoyed a close relationship with God (*Gn.* 5.18–19, 21–24). See also ENOCH, BOOKS OF.

• Umberto Cassuto, *A Commentary on the Book of Genesis*, pt.1, *From Adam to Noah*, Publications of the Perry Foundation for Biblical Research in the Hebrew University of Jerusalem (Jerusalem, 1988), pp. 282–286. Claus Westermann, *Genesis 1–11*, translated by John H. Scullion (Minneapolis, 1984), pp. 357–359. –SHALOM PAUL

ENOCH, BOOKS OF, literary works supposed to have been written by, or at the time of, *Enoch, Son of Jared, who—though of minor significance in the Bible—seems to have captured the imagination of the Bible's early readers. Enoch is reported to have "walked with God" and to have been "taken" by God (*Gn.* 5.24). The latter phrase was the starting point of many Second Temple period traditions concerning Enoch's heavenly journey.

The *First Book of Enoch* is preserved in its entirety only in Ethiopic, but Greek and Latin fragments are also extant, and numerous fragments of the original Aramaic text(s) were found among the *Dead Sea Scrolls. It is a composite work made up of several different sections, whose dates of composition range from the third century BCE to the first century CE. Parts of *1 Enoch* recount events in Enoch's life, including his involvement in the account of the fallen angels who were expelled from heaven, a story based in part on *Genesis* 6.1–4. Other sections of *1 Enoch* contain apocalyptic revelations, in some of which Enoch is taken on heavenly and earthly journeys and is taught the secrets of the universe, and in others of which he sees symbolic scenarios depicting the history of the world, and especially of the Jewish people, from the Creation to the final judgment. One of these historically minded apocalypses, the so-called "Animal Apocalypse," clearly was written in the wake of the Hasmonean revolt (see HASMONEANS) and is therefore contemporaneous with the *Book of *Daniel*. Several sections of *1 Enoch* have exerted a considerable influence not only on some of its (chronologically) later sections, but also on such works as the *Book of *Jubilees* and on some of the texts found among the *Dead Sea Scrolls. The popularity of this Enochic corpus is also attested by its mention in the *New Testament (*Letter of Jude* 14).

The *Second Book of Enoch* is a composite work, preserved only in two different Slavonic versions, clearly derived from a Greek version, which may in turn have been a translation from a Hebrew or Aramaic original. The date and place of composition are difficult to determine, and while an Egyptian Jew living in the first century BCE or CE would be a likely author, a later Christian author cannot be ruled out. In the first part of the book, Enoch describes the heavenly tour on which he was taken, and during which he learned the secrets of the universe, and exhorts his children to behave righteously and to observe various moral and halakhic precepts. This section ends with Enoch's translation to heaven. The second part of the work describes events following Enoch's death, including Methuselah's service as a priest, the miraculous birth of Melchizedek, and the Flood.

The *Third Book of Enoch* is a composite Hebrew work extant in several different recensions and probably compiled in the sixth or seventh century CE in Erets Yisra'el or in Babylonia. It describes the ascent of R. *Yishma'e'l ben Elisha' to heaven and his encounter with the archangel Metatron, who recounts how he was originally called Enoch and was taken into heaven where he was transformed into an angel. Enoch–Metatron takes R. Yishma'e'l around heaven and reveals to him the secrets of the universe and of the angelic world. In its style and subject matter, *3 Enoch* clearly belongs with the so-called *Heikhalot literature, with its many descriptions of God's heavenly court and the hierarchies of the angelic world and their daily liturgies and with its pseudonymous ascription of such traditions to important tannaitic figures such as R. Yishma'e'l.

• Philip S. Alexander, "3 (Hebrew Apocalypse of) Enoch," Francis I. Andersen, "2 (Slavonic Apocalypse of) Enoch," and Ephraim Isaac, "1 (Ethiopic Apocalypse of) Enoch," in *The Old Testament Pseudpigrapha*, edited by James H. Charlesworth, vol. 1 (Garden City, N.Y., 1983), pp. 223–315, 91–221, 5–89. Matthew Black, *The Books of Enoch or 1 Enoch: A New English Edition with Commentary and Textual Notes*, Studia in Veteris Testamenti Pseudepigrapha 7 (Leiden, 1985). Ithamar Gruenwald, *Apocalyptic and Merkavah Mysticism*, Arbeiten zur Geschichte des antiken Judentums und des Urchristentums, Bd. 14 (Leiden, 1980). David J. Halperin, *The Faces of the Chariot*, Texte und Studien zum Antiken Judentum 16 (Tübingen, 1988). Martha Himmelfarb, *Ascent to Heaven in Jewish and Christian Apocalypses* (New York and Oxford, 1993). George W. E. Nickelsburg, *Jewish Literature between the Bible and the Mishnah* (Philadelphia, 1981). Patrick A. Tiller, *A Commentary on the Animal Apocalypse of I Enoch*, Early Judaism and Its Literature, no. 4 (Atlanta, 1993). James C. VanderKam, *Enoch and the Growth of an Apocalyptic Tradition*, Catholic Biblical Quarterly, Monograph Series 16 (Washington, D.C., 1984). –GIDEON BOHAK

EPHOD, in the Torah, one of the ceremonial *priestly vestments, namely, the elaborate, apronlike outer garment described in *Exodus* 28.6–12 and 39.2–7 to be worn by Aaron, the high priest. Its two shoulder straps bore two lapis lazuli stones encased in golden frames; upon each stone were engraved the names of six of the tribes of Israel. Thus, the high priest symbolically represented the entire Israelite people when ministering "before the Lord" (*Ex.* 28.12). Two more golden frames, each with a golden chain descending from it, were attached to the shoulder straps; on these, the breastpiece containing the Urim and Thummim (see ORACLES) was suspended. The high priest's robe, worn together with the ephod, is also referred to as "the robe of the ephod" (*Ex.* 28.31, 29.5).

In the remaining books of the Bible, the term *ephod* refers to some unspecified religious article. Sometimes it appears to be a garment, such as the linen ephod worn by Samuel (*1 Sm.* 2.18) and by David (*2 Sm.* 6.14), which was not like the costly and intricate ephod of the high priest. Elsewhere, it is certainly not a vestment at all but an object of worship (*Jgs.* 8.27, 17.5, 18.14, 18.17) or an article for divination (*1 Sm.* 23.9, 30.7; *Hos.* 3.4). Although the exact meaning of the word *ephod* is unknown, it has Akkadian, Ugaritic, and Syrian cognates.

• Paul Carus, *The Oracle of Yahveh: Urim and Thummim, the Ephod, the Breastplate of Judgement* (Chicago, 1911). Julian Morgenstern, *The Ark, the Ephod, and the "Tent of Meeting"* (Cincinnati, 1945). Tsevi Natanzon, *Ḥoshen ve-Efod* (Bene Beraq, 1992). —BARUCH J. SCHWARTZ

EPHRAIM (Heb. Efrayim), Joseph's second son, born in Egypt; his mother was Asenath, daughter of Potipherah, priest of On (*Gn.* 41.50–52, 46.20). Before his death, *Jacob counted his grandsons Ephraim and Manasseh as his own heirs, which later led to their status as independent tribes, and blessed them both with fertility. He also placed his right hand on the head of the younger son, Ephraim, thereby granting him priority over his older brother, Manasseh (*Gn.* 48). Moses, too, in his blessings to the tribes before his death, blessed both Ephraim and Manasseh with fertility and recognized Ephraim's priority over Manasseh (*Dt.* 33.13–17). Ephraim's dominance over Manasseh in these blessings probably reflects the historical reality of early Manassehite numerical, political, or cultic superiority, which was later superseded by the Ephraimite tribe.

After the conquest of Canaan, the tribe of Ephraim received territory in the hills of Samaria. It was the tribe of *Joshua and the site of Shiloh, the sanctuary where the Ark of the Covenant was kept. It also took the lead in splitting the kingdom after the death of Solomon. Jeroboam of the tribe of Ephraim was the first king of the northern kingdom, which was sometimes known as Ephraim (cf. *Is.* 7.17).

• Nahum M. Sarna, *Genesis*, The JPS Torah Commentary (Philadelphia, 1989), pp. 289, 315, 324–330. —SIMEON B. CHAVEL

EPITAPH. See TOMBS.

EPSTEIN, JACOB NAHUM (1878–1952), scholar of Talmud and rabbinics. Born in Brest Litovsk, Poland, he received traditional religious training in eastern Europe before moving on to university study in Vienna and Bern. After earning his doctorate in Bern in 1912, Epstein published extensively in German over the next decade in the fields of geonic and Talmudic philology. In 1915 Epstein also began work on a monumental project: the production of a critical edition of the Mishnah. In 1923 Epstein began to teach at the Hochschule für die Wissenschaft des Judentums in Berlin. Two years later he was appointed to a professorship in Talmudic philology at the fledgling Institute of Jewish Studies of the Hebrew University of Jerusalem. In his opening lecture in Jerusalem, Epstein reiterated the need for a critical edition of the Mishnah. Though he never completed this task, he did publish a major two-volume work, *Mavo' le-Nusaḥ ha-Mishnah* (Jerusalem, 1948), which identified and cataloged discrete strands of the Mishnah. Two other preparatory works of his on the Mishnah were published posthumously, *Mevo'ot le-Sifrut ha-Tanna'im* (1957) and *Mevo'ot le-Sifrut ha-'Amora'im* (1962).

• Baruch M. Bosker, "Jacob N. Epstein's *Introduction to the Text of the Mishnah*," and "Jacob N. Epstein on the Formation of the Mishnah," in *The Modern Study of the Mishnah*, edited by Jacob Neusner, Studia Post-Biblica, vol. 23 (Leiden, 1973), pp. 13–26, 37–55. Moshe Schwabe et al., *Le-Zikhro shel Prof. Ya'aqov Naḥum Epshtain* (Jerusalem, 1952). —DAVID N. MYERS

EPSTEIN, YEḤI'EL MIKHAL (1829–1908), rabbi and halakhic authority. He was born in Bobruisk, Belorussia, and studied in Volozhin under R. Yitsḥaq of Volozhin. In 1874 he was appointed rabbi of Novogrudok, Belorussia, where he remained until his death. Epstein's fame rests with his *'Arukh ha-Shulḥan* (1884–1907), a comprehensive code of Jewish law that utilizes the framework of the *Shulḥan 'Arukh*. In his introduction, Epstein wrote that many difficult legal issues had arisen in the three hundred years since the publication of the *Shulḥan 'Arukh*, and, therefore, "anxiety and confusion have reappeared, particularly in this lowly generation in which there are few students of Torah." Epstein, therefore, undertook to compose a work that would summarize and amplify the opinions of the *Shulḥan 'Arukh* and present and decide among the various opinions advanced since its publication. Epstein also codified material relating to the Temple period and Erets Yisra'el in his *'Arukh ha-Shulḥan he-'Atid* (published posthumously from 1938 to 1969).

• Menachem Elon, *Jewish Law: History, Sources, Principles*, (Philadelphia, 1994), vol. 3, pp. 1448–1450. Barukh ha-Levi Epstein, *Meqor Barukh*, 4 vols. (Vilna, 1928), vol. 3, pp. 1163–1173. —ADAM MINTZ

EQUITY, the principle that governs the application of law to specific cases and ensures that fair results are reached. Its primary application is in civil rather than ritual law. Among the most significant principles used by Jewish law to encourage fairness is the concept of *lifenim mi-shurat ha-din*, "beyond the letter of the law," which allows a *beit din* to encourage, and in some cases compel, activity that is not normally considered legally obligatory in the name of equity. Other principles used to advance fairness include the *taqqanah*, *ḥerem beit din*, *minhag*, and *dinei shamayim*.

• Aaron Kirschenbaum, *Equity in Jewish Law: Halakhic Perspectives in Law: Formalism and Flexibility in Jewish Civil Law* (New York, 1992). Aaron Kirschenbaum, *Equity in Jewish Law: Beyond Equity: Halakhic Aspirationism in Jewish Civil Law* (New York, 1992). —MICHAEL BROYDE

ERETS YISRA'EL, (אֶרֶץ יִשְׂרָאֵל; Land of Israel), traditional name, since rabbinic times, of the land promised by God to Abraham and his descendants (hence, it was also called the Promised Land) and referred to as such in *Ezekiel* 40.2 and 47.18. The land was never occupied to the full extent of the frontiers indicated in the patriarchal covenant (*Gn*. 15.18–21). Other boundaries are described in *Numbers* 34.12 and in various biblical and Talmudic sources. The land was to be dedicated to the worship of God as its ultimate owner (*Lv*. 25.23) and was considered a divine gift, an expression of God's love for his people to be held by them as a sacred trust. It would cast them out if they followed the idolatrous and immoral practices of the peoples who had previously occupied it (*Lv*. 18.24–29). Israel's acknowledgment of this relationship was expressed through such rites as the bringing of the *first fruits (*Dt*. 26.1–11), the institutions of the **shemittah* and **yovel*, and classified in Talmudic literature as "commandments dependent on the Land" (*Qid*. 1.9), to be observed only in Erets Yisra'el, as opposed to the "commandments of the person" (*Sifrei* on *Dt*. 12.1), such as the Sabbath, dietary laws, and ethical precepts, which were applicable everywhere. Talmudic law, probably to maintain the economic viability of Jewish agriculture in the face of ruinous taxation imposed by the Roman authorities, restricted the application of the *agrarian laws to those areas that had been settled by the exiles who returned to Zion during the Second Temple period. The rabbis (*Ḥag*. 3b; *Yev*. 82b) reasoned that the "first sanctity" deriving from the biblical conquest had automatically lapsed with the destruction of the Temple and the exile. The "second sanctity," however, was viewed as permanent, since it stemmed not from conquest but from legal possession exercised under the mandate granted by Cyrus (*2 Chr*. 36.22–23). It excluded such areas as Beth-shean in the Jordan Valley and the Gaza region. The agrarian laws have only rabbinic authority since their biblical validity depended on the majority of the Jewish people residing in the land (*Ket*. 25a). These rabbinic rulings enabled Jewish farmers to work their fields during the sabbatical year, a precedent followed in modern Israel by those who strictly observe the agrarian laws. In contrast, Erets Yisra'el within its biblical boundaries possessed an intrinsic sanctity (*Jl*. 4.2; cf. *Kel*. 1.2) that made it a preferred place of residence for the living and of burial for the dead and the exclusive locale for prophesy. The religious supremacy of Erets Yisra'el scholars and congregations, irrespective of their erudition or numbers, was to be recognized by Jews everywhere (*Hor*. 51a). The insistence of the Talmud on the sanctity of the land was prompted by a desire to promote settlement and discourage emigration. A title deed to land purchased in Erets Yisra'el may, therefore, be written even on the Sabbath (by a non-Jew, *B. Q*. 80b), and spouses may be compelled to follow their partners to reside in Erets Yisra'el. Refusal to do so was a reason for divorce and forfeiture of the marriage settlement (*Ket*. 110a). The enforced *exile from Erets Yisra'el after 70 CE was regarded as the greatest calamity to befall the people, and numerous expressions of mourning were introduced into the liturgy and religious practice to express longing for the land. In the twelfth and thirteenth centuries, persecution and growing insecurity in western Europe prompted a wave of immigration to Erets Yisra'el led by prominent rabbis. However, other authorities maintained that in view of the dangers of travel and the difficulties involved in fulfilling the agrarian commandments the religious duty to reside in Erets Yisra'el no longer applied. Nevertheless, religious authorities have generally adopted a highly positive attitude toward resettling Erets Yisra'el or, failing that, toward visiting it on *pilgrimage. Nahmanides regarded the duty to dwell in Erets Yisra'el as a positive biblical commandment applicable for all time. Those buried in the Diaspora would try to have a bag of soil from Erets Yisra'el put in their grave. Classical *Reform Judaism, which regarded Judaism purely as a monotheistic, ethical religion with no national or territorial ingredient, accepted Diaspora existence as normative and deleted from its prayer books all references to a return to Erets Yisra'el. Contemporary Reform has reintroduced these formulas. The traditional and Conservative prayer books have always been centered around Erets Yisra'el, for example, the prayers for rain and dew (see TEFILLAT GESHEM; TEFILLAT TAL) are said in conjunction with the appropriate season in Erets Yisra'el. What may be regarded as a theology of the Holy Land was developed in the medieval period by *Yehudah ha-Levi, as well as by kabbalists and mystics, and in recent times, particularly, by R. Avraham Yitsḥaq ha-Kohen Kook (see KOOK FAMILY), whose disciples inspired *Religious Zionism, which has promoted the resettlement of Erets Yisra'el within its biblical boundaries. See also ZIONISM.

• Meir Bar-Ilan and Shelomoh Y. Zevin, eds., *Otsar Erets Yisra'el*, new ed. (Jerusalem, 1987). Martin Buber, *Bein 'Am le-'Artso* (Jerusalem, 1944). Yehezkel Kaufmann, *The Religion of Israel*, translated and abridged by Moshe Greenberg (New York, 1972). Zev Vilnay, *Ari'el: Entsiqlopedyah li-Yedi'at Erets Yisra'el* (Tel Aviv, 1984). Zvi Yaron, *The Philosophy of Rabbi Kook*, English version by Avner Tomaschoff (Jerusalem, 1991), pp. 208ff. on Erets Yisra'el. Yosef Zahavi, *Erets Israel in Rabbinic Lore*, translated by Aryeh Newman (Jerusalem, 1962).

—ARYEH NEWMAN

'EREV (עֶרֶב; eve), in popular usage, the day preceding the commencement of a holy day (so that *'erev Shabbat* is a Friday and *'erev yom tov* is the day before a festival). It is the eve inasmuch as the day in the Jewish *calendar commences with sunset. The period of holiness is inaugurated some time before sunset, and in Temple times (as in the State of Israel today) the shofar was sounded as a signal to cease work. The rabbis also advised people to eat abstemiously on the eves of Sabbaths and festivals so as to derive the maximum enjoyment from the evening meal. The Taḥanun prayer is omitted from the afternoon service on the eves of Sabbaths and festivals. On the eve of Ro'sh ha-Shanah, *seliḥot* are recited (including a special one for this occasion—*Zekhor Berit). The eve of Yom Kippur is a time for eating and also for asking forgiveness from others who may have been offended during the past year. The eve of Pesaḥ is *Ta'anit

Bekhorim; the eve of Ro'sh Ḥodesh is observed by some as a fast called *Yom Kippur Qatan.

• Robert Gordis, "An Unrecognized Biblical Use of *Ereb*," *Journal of Biblical Literature* 102 (1983): 107–108. —CHAIM PEARL

ERUSIN. See BETROTHAL; MARRIAGE.

ʿERUV (עֵרוּב; blending), the general term for three types of rabbinic enactments intended to promote the sanctity of the Sabbath. The first type is known as *ʿeruv teḥumim* (*ʿeruv* of boundaries), a legal device intended to ease certain Sabbath restrictions of rabbinic (but never of biblical) origin. According to the rabbinic interpretation of *Exodus* 16.29–30, which commands "each man to sit in his place" on the Sabbath, there is no biblical prohibition on walking outside the limits of one's place of residence on the Sabbath unless this distance exceeds twelve miles. Rabbinic law, however, places the limit at two thousand cubits (about two-thirds of a mile) from the point where the more heavily populated area of a locality ends. The rabbis made it possible for a person to go another two thousand cubits provided he had, before the Sabbath, placed food for two meals at the end of the permitted two thousand cubits. The location of the food would then, in theory, be considered his place of residence for the Sabbath, thus permitting him to go another two thousand cubits from that point. Hence it became possible to walk from one town to another whenever the distance between the two was less than four thousand cubits. An extension of this, *ʿeruv reshuyyot* (*ʿeruv* of domains), permits the stringing of a wire (attached to posts) round a whole area or town, which is then considered a single domain within which carrying is permitted. Every city in Israel is surrounded with such an *ʿeruv*, and others have been put up in certain places in the Diaspora.

The second type of *ʿeruv* is called *ʿeruv ḥatserot* (*ʿeruv* of courtyards). According to biblical law, one may carry things on the Sabbath from a house into a courtyard even if many other houses open onto it: as long as the courtyard is enclosed, it is considered a private domain. To promote the sanctity of the Sabbath, however, the rabbis prohibit such carrying unless the inhabitants of the courtyard symbolically make all their houses a single dwelling by each contributing some food to be placed in one of the houses belonging to the courtyard. Since there is now a "common" eating place, it is permissible to carry objects in the whole courtyard. The same procedure may be followed to make it possible to carry objects from all the courtyard into a common alleyway enclosed on at least three sides (and symbolically on a fourth), except that the food is placed not in the alleyway but in one of the courtyards. The name of this type of *ʿeruv* is *shitufei mova'ot* (partnership of alleyways).

The third type of *ʿeruv* is called *ʿeruv tavshilin* (*ʿeruv* of cooking) and is intended to safeguard the eminence of the Sabbath when preceded by a festival day. Ordinarily one may cook on a festival day only for that day. However, when such a day precedes the Sabbath, one is permitted to cook on that day for the Sabbath, provided one has symbolically begun the Sabbath preparation on the day preceding the festival by setting aside something cooked and something baked for the Sabbath and making an appropriate benediction. The laws are discussed in tractate *ʿ*Eruvin*.

• Yosef Gavriel Bechhofer, *Eruvin in Modern Metropolitan Areas*, 2d ed. (Skokie, Ill., 1995). Elimelech Lange, *Hilkhot ʿEruvin* (Jerusalem, 1972). Zekharyah Yeḥi'el ben Avigad Sharʿabi, *Sefer Yavo' Shiloh* (Jerusalem,

ʿERUVIN (עֵרוּבִין; Blendings), tractate in Mishnah order Moʿed, consisting of ten chapters, with related material in the Tosefta' and in both Talmuds. *ʿEruv* is a term utilized for various practices associated with the laws of Sabbath and festivals. *ʿEruvin* discusses the definition of a partition, which establishes a domain as private and permits carrying therein, followed by the laws governing two forms of *ʿeruvin*: *ʿeruv ḥatserot* and *ʿeruv tavshilin* (see ʿERUV).

The tractate was translated into English by I. W. Slotki in the Soncino Talmud (London, 1938).

• Chanoch Albeck, ed., *Shishah Sidrei Mishnah, Seder Moʿed* (Jerusalem, 1952). Philip Blackman, ed. and trans., *Mishnayot*, vol. 2, *Order Moʿed* (Gateshead, 1973). Pinhas Kehati, ed., *Mishnah: A New Translation with a Commentary, Seder Moʿed*, vol. 1, *Shabbat, ʿEruvin* (Jerusalem, 1990). Hermann Leberecht Strack, *Introduction to the Talmud and Midrash* (1931; Minneapolis, 1992). —AVRAHAM WALFISH

ESAU (Heb. ʿEsav), elder son of *Isaac and *Rebekah and twin brother of *Jacob. The personalities of Jacob and Esau in the *Book of Genesis* symbolize the biblical view of the character and origin of the two nations of Israel and Edom, which derived from a similar background but developed an enmity toward each other (Jacob is identified with Israel in *Gn*. 32.25–29 and Esau with Edom in *Gn*. 36.1). Esau is depicted as a hunter (*Gn*. 25.27) who sells his birthright to Jacob (*Gn*. 25.28–34). His anger at Jacob for having obtained their father Isaac's blessing through cunning results in Jacob's flight to Haran (*Gn*. 27); but on Jacob's return twenty years later, Esau shows only friendliness (*Gn*. 32). At the age of forty, Esau married two Hittite women and later the daughter of Ishmael (*Gn*. 26.34, 28.9). The rabbis depict Esau as the epitome of wildness and lust for power; the name Esau (or Edom) is used as an eponym for Rome and in medieval Hebrew literature for any anti-Jewish regime, Christianity in particular.

• Nahum M. Sarna, *Genesis*, The JPS Torah Commentary (Philadelphia, 1989), pp. 177–182. Claus Westermann, *Genesis 12–36*, translated by John J. Scullion (Minneapolis, 1985), pp. 410–419. —SHALOM PAUL

ESCHATOLOGY, doctrines concerning the fate of human beings after death (individual eschatology; see AFTERLIFE) or beliefs about the end of history (collective or cosmic eschatology). The word is derived from the Greek *eschaton* (end).

The united kingdom under David and Solomon (1000–922) could be seen as the fulfillment of God's covenant with Israel: Israel lived in peace and prosperity in the land promised to its fathers. But with the division of the kingdom, ongoing wars with neighbors and enemy incursions, as well as social and moral corruption, life for the Israelites looked much less golden. Amos, the first of the classical prophets (mid-eighth cent. BCE), provides the earliest biblical evidence for the expectation of a coming Day of Judgment (see YOM HA-DIN), a "*Day of the Lord" (*Am.* 5.18–20). The prophet rejects what was apparently the popular view of that day as the moment when the Lord would take vengeance on Israel's enemies and grant his people the peace and prosperity they lacked. Rather he insists that the Day of the Lord is a day of judgment for the people of Israel as well.

Later prophets follow Amos in claiming that God's judgment would not spare the people of Israel, but they emphasized the subsequent restoration. Isaiah of Jerusalem, a younger contemporary active in Judah, the southern kingdom, from the middle of the eighth through the beginning of the seventh century BCE, suggests that a righteous remnant of the people of Israel will survive the judgment and enjoy the new age. Other prophets also pictured a future reconciliation between God and the whole people or a pious and holy remnant.

The sack of Jerusalem by the Babylonians in 586 BCE overturned the basic assumptions of the southern kingdom: the divine inviolability of the house of David, of the house of the Lord, the Temple, and the City of the Lord, which was also the City of David. The prophet known as Deutero-Isaiah interpreted the conquest of Babylonia by the Persian king Cyrus in 538 BCE as an event fraught with eschatological significance. His prophetic interpretation seemed confirmed when Cyrus issued his decree permitting the exiles to return to their land and rebuild the Temple. But reality failed to measure up to the prophet's high hopes. The new Temple was a sad sight for those who remembered the first, and it stood in the midst of a divided community ruled by a Persian governor rather than a descendant of David.

The hope for the restoration of national sovereignty made eschatology a central concern of the Second Temple period as Hellenistic and Roman rulers followed the Persians, with only a century of independence under the Hasmoneans. Other subjects of the Hellenistic empire, particularly the Egyptians, produced prophecies about a new era in which a native king would be restored to the throne and proper order again established. Nevertheless, the content of Jewish eschatology was unique, because it was embedded in biblical traditions and prophetic utterance.

According to the eschatology of the Second Temple period, the course of history represented the unfolding of a plan determined by God. The *Book of Daniel*, for example, says that Israel had to be subjugated to four foreign kingdoms in succession before the establishment of "the kingdom of the holy ones of the Most High." Antiochus IV Epiphanes, the enemy at the time of the book's composition, is the last of the kings of the last kingdom. In the *Fourth Book of Ezra*, written several centuries later, after the destruction of the Second Temple by the Romans in 70 CE, a vision identifies the Roman empire as the last of the four kingdoms.

Responses to the belief in the imminent end of history were varied. The *Qumran community practiced an intensified version of the purity rules of the Bible. The earliest Christians introduced new practices in keeping with their belief that the Messiah had already appeared and inaugurated the end time. For others, the knowledge that the end was near inspired political and military action. According to Josephus, a number of messianic pretenders who led small groups of followers against the Romans toward the end of the Second Temple period and the Jewish revolt against the Romans from 66 to 70, which led to the destruction of the Second Temple, had eschatological components. The timing of the Bar Kokhba' Revolt between 132 and 135 seems also to reflect eschatological expectation: since the Second Temple was rebuilt roughly seventy years after the First Temple was destroyed, some Jews believed that the time was ripe for the establishment of the third and final temple as the seventy-year mark from the destruction of the Second Temple approached.

The belief in a future era of redemption is central to rabbinic thought, and it is expressed clearly in the liturgy of the synagogue as well as in rabbinic literature. The new era is always presided over by the *Messiah, who was not a constant feature of the eschatological scenarios of the prophets and the authors of the Second Temple period. Still, the rabbis remained cautious, which is not surprising in light of the unhappy outcome of the revolts against Rome. While the end was certain to come, its coming could not be forced by human beings.

No unified picture of the end of time emerges from the literature. Indeed, Gershom Scholem has suggested that there is a fundamental split in Jewish eschatology between "restorative" and "utopian" strands. The restorative strand comprises visions of an end that is possible in the world as we know it: Israel is established in its own land under a new Davidic king. The utopian strand, on the other hand, is not limited by the world as it is: the lion lies down with the lamb and death is abolished.

The third-century Babylonian rabbi Shemu'el insisted that the only difference between his age and the messianic era was that Israel would no longer be subjugated to the nations. He cites *Deuteronomy* 15.11, "The poor shall never cease from the midst of the land," as proof of his anti-utopian position. Such a position is less of an incitement to messianic activity than a more utopian one. Maimonides' picture of the messianic era in his legal code, the *Mishneh Torah*, comes from Shemu'el: the Messiah will be recognized as such because he will succeed in restoring the Jews to their homeland and rebuilding the Temple; there will be nothing supernatural about what he accomplishes; anyone who fails to restore Israel to its biblical state is not the Messiah. Maimonides' view is connected to his involvement in the controversy about a messianic pretender who had attracted many followers among the Jews of Yemen.

The most important of the messianic claimants of the Middle Ages was *Shabbetai Tsevi. The ideology of the Shabbatean movement was derived from the kabbalistic thought of Yitsḥaq *Luria, who believed that creation involved a cataclysm in which sparks of the divine were dispersed into the created world. By observing the commandments, a pious Jew helped to restore these sparks from their exile. When the restoration was completed, the world would be perfected and the exile of the Jews ended together with the exile of the divine. In Poland a century later, the Shabbatean Yaʿaqov *Frank (1726–1791) claimed to be the Messiah and led his followers to baptism in order to complete the work of Shabbetai Tsevi.

The end of the twentieth century provides a striking example of the vitality of such expectations in some quarters. In the years before the death of their seventh *rebbi*, Menaḥem Mendel Schneerson, the Lubavitcher Ḥasidim undertook a campaign to encourage nonobservant Jews to perform various Jewish rituals in an effort to speed the raising of the fallen sparks so that the *rebbi* could manifest himself as the Messiah. Some continue to believe that he is the Messiah even after his death. The Reform movement suggests that there will not be one Messiah; rather humans will be raised to their messianic potential and thereby enjoy the fruits of a messianic era.

• George W. Buchanan, *Revelation and Redemption: Jewish Documents of Deliverance from the Fall of Jerusalem to the Death of Naḥmanides* (Dillsboro, Ind., 1978). John J. Collins, *The Apocalyptic Imagination: An Introduction to the Jewish Matrix of Early Christianity* (New York, 1984). John J. Collins, *The Scepter and the Star: The Messiahs of the Dead Sea Scrolls and Other Ancient Literature* (New York, 1995). Paul D. Hanson, *The Dawn of Apocalyptic: The Historical and Sociological Roots of Jewish Apocalyptic Eschatology*, rev. ed. (Philadelphia, 1979). George F. Moore, *Judaism in the First Centuries of the Christian Era: The Age of the Tannaim*, 3 vols. (Cambridge, Mass., 1927–1932), vol. 2, pp. 323–376. Raphael Patai, *The Messiah Texts* (Detroit, 1979). E. P. Sanders, *Jesus and Judaism* (Philadelphia, 1985). Gershom Gerhard Scholem, *Major Trends in Jewish Mysticism* (New York, 1961). Gershom Gerhard Scholem, *The Messianic Idea in Judaism and Other Essays on Jewish Spirituality* (New York, 1971). Emil Schürer, *The History of the Jewish People in the Age of Jesus Christ*, revised and edited by Geza Vermes et al. (Edinburgh, 1973–1987), vol. 2, pp. 488–554. Efraim E. Urbach, *The Sages: Their Concepts and Beliefs*, translated by Israel Abrahams (Jerusalem, 1975), pp. 649–690.

—MARTHA HIMMELFARB

ESDRAS, BOOKS OF, several Jewish works in the Greek Septuagint and Latin Vulgate (see BIBLE TRANSLATIONS). Esdras is the Greek form of the biblical name Ezra. In the Septuagint, and in current scholarship, *1 Esdras* is the name given to a composite work containing materials from the biblical books of *Ezra*, *Nehemiah*, and *2 Chronicles*, as well as the extra-biblical story of Zerubbabel's wisdom as displayed in the court of Darius I, the Persian king. It remains uncertain when *1 Esdras* was composed and whether it was originally written in Hebrew or in Greek; the book was used by *Josephus Flavius, in approximately 90 CE. The *Second Book of Esdras* is the Hebrew Bible's **Ezra-Nehemiah*.

In the Vulgate, *1 Esdras* is the name given to the biblical *Book of Ezra*, *2 Esdras* to the *Book of Nehemiah*, and *3 Esdras* to the above-described *1 Esdras*. The *Fourth Book of Esdras*, which today is often called *2 Esdras*, when *Ezra* and *Nehemiah* are not counted as *1* and *2 Esdras*, respectively, is a work that falls into three distinct sections. The *Fourth Book of Esdras* 3–14 (known today as *4 Ezra*) is a complex apocalyptic work, originally written in Hebrew or Aramaic and translated into Latin from a Greek translation (only fragments of which survive). It is also preserved in several other languages, including Syriac, Ethiopic, Armenian, Georgian, and Arabic. Written shortly after the destruction of the Second Temple in 70 CE, it reflects the confusion and desperation of Jews who lived through tumultuous times and tried to reconcile their situation with the biblical promises for God's chosen people. About half of the work is devoted to the dialogues of Ezra, distressed by the destruction of the First Temple, with the angel Uriel, who comforts him by expounding on the meaning of this apparent calamity and promising that the end and the Jews' salvation are near. The second part of the work describes the complex symbolic visions revealed to Ezra, visions of Israel's future oppression, followed by eschatological upheavals and finally salvation with the coming of the savior *Messiah. Chapters 1–2 of *4 Esdras* (known today as *5 Ezra*) and chapters 15–16 (*6 Ezra*) are later Christian additions and are among the numerous Christian texts that bear Esdras's name.

• R. J. Coggins and Michael A. Knibb, *The First and Second Books of Esdras*, The Cambridge Bible Commentary (Cambridge, 1979). Bruce M. Metzger, "The Fourth Book of Ezra," in *The Old Testament Pseudepigrapha*, edited by James H. Charlesworth, vol. 1 (Garden City, N.Y., 1983), pp. 516–559. Jacob M. Myers, *I and II Esdras*, The Anchor Bible, vol. 42 (New York, 1974). Michael E. Stone, *Fourth Ezra*, Hermeneia Commentary (Minneapolis, 1990).

—GIDEON BOHAK

ESHET ḤAYIL (אֵשֶׁת חַיִל; A Woman of Worth), alphabetical acrostic from *Proverbs* 31.10–31 describing the ideal wife; recited by the husband in the home on Sabbath eve in the Ashkenazi and kabbalistic rites. The custom originated with the sixteenth-century kabbalists in Safed, for whom the term *eshet ḥayil* was a mystical metaphor for the Shekhinah. The practice of reciting Eshet Ḥayil has been discontinued in certain circles in the light of feminist objections that the reading stereotypes women as subservient homemakers. Reform liturgy suggests a parallel reading by women (*Ps*. 112.1–9) in honor of their husbands.

• A. Cohen, *Proverbs*, Soncino Books of the Bible, 2d. ed. (London, 1952). Tziporah Heller, *More Precious Than Pearls: Selected Insights into the Qualities of the Ideal Woman, Based on Eshes Chayil* (Jerusalem and New York, 1993). W. G. Plaut, *The Book of Proverbs: A Commentary* (New York, 1961).

ESNOGA, a word used among western Sephardim for a synagogue. That it appears for the first time in the Zohar is taken as evidence that this kabbalistic work was composed in northern Spain, in a Spanish-speaking, Jewish environment. In the Netherlands, the famous Portuguese synagogue in Amsterdam is commonly called the "Snoge."

• Judith C. E. Belinfante et al., eds., *The Esnoga: A Monument to Portuguese-Jewish Culture*, translated by John Rudge and Sammy Herman (Amsterdam, 1991).

ESSENES (Heb. Isiyyim), religious movement that flourished in Palestine from the mid-second century BCE to the destruction of the Temple in 70 CE. The derivation of the name is unclear but may be related to the Syriac equivalent of the Hebrew Ḥasidim (pious ones) or to the Aramaic word for healers (which parallels the Greek; see THERAPEUTAE). When the first *Dead Sea Scrolls were published in the early 1950s, most scholars were convinced that they originally belonged to an Essene library and that *Qumran was the site of an Essene settlement. Despite many challenges, this theory is still the most widely accepted explanation, given the many similarities between the documents found among the Dead Sea Scrolls and the descriptions of the Essenes by *Philo and *Josephus Flavius, as well as the location of the Qumran site itself, which fits well with Pliny the Elder's description of the Essenes' location.

The origins and early growth of the Essenes is still a subject of controversy, and it can only be definitely stated that the group emerged at some time during the second century BCE, a period of great political and religious change in Erets Yisra'el (see HASMONEANS). According to Philo and Josephus, whose descriptions are possibly tendentious, there were some four thousand Essenes scattered throughout the villages of Judea. The reliability of Josephus's account, which notes that there were two distinct groups among the Essenes, one practicing celibacy while the other permitted marriage, is still a matter of debate. According to these descriptions, the Essenes were a tightly knit, exclusive group, living together in communities and practicing communal ownership of wealth and goods. It was forbidden for an Essene to pass on the teachings of his sect to an outsider, and anyone wishing to join their number had to undergo a period of testing and examination. Discipline was strict, the most severe punishment being expulsion from the group, an act that, according to Josephus, was equivalent to a sentence of death by starvation if the expelled member continued to observe the peculiar dietary laws of the sect. The Dead Sea Scrolls present the Essenes as a group holding eschatological beliefs combined with a dualistic view of the world: even Israel is divided, by divine predestination, into two—the community of the elect and "children of darkness"—to be marked for salvation or for destruction in the apocalyptic events of the last days. The Essenes seem to have followed the 364-day solar calendar, known also from the *Book of *Jubilees*, which resulted in different festival dates from those observed by other Jews, including Yom Kippur. Essene *halakhah*, somewhat better known after the recent publication of **Miqtsat Ma'asei ha-Torah*, emerges as closely related to what the later rabbinic literature attributes to the *Sadducees, but the exact relationship between the Sadducees and the Essenes has yet to be elucidated. There are certain superficial similarities between early Christians and the Essenes, but the suggestion that *John the Baptist may have been an Essene is not generally accepted.

• Joseph A. Fitzmyer, *The Dead Sea Scrolls: Major Publications and Tools for Study* (1975; rev. ed. Atlanta, 1990). Elisha Qimron and John Strugnell, *Qumran Cave 4: Miqtsat Ma'ase ha-Torah*, Discoveries in the Judaean Desert 10 (Oxford, 1994). Emil Schürer, Geza Vermes, and Fergus Millar, *The History of the Jewish People in the Age of Jesus Christ* (Edinburgh, 1979), vol. 2, pp. 555–590. Geza Vermes and Martin D. Goodman, *The Essenes According to the Classical Sources* (Sheffield, Eng., 1989). Geza Vermes and Pamela Vermes, *The Dead Sea Scrolls: Qumran in Perspective* (Philadelphia, 1981).

—GIDEON BOHAK

ESTHER (Heb. Ester), heroine of the biblical *Book of Esther*, one of the *Ḥamesh Megillot in the *Hagiographa. There was opposition to its canonization, partly because God is nowhere mentioned in the book. The name *Esther*, derived apparently from the ancient Persian *stara* (star), occurs only in the *Book of Esther*. Esther's other personal name, Hebrew in origin, was Hadassah (*Est*. 2.7 only), derived from the Hebrew word for myrtle. In the Esther story, the Persian king *Ahasuerus ruled an empire that stretched from India to Ethiopia (1.1). During the third year of his reign, he gave an elaborate banquet, at which time he deposed his wife Vashti for her refusal to appear (1.3–8, 10–19). After a search, he finally selected as his next queen Esther, a Jew who hid her identity from him (2.1–4, 17). At the instigation of his chief minister, *Haman, who was frustrated by the refusal of Esther's relation *Mordecai to bow down to him, Ahasuerus, without even inquiring as to whose death sentence he was sealing, issued a decree of genocide against the entire Jewish people (3.1–15). The plot was eventually thwarted by Esther, leading to Ahasuerus having Haman and his sons executed and promoting Mordecai to the position of chief minister. Ahasuerus, under the influence of Esther, issued a decree allowing the Jews to defend themselves against their enemies. Their eventual victory led to the establishment of the holiday of *Purim (8.3–14, 9.5–10, 13–14). The *Book of Esther* contains some clearly authentic historical elements, such as the Hebrew name *Ahasuerus*, which is the same as the Persian name *Xerxes*, Other historically accurate background details include the extent of Xerxes' empire from India to Ethiopia (1.1), his winter palace at Susa (Shushan; 1.2), his seven princely advisers (1.14), the practice of showing obeisance before the king's high officials (3.2), the recording and rewarding of the king's "benefactors" (2.23, 6.8), the use of hanging as a means of capital punishment (2.23, 5.14, 7.10), and the many Persian loanwords throughout the text. These elements, together with the Hebrew style of *Esther* (closest to the book of *Chronicles*, composed c.400 BCE) and the sympathetic attitude of the author toward the Persian king (which best fits the Persian period until 330 BCE), have led scholars to the conclusion that *Esther* was written between 400 and 330 BCE. On the other hand, several elements must be considered at the very least historically unlikely and in some cases completely ahistoric; for example, a royal feast lasting 180 days (1.2–4) and royal proclamations written in all languages of the Persian empire rather than in the official language of the empire, Aramaic (1.22, 3.12, 8.9). Also, according to *Esther* 2.16 and 3.7 Esther was Xerxes' queen between his seventh and twelfth years, while according to the classical historian Herodotus (VII:114; IX:112), Amestris was queen at that time. Furthermore, Herodotus specifically indicates (III:84) that Persian queens could come only from one of the seven Persian noble families. Thus, both Esther's ascent to the throne as well as the very concept in *Esther* 2 of a royal beauty contest to select the new queen must be considered highly unlikely from a historical point of view.

Scholars (e.g., S. B. Berg, M. V. Fox) have asserted that reversal is the central theme of the story, whose plot is comprised of many coincidences and ironic moments. With respect to literary structure, the influence of reversal is perhaps somewhat more subtle, but in the end even more pervasive. Haman is introduced at the beginning of chapter 3, which is the first of three chapters (3, 4, and 5) in which everything that occurs points toward the strong likelihood that Haman will indeed succeed in his planned annihilation of the Jews. Then comes the turning point in *Esther* 6.1, after which all the previous negative events are reversed in favor of the Jews, leading to Haman's demise and the thwarting of his diabolical plot. Reversal also underlies the rabbinic dictum that one is permitted and even expected to get inebriated on Purim until one is no longer able to distinguish between "cursed be Haman" and "blessed be Mordecai" (*Meg.* 7b).

The purpose of including historically accurate elements must have been to provide *Esther* with an authentic historical background; thus, *Esther* can be categorized as a historical *novella*. Such a characterization, however, does not take into consideration the many humorous and ironic features of the book, such as the lavish and enduring royal parties (1.4); the king's letter ordering all men throughout the Persian empire to be masters in their own homes (1.22), as a result of which it is expected that "all wives will treat their husbands with respect, high and low alike" (1.20); and Haman's desperate attempt to plead for his life before the queen, which culminates in his unintentionally and haplessly falling on the queen's couch just as the king enters the room—an act to which the king responds "Does he mean to ravish the queen in my own palace?"—and the king's subsequent order for Haman's execution by hanging on the very gallows he had built to kill Mordecai (7.7–10). According to H. L. Ginsberg, the book was written "as a mock-learned disquisition to be read at the opening of a carnival-like celebration," whose express purpose was to turn the local Purim celebration of Persian Jewry into a holiday for Jews worldwide. The book is read in the synagogue on the eve and morning of the Purim festival. The regulations for its reading are contained in tractate *Megillah. It was to be read from a special scroll, which became a favorite subject for decoration by Jewish artists. Its message of the triumph of the Jews over their enemies appealed strongly to Jews persecuted throughout the Diaspora.

• Sandra B. Berg, *The Book of Esther: Motifs, Themes and Structure* (Missoula, Mont., 1979), pp. 103–113. Elias Bickerman, *Four Strange Books of the Bible: Jonah, Daniel, Koheleth, Esther* (New York, 1967), pp. 171–240. M. V. Fox, "The Structure of the Book of Esther," in *Isac Leo Seeligmann Volume*, edited by Alexander Rofe and Yair Zakovitch, vol. 3 (Jerusalem, 1983), pp. 291–303. Harold L. Ginsberg, *The Five Megilloth and Jonah: A New Translation* (Philadelphia, 1969), pp. 82–88. William W. Hallo, "The First Purim," *Biblical Archaeologist* 46 (1993): 19–26. Carey A. Moore, *Esther*, The Anchor Bible (New York, 1971). Carey A. Moore, "Esther, Book of," in *The Anchor Bible Dictionary*, edited by David N. Freedman et al., vol. 2 (New York, 1992), pp. 633–643.

—CHAIM COHEN

ESTHER, ADDITIONS TO BOOK OF, six passages that are found in the Greek translation of the *Book of *Esther* but not in the text preserved in the Hebrew Bible. These additions include a dream of Mordecai at the beginning of the story, in which the events about to happen are foretold in a symbolic manner, as well as the text of Haman's anti-Jewish edict and of Mordecai's own edict following Haman's downfall. From internal inconsistencies, it is evident that these textual units did not belong in the original *Book of Esther*, but it is less clear which additions were translated from Hebrew or Aramaic and which were originally composed in Greek. Dating each addition is equally difficult; probable dates range from the second century BCE to the first century CE.

• Carey A. Moore, *Daniel, Esther and Jeremiah: The Additions*, The Anchor Bible, vol. 44 (Garden City, N.Y., 1977), pp. 153–252.

—GIDEON BOHAK

ESTHER, FAST OF. See TAʿANIT ESTER.

ESTHER, SCROLL OF. See ESTHER; ḤAMESH MEGILLOT.

ESTHER RABBAH, a *midrash* on the *Book of *Esther*, from the collection called the *Midrash Rabbah, originally known by several other names: *Midrash Ahasuerus*, *Midrash Megillah*, or *Haggadat Megillah*. In the earliest printed editions, the *midrash* was divided into six chapters, while publishers in Vilna divided it into ten sections. Analysis of the *midrash*, based on the assumption that the existence of a proem reveals the beginning of a section, shows that the *midrash* should be divided into seven sections. A closer reading of the *midrash* shows that the seventh section is actually a separate *midrash*. The first *midrash*, consisting of six sections that explain the first two chapters of the biblical *Book of Esther*, is an early exegetical *midrash*; each section is opened by a classically styled proem. The proems that mark the beginning of the second *midrash* are not in the classical style, and the *midrash* itself is more a retelling of the biblical story of Esther than an exegetical *midrash*. The first part uses early sources, including the Targum Onkelos, while the second part shows an affinity with the *Book of Yosippon*, which was compiled in the tenth century.

Closely associated with *Esther Rabbah* is another *midrash* on the *Book of Esther*, *Abba' Guryon*, known by the words with which it begins, whose contents are almost identical to *Esther Rabbah*, on which it is clearly based. Because *Abba' Guryon* has, at times, better readings of the text than those to be found in the present edition of *Esther Rabbah*, it must be presumed that its editor had access to earlier manuscripts of *Esther Rabbah* than those that have survived.

Esther Rabbah was first published in Pesaro in 1519; it was translated into English by Maurice Simon (London, 1939) and Jacob Neusner.

• Jacob Neusner, ed. and trans., *Esther Rabbah I: An Analytical Translation*, Brown Judaic Studies, vol. 182 (Atlanta, 1989). Joseph Tabory, "Le-Gilgulo shel ha-Midrash la-Katuv 'Divrei Fi Ḥakham Ḥen,'" *Sidra'* 2 (1986): 151–155 (Hebrew). Joseph Tabory, "Mi-Bʿayot ha-Hadarah shel Ester Rabbah," *Sidra'* 1 (1985): 145–152.

—JOSEPH TABORY

ESTIMATES (Heb. *ʿarakhim*), sums of money to be given to the Temple in place of something that was dedicated by a vow but that cannot be sacrificed (*Lv.* 27). The possibility for such substitution, "redemption" money in biblical terms, enables a person symbolically to offer his own life or that of one of his dependents as a sacred gift, or to offer an animal even if he does not have one or cannot afford actually to put one to death; it also allows him to offer an impure animal, a home, or a field. Some of the monetary values are fixed by law; others are determined by the priest. In the case of real estate, the value is based on the field's productivity. After redeeming the dedicated item, thereby rescuing it from being sacrificed, the owner must add one-fifth of its value in order to regain possession. Fields that have been dedicated from one's ancestral allotment must be reclaimed before the jubilee year; otherwise, they become Temple property in perpetuity. The institution of *ʿarakhim* was a major source of much-needed revenue for the Temple. In rabbinic law, the possibilities for such donations and dedications are enlarged. The laws of estimates are in the Talmudic tractates *ʿ*Arakhin* and **Temurah*.

• Menahem Haran, *Temples and Temple-Service in Ancient Israel* (Winona Lake, Ind., 1985). —BARUCH J. SCHWARTZ

ETERNAL LIGHT. See NER TAMID.

ETHICAL CULTURE. See ADLER, FELIX.

ETHICAL WILLS, parting deathbed messages given most often by fathers to their children. The biblical example of Jacob (*Gn*. 49.33) and the various instances of last messages in the Talmud, such as the deathbed message of Yehudah ha-Nasi' (*Ket*. 103a–b), were verbal communications. In the Middle Ages, however, the custom developed of scholars writing testamentary dispositions to their children. Since these consisted not of worldly possessions but of ethical advice, they have been called ethical wills. Among the most famous ethical wills are those of R. Elʿazar ben Yehudah of Worms, R. Asher ben Yeḥi'el, his sons Yehudah and Yaʿaqov, and R. Avraham and R. Sheftel (father and son, respectively, of Yeshaʿyahu Horowitz). There is also at least one example of a mother writing an ethical will for her children, found in the *Memoirs* of Glueckl of Hameln (first published by David Kaufmann in 1896; translated into English by M. Lowenthal in 1932). Enjoining humility, piety, and ethical conduct of the highest degree, the ethical will became a distinctive literary genre. In modern times, the Holocaust was responsible for many poignant examples.

• Israel Abrahams, ed., *Hebrew Ethical Wills*, 2 vols. (Philadelphia, 1926). Jack Riemer and Nathaniel Stampfer, *Ethical Wills: A Modern Jewish Treasury* (New York, 1983).

ETHICS. The norms and principles of Jewish religious ethics are founded on theological presuppositions, including the existence of God, his purpose in creation, revelation, and the destiny of the soul in this world and in the hereafter. The question of the autonomy of ethics was much discussed by medieval philosophers: is an action right because God commanded it, or did God command it because it is intrinsically right? Some thinkers assert that ethics and religion are the same, while others hold that despite the overlap, there is an essential difference between them. Abraham, they suggest, was ready on purely religious grounds to obey God's command to sacrifice his son Isaac (*Gn*. 32), although on purely moral grounds he ought to have disobeyed. However, the analytical distinction between the realms of religion and ethics belongs to later philosophical development. The difference is not recognized in most ancient religions, where ceremonial, ethical, legal, and cultic precepts appear together (cf. the biblical Holiness Code in *Lv*. 19–20). The ethical element is prominent throughout the Bible. There is an urgent appeal to man's free will to choose the good, which is also his true blessing and happiness (*Dt*. 30.15–20); the divine will, as revealed in the Torah, is that man do "that which is good and right in the sight of the Lord your God" (*Dt*. 12.28). God is the advocate "of the fatherless and widow, and loves the stranger" (*Dt*. 10.18). The historical books of the Bible as well as the prophets interpret history in moral terms: prosperity and disaster are regarded as divine reward and punishment, respectively. History will end with the ultimate triumph of good over evil (See ESCHATOLOGY). The great literary prophets emphasize the ethical elements of religion even more strongly. Their criticism of sacrifices and ritual (cf. *Is*. 1.10–17; *Jer*. 7.9) is a passionate denunciation of ceremonial worship that is not matched by *social justice and purity of heart. The principles of prudence and common sense in *wisdom literature are ultimately based on the fear of God and the knowledge of his commandments. A similar tendency is discernible in Jewish *Hellenism, particularly in the writings of Philo of Alexandria: the moral life and the practice of virtue are nothing but conformity to the laws of the cosmos, which the Creator established from the very beginning and which he revealed in his Torah. The Talmud, though primarily a record of legal discussions, contains a detailed though unsystematic rabbinic ethics, both implicitly in its *halakhah* and explicitly in a wealth of moral dictums and maxims, as well as in parables and homiletic interpretations of scripture. Hillel's saying, "What is hateful to you, do not unto your fellow man," and R. ʿAqiva''s statement, "Love your neighbor as yourself—this is a basic principle of the Torah," are among the best-known of the rabbinic maxims, as is Mishnah tractate **Avot*, known as the *Ethics of the Fathers*. The *aggadah* is a treasury of ethical teachings, which, in general, eschews excesses and recommends a golden mean ("a man should spend no less than one tenth of his income on charity, and no more than one fifth, lest he become himself dependent on charity"), although the extreme and uncompromising ethics of the *ḥasid* (pious one) are also held up as exemplary. *Halakhah*, too, implicitly assumes ethical categories; for example, it distinguishes among "matters between man and God" and "matters between man and his fellow," and it says that the agent of certain actions "must be acquitted by the human court but is guilty according to heavenly law." The concept of **lifnim mi-shurat ha-din* implies an ethical norm of which the actual law is but the last limit.

Ethical literature as a distinct genre began to appear in the Middle Ages under the influence of Arabic thought. The earliest ethical treatise is the tenth, concluding chapter, "Man's Conduct," of Saʿadyah Ga'on's theological work *Emunot ve-Deʿot*, which was written in Arabic during the first half of the tenth century. Another example is Shelomoh ibn Gabirol's *Tiqqun Middot ha-Nefesh*. But the most important early work is Baḥya ben Yosef ibn Paquda''s *Ḥovot ha-Levavot*. (All three of these works were translated into Hebrew by Yehudah ibn Tibbon in the second half of the twelfth century.) Baḥya differed from his two predecessors in the radically spiritual and pietistic orientation of his teaching, and his work, written in the eleventh century, remains to this day one of the most influential manuals of spirituality and religious ethics.

The first ethical works in Hebrew were written in the twelfth century: *Hegyon ha-Nefesh*, four homilies on the nature of the soul, ethics, and repentance, by Avraham bar Ḥayya'; *Yesod Mora'*, by Avraham ibn Ezra; and *Sefer ha-Maddaʿ*, the first part of the *Mishneh Torah*, by Maimonides. These were followed in the thirteenth century by works of philosophers including Yaʿaqov ben Abba' Mari Anatoli and Shem Tov ben Yosef Falaquera. All of these works were marked by the philosophical rationalism dominant in Sephardi theology. A different, independent school of ethical teachings, known as that of the *Ḥasidei Ashkenaz, headed by Yehudah ben Shemu'el he-Ḥasid of Regensburg and his disciple Elʿazar ben Yehudah of Worms, developed in Germany during the second half of the twelfth century. The most comprehensive work of this school is *Sefer Ḥasidim*, which clearly addresses a distinct society of pietists who perceive their teachings as a spiritual preparation for the Crusader massacres. While the rationalist philosophers viewed ethics as an autonomous expression of the human capacity for good, the Ḥasidei Ashkenaz saw religion and ethics as divinely imposed demands that contradict human nature and test human devotion to God; every performance of a religious or ethical precept is a test, preparing one for the ultimate sacrifice, martyrdom.

In the first half of the thirteenth century, another school of ethics emerged in northern Spain. Although Yitsḥaq Saggi Nahor refused to allow his disciples to publish their kabbalistic teachings because he insisted that the *Kabbalah was strictly esoteric, his disciples produced a body of ethical work that included half-hidden kabbalistic messages and that presented an alternative to rationalist ethics. Nahmanides wrote several ethical treatises and homilies, as did Asher ben David. Among the most important works of this school were Yaʿaqov ben Sheshet Gerondi's *Ha-'Emunah ve-ha-Bittaḥon* and Yonah ben Avraham Gerondi's *Shaʿarei Teshuvah*, which became very popular and was the precursor for a whole genre of penitential literature. At the same time in Italy a non-kabbalistic ethical work based on traditional sources, *Maʿalot ha-Middot*, was written by Yeḥi'el ben Yequti'el Anav in Rome.

The expulsion of the Jews from Spain in 1492 and the resulting spiritual upheaval opened the way for the sixteenth-century kabbalists of Safed, whose work combined traditional ethics, philosophical ideas, the teachings of the Ḥasidei Ashkenaz, and kabbalistic concepts. Among the most important works of this new and vigorous ethical literature were *Tomer Devorah* by Mosheh ben Yaʿaqov Cordovero, *Re'shit Ḥokhmah* by Eliyyahu de Vidas, *Sefer Ḥaredim* by Elʿazar ben Mosheh Azikri, *Shaʿarei Qedushah* by Ḥayyim Vital, and *Shenei Luḥot ha-Berit* by Yeshaʿyahu Horowitz. Despite the great differences between them, all described the achievement of ethical perfection in the context of kabbalistic symbolism. In some respects these works can be compared to Christian and Sufi treatises on preparations for the mystical life, which emphasize individual spiritual perfection.

Kabbalistic ethical literature became increasingly popular in the seventeenth and eighteenth centuries. Many Shabbatean works were written in a similar style, including *Shevat Musar*, by Eliyyahu ha-Kohen of Smyrna, and the great collection of homilies, *Ḥemdat Yamim*, written by a group of Shabbateans in Turkey at the beginning of the eighteenth century. Modern Hasidic literature, which is largely composed in the form of ethical and homiletical treatises, is based on kabbalistic symbolism.

In the nineteenth century, the *Musar movement developed out of the conviction that the legal and ritualistic aspects of *halakhah* were overshadowing the ethical elements, almost to their exclusion. Meeting to study ethical texts and engage in self-criticism, followers of the Musar movement succeeded in introducing the study of ethics into the great European *yeshivot*. A late classic of Musar literature was *Messilat Yesharim* by Mosheh Ḥayyim Luzzatto. In the twentieth century Yisra'el Me'ir ha-Kohen's *Ḥafets Ḥayyim*, on the laws of talebearing and slander, achieved widespread popularity.

Emancipation raised ethical issues that had been irrelevant in the world of the ghetto. Today the study of Jewish ethics has been expanded to include such subjects as business ethics and *medical ethics. See also DEREKH ERETS.

• S. Daniel Breslauer, *Contemporary Jewish Ethics: A Bibliographical Survey* (Westport, Conn., 1985). Joseph Dan, *Jewish Mysticism and Jewish Ethics* (Seattle, 1987). Joseph Dan, *Sifrut ha-Musar veha-Derush* (Jerusalem, 1975). Marvin Fox, ed., *Modern Jewish Ethics: Theory and Practice* (Columbus, Ohio, 1975). Menachem Marc Kellner, *Contemporary Jewish Ethics* (New York, 1978). Isaak Heinemann, *Ta'amei ha-Mitsvot be-Sifrut Yisra'el* (Jerusalem, 1956). Max Kadushin, *Worship and Ethics: A Study in Rabbinic Judaism* (Evanston, Ill., 1964). Moritz Lazarus, *The Ethics of Judaism*, 2 vols. (Philadelphia, 1900–1901). Shalom Rosenberg in *Contemporary Jewish Religious Thought*, edited by Arthur A. Cohen and Paul Mendes-Flohr (New York, 1987), pp. 195–202. Daniel J. Silver, ed., *Judaism and Ethics* (New York, 1970). Shubert Spero, *Morality, Halakha and the Jewish Tradition* (New York, 1983). Isaiah Tishby and Joseph Dan, eds., *Mivḥar Sifrut ha-Musar* (Jerusalem, 1970). —JOSEPH DAN

ETHICS OF THE FATHERS. See AVOT.

ETHIOPIAN JEWS. See BETA ISRAEL.

ETIQUETTE. See DEREKH ERETS.

ETROG (אֶתְרוֹג; citron), one of the *four species carried and shaken in the *Sukkot synagogue service. The custom, which was well established in Second Temple times, is based on *Leviticus* 23.40, where the "fruit of a goodly tree" was traditionally interpreted as referring to the citron (in the lemon family); the rabbis proffer Midrashic explanations for that choice. The rabbis ruled that it had to be in perfect condition; therefore, to make sure that it was not damaged, it was usually wrapped in flax or cotton wool and kept in a special box (often the object of artistic decoration). In the Diaspora, societies were organized to send emissaries to purchase *etrogim*. At times, prices were so high that a single *etrog* was made to serve an entire community (or even a number of communities). Until the late nineteenth century, when they began to be cultivated in Erets Yisra'el (where they had grown in ancient times), the main source of *etrogim* was the Greek island of Corfu. The *etrog* featured widely as a Jewish symbol in classical times.

• Harry Abramowitz, "Some Retouched Dies of the Bar Kokhba Coinage," *Israel Numismatic Journal* 5 (1981): 38–43. Yehiel M. Stern, *Kashrut Arbaʿat ha-Minim* (Jerusalem, 1992), pp. 8–72, 178–199. Eliyahu Weisfisch, *Sefer Arbaʿat ha-Minim ha-Shalem* (Jerusalem, 1975), pp. 51–93. Michael Zohary, *Plants of the Bible* (Cambridge, 1982), p. 123.

ETTLINGER, YAʿAQOV (1798–1871), Talmudist and halakhic authority; pioneer of *Neo-Orthodoxy. One of the earliest Orthodox rabbis to attend university and preach in the vernacular, he served as rabbi and head of the *yeshivah* in Mannheim and, from 1836, as chief rabbi of Altona. A prolific author, Ettlinger was a staunch traditionalist and opponent of the Reform movement, and he founded pioneering Orthodox periodicals. He was also an activist supporter of the settlement of Erets Yisra'el. Through his own writings and those of his disciples, Samson Raphael Hirsch and Ezriel Hildesheimer, he exerted great influence on Orthodox Judaism in Germany. His major works are *ʿArukh la-Ner* (Talmudic *novellae*): on *Yevamot* (Altona, 1850), on *Makkot* and *Keritot* (Altona, 1855), on *Sukkah* (Altona, 1858), on *Niddah* (Altona, 1864), on *Ro'sh ha-Shanah* and *Sanhedrin* (Warsaw, 1873); *Bikkurei Yaʿaqov* (laws of Sukkot; Altona, 1836); *Binyan Tsiyyon* (*responsa*; Altona, 1868) and *Binyan Tsiyyon ha-Ḥadashot* (Vilna, 1874); and *Minḥat ʿAni* (homilies; Altona, 1874).

• Akiba Posner and Ernest Freiman, "Rabbi Jacob Ettlinger," in *Guardians of Our Heritage*, edited by Leo Jung (New York, 1958), pp. 231–243.

–JUDITH BLEICH

EULOGY (Heb. *hesped*). Eulogies are of ancient origin. Biblical examples include David's elegies for Saul and Jonathan (*2 Sm*. 1.17–27) and Abner (*2 Sm*. 3.33–34), and several eulogies, couched in a very distinctive style, are recorded in the Talmud. The Talmud refers to professional eulogizers and addresses the question of whether eulogies are in honor of the dead or to honor the mourners, deciding that they are for the sake of the dead (*San*. 46b). If a pious person before death asks not to be eulogized, the request is respected only in the home; however, there is a eulogy in the synagogue and at the cemetery. It was customary on 7 Adar, the traditional anniversary of Moses' death, to eulogize distinguished individuals who had died during the preceding year. On Sabbaths and during certain festival periods, eulogies are not permitted. In Sephardi communities, it became customary to deliver a eulogy in the form of a Talmudic discourse after the *sheloshim* (the thirty-day period of mourning). The rabbis warned against exaggeration in funeral addresses but said that the dead person's piety should be emphasized, both to comfort the mourners and to encourage those present to follow a virtuous path (*Ber*. 62a; *San*. 46b–47a). It is forbidden to eulogize those who have committed suicide or those who have been excommunicated.

• David N. Freedman, "On the Death of Abner," in *Love and Death in the Ancient Near East*, edited by John Marks and R. Good (Guildford, Conn., 1987), pp. 125–127. Elliot Horowitz, "Speaking of the Dead: The Emergence of Eulogy among Italian Jewry of the Sixteenth Century," in *Preachers of the Italian Ghetto*, edited by David Ruderman (Berkeley, 1992), pp. 129–162.

EUNUCH. See CASTRATION.

EUTHANASIA. Mercy killing is forbidden under Jewish law, and the killer of a dying individual is treated in exactly the same fashion as any other killer. Indeed, the Talmudic principle governing the dying is that individuals are treated as "living beings in all respects," and their legal capacity is not impaired by their physical state (minor tractate *Semaḥot* 1.1). The treatment of the dying is, however, governed by a distinction between precipitating death and removing an impediment to it. This distinction is articulated in early halakhic sources in the context of removing a pillow from under the head of a dying person, versus the prevention of a noise, which, apparently, disturbs the dying process and impedes death. According to R. Mosheh Isserles (*Shulḥan ʿArukh, Yoreh Deʿah* 339.1, gloss), pillow removal is forbidden because it precipitates death, whereas, noise prevention is permitted on the grounds that it is an indirect act, the only effect of which is to remove an impediment to the demise of the moribund person (*Yoreh Deʿah* 339.1). The general consensus among contemporary halakhic authorities is that futile medical treatment constitutes an impediment; hence, it may be withheld or even withdrawn. The maintenance of a patient's basic biological processes, that is, respiration, nutrition, and hydration, must, according to some Orthodox rabbis, be continued until the establishment of death. Most rabbis, however, including those within the Conservative and Reform movements, would permit the withholding or withdrawal of machines and medications that are artificially keeping the patient alive, and some would permit the withholding or withdrawing of artificial nutrition and hydration as well. *Halakhah*, in any case, does permit praying for the death of a suffering individual. Jewish criminal law provides that the killer of a person suffering from a fatal organic defect is not liable for the death penalty for homicide. Maimonides defines a fatal organic defect in terms of medical evidence as to the certainty of death within one year (*Hilkhot Rotseaḥ* 2.8). This provision has been used by some authorities to justify the choosing of one life over another in cases where only one person can be saved, and it may be applicable to some of the situations that face medical staff in emergency-ward triage. While this subject continues to be an issue of discussion in Reform Judaism, the movement allows for euthanasia.

• J. David Bleich, "The Quinlan Case: A Jewish Perspective," in *Jewish Bioethics*, edited by Fred Rosner and J. David Bleich (New York, 1979), pp. 266–277. Walter Jacob and Moshe Zemer, eds., *Death and Euthanasia in Jewish Law: Essays and Responsa* (Pittsburgh, 1995). Immanuel Jakobovits, *Jewish Medical Ethics* (New York, 1959), pp. 119–125. Daniel Sinclair, "Assisted Death: A Jewish Perspective," in *Must We Suffer Our way to Death? Cultural and Theological Perspectives on Death by Choice*, edited by Ronald Hamel and Edwin Dubose (Dallas, 1996), pp. 141–173. Daniel B. Sinclair, *Tradition and the Biological Revolution: The Application of Jewish Law to the Treatment of the Critically Ill* (Edinburgh, 1989), pp. 9–16. —DANIEL SINCLAIR

EVE (Heb. Ḥavvah), the first created woman. In the narrative of *Genesis*, Eve was created from the rib of Adam to be a "help meet for him" (*Gn*. 2.20–22). Adam called her *woman* (*ishah*; a play on the word *ish* [man], although actually from two different roots [*Gn*. 2.23]), which is to be regarded as a generic designation, due to its occurrence with the article, and not as a proper noun. Having allowed herself to be seduced by the serpent into eating the fruit forbidden to her by divine command and subsequently seducing Adam to commit the same sin, causing the couple to be expelled from the garden of Eden, she was sentenced to endure pains in childbearing and to be subordinate to her husband (*Gn*. 3.16), while her offspring would perpetuate the mortal antipathy toward the serpent (*Gn*. 3.15). She subsequently gave birth to Cain, Abel, Seth, and other unnamed children (*Gn*. 4.1–2, 4.25, 5.4), but there is no further mention of her. The derivation of the name Ḥavvah is uncertain and controversial. The narrative in *Genesis* associates the word with the root "to live" (*ḥ y h*; cf. *Gn*. 3.20: "the mother of all living"; cf. also the Septuagintal rendering for Eve: *Zōē* [life]). Rabbinical exegesis linked the name with the Aramaic word for serpent (*ḥivya'*; cf. *Gn. Rab*. 20.11). Other scholars have combined these two ideas by proposing a hypothetical root (*ḥ w y*) that combined the notions of life and serpent. Eve is the subject of many legends in the Apocrypha and in rabbinical *aggadah*. The rabbis did not propound a doctrine of original sin, and the taint of her wrongdoing was, in any case, removed by the Israelites' acceptance of the Torah. Eve is prominent in Jewish feminist writing because of both the patriarchal approach to the story and what are seen as the positive aspects of her rebelliousness.

• Ilana Pardes, *Countertraditions in the Bible: A Feminist Approach* (Cambridge, Mass., 1992), pp. 13–59. Howard N. Wallace, *The Eden Narrative*, Harvard Semitic Monographs, no. 32 (Atlanta, 1985), pp. 147–161. Claus Westermann, *Genesis 1–11* (Minneapolis, 1984), pp. 178–278. —MICHAEL JAMES WILLIAMS

EVEL RABBATI, minor tractate, appended to standard editions of the Talmud Bavli at the conclusion of tractate *ʿAvodah Zarah*, dealing with laws concerning death and mourning. It is euphemistically referred to as *Semaḥot* (Joys). Some scholars accept the view of certain ge'onim that *Evel Rabbati* is tannaitic. Other scholars, while recognizing the inclusion in *Evel Rabbati* of substantial bodies of original tannatic material, some of it unattested elsewhere, nonetheless date the final redaction of *Evel Rabbati* to the geonic period. There is evidence that indicates that an alternative version of this tractate existed and was utilized by several medieval scholars. A critical edition was published by Michael Higger (1931) and an annotated English translation with critical text by Dov Zlotnick (1966). —AVRAHAM WALFISH

EVEL ZUTARTI, minor tractate dealing with laws, teachings, and parables related to death, euphemistically called *Semaḥot de-Rabbi Ḥiyya'*. Inasmuch as it was never printed together with the Talmud Bavli, it was relatively neglected, although it was known and cited by several medieval scholars. *Evel Zutarti*, unlike **Evel Rabbati*, contains primarily—although not exclusively—aggadic material, yet evidence indicates that these two works originally were both part of a single tractate.

• Michael Higger, *Massekhet Semaḥot* (Jerusalem, 1970). —AVRAHAM WALFISH

EVEN HA-ʿEZER. See SHULḤAN ʿARUKH.

EVEN HA-SHETIYYAH (אֶבֶן הַשְּׁתִיָּה; the foundation rock), a tannaitic term understood in two ways in Talmudic times: "the rock from which the world was woven," and "the foundation rock." Both meanings are based on the belief that the world was created from the rock located in the Holy of Holies of the Temple in Jerusalem, and thus the center of the world. This concept is closely related to the image of Jerusalem and the Temple as located at the "navel of the world." The Holy Ark was placed on this rock, and during the Second Temple period, the high priest, upon entering the Holy of Holies on *Yom Kippur, placed the fire-pan on it. Muslim tradition identifies the rock, over which was built the Dome of the Rock, with the *even ha-shetiyyah*.

• Judah David Eisenstein, comp., *Otsar Midrashim* (1915; New York, 1988), p. 70a. Louis Ginzberg, *The Legends of the Jews*, vol. 5 (Philadelphia, 1925), pp. 14–16. Saul Lieberman, *Tosefta' ke-Feshutah*, vol. 4, *Seder Mo'ed* (1962; Jerusalem, 1993), pp. 772–773. Daniel Sperber, *Midrash Yerushalem* (Jerusalem, 1982), pp. 63–67. —DANIEL SPERBER

EVENING SERVICE. See MAʿARIV.

EVIDENCE, testimony received in legal proceedings in proof or disproof of the facts under inquiry. Whoever is in possession of direct knowledge of such facts is obliged (*Lv*. 5.1) to state them in testimony, and it became customary to issue a *ḥerem* against people who refused to testify. However, no legal decision can be arrived at in capital or civil cases in matters of atonement, sacrifices, those involving flagellation, or those relating to the promotion or demotion in the priesthood on the evidence of a single *witness (*Dt*. 19.15 and *Sifrei*). But while a single witness is insufficient, he must, nonetheless, attend court to testify, since in many instances his testimony may be joined to that of another of whom he is unaware, or his evidence might be sufficiently compelling to force the one testified against to substantiate his plea by oath (see VOWS AND OATHS). The inadequacy of a single witness extends only to the legal status of persons or property, but in deciding the ritual status of an object, his testimony is decisive. His evidence is also extremely important in the case of an *ʿ*agunah* (a deserted woman or a woman whose husband is suspected dead). The evidence of two witnesses bears the same weight as a hundred. When two witnesses are contradicted (*hakhḥashah*) by two others, the case is decided as if no witnesses were available for either side. Procedurally, the court is first addressed on the gravity of bearing *false witness, and then witnesses are cross-examined in order to ascertain their reliability and trustworthiness. Two types of cross-examination are added in criminal cases: *ḥaqirah*, to establish the exact time and place of the criminal act; and *bediqah*, to ascertain the exact nature of the crime. Once the testimony is recorded in court, it cannot be retracted. The litigant may, however, enter new evidence, in which event the court must retry the action. Persons who are known to earn their livelihood by gambling, who have no regard for the law, who are related to one of the litigants, who have some interest in the case, or, in most instances, who are women are invalidated from giving testimony in traditional Jewish law. Self-incrimination, except for admission of monetary liabilities, does not form valid ground for conviction since in Jewish law nobody can testify against himself. Circumstantial evidence (even of the most convincing nature), hearsay, or anything not actually heard or seen by the witness is invalid and inadmissable as evidence.

• Boaz Cohen, *Evidence in Jewish Law* (Brussels, 1965). Menachem Elon, *Jewish Law: History, Sources, Principles*, 4 vols. (Philadelphia, 1994).

EVIL. See GOOD AND EVIL.

EVIL EYE (Heb. *ʿayin ha-raʿ* or *ʿein ha-raʿ*), in popular folklore, the power, held by particular individuals, to harm others (humans, animals, plants) by looking at them. People with eyes that are unusual, because of their color, size, shape, or some defect, are suspected of having this power. Envy is the motivation usually attributed to the use of the evil eye, which has the effect of drying the liquids that are essential for life (water, blood, milk, etc.). Young children and pregnant women are particularly vulnerable. Belief in the evil eye existed in many ancient cultures, and its popularity still persists. Protective measures against the evil eye include the use of salt, *amulets, the colors red or blue, specific hand gestures, the verbal expression of the opposite of a positive personal attribute (for example, saying a person is ugly or unsuccessful, etc.), or the number five, which is believed to have holy qualities.

If one is struck by the evil eye, special rituals conducted by professional healers can remove its influence. The evil eye can be either inherited or developed as a skill. There are people considered naturally blessed and always protected from the effects of the evil eye, such as the biblical Joseph and all his descendants and, among animals, the fish. The evil eye is mentioned in classic Jewish sources, including the Mishnah, the Talmud and Midrash, the Zohar, and *Sefer Ḥasidim*. References to the evil eye are found in all Jewish communities, despite condemnation by Maimonides (*Hilkhot ʿAkkum* 11) and other authorities.

• Alan Dundes, ed., *The Evil Eye: A Folklore Casebook* (New York, 1982). Edward S. Gifford, *The Evil Eye: Studies in the Folklore of Vision* (New York, 1958). Siegfried N. Seligmann, *Die Zauberkraft des Auges und das Berufen* (Hamburg, 1922). Joshua Trachtenberg, *Jewish Magic and Superstition: A Study in Folk Religion* (New York, 1974).

—TAMAR ALEXANDER

EVIL INCLINATION. See YETSER HA-RAʿ AND YETSER HA-TOV.

EVIL SPIRITS. See DEMONS.

EVOLUTION, the theory, generally associated with Charles Darwin, that the various animal species arise from other and lower forms and that the higher forms of life (especially man) are but the latest link in the chain of development. Evolution provoked considerable controversy when first propounded in the nineteenth century and continues to exercise fundamentalist circles. Modern biological theories at first made little impact on Jewish thought. When scientific theories became more generally accepted, Orthodoxy still continued to reject them as heretical and as incompatible with the biblical account of *Creation. Attempts to interpret figuratively the biblical six days of Creation as geological ages or to "discover" Midrashic, aggadic, or medieval philosophical statements that apparently are consistent with an evolutionary theory did not go beyond homiletical apologetics; the basic philosophical issues of evolution—which do not involve the congruence or incongruence of the biblical and scientific chronologies but the transcendence or immanence of the creative act, the nature of purposiveness in the evolutionary process, and the moral implication of the survival factor—have so far not been tackled in Jewish thought. Although the Creation account of *Genesis* has traditionally been taken to be a mystery (see MAʿASEH BE-REʾSHIT) and creation itself understood as a supratemporal act, Orthodoxy has, nevertheless, tended to remain rigidly fundamentalist at the same time. Non-Orthodox thought on evolution has hardly moved beyond superficial commonplaces. A theological understanding of the doctrine of creation in the light of evolutionary biology is still seen by many as an outstanding challenge.

• Aryeh Carmell and Cyril Domb, eds., *Challenge: Torah Views on Science and Its Problems*, 2d rev. ed. (Jerusalem, 1978). Norbert M. Samuelson, *Judaism and the Doctrine of Creation* (Cambridge, 1994).

EVYATAR BEN ELIYYAHU HA-KOHEN (c.1040–1110), one of the last heads of the Palestinian academy (which had moved from Jerusalem to Tyre). He succeeded his father, Eliyyahu ben Shelomoh (whose family originated in Morocco) as *gaʾon in the year 1081. He was involved in a bitter struggle aimed at maintaining some vestiges of autonomy and communal authority for the Palestinian academy. His antagonist was the political head of Egyptian Jewry, David ben Daniyyeʾl ben ʿAzaryah, who was descended from the Babylonian dynasty of the *exilarchs and whose father had headed the Palestinian academy between 1052 and 1062. David denied the traditional authority of the Palestinian academy, not wishing it to be seen as the leading institution of the Jewish community in the Fatimid empire; he was ultimately rebuffed by Evyatar and his allies, but their triumph was short-lived; the Palestinian academy relocated in 1127 to Al-Fusṭāt and was absorbed into the Jewish community of Egypt. Evyatar's account of his struggle against David ben Daniyye'l is contained in *Megillat Evyatar* (published by Solomon Schechter in the *Jewish Quarterly Review* [1901–1902]), noteworthy for its evocation of the traditional stature and prerogatives of the Palestinian center and its academy; the one-sided picture presented by this source has now been supplemented by numerous documents from the period found in the Cairo *Genizah.

• Moshe Gil, *Erets-Yisra'el bi-Tequfat ha-Muslamit ha-Ri'shonah, 634–1099* (Tel Aviv, 1983). Moshe Gil, *A History of Palestine, 634–1099*, translated from the Hebrew by Ethel Broido (New York, 1992). Solomon Schechter, *Sa'adyana: Genizah Fragments of Writings of R. Sa'adyah Ga'on and Others* (Cambridge, 1903). —ROBERT BRODY

EXCOMMUNICATION, the exclusion of a person from membership in the *community and from its rights and privileges, issued by a *beit din*. It is mentioned in the Bible as a punishment imposed by Ezra (*Ezr*. 10.8). Excommunication is employed either as a punishment for transgressions or as a sanction to ensure obedience to communal enactments. The regulations governing excommunication are carefully detailed in the Talmud, and various safeguards were instituted from time to time to prevent the abuse of this powerful weapon.

Excommunication took three forms, of increasing severity. The mildest was *nezifah* (rebuke), which lasted for only one day in Babylonia and seven in Erets Yisra'el. The punishment consisted merely of the offender having to retire to his house and refrain from social intercourse. On expressing regret at his conduct, he was allowed to resume his normal life.

A stronger form of excommunication was *niddui* (banishment), which was imposed for a fixed period of seven days in the Diaspora and usually of thirty days in Erets Yisra'el, with the possibility of prolongation if the person was not prepared to change his conduct. During the period, the person excommunicated was regarded as a pariah. He was ostracized, except by the immediate members of his own family, and had to fulfill all the regulations appertaining to a mourner. His children could be denied circumcision, tuition, or attendance at worship.

Should these measures fail to bring him to penitence or conformity, the most extreme form of excommunication—the *ḥerem* (ban)—was imposed with solemn ceremonial. (The term *ḥerem* actually refers in its primary sense to property that must be forfeited, either for sacred purposes [*Lv*. 27.28] or because biblical law disallows contact with it; for example, idolatrous appurtenances from which no benefit may be derived. Thus, in Israel's "Holy Wars" [*Dt*. 7.23–26], no booty could be taken since it was *ḥerem* and had to be destroyed. Ezra uses the term in the sense of confiscation of property [*Ezr*. 10.8]. In the Talmud and subsequent Jewish literature, *ḥerem* refers to complete ostracism from the community.) This ban lasted for an indefinite period, and the person placed under the ban was denied every amenity of social and religious life apart from the barest necessities. During the Middle Ages, when Jews had no other legal means for enforcing conformity, the *ḥerem* became a powerful weapon. Thus, the phrase "*ḥerem* of Rabbenu Gershom," as applied to the famous enactments of Rabbenu Gershom ben Yehudah, including those outlawing polygamy and the divorce of a wife without her consent, meant that they contained the provision that in the absence of any other means of compelling obedience a person transgressing them would be placed in *ḥerem*. Such sanction proved sufficient to ensure adherence and could be canceled after a few days, with the transgressor expressing repentance and submission. Two notable examples of the invocation of the *ḥerem* by the Sephardi community of seventeenth-century Amsterdam concerned Uriel *Acosta and Baruch *Spinoza. Another was the imposition of the *ḥerem* on Ḥasidim by R. Eliyyahu ben Shelomoh Zalman of Vilna. In the eighteenth century, excommunication began to lose its significance as a result of its overuse by rabbis and the disintegration of the self-enclosed medieval Jewish community.

• Yosef Kaplan, "Deviance and Excommunication in the Eighteenth Century: A Chapter in the Social History of the Sephardi Community of Amsterdam," in *Dutch Jewish History*, edited by Jozeph Michman, vol. 3 (Jerusalem and Assen/Maastricht, 1993), pp. 103–116.

EXECUTION. See CAPITAL PUNISHMENT.

EXECUTION, CIVIL, the process in Jewish law by which debts and other moneys owed by one party to another are recovered. Essentially Jewish law recognizes that debts normally create two types of obligations, personal and property; thus any debt may be recovered from the property of the debtor. Biblical verses (*Ex*. 22.24–26), however, prevent the creditor from depriving the debtor of basic necessities or personal freedom. Involuntary slavery is limited to cases of theft. While there were a small number of medieval authorities who permitted the imposition of forced labor to repay certain debts, normative Jewish law rejected that ruling and prohibited such conduct. Jewish law also had an established procedure for addressing priorities of claim, preferential rights, and insolvency.

• Menachem Elon, "Execution," in *Principles of Jewish Law* (Jerusalem, 1975), pp. 621–633. —MICHAEL BROYDE

EXEGESIS. See BIBLE EXEGESIS; HERMENEUTICS.

EXILARCH (Aram. *resh galuta'* [head of the exile]), title of the head of Babylonian Jewry. The office of exilarch was hereditary, originating with King Jehoiachin, who was exiled to Babylon in 597 BCE. The purpose of the exilarchate was to maintain the continuity of Davidic rule; the importance of the position increased after the failure of the Bar Kokhba' Revolt (135 CE; see BAR KOKHBA', SHIM'ON), when the exilarch rivaled and eventually surpassed the authority of the parallel Erets Yisra'el institution of the *nasi'. The exilarch was responsible for the administration of justice in both civil and criminal cases in the Jewish community, necessitating close collaboration with the rabbis in both tannaitic and amoraic times, and he was responsible for the appointment of judges and of market overseers. He was treated with great honor by the caliph and in the Jewish community. A man called to the Torah reading in the synagogue would come to the platform on which the Torah was placed; when the exilarch was called, the Torah scroll was carried to him (Y., *Sot.* 22a). Under the ge'onim (see GA'ON), the influence of the religious authorities grew, and new exilarchs had to receive the approval of the heads of academies before their appointment was submitted to the caliph for approval. The Ashkenazi Sabbath morning-prayer ritual to this day carries a petition for the welfare of the *resh galuta'* in the *Yequm Purqan.

• Moshe Beer, *Ra'shut ha-Golah be-Bavel bi-Yemei ha-Mishnah veha-Talmud* (Tel Aviv, 1970). Avraham Grossman, *Ra'shut ha-Golah be-Bavel bi-Tequfat ha-Ge'onim* (Jerusalem, 1984). Jacob Neusner, *A History of the Jews in Babylonia*, 5 vols. (Leiden, 1965–1970). Jacob Neusner, *Israel's Politics in Sasanian Iran: Jewish Self-Government in Talmudic Times* (Lanham, Md., 1986).

EXILE (Heb. *galut, golah*), the enforced dwelling of the Israelites (Jews) outside the Holy Land. The Jewish people has lived in exile from Erets Yisra'el for a longer period than it has lived in it. Also, in periods not technically defined as exilic, such as the Second Temple period, the Jewish population in the Diaspora, especially that of Babylonia and Alexandria, was larger than it was in Erets Yisra'el. Rabbinic tradition distinguishes between two major exiles: the *Babylonian exile, and the exile following the destruction of the Second Temple in 70 CE. There was also an earlier Egyptian exile from the time of Jacob to the Exodus. From a historical viewpoint, however, there was continuity in the life and development of the Diaspora (Gr.; dispersion; i.e., Jewish residence outside the Holy Land) since the beginning of the sixth century BCE. The two exiles have decisively influenced Jewish religious and social development, and the seeds of many of the features characteristic of the second exile can already be detected in the brief first exile in Babylonia. Ezekiel's prophecies were uttered in Babylonia (cf. *Ez.* 1.1–2) and exhibit important effects of that exile: insistence on the need for personal, as distinct from national, righteousness (cf. *Ez.* 14); intimations of the foundation of the *synagogue, which as a "minor sanctuary" (*Ez.* 11.16) was subsequently to become a substitute for the "major sanctuary," the Temple; and the formulation of the motif of hope for an eventual return to Zion and the rebuilding of the Temple (*Ez.* 37). The rabbis noted other effects of the cultural contacts and influences to which Israel was exposed during the Babylonian exile, such as the adoption of the square or "Aramaic" script (*ketav Ashuri*) in place of the earlier Phoenician script (*ketav 'Ivri*), the adoption of Babylonian names for the Hebrew months, and the development of angelology. They interpreted the verse "So they read in the book of the law of God distinctly, and gave the sense, and caused them to understand the reading" (*Neh.* 8.8) as referring to the translation of the Hebrew text into Aramaic, thereby drawing attention to the adoption by the exiles of the vernacular of their country of exile. During the second exile, which lasted almost nineteen centuries, there was a vast extension of these developments. The synagogue became the center of worship, and R. Yoḥanan ben Zakk'ai deliberately transferred to it many of the rites and ceremonies that originally had belonged to the Temple (cf. *R. ha-Sh.* 4.1–3, *Suk.* 3.12). Morning and afternoon services took the place of the daily sacrifices while the *Musaf service commemorated the additional sacrifices on the days on which these used to be offered. The scriptural verses pertaining to the sacrifices for that particular day were combined with a fervent prayer for the restoration of Israel to its land and the rebuilding of the Temple. The synagogue *liturgy thus also served to keep alive the faith in the ultimate return. A great variety of external influences penetrated and enriched Jewish culture during the second exile. The adoption of the prevailing systems of Greek philosophy as preserved and developed by the Arabs, and the introduction of Arabic rhyme and meter by the medieval Hebrew poets, are among the outstanding examples. The use of the vernacular for literary purposes was particularly marked in the Muslim world, where Arabic was used by leading Jewish writers and thinkers. In Christian countries that particular influence was less marked, and rabbinic Hebrew remained the medium of religious literature. Life in the Diaspora profoundly affected ritual and civil law. With the destruction of the Temple, large areas of Jewish law, such as that pertaining to sacrifices, local and national government, and the agricultural laws that obtained only in Erets Yisra'el, became inoperative and subjects for study only, although this was passionately pursued with the double object of maintaining the belief in the restoration and of acquiring merit through study for its own sake. The area of practical Jewish law became correspondingly circumscribed. Until the advent of the modern era, exile was regarded variously as an unmitigated evil, a curse, a punishment for Israel's sins, and a redemptive suffering; in all cases as a provisional form of existence, which would be terminated by the ingathering of the exiles and messianic redemption. The latter either had to be patiently awaited or actively prepared for by piety and penitence. In early rabbinic and later mystical theology the notion of Israel's exile was complemented by that of God's own exile (*galut ha-shekhinah*—the exile of the divine presence). This doctrine implied both that God himself shared Israel's sufferings, and that, even in exile, Israel's communion with God was unbroken. Under the influence either of kabbalistic thought or of modern existentialist philosophy, exile has also been understood as a metaphor for alienation, the healing of which is a messianic utopia. Under the impact of the Enlightenment, influenced by the thinking of Baruch Spinoza and Moses Mendelssohn, certain circles—including nineteenth century Reform—universalized the concept of exile and identified as exile any imperfection in the human condition. The Jewish mission was defined as correcting these imperfections anywhere in the world; the Jews would not be redeemed solely through the achievement of Emancipation or through a return to Erets Yisra'el. Modern Zionism, however, continued the traditional attitude that exile was an evil to be overcome by the return to Erets Yisra'el. The Orthodox religious view of Zionism was articulated by R. Avraham Yitsḥaq Kook and his successor R. Isaac Herzog, who saw in statehood the beginning of redemption. With the establishment of the State of Israel in 1948 and the partial ingathering of the exiles, the problem of the historical, political, and social definition of exile came to the fore. Now that every Jew has the option to return to Israel, there is discussion as to whether the Diaspora Jewries should consider themselves as living in exile or not, with many maintaining that they are living in the Diaspora but not in exile.

• Peter R. Ackroyd, *Exile and Restoration: A Study of Hebrew Thought of the Sixth Century B.C.* (Philadelphia, 1968). Yitshaq Baer, *Galut*, translated by Robert Warshow (New York, 1947). Shaye J. D. Cohen, ed., *Diasporas in Antiquity* (Atlanta, 1993). Benzion Dinur, *Israel and the Diaspora* (Philadelphia, 1969). Arnold Eisen, *Galut: Modern Jewish Reflection on Homelessness and Homecoming* (Bloomington, Ind., 1986). Richard Elliot Friedman, *The Exile and Biblical Narrative* (Chico, Calif., 1981). Yeḥezq'el Kaufmann, *Golah ve-Nekhar* (Tel Aviv, 1962). Etan Levine, ed., *Diaspora: Exile and the Contemporary Jewish Condition* (New York, 1986).

EXILE, BABYLONIAN. See BABYLONIAN EXILE.

EXILES, INGATHERING OF THE, biblical concept, first expressed in *Deuteronomy* 30.3–5, that God will bring back to Erets Yisra'el those of his people scattered throughout other lands. According to the prophets, exile was a punishment for the people's sinfulness. When Ezekiel prophesied the eventual return of the Babylonian exiles to their native land, he addressed himself first to the Judean exiles and then extended his prophecy to include the exiles of the northern kingdom (the ten tribes) who had been dispersed over a century earlier (*Ez.* 37.16–28). Although there is disagreement in the Mishnah (*San.* 10.3) about whether or not the ten tribes are destined to return, the prevailing view is that the ultimate restoration will include the ten tribes (see TRIBES OF ISRAEL). It is this belief that explains the phrase *qibbuts galuyyot* (ingathering of the exiles), that is, the exiles of both Judah and Israel; the word *exile* refers to the condition, not the persons. According to the rabbis, the ingathering of the exiles was as significant as the creation of heaven and earth (*Pes.* 88a). Whenever the liturgy incorporates prayers for the ingathering of the exiles (in the Ahavah Rabbah, the tenth blessing of the ʿAmidah, the Birkat ha-Ḥodesh) the words "from the four corners of the earth" (cf. *Dt.* 30.4–5) are added, and the reference is to the messianic future. The ingathering of the exiles became a basic concept of modern *Zionism (rejected by some Orthodox, who believed it had to be effected not by human initiative but by divine intervention), and after 1948 the term was applied to the mass immigration to the State of Israel of Jews from over one hundred countries in the Diaspora. This return was regarded by religious Zionists as the beginning of the fulfillment of the biblical prophecy of redemption.

• "Exiles," *Parabola* 10.2 (1985): 3–119, theme issue on comparative studies. Hadassah Education Department, *The Theme of the Ingathering of the Exiles in the Bible* (New York, 1977)

EXISTENTIALISM, a modern movement in philosophy concerned with the understanding of human existence in its concreteness rather than as an object of understanding or theoretical abstraction. In spite of certain existentialist features of early philosophy (as in Socrates, Pascal), existentialism proper begins with the nineteenth-century Danish Protestant thinker Søren Kierkegaard. A basic attitude toward philosophy rather than a well-defined doctrine, existentialism encompasses atheistic thinkers (Heidegger, Sartre) as well as religious ones (e.g., Marcel). Franz *Rosenzweig, one of the greatest modern Jewish thinkers, was one of the founders of the existentialist philosophy. Many modern thinkers believe that existentialism provides better tools than classical philosophy for interpreting the significance of religion. Martin *Buber's "I and Thou" philosophy and his interpretations of the Bible have exerted wide influence as major expressions of a religious existentialism that sees in religion no objective system of doctrine or law but rather a relationship and mode of being realized in actual existence.

• William E. Kaufman, *Contemporary Jewish Philosophies* (New York, 1976).

EXODUS (Heb. *yetsi'at Mitsrayim*), the departure of the Israelite people from their enslavement to Pharaoh in Egypt. In the Bible, this event is related as an act of God's intervention in human affairs on his people's behalf, and the belief in God's role in the Exodus is a central tenet of the Jewish faith. In the first words of the *Ten Commandments, God presents himself as "YHVH your God, who brought you out of the land of Egypt" (*Ex.* 20.2).

According to the Bible, God told Abraham that his descendants would be enslaved in a foreign land, and only afterwards would they be set free in order to take possession of the land of Canaan, which he had promised them (*Gn.* 15.13–16). Later, as a result of the famine in the time of Joseph, the entire Israelite clan took up residence in Egypt, where they became a numerous people (*Gn.* 42–46), also part of the divine promise (*Gn.* 12.2, 15.5). Astounded by Israel's numbers, a "new king" of Egypt commandeered them into teams of forced laborers, setting over them cruel taskmasters and putting them to work on his construction projects. When this failed to weaken them, he decreed that all newborn Israelite males were to be drowned in the Nile.

Aroused by his people's suffering, God resolved that the time had come to keep his promise. Meanwhile, Moses, a Levite who was cleverly saved from the order of extermination, attained his manhood, discovered his Israelite identity, and fled to Midian (*Ex.* 2). There, God directed him, along with his brother Aaron, to announce to the people that the moment of their deliverance was near and to demand of Pharaoh that he set the Israelites free; at this juncture, the divine name, YHVH, was also revealed (see GOD, NAMES OF). Moses was warned that strategems, and ultimately force, would be necessary in order to get Pharaoh to comply (*Ex.* 3–7).

The mission to Pharaoh met with the expected refusal. Pharaoh was not even willing to allow the slaves to depart for an ostensibly brief period; thus, the ruse devised in order to quit Egypt by stealth did not succeed. The battle between God and Pharaoh ensued, taking the form of a series of miraculous plagues (*Ex.* 7–11; see PLAGUES OF EGYPT), at the culmination of which Pharaoh was forced to admit the superior might of God. In his suffering, Pharaoh begged the Israelites to leave his country as quickly as they could (*Ex.* 12); yet, when he realized what he had done, he pursued them with full military force. The climax of the story is the episode at the Red Sea; God miraculously split the sea in two, enabling the multitude of fleeing slaves to pass through on dry land, after which he reunited the waters, drowning Pharaoh and all his army. God then led his people safely through the Sinai Peninsula until they eventually reached Canaan (*Ex.* 14–15).

In biblical tradition, the Exodus marks the birth of the Israelite nation. It is an act of undeserved grace: it is not a reward for Israel's righteousness; rather, it is purely the fulfillment of a sovereign promise made by God. It thus serves to place Israel permanently in God's debt, since it owes its very existence to him. God's demand that Israel serve and obey him is founded on this (*Ex.* 19.1–6); compliance with his commands is due because of this act of salvation (*Dt.* 6.20–25).

The Exodus is also the source of Israel's love and gratitude to God; it is called a "redemption." God is pictured as Israel's close kinsman, showing familial concern for his kinfolk and relieving them from their hopelessness. The Exodus is the archetype of divine lovingkindness, the type of behavior Israel is expected to emulate. Over and over again, Israel is enjoined to recall its former condition of need; to be kind to the poor, the orphan, and the widow; and not to mistreat slaves or those without property. Numerous biblical passages recall and celebrate various miraculous facets of the Exodus; it would seem that in biblical times the retelling and embellishing of the tale had already become an accepted form of exhortation, chastisement, and praise (*Jos* 24.5–7; *Jgs.* 2.12, 6.8–13; *Ez.* 20.5–10; *Neh.* 9.9–12; *Ps.* 74.12–15, 78, 81.6–7, 104.34–39, 106, 114, 136.10–16; *Jer.* 11.1–8).

Although the appropriate historical context for the Exodus can probably be identified (the building projects of Ramses II, a generation or so before the known period of Israel's invasion of Canaan) and historical data from the mid-thirteenth century BCE can be adduced, outside of the Bible no corroboration for the actual events has been found. However, in view of the antiquity, weight, and quantity of biblical evidence, scholars tend to attach to the story a kernel of historical truth. Evidently a group of Israelite herdsmen were pressed into corvée by an Egyptian pharaoh, a bondage so traumatically different from their traditional way of life that it was never forgotten, and their eventual release from it was naturally attributed to the merciful aid of their ancestral God. Biblical tradition, here as elsewhere, would thus preserve an authentic, indelible memory, though many of the details may be gradual embellishments.

First among commemorative rituals, the annual *Pesaḥ offering was instituted to recall the Exodus each year on the date of its occurrence. In post-Temple times, this was replaced by the Pesaḥ *Seder. In both rituals, the liturgical retelling of the story of the Exodus figures prominently (see HAGGADAH OF PESAḤ), taking literally the instruction "You shall tell your son on that day: 'This is because of what the Lord did for me when I came out Egypt' " (*Ex.* 13.8).

• John Bright, *A History of Israel* (Philadelphia, 1972), pp. 103–139. Samuel E. Loewenstamm, *The Evolution of the Exodus Tradition* (Jerusalem, 1992). Benjamin Mazar, *The World History of the Jewish People*, 1st ser., vol. 3, *Judges* (London, 1971), pp. 69–93. Nahum Sarna, *Exploring Exodus: The Heritage of Biblical Israel* (New York, 1986). Yair Zakovitch, *"And You Shall Tell Your Son . . . ": The Concept of the Exodus in the Bible* (Jerusalem, 1991).

—BARUCH J. SCHWARTZ

EXODUS, BOOK OF (Heb. *Shemot*; [These Are] the Names [of]), the second book of the *Torah, whose Hebrew title is from the opening phrase of the book. The name *Exodus* (from Gr. *exodos*), referring to Israel's departure from Egypt, also appears in rabbinic literature. After a brief recapitulation of the Israelites' arrival in Egypt, the book, which is divided into forty chapters, narrates the Israelites' bondage to *Pharaoh (chap. 1); the birth and early years of *Moses (chap. 2); Moses' mission to Pharaoh (chaps. 3–6); the *plagues of Egypt and the *Pesaḥ sacrifice (chaps. 7–13); the departure from Egypt (see EXODUS) and the miraculous crossing of the sea (chaps. 14–15); and the first portion of the journey to Canaan, until the arrival at *Sinai (chaps. 16–18). The remainder of the narrative takes place while the Israelites are camped at Sinai: the theophany and giving of the *Ten Commandments (chaps. 19–20); the laws given to Moses and the *covenant made over them (chaps. 21–24); and the worship of the *golden calf, the renewal of the covenant, and the two sets of tablets (chaps. 32–34). Interspersed with the final portion is the account of how Moses received and carried out the detailed instructions for the building of the *Tabernacle (chaps. 25–30, 35–40); the narrative ends when, a year after the Exodus, the Tabernacle is completed. Thus, following two introductory chapters in the which Israelites develop into a numerous people, most of the book covers a time span of two crucial years in Israel's history in which its central formative events take place: its redemption from slavery, its covenant with God at Sinai, and the establishment of its central cultic institution. In Jewish tradition, the *Book of Exodus*—like all books of the Torah—was written by Moses under divine inspiration. Bible critics detect at least three distinct narrative sources (J, E, and P) running through the book and assign to each of them a section of the legal material.

The *Book of Exodus* consists of eleven weekly portions, read in the synagogue on successive sabbaths during the winter months. See also GIVING OF THE TORAH; PILLAR OF CLOUD AND FIRE; TABLETS OF THE LAW.

• Umberto Cassuto, *A Commentary on the Book of Exodus*, translated by Israel Abrahams (Jerusalem, 1967). Brevard S. Childs, *The Book of Exodus*, The Old Testament Library (Philadelphia, 1974). Moshe Greenberg, *Understanding Exodus* (New York, 1969). Nahum M. Sarna, *Exodus*, The JPS Torah Commentary (Philadelphia, 1991). Nahum M. Sarna, *Exploring Exodus* (New York, 1986).

—BARUCH J. SCHWARTZ

EXODUS RABBAH, aggadic *midrash* on the *Book of Exodus*, included in the compilation commonly referred to as *Midrash Rabbah (the main edition of which, with commentaries, was published in Vilna in 1878). Written almost entirely in Hebrew, it is a composite work. The first part, *Exodus Rabbah 1* (sections 1–14), covers chapters one through ten of the *Book of Exodus*; the second part, *Exodus Rabbah 2* (sections 15–52), is a *midrash* covering chapters twelve to the end. While *Exodus Rabbah 2* is an edition of the *Tanḥuma'-Yelammedenu *midrash* to *Exodus* and is thus an example of a homiletical *midrash*, *Exodus Rabbah 1* is an exegetical *midrash*, containing Midrashic comments on almost every verse. Each section (*parashah*) begins with one or more *petiḥot* (see Petiḥah), almost all of them anonymous. *Exodus Rabbah 1* is a relatively late redaction (c.10th cent.) of Midrashic material found mostly in the *Midrash Tanḥuma'* to *Exodus*, including several sections from the Talmud Bavli and perhaps material originating with the redactor himself. It is first cited by Spanish authors from the thirteenth century. It has been posited that the redactor of *Exodus Rabbah 1* was interested in creating an exegetical *midrash* that would bridge the gap between *Genesis Rabbah* and the tannaitic *midrash* to *Exodus* (*Mekhilta' de-Rabbi Yishma'e'l*), which begins only at *Exodus* chapter 12; this part was then supplemented by an edition of the Tanḥuma'-Yelammedenu *midrash* to the remaining chapters of *Exodus*.

Midrash Rabbah: Exodus (edited by H. Freedman and M. Simon, 3d ed. [London, 1961]) is an English translation of *Exodus Rabbah*. A critique of *Exodus Rabbah 1* was published in Jerusalem in 1984 (*Midrash Shemot Rabbah: Chapters 1–14*).

• Saul Lieberman, ed., *Midrash Devarim Rabbah*, 3d ed. (Jerusalem, 1974). Avigdor Shin'an, ed., *Midrash Shemot Rabbah: Derashot 1–14* (Tel Aviv, 1984). Leopold Zunz, *Ha-Derashot be-Yisra'el ve-Hishtalshelutan ha-Historit*, edited by Chanoch Albeck (1892; Jerusalem, 1974).

—PAUL MANDEL

EXORCISM, the expulsion of foreign spirits that have possessed an individual. Mention of exorcism is rare in early Jewish literature. In the Bible, the only clear examples are the possession of Saul by an evil spirit and its exorcism by David's playing the harp (*1 Sm.* 16.14–23) and in the Apocrypha in the *Book of Tobit*. The New Testament refers to the casting out of "unclean spirits." References in the Talmud are sparse. With the spread of Kabbalah and its doctrine of the *transmigration of souls, especially the variety defined as *'ibbur* (the impregnation of a living person or soul by another soul or spirit), the belief in exorcism became powerfully reinforced, notably in eastern Europe. A particular form of exorcism was the expulsion of a *dybbuk.

• Gedalyah Nigal, *Magic, Mysticism and Hasidism: The Supernatural in Jewish Thought*, translated by Edward Levin (Northvale, N.J., 1994), pp. 112–133.

—SHIFRA EPSTEIN

EYBESCHUETZ, YONATAN (c.1690–1764), Talmudist and kabbalist. Born in Kraków, Eybeschuetz was recognized as a Talmudic prodigy (*'illu'iy*). A student of R. Me'ir Eisenstadt, he attained prominence as a scholar, community rabbi, and *yeshivah* head in Prague in 1715, where he came into contact and conflict with R. David ben Abraham Oppenheim, the leading rabbinic figure of that city. From Prague, Eybeschuetz moved on to Metz in 1741 and Altona in 1750.

Eybeschuetz was instrumental in persuading the Christian authorities to allow the printing of the Talmud in Prague (1728–1739). This edition, from which all potentially anti-Christian passages were censored, aroused strong opposition from Oppenheim and other Talmudists, who decried it as a distortion of the true text and feared that its circulation would influence future printings of the Talmud. Ultimately, the edition's opponents succeeded in persuading the emperor to prohibit its further publication. These events are indicative of the controversies that filled Eybeschuetz's public life. On the one hand, he was respected as a brilliant Talmudic scholar. His *Urim ve-Tummim*, a two-part commentary on the *Ḥoshen Mishpat* section of the *Shulḥan 'Arukh*, and his *Kereti u-Feleti*, a commentary on the *Yoreh De'ah* section of the *Arba'ah Turim*, are regarded as classics of halakhic literature and are still widely published. He was also a popular preacher, whose sermons are collected in *Ya'arot Devash* and other works. He enjoyed widespread popularity in the communities in which he served. On the other hand, many rabbis suspected that Eybeschuetz was a follower of Shabbetai Tsevi. A kabbalistic text published in 1724, *Ve-'Avo' ha-Yom el ha-'Ayin*, was recognized by rabbinic consensus as a Shabbatean work; the book bears striking similarities to Eybeschuetz's *Shem 'Olam*. According to Eybeschuetz's leading opponent, R. Ya'aqov *Emden, amulets by Eybeschuetz that were opened in 1751 were found to contain Shabbatean mystical formulas. Though exonerated by Polish Jewry's Council of the Four Lands in 1753, Eybeschuetz remained a controversial figure. Modern scholars tend to accept as true the claims of his opponents that he was, in fact, a Shabbatean.

• Elisheva Carlebach, *The Pursuit of Heresy: Rabbi Moses Hagiz and the Sabbatian Controversies* (New York, 1990). Heinrich Graetz, *History of the Jews* (Philadelphia, 1949), vol. 5, pp. 246–271. Moses Perlmuter, *R. Yehonatan Aybeshits ve-Yaḥaso el ha-Shabta'ut* (Jerusalem, 1947). Raphael N. Rabinowitz, *Ma'amar 'al Hadpasat ha-Talmud* (Jerusalem, 1951), pp. 112–113.

—MARK WASHOFSKY

EZEKIEL (Heb. Yeḥezqe'l; 6th cent. BCE), prophet in the *Babylonian exile; son of Buzi, a member of the priestly house of Zadok. His prophecies are contained in the biblical book bearing his name. He was deported along with King Jehoiachin of Judah and a large group of Jerusalemites in 597 BCE to Babylon by the invading forces of Nebuchadnezzar (*2 Kgs*. 24.8–16; *Ez*. 1.1–3). The exiles were settled at Tel-abib on the river Chebar; there they were joined by later waves of deportees. Eventually they received the news of the siege and final destruction of Jerusalem (586). Ezekiel's call to prophesy came in July 593, and all of his preaching took place among the deported Jerusalemites. From July 593 until January 585, he spoke only of the impending downfall; these oracles were probably uttered in the privacy of his home. Once news of the fall arrived, Ezekiel spoke openly, primarily of the future restoration of Israel's land and Temple cult. He continued to prophesy until 571. Due to his background, Ezekiel's style and vocabulary are highly influenced by the Torah, particularly the Priestly tradition. His prophecy is rich in visionary experiences and symbolic actions, and his highly sophisticated, often daring, and always forceful use of language indicates that he composed his prophecies not only as orations but as literary works. The inescapable nature of God's punitive justice and overriding concern for divine sovereignty are the hallmarks of his message; they are probably also a reflection of his own pessimism and uncompromising integrity.

The *Book of Ezekiel* is the third book of the *Latter Prophets. It opens with the appearance of the divine chariot (chap. 1), a portent that God is about to abandon his Temple and city to destruction, and the call to prophesy (2.1–3.15), in which Ezekiel is warned that his pronouncements of doom will not change the people's behavior since they, like all previous generations, are incorrigible. In the prophecy of *Ezekiel* 3.16–21 (repeated in 33.1–9), God compares Ezekiel's task to that of a watchman; he is morally bound to sound the alarm whether the people listen or not. This is followed by the oracles of judgment (chaps. 4–24). The climax of this section is Ezekiel's visionary excursion to Jerusalem (chaps. 8–11), where—six full years before the city was actually destroyed—he witnesses the abominations of the Jerusalemites, their slaughter by divine messengers, the burning of the city, and God's departure. The historical surveys (chaps. 16, 20, 23) emphasize that God has lost patience with his people's uninterrupted sinfulness; the allegorical portrayal of the wanton Jerusalem (chap. 16) is the most outspoken. The prophet stresses that guilt is not passed from generation to generation (18.1–20); his intent is to show that although Israel's imminent punishment is not a case of inherited guilt, all generations have been equally sinful (chap. 20). When God informs Ezekiel that the siege of the city has begun, this period in Ezekiel's ministry ends (chap. 24). A series of oracles against foreign nations follows (chaps. 25–32). Then the news of the actual fall arrives in Babylon, vindicating Ezekiel (33.21–22). In the oracles that follow, Ezekiel announces God's intention to return Israel from captivity, reunite and resettle the tribes, reestablish the monarchy, and rebuild the Temple. All this, God will do not out of compassion or because Israel deserves it, but for the sake of his own holy name, which Israel has desecrated. God desires to rehabilitate his reputation, which has been tarnished by Israel's exile, in the sight of other nations. The exiles doubt they will ever be returned home, and this despair prompts the vision of chapter 37.1–14, in which a massive heap of dry bones comes back to life—affirming that the ingathering of the exiles, however unimaginable, will indeed take place. In the concluding vision (chaps. 40–48), Ezekiel is again transported to Jerusalem, where he is given a preview of the rebuilt Temple and the return of the divine presence to dwell in his city, now renamed YHVH Shammah (the LORD is there; 48.35).

Ezekiel's descriptions of the divine chariot became the basis for an entire branch of Jewish mysticism (see MA'ASEH MERKAVAH); the rabbis of the Talmud forbade untutored lay persons to delve too deeply into the study of these portions (*Ḥag.* 2.1). The vision of the dry bones (37.1–14) was taken by later Jewish sources as a scriptural basis for the belief in *resurrection (*San.* 92b). Since a number of legal provisions of the restored Temple cult contradict the Torah, some of the sages, though not doubting the book's authenticity or its sanctity, advocated removing it from circulation (*Shab.* 13b). The contradictions were resolved, however, and the book continued to be read. Though some of its harsher sections were not permitted to be read in the synagogue, a number of *haftarot* are taken from Ezekiel. The chariot vision is read on Shavu'ot to complement the theophany at Sinai, and the vision of the dry bones is read on Pesaḥ, a promise of a new exodus from exile.

• Leslie C. Allen, *Ezekiel 20–48*, Word Biblical Commentary, vol. 29 (Waco, Tex., 1990). Ellen Frances Davis, *Swallowing the Scroll: Textuality and the Dynamics of Discourse in Ezekiel's Prophecy*, Bible and Literature Series 21, Journal for the Study of the Old Testament, Supplement Series 78 (Sheffield, Eng., 1989). Julie Galumbush, *Jerusalem in the Book of Ezekiel*, Dissertation Series (Society of Biblical Literature), no. 130 (Atlanta, 1992). Moshe Greenberg, *Ezekiel 1–20*, The Anchor Bible, vol. 22 (Garden City, N.Y., 1983). Moshe Greenberg, Prolegomenon to Charles Cutler Torrey, *Pseudo-Ezekiel and the Original Prophecy* (repr. New York, 1970), pp. XI–XXXV. Paul Joyce, *Divine Initiative and Human Response in Ezekiel*, Journal for the Study of the Old Testament, Supplement Series 59 (Sheffield, Eng. 1989). *Interpretation*, vol. 38, no. 2 (1984): 117–208 (various articles). Jon Douglas Levenson, *Theology of the Program of Restoration of Ezekiel 40–48*, Harvard Semitic Monographs, no. 10 (Missoula, Mont., 1976). J. Lust, ed., *Ezekiel and His Book* (Leuven, 1986). Baruch J. Schwartz, "Repentance and Determinism in Ezekiel," *Proceedings of the Eleventh World Congress of Jewish Studies* (1994), pp. 123–130. Walter Zimmerli, *Ezekiel*, translated by Ronald E. Clements, edited by Frank Moore Cross and Klaus Baltzer, Hermeneia, vols. 1 and 2 (Philadelphia, 1979 and 1983).

—BARUCH J. SCHWARTZ

EZRA (5th cent. BCE), priest and *scribe (descendant of *Zadok), who was primarily responsible for a series of religious reforms laying the spiritual foundations of the new Judean commonwealth after the Babylonian exile. According to the traditional account (*Ezr.* 7–8), he returned to Jerusalem at the head of a group of exiles, with full powers from the Persian king Artaxerxes I to impose the law of the Torah on the community there (458 BCE) and, bearing the sacred vessels of the *Temple, set about effecting reforms in the religious as well as civic conditions then prevailing in Judah. Mixed marriages with heathen wives were annulled (probably completing the breach with the nascent *Samaritans; *Ezr.* 10.18–44) and a vigorous program was launched for observing the Sabbath and sabbatical year and expounding the Torah to the common people. Ezra also revived the practice of the thanksgiving Sukkah (*Neh.* 8.13–18). As the traditional founder of the *Keneset ha-Gedolah, Ezra laid the basis for the future form of Judaism. The Talmud also ascribes to him the introduction of the square Hebrew script. It says that he promulgated ten decrees including the Torah reading on the Sabbath *Minḥah service and in *Shaḥarit on Mondays and Thursdays (*Meg.* 31b).

The *Book of Ezra* (partly in Aramaic) appears tenth in the Hagiographa and is regarded as a single unit with the *Book of Nehemiah* (see EZRA-NEHEMIAH, BOOK OF). The narrative centers around the vicissitudes of the rebuilders of the Second Temple and is written from a priestly viewpoint. The relation of Ezra's activity to that of Nehemiah, as well as their respective dates, are a matter of controversy among modern biblical scholars. Rabbinic evaluation of Ezra's initiative during the critical period of transition from the prophetic to the Pharisaic era can be gathered from the Talmudic observation that, had not Moses preceded, God would have given the Torah through Ezra (*San.* 21b). Various traditions relate to his burial site, but the one most generally accepted places it near Basra, Iraq, which became a site of pilgrimage.

• J. Blenkinsopp, *Ezra–Nehemiah: A Commentary*, The Old Testament Library (Philadelphia, 1988). Yehezkel Kaufmann, *History of the Religion of Israel: Vol. IV, From the Babylonian Captivity to the End of Prophecy* (New York, 1977), pp. 324–358. H.G.M. Williamson, *Ezra, Nehemiah*, Word Biblical Commentary, vol. 16 (Waco, Tex., 1985).

– DAVID A. GLATT-GILAD

EZRA-NEHEMIAH, BOOK OF (Heb. *ʿEzra'-Neḥemyah*), the penultimate book in the Hagiographa section of the Hebrew Bible, originally referred to by the name *Ezra* alone. The first reference to the division of this book into separate books of *Ezra* and *Nehemiah* was made by the church father Origen (3d cent. CE). *Ezra-Nehemiah* is set in the period of Persian rule over Erets Yisra'el. The book's three major sections are *Ezra* 1–6, which covers the period from Cyrus's proclamation permitting Jews to return from exile in Babylonia to Jerusalem in order to rebuild the Temple (538 BCE), through the successful completion of the rebuilding project in the sixth year of Darius I (516); *Ezra* 7–10, which describes Ezra's mission and activities (beginning in 458); and *Nehemiah* 1–13, which describes Nehemiah's career (445–c.432). *Ezra-Nehemiah* brings together many diverse source materials. These include Aramaic documents, such as Tattenai's letter to Darius questioning the Jews' right to rebuild the Temple (*Ezr.* 5.6–17) and Artaxerxes' letter of commission to Ezra (*Ezr.* 7.12–26); selections from Ezra's autobiography (*Ezr.* 7.27–28, 8–9); and selections from Nehemiah's autobiography (most of *Neh.* 1.1–7.5, 12.27–13.31). The finished literary product reflects a carefully planned portrayal of the restoration process marked by a particular ideology. Each step of the process is supported by the reigning Persian king, whose favorable attitude toward the Jews, despite vehement opposition from local enemies, is a sign of divine providence (*Ezr.* 1.1–3, 6.14, 7.6, 7.27–28; *Neh.* 2.4–8). The ultimate goal of the restoration is the creation of a community that lives by the commandments of the Torah (*Neh.* 8.1–8, 10.29–30).

• Joseph Blenkinsopp, *Ezra-Nehemiah: A Commentary*, Old Testament Library (London, 1989). Tamara C. Eskenazi, *In An Age of Prose: A Literary Approach to Ezra-Nehemiah*, Society of Biblical Literature Monograph Series, no. 36 (Atlanta, 1988). Ralph W. Klein, "Ezra and Nehemiah in Recent Studies," in *Magnalia Dei: The Mighty Acts of God: Essays on the Bible and Archaeology in Memory of G. Ernest Wright*, edited by F. M. Cross, W. E. Lemke, P. D. Miller, Jr. (Garden City, N.Y., 1976), pp. 361–376. Hugh G. M. Williamson, *Ezra, Nehemiah*, Word Biblical Commentary, vol. 16 (Waco, Tex., 1985).

–DAVID A. GLATT-GILAD

EZRA OF GERONA (died c.1240), one of the earliest and most important kabbalists, who established the center for Kabbalah in the town of Gerona in Catalonia. He was the disciple of R. Yitsḥaq Saggi Nahor, the leader of the kabbalists in Provence. Ezra is one of the first writers to quote *Sefer ha-Bahir*, the earliest work of medieval Kabbalah. Together with his relative R. ʿAzri'el of Gerona (with whom he was often confused), he developed the main genres of kabbalistic creativity in the thirteenth century: commentaries on the *aggadot* in the Talmud, on the exegesis of biblical books (especially the *Song of Songs*), and on *Sefer Yetsirah*. He influenced considerably the kabbalistic works of Nahmanides, the leader of the Gerona kabbalists, and of other writers in that center. Rabbi Yaʿaqov ben Sheshet, another kabbalist of Gerona, presented arguments against some of his ideas. Ezra was quoted by later kabbalists, like R. Baḥya ben Asher at the end of the thirteenth century, and some of his ideas found their place in the Zohar.

• Gershom Gerhard Scholem, *Origins of the Kabbalah* (Princeton, 1987), pp. 370–378. Georges Vajda, *Le Commentaire d'Ezra de Gérone sur le Cantique des Cantiques* (Paris, 1969).

–JOSEPH DAN

ʿEZRAT NASHIM (עֶזְרַת נָשִׁים; women's courtyard), originally, a separate uncovered courtyard for women in the Temple in Jerusalem, located in the eastern sector. *Women were not permitted to go beyond the *ʿezrat nashim* into the main courtyard. The term was later used for the separate women's section of the synagogue, either a balcony or a section on the same level as, or slightly above, the men's section, partitioned off from the men's section by a **meḥitsah* (divider). There is no evidence of such a division in early synagogues, but it was well established in the medieval period. In the synagogues of Provence in the late Middle Ages, women were in a room under the synagogue with a grille in the ceiling through which they could hear the service. In Nürnberg, women had their own synagogue. In Poland, women were provided with an annex and a separate entrance. In some places, women had their own prayer leader in the *ʿezrat nashim*, who also preached on occasion. In some Muslim lands, there was no provision for women, who would sit outside the synagogue window and listen to the service. Abolishing separate seating for men and women was one of the earliest changes introduced by the *Reform movement into the synagogue service. At present, all Reform synagogues maintain seating with "family pews," and most Conservative synagogues have followed suit.

• Ismar Elbogen, *Jewish Liturgy: A Comprehensive History*, translated by Raymond P. Scheindlin (Philadelphia, New York, and Jerusalem, 1993), pp. 357–358. Leopold Löw, *Gesammelte Schriften*, vol. 4 (Szegedin, 1898), pp. 72–92.

–SHMUEL HIMELSTEIN

F

FAITH. The biblical concept of faith is expressed in the Hebrew term *emunah*, which is derived from a root meaning "firm" or "steadfast" and hence denotes, in a religious context, unwavering trust and confidence in God, rather than assent to theological propositions. *Isaiah* 7.9 uses the verb for a punning double-entendre: "if you will not have faith [in the sense of total trust] you will not be established." The word **amen* is derived from the same root. There is considerable overlap with the concept of **bittaḥon*.

In due course, however, and in response to a variety of aggressive cultural alternatives, a more self-conscious awareness of faith as belief in the truth of certain ideas and propositions developed. The Talmud shows an awareness that the Torah or, conversely, idolatry could be affirmed or denied (cf. *Sifrei* on *Dt*. 28), and that the holding of certain views rendered an individual a *kofer ba'iqqar* (one who denied the very basis). The Mishnah (*San*. 11.1) lists doctrines by the denial of which one forfeits one's share in "the world to come."

In the Middle Ages the encounter with two rival monotheistic religions, which themselves had encountered the challenge of rationalist philosophies inherited from Greece, demanded a "defense of the faith." On the philosophical level, the more serious problem was that of faith versus reason. Most philosophers after *Sa'adyah ben Yosef Ga'on agreed that certain tenets and even commandments were evident truths of reason, capable of rational proof, whereas others had to be accepted on the authority of *revelation. Moses *Maimonides, in his commentary on the Mishnah (*San*. 11.1), enumerated *thirteen principles (*'iqqarim*) of faith, which were subsequently reformulated in the form of a *creed ("I believe with perfect faith that. . . "); in this form, they found their way into some versions of the *prayer book. Maimonides' list was criticized on many counts by other philosophers, including Ḥasda'i ben Avraham *Crescas, Shim'on Duran (see Duran Family), Yosef *Albo, and Yitsḥaq Abravanel (see Abravanel Family), but there is little doubt that the discussion contributed greatly to the clarification of theological reflection. Faith as an expression of Jewish historical experience rather than rational philosophizing was propounded by *Yehudah ha-Levi. The view that Judaism was concerned primarily with conduct (praxis) was reformulated in the eighteenth century, in terms of universalist *Enlightenment rationalism, by Moses *Mendelssohn. Mendelssohn argued that religious truths were universal; the specificity of the "Mosaic Law" was in its commanding the Israelites what to do, or refrain from doing, rather than what to believe. Mendelssohn himself preferred to translate the opening phrase of the Thirteen Principles of Maimonides with "I am firmly convinced." *Reform Judaism sought to uncover a new basis of faith to replace the traditional observances and ritual laws that it regarded as no longer binding. Internal religious polemics between orthodox and rationalists, that is, progressives, tended to turn on questions of alleged facts (e.g., the Mosaic origin of the Pentateuch, the account of Creation in *Gn*. 1). The nature of faith itself (i.e., the act of faith and the nature of the "man of faith") rather than its contents, or, faith as a mode of life rather than as a matter of "I believe that . . . ," has become an increasingly central concern of modern thinkers (e.g., Martin *Buber, Abraham Joshua *Heschel, Yosef Dov Soloveichik [see Soloveichik Family]), especially under the impact of existentialist philosophy on the one hand and the Holocaust on the other.

• Eliezer Berkovits, *God, Man and History* (New York, 1959). Martin Buber, *Two Types of Faith* (New York, 1951). Isidore Epstein, *Faith of Judaism* (London, 1954). Julius Guttmann, *Philosophies of Judaism: The History of Jewish Philosophy from Biblical Times to Franz Rosenzweig* (New York, 1964). Abraham Joshua Heschel, *God in Search of Man* (New York, 1955). Abraham Joshua Heschel, *Man Is Not Alone* (New York, 1951). Louis Jacobs, *Faith* (New York, 1968). Louis Jacobs, *Principles of the Jewish Faith* (New York, 1964). Joseph Dov Soloveichik, *The Halakhic Mind* (New York, 1986). Joseph Dov Soloveichik, *The Lonely Man of Faith* (New York, 1992). Milton Steinberg, *Anatomy of Faith* (New York, 1960).

FAITH, ARTICLES OF. See Thirteen Principles of Faith.

FALAQUERA, SHEM TOV BEN YOSEF (c.1225–1295), philosopher and poet in Spain or southern France; author of many books aimed at reconciling Judaism with philosophy. His best-known work, *Moreh ha-Moreh* (1837), is a commentary on Maimonides' *Guide of the Perplexed*, which quotes extensively from Arab and Jewish philosophers. Falaquera wrote *Sefer ha-Ma'alot* (1557) and *Iggeret ha-Vikkuaḥ* (1875), a dialogue between a Talmudic scholar and a philosopher about the various degrees of intellectual perfection. His biblical commentary and an exegesis of the *aggadot* of the Talmud have been lost. His most important work, *De'ot ha-Filosofim* remains in manuscript. His work on psychology, *Sefer ha-Nefesh*, was published in 1978 by Raphael Jospe in a critical edition with an annotated translation in English.

• Steven Harvey, *Falaquera's Epistle of the Debate: An Introduction to Jewish Philosophy* (Cambridge, Mass., 1987). Raphael Jospe, *Tora and Sophia: The Life and Thought of Shem Tov ibn Falaquera* (Cincinnati, 1988).

—Francisco Moreno Carvalho

FALASHAS. See Beta Israel.

FALK, YA'AQOV YEHOSHU'A (1680–1756), Polish-born rabbi. He studied in various *yeshivot* before embarking on a career in trade. Personal tragedy (the death of his wife and daughter) led him to resume full-time study and a rabbinical career. He served in Lemberg (Lwów) and the surrounding region before becoming rabbi of Berlin in 1730, Metz in 1734, and Frankfurt am Main in 1741. He was bitterly opposed to Shabbateanism, excommunicating its adherents in Lemberg in 1722. He supported Ya'aqov *Emden against Yonatan *Eybeschuetz, issuing a ban against him—a stand that led to Falk's resignation from the Frankfurt rabbinate in 1751. Falk's fame rested on his volumes of *novellae* on the Talmud, *Penei Yehoshu'a* (published separately,

1730–1780; together, in Lemberg, 1809), distinguished from a work of the same name written by his grandfather by the subtitle *Appei Zutrei*. His aim was to resolve the problems raised by the tosafists in their commentary on Rashi.

• Ḥayyim Nathan Dembitzer, *Sefer Qelilat Yofi* (Jerusalem, 1988–1989; repr. of Kraków, 1892–1893), vol. 1, pp. 108–115. Bernhard Wachstein, "Seridim mi-Pinqaso shel Rabbi Ya'aqov Yehoshu'a Ba'al Penei Yehoshu'a," in *Studies in Jewish Bibliography and Related Subjects in Memory of Abraham Solomon Freidus* (New York, 1929), pp. 15–31.

—ADAM TELLER

FALK, YEHOSHU'A BEN ALEKSANDER HA-KOHEN (c.1555–1614), Polish halakhist known by the acronym Sma' from the title of his best-known work, *Sefer Me'irat 'Einayim*. Born in Lublin, Falk studied under Mosheh Isserles and Shelomoh Luria. Declining to accept rabbinical posts, he settled in Lemberg (Lwów), where, with the assistance of his wealthy father-in-law, he established a private *yeshivah*. He was a leading rabbinic authority and participated in the Polish Jewish autonomous body, the Council of the Four Lands, drawing up its regulations concerning credit and interest—*Hetter 'Isqa'* (published as *Qunteres 'al ha-Ribbit* [1962]). His famous *Sefer Me'irat 'Einayim* is a commentary on the **Shulḥan 'Arukh, Ḥoshen Mishpat*, today printed in all editions of the *Shulḥan 'Arukh*. This work is the fourth part of a larger commentary on the *Shulḥan 'Arukh* and the *Arba'ah Turim*, the other three parts of which are called *Perishah*, *Derishah*, and *Be'urim*. Most of his work (including the first three parts of his commentary) remains in manuscript, though some of his *responsa* have been published.

• Haim Hillel Ben-Sasson, *Hagut ve-Hanhagah* (Jerusalem, 1959). Yosef Buksboim, ed., *Sefer ha-Zikkaron: Li-Khevodo ule-Zikhro shel-Maran Rabbi Ya'aqov Betsalel Zolti . . .* (Jerusalem, 1986–1987), pp. 297–320. Jacob Elbaum, *Petiḥut ve-Histagrut: Ha-Yetsirah ha-Ruḥanit ha-Sifrutit be-Polin uve-'Artsot Ashkenaz be-Shilhe ha-Me'ah ha-Shesh-'Esreh* (Jerusalem, 1990).

—ADAM TELLER

FALLEN ANGELS. See ANGELS.

FALSE WITNESS. The prohibition "you shall not bear false witness against your neighbor" (*Ex*. 20.13) embraces all forms of slander, defamation, and misrepresentation, whether of an individual, a group, a people, a race, or a faith, but is primarily directed against the giving of false testimony in court. The biblical injunction to do to the false witness as he had proposed to do to his brother (*Dt*. 19.19) applies only if a second pair of witnesses state in court, "How can you testify? You were with us that day in another place." The punishment is, however, only carried out if the false testimony of the witness is proven prior to the execution of the sentence. See also EVIDENCE; WITNESS.

• Menachem Elon, *Jewish Law: History, Sources, Principles*, 4 vols. (Philadelphia, 1994). Johann J. Stamm, *The Ten Commandments in Recent Research* (London, 1970). Charles M. Swezey, "Exodus 20:16—'Thou Shalt Not Bear False Witness Against Thy Neighbor,'" *Interpretation* 34 (1980): 405–410.

FAMILY. From earliest biblical times, it was taken for granted that the family was an integral part of the social structure. The tribe was an extension of the family. The first of the six hundred thirteen commandments, "Be fruitful and multiply," was interpreted by the rabbis as implying the prime duty of rearing a family. The Bible inculcates respect for *parents (*Ex*. 20.12) and protection of *inheritance rights (e.g., *Dt*. 18.8, 21.15–17). The latter was of great importance in keeping the patrimony within the possession of the family, and even land that was sold reverted to the family in the jubilee year (see YOVEL). The execution of justice was also often entrusted to the family in early society, and in the event of a murder, for example, the next of kin was obligated to seek revenge on the murderer (see BLOOD AVENGER). Wisdom literature abounds with advice on familial happiness (e.g., *Prv*. 13.1, 15.5, 19.13). The *mother is the object of reverence and love, but her status was lower than that of her husband (see WOMEN). In biblical times, the family unit would often include concubines (especially when the wife was barren), but Judaism's tendency was toward the monogamy that became the rule among Western, and later also Eastern, Jewry. The Talmudic concept of the family set the tone for the rich Jewish family experience of the Middle Ages, when Jewish life, to a large extent, centered around the home, especially on Sabbaths and festivals. *Children were expected to honor (*Ex*. 20.12) and revere (*Lv*. 19.3) their parents, while the parents had obligations to rear and educate their children. Marital relations were strictly regulated by *halakhah*, and great stress was laid on **taharat ha-mishpaḥah* (family purity), which included shunning forbidden relationships and observing the relevant laws of ritual cleanness. Families were proud of their illustrious descent (*yiḥus*), originally from the line of David or the priests and later from distinguished scholars. See also FATHER; MARRIAGE; SHELOM BAYIT.

• Miriam Adahan, *The Family Connection: Understanding Your Loved Ones* (Southfield, Mich., 1995). Steven Bayme and Gladys Rosen, *The Jewish Family and Jewish Continuity* (Hoboken, N.J., 1994). Shaye J. D. Cohen, *The Jewish Family in Antiquity*, Brown Judaic Studies 289 (Atlanta, 1993). Leora W. Isaacs, *Jewish Family Matters: A Leader's Guide* (New York, 1994). Kalman Kaplan, ed., *The Family: Biblical and Psychological Foundations* (New York, 1984). Michael Kaufman, *Love, Marriage, and Family in Jewish Law and Tradition* (Northvale, N.J., 1992).

FAMILY PURITY. See TAHARAT HA-MISHPAḤAH.

FANO, MENAḤEM 'AZARYAH DA (1548–1620), Italian rabbi and kabbalist. He lived in various Italian cities and as a wealthy man was a patron of scholarship. His influence on medieval Jewish thought was largely through his work on Kabbalah, *'Asarah Ma'amarot* (first three parts [Venice, 1597]). One hundred thirty of his *responsa* were published in Venice in 1600. In his *Gilgulei Neshamot* (Prague, 1688) he described many figures in Jewish intellectual history. He thought the problem of evil would be solved when Satan made atonement and became a holy angel. His mystical thought influenced scholars in Safed and also in eastern Europe. His *Sefer Sefat Emet* (Lubaczów, 1898) was a noted source for the symbols of Jewish mysticism. He held that God has no name or attributes, and nothing can be said of him except that he exists. But his divinity is absolute, and he is the *Ein Sof who is beyond the imagination and thought.

• Yosef Avivi, in *Sefunot*, new series, 4.19 (1989): 347–376, for a bibliography of Fano's writings. Moshe Idel, "Major Currents in Italian Kabbalah between 1560–1660," in *Essential Papers on Jewish Culture in Renaissance and Baroque Italy*, edited by David B. Ruderman (New York, 1992), pp. 345–368. S. Rosenberg, in *Erets Yisra'el be-Hagut ha-Yehudit bi-Yemei ha-Beinayim*, edited by Moshe Halamish and Aviezer Ravitzky (Jerusalem, 1991), pp. 183–192. Y. L. Vidislavski, *Toledot Rabbenu Menaḥem ʿAzaryah mi-Fano* (Peterkov, 1903). —SHALOM BAR-ASHER

FASTS, periods of abstention from food as a sign of mourning or in expiation of sins. A major fast involves abstention from eating, drinking, sexual intercourse, and the wearing of leather footwear. The only fast in Mosaic law is *Yom Kippur, which concludes the ten-day period of repentance on 10 Tishrei. The phrase "you shall afflict your souls" (*Lv*. 23.27) was taken as a synonym for fasting and is the basis of the Talmudic word *taʿanit* (in preference to the biblical word *tsom*). Physical abstention is regarded not as an end in itself but as a means to spiritual affliction and self-abasement. This finds eloquent expression in the portrayal of the true fast in *Isaiah* 58, which was adopted not only as the prophetic reading for Yom Kippur but was probably read on the occasion of each public fast. The regulation of Yom Kippur specifically mentions that it shall be observed "from evening to evening" (*Lv*. 23.32), namely, for twenty-four hours. The only other fast to which this applies is *Tish'ah be-'Av, observed in commemoration of the destruction of the Temple. The period of abstention for all other fasts is from daybreak until nightfall. All statutory fasts, apart from Yom Kippur, are days of mourning in commemoration of tragic events in Jewish history. Four of them date back to the period of the First Temple or immediately after its destruction, as is evidenced by the reference to "the fast of the fourth month and the fast of the fifth and the fast of the seventh and the fast of the tenth" (*Zec*. 8.19). The query of the people whether fasting was still obligatory after the return (*Zec*. 7.3) and the prophecy that the fasts would be turned to "joy and gladness and cheerful feasts" (*Zec*. 8.19) prove that they were instituted to commemorate that tragic period. These fasts are 17 Tammuz (see SHIVʿAH ʿASAR BE-TAMMUZ), 9 Av (see TISHʿAH BE'-AV), 3 Tishrei (see TSOM GEDALYAH), and 10 Tevet (see ʿASARAH BE-TEVET). To these was later added 13 Adar (see TAʿANIT ESTER). All fasts falling on the Sabbath, except Yom Kippur, are observed on another day (generally the following Sunday). In addition to these statutory fasts, public and private (individual) fasts were also instituted. The former were to ward off threatened calamities, most frequently in the case of severe drought, and almost the whole of the tractate *Taʿanit* is devoted to the regulation of these fasts—which are days of supplication and a call to penitence in the hope that "repentance will nullify the evil decree." The purpose is conveyed in the standard words of admonition uttered by the head of the elders on these occasions: "Brothers, it is not written of the men of Nineveh that God saw their sackcloth and their fasting, but that God saw their works that they turned from their evil ways [*Jon*. 3.10]; and the prophet Joel says [2.13] 'Rend your hearts and not your garments'" (*Taʿan*. 2.1). Other common fasts were the firstborn fast on 14 Nisan (see TAʿANIT BEKHORIM); the fast observed by the bride and groom on their wedding day; the fast observed in certain kabbalistic circles on the eve of the new moon (see YOM KIPPUR QATAN); and fasts on a *yortsayt*. In the thirteenth century, some pietists fasted on the first Monday and Thursday of the month of Ḥeshvan and Iyyar to atone for possible overjoyful indulgences during the festivals of Pesaḥ and Sukkot. (For another set of fasts inaugurated after the 1492 expulsions from Spain, see SHOVAVIM TAT). Some sages condemned excessive fasting, and *Levi Yitsḥaq of Berdichev complained that the evil inclination encouraged fasting to deflect from genuine worship. Individual fasts were undertaken mostly as a result of evil *dreams. Some extremely pious Jews fast every Monday and Thursday (see SHENI VA-ḤAMISHI). According to *halakhah*, fasting is obligatory for males over thirteen and girls over twelve. Exceptions are made for the sick or when health might be endangered.

• Ismar Elbogen, *Jewish Liturgy: A Comprehensive History*, translated by Raymond P. Scheindlin (Philadelphia, New York, and Jerusalem, 1993), pp. 106–108. Eliyahu Kitov, *The Book of Our Heritage: The Jewish Year and Its Days of Significance* (Jerusalem and New York, 1978), pp. 317–338. Isaac Kline, *A Guide for Jewish Practice* (New York, 1992). Peter Knobel, ed., *Gates of the Season* (New York, 1983). S. Z. Leiman, "The Scroll of Fasts: The Ninth of Tebet," *Jewish Quarterly Review* 74 (1983): 174–195.

FAT. See ḤELEV.

FATALISM, the belief in the inexorable operation of fate, to which everything is subject. Fate can be conceived of as impersonal (e.g., a cosmic law to which even the gods are subject, the rule or influence of the stars [see ASTROLOGY], natural causality, etc.) or as personal. In the latter case it might be interpreted as the will of an omnipotent God. A certain tension between fatalism and indeterminacy owed to the freedom of action of humans and/or God exists in monotheistic religions (see DETERMINISM; FREE WILL). Generally speaking, Jewish theological tradition emphasizes the element of freedom: everything—or at least Israel—is directly subject to God's will, but God permits himself to be influenced by prayer, repentance, and good works. Other tendencies are also in evidence, but full-fledged fatalism could not develop in the religious climate of Judaism.

• David B. Burrell, *Freedom and Creation in the Three Traditions* (Notre Dame, 1993). Joseph Wochenmark, *The Concept of Fatalism in Judaism*, translated by Arnold W. Marque and edited by Seymour Cohen (Berkeley, 1977).

FATE. See PROVIDENCE.

FATHER (Heb. *av*; Aram. *abba'*). In the Bible, the basic family unit is designated "house of the father" (*Gn*. 24–38). In Jewish law, the rights of the father over his *children, as long as they are minors, are unbounded, and the Fifth Commandment enjoins children to respect their *parents. The father, however, has definite legal obligations toward his children, which are codified in the saying that "the father is obliged to circumcise his son, teach him Torah, teach him a trade, and marry him off" (*Qid.* 29b). There was originally no legal obligation on the father to provide for his children's material needs (instead, this was regarded as a moral duty); hence, the rabbinical application of the verse "Happy are they that keep justice, that do righteousness at all times" (*Ps.* 106.3) to the man who maintains his sons and daughters in their childhood (*Ket.* 50a). The second-century synod of Usha' made it obligatory upon a father to maintain his children during their minority (*Ket.* 49b). Only when parents order a child to transgress the precepts of Judaism must a child defy them. Later authorities ruled that a child could defy his or her father's objections to choice of a bride or groom (after the child has reached majority). Paternity requires no proof, and it is assumed that the husband of a married woman is the father of her child. In all cases, if a man says "this is my child," he is believed. In the case of the child of a Jew and a non-Jew, the child's Jewishness is determined by the status of the mother. In Jewish marriages, the child's communal standing is modeled after the father's; that is, the son of a priest is a priest regardless of whether the mother belongs to a priestly family or not (*Qid.* 3.12). A father can punish his childen only while they are minors (*Mo'ed Q.* 17a). His legal responsibility toward them generally ends upon their attaining their majority (see ADULT), which is the basis of the blessing uttered by the father at the *bar mitsvah* of his son: "Blessed be he who has relieved me of the responsibility for him." There is no provision in Jewish law for *adoption, and these regulations apply only to a natural parent. The use of "father" as a title of honor is rare in Judaism. It is said that only the three *patriarchs may be called father (*Ber.* 15b); in rabbinical literature Hillel and Shamm'ai (*'Eduy.* 1.4) and R. Yishma'e'l (Y., *R. ha-Sh.* 56a) are referred to as "the fathers of the world." On the other hand, during the tannaitic period a number of rabbis were given the honorific title (as distinct from a cognomen, common in amoraic times) of **abba'*, generally those who maintained a particularly high standard of saintliness and purity in their lives. The second in rank in the *Sanhedrin, after the *nasi'*, was given the title of *av beit din* (father of the court; *Ḥag.* 16b). The word is also applied to a teacher, and the Talmud regarded the father and son of the *Book of Proverbs* as teacher and disciple (*Ḥul.* 6a). God is seen as the father of the Jewish people and is frequently addressed as such in the liturgy (our father, our king, merciful father, etc.). See also FAMILY; INHERITANCE; MOTHER; PATRILINEAL DESCENT.

• James Barr, "Abba Isn't 'Daddy,'" *Journal of Theological Studies* 39 (1988): 28–47. Alfred W. Matthews, *Abraham Was Their Father* (Macon, Ga., 1981). Gordon E. Pruett, *As a Father Loves His Children: The Image of God as Loving Father in Judaism, Christianity, and Islam* (San Francisco, 1994). Devorah Steinmetz, *From Father to Son: Kinship, Conflict, and Continuity in Genesis* (Louisville, Ky., 1995).

FEAR OF GOD, or awe, is regarded as the basis of Jewish religious awareness and is repeatedly exhorted in the Pentateuch, for example, "And now, Israel, what does the Lord your God require of you, but to fear the Lord" (*Dt.* 10.12). Fear of God is the "beginning of knowledge" (*Prv.* 1.7) and the "beginning of wisdom" (*Prv.* 10.10). In biblical language the terms "fear" and "love" are close to each other in meaning. According to the Talmud the person who "possesses knowledge without fear of heaven is like a treasurer who possesses the outer keys but not the inner" (*Shab.* 31a–b; Talmudic literature uses the alternative phrase "fear of heaven" [*yir'at shamayim*]). The purity of motive that is demanded in the service of God is emphasized by Antigonus of Sokho who states that one should serve God without any thought of reward but "let the fear of heaven be upon you" (*Avot* 1.3). The rabbinic attitude is expressed in the statement of R. Shim'on ben El'azar, "Greater is he who acts from love than he who acts from fear" (*Sot.* 31a). Fear of heaven is entirely in humankind's hands, and the statement "everything is in the hands of heaven except for the fear of heaven" (*Ber.* 33b) is a key to the rabbinic doctrine of *free will. Fear of God is to be distinguished from fear of divine punishment, for as "fear and trembling" arise out of an awareness of the awesome and numinous quality of the divine majesty, it is closely allied to the complementary attitude of love of God. Impressive formulations of the sense of numinous awe in the presence of God are found in the liturgy for Ro'sh ha-Shanah and Yom Kippur (the first and last of the "Days of Awe," see YAMIM NORA'IM). Among the medieval philosophers, *Baḥya ben Yosef ibn Paquda' sees fear of God as an essential prerequisite to the love of God. He also distinguishes between two grades of fear of God: the lower being fear of punishment for sin, the higher being awe of God (*Ḥovot ha-Levavot* 10; a similar distinction is made in the *Zohar and by the eighteenth-century moralist Mosheh Ḥayyim *Luzzatto). *Maimonides suggests that fear of God leads to moral action and love of God leads to right thinking (*Guide of the Perplexed* 3.52). Although extensively discussed in medieval thought, the concept of fear of God is almost totally absent among modern Jewish thinkers.

• Adolf Büchler, *Studies in Sin and Atonement in the Rabbinic Literature of the First Century* (London, 1928). Louis Jacobs, *Jewish Values* (London, 1960), pp. 31–50. Byron L. Sherwin, "Fear of God," in *Contemporary Jewish Religious Thought*, edited by Arthur A. Cohen and Paul Mendes-Flohr (New York, 1987), pp. 245–254. Efraim Elimelech Urbach, *The Sages, Their Concepts and Beliefs* (Jerusalem, 1975), pp. 400–419.

FEAST. See ḤAGGIM; SE'UDAH.

FEINSTEIN, MOSHEH (1895–1986), Orthodox rabbi generally acknowledged as one of the outstanding Orthodox legal adjudicators of the twentieth century. Born in Uzda, Belorussia, Feinstein studied in *yeshivot* in Slutsk, Shklov, and Arntsishaw before being named rabbi of Luban, Belorussia. He remained in that post for sixteen years before fleeing Soviet oppression and immigrating to the United States in 1936. Settling on the Lower East Side of New York City, he was appointed *ro'sh yeshivah* (dean) of the Mesivta Tifereth Yerushalayim, a position he maintained until his death fifty years later. He was president of the Union of Orthodox Rabbis of the United States and Canada and chaired the American section of Agudat Israel's rabbinical council,

Mo'etset Gedolei ha-Torah. He also took a leadership role in the independent Orthodox educational system in Israel, Ḥinnukh 'Atsma'i.

Feinstein's greatest renown stemmed from a lifetime of responding to religious questions posed by Orthodox Jews in America and worldwide. His thousands of *responsa*, which deal with the widest range of human experiences and Jewish ritual problems and observances, have been compiled in his seven-volume *Iggerot Mosheh* (New York, 1959–1986). He also published several volumes of Talmudic *ḥiddushim* (*novellae*) and discourses under the title of *Dibberot Mosheh* (11 vols. [1946–1984]). These works serve as a major source for understanding twentieth-century Orthodox Jewry's encounter with modern science, technology, and politics.

• Daniel Eidensohn, *Yad Moshe: Index to the Igros Moshe of Rav Moshe Feinstein* (Brooklyn, N.Y., 1987). Shimon Finkelman, with Nosson Scherman, *Reb Moshe: The Life and Ideals of Ha Gaon Rabbi Moshe Feinstein* (Brooklyn, N.Y., 1986). Ira Robinson, "Because of Our Many Sins: The Contemporary Jewish World as Reflected in the Responsa of Moses Feinstein," *Judaism* 35 (1986): 35–46. Nosson Scherman, "Rabbi Moses Feinstein: An Appreciation," *Jewish Observer* (October 1986): 8–31.

–JEFFREY S. GUROCK

FEMINISM. Jewish feminism first arose in the United States in the early 1970s, as thousands of American Jewish women, already committed to enhancing women's roles and status in society, began to subject Judaism and the American Jewish community to feminist critique. With the exception of the short-lived Jewish Feminist Organization (1972–1974), feminist inroads continue to be made largely through communal and denominational efforts; the growing visibility of women in Jewish leadership roles; scholarly works written from feminist perspectives; the proliferation of conferences, classes, and lecture series on Jewish feminism and issues related to gender; and such magazines as *Lilith: The Independent Jewish Women's Magazine* (1976–present) and *Bridges: A Journal for Jewish Feminists and Our Friends* (1991–present).

Since the early 1990s, the Israel Women's Network has initiated and actively supported feminist efforts in Israel and has facilitated communication and coordinated action among Jewish feminists throughout the world. Outside of North America and Israel, Great Britain, with a Jewish population of over three hundred thousand, can claim the only other Jewish community in which feminist issues have consistently been placed on the communal agenda. Given their many religious and cultural differences, Jewish feminists do not share a common agenda. Some feminists have called for greater participation by women within religious life, though not necessarily equal access. Many of them, Orthodox or traditional Conservative, have attempted to create or facilitate public religious opportunities for girls and women from which traditionally they were exempt if not excluded; other Jewish feminists call for equal access to all aspects of Jewish life, including those rights and responsibilities (such as rabbinic ordination and cantorial investiture) formerly reserved for men, and the integration of women's experiences into Jewish life leading toward Judaism's eventual transformation. Still others are working toward a feminist Judaism, in which concepts of God, Torah, and Jewish peoplehood are reevaluated and re-created. See also WOMEN.

• Sylvia Barack Fishman, *A Breath of Life: Feminism in the American Jewish Community* (New York, 1993). Susannah Heschel, ed., *On Being a Jewish Feminist: A Reader* (1983; New York, 1994). Judith Plaskow, *Standing Again at Sinai: Judaism from a Feminist Perspective* (San Francisco, 1990). Letty Cottin Pogrebin, *Deborah, Golda, and Me: Being Female and Jewish in America* (New York, 1991). Barbara Swirski and Marilyn Safir, eds., *Calling the Equality Bluff: Women in Israel* (New York, 1991). Ellen M. Umansky and Dianne Ashton, eds., *Four Centuries of Jewish Women's Spirituality: A Sourcebook* (Boston, 1992), includes rituals, blessings, essays, and prayers by many contemporary Jewish feminists.

–ELLEN M. UMANSKY

FENCE AROUND THE LAW. See SEYAG LA-TORAH.

FESTIVAL PRAYERS. In their basic structure, festival prayers do not differ greatly from the daily prayers or the Sabbath liturgy; however, they are distinguished in four areas: scriptural readings; changes in number and content of obligatory prayers and additions; poetic embellishments (see PIYYUT); and musical aspects of the congregational service. The Torah and prophetic readings are taken from passages concerning the festival or containing a special theological message associated with the festival by the sages. The Five Scrolls (see ḤAMESH MEGILLOT) are read on relevant occasions: *Song of Songs* on the Sabbath during the week of Pesaḥ; *Ruth* on Shavu'ot; *Lamentations* on Tish'ah be-'Av; *Ecclesiastes* on Sukkot; and *Esther* on Purim. On festivals the number of services is increased from three to four with the addition of the *Musaf service and even a fifth, concluding service on Yom Kippur (*Ne'ilah); the intermediary benedictions of the daily *'Amidah are replaced by one benediction dedicated to the specific "holiness of the day," reducing the total number of benedictions to seven; and special additions are made to the 'Amidah, such as those in the Ro'sh ha-Shanah Musaf service (*Malkhuyyot, *Zikhronot, and *Shofarot) or the addition of the *confession in the Yom Kippur 'Amidah prayers (see 'AL ḤET'; ASHAMNU). The other sections of the liturgy for festivals do not differ essentially from the weekday version. *Pesuqei de-Zimra' is enlarged and followed by *Birkat ha-Shir, as on the Sabbath. *Hallel is recited after the morning service on the Shalosh Regalim, Ro'sh Ḥodesh, Ḥanukkah, and Yom ha-'Atsma'ut; *Kol Nidrei is recited at the solemn opening of Yom Kippur. Although the festival prayers have been elaborated with *piyyutim*, in recent times the tendency has been to reduce or omit them. Special cantillations for the reading of sections of the Torah (for example, the reading of the Ten Commandments on Shavu'ot) or special melodies for *piyyutim* or prayers also contribute to the special character of Jewish holy days. Festival prayers are printed in a special volume, the *Maḥazor*.

• Abraham P. Bloch, *The Biblical and Historical Background of the Jewish Holy Days* (New York, 1978). Ismar Elbogen, *Jewish Liturgy: A Comprehensive History*, translated by Raymond P. Scheindlin (Philadelphia, 1993), pp. 91–184. Abraham Z. Idelsohn, *Jewish Music: Its Historical Development* (New York, 1929).

–PETER LENHARDT

FESTIVALS. See ḤAGGIM.

FIFTEENTH OF AV. See TU BE-'AV.

FIFTEENTH OF SHEVAT. See TU BI-SHEVAT.

FINDING OF PROPERTY. See LOST PROPERTY.

FINES (Heb. *qenasot*). While any court can render a decision involving monetary statutes, the authority to levy a fine as a punishment for wrongdoing, such as is explicitly stated in the Bible (for example, "He whom God shall condemn shall pay double unto his neighbor"; *Ex*. 22.8), rests only with those judges who have received ordination in Erets Yisra'el from teachers themselves so ordained. Fines can be imposed only on the evidence of two witnesses; the admission of the defendant is insufficient (*Ket*. 42b–43a). In practice, certain categories of fines are levied by rabbinical courts up to the present, despite the fact that ordination has long ceased to exist. Generally the amount of the fine is fixed by the court, although in some cases it is fixed by law. Fines for which one can only become liable on conviction in court, but not when one freely admits to wrongdoing, are payable to the injured party and not to the court or the state. Later rabbinical courts, however, ruled that fines should be paid to the communal fund in the case of certain public misdemeanors. Fines could also be imposed for failure to observe public obligations (e.g., refusal to accept communal office).

• Menachem Elon, *Jewish Law: History, Sources, Principles*, 4 vols. (Philadelphia, 1994).

FINIALS. See TORAH ORNAMENTS.

FINKEL, NATAN TSEVI (1849–1927), Talmudic scholar and leader of the *Musar movement. He was born in Raseiniai, Lithuania, and was a disciple of Simḥah Zissel Broida, who was one of the outstanding students of Yisra'el *Salanter, founder of the Musar movement. Finkel devoted his life to the dissemination of Musar literature, stressing the importance of ethical behavior and the ability of man to elevate himself to greater heights. In 1882 he established a Musar *yeshivah* in *Slobodka, Lithuania, where hundreds of Talmudic scholars were educated. In 1924 he opened a branch in Hebron and moved there himself in 1925. His students called him the Sabba' (Grandad) of Slobodka. Finkel left no published works, but a number of his discourses were collected by students in *Or ha-Tsafun* (Jerusalem, 1959) and *Siḥot ha-Sabba' mi-Slobodka* (Tel Aviv, 1955).

• Lucy S. Dawidowicz, ed., *The Golden Tradition* (1967; repr. Northvale, N.J., 1989), pp. 179–185. Dov Katz, *Tenu'at Ha-Musar*, vol. 3 (Tel Aviv, 1974), repr. in English as *The Musar Movement*, translated by Leonard Oschry (Jerusalem, 1982). —ADAM MINTZ

FINKELSTEIN, LOUIS (1895–1991), scholar of rabbinical thought and chancellor of the *Jewish Theological Seminary of America in New York. Born to an Orthodox family in Cincinnati, Finkelstein gained his reputation as a leading Conservative rabbi, educator, and scholar. He earned his doctorate at Columbia University in 1918 and received his rabbinical ordination one year later from the Jewish Theological Seminary. He taught at the seminary and served as provost in 1937, president in 1940, and chancellor in 1951, raising the seminary to an international center for Jewish studies. He guided the Conservative movement to a preeminent role in Jewish religious life in the United States in the post–World War II years. He wrote and edited many books and articles exploring historical and sociological understandings of rabbinic Judaism. In his pioneering *Jewish Self-Government in the Middle Ages* (1924), Finkelstein traced the development of European rabbinical authority and the structuring of medieval Jewish life through synods and *taqqanot*. His other works include *The Pharisees* (2 vols. [1938 and 1966]) and *Akiba: Scholar, Saint and Martyr* (1936).

• *A Bibliography of the Writings of Louis Finkelstein* (New York, 1977). Moshe Davis, *The Emergence of Conservative Judaism* (Philadelphia, 1963). Herbert Parzen, *Architects of Conservative Judaism* (New York, 1964). Neil Gillman, *Conservative Judaism: The New Century* (New York, 1993). —EUGENE R. SHEPPARD

FIRE (Heb. *esh*). The use of fire as an element of ritual worship is common to all faiths. It was associated with the revelation of God to Abraham (*Gn*. 15.17) and Moses (*Ex*. 3.2 [the *burning bush] and *Ex*. 19.18). At the time of the Exodus and in the wilderness, God appeared in a pillar of fire (*Ex*. 31.13–22). In ritual practice, its use was limited to the fire on the altar for the burnt offering (*Lv*. 6.5) and the eternal light (**ner tamid*) that burned in the Temple (*Ex*. 27.20; *Lv*. 24.2). Both had to remain permanently alight. The lamp is regarded as the symbol of God's presence among his people (*Shab*. 22b), and most synagogues have a *ner tamid* for that symbolic reason. Aaron's two sons forfeited their lives for offering up on the altar "strange fire which he had not commanded them"; as a result "fire went forth from before the Lord and consumed them" (*Lv*. 10.1–2). Kindling a fire is singled out as a Sabbath prohibition (*Ex*. 35.3). While the rabbis ruled that a fire kindled before the Sabbath was permitted, the Sadducees and Karaites forbade even the existence of a fire on the Sabbath. The blessing over the *Havdalah candle praises God "who creates the lights of fire" (*Ber*. 52a) through which man becomes culturally creative during the six workdays. The use of Sabbath and Havdalah candles is not connected with the ritual use of fire in the Temple. See also CANDLES; MENORAH; OIL; SABBATH.

• Joshua Trachtenberg, *Jewish Magic and Superstition* (Cleveland, 1961).

FIRKOWITSCH, AVRAHAM (1785–1874), Karaite scholar. Born in Lutsk, Poland, Firkowitsch was a controversial figure in eastern European Jewish culture in the nineteenth century. He began to publish the writings of the early Karaite scholars, which he edited, sometimes changing or omitting sections in order to strengthen the Karaite position. He attempted to prove that it was the Karaites who had converted the Khazars to Judaism. His contempt for Talmudic Judaism is evident in his work *Massah u-Merivah* (1838). His views led to bitter disputes with rabbinical authorities, and he angered many Jews by seeking to curry favor with the Russian government, suggesting that the Jews should be encouraged to enter agriculture and should be removed from the areas near the western border in order to prevent smuggling.

He was commissioned by the governor-general of Crimea and the Historical Society of Odessa in 1839 to undertake expeditions in the Caucasus in order to uncover the origins of the Karaites. He acquired many valuable documents from the *genizot* (storehouses) of Jewish communities and sought to prove that the Karaites were descendants of the ten lost tribes, who had lived in Crimea from antiquity and could not be accused of any connection with the crucifixion of Jesus. Firkowitsch describes his discoveries and travels in his main work, *Avnei Zikkaron* (1872). The authenticity of much of Firkowitsch's material has been questioned; some documents were forged. However, he succeeded in stimulating interest in Karaite and Jewish history and literature and saved a large number of Karaite manuscripts in the east that would have been lost without his initiative. Most of them were gathered in Erets Yisra'el, Syria, and Egypt in 1843. He sold many of these manuscripts to the Saint Petersburg library.

• Adolf Jellinek, *Abraham Firkowitsch . . .* (Vienna, 1875). Hermann L. Strack, *A. Firkowitsch und seine Entdeckungen* (Leipzig, 1876).

—ADAM RUBIN

FIRMAMENT. See COSMOLOGY; CREATION.

FIRSTBORN (Heb. *bekhor*), a designation that applies to a father's firstborn male child, regardless of whether the child is his mother's firstborn. The Bible allots the firstborn a double portion of the inheritance from his father's estate (*Dt.* 21.17). This right does not apply to that which accrues posthumously to the estate. Since in Jewish law it is not the testator's will that determines to whom the *inheritance should go, a father cannot deprive his firstborn of his inheritance right. A father may, however, divide his property during his lifetime, thus equalizing his children's shares; the property is then a gift bestowed during the lifetime of the owner and does not infringe upon the laws of inheritance. According to some authorities, however, a father violates a religious precept if he does not make provision for his firstborn son to enjoy his *birthright, although the firstborn may voluntarily renounce his birthright (*B. B.* 124a). A child born after his father's death, although an inheritor, does not enjoy the right of primogeniture, and a child delivered by Caesarean section is likewise excluded (*Bekh.* 8:2). On receiving his double inheritance, the firstborn takes on double the obligations affecting the estate; thus, he is obligated to pay a double share in settling his father's outstanding debts. Kingship and other hereditary offices pass to the firstborn, provided he is suited for the tasks of office. See also BIRTHRIGHT; FIRSTBORN, REDEMPTION OF THE; TAʿANIT BEKHORIM.

• Barry J. Beitzel, "The Right of the Firstborn (Pî Shnayim) in the Old Testament (Deut. 21:15–17)," in *A Tribute to Gleason Archer*, edited by W. Kaise and R. Youngblood (Chicago, 1986), pp. 179–190. Nathan Gottlieb, *A Jewish Child Is Born: The History and Ritual of Circumcision, Redemption of the Firstborn Son, Adoption, Conversion and Choosing and Giving of Names* (New York, 1960).

FIRSTBORN, FAST OF THE. See TAʿANIT BEKHORIM.

FIRSTBORN, REDEMPTION OF THE (Heb. *pidyon ha-ben*), the obligation of a father to redeem his firstborn son from a priest by payment of a ransom of five shekels (*Nm.* 3.44–51) or its equivalent in goods. The commandment to redeem the firstborn refers to the firstborn male on the mother's side—"whatsoever opens the womb"—and applies to both man and beast (*Ex.* 13.1–16).

The redemption of a firstborn son is effected at a short religious ceremony on the thirty-first day after a child's birth (if that falls on a Sabbath or festival, the ceremony is postponed until the eve of the following day), and the occasion is a festive one. The ceremony was finalized in the geonic period. The father quotes *Numbers* 18.16 and *Exodus* 13.1, assures the priest that he prefers to give the priest money rather than his firstborn son, and recites two appropriate blessings. The ceremony is usually followed by a festive repast.

Prior to the construction of the Tabernacle, the firstborn male in each family was consecrated to the service of God, thus forming a priesthood of the firstborn, in return for the deliverance of the Hebrew firstborns during the night of the Exodus, when Egyptian firstborns were slain (*Nm.* 8.17). Tradition asserts (*Zev.* 112b) that the Israelite firstborns indeed served in the priesthood until the completion of the Tabernacle, whereupon they were exchanged for the tribe of Levi (*Nm.* 3.12–13). Priests and Levites are exempt from the obligation to redeem their firstborn since they are, in fact, consecrated to the service of God (*Nm.* 3.6–10). The firstborn sons of the daughters of priests or Levites are also not redeemed. The obligation of redemption does not apply in the case of a child who was preceded by a miscarriage or a stillbirth, or who was delivered by Caesarean section, since in these instances the child does not in fact "open the womb" of its mother.

The firstling of clean animals (that is, those from which sacrifices can be brought) are automatically consecrated at birth and, in Temple times, were to be sacrificed as peace offerings (*Nm.* 18.15–18; *Dt.* 15.19–23). The firstling of an ass is to be either redeemed or destroyed. Since the destruction of the Temple, the firstlings of animals are given to a priest and left to pasture. They may not be used nor may benefit be derived from them unless a blemish occurs that would have invalidated them for sacrifice, in which case they may be slaughtered for food. The laws of the firstborn are found in tractate **Bekhorot*. Since Reform Judaism rejects social class distinction, this ceremony is considered irrelevant for most Reform Jews; however, some families still choose to observe the ceremony or to change it to a ritual that is more compatible to the principles of Reform Judaism.

• Gedaly Oberlander, *Sefer Pidyon ha-Ben ke-Hilkhato* (Jerusalem, 1992). Dorothy Steiner, *Rites of Birth: Circumcision, Naming, Pidyon ha-Ben: An Annotated Bibliography* (Cincinnati, 1977). Yosef David Weisberg, *Sefer Otsar Pidyon ha-Ben*, 2 vols. (Jerusalem, 1993).

FIRST FRUITS (Heb. *bikkurim*). The biblical precept to bring the first ripe fruits, cultivated or wild, to the Temple (*Ex.* 23.19, 34.26; *Dt.* 26) applied, according to the Talmud, only in Temple times (since the first fruits, which had the sacred status of the *terumah*, were to be placed "before the altar of the Lord") and affected only the produce of Erets Yisra'el, in which the rabbis included Transjordan and Syria. First fruits could be brought only from the seven kinds of produce for which the Land of Israel was praised: wheat, barley, figs, vines, pomegranates, olives, and honey (*Dt.* 8.8). When the first fruits appeared in the field, they were to be tied with a marker and left to grow and ripen. They were then cut and brought with great ceremony to the Temple court. Psalms were chanted throughout the journey, which was made by as large a group of people as possible. The streets of Jerusalem were adorned, and those bringing the first fruits were profusely welcomed. The main occasion for bringing the fruits was the feast of *Shavu'ot (called the Festival of the First Fruits), but they could be brought until the following Ḥanukkah. Placed in a basket (*Dt.* 26.2), the copiously decorated fruit was presented to the priest, while the donor recited the confession prescribed in *Deuteronomy* 26.5–10, thereby expressing his faith in God, the owner of the land, and thanksgiving for allowing him to hold it in trust. The priest then touched the basket, and the fruit became his property. The entire ceremony was accompanied by the singing of Psalm 30 by the Levitical choir and followed by the peace offerings. After the destruction of the Temple, when first fruits could no longer be brought, the rabbis regarded acts of charity as a substitute (*Lv. Rab.* 24), especially those for the support of scholars (*Ket.* 106a). The relevant legislation is discussed in the Talmudic tractate **Bikkurim*. A modern celebration of the bringing of the first fruits has been introduced in some Israeli settlements.

• Joseph M. Baumgarten, "The Laws of Orlah and First Fruits in the Light of Jubilees, the Qumran Writings, and Targum ps-Jonathan," *Journal of Jewish Studies* 38 (1987): 195–202. John C. Reeves, "The Feast of First Fruits of Wine and the Ancient Canaanite Calendar," *Vetus Testamentum* 42 (1992): 350–361.

FIVE BOOKS OF MOSES. See BIBLE; TORAH.

FIVE SCROLLS. See ḤAMESH MEGILLOT.

FLAGELLATION. See FLOGGING.

FLESH (Heb. *basar*). The word is used in the Bible for the body as a whole; as a collective noun for mankind (*Is.* 66.16); figuratively, as the impressionable side of human nature (*Ez.* 35.26) or weakness (*Is.* 31.3); and as a type of food (*Dn.* 7.5). Originally forbidden to humans as food (*Gn.* 1.29–30), it was later permitted with qualifications (see MEAT). The dualistic opposition of flesh and spirit taught by some Jewish groups (such as the *Qumran community) and adopted by the *New Testament was not favored by rabbinic Judaism, which encouraged neither the mortification of flesh nor the ascription to it of inherent sinfulness. Although recognizing that human frailties stem from the nature of the *body and the temptations to which it is subject, the consensus of Jewish precept and teaching, far from negating the flesh, is directed to uplifting and sanctifying it.

• Daniel Boyarin, *Carnal Israel: Reading Sex in Talmudic Culture* (Berkeley, 1993). William D. Davies, "The Old Enemy: The Flesh and Sin," in *Paul and Rabbinic Judaism: Some Rabbinic Elements in Pauline Theology* (New York, 1967). Howard Eilberg-Schwartz, ed., *People of the Body: Jews and Judaism from an Embodied Perspective* (Albany, 1992).

FLOGGING (Heb. *malqot*), punishment by the infliction of lashes as provided for in *Deuteronomy* 25.1–3. Although the Bible prescribes a maximum of forty lashes, the rabbis interpreted this as a maximum of thirty-nine, one-third being administered on the chest and two-thirds upon the back. The number of lashes was determined by the *beit din* in accordance with the gravity of the offense. Flogging was the normal punishment for the active infringement of negative commandments for which no specific mention was made of a death penalty. It was also considered to be sufficient punishment for severe violations of commandments for which the punishment was traditionally decreed as **karet* (cutting off). Although there was no physical punishment for the failure to carry out a positive commandment, the rabbinical authorities administered such punishment for the general welfare of the community in all cases where they saw fit. Flogging has not been applied in modern times, and in the State of Israel corporal punishment was forbidden in 1950. The subject is fully discussed in the Talmudic tractate **Makkot*. Formerly, symbolic lashes were administered in synagogues to male congregants on the eve of Yom Kippur as an indication of contrition.

• Menachem Elon, *Jewish Law: History, Sources, Principles*, 4 vols. (Philadelphia, 1994).

FLOOD. The biblical account of the flood that God visited upon the earth because of human wickedness is told in *Genesis* 6.5–9.17. Only the righteous *Noah, his family, and representatives of the animal kingdom were allowed to escape in a floating ark. The Flood is described as a release of the primeval waters of chaos that had been restrained by the act of creation. Subsequently, God vowed never to repeat this punishment and proclaimed the *rainbow as a sign of his covenant (*Gn.* 9.12–17). Flood legends are known from many parts of the world. The biblical account shows many similarities to the Sumerian–Babylonian versions. Bible scholars maintain that *Genesis* 6–9 weaves two originally distinct versions into a single story, in which the ancient Oriental material was refashioned into a moral drama to express a monotheistic and universalist conception of history. The Midrash develops this view by describing in detail the sinfulness of antediluvian humanity and Noah's attempts to make them repent.

• Chaim Cohen, "The 'Held Method' for Comparative Semitic Philology," *Journal of the Ancient Near Eastern Society* 19 (1989): 9–23. Chaim Cohen, *Leshonenu* 53 (1989): 193–201, in Hebrew with an English summary. Chaim Cohen and Elisha Qimron, "Mabbul," in *'Olam ha-Tanakh: Be-Re'shit* (Tel Aviv, 1982), p. 59. Jack P. Lewis, "Flood," in *The Anchor Bible Dictionary*, vol. 2 (New York, 1992), pp. 798–803. S. Loewenstamm, "Mabbul," in *Entsiqlopedyah Miqra'it*, vol. 4 (Jerusalem, 1962). Abraham Malamat, *Mari and the Early Israelite Experience* (Oxford, 1989), p. 33.

FOLKLORE, popular traditions, including beliefs, customs, ritual practices, music, songs, dances, legends, and tales, originally oral but no longer exclusively so since the spread of literacy. Jewish folklore comprises traditions that are specifically cultivated and practiced by Jews. In a community spread around the world, these traditions also inevitably reflect the influence of the respective environments. The bearers of so-called "high" culture, whether literary, philosophical, theological, or halakhic, have tended to regard folklore as a debased, or at any rate lower, and primitive form of culture, often associated with magic, superstition, and non-Jewish and pagan traditions. Hence the term is sometimes used with a pejorative connotation, and many beliefs and *minhagim* (e.g., *Lag ba-ʿOmer, **kapparot*, *pilgrimages to tombs of holy rabbis, *dybbuk, *golem) were at first disapproved. Today, folklore is treated as a legitimate form of culture, and an increasing number of monographs, journals, and archival collections are devoted to the study of all aspects of Jewish folklore.

• Tamar Alexander and Galit Hasan-Rokem, eds., *Meḥqerei Yerushalayim be-Folqlor Yehudi* (Jerusalem, 1981–1996). Tamar Alexander-Frizer, *The Pious Sinner: Ethics and Aesthetics in the Medieval Hasidic Narrative*, Texts and Studies in Medieval and Early Modern Judaism 5 (Tübingen, 1991). Galit Hasan-Rokem, "Proverbs in Israeli Folk Narratives: A Structural Semantic Analysis," *FF Communications* 232 (Helsinki, 1982). Dov Noy, ed., *Meḥqerei ha-Merkaz le-Ḥeqer ha-Folqlor*, 7 vols. (Jerusalem, 1970–1995). Dov Noy, ed., *Studies in Jewish Folklore* (Cambridge, Mass., 1980). Haim Schwarzbaum, *Jewish Folklore Between East and West: Collected Papers* (Beersheba, 1989). Aliza Shenhar-Alroy, *Jewish and Israeli Folklore* (New Delhi, 1987). Joshua Trachtenberg, *Jewish Magic and Superstition: A Study in Folk Religion* (New York, 1974). Eli Yassif, *Sippur ha-ʿAm ha-ʿIvri: Toledotav, Sugav, u-Mashmaʿuto* (Jerusalem, 1994).

FOOD. Jewish culinary traditions date back three thousand years. The *dietary laws governing the selection, preparation, and consumption of all food were laid down in the Pentateuch. They are based on the concept of holiness and include permissible and forbidden foods and the laws of ritual slaughter, to which the rabbis added the ban on consuming meat and milk products together. Jews used ingredients available in the countries in which they lived, and considerable differences emerged between Ashkenazi and Sephardi traditions and nomenclatures.

Ceremonial foods in ancient Israel served as a means of expression of the relationship between humans and God and between the priestly tribe of Levi and the rest of the Israelite people.

Each act of dining, from the preparation of food to the recitation of *Birkat ha-Mazon, is carefully prescribed by Jewish law. The rituals surrounding Sabbath and festival meals express thanksgiving to God. *Wine is an essential component of festive meals.

Many food customs evolved that were linked to the holiday. The celebration of Ro'sh ha-Shanah includes partaking of honey and a fruit not previously eaten in that season to symbolize the hope for a sweet year ahead. Foods like *lekaḥ* (honey cake), *teyglakh* (boiled dough dipped in honey) and carrot *tsimmes* are also eaten. By placing the head of a fish on the table, Sephardim express the hope of being like the head and not the tail. During *Sukkot, the fall harvest festival, families dine in a specially constructed booth (see SUKKAH) and traditionally eat stuffed vegetables, as a symbol of plenty, such as *yaprak* (stuffed grape leaves), or *holishkes* or *praches* (stuffed cabbage). In Yemen, families would consume a sheep or an ox. During *Ḥanukkah, latkes (potato pancakes fried in oil) are eaten by most American Jews, while Sephardi Jews eat sweets fried in oil and dipped in honey, and Israelis eat *sufganiyyot* (jelly doughnuts), symbolic of the oil of the Ḥanukkah miracle. On *Purim, the last festival before Pesaḥ, when the yearly store of flour must be used up, *hamantashen* (triangular-shaped pastries filled with poppy seeds or fruit, traditionally believed to be in the shape of *Haman's hat) are eaten. For seven days (eight in the Diaspora) during Pesaḥ, dishes prepared with **matsah* (unleavened bread), symbolizing the Exodus from Egypt, and eggs, abundant in the spring and symbolic of fertility, are eaten.

Various symbolic dishes are part of the *Seder ceremony. Ashkenazim eat *knaidlach*, a *matsah* dumpling made with eggs and fat, in chicken soup. During Pesaḥ, Ashkenazim, but not Sephardim, refrain from eating rice. On *Shavuʿot, the feast of the first fruits and the time of the receiving of the Torah, dairy foods such as cheesecake and blintzes (thin pancakes, an Ashkenazi dish) filled with cheese are served.

The Sabbath is marked by the eating of **ḥallah* (two symbolic loaves of white bread often baked in a braided or twisted form) and the drinking of wine. Ashkenazim favor gefilte fish, which is prepared from a mixture of fish, bread or *matsah* crumbs, eggs, and seasonings simmered in a fish stock. Cooking is not allowed on the Sabbath; thus delicacies that could be prepared ahead, like chopped liver; kugel (baked sweet or savory pudding made from noodles, potatoes, or bread); and the eastern European *tsholent*, Moroccan *adafina*, and Iraqi *ḥamim* (all Sabbath stews of slow-baked meat, vegetables, and sometimes rice or barley) were devised by different communities. Many Moroccan communities start each of the Sabbath meals with fish, and there was a popular saying "Whoever eats fish will be saved from the judgment of Gehenna" (see GEIHINNOM).

• John Cooper, *Eat and Be Satisfied: A Social History of Jewish Food* (Northvale, N.J., 1993), includes bibliography. Gloria K. Greene, *The Jewish Festival Cookbook: An International Collection of Recipes and Customs* (London, 1988). Anita Hirsch, *Our Food: The Kosher Kitchen Updated* (New York, 1992). Joan Nathan, *Jewish Cooking in America* (New York, 1994). Batia Ploch and Patricia Cobe, *The International Kosher Cookbook* (New York, 1992). Devorah Wigoder, *The Garden of Eden Cookbook: Recipes in the Biblical Tradition* (New York, 1988).

—JOAN NATHAN

FORBIDDEN FOODS. See CLEAN AND UNCLEAN ANIMALS; DIETARY LAWS.

FORCED CONVERSION. See CONVERSION, FORCED.

FORGERY, any alteration in the text of a document, such as an erasure or the insertion of words between lines; this renders the document invalid. In order to detect possible changes in documents, rabbinic legislation established the type of paper, ink, and so forth that was to be used for certain documents (*Git*. 19a, 22–23; *B. B.* 162–167). In order to remove complications stemming from charges that an entire document has been forged, any document could be submitted to a rabbinic court for certification. Although forgery is considered a sin, it is not a criminal offense, and there is no prescribed punishment for it, although if a forged document is used as an instrument to commit *fraud, the perpetrator can be punished under that charge. At most, a person convicted of forgery is disbarred from serving as a witness.

• Menachem Elon, *Jewish Law: History, Sources, Principles*, 4 vols. (Philadelphia, 1994). Ira Robinson, "Literary Forgery and Hasidic Judaism: The Case of Rabbi Yudel Rosenberg," *Judaism* 40 (Winter 1991): 61–78. Norman Roth, "Forgery and Abrogation of the Torah: A Theme in Muslim and Christian Polemic in Spain," *Proceedings of the American Academy of Jewish Research* 54 (1987): 203–236. Elliot Wolfson, "Hai Gaon's Letter and Commentary on Aleynu: Further Evidence of Moses de León's Pseudepigraphic Activity," *Jewish Quarterly Review* 81 (1991): 365–409.

FORGIVENESS. God is proclaimed as "forgiving iniquity, transgression, and sin" (*Ex*. 34.6–7), and the sixth of the ʿAmidah blessings is a prayer for such forgiveness. The conditions for forgiveness are confession, repentance, and the resolution to abstain from repeating the transgression. Since the individual should imitate the attributes of God, forgiveness for injuries or offenses should be freely given by the injured party, but human forgiveness involves the added need for rectifying any wrong and appeasing the person injured. See also ATONEMENT.

• Elliot N. Dorff, "Individual and Communal Forgiveness," in *Autonomy and Judaism: The Individual and the Community in Jewish Philosophical Thought*, edited by Daniel H. Frank (Albany, 1992). Leonard S. Kravitz and Kerry M. Olitzky, *The Journey of the Soul: Traditional Sources on Teshuvah* (Northvale, N.J., 1995). Abraham Joshua Heschel, *God in Search of Man* (Northvale, N.J., 1987).

FORMER PROPHETS (Heb. *nevi'im ri'shonim*), originally the biblical term used in postexilic biblical works (*Zec*. 1.4, 7.7) to refer to the prophets who prophesied before the Babylonian exile. Later, however, Former Prophets became a designation for the historical books of *Joshua*, *Judges*, *Samuel*, and *Kings*, which were placed at the beginning of the Prophets, the second division of the Bible. See also BIBLE; LATTER PROPHETS.

–BARUCH J. SCHWARTZ

FORMSTECHER, SALOMON (1808–1889), German Reform rabbi and religious philosopher. In his main work, *Die Religion des Geistes* (1841), he developed a systematic philosophy in support of Jewish religious reform and integration into modern culture and society. Recasting the principles of Hegel and Schelling, he argued that Judaism is governed by an overarching idea—which affirms God to be a transcendent, pure moral being—whose extensive meaning is progressively revealed in time to all of humanity. In this process the pagan elements of human and culture sensibility, grounded in a "religion of nature," are gradually eliminated. Until such time that paganism is finally overcome, Judaism is to persist as a distinct entity so that it may secure the idea of the Religion of Spirit. Nonetheless, parallel to the progressive universalization of its animating idea, Judaism should undergo progressive change toward its ultimate union with the rest of humanity.

• Julius Guttmann, *Philosophies of Judaism* (Garden City, N.Y., 1966), pp. 308–313. Michael A. Meyer, *Response to Modernity: A History of the Reform Movement in Judaism* (New York, 1988), pp. 70–72. Nathan Rotenstreich, *Jewish Philosophy in Modern Times* (New York, 1968), pp. 16–20.

–PAUL MENDES-FLOHR

FORNICATION. See ADULTERY; SEX.

FOUND PROPERTY. See LOST PROPERTY.

FOUR CAPTIVES, the story of four famous rabbis who set sail from Bari in Italy during the tenth century, were captured by Muslims, and were ransomed by Jewish communities, where they established eminent rabbinic academies—Shemaryah ben Elḥanan in Alexandria, *Ḥushi'el ben Elḥanan in Kairouan, and *Mosheh ben Ḥanokh (with his son *Ḥanokh ben Mosheh) in Cordova (the identity of the fourth rabbi is not known). The story, which first appeared in Avraham *ibn Daud's *Sefer ha-Qabbalah*, is not believed to be true, but offered consolation for the declining authority of the Babylonian academies and the rising primacy of academies in North Africa and Spain.

• Abraham ben David, ha-Levi, ibn Daud, *Sefer ha-Qabbalah: The Book of Tradition*, critical edition with translation and notes by Gerson D. Cohen (Philadelphia, 1967).

FOUR CUPS (Heb. *arbaʿ kosot*), the four cups of wine obligatorily consumed during the course of the Pesaḥ *Seder service. Midrashic explanations of the custom variously link the four cups to four references to redemption in *Exodus* 6.6–7 or to four references to Pharaoh's cup in *Genesis* 40, to the four times the word *cup* is applied to punishments traditionally to be meted out to the nations of the world, and to the four times the word is used in connection with the consolations that Israel will eventually receive (Y., *Pes*. 10). The four cups are drunk after the sanctification (Qiddush), after the conclusion of the first part of the Seder, after *Birkat ha-Mazon, and following the conclusion of the second part of the service (see HAGGADAH OF PESAḤ).

• "Arba Kosot," in *Entsiqlopedyah Talmudit*, vol. 2 (Jerusalem, 1949), pp. 159–163. Baruch Bokser, *The Origins of the Seder: The Passover Rite and Early Rabbinic Judaism*, (Berkeley, 1984), pp. 62–65. Eliyahu Ki Tov, *The Book of Our Heritage* (Jerusalem, 1968), pp. 268–275.

FOUR QUESTIONS. See MAH NISHTANNAH.

FOUR SPECIES (Heb. *arbaʿah minim*), the four plants taken and waved during the morning service on *Sukkot. The Bible decrees: "you shall take on the first day the fruit of goodly trees, branches of palm trees, boughs of thick trees, and willows of the brook and rejoice before the Lord your God seven days" (*Lv*. 23.40). The Bible does not explain the injunction, although from *Nehemiah* 8.15–16, it appears that Nehemiah (and later the Sadducees and Karaites) interpreted the verse to refer to the species used in building the **sukkah*. Rabbinic tradition identified the "fruit of goodly trees" with the myrtle (*hadas*; *Suk*. 32b–33a). The four species are traditionally made up of one palm branch (*lulav), one *etrog, three sprigs of myrtle, and two *willow twigs. The Midrash offers a wealth of allegorical interpretations (for example, the qualities of the four species correspond to four types of Jews who make up the community, or the shapes of these species correspond to the organs of the human body—the heart, eye, lip, and spine). Modern scholars regard the four species as part of the ancient ritual of prayer for rain (see TEFILLAT GESHEM); rabbinic tradition also confirms that one of the main concerns of Sukkot was rain for the coming season. In the morning service, the *lulav* is held in the right hand and the *etrog* in the left (*Suk*. 37b). After reciting the appropriate benediction ("to take the *lulav*") during the *Hallel prayer on each day of the festival, the four species are waved in the four directions of the compass, as well as upward and downward, and a circuit is made with them around the synagogue (in Temple times, around the altar). In Temple times the waving was done on each day of the festival in the Temple but only on the first day elsewhere. After the destruction of the Temple it was ordained that the four species would be waved everywhere on all days of the festival, except the Sabbath (*Suk*. 3.12). On *Hosha'na' Rabbah seven circuits are made.

• Yehiel M. Stern, *Kashrut Arba'at ha-Minim* (Jerusalem, 1992). Eliyahu Weisfisch, *Sefer Arba'at ha-Minim ha-Shalem* (Jerusalem, 1975).

FRANCKEL, DAVID (1707–1782), rabbi and commentator on the Talmud Yerushalmi. Franckel was born in Berlin and was rabbi in Dessau until he was appointed chief rabbi of Berlin in 1743. Moses *Mendelssohn was Franckel's student, following him from Dessau to Berlin and eventually supporting him there. Franckel's commentary to the Talmud Yerushalmi, one of the two standard commentaries printed with it, is his most significant literary achievement. The commentary is comprised of two parts: the *Qorban ha-'Edah*, which is modeled after Rashi's commentary on the Talmud Bavli and explains the plain meaning of the text; and *Shirei Qorban*, which is modeled after the tosafistic commentaries, examines contradictions in the text, and offers *novellae*.

• Alexander Altmann, *Moses Mendelssohn: A Biographical Study* (Philadelphia, 1973).
—JOEL HECKER

FRANK, YA'AQOV (1726–1791), last of the pseudo-Messiahs who emerged in the wake of the messianic movement initiated in 1665 by followers of *Shabbetai Tsevi. Even after Shabbetai Tsevi's death, various groups of believers persisted, including the *Dönmeh in Turkey and secret societies in Poland and Galicia. Many of these groups embraced sexual license as part of a perverse mystical faith in the Messiah. Frank, who was born in Podolia, was brought up in one of these sects, became its leader, and eventually claimed to be the successor of Shabbetai Tsevi. He preached an antinomian doctrine and advocated a rapprochement with the Catholic church similar to the adoption of Islam by Shabbetai Tsevi and the Dönmeh (with whom Frank had personal contacts). After various disputations with the rabbis, in which Frank repudiated the Talmud, confessed a Trinitarian Judaism, and even repeated the blood libel, his followers, known as Frankists, took the decisive step of baptism in Lemberg (Lwów) in 1759. Frank himself insisted on being baptized in the Warsaw Cathedral with great pomp, having chosen Emperor Augustus III as his godfather. Accused of heresy against the church a year later, Frank was incarcerated and remained in prison for thirteen years, during which time he became known as the "suffering messiah" among his followers. In 1786 he settled in Offenbach near Frankfurt, where he and his daughter Eve presided over the secret headquarters of the sect and indulged in orgiastic rituals. After Frank's death, the sect ceased to exist, and the baptized Frankists completely merged with Polish society.

• Majer Balaban, *Le-Toledot ha-Tenu'ah ha-Franqit* (Tel Aviv, 1934–1935). Heinrich Graetz, *Frank und die Frankisten: Eine Sekten-Geschichte aus der letzten Halfte des vorigen Jahrhunderts* (Breslau, 1868). Alexander Kraushar, *Frank i frankisei polscy, 1726–1816*, 2 vols. (Kraków, 1895). Hillel Levine, ed., *Ha-"Kroniqah": Te'udah le-Toledot Ya'aqov Franq u-Tenu'ato* (Jerusalem, 1984). Arthur Mandel, *The Militant Messiah: Or, the Flight from the Ghetto: The Story of Jacob Frank and the Frankist Movement* (Atlantic Highlands, N.J., 1979).

FRANKEL, ZACHARIAS (1801–1875), rabbinical scholar; founder of the *Historical movement, which developed into *Conservative Judaism. Born in Prague, he served as rabbi in Teplitz (Teplice) and Dresden until his election in 1854 to the post of director of the Breslau Rabbinical Seminary, which he headed until his death. He was the author of many basic *Wissenschaft des Judentums works, notably *Darkhei ha-Mishnah*, a history of *halakhah* (which argued that the oral law derived from the rabbis and not from Sinai, causing an outcry among the Orthodox), and *Mavo' ha-Yerushalmi*, an introduction to the Talmud Yerushalmi. He established and edited the *Monatsschrift für Geschichte und Wissenschaft des Judentums*, which remained the central German journal of Jewish scholarship until the Nazi era.

While Frankel felt the need to introduce changes in Judaism, he was unsympathetic to the extreme measures adopted by Reform Judaism in his time, especially the replacement of Hebrew with German as the language of prayer (he withdrew from the 1845 Reform synod over this issue) and the omission of references to sacrifices and the return to Zion. At the same time, he advocated liturgical changes and the modernization of Jewish education. Frankel saw the Jewish people as the source of law and tradition, and his study of the development of *halakhah* was guided by his search for the elements that had promoted the Jewish people's vitality and those that had lost their relevance and should therefore be discarded. He regarded Hebrew and messianism as two of the main eternal elements in Judaism. He maintained the Sinaitic revelation but held that this had been supplemented by the oral Torah, which originates in the will of the people. Since it is of human origin, the oral Torah is not immutable; therefore, the sanctity of the Sabbath and the dietary laws repose not on their Sinaitic origin but on their expression over thousands of years in Jewish souls. His ethnic approach contrasted with the ethical emphasis of the reformers. These ideas formed the basis of the Positive Historical school of Judaism, which accepted adaptation to modernism, but only if rooted in tradition. Frankel's school did not become a movement in Germany, but his middle course between Orthodoxy and Reform provided the ideological underpinning for the Conservative movement when it emerged in the United States.

• Saul Phinehas Rabinowitz, *R. Zekharyah Frankel* (Warsaw, 1898), in Hebrew. Louis Ginzberg, "Zechariah Frankel," in *Students, Scholars, and Saints* (Philadelphia, 1928), pp. 195–216. David Rudavsky, *Modern Jewish Religious Movements* (New York, 1979), pp. 192–215.

FRANKISTS. See Frank, Ya'aqov.

FRAUD. Jewish law strongly condemns all forms of fraud and legislates appropriate punishments. A judgment of fraud annuls a contract, and the injured party is entitled to damages. The Bible strictly prohibits the use of false weights and measures (*Lv.* 19.35–36). Fraudulent representation and unfair profit are termed *ona'ah* (oppression). The rabbis apply the biblical prohibition "You shall not wrong one another" (*Lv.* 25.14) to transactions in which the profit obtained is so great that the overcharge is tantamount to fraud. Overcharging by the seller or underpayment by the purchaser by one-sixth of the market value constitutes grounds for canceling a transaction. This formula applies to transactions involving movable goods; the rule was not generally applied to real estate transactions, where the overcharge had to exceed 50 percent in order for the agreement to be annulled. A deal is regarded as fraudulent only when the seller conceals the profit margin. An individual selling personal property, because of the sentimental value attached to it, may sell it at any price (*B. M.* 51a). If an article for sale is defective, the purchaser must be informed prior to the sale, otherwise the transaction is considered fraudulent; any false description gives the buyer the right to have the contract annulled and the purchase money refunded. The term *ona'ah* was also applied to wounding another's feelings, considered to be a worse offense than monetary imposition (*B. M.* 58b); with the latter there exists the possibility of restitution, whereas the former offense cannot be completely nullified. The term *ona'ah* is also used in the extended sense, for example, of asking the price of an object with no intention of buying it, regardless of what price is quoted, or reminding a convert of an idolatrous past.

• Leo Jung, *Business Ethics in Jewish Law* (New York, 1987). Saul Wagschal, *Torah Guide for the Businessman* (Jerusalem and New York, 1990), pp. 3–26.

—SHMUEL HIMELSTEIN

FREEDOM. Although the word *freedom* means release from all arbitrary control or authority, it originally referred to the exemption or release from slavery, which was an accepted part of the economic and social system of the ancient (but not only the ancient) world. The supreme gift of national independence is symbolized by the *Exodus from slavery in Egypt (Pesaḥ is referred to as the feast of freedom). The Ten Commandments begin with the evocation of the fundamental historical experience of liberation: "I am the Lord your God who brought you out of the land of Egypt, out of the house of bondage," rather than with a theological statement such as, "I am the Lord your God, creator of heaven and earth." The gift of national freedom through the Exodus, meant to turn the Israelites from the slaves of Pharaoh into a nation of servants of God, served as a paradigm for all liturgical and spiritual evocations, such as the dictum of *Yehudah ha-Levi, "The servants of time are servants of servants; only the servant of God is truly free," as well as subsequent theoretical discussions of freedom, including such issues as *free will versus *predestination, divine foreknowledge, and causality.

• David B. Burrell, *Freedom and Creation in Three Traditions* (Notre Dame, 1993). Robert Gordis, *Judaism and Religious Liberty* (Los Angeles, 1964). Emmanuel Levinas, *Difficult Freedom: Essays on Judaism* (London, 1990).

FREEHOF, SOLOMON BENNETT (1892–1990), American Reform rabbi and scholar. Born in London, he came to the United States in 1903. In 1915 he began teaching liturgy at Hebrew Union College, Cincinnati, where he had been ordained. He then became rabbi of Congregation Kehillath Anshe Maarav in Chicago (1924–1934) and in 1934 rabbi of Rodef Shalom in Pittsburgh. He was the outstanding American Reform authority on Jewish law and headed the Responsa Committee of the Central Conference of American Rabbis (CCAR). His volumes of *responsa* guided the American Reform movement and linked its practices to the historic teachings of Jewish law. His many volumes of *responsa* include *The Responsa Literature* and *Treasury of Responsa* (repr. New York, 1973), *Reform Responsa* and *Recent Reform Responsa* (repr. New York, 1973), *Current Reform Responsa* (Cincinnati, 1969), *Modern Reform Responsa* (Cincinnati, 1971), *Contemporary Reform Responsa* (Cincinnati, 1974) and *New Reform Responsa* (Cincinnati, 1980). As chairman of the CCAR Committee on Liturgy, he was influential in the publication of the standard Reform prayer books, the *Union Prayer Book* (1940–1945) and the *Union Home Prayer Book* (1951). His writings on the Bible include commentaries on *Psalms* (1938), *Job* (1958) and *Isaiah* (1972). He was president of the World Union for Progressive Judaism from 1959 to 1964.

• Rodef Shalom Congregation (Pittsburgh), *Essays in Honor of Solomon B. Freehof* (Pittsburgh, 1964).

FREE WILL, the notion that men and women determine their own actions and are therefore morally responsible for them. Free will becomes a religious and philosophical problem in the light of the belief in divine omniscience or predestination of *providence (see Determinism; Fatalism). Although the contradiction is often transcended in actual religious experience (cf. *Jer.* 4.3ff.), it remained a serious problem for reflective thought. Attempts to solve it often tended to curtail either one's free will or God's omniscience and omnipotence. The former solution not only outrages one's moral sense, but also calls in question the justice of God in rewarding virtue and punishing sin. The limitation of God's sovereignty also entails serious theological difficulties. Philosophical discussions of free will oscillate between these two poles, one side maintaining that every being, including God, is determined by the necessity of its own being and cannot voluntarily do anything or leave it undone, and the other side asserting that God is not bound by necessity external to himself. Freedom of choice seems to be presupposed in the Bible (cf. *Dt.* 30.19) and, in particular, in prophetic preaching. According to Josephus, the *Sadducees denied the existence of divine providence and attributed everything to chance; the *Essenes, however, were absolute determinists and attributed everything to predestination and the will of God (see QUMRAN COMMUNITY); the *Pharisees asserted both the sovereignty of God and the freedom of the individual, holding that not all things are predestined and that in certain matters humans have freedom. Indeterminism and freedom in one's religious choice are asserted in such rabbinic statements as, "Everything is in the hands of God except the fear of God" (*Ber.* 33b) or "The eye, ear, and nostrils are not in man's power, but the mouth, hand, and feet are" (*Tanḥuma', Toledot*), meaning that external impressions are involuntary but actions, steps, and words arise from an individual's own volition. The Jewish philosophers generally follow the Pharisaic tradition, defending free will either at the price of limiting the scope of God's foreknowledge or by arguing that divine omniscience does not impinge on a person's free will. *Philo departed from Stoic thought and held that free will is a divine part of divine knowledge in such a way that it does not impinge on one's freedom. *Saʿadyah ben Yosef Ga'on and *Yehudah ha-Levi held that God's knowledge of human actions, past and future, did not prejudge or determine them in any way. *Baḥya ben Yosef ibn Paquda' saw free will as limited to the mental acts of decision and choice; external acts, however, he claimed, were determined. Ḥasda'i ben Avraham *Crescas alone among the Jewish philosophers, although aware of the demoralizing effect of his doctrine, denied free will in the interests of proving the sovereignty of God and his infinite attributes.

• Alexander Altmann, "The Religion of the Thinkers: Free Will and Predestination in Saadia, Bahya and Maimonides," in *Religion in a Religious Age*, edited by S. D. Goitein (Cambridge, Mass., 1974). David Winston in *Contemporary Jewish Religious Thought*, edited by Arthur A. Cohen and Paul Mendes-Flohr (New York, 1987), pp. 269–274.

FREE-WILL OFFERING (Heb. *nedavah*), one of the *sacrifices made by an individual as an act of spontaneous devotion (as distinct from one that is required in expiation for sin or impurity, in visiting the Temple on festival days, in payment of a vow, or in thanksgiving for some form of salvation). Free-will offerings could take two forms: the animal could be offered in its entirety, or it could be eaten as a sacred meal in celebration of God's lovingkindness. Thus, it is a subcategory of both the *burnt offering and the *peace offering. In the latter case, it was the least-sacred type of offering; not only could it be eaten over a two-day period (*Lv.* 7.16–17), but also certain imperfections in the animal were allowed (*Lv.* 22.23)—the only exception to the rule that sacrificial animals had to be without blemish.

• Baruch A. Levine, *Leviticus*, The JPS Torah Commentary (Philadelphia, 1989), pp.15–17, 42–47. Jacob Milgrom, *Leviticus 1–16*, The Anchor Bible (New York, 1991), pp. 202–225, 419–420.

—BARUCH J. SCHWARTZ

FRIEDLÄNDER, DAVID (1750–1834), communal leader and educator. Born into the wealthiest Jewish family in Königsberg, David Friedländer received a thorough Jewish and secular education. Soon after moving to Berlin, he married a banker's daughter in 1772 and established himself as a partner in a silk factory in 1776. His early reputation in the textile industry propelled him into a position of influence. A disciple of Moses Mendelssohn, Friedländer argued for emancipation through reform. Friedländer helped to establish the Free School in 1778, which he directed for twenty years, along with an adjacent Hebrew press and bookstore. He prepared numerous textbooks and translations. Frederick William II invited him to present the grievances of the Jewish community in 1787. In 1799 Friedländer, representing "some Jewish householders," penned an open letter to a prominent theologian, Wilhelm Abraham Teller, in which he offered to convert to Christianity so long as he and those he represented would not be expected to accept the dogmas of the church. Teller rejected Friedländer's conditions.

• Steven Lowenstein, *The Jewishness of David Friedländer and the Crisis of Berlin Jewry* (Ramat Gan, 1994). Michael A. Meyer, *The Origins of the Modern Jew: Jewish Identity and European Culture in Germany, 1749–1824* (Detroit, 1967), pp. 57–84.

—KERRY M. OLITZKY

FRINGES. See TALLIT; TSITSIT.

FUGITIVES. See ASYLUM.

FUNERAL ORATION. See EULOGY.

FUNERAL SERVICE. While there is no prescribed form for funerals (see BURIAL), the various branches of Judaism have delineated basic structures. The funeral service usually includes the recitation of psalms and passages from the Bible or rabbinic literature, a *eulogy, and the memorial prayer *El Male' Raḥamim. The funeral is most often conducted in a special funeral chapel and/or at the graveside; some still follow the older practice of conducting funerals at the home of the deceased. In the case of notables and among some Reform congregations, the service begins in the synagogue. Immediate burial is preferred in Judaism as a way of honoring the deceased. However, a funeral service may be delayed to allow a mourner to arrive.

At the graveside the coffin is borne by designated pallbearers, who stop seven times before reaching the grave while Psalm 91 is recited. (In Reform Judaism the practice of stopping seven times has been eliminated.) The coffin is then placed in the grave. Some follow the custom of covering the coffin with earth before the service continues. The prayer *Tsidduq ha-Din, which is an acclamation of God's justice, is recited (in some rites, it is said before the burial), followed by the recitation of the *Qaddish by the next of kin. Filling the grave is a *mitsvah*, and those present often participate. After the service at the graveside is concluded, the people in attendance form two rows through which the mourners pass and offer condolence with the words "May God comfort you among the mourners of Zion and Jerusalem." It is customary to wash one's hands and to pluck some blades of grass before leaving the cemetery. Traditionally, Orthodox Jews did not place flowers on the grave, but in modern times this has become a frequent practice.

• Hayyim Halevy Donin, *To Be A Jew* (New York, 1991). Hyman Goldin, *Hamadrikh: The Rabbi's Guide* (New York, 1956). Jules Harlow, ed., *Liqqutei Teffillah: A Rabbi's Manual* (New York, 1965). Isaac Klein, *A Guide to Jewish Religious Practice* (New York, 1992). Peter Knobel, "Rites of Passage," in *Judaism: A People and Its History*, edited by Robert Seltzer (New York, 1989). Maurice Lamm, *The Jewish Way in Death and Mourning* (New York, 1969). Simeon Maslin, ed., *Gates of Mitzvah: Shaarei Mitzvah, a Guide to the Jewish Life Cycle* (New York, 1979). David Polish, ed., *Maglei Tsedek: A Rabbi's Manual*, with notes by W. Gunther Plaut (New York, 1988). Tzvi Rabinowicz, *A Guide to Life: Jewish Laws and Customs of Mourning* (London, 1964).

—PETER KNOBEL

G

GABBA'I (גַּבַּאי; a collector, tax gatherer), a synagogue warden or treasurer. In Talmudic times, when it referred to tax gatherers, the term was one of opprobrium, as in *Ḥagigah* 3.6, "If *gabba'im* entered a house, the house is unclean." Similarly, the Talmud (*San.* 25b) states that *gabba'im* are disqualified from giving evidence, the reason being that, as tax collectors, the *gabba'im* collect more than the amount permitted them by law. *Gabba'ei tsedaqah*, on the other hand, collected and often distributed money for charitable causes, a position offered only to those of the highest probity. Family members of *gabba'ei tsedaqah* were able to marry into priestly families without the check into genealogy required of others (*Qid.* 4.5). The Talmud nevertheless required *gabba'ei tsedaqah* to collect and disburse funds in pairs to avoid even the faintest hint of suspicion. In the Middle Ages that rule was applied to administrators of the various societies of the *community (for example, the societies for caring for the dead, visiting the sick, charitable funds); administrators for the largest funds rotated office every month. In Erets Yisra'el there were *gabba'im* who headed each **kolel*, and there were also women with the title who cared for poor women and instructed women in ritual. Among the Ḥasidim, the term is applied to the person in charge of the court of the **rebbi*. Eventually, the term evolved to mean the synagogue treasurer and then to refer to the synagogue warden, even though the latter function often involves no financial aspect. See also PARNAS.

• Shlomo Eidelberg, *R. Yuzpa, Shammash di-Kehillat Varmaisa: 'Olam Yehudeyah ba-Me'ah ha-17* (Jerusalem, 1991), pp. 31–33. Ismar Elbogen, *Jewish Liturgy: A Comprehensive History*, translated by Raymond P. Scheindlin (Philadelphia, New York, and Jerusalem, 1993), p. 370.

—SHMUEL HIMELSTEIN

GABIROL. See IBN GABIROL, SHELOMOH.

GABRIEL. See ANGELS.

GAD, the name of two biblical figures. The earlier Gad was the seventh son of Jacob; son of Zilpah, the handmaiden of Jacob's wife Leah. One of the twelve tribes is descended from him. The original meaning of the word *gad* (good fortune, deity of luck) appears in the account of his naming (*Gn.* 30.11). Members of the tribe of Gad, most of whom were shepherds, dwelt east of the Jordan River in Jazer and Gilead, regions known for their livestock. They were required to be among the first to arm themselves and cross the Jordan in the conquest of Canaan (*Nm.* 32.1–33) as a condition of their land allotment. They subsequently constructed an altar near the Jordan as a sign of their allegiance to the worship of God (*Jos.* 22.26–34). The later Gad was a prophet at David's court who advised David to return to Judah and to build the altar on the threshing floor of Araunah (*1 Sm.* 22.1–5; *2 Sm.* 24.18).

• Nahum Sarna, *Genesis*, The JPS Torah Commentary (Philadelphia, 1989), p. 208. Claus Westermann, *Genesis 12–36*, translated by John J. Scullion (Minneapolis, 1985), p. 475.

—SHALOM PAUL

GALANTE FAMILY, family of rabbis and scholars originating in Spain, who settled in Italy, Turkey, Syria, and Erets Yisra'el.

Mosheh bar Mordekhai Galante (1540–1608), born in Rome and a pupil of Yosef Karo in Safed. He was one of the outstanding *poseqim* in Safed, where he served as *av beit din*. He wrote *responsa; Mafteaḥ ha-Zohar* (Venice, 1566), an index to Bible verses interpreted in the Zohar; and *Qohelet Yaʿaqov* (Safed, 1578), a commentary on *Ecclesiastes*.

Mosheh ben Yehonatan Galante (1620–1689), grandson of Mosheh bar Mordekhai; representative of the Jerusalem Jewish community before the Ottoman authorities and distinguished head of the Beit Yaʿaqov Yeshivah. He played a leading role in making Jerusalem a rabbinical center and traveled extensively throughout the Ottoman empire on behalf of the Jerusalem community. He was known as Ha-Magen (The Defender) after his (unpublished) book of a thousand *responsa, Elef ha-Magen*. His published works included *Zevaḥ ha-Shelamim* (Amsterdam, 1708), a commentary on the Torah.

• Abraham Elmaleh, "'Ha-Ri'shon le-Tsiyyon' ha-Ri'shon," in *Ha-Ri'shonim le-Tsiyyon* (Jerusalem, 1970), pp. 55–69. David Goldstein, "A Possible Autograph of Moses ben Mordecai Galante," *Studies in Bibliography and Booklore* 13 (1980): 17–19.

—SHALOM BAR-ASHER

GALUT. See EXILE.

GAMBLING. There are no references to games in the Bible, although lots were cast to make decisions, and on this basis Ya'ir Ḥayyim *Bacharach permitted raffles (*Ḥavvot Ya'ir* 61). It seems that only under Greek and Roman influence were games such as dice playing (*qubyah*) adopted and indulged in by Jews. The rabbis were strongly opposed to all forms of gambling, which although not classed as actual robbery (since appropriation against the will of the owner is an essential legal requirement for proving robbery in Jewish law) was considered closely akin to it; gambling debts could not be legally claimed. Although the general tendency of rabbinic law is to forbid all manner of gambling, careful distinction is made between those who indulge in it as a pastime and those for whom it is a profession (*San.* 24b). Professional gamblers were considered untrustworthy and invalid as witnesses, for "they waste their time in idleness and are not interested in the welfare of humanity" (*R. ha-Sh.* 1.8; *San.* 3.3). The *Shulḥan ʿArukh* permits gambling (*Ḥoshen Mishpat* 207.13, 370). The numerous communal enactments against gambling that are found in the medieval records of European Jewry show that gambling was fairly widely indulged in, and several instances of addiction are recorded (including Leone *Modena, despite the fact that in his youth he wrote an antigambling treatise). Debts incurred in gambling could not be recovered in a *beit din* (*Resp. Rashba'* 7, 445), and addicted gamblers were excluded from community activities. The custom of playing cards on

Ḥanukkah and other festive occasions was fairly widespread among Orthodox Jews in eastern Europe. In modern times, rabbis have discussed the morality of using synagogue premises for games of chance; this has usually been approved if charity or the synagogue benefits from the proceedings.

• Alfred Cohen, "Gambling in the Synagogue," *Tradition* 18.4 (1980): 319–326.

GAMLI'EL. It is often uncertain which Gamli'el is meant in the primary sources. The name can appear with no further qualifiers; sometimes the title "the Elder" is used for Rabban Gamli'el I, who was active during the time of the Second Temple. Some of the tosafists rely on this distinction and assume that when the name Gamli'el appears alone it is a reference to Gamli'el II of Yavneh; however, parallel texts exist in which "the Elder" appears in one version only. Historians, therefore, add another criterion: if the incident clearly occurred before the destruction of the Second Temple, the reference is to *Gamli'el the Elder. An additional difficulty is the confusion in texts between Gamli'el and *Shim'on ben Gamli'el, the latter name referring to one of two separate patriarchs. There are more than twenty-five such variants in Mishnah manuscripts alone.

Gamli'el II of Yavneh was the name of the son of the *nasi'* R. Shim'on ben Gamli'el and grandson of Gamli'el the Elder. He was born about twenty years before the destruction of the Temple in 70 CE. Most of his public activities took place after that time. He succeeded R. Yoḥanan ben Zakk'ai at Yavneh in about 80 CE. Since he was a *nasi'*, he should have assumed the patriarchate at Yavneh immediately after the fall of Jerusalem. He may have been kept out of office by the Romans and perhaps even hunted down by them in an attempt to eradicate all descendants of the ruling family; his father, Shim'on, in all probability was killed during the Great Revolt. It is possible that Gamli'el was in hiding for a number of years. No source records Gamli'el's participation in the academy at Yavneh with R. Yoḥanan, and only one source links them as teacher and disciple. When Gamli'el succeeded Yoḥanan at Yavneh, Yoḥanan retired to Beror Ḥayil.

At Yavneh, Gamli'el's main tasks were to reestablish the Sanhedrin and to strengthen the institution of the patriarchate (*nesi'ut*). A strong leader, he came into conflict with other sages at the academy, notably R. *Eli'ezer ben Hurqanos and R. *Yehoshu'a ben Ḥananyah. He was temporarily deposed but was reinstated after coming to terms with his antagonists.

Most of Gamli'el's important halakhic dictums dealt with the need for religious readjustment and a uniform *halakhah* after the destruction of the Temple. Many important ordinances were issued in his name fixing the liturgy (i.e., determination of the Pesaḥ Seder service [*Pes.* 10.5] and three daily prayers), incorporating elements reminiscent of the Temple ritual. He instituted a prayer against sectarians (*Birkat ha-Minim), to be recited in the daily 'Amidah. It was directed against Jewish-Christians and further distanced them from Judaism and the synagogue. He was well versed in the sciences, which he used in fixing the Jewish calendar. His knowledge of Greek made him a spokesman for Judaism in encounters with paganism and Christianity. The translation of the Bible into Greek by Aquila the Proselyte was undertaken in the Yavneh period; unlike the Septuagint, it followed the Masoretic Text closely. This, too, can be seen as the creation of a new norm to shore up rabbinic Judaism. Gamli'el did much to raise the prestige of the patriarchate through his frequent trips in Erets Yisra'el and abroad—to Beirut, Damascus, Tripoli, Antioch, Aleppo, and Rome. His dialogues with gentiles, which took place on these journeys, make up a major portion of the nonhalakhic traditions about him.

• Gedaliah Alon, *The Jews in Their Land in the Talmudic Age, 70–640 C.E.* (Jerusalem, 1980), pp. 86, 131, 253–287. Heinrich Graetz, *History of the Jews*, vol. 2 (Philadelphia, 1956), pp. 321–359. M. B. Lerner, "Rabban Gamaliel of Jabneh," in *The World of the Sages*, edited by Isaac Gottlieb, unit 4 (Ramat Gan, 1984). Shemuel Safrai, "The Era of the Mishnah and Talmud, 70–640," in *A History of the Jewish People*, edited by Haim Hillel Ben-Sasson (Cambridge, Mass., 1976), pp. 307–382.

–ISAAC B. GOTTLIEB

GAMLI'EL THE ELDER (died c.50 CE), head of the Sanhedrin during the rule of Caligula; grandson of *Hillel; also known as Rabban (Our Master) Gamli'el or Gamli'el I. There were six Palestinian patriarchs (1st–5th cent.) of the school of Hillel, and it is often unclear to which *Gamli'el the Talmud is referring. Gamli'el the Elder introduced important judicial reforms, including improving the legal status of women; for example, he permitted a woman to remarry even if there was only a single witness to her husband's death (*Yev.* 16.7). He also condemned discrimination against non-Jews, for example, in giving of charity to them. Among his pupils was *Paul (*Acts* 22.3), who mentions sympathetically Gamli'el's tolerance for the small Christian sect.

• Gershom Bader, *Encyclopedia of Talmudic Sages* (Northvale, N.J., 1988). Emil Cohn, "Rabban Gamaliel," in *Stories and Fantasies from the Jewish Past* (Philadelphia, 1961). Jeffrey A. Trumbower, "The Historical Jesus and the Speech of Gamaliel (Acts 5.35–9)," *New Testament Studies* 39 (1993): 500–517.

–ISAAC B. GOTTLIEB

GAN 'EDEN. See EDEN, GARDEN OF; PARADISE.

GANZFRIED, SHELOMOH (1804–1886), halakhic authority and chief rabbinical judge in Ungvár (Uzhgorod), Hungary. He was a leading spokesman for the separatist camp in the Orthodox struggle against Neology, but he is best known for his code of Jewish law, the *Qitsur Shulḥan 'Arukh* (1864), an abridgment based on Yosef Karo's **Shulḥan 'Arukh*, which summarizes in fluid, simple Hebrew the laws incumbent on the individual Jew. Generally, he included only those opinions that he held to be correct. In his lifetime, fourteen editions of the *Qitsur Shulḥan 'Arukh*, as well as a number of commentaries, had been published. The book's popularity reflects the decline in basic traditional Jewish study skills among laymen, who preferred the popularization to deeper study of the original. Additionally, its unequivocal nature echoes the Hungarian approach that demanded strict adherence to uniform practice.

• J. Katz, "The Changing Position and Outlook of Halachists in Early Modernity," in *Scholars and Scholarship: The Interaction between Judaism and Other Cultures*, edited by Leo Landman (New York, 1990), pp. 93–106. M. R. Lehman, "Teshuvat ha-Ga'on Rabbi Shelomoh Ganzfried be-ʻInyan Tiqqunim le-ʻQitsur Shulḥan ʻArukh' Shelo," *Sinai* 93 (1983): 53–58. J. L. Maimon, "Le-Toledot ha-Qitsur Shulḥan ʻArukh," in *Qitsur Shulḥan ʻArukh* (Jerusalem, 1950), pp. 13–15. —ADAM S. FERZIGER

GA'ON (גָּאוֹן; excellency, pride), title of the head of either of the two leading *academies in Babylonia, *Sura and *Pumbedita, following the period of the *savora'im. The beginning and end of the geonic period are difficult to date precisely, but the geonic period is considered to have extended from the mid-sixth to the mid-eleventh century. The title *ga'on* is an abbreviation of the designation *ro'sh yeshivat ga'on Yaʻaqov* (head of the academy that is the pride of Jacob). Although the *exilarch served as the official representative of the Jewish community vis-à-vis the Muslim authorities, the ge'onim, too, exercised considerable temporal power: the Jewish communities nearest Babylonia were divided into three *reshuyyot* (spheres of influence), of which one was controlled by the exilarch and one by each of the ge'onim (or their academies). In every district, the appropriate central authority was empowered to appoint (and, if necessary, to dismiss) local officials and to collect taxes from the Jewish populace; these comprised a major source of funding for the central institutions. The exilarch also played a leading role, at least on several occasions, in the selection of a new ga'on when the office became vacant.

The ge'onim did much to foster and develop Talmudic law and to enhance the status and authority of the *Talmud Bavli in particular. The geonic period saw the Talmud Bavli established as the recognized standard of halakhic authority throughout the Jewish world, at the expense of the ancient Palestinian center and its traditions. This victory, which was achieved only after a prolonged struggle, reflected a widespread recognition of Babylonian superiority in the halakhic realm.

In addition to transmitting and explicating the Talmudic text, the ge'onim were obliged to draw practical conclusions concerning questions that had been discussed without clear decisions having been reached, as well as questions that had not arisen in the Talmud and so had to be answered by analogy to earlier discussions.

The characteristic literary form of the period was the *responsum* (see RESPONSA), in which a ga'on (writing on behalf of and with the cooperation of the scholars of his academy) answered correspondents' queries, mostly on Talmudic and halakhic matters. These *responsa* were often copied and referred to by contemporary and later scholars, and not only by the original addressees. Geonic influence was felt most directly and profoundly in North Africa and Spain, where Jewish communities frequently corresponded with the Babylonian academies, but geonic writings were later accorded a semicanonical status even in areas such as France and Germany.

The earlier part of the geonic period saw the publication of three ambitious literary works, none of which (in all probability) was written by a ga'on. One of these was the *She'iltot*, a collection of homilies combining *halakhah* and *aggadah*, the redaction of which is attributed to *Aḥa' of Shabḥa. The other two are in the nature of systematic halakhic codes with some pretensions to comprehensiveness. The earlier of these, **Halakhot Pesuqot*, is traditionally but somewhat implausibly attributed to*Yehuda'i ben Naḥman Ga'on; the later **Halakhot Gedolot* was attributed to R. Shimʻon Kayyara, of whom virtually nothing is known.

Yehuda'i Ga'on, who trained in Pumbedita but from 760 headed the academy of Sura, is the earliest ga'on whose *responsa* have been preserved in significant numbers. He is also the earliest figure reported to have attempted to establish Babylonian hegemony in matters of *halakhah* and tradition, going so far as to instruct Palestinian Jews to abandon their ancestral customs in favor of Babylonian ones.

The ninth century saw a number of prominent ge'onim of both academies sending large numbers of *responsa* to the Diaspora. Perhaps the most prolific of these was *Natrona'i bar Hila'i, ga'on of the Sura academy; over five hundred of his *responsa* have been preserved. Equally famous is Natrona'i's rival and possible successor, *ʻAmram bar Sheshna', best known for his prayer book *Seder Rav ʻAmram*. Leading ge'onim of Pumbedita included Palto'i Ga'on (842–857), who is reported to have sent a copy of the Talmud to Spain.

The nature of the gaonate changed considerably in the tenth century, primarily as a result of the career of *Saʻadyah ben Yosef Ga'on, who became ga'on of Sura in 928. Saʻadyah's unconventional background and personality had far-reaching effects on the intellectual elite of Babylonia, most notably a broadening of their intellectual horizons to include non-Talmudic subjects such as Bible, poetry, and philosophy, and of their literary activities to include the writing of systematic works on these and other topics. Saʻadyah's most notable followers were *Shemu'el ben Ḥofni, ga'on of Sura, and *Ha'i Ga'on, Shemu'el's son-in-law and the head of the Pumbedita academy. Ha'i's father and predecessor as head of the academy, *Sherira' ben Ḥanina' Ga'on, is famous primarily for his epistle of 986, *Iggeret Rav Sherira' Ga'on*, which constitutes the most important source for the chronology of the geonic period and a major discussion of the evolution of Talmudic literature. Shortly after Ha'i's death the Babylonian academies lost their leading role in the Jewish world, and in the late ninth century they relocated to Baghdad but retained their traditional names. The head of an academy located in Baghdad continued to lay claim to the title of ga'on as late as the thirteenth century. A gaonate also emerged in Erets Yisra'el, although its early history is not clear. The Babylonians were dissatisfied with this use of the title ga'on and refrained from addressing the heads of the Erets Yisra'el community as such. The ga'on headed the *yeshivah* of Tiberias, which moved to Jerusalem, and he also directed all aspects, including economic, of the country's Jewish community. He was recognized by the non-Jewish rulers as the representative of the community. The gaonate was headed by a group of seven scholars (sometimes called the Great Sanhedrin) headed by the ga'on, with the *av beit din* as his deputy and successor. The senior positions were often hereditary and were usually held by members of three families, of whom the Ben Me'ir family was the most prominent. They appointed judges and community leaders in Erets Yisra'el and Syria. Few of the *responsa* of these ge'onim have survived, but many of their letters, often requesting support, have been found in the Cairo Genizah. After the Seljuk conquest in 1076, which brought great suffering to the Jews, the gaonate moved to Tyre and later to Damascus, where it came to an end. Egyptian Jews also founded a gaonate in the eleventh century, and it flourished for some decades in the twelfth century. The term ga'on continues in popular Jewish usage to describe an outstanding scholar.

• Shraga Abramson, *'Inyanot be-Sifrut ha-Ge'onim* (Jerusalem, 1974). Simḥa Assaf, *Tequfat ha-Ge'onim ve-Sifrutah* (Jerusalem, 1967). Robert Brody, ed., *Teshuvot Rav Natrona'i bar Hila'i Ga'on* (Jerusalem, 1994). Neil Danzig, *Mavo' le-Sefer Halakhot Pesuqot* (Jerusalem, 1993). Louis Ginzberg, *Geonica* (1909; Jerusalem, 1986). Tsvi Groner, *The Legal Methodology of Hai Gaon* (Chico, Calif., 1985). Henry Malter, *Saadia Gaon* (1921; Hildesheim, 1978). Samuel Abraham Poznanski, *Babylonische Geonim im nachgaonäischen Zeitalter* (Berlin, 1914).

—ROBERT BRODY

GA'ON OF VILNA. See ELIYYAHU BEN SHELOMOH ZALMAN OF VILNA.

GARDEN OF EDEN. See EDEN, GARDEN OF; PARADISE.

GAR'JI, MATTATYAHU (1844–1918), rabbi in Afghanistan. The Jewish community of Afghanistan was strengthened after 1839 by refugees from Mashhad in Persia (where the Jews had been forcibly converted to Islam), including several members of the Gar'ji family. They were among the rabbinical leaders in their new home. The Jews of Afghanistan had a vibrant Jewish life, maintained almost completely without contacts with the outside world, and produced a literature in Judeo-Persian and Hebrew. Gar'ji, who lived most of his life in Herāt, wrote many works, among them *Qorot Zemanim* (Jerusalem, 1913), describing the fate of the refugees from Mashhad, including their move to Erets Yisra'el, from the end of the nineteenth century and, most notably, *'Oneg Shabbat* on the Torah and Five Scrolls, divided according to the weekly synagogue readings. He also wrote a commentary on *Psalms* and sermons on the Talmud and *Pirqei Avot*.

• Reuben Kashani, ed., *Qorot Zemanim* (Jerusalem, 1970). Nehemiah Robinson, *Persia and Afghanistan and Their Jewish Communities* (New York, 1953).

—SHALOM BAR-ASHER

GARTEL. See COSTUME.

GEDALIAH, FAST OF. See TSOM GEDALYAH.

GEHENNA. See GEIHINNOM.

GEIGER, ABRAHAM (1810–1874), scholar and spiritual leader of *Reform Judaism in Germany. The outstanding intellectual figure among the early Reformers, he was animated by the desire to liberate Judaism from its ceremonialism, to link it with European traditions, to organize it on modern scientific lines, and to interpret it in the light of an ethical universality based on the prophets. His Reform principles and theological convictions are embodied in the prayer book that he published in 1854. It omits all references to angels, the resurrection of the dead, the restoration of the Temple, and the return to Zion. Geiger was opposed to the doctrine of Israel's election and all religious or national particularism. Among the innovations he introduced into the service were choral singing, confirmation exercises, and sermons in German. He favored the elimination of circumcision and the dietary laws but opposed the tendency in certain Reform circles to observe the Sabbath on Sundays. His scholarly activities were based on a historical–critical study of the evolution of Judaism. He believed that Judaism ought to become a world religion that would take the place of Christianity, which he maintained was marred by basic misconceptions.

Geiger was one of the most versatile and influential Jewish scholars of the nineteenth century. His initial research focused on the question of Jewish influence on Islam, which was followed by a long series of articles on various aspects of Jewish literature. Geiger's most renowned book was on the transmission of the Bible within Jewish tradition, *Urschrift und Übersetzungen der Bibel* (1857). As a professor at the *Hochschule für die Wissenschaft des Judentums, Geiger lectured on the whole course of Jewish history. Reflecting the fusion of his roles as critical scholar and Reform activist, he gave expression to a view of Judaism as ceaselessly and dynamically evolving, for instance, from a period of rigid legalism in medieval and early modern times to an age of liberation in the post-Enlightenment era.

• Ludwig Geiger, *Abraham Geiger: Leben und Lebenswerk* (Berlin, 1910). Ludwig Geiger, *Abraham Geiger's Nachgelassene Schriften*, 5 vols. (Berlin, 1875–1878). Michael A. Meyer, *Response to Modernity: A History of the Reform Movement in Judaism* (New York, 1988). Jakob J. Petuchowski, ed., *New Perspectives on Abraham Geiger: An HUC-JIR Symposium* (New York, 1975). Max Wiener, *Abraham Geiger and Liberal Judaism: The Challenge of the Nineteenth Century* (Philadelphia, 1962).

—DAVID N. MYERS

GEIHINNOM, valley (Gei ben Hinnom) outside the western wall of Jerusalem, mentioned in the Bible (*Jos*. 15.8, 18.16; *2 Kgs*. 23.10; *Jer*. 7.31; *Neh*. 11.30) as a valley through which ran the boundary between the tribes of Benjamin and Judah. It was the site of *Topheth, where child sacrifices were offered to *Molech. The valley also served for the incineration of the city's refuse and for dumping of animal carcasses and the bodies of criminals. Jeremiah prophesied (*Jer*. 7.32) that the valley would become a "valley of slaughter" and a burial place. Thus it assumed in post-biblical literature the connotation of hell, where the wicked are punished (in opposition to the garden of Eden, or paradise)—though no such allusion to it exists in the Bible itself, which refers to the abode of the dead only as Sheol (cf. *Gn*. 37.25). Some rabbis place Geihinnom (or hell) in the bowels of the earth (*'Eruv*. 19a); others, in the heavens or beyond "the mountain of darkness" (*Tam*. 32b). The form of punishment inflicted on the wicked is not clearly defined in the Talmud but is principally associated with fire. Maimonides interpreted the tradition of punishment of the wicked in Geihinnom as a denial of eternal life for them. The Zohar describes an upper Geihinnom and a lower Geihinnom; the dross of the soul that is not purged in the lower Geihinnom is finally removed in the upper Geihinnom. See also AFTERLIFE.

• Yehoash Biber, *Gei ben Hinnom ve-Naḥal Qidron* (Jerusalem, 1991). Samuel J. Fox, *Hell in Jewish Literature* (Northbrook, Ill., 1972).

GELILAH (גְּלִילָה; rolling), in the Ashkenazi rite, the honor accorded a person of rolling (i.e., closing) up and binding the Torah scroll and putting on the Torah ornaments after the Torah reading in the synagogue. One person first raises the scroll (**hagbahah*), whereupon another performs *gelilah*. In the eastern Sephardi rite, in which the Torah scroll is not tied, there is no *gelilah*. In Talmudic times, the person who read the last portion of the Torah would roll it up. In some congregations, *gelilah* is now performed by children.

• Ismar Elbogen, *Jewish Liturgy: A Comprehensive History*, translated by Raymond P. Scheindlin (Philadelphia, New York, and Jerusalem, 1993), p. 142. —SHMUEL HIMELSTEIN

GEMARA' (Aram.; גְּמָרָא; completion), the usual designation for the commentary and discussions on the *Mishnah that surround the latter on the printed page of the Talmud. The Mishnah together with the *gemara'* make up the *Talmud. There is both a Palestinian and a Babylonian *gemara'* to the Mishnah, but there are many tractates to which no *gemara'* has been preserved.

GEMATRIA. See GIMATRIYYAH.

GEMILUT ḤESED (גְּמִילוּת חֶסֶד), any act of kindness, consideration, or benevolence. Torah, worship, and *gemilut ḥesed* are the three foundations of the world (*Avot* 1.2), and *gemilut ḥesed* is one of the distinguishing characteristics of the Jewish people (*Yev*. 79a). In three respects *gemilut ḥesed* is superior to *tsedaqah* (acts of charity): *tsedaqah* can be given only in money or in kind; *gemilut ḥesed* can be given in personal service also. *Tsedaqah* can be given only to the poor; *gemilut ḥasadim* to both rich and poor. *Tsedaqah* can be performed only for the living; *gemilut ḥasadim* for the living and the dead (*Suk*. 49b). *Gemilut ḥesed* is unlimited in its applications and is listed among those actions by which "man enjoys the fruit in this world, while the stock remains to him in the world to come" (*Pe'ah* 1.1). *Gemilut ḥesed* is one of the attributes of God, who is described in the daily ʿAmidah as *gomel ḥasadim tovim* (bestower of loving-kindness). Because lending money to enable a person to become self-sufficient is *gemilut ḥesed* and is considered superior to almsgiving, which could humiliate the recipient, the term *gemilut ḥesed* was applied more specifically to the lending of money free of interest to those in need of temporary financial assistance. *Gemilut ḥesed* societies exist for this purpose.

• S. Romerowski, "Que signife le mot *ḥesed?*" *Vetus Testamentum* 40 (1990): 89–103. Robin L. Routledge, "*Ḥesed* as Obligation: A Re-Examination," *Tyndale Bulletin* 46 (1995): 179–196. Katharine D. Sakenfeld, *Faithfulness in Action: Loyalty in Biblical Perspective* (Philadelphia, 1985). —SHMUEL HIMELSTEIN

GENEALOGY. See YUḤASIN.

GENESIS, BOOK OF (Heb. *Be-Re'shit* [In the Beginning]; from the opening word of the book), the first book of the Torah, whose English title was taken from the Greek *genesis* (coming into being). The book, which is divided into fifty chapters, consists of four cycles, the first of which covers primeval history (1.1–11.26) and describes the *creation of the world and Israel's understanding of the origins of humanity (stories about *Adam and *Eve, *Noah, and the *Flood, etc.). The second cycle (11.27–22.24) presents the life story of *Abraham and centers around his relationship with God, the establishment of the *covenant, and Abraham's quest for an heir (realized by his son *Isaac). The third major unit is the *Jacob cycle (25.19–35.22), which details the trials and tribulations of the third of Israel's *patriarchs. There is no special cycle devoted to Isaac, whose character is the least developed of the three patriarchs. The final unit is the *Joseph story (37.1–50.26), which concentrates on Jacob's favorite son and the migration of the Israelites to Egypt. Small units of linking material (23.1–25.18, 35.23–36.43) provide minor details necessary to round out the stories of the patriarchs; they are placed between the Abraham and Jacob cycles and between the Jacob and Joseph cycles. The *Book of Genesis* lays the foundations for the historical accounts, teachings, and legislation of the subsequent books of the Bible. Major issues are the sovereignty and providence of the one God who created the world, who is the source of morality, and who guides Israel; the emergence of the peoples of the world; the special relationship of the patriarchs to God and the election of their seed to be God's people; and God's promise of the land of Canaan as Israel's ultimate home. The traditional Jewish view of the *Book of Genesis* is that it is of divine origin and was given by God to Moses at Sinai. Since the seventeenth century, critical scholars have rejected this view and have proposed various dates for the authorship and/or final redaction of *Genesis*. Several indications in the text point to a tenth-century BCE (Davidic–Solomonic) date. Such clues include the promise of kings descending from Abraham and Sarah (17.6, 17.16); Abraham's tithing to a priest of Salem (Jerusalem; 14.18–20); Abraham's sacrifice of a ram on "the mount of the Lord" (22.14), a phrase used elsewhere in the Bible only with reference to Jerusalem; Israel's rule over Edom (27.29); the latter's rebellion (27.40); the close relationship with Ammon and Moab (19.36–38); and the connection between Judah and royal rule (49.8–10). All of these reflect the historical, political, and theological developments of the united kingdom under David and Solomon. According to this view, the *Book of Genesis* presents the early history of Israel as filtered through the lens of an Israelite author (or authors) of the tenth century BCE.

• Umberto Cassuto, *A Commentary on the Book of Genesis*; pt. 1, *From Adam To Noah*, pt. 2, *From Noah to Abraham* (Jerusalem, 1961–1964). Gary A. Rendsburg, *The Redaction of Genesis* (Winona Lake, Ind., 1986).

Nahum M. Sarna, *Genesis*, The JPS Torah Commentary (Philadelphia, 1989). Nahum M. Sarna, *Understanding Genesis* (New York, 1970). Meir Sternberg, *The Poetics of Biblical Narrative* (Bloomington, Ind., 1985).

—GARY A. RENDSBURG

GENESIS APOCRYPHON, an Aramaic manuscript of the *Dead Sea Scrolls, found in Qumran, Cave 1, in 1947. The *Genesis Apocryphon* is a collection of patriarchal narratives based on the *Book of Genesis*. The material in its preserved twenty-two columns (only cols. 2 and 19–22 have been fully published) covers the narratives from Lamech to Abraham. In style, it is related to the Targum and the Midrash, while much of its content parallels the *Book of *Jubilees*. The *Genesis Apocryphon* manuscript dates from the late first century BCE to the early first century CE, while it was composed between the early and middle second century BCE. It was first published by Naḥman Avigad and Yigael Yadin (Jerusalem, 1956), and an English translation by Geza Vermes appeared in his *The Dead Sea Scrolls in English* (London, 1987).

• Joseph A. Fitzmyer, *The Genesis Apocryphon of Qumran Cave I*, 2d rev. ed., Biblica et Orientalia, 18a (Rome, 1971).

—SIDNIE WHITE CRAWFORD

GENESIS RABBAH, a collection of Midrashic-homiletic comments to *Genesis*, generally considered the earliest of the aggadic *midrashim*. Compiled in Erets Yisra'el in the fifth or sixth century CE, *Genesis Rabbah* includes an abundance of exegetical comments, parables, biblical narrative expansions, and aggadic stories transmitted by rabbinic sages of the Mishnaic and Talmudic periods. The passages, written in a mixture of Rabbinic Hebrew and Galilean Aramaic (with an influence of Greek vocabulary) are arranged in order of the verses of *Genesis*; almost every verse is expounded by one or more passages. The work is divided into 101 sections or *parashiyyot* (the numbering of sections varies slightly among the manuscripts and printed editions). These sections conform partially to the "open" and "closed" paragraphs of the Masoretic Text of the Torah, and partially to the *sedarim* of the *triennial cycle of Torah readings. Each section, with a few exceptions, commences with one or more *petiḥot* (proems): the *petiḥah* presents an exposition of a verse unconnected to *Genesis* (taken generally from the Hagiographa), which is subsequently related to the beginning verse of the section. The Midrashic material in *Genesis Rabbah*, serving as a prime example of rabbinic thought and exegesis, has numerous direct parallels in other early rabbinic works, especially the Talmud Yerushalmi. Many of the themes, legends, and exegeses in *Genesis Rabbah* may also be found in the apocryphal and pseudepigraphal literature as well as in the first-century CE Jewish authors Philo and Josephus, although a direct influence of these works on the Midrash is not generally assumed.

Two English translations of *Genesis Rabbah* are H. Freedman and M. Simon's *Midrash Rabbah*, volumes 1 and 2 (3d ed. [London, 1961]), and J. Neusner's *Genesis Rabbah: The Judaic Commentary on Genesis, A New American Translation* (3 vols. [Atlanta, 1985]).

• Chanoch Albeck, "Mavo' u-Mafteḥot," in *Midrash Be-Re'shit Rabba'*, 2d ed., edited by Julius Theodor and Chanoch Albeck, vol. 3 (Jerusalem, 1965). Michael Sokoloff, *Qit'ei Be-Re'shit Rabbah min ha-Genizah* (Jerusalem, 1982). Hermann Leberecht Strack, *Introduction to the Talmud and Midrash* (1931; Minneapolis, 1992). Leopold Zunz, *Ha-Derashot be-Yisra'el ve-Hishtalshelutan ha-Historit*, edited by Chanoch Albeck (1892; Jerusalem, 1974).

—PAUL MANDEL

GENESIS RABBATI, Midrashic anthology on *Genesis* composed by *Mosheh ha-Darshan of Narbonne (11th cent.), or at least emanating from his school. The existing text may be an abridgment of a more extensive anthology by Mosheh ha-Darshan. It draws heavily on **Genesis Rabbah* but also makes abundant use of the Mishnah, Talmud (primarily Bavli), Midrash Rabbah, Tanḥuma'-Yelammedenu, *Pesiqta'*, and *Pirqei de-Rabbi Eli'ezer*, among other works. Moreover, embedded in the Midrashic compilations are elements culled from apocryphal literature, such as *Jubilees*, *Enoch*, and the *Testaments of the Twelve Patriarchs* (which apparently Mosheh read in an improved Hebrew version). Subsequently, medieval authorities, such as Rashi and Natan ben Yeḥi'el of Rome (author of the *'Arukh*), cited it extensively. The work was published in Jerusalem in 1940 by Ḥanokh Albeck from the only known manuscript. It was mentioned and quoted by the thirteenth-century Spanish Dominican Raymund Martini as *Midrash Be-Re'shit Rabbah Major*.

• Chanoch Albeck, ed., "Mavo'," in *Midrash Be-Re'shit Rabbati* (1940; Jerusalem, 1967). Abraham Epstein, ed., *Moshe ha-Darshan mi-Narbonah* (Vienna, 1891).

—DANIEL SPERBER

GENETICS. The first reference to heredity may be in the biblical passage in which Jacob is granted a vision about "he-goats which leaped upon the flock [and] were streaked, speckled, and grizzled" (*Gn*. 31.10). He requests his wages in the form of speckled young, presumably because he had noticed how this characteristic was transferred from the parents to their offspring. The Talmud rules that a man may not marry a woman from a leprous or epileptic family for fear that these diseases will be passed on to their offspring (*Yev*. 64b). Marriage between spouses possessing diverse physical characteristics is encouraged (*Bekh*. 45b), and while marriages between uncles and nieces are approved (*Yev*. 63a), later authorities frown upon this practice.

• Immanuel Jakobovits, "Genetic Engineering," *Le'ela* 2.6 (1983): 1–5. Fred Rosner, "Genetic Engineering and Judaism" in *Jewish Bioethics*, edited by Fred Rosner and J. David Bleich (New York, 1979), pp. 409–420. Fred Rosner, "Test Tube Babies, Host Mothers and Genetic Engineering in Judaism," *Tradition* 19.2 (1981): 141–148.

—DANIEL SINCLAIR

GENIZAH (גְּנִיזָה; storing), a hiding place or storeroom, usually connected with a synagogue, for the depositing of worn-out sacred books and sacred objects, such as **tefillin*, which must not be destroyed according to Jewish law. It is also the place for storing books considered heretical but which contain the name of God and hence are too sacred to be burned. Present-day Orthodox custom is to give cemetery burial to all such documents, which are accumulated in a special place set aside in the synagogue. Reference is made in the Talmud to

R. Gamli'el's placing an Aramaic translation of the *Book of Job*, considered improper at the time, under the pillars of the building on the Temple mount. During the Middle Ages, a room was set aside in almost every synagogue as a *genizah* for old or imperfect books or ritual objects. Such synagogue hiding places for sacred works have often provided later generations with precious pages of books considered lost. The most famous such *genizah* is that discovered in the synagogue of Fostat, in Cairo (built in 882), which comprised two hundred thousand fragments, including part of the lost Hebrew version of *Ben Sira* (see WISDOM OF BEN SIRA) and other lost Hebrew works; extracts from *Aquila's Greek translation of the Bible; early Masoretic documents throwing light on Palestinian and Babylonian vocalization; the Zadokite fragments, which portray a halakhic system with affinities both to the Pharisaic tradition and to that of the Judean Desert sect (see DAMASCUS DOCUMENT); variant text readings of the Mishnah and Talmud; ancient liturgies and synagogue poetry from almost all places of known Jewish settlement at the time; works of lexicography; early mystical treatises; as well as miscellaneous secular documents and letters, many of which are extremely valuable as historical sources. The oldest known work in Yiddish (14th cent.) was also found in this *genizah*. The finds in the Cairo Genizah have thrown much new light on the history of the gaonate, the *Karaites, and the conditions of Jews in Erets Yisra'el and Egypt between 640 and 1100. A new kind of *genizah* has come to light more recently with the discovery of the *Dead Sea Scrolls.

• Joshua Blau and Stefan C. Reif, eds., *Genizah Research After Ninety Years: The Case of Judeo-Arabic* (Cambridge, 1992). Abraham Meir Habermann, *Ha-Genizah* (Jerusalem, 1943). Paul E. Kahle, *The Cairo Genizah* (London, 1947). Geoffrey A. Khan, "Twenty Years of Geniza Research," *Encyclopaedia Judaica Year Book* (Jerusalem, 1983–1985): 163–169. Stefan C. Reif, "Genizah Material at Cambridge University," *Encyclopaedia Judaica Year Book* (Jerusalem, 1983–1985): 170–171.

GENTILES (from Lat. *geni* or *genites* [family nation]), the common English translation for the Hebrew *nokhri* or *goy*, that is, members of non-Jewish nations. A *Jew is a person either born of a Jewish mother (the Reform movement has stated a Jewish parent of either sex) or who has accepted the Jewish faith by undergoing conversion; all others are gentiles. In Jewish law, gentiles are divided into different categories depending on their acceptance of various basic standards of conduct; of these divisions and subdivisions, the most important are *'*akkum* (a word made up of the initial letters of the Hebrew phrase for "a worshiper of stars and planets"—that is, an idolater or pagan) and those who have abandoned idolatry and accepted the belief in one God. According to rabbinic opinion (*'A. Z.* 64b) the latter type alone—that is, those who accept the seven *Noahic laws—can qualify for the status of a *ger toshav* (resident stranger) with defined rights in the community. The rabbis said "the pious of all the nations of the world have a share in the world to come," and these are identified by Maimonides as those who accept Noahic laws as divine revelation. As a result of this distinction, the extremely severe laws applying to heathens and idolaters in the Bible and Talmud are not held to apply to Christians or Muslims. Another consideration, however, came into play that deleteriously affected the relationship between Jews and gentiles. In their determined efforts to prevent assimilation and loss of identity as a small minority in the midst of a hostile majority, the rabbis deliberately set up barriers for the explicit purpose of preventing social intercourse with gentiles that could lead, among other things, to *intermarriage. The injunction in *Deuteronomy* 7.2–4, originally limited specifically to the seven Canaanite nations who inhabited Erets Yisra'el, was extended to include all gentiles, and decrees were enacted to erect barriers against this danger (see ḤUQQAT HA-GOYYIM). The partaking of meals with gentiles was forbidden, even when it did not infringe the dietary laws. Food cooked by gentiles was banned (*'A. Z.* 2.6), and the prohibition sometimes extended even to bread and oil. The prohibition against "non-Jewish wine," originally of a strictly ritual nature, was maintained and extended even after the ritual motivation had lapsed, for the purpose of minimizing Jewish–gentile conviviality. The modern period, starting with the Emancipation, has witnessed a revolution in relations between Jews and gentiles. Having emerged from ghetto conditions, Jews maintain close everyday contacts with gentiles; on one level, this has brought about the tendency to *assimilation; on another, it has encouraged a more liberal approach to gentiles from the religious aspect, including interfaith activities (see INTERFAITH RELATIONS).

• Zeev W. Falk, "On the Historical Background of the Talmudic Laws Regarding Gentiles," *Immanuel* 14 (1982): 102–113. Dov I. Frimer, "Israel, the Noahide Laws and Maimonides: Jewish Gentile Legal Relations in Maimonidean Thought," *Jewish Law Association Studies* 2 (1986): 89–102. Yehuda Gershuni, "Minority Rights in Israel," *Crossroads* 1 (1987): 19–33. Lawrence Schiffman, "Legislation Concerning Relations with Non-Jews in the Zadokite Fragments and Tannaitic Literature," *Religion Quarterly* 11 (1984): 379–389. Israel Ta-Shema, "Judeo-Christian Commerce on Christian Holy Days in Medieval Germany and Provence," *Immanuel* 12 (1981): 110–122. Efraim E. Urbach, "Self-Isolation or Self-Affirmation in Judaism in the First Three Centuries: Theory and Practice," in *Jewish and Christian Self-Definition*, edited by E. P. Sanders (Philadelphia, 1981), pp. 269–298, 413–417.

GER (גֵּר; sojourner, i.e., in a strange land), originally meaning a stranger dwelling in Erets Yisra'el (cf. *Lv.* 19.33–34), subsequently came to signify a convert to Judaism. Rabbinic law distinguished between the *ger toshav* (resident sojourner), who has renounced paganism and observes the seven *Noahic laws, and the *ger tsedeq*, the full "proselyte of righteousness," who is considered a Jew in every respect. See also GENTILES; PROSELYTE.

• Menachem Finkelstein, *Ha-Giyyur: Halakhah u-Ma'aseh* (Ramat Gan, 1994). Martin Goodman, *Mission and Conversion: Proselytizing in the Religious History of the Roman Empire* (Oxford, 1994).

GER, the Yiddish name (Heb. Gur) of the Polish town Góra Kalwaria, near Warsaw, and seat of a Hasidic dynasty established in 1859. The Ger Ḥasidim represented the largest Hasidic group in central Poland from the late nineteenth century until the destruction of Polish Jewry during World War II. The dynasty was founded by

Yitsḥaq Me'ir Rothenberg Alter (1799–1866), a follower of R. *Menaḥem Mendel of Kotsk. Rabbi Yitsḥaq Me'ir was well known as a Talmudist and is often referred to by the title of his work, *Ḥiddushei ha-Rim* (Warsaw, 1875–1891). He was succeeded by his grandson R. Yehudah Leib Alter (1847–1904), one of the most creative and original of the later Hasidic masters. His five-volume *Sefat Emet* (Piotrków-Kraków, 1905–1908) is still widely studied within Ger Hasidic circles and beyond. The third leader of Ger, R. Avraham Mordekhai Alter (1866–1948) was a key figure in the founding of *Agudat Israel and in the leadership of Polish Jewry during the period between the two world wars. He managed to escape the Holocaust and to reestablish the court of Ger in Jerusalem, where it continues to flourish.

• D. Assaf in *Tsaddiqim ve-'Anshei Ma'aseh*, edited by Rachel Elior, Yisrael Bartal, and Ḥonah Shmeruk (Jerusalem, 1994), pp. 369–371, for further bibliography. E. Bergman in *Tsaddiqim ve-'Anshei Ma'aseh*, edited by Rachel Elior, Yisrael Bartal, and Ḥonah Shmeruk (Jerusalem, 1994), pp. 111–117. Avraham Y. Bromberg, *Rebbes of Ger: Sfas Emes and Imrei Emes* (Brooklyn, N.Y., 1987). Max A. Lipshitz, "The Hassidic School of Gur," Ph.D. dissertation, University of Wisconsin, 1964.

—ARTHUR GREEN

GERIM, minor tractate, consisting of four chapters, compiled (probably in Palestine) during the period of the ge'onim, dealing with the laws regarding *proselytes. In order to convert to Judaism, the proselyte must agree to accept willingly both the persecutions and the commandments associated with Jewish peoplehood, male proselytes must be circumcised, and both male and female proselytes are subject to ritual immersion. *Gerim* also outlines the laws of a *ger toshav* (resident alien), who receives the right to dwell in Erets Yisra'el, among other privileges, after accepting certain fundamental theological and ethical principles. *Gerim* concludes with the admonition to treat the *ger* with consideration and special love and esteem.

• Shaye J. D. Cohen, "The Rabbinic Conversion Ceremony," *Journal of Jewish Studies* 41 (1990): 177–203. Michael Higger, *Seven Minor Treatises* (New York, 1930).

—AVRAHAM WALFISH

GERIZIM, MOUNT, the highest of the hills of Ephraim; south of Nablus, the ancient Shechem. According to *Deuteronomy* 11.29, Gerizim was the mountain from which six of Israel's tribes were to pronounce the blessings upon the observant; Joshua carried out this ceremony immediately upon conquering the region (*Jos.* 8.30ff.). Gerizim is fertile and endowed with natural water sources, in contrast to its arid neighbor Mount Ebal, which was designated for the curse. When the *Samaritans were denied participation in the building of the Second Temple, they built their own sanctuary on Gerizim, which was eventually destroyed by John Hyrcanus in 129 BCE. Gerizim remains the focal point in the ritual of the Samaritans who call it "the blessed mountain" and face in its direction when praying. The existence of the shrine on Mount Gerizim was a serious source of disagreement between the Jews and the Samaritans, who denied the sanctity of Jerusalem and refer to the sanctity of Gerizim at the end of their text of the Ten Commandments. Even after the destruction of the shrine, the Samaritans continued to observe their festivals on the mountain. Today the entire congregation dwells on the slopes during the Pesaḥ season, when a paschal lamb is still sacrificed.

• Yitzchak Magen, "Mount Gerizim and the Samaritans," in *Early Christianity in Context: Monuments and Documents*, edited by F. Manns and E. Alliata (Jerusalem, 1993), pp. 91–148.

GERONDI. See NISSIM BEN RE'UVEN; YONAH BEN AVRAHAM; ZERAḤYAH BEN YITSḤAQ HA-LEVI.

GEROUSIA (Gr.; council of elders). In the Roman period, the affairs of many Jewish communities in the empire—including Erets Yisra'el—were conducted by councils of elders. The *gerousia* of Jerusalem was headed by the high priest. Those chosen for the *gerousia* were selected for their learning and piety and were not necessarily old. Josephus applies this term to the seventy elders who were chosen to aid Moses (*Antiquities of the Jews* 4.8.14).

• Martin Goodman, *The Ruling Class in Judaea: The Origins of the Jewish Revolt* (Cambridge, 1987).

—SHMUEL HIMELSTEIN

GERSHOM BEN YEHUDAH (c.960–1028), leading halakhic authority in the Ashkenazi (Franco-German) community, surnamed Me'or ha-Golah (Light of the Diaspora). Little is known of his predecessors, and Talmudic thought in Ashkenaz effectively begins with Rabbenu Gershom, as he is usually called. It is difficult to separate his personal accomplishments from those of the Mainz school, to which he so significantly contributed. The commentary that bears his name, and which underlies the more famous commentary by *Rashi, was probably a multigenerational product of his school. Although many of the ordinances regulating Jewish life in Europe, such as the prohibition against polygamy and the requirement of mutual consent to a divorce, bear his name, some possibly antedate him and others clearly postdate him by centuries. Those who violated these regulations were subject to excommunication; hence, they were known as *ḥerem* (ban) of Rabbenu Gershom. His exegetical activities encompassed both *explication de texte* and the determination of correct readings. Attaching great importance to textual accuracy, he personally transcribed many of the classic texts, copies of which are cited authoritatively by his successors. Communally active, he wrote numerous *responsa*. At the same time, he composed liturgical poems and commented upon the liturgical works of his predecessors. Little is known of his personal life. He married a widow, Bona, the daughter of David (a copy of their marriage contract has survived), and had two children. Tradition has it that one son converted to Christianity, and R. Gershom went into mourning for him.

• Shlomo Eidelberg, "The Responsa of Rabbi Gershom ben Judah Me'or ha-Golah as a Source of the History of the Jews," Ph.D. dissertation, Yeshiva University, 1952. Marcus Lehmann, *Rabbenu Gershom: Me'or ha-Golah* (Brooklyn, N.Y., 1960).

—HAYM SOLOVEITCHIK

GERSONIDES. See LEVI BEN GERSHOM.

GER TSEDEQ. See PROSELYTE.

GERUSHIN (Aram.; גֵּרוּשִׁין; driving out, banishment, or expulsion), a technical term denoting *divorce. Among the kabbalists in sixteenth century Safed, *gerushin* also meant peregrinations undertaken for the purpose of sharing the "exile of the **shekhinah*" and gaining mystical illumination. The practice was cultivated especially by the circle of Mosheh ben Ya'aqov *Cordovero and Shelomoh *Alkabez, who wrote a description of these travels to the tombs of saints and of the illuminations experienced.

• Moses Cordovero, *Sefer Gerushin* (Jerusalem, 1961). Aharon Shabtai, *Gerushin* (Jerusalem, 1990), on divorce.

GESHEM. See TEFILLAT GESHEM.

GET. See DIVORCE.

GE'ULLAH (גְּאֻלָּה; Redemption), the name of various benedictions in the liturgy: one of the petitions in the weekday *'Amidah; a benediction following the *Shema' in the *Shaḥarit and *Ma'ariv prayers; and the benediction concluding the first part of the *Haggadah of Pesaḥ, which gives thanks for the redemption from Egypt. It expresses the central Jewish dogma of God's involvement in history. The Ge'ullah in the 'Amidah may be understood as a prayer for redemption not in the messianic sense but for deliverance from hardships and the troubles of the individual. The Talmud Bavli (*Pes.* 117b) rules that the Ge'ullah in the 'Amidah is to be concluded in the present tense (" . . . who redeems [or, the redeemer of] Israel"), but the Ge'ullah in the Shema' in the past (" . . . who has redeemed Israel"). This distinction was not made universally. In the old Palestinian rite the Ge'ullah after the Shema' was concluded " . . . the Rock of Israel and its Redeemer." Moreover, in the Ge'ullah of Pesaḥ eve, a petition for future redemption was inserted by R.*'Aqiva' ben Yosef, and in the Ge'ullah after the Shema', messianic prayers have been added in a variety of forms, mostly in **piyyut* style (see EMET VE-'EMUNAH AND EMET VE-YATSIV). This shows that, at least according to the Palestinian tradition, the main topic of the benediction was the possibility of redemption without any special distinction between past, present, and future. Poetic embellishments composed for insertion into the Ge'ullah of the Shema', especially on festivals, are also known as Ge'ullah.

• Ismar Elbogen, *Jewish Liturgy: A Comprehensive History*, translated by Raymond P. Scheindlin (Philadelphia, 1993), pp. 21–22, 42–43, 168–169. Jacob Freedman, *Polychrome Historical Haggadah for Passover* (Springfield, Mass., 1974), p. 62. Reuven Kimelman, "The Shema' and Its Blessings: The Realization of God's Kingship," in *The Synagogue in Late Antiquity*, edited by Lee I. Levine (Philadelphia, 1987), pp. 73–86.

—PETER LENHARDT

GEVIROL. See IBN GABIROL, SHELOMOH.

GEZERAH (גְּזֵרָה; decree), legal term paired with **taqqanah* referring to a halakhic directive that is not derived from scriptures or from previous legal decisions. It generally refers to a directive that obstructs a prohibited action, while a *taqqanah* calls for positive behavior. The power to make such decrees is derived for the former from *Leviticus* 18.30; for the latter, from *Deuteronomy* 17.11 or 30.7. *Gezerah* is also applied to a divine command for which no reason is apparent (e.g., the *red heifer; cf. *Nm. Rab.* 19.4). In nonlegal usage, the term came to mean an evil or anti-Jewish decree and, by extension, anti-Jewish persecutions and pogroms.

• Wilhelm Bacher, *Die exegetische Terminologie der jüdischen Traditionsliteratur* (Leipzig, 1905), pp. 12–13. Z. H. Chajes, *The Student's Guide Through the Talmud*, 2d ed. (New York, 1960), pp. 35–45.

—LOU H. SILBERMAN

GHETTO, section of a town enclosed by a separate wall and designated by law as an exclusive living quarter for the Jews (as distinct from a section chosen by Jews because of their preference for living together for religious, social, and security reasons). The term most probably derives from the name of the Jewish quarter established near a foundry in Venice in 1516. In spite of the degradation, overpopulation, and other dangers, Jewish life in the ghetto had its positive aspects, and there were many Jewish authorities who dreaded the demolition of its walls. In the enforced seclusion of the ghetto, the precepts of Judaism could be inculcated and observed with little or no interference from without, and the close communion among ghetto inhabitants fostered a highly developed morality. Life in the ghetto was regulated by Jewish law, including Jewish civil law; the age-old prohibition against taking one's lawsuits to a non-Jewish court could be and was rigidly enforced. As a result, a large section of *ḥoshen mishpat* (civil law), which was otherwise largely inoperative in the Diaspora, was fostered and applied.

• Ennio Concina, "Owners, Houses, Functions: New Research on the Origins of the Venetian Ghetto," *Mediterranean Historical Review* 6.2 (1991): 180–189. Elisabeth Crouzet-Pavan, "Venice Between Jerusalem, Byzantium, and Divine Retribution: The Origins of the Ghetto," *Mediterranean Historical Review* 6.2 (1991): 163–179. Lois C. Dubin, "The Ending of the Ghetto of Trieste in the Late Eighteenth Century," *Il mondo ebraico: gli ebrei tra Italia nord-orientale e Impero asburgico dal Medioevo all'eta contemporanea, A cura di Giacomo Todeschini e Pier Cesare Ioly Zorattini* (Pordenone, 1991), pp. 287–310. Benjamin C. I. Ravid, "The Establishment of the Ghetto Nuovissimo of Venice Jews in Italy," in *Studies Dedicated to the Memory of U. Cassuto*, edited by H. Beinart, (Jerusalem, 1988), pp. 35–54. Benjamin C. I. Ravid, "From Geographical Realia to Historiographical Symbol: The Odyssey of the Word 'Ghetto,'" in *Essential Papers on Jewish Culture in Renaissance and Baroque Italy*, edited by David B. Ruderman (New York, 1992), pp. 373–385. Benjamin C. I. Ravid, "New Light on the Ghetti of Venice," in *Shlomo Simonsohn Jubilee Volume: Studies on the History of the Jews in the Middle Ages and Renaissance Period*, edited by Daniel Carpi et al. (Tel Aviv, 1993), pp. 149–176. Cecil Roth, *History of the Jews in Italy* (Philadelphia, 1946). Daniel Schroeter, "The Jewish Quarter and the Moroccan City," in *New Horizons in Sephardic Studies*, edited by Yedida K. Stillman and George K. Zucker (Albany, 1993), pp. 67–81. Sandra Debenedetti Stow, "The Etymology of 'Ghetto': New Evidence from Rome," in *The Frank Talmage Memorial Volume* II, edited by Barry Walfish (Haifa, 1992), pp. 79–85.

GIANTS. Mythological giants rarely, if ever, occur in the Bible, though the descendants of the sons of God (*Gn.* 6.1–4) may have been such. *'Anaqim*, usually translated "giants," are mentioned among the inhabitants of Palestine and must have impressed the Israelites by their physical stature (cf. *Nm.* 13.22, 13.28, 13.32–33). The two giants whose measurements are specified in the Bible are Og of Bashan (*Dt.* 3.11) and Goliath (*1 Sm.* 17.4).

• Umberto Cassuto, *A Commentary on the Book of Genesis*, pt. 1, *From Adam to Noah*, Publications of the Perry Foundation for Biblical Research in the Hebrew University of Jerusalem (Jerusalem, 1989), pp. 290–301. Brevard S. Childs, *Myths and Reality in the Old Testament* (London, 1968), pp. 50–59. Claus Westermann, *Genesis 1–11*, translated by John J. Scullion (Minneapolis, 1984), pp. 363–383. —SHALOM PAUL

GIBEONITES. See NETHINIM.

GIDEON (c.12th cent. BCE), one of the judges of Israel; son of Joash the Abiezerite from the tribe of Manasseh and the town of Ophrah (*Jgs*. 6–8); also called Jerubbaal. Gideon coordinated a successful effort to drive marauding Midianites, Amalekites, and other eastern raiders from the west bank of the Jordan River. Later he had the Ephraimites block the Jordan River crossings, trap the Midianites, and annihilate them. Gideon diplomatically averted a potential civil war by placating the Ephraimites, who resented not being invited to join the original coalition of Naphtalites, Asherites, and Manassehites. He then pursued the remaining fugitives to the edge of the eastern desert, where he captured two Midianite princes, whom he eventually killed. On returning, he sacked Succoth and Penuel, Israelite cities on the east bank of the Jordan, for refusing to provide sustenance during the pursuit (*Jgs*. 7.15–8.21).

Gideon was invited to become the first ruler of Israel, but he declined, proclaiming instead, "I shall not rule over you, nor shall my son rule over you; the Lord alone shall rule over you." Nevertheless he continued to wield great economic and political power and named one of his sons *Abimelech (My Father Is King; *Jgs*. 8.22–31).

Despite destroying an altar to Baal, hewing Asherah's grove, and using the remains to dedicate an altar to YHVH, Gideon later instituted idolatrous worship involving an *ephod (*Jgs*. 6.25–27, 8.24–27).

• Louis H. Feldman, "Josephus' Portrait of Gideon," *Revue des études juives* 152 (1993): 5–28. Moshe Garsiel, "Homiletic Name Derivations as a Literary Device in the Gideon Narrative: Judges 5–8," *Vetus Testamentum* 43 (1993): 302–317. —SIMEON B. CHAVEL

GID HA-NASHEH (גִּיד הַנָּשֶׁה; sciatic nerve), a nerve that runs the length of a mammal's leg, which Jews are forbidden to eat. The prohibition on its consumption is derived from the biblical passage that describes Jacob's fight with a messenger or angel: "A stranger fought with him until before daybreak. When the stranger saw that he was unable to win, he touched Jacob's upper thigh and his hip became dislocated in the struggle . . . As a result of this incident, the children of Israel are forbidden to eat the sciatic nerve that runs from the hip down the leg" (*Gn*. 32.25ff.). A more complete discussion of the rules related to the sciatic nerve appears in *Ḥullin* 89b and in the *Shulḥan ʿArukh, Yoreh Deʿah* 65.5. Essentially, the biblical prohibition applies to both hind legs of kosher mammals. The prohibition does not extend to birds because they do not have hips. The sages prohibited eating the area directly above or below the sciatic nerve lest one accidentally eat the nerve itself.

• "Gid Hanasheh," in *Entsiqlopedyah Talmudit* (Jerusalem, 1947–), vol. 6, pp. 1–21. —MICHAEL BROYDE

GIFT, the transference to another of the rights enjoyed in a particular object or piece of property. Even though a gift is without payment, the laws of *sale apply. Such transfer becomes legally valid only when a *qinyan* (see ACQUISITION) has been effected. A verbal promise (except in the case of **heqdesh*) is not legally binding. An exception is made in the case of a dying person, whose gift is valid even without a *qinyan*. A gift may be given for a limited period of time, after which it reverts to the owner. It may also be subject to other conditions. The sending of gifts to friends forms part of the celebration of Purim. See also CHARITY; PRIESTLY PRIVILEGES.

• Menachem Elon, *Jewish Law: History, Sources, Principles*, 4 vols. (Philadelphia, 1994).

GIKATILLA, YOSEF BEN AVRAHAM (1248–c.1325), one of the most influential kabbalists during the period in which the Kabbalah reached its peak in medieval Spain. He was born in Castile and lived for many years in Segovia. His first teacher in Kabbalah was Avraham ben Shemu'el *Abulafia, and Gikatilla's early writings reflect the teachings of the Abulafia school, especially his *Ginnat Egoz*, devoted to the analysis of the Tetragrammaton and the Hebrew alphabet. Later, however, his views changed, and he joined R.*Mosheh de León's school. Gikatilla's later writings are among the clearest and most profound presentations of the system of the ten divine hypostases, the *sefirot* (which do not play a part in Abulafia's Kabbalah), and include *Shaʿarei Orah* and *Shaʿarei Tsedeq*, each describing the particular characteristics of the *sefirot* and their inner relationships. In *Shaʿarei Orah* Gikatilla also defined the nature of kabbalistic symbolism and the relationship between the supreme Godhead and the *sefirot* (he viewed the first *sefirah* as identical with the Godhead). Gershom Scholem discovered some evidence suggesting that Gikatilla participated in the authorship of the Zohar with R. Mosheh de León, but the extent of this is not clear.

• Shlomo Blickstein, "Between Philosophy and Religion: A Study of the Philosophical-Qabbalistic Writings of Joseph Giqatila, 1248–c.1322," Ph.D. dissertation, Jewish Theological Seminary of America, 1983. Gershom Gerhard Scholem, *Major Trends in Jewish Mysticism* (New York, 1995), chap. 5. —JOSEPH DAN

GILGAL, name of several places of religious significance in ancient Palestine; possibly marked originally by a heap (Heb. *gal*) of stones (cf. *Gn*. 31.46–47): (1) biblical site west of the Jordan, where Joshua set up twelve stones commemorating the Israelites crossing the river and where he circumcised the people (*Jos*. 4–5) and where Samuel judged the people and proclaimed Saul king (*1 Sm*. 11); (2) site near Mount Gerizim and Mount Ebal (*Dt*. 11.29–30); (3) site visited by Elijah and Elisha (*2 Kgs*. 2.1–2, 4.38–44); (4) site that is the residence of a Canaanite king (*Jos*. 12.23).

• Avraham Negev, *The Archeological Encyclopedia of the Holy Land*, rev. ed. (Nashville, 1986), p. 159. —SHALOM PAUL

GILGUL. See TRANSMIGRATION OF SOULS.

GILLUI ʿARAYOT. See INCEST.

GILLUI RO'SH. See COVERING OF THE HEAD.

GIMATRIYYAH (גִּימַטְרִיָּה; from Gr. *geōmetria*), the calculation of the numerical value of Hebrew words and the search for other words or phrases of equal value. The system was known in Babylonia and elsewhere and was apparently first used in Jewish circles during the Second Temple period. Since every Hebrew letter (as in some other alphabets) has a numerical value, words and phrases could be added to make sums. *Gimatriyyah* as a method of exegesis is mentioned in the *baraiyta'* of R. Eli'ezer ben Yosei ha-Galili on the "thirty-two hermeneutical rules" (see HERMENEUTICS) and was much used for aggadic and homiletical purposes; for example, Jacob's words to his sons, "go down (*redu*) to Egypt" (*Gn*. 42.2), are said to have initiated the Israelites' stay of 210 years in that country (the numerical value of *raish*, *dalet*, and *vav* equals 210). While many scholars were critical of *gimatriyyah* or took it as a kind of homiletical game, others considered it an important avenue to the hidden or implied meanings of scripture. Certain authorities, such as Moses Nahmanides, frowned on its overuse. Under the influence of letter mysticism, which played an important part in esoteric tradition, *gimatriyyah* became a major feature of kabbalistic exposition as well as of magical practice (e.g., in *amulets). *Gimatriyyah* was not common in the Zohar and early Spanish Kabbalah but entered kabbalistic thought in the late thirteenth century under the influence of the Ḥasidei Ashkenaz, who influenced its usage in the formulation of *halakhah*. Not all kabbalists used *gimatriyyah*, but for some it was a major aspect of their writing, and it was a favorite device of North African rabbis. Among followers of *Shabbetai Tsevi and in some Hasidic circles, it was a favorite tool of interpretation.

• Raymond Abellio, *Introduction à la théorie des nombres bibliques: Essai de numérologie kabbalistique* (Paris, 1984). Matityahu Glazerson, *Letters of Fire: Mystical Insights into the Hebrew Language*, translated by S. Fuchs (New York, 1991). Joshua Trachtenberg, *Jewish Magic and Superstition: A Study in Folk Religion* (New York, 1984).

GINZBERG, ASHER. See AḤAD HA-'AM.

GINZBERG, LOUIS (1873–1953), Talmudic and rabbinic scholar. Born in Kovno, Lithuania, Ginzberg attended the Lithuanian *yeshivot* of Slobodka and Tels, then studied history, philosophy, and ancient Near Eastern languages at the universities of Berlin, Strasbourg, and Heidelberg. In 1899 he immigrated to the United States, where he became an editor of the rabbinic section of the *Jewish Encyclopedia* in 1900; his many entries in that work are still regarded as authoritative. From 1903 to 1952, he taught Talmud at the *Jewish Theological Seminary of America. He was also a cofounder of the American Academy of Jewish Research. The major thrust of Ginzberg's scholarship focused on the origins of *aggadah*, *halakhah*, and geonic literature. His introductions, commentaries, and extended analyses of various texts opened scholarly and popular access to many basic works, notably the Talmud Yerushalmi, on which he wrote a commentary (3 vols. [1941]), and texts from the Cairo Genizah. In his *The Legends of the Jews* (7 vols. [Philadelphia, 1909–1938]), Ginzberg analyzed the origin and development of the legend in Midrashic literature by interweaving rabbinic, Hellenistic, early Christian, kabbalistic, and other textual sources.

• Boaz Cohen, *Bibliography of the Writings of Professor Louis Ginzberg* (New York, 1933). Eli Ginzberg, *Keeper of the Law: Louis Ginzberg* (Philadelphia, 1966). *Louis Ginzberg Jubilee Volume on the Occasion of His Seventieth Birthday* (New York, 1945), includes a bibliography of Ginzberg's writings (English section).

—EUGENE R. SHEPPARD

GITTIN (גִּטִּין; Bills of Divorce), tractate in Mishnah order Nashim, consisting of nine chapters, with related material in the Tosefta' and in both Talmuds, dealing with laws pertaining to *divorce. The biblical provision that divorce be effected by means of a *get* (bill of divorce; *Dt*. 24.1) is analyzed and expanded in exacting detail. *Gittin* stresses the unique nature of the *get* vis-à-vis other legal documents. Strict provisions govern all aspects of writing and delivering the *get*. Its writing must be explicitly authorized by the husband, and the *get* must sever entirely any relationship between husband and wife; hence, the husband may not attach conditions to the divorce that would restrict the woman's freedom after the divorce is effected.

The conditions of life in the Diaspora and Roman domination of Erets Yisra'el left their imprint on *Gittin*. The tractate regulates divorce proceedings for a woman whose husband has sent her a *get* from a Diaspora community far removed from the halakhic institutions in Palestine. Provisions are made for witnesses who sign their names in Greek and for dating the *get* in accordance with the reign of the Roman emperor.

The tractate in the Talmud Bavli was translated into English by Maurice Simon in the Soncino Talmud (London, 1936).

• Chanoch Albeck, ed., *Shishah Sidrei Mishnah, Seder Nashim* (Jerusalem, 1954). Philip Blackman, ed. and trans., *Mishnayot*, vol. 2, *Order Nashim* (Gateshead, 1973). Pinhas Kehati, ed., *Mishnah: A New Translation with a Commentary, Seder Nashim*, vol. 3, *Gittin, Qiddushin* (Jerusalem, 1989). Hermann Leberecht Strack, *Introduction to the Talmud and Midrash* (1931; Minneapolis, 1992).

—AVRAHAM WALFISH

GIVING OF THE TORAH (Heb. *mattan Torah*), the central event in the establishment of the covenant between God and the Israelite people, in the form of a body of divinely revealed legislation (religious, moral, criminal, and civil), endowing them with their distinct way of life; hence, also the close association of the concepts of *Torah and *halakhah*. Though some laws are said in the Bible to have been given to the Israelites before arriving at Sinai (the Sabbath command, given in the wilderness; the precepts concerning the Pesaḥ sacrifice, in Egypt) and even to the patriarchs (the command of circumcision), the full corpus of laws was given by God through the mediation of Moses at Mount Sinai. According to the biblical account, the giving of the law took place in stages. It began with a public theophany, at which God spoke to the entire people, proclaiming to them a sampling of the laws to be given subsequently (*Ex*. 19–20;

Dt. 5; see TEN COMMANDMENTS). Next, Moses ascended Sinai and received a body of legislation to be communicated to the people (*Ex.* 20–24). After he did so and the laws were committed to writing (see COVENANT, BOOK OF THE), a covenant ceremony was performed, and the people reaffirmed their commitment to the divine command. Following this, Moses reascended the mountain to receive the tablets of the Law. On this occasion Moses was given detailed instructions for the construction of a portable shrine (*Ex.* 25–30; see TABERNACLE) that would serve as a meeting place for God and Moses for the purpose of giving additional laws (*Ex.* 25.22). Moses was also given laws pertaining to the ritual to be performed at the shrine. Moses' final ascent to the mountaintop, for the purpose of having the second set of tablets inscribed by God, provided another occasion for God to communicate further laws to him (*Ex.* 34). Once the Tabernacle was erected, the prolonged process of continuous lawgiving commenced. On regular occasions, God spoke to Moses from the Holy of Holies, each time conveying to him the legislation pertaining to a specific topic. Each time, Moses verbally transmitted to the entire people what he had been commanded. This process continued even after the Israelites left Mount Sinai, extending into the forty years of wandering in the wilderness (*Lv.* and *Nm.*). In a final stage right before his death, and just prior to the entry into Canaan, Moses assembled the entire people and in a lengthy address conveyed to them a full body of legislation that was communicated to him by God at Sinai but that he had not yet disclosed to them (*Dt.* 5.20–26.19). He then committed the entire text to writing and deposited the Law with the Levites (*Dt.* 31). Thus, the greater part of *Exodus* 20 through *Deuteronomy* 26 consists of a series of laws that together make up "the Torah" in the strict sense of the word.

Rabbinic tradition tended to concentrate on the first phase—the epiphany at Sinai—in which the entire people participated (*Ber.* 58a). This event is described in superlative terms: the entire universe participated, generations unborn were present, and each individual heard the voice of God in a way suited to his or her own intellect.

The Bible mentions no festival in commemoration of the giving of the Law, because in the biblical view, it was a protracted process and could not be restricted to a single date. Later tradition, however, reckoned the theophany at Sinai to have taken place on 6 (or 7) Sivan. Thus *Shavuʿot, originally the wheat harvest and first-fruits festival (*Lv.* 23.9–14), became the festival of the giving of the Law. See also ORAL LAW; WRITTEN LAW.

• Jeffrey Jay Niehaus, *God at Sinai: Covenant and Theophany in the Bible and Ancient Near East*, Studies in Old Testament Biblical Theology (Grand Rapids, 1995). *Present at Sinai: The Giving of the Law*, commentaries selected by S. Y. Agnon, translated by Michael Swirsky, with an introduction by Judah Goldin (Philadelphia, 1994). J. J. Stamm, *The Ten Commandments in Recent Research* (London, 1970). Arie Toeg, *Mattan Torah be-Sinai* (Jerusalem, 1977). Moshe Weinfeld, "The Decalogue: Its Signficance, Uniqueness, and Place in Israel's Tradition," in *Religion and Law: Biblical-Judaic and Islamic Perspectives*, edited by E. R. Firmage, B. G. Weiss, and J. W. Welch (Winona Lake, Ind., 1990), pp. 3–47.

—BARUCH J. SCHWARTZ

GIYYUR. See PROSELYTE.

GLEANINGS. See LEQET, SHIKHḤAH, AND PE'AH.

GNOSTICISM (from Gk. *gnōsis* [knowledge]), a term describing the ideas and mystical theories—usually confined to a limited circle of initiates—of a number of sects that arose both within and around Judaism, Christianity, and paganism in the Roman world during the first and second centuries. The beginnings of gnosticism, however, seem to be earlier, and some scholars suggest that it originated in Jewish or Samaritan circles influenced by certain oriental ideas. While gnostic sects differed widely from each other in style of behavior and in theories, most shared a number of beliefs. Gnosticism distinguished between the "Supreme Divine Being" and the "Demiurge," a secondary power responsible for creation and involved in the material world. *Dualism—the belief that the world is ruled by two opposing principles—divided the heavenly powers into pairs—male and female, left and right, and so on; the "Supreme First Principle" was conceived as an all-good power, whereas the "Creator-Demiurge" was considered a lower, fallen, and imperfect being. Some Christian Gnostics, for example, Marcion, identified the "First Principle" with the New Testament "God of love," and the "Creator-God" with the Old Testament Law, which they labeled as evil. In contrast to the biblical tradition, which regarded creation as essentially good (*Gn.* 1.31), gnosticism considered the material universe the result of a primordial fall from a state of pure, that is, spiritual, being. The soul, too, is thought to be in exile in the lower and basically evil material world, into which it has fallen and from which it can be redeemed and returned to its celestial home by means of *gnōsis*, that is, secret knowledge. The sense of irreconcilable conflict between the sphere of *pneuma* (spirit) and the material world of creation made for some affinities between gnosticism and Neoplatonic philosophy. Some of the gnostic sects demonstrated their liberation from the material world (of which morals and the law form part) and the spiritual freedom that they had attained by theoretical and practical *antinomianism. The early church combated the Christian forms of gnosticism as a dangerous heresy. The Jewish struggle against gnosticism is reflected in liturgical and other regulations directed against the **minim*. However, in spite of its struggle against gnostic heresy, Judaism, and Jewish mysticism in particular (see HEIKHALOT; MAʿASEH MERKAVAH), absorbed certain gnostic themes and ideas. Tendencies of a gnostic character also appeared in medieval Kabbalah, for example in the *Zohar and particularly in the esoteric doctrines of Yitsḥaq *Luria.

• Robert McQueen Grant, *Gnosticism and Early Christianity* (New York, 1959). Gershom Scholem, *Jewish Gnosticism, Merkabah Mysticism and Talmudic Tradition* (New York, 1960). David M. Scholer, "Bibliographic Gnostica: Supplementum XXII," *Novum Testamentum* 36.1 (1994): 58–

GOD, the Supreme Being; the Creator of the universe; the Judge and Ruler of history; the Supreme Lawgiver and object of the religious attitudes of love, awe, reverence, obedience, and worship. The existence of God is presupposed in the Bible from the very first sentence, and no attempt is made to prove it. His power and love are immediately experienced. He is conceived not in philosophical or abstract terms, such as "First Cause," but in imaginative pictorial ideas, such as father, shepherd, judge, and king. Although ideas of God were present in the civilization in which the Bible came into being, the Israelite conception is unique. All others were based on mythological ideas, so that the gods were conceived to be subject to the laws of natural necessity. In the biblical idea of God, the Supreme Being has no mythological quality whatsoever. He has no body, no relative, no human needs. He is the Sovereign Lord of nature, which is completely dependent on him. There is no force that is independent of his sovereign will and does not do his bidding. He is completely independent, and there are no other divine beings to compete with him for lordship. These notions may have developed in stages, but ultimately they gave rise to the pure *monotheism of the Bible and later literature. There is a constant battle against *idolatry, which is the substitution of some nonabsolute force or entity for the Supreme God of the Bible. God and the world are distinct. He is the Creator of the world, which is completely subject to his will. Nature is orderly and regular, not because of any inherent law but because the Creator maintains that order under his covenant with creation. Man experiences the presence and power of God in seemingly contradictory ways. He is majestic, yet kind and compassionate. He punishes those who do wrong, yet he is quick to forgive. He is transcendent, beyond anything in the world, yet his wisdom is the source of human understanding. There is a special relationship between God and Israel. Israel is God's chosen people, not because of any special merit that the people of Israel possess, but because of God's own act of grace. Through God's relations to his people, his relationship to the world is also exhibited. Israel is to be God's witness. When Israel falls away from its task of being God's people, he sends prophets to admonish and chastise it. Through Israel, the rest of mankind will be brought to recognize God's sovereignty. Thus, Israel is the instrument of *redemption. Another aspect of God's love for Israel is his activity as a lawgiver to his people. Through *revelation God relates himself to man. Under the covenant of the Law (Torah) Israel is called to be a holy nation. The God of the Bible, however, is not a national God; he is the Lord of all nations. The fate of one people mirrors the universal facts of his kingship and fatherhood. His power and presence are experienced through great historical events like the *Exodus from Egypt. Humanity has been given the freedom to obey or to defy God. When individuals disobey, God metes out his *justice. In the end of days (see MESSIAH), people will possess a new heart and all the disharmonies of history will be banished. Thus, three aspects of God's relationship to the world are manifest in the Bible. Through *creation God calls the world into being; through revelation God speaks to humanity; and through redemption God will sanctify all existence.

Post-biblical literature reflects the beginning of philosophic influence on the formulation of the God idea in Judaism. This influence came by way of the Greek philosophers, whose view of God was abstract and impersonal. The earliest traces of philosophic formulations in speaking of God are found in the Apocrypha (see APOCRYPHA AND PSEUDEPIGRAPHA). The books originating in Palestine deal with the concept of God in substantially traditional terms. Differences stem from the terminology rather than the content of the ideas. In the Alexandrine Apocrypha some change of conception is evident, but even these include works whose theology is a restatement of biblical teachings. In the *Targum and *Septuagint translation of the biblical books there are evidences of an attempt to avoid *anthropomorphism. The writings of *Philo reveal a consistent effort to reinterpret the biblical view of God in philosophic traditions. These are the first attempts to harmonize the biblical and Greek philosophical traditions. Philo's synthesis exerted far-reaching effects on the subsequent history of *philosophy and theology in the West. Philo placed great stress on God's complete transcendence and posited the existence of intermediaries through which God influences creation. Of special importance is the *Logos. The personal, direct relationship between God and man was stressed in the Talmudic and Midrashic literature. Although the rabbis use circumlocutions for God in order to increase respect for his holy name (see GOD, NAMES OF), they brought the divine near to even the humblest heart. They would speak of God as suffering together with his children, weeping over the destruction of the Temple, and rejoicing over piety and good works, and they would even describe him as taking part in learned discussions or putting on **tefillin*. The rabbis were essentially carrying on the prophetic concept of God, but they expressed themselves in a more popular and picturesque way. As a reaction to the teachings of heretical sects and *Christianity, the rabbis laid great stress on the unity of God. Thus, the *Shemaʿ was considered the most important confession of faith, and it was incumbent on all Jews to recite it twice daily. The rabbis were especially careful to repudiate any suggestion that there were two powers (dualism) and insisted that God has no father, son, or brother (*Dt. Rab.* 2). Of special importance in rabbinic literature is God's role as the lawgiver. The Torah, which is God's gift to Israel, is highly exalted and even described as the purpose and instrument of creation. It is through the study of the Torah that individuals know the will of God. The best source for the study of rabbinic theology is the *liturgy, which contains all the basic teachings of the rabbis concerning the divine being.

Medieval Jewish thought developed under the influence of the rediscovery and development of Greek philosophy by the Arabs. Jewish theologians reinterpreted their faith in the light of the new philosophy, especially *Neoplatonism and *Aristotelianism. The philosophers of the Middle Ages were particularly concerned with such problems as the attributes of God (see GOD, ATTRIBUTES OF), the relation between divine foreknowledge and human freedom, and the presence of evil in the world (see Good and Evil). It was their aim to demonstrate that the biblical and Talmudic teachings about God were in conformity with rational thinking. Thus, they held that the existence of God could be logically proved. Since the Creator is the cause of all bodies, he himself must be beyond all matter. He is free of all human and natural properties. The absolute unity of God implies the spiritual nature of his essence. For were he not one, he would be many, and multiplicity is characteristic of corporeality; his oneness thus implies his incorporeality. Although God is abstract and transcendent, he is not inactive. He reveals himself to his prophets and directs the affairs of creation. Direct biblical expression about God, however, should be understood in a metaphorical sense. Jewish medieval philosophy tended generally to deny the possibility of saying anything valid about the essence of God, who is conceived as utterly transcendent to his creation and to human understanding. Only his existence could be asserted, along with certain qualities or attributes. The greatest medieval Jewish philosopher, Moses *Maimonides, was also the most extreme in stressing God's transcendence. He denied that humans had the capacity to say anything meaningful about God. The existence of God, it was true, could be proved. But the meaning and nature of this existence were beyond human comprehension. Everything said about God is allegorical, and all positive ways of describing him clothe essentially negative statements. Thus, when one says that God exists, the only real meaning of the statement is that his nonexistence is unthinkable. Maimonides is the exponent of the so-called "negative theology" that was then developed in other directions by the mystics. Other thinkers, like *Yehudah ha-Levi, felt the aridity of the abstract formulations of God's nature and stressed the experience of the divine action in history, especially in the crucial events in the annals of Israel. A bold solution of the problem of God's power and foreknowledge, and an individual's free will, is offered by Avraham *ibn Daud. He concluded that God restricts his omniscience and omnipotence deliberately so as to allow people freedom of choice. Another attempt to overcome the tension between the transcendent, absolutely unique God of philosophy and the vital, real, and dynamic God of religious experience was made in the medieval kabbalistic literature, which taught the doctrine of the two aspects of the Godhead: the infinite, inaccessible "mystery of hiddenness" (see Ein Sof) and the ten **sefirot* of divine manifestation. This profound and audacious conception often came under criticism for harboring the seeds of heretical deviations and, particularly, for coming dangerously close to polytheism.

Contemporary Jewish philosophy reflects the fundamental change in outlook that characterizes modern thought in general. Whereas medieval speculation was concerned with harmonizing revelation and reason (both elements being taken as authoritative), the period of the Enlightenment (see Haskalah) called the authority of revelation into question. The Jewish religion must be authenticated as a manifestation of the human spirit and be shown as significant within the larger framework of thought, be it conceived as universal reason (Hegel), the dialectic of the mind (Kant), or human existence as such (*existentialism). The first significant attack on the Jewish conception of God was made by Baruch *Spinoza, who denied the medieval attempt to derive the material world from a god who is wholly transcendent to it and propounded a thoroughgoing *pantheism. Moses *Mendelssohn taught that the basic ideas of religion—the existence of a personal God and the immortality of the individual soul—were universal possessions of humankind because of their reasonableness. They need not wait for revelation to be known, since they were manifest at all times and everywhere. Mendelssohn summed up his view in his famous phrase: "Judaism is not a revealed religion, but a revealed law." The rise of Kantianism accentuated the division between theoretical and practical reason. The proofs that Kant adduced to destroy rational theology led to the idea that religion was dependent on ethics and fundamentally an expression of practical reason. Hermann *Cohen produced the most impressive synthesis between Kantianism and Judaism. To him the idea of God is indispensable both to theoretical and to practical reason. It establishes the necessary link between the two spheres by ensuring the final realization of man's moral destiny within the natural order of being. The philosophy of Franz *Rosenzweig is an elaboration of Schelling's positive philosophy combined with modern existentialism. God, humanity, and the world are irreducible entities. The task of philosophy is to interpret the interrelation between God, humanity, and the world. God and people are united in and through speech. The term "speaking" as used by Rosenzweig means "speaking to a person in all earnestness and devotion." God speaks to humanity through revelation. He also calls the world into being through creation. This philosophy plays an important part in the thought of Martin *Buber. God cannot be known in his essence. He can only be addressed, when one turns to him in full devotion, in the full power of an "I" addressing a "Thou." Mordecai Menahem *Kaplan was influenced by naturalism. God is conceived as a "force" or a "power" within the physical universe that makes for humanity's *salvation. Hasidic mysticism, which was based largely on kabbalistic thought, at times came close to pantheism but generally remained orthodox.

• David Brusin, "The God of Abraham, Isaac, Jacob, and Mordecai M. Kaplan," *Reconstructionist* 50.6 (1985): 11–15, 35. Bruce D. Chilton, "God as 'Father' in the Targumim, in Non-Canonical Literatures of Early Judaism and Primitive Christianity, and in Matthew," *The Pseudepigrapha and Early Biblical Interpretation*, edited by James H. Charlesworth and Craig A. Evans (Sheffield, Eng., 1993), pp. 151–169. Elliot N. Dorff, "The Concept of God in the Conservative Movement," *Judaism* 40.4 (1991): 429–441. Rachel Elior, "The Concept of God in Hekhalot Literature," *Binah* 2 (1989): 97–129. Isaac Franck, "Maimonides and Aquinas on Man's Knowledge of God: A Twentieth Century Perspective," *Review of Metaphysics* 38.3 (1985): 591–615. Jerome I. Gellman, "The Love of God in Maimonides' Religious Philosophy," *Sobre la vida y obra de Maimonides*, edited by Jesus Pelaez del Rosal (Cordova, 1991), pp. 219–227. Isaac Husik, *A History of Mediaeval Jewish Philosophy* (New York, 1916). Joerg Jeremias, "Changes in the Conception of God in the Old Testament," *Old Testament Essays* 5 (1987): 129–151. William E. Kaufman, "Recent Jewish Theology," *Conservative Judaism* 43.2 (1990–1991): 83–89. Arthur Marmorstein, *The Old Rabbinic Doctrine of God* (New York, 1968). Sigfred Pedersen, "The Concept of God as Theme of Biblical Theology," in *New Directions in Biblical Theology: Papers of the Aarhus Conference, September 1992*, edited by Sigfred Pedersen (Leiden, 1994), pp. 243–266. Norbert M. Samuelson, "God: The Present Status of the Discussion," in *Frontiers of Jewish Thought*, edited by Steven T. Katz (Washington, D.C., 1992), pp. 43–59. Gershom Gerhard Scholem, *Major Trends in Jewish Mysticism* (New York, 1946). Byron L. Sherwin, *Toward a Jewish Theology: Methods, Problems, and Possibilities* (Lewiston, N.Y., 1991).

GOD, ATTRIBUTES OF. In the history of philosophy, discussions of attributes almost always concern the nature of *God. Attributes are permanent qualities of a substance that determine its nature, and they generally stand in contrast to accidents, the absence of which would in no way detract from the nature of a thing. In traditional Jewish texts like the Bible and the prayer book, God's attributes are set forth in unquestioned terms; that is, the conception of God as omnipotent, omniscient, eternal, and so on is never analyzed. The attributes merely attest to the sense of human dependence on a power that compels reverence and obedience. When they began to be analyzed, however, God's attributes became philosophical and theological issues with implications for the understanding of the nature of God, his unity, and his transcendence. Jewish philosophers beginning with *Saʿadyah ben Yosef Ga'on (9th cent.) have dealt with the difficult problem of how to assert anything positive about God. If it is assumed, as by most Jewish philosophers, that one cannot know what God is like and that God's absolutely transcendent nature cannot in any way be said to resemble a man's or a woman's nature or to be expressible in human terms, then it becomes impossible to talk meaningfully about God's attributes. Indeed, Gersonides (*Levi ben Gershom [14th cent.]) attacked the prevailing Maimonidean view that there is nothing in God's attributes susceptible to human grasp. Moses *Maimonides (12th cent.) had declared that assertions about God's thinking can have no real cognitive significance, since God thinks in a way unknown to humankind. This led Gersonides to the conclusion that if such be the case, a person cannot legitimately assert anything about God's attributes. To escape this conclusion, he challenged the premise and insisted that divine and human attributes were distinct merely in the measure of their perfection, not in their essence. This solution of Gersonides, however, was not generally accepted by medieval Jewish philosophers. The whole trend of Jewish philosophy was to seek a definition of God's attributes that would set them apart from any human associations. There was always the problem of finding something in God about which one could talk intelligibly; hence, the various divisions made by philosophers into those qualities that could be asserted about God and those that had to be treated obliquely. Saʿadyah, for example, denied that God possesses positive attributes except in regard to his existence, unity, power, and wisdom, which are one in fact, although not in humanity's thought about God. This objection against articulating any distinctive attributes that do not actually imply each other is respected throughout the Jewish philosophical tradition. *Baḥya ben Yosef ibn Paquda' (12th cent.), in making a distinction between the essential attributes and those that describe God's actions, lists the former as his existence, unity, and eternity. He hastens to add that they are really one. Moreover, even when affirmed positively, their real meaning is to negate the possibility of God's possessing the opposite attribute. Thus, God cannot be multiple or have parts; nor can he be in time. *Yehudah ha-Levi (12th cent.) lists three groups of attributes: the active ones (those indicating God's power to affect human fate); the relative ones (in which, for example, God's blessedness is set forth); and the negative (which include the essential attribute that can be expressed only negatively). Maimonides listed various kinds of positive attributes and concluded that none of them could legitimately be asserted of God, who can be described only negatively, that is, in terms not of what he is but of what he is not. Jewish thought down to the present day has shied away from definitive statements regarding the nature of God. See also THIRTEEN ATTRIBUTES.

• Giuseppa Saccaro Battisti, "Herrera and Spinoza on Divine Attributes: The Evolving Concept of Perfection and Infinity Limited to Only One Genre," *Italia* 3 (1985): 21–58. Lenn Evan, "Matter and Form as Attributes of God in Maimonides' Philosophy," in *A Straight Path: Studies in Medieval Philosophy and Culture: Essays in Honor of Arthur Hyman*, edited by Ruth Link-Salinger (Washington, 1988), pp. 86–97. Isaac Husik, *A History of Mediaeval Jewish Philosophy* (Philadelphia, 1916). Charles H. Manekin, "Belief, Certainty, and Divine Attributes in the 'Guide of the Perplexed,'" *Maimonidean Studies* 1 (1990): 117–141. Norbert M. Samuelson, "Divine Attributes as Moral Ideals in Maimonides' Theology," in *The Thought of Moses Maimonides*, edited by Ira Robinson (New York, 1990), pp. 69–67.

GOD, NAMES OF, may be either conceptual (e.g., God, Creator) or proper. The latter sort predominates in ancient literature, but the original significance of such names is not always easily determined. The choice of one name rather than another generally depends on its significance, the occasion, and the specific traditions of the user. *Bible criticism has taken the two most important biblical names of God, YHVH and Elohim, as indicative of two distinct biblical traditions. Of the two names, the Tetragrammaton, consisting of the letters *yud*, *heh*, *vav*, *heh*, is the most frequent in the Bible, and rabbinic tradition considers it the essential name of God. The name seems to be connected with the phrase *ehyeh asher ehyeh* (translated as "I am that I am" [*Ex.* 3.14]). Interpreted as denoting eternal existence, the phrase became the symbol of *monotheism. The holiest of names was never pronounced ("the Ineffable Name" [Shem ha-Meforash]), except once a year by the high priest in the Holy of Holies on Yom Kippur. According to a rabbinic tradition, once (or twice) in seven years the sages entrusted to their disciples the pronunciation of the Tetragrammaton (*Qid.* 71a), but the original pronunciation is now unknown; it is read as Adonai (my Lord), which was already used in the second century BCE. The combination in the Hebrew Bible of the consonants *y*, *h*, *v*, *h* and the vocalization for Adonai gave rise to the misnomer Jehovah. Yah (cf. Halleluyah) is thought to be a shortened form of YHVH. Other names of God mentioned in the Bible, but classified by the rabbis as "secondary," although historically primary, are El, Eloha, Elohim (a plural form, although used as a singular when applied to the God of Israel) with various suffixes, Shaddai (chiefly in *Jb.*), and Zebaoth (although the Talmud opines that the last is not a name of God but refers to the hosts of Israel of which God is the Lord). The word *elohim* is also found in a secular sense, referring not only to heathen gods (e.g., *Ex.* 20.3) but also to human judges (e.g., *Ex.* 22.7). The rabbis, considering the names of God as symbols of his relationship to his creatures, held that YHVH expressed his attribute of mercy (see COMPASSION), and Elohim referred to his attribute of *justice. Both the essential and secondary names of God must be written "in holiness," and once written they must not be erased. To avoid "taking the name of the Lord in vain," the custom developed of pronouncing and sometimes writing even the substitute for the Tetragrammaton, Adonai, as ha-Shem (the Name)—and, for sake of assonance, as Adoshem—and Elohim as Eloqim. Adonai is usually printed in prayer books as two *yuds*; the prohibition against erasure does not apply to this abbreviation.

Other names of God, which are descriptive rather than personal names and express divine attributes (such as Raḥum [Merciful]; ʿElyon [the Most High]; Shaddai [the Mighty One]), do not fall under the prohibition against erasure as they can be applied to mortals as well (*Shev.* 35a). According to some authorities, however (cf. *Sot.* 10a), the word *shalom* (peace) can occur as a divine name, in which case it belongs to the former category. The sanctity attached to the divine names and the prohibition of the Third Commandment against taking the name of the Lord in vain resulted in a growing disinclination to use the biblical names of God, and in the Talmudic period a series of circumlocutions evolved. The most common one, used almost exclusively in Midrashic literature, is *ha-Qadosh barukh hu'*, "the Holy One, blessed be he," and in Aramaic *Qudesha' berikh hu'*, sometimes expanded into "The Supreme King of kings, the Holy One, blessed be he." Next in popularity and occurring mainly in invocations, is Ribbono shel ʿOlam (Master of the Universe). Also frequent and possibly early is the name ha-Maqom (the Place), probably an abbreviation of "he who dwells in this place [the Temple]" but was later interpreted more theologically, explained as "He is the space of the world but the world is not his space" (*Gn. Rab.* 69.9) and translated as "the Omnipresent." Ha-Raḥaman (the All-Merciful) is a Mishnaic form of the biblical Raḥum (cf. in the *Birkat ha-Mazon). Another frequent Talmudic designation is the **shekhinah* (divine presence). Philosophical and kabbalistic literature added further designations that, however, were technical terms and mystical symbols (e.g., First Cause, *Ein Sof) rather than names. The medieval poets, too, coined many terms and epithets designating God. Esoteric tradition contains references to divine names composed of twelve, forty-two, and seventy-two letters, and the kabbalists considered the whole Pentateuch as a series of mystical names of God. This doctrine lent itself to the use of various combinations of Hebrew letters as powerful names of God for magical purposes, for example, in *amulets.

• Adrian Auret, "The Theological Intent of the Use of the Names of God in the Eighth-Century Memoir of Isaiah," *Old Testament Essays* 5.2 (1992): 272–291. Joseph M. Baumgarten, "A New Qumran Substitute for the Divine Name and Mishnah Sukkah, 4.5 [4Q266]," *Jewish Quarterly Review* 83 (1992): 1–5. Alexander Broadie, "Maimonides and Aquinas on the Names of God," *Religious Studies* 23 (1987): 157–170. James R. Davila, "The Name of God at Moriah: An Unpublished Fragment from 4QGenExod[a]," *Journal of Biblical Literature* 110 (1991): 577–582. Kees F. de Blois,"Translating the Names of God: Tryggve Mettinger's Analyses Applied to Bible Translation," *Bible Translator* 43 (1992): 406–414. Shaul Esh, *Der Heilige (Er Sie gepreisen)* (Leiden, 1957). Barbara E. Galli, "Rosenzweig and the Name for God," *Modern Judaism* 14 (1994): 63–86. Arthur Marmorstein, *The Old Rabbinic Doctrine of God: The Names and Attributes of God* (London, 1969), pp. 17–145. A. Murtonen, *A Philological and Literary Treatise on Old Testament Divine Names* (Helsinki, 1952).

GOD, PROOFS FOR THE EXISTENCE OF. The possibility, the necessity, and the desirability of providing rational proofs for the existence of *God have been permanent themes of theology. The Bible takes the existence of God for granted. The heavens declare his glory (*Ps.* 19.1), and only a spiritually deaf churl would say "there is no God" (*Ps.* 14.1, 53.2), an utterance that clearly expresses an irreligious disposition rather than a philosophical position. Contact with the philosophical culture of the Hellenistic age seems to have prompted *Philo to suggest that reflection on nature and on the human soul would provide evidence for the existence of God. In the Middle Ages, theological thinking was greatly stimulated and influenced by Arabic *philosophy, and the existence of God, reason versus faith, and rational insight versus revelation became central themes of investigation. The principle of causality asserted that since nothing can exist without a cause, there must be a first cause, and the created world must have a creator who could be shown to be all-wise and omnipotent. Only God is uncaused and self-existent. The teleological argument emphasized the design of the cosmic order and of its workings: there cannot be a watch without a watchmaker. The Aristotelian philosophers, who held that God's existence could be rationally proved, taught that God was beyond human comprehension. Said *Saʿadyah ben Yosef Ga'on, "If I knew him I would be he." Moses *Maimonides was the most radical in his insistence that only God's existence could be proved; positive attributes and anthropomorphisms were heresies. Others, such as Ḥasda'i ben Avraham *Crescas, rejected philosophical proofs; belief in God rested on the authority of *revelation. Even opponents of rationalist philosophy such as *Yehudah ha-Levi agreed that belief in God, though not a matter of rational proof, was not contrary to reason, even though essentially its evidence lay in experience, especially the historical experience of Israel during the Exodus and at Mount Sinai.

The modern tone for the discussion was set by Kant's demolition of the traditional medieval "proofs," and Jewish thinkers, too, have adapted their discourse. Reform theologian Kaufmann *Kohler held that for the religious consciousness God was not demonstrated by argument but was a fact of inner and outer experience. For Hermann *Cohen, God was, in Kantian style, a postulate of reason linking together logic and ethics. Franz *Rosenzweig saw God as one of three aspects of reality (the other two being the human person and the world) that could not be reduced. God for him was the affirmation of being. For Martin *Buber, God was the ultimate "thou," upon which all of our "I-Thou" relations exist. For Mordecai Menahem *Kaplan, belief in God ultimately served as an affirmation that life had value. Since Kant, the existence of God is generally a basic assumption of religious life.

• Jacob B. Agus, *Modern Philosophies of Judaism* (New York, 1941). Eliezer Berkovits, *God, Man, and History: A Jewish Interpretation* (Middle Village, N.Y., 1979). Hermann Cohen, *The Religion of Reason Out of the Sources of Judaism*, translated by Simon Kaplan (New York, 1972). Samuel S. Cohon, *Jewish Theology: A Historical and Systematic Interpretation of Judaism and Its Foundations* (Assen, 1971). Julius Guttmann, *Philosophies of Judaism* (Garden City, N.Y., 1966). Abraham Joshua Heschel, *God in Search of Man* (New York, 1955). John Hick, *Arguments for the Existence of God* (London, 1970). Isaac Husik, *A History of Mediaeval Jewish Philosophy* (Philadelphia, 1946). Louis Jacobs, *A Jewish Theology* (New York, 1973). Mordecai M. Kaplan, *The Meaning of God in Modern Jewish Religion* (New York, 1947). Kaufmann Kohler, *Jewish Theology* (Cincinnati, 1943). Arthur Marmorstein, *The Old Rabbinic Theology of God* (London, 1979). Franz Rosenzweig, *The Star of Redemption*, translated by William W. Hallo (New York, 1971). Colette Sirat, *A History of Jewish Philosophy in the Middle Ages* (Cambridge, 1990).

GODFATHER. See SANDAQ.

GOD FEARERS, a term applied to non-Jews in ancient times who observed some of the precepts of the Torah without fully converting to Judaism. In various Greco-Roman sources, reference is made to people who fear or worship God or heaven, but determining what exactly is implied by such references is extremely difficult, especially since the same words are also applied to devout Jews and to devout non-Jews worshiping their own gods. Nevertheless the convergence of evidence from many different sources—such as rabbinic literature (with references to *yir'ei shamayim* [fearers of heaven], that is, non-Jews who observe some Jewish precepts), *Josephus Flavius (who in several instances refers to non-Jews who adopt Jewish practices or join the Jews "in some way"), the *New Testament (where Paul is said to have preached to "Jews and God fearers" and to have been very successful among the latter), Roman writers (such as the satirist Juvenal, who ridicules Romans who "fear the Sabbath" and abstain from pork), and Roman-period inscriptions—clearly shows that both Jews and non-Jews were aware of the attraction that some non-Jews felt toward the Jewish way of life, an attraction that regularly fell short of full conversion. The extent of Jewish faith and practices adopted by such God fearers and their treatment by the local Jewish community may have varied greatly in different places and at different times. In some cases, however, such as in the city of Aphrodisias (in present-day Turkey), where a relevant inscription has recently been found, the synagogue seems to have consisted of two groups: born Jews and proselytes, on the one hand, and non-Jewish God fearers, on the other, so that the God fearers clearly were acknowledged by the Jewish community and partly incorporated into it.

• Martin Goodman, *Mission and Conversion: Proselytizing in the Religious History of the Roman Empire* (Oxford, 1994). J. Andrew Overman and Robert S. MacLennan, eds., *Diaspora Jews and Judaism: Essays in Honor of, and in Dialogue with, A. Thomas Kraabel* (Atlanta, 1992). Joyce Reynolds and Robert Tannenbaum, *Jews and God-Fearers at Aphrodisias: Greek Inscriptions with Commentary*, Cambridge Philological Society Supplementary Volume 12 (Cambridge, 1987), for the Aphrodisias inscription and its implications. Paul R. Trebilco, *Jewish Communities in Asia Minor*, Society for New Testament Studies Monograph Series 69 (Cambridge, 1991), pp. 145–166.

—GIDEON BOHAK

GO'EL. See REDEMPTION.

GOG AND MAGOG, the satanic powers who wage the great eschatological battle against the host of the righteous. The concept is derived from *Ezekiel* 38.2, where "Gog, of the land of Magog, the chief prince of Meshech and Tubal" is set to lead a savage horde of nations from the north against Israel. He and his army, the Bible says, will be defeated by the hand of the Lord on the mountains of Israel. Though Josephus (*Antiquities of the Jews* 1.6.1) identifies the Magog mentioned in the table of nations in *Genesis* 10.2 as the progenitor of the Scythians, it is possible that this figure reflects the historical Gyges, king of Lydia. Gog and Magog also appear in the Dead Sea Scrolls and are vividly portrayed in Talmudic literature, where the war against Gog and Magog is identified with the "messianic wars" preceding the advent of the Messiah. This idea of eschatological warfare against Gog and Magog is echoed in Christian (e.g., *Rv*. 20.7–9) and Islamic traditions. See also ESCHATOLOGY.

GOLAH. See EXILE.

GOLDEN CALF, molten image constructed by the Israelites at the foot of Mount Sinai after leaving Egypt. After the covenant was made, following the giving of the Law, *Moses was summoned by God to return to the mountaintop to receive the tablets of the Law (*Ex*. 24). However when Moses remained away for forty days, the impatient Israelites began to doubt that he would return. In response to their request for a visible god to lead them, Aaron gathered earrings and other gold ornaments (which the people willingly donated) and fashioned the calf. The people proclaimed, "This is your God, O Israel, who brought you out of the land of Egypt," thus directly transgressing the order of the Ten Commandments to have no other gods but the Lord. The Israelites worshiped the calf with sacrifice, feasting, and merriment, though they called the celebration "a festival for the Lord." Meanwhile on Mount Sinai, God revealed to Moses what had happened and announced his decision to destroy Israel. Moses implored him to forbear, came down from the mountain, and catching the people in the act of frenzied calf worship, smashed the tablets of the Law to the ground, thereby effectively canceling the covenant with God. (In the ancient Near East, legal agreements were symbolically canceled by the breaking of the tablets, clay or stone, upon which they were written.) He then ground down the calf, burnt it (suggesting that the calf was made of wood plated with gold), and mixed the dust with water, which he forced the people to drink, a form of trial by ordeal. Although Moses managed to forestall God's wrath, some three thousand Israelites were punished with death, after which a new covenant was made and new tablets inscribed (*Ex.* 32–34; *Dt.* 9–10). In rabbinic tradition the tribe of Levi did not participate in the worship of the golden calf, for which they were rewarded with the priesthood. The rabbis attempted to minimize Aaron's active role in the sin. Calf images were not unusual in ancient Canaanite worship. Calves were also installed by Jeroboam I at Dan and Bethel (*1 Kgs.* 12.28–30); these were condemned by Hosea (*Hos.* 8.6, 13.2). Thus, it does not seem that the golden calf was an imitation of Egyptian practice; rather, that the biblical account is a reflection of Canaanite forms of worship encountered by the Israelites. It has been suggested that the calf was not even a representation of the deity but instead symbolized the animal upon which the deity stood. This is supported by ancient Near Eastern iconography, which often pictures the deity standing erect upon the back of a bull. Miniature bronze calves have been discovered in archeological excavations in Israel.

• Herbert C. Brichto, "The Worship of the Golden Calf: A Literary Analysis of a Fable on Idolatry," *Hebrew Union College Annual* 54 (1983): 1–44. Umberto Cassuto, *A Commentary on the Book of Exodus*, translated from Hebrew by Israel Abrahams (Jerusalem, 1961–1967), pp. 407–410. Nahum M. Sarna, *Exploring Exodus* (New York, 1986), pp. 215–220. Lawrence E. Stager, "When Canaanites and Philistines Ruled Ashkelon," *Biblical Archaeology Review* 17.2 (1991): 24–37, 40–43.

—BARUCH J. SCHWARTZ

GOLDSTEIN, HERBERT (1890–1970), Orthodox rabbi in the United States. An innovator in the evolution of the American Orthodox synagogue in the twentieth century, Goldstein was born on New York City's Lower East Side, attended the city's public schools and Columbia University, and was ordained an Orthodox rabbi by R. Sholom E. Jaffe in 1912 before graduating from the Jewish Theological Seminary in 1913. In 1917 Goldstein became the founding rabbi of Harlem's Institutional Synagogue. This was the first Orthodox congregation consciously to integrate religious, educational, and social activities into its synagogue's life. Goldstein continued in that pulpit for the next fifty-three years, even when the congregation relocated in the 1930s and became the West Side Institutional Synagogue. Goldstein wrote *Forty Years of Study for a Principle: The Biography of Harry Fischel* (New York, 1928).

• Jeffrey S. Gurock, *When Harlem Was Jewish, 1870–1930* (New York, 1979). Aaron I. Reichel, *The Maverick Rabbi: Rabbi Herbert S. Goldstein and the Institutional Synagogue—A New Organizational Form* (Norfolk, Va., 1984).

—JEFFREY S. GUROCK

GOLEM. The word *golem* occurs once in the Bible (*Ps.* 139.16) and there refers to an embryo; in Medieval Hebrew the word was used to mean formless matter but later came to refer to a robot magically created. A man made of clay was brought to life by the insertion of a slip of paper with one of the mystic names of God under his tongue. The golem would then obey the behests of his creator. Ideas concerning the golem were variously associated with the magical interpretation of the **Sefer Yetsirah* and its letter mysticism and with the mystico-symbolic rituals practiced by the *Ḥasidei Ashkenaz. Tsevi Hirsch *Ashkenazi of Amsterdam seriously discussed whether a golem might be counted in the religious quorum of ten (*Resp.* no. 93), adding that his grandfather, R. Eliyyahu of Chełm, had fashioned such a creature. There was considerable fear that a golem might get out of hand (there were parallels in non-Jewish legend and fiction, from Goethe's *Sorcerer's Apprentice* to Mary Wollstonecraft Shelley's *Frankenstein*). In one version of the legend, the kabbalist creator removed the name of God from the golem, but the lifeless mass of clay fell on its maker and killed him. The golem legend has come to be associated (without historical foundation) with the famous R. *Yehudah Liva' ben Betsal'el of Prague. In Hebrew and in colloquial Yiddish the word *golem* designates a stupid person.

• Hayim Bloch, *The Golem: Legends of the Ghetto of Prague* (Vienna, 1925). Moshe Idel, *Golem: Jewish Magical and Mystical Traditions on the Artificial Anthropoid* (Albany, 1990). Gershom Gerhard Scholem, *On the Kabbalah and Its Symbolism*, translated by Ralph Manheim (New York, 1965). Byron L. Sherwin, *The Golem Legend: Origins and Implications* (Lanham, Md., 1985).

—JOSEPH DAN

GOMBINER, AVRAHAM ABELE (c.1637–1683), Polish Talmudist and *yeshivah* head in Kalisz, popularly known as the Magen Avraham (Shield of Abraham) after the title of his commentary to the **Shulḥan ʿArukh, Oraḥ Ḥayyim* (printed in standard editions).

Gombiner's work is more of a pure commentary on the *Shulḥan ʿArukh* than is *David ben Shemu'el ha-Levi's *Turei Zahav*, which is often a discussion of *Yaʿaqov ben Asher's *Arba'ah Turim*, and Gombiner seeks to uphold the *Shulḥan ʿArukh* over the *Turim* and to harmonize discrepancies between the views of Yosef *Karo and Mosheh *Isserles. Although its succinctness made it difficult to understand, *Magen Avraham* achieved great popularity in both eastern and western Europe, particularly among the leadership of the Hasidic movement.

Gombiner also wrote *Zayit Raʿanan* (Dessau, 1704), a commentary on the **Yalqut Shimʿoni*, which included sermonica on the first part of *Genesis*.

• Chaim Tchernowitz, *Toledot ha-Poseqim*, vol. 3 (New York, 1947), pp. 164–172.

—ELIJAH J. SCHOCHET

GOMEL, BIRKAT HA-. See BIRKAT HA-GOMEL.

GOOD AND EVIL. Reflections on good and evil pervade Jewish literature from its inception to the present. Yet, as with other complex philosophical questions, Jewish tradition offers no systematic treatment of the topic, only a vast array of sources from which the general contours of Jewish thought may be discerned.

Genesis 1 asserts unequivocally that God considered his creation "very good" (*Gn.* 1.31). This view and its corollary, that life is a blessing rather than a curse, is never seriously challenged. Against this background, the problem of evil is inescapable and, some would argue, irresolvable. The problem is particularly pressing in a religion that holds that the one God is not only good and benevolent but also omnipotent. The evident facts that life includes much suffering and that humans have the capacity to harm both themselves and others require explanation. On the whole, moral evil (sin and its consequences) has received more sustained attention than natural evil (natural disasters, birth defects, etc.). With respect to the former, two central themes, both biblical in origin, dominate. First, the good is defined as God's will, which is communicated through revelation, prophets, and authoritative teachers. Second, humans are endowed with free will (in rabbinic terminology, a good inclination and an evil inclination) either to obey or disobey and must suffer the consequences of their choice. These two notions lead to the view that any evil that befalls humans, collectively or individually, is a divine punishment for evil committed by them. The doctrine that the one omnipotent and benevolent God is the source of both good and evil found striking expression in the rabbinic injunction that "one should bless God for the evil that occurs just as one blesses God for the good" (*Ber.* 33b).

The difficulties inherent in this view, however, lead to a number of strategies for reconciling both God's goodness with the existence of evil and God's justice with life's apparent injustices. These include, but are not limited to, claims that all things are for the good, though they may not appear so (*Ber.* 60b); that there is an evil force, sometimes personified as Satan, who, though subservient to God, causes people to do or to experience evil (*Jb.* 1–2; *Ber.* 6a; *Gn. Rab.* 84.3); that the unmerited good and evil experienced in this life will be rectified in the *afterlife (*Ber.* 4a; *Ta'an.* 11a); that divine punishment is an indication of God's love and concern for the transgressor (*Am.* 3.2); that God causes the righteous to suffer as an "affliction of love," so that they will more intensively pursue certain virtues (*Ber.* 5a; *B. M.* 85a); that humans inherit the merits or demerits of their ancestors, and God treats them accordingly (*Ber.* 7a); and that the ways of God are mysterious, and humans cannot understand why the righteous and wicked fare as they do (*Hb.* 1.2–4; *Jb.* 35–42).

Efforts to formulate an adequate theory of theodicy were made by all major medieval philosophers. Maimonides defends the Aristotelian position that evil has no positive substance but is the absence, namely, the "privation," of good. He was also the first to distinguish natural evil from moral evil. The kabbalists, on the other hand, developed a doctrine of evil as a demonic counterworld: the "left emanation" or the "other side" (see SITRA' AḤRA'). In the modern period, in the aftermath of the Holocaust, the problem of evil has received new emphasis. See HOLOCAUST THEOLOGY.

• Eugene B. Borowitz, "Rethinking Good and Evil," *Moment* 9.9 (1984): 57–59. Daniel Boyarin, "Dialectics of Desire: The Evil Instinct Is Very Good," in *Reading Sex in Talmudic Culture* (Berkeley, 1993), pp. 61–76. Martin Buber, *Good and Evil* (New York, 1953). David B. Burrell, "Maimonides, Aquinas and Gersonides on Providence and Evil," *Religious Studies* 20.3 (1984): 335–351. Warren Zev Harvey, "Maimonides and Spinoza on the Knowledge of Good and Evil," *Binah* 2 (1989): 131–146. Stig Norin, "[On] F. Lindstroem, 'God and the Origin of Evil: A Contextual Analysis of Alleged Monistic Evidence in the Old Testament,' " *Vetus Testamentum* 35.2 (1985): 238–245. Shlomo Pines, "Truth and Falsehood Versus Good and Evil: A Study in Jewish and General Philosophy in Connection with the 'Guide of the Perplexed,' " in *Studies in Maimonides*, edited by Isadore Twersky (Cambridge, 1990), pp. 95–157. John F. A. Sawyer, "The Image of God, the Wisdom of Serpents and the Knowledge of Good and Evil," in *A Walk in the Garden: Biblical, Iconographical, and Literary Images of Eden*, edited by Paul Morris and Deborah Sawyer (Sheffield, Eng., 1992), pp. 64–73. Douglas M. Snyder, "Judaism and Freud: The Inclinations to Do Good and Evil," *Psychoanalysis and Contemporary Thought* 16.1 (1993): 103–122. J. Marvin Spiegelman, "The Jewish Understanding of Evil in the Light of Jung's Psychology," in *Judaism and Jungian Psychology* (Lanham, Md., 1993), pp. 61–84.

—LOUIS E. NEWMAN

GORDON, ELI'EZER (1840–1910), rabbi and scholar. At an early age, he was asked by R. Yisra'el *Salanter to succeed him in instructing young students in Kovno. In 1874 Gordon became rabbi of Kelme; ten years later he was appointed rabbi of *Tels and head of its prestigious *yeshivah*. An exponent of a rigorous logical and conceptual approach to the Talmud, Gordon was a pioneer of the *Musar movement. He played an active role in the creation of Keneset Yisra'el, an organization that sought to represent all Orthodox Jews. His *responsa, Teshuvot Rabbi Eli'ezer*, were published in two volumes (1912, 1940).

• Dov Katz, *The Musar Movement: Its History, Leading Personalities, and Doctrines*, translated by Leonard Oschry (Tel Aviv, 1975). Ze'ev Aryeh Rabiner, *Ha-Ga'on Rabbi Eli'ezer Gordon Zatsal* (Tel Aviv, 1968). Norman Solomon, *The Analytic Movement: Hayyim Soloveitchik and His Circle* (Atlanta, 1993), for a discussion of Gordon's approach to Talmudic interpretation.

—JACOB MESKIN

GOREN, SHLOMO (1917–1994), Israeli chief rabbi and halakhic authority. Born in Zambrów, Poland, he went as a child to Palestine to Kefar Ḥasidim, which his father helped to found. A Torah prodigy, he published his first work, *Netser ha-Qadosh*, on Maimonides' *Mishneh Torah*, when he was seventeen. He served in the Haganah (the Jewish paramilitary force) and fought in Israel's War of Independence. After the establishment of the State of Israel, he was appointed the first chief chaplain of the Israeli Defense Forces. A flamboyant figure, he participated in parachute jumps and sounded the shofar at the *Western Wall immediately upon its capture in 1967. As chief chaplain, he introduced a unified liturgy, used by soldiers of all backgrounds. He also made significant halakhic decisions related to modern army life. He gave permission to remarry to the widows (see 'AGUNAH) of soldiers killed in action whose bodies had not been found (for example, those drowned in boats or in submarines lost at sea). From 1968 to 1972, he was Ashkenazi chief rabbi of Tel Aviv. From 1972 to 1983, he was Ashkenazi chief rabbi of Israel. His liberal interpretations solved many of the problems relating to converts, *mamzerim* (see MAMZER), and post-mortem examinations. He also ruled that there were certain sections of the Temple mount where it was permissible for Jews to enter and pray, and he founded the Idra Rabbah Yeshivah facing the Western Wall. After stepping down as chief rabbi, he spoke out against giving land for peace and the evacuation of Jewish settlements. He was the author of many works, including a commentary on the Talmud Yerushalmi.

• Yitshak Alfasi, *Ha-Ma'alot li-Shelomoh: Sefer Zikkaron ba-Halakhah uva-Aggadah le . . . Shelomoh Goren* (Jerusalem, 1995). Obituary, *The London Times* (November 1, 1994), p. 21a.

GOSPELS. See NEW TESTAMENT.

GOSSIP. See SLANDER.

GOVERNMENT, PRAYER FOR. See HA-NOTEN TESHUʿAH LA-MELAKHIM; TEFILLAH LI-SHELOM HA-MEDINAH.

GOY (גּוֹי), a term used in the Bible for any nation including Israel. It subsequently came to mean the non-Jewish nations in general and finally a member of any such nation, that is, the non-Jew. See also GENTILE.

GRACE AFTER MEALS. See BIRKAT HA-MAZON.

GRACE BEFORE MEALS. See BIRKAT HA-MOTSIʾ.

GRACIAN, ZERAḤYAH (13th cent.), philosopher. A member of the prominent Spanish Gracian family, Zeraḥyah (also known as Zeraḥyah Ḥen) was born in Barcelona. He studied Islamic and Jewish philosophy under Yonah ben Avraham Gerondi and was a physician by profession. In 1277 he immigrated to Rome, where he lived until 1290. His native language was probably Arabic, and he translated a number of works from Arabic into Hebrew, facilitating the spread of Jewish philosophy in Italy. In addition he wrote commentaries on the Pentateuch (or portions of it), *Job, Proverbs*, and parts of Maimonides' *Guide of the Perplexed*. He was a devoted follower of Maimonides and a recognized authority on his teachings. His commentaries combine philological and philosophical interpretations.

• Moritz Steinschneider, in *Otsar Neḥmad*, vol. 2 (Vienna, 1857), pp. 121ff., 229–245. —STEVEN BALLABAN

GRAETZ, HEINRICH (1817–1891), historian. Born in eastern Prussia and given a traditional Jewish education, Graetz studied modern and classical languages and other subjects on his own. His crisis of faith was resolved with the help first of Samson Raphael Hirsch and then of Zacharias Frankel. In 1853 Graetz was appointed to the faculty of the Jewish Theological Seminary in Breslau. Graetz is best known for his erudite, dramatic, and highly opinionated eleven-volume *History of the Jews*, although he also published studies of biblical books and essays on the philosophy of Jewish history and Jewish ethics.

In his programmatic essay, "The Construction of Jewish History," which he wrote in 1846, Graetz asserted that the essence of Judaism originally took the form of a unique theoretical idea (a concept of deity in its transcendence totally opposed to paganism), but he sought to show that the concrete implications of the idea unfolded, in a somewhat Hegelian manner, in the various cycles of its historical experience. *History of the Jews* limned a vast panorama of the Jewish people as a living folk and not merely a religious association, as Graetz accused the Reform Jews of his day of advocating. His presentation emphasized Jewish achievements in literature, philosophy, and law, as well as the historic willingness of Jews to sacrifice life itself for the sake of Judaism's spiritual mission.

• Salo W. Baron, *History and Jewish Historians* (Philadelphia, 1964), pp. 263–275. Philip Bloch, "Memoir of Heinrich Graetz," in *History of the Jews*, by Heinrich Graetz (Philadelphia, 1891–1898), vol. 6, pp. 1–86. Jay M. Harris, *How Do We Know This? Midrash and the Fragmentation of Modern Judaism* (Albany, N.Y., 1995), pp. 175–190 and *passim*. Lionel Kochan, "The Messiah as the Spirit of History: Krochmal and Graetz," in *The Jew and His History* (New York, 1977), pp. 69–87. Michael A. Meyer, ed., *Ideas of Jewish History* (New York, 1974), pp. 217–244. —ROBERT M. SELTZER

GRAGER (Yi.; גראַגער), rattle sounded in the synagogue on Purim at each mention of the name of *Haman in the course of the reading of the *Book of Esther*. The *grager* dates back to thirteenth-century France and Germany. The custom among Oriental Jews was to stamp the feet or knock two stones together at the mention of Haman's name, but this has generally been superseded by the *grager* (although not in Persia).

• Shifra Epstein, "Purim: The Smiting of the Figures of Haman and Zeresh in Yemen," *Mankind Quarterly* 29.4 (1989): 401–416. Joseph Gutmann, "Purim in Jewish Art," in *Purim, the Face and the Mask: Essays and Catalogue of an Exhibition* (New York, 1979), pp. 21–24.

GRAIN OFFERING. See MEAL OFFERING.

GRAVE. See BURIAL; TOMBS.

GREAT ASSEMBLY. See KENESET HA-GEDOLAH.

GREAT SYNAGOGUE. See KENESET HA-GEDOLAH.

GREETINGS AND CONGRATULATIONS. The Bible contains a number of formal greetings. For example, Laban greets the servant of Abraham with the words "Come, blessed of the Lord" (*Gn*. 24.11); the *Book of Ruth* contains both the greeting "The Lord be with you" and the response "The Lord bless you" (*Ru*. 2.4); while the longest greeting is David's to Nabal, "All hail, and peace to you, and peace to your house, and peace to all that is yours" (*1 Sm*. 25.6). The word *peace* (*shalom*; cf. *Gn*. 43.27; *Ex*. 18.7; *Jgs*. 6.23) figures most frequently in Jewish greetings up to the present (*shalom ʿaleikhem*, "peace to you"). The Talmud goes to great lengths in detailing the etiquette of greetings and appropriate responses—such as who has to greet whom first and the proper point at which to reply. Readiness to be first in greeting is an act of special piety (*Avot* 4.20), while "he who fails to return a greeting is like a robber" (*Ber*. 6b).

Formal greetings are customary on the Sabbath. At the beginning of the Sabbath, people greet one another with *Shabbat shalom*, "a peaceful Sabbath"; or, among Ashkenazim, with the Yiddish *gut Shabes*, "good Sabbath." At the conclusion of the Sabbath, people wish each other *shavuʿa tov* (Heb.) or *gut vokh* (Yi.), "a good week." On festivals, *ḥag sameaḥ*, "a joyful festival" is the standard greeting. *Moʿadim le-simḥah*, "[may you have] festivals for rejoicing," was traditionally used by Sephardim, particularly on the Shalosh Regalim, and derives from the festival ʿAmidah. Today it is commonly used in Israel; the traditional reply is *ḥaggim u-zemannim le-sason*, "feasts and festal seasons for joy." Another (traditionally Ashkenazi) festival greeting is the Yiddish *gut yontef*, "good holiday." The specific Roʾsh ha-Shanah greeting is *le-shanah tovah tikatev ve-teḥatem*, "may you be inscribed and sealed for a good year."

On performing a religious duty, it is customary to utter the greeting *ḥazaq barukh*, "be strong, blessed"; among Ashkenazim, *yishar koḥakha* (*yashar koaḥ*), "may your strength increase" (*Shab*. 87a). *Yishar koḥakha* derives from a passage in the Talmud (*Shab*. 87a) where Reish Laqish, by a play on the word *asher* in *Exodus* 34.1, has God say approvingly to Moses, "*yishar koḥakha*" for smashing the tablets of the Law. These phrases are used as expressions of thanks to the preacher (after a sermon), priest (after the Birkat ha-Kohanim), or the performer of a *mitsvah*.

A customary welcome is *barukh ha-ba'*, "blessed is he who comes" (cf. *Ps*. 118.26). No greetings are made on Tishʿah be-'Av or in a house of mourning, where the visitor consoles the mourner with the phrase *ha-Maqom yenaḥem etkhem tokh she'ar avelei Tsiyyon vi-Yerushalayim*, "May the Almighty comfort you among the other mourners of Zion and Jerusalem." Among British Jews it is customary to wish mourners "long life."

The most frequent forms of congratulations have an astrological origin. In *mazzal tov*, "good luck," and *mazzal u-verakhah*, "luck and blessing," the word *mazzal* originally applied to a constellation of stars, while *besiman tov*, used among Sephardim, means "under a good sign." Among Sephardim, various congratulations are introduced with the word *tizkeh* ("may you be vouchsafed"—a long life, the performance of commandments, etc.). *Le-ḥayyim*, "to life," is said for a toast, and the birthday greeting is "may you live to 120 years" (cf. *Gn*. 6.3).

• Martin S. Cohen, "Synagogue Etiquette," *Ecumenism* 119 (1995): 21–22. Joseph A. Fitzmyer, "Aramaic Epistolography," *Semeia* 22 (1981): 25–57, discusses greetings in ancient Aramaic letters. Gerald Friedlander, *Laws and Customs of Israel* (London, 1949).

GRODZINSKI, ḤAYYIM ʿOZER (1863–1940), Lithuanian rabbi and leader of Orthodox Jewry. Though he was appointed at age twenty-four one of the rabbinic judges of Vilna, his authority extended far and wide, both as an interpreter of Jewish law and as a spokesman for Russian-Polish Jewry. Grodzinski was a founder and major leader of *Agudat Israel. In Poland between the two world wars he helped to organize the Vaʿad ha-Yeshivot in Vilna, an association devoted to raising funds for the financially strapped *yeshivot*. In the early 1930s, Grodzinski was officially named one of the rabbis of Vilna, after a prolonged public dispute over the nomination of Zionist leader R. Yitsḥaq Rubinstein to the post. Grodzinski's halakhic writings were collected in his still influential book of *responsa* on the **Shulḥan ʿArukh* entitled *Aḥiʿezer*.

• Aharon Sorski, *Rabban shel Yisra'el* (Bene Beraq, 1971).

—GERSHON BACON

GUARANTOR. See SURETY

GUARDIAN (Heb. *epitropos*, from Gr. *apotropos*), an individual who may be appointed for minors, mentally defective adults, or absentees. The major focus of the *halakhah* in this area is the administration of the ward's property and finances. A father is the natural guardian of his minor children, but he may also appoint another person as their guardian (*Git*. 52a). A guardian may be appointed by a court by virtue of its authority as "the father of orphans" (*Git*. 37a), and it will use this power in relation to orphans, or in cases in which either the father, or the guardian appointed by him, fails to act in the best interests of the ward (*B. Q*. 37a; Rema', *Ḥoshen Mishpat* 285.8). A mother must either be specifically appointed as a guardian or may undertake the responsibility for dependent minors, by virtue of which they become members of her household for all legal purposes (*Shulḥan ʿArukh, Ḥoshen Mishpat* 290.1). Although in principle in *halakhah* women are not appointed as guardians, later authorities agree that a woman who is "experienced in business matters and accustomed to going about in public" may be appointed by the court to act as a guardian if this would be in the best interests of the ward (Bayit Ḥadash, *Ḥoshen Mishpat* 290.3). The fiduciary powers of a guardian are limited to the prudent administration of the ward's estate, and all guardians, including the father of a minor, are subject to supervision by the court (*Git*. 52a). The court may set aside transactions entered into by a guardian in excess of his or her powers, and, in such a case, the guardian may be held personally liable for any loss suffered by the ward unless court approval was secured prior to the transactions in question (Rema', *Ḥoshen Mishpat* 290.13). A full report must be submitted at the termination of the guardianship, which ends automatically upon a minor achieving the age of majority. Guardians are not entitled to any remuneration for their services but may take compensation for limited personal expenses incurred in the course of the direct management of the ward's estate.

• H. Shanks, J. Greenfield, and S. Applebaum, "Israel Museum Exhibit Reveals Wife and Mother from Bar Kochba Period," *Biblical Archaeology Review* 7.4 (1981): 12. Eliav Shochetman, "On the Nature of the Rules Governing Custody of Children in Jewish Law," *Jewish Law Annual* 10 (1992): 115–157. Daniel Sinclair, "Jewish Law in the State of Israel," *Jewish Law Annual* 9 (1991): 251–257.

—DANIEL SINCLAIR

GUIDE OF THE PERPLEXED. See MAIMONIDES, MOSES.

GUILT OFFERING. See REPARATION OFFERING.

GUNZBERG, ARYEH LEIB BEN ASHER (c.1695–1785), Talmudist. In 1720 he moved to Minsk, where he founded and headed a *yeshivah* that attracted pupils from many parts of eastern Europe. Later he served as rabbi in Volozhin, and from 1765 he served as rabbi and head of a *yeshivah* in Metz. The most prominent of his disciples were Refa'el ha-Kohen of Altona and Ḥayyim ben Yitsḥaq Volozhiner. An outstanding casuist and eminent scholar, Gunzberg's classic halakhic work, *Sha'agat Aryeh* (Frankfurt an der Oder, 1755), and his *novellae*, *Turei Even* (Melz, 1781) and *Gevurot Ari* (Vilna, 1862), are essential links in the chain of analytic works that shaped the methodology that is the hallmark of Lithuanian Talmudic scholarship, and they are studied assiduously in *yeshivot* to this day. His *responsa*, with glosses by his son, Asher Löw, were published in Vilna in 1874.

• David Maggid, *Sefer Toledot Mishpeḥot Ginzburg* (St. Petersburg, 1899), pp. 32–52.

—JUDITH BLEICH

GUR. See GER.

GUTTMACHER, ELIYYAHU (1795–1874), rabbinic forerunner of modern Zionism. His rejection of passive messianism combined with his mystical pietism earned him the title Tsaddiq of Grodzisk, a village in the province of Posen (Poznań), where he officiated as rabbi. Unwittingly, he attracted large numbers of believers from eastern Europe in the efficacy of his prayers and amulets. He collaborated with R. Tsevi Hirsch *Kalischer, who had studied with him at the *yeshivah* of their mentor R. ʿAqiva' *Eger, in supporting agricultural settlement in Erets Yisra'el, which Guttmacher saw as the spiritual antidote to the ills of the Diaspora, exemplified for him in Reform Judaism and secularization. Nevertheless he regarded Jewish emancipation as a sign of the approaching redemption. His numerous *responsa* were noted for their compassion for the less fortunate, their Talmudic erudition, and their uncompromising opposition to any change in traditional customs. Some of his *novellae* were included in the standard Romm edition of the Talmud. His *responsa* were collected in *Adderet Eliyyahu* (2 vols., 1984).

• Salomon Schreiber, ed., *Iggerot Soferim* (Vienna, 1933), pp. 81–82. Nahum Sokolow, *Ḥibbat Tsiyyon* (Jerusalem, 1935), pp. 17ff.

—ARYEH NEWMAN

H

ḤABAD, an acronym formed from the Hebrew words for wisdom (*ḥokhmah*), understanding (*binah*), and knowledge (*da'at*); school of *Hasidism founded by R.*Shneur Zalman of Lyady. Its principal and most influential literary work, entitled *Liqqutei Amarim*, but better known as the *Tanya'*, expounds the doctrine of Ḥabad. The work's basic thought follows the Hasidic themes of *hitbonenut* (contemplation of the nature of the divine entity constantly present in the world), *devequt* (constant communion with and cleaving to God), *hitlahavut* (intensity of feeling at times bordering on ecstasy), and *kavvanah* (devotion, meditation, intent). Ḥabad's principle that "there is no place empty of him" has more than once provoked the charge of pantheism. The element in Ḥabad that distinguishes it from other Hasidic schools is its emphasis on the importance of intellectual effort in religious striving. The powers of contemplation, analysis, and understanding—the upper *sefirot*—must rule and guide the lower, emotional impulses. The result of such intellectual effort ought to be the intensification of the emotional aspects of prayer and religious effort. Partly through its emphasis on systematizing religious work and partly due to a succession of gifted leaders, Ḥabad Hasidism (as expressed by the Lubavitch movement) continued to win adherents even when other Hasidic schools began to weaken. In order to disseminate Ḥabad thought, as demanded by Shneur Zalman's teachings, the movement has become active in many parts of the world, attempting to counter the slackening of Jewish life by founding schools and orphanages, distributing literature, and promoting study groups and the observance of religious festivals. These efforts provoked opponents to charge Ḥabad with overt missionary activity. In recent years, Ḥabad engendered a messianic arousal centered on the person of R. Menaḥem Mendel Schneerson (see SCHNEERSOHN FAMILY), who, as the seventh master of Ḥabad, was perceived by many members of the movement as the promised Messiah.

• Rachel Elior, "The Contemplative Ascent to God," in *Jewish Spirituality*, vol. 2, *From the Sixteenth Century Revival to the Present*, edited by Arthur Green (New York, 1987), pp. 157–205. Rachel Elior, *The Paradoxical Ascent to God: The Kabbalistic Theosophy of Habad Hasidism* (Albany, 1993). Rachel Elior, *Torat ha-'Elohut ba-Dor ha-Sheni shel Ḥasidut Ḥabad* (Jerusalem, 1982). Louis Jacobs, *Seeker of Unity: The Life and Works of Aaron of Starosselje* (London, 1966). Louis Jacobs, ed. and trans., *Tract on Ecstasy*, by Dov Baer Schneersohn (London, 1963). Naftali Loewenthal, *Communicating the Infinite: The Emergence of the Habad School* (Chicago, 1990). Nissan Mindel et al., trans., *Liqqutei Amarim*, by Shneur Zalman of Lyady, 2d ed. (Brooklyn, N.Y., 1972). —RACHEL ELIOR

HABAKKUK (7th cent. BCE), prophet in the kingdom of Judah during the early period of Judah's submission to Babylonia. Little is known of Habakkuk's life or personal circumstances. In vivid language, he described the rise of the Chaldeans (Neo-Babylonians) to the position of the dominant world power, the ferocity of their military campaigns, and their unbridled cruelty. He probably prophesied after the collapse of the Assyrian empire between 614 and 609, and his utterances appear to reflect Nebuchadnezzar's defeat of Egypt in 605 BCE and subsequent invasion of Judah. Habakkuk's message focuses on the problem of theodicy: why does a righteous and at the same time omnipotent God allow evil (in this case the Neo-Babylonian empire) to rule the world? Habakkuk's dictum that "the righteous shall live by his faith" (2.4), implying that God would ultimately redeem the righteous, summarizes, according to the Talmud (*Mak.* 24a), the whole teaching of the Bible.

The *Book of Habakkuk* is the eighth book of the Minor Prophets. According to its superscriptions (1.1 and 3.1), it contains two major parts—"the oracle that Habakkuk the prophet saw" (chaps. 1–2) and the "prayer of Habakkuk the prophet." The oracle consists of five prophetic utterances: Habakkuk's initial complaint against violence and oppression, 1.1–4; God's answer—the Chaldeans are his instruments of punishment, 1.5–11; the prophet's second protest against the oppressor, 1.12–17; God's answer—the righteous shall live by his faith, whereas the wicked shall perish, 2.1–5; and five more oracles condemning the oppressors, 2.6–20. The "psalm" of Habakkuk (chap. 3) reinforces the message of the triumph of the righteous over evil with a theophanic description of God's defeat of oppressors, concluding with the prophet's statement of trust and faith in God. A commentary (called a *pesher*) on *Habakkuk* 1–2 has been found among the *Dead Sea Scrolls. *Habakkuk* 3 is read in the Diaspora as the *haftarah* portion on the second day of Shavu'ot, which commemorates the revelation of the Torah at Sinai (*Meg.* 31a).

• Umberto Cassuto, "Chapter III of Habakkuk and the Ras Shamra Texts," in *Biblical and Oriental Studies*, vol. 2 (Jerusalem, 1975), pp. 3–15. Donald E. Gowan, *The Triumph of Faith in Habakkuk* (Atlanta, 1976). Robert D. Haak, *Habakkuk*, Supplements to Vetus Testamentum, vol. 44 (Leiden, 1992). Theodore Hiebert, *God of My Victory: The Ancient Hymn in Habakkuk 3*, Harvard Semitic Monographs, no. 38 (Atlanta, 1986). J.J.M. Roberts, *Nahum, Habakkuk, and Zephaniah: A Commentary*, The Old Testament Library (Louisville, Ky., 1991). Marvin A. Sweeney, "Genre, Structure, and Intent in the Book of Habakkuk," *Vetus Testamentum* 41 (1991): 63–83. —MARVIN A. SWEENEY

ḤABIB. See IBN ḤAVIV FAMILY.

ḤADASH (חָדָשׁ; new), technical halakhic term for the new grain ripening in spring, which could not be eaten until "a sheaf of the first fruits" from the new harvest (*'omer) was offered by the priests in the Temple on the second day of *Pesaḥ, 16 Nisan (*Lv.* 23.14). Since the destruction of the Temple and the suspension of the *'omer* offering, eating *ḥadash* has been forbidden through 16 Nisan, but the prohibition lapses automatically on the eve of 17 Nisan.

HADASSI, YEHUDAH BEN ELIYYAHU (12th cent.), *Karaite scholar who was active in Constantinople and who followed the ascetic practices of the *Avelei Tsiyyon. His greatest work, *Eshkol ha-Kofer* (Gozlva, 1836), begun in 1148, is an encyclopedia of Karaite theology and law. It is not an original work but an eclectic summary of Karaite knowledge, reflecting how the achievements of the golden period of Karaite creativity in the tenth and eleventh centuries were transferred to a new environment in Byzantium. It is written partly in verse, in Hadassi's own unique and awkward Hebrew, which frequently makes it difficult to understand. *Eshkol ha-Kofer* is arranged according to the Ten Commandments and explains the *mitsvot* and their reasons. In addition, Hadassi included much information on natural phenomena, biblical exegesis, grammar, and philosophy, as well as attacks on Christianity and Islam; the book reveals how Byzantine Jews saw the world. In addition to *Eshkol ha-Kofer*, Hadassi wrote a work explicating the commandments in order of their appearance in the Bible, of which only a manuscript fragment survives, as well as some religious hymns that were included in the Karaite prayer book.

• Zvi Ankori, *Karaites in Byzantium: The Formative Years, 970–1100* (New York, 1959). D. Lasker, *Sefer ha-Yovel li-Shelomoh Pines*, edited by Moshe Idel et al. (Jerusalem, 1988), vol. 1, pp. 477–492. Sandor Scheiber, ed., *Jubilee Volume in Honour of Prof. Bernhard Heller* (Budapest, 1941), pp. 101–129.
—DAVID E. SKLARE

ḤAD GADYA' (Aram.; חַד גַּדְיָא; One Kid), Aramaic poem with ten stanzas recited at the close of the Pesaḥ *Seder service. Resembling a German folk song and composed on the cumulative pattern known to English readers from "The House that Jack Built," it was written by an unknown author, probably in the fifteenth century, and may have been included in the *Haggadah in order to amuse the children who were kept up late. It is not found in the Sephardi or Yemenite traditions. Literally, its theme is the retribution meted out for evil deeds, and various allegorical interpretations have been advanced by commentators. According to some it symbolizes the fate of the Jewish people among the nations; others have suggested that it describes the experiences of the soul in the human body from birth to judgment day.

• G. Jochnowitz, "Ḥad Gadya' in Judeo-Italian and Shuadit (Judeo-Provençal)," in *Readings in the Sociology of Jewish Languages*, edited by Joshua A. Fishman, (Leiden, 1985), pp. 241–245. Macy Nulman, *The Encyclopedia of Jewish Prayer* (Northvale, N.J., 1993), p. 145. Freddy Raphael, Robert Weyl, and Martine Weyl, "Trois 'Chants du Séder' des juifs d'Alsaçe," *Ethnologie française* 11.3 (1981): 271–278. Abraham Schwadron, "Un Cavritico: The Sephardic Tradition," *Journal of Jewish Music and Liturgy* 5 (1982–1983): 24–39. Abraham Schwadron, "Khad Gadya: The Italian Traditions," *Ninth World Congress of Jewish Studies*, vol. 2, Division D (Jerusalem, 1986), pp. 257–264. Ch. Szmeruk, "The Earliest Aramaic and Yiddish Version of the 'Song of the Kid' (Chad Gadya)," in *The Field of Yiddish: Studies in Language, Folklore and Literature*, edited by Uriel Weinreich (New York, 1954), pp. 214–218.

HADLAQAT NEROT. See KINDLING OF LIGHTS.

HADRAN (Aram.; הַדְרָן; "We returned"), word said aloud at the conclusion of the study of a Talmudic tractate and name of a prayer recited on that occasion, which is usually marked by an appropriate homily and a feast (Se'udat Mitsvah; see SE'UDAH) as mentioned in *Shabbat* 118b–119a.

• Samuel Kalman Mirsky, *Siyyumei ha-Massekhtot ba-Mishnah uva-Talmud ha-Bavli* (Brooklyn, N.Y., 1961).

ḤAFETS ḤAYYIM. See YISRA'EL ME'IR HA-KOHEN.

HAFQA'AT SHE'ARIM (הַפְקָעַת שְׁעָרִים; profiteering), charging prices deemed excessive relative to the norm. Profiteering is to be distinguished from the biblical prohibition against *ona'ah* (overreaching), which creates a framework for protecting the individual consumer against excessive prices charged by a deceitful vendor seeking to exploit the consumer's inferior knowledge of the true market value of the commodity being purchased. The sanctions applicable against the vendor in cases of overreaching are, therefore, designed to compensate the wronged consumer, by giving him the right to rescind the transaction (where the price paid was more than one-sixth in excess of market value) or to claim a refund of the excess (where the price paid was precisely one-sixth in excess).

The rabbinic prohibition against *hafqa'at she'arim*, on the other hand, represents a particular economic policy advocating conscious intervention in the markets as a whole, for the purpose of controlling prices of essential commodities. Such controls were deemed necessary for the protection of the weaker elements in society and were inspired by the general biblical injunction ". . . that your brother may live with you" (*Lv*. 25.36). Because the prohibition is an element of economic policy rather than a device for the protection of the individual consumer, it is applicable whether or not the purchaser protests.

Various opinions were expressed by the early sages as to the specific implementation of this policy, particularly with regard to whether the local authorities would actually fix permissible prices or merely make an objective determination as to what the current market prices were. The codes, following the position of Maimonides, decided in favor of active intervention: local authorities were empowered and obligated to fix the retail prices of essential commodities, such as flour, oil, wine, and the like, at amounts no more than one-sixth above the vendor's costs and were similarly empowered to apply sanctions against offenders as they saw fit.

Manipulative tactics that could result in artificial shortages and thus in unjustified higher prices, such as hoarding and excessive exports, were similarly prohibited.

• Menachem Elon, ed., *The Principles of Jewish Law* (Jerusalem, 1975), pp. 219–221. Aaron Levine, *Free Enterprise and Jewish Law* (New York, 1980), pp. 89–114. Nahum Rakover, *Ha-Mishar ba-Mishpat ha-'Ivri* (Jerusalem, 1987), pp. 28–32. Shlomo Yosef Zevin, ed., *Entsiqlopedyah Talmudit* (Jerusalem, 1981), vol. 10, pp. 41–49.
—BEN TZION GREENBERGER

HAFTARAH (הַפְטָרָה; conclusion [of the biblical lesson]), the reading from the prophetic books that follows *qeri'at ha-Torah* in the Shaḥarit service on Sabbaths and festivals; on fast days a *haftarah* is read during the afternoon service in the Ashkenazi rite, while on Yom Kippur and Tish'ah be-'Av a *haftarah* is read in both the morning and afternoon services. The person called to read the *haftarah* (the *maftir*) first reads a portion from the Torah (mostly a repetition of the last three verses of the day's reading). Unlike the reading of the Torah, which must be performed from a handwritten scroll, the *haftarah* may be read from a printed text; only a few congregations (mainly in Jerusalem) use scrolls of the prophetic books. The *maftir* usually reads the *haftarah* himself; in some congregations (including those in which the *haftarah* is read from a scroll), it is chanted by a reader. Before the readings a benediction is recited in praise of God "who has chosen true prophets"; another four benedictions follow the reading, one affirming faith in the eventual realization of the words of the prophets, two petitions of messianic content (for the rebuilding of Jerusalem and the coming of the Messiah), and one referring to the holiness and significance of the day (Sabbath or festival, respectively; this last blessing is omitted on fast days except on the morning of Yom Kippur). The custom of conducting regular public readings from the Prophets goes back to Second Temple times, possibly to the Hasmonean period. It has been suggested that it was introduced during the persecution of *Antiochus IV Epiphanes, when the public reading of the Torah was forbidden. Its purpose was to conclude the reading of the Torah—the main instrument for educating the people and strengthening their faith—with words of consolation and promises of messianic redemption. In later times the *haftarah* portion was no longer necessarily a prophecy of consolation but was instead suited to the occasion of its recitation. Thus on a festival, the *haftarah* is in some way connected with the day, while on Sabbaths it is chosen on the basis of its association with the Pentateuchal portion for that day. On Shabbat Sheqalim, Shabbat Zakhor, Shabbat Parah, and Shabbat ha-Ḥodesh (see SABBATHS, SPECIAL), the *haftarah* again refers to the specific occasion. On a Sabbath that is also the new moon, *Isaiah* 66, which refers to both the Sabbath and Ro'sh Ḥodesh, is read. On the three Sabbaths preceding 9 Av, *Jeremiah* 1 and 2 and *Isaiah* 1 are read because of their prophecies of wrath, while on the seven following Sabbaths, prophecies of consolation (taken from *Is.* 40ff.) are chosen in most rites. The chief rabbinate of the State of Israel has ordained the reading of *Isaiah* 10.32 and 11.12 for the annual Yom ha-ʿAtsma'ut service. On those Sabbaths when two Pentateuchal portions are read, the *haftarah* recited is generally that for the second portion. The *haftarah* varies according to different rites; current *haftarah* portions do not correspond with those mentioned in the Mishnah (*Meg.* 4.1–10, 31a). In many congregations, it is considered a special honor to be called to read the *haftarah*, and it is given, for instance, to a boy celebrating his *bar mitsvah* (and in non-Orthodox congregations, to a girl celebrating her *bat mitsvah*) or a bridegroom; in others (including Sephardi and ʿAdot ha-Mizraḥ), it is customary to call boys below the age of thirteen for *maftir* (but not for other parts of the reading). In the Talmudic period, a reading from the Hagiographa was incorporated into the Sabbath afternoon service. The *haftarah* is chanted to a special melody. In Reform congregations, it is often read rather than sung.

• Jacob Mann, *The Bible as Read and Preached in the Old Synagogue*, 2 vols. (Cincinnati, 1940). Pinchas Spiro, *Haftarah Chanting* (New York, 1994).

HAGAR, Egyptian handmaiden of *Sarah, concubine of *Abraham, and mother of *Ishmael. In accordance with common ancient Near Eastern family laws, Sarah offered Hagar to Abraham as a concubine when it became apparent that she herself was barren (*Gn.* 16). After Hagar became pregnant with Ishmael, she held her mistress in contempt, since her son would eventually receive the family inheritance. Sarah, in turn, forced Hagar to flee to the wilderness, where a messenger of God told her to return to her mistress and promised that her son would become the founder of a great nation. After the birth of Isaac (*Gn.* 21), Sarah demanded the expulsion of Hagar and Ishmael, lest Ishmael inherit Abraham's estate together with Isaac. (Parallel texts from Mesopotamia indicate that Isaac, though born later, would still be legally considered the firstborn.) When Hagar found herself without water in the wilderness of Beersheba, a messenger of God appeared to her, proclaimed his promise concerning Ishmael, and provided a well of water to sustain her and Ishmael. Some scholars regard the two episodes (*Gn.* 16 and 21) as different versions of the same story.

• Katheryn Pfisterer Darr, *Far More Precious Than Jewels: Perspectives on Biblical Women*, Gender and the Biblical Tradition (Louisville, Ky., 1991). JoAnn Hackett, "Rehabilitating Hagar: Fragments of an Epic Pattern," in *Gender and Difference in Ancient Israel*, edited by Peggy Lynne Day (Minneapolis, 1989), pp. 12–27. Nahum M. Sarna, *Understanding Genesis* (New York, 1966), pp. 127–129, 154–165. Phyllis Trible, *Texts of Terror: Literary–Feminist Readings of Biblical Narratives*, Overtures to Biblical Theology 13 (Philadelphia, 1984). —MARVIN A. SWEENEY

HAGBAHAH (הַגְבָּהָה; elevating), the act of raising the open Torah scroll to display its text to the assembled congregation. Among Sephardim this act precedes the Torah reading and is performed by an honorary official or member of an honorary brotherhood (*levantodores*). Among Ashkenazim it follows the Torah reading and is followed by *Gelilah. Upon seeing the open Torah scroll, congregants say: "And this is the Torah that Moses placed before the children of Israel (*Dt.* 4.44) at the commandment of the Lord by the hand of Moses (*Nm.* 9.23)." Sephardim recite *Deuteronomy* 4.24 and 33.4, and Reform Jews recite *Proverbs* 3.18.

• Ismar Elbogen, *Jewish Liturgy: A Comprehensive History*, translated by Raymond P. Scheindlin (Philadelphia, New York, and Jerusalem, 1993), p. 142. Benhard S. Jacobson, *The Sabbath Service* (Tel Aviv, 1981), pp. 268–270.

HAGGADAH. See AGGADAH.

HAGGADAH OF PESAḤ, literally, the "telling" of the Passover story, but by extension, the home liturgy for the first two nights of Pesaḥ (in Israel, and among Reform Jews, the first night only; see PESAḤ) that accompanies the ritual meal called the Seder (Order). A multifaceted literary corpus that has evolved over time, the recitation of the liturgy fulfills the obligation to retell the tale of the *Exodus (*Ex.* 13.8). The Seder began as a rabbinic version of first-century Greco-Roman ritualized meals called *symposia*, and gradually developed a larger and larger narrative accompaniment, which became fixed in the Haggadah.

Originally, the meal (introduced by the standard *Qiddush prayer and outfitted with standard blessings before and after eating) was followed by spontaneous questions to prompt discussion, a Midrashic recounting of the Exodus narrative, and a recitation of the ten plagues. The liturgy concluded with psalms of praise, called *Hallel, to observe the principle that the Seder progress in tone "from degradation to praise." By 200 CE, the meal had been postponed until the end of the liturgy, and set questions, called "the four questions" (*mah nishtannah*), replaced the spontaneous ones. In the Middle Ages, the role of asking these questions was given to children, in keeping with the Bible's instructions that the Exodus be retold "when your children ask you on that day" (*Ex.* 13.14).

Over time, a third-century Talmudic discussion of "degradation" was recast as a preamble to the Midrash. *'Avadim Hayinu (We Were Slaves) identified degradation as physical servitude, and Mi-Teḥillah (In the Beginning [Our Ancestors Were Idolaters]) defined it as an inner spiritual matter. Already, R. Gamli'el's first-century interpretation of biblical food symbols (the *pesaḥ*, or *paschal lamb, **matsah* and **maror*) had been appended, possibly to counter Christological interpretation by Jewish–Christians for whom the Seder recapitulated the Last Supper. The familiar song *Dayyenu has been variously dated but is sufficiently late as to have been considered optional in the tenth century.

The earliest extant written Haggadah text is a relatively complete fragment datable to eighth- or ninth-century Palestine. The version that became canonical for Jews worldwide is part of a ninth-century prayer book, *Seder Rav Amram*, by Amram Ga'on of Babylonia. Amram's text was expanded in Europe, following the Crusades. The concluding Hallel psalms had already been split with Psalm 113 and Psalm 114 preceding the meal and Psalm 115 through Psalm 118 following it, along with Psalm 136 (called the Great Hallel), which had been mandated in antiquity as a special psalm of thanksgiving for the night. This relatively spare after-dinner liturgy was now enhanced to reflect the millennial piety of the High Middle Ages, emphasizing an imminent messianic coming and the horror occasioned by the massacre of Rhineland Jewry in the First Crusade.

These factors led Jews on the Seder eve to expect the arrival of *Elijah to announce the Messiah. They would open the door for him, invoke revenge on their oppressors, and end by wishing one another "Next year in Jerusalem" (**la-shanah ha-ba'ah bi-Yerushalayim*). A series of concluding folk songs was also added over the years, notably *Addir Hu', an alphabetic acrostic celebrating God's might, and *Ḥad Gadya', which plays with the hierarchy of power in the animal kingdom, over which death alone rules—but below God's ultimate sovereignty.

The ambience of the meal is central to the Haggadah, not only because the Bible commands special foods, but because ever since its *symposium* origins, it has invested common foodstuffs with symbolic value. Today's ritual thus includes also **ḥaroset*, a sweet paste usually made from wine, fruit and nuts, originally a *symposium* hors d'oeuvre but reinterpreted to symbolize the mortar from which Israelite slaves made bricks, and *karpas*, greens, dipped in salt water, another hors d'oeuvre, reinterpreted to symbolize the green of new life mixed with tears of slavery. Common also are eggs, originally signifying eternal life, and potatoes, harvested from the earth, like greens, and introduced in countries where spring was late and greens were unavailable. The paschal lamb offering ceased with the Temple's destruction (70 CE), but symbolic reminders of it and of another festival sacrifice, the **ḥagigah*, remain arrayed, but uneaten, on the Seder tray in the form of a roasted shankbone and egg. A final piece of *matsah*, called the **afiqoman*, concludes the meal, and *four cups of wine are consumed to indicate God's saving presence four times in Jewish history. A dispute as to whether a fifth cup was obligatory—to symbolize deliverance at the end of time—led to the custom of filling but not drinking still another cup, subsequently called "Elijah's cup."

Fifteenth- and sixteenth-century Haggadot were outfitted with lavish illustrations. Sephardi artists painted entire biblical epics as visual textual preambles; Ashkenazi (German and Italian) painters drew a running visual commentary to the liturgy. With printing, the artistic tradition continued with woodcuts and copper plate drawings, and modern artists, too, find the Haggadah a favorite medium of expression. Orthodox Haggadot today contain the entire text as tradition has preserved it, whereas liberal Jews, particularly Reform, adapt the Haggadah more freely, dispensing with old readings now deemed irrelevant, translating prayers into the vernacular, and adding material reflective of Haggadah themes. New Haggadot frequently reflect on the Holocaust and the wonder of Israel's revival as a modern Jewish state. Special Haggadot include an Israeli army Haggadah; Haggadot from otherwise socialist/secular kibbutzim; "Freedom Haggadot" from the cold war to strengthen solidarity with Soviet Jews unable to celebrate Pesaḥ; and, more recently, women's Haggadot, marking the impact of *feminism in a Jewish context. With computer technology, more and more families compose their own Haggadot, altered annually to reflect the tradition that the Pesaḥ message of liberation speaks freshly to every generation.

• Debra Reed Blank, *"Sh'fokh Ḥamatkha'* and Eliyahu in the Haggadah: Ideology in Liturgy," *Conservative Judaism* 40:2 (1987): 73–86. Baruch M. Bokser, *The Origins of the Seder: The Passover Rite and Early Rabbinic Judaism* (Berkeley, 1984). E. D. Goldschmidt, *Haggadah shel Pesaḥ* (Jerusalem, 1977). Joseph Gutmann, in *Sefer Refa'el Mahler* (Merhavyah, 1974), pp. 29–38. David Weiss Halivni, in *Meḥqarim be-'Aggadah, Targumim, u-Tefillot Yisra'el le-Zekher Yosef Heinemann*, edited by Ezra Fleischer and Jakob Petuchowski (Jerusalem, 1981), pp. 66–74. Lawrence A. Hoffman, *Beyond the Text: A Holistic Approach to Liturgy* (Bloomington, Ind., 1987), pp. 86–148. Mendel Metzger, *La Haggada enluminee* (Leiden, 1973).

–LAWRENCE A. HOFFMAN

HAGGAHOT (הַגָּהוֹת; glosses), explanatory notes by Jewish scholars intended primarily to correct textual errors, provide short explanations and cross references, or call attention to difficulties in classical texts. Throughout Jewish history, scholars have written short glosses on books. This was especially the case with regard to works composed before the invention of printing, since they circulated in a variety of versions, and the one finally printed did not always represent the best possible text. Despite a series of warnings by such luminaries as Yaʿaqov ben Me'ir Tam, these marginal corrections were often inserted into the actual text, either by the scholar himself or by later copyists. Current editions of the Talmud contain many comments and corrections of ge'onim, Rashi, and R. Shelomoh Luria, the fact of which many traditional commentators have often been unaware. Other important examples of glosses on the Talmud are the notes of R. Yo'el ben Shemu'el Sirqes, R. Eliyyahu ben Shelomoh Zalman of Vilna, and R. ʿAqiva' Eger. Even many of R. Avraham ben David of Posquières' famous *hassagot* (animadversions) on Maimonides' *Mishneh Torah* are explanatory or neutral in content and would be better categorized as *haggahot*.

Haggahot literature also comprises glosses that are intended to supplement a work in various ways. An outstanding example is the thirteenth-century **Haggahot Maimuniyyot*, written by Me'ir ha-Kohen, which supplements Maimonides' code with the opinions of German and French scholars. The *haggahot* of R. Mosheh Isserles to R. Yosef Karo's *Shulḥan ʿArukh* are, historically speaking, the most significant *haggahot* ever written. Through his notes, Isserles incorporated the Ashkenazi tradition into Karo's code of Jewish law, enabling both Karo's work, together with Isserles's notes, to be accepted as the central work of Jewish law of the last few hundred years. Such widespread acceptance, by all segments of Jewry, illustrates the advantages of *haggahot* over full-fledged commentaries or codes, which are designed to be independent and which compete with one another rather than complement each other. *Haggahot* literature continues to be published today, including glosses on the Talmud, *Mishneh Torah*, and other Jewish classics. The popular Ashkenazi halakhic works, *Kitsur Shulḥan ʿArukh* and *Mishnah Berurah*, have been published with glosses recording Sephardi practices, allowing these works, too, to achieve acceptance throughout Jewry.

• Irving A. Agus, "R. Jacob Tam's Stringent Criticism of R. Meshullam of Melun, in Its Historical Setting," in *Essays on the Occasion of the Seventieth Anniversary of the Dropsie University*, edited by Abraham Isaac Katsh and Leon Nemoy (Philadelphia, 1979), pp. 1–10. David Dablitski, "Haggahot Maimuniyyot," *Tsefunot* 1 (1989): 49–59. Menahem Kasher, *Gemara' Shelemah* (Jerusalem, 1960), introduction. Isadore Twersky, *Rabad of Posquières* (Cambridge, 1962; rev. ed. Philadelphia, 1980), chap. 3.

—MARC SHAPIRO

HAGGAHOT MAIMUNIYYOT, a thirteenth-century halakhic work written by R. Me'ir ha-Kohen of Rothenburg, a student of R. *Me'ir ben Barukh of Rothenburg, consisting of supplemental notes (*haggahot*) to Moses *Maimonides' *Mishneh Torah*. Rabbi Me'ir ha-Kohen's main objective was to attach rulings of German and northern French scholars to the code of Maimonides, whose own post-Talmudic sources were, for the most part, from Sephardi sources. Moreover, other students from the school of R. Me'ir ben Barukh of Rothenburg, including R. Me'ir ha-Kohen's brother-in-law, R. *Mordekhai ben Hillel, also sought to introduce in their writings the pillars of Sephardi *halakhah*, such as Maimonides and Alfasi. *Haggahot Maimuniyyot* is divided into two sections: notes that are attached to the *Mishneh Torah* itself, and *Teshuvot Maimuniyyot*, which are appended to the end of each book of the *Mishneh Torah* and contain relevant Ashkenazi *responsa*. The work as a whole constitutes an important source for twelfth- and thirteenth-century medieval rabbinic literature from Germany and France, containing a number of attributed formulations that appear nowhere else. *Haggahot Maimuniyyot* is included in standard editions of the *Mishneh Torah* (the first part appeared in the Constantinople edition of 1509). There are numerous manuscript versions that have not yet been investigated thoroughly. Manuscript evidence suggests that the comments were originally added as glosses in the margins of the *Mishneh Torah*.

• Jose Faur, *ʿIyyunim be-Mishneh Torah leha-Rambam* (Jerusalem, 1978). Maurice-Ruben Hayoun, "Moses Maimonides (1138–1204) und Meir von Rothenburg (1215–1293)," in *Zur Geschichte der mittelalterlichen jüdischen Gemeinde in Rothenburgh ob der Tauber* (Rothenburg, 1993). Efraim E. Urbach, *Baʿalei ha-Tosafot* (Jerusalem, 1980), vol. 2, pp. 553–556.

—EPHRAIM KANARFOGEL

HAGGAI (6th cent. BCE), prophet in the kingdom of Judah during the period of restoration after the Babylonian exile; contemporary of *Zechariah. Haggai delivered four addresses to the postexilic Jewish community in Jerusalem over the course of three months during the fall of 520 BCE in support of efforts to build the Second Temple. This was a period of widespread political chaos within the Persian empire, during which Darius I fought to establish his control. Haggai maintained that the time had come to rebuild the Temple, that the nations would stream to Jerusalem to recognize God's sovereignty, and that *Zerubbabel, the Jewish governor of Judah under Persian rule and grandson of King Jehoiachin, would rule in Jerusalem. Haggai's role in rebuilding the Temple is noted in *Ezra* 5.1 and 6.14.

The *Book of Haggai* is the tenth book of the Minor Prophets. Haggai's first prophecy (1.1–11) contains an exhortation to rebuild the Temple and blames the anger of God, who brought on a drought, on their failure to do so. It continues (1.12–15) with a short narrative relating how the entire community along with its leaders, Zerubbabel (the governor) and Joshua (the high priest), took up the task of rebuilding the Temple. In Haggai's second prophecy (2.1–9) God consoles the people, telling them that although the Temple now being built is much less impressive than Solomon's, it will become even more glorious than the first. In his third prophecy (2.10–19), Haggai reiterates the prophetic note of the primacy of morality and reminds the people that the Temple does not confer holiness on those whose deeds are impure. The prophecy concludes with a promise of prosperity. Finally, *Haggai* 2.20–23 maintains that Zerubbabel will be recognized as God's "signet ring" or ruler at a time when the power of the nations will be overthrown.

According to rabbinic tradition, the book was edited by the Men of the *Keneset ha-Gedolah (*B. B.* 21a).

• Peter R. Ackroyd, *Exile and Restoration*, The Old Testament Library (London, 1968). R. J. Coggins, *Haggai, Zechariah, Malachi*, Old Testament Guides (Sheffield, Eng., 1987). Carol L. and Eric M. Meyers, *Hag-*

gai, Zechariah 1–8, The Anchor Bible, vol. 25B (Garden City, N.Y., 1987). David L. Petersen, *Haggai and Zechariah 1–8* (Philadelphia, 1984). Ralph L. Smith, *Micah–Malachi*, Word Biblical Commentary, vol. 32 (Waco, Tex., 1984). Hans Walter Wolff, *Haggai*, translated by Margaret Kohl (Minneapolis, 1988). —MARVIN A. SWEENEY

ḤAGGIM (חַגִּים; festivals). The Torah enumerates five festivals to be observed in the course of the year: the *Shalosh Regalim (the pilgrim festivals of *Pesaḥ, *Shavuʿot, and *Sukkot), the "day of blowing the trumpets" (see RO'SH HA-SHANAH), and *Yom Kippur, which, although observed as a fast, is included among the festivals. Ro'sh ha-Shanah and Yom Kippur are celebrated as purely religious occasions of judgment, atonement, and reconciliation with God, unlike the Shalosh Regalim, whose origins are historical and agricultural. Each of the Shalosh Regalim also has a liturgical name that does not appear in the Bible: the Season of Our Freedom (Pesaḥ), the Season of the Giving of Our Torah (Shavuʿot), and the Season of Our Rejoicing (Sukkot). Doubt is expressed in the Talmud about whether *Shemini ʿAtseret, with which the festival of Sukkot concludes (*Nm.* 29.35), is to be regarded as a separate festival or as the concluding day of Sukkot. During the period of the First Temple, *Ro'sh Ḥodesh, the new moon, was celebrated as a semifestival, but it has since completely lost its festive character. Ro'sh ha-Shanah is now observed both in Israel and in the Diaspora for two days; Yom Kippur, for one. The celebration of the other biblical festivals (the first and last day of Pesaḥ, Shavuʿot, the first day of Sukkot, Shemini ʿAtseret) has been extended in the Diaspora to two days (see YOM TOV SHENI SHEL GALUYYOT). Although the original reason for the extension no longer existed even in Talmudic times, the custom was retained, except in Reform Judiasm and in some Conservative circles. (*Beits.* 4b). On all these festivals (apart from the intermediate days; see ḤOL HA-MOʿED), abstention from work is obligatory. Yom Kippur, the "Sabbath of Sabbaths" (*Lv.* 23.32), is subject to the same prohibitions as the Sabbath. On the other festivals, unlike the Sabbath, carrying and the use of fire, both for cooking and other essential needs, are permitted. Shemini ʿAtseret (in the Diaspora, its second day) has developed as the special festival of *Simḥat Torah, on which the completion of the annual reading of the Torah in the synagogue is joyfully celebrated. To these major festivals a number of others have been added, to which the prohibition on work does not apply. These can be divided into full festivals, with their special ritual and liturgy, and semifestivals, which are little more than days commemorating events regarded as sufficiently significant to justify the omission of supplicatory prayers. To the former category belong *Ḥanukkah and *Purim (the latter, although its institution is recounted in the biblical *Book of *Esther*, has the character of a post-biblical festival). The minor post-biblical festivals (some of them now of folkloristic rather than liturgical consequence) include *Tu bi-Shevat, the traditional date of the death of Moses (7 Adar), *Lag ba-ʿOmer, *Pesaḥ Sheni, *Tu be-'Av, and *Hoshaʿna' Rabbah. In modern Israel, two further festivals have been added—*Yom ha-ʿAtsma'ut and *Yom Yerushalayim, which have received religious recognition from the Israel chief rabbinate. See also FESTIVAL PRAYERS.

• Theodor Gaster, *Festivals of the Jewish Year* (New York, 1953). Irving Greenberg, *The Jewish Way: Living the Holidays* (New York, 1993). Isaac Klein, *A Guide to Jewish Religious Practice* (New York, 1979), chaps. 4–18. Hayim Schoys, *Guide to Jewish Holy Days* (New York, 1964). Eliezer Schweid, *Sefer Maḥzor ha-Zemanim* (Tel Aviv, 1984). Michael Strassfeld, *The Jewish Holidays* (New York, 1985). Arthur Waskow, *Seasons of Our Joy* (New York, 1982). Shelomoh Z. Zevin, *Ha-Moʿadim be-Halakhah* (Tel Aviv, 1963).

ḤAGIGAH (חֲגִיגָה; festival offering), name of a sacrifice and of a Mishnaic tractate.

Sacrifice. Every worshiper was obliged to bring an animal sacrifice to the Temple on each of the *Shalosh Regalim. It had to be not less in value than two silver pieces. The lame, blind, sick, aged, and those incapable of going up to Jerusalem on foot were exempt from the obligation to bring the *ḥagigah*. After the prescribed parts (*Lv.* 3.15) had been offered on the altar, the remainder was consumed by the person who had brought the sacrifice. In order that the paschal lamb, consumed on the first night of Pesaḥ, be eaten to fulfill the religious commandment only and not to assuage hunger, a special *ḥagigah* was brought on the eve of Pesaḥ and served as the main course of the evening meal before the paschal lamb was served.

Tractate. *Ḥagigah* is the last tractate of Mishnah order Moʿed, consisting of three chapters, with related material in the Tosefta' and in both Talmuds. The tractate deals with the laws of pilgrimage to the Temple and with the sacrificial offerings that accompany the pilgrimage, particularly the *ḥagigah* offering. The latter half of the tractate discusses degrees of ritual purity and their correspondence to degrees of sanctity. The meticulous observance of these standards of purity caused a division between the Pharisaic community and the common folk (see ʿAM HA-'ARETS), yet these standards were relaxed on the festivals in order to enable all segments of the population to participate in the pilgrimage.

The laws of *ḥagigah* lacked a solid scriptural basis and served as a major source of halakhic controversy during Second Temple times. The sectarian overtones of this controversy serve as a point of departure for a discussion by the Mishnah and Talmud of the major ideas of early rabbinic mysticism.

The tractate in the Talmud Bavli was translated into English by Israel Abrahams in the Soncino Talmud (London, 1938).

• Chanoch Albeck, ed., *Shishah Sidrei Mishnah, Seder Moʿed* (Jerusalem, 1952). Philip Blackman, ed. and trans., *Mishnayot*, vol. 2, *Order Moʿed* (Gateshead, 1973). Pinhas Kehati, ed., *Mishnah: A New Translation with a Commentary, Seder Moʿed*, vol. 5, *Taʿanit, Megillah, Moʿed Qatan, Ḥagigah* (Jerusalem, 1991). Hermann Leberecht Strack, *Introduction to the Talmud and Midrash* (1931; Minneapolis, 1992). —AVRAHAM WALFISH

HAGIOGRAPHA, a term from Greek that refers to the third of the traditional tripartite divisions of the Bible, the Writings (Heb. Ketuvim), and the last to be canonized. It consists of *Psalms*, *Proverbs*, *Job*, *Song of Songs*, *Ruth*, *Lamentations*, *Ecclesiastes*, *Esther*, *Daniel*, *Ezra*, *Nehemiah*, *1 Chronicles*, and *2 Chronicles*.

• Thomas Henshaw, *The Writings: The Third Division of the Old Testament Canon* (London, 1963). S. Z. Leiman, *The Canonization of Hebrew Scriptures: The Talmudic and Midrashic Evidence*, 2d ed. (New Haven, 1991). Joseph Rosner, *The Story of the Writings* (New York, 1970).

–SHALOM PAUL

HAGIOGRAPHIES. There is no authentic Hebrew term for *hagiography*, though the practice of telling stories about great scholars and sages is prevalent in Hebrew literature. Joseph Dan has suggested using the term *shevaḥim* literature, because Hebrew collections of such narratives have been often called *shevaḥim* (from the Hebrew word meaning praise), like those dedicated to Yitsḥaq Luria and the Baʿal Shem Tov. Talmudic literature abounds with biographical material, historical and legendary, about the great Talmudic sages, especially the tanna'im, such as Hillel, R. Yoḥanan ben Zakk'ai, R. ʿAqiva', R. Eliʿezer ben Hurqanos, and many others. Talmudic and Midrashic clusters of such stories mark the beginnings of an independent literary genre. The eighth-century *midrash, Pirqei de-Rabbi Eliʿezer*, begins with two chapters dedicated to a legendary, miraculous biography of R. Eliʿezer, to whom the *midrash* is attributed. Hagiographies concerning ten noted tanna'im were gathered to create the narrative of the *Ten Martyrs, which is closely connected to the literature of the ancient mystics of the Talmudic period, the *yordei ha-merkavah*. Talmudic hagiography combines miraculous biography with ethical teaching, often including examples within the framework of the narrative.

Hebrew literature of the Middle Ages continued to relate and elaborate on narratives about the Talmudic sages (as well as, of course, biblical figures, within the continuous process of the retelling of the biblical and Talmudic narratives). Hagiographies written between the eighth and fifteenth century concerning central figures of Jewish culture are brief and scattered showing a reluctance to attribute miraculous biographies to medieval leaders. The one clear exception is the evolution of a hagiographic cycle around the leaders of Ashkenazi Jewry in the twelfth and thirteenth centuries, mainly around R. Yehudah ben Shemu'el he-Ḥasid and his father, R. Shemu'el. In the sixteenth century hagiography became a central genre of literary and religious expression. Rabbi Gedalyah ben David ibn Yaḥya', who wrote the sixteenth-century historical-hagiographic work *Shalshelet ha-Qabbalah*, was one of the first writers to present a cycle of stories about Rashi, Nahmanides, and others. Previously, stories about R. Yehudah ben Shemu'el he-Ḥasid and his circle had been collected, and they were later translated into Yiddish and published in the **Maʿaseh Book*. The best-known and most influential cycle was that around R. Yitsḥaq Luria, which evolved in the last years of the sixteenth century and was subsequently collected into *Shivḥei ha-'Ari* and *Toledot ha-'Ari*. A selection from the diary of Luria's disciple, R. Ḥayyim Vital, was published as *Shivḥei ha-Raḥu*. The Shabbatean movement of the seventeenth century created many narrative cycles around Shabbetai Tsevi and his prophet Natan of Gaza. The Hasidic collection of narratives *Shivḥei ha-Besht*, about the Baʿal Shem Tov, the founder of Hasidism, is probably the most developed and influential Hebrew hagiographic work. Following the success of this work (which was published in 1815), many Hasidic and non-Hasidic hagiographic collections were published, their heroes ranging from R. Shneur Zalman of Lyady to Maimonides, Yehudah Liva' ben Betsal'el of Prague, and Avraham ibn Ezra. The period between 1865 and 1914 marks the peak of creativity in this field, but hagiography has continued throughout the twentieth century; several such collections devoted to the rabbi of the Lubavitcher Hasidim, Menaḥem Mendel Schneerson (died 1994) have been published.

• Meir Benayahu, *Sefer Toledot ha-'Ari* (Jerusalem, 1967). Joseph Dan, "Sifrut ha-Shevaḥim," *Meḥqerei Yerushalayim be-Folklor Yehudi* 1 (1981): 82–100. Aryeh Wineman, "The Metamorphosis of Narrative Traditions: Two Stories from Sixteenth Century Safed," *AJS Review* 10 (1985): 165–180.

–JOSEPH DAN

ḤAGIZ FAMILY, family of Spanish origin that settled in Morocco and Erets Yisra'el, and in the sixteenth through the eighteenth century produced many rabbis and scholars.

Yaʿaqov Ḥagiz (1620–1674), rabbinic scholar. Raised in the Sephardi rabbinic tradition, he migrated in 1645 from North Africa to Verona, Italy, where he established a Hebrew printing press. From there he traveled to Venice and Leghorn, where he continued to publish. His early works were intended to integrate former Marranos into the Jewish community. His commentary on the Mishnah, *ʿEts ha-Ḥayyim* (Verona, 1645), reflected the emphasis in Sephardi rabbinic circles on Mishnah study. In 1658 he established the *yeshivah* Beit Yaʿaqov in Jerusalem, the most important Sephardi academy in Erets Yisra'el in the seventeenth century. His collection of *responsa, Halakhot Qetanot* (Venice, 1704), was one of the major halakhic works to emerge from his *yeshivah*. He hoped to ignite a spiritual revival of the Jewish community in Jerusalem, but his vision of building Jerusalem into a Jewish spiritual center turned into bitter disappointment at the eruption of the Shabbatean messianic movement, whose prophet, *Natan of Gaza, was his former disciple. He resolutely opposed the messianic movement from its inception. He translated Yitsḥaq Aboab's *Menorat ha-Ma'or* into Spanish (Leghorn, 1656).

Mosheh Ḥagiz (c.1671–1751), scholar and kabbalist; son of Yaʿaqov. He was born in Jerusalem and migrated to western Europe, where he became an outspoken critic of the Sephardi communities for their lack of respect for rabbinic authority and their breaches in observance of the law. Author and editor of many halakhic and kabbalistic works, his chief renown derived from his relentless pursuit of suspected Shabbateans, against whom he orchestrated three major rabbinic campaigns: between 1713 and 1715, against Neḥemyah *Ḥayon in Amsterdam; between 1725 and 1726 against Shabbatean emissaries in eastern Europe, including Yonatan *Eybeschuetz; and between 1730 and 1735 against the Italian writer and kabbalist Mosheh Ḥayyim *Luzzatto. *Shever Poshʿim* (London/Amsterdam, 1714) is an example of Ḥagiz's virulent anti-Shabbatean polemics. His major work, *Mishnat Ḥakhamim* (Wandsbek, 1733), a compendium of rabbinic lore, appealed for restoration of rabbinic authority in Jewish society. He returned to Erets Yisra'el in 1738.

• Raphael Biton, *Ḥayyav u-Mishnato shel Rabbi Yaʿaqov Ḥagiz* (Ramat Gan, 1983). Elisheva Carlebach, *The Pursuit of Heresy: Rabbi Moses Hagiz and the Sabbatian Controversies* (New York, 1990).

—ELISHEVA CARLEBACH

ḤAHAM. See Ḥakham.

HA-ḤINNUKH, SEFER. See Sefer ha-Ḥinnukh.

HA'I GA'ON (939–1038), ga'on of the Babylonian academy of *Pumbedita, which under his direction reached the zenith of its fame. A son of *Sherira' ben Ḥanina' Ga'on, Ha'i was appointed *av beit din* in 984 and succeeded to the office of ga'on upon his father's retirement in approximately 998. In addition to the traditional geonic activity of writing *responsa*, Ha'i followed a number of the precedents set by *Saʿadyah ben Yosef Ga'on; he wrote Judeo-Arabic monographs on selected legal topics, Hebrew liturgical poetry, and a Hebrew-Arabic dictionary entitled *Kitab al-Hawi*, covering Biblical and some Rabbinic Hebrew. Most of Ha'i's Arabic-language writings are still unpublished, but two of his major legal monographs were translated into Hebrew in his lifetime or shortly thereafter; these are *Sefer ha-Meqaḥ veha-Memkar* (on the law of sale; a Venice edition was published in 1602) and *Sefer Mishpetei Shevuʿot* (on judicial oaths; a Venice edition was published in 1602). At least one thousand of his *responsa* to queries from all parts of the Jewish world have been preserved. He was the author of prayers and *piyyutim*, notably five *seliḥot* for Tishʿah be-'Av. Ha'i was generally regarded as "the last of the ge'onim in time, but the first in eminence."

• Tsvi Groner, *The Legal Methodology of Ha'i Ga'on* (Chico, Calif., 1985). Tsvi Groner, "Reshimat Teshuvot Rav Ha'i Ga'on," *ʿAlei Sefer* 13 (1986). Esriel Erich Hildesheimer, *Mystik und Agada im Urteile der Gaonen R. Scherira und R. Hai* (Frankfurt am Main, 1931). Yehudah Leib Maimon, ed., *Rav Ha'i Ga'on* (Jerusalem, 1938).

—ROBERT BRODY

ḤAKHAM (חָכָם; wise man, sage), a term originally used in a general, descriptive sense (for example, in *Proverbs*) and applied to both Jews and non-Jews. Thus, the Talmud speaks repeatedly of *ḥakhmei ummot ha-ʿolam*, "the wise men of the nations of the world" (e.g., *Pes.* 93b). Subsequently *ḥakham* became a specific title in both Erets Yisra'el and Babylonia. In the tannaitic period, the office indicated by the title *ḥakham* was ranked third in the *Sanhedrin after the *nasi'* (president) and *av beit din* (head of the court of law) (*Hor.* 13b). The plural *ḥakhamim* is generally used in the Talmud to designate the majority of scholars as opposed to a single authority. In Sephardi communities, the title is given to fully ordained rabbis; in England, the chief Sephardi rabbi is called Haham. See also Ḥakham Bashi; Ḥazal.

—SHMUEL HIMELSTEIN

ḤAKHAM BASHI (chief sage), under Turkish rule, the title accorded a chief rabbi who was recognized by the government as the representative of the Jewish community. The *ḥakham bashi* was originally granted wide powers (later curtailed) by the authorities, including the right to judge Jews, collect taxes, appoint rabbis, and even impose punishments. The term was also employed for leading provincial rabbis. This title was held by the chief rabbis of Turkey (who resided in Constantinople) and Egypt, as well as by the Sephardi chief rabbi of Erets Yisra'el until 1918. The Turkish *ḥakham bashi* wore special gold and silver garments, and Muslims as well as Jews were required to show him respect.

• Simon Schwarzfuchs, *A Concise History of the Rabbinate* (Oxford and Cambridge, 1993).

—SHMUEL HIMELSTEIN

ḤAKHAM TSEVI. See Ashkenazi, Tsevi Hirsch.

HAKHNASAT KALLAH (הַכְנָסַת כַּלָּה; bringing in a bride [under the wedding canopy]), the provision of a dowry to a poor girl. According to a passage in the Talmud (*Suk.* 49b; see Rashi on *Suk.* 49b) the essential virtue of this good deed lay in the secret manner in which it was performed: the bride must not be put to shame. *Hakhnasat kallah* is one of the few good deeds that takes precedence even over the study of Torah (*Meg.* 3b). Since the Middle Ages special societies have existed for the purpose of *hakhnasat kallah*. The inclusion of this virtuous custom in the prayer-book version of Mishnah *Pe'ah* 1.2 as being one of those acts "the fruits of which a man enjoys in this world, while the stock remains for him in the world to come" has no basis in rabbinic literature but illustrates the great value attached to this act of charity.

• Yosef Freund, "The Marriage and the Dowry," *Jewish Bible Quarterly* 23 (1995): 248–251. Gesellschaft Hachnassath-Kallah, Berlin, *Statuten* (Berlin, 1905). Kerry M. Olitzky, *The Jewish Wedding Ceremony* (Hoboken, N.J., 1996). Wilhelmina C. Pieterse, *350 jaar Dotar* (Amsterdam, 1965), with an English summary.

HAKHNASAT OREḤIM. See Hospitality.

ḤAKIM, SHEMU'EL HA-LEVI IBN (c.1480–1547), rabbinical scholar. He came from a family of Spanish origin that had settled in Cairo. Around 1527, he moved to Constantinople. Faced with problems caused by the arrival of Jewish and Marrano refugees from Spain, he issued rulings on the laws of personal status. He showed tolerance both to the Marranos and especially to the *Karaites. He classed the latter as "inadvertent sinners," allowing intermarriage with them and recognizing Karaite divorce.

• Michael Corinaldi, *Ha-Maʿamad ha-'Ishi shel ha-Qara'im* (Jerusalem, 1984), pp. 116–121. Louis M. Epstein, *Marriage Laws in the Bible and Talmud* (Cambridge, Mass., 1942), pp. 214–219.

—SHALOM BAR-ASHER

HA' LAḤMA' ʿANYA' (Aram.; הָא לַחְמָא עַנְיָא; "This is the bread of affliction"), opening words of the introductory paragraph to the Seder service. The text is composite and varies slightly from rite to rite. In some rites, for example, it is preceded by the words "In haste did you go out of Egypt." Ha' Laḥma' ʿAnya' is very old, though its exact date and provenance are the subject of debate. The invitation to all that are hungry to come and partake of the Pesaḥ meal may presuppose that the Temple is no longer in existence, as does the conclusion to the passage, "Next year in Jerusalem . . . next year free."

• Joseph Elias, *Passover Haggadah: With Translation and a New Commentary*, 3d ed. (New York, 1994).

HALAKHAH (הֲלָכָה), a term that refers to the legal, as opposed to the nonlegal or aggadic (see AGGADAH), aspect of Judaism. It is also used to indicate a definitive ruling in any particular area of Jewish law. The Hebrew root of *halakhah* means "to go," and the Bible refers to the fulfillment of the Torah as the way in which the people "are to go" (*Ex.* 18.20). The use of the term *halakhah* may also serve as an indication of the dynamic quality of Jewish law.

The Written Law and Its Interpretation. The process of interpreting the written law begins in the Bible itself and reaches a high point with Ezra, who "interpreted the Torah" (*Ezr.* 7.10) in order to enable the people to "understand Scripture" (*Neh.* 8.1). The tanna'im continued this process, developing hermeneutical principles (see HERMENEUTICS) that were consolidated into the thirteen *middot* of R. Yishma'e'l ben Elisha' (*Sifra'*, Introduction). The consensus among rabbinic authorities is that laws derived by means of these *middot* are biblical in nature (see I. Herzog, *Main Institutions of Jewish Law* [1965–1967]). A debate arose between the schools of R. Yishma'e'l and R. 'Aqiva' regarding the extent to which new laws could be legitimately derived from superfluous words in the biblical text. According to the school of R. Yishma'e'l, "the Torah speaks in the language of men"; hence not every apparent semantic redundancy should be used as the basis for deriving a new law. The school of R.'Aqiva', however, rejected the idea that words in the Torah were there purely for literary effect and, as a result, derived halakhic rulings from particles such as *and* and *if*. Indeed, in a dramatic Talmudic passage, the view is recorded that the purpose of the decorative crowns attached to some of the letters in the Torah was to provide R. 'Aqiva' with grist for his hermeneutical mill (*Men.* 29b). The interpretation of the written law as a source for *halakhah* virtually ceased after the tannaitic period, and the focus of halakhic legal creativity shifted to the *Mishnah. This development is reflected in a significant change in the literary form of the *oral law. Prior to the redaction of the Mishnah, much of the rabbinic interpretation of scripture was recorded in the form of glosses to biblical passages, which are known by the generic term *midrash halakhah*. The Mishnah, however, sets out the oral law according to subject matter rather than biblical sources. Halakhic discussion since the Mishnah has, therefore, focused on the *Talmud rather than on the biblical text. There are two versions of the Talmud: the Talmud Yerushalmi and the Talmud Bavli. The latter became the more authoritative and is regarded as the final and overriding exposition of the oral law. The most powerful statement of the halakhic authority of the Talmud is found in Maimonides' introductory remarks to his *Mishneh Torah*: "All Israel is obliged to follow the matters stated in the Babylonian Talmud. Every city and every province are to be coerced to follow all the customs that the sages of the Talmud followed and to obey their decisions and follow their enactments since all the matters in the Talmud have been accepted by all Israel. And those sages who made the enactments or introduced the decrees or ordained the customs or decided the laws, teaching that the decision was so, were all the sages of Israel or the majority of them. And they heard by tradition the main principles of the whole Torah generation after generation reaching back to the generation of Moses our teacher."

Rules for deciding the *halakhah* in a Talmudic dispute are found in the Talmud itself and were refined and expanded by the savora'im, ge'onim, and *ri'shonim*. Of special significance is the principle of *hilkhata' ke-vatrai*, according to which the *halakhah* follows the rulings of the later authorities.

Rabbinic Legislation. The biblical source for the power of the rabbis to enact legislation is discussed in the Talmud (*Shab.* 21b), and Maimonides is of the view that it lies in the biblical charge to "act in accordance with the instructions given to you [by the Court]" and "not to deviate from that which they will tell you" (*Dt.* 17.10–11; *Hilkhot Mamrim* 1.1–2). Nahmanides opts for the less weighty verse: "Ask your father, he will inform you; your elders, they will tell you" (*Dt.* 32.7; Nahmanides' Glosses to Maimonides' *Sefer ha-Mitsvot, Shoresh* 1). A useful rule of thumb is that preventive enactments, such as *muqtseh* and not blowing the shofar on Ro'sh ha-Shanah when it falls on Shabbat, are called *gezerot* (see GEZERAH), whereas positive legislation, such as the *ketubbah* and Hillel's *perozbol*, is referred to by the term **taqqanah*. In general, rabbinic legislation may not come into conflict with a negative biblical commandment, although exceptions are made in the cases of *'agunot* and in cases where the maintenance of communal religious values are at stake (*Yev.* 16.17, 90b). The apparent contradiction between the power of the rabbis to legislate and the scriptural prohibition against adding to and subtracting from the Torah (*Dt.* 4.2, 13.1) is resolved, according to Maimonides, if it is made clear that the enactment is of rabbinic status only and that it is for the purpose of protecting or enhancing Torah law (*Hilkhot Mamrim* 2.9). In general, enactments must be accepted by the public before they become fully binding, but once they are widely accepted, they may not be overturned by a later court unless "it is greater in wisdom and numbers" than the enacting tribunal (*'Eduy.* 1.5; *Hilkhot Mamrim* 2.9). A significant body of medieval halakhah is devoted to communal enactments (**taqqanot ha-qahal*), which regulated much of the public and administrative affairs of Jewish communities in the Middle Ages and at the dawn of modernity. The creation of the chief rabbinate under the British Mandate in Palestine in 1921 prompted R. Avraham Kook, the Ashkenazi chief rabbi, to suggest the *taqqanah* as the means by which the gap between *halakhah* and modernity might be resolved. To this end, a number of *taqqanot* were passed, including the establishment of a Rabbinical Appeals Court and the raising of the legal age of marriage. After this early period, however, the Israeli chief rabbinate virtually ceased to enact *taqqanot*, with the sole exception of R. Isaac Herzog, who prepared detailed *taqqanot* on matters of inheritance in the early years of the State.

Custom. In the Talmud, custom (**minhag*) constitutes a means of resolving halakhic disputes in ritual matters (*Ber.* 45a; *Pes.* 66a) and is a source of *halakhah* in commercial and civil law (*B. M.* 74a). The principle that "custom overrides *halakhah*" is found only in the Jerusalem Talmud and is restricted to civil law. Customs in the ritual sphere that have no basis in *halakhah* ought, nevertheless, to be respected, provided that they do not conflict with any halakhic norm. Among the medieval authorities, R. Yaʿaqov ben Me'ir Tam stands out as a principled opponent of non-halakhic customs (*Tosafot, Ber.* 48a, *s.v. velet; B. B.* 2a, *s.v. bigvil*), and his attitude is echoed by the eighteenth-century authority R. Yeḥezqe'l *Landau of Prague (*Noda' bi-Yehudah, Yoreh Deʿah, Hilkhot Niddah* no. 54). Custom played an important role in the development of Orthodoxy, which regarded the maintenance of stringent customs as a prerequisite for the preservation of Jewish life in the post-Emancipation period.

Precedent. Notwithstanding any doctrine of binding precedent (**maʿaseh*) in the *halakhah*, the Talmud emphasizes the binding nature of decided cases (*Yev.* 46b) and the persuasive authority of practice (*R. ha-Sh.* 29b). The need to distinguish a precedent in terms of the facts of the case is a well-developed concept in Talmudic law (*B. B.* 130b; *B. M.* 36a). The importance of practical *halakhah* is an established principle in Jewish law and provides the basis for the significant normative authority enjoyed by **responsa* in halakhic literature.

Rational Principles. The principle that one life may not be preferred over another is derived from a **sevarah* (*San.* 74a), as is the procedural rule that in civil suits the burden of proof lies with the plaintiff (B. Q. 46b). Laws derived on the basis of *sevarah* possess biblical status.

Literary Sources of Halakhah. The two major sources of *halakhah* in post-Talmudic times are halakhic codes and rabbinic *responsa*. The most influential codes are the *Sefer ha-Halakhot* by R. Yitsḥaq Alfasi; the *Mishneh Torah* by Maimonides; *Pisqei ha-Ro'sh* by R. Asher ben Yeḥi'el; *Arbaʿah Turim* by R. Yaʿaqov ben Asher; and the *Shulḥan ʿArukh* by R. Yosef Karo, together with R. Mosheh Isserles's *Mappah*. The *Shulḥan ʿArukh* was chosen as the major code for expansion and development by later authorities, and this has remained the pattern in Orthodox circles. Rabbinic *responsa* constitute the dynamic side of halakhic literature and are the main source for the application of *halakhah* to the problems posed by modernity.

Halakhah and Ethics. The emancipation of European Jewry created a situation in which *halakhah* fell into disrepute in the eyes of many Jews eager to adapt to the ways of their non-Jewish environment. As a result, it was totally rejected as a way of life by the Reform movement. The Conservative movement maintains the belief that *halakhah* is central to Jewish life but seeks ways of bringing it into line with modern values. Orthodox Judaism strives to maintain its strong commitment to *halakhah* but recognizes the need to avoid falling into the trap of halakhic formalism. Modern Reform Judaism has developed a new interest in *halakhah* and has produced *responsa* on halakhic subjects from a Reform perspective. See also JEWISH LAW; MIDRASH.

• Eliezer Berkovits, *Not In Heaven: The Nature and Function of Halakha* (New York, 1983). J. David Bleich, *Contemporary Halakhic Problems*, 4 vols. (New York, 1973–1995). Zevi Chajes, *The Student's Guide Through the Talmud* (London, 1952). Dan Cohn-Sherbok, "Law in Reform Judaism: A Study of Solomon Freehof," *Jewish Law Annual* 7 (1988): 198–209. David Weiss Halivni, *Peshat and Derash: Plain and Applied Meaning in Rabbinic Exegesis* (New York, 1991). Bernard Jackson, ed., *The Halakhic Thought of R. Isaac Herzog* (Atlanta, 1991). Louis Jacobs, *A Tree of Life: Diversity, Flexibility, and Creativity in Jewish Law* (Oxford, 1984). Immanuel Jakobovits, *Jewish Law Faces Modern Problems* (New York, 1965). Lawrence Kaplan, "Rabbi Joseph B. Soloveitchik's Philosophy of Halakhah," *Jewish Law Annual* 7 (1988): 139–197. A. Lichtenstein, "Does Jewish Tradition Recognize an Ethic Independent of Halakhah?" in *Jewish Law and Legal Theory*, edited by Martin Golding (Aldershot, 1994), pp. 155–182. David Novak, "Natural Law, *Halakhah* and the Covenant," *Jewish Law Annual* 7 (1988): 43–67. Joel Roth, *The Halakhic Process: A Systemic Analysis* (New York, 1986). Efraim E. Urbach, *The Halakhah: Its Sources and Development* (Tel Aviv, 1986). –DANIEL SINCLAIR

HALAKHAH LE-MOSHEH MI-SINAI (הֲלָכָה לְמֹשֶׁה מִסִּינַי; a law [transmitted orally] to Moses from [Mount] Sinai), laws regarded by the Talmud, while never stated explicitly in scripture or derived from it, as having biblical authority. Since a number of these laws were clearly post-Mosaic, some medieval commentators noted that the term was also used to describe laws that were beyond any doubt, as if they had been given to Moses at Sinai. Shemu'el Safrai has shown that early rabbinic literature did not recognize a special category of laws given to Moses at Sinai and that the term is nothing more than a rabbinic flourish that originally was not meant to be taken literally. However, over time these laws were regarded as being in a class by themselves, irrefutable.

• *Entsiqlopedyah Talmudit* (Jerusalem, 1947–), vol. 9, pp. 365–387. S. Safrai, "Halakhah le-Mosheh mi-Sinai: Historyah o Teologyah?" in *Meḥqerei Talmud*, edited by Yaacov Sussman and David Rosenthal (Jerusalem, 1990), pp. 11–38. –MARC SHAPIRO

HALAKHOT GEDOLOT, a compilation of legal decisions from the geonic period. This ninth-century work is attributed by reliable authorities, including the last ge'onim (see GA'ON), to R. Shimʿon Qayyara', of whom almost nothing is known. (Many medieval authors, especially in the Franco-German sphere, mistakenly attributed it to the better-known *Yehuda'i ben Naḥman Ga'on.) The work incorporates a wide range of sources, most prominently the *responsa* of *Aha' of Shabḥa and **Halakhot Pesuqot*, large sections of which are copied verbatim. *Halakhot Gedolot* was widely cited by medieval authors and probably constituted their most important source for the teachings of the geonic period. It was first published in Venice in 1548 and, most recently, edited by E. Hildesheimer (Berlin, 1888–1892; repr. Jerusalem, 1971–1987).

• Neil Danzig, *Mavo' le-Sefer Halakhot Pesuqot* (New York, 1993).
–ROBERT BRODY

HALAKHOT PESUQOT, halakhic work from the geonic period. It was attributed to *Yehuda'i ben Naḥman Ga'on, but this attribution is problematic.

Written in a mixture of Hebrew and Aramaic, it was soon translated both into Hebrew (*Hilkhot Re'u*) and into Arabic and served as the basis of the slightly later **Halakhot Gedolot*. *Halakhot Pesuqot* represents the earliest known attempt to present a comprehensive digest of practical *halakhah* and combines abridged Talmudic passages with post-Talmudic formulations. Although the book was often quoted, it was not until 1911 that a partial manuscript was found in Yemen. It was published by Solomon Sassoon in 1950 (*Sefer Halakhot Pesuqot le-Rav Yehuda'i Ga'on*). The section "Hilkhot Terefot" was published by Mordecai Margaliot in *Talpioth* 8 (1963): 307–330.

• Neil Danzig, *Mavo' le-Sefer Halakhot Pesuqot* (Jerusalem, 1993). Leon Sclosberg, ed., *Sefer Halakhot Pesuqot o Hilkhot Re'u ha-Meyuḥasot le-Talmidei Rav Yehuda'i Ga'on* (1886; Jerusalem, 1967). Meyer Waxman, *A History of Jewish Literature* (New York, 1960). —ROBERT BRODY

HALAKHOT QETSUVOT, an anonymous medieval halakhic code written in Hebrew, erroneously attributed to *Yehuda'i ben Naḥman Ga'on. It is topically arranged and treats selected subjects (largely related to the Sabbath and holidays) briefly, without citing Talmudic sources. It presents an amalgamation of Babylonian and Palestinian halakhic traditions but also contains a number of egregious errors. The work is thought to have originated in Italy in the ninth century, but supporting evidence is weak. It was first published by C. M. Horowitz in 1881 and then by Mordecai Margaliot in *Sefer Halakhot Qetsuvot Meyuḥas le-Rav Yehuda'i Ga'on* (1942).

• Victor Aptowitzer, *Meḥqarim be-Sifrut ha-Ge'onim* (Jerusalem, 1941), pp. 27, 84, 91–95. —ROBERT BRODY

HALBERSTAM, ḤAYYIM (1797–1876), Hasidic master. While serving as rabbi in Rudnik (from 1817), Halberstam became a disciple of R. Naftali of Ropczyce. After 1830, when Halberstam was appointed communal rabbi of Nowy Sącz in Western Galicia, he began to conduct himself as a Hasidic master as well. His renown as a Talmudic scholar served to advance the growing acceptance of Ḥasidism among the Galician learned elite. Beginning in 1869, Halberstam conducted a campaign against the luxurious lifestyles of the Friedmann dynasty of Ruzhin. This controversy lasted some thirty years and caused great consternation and internal division within Hasidism. Halberstam's teachings are contained in *Divrei Ḥayyim* (Mukachevo, 1887–1888). He was the progenitor of an important Hasidic dynasty, the descendants of which include the rabbis of Sieniawa, Klausenburg, and Bobowa.

• *Entsiqlopedyah la-Ḥasidut*, vol. 2 (Jerusalem, 1986), pp. 542–549. Joseph Scheinberger, ed., *Sefer Otsar ha-Ḥayyim* (Brooklyn, N.Y., 1962). —ARTHUR GREEN

HA-LEVI, AVRAHAM. See AVRAHAM HA-LEVI.

HA-LEVI, YEHUDAH. See YEHUDAH HA-LEVI.

HALEVY, ISAAC (1847–1914), scholar of the oral law. Born in Ivenets (Belorussia), Halevy studied at and later became *gabba'i* of the Volozhin Yeshivah. After his Vilna tea business went bankrupt in 1895, Halevy briefly sojourned in Frankfurt, London, Paris, Pressburg, and Homburg, but in 1902 he settled in Hamburg, where he was appointed rabbi. An outspoken advocate of Orthodox Judaism, Halevy helped establish the *Agudat Israel in 1912, as well as the Frankfurt Jüdisch-Literarisch Gesellschaft in 1901. Halevy's contribution to scholarship, *Dorot ha-Ri'shonim* (6 vols. [1897–1964]), attempted to reestablish the centrality of tradition to Jewish scholarship and challenged the various nineteenth-century critical, historical conceptualizations of the rabbinic tradition (Naḥman Krochmal, Shelomoh Yehudah Leib Rapoport, Zacharias Frankel, Heinrich Graetz).

• Moses Auerbach, ed., *Sefer Zikkaron le-Rabbi Yitsḥaq Ayzik ha-Levy* (Bene Beraq, 1964). O. Asher Reichel, *Isaac Halevy: Spokesman and Historian of Jewish Tradition* (New York, 1969). —DIDIER Y. REISS

ḤALITSAH. See LEVIRATE MARRIAGE.

ḤALLAH (חַלָּה), name of a dough offering and of a Mishnaic tractate.

Dough Offering. *Ḥallah* is the part of the dough separated out as a gift for the priest (*Nm.* 15.7–21). Any dough made from the flour of wheat, barley, spelt, rye, or oats (*Ḥal.* 1.1), and no less in volume than approximately three pounds, twelve ounces, was subject to the laws of *ḥallah*. The amount to be separated out was one twenty-fourth of the "dough of the householder" or one forty-eighth of the "dough of the baker." *Ḥallah* had the same ritual status as the heave offering (**terumah*) and was originally obligatory in Erets Yisra'el only. In order that the precept should not be forgotten, however, the rabbis ordained its observance throughout the Diaspora. After the destruction of the Temple the separated portion could no longer be given to the priest; it was therefore burnt. Since it is usually the woman who bakes in the home, the dictate of *ḥallah* is enjoined particularly upon her (*Shab.* 2.7): she takes a tiny quantity of the dough (the size of an olive), as a symbolic reminder, throws it into the oven or fire to be burned, and recites a special blessing. The loaves baked for Sabbath and festival meals are called *ḥallot*, since their preparation provides one with the opportunity to perform the duty of separating out the *ḥallah* portion.

• Abraham Havivi, "Mishnah Hallah Chapter One: Translation and Commentary," in *Approaches to Ancient Judaism*, vol. 3, edited by William Green (Chico, Calif., 1981), pp. 149–184. —CHAIM PEARL

Tractate. The tractate *Ḥallah* is in Mishnah order Zera'im and consists of four chapters, with related material in the Tosefta' and in the Talmud Yerushalmi. It deals with the biblical command to separate *ḥallah* from "the first of your kneading trough" (*Nm.* 15.20) as a heave offering to God. Even though the taking of *ḥallah* is biblically mandated only "when you come into the land" (*Nm.* 15.18), the Mishnah requires its separation for dough produced in Erets Yisra'el from grain grown elsewhere. There is some controversy regarding dough produced outside Erets Yisra'el from Israel-grown grain. *Ḥallah* is an important source for the halakhic definition of the boundaries of the land of Israel, as well as the halakhic definition of bread.

The Mishnah tractate was translated into English by Herbert Danby in *The Mishnah* (Oxford, 1933).

• Chanoch Albeck, ed., *Shishah Sidrei Mishnah, Seder Zera'im* (Jerusalem, 1957). Philip Blackman, ed. and trans., *Mishnayoth*, vol. 1, *Order Zera'im* (Gateshead, 1973). Pinhas Kehati, ed., *Mishnah: A New Translation with a Commentary, Seder Zera'im*, vol. 3, *Ma'aser Sheni, Ḥallah, 'Orlah, Bikkurim* (Jerusalem, 1994). Hermann Leberecht Strack, *Introduction to the Talmud and Midrash* (1931; Minneapolis, 1992).

—AVRAHAM WALFISH

HALLEL (הַלֵּל; praise), a generic term for "praise with psalms," of which there are three known varieties: the Egyptian, the Great, and the Daily Hallel. The most widely known is the Egyptian Hallel (*Ps.* 113–118), so named because of the reference to the Exodus in *Psalms* 114.1. The Daily Hallel (*Ps.* 145–150) is recited every morning as part of the synagogue service, and the Great Hallel (*Ps.* 136) is featured as part of the Pesaḥ Seder along with the Egyptian Hallel (see *Pes.* 118a). The Egyptian Hallel is recited in the synagogue after the morning service on the *Shalosh Regalim and on Ḥanukkah. The custom originated in Temple times when Hallel was recited during the offering of the pilgrims' sacrifices on Pesaḥ eve, while the paschal lambs were being slaughtered, and again that night when they were eaten during the Seder (*Pes.* 5.7; 10.5–7; see HAGGADAH OF PESAḤ). Talmudic sources indicate different manners of reciting the Hallel, either antiphonally, with the reader and congregation chanting alternate verses, or by the reader reciting aloud the entire Hallel with the congregation responding "hallelujah" after each verse, as is still the practice in the Yemenite rite. Among Ashkenazi Jews, it is usual for the congregation to recite each chapter silently and for the reader to repeat the conclusions aloud, but some passages are sung jointly. The latter verses of Psalm 118 are read twice to preserve the symmetry that marks the first part of the psalm. In some congregations, the Hallel is also recited on Pesaḥ eve in the synagogue. From the second day of Pesaḥ on (outside Erets Yisra'el, from the third day), an abbreviated Hallel, omitting the first parts of Psalm 115 and Psalm 116, is used. This shorter version (known as Half Hallel) is also recited on Ro'sh Ḥodesh; Hallel was not read in ancient Israel on this occasion and is hence not obligatory. A benediction is recited before the reading of Hallel (though not on Pesaḥ eve) and after it; authorities differ as to whether the blessing should be recited or omitted on Ro'sh Ḥodesh. On Purim no Hallel is read because according to the Talmud the reading of *Esther* takes its place. It is also recited each day during Ḥanukkah. In most synagogues in the State of Israel today, Hallel is read on Yom ha-'Atsma'ut, although the recitation of the benediction on this occasion is disputed. On Sukkot the worshipers hold the *lulav* and *etrog* in their hand during Hallel and shake them while reciting *Psalms* 118.1–4, 25, and 29. It is customary for the congregation to stand during the recitation of Hallel. Genizah discoveries have shown that alternative psalms were used in the past. Alternative forms, especially in the Daily Hallel, are also to be found in modern usage.

• Ismar Elbogen, *Jewish Liturgy: A Comprehensive History*, translated by Raymond P. Scheindlin (Philadelphia, 1993). Reuven Hammer, *Entering Jewish Prayer: A Guide to Personal Devotion and the Worship Service* (New York, 1994). Lawrence A. Hoffman, *The Canonization of the Synagogue Service* (Notre Dame, 1979). Abraham Z. Idelsohn, *Jewish Liturgy and Its Development* (New York, 1932). Isaac Klein, *A Guide to Jewish Religious Practice* (New York, 1992). Abraham Millgram, *Jewish Worship* (Philadelphia, 1975). Stefan C. Reif, *Judaism and Hebrew Prayer: New Perspectives on Jewish Liturgical History* (Cambridge, 1993).

—PETER KNOBEL

HALLELUJAH ("Praise [ye] the Lord"), liturgical exclamation occurring at the beginning and end of many psalms; in the Talmudic period it served as a congregational response during the recitation of the Great *Hallel (*Suk.* 3.10). The word also has become an inseparable part of the Christian tradition of praise and worship.

• Joseph Heinemann, *Prayer in the Talmud: Forms and Patterns* (Berlin, 1977). Jacob Mann, *The Bible as Read and Preached in the Old Synagogue*, 2 vols. (New York, 1966–1971).

ḤALUQQAH (חֲלֻקָּה; distribution), financial support given from the end of the eighteenth century onward to pious Ashkenazi Jews in the four holy cities of Jerusalem, Hebron, Safed, and Tiberias. From the beginning of Second Temple times, Diaspora Jewry sent assistance to Jerusalem (*Ezr.* 1.6) and the custom endured in all periods of Jewish settlement in the *Holy Land. This was regarded as the continuation of the *shekel tax sent to the Temple. Thus in the Mishnaic period, leading rabbis traveled extensively to collect money for the Palestinian academies; *sheliḥei Tsiyyon* (emissaries of Zion) were sent abroad with a similar object in amoraic and geonic times. In 1623 Yesha'yahu Horowitz, chief Ashkenazi rabbi of Jerusalem, organized fixed help from communities in central Europe (see ME'IR BA'AL HA-NES). The modern concept of *ḥaluqqah* dates from the Hasidic immigration of 1777. The nineteenth century saw the proliferation in the four cities of small communities (*kolelim*) that distributed the money collected abroad. Special emissaries (see MESHULLAḤ; also known as *shadar* [*shaliaḥ de-rabbanan*]), many of them distinguished Torah scholars, were sent to Jewish communities throughout the world to solicit funds for the support of scholars, pious Torah students, and the poor of the Holy Land. By 1913, 80 percent of the Ashkenazi communities in Jerusalem lived on *ḥaluqqah*, and there were twenty-nine *kolelim*; for example, Kolel Austria-Galicia, Kolel Holland-Germany, and Kolel Pinsk. Support from Europe came to an end with World War II, but Orthodox Jews in the United States still contribute considerable funds to maintain pious Jews in Erets Yisra'el who devote themselves to rabbinical studies.

• Y. Barnay, *The Jews in Palestine in the Eighteenth Century: Under the Patronage of the Istanbul Committee of Officials for Palestine*, translated by Naomi Goldblum, Judaic Studies Series (Tuscaloosa, Ala., 1992). Menahem Mendel Eilbaum, *Erets ha-Tsevi*, Sifriyyah le-Toledot ha-Yishuv ha-Yehudi be-Erets Yisra'el (Vienna, 1882–1883; Jerusalem, 1982). Joseph Joel Rivlin and Benjamin Rivlin, eds., *Iggerot ha-Peqidim veha-Amarqalim me-Amsterdam*, 3 vols. (Jerusalem, 1965). Abraham Yaari, *Sheluḥei Erets Yisra'el: Ha-Sheliḥut meha-Arets la-Golah me-Ḥurban Bayit Sheni 'ad ha-Me'ah ha-Tisha' 'Esreh* (Jerusalem, 1950–1951).

ḤAMA' BAR ḤANINA' (3d cent.), Palestinian amora'. He resided in Sepphoris, where his father, the more prominent R. *Ḥanina' bar Ḥama', headed an academy. Both of them were wealthy, a subject sometimes alluded to in Talmudic anecdotes (Y., *Pe'ah* 8.9, 21b). Ḥama' is known especially for his aggadic interpretations (frequently transmitted by R. Levi, most notably in

Tanḥuma'-Yelammedenu); his halakhic teachings are less common (e.g., *Shab.* 147b). The saying "Great is repentance, for it brings healing to the world" (*Yoma'* 86a) is attributed to him.

• Wilhelm Bacher, *Die Agada der palästinensischen Amoräer* (1892–1899; Hildesheim, 1965). Aaron Hyman, *Toledot Tanna'im ve-'Amora'im* (1910; Jerusalem, 1987). —MICHAEL L. BROWN

HAMAN, chief minister of King Ahasuerus of Persia and Media. As related in the *Book of Esther*, Haman secured a royal decree for the destruction of the Jews, ultimately based on *Mordecai's refusal to bow down before him, but his scheme was frustrated by *Esther. Haman and his sons were hanged on the gallows he had prepared for Mordecai. Haman is the central object of scorn in the celebration of the holiday of Purim, and his name is traditionally greeted with derisive interruptions during the synagogal reading of the *Book of Esther*. Haman is identified as a descendant of Agag the Amalekite, and his name has become a term for Jew-baiters.

• Michael V. Fox, *Character and Ideology in the Book of Esther* (Columbia, S.C., 1991), pp. 178–184. Carey A. Moore, *Esther*, The Anchor Bible, vol. 7B (Garden City, N.Y., 1971). —SHALOM PAUL

HA-MAVDIL (הַמַּבְדִּיל; He Who Separates), **piyyut* recited at the end of the *Havdalah ceremony. It alludes to the opening formula of the Birkat ha-Mavdil and to themes of the Yom Kippur *Ne'ilah service. It includes a request for God's forgiveness for wrongdoing and for a manifold progeny. It may have been originally intended for the Ne'ilah service, where it is recited in the Algerian rite. Following the acrostic, it has been attributed to Yitsḥaq ben Ghayyat (Spain, 11th cent.), but this is by no means certain, and there are other versions or elaborations in the various rites.

• B. S. Jacobson, *The Sabbath Service: An Exposition and Analysis of its Structure, Contents, Language and Ideas* (Tel Aviv, 1981), pp. 410–417. —PETER LENHARDT

ḤAMESH MEGILLOT (חָמֵשׁ מְגִלּוֹת; Five Scrolls), the biblical books *Song of Songs, Ruth, Lamentations, Ecclesiastes*, and *Esther* (see also BIBLE). In ancient times, all biblical books were written on scrolls; these five (as well as the *Torah) are regularly written on scrolls even today. The reason for their special designation is that they are read aloud, annually, in the synagogue, on fixed occasions. The most important of the five is *Esther* (known simply as the Megillah), read on Purim evening and morning; according to the sages, this practice was ordained by Mordecai and Esther themselves. Almost as ancient is the mournful, public reading of *Lamentations* on the eve of Tish'ah be-'Av (and in some congregations also on the morning), in commemoration of the destruction of the Temple. The custom of reading the other three scrolls in the synagogue is not universal and developed gradually. The *Song of Songs*, traditionally viewed as an allegory of God's "marriage" to Israel, which commenced with the Exodus from Egypt, is read on the Sabbath during Pesaḥ; *Ruth* is read on Shavu'ot, in light of its connection with the barley harvest and also because of its association with David, who traditionally was born and died on this date; *Ecclesiastes* is read on the Sabbath of Sukkot because of the book's preoccupation, however cynical, with joy and gladness. Only *Esther* is required to be read from an actual scroll; the other four often are read from scrolls (particularly in Ashkenazi congregations in Israel) but are just as likely to be read from a printed Bible. Today, most printed Bibles arrange these five books according to the order of the occasions on which they are read, beginning with *Song of Songs*.

• Abraham Cohen, *The Five Megilloth: Hebrew Text, English Translation and Commentary*, Soncino Books of the Bible, vol. 12 (London, 1983). Meir Zlotowitz et al., eds., *The Five Megillos: A New Translation with Overviews and Annotations Anthologized from the Classical Commentators* (Brooklyn, N.Y., 1986). —BARUCH J. SCHWARTZ

ḤAMETS (חָמֵץ; leaven), an agent of fermentation and the subject of biblical prohibitions of a ritual nature. The *halakhah* defines *ḥamets* as dough that has been kneaded from flour and water and allowed to stand until it has soured. In commemoration of the *Exodus, when the Israelites in leaving Egypt could not wait until their dough leavened (*Ex.* 12.39), only unleavened foods are permitted during *Pesaḥ; for, "whosoever shall consume leaven, that soul shall be cut off from the congregation of Israel" (*Ex.* 15.19). *Ḥamets* was also barred in the Temple meal offering (cf. *Lv.* 2.11). For a dough to be considered *ḥamets*, it must have stood for approximately eighteen minutes, after which time it is presumed to have begun fermenting. According to biblical law, only dough made from the five kinds of grain (*ḥamesh minim*), wheat, barley, spelt, rye, and oats, is considered *ḥamets*. Ashkenazim prohibit rice, corn, and millet and also forbid a range of legumes, including beans and peas. Whisky and other alcoholic beverages made from the fermentation of any of the five species of grain are also prohibited on Pesaḥ. All *ḥamets* is to be removed before Pesaḥ; food prepared for Pesaḥ is rendered unfit for consumption if even the smallest amount of *ḥamets* falls into it. Shortly before Pesaḥ, a thorough search of one's premises is undertaken in order to ensure that no *ḥamets* remains there (see BEDIQAT ḤAMETS). Any *ḥamets* found is burned the following morning (see BI'UR ḤAMETS), after which no benefit may be derived from *ḥamets* until after the festival. *Ḥamets* that may unknowingly have remained is declared ownerless. Where there was a large amount of *ḥamets*, it was feared that the owner might not wholeheartedly nullify his possession of it or destroy it. The custom, therefore, arose of selling the *ḥamets* to a non-Jew for a nominal sum and repurchasing it after Pesaḥ.

• Eliyahu Kitov, *The Book of Our Heritage: The Jewish Year and Its Days of Significance*, rev. ed. (Jerusalem and New York, 1978), pp. 165–199.

ḤAMISHAH 'ASAR BE-'AV. See TU BE-'AV.

ḤAMISHAH 'ASAR BI-SHEVAT. See TU BI-SHEVAT.

HAMMURABI (r. 1792–1750), one of the eleven kings of the first dynasty of Babylon and one of the most celebrated of all ancient Mesopotamian monarchs. Like the other kings of this dynasty, he was of Amorite origin. The main historicopolitical achievement of Hammurabi and his dynasty was the elevation of the previously little known city-state of Babylon to the status of capital city and cultural metropolis of southern Mesopotamia (which eventually came to be known as Babylonia, while northern Mesopotamia was designated Assyria). The period of Hammurabi's reign is the best documented of any Babylonian king, and his numerous letters and the Code of Hammurabi have become standard texts for learning the classic Old Babylonian dialect of the Akkadian (Assyro-Babylonian) language. The Code of Hammurabi, written toward the end of his reign and the single most famous Old Babylonian document (one of the most important sources for comparative studies in biblical and ancient Near Eastern literature), is not a comprehensive law code, but a collection of almost exclusively casuistic laws on various subjects, one of twelve such collections written in Sumerian, Akkadian, and Hittite from approximately the end of the third millennium until the end of the eighth century BCE. In the epilogue to this text, Hammurabi claimed to have written the laws ("my precious words") in order to merit the title "the king of justice," thereby justifying his selection by the gods "so that the mighty not wrong the weak." The canonical nature of this text is evidenced by its having been recopied for use in the Mesopotamian scribal schools for more than a thousand years after Hammurabi's death.

• Jean Bottéro, "The 'Code' of Hammurabi," in *Mesopotamia: Writing, Reasoning, and the Gods* (Chicago, 1992), pp. 156–184. C. J. Gadd, "Hammurabi and the End of His Dynasty," in *The Cambridge Ancient History*, 3d ed., edited by I. E. S. Edwards et al. (Cambridge, 1973), vol. 2, pt. 1, pp. 176–227. Victor A. Hurowitz, *Īnu Anum sīrum: Literary Structures in the Non-Judicial Sections of Codex Hammurabi* (Philadelphia, 1994). S. A. Meier, "Ḥammurapi," *Anchor Bible Dictionary*, vol. 3 (New York, 1992), pp. 39–42. Shalom M. Paul, *Studies in the Book of the Covenant in the Light of Cuneiform and Biblical Law* (Leiden, 1970). Martha T. Roth, *Law Collections from Mesopotamia and Asia Minor* (Atlanta, 1995), pp. 1–10, 71–142. Georges Roux, *Ancient Iraq*, 2d ed. (Harmondsworth, Eng., 1980), pp. 184–207. H. W. F. Saggs, *The Greatness that Was Babylon* (New York, 1962). D. J. Wiseman, "Ḥammurapi," *New Bible Dictionary*, 2d ed. (Downers Grove, Ill., 1982), p. 451. —CHAIM COHEN

HA-MOTSI', BIRKAT. See BIRKAT HA-MOTSI'.

ḤANAN'EL BEN ḤUSHI'EL (c.990–1055), rabbinic scholar and commentator. He was born in Kairouan, North Africa, where he succeeded his father as head of the academy. His concise and lucid commentary on the Talmud, one of the first such works to be written, became a classic of Jewish literature and was much used by later commentators. He concentrated on summarizing the text and finding the *halakhah* without further commentary, a method that was copied by later North African and Spanish scholars. He paid careful attention to the text of the Talmud, studying all of the available manuscripts. Of his commentary on the Bible, only citations in other works have been preserved. Like his father (who may have been of Italian origin), he wrote and spoke Hebrew, not Arabic. Both wrote succinctly, and Ḥushi'el was able to summarize a whole page of the Talmud in a few sentences. Ḥanan'el often compared the Talmud Bavli and Talmud Yerushalmi, which was unusual for that time. Later generations called him ga'on, and Yitsḥaq *Alfasi regarded himself as a disciple of Ḥanan'el, who lived at the end of the geonic period and is regarded as one of the first of the *ri'shonim*. While Ḥanan'el's commentaries on the Talmud were very influential, they were only rediscovered in the nineteenth century, and the first selections were incorporated in the 1880 Vilna edition of the Talmud.

• Shraga Abramson, ed., *Perush Rabbenu Ḥanan'el la-Talmud* (Jerusalem, 1995). Israel Ta-Shema, *Zeraḥyah ha-Levi u-Venei Ḥugo* (Jerusalem, 1993), pp. 121–123. —SHALOM BAR-ASHER

HANANIAH, MISHAEL, AND AZARIAH, *Daniel's three companions at Nebuchadnezzar's court (who were given the Babylonian names Shadrach, Meshach, and Abed-nego), who underwent a three-year preparatory course before entering the king's service. At the termination of this period, during which they strictly abided by the dietary laws, eating only legumes, they were found to be ten times more skilled than all the king's magicians and soothsayers (*Dn.* 1). According to the narrative tale in *Daniel* 3, they were thrown into a fiery furnace when they refused the king's order to worship his image, but they were miraculously saved, totally unharmed. Two other tales, *The Prayer of Azariah* and the *Song of the Three Young Men*, which appear in the Apocrypha, have been preserved in the Catholic Bible.

• John Joseph Collins, *Daniel: A Commentary on the Book of Daniel, With an Essay by Adela Yarbro Collins*, edited by Frank Moore Cross, Hermeneia—A Critical and Historical Commentary on the Bible (Minneapolis, 1993), pp. 127–147, 176–207. —SHALOM PAUL

ḤANINA' BAR ḤAMA' (2d–3d cent.), Babylonian and Palestinian amora'. Born to a priestly family in Babylonia, he prospered as a honey trader (and also practiced medicine) before settling in Erets Yisra'el with his son *Ḥama' bar Ḥanina'. There he studied with R. Yehudah ha-Nasi', adhering to his teachings with such carefulness (Y., *Nid.* 2.7, 50b) that he once boasted that if the entire Torah were forgotten, he could recover it all through his sharpness (*Ket.* 103b). He was ordained by R. Ḥiyya' ben Abba', eventually succeeding R. Afes as the head of the Sepphoris academy. The academy was built through the generosity of Ḥanina'. He is mentioned hundreds of times in both Talmuds, and nearly sixty sages pass on teachings in his name. His foremost students include R. Yoḥanan bar Nappaḥa' (whom Ḥanina' claimed to have taught *aggadot* for the entire Bible, with the exception of only *Proverbs* and *Ecclesiastes*; Y., *Hor.* 3.4, 48b), Shim'on ben Laqish, and R. El'azar ben Pedat. He was blessed with exceptional longevity but lost a son and daughter at young ages. In one extraordinary instance he is credited with resurrecting the slain slave of the emperor (*'A. Z.* 10b), but he is not otherwise prominent as a miracle worker. His devotion to Erets Yisra'el was such that he was strongly opposed to anyone, especially a priest, leaving the land, even to perform a meritorious deed (Y., *Mo'ed Q.* 3.1, 81a). Although he emphasized the role of providence, he taught that piety was an individual choice, albeit influenced by divine destiny (*Ber.* 33b). He believed that Jerusalem was destroyed in 70 CE because the people failed to rebuke each other (*Shab.* 119b), a practice from which he did not shrink, occasionally angering the people of Sepphoris. He welcomed the Sabbath with the words "Let us go to greet the Queen Sabbath" (*Shab.* 119a) and he taught an interpretation of *Isaiah* 54.13, reading *bonayikh* (your builders) for *banayikh* (your sons), to mean that Torah scholars increase peace in the world (*Ber.* 64a), a saying that has been incorporated into the prayer book.

• Wilhelm Bacher, *Die Agada der palästinensischen Amoräer* (1892–1899; Hildesheim, 1965). Gershom Bader, *The Encyclopedia of Talmudic Sages*, translated from the Yiddish by Solomon Katz (Northvale, N.J., and London, 1988). Aaron Hyman, *Toledot Tanna'im ve-'Amora'im* (1910; Jerusalem, 1987). —MICHAEL L. BROWN

ḤANINA' BEN DOSA' (1st cent.), Palestinian *tanna' known for his asceticism and for his saintliness. Many miracles were ascribed to him, and his prayer and intercession (especially for the sick, cf. *Ber.* 34b) were considered to be of particular efficacy. Thus when the son of R. *Yoḥanan ben Zakk'ai became sick, Yoḥanan turned to his friend Ḥanina' ben Dosa' and requested that he pray for him. Ḥanina' ben Dosa' put his hand between his knees, prayed briefly, and the lad was healed. Virtually no halakhic traditions have come down in the name of Ḥanina' ben Dosa', only moral and ethical statements. One of his most famous ones, which characterizes his personality, is "He in whom the spirit of mankind finds pleasure, the spirit of God finds pleasure; but he in whom the spirit of mankind finds no pleasure, in him the spirit of God finds no pleasure" (*Avot* 3.13).

• Gershom Bader, *The Encyclopedia of Talmudic Sages*, translated from the Yiddish by Solomon Katz (Northvale, N.J., and London, 1988). Aaron Hyman, *Toledot Tanna'im ve-'Amora'im* (1910; Jerusalem, 1987). Mordecai Margaliot, ed., *Entsiqlopediyyah le-Ḥakhmei ha-Talmud veha-Ge'onim* (Jerusalem, 1946). —DANIEL SPERBER

ḤANINA' BEN TERADYON (2d cent.), Palestinian *tanna'; head of the academy at Sikhnin in Upper Galilee. A man of scrupulous honesty, he was entrusted with the allocation of charitable funds. He never stopped teaching the Torah, even after it had been forbidden by the Romans. Forewarned by his colleague R. Yosei ben Qisma', he nonetheless continued his educational activities until the Romans arrested him. As punishment, he was wrapped in a Torah scroll and burned alive. His daughter *Beruryah was the wife of R. *Me'ir.

• Herbert W. Basser, "Hanina's Torah, a Case of Verse Production or of Historical Fact?" in *Approaches to Ancient Judaism*, new series, vol. 1, edited by Jacob Neusner (Atlanta, 1990). —DANIEL SPERBER

ḤANINA' SEGAN HA-KOHANIM (c.50–90), tanna' who, from his title, would appear to have served as deputy *high priest. He himself explained this position as referring to the priest who would take over from the high priest should he become unfit for Temple service (*Yoma'* 39a). After the destruction of the Temple (70 CE), Ḥanina' cited several testimonies concerning priestly ritual and Temple service (e.g., *ʿEduy.* 2.1–2.3; *Zev.* 12.4; *Men.* 10.1). Having seen the internal strife in Jerusalem prior to its destruction, he declared: "Great is peace, which may be weighed against all the works of creation" (*Sifrei* on *Nm.* 42). He further declared that one should pray for the peace of the authorities, for without respect for authority "man devours his neighbor" (*Avot* 3.2). The most important pursuit, according to Ḥanina, is study of Torah, which protects a person from all manner of dangers (*Avot de-Rabbi Natan* 20).

• Wilhelm Bacher, *Die Agada der Tannaiten*, 2 vols. (Strassburg, 1966). —DANIEL SPERBER

HANNAH, mother of *Samuel; along with Peninnah, one of the two wives of Elkanah. She was barren and was constantly tormented by Peninnah, who was able to bear children. As a result, Hannah made a pilgrimage to the shrine at Shiloh, vowing that, were she to give birth, she would dedicate her son as a *Nazirite to the worship of God. *Eli, the priest of Shiloh, at first thought that the prayer she silently uttered was that of a drunken woman. Upon realizing her intent, he assured her that her prayer would be answered. She subsequently gave birth to Samuel and fulfilled her vow by bringing the child to the sanctuary at Shiloh when he was three years old (*1 Sm.* 1) and gave expression to her thankfulness by uttering a moving hymn to God (*1 Sm.* 2.1–10). Later she bore three more sons and two daughters (*1 Sm.* 2.21).

• Athalya, Brenner, ed., *A Feminist Companion to Samuel and Kings* (Sheffield, Eng., 1994), pp. 68–104. —SHALOM PAUL

HANNAH AND HER SEVEN SONS, a story originating in *2 Maccabees* and elaborated upon by the author of *4 Maccabees*, about a woman (her name is never mentioned) who, together with her seven sons, chose to die at the hands of *Antiochus IV Epiphanes (in c.167 BCE) rather than abandon the Jewish way of life. While the books of the *Maccabees* were preserved only by Christian copyists, the story of the mother and her seven sons appears several times in rabbinic literature. The nameless mother of *2 Maccabees* was given a name, Miriam, and the story of the family's martyrdom was transposed from the second century BCE to the Hadrianic persecutions of the second century CE. It is clear that the author of the tenth-century *Book of Yosippon* was familiar with the Latin translation of *2 Maccabees*, since the story appears within its original Maccabean context, and the woman's name is given as Hannah. *Yosippon*'s great popularity, as well as the story's appeal for subsequent generations of persecuted Jews, guaranteed the story of Hannah and her seven sons a wide diffusion in later Jewish literature and lore. Both the Western church and the Eastern church adopted Hannah and her sons as the "Maccabean saints," to whom an annual commemoration day was dedicated.

• Gerson D. Cohen, "Hannah and Her Seven Sons in Hebrew Literature," in *Studies in the Variety of Rabbinic Cultures* (Phliadelphia and New York, 1991), pp. 39–60. —GIDEON BOHAK

HANNOVER, NATAN NETAʿ (died 1683), chronicler of the 1648 Cossack massacres of Polish Jews. Born in Volhynia, he studied at the Ostróg Yeshivah before settling in Zasław. He fled the Chmielnicki rebellion in the Ukraine in 1648, going to Germany, Holland, and, in 1653, Italy, where he studied Kabbalah. There he published his Hebrew chronicle, *Yeven Metsulah*, in which he described the sufferings of the Jews in the first two years of the rebellion. He felt that these events were heralding the messianic era. He later published a Hebrew-

German-Latin-Italian phrase book, *Safah Berurah* (1660), and a kabbalistic prayer book, *Sha'arei Tsiyyon* (1662). In 1662 he was appointed rabbi of Jassy, Walachia, later moving to Ungarisch-Brod in Moravia, where he was killed by Turkish soldiers. His three major works greatly influenced Ashkenazi society, his prayer book serving as a conduit for the introduction of Lurianic prayers into the daily service. *Yeven Metsulah* remained popular for generations. There have been numerous editions of the text, the most recent one by Israel Halpern (Tel Aviv, 1966), and the book has often been translated into Yiddish (the best edition being that of Shatzky [Vilna, 1938]) and a number of other languages, including English (*Abyss of Despair*, translated by A. Mesch [1950]).

• William B. Helmreich's Introduction in *Abyss of Despair*, translated by Abraham J. Mesch, 2d ed. (New York, 1950; repr. New Brunswick, N.J., 1983). Jacob Shatzky, "Historish-kritisher araynfir tzum 'Yeven Metsule' fun R. Noson Neta Hanover," in *Gzeires Takh*, edited by Jacob Shatzky (Vilna, 1938), pp. 5–159. Chone Shmeruk, "Yiddish Literature and Collective Memory: The Case of the Chmielnicki Massacres," *Polin* 5 (1990): 173–183. *Sho'at Yehudei Uqra'inah bi-Tequfat ha-Tsorer Ḥmielnitsqi ba-Shanim 408–409 (1648–1649)*, documentary collection by Towiah Friedman (Haifa, 1983).

—ADAM TELLER

ḤANOKH. See ENOCH.

ḤANOKH BEN MOSHEH (died 1014), Spanish rabbinical scholar; son of *Mosheh ben Ḥanokh. He succeeded his father as rabbi of Cordova (c.965) and, in essence, as the chief rabbi of Muslim Spain. The appointment was a subject of competition, and the Umayyad ruler appears to have intervened to secure his appointment as *nasi'* and head of the *yeshivah*. He continued his father's efforts to establish a Torah center in Spain, which would be independent of the Babylonian authorities. In view of his great scholarship he was given the title ga'on. Some of his *responsa* are included in the geonic *responsa*.

• Gerson D. Cohen, ed., *A Critical Edition with a Translation and Notes of the Book of Tradition, Sefer ha-Qabbalah* (Philadelphia, 1967), pp. 63–78, 263–303.

—SHALOM BAR-ASHER

HA-NOTEN TESHU'AH LA-MELAKHIM (הַנּוֹתֵן תְּשׁוּעָה לַמְּלָכִים; "He who gives salvation to kings" [*Ps.* 144.10]), the customary formula for prayers for the government, which probably originated in Spain. The duty to pray for the welfare of the authorities in whatever land Jews happened to live was first stated by the prophet Jeremiah ("Seek the peace of the city whither I have caused you to be carried captive, and pray for it unto the Lord" [29.7]) and reinforced by the Mishnah ("pray for the welfare of the government" [*Avot* 3.2]). Prayer for the government as a regular feature of the synagogue service is first attested in the fourteenth century, but an earlier version is known from the eleventh-century Rhineland. Various changes have been introduced into the wording of the prayer as a result of political and other circumstances, such as the change from monarchies to republican forms of government. In many congregations the prayer, or part of it, is said in the vernacular (in the Spanish and Portuguese synagogue in Amsterdam, it is still recited in Portuguese). In the United States, the Orthodox retain the traditional form, but the non-Orthodox have adapted original versions (see TEFILLAH LI-SHELOM HA-MEDINAH). It is usually recited on Sabbaths and festivals after the reading of the Torah.

• S. D. Goitein, "Prayers from the Geniza for Fatimid Caliphs, the Head of the Jerusalem Yeshiva, the Jewish Community and the Local Congregation," in *Studies in Judaica, Karaitica and Islamica Presented to Leon Nemoy* (Ramat Gan, 1982), pp. 47–57. Philippe Landau, "Religion et patrie: Les Prières israélites pour la France," *Pardès* 14 (1991): 11–32. Charles S. Liebman, *Religion and Politics in Israel* (Bloomington, Ind., 1984). Marcel Marcus, "T'filah Lischlom Hamedina (Gebet für den Frieden des Staates); Gedanken zu einem Gebet," *Judaica* 40.1 (1984): 16–27. Barry Schwartz, "'Ha-Noten Teshu'ah': The Origin of the Traditional Jewish Prayer for the Government," *Hebrew Union College Annual* 57 (1987): 113–120.

ḤANUKKAH (חֲנֻכָּה; dedication), festival (also known as Ḥag ha-'Urim [the Festival of Lights]) commemorating the rededication of the Second Temple by *Judah the Maccabee on 25 Kislev 165 BCE, the third anniversary of its desecration by *Antiochus IV Epiphanes. The historical source for the festival is found in *1 Maccabees*. The concluding sentence of the special prayer for Ḥanukkah (*'Al ha-Nissim) inserted in the 'Amidah and Birkat ha-Mazon, "And thereupon your children came into the shrine of your house . . . and did light lamps in your holy courts, and appointed these eight days to be kept with praise and thanksgiving . . . and we thank your great name," accords with the statement in *1 Maccabees* 4.49: "and Judah and his brethren and the whole congregation of Israel ordained that the days of the dedication of the altar should be kept in their seasons from year to year for eight days from the 25th day of Kislev." Talmudic legend (*Shab.* 21b), in a poetic embellishment of the historical reason, states that the festival was instituted for eight days because the pure oil found in the Temple, though sufficient for one day only, miraculously burned for eight days until new supplies could be provided; in fact, the length of the festival was probably determined by analogy to the eight-day festival of Sukkot (*1 Mac.* 10). The emphasis placed by the rabbis on *Zechariah* 2.14–4.7 (the prophetical portion for the first Sabbath of Ḥanukkah, which includes the penultimate verse, "Not by might nor by power, but by my spirit, says the Lord of Hosts") is one example of the pronounced tendency on their part (possibly against the background of the dispute between the Pharisees and the Hasmoneans) to diminish the military aspect of the festival and concentrate instead on the aspect of the survival of religious values in the face of pagan and idolatrous opposition. In modern times, especially in the State of Israel, the opposite tendency is to be noted. The festival may also have been influenced by the eight-day dedication by *Solomon of the First Temple. The main feature of the celebration is the kindling of the eight-branched menorah (Mod. Heb. *ḥanukkiyah*) from a light placed in a ninth socket (*shammash*), followed almost everywhere by the singing of the *Ma'oz Tsur hymn (originally in the Ashkenazi rite only). Sephardim also recite Psalm 30. The lights are inserted on successive nights incrementally from right to left, but the actual lighting is from left to right; that is, beginning with the most recent addition.

The view of the school of Hillel that one light is kindled the first night and one successively added every following night prevailed over the opinion of the school of Shamm'ai that eight candles are lit on the first night and are thereafter decreased by one each night. Halakhically, in the absence of any males, the obligation to kindle the Ḥanukkah lights falls on females. The candelabrum should be kindled in a prominently visible place "to advertise the miracle" (cf. *Shab.* 23b). Ḥanukkah is the only nonbiblical festival on which the full *Hallel (*Ps.* 113–18) is recited, and the special scriptural reading consists of the passage that describes the gifts brought by the princes for the dedication of the Sanctuary in the wilderness (*Nm.* 7). Work is permitted during the festival, but not while the candles are burning. A number of children's games became popular (notably spinning the Ḥanukkah top—*dreidl* or *trendl* in Yiddish; *sevivon* in Hebrew), and the custom also developed of giving children monetary gifts (Ḥanukkah *gelt*) and presents. In the United States, the festival has become one of the most observed of Jewish holidays, especially for children, partly to present a parallel to Christmas, which falls in the same period of the year.

• Eliezer Don-Yehiya, "Hanukkah and the Myth of the Maccabees in Zionist Ideology and in Israeli Society," *Jewish Journal of Sociology* 34.1 (1992): 5–23. Ismar Elbogen, *Jewish Liturgy: A Comprehensive History*, translated by Raymond P. Scheindlin (Philadelphia, New York, and Jerusalem, 1993), p. 109. Theodor H. Gaster, *Purim and Hanukkah: Custom and Tradition* (New York, 1950), pp. 85–118. Philip Goodman, *The Hanukkah Anthology* (Philadelphia, 1976). Eliyahu Kitov, *The Book of Our Heritage: The Jewish Year and Its Days of Significance*, rev. ed. (Jerusalem and New York, 1978), pp. 271–314. Simon Maurice Lehrman, *A Guide to Hanukkah and Purim* (London, 1958), pp. 7–49. James C. VanderKam, "Hanukkah: Its Timing and Significance According to 1 and 2 Maccabees," *Journal for the Study of the Pseudepigrapha* 1 (1987): 23–40. S. Z. Zeitlin, *Studies in the Early History of Judaism* (New York, 1973), pp. 239–274.

ḤANUKKAH LAMP. See Ḥanukkah.

ḤANUKKAT HA-BAYIT. See Dedication.

HA-QADOSH BARUKH HU'. See God, Names of.

HAQDAMAH (הַקְדָּמָה; introduction). Jewish works began to carry introductions during the geonic period; the first known *haqdamah* appeared in *Halakhot Gedolot*. Introductions were very popular in medieval times, and there is even a famous introduction to the Talmud that was composed during this period and falsely attributed to Shemu'el ha-Nagid. Authors often discussed important methodological issues in introductions and explained what motivated them to compose their works. Some of these introductions are so significant that they are works in themselves. Especially notable are those introductions written by Maimonides. The *haqdamah* to his *Sefer ha-Mitsvot* provides a detailed explanation of his method of enumerating the commandments, without which the work as a whole would be incomprehensible. This introduction became the starting point for all later discussions of enumeration of the *mitsvot*. Maimonides' *haqdamah* to the tenth chapter of tractate *Sanhedrin* is of great theological significance. It is here that his famed *Thirteen Principles of Faith are found. The introductions of Yosef Karo and Mosheh Isserles to the *Shulḥan ʿArukh*, however, have been omitted in almost all editions of this work that have appeared in the last few hundred years. In modern times introductions continue to serve a valuable literary aid, and hardly any traditional works are published without them.

• Shemu'el ha-Nagid, *Hilkhot ha-Nagid*, edited by Mordechai Margaliot (Jerusalem, 1962). Moses Maimonides, *Haqdamot ha-Rambam la-Mishnah*, edited by Yitsḥaq Shailat (Jerusalem, 1992).

—MARC SHAPIRO

HAQHEL (הַקְהֵל; assemble), ceremony observed in Biblical times every seven years in the year following the **shemittah*. This is based on *Deuteronomy* 31.10–13: "And Moses commanded them saying, 'At the end of every seven years, at the set time of the year of release, at the feast of booths . . . Assemble the people, . . . so they may hear and learn to fear the Lord your God, and be careful to do all the words of this law . . . .' " The Mishnah (*Sot.* 7.8) connects this assembly with *Deuteronomy* 17.14–20 and describes a ceremony on the second day of *Sukkot* in which the king read selected verses of *Deuteronomy* from a Torah scroll and then blessed the people gathered in the Temple courtyard. In recent years, there has been an attempt to revive a symbolic form of this practice at the Western Wall.

• Ismar Elbogen, *Jewish Liturgy: A Comprehensive History*, translated by Raymond P. Scheindlin (Philadelphia, 1993).

—PETER KNOBEL

HAQQAFOT (הַקָּפוֹת; circuits), three types of processional circuits made on various ceremonial occasions.

Circuits around the *Bimah* in the Synagogue. During *Sukkot, a single circuit is made daily (except on the Sabbath); worshipers carry the *four species and are accompanied by the singing of the day's **hoshʿanot*, in commemoration of the daily festival circuit around the altar in the Temple (*Suk.* 4.5). On *Hoshʿana' Rabbah, there are seven such *haqqafot* recalling a similar custom in the Temple. On *Simḥat Torah (Ḥasidim outside Israel commence on Shemini ʿAtseret), members (among the Orthodox, only male) of the congregation, led by children carrying flags, participate in carrying all the Torah scrolls from the ark in seven (or more) *haqqafot*. These are held both on the eve and morning (among most Reform congregations, only on the eve) of Simḥat Torah. In Israel it is customary to have additional *haqqafot*, often in the open and to musical accompaniment, on the evening following Simḥat Torah. At the dedication of a new synagogue, seven *haqqafot* are made with the Torah scrolls.

Circuits at the Cemetery. In consecrating a new cemetery, an extension to an existing one, or a cemetery wall, seven *haqqafot* are made to the recitation of appropriate biblical passages. Sephardim make seven *haqqafot* around the grave prior to burial. In the past it was the custom to pray for the sick while circumambulating the cemetery.

Circuits at a Wedding. In many Orthodox Ashkenazi communities the bride is led around the bridegroom three (or seven) times during the wedding ceremony.

• Ismar Elbogen, *Jewish Liturgy: A Comprehensive History* (Philadelphia, 1993).

HA-RAḤAMAN. See Compassion; God, Names of.

ḤAREDIM (חֲרֵדִים; awestruck [at God's Word] ones [cf. *Ezr.* 10.3; *Is.* 66.5]), a term commonly reserved for those Orthodox Jews who claim not to make any compromises with contemporary secular culture or essential changes in the way they practice their Judaism from what tradition and *halakhah* have sanctified. Although Ḥaredim, constituting about 250,000 of Israel's Jews and about 105,000 of America's, appear to constitute a single group, they are subdivided into Ḥasidim, who follow particular charismatic rabbis (*rebbis*), and Benei Yeshivah, who identify with particular academies of Jewish learning and an academy's leading scholar (*ro'sh yeshivah*), students, and interpretive traditions. Sustaining their values and lifestyle, Ḥaredim believe, requires them to maintain a social solidarity among themselves and a cultural distance from (and often a hostility toward) the surrounding larger secular society. They use relatively simple mechanisms to accomplish this. These include dressing in ways that make them clearly stand apart from surrounding culture. For men, this means wearing beards and ear locks, as well as caftans and black hats; for women, it means modest clothing that covers most of their bodies and, for the married among them, a head covering that may range from a kerchief over a shorn head for the most extreme to a wig for those less so (variations are determined by sectarian affiliation). Ḥaredim also distinguish themselves by living in relatively insular communities and by speaking *Yiddish. They send their children to private Jewish schools, most often arrange their marriages, and are overwhelmingly endogamous.

• Menachem Friedman, "Ḥaredim Confront the Modern City," in *Studies in Contemporary Jewry II*, edited by P. Medding (Bloomington, Ind., 1986), pp. 74–96. Samuel Heilman, *Defenders of the Faith: Inside Ultra-Orthodox Jewry* (New York, 1992). Samuel Heilman and Menachem Friedman, "Fundamentalism and Religious Jews: The Case of the Ḥaredim," in *Fundamentalisms Observed*, edited by Martin E. Marty and R. Scott Appleby (Chicago, 1991). Wolf Zeev Rabinowitsch, *Lithuanian Hasidism*, translated by M. Dagut (New York, 1971).

—SAMUEL C. HEILMAN

ḤAROSET (חֲרֹסֶת), traditionally a mixture of ground apples, walnuts, almonds, cinnamon, and other spices combined into a thick paste with wine, but various recipes are used in different communities. *Ḥaroset* is one of the ingredients on the *Seder plate on Pesaḥ eve, serving as a dip for the bitter herbs. In ancient times *ḥaroset* was used as a vegetable dressing. The Talmud (*Pes.* 116a) states that the clay-like appearance of *ḥaroset* recalls the mortar used by the Israelite slaves in Egypt.

• Philip Goodman, *The Passover Anthology* (Philadelphia, 1971), p. 422. Eliyahu Kitov, *The Book of Our Heritage: The Jewish Year and Its Days of Significance*, rev. ed. (Jerusalem and New York, 1978), pp. 249–250.

HARVEST FESTIVALS. In biblical times the occasion of the harvest was one of merrymaking and dancing, as at the grape harvest (*Jgs.* 9.27; *Is.* 16.10; *Jer.* 48.33). All the *Shalosh Regalim are specifically referred to in the Bible as harvest festivals, and it has been suggested that this was their original significance among the ancient Canaanites. *Pesaḥ is the occasion for bringing "a sheaf of the first fruits of your harvest to the priest" (*Lv.* 23.10). Also called the Festival of the *ʿOmer, Pesaḥ is when the offering of barley was brought to the Temple. The holiday of *Shavuʿot marks the time when "you reap the harvest of your land" (*Lv.* 23.22), and the solemn ceremony of thanksgiving (*Dt.* 26) took place when the wheat ripened and the *first fruits were brought to Jerusalem. *Sukkot is referred to as "the harvest festival" and "the feast of ingathering, which is the end of the year, when you have gathered in your labors from the field" (*Ex.* 23.16; see also *Ex.* 34.22). In the Diaspora, the agricultural aspects of these festivals were overshadowed by the historical significance. In modern Israel, they have been revived, especially in rural settlements. See Kibbutz Festivals.

• Richard David Barnett, "From Arad to Carthage: Harvest Rites and Corn-Dollies," *Eretz-Israel* 20 (1989): 1–11.

ḤASDA'I CRESCAS. See Crescas, Ḥasda'i ben Avraham.

HA-SHEM. See God, Names of.

HASHGAḤAH. See Providence.

HASHKAMAH (הַשְׁכָּמָה; early rising), term used to denote an early morning service, ending before the commencement of the official morning prayers. The expression *hashkamat beit ha-midrash* signifies "timely attendance" at services (*Shab.* 127a).

HASHKAVAH. See Ashkavah.

HASHKIVENU (הַשְׁכִּיבֵנוּ; "Cause us [O Lord our God] to lie down [in peace]"), opening words of the second benediction following the evening *Shemaʿ (the first being the *Ge'ullah); a prayer for divine protection and peace during the night. The wording differs slightly in various rites, and there are certain differences between the weekday and the Sabbath and festival versions of the prayer, the latter being a Palestinian version (cf. Y., *Ber.* 4.5) and the former of Babylonian origin (cf. *Ber.* 4b, 9b). Hashkivenu has also been incorporated in the night prayers (see Qeri'at Shemaʿ ʿal ha-Mittah).

ḤASID (חָסִיד; pious man), a term occasionally applied to God, who loves righteousness and kindness (*Jer.* 3.12; *Ps.* 145.17). As a designation of a social group, the term first appears in the Second Temple period. The *First Book of the Maccabees* 2.42 mentions *Hasideans (Gr. Asidaioi [Pietists]), who opposed the Hellenizers and supported the Hasmonean Revolt. There are a variety of meanings for the word *ḥasid* as used in Talmudic literature. In legal contexts, a *ḥasid* is one who forgoes his rights and acts beyond the requirements of *halakhah*. Frequently, it refers to the pious and God-fearing without further qualification. At the end of the twelfth century and during the thirteenth century the term was applied in the Rhineland to pietistic groups known for their ascetic and penitential zeal. The *Ḥasidei Ashkenaz also cultivated esoteric doctrines that later emerged with kabbalistic currents. At the beginning of the eighteenth century, the followers of R. Yisra'el ben Eliʿezer Baʿal Shem Tov, who initiated a mystical revival reaching out beyond a spiritual elite and directed toward instilling piety into the life of the masses, were designated as Ḥasidim (see HASIDISM). This has become its common contemporary usage.

• Nelson Glueck, *Ḥesed in the Bible* (Cincinnati, 1967). Gershom Gerhard Scholem, "Hasidism in Medieval Germany," and "Hasidism: The Latest Phase," in *Major Trends in Jewish Mysticism* (New York, 1965), pp. 80–118; 325–350. Efraim E. Urbach, *The Sages: Their Concepts and Beliefs*, translated by Israel Abrahams (Cambridge, Mass., 1987).

—LOU H. SILBERMAN

ḤASID, YEHUDAH HE-. See YEHUDAH BEN SHEMU'EL HE- ḤASID.

HASIDEANS, an obscure Jewish group mentioned three times in *1* and *2 Maccabees*. Their name is derived from the Greek transliteration of the Hebrew word *ḥasidim* (pious ones). They are first referred to as having joined Mattathias and his followers in the rebellion against the religious persecution of *Antiochus IV Epiphanes (*1 Mc*. 2.41). The next references (*1 Mc*. 7; *2 Mc*. 14) relate that sixty of the Hasideans were treacherously murdered by *Alcimus, who considered them in the same camp as *Judah the Maccabee, which probably was not entirely accurate. In addition to these meager bits of evidence, Talmudic and Midrashic literature sometimes refer to the *ḥasidim ri'shonim* (the early pietists) and their strict obedience to the Torah, such as their refusal to kill even snakes or scorpions on the Sabbath and their practice of meditating for one hour before and after prayer (*Ber*. 5.1), which they would not interrupt "even if a serpent were to wind itself around their ankle" (T., *Ber*. 3.20; *Ber*. 32b). Modern scholarship has tended to conflate all these disparate data and reconstruct an early Jewish sect, thought by some to be the forerunner of the *Pharisees and the *Essenes, but it is equally possible that the term *ḥasidim* was loosely used to describe various groups of Jewish pietists, without any organizational or ideological links betweem them.

• Martin Hengel, *Judaism and Hellenism*, 2 vols. (Philadelphia, 1974), vol. 1, pp. 175–180, 224–227. John Kampen, *The Hasideans and the Origin of Pharisaism: A Study in 1 and 2 Maccabees*, Septuagint and Cognate Studies Series 24 (Atlanta, 1988), with extensive bibliography.

—GIDEON BOHAK

ḤASIDEI ASHKENAZ (חֲסִידֵי אַשְׁכְּנַז; the pious ones of Ashkenaz), a term that refers to the various circles of Jewish mystics and pietists in Ashkenaz—that is, Germany (mainly the Rhineland) and northern France—in the second half of the twelfth and thirteenth centuries. The term refers to several schools, most of them independent of each other, which developed different theologies and world views; many of their ideas and symbols were later absorbed by the *Kabbalah.

Among the main groups is the Kalonimos school, centered around Shemu'el ben Kalonimos (c.1130–1190), known as he-Ḥasid, ha-Qadosh, veha-Navi' (the Pious, the Saint, and the Prophet; see KALONIMOS FAMILY), his son *Yehudah ben Shemu'el he-Ḥasid (c.1150–1217), and their relative *Elʿazar ben Yehudah of Worms (c.1160–1230). This school produced the earliest commentaries on the prayers, a significant body of esoterical works, and a particular form of Hasidic ethics, expressed mainly in R. Yehudah's *Sefer Ḥasidim*. Elʿazar's work was continued by his disciples, among them *Avraham ben ʿAzri'el of Bohemia, author of the encyclopedic commentary on the *piyyutim*, *ʿArugat ha-Bosem* (completed c.1234), and *Yitsḥaq ben Mosheh of Vienna, author of the halakhic work *Or Zaruʿa*. In the second half of the thirteenth century, writers of the Kalonimos school integrated their teachings with those of the Kabbalah; among them was R. Mosheh ben Eliʿezer, the great-grandson of Yehudah ben Shemu'el he-Ḥasid, who wrote a mystical commentary on the **Shiʿur Qomah*.

The Unique Cherub circle based its teachings on a pseudepigraphous treatise, *Baraiyta' de-Yosef ben ʿUzzi'el*, the author of which was said to be the grandson of Ben Sira, son of the prophet Jeremiah. Other authoritative texts produced by members of the Unique Cherub school were the commentary on the *Sefer Yetsirah* by Pseudo-Saʿadyah and the writings of Elḥanan ben Yaqar of London, as well as two additional commentaries on the *Sefer Yetsirah* and a theological treatise, *Sod ha-Sodot*. This circle is distinguished from the other schools by its doctrine of the unique cherub, the power by which God is said to reveal himself to the prophets.

A third Ḥasidei Ashkenaz circle produced several anonymous mystical and ethical treatises, the most important being *Sefer ha-Ḥayyim*, written in approximately 1200, and *Sefer ha-Navon*, a commentary on the *Shemaʿ and **Shiʿur Qomah* written in approximately 1230.

These schools believed in intermediary divine powers that emanated from the supreme Godhead, the Creator, and served as subjects of divine revelation. This is in contrast to the beliefs of Talmudic scholars, such as Mosheh ben Ḥisda'i Taqu, who opposed theological speculation of any kind. The Ḥasidei Ashkenaz developed sophisticated concepts of divine immanence in the created world, while insisting on the complete transcendence of the supreme Godhead. They introduced new methodologies in biblical exegesis and the interpretation of prayers and *piyyutim* and used them to create diverse esoteric theologies concerning the divine world, the human soul, cosmology and cosmogony, and the ways by which an individual can approach God. Their ethical teachings are characterized by the demand of extreme devotion to every detail of the commandments and ethical precepts as a preparation for the ultimate religious experience, *qiddush ha-Shem*.

• Yitzhak F. Baer, "The Origins of Jewish Communal Organization in the Middle Ages," in *Binah*, vol. 1, *Studies in Jewish Thought*, edited by Joseph Dan (New York, 1989), pp. 57–95. Joseph Dan, "The Emergence of Jewish Mysticism in Medieval Germany," in *Mystics of the Book: Themes, Topics, and Typologies*, edited by Robert A. Herrera (New York, 1993), pp. 57–95. Joseph Dan, *Ḥasidut Ashkenaz* (Tel Aviv, 1992). Joseph Dan, *ʿIyyunim be-Sifrut Ḥasidut Ashkenaz* (Ramat Gan, 1975). Joseph Dan, *Torat ha-Sod shel Ḥasidut Ashkenaz* (Jerusalem, 1968). Ivan Marcus, *Pi-*

ety and Society: The Jewish Pietists of Medieval Germany (Leiden, 1981). Gershom Gerhard Scholem, *Major Trends in Jewish Mysticism* (New York, 1954), pp. 80–118.

—JOSEPH DAN

ḤASIDEI UMMOT HA-ʿOLAM (חֲסִידֵי אֻמּוֹת הָעוֹלָם; pious of the nations of the world), a term of rabbinic origin referring to righteous non-Jews. According to the Tosefta' (*San*. 13.2), such individuals do have a share in the world to come. Maimonides (*Hilkhot Melakhim* 8.11) defined the pious gentiles as those who adhere to the seven *Noahic laws which are binding on all humanity, provided they are motivated by faith in God and his revelation. Since World War II, the term has been applied to non-Jews who endangered themselves by helping Jews under Nazi rule.

• Arieh L. Bauminger, *The Righteous Among Nations* (Tel Aviv, 1990). Eric Silver, *The Book of the Just: The Silent Heroes Who Saved Jews from Hitler* (London, 1992).

HASIDISM, a religious renewal movement among eastern European Jews that began in approximately 1750. Started by a small group that gathered around R. Yisra'el ben Eliʿezer *Baʿal Shem Tov in an obscure corner of southeastern Poland, by the early nineteenth century Hasidism had conquered most of eastern European Jewry outside Lithuania and continues to be influential today. The movement's history may be divided into four periods.

1750–1815. Hasidism began as a mystical revival movement among Jews of Podolia and Volhynia who were critical of both the remote and elitist culture of Talmudic learning and the obscure, equally elitist, and highly ascetic kabbalistic traditions practiced in their day. Seeking an alternative, but without wholly rejecting the values of either, they were attracted to the message of the Baʿal Shem Tov. He taught of a God who was present throughout the universe, even, and perhaps especially, in the most unlikely of places. A person needed only to train his awareness to see everywhere the sparks of divine light that in each moment seek out the Jew to redeem them. The Jew's task is not to turn away from the world but to embrace all that surrounds him and encompass it in his devotional life, so that the sparks in all things might find in him a channel through which to reunite with their source in God. The same is true of fallen souls; they seek their **tiqqun* (redemption) through the prayers of others, so that they might be uplifted. These acts of reuniting the world with God constituted a typically revivalist simplification of complex kabbalistic doctrine, which Hasidism made accessible to ordinary and even unlettered Jews. The Baʿal Shem Tov taught that "God needs to be served in all ways," not only through the prescribed commandments but also in every act that a person performs and every word that he speaks. Among the Baʿal Shem Tov's disciples were some much more educated than he, including R. *Yaʿaqov Yosef ha-Kohen of Polonnoye, an important early theoretician of Hasidism, and R. *Dov Ber of Mezhirech, who became leader of the movement following the Baʿal Shem Tov's death in 1760. Dov Ber, or the Maggid as he is often called, extended the Baʿal Shem Tov's teachings into a cosmic philosophy, in which God and the divine word were the only true reality, corporeality serving as a veil that keeps us from fully knowing God's truth. The cultivation of *daʿat* (mindfulness), the chief goal of religious training, leads to the ability to see through that veil and to redeem oneself from the prison of falsehood. This mindfulness is most fully realized by the *tsaddiqim* (see TSADDIQ), a network of spiritual illuminati who are the rulers of each generation on the spiritual plane. Other Jews may seek intimacy with God through them, each Jew finding the particular *tsaddiq* to whose spiritual root his own soul belongs by its very nature. Thus Hasidism, which stood on one level for equalization, on another level insinuated a claim for a new elite, the *tsaddiq*, who stood on the highest rung and held the keys to divine blessing. Dov Ber was the great movement builder of Hasidism; he scattered his group of remarkable disciples throughout the Polish-Jewish world. By the time of his death in 1772, Hasidism had entered the public arena as a new religious movement, challenging the complacent authority of the wealthy and learned oligarchy that dominated Jewish life and calling forth a wave of bitter denunciation and opposition. The bans against Hasidism, mostly emanating from *Eliyyahu ben Shelomoh Zalman of Vilna (the Vilna Ga'on) and his disciples, first pronounced in 1772 and renewed throughout the closing decades of the eighteenth century, accused the Ḥasidim of being religious innovators, destroyers of tradition, madmen, fomenters of civic strife, and revolutionaries. While specific violations of law, either civil or religious, were hard to find, Hasidic disregard for venerable local custom was very much at issue. Ḥasidim had adopted certain practices as distinguishing badges of special piety. These, including the use of the Sephardi prayer rite, disregard for precise times of prayer, and the extra sharpening of knives for ritual slaughter, now became battle cries in the struggle against the new movement. In some places, especially in Lithuania, Hasidism was utterly defeated, but in most areas it was Ḥasidim who won the day, and by the opening decade of the nineteenth century Hasidism had taken deep root in the Ukraine, Belorussia, and Galicia. Large numbers of Jews were praying in the many Hasidic prayer rooms that had sprung up, traveling to obtain the blessings of Hasidic masters, and listening to the teachings and tales that were starting to constitute the growing body of Hasidic literature. The third generation of Hasidic leaders lived into the Napoleonic era. Hasidism by this time had taken on varied hues because of regional differences and because of the different personalities and emphases of the various masters. From the time of the Maggid's death in 1772, there was no central authority in the movement. Special mention should be made of the emergence of the *Ḥabad and Bratslav (see NAḤMAN OF BRATSLAV) schools, both of which took shape in this period.

1816–1881. As Hasidic leadership passed to the fourth generation, the movement neared the height of its powers. The *Mitnaggedim had at least formally ended their war on Hasidism, and the movement was free to grow and move into such new areas as Congress Poland and northeastern Hungary without organized opposition. The pattern of dynastic succession was firmly in place, ensuring some regularity in the passing of authority. The *tsaddiqim* were widely venerated, and their books were being published in increasing numbers. But the Maskilim (Enlighteners; see MASKIL) began their own war against Hasidism, which they depicted as backward, superstitious, and the source of Polish Jews' resistance to attempts to ameliorate their conditions through education or westernization. Rulers and government agencies supported most of these claims, and this set Hasidism and its leaders on a course of direct opposition to various governmental policies. As the Haskalah's influence began to be felt in Hasidic areas, a new conservatism and concern with support for both study and punctilious observance of the law became more commonplace in Hasidic circles. Leaders such as Tsevi Elimelekh of Dynów (1786–1841) and Menaḥem Mendel Schneersohn (see SCHNEERSOHN FAMILY) of Lubavich (1789–1866) wrote mystical justifications of the commandments, something that seemed unnecessary in earlier times. As Hasidic communities built and supported *yeshivot*, there appeared on the scene masters such as Ḥayyim *Halberstam of Sanz (1797–1876) and Yitsḥaq Me'ir Rothenberg Alter of *Ger (1799–1866), who were better known for their halakhic writings than for their Hasidic teachings. In some areas, Hasidism assumed a militant posture in defense of orthodoxy; such was the position of the *Maḥzike ha-Das, organized by the *Belz Ḥasidim in Galicia, and the *tsaddiqim* of Hungary in the battle against Reform. Varieties of Hasidism continued to grow and flourish, such as the intellectualist camp of Polish Hasidism, defined by the elitist circles of Przysucha and Kotsk and their later offshoots in Ger and *Izbica. The Ḥasidim of Zhidachov and Komarno made an attempt to appropriate kabbalistic learning that earlier Ḥasidim had ignored.

1882–1945. This was the period of Hasidism's decline and near obliteration. The pogroms of 1881 and the following years, economic changes, and finally war destroyed the *shtetl*, which had been the natural home of Hasidic piety. Immigration to the West as well as urbanization, industrialization, and secularization within eastern Europe placed masses of Jews in new and unfamiliar situations. New ideologies, including those of organized labor, socialist idealism, and Zionism spoke to the children of Ḥasidim more powerfully than did the *rebbi*s. Still, there remained some important and creative figures on the Hasidic scene, particularly in Poland; for example, R. Yehudah Leib Alter of Ger (1847–1904) and R. *Tsadoq ha-Kohen of Lublin (1823–1900). Developments following World War I, including the pogroms in the Ukraine, and the establishment of Soviet rule, had destructive effects on Hasidic life. During the interwar period, much of the remaining energy within the movement was focused on politics, centering on *Agudat Israel in Poland and on opposition to Zionism both in Europe and in Erets Yisra'el, where Hasidism had established an important presence. The Holocaust destroyed the remains of Hasidism almost completely, including thousands of Hasidic masters and their faithful disciples.

1946–Present. The few "brands plucked from the fire" of Hasidic life, as they called themselves, began to reorganize immediately after the war. Hasidic writings were published in the displaced-persons camps as early as 1946. Attempts were made to explain the calamity, with blame often assigned to assimilated Jewry, religious reform, or Zionism. Hungarian Ḥasidim, whose survival rate was somewhat higher than elsewhere, organized around R. Yo'el Teitelbaum (1888–1979) of *Satmar, who by 1947 had reestablished his court in the Williamsburg section of Brooklyn, New York, and had begun a vast private social service network for the rescue and resettlement of his followers. Rabbi Yo'el's preaching and writing continued the extreme anti-Zionism and uncompromising ultra-Orthodoxy of prewar Hungary, now taking the form of controversial active opposition to the Jewish state. Lubavitch Hasidism, established in the United States in 1940 by R. Yosef Yitsḥaq Schneersohn, began to create a far-flung educational system that included many thousands of Jews not from Lubavitch homes, some of whom joined the fast-growing movement. Under the leadership of R. Menaḥem Mendel Schneerson, beginning in 1950, Lubavitch became a tremendous international movement, reaching out to all Jews and seeking to make them more observant and committed to traditional Jewish life. In the last years of R. Menaḥem Mendel's life, there was an outburst of messianic fervor in Lubavitch Hasidism, many claiming that the *rebbi* himself was about to be revealed as the Messiah. The Lubavitch movement was denounced in other Orthodox circles. In the postwar period other Hasidic groups achieved prominence: Bobov, reorganized in Brooklyn by R. Shelomoh Halberstam; Belz and Ger, both centered in Jerusalem; and *Vizhnitz, centered in Bene Beraq. The Hasidic community has grown significantly in recent decades and has attracted outsiders, not a few of Sephardi descent, as well as some Jews from nonobservant backgrounds (see BAʿAL TESHUVAH). At the same time, *Neo-Hasidism, in its various manifestations, has brought aspects of the Hasidic heritage to many who live outside the Hasidic world.

Hasidic Literature. Hasidism was not initially a literary movement, and its teachings were spread first by word of mouth rather than by writing. Nevertheless, perhaps as many as ten thousand works have been published, from the first book in 1780 to the present. Hasidic literature may be divided into three types, each of which has its origins in the early oral teachings of the masters.

Teachings and homilies are the classic holy books, most of which take the form of homilies on the weekly Torah portions, passages from *Psalms* and the Five Scrolls, and selected Talmudic legends. The first to be published was *Toledot Yaʿaqov Yosef* by R. Yaʿaqov Yosef ha-Kohen of Polonnoye. Many collections of homilies were published posthumously by students or descendants after their masters' deaths. Though the homilies were always delivered in Yiddish, they were published in Hebrew, based on notes written by the master or summaries written by students. A small group were originally written as books in Hebrew and not culled from oral sermons. Classic among these is the *Tanya'* by *Shneur Zalman of Lyady. The Ḥabad school also is the source of many such writings.

From its earliest period, Hasidism cultivated the oral tale as an important vehicle for conveying its teachings. The Ba'al Shem Tov himself was a master storyteller, and the desire of Hasidism to bring its message to the uneducated masses of Ukrainian Jewry made this vessel a natural one. The body of Hasidic tales includes original stories, many based on actual events or conversations between masters and disciples; reworkings of older Jewish tales, now placed in a Hasidic setting; and tales based on folk motifs. The first printed collection of these tales is **Shivḥei ha-Besht*, published in Kopyś in 1814. Many of the most important collections were published only after 1900; their late publication dates as well as their fantastic content have led to much controversy among scholars as to their historical reliability.

Counsels, ethical wills, and spiritual "recipes," sometimes published as discreet units and sometimes appended to more formal teachings or tales, contain some of the most powerful Hasidic statements. Prayer, inward devotion, and the constant service of God are among their key themes.

• Joseph Dan, *Ha-Sippur ha-Ḥasidi* (Jerusalem, 1975). Simon Dubnow, *Toledot ha-Ḥasidut* (Tel Aviv, 1966). Immanuel Etkes, "Hasidism as a Movement—The First Stage," in *Hasidism: Continuity or Innovation*, edited by Bezalel Safran (Cambridge, Mass., 1988). Arthur Green, in *Back to the Sources*, edited by Barry W. Holtz (New York, 1984), pp. 361–401. Zeev Gries, *Sefer, Sofer, ve-Sippur be-Re'shit ha-Ḥasidut* (Tel Aviv, 1992). Zeev Gries, *Sifrut ha-Hanhagot* (Jerusalem, 1989). Gershon Hundert, ed., *Essential Papers on Hasidism: Origins to Present* (New York, 1991). Gedalyah Nigal, *Ha-Sipporet ha-Ḥasidit* (Jerusalem, 1981), further bibliography pp. 295–310. Rivka Schatz-Uffenheimer, *Hasidism as Mysticism* (New York, 1993). Elijah Judah Schochet, *The Hasidic Movement and the Ga'on of Vilna* (Northvale, N.J., 1994). Aharon Verthaim, *Law and Custom in Hasidism* (Hoboken, N.J., 1992). Joseph Weiss, *Studies in Eastern European Jewish Mysticism* (Oxford, 1985). Mordecai Wilensky, *Ḥasidim u-Mitnagdim* (Jerusalem, 1970).

—ARTHUR GREEN

HASKALAH (הַשְׂכָּלָה; Enlightenment), movement among the Jews of central and eastern Europe in the late eighteenth and nineteenth centuries to acquire modern European culture and secular knowledge. The Haskalah opposed the dominance of rabbinic Orthodoxy in Jewish life and culture and the restriction of education to Talmudic studies. Spreading eastward from Berlin (see MENDELSSOHN, MOSES), the Haskalah shared many of the values of the European Enlightenment and attempted to steer a middle course between unbending Orthodoxy and radical *assimilation. Through an emphasis on the importance of pure (Biblical) Hebrew as a literary medium, the Haskalah hoped to foster a specifically Jewish cultural consciousness. The character of Haskalah activity differed in various countries (Germany, Russia, Galicia, Lithuania). In eastern Europe, the Haskalah was tantamount to westernization, and its efforts to substitute modern schools for the traditional *ḥeder* were violently resisted by the Orthodox; Haskalah writers in Galicia countered with bitter satires, attacking the obscurantism, fanaticism, and superstitions of the Ḥasidim and the Talmudists (for example, Isaac Erter's satire *Mo'znei Mishqal*), but these writers also advanced historical research considerably in their scholarly periodicals (*Bikkurei ha-'Ittim*, 1820–1831; *He-Ḥaluts*, 1852–1889; *Kerem Ḥemed*, 1853–1857). To counteract excessive devotion to the Talmud and rabbinic theology, secular schools were founded and new pedagogic manuals of instructions written (by Hartwig Wessely in Berlin and Naphtali Herz Homberg in Galicia). Their severe rationalism notwithstanding, the Maskilim (proponents of the Haskalah) were animated by a romantic desire to return to nature (Y. L. Gordon) and by a high regard for manual labor (schools of arts and crafts were opened at Tarnopol in 1819 and in Odessa in 1826). Maskilim advocated an esthetic reform of the synagogue service and in literature exhibited both a particular interest in ancient heroes (Saul, Samson) and an inclination to romanticism and hedonism (translations of the pastoral poetry of Haller, Gessner, Kleist as well as verses in honor of wine, women, and love appeared in *Me'assef*, the first literary periodical [1784–1811] of the Maskilim). The opponents of the Haskalah feared that the movement would lead to the diminishment of historical Judaism; that it had too little regard for Jewish sentiment, tradition, and piety; and that its critical scholarship would undermine Orthodoxy and serve the purposes of Reform. By the end of the nineteenth century, the Haskalah had run its course. Some of its ideas and achievements were firmly established; others, however, became anachronisms. On the one hand, full cultural emancipation rendered a Hebrew Haskalah unrealistic; on the other hand, it became obvious that social emancipation had failed and that cultural reform would not stem the rising tide of antisemitism. Writers began to denounce the Haskalah as a betrayal of Jewish identity, but the growing awareness of Jewish nationhood as expressed in *Zionism was in many ways a result of the influence of the Haskalah, which had created a secular middle class faithful to historic tradition and Hebrew culture, yet alive to Western ideas.

• Frederique van Cleeff-Hiegentlich, "Reflections on the Relationship between the Dutch 'Haskalah' and the German 'Haskalah,'" in *Dutch Jewish History, Proceedings of the Symposium on the History of the Jews in the Netherlands, November–December 1982*, edited by Jozeph Michman, vol. 1 (Tel Aviv, Jerusalem, 1984), pp. 207–218. Emanuel Etkes, "The Gaon of Vilna and the Haskalah Movement: Image and Reality," *Binah* 2 (1989): 147–175. Amram Gamliel, "A Spark of Enlightenment among the Jews of Yemen," *Hebrew Studies* 25 (1984): 82–89. Emanuel S. Goldsmith, "Mordecai M. Kaplan and the Retrieval of the 'Haskalah,'" *Judaism* 37 (1988): 295–306. Arthur Hertzberg, "The Enlightenment and Western Religion," in *Interwoven Destinies: Jews and Christians through the Ages*, edited by Eugene J. Fisher (New York, 1993), pp. 134–142. Jacob Katz, ed., *Toward Modernity: the European Jewish Model* (New Brunswick, N.J., 1987). Frances Malino and David Sorkin, eds., "Mordechai Aaron Guenzburg: A Lithuanian Maskil Faces Modernity," in *From East and West: Jews in a Changing Europe, 1750–1870* (Oxford, 1990), pp. 126–147. Moshe Pelli, *The Age of Haskalah: Studies in Hebrew Literature of the Enlightenment in Germany* (Leiden, 1979). Jacob J. Schacter, "Haskalah, Secular Studies and the Close of the Yeshiva in Volozhin in 1892," *Torah u-Madda Journal* 2 (1990): 76–133. Yaacov Shavit, "A Duty Too Heavy to Bear: Hebrew in the Berlin Haskalah, 1783–1819—Between Classic, Modern, and Romantic," in *Hebrew in Ashkenaz: A Language in Exile*, edited by Lewis Glinert (New York, 1993), pp. 111–128. David Sorkin, "From Context to Comparison: The German Haskalah and Reform Catholicism," *Tel Aviver Jahrbuch fuer Deutsche Geschichte* 20 (1991): 23–58. David Sorkin, "Jews, the Enlightenment and Religious Toleration: Some Reflections," *Leo Baeck Institute Year Book* 37 (1992): 3–16.

HASKAMAH. See APPROBATION.

HASMONEANS, family name of the Hasmonean, or Maccabean, priestly dynasty. The Hasmonean name came to the fore when Mattathias, the elderly priest, escalated the revolt against the Seleucid ruler of Syria, *Antiochus IV Epiphanes, in 166 BCE. Upon the death of Mattathias, the revolt was led by his son, *Judah the Maccabee, who succeeded in capturing parts of Jerusalem and purifying the Temple. When Judah died in battle in 161 BCE, his brother Jonathan assumed the leadership of the anti-Seleucid forces, and proved an able military and political leader, utilizing conflicts within the Seleucid court in Antioch to enhance his power in Judah. In addition to his military position, Jonathan was appointed, in 152 BCE, high priest of the Jerusalem Temple, a post that seemed to have remained vacant since the death of *Alcimus, some seven years earlier. In 143 BCE, Jonathan was murdered by his opponents, and his place was assumed by his brother Simon. Simon's political maneuvers soon brought further gains, and Judah was exempted from paying tribute to the Seleucids, a de facto recognition of the Jews' independence. Simon continued to make military conquests in the regions around Judah and dislodged Seleucid supporters from their last stronghold in Jerusalem. Simon was succeeded in 135 BCE by his son John Hyrcanus I, who embarked upon further territorial conquests, forcing the non-Jewish populations of the conquered regions to adopt the Jewish way of life and destroying the Samaritan temple on Mount Gerizim. Hyrcanus was the first Hasmonean to issue coinage, a sign of full political independence, and his son Aristobulus I (died 103 CE), was the first to declare himself not only a high priest and head of the Jewish nation but also king. Upon Aristobulus's death, his powers were assumed by his brother Alexander Yannai (died 76 BCE), whose reign saw not only the expansion of the Hasmonean kingdom to its largest extent ever but also the eruption of a full-scale civil war between Yannai and his numerous opponents, who objected to his rule for religious, moral, and economic reasons. Following Yannai's death, his wife, Salome Alexandra, ruled, and her own death, in 67 BCE, brought about a fierce struggle between their two sons, Aristobulus II and Hyrcanus II, which ended in the conquest of Judah by the Romans (63 BCE). The period from 40 to 37 saw the brief reign of the Hasmonean Antigonus II, son of Aristobulus II, but Herod, having been nominated by the Roman king of Judaea (as the province was now called), soon took charge of his realm and eventually destroyed the remnants of the Hasmonean dynasty.

The Hasmonean period was a formative one in Jewish history. What began as a rebellion against the anti-Jewish measures of a Seleucid king soon turned into a war for political independence, and the war for independence led to the establishment of an expansionist Jewish state. Moreover, this period witnessed several major socioreligious developments: the transfer of high priestly power from its hereditary holders, the sons of Zadok, to a previously obscure priestly family, the Hasmoneans; the rapid Hellenization of the very dynasty whose forefathers had fought against the Jewish Hellenizers; and the forced conversions of the non-Jewish populations of Erets Yisra'el and their partial incorporation into Jewish society. Jewish independence brought with it much internal strife, and the Hasmonean period saw recurrent inner Jewish conflicts and massacres, as well as the emergence of the three main Jewish sects—the *Sadducees, *Pharisees, and *Essenes—sects that remained active on the Jewish scene long after the Hasmonean dynasty had ceased to exist.

• Elias Joseph Bickerman, *From Ezra to the Last of the Maccabees: Foundations of Post-Biblical Judaism* (New York, 1962), pp. 91–186. Shaye J. D. Cohen, *From the Maccabees to the Mishnah*, Library of Early Christianity, vol. 7 (Philadelphia, 1987). Martin Hengel, *Judaism and Hellenism: Studies in Their Encounter in Palestine during the Early Hellenistic Period*, translated by John Bowden (Philadelphia, 1981). Emil Schürer, Geza Vermes, and Fergus Millar, *The History of the Jewish People in the Age of Jesus Christ* (Edinburgh, 1973), vol. 1, pp. 137–286. Avigdor Tcherikover, *Hellenistic Civilization and the Jews*, translated by Shimon Applebaum (Philadelphia, 1959).

—GIDEON BOHAK

HASSAGAT GEVUL (הַסָּגַת גְּבוּל; overstepping of bounds), prohibition against encroachment on another's land or upon other economic and property rights.

The biblical prohibition is derived from the verse "You shall not remove your neighbor's landmark, which they of old time have set, in your inheritance which you shall inherit, in the land that the Lord your God gives you to possess" (*Dt*. 19.14). It applies to the fraudulent removal of boundary markers dividing adjoining parcels of land in Erets Yisra'el with the intent of enlarging one's own parcel by encroaching upon that of a neighbor. While such improper conduct would constitute a transgression of the more general prohibition against theft even in the absence of the concept of *hassagat gevul*, the sages interpreted the above verse as imposing an additional, particular prohibition intended to preserve the integrity of land ownership in Erets Yisra'el.

The reference to landmarks "which they of old time have set" was understood to mean that the prohibition was applicable not only to boundaries between individual parcels but also to boundaries between the territories of the various tribes of Israel: any readjustment of the boundaries between the tribes not in accord with the boundaries fixed by Joshua would be prohibited.

With the transitions that took place in the late Talmudic and post-Talmudic social and economic environment from an agararian, land-based economy to a commercial, capital-based economy, in which income-producing opportunities for Jews were severely restricted, the rabbis expanded the prohibition to encompass other forms of improper economic encroachments. While Talmudic sources defended the overriding principles of free enterprise against attempts to impose protectionist restraints upon free competition (as evidenced by rulings such as that of R. Huna' [*B. B.* 21b] that an artisan already operating in a particular courtyard could not prevent the entry of an additional artisan into the courtyard, even though such competition would certainly impact negatively upon his income), the codes adopt a more receptive approach to such restraints, in areas that were considered particularly worthy of protection. These included monopolies purchased from the authorities at considerable expense; the employment contracts of teachers, rabbis, and ritual slaughterers; residential leases; and copyright.

• Menachem Elon, ed., *The Principles of Jewish Law* (Jerusalem, 1975), pp. 340–346. Isaac Herzog, *The Main Institutions of Jewish Law*, 2d ed. (London, 1965), vol. 1, pp. 127–132. Nahum Rakover, *Ha-Mishpar ba-Mishpat ha-'Ivri* (Jerusalem, 1987), pp. 103–134. Shlomo Yosef Zevin, ed., *Entsiqlopedyah Talmudit* (Jerusalem, 1981), vol. 9, pp. 542–546.

—BEN TZION GREENBERGER

HASSAGOT (הַשָּׂגוֹת; criticisms), a genre of Jewish literature in which one author criticizes the work of another. *Hassagot* are generally directed to Jewish legal codes, although some critique writings on Jewish beliefs and philosophy.

Jewish legal codes claim to state the normative law that, theoretically, should apply to all observant Jews wherever they may live. In fact, Jewish communities in different locales often had their own regional practices and authorities. When a code ruled against these, *hassagot* were often written in defense of local tradition. Sometimes the code's format itself was the source of criticism. This was especially true in the case of Maimonides' *Mishneh Torah*. Maimonides consciously omitted the sources of the legal decisions in his code. This generated the heated criticism of Avraham ben David of Posquières, who stated that failure to provide such sources meant that no one could determine the accuracy or authority of Maimonides' views. He went on to point out what he considered flawed decisions throughout Maimonides' code. He is, therefore, called Ba'al ha-Hassagot (Master of Criticisms).

Other famous *hassagot* are those of R. Zeraḥyah ben Yitsḥaq ha-Levi Gerondi on Yitsḥaq Alfasi's code and Nahmanides' critique of Maimonides' *Sefer ha-Mitsvot*.

• Menachem Elon, *Jewish Law: History, Sources, Principles*, 4 vols. (Philadelphia, 1994). Isadore Twersky, *Rabad of Posquières: A Twelfth-Century Talmudist* (Cambridge, 1962). Isadore Twersky, *Rabbi Moses Nahmanides (Ramban): Explorations in His Religious and Literary Virtuosity* (Cambridge, Mass., 1983).

—MICHAEL CHERNICK

ḤATAM SOFER. See SOFER FAMILY.

ḤATAN. See BETROTHAL.

ḤATAN TORAH AND ḤATAN BE-RE'SHIT (חֲתַן תּוֹרָה; חֲתַן בְּרֵאשִׁית; bridegroom of the Torah and bridegroom of *Genesis*), titles of honor accorded two members of the congregation during the synagogue service on *Simḥat Torah (which in Israel coincides with *Shemini 'Atseret). At this service, the annual cycle of the reading of the Pentateuch is concluded and a new one immediately begun. The person called up to the reading of the last section of *Deuteronomy* (33.27–34.12) is called the *ḥatan Torah*, the person who is called up to the reading of the first section of *Genesis* (1.1–2.3) is called the *ḥatan Be-Re'shit*. Until the Middle Ages, one person read the two sections from a single scroll (as is still the Yemenite custom); today the portions of the two "bridegrooms" are read from separate scrolls. At one time the coveted honors of bridegroom were bestowed upon the rabbi and **parnas*, but now any worthy congregant may be honored (and in some congregations, women may be honored as *kallot ha-Torah* [brides of the Torah]). In certain places (such as Italy), the "bridegrooms" would be conducted to the synagogue to the accompaniment of flares and an orchestra, while in some Sephardi synagogues, the "bridegrooms" sit on special chairs of honor. In Sephardi congregations in England and the United States, the choice was made by election; the exposure involved sometimes made the chosen "bridegrooms" refuse the honor, for which they might be fined by the synagogue elders. The two "bridegrooms" usually entertain the congregation in celebration of the occasion.

• Ismar Elbogen, *Jewish Liturgy: A Comprehensive History* (Philadelphia, 1993).

ḤATIMAH (חֲתִימָה; sealing). *Benedictions begin either with the *petiḥah*, the full benediction formula, which includes the divine name and the affirmation of the divine kingship: "Blessed are You, O Lord our God, Sovereign of the universe"; or they begin with the *ḥatimah*, a shortened formula: "Blessed are You, O Lord." Both formulas then conclude with the mention of the activity for which the deity is being praised or thanked. The *ḥatimah* is derived from *Psalms* 119.12; the *petiḥah* is ascribed by the Talmud to the Men of the Keneset ha-Gedolah. Often prayers open with the *petiḥah* and conclude with the *ḥatimah*, which summarizes the content of the prayer. Sometimes the *petiḥah* is omitted.

• Ismar Elbogen, *Jewish Liturgy: A Comprehensive History*, translated by Raymond P. Scheindlin (Philadelphia, 1993). Joseph Heinemann, *Prayer in the Talmud: Forms and Patterns* (Berlin, 1977). Abraham E. Millgram, *Jewish Worship* (Philadelphia, 1971), pp. 91ff.

—A. STANLEY DREYFUS

HATRA'AH. See WARNING.

HATRED. The Bible commands "You shall not hate your brother in your heart" (*Lv*. 19.17). Any hostile feeling amounts to hatred. Hatred of evildoers or of the enemies of God, which often finds eloquent expression in the Bible (e.g., *Ps*. 139.21–22), is considerably toned down by the rabbis, who emphasize the duty of hating not the sinner but the sin; hence the ideal course is to prevail upon the evildoer to repent. Groundless hatred is considered by the rabbis to be the greatest of all social vices. "The First Temple is said to have been destroyed because of the commission of the three cardinal sins of Judaism—idolatry, immorality, and murder—but the Second Temple because of the prevalence of groundless hatred" (*Yoma'* 9b). Hatred will ruin one's life (*Avot* 2.16) and is even equated with murder (*Derekh Erets Rabbah* 11).

• Eugene W. Brice, "A Study of Hatred and Anger in Old Testament Man," Ph.D. dissertation, Yale University, 1962.

HATTARAT HORA'AH. See ORDINATION.

HATTARAT NEDARIM. See VOWS AND OATHS.

ḤATUNNAH. See BETROTHAL.

HAVDALAH (הַבְדָּלָה; Differentiation [Between the Holy and Secular]), prayer recited at *motsa'ei* (conclusion) Shabbat and festivals to indicate the distinction between the sacred day that has ended and the weekday that is beginning. Havdalah corresponds to *Qiddush, which proclaims the sanctity of the Sabbath day at its beginning. According to *halakhah*, no work should be done and no food consumed after nightfall until Havdalah has been recited. One form of Havdalah is incorporated as part of the fourth benediction of the *ʿAmidah of Maʿariv; but Havdalah is recited again over a cup of wine (or, in its absence, over another liquid) as a separate benediction at the end of the Maʿariv service and then at home (it is unclear whether Havdalah originated in the home or the synagogue). According to the Talmud, Havdalah was instituted by the Men of the *Keneset ha-Gedolah, but scholars have suggested that it was initiated as part of dining practices in the Greco-Roman period (*Ber*. 33b). The prayer enumerates the differences between "holy and profane," between "light and darkness," between "Israel and the gentiles," and between the Sabbath and the weekdays. As part of the ceremony, it is customary also to recite a benediction over *spices (in a special spice box) and over the light of a candle (*Ber*. 8.5–6, 52a). If a festival follows directly upon the Sabbath, a special form of Havdalah is combined with the Qiddush (see YAQNEHAZ). In several versions of the Havdalah service *Elijah is mentioned prominently; according to a belief that originated after the Crusades, Elijah's advent as harbinger of the Messiah (see *Mal*. 3.23) would occur on a Saturday evening after the conclusion of the Sabbath. In certain communities, such as Morocco and Syria, participants would place drops of wine from the cup over which Havdalah was recited on the backs of their necks and in their pockets for good luck in the coming week.

• Ismar Elbogen, *Jewish Liturgy: A Comprehensive History*, translated by Raymond P. Scheindlin (Philadelphia, New York, and Jerusalem, 1993), pp. 41–42, 118, 123. Joseph Gutmann, ed., *Beauty in Holiness: Studies in Jewish Customs and Ceremonial Art* (New York, 1970), pp. 204–280. Jacob Z. Lauterbach, *Studies in Jewish Law, Custom and Folklore* (New York, 1970), pp. 75–132. Macy Nulman, *The Encyclopedia of Jewish Prayer* (Northvale, N.J., and London, 1993), pp. 169–171. Zvi A. Yehuda, "The Ritual and the Concept of 'Havdalah,'" *Judaism* 43.1 (1994): 78–86.

ḤAVER (חָבֵר; companion), term or title used to denote a scholar or pious man. A disciple who reached a standard of scholarship almost equal to that of his master was referred to as a *talmid ḥaver* (*Ber*. 27b). During the Second Temple era, the term was bestowed upon members of a Pharisaic association that observed the Levitical rules prescribed for the handling of sacred food and that was punctilious in the matter of tithes and ritual purity; the opposite of *ḥaver* in this context is *ʿ*am ha-ʾarets*. In amoraic times, *ḥaver* became synonymous with **talmid ḥakham* (*B. B*. 75a). In Babylonia the title *ḥaver* was given to each of three rabbis who sat in the front row of sages in the academy, but at the end of the geonic period the title was extended to sages outside the academy; the title was also given to scholars in the Arabic-speaking world. In the sixteenth century the title *ḥaver* was conferred upon young scholars. According to R. Mosheh Sofer (1762–1839), it was customary in Germany to confer the title *ḥaver* on learned individuals who were not ordained rabbis. He states that in Moravia, however, a rabbi with fewer than ten students in his college could not confer the title of *ḥaver* without the permission of his district rabbi. In eastern Europe, outstanding scholars were called *ḥaver* and entitled to special privileges. The conferment of the title *ḥaver* was in vogue in Germany up to the 1930s and is still in use in various communities of German Jews in the United States.

• Chaim Rabin, *Qumran Studies* (London, 1957), a comparison of the Qumran community and *ḥaverim*. —SHMUEL HIMELSTEIN

ḤAVURAH (חֲבוּרָה; company or society), a small group of Jews who meet together in religious fellowship. The concept originated in Second Temple times among Pharisees and Essenes. In the United States in the late 1960s *ḥavurot* arose as gatherings for worship, study, and fellowship. *Ḥavurot* initially served as alternatives to the established Jewish modes of worship in America and came about in reaction to what their members conceived of as the formal, cold, unegalitarian atmosphere of synagogues at the time. Ḥavurot Shalom, the first *ḥavurah*, was founded in Somerville, Massachusetts, in 1968; among its founders were Zalman Schachter, a leader in the Renewal movement, of which the *ḥavurah* was one manifestation, and Arthur Green, who later served as president of the Reconstructionist Rabbinical College. The second *ḥavurah* was started in New York in 1970. Other *ḥavurot* soon emerged in other cities, usually in university communities. The *ḥavurot* did not employ rabbis; they emphasized equality of participants, experimented in worship, and strove toward spirituality and meaning in Jewish practice. In the 1980s *ḥavurot* entered the mainstream. Hundreds of *ḥavurot* were established throughout the United States and other countries. Many of them are not intended for worship but rather for study and socializing and often operate in conjunction with established synagogues. The rise of *ḥavurot* was part of a larger movement of revival within American Judaism that manifested, among other things, a quest for more knowledge of Judaism as well as for experiencing the spiritual dimensions of religious life.

• Jacob Neusner, ed., *Contemporary Judaic Fellowship in Theory and in Practice* (New York, 1972). Riv-Ellen Prell, *Prayer and Community: The Ḥavurah in American Judaism* (Detroit, 1989). —YAAKOV ARIEL

ḤAYON, NEḤEMYAH (c.1655–1730), kabbalist with strong Shabbatean tendencies. A descendant of a Sephardi family from Bosnia, Ḥayon was born in Sarajevo and brought up in Jerusalem, and he later traveled in the Balkans and Italy. Having received the pamphlet *Raza' Mehemanuta'* (The Secret of Faith) attributed to *Shabbetai Tsevi, he changed its name to *Mehemanuta' de-Khula'* (The Secret of All), on which he wrote his commentary *ʿOz le-Elohim* (Berlin, 1713). Ḥayon criticized both Avraham *Cohen de Herrera and Avraham Miguel Cardoso (see CARDOSO FAMILY) for their metaphorical interpretations of Yitsḥaq *Luria's doctrine of **tsimtsum* (contraction), accusing them of introducing Platonic concepts into Lurianic Kabbalah. Ḥayon's doctrine concerning the three *partsufim* (faces) of the deity was adjudged by his opponents to be Shabbatean. In Amsterdam he at first enjoyed the patronage of the Sephardi *ḥakham* Shelomoh ben Yaʿaqov *Ayllon (who was also accused of being a Shabbatean) but was persecuted by Tsevi Hirsch *Ashkenazi, the rabbi of the Ashkenazi congregation. The controversy developed into an Ashkenazi–Sephardi dispute, in which other communities (London, Leghorn, Hamburg, Smyrna, and Constantinople) became involved. Finally losing Ayllon's support, Ḥayon was forced to leave for North Africa, where he wandered for the rest of his life.

• Elisheva Carlebach, *The Pursuit of Heresy: Rabbi Moses Hagiz and the Sabbatian Controversies* (New York, 1990). —NISSIM YOSHA

ḤAYYAT, YEHUDAH (c.1450–1510), a leading kabbalist in the age of the expulsion of the Jews from Spain, when the Kabbalah ceased to be studied only in closed, esoteric circles and became a central component of Jewish culture. Ḥayyat's best-known work is *Minḥat Yehudah*, which is a commentary on **Maʿarekhet ha-'Elohut*. It was printed, together with the text, in Ferrara in 1557, and again in Mantua in 1558. Ḥayyat wrote the commentary at the request of R. Yosef Yaʿbets, one of the leaders of Spanish Jewry, who settled in Italy after the expulsion and wrote treatises indicating his belief in imminent messianic redemption. Ḥayyat's system is based on the Zohar and the teachings of R. Menaḥem Recanati. Reflecting the ideological norms of the age of the expulsion, Ḥayyat opposes philosophical presentations of Judaism, and his long quotations from the Zohar present a concept of Jewish theosophy that is intended to replace medieval rationalism. *Maʿarekhet ha-'Elohut* with Ḥayyat's commentary became one in the minds of many readers, and together they influenced subsequent kabbalists, as well as nonkabbalists who used the work as a source for the basic concepts of the Kabbalah.

• Gershom Gerhard Scholem, *Kabbalah* (New York, 1974). —JOSEPH DAN

ḤAYYIM AL-ḤAKHAM. See YOSEF ḤAYYIM BEN ELIYYAHU AL-ḤAKHAM.

ḤAYYIM BEN BETSAL'EL (c.1520–1588), Talmudic scholar, halakhist, and grammarian. He was born in Poznań and was the older brother of R. *Yehudah Liva' ben Betsal'el. He studied with R. Yitsḥaq ha-Sefardi, who greatly influenced him, with R. Shelomoh Luria, with R. Shalom Shakna of Lublin, and with R. Mosheh Isserles, and he served as rabbi of Worms and Friedberg.

His best-known work, *Vikkuaḥ Mayim Ḥayyim* (Amsterdam, 1712), contains a strong critique of the writings of both R. Yosef Karo and R. Mosheh Isserles. The former claimed (in the introduction to his *Beit Yosef*) that he was not great enough to decide between the earlier authorities but then proceeded to do just that. Rabbi Ḥayyim criticized Isserles's *Torat Ḥattat* (which dealt with the dietary laws) for unintentionally leading people astray, maintaining that it should have been restricted to the use of qualified scholars (a strategy that he had apparently adopted himself in regard to a similar kind of work that he had written). He also chided Isserles for not sufficiently delineating the weight of German custom, which was particularly authoritative; for introducing a new category of leniency; and for setting aside well-based legal practices in favor of custom.

Rabbi Ḥayyim composed a work on Jewish ethics entitled *Sefer ha-Ḥayyim* (Kraków, 1593) and a work on Hebrew grammar called *ʿEts Ḥayyim*. In a comment, which accords with his brother's views, R. Ḥayyim attributes the relative neglect of the study of Hebrew grammar to the fact that even the most pious Ashkenazi scholars confined themselves to the study of the Talmud. Like his brother, R. Ḥayyim wrote a supercommentary, *Be'er Mayim Ḥayyim*, on Rashi's commentary to the Torah. His ethical works were popular in Hasidic circles.

• Haim H. Ben-Sasson, *Hagut ve-Hanhagah* (Jerusalem, 1959). Jacob Elbaum, *Petiḥut ve-Histagrut* (Jerusalem, 1990). Asher Siev, *Ha-Rema'* (Jerusalem, 1956), pp. 47–49. —EPHRAIM KANARFOGEL

ḤAYYIM BEN YITSḤAQ OF VIENNA (13th cent.), rabbinic scholar, tosafist, and legal authority; son of *Yitsḥaq ben Mosheh of Vienna. He is often referred to as R. Ḥayyim Or Zaruʿa after his father's well-known halakhic work. Rabbi Ḥayyim composed an abridged version of that work entitled *Qitsur Or Zaruʿa* or *Simmanei Or Zaruʿa*. He studied with R. Me'ir ben Barukh of Rothenburg and later with R. Asher ben Yeḥi'el. He lived in several German cities, including Regensburg, Neustadt, and Cologne. A collection of his *responsa* (Leipzig, 1865) has survived. In it, he describes aspects of the curriculum and travel practices of *yeshivah* students in his day. He based his legal decisions on the teachings of leading rabbinic scholars in northern France and Germany. Rabbi Ḥayyim also composed homilies on the halakhic regulations of festivals.

• Noah Goldstein, "Rabbi Ḥayyim Eliezer ben Isaac Or Zaruʿa: His Life and Work, and a Digest of His Responsa," D.H.L. dissertation, Yeshiva University, 1959. Isaac S. Lange, ed., *Pesuqei Halakhah shel R. Ḥayyim Or Zaruʿa* (Jerusalem, 1972). Efraim E. Urbach, *Baʿalei ha-Tosafot* (Jerusalem, 1980), vol. 1, pp. 442–445, and index. —EPHRAIM KANARFOGEL

ḤAYYIM OF VOLOZHIN. See VOLOZHINER, ḤAYYIM BEN YITSḤAQ.

ḤAZAL (חֲזַ״ל), word formed by the initials of the phrase *ḥakhameinu zikhronam li-verakhah*, "our sages of blessed memory." Like *razal* (*rabboteinu zikhronam li-verakhah*, "our masters of blessed memory"), it refers to the teachers of the Talmudic period.

ḤAZAQ (חֲזָק; "Be strong!"), exclamation (usually *ḥazaq ḥazaq ve-nitḥazzeq*, "be strong and encouraged!") made by the congregation to the reader at the completion of the synagogal reading of the Torah; to someone for a successful achievement; and among Ashkenazim, to a **bar mitsvah* after his reading of the **haftarah*. The term *ḥazaq* was inspired by the congratulation *ḥazaq ve-'emats*, "be strong and courageous," found in *Deuteronomy* 31.7, 23, and *Joshua* 1.6–9. Sephardim and Eastern Jews congratulate one who has performed a **mitsvah* in the synagogue with the phrase *ḥazaq u-varukh*, "be strong and blessed."

ḤAZAQAH (חֲזָקָה; taking hold), the presumptive right of one in possession of property to retain ownership until such right is disproved (usucapion). *Ḥazaqah* is an important principle of Jewish law and is one of the bases for the Jewish legal theory of ownership and possession as well as personal and ritual status. The state of a thing or person as it is known to have last existed forms the presumption in law for all questions involving present status. For example, the undisturbed possession of land for a period of three years creates the presumption of a legal title. The transfer of land is effected by means of an act of *acquisition (*qinyan*), also called *ḥazaqah*. In the course of time, the right of *ḥazaqah* had many applications in Jewish law, such as the right to a certain seat in a synagogue. In Italy, the term *jus gazaga* (from Latin *jus* [law], and *ḥazaqah*) was applied during the ghetto period to the rights of Jewish tenants in houses they were not permitted to own. Throughout the ages, the rabbis have been stringent in their rulings concerning *ḥazaqah* to protect internal communal order and to regulate relations with non-Jews.

• Menachem Elon, *Jewish Law: History, Sources, Principles*, 4 vols. (Philadelphia, 1994).

HAZKARAT NESHAMOT. See EL MALE' RAḤAMIM.

ḤAZON ISH. See KARELITZ, AVRAHAM YESHAʿYAHU.

ḤAZZAN. See CANTOR.

ḤAZZAN, YISRA'EL MOSHEH (1807–1863), rabbinical authority. Born in İzmir, he was taken in 1811 by his father to Jerusalem, where he studied in the *yeshivah* of his grandfather, the noted scholar Yosef Refa'el Ḥazzan. He soon won a reputation for his scholarship and eventually became a member of the *beit din* of R. Yaʿaqov Finzi. However, he became involved in disagreements with Finzi, which was one of the reasons he was sent abroad on missions to Sephardi communities in western Europe (spending some time in London, where he wrote against the Reform movement) and North America. From 1847 to 1862, he served as *av beit din* in Rome, Corfu, and Alexandria. His interests included philosophy and the works of the geonic period. Ḥazzan strongly opposed stringent practices and decisions that were unsupported in the Bible and rabbinic literature. In his various community appointments, he emphasized the importance of the Hebrew language.

• Jose Faur, *Rav Yisra'el Mosheh Ḥazzan: Ha-'Ish u-Mishnato* (Haifa, 1978), with an English introduction. —SHALOM BAR-ASHER

ḤAZZANUT. See CANTORIAL MUSIC.

HEAD COVERING. See COVERING OF THE HEAD.

HEALTH. The Talmud derives the obligation to preserve one's health from the biblical mandate "to take heed and preserve your soul" (*Dt*. 4.9). A number of unhygienic and dangerous activities, including the drinking of contaminated water and entering unsafe buildings, are proscribed on the basis of this mandate (Maimonides, *Hilkhot Rotseaḥ* 12.4–15). It is, however, permitted to engage in dangerous activities for the sake of earning a living (*B. M.* 112a). The biblical verse "And you shall keep my statutes and judgments which a man will do and live by them" (*Lv*. 18.5) is the source for the principle that the preservation of life overrides the performance of the *mitsvot* (*Yoma'* 85b). Hence, it is forbidden to desist from a lifesaving activity on the grounds that it involves a breach of Jewish law, with the exception of the three cardinal offenses of homicide, idolatry, and forbidden sexual relations (*San*. 4a). In all other cases, the saving of life takes precedence over the *mitsvot*, and an individual who insists on fasting on Yom Kippur against medical advice or refuses vital medical therapy on the Sabbath is considered a "pious fool," whose deeds are without any religious merit. Indeed, it is permitted to force an individual to receive lifesaving medical therapy, provided that it is not medically uncertain, highly risky, or unlikely to be of any benefit if administered in a coercive manner. Many biblical and Talmudic laws deal directly with the preservation of life and health, for example, isolation of lepers and quarantine (*Lv*. 12–15); military hygiene (*Dt*. 23.10–15); bodily cleanliness (*ʿA. Z.* 20b); and exercise (*Ket*. 111a). Other laws are commonly understood as measures designed in part to enhance health. Thus, the separation imposed by the laws of *niddah* ensures that a woman has fully recovered from her menstruation and regained her vitality before renewing intercourse. Circumcision, observance of the dietary laws, washing the hands before meals, various ablutions and instructions regarding personal habits, as well as a general insistence upon moderation in all things were seen as contributing to the physical well-being of those who performed them. The rabbis legislated in the area of public health and imposed restrictions upon building and the raising of certain types of livestock in order to protect the health of the community. Under Talmudic law, "matters prohibited because of danger to life and health are treated more stringently than things merely forbidden by the law" (*Ḥul*. 10a). Modern issues such as smoking and drug abuse figure in the contemporary halakhic literature on the preservation of health, and mental health is taken into account in decisions on matters ranging from abortion to plastic surgery.

• David M. Feldman, *Health and Medicine in the Jewish Tradition* (New York, 1986). Immanuel Jakobovits, *Jewish Medical Ethics* (New York, 1959), pp. 73–98. Fred Rosner, *Medicine in the Bible and the Talmud* (New York, 1977). Moshe Halevi Spero, *Judaism and Psychology: Halakhic Perspectives*, The Library of Jewish Law and Ethics, vol. 7 (New York, 1980). —DANIEL SINCLAIR

HEART (Heb. *lev*), a word used frequently in a figurative sense in scriptures; rarely does it refer to the bodily organ (*2 Sm*. 18.14). *Lev* may mean good cheer (*Ps*. 22.27); may be the site of the feeling of fear (*Ps*. 27.3) or courage (*Ez*. 22.14); or it may be considered the organ of thought (*Jer*. 3.16) or memory (*Ps*. 31.13). It is thus a collective concept for the human condition and character. When Saul is anointed ruler, he is said to receive another heart so that he can carry out his duties (*1 Sm.* 10.9). An individual in want, distress, or burdened with guilt is spoken of as having a broken heart healed by God. In rabbinic thought, the heart is also the organ to which all the manifestations of reason and emotion are ascribed. In *Ecclesiastes Rabbah* 1.16 there is an extensive catalog of all aspects of the heart's activities, both positive and negative: "the heart rejoices, the heart weeps, the heart loves, the heart hates (cf. *Pesiqta' de-Rav Kahana'* 16). See also TRANSPLANTS.

• C. A. Briggs, "A Study in the Use of *Lev* and *Levav* in the Old Testament," in *Semitic Studies in Memory of A. Kohut* (Berlin, 1897), pp. 95–105. Solomon Schechter, *Some Aspects of Rabbinic Theology* (New York, 1936), pp. 255–256. —LOU H. SILBERMAN

HEAVEN (Heb. *shamayim*), the upper region of the universe according to traditional *cosmology. "In the beginning the Lord created the heavens and the earth" (*Gn.* 1.1), but "the heavens are the heavens of the Lord and the earth he has given to the sons of man" (*Ps.* 115.16). Heaven is thus the abode of God and the celestial beings, while man has been given the earth for his habitation. The only specific mention made in the Bible of an ascension to heaven is that of Elijah (*2 Kgs.* 2.11); otherwise the Bible is geocentric in its outlook. During the Second Temple and Talmudic periods, the idea developed of heaven as the abode of the righteous after death. Not infrequently descriptions of this heaven of the souls are influenced by descriptions of the post-messianic, eschatological "world to come" (see ʿOLAM HA-ZEH AND ʿOLAM HA-BAʾ), but ultimately the celestial abode of the souls was identified with the heavenly garden of *Eden (or *paradise). Later Midrashic and kabbalistic literature depicted in great detail the life of the righteous in heaven, which has always been the popular symbol of immortality. Modernist thinking (including Reform theology) tends to the philosophical view that heaven refers to a spiritual state rather than a specific place. See also AFTERLIFE.

• Victor Aptowitzer, *The Celestial Temple as Viewed in the Aggadah* (Jerusalem, 1987). Ella Belfer, *The Jewish People and the Kingdom of Heaven: A Study in Jewish Theocracy* (Ramat Gan, 1986). Martha Himmelfarb, *Ascent to Heaven in Jewish and Christian Apocalypses* (New York, 1993).

HEAVE OFFERING. See TERUMAH.

HEBREW LANGUAGE (Heb. ʿIvrit), a branch of the Canaanite group of Semitic languages, possibly adopted by the Israelites after their settlement in Erets Yisra'el. The designation Hebrew for the language is late, and in biblical times the language was known as Yehudit ([Jewish] *2 Kgs.* 18.26). Different forms of Hebrew developed at various periods (Biblical Hebrew, Mishnaic Hebrew, etc.), and the language, even when used for liturgical and literary purposes only, continually absorbed outside influences, particularly from vernaculars currently in use among Jews (Aramaic, Greek, Arabic, etc.). As the language in which the Bible was written, Hebrew became for the rabbis *leshon ha-qodesh* (the holy tongue) and is commonly known by this name in rabbinic literature, which is often extravagant in its praise of the language (for example, Hebrew is "the language spoken by the angels," *Ḥag.* 16a). Many rabbinic statements on the importance of teaching Hebrew as a language (for example, "When the child begins to speak, his father should speak to him in the holy tongue . . . and if he does not speak to him in the holy tongue . . . it is as though he had buried him," *Sifrei* on *Dt.* "ʿEqev" 46; or, "He who dwells in the Land of Israel permanently, eats his food in a state of ritual purity, speaks in the holy tongue, and reads the Shemaʿ morning and evening is certain of the life of the World to Come," Y., *Shab.* 1) were clearly meant to counteract tendencies to neglect Hebrew in favor of the current vernacular. To the rabbis, the language was invested with a special sanctity. As a result, the tendency developed, especially during the Middle Ages, to confine its use to sacred purposes, such as prayer, study, or correspondence of a religious nature. This tendency manifested itself again in the bitter opposition of some religious elements in Erets Yisra'el to the activities of Eliʿezer Ben-Yehudah (1858–1922), whose aim was to make Hebrew the vehicle of ordinary communication. The value of Hebrew was further enhanced by certain Midrashic and mystical traditions, as a result of which a mystical theology of the Hebrew language developed and proved of great importance in kabbalistic speculation and practice (see ALPHABET, HEBREW). Although Hebrew continued to be used by medieval Jewry and, indeed, served as the Jewish lingua franca, significant differences in the attitude to the language developed among different groups. Medieval Spanish Jews preferred Arabic not only for oral communication but also for philosophical, theological, and at times even halakhic writing; Hebrew served as a purely literary medium, mostly for poetry, and Spanish writers insisted on purity of diction and rigid adherence to the forms and syntax of classical Biblical Hebrew and grammar, opposing innovations and the introduction of post-biblical terms. The Franco-German scholars, on the other hand, were never averse to allowing Mishnaic Hebrew and even Aramaic into their vocabulary and regarded Hebrew as the sole medium for written communication and literature. Hebrew became established as the only language acceptable for liturgical purposes, although Talmudic law (*Sot.* 7.1) explicitly permits the use of the vernacular for prayer (including the Shemaʿ and the ʿAmidah). In modern times the vernacular has reappeared in the synagogue both for the sermon and, to greater or lesser degrees, in Reform and Conservative services. Under the impact of Ben-Yehudah and others, Hebrew became the language of the *yishuv* (the modern Jewish community in Erets Yisra'el) and of the State of Israel. Since the time of the *Haskalah, Hebrew has been the language of a secular literature. It is widely studied as a living language in the Diaspora, and only a small group of Ḥaredim refuse to use it for everyday speech because of its holiness. Variant pronunciations of Hebrew developed regionally. Yemenite pronunciations (they pronounce the letter *vav* as "w" and *taf* as "th") are probably the closest to the spoken Hebrew of Bible times. Sharp differences can be distinguished between the Hebrew of the Ashkenazim and the Hebrew of the Sephardim. In modern Erets Yisra'el, the Sephardi pronunciation was adopted as standard, and, as a result, some Ashkenazi synagogues in the West now pray using Sephardi pronunciation.

• Abba Bendavid, *Leshon Miqra' u-Leshon Ḥakhamim* (Tel Aviv, 1967–1971). Ḥemdah Ben-Yehudah, *Ben-Yehudah, Ḥayyav u-Mif'alo* (Jerusalem, 1990). William Chomsky, *Hebrew: The Eternal Language*, 1st. ed (Philadelphia, 1957). Edward Y. Kutscher, *A History of the Hebrew Language* (Jerusalem, 1982). Shelomoh Morag, ed., *Ha-'Ivrit bat-Zemannenu* (Jerusalem, 1987). Chaim Rabin, *A Short History of the Hebrew Language* (Jerusalem, 1973). Michael Riegler, comp., *Reshimat Sefarim, Ma'amarim va-'Avodot Doqtor 'al ha-'Ivrit be-Yameinu be-Nikhtevu 'Ivrit ve-Ra'u Or be-Yisra'el ba-Shanim 708–740 (1948–1980)* (Jerusalem, 1984). Nahum H. Waldman, *The Recent Study of Hebrew*, Bibliographica Judaica, no. 10 (Cincinnati, 1989).

HEBREWS (Heb. 'Ivrim), term describing the children of Israel, used when the Israelites refer to themselves when addressing others (e.g., *Jon*. 1.9), when others refer to the Israelites (e.g. *Gn*. 39.14, 17), and when the Israelites are differentiated from other ethnic groups (e.g., *Gn*. 14.13; *Ex*. 2.11). Some have derived the origin of the name from Eber, the grandson of Shem, one of the ancestors of Abraham, while others trace it to the Hebrew word *'ever* (the other side), referring to the district on the other side of the Jordan or, perhaps, the Euphrates. It also has been suggested that the term is connected with the diverse group of people with an inferior social status known throughout the ancient Near East in the second millennium BCE as the Ḫab(p)iru or 'Apiru. Although *Israelite* and, later, **Jew* became the usual terms, in popular parlance Jews are still sometimes referred to as Hebrews.

• Moshe Greenberg, *The Ḫab/piru*, American Oriental Series, vol. 39 (New Haven, 1955). Oswald Loretz, *Habiru-Hebräer: Eine soziolinguistische Studie über die Herkunft des Gentiliziums 'ibrî vom Appelativum ḥabiru*, Beiheft zur Zeitschrift für die altestamentliche Wissenschaft 160 (Berlin and New York, 1984). Nadav Na'aman, "Ḫabiru and Hebrews: The Transfer of a Social Term to the Literary Sphere," *Journal of Near Eastern Studies* 45 (1986): 271–288. —MICHAEL JAMES WILLIAMS

HEBREW SCHOOLS. See EDUCATION.

HEBREW THEOLOGICAL COLLEGE, educational institution located in Skokie, Illinois. It was founded in 1921 and serves over five hundred students. The College offers academic and professional educational programs to advance scholarship in Jewish law and culture in accordance with the principles of Orthodox Judaism. Bet Midrash students focus on intensive Talmud study as well as courses in Bible, Jewish history, Jewish philosophy, and Hebrew. The Anne M. Blitstein Institute for Women similarly provides opportunities for women to develop advanced skills as Jewish scholars. Hebrew Theological College also offers courses in the liberal arts and sciences, allowing students to combine their Jewish studies with a general education leading to a bachelor's degree in Judaic studies. Rabbinic ordination and professional certification in selected areas are options for qualified students.

HEBREW UNION COLLEGE–JEWISH INSTITUTE OF RELIGION, Reform religious seminary with campuses in Cincinnati, New York, Los Angeles, and Jerusalem. Hebrew Union College (HUC) was founded in 1875 by Isaac Mayer *Wise in the basement of a Cincinnati temple with a student body of fourteen. By 1881 a building had been acquired, but expansion was rapid, and in 1913 an eighteen-acre campus was dedicated. A dormitory was opened in 1924; the library building in 1931 (both of these were largely expanded in the 1960s; a manuscripts and rare books wing was added to the library). In 1988 the campus was further expanded by the addition of a conference hall and museum exhibit space.

In New York City, independent of HUC, Stephen S. *Wise, established another Reform rabbinical seminary, in 1922, the Jewish Institute of Religion (JIR). Situated on West 68th Street, it adjoined Wise's Free Synagogue. In 1950, the year after Wise's death, HUC and JIR merged. A building was constructed in the New York University area and dedicated in 1979.

The post–World War II growth of the Jewish community on the West Coast led to the establishment by HUC in 1947 of a college of Jewish Studies in Los Angeles, and by 1954 a pre-rabbinic program had been inaugurated. A campus was dedicated in 1971.

In Jerusalem, a two-acre site was acquired in 1954, but construction on the property was delayed by various problems, including opposition from Orthodox circles in Israel. The campus was dedicated in 1963. It was made obligatory for rabbinical students on the American campuses to spend a year in Israel. A further two acres were acquired in 1983, and additional buildings erected.

Since its establishment, HUC–JIR has graduated some two thousand rabbis—since the 1970s, many of them women. In recent decades, women have also made up a large proportion of students in the School of Sacred Music, founded in 1948 in New York City, from which almost three hundred cantors have been graduated.

Among the other activities on the campuses are the Schools of Education for the training of educators; the School of Communal Service, on the Los Angeles campus; a School for Graduate Study, for both Jewish and Christian clergy, founded in 1947 in Cincinnati; the School of Biblical Archaeology in Jerusalem; the American Jewish Archives in Cincinnati; and museums and libraries on all campuses.

Wise served as president until 1900. He was succeeded by Moses Mielziner (acting president, 1900–1903), Kauffmann Kohler (1903–1921), Julian Morgenstern (1921–1947), Nelson Glueck (1947–1971), Alfred Gottschalk (1971–1994, Chancellor, 1994), and Shelden Zimmerman (1995–). See also REFORM JUDAISM.

• Michael A. Meyer, "A Centennial History," in *Hebrew Union College–Jewish Institute of Religion at One Hundred Years*, edited by Samuel E. Karff, pt. 1 (Cincinnati, 1976). David Philipson, "The History of the Hebrew Union College," in *Hebrew Union College Jubilee Volume, 1875–1925*, edited by David Philipson et al. (1925; repr. New York, 1968).

HEBRON (Heb. Ḥevron), town, also called Kirjath-arba in the Bible (*Jos*. 14.15), in the Judean hills, south of Jerusalem; a Levitical city and a city of refuge (*Jos*. 21.13; *1 Chr*. 6.42). Hebron is the place where *Sarah died (*Gn*. 23.1–2); the cave of *Machpelah was located nearby. Hebron was visited by the spies sent by Moses to the land of Canaan (*Nm.* 13.22) and given to Caleb son of Jephunneh (*Jos.* 15.13; *Jgs.* 1.20). Hebron was David's original royal city, where he was anointed king of Judah (*2 Sm.* 2.1–4) and, later, king over all Israel (*2 Sm.* 5.1–3). Around the time of the Babylonian exile, the city was conquered by the Edomites (Idumeans) but in the time of the Hasmoneans it was again Jewish. Thereafter Jewish settlement in the city was continuous for most of the period up to the time of the Crusaders. The cave of Machpelah, which under the Arabs had been a mosque—with an adjoining synagogue—became a church. Jewish settlement was renewed in the thirteenth century although Jews were barred from entering Machpelah until 1967. The Jewish community was small until the Ottoman conquest, when it was augmented by the arrival of refugees from Spain. During subsequent centuries Hebron was a noted spiritual center, with distinguished rabbinical authorities and scholars, many of them influenced by mysticism. In the nineteenth century it became a home to a significant community of *Ḥabad Ḥasidim. In recent centuries Hebron—along with Jerusalem, Safed and Tiberias—has come to be regarded as one of the four *holy cities. In the early twentieth century, distinguished *yeshivot* were founded there, including in 1925 the *Slobodka Yeshivah from Lithuania. Arab riots in 1929 and 1936 led to the demise of the community. After 1967, a small number of Jews settled in Hebron.

• Oded Avissar, ed., *Sefer Ḥevron* (Jerusalem, 1970). Amikam Elad, "Pilgrims and Pilgrimage to Hebron (al-Khalil) during the Early Muslim Period (638?–1099)," in *Pilgrims and Travelers to the Holy Land*, Studies in Jewish Civilization 7, edited by Bryan F. LeBeau and Menaham Mor (Omaha, Neb., 1996). Eleanor K. Vogel and Brooks Holtzclaw, "Bibliography of Holy Land Sites, Part II," *Hebrew Union College Annual* 52 (1981): 35.

—FERN SECKBACH

ḤEDER (חֶדֶר; room), name popularly applied to an elementary religious school of the type prevalent in eastern Europe from the seventeenth century until World War II, often situated in a single room in the teacher's house. Education in a *ḥeder* was limited to males. Similar schools were found in Sephardi and Eastern communities. A frequent Talmudic appellation for schoolchildren, "children of the house of their teacher" (*tinoqot shel bet rabban*), suggests that a similar system existed in Talmudic times. Study hours in the *ḥeder* were long, and the teacher rarely had any pedagogical training. A minor official connected with the system was the *belfer* (from *behelfer* [assistant]), who conducted the children from their homes to the *ḥeder*. Students would study in a *ḥeder* from as early as three years old until the age of thirteen, at which time those with the ability to continue their studies would proceed to a **yeshivah*, while the rest would start to work. Much of the study in the *ḥeder*, especially in the case of the younger students, was by rote. In eastern Europe instruction was in Yiddish. The youngest students were primarily taught reading, with the prayer book as their basic text; the aim was to enable them to recite the prayers by themselves. Older students would be taught the Torah with Rashi's commentary, while the oldest students might study the Mishnah and the Talmud. Under the influence of the Haskalah movement in the nineteenth century, an attempt was made to modernize the *ḥeder* system by the institution of the *ḥeder metuqqan* (improved *ḥeder*). In Western countries, compulsory secular elementary education relegated Jewish studies for boys and girls to afternoon and Sunday "Hebrew schools." The tendency now is toward other forms of Jewish *education for children (day schools), and the traditional *ḥeder* is to be found only in strictly Orthodox circles. In England and South Africa, the supplementary afternoon Hebrew school is still known as a *ḥeder*. See also TALMUD TORAH.

• Miriam Gillis-Carlebach, "Various Types of Heder in Eretz Israel in the Nineteenth Century: Similarities, Differences, and Trends in Development," *Proceedings of the Tenth World Congress of Jewish Studies*, division B, vol. 1, pp. 289–296. Anne Sheffer, "Beyond Heder, Haskalah, and Honeybees: Genius and Gender in the Education of Seventeenth- and Eighteenth-Century Judeo-German Women," in *Recovering the Role of Women: Power and Authority in Rabbinic Jewish Society*, edited by Peter Haas (Atlanta, 1992), pp. 85–112. Steven Singer, "Jewish Education in the Mid-Nineteenth Century: A Study in the Early Victorian London Community," *Jewish Quarterly Review* 77 (1986–1987): 163–178. Steven Zipperstein, "Transforming the Heder: Maskilic Politics in Imperial Russia," in *Jewish History: Essays in Honour of Chimen Abramsky*, edited by A. Rapoport-Albert and S. Zipperstein (London, 1988).

—SHMUEL HIMELSTEIN

HEDYOT. See LAYMAN.

ḤEFETS BEN YATSLIAḤ (c.11th cent.), Babylonian scholar, a native of Mosul. His Arabic-language *Sefer ha-Mitsvot* was one of the most important works on the commandments. The precepts were divided into some thirty-six thematic sections or chapters, each of which was further divided into positive and negative commandments. Biblical and rabbinic sources were quoted in order to characterize and define each commandment in turn. This book served to a considerable extent as the basis of Maimonides' *Book of the Commandments* (Maimonides avers that this youthful work contains errors that he attributes to having been unduly influenced by Ḥefets). Only fragments of *Sefer ha-Mitsvot* are known. Several scholars attributed to Ḥefets another work, cited by medieval European scholars under the title *Sefer Ḥefets*, but this attribution appears to be mistaken.

• Neil Danzig, "The First Discovered Leaves of 'Sefer Ḥefets,' " *Jewish Quarterly Review* 82 (1991). Benzion Halper, ed., *A Volume of the Book of Precepts by Ḥefets ben Yatsliaḥ* (1915; Tel Aviv, 1972). Moshe Zucker, "Qeta'im Ḥadashim mi-Sefer ha-Mitsvot le-Rav Ḥefets ben Yatsliaḥ," *Proceedings of the American Academy for Jewish Research* 24 (1960–1961): 1–68 (Hebrew section).

—ROBERT BRODY

HEFQER (הֶפְקֵר; unclaimed property), a term designating ownerless property. *Property may become ownerless by voluntary formal renunciation on the part of the owner in the presence of three persons; by compulsory renunciation by the owner of his right to the property, as ordered by a court; by the death of a proselyte who leaves property but no Jewish heirs; or by being lost by its owner who despairs of recovering it. Property found in deserts or at sea is treated as ownerless. *Hefqer* becomes the property of the first person to acquire it by the usual means (see ACQUISITION). *Hefqer* is not subject to the law of tithing, nor is it subject to the laws benefiting the poor. In Israel, ownerless property belongs to the state.

• Menahem Elon, *Jewish Law: History, Sources, Principles*, 4 vols. (Philadelphia, 1994).

HEFQER BEIT DIN. See CONFISCATION.

HEIKHAL. See ARON HA-QODESH; TEMPLE.

HEIKHALOT (הֵיכָלוֹת; temples, palaces, halls), term designating a type of esotericism, also known as Merkavah mysticism (see MAʿASEH MERKAVAH), as well as the literature in which it is found. The main theme is the ecstatic ascent to the celestial realms and palaces, climaxing with the vision of the *throne of God. In addition to these visionary accounts, Heikhalot literature also contains magic (e.g., "The Sword of Moses," "The *Havdalah* of Rabbi ʿAqiva'") and cosmological (*Seder Rabba' de-Ve-Re'shit*) texts. Because of certain similarities with contemporary phenomena in the Hellenistic world, this literature has sometimes been labeled as "gnostic." The extant texts were probably composed in Babylonia between the third century and the seventh century. Among the texts that can be classified as mystical are the "Lesser Heikhalot," in which the ascension of R ʿAqiva' plays a central role; the "Greater Heikhalot," which contains the story of the *Ten Martyrs and the ascension of R. Yishmaʿe'l; the **Shiʿur Qomah*, with its highly anthropomorphic description of the dimensions of the Creator God; and the *Sefer Heikhalot*, also known as *3 *Enoch*, with its description of the elevation of Enoch and his transformation into *Metatron. These treatises exhibit features not found elsewhere, such as the use of the term *heikhalot* for the celestial and divine halls and realms, the interpretation of the *Song of Songs* in terms of *Shiʿur Qomah* notions, the ecstatic ascent and descent, and the emphasis on direct individual experience rather than on the exegesis of canonical texts. The texts show a concern for the "perils of the soul" that attend the mystical vision and are replete with instructions on how to avoid the dangers represented by the angelic guardians and celestial gatekeepers. The texts also report the hymns sung by the celestial choirs and heard by the visionary. Some of these Heikhalot hymns were later included in the prayer book.

• Joseph Dan, *Ancient Jewish Mysticism* (Tel Aviv, 1993). Rachel Elior, "The Concept of Angels in Hekhalot Literature," *Jewish Studies Quarterly* 1 (1993–94): 1–50. Ithamar Gruenwald, *Apocalyptic and Merkavah Mysticism* (Leiden, 1980). Peter Schäfer, *Hekhalot-Studien* (Tübingen, 1988). David Halperin, *The Faces of the Chariot: Early Jewish Responses to Ezekiel's Vision* (Tübingen, 1988). Peter Schäfer, *The Hidden and Manifest God: Some Major Themes in Early Jewish Mysticism* (Albany, N.Y., 1992). Peter Schäfer, *Synopse zur Hekhalot-Literatur* (Tübingen, 1981). Gershom Gerhard Scholem, *Jewish Gnosticism, Merkabah Mysticism and Talmudic Tradition*, 2d ed. (New York, 1965). Gershom Gerhard Scholem, *Major Trends in Jewish Mysticism* (New York, 1954), pp. 40–79.

HEIR. See INHERITANCE.

HEKHSHER (הֶכְשֵׁר; approbation), document signed by an authorized rabbi asserting that a product, usually food, is *kasher* (ritually fit). The main foods requiring such certification are poultry or meat or their derivatives, the preparation of which is supervised by a **mashgiaḥ*. After ensuring that the meat has been properly slaughtered and its organs inspected, the *mashgiaḥ* affixes a sign, usually a lead seal, to the animal's foot. Before Pesaḥ a variety of foods is given a *hekhsher* (usually printed on the packaging), to show that they have been properly prepared. Today *hekhsherim* are also given to dairy products, fruits and vegetables (signifying that the laws of **ʿorlah* and **shemittah* have been properly observed), and flour products (having to do with the law of **ḥadash*). Certificates of *hekhsher* issued by the rabbinate are also issued to and displayed in kosher restaurants. The term *hekhsher* is used popularly to refer to any seal of approval.

• Isidor Grunfeld, *The Jewish Dietary Laws*, 2 vols. (London, 1982).

HELENA. See ADIABENE.

ḤELEV (חֵלֶב; fat), in biblical usage certain portions of the intestinal fat of oxen, sheep, and goats offered upon the altar (*Lv.* 3.3–17). Like *blood, *ḥelev* was forbidden to the Israelites (*Lv.* 7.23). Maimonides (*Hilkhot Ma'akhalot Asurot* 7.5) explains the distinction between intestinal fat (*ḥelev*), which is forbidden to be eaten, and animal fat (*shuman*), which is part of the sinews and is permitted to be eaten.

• Isidor Grunfeld, *The Jewish Dietary Laws*, 2 vols. (London, 1982). Jacob Milgrom, *Studies in Cultic Theology and Terminology* (Leiden, 1983).

HELL. See GEIHINNOM.

HELLENISM. While there is little reason to believe that Alexander the Great or his successors, such as the Ptolemies in Egypt or the Seleucids in Syria–Babylonia, deliberately sought to Hellenize the indigenous populations under their control, they nevertheless contributed greatly to the process. The founding of new cities, built entirely on a Greek model (Alexandria, Antioch, and many more), the encouragement of Greek immigration to the newly conquered lands, and the tendency to conduct official businesses in the conquerors' language all contributed greatly to the spread of Greek culture in regions far outside the Greek homeland. The Jews, like all their neighbors, were exposed to a culture that was not unknown to them—contacts with Greece had preceded Alexander by several centuries—but that now loomed larger than ever before. Chronologically, the first to be Hellenized were communities in the Diaspora, such as Egypt, in which the Jews quickly abandoned their ancestral language and adopted Greek as their main means of expression. From the third century BCE onwards, Egyptian Jews conducted not only their everyday business but also their religious life in Greek, including the use of a Greek translation of the Torah (see SEPTUAGINT). However, abandoning the ancestral language did not necessarily mean abandoning ancestral behavior, beliefs, and identity. No doubt many chose to abandon the traditional way of life and to leave the community, but others continued to maintain their Jewish identity and to observe their unique customs. In Judea, densely populated by Jews and, due to its geographical location and character, relatively unattractive to Greek settlers, the process of Hellenization seems to have been much slower than in Egypt or the cities of the Mediterranean coast. Nevertheless, Judea was not immune to Hellenistic influences, and this tension was one of the leading factors behind the events that led to the Maccabean Revolt. However, the success of the revolt only served to increase the pace of Hellenization, since the victorious *Hasmoneans quickly adopted many of the trappings of neighboring Hellenistic dynasties. The Roman conquest of Jerusalem in 63 BCE, the reign of Herod (37–4) and his descendants, and the direct Roman rule that followed, all contributed to the further spread of Hellenism among the Jews of Erets Yisra'el. Greek-speaking communities were to be found throughout the Roman empire, while in Erets Yisra'el itself, many Jews seem to have been bilingual, and even trilingual, using Greek, Aramaic, and Hebrew. The impact of Hellenism on Hebrew can be gauged from the vocabulary in rabbinic literature: numerous Greek words entered the Hebrew language (and many are still commonly used in modern Hebrew), as did many concepts, legends, and theories, whose Hellenistic origin is indisputable. At the same time the rabbis opposed too close an acquaintance with, and study of, Greek culture, which they saw as pagan and idolatrous, by definition the antithesis of Judaism. The upper classes, however, adopted a thoroughgoing Hellenistic style of life, which was often assimilationist. The impact of Hellenistic culture on Greek-speaking Jewry is even more marked (see LETTER OF ARISTEAS; PHILO; WISDOM OF SOLOMON). Gentile Hellenism, which regarded Jewish monotheism and the worship of an invisible God as tantamount to atheism, also produced the first historic expressions of both literary and practical (anti-Jewish riots) antisemitism. As a result much Jewish Hellenistic writing, whether philosophical (see PHILO) or historical (see JOSEPHUS FLAVIUS), was apologetic and propagandist in character, attempting to demonstrate the excellence and even superiority of Jewish laws and teachings. This literature, however, does not seem to have made an impression on the Greeks. The Judeo-Greek culture of the Diaspora eventually died out, for reasons that are not entirely clear, and its fruits were preserved solely by the Christian church.

• William David Davies and Louis Finkelstein, eds., *The Cambridge History of Judaism*, vol. 2, *The Hellenistic Age* (Cambridge, 1989). Louis H. Feldman, "Hellenism and Hebraism Reconsidered," *Judaism* 43 (1994): 115–126. Martin Hengel, *Jews, Greeks and Barbarians: Aspects of the Hellenization of Judaism in the Pre-Christian Period*, trans. of German ed. of 1976 (Philadelphia, 1980). Martin Hengel, *Judaism and Hellenism: Studies in Their Encounter in Palestine During the Early Hellenistic Period*, trans. of 2nd rev. and enl. German ed. of 1973 (Philadelphia, 1981). Saul Lieberman, *Greek in Jewish Palestine* (New York, 1942). Saul Lieberman, *Hellenism in Jewish Palestine* (New York, 1962). Abraham Schalit, ed., *The World History of the Jewish People*, vol. 6, *The Hellenistic Age* (Jerusalem, 1972). Avigdor Tcherikover, *Hellenistic Civilization and the Jews* (Philadelphia, 1959).

—GIDEON BOHAK

HELLER, MESHULLAM FEIBUSH (died 1795), Galician Hasidic master and author. A descendant of Yom Tov Lipmann Heller, his major teachers were the early Hasidic masters Menaḥem Mendel of Peremyshlany and Yeḥi'el Mikha'el of Zloczów. In two important pastoral letters written in 1777, he interpreted the teachings of Dov Ber of Mezhirech, whose radical practices he restricted to great masters alone. Ordinary Hasidim, he believed, should follow a path of humility, sincerity, and faith in the powers of the masters. First published in the Hasidic anthology *Liqqutim Yeqarim* (Lwów, 1792), his letters have been frequently reprinted and issued under several titles, including *Yosher Divrei Emet* (Mukachevo, 1905).

• Louis Jacobs, *Hasidic Prayer* (New York, 1973). Miles Krassen, " 'Devequt' and Faith in Zaddiqim: The Religious Tracts of Meshullam Feibush Heller of Zbarazh," Ph.D. dissertation, University of Pennsylvania, 1990.

—MILES KRASSEN

HELLER, YOM TOV LIPMANN (1579–1654), rabbi and communal leader. Born in Wallerstein, Bavaria, Heller studied under *Yehudah Liva' ben Betsal'el of Prague. Heller's rabbinic career was turbulent. While in Prague, he was accused by his enemies of unfairly imposing taxes upon the poor to satisfy the government's demand that Bohemian Jewry help defray expenses incurred during the Thirty Years' War. Heller was also accused by some Jews of defaming Christianity, and a death sentence, later commuted to imprisonment and a heavy fine, was imposed upon him by the gentile authorities. Later in his career, while at Vladimir-Volynski, he became embroiled in controversy arising from his strong stand against those rabbis guilty of obtaining their rabbinic positions by illegal means.

Heller was a prolific and versatile writer. His principle work, *Tosafot Yom Tov* (Prague, 1614–1617), a commentary to the Mishnah, elucidated the earlier commentary of ʿOvadyah of *Bertinoro and sought to correct texts, supply sources, and provide halakhic analyses and conclusions. Heller also wrote kabbalistic commentaries, a three-volume commentary to the code of *Asher ben Yeḥi'el (*Maʿadenei ha-Melekh* [Prague, 1619, 1628]), *responsa*, sermons, and several liturgical poems mourning the persecutions suffered by the Jews of Prague in 1618 and by the Jews of the Ukraine in 1648 at the hands of anti-Jewish mobs. Heller's autobiography, *Megillat Eivah* (Breslau, 1818), has been translated into German and Yiddish.

• Israel David Bet-Halevi, *Toledot Rabbenu Yom-Tov Lippman Heller* (Tel Aviv, 1954). Joseph M. Davis, "R. Yom Tov Lipmann Heller, Joseph b. Isaac haLevi and Rationalism in Ashkenazic Jewish Culture," Ph.D. dissertation, Harvard University, 1990. Benzion Katz, *Rabbanut, Ḥasidut, ve-Haskalah*, vol. 1 (Tel Aviv, 1956), pp. 91–97. Judah Leib Maimon, ed., *Li-Khevod Yom Tov* (Jerusalem, 1956). Chaim Tchernowitz, *Toledot ha-Poseqim*, vol. 3 (New York, 1947), pp. 127ff.

—ELIJAH J. SCHOCHET

ḤEMDAT YAMIM, eighteenth-century anonymous ethical work dealing with the practices and behavior required of a pious Jew during the holy days of the religious year. The book consists of sermons that offer interpretations of biblical and rabbinic citations for inspiration and instruction. Indicating the influence of Lurianic Kabbalah, pious deeds are viewed as a reflection of events in the divine realm; some scholars have found Shabbatean allusions in *Ḥemdat Yamim*. The work has had a strong influence on modern Hebrew literature, especially the style of S. Y. Agnon. The first edition appeared in Smyrna in 1731 and 1732.

• Isaiah Tishby, *Netivei Emunah u-Minut* (Tel Aviv, 1964), pp. 108–168. Abraham Yaari, *Taʿalumat Sefer* (Jerusalem, 1954), includes bibliography.

HEMEROBAPTISTS (Gr.; Daily Bathers), a Jewish sect, mentioned by the church fathers as late as the third century CE, observing ritual immersion (see MIQVEH) every morning. Daily *ablutions were practiced by several Jewish groups (including the *Essenes), and the Hemerobaptists may be identical with one of them, possibly with the *tovelei shaḥarit* (dawn bathers) mentioned in the Talmud (*Ber.* 22a).

• Marcel Simon, *Jewish Sects at the Time of Jesus* (Philadelphia, 1980).

HEQDESH (הֶקְדֵּשׁ; consecrated property), property dedicated to the Temple. In post-Talmudic times the term *setam heqdesh* came to mean any property set aside for charitable purposes or for the fulfillment of a *mitsvah*.

Property could be imbued with different degrees of sanctity: intrinsic sanctity (*qedushat ha-guf*) for objects dedicated to the altar and ritually fit for sacrifice and which could not be redeemed; and monetary sanctity (*qedushat damim*) for objects consecrated to the Temple treasury for the Temple upkeep. Into a third category fell objects dedicated to the altar but unfit for sacrifice because of blemish. These could be redeemed, and when they were redeemed, they returned to their secular status. According to a special ruling, an oral statement was sufficient to effect a transfer of property from an individual to Temple ownership (*Qid.* 1.6, 28b, 29a).

• Isaac Herzog, *The Main Institutions of Jewish Law*, 2d ed. (London, 1965–1967). —DANIEL SPERBER

ḤEREM. See EXCOMMUNICATION.

ḤEREM BEIT DIN (חֵרֶם בֵּית דִּין), legal term used to denote an *excommunication, ostracism, or shunning authorized by a Jewish court of law as a form of deterrence or punishment against a member of the Jewish community who violates the ordinances of the community. Jewish law recognizes three different levels of *ḥerem beit din* (*niddui, shamta'*, and *ḥerem*), each denoting a particular form of exclusion from the Jewish community. There was significant dispute among later commentators regarding the nature of *ḥerem beit din*. Some argued that *ḥerem* was a form of judicial punishment mandated for a violation of Jewish law; most argued that *ḥerem* was a form of deterrence designed to prevent prospective violations of Jewish law. For example, R. Mosheh Isserles (*Shulḥan ʿArukh, Yoreh Deʿah* 334.1) permitted an innocent party to be placed in *ḥerem* to deter an ongoing violation of Jewish law by one close to the innocent party. In pre-Emancipation Jewish communities, *ḥerem* was a very effective device for enforcing communal unity and suppressing dissent. *Ḥerem* is no longer an effective method of preventing improper conduct but is used as a means of expressing communal disdain for a person's behavior.

• Michael J. Broyde, "Forming Religious Communities and Respecting Dissenter's Rights: A Religious Human Rights Approach to a Tort Law Problem," in *Religious Human Rights in the World Today: Legal and Religious Perspectives*, edited by John Witte (The Hague, 1996). —MICHAEL BROYDE

ḤEREM DE-RABBENU GERSHOM. See GERSHOM BEN YEHUDAH; POLYGAMY.

ḤEREM HA-YISHUV (חֵרֶם הַיִּשּׁוּב; ban on settlement), ban on Jews joining an existing community. In the Middle Ages, when Jewish settlement and employment were severely restricted, many Ashkenazi Jewish communities enacted regulations forbidding any outsider from living in their communities without obtaining prior permission. On the other hand, there were clear criteria whereby one who was not a resident could become one; for example, by buying, renting, or inheriting property in the town. Similarly, one who had been permitted to remain temporarily in a particular community could after a certain period of time claim permanent residence. Underlying these regulations was the premise that the community belonged to its residents, and that as such they could make decisions necessary to maintain their livelihoods. The *ḥerem ha-yishuv* was opposed by leading rabbinic authorities, who said it was unethical to deny aid to fellow Jews, except, according to rabbinic authorities, to those Jews who had failed to pay community taxes. The ban disappeared in the eighteenth century.

• John Edwards, trans., *The Jews in Western Europe, 1400–1600* (Manchester, 1994). R. P. Hsia and H. Lehmann, eds., *In and Out of the Ghetto: Jewish–Gentile Relations in Late Medieval and Early Modern Germany* (Washington, D.C., 1995).

HERESY, a term defined as a departure from orthodox belief. Various appellations are used for heretics. The generic name is **minim* (sectarians), and refers to those who depart in their conduct and beliefs from the norms of Judaism; the term covers a multitude of sinners and in specific context can refer to Gnostics, Judeo-Christians, Sadducees, and others. Alternate names for heretics are *apiqorsim* (Epicureans; see APIQOROS), *koferim be-ʿiqqar* (deniers of the root)—which originally referred to those who denied God and later to a principle of faith—and *mumarim* (those who have changed; see APOSTASY). The usual and practically only punishment foretold for heretics is that they "forfeit their share in the world to come," that is, their punishment is in the hands of God and comes after their death, not by human courts during their lifetime. Thus, the Mishnah (*San.* 10.1) enumerates among those who forfeit their share in the world to come those who deny the doctrine of resurrection, or the divine origin of the Torah, while R. Elʿazar ha-Modaʿi specifies he "who profanes sacred things, puts his fellow to shame in public, despises the festivals, nullifies the covenant of Abraham, and makes the Torah bear a meaning other than its true one" (*San.* 3.15). Rabbinic authorities have never set up courts comparable to the Inquisition for trying heretics, though severe sanctions such as the *ḥerem* were applied at certain periods to deviants whose doctrines and behavior might bring internal or external harm to the Jewish community. Outstanding victims of such sanctions in the seventeenth century were Baruch *Spinoza and Uriel *Acosta in Amsterdam. Writings belonging to heretics were not to be rescued from a conflagration on the Sabbath, and R. *Tarfon went so far as to declare that he would deliberately commit them to the flames (*Shab.* 116b). Whereas norms of behavior were spelled out in detail by the *halakhah*, matters of faith were not sufficiently systematized to permit the establishment of generally accepted categories of heresy (see CREED). In this respect, the attempt of Maimonides to lay down the *Thirteen Principles of Faith, the denial of which would place those who rejected them outside the pale of Judaism, represented a departure from the Jewish norm and was not allowed to go unchallenged.

• Zeev Gries, "Heresy," in *Contemporary Jewish Religious Thought*, edited by Arthur A. Cohen and Paul Mendes-Flohr (New York, 1987), pp. 339–352.

HERMAPHRODITE. See ANDEROGINOS.

HERMENEUTICS (Heb. *middot*), rules for interpreting the biblical text for halakhic and aggadic purposes. The rules of hermeneutics are traditionally held to be as old as the text itself. Their origin is unknown, but they were first classified by *Hillel, who formulated seven exegetical principles by which the Bible is to be expounded (T., *San.*, end of chap. 7): *qal va-ḥomer*, an inference that permits deductions from a minor to a major case; *gezerah shavah*, an inference based on word analogy (if two biblical passages contain words with similar or identical meanings, both laws, although different in themselves, are subject to the same application); *binyan av mi-katuv eḥad*, principles derived from a single verse and applied to a group of biblical passages; *binyan av mi-shenei ketuvim*, principles derived from two verses and applied to a group of biblical passages; *kelal u-ferat u-ferat u-kelal*, limitations of a general principle derived from a particular principle, and vice versa; *ka-yotse' bo be-maqom aḥer*, principles derived by virtue of similar passages; and *davar ha-lamed me-ʿinyano*, deduction from context.

Rabbi Yishmaʿe'l ben Elishaʿ expanded these principles to thirteen (*Sifra'*; *Zev.* 50a–51a; also included in the Shaḥarit service) and R. Eliʿezer ben Yosei ha-Galili (according to post-Talmudic literature) expanded them to thirty-two. Most of R. Eliʿezer's principles are intended for aggadic interpretation, but some are valid for halakhic interpretation and appear also in the rules of Hillel and Yishmaʿe'l. Other methods of biblical hermeneutics applied at different times included **gimatriyyah*, **notariqon*, and interpretations of apparently superfluous words, prefixes, and suffixes. This last method characterized the approach of R. ʿAqiva', who derived halakhic rules from formal details of the biblical text, such as seemingly superfluous letters or the meaningless word *et* (*Pes.* 22b). This approach was opposed by R. Yishmaʿe'l, who held that "the Bible speaks in the language of men"; that is, the biblical text uses human speech and cannot form the basis of legal deductions. Rabbi Yishmaʿe'l's viewpoint generally prevailed, and later rabbis taught that "nothing can override the plain meaning of the text" (*Shab.* 63a). Me'ir Leibush *Malbim, in the introduction to his commentary on the *Sifra'*, suggested that all the rules of interpretation are implied in the text and can be deduced from the unique logical syntax of the Hebrew language.

• Louis Jacobs, *The Talmudic Argument: A Study in Talmudic Reasoning and Methodology* (Cambridge, 1984). Jacob Neusner, *Talmudic Dialectics* (Atlanta, 1995). Elliot R. Wolfson, *Along the Path: Studies in Kabbalistic Myth, Symbolism, and Hermeneutics* (Albany, 1995). Irving M. Zeitlin, *Ancient Judaism: Biblical Criticism from Max Weber to the Present* (Cambridge, 1984).

HERTZ, JOSEPH HERMAN (1872–1946), chief rabbi of the United Hebrew Congregations of the British empire. Born in Slovakia, Hertz grew up in New York City, where he was the Jewish Theological Seminary of America's first graduate in 1894. He served as rabbi of Johannesburg, South Africa from 1896 to 1911, before being elected Great Britain's chief rabbi in 1913 in succession to Hermann Adler (see ADLER FAMILY). A religious champion of Zionism, Hertz played a notable part in securing the Balfour Declaration in 1917 and was an incisive critic of British government policy under the Mandate. Between the two world wars, he also opposed the growth of Liberal Judaism, helped eliminate a calendar reform threat to Sabbath observance, fought antisemitism at home and abroad, and organized the rescue of Jews from Nazi persecution. An influential popularizer of Jewish knowledge, his publications include *A Book of Jewish Thoughts* (London, 1917), *The Pentateuch and Haftorahs* (Oxford, 1929–1936), *Sermons, Addresses, and Studies* (Surrey, 1938), and *The Authorised Daily Prayer Book with Commentary* (London, 1942–1945).

• Geoffrey Alderman, *Modern British Jewry* (Oxford and New York, 1992). Richard Bolchover, *British Jewry and the Holocaust* (Cambridge, 1993). Isidore Epstein, ed., *Joseph Herman Hertz, 1872–1946, In Memoriam* (London, 1947). *Essays in Honour of the Very Rev. Dr. J. H. Hertz, Chief Rabbi of the United Hebrew Congregations of the British Empire, on the Occasion of His Seventieth Birthday, September 25, 1942*, edited by Isidore Epstein, Ephraim Levine, and Cecil Roth (London, 1942), pp. 1–14, 261–270. V. D. Lipman, *A History of the Jews in Britain Since 1858* (New York, 1990).

—GABRIEL A. SIVAN

HERZOG, ISAAC (1888–1959), rabbinic scholar; chief rabbi of Israel from 1937 through 1959. Born in Łomża, Poland, Isaac Herzog immigrated to England at the age of nine. He was rabbi of Belfast from 1916 to 1919, served as chief rabbi of the Irish Free State between 1922 and 1937, succeeded R. Avraham Yitsḥaq ha-Kohen Kook as chief rabbi of Palestine, and became the first chief rabbi of the State of Israel. He was recognized as one of the great rabbinical authorities of his time, and he wrote many books and articles dealing with halakhic problems surrounding the Torah and the state. Herzog's writings helped shape the attitude of the Religious Zionist movement toward the State of Israel. He was the author of *Main Institutions of Jewish Law* (1965–1967), *Heikhal Yitsḥaq* (1960–1972), *Tekhuqah le-Yisra'el ʿal pi ha-Torah* (1989), *Pesaqim u-Ketavim* (1989–1991), and *The Royal Purple and the Biblical Blue* (1987).

• Geulah Bath Yehudah, "Yitzhak Eizik Halevi Herzog, 1888–1959," in *Men of the Spirit*, edited by Leo Jung (New York, 1964), pp. 125–138. Shmuel Avidor Hacohen, *Yaḥid be-Doro* (Jerusalem, 1980). Joseph Safran, "Harav Dr. Yitsḥaq Eizik ha-Levi Hertsog," in *Ḥokhmat Yisra'el be-*

Maʿarav Eiropah, edited by Simon Federbusch, vol. 3 (Jerusalem, 1965), pp. 127–149. Shelomoh Yosef Zevin, "Isaac Herzog's Halakhic Decisions and Lectures," in *Men of the Spirit*, edited by Leo Jung (New York, 1964), pp. 141–145.

—ELIAV SHOCHETMAN

HESCHEL, ABRAHAM JOSHUA (1907–1972), religious philosopher. Born in Poland into a distinguished Hasidic family, he studied at the University of Berlin and taught Talmud at the Hochschule für die Wissenschaft des Judentums. In 1939 he escaped to England and then moved to the United States, where he taught first at Hebrew Union College in Cincinnati and from 1946 at the Jewish Theological Seminary of America in New York. Heschel's books cover a wide range of thought, philosophic and mystic. He wrote *The Prophets* (1962) on a biblical theme, *Maimonides* (German, 1935; English, 1982) on the famous medieval philosopher, *A Passion for Truth* (1973) on the Hasidic thinker Menaḥem Mendel of Kotsk, and *The Earth Is the Lord's* (1949) on the lost legacy of Polish Jewry. He is best known for his theological writings, often written in a poetic style with strong mystical influences, which include *Man Is Not Alone* (1951), *Man's Quest for God* (1954), *God in Search of Man* (1955), *The Sabbath* (1951), and *Israel: An Echo of Eternity* (1969). Heschel became deeply involved in the civil rights movement in the United States. He was also a leading figure in the growing Jewish–Christian interfaith movement and was active behind the scenes during the Second Vatican Council.

In his major work, *God in Search of Man*, Heschel asserts that the religious life of contemporary Jews is without fervor and inner conviction, a form of religious behaviorism. There is a need to rediscover the paths that lead to an awareness of God's presence in the world and in one's own life. The paths to such awareness are not those of rational argument but of existential decision making. Reason, however, can function to clarify the alternatives among which we must choose.

According to Heschel, the first of the three such paths is that of reawakened religious emotions, the experiences of awe and reverence. These lead to an awareness of the grandeur of natural and human existence, of their mystery, and of their allusiveness to an ineffable reality. The second path to God is through the Torah: God's voice can be heard addressing us in the words of the Torah. The Torah is written not in descriptive language but in evocative language, proclaiming mysteries rather than explaining facts. There is a human element as well as a divine element in the revelatory experience: the words of Torah are the prophets' own in response to the intiative of God. We must put aside preconceptions and open ourselves to the actual content of the biblical message: that God's omnipotence is restrained; that God needs humans as much as they need to be needed; that without human cooperation the goals of redemption cannot be achieved; and that God, too, experiences emotions. The pathos of God is God's loving concern for creatures, God's suffering together with creatures who are in pain, and God's anger at the moral failures of human beings.

The third path to the awareness of the presence of God is through the life of *mitsvot*, which begins as an experiment in living. The *mitsvot* can evoke experiences of the sublimity and mystery of existence. Moreover, the discipline of the *mitsvot* enables people to control their darker impulses. We can become God's proxy in bringing redemption to the world by ridding the world of violence and oppression.

• Edward K. Kaplan, *Holiness in Words: Abraham Joshua Heschel's Poetics of Piety* (West Fulton, N.Y., 1996). Harold Kasimow, *No Religion Is an Island: Abraham Joshua Heschel and Interreligious Dialogue* (Maryknoll, N.Y., 1991). Fritz Rothschild, ed., *Between God and Man: An Interpretation of Judaism from the Writings of Abraham J. Heschel* (New York, 1959).

—SOL TANENZAPF

ḤESHBON HA-NEFESH (חֶשְׁבּוֹן הַנֶּפֶשׁ; accounting of the soul), an individual's examination of conscience concerning obligations to God and to other humans. The concept is prevalent in the ethical literature of the Middle Ages, and it is the subject of the eighth section of *Ḥovot ha-Levavot* by *Baḥya ben Yosef ibn Paquda'. This reckoning should be made every day, but especially during the month of Elul and the *ʿAseret Yemei Teshuvah as a prerequisite to genuine repentance and self-improvement. The wedding day is also a time for *ḥeshbon ha-nefesh*, and the bride and groom traditionally fast until the ceremony.

• Shmuel Y. Agnon, *Days of Awe: Being a Treasury of Traditions, Legends, and Learned Commentaries Concerning Rosh ha-Shana, Yom Kippur, and the Days Between* (New York, 1948).

ḤESHVAN (חֶשְׁוָן), second month of the religious calendar, eighth month of the civil calendar, also referred to as Marḥeshvan; known in the Bible as Bul. It has twenty-nine or thirty days, and its zodiac sign is Scorpio. Ashkenazim outside Erets Yisra'el incorporate a daily prayer for rain into the ʿAmidah from 7 Ḥeshvan until Pesaḥ; elsewhere the prayer is recited from immediately after Sukkot. Ḥeshvan is the only month in the Jewish calendar that does not contain any festival or fast observance. The name *Marḥeshvan* in Babylonian means eighth month, but *mar* also means both drop, which relates to the fact that it is the beginning of the rainy season, and bitter, because it is a month with no observances.

• Nathan Bushwick, *Understanding the Jewish Calendar* (New York, 1989). George Zinberg, *Jewish Calendar Mystery Dispelled* (New York, 1963).

—CHAIM PEARL

HESPED. See Eulogy.

HESSAḤ HA-DAʿAT (הֶסַּח הַדַּעַת; "removal of one's mind"), phrase used in Jewish religious law to convey the idea of a lack of attentiveness during the performance of religious duties, which because of their importance demand special mental awareness. As a result of *hessaḥ ha-daʿat*, such actions become invalid, that is, if the person performing them allows his attention to wander. Typical examples include the need to keep one's mind alert in the separation of heave offerings, in the rituals appertaining to ritual uncleanness, and in the preparation of the ashes of the *red heifer. Different aspects of *hessaḥ ha-daʿat* are combined in a statement of

R. Ze'ira' (*San*. 97a): "A lost article, the Messiah, and [the bite of] a scorpion appear with *hessah ha-da'at*." The first instance merely means "absent-mindedness"; the other two mean that they come when least expected.

• Howard Eilberg-Schwartz, "The Human Will in Judaism: The Mishnah's Philosophy of Intention," Ph.D. dissertation, Brown University, 1986.

HESTER PANIM (הֶסְתֵּר פָּנִים), the hiddenness of God. The phrase *hester panim* is used with reference to the question of theodicy. In the biblical context, God's hiddenness can be a manifestation of divine judgment in response to human sinfulness or a test of worthiness, or it can be used liturgically as supplication on the part of suffering innocents lamenting their abandonment by God. In the twentieth century, God's silence in the Holocaust has prompted discussion of the meaning of such silence (see HOLOCAUST THEOLOGY). The term suggests a dialectic between God's presence and absence, and that the return of his presence is ultimately hoped for.

• Martin Buber, *Eclipse of God: Studies in the Relation between Religion and Philosophy* (New York, 1952). André Neher, *The Exile of the Word: From the Silence of the Bible to the Silence of Auschwitz* (Philadelphia, 1981).

—JOEL HECKER

HETTER. See DISPENSATION.

HETTER HORA'AH. See ORDINATION.

ḤEVRAH (חֶבְרָה; association), society for the performance of a religious, educational, or philanthropic function within the Jewish *community. Since the fourteenth century such societies have played an essential role within the autonomous Jewish community, and some of them continued to exist within the voluntary community after *autonomy ended. The **ḥevrah qaddisha'*, concerned with the care and burial of the dead, remains an essential institution. Other associations included groups for the upkeep of the synagogue, caring for the sick (*biqqur ḥolim*), dowering poor brides, and ransoming captives. Educational societies provided **talmud Torah* classes for younger children, and others met for Talmud study and the recitation of psalms.

• Salo Wittmayer Baron, *The Jewish Community: Its History and Structure to the American Revolution* (Westport, Conn., 1972). Sylvie Anne Goldberg, "De l'origine de la Hèvrah Qadichah: Rachi au service de la Wissenschaft des Judentums," in *Rashi 1040–1990: Hommage à Ephraim E. Urbach*, edited by Gabrielle Sed-Rajna (Paris, 1993), pp. 751–757. Jacob Rader Marcus, *The Jew in the Medieval World* (Cincinnati, 1938), pp. 446–449. Mark Wischnitzer, *A History of Jewish Crafts and Guilds* (New York, 1965).

ḤEVRAH QADDISHA' (Heb. and Aram.; חֶבְרָה קַדִּישָׁא; holy society), referred originally to the Jewish community as a whole (as in the Sabbath morning *Yequm Purqan prayer) or to different Jewish community organizations that assumed responsibility for various communal needs. In the fourteenth century, five such societies existed in the French city of Perpignan, dealing respectively with the school, the sick, lighting in the synagogue, general welfare needs, and burial of the dead. Subsequently, however, the term *ḥevrah qaddisha'* came to be applied almost exclusively to the "brotherhood" and "sisterhood" that undertook to perform the religious task of burying the dead in accordance with Jewish law. The respect due to the dead and the strict prohibition against deriving any material benefit from a dead body combined to make this a sacred, voluntary duty. Although there are references to such groups in earlier times (*Mo'ed Q*. 27b), R. Yehudah Liva' ben Betsal'el of Prague is credited with founding the first formal *ḥevrah qaddisha'*; by the seventeenth century it had become a recognized institution. Members were often present to hear deathbed confessions, to provide the funeral repast, and to comfort the mourners. The *ḥevrah qaddisha'* held an annual banquet, either on 7 Adar or on 15 or 20 Kislev, preceded by a service at which special *seliḥot* (penitential prayers) were recited, asking for forgiveness if the members had been remiss in showing proper respect for the dead. Among Sephardim, the *ḥevrah qaddisha'* is called the Society of Lavadores ("those who wash," i.e., the body), or *ḥevrah qaddisha' ḥesed ve-'emet*, "burial society of loving kindness and truth." In many Western countries, the role assumed by the voluntary *ḥevrah qaddisha'* has been either augmented or replaced by commercial funeral directors. Religious persons, though, always seek to have a *ḥevrah qaddisha'* take care of the religious preparations and the funeral itself.

• Jacob Z. Lauterbach, "Burial Practices," in *Studies in Jewish Law, Custom, and Folklore* (New York, 1970). Mareleyn Schneider, *History of a Jewish Burial Society: An Examination of Secularization* (Lewiston, N.Y., 1991).

HEZEKIAH (Heb. Ḥizqiyyah), king of Judah (r. 727–698), described by the biblical books as a righteous king, who, with the encouragement of the prophet Isaiah, instituted a religious reform that included the eradication of all idolatrous elements from Israelite worship (some of which Hezekiah's father, Ahaz, had introduced even into the Temple in Jerusalem), the cleansing and sanctifying of the Temple, and the restoration of the Temple cult (*2 Kgs*. 18.3–4, *2 Chr*. 29–30). In his zeal to eradicate all idols, he also destroyed the brazen serpent (*Nehushtan) of Moses (*2 Kgs*. 18.4; cf. *Nm*. 21.4–9). *Proverbs* makes reference to the period of Hezekiah as one of royally sponsored literary activity (*Prv*. 25.1). In order to gain political independence, in 701 BCE he rebelled against Sennacherib, king of Assyria, who thereupon besieged Jerusalem. Preparing for the upcoming assault, Hezekiah had a tunnel (still existent) constructed to bring the waters of the Gihon spring into the walls of the city to ensure adequate water supply (*2 Kgs*. 20.20; *2 Chr*. 22.30; *Is*. 22.9–11). The famous Siloam inscription, discovered carved into the rock inside the tunnel, describes the digging of the tunnel by two teams starting at opposite ends and meeting in the middle. According to the biblical account, Jerusalem was spared when a plague broke out in the Assyrian army and the siege was lifted (*2 Kgs*. 18.35; *2 Chr*. 32.21; *Is*. 37.36). Nevertheless the Assyrian king did exact a high tribute from Hezekiah (*2 Kgs*. 18.13–16), who was described as a "bird in a cage" in Sennacherib's own inscription recording the siege. The Talmud depicts Hezekiah as an ideal king, originally destined to be the Messiah (*San*. 94a; *Sg. Rab*. 4.8). According to one rabbinic opinion, the books of *Isaiah*, *Proverbs*, *Song of Songs*, and *Ecclesiastes* were written (probably meaning edited or published) by Hezekiah and his colleagues (*B. B.* 15a).

• Mordechai Cogan and Hayim Tadmor, *II Kings: A New Translation with Introduction and Commentary*, The Anchor Bible, vol. 11 (Garden City, N.Y., 1988), pp. 215–263. Paul K. Hooker, "The Kingdom of Hezekiah: Judah in the Geo-Political Context of the Late Eighth Century BCE," Ph.D. dissertation, Emory University, 1993. –DAVID A. GLATT-GILAD

ḤIBBUT ʿARAVAH. See HOSHAʿNAʾ RABBAH.

ḤIBBUT HA-QEVER (חִבּוּט הַקֶּבֶר; torture of the grave), a folk belief that people are judged in the grave during the first three days after burial by being tortured by the *angel of death or other demonic beings unless they remember their names. That is why people were encouraged to memorize biblical verses beginning and ending with the initial and final letters of their names. The idea occurs in early eschatological *aggadah* (in *Ḥibbut ha-Qever*, also known as *Midrash Rabbi Yitsḥaq ben Parnaq*) and was developed by the kabbalists, notably Yitsḥaq *Luria in his *Sefer ha-Kavvanot*. Those who practice charity, hospitality, and devotion in prayer are said to be exempt from the test, as are those who live in Erets Yisraʾel and those who die on the Sabbath eve. Others who are spared this torture include sages and those who have lived in penury or affliction (e.g., Yeshaʿyahu Horowitz, *Shenei Luḥot ha-Berit* II 146a).

• Jacob Z. Lauterbach, "The Belief in the Power of the Word," in *Studies in Jewish Law, Custom, and Folklore* (New York, 1970), pp. 143–158.

ḤIDDUSHIM (חִדּוּשִׁים), a genre of rabbinic literature, also referred to as *novellae*, usually devoted to the discussion of Talmudic materials, although the term is also used to describe biblical commentary (by Moses *Nahmanides, for example). Broadly speaking, *ḥiddushim* proceed beyond the commentary of *Rashi, who provides a running exposition of the Talmudic text, to consider problems that arise from a study of the pericope as a whole or other, related, Talmudic materials. The solutions offered often posit new legal doctrine, contributing to the history of halakhic ideas as well as to the process of halakhic decision making. The twelfth-century tosafists of Germany and France (see TOSAFOT) were among the pioneers of the genre, as were Yosef ben Meʾir *ibn Migash of Spain and *Avraham ben David of Posquières of Spain. The tosafist method was further refined in thirteenth- and fourteenth-century Spain by Nahmanides, Shelomoh ben Avraham *Adret, *Yom Tov ben Avraham Ishbili, and others. In its earliest stages, the term *novellae* was often not attached to the work in question but was appended later, when it became clear that the material, in fact, belonged to the genre. *Ḥiddushim* were not devoted to Talmudic *halakhah* alone; classic *novellae* were written on Talmudic *aggadah* (see EDELS, SHEMUʾEL ELIʿEZER) and on Moses *Maimonides' *Mishneh Torah*. Indeed this genre has thrived even in the twentieth century in the work of Ḥayyim Soloveichik (see SOLOVEICHIK FAMILY) and R. Meʾir Simḥah of Dvinsk, who composed major *novellae* on the *Mishneh Torah*. Moreover, *novellae* are often found in other genres of rabbinic literature such as *responsa* and commentary, for example, the *Shaʾagat Aryeh* of Aryeh Leib ben Asher *Gunzburg. Both the *Urim ve-Tummim* (Yonatan *Eybeschuetz), and *Ketsot ha-Ḥoshen* (Aryeh Leib ha-Kohen), ostensibly commentaries on the *Shulḥan ʿArukh*, are in essence *novellae* on topics of civil law appended to *Ḥoshen Mishpat*.

Despite the medieval origins of the genre, the term *ḥiddushim* and the concept behind it are firmly anchored in the early Talmudic worldview, which frequently asserts that "there is no study house without a new idea [*ḥiddush*]," and which describes various laws as "*novellae* of the sages" (*ḥiddush . . . soferim*). Nahmanides introduced his *Milḥamot* by claiming that it fulfilled the "obligation . . . of searching . . . the Torah . . . and revealing its secrets. . . . This book does not say anything new which had not been said before . . . but merely explains the words of its predecessors." In modern times, R. Yosef Baer Soloveichik has placed the *ḥiddush* at the heart of his description of the creative halakhic personality. See also PILPUL.

• Avraham Grossman, "Reʾshitan shel 'ha-Tosafot,'" in *Rashi: ʿIyyunim be-Yetsirato*, edited by Zvi Arie Steinfeld (Ramat Gan, 1993), pp. 57–68. Dov Rappel, *Ha-Vikkuaḥ ʿal ha-Pilpul* (Jerusalem, 1979). Yochanan Silman, "Torah Yisraʾel le-Or Ḥiddusheha: Berur Finominologi," *Proceedings of the American Academy for Jewish Research* 57 (1990–1991): 49–67. –GERALD J. BLIDSTEIN

ḤIDQAʾ, FEAST OF RABBI. See SEʿUDAT RABBI ḤIDQAʾ.

HIGHER CRITICISM. See BIBLE.

HIGH HOLIDAYS. See YAMIM NORAʾIM.

HIGH PLACE (Heb. *bamah*), cultic installation existing in biblical times, used by Canaanites in the worship of their gods as well as by Israelites in their worship. A high place was probably a raised platform of earth and stones, specially constructed for sacrifice, and not necessarily located on a naturally high spot. It was not a temple or shrine; it did not have any of the features of an abode for the deity, any symbols of the divine presence, or an official priesthood. Rather it consisted of a platform, an altar, and a nearby facility, probably a small chamber, in which the sacrificial meal was held (*1 Sm.* 9). Thus it stands somewhere between the local houses of God, or shrines, and field altars, but closer to the latter. Several possible high places have been identified in archeological excavations in Israel. The Bible speaks approvingly of the high places that existed before the Temple was built (*1 Kgs.* 3.4) but thereafter, in accord with *Deuteronomy*, views all worship at high places, and indeed their very existence, as sinful. The *Book of Kings* connects the prolonged failure to centralize the cult as a cause of the eventual fall of the kingdom and, therefore, views with favor only those kings of Judah who destroyed the high places: Hezekiah and Josiah (*2 Kgs.* 18.3–4, 22.1ff.). The Mishnah (*Zev.* 14.4–8) devised an elaborate historical theory, according to which high places were originally permitted, prohibited during the wilderness wanderings, permitted again when the Israelites arrived in Canaan, banned again when the Tabernacle was set up in Shiloh, permitted after it was destroyed, and prohibited for all time when the Temple was built.

• Menahem Haran, *Temples and Temple-Service in Ancient Israel* (Oxford, 1978), pp. 13–25. Beth Alpert Nakhai, "What's a Bamah? How Sacred Space Functioned in Ancient Israel," *Biblical Archaeology Review* 20.3 (1994): 18–29, 77–78.

—BARUCH J. SCHWARTZ

HIGH PRIEST (Heb. *ha-kohen ha-gadol; Nm.* 35.25, 28; *Jos.* 20.6), chief officiant in the Temple in ancient Israel. The name parallels the Ugaritic *rb khnm*. Short for "the highest priest among his brothers" (*Lv.* 21.10), he is also called *ha-kohen ha-mashiaḥ* (the anointed priest; *Lv.* 4.3, 6.15), since he alone has the anointing oil poured on his head (*Ex.* 29.7; *Lv.* 8.12, 21.10), and *[ha-]kohen ha-ro'sh* (the head priest; e.g., *2 Kgs.* 25.18). *Aaron, the brother of Moses, was ordained at God's command as the first high priest (*Ex.* 28.1ff.); upon his death God appointed his son Eleazar in his place (*Nm.* 20.22–29). Later, Eleazar's son Phinehas, in recognition of his zealousness on God's behalf (see *Nm.* 25.1–9), was given a divine "promise of eternal priesthood" (*Nm.* 25.13). Since Phinehas served later as high priest (*Jos.* 22.13ff.; *Jgs.* 20.28), this may mean that the high priesthood was thenceforth to remain among his descendants. This interpretation is reflected in *1 Chronicles* 5.29 and following, according to which David and Solomon's chief priest Zadok, from whom the high priests of First Temple times were descended, was a descendant of Phinehas. This may be a late tradition, however, since the high priesthood is said to have been given to Zadok after having been taken away from the house of Eli (*1 Kgs.* 2.27).

In the Torah the high priest is pictured not as a public official, nor as a teacher or leader, but rather as a divinely designated, sacred representative of the Israelite people. Virtually his entire function is ceremonial. Dressed in the *priestly vestments, he embodies the body politic, serving in God's earthly abode, paying uninterrupted homage to the enshrined deity on behalf of the Israelite tribes, and calling his attention to their needs in the daily *tamid* sacrifice. He is consecrated for this task by investiture (*Lv.* 8), having the priestly vestments placed upon him. In addition, he is responsible for the purgation of sins and impurities that penetrate the Tabernacle and its inner sanctum (*Lv.* 4.3–21), which means he is the sole officiant in the annual Yom Kippur ceremonies, purifying the Tabernacle and driving away Israel's sins. On this occasion he enters the Holy of Holies (see TEMPLE), the only time this is permitted, which constitutes the climax of the ritual year (*Lv.* 16). He also administers the divine oracle, the Urim and Thummim (see ORACLES). Because he belonged to the innermost sphere of sanctity, the high priest was subject to a greater number of restrictions than other priests; he had to marry a woman not previously married and was forbidden to come into contact with the corpses of even his own closest relatives (see IMPURITY) or to mourn the dead (*Lv.* 21).

Some of the high priests who served in First Temple times are mentioned by name, such as Jehoiada (*2 Kgs.* 11.4ff.) and Hilkiah (*2 Kgs.* 22.4ff.). High priests took on more administrative tasks in the Temple, and occasionally the position became one of political influence. In early Second Temple times, the high priest was the religious and political head of the nation and was recognized as such by foreign rulers; later he also served as head of the *Sanhedrin. Eventually the high priesthood was taken over by the *Hasmoneans, who combined the office with that of king, to the dismay of the *Pharisees. Under Roman rule, from the time of Herod, appointments were made at the whim of the ruler, and there is evidence that in the disputes dividing religious sects in early rabbinic Judaism the high priests were often of the Sadducean faction. See also PRIESTHOOD.

• Gedalia Alon, *Jews, Judaism and the Classical World: Studies in Jewish History in the Times of the Second Temple and Talmud*, translated by Israel Abrahams (Jerusalem, 1977), pp. 48–88. Menahem Haran, *Temples and Temple-Service in Ancient Israel* (Winona Lake, Ind., 1985), pp. 84–103, 205–221 and *passim*. Jacob Milgrom, *Leviticus 1–16*, The Anchor Bible, vol. 3 (New York, 1991), pp. 493–595. Jacob Milgrom, *Numbers: Ba-Midbar*, The JPS Torah Commentary (Philadelphia, 1990), pp. 169–171, 216–218, 484–486. James C. VanderKam, "Jewish High Priests of the Persian Period," in *Priesthood and Cult in Ancient Israel*, edited by Gary A. Anderson and Saul M. Olyan, Journal for the Study of the Old Testament, Supplement Series 125 (Sheffield, Eng., 1991), pp. 67–91.

—BARUCH J. SCHWARTZ

HILDESHEIMER, EZRIEL (1820–1899), scholar and leader of Orthodox Jewry in Germany. He officiated as rabbi in Eisenstadt (Hungary, now Austria), where he founded a rabbinical school that was the first *yeshivah* to combine secular with religious studies and to teach not in Yiddish but in the vernacular languages (German and Hungarian). For these innovations, Hildesheimer found himself the object of bitter attacks by most Orthodox Hungarian rabbis, especially among the Ḥasidim. In 1869 he moved to Berlin to head the *Adass Jisroel congregation, where he founded a modern religious school for boys and girls. He was one of the foremost opponents of Reform, especially of the activities of Abraham Geiger. In 1873 he founded, and directed until his death, the *Berlin Rabbinical Seminary (long known in popular parlance as the Hildesheimerseminar) for the training of modern Orthodox rabbis, prompted in part by the need to counter the Reform *Hochschule für die Wissenschaft des Judentums. In 1870 he founded the weekly Orthodox journal *Jüdische Presse* and was an active supporter of renewed Jewish settlement in Erets Yisra'el. His most notable work, **Halakhot Gedolot*, was a translation of a Vatican manuscript. His collected essays, *Gesammelte Aufsätze* were published in German (1923) and his *responsa* were published in Hebrew (1969, 1976).

• Gustav Karpeles, *Dr. Israel Hildesheimer: Eine biographische Skizze* (Frankfurt am Main, 1870). I. Unna, in *Jewish Leaders*, edited by L. Jung (New York, 1953), pp. 213–232.

ḤILLAZON (חִלָּזוֹן), conchiferous marine animal, the blue blood of which was used for dying the blue cord of the **tsitsit* as prescribed in *Numbers* 15.38 (*Men.* 44a). The *ḥillazon* was very scarce and supposedly appeared only once every seventy years. For this reason the rabbis allowed its use to be dispensed with. According to *Sanhedrin* 91a, the *ḥillazon* snail was also found in the mountains, but the ritually prescribed species was caught near the coast in territory held by the tribe of Zebulun (*Meg.* 6a). Rabbi Yosef described the *ḥillazon* fishing area as extending from Tyre in Phoenicia down to the Bay of Haifa. According to the Zohar, the *ḥillazon* could also be found in the Sea of Galilee. It was identified by Gershon Ḥanokh Leiner with the cuttlefish, by Isaac Herzog with the snails *Janthina pallida* and *Janthina bicolor*, and by other researchers with the *Murex* snails found along the eastern Mediterranean littoral.

• Menaḥem Burshtin, *Ha-Tekhelet* (Tel Aviv, 1987). Isaac H. Herzog, *The Royal Purple and the Biblical Blue*, edited by E. Spanier (Jerusalem, 1987). Menahem M. Kasher, in *The Leo Jung Jubilee Volume* (New York, 1962). Gershon H. Leiner, *Tekhelet ba-Tsitsit be-Yamenu* (Tel Aviv, 1953).

HILLEL (1st cent. BCE), early tanna', rabbinic authority, and Pharisaic leader. He and his colleague Shamm'ai are the last of the "pairs" (of scholars) presented in *Avot* 1. He is the first of the patriarchs, a line of moderate Pharisaic sages who presided over the Sanhedrin and represented Palestinian Jewry to the Roman authorities. The added appellation "the Elder" (*ha-Zaqen*) attests to his importance.

Hillel came from Babylonia and was appointed *nasi'* around 30 BCE, probably by Herod. He earned the position, according to the Talmud, by interpreting biblical verses about the paschal sacrifice, thereby solving a halakhic problem. Hillel is elsewhere presented as an early expositor of the scriptures and a founder of the Midrashic method; he is credited with "seven rules of hermeneutics" (*middot*). His famous dictum to the prospective proselyte, "What is detestable to you do not inflict upon your fellow man," is a *midrash* of the verse "Love thy neighbor as thyself" (*Lv.* 19.18). He also used the Midrashic technique of the parable.

Hillel differed with Shamm'ai on three or four issues of law, but the number of halakhic disputes widened among their disciples, called the House of Hillel (Beit Hillel) and the House of Shamm'ai (Beit Shamm'ai). Hillel comes across from the sources as both modest and tolerant; Shamm'ai is presented as fastidious and strict in presenting the Law. Thus, Hillel was prepared to teach the proselyte who demanded to know the entire Torah "while standing on one leg," while Shamm'ai banished him.

Mishnaic sources record two regulations (*taqqanot*) that Hillel instituted: the **perozbol*, a legal instrument to prevent the cancellation of debts during the sabbatical year, thereby encouraging people to lend money to the poor (*Shevi'it* 10.3); and a regulation allowing one who sold his home to redeem it (*Lv.* 25.30) by depositing the purchase price with the Temple authorities when the buyer was not available (*'Arakh.* 9.4). Both regulations are evidence of the ability to adapt the law to prevailing economic circumstances.

Hillel taught, "Be among the disciples of Aaron—love peace and pursue it, love all men and draw them close to the Torah" (*Avot* 1.12). Possibly a democratic view of who could study Torah emerges from here, as opposed to a more elitist concept associated with the Sadducees. The mention of Aaron, the high priest, in this context, when that office was often identified as an elite position controlled by the Sadducees, is not without significance. He also taught, "He who wishes to raise his name lowers it; he who does not seek the law does not deserve to live. He who uses the crown of the Torah for his own ends, perishes" (*Avot* 1.13). His personal exemplary behavior, his role as innovator in biblical interpretation and as a teacher of Torah who founded a school, and his position as *nasi'* all mark him as a central figure in the history of *halakhah*. Indeed, it is said of Hillel that like Ezra, who also came from Babylonia to Jerusalem, he restored the Torah, which had been neglected. See also BEIT HILLEL AND BEIT SHAMM'AI.

• Nahum Norbert Glatzer, *Hillel the Elder* (New York, 1956). William Scott Green, ed., *Persons and Institutions in Early Rabbinic Judaism*, Brown Judaic Studies, no. 3 (Missoula, Mont., 1977). Jacob Neusner, *The Rabbinic Traditions about the Pharisees before 70*, 3 vols. (Leiden, 1971). Emil Schürer, *The History of the Jewish People in the Age of Jesus Christ, 175 B.C.–A.D. 135*, a new English version, revised and edited by Geza Vermes, Fergus Millar, and Martin Goodman, vol. 2 (Edinburgh, 1979), pp. 356–369.

–ISAAC B. GOTTLIEB

HILLEL (4th cent. CE), known as Hillel II, patriarch of Palestinian Jewry. According to a tradition cited by Nahmanides, in the year 358 Hillel II abolished the proclamation of a new month by observation of the new moon (see RO'SH ḤODESH) and substituted for it a permanent *calendar based on complicated but very exact calculations. After adopting this calendar, Diaspora Jews no longer had to depend on Erets Yisra'el for the fixing of dates; it remains the standard Jewish calendar to this day. Hillel II corresponded with the Roman emperor Julian (later called "the Apostate" by the church), who addressed him with particular affection.

• Aaron Hyman, *Toledot Tanna'im ve-'Amora'im* (1910; Jerusalem, 1987).

–DANIEL SPERBER

HILLEL, SCHOOL OF. See BEIT HILLEL AND BEIT SHAMM'AI.

HILLEL BEN SHEMU'EL (c.1220–1295), physician and Talmudist; the first Jewish philosopher in Italy. He translated many treatises on medicine from Latin into Hebrew. Hillel took an important part in the counterattack of the supporters of Maimonides against their opponents during the years 1289 and 1290 (see MAIMONIDEAN CONTROVERSY) and sought to harmonize Neoplatonic philosophical concepts with the standard religious ideas on the immortality of the individual soul, personal reward and punishment, and the literal acceptance of miracles. His book *Tagmulei ha-Nefesh*, completed in 1291, shows the strong influence of Christian scholasticism. He also wrote a commentary on the twenty-five Aristotelian propositions postulated in Maimonides' *Guide of the Perplexed* and three dissertations on the question of free will, the relation of death to Adam's fall, and fallen angels.

• Isaac Husik, *A History of Mediaeval Jewish Philosophy* (Philadelphia, 1944), pp. 312–327. Giuseppe Sermoneta, ed., *Hillel ben Shemu'el of Verona: Sefer Tagmulei ha-Nefesh* (Jerusalem, 1981).

–FRANCISCO MORENO CARVALHO

HILLULA' (Aram.; הִלּוּלָא; festivity), a pilgrimage to and celebration at the tomb of a saintly and charismatic rabbi on the anniversary of his death. Local, regional and even national pilgrimages brought masses of Jews to venerated gravesites, especially in southern Morocco. The tombs of R. Yaʿaqov Abi-Ḥasira, R. Amram ben-Diwan, and R. David u-Mosheh were frequented by Muslims as well as by Jews. Some "saints," like the aforementioned, were historic personalities. Others were legendary. The *hillula'* celebration was marked by ecstatic prayer, feasting, and entertainment and formed an integral part of Moroccan Jewish folk religion. In Israel a *hillula'* is observed annually for R. *Me'ir Baʿal ha-Nes and, on *Lag ba-ʿOmer, at the reputed grave of R. Shimʿon bar Yoḥ'ai on Mount Meron. In Kabbalistic and Hasidic literature, the death of a **tsaddiq* is called a *hillula'*, because his soul enters before God like a bride enters under the wedding canopy (in Aramaic the term means a wedding celebration). The Zohar (*Devarim* 296) relates that when Shimʿon bar Yoḥ'ai died, a voice was heard saying "ascend and gather" at R. Shimʿon's *hillula'*.

• Issachar Ben-Ami, "The Folk Veneration of Saints among Moroccan Jews: Traditions, Continuity and Change: The Case of the Holy Man, Rabbi David u-Moshe," in *Studies in Judaism and Islam*, edited by Shelomoh Morag, Issachar Ben-Ami and Norman Stillman (Jerusalem, 1981), pp. 283–345. Alex Weingrod, *The Saint of Beersheba* (Albany, N.Y., 1990).

—JANE S. GERBER

ḤILLUL HA-SHEM (חִלּוּל הַשֵּׁם; profanation of the [divine] Name), an action or remark that brings disgrace upon the Jewish community, and, hence, upon God (cf. *Lv*. 22.32). The special emphasis placed upon *ḥillul ha-Shem* in Jewish thought derives from the concept that the honor of God is so bound up with the Jewish people that any praiseworthy act on the part of a Jew adds to the glory of God (see QIDDUSH HA-SHEM), and any unworthy or dishonorable act detracts from that glory and causes a profanation, not only of the good name of the Jew, but of God himself. This is particularly serious when the transgression is committed publicly (*Qid*. 40a). Consequently *ḥillul ha-Shem* is usually associated with a disreputable act by a Jew against a non-Jew. If a Jew steals from a non-Jew, it is regarded as a more heinous offense than if a Jew steals from a fellow Jew, since it brings upon him the added sin of *ḥillul ha-Shem*. In some instances *ḥillul ha-Shem* was punished by excommunication. A person publicly regarded as a representative of the Jewish people must be particularly careful to ensure that his conduct is above reproach. Thus, Rav said that were he to purchase meat and not pay the butcher immediately (that is, use his rabbinic reputation to buy on credit), he would be guilty of *ḥillul ha-Shem* (*Yoma'* 86a). According to one Talmudic view, the sin was so grave that it could not be expiated by atonement or repentance but only by death (*Yoma'* 86a).

• E. Borowitz, "Ḥillul Hashem: A Universalistic Rubric in Halakhic Ethics," in *Studies in Jewish Philosophy: Collected Essays of the Academy for Jewish Philosophy, 1980–1985*, edited by Norbert Samuelson (Lanham, Md., 1987). Jacob Milgrom, "Kiddush Hashem and Ḥillul Hashem in the Jewish State," *Conservative Judaism* 40 (1988): 30–35. Henriette Salomon, *Dédicace, consecration, profanation des temples en droit romain* (n.p., 1945).

ḤILLUL SHABBAT (חִלּוּל שַׁבָּת), desecration or profanation of the *Sabbath. Observance of the Sabbath is considered so fundamental that its profanation is compared to transgression of the entire Torah. Some authorities ruled that wine touched by a desecrator of the Sabbath is regarded as if it were touched by a non-Jew and is, therefore, unfit for Jewish use. In biblical law, the desecration of the Sabbath was punishable by death. If unintentional, the offender had to bring a sin offering to the Temple. The deliberate performance of one of the thirty-nine types of work prohibited on the Sabbath constituted *ḥillul Shabbat*. The duty of saving human life, however, overrides the prescription of Sabbath observance.

• Abraham Joshua Heschel, *The Sabbath: Its Meaning for Modern Man* (New York, 1995).

—CHAIM PEARL

HINNENI HE-ʿANI MI-MAʿAS (הִנְנִי הֶעָנִי מִמַּעַשׂ; "Here am I, poor in deeds"), opening words of a **reshut* for the **sheliaḥ tsibbur* before the *Musaf service on the High Holy Days in the Ashkenazi rite; of unknown but obviously early modern provenance. It explains the role of the *sheliaḥ tsibbur* and his responsibility in spite of his inadequacies. Its cantorial elaborations made it popular so that even when the Musaf service was omitted in Reform congregations, it was preserved as a solemn opening for the *Ro'sh ha-Shanah eve service.

• Stefan C. Reif, *Judaism and Hebrew Prayer: New Perspectives on Jewish Liturgical History* (Cambridge, 1993), p. 246. Morris Silverman, *High Holiday Prayerbook* (Hartford, Conn., 1939), p. 124.

—PETER LENHARDT

HIRING (Heb. *sekhirut*), transactions by which an interested party contracts for the use of property or the labor power and skill of an individual. The hiring of a laborer is governed by the general considerate relationship between master and servant, employer and employee, outlined in the Talmud and based on biblical legislation (e.g., *Lv*. 25.43). Hiring and the letting of property are subject to the laws of sale (*B. M.* 56b), in regard to the manner of acquisition and concerns about deceit or overcharge. The liability of the lessee extends only to neglect but not to damage incurred in the normal use of the property hired. If no definite date has been agreed upon for termination of the lease, the type of property hired, the season of the year, and local custom (*B. M.* 101b) are taken into consideration.

• Menachem Elon, *Jewish Law: History, Sources, Principles*, 4 vols. (Philadelphia, 1994).

HIRSCH, SAMSON RAPHAEL (1808–1888), German rabbi and author; leading exponent of *Neo-Orthodoxy. Born and educated in Hamburg, where his religious outlook was greatly influenced by Isaac *Bernays and Yaʿaqov *Ettlinger, he also studied at the University of Bonn prior to becoming *Landesrabbiner* of Oldenburg in 1830. It was there, over the next eleven years, that Hirsch formulated his own traditionalist response to modernity, writing the two works that constituted the basis of his ideology, *Neunzehn Briefe über Judentum* (Altona, 1836) and *Choreb, oder Versuche über Jissroels Pflichten in der Zerstreuung* (Altona, 1837). Unlike the advocates of *Reform Judaism, he took a literalist approach to the biblical narrative and divine revelation, insisting that the written and oral law are eternally authoritative for all Jews and not subject to the dictates of convenience or fashion. At the same time, however, Hirsch differed with the traditionalist Orthodox leaders, such as Mosheh Sofer (see SOFER FAMILY) of Pressburg, in his readiness to harmonize traditional Judaism with modern life in dress, speech, forms of worship, and a positive attitude toward the society and culture of nineteenth-century Europe.

After occupying posts in Emden and Nikolsburg, Moravia (1841–1851), Hirsch was invited to head the Israelitische Religionsgesellschaft, a small group of like-minded Orthodox Jews who rejected the Reform-dominated community in Frankfurt am Main. As a gifted writer, educator, and preacher, he devoted the rest of his life to making the new-style *Orthodoxy respectable, to expanding the membership and ramiform activities of his independent congregation, and to fostering the growth of similar (*Adass Jisroel) communities outside Frankfurt.

Hirsch devised a new meaning for the rabbinic concept of *Torah im derekh erets* (*Avot* 2.2): Torah Judaism in harmony with secular culture. This became the watchword of his Orthodox modernism. Hirsch developed these ideas further in his monthly *Jeschurun* (1854–1870), as well as in his annotated Pentateuch (Frankfurt am Main, 1867–1878; translated by Isaac Levy [London, 1956–1962]), *Psalms* (Frankfurt am Main, 1883; translated by Gertrude Hirschler, 2 vols. [Jerusalem and New York, 1960–1966]), and daily prayer book entitled *Siddur Tefillot Yisra'el: Israels Gebete übersetzt und erläutert* (Frankfurt am Main, 1895). Hirsch divided the biblical laws into six categories: *torot*, or doctrines, namely, the principles of Jewish faith that have been historically revealed; *mishpatim*, or principles of justice between individuals; *ḥuqqim*, or statutes, a category defined by the rabbis as laws whose motivation is not apparent to human reasoning and that, according to Hirsch, ensure justice to all creatures; *'edot*, or testimonials, the symbolic actions, such as ceremonials, festivals, and fasts meant to train Israel; *mitsvot*, or commandments, such as family and communal obligations and penitence; and *'avodah*, or worship, which embraces all aspects of worship. The Torah was given in the wilderness to show that Jewish nationhood does not depend on a particular land and that the Jewish mission can be accomplished in exile. Nothing matters but the Torah, which is meant to teach the observance of religious law and not philosophical truths. The ideal individual is the *Mensch-Jissroel* (that is, the Torah-observant Jew).

Thanks to the prolonged efforts of Eduard Lasker, a Jewish deputy in the Prussian *Landtag* (parliament), an *Austrittsgesetz* (law of secession) was passed in 1876, enabling Hirsch's congregation and others like it to become self-supporting, with no legal or financial obligations to the Reform-controlled communities that denied them a budget. This measure plunged Hirsch into an ideological dispute with those Orthodox leaders (such as Seligmann Baer *Bamberger) who felt that the interests of traditional Judaism should be defended within—not outside—the general communal framework. It also created a rift within the Neo-Orthodox camp, between militant separatists and their more tolerant, nonisolationist opponents.

Hirsch was criticized in his later years for giving too little weight to Jewish national solidarity and too much to Diaspora-centered universalism. He was highly legalistic, hostile toward modern Jewish scholarship, and inspired the inward-looking **Austrittsgemeinde* mentality of his *Breuer family descendants. On the other hand, he made it possible for Orthodox Jews to play a constructive role in general society. His collected works were published in six volumes as *Gesammelte Schriften* (Frankfurt am Main, 1902–1912).

• Mordekhai Breuer, *Jüdische Orthodoxie im deutschen Reich 1871–1918* (Frankfurt am Main, 1986), pp. 61–82. Mordekhai Breuer, "Samson Raphael Hirsch," in *Guardians of Our Heritage*, edited by Leo Jung (New York, 1958), pp. 265–299. Bernard Drachman, trans., *The Nineteen Letters of Ben Uziel* (New York, 1899); rev. ed. by Jacob Breuer (New York, 1960). Isidor Grunfeld, trans., *Horeb: Essays on Israel's Duties in the Diaspora*, 2 vols. (London, 1962). Isidor Grunfeld, ed. and trans., *Judaism Eternal*, 2 vols. (London, 1959–1966), includes a complete list of Samson Raphael Hirsch's publications in vol. 1, pp. xlix–lxi. Isidor Grunfeld, *Three Generations: The Influence of Samson Raphael Hirsch on Jewish Life and Thought* (London, 1958), contains extensive bibliographical data. Gertrude Hirschler, trans., *The Hirsch Siddur: The Order of Prayers for the Whole Year* (Jerusalem and New York, 1969). Karin Paritzky, trans., *The Nineteen Letters* (Jerusalem, 1995), rev. and with a commentary by Joseph Elias. Hermann Schwab, *The History of Orthodox Jewry in Germany* (London, 1950). Noah H. Rosenbloom, *Tradition in an Age of Reform: The Religious Philosophy of Samson Raphael Hirsch* (Philadelphia, 1976).

—GABRIEL A. SIVAN

HIRSCH FAMILY, leading Reformers in Germany and the United States in the late ninteenth and early twentieth centuries.

Samuel Hirsch (1815–1889), Reform rabbi and philosopher of Judaism. Born in Prussia, he studied at the Universities of Berlin, Bonn, and Leipzig. He served as a rabbi in Dessau before becoming chief rabbi of Luxembourg from 1843 to 1866. Subsequently he immigrated to the United States, where he succeeded David *Einhorn as rabbi of Temple Keneseth Israel in Philadelphia. Prominent in the Reform movement both in Germany and in the United States, he presided over the first American rabbinical conference in Philadelphia in 1869 and was an influential voice in the formulation of the *Pittsburgh platform of 1885. In 1842, he published *Die Religionsphilosophie der Juden*, in which he contrasted Judaism with Christianity. Although influenced by Hegel, Hirsch rejected his view that Judaism was a less-elevated religion than Christianity, arguing instead that both should be regarded as "absolute religion." The mission of Christianity was to proclaim the one true God to the pagan world, while Judaism was an "intensive" religiosity—a way of living centered on God. Hirsch stressed the importance of human freedom in confronting the world of nature, and he interpreted the *'aqedah story as Abraham's conscious rejection of child sacrifice. In his own ministry, Hirsch was totally committed to the ideal of social justice.

Emil Gustave Hirsch (1851–1923), Reform rabbi; son of Samuel Hirsch. Emil served as a rabbi in Baltimore, in Louisville, and, from 1880 until his death, in Chicago, at Temple Sinai. A leader of radical Reform, he emphasized the ethical message of Judaism, especially social justice. He put his theories into practice in public life in Chicago, where he worked for laws protecting women and guaranteeing workers' compensation. He edited the Bible section of the *Jewish Encyclopedia*.

• **Samuel Hirsch**: Julius Guttmann, *Philosophies of Judaism* (New York, 1964), pp. 313–321. Walter Jacob, *Christianity through Jewish Eyes: The Quest for Common Good* (New York, 1974), pp. 51–56. David Philipson, *Reform Movement in Judaism* (New York, 1907). W. Gunther Plaut, *The Rise of Reform Judaism: A Sourcebook of Its European Origins* (New York, 1963). Nathan Rotenstreich, *Jewish Philosophy in Modern Times: From Mendelssohn to Rosenzweig* (New York, 1968), pp. 120–136. **Emil Gustave Hirsch**: David Einhorn Hirsch, *Rabbi Emil G. Hirsch: The Reform Advocate* (Chicago, 1968). —LAVINIA COHN-SHERBOK

ḤISDA' (c.217–310), Babylonian amora'. He and his colleague R. *Huna'—both disciples of *Rav—were called "the pious men of Babylonia" or "the Elders of *Sura" and increased the prestige of the Sura academy, which Ḥisda' was instrumental in rebuilding in the year 293. Many of his aggadic and halakhic dicta are quoted in both the Talmud Yerushalmi and the Talmud Bavli. The prayer recited on setting out on a journey (*Ber.* 29b), *Tefillat ha-Derekh, is ascribed to him. He excelled in penetrating analysis, while his colleague R. Sheshet was famed for the breadth of his knowledge (*'Eruv.* 67b). Ḥisda' was extremely orderly in his study (*Sot.* 39b) and used mnemonic devices to aid memorization (*'Eruv.* 54b); many of these mnemonic devices have survived in editions of the Talmud. Ḥisda' believed that the destruction of the Temple altered nature and that climate and wind directions were adversely affected (*Ber.* 79a).

• Gershom Bader, *The Encyclopedia of Talmudic Sages*, translated from the Yiddish by Solomon Katz (Northvale, N.J., and London, 1988). Aaron Hyman, *Toledot Tanna'im ve-'Amora'im* (1910; Jerusalem, 1987). Mordecai Margaliot, ed., *Entsiqlopediyyah le-Ḥakhmei ha-Talmud veha-Ge'onim* (Jerusalem, 1946). —DANIEL SPERBER

HISTORICAL MOVEMENT, a school of religious thought in nineteenth-century Germany which sought to take a middle path between the *Reform and the *Orthodox, preserving the authority of Jewish law and tradition while recognizing its ongoing development throughout history and its consequent need to be open to change. It arose in response to the challenge of modernity and the substantial changes in Jewish practice advocated by the Reformers. Also known as the "Positive-Historical School," the movement was allied with emerging trends in modern Jewish scholarship (see WISSENSCHAFT DES JUDENTUMS). Instead of understanding Jewish tradition solely as it understood itself, as reflected in traditional commentaries, the new approach sought to place Jewish texts in their historical context through applying the tools of critical research—cross-cultural studies, linguistic analysis, archaeology, and so forth. The authority of Jewish law, then, derived primarily from the Jewish community's adherence to it, as it evolved in response to changing historical circumstances. This orientation made historical study and historical identity central in defining and motivating Jewish commitment. It was intended that these innovations would lead, in the words of Zacharias *Frankel, the prime founder of this movement, to "moderate reform." This position gradually became the dominant one in Germany, where it also came to be known as Liberal Judaism. In the United States, it formed the ideological foundation for the *Conservative movement. In Israel, it is known as the Masorti movement.

• Moshe Davis, *The Emergence of Conservative Judaism* (Philadelphia, 1963). Daniel H. Gordis, "Positive-Historical Judaism Exhausted: Reflections on a Movement's Future," *Conservative Judaism* 47.1 (Fall 1994): 3–18, with responses in the Spring 1995 issue. Ismar Schorsch, *From Text to Context: The Turn to History in Modern Judaism*, The Tauber Institute for the Study of European Jewry Series, vol. 19 (Hanover, N.H., 1994). Mordecai Waxman, ed., *Tradition and Change: The Development of the Conservative Movement* (New York, 1958). —ELLIOT NELSON DORFF

HISTORIOGRAPHY. The history of Judaism commences and receives its most sweeping articulation not in post-biblical interpretation but in the Bible itself. The Bible is both the foundational text of Judaism and the originating point of Jewish historical writing. One of the defining features of biblical historiography is the ascription of divine meaning to historical acts rather than simply the recording of past deeds and events. Thus, the Pentateuch describes the role of God in shaping the historical experience of the Israelites. Moreover, with varying degrees of specificity, the Hebrew Bible records the chief events in ancient Jewish memory: the emergence of the Israelite patriarchs, settlement in and Exodus from Egypt, Sinaitic revelation, conquest of and settlement in Canaan/Erets Yisra'el, the rise and fall of kingship in Erets Yisra'el, and the causes and consequences of exile to Babylonia. The cumulative effect is a grand historical narrative describing the birth and transformation of a major world religion, as well as of a fledgling nation. In **Samuel*, **Kings*, and **Chronicles*, this narrative rests on a rather detailed political history, replete with succession struggles, court intrigues, and military victories and defeats.

This kind of history largely disappeared from post-Biblical Jewish writing. The most important ancient exception was the first-century Jewish soldier and writer, *Josephus, whose historical works, *Antiquities of the Jews* and *The Jewish War*, demonstrate a grasp of political and social context reminiscent of contemporaneous Greco-Roman historians. However, after Josephus, Jewish writers spent little time chronicling the political travails of their people. After the fall of the Second Temple, Jews no longer possessed political and territorial sovereignty, and were increasingly subject to geographic dispersion. In this post–Second Temple age, Jewish scholars devoted much effort to the elaboration of enduring legal norms and precepts. The need to fashion a new religious-legal authority and the lack of territorial sovereignty dampened the impulse to write history. That is not to suggest that Jews in late antiquity and medieval times lacked a sense of historical consciousness. They remained highly cognizant of the world around them and developed new "sites of memory"—rituals, liturgy, fast and feast days—to recall past events of religious import.

The specific work of historical chronicling, however, was not commonplace. One of the few works of history to circulate in medieval European Jewish circles was the *Sefer Yosippon*, a Hebrew account of the Second Temple period attributed to Josephus but probably written by a tenth-century Italian Jew. Other sources of Jewish historical writing in the Middle Ages were the Hebrew "chains of tradition" (*shalshelot ha-qabbalah*), containing lists of rabbinic luminaries responsible for the transmission of Jewish law over the ages. An impressive example of this genre was *Sefer ha-Qabbalah*, written by the twelfth-century Spanish philosopher Avraham *ibn Daud.

An important stimulus to Jewish historical writing in pre-modern times, where it existed, was persecution and tragedy. For example, the devastating effect of the Crusades on central European Jewry prompted a number of Jews to write Hebrew chronicles detailing the extent of destruction and sanctifying the suffering of their coreligionists (12th cent.). Similarly, the expulsion of the Jews from Spain in 1492 impelled various Jews in the sixteenth century to write accounts of Jewish history leading up to the Spanish expulsion. These include Solomon ibn Verga's *Shevet Yehudah*, Samuel Usque's Portuguese volume *Consolaçam as tribulaçoens de Israel*, and Yosef Ha-Kohen's *ʿEmeq ha-Bakha'*. In addition to these books, several other important works of Jewish historiography were produced in the sixteenth century that bore the traces of contemporaneous non-Jewish intellectual currents, in particular an incipient Renaissance historicism. Among the most notable of these were ʿAzaryah ben Mosheh dei *Rossi's *Me'or ʿEinayim*, a work that demonstrates a new critical spirit in analyzing Jewish historical sources, and David Gans's *Tsemaḥ David*.

Some historians have pointed to this crop of sixteenth-century texts as the beginning of modern Jewish historiography. To a great extent, Jewish historical writing until this period sought to emphasize the unbroken continuity of Jewish history, as well as to explain Jewish tragedy as part of a divine scheme. In this respect, Jewish history was *Heilsgeschichte*, sacred history whose recording was intended to edify and fortify. Anticipations of a more prosaic sense of history can, in fact, be found in sixteenth-century writers such as ibn Verga and ʿAzaryah dei Rossi. However, a mundane sense of historical causality took root only later, with the important changes in political order and religious attitudes that characterized European society in the eighteenth and nineteenth centuries.

Interestingly, the first systematic history of the Jews in modern times was written by a French Huguenot scholar, Jacques Basnage. Set against the backdrop of Protestant criticism of Catholicism, his seven-volume *Histoire du peuple juif depuis Jésus Christ jusqu'à présent* (1706–1711) reflects a new tolerance toward Jews and their history. At the same time, it is clear that Basnage's primary aim was not to edify the Jewish masses with tales of their past. By contrast, this ambition can be said to mark the new spate of biographical and historical writing among Jewish Enlightenment figures, or Maskilim, in the late eighteenth century. Centered in Berlin, in the 1780s, the Maskilim published a Hebrew journal, *Ha-Me'assef*, that reflected their reverential attitude toward the Jewish past.

An important new stage in Jewish historiography commenced in 1819 with the creation of the Verein für Kultur und Wissenschaft der Juden (Society for the Culture and Science of the Jews) in Berlin. Members of the Verein applied their recently acquired university training in history, philology, and theology to the study of Jewish sources. Infused with a commitment to scientific study, they sought to claim control over these sources from those whom they regarded as uncritical Jewish traditionalists and biased Christian scholars. One of the most distinguished members of this group was Leopold *Zunz (1794–1886), who wrote many seminal studies in German on Jewish literature, liturgy, and ritual. Zunz's childhood friend, I. M. Jost (1793–1860), published in the 1820s a nine-volume history of the Jews, *Geschichte der Israeliten*, noteworthy for its dispassion and integrationist thrust. From the next generation of scholars in Germany came the most important Jewish historian of the century, Heinrich *Graetz (1817–1891). Given the prevailing legal and social barriers, Graetz could not find employment in a German university. Rather, he and other scholars of *Wissenschaft des Judentums taught in the new rabbinical seminaries that arose in various Jewish communities in central Europe.

A related though distinct tradition of scholarship known as Ḥokhmat Yisra'el (see WISSENSCHAFT DES JUDENTUMS) developed throughout the nineteenth century. Its main advocates—Shelomoh Yehudah Leib *Rapoport, Naḥman *Krochmal, and Shemu'el David *Luzzatto—wrote in Hebrew and regarded their work as continuous with traditional Jewish scholarship. In this respect, they differed from their German-Jewish colleagues who hoped to attain a new position of critical distance from the past. Nevertheless, both sets of scholars remained largely focused in their research endeavors on the religious and literary development of Judaism.

In the late nineteenth and early twentieth centuries, the Russian-Jewish historian, Simon *Dubnow, attempted to introduce a "sociological corrective" to previous Jewish historiography. Dubnow's multi-volume *Weltgeschichte des jüdischen Volkes* revealed his innovative periodization of Jewish history, based on shifting centers of influence, as well as an emphasis on the material condition of the Jewish community throughout history. This new emphasis was replicated by other scholars, particularly those who had come to identify the Jews more as a nation than as a religious group. Eastern European researchers such as Meir Balaban (1877–1942), Jacob Lestschinsky (1876–1966), and Ignacy

Schiper (1886–1943) produced important studies, often in Yiddish, of Jewish communal, demographic, and economic history prior to World War II. Meanwhile, at the Hebrew University in Jerusalem, a cadre of transplanted Europeans began in the 1920s to advance a new framework for Jewish history that stressed the national dimensions of the Jewish past. This group of scholars, whose most notable first-generation representatives were Yitzhak *Baer, Benzion Dinur (1884–1973), and Gershom Gerhard *Scholem, opened a new chapter in the intellectual and institutional history of Jewish historical scholarship. Scholem, in particular, exerted a dominant influence on Jewish studies internationally as a result of his magisterial research into the history of Jewish mysticism. In part due to the labors of this founding generation of Jerusalem scholars, the largest center of Jewish scholarship in the world now exists in Israel.

The other major world center of Jewish historiography is the United States. The dominant figure among Jewish historians in twentieth-century America has been Salo Wittmayer Baron (1895–1989), whose monumental *Social and Religious History of the Jews* was the latest and perhaps last multi-volume narrative of Jewish history to be written by one person. Like Simon Dubnow before him, Baron was intensely interested in the social, economic, and communal aspects of Jewish history. He also fought to overturn what he called the "lachrymose conception" of Jewish history, which is characterized by the tendency to reduce that history to a series of unending persecutions and attacks. Many contemporary historians of the Jewish past have affirmed Baron's charge and have attempted to incorporate new methods in social and cultural history into an expanded reading of the Jewish past. The methodological expansion of Jewish history has yielded many new research possibilities. Especially notable in recent decades is the work of historians such as Paula Hyman, who seeks to weave the experience of Jewish women into the narrative of Jewish history.

Even with general scholarly consensus to overturn the "lachrymose conception" of Jewish history, the enormous impact of the Holocaust has proved to be an important countervailing force in Jewish studies over the past half-century. Both in scholarly and popular perception, it has been quite common to associate Jewish history with martyrdom and tragedy. At the same time, the Holocaust has generated a tremendous body of new historical scholarship that now forms an academic subfield of its own, Holocaust studies. It may also be due to the Holocaust, with its challenge to conventional moral and philosophical assumptions, that a new introspective turn has been taken in Jewish historiography. Beginning in 1982, with the publication of Yosef Hayim Yerushalmi's *Zakhor*, Jewish historians have been reflecting upon the relationship between their scholarly endeavors and Jewish collective memory. With unprecedented reflexivity, they have started to study the history of their own profession in an attempt to understand the balance between scholarly and extra-scholarly (i.e., existential and ideological) considerations in their work.

• David Berger, "Religion, Nationalism, and Historiography: Yehezkel Kaufmann's Account of Jesus and Early Christianity," in *Scholars and Scholarship: The Interaction between Judaism and Other Cultures*, The Bernard Revel Graduate School Conference Volume, edited by Leo Landman (New York, 1990), pp. 149–168. Robert Chazan, *In the Year 1096: The First Crusade and the Jews* (Philadelphia, 1996). Shaye J. D. Cohen, "History and Historiography in the 'Against Apion' of Josephus," in *Essays in Jewish Historiography: In Memoriam Arnaldo Dante Momigliano, 1908–1987*, edited by Ada Rapoport-Albert (Middletown, Conn., 1988), pp. 1–11. Shaye J. D. Cohen, *Josephus in Galilee and Rome: His Vita and Development as a Historian* (Leiden, 1979). Lynn Davidman and Shelly Tenenbaum, eds., *Feminist Perspectives on Jewish Studies* (New Haven, 1994). Jose Faur, "Jewish and Western Historiographies: A Post-Modern Interpretation," *Modern Judaism* 12.1 (1992): 23–37. Amos Funkenstein, *Perceptions of Jewish History* (Berkeley, 1993), pp. 208–219. Eleazar Gutwirth, "The Expulsion from Spain and Jewish Historiography," in *Jewish History: Essays in Honour of Chimen Abramsky*, edited by Ada Rapoport-Albert and Steven J. Zipperstein (London, 1988), pp. 141–161. Paula E. Hyman, "The Ideological Transformation of Modern Jewish Historiography," and Ivan G. Marcus, "Medieval Jewish Studies: Toward an Anthropological History of the Jews," in *The State of Jewish Studies*, edited by Shaye J. D. Cohen and Edward L. Greenstein (Detroit, 1990), pp. 143–157, 113–127. Lionel Kochan, *The Jew and His History* (Chico, Calif., 1977). Michael A. Meyer, *Ideas of Jewish History* (New York, 1972). Michael A. Meyer, *The Origins of the Modern Jew: Jewish Identity and European Culture in Germany* (Detroit, 1967). Michael L. Morgan, *Dilemmas in Modern Jewish Thought: The Dialectics of Revelation and History* (Bloomington, Ind., 1992). Michael L. Morgan, "Overcoming the Remoteness of the Past: Memory and Historiography in Modern Jewish Thought," *Judaism* 38.2 (1989): 160–173. David N. Myers, *Re-Inventing the Jewish Past: European Jewish Intellectuals and the Zionist Return to History* (New York, 1995). David Nathan Myers, "The Scholem–Kurzweil Debate and Modern Jewish Historiography," *Modern Judaism* 6.3 (1986): 261–286. Nathan Rotenstreich, *Tradition and Reality: The Impact of History on Modern Jewish Thought* (New York, 1972). Ismar Schorsch, *From Text to Context: The Turn to History in Modern Judaism* (Hanover, N. H., 1994). Lester Segal, *Historical Consciousness and Religious Tradition in Azariah de'Rossi's Me'or 'Einayim* (Philadelphia, 1989). Y. Efraim Shmueli, "The Jerusalem School of Jewish History (A Critical Evaluation)," *Proceedings of the American Academy for Jewish Research* 53 (1986): 147–178. John T. Squires, "Hellenistic Historiography and Philosophy in Josephus' Account of Jewish History," *Menorah: Australian Journal of Jewish Studies* 4.1–2 (1990): 148–157. Yosef Hayim Yerushalmi, *Zakhor: Jewish History and Jewish Memory* (Seattle, 1982).

—DAVID N. MYERS

HITLAHAVUT (הִתְלַהֲבוּת; enthusiasm), a term meaning religious ecstasy. In Hasidism, the profound *joy in God is rooted in an inner fervor—*hitlahavut*—from which one can achieve complete self-effacement. Yisra'el ben Eli'ezer *Ba'al Shem Tov stressed the importance of *hitlahavut* in prayer, and it is believed that each word of prayer requires concentration (*kavvanah*; see INTENT) to the extent that one loses consciousness of the self in religious enthusiasm.

HITTITES, a people of the ancient Near East, named as offspring of Heth, Canaan's second son (*Gn.* 10.15), who inhabited central Anatolia, with their capital at Hattushash (modern Bogazköy). The Hittites, who had a well-developed pantheon and an extensive literature, including a comprehensive legal collection, controlled Asia Minor from the seventeenth through the thirteenth century BCE, but their empire disintegrated under the pressure of the massive immigration of the Sea Peoples. The many city-states that resulted eventually fell to Assyria. The Bible scarcely mentions the great Hittite empire (cf. *Jos.* 1.4), although it makes a number of references to the Hittite kingdoms in Syria (e.g., *2 Kgs.* 7.6). Biblical references to Hittites in Canaan indicate that they dwelt in and around the hill country of Judah (e.g., *Nm.* 13.29; *Jos.* 11.3), perhaps as migrants from the once powerful Hittite empire, fully assimilated into the surrounding population.

Ephron the Hittite sold Abraham the cave of Machpelah, in which he buried his wife *Sarah (*Gn.* 23). Esau married two Hittite women (*Gn.* 26.2). The destruction of the Hittites was ordered along with all the other Canaanite peoples (*Dt.* 20.17), though they did intermarry with Israelites (*Jgs.* 3.5–6). David, after his liaison with Bath-sheba, had her husband, Uriah the Hittite, one of his thirty warriors, dispatched to his death in battle (*2 Sm.* 11). King Solomon had Hittite women among his harem (*1 Kgs.* 11.1).

• F. F. Bruce, *The Hittites and the Old Testament* (London, 1947). O. R. Gurney, *The Hittites*, 2d ed. (Baltimore, 1954). James G. Macqueen, *The Hittites and Their Contemporaries in Asia Minor*, rev. ed. (New York, 1986).
—MICHAEL JAMES WILLIAMS

ḤIVI AL-BALKHI (9th cent.), "heretical" polemicist and critic. Born in Balkh (in present-day Afghanistan), he lived in Persia. He expressed his views in his "two hundred critical comments on the Bible." The book itself is lost, but its contents can be reconstructed from the polemical rejoinders it provoked, notably from *Sa'adyah ben Yosef Ga'on, which testify to the impact made by the book at the time. Ḥivi seems to have been influenced by gnostic trends.

• Israel Davidson, *Saadia's Polemic against Hiwi al-Balkhi* (New York, 1915). Moshe Gil, *Ḥivi ha-Balkhi ha-Kofer mi-Khurson* (Tel Aviv, 1966). Judah Rosenthal, *Hiwi al-Balkhi: A Comparative Study* (Philadelphia,

ḤIYYA' (2d–3d cent.), a Palestinian *tanna', coredactor, along with his disciple R. Hosha'yah, of the *Tosefta'. Born in Kafri, in Babylonia, Ḥiyya' is regarded as one of the leading authorities of the last generation of tanna'im. He settled in Tiberias, where he became a colleague of R. *Yehudah ha-Nasi'. He also encouraged the development of centers of learning in Babylonia, perhaps out of fear for the future of Palestinian Jewry during this period of hardship and turmoil in the Roman empire.

• Gershom Bader, *The Encyclopedia of Talmudic Sages*, translated from the Yiddish by Solomon Katz (Northvale, N.J., and London, 1988). Aaron Hyman, *Toledot Tanna'im ve-'Amora'im* (1910; Jerusalem, 1987). Mordecai Margaliot, ed., *Entsiqlopediyyah le-Ḥakhmei ha-Talmud veha-Ge'onim*, revised and updated by Yehuda Eisenberg (Tel Aviv, 1995).
—DANIEL SPERBER

ḤIYYA' BEN ABBA' (3d–4th cent.), Palestinian amora'. He is sometimes designated as Ḥiyya' II ben Abba', to distinguish him from R. Ḥiyya' (ben Abba') the Elder, the contemporary of R. Yehudah ha-Nasi'. Born into a priestly family in Babylonia, he moved to Erets Yisra'el as a youth, where he studied with R. Ḥanina' and R. Yehoshu'a ben Levi, before becoming the most prominent student of R. Yoḥanan (*Ber.* 38b). Several of his sons were also prominent amora'im. He is mentioned hundreds of times in the two Talmuds and in the Midrash. He was appointed as an emissary of R. Yehudah ha-Nasi' II and traveled widely throughout Erets Yisra'el and the Diaspora. Known especially as a halakhic scholar, a Talmudic account relates that in one city R. *Abbahu's aggadic teaching drew a large crowd while the halakhic discourse of R. Ḥiyya' was sparsely attended, prompting a conciliatory R. Abbahu to compare aggadic lore to cheap merchandise while likening *halakhah* to precious stones (*Sot.* 40a). There are, however, numerous Midrashic comments preserved in the name of R. Ḥiyya', among which are his oft-quoted interpretation of *Jeremiah* 16.11; that is, that God would rather that his people forsake him than his Torah, since through keeping his laws they would return to him (Y., *Ḥag.* 1.7, 76c).

• Wilhelm Bacher, *Die Agada der palästinensischen Amoräer* (1892–1899; Hildesheim, 1965). Wilhelm Bacher, *Die Agada der babylonischen Amoräer* (1913; Hildesheim, 1967). David C. Kraemer, *Responses to Suffering in Classical Rabbinic Literature* (New York, 1995).
—MICHAEL L. BROWN

HOCHSCHULE FÜR DIE WISSENSCHAFT DES JUDENTUMS (Ger.; High School for Jewish Studies), institute for Jewish studies and for the training of Reform rabbis opened in Berlin in 1872; from 1883 to 1920 it was also known as Lehranstalt für die Wissenschaft des Judentums. The Hochschule, which was founded according to the "scientific approach" to Jewish law advocated by Abraham *Geiger, one of the school's first teachers, remained in existence until it was closed by the Nazis in 1942. Its last head was Leo *Baeck.

• Leo Baeck et al., *Festschrift zum 50 jahrigen Bestehen der Hochschule für die Wissenschaft des Judentums in Berlin* (Berlin, 1922). Israel O. Lehman, *Lehrer und Schulere an der Hochschule für die Wissenschaft des Judentums in Berlin* (St. Gallen, 1972).

HODAYOT. See THANKSGIVING PSALMS.

HOFFMANN, DAVID TSEVI (1843–1921), Bible and Talmud scholar, lecturer, and, from 1899, principal of the *Berlin Rabbinical Seminary. Hoffmann was a vigorous champion of Orthodoxy both against Reform and against antisemitic attacks on the Talmud and the *Shulḥan 'Arukh*. He wrote a two-volume work that critically examined the Graf-Wellhausen theories of biblical criticism (see BIBLE) and purported to show the unity of the Pentateuch. He applied these ideas in more detail in his works on *Leviticus* (2 vols. [1905, 1906]) and *Deuteronomy* (1913, 1922).

His biography of the Talmudic rabbi Mar Shemu'el (1873) was one of the first scientific historical works by an Orthodox scholar on the Talmudic period and aroused opposition in the Orthodox world. His *Die erste Mischna und die Controversen der Tannaim* (1882) showed that entire passages of the *Mishnah had been composed before the destruction of the Second Temple. *Zur Einleitung in die halachischen Midraschim* (1887) demonstrated that contradictions in halakhic *midrashim* derived from the existence of two competing schools—those of R. 'Aqiva' and R. Yishma'e'l—and from their separate sets of *midrashim* on *Exodus*, *Leviticus*, *Numbers*, and *Deuteronomy*. Hoffmann's *responsa* were collected in the three-volume *Melammed le-Ho'il* (1926–1932).

• Louis Ginzberg, *Students, Saints, and Scholars* (New York, 1928), pp. 252–262. Alexander Marx, *Essays in Jewish Biography* (New York, 1947), pp. 185–222.

HOLDHEIM, SAMUEL (1806–1860), German Reform rabbi and religious philosopher. Under his tutelage, the Berlin congregation, which he served from 1847 until his death, became the center of Reform Judaism's most radical and revolutionary expression. He held that with their integration into the modern world, Jews should strive to reduce the barriers between themselves and "non-Jewish monotheists" and, concomitantly, to eliminate the national, particularistic aspects of traditional Judaism. In this spirit, his reforms included the transference of the Sabbath from Saturday to Sunday, and the sanctioning of intermarriage. Theologically, he justified these innovations by making a distinction between the eternal religious and ethical teachings of Judaism, and its ceremonial laws embodying ultimately transitory political and national principles. Although his following in Germany was limited, his disciples in the United States exercised a major influence on the direction that Reform Judaism was to take in that country in the nineteenth and early twentieth centuries. He wrote *Über die Autonomie der Rabbinen und das Prinzip der jüdischen Ehl* (1843).

• Paul Mendes-Flohr and Jehuda Reinharz, *The Jew in the Modern World: A Documentary History*, 2d ed. (New York, 1995), pp. 183–187. Michael A. Meyer, *Response to Modernity: A History of the Reform Movement in Judaism* (New York, 1988), pp. 80–84. Jakob J. Petuchowski, *Prayerbook Reform in Europe: The Liturgy of European Liberal and Reform Judaism* (New York, 1968), index. —PAUL MENDES-FLOHR

ḤOL HA-MOʿED (חוֹל הַמּוֹעֵד; the weekday of the festival), the intermediate days of the festivals of Pesaḥ (days three through six in the Diaspora, days two through six in Israel) and Sukkot (days three through seven in the Diaspora, days two through seven in Israel). The pertinent regulations treat these days as a combination of weekday and festival. Only urgent work should be performed, although normal work is permitted if done with a distinguishing difference. *Mourning is restricted, while marriages are not performed since one does not "commingle one joy with another." A special prayer, *Yaʿaleh ve-Yavo', is inserted in the ʿAmidah and Birkat ha-Mazon; *Hallel is recited (Half Hallel on Pesaḥ), as is Musaf; and special scriptural passages are read. There is a difference of opinion as to whether **tefillin* should be donned; Sephardim and Ḥasidim do not, while Mitnaggedim do, but without reciting the customary blessing. In Israel, where the festive aspect of these days is more pronounced than elsewhere, the custom of not donning *tefillin* is almost universal. The Talmudic tractate **Moʿed Qatan* is devoted to the regulations governing *ḥol ha-moʿed*.

• Yequti'el Farqash, *Sefer Ḥol ha-Moʿed ke-Hilkhato* (Brooklyn, N.Y., 1987). S. Wagschal, *The Practical Guide to the Care of Children on Shabbos and the Laws of Yom Tov and Chol Hamoed*, rev. and enlarged ed. (Jerusalem and New York, 1993). G. Zinner, *Sefer Nit'e Gavri'el: Hilkhot ʿErev Pesaḥ she-Ḥal be-Shabbat* (Brooklyn, N.Y., 1994). Dovid Zucker and Moshe Francis, *Chol HaMoed: Comprehensive Review of the Laws of the Intermediate Days of the Festivals* (Lakewood, N.J., 1981).

HOLIDAYS. See ḤAGGIM.

HOLINESS (Heb. *qedushah*). In an ethical sense, holiness signifies the attainment of moral purity and perfection through right conduct and especially by imitating the divine attributes (see IMITATION OF GOD). Essentially holiness is an attribute of God, who alone is "holy with every form of holiness" (Y., *Ber*. 9a), and the most common epithet for God in rabbinical literature is "The Holy One, blessed be He." Man attains holiness to the extent that he consciously models his life and conduct on the known attributes of God: "As he is merciful, so be you merciful; as he is gracious, be you gracious" (*Shab*. 133b). Originally, however, holiness was not an ethical term; the basic concept is rather one of "separateness," the divine attribute of being apart from that which is not divine. As a result of the *covenant with God, Israel, too, became "separate" (*Ex*. 19.6; *Dt*. 7.6) and accepted a state of holiness that was to inform henceforth all its activities and even to have physical implications (see HOLY CITY; HOLY LAND; HOLY PLACE). Israel is separated as a holy people; the priests and Levites are separated as a holy caste responsible for the Temple ritual; the Sabbath is separated as a holy day; the Temple itself was out of bounds to profane access, and objects belonging to it, including, for example, sacrificial animals, were holy; that is, separate from profane use. The obligation of holiness falls on the individual as part of a holy people, and any shortcomings on the part of the individual reflect on the entire people. Failures in the ceremonial sphere cause a state of ritual impurity that must be expurged by a prescribed ritual. Apart from ceremonial holiness, greater stress came to be laid on holiness in the ethical sense as it affected personal character. The prophets clashed with the priesthood over the question of emphasis; they did not negate ceremonial holiness but proclaimed it meaningless without concomitant ethical holiness. The rabbinic code was devoted to sanctifying all of human life, and with this object in mind a daily routine was prescribed by which the Jew would always feel himself part of a holy people. More specifically, the rabbis on occasion connected holiness with the prohibition against sexual license, interpreting the verse "You shall be holy" (*Lv*. 19.2) as "you shall be separated from sexual immorality" (see RASHI) and adding that the word was always employed in connection with this aspect of right living (*Sifra'*). Accordingly, Maimonides gives the title *Qedushah* to the fifth book of his code, which deals with sexual relationships. Similarly the rabbis connect holiness with the dietary laws because of the juxtaposition (both in *Lv*. 11.45 and *Lv*. 20.26) of the prohibition against unclean animals, birds, and insects with the commandment to be holy. Nevertheless the separation implicit in holiness is by no means to be regarded as a withdrawal from the world and its temptations, and Judaism has in the main opposed reclusion and extreme asceticism. It insists on the attainment of holiness by remaining separate from contaminating things but still living in their presence. It is this idea that runs through *Leviticus* 19—the so-called "Chapter of Holiness." The words "You shall be holy" are the keynote to the chapter, and the various precepts must be read in connection with it. Holiness is not so much an abstract or a mystic idea as a regulative principle in the everyday life of men and women. It is attained not by flight from the world, nor by renunciation of human relationship of family or station, but by the spirit in which the obligations of life in its simplest and commonest details are fulfilled. According to the rabbis, man has only to set his feet on the road to holiness to receive divine aid in its attainment: "If a man sanctify himself a little, he becomes sanctified much; if he sanctify himself below, he becomes sanctified from on high" (*Yoma'* 39a). The classical exposition of the ladder of virtues by which man rises to holiness was set forth in Mosheh Ḥayyim Luzzatto's *Mesillat Yesharim*. See also SANCTIFICATION.

• Allen Grossman, "Holiness," in *Contemporary Jewish Religious Thought*, edited by Arthur A. Cohen and Paul Mendes-Flohr (New York, 1987), pp. 389–397. Israel Knohl, *Sanctuary of Silence: The Priestly Torah and the Holiness School* (Minneapolis, 1995). Joseph Dov Soloveitchik, *Halakhic Man*, translated by Lawrence Kaplan (Philadelphia, 1983).

HOLINESS CODE, the laws in *Leviticus* 17–26 (and similarly styled laws in a few other places in the Torah). According to scholars, the Holiness Code is a distinct substratum in the Priestly source, one of the originally separate documents from which the Torah was composed in view of critical biblical scholarship. See also BIBLE.

• Israel Knohl, *The Sanctuary of Silence* (Minneapolis, 1995). Baruch A. Levine, *In the Presence of the Lord*, Studies in Judaism in Late Antiquity, vol. 5 (Leiden, 1974). —BARUCH J. SCHWARTZ

HOLOCAUST. See BURNT OFFERING.

HOLOCAUST, RELIGIOUS RESPONSES DURING THE. For a Jew to maintain religious observances under the circumstances of the Holocaust became a supreme *mitsvah*, seen as a form of *qiddush ha-ḥayyim* (sanctification of life). Despite the circumstances, Jews found ways to pray together and to observe the life and annual festival cycles. Circumcisions were performed in the ghettos despite the risks involved. Observant women sought immersion in the *miqveh* in the Warsaw Ghetto. Jewish burial societies (see ḤEVRAH QADDISHA') struggled to ensure ritually proper burials under the most hostile conditions for those who died in the ghettos and on forced marches from starvation, beatings, and shootings. In the camps, where prayer books or study texts were not available, fragments from scripture, liturgy, or the Talmud were reproduced by hand.

The struggle to maintain a normal pattern of religious activity led to a **responsa* literature. The replies of rabbinic authorities to ritual questions and ethical dilemmas reflect the effort to maintain the faith. Among the notable *responsa* were those by R. Tsevi Hirsh Meisels (*Meqadshe ha-Shem*), R. Efrayyim Oshry (*Mi-Ma'amaqim*), and R. Yehi'el Weinberg (*Seridei Esh*). See also HOLOCAUST THEOLOGY.

• Rachel Auerbach, *Be-Ḥutsot Varshah, 1939–1943* (Tel Aviv, 1954). Bruno Bettelheim, *The Informed Heart* (Glencoe, Ill., 1960). Lucy S. Dawidowicz, *The War Against the Jews, 1933–1945* (London, 1975). Mordecai Eliav, ed., *Ani Ma'amin: 'Eduyot 'al Ḥayehem u-Motam shel Anshei Emunah bi-Yemei ha-Sho'ah* (Jerusalem, 1969). Issar Frankel, *Yeḥidei Segulah* (Tel Aviv, 1955). Shimon Huberband, *Kiddush Hashem: Jewish Religious and Cultural Life in Poland during the Holocaust* (Hoboken, N.J., 1987). Efroim Oshry, *Responsa from the Holocaust* (New York, 1983). Pesach Schindler, *Hasidic Responses to the Holocaust in the Light of Hasidic Thought* (Hoboken, N.J., 1990). Nissan Wolpin, ed., *A Path Through the Ashes: Penetrating and Inspiring Stories of the Holocaust from a Torah Perspective* (Brooklyn, N.Y., 1986).

HOLOCAUST THEOLOGY. While World War II was still raging, the question was already being asked: How could an omnipotent and merciful God, who had entered into a special covenant with his chosen people, have allowed this to happen? In 1944 Reform rabbi and Hebrew University chancellor Judah L. Magnes quoted R. *Levi Yitsḥaq of Berdichev, who addressed God: "I do not ask why I suffer but only do I suffer for your sake?" Many Orthodox rabbis said that for those with faith there are no questions; for those without faith there are no answers. Rabbi Issachar Jacobsohn urged: "We must give up the idea of arriving at a rational explanation of the Holocaust in order to remain believers."

Some Orthodox authorities found an explanation for the Holocaust in the traditional belief that suffering must be the result of sinfulness. They blamed the calamities visited upon the Jewish people on their faithlessness to the divine covenant, sometimes linking their accusations to post-emancipatory developments, notably the emergence of Reform and Conservative Judaism, while others blamed Zionists, who refused to await the messianic age when the Jews would miraculously be returned to their land. One Hungarian Orthodox rabbi, Issachar Shelomoh Teichtal, in his *Em ha-Banim Semeḥah* (Budapest, 1943), blamed the Holocaust on the Orthodox leaders' sin of anti-Zionism. Since they had rejected the chance to end the exile, the exile had finished them.

In the years following the Holocaust, Jewish thought has been dominated by Holocaust theology and its implications. Leading Jewish thinkers who survived the Holocaust reexamined their attitudes. Leo *Baeck shifted his prewar emphasis on Judaism (*This People Israel* [1965]) to stress Jewish peoplehood and his belief in Jewish rebirth, exemplified by the emergence of the State of Israel. Martin *Buber asked whether it was still possible to enter into a relationship or dialogue with God and found his answer in the concept of the "eclipse of God" (a variation on the old Jewish theme of **hester panim*; *The Eclipse of God* [1952]). This theory found its critics, among them Israeli philosopher Eliezer Schweid, who wrote that *hester panim* was a punishment and that no sin could deserve the punishment of the Holocaust; if any event warranted divine intervention, this was surely it. To say that at that very moment God turned his face away in order to allow man freedom was a theological prevarication (*Holocaust and Genocide Studies* 3, no. 4 [1988]). To Schweid, the problem raised by the Holocaust is not the justification of God but the justification of religion; the implications are more severe for Christians than for Jews because of the historical ethical failure of Christianity.

One subject that has been widely debated is the uniqueness of the Holocaust. Elie Wiesel wrote, "In the beginning was the Holocaust," and called it a new Jewish Sinai, a revelatory event, in which context all Jewish thought must now be set. In the words of Immanuel Jakobovits, however, "The size of suffering can hardly affect its justice or meaning. A single baby's cot death [crib death] may theologically be no less baffling than the deliberate genocide of millions." United States theologian Eugene Borowitz denied that the Holocaust is the Sinai of our time; he argues that the terms of the covenant are unchanged after the Holocaust and that God still acts in history. Others have drawn distinctions between the Holocaust's historical uniqueness and its theological uniqueness.

Another view was advanced by Richard Rubenstein, in line with the fashionable "Death of God" theology. In his *After Auschwitz* (1966) Rubenstein held that the Holocaust refuted the existence of God and of meaning in the universe. All attempts to justify God's part in the Holocaust are ultimately meaningless, and to say that God's ways are beyond comprehension is an insult to human judgment and dignity. At the same time, Rubenstein emphasized the supreme value of life and the importance of the Jewish religious community. Irving Greenberg believes that the Holocaust shattered the covenant and suggests that faith in a covenant of redemption be replaced by a new covenant to be formulated in terms of empowerment. The lesson of the Holocaust is that powerlessness is immoral, because it is not compatible with survival. The existence of the State of Israel validates continuing faith in God and constitutes a redeeming act, which matches the great catastrophe. Another lesson is that the embrace of modernity was a profound blunder, and Jews must learn to resist the absoluteness of the secular.

Emil Fackenheim says that God was present in Auschwitz, where he issued his 614th commandment—the obligation of survival. Individual Jews may deny God, but the Jewish people cannot, for their reality is his. It is no longer useful to distinguish between religious and secular Jews—any Jew who contributes to Jewish continuity fulfills the new, supreme commandment (*The Jewish Return into History* [1978]).

Orthodox rabbi Eliezer *Berkovits holds that God's hiddenness creates the possibility for autonomous human action and leaves man the choice between good and evil. United States theologian Arthur A. Cohen concluded that God does not have the power to interfere in human affairs. He calls for the redefinition of the God concept, noting that "what is taken as God's speech is really always man's hearing" and that God is not a direct causal agent in human affairs.

For many thinkers, the establishment of the State of Israel was the answer to the theological problem of the Holocaust. To Fackenheim, the Jew in the State of Israel bears witness to the voice of Auschwitz in a way that is impossible in the Diaspora. Elie Wiesel, however, argues that any link between the Holocaust and Israel diminishes both—they are two different mysteries, one historic, the other messianic. To Schweid, theologians who seize upon the State of Israel are trying to escape from a very real dilemma. Two noted theologians, Abraham Joshua *Heschel and André *Neher, felt that in view of the enormity of the events of the Holocaust the only course for man is silence.

• Eugene B. Borowitz, *How Can a Jew Speak of Faith Today?* (Philadelphia, 1969). Helga B. Croner and Leon Klenicki, eds., *Issues in the Jewish–Christian Dialogue*, Studies in Judaism and Christianity (New York, 1979). Eva Fleischner, ed., *Auschwitz, Beginning of a New Era? Reflections on the Holocaust: Papers Given at the International Symposium on the Holocaust, Held at the Cathedral of Saint John the Divine, New York City, June 3–6, 1974* (New York, 1977). Menachem Friedman, "The Haredim and the Holocaust," *Jerusalem Quarterly* 53 (Winter 1990): 86–114. Steven T. Katz, *The Holocaust in Historical Context*, vol. 1, *The Holocaust and Mass Death before the Modern Age* (New York, 1994). Abraham J. Peck, ed., *Jews and Christians after the Holocaust* (Philadelphia, 1982). Jonathan Sacks, *Crisis and Covenant: Jewish Thought after the Holocaust*, Sherman Studies of Judaism in Modern Times (Manchester and New York, 1992). Norman Solomon, "Does the Shoah Require a Radically New Jewish Theology?" in *Remembering for the Future*, vol. 3, Papers and addresses delivered at the International Conference—Remembering for the Future, Oxford, Eng., 1988 (Oxford, 1989).

HOLY CITY, the traditional term for *Jerusalem. All cities that were believed to have been surrounded by walls at the time of the conquest of Erets Yisra'el by Joshua are also invested with a special holiness, though less so than Jerusalem. The Mishnah (*Kel.* 1.6–9) speaks of the ten concentric circles of geographical holiness that radiate out from Jerusalem and the various parts of the Temple, including the Holy of Holies. Beginning in the seventeenth century, three other cities in Erets Yisra'el came to be regarded as holy—*Hebron, because of its association with the patriarchs and matriarchs; *Tiberias, because it had become the religious focus of the country after the Bar Kokhba' Revolt; and *Safed, because it was the center of the kabbalists in the sixteenth century.

HOLY DAYS. See Ḥaggim.

HOLY, HOLY, HOLY. See Qedushah.

HOLY LAND (Heb. Erets ha-Qodesh). According to *Kelim* 1.6, "The Land of Israel is holier than any other land." This statement is true not only for Jews but also for Christians and, to a lesser extent, Muslims. The phrase "Holy Land" or "holy soil" is applied only once in the Bible to Erets Yisra'el (*Zec.* 2.16), but it is nevertheless clearly regarded as the land "which the Lord your God cared for" (*Dt.* 11.12) and is holy in the sense of being selected and set apart for the *chosen people. Promised by God to the descendants of Abraham in a secured covenant (*Gn.* 17.8), it became the "Promised Land." Legally, its sanctity was expressed in the fact that certain commandments could be fulfilled only in Israel. Consequently the question was raised whether the sanctity with which it was endowed after the conquest by Joshua ceased with the Babylonian exile and whether all the land or only those portions that were occupied by the returned exiles was endowed with a permanent sanctity (*ʿEduy.* 8.6; *Ḥul.* 7a). Over and above these legal considerations however, the sentiment of the Jewish people invested the land with imperishable holiness. The Talmud (e.g., *Ket* end.) provides many examples of the manner in which the rabbis gave expression to their love for the Holy Land. This love was echoed throughout Jewish literature, both lyrical and doctrinal, and finds its most vivid expression in the liturgy. Rabbinic and kabbalistic texts did not recoil from the most extravagant statements in glorifying the Holy Land, the merit of dwelling in it, and the spiritual graces (prophecy in particular) attainable in it. The holiness of the land led to the custom of taking to Israel for burial the remains of those who died abroad, and the rabbis said, "Whoever is buried in the Land of Israel is as if he were buried beneath the altar." The custom elicited a vigorous protest from R. Yehudah ha-Nasi' (2d. cent. CE), despite the fact that its first instances are those of the biblical Jacob and Joseph (*Gn. Rab.* 96.8). Throughout the centuries it was customary for Jews in the Diaspora to be buried with earth brought from the Holy Land. See also ZIONISM.

• Yehoshua Ben-Arieh and Yaacov Ariel, "Western Societies and the Holy Land," in *Teaching Jewish Civilization*, edited by Moshe Davis (New York, 1995), pp. 152–154. Gershon Greenberg, *The Holy Land in American Religious Thought, 1620–1948: The Symbiosis of American Religious Approaches to Scripture's Sacred Territory* (Lanham, Md., and Jerusalem, 1994). Walter C. Kaiser, "The Promised Land: A Biblical–Historical View," *Bibliotheca Sacra* 138 (1981): 302–312. Jerome Murphy-O'Connor, *The Holy Land: An Archaeological Guide*, 3d ed. (New York, 1992). Robert Wilken, *The Land Called Holy: Palestine in Christian History and Thought* (New Haven, 1992).

HOLY OF HOLIES. See TEMPLE.

HOLY PLACE. Every spot where God manifests himself becomes holy. Moses was bidden at the bush, "Do not come closer; remove your sandals from off your feet, for the place on which you stand is holy ground" (*Ex.* 3.5). Mount Sinai was a holy place for the period of the revelation only, during which time the people were forbidden to set foot there (*Ex.* 19.23). The *Temple likewise was holy, and gentiles and those in a state of ritual impurity were forbidden to enter it. The holiest of all places in Jewish tradition was the *Holy of Holies, which was barred to all but the high priest, and even he could enter only on Yom Kippur. Subsequent Jewish tradition has maintained the holiness of the Temple site, which should, therefore, not be visited in Orthodox tradition, because of the irremovable ritual impurity attached to individual Jews in the post-Temple period. Among Eastern Jews, even outside Erets Yisra'el, various locations have been invested with the sanctity of a holy place as the real or reputed sites of the graves of outstanding biblical and post-biblical figures. In many instances regular *pilgrimages take place to these shrines on specific days. Thus in Hamadan, Persia, the reputed graves of Esther and Mordecai were visited at the end of every month and on Purim; the Babylonian Jews venerated the site of the traditional grave of Ezra at Shatt al-Arab at the confluence of the Tigris and Euphrates rivers, and at Alkush, near Mosul, the grave of the prophet Nahum is venerated. In Israel, Mount Meron near Safed—the reputed burial place of R. Shimʿon bar Yoḥ'ai, the traditional author of the Zohar—has become the site of a mass celebration on Lag ba-ʿOmer, although the custom was strongly denounced as near idolatry by many authorities, from the sixteenth century rabbis of Safed to R. Mosheh *Sofer in the nineteenth century. Many sites in Galilee were purportedly identified as the graves of distinguished Talmudic rabbis by the sixteenth-century Lurianic kabbalists in Safed and became the objects of the accepted tour of Orthodox pilgrims. The reputed grave of King David on Mount Zion is particularly ven erated by *ʿAdot ha-Mizraḥ. Other traditional holy places are the cave of *Machpelah in Hebron and the Tomb of Rachel on the road from Jerusalem to Bethlehem, and the *Western Wall in Jerusalem. Frequent interreligious and intrareligious conflicts over the holy sites of Jews, Christians, and Muslims have occurred throughout the history of the Holy Land. To some extent these conflicts were regulated by an Ottoman document known as the "Status Quo," recognized by subsequent régimes, although friction has continued over disputed sites. In 1967 the Israeli parliament passed a law guaranteeing respect for the holy sites of all faiths.

• Bryan F. LeBeau and Menahem Mor, eds., *Pilgrims and Travelers to the Holy Land*, Studies in Jewish Civilization 7 (Omaha, Neb., 1996). Jonathan Z. Smith, *To Take Place: Toward Theory in Ritual* (Chicago, 1987).

HOLY SCRIPTURES. See BIBLE.

HOLY SPIRIT. See RUAḤ HA-QODESH.

HOLY TONGUE. See HEBREW LANGUAGE.

HOMBERG, HERZ (1749–1841), Haskalah educator. Born in Lieben (Bohemia), he studied at *yeshivot* in Prague, Bratislava, and Głogów. In Breslau, Berlin, and Hamburg he acquired knowledge of languages and mathematics, as well as an interest in pedagogy. Homberg was held in high regard by Moses Mendelssohn, who, in 1779, hired him to tutor his son Joseph and, in 1782, invited him to contribute to his German Bible translation *Bi'ur*. Homberg taught in Gorizia and Trieste and in 1787 was appointed superintendent of the Galician-Jewish school district, where he established over a hundred German-language schools, including a teachers' seminary. He recommended that civil rights be extended to Jews only on condition that they be thoroughly acculturated and that traditional educational institutions and "superstitious" Jewish texts be abolished. His own text, *Benei Zion* (1812), was made mandatory reading in all Hapsburg Jewish schools. Homberg's pedagogic dogmatism and willing collaboration with non-Jewish authorities, however, met with the fierce opposition of the local Jewish community, and he was forced to leave Galicia. After a dozen years as Jewish book censor in Vienna, Homberg became a teacher of religion and ethics in Prague in 1814.

• Mordechai Eliav, *Ha-Ḥinnukh ha-Yehudi be-Germanyah* (Jerusalem, 1958). Ruth Kestenberg-Gladstein, *Neuere Geschichte der Juden in den böhmischen Ländern* (Tübingen, 1969). Joseph Klausner, *Historyah shel ha-Sifrut ha-ʿIvrit ha-Ḥadashah* (Jerusalem, 1952), pp. 211–223. William McCagg, *A History of Habsburg Jews, 1670–1918* (Bloomington, Ind., 1992).

—DIDIER Y. REISS

HOME. See FAMILY.

HOMICIDE. "You shall not murder" (*Ex.* 20.13) is one of the Ten Commandments; willful murder is a capital crime for which no expiation is possible other than the forfeiture of the life of the murderer (*Nm.* 35.31–33; see CAPITAL PUNISHMENT). Failure to expiate the crime of murder renders society guilty (*Dt.* 19.10) and the land polluted (*Nm.* loc. cit.). Thus, even in a case where the murderer is unknown, the Bible ordains the ceremony of *ʿeglah ʿarufah* (*Dt.* 21.1–9), in order to free society from the taint of innocent blood shed in its midst. The prohibition against homicide was formally and explicitly enjoined upon Noah (see NOAHIC LAWS)—"Whosoever sheds man's blood, by man shall his blood be shed, for in the image of God made he man" (*Gn.* 9.6)—and is already presupposed in the original order of creation as implied in the story of Cain's murder of his brother Abel (*Gn.* 4.8–16). The capital punishment suffered by the murderer serves both as an expiation for the community at large and as *atonement for the criminal, provided repentance and a full confession are made. The only instances of what might be called justifiable homicide are: self-defense, which applies not only when one's life is directly threatened but also when there exists reasonable certainty that one's life might be in danger (see BURGLARY; this also applies in the case of war); when one pursues another with the intention of taking that individual's life (*rodef*), it is justifiable for anyone to prevent the attempted crime, even by taking the pursuer's life; and when one sees another pursuing a victim with the intention of committing rape, adultery, incest, or an unnatural sexual act, one is obligated to prevent the crime by taking the assailant's life.

In these instances the assailant is intent upon a crime that is punishable by death or excision (**karet*); the taking of a life is condoned only where other means, such as wounding, prove ineffective in preventing the crime. If such means could have been attempted but were not, the rescuer is considered a murderer (*San.* 74a). However, the punishment of the rescuer is left to divine intervention and not to a human court. Moreover, once the crime has been committed, it is forbidden to take the law into one's own hands. Accidental manslaughter is punished by banishment to one of the forty-eight cities of refuge (see ASYLUM). The court trying a case of murder must consist of no less than twenty-three fully qualified judges (*San.* 26b). While the court may acquit by a simple majority vote, a majority of at least two votes is necessary for a conviction. In the event the accused is sentenced to death, the judges must fast until evening. Circumstantial *evidence, even of the most compelling kind, is not acceptable in court. To be convicted, the intention of both the act and its result must be proved and the death of the victim must have resulted from the direct and immediate blow of the accused. If, after summing up the evidence, one of the judges is unable to render a decision, two more judges are added to the bench, a new trial commenced, and the previous proceedings rendered void. In rabbinic law, capital punishment can be imposed only after the fulfillment of conditions so stringent (e.g., two eyewitnesses must have forewarned the murderer of the gravity of the crime he was about to commit [see WARNING]; the Sanhedrin must be sitting in the Temple) that a death sentence was an extremely rare event. When carried out, execution for homicide was by means of the sword. If the crime of homicide was proved but the requisite conditions for the death penalty had not been fulfilled, rabbinic law provides for lengthy *imprisonment. In the State of Israel, homicide is not punishable by death. See also ABORTION; EUTHANASIA.

• Mieke Bal, *Death and Dissymmetry: The Politics of Coherence in the Book of Judges* (Chicago, 1988). Hermann Schulz, *Das Todesrecht im Alten Testament* (Berlin, 1969). Johann J. Stamm, *The Ten Commandments in Recent Research*, translated by M. E. Andrew (London, 1970).

HOMILETICS. While it is debatable whether the orations of Moses and the prophets should be considered sermons, the Levites' explication of Torah verses read at a public gathering (*Neh.* 8.7–9) appears to be a model emulated by subsequent preachers. Jewish synagogue oratory continued through the Hellenistic and Roman periods; some examples may have been preserved in early Christian sources (e.g., *Mt.* 5.1–7.27—the Sermon on the Mount—and *Acts* 13.16–41).

Rabbinic literature contains many references to the obligation of preaching, especially in connection with holidays (*Meg.* 32a), and to the actual circumstances of sermon delivery (*Gn. Rab.* 98.11). Distinctive homiletical forms were developed. Aggadic *midrashim* contain extensive material based on synagogue sermons (*derashot*; see AGGADAH; MIDRASH). Yet the vast rabbinic literature has apparently not preserved even a single text of a sermon as actually delivered, in contrast to the hundreds of recorded sermons delivered by the church fathers. The reason for this absence (beyond the prohibition of transcribing what was said on the Sabbath) has not been satisfactorily explained.

Documents in the Cairo Genizah show that preaching continued throughout the early Middle Ages in Islamic lands. The earliest extant collections of sermons date from thirteenth-century southern Europe. These model sermons reflect a continuity of form from the rabbinic period. Beginning with a verse from the Hagiographa, they explore different meanings of that verse before applying it to the Torah lesson for the week. They then proceed to a discussion of various topics pertaining to the lesson.

A different form, clearly influenced by medieval Christian homiletics, emerges in the late fifteenth century. The preacher begins with a verse from the Torah lesson (the *nose'* [theme]), often followed by a rabbinic dictum (*ma'amar*). In sermons for special occasions, an elaborate formal introduction is used. The preacher then focuses on a particular issue (the *derush*). Sometimes a series of problems (*sefeqot*) is raised and eventually resolved.

As for content, holiday sermons frequently reviewed and explained the detailed obligations that Jews had to fulfill. The nonlegal components were generally grounded in exegesis of biblical verses and rabbinic statements, including imaginative puns on the Hebrew wording of proof texts. Jewish preachers (e.g., Yaʿaqov Anatoli, 13th cent.) began to use philosophical material, giving allegorical interpretations of biblical stories and discussing philosophical problems. Citations of Aristotle became frequent, and some sermons employed philosophical modes of reasoning such as the syllogism and the scholastic "disputed question" (Yosef and Shem Tov ibn Shem Tov, 15th cent.). These developments aroused opposition, but attempts to suppress them were unsuccessful.

Despite a greater reluctance to discuss kabbalistic material from the pulpit, some preachers did so (Yehoshuʿa ibn Shu'eib, early 14th cent.). The noted Talmudist Yitsḥaq Aboab (late 15th cent.) incorporated both technical philosophy and kabbalistic literature into his sermons. Preachers criticized the religious shortcomings of the community. In times of disaster, they turned to exhortation and solace. Parables serving as vivid illustration of a difficult point were used for their didactic and entertainment value. Beginning in the fifteenth century, the *eulogy (*hesped*) became an increasingly important genre of Jewish homiletics.

In lands of the Mediterranean basin and in the Sephardi Diaspora, many rabbis preached each Sabbath. Writings by Shelomoh ha-Levi in Salonika (16th cent.), Saul Levi Morteira in Amsterdam (17th cent.), and Isaac Cantarini in Padua (17th cent.) include the sermons they delivered each week over many years. In northern and eastern Europe, preaching was the primary responsibility of specialists appointed to the position of **maggid*. There were also itinerant preachers, some of whom were treated with disdain, while others (e.g., Yaʿaqov Krantz, the Maggid of Dubno, 18th cent.), achieved enormous renown. In eastern Europe and elsewhere, leading rabbis preached twice a year—on Shabbat Shuvah (before Yom Kippur) and Shabbat ha-Gadol (before Pesaḥ). These sermons were usually lengthy expositions of halakhic themes.

In the nineteenth century, preaching became a part of the controversy over the new Reform movement in Germany. While sermons had always been delivered in the vernacular, the Reformers' innovation made the German sermon a central part of the worship service; their preaching emphasized edification rather than exegesis. In twentieth-century America, weekly sermons prevailed in modern Orthodoxy and in the Conservative and Reform movements, and homiletics became part of the syllabus of rabbinical seminaries. Some of the most influential rabbis in American Jewish life, including Stephen S. Wise, Abba Hillel Silver, Solomon Freehof, Israel Levinthal, Milton Steinberg, Joseph Lookstein, were celebrated as preachers.

• Israel Bettan, *Studies in Jewish Preaching* (Cincinnati, 1939). Joseph Dan, *Sifrut ha-Musar veha-Derush* (Jerusalem, 1975). Joseph Heinemann with Jakob Petuchowski, *The Literature of the Synagogue*, pt. 2, *Sermons* (New York, 1975). David Ruderman, ed., *Preachers of the Italian Ghetto* (Berkeley, 1992). Marc Saperstein, *Jewish Preaching 1200–1800* (New Haven, 1989). Marc Saperstein, *"Your Voice Like a Ram's Horn": Themes and Texts in Traditional Jewish Preaching* (Cincinnati, 1996). Henry Sosland, *A Guide for Preachers on Composing and Delivering Sermons: The Or ha-Darshanim of Jacob Zahalon* (New York, 1987). Leopold Zunz, *Ha-Derashot be-Yisra'el*, edited by Hanokh Albeck (Jerusalem, 1974); a translation, with supplementary material, of Zunz's classic *Die Gottesdienstlichen Vortrage der Juden: Historisch Entwickelt*, 2d ed. (Frankfurt, 1892).

—MARC SAPERSTEIN

HOMOSEXUALITY. Male homosexual relations, specifically in a Canaanite context, are prohibited in *Leviticus* 18.22 and 20.13. Rabbinic sources extend this prohibition to all contexts (*San*. 53a and following; *Yev*. 83b; *Ker*. 2a and following; *Ned*. 51a), and they also forbid female homosexual sex (*Shab*. 65a; *Yev*. 76a; *Sifrei* 98; *Mishneh Torah*, "Laws of Forbidden Intercourse" 21.8; *Shulḥan ʿArukh, Even ha-ʿEzer* 20.2). Male homosexual relations were considered an abomination to be punished by death (*Lv*. 20.13), although the incidence of homosexuality was thought to be so rare that the Talmud states, and Maimonides concurs, that Jews were not suspect of the practice (*Qid*. 82; *Yad*, Issurei Bi'ah 22.2). However, the sixteenth-century *Shulḥan ʿArukh* asserts that "in these generations, when sexual licentiousness is rampant, a man should distance himself from lying together with another man" (*Shulḥan ʿArukh, Even ha-ʿEzer* 24.1). In recent years, many Jews have challenged the traditional Jewish stance. In general, the Reform and Reconstructionist movements have been more accepting of homosexuality than has the Conservative movement. The rabbis of the Reform movement passed a resolution in 1977 that "encourage[s] legislation which decriminalizes homosexual acts between consenting adults and prohibits discrimination against them as persons." In 1991 and 1992 the rabbinic and synagogue arms of the Conservative movement passed similar resolutions. In 1996, same-sex civil marriages were endorsed by the U.S. Reform rabbinical organization. Conservative rabbinic rulings have forbidden officiating at commitment ceremonies for homosexuals; Reconstructionist and many Reform rabbis, and a few Conservative rabbis, are willing to perform them. Sexually active homosexuals have been accepted into the rabbinical and cantorial schools of the Reform and Reconstructionist movements though not into those of the Conservative movement. Also, synagogues with special outreach to homosexuals have gained affiliation with the Reform and Reconstructionist synagogue organizations but not with the Conservative synagogue association. The Orthodox have continued to denounce homosexual sex while accepting the homosexual as a full, but sinning, Jew.

• Bradley Shavit Artson "Gay and Lesbian Jews: An Innovative Jewish Legal Position" *Jewish Spectator* (Winter 1990): 6–14. Elliot Dorff, *"This Is My Beloved, This Is My Friend": A Rabbinic Letter on Intimate Relations* (New York, 1996), part D. Walter Jacob, ed., *American Reform Responsa* (New York, 1983), pp. 49–54. Walter Jacob, ed., *Contemporary American Reform Responsa* (New York, 1987), pp. 88–90, 296–298. Norman Lamm, "Judaism and the Modern Attitude to Homosexuality," *Encyclopedia Judaica Yearbook* (Jerusalem, 1974), pp. 194–205. Yaakov Levado, "Gayness and God: Wrestlings of an Orthodox Rabbi," *Tikkun* 8.5 (September/October 1993): 54–68, 89, with a roundtable of responses.

—ELLIOT NELSON DORFF

ḤONI HA-MEʿAGGEL (died 65 BCE), a pietist (*ḥasid*), known as the Circle-Drawer or the Roof-Roller; a scrupulous observer of the Law, who also performed some good deeds that are said to have been accomplished through extraordinary powers of prayer or as miracles. All the sources (Mishnah, Tosefta', Talmud, *Megillat Taʿanit*, Josephus) record a single story about his power to bring rain in times of drought. According to the Mishnah version (*Taʿan*. 3.8): "Once it happened that they said to Ḥoni the Circle-Drawer, 'Pray that rain may fall' . . . He prayed but no rain fell. What did he do? He drew a circle and stood within it, and said before God, 'Master of the Universe, your children have set their faces to me, for that I am as a son of the household before you. I swear by your great name that I will not stir hence until you will have compassion upon your children.' Rains commenced to trickle. He said, 'Not for such rain did I pray, but for rain which will fill the cisterns, pits, and caves.' " The Mishnah relates that he then prayed for adjustment of the rainfall until it was satisfactory. Later, the sage Shim'on ben Shetaḥ, according to tradition president of the Sanhedrin, said to him, "Had you not been Ḥoni, I would have excommunicated you [for importuning God in this manner of prayer], but you act before the Lord like a son who importunes before his father, and he fulfills his desires."

Ḥoni's death account is preserved in rabbinic sources and in Josephus. During a conflict between John Hyrcanus and his brother Aristobulus, Ḥoni was told to place a curse on Aristobulus and his followers. When he refused, he was stoned to death. According to legend, Ḥoni slept for seventy years and on awakening prayed for death rather than living in a strange world.

• Judah Goldin, "On Ḥoni, The Circle Maker—A Demanding Prayer," *Harvard Theological Review* 56 (1963): 233–237; repr. in *Studies in Midrash and Related Literature*, by Judah Goldin, JPS Scholars of Distinction Series (Philadelphia, 1988). William Scott Green, "Palestinian Holy Men: Charismatic Leadership and Rabbinic Tradition," in *Aufstieg und Niedergang der römischen Welt*, edited by Hildegard Temporini and Wolfgang Haase (Berlin and New York, 1979), pp. 619–647. M. B. Lerner, "Ḥoni Ha-Me'aggel and Simeon b. Shetaḥ," in *The World of the Sages*, edited by Isaac B. Gottleib, unit 2 (Ramat Aviv, 1983).

—ISAAC B. GOTTLIEB

HONOR (Heb. *kavod*). [*For the theological use of the term* kavod, *see* KAVOD.] In the first place, honor is due to God, the source of all honor (*Prv.* 3.9; *Mal.* 1.6), and, according to the Bible, also to parents (*Ex.* 20.12), the Sabbath (*Is.* 18.13), the aged (*Lv.* 19.32), and the God-fearing (*Ps.* 15.4). The rabbis also emphasize the honor due to one's teacher, since "the father only ensures him life in this world, while the teacher brings him to the life of the world to come" (*B. M.* 33a). The rabbinic saying "Let the honor of your friend be as dear to you as your own" (*Avot* 2.15) enjoins both the duty of self-respect and the honor due to others. The honor of others takes precedence even over the observance of a negative *mitsvah* (*Ber.* 19b). Honor is to be paid to royalty (*Ex. Rab.* 4), the patriarch (*Ket.* 17a), scholars, and the Torah. The Talmud discusses whether a person can renounce the honor that is due him and concludes that a king (*Ket.* 17a) and a teacher (*Qid.* 32b) may not. At the same time, the rabbis repeatedly and severely condemned the seeking of honor: "Honor flees from him who pursues it, but it pursues him who flees from it" (*'Eruv.* 13b). It is an expression of respect, and a person can be punished for offending another's honor.

HORA'AT SHA'AH (הוֹרָאַת שָׁעָה; teaching for the hour), the temporary suspension of biblical prohibitions in cases of emergency. The Talmudic source for this power of the court is the action taken by Elijah in offering sacrifices on Mount Carmel rather than in the Temple in Jerusalem (*1 Kgs.* 18.19–46). Although this deed contravened two biblical prohibitions, it was permitted, since its purpose was to restore the people to faith and save many Jews from falling into sin (*Yev.* 90b). Maimonides provides a medical parable for this judicial function: "Just as a physician amputates a hand or foot to save a life, so a court in appropriate circumstances may decree a temporary violation of some of the commandments so that their totality will be preserved" (*Hilkhot Mamrim* 2.4).

• Menachem Elon, *Jewish Law: History, Sources, Principles* (Jerusalem, 1975). Emanuel Quint and Neil Hecht, *Jewish Jurisprudence: Its Sources and Modern Applications* (New York, 1980), pp. 139–213.

—DANIEL SINCLAIR

HORAYOT (הוֹרָיוֹת; Rulings), last tractate of Mishnah order Neziqin, consisting of three chapters, with related material in the Tosefta' and both Talmuds. The tractate deals with the different sin offerings required to expiate transgressions of the community, the high priest, or the king (*Lv.* 4). According to *Horayot*, the special sin offerings of the community and of the high priest are brought only when the transgression is committed as a result of a mistaken halakhic ruling, hence the name of the tractate. The laws of sacrifices serve as point of departure for an in-depth analysis of the procedures used by the *Sanhedrin to issue rulings and of the character of the Sanhedrin's authority.

Following a comparative analysis of the positions of high priest and king, the tractate concludes with a hierarchy of the different levels of sanctity of the Jewish people. The final words of the tractate express the superiority of personal merit over inherited rank: "A *mamzer* Torah scholar takes precedence over an ignorant high priest."

The tractate was translated into English by Herbert Danby in *The Mishnah* (Oxford, 1933).

• Chanoch Albeck, ed., *Shishah Sidrei Mishnah, Seder Neziqin*, 2d ed. (Jerusalem, 1956). Philip Blackman, ed. and trans., *Mishnayot*, vol. 4, *Order Neziqin* (Gateshead, 1973). Pinhas Kehati, ed., *Mishnah: A New Translation with a Commentary, Seder Neziqin*, vol. 4, *'Avodah Zarah, Avot, Horayot* (Jerusalem, 1987). Hermann Leberecht Strack, *Introduction to the Talmud and Midrash* (1931; Minneapolis,1992).

—AVRAHAM WALFISH

HOREB. See SINAI, MOUNT.

ḤORIN, AHARON BEN KALMAN. See CHORIN, AHARON BEN KALMAN.

HOROWITZ, PINḤAS BEN TSEVI HIRSH (c.1730–1805), German rabbi. Born in Poland, Horowitz gained wide note as an antagonist of the prominent R. Yeḥezqe'l Landau of Prague in a controversy over the validity of a bill of divorce. Horowitz's reputation as an outstanding halakhist earned him an appointment, in 1771, as rabbi of Frankfurt, where he soon was embroiled in the conflict between the town authorities and R. Natan Adler over the latter's Hasidic tendencies. Horowitz, despite his own Hasidic leanings and his friendship with Adler, joined the ban because of the latter's refusal to accept communal discipline. He also opposed Moses Mendelssohn's German translation of and commentary on the

Bible, *Biʿur*, charging that Mendelssohn systematically rejected the traditional rabbinic understandings of the biblical text. Horowitz was the author of *Sefer Hafla'ah*, a pilpulistic commentary to the Talmudic tractates *Ketubbot* and *Qiddushin*.

• Marcus Horovitz, *Rabbanei Frankfurt* (Jerusalem, 1972), pp. 144–178.
—MARK WASHOFSKY

HOROWITZ, YAʿAQOV YITSḤAQ. See YAʿAQOV YITSḤAQ, HA-ḤOZEH MI-LUBLIN.

HOROWITZ FAMILY, a family of Polish scholars.

Avraham ben Shabbetai Sheftel Horowitz (c.1550–1615), Polish scholar and moralist. A student of Mosheh Isserles, he lived in Kraków, Lemberg (Lwów), where he was *dayyan*, and Prague, where he died. In his youth, he was attracted to philosophy and secular study, perhaps under the influence of Sephardi tradition. In 1557 he wrote two moralistic works, *Ḥesed Avraham* and *Berit Avraham* (Kraków, c.1602), a commentary on Maimonides' *Shemoneh Peraqim*. In 1559 he wrote a pamphlet attacking the rabbi of Poznań for preaching against Maimonides. Later, he returned to Ashkenazi tradition and was influenced by the kabbalistic ideas then spreading. His work *ʿEmeq Berakhah* (Kraków, 1597), a halakhic exposition on the benedictions, and the revised edition of his 1557 books (1602), reveal this changed emphasis. He is best known for his ethical will *Yesh Noḥalin* (1615), to which his sons and grandson added notes (Amsterdam, 1701).

Yeshaʿyahu Horowitz (c.1570–1626), Polish rabbi and kabbalist, known as Shelah after the acronym of his main work; son of Avraham ben Shabbetai Sheftel. He studied under his father and at *yeshivot* in Lublin and Lemberg before serving as rabbi in Dubno and, in 1606, Frankfurt am Main. In 1614 he was appointed rabbi of Prague, and in 1621 he went to Jerusalem, where he became rabbi of the Ashkenazi community. He died in Tiberias and was buried close to Maimonides. Horowitz wrote kabbalistic notes on his father's *ʿEmeq Berakhah*; they were published together in Kraków in 1597. In his youth, he wrote a commentary on the medieval halakhic text, *Mordekhai*, part of which was published after his death (*Bigdei Yeshaʿ* [Kraków, 1757]). His most important work was the compendium *Shenei Luḥot ha-Berit*, which he compiled while in Jerusalem. The major purpose of this extensive and multifaceted book was the presentation of *halakhah* as a basis for spiritual life. The work is divided into two parts; the first, arranged in order of the Talmudic tractates, contains the laws pertaining to the sequence of festivals in the calendar, while the second part presents the laws in the order in which they appear in the Torah. It concludes with a section on Talmudic methodology and hermeneutics and an ethical passage dedicated to his children.

Horowitz's use of the sources was remarkably wide, and though opposed to the study of the Greek philosophers, he did quote works of Jewish philosophy. He approved of halakhic compendia as a study tool, and although he felt that Shelomoh Luria's work on the dietary laws was superior, he agreed that Mosheh Isserles should be followed as the accepted authority. An important halakhist, he took an independent and often innovative stance on questions of Jewish law, opposing accepted customs inconsistent with *halakhah* and advocating new customs, particularly under kabbalistic auspices. Horowitz was heavily influenced by the kabbalistic thought of Yitsḥaq Luria, Mosheh Cordovero, and Yosef Karo, and although not an original thinker as a kabbalist, he was able to harmonize the thought of early mystics, the Zohar, and the later Safed masters. According to Horowitz, humans were created with free will to choose between good and evil, since all potentialities are contained within the Creator. The aim of humanity is to achieve mystical union with God by achieving perfection through study, contemplation, and adherence to his precepts. Revelation is an ongoing process. Horowitz saw *qiddush ha-Shem* (martyrdom) as an expression of the human ability to cleave to God even when physically prevented from fulfilling God's precepts, and he prescribed a special preparatory prayer to be recited by those about to face such a fate. He also proposed a new educational system for Ashkenazi society: the systematic and grammatical study of the entire Bible, followed by step-by-step study of the entire Mishnah and the Talmud, advancing to the later halakhic authorities. The intellectual and moral elite could progress to studying the Zohar, but Horowitz was of the opinion that the secrets of mysticism should be transmitted orally and not made generally available.

His other published works include a prayer book and commentary (*Shaʿar Shamayim* [Amsterdam, 1717]), notes on the Zohar (1882), and *novellae* (Kraków, 1729). *Shenei Luḥot ha-Berit* was extremely influential among the Jews of eastern Europe for many generations, playing a role in the early development of Hasidic thought. The authoritative edition of *Shenei Luḥot ha-Berit* was published in Amsterdam in 1648.

• **Avraham ben Shabbetai Sheftel Horowitz:** Haim H. Ben-Sasson, *Hagut ve-Hanhagah* (Jerusalem, 1959), *passim*. Y. Elboim, "R. Avraham Horowitz ʿal ha-Teshuvah," in *Meḥqarim be-Qabbalah, be-Filosofiyah Yehudit uve-Sifrut ha-Musar veha-Hagut—Mugashim li-Yeshaʿyah Tishby*, edited by Joseph Dan and Joseph Hacker (Jerusalem, 1986), pp. 537–567. **Yeshaʿyahu Horowitz:** Haim H. Ben-Sasson, *Hagut ve-Hanhagah* (Jerusalem, 1959), *passim*. Eugene Newman, *Life and Teachings of Isaiah Horowitz* (London, 1972). Elliott Wolfson, "Hashpaʿat ha-'Ari ʿal ha-Shelah," in *Meḥqerei Yerushalayim be-Maḥshevet Yisra'el*, edited by Rachel Elior and Y. Liebes, vol. 10 (Jerusalem, 1992), pp. 423–448.
—ADAM TELLER

HOSANNA. See HOSHAʿNOT.

HOSEA (Heb. Hosheʿa; 8th cent. BCE), son of Beeri; a prophet from the northern kingdom of Israel who, according to the superscription of the biblical *Book of Hosea*, prophesied during the reigns of Uzziah, Jotham, Ahaz, and Hezekiah, kings of Judah, and of Jeroboam II, king of Israel, prior to the Assyrian invasions of Israel under Tiglath-pileser III (745–727). Hosea is the only prophet to have come originally from northern Israel, which explains the distinctive character and difficulties of his language. Hosea's message centers around a condemnation of the northern kingdom of Israel for its religious infidelity to God and its willingness to enter into a political alliance with Assyria to carry out trade with Egypt (cf. 7.8–11; 8.9; 12.1). To this end, Hosea condemns the monarchy, and the priests in particular, for not teaching the true knowledge of God. Hosea underscores his message with his marriage to Gomer, daughter of Diblaim, described as a "woman of harlotry" (1.2). He has three children with her, each of whom represents a different aspect of the broken relationship between Israel and God. Thus, his first son, Jezreel, calls to mind the bloody revolt in Jezreel against the Omrides, which brought the Jehu dynasty to power in Israel (1.4–5); daughter Lo-ruhamah (Not Pitied) symbolizes the Lord's lack of pity for the people (1.6–7); and Hosea's second son, Lo-ammi (Not My People), symbolizes God's rejection of the people (1.8–9). In chapter 3, Hosea is also commanded to love an adulterous woman, symbolizing God's love for Israel who, in turn, consorts with other gods. The prophet envisions a return to an ideal state in the relationship between Israel and God (3.5). According to the Talmud, Hosea was greater than his contemporaries Isaiah, Amos, and Micah (*Pes.* 87a).

The *Book of Hosea* is the first book of the Minor Prophets and is composed of three major parts. Chapters 1–3 contain a mixture of narrative and poetic material that describes and reflects upon the meaning of Hosea's marriage to Gomer, apparently a cultic prostitute; her infidelity to Hosea symbolizes Israel's broken relationship with God, its spouse. Chapters 4–13 consist of a series of poetic speeches in which the prophet condemns the superstitious people, the corrupt priests, and the Israelite monarchy for their failure to display proper "knowledge of God" and for relapses into idolatry (4.1). This section also contains many allusions to Israel's past ideal relationship with God. The final section in *Hosea* 14 is an impassioned plea to the people to return to God from their iniquity and idolatry because they will not be saved by Assyria. The presence of various statements throughout the book that address Judah as well as the northern kingdom of Israel have led some scholars to conclude that the redaction of the book took place in Judah (dating varies from the late 8th cent. to the post-exilic period).

• Francis I. Anderson and David Noel Freedman, *Hosea*, The Anchor Bible, vol. 24 (Garden City, N.Y., 1980). Martin J. Buss, *The Prophetic Word of Hosea: A Morphological Study*, Beihefte zur Zeitschrift für die alttestamentliche Wissenschaft, 111 (Berlin, 1969). Grace I. Emmerson, *Hosea: An Israelite Prophet in Judaean Perspective*, Journal for the Study of the Old Testament, Supplement Series 28 (Sheffield, Eng., 1984). Robert Gordis, "Hosea's Marriage and Message: A New Approach," in *Poets, Prophets, and Sages: Essays in Biblical Interpretation* (Bloomington, Ind., 1971), pp. 230–254. Philip J. King, *Amos, Hosea, Micah: An Archaeological Commentary* (Philadelphia, 1988). James Luther Mays, *Hosea: A Commentary*, Old Testament Library (Philadelphia, 1969). Gale A. Yee, *Composition and Tradition in the Book of Hosea*, Dissertation Series (Society of Biblical Literature), no. 102 (Atlanta, 1987).

—MARVIN A. SWEENEY

HOSHAʿNAʾ RABBAH (הוֹשַׁעְנָא רַבָּה), the seventh day of *Sukkot, falling on 21 Tishrei, and the last day of **ḥol ha-moʿed*. During Sukkot in Temple times the people made daily circuits round the altar, waving the *four species (or just the willow; there is disagreement over this) and crying *"hoshaʿnaʾ"* (see Hoshaʿnot); on the seventh day they circuited seven times. In late sources the day was therefore called Hoshaʿnaʾ Rabbah, namely, "the Great Hoshaʿnaʾ." *Simḥat Beit ha-Shoʾevah, a ritual of great merrymaking (*Suk.* 53a), took place during Sukkot, while Hoshaʿnaʾ Rabbah itself was the occasion for the beating of the willow branches (*ḥibbut ʿaravah*; possibly the remnant of an earlier rite calling on the "waters below" to respond to the "waters above," the subject of Sukkot prayers that were the climax of the festival, although they were opposed by the Sadducees and Boethusians because of the absence of scriptural authority). During the Middle Ages a sober note was introduced into the celebrations by identifying Hoshaʿnaʾ Rabbah with the last day of judgment and the culmination of the period of self-examination and repentance that begins three weeks earlier on Roʾsh ha-Shanah. This aspect is especially stressed in Sephardi practice. There was a popular belief that on Hoshaʿnaʾ Rabbah God issued notes with the fate of every individual for the coming year. A common Ashkenazi greeting was *gute kvitl* (Yi.; good note). The synagogue service combines the *ḥol ha-moʿed* ritual together with a sevenfold circuit of the bimah with the four species, while appropriate *hoshaʿnaʾ* hymns are recited accompanied by the blowing of the shofar. In the Ashkenazi rite the penitential character of the day is emphasized by the reader's wearing of the white robe of the *ʿAseret Yemei Teshuvah and by the recitation of the preliminary psalms read on Sabbaths and festivals. The beating of the willow branches continues the Temple custom. Such importance was attached to this day that the calendar was eventually adjusted so that Hoshaʿnaʾ Rabbah would never fall on a Sabbath when the carrying of the willows would be forbidden. David ben Yosef *Abudarham (14th cent.) mentions the custom, which still prevails among pious Jews, of staying up on the night of Hoshaʿnaʾ Rabbah. The kabbalists evolved a special order of service for the occasion, which included the reading of the *Book of Deuteronomy* and the *Book of Psalms* and passages from the Zohar (the selection of readings was changed by the seventeenth-century authority Yeshaʿyahu Horowitz to resemble the readings in the **tiqqun* for *Shavuʿot). A number of superstitions arose, and it was widely believed that a person who was to die during the coming year would not see the shadow of his head on the night of Hoshaʿnaʾ Rabbah.

HOSHAʿNOT (הוֹשַׁעְנוֹת; from *hoshaʿnaʾ*, "O deliver" [*Ps.* 118.25]), prayers recited on the festival of Sukkot during the **haqqafot* (circuits) around the synagogue (originally around the Temple altar). Written in the form of litanies, the *hoshaʿnot* consist of a large number of brief lines (usually arranged alphabetically), each of which opens and concludes with the response *hoshaʿnaʾ* spoken by the congregation. *Hoshaʿnot* are generally simple in form, addressing God by different epithets or beseeching him for deliverance "because of your truth, because of your covenant . . . "; some *hoshaʿnot* in use today, however, were composed by well-known *payyetanim* such as Elʿazar Kallir, and are more complex. Originally, the *hoshaʿnot* were prayers for rain (see TEFILLAT GESHEM) recited on Sukkot because it marks the approaching rainy season in Erets Yisra'el, but rain is not explicitly mentioned in all *hoshaʿnot* as the desired object. The word *hoshaʿna'* was also popularly applied to the willow branch carried on *Hoshaʿna' Rabbah.

• Ismar Elbogen, *Jewish Liturgy: A Comprehensive History*, translated by Raymond P. Scheindlin (Philadelphia, New York, and Jerusalem, 1993). Macy Nulman, *The Encyclopedia of Jewish Prayer* (Northvale, N.J., and London, 1993), pp. 179–180.

HOSHAʿYAH RABBAH (3d cent.), Palestinian amora', disciple of R. *Ḥiyya'. A celebrated authority on the Mishnah and editor of *baraiytot*, it was said that "Any *baraiyta'* that was not studied and formulated in the academy of Rabbi Ḥiyya' and Rabbi Hoshaʿyah is not authoritative, and should not be brought as evidence in the discussions of the academy" (*Ḥul.* 141b). He was equally prominent as an aggadic teacher. His homilies (of which the opening chapter of *Genesis Rabbah* is one—hence, the whole *midrash* has been attributed to him) reflect the religious discussions between Jews and Christians in Caesarea, where Hoshaʿyah had his academy. Most leading Palestinian amora'im of the next generation were his disciples. His famous statements include "Customs can annul law" (Y., *R. ha-Sh.* 7.1) and "The Lord was gracious unto Israel in that he scattered them among the nations"(*Pes.* 87b, which means, according to Rashi, that they could not be annihilated in one blow).

• Chanoch Albeck, *Mavo' la-Talmudim* (Tel Aviv, 1987). Wilhelm Bacher, *Die Agada der paläestinensischen Amoräer* (Strassburg, 1892–1899). Aaron Hyman, *Toledot Tanna'im ve-'Amora'im* (1910; Jerusalem, 1987).

ḤOSHEN MISHPAT. See SHULḤAN ʿARUKH.

HOSPITALITY (Heb. *hakhnasat oreḥim* [bringing in guests]). Few social virtues rank higher on the scale of merit than hospitality, which is included among "those things of which a man enjoys the fruit in this world while the principal remains with him in the world to come" (*Shab.* 127a; *Pe'ah* 1.2). Abraham's welcoming of the three travelers in *Genesis* 18.1–8 typifies the virtue of hospitality in Jewish lore. The Bible, which offers many instances of hospitality to travelers (e.g., *Jgs.* 13.15; *2 Kgs.* 4.8–11), bases the requirement of hospitality on Israel's experiences as strangers in a strange land (*Lv.* 19.34). The phrase now incorporated into the Pesaḥ Seder—"Let all who hunger enter and eat"—was originally the invitation uttered before all meals by R. Huna' (*Taʿan.* 20b). Hospitality is to be extended to everyone, including the poor, the ignorant, the stranger, and those of lower social status than the host: "Let your house be open wide, and let the poor frequent it" (*Avot* 1.5). The laws of hospitality and the duties of both host and guest are elaborated in rabbinic literature. The host should always have a cheerful countenance in order to make his guests feel at home: he should serve the guests himself: various dishes should be placed on the table so as not to embarrass the fastidious guest. The guest is required to express his thanks to the host; therefore, the privilege of reciting Birkat ha-Mazon is given to him "in order that he may thereby invoke the blessing of God on his host" (*Ber.* 58a). In addition, "the good guest also says 'Blessed be the host, may he be remembered for good' " (Y., *Ber.* 9). When a learned company was assembled and speeches were delivered in a private home, "they opened their discourse with praise of the host" (*Ber.* 68a). During the Middle Ages, hospitality was extended to itinerant mendicants and traveling scholars; a Jew visiting a synagogue in a strange town would naturally be invited to the homes of the congregants for meals. *Hakhnasat oreḥim* societies were established to provide shelter for travelers.

• Helen Latner, *The Book of Modern Jewish Etiquette* (New York, 1981). C. G. Montefiore and H. Loewe, "On Charity," in *A Rabbinic Anthology* (London, 1938), chap. 16, pp. 412–439. Meir Wikler, *Aishel: Stories of Contemporary Jewish Hospitality* (Jerusalem, 1994).

HOST OF HEAVEN. God is frequently described as the "Lord of Hosts," the reference being sometimes to human armies (e.g., *Ex.* 7.4, 12.41), to the stars (*Dt.* 4.19; *Is.* 40.26), to the angels (*Jos.* 5.14ff.), or to cosmic powers generally (*Gn.* 2.1). The "host of heaven" may have originally referred to the stars, regarded as arrayed in battle order (cf. *Jgs.* 5.20, "the stars in their courses fought against Sisera."). In ancient Mesopotamian religion the heavenly host was the object of worship (cf. *ʿavodat kokhavim* [worship of the stars], one of the rabbinic terms for paganism). The gods were considered as naturally residing in heaven, each of the major stars and other heavenly bodies being identified with a different prominent deity, as were the three individual sections of the horizon. In biblical theology, the creation and the nature of the host of heaven are emphasized as part of the monotheistic polemic against polytheism: the God of Israel, as the one true God, himself created all the heavenly bodies. This miraculous feat was considered major evidence that the God of Israel was the creator of the universe (e.g., *Ps.* 136.4–9; *Jb.* 9.9–10). It was absolutely forbidden to worship the stars and the heavenly bodies (see *2 Kgs.* 21.3–5, 23.5; *Jer.* 19.2; *Zep.* 1.5) as independent deities (e.g., *Ex.* 20.3; *Dt.* 5.8; *2 Kgs.* 23.5; *Jer.* 19.13; *Am.* 5.26). On the other hand, popular religion already considered the heavenly bodies as representing living beings. Thus the stage was set for the process of demythologization, according to which the host of heaven became identified with the *angels, God's usually subservient assistants and members of his heavenly entourage (see *1 Kgs.* 22.19; *Jb.* 38.7; *2 Chr.* 18.18; and cf. *Is.* 6). He counted and ordered them as well as determined their names (*Is.* 40.26; *Ps.* 147.4), and it was within his power to extinguish their light (*Jb.* 9.7; cf. 38.31). Their function was to serve and praise God (*Is.* 40.26; *Ps.* 8.2, 4, 148.1–6) as his very own heavenly host (*Ps.* 115.15–16).

• E. Theodore Mullen, "Hosts, Host of Heaven," in *The Anchor Bible Dictionary*, vol. 3 (New York, 1992), pp. 301–304. Otto Neugebauer, *A History of Ancient Mathematical Astronomy* (Berlin, 1975). Erica Reiner, *Astral Magic in Babylonia* (Philadelphia, 1995). Erica Reiner and David Pin-

gree, *Babylonian Planetary Omens: Part 2* (Malibu, Calif., 1981), pp. 2–22. F. Rochberg-Halton in *Entsiqlopedyah Miqra'it*, vol. 8 (Jerusalem, 1982).
—CHAIM COHEN

ḤOVAH. See Duty.

ḤOZER BI-TESHUVAH. See Ba'al Teshuvah.

ḤULLIN (חוּלִּין;), name of things that are profane and of a Mishnaic tractate.

Profane Things. *Ḥullin* denotes anything that is not holy, that is, reserved for priestly or ritual use. More particularly it refers to profane food, food to which the rules of Levitical purity do not apply (unlike meat, the *terumah* offering, etc.; *Ter.* 11.5).

Tractate. The tractate *Ḥullin* is in Mishnah order Qodashim and consists of twelve chapters, with related material in the Tosefta' and Talmud Bavli. The tractate deals with the laws concerning the *ritual slaughter of animals for profane use, and in addition, it includes prescriptions relating to the preparation of meat and poultry. *Ḥullin* stresses the differences between the laws relating to food from consecrated and unconsecrated animals. However, many points of contact may be noted: disqualification of slaughter due to improper intent, concern for maternal sensibility, the importance of proper disposition of blood, and the setting aside of a priestly portion. *Ḥullin* is one of the main sources for the *dietary laws.

An English translation by Eli Cashdan appears in the Soncino Talmud (London, 1948).

• Chanoch Albeck, ed., *Shishah Sidrei Mishnah, Seder Qodashim* (Jerusalem, 1956). Philip Blackman, ed. and trans., *Mishnayot*, vol. 5, *Order Qodashim* (Gateshead, 1973). Pinhas Kehati, ed., *Mishnah: A New Translation with a Commentary, Seder Qodashim*, vol. 1, *Zevaḥim, Menaḥot, Ḥullin* (Jerusalem, 1994). Hermann Leberecht Strack, *Introduction to the Talmud and Midrash* (1931; Minneapolis, 1992).
—AVRAHAM WALFISH

HUMAN BEING. The Bible generally uses the term *adam* to refer to any member of the human species, as is implied by its original use as the name of the first man, and the term is etymologically connected with the word for earth (*adamah; Gn.* 1.26). Other names are *ish, enosh* (an archaic form of *ish*) and *gever*, the last suggesting masculine qualities. Human beings are considered the highest creation (*Gn.* 1.28) and are insignificant only when compared to *God. The contrast between human majesty in one sphere and insignificance in another is expressed by the Bible: "What is man that you are mindful of him, and the son of man that you visit him? Yet you have made him little less than the angels, and have crowned him with glory and honor. You made him to have dominion over the work of your hands and have put all things under his feet." (*Ps.* 8.4–6). In the biblical account of creation, the creation of humans (male and female) along with that of other living creatures, took place on the sixth day; though placed in the same physical category with the other living creatures, the human claim to preeminence rests on the statement that human beings were created "after the image and likeness of God" (*Gn.* 1.26–27). In their statement, "Beloved is man, for he was created in the image of God; still greater was the love in that it was made known to him that he was created in the image of God" (*Avot* 3.15), the rabbis wished to emphasize that humans are endowed not only with special dignity but also with the consciousness of this dignity. There is no initial distinction between one person and another, and the opening sentence of *Genesis* 5.1 ("This is the book of the generations of *adam*") is held by the rabbis to convey the "fundamental principle" of the common descent of all humankind. The biblical account of the creation of humankind (*Gn.* 1.27), "And God created man in his image . . . male and female he created them," emphasizes that this image is constituted only by man and woman together. Subsequent formulations and elaborations of the idea of the human being by Hellenistic thinkers, Talmudic *aggadah*, medieval philosophy, Kabbalah, and modern writers have relied on the theories and terminologies of contemporary philosophies. See also Afterlife; Resurrection; Soul; Yetser ha-Ra' and Yetser ha-Tov.

• Haim Hermann Cohn, *Human Rights in the Bible and the Talmud*, translated by Shmuel Himelstein (Tel Aviv, 1989). Frederick E. Greenspahn, ed., *The Human Condition in the Jewish and Christian Traditions* (Hoboken, N.J., 1986). David Hartman, *A Living Covenant* (New York, 1985), pt. 1. Abraham Joshua Heschel, *Man's Quest for God* (New York, 1954). Milton Ridvas Konvitz, ed., *Judaism and Human Rights* (New York, 1972). Raphael Patai, *Man and Temple in Ancient Jewish Myth and Ritual* (New York, 1967).

HUMANISTIC JUDAISM, philosophy and movement that views Judaism as the cultural creation of the Jewish people rather than in theological–religious terms. It has its roots in the Haskalah, in the secular nationalism of the last one hundred years, in the democratic revolution of modern times, and in the Holocaust experience. It maintains that reason is the best method for the discovery of truth, that it is in our power to solve human problems, and that ethical guidelines derive from the human quest for renewal, justice, and happiness. Jews and non-Jews alike must rely on themselves and on each other in the struggle for their ideas. Its worldview centers around the autonomous human and not a God figure. Hence, neither God-language nor worship are appropriate to a humanistic style of life. Humanistic Jews study Jewish history and culture from a naturalistic perspective, cultivate Jewish languages, celebrate holidays in a humanistic spirit, mark life cycle events with secular poetry and music, respond ethically to personal needs and social issues, and organize communities in which these activities can be done cooperatively. The kibbutz movement in Erets Yisra'el formulated an ideology, ethic, and practice based on humanistic values and Jewish cultural traditions (see Kibbutz Festivals).

Many Humanistic Jewish communities are served by certified leaders. In ascending order of training the titles of these leaders are *madrikh* (guide), senior leader, and rabbi. The International Institute for Secular Humanistic Judaism (Jerusalem and Detroit) provides the training. The International Federation of Secular Humanistic Jews, founded in 1985, has affiliates in nine national organizations, including in the United States, Belgium, and Israel. Humanistic Judaism has existed as an organized movement since the mid-1960s.

• International Institute for Secular Humanistic Judaism, *Judaism in a Secular Age: An Anthology of Secular Humanistic Jewish Thought* (Hoboken, N.J., 1995). Sherwin Wine, *Celebration: A Ceremonial and Philosophic Guide for Humanists and Humanistic Jews* (Buffalo, N.Y., 1988). Sherwin Wine, *Humanistic Judaism* (Buffalo, N.Y., 1978). Sherwin Wine, *Judaism Beyond God* (Hoboken, N.J., 1995).

—SHERWIN T. WINE

HUMILITY. The Talmud says (*Mak.* 24a) that the verse "What does the Lord require of you but to do justly, to love mercy, and to walk humbly with your God" (*Mi.* 6.8) contains within it the entire Torah, and the rabbis described the third of its prescriptions, humility, as the outstanding virtue. The greatest of prophets, Moses, is singled out as being "exceedingly humble, above all the men that were upon the face of the earth" (*Nm.* 12.3). Humility is regarded as the outstanding characteristic of the "disciples of Abraham," in contrast to the "disciples of Balaam" (*Avot* 5.21). However, humility must not be confused with servility, which is considered a vice, despite the statement "Be exceedingly lowly in spirit" (*Avot* 4.4). The virtue of humility is ascribed even to God: "In every passage where mention is made of the greatness of God, it is combined with mention of his humility. This is written in the Pentateuch, repeated in the Prophets, and stated for a third time in the Hagiographa" (*Meg.* 31a).

• Samuel H. Dresner, *Prayer, Humility and Compassion* (Philadelphia, 1957).

ḤUMMASH, popular term for the *Torah derived from *ḥamishah ḥumshei Torah* (five-fifths of the Torah). Originally each *ḥummash* referred to one-fifth of the five books of the Torah; later the term came to be used to designate a printed volume containing one of these five books; and still later as a name for a volume containing the entire five books, used in the synagogue by the congregation to follow the public reading.

—BARUCH J. SCHWARTZ

ḤUMRA' (Aram.; חוּמְרָא; severity), in cases of halakhic doubt, the stricter of two possible rulings. Although indiscriminate preference for the more lenient ruling is condemned by the rabbis, they deny any virtue to a *ḥumra'* for its own sake. When there are doubts regarding biblical law, the stricter ruling applies; in matters of rabbinic law, the more lenient solution (*qulla'*) should be adopted. Rabbinic law provides further directives as to when and to what extent doubts, mitigating circumstances, the nature of the issue, and so forth should affect the ruling. The term *ḥumra'* was later applied to stringencies that pious individuals took upon themselves over and above accepted interpretations.

• Sara Epstein Weinstein, "Rabbinic Criticism of Self-Imposed Religious Stringency," Ph.D. dissertation, New York University, 1994.

HUNA', Babylonian amora', who died in 297 according to *Iggeret Rav Sherira' Ga'on*. Best known of the many Talmudic sages named Huna', he is sometimes confused with R. Huna' the exilarch, who was, according to some sources, his grandfather. Both Talmuds make frequent mention of his halakhic and aggadic teachings and also preserve numerous personal anecdotes regarding his life and death that attest to his great stature as a "pillar of the Talmud." In eulogizing him, R. *Abba' claimed that the **shekhinah* (divine presence) would have rested on him had he not lived in Babylon (*Mo'ed Q.* 25a). Huna' studied with *Rav in *Sura, becoming one of the principal transmitters of Rav's teachings (cf. *Nid.* 24b; *Bekh.* 45b). He eventually succeeded Rav as leader of the Sura academy, reportedly holding the position for forty years (according to Sherira' Ga'on). During this time the academy thrived (cf. *Ket.* 106a), surpassing the scholarship of Erets Yisra'el (cf. *Git.* 6a). He was not, however, officially recognized as academy head until the death of Shemu'el, leader of the *Nehardea academy. At that time, Huna' became acknowledged as the leading sage in Babylon, a reputation that extended even to Erets Yisra'el upon the death of R. Yoḥanan (cf. Y., *Ḥag.* 1.8, 76c). He was known in his earlier years for his devotion to study in spite of his poverty (*Meg.* 27b). He later became wealthy and was fabled for his generosity (cf. *Meg.* 27a–b; *Ta'an.* 20b).

• Wilhelm Bacher, *Die Agada der babylonischen Amoräer* (1913; Hildesheim, 1967). Israel Konovitz, comp., *Ma'arakhot ha-'Amora'im*, vol. 3, *Rav Huna' . . . Rav Ḥisda'* (Jerusalem, 1977). —MICHAEL L. BROWN

ḤUPPAH (חוּפָּה; canopy), originally the bridal chamber in which a marriage was consummated (see *Jl.* 2.16; *Ps.* 19.6) and in which the nuptials continued for seven days. The word now refers to the canopy, symbolizing the chamber, under which the wedding ceremony takes place. Canopies range in form from richly embroidered baldachins to a simple **tallit* attached to four poles. The word *ḥuppah* is popularly employed to mean the wedding ceremony. In some communities a new *Sefer Torah is brought to the synagogue under a *ḥuppah*.

• S. B. Freehof, "The Huppah," in *In Time of Harvest: Essays in Honor of Abba Hillel Silver*, edited by Daniel J. Silver (New York, 1963).

ḤUQQAT HA-GOYYIM (חֻקַּת הַגּוֹיִים; statute of the gentiles), non-Jewish practices, which the rabbis, expanding upon the law in *Leviticus* 18.3 and 20.23, forbade the Jews to copy, especially if these involved lewdness or loose morality or the manner in which the gentiles conducted their religious rites. Jews were prohibited from wearing a specifically gentile *costume, including even the manner of dressing one's hair (see *Shab.* 67a–b; *San.* 74a–h), and they were forbidden to attend circuses and stadiums (see Rashi on *Lv.* 18.3). The ban on idolatrous rites also extended to customs that "have become part of their folly," such as superstitious practices (see *tosafot* on *San.* 52a). From Talmudic times, heathen customs and superstitions were called "Amorite ways" (*darkhei ha-'Emori*) and were strictly forbidden, although some folk customs were retained among the people. Maimonides denounced all "those heathen follies" (*Hilkhot 'Akkum* 11, 16). Orthodox Jews condemned many of the innovations of *Reform Judaism because of the dangers they saw in adopting non-Jewish habits. On the other hand, Jewish religious practice has always been influenced by its environment; liturgical music and synagogue architecture are two examples. However, a line is drawn when practices, while harmless in themselves, are regarded as contravening Jewish symbolism and spirit, as in the introduction of Christmas trees into Jewish homes.

• David Novak, *The Image of the Non-Jew in Judaism: An Historical and Constructive Study of the Noahide Laws* (New York, 1983). Christiana Van Houten, *The Alien in Israelite Law*, Journal for the Study of the Old Testament, Supplement Series 107 (Sheffield, Eng., 1981).

HUSBAND. See MATRIMONY.

ḤUSHI'EL BEN ELḤANAN (died c.1027), North African rabbinical scholar. Born in Italy, he arrived in Kairouan (near Tunis) in 1105. He was one of the *four captives of the popular legend who introduced Talmudic studies into various Mediterranean countries. He became the head of the Kairouan *beit midrash*, the highest judicial position in North Africa at that time. His titles were *mu'alam* (teacher) and *reish bei rabbanan* (head of the *yeshivah*). While his focus of study was the Talmud Bavli and the geonic halakhic literature, Ḥushi'el introduced study of the Talmud Yerushalmi to Kairouan. He attracted many students from east and west, including the head of the Jerusalem Yeshivah, R. Natan ben Avraham, who brought Ḥushi'el's study methods to Palestine and Egypt. Ḥushi'el was a pioneer in bringing Talmudic studies from Babylonia to North Africa. His son was *Hanan'el ben Ḥushi'el.

• Menaḥem Ben-Sasson, "Ḥevrah ve-Hanhagah bi-Qehillot Yisra'el be-'Afriqah ha-Tsefonit bi-Yemei ha-Beinayim: Kiro'an 800–1057," Ph.D. dissertation, Hebrew University, 1983, pp. 150–158.

–SHALOM BAR-ASHER

HUTNER, YITSḤAQ (1906–1980), rabbi and educator. He was born in Warsaw and educated in the Slobodka Yeshivah (both in Europe and Erets Yisra'el) and at the University of Berlin. In 1935 he immigrated to the United States and in 1939 became the head of Yeshiva Rabbi Chaim Berlin in New York City. In 1950 he founded and headed Kolel Gur Aryeh for advanced rabbinic studies.

Hutner published extensively on rabbinic subjects. His collected discourses, entitled *Paḥad Yitsḥaq* have been issued in thirteen volumes (1964–1991). They reflect the influence of both Hasidic and Mitnaggedic traditions. He was particularly known for his approach to the apparent contradictions between Torah and philosophy.

• Yosef Buksboim, ed., *Sefer ha-Zikkaron le-Maran Ba'al ha-Paḥad Yitsḥaq* (Jerusalem, 1983–1984). Hillel Goldberg, *Between Berlin and Slobodka: Jewish Transition Figures from Eastern Europe* (Hoboken, N.J., 1989), pp. 63–87. Hillel Goldberg, "Rabbi Isaac Hutner: A Synoptic, Interpretive Biography," *Tradition* 22.4 (Winter 1987): 18–46.

–IRA ROBINSON

HYGIENE. See CLEANLINESS; HEALTH.

HYMN OF GLORY. See SHIR HA-KAVOD.

HYMN OF UNITY. See SHIR HA-YIḤUD.

HYMNS. See PIYYUT; ZEMIROT.

HYPOCRISY. The Talmud states that God detests the hypocrite as "he who says one thing in the heart and another with his lips" (*Pes.* 113b). Hypocrisy is frequently condemned by the rabbis, and Gamli'el II forbade any student "whose inside is not like his outside" to enter his academy (*Yoma'* 72b). A classic warning against the hypocrite is the deathbed advice of the Sadducee king Alexander Yannai to his Pharisee wife Salome Alexandra, "Fear neither those who are Pharisees nor those who are not, rather fear those hypocrites who pretend to be Pharisees, who act like Zimri and want the reward of Pinchas" (*Sot.* 22b, in reference to *Nm.* 25).

• Seymour Cohen, *The Ways of the Righteous: Orchot Tzaddikim* (New York, 1982). Richard A. Freund, ed., *Understanding Jewish Ethics* (San Francisco, 1990). Zelig Pliskin, *Guard Your Tongue* (Brooklyn, N.Y., 1975).

I

IBN AKNIN, YOSEF BEN YEHUDAH (c.1150–1220), philosopher. He was born in Barcelona but from an early age lived in Fez. Almost nothing is known of his life. Three of his works are: *Sefer ha-Musar*, a Hebrew commentary on *Avot; Tibbal-nufus*, in Arabic on psychology; and an Arabic philosophical commentary on the *Song of Songs* called *Inkishaf al-asrar watuhar al-anwar* (with Hebrew translation by Abraham S. Halkin [Jerusalem, 1964]). In this last book, which was influenced by the Arabic philosopher al-Farabi, Ibn Aknin explains the emanation of the intellects from God. He interprets the *Song of Songs* as an allegorical account of the love of the human soul and the "active intellect"—the divine lover asks the beloved, the soul, to acquire knowledge and to separate itself from matter so that it can unite with the active intellect. In his commentary, Ibn Aknin interprets the literal meaning of the text, the rabbinical-Midrashic meaning, and the traditional meanings of the text as an allegory of the relationship between God and Israel. Ibn Aknin also wrote a Hebrew introduction to the Talmud.

• A. S. Halkin, "Ibn Aknin's Commentary on the Song of Songs," in *Alexander Marx: Jubilee Volume on the Occasion of His Seventieth Birthday* (New York, 1950), pp. 389–424. Tony Levy, "Mathematiques et penseurs juif medievaux: L'Example de Maimonide (1138–1204) et de Joseph ibn Aknin (c. 1150–1220)," in *Judaisme, sciences et techniques*, edited by Doris Bensimon (Paris, 1989), pp. 45–61.

–FRANCISCO MORENO CARVALHO

IBN ATTAR, ḤAYYIM. See ATTAR FAMILY.

IBN ATTAR, YEHUDAH. See ATTAR FAMILY.

IBN AVI ZIMRA, DAVID BEN SHELOMOH. See DAVID BEN SHELOMOH IBN AVI ZIMRA.

IBN BAKUDA', BAḤYA BEN YOSEF. See BAḤYA BEN YOSEF IBN PAQUDA'.

IBN BAL'AM, YEHUDAH (11th cent.), Spanish biblical commentator and Hebrew grammarian. He was born in Toledo, but spent most of his life in Seville. Ibn Bal'am wrote his commentaries on the Pentateuch, *Kitab al-Tarjih*, and on the Prophetic books, *Nuqat al-Miqra*, in Arabic. The former explains both narrative and legal passages in light of the writings of Ha'i Ga'on, while the commentary on the Prophetic books draws on the lexicography and linguistic analyses developed by Ibn Janaḥ and Ibn Ḥayyuj. Ibn Bal'am's exegetical writings, recovered in the nineteenth century, constitute a significant source for the development of biblical commentaries from Sa'adyah ben Yosef Ga'on to Avraham ibn Ezra. In addition to his biblical commentaries, he wrote three works in Arabic on Hebrew grammar.

• S. Abramson in *Henoch Yalon Jubilee Volume*, edited by Saul Lieberman (Jerusalem, 1963), pp. 51–149, Salomon Fuchs, *Studien über Abu Zakaria Jachja (R. Jehuda) Ibn Bal'am* (Berlin, 1893). Moshe Goshen-Gottstein, *Perush R. Yehudah ibn Bal'am le-Sefer Yesha'yahu* (Ramat Gan, 1992).

–MICHAEL A. SIGNER

IBN DAUD, AVRAHAM (c.1110–1180), Spanish philosopher, historian, physician, and astronomer; known by his initials as Ravad. He was born in Cordova, Spain; fled from the Almohade persecutions to Castile in 1146; and lived in Toledo, where he died a martyr. The first thoroughgoing Jewish Aristotelian, he tried to show in his major philosophical work, *Emunah Ramah*, composed between 1160 and 1161 (of which only two Hebrew translations from the 14th-cent. Arabic original have survived), that science and religion were not at variance and that the distinctive doctrines of traditional Judaism were in complete harmony with Aristotelian philosophy. He followed the Islamic Aristotelians in his proofs of the existence of God and in his interpretation of prophecy (which, however, he limited in accordance with rabbinic teaching to the Jewish people in Erets Yisra'el). Prophecy is the highest attainment of the human spirit and derives solely from pure intellect without the participation of imaginative faculties. The problem of free will is solved by Ibn Daud with the traditional argument that God limits his own omniscience. In his discussion of the soul, Ibn Daud follows the Arab Aristotelian philosopher, Avicenna. He departs from Aristotle in denying the eternity of matter and upholding the doctrine of creation *ex nihilo*. The Bible contains the highest ethical precepts, and these are not contradicted by philosophical speculation. The goal of humans is conceived in Aristotelian fashion as intellectual perfection and knowledge, which is in turn identified with faith. Ibn Daud also wrote *Sefer ha-Qabbalah*, relating the chain of rabbinic tradition from Moses to his own time. Primarily undertaken to refute Karaite denials of such a tradition, the work is of major importance for our knowledge of the history of Spanish Jewry. He also wrote histories of the Second Temple and of Rome. *Emunah Ramah* was published by Simon Weil in 1852 with a German translation (republished in Frankfurt, 1982). An English translation with commentary was published by Norbert M. Samuelson (*The Exalted Faith* [Rutherford, 1986]). *Sefer ha-Qabbalah* was published in Hebrew and English by Gerson Cohen (Philadelphia, 1967).

• Gerson D. Cohen, Introduction to *A Critical Edition with a Translation and Notes of the Book of Tradition, Sefer ha-Qabbalah* (Philadelphia, 1967). Amira Eran, *Meqorotov ha-Filosofiyyim shel Avraham ibn Daud be-Sifro Al 'Aqidah al-Rafi'ah* (Jerusalem, 1990). Eleazar Gutwirth "L'Accueil fait à Abraham Ibn Daud dans l'Europe de la Renaissance," in *Tolède et Jerusalem: Tentative de symbiose entre les cultures espagnole et judaique* (Lausanne, 1992), pp. 97–110. Isaac Husik, *A History of Mediaeval Jewish Philosophy* (Philadelphia, 1940), pp. 197–235.

–FRANCISCO MORENO CARVALHO

IBN EZRA, AVRAHAM (1089–1164), Bible commentator, poet, grammarian, philosopher, and astronomer. He was responsible for the transmission of the literary, philosophical, and cultural achievements of the Jewish community in Spain to Jewish communities in northern Europe. As did the Kimḥi and Ibn Tibbon families, Ibn Ezra translated significant works in Arabic about the Hebrew language into Hebrew. In his voluminous biblical commentaries, he provided access to Saʿadyah ben Yosef Ga'on and to the commentator Mosheh ben Shemu'el ha-Kohen Gikatilla for Hebrew readers.

Ibn Ezra's life can be divided into two periods. From 1089 to 1140, he lived in Spain. From there, he traveled throughout North Africa as far as Egypt. He had a significant friendship with Yehudah ha-Levi. Of Ibn Ezra's four children, only one is known, Yitsḥaq. It seems to have been the conversion of Yitsḥaq to Islam that sent Ibn Ezra in exile from Spain. The second period, from 1140 until his death in 1164, was a time of wandering. Ibn Ezra traveled first to Italy, where he lived in Rome, Lucca, Mantua, and Verona. By 1147 he had left Italy for Provence, where he visited Narbonne and Béziers. He then went north to Normandy, where he lived in Rouen and Dreux. By 1158 he had reached London. After 1161 he returned to southern France. The precise location of his death remains unknown.

As a poet, Ibn Ezra was the last link in the chain of great religious poets of Spain that began with Yosef ben Yitsḥaq ibn Abitur. Ibn Ezra had a complete mastery of the structure of Arabic poetry. He was the first of the Spanish poets to write disputations between animals and other inanimate objects. In addition, he developed rhythmic and rhymed riddles on letters and numbers.

His poetry focuses on ordinary things, such as food and lodging. However, it is also filled with humor, irony, and satire. Many poems provide a window into Ibn Ezra's stormy relationships with his literary patrons. There is also a large corpus of religious poetry that reveals Ibn Ezra's intense longing for a mystical encounter with God. These religious themes recur in his poem *Ḥai ben Meqits*, which describes a journey from the created world into the heavenly spheres to behold the Creator. Ibn Ezra's poetic abilities are also evident in the rhymed introductions to his biblical commentaries.

He is best known for his biblical commentaries, which cover almost the entire scripture, with the exception of *Samuel, Kings, Jeremiah, Ezekiel, Proverbs, Ezra, Nehemiah*, and *Chronicles*. Some of these commentaries exist in two versions. The style of the commentaries is often cryptic, indicating that they may simply provide his own random notes.

Ibn Ezra emphasized the role of human reason in understanding the divine revelation of the Pentateuch and the Prophets. He scrutinized biblical language and grammar as a point of departure. He believed the grammarian was in danger of error without a correct understanding of rabbinic tradition. *Karaite scholars, for example, might have applied the rules of grammar to scripture, but since they did not believe in the interpretations of the rabbis, their interpretations were incorrect. The limits set by the rabbis did not prevent Ibn Ezra from raising questions about chronological inconsistencies in the Bible. Later thinkers, such as Baruch Spinoza and Naḥman Krochmal, would point to Ibn Ezra's questions as a foreshadowing of modernity. Closer scrutiny of Ibn Ezra's resolutions to these questions indicates that they do not constitute a radical departure but fall within the broad range of opinions contained within classic rabbinic literature.

In addition to the linguistic elements of his biblical commentaries, Ibn Ezra also wrote philosophical digressions on subjects like the name of God, miracles, and astronomy. His *Yesod Mora'* is a treatise on the meaning of the biblical commandments. His approach to philosophical matters was influenced by the Neoplatonism of Shelomoh ibn Gabirol.

• Michael Friedlander, ed. and trans., *The Commentary of Ibn Ezra on Isaiah* (New York, 1960). Michael Friedlander, *Essays on the Writings of Abraham ibn Ezra* (London, 1877; repr. Jerusalem, 1963), vol. 4. Hermann Greive, *Studien zum jüdischen Neoplatonismus: Die Religionsphilosophie des Abraham ibn Ezras* (Berlin, 1973). Isaac Husik, *A History of Mediaeval Jewish Philosophy* (Philadelphia, 1944), pp. 187–196. Raphael Levy, *The Astrological Works of Abraham ibn Ezra* (Baltimore, 1927). Uriel Simon, *Four Approaches to the Book of Psalms: From Saadia to Abraham ibn Ezra* (Albany, 1991). H. Norman Strickman, trans., *The Secret of Torah: A Translation of Abraham ibn Ezra's Yesod Mora ve-Sod ha-Torah* (Northvale, N.J., 1995). H. Norman Strickman and Arthur Silver, trans., *Abraham ibn Ezra's Commentary on the Pentateuch: Genesis* (New York, 1988). Isadore Twersky and Jay M. Harris, eds., *Rabbi Abraham ibn Ezra: Studies in the Writings of a Twelfth-Century Jewish Polymath* (Cambridge, Mass., 1993).

—MICHAEL A. SIGNER

IBN EZRA, MOSHEH (1070–1138), Spanish philosopher and poet. Born into a distinguished family, his life was marked by sorrows and misfortune. His major philosophic work, *Arugat ha-Bosem*, dealing with the familiar problems of medieval philosophy (e.g., divine attributes, creation, nature, and the intellect), suggests a knowledge of Greek and Latin in addition to the standard acquaintance with Arabic thought. However, his fame rests mainly on his religious and secular poetry. A great part of his 220 sacred compositions are scattered throughout the Sephardi *prayer book, especially the liturgy for Ro'sh ha-Shanah and Yom Kippur. In these poems he calls upon people to search themselves, to consider the emptiness of life and the vanity and illusion of mundane pleasures. His poetic paraphrase of the *Book of Jonah* was adopted in the Avignon rite for Yom Kippur.

• Joseph Dan, "Meaningful Rhyme in the Poetry of Spain (Selected Examples from the Sacred Poetry of Rabbi Moses ibn Ezra)," *Jewish Quarterly Review* 76.3 (1986): 169–189. Paul Fenton, *Philosophie et exégèse dans le Jardin de la métaphore de Moise Ibn Ezra, philosophe et poète andalou du XIIe siècle* (New York, 1996). Jan D. Katzew, "Moses Ibn Ezra and Judah Halevi: Their Philosophies in Response to Exile," *Hebrew Union College Annual* 55 (1984): 179–185. Arie Schippes, "Two Andalusian Poets in Exile: Reflections on the Poetry of Ibn Ammar . . . and Moses Ibn Ezra . . .," in *The Challenge of the Middle East: Middle Eastern Studies at the University of Amsterdam*, edited by Ibrahim A. El-Sheikh et al. (Amsterdam, 1982), pp. 112–121. Israel Zinberg, *A History of Jewish Literature*, translated and edited by Bernard Martin (Cleveland, 1972–1978).

IBN FALAQUERA, SHEM TOV BEN YOSEF. See FALAQUERA, SHEM TOV BEN YOSEF.

IBN GABIROL, SHELOMOH (c.1021–1058), Spanish philosopher and poet. Little is known of his life after he left Saragossa at the age of sixteen. He seems to have suffered from melancholia and loneliness, and to have died young. His chief philosophical work, *Meqor Ḥayyim*, written in Arabic, has survived only in a Latin translation, *Fons vitae*, and in a few Hebrew excerpts translated by Shem Tov Falaquera in the thirteenth century. The *Fons vitae* was known to Christian scholastics, who never suspected it to be the work of a Jewish author, since it had no specifically Jewish context and was neglected by Jews. It was only in 1845 that the French scholar Solomon Munk discovered that its author, "Avicebron," was identical with Ibn Gabirol. The work represents the climax of the Neoplatonic tradition in medieval Jewish philosophy. The initial question, how a material world could derive from an utterly spiritual Being, is answered in Neoplatonic fashion: by way of emanation from the Creator. From the divine will, which is, in essence, identical with the Godhead yet also separate from it in its outward action, there proceeded the two basic principles of "general matter" and "general form." The chain of emanations ends with the corporeal world, in which, however, the initial divine will is still present. Since man is a *microcosm partaking of both the intelligible and the corporeal worlds, he is able to grasp the immaterial, spiritual forms in things by his own powers and is not dependent, as Arab thinkers asserted, on an external intelligence for his illumination. By means of this conception of matter, Ibn Gabirol attempted to reconcile the Arab view of matter as metaphysically self-subsistent with the Jewish view of a transcendental God who created the world by an act of his divine will. Ibn Gabirol's doctrine of the will subsequently, although indirectly, influenced the kabbalistic doctrine of divine emanation. His ethical work, *Tiqqun Middot ha-Nefesh* is the first work of its kind by a Jewish philosopher, inasmuch as it presents an ethical system independent of any specific religious tradition. Ibn Gabirol also ranks among the greatest Hebrew poets. His secular poetry deals with the standard themes of wine, friends, life, and love, as well as with loneliness and sorrow; it expresses both a *joie de vivre* and despair at the vanity of life and worldly striving. In his religious poetry, personal sorrow and joy have been transmuted into Israel's sorrow in its exile and joy in its communion with God. Many of Ibn Gabirol's penitential prayers have found their way into the prayer book, and his powerful hymns on the glory of the divine majesty form part of the Sephardi liturgy for the High Holy Days. His greatest poem, "Keter Malkhut," is frequently recited as a private devotion after the evening service on Yom Kippur.

• Fernand Brunner, *Platonisme et aristotélisme: La Critique d'Ibn Gabirol par St. Thomas d'Aquin* (Louvain, 1965), includes bibliography. Israel Davidson, ed., *Selected Religious Poems of Solomon Ibn Gabirol* (New York, 1973). Raphael Loewe, *Ibn Gabirol* (London, 1989). Jefim Schirmann, *Ha-Shirah ha-ʿIvrit bi-Sefarad uve-Provans* (Jerusalem, 1956–1959). Jacques Schlanger, *La philosophie de Salomon Ibn Gabirol* (Leiden, 1968). Adena V. Tanenbaum, "Poetry and Philosophy: The Idea of the Soul in Andalusian Piyyut," Ph.D. dissertation, Harvard University, 1993. Stephen S. Wise, ed. and trans., *The Improvement of Moral Qualities: An Ethical Treatise of the Eleventh Century by Solomon ibn Gabirol* (New York, 1966). Dov Yarden, *Shirei Ḥol shel Shelomoh ibn Gabirol* (Jerusalem, 1975). Israel Zangwill, trans., *Selected Religious Poems of Solomon ibn Gabirol* (Philadelphia, 1923).

IBN GIKATILLA, YOSEF BEN AVRAHAM. See GIKATILLA, YOSEF BEN AVRAHAM.

IBN ḤAVIV FAMILY, scholars of Spanish origin.

Yaʿaqov ben Shelomoh ibn Ḥaviv (c.1450–1516), Talmudist. After the expulsion from Spain, he settled in Salonika, where he served as rabbi. There he compiled *ʿEin Yaʿaqov*, a comprehensive collection of the aggadic sections of the Talmud Bavli (and some from the Talmud Yerushalmi) with relevant commentaries, including his own. In his lifetime the sections devoted to the orders Zeraʿim and Moʿed were published. He also wrote comments on part of Yaʿaqov ben Asher's *Arbaʿah Turim*, some of which are cited by Yosef Karo in the *Shulḥan ʿArukh*.

Levi ibn Ḥaviv (c.1484–1545), son of Yaʿaqov; the leading sage in Jerusalem in his time. He left Salonika and settled in Jerusalem in 1525. He was soon elected chief rabbi of the city and completed his father's *ʿEin Yaʿaqov*, which was first published in full in Salonika in 1516 and has been reprinted over a hundred times. It became an extremely popular work among all sections of Jewry and was studied by groups specially formed for the purpose.

Levi was the leading opponent of Yaʿaqov *Berab's attempt to revive *ordination. He published a series of pamphlets against Berab after Berab ordained four of his pupils and was responsible for thwarting the scheme. His *responsa* were published in Venice in 1565.

• M. Benayahu, "Ḥiddushah shel ha-Semikhah bi-Tsefat," in *Sefer Yovel le-Yitsḥaq Baer*, (Jerusalem, 1960), pp. 248–269. Avraham Vinberg et al., eds., *Shiʿurim be-Haggadot Ḥazal: "ʿEin Yaʿaqov"* (Bene Beraq, 1995).

–SHALOM BAR-ASHER

IBN ḤAYYIM, AHARON (1555–1632), rabbinical scholar born in Fez, Morocco, and descended from Spanish exiles. He studied with Yosef Almosnino (see ALMOSNINO FAMILY) and was a member of the *beit din* of his teacher Vidal ha-Tsarefati. He was apparently a leading authority in Fez and Marrakesh, the two main communities of Spanish and Portuguese exiles. In 1608 he left Fez for Venice and after three years moved to Egypt. He lived his latter years in Jerusalem.

A scholar by nature, his best-known works were *Middot Aharon* (Venice, 1609) on the thirteen hermeneutical rules expounded by R. Yishmaʿeʾl ben Elishaʿ and *Qorban Aharon* (Dessau, 1742) on *Sifraʾ* (on the *Book of Leviticus*). He laid down limits for the application of *a fortiori* arguments derived from the internal relationship between laws. Of his biblical and Talmudic commentaries, only his *Lev Aharon* on *Joshua* and *Judges* has been published (most recently in Jerusalem in 1984).

• M. Amar, "Toledot Rabbi Aharon Ibn Ḥayyim ve-Yetsirato," in Aharon Ibn Ḥayyim, *Sefer Lev Aharon* (Jerusalem, 1983), introduction, pp. 1–8.

–SHALOM BAR-ASHER

IBN LATIF, YITSḤAQ (c.1228–1290), Spanish kabbalist and philosopher. Unlike other kabbalists, he was an admirer of Maimonides, though his philosophy was of a Neoplatonic character and clearly indebted to Shelomoh *ibn Gabirol's *Meqor Ḥayyim*, which he knew in the original Arabic. His emphatic rejection of the doctrine of transmigration of souls rendered him suspect in the eyes of some kabbalists. His writings influenced many medieval and modern thinkers.

• S.O.H. Wilensky, "Isaac Ibn Latif: Philosopher or Kabbalist?" in *Jewish Medieval and Renaissance Studies*, edited by Alexander Altmann (Cambridge, Mass., 1967).

IBN MIGASH, YOSEF BEN ME'IR (1077–1141), Spanish Talmudic scholar. In Lucena he was the favorite pupil of Yitsḥaq *Alfasi, who chose him to be his successor as head of the academy. He was accepted as the highest rabbinic authority throughout Spain. He was the teacher of Maimon, father of Moses *Maimonides, who mentions him with great respect and esteem. He also influenced R. *Zeraḥyah ben Yitsḥaq ha-Levi Gerondi. *Yehudah ha-Levi composed for Ibn Migash a poem to be sent to the rabbis of Narbonne. Few of Ibn Migash's writings have survived; they include *novellae* to tractates *Bava' Batra'* and *Shevu'ot* and *responsa*. On the question of whether decisions of rabbinic law should be based strictly on the Talmud or whether it was necessary also to consult geonic literature, he decided that it was forbidden to make decisions without consulting the ga'onim, believing that one must take living traditions into consideration. Ibn Migash's works played an important role in the development of Talmud study in Spain and Provence.

• A. L. Grayevski, *Rabbenu Yosef ha-Levi Ibn Migash* (Jerusalem, 1963). Y. Ta-Shema, "Yosef Ibn Migash," in *Rabbi Zeraḥyah ha-Levi Ba'al ha-Ma'or u-Venei Ḥugo* (Jerusalem, 1992), p. 173. –SHALOM BAR-ASHER

IBN MOḤA', REFA'EL MAS'UD (1781–1876), rabbi and halakhist in Marrakesh, Morocco. He headed the *beit din* in Marrakesh and maintained close links with rabbinic authorities in northern Morocco, whom he often cites in his *responsa*. He disseminated Torah study not only in his own community but in the large Atlantic coastal towns of Essaouira (Mogador) and Safi. He offered original interpretations to the Bible, *aggadah*, and *halakhah*. Many of his most notable works were written while he was still a youth. He cites rabbinical sages not only in Muslim lands but also in Europe, with whose writings he was well acquainted.

• Yehudah Edri and Ya'aqov Alḥar'ar, "Ha-Rav Refa'el Mas'ud Ibn Moḥa'," in *Sefer Parfara'ot la-Ḥokhmah* (Jerusalem, 1984), pp. 1–8. –SHALOM BAR-ASHER

IBN PALQUERA, SHEM TOV BEN YOSEF. See FALAQUERA, SHEM TOV BEN YOSEF.

IBN PAQUDA', BAḤYA BEN YOSEF. See BAḤYA BEN YOSEF IBN PAQUDA'.

IBN SHEM TOV FAMILY, family of Spanish kabbalists, theologians, and philosophers, whose activities spanned three generations.

Shem Tov ibn Shem Tov (c.1380–1441), author of the anti-philosophical work *Sefer ha-'Emunot* (Ferrara, 1556; reprinted in Jerusalem in 1969), which attacked Greek scholarship, Aristotelian philosophy, and those Jewish authors who used them in their writings, particularly Maimonides. Shem Tov's opposition to philosophy was partly a result of the large number of Jews who converted to Christianity in the decades following the massacres of 1391, which he attributed to the spread of philosophy. In place of philosophy, Shem Tov advocated a mixture of biblical literalism and Kabbalah.

Yosef ben Shem Tov ibn Shem Tov (c.1400–1480), son of Shem Tov ibn Shem Tov. A participant in religious disputations in the courts of John II and Henry IV of Castile, he accepted the philosophers, including Aristotle and Maimonides. His tolerance for philosophy was based upon his reinterpretation of their doctrines and his reliance upon apocryphal works attributed to them. In his commentary on Aristotle's *Nicomachean Ethics*, he wrote that Aristotle believed that the highest good of human beings was to be achieved in the next life. In the same commentary, Yosef ben Shem Tov mentions a work discovered in Egypt and attributed to Aristotle, in which Aristotle rejects his doctrine of the prior eternalness of the universe. Although Yosef wrote commentaries on several philosophical works, he is best known for his *Kevod Elohim* (Ferrara, 1556). In it he subordinated philosophy to traditional observance of the commandments. According to his understanding, while philosophy assisted the Jew in achieving the ultimate good, reliance on scripture took precedence, leading to the greatest good. Moreover, he advised that the study of philosophy be delayed until the student has reached a suitable age. Yosef spent the last years of his life as an itinerant preacher, and some of his sermons have survived, as has a handbook on preaching that he composed. He died a martyr.

Yitsḥaq ben Shem Tov ibn Shem Tov (flourished c.1461–1490), another son of Shem Tov ibn Shem Tov. He was more philosopher than theologian and apparently taught philosophy for several decades. He wrote a number of commentaries on Arabic philosophers, as well as a commentary on Maimonides' *Guide of the Perplexed*.

Shem Tov ben Yosef ibn Shem Tov (flourished c.1461–1489), son of Yosef ben Shem Tov ibn Shem Tov; author of a commentary on Maimonides' *Guide of the Perplexed* and a book of sermons titled *Derashot ha-Torah* (Salonika, 1525).

• Isaac Husik, *A History of Mediaeval Jewish Philosophy* (New York, 1916), pp. 429–430. Colette Sirat, *A History of Jewish Philosophy in the Middle Ages* (Cambridge, 1990), pp. 346, 381–384, 448, 451–452. –STEVEN BALLABAN

IBN TIBBON FAMILY, family of translators who lived in southern France. Their activities spanned four generations during the twelfth and thirteenth centuries. Their translations made major works of Greek, Islamic, and Jewish philosophy available in Arabic accessible to the European Jewish communities of France and Germany, and through them, to the larger intellectual communities of Europe. Pioneers in the art of translation, the Ibn Tibbons developed the Hebrew idiom for rendering Arabic philosophical terminology.

Yehudah ben Sha'ul ibn Tibbon (c.1120–1190), a physician by profession; known as "the father of translation." He moved from Granada, Spain, where he was born, to Lunel in southern France. Among other works, he translated Sa'adyah ben Yosef Ga'on's *Emunot ve-De'ot*, Yehudah ha-Levi's *Kuzari*, and Shelomoh ibn Gabirol's *Tiqqun Middot ha-Nefesh*. In his introduction to *Ḥovot ha-Levavot*, by Baḥya ben Yosef ibn Paquda', Yehudah explains the superiority of the Arabic language because of its breadth and diversity, as well as its widespread use by Jews in Islamic countries. This translation, which may have been Yehudah's first, was commissioned by the head of Lunel's Jewish community,

R. Meshullam ben Yaʿaqov of Lunel, and was completed around 1160.

Shemu'el ben Yehudah ibn Tibbon (c.1150–1230), son of Yehudah ben Sha'ul; best known for his translations of Maimonides' *Guide of the Perplexed*, which included a glossary of philosophical terms in an appendix; for his introduction to Mishnah tractate *Avot* (known as *Shemonah Peraqim*) and the tenth chapter of Mishnah *Sanhedrin* (known as *Pereq Ḥeleq*); and for his *Treatise on Resurrection, Epistle on Resurrection*, and *Epistle to Yemen*. Shemu'el's correspondence with Maimonides has also survived. He composed a commentary on the biblical book *Ecclesiastes* and a commentary on *Genesis* 1.9 called *Ma'amar Yiqavu ha-Mayim* (Pressburg, 1837).

Mosheh ben Shemu'el ibn Tibbon (fl. 1240–1283), son of Shemu'el ben Yehudah. The most prolific member of the family, he translated works in a wide variety of disciplines, including medicine, science, philosophy, and mathematics by non-Jewish as well as Jewish authors. He also wrote a philosophical commentary on the *Song of Songs* and a number of other works that have not survived.

Yaʿaqov ben Makhir (c.1236–1307), known as Don Prophet Tibbon, Profatius, and Profacius Judaeus; grandson of Shemu'el ben Yehudah. He translated mathematical and astronomical works.

• Isidore Loeb, *Un procès dans la famille des Ibn Tibbon, Marseille, 1235–1236* (Paris, 1886). Ernest Renan and Adolf Neubauer, *L'Histoire littéraire de la France*, vol. 27 (Paris, 1877), pp. 572–575; 593–623. Georges Vajda, *Recherches sur la philosophie et la Kabbale dans la pensee juive du Moyen Âge* (Paris, 1962). —STEVEN BALLABAN

IBN ZERAḤ, MENAḤEM. See MENAḤEM BEN AHARON BEN ZERAḤ.

IBN ZIMRA, DAVID BEN SHELOMOH. See DAVID BEN SHELOMOH IBN AVI ZIMRA.

IBN ZUR, YAʿAQOV (1672–1753), known by the acronym Yavets; Moroccan religious leader. Born in Fez, he was appointed *dayyan* (judge) in the rabbinical court at the age of thirty-one and served there for almost fifty years, except for a period of exile in Meknes. His public and literary activities greatly influenced Moroccan Jewry and its communal and legal structure. He was noted for the courage of his leadership and legal decisions. His edicts that a single *dayyan* had as much authority to make decisions as three *dayyanim*, and that a ruling handed down in one place could not be challenged in another, strengthened the status of small communities. Yaʿaqov ibn Zur codified the *taqqanot* (enactments) of Moroccan Jewry, beginning with those passed at the time of the Spanish expulsion, and these became a basic source of reference for rabbinic judges. Before his death, he ordained five *dayyanim* in Fez, who constituted the largest *beit din* known in Morocco at that time. The rulings of Yaʿaqov ibn Zur covered all facets of life: he banned parents from taking children of ages six or seven out of school; he guaranteed compensation to the affluent for arbitrary seizures and arrests; and he defined the functions of court officials, scribes, and ritual slaughterers as well as exempting them from taxes.

• Binyamin Bar-Tikvah, ed., *Piyyutei R. Yaʿaqov ibn Tsur* (Jerusalem, 1988), includes bibliography and English summary. —SHALOM BAR-ASHER

IDOLATRY, the worship of physical representations of gods, generally symbolizing the forces of nature, and of the powers that they represent; often treated as synonymous with paganism. Jewish tradition finds the first protest against idols in Abraham's iconoclastic revolt against his idolatrous father, Terah. *Monotheism has ever since become synonymous with the negation of idol worship: "You shall have no other gods before me. You shall not make for yourself a graven image or any likeness of anything that is in the heaven above or in the earth below . . . you shall not bow down to them or serve them." Biblical literature is replete with references to Israel's reversion to idolatrous foreign cults, and the struggle against such practices constitutes one of the major features of biblical history (see GOLDEN CALF for a notable lapse). Legal prohibitions, passionate denunciation, and scathing sarcasm (particularly by Deutero-Isaiah) were among the weapons that the Law and the prophets directed against idolatry and its attendant moral and spiritual degradation (orgiastic promiscuity, human sacrifices, necromancy, magic, divination, etc.). The most frequently mentioned idols in the Bible are the Canaanite Baal and Astarte; references are often couched in the form of derogatory epithets such as: "vanity," "iniquity," "abomination," "carcasses," and so forth. In the northern kingdom of Israel, Jeroboam placed idols of bulls in the sanctuaries at Bethel and Dan. It was only during the Babylonian exile (586–516) that Israel was effectively weaned from idol worship. The varied attempts at reintroducing pagan cults into Judea during the Greco-Roman period met with the physical opposition of the Jewish masses. The Talmud devotes an entire tractate—*ʿ*Avodah Zarah*—to the regulation of the social and commercial intercourse between Jews and heathens. Idolatry, together with incest and murder, was a cardinal sin that must not be transgressed even to the extent of forfeiting one's life. The *wine of a gentile may not be drunk out of fear that it was prepared as a libation to an idol. The problem as to which of the non-Jewish religions were to be considered as idolatrous has been discussed by medieval and later halakhists and theologians. Islam was generally considered a genuinely monotheistic religion, but many authorities classified Christianity as idolatry (because of its doctrines of the Incarnation and the Eucharist and its use of images). Others held that Christianity, while not a "pure monotheism," was not idolatrous either, since strict monotheism was enjoined on Israel only, and so Christians need not be considered as idolaters. Some authorities also distinguished between Roman Catholic and Protestant forms of Christianity, the latter being considered as less idolatrous.

• Robert Merrihew Adams, "Idolatry and the Invisibility of God," in *Interpretation in Religion*, edited by Shlomo Biderman and Ben-Ami Scharfstein (Leiden, 1992), pp. 39–52. William Adler, "Abraham and the

Burning of the Temple of Idols: Jubilees' Traditions in Christian Chronography," *Jewish Quarterly Review* 77.2–3 (1986–1987): 95–117. Lionel E. Kochan, "Towards a Rabbinic Theory of Idolatry," *Jewish Law Annual* 8 (1989): 99–113. Mark Moore,"Jeroboam's Calves: Idols or Imitations?," *Bible Translator* 41.4 (1990): 421–424. Karl-Gustav Sandelin, "The Danger of Idolatry According to Philo of Alexandria," *Temenos* 27 (1991): 109–150. Sacha Stern, "The Death of Idolatry?," *Le'ela* 35 (1993): 26–28.

IDRA', name of three kabbalistic works (*Idra' Rabba'*, *Idra' Zuta'*, and *Idra' de-Vei Mashkena'*) incorporated into the *Zohar and containing its most fundamental and revered doctrines. The date of composition is unknown, but in its final form, the *Idra'* dates from the first part of the thirteenth century. The kabbalists introduced *Idra' Rabba'* and *Idra' Zuta'* into certain liturgies (e.g., the Tiqqun for Shavu'ot and Hosha'na' Rabbah). Many commentaries have been written on all three works.

• Gershom Gerhard Scholem, *Major Trends in Jewish Mysticism* (New York, 1995). Isaiah Tishby et al., *The Wisdom of the Zohar: An Anthology of Texts*, 3 vols. (London, 1991).

IGGERAT BAT MAḤALAT, in popular mythology, a demon queen controlling a hundred eighty thousand angels of destruction, who travels about in her chariot seeking to harm living creatures. According to the Talmud, R. Ḥanina' ben Dosa' was able to limit her activities to the Sabbath eve and Wednesdays, while the amora' Abbayei endeavored to banish her altogether but was not completely successful (*Pes*. 112b). According to the Zohar, Iggerat will exist until the messianic era, when God will destroy the spirit of uncleanness.

• Louis Ginzberg, ed., *Legends of the Jews*, vol. 5 (Philadelphia, 1937–1966), p. 39. Joshua Trachtenberg, *Jewish Magic and Superstition: A Study in Folk Religion* (New York, 1974), p. 36. –SHIFRA EPSTEIN

IGGERET, a *responsum* by Rav *Sherira' ben Ḥanina' (10th cent. CE), head of the Talmudic academy of Pumbedita in Babylonia, to an inquiry from *Nissim ben Ya'aqov ben Nissim ibn Shahin concerning the origins of the Mishnah, the Talmud, and other works of classic rabbinic literature. The answer of Sherira', which draws heavily upon the archives of his academy, provides a running history of the oral Torah and is an indispensable source for knowledge of the savoraic and geonic periods. His remarks on the redaction of the Talmud Bavli have served as the focal point for scholarly debate on that subject for centuries. First printed in Constantinople in 1566, *Iggeret* exists in two manuscript versions, the "French" and the "Spanish," distinguished from each other by considerations of orthography and content. The "French" version is considered the more reliable.

• Jacob E. Ephrathi, *Tequfat ha-Savora'im ve-Sifrutah* (Petaḥ Tiqvah, 1973). Jacob Nahum Epstein, *Mevo'ot le-Sifrut ha-'Amora'im* (Jerusalem, 1962), pp. 610–615. –MARK WASHOFSKY

IGGERET HA-QODESH, a short treatise on the proper meaning and conduct of sexual relations written in the early thirteenth century in Spain by a still unidentified kabbalist. It became enormously influential in subsequent centuries in defining Jewish attitudes toward sexuality, but it also bears some similarities to medieval Christian and Moslem treatises on sexual conduct.

The *Iggeret* denounces Maimonides for denigrating the sense of touch and argues that marital intercourse, when properly conducted, is holy. Following kabbalistic doctrine, the correct union of husband and wife fosters the union of the male and female emanations of God. Proper union, which is intended for the procreation of holy souls, requires that the thoughts of the partners be directed toward the divine; if their thoughts are directed only toward the pleasure of the body, the sex act becomes idolatrous. Going far beyond earlier Talmudic law, *Iggeret ha-Qodesh* placed much greater weight on intentionality and made sexuality a matter of cosmic importance. It was edited and translated into English by Seymour J. Cohen (New York, 1976).

• David Biale, *Eros and the Jews: From Biblical Israel to Contemporary America* (New York, 1992), pp. 101–109. Charles Mopsik, *Lettre sur la sainteté: Le Secret de la relation entre l'homme et la femme dans la cabale* (Lagrasse, 1986). –DAVID BIALE

'IKKUV HA-TEFILLAH (עִכּוּב הַתְּפִילָּה; delaying of prayer), a custom, also called *'ikkuv ha-qeri'ah*, that arose among Ashkenazi Jewry in the Middle Ages, whereby a person who felt that he (or she—the right was available to all) had been wronged could call a delay in either the prayers or the Torah reading in the synagogue in order to voice the grievance. The wrong might be moral or legal, and the complaint could be against an individual or the communal authorities. The source for this custom is attributed to a decree by R. *Gershom ben Yehudah permitting a person who felt wronged by the community and who had exhausted all other avenues the right to call a halt in the prayers and explain to the entire congregation how the wrong had occurred. Should community authorities not respond, the person had the right to delay the prayers for the following two days as well. If still not satisfied, the offended could cause prayers in all the synagogues in the city to be delayed. As a counterweight, should the leaders of the community declare that the person's charges were baseless, they had the right to cancel the delay. Although various measures were adopted to curtail the overuse of *'ikkuv ha-tefillah*, the authorities generally made special provision for widows and orphans to be heard. Although there are still isolated cases of *'ikkuv ha-tefillah*, it has all but died out. This practice is also referred to as *bittul ha-tamid*, "the cancellation of the daily sacrifice" (which was offered in the Temple).

• Irving A. Agus, *The Heroic Age of Franco-German Jewry* (New York, 1969), pp. 204–207. Avraham Grossman, "Re'shito vi-Yesodotav shel Minhag 'Ikkuv ha-Tefillah," *Mileit* 1 (1983): 199–219.

–SHMUEL HIMELSTEIN

ILLEGITIMACY. Jewish law does not subject children born out of wedlock to any deprivation of status or rights. The product of an adulterous or incestuous union, however, is a **mamzer* and is forbidden to marry any person other than another *mamzer* or a convert. Aside from the *mamzer*, there are a number of other cases in which individuals are subject to restrictions in the area of personal status. An **asufi* is a child found abandoned in a public place and whose parents cannot be identified. Such an individual is of doubtful status in relation to both religious identity and *mamzerut* and, hence, may not marry anyone at all. Any evidence of care for the *asufi*'s survival will tip the scales in favor of legitimacy since it is assumed that such care would be lavished only on a child of untainted lineage (*Qid.* 73b–74a). A *shetuqi* is the child of an unmarried Jewish woman who cannot or will not reveal the identity of the father. In the absence of a clear majority of Jews of perfect lineage in the vicinity of its birth, the child is likely to be declared a "doubtful *mamzer*." The mother's declaration of paternity is definitive in the case of a *shetuqi* and she can remove any suspicion of *mamzerut* from her offspring by declaring the father to be a legitimate Jew or a gentile. In the latter case, the child takes its status from the mother (*Qid.* 69a, 74a). The male offspring of a *kohen* and a woman forbidden to him in marriage is called a *ḥalal* and is disqualified from the priesthood. Halakhic problems relating to the status of "doubtful *mamzerut*" have also arisen in relation to Karaites and Ethiopian Jews (see BETA ISRAEL).

• Shoshana Matzner-Bekerman, *The Jewish Child: Halakhic Perspectives* (New York, 1984).

—DANIEL SINCLAIR

ILLNESS. See MI SHE-BERAKH LE-ḤOLIM; SICK, VISITING THE.

IMAGES. See IDOLATRY.

IMITATION OF GOD. Although the desire to be "like unto God" (cf. *Gn.* 3.5) is considered a sinful disregard of human limitations, certain of the attributes of God should, according to the rabbis, be taken as models for human behavior. Although the literal fulfillment of the biblical commandment (e.g., *Dt.* 10.20, 13.15) to "cleave" to God is impossible, yet man should "cleave to his qualities." Elaborating on *Leviticus* 19.2 ("You shall be holy for I the Lord am holy"), the rabbis taught, "As he is merciful and gracious, so be you merciful and gracious" (*Mekhilta'* 37a); similarly R. Ḥama' bar Ḥanina' said, "Follow the attributes of God; as he clothes the naked, so do you clothe the naked; as he visits the sick, so do you visit the sick; as he comforts the mourners, so do you comfort the mourners; and as he buries the dead, so do you" (*Sot.* 14a). These and other texts show that it is God's qualities of mercy, compassion, and lovingkindness that are held up for imitation. In the moral teaching of the kabbalist mystics, the concept of imitation of God is correlated in great detail to the various aspects of the deity known as the *sefirot*. In general, however, Jewish piety was more influenced by the ideal of the Godly life practiced with a sense of the presence of God (cf. *Ps.* 16.8 ["I have set the Lord always before me"] or *Prv.* 3.6 ["In all your ways acknowledge him"]) rather than of the imitation of God.

• Arthur Marmorstein, "The Imitation of God (Imitatio Dei) in the Haggadah," in *Studies in Jewish Theology* (London, 1950).

IMMERSION. See MIQVEH.

IMMORTALITY. See AFTERLIFE.

IMPRISONMENT, always mentioned in the Torah as a temporary measure pending a decision on appropriate punishment (cf. *Lv.* 24.10–23 and *Nm.* 15.32–36); nowhere is imprisonment considered by the Torah as a form of punishment, and offenders were at most placed in custody until the court could attend to their case and decide their ultimate penalty. The experience of Jeremiah (*Jer.* 37.15; cf. *2 Chr.* 16.7–10; *1 Kgs.* 22.26–28) possibly indicates the use of imprisonment for political offenders during a later period. Nonetheless, penal institutions did exist in ancient times, and the rabbis legislated imprisonment as a punishment in the case of certain offenses for which no other penalty is prescribed in the Bible or for which circumstances demanded particular measures. As provided for in the Talmud, imprisonment is extremely severe and is for life. The prisoner is to be incarcerated in a narrow cell and receive a scant diet. Imprisonment was applied to the incorrigible offender (*San.* 9.5), but only in cases where the culprit had already received corporal punishment for transgression of a prohibition involving excision (*karet*); when the court was certain that the culprit was guilty of murder but was unable to pronounce a death sentence because of legal technicalities (if there is insufficient evidence in law to convict and execute a culprit in crimes other than murder, but that also involve capital punishment, the accused is, nonetheless, acquitted); to one found guilty of causing a murder by hiring an assassin; and as detention during judicial investigation and prior to execution. In post-Talmudic times, imprisonment was a common punishment imposed by Jewish courts in the framework of Jewish *autonomy. Sometimes the community had its own prison; if not, the person sentenced would be handed over to the non-Jewish authorities for the imposition of the punishment. From the fourteenth century on, imprisonment was applied for a variety of offenses ranging from sexual crimes to gambling. Imprisonment for debt, previously rejected by the rabbis, was instituted by communities, although this development was sharply disputed by rabbinic authorities. The subject was also debated in the State of Israel before a 1967 law allowed imprisonment for debt in certain extreme cases, but for a maximum of twenty-one days.

• Menachem Elon, *Jewish Law: History, Sources, Principles*, 4 vols. (Philadelphia, 1994).

IMPURITY (Heb. *tum'ah*). Ritual impurity results from a flux issuing from a man or woman (*Lv.* 15.2, 25); menstruation (*Lv.* 15.19); childbirth (*Lv.* 12.2); leprosy (*Lv.* 13.1ff.); and semen (*Lv.* 15.15). Contact with a corpse (*Nm.* 19.11); carrion (*Lv.* 11.26, 39); creeping things (*Lv.* 11.29–31); the burning of the red heifer (*Nm.* 19.7); the burning of certain sacrifices (*Lv.* 4.12, 4.21, 4.26; 16.27–28); or the scapegoat as it is led away (*Lv.* 16.26) also creates a state of ritual impurity. Those impurities mentioned specifically in the Pentateuch are called *avot ha-tum'ah*. Items rendered impure by *avot ha-tum'ah* are called *ri'shon le-tum'ah* (first degree of impurity); items rendered impure by *ri'shon le-tum'ah* are called *sheni le-tum'ah* (second degree impurity). Most authorities rule that *tum'ah* expires at the fourth level, but some contend that it expires at the third or fifth. Holy objects (e.g., sacrificial meat, heave offerings) that are defiled become unfit for consumption and must be burned. A state of impurity lasts for varying periods and is removed by immersion in the *miqveh, by offering sacrifices for more serious cases, and in some cases also by the sprinkling of the ashes of the red heifer (*Nm.* 19). A person in a state of impurity is not allowed to touch holy objects, enter the Temple precincts, partake of sacred foods, or (in the case of a menstruating woman, a woman after childbirth, or a woman with a flux of blood) have marital contact. Leprosy precludes normal intercourse with other people. The biblical laws of ritual purity (*tohorah*) and impurity are set out mainly in the *Book of Leviticus*; in the Talmud the entire order *Tohorot is devoted to the subject. Much attention is paid to the impurity of vessels, clothes, and food. Most of the relevant laws ceased to apply after the destruction of the Temple, and all Jews are now regarded as being in a state of ritual impurity. For this reason many Orthodox Jews will not approach the Temple mount in Jerusalem, for which full ritual purity is essential. See also ABLUTION; HOLINESS; NIDDAH.

• Shimon D. Eider, *Halachos of Niddah* (Lakewood, N.J., 1981–). Hannah K. Harrington, *The Biblical Foundations of the Impurity Systems of the Qumran Sectaries and the Rabbis* (Atlanta, 1993). Aryeh Kaplan, *Waters of Eden: An Exploration of the Concept of Mikvah* (New York, 1984). Jacob Neusner, *A History of the Mishnaic Law of Purities* (Leiden, 1974–1977). Jacob Neusner, *Purity in Rabbinic Judaism* (Atlanta, 1994).

INCENSE (Heb. *qetoret*) Fragrant incense was to be offered twice daily on the gold-plated incense altar inside the Tabernacle (*Ex.* 30.1–10). A similar, but larger, gold altar was erected in Solomon's Temple (*1 Kgs.* 6.20, 22, 7.48) for the burning of incense, as well as in the Second Temple. Incense was used throughout the ancient world (as an inhalant or for cosmetic purposes) by kings and on special occasions. Its use in the Tabernacle symbolized obeisance to the deity, perceived to be enshrined in his earthly abode. The incense used in the Tabernacle consisted of four ingredients (*Exodus* 30.34), the most precious being pure frankincense. The Talmud (*Ker.* 6a) mentions seven additional ingredients, including one called *ma'aleh 'ashan*, which caused the smoke to rise in a straight column. Rabbinic tradition states that extraordinary care was taken in the preparation of the incense, and the repetition in the phrase "pound well, well pound" indicates the belief that "noise [possibly meaning the regular rhythm] is beneficial to the fragrance." The recipe for the altar incense was not to be used for any other purpose (*Ex.* 30.37–38), and the rabbis considered the omission of even one ingredient a capital offense. A special ceremony took place annually on *Yom Kippur, when the high priest entered the Holy of Holies (*Lv.* 16.12–13) in a cloud of smoke, carrying a censer filled with incense taken from the altar. The stated purpose was to screen himself from the "fatal" presence of the deity; but the rabbis tended to reject this explanation (*Yoma'* 5.1–2). Incense was probably offered, in censers and not on altars, as part of the Israelite cult in biblical times (cf. *Nm.* 17.11), but with the centralization of the cult, this practice fell into desuetude. Though incense plays no part in post-Temple worship, its role in ancient times and its symbolic significance as a spiritual rising to God are recalled in the references to it included in the daily prayer service (see PITTUM HA-QETORET).

• M. D. Fowler, "Excavated Incense Burners," *Biblical Archaeologist* 47 (1984): 183–186. Menahem Haran, *Temples and Temple-Service in Ancient Israel* (Winona Lake, Ind., 1985), pp. 205–245. Jacob Milgrom, *Leviticus 1–16*, The Anchor Bible, vol. 3 (New York, 1991), pp. 1014–1015, 1028–1030. Kjeld Nielsen, *Incense in Ancient Israel*, Supplements to Vetus Testamentum, no. 38 (Leiden, 1986). —BARUCH J. SCHWARTZ

INCEST (*gillui 'arayot*). The family relationships that constitute incest in the biblical view are specified in *Leviticus* 18.6–18. The list includes only primary relationships, such as parents and sisters-in-law. The rabbis extended this list with twenty additional relationships, including secondary relationships, such as a paternal grandmother and a son's daughter-in-law (*Yev.* 21a). Primary incest carries either the death penalty or **karet*. In some cases both penalties are prescribed (*Ker.* 1.1). Only the product of primary incest is a **mamzer*. Whereas there can be no valid marriage among the primary degrees of consanguinity, marriages among secondary degrees are valid, and require a legal divorce in the event of their termination. Incest is one of the three cardinal offenses which a person may not commit even in order to save himself from certain death (*San.* 74a). According to some authorities, however, a woman, being the passive partner, may submit to incest rather than suffering death (Rema', *Yoreh De'ah* 157.1). See also MARRIAGES, PROHIBITED; SEXUAL OFFENSES.

• H. Cohn, "Incest," in *The Principles of Jewish Law*, edited by Menachem Elon (Jerusalem, 1975), pp. 487–488. —DANIEL SINCLAIR

INCLINATION, GOOD AND EVIL. See GOOD AND EVIL.

INDEMNITY. Injury to another's person is considered equivalent to damage inflicted upon the person's property (*San.* 2b), and in both instances financial compensation and restitution are obligatory. In cases of personal injury, indemnity consists of payment based on the injury itself, pain suffered, medical expenses arising from the injury, loss of earnings incurred, and indignity suffered. In estimating the amount due for indignity suffered, the sensitivity of the victim, the circumstances surrounding the incident, and the standing and intention of the perpetrator are all taken into account. A halakhic principle states that two punishments cannot be meted out for a single offense; therefore, one who is obligated to pay an indemnity receives no corporal or other punishment. Crimes punishable by monetary indemnity are not considered criminal offenses.

• Menachem Elon, *Jewish Law: History, Sources, Principles*, 4 vols. (Philadelphia, 1994).

INDEPENDENCE DAY, ISRAEL. See YOM HA-'ATSMA'UT.

INFERTILITY. See BARRENNESS.

INFORMING. See DENUNCIATION.

INGATHERING OF THE EXILES. See EXILES, INGATHERING OF THE.

INHERITANCE. The biblical order of inheritance is the deceased man's son, daughter, brothers, father's line and the next of kin (*Nm.* 27.8–11). A daughter succeeding to her father's estate was required to marry into her father's tribe so that "the inheritance of the Children of Israel shall not move from tribe to tribe" (*Nm.* 36.6–7). The Talmud, however, confines this requirement to the generation entering the Promised Land (*B. B.* 120a). It is settled law that a husband inherits from his wife, although the question of whether or not this is a biblical rule is disputed (Maimonides, *Laws of Inheritance* 1.8). Under Talmudic law, a father inherits from his son (*B. B.* 8:2). Jewish law operates with a parentelic system of succession, that is, all the kin of the deceased in the agnate (paternal) line stand to inherit along both descending and ascending branches. A mother does not inherit from her sons, nor do her brothers or other relatives. Sons do, however, inherit from their mothers (*B. B.* 8.1). *Mamzerut* does not detract from inheritance rights under Jewish law (*Yev.* 2.5). The right of primogeniture applies under biblical law (*Dt.* 21.16–17), and if the firstborn son predeceases his father, then the double share is passed on to his heirs. A firstborn's double portion is equivalent to the portions of two ordinary heirs and it is taken out of the estate assets at the time of the father's death; future earnings are not taken into account (*B. B.* 142b). The right of inheritance carries with it the obligation to pay any debts owed by the deceased, and the firstborn's double portion includes debts as well as assets (*B. B.* 124a). Various *taqqanot* were introduced, from the Talmudic period onwards, for the purpose of ameliorating the bias toward the male line in inheritance law. Under the Mishnaic *taqqanah* of *ketubbat benin dikhrin*, the sons of a wife who predeceased her husband would be the sole inheritors of their mother's *ketubbah* and dowry. These assets would not be shared with other sons of the father upon his death (*Ket.* 52b). In the Middle Ages, the trend toward restricting the inheritance of a woman's dowry to her sons and other relatives continued, and even the husband was generally limited to only one-half of her estate (Rema', *Even ha-'Ezer* 118.80). A wife is not a legal heir to her husband's estate (*B. B.* 8.1), but is entitled to receive her ketubbah, the dowry increment, and any property designated as hers which she brought into the marriage. Daughters must be maintained out of their dead father's estate and if there is not enough property for both inheritance and maintenance purposes, then the daughters receive maintenance and the sons "go begging for a living" (*Ket.* 4.6). If there are no sons but only daughters, then they simply share the estate (*Shulḥan 'Arukh, Even ha-'Ezer* 112.18). Sons are obliged to give their deceased father's daughters part of the estate as a dowry. The size of the dowry portion is worked out on the basis of the amount the father would have given to his daughters had he still been alive. If no such estimate is possible then the amount is fixed at one-tenth of the estate (*Ket.* 68a). In Ashkenazi communities, the custom arose of writing a deed at the time of a daughter's marriage in which her father undertook to pay her a large sum one hour prior to his death, with a condition exempting his sons from paying the debt if they gave her half of all the assets (Rema', *Ḥoshen Mishpat* 28.1.7).

• Menachem Elon, *Jewish Law: History, Sources, Principles* (Philadelphia, 1994). Ben Tzion Greenberger, "Rabbi Herzog's Proposals for *Takkanot* in Matters of Inheritance," in *The Halakhic Thought of R. Isaac Herzog*, edited by Bernard Jackson, Jewish Law Association Studies, vol. 5 (Atlanta, 1991), pp. 57–112. Isidor Grunfeld, *The Jewish Law of Inheritance: Problems and Solutions in Making a Jewish Will* (Jerusalem, New York, and Oak Park, Mich., 1987). Moses Mielziner, *The Rabbinical Law of Hereditary Succession* (Cincinnati, 1900). Reuven Yaron, *Gifts in Contemplation of Death in Jewish and Roman Law* (Oxford, 1960).

—DANIEL SINCLAIR

INITIALS. See ABBREVIATIONS.

INJURY. See TORTS.

INNOCENCE. In Jewish law, a person is presumed innocent until proved guilty. Neither hearsay nor circumstantial *evidence (especially in capital cases) is allowed to undermine the presumption. In criminal cases, the presumption of innocence is so strong that the accused must virtually have surrendered to the consequences of the act in front of witnesses in order to be found guilty (see WARNING), while self-incrimination has no validity in law. A presumption of innocence is grounded in the essential trustworthiness and moral dignity ascribed to the individual.

• Menachem Elon, *Jewish Law: History, Sources, Principles*, 4 vols. (Philadelphia, 1994).

INQUISITION, an ecclesiastical court ("Holy Office") set up by the Catholic church for the trial of heretics; that is, those who had abandoned the religious tenets and beliefs of the Catholic faith in which they had been brought up or that they had adopted. It first became prominent in Europe in the thirteenth century when it was established to deal with the heretical Albigenses in southern France. Its operation was mainly entrusted to the Dominicans. It had no jurisdiction over persons other than members of the church, including such Jews as had, voluntarily or otherwise, formally adopted Christianity. These were regarded as guilty of heresy when reverting to Jewish practice and belief. The Inquisition is best known for its relentless pursuit of the descendants of converted Jews in Spain in the late fifteenth century and afterward. It was introduced into the united kingdoms of Castile, Aragon, and Navarre by Ferdinand and Isabella and lasted for nearly 350 years, from the first auto-da-fé held in Seville in 1481 until its final abolition in 1834. Both the Spaniards and the Portuguese carried it to their overseas possessions in America and India. In northern Portugal alone, over nine hundred communities were victimized by the Inquisition between 1565 and 1595, and estimates are given that the Spanish Inquisition sentenced over thirty thousand *Marranos to be burned at the stake, with another sixteen thousand punished *in absentia* by being burnt in effigy.

• Haim Beinart, *Conversos on Trial: The Inquisition in Ciudad Real*, translated by Yael Guiladi (Jerusalem, 1981). Haim Beinart, *The Records of the Inquisition: A Source of Jewish and Converso History* (Jerusalem, 1967). Eleanor Hibbert, *The Spanish Inquisition: Its Rise, Growth, and End* (New York, 1967). Benzion Netanyahu, *The Origins of the Inquisition in Fifteenth-Century Spain* (New York, 1995).

INSANITY, the state of being permanently deranged. One who suffers temporary, occasional, or periodic bouts of insanity or epileptic fits is considered sane and responsible during his lucid periods (Y., *Ter.* 81). Examples of the symptoms of insanity given by the rabbis include going out alone at night, sleeping in a cemetery, tearing one's garments, or destroying all that one has been given (*Ḥag.* 3b; *Ter.* 1.3). It is not necessary for all of the symptoms to be present, and a rational explanation must be lacking for the symptoms. A generally muddle-headed and irresponsible demeanor is also considered evidence of insanity. People suffering from insanity are free from all religious obligations or punishment and are not responsible in law for any tort committed by them. Their dealings have no legal validity, and they are classed together with the deaf and dumb mute and the minor. They are, however, to be compensated for any wrongful act committed against them or their property (*B. Q.* 87a). If adjudged dangerously insane, they may be placed in protective custody in order to safeguard others. They are, however, to be periodically examined, and upon recovery, their civil rights are fully reinstated. Insane persons cannot marry, since the consent of both parties is necessary. A man who becomes insane after marriage cannot give his wife a bill of divorce (*Git.* 71b); a woman who becomes insane after marriage legally can be divorced, but the rabbis forbade such an action on humanitarian grounds, though in special cases they permitted the husband to take a second wife upon receiving permission from a hundred rabbis (*Shulḥan ʿArukh, Even ha-ʿEzer* 1.10).

• Tzvi Marx, *Halakha and Handicap: Jewish Law and Ethics on Disability* (Jerusalem and Amsterdam, 1992). Julius Preuss, *Biblical and Talmudic Medicine*, edited and translated by Fred Rosner (New York, 1993). Moshe Halevi Spero, *Handbook of Psychotherapy and Jewish Ethics* (Jerusalem, 1986).

INSPIRATION, the condition of being directly under divine influence so that the spirit of God enters into an individual. Since inspiration emanates from God, it is free from human error. Biblical prophecy is a classical example of inspiration, and as a result the one criterion in selecting and determining the biblical canon was whether the books under review were "composed under divine inspiration" (*Meg.* 7a). However, inspiration was not confined to the prophets. Bezalel, the architect of the Sanctuary in the wilderness, was "filled with the spirit of God" (*Ex.* 31.3, 35.1); it came to the heathen prophet Balaam to enable him to utter his prophecies (*Nm.* 24.2); and it also descended on seventy elders (*Nm.* 11.17) and enabled them to prophesy. Although inspiration is considered to have ceased with the last prophets—Haggai, Zechariah, and Malachi—(*San.* 11a), the Talmud does not hesitate to ascribe inspiration to the authoritative Aramaic translation of the Bible by Yonatan ben ʿUzzi'el (*Meg.* 3a), as Philo does to the Septuagint (*Vita Moysis* 2.7; *Letter of Aristeas* 305–317). Although nowhere in the Talmud is there explicit mention of different degrees of inspiration between the Pentateuch, the Prophets, and the Hagiographa—all having been "composed under divine inspiration"—such a difference is implicit in a comparison of the manner in which Moses received the divine message with that of the later prophets: "If there be a prophet among you, I the Lord will make myself known to him in a vision, and will speak with him in a dream. Not so my servant Moses. . . . With him will I speak mouth to mouth, even manifestly and not in dark speeches" (*Nm.* 12.6–8)—that is, inspiration came to the other prophets while their cognitive faculties were in a state of suspended animation (in trances, in dreams, and in ecstasy), whereas Moses alone was inspired while in full possession of his normal cognitive faculties. This difference is succinctly expressed by the rabbinic statement that whereas other prophets saw God "through nine glasses," Moses saw him "through one lens" or "through a clear lens" (*Lv. Rab.* 1.14). Maimonides, on the other hand, specifically lays down three descending degrees of inspiration for the three sections of the Bible (*Guide of the Perplexed* 2.45). The belief in the descent or action of the Holy Spirit or other celestial agencies was common among charismatic mystics and kabbalists. Orthodox Judaism still holds to a strict belief in the verbal inspiration of the Pentateuch and rejects the modern critical study of the text. Conservative and Reform Jews believe that an honest reading of the Torah requires that it be placed in its historical context. Such a reading finds that the text itself is composed of at least four documents (the documentary hypothesis), which were committed to writing at different times and places. While this history of the transmission of the Torah makes some Jews (especially Reconstructionists) believe that the entire Torah was written by human beings without divine inspiration, that is not the majority view. Some Conservative and Reform Jews believe that God spoke words at Sinai; it is just that the record we have in hand was written by human beings in varying time periods and therefore is subject to the normal historical analysis through which every human document can be better understood. Other Conservative and Reform Jews believe that Moses and the later authors who wrote in his name were inspired by God to write the words included in the Torah in a process of inspiration similar to that of a great poet or musician. They then suggest various reasons as to why the inspiration contained in the Torah is more authoritative than any other inspiration. Still others believe that human beings wrote the Torah in response to their experiences with God in an effort to articulate the substance and import of those experiences for them and their religious community. These varying theories of both the authorship of the Torah text and the process of inspiration that produced it have major implications for the meaning and authority of the Torah, issues addressed by the ideologies of all modern movements. See also REVELATION.

• Philip Goodman, ed., *A Treasury of Jewish Inspiration* (New York, 1962). Abraham Joshua Heschel, "Prophetic Inspiration," in *To Grow in Wisdom: An Anthology*, edited by Jacob Neusner (Lanham, Md., 1990).

INSULT is regarded as an injury in Jewish law and as such requires compensation. In cases of bodily injury, the insult, or shame (*boshet*), involved is considered an additional count in determining the extent of damages; for example, the shame endured by one who has been maimed or the shame suffered by the family of a female who has been raped. The compensation for insult "is in accordance with the standing of him that inflicts the indignity and him that suffers the indignity" (*Ket*. 3.7). Insulting a scholar or displaying insulting behavior in court was usually dealt with by rebuke and partial ostracism of the culprit. The rabbis decreed that "one who insults his fellow in public has no share in the world to come" (*B. M.* 58b).

• Kevin Cathcart, "*Boset* in Zephaniah 3:5," *Journal of Northwest Semitic Languages* 12 (1984): 35–39. Menachem Elon, *Jewish Law: History, Sources, Principles*, 4 vols. (Philadelphia, 1994).

INSURANCE. The insurance contract is not referred to as a distinct legal vehicle in the biblical or Talmudic literature, although there is mention in the Talmud of what was, in effect, a mutual insurance arrangement within guilds or professional associations. In that instance, the risk of loss of a vessel or of pack-animals was spread among all members of the group, and any loss suffered by one member of the group would be compensated by the group as a whole. As the concept of insurance developed in the general commercial environment of the post-Talmudic Diaspora, a need arose to examine the various insurance-related devices from the perspective of Jewish law, in order to determine whether the use of such devices involved any halakhic prohibitions, primarily that of *ribbit* (usury); and whether their use could be recognized as binding based on existing doctrines, such as bailment (where the shipper acts as insurer), surety (where the insurer is a third party), and commercial custom (*situmta'*).

A classic example of an early form of insurance was the maritime loan, whereby the shipping agent received a loan to finance the purchase of the vessel or the goods, and agreed that upon safe arrival at his destination, he would repay the loan plus an additional sum (in effect, an insurance premium), calculated as a percentage of the loan, in consideration of the lender's assumption of the risk in the event that the ship or the goods were lost en route. Most authorities ruled that such an arrangement was tainted by the *ribbit* prohibition, since the additional sum being paid by the borrower, while designated as "insurance," constituted, in effect, the payment of interest.

The first mention of modern insurance, where a premium is paid in advance to cover the risk of loss, is to be found in the precedent-setting *responsa* of R. Yitsḥaq bar Sheshet of Spain in the fourteenth century. He ruled, as have many halakhic authorities down to the present time, that no comparable problem of *ribbit* exists in the standard insurance contract, since the premium is not related to a loan of any kind, and the contract was indeed binding under accepted Jewish legal principles. Similar rulings are to be found in the *responsa* literature regarding fire, theft, health and life insurance policies.

• Stephen M. Passamaneck, *Insurance in Rabbinic Law* (Edinburgh, 1974). Menachem Slae, *Ha-Bittuaḥ ba-Halakhah* (Tel Aviv, 1980).

—BEN TZION GREENBERGER

INTELLECT. The exact meaning of the term (Gr. *nous*, Lat. *intellectus*, Arab. *'aql*, Heb. *sekhel*) and its synonyms (in Hebrew, e.g., *da'at*, *binah*, *tevunah*) vary according to the context and the vocabulary of writers. Aristotelian philosophy spoke of "separate intellects," meaning spiritual and non-material entities derived from the highest being; hence angels came to be called, in medieval philosophical Hebrew, "separate intelligences" (*sekhalim nifradim*). Alexander of Aphrodisias (c.200) defined Aristotle's "active intellect" as that aspect of the deity with which the highest part of the human soul could be in touch. The term thus acquired a very specific technical meaning with obvious religious implications: knowledge of God equals communion with God. Human perfection, the attainment of prophecy, perhaps even immortality, were due to contact with the divine active intellect, whereby the highest potentiality of the *soul could become realized in "acquired intellect." This doctrine became dominant in philosophy through the influence of Moses *Maimonides and was echoed by his followers, such as Yosef ben Abba' Mari *Caspi and *Levi ben Gershom. The doctrine as well as the rationalistic approach underlying it, which appeared to put a premium on intellectual understanding rather than the love of God, were opposed by the critics of Aristotelianism, such as Ḥasda'i ben Avraham *Crescas.

• Kalman Bland, ed. and trans., *The Epistle on the Possibility of Conjunction with the Active Intellect by Ibn Rushd with the Commentary of Moses Narboni* (New York, 1982). Philip David Bookstaber, *The Idea of Development of the Soul in Medieval Jewish Philosophy* (Philadelphia, 1950). Seymour Feldman, ed. and trans., *Levi ben Gershom: The Wars of the Lord* (Philadelphia, 1984). Norbert Samuelson, *The Exalted Faith of Abraham ibn Daud* (London, 1986).

INTENT, corresponds to two Hebrew terms, *kavvanah* and *ẓadon*.

Kavvanah means intent, in both a legal and moral sense, and devotion, in the sense of spiritual concentration, particularly accompanying religious exercises or the performance of a commandment with a view to establishing **devequt* (communion) with God. The Talmudic discussion of whether "the performance of a commandment requires *kavvanah*" (*'Eruv*. 95b) and the rabbinic statement that *kavvanah* is essential to *prayer (in particular the Shema', cf. *Ber*. 16a) both refer to the general intent of one's actions. "When standing in prayer one should direct one's mind to God" (*Ber*. 31a). According to the Mishnah (*Ber*. 5.11), the early Hasideans waited an hour before reciting the 'Amidah so as to be in the appropriate frame of mind (*Ber.* 5.1). Maimonides ruled that prayer without *kavvanah* was not accounted as prayer and that if a person prayed without *kavvanah* he should repeat the prayer with *kavvanah* (referring apparently to the first section of the ʿAmidah). The person praying should empty his heart of all other thoughts "and regard himself as though standing in the divine presence" (*Hilkhot Tefillah* 4.15; cf. *Guide of the Perplexed* 3.51). Medieval mystics developed the concept of *kavvanah* to mean systematic meditation during prayer; this method reached its height in the kabbalistic system of Yitsḥaq *Luria. Moralists and spiritual writers (such as Natan Netaʿ Hannover and Yeshaʿyahu Horowitz) composed special prayers to be recited before the performance of specific ritual obligations (donning *tefillin*, counting the ʿOmer, entering the synagogue, etc.) with the purpose of giving expression to the spiritual meaning underlying the outward action. These prescribed meditations are called *kavvanot*.

Zadon is a legal term; to be culpable in law, intention (*zadon*) must be proven (see Warning). Where such intention is lacking, the Bible imposes compensatory ritual obligations in a limited number of cases (mainly those concerned with the performance of ritual, with purity, and with prohibitions involving excision from the community).

• Howard Eilberg-Schwartz, *The Human Will in Judaism: The Mishnah's Philosophy of Intention* (Atlanta, 1986). Gershom Gerhard Scholem, "The Concept of *Kavvanah* in the Early Kabbalah," in *Studies in Jewish Thought*, edited by A. Jospe (Detroit, 1981), pp. 162–180. Tzvee Zahavy, "Kavvanah for Prayer in the Mishnah and the Talmud," in *Religion, Literature, and Society in Ancient Israel, Formative Judaism, and Christianity*, edited by Jacob Neusner et al. (Lanham, Md., 1987).

INTERCALATION. See Calendar.

INTEREST. See Moneylending.

INTERFAITH RELATIONS. The modern interfaith movement is based on a number of principles which distinguish it from other attempts at interreligious exchange in the past. It is conceived of as an open encounter between believers of different faiths whose intention is to listen to each other, to understand each other, and to work together. The dialogue takes place on the basis of full equality between the partners. An important aspect of interfaith dialogue is that it is not intended to convert the other to one's own beliefs, and an effort is made to exclude any attitude of triumphalism, which has so often in the past characterized religious attitudes.

The emergence of the Christian ecumenical movement was one of the decisive reasons for the development of the modern interfaith movement. The division of the Christian churches was increasingly felt by a great number of believers to be no longer acceptable. This conviction led to the creation of a movement aimed at the restoration of Christian unity; it found its expression notably in the formation, in 1948, of the World Council of Churches, to which today several hundred Protestant and Orthodox churches belong. At the Second Vatican Council in Rome, the Roman Catholic church decided to join the ecumenical movement, while maintaining its full organizational independence. Religious dialogue between the various Christian churches and communities has become one of the most important methods in trying to overcome the present divisions and in preparing the way toward achieving a greater measure of Christian unity.

Another important factor in opening the way to interreligious dialogue with Jews was the recognition by large Christian circles of the silence and passivity of the Christian churches in the face of the brutal anti-Jewish persecutions by the Nazis, and during the whole period of the Holocaust, and the necessity to understand the consequences of this dismal failure. This led to a reexamination of the basic teachings by the Christian churches on Jews and Judaism, and to the gradual elaboration of a new Christian theology on Judaism. The "Declaration on the Relationship of the Church to non-Christian Religions" (*Nostra aetate*, no. 4) of the Ecumenical Council Vatican II states: "Since the spiritual patrimony common to Christians and Jews is thus so great, this Second Synod wishes to foster and recommend that mutual understanding and respect which is the fruit above all of biblical and theological studies, and of brotherly dialogues." The new attitudes were developed in two further documents: *Guidelines* for implementing *Nostra aetate* (1975) and *Notes on the Current Way to Present Jews and Judaism in Preaching and Catachesis* (1985). The International Council of Christians and Jews and the national groups affiliated with it have been the pioneers of the dialogue between Christians and Jews. The participants in these meetings did not speak officially on behalf of their churches or communities but they prepared the ground, on a voluntary basis, for a new Christian–Jewish relationship.

A further development was the institution of official consultations between the churches and representatives of the world Jewish community. The first such encounter of a real international character was arranged in 1968, between the World Council of Churches and representatives of the world Jewish community. This led to regular meetings in the following years. Similar encounters took place in various countries on the national level. They were followed, on the Catholic side, by the establishment in 1970 of an International Catholic–Jewish Liaison Committee, the official dialogue organ between the Catholic church and the Jewish community, which since its formation has met regularly. The consultations with the World Council also continued and produced the document, "Ecumenical Considerations on Jewish–Christian Dialogue," published by the Executive Committee of the World Council of Churches on 16 July 1982. In addition, special meetings between the representatives of the various confessional families belonging to the World Council and representatives of the Jewish community have taken place since 1976. This was notably the case with regard to the Lutheran World Federation, the Anglican Communion, and the Orthodox churches. The top-level documents and meetings have been reflected also at a grass-roots level (though not everywhere). In the United States, for example, interfaith activities have become common in most larger communities. Attempts have also been made to extend the Christian–Jewish dialogue to the Muslim community. While several such meetings have taken place—mostly on a regional or national level—the political climate so far has not allowed a real breakthrough in this field.

In a world in which religious pluralism has become a reality, the interfaith movement has led to a series of interconfessional meetings, in which major political and social problems have been discussed and in which solutions for the burning questions with which the world is confronted have been sought. Not all of these initiatives have come from the West; important suggestions have originated from leaders of the Eastern religions in India, Japan and other Far Eastern countries. Most of the conferences have had as a major topic the problem of maintaining peace in a divided world. The World Conference on Religions and Peace has made this issue its major concern, and holds regular meetings on the international and regional level to this effect. Other groups have chosen different items for discussion. Interesting initiatives have been undertaken in the fields of social justice and ecology. In general, Jews have welcomed the dialogue. The main objection comes from the strictly Orthodox community, which refuses to participate, and there is a suspicion in certain Orthodox circles that Christians retain a hidden missionizing agenda. Many Orthodox Jews follow the guidelines established by R. Yosef Dov *Soloveichik, according to which interreligious dialogue may not include theological issues but must be restricted to subjects of common social concern.

• Helga Croner, ed., *More Stepping Stones to Jewish–Christian Relations: An Unabridged Collection of Christian Documents, 1975–1983* (New York, 1985). Helga Croner, ed., *Stepping Stones to Further Jewish–Christian Relations* (London and New York, 1977). *Fifteen Years of Catholic–Jewish Dialogue, 1970–1985: Selected Papers* (Vatican City, 1988). *Jewish Christian Dialogue: Six Years of Christian–Jewish Consultations*, published by the International Jewish Committee on Interreligious Consultations and the World Council of Churches Sub-Unit on Dialogue with the People of Living Faiths and Ideologies (Geneva, 1975). Leon Klenicki and Geoffrey Wigoder, eds., *A Dictionary of the Jewish–Christian Dialogue*, expanded ed. (New York, 1995). Malcolm Lowe, ed., "Orthodox Christians and Jews on Continuity and Renewal: The Third Academic Meeting between Orthodoxy and Judaism" *Immanuel* 26–27 (1994): 7–249. James Parkes, *Prelude to Dialogue* (London, 1969). John Pawlikowski, *What Are They Saying About Christian–Jewish Relations* (New York, 1980). Geoffrey Wigoder, *Jewish–Christian Relations since the Second World War* (Manchester, 1988).

—GERHART M. RIEGNER

INTERMARRIAGE, marriage between a Jew and a non-Jew. In an alternative contemporary usage, intermarriage refers to any marriage of a Jew to someone who was born a non-Jew, with "conversionary marriage" used when the originally non-Jewish partner converts to Judaism and "mixed marriage" used when the non-Jewish partner remains a non-Jew. Since intermarriage is still most widely understood in its original sense, it will be so used here.

Intermarriage was always discouraged among Jews (*Dt.* 7.3–4) and was forbidden by Jewish law by the Second Temple period. When *Ezra returned from exile, he found extensive intermarriage with pagan women and got a promise that they would be banished (*Ezr.* 9–10). Indeed, intermarriages have no standing in Judaism's legal system. Since the children of invalid marriages acquire their mother's legal status, the children of intermarriages, according to Jewish law, are Jewish only if their mothers are Jewish. This matter is complicated, however, by two factors: the decision of the Reform movement, in 1983, to recognize as Jewish any child of intermarriage who publicly and formally identifies as a Jew, regardless of which parent is Jewish (see PATRILINEAL DESCENT); and the fact that open, democratic societies treat *Jewish identity as a personal option, rather than as a collective status over which a recognized group has formal control.

The opposition to intermarriage in Jewish history flows from Judaism's definition of Jewishness as familial, that is, not as a consequence of any given belief or specific act, but rather as descent from Abraham through Isaac and Jacob. A non-Jew who wishes to join the covenantal relationship does so by symbolically becoming a child of those same ancestors (see PROSELYTE). Opposition to intermarriage also has sociological roots, based on the view that Jewish identity is transmitted through socialization in the context of family life, with the result that the children of intermarried couples are not likely to be Jewish in the sociocultural sense, regardless of their status in Jewish law.

Until recently, intermarriage was seen, accurately in most cases, as a rebellion against or at least as a quiet renunciation of Jewishness, and the response by relatives, friends, and the Jewish community was usually severe. Intermarried Jews were often totally shunned, even treated symbolically as having died.

In more recent decades, there have been major changes. For most Jews, the scope and content of Jewish identity have changed. (The exceptions are, generally, the very traditional and, less frequently, those religious liberals whose lives are pervasively and profoundly shaped by their Jewishness.) The diminution of the scope of Jewishness in most Jews' lives has allowed intermarriage to be compatible with their continued Jewish identity. As a result, the rate of intermarriage has soared to the point that, according to recent studies, more than half of American Jews who now marry choose non-Jewish spouses. Intermarriage is much more widely accepted among Jews than ever before, not only in Diaspora communities, but in Israel as well. While intermarriage is still spoken of as a problem by Jewish organizations and communal leaders, most of them, especially the non-traditional, tend to emphasize cordiality and outreach over the application of negative sanctions. Many Jewish organizations (including liberal synagogues) now have significant numbers of intermarried Jews and their non-Jewish spouses among their members, and, therefore, it is not easy for these organizations, despite their official position, to conduct programs that explicitly discourage intermarriage or even convey convincingly the importance of marrying within the Jewish faith.

A number of Reform rabbis are prepared to officiate at

intermarriages so as not to alienate the Jewish participant from the community and in the hope that children of such marriages will be brought up as Jews. Reconstructionist rabbis officiate if the marriage is under secular auspices but not in a church.

• American Jewish Committee, *The Intermarriage Crisis: Jewish Communal Perspectives and Responses* (New York, 1991). Steven Bayme and Gladys Rosen, eds., *The Jewish Family and Jewish Continuity* (Hoboken, N.J., 1994). Egon Mayer, *Intermarriage and Rabbinic Officiation* (New York, 1989). Ellen Jaffe McClain, *Embracing the Stranger: Intermarriage and the Future of the American Jewish Community* (New York, 1995). Roy A. Rosenberg, *Happily Intermarried: Authoritative Advice for a Joyous Jewish–Christian Marriage* (New York, 1988). Susan W. Schneider, *Intermarriage: The Challenge of Living with Differences between Christians and Jews* (New York, 1989). —MERVIN F. VERBIT

INTERMEDIATE DAYS. See Ḥol ha-Moʿed.

ʿIR HA-NIDDAḤAT (עִיר הַנִּדַּחַת; a city led astray), an Israelite city that worshiped deities other than the Lord, YHVH (*Dt*. 13.13–19). The Bible holds that Israel's very existence is predicated upon exclusive loyalty to the Lord and views the worship of other deities by Israelites as a crime exposing the entire nation to disaster. Therefore, Israelites who worship deities other than the Lord are subject to capital punishment. If the authorities hear that an Israelite city has been led astray, the report is to be investigated carefully; if confirmed, the city's population is to be executed, its contents completely destroyed, and the city itself never to be rebuilt. This law reflects the concept that God is Israel's king and that worshiping other gods is high treason. It has parallels in ancient treaties and similar texts requiring that sedition against the sovereign, by individuals and cities, be reported and punished. Talmudic exegesis holds that the authorities may not seek out such cases on their own but may investigate only if the crime is reported to them by others; the townspeople must be given a chance to reform, and only the guilty are to be punished. The rabbis interpreted the law narrowly and imposed stringent procedural safeguards on the investigation. Because the combination of circumstances they required for applying the law would rarely occur, some held that it was never expected to be applied but was stated in the Torah only to show the gravity of the crime.

• Paul-Eugene Dion, "Deuteronomy 13: The Suppression of Alien Religious Propaganda in Israel during the Late Monarchical Era," in *Law and Ideology in Monarchic Israel*, edited by Baruch Halpern and D. W. Hobson (Sheffield, Eng., 1991), pp. 147–216. Jeffrey H. Tigay, *Deuteronomy*, The JPS Torah Commentary (Philadelphia, 1996). Moshe Weinfeld, *Deuteronomy and the Deuteronomic School* (Oxford, 1972), pp. 91–100. —JEFFREY H. TIGAY

ISAAC (Heb. Yitsḥaq), second of the three *patriarchs; son of *Abraham and *Sarah. Both Abraham and Sarah laughed (*tsaḥaq*) with incredulity when God's angel promised them a son in their old age (*Gn*. 17.17, 18.12); hence, the biblical derivation of Isaac's name. Unlike his half brother Ishmael, Isaac was to be the heir of God's promise to Abraham. Isaac was circumcised at the age of eight days. His supreme trial was the *ʿ*aqedah*. Although this was primarily the story of Abraham's willingness to sacrifice his beloved son at God's bidding (*Gn*. 22.1–19), Isaac's consent to be bound to the altar and sacrificed became symbolic of *qiddush ha-Shem*, the willingness to forfeit one's life for the glory of God. At the age of forty, Isaac married *Rebekah, who bore him *Esau and *Jacob. In old age, he lost his eyesight, and his wish to bestow the patriarchal blessing upon Esau was redirected to Jacob through a ruse of Rebekah. He died at the age of one hundred eighty and was buried by Jacob and Esau in the patriarchal tomb, the cave of *Machpelah (*Gn*. 35.28–29). Isaac's filial loyalty is depicted in many *midrashim* as well as in Islamic lore. Rabbinic tradition credits Isaac with the introduction of the custom of praying each afternoon.

• Nahum M. Sarna, *Understanding Genesis* (New York, 1966), pp. 154–180, 392–394. Claus Westermann, *Genesis 12–36*, translated by John J. Scullion (Minneapolis, 1985), pp. 330–577. —SHALOM PAUL

ISAAC, BINDING OF. See ʿAqedah.

ISAIAH (Heb. Yeshaʿyahu; 8th cent. BCE), son of Amoz; a prophet active in Jerusalem during the reigns of four kings of Judah, Uzziah, Jotham, Ahaz, and Hezekiah (cf. *2 Kgs*. 19–20; *2 Chr*. 26.22, 32.20, 32). Isaiah's sophisticated literary style and easy access to the Judean kings suggest that he was well educated and well connected. He prophesied during the rise of the Neo-Assyrian empire under Tiglath-pileser III and his expansion into the Syro-Israelite region. Major events presupposed in Isaiah's work include the Syro-Ephraimite War (735–732), the fall of the northern kingdom of Israel (722–721), Hezekiah's revolt (705–701), and Sennacherib's siege of Jerusalem (701). Isaiah's prophetic message emphasized the divine guarantee of Jerusalem's security and of eternal rule by the house of David. Isaiah did not hesitate to criticize monarchs when they deviated from what he considered the principles of Davidic rule. Since God, in keeping with his promise, would defend Jerusalem, Isaiah opposed alliances with foreign nations and censured Ahaz for considering an alliance with Assyria when Judah was threatened by Aram and Israel during the Syro-Ephraimite War (chap. 7). Isaiah gave his children symbolic names to illustrate his message. Shear-yashub (A Remnant Will Return) accompanied his father when Isaiah attempted to convince Ahaz to rely on God alone during the Syro-Ephraimite crisis (7.3) and to assure Ahaz that a remnant of Judah would survive, although Shear-jashub's name signifies the remnant of Israel that will return to God (and Davidic rule) following the Assyrian invasions in *Isaiah* 10.20–26. Likewise, Isaiah named another son Mahar-shalal-hash-baz (The Spoil Speeds, the Prey Hastens) to symbolize the defeat of Damascus and Samaria at the hands of the Assyrians during the Syro-Ephraimite War. Another child was named Immanuel (God Is with Us) to signify God's promise of security to Ahaz (7.14). The noun *ʿalmah* (young woman [7.14]), referring to Immanuel's mother, was interpreted by Christian tradition (*Mt*. 1.18–25) as "virgin," and, hence, as a prophecy of the virgin birth of the messianic Son of David. Isaiah criticized Hezekiah for entering alliances with Egypt (chaps. 30–31) and the Babylonians (chap. 39) in preparation for his revolt against Sennacherib, king of Assyria from 705 to 701. *Isaiah* 36–39, however, reports that Hezekiah placed total trust in God during Sennacherib's siege of Jerusalem in 701, which was ended by what was seen as divine intervention that destroyed the Assyrian invaders. According to the pseudepigraphous book, *The Martyrdom of Isaiah* (5.11), the prophet was put to death by King Manasseh when the latter purged Judah of opponents to his syncretistic policies. *Isaiah* 6.3, which portrays the seraphim flying about chanting "Holy, holy, holy is the Lord of hosts, the whole earth is full of his glory" in Isaiah's powerful vision of his commission to the prophetic ministry, is the basis of the *Qedushah prayer in Jewish (and the parallel Sanctus in Christian) liturgy.

The *Book of Isaiah* is the first of the Latter Prophets, although one opinion places *Isaiah* after *Jeremiah* and *Ezekiel* (*B. B.* 14b). According to the superscription in *Isaiah* 1.1, the entire book is attributed to Isaiah ben Amoz, but references to the sixth-century Persian monarch Cyrus II (44.24, 45.1), the Babylonian exile, and the return to Zion have led scholars, beginning with hints by Avraham *ibn Ezra, to conclude that chapters 40–66 were written by a later prophet. Scholarly consensus holds that only *Isaiah* 1–39 contains material from the eighth-century BCE prophet, and even these chapters may contain much later material. Examples include the Hezekiah narratives in *Isaiah* 36–39, which are drawn largely from *2 Kings* 18–20; *Isaiah* 24–27, which appears to be an early form of apocalyptic literature dating to the sixth-century BCE or later; and the oracle against Babylon in *Isaiah* 13–14, which posits the downfall of Babylon, the dominant power of the sixth century (this prophecy, however, may actually refer to Assyria and the demise of one of its kings). *Isaiah* 40–66 reflects the work of an anonymous prophet living in Babylon during the sixth century BCE, designated as Deutero-Isaiah or Second Isaiah, who prophesied that the impending fall of Babylon to Cyrus would signal the return of exiled Jews to Jerusalem. This prophet engaged in an extensive polemic against idols and their worshipers and envisioned the eventual recognition of God's sovereignty by all the nations. Deutero-Isaiah's oracles are characterized by a flowing, picturesque, poetic style, in contrast to the shorter strophic style of *Isaiah* 1–39 (First Isaiah); the presence of Babylon rather than Assyria; his employment of the literary genre of a trial between Israel and its God against the idols and their worshipers; the emphasis on foreign nations' acceptance of God's teachings instead of depiction of their defeat; the glory of the new Jerusalem; the extensive use of traditions from the Pentateuch and literary influences of earlier prophets and psalms. Christian theology interpreted the so-called "suffering servant" of the Second Isaiah (52.13–53.12) as a precursor to Jesus despite the identification of the servant as the people of Israel throughout these chapters. According to many scholars, *Isaiah* 56–66 reflects a different literary style and different concerns, prompting them to identify it as the work of Trito-Isaiah or Third Isaiah (late 6th to late 5th cent.) with a Judean setting. The presence of various authors within the *Book of Isaiah* is generally accepted, and scholars feel that the book was shaped over the course of some four centuries into a relatively coherent whole. *Isaiah* 1–33 focuses on the impending judgment against both Israel and Judah followed by a restored Jerusalem as the center of God's worldwide sovereignty. The second half of *Isaiah* presents contrasting images of the downfall of evil, represented by Edom, and the return of Israel to Zion in a new Exodus through the wilderness (chaps. 34–35); an extended argument that God is the master of creation who is raising up Cyrus and restoring Zion (chaps. 40–54); and exhortational material that calls upon Jews to hold firm to the covenant until the last elements of evil in the world are defeated (chaps. 55–56). One complete scroll of the *Book of Isaiah* and another fragmentary one were found at Qumran among the *Dead Sea Scrolls. *Isaiah* is the single most used source for prophetic readings (*haftarot*) in the synagogue, including all seven "*haftarot* of consolation" read in the weeks between Tishʿah be-'Av and Ro'sh ha-Shanah.

• Peter R. Ackroyd, *Studies in the Religious Traditions of the Old Testament* (London, 1987). R. E. Clements, *Isaiah 1–39*, New Century Bible Commentary (Grand Rapids, 1980). R. E. Clements, *Isaiah and the Deliverance of Jerusalem: A Study of the Interpretation of Prophecy in the Old Testament*, Journal for the Study of the Old Testament, Supplement Series 13 (Sheffield, Eng., 1980). Yehoshua Gitay, *Isaiah and His Audience: The Structure and Meaning of Isaiah 1–12*, Studia Semitica Neerlandica 30 (Assen/Maastricht, 1991). Abraham Joshua Heschel, *The Prophets* (New York, 1969). Stuart A. Irvine, *Isaiah, Ahaz, and the Syro-Ephraimitic Crisis*, Dissertation Series (Society of Biblical Literature), no. 123 (Atlanta, 1990). Otto Kaiser, *Isaiah 1–12*, translated by John Bowden, 2d ed., The Old Testament Library (Philadelphia, 1983). Otto Kaiser, *Isaiah 13–39*, translated by R. A. Wilson, The Old Testament Library (Philadelphia, 1974). Peter Machinist, "Assyria and Its Image in First Isaiah," *Journal of the American Oriental Society* 103 (1983): 709–737. Roy F. Melugin, *The Formation of Isaiah 40–55*, Beihefte zur Zeitschrift für die alttestamentliche Wissenschaft 141 (Berlin, 1976). Christopher R. Seitz, *Zion's Final Destiny: The Development of The Book of Isaiah: A Reassessment of Isaiah 36–39* (Minneapolis, 1991). Marvin A. Sweeney, *Isaiah 1–39: With an Introduction to Prophetic Literature*, The Forms of the Old Testament Literature 16 (Grand Rapids, 1995). Marvin A. Sweeney, "A Philological and Form-Critical Reassessment of Isaiah 8.16–9.6," *Hebrew Annual Review* 14 (1994): 215–231. Claus Westermann, *Isaiah 40–66: A Commentary*, translated by David M. G. Stalker, The Old Testament Library (Philadelphia, 1969). J. William Whedbee, *Isaiah and Wisdom* (Nashville, 1971).

—MARVIN A. SWEENEY

ISAIAH, ASCENSION OF. See Ascension of Isaiah.

ISHBILI, YOM TOV BEN AVRAHAM. See Yom Tov ben Avraham Ishbili.

ISHMAEL (Heb. Yishmaʿe'l), elder son of Abraham. His mother was *Hagar, Sarah's Egyptian handmaiden and Abraham's concubine (*Gn.* 16.15). Ishmael was circumcised by Abraham at the age of thirteen, an age at which the ceremony is still practiced among many Arab peoples. Expelled from his home because of Sarah's jealousy, he fled with his mother to the desert and became an archer. Ishmael married an Egyptian wife (*Gn.* 21.20–21), and his daughter married Esau (from them the heads of the Edomite families were traditionally descended; *Gn.* 25.13–15). Ishmael died at the age of one hundred thirty-seven (*Gn.* 25.17). Arabs trace their ancestry to Ishmael, and in Islam, he is regarded as a prophet. In the Qur'an (*Sura* 37.99–110), he (and not Isaac) is identified as the son about to be sacrificed by

Abraham. In medieval Hebrew usage, Ishmael represents the Muslim world (i.e., the Arabs and later the Turks).

• Israel Eph'al, *The Ancient Arabs* (Jerusalem and Leiden, 1982), pp. 233–240. Nahum M. Sarna, *Understanding Genesis* (New York, 1966), pp. 155–157.

—SHALOM PAUL

ISLAM, the religion founded by *Muḥammad (c.570–632), the spiritual development of which owed much to Jewish as well as Christian contacts and influences. Jewish elements are much in evidence in the *Qur'an, as well as in certain beliefs and institutions of Islam, particularly in its uncompromising *monotheism, which made many medieval Jewish authorities think more highly of Islam than of Christianity. Muḥammad became hostile to the Jews when he was unable to convert them to his religion, but he did not consider them on the same standing as pagans. Jews and Christians, in fact all "peoples of the book" (i.e., peoples with holy scriptures brought by messengers of God, recognized by Islam as precursors of Muḥammad), were to be tolerated, though regarded as inferior and made to suffer various indignities and disabilities (see DHIMMI). Islam, in its turn, profoundly affected Judaism, and both Jewish medieval philosophy and ascetic piety (see, for example, BAḤYA BEN YOSEF IBN PAQUDA') are indebted to the influence of Muslim thinkers and mystics (see SUFISM). The opening of the Shahadah (Confession of Faith, the first of the five pillars of Islam), "there is no God but Allah," is the Islamic counterpart of the *Shema' (cf. *2 Sm.* 22.32, "For who is God save the Lord," and *Ps.* 18.32, "There is no God but the Lord"). Muslim orthodoxy does not recognize saints serving as mediators between the individual and the Creator, and it has no priesthood. Any competent man of good character may conduct the prayer service. Religious leadership rests with scholars and teachers of the law; the central Muslim concept of *shari'a* resembles the **halakhah* of Judaism. The second pillar of Islam is the obligation to pray five times daily—at sunrise, midday, midafternoon, sunset, and at night before retiring—and some scholars have suggested that the Arabian Jews also used to pray five times a day. At first, Muslims turned toward Jerusalem when praying, but Muḥammad later changed the direction to Mecca. Even so, Jerusalem remains, after Mecca and Medina, the third most holy city of Islam, and according to one tradition, a single prayer in Jerusalem outweighs a thousand prayers elsewhere. The hours of prayer are announced by a crier (*muezzin*) from the tower of the mosque, a practice reminiscent of the custom followed in the Temple of Jerusalem, where according to the Talmud an appointed crier used to announce: "Arise, priests to your service, Levites to your platforms, and Israelites to your stands." Instead of the Jewish Sabbath or the Christian Sunday, Muḥammad chose Friday as a day of assembly (possibly influenced by the practice of Arabian Jews to begin the observance of the Sabbath early on Friday), but he did not declare it a day of rest; work is permitted and the day is merely marked by special congregational services and sermons. The third pillar, *zakat* (alms) to the poor, the widowed, and the orphaned, was originally left to individual charity but subsequently became a fixed tax. All Muslims must make a pilgrimage to Mecca at least once in their lifetimes (this is the fourth pillar of Islam), unless physically or financially unable to do so. For regular corporate worship, Muslims pray in mosques, which are similar to the synagogues that most likely served as their models. At first, Muḥammad instituted a fast on the tenth day of the Muslim calendar year ('Ashura', Fast of the Tenth), obviously in imitation of Yom Kippur, observed on 10 Tishrei, but he subsequently revoked the obligation. Instead, he instituted the fast of the month of Ramadan (the ninth month of the Muslim lunar year), which is observed for thirty days, from sunrise to sunset, and is considered the fifth pillar of Islam. Muslims practice circumcision and refrain from the consumption of blood, pork, or the flesh of any animal that "dies of itself." *Jihad* (struggle), that is, holy war, is a duty incumbent upon Muslims but not counted among the pillars of Islam. Followers of Muḥammad share the hope of spreading Islam to the non-Muslim world. This concept requires of Muslims that they subdue the infidel, and they who die in the war for Allah are considered martyrs and guaranteed entry into paradise. Jews under Islam have known occasional periods of fanatical persecution but also of great cultural flowering (such as the golden age of Spanish Jewry). On the whole, Jewish life in the Middle Ages was less precarious under Muslim than under Christian rule. The extent to which Jews shared the culture of their Muslim neighbors is illustrated by the number of Jewish classics (philosophical, ethical, and even halakhic) written in Arabic, as well as by the influence of Muslim thinkers that these works exhibit. In the twentieth century the Muslim–Jewish relationship in many lands deteriorated as a result of Muslim hostility to Zionism and the growth of Islamic fundamentalism. Most Jews living in Muslim lands left them after 1948, notably for the State of Israel.

• Mark R. Cohen, *Under Crescent and Cross* (Princeton, 1994). Henry Corbin, *History of Islamic Philosophy*, translated from French by Liadain Sherrard (London, 1993). Solomon D. Goitein, *Studies in Islamic History and Institutions* (Leiden, 1966). Ignác Goldziher, *Introduction to Islamic Theology and Law*, translated from German by Andras and Ruth Hamori, Modern Classics in Near Eastern Studies (Princeton, 1981). James Heyworth-Dunne, *A Basic Bibliography on Islam*, Muslim World Series, no. 4 (Cairo, 1952). Elie Kedourie, *Islam in the Modern World*, 1st American ed. (New York, 1981). Erwin I. J. Rosenthal, *Judaism and Islam* (London and New York, 1961). Joseph Schacht, *An Introduction to Islamic Law* (Oxford, 1964). Naphtali Wieder, *Hashpa'ot Islamiyyot 'al ha-Pulḥan ha-Yehudi* (Oxford, 1947).

ISRAEL (Heb. Yisra'el), name of honor (meaning God Fights, or He for Whom God Fights, or He Who Fights with God) bestowed upon the patriarch *Jacob after his nocturnal struggle near the brook of Jabbok (*Gn.* 32.24–32). The name was also applied to the whole of Jacob's descendants (the children of Israel or the *Israelites; *Ex.* 1.9). With the dvision of the kingdom after the death of Solomon, the name was used to designate the northern portion only (the southern part was called Judah). The land of Canaan became known as the Land of Israel (see

ERETS YISRA'EL). When the Jewish state was established in 1948, it was named the State of Israel. See also ISRAEL, KINGDOM OF.

• Abraham Arazy, "The Appellations of the Jews (Ioudaios, Hebraios, Israel) in the Literature from Alexander to Justinian," Ph.D. dissertation, New York University, 1977. Peter J. Tomson, "The Names Israel and Jew in Ancient Judaism and in the New Testament [part] I," *Bijdragen: Tijdschrift voor filosofie en Theologie* 47 (1986): 120–140.

ISRAEL, KINGDOM OF, the northern Israelite kingdom during the period of the divided monarchy (c.928–722). After Solomon's death, his son Rehoboam could not mend regional differences and discontent in his kingdom, especially among non-Judahites (*1 Kgs*. 12). David and Solomon's united monarchy was split into two nations, the kingdom of Judah (see JUDAH, KINGDOM OF) and the kingdom of Israel under the leadership of Jeroboam (who had led an unsuccessful revolt against Solomon). The northern tribes comprised the larger territory of Israel. Manasseh, Issachar, Zebulun, Naphtali, Ashar, and Dan were in Galilee, and Reuben, Gad, and part of Manasseh were east of the Jordan. The border between the two kingdoms shifted during the next fifty years as a result of repeated warfare. It became fixed in the mid-ninth century when relations between the two nations improved. The geographical area of Israel, however, continued to change throughout its history depending on the political situation between Israel, the Aramean and Transjordanian kingdoms, and Assyria. In its two centuries of existence, Israel was ruled by nineteen kings from a number of dynasties, none of the lineage of David. Several kings, including the first, Jeroboam, were anointed by prophets. Jeroboam established Israel's capital first at Shechem and then at Penuel. He set up golden calves at Dan and Bethel and designated those shrines as substitutes for the Jerusalem Temple. His religious institutions remained the objects of prophetic rebuke until the demise of the kingdom. Israel's history was marked by civil war, palace revolts, and assassinations, although a few powerful kings brought periods of stability and prosperity to the nation. The Omride dynasty was one of the most successful. Omri (882–871) founded the city of Samaria at a strategic location on Mount Ephraim and moved his capital there from Tirzah. His son Ahab (873–852) married a Phoenician princess, Jezebel, thereby establishing close ties with her homeland, a nation known for its craftsmen and master builders. He expanded Samaria and succeeded militarily. Assyrian documents referred to Israel as "the House of Omri" long after his dynasty ceased to exist. Jeroboam II (789–748), the longest reigning of Israel's kings, expanded its borders up to Damascus, Syria. Samaria reached the zenith of its growth and prosperity during his reign.

Following the death of Jeroboam II a combination of internal anarchy and Assyrian imperialism set in motion Israel's downfall. The Assyrian ruler Tiglath-pileser's conquest of the West (734–732) included most of Israel's territory. Only Samaria and its environs remained; its king, Hoshea, was an Assyrian vassal. Hoshea soon conspired with the Egyptians against Assyria (*2 Kgs*. 17), and Samaria was conquered by Shalmaneser V in 722. Shalmaneser's successor, Sargon II, returned to Samaria in 720 and exiled the population to Assyrian lands (see ASSYRIAN EXILE). Samaria then became an Assyrian provincial administrative center. Captives from other nations, later known as *Samaritans, were settled in Samaria. Based on the striking growth of Jerusalem at that time, it seems that many northerners fled into Judah before the deportations. See also TRIBES OF ISRAEL.

• Yohanan Aharoni, *The Land of the Bible: A Historical Geography*, 2d ed., rev. and enl. (Philadelphia, 1979). Gösta W. Ahlström, *The History of Ancient Palestine* (Minneapolis, 1993). Amnon Ben-Tor, ed., *The Archaeology of Ancient Israel*, translated by R. Greenberg (New Haven, 1992). John Bright, *A History of Israel*, 3d ed. (Philadelphia, 1981). Mordechai Cogan and Hayim Tadmor, *II Kings*, The Anchor Bible, vol. 11 (Garden City, N.Y., 1988). John Gray, *I and II Kings: A Commentary*, 3d fully rev. ed., The Old Testament Library (London, 1977; 1985 printing). Abraham Malamat, ed., *The Age of the Monarchies: Political History*, The World History of the Jewish People, vol. 4, pt. 1; *The Age of the Monarchies: Culture and Society*, The World History of the Jewish People, vol. 4, pt. 2 (Jerusalem, 1979). Amihay Mazar, *Archaeology of the Land of the Bible: 10,000–586 B.C.E.* (New York, 1990).

—NILI SACHER FOX

ISRAEL, LAND OF. See ERETS YISRA'EL.

ISRAEL, PRAYER FOR STATE OF. See TEFILLAH LI-SHELOM HA-MEDINAH.

ISRAEL, STATE OF, JEWISH RELIGIOUS LIFE IN. Israel was founded as a Jewish state, and over 80 percent of its population is Jewish. The religious establishment in Israel is exclusively in Orthodox hands, along the lines set up by the British when they founded the *chief rabbinate in 1920 (at which time there were no non-Orthodox religious institutions). There is no separation of state and religion. Matters of personal status (notably marriage and divorce) are governed by the religious laws of each community (Jewish, Muslim, Druzian, Christian). This means, for example, that there is no provision in Israel for marriages between couples of different faiths, although such marriages contracted outside Israel are recognized by the state. Rabbinical courts are recognized by the state, and their judges and functionaries are state officials. A Ministry of Religions supervises the rabbinical courts and is responsible for other aspects of religious life (such as the upkeep of synagogues). The question of membership is not easily settled in cases where individuals want to separate religion and nationality (for example, by being a Christian Jew). Israeli secular courts have ruled that one cannot be a Jew by nationality and a Christian by religion in Israel (see JEW, WHO IS A?, CONTROVERSY).

*Ashkenazim and *Sephardim in Israel each have their own chief rabbi and rabbis at the local level. However, there are unifying tendencies in courts of law and in prayer rites (such as the unified rite adopted by the army). Because of the historical anti-Zionism of the Reform movement, Reform communities and institutions only emerged after the establishment of the state, and although the Conservative movement was not anti-

Zionist, few Conservative Jews lived in Israel before it achieved statehood. Both now have rabbinical seminaries and a network of synagogues. However, their rabbis are not allowed to act as marriage registrars. There is a plethora of *synagogues throughout the country, reflecting the diverse origins of the Jewish population. The synagogue is almost exclusively a house of prayer, as the educational and communal functions it assumed in the Diaspora are met in Israel by different institutions.

Within the Jewish population, there is a clear dividing line between two subcultures—the religious and the secular (*ḥiloni*). Orthodox Jews are in the minority, and their numbers have been estimated at less than one-third of the total Jewish population. However, religion is very much a part of everyday political discourse in Israel, and both the more moderate Orthodox and the *Ḥaredim have their own political parties and representation in the Knesset (see RELIGIOUS PARTIES IN ISRAEL). The religious parties have been members of nearly all government coalitions, and in return for their support of the government, they have obtained key religious legislation. For example, dietary laws are observed in the army and in government institutions, while the raising of pigs and the selling of pork are forbidden by law (except in a few areas where Christians predominate).

The language of Israel is Hebrew, which incorporates much terminology from religious sources. The Sabbath and festivals are official days of rest: the Pesaḥ *Seder is almost universally observed, while all traffic ceases on *Yom Kippur. The traditional rites of passage are observed by all. The Jewish state school system in Israel is divided into two parallel subsystems, one religious and the other secular. Even secular schools teach Bible, Jewish history, Jewish law, and Jewish literature. Ḥaredim introduced an independent school system that now receives financing from the state. Israel is today the leading center of **yeshivah* education (*yeshivah* students are exempted from military service). A recent development has been the establishment of a small network of schools for religious, non-Orthodox education.

Prior to the establishment of the State of Israel, the Ḥaredim had been extremely anti-Zionist. A tiny group known as the *Neturei Qarta' still refuses to recognize the Jewish state. The more moderate Orthodox (*datiim*) participated in the Zionist endeavor (see RELIGIOUS ZIONISM) and hailed the foundation of the state as "the beginning of redemption." The term *masorti* (traditional) denotes those who are partially observant, and in Israel the Conservative movement is known as the Masorti movement.

One of the consequences of the Six-Day War was the settlement of the newly acquired areas of Erets Yisra'el by Orthodox Jews, who were determined that these should remain under Jewish control, motivated by the belief that Jewish law forbids the relinquishment of any part of the historic land of Israel. This resulted in a far greater involvement of religious Jews in matters connected with security and foreign policy.

• S. Zalman Abramov, *Perpetual Dilemma: Religion in the Jewish State* (Rutherford, N.J., 1976). Benjamin Beit-Hallahmi, *Despair and Deliverance: Private Salvation in Contemporary Israel* (Albany, N.Y., 1992). Charles S. Liebman, *Civil Religion in Israel: Traditional Judaism and Political Culture in the Jewish State* (Berkeley, 1983). Charles S. Liebman, *Religion and Politics in Israel* (Bloomington, Ind., 1984). Ira Sharansky, *Israel and Its Bible: A Political Analysis* (New York, 1996).

—BENJAMIN BEIT-HALLAHMI

ISRAEL, STATE OF, THEOLOGICAL ASPECTS. The topic is usually discussed among Religious Zionists in terms of messianism. The institutionally sanctioned prayer for the state, recited in synagogues around the world, refers to "the first flowering of our redemption." This view, largely as it developed under the influence of the chief rabbi Avraham Yitsḥaq ha-Kohen Kook (see KOOK FAMILY), adopts a naturalistic understanding of the messianic process. The fact that no overt miracles are involved suggests that the Jewish people, working within the order of nature and history, can play a positive role in the messianic advent. The State of Israel is seen as a decisive stage of that process. Furthermore, given the way in which the history of the State of Israel seems to mirror so many prophetic promises concerning redemption (victory against overwhelming odds in war; ingathering of the dispersed of Israel; the greening of the desert; etc.), Religious Zionists have become convinced that Israel is the **atḥalta' di-ge'ullah* (the beginning of the redemption).

Those who deny both the messianic character and the theological significance of the State of Israel on religious grounds generally represent ultra-Orthodox (*ḥaredi*) understandings of messianism, according to which the messianic advent will be accompanied by overt miracles. Furthermore, *ḥaredi* thinkers tend to claim that repentance on the part of the whole people is a precondition and not a consequence of that event. They also expect the wars of Armageddon and the "great and terrible Day of the Lord" as necessary parts of the traditional messianic scenario. Since the State of Israel satisfies none of these criteria it is devoid of messianic and, therefore, theological, significance. Some (e.g., Satmar Ḥasidim) even maintain that in attempting to encroach on God's prerogative, "ungodly" Zionism reveals itself as the work of Satan. It was this Satanic Zionism that brought down upon the people God's wrath, which found its expression in the horrors of the Holocaust.

Orthodox Zionists and ultra-Orthodox non- or anti-Zionists are further divided over two other issues, both having messianic implications. From the Zionist perspective, the Holocaust marks a caesura in Jewish history. Since the fall of Jerusalem in 70 CE, Jews have behaved as if there was a de facto agreement with the powers of the world, under which they renounced all claims to political power in return for tolerated existence. The Holocaust marked the end of that arrangement. For the first time, the people as a whole was threatened with extinction. The gentile powers can no longer be relied upon to guarantee the mere existence of Jews and Judaism. In consequence, Israel must reenter the world of history and once again become actors upon its stage. For Orthodox Zionism, this is God's will, and the State of Israel is the way in which it is realized.

Ultra-Orthodox thinkers, on the other hand, tend to see the Holocaust as one more in a series of pogroms that Jews have suffered throughout history. Without minimizing the horrors of the Holocaust, they do not see it as different in kind from other persecutions: quantitatively greater, qualitatively the same. Hence, there are no new lessons to be learned from it. Gentiles have always hated Jews and will always hate Jews. They always have and always will seek to destroy Israel, until God ushers in the messianic era. According to this view, conclusions drawn from the Holocaust are simply a misreading of history, and relating these conclusions to messianism compounds the mistake, which can at best be excused as an act of immaturity, and at worst must be condemned as a revolt against God. See also HOLOCAUST THEOLOGY.

• David Hartman, *Conflicting Visions: Spiritual Possibilities of Modern Israel* (New York, 1990). Jacob Katz, "Israel and the Messiah," *Commentary* 73 (January 1982): 31–41. Menachem Kellner, "Jews and their Messiahs," *Jewish Quarterly* 41.3 (1994): 7–13. Menachem Kellner, "Messianic Postures in Israel Today," *Modern Judaism* 6 (1986): 197–209. Lionel Kochan, *Jews, Idols and Messiahs: The Challenge from History* (Oxford, 1990). Yeshayahu Leibowitz, *Judaism, Human Values, and the Jewish State* (Cambridge, Mass., 1992). Aviezer Ravitzky, "'Forcing the End:' Zionism and the State of Israel as Antimessianic Undertakings," in *Jews and Messianism in the Modern Era: Metaphor and Meaning*, Studies in Contemporary Jewry, vol. 7, edited by Jonathan Frankel (New York, 1991), pp. 34–67. Aviezer Ravitzky, *Messianism, Zionism, and Jewish Religious Radicalism* (Chicago, 1996). Marc Saperstein, ed., *Essential Papers on Messianic Movements and Personalities in Jewish History* (New York, 1992). Eliezer Schweid, "Jewish Messianism: Metamorphoses of an Idea," *Jerusalem Quarterly* 36 (1985): 63–78.

—MENACHEM KELLNER

ISRAELI, YITSḤAQ (c.855–955), North African philosopher who lived in Kairouan, where he was court physician. His medical writings, for which he was best known, were influential for many centuries, while his philosophical works gained the attention of Christian scholars. His most famous philosophical book, *Sefer ha-Gevulim*, defines and sometimes discusses major philosophic concepts. Other works include *Sefer ha-Yesodot*, which discusses Aristotle's theories of the elements, and *Sefer ha-Ruaḥ veha-Nefesh*, the only book in which he refers to the Bible and which he wrote specifically for Jewish readers. His books were written in Arabic, but his philosophical works are known only in Hebrew and Latin translations. Israeli was a pioneer of Jewish Neoplatonic thought and influenced later medieval Jewish thinkers. He himself was influenced by the works of the Arabic philosopher al-Kindi and by other Neoplatonic writings no longer known, and he also introduced a number of Aristotelian ideas, such as the tripartite division of the soul into the vegetable, animal, and rational, into his works. While seeking to synthesize religious and philosophical concepts, for example combining the biblical account of creation with Neoplatonic ideas of emanation, his emphasis is on the philosophical approach.

• Alexander Altmann and S. M. Stern, eds. and trans., *Isaac Israeli, A Neoplatonic Philosopher of the Early Tenth Century: His Works Translated with Comments and an Outline of His Philosophy* (London, 1958). Isaac Husik, *A History of Mediaeval Jewish Philosophy* (Philadelphia, 1944), pp. 1–16. Harry A. Wolfson, *Studies in the History of Philosophy and Religion*, vol. 1 (Cambridge, 1973).

—FRANCISCO MORENO CARVALHO

ISRAEL INDEPENDENCE DAY. See YOM HA-ʿATSMA'UT.

ISRAELITE, a descendant of *Jacob (who was given the name *Israel, *Gn*. 32.29). Israelites were also known as the children of Israel and as the Twelve Tribes. After the death of Solomon, the term *Israelite* was limited to the inhabitants of the northern kingdom of Israel (in contrast to the Judahites in the south), but following the end of the northern kingdom in 722 BCE, *Israelite* was almost entirely superseded by **Jew*, derived from Judah. Because of the derogatory associations connected with the word *Jew* during and after the *Emancipation, Western and assimilated Jews, in particular, revived the term *Israelite* as a less offensive substitute; in certain languages, such as French and Italian, *Israelite* remains the accepted term. In a purely liturgical context, an Israelite is a Jew who is neither a priest nor a Levite (see QERI'AT HA-TORAH). A citizen of the State of Israel is called an Israeli, a term that designates nationality and citizenship but not faith.

• H. H. Ben-Sasson, ed., *A History of the Jewish People* (Cambridge, Mass., 1976). Ehud Ben Zvi, "Inclusion in and Exclusion from Israel as Conveyed by the Term 'Israel' in Post-Monarchic Biblical Texts," in *The Pitcher Is Broken: Memorial Essays for Gosta W. Ahlstrom*, edited by Steven W. Holloway (Sheffield, Eng., 1995). James M. Miller, *A History of Ancient Israel and Judah* (London, 1986). Robert M. Seltzer, *Jewish People, Jewish Thought: The Jewish Experience in History* (New York, 1980).

ISRAELITISCH-THEOLOGISCHE LEHRANSTALT, rabbinical and teachers' seminary established in Vienna in 1893. Adolf Schwarz was its first rector, and under his guidance it developed into one of the most important rabbinical seminaries in Europe, combining traditional rabbinic studies with general education. Many noted scholars, among them Samuel Krauss, Meir Friedmann, and Victor Aptowitzer, taught at the seminary, which closed in 1938 after the Nazi occupation of Austria.

• Steven Beller, *Vienna and the Jews, 1867–1938: A Cultural History* (Cambridge, 1989). *Jahresbericht der Israelitich-Theologeschen Lehranstalt in Wien für das Schuljahr . . .* (Vienna, 1894–1932).

ISRU ḤAG (אִסְרוּ חַג; bind the festival), the day after the Shalosh Regalim. The Talmud comments: "To add a day to the festival and honor it with feasting, is as if to have offered a sacrifice at the altar" (*Suk*. 45b). The day is considered a minor festival for liturgical purposes, and no supplicatory or penitential prayers are said; fasting and funeral eulogies are prohibited. This custom, expressive of the reluctance with which the passing of the festival is viewed, possibly goes back to a more ancient custom—deduced from *Deuteronomy* 16.7—of remaining an extra night in Jerusalem at the conclusion of a festival (*Ḥag*. 16a). In the Talmud Yerushalmi (*ʿA. Z.* 1.1) the day is called *berei de-moʿada'*, "the son [offshoot] of the festival."

• Ismar Elbogen, *Jewish Liturgy: A Comprehensive History* (Philadelphia, 1993).

ISSACHAR (Heb. Yissakhar), Jacob's fifth son from Leah and one of the Israelite tribes. The name is apparently derived from two words: *ish* (man) and *sakhar* (recompense). The meaning of the name is explained in the story of Issachar's birth (*Gn*. 30.8) and in Jacob's blessing of Issachar (*Gn*. 49.15).

The land of Issachar extended mostly from the highlands north of Jezreel to Mount Tabor in the north and the Jordan River in the east. The western border is not clearly known (*Jos*. 49.17–23). It seems that the valley areas of Issachar were not conquered by the tribe until a later period, since the Canaanites with their chariots were too difficult to defeat for a long time. Therefore, it is likely that the sons of Issachar (and parts of the tribe of Zebulun) were subjected to the Canaanites, a reflection of which can be found in *Genesis* 49.15: ". . . so he bowed his shoulder to bear, and became a slave at forced labor." Men from the tribe of Issachar participated in the war against the Canaanites (*Jgs*. 5.15). The land of Issachar is mentioned as a separate county in the time of King Solomon (*1 Kgs*. 4.17), which may reflect the stabilization of the status of the tribe of Issachar in their land. The judge Tola, son of Puah, was from the tribe of Issachar and so was Baasha, the third king of Israel (the northern kingdom, 906–883).

• Zvi Gal, "The Settlement of Issachar: Some New Observations," *Tel-Aviv* 9 (1982): 79–86. Nahum M. Sarna, *Genesis*, The JPS Torah Commentary (Philadelphia and New York, 1989), pp. 338–340.

—ZE'EV KAINAN

ISSERLEIN, YISRA'EL BEN PETAḤYAH (1390–1460), German rabbi who figured prominently in the intellectual and cultural renaissance that followed the period of decline associated with the Black Death persecutions of 1348 and 1349. Born in Regensburg, he served as rabbi for many years in Wiener Neustadt. Recognized during his lifetime as an outstanding halakhic authority, he is frequently cited as a source for the legal rulings of R. Mosheh Isserles, appended to the *Shulḥan ʿArukh*, decisions that in turn exerted enormous influence upon subsequent Ashkenazi halakhic practice. Isserlein, nonetheless, held a rather restrictive view of rabbinic authority. He was well known for his opposition to the attempts by some rabbis to enforce their decrees upon communities that did not accept them. In his view, even the *gedol ha-dor* (the greatest scholar of his time) has no power to enact legislation that the majority of the community cannot abide. Among Isserlein's best-known works is *Terumat ha-Deshen* (Venice, 1519), a collection of halakhic *responsa*, which some (though not all) authorities regard as answers to questions that Isserlein himself composed rather than to inquiries received from others. His *Pesaqim u-Khetavim* (Venice, 1519) and *Leqet Yosher* (1903–1904) are collections arranged by his students. The former primarily contains *responsa* and halakhic decisions, while the latter emphasizes many of Isserlein's own personal religious practices (*minhagim*).

• Yedidya Dinari, *Ḥakhmei Ashkenaz be-Shilḥei Yemei ha-Beinayim* (Jerusalem, 1984). Shlomo Eidelberg, *Jewish Life in Austria in the XVth Century as Reflected in the Legal Writings of Rabbi Israel Isserlein and His Contemporaries* (Philadelphia, 1962). Menachem Elon, *Jewish Law: History, Sources, Principles* (Philadelphia, 1994), pp. 1516–1517.

—MARK WASHOFSKY

ISSERLES, MOSHEH (c.1525–1572), Polish halakhic authority and codifier; popularly known by the acronym Rema'. Born in Kraków and educated at the *yeshivah* of Shalom Shakna in Lublin, Isserles was an acknowledged halakhic authority while still a youth.

His principal halakhic works established him as Yosef Karo's counterpart in the Ashkenazi community. *Darkhei Mosheh*, Isserles's commentary to the *Arbaʿah Turim*, presents Ashkenazi legal precedents not found in Karo's *Beit Yosef*. Karo codified mainly Sephardi usage, for which his works were criticized among Ashkenazim. Therefore, after Karo produced the **Shulḥan ʿArukh*, Isserles published the supplementary *Mappah*, providing Ashkenazi rulings and customs. Although Isserles frequently contested Karo's views, by appending his own notes and glosses to Karo's work (printed in all standard editions), he rendered the *Shulḥan ʿArukh* an acceptable code of law for Ashkenazim, and one to which future generations of Ashkenazi halakhists added their own commentaries. The eventual emergence of Karo's *Shulḥan ʿArukh* as the definitive code of law for world Jewry was therefore due in no small part to Mosheh Isserles. Isserles's glosses uphold the authority of *minhagim* (customs)—"the **minhag* is the law" (*Darkhei Mosheh* on *Arbaʿah Turim, Yoreh Deʿah* 116)—thereby placing the legal decisions of **aḥaronim* (later generations of rabbis) along with current practices on a level equal to that of earlier authorities.

Isserles wrote a treatise entitled *Torat ha-Ḥattat* (Kraków, 1569), following the structure of Yitsḥaq ben Me'ir *Dueren's *Shaʿarei Dura'*, and he composed glosses to several Talmudic tractates, as well as to Yaʿaqov ben Yehudah *Weil's *Sheḥitah u-Vediqah* and Asher ben Yeḥi'el's *Ro'sh*. In addition, Isserles wrote ninety-one *responsa* (Kraków, 1640). His principal non-halakhic works were *Meḥir Yayin*, a philosophical–allegorical interpretation of the *Book of Esther*, and *Torat ha-ʿOlah*, a philosophical analysis of the Temple's structure and appurtenances and of the relationship of the sacrificial cult to the nature of man and the universe.

Although Isserles was not an ardent kabbalist and ruled against the Zohar whenever it contravened halakhic precedent and practice, he did incorporate kabbalistic observations into the *Torat ha-ʿOlah* and left behind an unpublished commentary on the Zohar, as well as a kabbalistic treatise entitled *Yesodei Sifrei ha-Qabbalah*. He also composed notes to Maimonides' *Guide of the Perplexed* and commentaries to aggadic portions of the Talmud and to the *Song of Songs*.

Isserles's designation as the "Maimonides of Polish Jewry" was meant to imply similarities between the two in their mastery of both sacred and secular studies. However, Isserles's approval of the study of philosophy earned him caustic rebukes from Shelomoh Luria and Eliyyahu ben Shelomoh Zalman, the Vilna Ga'on.

Isserles also had his critics in the area of *halakhah*. His *Torat ha-Ḥattat* was attacked by *Ḥayyim ben Betsal'el and Yom Tov Lipmann *Heller. Heller also criticized Isserles's glosses on the *Shulḥan ʿArukh* for neglecting German–Jewish customs and warned that such codes of law were dangerous because they discouraged the study of the true sources, the Talmud and the *ri'shonim*.

Such criticism notwithstanding, Isserles is the preeminent Ashkenazi codifier–annotator, whose rulings generally came to be accepted as authoritative by subsequent generations.

He lived in Kraków where a synagogue was named after him during his lifetime. The synagogue still stands, with his tomb in the courtyard.

• Yonah Ben-Sasson, *Mishnato ha-ʿIyyunit shel ha-Rema'* (Jerusalem, 1984). Asher Siev, "Li-Demuto ha-Ruḥanit shel Rabbenu ha-Rema'," in *Sefer Ziqqaron li-Shemu'el Belkin*, edited by Moshe Carmilly (New York, 1981), pp. 148–154. Asher Siev, *Rabbi Mosheh Isserles: Ramo* (New York, 1972). Chaim Tchernowitz, *Toledot ha-Poseqim*, vol. 3 (New York, 1947), pp. 37–73. —ELIJAH J. SCHOCHET

ISSUR VE-HETTER (אִסּוּר וְהֶתֵּר; prohibited and permitted), the classical Jewish legal term denoting ritual law. The rules governing *issur ve-hetter* differ in certain ways from other fields of Jewish law, such as financial cases. Thus, for example, mutually agreed upon conditions in violation of Jewish law have no impact in the areas of ritual law or criminal law but are valid in the area of financial law. The Talmud (*Ber*. 19b; *Ket*. 40b) states that neither analogies from ritual matters to financial matters nor the reverse are generally accepted to prove law. So, too, the role of secular law is vastly curtailed in ritual law, whereas **dina' de-malkhuta' dina'* is a valid source of financial law. Finally, Talmudic methodology appears to be different in these two areas in that financial law is driven by the more classical forms of legal reasoning, whereas ritual law is more closely governed by the hermeneutic rules of the Talmud.

While most areas of law intuitively divide between ritual and financial law, this is not always the case. Thus, the rules governing usury fall under ritual law, whereas certain portions of the laws governing redemption of the firstborn are regarded as financial matters. Charity laws are regulated by both sets of principles, and the proper status of inheritance laws is subject to dispute.

• Arnold Cohen, *An Introduction to Jewish Civil Law* (Jerusalem and New York, 1991), pp. 11–27. Menachem Elon, *Jewish Law: History, Sources, Principles* (Philadelphia, 1994), pp. 11–141. —MICHAEL BROYDE

IYYAR (אִיָּר), second month of the Hebrew civil calendar and eighth of the religious; the zodiac sign for Iyyar is Taurus. It has twenty-nine days and is referred to in the Bible as the month of Ziv. Special days in this month are *Yom ha-ʿAtsma'ut on 5 Iyyar, *Pesaḥ Sheni on 14 Iyyar, *Lag ba-ʿOmer on 18 Iyyar, and *Yom Yerushalayim on 28 Iyyar.

• Nathan Bushwick, *Understanding the Jewish Calendar* (New York, 1989). George Zinberg, *Jewish Calendar Mystery Dispelled* (New York, 1963). —CHAIM PEARL

ʿIYYUN CIRCLE, a term denoting a circle that produced a few dozen relatively short theosophical treatises. The earliest date from either late twelfth-century Provence or mid-thirteenth-century Castile. These anonymous or pseudonymous works were presumably composed by many different individuals. It is unknown whether the authors had personal contact with each other, but their writings all exhibit the influence of one or both of two pivotal texts: *Sefer ha-ʿIyyun*, attributed to R. Ḥamma'i, and *Maʿayan ha-Ḥokhmah*, ascribed to Moses. The first two recensions of *Sefer ha-ʿIyyun* delineate ten divinely emanated *koḥot* (powers) beginning with Primordial Wisdom and Marvelous Light; two later recensions discuss thirteen powers. *Maʿayan ha-Ḥokhmah* presents a cosmogony using distinct, yet interrelated, sequences of primal letters or cosmic ethers and lights. Neither *Sefer ha-ʿIyyun* nor *Maʿayan ha-Ḥokhmah* refer to the *sefirot*. Later writings, however, synthesized kabbalistic terminology with the ʿIyyun Circle's concepts.

• Gershom Gerhard Scholem, *Origins of the Kabbalah* (Princeton, 1987), pp. 309–364. Mark Verman, *The Books of Contemplation* (Albany, 1992). Mark Verman, "The Evolution of the Circle of Contemplation," in *Gershom Scholem's Major Trends in Jewish Mysticism Fifty Years After*, edited by Peter Schäfer and Joseph Dan, (Tübingen, 1993), pp. 163–177. —MARK VERMAN

IZBICA, nineteenth-century Polish Hasidic dynasty founded by R. Mordekhai Yosef Leiner (1800–1854). Leiner was the preeminent student of Menaḥem Mendel of Kotsk until an ideological estrangement led to Leiner's move to Izbica (1840). Leiner advocated a pluralistic, egalitarian approach to Judaism that encouraged idiosyncratic interpretation of the divine will and individual criteria for the fulfillment of the divine commandments. He argued against the search for unequivocal truth and denied an authoritative reading for the holy scripture. Further, since the omnipotent divine will is concealed within the illusions of reality, all human deed is inconsequential. Leiner wrote *Beit Yaʿaqov* (Warsaw, 1890). He was succeeded by his son Yaʿaqov Leiner of Radzyń and his grandson Gershon Henikh of Radzyń, who published his grandfather's teachings in *Mei ha-Shilloaḥ* (vol. 1 [Venice, 1860]; vol. 2 [Lublin, 1922]).

• Rachel Elior, in *Tarbiz* 62 (1993): 381–402. Morris Faierstein, *All Is in the Hands of Heaven: The Teachings of Rabbi Mordecai Joseph Leiner of Izbica* (Hoboken, N.J., 1989). Joseph Weiss, "A Late Jewish Utopia of Religious Freedom," in *Studies in Eastern European Jewish Mysticism*, edited by David Goldstein (New York, 1985), pp. 209–248. —RACHEL ELIOR

J

JABNEH. See YAVNEH.

JACHIN AND BOAZ (Heb. Yakhin; Boʿaz), names of two bronze pillars that flanked the entrance of the porch of Solomon's Temple—Jachin on the right, Boaz on the left (*1 Kgs*. 7.21–23). Their exact significance is uncertain, as they appear not to have been part of the Temple structure itself. According to Jewish tradition, the pillars were symbolic of God's presence as a pillar of fire and a pillar of cloud in the wilderness. Their names could signify words from a dynastic inscription: Jachin (Heb. *kun*), "He will establish"; Boaz (Heb. *ʿoz*), "in strength."

• John Gray, *I and II Kings: A Commentary*, 3d fully rev. ed., The Old Testament Library (London, 1977; 1985 printing). Carol L. Meyers, "Jachin and Boaz in Religious and Political Perspective" *Catholic Biblical Quarterly* 45 (1983): 167–178.

—NILI SACHER FOX

JACOB (Heb. Yaʿaqov), Israelite patriarch, son of *Isaac and *Rebekah, also called *Israel (*Gn*. 32.29). The third and eponymous forefather of the Jewish people, he was the younger twin of *Esau. The two traditional folk etymologies of the name derive from Jacob's gripping Esau's heel (*ʿeqev*) at birth (*Gn*. 25.26) and Esau's later charge that "he has supplanted me [*va-yaʿqeveni*] these two times" (*Gn*. 27.36). The narratives concerning Jacob form one of the main components of *Genesis*. Jacob himself characterized the years of his life as "few and difficult" (*Gn*. 47.9). His struggles began in the womb of his mother, Rebekah, where he wrestled with his brother, Esau—a condition divinely explained as indicating that the older twin would serve the younger (*Gn*. 25.21–23). While Esau was described as red, hairy, a skillful hunter, and a man of the open field, Jacob was portrayed as reserved, tending his flocks, and tilling the fields (*Gn*. 25.25–27). Jacob later exploited this difference both when he extracted the birthright from the famished Esau for a pottage of lentils (*Gn*. 25.29–34) and when, under the direction of Rebekah, he secured the blessing of the firstborn through deceiving his father, Isaac (*Gn*. 27.1–40). Rebekah then intervened and sent him off to her brother Laban in Mesopotamia. At the outset of his journey, Jacob received a revelation from God at Bethel in which he saw a ladder reaching up to heaven. God promised him divine protection as well as eventual possession of the country. While abiding with Laban he was deceived into marrying Laban's eldest daughter, *Leah, rather than *Rachel, the younger daughter whom he wished to marry (*Gn*. 29.14–30). Jacob continued working for Laban for a period of twenty years in order to eventually marry Rachel and to provide for his own family, which numbered twelve sons and one daughter. During that time, Jacob prospered despite Laban's repeated attempts to profit at his expense (*Gn*. 30.25–43). Eventually Jacob fled from Laban's authority to return to the land of Canaan (*Gn*. 31). En route, however, after preparing gifts to assuage Esau (*Gn*. 32.3–21), he wrestled with God (or a divine being) at Peniel near the ford of the Jabbok River and received the blessing of a new name: Israel (*Gn*. 32). In his later years Jacob was deprived of his son Joseph through the machinations of his other sons (*Gn*. 37). The family was later reunited, however, by the agency of Joseph himself, who, as vizier of Egypt, settled them in the region of Goshen during a time of famine (*Gn*. 42–47.12). After blessing his sons (*Gn*. 49; see JACOB, BLESSING OF), Jacob died in Egypt at the age of 147 but was carried in a solemn procession to the land of Canaan to be buried with Abraham, Sarah, Isaac, Rebekah, and Leah in the cave in the field of Machpelah (*Gn*. 49.29–50.14). In biblical literature the name Jacob appeared very often as an epithet for Israel (e.g., *Nm*. 23.7; *Dt*. 33.4). Jacob's many trials are treated in rabbinic literature as symbolic of the plight and struggles of the Jewish people. The rabbis ascribed to Jacob the introduction of the evening prayer, Maʿariv (*Ber*. 26b). See also TRIBES OF ISRAEL.

• James Stokes Ackerman, "Joseph, Judah, and Jacob," in *Literary Interpretations of Biblical Narratives*, edited by Kenneth R. R. Gros Louis, with James Stokes Ackerman and Thayer S. Warshaw, vol. 2 (Nashville, 1982), pp. 85–113. Joyce G. Baldwin, *The Message of Genesis 12–50: From Abraham to Joseph*, The Bible Speaks Today (Leicester, 1986). Ronald S. Hendel, *The Epic of the Patriarch: The Jacob Cycle and the Narrative Traditions of Canaan and Israel*, Harvard Semitic Monographs, no. 42 (Atlanta, 1987). William McKane, *Studies in the Patriarchal Narratives* (Edinburgh, 1979). Nahum M. Sarna, *Understanding Genesis* (New York, 1966), pp. 181–231.

—MICHAEL JAMES WILLIAMS

JACOB, BLESSING OF, the words of the dying patriarch Jacob, contained in *Genesis* 49. E. A. Speiser has termed it "The Testament of Jacob," because most of the sayings are curses rather than blessings (e.g., *Gn*. 49.3–4, 5–7; and cf. Ibn Ezra and Ḥizquni on *Gn*. 49.1). It is part of the corpus of early Israelite poetry, apparently dating from the Mosaic period in the thirteenth century BCE until the end of the united kingdom around 921 BCE. While the various sayings in the Testament of Jacob refer to, and may well have been composed in, diverse periods (e.g., the passage concerning Simeon and Levi [5–7] can refer only to the rape of Dinah [*Gn*. 34] in the patriarchal period; while the passage concerning Judah [8–12] apparently dates from the period of the united monarchy), the composition as a whole can not be earlier than the date of the composition of its latest components, namely the period of the united kingdom in the tenth century BCE.

• William F. Albright, *Yahweh and the Gods of Canaan* (New York, 1968), pp. 1–52, 265c, 275ee. Frank M. Cross, *Canaanite Myth and Hebrew Epic* (Cambridge, Mass., 1973). Frank M. Cross and David N. Freedman, *Studies in Ancient Yahwistic Poetry*, 2d ed. (Missoula, Mont., 1975), pp. 3–12, 69–93, 181–187. Stephen A. Geller, *Parallelism in Early Biblical Poetry* (Missoula, Mont., 1979). Donald W. Goodwin, *Text-Restoration Methods in Contemporary U.S.A. Biblical Scholarship* (Naples, 1969). Victor P. Hamilton, *The Book of Genesis: Chapters 18–50* (Grand Rapids, 1995), pp. 644–689. Edward Y. Kutscher, *A History of the Hebrew Language* (Jerusalem, 1982), pp. 79–80. *ʿOlam ha-Tanakh: Be-Re'shit* (Tel Aviv, 1982), pp. 247–254. David A. Robertson, *Linguistic Evidence in Dating Early Hebrew Poetry* (Missoula, Mont., 1972). Nahum M. Sarna, *Genesis*, The JPS Torah Commentary (Philadelphia, 1989), pp. 331–346, 371–372. Ephraim A. Speiser, *Genesis*, The Anchor Bible (Garden City, N.Y., 1964), pp. 361–372. Moshe Weinfeld, *Sefer Be-Re'shit* (Tel Aviv, 1975), pp. 298–314. Gordon Wenham, *Genesis 16–50*, Word Biblical Commentary (Waco, Tex., 1994), pp. 466–487. Claus Westermann, *Genesis 37–50* (Minneapolis, 1986), pp. 195–198, 215–244. —CHAIM COHEN

JACOBSON, ISRAEL (1768–1828), financier and pioneer of Reform Judaism. Born in Halberstadt, Germany, he received an Orthodox education. Influenced by Moses Mendelssohn and the Haskalah, he saw a need to train Jews for vocations and opened a school in Seesen. His suggestion to Napoléon to establish a supreme Jewish council headed by a patriarch headquartered in Paris (1806) probably influenced Napoléon's idea for a Sanhedrin (see SANHEDRIN, FRENCH). Jacobson convened a gathering of Jewish notables in Kassel in 1808 to introduce religious reforms; he built a synagogue there, the services of which included sermons in German as well as confirmation rites (1810). Officiating in the robes of a Protestant clergyman, he dedicated the school the following year with the ringing of bells and singing of German hymns accompanied by organ music. After the fall of Napoléon and the breakup of Westphalia, Jacobson moved to Berlin, where he continued to work for religious reform. For his son's *bar mitsvah* in 1815, Jacobson opened a Reform synagogue in his house. Due to lack of space, he later moved the synagogue to the home of Jacob Hertz Beer, where Leopold Zunz and Eduard Kley preached. The holding of prayer meetings in private homes was a practice typical of upper-class German Jews of the period. Responding to pressure by Orthodox rabbis who argued for the closure of Jacobson's synagogue, the government prohibited all private, home-based synagogues in 1823.

• Jacob Rader Marcus, *Israel Jacobson: The Founder of the Reform Movement in Judaism* (Cincinnati, 1972). —KERRY M. OLITZKY

JAFFE, MORDEKHAI BEN AVRAHAM (c.1535–1612), codifier and Talmudist known as the Baʿal ha-Levushim (Author of the *Levushim*). Born in Prague, Jaffe studied under Shelomoh *Luria and Mosheh *Isserles in Poland, where he also became well versed in mathematics, astronomy, philosophy, and Kabbalah. Upon his return to Prague, Jaffe headed the local *yeshivah*, but his disappointment with the emphasis placed upon **pilpul* there led him to devote himself primarily to literary endeavors.

Jaffe composed a code of law, the *Levushim* (found in most standard editions of the *Arbaʿah Turim* by Yaʿaqov ben Asher), over the span of half a century. Shorter in length than Yosef *Karo's copious *Beit Yosef* but longer than his concise **Shulḥan ʿArukh*, Jaffe's code incorporates parts of the *Arbaʿah Turim* omitted by Karo and includes numerous customs practiced by Polish and German Jewry. Jaffe's code supplies rationales for many religious observances as well as kabbalistic insights. Five of the ten sections of *Levushim* deal with the legislation of the *Arbaʿah Turim*; the remaining five sections include sermons, comments on *Rashi's and Menaḥem Recanati's commentaries to the Pentateuch, and Jaffe's own commentary to Maimonides' *Guide of the Perplexed*. Although the *Levushim* proved to be a popular code of law during Jaffe's lifetime, it was eclipsed in ensuing years by the popularity of the *Shulḥan ʿArukh*.

Jaffe served as a rabbi in both eastern and western European Jewish centers, most notably Grodno, Lublin (where he played an active role in the deliberations of the Jewish autonomous body, the Council of the Four Lands), Prague, and Poznań.

• Samuel Aba Horodezky, *Le-Qorot ha-Rabbanut* (Warsaw, 1911), pp. 145–174. Lawrence Kaplan, "Rabbi Mordekhai Jaffe and the Evolution of Jewish Thought in Poland in the Sixteenth Century," in *Jewish Thought in the Sixteenth Century*, edited by Bernard Dor Cooperman (Cambridge, Mass., 1983), pp. 266–282. —ELIJAH J. SCHOCHET

JAGEL, AVRAHAM BEN ḤANANYAH DEI GALICCHI (1553–c.1623), philosopher and scientist. He was born at Monselice, northern Italy, and lived in various towns in Italy. His *Leqaḥ Tov* (Venice, 1595) was written under the influence of the Christian catechism as a dialogue between a rabbi and a student. He bases Judaism on Maimonides' *Thirteen Principles of Faith and posits faith, hope and charity (i.e., love) as the basis of righteous conduct. Jagel combined a broad secular knowledge with Jewish tradition and sought to link the sciences to the sources of Judaism. His *Beit Yaʿar ha-Levanon*, written in 1579 (unpublished), is an encyclopedic work of the sciences of his day. One of its main themes was magic, which Jagel held had been part of Jewish tradition since the time of Abraham. His ethical work, *Gei' Ḥizzayon*, was written when he was twenty-five. In an imitation of Dante, the author describes how he was guided through the afterworld by his father's spirit. From the spirits, he hears moral tales; many of them are Renaissance *novellae* which are given a Jewish coloring. The work was written in rhymed prose. It was translated into English by David R. Ruderman (*A Valley of Vision* [Philadelphia, 1990]).

• David B. Ruderman, *Kabbalah, Magic, and Science: The Cultural Universe of a Sixteenth-Century Jewish Physician* (Cambridge, Mass., 1988). —FRANCISCO MORENO CARVALHO

JAHRZEIT. See YORTSAYT.

JASHAR, BOOK OF. See BOOK OF JASHAR.

JEDID AL-ISLAM, a Persian Jew forcibly converted to Islam. The first forced conversion under Shah Abbas I (1588–1629) was followed in 1656 by the mass conversion of all Persian Jews by Shah Abbas II (1642–1666). These new Muslims were allowed to revert to Judaism only to be persecuted once again in the eighteenth century. Another forced conversion occurred in the city of Mashhad, site of Iran's most important Shiite shrine, in 1839. These converts continued to practice Judaism in utmost secrecy, while scrupulously performing the rites of Islam publicly. They lived separately in their own quarter and married exclusively among themselves. While prohibited from reverting to Judaism, they eventually immigrated to neighboring countries and later to Israel and the United States, where they have formed Mashhadi congregations that retain some of the unique practices forged under the adverse conditions of crypto-Judaism.

• Itzhak Ben-Zvi, *The Exiled and the Redeemed*, translated by Isaac A. Abbady (Philadelphia, 1957), pp. 112–119. Laurence D. Loeb, *Outcaste: Jewish Life in Southern Iran* (New York, 1977). Amnon Netzer, ed., *Mekhon Ben-Tsevi le-Ḥeqer Kehilot Yisra'el ba-Mizraḥ* (Jerusalem, 1985).

—JANE S. GERBER

JEHOIADA (Heb. Yehoyada'), chief priest in the Temple during the reigns of Athaliah and Joash of Judah (c.842–798). Jehoiada was responsible for restoring Judah's monarchy to the house of David (*2 Kgs*. 11). Following the death of Ahaziah, the king's mother, Athaliah (Ahab's daughter), murdered the royal heirs and usurped the throne. Jehosheba, Jehoiada's wife and Ahaziah's sister, saved the sole living prince, Joash, and hid him in a Temple chamber. In the seventh year of Athaliah's reign, Jehoiada successfully carried out a revolt against the queen. He crowned Joash, put Athaliah to death, tore down the house of Baal, and killed its priest, Mattan. The Temple of God was purified, and a chest was installed to collect donations for Temple repairs. Jehoiada is credited for Joash's exemplary behavior (*2 Kgs*. 12.3). After his mentor's death, Joash accepted idolatrous practices and even murdered Jehoiada's son Zechariah when he reproached the king for his behavior (*2 Chr*. 24.17–22).

• Mordechai Cogan and Hayim Tadmor, *II Kings*, The Anchor Bible, vol. 11 (Garden City, N.Y., 1988). John Gray, *I and II Kings: A Commentary*, 3d fully rev. ed., The Old Testament Library (London, 1977; 1985 printing). Sara Japhet, *I and II Chronicles: A Commentary*, The Old Testament Library (Louisville, Ky., 1993). Jacob Martin Myers, *II Chronicles*, The Anchor Bible, vol. 13 (Garden City, N.Y., 1965). —NILI SACHER FOX

JEHOVAH. See God, Names of.

JELLINEK, ADOLF (1821–1893), rabbi, preacher, scholar; officiated in Leipzig and, from 1856, in Vienna. The most celebrated Jewish preacher of the period (he always referred to himself by the title "preacher" [*Prediger*] and not "rabbi"), his brilliant sermons—noteworthy for their Midrashic exposition—attracted large congregations, including many non-Jews. Over two hundred of his sermons were published and greatly influenced Jewish homiletics. He inclined toward moderate Reform Judaism and opposed Zionism. As a scholar, he belonged to the modern school of the *Wissenschaft des Judentums. His extensive researches covered many fields, in particular medieval Jewish philosophy (he wrote on Thomas Aquinas in Jewish literature). A pioneer in Jewish scholarly research into mysticism and one of the few Wissenschaft scholars to approach it with true respect, he was the first to show scientifically that *Mosheh de León was the author of the *Zohar. He edited from manuscript many of the smaller and apocryphal *midrashim*, publishing ninety-nine of these in his *Beit ha-Midrash* (6 vols. [1853–1878, 1938]). He also was the author of many bibliographical works.

• Moses Rosenmann, *Adolf Jellinek* (Vienna, 1931), in German with full bibliography. Marsha L. Rozenblit, "Jewish Identity and the Modern Rabbi: The Cases of Isak Noa Mannheimer, Adolf Jellinek, and Moritz Guedemann in Nineteenth-Century Vienna," *Leo Baeck Institute Year Book* 35 (1990): 103–131.

JEPHTHAH (Heb. Yiftaḥ), one of the Israelite judges. Because he was the son of a harlot, he was driven out of the house by his half brothers and subsequently gathered a band of mercenaries in the land of Tob (probably in the northern part of modern Jordan; *Jgs*. 11.1–3).

After the Ammonites attacked the Gileadites, Jephthah, who was a Gileadite, came to their rescue at the request of the elders of Gilead. Before the battle, Jephthah vowed to sacrifice whomever he first met when he returned home victorious from the battlefield. When he did return from battle, it was his own daughter who came out first to greet him, and he was obliged to offer her as a sacrifice, but the text is vague about her actual fate. Some scholars contend that she was not sacrificed but was forced to live in confinement. After his victory over the Ammonites, Jephthah went on to suppress an Ephraimite force in Gilead, an incident that probably reflects the Ephraimite aspirations in Transjordan and Gilead (*Jgs*. 12.1–6).

Jephthah served as a judge for six years and was buried in the region of Gilead (*Jgs*. 12.7).

• Robert G. Boling, *Judges*, The Anchor Bible (Garden City, N.Y., 1975), pp. 196–214. J. Alberto Soggin, *Judges*, Old Testament Library (London, 1981), pp. 201–222. Phyllis Trible, "A Daughter's Death: Feminism, Literary Criticism and the Bible," *Michigan Quarterly Review* 22 (1983): 177–189. —ZE'EV KAINAN

JEREMIAH (Heb. Yirmeyahu; born c.645 BCE, died after 582), prophet during and following the last years of the monarchy of the kingdom of Judah; son of Hilkiah, a priest of the line of *Eli from Anathoth, a village a few miles northeast of Jerusalem. Jeremiah's prophetic career began in the thirteenth year of the reign of King *Josiah (626 BCE), and continued through the reigns of Kings Jehoahaz, Jehoiakim, Jehoiachin, and Zedekiah to the Babylonian destruction of Jerusalem in 586 and the assassination of the Judean governor Gedaliah in 582. Jeremiah prophesied during the years of the collapse of the Assyrian empire and the rise of the Neo-Babylonian empire, whose king Nebuchadnezzar destroyed Judah. Jeremiah was an early supporter of the reform measures taken by Josiah to purify Jewish religious practice according to the principles laid down in *Deuteronomy*. Following Josiah's death in battle in 609 and the collapse of his restoration program, Jeremiah became convinced that God would punish his people, and he contested the general belief, rooted in the prophecies of Isaiah, in the inviolability and divine security of Jerusalem. Although Jeremiah was banned from the Temple after nearly being executed for sedition (chap. 26), he sent his scribe *Baruch ben Neriah to read his sermons publicly (chaps. 36 and 45). The king, Jehoiakim, destroyed the scroll, which was then redictated by Jeremiah to Baruch. At the time of the Babylonian victory over Egypt at Carchemish in 605, Jeremiah appeared at the royal court in Jerusalem with a yoke on his back arguing that Judah would submit to Babylon for a period of seventy years, in contrast to the (according to Jeremiah, false) prophet Hananiah, who foretold that God would deliver Jerusalem within two years (chaps. 27–28). After the exile of Jehoiachin and the leading citizens of Judah in 597, Jeremiah wrote a letter to the exiles encouraging them to accept exile as God's will (chap. 29). Many considered Jeremiah a traitor, since he urged the people to submit to Babylon. For this he was constantly persecuted, placed in stocks, and put under house arrest. During a lull in the Babylonian siege of Jerusalem in 588, Jeremiah was arrested for treason when he attempted to leave the city to settle a family property matter (chap. 37). Although he was imprisoned, an Ethiopian eunuch named Ebed-melech saw to his welfare, and Zedekiah continued to consult with Jeremiah throughout the rest of the siege (chaps. 37–38). After the fall of Jerusalem, the Babylonians placed Jeremiah under the care of Gedaliah, whom they appointed governor of Mizpah (chap. 39). Following Gedaliah's assassination in 582, Jeremiah urged the remaining population to stay in Judah and rebuild the devastated land, despite the prospects of Babylonian vengeance (chaps. 40–44), but he was taken by force to Egypt, where he lived out his days. He never married, in order to symbolize the destruction that was coming upon his people (chap. 16). His actions and words were very unpopular in Judah, which prompted a great deal of opposition against him. Jeremiah waged an ongoing battle against the false prophets (23.25) who deceived the people into thinking that the times were ones of peace and welfare (7.14). He complained bitterly about his rejection by many in his society. At times, he even charged that God had deceived him, and he cursed the day that he was born (chap. 20). Despite his prophecy of judgment, Jeremiah portrayed a future restoration of Judah and Israel in which the Lord's Torah would be written upon the hearts of the people (chaps. 30–31). He therefore purchased land in his native Anathoth in anticipation of the future restoration (chap. 32). According to rabbinic tradition, Jeremiah wrote the *Book of Jeremiah*, *Kings*, and the *Book of Lamentations* (*B. B.* 15a).

The *Book of Jeremiah* is the second book of the Latter Prophets, although a minority of rabbis considered it to be the first (*B. B.* 14b). There are two extant versions: the Hebrew (the Masoretic Text) and the Greek (the Septuagint). Many scholars believe that the Greek version was a translation from a Hebrew edition of *Jeremiah* that predates the Masoretic Text. The Greek text is approximately one-eighth shorter than the apparently expanded Masoretic Text, and the arrangement of the two versions differs substantially after *Jeremiah* 25.13a. Portions of at least four Hebrew *Jeremiah* manuscripts were discovered among the Dead Sea Scrolls; three of the manuscripts are proto-Masoretic, while one corresponds much more closely to the Greek text. The book contains a mixture of prose and poetry, and some scholars argue that the prose sections may reflect the work of Baruch. An early edition, which may incorporate some of Jeremiah's original discourses in the Temple, is suggested in the present version of chapters 1–20. Within these chapters appear the account of Jeremiah's call to prophesy (chap. 1); prophecies from his early years that focus on the themes of religious harlotry and the "foe from the north" (chaps. 2–10); and oracles concerning Judah and Jerusalem that are built around the prophet's so-called confessions (chaps. 11–20). *Jeremiah* 21–23 is an appendix to chapters 1–20 and focuses on Judah's kings and prophets. A prose section, chapters 24 and 25, presents the prophet's life in relation to the last years of the kingdom of Judah. Included is the "Book of Comfort," chapters 30–33, which appears to be a reworked version of Jeremiah's early oracles that point to the ultimate restoration of the land. The oracles against the nations appear in chapters 46–51. A historical narrative drawn largely from *2 Kings* 24.18–25.30, which describes the Babylonian destruction of Jerusalem and the exile of the population, concludes the book.

• Sheldon H. Blank, *Jeremiah: Man and Prophet* (Cincinnati, 1961). John Bright, *Jeremiah*, The Anchor Bible, vol. 21 (Garden City, N.Y., 1965). Robert P. Carroll, *Jeremiah: A Commentary*, The Old Testament Library (Philadelphia, 1986). Abraham Joshua Heschel, *The Prophets* (New York, 1962). William Lee Holladay, *Jeremiah*, Hermeneia—A Critical and Historical Commentary on the Bible, 2 vols. (Philadelphia, 1986, and Minneapolis, 1989). J. Gerald Janzen, *Studies in the Text of Jeremiah*, Harvard Semitic Monographs, vol. 6 (Cambridge, Mass., 1973). Elmer A. Leslie, *Jeremiah* (Nashville, 1954). Jack R. Lundbom, *Jeremiah: A Study in Ancient Hebrew Rhetoric*, Dissertation Series (Society of Biblical Literature), no. 18 (Missoula, Mont., 1975). William McKane, *A Critical and Exegetical Commentary on Jeremiah*, vol. 1, *Jeremiah 1–25*, International Critical Commentary, vol. 11 (Edinburgh, 1986). Ernest W. Nicholson, *Preaching to the Exiles: A Study of the Prose Tradition of the Book of Jeremiah* (New York, 1970). Thomas W. Overholt, *The Threat of Falsehood: A Study in the Theology of the Book of Jeremiah*, Studies in Biblical Theology, 2d series, 16 (Naperville, Ill., 1970). Leo G. Perdue and Brian Kovacs, eds., *A Prophet to the Nations: Essays in Jeremiah Studies* (Winona Lake, Ind., 1984). John Skinner, *Prophecy and Religion: Studies in the Life of Jeremiah* (Cambridge, 1922). Mark S. Smith, *The Laments of Jeremiah and Their Contexts*, Monograph Series (Society of Biblical Literature) no. 42 (Atlanta, 1990). Jeremiah Unterman, *From Repentance to Redemption: Jeremiah's Thought in Transition*, Journal for the Study of the Old Testament, Supplement Series 54 (Sheffield, Eng., 1987).

—MARVIN A. SWEENEY

JERUSALEM (Heb. Yerushalayim), ancient capital of the Davidic kingdom; spiritual capital of Judaism throughout the ages. It is first mentioned in the Ebla documents and Egyptian execration texts (c.2000 BCE). Although referred to 656 times in the Bible, in the Pentateuch it is linked only with Salem, mentioned at the time of Abraham (*Gn.* 14.8). Later legend identified Mount *Moriah, site of the *'*aqedah*, with the *Temple mount. After *Joshua's conquest of Canaan, the Jebusites retained Jerusalem (*Jgs.* 1.21), situated in hill country, until *David captured it. Anointed king of all Israel, David, in a move aimed at unifying the nation, chose it as his capital over *Hebron (*2 Sm.* 5.5). His choice was probably dictated by its strategic site, its central location, and its non-identification with any of the tribes. It was subsequently referred to as the City of David. In addition to being the political capital, Jerusalem's role as spiritual center was immeasurably enhanced by David's act of bringing the *Ark of the Covenant into the city (*2 Sm.* 6) and by the building of the *Temple under *Solomon (*1 Kgs.* 6ff.). During Temple times the city was the goal of *pilgrimage on the occasion of the three annual pilgrim festivals (see SHALOSH REGALIM). After the Israelite kingdom split in two, Jerusalem remained the capital of the kingdom of *Judah. During the period of the Second Temple, pilgrims flocked to Jerusalem not only from the land of Israel but from Diaspora communities near and far. Jerusalem received distinct treatment in Jewish law. It was the holiest place on earth, and the Holy of Holies was the holiest place in Jerusalem. This led to a series of laws applicable solely in Jerusalem (*B. Q.* 82b; *Kel.* 1.6ff). After the exile of 70 CE, Jerusalem retained its centrality in the Jewish mind. Scattered Jews faced Jerusalem when praying, prayed for the restoration of *Zion, and concluded the Seder service and the Yom Kippur liturgy with the yearning prayer, "Next year in Jerusalem." Many folk customs were linked to mourning over the destruction of the city. An often imaginary Jerusalem was a central feature of folk art. Believing that the Messiah would appear in Jerusalem, Jews went there to die and be buried on the Mount of Olives in anticipation of the resurrection of the dead. After the State of Israel was established, Jerusalem was proclaimed its capital.

• Abraham S. Halkin, ed., *Zion in Jewish Literature* (New York, 1961). Reuven Hammer, *The Jerusalem Anthology* (Philadelphia, 1995). Avraham Holz, *The Holy City: Jews on Jerusalem* (New York, 1970). Lee I. Levine, ed., *The Jerusalem Cathedra: Studies in the History, Archaeology, Geography, and Ethnography of the Land of Israel*, 3 vols. (Jerusalem and Detroit, 1981–1983). Amnon Linder, "Jerusalem as a Focus of Confrontation between Judaism and Christianity," in *Vision and Conflict in the Holy Land*, edited by Richard I. Cohen (Jerusalem and New York, 1985). James D. Purvis, *The Holy City: A Bibliography* (Metuchen, N.J., and London, 1988–1991). Zev Vilnay, *Legends of Jerusalem* (Jerusalem, 1995).

—FERN SECKBACK

JERUSALEM DAY. See YOM YERUSHALAYIM.

JERUSALEM TALMUD. See TALMUD.

JESUS (c.4 BCE–30 CE), founder of *Christianity. The name *Jesus* is the Greek form of the Hebrew name *Yehoshuʿa*; *Christ* is the Greek equivalent of *messiah* (anointed one). The only source of knowledge about Jesus' life and teaching is the *New Testament, which was written in the late first and early second centuries and apparently often reflects the beliefs and struggles of the nascent church rather than those of Jesus' own day. Jewish references to Jesus (for example, in the Talmud and **Toledot Yeshu*) are late and merely polemical; there is also a reference in Josephus (*Antiquities of the Jews* 18.3.3.63–64). It appears that Jesus was a Galilean Jew who, as a young adult, was influenced by *John the Baptist. John preached *baptism and repentance in preparation for the immediate advent of the kingdom of God. During this period, Jesus also may have absorbed some sectarian influences (see ESSENES). He became a wandering teacher, roaming the country with a small band of followers, preaching in the synagogues, and urging the people to repent because the kingdom of God was at hand. New Testament accounts of Jesus' clashes with the *Pharisees and his diatribes against the Jews probably reflect growing Christian hostility against the Jews, who rejected the claims of the young church. The Pharisees evidently resented the authority that Jesus claimed and the liberties that he took regarding the law far more than they minded the insistence (which he shared with other moralists and teachers) that intention and right spirit were more important than outward performance. In spite of these conflicts, Jesus' sayings resemble contemporary rabbinic teaching, and he essentially belonged to the Pharisaic rather than the Sadducean or sectarian tradition, both in his observance of the law and in his acceptance of specifically Pharisaic doctrines (e.g., the resurrection of the dead). Ultimately, it was his conception of his messianic mission and destiny that was decisive. Jesus lived in the intense apocalyptic expectation of contemporary Jewish sectarian *eschatology and apparently believed himself called to the messianic role of the *Son of Man. In the course of his short ministry, he seems to have concluded that his task also involved suffering and dying. After a messianic entry into Jerusalem just before Pesaḥ in 30 CE, he was arrested as a potential revolutionary and executed (by crucifixion) by order of the Roman procurator Pontius Pilate, probably at the instigation of Jewish circles who feared the Roman reactions to messianic agitation. For some time, his disciples and their followers, who believed that Jesus had risen from the dead and ascended into heaven, existed as a sect within the main body of Jewry (see JEWISH CHRISTIANS) but soon established a distinct, and for a long time hostile, religion. Although the life and teachings of Jesus have exercised a great influence on the course and development of Western civilization, they had no direct effect on Jewish thought; nevertheless, their reconstruction by New Testament scholarship helps to illuminate the religious movements and messianic ferment in Judaism at the end of the Second Temple period. Over the past century, there has been considerable Jewish scholarship concerning Jesus (J. Klausner, D. Flusser, G. Vermes). After World War II, Western Christianity became increasingly conscious of the Jewishness of Jesus, his totally Jewish milieu, and the Jewish inspiration of his teachings. Research into the *Qumran community has shown that much of Jesus' teaching previously thought to derive from Hellenistic sources can be traced to Jewish sectarianism.

• Markus Barth, *Jesus the Jew* (Atlanta, 1978). John Westerdale Bowker, *Jesus and the Pharisees* (Cambridge, 1973). James H. Charlesworth, *Jesus within Judaism* (New York, 1989). Haim Hermann Cohn, *The Trial and Death of Jesus* (New York, 1972). David Flusser, *Jesus* (New York, 1969). Paula Fredriksen, *From Jesus to Christ* (New Haven, 1988). Joseph Klausner, *Jesus of Nazareth*, translated by Herbert Danby (New York, 1925). E. P. Sanders, *Jesus and Judaism* (Philadelphia, 1985). Samuel Sandmel, *We Jews and Jesus* (New York, 1965). Geza Vermes, *Jesus the Jew* (London, 1973). Geza Vermes, *Jesus and the World of Judaism* (Philadelphia, 1983).

JETHRO (Heb. Yitro), father-in-law of Moses and priest of Midian. After Moses, having fled from Egypt to Midian, saved Jethro's seven daughters from being molested by shepherds, Jethro gave his daughter Zipporah to Moses in marriage. In this account, Jethro is called Reuel (*Ex.* 2.16–22); in *Exodus* 3.1, he is called Jethro; and in *Numbers* 10.29, Hobab. These are three variant traditions referring to the same individual. Jethro later blessed the Lord, offered him sacrifices, and gave Moses advice on how to lighten his judicial burden by hearing only the most difficult of cases, while appointing God-fearing men to handle the rest (*Ex.* 18.1–24).

• Jacob Milgrom, *Numbers*, The JPS Torah Commentary (Philadelphia, 1990), pp. 78–79. Nahum M. Sarna, *Exodus*, The JPS Torah Commentary (Philadelphia, 1991), pp. 12, 98–101.

—SHALOM PAUL

JEW (Heb. Yehudi), originally a tribal definition meaning a member of the tribe of *Judah. With the division of the kingdom during the reign of Rehoboam, the southern kingdom, consisting of the two loyalist tribes of Judah and Benjamin, took the single name Judah. Thus the word *Yehudit* (Hebrew) in *2 Kings* 18.28 means, in its context, "the language of the kingdom of Judah." With the disappearance of the northern kingdom of Israel and the exile of its population, Judah alone remained to perpetuate the Israelite faith and nationality. During the Babylonian exile, the Judean exiles retained their communal identity. After their return to Jerusalem following the declaration of Cyrus II, they came to be called by the name *Yehudi*. The word became synonymous with the "descendants of Abraham" and is found in *Esther* 2.5 referring to "Mordecai . . . a Benjamite." Hence, *Jew* developed into a common appellation (from the Gr. *Ioudaios* and the Lat. *Judaeus*, from which the word *Judaism* was derived to designate the faith of the Jew). In rabbinical sources the term is used in a purely homiletical as well as in a legal–theological sense; a statement such as "anyone who repudiates idolatry is called a Jew" (*Meg.* 18a) has homiletical significance only, whereas rabbinic law defines a Jew as either a person born of a Jewish mother or one who has been converted to Judaism (see PROSELYTE). The origin of the rule that a child born of a Jewish father and a non-Jewish mother is not considered a Jew is obscure, but scriptural authority is adduced from *Nehemiah* 10.29, where it is said that Ezra obligated those Jews who had married foreign wives to put them away together with their children. The child of a Jewish mother, on the other hand, even if the father is not Jewish, has all the rights and privileges of a Jew. Whether, or the extent to which, a Jew can lose his Jewish character and the rights and responsibilities entailed by it has been a matter of controversy. The Talmudic statement "an Israelite, even though he sins, remains an Israelite" (*San.* 44a) has been interpreted so widely as to include even the sin of apostasy, but different authorities have held varying views regarding the loss of certain rights. Later authorities ruled that a repentant apostate who wishes to return to his original faith must go through a ceremony of readmission; nevertheless, failure to do so would not deprive him of his character as a Jew. The non-Jew who wishes to become a Jew has, after undergoing a course of instruction, formally to take upon himself the obligations of Judaism, and in the case of a male to undergo ritual *circumcision. All converts, in addition, have to undergo immersion in a ritual bath (**miqveh*) and come before a properly constituted court. Such a convert is in every respect a Jew and is considered to be on a par with natural-born Jews. The convert suffers from practically no disabilities, except that a female convert cannot marry a priest. Reform Judaism modified and sometimes abolished the Talmudic rules and rituals concerning conversion and in recent years has accepted as Jews those born of a Jewish father and a non-Jewish mother (see PATRILINEAL DESCENT). This has led to conflicts with other branches of Judaism, especially Orthodox Judaism, which in many cases will not recognize as Jews those considered as such by Reform (and often by Conservative) Jews. Bitter controversies have erupted over the interpretation of the *Law of Return (see JEW, WHO IS A?, CONTROVERSY). In the post-Emancipation world, Jewish identity is no longer based exclusively upon religious practice or belief, and many of those who consider themselves or are considered Jews are not religiously observant (see JEWISH IDENTITY). Prior to the Holocaust there were almost seventeen million Jews in the world. Almost six million were killed during World War II, and today, the world Jewish population is approximately thirteen million people.

• Shaye J. D. Cohen, "Crossing the Boundary and Becoming a Jew," *Harvard Theological Review* 80 (1987): 14–33. Shaye J. D. Cohen and E. S. Frerichs, eds., *Diasporas in Antiquity*, Brown Judaic Studies (Atlanta, 1993). Martin Goodman, *Who Was a Jew?* (Oxford, 1989). Lawrence H. Schiffman, *Who Was a Jew?: Rabbinic and Halakhic Perspectives on the Jewish Christian Schism* (Hoboken, N.J., 1985). Robert M. Seltzer, *Jewish People, Jewish Thought: The Jewish Experience in History* (New York, 1980).

JEW, WHO IS A?, CONTROVERSY. Jewish law (*halakhah*) defines a Jew as a person born of a Jewish mother or one who has converted to Judaism. In the State of Israel it became essential to formulate a legal definition of a Jew as a result of the adoption in 1950 of the *Law of Return, which granted Jews the right to immigrate to Israel and immediately receive citizenship. This became a major issue following the considerable immigration from Poland in 1956 and 1957, which included a high proportion of mixed marriages, in which the wife was generally the non-Jewish partner. The question arose as to how to register children of such marriages should both parents request that they be registered as Jews. The dispute led to a government crisis when the minister of the interior instructed that anyone who declared himself to be a Jew should be registered as such, as a result of which decision the religious parties left the coalition government. Prime Minister David Ben-Gurion sought the advice of scholars throughout the world in search of a solution. The replies were diverse. Orthodox authorities insisted on *halakhah* and criticized Ben-Gurion for even seeking non-Orthodox opinions. Israeli Supreme Court justice Haim Cohn responded that once jurisdiction in the country had been split between religious and secular authorities, inconsistencies were unavoidable; a Jew for the purpose of citizenship registration could not be the same as a Jew according to rabbinical tradition, and therefore the parents' wishes should be respected. The majority of respondents recognized the link between nationality and religion and recommended the maintenance of traditional categories, at least for the time being. In 1959 Ben-Gurion revoked the directive of the interior minister, and the following year new directives were issued according to halakhic guidelines. In 1962, Brother Daniel Rufeisen, a converted Jew who had become a Catholic monk, claimed citizenship under the Law of Return, saying he was a Jew by birth and remained a Jew halakhically (according to the halakhic prescription that however much a Jew may stray, he remains a Jew). The Israeli Supreme Court ruled that *Jew* for the purposes of the Law of Return referred to those traditionally regarded by Jews as such and did not apply to a convert to Christianity. In the Shalit case, a Jewish father with a non-Jewish wife sought to have his Israeli-born children registered as Jews. A political controversy was triggered when the Supreme Court ruled that a registration officer was bound to honor the request of the parents, as a result of which in 1970 the Law of Return was amended to set aside the halakhic definition as the criterion.

The Indian *Bene Israel and the Ethiopian *Beta Israel were not originally recognized by the Israeli rabbinate because of doubts about the Jewish origins of these communities. The problems concerning the Bene Israel were eventually resolved; the halakhic identity of the Beta Israel remains under dispute.

The State of Israel has always recognized non-Orthodox conversions contracted outside Israel and registered such converts as Jews, though they are not recognized as Jews in the rabbinical courts, which have jurisdiction over all matters of personal status (including marriage and divorce). In the 1980s, Orthodox Jews proposed that only converts who had undergone an Orthodox conversion be recognized as Jews and not those who had converted under Conservative or Reform auspices. The storm of opposition aroused in the Diaspora, notably in the United States, persuaded the Israeli premier not to act on the demand. It has remained, however, on the agenda of the religious parties. In 1985 a Reform convert from the United States who had moved to Israel appealed to the Supreme Court when the Interior Ministry refused to register her as a Jew. She won the appeal. The issue arose again in 1995 when the Israeli Supreme Court recognized the legitimacy of Reform and Conservative conversions inside Israel. The religious parties fought to overturn the ruling.

The question of who is a Jew also arose in the United States, heightened by the proliferation of mixed marriages. Thousands of conversions were performed by non-Orthodox authorities. The problem was exacerbated in the mid-1980s by the acceptance of *patrilineal descent by the Reform and Reconstructionist movements as an acceptable criterion for creating a presumption of Jewishness for children of an interfaith marriage. Thus a considerable and growing number of children of non-Jewish mothers or of parents whose conversions have been conducted under non-Orthodox auspices are not accepted as Jews in Orthodox circles. This means, for example, that they could not have an Orthodox marriage without undergoing an Orthodox conversion.

• S. Z. Abramov, *Perpetual Dilemma: Jewish Religion in the Jewish State* (New York, 1976). Sidney Goldstein, "Profile of American Jewry: Insights from the 1990 National Jewish Population Survey," *American Jewish Year Book* (1992), pp. 77–176. Irving Greenberg, "Will There Be One Jewish People by the Year 2000?" *Perspectives* (June 1985). Sidney B. Hoenig, ed., *Jewish Identity: Modern Responsa and Opinions on the Registration of Children of Mixed Marriages* (New York, 1965). Charles S. Liebman, ed., *Religious and Secular: Conflict and Accommodation between Jews in Israel* (Jerusalem, 1990). Charles S. Liebman and Steven M. Cohen, *Two Worlds of Judaism: The Israeli and American Experiences* (New Haven, 1990). Jonathan Sacks, *One People? Tradition, Modernity, and Jewish Unity* (London, 1993).

JEWISH CHRISTIANS. The abrogation, called "fulfillment," of the Law proclaimed by *Paul (see CHRISTIANITY) led to adoption of the new faith by many gentiles. Most of the Jewish followers of *Jesus, however, who had scrupulously maintained the ritual and ceremonial regulations of Judaism, continued to do so and became Jewish Christians; that is, Jews who observed the Law while believing in Jesus. The varying extent of their belief differentiates the two main sects of these Jewish Christians, the *Ebionites and the Nazarenes. The former believed in Jesus' messianic character but denied his divinity and miraculous birth, while maintaining the continued validity of the Law, which they observed. The Nazarenes accepted Jesus' divinity and maintained that the Law was binding on Jews only. It was in order to drive the Jewish Christians from the Jewish religious communion that the patriarch *Gamli'el II instructed R. Shemu'el ha-Qatan to compose the imprecation that became an additional paragraph to the existing *ʿAmidah (c.100 CE; see BIRKAT HA-MINIM).

In modern times, attempts have been made by Jewish converts to Christianity to reestablish the concept of Jewish Christians (or Hebrew Christians). Over a hundred such groups are in existence including Beth Sar Shalom (founded in 1894), Ariel Ministries, Beth Yeshua, and Emmanu-el. The best-known Hebrew Christian group is Jews for Jesus, founded in 1970. They have active proselytization programs and teach that Jews who accept Jesus as Messiah are not giving up their Judaism but are fulfilling it; without this, Judaism remains incomplete. The groups have missions in various parts of the world, including Israel. Jews do not accept members of these groups as Jewish and maintain that a person who accepts Jesus as Messiah is simply a Christian. A number of court rulings in Israel have rejected claims by Hebrew Christians to be regarded as Jews. See also APOSTASY.

• Terrance Callan, *Forgetting the Root* (New York, 1986). Jean Daniélov, *Theology of Jewish Christianity* (London and Chicago, 1964). Richard N. Longenecker, *The Christology of Early Jewish Christianity* (London, 1970). M. R. Rudin, "Cults and Missionaries," *Encyclopedia Judaica Year Book* (1986–1987): 80–90. Hans Joachim Schoeps, *Jewish Christianity* (Philadelphia, 1969). Hugh Joseph Schonfield, *The History of Jewish Christianity: From the First to the Twentieth Century* (London, 1936).

JEWISH IDENTITY. In the biblical period, Jewish identity meant belonging to the Jewish community as a religio-national entity. The stranger (*ger*) was naturalized into this community by choosing to live its life. At the very beginning of Jewish history, during the Exodus from Egypt, a substantial number of strangers chose to accompany the Jews into the desert (*Ex.* 12.48; *Lv.* 24.10). During the conquest of Canaan, remnants of the earlier inhabitants of the land of Canaan remained resident among the Jews (*1 Kgs.* 9.20–21), and, from time to time, some refugees from nearby peoples also came into the land of Israel (*Is.* 16.4, 24.14–15). Marriage with *gerim* was expressly permitted with the exception of those descended from Ammonites and Moabites and, for three generations, from Edomites and Egyptians (*Dt.* 23.4–9). The first important change in these attitudes occurred after the Babylonian exile. The handful of Jews who returned under Zerubbabel and Ezra in the sixth and fifth centuries BCE were now an embattled minority, even in the very heart of their own settlement, in Jerusalem and the land nearby. Ezra chose the uncompromising path of ordering all of those who wanted to remain faithful as Jews to "put away" their foreign wives (*Ezr.* 9–10).

Because of the remarkable success that ancient Jews had had in converting others, new formulations of Jewish identity arose. The Hasmoneans, in the first century BCE, forced Idumeans and a number of other border communities to convert to Judaism (it is not entirely clear whether these conversions were conducted with more formality than those of the ancient biblical *gerim*). In the Diaspora there was an increasing number, perhaps millions by the first century, of *sebomenoi* (*metuentes, yere'im* [God fearers]), gentiles who had not gone the whole route toward conversion. Most half-Judaized gentiles remained in that estate and were regarded not as Jews but as sympathizers. The earliest Pauline Christians, those gentile converts to the new religion who had not first become Jews according to the law, were not regarded by anyone as Jews. The Jewish Christians, especially the circle in Jerusalem and the Holy Land in the first century, were much more of a problem. Whatever may have been the exact beliefs of these *Ebionites, their exclusion from the Jewish community did not occur primarily for halakhic reasons. By their own choice these Jewish Christians left Jerusalem and emigrated to Pella in Transjordan at the beginning of the war of 66–70. They separated themselves from the national destiny of the Jews. For some years the Jewish Christian group remained in an intermediate position, but those who did not participate in the Bar Kokhba' Revolt (c.132–135) could no longer lay any claim on being Jewish. Official Christianity was by then largely gentile, and the new religion was systematically excluding all traces of the preeminence of Jews.

The most complicated example of the interweaving of internal and external forces was that of Marranism (see MARRANOS). On occasion, both Islam and Christianity forced Jews to apostatize. This occurred in such places as Yemen and North Africa, in the early centuries of Islam, and, from late antiquity throughout the Middle Ages, especially in the Iberian Peninsula, in the case of Christianity. Under Islam, forced apostates were usually allowed to return to Judaism within one generation. Those who chose not to do so usually rapidly assimilated. Under Christianity, the situation was different. The majority that had forced the conversions looked upon the newcomers with suspicion for many generations, certainly for longer than any intensity of Jewish feeling or affirmation lasted among the Marranos themselves. Those who chose to remain Marranos had, in one or two generations, little Jewish loyalty and observed even fewer secret Jewish practices than supposed. Remaining Jewish loyalties were evoked into new vigor in sixteenth-century Spain, not so much by memories of the past as by the persecution of the Inquisition. Attacks continued in the seventeenth and eighteenth centuries in the name of the doctrine of *limpieza de sangre* (purity of blood), under which new Christians of even partial Jewish ancestry were barred from the highest offices of state and church; there was, therefore, new reason for people who had ceased to be Jewish except by the accident of birth to return, as it were, to Judaism. This was a difficult and sometimes tragic journey into a strange and constricting world. Until the dawn of the modern era, the definition of Jewish identity was not a problem. A Jew was defined by *halakhah*, as one who was born of a Jewish mother (or who converted to Judaism) and who, in actual practice, regarded himself and was regarded as belonging to the Jewish community.

*Emancipation cast a new light on the whole question of Jewish identity. With the creation of the modern secular state, the decision to uphold one's religion became purely voluntaristic. At the height of nineteenth-century liberalism in Europe and America, some Jews simply ceased to maintain Jewish associations of any kind. On the other hand, it was possible for Jews to feel a strong sense of Jewish identity on the basis of minimal or no association, even after every vestige of religious faith and practice had evaporated. Increasingly there arose the institutions of the voluntaristic Jewish community of the modern era, these bodies who regarded it as their task to serve all who claimed to be Jews, especially at moments of danger or when such people needed social services. Indeed, these voluntaristic associations to alleviate suffering became increasingly the building blocks of Jewish communal organization.

The new definition was that Jews were not a religion but a people. Just as it was possible in the modern age of doubt to cease being Anglican yet remain English, so it was possible to cease believing in Judaism yet remain Jewish. Theoreticians of Diaspora nationalism, such as Simon Dubnow, opted for Jewish communal organization, an international Jewish parliament, and national institutions of culture and education to maintain the national ethos. The Yiddishist movement that arose at the beginning of the twentieth century placed emphasis on Yiddish as the spoken and living language of world Jewry (at least before 1939) and aimed at preserving a secular national culture in that language. The most important national movement, Zionism, proposed to normalize the Jewish people by concentrating them in their own land and reviving the Hebrew language.

In the 1980s, the Reform movement agreed to regard someone either of whose parents were Jewish as a Jew by birth (see PATRILINEAL DESCENT). For religious Jews, the question of Jewish identity continues to be decided by *halakhah*. The overarching institutions of world Jewry determine their policy by broader and more amorphous considerations of history and situation. So, when the last remaining, completely de-Judaized, almost entirely intermarried Communists of Jewish parentage in Poland were purged in 1968, the Israeli government provided them with the necessary exit passports even though few were going to Israel, and the world Jewish social-service budget took care of the overwhelming majority who opted to go to other countries. Beginning in the 1970s, equally flexible standards were applied to those who were leaving the Soviet Union as Jews and more recently, in the 1980s, to the *Beta Israel from Ethiopia. Those who suffer as Jews remain part of world Jewish concern. In the broadest sense, significant elements of world Jewry in the modern era have defined, and are defining, Jewish identity as a community of history and destiny. See also JEW, WHO IS A?, CONTROVERSY.

• Bernard J. Bamberger, *Proselytism in the Talmudic Period* (Cincinnati, 1939). Calvin Goldscheider and Alan S. Zuckerman, *The Transformation of the Jews* (Chicago, 1984). Simon N. Herman, *Israelis and Jews: The Continuity of an Identity* (Philadelphia, 1970). Simon N. Herman, *Jewish Identity: A Social Psychological Perspective* (Beverly Hills, Calif., 1977). Arthur Hertzberg, *The Jews in America* (New York, 1989). Baruch Litvin and S. B. Hoenig, *Jewish Identity* (New York, 1965).

—ARTHUR HERTZBERG

JEWISH INSTITUTE OF RELIGION. See HEBREW UNION COLLEGE–JEWISH INSTITUTE OF RELIGION.

JEWISH LANGUAGES refers variously to the *Hebrew language, to languages at some time spoken by most Jews (*Aramaic, Greek), and to about twenty Judeo-Xenic (from Gr. *xenos* [foreign]) languages used by Jews in the Diaspora, including *Judeo-Arabic, Judeo-Berber, Judeo-German (*Yiddish), Judeo-Greek, *Judeo-Persian, Judeo-Tatar, Judeo-Catalan, Judeo-French, Judeo-Italian, Judeo-Portuguese, Judeo-Provençal, and *Judeo-Spanish (Ladino or Judezmo). The last six named may have descended from Judeo-Latin. Judeo-Xenic languages originated in the language of the larger community, with an admixture of religious and cultural lexicon, and occasionally grammatical or syntactic features from Hebrew, Aramaic, or other languages; were mostly reduced to writing, always with Hebrew letters (Ladino is now written using the Latin alphabet); have in many cases produced considerable religious (Bible translations and dictionaries) and secular (poetry, philosophy) literature; and have at times been used as secret languages (some like the North African Lashon have had only that purpose). With respect to provenance, number of speakers, and literature, the most important Judeo-Xenic languages are Judeo-Arabic, Ladino, and Yiddish. Yiddish was previously spoken by three-fourths of the world's Jews. Because of the Holocaust, migration to the State of Israel, and assimilation, all Judeo-Xenic languages are on the decline or have disappeared.

• Joshua A. Fishman, ed., *Readings in the Sociology of Jewish Languages*, vol. 1 (Leiden, 1985). David L. Gold, ed., *Jewish Linguistic Studies* (Haifa, 1989). Herbert H. Paper, ed., *Jewish Languages, Theme and Variations* (Cambridge, Mass., 1978).

—DENNIS M. DREYFUS

JEWISH LAW. The term *Jewish law* is a translation from the German *jüdisches Recht* and is identified with the nineteenth-century scholarly enterprise of highlighting the legal quality of the *halakhah* and demonstrating its similarity to other systems of law. The Hebrew form of the term, *mishpat ʿIvri*, was coined by a group of Jewish legal scholars in Russia, shortly after the issuing of the Balfour Declaration by the British government in 1917. The major goals of this group, which became known as the Mishpat Ivri Society, were the preparation of a legal system for a future Jewish state based upon *halakhah* and the establishment of a research institute for this purpose in Jerusalem. The method proposed by the society for achieving its first goal was to separate the legal aspects of the *halakhah* from its purely religious elements and to "prepare Jewish law to exist as a secular legal system" (*Ha-Mishpat ha-ʿIvri* [Moscow, 1918]).

Halakhah as a Legal System. Notwithstanding the overall unity of its religious and legal elements, the *halakhah* makes a number of basic distinctions between these two areas. Religious laws, such as Sabbath observance and the dietary laws, are known as **issur ve-hetter* and are distinguished from *civil law and criminal law (*penal law), which are termed *dinei mamonot* and *dinei nefashot*, respectively. Religious law is generally less amenable to rabbinic legislation than civil law, and the maxim that "custom overrides law" is restricted to the realm of civil matters. The rule that the "law of the land is the law" (**dina' de-malkhuta' dina'*) has no application in the area of religious law but is highly significant in civil law. *Dinei mamonot* is, therefore, an identifiable body of *halakhah* that corresponds to a substantial part of the subject matter of modern legal systems and displays much of the flexibility and capacity for development associated with them. It is this body of legal doctrine that is the object of study in the discipline of Jewish law and with which the Mishpat Ivri Society was concerned.

The Jewish Judicial System. Biblical law provides detailed instructions for the establishment of a judicial system (*Ex.* 18.21–27; *Dt.* 16.18), and Jewish courts (see BEIT DIN) have existed in all Jewish communities, even in the absence of political sovereignty, and in all countries of the Diaspora. Jewish judicial *autonomy was a consistent feature of Jewish life until the Emancipation and constituted one of the major privileges of Jewish communities in their medieval charters. The jurisdiction of the Jewish courts extended to all aspects of private and communal life, and in Spain it included the power to administer *capital punishment, particularly in cases of informers. The wide range of issues dealt with by the Jewish courts in pre-Emancipation times is manifested in the **responsa* literature of this period, the bulk of which is devoted to civil, criminal, and public administrative law. Sanctions available to Jewish courts included attachment of property, *fines, corporal punishment (see FLOGGING), and, most important of all, the *ḥerem* (*excommunication). Internal discipline was also effected by means of the prohibition against non-Jewish courts (*Git.* 88b), and a Jew who took his case to a gentile tribunal in defiance of the Jewish court was "deemed to have reviled and blasphemed and rebelled against the Torah of Moses our teacher" (Maimonides, *Hilkhot Sanhedrin* 26.7). Only in exceptional circumstances was recourse to a non-Jewish court permitted, and even in the post-Emancipation period, religious Jews continued to take their civil disputes to rabbinical courts rather than to the general courts of the countries in which they lived.

Matters of Personal Status in Israeli Law. Upon its establishment in 1948, the State of Israel adopted the legal system in force during the British Mandate. Matters of personal status, which consist mainly of marriage and divorce, were decided by the religious courts of the parties concerned; other legal issues were governed by an amalgam of English, Ottoman, and Muslim law, together with a number of Mandatory ordinances. Under the Rabbinical Courts Jurisdiction (Marriage and Divorce) Law of 1953, Jewish citizens and residents are subject to the sole jurisdiction of the rabbinical courts in these areas. The religious courts also enjoy a limited concurrent jurisdiction with the general courts in *maintenance cases and in cases involving other aspects of personal-status law. In these other areas of personal-status law, however, the religious courts are not empowered to rule based solely on *halakhah* without reference to Israeli legislation. Judicial review of a religious court is also available if the court ignores the requirements of natural justice, such as denying one party the right to a court hearing. In general, the trend in Israeli law is to restrict the jurisdiction of the rabbinical courts to marriage and divorce and to place the rest of personal-status law in the hands of the secular courts. There are, nevertheless, examples of the incorporation of halakhic principles into secular personal-status law, an outstanding example being the provision in the Succession Law of 1965 that "the fact that a child is born out of wedlock shall have no effect upon succession rights." This principle, which was certainly unique to Israeli law in 1965, was based squarely upon the halakhic rule that illegitimate offspring (*mamzerim*) do not suffer any disadvantage with respect to rights of succession (*Shulḥan ʿArukh, Ḥoshen Mishpat* 76.6). A striking illustration of the purely secular character of Israeli personal-status law in areas outside of marriage and divorce is the definition of Jewish identity under the *Law of Return of 1950. (See also Jew, Who Is a?, Controversy.)

Jewish Law in Areas Other than Personal Status. There is no legal recognition in Israel of the binding force of *halakhah* outside the rubric of matters of personal status. Even those laws that deal entirely with issues of a purely halakhic or religious nature, such as the official status of the Sabbath and festivals or pig breeding and missionary activities by non-Jews, are all administered by secular authorities and applied by the courts without any reference to *halakhah*. The rules and principles of Jewish law are, nevertheless, often referred to in the course of parliamentary debates on proposed legislation, and it is routine practice for all draft bills to be sent to the deputy attorney general and advisor on Jewish law, whose comments are, on occasion, incorporated into the preamble to the final law. One example of such a law is the Wages Protection Law of 1958, which requires employers to pay their workers on time. The principle of prompt payment is found in the Bible (*Lv.* 19.13; *Dt.* 24.15) and is discussed in the Talmud and codes (*B. M.* 11a–112a). These sources were referred to in the Knesset deliberations, and the preamble to the law mentions its halakhic background. Nevertheless, none of the sections of the actual law is based upon halakhic principles, and the detailed provisions that they incorporate are to be found in many modern legal systems. Moreover, in the course of the Knesset discussion, the suggestion that "any problem arising in relation to the implementation of this law be resolved by reference to Jewish law" was summarily dismissed by the minister of justice on the grounds that it was neither practical nor wise.

With regard to case law, the judiciary has proved to be a far more fertile ground for the incorporation of Jewish law than the legislature. Judges have referred to the *halakhah* for the purpose of elucidating legal terms and concepts. In some cases, Jewish law has played a pivotal role in actual decisions. One of the most dramatic cases is that of *Moshe Cohen v. State of Israel* (Cr.A. 91/80 P.D. 35(3) 281), in which the petitioner was charged with the *rape of his wife. The relevant section of the 1977 Penal Law defines rape as "illegal" intercourse. The common law position was that a husband could not have "illegal" intercourse with his wife since intercourse constituted one of the basic conditions of the marriage agreement entered into by both parties. The origin of this position lies in the Christian concept of the conjugal debt owed by a wife to her husband. The prosecution argued that the term *unlawfully* should be interpreted in the light of the petitioner's personal law, which in Cohen's case was Jewish law. Upon examination of the relevant sources it became evident that the *halakhah* forbids the use of force in the context of marital intercourse (*ʿEruv.* 100b; Maimonides, *Hilkhot Ishut* 15.17; *Shulḥan ʿArukh, Even ha-ʿEzer* no. 25.2), although there is no criminal sanction against a husband who disregards this prohibition. The court held that it was permissible to extrapolate from the realm of pure halakhic prohibitions to the criminal law, and Moshe Cohen was found guilty of raping his wife. Justice Bekhor commented on the progressive approach of Jewish law in this area, and contrasted the positive attitude toward female sexual fulfillment in Jewish sources with the generally negative one found in many Christian writings. The law has since been changed in both the United Kingdom and the United States in favor of the wife. In this case, *halakhah* was applied in order to achieve a result that was morally progressive, and it is in this type of enterprise that the courts have excelled at drawing inspiration from the *halakhah*. Another case of this nature is *Becker v. Eilat* (H.C. 172\78, P.D. 32(3) 372), in which the petitioner was a road-safety expert who had been summoned to testify in a homicide case. He declined to take the witnesses' oath on the Bible because he was an agnostic. Under existing law, a witness could be excused from taking an oath on the grounds of "religion" or "conscience." Moreover, the petitioner's request to be excused from taking the oath was not made in "good faith" as required by the law. The high court reversed the lower court's decision both in terms of the interpretation of the exemption qualifications and the issue of "good faith." Justice Elon pointed out that under Jewish law there is no witnesses' oath, since all witnesses are subject to the biblical prohibition against "bearing false witness against your neighbor" (*Ex.* 20.13; *Dt.* 5.17). According to Talmudic law, witnesses are warned about the terrible consequences of lying to the court, but there is no formal oath to tell the truth. A change occurred in the Middle Ages, possibly under non-Jewish influence, and the court was given discretion to impose an oath should it feel that this step was necessary for the establishment of the truth. This approach was recommended to the Israeli legislature by Justice Elon as being commensurate with the demands of both justice and the Jewish tradition in a modern context. Shortly after this decision the law was changed, and under the Evidence Law Amendment (Warning of Witnesses and Removal of Oath) of 1980 there is no mandatory witnesses' oath in Israeli courts. Instead, the witness is warned to tell the truth, and the judge has the discretion to impose an oath if this step would facilitate truthful evidence. The witness preserves the right to request exemption from such an oath on grounds of "conscience" and "religion," provided that the request is made in "good faith." In both of these cases, the results obtained under the inspiration of Jewish law were acceptable under general jurisprudence and morality. Where this is not the case, the court is very firm in its rejection of *halakhah* as a source for considering the solution to the problem with which it is dealing. Notwithstanding its lack of official status, Israeli courts have turned to Jewish law for guidance with respect to general issues of morality and justice from the early days of the establishment of the state.

One of the elements of mandatory law incorporated into Israeli law was article 46 of the Palestine Order in Council (1922). It provided that legal problems to which there were no solutions in the existing law be solved by reference to the principles of canon law and equity as they were applied in England. Although this link with English law was severely restricted by Israeli courts in the early years of the state, it was not officially severed until 1980, with the passage of the Foundations of Law Act. According to this act, a court that is unable to find an answer to a legal problem in "legislation, case-law or by way of analogy shall decide the case in the light of the principles of freedom, justice, equity and peace of the heritage of Israel." The scope of this law is a matter of debate, but it does provide an official basis for the use of halakhic material in cases where the result accords with the principles of freedom, justice, equity, and peace specified in the law. Among the issues discussed and informed by Jewish law in recent years are kidney transplants from mentally incompetent patients; protection of privacy and the status of evidence obtained by nonconsensual medical procedures; conscientious objection; prisoners' rights to marital relations and judicial bias; and issues of ethical significance (see Israel, State of, Jewish Religious Life in).

The Mishpat Ivri movement has been criticized on the grounds that its work constitutes a secularization of *halakhah*. One reason for this charge is the fact that the areas of *halakhah* chosen by the proponents of the movement for purposes of both academic research and practical application to the legal system of the State of Israel are confined to civil and criminal matters. The field of religious law is almost entirely neglected, notwithstanding the fact that it includes procedural matters such as the laws of evidence and judicial discretion, which apply to all areas of *halakhah*. Another critique is that the unique feature of *halakhah* is its concept of justice and righteousness rather than its substantive solutions to particular legal problems. Only a judge steeped in the traditional ethos of the *halakhah* is in a position to elucidate this feature of *halakhah* in the case before him and apply it. It is also argued by critics of Mishpat Ivri that the research methodology used by its principal champions is historical rather than normative, and yet they claim that the results of this research should be applied in the legal system of the State of Israel, which is, after all, a normative legal system.

The defenders of Mishpat Ivri maintain that the distinction between civil and religious law is an internal one and that the former is traditionally much more flexible than the latter. Mishpat Ivri also is presented as the process of analyzing *halakhah* (*lamdanut*) rather than deciding it (*pesiqah*). Both the selective nature of Mishpat Ivri and the secular context in which it operates are compatible with the division between civil and religious law and the distinction between *lamdanut* and *pesiqah* in classical halakhic thinking. This argument is also valid in the context of research methodology, since it justifies the adoption of an analytical, as opposed to a strictly normative, approach to law.

• Haim Cohn, *Jewish Law in Ancient and Modern Israel* (New York, 1971). David Daube, *Ancient Jewish Law* (Leiden, 1981). Elliot Dorff and Arthur Rosett, *A Living Tree: The Roots and Growth of Jewish Law* (New York, 1988). Menachem Elon, *Jewish Law: History, Sources, Principles* (Philadelphia, 1994). D. Frimer, "Israel Civil Courts and Rabbinical Courts Under One Roof," *Israel Law Review* 24 (1990): 553–559. Louis Ginzberg, *On Jewish Law and Lore* (New York, 1970). Martin Golding, ed., *Jewish Law and Legal Theory* (Aldershot, 1994). Neil S. Hecht et al., eds., *An Introduction to the History and Sources of Jewish Law* (Oxford, 1996). Isaac Herzog, *The Main Institutions of Jewish Law*, 2d ed. (London, 1965). Bernard Jackson, "Jewish Law or Jewish Laws," *Jewish Law Annual* 8 (1989): 15–34. *Jewish Law Annual*, vols. 1–11 (1980–1994). Aaron Kirschenbaum, *Equity in Jewish Law* (New York, 1991). Mendell Lewittes, *Principles and Development of Jewish Law* (New York, 1987). Brahyahu Lifshitz, "Israeli Law and Jewish Law: Interaction and Independence," *Israel Law Review* 24 (1990): 507–524. Samuel Mendelsohn, *The Criminal Jurisprudence of the Jews* (New York, 1991). Dale Patrick, ed., *Thinking Biblical Law* (Atlanta, 1989). Emanuel Quint and Neil Hecht, *Jewish Jurisprudence* (Chur, Switzerland, 1980). Pinhas Shifman, "Family Law in Israel: The Struggle Between Religious and Secular Law," *Israel Law Review* 24 (1990): 537–552. Shmuel Shilo, "The Contrast Between *Mishpat Ivri* and *Halakah*," *Tradition* (1982): 91–100. Eliav Shochetman, "Israeli Law and Jewish Law: Interaction and Independence: A Commentary," *Israel Law Review* 24 (1990): 525–536. Moshe Silberg, *Talmudic Law and the Modern State* (New York, 1973).

—Daniel Sinclair

JEWISH OATH. See Oath More Judaico.

JEWISH RECONSTRUCTION FOUNDATION. See Reconstructionism.

JEWISH RELIGION. More than three thousand years ago the Jewish religion originated in the Near East among the Hebrews. From the patronymic of a patriarchal ancestor, loosely associated clans came to be called the children of Israel. The dominant self-understanding of the people of Israel since biblical times is expressed through the concept of a *covenant or alliance with *God, a relationship analogous to the family bond but more contractual in character, in this case established by divine initiative (see CHOSEN PEOPLE). Many of the central theological terms (e.g., *ḥesed, go'el*) indeed derive from the traditional kinship vocabulary. The *Shema' (*Dt.* 6.4–9), which in the course of time became the self-identifying expression of the Jewish faith, is not so much a theoretical proclamation of monotheism as the living "acceptance of the yoke of the kingdom of heaven" (in rabbinic language) implicit in the covenant relationship and elaborated in the divine commandments (see MITSVAH) set forth in the *Torah, the quintessence of the Mosaic revelation. The study of Torah (see TALMUD TORAH) is in itself a spiritual practice.

The frequent invasions of the Jewish homeland and the severe oppression, persecution, and dispersion of Jews to the four corners of the earth tested the strength and flexibility of Judaism to survive creatively. Among the most decisive developments that took place after the destruction of the Second Temple and the cessation of the sacrificial cult administered by the hereditary priesthood was the emergence of new patterns of religious authority and organization devised by the rabbis, with the *synagogue replacing the Temple as the focus of the ritual. Devotion to Jerusalem (Zion) and its eventual restoration remained a potent symbol, embracing both the promise of national redemption from exile and oppression and a messianic vision of an end to violence and injustice. Over the centuries, a vast body of religious teaching has grown up. The most important, authoritative, and influential rabbinic text is the *Talmud. Alongside this major rabbinic corpus there also developed a body of ethical literature (see ETHICS) as well as a continuous mystical stream (see KABBALAH).

Jewish worship (see LITURGY), the holidays (see ḤAGGIM), and rituals marking the life cycle recapitulate the archetypal themes of Judaism and form a metanarrative that spans the creation of the universe by God, God's covenant with the patriarchs, the liberation from bondage in Egypt, the revelation at Mount Sinai, and the coming redemption of Israel and the world with the establishment of the kingdom of God.

In accordance with this paradigm, the creation of the world and its moral order is celebrated as a spiritual renewal at the beginning of the year, starting with *Ro'sh ha-Shanah, followed by a ten-day period of introspection culminating with *Yom Kippur. *Sukkot, *Pesaḥ, and *Shavu'ot, the three biblical pilgrimage festivals (*Shalosh Regalim) combine references to the natural and agricultural rhythms with the commemoration of events of historical significance. The weekly *Sabbath liturgy stresses the three themes of Judaism: *Creation, the Sinaitic *revelation of the Torah, and ultimate *redemption. Life is shaped not only by the religious calendar but by the daily observance of a variety of *mitsvot*, among the more conspicuous of which are the *dietary laws.

Although Judaism does not lack theological *dogmas, and although at times acrimonious doctrinal *controversies have arisen, Jews do not classify themselves into credal denominations in the manner familiar to Christians, for example. There are positions reflecting varying understandings of revelation and of the authority of the received Torah, as well as differing responses to the encounter with the modern world. The most liberal of these is usually designated as *Reform Judaism, which, in the nineteenth century, responded to modernity by the adaptation of Western styles of worship and considerable modification of forms of observance, invoking the concept of "continuous revelation." *Orthodoxy cleaves to the entire body of Jewish observance as authoritative and unchangeable, except through the hermeneutic procedures held to be revealed together with the Torah. But the spectrum of Orthodoxy, too, is wide and varied, ranging from the rejection of secular *Zionism to an extreme and quasi-messianic *nationalism, from non-mystical halakhic rigorism and fundamentalism to a revived appeal of *Hasidism (as in the Lubavitch Ḥabad movement). *Conservative Judaism seeks a middle ground between Orthodoxy and Reform, while *Reconstructionism, a specifically American phenomenon that stresses Judaism as a civilization, has been open both to naturalistic theology and to neomystical themes and observances.

• Haim H. Ben-Sasson, ed., *A History of the Jewish People* (Cambridge, Mass., 1976). Eugene Borowitz, *Liberal Judaism* (New York, 1984). Reuven Bulka, *Dimensions of Orthodox Judaism* (New York, 1983). Abraham Joshua Heschel, *Man is not Alone: A Philosophy of Religion* (New York, 1995). Louis Jacobs, *A Jewish Theology* (New York, 1974). Isaac Klein, *A Guide to Jewish Religious Practice* (New York, 1979). George Foot Moore, *Judaism in the First Centuries of the Christian Era*, vol. 3 (Cambridge, Mass., 1954). Robert M. Seltzer, *Jewish People, Jewish Thought: The Jewish Experience in History* (New York, 1980).

JEWISH SCIENCE, a philosophy of Judaism that emphasizes God's goodness, the efficacy of personal prayer, and the human capacity to activate the Divine Mind, or power of healing, within us. As conceived by Reform rabbi Alfred Geiger Moses in *Jewish Science: Divine Healing in Judaism* (1915), it sought to awaken religiously apathetic Jews to Judaism's spiritual possibilities and, subsequently, stem the tide of Jews attracted to Christian Science. Efforts by Bertha Strauss and Lucia Nola Levy of New York City led to the creation of the Society of Jewish Science in 1922, under the leadership of Reform rabbi Morris Lichtenstein. The most successful of several Jewish Science groups formed during the 1920s, the society brought its optimistic message to thousands of American Jews through such publications as Lichtenstein's *Jewish Science and Health* and the monthly *Jewish Science Interpreter*. Led by Lichtenstein, until his death in 1938, and his wife Tehilla, from 1938 until 1973, the society continues to exist.

• Morris Lichtenstein, *How To Live: Jewish Science Essays* (New York, 1929). Morris Lichtenstein, *Jewish Science and Health: The Text Book of Jewish Science* (New York, 1925). Tehilla Lichtenstein, *Applied Judaism: Selected Jewish Science Essays*, edited by Doris Friedman (New York, 1989). Alfred Geiger Moses, *Jewish Science: Divine Healing in Judaism* (Mobile, 1916); rev. and repub. as *Jewish Science: Psychology of Health, Joy, and Success, or the Applied Psychology of Judaism* (New Orleans, 1920).

—ELLEN M. UMANSKY

JEWISH STUDIES. Critical Jewish scholarship in the twentieth century owed much to the methodological advances made by the nineteenth-century founders of *Wissenschaft des Judentums. At the same time, the field of modern Jewish studies has changed dramatically. By the turn of the twentieth century, Jewish scholars in Germany and eastern Europe had begun to expand the scope of research by moving away from an exclusive emphasis on literary history to the study of social, economic, and local history. An important figure in challenging the earlier emphasis of German-Jewish scholars was the Russian-Jewish historian, *Simon Dubnow, author of a multivolume history of the Jewish people, who called for a sociological corrective to the historicophilological approach. This attitude reflected the broader tendency of many eastern European scholars to focus on the material aspects of Jewish existence using the disciplines of social and economic history, demography, and sociology. From 1925, the clearinghouse for scholarship of this nature became the Yiddish Scientific Institute (YIVO) based in Vilna. Around the time that YIVO was founded, another center of advanced Jewish learning opened in Jerusalem. The Institute of Jewish Studies of the new Hebrew University provided a home to immigrant scholars from eastern and central Europe. Most of these immigrants shared the belief that the establishment of a Jewish national university in Palestine offered the prospect of overcoming the biases and limitations of previous scholarship, and in fact new emphases, not without biases of their own, developed among the Jerusalem scholars, who included Gershom Gerhard *Scholem, Yitzhak *Baer, Benzion Dinur, and Yehezkel *Kaufmann. Scholem's pioneering research on Jewish mysticism created an entirely new field of study. Dinur developed a "Palestinocentric" historiographical approach, in which Erets Yisra'el stood at the center of all Jewish history. Through their efforts, and partly due to the death of so many Jewish scholars in Europe during the Holocaust, the Hebrew University became the cradle of a new style of Jewish scholarship.

Since the end of World War II, the United States has emerged as a major center of Jewish studies. A central role was played by the three rabbinical seminaries affiliated with the Conservative, Orthodox, and Reform movements. Another, and increasingly significant, venue developed in American universities. The origins of Jewish studies in American universities extend back to the late nineteenth century, when Jewish professors were invited to teach in departments of Semitic languages. In the latter half of the 1920s, the first two explicit Jewish studies appointments were made at Harvard (Harry Austryn *Wolfson) and Columbia (Salo W. Baron). From the 1970s, there has been a proliferation of Jewish studies in various departments of American universities (religious studies, history, Near Eastern languages). This development has encouraged a greater openness to new methodological approaches and interdisciplinary research. A similar pattern for Jewish studies can be seen, though on a smaller scale, in France, England, Germany, Russia, and South America.

• Salo W. Baron, *The Contemporary Relevance of History: A Study in Approaches and Methods* (New York, 1986). Moshe Davis, ed., *Teaching Jewish Civilization: A Global Approach to Higher Education* (New York, 1995). Simon Dubnow, *Nationalism and History: Essays on Old and New Judaism* (Philadelphia, 1958). Leon A. Jick, ed., *The Teaching of Judaica in American Universities* (New York, 1970). David N. Myers, *Re-Inventing the Jewish Past: European Jewish Intellectuals and the Zionist Return to History* (New York, 1995). Paul Ritterband and Harold Wechsler, *Jewish Learning in American Universities: The First Century* (Bloomington, 1994). Efraim Shmueli, *Seven Jewish Cultures: A Reinterpretation of Jewish History and Thought* (New York, 1990). —DAVID N. MYERS

JEWISH THEOLOGICAL SEMINARY OF AMERICA, the rabbinical seminary of the *Conservative movement, situated in New York City. It was founded in 1887 by Sabato *Morais with the objective of training rabbis and teachers in traditional Judaism in order to combat the challenge of radical *Reform Judaism. It was reorganized in 1902 after the arrival in the United States of Solomon *Schechter, who assumed the presidency and made the seminary into one of the outstanding theological schools in the Jewish world and the cradle of *Conservative Judaism. He assembled a faculty of world-renowned scholars, expanded the library, and founded the Teachers Institute. Schechter was succeeded by Cyrus Adler (1914–1940) and Louis *Finkelstein (1940–1972). Under the latter's long chancellorship, the seminary and the Conservative movement flourished. In the seminary itself a creative tension existed between teachers such as Saul *Lieberman and Abraham Joshua *Heschel, who were in the more conservative wing of the movement, and Mordecai Menahem *Kaplan, who was more liberal. Finkelstein was succeeded by Gerson Cohen (1972–1986) and Ismar Schorsch (1986–).

The New York campus houses the Rabbinical School, the Graduate School, the Cantors' Institute, and other institutes, as well as the library with its 270,000 volumes, 15,000 manuscripts and codices, and 40,000 **genizah* fragments. Affiliated with the seminary are the *University of Judaism in Los Angeles, the Beit Midrash in Jerusalem, the Jewish Museum in New York, and the *Seminario Rabínico Latinoamericano in Buenos Aires. The seminary is now operating programs in the former Soviet Union. It also pioneered Jewish broadcasting on radio and television, notably through its *Eternal Light* and *Frontiers of Faith* programs.

• Nina Beth Cardin and David Wolf Silverman, eds., *The Seminary at 100: Reflections on the Jewish Theological Seminary and the Conservative Movement* (New York, 1987). Neal Gillman, *Conservative Judaism: The New Century* (New York, 1993).

JEWS' COLLEGE, training institution for Orthodox rabbis for the British Commonwealth. Established in London in 1855, it originally included a day school, which was separated from the college in 1860 and closed in 1879. Jews' College now includes a training section for cantors and is a recognized college of the University of London. Among those who have served as its principal are Michael Friedlander, Adolf Büchler, Isidore Epstein, H. J. Zimmels, and Jonathan Sacks.

• Isidore Harris, ed., *Jews' College Jubilee Volume* (London, 1906). Albert Montefiore Hyamson, *Jews' College, London, 1855–1955* (London, 1955).

JEZEBEL (Heb. Iyzevel), daughter of the Phoenician king, Ethbaal; wife of *Ahab, king of Israel (9th cent.

BCE; *1 Kgs*. 16.31), and mother of King Ahaziah and King Jehoram. Jezebel's marriage to Ahab helped him, politically and commercially, but it also entailed alien religious influence and the introduction of foreign cults (*1 Kgs*. 18.4, 13, 19, 19.1, 21.11, 23; *2 Kgs*. 9.7, 10, 22, 30, 36–37). Her sponsorship of Baal and Asherah worship, together with her royal origins and personal influence, made her into a bitter enemy of the prophets *Elijah and *Elisha. Though she acted as a reigning queen, the Bible never refers to her by that title. She was, however, called *gevirah* (lady) after her husband's death (*2 Kgs*. 10.13), probably acting as regent after her second son, Jehoram, was killed by Jehu (*2 Kgs*. 9.14, 28). She also planned Naboth's killing (*1 Kgs*. 21) with legal skill and determination. She was killed by Jehu, who was determined to eradicate the cult of Baal in Samaria (2 *kgs*. 9.30–37). She is depicted as merciless, unscrupulous, and cruel, and later Jewish and Christian traditions, from the New Testament (*Rv*. 2.20) onward, made her name a symbol of depravity.

• Zafrira Ben-Barak, "The Status and Right of the *Gebira*," *Journal of Biblical Literature* 110 (1991): 23–34. T. Pippin, "Jezebel Re-Vamped," in *A Feminist Companion to Samuel and Kings*, edited by Athalya Brenner (Sheffield, Eng., 1994), pp. 196–206. —ATHALYA BRENNER

JHWH. See GOD, NAMES OF.

JOB, a man of exemplary righteousness, mentioned together with Noah and Daniel (*Ez*. 14.14, 20). He also appears as the hero of the biblical work (the third book of the Hagiographa) that bears his name. The prologue of the *Book of Job* (chaps. 1–2), in prose, portrays the righteous ways of Job, who lived and prospered in the land of Uz. In the celestial council Satan cynically attributes Job's exemplary piety to his good fortune, and he is granted a free hand to test Job's faith in God. Visited by a series of increasingly heavy misfortunes and ills, Job is reduced to the depths of agony and despair but withstands the temptation to "curse God." There follows a series of poetically phrased discourses on the possible causes and significance of Job's suffering, delivered in the form of a discussion between Job and his four friends (Eliphaz, Bildad, Zophar, and Elihu), most of whom maintain the traditional, popular view that suffering must be a consequence of sin, while Job insists that he is not conscious of having committed any wrong that would be deserving of such unbearable punishment (chaps. 3–37). Finally God answers Job out of a whirlwind, in an overpowering manifestation of his inscrutable omnipotence (chaps. 38–41). The book concludes with an epilogue (chap. 42) in which Job regrets his presumption in doubting God's ways; his health and vigor are restored and his former fortune doubled. The setting and characters of the book are all non-Israelite, thus stressing the anonymous author's universalist conception of his central theme: innocent suffering and God's justice. The precise interpretation of the book's argument depends in part on one's views regarding the nature and composition of the text. Many scholars consider Elihu's speeches (chap. 32–37) a later addition. But it is generally agreed that God does not offer any rational answer to Job's problem of innocent suffering. While disavowing the theological explanations of Job's friends, God humbles Job and forces him to realize that man cannot presume to ask God any questions. The book exhibits a unique combination of audacity and profound faith, climaxed by Job's affirmation: "But as for me, I know that my redeemer liveth, and that he shall stand up over my dust at the last" (19.25). Scholars differ as to the date of the book but agree that it belongs to the school of *wisdom literature. Some scholars claim that the book contains Edomite and Aramaic elements. Talmudic views varied. Some rabbis suggested Mosaic authorship for the book (*B. B*. 14b) and held Job to be a contemporary of Abraham; others thought that "Job never existed but was a parable" (*B. B*. 15a; *Gn. Rab*. 57). According to the Talmud, the book was read by the high priest shortly before Yom Kippur, and it is still read by Sephardim on Tish'ah be-'Av. The *Book of Job* is one of the few biblical texts whose study is permitted during the period of mourning.

• Nahum N. Glatzer, *The Dimensions of Job: A Study and Selected Readings* (New York, 1975). Robert Gordis, *The Book of God and Man: A Study of Job* (Chicago, 1978). Marilyn Lundberg, "'So That Hidden Things May Be Brought to Light': A Concept Analysis of the Yahweh Speeches in the Book of Job," Ph.D. dissertation, Claremont Graduate School, 1995. Marvin Pope, *Job*, Anchor Bible, 3d ed. (New York, 1973).

JOB, TESTAMENT OF. See TESTAMENT OF JOB.

JOEL (Heb. Yo'el), prophet in the kingdom of Judah of whom very little is known. The *Book of Joel* states the name of his father, Pethuel, but provides no information concerning the historical context in which Joel lived (1.1). Most scholars place him in postexilic Judah between the late sixth and fifth centuries BCE. The imagery of the prophet's message in his portrayal of the apocalyptic battle that will bring about the destruction of God's enemies among the nations and the full restoration of Jerusalem appears to have been prompted by a severe locust plague, which serves as a metaphor for the destruction and natural catastrophe that will precede new growth. Fundamental to Joel's preaching is the concept of the "Day of the Lord" (3.4), considered as the day of God's judgment of the wicked.

The *Book of Joel* is the second of the Minor Prophets. The Hebrew version is divided into four chapters, whereas the Greek is divided into three; Christian versions are generally based upon the Greek. Many scholars have interpreted the book as an example of prophetic liturgy, designed for a service of repentance in the Temple at a time of calamity. The structure of the book includes two basic parts. *Joel* 1–2 (Greek and Christian translation 1.1–2.27) contains community lamentations over a severe locust plague that is destroying the land, calls to repentance, and an oracle of deliverance. *Joel* 3–4 (Greek, 2.28–3.21) projects a future apocalyptic scenario in which God will defeat the enemies of Judah and Jerusalem on the "Day of the Lord" in a great cosmic battle in the "valley of decision" at the Valley of Jehoshaphat. The book concludes with a promise of protection from all future attacks and a blessing of fertility for the land. Joel's prophecy that in the future all people will be prophets (2.28–29) provided the background for the New Testament account (*Acts* 2.14–21) of the descent of the Holy Spirit on the early church, as well as of prophetic mass phenomena in the seventeenth-century messianic movement centered around *Shabbetai Tsevi.

• Gösta W. Ahlström, *Joel and the Temple Cult of Jerusalem*, Supplements to Vetus Testamentum, vol. 21 (Leiden, 1971). Arvid Schou Kapelrud, *Joel Studies* (Uppsala and Leipzig, 1948). Graham S. Ogden, "Joel 4 and Prophetic Responses to National Laments," *Journal for the Study of the Old Testament* 26 (1983): 97–107. Willem S. Prinsloo, *The Theology of the Book of Joel*, Beinheft zur Zeitschrift für die altestamentliche Wissenschaft 163 (Berlin and New York, 1985). John Merlin Powis Smith, William Hayes Ward, and Julius A. Bewer, *A Critical and Exegetical Commentary on Micah, Zephaniah, Nahum, Habakkuk, Obadiah and Joel*, International Critical Commentary, vol. 13, pt. 2 (New York, 1911). Douglas K. Stuart, *Hosea–Jonah*, Word Biblical Commentary, vol. 31 (Waco, Tex., 1987). Hans Walter Wolff, *Joel and Amos*, Hermeneia—A Critical and Historical Commentary on the Bible, translated by Waldemar Janzen, S. Dean McBride, and Charles A. Muenchow (Philadelphia, 1977).

—MARVIN A. SWEENEY

JOHN THE BAPTIST (died c.29 CE), ascetic preacher who exercised a powerful influence on *Jesus. Possibly connected with the *Essene sect, he lived as a hermit in the desert until about 15 CE, when he emerged from his seclusion in order to preach the need for repentance in view of the imminent advent of the kingdom of God. *Baptism, which he (like many others) regarded as of supreme importance, was to be the sign of that repentance; repentance, and not the ethnic factor of belonging to the Jewish people, was the key to salvation (*Mt.* 3.7–10). Among those who answered the call, according to the *New Testament, was Jesus, in whom John saw the Messiah, who would bring about the kingdom of God. Christian tradition casts him in a role similar to that of *Elijah in Judaism—the forerunner of the Messiah. According to the Gospels, he was beheaded by Herod Antipas at the request of Herod Antipas's wife's daughter, having offered to reward her dancing with whatever she wished (*Mt.* 14.6–12; *Mk.* 6.21–28). Modern scholarship has found parallels between John's teachings and that of the *Dead Sea Scrolls. However, there are also significant differences, and John may have been influenced by another sect, of which there were many.

• Otto Betz, "Was John the Baptist an Essene?," *Bible Review* 6.6 (1990): 18–25. Hermann Lichtenberger, "The Dead Sea Scrolls and John the Baptist: Reflections on Josephus' Account of John the Baptist," in *The Dead Sea Scrolls. Forty Years of Research*, edited by Devorah Dimant and Uriel Rappaport (Leiden and Jerusalem, 1992), pp. 340–346. Ramsey Michaels, "Paul and John the Baptist: An Odd Couple?," *Tyndale Bulletin* 42 (1991): 245–260.

JOINT OWNERSHIP. See PARTNERSHIP.

JONAH (Heb. Yonah; 8th cent. BCE), son of Amittai; Jonah is mentioned in *2 Kings* 14.25 as a prophet from Gath-hepher in Galilee, whose message supported King Jeroboam II's expansion of Israelite borders "from the entrance of Hamath as far as the Sea of Arabah." The figure of the historical Jonah was adopted as the name of the prophet in the *Book of Jonah*, but this book is seen by scholars as a parable, legendary fiction that has little to do with the actual prophet. The book is dated by some scholars, on linguistic grounds, to the Second Temple period. Because of its emphasis on God's sovereignty over all nations and his forgiveness after genuine repentance, the book is read as the prophetic portion during the afternoon service on Yom Kippur.

• James Stokes Ackerman, "Satire and Symbolism in the Song of Jonah," in *Traditions in Transformation: Turning Points in Biblical Faith*, edited by Baruch Halpern and Jon Douglas Levenson (Winona Lake, Ind., 1981), pp. 213–246. E. J. Bickerman, *Four Strange Books of the Bible* (New York, 1984). Mordechai Cogan, *'Ovadyah: 'Im Mavo' u-Ferush*; Uriel Simon, *Yonah: 'Im Mavo' u-Ferush*, Miqra' le-Yisra'el (Tel Aviv and Jerusalem, 1992). Edwin Marshall Good, *Irony in the Old Testament*, 2d ed., Bible and Literature Series 3 (Sheffield, Eng., 1981). James Limburg, *Jonah: A Commentary*, The Old Testament Library (Louisville, Ky., 1993). Jonathan Magonet, *Form and Meaning: Studies in Literary Techniques in the Book of Jonah*, 2d ed., Bible and Literature Series 8 (Sheffield, Eng., 1983). Jack N. Sasson, *Jonah*, The Anchor Bible, vol. 24B (New York, 1990).

—MARVIN A. SWEENEY

JORDAN RIVER (Heb. Yarden; from the root *yarad* [descend]), the largest river in Erets Yisra'el. From the foothills of Mount Hermon, the river winds its way along the Great Rift Valley through the Sea of Galilee to the Dead Sea, 1,292 feet below sea level. For the Israelites under Joshua, the crossing of the Jordan in miraculous circumstances heralded the first stage of the predestined conquest of Canaan (*Jos.* 3.15–17). The river figures in a number of biblical narratives, while in the Second Temple period a number of sects centered their baptismal rites around the Jordan (see ESSENES; JOHN THE BAPTIST). The river is prominent in both Jewish and Christian tradition and folklore.

• Nelson Glueck, *The River Jordan* (New York, 1968).

JOSEPH (Heb. Yosef), elder son of Jacob and Rachel. The narratives concerning Joseph are related in *Genesis* 37–50 and form the transition between the stories of the patriarchs and the Israelite enslavement in Egypt. The account begins with the abduction of Joseph and his subsequent sale into slavery in Egypt by his brothers, who resented the fact that he was both a dreamer and the favored son of their father, Jacob. Joseph was sold to Potiphar, one of Pharaoh's officials, who recognized the blessing of God on Joseph and placed him over his entire household. In an episode with clear parallels to the Egyptian *Tale of Two Brothers*, Potiphar's wife unsuccessfully attempted to seduce Joseph. Having been rebuffed, she charged Joseph with attempting to rape her, and Joseph was imprisoned. In prison, Joseph again found favor and was placed in charge of all the prisoners. Among these were two of Pharaoh's officials, his chief butler and his chief baker. Joseph's correct interpretation of their respective dreams led to an invitation to interpret those of Pharaoh. Joseph revealed to Pharaoh that his dreams concerned a future period of seven years of abundance followed by a period of seven years of famine, and he advised Pharaoh on how to provide for the lean years by making adequate provisions during the bountiful years. Joseph's ability pleased Pharaoh, and he elevated Joseph to the position of vizier, as which he administered the accumulation and distribution of grain during the periods of abundance and famine. He also gave Joseph an Egyptian name, Zaphnath-paaneah.

During the famine, Joseph's brothers came to Egypt to buy grain. Having the advantage of recognizing his brothers without their recognizing him, Joseph perpetrated a series of deceptions on them that finally resulted in a restoration of family unity. At Joseph's invitation, and with Pharaoh's consent, the entire family traveled to Egypt, where they were settled in the region of Goshen and were regularly supplied with food. Before Jacob died in Egypt, he blessed Joseph's sons, Ephraim and Manasseh, who had been born to Joseph in Egypt by Asenath, daughter of Potiphera, priest of On. These sons were henceforth reckoned as Jacob's. After burying his father at the family burial place in Canaan, Joseph returned to Egypt, where he remained until his own death at what was considered the ideal life span for an Egyptian, 110 years. Joseph was embalmed in Egypt, but his remains were later carried along with the Israelites during the Exodus for interment in Canaan near Shechem (*Ex.* 13.19; *Jos.* 24.32). In biblical literature the name Joseph (or house/children of Joseph) denotes the tribes Manasseh and Ephraim (e.g., *Jos.* 17.14–17; *1 Kgs.* 11.28) or the kingdom of the northern tribes (e.g., *Am.* 5.6, 6.6). In rabbinic tradition, he was known as "Joseph the Righteous."

• W. Lee Humphreys, *Joseph and His Family: A Literary Study*, Studies on the Personalities of the Old Testament (Columbia, S.C., 1988). Eric I. Lowenthal, *The Joseph Narrative in Genesis* (New York, 1973). Donald B. Redford, *A Study of the Biblical Story of Joseph, Genesis 37–50*, Supplements to Vetus Testamentum, vol. 20 (Leiden, 1970). Nahum M. Sarna, *Understanding Genesis* (New York, 1966), pp. 211–231.

–MICHAEL JAMES WILLIAMS

JOSEPH, JACOB (1848–1902), Orthodox rabbi in the United States who championed the goal of transplanting east European Orthodoxy to the United States and preached immigrant resistance to Americanization. Born in Krozhe, Lithuania, R. Joseph was a disciple of Rabbis Hirsch Leib Berlin and Yisra'el Salanter and, a respected Talmudist and renowned *maggid* (preacher), served in various Lithuanian communities. He was brought to New York City's Lower East Side in 1888 by the Association of American Orthodox Hebrew Congregations and was installed there as that city's Orthodox chief rabbi. He advocated a separatist, all-day *yeshivah* education for young men, although most immigrant parents sent their sons and daughters to public schools. He called for scrupulous observance of the Sabbath, although most immigrants did not honor the day of rest. He fought for strict controls over the kosher meat industry, but local butchers and competing rabbis undermined his authority. Although the experiment of appointing a chief rabbi in New York was a failure, the *Union of Orthodox Rabbis of the United States and Canada was founded at the time of R. Joseph's death and attempted to achieve many of the goals R. Joseph had set for himself. He was the author of *Le-Veit Yaʿaqov* (Vilna, vol. 1, 1872; vol. 2, 1888).

• Leonard Dinnerstein, "The Funeral of Rabbi Jacob Joseph," in *Anti-Semitism in American History*, edited by David A. Gerber (Urbana, Ill., 1986), pp. 275–301. Judah David Eisenstein, *Otsar Zikhronotai* (New York, 1929), pp. 252–271. Jeffrey S. Gurock, "How 'Frum' Was Rabbi Jacob Joseph's Court? Americanization Within the Lower East Side's Orthodox Elite, 1886–1902," *Jewish History* (Winter 1994), pp. 1–14.

–JEFFREY S. GUROCK

JOSEPH AND ASENATH, pseudepigraphous work extant in four different Greek recensions, as well as in Syriac, Armenian, Latin, Slavonic, Modern Greek, and Romanian. It was written in Greek by an Egyptian Jew, perhaps connected with the Temple of *Onias in Heliopolis, sometime between the second century BCE and the early second century CE. The work recounts how Asenath, the beautiful virgin daughter of the high priest of Heliopolis, fell in love with the handsome Joseph and asked to marry him (cf. *Gn.* 41.45). When Joseph refused to marry an idolatrous woman, she repented of her idolatry and was visited by an angelic being, who revealed many secrets to her and promised her that her wish would be fulfilled. Following her marriage to Joseph, conducted by Pharaoh himself, Pharaoh's son, aided by four of Joseph's brothers, tried to kill Joseph and kidnap Asenath. The wicked plot failed, Pharaoh's son died, and Joseph ruled Egypt for forty-eight years.

• For a translation of one of the Greek versions with brief notes, see Christoph Burchard, "Joseph and Aseneth," in *The Old Testament Pseudepigrapha*, edited by James H. Charlesworth, vol. 2 (Garden City, N.Y., 1985), pp. 177–247. For a detailed introductory survey, see Christoph Burchard, "The Present State of Research on Joseph and Aseneth," in *New Perspectives on Ancient Judaism*, edited by Jacob Neusner et al., vol. 2 (Lanham, Md., 1987), pp. 31–52.

–GIDEON BOHAK

JOSEPHUS FLAVIUS (c.38–100), politician, soldier, and historian. During the Great Revolt against the Romans he was commander in Galilee, but when his fortress, Jotapata, was conquered, he went over to the Romans and changed his name (from the Heb. Yosef ben Mattityahu ha-Kohen), adopting the name of Vespasian's family, Flavius. Josephus accompanied Vespasian and Titus during the siege of Jerusalem and later lived in Rome, where he wrote books on Jewish history (*The Jewish War* and *Antiquities of the Jews*), a defense of the Jewish people (*Against Apion*, an anti-Jewish Alexandrian writer), and an autobiographical work called *The Life*. His writings, which cannot always be implicitly trusted, are an important source of knowledge about the religious scene at the end of the Second Temple period. All discussions regarding the Pharisees, Sadducees, Essenes, and Qumran community must take Josephus into account. In order to make them comprehensible to his readers, he presented the various sects as Greek philosophical schools. His *Antiquities of the Jews* was written to teach non-Jews about the Jewish people and their beliefs, in the conviction that such knowledge would contribute to a diminution in anti-Jewish prejudice. He told the story of the Jews from biblical times, with Midrashic embellishments, always attuned to the Hellenistic mentality.

• Shaye J. D. Cohen, *Josephus in Galilee and Rome: His Vita and Development as a Historian* (Leiden, 1979). Louis H. Feldman, *Josephus and Modern Scholarship, 1937–1980* (Berlin, 1984). Louis H. Feldman, *Josephus: A Supplementary Bibliography* (New York, 1986). Tessa Rajak, *Josephus: The Historian and His Society* (Philadelphia, 1984).

JOSHUA (Heb. Yehoshuʿa) Moses' aide and subsequently his successor as leader of the children of Israel. An Ephraimite originally called Hoshea (*Nm.* 13.6, 8; *Jos.* 19.49–50), Joshua first appears in a military role, defeating the Amalekites while Moses' hands are raised toward heaven (*Ex*. 17.8–13). As a ministering servant to Moses, Joshua plays a supporting role during the golden calf episode (*Ex*. 32.17, 33.11) and at the "graves of lust" fiasco (*Nm*. 11.28). As one of the two spies, along with Caleb, who did not give a slanderous report about Erets Yisra'el, Joshua is promised that he will enter that land (*Nm*. 14.30). Toward the end of the period of wandering in the desert, Joshua is formally installed as Moses' successor (*Nm*. 27.15–23, *Dt*. 31.7–8). The *Book of Joshua*, first book of the *Former Prophets, traces Joshua's illustrious career spanning the conquest of Canaan (chaps. 1–12), the division of the land among the Israelite tribes (chaps. 13–21), and his final acts and exhortations, including a landmark covenant renewal ceremony at Shechem (chaps. 22–24).

The historical value of much of the material in *Joshua* has been the focus of scholarly debate. At the heart of this controversy is the nature of the Israelite occupation of Canaan. On the one hand, verses that can be characterized as editorial summaries describe a total and swift conquest of the entire land (e.g., *Jos*. 10.40–42, 11.16–20, 21.41–43; see also the impressive list of 31 defeated kings in *Jos*. 12). On the other hand, verses such as *Joshua* 16.10 and 17.11–13 (cf. *Jgs*. 1.27ff.) indicate that even the conquest of the tribal allotments in the heartland (as opposed to the remaining land on the periphery; see *Jos*. 13.1–6) was less than complete. The gradual nature of the conquest appears from the summary of these events in *Judges* 1.1–2.5. Complicating matters even further is the archaeological evidence, which casts grave doubts on the Bible's accounts of the destruction of Jericho and Ai. In light of these complexities, scholars have tended to treat the materials in *Joshua* as a combination of local Benjamite or Ephraimite legends and hero stories, scattered authentic notices delineating the limits of Israelite control, and later Deuteronomic (7th cent. BCE) editorial statements that describe the conquest in sweeping and idealistic terms. The Deuteronomic editors were also responsible for portraying Joshua as one who scrupulously fulfilled Moses' instructions as reflected in the Torah (*Jos*. 1.7–8, 8.30–35, 11.12–15, 23.6).

• Y. Aharoni, "The Settlement of Canaan," in *Judges*, The World History of the Jewish People, vol. 3, edited by Benjamin Mazar (Tel Aviv and New Brunswick, 1971), pp. 94–128. Robert G. Boling, ed., *Joshua: A New Translation with Notes and Commentary*, The Anchor Bible, vol. 6 (Garden City, N.Y., 1982). Yehezkel Kaufmann, *The Biblical Account of the Conquest of Palestine*, translated by M. B. Dagut (Jerusalem, 1953). J. Maxwell Miller, "The Israelite Occupation of Canaan," in *Israelite and Judaean History*, edited by John H. Hayes and J. Maxwell Miller (Philadelphia, 1977), pp. 213–284. Robert Polzin, *Moses and the Deuteronomist: Deuteronomy, Joshua, Judges*, A Literary Study of the Deuteronomic History, pt. 1, Indiana Studies in Biblical Literature (New York, 1980; repr. Bloomington, Ind., 1993). J. Alberto Soggin, *Joshua: A Commentary*, Old Testament Library, translated by R. A. Wilson (London, 1972).

—DAVID A. GLATT-GILAD

JOSIAH (Heb. Yo'shiyyahu; 640–609), king of Judah. Josiah ascended the throne at the age of eight, following the assassination of his father, Amon. As the Assyrian empire crumbled, Josiah strengthened Judah and expanded its frontiers to the north to include almost all of the former territory of the northern kingdom of Israel. His most important legacy was the extensive and unprecedented religious reform he undertook to wipe out all vestiges of Canaanite and Assyrian idolatry and to centralize worship in the Temple. According to *2 Chronicles* 34, the bulk of this reform took place in Josiah's twelfth year. However, according to *2 Kings* 22–23, the impetus for Josiah's reform came in the wake of the discovery of a Law book (identified by many scholars as the *Book of *Deuteronomy*), which came to light during the course of Temple repairs in Josiah's eighteenth year. One possible way of accounting for the chronological discrepancy is that those aspects of the reform that related to the removal of foreign cults were initiated in Josiah's twelfth year, whereas the centralization of the cult in Jerusalem took place only in Josiah's eighteenth year. *2 Kings* and *2 Chronicles* concentrate on different aspects of the reform in order to highlight variant historiographic purposes. The *Second Book of Chronicles* seeks to emphasize Josiah's youthful enthusiasm in undoing the cultic sins of the past, whereas *2 Kings* wishes to underscore the crucial influence of the Deuteronomic code on Josiah's actions. His exemplary righteousness is celebrated especially in *2 Kings*, which describes him as unequaled among all the kings in his fervor of returning to the Lord "with all his heart, with all his soul, and with all his might" (*2 Kgs*. 23.25; cf. *Dt*. 6.5). Many recent scholars posit an earlier, preexilic version of *Kings*, which came to a climactic finale with the religious achievements of Josiah. One element of Josiah's reform, described at length in *2 Chronicles*, is his observance of a national Pesaḥ festival in Jerusalem, the likes of which had not been observed since the period of the Judges. Josiah's modesty and program of social justice is noted favorably by the prophet Jeremiah (*Jer*. 22.15–16). Ultimately, Josiah met a tragic death in the battle of Megiddo in 609 BCE at the hands of the Egyptian pharaoh Necho II, who was on his way to Carchemish in order to bolster the faltering Assyrian army against the rising Babylonians. Josiah's death is accounted for theologically in *2 Chronicles* 35.21–22 by his refusal to heed a divine message to stay out of Necho's path. In rabbinic literature, Josiah's death is explained as resulting from the duplicity of his generation (*Lam. Rab*. 1.53).

• Mordechai Cogan and Hayim Tadmor, *II Kings*, The Anchor Bible, vol. 11 (Garden City, N.Y., 1988), pp. 277–302. Frank Moore Cross, *Canaanite Myth and Hebrew Epic: Essays in the History of the Religion of Israel* (Cambridge, Mass., 1973), pp. 274–289. Norbert Lohfink, "The Cult Reform of Josiah of Judah: 2 Kings 22–23 as a Source for the History of Israelite Religion," in *Ancient Israelite Religion: Essays in Honor of Frank Moore Cross*, edited by Patrick D. Miller, Paul D. Hanson, and S. Dean McBride (Philadelphia, 1987), pp. 459–475. John William McKay, *Religion in Judah under the Assyrians, 732–609 B.C.*, Studies in Biblical Theology, 2d ser., vol. 26 (Naperville, Ill., 1973).

—DAVID A. GLATT-GILAD

JOURNEY, PRAYER ON SETTING OUT ON A. See TEFILLAT HA-DEREKH.

JOY. A spirit of joy is regarded as an essential prerequisite to the true worship of God. "Serve the Lord with joy [Heb. *simḥah*], come before him with exulting" (*Ps*. 100.2). The Midrash (*Sg. Rab*. 1.4) enumerates ten words used in the Bible to express Israel's joy. The rabbis said "The divine presence does not rest upon a man while he is in a state of gloom . . . but is manifested only through the joy with which he fulfills the commandments" (*Shab.* 30b) and "The Holy Spirit descends only upon a joyful heart" (Y., *Suk.* 5.1). The truest source of joy is said to be the fulfillment of the commandments, in particular, family celebrations (such as circumcision and *bar mitsvah* ceremonies and especially weddings), marriage ("he who dwells without a wife dwells without joy"—*Yev.* 62b), and the observance of Sabbath and festivals. The water-libation ceremony in the Temple was described as a ceremony of such joy that "he who has not seen it has not seen true joy" (*Suk.* 5.1), and the celebration of *Simḥat Torah in the synagogue is to this day a public demonstration of the conviction that "the precepts of the Lord are right, rejoicing the heart" (*Ps.* 19.8). The Ḥasidim have made joyful enthusiasm (*hitlahavut*) a central feature of their worship.

• Shloma Majeski, *The Chassidic Approach to Joy* (Brooklyn, N.Y., 1995). Arthur I. Waskow, *Seasons of Our Joy: A Modern Guide to the Jewish Holidays* (Boston, 1990).

J SOURCE. See Yahvist Source.

JUBILEE. See Yovel.

JUBILEES, BOOK OF, pseudepigraphous work. Originally written in Hebrew, it is extant in its entirety only in an Ethiopic translation, but numerous Hebrew fragments of several manuscripts have been found among the *Dead Sea Scrolls, attesting its Hebrew origins; parts of Greek and Latin versions were preserved through Christian transmitters. It was composed some time in the second century BCE or possibly even earlier. The *Book of Jubilees* recasts *Genesis* and the first chapters of *Exodus* in the form of an angelic revelation to Moses and amends the biblical stories. Many biblical passages are entirely omitted, while others are expanded either by the addition of narratives concerning the biblical characters or by the incorporation of numerous halakhic injunctions. The historical account is divided into jubilee periods (periods of 49 years) that set the chronology of biblical events, and the work emphasizes the importance of observing a 364-day solar *calendar, the same calendar that appears in some of the Dead Sea Scrolls. The explicit reference in the Qumran scrolls to "the book of the divisions of the times into their jubilees and their weeks," the community's insistence on the observance of the solar calendar, and the existence of Hebrew fragments of the text in Qumran suggest that the book is not a Qumranic composition but was already accepted as an authoritative text.

• Gene L. Davenport, *The Eschatology of the Book of Jubilees*, Studia Post-Biblica 20 (Leiden, 1971). Annie Jaubert, *The Date of the Last Supper*, translated by I. Rafferty (Staten Island, N.Y., 1965), pp. 15–30, includes calendrical discussion. James C. VanderKam, *Textual and Historical Studies in the Book of Jubilees*, Harvard Semitic Monographs 14 (Missoula, Mont., 1977). Orval S. Wintermute, "Jubilees," in *The Old Testament Pseudepigrapha*, edited by James H. Charlesworth (Garden City, N.Y., 1985), vol. 2, pp. 35–142. —Gideon Bohak

JUDAH (Heb. Yehudah), the fourth son of *Jacob by his wife *Leah, and the eponym of the largest Israelite tribe and its territory, which after Solomon's death formed the major part of the southern kingdom, also known as Judah (see Judah, Kingdom of). Judah plays a prominent role in the Joseph cycle (*Gn.* 37–44). Jacob's blessing anticipates the leadership of Judah in the tribal confederacy and that tribe as the source of a monarchy (*Gn.* 49.8–11; cf. also *1 Chr.* 5.1–2). *Genesis* 38 provides the earliest history of the tribe and its marital alliances with the local Canaanites living in the coastal plain.

Of the three surviving lines (*1 Chr.* 2; 4.1–23), Shelah's descendants continued to reside around Lachish and Mareshah probably until they were exiled in Sennacherib's campaign in 701 (*Mi.* 1.10–15). Perez, centered in the Judean hills, became the dominant branch, from which came the clans of *Caleb (*Hebron) and Ramephrath (*Bethlehem). *David, of the Perezite clan of Ram, united the Judean and allied southern clans, and established his kingdom at Hebron. After Solomon's death and the secession of the northern kingdom of Israel, the kingdom of Judah continued under the Davidic dynasty until its destruction by Nebuchadnezzar in 586 BCE. The extent of its territory varied depending on the political fortunes of its kings. *Joshua* 15.21–62, as well as an additional passage found in the Septuagint, presents the administrative subdivision of the kingdom, probably dating from the eighth century BCE.

Under Persian rule, the small province of Medinat Yehud extended from Bethel in the north to Bethsur in the south, from Jericho and Ein Gedi in the east to the higher plateau of the Shephelah in the west (Keilah, Zanoah, Adullam). At this time, the term *Jew* came into vogue (*Est.* 2.5). The earliest appointed governors Sheshbazzar, *Zerubbabel, Elnathan and Hananiah were probably members of the Davidic family. The later governor *Nehemiah (445–432) came from an old Jerusalemite family. He rebuilt the city walls and gave new stature to the old capital of Judah. In the fourth century BCE, the first Jewish coinage bears the name *yhd* in Paleo-Hebrew script.

After the destruction of the Second Temple in 70 CE and the loss of Jewish autonomy, Vespasian and his son Titus celebrated their victory through the series of coins called "Judea Capta," which depicted the defeated Jewish people among the spoils of war. It was at this time, also, that the Romans changed the name of the province from Judea to Palestina, the Greek term for Philistia, on the Mediterranean coast.

• Yohanan Aharoni, *The Land of the Bible: A Historical Geography* (Philadelphia, 1979). Aaron Demsky, "The Clans of Ephrath: Their Territory and History," *Tel Aviv* 13–14 (1986–1987): 46–59. Aaron Demsky, "Pelekh in Nehemiah 3," *Israel Exploration Journal* 33 (1983): 242–244. Abraham Malamat, *Yisra'el be-Tequfat ha-Miqra'* (Jerusalem, 1983). Benjamin Mazar, *The Mountain of the Lord* (Garden City, N.Y., 1975). Avi Ofer, "The Judaean Hill Country: From Nomadism to a National Monarchy," in *From Nomadism to Monarchy: Archaeological and Historical Aspects of Early Israel*, edited by N. Na'aman and I. Finkelstein, rev. ed. (Jerusalem, 1994). Roland de Vaux, "The Settlement of the Israelites in Southern Palestine and the Origins of the Tribe of Judah," in *Translating and Understanding the Old Testament*, edited by Harry T. Frank and W. L. Reed (Nashville, 1970), pp. 108–134. —Aaron Demsky

JUDAH, KINGDOM OF, the southern kingdom during the period of the divided monarchy (c.928–586). After Solomon's death, his son Rehoboam could not mend regional differences and quell discontent in his kingdom, especially among non-Judahites (*1 Kgs.* 12). David and Solomon's united monarchy was split into two nations, the kingdom of Israel (see ISRAEL, KINGDOM OF) and the kingdom of Judah. The northern tribes comprised the larger territory of Israel; Judah, Benjamin, and Simeon formed the Judean kingdom. The border between the two kingdoms shifted during the next fifty years as a result of repeated warfare. It became fixed in the mid-ninth century when relations between the two nations improved. The geographical area of Judah, however, continued to change throughout its history, depending on the political designs of the major Near Eastern powers, primarily Egypt, Assyria, and Babylon. With variations, it included small sections of coastal plain, the Shephelah (foothills region), the Judean hill country, the wilderness west of the Dead Sea, the Arabah (south of the Dead Sea), and parts of the Negev. In its three and a half centuries of existence, Judah was ruled by twenty monarchs. All except one, Queen Athaliah, were of the lineage of David. *Jerusalem, the site of the Temple and the king's chief residence, remained the capital throughout its history. Jerusalem was the largest urban center, well fortified, and made up of a lower city and an acropolis where the palace and Temple stood. By the end of the eighth century BCE Jerusalem covered an area of about a hundred fifty acres, ten times the size of the Canaanite city conquered by David. Much of its expansion can be attributed to an influx of Israelites from the northern kingdom at the time of its demise (722 BCE). Lachish, situated in the Shephelah, was the second largest city in Judah, a fortified administrative center with a palace fort, numerous store buildings, and a residential section. Small administrative centers, such as Beersheba in the northern Negev and Arad in the eastern Negev, were located in more sparsely settled areas. A number of seals belonging to officials and inscriptions bearing correspondences from these and other sites evidence a centralized administrative system of government.

Judah's modest size did not prevent its kings from clashing with larger nations and forming political alliances against the giant empires of the day. By the mid-eighth century, the Judean kingdom became an Assyrian vassal. Hezekiah (727–698), hoping to restore independence, formed an anti-Assyrian coalition. In response, Sennacherib, king of Assyria, marched against Judah in 701, devastating most of its cities. Although Jerusalem survived by paying an exorbitant tribute, the kingdom was much reduced and weakened (*2 Kgs.* 18–19). Judah was able to recover in the latter half of the seventh century, partly because of Assyria's decline. Josiah (639–609) expanded Judah's borders into Philistia and northern Israel. However, he lost his life and Judah's independence in a battle against Pharaoh Necho. Judah became first an Egyptian and then a Babylonian vassal. Jehoiakim's revolt against Babylon precipitated the first exile in 597 BCE. When Zedekiah rebelled (c.589), Nebuchadnezzar laid siege to Jerusalem. In 586 the city fell, the Temple was razed, and many Judeans were exiled to Babylon. The kingdom of Judah came to an end and the Davidic monarchy was never restored. See also TRIBES OF ISRAEL.

• Yohanan Aharoni, *The Land of the Bible: A Historical Geography*, 2d ed. (Philadelphia, 1979). Gösta W. Ahlström, *The History of Ancient Israel* (New Haven, 1992). Amnon Ben-Tor, ed., *The Archaeology of Ancient Israel*, translated by R. Greenberg (New Haven, 1992). John Bright, *A History of Israel*, 3rd ed. (Philadelphia, 1981). Mordechai Cogan and Hayyim Tadmor, *II Kings*, The Anchor Bible, vol. 11 (Garden City, N.Y., 1988). John Gray, *I and II Kings: A Commentary*, 3d fully rev. ed., The Old Testament Library (London, 1977, 1985 printing). Abraham Malamat, ed., *The Age of the Monarchies: Political History*, The World History of the Jewish People, vol. 4, pt. 1; *The Age of the Monarchies: Culture and Society*, The World History of the Jewish People, vol. 4, pt. 2 (Jerusalem, 1979). Amihay Mazar, *Archaeology of the Land of the Bible: 10,000–586 B.C.E.* (New York, 1990).

—NILI SACHER FOX

JUDAH THE MACCABEE (died 161 BCE), one of the five sons of the priest Mattathias of Modin and military leader in the rebellion against the Syrian Seleucids. How Judah came to be known as "Maccabaeus," a name probably related to the Hebrew word for hammer, is unclear; one explanation is that he was born with a hammer-shaped head. After the death of his father (c.166 BCE), Judah assumed command of the Jewish rebels and repeatedly defeated the Seleucid forces sent against him. By 164 he was able to liberate Jerusalem and reconsecrate the Temple, events commemorated in the *Ḥanukkah celebration. The Seleucids were forced to repeal their anti-Jewish measures (see *ANTIOCHUS IV EPIPHANES) and grant the Jews complete religious freedom, but by now it was too late to turn the wheel back. Judah led several campaigns against Idumea, Ammon, Galilee, Gilead, and Ashdod, aimed at relieving the oppressed Jewish communities there and at consolidating his own power in Judea and its environs. He also waged a constant war against those Jews who supported the Seleucids, including *Alcimus, the newly consecrated high priest. When Alcimus asked the Seleucid authorities for help, they sent a large army against Judah, but he was able to defeat their forces and kill their commander, Nicanor. Wanting to ensure that there would be no further Seleucid aggression, Judah sent emissaries to Rome to sign a treaty of friendship between the Jews and the Romans. The Seleucids, however, quickly dispatched a large military force to Judea, and in the ensuing battle, Judah's forces were routed, and he was killed. Upon Judah's death, the command of the anti-Seleucid Jewish forces was taken over by his brother Jonathan (see HASMONEANS). The main sources for the history of Judah are *1 Maccabees* and *2 Maccabees*. His piety, qualities of leadership, and military genius have made him one of the great Jewish heroes.

• Bezalel Bar-Kochva, *Judas Maccabaeus: The Jewish Struggle Against the Seleucids* (Cambridge and New York, 1989). Martin Hengel, *Judaism and Hellenism*, translated from German by John Bowden, 2 vols. (Philadelphia, 1974). Emil Schürer, Geza Vermes, and Fergus Millar, *The History of the Jewish People in the Age of Jesus Christ, 175 B.C.–A.D. 135*, vol. 1 (Edinburgh, 1973), pp. 164–173. Avigdor Tcherikover, *Hellenistic Civilization and the Jews*, translated from Hebrew by S. Applebaum (Philadelphia, 1959).

—GIDEON BOHAK

JUDAISM. See JEWISH RELIGION.

JUDAIZING SECTS, designation of groups of non-Jews who at various times adopted certain Jewish beliefs or observances (for example, the Sabbath, dietary laws). References to this behavior are even found in the biblical text (e.g., *Est.* 8.17), though it is unclear whether people were pretending to be Jews or actually converting to Judaism. In the Roman period, a number of people, in reaction to the paganism of this time, became *sebomenoi* (*God fearers) and adopted certain Jewish customs. The early church, following the teaching of Paul, opposed believers in Jesus who insisted on the continued validity of the law. These Judeo-Christian groups finally disappeared, but the term *Judaizers* was often applied to dissidents; its use was particularly frequent in Reformation controversies. The term should not be applied to groups that converted (see BETA ISRAEL; KHAZARS), although the borderline between Judaizing and conversion is often fluid.

Of considerable historical interest are the Judaizing sects that arose in eastern Europe. In the late fifteenth and early sixteenth centuries, heretical groups in Novgorod and Moscow, described as "atheist" and "Judaizing" (*zhidovomudrstuyshchiye* was one of the terms of opprobrium used against them), were persecuted and destroyed by the Orthodox church. Within one hundred years, however, Judaizing tendencies—stemming from the Reformation—took hold of anti-Trinitarian splinter groups throughout Europe. Unlike the milder "Old Testament" Puritans, the Huguenots, or the Hungarian Calvinists, the sectarians of Poland and Lithuania headed by Szymon Budny (c.1530–1593) combined a belief in the Messiahship of Jesus with adherence to Mosaic law. Their counterparts in Transylvania, under the leadership of Simon Péchi (c.1567–c.1639), moved even closer to Judaism and came to be known as the Szombatos or Somrei Sabat (Sabbatarians). Prior to its repression after 1638, this movement had gained at least twenty thousand adherents.

During the eighteenth century, Judaizing groups reappeared. The *Subbotniki, the Sabbath-keeping sect of an offshoot of the Dukhobors, gave rise to a third sect known as the Gery (True Proselytes) which, like the Hungarian Szombatos, went underground and managed to survive. A large proportion of these Sabbatarians merged with the Hungarian and Russian Jews; others were absorbed in Erets Yisra'el. The Abrahamites in eighteenth-century Bohemia adopted many Jewish customs and were persecuted—some were executed—until the Patent of Toleration in 1781 enabled them to emerge from the underground. They later disintegrated.

New Judaizing sects, often claiming descent from the ten lost *tribes of Israel, have appeared in recent years in southern Africa, Latin America, the United States, India, and Japan. They include genuine proselytes and fringe groups such as the Black Hebrews, some of whom emigrated from the United States and now live as a sectarian community in Israel.

• Morris Lounds, *Israel's Black Hebrews: Black Americans in Search of Identity* (Washington, D.C., 1981). Louis I. Newman, *Jewish Influence on Christian Reform Movements* (1925; repr. New York, 1966). Antal Pirnat, *Die Ideologie der Siebenbürger Antitrinitarier in den 1570er Jahren* (Budapest, 1961). Joyce Reynolds, *Jews and God-fearers at Aphrodisias* (Cambridge, 1987). George H. Williams, *The Radical Reformation* (Philadelphia, 1962).

—GABRIEL A. SIVAN

JUDEO-ARABIC, dialect spoken and written, in Hebrew characters, by Jews in Islamic lands based on the Arabic language. With the Arab conquests of the seventh century, Jews under Arab rule began in many places to speak Arabic. The vernacular, retaining an element of Hebrew and Aramaic vocabulary and grammar, developed in the eighth century into Judeo-Arabic. Unlike in Ashkenazi Europe, where Hebrew remained the literary language of Jews, beginning in the ninth century Judeo-Arabic produced a rich religious and secular literature, although poetry and halakhic works for the most part continued to be written in Hebrew. Medieval Arabic literature is linguistically conservative, providing few clues to the spoken language of the time. Judeo-Arabic, therefore, representing the middle Arabic vernacular from which modern dialects are descended, is a valuable linguistic resource, exhibiting the evolving weakening of prefinal vowels and the loss of final ones, the loss of case endings, and the glottal stop. A rich literature in Judeo-Arabic appeared in the medieval period, including most of the classic works of Jewish philosophy. Judeo-Arabic, once spoken from Spain to Iraq, continues in use in pockets of the Middle East and North Africa.

• Joshua Blau, *Diqduq ha-ʿAravit ha-Yehudit shel Yemei ha-Beinayim* (Jerusalem, 1980). Joshua Blau and Stefan C. Reif, eds., *Genizah Research after Ninety Years: The Case of Judaeo-Arabic* (Cambridge, 1992). Benjamin H. Hary, *Multiglossia in Judeo-Arabic: With an Edition, Translation, and Grammatical Study of the Cairene Purim Scroll* (Leiden, 1992).

—DENNIS M. DREYFUS

JUDEO-PERSIAN, name of the form of Modern Persian written in the Hebrew alphabet. The very earliest examples of the Modern Persian language (Farsi), from the eighth century CE, are written in the Hebrew alphabet. Until recently, Persian-speaking Jews in Iran, Afghanistan, and the central Asian provinces of Uzbekistan and Tajikistan were only literate in the Hebrew alphabet. The earliest Judeo-Persian translation of the Bible is an incomplete Pentateuch dated to 1319 from a manuscript in the British Library. In the fourteenth century, the Jewish poet Shahin of Shiraz composed a number of extensive poems, including an account in rhymed couplets of stories from the *Book of Joshua* to the coronation of King David and a poetic work with the teachings of the *Pirqei Avot*. At the end of the nineteenth century, the noted Bukharan rabbi Shimon Ḥakham, living in Jerusalem, arranged to edit and print many works in Judeo-Persian, in a form that reflected the central Asian variety of the language, which in modern times is called Tajiki. He also translated and published the entire Pentateuch, the Former Prophets, and much of *Isaiah*. He edited and printed the works of Shahin, adding his own compositions in prose on a number of subjects, such as an extensive biography of Moses entitled *Musa-nama*. In addition, there exist numerous examples of the works of many non-Jewish Persian poets whose poems are transcribed into the Hebrew alphabet for the benefit of Jewish readers. Major collections of Judeo-Persian books and manuscripts are to be found in the British Library, the library of the Jewish Theological Seminary of America, the Royal Danish Library, and the libraries of the Hebrew Union College–Jewish Institute of Religion in Cincinnati, the Hebrew University of Jerusalem, and the Ben-Zvi Institute in Jerusalem.

• Jes P. Asmussen and Herbert H. Paper, *The Song of Songs in Judeo-Persian*, Det Kongelige daske videnskabernes selskab, Historisk-filosofiske skrifter 9.2 (Copenhagen, 1977). Herbert H. Paper, *A Judeo-Persian Pentateuch* (Jerusalem, 1972). David Yeroushalmi, *The Judeo-Persian Poet Emrani and His Book of Treasure* (Leiden, 1995).

—HERBERT H. PAPER

JUDEO-SPANISH, also known as Ladino, Judeo-Spaniol, or Judezmo. When the Jews were expelled from Spain at the end of the fifteenth century, the Castilian language was still in its formative stages of development. Sephardi Jews took this medieval Spanish with them, preserving its irregularities of pronunciation, spelling, grammatical forms, and morphology.

Some of the dispersed Sephardi communities retained ties with Spain, keeping abreast of developments in Spanish culture, including linguistic advances. In Morocco the Judeo-Spanish language, known as Ḥakétia, possessed more modern Spanish words and fewer loan words from Hebrew or Arabic. More distant communities, such as those of the Ottoman empire, gradually became removed from the developments of the language that came to be known as Spanish, retaining older forms or archaisms with a larger reservoir of loan words from the surrounding languages of Greek (in Salonika), Serbo-Croatian (in Monastir), Turkish (in the Ottoman empire), and Arabic, as well as French, Italian, Bulgarian and Romanian. The gap between Judeo-Spanish and its Castilian mother tongue widened with time, and various forms of Judeo-Spanish arose. The closer the relations were with Spain, the more likely the parallels between the languages. The Judeo-Spanish language was both a written (primarily in Hebrew characters) and a spoken language.

A body of Judeo-Spanish literature developed over the centuries. This literature was of two types: first, literature preserving medieval ballads (*romansas*), proverbs (*refrenes*), and folk songs; second, new rabbinic literature. The classic of Ladino literature, *Meʿam Loʿez*, a popular encyclopedia of biblical and rabbinic traditions, was composed by Yaʿaqov *Culi in 1730. Culi combined biblical explanations in his commentary to the *Book of Genesis* with folk tales and anecdotes, as well as practical advice and information on a variety of subjects. His work became extremely popular among the Jews of the Ottoman empire. After Culi's death in 1732 others continued composing commentaries on the books of the Bible.

In the nineteenth century a renaissance of Judeo-Spanish occurred in the Balkans and the Near East, as publishing houses produced dozens of translations of European and Jewish books. A lively Judeo-Spanish press disseminated modern Jewish and Western ideologies in the Balkans, Palestine, Egypt, and Europe.

The decline of Judeo-Spanish began in the twentieth century: the Alliance Israélite Universelle schools opposed the use of Judeo-Spanish in favor of French as a means of modernizing Near Eastern Jewry, while the emergent Turkish Republic required that Jews use the Turkish language. The Nazi onslaught in World War II engulfed the Balkan communities. Most of the Sephardi Jews of Europe who survived the Holocaust (e.g., in Bulgaria) immigrated to Israel or France and South America. After five hundred years Judeo-Spanish has largely ceased to be a living language and is on the verge of extinction.

• Samuel Armistead and Joseph Silverman, *The Judeo-Spanish Chapbooks of Yacob Abraham Yona* (Berkeley, 1971). David N. Barocas, *A Study on the Meaning of Ladino, Judezmo and the Spanish-Jewish Dialect* (New York, 1976). Mair Jose Benardete, *Hispanic Culture and Character of the Sephardic Jews*, 2d ed. (New York, 1982). Moshe Lazar, ed., *The Sephardic Tradition: Ladino and Spanish-Jewish Tradition* (New York, 1972). Denah Lida, "Ladino Language and Literature," in *Jewish Languages: Theme and Variations*, edited by Herbert H. Paper (Cambridge, Mass., 1978). Denah Lida, "Language of the Sephardim in Anglo-America," in *Sephardim in the Americas*, edited by Martin Cohen and Abraham Peck (Tuscaloosa, Ala., 1993).

—JANE S. GERBER

JUDGE. According to the biblical account, the *elders of the twelve tribes served as judges before the settlement of Canaan. Acting upon the advice of *Jethro, Moses appointed judges at various levels (*Ex.* 18.25–26). Afterward, the function of supreme judge was occasionally merged with that of the leader (see JUDGES, BOOK OF), king, priest, or prophet. The Bible insists on the impartiality of a judge, saying on the one hand that he should not favor the rich and, on the other hand, that in his mercy, he should be moved to show favoritism to the underprivileged. Bribing a judge (see BRIBERY) was a particularly heinous offense (*Ex.* 23.3–8). See also DAYYAN.

• Lawson G. Stone, "From Tribal Confederation to Monarchic State: The Editorial Perspective of the Book of Judges," Ph.D. dissertation, Yale University, 1988.

JUDGES, BOOK OF (Heb. *Sefer Shofetim*), second book of the second part of the Bible (the Prophets); a direct continuation of the *Book of Joshua*, describing Israel's varying fortunes from the death of Joshua to the rise of the prophet Samuel. The period was characterized by general instability and lack of cohesion among the tribes: "In those days there was no king in Israel; every man did what was right in his own eyes" (21.25). The judges were not judges in the legal sense (except for Deborah; 4.45), but were inspired leaders, arising in moments of severe crises and impelled to action by the spirit of God. As temporary leaders in war, their influence rarely exceeded local or tribal boundaries. There were twelve judges, six major ones (Othniel, *Ehud, *Deborah, *Gideon [with his son *Abimelech], *Jephthah, and *Samson) and six minor ones (Shamgar, Tola, Jair, Ibzan, Elon, and Abdon). *Judges* consists of three parts. The first is an account of the conquest of Canaan

(1–2.5). This account, which explains the conquest as a series of independent battles fought by the warrior tribes for their own individual portion of land, differs from that of the *Book of Joshua* (chaps. 1–11), which presents an ideological picture of the conquest of Canaan as a sweeping military achievement in which all the tribes appear to be acting in unison. The second part of the *Book of Judges* consists of the stories of the judges (2.6–16.31); and the third part is an appendix that tells the stories of the migration of the tribe of Dan, of Micah's sanctuary and its idol, and of the war of the tribes against Benjamin following the outrage at Gibeah (chaps. 17–21). The purpose of the book is to present Israel's vicissitudes in Canaan in terms of an alternating rhythm of apostasy (as a result of the failure to exterminate the Canaanite population), foreign oppression, return to God, deliverance through a judge, reversion to idolatry, and so on (2.6–3.6). Rabbinic tradition ascribes the authorship of *Judges* to Samuel.

• Robert G. Boling, *Judges*, The Anchor Bible, vol. 6A (Garden City, N.Y., 1975). Athalya Brenner, ed., *Judges: A Feminist Companion to Judges* (Sheffield, Eng., 1993). J. Alberto Soggin, *Judges*, The Old Testament Library (Philadelphia, 1981). –SHALOM PAUL

JUDGMENT, DAY OF. See YOM HA-DIN.

JUDITH, apocryphal book relating the story of Judith and Holofernes. Nebuchadnezzar, king of Assyria, enraged at the peoples of the western parts of his empire for refusing to help him in a military campaign, sent his general Holofernes with a large army to subdue the stubborn nations and destroy their ancestral shrines, so that Nebuchadnezzar alone would be worshiped as god. The Jews, terrified by the advance of Holofernes, fortified the mountain passes leading to Jerusalem. Holofernes laid siege to the Jewish village of Bethulia, "which is opposite Esdraelon, facing the plain near Dothan" (*Judith* 4.6). Judith, a pious and beautiful widow, left Bethulia, befriended Holofernes, seduced him, and cut off his head. When the Assyrians learned of their commander's death, they panicked and dispersed, chased by the jubilant Jews. The story contains many contradictions and historical anachronisms, and while it may reflect some historical events of the fourth century BCE, it may also be a purely fictional creation. Preserved in a Greek version, it probably was written in Hebrew, and given its obvious relevance for the period of the Maccabean Revolt, a date in the second half of the second century BCE seems most plausible. Some late Hebrew *midrashim* contain the same story, but they probably represent medieval retranslations from the Vulgate and do not preserve the lost Hebrew original of the work.

• Toni Craven, *Artistry and Faith in the Book of Judith*, Society of Biblical Literature, Dissertation Series, no. 70 (Chico, Calif., 1983). Yehoshua M. Grintz, *Sefer Yehudit* (Jerusalem, 1957). Carey A. Moore, *Judith: A New Translation with Introduction and Commentary*, The Anchor Bible, vol. 40 (Garden City, N.Y., 1985). James C. VanderKam, ed., *No One Spoke Ill of Her: Essays on Judith* (Atlanta, 1992). –GIDEON BOHAK

JUS TALIONIS, the law of retaliation. The Bible states "An eye for an eye, a tooth for a tooth, a hand for a hand" (*Ex*. 21.24–5; *Lv*. 24.20; *Dt*. 19.21) as the punishment to be inflicted upon one who has caused bodily injury to another. There is no evidence that this was ever applied literally (although according to an early source, the Sadducees maintained that it should be so interpreted), and in rabbinical law it was interpreted to mean that appropriate monetary compensation for personal injury, or financial restitution in cases of damage to property, would have to be made. The only exception to this rule was in the case of murder, where the life of the murderer is forfeit (see HOMICIDE). However, even in the case of murder, the practice (found in some ancient codes) of exacting vengeance from the children of the criminal is expressly prohibited—"The fathers shall not be put to death for the children neither shall the children be put to death for the fathers; every man shall be put to his death for his own sin" (*Dt*. 24.16).

• Calum M. Carmichael, "Biblical Laws of Talion," *Hebrew Annual Review* 9 (1985): 107–126. Raymond Westbrook, "Lex Talionis and Exodus 21:22–25," *Revue biblique* 93 (1986): 52–69.

JUSTICE, a divine attribute, expressed in God's intolerance of evil and his punishment of sin. Rabbinic literature frequently refers to the tension between God's justice (expressed by the divine name Elohim) and his *compassion (expressed by the Tetragrammaton; see GOD, NAMES OF). A corollary to the doctrine of divine justice is the belief in *reward and punishment. Divine justice must be reflected in human justice: "What does the Lord require of you but to do justly, to love mercy, and to walk humbly with your God" (*Mi*. 6.8). The passion for justice is the basis of the demand for social righteousness on the part of the prophets and can be regarded as the keynote of biblical legislation. The injunction "Justice, justice shall you pursue, that you may live to inherit the land that the Lord your God gives you" (*Dt*. 16.20) expresses the legal basis and "the Holy God is sanctified by justice" (*Is*. 5.15) its ethical basis. This insistence on justice as the foundation of Judaism is emphasized not only by contrasting it with injustice but by insisting, in deliberately hyperbolic language, on its superiority over two other supreme virtues, *peace and compassion. Rabbi Shim'on ben Gamli'el said, "By three things is the world preserved—by truth, justice, and peace" (*Avot* 1.18). The rabbis, however, make Moses the prototype of strict justice and Aaron the prototype of peace (*San*. 6b), interpreting Aaron's sin in making the golden calf as one of preferring peace to justice (*Ex. Rab*. 41.6). Similarly the rabbis were at great pains to define the precise bounds of justice and mercy. The world depends on justice (*Ex. Rab*. 30.15), but it cannot exist if governed solely by justice. Justice must, therefore, be tempered by mercy, but the element of mercy must not be permitted to deflect the straight course of justice and can only modify the verdict. This is strikingly exemplified by the injunction, "You shall not favor a poor man in his cause" (*Ex*. 23.3), which, in its unbending insistence on the strictest impartiality, signifies that even a wrongful verdict to favor the poorer party in a suit on the grounds that the rich man would not thereby be harmed is an act of injustice. The proscription "You shall not wrest justice; you shall not respect persons; neither shall you take a gift" (*Dt.* 16.19) was practiced to an extraordinary extent by the rabbis. Anything that might be interpreted as showing favor to one party against the other, anything that might, even unconsciously, influence a judge one way or the other, was rigidly forbidden.

• Doron Horowitz, *The Jewish Concept of Justice: A Bibliography and Catalogue* . . . (London, 1972). Norman Lamm, *Freedom and Constraint in the Jewish Judicial Process* (New York, 1979). Jacob Neusner, *The Yerushalmi—The Talmud of the Land of Israel: An Introduction* (Northvale, N.J., 1993). Hayyim Shain, *Ha-Tsedeq ba-Mishpat ha-'Ivri* (Tel Aviv, 1994).

K

KABBALAH (from the root *q b l* [receive]), tradition as defined from the point of view of the recipient. From the point of view of those passing it on, it would be **masorah*, the exact equivalent of the English *tradition*. The term originally referred to tradition in general, but especially to halakhic rules for which there was no explicit scriptural warrant and which were therefore said to be a "kabbalah from Moses on Mount Sinai." The new type of esoteric theosophical teaching that appeared in the twelfth and thirteenth centuries in Provence and northern Spain was at first simply called secret or hidden teaching, but before long it came to be designated as Kabbalah. Its terminology, symbolism, and conceptual structure are better described as a form of esotericism rather than mysticism, though elements of the latter are not absent and sometimes even prominent. The first literary expression of this new doctrine was the **Sefer ha-Bahir*. The literary culmination of the new teaching, the *Zohar, soon established itself as the authoritative and canonical kabbalistic text. The Kabbalah became the dominant form of Jewish mystical theology and was subsequently, and erroneously, identified with Jewish mysticism as such. At first cultivated in closed esoteric circles, it later spread more widely and, especially after the sixteenth century, gradually came to dominate popular belief and religious practice. This development was abetted by the increasingly messianic character of the later Kabbalah.

The salient features of this system are the notion of an utterly hidden and therefore completely inaccessible Godhead (*Ein Sof) and its manifestation in a complex and dynamic structure of ten emanations (the **sefirot*). A particularly important feature of this system is the female character of the tenth *sefirah*, the *Shekhinah, and the view that the unity of the Godhead is consummated by the union of the male and female elements within it. The human being (male-and-female) is the "image of God" by virtue of its analogy to the *sefirot*. Divine manifestation means both *creation and *revelation, and hence it is through the created order and the revealed *Torah, that the Godhead-in-the-*sefirot* is accessible in meditation and religious performance. Central to kabbalistic piety is its relation to the commandments, which are given not an ethical but an esoteric and mystical interpretation with a theurgical character. Meditation on the *sefirot* also serves as a mystical "ladder of ascent." This, combined with the proper performance of the commandments, enables man to take an active part in the life of the Godhead by assisting the union of the *sefirot* in general, and, in particular, of the sixth *sefirah*, Tiferet (representing the male *sefirot*), with the tenth, female *sefirah*, Malkhut, or Shekhinah. Whether the doctrine of emanations also leads to a pantheistic conception of the cosmos is a much debated question that flared up also among non-Jewish scholars in the eighteenth century in connection with the so-called Spinoza controversy. The problem of evil is dealt with in terms of negative emanations (see LILITH; SAMAEL; SITRA' AḤRA'), which constitute a powerful demonology. The kabbalists also adopted the doctrine, hitherto considered as heretical, of the *transmigration of souls (*gilgul*).

The origins of this system and the historical and geographical reasons for its emergence in twelfth-century Provence are still obscure. Certain similarities with gnostic doctrines of late antiquity are suggestive, but there is no evidence of their secret, "underground," transmission, and no convincing explanation for their surfacing at that time and place. None of the explanations offered (e.g., as a reaction to the excessive philosophical rationalism of the period) adequately accounts for the phenomenon.

There were eight main phases of the development of the Kabbalah. *Sefer ha-Bahir* represents the early kabbalistic traditions and served as an authoritative source of the concepts of the *sefirot* and the feminine element in the divine world. The second phase comprises the schools of kabbalists in Provence, centered around the figure of Yitsḥaq Saggi Nahor (Isaac "the Blind"). This center flourished at the end of the twelfth century and the beginning of the thirteenth. The third phase comprises the Gerona circle, which united the traditions of the *Bahir* and Yitsḥaq and his school, systematized them, and reinterpreted many philosophical terms in light of the new teachings; it also developed a specific kind of ethical literature in which the kabbalistic message is hidden. The most prominent figures in this school were Ezra of Gerona, ʿAzri'el, Nahmanides, Asher ben David (who came from Provence, a nephew of Yitsḥaq Saggi Nahor), and Yaʿaqov ben Sheshet. The fourth phase comprises the school of the Kohen brothers, Yaʿaqov and Yitsḥaq, and their disciple, Mosheh of Burgos, who flourished in Castile in the second half of the thirteenth century. These thinkers had a profound influence on the circle that produced the Zohar and on the school of Shelomoh ben Avraham Adret at the end of the thirteenth century and the beginning of the fourteenth.

The fifth phase comprises the school of Avraham Abulafia, whose teachings Gershom Scholem terms "ecstatic" or "prophetic" Kabbalah. Abulafia traveled to many Jewish communities, spreading his unique ideas and establishing a tradition that is in many aspects different from that of the Geronese and Castilian schools.

The medieval Kabbalah reached its peak in the age of the Zohar, in the last decades of the thirteenth century and beginning of the fourteenth century. This is the period in which Mosheh de León wrote the Zohar and his numerous kabbalistic treatises, and in which his colleague, Yosef Gikatilla, wrote some of the most influential kabbalistic works. Several other prominent kabbalists belong to this age, among them David ben Yehudah he-Ḥasid, Yosef of Shushan, and Yosef ben Shalom Ashkenazi. The anonymous *Sefer ha-Temunah* probably also belongs to this period. Parallel to the group connected to the Zohar was the school of Shelomoh ben Avraham Adret, centered in Catalonia.

In the fourteenth and fifteenth centuries, kabbalistic schools appeared in Italy, in Greece, and in Erets Yisra'el. The spread of the Kabbalah in central Europe, which started in the second half of the thirteenth century, continued. In the second half of the fifteenth century, new kabbalistic schools appeared in Spain, influenced by the persecutions and expressing the messianic hopes of the age. The end of this century saw the development of the Christian Kabbalah in Italy and Germany.

In the sixteenth century, after the expulsion of the Jews from Spain, the Kabbalah emerged out of the esoteric circles in which it had been studied and experienced to become the dominant theology of most Jewish communities. The main centers were in Italy and Erets Yisra'el, especially Safed (see LURIA, YITSḤAQ). In the early modern period, the Kabbalah became a central element in Jewish culture as a whole, shaping major historical and cultural events, such as the Shabbatean messianic movement (see SHABBETAI TSEVI) and modern *Hasidism. See also MYSTICISM.

• Joseph Dan, *Gershom Scholem and the Mystical Dimension in Jewish History* (New York, 1987). Joseph Dan and Frank Talmage, eds., *Studies in Jewish Mysticism* (Cambridge, Mass., 1982). Efraim Gottlieb, *Meḥqarim be-Sifrut ha-Qabbalah*, edited by Joseph Hacker (Tel Aviv, 1976). Moshe Idel, *Kabbalah: New Perspectives* (New Haven, 1988). Peter Schäfer and Joseph Dan, eds., *Gershom Scholem's Major Trends in Jewish Mysticism: 50 Years After* (Tübingen, 1993). Gershom Gerhard Scholem, *Kabbalah* (Jerusalem, 1974). Gershom Gerhard Scholem, *Major Trends in Jewish Mysticism* (New York, 1954). Gershom Gerhard Scholem, *On the Kabbalah and Its Symbolism* (New York, 1965). Gershom Gerhard Scholem, *On the Mystical Shape of the Godhead: Basic Concepts in Kabbalah* (New York, 1991). Isaiah Tishby, *Ḥiqrei Qabbalah u-Sheluḥoteha*, 3 vols. (Jerusalem, 1982–1993). Isaiah Tishby et al., eds., *The Wisdom of the Zohar*, 3 vols. (Oxford, 1989).

KAFAḤ, YIḤYA' BEN SHELOMOH (1850–1931), Yemenite rabbinical authority who came to symbolize modern trends within Yemenite Judaism. He stood at the center of a dispute around the Kabbalah in which, under the impact of European scholars, he denied the traditional ascription of the authorship of the *Zohar to Shimʿon bar Yoḥ'ai and went so far as to say that kabbalistic literature is alien to Torah. His extreme views found followers among the young and the affluent, and especially among those close to the Ottoman authorities who had been open to rationalist influences, but were sharply opposed by most of the community. In order to disseminate his views, Kafaḥ founded the Dardaʿ (Generation of Knowledge) movement.

This ideological struggle, which involved social, economic, and personal considerations, produced several polemical works for and against the Kabbalah. Kafaḥ put forward his views in *Sefer Milḥamot ha-Shem* (1931). In his *beit midrash* he advocated the literal interpretation of the Torah as against the homiletic, allegorical, or mystical ones. Up to that time, Jewish scholarship in Yemen did not extend beyond Maimonides' *Mishneh Torah* and had not even reached the *Shulḥan ʿArukh*. Under the influence of Kafaḥ, Maimonides' *Guide of the Perplexed*, Yehudah ha-Levi's *Kuzari*, and *Ḥovot ha-Levavot* of Baḥya ben Yosef ibn Paquda' began to be studied, along with works of the *ri'shonim* who were not influenced by kabbalistic literature. The sages of Sana published *Emunat ha-Shem* (1937) to combat Kafaḥ's views.

• Y. T. Langermann, *Ha-Madaʿim ha-Meduyaqim be-Qerev Yehudei Teiman* (Jerusalem, 1987), pp. 1–5. Joseph Tovi, "Jewish Centers in Asia," in *Toledot ha-Yehudim be-'Artsot ha-'Islam*, edited by Samuel Ettinger (Jerusalem, 1981), in Hebrew.

—SHALOM BAR-ASHER

KAHANEMAN, YOSEF (1888–1969), also known as the Ponevezher Rav, rabbi, educator, and builder of educational institutions. In 1916 he became head of the *yeshivah* in Grodno, Lithuania, and three years later became rabbi of Ponevezh, soon opening a *yeshivah* there. In addition to Kahaneman's numerous communal and educational projects, he was also prominent in *Agudat Israel and was elected to a seat in the Lithuanian parliament. Kahaneman settled in Palestine in 1940, where he began to build a network of Jewish educational institutions. In 1944 he reestablished the Ponevezh Yeshivah in Bene Beraq and went on to organize many schools in the vicinity linked to the *yeshivah*.

• Shemuel Kol, *Eḥad be-Doro*, 2 vols. (Tel Aviv, 1970).

—JACOB MESKIN

KALAM, (Arab.; speed, or word), a form of Islamic scholasticism that appeared formally in the eighth century. The founder of the movement was Wasil b. ʿAta' (died 748). The establishment of the movement centered on the question of free will and the free moral choice of the individual. The practitioners of the Kalam were termed Mutakallimun; the earliest school was known as Muʿtazilah (Separatist), because Wasil separated himself from orthodoxy. This school remained highly influential, particularly in Jewish circles. The main doctrines that characterized the group were free will; atomism, the principle that the world is formed from indivisible atoms that are created and arranged by God at every instant and the denial of necessary causation; the creation of the Qur'an, along with the rest of the universe; the absolute unity and incorporeality of God, to whom no attributes may be ascribed; and the perfect justice of God. The two latter occupied the Muʿtazili to such a degree that they were also known as "the people of unity and justice." The Muʿtazili enjoyed their greatest popularity during the caliphate of al-Maʿmun, who in 833 declared their position on the Qur'an to be official doctrine and instituted an inquisition against those who denied it. In 847 the caliph al-Mutawakkil restored orthodox belief, and in particular the belief in the eternity of the Qur'an. The Kalam had a lasting influence on Jewish theology. Works by prominent members of the Karaite sect such as David ibn Marwan Muqammis, Yosef Basir, and Yeshuʿa ben Yehudah are almost indistinguishable from those of their Islamic counterparts. Among the Rabbanites, the most noted philosopher to apply the methods and arguments of the Mutakallimun was Saʿadyah ben Yosef Ga'on, in his *Emunot ve-Deʿot*.

• Majid Fakhry, *A History of Islamic Philosophy*, 2d ed. (New York, 1983), pp. 42–65. Julius Guttmann, *Philosophies of Judaism* (New York, 1964). Harry Austryn Wolfson, *The Philosophy of the Kalam* (Cambridge, Mass., 1976). Harry Austryn Wolfson, *Repercussions of the Kalam in Jewish Philosophy* (Cambridge, Mass., 1979).

KALISCHER, TSEVI HIRSCH (1795–1874), rabbinic forerunner of modern Zionism who flourished in the western Polish province of Posen (Poznań) annexed by Prussia. A disciple of R. ʿAqiva' *Eger and for fifty years rabbi of Thorn (Toruń), a major Jewish community in the region, which he insisted on serving in an honorary capacity, Kalischer became the most prominent and active promoter of practical Zionism of his day, influencing both the English-Jewish leader Sir Moses Montefiore and the leaders of the newly established French-Jewish philanthropic organization Alliance Israélite Universelle to promote Jewish settlement in Erets Yisra'el. He prevailed on the latter to found the agricultural school of Miqveh Yisra'el, near Jaffa in 1870; organized societies for the settlement of the country; and convened an embryonic Zionist conference, mainly attended by rabbinic supporters, at Thorn in 1860. Although an author of halakhic, philosophic, and homiletic writings, Kalischer's most influential work was a booklet entitled *Derishat Tsiyyon* (1862), which became a classic, outlining his Religious Zionist program and citing the relevant rabbinic texts. He maintained that the Messiah would come only after large numbers of Jews had settled in Erets Yisra'el and opposed the prevalent Orthodox view that Jews had to await the arrival of the Messiah to return to the Holy Land. He advocated the restoration of the biblical sacrificial cult but nevertheless emphasized the essential rational basis of Judaism, combining a rigid Orthodoxy with a permissive approach to the conversion of the children of mixed marriages. His Zionist writings, including his letters, were published by I. Klausner (1947, with bibliography). His halakhic publications included *Emunah Yesharah* (2 vols. [1843, 1871]) and *Moznayyim le-Mishpat* (2 vols. [1855]).

• Arthur Hertzberg, ed., *The Zionist Idea* (New York, 1960), pp. 108–114. I. Klausner, ed., Introduction to *Ha-Ketavim ha-Tsiyoniyyim shel Tsevi Kalisher* (Jerusalem, 1947). Jody Elizabeth Myers, "Zevi Hirsch Kalischer and the Origins of Religious Zionism," in *From East and West: Jews in a Changing Europe, 1750–1870*, edited by Frances Malino and David Sorkin (Oxford, 1991), pp. 267–294. Jody Elizabeth Myers, "Seeking Zion: The Messianic Ideology of Zevi Hirsch Kalischer, 1795–1874," Ph.D. dissertation, University of California at Los Angeles, 1985. Moshe Weiss, *Rabbi Zvi Hirsch Kalisher, Founder of Modern and Religious Zionism* (New York, 1969).

—ARYEH NEWMAN

KALLAH. [*This entry discusses the minor tractate* Kallah; *for a discussion of brides, see* BETROTHAL.] This minor tractate, printed in standard editions of the Talmud Bavli, probably dates from early geonic times. It deals with laws concerning marriage and sexual relations, many of which seem to be based on tannaitic and amoraic teachings, and it derives its name from its opening regarding the prohibition of a bride to her husband prior to the recitation of the marriage blessing. *Kallah* seems to have no connection with the *Massekhet Kallah* mentioned in the Talmud Bavli, which refers to the tractate, different each year, studied during the *kallah* study months in Babylonia (see KALLAH MONTHS). *Kallah* is followed, in standard Talmud Bavli editions, by the minor tractate *Kallah Rabbati*, written in Aramaic, which elaborates on the *baraiytot* of *Kallah* and other sources in quasi-Talmudic style. It was published by Michael Higger (New York, 1936; reprinted in Jerusalem, 1970).

—AVRAHAM WALFISH

KALLAH MONTHS, the months of Adar and Elul, during which study conventions were held in the Babylonian *academies at the time of the ge'onim and perhaps even earlier during the time of the amora'im. The conventions were attended by a large number of scholars and students who did not reside in the vicinity of the academies. The choice of Adar and Elul, which fall immediately before the spring and autumn seasons, respectively, enabled farmers to attend, since they were comparatively free from agricultural duties during these months. Regular members of the academy, who received stipends, were expected to study a specific tractate during the five months between one *kallah* month and the next and were examined by the head of the academy during the *kallah* month. The discussion of queries addressed to the ga'on and scholars of the academy, although not restricted to these months, seems also to have featured prominently in these gatherings.

• Chanoch Albeck, *Mavo' la-Talmudim* (Tel Aviv, 1987). Simḥa Assaf, *Tequfat ha-Ge'onim ve-Sifrutah* (Jerusalem, 1967). Isaiah Gafni, *Yehudei Bavel bi-Tequfat ha-Talmud* (Jerusalem, 1990). David Mordecai Goodblatt, *Rabbinic Instruction in Sasanian Babylonia* (Leiden, 1975). Adolf Neubauer, *Mediaeval Jewish Chronicles and Chronological Notes* (1887–1895; Jerusalem, 1967). Solomon Schechter, *Saadyana: Genizah Fragments of Writings of R. Saadya Gaon and Others* (Cambridge, 1903).

—ROBERT BRODY

KALLIR, ELʿAZAR (6th–7th cent.), the most famous and influential of the early liturgical poets. He refers to his home town as Qiryat Sefer (cf. *Jgs.* 1.11), which is not precisely identified but may be Sepphoris in Galilee. His voluminous *oeuvre* is the climax of the classical **piyyut* in Erets Yisra'el, at the end of the Byzantine period, and contains elaborate *piyyutim* for almost every special liturgical occasion. Kallir developed the poetic tradition of his forerunners (e.g., *Yann'ai) into a personal, highly complex style. His poetry is full of Midrashic allusions, and his Hebrew showed daring innovation and departures from accepted usage. However, his meanings are often obscure, and his compositions were often criticized (e.g., by Avraham ibn Ezra) for their intricacy and artificiality. Nevertheless, his elaborate and often enigmatic style set standards in Jewish liturgical poetry for almost half a millennium, especially north of the Mediterranean, until the rise of the Spanish school. Some two hundred of his compositions may be found in editions of the Ashkenazi **maḥazor*. Others have been published by modern scholars, many of them discovered in the Cairo *Genizah.

• T. Carmi, ed. and trans., *The Penguin Book of Hebrew Verse* (New York, 1981), pp. 221–232. Jakob J. Petuchowski, *Theology and Poetry: Studies in the Medieval Piyyut* (London and Boston, 1977), *passim*. Leopold Zunz, *Literaturgeschichte der synagogalen Poesie* (Berlin, 1865), pp. 29–64.

—PETER LENHARDT

KALONIMOS BEN KALONIMOS (1286–after 1328), Provençal author and translator. In his *Iggeret ha-Hitnatselut ha-Qatan* (Jerusalem, 1966), he explained why he left his native Provence to study under Shelomoh ben Avraham Adret (Rashba') in Barcelona. In most of his works Kalonimos ben Kalonimos was critical of Provençal society and his contemporaries. His *Even Boḥan* (Naples, 1489; Tel Aviv, 1956) satirized the moral life, social positions, and religious abuses of Provençal Jewry. Kalonimos complained, for example, that Jewish festivals were observed in their externals—food and festivities—while their real significance was ignored. He also wrote *Massekhet Purim* (Pesaro, 1513), a parody of a Talmud tractate and its rabbinical argumentation for the festival of Purim; *Iggeret Musar* (Jerusalem, 1936), an ethical work to his son; and *Teshuvah*, a polemic against the philosophical views of Yosef ben Abba' Mari Caspi (Munich, 1879). Among Kalonimos's significant translations into Hebrew were Ibn Ridwan's *Principles of Medicine*, Archimedes' *On the Sphere and Cylinder*, Galen's *De clysteribus et colica liber*, Ibn Sankh's *Cylinder and Cone*, and Ptolemy's *Hypothesis*. Of special note is Kalonimos's Latin translation of Averroës's *Destructio destructionis*.

• Abraham M. Habermann, ed., *Even Boḥan* (Tel Aviv, 1956), pp. 163–187. Meyer Kayserling, *Leben Kalonymos ben Kalonymos* (Leipzig, 1879).

—SHLOMO H. PICK

KALONIMOS FAMILY, prominent German-Jewish family from the ninth through the thirteenth century. Several sources, all stemming from the *beit midrash* of R. El'azar ben Yehudah of Worms, describe how in 917 CE "King Karl" (i.e., Charlemagne) brought the Kalonimos family from Lucca in northern Italy to Mainz. The most likely possibility is that the migration did take place in 917, although Conrad I was the king of Germany at that time.

The Kalonimides were adepts in liturgical poetry and esoteric teachings, in addition to being authorities on rabbinic literature. They were largely responsible for bringing mystical teachings from Italy to Germany. Through the First Crusade, along with several other elite families, they provided both the spiritual and temporal leadership of the main Rhineland communities of Mainz and Worms, even directing the martyrdom that took place at the time of the First Crusade. Rabbi Shemu'el he-Ḥasid, R. Yehudah ben Shemu'el he-Ḥasid, and R. El'azar of Worms, who molded the *Ḥasidei Ashkenaz in the twelfth and thirteen centuries, all belonged to this family (R. Yehudah was the major teacher of R. El'azar of Worms and the source from whom R. El'azar received the family chain of tradition and history). They and their circle attempted to retain aspects of the cultural and spiritual milieu of the pre-Crusade period in the face of tosafistic dialectic and inquiry and a changing Ashkenazi society.

• Joseph Dan, *Torat ha-Sod shel Ḥasidut Ashkenaz* (Jerusalem, 1968), pp. 14–20, 50–51. Avraham Grossman, *Ḥakhmei Ashkenaz ha-Ri'shonim* (Jerusalem, 1981).

—EPHRAIM KANARFOGEL

KAPLAN, MORDECAI MENAHEM (1881–1983), U.S. rabbi; founder of *Reconstructionism. The son of an Orthodox rabbi, Kaplan, who arrived with his family in the United States at age nine, was ordained at the Jewish Theological Seminary of America, where he became founding dean of the Teachers Institute in 1909. He taught at the seminary for over five decades and influenced generations of Conservative rabbis. He was one of the founders of the New York Kehillah; he organized the first synagogue center, the Jewish Center, in 1917; and he founded the Society for the Advancement of Judaism in 1922, *The Reconstructionist* magazine in 1935, and the Jewish Reconstructionist Foundation in 1940. Kaplan's first major work, *Judaism as a Civilization* (New York, 1934), criticized all current Jewish approaches as based on an inadequate understanding of Jewish civilization. Drawing upon American philosophical pragmatism, the cultural Zionism of 'Aḥad ha-'Am, and the sociology of Durkheim and Gittings, Kaplan defined Judaism as the "evolving religious civilization of the Jewish people," one that has been continuously adapted to the historical contexts in which Jews have found themselves. He argued that Jewish survival in modern Western culture similarly depends on the reconstruction of Jewish life in response to unprecedented challenges. Judaism is more than a faith or an ethic, he asserted. Jewish civilization, in all of its historical stages, has included the totality of Jewish culture: land, language, polity, arts. It has been transmitted in the context of Jewish communities that have been governed by Jewish law, and in which the language, culture, and governance have all been Jewish. Thus, he saw the political emancipation of the Jews as a critical challenge, since citizens of nations now had a choice about living in Jewish communities and, in any case, were integrated into the greater national culture. He sought to reconstruct Judaism in America to make it speak to the concerns of modern Jews. To do so, he articulated a theology of religious naturalism, defining God as "the process that makes for salvation" and not a miraculous intervener in history. He saw Jewish religion as embracing the cumulative quest of the Jewish people for a meaningful existence. He remained traditional in his ritual practice and developed a method of revaluation, in which the values and insights embedded in seemingly arcane rituals are abstracted and then expressed in a contemporary idiom. Thus, the practices are preserved while the intention is reinterpreted. The *Sabbath Prayer Book* (Jewish Reconstructionist Foundation, 1945) and other liturgical works that Kaplan coedited retain most of the words of the traditional liturgy, but the text has been changed to avoid affirming belief in the Jews as the chosen people, resurrection of the dead, or a personal Messiah. Kaplan introduced the **bat mitsvah* ceremony in the early 1920s. His other writings include *The Meaning of God in Modern Jewish Religion* (1937); *A New Zionism* (1955); and *The Religion of Ethical Nationhood: Judaism's Contribution to World Peace* (1970).

• Ira Eisenstein and Eugene Kohn, eds., *Mordecai M. Kaplan: An Evaluation* (New York, 1952). Emanuel S. Goldsmith and Mel Scult, eds., *Introduction to Dynamic Judaism: The Essential Writings of Mordecai M. Kaplan* (New York, 1985). Emanuel S. Goldsmith, Mel Scult, and Robert M. Seltzer, eds., *The American Judaism of Mordecai M. Kaplan* (New York, 1990). Mel Scult, *Judaism Faces the Twentieth Century: A Biography of Mordecai M. Kaplan* (Detroit, 1993).

—JACOB J. STAUB

KAPPARAH. See ATONEMENT.

KAPPAROT (כַּפָּרוֹת, expiations), a custom performed on the morning preceding Yom Kippur (or before), by which the sins of an individual are symbolically transferred to a live fowl. The fowl is taken in the right hand, and verses are recited from *Psalms* (107.17–20) and *Job* (33.23–24). After the recitation, the fowl is waved around the head while the following is said three times: "This is my substitute, this is my redemption. This rooster shall be killed, while I shall be admitted to and allowed a long, happy, and peaceful life." A cock is used by a man, a hen by a woman. Nowadays many who practice *kapparot* use eighteen coins (in Hebrew the numerical value of the word *life*) instead of a fowl. The fowl or the money is then given to charity. The custom may be ancient but is not mentioned before the geonic period (9th cent.) and may have arisen in Babylonia, where an analogous ritual of casting a basket filled with seeds into a river was sometimes performed. Several authorities (e.g., Shelomoh ben Avraham Adret, Nahmanides) opposed the practice because of its pagan character, and even the sixteenth-century codifier and kabbalist Yosef Karo dismissed it as a "foolish practice," but because of the weight of opinion and tradition, and kabbalistic influence in particular, the custom is still practiced in certain circles. The negative ruling in the first edition of Karo's *Shulḥan ʿArukh* (Venice, 1565) was omitted in all later printings of the work.

• Jacob Z. Lauterbach, "The Ritual for the Kapparot Ceremony," in *Studies in Jewish Law, Custom, and Folklore* (New York, 1970).

KARA, YOSEF (born c.1065), northern French commentator on the Bible and on **piyyutim*. He lived in Worms and Troyes, and studied with both his paternal uncle Menaḥem ben Ḥelbo and with Rashi. He wrote commentaries on almost all the books of the Bible, although many of these have not been printed. These commentaries reveal his focus on the **peshat* method of interpretation, in which reference to rabbinic literature is avoided when explaining difficulties in biblical language. Kara engaged in debate with Christian scholars, and his *responsa* are included in collections of Jewish polemics. He also wrote commentaries on the religious poetry used by Franco-German Jewry.

• Moshe Ahrend, *Le Commentaire sur Job de Rabbi Yosef Qara* (Hildesheim, 1978). Avraham Grossman, *Ḥakhemei Tsarefat ha-Ri'shonim* (Jerusalem, 1995). Sara Japhet, "The Nature and Distribution of Medieval Compilatory Commentaries in the Light of Rabbi Joseph Kara's Commentary on the Book of Job," in *The Midrashic Imagination: Jewish Exegesis, Thought and History*, edited by Michael Fishbane (Albany, N.Y., 1993), pp. 98–130. —MICHAEL A. SIGNER

KARAITES (Scripturalists), a religious group that developed a system of Jewish law independent of the Talmud. Karaite roots may be traced to eighth-century Babylonia when, according to rabbinic (i.e., non-Karaite) traditions, *ʿAnan ben David is said to have founded the new religion after having failed to obtain the position of exilarch. Karaites claim that their form of Judaism is the original one and that evidence of its premedieval existence can be found among certain Second Temple groups (such as the one known today as the *Qumran community). ʿAnan, according to Karaite belief, merely revitalized this ancient Jewish group. Whatever ʿAnan's actual role, most scholars agree that Karaism as it has developed since the ninth century has very little to do with ʿAnan's teaching and that ʿAnan was apparently appropriated (because of his presumed Davidic lineage) by later Karaites in an attempt to give the group greater legitimacy.

Strong Karaite communities developed in the early Middle Ages, but they were never as great a threat to rabbinic Judaism as is commonly believed (*Saʿadyah ben Yosef Ga'on is credited with repulsing this threat). Karaism flourished between the late ninth century and the eleventh century. During that golden age, Karaite practices and beliefs were firmly established by such luminaries from Erets Yisra'el as Daniyye'l ben Mosheh al-*Qumisi (who called for immigration to Erets Yisra'el); *Salmon ben Yeruḥim and *Sahl ben Matsliaḥ (Karaite propagandists); *Yefet ben ʿAli (foremost Karaite commentator on the Bible whose work influenced such Rabbinites as Avraham *ibn Ezra); and Yosef ben Avraham *Basir and his student *Yeshuʿa ben Yehudah (philosophers and legal authorities).

As a result of the destruction of the Karaite community in Erets Yisra'el in the wake of the First Crusade in 1099, the Karaite center of activity moved to Byzantium, where it remained until the sixteenth century. Migration patterns brought Karaites to the Crimean peninsula and eventually to Lithuania and parts of Poland. Whereas Karaites in Muslim countries maintained their identity as part of the Jewish people, Karaites in Christian Europe, beginning in the late eighteenth century in czarist Russia, denied their affinity to Jews, mainly in order to avoid restrictions placed upon Jews. By the time of the Holocaust, Karaites in Europe had forged a sufficiently separate identity to escape much of the persecution. This separate identity, however, has brought with it an almost total dissolution of Karaism in eastern Europe.

The one remaining significant Karaite community is in Israel, made up mostly of immigrants from Egypt (where the ancient Karaite community has been reduced to a handful of individuals). Their number is estimated at between twenty thousand and twenty-five thousand people in Israel with major centers in Ramla and Ashdod. Small communities also can be found in İstanbul, Turkey; France; and the United States (mostly in the San Francisco Bay area).

Major differences in practice exist between Karaites and Rabbinites. The Karaite calendar is calculated according to the actual phases of the moon, resulting in slight differences in dates from the Rabbinite calendar; there is no restriction on which day of the week a holiday can fall (except for Shavuʿot, which is always on Sunday), and biblical holidays (including Ro'sh ha-Shanah) are observed for only one day both in and out of Erets Yisra'el. Ḥanukkah is not recognized since it is a postbiblical holiday. Milk and meat are not eaten at the same meal; however, the same dishes are used. Since the fifteenth century, Karaites have allowed the kindling of lights before the Sabbath (without a blessing) to provide light on the Sabbath, but they still prohibit sexual relations and the preparation of hot food on the Sabbath. The Karaite liturgy is totally different from the Rabbinite one, and prayer is marked by removal of shoes and full genuflection in synagogues devoid of chairs. *Tefillin* are not worn.

Because of different marriage and divorce laws, intermarriage between Karaites and Rabbinites, though it has occurred, has always been problematic. To this day, Ashkenazim, following the ruling of R. Mosheh *Isserles (16th cent.), generally refrain from such intermarriages. Sephardim, however, may follow the ruling of *David ben Shelomoh ibn Avi Zimra (16th cent.), who permitted such unions. In Israel today Karaites have no de jure control over personal status, but the state informally recognizes Karaite marriages and divorces as long as both partners are Karaites and willing to accept the authority of the Karaite court.

• Zvi Ankori, *Karaites in Byzantium* (New York, 1968). Haggai Ben-Shammai, "Between Ananites and Karaites: Observations on Early Medieval Jewish Sectarianism," *Studies in Muslim-Jewish Relations* 1 (1993): 19–29. Philip Birnbaum, ed., *Karaite Studies* (New York, 1971). Bruno Chiesa and Wilfrid Lockwood, *Yaqub al-Qirqisani on Jewish Sects and Christianity* (Frankfurt am Main, 1984). Daniel J. Lasker, "Rabbinism and Karaism: The Contest for Supremacy," in *Great Schisms in Jewish History*, edited by Raphael Jospe and Stanley M. Wagner (New York, 1981), pp. 47–72. Phililp E. Miller, *Karaite Separatism in Nineteenth-Century Russia* (Cincinnati, 1993). Leon Nemoy, L., *Karaite Anthology* (New Haven, 1952). Nathan Schur, *History of the Karaites* (Frankfurt am Main and New York, 1992). Georges Vajda, *Al-Kitab al-Muhtawi de Yusuf al-Basir* (Leiden, 1985).

—DANIEL J. LASKER

KARAKASANI. See QIRQISANI, YAQUB.

KARELITZ, AVRAHAM YESHAʿYAHU (1878–1953), Talmudic scholar, popularly known as the Ḥazon Ish (Vision of a Man; *ish* [man] being an acronym of his name), after the title of his published writings. Born in Kosov, in the Russian province of Grodno, Karelitz received his education from his father, the town rabbi. He never held any official position, but devoted himself entirely to Talmudic study, supporting himself first from the proceeds of a store run by his wife, and later from the sale of his books. In 1911 his first work, on a section of the *Shulḥan ʿArukh, Oraḥ Ḥayyim*, appeared anonymously under the title *Ḥazon Ish*, and made a strong impact on the rabbinic world in general and in particular on R. Ḥayyim ʿOzer Grodzinski, communal rabbi of Vilna and the leading rabbinic authority in eastern Europe. When Karelitz moved to Vilna in 1920, he was consulted by Grodzinski on all religious and communal matters. In 1933, Karelitz moved to Erets Yisra'el and settled in Bene Beraq. He quickly emerged as the unchallenged spiritual authority of the Ḥaredi (non-Zionist strictly Orthodox) community in the country, and, after the death of Grodzinski in 1940, of the Ḥaredi community the world over.

Karelitz's twenty-three volumes of halakhic writings (Vilna [vols. 1–7] and Jerusalem [vols. 8–23], 1911–1953) are characterized by their practical orientation. Soon after settling in Bene Beraq, he issued rulings on such issues as the proper mode of observance of the Jewish agricultural laws (in particular the laws of the sabbatical year), the problem of milking on the Sabbath, and the determination of the international date line. These rulings were accepted as binding by the Ḥaredi community, and even influenced circles of the non-Ḥaredi Orthodox. Karelitz also guided the Ḥaredi community in its relationship with the newly established State of Israel. While strongly opposed to Zionism, including Religious Zionism, Karelitz urged the Ḥaredi camp to accept the state *de facto* and participate in Israeli elections in the Knesset in order to further its religious interests.

In his collection of letters, *Kovets Iggerot* (3 vols. [Bene Beraq, 1954–1956, 1990]) and his pietistic work, *Emunah u-Vittaḥon* (Bene Beraq, 1954), Karelitz contended that the only path to ethical and spiritual perfection is exclusive devotion to Torah study, in particular the study of Jewish law, and by the unreserved submission to, and precise observance of, the rigorous and uncompromising demands of that law.

• Shlomo Cohen, ed., *Pe'er ha-Dor* (Bene Beraq, 1966), a somewhat hagiographical biography. Raphael Halperin, *Bi-Meḥitsat he-"Ḥazon Ish"* (n.p., 1991). Shimon Finkelman, *The Chazon Ish: The Life and Ideals of Rabbi Yeshayah Karelitz* (New York, 1989), based primarily on *Pe'er ha-Dor*. Lawrence Kaplan, "The Hazon Ish: Haredi Critic of Traditional Orthodoxy," in *The Uses of Tradition: Jewish Continuity in the Modern Era*, edited by Jack Wertheimer (New York, 1992), pp. 145–173.

—LAWRENCE J. KAPLAN

KARET (כָּרֵת; cut off), a divinely imposed punishment for violations of Jewish law that usually involve transgressions that occur in private without the presence of witnesses. The punishment is left to God, not human beings, and the term *karet* refers to being cut off from God and the ability to communicate with him. There is a difference of opinion as to whether it consists of premature death or childlessness (see *Lv*. 20.20). Examples of such transgressions include consuming blood (*Lv*. 7.25), committing certain sexually deviant acts (*Lv*. 20.17), not sanctifying Yom Kippur (*Lv*. 23.29), and not eating *matsah* on Pesaḥ (*Ex*. 12.15). Others note that this spiritual excommunication must be linked to the failure to circumcise (*Gn*. 17.13), which is also punished by *karet*. Avraham ibn Ezra (commenting on *Lv*. 15.29) notes that because of the severity of these crimes, the threat of *karet* is license for capital punishment.

• "Issur Karet," in *Entsiqlopedyah Talmudit* (Jerusalem, 1947–), vol. 2, p. 18. Philip D. Stern, *The Biblical Herem: A Window on Israel's Religious Experience*, Brown Judaic Studies 211 (Atlanta, 1991).

—MICHAEL BROYDE

KARLIN, name of a Hasidic dynasty with its center in Karlin and Stolin near Pinsk. Its founder was Aharon the Great (1736–1772), who was a disciple of Dov Ber of Mezhirech. The descendants and disciples of R. Aharon founded other, related Hasidic dynasties, such as those from Lyakhovichi, Kobrin, and Slonim. While most of these Ḥasidim and their leaders were killed in the Holocaust, some groups continue to have adherents in the United States and Israel. The heyday of the Karlin Ḥasidim was during the period of R. Aharon ben Asher (1802–1872), when as many as three or four thousand Ḥasidim would come to Karlin on the Shalosh Regalim.

• Aharon ben Ya'aqov of Karlin, *Tsava'ah* (Warsaw, 1878). Wolf Zeev Rabinowitsch, *Lithuanian Hasidism* (New York, 1971).

—GERSHON DAVID HUNDERT

KARO, YOSEF (1488–1575), Talmudic authority, codifier of rabbinic law, and kabbalist. Born (probably in Portugal) of a Toledo family of eminent rabbinic scholars, he was orphaned as a child and brought up by his uncle Yitsḥaq, who had himself lost all his children. He seems to have left the Iberian Peninsula at an early age, but it is impossible to reconstruct his movements and places of study; he may have studied in Egypt in the academy of R. Ya'aqov *Berab, to whom he refers as "my master" and from whom he received *ordination in 1538. The early part of his career was spent in Greece (then part of the Ottoman empire), Adrianople, Nicopolis, and possibly Salonika, where he was in close contact with leading scholars, pietists, and kabbalists, including Yosef Taitazak, Mosheh ben Ya'aqov Cordovero, and Shelomoh Alkabez, and where he soon gained a reputation as a leading rabbinic authority. In 1522 he began writing his monumental *Beit Yosef*, on which he continued to work after settling in Safed in Upper Galilee in 1536. The work was finished in 1542, but Karo devoted more years to a revision of this *magnum opus*, which confirmed his standing as the most eminent scholar and rabbinic authority of his age. The *Beit Yosef* is written in the form of a commentary on the code of *Ya'aqov ben Asher, the *Arba'ah Turim*, which (unlike Maimonides' code, *Mishneh Torah*) does not simply state rabbinic law, paragraph by paragraph, but summarizes the views of earlier authorities. Hence, Ya'aqov ben Asher's code lent itself admirably as a basis for a detailed critical survey and digest of the whole immense corpus of halakhic literature, on the basis of which Karo then formulated his definitive rulings. It has been frequently published in editions of the *Arba'ah Turim*. These were presented again, in simpler form and without discussion, in his shorter code **Shulḥan 'Arukh*, which, being accessible to laymen, soon established itself as the standard formulation of rabbinic law and religious observance for subsequent generations, including present-day Orthodoxy, especially after R. Mosheh *Isserles of Kraków added glosses incorporating divergences in Ashkenazi customs. Karo also wrote a commentary, *Qesef Mishneh* (Venice, 1574–1575), on the code of Maimonides. His legal *responsa* were printed posthumously (Salonika, 1598, 1791). In Safed, Karo was soon recognized as the leading authority of this remarkable community, although most of the time he was also engaged in fierce controversies with another halakhic authority, Mosheh di Trani (see TRANI FAMILY). Karo was also involved in the great controversy triggered by Berab's abortive attempt to renew ordination.

Karo was a central figure in the circle of kabbalistic pietists and charismatics that had formed in Adrianople, Salonika, and other centers in Turkey and flourished in Safed and that combined extreme asceticism with messianic yearning. The meteoric career of Shelomoh *Molkho (whom Karo may have met in Salonika), his intense charismatic life, and his martyr's death at the stake profoundly influenced Karo's spiritual life, which was marked by an unusual yearning for martyrdom. Over more than four decades, Karo maintained he was visited, mostly at night, by a celestial mentor (**maggid*), identified as the personified *Mishnah as well as **shekhinah*. Karo wrote down these revelations in an intimate mystical diary. A minor part that survived was published in edited form under the title *Maggid Meisharim* (Amsterdam, 1708). The authenticity of this diary has been disputed by many historians who do not accept the idea that the lucid legalist scholar also was the subject of nocturnal heavenly visitations.

• Boaz Cohen, *The Shulhan Aruk as a Guide for Religious Practice Today* (New York, 1940). Hirsch L. Gordon, *The Maggid of Caro* (New York, 1949). Miri Peer, *The Story of Maran Bet Yosef: R. Yosef Caro, Author of the Shulhan Arukh* (Brooklyn, N.Y., 1986). R. J. Zwi Werblowsky, *Joseph Karo: Lawyer and Mystic*, 2d ed. (Philadelphia, 1977).

KASHER (כָּשֵׁר; fit, proper; Ashkenazi pronunciation, *kosher*), food prepared in accordance with the *dietary laws; in this sense, the opposite of **terefah*. The term can be used to designate the ritual fitness of any object according to Jewish law, such as a *shofar, **tefillin*, a **lulav*, or a **miqveh*. *Kasher* is also used as a verb; one is said, for example, to *kasher* vessels, and the ritual preparation of meat is also commonly described as koshering. In many states of the United States, in some European countries, and in the State of Israel, the term is legally protected, and merchants or food dispensers who advertise their products as *kasher* may be prosecuted if they violate the rabbinic requirements. A modern development has been the introduction of degrees of *kashrut* (i.e., the state of being *kasher*). The strictly Orthodox insist on their food products being *glatt-kosher* or *kosher le-mehadderin*, terms attesting to an even more meticulous supervision. In the United States, foods classified as "kosher-style" resemble familiar Jewish products but have not necessarily been produced under rabbinic supervision.

• Seymour E. Freedman, *The Book of Kashruth* (New York, 1970). Ruth B. Waxman, ed., "Some Current Aspects of Kashrut: Law and Practice," *Judaism* 39 (1990): 389–403.

KASHER, MENAḤEM (1895–1983), scholar of Talmudic and rabbinic literature. Born in Warsaw, Kasher studied under prominent rabbis in Poland and was ordained in 1915. He moved to Palestine in 1925 as an emissary of the Ger Hasidic dynasty, on whose behalf he founded the *yeshivah* Sefat Emet in Jerusalem, which he headed for two years.

Kasher was a prolific scholar, producing several comprehensive anthologies. His best-known work is the *Torah Shelemah*, an encyclopedia of the Talmud and Midrash, in which material from the oral law is collected and organized according to biblical verse, together with notes and supplemental material. Between 1927 and 1992, forty-three volumes were published. Other important compilations include *Haggadah Shelemah* (1956), devoted to the Pesaḥ Haggadah with variant readings, notes, and relevant homiletic comments; and *Gemara' Shelemah* (1960), which contains manuscripts and medieval commentaries dealing with the first nine pages of the Talmudic tractate *Pesaḥim*.

Kasher also wrote extensively about the halakhic aspects of such contemporary issues as artificial insemination and autopsies. Many of these writings appeared in *No'am*, an annual publication that was founded in 1958 and edited by Kasher.

• Aaron Greenbaum, "Architect and Builder: The Life of Harav Menachem M. Kasher," in *Sages and Saints*, edited by Leo Jung (Hoboken, N.J., 1987), pp. 231–272. Getzel Kressel, *Leksikon ha-Sifrut ha-'Ivrit ba-Dorot ha-Aḥaronim*, vol. 2 (Merḥavyah, 1965–1967), pp. 155–156.

—ADAM RUBIN

KASHRUT. See DIETARY LAWS.

KASOVSKY, CHAYIM YEHOSHU'A (1873–1960), scholar of rabbinics. Born in Jerusalem, Kasovsky studied at the local Ets Ḥayyim Yeshivah. He compiled concordances for the Mishnah (4 vols. [1927–1960]), Tosefta' (6 vols. [1932–1961]), and Targum Onkelos (2 vols. [1933–1940]). Six volumes of his concordances to the Talmud Bavli appeared in his lifetime, and the work was continued by his son Binyamin Kasovsky in over thirty additional volumes. His other son, Mosheh, published a concordance of the Talmud Yerushalmi.

• Avraham Ḥ. Elḥanani, *Siḥat Sofrim* (Jerusalem, 1960), pp. 228–236. Yitsḥaq Raphael, *Ri'shonim ve-'Aḥaronim* (Tel Aviv, 1957), pp. 421ff.

—DIDIER Y. REISS

KASPI, YOSEF BEN ABBA' MARI. See CASPI, YOSEF BEN ABBA' MARI.

KATZ, AVRAHAM BEN ALEKSANDER (died 1810), Hasidic rabbi. A disciple of Dov Ber of Mezhirech, Hasidic legend has it that he had previously been a student of the Vilna Ga'on. By 1768 Avraham was the leader of a group of Ḥasidim in a province of Vitebsk, Belorussia. He was a leading participant in the meeting of Hasidic leaders in the aftermath of the bans of excommunication in 1772. In 1777 he joined Menaḥem Mendel of Vitebsk at the head of some three hundred Jews who immigrated to Palestine, settling first in Safed and later in Tiberias. Menaḥem Mendel and Avraham continued to instruct the followers they had left behind in epistles, and their Ḥasidim in Europe in turn raised funds to support the colony in Galilee.

Avraham stressed the centrality of continuous attachment to divinity and the value of simple faith. He and his followers were accused (by Shneur Zalman of Lyady in the course of a dispute many years later) of provoking the first bans of excommunication by their extreme behavior—turning somersaults in the streets and mocking and insulting the rabbis—thus helping to create the division between Ḥasidim and *Mitnaggedim. His criticism of Shneur Zalman's book, *Tanya'* ("too much oil may extinguish the flame"), probably contributed to the crystallization of Ḥabad as a distinct Hasidic group. His *Sefer Ḥesed le-'Avraham* was published in Lwów in 1851.

• Ze'ev Gries, "Mi-Mitos le-'Etos: Qavim le-Demuto shel R. Avraham Kalisker," *Umah ve-Toledoteha* 2 (1984): 117–146.

—GERSHON DAVID HUNDERT

KATZENELLENBOGEN, ME'IR BEN YITSḤAQ (1473–1565), Italian rabbinic scholar; also known as Maharam of Padua. His halakhic writings emphasize the teachings of the *ri'shonim*; his *responsa* are succinct, analytical, and clear and do not enter into *pilpul*, although he was a pupil of Ya'aqov *Pollak, a noted pilpulist. Katzenellenbogen was a recognized *poseq* while still a student in Padua, where he continued as rabbi and *av beit din* of the Venetian republic. He was noted for his moderation and modesty and the fatherly interest he took in the students of his *yeshivah* in Padua. He advised his colleagues not to reach their decisions hastily and to be respectful of their fellow judges and of the public, while at the same time standing firm once decisions were reached. He strengthened the ability of the courts to arbitrate disputes. His *responsa* were published with those of his teacher Yehudah *Mintz (Venice, 1553). Katzenellenbogen issued *taqqanot*, including one in which he ruled that *semikhah* should be given by three sages so as to strengthen the authority of the newly ordained rabbi.

• Robert Bonfil, *Rabbis and Jewish Communities in Renaissance Italy* (London, 1993), pp. 150–155, 220–230. S. Schwarzfuchs, "I Responsi di Rabbi Meir da Padova come fonte storica," in *Scritti in memoria di Leone Carpi*, edited by D. Carpi (Milan, 1967), pp. 112–132.

—SHALOM BAR-ASHER

KAUFMANN, DAVID (1852–1899), scholar of Jewish philosophy. Born in Moravia, he studied at the Breslau Rabbinical Seminary and received a Ph.D. from the University of Leipzig in 1874 with a dissertation on religious philosophy. In 1877 he was appointed professor at the Budapest Rabbinical Seminary, where he remained until his death. Kaufmann was a prolific scholar who wrote twenty-six books and over five hundred articles and reviews on many areas of Jewish scholarship. He is noted for his influential study of Jewish and Muslim religious philosophy in the Middle Ages, *Geschichte der Attributenlehre in der jüdischen Religionsphilosophie des Mittelalters von Saadja bis Maimuni* (1877–1878). He discovered and published the memoirs of Glückel of Hameln, one of the most important sources documenting Jewish social life in the seventeenth century. Kaufmann was also a pioneering scholar of Jewish art, cofounding the Gesellschaft für Sammlung und Konservierung von Kunst- und historischen Denkmälern des Judentums in Vienna in 1896.

• Ferdinand Rosenthal, in *Gedenkbuch zur Erinnerung David Kaufmann* (1900; repr. New York, 1980). Marcus Brann, in *Gesammelte Schriften*, by David Kaufmann (Frankfurt am Main, 1908).

—GAVRIEL D. ROSENFELD

KAUFMANN, YEHEZKEL (1889–1963), historian, biblical scholar, and essayist on Jewish nationalism and Zionist ideology. Born in the Ukraine, Kaufmann studied in Odessa, Saint Petersburg, and Berne and in 1928 immigrated to Palestine, where he taught at the Re'ali School in Haifa and, after 1949, at the Hebrew University of Jerusalem. His first major work, *Golah ve-Nekhar* (1929–1930), is an interpretation of the forces and dilemmas in Jewish survival from the perspective of historical sociology. His *Toledot ha-'Emunah ha-Yisra'elit* (8 vols. [1937–1956]; translated and abridged by Moshe Greenberg as *The Religion of Israel* [Chicago, 1960]) is an explication of the historical uniqueness and antiquity of Israelite monotheism.

According to Kaufmann, Israelite radical monotheism was not a gradual evolution of paganism but a revolutionary intuition of Israelite culture from the time of Moses, which gave rise to a religion devoid of true mythology and possessing no theogony or theomachy. The prophetic misinterpretation of idols as fetishes made by human hands was a result of this monotheistic understanding of the world, one way in which the classical prophets from Amos on developed the implications of biblical faith. The universalistic potential of biblical ideas was actualized in Jewish proselytism of the late Second Temple period. Christianity developed out of the individualistic side of first-century apocalyptic Judaism, gradually severing its bond from the Jewish people but not from its monotheistic roots.

Contrary to the Jewish secular nationalists of his time, Kaufmann believed it was religion and not a supposed national will to survive that preserved the Jewish people in exile throughout the centuries. But religion, he held, could no longer serve that function in modern times. The painful need for an end to Jewish alienation could be resolved only with the creation of a Jewish homeland.

• David Berger, "Religion, Nationalism, and Historiography: Yehezkel Kaufmann's Account of Jesus and Early Christianity," in *Scholars and Scholarship: The Interaction between Judaism and Other Cultures, The Bernard Revel Graduate School Conference Volume*, edited by Leo Landman (New York, 1990), pp. 148–168. Menahem Haran, ed., *Sefer ha-Yovel li-Yeḥezq'el Koifman* (Jerusalem, 1960). Jon D. Levenson, "Yehezkel Kaufmann and Mythology," *Conservative Judaism* 36.2 (Winter 1982–1983): 36–43. Ehud Luz, "Jewish Nationalism in the Thought of Yehezkel Kaufmann," in *Studies in Jewish Thought*, vol. 2, edited by Joseph Dan (New York, 1989). —ROBERT M. SELTZER

KAVOD (כָּבוֹד), a term with social, moral, and theological implications derived from the Hebrew root for *weight*, meaning honor, respect, reverence, importance, distinction, or glory. A person gives *kavod* (honor) to God (*Jos*. 7.19), and God is the *kavod* (glory) of those who believe in him (*Ps*. 3.4); Israel was created for God's *kavod*, that is to glorify him (*Is*. 43.7). More particularly, the term refers to God's power and majesty and is often connected with the appearance of divine light: "The glory [*kavod*] of the Lord was like devouring fire" (*Ex*. 24.17); "so was the appearance of the brightness round about. That was the appearance of the likeness of the glory [*kavod*] of the Lord" (*Ez* 1.28). As the visible and luminous manifestation of the divine, the *kavod* was considered by some medieval schools as a distinct creation. The doctrine of the "created *kavod*" draws on the philosophical theology of *Sa'adyah ben Yosef Ga'on and was further developed by the *Ḥasidei Ashkenaz. The new Jewish Publication Society translation of the Bible uses the word *presence* in place of the earlier *glory* in many instances where the nature of the divine appearance is not specified. See also THRONE OF GOD.

• Samuel S. Cohen, *The Jewish Idea of God* (Cincinnati, 1939). Ludwig Köhler et al., eds., *Hebräisches und Aramäisches Lexikon zum Alten Testament* (Leiden, 1974), vol. 2, pp. 436–437. Arthur Marmorstein, *The Old Rabbinic Doctrine of God: I. The Names and Attributes of God* (New York, 1968). Harry M. Orlinsky, *The Torah: Notes on the New Translation of Torah* (Philadelphia, 1969), p. 171. —LOU H. SILBERMAN

KAVVANAH. See INTENT.

KAZARS. See KHAZARS.

KAZYONNY RAVVIN (Rus.; official rabbi), government-appointed official in czarist Russia responsible for regulating Jewish communal life. In its attempt to "modernize" and control the Jews of Russia, the Russian government in 1857 ordered all Jewish communities to elect rabbis in accordance with criteria set by the government. In practice, anyone who had a few years of formal schooling in a Russian primary school could apply for such a post, even if his religious training was rudimentary. These "rabbis" had almost no influence, devoid as most were of the requisite rabbinic training. Furthermore, the fact that they had to be reelected periodically to their posts left them open to the manipulation of various individuals and groups, further decreasing their influence. Among the Jews, these officials were referred to—generally contemptuously—as *rabbanim mi-ta'am*, "rabbis on behalf [of the authorities]." The "rabbis" nevertheless played a certain role in representing their communities to the Russian authorities, keeping records of births, marriages, and deaths, and even delivering addresses praising the czar. The office was abolished with the Russian Revolution of 1917.

• Simon Schwarzfuchs, *A Concise History of the Rabbinate* (Oxford and Cambridge, 1993), pp. 135–137. Azriel Shohat, *The Crown Rabbinate in Russia: A Chapter in the Cultural Struggle Between Orthodox Jews and the Maskilim* (Haifa, 1975). —SHMUEL HIMELSTEIN

KELAL YISRA'EL (כְּלָל יִשְׂרָאֵל; community of Israel), a phrase, though rarely found in rabbinical sources, that is widely used to convey the concept of what has been called "catholic Israel," that is, the totality of the Jewish people as one indivisible unit with a common destiny. The rabbis stress that "all Jews are responsible for each other" (*Shev*. 39a). The underlying idea is expressed in a Midrash that compares the *four species to the four types of Jews who make up the community—those who have both Torah and good works, those who possess only one or the other of them, and those who are completely devoid of any virtue. "Yet I cannot destroy them," the Midrash has God say; "let them all be bound together and they will complement one another and atone for one another" (*Lv. Rab*. 30.9–12). The concept of *kelal Yisra'el* played a central role in the thought of Solomon *Schechter and in Conservative Judaism.

KELIM (כֵּלִים; Vessels), first tractate in Mishnah order Tohorot, consisting of thirty chapters, with related material in the Tosefta'. There is no corresponding *gemara'* in either the Talmud Bavli or Yerushalmi. The tractate opens with a general introduction to the laws of ritual impurity, listing ten ascending levels of impurity, culminating in the most severe of all sources of impurity, the body of a dead person. The first chapter continues with a list of ten ascending levels of impurity that emanate from the human body and then enumerates the ten ascending levels of sanctity within Erets Yisra'el, which correspond to the levels of purity and sanctity demanded of one who would enter the Temple and finally the Holy of Holies.

The other twenty-nine chapters of the tractate deal with the minutely detailed laws governing the ritual uncleanness contracted by various types of utensils, as stipulated in *Leviticus* (11.32ff.) and *Numbers* (19.14ff.). *Kelim* follows the biblical differentiation among wooden, clay, and metal utensils, regarding conditions both for the contraction of impurity and for the purification process. The meticulous attention devoted by *Kelim* to classification of a broad array of utensils attests to the vitality and significance of the laws of ritual impurity in the daily lives and households of Jews during the Mishnaic period. The laws of impurity imbued even mundane activities, such as eating, with a sense of sanctity and regulated social groupings within the Jewish community and social intercourse among them. *Kelim* is a rich source of information on the everyday life and realia of the Mishnaic period.

Kelim was translated into English by Herbert Danby in *The Mishnah* (Oxford, 1933).

• Chanoch Albeck, ed., *Shishah Sidrei Mishnah, Seder Tohorot* (Jerusalem, 1958). Philip Blackman, ed. and trans., *Mishnayoth*, vol. 5, *Order Taharoth* (Gateshead, 1973). Yehoshua Brand, *Kelei ha-Ḥeres be-Sifrut ha-Talmud* (Jerusalem, 1953). Jacob Nahum Epstein, *Mevo'ot le-Sifrut ha-Tanna'im* (Jerusalem, 1957). Hermann Leberecht Strack, *Introduction to the Talmud and Midrash* (1931; Minneapolis, 1992).

—AVRAHAM WALFISH

KENESET HA-GEDOLAH (כְּנֶסֶת הַגְּדוֹלָה; Great Assembly), according to rabbinic tradition, a gathering originally convened by Ezra and his associates in order to promulgate various rulings and conclude a covenant as reported in *Nehemiah* 8–10. According to *Avot* 1.1, the Men of the Great Assembly, followed by Shim'on ha-Tsaddiq (fl. 200), came between the prophets and the pairs (the immediate forerunners to the tannaitic sages; see ZUGOT). On the basis of this and related Talmudic traditions, the Keneset ha-Gedolah has been described as a spiritual and legislative institution of supreme authority that governed the postexilic community of Erets Yisra'el throughout the Persian period (approximately 300 years). In the absence of historical sources for the Persian period, this account cannot be substantiated, and even relatively late Talmudic traditions do not support it. In the earliest rabbinic texts, the term refers only to the Great Assembly mentioned in *Nehemiah* 8–10, a single transitional generation (hence, the rabbinic phrase "the generation of the Men of the Great Assembly") bridging the worlds of biblical and post-biblical Judaism that lasted only thirty-four years. The Talmudic sages attributed a number of key enactments to the Men of the Great Assembly: they are said to have composed the books of *Ezekiel*, *Daniel*, *Esther*, and the twelve Minor Prophets; to have instituted the 'Amidah and its thrice daily repetition, Qiddush and Havdalah, and the benedictions before the performance of commandments and before and after meals; and to have initiated the public reading of the Torah at specified times. Finally, they are credited with the threefold division of the oral law into the fields of *midrash*, *halakhah*, and *aggadah*. These traditions reflect the assumption of the Talmudic sages that the final form of the biblical text and the characteristic elements of later Pharisaic–rabbinic Judaism came into being during the Persian period. Some scholars view the assembly in *Nehemiah* 8–10 as a model for assemblies throughout the Persian period or the forerunner of institutions known from the Second Temple period, for example, the **gerousia* or the Hasmonean *ḥever*.

• Matty Cohen, "La Maxime des hommes de la Grande Assemblée: Une Reconsidération," in *Hellenica et Judaica*, edited by A. Caquot, M. Hadas-Lebel, and J. Riaud (Leuven, Belgium, 1986), pp. 281–296. Louis Finkelstein, *Ha-Perushim ve-'Anshei Keneset ha-Gedolah* (New York, 1950). Hugo Mantel, *Anshei Keneset ha-Gedolah* (Tel Aviv, 1983). George Foot Moore, *Judaism in the First Centuries of the Christian Era, the Age of the Tannaim*, vol. 1 (Cambrige, 1927), pp. 31–34.

—CHRISTINE E. HAYES

KENESET YISRA'EL (כְּנֶסֶת יִשְׂרָאֵל; assembly [cf. Gr. *ekklēsia*] of Israel), a phrase often used homiletically in the Midrash as a synonym for the Jewish people as a collective whole, usually in a spiritual sense. More or less identical with "Israel," *kenest Yisra'el* is used to emphasize the characteristics that distinguish the Jewish people as a separate entity and in its special relationship with God. Midrashic literature abounds in references portraying *keneset Yisra'el* as speaking to or pleading before God, and interprets the **Song of Songs* as a dialogue of love between God, the groom; and *keneset Yisra'el*, the bride. The rabbinic concept of an earthly community that is at the same time spiritual and heavenly seems to have influenced the Christian theological concept of "church." The symbol of *keneset Yisra'el* also played an important role in Kabbalah, where it is identified with the tenth *sefirah* (see SEFIROT), the *Shekhinah.

KEREM BE-YAVNEH. See YAVNEH.

KERITOT (כְּרִיתוֹת; Excisions), tractate in Mishnah order Qodashim, consisting of seven chapters, with related material in the Tosefta' and the Talmud Bavli. The tractate deals with the laws of sin offerings (see PURIFICATION OFFERING), which are required as atonement for those who have inadvertently transgressed prohibitions bearing the divine punishment of **karet* (excision). Biblical law mandates different forms of sin offerings for different transgressions (*Lv*. 4–5) as well as sin offerings that serve as part of a process of purification, such as the sin offering of a woman who has given birth (*Lv*. 12.5–8). *Keritot* defines those occasions for which one is obligated to make a sacrifice, concentrating on issues such as multiple births and multiple or combined transgressions. *Keritot* analyzes the role of objective and subjective factors in defining a series of transgressions as one continuous act or as discrete actions.

The Talmud tractate was translated by Israel Porush in the Soncino Talmud (London, 1948).

• Chanoch Albeck, ed., *Shishah Sidrei Mishnah, Seder Qodashim* (Jerusalem, 1956). Philip Blackman, ed. and trans., *Mishnayoth*, vol. 5, *Order Kodashim* (Gateshead, 1973). Hermann Leberecht Strack and Günter Stemberger, *Introduction to the Talmud and Midrash*, rev. and updat. ed., translated by Markus Bockmuehl (Minneapolis, 1992).

—AVRAHAM WALFISH

KETER (כֶּתֶר; crown). In the Bible, the word is found only in the *Book of Esther* (1.11, 2.17, 6.8), referring to the royal diadem. It came to be used metaphorically for the highest virtues (cf. "crowning glory" in English), a symbol of excellence. *Avot* 4.17 lists the "crown of the Torah," the "crown of royalty," and the "crown of priesthood" but finds that the "crown of a good name" outweighs the others. The *keter Torah* (crown of the Torah) is the symbol of learning. Unlike the crown of royalty and the crown of priesthood, the *keter Torah* can be acquired by anyone, regardless of birth or descent. This phrase is also applied to the ornate crowns that decorate the synagogal Torah scrolls. The *keter Torah*, usually made of silver, has two sockets into which the tops of the Torah rollers are inserted.

Keter malkhut (crown of royalty) is a phrase representing the enthronement of God by angels and human beings, not so much through their acceptance of his sovereignty but by "crowning" him with praise. The Talmud (*Ḥag*. 13b) describes Sandalfon, one of the archangels, as standing behind the divine chariot and "binding crowns on the head of his maker." Similarly *Yalqut Yeshaʿyahu* 272 states, "Daily the heavenly angels crown the holy one, blessed be he, with the threefold **qedushah*" (see *Is*. 6.3), and a *midrash* states that the angels take the words of prayer and praise uttered by Israel and weave them into a crown for the supreme king of kings (*Ex. Rab*. 21.4). Shelomoh *ibn Gabirol titled his great poem in praise of God "Keter Malkhut"; other poets used the same title for similar compositions. Keter Malkhut poems, particularly Ibn Gabirol's, are frequently recited after the evening service of Yom Kippur.

Precious Bible manuscripts, carefully written and revised, were also called *ketarim* by Jews in the Muslim world, the best known being the tenth-century *Keter of Aleppo*, the oldest copy of the authorized Masoretic Text of the Bible.

• Joseph L. Blau, "On the Supposedly Aristotelian Character of Gabirol's *Keter Malkut*," in *Salo Wittmayer Baron: Jubilee Volume*, 2 vols. (Jerusalem, 1975), pp. 219–228. Abram Kanof, *Jewish Symbolic Art* (Jerusalem, 1990), includes discussion of Torah-scroll crowns. Daniel C. Matt, "David ben Yehudah Hehasid and his *Book of Mirrors*," *Hebrew Union College Annual* 51 (1980): 129–172, discusses kabbalistic use of the term *keter*. Efraim E. Urbach, *The Sages, Their Concepts and Beliefs* (Cambridge, Mass., 1987), on Torah study as a "crown."

KETUBBAH (כְּתֻבָּה; writ), a legal document containing a statement of the obligations that the bridegroom undertakes toward his bride and that in rabbinic law is a prerequisite to marriage. The Aramaic language in which it is composed indicates its post-biblical origin. In biblical times the husband acquired the bride by paying a sum of money (*mohar*). At some stage (possibly during the Babylonian exile or following the return to Jerusalem in the 6th cent. BCE) the document was instituted for the economic protection of a divorced or widowed woman. Initially the text was not fixed, since the economic clauses varied with each case. The oldest known *ketubbah* was discovered in the Jewish settlement of Elephantine and dates from 440 BCE, while a second-century CE example has been found among the Dead Sea Scrolls. The first specific literary reference to a marriage document is in *Tobit* 7.19. Rabbi Shimʿon ben Shetaḥ (2d cent. BCE) is said to have had a hand in the formulation of the document (*Ket*. 82b), which has essentially remained unchanged through the ages. Only the date is written in Hebrew, though in some periods a translation was appended, and today a summary in the vernacular is often read by the officiant. The Talmud discusses whether the institution of the *ketubbah* rests on biblical or rabbinic authority (*Ket*. 11). Originally it was not read aloud but was given to the bride (*Shulḥan ʿArukh, Even haʿEzer* 66.1), who kept it as a statement of her rights; subsequently, it became customary to read it aloud as part of the wedding ceremony (*Shulḥan ʿArukh, Even ha-ʿEzer* 62.6).

The financial obligations assumed by the husband in the *ketubbah* were also meant to serve as an impediment to hasty divorce (*Ket*. 11a). Under the terms of the *ketubbah* the husband is legally responsible for the proper support of his wife; in the event of divorce, she is to receive monetary compensation and in the case of widowhood has a claim on his estate.

The *ketubbah* is prepared before the wedding ceremony. Formerly the officiating rabbi wrote it out shortly before the beginning of the ceremony. In modern times, the form is usually printed, leaving the date and other relevant details to be filled in. It is traditionally signed by two male witnesses not related to the bride, the groom, or each other; in some communities (including Israel), it is also signed by the bridegroom. The groom performs an act of *qinyan* (see ACQUISITION) as well, a symbolic acceptance of the listed obligations. The bride or her family keeps the *ketubbah* as legal proof of her husband's obligations toward her. In certain Muslim lands, it was customary to add to the *ketubbah* a second legal document recording a special gift by the groom to his bride. In Morocco, the distinguished genealogies of the couple were frequently appended to the document.

Under the provisions of the *ketubbah* the minimum amount payable to a widow or divorcee who was a virgin at the time of marriage was two hundred *zuzim*. Estimates suggest that this was sufficient to support a family for one year. If the bride had been a widow or divorcee, the amount payable was one hundred *zuzim*. The *ketubbah* also specified the dowry and the *tosefet* (addition) that the bridegroom undertook to repay in the event of divorce (or decease), beyond the legal requirements. The custom at present is to double the amount of the dowry for a previously unmarried woman (always the equivalent of a hundred silver pieces; fifty silver pieces for divorcees or widows). Both the real and personal property of the husband are under lien to the wife should a *ketubbah* settlement become necessary.

The tradition of adding *tena'im* (conditions) has been revived in modern times, and the Israeli chief rabbinate has sanctioned several such appendices. The Rabbinical Assembly of the Conservative movement has introduced a *ketubbah* in English containing an additional clause in which the bride and groom pledge to appear before a rabbinic court in the event of any dispute between them. The purpose of this provision is to enable the rabbinic authorities to counsel couples in marital difficulty and to ensure that all regulations concerning *divorce will be followed if the marriage is eventually dissolved. The couple also undertake to abide by decisions of the rabbinic court, thereby preventing problems that arise when a husband refuses to grant his wife a divorce to which she is entitled. In recent years, egalitarian marriage certificates have been introduced, specifying mutual obligations and omitting the traditional financial and legal details.

The *ketubbah* became one of the favorite objects of Jewish art. Illuminated marriage contracts are to be found from many lands, and there is evidence that the artists were often non-Jews. Most historical *ketubbot* are from Sephardi communities in Europe (examples from Italy and Holland are outstanding) and North Africa, but there are some Ashkenazi examples from eastern Europe. European examples often portray appropriate biblical scenes and sometimes even the bride and groom. Other favorite motifs include cherubim and kissing birds, as well as traditional Jewish symbols. *Ketubbot* from Muslim lands tend to be written on paper, not parchment as was usual elsewhere. The ornamentation is often nonrepresentational. Recent decades have seen a renaissance of illuminated *ketubbot*. Sometimes the bride and groom design and execute their own *ketubbah*. The regulations concerning the marriage document are codified in Talmud tractate **Ketubbot*.

• Eliyahu Hayim Bar Shalom, *Mishpat ha-Ketubbah*, 2 vols. (Bene Beraq, 1994–1995). David Davidovitch, *The Ketuba: Jewish Marriage Contracts Through the Ages* (New York, 1985). Mordechai Akiva Friedman, *Jewish Marriage in Palestine: A Cairo Genizah Study* (Tel Aviv and New York, 1980–1981). Moses Gaster, *The Ketubah: A Chapter from the History of the Jewish People* (Berlin, 1923). A. Leo Levin and Meyer Kramer, *New Provisions in the Ketubah: A Legal Opinion* (New York, 1955). Shalom Sabar, "The Beginnings and Flourishing of Ketubbah Illustration in Italy: A Study in Popular Imagery and Jewish Patronage during the Seventeenth and Eighteenth Centuries," Ph.D. dissertation, University of California at Los Angeles, 1987. Shalom Sabar, *Mazal Tov: Illuminated Jewish Marriage Contracts From the Israel Museum Collection* (Jerusalem, 1993). Shalom Sabar, "The Use and Meaning of Christian Motifs in Illustrations of Jewish Marriage Contracts in Italy," *Jewish Art* 10 (1984): 47–63.

KETUBBOT (כְּתֻבּוֹת; Marriage Contracts), tractate in Mishnah order Nashim, consisting of thirteen chapters, with related material in the Tosefta' and both Talmuds Bavli and Yerushalmi. The tractate deals with the marital and financial rights and obligations of husband and wife, focusing particularly on those obligations contained in the **ketubbah* document. The most basic stipulation in the *ketubbah* is the *dowry payment from husband to wife, corresponding to the biblical *mohar* (*Gn*. 34.12; *Ex*. 22.16). In rabbinic times, this payment was made after dissolution of the marriage and served to protect the wife against hasty or arbitrary divorce (*Ket*. 39b). Virginity was highly prized, ensuring the purity and primacy of the bond between husband and wife; hence, the fixed bridal sum for a virgin was set at two hundred *zuzim* (approximately 960 grams of silver), while the sum for a nonvirgin was set at one hundred *zuzim* (approximately 480 grams). Other *ketubbah* stipulations include the right of the wife to financial support and conjugal relations at reasonable intervals, depending on the husband's profession, and the right of the husband to expect the wife to manage household affairs and to maintain decent standards of modesty. The regulation of rights, obligations, and expectations within the marriage was regarded as an essential component of marital stability, leading R. Me'ir to remark that a husband who tampered with the financial obligations mandated by the *ketubbah* was regarded as though he were engaging in fornication (*Ket*. 5.1).

• Chanoch Albeck, ed., *Shishah Sidrei Mishnah, Seder Nashim* (Jerusalem, 1954). Philip Blackman, ed. and trans., *Mishnayoth*, vol. 2, *Order Nashim* (Gateshead, 1973). Jacob Nahum Epstein, *Mevo'ot le-Sifrut ha-Tanna'im* (Jerusalem, 1957). Pinhas Kehati, ed., *Mishnah: A New Translation with a Commentary, Seder Nashim*, vol. 3, *Gittin, Kiddushin* (Jerusalem, 1989). Hermann Leberecht Strack, *Introduction to the Talmud and Midrash* (1931; Minneapolis, 1992). Abraham Weiss, *Hithavvut ha-Talmud bi-Shelemuto* (New York, 1943).

—AVRAHAM WALFISH

KETUVIM. See HAGIOGRAPHA.

KHAZARS, a tribe of Turkish origin that lived along the lower Volga region. From the eighth through the tenth century, they reached the zenith of their power, and during this period a Judaizing movement took place among them. King Bulan, together with some four thousand nobles, adopted the Jewish faith, probably about 730, and although Muslims, Christians, and pagans formed the great majority of the population and were granted internal autonomy, the state religion was Judaism.

Ḥisdai ibn Shaprut, vizier to ʿAbdar-Raḥman III of Cordova, is said to have established contact with the then reigning king Joseph by sending him a letter written by Menaḥem ben Saruq (c.960). In his reply, the king gave details concerning the conversion of his ancestor and other information about the state. Doubts have been expressed about the authenticity of the letters. They appear as a preface to *Yehudah ha-Levi's *Kuzari* (i.e., Khazars, which uses the historical incident of the king's conversion as the framework for an imaginary dialogue between the king and a Jewish sage). The power of the Khazars declined following a Russian attack in 965 and was broken by Archduke Jaroslav in 1083. The Khazars disappeared following the Tatar invasion of 1237.

• Norman Golb, *Khazarian Hebrew Documents of the Tenth Century* (Ithaca, N.Y., 1982). Peter B. Golden, *Khazar Studies: An Historico-Philological Inquiry into the Origins of the Khazars* (Budapest, 1980). Arthur Koestler, *The Thirteenth Tribe: The Khazar Empire and Its Heritage* (New York, 1976).

KIBBUTS GALUYYOT. See EXILES, INGATHERING OF THE.

KIBBUTZ FESTIVALS. The early nature festivals of the kibbutz originated in the 1930s. Ancient agricultural celebrations were renewed by tying them into the Zionist values of tilling the soil and settling on the land. Appropriate ceremonies, which linked the biblical and post-biblical past, when Jewish farmers worked the land, with contemporary settlers, included attempts to celebrate a water drawing festival, a sheep-shearing festival, an ʿ*omer*-cutting ceremony, and a love festival on Tu be-'Av. In most cases, these did not stand the test of time. Experience showed that only the traditional holidays with a continuous history of practice could be successfully adapted to the secular kibbutz society.

Festivals are observed on the Israeli kibbutzim without synagogues, rabbis, cantors, or prayer (with the exception of Orthodox kibbutzim, which follow traditional observance). Pesaḥ, the festival of freedom, is the holiday that has been most successfully absorbed into kibbutz life, with many kibbutzim writing their own Haggadot (see HAGGADAH OF PESAḤ). The High Holy Days lack the historical and national perspective of the Shalosh Regalim or of Ḥanukkah and Purim. Indeed, Ro'sh ha-Shanah and Yom Kippur were not initially observed at all.

Agricultural values, though still strong, are being eroded by the growth of industry in Israel. Today the entire Jewish calendar is being progressively included in the kibbutz festival cycle as questions of Jewish identity increasingly appear on the kibbutz agenda.

• Joseph R. Blasi, *The Communal Experience of the Kibbutz* (New Brunswick, 1986). Ernest Krausz, ed., *The Sociology of the Kibbutz* (New Brunswick, 1983). David Leichman and Idit Paz, eds., *Kibbutz: An Alternative Lifestyle* (Tel Aviv, 1994). Charles S. Liebman and Eli'ezer Don-Yiḥya, *Civil Religion in Israel: Traditional Judaism and Political Culture in the Jewish State* (Berkeley, 1983). Shalom Lilker, *Kibbutz Judaism: A New Tradition in the Making* (New Brunswick, 1986). Nissan Rubin, "Death Customs in a Non-Religious Kibbutz: The Use of Sacred Symbols in a Secular Society," *Journal for the Scientific Study of Religion* 25.3 (1986): 292–303.

–SHALOM LILKER

KIDNAPPING. The biblical law "He that steals a man, and sell him, or if he be found in his hand, he shall surely be put to death" (*Ex.* 21.16; cf. *Dt.* 24.7) marks kidnapping as a capital offense. The Talmud, as well as some modern scholars, considers the eighth commandment of the Decalogue to refer not to the stealing of property but to kidnapping (*San.* 86a). To be subject to capital punishment the following four conditions had to be present: the kidnapper had actually to have taken the abducted person into his possession or domain, thus depriving that person of personal liberty; the kidnapper had to have sold the captive as a slave; the sale had to have been to a stranger (if the kidnapped person was sold to a relative, the thief was not culpable since the victim had not been deprived of association with family); and the kidnapper must have treated the victim as a slave before any sale. Each stage had to be attested to by at least two witnesses (*San.* 85b).

• Menachem Elon, *Jewish Law: History, Sources, Principles*, 4 vols. (Philadelphia, 1994).

–MICHAEL BROYDE

KIL'AYIM (כִּלְאַיִם), name of laws prohibiting various mixtures and of a Mishnaic tractate.

Laws. The laws of *kil'ayim* concern the sowing, grafting, breeding, or mixing of diverse kinds of seeds, trees, animals, or fabrics, which are prohibited by the Bible (*Lv.* 19.19; *Dt.* 22.9–11). The relevant laws fall under four major headings, the first of which applies only in Erets Yisra'el.

The first set of laws is known as *zera'im* (seeds). Under these rules, it is forbidden to plant together two types of seed that differ in name, appearance, or taste. The prohibition applies only to seed normally planted for food but not to seed usually planted for medical use. The space to be left unplanted between different kinds of seed varies with the plant in question. The grafting of trees is also regulated by laws in this category.

The next heading of laws is *kerem* (vine). These regulations, which are stricter than those of *zera'im*, concern the planting of two kinds of seed together with the vine; it is forbidden to derive any benefit whatsoever from the product (*Qid.* 56b).

The next group is called *behemah* (animal). It is forbidden to crossbreed any two species of animal; nor may two species of animal be tied or yoked together for purposes of work, such as plowing or pulling (*Dt.* 22.10).

The final heading is *sha'atnez* (mingling of fabrics). Garments containing a mix of wool and linen are forbidden to be worn. Any intermingling whatsoever of hackled, spun, or woven wool with linen renders the cloth or garment *sha'atnez*. Exceptions to this are the priestly garments, of which the girdle contained both wool and linen, and **tsitsit* (fringes), which in former times were made by adding a woolen thread even to a linen garment.

The laws of *kil'ayim* are among those called *ḥuqqim* in the Bible (*Lv.* 19.19). *Ḥuqqim* are interpreted by the rabbis as divine decrees, whose explanations are beyond human comprehension. The prohibition against *kil'ayim* may be related to the Creation account in *Genesis*, according to which each plant and animal species was created "according to its kind." Mixing species, therefore, is a sin against the divinely instituted order of creation.

• Calum Carmichael, "Forbidden Mixtures," *Vetus Testamentum* 32 (1982): 394–415. Yehuda Feliks, *Kil'ei Zera'im ve-Harkavah* (Tel Aviv, 1967). Isidor Grunfeld, "Kilayim—Diverse Kinds," in *The Jewish Dietary Laws* (London and New York, 1972), vol. 2, pp. 45–55. Irving Mandelbaum, *A History of the Mishnaic Law of Agriculture: Kilayim: Translation and Exegesis* (Chico, Calif., 1982). Solomon ben Joseph Sirillo, ed., *Masekhet Kil'ayim min Talmud Yerushalmi, Seder Zera'im* (Jerusalem, 1951).

Tractate. The tractate *Kil'ayim* is in Mishnah order Zera'im and consists of nine chapters, with related material in the Tosefta' and the Talmud Yerushalmi. The tractate discusses and expands upon the biblical prohibitions against mixing plants, animals, or clothing of different species (*Lv.* 19.19; *Dt.* 22.9–11). *Kil'ayim* identifies which plants, animals, or clothing are regarded as exemplars of one species and which are of different species. The bulk of the tractate deals with the degree and nature of the separation required in order for different species not to be regarded as mixed. The separation required by the principles of *kil'ayim* depends, to a great extent, on agricultural practices and customs. Special attention is devoted in *Kil'ayim* to regulations concerning vineyards, both because of their agricultural centrality in Erets Yisra'el and because of the special severity attached by the rabbis to mixing the species of the vineyard.

The Mishnah tractate was translated by Herbert Danby in *The Mishnah* (Oxford, 1933).

• Chanoch Albeck, ed., *Shishah Sidrei Mishnah, Seder Zera'im* (Jerusalem, 1957). Philip Blackman, ed. and trans., *Mishnayoth*, vol. 1, *Order Zeraim* (Gateshead, 1973). Jacob Nahum Epstein, *Mavo' le-Nusaḥ ha-Mishnah*, 2d ed. (Tel Aviv, 1964). Jacob Nahum Epstein, *Mevo'ot le-Sifrut ha-Tanna'im* (Jerusalem, 1957). Jehuda Feliks, *Ha-Ḥaqla'ut be-Erets Yisra'el bi-Tequfat ha-Mishnah veha-Talmud* (Tel Aviv, 1963). Jehuda Feliks, *Kil'ei Zera'im ve-Harkavah: Massekhet Kil'ayim* (Tel Aviv, 1967). Pinhas Kehati, ed., *Mishnah: A New Translation with a Commentary, Seder Zera'im*, vol. 2, *Dema'i, Kil'ayim, Shevi'it* (Jerusalem, 1992). Irving J. Mandelbaum, "Scripture and the Interpretation of Mishnah: The Case of Tractate Kil'ayim," *World Congress of Jewish Studies* 9C (1986): 15–22.

Hermann Leberecht Strack, *Introduction to the Talmud and Midrash* (1931; Minneapolis, 1992). —AVRAHAM WALFISH

KI LO NA'EH. See ADDIR BI-MELUKHAH.

KIMḤI FAMILY, grammarians, translators, and Bible commentators. They moved to Narbonne (in southern France) from Spain. They engaged in disputation with Christians, both of the Catholic church and heretics, as well as with Jews who opposed the introduction of philosophical learning into Judaism.

Yosef Kimḥi (c.1105–1170), wrote *Sefer ha-Berit* (Constantinople, 1710) to defend Jewish interpretation of the Bible against Christian typological exegesis. This is one of the first systematic treatises against Christianity written in Europe. He wrote works on Hebrew grammar, *Sefer ha-Zikkaron* (1888) and *Sefer ha-Galui* (1887), which made the linguistic achievements of Jewish grammarians who wrote in Arabic, such as Ibn Ḥayyuj and Ibn Janaḥ, available to Hebrew readers. His biblical commentaries emphasized the use of *peshat*, or the plain meaning of the text, as opposed to the more homiletically oriented exegesis, such as that of *Mosheh ha-Darshan, which had been traditional in Provence. He wrote commentaries on the Pentateuch, the Prophets, *Job*, and *Proverbs*. Many of his comments are known through the writings of his students, such as his son David and Menaḥem ben Shimʿon of Posquières. His career as a biblical exegete parallels that of Avraham ibn Ezra, whom he knew and who cited him in his own commentaries. Yosef Kimḥi also translated *Ḥovot ha-Levavot*, by *Baḥya ben Yosef ibn Paquda', into Hebrew. His philosophical interests are also in evidence in his verse anthology *Sheqel ha-Qodesh* (pub. 1919), a reworking of ethical sayings from Shelomoh ibn Gabirol's *Mivḥar ha-Peninim*.

Mosheh Kimḥi (died c.1190), following the method of his father, Yosef, concentrated on Hebrew grammar and linguistic studies. He wrote a grammar book, *Mahalakh Shevilei ha-Daʿat* (Pesaro, 1508), and a treatise devoted to the more theoretical dimensions of language, *Sekhel Tov* (1894). His biblical commentaries on *Proverbs* and *Job* follow the *peshat* orientation of his father.

David Kimḥi (c.1160–1235), also son of Yosef and known as Radaq, wrote a systematic treatise on the textual criticism of the Bible, *Et Sofer* (Lyck, 1864), which describes manuscript variations of the problems of the Masorah. He also wrote a grammar book, *Sefer ha-Mikhlol* (Constantinople, 1532), containing both a dictionary and a description of Hebrew grammatical rules. He wrote commentaries on *Genesis*, all the Prophetic books, *Psalms, Proverbs*, and *Chronicles*. These commentaries reflect the linguistic orientation that was developed in the Arabic-speaking Jewish world. They also have a strong rationalist approach, which he learned from the Jewish philosophical tradition, particularly from the writings of Maimonides. He argued that rationalist views of the miracles in scripture or prophecy were simply an extension of the original efforts of the classical rabbis. For him, philosophy was one more way to reclaim the correct interpretation of scripture. Toward that end, he wrote allegorical commentaries on the *Genesis* narratives of the garden of Eden, and of Cain and Abel, as well as on the first chapter of *Ezekiel*. These allegorical commentaries demonstrate his affinity for Maimonidean interpretation. Like his father, he engaged in polemics with Christians. His commentary on *Psalms* contains significant treatments of Christian interpretations of *Psalms*, which reveal, from Kimḥi's point of view, an insufficient knowledge of Biblical Hebrew grammar and syntax.

• Beryl D. Cohon, "Moses Kimchi as Exegete and Grammarian; with Special Reference to His Commentary on Proverbs," rabbinic thesis, Hebrew Union College, 1925. Frank E. Talmage, *David Kimḥi: The Man and the Commentaries* (Cambridge, Mass., 1975). Frank E. Talmage, ed. and trans., *The Book of the Covenant of Joseph Kimhi* (Toronto, 1972). —MICHAEL A. SIGNER

KINDLING OF LIGHTS (Heb. *hadlaqat nerot*). Lights are kindled by women at the onset of Sabbaths and festivals and indicate the approach of a day of light and cheerfulness. The kindling of lights is one of the three commandments that *women are obliged to perform, but in the absence of women the obligation falls on men. Maimonides (*Hilkhot Shabbat* 5.1) stressed the importance of the obligation and wrote that even if there is nothing to eat, the light must be lit, because this is the essence of "Sabbath delight" (*ʿoneg Shabbat*). A section of the tractate *Shabbat* (2) is devoted to the question of which oil may be used for the light; later, candles were substituted for oil lamps. It has been suggested that the custom arose to protest against the Babylonian belief in the Sabbath as an unlucky and gloomy day when no fire or light was lit. In Roman times, the lighting of Sabbath lamps was a distinguishing feature of Jewish homes, and the younger Seneca condemned Romans for imitating the custom (*Epistulae* 95.47). It is customary to kindle two lights; this has been associated homiletically with the two versions of the Sabbath commandment (*Ex*. 20.8 and *Dt*. 5.12) but may originate in the necessity of having one light in the living room and one in the kitchen. Some, however, light candles according to the number of persons in the family. The kindling of these lights constituted one of the major practical differences between the Karaites and the Rabbanites; the former would not allow a light to burn, even if kindled prior to the Sabbath, and sat in darkness throughout the Sabbath eve. Other occasions for the kindling of lights are Ḥanukkah, the anniversary of the death of a near relative (*yortsayt*), and on Yom Kippur. See also CANDLES.

• Abraham Ezra Millgram, *Sabbath, the Day of Delight* (Philadelphia, 1993).

KINGDOM OF HEAVEN (Heb. *malkhut shamayim*), an eschatological concept referring to a future state of perfection of the world, free from sin and suffering, in which all shall live in accordance with the divine will. *Heaven* is a metonymy for *God*; the term thus refers not to a heavenly realm but to the kingdom of God on earth. The Israelite prophets not only regarded history as the scene of divine action rather than as a fortuitous series of events but also envisaged a glorious consummation.

The present sinful and imperfect order would come to an end on the terrible *Yom ha-Din (see DAY OF THE LORD), after which God would create a "new heaven and a new earth," and all creatures would be at peace with one another, with nature, and with God, just as they were in the garden of *Eden. Originally, the concept of the kingdom of heaven was not identical with the messianic idea. However, the two eschatological concepts fused to some extent, until practically no distinction was made between the kingdom of heaven and the "Days of the *Messiah." Pseudepigraphous literature abounds in detailed descriptions of this new world, and the notion as well as the expectation of the imminent advent of the kingdom of heaven occupied a central position in the teachings of Jesus. Members of the Qumran community believed that they were members of the community of the elect, destined to inherit the kingdom of heaven. The Qumran community, like the early Christians, believed the kingdom of heaven to be at hand and saw themselves as active participants in the eschatological drama that had already begun to unfold. In contrast to the sectarians, the Pharisees saw themselves as still living in *ʿolam ha-zeh* (see ʿOLAM HA-ZEH AND ʿOLAM HA-BAʾ). In Talmudic literature the concept of the kingdom of heaven is at times vague and ambiguous. In many instances it is equated with the "Days of the Messiah"; at other times it means a completely new age (*ʿolam ha-baʾ*). The reign of the Messiah still belonged to this world. After the messianic era had come to an end, there would be a general *resurrection of the dead, followed by the great judgment of all mankind and the establishment of a new creation cleansed of all unrighteousness, namely, the kingdom of heaven. The distinction between the two eschatological eras, which implies that the political and social redemption of Israel and mankind were the penultimate and not the ultimate goal of history, was also maintained by medieval theologians. The idea of the kingdom of heaven connects ultimate perfection with a profound and radical transformation of the cosmos as a whole. See also APOCALYPSE; ESCHATOLOGY.

• Marc Z. Brettler, *God Is King* (Sheffield, Eng., 1989). Martin Buber, *Kingship of God*, translated by Richard Scheimann (New York, 1967). Odo Camponovo, *Königtum Königsherrschaft und Reich Gottes in den frühjüdischen Schriften*, Orbis Biblicus et Orientalis, no. 58 (Freiburg, 1984). Warren Zev Harvey, "Kingdom of God," in *Contemporary Jewish Religious Thought*, edited by Arthur A. Cohen and Paul Mendes-Flohr (New York, 1987), pp. 524–525. Martin Hengel and Anna Maria Schwemer, eds., *Königsherrschaft Gottes und himmlischer Kult*, Wissenschaftliche Untersuchungen zum Neuen Testament, no. 55 (Tübigen, 1991).

KINGS, BOOK OF (Heb. *Sefer Melakhim*), the last book in the Former Prophets section of the Bible. It recounts Israel's history during a four-hundred-year period from the end of the reign of David, the reign of Solomon, and the building of the Temple, the political division of the united kingdom under King Rehoboam, and the subsequent history of the two separate lines of kings in both Israel and Judah to the demise of the northern kingdom of Israel in 722 BCE and the destruction of Judah and the First Temple in 586 BCE, ending with King Jehoiachin's release from Babylonian imprisonment in 561. An important section of the *Book of Kings* is also dedicated to the narratives of the prophets Elijah and Elisha (*1 Kgs*. 17–*2 Kgs*. 9). Following the Septuagint, *Kings* is divided into two books, *1 Kings* and *2 Kings* (corresponding to *3 Kings* and *4 Kings* in the Septuagint, where *1 Samuel* and *2 Samuel* appear as *1 Kings* and *2 Kings*). Authorship of *Kings* is ascribed by the Talmud to Jeremiah (*B. B.* 15a). Modern critics believe the writing of its sources began as early as the end of Solomon's reign. These sources include official royal chronicles and temple archives that are no longer extant, for example, the *Book of the Annals of Solomon* (*1 Kgs*. 11.41) and the *Books of the Annals of the Kings of Judah* (*1 Kgs*. 14.29, 15.7, etc.). The final editing of the book took place in the exilic period (mid-6th cent. BCE). The prevalence of a strong Deuteronomic influence in the book has been pointed out by many scholars. This influence is most pronounced in the book's invariable tendency to evaluate the kings of both Israel and Judah in accordance with their degree of adherence to the "centralization of cult" reform, introduced by King Josiah of Judah (*2 Kgs*. 22–23), namely, the Deuteronomic requirement that all legitimate sacrificial worship be conducted at the central sanctuary (*Dt*. 12). Another typically Deuteronomic conception that finds expression in *Kings* is the inevitability of the prophetic word being fulfilled (*1 Kgs*. 12.15, 15.29, 16.12; *2 Kgs*. 1.17, 17.23; cf. *Dt*. 18.14–22). The theological viewpoint of *Kings* occasionally obscures the accomplishments of those kings who were deemed to be wicked according to the book's strict religious standards. For example, the Omride dynasty in Israel exerted a powerful military influence in the whole region of ancient Syria and Erets Yisraʾel, as is known from Mesopotamian sources. However, its legacy in *Kings* is one of continuous failure in upholding God's covenant. Ultimately, *Kings* seeks to provide a theodicy that accounts for the destruction of both the northern and southern kingdoms along with the First Temple.

• Brevard S. Childs, *Introduction to the Old Testament as Scripture* (Philadelphia, 1979), pp. 281–301. Mordechai Cogan and Hayim Tadmor, *II Kings*, The Anchor Bible, vol. 11 (Garden City, N.Y., 1988). John Gray, *I and II Kings: A Commentary*, 3d fully rev. ed., The Old Testament Library (London, 1977; 1985 printing). Stephen L. McKenzie, *The Trouble with Kings: The Composition of the Books of Kings in the Deuteronomistic History*, Supplements to Vetus Testamentum, vol. 42 (Leiden, 1991). James A. Montgomery, *A Critical and Exegetical Commentary of the Book of Kings*, The International Critical Commentary, vol. 9 (Edinburgh, 1960). Gerhard von Rad, "The Deuteronomistic Theology of History in the Books of Kings," in *Studies in Deuteronomy*, translated by David Stalker, Studies in Biblical Theology, no. 9 (London, 1963, pre. of 1953 ed.), pp. 74–91.

—DAVID A. GLATT-GILAD

KINGSHIP, first instituted in Israel at the end of the period of the judges (unlike most other ancient Near Eastern societies, in which kingship was conceived of as coming from God at the time of creation). At that time, the Israelites were confronted with the invasion of the better-organized and better-equipped Philistines and were unable to withstand such an attack without a unified resistance under the leadership of a single military leader. During this crisis, the prophet Samuel, at the command of God, anointed Saul as the first king of Israel. Samuel's personal reluctance about the institution of kingship was based on the theology that God alone was the sole ruler of the people, and he gave voice to his opposition by warning the people of the prerogatives that the king would take for himself (*1 Sm.* 8). He also reflected the sentiment of many of the Israelites who were unwilling to forgo their own autonomous tribal affinities. *Deuteronomy* 17.15–20 states that the king must be an Israelite, and he is warned not to take too many wives, too much silver and gold, or too many horses for himself. He is also commanded to write a copy of the law and to read it, so that "his heart be not lifted up against his brethren." After the schism of the united kingdom, there were frequent changes of dynasties in the northern kingdom of Israel; however, the southern kingdom of Judah remained faithful to the ideology that kingship was hereditary in the house of David. For this reason the first Hasmonean rulers, who were not of Davidic descent, did not adopt the title of king, and when Alexander Yannai took the title, he was criticized for flaunting the Jewish tradition. Prayers are still recited for the restoration of the Davidic line in one of the blessings of the *haftarah* in the synagogue service on the Sabbath. Many prayers stress the kingdom of God (see KINGDOM OF HEAVEN; MALKHUYYOT).

• Henri Frankfort, *Kingship and the Gods: A Study of Ancient Near Eastern Religion as the Integration of Society and Nature* (Chicago, 1978). Baruch Halpern, *The Constitution of the Monarchy in Israel* (Chico, Calif., 1981). Tomoo Isida, *The Royal Dynasties in Ancient Israel* (Berlin, 1977). Keith W. Whitelam, *The Just King: Monarchical and Judicial Authority in Ancient Israel* (Sheffield, Eng., 1979). —SHALOM PAUL

KIPPAH (כִּיפָּה), the skullcap (as distinct from the hat) worn as a *covering of the head in accordance with Orthodox Jewish custom. The Yiddish equivalent is *yarmulke*, a word of Slavic origin but uncertain derivation. *Kappel* (from the Italian *cappella* [hat]) is also used in Yiddish.

KISLEV (כִּסְלֵו), third month of the civil calendar, ninth in the religious. The name is of Akkadian/Babylonian origin and is first mentioned in the Bible in *Zechariah* 7.1 and *Nehemiah* 1.1. It has twenty-nine or thirty days, and its zodiac sign is Sagittarius. *Ḥanukkah commences on the twenty-fifth day of the month. In early times, if the new moon (see RO'SH ḤODESH) of Kislev arrived and no rain had yet fallen, the religious authorities called for a fast of petition (*Ta'an.* 1.5).

• Nathan Bushwick, *Understanding the Jewish Calendar* (New York, 1989). George Zinberg, *Jewish Calendar Mystery Dispelled* (New York, 1963). —CHAIM PEARL

KISSING. The rabbis approved of three types of kisses: kisses given to a man when he is appointed to a position of honor; kisses of meeting and parting; and kisses between relatives. Other kissing was considered by the rabbis to be either "shameful" or "silly" (*Ex. Rab.* 5.1). Sacred articles are kissed as a sign of respect, for example, the *tallit* or *tsitsit* (cf. *Nm.* 15.37–41), the Torah scrolls, the **mezuzah*, or a religious book that has fallen to the ground. Among Sephardim, children kiss their parents' hands after receiving a parental blessing, and among Jews in Muslim lands it is customary to kiss the hand of the **ḥakham* in salutation. The peaceful surrender of one's soul to God is called "death by the kiss [of God]" on the basis of the literal translation of *Deuteronomy* 34.5, a privilege accorded only to the most pious (*Ber.* 8a). Later rabbis disapproved of men kissing relatives other than their mothers, wives, daughters, or sisters, and a man was forbidden to kiss his wife during her period of impurity.

• John Ellington, "Kissing in the Bible: Form and Meaning," *Bible Translator* 41.4 (1990): 409–416. Louis M. Epstein, *Sex Laws and Customs in Judaism* (New York, 1967), pp. 105–109.

KITEL (Yi.; קיטל), the white garment traditionally worn in some Ashkenazi rites by the officiant and members of the congregation during prayer on the Yamim Nora'im (High Holidays), by the officiant and devout congregants during the Musaf service on the first day of Pesaḥ (when Tefillat Tal is recited) and the eighth day of Sukkot (during Tefillat Geshem on Hosha'na' Rabbah), by the celebrant at the *Seder table, and in some communities by the groom during the marriage ceremony (where it is usually presented to him by his bride). Formerly it was worn every Sabbath and at all solemn occasions (cf. Y., *R. ha-Sh.* 1.3). The color white is associated with symbolic purity (and hence forgiveness of sins), integrity, and piety. The *kitel* is also part of the clothing in which the dead are buried.

• Vera Baviskar et al., *The Language and Cultural Atlas of Ashkenazic Jewry* (Tübingen, 1992). H. J. Zimmels, *Ashkenazim and Sephardim* (London, 1958).

KLATZKIN, JACOB (1882–1948), Hebrew publicist and philosopher. A son of a renowned Russian rabbi, he received a thorough traditional education. At the age of eighteen he went to Germany to study philosophy. Concurrent with his studies, he abandoned strict religious practice and joined the Zionist movement. In 1909 he was appointed the editor of the prestigious organ of the German Zionist movement, *Die Welt*. Together with Nahum Goldmann, he founded the Eschkol Publishing House, which sponsored the monumental *Encyclopaedia Judaica*, of which ten volumes appeared before Hitler came to power. Thereupon he left Germany and settled in Switzerland, where he lived until the end of his life; during the war he resided temporarily in the United States.

A disciple of the iconoclastic philosopher and psychologist Ludwig Klages (1872–1956), Klatzkin followed his master in repudiating both reason and the life of the spirit. Celebrating a biologically grounded life-force expressed in fundamental human instincts, he called upon his fellow Jews, enfeebled by a surfeit of spirit, to affirm the liberating vitality of that life-force. In the *exile (*galut*), the Jews' abnormal existence had caused them to become estranged from their instincts, and develop a compensatory, but ultimately unhealthy, spiritual culture. The return to Zion would allow Israel to reestablish a natural, wholesome relationship to its institutional life. By virtue of the "normalization" of their existence, Jews would be freed from the life-denying effects of a spiritual vocation and revitalized through the reacquisition of the natural parameters of peoplehood: a land and language of their own. The attainment of these conditions would not only promote the revitalization of the Jews as a normal people, but also ensure their survival, especially now that religion, which hitherto held the people together, was being increasingly corroded by the secularizing forces of the modern world. It thus follows, Klatzkin argued, that Jewish existence in the *galut*, where the Jews are bereft of a land and language of their own, is not only undignified but destined to disappear. His philosophical writings included *Sheqiʿat ha-Ḥayyim* (1925), *Der Erkenntnistrieb als Lebens und Todesprinzip* (1935), and *Krisis und Entscheidung im Judentum* (1921). A volume of his writings in English is entitled *In Praise of Wisdom* (New York, 1943).

• Eli Ginzberg, *Keeper of the Law: Louis Ginzberg* (Philadelphia, 1966), pp. 270–272. Arthur Hertzberg, *The Zionist Idea: A Historical Analysis and Reader* (Cleveland, 1959), pp. 314–327. Walter Laqueur, *A History of Zionism* (London, 1972), pp. 170–171, 262f., 390f.

—PAUL MENDES-FLOHR

KLOYZ (Yi.; קלויז; enclosure; also Ger. *Klaus* from Lat. *claustrum* [cloister]), a kind of **beit midrash*, usually serving as a synagogue as well, in which the Talmud was studied by adults. The term was used in central and eastern Europe as far back as the seventeenth century. The Ḥasidim often referred to their synagogue as a *kloyz*. Among Sephardim, the corresponding institution was known as *hesger* (enclosure).

KLUGER, SHELOMOH (1785–1869), Galician rabbi and halakhic authority; known by the acronym Maharshaq. After short terms as communal rabbi in two small towns, in 1820 Kluger accepted the post as communal preacher (*maggid*) and head of the rabbinic court in Brody, where he served with distinction for almost half a century. His encyclopedic knowledge of Talmudic literature and keen analytical skills earned him a reputation as one of the leading interpreters of Jewish law of his generation. Kluger's independent mind and his uncompromising attitude toward what he regarded as breaches of Jewish law or custom brought him on occasion into conflict with Enlightenment-influenced communal leaders in Brody (over, for example, the issue of transporting a corpse to burial in a hearse rather than carrying the deceased's remains in a litter) or his rabbinic contemporaries (over the issue of machine-made *matsot*). Kluger was a prolific author. Only a small portion of his writings was published, but many have survived in manuscript. Included among his works are *Ha-'Elef Lekha Shelomoh* and *Tuv Taʿam va-Daʿat* (*responsa*); *Avodat* and *Nidrei Zerizin* (Talmudic *novellae*); and *Ḥokhmat Shelomoh* (a commentary on the *Shulḥan ʿArukh*).

• Judah Aaron Kluger, *Toledot Shelomoh* (Jerusalem, 1955). Meir Wunder, *Me'orei Galitsyah* (Jerusalem, 1990), vol. 4.

—GERSHON BACON

KNEELING. See PROSTRATION.

KOHEN. See PRIESTHOOD.

KOHEN, SHABBETAI BEN ME'IR HA-. See SHABBETAI BEN ME'IR HA-KOHEN.

KOHEN, YISRA'EL ME'IR HA-. See YISRA'EL ME'IR HA-KOHEN.

KOHLER, KAUFMANN (1843–1926), American Reform rabbi. Born and educated in Germany, he initially supported Neo-Orthodoxy, but his doctoral thesis was far-reaching in its critical attitude toward the Bible, and, realizing that he could not obtain an Orthodox rabbinical position in Europe, he moved to the United States and became rabbi of Detroit's Reform Congregation Beth El. Later he served in Chicago and in 1879 succeeded his father-in-law, David *Einhorn, as rabbi of Congregation Beth El in New York. In 1903 Kohler moved to Cincinnati, where he served as president and professor of theology at Hebrew Union College, retiring in 1921. He supported the radical Reform advocated by Einhorn. In Kohler's major work, *Jewish Theology* (New York, 1918), he stated, "Judaism is nothing less than a message concerning the one and holy God and one undivided humanity, a message entrusted by divine revelation to the Jewish people." The Jewish people had the mission to teach the world ethical monotheism. Kohler found no place for Zionism in his system, nor could he find much justification for the rituals of traditional Judaism. He regarded legalism and nationalism as perversions of true Judaism, the essence of which he found in what he believed to be prophetic universalism. He attributed Jewish survival to the religious genius of the Jewish people and considered (influenced by Kant) the idea of God a postulate to man's moral conscience.

A long controversy with Alexander *Kohut, whose views were more traditional, led Kohler to convene a conference of Reform rabbis in Pittsburgh in 1885, at which his declaration of principles became the basis of the *Pittsburgh platform that was to guide American Reform for the next half-century. In his later years he became more open to religious ritual but remained strongly anti-Zionist.

Kohler was a major figure in the editing of the *Jewish Encyclopedia* (1901–1906), heading its theology and philosophy departments and writing many of its entries. He was also one of the editors of the Jewish Publication Society's translation of the Bible (1917), and the society published his translation of the *Book of Psalms* (Philadelphia, 1903). A bibliography of his writings up to 1913 appeared in *Studies in Jewish Literature in Honor of Prof. Kaufmann Kohler* (Berlin, 1913).

• Samuel Solomon Cohon, "Kaufmann Kohler the Reformer," in *Mordecai M. Kaplan: Jubilee Volume on the Occasion of His Seventieth Birthday*, edited by Moshe Davis (New York, 1953). Karla Ann Goldman, *Beyond the Gallery: The Place of Women in the Development of American Judaism*, Ph.D. dissertation, Harvard University, 1993. Shuly Rubin Schwartz, *The Emergence of Jewish Scholarship in America*, Monographs of the Hebrew Union College, no. 13 (Cincinnati, 1991). *Studies in Jewish Literature, Issued in Honor of Professor Kaufmann Kohler . . . 1913* (Berlin, 1913), contains several articles about Kaufmann Kohler including biographical information.

KOHUT, ALEXANDER (1842–1894), rabbi and scholar. A native of Hungary, he served as rabbi in congregations in Hungary and emigrated to the United States in 1885 to become rabbi of congregation Ahabath Chesed in New York City. He helped to inspire a revival of traditional Judaism in America and was one of the founders of the *Jewish Theological Seminary of America, where he was professor of Midrash and Talmudic methodology. He combined the traditionalist and progressive wings of the *Historical movement, which was reflected in his work *The Ethics of the Fathers* (1885). His main scholarly work was a revised and augmented edition of *Natan ben Yeḥi'el's talmudic dictionary *'Arukh ha-Shalem*, which he had conceived in his youth; it was published in eight volumes (1870–1892).

• Edward D. Coleman, *A Bibliography of George Alexander Kohut* (New York, 1935). Moshe Davis, *Emergence of Conservative Judaism* (Westport, Conn., 1963). George Alexander Kohut, *Concerning Alexander Kohut: A Tentative Bibliography* (Budapest, 1927).

KOIDONOVER FAMILY, a prominent Lithuanian family.

Aharon Shemu'el Koidonover (c.1614–1676), Lithuanian rabbi. He studied at Brisk but fled to Vilna in 1648 as a result of the Chmielnicki uprising. There he served on the rabbinic court with other distinguished scholars, including *Shabbetai ben Me'ir ha-Kohen and Mosheh ben Yitsḥaq Yehudah *Lima. In 1656 he moved to Kurów near Lublin, where two of his daughters were massacred by Cossacks. He left Poland, serving as rabbi in, among other places, Nikolsburg, Fürth, Frankfurt, and Hamburg, where, in 1669, he drew up a series of communal regulations. At the end of his life, he returned to Poland and was appointed rabbi of Kraków.

An important halakhist, Koidonover emphasized primary sources rather than later commentators. His major work, *Birkat ha-Zevaḥ* (Amsterdam, 1669), consists of *novellae* and a commentary on Qodashim and includes an autobiographical introduction. His other works, posthumously published by his son, are *Emunat Shemu'el* (Frankfurt, 1682), *responsa* dealing particularly the question of the *'*agunah*; *Birkat Shemu'el* (Frankfurt, 1682), sermons demonstrating kabbalistic influences; and *Tif'eret Shemu'el* (Frankfurt, 1696), *novellae* on the Talmud and halakhic codes. His work on questions of divorce and levirate marriage has survived in manuscript.

Tsevi Hirsch Koidonover (died 1712), Lithuanian moralist. Born in Vilna, son of Aharon Shemu'el Koidonover, he studied under Yosef ben Yehudah of Minsk. While a child, Koidonover and his family suffered during the Polish wars of 1659 and fled to central Europe. He returned to Vilna but, after imprisonment on a false charge, moved to Frankfurt, where he published his homiletical work *Kav ha-Yashar* (1705). Drawing heavily on his teacher's *Yesod Yosef*, *Kav ha-Yashar*'s readable style and mixture of homily, realistic detail, and folklore made it one of the most popular works of its genre. Koidonover was influenced by Kabbalah, and his biting social criticism was accompanied by graphic details of the terrors awaiting the sinner in the next world. *Kav ha-Yashar* was translated into Yiddish (Frankfurt, 1709) and Ladino (Constantinople, 1724) and often appeared in bilingual editions.

• **Aharon Shemu'el Koidonover:** Marcus Horovitz, *Frankfurter Rabbinen* (Jerusalem, 1969), pp. 87–90. Isaac Markon, "Bemerkungen zum Bericht des R. Jakob Emden über die wilnaer Flüchtling im XVII Jahrhundert," in *Studies in Jewish Bibliography and Related Subjects in Memory of Abraham Solomon Freidus, 1867–1923* (New York, 1929), pp. 373–376. **Tsevi Hirsch Koidonover:** Israel Zinberg, *A History of Jewish Literature*, translated and edited by Bernard Martin, vol. 6 (Cleveland, 1975), pp. 155–173.

–ADAM TELLER

KOL BO (כָּל בּוֹ; everything within), an encyclopedia or compendium. The term is applied particularly to two works. The first is a ritual compendium, containing, apart from the usual laws (based mainly on Moses *Maimonides' *Mishneh Torah*), a number of religious enactments, legends, and other additions, written around the beginning of the fourteenth century, the authorship of which is unknown. The first edition was printed in Naples in 1490 and 1491. The second work is a large comprehensive folio prayer book designed for the use of the officiant; it includes the complete and unabridged liturgy with all *piyyutim* for every weekday, Sabbath, festival, and fast.

KOLEL (כּוֹלֵל; comprehensive), a term applied nowadays to a higher level *yeshivah*, generally (but not exclusively) for married students who devote their time to Talmudic study. In many cases, these students are granted a modest stipend to enable them to help support their families. In Israel, much of the money used to pay such stipends is derived from government sources, to a large extent funneled through the Ministry of Religious Affairs. The first *kolel* was founded by R. Yisra'el *Salanter in Kovno (Kaunas) in 1878. The term *kolel* was also applied from the late nineteenth century by Ashkenazi Jews in Erets Yisra'el to groups of Jews in the four "*holy cities" of Jerusalem, Hebron, Safed, and Tiberias who received support from compatriots in their native European countries, thereby enabling those in Erets Yisra'el to devote all their time to Talmudic study. See also ḤALUQQAH.

–SHMUEL HIMELSTEIN

KOL NIDREI (כָּל נִדְרֵי; All Vows), title and opening words of a declaration recited by the *shaliaḥ tsibbur* on behalf of the public at the commencement of the *Yom Kippur eve service. It states that all kinds of vows made before God unwittingly or rashly during the year (and hence unfulfilled) shall be considered null and void. Thus, from the outset of the solemn day the worshipers might remove from themselves the guilt of any vow that they had unintentionally failed to observe. The declaration dates from the geonic period and persisted despite the opposition of almost all leading ge'onim, *ri'shonim*, and *aḥaronim*. Kol Nidrei is recited in Aramaic in most rites, in Hebrew in others (e.g., Roman and Byzantine). In its original version, it referred to vows made during the preceding year; R. Tam altered the formulation to refer to the forthcoming year, thereby anulling its pseudo-legal character. This version became customary among Ashkenazim. Italians still use the original version. Sephardim and most congregations in Israel combine both forms. Because of its position at the opening of the service on the most sacred day of the liturgical year, it has been charged with strong religious sentiments. During its recitation, the ark is opened and two Torah scrolls taken out, one held on each side of the reader. It is recited three times. In the Ashkenazi rite, it is chanted to a melody derived from the **mi-Sinai* repertoire. The impact of this ceremony has been so great that despite all halakhic or rationalistic criticism in Orthodox and Reform circles alike, its name is generally used to refer to the entire eve of Yom Kippur. Classical Reform replaced it with Psalm 103 or Psalm 110, but the modern tendency has been to reinstate it.

• Shmuel Y. Agnon, ed., *Days of Awe: A Treasury of Jewish Wisdom for Reflection, Repentance, and Renewal on the High Holy Days*, translated by Maurice T. Galpert (New York, 1995). Abraham Besdin, "Why is Kol Nidre Associated with Yom Kippur," in *The Jacob Dolinitzky Memorial Volume*, edited by Morris C. Katz (Skokie, Ill., 1982), pp. 54–58. Ismar Elbogen, *Jewish Liturgy: A Comprehensive History*, translated by Raymond P. Scheindlin (Philadelphia, 1993), pp. 128, 311. Philip Goodman and Ellen Frankel, eds., *The Yom Kippur Anthology* (Philadelphia, 1992). Michele Kohn, "The Theories of Origins of the Kol Nidre Chant," master's thesis, University of Oregon, 1981.

–PETER LENHARDT

KOOK FAMILY, proponents of *Religious Zionism.

Avraham Yitsḥaq ha-Kohen Kook (1865–1935), religious thinker; first Ashkenazi chief rabbi of Palestine. Born in Griva, Latvia, his mother's family had leanings toward Hasidism, while his father's family had leanings toward Mittnagedism. In his youth, Kook studied in Lithuanian *yeshivot* and served as rabbi in Zaumel, Lithuania, and Bauska, Latvia. In 1904 he moved to Erets Yisra'el and was appointed rabbi of Jaffa, but, in fact, he was accepted as the rabbi of the entire new Jewish settlement of Erets Yisra'el. Rav Kook was simultaneously a highly revered and controversial personality. He was a spiritual and halakhic authority who laid the foundations for a Religious Zionism that was not restricted to the political pragmatism of the Mizrachi movement, but instead regarded Zionism as a movement of overall Jewish renascence.

In 1914 he was caught in Europe by the outbreak of World War I and stayed in Germany and in Saint Gall, Switzerland, until 1916, after which time he accepted a temporary position as the rabbi of the Maḥzike ha-Das community in London. While in London he became involved in political efforts to obtain the Balfour Declaration. After the war, the British mandatory authorities established the chief rabbinate, and he was appointed the first Ashkenazi chief rabbi in 1921. He established a *yeshivah* in Jerusalem (Yeshivat Merkaz ha-Rav), and his students played a leading role in Religious Zionism. In his *yeshivah*, stress was laid on the agrarian laws and the Temple ritual that had been neglected in the Diaspora. He praised the secular pioneers who were building Palestine for performing a holy mission; he believed that all Jewish souls possessed a religious character. His views were attacked by some Orthodox Jews.

His legacy encompasses many disciplines: Jewish law, philosophy, mysticism, and poetry. He refrained from adopting either kabbalistic or philosophic language. Instead he created a "new" language, freely utilizing kabbalistic and philosophic concepts, while vesting them with new meaning. Rav Kook perceived reality as an absolute unity and as the incarnation of divinity that becomes progressively clearer with the march of history. His worldview was characterized by openness, tolerance, and pluralism. He perceived the return of the Jewish people to their land as an important and central link in the process of the redemption of the entire world.

Tsevi Yehudah Kook (1891–1982), son of Avraham Yitsḥaq Kook. He succeeded his father as head of Yeshivat Merkaz ha-Rav and became leader and ideologist of the activist circles of Religious Zionism. After his father's death, he devoted himself to editing and publishing his writings. He regarded the State of Israel as the beginning of the redemptive process and believed that its institutions, including the army, were vested with intrinsic holiness. After the Six-Day War, he was adamantly opposed to any kind of territorial compromise and became the spiritual leader of the Gush Emunim movement, established by his students and based on the idea of Israel's divine right to the land within its biblical borders.

• **Avraham Yitsḥaq ha-Kohen Kook**: Jacob Agus, *High Priest of Rebirth: The Life, Times, and Thought of Abraham Isaac Kuk* (New York, 1972). Yosef Ben-Shelomoh, "Shelemut ve-Hishtalmut be-Torat ha-'Elohim shel ha-Rav Kook," *'Iyyunim* 33 (1984): 289–309. Samuel Hugo Bergman, *Faith and Reason: An Introduction to Modern Jewish Thought* (New York, 1968). Benjamin Ish Shalom, *Rav Avraham Itzhak HaCohen Kook: Between Rationalism and Mysticism*, translated by Shalom Carmy and Bernard Casper (New York, 1993). Benjamin Ish Shalom and Shalom Rosenberg, eds., *The World of Rav Kook's Thought* (Jerusalem, 1991). Eliezer Schweid, *Ha-Yehudi ha Boded veha-Yahadut* (Tel Aviv, 1974). **Tsevi Yehudah Kook:** Richard L. Hoch, "The Politics of Redemption: Rabbi Tzvi Yehudah ha-Kohen Kook and the Origins of Gush Emunim," Ph.D. dissertation, University of California, Santa Barbara, 1994. Nathan Rotenstreich, *Jewish Philosophy in Modern Times* (New York, 1968).

–BENJAMIN ISH SHALOM

KORAH, a Levite, son of Izhar, son of Kohath, who, supported by other Levites and Israelites, led a rebellion in the wilderness against Moses and Aaron. The account of the rebellion in *Numbers* 16 seems to be a combination of three separate traditions regarding challenges against the authority of Moses as the leader of the Israelites and against the preferred status of Aaron and his family in all cultic matters. One of the traditions concerns Dathan and Abiram, members of the tribe of Reuben, and reflects the bitter feelings of the Reubenites, who, though members of the oldest tribe of Israel, were not accorded the honor due to them because of their impetuous behavior as narrated in *Genesis* 49.3–4. They were punished by being swallowed up by the earth (see also *Ps*. 106.17). The second tradition concerns the 250 Israelites (described as "chosen by the assembly, well known men"; *Nm*. 16.2) who revolted against the exclusive leadership of Moses; they were consumed by divine fire. The third, and apparently the latest, tradition was the challenge of Korah and other Levites against the privileges of the Aaronite order and their exclusive right to conduct the Lord's service. Korah argued that all the Levites deserved to serve the Lord, not only Aaron's family and Moses, the descendants of Amram, the firstborn son of Kohath. At first, Moses suggested that a divine sign should determine who shall "come near to the Lord" (*Nm.* 16.4–7), but according to *Numbers* 16.8–11, Moses did not entertain Korah's claim at all. *Numbers* 16.16 and following describe the divine test. The final redaction of the text merged the three traditions into one story but did not eliminate the inner textual problems. The story emphasizes the privileged status of the priests (from the house of Aaron) over that of the Levites and the rest of the Israelites. These traditions are all merged into one short account in *Numbers* 26.9–11.

The sons of Korah, a family of Levites (*Nm.* 26.58), are mentioned in the titles of eleven psalms (*Ps.* 42, 44–49, 84, 85, 87, 88). The statement in *Numbers* 26.11 that "the children of Korah did not die" may be interpreted as a late editorial comment intended to explain their occurrence in later biblical passages (cf. *1 Chr.* 6.22). The Korahites are also mentioned among the mighty men of David in *1 Chronicles* 12.7. The name *Benei Korah* (Sons of Korah) found on an ostracon in the excavations in Arad in a room near the temple entrance, dated to the end of the eighth century BCE, may refer to a family of priests who served in the Arad temple.

• Baruch A. Levine, *Numbers 1–20*, The Anchor Bible (Garden City, N.Y., 1993), pp. 405–432. Jacob Milgrom, *Numbers*, The JPS Torah Commentary (Philadelphia, 1990), pp. 129–139, 414–423. Gunther Wanke, *Die Zionstheologie der Korchiten in ihrem traditionsgeschichtlichen Zusammenhang*, Beihefte zur Zeitschrift für die alttestamentliche Wissenschaft 97 (Berlin, 1996). —ZE'EV KAINAN

KORAN. See QUR'AN.

KOSHER. See DIETARY LAWS; KASHER.

KOTEL HA-MAʿARAVI. See WESTERN WALL.

KOTLER, AHARON (1892–1962), rabbi and *ro'sh yeshivah*. He was born in Sislowitz, Lithuania, and studied at the Slobodka *yeshivah*. In 1914 he assisted his father-in-law, R. Isser Zalman Meltzer, at the *yeshivah* Ets Ḥayyim in Slutsk, later transferred to Kletsk. In 1921 he succeeded R. Meltzer as *ro'sh yeshivah* and continued in this role until World War II. He fled Europe and reached the United States, via Japan, in 1941.

In the United States, he was active in the Vaʿad ha-Hatsalah, an organization that rescued Jews from Nazi-occupied Europe. In 1943 he founded the Beth Midrash Govohah in Lakewood, New Jersey. This institution, with which Kotler was closely identified, became one of the most prominent *yeshivot* in the world.

In 1954 Kotler became president of the Supreme Council of Agudat Israel. He also served on the presidium of the Union of Orthodox Rabbis of the United States and Canada and was a leader of the independent Orthodox educational system in Israel (Ḥinnukh ʿAtsma'i). He wrote *Mishnat Rabbi Aharon* (4 vols. [1975–1986]) and *Osef Ḥiddushei Torah* (1983).

• A. Avi-Shefer, *Maran ha-Ga'on Rabbi Aharon Kotler* (Jerusalem, 1963–1964). Alex J. Goldman, *The Greatest Rabbis' Hall of Fame* (New York, 1987), pp. 257–273. —IRA ROBINSON

KOTSK, MENAḤEM MENDEL. See MENAḤEM MENDEL OF KOTSK.

KOZIENICE, YISRA'EL BEN SHABBETAI. See YISRA'EL BEN SHABBETAI HAPSTEIN KOZIENICE.

KRANZ, YAʿAQOV BEN WOLF (1741–1804), Lithuanian preacher who achieved great fame as the Maggid (preacher) of Dubno, the city in which he served for a number of years. Kranz was very close to the renowned R. Eliyyahu ben Shelomoh Zalman of Vilna, the Vilna Ga'on, who was greatly impressed with Kranz's incisive parables and, according to legend, even asked Kranz to point out his faults. Kranz's major works, all published posthumously, are *Mishlei Yaʿaqov* (parables [Kraków, 1886]), *Ohel Yaʿaqov* (homilies [1859–1863]), and *Sefer ha-Middot* (ethics and theology [Vilna, 1860]). Kranz's works have been republished many times.

• Jacob Kranz, *The Maggid of Dubno and His Parables*, compiled by Benno Heinemann (New York, 1967). —MARC SHAPIRO

KRAUSS, SAMUEL (1866–1948), scholar of Jewish history and literature. Born in Ukk, Hungary, Krauss studied at both the Jánosháza Yeshivah and at Salomon Breuer's *yeshivah* (see BREUER FAMILY) at Pápa before receiving his ordination from the Budapest Rabbinical Seminary in 1894. He also studied at the Universities of Budapest and Berlin and received his Ph.D. from the University of Giessen in 1893. He taught at the Budapest Lehrerseminar until moving to the Israelitisch-Theologische Lehranstalt in Vienna in 1905, where he became the head in 1932. In 1938 he moved to Cambridge, England. A prolific writer in five languages (his bibliography contains over thirteen hundred items), he wrote on philology, history, Bible, Talmud, Christianity, and medieval Hebrew literature. Krauss's main works include *Griechische und lateinische Lehrwörter in Talmud, Midrasch und Targum* (2 vols. [1898–1899]), *Talmudische Archaeologie* (3 vols. [1910–1912]), and *Synagogale Altertümer* (1922), which provided important sociohistorical information about life in the Talmudic period. Krauss also collaborated on the Hungarian translation of the Bible and contributed hundreds of articles to various encyclopedias.

• Eliyahu Ashtor, *Bibliographie der Schriften Prof. Samuel Krauss, 1887–1937* (Vienna, 1937). Eliezer R. Malachi's bibliography in *Qorot Batei ha-Tefillah be-Yisra'el*, by Samuel Krauss (New York, 1955), pp. 324–332. —DIDIER Y. REISS

KROCHMAL, NAḤMAN (1785–1840), historian and philosopher. Known by the acronym Ranak, Krochmal was born in Brody and lived all his life in that area. He was self-educated in philosophy, particularly in the works of Maimonides, Avraham ibn Ezra, Vico, Herder, Kant, Schelling, and Hegel. In his lifetime, Krochmal's reputation spread among participants of Wissenschaft des Judentums and, after he died, his philosophical speculations and historical researches were sent to Leopold Zunz, who edited and published them in 1851 as *Moreh Nevukhei ha-Zeman*.

Like Hegel, Krochmal believed that God or the Absolute Spirit is an infinite, supersensual reality in which everything subsists and that generates all finite particulars. Religious representations are a form of knowledge, differing from the ideas of philosophy primarily in their degree of abstraction and conceptual necessity. All religions conceive of some aspect of the spiritual, using images or imaginative language, rather than abstract concepts. Biblical prophecy truly grasped the infinite, unified nature of the Absolute, so that for Krochmal, the Torah of ancient Israel was the religion of the Absolute Spirit.

Like Vico and Herder, Krochmal viewed each nation as having its distinctive folk spirit and as passing through an organic cycle of birth, growth, maturity, decline, and death. The Jewish people, however, has experienced at least three such cycles, undergoing periodic regeneration as the latent teachings of Torah were further actualized. The first cycle began with the biblical patriarchs and concluded with the Babylonian exile; the second comprised the centuries of the Second Temple, from the biblical return to Zion to the Roman conquest; the third was the Middle Ages. Scholars disagree as to whether Krochmal believed a fourth, modern, cycle had begun.

Krochmal described the *halakhah* of the oral law as a unified system, the growth of which could be understood developmentally as various generations of sages interpreted Jewish law by exegetical rules and other means. Although the moral teachings and parables of the ancient rabbis were directed mainly to the general Jewish public, the underlying structure of the *aggadah* (the nonlegal parts of rabbinic lore) was philosophical.

Krochmal was a philosopher of Judaism in the idealist tradition and an intellectual precursor of Jewish spiritual nationalism.

• Julius Guttmann, *Philosophies of Judaism*, translated by David W. Silverman (New York, 1964), pp. 321–344. Jay M. Harris, *Nachman Krochmal: Guiding the Perplexed of the Modern Age* (New York, 1991). Michael A. Meyer, ed., *Ideas of Jewish History* (New York, 1974), pp. 189–214. Simon Rawidowicz, "Was Nachman Krochmal a Hegelian?" in his *Studies in Jewish Thought*, edited by Nahum N. Glatzer (Philadelphia, 1974). Nathan Rotenstreich, *Tradition and Reality: The Impact of History on Modern Jewish Thought* (New York, 1972), pp. 37–48. Shalom Spiegel, *Hebrew Reborn* (Philadelphia, 1930), pp. 93–118.

—ROBERT M. SELTZER

KUTIM, minor tractate, printed in standard editions of the Talmud Bavli at the end of tractate *ʿAvodah Zarah*, based largely on tannaitic sources. It deals with the status of the *Samaritans, who were taken by Sennacherib, the Assyrian king, from Cuthah (near Babylonia) and resettled in Samaria after the exile of the ten northern tribes. They began observing Jewish customs—but without abandoning their idolatrous beliefs—in order to propitiate the god of the land, who had set lions upon them; hence, rabbis of the tannaitic period debated about whether they were true proselytes or "proselytes of lions" (*Qid.* 75b). Their ambivalent status in Jewish law is reflected in the tractate's introductory pericope: "The usages of the Samaritans are at times like those of the heathens, at times like those of the Israelites. . . ." *Kutim* was published by Michael Higger in *Seven Minor Tractates* (New York, 1930).

—AVRAHAM WALFISH

KUZARI, BOOK OF. See Yehudah ha-Levi.

KVITL (Yi.; קוויטל), a petition offered to a Hasidic rabbi, placed near the grave of a saint, or inserted between the stones of the *Western Wall. In the Hasidic context, the offering of a *kvitl* to a Hasidic master is an act of fealty, a statement that the petitioner believes the holiness of the **tsaddiq* or the merit of his ancestors will suffice to bring his prayers before God. Typically a *kvitl* is accompanied by a monetary gift known as a *pidyon* (short for *pidyon nefesh* [redemption of the soul]), serving to bind the *tsaddiq* to the concerns of the petitioner. Popular leaders of Hasidism accept petitions for healing, and they are especially thought to be helpful concerning issues of childbearing. Some Hasidic masters, including those of *Lubavich and Bratslav (see Naḥman of Bratslav), accepted petitions only for help in the spiritual growth of their disciples.

• Louis Jacobs, *Hasidic Prayer* (New York, 1972), pp. 132f. Aaron Wertheim, *Halakhot ve-Halikhot ba-Ḥasidut* (Jerusalem, 1960), pp. 161–164.

—ARTHUR GREEN

L

LAʿAZ (לַעַז), originally a term meaning foreign language. In the Talmud the word was used to mean a language current among Jews, specifically Greek (*Meg*. 2.1, 18a; *Sot*. 49b; Y., *Sot*. 7.1). By the early Middle Ages, however, it signified the Latin or Romance equivalent of a Hebrew word or phrase, diacritical marks indicating how the transliterated form was pronounced. *Rashi introduced several thousand *leʿazim* into his commentaries on the Bible and Talmud, with the result that *be-laʿaz* was taken to mean "[a gloss] in Old French." Commenting on *Jeremiah* 2.22, for example, Rashi explains that *borit* is equivalent to the Old French *sabon* (soap). His contemporary *Natan ben Yeḥi'el of Rome and other medieval scholars also relied on vernacular glosses to clarify the Hebrew text. Their *leʿazim* refer to many aspects of daily life and have therefore promoted Romance philology and helped to preserve pronunciations. According to a popular misinterpretation, *be-laʿaz* is the acronym of *bi-leshon ʿam zar* (in a foreign tongue).

• David S. Blondheim, *Les Parlers judéo-romans et la Vetus latina* (Paris, 1925). Mochè Catane, *Otsar ha-Laʿazim: Ha-Milim ha-Tsarfatiyyot shebe-Feirushei Rashi ʿal ha-Talmud* (Jerusalem, 1988). Arsène Darmesteter, *Les Gloses françaises de Raschi dans la Bible* (Paris, 1909).

—GABRIEL A. SIVAN

LABOR. The Bible and rabbinic tradition generally take a positive attitude toward the dignity and social value of labor. Rabbi Shimʿon bar Yoḥ'ai stated that the phrase "six days shall you work" is a commandment as binding as the phrase that follows, "and on the seventh you shall rest" (*Mekhilta'* on *Ex*. 20.9–10). Even Adam was enjoined to work in the garden of Eden (*Gn*. 2.15), and such biblical verses as "when you eat of the labor of your hands, happy shall you be and it will be well with you" (*Ps*. 128.2); "sweet is the sleep of the laborer whether he eat little or much" (*Eccl*. 5.13); and "go to the ant you sluggard" (*Prv*. 6.6) emphasize the value of labor. Until the Middle Ages, rabbis earned their living from their occupations, and the trades of various Talmudic rabbis can be gauged from their names, such as Yoḥanan the Shoemaker and Yitsḥaq the Blacksmith. The rabbis said "idleness leads to immorality . . . and to degeneration" (*Ket*. 5.5), "he who does not teach his son a trade teaches him brigandage" (*Qid*. 29a), "great is labor for it lends dignity to man" (*Ned*. 49b), and "the man who lives from the labor of his hands is greater than one who fears heaven" (*Ber*. 8a). A difference of opinion developed over the question of whether one was entitled to abandon work in order to devote one's self to sacred study. Against the opinion of R. Gamli'el that "study without labor must be futile and lead to sin" (*Avot* 2.2), the view was advanced that in the case of the truly righteous "their labor is performed for them by others" (*Ber*. 35b). In answer to the injunction of R. Me'ir to the effect that "a man should always teach his son a light and clean trade," R. Nehora'i said "I eschew every trade in the world and will teach my son only Torah" (*Qid*. 4.14). The rights of the laborer laid down in the Bible are reinforced in the Talmud. Whereas the Bible legislates simply that the day laborer should be paid at the end of the day's work (*Lv*. 19.3; *Dt*. 24.5), the Talmud specifies that a breach of this rule contravenes four distinct biblical commandments (*B. M*. 111a). Moreover, wages were to be paid in money and not in goods (*B. M*. 10.5), and an employer could not make his laborers work outside the agreed working hours (*B. M*. 3.1). In the legal sphere, the general rule that one cannot establish a financial claim merely by swearing to it was set aside in the case of a laborer, who could establish a claim by swearing that wages had not been received (*B. M*. 9.13). In modern rabbinic law, attempts have been made to cope with recent developments that affect the character of labor, wages, the relationship between labor and management, and so on. See also SOCIAL JUSTICE.

• Moses Auerbach, *Labor, Crafts, and Commerce in Ancient Israel* (Jerusalem, 1994). Michael S. Perry, *Working Paper on Labor Rights in the Jewish Tradition* (New York, 1993). Miriam Peskowitz, " 'The Work of Her Hands': Gendering Everyday Life in Roman-Period Judaism in Palestine, 70–250 CE, Using Textile Production as a Case Study," Ph.D. dissertation, Duke University, 1993.

LADINO. See JUDEO-SPANISH.

LAG BA-ʿOMER (ל״ג בָּעֹמֶר; Thirty-third [Day] of the ʿOmer), a minor festival that falls on 18 Iyyar, the thirty-third day of the seven-week period of the counting of the *ʿOmer, which extends from the second day of Pesaḥ to Shavuʿot (*Lv*. 23.15). On Lag ba-ʿOmer the semimourning of the ʿOmer period is lifted, and weddings, haircuts, and so on are permitted. Among Sephardim, the ban is lifted only on the following day but—unlike among Ashkenazim—is not imposed for the rest of the ʿOmer period. The reason for the institution of Lag ba-ʿOmer is obscure. A Talmudic passage (*Yev*. 62b) that tells of the plague that killed the twenty-four thousand disciples of R. *ʿAqiva' ben Yosef during the ʿOmer period provides the rationale for the mourning observed and is taken as a reference to the disasters of the Bar Kokhba' Revolt (see BAR KOKHBA', SHIMʿON); this passage, however, makes no mention of Lag ba-ʿOmer, though one complicated gloss on the statement, "the plague ceased at the middle of the period to Shavuʿot," relates it to Lag ba-ʿOmer, which subsequently became known as the Scholars' Festival. Hence it became customary to grant students a holiday on this day. Some writers suggest that after a series of defeats, Bar Kokhba' secured a victory over the Romans on that date, which was henceforth celebrated, but owing to continued Roman rule, the real reason could not be publicly revealed and was eventually forgotten. Others have connected it with the taking up of arms at the outbreak of the first revolt against Rome (66 CE). According to another view the day was selected because only thirty-two of the forty-nine days of the ʿOmer period are days of mourning when *Taḥanun is said; the thirty-third day, therefore, marks the lifting of the ban. In the synagogue service, Taḥanun is not recited. According to other traditions, the great Flood commenced on this day, and, in the time of Moses, manna began to fall from heaven. A later tradition established Lag ba-ʿOmer as the date of death of R. Shimʿon bar Yoḥ'ai, to whom the *Zohar is attributed, and hence it came to be celebrated in particular by kabbalists. R. Shimʿon's burial place—Meron in Galilee—has remained the scene of a picturesque ceremony on this day (*Hillula' de-Rabbi Shimʿon bar Yoḥ'ai), when Ḥasidim and others bring their young sons for their first haircut, light bonfires, and dance through the night. The ceremony incurred the displeasure of many of the sixteenth-century kabbalists of Safed, who wished—unsuccessfully—to ban it because of its folkloristic, semipagan character. This displeasure was echoed as late as the nineteenth century by R. Mosheh Sofer, without detriment, however, to the popularity of the festival. In Europe it was customary for children to play in the fields with bows and arrows, perhaps as a reminder of the Jewish–Roman war. Lag ba-ʿOmer is also an occasion in Israel for lighting bonfires, even among the nonobservant. Among western and certain other Sephardim, the day is known as Lag la-ʿOmer.

• Ismar Elbogen, *Jewish Liturgy: A Comprehensive History*, translated by Raymond P. Scheindlin (Philadelphia, 1993). Theodor H. Gaster, *Festivals of the Jewish Year* (New York, 1978).

LAMDAN (from Heb. *lamad* [learn]), a Talmudic scholar; usually a layman who has acquired competence in Talmudic studies. –SHMUEL HIMELSTEIN

LAMED VAV (לָמֶד וָו; Hebrew letters for the number thirty-six), legendary group of righteous whose piety saves the world. According to a statement by *Abbayei (*San*. 97b; cf. *Suk*. 45b), "the world must contain not less than thirty-six righteous individuals who are vouchsafed the sight of the divine presence." The Talmud also says that these thirty-six individuals differ from other righteous persons in that they behold the divine presence with special clarity. On this basis arose the legend of the *lamed vav tsaddiqim* (thirty-six righteous individuals), men usually of humble vocation who do not know of the existence of the others and whose special spiritual gifts are not generally recognized or appreciated but by whose merit the world exists. In times of crisis and danger they reveal themselves and bring salvation to the people. According to the *Tiqqunei Zohar* (chap. 21), there are two such groups of thirty-six secret saints, one for Erets Yisra'el and one for elsewhere. The legend forms the basis for numerous Jewish folk tales, including many in kabbalistic and Hasidic sources. The Yiddish term *lamed-vovnik* is used for a saintly individual.

• Gershom Gerhard Scholem, "Die 36 verborgenen Gerechten in der jüdischen Tradition," in *Judaica*, vol. 1 (Frankfurt am Main, 1963).

LAMENTATION. See QINAH.

LAMENTATIONS, BOOK OF (Heb. *Eikhah*, after its opening word; in the Talmud, called *Kinot* [Dirges]), sixth book in the Hagiographa section of the Bible and third of the Five Scrolls (see ḤAMESH MEGILLOT). Traditionally ascribed to the prophet Jeremiah (on the basis of *2 Chr*. 35.25), the book is placed in the Septuagint version after the *Book of Jeremiah*. It consists of five chapters, of which the first four, written acrostically according to the alphabet (the third chapter contains a triple acrostic, each letter appearing three times at the beginning of a verse), elegiacally bemoan Israel's sorrowful plight during the siege and fall of Jerusalem in 587 and 586 BCE. In the fifth chapter (not an acrostic, but consisting of twenty-two verses, equivalent to the number of the letters in the Hebrew alphabet) the plaint fuses into a prayer for Israel's redemption. The prevalent motif is that a causal connection exists between divine punishment (graphically described in the plight of dying children and the ultimate resort to cannibalism) and the sins of the people—prophets and priests included. Nevertheless, with the exception of 4.13, the sins of the people are not spelled out specifically, and God's judgment in bringing on the destruction is regarded as exceptionally severe (e.g., 3.43, 5.7). This is one reason why critical scholarship denies the book's sole authorship to Jeremiah, who viewed the destruction as inevitable and fully justified (*Jer*. 5.7–9, 9.1–5, 11–13) and who foresaw the failure of foreign alliances (*Jer*. 2.18, 37.5–10), whereas the author of *Lamentations* expressed the frustrating reliance on outside help (4.17). Nevertheless, the book was most likely composed close in time to the catastrophic events it describes. From a literary-generic point of view, *Lamentations* resembles Sumerian elegies that were written over cultic centers destroyed by the god of the city. The book is read in the synagogue during the evening and morning services on Tishʿah be-'Av, the traditional anniversary of the destruction of the Temple.

• W. C. Gwaltney, "The Biblical Book of Lamentations in the Context of Near Eastern Lament Literature," in *Scripture in Context II: More Essays on the Comparative Method*, edited by William W. Hallo, J. Moyer, and L. Perdue (Winona Lake, Ind., 1983), pp. 191–211. Delbert R. Hillers, *Lamentations*, 2d rev. ed., The Anchor Bible, vol. 7A (New York, 1972). Yehezkel Kaufmann, *The Religion of Israel: From Its Beginnings to the Babylonian Exile*, translated from the Hebrew and abridged by Moshe Greenberg (Chicago, 1960), pp. 408–409. –DAVID A. GLATT-GILAD

LAMENTATIONS RABBAH, an aggadic *midrash* to the *Book of *Lamentations*, included in the collection commonly referred to as the *Midrash Rabbah. Compiled in Erets Yisra'el in the fifth or sixth century CE, *Lamentations Rabbah* contains exegetical comments, parables, and stories, written in Hebrew and Aramaic, and follows the order of the verses of the biblical book. The *midrash* is prefaced by thirty-six *petiḥot* (see PETIḤAH), most of them concluding with a reference to the first verse of *Lamentations*. The biblical book laments the destruction of the First Temple and the calamities that befell the Jewish people at the time, especially in Jerusalem; *Lamentations Rabbah* expounds on these and other calamities, often referring, obliquely or directly, to the destruction of the Second Temple and the Bar Kokhba' Revolt (see BAR KOKHBA' SHIMʿON). Much historical material relating to these periods is included—albeit in aggadic garb—in the *midrash*, some of which has parallels in Josephus's historical accounts.

• Juan José Alarcón Sainz, "Los Mesalim de los proemios de Lamentaciones Rabbah (LamR)," *Miscelánea de Estudios Arabes y Hebraicos* 39.2 (1990): 39–46. Juan José Alarcón Sainz, "Vocablos griegos y latinos en los 'Proemios (Petîhôt) de Lamentaciones Rabbah,' " *Sefarad* 49.1 (1989): 3–10. Salomon Buber, ed., *Midrash Eikhah Rabbah* (Vilna, 1899). Harry Freedman and Maurice Simon, *Midrash Rabbah*, vol. 7, *Deuteronomy, Lamentations* (London, 1961). Michael Krupp, "Die jemenitische Version des 'Midrasch Echa,' " in *Die Hebräische Bibel und ihre zweifache Nachgeschichte: Festschrift für Rolf Rendtorff*, edited by Erhard Blum (Neukirchen-Vluyn, 1990). *Midrash Rabbah* (Vilna, 1878). Jacob Neusner, ed. and trans., *Lamentations Rabbah: An Analytical Translation*, Brown Judaic Studies, vol. 193 (Atlanta, 1989). Chaim Raphael, *The Walls of Jerusalem: An Excursion into Jewish History* (New York, 1968). Hermann Leberecht Strack, *Introduction to the Talmud and Midrash* (1931; Minneapolis, 1992). Leopold Zunz, *Ha-Derashot be-Yisra'el ve-Hishtalshelutan ha-Historit*, edited by Chanoch Albeck (1892; Jerusalem, 1974).

–PAUL MANDEL

LAMP. See CANDLES; MENORAH.

LAMPRONTI, YITSḤAQ ḤIZQIYYAHU BEN SHEMU'EL (1679–1756), Italian rabbi, scholar, and physician. He practiced medicine in Ferrara, where (from 1743) he was rabbi and head of the *yeshivah*. He is best known for his *Paḥad Yitsḥaq*, an extensive halakhic encyclopedia that appeared in two editions, one consisting of a hundred twenty volumes, the other of thirty-five volumes. The articles in this work are generally exhaustive dissertations on their subjects and are valuable for their quotations of rabbinic *responsa* (especially from Italy) and other often unpublished sources. The work was published up to the letter *mem* in Italy between 1750 and 1840 and was completed in Germany between 1864 and 1887.

• Benedetto Levi, *Toledot ha-Rav ha-Gadol Yitsḥaq Lampronti* (Lyck, 1871). David B. Ruderman, "Contemporary Science and Jewish Law in the Eyes of Isaac Lampronti and His Rabbinic Interlocutors," in *Jewish Thought and Scientific Discovery in Early Modern Europe* (New Haven, Conn., 1995). H. A. Savitz, *Doctor Isaac Lampronti, 1679–1757, Rabbi, Physician, Teacher, Preacher, and Encyclopaedist* (Turin, 1962).

–JEFFREY R. WOLF

LAMPS, SABBATH. See KINDLING OF LIGHTS.

LANDAU, YA'AQOV, (15th cent.) Talmudist. Little is known of his life except that he was born and educated in Germany and later lived and worked in Italy. He is known for his work *Ha-'Agur*, which surveys Ashkenazi scholarship on two books of the *Arba'ah Turim* of Ya'aqov ben Asher—*Oraḥ Ḥayyim* and *Yoreh De'ah*. It offers an abridgment and the halakhic decisions designed for the nonscholar and was often cited by Yosef Karo. *Ha-'Agur* was the first rabbinical work to contain *haskamot* (see APPROBATION) from other rabbis.

• Mosheh Hershler, introduction to *Ha-'Agur ha-Shalem* (Jerusalem, 1960).

LANDAU, YEḤEZQE'L (1713–1793), known from his most famous work as Noda' bi-Yehudah; Polish-born rabbi and halakhist. Born to a leading rabinical family in Opatów, he was educated in Ludmir (Vladimir-Volynskiy) and in Brody, where he also served as *dayyan*. In 1745 he was appointed rabbi in Jampol, serving for ten years until his appointment to the prestigious Prague rabbinate, where he remained until his death. His *yeshivah* in Prague soon became one of the most important such institutions in central Europe. Conservative in viewpoint, he took a public stand on many of the burning issues of his day. He was fiercely opposed to Shabbateanism and Frankism, though he adopted a conciliatory stance in the Emden–Eybeschuetz controversy of 1752, arguing that Eybeschuetz was being misrepresented—a position that was influential in winning Landau his Prague appointment. He was also opposed to the new Hasidism of his day, the innovations of which he suspected were influenced by Shabbateanism. Though open to the study of secular subjects within a traditional Jewish framework and cautiously supportive of the foundation of a new Jewish school in Prague in 1782, he was hostile to the Berlin Haskalah, attacking the publication of Wessely's *Divrei Shalom ve-'Emet* (1782) and excoriating Mendelssohn's Bible translation (1783). Aware of the changing legal status of Bohemian Jewry, he attempted to instill patriotic feeling in the Jewish community, while using his connections with the authorities (including the emperor) to ensure that new legislation harmed as little as possible the framework of Jewish traditional and, in particular, family life. When Jews were first recruited into the Austrian army, he addressed them in 1789, urging both loyalty to the country and adherence to Jewish law.

As a halakhist, his reputation was based on his extensive collection of 855 *responsa*, *Noda' bi-Yehudah* (vol. 1 [Prague, 1776]; vol. 2 [Prague, 1811]). These halakhic enquiries were addressed to him from every part of the Jewish world, and in his responses, he demonstrated his mastery of the sources and his incisive analytical skill, sometimes tending toward leniency in his decisions (for which reason some were rejected by later authorities). He was also a gifted preacher and wrote extensively. Among his more important works are *Tsiyyun le-Nefesh Ḥayyah*, *novellae* on various tractates of the Talmud (Prague, 1783, 1791, 1799, 1959); *Ahavat Tsiyyon*, *Shivat Tsiyyon*, and *Derush le-Tsiyyon*, three volumes of sermons, eulogies, and *novellae* (1826); *Dagul me-Revavah*, notes on the *Shulḥan 'Arukh* (Prague, 1794); and *Das mosaisch-talmudische Eherecht*, describing Jewish family law and comparing it with legislation introduced by Emperor Joseph II (1903).

• Leon Gellman, *Ha-Noda' bi-Yehudah u-Mishnato* (Jerusalem, 1961). Yekuthiel Aryeh Kamelhar, *Mofet ha-Dor* (1903); repr. in *Sefer Doresh le-Tsiyyon*, by Ezekiel ben Judah Landau, pt. 4 (New York, 1984). Shnayer Z. Leiman, "When a Rabbi Is Accused of Heresy: R. Ezekiel Landau's Attitude Toward R. Jonathan Eibeschuetz in the Emden–Eibeschuetz Controversy" in *From Ancient Israel to Modern Judaism: Essays in Honor of Marvin Fox*, edited by Jacob Neusner et al., 4 vols. (Atlanta, 1989), vol. 3, pp. 179–194. Solomon Wind, "Ezekiel Landau," in *Jewish Leaders*, edited by Leo Jung (New York, 1953), pp. 77–98.

–ADAM TELLER

LANDESRABBINER (Ger.; land rabbi), title given to rabbis appointed or recognized by the government from the seventeenth century on in Germany and Austria. Their jurisdiction extended over the political unit known as a *Land*, of which there were many in Germany. Their function was often civic and representative (in the nineteenth century, they were generally expected to Germanize the Jews) rather than strictly religious.

LAND LAWS. See AGRARIAN LAWS.

LANDLORDS. See TENANCY.

LAND OF ISRAEL. See ERETS YISRA'EL.

LA-SHANAH HA-BA'AH BI-YERUSHALAYIM (לַשָּׁנָה הַבָּאָה בִּירוּשָׁלָיִם; "Next year in Jerusalem"), a wish traditionally expressed at the conclusion of the Pesaḥ *Seder and, in most rites, at the concluding service of *Yom Kippur. The recitation of the phrase on these two occasions reflects a Talmudic dispute as to whether redemption will come in the month of Nisan or Tishrei (*R. ha-Sh.* 11a). In the State of Israel, the wording is *bi-Yerushalayim ha-benuyyah*, "next year in rebuilt Jerusalem" (cf. *Ps.* 122.3).

• Macy Nulman, *The Encyclopedia of Jewish Prayer* (Northvale, N.J., and London, 1993), pp. 228.

LASHON HA-RAʿ. See SLANDER.

LATTER PROPHETS (Heb. *nevi'im aḥaronim*), term used to refer to the prophetic books of *Isaiah*, *Jeremiah*, *Ezekiel*, and the twelve *Minor Prophets, in order to distinguish them from the historical books of *Joshua*, *Judges*, *Samuel*, and *Kings*, often referred to as the *Former Prophets. In this usage, the terms *former* and *latter* simply refer to the order of the books in the biblical collection. See also BIBLE. —BARUCH J. SCHWARTZ

LAUTERBACH, JACOB ZALLEL (1873–1942), rabbinic scholar. Born in Monasterzyska, Galicia, Lauterbach was ordained at the Berlin Rabbinical Seminary. In 1902 he received his Ph.D. from the University of Göttingen, where he studied with Julius Wellhausen. In 1904 Lauterbach moved to New York, becoming an editor of the *Jewish Encyclopedia*, to which he contributed two hundred sixty entries. Lauterbach served as rabbi for both traditional and Reform congregations and, from 1911 to 1934, taught at the Hebrew Union College in Cincinnati. His scholarly work centered mainly on the history of the Pharisees but also explored the literary history of the Talmud as well as Jewish customs and folklore. He published a translation of the tannaitic *midrash Mekhilta' de-Rabbi Yishmaʿe'l*. Several of his essays were published after his death (*Rabbinic Essays* [Cincinnati, 1951]).

• Lewis M. Barth in *Hebrew Union College–Jewish Institute of Religion at One Hundred Years*, edited by Samuel E. Karff (Cincinnati, 1976), pp. 317–382. —DIDIER Y. REISS

LAVER, a bowl for washing hands. Priests were required to wash their hands and feet before entering the sacred precincts to perform their cultic duties; for this reason the instructions for building the Tabernacle concluded with the command to fashion a bronze Laver or wash basin (*kiyyor*) filled with water and to place it in the Tabernacle courtyard between the altar and the entrance to the Tabernacle (*Ex.* 30.18). According to *Exodus* 38.8, the Laver was fashioned out of the mirrors of the women who congregated at the entrance of the Tent of Meeting, making the Laver a specifically feminine contribution to the construction of the Tabernacle. In the First Temple, the function of the Laver was served by the immense *Brazen Sea. There was also a laver in the Second Temple. Some synagogues have lavers, often ornamental, at which worshipers wash their hands before entering the sanctuary and at which the priests wash before pronouncing the Birkat ha-Kohanim.

• Menachem Haran, *Temples and Temple-Service in Ancient Israel* (Oxford, 1978). Albert Zuidhoff, "King Solomon's Molten Sea and *Pi*," *Biblical Archaeologist* 45 (1982): 179–184. —BARUCH J. SCHWARTZ

LAW. See HALAKHAH; TORAH.

LAW, CIVIL. See CIVIL LAW.

LAW, CODIFICATION OF. See CODIFICATION OF LAW.

LAW, ORAL. See ORAL LAW.

LAW, READING OF. See QERI'AT HA-TORAH.

LAW, REJOICING OF. See SIMḤAT TORAH.

LAW, SCROLL OF. See SEFER TORAH.

LAW, TABLES OF. See TABLETS OF THE LAW.

LAW COURT. See BEIT DIN.

LAW OF RETURN, an Israeli law adopted in 1950 stating that "every Jew has the right to immigrate to the State of Israel" and may immediately obtain an immigrant certificate. From the religious viewpoint, this has engendered a series of controversies over the definition of who is a Jew (See JEW, WHO IS A?, CONTROVERSY). In 1958, the minister of the interior decided that any new immigrant who made a sincere profession of Judaism was covered by the Law of Return. This enraged the National Religious Party (NRP), which resigned from the coalition government over the issue. Eventually, the Interior Ministry was entrusted to the hands of the NRP, and an amendment to the law was accepted in 1970 by which a Jew was defined according to *halakhah*: as "a person born of a Jewish mother or who has become converted to Judaism and is not a member of another religion." The nature of the conversion was not specified, but the *Agudat Israel party insisted that only conversions "according to *halakhah*" should be accepted, and not those by Conservative or Reform courts. This led to a crisis in 1988 when Agudat Israel postulated that such an amendment be adopted as a condition of its joining the government. The prime minister designate was willing to accept the demand, but this led to an outcry in the Diaspora, notably in the United States, and the amendment was not adopted. The 1970 amendment extended the Law of Return to cover "a child or grandchild of a Jew, the spouse of a Jew, the spouse of a child of a Jew, and the spouse of a grandchild of a Jew, except for a person who has been a Jew and voluntarily changed his religion." A further controversy arose in the 1990s as a result of large-scale immigration from the former Soviet

Union and, to a smaller extent, from Ethiopia. It was estimated that a fifth of the immigrants from the former Soviet Union from 1989 through 1995 were non-Jews who fell into these categories (a consequence of widespread intermarriage) and that over a hundred thousand new immigrants to Israel were non-Jews who qualified under the amended Law of Return.

• John W. Montgomery, "When Is a Jew Not a Jew?" *Law and Justice* 118–119 (1993): 108–110. Nancy C. Richmond, "Israel's Law of Return: Analysis of Its Evolution and Present Application," *Dickenson Journal of International Law* 12 (1993): 95–133.

LAWS OF NOAH. See NOAHIC LAWS.

LAYMAN (Heb. *hedyot*), term used in Temple times to designate a private person, as opposed to a member of royalty or the priesthood. It is also found as an appellation for an ignorant man, one of low character or poor manners, and the unskilled as opposed to the skilled worker. Thus, *leshon hedyot* means popular, everyday, or vulgar parlance; *kohen hedyot* refers to an ordinary priest. With the destruction of the Temple, most distinctions between laymen and priests disappeared. See also PRIESTHOOD.

LAZARUS, MORITZ (1824–1903), philosopher and psychologist. Born in Poznań, he studied history and philosophy at the University of Berlin, from which he received his Ph.D. in 1850. In 1860 he was appointed professor at the University of Berne, and in 1874 he received an appointment at the University of Berlin. Along with Heymann Steinthal, Lazarus is noted for founding the discipline of *Völkerpsychologie*, the study of the psychological character of nations. From 1859 to 1890 he edited the journal *Zeitschrift für Völkerpsychologie und Sprachwissenschaft*. Lazarus's most noted Jewish work was his *Ethik des Judentums* (1898; English translation by Henrietta Szold, 2 vols. [1900–1901]). This Kantian work stressed the universal rather than the particularist elements of Jewish morality, a point that was criticized by Jewish scholars such as Hermann Cohen, who instead emphasized the historical evolution of a distinct Jewish morality. Lazarus's autobiography, *Aus Meiner Jugend, Autobiographie* was published in 1913.

• Nahida Ruth Lazarus and Alfred Leicht, eds., *Moritz Lazarus' Lebenserinnerungen* (Berlin, 1906). —GAVRIEL D. ROSENFELD

LEAH, eldest daughter of Laban; Jacob's first wife, who bore him six sons—Reuben, Simeon, Levi, Judah, Issachar, and Zebulun—and one daughter, Dinah; third matriarch of Israel. Leah became Jacob's wife only after her father substituted her as a bride for *Rachel, her younger sister, for whom Jacob had worked for seven years. He then had to work for an additional seven years for Rachel's hand. Leah also gave Jacob her handmaid Zilpah, who bore him two children, Gad and Asher. Leah, along with Rachel and their children, returned to Canaan with Jacob when he fled from her father's house in Padan-aram (*Gn.* 29–31, 33.1–7). The names of both Rachel and Leah were invoked as a blessing to brides on their wedding day (*Ru.* 4.11), a custom still practiced today at Jewish weddings before the bride is led to the wedding canopy.

• Nahum M. Sarna, *Genesis*, The JPS Torah Commentary (New York, 1989), pp. 206–226. Claus Westermann, *Genesis 12–36*, translated by John J. Scullion (Minneapolis, 1985), pp. 461–501. —SHALOM PAUL

LEAP YEAR. See CALENDAR.

LEAVEN. See ḤAMETS.

LEAVEN, SEARCH FOR. See BEDIQAT ḤAMETS.

LECTIONARY CYCLE. See QERI'AT HA-TORAH.

LEESER, ISAAC (1806–1868), Orthodox religious and communal leader. Leeser was born in Neuenkirchen, Westphalia, Germany, and as a youth was influenced by R. Abraham Sutro, an outspoken opponent of Reform Judaism. Arriving in America in 1824, Leeser first served as a *ḥazzan* in Richmond, Virginia, before being called in 1829 to Philadelphia's Mikveh Israel, where he remained until 1850. In 1857 he was elected head of Congregation Beth El Emeth in Philadelphia and remained its *ḥazzan* until his death in 1868.

While in Philadelphia, Leeser endeavored to modernize congregational ritual to make Orthodox Judaism more intelligible and attractive to laypeople who were assimilating or aligning with Reform Judaism. He introduced the weekly English sermon and struggled to institutionalize it in Mikveh Israel. The founder of the first Jewish Publication Society of America, he translated both the Sephardi and Ashkenazi prayer books into English and in 1845 published the first Jewish translation of the Bible in English, on which he had worked for seventeen years. Through his newspaper, the *Occident*, Leeser attempted both to promote Orthodoxy and to unify all American Jews. Toward that end, he was also instrumental in the founding in 1859 of the Board of Delegates of American Israelites. In 1867 Leeser founded Maimonides College, the first serious attempt at creating a rabbinical seminary in America.

• Moshe Davis, *The Emergence of Conservative Judaism: The Historical School in Nineteenth-Century America* (Philadelphia, 1965). Moses Legis Isaacs and Nancy Isaacs Klein, "Isaac Leeser and the Occident," in *Guardians of Our Heritage, 1724–1953*, edited by Leo Jung (New York, 1958), pp. 247–261. Lance Jonathan Sussman, *Isaac Leeser and the Making of American Judaism*, American Jewish Civilization Series (Detroit, 1995). —JEFFREY S. GUROCK

LEGACY. See INHERITANCE.

LEGEND. See AGGADAH.

LEHRENSTALT FÜR DIE WISSENSCHAFT DES JUDENTUMS. See HOCHSCHULE FÜR DIE WISSENSCHAFT DES JUDENTUMS.

LEIBOWITZ, YESHA'YAHU (1903–1994), scientist, philosopher, and theologian. Born in Riga, he studied in Berlin and Basel. In 1935 he joined the Hebrew University of Jerusalem, where he became professor of organic and biological chemistry and of neurophysiology. Judaism, according to Leibowitz, found its expression through the ages in the practice of the *mitsvot* and not necessarily in credos on which the sages of Israel did not unanimously agree. *Halakhah* and not the Bible is the distinctive mark of Judaism and the Jewish people. Leibowitz considered man's willingness and ability to choose religion as the culmination of freedom. Religion is not a means for achieving a goal, but is the goal itself; this is why one should not look for reasons for the *mitsvot*. The real believer should not expect any reward for fulfilling the *mitsvot*—their very observance is the reward. Leibowitz defined Judaism as a theocentric religion, requiring its believer to serve God for the sake of serving him. He made a complete distinction between religion and science. In his view, the findings of science are compelling, while religion is a matter of choice; these two paths will never cross. He therefore rejected the apologetic writings that try to explain miraculous events in the Bible on scientific principles.

Ethics, Leibowitz believed, might be in conflict with religious commands (for example, the sacrifice of Isaac). Therefore, he did not define himself as a humanist, even though many of his ideas, particularly those regarding politics and Arab–Jewish relations, were seen as humanistic. He believed that human history should not be interpreted on the basis of divine intervention but on the basis of human behavior, including all human atrocities. Thus, he avoided the necessity of finding a theological explanation for the Holocaust. Leibowitz saw in the State of Israel a mere political entity with no religious significance. He doubted the possibility of a halakhic state and advocated the complete separation between church and state. Regarding the messianic idea, he said "Any actual Messiah is a false Messiah." Like Maimonides, he thought that Jews should concentrate not on the world to come but on their duties in this world.

Leibowitz advocated the full participation of women in learning Torah but rejected their struggle for equality in the fulfillment of time-bound *mitsvot* as meaningless from a religious point of view. His writings include *Yahadut, ʿAm Yehudi u-Medinat Yisraʾel* (Jerusalem, 1975); *Siḥot al-Shemonah Peraqim le-Rambam* (Jerusalem, 1986); and *Emunah, Historiyyah ve-ʿArakhim* (Jerusalem, 1982).

• *Yeshaʿyahu Leibovits al-ʿOlam u-Meloʾo: Siḥotʿim Michael Shashar* (Jerusalem, 1987).

—MICHAEL SHASHAR

LEIL SHIMMURIM (לֵיל שִׁמּוּרִים; night of watching), name given by the Bible (*Ex*. 12.42) to the night of the *Exodus and, hence, to the first night (in the Diaspora the first two nights) of Pesaḥ. Because the night was thought to be under special divine protection, doors were often left unlocked and night prayers omitted. Some scholars suggest that the term *leil shimmurim* is similar to the Bedouin *samarum* (the practice of staying up all night and telling stories) and refers to the custom of staying awake all night and recounting the Exodus from Egypt.

• Eliyahu Kitov, *The Book of Our Heritage: The Jewish Year and Its Days of Significance*, rev. ed. (Jerusalem and New York, 1978), pp. 312–328.

LEINER, MORDEKHAI YOSEF. See IZBICA.

LEKHAH DODI (לְכָה דוֹדִי; "Come my beloved"), introductory words of a sixteenth-century composition (one of the last to be included in the prayer book) sung at the inauguration of the Sabbath. The author's name, Shelomoh *Alkabez, is given in acrostic in eight of the nine stanzas. Incorporating many biblical phrases, particularly from *Isaiah*, the poem personifies the Sabbath as a bride (cf. *Shab*. 199a) symbolically welcomed by the congregation's bowing toward the entrance during the last stanza. It is a remnant of a more elaborate processional greeting of the Sabbath renewed by Alkabez, who, with his fellow kabbalists, went out to the countryside around Safed to welcome "Sabbath the bride." Replete with references to the peace and joy of the Sabbath and the larger peace and joy of messianic times and the restoration of Jerusalem and Israel, Lekhah Dodi was quickly adopted in all rites. The hymn is sung after the introductory Psalm 29.

• Macy Nulman, *The Encyclopedia of Jewish Prayer* (Northvale, N.J., and London, 1993), pp. 223–224.

LEKHU NERANNENAH (לְכוּ נְרַנְּנָה; "Come, let us exult"), the opening words of Psalm 95, and hence of the group of six psalms (95–99 and 29) recited in the Ashkenazi rite for the inauguration of the Sabbath at the beginning of the Friday evening service. Initially, only Sephardi congregations began with Psalm 29 but eventually most Jewish liturgies came to include all six psalms. The six psalms, which describe the grandeur of God's work in nature and his righteous judgment of the world, were said to correspond to the six working days of the week. They are followed in the liturgy by *Lekhah Dodi and Psalm 92, the Sabbath Psalm. The custom of reciting this group of psalms was introduced by the kabbalists of Safed in the sixteenth century. Previously, the beginning of the Sabbath eve service had been the same as on weekdays.

• Macy Nulman, *The Encyclopedia of Jewish Prayer* (Northvale, N.J., and London, 1993), pp. 224–226.

LEO BAECK COLLEGE, British non-Orthodox rabbinical college. The Leo Baeck College, which opened in 1956, was the successor to the Berlin Hochschule, which was destroyed in the Nazi period. It is sponsored jointly by the two British progressive movements, the Reform Synagogues of Great Britain and the Union of Liberal and Progressive Synagogues of Great Britain. Since 1982 the college has been housed in the Sternberg Centre for Judaism in North Finchley, London. Besides preparing rabbis for pulpits in Europe and the British Commonwealth, it provides teacher training and awards bachelor's and master's degrees in Jewish studies.

• Ellen Littmann, "The First Ten Years of the Leo Baeck College," in *Reform Judaism*, edited by Dov Marmur (London, 1973), pp. 160–180.

—LAVINIA COHN-SHERBOK

LEÓN, MOSHEH DE. See MOSHEH DE LEÓN.

LEON OF PARIS. See YEHUDAH BEN YITSḤAQ.

LEPROSY, an affection of the skin or other surfaces that renders a person or object unclean (see IMPURITY), referred to in the Bible as *tsoraʿat*. Signs of leprosy, which may appear on persons, walls of houses, or in fabrics, are described at length in *Leviticus* 13. Upon being pronounced as leprous by a priest, the affected person or object was quarantined until the scourge disappeared. Upon being healed, a leper had to undergo a cleansing ceremony and bring special offerings to the Temple (*Lv*. 14). The rabbis suggested that leprosy was the punishment for scandalmongering and *slander, as evidenced in the instances of Moses speaking against Israel (*Ex*. 4.1–8) and Miriam speaking against Moses (*Dt*. 24.8–9). The laws concerning leprosy are discussed in Talmud tractate **Negaʿim*.

• Jacob Neusner, "The Leper: Leviticus 13:1–14:57," in *Sifra: The Rabbinic Commentary on Leviticus—An American Translation*, Brown Judaic Studies, no. 102 (Atlanta, 1985), pp. 7–140.

LEQAḤ TOV, *midrash* on the Torah and the Five Scrolls composed in Germany at the end of the eleventh century by the Balkan scholar *Toviyyah ben Eliʿezer. It contains allusions to contemporary historical events, specific reference to the martyrs of the First Crusade of 1096, ideas culled from early (now lost) aggadic *midrashim*, and early mystical literature. The author frequently explains anthropomorphic verses and statements as parables, using the rabbinic phrase, "The Torah speaks in the language of humans," a reflection of the author's ongoing dispute with the Karaites, which frequently finds expression throughout this work. *Leqaḥ Tov* is also known as *Pesiqta' Zutarta'* and was often confused with other compilations. *Leqaḥ Tov* on *Genesis*, *Exodus*, and *Esther* was published by Solomon Buber (1884–1896); on *Leviticus*, *Numbers*, and *Deuteronomy* by Me'ir Katzenellenbogen (1884); on *Song of Songs* and *Lamentations* by A. W. Greenup (1909); and on *Ruth* by I. Bamberger (1887).

• Louis Ginzberg, ed., *Ginzei Schechter* (1928–1929; Jerusalem 1969). Leopold Zunz, *Ha-Derashot be-Yisra'el ve-Hishtalshelutan ha-Historit*, edited by Chanoch Albeck (1892; Jerusalem, 1974). –DANIEL SPERBER

LEQET, SHIKHḤAH, AND PE'AH (לֶקֶט; שִׁכְחָה; פֵּאָה), three parts of the harvest that the farmer was instructed to leave for the poor; they are known as *mattenot ʿaniyyim*, "gifts to the poor" (see AGRARIAN LAWS).

Leqet (gleaning) referred to stalks dropped by the harvesters that may not be retrieved (*Lv*. 19.9–10). The same applied to grapes that fell while being gathered in the vineyard (for which the technical term was *peret*). The most well-known example of gleaning is the story of Ruth in the fields of Boaz (*Ru*. 2), in which the gleaners are pictured as following the reapers to gather up what was left. Gleaning is limited to cornfields, orchards, and vineyards and may not take place in vegetable gardens. The owner of the field may derive no benefit from the gleanings nor should he discriminate among or help the gleaners. Gleaners are exempt from the obligation of tithing.

Shikhḥah (a forgotten thing) refers to the sheaves that the landowner and his workers had overlooked during reaping and that may not be retrieved but must be left for the poor to gather (*Dt*. 24.19). The Bible refers to cut sheaves, but the rabbis applied the ruling also to uncut corn (*Pe'ah* 6.7) or to trees that had been overlooked (*Pe'ah* 7.1).

Pe'ah (corner) refers to corners of fields that should not be reaped but left for the poor (*Lv*. 19.9–10, 23.22). Although halakhically the obligation is met by leaving a single stalk for the poor, the rabbis ordained that at least one-sixtieth of the harvest should be left and that this proportion should be increased in the event of a good crop or a large number of poor gleaners.

The rabbis applied these laws only in Erets Yisra'el, but the custom was also observed in Babylonia and elsewhere. Although originally the laws were intended for the Jewish poor, they were later extended to apply also to the non-Jewish poor (*Git*. 5.8). The subject is discussed in the Talmudic tractate *Pe'ah*.

• Roger Brooks, *Support for the Poor in the Mishnaic Law of Agriculture: Tractate Peah*, Brown Judaic Studies, no. 43 (Chico, Calif., 1983).

LETTER MYSTICISM. The view that the letters of the Hebrew *alphabet are vehicles of God's essence and creative power underlies both mystical speculation and practical magic (see AMULETS). Human language, as used for communication, is different from divine language, which is a manifestation of the infinite wisdom of God and the instrument by which the world was created. Since divine power inheres in the letters on which language is based, the semantic aspect of language is merely one among many. Language as sound and, especially, written language as pictures are important means of unraveling divine secrets. Speculation concerning the shapes of the letters began in late antiquity and is contained in texts such as the **Alphabet of Rabbi ʿAqiva'*, an esoteric, Midrashic anthology compiled at the beginning of the geonic period. The earliest kabbalistic work, **Sefer ha-Bahir*, also discusses the shapes of the letters and of the vocalization marks. In the second half of the thirteenth century, R. Yaʿaqov ben Yaʿaqov of Castile wrote a commentary on the shapes of the letters, and his brother, R. Yitsḥaq, wrote a commentary on the shapes of the *teʿamim*, the marks indicating the tunes to which scripture should be recited. The subject figures prominently in the Zohar. According to the fourteenth-century *Sefer ha-Temunah*, the image of the alphabet reflects the image of God. Many kabbalistic writings concentrate in particular on the letters that constitute the Tetragrammaton, regarded as the closest possible representative of the essence of God in the created world.

• Sh. Z. Kahana, *Ha-'Otiyyot ve-Sodotehen* (Jerusalem, 1985). –JOSEPH DAN

LETTER OF ARISTEAS, a Greek work written by a Jewish author probably in the second half of the second century BCE. It recounts how Ptolemy II, king of Egypt (285–246), wishing to have every possible book included in his Alexandrian library, decided to commission a Greek translation of the Hebrew Torah. He sent messengers to the high priest in Jerusalem, who sent the king seventy-two men, six from each tribe, to prepare the translation. Following a series of royal banquets, during which the king was impressed by the Jews' sagacity and good manners, the translators set to work, completing the whole translation in seventy-two days. The translation was subsequently approved not only by the king but also by the Jewish community of Alexandria, whose members vowed never to alter it in any way. The *Letter of Aristeas*, besides supplying an account of the origin of the *Septuagint, which may contain a grain of truth, provides an excellent example of the fruitful fusion of Jewish and Greek cultures. Its various Jewish protagonists, whether coming from Jerusalem or from Alexandria, take pride in their loyalty to their ancestral religion but are, nevertheless, open to the Greek culture around them and are willing to adopt many of its elements.

• Moses Hadas, *Aristeas to Philocrates* (New York, 1951). Emil Schürer, *The History of the Jewish People in the Age of Jesus Christ, 175 B.C.–A.D. 135*, new English version revised and edited by Geza Vermes and Fergus Millar, vol. 3.1 (Edinburgh, 1973), pp. 677–687. R. J. H. Shutt, "Letter of Aristeas," in *The Old Testament Pseudepigrapha*, edited by James H. Charlesworth, vol. 2 (Garden City, N.Y., 1983), pp. 7–34.

—GIDEON BOHAK

LETTING. See HIRING.

LEV, YOSEF BEN DAVID IBN (c.1505–1580), halakhist born in Monastir (Bitola, Yugoslavia); known by the acronym Maharival. By 1535 Lev had arrived in Salonika, where his fame as a legal authority became firmly established. In 1550 he moved to Constantinople, where he taught in the *yeshivah* endowed by Donna Gracia Mendes, a great patron of Jewish scholarship. He wrote the *responsum* that provided the legal basis for the boycott of the port of Ancona in Italy engineered by Donna Gracia in retaliation for the burning of Marranos at the stake. Three volumes of Lev's *responsa* were published during his lifetime and a fourth shortly thereafter (they were published together in Amsterdam in 1726; new edition, Jerusalem, 1959–1960). Each volume also contains *novellae* on tractates of the Talmud.

• Samuel Morell, *Precedent and Judicial Discretion: The Case of Joseph ibn Lev* (Atlanta, 1991).

—SAMUEL MORELL

LEVAYAH. See BURIAL.

LEVI. See LEVITES.

LEVIATHAN, primeval sea monster mentioned in five different contexts (*Is*. 27.1; *Ps*. 74.13–14, 104.25–26; *Jb*. 3.8, 40.25–41.26), all of which are reminiscent of the demythologized battle between God and his rebellious helpers in the primordial era (see BEHEMOTH). The special reference to God's creation of Leviathan in *Psalms* 104.25–26 was probably intended to eliminate any doubt that this dragonlike creature was in any way an independent deity in biblical theology (cf. the creation of the *tanninim* in *Gn*. 1.21 and the parallelism or association between these two terms in *Is*. 27.1 and *Ps*. 74.13–14). In *Isaiah* 27.1 and *Psalms* 74.13–14, Leviathan, the many-headed sea serpent vanquished by the God of Israel in primordial times, allegorically symbolizes the forces of evil in the First Temple period (cf. *Is*. 51.9 from a later period). This symbol of evil and militancy, however, is ultimately derived from ancient, Northwest Semitic mythology, as specifically demonstrated by the Ugaritic literature of the fourteenth through the thirteenth century BCE; for example, "If you smite Lothan [the Ugaritic equivalent of Leviathan], the elusive serpent, destroy the twisting serpent, Shalyat of the seven heads" (KTU 1.5:I:1–3, 27–30). The description of Leviathan in *Job* 41.11–14 as a scaly monster of supernatural strength, breathing smoke from his nostrils and with flames blazing from his mouth, is a demythologized depiction of a dragonlike creature created by God to serve him, but against whom God was later forced to fight in the primordial era.

According to the Talmud (*B. B.* 74b), Leviathan was among the sea monsters mentioned in *Genesis* 1.21. Plotting to destroy the world, he was slain by the Lord, and his flesh was cut up and preserved as sustenance for the righteous in the world to come. Leviathan symbolizes the forces of chaos and evil defeated by the power of good. The kabbalists found esoteric significance in the story of Leviathan, identifying the male and female of the species with *Samael and *Lilith. Maimonides suggested that the Leviathan legends were veiled prophecies referring to future events.

• Chaim Cohen, "Leviathan," in *The Illustrated Dictionary and Concordance of the Bible*, edited by Geoffrey Wigoder et al. (New York, 1986), pp. 620–621. Chaim Cohen in *Sefer H. M. Y. Gevaryahu*, vol. 2 (Jerusalem, 1989), pp. 74–81, in Hebrew. Chaim Cohen, *Biblical Hapax Legomena in the Light of Akkadian and Ugaritic* (Missoula, Mont., 1978), pp. 50–51, 97–100. A. Cooper and M. H. Pope in *Ras Shamra Parallels: The Text from Ugarit and the Bible*, Analecta Orientalia 51, vol. 3, edited by Stan Rummel (Rome, 1981), pp. 369–383, 388–391, 424–428, 441–444. Robert Gordis, *The Book of God and Man: A Study of Job* (Chicago, 1978), pp. 569–572. Marvin H. Pope, *Job*, Anchor Bible, 3d ed. (New York, 1973), pp. 329–346. Naphtali H. Tur-Sinai, *The Book of Job: A New Commentary* (Jerusalem, 1967), pp. 562–575. Mary K. Wakeman, *God's Battle with the Monster: A Study in Biblical Imagery* (Leiden, 1973), pp. 62–68.

—CHAIM COHEN

LEVI BEN AVRAHAM BEN ḤAYYIM (c.1245–1315), French philosopher, encyclopedist, and scholar of the secular sciences. Born in Villefranche-de-Conflent, he lived in Perpignan, Montpellier, Narbonne, Béziers, and finally Arles, where he died. His life was made more difficult by the combination of poverty and persecution by his anti-Maimonist opponents, particularly R. Shelomoh ben Avraham Adret, whom he angered with his allegorical interpretations of scripture. Levi ben Avraham was the author of two extensive works. The first, *Battei ha-Nefesh veha-Leḥashim* is an encyclopedia of the physical and metaphysical sciences, logic, and ethics. Begun in Montpellier in 1276, it consists of 1,846 lines in ten chapters, written entirely in rhyming prose. The second work, *Livyat Ḥen*, was also an encyclopedic work. It contained his more controversial statements on scripture and aroused the opposition of Adret in 1305. *Livyat Ḥen* incorporated three minor works by Levi ben Avraham: *Sodot ha-Torah, Sefer ha-Tekhunah*, and *Shaʿar ha-Arbaʿim be-Koḥot ha-Kokhavim*, covering astronomy, astrology, and metaphysics.

• Ernest Renan and Adolf Neubauer, *Les Rabbins français du commencement du quatorzième siècle* (Paris, 1877), pp. 628–674. Colette Sirat, *A History of Jewish Philosophy in the Middle Ages* (Cambridge, 1990), pp. 243–247.

—STEVEN BALLABAN

LEVI BEN GERSHOM (1288–1344), Provençal Bible commentator, philosopher, talmudist, mathematician, and astronomer; known as Gersonides or by his initials as Ralbag. Levi attempted to solve contradictions between Ptolemy's system and his own astronomical observations, and he invented an instrument to measure the angular distance between two stars, called Jacob's staff, which proved very useful during the following centuries in navigation. He also perfected a camera obscura and propounded an original hypothesis for the movement of the stars. His *Milḥamot Adonai* discusses the major philosophical and theological problems of his time, both supplementing Moses *Maimonides and criticizing him on many points. This work, finished in 1329 (Riva, 1526), is composed of six volumes. Volume one deals with the question of the immortality of the soul; volume two is dedicated to the question of prophecy; volume three to God's knowledge; volume four to divine providence; volume five to astronomy and mathematics (this part of the work, composed of 136 chapters, was not published in printed editions of the book); and volume six to the question of the eternity of the world versus creation *ex nihilo*. Although Levi exhibited a formal attachment to traditional Jewish doctrines, his thinking was more radically Aristotelian than that of most of his predecessors, and he was greatly influenced by the Arab philosopher Averroës, on several of whose works Levi wrote supercommentaries. Whereas Maimonides, where necessary, gave precedence to revelation over Aristotelian doctrine, Levi endeavored to adapt traditional concepts to Averroistic rationalism; thus he differs from Maimonides in holding that the world was created of eternal matter and not *ex nihilo*. Levi believed that divine providence is concerned with universals but not individuals, since God cannot know particulars. Immortality depends on the degree of philosophical knowledge that the soul absorbs as a result of its contact with the active intellect; the most advanced stage of this contact is prophecy. Miracles are possible for God, who created the world from formless primal matter by an act of divine will. Levi's Bible commentaries tend to the philosophical and ethical rather than to plain exposition of the text; his endeavor to interpret rationally every detail in the sacred text led him to make far-reaching use of allegory. Levi, who was one of the last Jewish Aristotelians, aroused much controversy, and his views were attacked by Ḥasda'i ben Avraham *Crescas, who even found some of them heretical. *Milḥamot Adonai* was translated into English as *The Wars of the Lord* by Seymour Feldman (Philadelphia, 1984).

• Gilbert Dahan, ed., *Gersonide en son temps: Science et philosophie medievales* (Louvain, 1991). Gad Freudenthal, ed., *Studies on Gersonides, a Fourteenth-Century Jewish Philosopher–Scientist* (Leiden, 1992). Warren Zev Harvey, "The Philosopher and Politics: Gersonides and Crescas," *Scholars and Scholarship*, edited by Leo Landman (New York, 1990), pp. 51–65. Menachem Kellner, "Introduction to the Commentary on Song of Songs Composed by the Sage Levi ben Gershom, An Annotated Translation," in *From Ancient Israel to Modern Judaism: Intellect in Quest of Understanding, Essays in Honor of Marvin Fox*, edited by Jacob Neusner, 4 vols. (Atlanta, 1989), vol. 2, pp. 187–205.

—FRANCISCO MORENO CARVALHO

LEVI BEN ḤAVIV. See IBN ḤAVIV FAMILY.

LEVI BEN SISI (3d cent.), amora'. He is referred to in the Talmud Bavli simply as Levi. A student of Yehudah ha-Nasi', he also collected and compiled tannaitic traditions. Because they do not appear in the Mishnah of Yehudah ha-Nasi', they are sometimes referred to as "the Mishnah of Levi" and are considered *baraiytot* (see BARAIYTA'). The Talmud refers to a tractate *Qiddushin* "of Levi's academy" (*Qid.* 76b). Thus, Levi represents a bridge between the tannaitic and amoraic periods.

After the death of Yehudah ha-Nasi', Levi studied with Ḥanina' bar Ḥama'. After Ḥanina' became head of the academy, Levi went to Babylonia and settled in Nehardea. There he became the colleague of Abba' bar Abba'. Levi is most often found in dispute with Rav, a major first-generation Babylonian amora'.

• Chanoch Albeck, *Mavo' la-Talmudim* (Tel Aviv, 1987).

—MICHAEL CHERNICK

LEVI BEN YEFET (10th–11th cent.), *Karaite scholar; known in Arabic as Abu Saʿid. He was the son of exegete Yefet ben ʿAli and lived in Jerusalem. He was recognized as an authority on religious law, and his Arabic code of law, translated into Hebrew as *Sefer ha-Mitsvot*, was widely used by later Karaite authors. He taught Yeshuʿa ben Yehudah, who became an important authority. Levi also wrote *Nukat*, a commentary on some books of the Bible; an abridgment of David Alfasi's *Jamiʿ al-Alfaz*; a book discussing the disagreements about legal matters between his father and Sahl ben Matsliaḥ; an abridgment of the biblical commentary of Sahl ben Matsliaḥ; a work on the masoretic differences between Aharon ben Mosheh Ben Asher and Mosheh ben David Ben Naftali; and also, evidently, a work of Kalam theology called *Kitab al-Niʿma*. If Levi were indeed the author of this last book, he would have been the first fully to introduce this school of thought into Karaism. Only small fragments of his code of law have been published, although large parts of it and his other works exist in manuscript.

• Haim H. Ben-Sasson in *Salo Wittmayer Baron Jubilee Volume* (Jerusalem and New York, 1975), pp. 71–90. Haggai Ben-Shammai, *Shenaton ha-Mishpat ha-ʿIvri* 11–12 (1984–86): 99–133. Samuel Poznanski, *Karaite Literary Opponents of Saadiah Gaon* (London, 1908), no. 15.

—DAVID E. SKLARE

LEVIRATE MARRIAGE (Heb. *yibbum*). Biblical law requires the brother of a deceased, childless man to marry the *widow in order that the "firstborn will succeed in the name of the dead brother, and his name will not be blotted out of Israel." If the levir (*yavam*) does not wish to marry the widow (*yevamah*) then the ceremony of *ḥalitsah* must take place before she may remarry (*Dt.* 25.5–10). In the Talmud, the scope of *yibbum* is confined to paternal brothers and to cases in which there is no child of either sex, including a *mamzer* (*Yev*. 22b, 17b). In principle, the obligation to fulfill the *mitsvah* of *yibbum* devolves upon the oldest surviving brother, but in practice any brother may perform it (*Yev*. 24a). Prior to *yibbum* or *ḥalitsah*, the widow is known as a *shomeret yavam*. If she marries someone else, the marriage is prohibited but valid, and the offspring are not *mamzerim* (*Yev*. 13b). Where a levirate marriage would constitute a prohibited but valid union, *ḥalitsah* is still required (*Yev*. 16a). The obligation of *yibbum* applies even to a *yavam* whose birth preceded his brother's death by as little as one day. In such a case, the widow must wait until he comes of legal age in order that he may either marry her or give her *ḥalitsah* (*Yev*. 105b). Biblical law does not require a formal marriage ceremony between *yavam* and *yavamah*, but the rabbis insisted upon such a wedding, which is know as *qiddushei ma'amar* (*Yev*. 4.7). The issue of the precedence of *ḥalitsah* over *yibbum* was debated in the Talmud (*Yev*. 39a–b), and, in the Middle Ages, it resolved itself into a division between Sephardim and Ashkenazim. The former tended to favor *yibbum*, both in order to spare the *yavam* the indignity of *ḥalitsah* and for kabbalistic reasons concerned with the welfare of the dead brother's soul (*Resp. Bet Yosef*, end). A *taqqanah* of the Israeli chief rabbinate in 1950 brought the practice to an end in Erets Yisra'el, even among Sephardi Jews. Ashkenazi authorities followed the view of Abba' Sha'ul (*Yev*. 39b) to the effect that *ḥalitsah* takes precedence. The reason behind this view is that since *yibbum* normally constitutes a forbidden marriage, it is only permitted if performed solely for the purpose of the *mitsvah* of continuing the dead man's line. Any other motivation brings *yibbum* dangerously close to *incest. The additional fact that polygamy was banned by Ashkenazi communities, following the *taqqanah* of R. Gershom, led to the gradual disappearance of *yibbum* among these communities. *Ḥalitsah* takes place before a court of five judges and consists of the *yevamah* reading the relevant biblical passage; drawing off the levir's right shoe, which is made especially for the purpose of *ḥalitsah* and the design of which is specified by the *halakhah*; and spitting on the ground in front of him as a sign of contempt and rebuke for shirking the duty of perpetuating his brother's name. Following *ḥalitsah*, the widow may not marry the levir or any of his brothers, and she is forbidden to a priest. In the modern period, the problem of the apostate levir was one motivation for the development of the concept of conditional marriage, and the problem of absent, recalcitrant, or minor levirs gave rise to a range of prenuptial legal instruments designed to avert the need for *ḥalitsah* in such circumstances. Under Israeli law, a recalcitrant levir may be imprisoned, and *ḥalitsah* may be compelled, in an approach similar to that used to obtain a *get* from a recalcitrant husband. Conservative and Reform Judaism do not recognize levirate marriage, although in some Conservative circles the need for *ḥalitsah* is discussed.

• R. Aharoni, "The Levirate and Human Rights," in *Jewish Law and Current Legal Problems*, edited by Nahum Rakover (Jerusalem, 1984), pp. 67–76. Menachem Elon, *Jewish Law: History, Sources, Principles* (Philadelphia, 1994), pp. 197–199, 389–390, 830–831, 1599–1600. Isaac Klein, *Responsa and Halakhic Studies* (New York, 1975), pp. 13–21. Donald Leggett, *The Levirate and Goel Institutions in the Old Testament with Special Attention to the Book of Ruth* (Cherry Hill, N.J., 1974). Dale Manor, "A Brief History of Levirate Marriage as it Relates to the Bible," *Restoration Quarterly* 27 (1984): 129–142. I. Mattuck, "The Levirate Marriage in Jewish Law," in *Studies in Jewish Literature in Honour of Kaufmann Kohler*, edited by David Philipson (Berlin, 1913), pp. 210ff.

—DANIEL SINCLAIR

LEVITA, ELIYYAHU (c.1468–1549), scholar. Born in Germany, Eliyyahu Levita lived in Italy, where he taught Hebrew to Christians, ecclesiastics, and humanists. In addition to important works—many of which were translated into Latin—on Hebrew grammar, biblical language, and *Masorah (his work *Masoret ha-Masoret* [Venice, 1538; English translation by C. D. Ginsburg (1867; repr. 1968)] lucidly explains masoretic tradition and terminology and influenced scientific Bible study among Jewish and non-Jewish Renaissance circles), he also wrote a Talmudical lexicon (*Tishbi* [Isny, 1541]), an Aramaic dictionary (*Meturgeman*), and a Bible concordance and translated from Hebrew into Yiddish (notably the *Book of Psalms*).

• G. E. Weil, *Elie Lévita, humaniste et massorète, 1469–1549*, Studia Postbiblica, vol. 7 (Leiden, 1963). Israel Zinberg, *A History of Jewish Literature*, vol. 4, *Italian Jewry in the Renaissance Era*, translated and edited by Bernard Martin (Cincinnati and New York, 1974), pp. 43–55.

LEVITES (Heb. Leviyyim), descendants of the ancient tribe of Levi, third of the twelve sons of Jacob. In biblical times, the Levites, to whom Moses himself belonged, were never a unified group assigned to a particular geographic region (*Gn*. 49.7; *Nm*. 18.24; *Dt*. 10.8–9; *Jos*. 13.33) but were indigent religious functionaries dispersed throughout the countryside.

According to the non-Priestly tradition, the privileges of priesthood were given to the entire tribe of Levi, in recognition for its faithfulness to God in the wilderness (*Ex*. 32.25–29; *Dt*. 10.6–9, 33.8–11). Their duties included providing cultic instruction; carrying the Ark; officiating at Temple sacrifice; and receiving the sacred portions of offerings, tithes, and firstborn animals. This role could be performed at local shrines as well as at the central Temple; any member of the tribe of Levi who presented himself at such a location could serve as a priest. *Deuteronomy* agrees, though it does not recognize the legitimacy of local shrines (*Dt*. 17.9, 17.18, 18.1, 21.5, 24.8). It views the provincial Levites as a class of unfortunates to be sustained by the alms of other Israelites (*Dt*. 12.12, 18–19, 14.27, 16.11, 14), including the third-year tithe (*Dt*. 14.28–29), and allows them to join their fellow Levites at the central Temple and serve there as full priests (*Dt*. 18.6–8). This law probably reflects historical development: following the centralization of worship in Jerusalem under King *Josiah, some local Levites were probably permitted to come to Jerusalem (*2 Kgs*. 23.8).

The Priestly literature differs. It maintains that the tribe is composed of two classes: priests (descendants of *Aaron; see PRIESTHOOD), and the remainder of the Levites. The insurrection of Korah (*Nm.* 16–17) established the primacy of the priests over the Levites. The latter were dedicated to God as a substitute for the Israelite *firstborn, who belonged to God from the moment he spared them in Egypt (*Nm.* 3.5–51); they were then consecrated by a special ceremony (*Nm.* 8). The priests alone officiated in the *Tabernacle; the Levites were not permitted to come into contact with the most holy objects. They were assigned the secondary tasks of erecting, dismantling, and carrying the Tabernacle and the sacred objects; forming a human guard, preventing nonpriests from encroaching upon the Tabernacle precincts by surrounding it both in camp and on the march; and assisting the priests with general duties (*Nm.* 18.2). It has been suggested that the name Levi comes from the Hebrew *nilvah* (accompany). They were eligible for the first task from age twenty (*1 Chr.* 23.24), twenty-five (*Nm.* 8.24), or thirty (*Nm.* 4.3) until age fifty. Even those Levites above the age of fifty were not exempt from guard duty (*Nm.* 8.25–26). After entering Erets Yisra'el, the Levites resided in the *Levitical cities, since they were not given any residential or farm land (*Nm.* 18.21–24).

During the time of the First Temple, following the centralization of worship, in particular, nonpriestly Levites became a distinct class. They continued to perform sacred guard duty and assisted in the Temple service. In time they assumed responsibility for all musical aspects of worship: singing of psalms of prayer and praise, and instrumental accompaniment first reflected in *Kings* and stressed in *Chronicles*. By Second Temple times, the Levites were few in number (*Ezr.* 2.36–39, 8.15–19; *Neh.* 11.3–24), indicating that the actual composition of the Levitical tribe had changed over the centuries. Nevertheless the distinction between priests and (all other) Levites is rigorously maintained by Ezekiel (though not by Malachi) as well as in post-biblical Jewish tradition down to the present. Second Temple practice, as reflected in *Ezra*, *Nehemiah*, and *Chronicles*, as well as rabbinic law institutionalized the separation, further dividing Levites (like the priests) into twenty-four divisions that functioned in rotation throughout the year. Virtually all cultic functions and privileges, including tithes, were removed from the Levites. They served as gatekeepers, and the main emphasis was placed on their musical role, performing "song and psalmody" as a prominent feature of the Temple service (for example, the festival Musaf prayer). Even in post-Temple Judaism, the identity of Levitical families and their secondary status to that of the priests have been preserved; a priest is still called first to the reading of the Torah, followed by a Levite; Levites still perform the ritual washing of the hands of the priests when the latter are to pronounce *Birkat ha-Kohanim in the synagogue.

• Menahem Haran, *Temples and Temple-Service in Ancient Israel* (Oxford, 1978), pp. 58–111. Samuel E. Loewenstamm, *From Babylon to Canaan* (Jerusalem, 1992), pp. 55–65. J. Gordon McConville, *Law and Theology in Deuteronomy*, Journal for the Study of the Old Testament, Supplement Series 33 (Sheffield, Eng., 1984), pp. 124–153. Jacob Milgrom, *Numbers*, The JPS Torah Commentary (Philadelphia, 1990), pp. 14–32, 61–66, 154–157, 341–344, 369–371, 432–436. Jacob Milgrom, *Studies in Levitical Terminology*, vol. 1, *The Encroacher and the Levite* (Berkeley, 1970). Julia M. O'Brien, *Priest and Levite in Malachi*, Dissertation Series (Society of Biblical Literature) 121 (Atlanta, 1990), pp. 1–26.

—BARUCH J. SCHWARTZ

LEVITICAL CITIES, towns set apart for members of the tribe of Levi. According to the Priestly tradition in the Bible, God instructed Moses to select forty-eight walled cities from the territories of the tribes and assign them to the *Levites (*Nm.* 35.1–8). These towns were to include the six *asylum cities; according to rabbinic law, all forty-eight became cities of asylum. Since the Levites, as a sacerdotal tribe, were given no residential or farm land, their city homes were their sole residences. They were inalienable: according to *Leviticus* 25.32–34, the Levite who sold his house could, unlike other Israelites (*Lv.* 29–31), purchase it back even after a year had elapsed, and in any case it would revert to him in the jubilee (see YOVEL). The Levites were also entitled to pasture their flocks in a two-thousand-cubit square around the assigned towns; some commentators believe that the amount of pasture land expanded as the town grew. This land, however, was not for cultivation and remained the property of the tribe in whose territory it was located. For their livelihood, the Levites depended on tithes, not agriculture. Probably the towns themselves were not exclusively Levite; the local tribe must have also made up a portion of the population. The actual list of towns, including ten on the east side of the Jordan and thirteen that are exclusively priestly cities, is given in *Joshua* 21; it appears again with minor differences in *1 Chronicles* 6.

• Menahem Haran, *Temples and Temple-Service in Ancient Israel* (Oxford, 1978), pp. 84–131. Jacob Milgrom, *Numbers*, The JPS Torah Commentary (Philadelphia, 1990), pp. 288–290, 502–504. Jacob Milgrom, "The Levitic Town: An Exercise in Realistic Planning," *Journal of Jewish Studies* 33 (1982): 185–188. John R. Spencer, "The Levitical Cities: A Study of the Role and Function of the Levites in the History of Israel," Ph.D. dissertation, The University of Chicago, 1980.

—BARUCH J. SCHWARTZ

LEVITICUS, BOOK OF (Heb. *Va-Yiqra'* [And (the Lord) Called]), third book of the Torah, whose Hebrew title is from the opening phrase of the book. It was also called *Torat Kohanim* (Instruction for the Priests) in rabbinic times; hence, its Greek name *Levitikon* (Things Pertaining to the Levites; i.e., the priests, who are from the tribe of Levi). *Leviticus* takes up the biblical narrative from the time the divine presence enters the Tabernacle on the first day of Nisan in the year following the Exodus. From within, God calls to Moses and imparts to him, in a series of encounters, the laws pertaining to sacrifice (chaps. 1–7), priestly sobriety (10.8–11), permitted and forbidden foods (chap. 11), the purification and atonement following physical defilement (chaps. 12–15), the annual Yom Kippur, on which the Tabernacle is cleansed of Israel's impurities (chap. 16), prohibitions against blood and profane slaughter (chap. 17), sexual crimes (chaps. 18 and 20), miscellaneous regulations assuring Israel's holiness (chap. 19), the qualifications for priestly service (chap. 21) and for sacrificial animals (chap. 22), the weekly Sabbath and annual festivals (chap. 23), the oil for the Tabernacle lamp (24.1–4), the showbread (24.5–9), the principle of an eye for an eye in damages (24.17–22), and the sabbatical and jubilee years, including laws of slavery and property rights (chap. 25). This last divine address concludes with a lengthy speech promising reward for compliance and punishment for failure to obey (26.3–45), after which there follows a summary (26.46). Thereafter, the laws of vows and tithes (chap. 27) are appended. The only events that interrupt the lawgiving are the dedication of the priesthood (chap. 8) and of the Tabernacle (chap. 9), the crime and immediate death of Aaron's sons (10.1–7, 12–20), and the crime of the blasphemer and his execution (24.10–16, 23). The lawgiving takes about one and a half months, after which the preparations for leaving Sinai commence (*Nm.* 1). Bible critics assign *Leviticus* to the Priestly source and agree that chapters 17–26, along with some other passages, belong to a distinct literary stratum (the *Holiness Code) that may be later than the kernel of the Priestly document. *Leviticus* is divided into ten weekly portions, read in the synagogue from early spring until before Shavu'ot. In Talmudic times, it was customary for small children to begin their study of the Bible with *Leviticus*, on the grounds that it is fitting for the pure (i.e., children) to engage in the study of purity (i.e., the laws of purification and atonement). See also ATONEMENT; DIETARY LAWS; IMPURITY; LEVITES; PRIESTHOOD; PRIESTLY CODE; SACRIFICES.

• John E. Hartley, *Leviticus*, Word Biblical Commentary, vol. 4 (Dallas, 1992). Israel Knohl, *The Sanctuary of Silence* (Minneapolis, 1995). Baruch A. Levine, *Leviticus*, The JPS Torah Commentary (Philadelphia, 1989). Jacob Milgrom, *Leviticus 1–16*, The Anchor Bible, vol. 3 (New York, 1991).

—BARUCH J. SCHWARTZ

LEVITICUS RABBAH, an aggadic *midrash* to the *Book of *Leviticus*, included in the compilation commonly referred to as *Midrash Rabbah. Compiled in Erets Yisra'el in approximately the fifth century CE, *Leviticus Rabbah* contains exegetical comments, parables, and stories—many containing popular and folkloristic elements—in Rabbinic Hebrew and Galilean Aramaic, relating to verses in the *Book of Leviticus*; these are divided into thirty-seven sections (*parashiyyot*). Unlike other compilations of the period (see GENESIS RABBAH), the Midrashic comments contained in a *parashah* of *Leviticus Rabbah* are related to only a few selected verses from the relevant biblical pericope. Each section typically includes several, usually lengthy, *petiḥot* (see PETIḤAH), followed by a collection of comments and stories, which, while formally expounding one or more verses from the pericope, often coalesce around a single theme. Many sections conclude with a message of comfort concerning personal or national salvation. For these reasons *Leviticus Rabbah* is described as a homiletical *midrash* as opposed to an exegetical *midrash*, as exemplified by *Genesis Rabbah*. Many parallels to the *midrash* are found in other rabbinic works, especially the Talmud Yerushalmi, *Genesis Rabbah*, and *Pesiqta' de-Rav Kahana'*; the last includes entire sections almost identical with those in *Leviticus Rabbah*.

• Chanoch Albeck, "Midrash Vayyiqra' Rabbah," in *Louis Ginzberg Jubilee Volume* (New York, 1946), Hebrew section. Harry Freedman and Maurice Simon, eds. and trans., *Midrash Rabbah* (London, 1961). Mordecai Margulies, ed., *Midrash Va-Yiqra' Rabbah* (Jerusalem, 1953–1960). Jacob Neusner, *Judaism and Scripture: The Evidence of Leviticus Rabbah* (Chicago, 1986). Hermann Leberecht Strack and Günter Stemberger, *Introduction to the Talmud and Midrash*, rev. and updat. ed., translated by Markus Bockmuehl (Minneapolis, 1992). Leopold Zunz, *Ha-Derashot be-Yisra'el ve-Hishtalshelutan ha-Historit*, edited by Chanoch Albeck (1892; Jerusalem, 1974).

—PAUL MANDEL

LEVI YITSḤAQ OF BERDICHEV (1740–1809), Hasidic master. He was among the leading disciples of *Dov Ber of Mezhirech, and his notebooks of his master's writings are the source for several published collections of Dov Ber's teachings. Levi Yitsḥaq served briefly as rabbi of Ryczwol, and later in Zelechów and in Pinsk. He had to leave both of the latter communities because of opposition to Hasidism. Publicly identified as a leader of the new movement, Levi Yitsḥaq engaged in a debate with R. Avraham Katzenellenbogen in 1781, and both parties claimed victory. In 1785 Levi Yitsḥaq became both communal rabbi and Hasidic *rebbi* of Berdichev, a major Jewish community in the Ukraine, where he remained until his death. He was the leading representative of the Mezhirech school of Hasidism in that area. His own book, *Qedushat Levi* (Berdichev, 1811), is a collection of homilies that continues Dov Ber's line of thought, including the insubstantiality of the corporeal world, the possibility of worshiping God through all things, and the identity of Torah with the essential, innermost self of every Jew. The figure of the *tsaddiq* is to be found quite frequently in the *Qedushat Levi*, though somewhat less prominently than in the writings of some others in the Mezhirech school. Other teachings are included in *Shemu'ah Tovah* (Warsaw, 1938). There are several Yiddish collections of tales exclusively devoted to him: *Niflo'os Qedushas Levi* (Bilgoraj, 1911), *Niflo'os Beys Helevi* (Piotrków, 1911), and *Melits Yoisher* (Lwów, 1929), and he figures prominently in many other collections. After Yisra'el ben Eli'ezer *Ba'al Shem Tov, Levi Yitsḥaq is the favorite Hasidic master in the Jewish folk imagination. Such widespread veneration is said to stem from his love for all Israel, including both the simple and the sinners, and his willingness to carry their cases before God, even arguing with heavenly justice and daring to reprove God for the sufferings of Israel.

• Samuel Dresner, *Levi Yitzhak of Berditchev* (New York, 1974). Shalom Guttman, *Tif'eret Beit Levi* (Jassy, 1909).

—ARTHUR GREEN

LEWANDOWSKI, LOUIS (1821–1894), composer and the first Jewish choral director. He left his native Poland at the age of twelve, following the death of his mother, and became a boy soprano under Cantor Ascher Lion of Berlin. With financial support from Alexander Mendelssohn (a Jewish cousin of Felix), Lewandowski became the first Jew to study at the Berlin Academy of Fine Arts. In 1840, he returned to serve Cantor Lion as choir director at the Old Synagogue in Berlin. Lion was succeeded by Cantor Abraham J. Lichtenstein, who inspired Lewandowski to arrange synagogue song for four-part singing. In 1866, after studying with Salomon *Sulzer in Vienna, Lewandowski was named choral director of the

New Synagogue in Berlin. Lewandowski's *Kol Rinah u-Tefillah* for solo and two-part chorus was published in 1871; his *Todah Ve-Zimrah* (1876–1882), featuring works for solo, congregational singing, and four-part chorus (with optional organ accompaniment), included compositions for the entire calendar year. Lewandowski's solo recitatives are reminiscent of the eastern European tradition of his youth, which he studied further with immigrant cantors from the region. His choral works, much in the style of Felix Mendelssohn, are more Western in flavor.

• M. Davidsohn, "Louis Lewandowsky," in *Proceedings of the Fifth Annual Convention of the Cantors Assembly* (New York, 1952), pps. 30–34. Abraham Z. Idelsohn, *Jewish Music in Its Historical Development* (New York, 1929; repr. New York, 1967; Westport, Conn., 1981), pps. 269–284.

—MARSHA BRYAN EDELMAN

LEX TALIONIS. See JUS TALIONIS.

LIBATION (Heb. *nesekh*), offering of wine or oil. Each of the animal *sacrifices in the Temple was accompanied by a *meal offering and a libation (*Nm*. 15.1–16) of wine, which was poured into a bowl in the southwest corner of the *altar, from where it flowed through a shallow cavity into the depths of the altar foundation (*Suk*. 48a). In the case of a lamb, the libation consisted of a quarter *hin* of wine; for a ram, a third of a *hin*; and for an ox, a half *hin*. Sometimes the sacrifice (especially a meal offering) was offered with *oil, which was either poured over the sacrifice or in which the sacrifice was soaked. During Sukkot, when prayers for rain (see TEFILLAT GESHEM) are offered, water libation formed part of the Temple service.

• Menahem Haran, *Temples and Temple-Service in Ancient Israel* (Oxford, 1978), pp. 216–217.

—SHALOM PAUL

LIBEL. See SLANDER.

LIBERAL JUDAISM. See REFORM JUDAISM.

LIBERTY. See FREEDOM.

LIEBERMAN, SAUL (1898–1983), Talmudic scholar. Born in Motol, Belorussia, Lieberman attended the *yeshivot* of Malch and Slobodka as well as the University of Kiev. Immigrating to Jerusalem in 1928, he concluded his studies of Talmudic philology and Greek language and literature at Hebrew University. He lectured at Hebrew University and was affiliated with the Mizrachi Teachers' Seminary and the Harry Fischel Institute for Talmudic Research until 1940, when he joined the faculty of the Jewish Theological Seminary of America in New York. A preeminent Talmud scholar, Lieberman attracted and trained scores of students in both Israel and the United States. His scholarship addressed all aspects of Jewish life in Palestine during Talmudic times: his *Greek in Jewish Palestine* (1942) and *Hellenism in Jewish Palestine* (1950) discussed the role of Hellenistic culture; his controversial *Talmudah shel Keisaryah* (1931) suggested a new chronology for the compilation of the Jerusalem Talmud; and his *Tosefet Ri'shonim* (4 vols. [1937–1939]) and *Tosefta' ki-Feshutah* (10 vols. [1955–1967]) introduced the Tosefta' to modern critical study.

• Shamma Friedman, ed., *Sefer ha-Zikkaron le-Rabbi Sha'ul Liberman* (Jerusalem and New York, 1993).

—DIDIER Y. REISS

LIEN. A debtor's personal obligation to repay his creditor automatically creates a lien upon the debtor's real property, referred to variously as *aḥarayut* or *shi'bud nekhasim*, thereby encumbering the property in the creditor's favor until the loan is repaid or the debtor is released by the creditor. The lien attaches to all of the debtor's property, including property acquired by the debtor after the date of the loan, unless the parties restrict the lien to specific assets.

The lien follows the property into the hands of subsequent purchasers, but only if the debt transaction creating the lien was consummated in writing, thereby achieving a level of publicity deemed sufficient to put subsequent purchasers on notice about the lien. The creditor is restricted from collecting the debt from a subsequent purchaser so long as the debtor himself possesses sufficient assets to repay the debt, and he must levy against later purchasers before he may turn to earlier ones.

• Menachem Elon, ed., *The Principles of Jewish Law* (Jerusalem, 1975), pp. 287–294. Isaac Herzog, *The Main Institutions of Jewish Law*, 2d ed. (London, 1965), vol. 1, chap. 20, pp. 345–360.

—BEN TZION GREENBERGER

LIFE is considered God's supreme blessing, sanctified, breathed into humans by God himself (*Gn*. 2.7). The Torah itself is a "tree of life" (*Prv*. 3.18), and by giving it to Israel, God has planted eternal life in our midst. The purpose of the commandments is "that man shall live by them" (*Lv*. 18.5), a phrase to which the rabbis added "and not die by them" (*Yoma'* 85b). Hence, all laws—with the exception only of the cardinal sins of idolatry, bloodshed, and illicit sex (incest and adultery)—are liable to suspension in case of *danger to life (*San*. 74a). As long as there is life there is hope, and "a living dog is better than a dead lion" (*Eccl*. 9.4). The biblical emphasis on life in this world (see *Ps*. 115.17, "The dead praise not the Lord, neither any that go down into silence") was generally maintained in Jewish tradition, in spite of the increasing importance of belief in an afterlife, which was perceived as the true life eternal. The positive attitude toward physical life is also attested by the ʿAmidah's dogmatic affirmation of the bodily resurrection of the dead, rather than the expectation of eternal life of the soul in a spiritual realm. The infinite value of every human life is solemnly asserted in the court's instruction to witnesses in capital trials: "Whoever destroys one life is as if he destroyed a whole world, and whoever preserves one life is as if he preserved a whole world" (*San*. 4.5). Hastening death even by one minute is considered tantamount to bloodshed, and rabbinic law prohibits *euthanasia.

• A. S. Abraham, *The Comprehensive Guide to Medical Halacha* (Jerusalem, 1996). Natalia Berger, ed., *Jews and Medicine: Religion, Culture, Science* (Tel Aviv, 1995), museum exhibition catalogue. Barry D. Cytron, *When Life Is in the Balance: Life and Death Decisions in Light of the Jewish Tradition*, 2d ed. (New York, 1994).

LIFE, BOOK OF. See BOOK OF LIFE.

LIFE, DANGER TO. See DANGER.

LIFNIM MI-SHURAT HA-DIN (לִפְנִים מִשּׁוּרַת הַדִּין; inside the line of justice). The common equivalent of this Talmudic concept is the notion of going beyond the letter of the law in order to do the right and good deed (*Dt.* 6.18) and not to rest content with the mere fulfillment of the literal requirements of the law. The concept is derived from the biblical injunction to follow the "practices of the Torah" (*Ex.* 18.20), which is interpreted by R. El'azar to refer to *lifnim mi-shurat ha-din* (*Mekhilta'*, *Yitro* 2, 198). The Talmud cites as examples of *lifnim mi-shurat ha-din* the restoration of lost property to its owners when the law does not so require (*B. M.* 24b) and the payment of compensation for damage caused as a result of erroneous expert advice for which, by law, there is generally no liability. This type of ethical behavior is not legally required, but the court may, in certain cases, enforce obligations which fall under this rubric.

• Menachem Elon, *Jewish Law: History, Sources, Principles* (Philadelphia, 1994), pp. 155–167. Aaron Kirschenbaum, *Equity in Jewish Law* (New York, 1991), pp. 109–135. —DANIEL SINCLAIR

LIGHT. In addition to its physical properties, light serves almost universally as a symbol of life, blessing, peace, knowledge, understanding, redemption, the soul, and good; whereas darkness represents chaos, death, ignorance, sin, suffering, and evil. God's first creation was light (*Gn.* 1.3–4), and in later theology, God himself was defined as light and the source of light. The Torah, too, is "a light," and to be blessed is to "walk in the light of God's face." In the Second Temple period the theology of light was further developed. Sectarian circles (see QUMRAN COMMUNITY) expressed the opposition between God's elect and the reprobate as one between the children of light and the children of darkness; this usage subsequently passed into the New Testament. Hellenistic philosophers, *Philo in particular, and Neoplatonists made much use of light symbolism when speaking of spiritual and divine realities. In mystical literature both the symbolism and the experience of higher, heavenly (viz., spiritual) light played an important role. Kabbalistic writers, especially, use light synonymously with divine substance, spiritual essence, and the like and describe cosmic and mystical processes in terms of the emanation and retraction (**tsimtsum*) of supernal lights. The symbolic significance of light is reflected by the frequent ritual use of lights, in particular of *candles and candelabra. From the *Menorah in the Temple to the Sabbath lamp and the lights of Ḥanukkah, from the **ner tamid* in the synagogue to the medieval custom of lighting a candle for the soul of the deceased (in the mourning period and on the **yortsayt*), Jewish thought and practice share the perennial symbolic significance of light.

• Erwin R. Goodenough, *By Light, Light: The Mystical Gospel of Hellenistic Judaism* (New Haven, 1935). Yigael Yadin, *The Scroll of the War of the Sons of Light against the Sons of Darkness* (London, 1962).

LIGHT, PERPETUAL. See NER TAMID.

LIGHTS, FEAST OF. See ḤANUKKAH.

LIGHTS, KINDLING OF. See KINDLING OF LIGHTS.

LILIENTHAL, MAX (1815–1882), rabbi and educator. Born in Munich, he was appointed preacher and Jewish school director in Riga in 1839, working with the czarist government in its plan to found state Jewish schools that would combine religious and secular education. The Jewish community, the Ḥasidim in particular, felt that the object of the czarist proposal was to undermine traditional Jewish education and encourage assimilation and conversion to Christianity. Despite the opposition of Lithuanian Jewry, Lilienthal continued to promote the scheme. In 1842 he was invited to be rabbi of Odessa, but now suspicious himself about the motivations of the government, which was issuing anti-Jewish legislation, he resigned his post in 1844 and immigrated to the United States. There he officiated as a rabbi first in New York City and then, in 1854, in Cincinnati, where he served the Bene Israel congregation and taught at Hebrew Union College. He was a moderate reformer who worked with Isaac Mayer *Wise in disseminating Reform Judaism in the Midwest. Lilienthal adopted a universalistic Judaism, opposing the belief in a return to Zion. He was president of the *beit din* of the American association of rabbis formed by himself and Wise and wrote extensively in the Jewish press.

• Kerry M. Olitzky, Lance Jonathan Sussman, and Malcolm H. Stern, eds., *Reform Judaism in America* (Westport, Conn., 1993), pp. 128–130. David Philipson, ed., *Max Lilienthal, American Rabbi: Life and Writings* (New York, 1915).

LILITH (Heb. Lilit), an ancient (possibly Sumerian) name for a goddess, which occurs once in the Bible. Because of the similarity of the name Lilith to the word *laylah* (night), the name came to be interpreted as referring to a nocturnal spirit. In Talmudic legend she is described as the first wife of Adam, before Eve, and as the mother of demons born from this union. She plays a principal role in a ninth-century narrative cycle, the *Pseudo-Ben Sira* or the *Alphabet of Ben Sira*: as Adam's first wife, created, like him, from the earth, she demanded equality with him. When he refused, she ran away and united with "the great demon." Three angels pursued her by God's command: Sanoy, Sansanoy, and Samangelof (probably a parody of Heikhalot angelic names). They let her go when she promised not to harm babies protected by amulets carrying their names. Following this story, Lilith became a demon who harms babies and young children. She also began to appear as the sexual temptress of pious individuals. In the kabbalistic system of R. Yitsḥaq ben Ya'aqov ha-Kohen of Castile, formulated in his *Ma'amar 'al ha-'Atsilut* in the second half of the thirteenth century, Lilith is the spouse of *Samael and the feminine counterpart of the *Shekhinah in the system of evil powers. He also distinguished between the "elder Lilith," who is Samael's wife, and "the younger Lilith," who is the wife of *Asmodeus and a lower power in the system of evil, but coveted by Samael. Lilith is described in this treatise as "half woman, half fire." The Zoharic mythology adopted all these motifs and added many others. Subsequently Lilith became a central figure of evil in popular and folkloristic tales. A popular Jewish feminist magazine has been entitled *Lilith*.

• Aviva Cantor, "The Lilith Question," in *On Being a Jewish Feminist: A Reader*, edited by Susannah Heschel (New York, 1983), pp. 40–50. Joseph Dan, "Samuel, Lilith and the Concept of Evil in Early Kabbalah," *AJS Review* 5 (1980): 17–40. Judith Plaskow, "The Jewish Feminist: Conflict in Identities," in *The Jewish Woman: New Perspectives*, edited by Elizabeth Koltun (New York, 1976), pp. 8–10. Judith Plaskow, *Standing Again at Sinai: Judaism from a Feminist Perspective* (San Francisco, 1990), pp. 54–55. Eli Yassif, *Sippurei Ben Sira bi-Yemei ha-Beinayim* (Jerusalem, 1983).

—JOSEPH DAN

LIMA, MOSHEH BEN YITSḤAQ YEHUDAH (1610–1666), Lithuanian rabbinical scholar. After serving as rabbi in Slonim, he was appointed *av beit din* in Vilna, where his colleagues were R. *Shabbetai ben Me'ir ha-Kohen and R. Efrayim ben Yaʿaqov ha-Kohen. The Lithuanian rabbis had rejected the pilpulistic approach to Talmudic study common in Poland and were adopting new and less dialectical approaches. Lima wrote *Ḥelqat ha-Meḥoqeq* (Kraków, 1670) on *Shulḥan ʿArukh, Even ha-ʿEzer*, dealing with laws of personal status. It was criticized by R. Shemu'el ben Uri Shraga Phoebus in his *Beit Shemu'el*, but the two men collaborated on *Qunteres ha-ʿAgunot*, dealing with the laws of *ʿagunot* (incorporated into standard editions of the *Shulḥan ʿArukh*). Unlike Ashkenazi commentators (but like the Sephardim), they based their decisions on later commentators without going back to the Talmud and geonic literature.

• Ḥayyim Biton, *Sefer Lev Ḥayyim* (Jerusalem, 1992). J. L. Joachimsthal, *Reshimat Sefarim: Catalog der reichhaltigen Sammlungen hebraischer und jüdischer Bücher Handschriften . . . nachgelassen von Meijer Lehren, Akiba Lehren und Moses de Lima* (Amsterdam, 1899).

—SHALOM BAR-ASHER

LIMITATION OF ACTIONS, or statutes of limitations, are essentially not part of Jewish jurisprudence. The Talmud, for example (*Ket*. 104a), affirms that a creditor may seek to recover a debt at any time.

There were a number of classical exceptions to this rule. The Talmud recounts that there is a twenty-five year statute of limitations on the collection of a *ketubbah* payment (*Ket*. 104a). A two-year statute of limitations was placed on the right of a widow to collect maintenance from the estate of her late husband (*Ket*. 96a).

In certain circumstances, Jewish law would view the delay in bringing a lawsuit for the collection of a debt as a presumption that the debt was not, in fact, valid, although this is closer to the modern legal doctrine of estoppel than to limitation of actions (see *Shulḥan ʿArukh, Ḥoshen Mishpat* 61.0 and 98.1).

• Menachem Elon, *Jewish Law: History, Sources, Principles* (Philadelphia, 1994), pp. 1724–1727. Menachem Elon, ed., *Principles of Jewish Law* (Jerusalem, 1975), pp. 596–599.

—MICHAEL BROYDE

LIPKIN, YISRA'EL. See SALANTER, YISRA'EL.

LIQQUT ʿATSAMOT (לִקּוּט עֲצָמוֹת; gathering of the bones), the collection of bones for final burial. In ancient Erets Yisra'el, the deceased were not immediately buried in the ground. They were placed in burial chambers until their bodies were reduced to skeletons. Then, after a year, the bones were removed by the children of the deceased and buried. Mourning rites were observed on that day with the omission of formal acts of comforting the mourners and a full eulogy. However, it was permitted to offer words of praise. The bones were treated with reverence, and the ceremony could not take place on the intermediate days of the festivals, since it was incompatible with the joy of festival times.

• Maurice Lamm, *The Jewish Way in Death and Mourning* (New York, 1969). Eric Meyers, *Jewish Ossuaries: Rebirth and Reburial: Secondary Burials in Their Ancient Near Eastern Setting*, Biblica et Orientalia 24 (Rome, 1971).

—PETER KNOBEL

LITURGICAL RESPONSES. See RESPONSES, LITURGICAL.

LITURGY (in the Septuagint, Gr. *leitourgia* [service, worship]), the public prayer service. In biblical times the divine service par excellence was the one performed by the *priesthood with *sacrifices and the singing of psalms by the *Levites at the Jerusalem *Temple. Only at the end of the Second Temple period was there an increasing participation of the ordinary worshiper in Temple liturgy (see MAʿAMAD). Also at that time, a new focus of worship, that of studying Torah on the Sabbath, became a regular phenomenon in Jewish religious practice. Only after the destruction of the Temple in 70 CE did Jewish liturgy center in the *synagogue, combining reading of the Bible with fixed prayers (see ʿAMIDAH; SHEMAʿ), which were the main features of liturgy in Talmudic times, framed by either *silent prayer or public readings (see PESUQEI DE-ZIMRAʾ). Until the third century, the statutory prayers were allowed to be recited in any language, but Greek was the most popular. From then on, the dominant language used in the liturgy was Hebrew, with a few Aramaic exceptions, such as the *Qaddish. Only in the nineteenth century was the vernacular reintroduced into Reform liturgy. After the Talmudic period, Jewish liturgy was expanded with the introduction of poetic embellishments of the prayers, the *piyyut*. This innovation originated in late Byzantine Erets Yisra'el, and from there spread to Europe, where it flourished from the sixth through the thirteenth century. The dominance of the Babylonian center in the geonic period is reflected in the codification of the liturgy in the eighth to the eleventh century. This step involved fixing the wordings of the prayers, providing instructions in ceremonial law, and determining a selection of *piyyutim*. Out of these efforts the first *prayer books were created. In the following centuries, Jewish liturgy maintained a basic unity in structure and in its main features, inherited from former periods, but also exhibiting a rich variety of regional rites, defined by differences in wording, the selection of the poetic parts, and details in ritual. Printing (which led to standardization), *codification of law, and the spread of Jewish mysticism (*Kabbalah) had a growing influence on liturgy. At the beginning of the nineteenth century in Europe, the growing stress on devotion found its expression in the introduction of new forms focusing on the experience of the participant (see HASIDISM; REFORM JUDASIM). In Israel, developments in the liturgy are characterized by mutual influences.

Jewish liturgy is not only defined by the text itself (see MAḤAZOR), but by nearly two thousand years of evaluation of it in various disciplines; this has produced a large literature on the subject. The main focuses of traditional approaches are the halakhic, defining liturgy as the performance of divine prescriptions according to written and *oral law (see HALAKHAH); the philosophical, asking the question (in Talmudic times) how can I worship God and (in the Middle Ages) who am I that I should worship God?; and the mystical, regarding prayer as an act of communication. Modern scientific approaches, pioneered by the *Wissenschaft des Judentums movement in the early nineteenth century, include the philological, based on textual and historical research; the literary, seeing liturgy as text and examining the relationship of form and content; and the anthropological, seeing the liturgy as ceremony, involving social and psychological issues, and regarding such phenomena as *music and synagogue art as integral parts of Jewish liturgy. Under the influence of the Enlightenment and Emancipation, the various non-Orthodox trends have introduced modifications of the traditional liturgy, including abbreviations and omission of prayers felt to be incompatible with their beliefs.

• Ismar Elbogen, *Jewish Liturgy: A Comprehensive History*, translated by Raymond P. Scheindlin (Philadelphia, 1993). Moshe Greenberg, *Biblical Prose Prayer: As a Window to the Popular Religion of Ancient Israel*, The Taubman Lectures in Jewish Studies, 6th ser. (Berkeley, 1983). Menahem Haran, *Temples and Temple-Service in Ancient Israel* (Winona Lake, Ind., 1985). Joseph Heinemann, *Prayer in the Talmud: Forms and Patterns*, Studia Judaica 9 (Berlin and New York, 1977). Lawrence A. Hoffman, *Beyond the Text: A Holistic Approach to Liturgy* (Bloomington and Indianapolis, 1987). Lawrence A. Hoffman, *The Canonization of the Synagogue Service* (Notre Dame, 1979). Lawrence A. Hoffman, ed., *Sha'are Binah: Gates of Understanding* (New York, 1977). Moshe Idel, *Kabbalah: New Perspectives* (New Haven, 1988). Louis Jacobs, *Hasidic Prayer* (New York, 1973). Stefan C. Reif, *Judaism and Hebrew Prayer: New Perspectives on Jewish Liturgical History* (Cambridge, 1993). Joseph Tabory, *Reshimat Ma'amarim be-'Inyenei Tefillah u-Mo'adim* (Jerusalem, 1992–1993).

—PETER LENHARDT

LOANS. The injunction to lend money to one in need is a positive precept (*Ex.* 22.24; *Lv.* 25.36), while the refusal to grant a loan involves the transgression of a prohibition. The Bible warns against refusing to lend money at the approach of the **shemittah*, during which debts were relaxed (see PEROZBOL). The rabbis enacted several ordinances to facilitate borrowing and regarded the lending of money as more important than charity (*Shab.* 63a), since it enables the borrower to stand on his own feet without feeling shame or humiliation. As potential recipients of loans, the poor take precedence over the rich, relatives over strangers, local persons over those from other towns. Where no date for repayment is stipulated, the normal loan period is thirty days, and repayment may not be claimed before the end of this period (*Mak.* 3b). Upon default of the borrower, no claim may be made against the guarantor before the thirty-day period ends. A loan contracted without recourse to a written deed is secured only by the movable property of the borrower; a loan contracted by deed is secured also by his immovable property. No interest may be demanded or offered between a borrower and lender who are both Jews (*Ex.* 22.24). See also MONEYLENDING.

• Menachem Elon, *Jewish Law: History, Sources, Principles*, 4 vols. (Philadelphia, 1994). Shelly Tennenbaum, "Immigrants and Capital: Jewish Loan Societies in the United States, 1880–1940," Ph.D. dissertation, Brandeis University, 1986.

LOGOS (Gr.; word, speech, reason), in Jewish theology, the word of God by which the universe was created. Although in a sense an aspect of the divine, the Logos often appears as a separate entity, namely, a half-personal *emanation of God. The concept was appropriated by *Philo in order to bridge the gap between the transcendent God of Judaism and the divine principle experienced by human beings. This view of the Logos as a mediating principle between God and material creation could link up with biblical references to the creative "Word of God," by which the heavens were made (*Ps.* 33.6) and with the concept of *meimra'* (Aram.; word) in *Targum literature (especially as it appears in Targum Onkelos). In *Proverbs*, *Job*, and in certain apocryphal books the concept of divine *wisdom (*ḥokhmah*) has some of the qualities of the Logos. Early Christianity took up the notion of Logos and in the *Gospel of John* (1.1), the Logos as an eternal, divine principle is said to have been made flesh in the person of Jesus. This emphasizes the redemptive function of the Logos as an exclusive vehicle of salvation, rather than its creative or revelatory function. As such, it became a major feature of Christian theology, and this fact possibly contributed to the disappearance of the whole Philonic tradition from Jewish thought. In "kabbalistic literature," concepts similar to that of Logos reappear in the doctrine of **sefirot*.

• Henry A. Fischel, ed., *Essays in Greco-Roman and Related Talmudic Literature* (New York, 1977). David Winston, *Logos and Mystical Theology in Philo of Alexandria* (Cincinnati, 1985).

LONZANO, MENAḤEM (c.1550–1623), kabbalist, poet, and rabbinical editor, who lived and wrote in Constantinople, Safed, Venice, and Jerusalem. He wrote and published Midrashic commentaries and linguistic notes on the Talmud, as well as prayers and moralistic poetry. He criticized Yitsḥaq *Luria's interpretation of the esoteric parts of the Zohar and became a controversial figure among the kabbalists, who attacked him for such an audacious attitude. Lonzano traveled through many Mediterranean towns in his search for kabbalistic manuscripts to be studied and published. He opposed the poet Yisra'el ben Mosheh *Najara for his erotic descriptions of the relationship between the God of Israel and his people, accusing Najara of sacrilege.

• Shaul Chana Kook, *'Iyyunim u-Meḥqarim* (Jerusalem, 1959), pp. 241–245. Gershom Gerhard Scholem, *Kitvei ha-Yad ha-'Ivriyyim*, vol. 1, *Kabbalah* (Jerusalem, 1930), pp. 241–245. —NISSIM YOSHA

LOOKSTEIN, JOSEPH (1902–1979), Orthodox rabbi in the United States. A proponent of the harmonization of Orthodoxy with American culture, Lookstein was born in Mogilev, Russia, and grew up on the Lower East Side of New York City and in the Brownsville section of Brooklyn. He was ordained at the Rabbi Isaac Elchanan Theological Seminary in 1926 and subsequently earned advanced degrees in sociology from Columbia University. Lookstein served Congregation Kehilath Jeshurun for fifty-three years (from 1926 to 1979). As a professor of sociology, practical rabbinics, and homiletics at Yeshiva Rabbi Isaac Elchanan, he stressed the importance of decorum and sermonics to his students. In 1936 he founded the Ramaz School, a leading integrated Orthodox day school, and served as its principal. In 1958 he was appointed acting president of Bar-Ilan University in Israel and subsequently served as its president. His books include *Judaism in Theory and Practice* (New York, 1931) and *Faith and Destiny of Man* (New York, 1967).

• Jeffrey S. Gurock, "Resisters and Accommodators: Varieties of Orthodox Rabbis in America, 1886–1983," *American Jewish Archives* (November 1983): 138–140. Jeffrey S. Gurock, ed., "The Ramaz Version of Orthodoxy," in *Ramaz: School, Community, Scholarship and Orthodoxy* (Hoboken, N.J., 1989), pp. 40–82. Jenna Weissman Joselit, *New York's Jewish Jews: The Orthodox Community in the Interwar Period* (Bloomington, Ind., 1990). Leo Landman, ed., *Rabbi Joseph H. Lookstein Memorial Volume* (New York, 1980).
—JEFFREY S. GUROCK

LOST PROPERTY. The finder of lost property is required to seek its owner and restore the property (*Dt.* 22.1–3). Even the property of one's enemy is to be returned (*Ex.* 23.4). With the exception of certain articles that lack any identification mark and that their owner would presumably despair of finding as soon as he knew they were lost (e.g., scattered coins), advertisement of the found property is to be made (in post-Temple times, this was done in the academy, the synagogue, or study center). The announcement is to be worded in general terms, and the applicant must be able to prove his ownership by describing marks of identification. The lost article is to be kept in good order by the finder until claimed; the finder is considered in law a bailee and is not entitled to a reward. A finder who knows the identity of the owner but does not inform him is guilty of a severe crime and is punished accordingly. If the owner does not claim the property, the finder is regarded as the owner. Regulations vary according to the kind of property lost and found (for example, animals whose upkeep involves expense for the finder). The subject is discussed in detail in tractate **Bava' Metsi'a'*.

• Moshe Goldberger, *Hashovas Aveidah: The Laws of Returning Lost Possessions*, with *responsa* by Moshe Feinstein (Staten Island, N.Y., 1980). Michael Wygoda, *Hashavat 'Avedah* (Jerusalem, 1991).

LOST TEN TRIBES. See TRIBES OF ISRAEL.

LOT, grandson of Terah and son of Haran, Abraham's younger brother. Lot migrated with Abraham's family to Canaan from Haran and accompanied him in his journey in Canaan and Egypt (*Gn.* 12.10–20, 13.1). Upon their return from Egypt, Abraham's and Lot's shepherds quarreled, leading Abraham to suggest that they separate from one another. Lot chose to dwell in the then fruitful Jordan plain in Sodom, whereas Abraham remained in the mountain area, in Hebron.

In *Genesis* 14, Lot was rescued by Abraham and his 318 men after being taken captive in battle. Before God destroyed the cities of Sodom and Gomorrah, he sent two emissaries to rescue Lot and his family (*Gn.* 19.1–29). During their escape from Sodom, Lot's wife disobeyed the angel's orders, looked back at the destruction, and was turned into a pillar of salt. After the destruction of the cities, Lot and his two daughters found refuge in a cave nearby. The daughters, believing that they were the only survivors left in the world, got Lot drunk with wine and each one cohabited with him. Their sons were given the pejorative names Moab (From the [Same] Father) and Ben-ammi (Son of the [Same] Clan), the ancestors of the Transjordanian peoples, the Moabites and the Ammonites.

This story explains the biblical ethnic view that the Moabites and the Ammonites were related to the ancestors of the Israelite nation (*1 Sm.* 22.3–4; *Ruth* 4.17–21; *Nm.* 21.24) but that their births were the result of incest. This tradition is later mentioned in *Deuteronomy* 2.9–19, where Moab and Ammon are called "children of Lot" (see also *Ps.* 83.9).

• Nahum M. Sarna, *Genesis*, The JPS Torah Commentary (Philadelphia, 1989), pp. 134–160. John Skinner, *Genesis*, International Critical Commentary (Edinburgh, 1910), pp. 306–314. Ephraim A. Speiser, *Genesis*, The Anchor Bible (New York, 1964), pp. 138–146.
—ZE'EV KAINAN

LO' TA'ASEH (לֹא תַעֲשֶׂה; do not do), a negative commandment; a term generally used to refer to a negative biblical commandment. Jewish law generally divides biblical obligations into positive and negative commandments. Within the category of negative commandments are those that prohibit activity (for example, "do not murder," *Ex.* 20.13) and those that compel activity ("do not stand by while one's neighbor's blood is shed," *Lv.* 19.16). Yet other negative commandments are connected to positive commandments, such as the prohibition against stealing, which is linked with the positive obligation to return what one has stolen. According to medieval calculations, there are 365 negative commandments among the 613 *mitsvot* in the Pentateuch. See also 'ASEH; COMMANDMENTS, 613; MITSVAH.

• Charles B. Chavel, *The Commandments: Sefer ha-Mitzvoth of Maimonides*, 2 vols. (London, 1976), introduction.
—MICHAEL BROYDE

LOTS. The casting of lots as a means of making decisions is documented in the Bible and in post-biblical literature. In the Bible lots were used to single out one or more members of a group; for example, in the election of a king (*1 Sm.* 10.20–21), the designation of the scapegoat for Yom Kippur (*Lv.* 16.8–10), or the designation of 14 Adar as the day on which the Persians would murder the Jews (*Est.* 3.7). In addition, lots were used to divide booty or conquered territory (*Is.* 17.14; *Na.* 3.10); for example, the apportioning of the land of Canaan (*Nm.* 26.52–56; *Jos.* 14–19). The casting of lots was understood to reflect divine will and was also used as a means of communicating with God in connection with the Urim and Thummim (*1 Sm.* 14.41–42; see ORACLES).

According to the Talmud, priestly roles were determined by lot (*Yoma'* 2.3–4), and the method of casting lots was described in some detail. The lots were placed in an urn and shaken, and one was taken in each hand. If the one marked "for the Lord" turned up in the right hand, it was considered a positive sign (*Yoma'* 3.9, 4.1). Josephus reports that the defenders of Masada chose ten of their number to kill the remaining survivors as part of a suicide pact, so that they would not be captured by the Romans. The Israeli archaeologist Yigael Yadin, who excavated the site at Masada, found marked ostraca that he suggested were these original lots.

• Yigael Yadin, *Masada: Herod's Fortress and the Zealot's Last Stand* (New York, 1966).

—PETER KNOBEL

LOTS, FEAST OF. See PURIM.

LOVE (Heb. *ahavah*). The love between men and women is frequently referred to in the Bible (*Gn.* 29.18, 29.20; *Dt.* 21.5; *Jgs.* 16.4), but the same word is also applied to relationships such as those between parents and children, between a person and fellow human beings (*Lv.* 19.18, 19.34), and between the individual and God (*Dt.* 6.5, 11.1, 13.4). It was the allegorical interpretation of erotic love as spiritual love that was responsible for the inclusion, or the retention, of the *Song of Songs* in the biblical canon. The prophets frequently use the image of matrimonial love to describe the relationship between God and Israel, most dramatically by Hosea; the prophets also describe the love between God and Israel as the love of a father for his son. In rabbinic literature the idea of the love of God as a supreme religious value is further developed, and in the Middle Ages the love of God acquired mystical connotations. According to the Talmud, the highest form of service to God is service "out of love," contrasted with "service out of fear" (*Ned.* 31a). God's love for Israel as expressed in his election of the people and especially in his granting them the Torah is an overriding theological concept. The benediction preceding the recitation of the Shemaʿ, which thanks God for the gift of the Torah and the commandments, is known technically as Ahavah (that is, God's love of Israel). The section of Maimonides' *Mishneh Torah* enumerating the laws of prayer, recitation of the Shemaʿ, *tefillin*, and circumcision has the heading "Ahavah" (commandments that express Israel's love of God). In most medieval manuals on the spiritual life, the central chapter is that on love.

Some medieval writers imply that love of God necessarily excludes love of created beings, but the mainstream of rabbinic tradition holds that in the love of God the natural forms of love (between spouses, family members, fellow humans) are hallowed. Love of God and love of one's fellow human beings are the natural bases of Jewish ethics. *Ahavat Yisra'el* (love of Israel), an all-embracing love, is regarded as a great virtue by the rabbis. *Ahavat Yisra'el* later became an important Hasidic concept. Love of one's fellow human beings is enjoined not only toward Jews (*Lv.* 19.18) but also toward the stranger (cf. *Lv.* 19.34; *Dt.* 10.19). Hillel's dictum (*Avot* 1.12) "Be as the disciples of Aaron, loving peace and pursuing peace" continues, "loving your fellow beings and drawing them near to the Torah."

• Jerome Eckstein, *Metaphysical Drift: Love and Judaism*, Revisioning Philosophy, vol. 10 (New York, 1991). Steven Harvey, "Love," in *Contemporary Jewish Religious Thought*, edited by Arthur A. Cohen and Paul Mendes-Flohr (New York, 1987), pp. 557–561. Leo Jung, *Love and Life* (New York, 1979). Hebreo Léon, *The Philosophy of Love*, translated into English by F. Friedeberg-Seeley and Jean H. Barnes (London, 1937). Joseph Litvin, *Yismaḥ Yisra'el ʿal Ahavat Yisra'el ve-'Erets Yisra'el* (London, 1958).

LÖW FAMILY, Hungarian family of scholars.

Leopold Löw (1811–1875) was the first Reform rabbi in Hungary and became one of the most forceful spokesmen of religious reform, involved in bitter controversies with the Orthodox. In 1850 he became rabbi of Szeged, where he served until his death. An outstanding preacher, he was the first rabbi to give sermons in Hungarian. He edited a scholarly journal, *Ben Chananja*, from 1858 to 1867 and published studies in which he sought to show that Judaism as a religion was always evolving.

Immanuel Löw (1854–1944), followed his father Leopold as rabbi of Szeged and was also a distinguished preacher in Hungarian. A noted scholar, he wrote on Talmudic *realia* and lexicography. His best-known work, *Die Flora der Juden* (4 vols. [1924–1934]), applies modern botanical knowledge to the Bible, Talmud, and rabbinical literature to identify and describe the flora mentioned in different ages.

• **Leopold Löw**: William Noah Loew, *Leopold Loew: A Biography* (New York, 1912). **Immanuel Löw**: for a bibliography of the writings of Immanuel Löw, see *Festschrift Immanuel Löw* (Breslau, 1934). Sander Scheiber, ed., *Semitic Studies in Memory of Immanuel Löw* (Budapest, 1947).

LUBAVICH, Belorussian town near Mogilev; name of a Hasidic dynasty. Until 1915 Lubavich was the chief seat of the *Schneersohn family, leaders of *Ḥabad Hasidism. Lubavich viewed itself as the intellectual capital of the Hasidic world, where the study of Jewish mysticism, as recast in the teachings of Ḥabad, was carried out in an intensive and systematic way. After their exile from Lubavich, the Schneersohns lived for twenty-five years in various cities in Russia and Poland, directing the most important network of resistance to the destruction of religious Jewry by the Soviet authorities. Since the move of R. Yosef Yitsḥaq Schneersohn to the United States in 1940, and especially under the leadership of his successor, R. Menaḥem Mendel Schneerson (died 1994), Lubavitch has become a worldwide movement for the promulgation of Ḥabad Hasidic teachings.

• Roman A. Foxbrunner, *Habad: The Hasidism of R. Shneur Zalman of Lyady* (Tuscaloosa, Ala., 1992). Avraham H. Glitsenshtain, *Rabbi Shemu'el Sheneursohn mi-Lyubavitsch* (Brooklyn, N.Y., 1985).

—ARTHUR GREEN

LUBLIN, SEER OF. See YAʿAQOV YITSḤAQ, HA-ḤOZEH MI-LUBLIN.

LUDOMIR, MAID OF. See WERBERMACHER, ḤANNAH RAKHEL.

LUḤOT HA-BERIT. See TABLETS OF THE LAW.

LULAV (לוּלָב; sprout), rabbinic term for the palm branch used together with other vegetable species on Sukkot. Because the *lulav* is the most conspicuous of the *four species (see *Lv*. 23.40), the term is used in the benediction to refer to the whole. The *lulav* is taken in the hand after the morning service ʿAmidah and waved in the air at designated points in the Hallel service (except on Sabbaths). It is also carried in the **hoshaʿnot* procession (**haqqafot*) and, in the Sephardi rite, during the additional service. The *lulav*, with the myrtle and the willow, is held in the right hand, the **etrog* in the left.

• Yehiel M. Stern, *Kashrut Arbaʿat ha-Minim* (Jerusalem, 1992), pp. 133–176. Eliyahu Weisfisch, *Sefer Arbaʿat ha-Minim ha-Shalem* (Jerusalem, 1975), pp. 3–18. Michael Zohary, *Plants of the Bible* (Cambridge, 1982), pp. 60–61.

LURIA, SHELOMOH (c.1510–1573), known by the acronym Maharshal (from Morenu ha-Rav Shelomoh Luria); Polish-Lithuanian Talmudist. Born in Poznań, he studied under his grandfather Isaac Kloiber and served as rabbi in the Lithuanian communities of Brześć and Ostróg before being appointed, in 1559, rabbi of Lublin, where he remained until his death. Conservative in outlook, he opposed the place of *pilpul* in the *yeshivah* curriculum, the study of philosophy, and the codification of *halakhah*, such as that produced by his rival Mosheh Isserles. He stressed the need to return to the Talmudic text in halakhic decision-making, demonstrating his method in his monumental, but uncompleted work *Yam shel Shelomoh* (published in parts: on *B. Q.* [Prague, 1616–1618]; on *Ḥul.* [Kraków, 1633–1635]). This rational commentary on the Talmud described the development of the *halakhah* from its origin until Luria's day. In his notes, *Ḥokhmat Shelomoh* (Kraków, 1582 or 1587), now printed in most editions of the Talmud, he used textual criticism to establish the correct readings for corrupt passages. In his later years, he composed other halakhic commentaries and a critical commentary on the liturgy, which served as a major source for Shabbetai Sofer's prayer book. Luria wrote many *responsa* that have been published (Lublin, 1574–1575; edited by S. Hurwitz [1938]), though his independent stance brought him into conflict with the dominant rabbinic figures of his day, Shalom Shachna' and Mosheh Isserles. Not widely popular, Luria's work was "rediscovered" by nineteenth-century Lithuanian *yeshivot*.

• S. Assaf, "Mashehu le-Toledot Maharashal," in *Louis Ginzberg: Jubilee Volume on the Occasion of His Seventieth Birthday*, edited by Alexander Marx et al. (New York, 1945), pp. 45–63 (Heb. vol.). M. Raffeld, "Ha-Maharshal veha-Yam shel Shelomoh," Ph.D. dissertation, Bar-Ilan University, 1990. Stefan C. Reif, "Some Observations on Solomon Luria's Prayer Book," in *Tradition and Transition: Essays Presented to Chief Rabbi Sir Immanuel Jakobovits to Celebrate Twenty Years in Office*, edited by Jonathan Sacks (London, 1986), pp. 245–257. —ADAM TELLER

LURIA, YITSḤAQ (1534–1572), kabbalist (see KABBALAH) and one of the most influential figures in the history of Jewish spirituality. Born in Jerusalem and brought up in Egypt, he acquired a reputation for halakhic and kabbalistic scholarship, but otherwise little is known about his early years. He settled in Safed in 1570 and died in the plague of 1572. These two years, about which no reliable details are known, laid the foundations for the subsequent explosion of legend, hagiography, and doctrinal innovation known as Lurianism. Luria appears to have collected around him a band of devoted disciples who had to pledge not to divulge the new esoteric teachings to outsiders. The first known reliable document is a solemn contract in which several disciples pledge not to discuss or commit to writing any of the master's teaching except in the presence of Ḥayyim Vital (see VITAL FAMILY), who had drawn up the contract in an effort to establish his claim to be the spiritual heir and sole repository of canonical Lurianism. In spite of the intended secrecy, pirated copies of Vital's "canonical" writings as well as other, and on some points divergent, versions of the master's doctrine began to circulate and were eagerly spread. According to legend, Luria himself had hardly written anything because the rush of inspiration was so powerful that it could not be reduced to writing. The vast corpus of Lurianic literature was composed by his disciples and by kabbalists influenced by them; it is still inadequately analyzed and any account of the Lurianic revolution is therefore provisional and incomplete. Luria's fame as a charismatic man of God spread through hagiographic epistles and books (such as *Shivḥei ha-'Ari* and *Toledot ha-'Ari*) long before his doctrines. His name entered Jewish tradition in the form of an acrostic of his Hebrew names ("the divine Rabbi Yitsḥaq"), the Ari (Lion), and his disciples were referred to as "the lion's cubs."

The revolutionary aspect of Lurianism resides in the notion that perfection is not in the past, not even in the eternal Godhead before creation, but in the future. The achievement of perfection is the purpose of all existence, the divine realm as well as the created order. Luria addressed the problem of the purpose of existence in a more radical manner than other theologians. Whereas the early Spanish Kabbalah was concerned mainly with the spiritual achievements of the individual, Lurianism transformed the Kabbalah into a teleological and history-oriented system, teaching the meaning of exile and messianic expectation not only on the level of the individual but also on that of the community of Israel. In Lurianism, mystical life thus acquires a redemptive and potentially messianic quality.

Luria utilized an ancient term, **tsimtsum*, found in Talmudic literature and in the writings of the *Ḥasidei Ashkenaz but gave it a novel twist. If God is All in All, how is a non-divine existence, such as creation, possible? According to Luria's theological mythology, the Godhead "retracted" and "withdrew itself into itself" so as to create an empty space in which creation could take place. This process is said to be cathartic, since the new vacuum (*tehiru*, Aramaic for *empty*) contained residues (*reshimu*) of elements in the primordial Godhead that would develop later into forces of evil. During the following process of creation, however, a major catastrophe occurred. The vessels (*kelim*), or channels, were not able to contain the power of the divine light that flowed through them, and so they collapsed (*shevirat ha-kelim*;

see BREAKING OF THE VESSELS). This brought into being a new independent realm, into which fell many divine lights and sparks (*nitsotsot*), which are held captive by the powers of evil until they are raised again in a process that is the ultimate meaning and purpose of history. Creation is thus out of joint from its very beginning and it is Israel's, and especially the kabbalist's, duty to set it right (see TIQQUN ʿOLAM). The way to do this involves the practice of the proper intentions and meditations, in both daily life and especially in ritual actions (see INTENT). The raising of the sparks is thus the inner purpose of everything. All historical events, from Adam and the garden of Eden to the theophany on Mount Sinai and the sin of the golden calf and beyond, were interpreted as failed attempts to bring about this *tiqqun*. The Lurianists created several mystical rituals and also re-edited the *prayer book. It has been suggested that the Lurianic Kabbalah was a response to the traumatic experience of the expulsion from Spain. The symbolism and terminological apparatus of Lurianic thought was taken up by both *Hasidism and non-Hasidic kabbalists of the eighteenth century.

• Joseph Avivi, *Binyan Ari'el: Mevo' Derushei ha-'Elohi Rabbi Yitsḥaq Luria* (Jerusalem, 1987). Meir Benayahu, *Sefer Toledot ha-'Ari* (Jerusalem, 1967). Joseph Dan, *Gershom Scholem and the Mystical Dimension in Jewish History* (New York, 1987), pp. 244–285. Gershom Gerhard Scholem, *Kabbalah* (Jerusalem, 1974), pp. 420–428 *et passim*. Gershom Gerhard Scholem, "Kabbalah and Myth," in *On the Mystical Shape of the Godhead* (New York, 1991). Gershom Gerhard Scholem, *Major Trends in Jewish Mysticism* (New York, 1954), pp. 244–286. David Tamar, *Meḥqarim be-Toledot ha-Yehudim be-'Erets Yisra'el uve-'Artsot ha-Mizraḥ* (Jerusalem, 1981), pp. 70–85. Isaiah Tishby, *Torat ha-Raʿ veha-Qelippah be-Qabbalat ha-'Ari* (Jerusalem, 1984).

LURIANIC KABBALAH. See LURIA, YITSḤAQ.

LUTHERANISM. See PROTESTANTISM.

LUTSKI, SIMḤAH YITSḤAQ BEN MOSHEH (died 1766), Karaite scholar and bibliographer. He was born in Lutsk, but he was brought to Chufut-Kale in the Crimea in approximately 1751 by Mordekhai ben Berakhah, the leading Crimean Karaite, in order to raise the level of Karaite education there. Simḥah Yitsḥaq wrote at least twenty-two books on theology, philosophy, religious law, and Kabbalah. Of these, only three have been published: *Or ha-Ḥayyim*, a commentary on the philosophical work of Aharon ben Eliyyahu; *ʿEts Ḥayyim* (published together with *Or ha-Ḥayyim* [Yevpatoriya, 1847]), in which Simḥah Yitsḥaq's kabbalistic tendencies found expression; and *Oraḥ Tsaddiqim* (Vienna, 1830), a short history of the Karaites and the dispute with the Rabbanites, together with the first bibliography of Karaite literature. Simḥah Yitsḥaq also wrote religious hymns, five of which found their way into the Karaite prayer book.

• Jacob Mann, *Texts and Studies in Jewish History and Literature*, vol. 2 (Cincinnati, 1935).

—DAVID E. SKLARE

LUTSKI FAMILY, Karaite scholars from the town of Lutsk, Volhynia, which was part of Poland until the end of the eighteenth century, when it came under Russian rule.

Yosef Shelomoh ben Mosheh Lutski (c.1777–1844), Karaite author born in Kukizov near Lwów. He lived in Lutsk until 1802, when he moved to Yevpatoriya in the Crimea and was appointed *ḥazzan* of the community. In 1827 he traveled with the *ḥakham* Simḥah Babovich to Saint Petersburg in a successful effort to seek an exemption for the Karaites from the compulsory military service imposed on the Jews by Nicholas I. Their journey and activities were described by Lutski in *Iggeret Teshuʿat Yisra'el* (Yevpatoriya, 1840; English translation, Philip E. Miller, *Karaite Separatism in Nineteenth-Century Russia: Joseph Solomon Lutski's Epistle of Israel's Deliverance* [1993]). He also wrote *Sefer ha-Ḥinnukh le-Petaḥ Tiqvah*, a teaching manual (Constantinople, 1831), and *Tirat Kesef*, a supercommentary on *Sefer ha-Mivḥar* by Aharon ben Yosef ha-Rofe' (they were printed together [Yevpatoriya, 1835]). A number of his religious hymns and prayers were incorporated into the Karaite prayer book.

Avraham ben Yosef Shelomoh Lutski (1792–1855), poet and scholar; son of Yosef Shelomoh. Born in Lutsk, he moved to Yevpatoriya with his father, who later sent him to Constantinople, where he was in the service of a Karaite merchant whose daughter he later married. During these years, he studied rabbinic literature with Rabbanite scholars and learned a number of languages. In 1835 he was chosen to be *ḥazzan* and rabbi of the community of Yevpatoriya, but he refused. He established a Karaite school there in 1844, which produced many of the future leaders of the Crimean Karaite community. Among his works are *Iggeret Zug ve-Nifrad*, a decision concerning marriage law in which he disagreed with most of the authorities of his time (Yevpatoriya, 1837); a Turkish translation of the play *Melukhat Sha'ul* by Yosef Tropplowitz; *Mishlei Musar*, a translation into Judeo-Tatar of ethical stories; and *Shoshanim ʿEdut le-'As-saf*, a collection of poems, letters, lamentations, sermons, and eulogies.

• Jacob Mann, *Texts and Studies in Jewish History and Literature*, vol. 2 (Cincinnati, 1935), on both Lutskis. Philip E. Miller, ed. and trans., *Karaite Separatism in Nineteenth-Century Russia: Joseph Solomon Lutski's Epistle of Israel's Deliverance*, Monographs of the Hebrew Union College, no. 16 (Cincinnati, 1993), on Yosef. Samuel Poznanski, *Karaite Literary Opponents of Saadiah Gaon* (London, 1908), on Yosef.

—DAVID E. SKLARE

LUZZATTO, MOSHEH ḤAYYIM (1707–1747), Italian mystic known by the acronym Ramḥal; head of a messianic secret society and author of ethical works, allegorical plays, and liturgical poetry. Luzzatto is recognized as one of the leading kabbalists of the eighteenth century. He wrote the most influential Jewish ethical work of modern times, *Mesillat Yesharim*, and is considered by many as one of the founders of modern Hebrew literature.

Luzzatto was born and raised in Padua. Besides acquiring a traditional Jewish education, he was in close touch with Italian culture. One of his early works is a treatise on rhetoric, *Leshon Limmudim* (Mantua, 1727). In 1727, he experienced a mystical revelation, in which a *maggid*, a messenger from the divine world, appeared to him, and from then on such experiences occurred frequently. The *maggid* instructed him to write kabbalistic works, and in the next few years, Luzzatto wrote several mystical treatises, many of them in the form and language of the *Zohar, calling them *Zohar Tinyana'* (sections published in Warsaw in 1889 and Jerusalem in 1958). Redemption is the main theme of these works. A circle of disciples, motivated by messianic enthusiasm, gathered around him, including Mosheh David Valle, seen as the Messiah, Son of David, who wrote an extensive biblical commentary identifying himself as the messianic hero of the biblical texts, and Yequti'el Gordon of Vilna, who later spread Luzzatto's teachings in eastern Europe. It seems that this group regarded *Shabbetai Tsevi as the Messiah, Son of Joseph, destined to be killed during the messianic upheavals. Luzzatto himself was regarded as the reincarnation of Moses, the supreme power in the messianic structure. Luzzatto viewed his own marriage (1731) as the culmination of the messianic process and the union of the male and female elements in the divine world; he explained it in detail in his commentary on his marriage contract.

Information concerning this group reached R. Mosheh Ḥagiz, who suspected that it was a Shabbatean conspiracy and brought his accusations before the court of the rabbis of Venice. Yesha'yahu Basan, Luzzatto's teacher, tried to defend his pupil, and a controversy arose. In 1730, Luzzatto accepted the rabbis' demand that he stop writing kabbalistic texts dictated by the *maggid* and hand over his previous writings to Basan for safekeeping. However, the accusations did not cease, and Luzzatto was forced to leave Padua in 1735, migrating to Amsterdam. His exile, however, did not prevent the Venice rabbinical court from ordering his works to be burned.

In Amsterdam, Luzzatto concentrated on completing his ethical works, especially the *Mesillat Yesharim* (Amsterdam, 1740; English translation by Mordecai M. Kaplan [1936]). Based on the *Baraiyta' de-Rabbi Pinḥas ben Ya'ir* (*Sot.* 9.15), it described the path of ethical and spiritual ascension of the individual, until, with the help of God, sanctity is reached. In this and other works, Luzzatto refrained from using kabbalistic terminology, because of the court's prohibition, but the mystical dimension is evident. His two other major ethical treatises are *Derekh ha-Shem* (Amsterdam, 1896), and *Da'at Tevunot* (Warsaw, 1886). He wrote many poems and letters, besides his allegorical plays, *La-Yesharim Tehillah* (Amsterdam, 1743) and *Migdal 'Oz* (Leipzig, 1837). In 1743 he immigrated to Erets Yisra'el and settled with his family in Acre, where, in 1747, they all died in a plague.

Luzzatto's works were influential in both Hasidic and non-Hasidic circles. The *Musar movement made the study of his ethical works compulsory in their academies (see HASIDISM), and Maskilim (see HASKALAH) viewed his plays and poetry as an early expression of their own literary creativity.

• Elisheva Carlebach, "Redemption and Persecution in the Eyes of Moses Hayim Luzzatto and His Circle," *Proceedings of the American Academy for Jewish Research* 54 (1987): 1–29. Batya Gallant, "The Alleged Sabbateanism of Rabbi Moshe Hayyim Luzzatto," *Tradition* 22.3 (1986): 44–53.

—JOSEPH DAN

LUZZATTO, SHEMU'EL DAVID (1800–1865), known by the acronym Shadal; Italian scholar. Luzzatto began teaching at the Padua Rabbinical College in 1828 and published studies on Jewish history and literature as well as on religious philosophy. He maintained the Mosaic authorship of the Bible and the unity of the *Book of Isaiah*. His commentaries on the Bible, utilizing his knowledge of Semitic languages and later Jewish and non-Jewish sources, are conservative, though not Orthodox, and scientific, though expressing opposition to what was called Higher Criticism. In his basic outlook, he was a romantic and contrasted his idea of a "Judaism of feeling" to the rationalism of Maimonides (he regarded philosophy as a negative phenomenon) as well as to the theosophy of the kabbalists. He distinguished two bases of world civilization—the Hellenistic, which had given the world philosophy and the arts and sciences; and Judaism, the contributions of which included religion, ethics, altruism, and the love of the good. Luzzatto is counted among the fathers of *Wissenschaft des Judentums. He translated much of the Bible into Italian and wrote many books and over three hundred articles in Hebrew and Italian on a variety of topics of Jewish study. They included editions of the prayer book, works on Hebrew grammar and philology, and a partial edition of the poems of *Yehudah ha-Levi. A bibliography of his writings by I. Luzzatto, *Catalogo ragionato con riferimenti agli altri suoi scritti e inediti*, appeared in Padua in 1881.

• Noah H. Rosenbloom, *Luzzatto's Ethico-Psychological Interpretation of Judaism* (New York, 1965). Peter Slymovics, "Romantic and Jewish Orthodox Influences in the Political Philosophy of S. D. Luzzatto," *Italia* 4.1 (1985): 94–126. Meyer Waxman, *History of Jewish Literature* (New York, 1961), pp. 389–399, 489–500.

LUZZATTO, SIMONE (1583–1663), Italian rabbi; contemporary of Leone *Modena and chief rabbi of Venice following Modena's death. An outstanding halakhist, Luzzatto wrote a number of *responsa*, many of which exist in manuscript and have yet to be collected in a single volume. Among his other works are *Discorso circa il stato degli hebrei* (1638), a plea for tolerance of the Jews written in a spirit of rationalism usually associated with a later era, and *Socrate oivero dell'humano sapere* (1651), written in the voice of Socrates, on the insufficiency of human reason without the assistance of divine revelation.

• Cecil Roth, *History of the Jews in Venice* (Philadelphia, 1930), pp. 227–231.

—MARK WASHOFSKY

LYING. Any act of lying, even those forms less serious than bearing *false witness or committing *perjury, is considered a violation of both a prohibition—"You shall not lie to one another" (*Lv.* 19.11)—and a positive precept (*Ex.* 23.7)—"Distance yourself from a false matter"—and is an offense to the God whose "seal is truth" and of whom it is said that he "lies not" (*1 Sm.* 15.29; *Ps.* 89.34–35). The Talmud abounds in condemnations of lying, including "Liars cannot behold the glory of God" (*Sot.* 42a). Lying "is the equivalent [in severity] of idolatry" (*San.* 92a) and the equivalent of theft (T., *B. Q.* 7.8).

Telling young children that they will be given something and then not giving them those objects is forbidden, because that teaches them to lie (*Suk.* 46b). "God hates the man who speaks one thing with his mouth and another in his heart" (*Pes.* 113b). The punishment of liars is that they are not believed when they speak the truth (*San.* 89b). Occasionally, to preserve family harmony, lying may be permitted. Rabbi Yonah ben Avraham Gerondi lists the following nine types of lies: untruths spoken in the course of business dealings; lying without intending or causing harm; lying with an eye to some future benefit; deliberate falsification of facts heard; a promise made with the intention of not keeping it; a promise made and left unfulfilled; causing another to assume that one has done him a favor; priding oneself on qualities one does not possess; and the falsehoods of children who, while not lying deliberately, nonetheless do not speak the truth.

• Richard A. Freund, "Lying and Deception in the Biblical and Post-Biblical Judaic Tradition," *Scandinavian Journal of the Old Testament* 1 (1990): 45–61. O. Horn Prouser, "The Truth about Women and Lying," *Journal for the Study of the Old Testament* 61 (1994): 15–28.

–SHMUEL HIMELSTEIN

M

MA'AMAD (מַעֲמָד; status, position). During the Second Temple period, the *ma'amadot* were the Israelites (i.e., those who were not priests or Levites) designated to represent the entire community when the daily communal sacrifice was offered in the Temple (*Ta'an.* 4.2). The country was divided into twenty-four districts (*ma'amadot*), and delegations (also *ma'amadot*) from each district served in weekly rotations. This division corresponded to the twenty-four divisions of priests and Levites (*mishmarot* [guards]) that officiated in the Temple, also in rotation. Since only a token number of Israelites could be present in Jerusalem, the others whose turn it was to be present gathered in their towns to offer prayers, the possible forerunner of synagogue worship. The Mishnah reports that members of the *ma'amad* on duty were required to recite texts from *Genesis* 1, to fast from Monday to Thursday (*Ta'an.* 4.2–3), and to refrain from cutting their hair or washing their clothes (*Ta'an.* 2.7). In the post-Talmudic period, the memory of the *mishmarot* and *ma'amadot* was long preserved in references found in rabbinic and Karaite liturgy. In Sephardi, and more particularly in western Spanish-Portuguese synagogue usage, the term came to refer to the board or governing body of the synagogue elected by the *yeḥidim* (members). The *ma'amad* wielded great power within the synagogue, controlling, among other things, marriage and divorce, granting permission for one synagogue member to sue another, and determining which religious or political books might be published. No one had the right to refuse any assignment imposed on him by the *ma'amad* or its president, and anybody who declined to serve on the *ma'amad* when elected had to pay a fine. Because appointment to the *ma'amad* between elections (when a member died or resigned) was made by the remaining members and former members of the *ma'amad*, many of the positions became almost hereditary.

• Samuel Klein, *Erets Yehudah* (Tel Aviv, 1939), pp. 202–219. Jacob Liver, *Peraqim be-Toledot ha-Kehunnah veha-Leviyyah*, Sidrat Sefarim le-Ḥeqer ha-Miqra' mi-Yesodo shel S. Sh. Peri (Jerusalem, 1968), pp. 33–52. Shemuel Safrai, "The Temple," in *The Jewish People in the First Century*, edited by Shemuel Safrai and Menahem Stern (Assen, 1976), pp. 870–873.

—CHRISTINE E. HAYES

MA'ARAVOT (מַעֲרָבוֹת), a sequence of six prayer poems (*piyyutim*) inserted into the four benedictions before the 'Amidah in the evening service (*Ma'ariv) for the *Shalosh Regalim, in the Ashkenazi liturgy. They describe the particular holiday, its laws and its customs. Originally, *ma'aravot* were included in the evening services of Ro'sh ha-Shanah and Yom Kippur, but they were later removed in order to avoid unduly prolonging the service. Nowadays, they are often omitted from the Orthodox service. They are not included in the Sephardi liturgy, nor have they been retained in non-Orthodox prayer books.

• Ismar Elbogen, *Jewish Liturgy: A Comprehensive History*, translated by Raymond P. Scheindlin (Philadelphia, 1993), p. 170. Abraham Z. Idelsohn, *Jewish Liturgy and Its Development* (New York, 1967), p. 40.

—A. STANLEY DREYFUS

MA'AREKHET HA-'ELOHUT, an anonymous treatise that was probably written in Spain in the beginning of the fourteenth century by a kabbalist who belonged to, or was heavily influenced by, the school of kabbalists around R. Shelomoh ben Adret (Rashba'). One of the best-known and most influential works of the Kabbalah, the treatise is a brief, systematic, theosophical presentation of a kabbalistic worldview. Its opening chapters address the unity of God, oppose anthropomorphic terms that had been used in describing him, and present a system of the divine *sefirot* that argues that the first *sefirah* should not be identified with the Godhead (Ein Sof). The author drew extensively upon the terminology and concepts of the Gerona school of kabbalists. The work was printed in Ferrara in 1557, and again in Mantua in 1558, beginning the practice of printing kabbalistic texts. Many commentaries were written on *Ma'arekhet ha-'Elohut*, two of which were printed with it, becoming part of the work as it was used in later Kabbalah.

• E. Gottlieb in *Sefer Zikkaron le-Vinyamin Deh-Fris* (Tel Aviv, 1968), pp. 295–304. Gershom Gerhard Scholem, *Kabbalah* (New York, 1974).

—JOSEPH DAN

MA'ARIV (מַעֲרִיב), the evening service, also called 'Arvit (from *'erev* [evening]), recited daily after nightfall and named after one of the opening words of its first prayer. Although it is to be recited by the midpoint of the night, if this is not possible, it may be said until dawn. Its institution was ascribed by the rabbis (*Ber.* 26b) to the patriarch Jacob (on the basis of *Gn.* 28.11). Opinions in the Talmud differ as to whether reciting the Ma'ariv *'Amidah is obligatory or optional; the accepted ruling is that it is optional, unlike in *Shaḥarit and *Minḥah, which correspond to the two daily communal sacrifices in the Temple. The established custom is, nevertheless, to recite the Ma'ariv 'Amidah daily, but it is not repeated by the reader. Biblical verses adduced to support a third daily prayer service include *Psalms* 55.18 and *Daniel* 6.11. Ma'ariv consists of two parts, which correspond to the two main parts of Shaḥarit: the *Shema' and its benedictions, and the 'Amidah. The recital of the Shema' each morning and evening is prescribed by the earliest law (*Dt.* 4.7), although according to ancient Palestinian custom, only the first two passages were recited at night. The benedictions before and after the Shema' follow the same scheme as the morning benedictions, though their wording is different. *Barekhu (preceded by *Ps.* 78.38 and 20.10) is followed by Ma'ariv 'Aravim ("Blessed . . . who brings on the evening twilight") instead of *Yotser, Ma'ariv 'Aravim is followed by Ahavat 'Olam, and the Shema' and the *Ge'ullah are followed by *Hashkivenu, a typical evening petition for peace and protection during the night. On weekdays another benediction, composed of a collection of Bible verses beginning with *Psalms* 135.21, is recited in most Ashkenazi congregations; it is of post-Talmudic origin. The Short *Qaddish precedes the 'Amidah, while the Full Qaddish and *ʿAlenu follow it. On Sabbath eve (when the service is preceded by *Qabbalat Shabbat), the reader recites one single benediction following the ʿAmidah containing *Magen Avot (probably an early Palestinian form of the ʿAmidah) and concluding "Blessed . . . who sanctifies the Sabbath." Otherwise Maʿariv for Sabbaths and festivals is no different from that of weekdays (except for the ʿAmidah) in most rites; only the conclusion of Hashkivenu has a different wording and is followed (in most congregations) by Bible verses appropriate to the day (e.g., *Ex.* 31.16–17 for Sabbath). In some congregations, however, it is customary on festivals to interpolate **maʿaravot* into each of the benedictions of the Shemaʿ. It also became customary to recite *Qiddush (originally for homeless strangers who slept in the synagogue) and either *Yigdal or *Adon ʿOlam on Sabbath and festival eves. On Saturday nights, Maʿariv is preceded by Psalm 144 and Psalm 67, while Psalm 91 is interpolated following the ʿAmidah together with other prayers and *Havdalah. Maʿariv on Yom Kippur is extended by the recitation of special *piyyutim* (see PIYYUT) after the ʿAmidah.

• Ismar Elbogen, *Jewish Liturgy: A Comprehensive History* (Philadelphia, 1993). Joseph Heinemann and Jakob Petuchowski, *Literature of the Synagogue* (New York, 1975). Joseph Heinemann, *Prayer in the Talmud: Forms and Patterns* (Berlin, 1977).

MAʿASEH (מַעֲשֶׂה; incident; referred to as *ʿuvda'* by the Talmud [*B. M.* 70a] and as *maʿaseh rav* by many), an instance in which an esteemed person or group of people performs an action that creates a legal precedent. Maimonides observes that "Tradition and precedent [*maʿaseh*] are important foundations of decision making and may be relied on." On the other hand, the Talmud recognizes the ease with which a *maʿaseh* can be misunderstood. It states, "One may not learn a normative rule from study or from a *maʿaseh*, unless the case is specifically stated to be a normative practice" (*B. B.* 130b).

Responsa literature is a manifestation of the Talmud's preference for developing legal rules based upon real cases, not merely based on abstract restatements of Jewish law. This has prompted a number of authorities, led by R. Yaʿaqov ben Mosheh ha-Levi Molin, to state that *responsa* literature is of greater value in determining normative rules than any other form of legal literature.

• Menachem Elon, *Jewish Law: History, Sources, Principles*, 4 vols. (Philadelphia, 1994), pp. 945–978. "Halakhah," in *Entsiqlopedyah Talmudit* (Jerusalem, 1947–), vol. 9, pp. 272–275. —MICHAEL BROYDE

MAʿASEH BE-RE'SHIT (מַעֲשֵׂה בְּרֵאשִׁית; act of creation), rabbinic term derived from the first word of the Hebrew Bible and designating an esoteric discipline of mystical cosmogony. In the Mishnah (*Ḥag.* 2.1), the term is used to refer to homiletical exegesis of the biblical chapters dealing with the subject of *Creation, mainly the first chapters of *Genesis*. The Talmuds, especially *Ḥagigah* 2, as well as the Tosefta', include several homilies and stories on the subject. The largest collection of stories of this genre is contained in the beginning of *Genesis Rabbah*, but others appear frequently in classical and late *midrashim*. In Talmud Bavli, the relevant section of *Ḥagigah* follows the Mishnah and prohibits dealing (at least in public) with "what is below and what is above, what is before and what is after," quoting *Ben Sira'*. The esoteric interpretation of the first chapter of *Genesis* was not to be taught in public, but could be transmitted from master to disciple only "under four eyes" (*Ḥag.* 2.1), because of the dangers of heretical misunderstanding. Several treatises dedicated specifically to the subject were composed in the late Talmudic and the geonic periods: the *Baraiyta' de-Maʿaseh Be-Re'shit, Midrash Qonen, Midrash Tadshe'*. The **Sefer Yetsirah* can be included in the Maʿaseh Be-Re'shit literature of late antiquity.

Maimonides and other rationalist thinkers interpreted the Mishnaic terms as referring to the study of physics (and*Maʿaseh Merkavah to metaphysics). Medieval Jewish mystics and esotericists devoted much effort to the study of this subject, especially in the numerous commentaries on the *Sefer Yetsirah* written by kabbalists and Ashkenazi Ḥasidim in the thirteenth century. In the Kabbalah, the term acquired specific mystical significance: it sometimes denoted not only the creation of the universe, but the emanation of the divine hypostases, the **sefirot*. The detailed study of this process, in the Zohar and other kabbalistic works, served not only as a description of the past, but it also had a mystical purpose: the knowledge of the secrets of creation can provide the mystic with a means to ascend to the Deity, and return to the primordial perfection of the divine world. See also HEIKHALOT; ḤASIDEI ASHKENAZ; KABBALAH.

• Gershom Gerhard Scholem, *Origins of the Kabbalah* (Princeton, 1987), pp. 210–214 et passim. Efraim E. Urbach, *The Sages: Their Concepts and Beliefs* (Jerusalem, 1975), pp. 184–213. —JOSEPH DAN

MAʿASEH BOOK (Yi. *Mayseh Bukh*; Story Book), a collection of anonymous Yiddish stories and folktales that first appeared in the latter part of the sixteenth century. The stories, of an ethical nature, are drawn from Talmudic and Midrashic *aggadah* (with much additional embellishment), as well as medieval legends of both Jewish and non-Jewish origin, but in all cases given a religious application.

• Moses Gaster, trans., *Maʿaseh Book: Book of Jewish Tales and Legends*, 2 vols. (Philadelphia, 1934). Israel Zinberg, *History of Jewish Literature*, vol. 5 (Cleveland, 1974), pp. 173–205. —SHIFRA EPSTEIN

MAʿASEH MERKAVAH (מַעֲשֵׂה מֶרְכָּבָה; work of the chariot), Mishnaic term (*Ḥag.* 2.1) denoting the Midrashic exposition of the vision of the celestial chariot described in *Ezekiel* 1, parallel to *Maʿaseh Be-Re'shit, the Midrashic exposition of *Genesis* 1–2. The term was extended to include any discussion or description of the celestial realms and later was identified by Maimonides with *metaphysics and by many Jewish writers with mystical speculation and theosophy. Several treatises that expound on the esoteric speculations of the Talmud, known as *Heikhalot and Merkavah literature, have the term *merkavah* in their titles and greatly expand on Ezekiel's description. According to *Re'uyyot Yeḥezqe'l*, for instance, Ezekiel saw seven chariots when looking into the waters of the river Chebar, as one firmament after another opened above him to reveal the chariot in each of them. The Merkavah texts served as the basis for the mystics of Europe: Elʿazar ben Yehudah of Worms wrote a treatise entitled *Sod ha-Merkavah*, and the kabbalists of Spain and Provence, especially the writers of **Sefer ha-Bahir* and the *ʿIyyun Circle, used Merkavah terminology as a source for their mystical symbolism. Maʿaseh Merkavah, which is essentially a Midrashic activity, differs from *yeridah le-merkavah* (descending to the chariot), which is the term used for the actual mystical activity of ascension to the divine palaces (*heikhalot*) described in several ancient texts. The "descenders" used *Ezekiel* imagery, but their main sources and symbols were taken from the *Song of Songs* and other texts. Echoes of Merkavah traditions are also present in the liturgical poetry (*piyyutim*) of both Spanish and Ashkenazi authors.

• Joseph Dan, *The Revelation of the Secret of the World: The Beginning of Jewish Mysticism in Late Antiquity* (Providence, R.I., 1992). David J. Halperin, *The Merkabah in Rabbinic Literature*, American Oriental Series, vol. 62 (New Haven, 1980). Peter Schaefer, *The Hidden and Manifest God*, translated by Audrey Pomerance, SUNY Series in Judaica (Albany, N.Y., 1992).

—JOSEPH DAN

MAʿASER. See TITHES.

MAʿASER SHENI (מַעֲשֵׂר שֵׁנִי; Second Tithe), tractate consisting of five chapters in Mishnah order Zeraʿim, with related material in the Tosefta' and in the Talmud Yerushalmi. Biblical law describes several *tithes that rabbinic law elaborates and organizes into a comprehensive seven-year cycle. Tithes that were offered to priests and Levites were taken annually (except in the seventh sabbatical year when no tithes were taken), whereas *maʿaser sheni*, which was used to celebrate the pilgrimage to the Temple, was taken only during the first, second, fourth, and fifth years of the cycle. *Maʿaser ʿani* (the poor person's tithe), which was distributed to the disadvantaged in the third and sixth years of the cycle (*Dt.* 14.28–29), was understood by rabbinic law—in contradistinction to other halakhic traditions during Second Temple times—as a replacement for *maʿaser sheni*.

Tractate *Maʿaser Sheni* deals with the laws governing the proper use and consumption of *maʿaser sheni* and of *kerem revaʿi* (produce of a vineyard during its fourth year), whose sanctity is regarded as equivalent to that of *maʿaser sheni*. *Maʿaser sheni* must be eaten within the Temple environs, including the walled city of Jerusalem (*Meg.* 1.11), and may not be consumed when either it or the eater is ritually impure. The sanctity of *maʿaser sheni* requires that it not be used for commercial purposes.

Not all produce from every part of Erets Yisra'el could be transported to Jerusalem; hence, *maʿaser sheni* could be redeemed, removing sanctity from the produce to the coins, whose sanctity would then be transferred to food items purchased during the pilgrimage to Jerusalem (*Dt.* 14.24–26). Discussion of the conditions governing consumption and redemption of *maʿaser sheni* led the tractate to deal with the halakhic boundaries of the sanctity of the Temple and of Jerusalem. The tractate concludes with the law of confession of tithes (*Dt.* 26.12–15) in which the farmer, in effect, says to God: "We have fulfilled what you have decreed upon us, now you need to fulfill what you have promised us" (*Maʿas. Sh.* 5.13).

An English translation of the Mishnah tractate is in Herbert Danby's *The Mishnah* (Oxford, 1933).

• Chanoch Albeck, ed., *Shishah Sidrei Mishnah, Seder Zeraʿim* (Jerusalem, 1957). Philip Blackman, ed. and trans., *Mishnayoth*, vol. 1, *Order Zeraim* (Gateshead, 1973). Pinhas Kehati, ed., *Mishnah: A New Translation with a Commentary, Seder Zeraim*, vol. 4, *Maʿaser Sheni, Hallah, Orlah, Bikkurim* (Jerusalem, 1994). Hermann Leberecht Strack and Günter Stemberger, *Introduction to the Talmud and Midrash*, rev. and updat. ed., translated by Markus Bockmuehl (Minneapolis, 1992).

—AVRAHAM WALFISH

MAʿASROT (מַעַשְׂרוֹת; Tithes), tractate consisting of five chapters in Mishnah order Zeraʿim, with related material in the Tosefta' and in the Talmud Yerushalmi. Several annual *tithes were required by biblical law for distribution to the priests, to the Levites (*Nm.* 18.12, 21ff.), and to the poor (*Dt.* 14.28–29) as well as for celebrating the pilgrimage to the Temple (*Dt.* 14.22ff.).

Maʿasrot deals with the regulations defining the kind of produce that is subject to the laws of tithing. Listing the different stages of growth that render various forms of produce subject to tithing, *Maʿasrot* forbids such produce for consumption when either it has been processed so that it is marketable or it is consumed in a manner or context characteristic of a fixed meal rather than of a snack. The requirement to tithe one's produce prior to its consumption reflects the devotion due to God and, perhaps, the continued devotion to the idea of Temple service; even after the destruction of the Temple rendered obsolete the original social context in which these laws were promulgated, Mishnaic law regarded untithed produce as forbidden for consumption.

The Mishnah tractate was translated into English by Herbert Danby in *The Mishnah* (Oxford, 1933).

• Chanoch Albeck, ed., *Shishah Sidrei Mishnah, Seder Zeraʿim* (Jerusalem, 1957). Philip Blackman, ed. and trans., *Mishnayoth*, vol. 1, *Order Zeraim* (Gateshead, 1973). Pinhas Kehati, ed., *Mishnah: A New Translation with a Commentary, Seder Zeraim*, vol. 3, *Terumot, Maʿasrot* (Jerusalem, 1993). Hermann Leberecht Strack and Günter Stemberger, *Introduction to the Talmud and Midrash*, rev. and updat. ed., translated by Markus Bockmuehl (Minneapolis, 1992).

—AVRAHAM WALFISH

MACCABEES. See HASMONEANS.

MACCABEES, BOOKS OF THE, four separate apocryphal books. The *First Book of the Maccabees* is primarily a historical account of the Maccabean Revolt, covering the period between 175 and c.135, that is, from the events preceding the persecution under *Antiochus IV Epiphanes to the death of Simon, last of the Hasmonean brothers. It was written in Hebrew during the latter part of the second century BCE but is preserved only in a Greek translation. Its anonymous author emerges as an ardent admirer of the *Hasmoneans, described as "those through whom salvation was granted to Israel" (*1 Mc.* 5.62), and seems to have had access to much reliable historical information, which he presented in a manner deeply influenced by biblical historiographical models.

The *Second Book of the Maccabees* is, according to its author, a condensed version of Jason of Cyrene's (otherwise lost) history of the Maccabean Revolt. In contrast to *1 Maccabees*, this book focuses on the career of *Judah the Maccabee alone, ignoring Judah's father, Mattathias, and ends with Judah's victory over Nicanor, the Syrian general, in 161 BCE. The *Second Book of the Maccabees* devotes much space to detailed descriptions of the suffering of the Jews under Antiochus IV Epiphanes and to God's intervention in various historical events. Written in Greek in the second century BCE (after 160), *2 Maccabees* follows many of the conventions of contemporary Greek historiography. Both *1 Maccabees* and *2 Maccabees* are part of the Apocrypha (see APROCRYPHA AND PSEUDEPIGRAPHA).

The *Third Book of the Maccabees* is in no way connected with the history of the Maccabees but relates the wonderful deliverance of the Temple from profanation at the hands of Ptolemy Philopator (r. 221–205) and Ptolemy's subsequent attempt to destroy the Jewish population of Alexandria. Ptolemy's plot failed, and the Egyptian Jews instituted a yearly festival to commemorate their miraculous deliverance. Written in Greek by an Alexandrian Jew, probably in the first century BCE or the first century CE, *3 Maccabees* may be conflating two different historical episodes, one of which seems to be described by *Josephus Flavius as having occurred around 145 BCE (*Against Apion* 2.53–55).

The *Fourth Book of the Maccabees* is a philosophical work, aimed at finding out "whether devout reason is absolute master over the passions (*4 Mc.* 1.1). To demonstrate that this indeed is so, *4 Maccabees* adduces several examples, taken from *2 Maccabees*, of Jews who chose to die under horrible torture rather than renounce their ancestral beliefs and customs. The *Fourth Book of the Maccabees* was written in Greek by a Jewish writer, whose geographical location is unknown, some time in the first century BCE or the first century CE.

• H. Anderson, "3 Maccabees," in *The Old Testament Pseudepigrapha*, edited by James H. Charlesworth, vol. 2 (Garden City, N.Y., 1983), pp. 509–529. H. Anderson, "4 Maccabees," in *The Old Testament Pseudepigrapha*, edited by James H. Charlesworth, vol. 2 (Garden City, N.Y., 1983), pp. 531–564. John R. Bartlett, *The First and Second Books of the Maccabees* (Cambridge, 1973). Jonathan A. Goldstein, *I Maccabees*, The Anchor Bible, vol. 41 (Garden City, N.Y., 1976). Jonathan A. Goldstein, *II Maccabees*, The Anchor Bible, vol. 41A (Garden City, N.Y., 1983). Moses Hadas, *The Third and Fourth Books of Maccabees* (New York, 1953).

—GIDEON BOHAK

MACHPELAH, CAVE OF, cave near Hebron. When Sarah died at Hebron, Abraham approached the local dignitaries desiring to buy a plot for her burial. Negotiations took place with Ephron the Hittite, who sold the cave of Machpelah to Abraham for four hundred silver shekels (*Gn.* 23). In this cave were also buried the three patriarchs and their wives (except Rachel) (*Gn.* 23.19, 25.9, 49.31, 50.13). In Byzantine times, a church was built on the site, and later a synagogue; and since the twelfth century, a mosque has occupied the site. In recent years, the location has been the scene of particularly intense rivalry and conflict between Muslims and Jews.

• Nahum M. Sarna, *Genesis*, The JPS Torah Commentary (Philadelphia, 1989), pp. 156–161. Claus Westermann, *Genesis 12–36*, translated by John J. Scullion (Minneapolis, 1985), pp. 369–376. —SHALOM PAUL

MAFTIR (מַפְטִיר; one who completes), the last verses (at least three in number) of the weekly Sabbath and festival reading from the Torah scroll; popularly also applied to the person called for this reading. On a regular Sabbath, the last few verses of the weekly portion are repeated, and these are called the *maftir*. On special Sabbaths (see SABBATHS, SPECIAL) and festivals, the *maftir* is taken from a passage relevant to that particular day and is read from a second scroll.

The person called to the Torah for the *maftir* reading recites the Torah blessings before and after the reading and usually goes on to read the *haftarah*. A boy making his *bar mitsvah* (and, in non-Orthodox synagogues, a girl making her *bat mitsvah*) will generally celebrate the religious occasion by reading the *maftir* and *haftarah*. In Sephardi synagogues, a minor may be called to the reading of the *maftir*, but only on a regular Sabbath.

• Ismar Elbogen, *Jewish Liturgy: A Comprehensive History*, translated by Raymond P. Scheindlin (Philadelphia, New York, and Jerusalem, 1993), pp. 143–149.

—CHAIM PEARL

MAGEN AVOT (מָגֵן אָבוֹת; "Shield of our forefathers"), opening words of an abbreviated form of the seven benedictions of the Friday evening *ʿAmidah (hence, also known as Meʿein Shevaʿ [an abstract of the seven benedictions]), recited by the cantor after the ʿAmidah. It was widely held (Maimonides, *Hilkhot Tefillah* 9.10–11) that it was originally instituted to enable latecomers to conclude their prayers and return home with the other congregants (since synagogues were situated outside towns, and it was dangerous to be out alone at night; see Rashi on *Shab.* 24b), but this theory is now considered as questionable. It has been suggested that Magen Avot is an early Palestinian form of the ʿAmidah.

• Joseph Heinemann, *Prayer in the Talmud: Forms and Patterns* (Berlin, 1977).

MAGEN DAVID (מָגֵן דָּוִד; shield of David), symbol consisting of two superimposed equilateral triangles, forming a hexagram. It was used for decoration and as a magical sign in many civilizations and in various parts of the world, but it was not known as a specifically Jewish symbol in biblical and Talmudic times. Where it appears in Jewish contexts, as in synagogues and on tombstones, it had a purely ornamental function. The phrase itself appears in the third benediction after the reading of the *haftarah*, where it is a designation for God. According to the authoritative study by Gershom Scholem, Jewish groups took over the designation *seal of Solomon* from Islamic magic sources. As a lucky sign it appeared on magical versions of the *mezuzah* from the tenth century. It is uncertain whether the term *shield of David* arose in Islamic or Jewish mystical circles. Although appearing in a number of Jewish contexts, it first had an official Jewish usage in Prague, probably as a heraldic symbol, and spread from there in the seventeenth century to other European countries. Some kabbalistic circles called it the "shield of the Son of David," referring to the Messiah, and it was adopted as a symbol by followers of *Shabbetai Tsevi. However, it only became widespread in the nineteenth century when central European Jews were looking for a striking symbol that would represent Judaism as the cross did Christianity. It had the advantage over the traditional *menorah* as being less particularistic (the latter was connected with the Temple worship). From Europe it spread to Muslim lands, and virtually no synagogue was without a representation of the *magen David*. It was adopted by the Zionist organization at the First Zionist Congress in 1897 and was subsequently incorporated in the flag of the State of Israel. In Israel the Red Shield of David corresponds to the Red Cross and Red Crescent. It formed the allegorical basis of Franz *Rosenzweig's major philosophical work, *Der Stern der Erloesung* (1921; *The Star of Redemption* [1971]). The Nazis used it on the identifying badge that Jews had to wear throughout Europe.

• Gershom Gerhard Scholem, *Kabbalah* (New York, 1974), pp. 362–368. Gershom Gerhard Scholem, *Magen-David: Toldotav shel Semel* (Jerusalem, 1949–1950). Gershom Gerhard Scholem, *The Messianic Idea in Judaism and Other Essays on Jewish Spirituality* (New York, 1971), pp. 257–281.

MAGGID (מַגִּיד), popular preacher or a technical term for a heavenly agent in mystical literature.

Popular Preacher. Known to have existed as far back as the eleventh century in France and Germany, the name and institution of the *maggid* became a characteristic feature of the Russian and Polish communities. From the seventeenth century on, the rabbis preached twice a year only (on the Sabbaths preceding Pesaḥ and Yom Kippur); the preaching throughout the year for purposes of edification, instruction, and repentance was left to the *maggid*, the larger congregations often appointing a permanent *maggid* along with a rabbi (e.g., R. Yaʿaqov ben Wolf *Kranz, the celebrated *maggid* of Dubno). The Hasidic leader *Dov Ber of Mezhirech was universally known as "the Maggid" (because the term occurred in the title of one of his books), but most of the *maggidim* were associated with the *Mitnaggedim. The manner of their preaching was characterized by a distinctive sing-song delivery. It was mainly by means of wandering preachers that *Hasidism was spread in the eighteenth century.

Heavenly Agent. A *maggid* (voice, angel, or spirit) would communicate supernatural illumination to the mystic. In the sixteenth century, maggidism was considered as one of the normal forms of charismatic life (which included the appearance of the prophet Elijah or celestial angels and inspiration by the holy spirit). The term *maggid* usually referred to a heavenly voice speaking through the mouth of the mystic. Many kabbalists had *maggidim*, the best-known instance being that of R. Yosef *Karo.

• Paysach J. Krohn, *In the Footsteps of the Maggid: Inspirational Stories and Parables about Eminent People of Yesterday and Today*, ArtScroll Series (Brooklyn, N.Y., 1992). Shlomo Pines, "Le Sefer ha-Tamar et les Maggidim des Kabbalistes," in *Hommage à Georges Vajda*, edited by G. Nation and C. Touati (Louvain, Belgium, 1980). Marc Saperstein, *Jewish Preaching, 1200–1800: An Anthology* (New Haven, 1989).

MAGIC, ritual acts, including the pronouncing of spells, performed for the purpose of influencing things and events beyond the ordinary range of human capacity by means of resort to occult powers. The Bible forbids the practice of magic; the penalty for transgressing this prohibition is death. Sorcerers are usually referred to in the feminine, and the Talmud implies (*San*. 67a) that magic was mostly practiced by women. The most complete list of the various forms of magic is to be found in *Deuteronomy* 18.10–11. The story of Saul and the "witch" (more accurately, necromancer; *1 Sm*. 28) illustrates the extent to which magic was practiced in early times, despite the biblical prohibition. The Talmud, however, seems to differentiate between what might be called "black magic" and "white magic," depending on the source of the occult powers. Thus, on the basis of *Joshua* 13.22, "Balaam the soothsayer" is considered a sorcerer by the Talmud (*San*. 106a–b); other magical acts, for example those ascribed to R. Ḥanina' and to R. Oshaʿyah (*San*. 65b) were held to be unobjectionable. The prohibition against magic as an "abomination unto the Lord" (*Dt*. 18.12) does not necessarily imply denial of its efficacy, though rationalist thinkers including Maimonides (*Hilkhot ʿAvodah Zarah* 11.15) dismissed it as a foolish superstition. Some medieval authorities even interpreted the story of Saul in *1 Samuel* 28 as the account not of an actual event but of a dream. Nevertheless, folk belief in magic persisted until a late date, and ancient magical traditions (spells, amulets) and belief in the power of combinations of letters constituting divine names were further strengthened by the Kabbalah. Exorcism of evil spirits has been practiced up to modern times. See also AMULETS; DEMONS; WITCHCRAFT.

• Joseph Naveh and Shaul Shaked, *Magic Spells and Formulae: Aramaic Incantations of Late Antiquity* (Jerusalem, 1993). Stephen Sharot, *Messianism, Mysticism, and Magic: A Sociological Analysis of Jewish Religious Movements* (Chapel Hill, N.C., 1982). Michael D. Swartz, *Scholastic Magic: Ritual and Revelation in Early Jewish Mysticism* (Princeton, 1996). Joshua Trachtenberg, *Jewish Magic and Superstition: A Study in Folk Religion* (New York, 1977).

MAGOG. See GOG AND MAGOG.

MAḤALOQET (מַחֲלֹקֶת; division), a term that signifies both dissension and difference of opinion. The former is deplored by the rabbis, who rule, for instance, that a man coming to a new locality must abide by local custom, even if he disagrees with it, "lest he cause *maḥaloqet* (*Pes*. 4.1). One may speak badly of people who cause *maḥaloqet* (Y., *Pe'ah* 1), for they are the emissaries of Satan (*Git*. 52a). On the other hand, a genuine difference of opinion (for example, the many variant Talmudic interpretations of the tanna'im and amora'im), based upon principle, especially regarding the elucidation of the meaning of scripture, is also called *maḥaloqet*. The two kinds of *maḥaloqet* are exemplified in *Avot* 5.19: the former by the story of Korah and Moses (*Nm*. 16); the latter, "*maḥaloqet* for the sake of heaven," by the controversies between Hillel and Shamm'ai.

• Menachem Elon, *Jewish Law: History, Sources, Principles*, 4 vols. (Philadelphia, 1994).

MAHARAL. See YEHUDAH LIVA' BEN BETSAL'EL.

MAHARAM. See Me'ir ben Gedalyah of Lublin.

MAHARIL. See Molin, Ya'aqov ben Mosheh ha-Levi.

MAHARIVAL. See Lev, Yosef ben David ibn.

MAḤAZOR (מַחֲזוֹר; cycle), a term first used for lists of special synagogal readings from the Torah and the Prophets or for collections of poetic embellishments of the public prayers (see Piyyut) arranged according to the Torah-reading cycle or the cycle of the liturgical year. In the Middle Ages, *maḥazor* became a name for a comprehensive *prayer book, like a *siddur*, for all liturgical occasions of the year (e.g., *Maḥazor Vitry*). Only in the Ashkenazi sphere and especially since the advent of printing has the *maḥazor* become more and more identified with the *festival prayers, in contrast to the *siddur*, the prayer book for daily and weekly use. In medieval northern Europe and Italy the *maḥazor* became a major object of book illumination. Sephardim call their prayer books for the Shalosh Regalim *mo'adim*.

• Malachi Beit-Arie, ed., *Worms Maḥzor*, vol. 1 (Vaduz, Liechtenstein, 1985). A. van der Heide and E. van Voolen, eds., *The Amsterdam Mahzor: History, Liturgy, Illumination* (Leiden, 1989). Gabrielle Sed-Rajna, *Le Mahzor enluminé: Les Voies de formation d'un programme iconographique* (Leiden, 1983). —PETER LENHARDT

MAḤAZOR VITRY. See Simḥah ben Shemu'el of Vitry.

MAH NISHTANNAH (מַה נִּשְׁתַּנָּה; "How does [this night] differ?"), the opening words of the four questions (*arba' qushyot*) asked at the Pesaḥ Seder, usually by the youngest child. Originally the Haggadah was recited after the meal, and the questions were prompted by what the child had already observed. The Mishnah (*Pes*. 10.4, 116a) reflects both the earlier custom of leaving it to the child's spontaneous curiosity to inquire about the meaning of the Seder ceremonies and the later use of a formalized version of the four questions, to which the leader of the Seder replies with the recital of the Haggadah, telling the story of the Exodus from Egypt. The questions relate to the use of unleavened bread, bitter herbs, the dipping of herbs, and the custom of reclining (there are differences in order in some rites). Palestinian recensions of the Mishnah point to early three-question versions. Not all homes used the same questions, and until the late medieval period the four-question set was asked by the leader of the Seder, not a child.

• Nahum Glatzer, *The Schocken Passover Haggadah* (New York, 1996). Philip Goodman, ed., *The Passover Anthology* (Philadelphia, 1993).

MAH TOVU (מַה טֹּבוּ; How Goodly), title and opening words of the prayer recited in the Ashkenazi rite upon entering the synagogue. It is composed of biblical verses all taken from *Psalms* and mentioning prayer or a house of prayer, the one exception being the quotation from *Balaam, "How goodly are your tents, O Jacob, your dwellings, O Israel" (*Nm*. 24.5), though this too is interpreted (*San*. 105b) as referring to the synagogue and *beit midrash*. In the Sephardi rite, one verse (*Ps*. 5.8) is generally said upon entering and another (*Ps*. 5.9) upon leaving the synagogue. Mah Tovu was set to music and was sung in many synagogues as a major choir piece.

• Ismar Elbogen, *Jewish Liturgy: A Comprehensive History*, translated by Raymond P. Scheindlin (Philadelphia, 1993), pp. 76–77.

MAḤZIKE HA-DAS (Upholders of the Faith), name first adopted by an organization established in 1879 to promote strict *Orthodoxy and combat modernism in Galicia. The organization held conferences, published a Hebrew-language weekly (*Qol Maḥziqei ha-Dat*), and drew mass support from Hasidic Jews loyal to Yehoshu'a Roqeaḥ, the rabbi of Belz. As titular head of this movement, Shim'on Sofer of Kraków, a son of Mosheh (Ḥatam) Sofer (see Sofer Family), was elected to the Austrian parliament. Transformed into a conservative, anti-Zionist party, the Maḥzike ha-Das competed with Agudat Israel in pre-Hitler Poland. Its Lithuanian counterpart, nicknamed Ha-Lishkah ha-Sheḥorah (the Black Bureau), waged an all-out campaign against Zionism in czarist Russia between the years 1890 and 1903.

Machzike Hadath was also the name given to an independent religious community founded in London's East End (1891) by eastern European Jews dissatisfied with the "compromising Orthodoxy" of Hermann Adler and the United Synagogue. After conducting a prolonged and successful campaign against their standards of *sheḥitah*, Machzike Hadath was headed for a time (1916–1919) by A. Y. Kook, the future Ashkenazi chief rabbi of Palestine. There are other Maḥzike ha-Das communities in Antwerp, Copenhagen, Toronto, and Vienna.

• Lucy S. Dawidowicz, ed., *The Golden Tradition: Jewish Life and Thought in Eastern Europe* (Northvale, N.J., 1989), pp. 192–200. Masha Greenbaum, *The Jews of Lithuania* (Jerusalem, 1995), pp. 135–139. Bernard Homa, *A Fortress in Anglo-Jewry: The Story of the Machzike Hadath* (London, 1953). —GABRIEL A. SIVAN

MAḤZOR. See Maḥazor.

MAIMON BEN YOSEF (died c.1165), Spanish rabbinical scholar and authority; the father and teacher of Moses *Maimonides. He was a *dayyan* in Cordova until forced to flee as a result of the edict of forced conversion issued by the Almohades in 1145. After ten years of wandering, he and his family reached Fez in North Africa. After a few years, he went with his sons to Erets Yisra'el and died either there or in Egypt. He was a distinguished and influential scholar. His *Iggeret ha-Neḥamah* (original Arabic in *Jewish Quarterly Review* 2 [1890]: 62–66, 335–369; Heb. translation by B. Klar [1945]) was directed especially to forced converts to Islam. He wrote that Islam is not to be regarded as idolatry; he was therefore opposed to martyrdom as a means of avoiding forced conversion to Islam. His other works include Talmud commentaries, which are known from citations in the writings of Maimonides.

• Isak Munz, *Maimonides, the Rambam: The Story of His Life and Genius* (Boston, 1935). —SHALOM BAR-ASHER

MAIMONIDEAN CONTROVERSY, a theological controversy that raged from the end of the twelfth to the fourteenth century, ostensibly over the writings of Moses *Maimonides, whose immense authority as a halakhist and codifier also gave his philosophical work a prestige and influence that could not be ignored. In actual fact it was a clash between traditional, fideistic orthodoxy and rationalist, philosophical (mainly Aristotelian) theology. The first criticism of Maimonides—during his lifetime—was directed at his halakhic method and rulings rather than his philosophy. Three decades after his death, his theology, especially his reserved attitude to the doctrine of the *resurrection of the dead, came under heavy attack in southern France (Provence), more particularly in rabbinic circles close to the emerging Kabbalah, whose members did not shrink from enlisting the help of the Inquisition to burn the "heretical" writings of Maimonides in 1232. This manifestation of extreme fanaticism, however, shocked Jewry to such an extent that the controversy subsided for some time. It flared up again early in the fourteenth century and focused on the allegorical, that is, "rationalist," interpretation of biblical texts. The leading rabbinic authority in Spain, R. Shelomoh ben Avraham *Adret of Barcelona, gave formal expression to the feeling of unease regarding the dangers implicit in the teachings of the by now generally revered Maimonides by issuing a ban in 1305 prohibiting the study of philosophy by students under the age of twenty-five.

The issues that formed the crux of the Maimonidean controversy did not die with Adret's ban, but changing circumstances, both external (including the increasingly aggressive Christian attempts to bring about the conversion of Jews in Iberia) and internal (such as the rise of Kabbalah) led to a softening of the intensity of the debates. For all intents and purposes, the issue died with the expulsion of the Jews from Spain in 1492.

• Marc Saperstein, "The Conflict over the Rashba's *Herem* on Philosophical Study: A Political Perspective," *Jewish History* 1 (1986): 27–38, contains further bibliography. Bernard Septimus, *Hispano-Jewish Culture in Transition: The Career and Controversies of Ramah* (Cambridge, Mass., 1982). Daniel Jeremy Silver, *Maimonidean Criticism and the Maimonidean Controversy: 1180–1240* (Leiden, 1965). Israel Zinberg, *A History of Jewish Literature*, vol. 3 (Philadelphia, 1973), pp. 55–77.

—MENACHEM KELLNER

MAIMONIDES, ABRAHAM BEN MOSES. See AVRAHAM BEN MOSHEH BEN MAIMON.

MAIMONIDES, MOSES (1135–1204), philosopher and codifier. Born in Spain into a distinguished family, he lived most of his life in Egypt, where he was physician to the court and leader of the Jewish community. Moses Maimonides is the Latinized form of Mosheh ben Maimon, and he is known by his acronym as Rambam. At the age of twenty-three he composed a treatise on logic. At the age of thirty he completed his commentary on the Mishnah, in which, unlike *Rashi, who explains each sentence separately, he gave a short review of the Talmudic treatise on the Mishnah, explained individual words, and determined the law, so that the student could obtain a clear picture of the whole subject. His commentary, written in Arabic, was widely appreciated, and several Hebrew translations were produced. As an introduction to his major work *Mishneh Torah*, Maimonides wrote *Sefer ha-Mitsvot*, consisting of an enumeration and definition of the 613 *mitsvot*. This work, too, was written in Arabic, while the *Mishneh Torah* was written in Mishnaic Hebrew. His objective in all his halakhic work was to define the law as it stood, in the most concise manner possible. Drawing upon the whole range of rabbinic literature, where subjects occur in the most unexpected contexts, Maimonides sifted his material from the "*sea of the Talmud," grouped it under appropriate headings, and extracted the final *halakhah* from the labyrinth of numerous and complicated discussions. Maimonides rejected customs based on a belief in demons or other superstitions; he expressed his stance on the matter with the motto "Man should never cast his sound reason behind him, for the eyes are in front and not in back." His work, the first of its kind, provoked much criticism, both because it codified the whole oral law and especially because it did so without indicating sources. R.* Avraham ben David of Posquières was its most outspoken opponent, and Maimonides, in a letter to one of his critics, expressed regret at not having listed out-of-the-way sources in a separate work. He indicated that he intended to compile such a reference book, though he never did. Numerous attempts have been made by later scholars to trace Maimonides' sources and reconstruct the arguments that led to his decisions. Nevertheless, many passages in the *Mishneh Torah* still remain unaccounted for, and very often its decisions run counter to the Talmud itself. It appears that Maimonides occasionally deviated from the opinion of early teachers, following instead the plain meaning of the biblical text (see *Hilkhot Ned*. 12.1); he also added laws not mentioned in any source but which accorded with his medical knowledge and could be deduced from the Mishnah (e.g., *Hilkhot Sheḥitah* 8.23). Maimonides included in his legal code a number of theological and philosophical ideas, as well as moral and practical rules, which, he held, formed part of the aggadic teaching of the oral law. The *Mishneh Torah* became a standard work of Jewish law and a major source for subsequent codes. The standing of Maimonides as a communal leader and rabbinic authority is evident from the epistles he addressed to Yemen and other parts of the Diaspora. Even more significant, in many respects, was Maimonides' philosophical *Guide of the Perplexed* (*Moreh Nevukhim*), thus entitled because it was intended neither for the ordinary pious folk, nor for those who occupied themselves exclusively with the study of Torah, but for those who followed both Torah and philosophy and who were "perplexed" by the contradictions between the teachings of the two. In interpreting the Torah in the light of philosophy, Maimonides rejects the literal understanding of certain texts, particularly *anthropomorphism. Phrases ascribing human qualities to God merely represent human language used by the Torah as metaphors for his actions. Faith is, ideally, a matter of conviction based on philosophical understanding. Maimonides' reconciliation of philosophy with Jewish tradition was based on his assumption that Aristotle's philosophy was the truth. However, he rejected the Aristotelian theory of the eternity of the universe, which he held to be unproved, and accepted the biblical doctrine of *creatio ex nihilo*. Prophecy, according to Maimonides, is that state of intellectual and moral perfection in which the human mind becomes illuminated by "active intellect" proceeding from God. All prophets received the divine message in a vision; only the prophecy of Moses came immediately from God. To know God and his relationship to creation, one must understand the nature of the universe and its parts. Man's free will is not affected by God's omniscience and foreknowledge; hence man remains responsible for his actions. The divine commandments are not arbitrary decrees but serve a rational purpose: to develop and perfect man's moral and intellectual potentialities, though some precepts are beyond human understanding. Maimonides defined certain propositions as prerequisites of Jewish religion. His list became known as the *Thirteen Principles of Faith and found its way into the liturgy in poetical form (*Yigdal). The *Guide of the Perplexed* was twice translated into Hebrew soon after its composition and thus came immediately to the notice of Jewish communities outside the Arab world. A Latin translation brought it to the notice of Christian scholastics as well. The *Guide* dominated the subsequent development of Jewish thought, although immediately upon its publication it provoked a storm of protest. Maimonides and his followers were accused of excessive rationalism, bordering on—or at least encouraging—heresy, and of undermining the belief in revelation, and thus the basis for following Jewish law. For over a century the conflict between Maimonists and anti-Maimonists almost rent Judaism into two camps (see MAIMONIDEAN CONTROVERSY), but ultimately the name of Maimonides became established as the symbol of the pure and orthodox faith. The popular evaluation was expressed by the later inscription on his tombstone: "From Moses to Moses there was none like unto Moses."

• Jacob I. Dienstag, ed., *Studies in Maimonides and St. Thomas Aquinas* (New York, 1975). Marvin Fox, *Interpreting Maimonides: Studies in Methodology, Metaphysics, and Moral Philosophy* (Chicago, 1990). Isaac Husik, *A History of Mediaeval Jewish Philosophy* (New York, 1916), pp. 236–311. *Maimonidean Studies* (1990–). Fred Rossner and Samuel Kottek, eds., *Moses Maimonides: Physician, Scientist, and Philosopher* (Northvale, N.J., 1993). Colette Sirat, *A History of Jewish Philosophy in the Middle Ages* (Cambridge, 1990), pp. 157–203. Isadore Twersky, *Introduction to the Code of Maimonides: Mishneh Torah* (New Haven, 1980). David Yellin and Israel Abrahams, *Maimonides: His Life and Work* (Philadelphia, 1903).

MAINTENANCE. A husband's obligation to provide his wife with food and clothing is a biblical law (*Ex.* 21.10), and it is extended by the Talmud to a number of other areas, including medical expenses and the use of the matrimonial home throughout widowhood (*Ket.* 46b–47a, 52b). Under rabbinic law, a husband is also required to provide funds for the maintenance of a domestic household and for any regular expenses of a personal nature incurred by his wife (*Shulḥan ʿArukh, Even ha-ʿEzer* 70.3). In return for her maintenance, the husband is entitled to his earnings for work done outside the home (*Ket.* 58b). The *beit din* is obliged to force a husband to maintain his wife in accordance with his potential earning capacity and not merely with his actual earnings (Rema', *Even ha-ʿEzer* 70.3). A husband who is, however, unable to work and lives in penury for reasons beyond his control is only obliged to share what little he has with his wife (Pitḥei Teshuvah, *Even ha-ʿEzer* 70.2). Normally, the obligation to maintain only applies if the wife lives in the matrimonial home. If the husband is responsible for his wife leaving the home, her claim for maintenance is unaffected by her departure from the common dwelling (Rema', *Even ha-ʿEzer* 70.12). A widow may choose between receiving maintenance from her husband's estate or collecting the lump sum in her *ketubbah*. There is a fundamental difference between Sephardi and Ashkenazi authorities with regard to the question of whether the choice in this situation is the widow's or the heirs' (*Shulḥan ʿArukh, Even ha-ʿEzer* 93.3). Under Talmudic law, the maintenance of children is obligatory only until they reach the age of six years. It is, however, regarded as an act of cruelty to refuse to maintain children beyond this age (*Ket.* 49b). In any case, there is a general obligation to support all close relations under the laws of charity (*Shulḥan ʿArukh, Even ha-ʿEzer* 71.1; *Yoreh Deʿah* 254.4). Daughters are entitled to receive maintenance from their dead mother's *ketubbah* out of the estate of their deceased father (*Ket.* 52b).

• Rachel Biale, *Women and Jewish Law: An Exploration of Women's Issues in Halakhic Sources* (New York, 1984). E. Westreich, "A Father's Obligation to Maintain His Children in Jewish Law," *Jewish Law Annual* 10 (1992): 177–212.

—DANIEL SINCLAIR

MAJORITY. See ADULT.

MAKHSHIRIN (מַכְשִׁירִין; Render Susceptible [to Ritual Impurity]), tractate in Mishnah order Tohorot, with related material in the Tosefta'. There is no *gemara'* in either Talmud. According to biblical law, foods are rendered susceptible to ritual contamination only after coming into contact with water (*Lv.* 11.34, 38). The laws governing the role of liquids in transmission of impurity were a major point of sectarian contention during Second Temple times, which helps to explain why the Mishnah devoted an entire tractate of six chapters to this subject.

The opening and closing laws of the tractate highlight its dominant conceptual theme: intention. The opening law of the tractate establishes intention as an essential component of the contact made between the liquid and the food. A discussion of the seven liquids that render food susceptible to impurity closes *Makhshirin*.

The focus on intention is characteristic of Pharisaic *halakhah* and is absent from the halakhic traditions of other sects, which tended to be much stricter in defining the laws of impurity. Much of the tractate is devoted to defining the boundaries between intended and unintended contact between food and liquid. In a series of disputes between *Beit Hillel and Beit Shamm'ai, Beit Hillel leniently requires a higher degree of intention than does Beit Shamm'ai in order to render food susceptible to impurity.

An English translation of the Mishnah tractate is in Herbert Danby's *The Mishnah* (Oxford, 1933).

• Chanoch Albeck, ed., *Shishah Sidrei Mishnah, Seder Tohorot* (Jerusalem, 1958). Philip Blackman, ed. and trans., *Mishnayoth*, vol. 5, *Order Taharoth* (Gateshead, 1973). Hermann Leberecht Strack and Günter Stemberger, *Introduction to the Talmud and Midrash*, rev. and updat. ed., translated by Markus Bockmuehl (Minneapolis, 1992).

—AVRAHAM WALFISH

MAKKOT (מַכּוֹת; Flogging), tractate consisting of three chapters in Mishnah order *Neziqin, with related material in the Tosefta' and in both Talmuds. *Makkot*, which was originally the end of tractate **Sanhedrin*, concludes *Sanhedrin*'s discussion of the laws of *capital punishment by dealing with several ancillary topics: the laws of false witnesses (*Dt.* 19.15–21), who are sometimes put to death; the exile of unintentional murderers to cities of refuge (*Nm.* 35.9–28; *Dt.* 19.1–10); and *flogging (*Dt.* 25.1–3), from which the name of the tractate is derived.

The biblical provision that a false witness be punished "as he intended to do to his friend" (*Dt.* 19.19) served as a major point of contention between Pharisees and Sadducees (*Mak.* 1.6, 5b), especially regarding capital cases. According to Pharisaic law, followed by *Makkot*, false witnesses are punished after their testimony has led to conviction of the defendant and prior to his actual execution. False testimony thus emerges as a unique case in Jewish law, in which a transgressor is punished for criminal intent, although the crime was not successfully executed. *Makkot* discusses the conditions for punishing false witnesses and the manner of punishment of witnesses to whom the principle of an "eye for an eye" (*Dt.* 19.21) is inapplicable.

The laws regarding the exile of murderers to cities of refuge focus on the legal determination of different levels of intent and of negligence as well as on the manner and conditions of the penalty of exile. *Makkot*'s discussion reflects the dual character of exile as protection of the person who has committed manslaughter from the blood avenger (*Nm.* 35.26–27; *Mak.* 2.7) and as atonement for criminal negligence (*Mak.* 2b).

Makkot lists transgressions for which the penalty of flogging is prescribed and describes the manner in which the flogging is carried out, stressing the care that must be taken to avoid the criminal's accidental death. The sages' aversion to carrying out capital punishment is underscored by *Makkot*'s characterization of any court that executed more than one criminal every seven (and, in one tradition, seventy) years as a "destructive court" (*Mak.* 1.10). The redactor of *Makkot* emphasizes the merciful and affirmative thrust of Jewish law (*Mak.* 1.7, 3.15) by concluding the Mishnaic discussion of punishments with the declaration that the plenitude of commandments stems from God's desire "to benefit Israel" (*Mak.* 3.16).

The Talmud Bavli tractate was translated into English by H. M. Lazarus in the Soncino Talmud (London, 1935).

• Chanoch Albeck, ed., *Shishah Sidrei Mishnah, Seder Nezikin* 2d ed. (Jerusalem, 1956). Philip Blackman, ed. and trans., *Mishnayoth*, vol. 4, *Order Nezikin* (Gateshead, 1973). Pinhas Kehati, ed., *Mishnah: A New Translation with a Commentary, Seder Nezikin*, vol. 3, *Makkot, Shevuot, Eduyot* (Jerusalem, 1988). Hermann Leberecht Strack and Günter Stemberger, *Introduction to the Talmud and Midrash*, rev. and updat. ed., translated by Markus Bockmuehl (Minneapolis, 1992).

—AVRAHAM WALFISH

MALACHI (Heb. Mal'akhi), postexilic prophet in the kingdom of Judah whose oracles appear in the book named after him. The existence of a prophet by this name is disputed because the name literally means "my messenger" and may be derived from the statement in *Malachi* 3.1, "Behold, I send my messenger to prepare the way before me." Furthermore, *Malachi* 2.7 identifies the priest as "the messenger of the Lord of Hosts." The Talmud as well as the Aramaic Targum Jonathan consider Malachi a proper name (*Meg.* 15a) and identify him with Ezra the scribe (*R. ha-Sh.* 19b). The message of the prophet presupposes the destruction of Edom and the rebuilding of the Temple in the late sixth and early fifth centuries BCE. He portrays a period of decline in the Jewish community in which intermarriage and lax Temple observance are prevalent. He exhorts the priests and the people to maintain the Torah and covenant with God, comparing that with marriage and marital fidelity. Just as he rejects divorce, so he rejects infidelity to the covenant. He foresees the "Day of the Lord," preceded by the appearance of the prophet Elijah, when God will punish the wicked and restore the righteous (KJV, *Mal.* 4.5–6).

The *Book of Malachi* is the twelfth and last book of the Minor Prophets. A characteristic stylistic feature of Malachi's prophecies is the employment of disputation speeches. The book consists of the preamble (1.1–5), in which God assures the people of his permanent relationship with them; a rebuke of the priests for treating the Temple disrespectfully (1.6–2.9); a denunciation of mixed marriages and divorce (2.10–16); a promise of divine retribution for those who engage in sorcery, adultery, perjury, and exploitation of the weaker classes (2.17–3.5); an accusation against the people for defrauding God of the payment of tithes (3.6–12); a condemnation of those who charge that the wicked and arrogant are not punished (3.13–4.3); and an exhortation to the people to be mindful of the Torah of Moses (4.4–6), for the prophet Elijah is about to come and herald the final "Day of the Lord." The closing verses of *Malachi* have also been interpreted as the conclusion of the entire prophetic section of the Bible. The book is commonly dated to the mid-fifth century BCE.

• R. J. Coggins, *Haggai, Zechariah, Malachi*, Old Testament Guides (Sheffield, Eng., 1987). Beth Glazier-MacDonald, *Malachi: The Divine Messenger*, Dissertation Series (Society of Biblical Literature) no. 98 (Atlanta, 1987). Andrew E. Hill, "Dating the Book of Malachi: A Linguistic Reexamination," in *The Word of the Lord Shall Go Forth: Essays in Honor of David Noel Freedman in Celebration of His Sixtieth Birthday*, edited by Carol L. Meyers and M. O'Connor (Winona Lake, Ind., 1983), pp. 77–89. Gordon Paul Hugenberger, *Marriage as a Covenant: A Study of Biblical Law and Ethics Governing Marriage, Developed from the Perspective of Malachi*, Supplements to Vetus Testamentum, vol. 52 (Leiden, 1994). Julia M. O'Brien, *Priest and Levite in Malachi*, Dissertation Series (Society of Biblical Literature) no. 121 (Atlanta, 1990). David L. Petersen, *Late Israelite Prophecy*, Monograph Series (Society of Biblical Literature) no. 23 (Missoula, Mont., 1977). Ralph L. Smith, *Micah–Malachi*, Word Biblical Commentary, vol. 32 (Waco, Tex., 1984).

—MARVIN A. SWEENEY

MALAKH, ḤAYYIM (c.1655–1717), radical Shabbatean kabbalist. Born in Poland, he adhered to Shabbateanism under the influence of mystic Yehoshuʿa Heshel *Tsoref of Vilna. In 1690 Malakh moved to Italy, where he associated with the clandestine Shabbatean activists Avraham Rovigo and Binyamin ha-Kohen, from whom he received the esoteric writings of Natan of Gaza. In Poland, Malakh spread Shabbatean ideas and later stayed in Adrianople with Shabbetai Tsevi's secretary Shemu'el Primo. In 1700 Malakh joined *Yehudah Ḥasid ha-Levi's group, which went to Jerusalem in expectation of the imminent advent of the Messiah. After Yehudah's sudden death, Malakh led the group but was expelled from Jerusalem by the rabbis. He moved to Salonika where he maintained contacts with the apostates of the *Dönmeh sect. In Podolia, Poland, he led the radical Shabbatean sect from which the Frankist movement emanated. None of his writings survived. He was strongly opposed by Avraham Miguel Cardoso (see CARDOSO FAMILY), the Shabbatean thinker, who rejected the radical Shabbateans' antinomianism and belief in the apotheosis of the Messiah.

• Elisheva Carlebach, *The Pursuit of Heresy: Rabbi Moses Hagiz and the Sabbatian Controversies* (New York, 1990). David Kohn, *Toledot ha-Mequbbalim, ha-Shabbeta'im veha-Ḥasidim*, vol. 2 (Odessa, 1913), pp. 175–180. —NISSIM YOSHA

MAL'AKH HA-MAVET. See ANGEL OF DEATH.

MALBIM, ME'IR LEIBUSH (1809–1879), rabbi, preacher, and biblical commentator. Malbim was born in Volochisk, Volhynia. He studied in Warsaw, and eventually became the rabbi of Bucharest and then the chief rabbi of Romania in 1858, where he was involved in the battles over religious reform. His strong anti-Reform stand led to his dismissal from that position. Malbim's biblical commentaries on *Esther* (1845), *Isaiah* (1849), *Leviticus* and *Song of Songs* (1860), and other books of the Bible (1867–1876), contain his polemics against modern methods of Bible study. Against the reformers, Malbim asserted that the words of the rabbis in the oral law were given from heaven, that there were no superfluous words in scripture, and that the rabbis had developed the basic foundations of grammar and logic. His commentaries achieved great popularity. In addition to his biblical commentaries, Malbim composed treatises on Talmudic law, commentaries on rabbinic codifications, and works on language, poetry, and logic.

• Eliezer Parkoff, *Fine Lines of Faith: A Study of the Torah's Outlook on Human Suffering Based on the Malbim's Commentary to Iyov* (Jerusalem and Spring Valley, N.Y., 1994). Noah Rosenbloom, *Ha-Malbim: Parshanut, Filosofiyah Maddaʿ u-Mistorin be-Khitvei ha-Rav Me'ir Leybush Malbim* (Jerusalem, 1988). Yehezkel Rotenberg and Aharon Sorski, eds., *Sefer ha-Malbim: Me'ah Shanah li-Fetirato*, by Meir Malbim (Bene Beraq, 1979). —MICHAEL A. SIGNER

MALKHUT SHAMAYIM. See KINGDOM OF HEAVEN.

MALKHUYYOT (מַלְכֻיּוֹת; Sovereignties), first of the middle three sections (the other being *Zikhronot and *Shofarot) of the *ʿAmidah additional service of the *Ro'sh ha-Shanah liturgy, devoted to the theme of God's sovereignty. The theme is expressed by appropriate biblical verses—three each from the Pentateuch, the Prophets, and the Hagiographa, with the concluding verse from the Pentateuch (as laid down in *R. ha-Sh.* 4.6)—*ʿAleinu, and a prayer. After Malkhuyyot, the *shofar is sounded (except on a Sabbath)—in the Sephardi rite, during both the silent ʿAmidah and its repetition by the cantor; in the Ashkenazi rite, during the repetition only.

• Eliezer Eliner, "Die Auswahl und Anordnung der Pesukim von 'Malchiot' in der Synagoge," *25 Jahre Judische Schule Festschrift* (Jerusalem, 1980), pp. 53–55. Macy Nulman, *The Encyclopedia of Jewish Prayer* (Northvale, N.J., 1993), pp. 235–236. L. A. Rosenthal, "Malkhijot R. Johanan b. Nuri's," *Festschrift zum siebzigsten Geburtstage David Hoffmann's*, edited by Simon Eppenstein et al. (Berlin, 1914), pp. 234–240.

MALQOT. See FLOGGING.

MALSHIN. See DENUNCIATION.

MAMRAM (Hebraized form of Lat. *membrana* [parchment]), promissory note; first described by Jewish authorities in sixteenth-century Poland. It was designed to allow a person to write out authorization to another to pay the bearer of the note a fixed amount of money, and in certain ways was similar to a bond or a check. It is first described in the halakhic literature by R. Mordekhai ben Avraham Jaffe in his work *Levushim*, although some believe it dates to the fourteenth century.

• J. David Bleich, "Survey of Recent Halakhic Literature: Checks," *Tradition* 24 (Fall 1989): 74–83. Abraham M. Fuss, "Assignability of Debt and Negotiable Instruments in Jewish Law," Diné Israel 12 (1984–1985): 19–37. —MICHAEL BROYDE

MAMZER (מַמְזֵר), the product of an adulterous or an incestuous union. Under biblical law it is forbidden for a *mamzer* to marry another Jew (*Dt.* 23.3; *Shulḥan ʿArukh, Even ha-ʿEzer* 4.13). Marriage between two *mamzerim* is permitted, as is a marriage between a *mamzer* and a convert, and their children will be *mamzerim* (*Yev.* 45b, 79b; *Shulḥan ʿArukh, Even ha-ʿEzer* 4.22–24). If, despite the prohibition, a Jew contracts a marriage with a *mamzer*, the offspring is a *mamzer* since the rule is that in prohibited unions, the children adopt the status of the "tainted" parent. The child of a *mamzer* and a non-Jewish woman will, however, be a non-Jew (*Qid.* 67a) and the product of an adulterous union between a Jewish woman and a non-Jewish man is not a *mamzer* (*Yev.* 45b). Although the term *mamzer* is often translated as "bastard," under Jewish law, a child born out of wedlock is in fact not a *mamzer*, and his or her personal status is legally unimpeachable. Except with regard to marriage, a *mamzer* does not suffer from any legal disadvantage. The *inheritance rights of a *mamzer* are the same as those of any other heir and he may be appointed to high public office. According to the Mishnah, "a scholarly *mamzer* takes precedence over an ignorant High Priest" (*Hor.* 3.8). It is a general principle of rabbinic law that the creation of *mamzerim* ought to be avoided and, in practice, various methods are used in order to ensure that the taint, if it has been established in a particular family, does not persist throughout the generations. See also ADULTERY; INCEST.

• J. David Bleich, *Contemporary Halakhic Problems* 1 (New York, 1977), pp. 159–176. David Weiss-Halivni, "Can a Religious Law Be Immoral?" in *Perspectives on Jews and Judaism: Essays in Honor of Wolfe Kelman*, edited by Arthur A. Chiel (New York, 1978), pp. 165–170. Moshe Zemer, "Purifying Mamzerim," *Jewish Law Annual* 10 (1992): 101–114.

—DANIEL SINCLAIR

MAN. See HUMAN BEING.

MAN, SON OF. See SON OF MAN.

MANASSEH (Heb. *Menasheh*), *Joseph's firstborn son and the name of one of the twelve tribes of Israel. Manasseh and *Ephraim were born to Joseph and his Egyptian wife, Asenath, in Egypt. Although Manasseh was the elder son, *Jacob put Ephraim first in his blessing (*Gn.* 48.20). Joseph was allotted two tribal territories, one for each of his sons. The territories of Manasseh and Ephraim were located in the central hill country; Manasseh's lay north of Ephraim's, half of it west of the Jordan River, half on its eastern bank. The earliest Israelite settlement sites are found in the territories of Manasseh and Ephraim. Mount Ebal in Manasseh was perhaps the site of the first Israelite cult center (*Jos.* 8.30). In the Midrash, Manasseh is identified as the interpreter between Joseph and his brothers (*Gn. Rab.* 91.8).

• Yohanan Aharoni, *The Land of the Bible: A Historical Geography*, 2d ed., translated by A. F. Rainey (Philadelphia, 1979). John Bright, *A History of Israel*, 3d ed. (Philadelphia, 1981). Israel Finkelstein, *The Archaeology of the Israelite Settlement*, translated by D. Saltz (Jerusalem, 1988). Amihay Mazar, *Archaeology of the Land of the Bible: 10,000–586* BCE *(New York, 1990)*.

—NILI SACHER FOX

MANASSEH, PRAYER OF. See PRAYER OF MANASSEH.

MANASSEH BEN ISRAEL (1604–1657), Marrano-born Dutch scholar. His family left Portugal for the freedom of Amsterdam, where they embraced Judaism and where Manasseh embarked on a multifaceted career. He served the Sephardi communities of Amsterdam as chief preacher, rabbi, schoolteacher, and principal, and he founded the city's first Hebrew printing press. Manasseh wrote many works in Hebrew, Spanish, Portuguese, and Latin. Some were addressed to the needs of returning Marranos (*Thesouro dos dinim; Nishmat Ḥayyim*). Other works include *Conciliador* (1632), on the reconciliation of apparent contradictions between biblical passages; *De creatione problemata* (1635), on creation; and *De resurrectione mortuorum* (1636), on resurrection. Manasseh had a wide reputation among learned Christians, who came to hear him preach, corresponded with him, and cultivated his personal acquaintance; these included the jurist Hugo Grotius and Rembrandt, who painted his portrait. In his *Miqveh Yisra'el* (1650), Manasseh lent credibility and millenarian significance to the purported discovery of the ten lost tribes in South America.

In 1655 Manasseh traveled to England, where he petitioned Oliver Cromwell to readmit Jews. While the terms of Manasseh's petition were never formally granted, it paved the way for the eventual return of open Jewish life to England. While there he wrote a polemical defense of Judaism, *Vindiciae Judaeorum* (1656), a response to a work by William Prynne, who was opposed to the return of Jews to England.

• Yosef Kaplan et al., eds., *Menasseh ben Israel and his World* (Leiden, 1989). Cecil Roth, *A Life of Menasseh ben Israel: Rabbi, Printer, and Diplomat* (Philadelphia, 1934), contains a comprehensive bibliography of Manasseh's writings. Lucien Wolf, *Menasseh ben Israel's Mission to Oliver Cromwell* (London, 1901).

—ELISHEVA CARLEBACH

MANICHAEISM, dualistic religion, incorporating elements of gnosticism, founded by Mani (c.216–276). Mani seems to have spent part of his youth in Judeo-Christian circles (see EBIONITES) and was active mainly in the Persian empire, where, after initial successes, he was finally martyred by order of the Sassanian king Bahrām I. Manichaeism was a missionary religion and seems to have had wide appeal, gaining adherents in North Africa, the Near East, Persia, Central Asia, and even China before being brutally stamped out. Scholars detect Manichaean influence in various medieval gnostic-dualistic heresies, including the Albigenses (Catharans) in twelfth-century southern France. The possibility of Catharan influence on *Kabbalah, particularly the doctrine of *transmigration, exists, but there is no conclusive evidence. The polemics of *Sa'adyah ben Yosef Ga'on (882–942) against dualistic beliefs and also against the belief in transmigration were probably directed at Jewish proponents of Manichaeism.

• Peter Bryder, ed., *Manichaean Studies* (Lund, 1988). Samuel N. C. Lieu, *Manichaeism in Mesopotamia and the Roman East* (Leiden, 1994). Gedaliahu A. G. Stroumsa, *Savoir et salut* (Paris, 1992). Geo Widengren, *Mani and Manichaeism* (London, 1982).

MANNA, food miraculously provided for the Israelites during their wandering in the wilderness (*Ex.* 16.4–35). It is described as a thin layer of seedlike substance, akin to hoarfrost (*Ex.* 16.14) or coriander seed, suitable for varied processing (*Nm.* 11.6–8). A double portion was gathered every Friday, the only time manna remained fresh until the next day (from which derives the custom of placing two loaves on the Sabbath-eve table). Only when the Israelites had crossed the Jordan River did manna cease to appear, but as a memorial, a jar of manna was placed in the Sanctuary. Its spiritual significance was explained in the passage " . . . and gave you manna to eat . . . in order to teach you that man does not live on bread only, but that man may live on anything that the Lord decrees . . . " (*Dt.* 8.3). The rabbis suggested that manna was created on the first Sabbath eve (*Avot* 5.9).

The physical nature of the manna was a perplexing question for the Israelites themselves; the Hebrew phrase in *Exodus* 16.15, *man hu'*, means both "what is it?" and "it is manna." The metaphorical descriptions "food from heaven" (*Ex.* 16.4) and "heavenly grain" (*Ps.* 78.24, cf. *Ps.* 105.40) are figurative and expressive but tell nothing of the physical properties of the manna. *Exodus* 16 and *Numbers* 11 provide some physical details, but several of the technical terms involved are themselves enigmatic, since they occur hardly anywhere else in the Bible. After comparison with other ancient Near Eastern texts, the manna may be described as an edible substance, white in color, abundant and fine like frost on the ground, with a sweet, rich, creamy taste, generally similar in nature to the seed of the more common (white) coriander herb.

• F. S. Bodenheimer, "The Manna of Sinai," in *The Biblical Archaeologist Reader*, vol. 1, edited by David M. Freedman and G. E. Wright (New York, 1961), pp. 76–80. Chaim Cohen and Daniel Sivan, *The Ugaritic Hippiatric Texts: A Critical Edition* (New Haven, 1983), pp. 38–39, 56–57. Paul Maiberger, *Das Manna: Eine literarische, etymologische und naturkundliche Untersuchung* (Wiesbaden, 1983). Joel C. Slayton, "Manna," in *The Anchor Bible Dictionary*, edited by David N. Freedman et al., vol. 4 (New York, 1992), p. 511. —CHAIM COHEN

MANNERS. See DEREKH ERETS.

MANNHEIMER, ISAAC NOAH (1793–1865), preacher whose name is associated with the Wiener *minhag* (Viennese rite), a compromise between *Orthodoxy and *Reform Judaism. The son of a Hungarian cantor, Mannheimer was born and educated in Copenhagen, where he endeavored to promote a reformed style of worship between 1817 and 1820. When Vienna's elegant new Stadttempel (City Temple) was consecrated in 1826, Mannheimer, director of the religious school (i.e., minister-preacher), officiated. Initially, his reluctance to antagonize most regular worshipers deflected him from his original path. By 1830, however, Mannheimer had become ideologically more conservative. Together with Salomon *Sulzer, the Stadttempel's young cantor-composer, he developed an aesthetically "improved" choral service with German-language sermons but few changes in the traditional liturgy. Prayers were recited in Hebrew, those expressing the hope for Israel's national restoration in Zion were retained, and organ music was excluded on Sabbaths and festivals. While this form of worship did not satisfy more-Orthodox Jews, it prevented a split in the community and—as the Wiener *minhag*—was adopted by many congregations throughout the Habsburg empire. Though not an ordained rabbi, Mannheimer excelled as a preacher and became renowned for his pastoral and philanthropic work. In later years he vigorously defended circumcision, boycotted Reform congresses in Germany, and issued a prayer book with translation (1840) that appeared in several editions. During the revolutions of 1848, he was elected to parliament and called for Jewish emancipation and the abolition of capital punishment.

• Michael A. Meyer, *Response to Modernity: A History of the Reform Movement in Judaism* (New York, 1988), pp. 144–151. Moses Rosenmann, *Isak Noa Mannheimer, Sein Leben und Wirken* (Vienna and Berlin, 1922). Kurt Schubert, ed., *Der Wiener Stadttempel 1826–1976* (Eisenstadt, 1978). Robert S. Wistrich, *The Jews of Vienna in the Age of Franz Joseph* (Oxford, 1989), pp. 98–106. —GABRIEL A. SIVAN

MANSLAUGHTER. See HOMICIDE.

MANTLE OF THE LAW. See TORAH ORNAMENTS.

MANUAL OF DISCIPLINE. See RULE OF THE COMMUNITY.

MA'OZ TSUR (מָעוֹז צוּר; O Fortress, Rock [of My Salvation]), hymn sung on *Ḥanukkah after the kindling of lights in the Ashkenazi ritual, but not the Sephardi one (although now widely sung by all communities in Israel). Ma'oz Tsur was composed by a certain Mordekhai (possibly 13th cent.), whose name appears in acrostic. Originally intended for the home, the song has been also transferred to the synagogue. Its stirring tune, adapted from an old German folk song, forms a fitting accompaniment to its theme of the Jewish people's salvation from the oppression of the Egyptians, Babylonians, Haman, and the Syrian Greeks.

• Israel Davidson, *Thesaurus of Medieval Jewish Poetry*, 4 vols. (New York, 1970). Macy Nulman, *The Concise Encyclopedia of Jewish Music* (New York, 1975), pp. 162–163. Macy Nulman, *The Encyclopedia of Jewish Prayer* (Northvale, N.J., and London, 1993), pp. 236–237. Ismar Schorsch, "A Meditation on 'Maoz Zur,'" *Judaism* 37.4 (1988): 459–464.

MAPPAH (מַפָּה; cloth), a word used for various types of coverings: (1) a binder wound around the Torah scroll in the Ashkenazi custom (see TORAH ORNAMENTS); (2) a cover, often elaborately decorated, for the reading desk; (3) a cover placed over the Torah scroll between sections of the Torah reading in the synagogue (*'aliyyot*); (4) the name of glosses on Yosef Karo's *Shulḥan 'Arukh* by Mosheh *Isserles, specifying Ashkenazi customs and practices.

• C. Grossman, "Womanly Arts: A Study of Italian Torah Binders," *Journal of Jewish Arts* 7 (1980): 35–43.

MAR (Aram.; מָר; master), honorific title given in Babylonia to the exilarchs and to some amora'im; for example, a son quoting his scholarly father was told to refer to him as "my father, my *mar*" (*Qid*. 31b). Sometimes the title was used in preference to "Rabbi," notably for the scholars Mar *Shemu'el, Mar Zutra' (6th cent. exilarch), and Mar 'Ukba' (10th cent. exilarch). In the course of a Talmudic discussion, when the words "*mar* said" are used, the meaning is "one [of the disputants mentioned earlier] said." In Modern Hebrew, "Mar" is used as "Mr." —SHMUEL HIMELSTEIN

MARBITS TORAH (מַרְבִּיץ תּוֹרָה; Torah teacher), a type of communal religious leader in Mediterranean lands from the sixteenth through the eighteenth century. When the Spanish refugees reached the Ottoman empire at the end of the fifteenth century, they called their local spiritual leaders *marbits Torah*. His authority was limited to a single community or province. Though a highly respected figure, there were often conflicts between the *marbits Torah* and the communities over halakhic issues, the heredity of the position, and the salary. The position was known in Turkey and Italy until the end of the seventeenth century and was still in existence in Tangiers at the end of the eighteenth century.

• Meir Benayahu, *Marbits Torah* (Jerusalem, 1953). —SHALOM BAR-ASHER

MARGALIT, MOSHEH (c.1719–1780), rabbi and Talmudic commentator. Margalit was born near Kovno, Lithuania, and later served as rabbi in several Lithuanian communities. He wrote one of the most important commentaries on the Talmud Yerushalmi. Part one, entitled *Penei Mosheh*, gives a running explanation of the text; the second part, *Mar'eh ha-Panim*, notes the differences between the Talmud Yerushalmi and the Talmud Bavli, and here Margalit shows great textual acumen, offering numerous emendations, based in part on evidence from the Tosefta'. Together with David Franckel's *Qorban ha-'Edah*, Margalit's commentary continues to appear in almost every edition of the Talmud Yerushalmi. Margalit enrolled at the University of Frankfurt in 1779, shortly before his death, in order to study botany, presumably to understand better the Jewish agricultural laws. The tradition that Eliyyahu ben Shelomoh Zalman of Vilna was, in his youth, Margalit's student is almost certainly apocryphal, and the former knew nothing of Margalit's commentaries, many of which were not published until after his death. Margalit wrote commentaries on the Torah and a few tractates of Talmud Bavli, but they were never published.

• Louis Ginzberg, *On Jewish Law and Lore* (New York, 1970), pp. 42–44.

—MARC SHAPIRO

MARGOLIES, MOSES ZEVULUN (1851–1936), Orthodox rabbi in the United States. He was born in Kroja, Russia, and attended *yeshivot* in Białystok and Kovno before serving as rabbi in Slobodka from 1877 to 1899. He then migrated to America and served as Boston's unofficial chief rabbi until 1905, when he moved to New York's Congregation Kehilath Jeshurun, where he served until his death.

Although he was a leader of the *Union of Orthodox Rabbis of the United States and Canada, which actively opposed immigrant religious acculturation, Margolies supported the *Union of Orthodox Jewish Congregations of America, the modernization of the Rabbi Isaac Elchanan Theological Seminary, and the modern *Talmud Torah* movement, all of which promoted Americanized Orthodoxy. The Ramaz School in New York is named for him (using his acronym).

• Jeffrey S. Gurock, "Resisters and Accommodators: Varieties of Orthodox Rabbis in America, 1886–1983," *American Jewish Archives* (November 1983): 120–125. Jenna Weissman Joselit, *New York's Jewish Jews: The Orthodox Community in the Interwar Years* (Bloomington, Ind., 1990), pp. 60–65. Haskel Lookstein, "Rabbi Moses Zebulon Margolies—High Priest of Kehilath Jeshurun," in *Congregation Kehilath Jeshurun Diamond Jubilee Year Book* (New York, 1946), pp. 48–51.

—JEFFREY S. GUROCK

MARḤESHVAN. See ḤESHVAN.

MAROR (מָרוֹר; bitter herb), bitter herb eaten at the *Seder service. The regulations for the paschal lamb include the injunction, "With unleavened bread and with bitter herbs shall they eat it" (*Ex*. 12.8). Originally a condiment eaten with meat, *maror* was invested with symbolic significance as a memorial of the fact that the Egyptians "embittered the lives" of the children of Israel (*Ex*. 1.14). With the destruction of the Temple, the paschal sacrifice ceased, but both unleavened bread and bitter herbs became an integral part of the Seder service. The *Haggadah is to be recited only "when **matsah* and *maror* are lying before you," and the *maror* is ceremoniously eaten twice, once with **haroset* and once with *matsah* in the form of a sandwich in recollection of the custom of *Hillel, who made a sandwich of the paschal offering together with *matsah* and *maror*. The Mishnah (*Pes*. 2.5) lists five plants that may be used for the bitter herb: *ḥazeret* (lettuce), *'olshin* (chicory), *tamkha'* (identification uncertain), *ḥarḥavinah* (a plant of the Umbelliferae family), and *maror* (possibly *Sonchus oleraceus*; Arab. *murar*). In eastern Europe it became customary to use the root of horseradish. According to the custom of Yitsḥaq ben Shelomoh *Luria, followed by the Sephardim, the *maror* is in the center of the Seder plate; according to R. *Eliyyahu ben Shelomoh Zalman, the Vilna Ga'on, followed by Ashkenazim, it is at the top of the plate.

• Baruch Bokser, *The Origins of the Seder: The Passover Rite and Early Rabbinic Judaism* (Berkeley, 1984). William Braude, "The Two Lives of Hillel's Sandwich," in *A Rational Faith: Essays in Honor of Rabbi Levi A. Olan*, edited by Jack Bemporad (New York, 1977), pp. 51–60. Arthur Schaffer, "The History of Horseradish as the Bitter Herb of Passover," *Gesher* 8 (1981): 217–237.

MARRANOS, crypto-Jews of Spain and Portugal, forcibly converted to Christianity in the fourteenth and fifteenth centuries. Beginning with violent anti-Jewish persecutions in 1391, followed by anti-Jewish legislation, compulsory conversionary sermons in synagogues, and a religious disputation in Tortosa in the early fifteenth century, over one hundred thousand Jews in Spain either reluctantly sought baptism or were forcibly converted to Christianity. They were known as *conversos* or New Christians. Some became sincere Christians, while others continued to adhere to Jewish practices in secret. The latter were soon derisively called Marranos, meaning swine. The Marranos of the Balearic Islands were known as *Chuetas. The converts hoped to weather the storm and return to Judaism, only to discover that their baptism was considered indelible by church authorities and that any further practice of Judaism would be regarded as the criminal offense of Judaizing or heresy. With their conversions, these former Jews were no longer barred from many areas of the Iberian economy or society, and they soon distinguished themselves in commerce, statecraft, and even within the church. They constituted a discernible and influential class of society.

In 1449 anti-Jewish popular sentiments were deflected into anti-Marrano riots. Laws were promulgated barring New Christians from advancement on the basis of their origins (racial laws known as *limpieza de sangre* [purity of blood]). In 1480 the Inquisition was established in the kingdom of Aragon; New Christians, particularly wealthier families, were its major target at first. The ranks of the Marrano population swelled with the expulsion of Jews from Spain in 1492 and the forced conversion of the Jewish community of Portugal in 1497.

Many of the latter were exiles from Spain who had chosen immigration over conversion only a few years previously. The Inquisition was introduced into Portugal in 1540. Marranism virtually ceased in Spain by the middle of the sixteenth century. Upon the annexation of Portugal by Spain in 1580, thousands of Marranos from Portugal fled back to Spain, assured by the authorities that the Spanish Inquisition would not try them for "crimes" committed in Portugal. Spanish society once again faced the issue of crypto-Judaism. With the passage of time traces of Judaism grew fainter among the Marranos. They constituted a secret society pervaded by fear of detection and Inquisitorial prosecution. After 1540, the Portuguese Inquisition was especially zealous in ferreting out Marranos. Eventually many Marranos escaped to England, Holland, France, the Ottoman empire, or the New World (where the Inquisition followed them) and returned to Judaism. They formed a diaspora stretching from Brazil to Goa, linked by family ties, shared tragedy, and often commerce. Rabbinical authorities tended to be lenient with these former Marranos, regarding them as Jews who were not to be reminded of their tragic past. Crypto-Judaism persisted in the Iberian Peninsula for centuries. Deprived of rabbinical authorities, access to knowledge of Hebrew, and access to post-biblical sources, as well as the sustenance of a living community, it became a radically altered religion. Nevertheless, Marranos and their descendants, who had long since forgotten why they retained some of their distinctive practices, continued to be stereotyped and stigmatized despite their strict adherence to Catholicism. Until its abolition in Portugal in the eighteenth century and in Spain in the nineteenth century, the Inquisition continued to prosecute Marranos. Remnants of Marrano practices persist in northeastern towns and villages in Portugal. Recently an entire community of Marranos in Belmonte, Portugal, returned to Judaism.

• Haim Beinart, *Conversos on Trial: The Inquisition in Ciudad Real* (Jerusalem, 1981). Benzion Netanyahu, *The Marranos of Spain* (New York, 1966). Benzion Netanyahu, *The Origins of the Inquisition in Fifteenth Century Spain*, 2 vols. (New York, 1995). Cecil Roth, *History of the Marranos* (Philadelphia, 1932). Yosef Yerushalmi, *From Spanish Court to Italian Ghetto: Isaac Cardoso: A Study in Seventeenth-Century Marranism and Jewish Apologetics* (Seattle, 1971).

–JANE S. GERBER

MARRIAGE. The married state is emphatically regarded in Judaism as a social, moral, and religious ideal, and as a necessary condition of spiritual perfection. *Celibacy was frowned upon, and even ascetic and mystical writers never suggested that the perfect life was possible without marriage. The rabbis eloquently extolled the virtues of marriage: "He who dwells without a wife dwells without joy, without blessing, without good, and without happiness" (*Yev*. 62b); and "He who has no wife is less than a man" (*Yev*. 67a). Marriage is a religious duty, as the first biblical commandment enjoined: "Be fruitful and multiply" (*Gn*. 1.28); the purpose of marriage is procreation, and ten years of childless marriage was regarded as a valid and natural cause for *divorce. Although monogamy was envisaged as the ideal state (see *Gn*. 1 and 2) and seems to have been the norm, the legal system presupposed *polygamy. It was not until the time of R. *Gershom ben Yehudah (c.960–1028) that monogamy became legally binding upon Ashkenazi Jews, but the decree enforcing it seems to have been the legal formulation of existing practice rather than a reform. The ideal relationship between God and Israel is depicted by the biblical prophets, as well as in later aggadic literature and liturgical poetry, not so much in the language of erotic love (as in the allegorical exegesis of the *Song of Songs*) as in imagery drawn from the marriage bond between husband and wife. See also BETROTHAL; MATRIMONY.

• Rachel Biale, ed., *Women and Jewish Law: The Essential Texts, Their History, and Their Relevance for Today* (New York, 1995). Sergio Della Pergola, *Recent Trends in Jewish Marriage* (Jerusalem, 1989). Louis M. Epstein, *The Jewish Marriage Contract: A Study in the Status of the Woman in Jewish Law* (New York, 1927). Norman Lamm, *A Hedge of Roses: Jewish Insights into Marriage and Married Life*, 2d ed. (New York, 1968).

MARRIAGE BROKER. See SHADDEKHAN.

MARRIAGE CONTRACT. See KETUBBAH.

MARRIAGES, PROHIBITED. There are two main categories of prohibited marriages in Jewish law: void and valid. The former category consists of adulterous unions, incestuous unions, and unions with non-Jews. In the case of adultery (on the wife's part) and incest the offspring are *mamzerim* (see MAMZER). While an adulterous woman must be divorced by her husband, such a step does not need to be taken in the case of incest or in the case of marriage with a non-Jew since these marriages are void *ab initio*. The halakhic status of the children of mixed marriages is determined by the matrilineal principle. Valid prohibited marriages are generally those involving lesser biblical offenses than incest and unions between the secondary degrees of consanguinity prohibited by the rabbis (*Shulḥan ʿArukh, Even ha-ʿEzer* 44.6–7). In the case of such marriages, pressure is applied to the couple to secure a divorce, even if they were unaware of the prohibition at the time of their nuptials. Examples of valid prohibited marriages include an adulteress and her lover, even after the woman's divorce from her husband or his death (*Yev*. 24b); a priest and a woman whom he is forbidden to marry (Rema', *Even ha-ʿEzer* 3.6); marriage between a divorcée who has remarried and her first husband, after her second husband has divorced her or died, (*Dt*. 24.4); and a bigamous union under the decree of R. Gershom. In general, if the husband was unaware at the time of marriage that his wife was prohibited to him, then both parties will be exempt from their marital obligations under the law. Voluntary obligations such as the *tosefet ketubbah* (see ALIMONY) will, however, remain in force (*Shulḥan ʿArukh, Even ha-ʿEzer* 116.1–3). Where the husband was aware of the impediment at the time of marriage, a balance is struck between compelling him to fulfill all the obligations imposed upon him by the law and creating a situation in which the couple will be encouraged to divorce. The wife's knowledge is of no legal significance in this area of Jewish law. In most cases where the principle of equality is at issue, the Reform movement rejects the notion of a prohibited marriage.

• Menachem Elon, *Jewish Law: History, Sources, Principles*, 4 vols. (Philadelphia, 1994), pp. 1771–1784. Louis Epstein, *Marriage Laws in the Bible and the Talmud* (Cambridge, Mass., 1967). Mendell Lewittes, *Jewish Marriage: Rabbinic Law, Legend, and Custom* (Northvale, N.J., 1994), pp. 19–27. —DANIEL SINCLAIR

MARTYRDOM. The Hebrew idiom for martyrdom is *qiddush ha-Shem* (death for "the sanctification of the Name [of God]"; see *Lv*. 22.32), a term stemming from the belief that any worthy action on the part of a Jew that enhances the prestige of Judaism in the eyes of gentiles thereby also "sanctifies" the name of God as embodied in his revelation and covenant to Israel (similarly, its opposite, **ḥillul ha-Shem*, an unworthy act, desecrates the Name). *Qiddush ha-Shem* came to have the more specific meaning of martyrdom, since the sacrifice of one's life for God's Torah was regarded as the ultimate sanctification of God's name. This supreme act of faith was final proof of man's willingness to "Love the Lord your God with all your soul (*Dt*. 6.5)—even though he take your soul" (*Ber*. 61b). The ideal of martyrdom in Judaism has its roots in the *ʿ*aqedah*, God's test of Abraham through a command to offer up his only son Isaac; in that case, the supreme sacrifice was not exacted, and essentially martyrdom thus represents the willingness to make such a sacrifice. The martyr "sanctifies the name of God in public" and he is called *qadosh* (holy one). On the other hand *suicide, the deliberate throwing away of life without reason, is regarded as the most heinous of crimes, and the various regulations in Talmudic and post-Talmudic literature attempting to establish those instances when martyrdom is justified are designed to show, as far as possible, the frontiers between the two acts. The duty of preserving life is paramount in Judaism, and it is a general rule that in order to save life one may transgress all the commandments of the Torah with the exception of the three cardinal sins of idolatry, shedding of innocent blood, and major sexual transgressions (adultery and incest). In the case of these three, one should endure martyrdom rather than transgress. However, in times of religious persecution, when the observance of the Torah becomes a public demonstration of religious loyalty, the Jew was obliged to submit to martyrdom rather than transgress even the most insignificant commandment (*San*. 74a). During the Middle Ages, mostly in connection with the massacres that accompanied the *Crusades, whole communities underwent self-immolation at the behest of their leaders rather than submit to baptism (the example of the Jewish community of York in 1190 is outstanding). These tragic episodes are usually regarded as the classic examples of martyrdom in Jewish thought and history, and to this day a prayer is recited on the Sabbath for "the holy congregations who laid down their lives for the sanctification of the divine name," and Sephardi communities recite a special memorial prayer (Hashkavah) in memory of the victims of the Inquisition. According to Jewish law, the wife of a martyr may not remarry. Medieval pietists and especially the kabbalists recommended that when faced with martyrdom, it should be met in contemplation while reciting the *Shemaʿ. The ʿAleinu prayer was also often recited by martyrs. See also MEMORBUKH; TEN MARTYRS.

• Ronal E. Agus, *The Binding of Isaac and Messiah: Law, Martyrdom, and Deliverance in Early Rabbinic Religiosity* (Albany, 1988). Arthur J. Drodge and James D. Tabor, *A Noble Death: Suicide and Martyrdom among Christians and Jews in Antiquity* (San Francisco, 1992), an unconventional interpretation. Hayim I. Kolits, *Rabbi Akiva: Sage of All Sages* (Woodmere, N.Y., 1989). Moses Maimonides, *Epistles of Maimonides: Crisis and Leadership*, edited and translated by Abraham Halkin and David Hartman (Philadelphia, 1993). Shalom Spiegel, *The Last Trial: On the Legends and Lore of the Command to Abraham to Offer Isaac as a Sacrifice: The Akedah*, translated by Judah Goldin (Woodstock, Vt., 1993).

MARTYRS, TEN. See TEN MARTYRS.

MASHGIAḤ (מַשְׁגִּיחַ; supervisor), a title applied to two types of religious supervisors. A *mashgiaḥ* is assigned by a rabbinic authority to supervise the *kashrut* of food products and in this role is known in Hebrew as a *mashgiaḥ kashrut*. This person is responsible for ensuring that the food products of a factory, store, restaurant, or hotel are in compliance with the *dietary laws. Besides being a halakhic expert on *kashrut*, the *mashgiaḥ* must be God-fearing and trustworthy. The ignorant and those motivated solely by financial gain are precluded from serving as *mashgiaḥ*. A *mashgiaḥ* is also assigned in a **yeshivah* to supervise the spiritual development and well-being of the students; this person is known as the *mashgiaḥ ruḥani*.

MASHIAḤ. See MESSIAH.

MASHIV HA-RUAḤ U-MORID HA-GESHEM (מַשִּׁיב הָרוּחַ וּמוֹרִיד הַגָּשֶׁם; "[He] who causes the wind to blow and the rain to fall"), phrase (taken from *Taʿan*. 1.1) introduced in all rites as part of the second benediction of the ʿAmidah. The onset of the fall and winter rainy season in Erets Yisra'el is marked by strong winds. The phrase is recited between *Shemini ʿAtseret (when first recited in the prayer for rain [see TEFILLAT GESHEM]) and the first day of *Pesaḥ, after which the Sephardi (but not the Ashkenazi) rite replaces it with *morid ha-tal*, "[He] who causes the dew to fall" (see TEFILLAT TAL). In Israel, most Ashkenazim follow the Sephardi practice.

• Ismar Elbogen, *Jewish Liturgy: A Comprehensive History*, translated by Raymond P. Scheindlin (Philadelphia and New York, 1993), p. 39, s.v. index. Joseph Heinemann, "La-Verur Peshutan shel Mishnayyot Aḥadot: She'elat Geshem ve-Hazkarat Geshamim ba-Golah uve-'Erets Yisra'el," in *ʿIyyunei Tefillah* (Jerusalem, 1981). Eliyahu Ki Tov, *The Book of Our Heritage* (Jerusalem, 1978), pp. 212–214.

MASKIL (מַשְׂכִּיל; intelligent, knowing), originally, particularly in Sephardi usage, a title of honor for a learned man. In the Middle Ages, the term also meant (depending on the circle in which it was used) either a philosopher or a kabbalist. In the nineteenth century, the term came to designate a follower of the *Haskalah (Enlightenment) movement; hence it had a pejorative implication when used by the Orthodox.

MASORAH (מָסוֹרָה; traditional text), a term that in the narrow and technical sense refers to an apparatus for the writing and reading of the biblical text (see BIBLE TEXT). The Masoretic Text is written around the consonantal framework of the biblical text as handed down for centuries by the schools of the Masoretes. There is no consensus concerning the vocalization of the word *masorah* and its exact meaning. According to some, it derives from the root *asar* (fetter; cf. *masoret*, *Ez*. 30.37); more likely the word derives from the verb *masar* (hand down, in the sense of traditional transmission). In the wider sense of the term, the Masorah consists also of the *vocalization, *accents, and certain other elements of the text. The Masorah had its origin in the period of the *soferim* (see SOFER), though some of its earliest features may date back to the time of *Ezra. The purpose of the Masoretes was to safeguard the integrity of the biblical text and to facilitate its study. Since scriptures as a whole, and the Torah in particular, were regarded as divinely inspired and considered the ultimate source of Jewish doctrine and observance, the slightest change could have far-reaching consequences (cf. *ʿEruv*. 13a). In order to achieve uniformity, the Masoretes compiled, first orally and subsequently in writing, numerous notes and rules with which to "fence round" the correct text and especially the exact spellings of the words—hence, the various masoretic treatises laying down the rules of spelling (full or defective) and marginal notes in Aramaic regarding the exceptions to these rules. As an additional precaution, the Masoretes would note how many times a certain spelling occurred in a given biblical book or in the Bible as a whole. Originally, it seems, the Bible was written in continuous script. The Masoretes, therefore, also directed their attention to such details of the text as the division into words, sentences, and paragraphs; vocalization and accents; and determining which letters must be written large (*Gn*. 1.1), small (*Lv*. 1.1), suspended (*Jgs*. 18.30), inverted (*Nm*. 10.35 ff.), or dotted (*Dt*. 29.28). The Masorah counted the letters, words, and verses in the individual books and in the Bible as a whole and printed out differences between pronunciation (*qeri* [what is read]) and spelling (*ketiv* [what is written]). The term *sevirin* (what could be suggested) referred to possible but not acceptable alternatives, though the text was left unchanged. The Masorah also mentions corrections of the scribes (**tiqqunei soferim*), which, however, seem to represent Midrashic exegesis rather than emendations. These masoretic notes are placed on the side margins (Minor Masorah), while the notes on the tops and bottoms of pages (Major Masorah) list in detail the particulars mentioned by way of allusion in the Minor Masorah. Still longer annotations, included in medieval manuscripts and the Second Rabbinic Bible (Venice, 1525–1526), are reserved for the end of the Bible (Final Masorah). The Masoretes worked over many centuries (probably from 500 until 1000), especially in Erets Yisra'el but also in Babylonia and elsewhere. The accepted text was determined by Aharon ben Mosheh ben Asher of the school of Tiberias. The masoretic apparatuses were developed far beyond the activity of the first generations of Masoretes into collections of notes written in separate volumes or handbooks of detailed observations on the biblical text, above all, about spelling, including **Okhlah ve-Okhlah*; *Minḥat Shai*, by Shelomoh Yedidyah (16th cent.); and *Masoret ha-Masoret*, by Eliyyahu *Levita (1538). The precise form of the Masorah, which was culled from various manuscripts by Yaʿaqov Ḥayyim ibn Adoniyahu for the Second Rabbinic Bible, has become the accepted text of the Masorah, although scholars prefer to use the Masorah of individual manuscripts, such as that of the Aleppo Codex published by Loewinger (1977) or that of the Codex Leningrad B19[A] published by Weil (1971).

• Mordechai Breuer, *Keter Aram Tsovah veha-Nusaḥ ha-Mekubbal shel ha-Miqra'* (Jerusalem, 1976). Menachem Cohen, *Miqra'ot Gedolot ha-Keter*, vol. 1, *Joshua, Judges* (Ramat Gan, 1992). Christian D. Ginsburg, *Introduction to the Massoretico-Critical Edition of the Hebrew Bible* (London, 1897; repr. New York, 1966). Israel Yeivin, *Introduction to the Tiberian Masorah*, translated from Hebrew and edited by E. J. Revell, Society of Biblical Literature, Masoretic Studes 5 (Missoula, Mont., 1980).

MASORETIC ACCENTS. See ACCENTS.

MASSEKHET (מַסֶּכֶת; Aram. *masekhta'*; woven fabric), a tractate of the Mishnah or of other rabbinic works (Tosefta', Talmud, Mekhilta'). Usually a *massekhet* deals with a specific subject and is subdivided into chapters, with the exception of *ʿEduyyot*, which is organized associatively. Originally the Mishnah had sixty tractates (*Sg. Rab*. 6.9; *Nm. Rab*. 18.21), but the division of tractate *Neziqin* into three subsections and the separation of *Makkot* from *Sanhedrin* raised the number to sixty-three. The Talmud Yerushalmi has thirty-nine tractates; the Talmud Bavli thirty-seven. —AVRAHAM WALFISH

MATMID (מַתְמִיד; from Heb. *tamid* [perpetual]), one who persists, particularly in his study of the Talmud. Among those studying in *yeshivot*, the *matmid* has always been the most admired of all students, a true *matmid* may spend as many as eighteen hours a day, or more, poring over the Talmud texts, leaving his books only for the three daily prayer services, meals, and a few hours of sleep. The fervent student who devotes days and nights to Talmudic learning has been immortalized in Hebrew literature by Ḥayyim Naḥman Bialik's poem Naḥman ha-Matmid. —SHMUEL HIMELSTEIN

MATRIARCHS (Heb. *immahot*), *Sarah, *Rebekah, *Leah, and *Rachel, the wives of the three *patriarchs. Unlike the patriarchs they are not mentioned in the traditional daily prayers, but they are now named along with the patriarchs in many non-Orthodox congregations and prayer books. Prayers for women who are ill and women after childbirth invoke the matriarchs, and blessings for girls mention their names. Rabbinic legends contain many stories about the four matriarchs, extolling their virtues.

• Catherine Chalier, *Les Matriarches: Sarah, Rébecca, Rachel et Léa* (Paris, 1985). Samson Raphael Hirsch, *Ha-'Ishah ha-Yehudit* (Jerusalem, 1979). Carol L. Myers, *Discovering Eve: Ancient Israelite Women in Context* (New York, 1988). —SHALOM PAUL

MATRILINEAL DESCENT. See PATRILINEAL DESCENT.

MATRIMONY. Matrimonial law developed in the patriarchal society of the ancient Middle East. The husband was the dominant party in the relationship, though the wife had a high status in the home and already in the stories of the *matriarchs often played an independent role. The biblical precedent set the tone for Talmudic law, codified in Maimonides' *Mishneh Torah* and in the *Shulḥan ʿArukh* (*Hilkhot Ishut* 12.1–4; *Shulḥan ʿArukh, Even ha-ʿEzer* 69.1–3). The husband was obligated to provide sustenance, clothing, and housing. He was also to decide where the couple would live, although if either wished to live in Erets Yisra'el and the other objected, such an objection was grounds for divorce. The husband was to cohabit with his wife (see SEX), to provide her a **ketubbah*, to be responsible for her medical needs, to ransom her from captivity, and to ensure that she had a proper burial. Allowance was also to be made for her maintenance in the event of his death. The husband was entitled to inherit his wife's property (see INHERITANCE). Reform Jews do not recognize these laws as binding; Conservative congregations have modified them in accord with modern outlooks.

Jewish literature abounds with expressions of *family values and of the unique nature of the husband–wife relationship (see WOMEN), seen as fundamental and integral to the whole structure of Judaism. God's presence dwells in a home that is loving and pure (*Sot*. 17a). See also BETROTHAL; MARRIAGE.

• Menachem Elon, *Jewish Law: History, Sources, Principles*, 4 vols. (Philadelphia, 1994). Ignaz Maybaum, *The Jewish Home* (London, 1945). Ben-zion Schereschewsky, *Dinei Mishpaḥah* (Jerusalem, 1967).

MATSAH (מַצָּה), unleavened bread. Since it does not require fermentation of the dough, *matsah* can be baked hurriedly and is therefore specified as the bread prepared for unexpected visitors (cf. *Gn*. 19.3). For the same reason it became the bread of the *Exodus: "And they baked unleavened cakes of the dough . . . for it was not leavened, because they were thrust out of Egypt and could not tarry" (*Ex*. 12.39). It therefore also became known as "the bread of affliction." As a result, the main ritual in the observance of Pesaḥ (also called the Festival of Matsot), is the prohibition against eating any **ḥamets* (leaven) and the religious duty of eating *matsah*. The two regulations are not identical; the positive duty of eating *matsah* applies only on the first night (the first two nights in the Diaspora), when the eating of *matsah* is a central feature of the *Seder, while the prohibition against leaven applies to the whole period of the festival. *Matsah* may be eaten all year, but it became a custom not to eat it in the period preceding Pesaḥ. The principal regulation concerning the baking of *matsah* is that the ingredients be only specially prepared flour (made from one of the "five species of grain," that is, wheat, rye, barley, oats, spelt; cf. *Pes*. 35a) and cooled water. The addition of salt is prohibited for no clear reason, and the dough must be continuously kneaded and baked with such rapidity as to prevent any possibility of fermentation. Eighteen minutes is usually regarded as the maximum amount of time. Normally it is sufficient to exercise care that the flour does not come into contact with moisture from the time of the grinding of the grain. In view of the positive obligation of eating *matsah* on the first night, many strictly Orthodox Jews bake a specially prepared *matsah* for that occasion. This is called *shemurah matsah* or *matsah shemurah* (i.e., *matsah* that has been specially guarded), and the flour for this *matsah* is supervised from the time the grain is harvested. Spiritually and allegorically, leaven is regarded as the symbol of impurity and *matsah* that of purity (*Ber*. 17a). All the meal offerings in the Temple were of *matsah* and were disqualified in the event of fermentation. The laws concerning *matsah* are to be found in the tractate *Pesaḥim*, in *Hilkhot Ḥamets u-Matsah* in Maimonides' *Mishneh Torah*, and in the *Shulḥan ʿArukh* (*Oraḥ Ḥayyim* 53–462).

• Yoel Ben-Nun, "Ḥamets u-Matsah be-Pesaḥ, be-Shavuʿot uve-Qorbonot ha-Leḥem," *Megadim* 13 (1991): 25–45. Avi Nilsson Ben-Zvi, "Passover Traditions and the Baking of Matzah Among Göteborg Jews," *Israel Museum Journal* 3 (1984): 68–74. Yehudah Felix, "Li-She'eilat Zihuyah shel Shibbolet Shuʿal," *Sefer ha-Yovel Minḥah le-'Ish*, edited by Itamar Warhaftig (Jerusalem, 1991), pp. 171–178. Shalom Y. Gross, *Laws and Customs of Passover Matzah* (Brooklyn, N.Y., 1981). I. Lerner, "Modern Matzo Manufacture," *L'eylah* 2.7 (1984): 8–11. Yisrael Ta-Shema, "Matzah Meluḥah be-Pesaḥ: Le-Tiv'am u-Muvanam shel Minhagei Ashkenaz ha-Qedumim," in *Minhag Ashkenaz ha-Qadmon* (Jerusalem, 1992), pp. 249–259.

MATSEVAH (מַצֵּבָה; monument), originally, a raised stone. According to the Bible, *matsevot* served as memorial stones for the dead (*Gn*. 35.20; *2 Sm*. 18.18) and commemorated treaties or border agreements (*Gn*. 31.45–52; *Jos*. 4.4–9). They were connected with the worship of the Lord, as is clear from the early narratives of Jacob at Bethel (*Gn*. 28.18, 22, 35.14). In general, however, they were viewed negatively, since they were also employed as part of the cultic worship of other gods, especially the Canaanite-Phoenician Baal (*1 Kgs*. 14.23; *2 Kgs*. 3.2). Thus, the Israelites were commanded to destroy them (*Ex*. 23.24, 34.13; *Dt*. 7.5, 12.3) and were prohibited from using them (*Dt*. 16.22). They have been identified with the larger stones or groups of stones found in archeological excavations throughout Israel dating from many of the early periods. In Jewish usage, the term subsequently signified a tombstone (see TOMBS).

• Shalom M. Paul and William G. Dever, eds., *Biblical Archaeology* (Jerusalem, 1973), pp. 271–275.

—SHALOM PAUL

MATTAN TORAH. See GIVING OF THE TORAH.

MATTATHIAS. See HASMONEANS.

MAYIM AḤARONIM (מַיִם אַחֲרוֹנִים; latter waters), the washing of hands after meals. Before beginning a meal at which bread is served, the hands must be washed and the appropriate blessing recited. The water used for this first ablution is called *mayim ri'shonim* (first waters). After the meal it is customary, though not obligatory, to dip the hands into a vessel containing *mayim aḥaronim* in order to cleanse the hands before reciting the *Birkat ha-Mazon. No blessing is recited over this post-prandial washing (*Shulḥan ʿArukh, Oraḥ Ḥayyim* 181.f).

• Philip Birnbaum, *A Book of Jewish Concepts* (New York, 1964), p. 414.

—A. STANLEY DREYFUS

MAZZAL (מַזָּל), literally, a "constellation," the word has come to mean "luck." *Astrology is based on the belief that the fate of each person is determined by the constellation under whose influence he or she was born; hence, the Talmudic dictum *ein mazzal le-Yisra'el*, namely, Israel is ruled by divine providence and is not subject to the rule of the stars (i.e., fate). The word *mazzal* now is completely devoid of any such astrological significance. Since fortune can be either good or bad, the Talmud differentiates between *mazzal tov* (good luck) and *mazzal bish* (bad luck). Today *mazzal tov* is a formal expression of congratulation (see GREETINGS AND CONGRATULATIONS).

• James H. Charlesworth, "Jewish Interest in Astrology during the Hellenistic and Roman Period," in *Aufstieg und Niedergang der römischen Welt*, section II, vol. 2, pt. 2 (Berlin, 1987), pp. 926–950. Wolfgang Hubner, *Zodiacus Christianus: Jüdisch-christliche Adaptationen des Tierkreises von der Antike bis zur Gegenwart* (Königstein, 1983).

—SHIFRA EPSTEIN

MAZZIQ. See DEMONS.

MEAL OFFERING (Heb. *minḥah*), one of the *sacrifices; also called a cereal or grain offering. The word *minḥah* actually means gift, in the sense of a tribute paid to a superior (e.g., *Gn*. 32.14, 22) or a ruler (e.g., *Jgs*. 3.15ff.; *1 Sm*. 10.27), and could be used to refer to sacrifices in general (*Gn*. 4.3; cf. *1 Sm*. 26.19; *1 Kgs*. 18.36). Usually, however, the *minḥah* is a specific type of sacrifice: a cereal offering, as opposed to an animal sacrifice. The ingredients of the *minḥah* are semolina and oil. The various types are enumerated in *Leviticus* 2. The simplest is the uncooked mixture, requiring the addition of frankincense. The remaining types all involve some preparation of unleavened cakes: oven-baked (as loaves or wafers), griddle-toasted (and crumbled), and pan-fried. Only a small, representative portion (*azkarah*) was placed on the altar, the larger remainder was eaten by the priest (*Lv*. 6.11, 7.9). Conceptually, it was as though God had given the priests a portion of his own gift of food (*Lv*. 6.9–11). A special meal offering was made by the high priest (*Lv*. 6.12–16), according to some authorities, daily; according to others, on the day of his investiture. An individual would be moved to make a meal offering for a multitude of reasons, among them reverence, homage, gratitude, and propitiation. The meal offering shared the same functions as the *burnt offering for those whose means did not enable them to offer an animal. In the public sacrificial system, meal offerings accompanied the daily, Sabbath, Ro'sh Ḥodesh, and festival offerings (*Nm*. 15.1–16, 28–29). The public *minḥah*, especially that which was part of the daily evening sacrifice, eventually gave its name to the afternoon prayer service (see MINḤAH). The laws of the meal offering as expounded by the rabbinic authorities are found in tractate **Menaḥot*.

• Gary A. Anderson, *Sacrifices and Offerings in Ancient Israel: Studies in Their Social and Political Importance*, Harvard Semitic Monographs, no. 41 (Atlanta, 1987), pp. 27–75. Baruch A. Levine, *Leviticus*, The JPS Torah Commentary (Philadelphia, 1989), pp. 9–14. Jacob Milgrom, *Leviticus 1–16*, The Anchor Bible, vol. 3 (New York, 1991), pp. 177–202, 382–401.

—BARUCH J. SCHWARTZ

MEʿAM LOʿEZ. See CULI, YAʿAQOV.

MEAT (Heb. *basar*), animal flesh, as opposed to the bones, sinews, horns, or hoofs of an animal. The flesh of fowl and birds is considered meat in rabbinic law but not in the Bible. The flesh of fish or permitted insects is not considered meat, nor is blood or forbidden fat. Certain parts of the hide or skin are considered meat, though not after they have been made into leather (*Ḥul*. 122a). Meat is mentioned in halakhic discussion in a variety of contexts; for example, in connection with the laws regarding the paschal lamb (*Ex*. 12.8), sacrificial flesh (*Ex*. 29.33), meat torn from a living animal (see EIVAR MIN HA-ḤAI), permitted and forbidden animals (*Lv*. 11), defects that render flesh unfit for consumption (see TEREFAH), the impurities to which flesh is subject (e.g., *Dt*. 14.21), flesh from which no benefit may be derived (e.g., *Ex*. 21.28), the prohibition against cooking meat and milk together (based on *Ex*. 23.19, etc.), the preparation of the meat of permitted animals for consumption, or the determination of what is considered meat as far as vows are concerned (*Ned*. 54b). Only the meat of permitted animals (*Lv*. 11) that have been ritually slaughtered (see RITUAL SLAUGHTER) may be eaten. Since, however, the Bible forbids the consumption of certain fats and blood (*Lv*. 3.17), the meat after slaughter must be porged (see NIQQUR) in order to rid it of forbidden fat and must be made *kasher* in order to rid it of any remaining blood. This is done by soaking the meat in water for a half hour and then covering it lightly with salt (*meliḥah*). The salt must be of a fairly coarse variety so that it will not melt on contact with the meat. Liver must be broiled directly over a flame in order to be rendered *kasher*. Meat may not be cooked together with milk or in utensils in which dairy foods have been cooked. Such cooking renders the meat and utensils forbidden, and no benefit may be derived from either. Although the Bible says, "You shall not seethe a kid in its mother's milk" (*Ex*. 23.19), all permitted animals and fowl are included in the meat–milk prohibition. Milk may not be eaten after the partaking of meat; custom varies as to the period of time that should elapse (see DIETARY LAWS). Meat is considered both a substantial food and one that gives joy. It is therefore to be eaten on the Sabbath and festivals. For the same reason, it is not eaten by the mourner on the day of the burial, nor is it eaten during periods of national mourning, such as the nine days that culminate in the fast of Tishʿah be-'Av.

• Seligmann B. Bamberger, *Hilchoth Melicho: Laws for the Preparation and Salting of Meat According to Halacha* (New York, 1958). Isidor Grunfeld, *The Jewish Dietary Laws*, 2 vols. (London, 1982).

MEDICAL ETHICS. The role of the physician, birth control, feticide, and the treatment of the dying are among the issues that have been dealt with in classical

Jewish law and that have been analyzed by halakhists over the centuries. Medical law is a major field of research for modern halakhists as a result of the universal concern with the moral implications of contemporary medicine and biotechnology. The extensive modern literature in this field includes discussions of fetal reduction in artificially assisted reproduction, surrogacy, the mapping of the human genome, the implications of genetic research and therapy, the use of fetal tissue, the treatment of patients in a persistent vegetative state, allocation of costly medical resources, confidentiality between doctor and patient, and professional ethics. The focus of Jewish medical law, which is distinct from Jewish medical ethics, is the nature and scope of relevant halakhic rules and principles. The wishes of the patient, therefore, are only relevant in the interstices of halakhic doctrine; they do not in themselves constitute a halakhically valid norm in biomedical decisions. However, in cases of medical uncertainty or high risk treatment or in cases in which depriving the patient of his or her autonomy is likely to affect health in an adverse manner, the relevant principle in Jewish law is that the patient's wishes are to be respected. The preservation of life, according to Jewish tradition, constitutes the fulfillment of a divine commandment, and only the prohibitions against the three major transgressions of homicide, idolatory, and forbidden sexual relations override the obligation to save life (*San.* 74a). Under Jewish law, a fetus is only endowed with full legal status, for purposes of criminal law, once it has emerged from the womb; hence, therapeutic abortion is generally treated in a lenient manner in the Jewish tradition (*Ohal.* 7.6). Such enterprises as the mapping of the human genome and research using genetic material need not clash with halakhic norms, as long as the research is orientated in a therapeutic direction. There are a number of institutions in various countries devoted to research in Jewish medical law and ethics, and there exist a number of publications, such as *Assia*, which are devoted solely to matters of *halakhah* and medicine. See also MEDICINE.

• Elliot N. Dorff, *Choose Life: A Jewish Perspective on Medical Ethics* (Los Angeles, 1985). *Entsiklopedyah Hilkhatit Refu'it*, edited by Avraham Steinberg, vols. 1–4 (Jerusalem, 1988–1994). David M. Feldman, *Health and Medicine in the Jewish Tradition* (New York, 1986). Immanuel Jakobovits, *Jewish Medical Ethics* (New York, 1959; repr. 1975). Fred Rosner and J. David Bleich, eds., *Jewish Bioethics* (New York, 1979). Daniel B. Sinclair, *Tradition and the Biological Revolution: The Application of Jewish Law to the Treatment of the Critically Ill* (Edinburgh, 1989). Moshe David Tendler, *Medical Ethics* (New York, 1981). –DANIEL SINCLAIR

MEDICINE. The first biblical reference to illness is in *Genesis* 48.1; the word *rofe'* (healer, doctor) appears first in *Genesis* 50.2, but it is applied there to Joseph's Egyptian servants who embalmed his father, Jacob. God is the healer who heals Israel (*Ex.* 15.26), and he promises to prevent diseases among the people if they keep his commandments (*Ex.* 23.25). Since it is God who smites with illness and who alone heals (see *1 Sm.* 2.6), the practice of medicine became a theological problem, since it represented an attempt to interfere with the ways of God. King Asa was reproved for seeking healing not from God but from physicians (*2 Chr.* 16.12). The Talmud deduces from *Exodus* 21.19 that the healing profession is religiously legitimate, but the problem continued to exercise thinkers throughout the Middle Ages when Jews were among the most renowned doctors. Moses *Maimonides, himself a physician, ruled that medical intervention was a religious duty and that every individual was obliged to care for his health in order to serve God (*Mishneh Torah, Hilkhot De'ot* 3.3). Other authorities (e.g., Nahmanides in his commentary on *Lv.* 26.11, Avraham ibn Ezra on *Ex.* 21.19) held different opinions; for example, that permission to seek and to dispense medical care applies to those on a lower spiritual level, that is, the majority, in consideration of their inability to abandon themselves completely to God's providence. The *Shulḥan ʿArukh* (*Yoreh Deʿah* 336) conforms with Maimonides' view that a physician who withholds his services is shedding blood.

According to the Talmud, a scholar, who should be aware of the obligation to care for one's life, may only live in a city where there is a physician and a surgeon (*San.* 17b). Of special historical interest are many passages in the Talmud testifying to some advanced medical knowledge. Such passages include references to anesthesia (a "sleeping drug") for surgical operations (*B. M.* 83b), amputations (Y., *Naz.* 9.5), artificial teeth and limbs (*Shab.* 6.5, 8), Caesarean sections on living mothers and in subsequent childbirths (*Bekh.* 8.2), and the feasibility of artificial human conception by impregnation through sperm in tub water (*Ḥag.* 15a)—the latter two being the first such references known in the history of medicine. The legal codes devote chapters to the laws of the physician, listing his responsibilities, including visiting and praying for the sick (*Yoreh Deʿah* 335), liabilities, claims to payment (*Yoreh Deʿah* 336), and the conditions under which the Sabbath and other precepts may be violated to protect life and health (*Oraḥ Ḥayyim* 228–230, 618, etc.). The Talmud also deals with *abortion, *birth, *circumcision, and *sterilization. Many of the best-known rabbis, philosophers, poets, and grammarians of the Middle Ages were physicians by occupation. Jews have continued to play a prominent part in all branches of medical research and practice. Certain medical developments have raised halakhic concerns, among them the need for *autopsies and dissections both for establishing the causes of death and for the training of medical students.

• Natalia Berger, ed., *Jews and Medicine: Religion, Culture, Science* (Tel Aviv, 1995). Harry Friedenwald, *The Jews and Medicine*, 2 vols. (Baltimore, 1944–1946). Immanuel Jakobovits, *Jewish Medical Ethics* (New York, 1959). Nathan Koren, *Jewish Physicians: A Biographical Index* (Jerusalem, 1973). Julius Preuss, *Biblical and Talmudic Medicine*, edited and translated by Fred Rosner (New York, 1978). Fred Rosner, *Medicine in the Bible and the Talmud: Selections from Classical Sources* (New York, 1995). –FRANCISCO MORENO CARVALHO

MEDINA, SHEMU'EL DE (1506–1589), known by the acronym Rashdam; rabbinical authority and community leader in his native Salonika, where he served as *dayyan*. He was a student of Yosef *Taitazak and was rabbi of two of the most important communities in Salonika. Medina was consulted on halakhic matters by many communities from all parts of the Ottoman empire and beyond, such as Italy and France. He was immersed in *halakhah* and took no interest in kabbalistic literature or philosophy. Many of his *responsa* became generally accepted decisions not only in the Ottoman empire but also in eastern Europe and have been quoted in modern times by judges in Israel. His authority and powerful personality were widely respected, and he was called on to decide disputes in the Salonikan and other communities. A selection of his *responsa* was published in his lifetime (Salonika, 1585?–1587) and a more comprehensive selection, consisting of 626 *responsa*, appeared after his death (Venice and Salonika, 1594–1595). He headed a large *yeshivah*, and his best-known student was Avraham ben Mosheh di Boton (see BOTON FAMILY).

• Leah Bornstein, ed., *Index to the Responsa of Rabbi Shemu'el de Medina* (Ramat Gan, 1979). Morris S. Goodblatt, *Jewish Life in Turkey in the XVIth Century as Reflected in the Legal Writings of Samuel de Medina* (New York, 1952).

–SHALOM BAR-ASHER

MEDINI, ḤAYYIM ḤIZQIYYAHU (1833–1905), rabbi and halakhist. Born in Jerusalem, he served as a rabbi for many years in Constantinople and in the Crimea before returning to Erets Yisra'el in 1899. Turning down the possibility of the appointment as chief rabbi of the Sephardi community, he accepted a rabbinical position in Hebron. Medini is best known for his *Sedei Ḥemed* (18 vols. [Warsaw, 1891–1912]), an encyclopedia of *halakhah* that deals with individual legal topics and with the rules of halakhic decision making. The work is used widely in Talmudic studies.

• Me'ir Benayahu in *Ḥemdat Yisra'el*, edited by Abraham Elmaleḥ (Jerusalem, 1945), pp. 183–212. Menachem Elon, *Jewish Law: History, Sources, Principles* (Philadelphia, 1994), pp. 1552–1553.

–MARK WASHOFSKY

MEDITATION. Jewish meditation entails deep reflection and contemplation of God. A frequently used Hebrew term connoting this is *hitbodedut* (self-isolation). It refers to withdrawal from social interactions and a turning inward. The Hebrew Bible is replete with spiritual directives that formed the basis of Jewish meditation. "For you, who adhere to the Lord, your God, are all alive today" (*Dt.* 4.4). From this the rabbis deduced that attachment (**devequt*) to God is life-sustaining and will ultimately result in resurrection (cf. *San.* 90b). The seminal formulation of *devequt* is: "I have continuously placed [*shivviti*] the Lord before me" (*Ps.* 16.8). The sages commented that "one who prays should perceive the divine presence before him" (*San.* 22a). These verses gave rise to various meditations in which the divine name is visualized, including R. Yitsḥaq ben Shemu'el of Acre's technique, wherein YHVH is imagined to be written infinitely large, while the heart focuses on the Ein Sof (the Infinite).

There are indications that biblical figures engaged in meditation. According to *Genesis* 24.63, Isaac ventured into the fields at sunset "*la-suaḥ*" (to meditate). Isaac served as a model for others to meditate outdoors. In the post-biblical period, various Jewish groups were involved in meditation: the Ḥasidim Ri'shonim (ancient pietists; *Ber.* 32b), the *Therapeutae, who included women and were discussed by Philo, and the *Heikhalot mystics.

Jewish meditation has been practiced publicly during the daily liturgy, as well as privately. The most significant communal meditation pertains to the recitation of the *Shemaʿ. *Berakhot* 13b recommended the protracted pronunciation of the climactic word *eḥad* (one). Each of its letters has been assigned a special significance and accompanying head movement. Kabbalists, like R. *Ezra of Gerona, associated these letters with aspects of the *sefirot*. Representative of normative *halakhah* is R. Yehoshuʿa Falk's summary: "When reciting the *alef*, one should consider that God is one; at the *ḥet*, that he is united in the seven heavens and on earth, which makes eight; and, the *dalet* alludes to the four directions" (*Arbaʿah Turim, Oraḥ Ḥayyim* 61.9).

Although the frequency and duration of private meditation is an individual decision, Hasidic masters—including R. Mordekhai of Chernobyl and R. Naḥman of Bratslav—encourage their followers to undertake *hitbodedut* for an hour or more daily.

Rabbi Ḥayyim Vital compiled the most comprehensive premodern anthology of meditative techniques in the long-suppressed fourth chapter of his *Shaʿarei Qedushah*. Among the texts quoted is *Shaʿar ha-Kavvanah*, in which the adept visualizes that he is light and is surrounded by celestial lights. Vital and R. Yehudah al-Botini publicized Avraham Abulafia's methods, in which divine names are chanted and their vocalization is accompanied by head movements. Vital also disseminated the practice of *yiḥudim* (unifications), wherein names representing different elements of the divine realm are interwoven and contemplated during prayers.

• Yitzhak Buxbaum, *Jewish Spiritual Practices* (Northvale, N.J., 1990). Arthur Green, ed., *Jewish Spirituality*, World Spirituality, vols. 13–14 (New York, 1987). Moshe Idel, *The Mystical Experience in Abraham Abulafia* (Albany, 1988). Aryeh Kaplan, *Meditation and Kabbalah* (Northvale, N.J., 1995). Zalman Schachter-Shalomi, *Fragments of a Future Scroll: Hassidism for the Aquarian Age* (Germantown, Pa., 1975). Mark Verman, "The Development of Yihudim in Spanish Kabbalah," *Jerusalem Studies in Jewish Thought* 8 (1989): 25–41. Ḥayyim ben Yosef Vital, *Ketavim Ḥadashim me-Rabbenu Ḥayyim Vital* (Jerusalem, 1988). R. J. Zwi Werblowsky, *Joseph Karo: Lawyer and Mystic* (Philadelphia, 1977).

–MARK VERMAN

MEʿEIN SHEVA'. See MAGEN AVOT.

MEGILLAH (מְגִלָּה;), name of an *Esther* scroll and of a Mishnaic tractate.

Esther Scroll. Magillah is a common designation for a handwritten parchment scroll of the *Book of Esther* (see ESTHER; ḤAMESH MEGILLOT), read in the synagogue on *Purim. The illuminaion of such scrolls has been a favorite Jewish art form. See also SCROLLS.

–BARUCH J. SCHWARTZ

Tractate. The tractate *Megillah* consists of four chapters in Mishnah order Moʿed, with related material in the Tosefta' and in both Talmuds. It derives its name from the scroll of *Esther*, the biblical source for Purim. The rabbis understood the biblical mandate to "commemorate" the two days of Purim (*Est.* 9.28) as a requirement to read the scroll of *Esther* as part of the festivities (*Meg.* 17a, 18a). The tractate deals with the rules for celebrating Purim, primarily the reading of the Megillah, as well as with the synagogal reading of the Torah and laws concerning the sanctity of the synagogue and the public prayer services. *Megillah*'s hierarchy of sanctified objects (3.1) focuses the sanctity of the synagogue on the ark housing the Torah scrolls, much as the sanctity of the Temple focused on the Ark housing the tablets of the Law during biblical times (*Ex.* 25.21–22; *1 Kgs.* 8.3–10).

• Chanoch Albeck, ed., *Shishah Sidrei Mishnah*, Seder Mo'ed (Jerusalem, 1952). Philip Blackman, ed. and trans., *Mishnayoth*, vol. 2, *Order Moed* (Gateshead, 1973). Pinhas Kehati, ed., *Mishnah: A New Translation with a Commentary, Seder Moed*, vol. 5, *Ta'anit, Megillah, Moed Katan, Haggigah* (Jerusalem, 1991). Joseph Rabbinowitz, ed. and trans., *Mishnah Megillah* (London, 1931). Hermann Leberecht Strack and Günter Stemberger, *Introduction to the Talmud and Midrash*, rev. and updat. ed., translated by Markus Bockmuehl (Minneapolis, 1992).
—AVRAHAM WALFISH

MEGILLAT ESTER. See ESTHER; ḤAMESH MEGILLOT.

MEGILLAT TA'ANIT, an ancient tannaitic chronicle compiled at the beginning of the Common Era and recording thirty-five anniversaries of glorious deeds or joyous events in the Second Temple period (*Ta'an.* 2.8). Public mourning was forbidden on most of these days; public fasting, on all of them. The scroll, written in Aramaic with Hebrew additions, is divided into twelve chapters coinciding with the months of the year and enumerating the appropriate events. The significance of the dates lapsed in the course of time, and, since the third century, days recorded in *Megillat Ta'anit* are no longer marked in the calendar.

• Solomon Zeitlin, *Megillat Ta'anit as a Source for Jewish Chronology and History in the Hellenistic and Roman Periods* (Philadelphia, 1922).

MEGILLOT, FIVE. See ḤAMESH MEGILLOT

MEḤILAH (מְחִילָה; forgiveness), the waiver or renunciation of a claim or right. No specific formalities or considerations are required; one possessing a claim or right, even in written form, may validly waive it by parole. A waiver may similarly be inferred from a creditor's statements or actions. One exception to this rule is a case in which the creditor continues to hold the debtor's written note or his pawn. A written waiver is required, for doubt would otherwise exist as to the genuineness of the creditor's intent.

In principle, the waiver of a future right is equally as valid as that of a present right. However, such a waiver cannot be effected where to do so would contradict the general principle that one cannot exercise legal control over a *devar she-lo' ba' la-'olam*, "something that has not yet come into existence." In order for an attempted change in a right or obligation to be effective, there must exist some present nexus between the right and the party seeking to make such change. Thus, a prospective husband could not validly waive his future right to usufruct in his wife's estate until after betrothal, which, while not creating a present right to usufruct, is deemed to have established a sufficient basis to allow a valid waiver even before the marriage is finalized.

• Menachem Elon, ed., *The Principles of Jewish Law* (Jerusalem, 1975), pp. 307–309. Isaac Herzog, *The Main Institutions of Jewish Law*, 2d ed. (London, 1965), vol. 2, pp. 229–233. —BEN TZION GREENBERGER

MEḤITSAH (מְחִיצָה; partition), a division in the synagogue separating men from women during public prayer. In the Temple there was a separate courtyard for women, and the Mishnah (*Suk.* 5.2) records the special care taken to maintain the separation of the sexes, especially during Sukkot, when the Temple festivities attracted large crowds of worshipers. However, there is no clear recorded reference in ancient times to a *meḥitsah* in synagogues. Archaeological evidence is ambiguous, but by the beginning of the Middle Ages, the *meḥitsah* had become a recognized feature (see 'EZRAT NASHIM). The *meḥitsah* takes various forms when the women are not in a balcony but on the same level as the men; iron or wooden grilles or curtains are common. It was customary in Sephardi synagogues to open the curtain during the reading of the Torah. Attempts by worshipers to remove the *meḥitsah* in synagogues that had been founded as Orthodox and whose charters stated that they must remain Orthodox have gone to the civil courts in the United States, where, in most instances, the rulings stipulated that the *meḥitsah* had to be kept in place. Reform and Conservative synagogues dispense with the *meḥitsah*, although there are Conservative synagogues in which men and women sit on opposite sides of a dividing aisle.

In *halakhah*, *meḥitsah* is a technical term for a division (e.g., a wall or fence) that creates a separate domain; to be legally effective it must be at least ten handbreadths (approx. 40 inches) in height.

• Hannah Safrai, "Women and the Ancient Synagogue," in *Daughters of the King: Women and the Synagogue*, edited by Susan Grossman and Rivka Haut (Philadelphia, 1992), pp. 39–49. *The Sanctity of the Synagogue: The Case for Mechitzah . . .* , edited by Baruch Litvin; 3d rev. ed., edited by Jeanne Litvin and Melvin Teitelbaum (Hoboken, N.J., 1987).
—SHMUEL HIMELSTEIN

ME'IL. See TORAH ORNAMENTS.

ME'ILAH (מְעִילָה; Misappropriation), tractate consisting of six chapters in Mishnah order *Qodashim, with related material in the Tosefta' and in the Talmud Bavli. It deals with the laws concerning the secular use of objects consecrated to the Temple, which are subject to the penalty of a *reparation offering. In addition, the value of the item together with an additional fifth of the value must be repaid to the Temple (*Lv.* 5.14–16). The tractate lists the kinds of items and forms of consecration that are subject to the laws of *me'ilah*, differentiating between those items that were actually utilized in the Temple service and those that were used for maintenance of the Temple structure. The former retained their sanctity even after being misappropriated for secular use, whereas the latter were considered profaned by secular use and therefore not subject to repeated violations (*Me'il.* 5.3).

An English translation of the tractate appears in the Soncino Talmud (London, 1948).

• Chanoch Albeck, ed., *Shishah Sidrei Mishnah, Seder Qodashim* (Jerusalem, 1956). Philip Blackman, ed. and trans., *Mishnayoth*, vol. 5, *Order Kodashim* (Gateshead, 1973). Hermann Leberecht Strack and Günter Stemberger, *Introduction to the Talmud and Midrash*, rev. and updat. ed., translated by Markus Bockmuehl (Minneapolis, 1992).

—AVRAHAM WALFISH

MEIMRA'. See Logos.

ME'IR (2d cent.), tanna', pupil of R. *ʿAqiva' ben Yosef. During the Hadrianic persecution following the failure of the *Bar Kokhba' Revolt in 135, Me'ir was secretly ordained and was a prominent member of the Sanhedrin established at Usha' in Galilee. Me'ir had a brilliant intellect and was said to have been able to adduce a hundred fifty reasons for declaring an object unclean and another hundred fifty reasons for declaring it clean. He is the authority whose opinions are most frequently found in tannaitic literature. His teaching formed an important basis for the compilation of the *Mishnah by R. Yehudah ha-Nasi', so that traditionally a Mishnaic teaching, the source of which was not specifically named, was ascribed to Me'ir (*San.* 86a). Nonetheless, in controversies with his contemporaries, Me'ir's opinions were not followed. The reason given by the later amora'im for this anomaly is that, precisely because of his brilliant argumentation, it is difficult to know whether he was seriously disagreeing with or merely debating the issues (*ʿEruv.* 13b). He was famous for his parables and fables. Nothing is known of his origins; the name of his father is nowhere given, but he may have come from Asia Minor. Me'ir was a professional scribe of the highest quality. He is described as a man of humility and resignation. His wife *Beruryah is also quoted as a Talmudic authority. Toward the end of his life, he left the Sanhedrin as a result of his opposition to the patriarch R. *Shimʿon ben Gamli'el; Me'ir's further statements are introduced as the remarks of "the others" (*aḥerim*). Perhaps it is for this reason that his opinions were not held as authoritative.

• M. Friedman, " ʿIyyunim be-Midrasho shel R. Me'ir," *Teʿudah* 4 (1986): 79–92. Israel Konovitz, *Rabbi Meir: Collected Sayings in Halakah and Aggadah in the Talmudic and Midrashic Literature* (Jerusalem, 1967).

—DANIEL SPERBER

ME'IR BAʿAL HA-NES, name associated with various rabbis, most popularly with the tanna' *Me'ir (*ʿA. Z.* 18a–b). A celebration is held at his grave in Tiberias each year on Pesaḥ Sheni (14 Iyyar), and he is venerated by both Ashkenazi and Sephardi Jews. The name Me'ir Baʿal ha-Nes became widespread only in the eighteenth century, when collections throughout the world for charitable causes in the Holy Land were made in boxes labeled "The Charity of R. Me'ir Baʿal ha-Nes." Many rabbis condemned the annual celebration and the association of the collection box with a legendary figure.

• Yizhar Hirschfeld, *A Guide to Antiquity Sites in Tiberias* (Jerusalem, 1992).

ME'IR BEN BARUKH OF ROTHENBURG (died 1293), German rabbinic authority; died in prison in Alsace, having refused to allow the Jewish community to ransom him and thereby encourage future extortion on the part of the rulers. With his death, the martyrdom of one pupil, R. *Mordekhai ben Hillel (1297), and the flight of another, R. *Asher ben Yeḥi'el, to Spain in 1305, the period of the German tosafists came to an end. Me'ir himself was not an original glossator (tosafist) of note, but rather a *poseq* (see Poseqim), the greatest produced by the Ashkenazi (Franco-German) community of the Middle Ages, and his rulings were viewed for centuries as authoritative. Sensing, perhaps, the impending fate of his community, he began in his academy to gather the *responsa* literature of the Ashkenazi community of the preceding three hundred years. These collections were assiduously copied in the later Middle Ages, and six volumes were subsequently published. Often going under his name, these influential compilations further enhanced Me'ir's fame. Unlike other Ashkenazi tosafists, who were wholly indifferent to Maimonides' code, Me'ir sought to integrate it with tosafist culture. His pupil, Me'ir ha-Kohen, wrote glosses on all fourteen volumes of Maimonides' work, seeking to provide for that code what Mosheh Isserles was later to do for Yosef Karo's *Shulḥan ʿArukh*, namely, to amend a Sephardi code and render it authoritative in Ashkenaz. Me'ir also wrote liturgical poems, the best known of which, composed after the burning of the Talmud in Paris in 1242, became part of the liturgy of Tishʿah be-'Av.

• Irving A. Agus, *Rabbi Meir of Rothenburg: His Life and His Works as a Source for the Religious, Legal, and Social History of the Jews in Germany in the Thirteenth Century*, 2d ed., 2 vols. (New York, 1970). Shemuel Argaman, *The Captivity of the Maharam: A Narrative of the Events Surrounding the Arrest and Captivity of the Maharam of Rothenburg* (New York, 1990).

—HAYM SOLOVEITCHIK

ME'IR BEN GEDALYAH OF LUBLIN (1558–1616), Talmudist and *yeshivah* head, known as Maharam (an acronym of Moreinu ha-Rav Me'ir, "Our Teacher Rabbi Me'ir") of Lublin. He attracted hundreds of students to his Kraków and Lublin academies. He wrote *Me'ir ʿEinei Ḥakhamim* (Venice, 1619; in many standard editions of the Talmud), a commentary on many Talmudic tractates, focusing in particular on the interpretations of Rashi and the tosafists. An independent thinker, Me'ir ben Gedalyah of Lublin criticized the authority of the *Shulḥan ʿArukh*, deeming it to be a collection of rulings rather than a cohesive halakhic work. At times, he preferred the views of later authorities over the more traditionally accepted views of Maimonides and the tosafists. His collection of 140 *responsa*, *Manhir ʿEinei Ḥakhamim* (Venice, 1618), provides valuable information about Jewish communal life in sixteenth- and seventeenth-century Poland. He exhibited great leniency in dealing with the problems of *ʿagunot* (see ʿAgunah) and the socially and economically disadvantaged.

• S. M. Chones, *Sefer Toledot ha-Poseqim* (New York, 1945–1946), pp. 366–371. Samuel A. Horodetzky, *Le-Qorot ha-Rabbanut* (Warsaw, 1911), pp. 175–182. S. B. Nissenbaum, *Le-Qorot ha-Yehudim be-Lublin* (Lublin, 1899).

—ELIJAH J. SCHOCHET

ME'IR BEN SHEMU'EL (c.1060–1135), rabbinic scholar, tosafist. He studied in Worms with R. Yitsḥaq ha-Levi during the period prior to the First Crusade. He also studied with the scholars of Lorraine, with R. Eliʿezer ben Natan of Mainz, and with Rashi, whose daughter Yokheved he married. Three of his sons, who were also his students, Shemu'el, Yitsḥaq, and Yaʿaqov Tam, became well-known through their biblical and Talmudic commentaries and *tosafot*, while his son-in-law was Shemu'el of Vitry, father of the important tosafist Yitsḥaq of Dampierre. Rabbi Me'ir himself wrote commentaries and *tosafot* to the Talmud, some of which are incorporated into the standard editions of Rashi and *tosafot*. It is likely that he played a crucial role in the transmission of the Talmudic dialectics that were produced at Worms in the last quarter of the eleventh century (found, for example, in the so-called Rashi commentary to tractate *Nazir*), which were then further developed and expanded by R. Tam and Yitsḥaq of Dampierre. Rabbi Me'ir lived mainly in the northern French town of Ramerupt and was known in tosafistic literature as Ha-Yashish (The Venerable One) or Avi ha-Rabbanim (Father of the Rabbis). He introduced certain changes in the *Kol Nidrei prayer and was responsible for its final formulation.

• Avraham Grossman, *Ḥakhmei Tsarefat ha-Ri'shonim* (Jerusalem, 1995). Ephraim Kanarfogel, *Jewish Education and Society in the High Middle Ages* (Detroit, 1992), pp. 69–70. Efraim E. Urbach, *Baʿalei ha-Tosafot* (Jerusalem, 1980), vol. 1, pp. 41–45.

—EPHRAIM KANARFOGEL

ME'IRI, MENAḤEM (1249–c.1316), Talmudist from Perpignan, in southern France. His first significant work, written in his youth, was *Ḥibbur ha-Teshuvah* (New York, 1950), a compendium of writings dealing with repentance. His *magnum opus* was *Beit ha-Beḥirah*, about twenty published volumes, noted for their expositions of Talmudic passages with definitive halakhic decisions. In this work, he employed the Talmud Yerushalmi extensively. His introduction to *Avot* contains a significant essay tracing the chain of tradition from Moses to his own day. He wrote commentaries to the biblical books of *Psalms* (Jerusalem, 1936) and *Proverbs* (Portugal, 1492; Jerusalem, 1937) based upon the ethical and wisdom literature of the Middle Ages, *midrashim*, and the works of noted grammarians. His *Kiryat Sefer* (İzmir, 1863–1881) contains the laws of writing a Torah scroll, while *Magen Avot* (London, 1909) defended local Provençal customs against criticism by Moses Nahmanides' disciples who had emigrated to Perpignan. Although Me'iri communicated extensively with R. Shelomoh ben Avraham *Adret, he did not accept the latter's ban on philosophy and maintained his independence of mind and freedom from intervention by outside rabbis. His rationalistic outlook is evidenced by his denial of the existence of evil spirits and of the efficacy of amulets and astrology, which—he said—contradicted human free will.

• Henri Gross, *Gallia judaica: Dictionnaire géographique de la France d'après les sources rabbiniques* (Paris, 1897; repr. Amsterdam, 1969), with a supplement by Simon Schwarzfuchs. Menahem ben Solomon Meiri, *Seder ha-Qabbala le-Rabbeinu Menaḥem ha-Meiri*, edited by Shelomoh Zalman ben Shalom Havlin (Jerusalem, 1991). Samuel Kalman Mirsky, *Ben Sheqi'ah li-Zeriḥah* (New York, 1951), pp. 83–115 (Hebrew).

—SHLOMO H. PICK

MEKHILTA' DE-RABBI SHIMʿON BAR YOḤ'AI, tannaitic *midrash* on the *Book of Exodus* (beginning with *Ex* 3.1) from the school of R. ʿAqiva'. The precise scope of the work is not clear, as it has only been preserved in fragmentary form. It is essentially a halakhic *midrash*, although parts of the work are aggadic in nature, and its *aggadah* closely resembles that in the parallel tannaitic *midrash*, *Mekhilta' de-Rabbi Yishmaʿe'l*. *Mekhilta' de-Rabbi Shimʿon bar Yoḥ'ai* is apparently one of the latest halakhic *midrashim*, although it cannot be dated with certainty. It is written in Rabbinic Hebrew.

• Jacob Nahum Epstein, *Mevo'ot le-Sifrut ha-Tanna'im* (Jerusalem, 1957). Hermann Leberecht Strack and Günter Stemberger, *Introduction to the Talmud and Midrash*, rev. and updat. ed., translated by Markus Bockmuehl (Minneapolis, 1992).

—LEIB MOSCOVITZ

MEKHILTA' DE-RABBI YISHMAʿE'L, tannaitic *midrash* on *Exodus*, produced by the school of R. Yishmaʿe'l ben Elishaʿ. The *Mekhilta'* presents a running commentary on *Exodus* 12.1–23.19 and concludes with two sections on the Sabbath (on *Ex*. 31–35). Fragments of another *Mekhilta'* on *Exodus*, from the school of R. ʿAqiva' (the so-called **Mekhilta' de-Rabbi Shimʿon bar Yoḥ'ai*), have also been preserved.

Mekhilta' de-Rabbi Yishmaʿe'l is first mentioned by name in geonic literature and was apparently unknown, at least in its present form, to the rabbis of the Talmud (although the Talmuds Bavli and Yerushalmi contain similar material). Nevertheless, the work is evidently of Palestinian provenance and was apparently redacted no later than the third century CE. The *Mekhilta'* is written in Rabbinic Hebrew and contains some Latin and Greek words. While the *Mekhilta'* is essentially a halakhic *midrash*, large parts of it deal with aggadic matters. A critical edition in light of *genizah* fragments was published by M. Kahana in *Tarbiz* 55 (1986): 545–587, and an English translation was done by J. Z. Lauterbach in 1933.

• Chanoch Albeck, *Mavo' la-Talmudim* (Tel Aviv, 1987). Daniel Boyarin, "Analogy vs. Anomaly in Midrashic Hermeneutic: Tractates Wayyassa and Amaleq in the Mekilta," *Journal of the American Oriental Society* 106.4 (1986): 659–666. Norman J. Cohen, "Analysis of an Exegetic Tradition in the 'Mekhilta de-Rabbi Ishmael': The Meaning of 'amanah' in the Second and Third Centuries," *AJS Review* 9.1 (1984): 1–25. Jacob Nahum Epstein, *Mevo'ot le-Sifrut ha-Tanna'im* (Jerusalem, 1957). Arie C. Kooyman, "Er was eens een koning: over de functie van parabels in de Mechilta van Rabbi Isjmael," *Ter Herkenning* 23.1–2 (1995): 5–20. Jacob Zallel Lauterbach, ed. and trans., *Mekilta de-Rabbi Ishmael* (Philadelphia, 1933–1935). Hermann Leberecht Strack, *Introduction to the Talmud and Midrash* (1931; Minneapolis, 1992). Leopold Zunz, *Ha-Derashot be-Yisra'el ve-Hishtalshelutan ha-Historit*, edited by Chanoch Albeck (1892; Jerusalem, 1974).

—LEIB MOSCOVITZ

MELAMMED (מְלַמֵּד; teacher), usually a teacher of small children (*melammed dardeqei* or *melammed tinoqot*). The Talmud stresses the *melammed*'s importance. In the course of time, because the term was applied to those on the lowest rung of the teaching profession, it came to have a certain derogatory meaning.

—SHMUEL HIMELSTEIN

MELAVVEH MALKAH (מְלַוֵּה מַלְכָּה; Accompanying the [Sabbath] Queen), a festive meal and celebration conducted at the termination of the Sabbath and lasting as long as possible in order to retain the Sabbath atmosphere after its conclusion. Just as the Sabbath is welcomed in song as a bride and as a queen (the Sephardi version of *Lekhah Dodi contains a kabbalistic addition ending "Come, O bride, come, O Sabbath queen"), so it is also solemnly bid farewell. Kabbalistic and Hasidic practice (based on the belief of Yitsḥaq ben Shelomoh *Luria that at the close of the Sabbath wicked souls return to Geihinnom and Sabbath angels to heaven) enhanced the observance of the custom. Authority for the Melavveh Malkah meal is found in the Talmud (*Shab*. 119b) where R. Ḥanina' enjoins laying the table on Sabbath night even if one is not hungry. Special **zemirot* have been composed for this celebration, of which the most important is in praise of the prophet Elijah, who, according to a popular belief, sits on this night under the tree of life and records the merits of those who have faithfully observed the Sabbath (Ya'aqov ben Mosheh ha-Levi Molin, *Hilkhot Shabbat*, end). The Melavveh Malkah is also identified with the feast of R. Ḥidqa' (see SE'UDAT RABBI ḤIDQA').

• C. Y. Friedman, ed., *Seder Melavveh Malkah* (Brooklyn, N.Y., 1994), includes bibliography. Abraham Joshua Heschel, *The Sabbath: Its Meaning for Modern Man* (New York, 1995).

MELIḤAH. See MEAT.

MEMORBUKH, martyrology containing a list of the countries and localities in which massacres took place during the Middle Ages, together with the names of the martyrs (usually confined to scholars and communal leaders) who lost their lives on those occasions. In many European synagogues, on all occasions upon which the memorial prayer for the dead was recited, the martyrologies were solemnly read out loud. The word *memorbukh* is a Yiddish translation of a phrase in *Malachi* ("and a book of rememberance was written before him for them that feared the Lord"—3.16).

MEMORIAL LIGHT (Heb. *ner zikkaron*), a light kindled, usually for twenty-four hours, to commemorate the death of a family member. The custom is supported by the verse, "The soul of man is the lamp of the Lord" (*Prv*. 20.27). Although it is usual to light special wax candles that last for an entire day, it is permitted to use an electric light (*Gesher ha-Ḥayyim*, vol. 1, pp. 198, 343). In recent years, specially designed electrical memorial lamps have become available. The lighting of memorial lights is post-Talmudic and may have originated in medieval Germany. It is customary to kindle memorial lights on the **yortsayt* (anniversary of the death of a close relative), during the **shiv'ah* (the seven days of mourning for a close family member), and on *Yom Kippur eve when one memorial light, called the *ner neshamah* (soul light), commemorates all deceased family members (*Oraḥ Ḥayyim* 610.3). Some people observe the custom of keeping a memorial light kindled throughout the entire year of mourning following the death of a parent. Many people now light a memorial light on Yom ha-Sho'ah, the day that commemorates the murder of millions of Jews during the Nazi Holocaust, and in Israel on Yom ha-Zikkaron (4 Iyyar), special flames are lit in public ceremonies that memorialize those who have fallen in Israel's defense.

• Isaac Klein, *A Guide to Jewish Religious Practice* (New York, 1979). Yeḥi'el Mikha'el Tuktsinski, *Gesher ha-Ḥayyim* (Jerusalem, 1960).

—CHAIM PEARL

MEMORIAL SERVICE. See YIZKOR.

MENAḤEM AV. See AV.

MENAḤEM BEN AHARON BEN ZERAḤ (c.1310–1385), Spanish codifier. Born in Estalla, Navarre, he moved to Toledo after the 1328 anti-Jewish outbreaks, in which all of his family was killed and he himself was severely injured. He studied with Yosef ben Shu'ayb and Yehudah, son of Asher ben Yeḥi'el (the Ro'sh). He belonged to a group of sages whose philosophy was influenced by Shelomoh ben Avraham Adret and whose halakhic outlook was influenced by the Ashkenazi traditions of the Asher ben Yeḥi'el. Like his friend Me'ir Aldabi, Menaḥem used scientific sources and his writings had lexical value. His main work, *Tsedah la-Derekh* (Ferrara, 1554; Warsaw, 1880), was a legal code meant for study in the *batei midrash* in Spain. It combines philosophy, halakhic methodology, and logic. Its subject matter concerns everyday life, including a discussion of bigamy, a subject on the communal agenda in those days, and a practice of which Menaḥem disapproved. In his *Or Torah*, he emphasized the importance of education for women.

• M. A. Friedman, "Menahem ben Aaron Ibn Zerah's Anti-Polygamy Torah Commentary from the Geniza," in *Minḥah le-Naḥum: Biblical and Other Studies presented to Nahum M. Sarna*, edited by Marc Brettler and Michael Fishbane, Journal for the Study of the Old Testament, Supplement Series 154 (Sheffield, Eng., 1993), pp. 108–116.

—SHALOM BAR-ASHER

MENAḤEM MENDEL BEN YOSEF OF RYMANÓW (died 1815), Hasidic master and author. As one of the three principal disciples of Elimelekh of Lyzhansk, he was an important Hasidic leader in Poland. He is best known for his asceticism and mystical support for Napoléon, whose wars he identified with the battles of Gog and Magog, a tradition associated with the advent of the messianic age. His writings and sermons were posthumously published, notably *Sifrei ha-Rahak Rabbi Menaḥem Mendel me-Rymanów* (Jerusalem, 1985).

• Martin Buber, *Tales of the Hasidim* (New York, 1947). Martin Buber, *For the Sake of Heaven: A Chronicle* (New York, 1969).

—MILES KRASSEN

MENAḤEM MENDEL OF KOTSK (1787–1859), Hasidic master; the outstanding figure among the disciples of *Ya'aqov Yitsḥaq and *Simḥah Bunem of Przysucha. Upon the latter's death in 1827, his closest followers looked to R. Mendel to lead what had become a distinct school of Polish Hasidism. First in Tomaszów, and from 1829 in Kotsk, there gathered around R. Mendel an assemblage of bright and learned young men, the likes of which Hasidism had not seen since the court of *Dov Ber of Mezhirech. The radical search for truth that R. Mendel demanded of his disciples meant an overthrow of convention and a challenging of all tokens of piety not specifically required by Jewish law. Miracles and claims of mystical experience were scoffed at by the Kotsker, who was a rationalist and a legalist within the Hasidic camp. Though some of his values appear contrary to Hasidism, the pursuit of truth became an expression of ecstatic passion. After 1840, R. Mendel became extremely reclusive, and for the last nineteen years of his life he was mostly isolated from his disciples. One of his most important disciples, R. Mordekhai Yosef Leiner, left him for ideological reasons and founded his own Hasidic court at *Izbica. The Kotsker had always insisted on the unique responsibility of each individual, however, and the disciples carried on their tasks of study and devotion without him. After Kotsker's death most of his disciples followed the Ger or Aleksander schools.

• Abraham Joshua Heschel, *Kotsk: In Gerangel far Emesdikeyt* (Tel Aviv, 1973). Yaacov Levinger, "Amarot Otentiyyot shel ha-Rabbi mi-Kotsk," *Tarbiz* 55 (1986): 109–135. Yaacov Levinger, "Torato shel ha-Rabbi mi-Kotsk," *Tarbiz* 55 (1986): 413–431. —ARTHUR GREEN

MENAḤEM MENDEL OF VITEBSK (1730–1788), Hasidic master and author. He was a leading disciple of Dov Ber of Mezhirech and led a Hasidic group in Minsk. After his master's death in 1772, he became the principal Hasidic leader in Belorussia and Lithuania. Along with his younger colleague, Shneur Zalman of Lyady, he unsuccessfully attempted to justify Hasidism to Eliyyahu ben Shelomoh Zalman, the Vilna Ga'on. In 1777 accompanied by two of his closest associates, Avraham of Kalisk and Yisra'el of Polotsk, he led a large group to Erets Yisra'el. He settled in Tiberias and became leader of the Hasidic community there, while continuing to exercise his authority over the Ḥasidim in Belorussia and Lithuania through correspondence. As a thinker, he was faithful to the extreme spiritual teachings of Dov Ber. Prayer has as its goal only *devequt*, cleaving to God by means of a contemplative ascent that results in a nullification of one's sense of individuality. Thus the verse "He shall do the will of those that fear him" (*Ps.* 145.19) is interpreted to mean that the one who prays contemplatively will be permitted to remain on a spiritual plateau even when compelled to descend to the mundane world. Believing that the ecstatic connection to God was paramount, he struggled in his teachings to justify the necessity for physically performing the commandments. He was the author of *Peri ha-'Arets* (Jerusalem, 1987).

• Martin Buber, *Tales of the Hasidim* (New York, 1946). Roman Foxbrunner, *Habad: The Hasidism of R. Shneour Zalman of Lyady* (Tuscaloosa, Ala., 1992). Rivka Schatz Uffenheimer, *Hasidism as Mysticism* (Princeton, 1993). —MILES KRASSEN

MENAḤOT (מְנָחוֹת; Meal Offerings), second tractate, consisting of thirteen chapters, in Mishnah order Qodashim, with related material in the Tosefta' and in the Talmud Bavli. It deals with the regulations concerning *meal offerings, serving as a sequel to the treatment of animal and fowl sacrifices in tractate *Zevaḥim*. Just as *Zevaḥim* opened with the requirement of intent and closed with a historical-geographical survey of the sanctuaries leading to the Temple in Jerusalem, so, too, *Menaḥot* opens with the requirement of intention in the central procedures of meal offerings and concludes with the status of priests who had served in the Temple of Onias in Elephantine, which was not recognized by the sages as a legitimate place of worship (see YEB). The discussion of various types of meal offerings includes a description of the ʿOmer service, whose performance on the second day of Pesaḥ was accompanied by great public fanfare, in order to underscore the rabbinic acceptance of the Pharisaic timing of the offering, as opposed to that of the Boethusians (*Men.* 10.3). *Menaḥot* closes with the declaration (13.11): "It matters not whether one offers much or little—providing that one directs his thoughts towards heaven."

An English translation of the tractate appears in the Soncino Talmud (London, 1948).

• Chanoch Albeck, ed., *Shishah Sidrei Mishnah, Seder Qodashim* (Jerusalem, 1956). Philip Blackman, ed. and trans., *Mishnayoth*, vol. 5, *Order Kodashim* (Gateshead, 1973). Pinhas Kehati, ed., *Mishnah: A New Translation with a Commentary, Seder Kodashim*, vol. 1, *Zevaḥim, Menaḥot, Ḥullin* (Jerusalem, 1994). Hermann Leberecht Strack and Günter Stemberger, *Introduction to the Talmud and Midrash*, rev. and updat. ed., translated by Markus Bockmuehl (Minneapolis, 1992). —AVRAHAM WALFISH

MENAQQER. See NIQQUR.

MENDELSSOHN, MOSES (1729–1796), German philosopher, communal leader, proponent of Jewish *emancipation, biblical scholar, and translator. Born in Dessau, the son of a Torah scribe, Mendelssohn received a traditional Talmudic education. In 1743 when Mendelssohn's teacher, R. David *Franckel, became chief rabbi of Berlin, Mendelssohn followed him there to pursue his studies. While continuing his study of Talmud and medieval Jewish philosophy, Mendelssohn mastered German, Greek, Latin, French, and English, and turned to the study of modern philosophy, particularly the writings of the English philosopher, John Locke, and the German philosophers, Gottfried Leibniz and Christian Wolff.

With his first work, *Philosophical Dialogues* (1755), Mendelssohn emerged as one of the leading and most eloquent spokesmen of German enlightenment philosophy. His reputation was cemented by his *Treatise on Metaphysical Evidence* (1763), which won the essay competition of the Berlin Royal Academy (Immanuel Kant received second place of honor), and by his *Phaedon* (1767). The latter was modeled on Plato's dialogue by that name and earned him the accolade of "the German Socrates." Mendelssohn professed himself particularly indebted to the Leibniz–Wolffian school, for having rationally demonstrated the fundamental truths of natural religion, namely, God's existence, his providence, and the immortality of the soul. In *Phaedon*, he drew upon Leibniz and Wolff to prove that the soul is immortal. In addition, arguing for God's goodness, he contended that God must necessarily guarantee that the soul after death will advance along the path to self-perfection and happiness. In his last metaphysical work, *Morgenstunden* (1785), Mendelssohn focused on proofs for the existence of God, in particular the ontological proof. Mendelssohn wrote on a wide variety of subjects, including aesthetics and psychology.

In the late 1750s, Mendelssohn published a Hebrew weekly (*Qohelet Musar*), of which only two issues appeared. In addition, he wrote a Hebrew commentary on Maimonides' *Treatise on Logic*. Although he devoted most of his efforts in the 1760s to his metaphysical works and literary essays, he did not completely abandon his Hebrew writings. In 1768, he wrote a Hebrew commentary on *Ecclesiastes*, and, in 1769, a Hebrew essay on the immortality of the soul (published after his death), partially based on *Phaedon*. That same year, he was publicly challenged by a Swiss pastor, Johann Lavater, either to refute an apologetic treatise purporting to prove the truth of Christianity or to convert. Mendelssohn, who had always hoped to avoid having his commitment to Judaism made into a public issue, was shaken by the challenge. True to his principles, he refused to engage in religious polemic, but simply replied that his continued commitment to traditional Judaism was not incompatible with his devotion to rational inquiry. In the 1770s, Mendelssohn made use of his growing reputation as a philosopher to deflect anti-Jewish measures in Germany and Switzerland. For the use of Prussian courts he wrote a précis of Jewish laws bearing upon property rights, somewhat misleadingly titled *Ritual Laws of the Jews* (1778). Mendelssohn's translation of the Pentateuch into German (using the Hebrew alphabet), together with a Hebrew commentary (*Bi'ur*), written in collaboration with a group of scholars, was published in the early 1780s. The translation, written in an elegant High German, and the *Bi'ur*, a skillful distillation of the tradition of medieval plain sense exegesis, supplemented with contemporary poetic and aesthetic observations, together led to a revival of biblical studies among Jews of the time; the work as a whole was described by many young Jews as their first way station along the road to Enlightenment. At the same time, it aroused the opposition of many traditionalist rabbis and narrowly escaped being banned.

In 1781 Mendelssohn, in connection with efforts to protect the Jews of Alsace, prevailed upon the German statesman and scholar, C. W. Dohm to write his pathbreaking treatise, *On the Civic Improvement of the Jews*. In 1782 in the "Preface" to the German translation of *Vindiciae Judaeorum* (written by the Amsterdam rabbi and philosopher *Manasseh ben Israel), Mendelssohn praised Dohm's treatise but criticized his suggestion that the Jewish community should be permitted to retain the right of religious excommunication. In a similar fashion, Mendelssohn also denied the state's right of coercion in matters of conscience. In response to these assertions there appeared an anonymous brochure, *The Searching for Light and Right*, in which the author, recently identified as August Cranz, a journalist of dubious reputation, asked Mendelssohn how he could combine his opposition to coercion in matters of religion with his continued adherence to Mosaic law, which would appear to sanction coercion. In reply, Mendelssohn, in 1782 and 1783, wrote his classic work, *Jerusalem, or On Religious Power and Judaism*. In the first section of the work Mendelssohn reaffirmed and elaborated upon his opposition to coercion in matters of conscience, grounding this opposition in the principle of natural law, while in the second section he sought to show that such opposition is in harmony with "authentic" Judaism. In this connection he presented a theory of Judaism in which he sought to differentiate between the eternal truths of natural religion, based solely upon reason and binding upon everyone, and the supernatural revelation of the law, binding upon Jews alone. For Mendelssohn, the original Mosaic constitution no longer holds, and while Mosaic ceremonial law is still binding on account of its religious significance, it has lost the civil status it once possessed. As a result, the ceremonial law may not be imposed through coercion, nor does it serve as a bar against the Jews' civic and political loyalty to the states in which they live.

Mendelssohn has often been called the first modern Jew. His pioneering attempt to combine enlightenment philosophy with traditional Judaism, continued observance of the law with participation in the intellectual streams of European culture, and loyalty to the Jewish community with political emancipation and liberalism has been epochal. In 1886 the centenary of Mendelssohn's death was commemorated by all sections of German Jewry, all of which hailed him as their spiritual godfather.

• Alexander Altmann, *Die trostvolle Aufklärung* (Stuttgart, 1982). Alexander Altmann, *Moses Mendelssohn: A Biographical Study* (University, Ala., 1973). Alexander Altmann, "Moses Mendelssohn's Conception of Judaism Re-examined," in *Von der Mittelalterlichen zur Modernen Aufklärung* (Tübingen, 1987), pp. 238–249. Alexander Altmann, *Moses Mendelssohns Fruhschriften zur Metaphysik* (Tübingen, 1969). Allan Arkush, trans., *Jerusalem: Or, On Religious Power and Judaism*, with an introduction and commentary by Alexander Altmann (Hanover, N.H., 1983). Allan Arkush, *Moses Mendelssohn and the Enlightenment* (Albany, N.Y., 1994), contains an up-to-date bibliography. Fritz Bamberger et al., eds., *Gesammelte Schriften: Jubiläumsausgabe*, 7 vols. (Berlin, 1929–1938), an incomplete edition of Mendelssohn's writings; a completed edition, edited by Alexander Altmann and Eva Engel, is almost completed (Stuttgart, 1971–). Fritz Bamberger, "Mendelssohn's Concept of Judaism," in *Studies in Jewish Thought*, edited by Alfred Jospe (Detroit, 1981), pp. 343–361. Edward Breuer, "Politics, Tradition, and History: Rabbinic Judaism and the Eighteenth-Century Struggle for Civil Equality," *Harvard Theological Review* 85 (1992): 357–383. Arnold Eisen, "Divine Legislation as 'Ceremonial Script': Mendelssohn on the Commandments," *AJS Review* 15 (1990): 239–267. Julius Guttmann, "Mendelssohn's *Jerusalem* and Spinoza's *Theologico-Political Treatise*," in *Studies in Jewish Thought*, edited by A. Jospe (Detroit, 1981), pp. 361–386. Eva Jospe, ed., *Moses Mendelssohn: Selections from His Writings* (New York, 1975). David Sorkin, "The Case for Compassion: Moses Mendelssohn and the Religious Enlightenment," *Modern Judaism* 14:2 (1994): 121–138.

—LAWRENCE J. KAPLAN

MENDES, HENRY PEREIRA (1852–1937), U.S. spiritual leader, communal activist, and author. Born in Birmingham, England, he served as rabbi of the Sephardi congregation in Manchester from 1874 to 1877 and then moved to Congregation Shearith Israel, the historic Spanish and Portuguese Synagogue of New York City, which he served until 1920, when he was named rabbi emeritus. He held a medical degree from New York University.

Mendes was the leading spokesman for Sephardi Jewry in the United States, a founder and first president of the *Union of Orthodox Jewish Congregations of America in 1898, and acting president of the *Jewish Theological Seminary of America from 1897 to 1902. He was a leader in Zionist and humanitarian causes.

A prolific author, he promoted traditional Jewish observances and values in the modern context. He wrote *The Jewish Religion Ethically Presented* (New York, 1905).

• Moshe Davis, *The Emergence of Conservative Judaism* (Philadelphia, 1963). David de Sola Pool, *H. Pereira Mendes: A Biography* (New York, 1938). David de Sola Pool and Tamar Pool, *An Old Faith in the New World* (New York, 1955), pp. 192–201. –MARC D. ANGEL

MENORAH (מְנוֹרָה; candelabrum). The design of the *menorah* was revealed to Moses on Mount Sinai. It consisted of seven branches, three on each side of the central shaft, each of which was ornamented with carvings of almond-blossom cups, divided into a knop and flowers. (A depiction of a *menorah* was discovered on the wall of a villa from Second Temple times in the Jewish Quarter in Jerusalem.)

The Tabernacle Menorah, formed from one ingot of gold, was situated in front of the veil on the south side of the Tabernacle (*Ex*. 25.31–40, 26.36, 40.24). In Solomon's Temple, there were ten golden candelabra in the large hall of the Temple, five to the right and five to the left of the entrance to the Holy of Holies (*1 Kgs*. 7.49). These were destroyed by the Babylonians (*2 Kgs*. 24.13) and do not appear in Ezekiel's vision of the Temple (*Ez*. 41.14). The Arch of Titus in Rome depicts what purports to be the Menorah of the Second Temple. It has a double-octagon base, but recent research has proved almost conclusively that this is an imaginative reconstruction since the Temple Menorah stood on three legs. Reproduction of the Temple Menorah or its use outside the Temple was forbidden. After the destruction of the Second Temple, traces of the Menorah disappeared, although legends abounded. The first-century philosopher *Philo interpreted the symbolism of the *menorah*, linking it to the seven planets, the cyclic quality of life, and the concept of time. The seven-branched *menorah* became one of the most familiar Jewish symbols and is frequently found in synagogue decorations and tombs from the first century CE on. In Kabbalah, the *menorah* symbolized the tree of life, and its seven branches were held to represent the planets, the firmament, and the days of Creation. The eight-branched Ḥanukkah candelabrum (*ḥanukkiyyah*) was modeled after the Temple Menorah.The Talmud forbids any attempt to replicate the Menorah of the Temple, and few three-dimensional examples are found in Jewish art before modern times. During the Emancipation, many Jews found the *menorah* too particularistic, and it was replaced by the **ma-gen David* as the central Jewish symbol. The *menorah* reemerged as a Zionist symbol, and the relief on the Arch of Titus was copied in the emblem of the State of Israel.

• Israel Museum, *Adrikhalut bi-Menorat ha-Ḥanukkah* (Jerusalem, 1978), exhibition catalogue. Carol L. Meyers, *The Tabernacle Menorah: A Synthetic Study of a Symbol from the Biblical Cult* (Missoula, Mont., 1976). Shalom M. Paul and William G. Dever, eds., *Biblical Archaeology* (Jerusalem, 1973), pp. 252–255. Jens Voss, *Die Menora: Gestalt und Funktion des Leuchters im Temple zu Jerusalem*, Orbis Biblicus et Orientalis 128 (Freiburg, 1993). Leon Yarden, *The Tree of Light: A Study of the Menorah* (Ithaca, N.Y., 1971). Jacob Zwarts, *Die Zevenarmige Kandelaar in de Romeinse Diaspora* (Utrecht, 1935). –SHALOM PAUL

MENSTRUATION. Sexual intercourse with a menstruant or *niddah* is forbidden under biblical law and the penalty is **karet* (*Lv*. 20.18). The Bible distinguishes between a *niddah* (menstruant), who becomes pure after the cessation of her menstrual discharge and a *zavah* (discharging blood outside her menstrual period), who must wait until seven bloodless days have passed before she is restored to purity (*Lv*. 15.19–32). In the course of time, this distinction was lost and during the tannaitic period the practice of waiting seven "clean days" after any menstrual discharge was universally accepted (*Nid*. 66a). On the evening of the conclusion of this seven day period, the woman immerses herself in a ritual bath (**miqveh*) and is then permitted to her husband (*Shulḥan 'Arukh, Yoreh De'ah* 197.1–5). Any bleeding or spotting during the seven clean days cancels the whole sequence and the seven day period must be recommenced once the discharge has ceased (*Shulḥan 'Arukh, Yoreh De'ah* 140.1, 196.10). It is accepted *halakhah* that a woman does not begin counting the seven clean days until at least five days have elapsed since the onset of her menses and the first day of bleeding is included in this period (Rema', *Yoreh De'ah* 196.11). In practice, therefore, an observant married couple will abstain from intercourse for a minimum of twelve days per menstrual cycle, regardless of the duration of bleeding or spotting. If a woman's first day of menstruation occurs between Saturday night and Sunday evening, she must wait until Thursday when, if the bleeding has ceased, she performs an internal examination before sunset to verify this fact and begins the seven day period that night. Internal examinations are performed every day and if no further discharge occurs, she immerses in a *miqveh* on the following Thursday evening, after which sexual relations can be resumed (*Shulḥan 'Arukh, Yoreh De'ah* 196.4–5). The idea behind this separation is expressed by R. Me'ir: "If a husband is with his wife constantly, he will come to loathe her, therefore, the Torah provided that she should be separated from him . . . and, thereafter, she will be as dear to him as at the moment she entered the bridal chamber" (*Nid*. 31b). Conservative Judaism has proposed reducing the minimum number of days from twelve to eleven and, in general, does not lay great stress on the observance of the menstruation laws. Reform Judaism has abolished them.

• Rachel Biale, *Women and Jewish Law: An Exploration of Women's Issues in Halakhic Sources* (New York, 1984), pp. 147–174. Moshe Meiselman, *Jewish Woman in Jewish Law* (New York, 1978), pp. 116–129. Moshe Tendler, *Pardes Rimonim: A Marriage Manual for the Jewish Family* (Jerusalem, 1970). –DANIEL SINCLAIR

ME'OT ḤITTIM (מְעוֹת חִיטִּים; contribution for wheat), money distributed on the eve of Pesaḥ to the poor, enabling them to make the requisite preparations for the festival. The Mishnah and Talmud saw this provision for the needy as a communal obligation, and in medieval times *meʿot ḥittim* was accepted as a communal tax. Although monetary gifts have largely supplanted gifts in kind, it is still the practice of some communal organizations and individuals to supply those in need with unleavened bread and wine for the festival.

• Eliyahu Kitov, *The Book of Our Heritage: The Jewish Year and Its Days of Significance*, rev. ed. (Jerusalem and New York, 1978), pp. 143–146.

MERCY. See COMPASSION.

MERITS, rabbinic doctrine that by performing those works commanded by and pleasing to God (meritorious works), one may obtain divine favor, which benefits not only the individual but also others (one's descendants, one's city or people, even the world). Merit (*zekhut*) is not negative (avoidance of sin) but positive (obedience of the laws and commandments of God). The conception of solidarity that underlies the doctrine of merits also implies, albeit to a lesser degree, a doctrine of demerits; the consequence of sin may fall not only on the sinner but on others as well. The doctrine of *zekhut* developed naturally out of the biblical notion that God responds to appropriate human behavior and has been frequently criticized by Christian writers as exemplifying the character of Judaism as a religion of works. See also ZEKHUT AVOT.

• Martin Abegg, "Paul, 'Works of the Law,' and MMT," *Biblical Archaeology Review* 20 (November–December 1994): 52–55, 82. Arthur Marmorstein, *The Doctrine of Merits in Old Rabbinical Literature* (New York, 1968). E. P. Sanders, *Paul and Palestinian Judaism: A Comparison of Patterns of Religion* (Minneapolis, Minn., 1989).

MERITS OF THE ANCESTORS. See ZEKHUT AVOT.

MERKAVAH. See MAʿASEH MERKAVAH.

MESHULLAḤ (מְשֻׁלָּח; messenger), an emissary accredited by the patriarch of the Jewish communities in Erets Yisra'el (termed *apostoli* by the Roman rulers) whose function was to collect funds to support the Talmudic academies of Erets Yisra'el after the destruction of the Temple. Originally designated in the Talmud (Y., *Ḥag.* 1.8) as a *shaluaḥ* or *sheliaḥ Tsiyyon* (emissary of Zion; *Beits.* 25b), these emissaries were also charged with the task of providing spiritual leadership and appointing religious functionaries for the Diaspora communities. They were the precursors of the *shadarim* (acronym of *sheluḥa' de-rabbanan* [Aram.; emissary of the rabbis]), emissary–scholars sent by the *yeshivot* of the Holy Land to raise money in the Diaspora through the medieval period until the rise of modern Zionism in the late nineteenth century. Besides collecting funds, the *shadarim* contributed to the maintenance of Hebrew and rabbinic scholarship, as well as to religious revivals in the communities that they visited and that extended as far as Australasia and the New World. Improved forms of communication and the development of banking facilities led to the decline of this ancient institution. On the other hand, in eastern Europe, particularly in Lithuania and Poland, the emergence of the central rather than local *yeshivah*, whose archetype was the *Volozhin Yeshivah, which drew students from all parts of the Diaspora, saw the revival of the *meshullaḥ*, who was sent out principally as a fund-raiser but acted also as an itinerant preacher or **maggid*. His spiritual influence was, however, limited to the Yiddish-speaking immigrant generation that had fled eastern Europe to settle in western Europe, South Africa, and the Americas.

• Jacob Saphir, *Even Sappir: Massa'otav ha-Mufla'im shel Yaʿaqov Safir ha-Levi be-Teiman* (Beersheva, 1990), Hebrew journal of a nineteenth-century Jerusalem *meshullaḥ* to the Far East, English excerpts appear in *The Jews in Victoria in the Nineteenth Century*, by Lazarus Goldman (Melbourne, 1954), p. 162. Abraham Yaari, *Sheluḥei Erets Yisra'el: Toledot ha-Sheliḥut meha-'Arets la-Golah me-Ḥurban Bayit Sheni ʿad ha-Me'ah ha-Teshaʿ Esreh* (Jerusalem, 1951), includes an extensive Hebrew and non-Hebrew bibliography. —ARYEH NEWMAN

MESHULLAM BEN MOSHEH (c.1175–1250), scholar of Béziers in southern France and maternal grandson of *Meshullam ben Yaʿaqov of Lunel. His nephew was Me'ir ben Shimʿon ha-Meʿili of Narbonne, author of *Ha-Me'orot*. Meshullam was opposed to the study of Kabbalah and supported his nephew's opposition to kabbalistic works. Meshullam corresponded with Moses Nahmanides about halakhic matters and about the Maimonidean controversy during the 1230s. One of Meshullam ben Mosheh's most famous students was Yedayah ben Avraham Bedersi, who left an account of his mentor's wisdom and the program of study in Meshullam's academy. Meshullam is best known for his *Sefer ha-Hashlamah*, the purpose of which was to complete Yitsḥaq *Alfasi's code. Meshullam based his work upon the works of earlier Provençal scholars. In it, he explicated the difficult passages of Alfasi's code, added laws that had been left out, updated it with Provençal traditions, and defended it from its critics. He also wrote critical notes to Maimonides' *Mishneh Torah*.

• Henrich Gross, *Gallia judaica: Dictionaire géographique de la France d'après les sources rabbiniques* (Paris, 1897; repr. Amsterdam, 1969), with a supplement by Simon Schwarzfuchs. Judah Lubetzki, ed., *Sefer ha-Hashlamah le-Seder Neziqin*, vol. 1 (Paris, 1885). Isadore Twersky, *Rabad of Posquières: A Twelfth-Century Talmudist* (Philadelphia, 1980). —SHLOMO H. PICK

MESHULLAM BEN YAʿAQOV OF LUNEL (c.1090–1160), Provençal scholar. Among his halakhic essays is *Issur ve-Hetter* (published by Y. Kafaḥ in *Teshuvot ha-Rabad* [Jerusalem, 1962]), in which he criticized prevalent Provençal ritual slaughtering customs and maintained that they were not in accordance with halakhic literary sources. As a philanthropist, he maintained an academy in Lunel, to which students flocked from southern France and northern Spain. He was the patron of Avraham ben David of Posquières and Zeraḥyah ben Yitsḥaq ha-Levi, who were among his outstanding students. Consequently, Lunel became famous as a significant center of study, and its scholars were known as the sages of Lunel. Meshullam was also prominent in secular studies. He sponsored the translation of books on grammar, theology, rhetoric, ethics, and parables. He himself wrote books on parables of wisdom and ethics that are no longer extant.

• Benjamin Ze'ev Benedikt, *Merkaz ha-Torah be-Provence* (Jerusalem, 1985). Israel Ta-Shema, *Rabbi Zeraḥyah ha-Levi—Ba'al ha-Ma'or u-Venei Ḥugo: Le-Toledot ha-Sifrut ha-Rabbanit be-Provence* (Jerusalem, 1992). Isadore Twersky, *Rabad of Posquières: A Twelfth-Century Talmudist* (Philadelphia, 1980).

—SHLOMO H. PICK

MESHUMMAD. See APOSTASY.

MESIRAH. See DENUNCIATION.

MESIVTA'. See YESHIVAH.

MESSER LEON FAMILY, family of Jewish scholars.

Yehudah ben Yeḥi'el Messer Leon (c.1425–c.1495), Italian physician, halakhist, and philosopher. He was born in the town of Montecchio, and lived at various times in Ancona, Bologna, Padua, Venice, and Mantua. In the wake of a dispute with Yosef *Colon, he was expelled from Mantua (c.1475) and settled in Naples. He was a distinguished physician, in recognition of which he was knighted and granted the title Messer by Emperor Frederick III in 1452. His stature was enhanced in 1469 when the same ruler granted him doctoral degrees in medicine and philosophy, allowing him to treat Christians and to grant doctoral degrees to others.

Intellectually, Messer Leon stood on the cusp of the Middle Ages and Renaissance. His philosophic writings, many of which are supercommentaries on Aristotle, Porphyry, and Maimonides, stand within the medieval scholastic tradition. Yet he is best known for *Nofet Tsufim* (Mantua, 1475), the first Hebrew book published in its author's lifetime, which demonstrates the conformity of the Bible with classical rhetoric. This concern with grammar and rhetoric demonstrates his openness to contemporary Italian humanism. Nevertheless, despite Renaissance traits, recent scholarship has characterized *Nofet Tsufim* as a medieval work in structure and argument.

Messer Leon's halakhic careeer was marked by controversy. While Italian halakhic practice was based upon the *Mishneh Torah* of Maimonides, Messer Leon taught and advocated the adoption by Italian Jewry of the stricter Ashkenazi tradition embodied in Ya'aqov ben Asher's *Arba'ah Turim* and represented by the French and German scholars migrating into northern Italy. Moreover, his rabbinic scholarship, adumbrated by his standing as physician and philosopher, convinced him of his preeminent rabbinic authority. These two factors led him to issue two highly controversial bans in 1455. The first called for the adoption of Ashkenazi strictures in the area of family law. The second banned the Torah Commentary of Gersonides as a measure to protect the Ashkenazim of northern Italy from its influence, which he regarded as subversive and contrary to normative Jewish scholastic thought.

David ben Yehudah Messer Leon (c.1470–1536), son of Yehudah and rabbi in Valena, Albania; after controversies around his halakhic rulings, he retired to Salonika. Like his father, he preferred the halakhic methods of the Ashkenazi to the Sephardi rabbinical scholars. He brought a broad knowledge of general culture, notably philosophy, to his writings on Jewish subjects.

• Alexander Altmann, in *Essays in Jewish Intellectual History* (Hanover, N. H., 1981), pp. 97–118. S. Assaf, in *Minḥah le-David:... R. David Yellin* (Jerusalem, 1935), pp. 226–228. Robert Bonfil, "Introduction," in *Nofet Tsufim*, by Judah ben Jehiel (Jerusalem, 1981), pp. 7–69. Robert Bonfil, *Rabbis and Jewish Communities in Renaissance Italy* (London, 1993). D. Carpi, in *Studi sull'ebraismo italiano: In memoria di Cecil Roth*, edited by Elio Toaff (Rome, 1974), pp. 39–62. Isaac Husik, *Judah Messer Leons' Commentary on the "Vetus Logica," a Study Based on Three Manuscripts* (Leiden, 1906). Isaac Rabinowitz, ed., *Judah Messer Leon: The Book of the Honeycomb's Flow* (Ithaca, 1983), pp. xv–lxx. Isaac Rabinowitz, in *Studies in Jewish Bibliography, History, and Literature in Honor of Edward Kiev*, edited by Charles Berlin (New York, 1972), pp. 399–406. Shalom Rosenberg, "Logiqah ve-'Ontologyah ba-Filosofyah ha-Yehudit ba-Me'ah ha-14," Ph.D. dissertation, Hebrew University, 1973. Moritz Steinschneider, *Die hebraischen Ubersetzungen des Mittelalters und die Juden als Dolmetscher* (Berlin, 1893), pp. 76–86. Hava Tirosh-Rothschild, *Between Worlds: The Life and Thought of Rabbi David ben Judah Messer Leon* (Albany, 1991), pp. 24–33.

—JEFFREY R. WOOLF

MESSIAH. The verb *m sh ḥ* (anoint [with oil]) is used in Biblical Hebrew in connection with material objects as well as persons. The noun *mashiaḥ* (anointed), which is the source of the English word *messiah*, in due course came to mean a consecrated person charged with a special mission from God (kings, prophets, priests; in one case even the gentile king Cyrus, founder of the Persian empire, is given this title [see *Is*. 45.1]). More specifically, the term signified the kings of the Davidic dynasty ("David and his seed"), and in particular the future "Son of David," who would deliver Israel from foreign bondage, restore the glories of a former golden age, and inaugurate the ingathering of Israel and God's kingdom of righteousness and peace. From its original Jewish context the term passed into general usage and the term *messianism* is often used to refer, broadly, to beliefs or theories regarding an ultimate improvement of the state of humanity and the world, or a final consummation of history.

Visions of a happy and blessed future were already expressed by the biblical prophets, especially as the sense of the fulfillment of God's *covenant with his people—living in the land that was promised to the fathers in peace and prosperity—was gradually undermined by negative experiences: the division of the kingdom, the ravages of wars and enemy incursions, and social and moral corruption. The prophets described a vision of a severe judgment, which would be followed by a glorious future, at least for a righteous remnant. However, "messianic" terminology in the eschatological sense is absent from these prophecies even when the reference is clearly to an ideal future king. The message of the prophet known as Deutero-Isaiah is definitely eschatological in character, though not messianic in its vocabulary, and the idea of a Davidic king is absent in this particular case. The usual association of the messianic idea with the Davidic kingship ideology is also illustrated by the Davidic pedigree assigned to Jesus by the writers of the Gospels (*Mt*. 1.1–17). Messianic terminology, and many of the expectations and hopes expressed by it, developed in the postexilic period and in response to varying historical situations. Thus, the rebuilding of the Temple became a central feature of the "messianic complex" after its destruction. The failure of *Zerubbabel to restore the kingdom of Judah moved the restoration of the Davidic dynasty into the eschatological realm. The period of persecution under Antiochus Epiphanes preceding the Maccabean Revolt seems to have stimulated messianic ferment and contributed to the development of *apocalyptic speculation. Various eschatological ideas (the messianic age, the *kingdom of heaven, the last judgment, the *resurrection of the dead, etc.) were held by different groups in different combinations and with varying emphases already in Second Temple times. The group known as the *Dead Sea (or Qumran) sect held a doctrine (found also in later sects) of a messianic pair: a priestly Messiah of the house of Aaron and a royal Messiah of the house of David. This detail may serve as illustration that the "anointed" one was not necessarily thought of as a savior (as for example, in later Christian thought) but rather as a symbolic figure presiding over an ideal, divinely willed and "messianic" socio-religious order. For others, the "Son-of-David" messianism, with its political or even military implications, was overshadowed by apocalyptic notions of a more mythological character, such as the *"Son of Man" who will descend from heaven to save the elect. Both early rabbinic and medieval Jewish thought exhibit much variety in the elaboration of messianic doctrine, ranging from the apocalyptic and kabbalistic end of the scale to more rationalist thinkers, such as Moses *Maimonides, who emphasized the non-miraculous nature of the messianic era. Medieval Jewish thought was largely concerned with interpreting and harmonizing the different, and occasionally conflicting, traditions enshrined in aggadic literature. A fundamental question was which prophecies should be taken literally and which metaphorically. The heterogeneity of the material also suggested a distinction between two different dispensations: a more this-worldly messianic age (ingathering of the dispersed, restoration of the Davidic kingdom, delivery from bondage, rebuilding of the Temple) and the eschatological "end of days" (day of judgment, resurrection of the dead).

To what extent revolts and uprisings, such as the Bar Kokhba' Revolt, were "messianic" in character has to be examined in detail in every case. The disastrous failure of uprisings had two significant consequences. It strengthened the element of "apocalyptic" catastrophe in the eschatological scheme: the final consummation would be preceded by great suffering (the messianic woes, *ḥevlei mashiaḥ*); moral degeneracy; wars and cosmic upheavals (Armageddon, *Gog and Magog); and a messianic "Son of Joseph" (possibly an indirect reference to the ten tribes), who would heroically fall in battle against the forces of evil before the ultimate triumph of the victorious Son of David. Another result was an increasingly quietistic emphasis, accompanied by warnings against attempts "to force the end." Messianic faith came to mean patient waiting, and "calculating the end" by means of interpreting certain biblical numbers (e.g., in the *Book of Daniel*) was discouraged by the rabbis, though the prohibition was not always obeyed. *Redemption, the rabbis asserted, will be brought about by God in his own time and not by human activity, though its advent could be hastened by ascetic piety, strict observance of the law, penitence and mystical meditation.

Nevertheless the strength and intensity of faith, hope, and yearning, drawing on biblical and rabbinic tradition as well as on the daily prayer book, in combination with constant suffering, persecution and humiliation, and, occasionally, large-scale massacres, frequently produced messianic outbursts. There has been a number of messianic pretenders, also known as "false Messiahs" or "pseudo-Messiahs," in Jewish history, as well as various announcers of the imminent arrival of the Messiah. Most of the movements generated by such individuals were short-lived and of local or regional extent only. The list of pretenders includes *Abu ʿIssa al-Isfahani and his disciple Yudghan in the eighth century; David *Alroy in twelfth-century Persia; the propagandists of the agitation among the Jewries of western Europe in the eleventh and twelfth centuries; and the twelfth-century Yemenite pretender who caused Maimonides to write his *Epistle to Yemen*. The best known of all false Messiahs, whose impact extended beyond the local level, was the pretender *Shabbetai Tsevi, in the seventeenth century. The Sabbataian debacle and its demoralizing aftermath, involving secret adherence and heresy-hunting on the one hand, apostasy and nihilism on the other, cast a cloud over all forms of overt messianic enthusiasm (see *DÖNMEH; *EMDEN, YAʿAQOV; *EYBESCHUETZ, YONATAN; *FRANK, YAʿAQOV).

The faith in an ultimately redeemed world of peace and justice, and in a messianic future for mankind (as distinct from faith in a personal Messiah), is shared by most trends in modern Jewry. Classical Reform rejected the concept of a personal Messiah, substituting the conviction that humankind was moving toward a messianic era of perfect peace and justice. Similarly, Conservative thinkers have adopted the concept of a messianic period to be achieved without supernatural intervention. Post-Enlightenment secularism identified messianism with either the social and political goals of tolerance, liberalism and full emancipation or, alternatively, socialism, and rejected Zionist nationalism in favor of universalist ideas. Contemporary attitudes toward nationalism and messianism are changing. While secularists might support a Jewish national identity without messianic expectations, Religious Zionism has undergone an ideological messianization. The prayer sanctioned by the chief rabbinate of Israel, and recited also in synagogues in the Diaspora, defines the State of Israel as "the beginning of the sprouting of our redemption," wording which implies that the messianic era has begun and that the State of Israel constitutes the beginning of the messianic process. *Ḥabad (Lubavitch) Hasidism has attracted attention in recent years for its explicit expectation of the imminent advent of the Messiah. The implicit suggestion is that the Messiah may be their leader, R. Menaḥem

Schneerson, who died in 1994. See also ESCHATOLOGY; KABBALAH.

• John J. Collins, *The Scepter and the Star: The Messiahs of the Dead Sea Scrolls and Other Ancient Literature* (New York, 1995). Joseph Klausner, *The Messianic Idea in Israel* (New York, 1955). Raphael Patai, *The Messiah Texts* (Detroit, 1979). Aviezer Ravitzky, *Ha-Qets ha-Megulleh u-Medinat ha-Yehudim* (Tel Aviv, 1993). Marc Saperstein, ed., *Essential Papers on Messianic Movements and Personalities in Jewish History* (New York, 1992), an anthology of some of the most important scholarship on Jewish messianism. Gershom Gerhard Scholem, *The Messianic Idea in Judaism and Other Essays on Jewish Spirituality* (New York, 1971). Gershom Gerhard Scholem, *Sabbatai Ṣevi: The Mystical Messiah, 1626–1676* (Princeton, 1973). Abba Hillel Silver, *A History of Messianic Speculation in Israel from the First through the Seventeenth Centuries* (New York, 1927; repr. Gloucester, Mass., 1978).

MESSIANIC MOVEMENTS. See MESSIAH.

METAPHYSICS, the philosophical study of the nature of being. Jewish philosophers have tended to define and defend their faith in the light of current general philosophical positions. In the first century, for example, *Philo of Alexandria interpreted the Torah as using a Platonic world view, and his writings were also influenced by contemporary Stoicism. Similarly *Saʿadyah ben Yosef Ga'on was indebted to Aristotelian as well as Muslim Kalam philosophy. In his *Emunot ve-Deʿot*, he argued that basic theological concepts are subject to rational analysis and that human reason is a legitimate source of religious knowledge. Shelomoh *ibn Gabirol understood Judaism in the light of Neoplatonism, while Moses *Maimonides was an Aristotelian. His *Guide of the Perplexed* was intended as a response to the difficulties of educated Jews who were troubled by the apparent contradictions between rabbinic Judaism and current philosophy.

Other Jewish thinkers, however, were skeptical of metaphysics. In his *Kuzari*, *Yehudah ha-Levi attempted to demonstrate the inadequacy of Aristotelian philosophy and argued for the superiority of religious revelation. Similarly Ḥasda'i ben Avraham Crescas, in his *Or Adonai*, argued strongly against the metaphysics of Maimonides and maintained that the only certainty lay in trusting in the authority of scripture.

• Hermann Cohen, *Religion of Reason: Out of the Sources of Judaism*, translated by Simon Kaplan (New York, 1972). Steven T. Katz, ed., *Jewish Philosophers* (New York, 1975). Leo Strauss, "The Mutual Influence of Theology and Philosophy," in *The Independent Journal of Philosophy* 3 (1980). A. Vdoff, "Metaphysics," in *Contemporary Jewish Religious Thought*, edited by Arthur A. Cohen and Paul Mendes-Flohr (New York, 1988).

METATRON, in Talmudic, Midrashic, and mystical literature the name of one of the supreme powers in the divine realm. He is often associated with the *sar ha-panim* (the prince of the countenance), meaning the power standing face to face with God (while others are to his left, to his right, or behind him). Talmudic literature associates Metatron with the angel sent by God to guide the Israelites in the wilderness, "for my name is in him" (*Ex.* 23.21). The name is probably based on the Greek *tetra* (four), referring to the Tetragrammaton, God's four-letter holy name (though other explanations have been offered, based on the references to Metatron as a "messenger"). According to *Ḥagigah* 15a, the sage *Elishaʿ ben Avuyah lapsed into heresy when in his vision he saw Metatron sitting on a throne in the seventh heaven and judging the world; this led him to the belief that "there are two powers in heaven." Metatron may also be associated with the *sar ha-ʿolam*, the prince of the world, an opaque Midrashic reference to a probably demiurgic power. The most detailed description of him in mystical literature is found in the Hebrew *Apocalypse of Enoch*, in which the gradual transformation of Enoch ben Jared (*Gn.* 5.18–19) into the power Metatron is described, after which he guides R. Yishmaʿe'l on a tour of divine worlds. Metatron is called *naʿar* (youth or servant; *3 En.*), the same appellation that is found in gnostic treatises. Gershom Scholem identified him with the angel Yahoel mentioned in the *Apocalypse of Abraham*. Medieval kabbalists identified Metatron with different aspects of the divine realm, most often with the *Shekhinah.

• Joseph Dan, *The Ancient Jewish Mysticism* (Tel Aviv, 1993), *passim*. Ithamar Gruenwald, *Apocalyptic and Merkavah Mysticism* (Leiden, 1980), pp. 235–241 *et passim*. Hugo Odeberg, *3rd Enoch or the Hebrew Book of Enoch*, 2d ed. (New York, 1873), pp. 79–147. Peter Schäfer, *The Hidden and Manifest God: Some Major Themes in Early Jewish Mysticism* (Albany, N.Y., 1993), *passim*. Gershom Gerhard Scholem, *Jewish Gnosticism, Merkabah Mysticism and Talmudic Tradition*, 2d ed. (New York, 1965), pp. 43–56 *et passim*. —JOSEPH DAN

METEMPSYCHOSIS. See TRANSMIGRATION OF SOULS.

METIVTA'. See YESHIVAH.

METURGEMAN (Aram.; מְתֻרְגְּמָן; interpreter), in early times, the translator of the Torah and Prophets into the vernacular (*Aramaic) when these were read in public in the synagogue service. His translation accompanied the reading (verse by verse for the Torah; three verses at a time for the Prophets) and consisted of the officially approved Aramaic version of the Bible (see TARGUM). He was not allowed to read his translation from a written text or to speak louder than the reader of the Hebrew so as to emphasize the primacy of the latter. On occasions the *meturgeman* not only translated but added explanation as well. During the Talmudic period, the *meturgeman* acted as a spokesman for the teachers when they lectured in public. The teacher would speak quietly to the *meturgeman* who then repeated the discourse to the audience in a loud voice (*Qid.* 31b; *Sot.* 40a). The office of *meturgeman* is still extant among Yemenite Jews.

• Avigdor Shinan, "Sermons, Targums and the Reading from Scriptures in the Ancient Synagogue," in *The Synagogue in Late Antiquity*, edited by Lee I. Levine (Philadelphia, 1987), pp. 97–110.

MEZONOT. See MAINTENANCE.

MEZUMMAN. See BIRKAT HA-MAZON.

MEZUZAH (מְזוּזָה; doorpost), small parchment (from the skin of a clean animal) on which are inscribed the first two paragraphs of the *Shemaʿ (*Dt.* 6.4–9, 11.13–21). The parchment is rolled tightly and placed in a small case, many of which have a small aperture through which the word *Shaddai* (Almighty), inscribed on the back of the scroll (homiletically explained as an acronym for *shomer delatot Yisra'el* [guardian of the doors of Israel]), can be seen. This seems to confirm the *mezuzah*'s original apotropaic purpose. *Mezuzot* are affixed to doorposts in the home in accordance with the prescription in *Deuteronomy* 6.9. Only a qualified scribe (**sofer setam*) may write a *mezuzah*, and it is to be written with the same care used in the writing of a Torah scroll. The *mezuzah* is nailed in a sloping position (the top pointing inward; the bottom outward) on the upper right-hand doorpost of the entry to the home and each of its rooms used for human habitation. The sloping position was a compromise reached by *Rashi, who held that it should be vertical, and by his grandson, *Yaʿaqov ben Me'ir Tam, who maintained that it should be horizontal. In ancient times a hollow was constructed in the doorpost, and the *mezuzah* was placed inside. A special blessing is recited when securing the *mezuzah* to the door. While some interpret *mezuzot* as protective *amulets, the *mezuzah* has also been described as the sanctification of the home by the continual reminder of God's omnipresence. Among pious Jews, it became customary to kiss the *mezuzah* upon entering or leaving a room. *Mezuzot* are to be checked twice every seven years to confirm their continued fitness. For *Karaites, the *mezuzah* is optional and consists of a plate in the shape of the two tablets of the Torah without any script. Rabbi *Me'ir ben Barukh of Rothenburg wrote, "No demon can have power over a house upon which the *mezuzah* is affixed." Names, verses, and figures were added by mystics and kabbalists, but Moses *Maimonides insisted upon not tampering with the text. The *mezuzah* case has been one of the objects of Jewish ritual artistic expression, especially since the eighteenth century. For example, in North Africa *mezuzot* covers were elaborately embroidered, and in the center appeared the name of the woman who embroidered the cloth or the recipient. Today, *mezuzot* are often carried or worn around the neck as charms.

• Belle Rosenbaum, *Upon Thy Doorposts: The Law, Lore, the Love of Mezuzot* (Hackensack, N.J., 1995). David Rothstein, "From Bible to Murabbaat: Studies in the Literary, Textual and Scribal Features of Phylacteries and Mezuzot in Ancient Israel and Early Judaism," Ph.D. dissertation, University of California at Los Angeles, 1992.

MICAH (fl. 8th cent. BCE), prophet from the southern kingdom of Judah, whose collection of prophecies, directed against both Samaria and Judah, comprises the sixth book in the collection of the Twelve Minor Prophets. He began to preach shortly before the fall of Samaria and was a later contemporary of Hosea and Isaiah. The seven chapters of the prophetic work may be divided into three sections. Chapters 1.1–3.12 are characterized by words of condemnation, in which the prophet denounces deeds of oppression, dishonest business practices, and idolatry, which eventually will bring about the downfall of Samaria (1.6). He also levels attacks against the prophets of his day, who cry "peace" only when they are paid for their oracles, and against the leaders of the people, who are guilty of perversions of justice, which will culminate in the destruction of Jerusalem (3.12). This is the first prophecy of its kind, and its repercussions were heard over a century later when Jeremiah was almost put to death for uttering a similar threat (*Jer.* 26.18), only to be saved because of Micah's prophecy. The second section, chapters 4–5, commences with a quote from *Isaiah* (*Is.* 2.2–4) predicting a reign of universal peace, with nations streaming to Jerusalem, which is portrayed as an international court of law from which God will issue instructions, thereby resolving all international disputes (4.1–4). Micah envisions the eventual destruction of Israel's enemies and the ingathering of exiles, presided over and shepherded by a descendant of David from Bethlehem (5.1–5), as well as the final extermination of idols (5.9–14). The final section, chapters 6–7, contains oracles of both condemnation and consolation, including Micah's famous pronouncement, "He has told you, O man, what is good and what the Lord requires of you: Only to do justice and to love goodness, and to walk modestly with your God" (6.8). The book concludes with a prayer for forgiveness and consolation, culminating with words that later were incorporated in the New Year custom of *Tashlikh, appealing to God to hurl people's sins "into the depths of the sea" (7.18–20).

• Delbert R. Hillers, *Micah*, Hermeneia Commentary (Philadelphia, 1984). Yehezkel Kaufmann, *The Religion of Israel* (Chicago, 1960), pp. 395–398. James L. Mays, *Micah*, The Old Testament Library (Philadelphia, 1976). Hans W. Wolff, *Micah the Prophet* (Philadelphia, 1981).

—SHALOM PAUL

MICHAEL (Who Is Like unto God), one of the four archangels; one of the few named angels in the Bible (*Dn.* 12.1). It is said that he is composed of snow, while Gabriel is composed of fire (*Dt. Rab.* 5). Michael figures prominently in apocryphal and aggadic literature, in which he is variously described as God's viceregent; celestial high priest, who sacrifices the souls of the righteous on the altar before God (*Midrash ʿAseret ha-Dibberot* 1); protector and advocate of Israel (*Yoma'* 77a); and keeper of the heavenly keys. As *Satan's main adversary, Michael also has certain eschatological functions (e.g., calling the dead to the Resurrection).

• Wilhelm Lueken, *Michael: Eine Darstellung und Vergleichung der jüdischen und der morgenlandisch-christlichen Tradition vom Erzengel Michael* (Göttingen, 1898). Benedikt Otzen, "Michael and Gabriel: Angelological Problems in the Book of Daniel," in *The Scriptures and the Scrolls*, edited by F. García-Martínez et al., eds. (Leiden, 1992), pp. 114–124.

MICROCOSM. The view that the human being represented an epitome or "miniature version" of the larger universe was widely held in the Middle Ages, and correspondences were asserted between the human organism, the cosmos, and even the Deity in whose image humans were said to have been fashioned. Hence, by knowing one's self, one might also arrive at a better knowledge of God, and the exhortation "know yourself O men, and you shall know your Lord" was taken over from Muslim philosophers by Jewish thinkers. The microcosm-macrocosm analogy was elaborated in Midrashic and philosophical works, of which Yosef ben Yaʿaqov ibn Zaddik's *ʿOlam Qatan* (i.e., microcosm) is one of the best known. The microcosm idea was developed and taken to great lengths by the kabbalists in their doctrine of *sefirot. See also ADAM QADMON.

MIDDAH KE-NEGED MIDDAH (מִדָּה כְּנֶגֶד מִדָּה; measure for measure), a term commonly used to describe the method of punishment that is exacted by God directly. One of the earliest references to this concept is found in Mishnah tractate *Sotah* 8b-9a, "The ways a person measures himself [conducts himself] is how he is measured from above," and the Mishnah continues with several examples of *middah ke-neged middah* as a form of *divine punishment. The Talmud seems to infer that this type of punishment is implied in Isaiah's comment "by measure and by exile, you contend with them" (*Is.* 28.7). The Talmud notes that the story of Purim contains within it the theme of *middah ke-neged middah* (*Meg.* 12b); it uses this principle to note that certain people will not participate in the resurrection of the dead because they did not believe that the Almighty would resurrect the dead and that all of the attributes of the Lord are measure for measure (*San.* 80a).

Middah ke-neged middah is not a normative Jewish principle of punishment but is limited to explaining the conduct of God.

• Shmuel Lenshtam, "Middah ke-Neged Middah," in *Entsiqlopedyah Miqra'it* (Jerusalem, 1950–), vol. 4, pp. 840–846. Saul Lieberman, "On Sins and Their Punishments," in *Texts and Studies* (New York, 1974), pp. 29–56. —MICHAEL BROYDE

MIDDAT SEDOM (מִדַּת סְדוֹם), when one person denies another a legal benefit, which could have been given without cost or detriment of any kind. The rabbis criticized such behavior as reflecting the immorality of the biblical Sodom, and characterized it as *middat Sedom* (a quality of Sodom). For example, if upon the dissolution of a partnership in land one partner requests to take his share in a given location, in order to maintain continuity with adjoining parcels owned by him individually, and if all potential shares are in all respects of equal value, the other partners would be guilty of *middat Sedom* if they refused. The rabbis implemented this moral judgment by imposing a legal obligation upon the uncooperative party to grant the benefit, stating that "one can be compelled to act against the quality of Sodom."

• Nahum Rakover, *Osher ve-Lo' be-Mishpat* (Jerusalem, 1987), pp. 20–22. Shlomo Yosef Zevin, ed., *Entsiqlopedyah Talmudit* (Jerusalem, 1981), vol. 15, pp. 409 et seq. —BEN TZION GREENBERGER

MIDDOT (מִדּוֹת; Measurements). [*This entry discusses the tractate* Middot; *for a discussion of hermeneutics, see* HERMENEUTICS.] Tractate *Middot* consists of five chapters in Mishnah order Qodashim, with no *gemara'* in either Talmud, describing the layout and structure of the Second *Temple. Opening with a list of places where the honor guard of priests and Levites took their posts for the night watch, *Middot* enumerates the gates, sections, and offices of the Temple, detailing the measurements of each section. *Middot* intersperses several remarks regarding the symbolic significance of some of the structures discussed: a doorway to the north of the main entrance to the Temple hall remained forever closed "because the Lord God of Israel enters through it [*Ez.* 44.2]" (*Mid.* 4.2); the fifteen stairs leading from the women's courtyard to the Israelite courtyard correspond to the fifteen songs of ascension in Psalms 120–134; and the Temple hall is called Ariel (Lion of God; *Is.* 29.1) due to its trapezoidal structure, similar to "the lion, which is narrow in the rear and broad in the front" (*Mid.* 4:7). Concluding its description with the "office of hewn-stone," where the Sanhedrin supervised the ritual fitness of the priests, *Middot* closes with a paean to God, who chose the sons of Aaron to serve before him in the Holy of Holies.

An English translation of the tractate by Herbert Danby is in *The Mishnah* (Oxford, 1933).

• Chanoch Albeck, ed., *Shishah Sidrei Mishnah, Seder Qodashim* (Jerusalem, 1956). Philip Blackman, ed. and trans., *Mishnayoth*, vol. 5, *Order Kodashim* (Gateshead, 1973). Frederick James Hollis, *The Archaeology of Herod's Temple: With a Commentary on Tractate Middoth* (London, 1934). Asher Selig Kaufman, ed., *Massekhet Middot*, Ha-Miqdash bi-Yerushalayim, pt. 1 (Jerusalem, 1991). Hermann Leberecht Strack and Günter Stemberger, *Introduction to the Talmud and Midrash*, rev. and updat. ed., translated by Markus Bockmuehl (Minneapolis, 1992). —AVRAHAM WALFISH

MIDDOT, THIRTEEN. See THIRTEEN ATTRIBUTES.

MIDIANITES, tribes of nomads and shepherds in the southern part of Canaan and northern Arabia. According to *Genesis* 25.2 (cf.*1 Chr.* 1.32), Midian was the son of Keturah, Abraham's wife. The Midianites dwelled in the same area as the rest of Abraham's descendants (other than Isaac), south and southeast of Canaan. The Midianites are mentioned as merchants (*Gn.* 37.28) and as shepherds (*Ex.* 3.1). In the first chapters of *Exodus*, Moses finds refuge with Jethro, "priest of Midian," described as a host and an ally to Moses and the people of Israel (*Ex.* 18; *Nm.* 10.29). Moses also marries Jethro's daughter, Zipporah. In contrast, the Midianites are mentioned as enemies of Israel during their wandering in the wilderness and allies of Balak, king of Moab (*Nm.* 22.4, 7), and also in the story of Baal-peor (*Nm.* 25). Hostilities between Israel and the Midianites are also evident in Canaan, where "the hand of Midian prevailed over Israel" (*Jgs.* 6.2). Gideon saved the Israelites, and the great victory was engraved in the historical memory of the nation. Reflections of this event can be found in *Psalms* (83.10) and *Isaiah* (9.3, 10.26). The peoples of Midian were apparently organized in a five-tribe alliance (*Nm.* 31.8; *Jgs.* 8.5; cf. *Gn.* 25.4). The names of the Midianite leaders (*Nm.* 31.8; *Jos.* 13.21; *Jgs.* 8.12) seem to be of Semitic origin (except Hur [*Nm.* 31.8], which is an Egyptian name; see also *Ex* 17.10, 12). After the Midianite alliance collapsed, some Midianite tribes remained in the area east of the Gulf of Aqaba, where the name Midian is mentioned in Hellenistic sources near the oasis of el-Baddai.

• Baruch A. Levine, *Numbers 1–20*, The Anchor Bible (New York, 1993), pp. 67–90, 334–335. Jacob Milgrom, *Numbers*, The JPS Torah Commentary (Philadelphia, 1989), pp. 78–80. —ZE'EV KAINAN

MIDNIGHT TIQQUN. See TIQQUN.

MIDRASH (מִדְרָשׁ), the discovery of meanings other than literal in the Bible; derived from the root *darash* (inquire), denotes the literature that interprets scripture in order to extract its full implications and meaning. These interpretations often formed a response to the need of a particular age or environment. The term *midrash* is found in the Bible (cf. *2 Chr.* 13.22, 24.27). It is supposed by Jewish tradition that some kind of *midrash*, in the form of a commentary on the Hebrew Bible—particularly its legal portions—must have existed from earliest times. Indeed it would seem to be required by the *written law, which often omits the details of those observances covered by some general command or prohibition. Thus, the method of slaughtering animals or the kinds of work forbidden on the Sabbath are never specified. In such cases scripture often uses the phrase "as the Lord commanded Moses" to indicate the details of the law. This would suggest the existence of a more detailed legislation, completing and complementing the written word of scripture. Like other branches of the *oral law, therefore, *midrash* goes back to very early origins. It appears that with the return from Babylon, the *soferim* headed by *Ezra, who were both scribes and scholars, began to study the traditional interpretation of the written law and apply it to the everyday needs of the community (cf. *Ezr.* 7.6, 10.11). They seem to have continued in this function up to the time of *Shim'on ha-Tsaddiq, who was both the last of the *soferim* and the first of the teachers of the Mishnah. Later, *midrash* was committed to writing. The very early *midrashim* originated with the same teachers whose sayings are preserved in the Mishnah, and they are for the most part halakhic *midrashim*, that is, they deal with the Mosaic law. A second type of *midrash*, the aggadic *midrash*, expounds the nonlegal parts of scripture, and although traces of this genre are also to be found early, its great period of efflorescence began after the Mishnaic era and continued as late as the twelfth and thirteenth centuries. Aggadic *midrashim* range over the whole of scripture, and their subject matter includes theology, ethical teaching, exhortation, popular philosophy, imaginative exposition, legend, allegory, animal fables, and so on (see AGGADAH). Halakhic *midrash* and aggadic *midrash* denote different genres of *midrash*, as well as collections of Midrashic works. Halakhic *midrash* applies to the various Midrashic compilations of the tannaitic period. This includes writings on the books *Exodus*, *Leviticus*, *Numbers*, and *Deuteronomy* (which also contain aggadic *midrash* in different degrees). Aggadic *midrash* applies to all Midrashic collections from the amoraic period and after, which contain almost exclusively comments of aggadic nature. As a whole, *Midrashic literature contains some of the most distinctive features of rabbinic Judaism. It was a way of delving more deeply than the literal meaning of the word of scripture and a method of linking the various parts of the Bible together by the discovery of typological patterns, verbal echoes, and rhythms of repetition. This last function is expressed in the phrase, "the happenings of the Fathers are a sign to their posterity." Thus, the exile of Jacob and his flight from his brother Esau became a symbol for all subsequent Jewish exile and wandering, both in the biblical and post-biblical periods. The aggadic *midrashim* in particular were an instrument for imparting contemporary relevance to biblical events. In this respect the function of *midrash* is the opposite of *peshat*, which aims at reconstructing the literal meaning of scripture, its local setting, and original system of reference. The balance between *midrash* and *peshat* is basic to the rabbinic mentality in its approach to scripture. Whereas the *peshat* performed its rigorous office of research into the exact meaning of scripture as far as the available historical and lexicographical knowledge allowed, *midrash* made possible a vivid application of the scriptural word to a later situation or a later system of ideas. It operated according to certain hermeneutic laws of interpretation (see HERMENEUTICS) that were, however, never strictly applied, and frequently the rabbis allowed themselves to indulge in far-fetched interpretations and narratives that were clearly intended to delight the fancy as well as to instruct. Unlike *halakhah*, where a clear and unequivocal ruling is required, inconsistencies in aggadic dicta are taken for granted.

• Daniel Boyarin, *Intertextuality and the Reading of the Midrash* (Bloomington, Ind., 1990). Lee Haas, "Bibliography on Midrash," in *The Study of Ancient Judaism*, edited by Jacob Neusner (New York, 1981), vol. 1, pp. 93–103. David Halivni, *Midrash, Mishnah and Gemara: The Jewish Predilection for Justified Law* (Cambridge, Mass., 1986). Barry W. Holtz, "Midrash," in *Back to the Sources: Reading the Classic Jewish Texts*, edited by Barry W. Holtz (New York, 1984), pp. 177–211. Rimon Kasher, "The Interpretation of Scripture in Rabbinic Literature," in *Mikra: Text, Translation, Reading and Interpretation of the Hebrew Bible in Ancient Judaism and Early Christianity*, edited by Martin J. Mulder, Compendia Rerum Iudaicarum ad Novum Testamentum, Section II, 1, Jewish Writings of the Second Temple Period (Philadelphia, 1988), pp. 547–594. James L. Kugel and Rowan A. Greer, *Early Biblical Interpretation* (Philadelphia, 1986). Hananel Mack, *The Aggadic Midrash Literature* (Tel Aviv, 1989). Gary G. Porton, "Defining Midrash," in *The Study of Ancient Judaism*, edited by Jacob Neusner (New York, 1981), vol. 1, pp. 55–92. Meir Rafeld and Joseph Tabory, comps., *Peraqim mi-Tokh Madrikh Bibliographi le-Torah she-be-'al-Peh: A. Midreshei Halakhah; B. Sifrut ha-'Aggadah* (Ramat Gan, 1992), with multilingual bibliography.

MIDRASH HA-GADOL, a thirteenth-century Yemenite Midrashic compilation on the Torah, compiled by David ben 'Amram of Aden. Written in a clear Hebrew prose, divided up according to the weekly Torah readings, each section is prefaced with a proem in rhymed verse. The author-compiler did not indicate his sources (unlike the otherwise similar **Yalqut Shim'oni*) and at times combined more than one source into a smoothly continuous unit. The work preserves many otherwise unknown early sources in an accurate transmission. With the aid of this work, scholars were able to reconstruct large portions of the lost *Mekhilta' de-Rabbi Shim'on bar Yoḥa'i* and the *Sifrei Zuta'* and also the *Mekhilta' de-Rabbi Yishma'e'l* on *Deuteronomy*, otherwise called *Midrash Tanna'im*. *Midrash ha-Gadol* also preserved accurate readings of early Midrashic texts and Talmudic sources. The compiler made copious use of Maimonides, thus *Midrash ha-Gadol* is important for Maimonidean studies. It first came to scholarly notice in the second half of the nineteenth century and has been published in a critical edition by a number of scholars: *Genesis* and *Exodus* by M. Margaliot (Jerusalem, 1947, 1956); *Leviticus* by A. Steinsaltz (1975); *Numbers* by Z. M. Rabinowitz (1967); *Deuteronomy* by S. Fisch (1972).

—DANIEL SPERBER

MIDRASHIC LITERATURE. Whereas halakhic *midrashim* aim at extracting the practical law from the scriptures, aggadic *midrashim* penetrate into their ethical and moral background (see MIDRASH). Midrashic interpretations were current from earliest times (cf. *Neh*. 8.8), but they really began to flourish in the tannaitic period, when teachers expounded the weekly portions of the Pentateuch and Prophets on Sabbaths and festivals during the service in the synagogue (cf. *Ber*. 28a). At first these expositions were recorded in several booklets called *Sifrei de-'Aggadeta'*—even before the **halakhah* and *gemara'* were committed to writing (cf. *Git*. 60a). Subsequently, they were unified and edited in complete works. Some of these *midrashim* have been lost in the course of time. The principal halakhic *midrashim* extant today are *Sifrei* on *Numbers* and *Deuteronomy*, *Sifra'* on *Leviticus*, and **Mekhilta'* on *Exodus*, but Maimonides (in the introduction to *Mishneh Torah*) speaks of *Mekhilta'* on the last four books of the Pentateuch by R. Yishmaʿe'l and another *Mekhilta'* by R. ʿAqiva'. It is now clear that the latter is identical with the *Mekhilta' de-Rabbi Shimʿon bar Yoḥ'ai* and *Sifrei Zuta'*, which originated in the school of R. ʿAqiva'. The ancient *midrashim* and the *Mishneh, Tosefta', and each *Talmud, although mainly halakhic, also contain much aggadic material. The principal *midrashim* of the amoraic period, almost all of which originated in Erets Yisra'el, are those included in *Midrash Rabbah (a collection of unrelated *midrashim* to the Pentateuch and the Five Scrolls of different periods and genres) and in the *Tanḥuma'-Yelammedenu collections; the *Pesiqta' de-Rav Kahana'* and *Pesiqta' Rabbati*, consisting of Midrashic comments on readings from the Pentateuch and prophetic lessons assigned to holidays and special Sabbaths; and *midrashim* on other books of the Bible, such as *Samuel*, *Psalms* (also known as *Shoḥer Tov*) and *Proverbs*. Classic Midrashic literature came to a close in the late tenth or early eleventh century. Important compilations of Midrashic literature, both halakhic and aggadic, include *Yalqut Shimʿoni* and *Midrash ha-Gadol*, the authors of which have preserved invaluable and otherwise unknown *midrashim*.

• Richard S. Sarason, "Toward a New Agendum for the Study of Rabbinic Midrashic Literature," in *Studies in Aggadah, Targum and Jewish Liturgy in Memory of Joseph Heinemann*, edited by Jakob J. Petuchowski and Ezra Fleischer (Jerusalem, 1981), pp. 55–73, includes select bibliography.

MIDRASH PROVERBS. See PROVERBS, MIDRASH.

MIDRASH RABBAH, a collection of aggadic *midrashim* to the Pentateuch and the Five Scrolls. The appellation *Rabbah* (Great), the origin and meaning of which are obscure, originally applied to only some of these *midrashim* (notably *Genesis Rabbah*) and then to all the *midrashim* on the Pentateuch; finally, as a result of the inclusion of all ten *midrashim* in one edition (Venice, 1545), the term came to be applied to the entire collection. Despite their appearance together, however, the *midrashim* so named are separate works, originating in different periods and organized in different ways. *Genesis Rabbah* is generally considered to be the earliest compilation (completed c.5th cent. CE); from a slightly later date are *Leviticus Rabbah* and the *midrashim* to the Five Scrolls. All of these are examples of classical aggadic *midrashim*, compiled in Erets Yisra'el, and were written in a mixture of Rabbinic Hebrew and Galilean Aramaic. Originating from a later period are the *midrashim* to *Exodus*, *Numbers*, and *Deuteronomy*, which are related to—and at times are identical with—the *Tanḥuma'-Yelammedenu collection of *midrashim*; these were written almost completely in Hebrew. Several of the *midrashim* (those to *Exodus*, *Numbers*, and *Esther*) are, in their present form, a composite of two works from different periods. Viewed together, the *midrashim* in Midrash Rabbah present a compendium of rabbinic exegesis and lore on the books of the Bible that were most often read and studied in the synagogue and study hall throughout the Mishnaic, Talmudic, and late Byzantine periods. Of the many commentaries that appear in standard editions of Midrash Rabbah, of special note are *Mattenot Kehunnah* by Yissakhar Berman Ashkenazi (Poland, 16th cent.), *Yefei To'ar* and *Yefei ʿAnaf* by Shemu'el Yaffe Ashkenazi (Constantinople, 16th cent.), and *Maharzev*—a contraction for Maharenu ha-Rav Ze'ev Wolf Einhorn (Vilna, 19th cent.). See also entries on the individual *midrashim*.

• Harry Freedman and Maurice Simon, *Midrash Rabbah* (London, 1961). *Midrash Rabbah* (Vilna, 1878). Hermann Leberecht Strack, *Introduction to the Talmud and Midrash* (1931; Minneapolis, 1992). August Wuensche, ed. and trans., *Bibliotheca Rabbinica* (Leipzig, 1880–1885). Leopold Zunz, *Ha-Derashot be-Yisra'el ve-Hishtalshelutan ha-Historit*, edited by Chanoch Albeck (1892; Jerusalem, 1974).

—PAUL MANDEL

MIDRASH SHEMU'EL. See SAMUEL, MIDRASH.

MIDRASH TADSHE', pseudepigraphous *midrash*, also called *Baraiyta' de-Rabbi Pinḥas ben Ya'ir* after the second-century tanna' to whom the work was ascribed. In both content and method it resembles certain late Second Temple works, upon which it clearly drew, such as *Jubilees* and works by Philo. *Midrash Tadshe'* opens with a commentary on "Let the earth bring forth grass" (*tadshe' ha-'arets*; *Gn*. 1.11), hence its title. *Midrash Tadshe'* contains speculations on the mystical significance of numbers along lines developed in **Sefer Yetsirah*, as well as astrological matter. It has been suggested that its author could possibly have been the eleventh-century southern French scholar *Mosheh ha-Darshan. It was first published by Adolph Jellinek (*Beit ha-Midrash* 3 [1928]: 164–193).

—DANIEL SPERBER

MIDRESHEI ESHET ḤAYIL, *midrashim* on the biblical acrostic poem Eshet Ḥayil (*Prv*. 31.10–31). One group of these *midrashim* interprets each verse as referring to a different female biblical personality. One of the editions, redacted no later than 1270, has been erroneously appended in various manuscripts and printed editions to *Midrash Proverbs*. Recently, a critical edition based on the twelve extant manuscripts has been prepared (Yael Levine Katz, "Midreshei Eshet Ḥayil," Ph.D. dissertation, Bar-Ilan University, 1993). Four editions from Yemen have been preserved in their entirety, the earliest appearing in the *Midrash ha-Gadol* of the thirteenth century, and there are six *genizah* fragments extant of undetermined date. The various editions share, for the most part, a common tradition with regard to the women included, though they differ considerably in content. These *midrashim* draw upon the vast corpus of Talmudic and Midrashic literature but also incorporate sources of unknown origin. They employ the hermeneutic methods of classical *midrashim*. The women in the first eight *derashot* are presented in chronological order: Noah's wife, Sarah, Rebekah, Leah, Rachel, Pharaoh's daughter, Jochebed, and Miriam. The remaining women are drawn from the Prophets and Hagiographa, although they do not appear in chronological order. After identifying the women, many of the *derashot* proceed to extol their virtuous deeds. Several acted on behalf of their husbands. Pharaoh's daughter rescued Moses. A number of *derashot* offer no further details about the women, focusing instead on their sons or on other male figures. Various *derashot* mention the rewards the women reaped for their good deeds.

Another group of these *midrashim* interprets the proverbial poem as referring to a singular biblical personality, Sarah. Three known editions of these *midrashim* are extant, the earliest of which dates to the ninth or tenth century.

• Mordecai Margulies, ed., *Midrash ha-Gadol* (Jerusalem, 1947). Burton Lyle Visotzky, "Midrash Eishet Ḥayil," *Conservative Judaism* 38 (1986). Solomon Aaron Wertheimer, ed., "Midrash Eshet Ḥayil," in *Battei Midrashot* (Jerusalem, 1980). —YAEL LEVINE KATZ

MILAH. See CIRCUMCISION.

MILK (Heb. *ḥalav*). The only halakhic restrictions on the consumption of milk are that it be drawn from a permitted species of animal and that milk or milk products not be mixed or cooked together with *meat or meat products; it is strictly forbidden even to derive benefit from such a mixture (see DIETARY LAWS). To prevent any doubts regarding a possible admixture of milk from prohibited (unclean) species, an animal should be milked either by a Jew or in the presence of a Jew (see MASHGIAḤ). Breast milk may be imbibed only by a suckling but not by a child already weaned or by an adult.

• Abraham ben Jehiel Michal Danzig, *The Laws of Meat and Milk*, translated by Jeffrey R. Cohen (New York, 1991). Binyomin Forst, *The Laws of Kashrus: A Comprehensive Exposition of Their Underlying Concepts* (Brooklyn, N.Y., 1993).

MILLENNIUM, the one-thousand-year period of messianic rule that is to precede the last judgment and the world to come. Though the idea of a messianic period is found in the pseudepigrapha, in rabbinic literature, and in Christian writings, there were many, and conflicting, calculations of when it would begin and how long it would last. In *4 Ezra* 7.26–31, for example (see ESDRAS, BOOKS OF), the days of the Messiah are expected to last four hundred years, while in *Sanhedrin* 99a different rabbis estimate the duration of the period at forty, seventy, four hundred, or a few thousand years. The term *millenarianism* is often used to refer to such eschatological expectations, regardless of the exact numerical calculations involved. The concept of one thousand years as the duration of the messianic era may have been derived from the idea of a world week, each day of which was to be a thousand years long. Such a notion, which is found, for example, in the Slavonic *Apocalypse of Enoch*, recurs in rabbinic sources, where it is also connected with *Psalms* 90.4 ("For a thousand years in your sight are but as yesterday"), interpreted to mean that God's day is a thousand years; just as the days of Creation were six in number, so will the world last for six thousand years, the seventh day being the thousand year reign of the Messiah (cf. *San*. 97a). The expectation of such a reign was very much alive in the early church (cf. *Rv*. 20.4–6), and subsequently in millenarian or chiliastic Christian movements.

• Norman Cohn, *The Pursuit of the Millennium: Revolutionary Millenarians and Mystical Anarchists of the Middle Ages* (London, 1957; repr. New York, 1970). Michael St. Clair, *Millenarian Movements in Historical Context* (New York, 1992). —GIDEON BOHAK

MIMUNAH (מִימוּנָה), name, of uncertain origin, of a celebration observed by Jews of North Africa and certain other *ʿAdot ha-Mizraḥ on the day following the conclusion of *Pesaḥ. It is a family festival observed in the home and at communal picnics with a strong emphasis on food, music, and traditional costumes. In Israel it has become a popular holiday among Jews of North African origin.

• Eliyahu R. Martsiano, *Ḥag ha-Mimunah* (Jerusalem, 1991).

MIN. See MINIM.

MINHAG (מִנְהָג; custom), a term with two distinct meanings in Jewish tradition, a post-biblical religious custom and a traditional liturgical rite.

A Post-Biblical Religious Custom. Customs not introduced by a rabbinical authority or based on biblical writ often became sacred by virtue of long usage. Accepted custom is one of the formative factors in the development of Jewish law and religious observance. This applies both to local *minhag*, that is, customs that obtain in one locality only, as well as to customs that have been adopted universally. *Minhagim* are less binding than formal legal enactments, though in the event of conflict, custom can take precedence over law (Y., *Yev*. 12.1). The institution of a second day of festivals (see YOM TOV SHENI SHEL GALUYYOT) in the Diaspora is a striking example of an obsolete law surviving merely because it qualified as a custom. Originally the second day was instituted because of doubt over the exact day of a festival, since the emissaries of the Sanhedrin could not reach the Jews in the Diaspora in time to notify them of the date of the new moon. When the calendar became fixed by astronomical calculations, this consideration no longer applied. The Talmud Bavli asked, "now that we are acquainted with the calendar, why do we observe two days?" and answered, "Because they sent a directive from Palestine stating, 'Adhere to the *minhag* of your ancestors that has been transmitted to you'" (*Beits*. 4b). The *covering of the head is another example of an early custom that became solidly entrenched in traditional practice. Two widespread *minhagim* are the practice of eating apples and honey on Ro'sh ha-Shanah and the **kapparot* rites before Yom Kippur.

According to rabbinic law, local custom is binding not only upon natives of the land but also upon all those who take up residence there, though they come from places where a particular custom may not obtain (*Suk*. 3.11). Discussing the different *minhagim* regarding the permissibility of work on the eve of Pesaḥ, the Mishnah lays down the general rule that "in order to obviate conflicts, no one should depart from local *minhag*," and a person should observe the strict custom of his hometown and the place he is visiting (*Pes*. 4.1). The Talmud records many differences in custom between the provinces of Judea and Galilee. The varieties of rituals that have developed in various communities are generally referred to as the *minhag* of such and such a group or community. The rabbinic attitude is summarized in the statement, "Custom is Torah" (*tosafot* to *Men*. 20b). Occasionally authoritative and powerful voices were raised in protest against slavish adherence to senseless or even objectionable customs. Thus, Maimonides did not hesitate to say of a prevalent custom, "This is not a *minhag*, but an error, and even smacks of heresy." Rabbi Yaʿaqov ben Me'ir Tam declared a certain custom "stupid," adding that the letters of the word *minhag* read backward as Gehinnom (hell) and that sages need not necessarily uphold foolish customs. Many customs entered Jewish usage from non-Jewish practices, but some of these were subsequently banned by the rabbis (see Ḥuqqat ha-Goyyim).

A Traditional Liturgical Rite. The basic foundations of the *liturgy, especially of the Shaḥarit (morning) service, are laid down in Talmud tractate **Berakhot*. Over the course of centuries, however, individual additions and modifications have been made and considerable and significant differences have developed in the rites of various countries and sects, most notably between the Ashkenazi ritual, which evolved from Palestinian practices, and Sephardi ritual, which evolved from Babylonian usage. Within these broad divisions, however, there are many variations of local *minhagim*: Byzantine, Italian, Avignon, Polish, German, Eastern Jewish, and Yemenite. Ḥasidim have adopted the ritual of Yitsḥaq Luria (*Nussaḥ Ari*), which varies slightly from standard Sephardi usage, while the Jerusalem *minhag* is based upon the meticulous regulations for prayer laid down by R. Eliyyahu ben Shelomoh Zalman of Vilna (the Vilna Ga'on), whose disciples (*perushim*) established the modern Ashkenazi community of Jerusalem. The greatest difference between the various rites is the choice of High Holy Day **piyyutim* (originally for other festivals as well). Considerable modification of the traditional liturgy has been introduced under Reform, Conservative, and Reconstructionist influence. Efforts have been made in the State of Israel (especially in the army) to consolidate a unified prayer rite, acceptable to all communities.

• Abraham P. Bloch, *The Biblical and Historical Background of Jewish Customs and Ceremonies* (New York, 1980). Abraham Chill, *The Minhagim* (New York, 1980). Haim H. Cohn, "Practice and Procedure," in *Principles of Jewish Law*, edited by Menachem Elon (Jerusalem, 1975), pp. 574–584. Menachem Elon, "Minhag," in *Principles of Jewish Law*, edited by Menachem Elon (Jerusalem, 1975), pp. 91–110. Joel Roth, "On Custom in the Halakhic System," in *The Halakhic Process: A Systemic Analysis* (New York, 1986), pp. 205–230.

MINHAGIM BOOKS. Books devoted to *minhagim* (customs; see Minhag) can be divided into three categories: collections of *minhagim* of various communities or of important individuals; *minhagim* related to specific subjects such as wedding or festival customs; and studies of *minhagim* that are meant to explain their background and origin. Books of *minhagim* are antithetical to the nature of customs; *minhagim* represent life patterns of societies and individuals that, by their very nature, are not recorded in books. The necessity for *minhagim* books arose from contacts between communities that had different customs. Collections of their *minhagim* showed, on the one hand, that it was legitimate for each community to follow a different custom and, on the other hand, that each set of customs was authoritative in its own locale. One of the earliest lists of such customs, a comparison of the differences in marriage customs between Judah and Galilee, appears in the Tosefta' (*Ket*. 1.4). The earliest extant work of significant size (*Sefer ha-Ḥilluqim*, edited by M. Margaliot [Jerusalem, 1938]) lists the differences between Palestinian and Babylonian liturgical customs and was compiled in the geonic period. Provence, in southern France, was an area in which Ashkenazi and Spanish scholars frequently met, and several collections of *minhagim* were composed there. The earliest account of different customs in European communities is *Sefer ha-Manhig* (critical ed. [Jerusalem, 1978]) by R. *Avraham ben Natan of Lunel. Around 1200 R. *Asher ben Sha'ul of Lunel compiled a collection of the customs of Lunel and Narbonne, which included sources for the *minhagim* and was an attempt to protect customs that were falling into disuse. Of great importance is the work of Menaḥem *Me'iri (1249–1316), also of Provence, published under the title *Magen Avot*, which defended Provençal customs against the authority of Spanish scholars who tried to impose the Spanish *minhag*. A modern work on the study of *minhagim* is the ongoing series by Daniel Sperber entitled *Minhagei Yisra'el*. This series contains chapters that discuss the meaning and significance of customs, the patterns of their development, and the history of individual customs.

• Ronald A. Brauner, "Some Aspects of Local Custom in Tannaitic Literature," in *Jewish Civilization, Essays and Studies, Jewish Law*, edited by Ronald A. Brauner, vol. 2 (Philadelphia, 1981), pp. 43–54. M. Rapeld and J. Tabory, "Custom, Its Offshoots and Research: A Selected Bibliography," in *Minhagei Yisra'el: Meqorot ve-Toledot*, by Daniel Sperber, vol. 4 (Jerusalem, 1994). Eli Yassif, *Jewish Folklore: An Annotated Bibliography* (New York, 1986).

–Joseph Tabory

MINḤAH (מִנְחָה; Offering). [*This entry discusses the prayer service; for a discussion of the offering, see* Meal Offering.] The Minḥah service is the second of the three daily prayer services. After the destruction of the Second Temple, the *Shaḥarit and Minḥah services were regarded as statutory, corresponding to the *tamid* offering (see PERPETUAL OFFERING) in the Temple, while the evening *Maʿariv prayer service was not initially obligatory. Minḥah is recited any time during the afternoon until sunset and corresponds to the daily evening sacrifice in the Temple (in practice several hours before sunset). Its institution is ascribed by the Talmud (*Ber.* 26b) to the patriarch *Isaac (on the basis of *Gn.* 24.63). Minḥah consists mainly of the *ʿAmidah (preceded and followed by *Qaddish), which is recited silently by the worshipers and then repeated aloud by the reader. An alternative custom is to have the reader recite aloud the first benediction (including *Qedushah) and the last three benedictions, while the middle section is said silently. It is customary to recite *Ashrei (Psalm 145) by way of opening (Sephardim first recite *Qorbanot, an account of the Temple sacrifices) and to conclude with *ʿAleinu. On Sabbaths, Yom Kippur, and other public fasts a short reading from the Bible precedes the ʿAmidah; on Sabbaths, the first part of the following week's portion is read. On fast days, a prophetical reading is also recited in some rites. The ʿAmidah for Minḥah is the same as that for Shaḥarit, but no Birkat ha-Kohanim is pronounced, except on fast days (by the reader in the Diaspora; by *kohanim* in Erets Yisra'el); in the Ashkenazi rite Shalom Rav is substituted in the last benediction for Sim Shalom. In many synagogues Minḥah is recited late in the afternoon and followed immediately (or after a short interval) by the Maʿariv service. In geonic times an abbreviated form of the ʿAmidah was widely used. For Minḥah, the reader wears the **tallit*; the congregation dons the *tallit* for Minḥah only on Yom Kippur and Tishʿah be-'Av (and in some western Sephardi congregations on every fast day).

• Ismar Elbogen, *Jewish Liturgy: A Comprehensive History*, translated by Raymond P. Scheindlin (Philadelphia, 1993).

MINIM (מִינִים), term used in the Talmud and Midrash for sectarians, heretics, or Gnostics. Although the etymology of *minim* is unknown, it may derive from Mani (founder of Manichaeism) or by way of abbreviation from *ma'amin Yeshu notseri* (believer in Jesus the Nazarene). Although the precise meaning of *minim* varied with the circumstances—it is used in Talmudic and Midrashic sources for Sadducees, Samaritans, Judeo-Christians, and other heretical sectarians—there is no doubt that it later came to mean Judeo-Christians in particular. The Talmud (Y., *San.* 10.6) states that at the time of the destruction of the Temple there were twenty-four kinds of *minim*. "The writings of the *minim*," said R. Tarfon, "deserve to be burned, even though they may contain the name of God, for sectarianism is more dangerous than paganism" (*Shab.* 116a). A prayer against the *minim*, which was added to the ʿAmidah, was composed by Shemu'el ha-Qatan at the request of the *nasi'*, R. Gamli'el, as part of the Jewish struggle against Christianity, which at the time was considered a Jewish sect (see BIRKAT HA-MINIM). The wording of the prayer underwent repeated changes for fear of censorship and to obviate anti-Jewish criticism; thus, *malshinim* (informers) was substituted for *minim*. Maimonides (*Mishneh Torah, Teshuvah* 3.7) enumerates five classes of *minim* (in the sense of "heretics") who have no share in the world to come: those who deny the existence of God and his providence; those who believe in several gods; those who attribute to God form and figure; those who believe in the eternity of matter from which God created the world; and those who worship stars, planets, and so on, believing that these act as intermediaries between human beings and God. *Minim* were disqualified from performing any religious or ritual functions, and their relatives were forbidden to mourn their death and instead instructed to rejoice (*Semaḥot* 2.10). See also HERESY.

• Alan F. Segal, *Two Powers in Heaven: Early Rabbinic Reports about Christianity and Gnosticism*, Studies in Judaism in Late Antiquity, vol. 25 (Leiden, 1977).

MINISTER. See RABBI AND RABBINATE.

MINOR PROPHETS, the twelve short prophetic books grouped together in the Bible as the fourth book of the Latter Prophets, following the three "major" prophets, *Isaiah*, *Jeremiah*, and *Ezekiel*. The Minor Prophets is commonly known as Terei ʿAsar, Aramaic for "The Twelve," and includes **Hosea*, **Joel*, **Amos*, **Obadiah*, **Jonah*, **Micah*, **Nahum*, **Habakkuk*, **Zephaniah*, **Haggai*, **Zechariah*, and **Malachi*. The arrangement of the books was determined by a combination of their length, chronological sequence as perceived in rabbinic tradition, and lexical associations (*B. B.* 14b). The collection may well have been edited as a distinct book by the time of Ben Sira (c.180 BCE; cf. *Ben Sira* 44–49). A Hebrew text of the Minor Prophets from Second Temple times was found at Wadi Murabbaʿat and a Greek version at Naḥal Ḥever in the Judean Desert.

• Paul R. House, *The Unity of the Twelve*, Journal for the Study of the Old Testament, Supplement Series 97 (Sheffield, Eng., 1990). James Nogalski, *Literary Precursors to the Book of the Twelve*, Beihefte zur Zeitschrift für die alttestamentliche Wissenschaft 217 (Berlin and New York, 1993).

—MARVIN A. SWEENEY

MINORS. See ADULT; CHILDREN; DEAF, RETARDED, AND MINORS.

MINOR TRACTATES, several tractates not included in the Talmudic canon; also known as *toseftot* (additional tractates) or *ḥitsonot* (external tractates). The existence of such tractates is attested in a number of medieval sources, such as *Numbers Rabbah* 18.21, which Midrashically explains *Song of Songs* 6.8, "and damsels without number," as "external mishnah." The appellation "minor," first used in the ninth-century geonic work *Halakhot Gedolot* (Venice edition, p. 143b), alludes to their extracanonical status and inferior authority (see *Iggeret Rav Sherira' Ga'on*, French recension, p. 47), rather than to their size. It is unclear exactly which works are referred to by these names. Normally the minor tractates are identified with the fourteen tractates published together following tractate *Avot* in the Romm (Vilna, 1886) edition of the Talmud Bavli. However early traditions refer to "seven minor tractates" or, occasionally, to "nine external tractates." The lack of a clear tradition regarding the identity of the minor tractates is a sign of their relative neglect, although later medieval authorities occasionally relied on their halakhic rulings.

While the minor tractates all seem to be of Palestinian origin, the nature of their content and the dates of their redaction vary widely. The aggadic *Avot de-Rabbi Natan* was apparently redacted during or soon after the tannaitic period, whereas most of the other minor tractates, both halakhic and aggadic, appear to have been compiled during the savoraic or early geonic periods. This dating helps to give a picture of the halakhic activity in Palestine in the centuries following the redaction of the Talmud Yerushalmi.

The minor tractates include *Avot de-Rabbi Natan*, **Soferim*, *Semaḥot* (**Evel Rabbati*), **Kallah*, *Kallah Rabbati*, **Derekh Erets Rabbah*, and *Derekh Erets Zuta'*; a second group of seven minor tractates, organized topically, includes **Gerim*, **Kutim*, *ʿ*Avadim*, *Sefer Torah*, *Tefillin*, *Tsitsit*, and *Mezuzah*. A critical edition of *Avot de-Rabbi Natan* was produced by Solomon Schechter, and Michael Higger produced scholarly editions of all of the remaining minor tractates. Higger's editions of the seven minor tractates and of *Derekh Erets* contain an English translation. Abraham Cohen produced a translation entitled *The Minor Tractates of the Talmud* (London, 1965; 2d ed. [1971]).

• Myron B. Lerner, "The External Tractates," in *The Literature of the Sages*, edited by Shemuel Safrai (Assen and Philadelphia, 1987), pt. 1, pp. 367–403. Hermann Leberecht Strack and Günter Stemberger, *Introduction to the Talmud and Midrash*, rev. and updated ed., translated by Markus Bockmuehl (Minneapolis, 1992). —AVRAHAM WALFISH

MINTZ, MOSHEH (15th cent.), rabbinic scholar and authority, communal leader. He studied with R. Yisra'el ben Petaḥyah Isserlein and with R. Yaʿaqov ben Yehudah Weil, and he served as rabbi in Würzburg, Mainz, Landau, Ulm, Bamberg, Nürnberg, and Poznań. He was forced to abandon a planned immigration to Erets Yisra'el for reasons that are unclear.

Mintz is best known for his collection of *responsa*, which center on civil and matrimonial law. He was heavily involved in the enactment of communal legislation, and he writes of *taqqanot* of which he approved and of those with which he could not agree. Several of his *responsa* deal with contemporary prayer and educational practices, and they serve as an important source for the history of the *yeshivot* of Germany during the fifteenth century. He was involved in a number of controversies concerning the appointments of communal rabbis and academy heads. Mintz referred to and prescribed penitential regimens (*tiqqunei teshuvah*), which had been developed by the Ḥasidei Ashkenaz.

• Yedidya Dinari, *Ḥakhmei Ashkenaz be-Shilḥei Yemei ha-Beinayim* (Jerusalem, 1984). Jacob Elbaum, *Teshuvat ha-Lev ve-Qabbalat Yissurim* (Jerusalem, 1993), pp. 21–24. Israel Yuval, *Ḥakhamim be-Doram: Ha-Manhigut ha-Ruḥanit shel Yehudei Germanyah be-Shilḥei Yemei ha-Beinayim* (Jerusalem, 1988). —EPHRAIM KANARFOGEL

MINTZ, YEHUDAH (c.1408–1506), Italian rabbi, born in Mainz, from where his family took its name. A student of R. Yisra'el ben Petaḥyah Isserlein, Mintz settled in Padua, where he headed a renowned *yeshivah* and was recognized as one of the outstanding halakhic scholars of Italy. The *taqqanot* (enactments) he imposed upon his community with the approval of the local nonrabbinic leadership testify that, like other communal rabbis of the period in Italy, Mintz exercised a significant degree of rabbinic authority. Sixteen of his *responsa* were published in 1553 by R. Me'ir ben Yitsḥaq Katzenellenbogen, the husband of Mintz's granddaughter.

• Robert Bonfil, *Rabbis and Jewish Communities in Renaissance Italy* (Oxford, 1990). Isaac H. Weiss, *Dor Dor ve-Dorshav* (Vienna, 1871–1891) vol. 5, pp. 280–282. —MARK WASHOFSKY

MINYAN (מִנְיָן; counting; hence, quorum), the requisite number of adult Jewish males (i.e., aged 13 or older) for a quorum for various liturgical purposes. Particular parts of the communal prayer, such as *Qaddish, *Qedushah, *Barekhu, the *Birkat ha-Kohanim, and the reader's repetition of the *ʿAmidah, may only be recited in the presence of a *minyan*. The reading of the Torah and of the **haftarah* also require a *minyan*. A *minyan* is also needed for *Shevaʿ Berakhot at the marriage feast, while the presence of a *minyan* at the *Birkat ha-Mazon requires a change in the text of the invocation to grace. Ten adult males are considered a "community," and thus their presence together permits the recital of the communal prayers. The number of adult males present is the determinant: fewer than ten males, even in a synagogue, may not recite the communal prayers together, while ten or more adult males, even if gathered in a locale other than the synagogue, may recite these prayers. Various explanations have been proposed for the origin of the quorum of ten. For example, of the twelve spies sent by Moses to scout out the land of Canaan, ten came back with a negative report. These ten are referred to as "this evil community" (*Nm.* 14.27), from which the rabbis deduced that a "community" consists of at least ten adult males. Another explanation refers to the ten righteous men who could have saved Sodom (*Gn.* 18.32). In areas where it was difficult to raise a quorum, the community would pay "*minyan* men" or **batlanim* to attend services regularly. If a full quorum was not present, the rabbis counted nine adults and a boy as a *minyan*. Reform Judaism counts *women worshipers in the quorum, while Conservative practice (since 1973) permits women to be counted but leaves the decision to individual congregations.

• Ismar Elbogen, *Jewish Liturgy: A Comprehensive History*, translated by Raymond P. Scheindlin (Philadelphia, New York, and Jerusalem, 1993), pp. 375–376. —SHMUEL HIMELSTEIN

MIQTSAT MAʿASEI HA-TORAH, one of the *Dead Sea Scrolls. Six copies (4Q394–399) of the document known as *MMT* were found in Cave 4 at Qumran. The overlapping fragments allowed the editors to reconstruct some 130 lines of the original text. As it stands, the reconstructed text consists of three sections: a solar 364-day calendar, a section of some twenty legal disputes, and an admonitory letter. Originally the editors believed that this letter was written by the founder of the Dead Sea sect, the *Teacher of Righteousness, to his enemy, the Wicked Priest. While one of the two editors

(Elisha Qimron) believes it to be a letter or epistle, the other (John Strugnell) questions its genre. The halakhic stance of the three diverse groups represented in *MMT* on various legal matters (e.g., poured liquid and purity after immersion) are reminiscent of the arguments between the Sadducees ("we") and Pharisees ("they") in rabbinic literature (esp. *Yad.* 4).

• Joseph M. Baumgarten, "Disqualifications of Priests in 4Q Fragments of the Damascus Document, a Specimen of the Recovery of pre-Rabbinic Halakha" in *The Madrid Qumran Congress: Proceedings of the International Congress on the Dead Sea Scrolls, Madrid 18–21 March 1991*, edited by Julio C. Trebolle Barrera and Luis Vegas Montaner (Leiden, 1992), vol. 2, pp. 502–513. Elisha Qimron and John Strugnell, eds., with Ya'akov Sussman and Ada Yardeni, *Miqsat Ma'asé ha-Torah*, Discoveries in the Judaean Desert, vol. 10 (Oxford, 1994). Lawrence H. Schiffman, "The Temple Scroll and the System of Jewish Law of the Second Temple Period" in *Temple Scrolls Studies*, edited by George J. Brooke (Sheffield, Eng., 1989), pp. 239–255.

—TIMOTHY H. LIM

MIQVA'OT (מִקְוָאוֹת; Ritual Baths), tractate consisting of ten chapters in Mishnah order *Tohorot, with related material in the Tosefta' but with no *gemara'* in either Talmud. It deals with the rules pertaining to purification by means of ritual immersion. Biblical law provides for ritual purification—"he shall bathe all his flesh in water" (*Lv.* 15.16); for more extreme forms of impurity, the Bible says, "he shall bathe his flesh in living waters" (*Lv.* 15.13). *Miqva'ot* defines these forms of immersion, requiring for both of them water from a natural source that has not been sullied by human intervention. "Living waters" is understood to mean fresh spring water, which purifies while in motion, so long as its flow has not been interrupted by a vessel; whereas a **miqveh* purifies only so long as its waters are stationary. The rabbis understood the provision to bathe "all his flesh" (*Lv.* 15.16) to mean that there should be no impediment separating any part of the body, or any part of a ritually immersed vessel (*Nm.* 31.23), from the purifying waters. Tractate *Miqva'ot* pronounces the special presumption of purity attached to baths found in Erets Yisra'el (*Miq.* 8.1).

An English translation of the Mishanat tractate is found in Herbert Danby's *The Mishnah* (Oxford, 1933).

• Chanoch Albeck, ed., *Shishah Sidrei Mishnah, Seder Tohorot* (Jerusalem, 1958). Philip Blackman, ed. and trans., *Mishnayoth*, vol. 5, *Order Taharoth* (Gateshead, 1973). Hermann Leberecht Strack and Günter Stemberger, *Introduction to the Talmud and Midrash*, rev. and updat. ed., translated by Markus Bockmuehl (Minneapolis, 1992).

—AVRAHAM WALFISH

MIQVEH (מִקְוֶה; collection [of water]), a collection of water for the purpose of immersion for ritual purification. It is first mentioned in *Leviticus* 11.36 which states in reference to purification after ritual impurity for individuals and utensils: "Only a spring, cistern, or collection [*miqveh*] shall be cleansing." In Temple times this law was applied to a variety of causes of *impurity. Subsequently it was applied primarily to women after *menstruation. In order for a *miqveh* to be fit for use it must be built on site and not transported to it in prefabricated form. The minimum amount of valid water required for a *miqveh* is forty *se'ah*, which corresponds to the volume of one square cubit by three cubits (*'Eruv.* 4b; *Tosafot Ḥag.* 11a, s.v. berum; *Shulḥan 'Arukh, Yoreh De'ah* 201.1). Since there is a dispute among halakhic authorities with regard to the size of the biblical cubit (*amah*), the modern equivalent of forty *se'ah* ranges from 250 to 1,000 liters of water. A *miqveh* must also be completely watertight and may not, therefore, be emptied through a hole in the floor. Instead, it is generally emptied from above, by hand, vacuum, or electric pump. Drawn water (*mayim she'uvim*) is unfit for *miqveh* use (*Miq.* 4.1). Natural spring water, rainwater, snow and melted ice are all valid for the purposes of filling a *miqveh*, but care must be taken that no vessel interferes with the flow of the water from its point of origin to the *miqveh*. This is because contact with any such vessel, for example, a pump or meter, may easily render the water impure. In order to solve this problem, nonmetal pipes free of any special fittings are used, the last section of which consists of a special trough of absorbent concrete generally resting on either compact earth or gravel. A small hole connects this trough to the *miqveh*. The process of transporting valid water in this fashion is known as *hamshakhah*. In practice, the *miqveh* usually consists of at least two chambers, one of which is a storage tank and the other the immersion pool. The valid water is stored in the tank which is connected to the immersion pool through a small round hole in the wall separating the two structures. This is made possible by the Mishnaic principle that once it contains forty *se'ah* of valid water, a *miqveh* is not rendered unfit by virtue of the addition of regular water (*Miq.* 3.1; Maimonides, *Hilkhot Miqva'ot* 4.6). It is, therefore, possible to mix valid water with regular water and to maintain a large immersion pool by means of the contact hole. This method is known as *hashaqah*. The other accepted method is to mix both valid water and regular water in a special tank and to fill the immersion pool with a combination of different types of water (*zeri'ah*). It is not uncommon to combine both methods in order to ensure a large supply of immersion water that can be changed at regular intervals. In order to ensure its watertightness, a modern *miqveh* is built of poured concrete, strengthened with steel bars and a dry mix of cement and iron aggregate. The cement is waterproofed by adding to it an expanding clay material or pulverized rock that swells and forms a jelly-like substance when touched by water. There are special procedures for the filling, heating and draining of a *miqveh*. *Miqva'ot* answering to the halakhic requirements for their construction have been discovered as early as the Second Temple period and throughout the Middle Ages, in both Ashkenazi and Sephardi countries. There are many references in the Talmud to the ubiquitousness of *miqva'ot*, especially in Jerusalem and in the Temple environs. In addition to menstruant women, women after childbirth, and converts, the *miqveh* is used for spiritual ablution and the ritual purification of utensils. In Talmudic times it was also used by men, after intercourse or other emissions of sperm, but this custom was almost totally abandoned subsequently. Maimonides emphasizes the spiritual nature of *miqveh* immersion and states categorically that "uncleanliness is not mud or filth which water can remove but is dependent upon the intention of the heart. Therefore, the sages said: If a man immerses himself but lacks special intention, then it is as though he has not immersed himself at all" (*Hilkhot Miqva'ot* 11.12). Regular immersion in a *miqveh* is a practice of some pious ascetics, and it is a hasidic custom for men to immerse themselves before the Sabbath. The Conservative movement upholds the principle of ritual immersion, although it is not widely observed, except for converts. Reform Judaism does not accept the need for the *miqveh* with an exception, especially outside the United States, for converts. See also TAHARAT HA-MISHPAḤAH.

• Aryeh Kaplan, *Waters of Eden: An Exploration of the Concept of Mikvah* (New York, 1982). Isaac Klein, *A Guide to Jewish Religious Practice* (New York, 1979), pp. 518–522. Mendell Lewittes, *Jewish Marriage: Rabbinic Law, Legend, and Custom* (Northvale, N.J., 1994), pp. 126–128. David Miller, *The Secret of the Jew* (San Francisco, 1930). Shmuel Rubenstein, *The Mikvah Anthology* (New York, 1968).

–DANIEL SINCLAIR

MIR, a small town in Lithuania famous for its *yeshivah*. The *yeshivah*, which was founded in approximately 1815 and flourished until World War II, blended Talmudic scholarship with the Musar teachings of R. Yisra'el *Salanter. During World War II, most of the *yeshivah*'s students managed to flee through Siberia to Japan and ultimately to Shanghai, China, where they reconstituted the *yeshivah*. To meet the dearth of Jewish religious works in that part of the world, the Shanghai Yeshivah reprinted many of the classics. After the war, teachers and students were able to migrate to various Western countries, especially the United States and Israel, where they founded successor schools to the original *yeshivah*.

–SHMUEL HIMELSTEIN

MIRACLES. The more fully developed concept of miracles presupposes a fixed natural order from which the miraculous event is a departure. The religious belief in miracles assumes that God can, for various purposes, set aside the order of nature that he has created, so as to reveal his saving presence or his omnipotence. Many miracles are recorded in scripture, mainly in connection with the history of the Jewish people, including the splitting of the sea after the *Exodus from Egypt, the divine revelation at Sinai, Joshua's stopping of the sun, or the miracles performed by Elijah and Elisha. Miracles are also recorded in rabbinic literature, though the rabbis do not offer a systematic theory or doctrine of the phenomenon. Thus the Mishnah lists a number of miraculous things that were created on the eve of the first Sabbath, that is, before the work of creation ended, and of miraculous phenomena in the Temple. The Talmud recounts miracles performed by saintly men (e.g., *Ḥoni ha-Me'aggel, *Ḥanina' ben Dosa'), and many Talmudic rabbis are described as "experienced in miracles." However, not everything called a miracle by the rabbis is a spectacular or manifestly supernatural event, and the term is sometimes used to denote God's salvation in everyday matters, such as the finding of daily bread or recovery after an illness, as in the language of the *'Amidah prayer, "the miracles that are daily with us—morning, noon, and night." The rabbis emphasize that man is surrounded at all times by miracles, many of which he is not even aware. Both usages of the term, however, refer to the work of God, either directly executed by him or through the mediation of a human or natural agency. With the development of the philosophical concepts of natural order and causality, it became increasingly difficult to defend miracles, and the more rationalist medieval thinkers, such as Moses *Maimonides and *Levi ben Gershom, tried to reduce the significance of even biblical miracles to a minimum, explaining most of them as symbolic allegories or dreams. This cautious rationalism of the philosophers stands in marked contrast to the belief in miracles that characterizes popular religion and certain forms of mysticism. Belief in miracles has often bordered on *magic and superstition, and it flourished in the Hasidic movement, which ascribed the power to work miracles to the saintly leader or **tsaddiq*. See also BA'AL SHEM.

• Allan Arkush in Arthur A. Cohen and Paul Mendes-Flohr, eds., *Contemporary Jewish Religious Thought* (New York, 1987), pp. 621–625. Isaac Husik, *A History of Medieval Jewish Philosophy* (Philadelphia, 1994), pp. 358–361. Mordecai M. Kaplan, "Introduction," in *The Meaning of God in Modern Jewish Religion* (New York, 1947). Kaufmann Kohler, "Miracles and the Cosmic Order," in *Jewish Theology* (Cincinnati, 1943), chap. 27. Franz Rosenzweig, "On the Possibility of Experiencing Miracles," in *The Star of Redemption*, translated by William W. Hallo (New York, 1971). Solomon Schechter, "On the Study of the Talmud," in *Studies in Judaism* (Philadelphia, 1945).

MIRIAM (Heb. Miriyam), sister of *Aaron and *Moses (*Nm.* 26.59; *Mi.* 6.4; *1 Chr.* 6.3), who is also called a prophet (*Ex.* 15.20). She helped to save the life of Moses in his infancy (*Ex.* 2.4–8). A competition over leadership and the status of a prophet seems to inform the incident in *Numbers* 12, where Moses' superiority as prophet and leader is challenged on two counts: his marriage to a Cushite woman and Miriam and Aaron's claim that their own prophetic powers are analogous to his. When God supports Moses' superiority as prophet and leader, Miriam is punished by a skin disease, and only after a period of isolation does she rejoin the camp. Another indication of her prominence is the attribution of a victory song to her and a women's choir (*Ex.* 15.20–21) after the Israelites crossed the Sea of Reeds (*Ex.* 14), paralleling the recital of a poem by Moses and the [male] Israelites (*Ex.* 15.1–19).

• Bernhard W. Anderson, "The Song of Miriam Poetically and Theologically Considered," in *Directions in Biblical Hebrew Poetry*, edited by Elaine R. Follis (Sheffield, Eng., 1987), pp. 285–96. J. Gerald Janzen, "Song of Moses, Song of Miriam: Who Is Seconding Whom?" *Catholic Biblical Quarterly* 54 (1992): 211–220. Ilana Pardes, *Countertraditions in the Bible: A Feminist Approach* (Cambridge, Mass., 1992). Phyllis Trible, "Bringing Miriam Out of the Shadows," *Bible Review* 2 (Feb 1989): 14–25, 34.

–ATHALYA BRENNER

MI SHE-BERAKH (מִי שֶׁבֵּרַךְ; "He who blessed"), the opening words of a synagogal prayer, in various forms, in which God's blessing is requested for any individual(s). Its recitation is customary in most rites during the **qeri'at ha-Torah* (reading of the Torah); it is offered by the reader for each person called to the reading, after which that person may request prayers to be added in honor of his (or, in non-Orthodox congregations, her) relations or anyone else. The prayer frequently (although less so today) states that the one requesting it has vowed a sum for charity. Special formulas are introduced for sick people, baby namings, boys at the time of their circumcision, and so on. Variations were also composed to fit different historical circumstances. A general Mi she-Berakh prayer dating from the geonic period calls on God to bless members of the congregation—together with other congregations—and is recited in the morning prayer service on Sabbaths and festivals. While the traditional version of Mi she-Berakh refers to the three *patriarchs, the Sephardi rite has a parallel version for the blessing of women that invokes the four matriarchs. In Israeli synagogues an additional Mi she-Berakh prayer has been added for the welfare of the country's soldiers.

• Ismar Elbogen, *Jewish Liturgy: A Comprehensive History*, translated by Raymond P. Scheindlin (Philadelphia, 1993). Abraham Idelsohn, *Jewish Liturgy and Its Developement* (New York, 1932). Macy Nulman, *The Encyclopedia of Jewish Prayer* (Northvale, N.J., 1993).

MI SHE-BERAKH LE-ḤOLIM (מִי שֶׁבֵּרַךְ לְחוֹלִים; He Who Blesses the Sick), a common form of prayer for the sick. In addition to the eighth benediction of the weekday *ʿAmidah, which is a petition for the healing of the sick, any individual may offer prayers for sick friends or relatives. These can be added to the above benediction or else to the sixteenth benediction of the ʿAmidah (which is used freely as a framework into which personal requests may be inserted). Prayers for the sick may also be offered in the synagogue after the reading of the Torah; it is usual for the person requesting such a prayer to vow an offering to charity (see MI SHE-BERAKH). It is also customary to read psalms for the sake of the sick. Prayers to be recited by a sick person, incorporating psalms and a brief confession of sin, were composed for those who were gravely ill, as were special prayers including the solemn change of *name.

• Jeffrey Glickman, "The Prayers and Praxis of Healing for the Contemporary Rabbinate," thesis, Hebrew Union College, 1987. Hirshel L. Jaffe, *Gates of Healing* (New York, 1988). Joseph S. Ozarowski, *To Walk in God's Ways: Jewish Pastoral Perspectives on Illness and Bereavement* (Northvale, N.J., 1995).

MISHKAN. See TEMPLE.

MISHMAROT. See MAʿAMAD.

MISHNAH (מִשְׁנָה; oral instruction), oral law compilation dating from approximately 200 CE, which serves as the foundation text for Talmudic law and tradition. The Hebrew verb *shanah* (repeat) came to be applied specifically to the repetition and memorization of oral traditions, hence to the study of oral law. The term *mishnah* may designate the method of oral study (in contradistinction to *miqra'*, that is, study of scripture), a specific unit of oral instruction, or a compilation of oral instruction. A sage who expounded *mishnah* was designated in Talmudic literature as a tanna', deriving from the root *teni*, the Aramaic equivalent of the Hebrew *shanah*. During the second century, *mishnah* collections abounded among the sages of Erets Yisra'el. However, by the turn of the century, one collection, that of R. *Yehudah ha-Nasi'—known as Rabbi—had achieved recognition as the authoritative compilation. From that time forward, the term *Mishnah* referred to this compilation, and material from all other compilations came to be known as *baraiytot* (external *mishnayyot*; from Aram. *bar* [outside]).

The Mishnah consists of six *sedarim* (orders), each of which deals with a major division of the oral law: *Zeraʿim (Seeds), *Moʿed (Appointed Time), *Nashim (Women), *Neziqin (Damages), *Qodashim (Holy Things), and *Tohorot (Purities). Each of these divisions is subdivided into *massekhtot* (tractates; from *massekhet* [woven fabric]), which in turn are divided into chapters and into individual pericopes, called *halakhot*, or more popularly, *mishnayyot*. Because of the frequently illogical nature of the division of Mishnah into chapters and *halakhot*, J. N. Epstein has argued that these divisions are not an organic part of the original Mishnah composition but that they were introduced by the Mishnah reciters of post-Mishnaic times, who needed to break Mishnah into smaller units for purposes of ease in memorization and recitation. However, more recent scholarship has suggested that these divisions are significant in understanding the literary and conceptual structure of Mishnah.

Most scholars, following *Iggeret Rav Sherira' Ga'on* (10th cent.), understand the Mishnah to be the product of successive stages of redaction, originating around the time of the destruction of the Second Temple, prior to which oral law was transmitted from master to disciple without fixed formulations or fixed order. The late Second Temple origin of Mishnaic forms is based partly on external evidence, such as Talmudic statements (Y., *Yoma'* 2.3, 39d; *Yoma'* 16a) attributing tractates *Tamid* and *Middot* to tanna'im who lived at the end of the Second Temple period and a statement in the Tosefta' (T., *ʿEduy.* 1.1) that may be understood as attributing tractate *ʿEduyyot* to the high court of Yavneh. Internal evidence is also cited, such as the list of names of Temple functionaries in *Sheqalim* 5.1, which appears to portray the situation existing most probably at the time immediately preceding the Second Temple's destruction.

In the initial stages of formulating and organizing the oral law, the Mishnaic arrangement of material, based on form and content, contended for supremacy with the Midrashic arrangement, based on associating oral traditions with scriptural verses, arranged according to the order of the Torah. A central figure in the history of Mishnah redaction was R. ʿAqiva', whose major contributions to both forms of arranging oral law generated intensive work by his disciples. Rabbi Me'ir's Mishnah arrangement served as the main basis for the Mishnah of Yehudah ha-Nasi'.

Since the medieval period, there have been two schools of thought, based on two conflicting versions of *Iggeret Rav Sherira' Ga'on*, about whether the Mishnah was redacted orally or was committed to writing. Current scholarly opinion follows the view of Saul Lieberman, who argued that even though there may have been written exemplars of Mishnah, it was transmitted orally throughout the Talmudic and most of the geonic periods and was first published in written form during the geonic period.

Following the widespread acceptance of the Mishnah of R. Yehudah ha-Nasi', the emphasis of the study of oral law shifted to the interpretation and application of the Mishnah, together with other tannaitic materials, focusing not on the mere formulation of the law, as in Mishnah, but on the dialectical and hermeneutical principles on which the law is based (see TALMUD).

Inasmuch as the Mishnah's formulations and structures do not correspond to those that would be expected in a legal codex, scholars have debated issues of the logic and purpose of Mishnaic redaction. Some, such as J. N. Epstein and E. E. Urbach, have sought explanations based on higher criticism for divergences in the Mishnah from the logical order one would expect. Others, such as H. Albeck and A. Goldberg, have suggested that the Mishnah was designed not as a legal code but as an educational device, such that its order is dictated by educational concerns, for example, ease in memorization. Some recent scholars suggest that Mishnaic forms and principles reflect the conceptual foundations of the Mishnah's halakhic thinking. The frequent aggadic pronouncements and anecdotes within the Mishnah, which are interwoven with the halakhic material in a highly sophisticated literary manner, may be seen as supporting this last viewpoint.

There are frequent differences between the text of the Mishnah as preserved in the Talmud Bavli and the Talmud Yerushalmi and in manuscript versions of the Mishnah, which modern linguistic scholarship has traced to Palestinian and Babylonian versions of Mishnaic Hebrew. Insofar as the Mishnah was not, in the Babylonian tradition, studied as an independent text but rather as a part of Talmud study, the Babylonian version of the Mishnah was preserved primarily in manuscripts of the Talmud Bavli. The Palestinian version has been best preserved in three complete Mishnah manuscripts, known as the Kaufman MS (in the library of the Hungarian Academy of Sciences), the Parma MS 138, and the Cambridge MS 73 (published by W. H. Lowe as *Matnita' de-Talmuda' di-Venei Ma'arav'a*). The *editio princeps* of the Mishnah is the Naples edition of 1492, containing Maimonides' commentary. Modern editions are based on the Mishnah text as corrected by R. Yom Tov Lipmann Heller, who printed the Mishnah together with his commentary, *Tosafot Yom Tov*, in Prague from 1614 through 1617. There is as yet no critical edition of the Mishnah as a whole, although critical editions exist for Zera'im, as well as for several tractates from other Mishnah orders. Other important Mishnah commentators include: R. 'Ovadyah Bertinoro (15th cent.), R. Shelomoh Adeni (*Melekhet Shelomoh*, 17th cent.), R. Yisra'el Lipschutz (*Tif'eret Yisra'el*, 19th cent.), and H. Albeck (1958–1959). English translations include those by H. Danby (1933), P. Blackman (1951–1956), and J. Neusner (1988). In addition, the Mishnah may be found in English translation in the Soncino Talmud translation, as well as in a recent English translation of the commentary to the Mishnah by P. Kehati.

• Chanoch Albeck, *Mavo' la-Mishnah* (Jerusalem, 1959). Jacob Nahum Epstein, *Mavo' le-Nusaḥ ha-Mishnah*, 2d ed. (Tel Aviv, 1964). Jacob Nahum Epstein, *Mevo'ot le-Sifrut ha-Tanna'im* (Jerusalem, 1957). Abraham Goldberg, "The Mishna: A Study Book of Halakhah," in *The Literature of the Sages*, edited by Shmuel Safrai (Assen and Philadelphia, 1987), pt. 1, pp. 211–262. David Weiss Halivni, *Midrash, Mishnah, and Gemara: The Jewish Predilection for Justified Law* (Cambridge, Mass., 1986). Jacob David Herzog, ed. and trans., *Mishnah* (Jerusalem, 1945). Benjamin Manasseh Lewin, ed., *Iggeret Rav Sherira' Ga'on* (1921; Jerusalem, 1982). Saul Lieberman, *Hellenism in Jewish Palestine* (1950; New York, Jacob Neusner, *A History of the Mishnaic Law of Purities*, pt. 21, *The Redaction and Formulation of the Order of Purities in Mishnah and Tosefta* (Leiden, 1977). Jacob Neusner, *Judaism: The Evidence of the Mishnah* (Chicago and London, 1981). 1994). Hermann Leberecht Strack and Günter Stemberger, *Introduction to the Talmud and Midrash*, rev. and updat. ed., translated by Markus Bockmuehl (Minneapolis, 1992). Yaacov Sussman, "Kitvei Yad u-Mesorot Nusaḥ shel ha-Mishnah," *World Congress of Jewish Studies* 7 (1981). Dov Zlotnick, *The Iron Pillar: Mishnah; Redaction, Form, and Intent* (Jerusalem, 1988).

—AVRAHAM WALFISH

MISHNEH TORAH. See MAIMONIDES, MOSES.

MI-SINAI (מִסִּינַי; from Sinai), a body of fixed melodies constituting a significant segment of Ashkenazi synagogue tradition that emerged in southwest Germany between the eleventh and fifteenth centuries. The term is used interchangeably with the Yiddish expression *scarbova niggunim*. Ya'aqov ben Mosheh ha-Levi *Molin, a renowned fourteenth-century rabbinic authority and *ḥazzan*, decreed that local custom and universal Jewish traditional melodies may not be changed.

Most of the *mi-Sinai* melodies are associated with the High Holy Days and festivals. The melody that pervades the High Holy Day Ma'ariv service, the chant for Kol Nidrei, and the melody for the Qaddish preceding the prayers for rain and dew (among others) became familiar tunes. The liberal reforms of the nineteenth century removed traditional *nussaḥ* from the vocabulary of synagogue music, but the *mi-Sinai* melodies retained their place in the service, even when the texts associated with them were translated or otherwise altered.

• Eric Werner, *A Voice Still Heard: The Sacred Songs of the Ashkenazic Jews* (University Park, Pa., 1976), pp. 26–45.

—MARSHA BRYAN EDELMAN

MITNAGGEDIM (מִתְנַגְּדִים; opponents), a term for opponents of Hasidism. The first bans of excommunication against Ḥasidim were issued in 1772 by *Eliyyahu ben Shelomoh Zalman of Vilna, the Vilna Ga'on. A second wave of bans followed the year after the first Hasidic publication, *Toledot Ya'aqov Yosef* (1780). A third cycle of excommunications ensued after the expansion of Hasidic influence and the publication of the *Tanya'* by Shneur Zalman of Lyady in 1796. In this last phase, the Ḥasidim and then their opponents sought to enlist the support of Russian government officials. During the 1790s, pamphlets attacking Hasidism were written by two itinerant preachers and zealous opponents of the movement, David of Maków and Israel Löbel of Sluck.

A pamphlet published in 1772 contained most of the key objections of the Mitnaggedim to Hasidic practice: the displacement by simple piety of Talmudic erudition in the hierarchy of values; the establishment of separate places of prayer where a different liturgy was followed and the fixed times of prayer sometimes were not fixed; changes in the method of ritual slaughter of animals (*sheḥitah*); excessive lightheartedness ("all their days are like holidays") and consumption of alcohol; a certain Shabbatean aroma; attribution of supernatural powers to their leaders, who bilked their followers of contributions; and the hubris of the Ḥasidim, who "have little of the bread of oral Torah," yet "enter the rose garden of the Kabbalah." On a different plane, there was the Mitnaggedic perception of the theological dangers associated with Hasidic doctrine and practice: the notion that divinity could be worshiped through material deeds; that "strange thoughts" could be elevated; and that God should be sought through both the evil and the good inclination. In a word, the almost pantheistic teachings of the Hasidic leaders tended toward the confusion of the realms of the sacred and the profane, of good and evil.

During the nineteenth century, the challenge of modernizing trends of thought muted the divisions within the traditional community; being a Mitnagged became merely a private preference within Orthodoxy.

• Gershon Hundert, *Essential Papers on Hasidism: Origins to Present* (New York, 1991). Norman Lamm, *Torah Lishmah: Torah for Torah's Sake in the Works of Rabbi Hayyim of Volozhin and His Contemporaries* (New York, 1989). Gloria Pollack, *Eli'ezer Zweifel and the Intellectual Defense of Hasidism* (Hoboken, N.J., 1995). Elijah Judah Schochet, *The Hasidic Movement and the Ga'on of Vilna* (Northvale, N.J., 1994). Mordecai Wilensky, *Ḥasidim u-Mitnaggedim: Le-Toledot ha-Pulmus she-Beineihem ba-Shanim 532–535*, 2 vols. (Jerusalem, 1970).

—GERSHON DAVID HUNDERT

MITSRANUT (מִצְרָנוּת; abutter's rights). In Jewish law, one who owns a property has the right to purchase the property abutting it from the neighbor when the neighbor wishes to or is forced for some reason to sell (*B. M.* 108a). The neighbor may be compelled to sell to the abutter at the market price; the neighbor may not demand a higher price from an abutter merely because the abutter may be more anxious to buy. On the other hand, Talmudic sages rule that the abutter must purchase the land for personal use and not merely to take advantage of a pressing financial need of the neighbor. When multiple neighbors abut, the one who plans to use the land in the same manner as the seller has precedence.

• Shalom Albeck, *Dinei ha-Mamonot ba-Talmud* (Tel Aviv, 1976). Menachem Elon, *Jewish Law: History, Sources, Principles*, 4 vols. (Philadelphia, 1994). Raymond Westbrook, *Property and Family in Biblical Law*, Journal for the Study of the Old Testament, Supplement Series 113 (Sheffield, Eng., 1991).

—MICHAEL BROYDE

MITSVAH (מִצְוָה; commandment), religious *duty or obligation; the term also came to be used to mean good deed. The word applies especially to the biblical "commandments and the statutes and the ordinances which I command you" (*Dt.* 7.11), which in their totality make up the *Torah. They form the basis of *Jewish law (**ha-lakhah*) and behavior. The number of biblical *mitsvot* is 613 (see COMMANDMENTS, 613), consisting of 365 prohibitions (*mitsvot lo' ta'aseh* or *l'av*) and 248 positive precepts (*mitsvot 'aseh*). In addition to the biblical *mitsvot* (known as *de-'oraita'* [from the Torah]), there are innumerable *mitsvot* of rabbinic origin (*de-rabbanan*; *Pes.* 10a; *Suk.* 44a). Some of these rabbinic ordinances are treated as if they had divine authority, and the blessing recited prior to their performance contains the formula otherwise confined to biblical precepts ("Blessed are you, our God, who has sanctified us with his commandments and commanded us to . . . "). These include the *mitsvot* of washing the hands before meals, kindling the Sabbath and festival lights, making the *'eruv*, reciting Hallel on festival days, lighting the Ḥanukkah lights, and reading the scroll of *Esther* on Purim. The rabbis allow that there may be differences of importance between various *mitsvot* (of certain *mitsvot*, such as *tsitsit* [*Ned.* 25a], circumcision [*Ned.* 32a], and charity [*B. B.* 9a], it is said that their performance is equal to the observance of the entire Torah) but nevertheless enjoin that one must "be as heedful of a light *mitsvah* as of an important one, for you never know the reward for the performance of a *mitsvah*" (*Avot* 2.1). Many classifications of *mitsvot* exist, such as those between humans and God and those between one human and another. *Mitsvot* are also classified by the severity of punishment legislated for their transgression (capital punishment, flogging, sacrifice, etc.). Another distinction is made between *mitsvot* that can be observed at any time and those that must be fulfilled at a fixed hour (women are exempt from the latter because of household duties). Another considerable category of *mitsvot* consists of those that can be performed only in Erets Yisra'el.

The opposite of a *mitsvah* is an *'averah* (transgression; see SIN). The rabbis said that a *mitsvah* that is fulfilled through an *'averah* is reckoned as an *'averah* (*Suk.* 30a); that is, with regard to *mitsvot*, the end does not justify the means. Liability for the performance of *mitsvot* starts with the attainment of one's religious majority: for a boy, his **bar mitsvah*; for a girl her **bat mitsvah*. A father is obligated to prepare his children for this responsibility.

A person already engaged in performing a *mitsvah* is exempt from performing another one that should be done at the same time (*Ber.* 4a). The sages suggested that *mitsvot* should be performed aesthetically (in the biblical phrase "This is my God and I will glorify him" [*Ex.* 15.2], glorify can also be interpreted as beautify). From this derived the traditions, for example, of decorating the *sukkah* or making Torah scrolls beautiful (*Shab.* 133b), which inspired Jewish ritual *art. Whether a *mitsvah* requires *kavvanah* (*intent), or whether the mere act is sufficient in itself, is a matter of dispute in the Talmud (*Ber.* 13a).

The question of the meaning and purpose of the *mitsvot* gave rise to reflection and discussion in Talmudic literature and in medieval and subsequent Jewish thought. A distinction was made between *ḥuqqim* (ordinances or laws), for which no rational explanation could be given, and commandments, for which reasons could be adduced and that would be observed even without divine revelation as expressions of natural morality (for example, honoring one's parents or the prohibitions against murder, theft, and dishonesty; see COMMANDMENTS, REASONS FOR).

Starting with Maimonides' *Sefer ha-Mitsvot* (12th cent.), which divided the *mitsvot* into fourteen categories following the divisions of books in his *Mishneh Torah*, various works were written listing the *mitsvot*, including *Sefer Mitsvot Gadol* by Mosheh ben Ya'aqov of Coucy (13th cent.) and the shorter *Sefer Mitsvot Qatan* by Yitsḥaq ben Yosef of Corbeil (13th cent.). See also 'ASEH; LO' TA'ASEH

• Gersion Appel, *A Philosophy of Mitzvot* (New York, 1975). Benjamin Blech, *Understanding Judaism: The Basics of Deed and Creed* (New York, 1991). Abraham Chill, *The Mitzvot: The Commandments and Their Rationale* (Jerusalem, 1974). Samson Raphael Hirsch, *Horeb: A Philosophy of Jewish Laws and Observations*, translated by Isidor Grunfeld (London, 1962). Herbert Samuel Goldstein, *Between the Lines of the Bible: A Modern Commentary on the 613 Commandments* (New York, 1959). Moses Maimonides, *Sefer Hamitzvoth: The Book of Mitzvoth*, translated by Shraga Silverstein (New York, 1993). Yeshayahu Leibowitz, "Commandments," in *Contemporary Jewish Religious Thought*, edited by Arthur A. Cohen and Paul Mendes-Flohr (New York, 1987), pp. 67–80.

MIXED KINDS. See KIL'AYIM.

MIXED MARRIAGE. See INTERMARRIAGE.

MIZMOR (מִזְמוֹר; song), a word that occurs in the superscriptions of more than a third of all psalms, and, hence, is synonymous with *psalm*. See also ZEMIROT.

—SHALOM PAUL

MIZRACHI. See RELIGIOUS PARTIES IN ISRAEL.

MIZRAḤ (מִזְרָח; east), a plaque, often highly artistic, frequently with only the word *mizraḥ* on it, hung on the eastern wall of a synagogue or in a private home when west of Erets Yisra'el, indicating the direction of Jerusalem. Jewish law requires the worshiper when standing in prayer, and especially when reciting the 'Amidah, to face Jerusalem. This is in fulfillment of Solomon's prayer at the dedication of the First Temple: "They shall pray to you toward their land which you gave their fathers, the city which you have chosen and the house which I have built to your name" (*1 Kgs*. 8.48). Arks in synagogues that are to the west of Erets Yisra'el are traditionally built on the eastern wall, so that worshipers will face the ark and, by extension, Jerusalem, when they pray. To avoid the accusation of worshiping the sun by turning east, the *Shulḥan 'Arukh* advocates turning in a south easterly direction (*Oraḥ Ḥayyim* 94.2). Because of the significance of the east in Jewish ritual, the most prized seats in synagogues were generally those "on the *mizraḥ* wall," and these were often reserved for the rabbi and dignitaries.

• F. Landsberger, "The Sacred Direction in Synagogue and Church," *Hebrew Union College Annual* 28 (1957): 181–203; reprinted in *The Synagogue: Studies in Origins, Archaeology and Architecture*, edited by Joseph Gutmann (New York, 1975), pp. 239–261. —SHMUEL HIMELSTEIN

MIZRAḤI, ELIYYAHU (1450–1526), rabbi in Constantinople. Born in Constantinople to a Romaniot family (i.e., of Turkish, not Spanish, origin), he was recognized at the end of the century, after the death of Mosheh Capsali, by both the Romaniot and Sephardi Jews as the supreme authority in the Ottoman empire. Highly regarded for his comprehensive general knowledge and for his halakhic expertise, he also welcomed the refugees from Spain, whose contribution to Jewish culture he greatly appreciated. His approach to the community was democratic; he rejected conferring any special status on the rich and the learned. He ruled that taxation should be based on socioeconomic considerations. He advocated a rapprochement with the Karaites, despite their rejection of rabbinic teachings, and taught them the oral law, although he strictly prohibited intermarriage between Rabbanites and Karaites. His best-known work is his supercommentary on Rashi (Venice, 1527). He also wrote a book on mathematics, *Sefer ha-Mispar* (Constantinople, 1533), and was versed in Greek and Arabic philosophy. He opposed Kabbalah, especially as a basis for halakhic decisions. In his *responsa* (Constantinople, 1560) he describes his busy daily life, including his rabbinic duties, heading a *yeshivah*, and teaching.

• J. R. Hacker, "Ottoman Policy toward Jews," in *Christians and Jews in the Ottoman Empire: The Functioning of a Plural Society*, edited by Benjamin Braude and Bernard Lewis (New York, 1982), pp. 117–126.

—SHALOM BAR-ASHER

MLOKHIM BUKH, a major Yiddish poetic work, setting biblical narrative in a European form, in the manner of the *_Shemu'el Bukh_. Believed to have been composed in the fifteenth century, and framed in Nibelungen (Hildebrand) stanza, the *Mlokhim Bukh* comprises stories derived from *1* and *2 Kings*, culminating in the destruction of Jerusalem by Nebuchadnezzar. The anonymous author draws copiously from later Jewish sources as well as his own sense of humor. The language employed is sophisticated and forward-looking. The first printed edition is from Augsburg in 1543.

• Max Erik, *Di geshikhte fun der yidisher literatur: fun di eltste tsaytn biz der haskalah-tekufah*, (Warsaw, 1928; repr. New York, 1979), pp. 121–122, 222. Lajb Fuks, *Das Altjiddische Epos Melokim-Buk*, 2 vols. (Assen, 1965). Chone Shmeruk, *Prokim fun der yidisher literatur-geshikhte* (Tel Aviv, 1988), pp. 97, 118, 160, 179, 183, 194, 197, 198. —DOVID KATZ

MNEMONICS, actual or artificial words used as aids in memorizing. A favorite approach was creating an *acronym, by which the initial letters of various words would form a single word (see ABBREVIATIONS). Mnemonics were important in the transmission of oral traditions and the liturgy at a time when the ordinary worshiper did not have a prayer book. Mnemonics were common both in literary compositions (for example, alphabetic and other *acrostics in *Psalms* and *Lamentations* and in *_piyyut_) and for memorizing halakhic discussions and conclusions (cf. *_yaqnehaz_ or—a nonhalakhic example—the three meaningless words quoted in the *Seder service, which constitute a mnemonic for the Ten Plagues [see PLAGUES OF EGYPT]). Mnemonics are also used as a device for remembering grammatical rules (e.g., *bagad kefat* to indicate the letters that take a *dagesh lene*). The rabbis advocated the use of mnemonics for study and suggested that the scholars of Judah remembered what they had learned while those of Galilee forgot because the former used mnemonics ('*Eruv*. 53–54).

• Birger Gerhardsson, *Memory and Manuscript: Oral Tradition and Written Transmission in Rabbinic Judaism and Early Christianity* (Lund, 1964). Frances Yates, *The Art of Memory* (London, 1992).

MOAB. See AMMON AND MOAB.

MO'ADIM LE-SIMḤAH. See GREETINGS AND CONGRATULATIONS.

MODEH ANI (מוֹדֶה אֲנִי; I Give Thanks), a short prayer said immediately upon waking in the morning. It does not appear in medieval sources and seems to have been composed in the seventeenth century to replace Elohay Neshamah (O My God, the Soul That You Gave Me), which is mentioned in the Talmud, and which was transferred to the Morning Benedictions (*Birkhot ha-Shaḥar). Modeh Ani does not mention the divine name and could be recited while still in bed and before performing the prescribed morning ablutions. It expresses thanks to the "living and eternal king" for the return of one's soul after sleep and welcomes the presence of God upon waking.

• Ismar Elbogen, *Jewish Liturgy: A Comprehensive History* (Philadelphia, 1993).

MODENA, AHARON BERAKHYAH. See AHARON BEREKHYAH BEN MOSHEH OF MODENA.

MODENA, LEONE (1571–1648), Italian rabbi and a versatile writer; also known as Yehudah Aryeh. His literary achievements were especially outstanding, and he was one of the most colorful figures in the Venice ghetto. In his apologetic work *Historia de' riti Ebraici* (Paris, 1637), he wrote as a proud resident of the ghetto but was also influenced by external culture, advocating the introduction of polyphony into synagogue music. He also advocated the harmonization of Jewish and Catholic sensibilities. His sermons attracted distinguished gentile audiences, and helped to alter Christian stereotypes of Judaism by explaining Jewish ritual. His *Ḥayyei Yehudah* was translated into English by Mark R. Cohen as *The Autobiography of a Seventeenth-Century Venetian Rabbi: Leon Modena's Life of Judah* (Princeton, 1988). Modena's *responsa, She'elot u-Teshuvot Ziqnei Yehudah*, were edited by Shelomoh Simonson (Jerusalem, 1956).

• Howard Adelman, "Success and Failure in the Seventeenth Century Ghetto of Venice: The Life and Thought of Leon Modena," Ph.D. dissertation, Brandeis University, 1985. Marc R. Cohen, "Leone da Modena's Ritti, a Seventeenth-Century Plea for Social Toleration of Jews," in *Essential Papers on Jewish Culture in Renaissance and Baroque Italy*, edited by David B. Ruderman (New York, 1992), pp. 429–473. E. Horowitz, "The Eve of the Circumcision: A Chapter in the History of Jewish Nightlife," in *Essential Papers on Jewish Culture in Renaissance and Baroque Italy*, edited by David B. Ruderman (New York, 1992), pp. 554–588.

—SHALOM BAR-ASHER

MO'ED (מוֹעֵד; Appointed Time), second order of the Mishnah, dealing with the laws of Sabbath and festivals. It has twelve tractates, each of which has related material in the Tosefta' as well as in both Talmuds (except **Sheqalim*, which lacks *gemara'* in the Talmud Bavli). The twelve tractates are **Shabbat*, **'Eruvin*, **Pesaḥim*, **Sheqalim*, **Yoma'*, **Sukkah*, **Beitsah*, **Ro'sh ha-Shanah*, **Ta'anit*, **Megillah*, **Mo'ed Qatan*, and **Ḥagigah*.

—AVRAHAM WALFISH

MO'ED QATAN (מוֹעֵד קָטָן; Minor Appointed Time), tractate consisting of three chapters in Mishnah order *Mo'ed, with related material in the Tosefta' and both Talmuds. An early name for the tractate, taken from its first word, was *Mashqin*. The name *Mo'ed Qatan* (in early sources, simply *Mo'ed*) refers to the subject of the tractate, the laws of *mo'ed*, a term used in *Mo'ed Qatan* to indicate the intermediate days of Pesaḥ and Sukkot. Whereas biblical law characterizes only the first and the last days of these festivals as days of refraining from work (*Lv*. 23.39; cf. *Lv*. 23.7–8), the rabbinic tradition characterizes the intermediate days as **ḥol ha-mo'ed* (the secular portion of the appointed time), requiring a partial restriction of work activities during these days as well. *Mo'ed Qatan* outlines the categories of work that are exempted from this prohibition, including activities that are essential to prevent financial loss, as well as activities that are necessary for public welfare or for proper enjoyment of the festival. The prohibition of mourning the death of a relative during the festival leads *Mo'ed Qatan*, particularly in the Talmud, into a lengthy excursus on the laws of mourning.

The Talmud Bavli tractate was translated into English by H. M. Lazarus in the Soncino Talmud (London, 1938).

• Chanoch Albeck, ed., *Shishah Sidrei Mishnah, Seder Mo'ed* (Jerusalem, 1952). Philip Blackman, ed. and trans., *Mishnayoth*, vol. 2, *Order Moed* (Gateshead, 1973). Pinhas Kehati, ed., *Mishnah: A New Translation with a Commentary, Seder Moed*, vol. 5, *Ta'anit, Megillah, Moed Katan, Haggigah* (Jerusalem, 1991). Hermann Leberecht Strack and Günter Stemberger, *Introduction to the Talmud and Midrash*, rev. and updat. ed., translated by Markus Bockmuehl (Minneapolis, 1992).

—AVRAHAM WALFISH

MOHAMMED. See MUḤAMMAD.

MOHEL (מוֹהֵל; circumciser), a person authorized to perform a *circumcision. The duty to circumcise a newborn male rests with the father, but the actual execution is entrusted to a person duly trained and declared competent both in theory and practice. The *mohel* thus acts as the agent of the parent. Although according to law any competent Jew may perform a circumcision, preference is given to one of genuine piety who performs the act "for the sake of heaven." According to Maimonides (*Hilkhot Milah* 2.1), a woman, a non-Jew, or even a competent minor may act as *mohel* where no competent male Jew is available. The Talmud states that a "sage should be able to perform ritual slaughter and circumcision" (*Ḥul*. 9a). Reform Jews often have medical doctors perform circumcisions.

• Michael A. Grodin, "Professional Issues for the Physician Mohel," *Conservative Judaism* 42 (1990): 46–53. Paysach J. Krohn, *Bris Milah: Circumcision, the Covenant of Abraham: A Compendium* (Brooklyn, N.Y.,

MOHILEVER, SHEMU'EL (1824–1898), Russian Zionist and rabbi of Bialystok. He used his considerable rabbinic reputation, enhanced by his wide general knowledge, to unite both secular and Orthodox nationalists in founding the pre-Herzlian Zionist movement of Ḥibbat Tsiyyon in Warsaw in 1882, convening the first conference of the Ḥovevei Tsiyyon at Kattowitz in 1884. He succeeded in persuading the Parisian philanthropist Baron Edmond de Rothschild to support their agricultural settlements, monitoring their progress himself in a visit to Palestine in 1890. He headed a rabbinic campaign in 1882 calling on the Jewish masses fleeing from the Russian pogroms to the West to settle instead the ancestral homeland, echoing a Midrashic statement to the effect that God preferred his children to live in their land even without due observance of the Torah than have them observe it properly in the Diaspora. In 1893 he founded Merkaz Ruḥani to spread Zionism among Orthodox Jewry from which the Religious Zionist movement Mizrachi took its name. He enthusiastically supported the political Zionist leader Theodor Herzl and helped him organize the First Zionist Congress in 1897. His message of Zionist ecumenism sent to the congress, which he was too ill to attend, deeply impressed the delegates.

• Mordecai Ben Zvi, *Rabbi Samuel Mohilever* (London, 1945). *Ha-Ga'on Rabbi Shemu'el Mohilever: She'elot u-Teshuvot ve-Ḥiqrei Halakhah*, Responsa and Halakhic Studies, 2 vols. (Jerusalem, 1974 and 1980). Arthur Hertzberg, ed., *The Zionist Idea* (Cleveland, 1959), pp. 398–405. Leo Jung, ed., *Men of the Spirit* (New York, 1964), pp. 417–436. Nahum Sokolow, *Ḥibbat Zion* (Jerusalem, 1935), pp. 221–225.

—ARYEH NEWMAN

MOLECH, Semitic deity worshiped in biblical times, known from Ugaritic and Mesopotamian sources as Malik. It is likely that Molech figured among the chtonic gods, that is, those associated with death and the underworld. According to biblical tradition, Molech was worshiped by means of child sacrifice, a practice abhorred and strictly forbidden by Israelite belief and law (*Ez*. 16.21, 20.26, 31, 23.39; *Ps*. 106.37–38). Child sacrifice is condemned in the Bible, without mention of the god Molech, as a characteristically repulsive form of Canaanite religion, to be shunned by the Israelites (*Dt*. 12.30–31, 18.10); explicit prohibitions against the worship of Molech are found in *Leviticus* 18.21 and 20.2–5. Sacrificing to Molech is called "whoring after" him; it desecrates God's name and pollutes his sanctuary. The penalty is death by stoning for the perpetrator and all of his followers; if the court fails to carry out the sentence, the perpetrator and his family are liable to divine punishment. Though the idolatrous practice of child sacrifice seems to have been introduced into Judah under the reign of Ahaz (*2 Kgs*. 16.3, *2 Chr*. 28.3) and is referred to in connection with Manasseh as well as Hoshea, king of Israel (*2 Kgs*. 17.7–12, 21.6; *2 Chr*. 33.6), the god Molech is mentioned by name in this connection only from the time of Josiah (*2 Kgs*. 23.10). There seems to have arisen then an institutionalized Molech cult, centered at Topheth in Gei Ben Hinnom near Jerusalem, and despite Josiah's efforts to eliminate it, it may have continued for some time. Some Israelites seem to have seen it as an acceptable form of worshiping the God of Israel; others connected it with Baal (*Jer*. 7.31–32, 19.5–6, 32.35). According to some rabbinic interpretation, and a few modern scholars, the burning of children in fire to Molech was symbolic rather than real. Molech is not to be identified with Milcom, god of the Ammonites; though the biblical text mistakenly confused them once (*1 Kgs*. 11.7), they are everywhere else kept distinct.

• John Day, *Molech: A God of Human Sacrifice in the Old Testament*, University of Cambridge Oriental Publications, no. 41 (Cambridge, 1989). George C. Heider, *The Cult of Molek*, Journal for the Study of the Old Testament, Supplement Series 43 (Sheffield, Eng., 1985). Geza Vermes, "Leviticus 18:21 in Ancient Jewish Bible Exegesis," *Studies . . . in Memory of Joseph Heinemann* (Jerusalem, 1981), pp. 108–124.

—BARUCH J. SCHWARTZ

MOLIN, YA'AQOV BEN MOSHEH HA-LEVI (c.1360–1427), German rabbi; also known as the Maharil or Mahari Siegel. He was prominent in rebuilding the Jewish community following the Black Death persecutions of 1348 and 1349. Born in Mainz, he studied there with his father and with R. Avraham Klausner and R. Shalom ben Yitsḥaq in Vienna. Molin became the rabbi of Mainz upon his father's death and served there for the rest of his life; his *yeshivah* attracted many students. He was a renowned exponent of *minhag Ashkenaz*, the customary religious practices of central European Jewry. His version of *minhag Ashkenaz* is preserved largely in *Sefer [Minhagei] ha-Maharil* (Sabionetta, 1556), compiled by his student R. Zalman of Saint Goar. The book, which served as a major source for the rulings of R. Mosheh Isserles in his glosses on the *Shulḥan 'Arukh*, also contains some of the teachings of Molin's teacher, R. Shalom, and of his student, R. Ya'akov ben Yehudah Weil. Molin was the author of numerous halakhic *responsa*, which have appeared in several recensions, most recently in a critical edition published by Yitsḥaq Satz in 1979; others remain in manuscript.

• Yedidyah Dinari, *Ḥakhmei Ashkenaz be-Shilhei Yemei ha-Beinayim* (Jerusalem, 1984). Leopold Greenwald, *Maharil u-Zemano* (New York, 1944). Sidney Steiman, *Custom and Survival: The Life and Work of Rabbi Jacob Molin . . .* (New York, 1963).

—MARK WASHOFSKY

MOLKHO, SHELOMOH (c.1500–1532), kabbalist, messianic enthusiast, and martyr. Born to a Marrano family in Portugal, he attained a high position at court but returned to Judaism after his meeting in 1525 with David *Re'uveni. He circumcised himself and subsequently experienced visions. From Lisbon, Molkho escaped to Salonika where he joined Shelomoh *Alkabez and other followers of kabbalist Yosef *Taitazak. From Turkey, Molkho went to Italy. Convinced that he was the Messiah, he spent thirty days in Rome in prayer and fasting among the beggars in front of the pope's palace, in fulfillment of a Talmudic legend recounting the suffering of the Messiah. This and other messianic gestures alarmed some Jewish leaders, but many Jews and Christians revered Molkho as a man of God and a prophet, especially when his predictions about the flooding of Rome by the Tiber in 1530 and the earthquake in Lisbon in 1531 came to pass. Even Pope Clement VII was greatly impressed by Molkho and protected him from the Inquisition. From Italy Molkho traveled to Regensburg with David Re'uveni to seek an audience with Emperor Charles V to persuade him to arm Marranos to fight against the Turks in Palestine. Charles V had both of them arrested and delivered to the Inquisition. Molkho was burned at the stake in Mantua. His kabbalistic homilies are printed in his *Sefer ha-Mefo'ar* (first published as *Derashot* [Salonika, 1529]), which includes his forecast that the Messiah would appear in the year 1540.

• Abraham M. Habermann, *Sippur Rabbi Yosi Dilah Reynah u-Ma'aseh Nora' mi-Shelomoh Molkho* (Jerusalem, 1942–1943). Julius Voos, *David Reubeni und Salomo Molcho: Ein Beitrage zur Geschichte der messianischen Bewegung im Judentum in der ersten Hälfte des 16 Jahrhunderts* (Berlin, 1933).

MOLOCH. See MOLECH.

MONASTICISM is practically unknown among Jews, although it plays an important role in Christianity and other religions. The only examples in mainstream Jewish history date from the late Second Temple period among the *Essenes, the *Qumran community (identified by many scholars with the Essenes), and the *Therapeutae. *Celibacy is frowned upon by Judaism, and extreme ascetic tendencies (see ASCETICISM), though widespread at certain periods in pietistic circles, were generally counteracted by the social and world-affirming orientation of the Jewish tradition. In general, the idea of monasticism, which requires withdrawal from the world in order to achieve spiritual perfection, is contrary to the Jewish demand of hallowing life in the world by the discipline of *sanctification.

• F. C. Conybeare, *Philo: About the Contemplative Life, with a Defense of Its Genuineness* (Oxford, 1895). Geza Vermes and Martin D. Goodman, eds., *The Essenes According to the Classical Sources* (Sheffield, Eng., 1989).

MONDAYS AND THURSDAYS. See SHENI VA-ḤAMISHI.

MONEYLENDING. Any charging of interest is strictly forbidden in the Bible (*Ex.* 22.24; *Lv.* 25.36–37; *Dt.* 23.20–21). There are two words used for interest, both found in *Leviticus* 25.36—*neshekh* (biting) and *tarbit* (increase). The Mishnah (*B. M.* 5.1) differentiates between the two, saying that the former refers to a direct addition to the money or produce lent, the latter to an increase in the value of the produce. The prohibition against interest seems to have been frequently disregarded in biblical times; *Psalms* 15.5 enumerates among the qualities of the virtuous man that "he puts not out his money on interest." The law against both accepting and paying interest applies only to Jews, non-Jews being explicitly excluded from the prohibition (*Dt.* 23.21). Jews circumvented the law by using non-Jews as straw men (cf. *B. M.* 5.6). The biblical prohibition against moneylending reflects the simple economy of an agricultural society where *loans were needed to provide immediate relief in moments of distress (e.g., failure of crops). The rabbis saw the taking of interest as the transgression of a negative commandment and even developed the concept of *avaq ribbit* (dust of interest) to prevent the lender from receiving any advantage from a loan, even if he did not receive actual interest. With the development of a money economy, industry, and trade, the ancient prohibitions became economically obsolete. Unable to disregard a plain biblical prohibition, Jewish practice evolved—against long resistance—the legal fiction known as *hetter 'isqa'*, by which a loan is contracted in the form of a partnership. Although this procedure is considered legitimate for business transactions and investments, loans to a fellow man in need should be free of interest (see GEMILUT ḤESED). The Catholic church in the Middle Ages enforced a prohibition against moneylending between Christians; hence, the Jews, debarred from other occupations, often became moneylenders and usurers. The financial operations of all banks in Israel are covered by a general *hetter 'isqa'*.

• Joseph Shatzmiller, *Shylock Reconsidered: Jews, Moneylending, and Medieval Society* (Berkeley, 1990).

MONOGAMY. See POLYGAMY.

MONOTHEISM, belief in, and worship of, one *God. Monotheism is the decisive characteristic of the Israelite conception of God, although different stages of development and definition are discernible. The composition of the term (Gr. *monos* and *theos*) indicates that monotheism is a form of theism, that is, belief in a personal, divine being, but biblical monotheism differs from polytheistic paganism not only quantitatively in the number of gods professed but also qualitatively in its understanding of God as absolutely above nature and in complete mastery of it. The world and its individual parts—stars, sun, earth, and sea—exist solely by God's will; they tremble before him and perform his bidding. The biblical conception of God is nonmythological: God was not born, does not beget other divinities, and is independent of matter or other beings. He cannot be coerced by magic, is omnipotent, and depends on no sacrificial cult to sustain his being. At the same time he enters into a direct, personal relationship with his creatures, is concerned with their plight, and even elects individuals or groups for special purposes. This idea of God is different from philosophical monotheism; it is an original religious intuition rather than the result of intellectual speculation, although the precise moment in the history of Israel at which it came into full blossom is difficult to determine. The rabbis of the Talmudic period ascribed the monotheistic revolution to Abraham. Critical scholarship associated the emergence of monotheism with the literary prophets, but some modern scholars accept the biblical account according to which the monotheistic intuition was arrived at by Moses (cf. *Ex.* 20.1–6), possibly in the experience of the burning bush, which was not only a prophetic calling but a revelation of the divine name (*Ex.* 3.14). Whereas in the Pentateuch God demands obedience to a law that is at once ritual and moral; that is, without sharp distinction between the two, prophetic monotheism becomes emphatically moral and at times antiritualistic. The biblical historians do not recognize a gradual evolution of ethical monotheism, but rather a gradual falling away from Israel's pristine faith. Even in the days of Moses there was occasional backsliding, as when the *golden calf was manufactured to serve as a material symbol of God. After the conquest of Canaan, the influence of the local population and its religious cults made itself felt. The *Book of Judges* describes alternate cycles of faith and faithlessness. The sporadic worship of Baal was followed by a resurgence of monotheism in the time of Saul, David, and Solomon, but *syncretism and *idolatry held sway again from then until the Babylonian exile. After the exile, idolatry diminished among Jews, and Ezra and his successors, unlike the prophets, no longer found it necessary to inveigh against it. Subsequently, the main stages in the history of Jewish monotheism were the struggle of the rabbis against the dualistic tendencies of *gnosticism and the attempts of the medieval philosophers to formulate a monotheism free from the taint of *anthropomorphism. All formulations of the Jewish *creed stressed monotheism, which was the second of Maimonides' *Thirteen Principles of Faith. Medieval apologists frequently contrasted the pure and uncompromising monotheism of Judaism with what seemed to them the polytheism implicit in the Christian doctrine of the Trinity. The kabbalistic doctrine of God (see SEFIROT) has been criticized by its opponents as a departure from strict Jewish monotheism, but the kabbalists held that their mystical theology, which described the dynamic unity of the Godhead in symbolic language, was perfectly monotheistic. Under the influence of Enlightenment rationalism, which emphasized the moral aspects of religion to the neglect of its ritual and irrational aspects, Jewish modernists often described their religion as "ethical monotheism" (see SHEMAʿ).

• Diana Edelman, *The Triumph of Elohim: From Yahwisms to Judaisms* (Kampen, 1995). Edith Engel and Henry Engel, *One God: Peoples of the Book* (New York, 1990). Sigmund Freud, *Moses and Monotheism*, translated by Katherine Jones (New York, 1959), a controversial interpretation. Lenn E. Goodman, *The God of Abraham* (New York, 1996). Larry Hurtado, *One God, One Lord: Early Christian Devotion and Ancient Jewish Monotheism* (Philadelphia, 1988).

MONTAGU, LILIAN (1873–1963), British social worker and progressive Jewish leader. A daughter of Baron Swaythling, she was by birth a member of the small, interrelated Anglo-Jewish aristocracy. She was closely involved with the activities of the Women's Industrial Council and the National Council of Women and served as president of both the West Central Jewish Club and the West Central Jewish Day Settlement. With Claude Montefiore, she was a founder of the Union of Liberal and Progressive Synagogues of Great Britain, the more reformed branch of British non-Orthodox Judaism, and was the first chair of its main synagogue, the Liberal Jewish Synagogue of St. John's Wood, London. She wrote *Thoughts on Judaism* in 1943.

• Eric Conrad, *Lily H. Montagu: Prophet of a Living Judaism* (New York, 1953). Ellen M. Umansky, *Lily Montagu and the Advancement of Liberal Judaism* (New York, 1983). —LAVINIA COHN-SHERBOK

MONTEFIORE, CLAUDE GOLDSMID (1858–1938), English scholar, theologian, and leader of the *World Union for Progressive Judaism. He was educated at Oxford and the Hochschule für die Wissenschaft des Judentums in Berlin. A man of means, he took Solomon *Schechter to England as his private tutor. He founded, funded, and edited, together with Israel Abrahams, the scholarly journal the *Jewish Quarterly Review*. He also founded the Jewish Religious Union, which brought radical Reform to England. From 1926 to 1938 he headed the World Union for Progressive Judaism. He wrote many works on Jewish and Christian topics and was one of the first Jewish scholars to write sympathetically of Jesus and the New Testament, notably in his *Synoptic Gospels* (2 vols. [1909]), a commentary on the New Testament utilizing Jewish sources, and *Judaism and St. Paul* (1914). Together with Herbert Loewe, he published *A Rabbinic Theology* (1938), in which the two men, in addition to presenting a systematized account of rabbinic teachers, conducted an Orthodox–Reform dialogue on the subject matter. Montefiore's emphasis on the universalism of Judaism led him to oppose Zionism as a narrow nationalist particularism. He argued for a progressive Judaism that was ethically compatible with other world religions and collaborated with the Catholic thinker Baron Friedrich von Hügel.

• Norman Bentwich, *Claude Montefiore and His Tutor in Rabbinics: Founders of Liberal and Conservative Judaism* (Southampton, Eng., 1966), with bibliography. Edward Kessler, *An English Jew: The Life and Writings of Claude Montefiore* (London, 1989). Joshua B. Stein, *Claude Goldsmid Montefiore on the Ancient Rabbis: The Second Generation of Reform Judaism in Britain* (Missoula, Mont., 1977). —EUGENE R. SHEPPARD

MONTH. See CALENDAR.

MOON. According to *Genesis* 1.16, the moon was the "lesser light," created together with the *sun on the fourth day of Creation. The moon was regarded throughout the Middle East as a deity; for example, in Ur and Haran, where Abraham spent his early years. Moon worship was, however, strictly forbidden to the Israelites (*Dt.* 4.19, 17.3). Nevertheless under Assyrian influence, King Manasseh of Judah introduced the moon cult (*2 Kgs.* 21.3–5), but the altars he built were destroyed by Josiah (*2 Kgs.* 23.12). In popular belief, the moon was thought to influence fertility, and women wore moon-shaped pendants (*Is.* 3.18); the moon was also seen as a symbol of permanence (*Ps.* 72.7). The lunar cycle formed the basis of the monthly *calendar reckoning, and the proclamation of the new moon (see RO'SH ḤODESH) was a prerogative of the *Sanhedrin. Two major festivals, Pesaḥ and Sukkot, begin on the night of the full moon. The monthly ceremony of blessing the moon (*Qiddush Levanah) generally takes place between the third and fifteenth day of each month when the light of the moon is regarded as being at its strongest. In superstitious beliefs, an eclipse of the moon was regarded as a bad omen (*Suk.* 29a), and it was believed that the waning and waxing of the moon could affect the human mind, while the period of a waxing moon was deemed auspicious for marriages.

• Joshua Trachtenberg, *Jewish Magic and Superstition* (New York, 1939).

MOON, BLESSING OF THE. See QIDDUSH LEVANAH.

MOON, NEW. See RO'SH ḤODESH.

MORAIS, SABATO (1823–1897), American rabbi and communal leader. Born in Leghorn, Italy, Morais served as director of the orphans' school of the Spanish and Portuguese congregation in London. Following five years of service in England, he became the spiritual leader of Congregation Mikveh Israel in Philadelphia in 1851, succeeding Isaac Leeser. Morais served Mikveh Israel for forty-seven years until his death.

He was an eloquent spokesman for American Orthodoxy, well-known for his conciliatory spirit; for example, in unifying Sephardim and Ashkenazim. He was the founding president of the *Jewish Theological Seminary of America (1887–1897) and wrote numerous articles on various aspects of Jewish life and culture. He was a noted Hebraist and biblical scholar. He wrote *Italian Hebrew Literature* (New York, 1926; repr., 1970).

• Moshe Davis, *The Emergence of Conservative Judaism* (Philadelphia, 1965). Henry Samuel Morais, *The Jews of Philadelphia* (Philadelphia, 1894). —MARC D. ANGEL

MORALISTS. See ETHICS; MUSAR MOVEMENT.

MORDECAI (Heb. Mordekhai), a descendant of a Benjamite family of Babylonian exiles who saved Persian Jewry from the anti-Jewish scheme of *Haman, the vizier of King Ahasuerus, when he bid Queen *Esther, his daughter by adoption, to intercede with the king. According to the *Book of Esther*, Mordecai became viceroy of Persia and conferred considerable benefits upon his brethren. To mark the celebration of the victory of the Jews over their enemies, Mordecai sent letters to all of the Jewish communities to celebrate annually on 13 and 14 Adar, which is the holiday of Purim. Talmudic *aggadah* identified Mordecai with the prophet Malachi (*Meg.* 10b).

• Michael V. Fox, *Character and Ideology in the Book of Esther* (Columbia, S.C., 1991), pp. 185–195. Carey A. Moore, ed. and trans., *Esther* (Garden City, N.Y., 1971). —SHALOM PAUL

MORDEKHAI BEN HILLEL (d.1298), German rabbi and halakhist; student of R. Me'ir ben Barukh of Rothenburg. He is known chiefly for his *Sefer ha-Mordekhai*, a digest of the halakhic teachings of his master and of the Ashkenazi sages of earlier generations based loosely upon *Halakhot* by R. Yitsḥaq Alfasi. *Sefer ha-Mordekhai* underwent significant alteration at the hands of students and copyists and exists in two primary recensions, the Rhenish and the Austrian, based on the dominant traditions in each. The book was widely quoted by subsequent authorities, both Sephardi and Ashkenazi. It was printed in the very first edition of the Talmud (Soncino, 1483–1484) and also appeared separately (Riva di Trento, 1559–1560).

• Menachem Elon, *Jewish Law: History, Sources, Principles* (Philadelphia, 1994), pp. 1249–1250. Efraim E. Urbach, *Ba'alei ha-Tosafot* (Jerusalem, 1980), pp. 556–561. —MARK WASHOFSKY

MOREDET (מוֹרֶדֶת; rebellious wife), a wife who persistently refuses to cohabit with her husband. She may be divorced by her husband after a period of twelve months and also forfeits her *ketubbah*. The twelve-month period is designated by the Talmud as a "cooling off" period aimed at allowing the wife to reconsider her "rebelliousness" in case it was prompted by sudden anger which she later regrets (*Ket.* 63b). Under early Talmudic law, there were certain procedural distinctions between a wife who refused to engage in sexual relations with her husband as a result of anger and one who claimed that her husband was physically repulsive to her. In later times, however, the *halakhah* governing both types of *moredet* followed the same procedure; that is, a twelve-month mandatory waiting period and divorce without a *ketubbah* (*Shulḥan 'Arukh, Even ha-'Ezer* 77.2). Though it was Maimonides' view that, in the case of physical repulsiveness, pressure ought to be applied to the husband to divorce his wife, following the mandatory twelve-month period, on the grounds that "she is not like a captive to have to submit to intercourse with a man whose physical presence she finds unbearable" (*Law of Marriage* 14.18), this was not accepted by the majority of authorities (Rema', *Even ha-'Ezer* 77.2–3).

• Menachem Elon, *Jewish Law: History, Sources, Principles*, 4 vols. (Philadelphia, 1994), pp. 658–665, 851. Shlomo Riskin, *The Rebellious Wife, the Agunah and the Right of Women to Initiate Divorce in Jewish Law: A Halakhic Solution* (New York, 1989). —DANIEL SINCLAIR

MOREH, ḤAYYIM (1872–1945), Persian rabbi. With the revival of rabbinical learning in Persia at the beginning of the twentieth century, Ḥayyim Moreh was its most distinguished representative. His special interest was the education of the Jewish community. He published *Derekh Ḥayyim* (Teheran, 1919) in Judeo-Persian, a review of Jewish history; *Gedulat Mordekhai* (Teheran, 1934), a collection of post-biblical texts translated into Judeo-Persian; and *Yedei Eliyahu* (Teheran, 1929), a work on ethical conduct.

• David Benvenisti, *Darko shel Moreh: Pirqei Ḥayyim be-Hora'ah* (Jerusalem, 1990). —SHALOM BAR-ASHER

MOREH NEVUKHIM. See MAIMONIDES, MOSES.

MOREH TSEDEQ. See TEACHER OF RIGHTEOUSNESS.

MORE JUDAICO. See OATH MORE JUDAICO.

MORENU (מוֹרֵנוּ; our teacher), title originally bestowed in Germany (14th cent.) upon exceptionally learned men and upon Torah scholars on their wedding day. *Morenu* may originally have applied to those learned in the laws of marriage and divorce. Some communities required knowledge of the entire Talmud and *Shulḥan 'Arukh* before one could be granted the title. In some communities, the title could be revoked if the recipient proved unworthy by his conduct. In more recent times in eastern Europe, the title was used broadly as an honorific, though in Germany it was bestowed only by a rabbi upon exceptionally learned and pious laymen.

—SHMUEL HIMELSTEIN

MORIAH, a land described in *Genesis* 22.2 as a mountainous area, a three-day journey from Beersheba, where Abraham was commanded to sacrifice his son Isaac. According to later Jewish tradition, Moriah was identified as the hilltop in Jerusalem where Solomon built the Temple (*2 Chr.* 3.1). This identification is also found in the *Book of Jubilees* (18.13) and is accepted by Josephus (*Antiquities of the Jews* 1.13.2.226), the Targum, and the Talmud (*Ta'an.* 16a).

• Nahum M. Sarna, *Genesis*, The JPS Torah Commentary (Philadelphia, 1989), pp. 391–392. —SHALOM PAUL

MORNING. Despite the fact that in the Bible the morning actually begins at sunrise (cf. *Jgs.* 9.33, "And it shall be in the morning when the sun rises"), halakhically, morning is considered to begin with the appearance of the morning star, even though the sun has not yet risen. This dawn is referred to as "the morning of the night" (*Yoma'* 20b); that is, the sign of morning that marks the end of the night. There is a difference of opinion in the Talmud as to when morning ends. According to the majority opinion it continues until midday, but R. Yoḥanan ben Zakk'ai holds that it extends only to the end of the fourth hour—the hour in this case being a twelfth part of the period of daylight (*Ber.* 26b–27a) and, hence, variable with the seasons. The obligatory morning reading, or the Shema', can be carried out from the beginning of daylight until a quarter of the day, that is, a quarter of the hours of daylight, depending on the season of the year. See also DAY AND NIGHT.

• Joseph Ascoly, *The Calendar* (Tallahassee, 1990). Ellen Robbins, "Studies in the Prehistory of the Jewish Calendar," Ph.D. dissertation, New York Unversity, 1989. —CHAIM PEARL

MORNING BENEDICTIONS. See BIRKHOT HA-SHAḤAR.

MORNING SERVICE. See SHAḤARIT.

MOSCATO, YEHUDAH (c.1530–1593), Italian rabbinical authority and preacher. Born in Osimo, he had to leave when the Jews were expelled in 1569 and went to Mantua, where he became chief rabbi. He was steeped in classical, medieval, and Renaissance literature and had a fine Hebrew style. His major works were *Qol Yehudah* (Venice, 1594), a commentary on Yehudah ha-Levi's *Kuzari*, and a sermonic collection, *Nefutsot Yehudah* (Venice, 1589). Impressed by classical rhetoric, he looked for similar features in biblical and rabbinic sources. An excellent writer and preacher, he modeled himself on Greek and Roman philosophers such as Plato and Seneca. In his sermon on music, for example, Moscato demonstrates how the fundamental concepts of Renaissance music were based on the terms and formulas found in the *Book of Psalms*. He drew on his extensive knowledge of Torah, Philo, and Kabbalah in order to identify ethical ideas common to different cultures. He was fond of syncretistic etymology, and he saw Hebrew as the original language of the human race, a natural bridge between civilizations.

• Alexander Altmann, "Ars Rhetorica as Reflected in Some Jewish Figures of the Italian Renaissance" in *Essential Papers on Jewish Culture in Renaissance and Baroque Italy*, edited by David B. Ruderman (New York, 1992), pp. 62–84. Robert Bonfil, *Rabbis and Jewish Communities in Renaissance Italy* (London, 1993), pp. 298–316. Elliot Horowitz, "The Way We Were: Jewish Life in the Middle Ages," *Jewish History* 1 (1986): 75–90. Cecil Roth, *The Jews in the Renaissance* (Philadelphia, 1959), pp. 21–43, 271–304. Moses A. Shulvass, *Ḥayyei ha-Yehudim be-'Italyah bi-Tequfat ha-Renesans* (New York, 1955), pp. 37–314. —SHALOM BAR-ASHER

MOSER. See DENUNCIATION.

MOSES (Heb. Mosheh), founder and leader of the Israelite nation. The Bible portrays Moses as the greatest of all prophets (a belief formulated in Maimonides' *Thirteen Principles of Faith), who, alone among men, knew God "face to face" (*Ex.* 33.11) and whom God chose to be the mediator of his revelation on Mount Sinai and the leader who would transform a horde of slaves into a potential "kingdom of priests" and "a treasured people" (*Ex.* 19.5–6). Moses' life, from birth to death, is depicted as an integral part of the divine design of redemption. According to the biblical account, the future liberator of Israel, son of Amram and Jochebed of the tribe of Levi, was born at the height of the Egyptian persecution (probably in the 13th cent. BCE), when Hebrew male infants were drowned at birth. After a period of concealment, Jochebed placed Moses in a basket among the Nile reeds, entrusting his life to providence, a well-known example of the widespread motif of the abandoned hero. Moses was rescued by Pharaoh's own daughter and brought up in the royal palace. But heredity triumphed over environment; when seeing an Egyptian taskmaster mistreat a Hebrew, Moses slew the Egyptian.

The next day he beheld an Israelite smiting a fellow Israelite. When he intervened, his Hebrew brother betrayed him, and he had to flee to Midian, where he married Zipporah, the daughter of *Jethro, priest of Midian (*Ex.* 2). At the age of eighty, he was vouchsafed a theophany in the form of a *burning bush that was not consumed, and in which the God of his fathers laid upon him the mission to lead his people out of Egypt. In vain Moses attempted to resist the call (*Ex.* 3), but finally accepting the divine charge, he appeared, together with his brother Aaron, before Pharaoh and demanded in the Lord's name, "Let my people go!" Ten plagues (see PLAGUES OF EGYPT) reinforced his demand; the last plague, the slaying of the Egyptian firstborn, brought the Hebrews freedom (*Ex.* 7–11). The urgency with which the Israelites left Egypt was matched by the haste with which Pharaoh sought to recapture his erstwhile bondmen, whom he overtook at the shore of the Sea of Reeds, misnamed the Red Sea. There an event occurred that left an indelible mark on Jewish tradition: the Israelites crossed dry-shod, while the pursuing Egyptians were drowned (*Ex.* 14–15). The *Exodus was the beginning of the journey that was to lead the Israelites to the Promised Land. The next major event was the giving of the Torah at Mount *Sinai. There the *Ten Commandments, and other legislation, were promulgated, and Moses bound the people in a solemn covenant to the Lord (*Ex.* 19–24). He also built the first national sanctuary, the *Tabernacle or Tent of Meeting, which was to serve as the visible symbol of the invisible God's presence in their midst (*Ex.* 25ff.). The unique theophany at Mount Sinai was followed by the anticlimactic sin of the *golden calf. In a burst of anger, Moses shattered the *tablets of the Law but subsequently interceded with God, obtained his pardon for the people, and carved the tablets anew (*Ex.* 32–34). The camp, however, continued to simmer with rebellion. The tragic climax came when ten of the twelve spies sent to reconnoiter the Promised Land brought back a discouraging report, saying that the Israelites would be unable to defeat the Canaanites (*Nm.* 13–14). Moses led Israel for forty years through the wilderness, until the elder generation died and a new generation had grown up. After annexing the lands of Sihon and Og in Transjordan, Moses' work drew to its close (*Nm.* 21). The Lord forbade him to cross the Jordan in punishment for an act of disobedience (*Nm.* 20.1–13). In three valedictory addresses, delivered on the Plains of Moab, Moses reviewed the story of the Exodus and recapitulated the terms and the laws of the covenant. Then, having exhorted and blessed his people (see MOSES, SONG OF), he died on Mount Nebo in the land of Moab, "but no one knows his burial place to this day" (*Dt.* 34.6) so that no cult could ever become attached to his person. The *aggadah* embellished the biography of Moses more than that of any other biblical personage. But through all the variegated and often contradictory legends runs the assumption that in spite of his unique career as the faithful "servant of God," Moses always remained a mortal, fallible human being. In modern times the historicity of Moses—and the Exodus tradition as a whole—has been challenged; but many scholars agree that some of the tribes were in fact enslaved in Egypt and freed, that the Israelite religion was founded in law by a solemn covenant, and that a heroic figure like Moses played a central role in these events. However, no critical hypothesis can in any way affect the towering image of Moses as it has developed in biblical, rabbinic, and kabbalistic tradition. Both a historical personality and a spiritual symbol, Moses represents the passionate and self-sacrificing leader, liberator, intercessor, lawgiver, teacher (Mosheh Rabbenu [Moses Our Master]), "faithful shepherd," founder of Judaism, and prophet of monotheism. Tradition attributes to him the authorship of the entire Torah and regards him as the fountainhead of the oral law. Eschatological speculation also ascribed to him a role in the future, messianic redemption.

• Martin Buber, *Moses: The Revelation and the Covenant* (New York, 1958). Umberto Cassuto, *A Commentary on the Book of Exodus*, translated by Israel Abrahams (Jerusalem, 1967). Brevard S. Childs, *The Book of Exodus: A Critical, Theological Commentary*, The Old Testament Library (Philadelphia, 1974). Solomon Goldman, *From Slavery to Freedom* (Philadelphia, 1949). Moshe Greenberg, *Understanding Exodus* (New York, 1969). André Neher, *Moses and the Vocation of the Jewish People* (New York, 1959). Nahum M. Sarna, *Exploring Exodus: The Heritage of Biblical Israel* (New York, 1986).

—SHALOM PAUL

MOSES, ASSUMPTION OF. See ASSUMPTION OF MOSES.

MOSES, BLESSING OF, the poetic blessing uttered by *Moses in bidding farewell to the children of Israel (*Dt.* 33). Moses viewed Israel's history from the perspective of later times, after the people had settled in the Promised Land. The core of the poem is the blessings of the individual tribes, in which Moses describes the lives of the tribes in their territories, focusing primarily on the resources and abundance they enjoy and their security and military prowess (*Dt.* 33. 6–25). Framing this core are an exordium and a coda (*Dt.* 33.2–5 and 26–29, respectively) that speak of the people as a whole, placing their security and prosperity in the broader context of God's benefactions to Israel. Moses' blessing has little in common with the rest of *Deuteronomy*, and critical scholars suggest that it was probably composed independently of *Deuteronomy*. Its psalmodic style indicates that it originally had a liturgical function and was perhaps recited at a festival at which all the tribes, or their representatives, gathered. From its language and content, it seems to have been composed sometime between Israel's settlement in the Promised Land, in approximately 1200 BCE, and the exile of the northern tribes in 721 BCE. It would have been incorporated into *Deuteronomy* because it was attributed to Moses and, by looking back on a successful conquest of the Promised Land, because it foretells the conquest. As one of the last two chapters in the Torah, the blessing is read in the synagogue on *Simḥat Torah.

• Umberto Cassuto, *Biblical and Oriental Studies*, translated by Israel Abrahams (Jerusalem, 1973), vol. 1, pp. 47–70. Frank Moore Cross and David Noel Freedman, *Studies in Ancient Yahwistic Poetry*, Society of Biblical Literature, Dissertation Series, no. 21 (Missoula, Mont., 1975), pp. 97–122. Otto Eissfeldt, *The Old Testament: An Introduction* (New York, 1965), pp. 227–231. Alexander Rofé, *Mavo' le-Sefer Devarim* (Jerusalem, 1988), vol. 1, chap. 20.

—JEFFREY H. TIGAY

MOSES, SEAT OF. In *Matthew* 23.2 Jesus refers to the scribes and Pharisees as "sitting in the seat of Moses"; a further reference to the seat of Moses is found in the *Pesiqta' de-Rav Kahana'* 12, quoted in the name of the fourth-century R. Aḥa'. Opinions differed as to the significance of the term—some scholars maintained that the reference was to a place of honor; others, that it was the stand on which the Torah scroll was placed during the service. Examples of seats designated for the most distinguished elder and placed close to the ark have been discovered in ancient synagogues in Dura-Europos, Hammath (near Tiberias), and Chorazin. A *bimah* referred to as "the seat of Moses" was found in the synagogue in K'ai-feng, China, and described as "a large elevated seat in the middle of the synagogue, from which the Torah is read every Sabbath day."

• Lee I. Levine, ed., *The Synagogue in Late Antiquity* (Philadelphia, 1987), pp. 12, 25.

—SHMUEL HIMELSTEIN

MOSES, SONG OF, poem in *Deuteronomy* 32.1–43, known in Hebrew as Ha'azinu (Give Ear) from its opening word. The poem describes the history of God's relations with Israel, emphasizing God's kindness and faithfulness, Israel's betrayal of him after settling in the Promised Land by worshiping other deities, and his decision to send an enemy to punish Israel but not to obliterate her, lest the enemy infer that its own gods, and not God (YHVH), gave it victory. The poem concludes by inviting listeners to celebrate God's deliverance of Israel and his punishment of the enemy. According to *Deuter-*

onomy 31.16–30, this poem was to be memorized by the people in order to serve as a "witness," warning Israel in advance and then attesting to God's justice and Israel's guilt when punishment came. Critical scholarship considers the poem post-Mosaic since it refers to the settlement in the Promised Land and Israel's apostasy as past events, is addressed to the guilty generation, and describes the ultimate punishment of the enemy as imminent. Language and content suggest that the poem was composed prior to the fall of the northern kingdom of Israel, in approximately 721 BCE, perhaps as early as the period of the judges (c.1200–1020) or shortly thereafter. It was probably composed after a particular invasion to offer an explanation and hope of deliverance. It could have been incorporated into *Deuteronomy* because it explained the disaster in theologically meaningful terms. In Second Temple times, the Levites read parts of the poem in the Temple while the additional sacrificial offering (*musaf*) was being made on the Sabbath. Nowadays, it is read on the Sabbath between Ro'sh ha-Shanah and Yom Kippur. In the Sephardi liturgy, it is recited during the morning service on 9 Av, the anniversary of the destruction of both Temples.

• Umberto Cassuto, *Biblical and Oriental Studies*, translated by Israel Abrahams (Jerusalem, 1973–1975), vol. 1, pp. 41–46, 95–100. Otto Eissfeldt, *The Old Testament: An Introduction* (New York, 1965), pp. 226ff. Yehezkel Kaufmann, *Toledot ha-'Emunah ha-Yisre'elit*, 4 vols. (Jerusalem, 1955), vol. 2, pp. 287–290. Alexander Rofé, *Mavo' le-Sefer Devarim* (Jerusalem, 1988), vol. 1, chap. 20. Jeffrey H. Tigay, *Deuteronomy*, The JPS Torah Commentary (Philadelphia, 1996), esp. excursuses 30–31.

—JEFFREY H. TIGAY

MOSES, SONS OF, legendary Jewish tribe, having their own independent kingdom in some faraway country. According to the ninth century traveler *Eldad ha-Dani, they lived beyond the river *Sambatyon. The legend of the sons of Moses is similar to that of the ten lost tribes (see TRIBES OF ISRAEL).

• Louis Ginzberg, *Legends of the Jews* (Philadelphia, 1946), vol. 4, pp. 317–318; vol. 6, pp. 407, 409.

MOSHAV ZEQENIM. See AGED.

MOSHEH BEN ḤANOKH (died c.965), Spanish rabbi. He was one of the four rabbis who, according to a famous story (see FOUR CAPTIVES), were captured by pirates in the Mediterranean and sold to foreign lands, where they spread rabbinic learning. Mosheh brought Talmudic knowledge to Spain, where he founded a *yeshivah*. Separating truth from legend, it appears that Mosheh reached Spain after 950 and established a *yeshivah* in Cordova. His authority was regarded as no less than that of the Babylonian ge'onim, and with his arrival the rabbis of Spain curtailed their dependence on the Babylonian academies. Many of Mosheh's *responsa* have survived. He was the father of *Ḥanokh ben Mosheh.

• Eliyahu Ashtor, *The Jews of Moslem Spain* (Philadelphia, 1992). Gerson D. Cohen, ed. and trans., *A Critical Edition with a Translation and Notes on The Book of Tradition (Sefer ha-Qabbalah)* (Philadelphia, 1967), pp. 64f., 200f.

MOSHEH BEN MAIMON. See MAIMONIDES, MOSES.

MOSHEH BEN NAḤMAN. See NAHMANIDES, MOSES.

MOSHEH BEN YAʿAQOV OF COUCY (13th cent.), codifier and preacher. He is best known for his code *Sefer Mitsvot Gadol*, popularly known by its acronym as *Semag*; arranged according to the 613 commandments, it presents the Jewish law applicable to each of them. Maimonides' *Mishneh Torah* served as the major source for the work, but Mosheh of Coucy added and gave precedence to his native French and German Jewish traditions. *Semag* achieved wide popularity and was one of the first Hebrew incunabula (it was published before 1480). As an itinerant preacher, Mosheh of Coucy traveled from France to Spain to urge Spanish Jewry to repent. Lax sexual morality in Spain and the abandonment of Torah study and daily ritual practices prompted his mission. In 1240 he participated in the Disputation of *Paris.

• Chaim Tchernowitz, *Toledot ha-Poseqim*, vol. 2 (New York, 1946–1947), pp. 87–92. Efraim E. Urbach, *Baʿalei ha-Tosafot* (Jerusalem, 1955), pp. 384–395.

—MICHAEL CHERNICK

MOSHEH BEN YEHOSHUʿA OF NARBONNE (died 1362), philosopher. He was born in Perpignan, where he was educated in Bible, rabbinic literature, medicine, and philosophy. In 1344 he moved to Spain and lived in several cities, dying in Soria. An accomplished physician and philosopher, he was the author of over twenty works, including a medical treatise (*Oraḥ Ḥayyim*) as well as numerous commentaries on Arabic and Jewish philosophy, most notably his commentary on Maimonides' *Moreh Nevukhim* (Vienna, 1852; repr. Jerusalem, 1961) and three works that detail his own opinions on the philosophic questions of his day: *Iggeret Shiʿur Qomah, Ma'amar ha-Beḥirah*, and *Pirqei Mosheh*. He knew Arabic and probably Latin as well. His writings combine philosophy, astrology, and Kabbalah.

• Alexander Altmann, "Moses Narboni's 'Epistle on Shi'ur Qoma,'" in *Jewish Medieval and Renaissance Studies* (Cambridge, Mass., 1967), pp. 225–288. Kalman P. Bland, ed. and trans., *The Epistle on the Possibility of Conjunction with the Active Intellect by Ibn Rushd with the Commentary of Moses Narboni* (New York, 1982). Maurice R. Hayoun, "L'Épître du libre arbitre de Moïse de Narbonne," in *Revue des études juives* 141 (1982): 139–167. Alfred L. Ivry, ed., *Ma'amar bi-Shelemut ha-Nefesh* (Jerusalem, 1977). Colette Sirat, *A History of Jewish Philosophy in the Middle Ages* (Cambridge, 1990), pp. 332–341, 444–445.

—STEVEN BALLABAN

MOSHEH BEN YOSEF HA-LEVI (fl. 13th cent.), philosopher. His principal work, *Ma'amar Elohi*, was originally written in Arabic in Seville. According to Neubauer (Catalogue of Hebrew Manuscripts in the Bodleian Library, no. 1324.5), he relied exclusively on Islamic philosophers such as al-Farabi and Averroës. He was well regarded by several Spanish-Jewish philosophers, including Yitsḥaq Abravanel, Ḥasda'i ben Avraham Crescas, and Yosef Albo, all of whom cite him. His treatise deals with the motion of the outermost sphere and the First Cause, which Mosheh contends is the active intellect. Three manuscripts of his work are known to exist, one of which is accompanied by a commentary that is often abusive of his opinions.

• Colette Sirat, *A History of Jewish Philosophy in the Middle Ages* (Cambridge, 1990), p. 266. Harry A. Wolfson, "Averroës' Lost Treatise on the Prime Mover," in *Studies in the History of Philosophy and Religion*, edited by Isadore Twersky and George H. Williams (Cambridge, Mass., 1973), vol. 1, pp. 402–429. —STEVEN BALLABAN

MOSHEH DE LEÓN (c.1240–1305), the leading kabbalist in Spain in the last decades of the thirteenth century and the principal author of the most important work of the *Kabbalah, the *Zohar. He was born in León, Castile, and spent many years in other communities in Castile, among them Guadalajara, Avila, Valladolid and Arevalo, where he died. During his travels he met adherents of the various kabbalistic schools of the time. He was familiar with the teachings of the Gerona school, Avraham ben Shemu'el Abulafia, and the Kohen brothers (see KABBALAH; YITSḤAQ BEN YAʿAQOV OF CASTILE). Some of the great kabbalists of the day were his personal friends, among them R. Yosef ben Avraham *Gikatilla, Yosef ben Todros *Abulafia, and Yitsḥaq ibn Sahulah. He was familiar with the teachings of Maimonides, and the *Guide of the Perplexed* was one of his sources of inspiration.

Mosheh de León wrote many kabbalistic treatises in Hebrew. The exact sequence of the writing of the Hebrew works, and their chronological and ideological relationship to the Zohar (which was written in Aramaic), has been presented in different ways by the modern scholars Gershom Scholem, Isaiah Tishby, and Alexander Altmann. According to Scholem, almost all the Hebrew works were written after the completion of the Zohar, which he dated to c.1291, and were intended to publicize the teachings of the Zohar. Tishby believed that Mosheh de León continued to write portions of the Zohar until his death and that the Hebrew works were written parallel to the Zohar. Altmann pointed out that there is evidence that some of the Hebrew works were written before the main part of the Zohar.

The most important of his Hebrew works are *Ha-Nefesh ha-Ḥakhamah*, concerning the nature of the soul; *Sefer ha-Rimmon*, a kabbalistic presentation of the reasons for the commandments; *Maskiyyot Kesef*, commentary on the prayers; *Sheqel ha-Qodesh*, on the **sefirot*; at least two commentaries on the ten *sefirot*; and collections of *responsa* on kabbalistic matters. All these works use terminology and ideas very close to those of the Zohar, and sometimes whole sentences and paragraphs seem to be Hebrew versions of passages in the Zohar.

Concerning the nature of his work, Mosheh de León insisted that the Zohar sections which he published were copied from an old manuscript which reached him from Erets Yisra'el; he offered to show this manuscript to R. Yitsḥaq ben Shemu'el of Acre, but he died before this could be done. His widow and daughter claimed that there was no such manuscript, and that Mosheh wrote "from his head." No evidence of the existence of a manuscript of the Zohar before Mosheh de León's has been found, and he should be regarded as an original, visionary and creative mystic.

• Gershom Gerhard Scholem, *Major Trends in Jewish Mysticism* (New York, 1954), chap. 5. Isaiah Tishby et al., eds., *The Wisdom of the Zohar*, vol. 1 (Oxford, 1989), pp. 1–92. —JOSEPH DAN

MOSHEH HA-DARSHAN (11th cent.), teacher and scholar of aggadic midrash; from Narbonne, France. He is quoted by Natan ben Yeḥi'el of Rome (who was his student) in his *ʿArukh* and by Rashi. Medieval Midrashic works based on Mosheh ha-Darshan's interpretations or those of his school include: *Genesis Rabbati, Numbers Rabbah* (Part 1, *Ba-Midbar* and *Naso'*), and *Midrash Aggadah* (edited by Solomon Buber [1894]). Steven Ballaban (Ph.D. dissertation, Hebrew Union College, 1995) suggests that he originally came from Nisibis in Persia, bringing to the West early traditions that were still circulating in the East.

• Abraham Grossman, *Ḥakhmei Tsarfat ha-Ri'shonim* (Jerusalem, 1995). Hananel Mack, "Midrash be-Midbar Rabbah," Ph.D. dissertation, The Hebrew University of Jerusalem, 1991. —MARC BREGMAN

MOSHEH ḤALFON HA-KOHEN (1874–1949), leading rabbinical authority in Djerba, an island off the coast of Tunisia with an ancient Jewish community. He served as rabbi and from 1935 to 1949 headed the Djerba *beit din*. He issued *responsa* on current questions and issued *taqqanot* for his community. Author of twenty-eight works, some published, some still in manuscript, he was particularly involved in educational programs, preparing curricula for rabbinical teachers, homiletic criteria, and a reader for Talmud study. He insisted on the comprehensive study of the Talmud and the *aggadah*.

• Abraham L. Udovitch and Lucette Valensi, *The Last Arab Jews: The Communities of Jerba, Tunisia* (Chur, Switzerland, and New York, 1984). —SHALOM BAR-ASHER

MOSHEH ḤAYYIM EFRAYIM OF SUDYLKOW (c.1748–1788), Hasidic author. Rabbi Efrayim, as he is called, was the elder son of Yisra'el ben Eliʿezer *Baʿal Shem Tov's daughter *Odel. Almost nothing is known of his life. He was rabbi of Sudylkow and is known for his book *Degel Maḥaneh Efrayim* (Korzec [Korets], 1810). Some have sought in this work a direct version of the Baʿal Shem Tov's teachings, that is, one relatively uninfluenced by either *Yaʿaqov Yosef ha-Kohen of Polonnoye or *Dov Ber of Mezhirech, but it is difficult to determine whether this is the case. Rabbi Efrayim devoted much attention to key themes of his grandfather's thought: the uplifting of sparks, the raising up of distracting thoughts, and the study of Torah for the sake of God. His book also contains important quotations from other early figures of Hasidism. A brief dream diary is appended to the work.

• Mattathias Y. Guttman, *Geza' Qodesh: Pe'ulotehem ve-Toratam shel Rabbi Efrayim mi-Sudilkov ve-Rabbi Barukh mi-Mezhibuh* (Tel Aviv, 1950). —ARTHUR GREEN

MOSHEH LEIB OF SASOV (1745–1807), Hasidic master. Although considered a disciple of *Dov Ber of Mezhirech and *Elimelekh of Lyzhansk, his principal teacher was Shemu'el Shmelke Horowitz of Nikolsburg, and his leading disciples were Menaḥem Mendel of

Kosov and Tsevi Hirsh of Zhidachov. He also had a profound influence on the young *Ya'aqov Yitsḥaq of Przysucha. Several collections of Moshe Leib's teachings were published posthumously and include both halakhic and Hasidic subjects. As a Hasidic teacher, his approach tended toward the early Hasidic extreme of viewing the material world as not ultimately real. Nevertheless, in many tales told concerning him, an active, compassionate approach toward relieving the sufferings of others predominates. His teachings appear in *Ḥiddushei ha-Ramal* (Brooklyn, N.Y., 1991).

• Martin Buber, *Tales of the Hasidim* (New York, 1946). Rivka Schatz Uffenheimer, *Hasidism as Mysticism* (Princeton, 1993).

—MILES KRASSEN

MOTHER (Heb. *em*; Aram. *imma'*). Although legally "the *father takes precedence over the mother in all matters" (*Ker*. 28a), both the Bible and Talmud insist with unvarying emphasis upon the equal rights of both *parents in the moral and ethical sphere. The Fifth Commandment, which enjoins the duty of honoring one's parents, mentions the father before the mother; in *Leviticus* 19.3, which enjoins fear (or reverence) for one's parents, the mother is mentioned before the father. This difference in phraseology forms the basis for the rabbinic statement that since God knows that the natural tendency of a child is to honor the mother more than the father and fear the father more than the mother, the order in each case is reversed in order to teach the duty of equal reverence and honor to both parents (*Qid*. 30b–31a). Similarly, the dire punishment for smiting or cursing parents specifically mentions both father and mother (*Ex*. 21.15–17). The four mothers, or *matriarchs (Sarah, Rebekah, Rachel, and Leah), rank equally in Jewish sentiment with the three patriarchs (Abraham, Isaac, and Jacob). In valid marriages the child is accorded the status of his father (for example, the son of a priest and an Israelite mother is a priest; the son of an Israelite father and the daughter of a priest is an Israelite [*Qid*. 3.12]), but with regard to mixed marriages, the child receives the status of the mother (the son of a non-Jewish father and a Jewish mother is considered Jewish). Only the woman bearing the child is regarded as the mother, since *adoption has no validity in Jewish law. The Talmud contains many stories of the extreme respect paid by the rabbis to their mothers; it is related of one rabbi that "when he heard his mother's footsteps, he used to remark, 'I stand up before the divine presence' " (*Qid*. 31b), and several medieval rabbis declared that their best teachers had been their mothers. Throughout Jewish history, the mother has symbolized home and *family life, which centered around her and which, to a great extent, was regarded as her responsibility. See also PATRILINEAL DESCENT; WOMEN.

• Eliezer Berkovits, *Jewish Women in Time and Torah* (Hoboken, N.J., 1990). Pieter Arie Hendrik de Boer, *Fatherhood and Motherhood in Israelite and Judean Piety* (Leiden, 1974). Mayer I. Gruber, *The Motherhood of God and Other Studies*, South Florida Studies in the History of Judaism, vol. 57 (Atlanta, 1992). Michael Kaufman, *The Woman in Jewish Law and Tradition* (Northvale, N.J., 1993).

MOTSA'EI SHABBAT. See HAVDALAH; SABBATH.

MOUNT OF OLIVES, mount east of Jerusalem and overlooking the city. The Kidron Valley separates it from the Temple mount. In Second Temple times, the *red heifer was burned on its crest (*Mid*. 2.6) and a bridge connected it to the Temple. It was regarded as holy by both Jews and Christians, based on the prophecy in *Zechariah* 14.3–4. On it was lit the first of the chain of beacons that brought the official confirmation of the sighting of the new moon to the Diaspora (see RO'SH ḤODESH; *R. ha-Sh*. 2.4). In the tenth century, the hill (or part of it) was in Jewish possession and was the site of pilgrimages and prayers. From the hill, the Jews could see into the Temple area, although they were not allowed access to it. On *Hosha'na' Rabbah, seven festive circuits were made round the Mount of Olives. By the Second Temple period, the Mount of Olives was a Jewish burial place; from the Middle Ages onward, it became a major Jewish cemetery. This was linked to the tradition that at the end of days the Messiah would appear on the Mount of Olives, and there Elijah would blow the trumpet heralding the resurrection of the dead; while all other bodies will have to roll from their burial place, those on the Mount of Olives would merely have to arise. Special *piyyutim* were composed for recitation upon ascending the Mount of Olives.

• Dan Bahat, *The Illustrated Atlas of Jerusalem* (New York, 1990).

MOUNT ZION. See ZION.

MOURNERS FOR ZION. See AVELEI TSIYYON.

MOURNING (Heb. *avelut*). Mourning rites are undertaken in times of both individual loss and national calamity (*Jos*. 7.6). The first mention of mourning in the Bible is that of Abraham weeping for his wife Sarah (*Gn*. 23.2). The injunction to Ezekiel after losing his wife bidding him to refrain from excessive lamentation, "you shall not mourn or weep nor shall your tears run down. Sigh, but not aloud; make no mourning for the dead. Bind on your turban, and put your shoes on your feet; do not cover your lips, nor eat the bread of mourners" (*Ez*. 24.16–17), is the basis for the rites of mourning. The Bible mentions many other such rites, some approvingly, such as rending one's garments (still symbolically observed), wearing sackcloth, and placing earth or ashes upon the head; and others negatively, such as cutting one's flesh or making oneself bald by tearing out one's hair. It was customary in Talmudic times to hire professional mourners to lament and wail (*Jer*. 9.16ff.). The Bible admonishes mourners against excessive grief, particularly that involving bodily affliction. Various periods for observing mourning are mentioned in the Bible, from thirty days (for Moses, *Dt*. 34.8) to seven (for Saul, *1 Sm*. 31.13). The Egyptians devoted seventy days of mourning to Jacob, who was also mourned for seven more days at the threshing floor of Atad (*Gn*. 50.3, 10).

Mourning rites are undertaken for immediate relatives, that is, one's father, mother, son, daughter, brother, sister, or spouse. These are the relatives on whose behalf a priest is obliged to defile himself in mourning (*Lv*. 21.2–3). The biblical obligation to mourn is derived from the remarks of Aaron (Maimonides on *Lv*. 10.3), but it extends only to the *onen*, that is, to the mourner on the day of death and burial of a relative (see ANINUT). Upon returning from the *burial, the first food is provided for the mourner by others (Seʿudat Havra'ah; see SEʿUDAH). The rabbis determined the period of mourning based on the different periods mentioned in the Bible, each suggesting a lesser degree of mourning: "Three days for weeping, seven days for eulogy, thirty days for pressing garments and haircutting" (*Moʿed Q*. 27b). The general rabbinic attitude toward mourning is reflected in the statement "it is forbidden to overstress mourning for the departed" (*Moʿed Q*. 27b), and the Talmud rules that "the law in matters pertaining to mourning is decided in accordance with the more lenient opinion" (*Moʿed Q*. 26b). See also SHELOSHIM; SHIVʿAH; YORTSAYT.

• Hayyim Halevy Donin, *To Be a Jew: A Guide to Jewish Observance in Contemporary Life* (New York, 1991). Hyman Goldin, *Hamadrikh: The Rabbi's Guide* (New York, 1956). Jules Harlow, ed., *Liqqutei Tefillah: A Rabbi's Manual* (New York, 1965). Judith Hauptman, "Death and Mourning: A Time for Weeping, a Time for Healing," in *Celebration and Renewal*, edited by Rela M. Geffen (Philadelphia, 1993), pp. 226–251. Isaac Klein, *A Guide to Jewish Religious Practice* (New York, 1992). Peter Knobel, "Rites of Passage," in *Judaism: A People and Its History*, edited by Robert Seltzer (New York, 1987). Maurice Lamm, *The Jewish Way in Death and Mourning* (New York, 1969). Simeon Maslin, ed., *Gates of Mitzvah: Shaarei Mitzvah, A Guide to the Jewish Life Cycle* (New York, 1979). David Polish, ed., *Magle Tsedek: Rabbi's Manual*, with notes by W. Gunther Plaut (New York, 1988). Tzvi Rabinowicz, *A Guide to Life* (London, 1964). Jack Riemer, ed., *Jewish Reflections on Death* (New York, 1976). Hayim Shoys, *The Lifetime of a Jew throughout the Ages of Jewish History* (Cincinnati, 1950).

—PETER KNOBEL

MOVABLE PROPERTY. Because of a debtor's inability to conceal land from a creditor, only land was considered suitable to stand as security for debt. Thus, the older sources classify immovable property as *nekhasim she-yesh lahem aḥarayut* (property that is a security), and movable property as *nekhasim she-'ein lahem aḥarayut* (property that is not a security). In time, a more general classification was adapted, which distinguished between *mitaltelim* (movables) and *qarqaʿ* (land). Movable property was further subclassified as either *kelim* (vessels; utensils, intended for repeated use) or *perot* (fruits; consumables).

Property that is physically movable but is on or under the surface of the ground in its natural state, such as rocks and minerals, is classified as land rather than as movable property. This classification applies also to fruits and vegetation, but there remains a difference of opinion as to when the attachment of produce to the soil may be deemed severed. One opinion is that its classification as land holds only so long as the produce has not yet ripened sufficiently to be fit for harvesting, while other authorities have ruled that all unharvested produce, so long as it remains physically attached to its source of growth, remains classified as land; the latter position is based on the principle *kol ha-meḥubbar le-qarqaʿ ke-qarqaʿ*, all that is connected to *qarqaʿ* is deemed *qarqaʿ*.

• Shalom Albeck, *Dinei ha-Mammonot ba-Talmud* (Tel Aviv, 1976), pp. 96–99, 110, 145, 166, 252, 257. Menachem Elon, ed., *The Principles of Jewish Law* (Jerusalem, 1975), pp. 197, 205, 215, 590. Asher Gulak, *Yesodei ha-Mishpat ha-ʿIvri*, vol. 1 (Tel Aviv, 1966), pp. 92–106. Isaac Herzog, *The Main Institutions of Jewish Law*, 2d ed. (London, 1965), vol. 1, pp. 77–117, 163–200, 225 273, 345–360.

—BEN TZION GREENBERGER

MUELHAUSEN, YOM TOV LIPMANN (15th cent.), Bohemian rabbi, philosopher, kabbalist, and theologian. Active in various communities including Erfurt and Kraków, he served as head of the rabbinical court in Prague. During his lifetime, that city became a center of the revival of interest in the philosophy of Maimonides, a revival sparked by the arrival of exiles from Provence in the wake of the persecutions of 1348 and 1349 and by the general intellectual ferment surrounding the Hussite rebellion in Bohemia. Muelhausen criticized those rabbis who ignored Maimonides' philosophical writings. He believed that philosophy deserved an honored place in rabbinic study and held the opinion that Maimonides was, in fact, a kabbalist who expressed his mystical ideas through philosophic rhetoric. A noted theological disputant, Muelhausen wrote *Sefer ha-Nitsaḥon* (Amsterdam, 1701), a work designed to offer its reader the tools to defend Jewish belief against the attacks of Christian critics. Among his halakhic writings is *Tiqqun Sefer Torah*, on the laws of the scribe and the Torah scroll.

• Judah Kaufman, *R. Yom Tov Lipmann Mihlhoizn* (New York, 1926). Israel Zinberg, *A History of Jewish Literature* (Philadelphia, 1972), vol. 3, pp. 148–150.

—MARK WASHOFSKY

MUḤAMMAD (570–632), founder of *Islam; he grew up in Mecca and was familiar with both Jews and Christians, by whose traditions and lore he was considerably influenced. At first Muḥammad had no intention of establishing a new religion. Considering himself the messenger and prophet of God (Allah) to the Arabs, he wished to convert his people to monotheism and to warn them of God's wrath on the Day of Judgment. He believed his revelations to be identical with those given by earlier prophets to Jews and Christians and was therefore disappointed when they rejected his claims. He consequently accused them of intentionally deleting predictions of his advent from the Bible. Rejected at first by his own people, he attempted to win the approval of the large Jewish community, especially that of Medina. In 622, after failing to gain the support of the Meccans, he made his famous flight (Hijrah) to Medina and proclaimed Islam as a new faith, leaning heavily on Judaism for its formulation. However, embittered by the refusal of the Jews to recognize him, he cruelly attacked several Jewish tribes, killing the men and enslaving the women and children in 625. Nevertheless, Muḥammad legislated that Jews, like Christians, should not be forced to embrace Islam, but like other "Peoples of the Book," they should be permitted to practice their religion while suffering certain ignominies. See also DHIMMI; QU'RAN.

• Karen Armstrong, *Muhammad: A Biography of the Prophet* (London, 1995). Muhammad Ibn Ishaq, *The Making of the Last Prophet: A Reconstruction of the Earliest Biography of Muhammad*, translation of part of *Sirat Rasul Allah*, by Gordon D. Newby (Columbia, S.C., 1989). Seyyed Hossein Nasr, *Muhammad, Man of God* (Chicago, 1995). F. E. Peters, *Muhammad and the Origins of Islam* (Albany, 1994).

MUKAMMIS, DAVID IBN MARWAN (9th–10th cent.), a Babylonian philosopher also known as David ha-Bavli. He was one of the first thinkers to introduce the philosophy of the Arab Kalam school into Jewish thought. His *ʿEsrim Peraqim* (translated into English by Sarah Stroumsa [Leiden, 1989]) deals primarily with proofs for the existence of God, clearly following the Kalam doctrine of divine attributes, which stresses their difference from human attributes. God's attributes are identical with his being and cannot affect his unity. Two of Mukammis's tractates are polemic attacks on Christianity for maintaining that God has form, a view inconsistent with pure monotheism; another tractate (now lost) argued against Islam. Mukammis, who wrote in Arabic, cites Greek and Arab authorities. Excerpts from *ʿEsrim Peraqim* were translated into Hebrew. They were quoted by Yehudah ben Barzillai al-Bargeloni in his commentary on *Sefer Yetsirah*. Mukammis is cited in works of medieval Jewish thinkers, including Baḥya ben Yosef ibn Paquda', Mosheh ibn Ezra, and Yaʿaqov ben Shelomoh Sarfati, as well as some Karaites. According to Yaqub Qirqisani, Mukammis translated a commentary on *Genesis* called *Book of Creation* and a commentary on *Ecclesiastes* from Christian sources, to whom he was close during part of his life.

• Sarah Stroumsa, ed. and trans., *Dawud ibn Marwan al-Muqammis' Twenty Chapters (Ishrun Maqala)* (Leiden, 1989), see introduction. Georges Vajda, "Le Problème de l'unité de Dieu d'après Dawud Ibn Marwan Al-Muqammis," in *Jewish Medieval and Renaissance Studies*, edited by Alexander Altmann (Cambridge, Mass., 1967), pp. 49–73.

—FRANCISCO MORENO CARVALHO

MUMAR (מוּמָר; apostate), one who has forsaken Judaism for a different faith (also called *meshummad*). At the behest of Christian censors, *mumar* has often been substituted for the original *meshummad* to be found in the rabbinic texts. See also APOSTASY.

MUQTSEH (מֻקְצֶה; set aside, excluded), objects that cannot be moved on Sabbaths and festivals. The Talmud enumerates twelve categories of *muqtseh*, including objects whose nature renders them unfit for use on the Sabbath (for example, tools or money, because of their connection with secular work); objects not normally used at all (for example, broken crockery or pebbles); *nolad*, that is, objects that were not in existence or were inaccessible at the commencement of the Sabbath (for example, a newly laid egg or fruit fallen from a tree on the Sabbath); and any object that at the commencement of the Sabbath served as a base for an object forbidden on the Sabbath (for example, a tray upon which the Friday night candles were placed). Although it is forbidden to move a *muqtseh* object directly, it may be moved indirectly; for example, broken crockery may be cleared away by the use of a broom.

• Yisroel Pinchos Bodner, *The Halachos of Muktza* (Lakewood, N.J., 1981).

MURDER. See HOMICIDE.

MUSAF (מוּסָף; Supplement), the name for the additional Temple sacrifice prescribed for Sabbath and festivals (see BURNT OFFERING); in the liturgy it is the name for the additional Sabbath and festival (Ro'sh Ḥodesh, the Shalosh Regalim, Ro'sh ha-Shanah, Yom Kippur) service. It is usually recited immediately after Shaḥarit and consists of the *ʿAmidah and various concluding prayers, including the *Qaddish. The Musaf ʿAmidah is first recited silently by the congregation and then repeated aloud by the reader. It contains only one intermediate benediction referring to the special significance of the day, and special mention is made of the Musaf sacrifices in the Temple. On Ro'sh ha-Shanah, the Musaf ʿAmidah contains three intermediate blessings: Malkuhyyot, Zikhronot, and Shofarot. Numerous and sometimes voluminous poetic embellishments (see PIYYUT) were written for the Musaf ʿAmidah, but the recent tendency has been to reduce or discard them. On Yom Kippur, the *ʿAvodah, a poetic description of the atonement service in the Temple, introduced by a detailed story of the creation of the world that demonstrates the cosmic dimension of the act of worship, is recited during the repetition of the Musaf ʿAmidah. On the first day of Pesaḥ a prayer for dew (*Tefillat Tal) is inserted into the Musaf ʿAmidah; on Shemini ʿAtseret a similar prayer for rain (*Tefillat Geshem) is inserted. In the Ashkenazi rite, the priests recite *Birkat ha-Kohanim (*Nm.* 6.22–24) before the repetition of the last blessing on festival days, whereas in Erets Yisra'el Birkat ha-Kohanim is said on all occasions when Musaf is recited. This emphasizes the way in which the Musaf service was designed to resemble the Temple service and its ideal of worship by offerings. The Musaf is subject to altered formulations or to omission in Reform congregations.

• Ismar Elbogen, *Jewish Liturgy: A Comprehensive History*, translated by Raymond P. Scheindlin (Philadelphia, 1993), pp. 91–128, 170–176. Abraham Millgram, *Jewish Worship* (Philadelphia, 1971). Jakob J. Petuchowski, *Prayerbook Reform in Europe: The Liturgy of European Liberal and Reform Judaism* (New York, 1968), pp. 240–264.

—PETER LENHARDT

MUSAR LITERATURE. See ETHICS; MUSAR MOVEMENT.

MUSAR MOVEMENT, nineteenth-century movement founded by R. Yisra'el *Salanter in Lithuania to promote the deliberate pursuit of piety (*musar* means ethics) in the spirit of *halakhah* among the masses. The movement has been viewed historically as the answer of *Mitnaggedim (opponents of Hasidism) to the various weaknesses in the social and religious fabric of Lithuanian Jewry (e.g., arid intellectualism and the gap between elitist Talmudic scholars and the masses) highlighted by the rise of Hasidism. It has also been understood as Salanter's attempt to fortify Jewish tradition in Lithuania from within, to aid it in withstanding the pervasive influence of the Haskalah (the Jewish Enlightenment movement).

Although the Musar movement never achieved the widespread popular appeal envisioned by Salanter, it did gain a foothold in the Lithuanian-style Talmudic academies, where it branched into several streams, each of which stressed some aspect of Salanter's teachings, thereby lending them new directions and interpretations. The most prominent schools are those of R. Simḥah Zissel of Kelme (1829–1898), R. Yosef Yozel Hurwitz of Novogrudok (1848–1890), and R. Natan Tsevi Finkel of Slobodka (1849–1927). Later representatives include R. Yosef Bloch (1859–1930) of the Tels Yeshivah and R. Eliyyahu Dessler (1892–1954) of the Gateshead Kolel in England, who later served as a *mashgiaḥ ruḥani* (spiritual guide) of the Ponevezh Yeshivah in Israel.

Initially the Musar movement encountered sharp opposition from some of the traditional *yeshivah* leadership, who felt that the new emphasis on conscious spiritual exercise detracted from the primacy of Torah learning as the supreme religious activity. But by the beginning of the twentieth century, Musar had become a prevailing trend in the Lithuanian *yeshivot*.

To this day many *yeshivah* students regard themselves as disciples of this or that variant of Musar and conduct their lives in accordance with its teachings. The vitality of the movement continues more indirectly in the very structure of contemporary Lithuanian-style *yeshivot*, in their more or less universal acceptance of periodic Musar sessions as an integral part of the curriculum and in the general practice of appointing a *mashgiaḥ ruḥani* as an indispensable member of the educational staff, whose task is to offer *siḥot Musar* (Musar talks) and to supervise the spiritual development of each student, as distinct from his intellectual growth. The development and significance attached to what has come to be known as *yeshivah* ideology (*yeshivishe hashkofah*), the set of beliefs and attitudes most conducive to ensuring normative behavior, can also be attributed to the influence of Musar teachings. In addition to the living influence of the Musar movement within the confines of the *yeshivot*, at least a hundred books have been produced since the original writings of Salanter, which are usually transcripts of the discourses of subsequent generations of Musar leaders who have built upon his teachings.

• I. Etkes, *Rabbi Israel Salanter and the Musar Movement: Seeking the Torah of Truth* (Philadelphia, 1993), contains extensive bibliographic resources. Dov Katz, *Tenu'at ha-Musar: Toledoteha, Ishehah ve-Shitoteha*, 6 vols. (Jerusalem and Tel Aviv, 1945–1974), the most comprehensive study of the movement to date. Mordechai Pachter, ed., *Kitvei Rav Yisra'el Salanter* (Jerusalem, 1972), introduction, pp. 7–71. Tamar Ross, "Ha-'Adam ve-Koakh Beḥirato ha-Musarit be-Maḥshevet ha-Rav Dessler," *Da'at* 12 (Winter 1984): 111–126. Tamar Ross, "Ha-Megamah ha-'Anti-ratsionalit bi-Tenu'at ha-Musar," *Alei Shefer: Meḥqarim be-Sifrut he-Hagut ha-Yehudit: Muggashim li-Khevod ha-Rav Dr. Aleksander Safran*, edited by Moshe Halamish (Ramat Gan, 1990), pp. 145–162. Tamar Ross, "Tenu'at ha-Musar ve-ha-Ba'yah ha-Hermenoytit be-Talmud Torah," *Tarbitz* 59 (1990): 191–214. J. J. Weinberg, in *Men of the Spirit*, edited by Leo Jung (New York, 1964), pp. 213–283.

—TAMAR ROSS

MUSIC. From the earliest recorded references, it is apparent that music has played an integral role in Jewish religious life. Temple and synagogue worship, home-based rituals and life-cycle celebrations of all Jewish communities have used music in styles and genres reflecting the variety of cultures into which Jews have come in contact. The biblical identification of Jubal as "father of those who handle the harp and the pipe" (*Gn.* 4.21) provides the first clue that music was to play an important role in Jewish life. Biblical figures including Moses (Song of Moses, *Ex.* 15.1–18) and Deborah (*Jgs.* 5.2–31) express their gratitude for divine help through song; other biblical references note the use of music in celebrating military victory (e.g., *Jgs.* 11; *1 Sm.* 18.6). *Psalms* extols God for a variety of blessings bestowed on the Israelite nation, and Psalm 150 exhorts "everything that has breath" to praise God using all manner of musical instruments. The first regular use of music in national religious life appears in the context of the *Temple in Jerusalem.

King David appointed the *Levites to preside over elaborate musical ceremonies surrounding the placement of the Ark of the Covenant in Jerusalem (*1 Chr.* 15.16–25). Later, when the Jerusalem Temple became the center of Israel's spiritual life, sacrificial rites were accompanied by the choral chanting of antiphonal and responsorial psalms and other passages, and a Temple orchestra of harps and lyres. (By the time of the Second Temple, a water-powered organ, trumpets, and flutes had been added). A minimum of twelve singers and twelve stringed instruments accompanied daily rites, while seemingly unlimited numbers of musicians enhanced the ritual on festive occasions; some four thousand singers and one hundred twenty trumpeters presided at the Temple's dedication (*2 Chr.* 5.12–13).

Following the destruction of the Second Temple in 70 CE, the rabbis imposed a national state of mourning, proscribing the use of instruments and attempting to forbid vocal music as well. Unable to enforce fully the latter ban, the rabbis did nevertheless successfully curtail Jewish musical expression: only perfunctory chants were permitted to accompany synagogue rites, and fully joyous musical displays were allowed only for weddings and for the dedication of synagogues and Torah scrolls.

Despite these limitations, evolving synagogue rites invited the creation of certain musical forms. The application of particular modes and patterned motives came to be known as **nussaḥ*, which, together with the public chanting of specified biblical books (cantillation; see ACCENTS; CANTORIAL MUSIC), defined the musical parameters of Jewish worship. At the same time, the aftermath of the Temple's destruction saw the dispersion of the Jewish people throughout the nations, and this brought Jewish ritual practice into contact with a vast repertoire of musical influences. As each community borrowed both consciously and subconsciously from its surrounding culture, Jewish music took on increasing diversity. The one unified musical tradition of the Jerusalem Temple yielded to hundreds of local variants.

Over time, three overarching ethnic traditions emerged within the Diaspora. Those Jews who remained in the Middle East experienced the least challenge to their existing customs. Surrounded by a similarly inclined Muslim community, the 'Adot ha-Mizraḥ exploited the improvisational possibilities of melodies influenced by Arabic *maqamot* (rhymed prose). The musical repertoire of the 'Adot ha-Mizraḥ focused on liturgical song and the chanting of quasi-liturgical poetry, and, honoring the prohibition against the use of instruments, they developed elaborate rhythmic accompaniments to Sabbath songs and life-cycle ceremonies.

Jews who made their way to the Iberian Peninsula brought with them the traditions of the Middle East, but those came under Western influence with the flowering of secular culture in Europe. The Spanish *romancero* dominated musical life and entered the repertoire of Sabbath table songs and synagogue chants, even over rabbinic objection. The expulsion of the Jews from Spain in 1492 saw a bifurcation of Sephardi musical traditions. Those whose exile took a more southern route (into the Balkan and Mediterranean countries) maintained the Eastern flavors of their forebears, favoring melismatic melodies over harmonic invention. Others, whose paths took them to Amsterdam and from there to England and South America, perpetuated a less ornate ritual tradition; their hymns and liturgical tunes combined the flowing melodies of their Eastern roots with the Western penchant for regular metrical patterns and harmonic accompaniment.

The first challenge to the notion that Jewish religious music must necessarily be limited to simple chants came from the Italian composer Salamone *Rossi in the early seventeenth century. A court musician, Rossi was eager to exalt his God with all the musical expertise at his disposal. His friend R. Leone *Modena, himself an amateur musician, issued a *responsum* in 1605 that permitted unaccompanied choral singing in the synagogue, and Rossi later published thirty-three settings of liturgical texts for combinations of three to eight voices. By the end of the seventeenth century, vocal and instrumental works by both Jewish and gentile composers were accepted ingredients in the celebration of synagogue dedications, the founding of fraternal societies, and the observance of special Sabbaths and festivals in Sephardi communities in Italy, France, and Amsterdam. In some cases, the regular performance of such works resulted in their assimilation into the popular liturgy, albeit in folklore form.

Between the eleventh and fifteenth centuries, the musical motives and styles of German plainsong provided the inspiration for Ashkenazi *nussaḥ* and for the **mi-Sinai* melodies that became an integral part of the musical culture of Jewish communities from central and eastern Europe. While many of these new traditions emulated the Western penchant for metrical melodies built of disjunct intervals, the hazzanic recitative and at least some of the newly popular melodies of these Ashkenazi communities retained the ornate, melismatic singing of the East. From the sixteenth to the eighteenth century, itinerant *ḥazzanim* carried this music throughout the region, often with boy sopranos and bass accompanists in tow, giving concerts and making themselves available to officiate at services on festivals and special Sabbaths. In eastern Europe, Ḥasidim stressed the role of music in prayer and other religious contexts. Many hasidic leaders created *niggunim* (see NIGGUN) for their followers to sing.

In the aftermath of political emancipation and the Enlightenment in the late eighteenth and early nineteenth centuries, French and German Jews were exposed to a variety of new musical forms. Bach, Mozart, and Beethoven provided new cultural standards, and the seemingly backward Eastern nuances of monophonic synagogue song (and the inability of Western music to accommodate them for harmonic purposes) were driven entirely from the musical vocabulary of new Reform congregations. Having declared most of rabbinic law irrelevant to modern times, the path was paved for *cantors in modern temples to produce their own music, complete with the accompaniment of *organs. Many cantors were musically untrained. Salomon *Sulzer (1804–1890) provided the direction that Reform music needed. A talented musician with a traditional religious background, Sulzer served as cantor in the Stadttempel of Vienna from 1826; his *Shir Tsiyyon* (published in 1840 and 1866) contained musical settings for every text of the liturgical year, which were eagerly adopted by contemporary cantors. Compositions by Sulzer and his student, Louis *Lewandowski, a choral conductor from Berlin, retain a significant role in Ashkenazi services to the present.

While not adopting the liberal reforms of their German coreligionists, composers from eastern Europe also began writing works for (male) choirs featuring virtuosic hazzanic performances. The turn of the century marked the golden age of *ḥazzanut*, in which gifted cantor-composers performed their own works, popularizing cantorial music outside the synagogue as well as within it. The wave of east European immigrants to North American shores in the period from 1880 to 1920 brought this new tradition with it, providing an alternative to the music of Reform and even gentile composers that had predominated in America since the German immigration of the mid-nineteenth century. Josef *Rosenblatt, Gershon Sirota, and the Kussevitsky brothers were among the many whose concertizing on both sides of the Atlantic brought renown to themselves and new opportunities for the music of their tradition.

The American synagogue underwent profound changes in the period following World War II. As the numbers of Orthodox congregations dwindled, the musical styles of the Reform and the Conservative movements gained prominence. Worshipers eager for a more active role in the prayer experience encouraged the creation of singable congregational melodies, and the somewhat exclusive role of the cantor and choir was diminished. This trend accelerated in the aftermath of the Six-Day War in 1967, with a strong identification with the music of Israel, in particular, and various new forms of Jewish music in general. The coincident attempt to attract younger worshipers to synagogues saw the emulation of jazz, folk, and rock genres in new liturgical settings. The newly accepted voice of Jewish women as cantors and composers has also brought new dimensions to ancient views of music and spirituality.

• A. W. Binder, "Jewish Music: An Encyclopedic Survey," in *Studies in Jewish Music: Collected Writings of A. W. Binder*, edited by Irene Heskes (New York, 1971). Irene Heskes, *Passport to Jewish Music: Its History, Traditions, and Culture* (Westport, Conn., 1994). Abraham Zebi Idelsohn, *Jewish Music in Its Historical Development* (New York, 1929; repr. New York, 1967; Westport, Conn., 1981). Joseph A. Levine, *Synagogue Song in America* (Crown Point, Ind., 1989). Macy Nulman, *The Concise Encyclopedia of Jewish Music* (New York, 1975). Aron Marko Rothmuller, *The Music of the Jews: An Historical Perspective*, rev. ed. (Cranbury, N.J., 1967). Alfred Sendrey, *Music in Ancient Israel* (New York, 1969). Amnon Shiloah, *Jewish Musical Traditions* (Detroit, 1992). Eric Werner, "Jewish Music, Liturgical," in *The New Grove Dictionary of Music and Musicians*, edited by Stanley Sadie (New York, 1980), vol. 9, pp. 614–634. Eric Werner, *A Voice Still Heard: The Sacred Songs of the Ashkenazic Jews* (University Park, Pa., 1976). Eric Werner, *The Sacred Bridge: The Interdependence of Liturgy and Music in Synagogue and Church during the First Millennium* (New York, 1959; repr. New York, 1984).

—MARSHA BRYAN EDELMAN

MUSIC, CANTORIAL. See CANTORIAL MUSIC.

MYRTLE. See FOUR SPECIES.

MYSTICISM (from Gr. *muein* [close]), originally, in religious terminology, secret teachings or rituals which the initiated (*mystes*) was not allowed to divulge to others. The term is now generally taken to refer to the inner, more intense and spiritual dimension of religious life on the intellectual (e.g., knowledge of God) or experiential (e.g., union or communion with God) level. Mystical traditions can be found, in varying degrees and in a variety of forms, in most of the known religious traditions. Traditional Hebrew has no equivalent term rendering this specific sense. Some of the experiences recounted by the prophets, in *Psalms*, and in later literature are sometimes described as "mystical," but this obscures a decisive difference between mysticism and biblical prophecy: the latter was never sought for its own sake. The prophets were, often against their will, recipients of a message from God which they had to transmit to the people. Some prophets received the message by means of visions. The non-prophetic type of visionary experience or revelation seems to have developed in the Second Temple period (see APOCALYPSE; APOCRYPHA AND PSEUDEPIGRAPHA; ENOCH; EZRA.) The Mishnah (*Ḥag.* 2.1) mentions two esoteric disciplines, *Maʿaseh Merkavah and *Maʿaseh Be-Re'shit (see HEIKHALOT). The medieval terms *torat ha-sod* or *torat ha-nistar*, that is, secret, hidden, and "esoteric" lore that must not be divulged, seem to be closer to the original meaning of the Greek word. Whether the cosmogonic speculations and teachings of the **Sefer Yetsirah* should be considered as mystical is an open question, but there is no doubt that the book greatly influenced later mystical literature. Many mystical systems aspire to the total union of the soul with, and its absorption in, the Godhead as the highest goal. It has been argued that God's utter transcendence was so basic a tenet of Judaism that it inhibited on both the theoretical and the experiential level the more extreme forms of mystical union. **Devequt* therefore meant close adherence to and communion with God. While this observation seems correct as a general characterization, there is evidence of contemplatives and mystics experiencing more radical forms of ecstasy and mystical union. The extant accounts of mystical experiences cover a wide gamut, ranging from the Maʿaseh Merkavah–type of awe and trembling at the vision of the divine glory to the illuminations and light-experiences of the so-called ecstatic and prophetic Kabbalah associated with Avraham *Abulafia.

Forms of spiritual life that were neither ecstatic nor visionary but rather ascetic and contemplative were influenced, especially in Muslim Spain, by *Sufism, with *Baḥya ben Yosef ibn Paquda' being the most influential representative of this trend. A different type of theological speculation, devotional life, and mystical piety developed in Germany and western Europe, in the twelfth century (see ḤASIDEI ASHKENAZ). R. *Yehudah ben Shemu'el he-Ḥasid and R. *Elʿazar ben Yehudah of Worms taught an other-worldly asceticism, humility, and equanimity in the face of worldly joys and trials, and the importance of mystical *kavvanot* (devotions, intentions) accompanying prayer. Their theological speculations centered on the divine light of the "Created Glory" and the mystery of the *cherubim as the manifestations of the otherwise utterly hidden and transcendent *God.

A new spiritual movement, the origins of which are still obscure, emerged in the twelfth century in rabbinic–pietistic circles in the Languedoc area of Provence (southern France), where its first major text, the **Sefer ha-Bahir*, made its appearance. From there it passed to northern Spain, where its further evolution culminated in the *Zohar. This particular theosophical system was subsequently called *Kabbalah. Opposed at first as a near-heretical innovation by Talmudic orthodoxy, it nevertheless succeeded in gradually dominating all forms of mystical speculation and practice, and as a result the term, which strictly speaking applies to only one phase of medieval Jewish spirituality, erroneously came to be used as synonymous with Jewish mysticism in general. In the sixteenth century, that is, after the expulsion from Spain and probably not unrelated to that traumatic event, Yitsḥaq *Luria developed a novel form of Kabbalah which, unlike most forms of mysticism which are supratemporal and hence ahistorical, gave the process of creation and history a mystical interpretation with a powerful messianic charge. The seventeenth century messianic movement unleashed by *Shabbetai Tsevi had Lurianic Kabbalah as its background. Lurianic concepts and terminology also permeate *Hasidism, the novel form of eighteenth century mystical revival in eastern Europe initiated by Yisra'el ben Eliʿezer *Baʿal Shem Tov. The mystical theology of R. Avraham Kook (see KOOK FAMILY) also bears the imprint of the kabbalistic heritage.

• Dan Cohn-Sherbok, ed., *Jewish Mysticism: An Anthology* (Oxford, 1995). Joseph Dan, *The Ancient Jewish Mysticism* (Tel Aviv, 1993). Joseph Dan, *Jewish Mysticism and Jewish Ethics*, 2d ed. (Northvale, N.J., 1996). Gershom Gerhard Scholem, *Major Trends in Jewish Mysticism* (New York, 1954), pp. 1–39. Margaret Smith, *Studies in Early Mysticism in the Near and Middle East* (Oxford, 1995).

N

NAHAWENDI, BINYAMIN. See BINYAMIN BEN MOSHEH NAHAWENDI.

NAḤEM (נַחֵם; Comfort), prayer instituted in amoraic times and recited in the afternoon service ʿAmidah on Tishʿah be-'Av asking for comfort for those who mourn Zion and for the rebuilding of the city. The original version appears in the Talmud Yerushalmi (Y., *Ber.* 4.1) and underwent various changes in geonic and later prayer books. Yosef *Karo suggested that it is recited at the afternoon service to correspond to the time of the actual destruction of the Temple.

• Macy Nulman, *The Encyclopedia of Jewish Prayer* (Northvale, N.J., and London, 1993), p. 254.

NAḤMAN BAR YAʿAQOV (3d–4th cent.), Babylonian amora'. Born in Nehardea, his father was the scribe of R. Shemu'el. His primary teacher was R. Abba' ben Avuha. He married Yalta', the daughter of R. Abbahu, the exilarch. Known as one of "the pious ones of Babylonia," he is mentioned countless times in the Talmud Bavli and frequently in the Talmud Yerushalmi. As a highly regarded *dayyan* (R. Huna' considered him Shemu'el's equal in civil matters), his opinions in legal disputes were viewed as authoritative by sages in subsequent generations (*Ket.* 13a). He regarded himself as an expert in judgment, whose opinion could outweigh that of the majority (*San.* 5a), but he was respected for answering questions honestly with, "I don't know" (*Shab.* 66a; cf. also *ʿEruv.* 16b).

• Wilhelm Bacher, *Die Agada der babylonischen Amoräer* (1913; Hildesheim, 1967). Aaron Hyman, *Toledot Tanna'im ve-'Amora'im* (1910; Jerusalem, 1987). Jacob Neusner, *A History of the Jews in Babylonia* (Leiden, 1969).
—MICHAEL L. BROWN

NAḤMAN BEN YITSḤAQ (died 356), Babylonian amora'. He is sometimes mistaken in the sources (in particular, the Talmud Yerushalmi) for his contemporary R. Naḥman bar Yaʿaqov, since both are often referred to without patronymic. His teachers included his uncle, R. Aḥa' ben Yosef, and R. Ḥiyya' ben Avin. Referred to as one of the masters of the Masorah (e.g., *Yoma'* 38b), he is mentioned frequently in the Talmud in halakhic matters; he taught that "a legal ruling should be as clear as a day when the north wind blows" (*ʿEruv.* 65a). He served as the principal lecturer at the semiannual **kallah* month sessions in the academy of Rava' in Maḥoza and was the head of the academy in Pumbedita from 352 to 356 (according to the *Iggeret Rav Sherira' Ga'on*). The Talmud records that his mother, having been warned by astrologers that her son would be a thief, determined that his head would always be covered "so that the fear of Heaven may be upon you" (*Shab.* 156b). This account was later used in the argument for covering the head. He taught that a transgression performed with good intentions was better than a precept performed with evil intentions (*Naz.* 23b) and that where there is rejoicing, there must also be reverence (lit., trembling; cf. *Ber.* 30b to *Ps.* 2.11).

• Wilhelm Bacher, *Die Agada der babylonischen Amoräer* (1913; Hildesheim, 1967). Aaron Hyman, *Toledot Tanna'im ve-'Amora'im* (1910; Jerusalem, 1987).
—MICHAEL L. BROWN

NAHMANIDES, MOSES (1194–1270), biblical exegete, kabbalist, halakhist, poet, and physician; also known as Mosheh ben Naḥman, Naḥmani, Ramban, and Bonastrug da Porta. Nahmanides was an intellectual and communal leader of the Jewish community in Catalonia during a crucial period of change. His writings reflect a major synthesis of the two most significant schools of thought: the dialectical tradition of northern French Jewry and the analytic-praxis orientation of Andalusian Jewry.

The broad scope of Nahmanides' learning enabled him to work for peace and stability within communities which were torn by conflicting ideas, originating both from within the Jewish world and from the larger Christian society. In 1232 he attempted to resolve a conflict over the use of the writings of Maimonides (see MAIMONIDEAN CONTROVERSY). He attempted to influence the rabbis of northern France not to enforce a ban, declared by rabbis in southern France, on the study of the writings of Maimonides and other philosophy. He suggested a program of studies that would regulate the study of philosophy, by restricting the age when students could begin to engage in philosophical studies. Because of the heightened emotions on the part of rabbis in southern France and Spain, Nahmanides was unsuccessful in preventing the bans.

Between 1263 and 1265, Nahmanides as the representative of Catalonian Jewry, was called upon by King James I (1213–1267) with regard to the attempts by the mendicant orders to establish their campaign to evangelize the Jewish communities by preaching in synagogues. King James invited Nahmanides to defend the Talmud against the accusations of Pablo Christiani, a Dominican friar, who sought to demonstrate that passages in rabbinic literature revealed Christian truth (see BARCELONA, DISPUTATION OF). Afterwards Nahmanides summarized his view of the issues raised in the debate, in his book *Sefer ha-Vikkuaḥ*. In this book, he defended his proposition that although the legal portions of the Talmud were obligatory upon all Jews, the speculative views of the *aggadah* were not. The stories and explanations contained in the *aggadah* provided useful teachings, but no Jew was obliged to believe them. By April 1265, the Dominicans requested Pope Clement IV to ask the king to punish Nahmanides for the views expressed in *Sefer ha-Vikkuaḥ*. With the help of the king, Nahmanides left Spain for Erets Yisra'el. After his arrival there in 1267, Nahmanides proceeded to Jerusalem, where he found the community in ruins. His letter to his son Naḥman elaborates on his sorrow at the sad state of the Jews in Jerusalem, and on his efforts to acquire property for a synagogue, set up a *yeshivah*, and organize the community. One year later Nahmanides moved to Acre, where he succeeded R. Yeḥi'el ben Yosef of Paris as head of the community.

Nahmanides' literary productivity was prolific. More than fifty authentic works of his are extant. The majority are in genres which relate to Talmudic and legal literature. In the genre of *Bible exegesis, Nahmanides wrote commentaries on the Pentateuch, on the messianic passages in *Daniel* (called *Sefer ha-Ge'ullah*), and on the *Book of Job*. His Pentateuch commentary, which received its final form after he moved to Erets Yisra'el, reveals respect for the writings of Rashi and Avraham ibn Ezra, but moves beyond their interests in linguistic matters and the synthesis of classical rabbinic literature with the text of scripture. In Nahmanides' commentary, both the plain meaning of the text and the deepest meaning of its laws and narratives—its mystical dimension—are explicated. The description of the creation of the world in the early chapters of *Genesis* reveals the six ages of world history and the future day of the Lord, and the sequence of the Pentateuchal narratives reveals the meaning of Israel's existence. He opposed Maimonides' attempt to provide rational explanations of miracles wholly within the natural order. Miracles are manifest proof of the reality of God's action within creation. The Pentateuch commentary is the primary source for Nahmanides' kabbalistic thinking. Despite his insistence on Kabbalah as esoteric knowledge, which ought to be confined only to a few initiates, his commentary was the first to reveal theosophic doctrines by explication of Talmudic *aggadah*.

Nahmanides' concern with theodicy, on the level both of the individual and of the people of Israel, is expressed in the commentary on *Job* and the *Sefer ha-Ge'ullah*. The suffering of the individual may be explained, according to the Job commentary, by the doctrine of transmigration of the soul (*gilgul nefashot*). Israel's suffering in exile among the nations of the world will ultimately be rectified through the coming of the Messiah. In *Sefer ha-Ge'ullah*, Nahmanides provided a sustained commentary on the messianic passages in *Daniel*, and arrived at a date for the arrival of redemption.

Nahmanides' extensive halakhic writings reveal his mastery both of the Talmudic text and of the history of post-Talmudic dialectical and juridical traditions. In his *novellae* (*ḥiddushim*) on the three most frequently studied orders of the Mishnah—Mo'ed, Nashim, and Neziqin—he utilized the sources of the Spanish community, in combination with the dialectical methods of the northern French tosafists. He also incorporated the teachings of the halakhists of Provence. Nahmanides also wrote works of criticism in which he defended earlier legal authorities against later views. Some of his monographs codified significant areas of Jewish law: *Dinei de-Garmei*, on the laws regarding disturbances to neighbors; *Mishpetei ha-Ḥerem*, on the application of, and release from, the ban administered by the community; and *Torat ha-'Adam*, on the laws relating to illness and death.

• Robert Chazan, *Barcelona and Beyond: The Disputation of 1263 and Its Aftermath* (Berkeley, 1992). Marvin Fox, "Nachmanides on the Status of Aggadot: Perspectives on the Disputation at Barcelona, 1263," *Journal of Jewish Studies* 40 (1989): 95–109. Amos Funkenstein, "Nahmanides' Symbolical Reading of History," in *Studies in Jewish Mysticism*, edited by Joseph Dan and Frank Talmage (Cambridge, Mass., 1982), pp. 129–150. Isadore Twersky, ed., *Rabbi Moses Nahmanides (Ramban): Explorations in His Religious and Literary Virtuosity* (Cambridge, Mass., 1983). Elliot R. Wolfson, "By Way of Truth: Aspects of Naḥmanides' Kabbalistic Hermeneutic," *AJS Review* 14 (1989): 103–178.

—MICHAEL A. SIGNER

NAḤMAN OF BRATSLAV (1772–1810), Hasidic master. One of the most enigmatic figures in the history of Hasidism, R. Naḥman has long been viewed with suspicion by Ḥasidim outside the Bratslav camp, while he has been the subject of intense fascination for moderns attracted to the Hasidic world. A great-grandson of Yisra'el ben Eli'ezer *Ba'al Shem Tov, Naḥman grew up during the period when his uncle *Barukh of Medzhibozh was working to create the first Hasidic dynasty. Since R. Baruch had no sons, Naḥman would have been the natural dynastic heir to the Ba'al Shem Tov's mantle. But even in his youth the deeply introspective Naḥman felt that he would not be fit to lead others until he had become a perfect **tsaddiq*. This required constant struggle against the dark forces of temptation, doubt, and depression that ever sought to overwhelm him. He also came to see the Hasidism of his uncle's court as superficial and inauthentic. It was only after a dramatic and transforming journey to Erets Yisra'el between 1798 and 1799 that Naḥman felt prepared to accept disciples, of whom he required an unusually high degree of intense mortification, self-examination, and loyalty to himself as master. There was a deep communion of soul between Naḥman and his disciples that formed the very essence of Bratslav Hasidism. Binding themselves to their master, they gained the ability through him to overcome the obstacles that stood before them. In his more elated moments, Naḥman came to see himself as the *tsaddiq ha-dor*, the unique figure within his generation who could solve the world's ills. Naḥman's Ḥasidim, unlike others, refused to crown another master upon his death from tuberculosis at the age of thirty-eight (he did have a son in 1806). They remain forever his personal disciples; it is he and he alone who can help them in their constant struggles for perfection. Signs posted in Bratslav prayer rooms still ask that prayers recited there be bound especially to the soul of this singular master. Naḥman insisted that his disciples engage in daily *hitbodedut* (a state of being alone), which in his case meant an hour-long conversation with God in which the Ḥasid, speaking aloud and in his native language, would "break his heart" before God. Naḥman's teachings are collected in *Liqqutei Moharan* (Ostròg, 1809; Mogilev, 1811). Naḥman is the first (and perhaps the only) Hasidic master to make room for doubt and questioning, even of the most basic sort, within the religious life. Naḥman is the author of the fantastic *Sippurei Ma'asiyot* (Ostróg, 1816), a collection of thirteen stories that sought to create in their hearers a new sort of sacred imagination. His stories have been hailed as classics of Jewish literature. Along with his teachings, these are still studied and venerated by Bratslav Ḥasidim, today centered in Jerusalem. Rabbi Naḥman's grave in Uman, Ukraine, has again become a pilgrimage site, especially on Ro'sh ha-Shanah.

• Arthur Green, *Tormented Master: A Life of Rabbi Naḥman of Bratslav* (New York, 1979). Mendel Piekarz, *Ḥasidut Braslav* (Jerusalem, 1972). Joseph G. Weiss, *Meḥqarim be-Ḥasidut Braslav* (Jerusalem, 1974).

—ARTHUR GREEN

NAḤOTEI (Aram.; נָחוֹתֵי; those who descend), sages who traveled from Erets Yisra'el to Babylonia, that is, sages who descended from the Holy Land to a place of lesser spiritual status. Their travels may have been for business reasons or for the purpose of studying with Babylonia's rabbinic scholars. Babylonian scholars who went to Erets Yisra'el to study the teachings and traditions of its academies, and who then reported them back to Babylonia, are also called *naḥotei*. They are primarily significant for their transmission of amoraic traditions between the two main centers of the Talmudic period and are credited with maintaining a living connection between the rabbinic circles of Erets Yisra'el and those of Babylonia. The *naḥotei* were active in the third and fourth centuries CE, and the best-known *naḥotei* include ʿUlla, Dimi, and Ravin.

• Nosson Dovid Rabinowich, ed. and trans., *The Iggeres of Rav Sherira Gaon* (Jerusalem, 1988). Adin Steinsaltz, *The Essential Talmud* (New York, 1976).

—MICHAEL CHERNICK

NAHUM (Heb. Naḥum; 7th cent. BCE), prophet in the kingdom of Judah. The superscription of the *Book of Nahum* identifies him as an "Elkoshite" (1.1), although the location of this place is unknown. The seventh book of the Minor Prophets, *Nahum* emphasizes God's action in history by describing the fall of Nineveh, the capital of Assyria, in 612 BCE, as a divine act. The book is divided into two parts: God's holiness and judgment against Assyria (vv. 2–10 contain in Hebrew a partially preserved alphabetical acrostic) and consolatory promises of protection to Judah (1.2–15); and a long vivid description of the downfall, sacking of, and curse upon Nineveh, which ends with a song taunting the doomed city (chaps. 2–3). Similar to the tradition preserved by the Greek historians Diodorus and Xenophon, *Nahum* 2.7 assumes that a flood (of the Tigris) was a major factor in the fall of the city. A *pesher or commentary on the *Book of Nahum* was found among the Dead Sea Scrolls. In addition, *Nahum* is represented in the Hebrew Minor Prophets scroll from Wadi Murabbaʿat and the Greek Minor Prophets scroll from Naḥal Ḥever in the Judean desert.

• Kevin J. Cathcart, *Nahum in the Light of Northwest Semitic*, Biblica et Orientalia, no. 26 (Rome, 1973). Richard J. Coggins, *Israel among the Nations: A Commentary on the Books of Nahum and Obadiah*, International Theological Commentary (Grand Rapids, 1985). Alfred Ossian Haldar, *Studies in the Book of Nahum*, Uppsala universitets arsskrift, 1946:7 (Uppsala, 1947). J.J.M. Roberts, *Nahum, Habakkuk, Zephaniah: A Commentary*, Old Testament Library (Louisville, Ky.,1991). Marvin A. Sweeney, "Concerning the Structure and Generic Character of the Book of Nahum," *Zeitschrift für die alttestamentliche Wissenschaft* 104 (1992): 364–377.

—MARVIN A. SWEENEY

NAḤUM OF CHERNOBYL (c.1730–1797), Hasidic author. He was a disciple of *Dov Ber of Mezhirech and progenitor of the Twersky dynasty (see TWERSKY FAMILY). He lived a life of simplicity and poverty, traveling to preach in towns in the northern and western Ukraine. His teachings are collected in *Me'or ʿEinayim* (1798), considered one of the classics of Hasidic literature. Though a disciple of Dov Ber, many of Naḥum's homilies reflect the somewhat simpler mysticism of Yisra'el ben Eliʿezer *Baʿal Shem Tov. The presence of God everywhere and at all times and the human obligation to serve God in every way, both through the commandments and beyond them, are the key themes of Naḥum's work. There is also a great emphasis in his homilies on the cultivation of *daʿat* (mindfulness) as the chief purpose of religious life.

• *Beit Tsernobil: Beit Naḥum* (Warsaw, 1927). Arthur Green, ed. and trans., *Upright Practices: The Light of the Eyes* (New York, 1982).

—ARTHUR GREEN

NAḤUM OF GIMZO (1st–2d cent.), tanna' noted for his learning, poverty, and pious resignation in the face of misfortune (which he accepted with the phrase *gam zu le-tovah*, "this too is for the best," a pun on the name of his Judean village, Gimzo, near Lydda). Several miraculous events are reported as having happened to him, as a result of his extreme piety. His teachings became influential through his pupil R. *ʿAqiva', who was responsible for the general acceptance of Naḥum's methods for the halakhic interpretation of scripture (see HERMENEUTICS).

• Gershom Bader, *The Encyclopedia of Talmudic Sages*, translated by Solomon Katz (Northvale, N.J., 1993), pp. 172–174, 258.

—DANIEL SPERBER

NAJARA, YISRA'EL BEN MOSHEH (c.1555–1628), rabbi, kabbalist, and poet in Erets Yisra'el. The outstanding Jewish poet of his period, he composed sacred and secular poems in Hebrew and Aramaic, restoring *piyyut* to its former importance. His main themes were praise for God, laments for the sufferings of Israel, and longing for redemption. His poetic description of the mystical union between God and Israel often resorted to erotic imagery that was condemned by other rabbis. Several hundred of his religious poems are extant, including *piyyutim* for each Sabbath and festival. Many passed into the liturgy, particularly in Italy and Muslim lands. Best known is *Yah Ribbon ʿOlam, which was incorporated into the Sabbath *zemirot* in all rites. The outstanding collection of his poems is *Zemirot Yisra'el*.

• Tovah Bari, "Beḥinot Tsurah ve-Tokhen be-Shirei "Olat Ḥodesh' le-Yisra'el Nag'arah," master's thesis, Hebrew University of Jerusalem, 1983. Gershom Gerhard Scholem, *Shir shel Yisra'el Najarah be-fi ha-Shabta'im* (Jerusalem, 1948–1949).

NAMES. In many ancient cultures names had a significance for which no parallel exists in the present day. Names represented one's essence, and a person was often given a new name upon entering a new phase of life. The earlier books of the Bible often explain why individuals were called by certain names or why the names of Abram, Sarai, Jacob, and Hoshea were changed to Abraham, Sarah, Israel, and Joshua, the change of name symbolically investing a person's life with new significance. Names of gods often formed a part of personal names, and it was not uncommon at first also for Israelite names to contain the element *baal* (see BAAL WORSHIP), although this was discontinued under the influence of monotheism, when the elements *el, eli*, and *yeho* were substituted. Rabbinic literature abounds in etymologies for the names of biblical persons, places and even animals (who were named by Adam; *Gn*. 2.19–20). Rabbinic law requires meticulous care in the correct spelling of all names in documents, particularly in bills of divorce, which would be invalidated by a misspelling or an omission. A Jew is known by a Hebrew name plus the name of the father (X son or daughter of Y) and in this form is "called up" to the reading of the Law in the synagogue. A growing custom in the West is to add the mother's name. A baby boy is named at the circumcision ceremony and a girl in the synagogue shortly after her birth. The Talmud states that "the majority of Jews in the Diaspora adopt the non-Jewish names of their environment" (*Git*. 11a), but the rabbis saw special virtue in the fact that "the children of Israel did not change their names in Egypt; as Reuben and Simeon they descended and as Reuben and Simeon they went out." During the period of the Second Temple, certain non-Jewish names (e.g., Alexander, Hyrcanus) became accepted among Jews. Rabbi El'azar states that a person's name is determined by God and influences his destiny (*Ber*. 7b). For this reason, names of biblical persons of ill-fate were avoided (*Gn. Rab*. 49.1). The notion of a connection between name and essence also underlies the rabbinic statement (*R. ha-Sh*. 16b) that a change of name was one of the four things that could avert the evil decree. This gave rise to the ritual of changing the name of a gravely ill person, usually by adding an auspicious name such as Ḥayyim (Life) or Yehoshu'a (Salvation). This custom is still extant in Orthodox circles; the change is conferred at a short ceremony in which charity is donated on behalf of the invalid, a blessing is recited, a formula (which differs in the Ashkenazi and Sephardi rites) is read announcing the new (additional) name, and a prayer is recited asking for "new life" for the bearer of the new name. The custom originally had a superstitious element in the belief that the change of name would mislead the angel of death. See also GOD, NAMES OF.

• Jeaneane D. Fowler, *Theophoric Personal Names in Ancient Hebrew: A Comparative Study*, Journal for the Study of the Old Testament, Supplement Series 49 (Sheffield, Eng., 1988). Heinrich W. and Eva H. Guggenheimer, *Jewish Family Names and Their Origins: An Etymological Dictionary* (Hoboken, N.J., 1992). Benzion C. Kaganoff, *A Dictionary of Jewish Names and Their History* (New York, 1977). Jacob Z. Lauterbach, "The Naming of Children in Jewish Folklore, Ritual and Practice," in *Studies in Jewish Law, Custom and Folklore* (New York, 1970), pp. 30–74. Michael H. Silverman, *Religious Values in the Jewish Proper Names at Elephantine* (Kevelaer, 1985).

NAMES OF GOD. See GOD, NAMES OF.

NAPHTALI, the sixth son born to Jacob and the second son of Bilhah, Rachel's maidservant, and the eponymous ancestor of the tribe and territory of that name. Rachel gave Naphtali his name to reflect her trials with her sister Leah: "With wrestlings of God I have wrestled [*naftulei elohim niftalti*] with my sister, and I have prevailed" (*Gn*. 30.8). During the period of the Judges, the tribe of Naphtali fought, sometimes unsuccessfully, against the local Canaanites (*Jgs*. 1.33). Its most noted campaign occurred at Mount Tabor under the leadership of the military figure Barak ben Avinoam. Supported by the prophet and judge *Deborah, Barak defeated the northern Canaanite confederation led by Sisera, the general of Jabin who was the king of Hazor, a major city-state in the territory of Naphtali (*Jgs*. 4–5). The territory of Naphtali was bordered in the north by Dan, to the east by the Jordan River, in the west by Asher, and to the south by Lake Kinneret and the territory of Issachar–Zebulun (*Jos* 19.32–39). The city of Kedesh-naphtali was the northernmost Cisjordanian city of refuge (see ASYLUM). During the Solomonic monarchy, Naphtali was an administrative district, governed by the king's son-in-law, an indication of its importance for the Israelite kingdom. Situated on the northern border, it was conquered by Ben-hadad I, the king of Damascus (*1 Kgs*. 15.20). The Assyrian monarch, Tiglath-pileser III captured "all the land of Naphtali and carried off the people captive to Assyria" (*2 Kgs*. 15.29). The Second Temple author of the apocryphal *Book of *Tobit* identifies its hero as a Naphtalian exile dwelling in Nineveh in the time of Sennacherib.

• Yohanan Aharoni, *The Land of the Bible: A Historical Geography* (Philadelphia, 1967). J. W. Hirschberg, ed., *Kol Erets Naftali* (Jerusalem, 1967). Benjamin Mazar, "Kol Erets Naftali," in *'Arim u-Gelilot be-'Erets Yisra'el* (Jerusalem, 1975), pp. 203–213.

—AARON DEMSKY

NAQQEDANIM (נַקְדָנִים; punctuators), scholars who punctuated and accented biblical manuscripts. They were the successors of the Masoretes (see MASORAH), whose work they conserved. The *naqqedanim* flourished from the ninth century until the invention of printing.

NASHIM (נָשִׁים; Women), third order of the Mishnah, dealing with laws concerning betrothal, marriage, divorce, and marital relationships. It has seven tractates: **Yevamot*, **Ketubbot*, **Nedarim*, **Nazir*, **Sotah*, **Gittin*, and **Qiddushin*. All have related material in the Tosefta' and both Talmuds.

—AVRAHAM WALFISH

NASI' (נָשִׂיא; prince, or patriarch), title given to authority figures from the biblical period forward. In biblical texts, clan heads, tribal leaders, and kings are referred to as *nasi'*. At Qumran, the term appears with a monarchic meaning or in reference to the leader of the sect. Second-century CE coins and documents refer to Shim'on *Bar Kokhba' as *nesi' Yisra'el*. In rabbinic sources, *nasi'*, an official title meaning patriarch, is applied first to one of each of the **zugot* (pairs), beginning with *Yosei ben Yo'ezer (c.160 BCE), then to the presiding officer of the *Sanhedrin in the Temple, and finally, through the amoraic period, to the head of the court. Most scholars agree that the rabbinic usage in the early period is anachronistic. Some date the patriarchate to Hillel (c.30 CE), others to Gamli'el the Elder (fl. 85 CE), and still others to R. Yehudah ha-Nasi' (fl. 190 CE). Certainly the patriarchate was not fully established until R. Yehudah ha-Nasi', who was recognized as the political head of the Jewish community by the Roman authorities and supported with money, land, and other privileges. Rabbinic sources describe the varied activities of the *nasi'*: he presided over the Sanhedrin; he and his court determined the calendar by proclaiming the new moon and leap years; and he proclaimed national fast days in emergencies, led certain public prayers, ordained scholars, and appointed judges. The *nasi'* dispatched emissaries to the Diaspora in order to teach, collect funds, and set up courts. The court of the *nasi'* possessed legislative powers, and ordinances issued by the court (*taqqanot*) were credited to the presiding *nasi'*. Hillel II's formulation of the principles of the calendar (c.350 CE) was the last great *taqqanah* of the *nesi'im*. A tradition attributing Davidic lineage to the patriarchs led to messianic speculation regarding them. Some rabbinic figures attacked this position, as did the church fathers in the Byzantine period. The office, which was held by descendants of Hillel, was abolished by the authorities in Palestine in 425 CE. In the Middle Ages, the term *nasi'* was applied to the lay leader of the Jewish community, both within and outside Erets Yisra'el, though at times its usage was honorific. Karaites also used the term to designate their leaders, and in Modern Hebrew, *nasi'* means president.

• Samuel Abramsky, *Bar Kokhva', Nesi' Yisra'el* (Tel Aviv, 1961). Gedaliah Alon, *The Jews in Their Land in the Talmudic Age*, translated by Gershon Levi (Jerusalem, 1980–1984), vol. 2, pp. 456–466, 626–628, 663–673, 705–737. David M. Goodblatt, "Re'shitah shel ha-Nesi'ut ha-Erets-Yisra'elit ha-Mukeret," in *Meḥqarim ba-Toledot 'Am Erets Yisra'el* (Haifa, 1978), vol. 3, pp. 89–102. Hugo Mantel, *Studies in the History of the Sanhedrin* (Cambridge, 1961). Ben Tsiyon Rosenfeld, "The Crisis of the Patriarchate in Eretz Israel in the Fourth Century," *Zion* 53 (1988): 239–257. Zvi Taubes, *Ha-Nasi' ba-Sanhedrin ha-Gedolah* (Vienna, 1925). Solomon Zeitlin, *Religious and Secular Leadership* (Philadelphia, 1943), pp. 7–15. —CHRISTINE E. HAYES

NATAN BEN YEḤI'EL OF ROME (1035–1106), Talmudic lexicographer and, along with his brothers, head of the Roman Talmudic academy. His *'Arukh* was one of the few medieval dictionaries of the Talmud and Midrash. A comprehensive and alphabetically arranged work, it explains unclear words in a variety of languages, while also elucidating many difficult passages in rabbinic literature. It is a unique source of geonic and early Ashkenazi literature, containing sources otherwise unknown. Among these are sections of the *Mainz Commentaries* on the Talmud, which served as a basis for Rashi's commentary. The *'Arukh* also preserves variant readings of many classic rabbinic works, as well as important information on contemporary customs. The work was extensively cited in medieval literature and provided one of the bases of subsequent Talmudic lexicography. First published in Rome in 1469, it was edited with an introduction by A. Kohut under the title *Arukh Completum* (Vienna, 1878–1892).

• I. A. Agus, in *World History of the Jewish People*, vol. 2, 2d ser., *The Dark Ages*, edited by Cecil Roth (New Brunswick, N.J., 1966), pp. 182–184. Avraham Grossman, *Ḥakhmei Ashkenaz ha-Ri'shonim* (Jerusalem, 1989). Samuel Krauss, *Additamenta ad Librum Aruch Completum Alexandri Kohut* (Vienna, 1937). —JEFFREY R. WOOLF

NATAN BEN YITSḤAQ HA-KOHEN HA-BAVLI (10th cent.), chronicler. He is known for his account of Babylonian Jewry's primary governing institutions, the gaonate and the exilarchate. Theoretically, the gaonate had legislative and judicial authority, while the exilarchate was the executive power; in fact, some of these powers overlapped. The gaonate was divided between the academies of Sura and Pumbedita, although during Natan's time, Sura was the stronger center.

Natan's account gives some information about the exilarch 'Uqba', who left Baghdad for North Africa. It focuses in greater detail, however, on the disputes between the ga'on Kohen Tsedeq and the exilarch David ben Zakk'ai (909–916), and between David ben Zakk'ai and Sa'adyah Ga'on (c.930). The disputes centered on both political and financial prerogatives, according to Natan. His account also describes in some detail the exilarch's "reception Sabbath," attended by the ge'onim of Sura and Pumbedita and their entourages, and the hierarchical arrangements of the geonic academies.

While Natan ha-Bavli's account is relatively short, it is one of the few reports about the later geonic period. It has been used by modern scholars, like Louis Ginzberg, to reconstruct the relationship between the gaonate and the exilarchate.

• Louis Ginzberg, *Geonica*, vol. 1 (New York, 1909), pp. 22–37, 55–66. Jacob R. Marcus, *The Jew in the Medieval World* (New York, 1938), pp. 287–292 —MICHAEL CHERNICK

NATAN HA-BAVLI (2d–3d cent.), fourth- through fifth-generation tanna'. Rabbi Natan migrated from Babylonia to Erets Yisra'el, where he served as *av beit din* of the Sanhedrin during R. Shim'on ben Gamli'el's presidency (*Hor.* 13b). The Talmud identifies Natan and Yehudah ha-Nasi' as the last of the tanna'im (*B. M.* 86b). Many scholars believe that Natan was an exilarch's son. He is mentioned only twice in the Mishnah (*Ber.* 9.5 and *Sheq.* 2.5); however, he appears frequently in the Tosefta', *Mekhilta'*, and *Sifrei* on *Numbers*. An extracanonical tractate similar to *Avot* is attributed to him: **Avot de-Rabbi Natan*. Modern scholars have revised their assessment of the state and nature of rabbinic learning in Babylonia during the tannaitic period based on R. Natan's scholarship.

• Gershom Bader, *The Encyclopedia of Talmudic Sages*, translated from the Yiddish by Solomon Katz (Northvale, N.J., and London, 1988). Menahem Ben-Sasson, "Ha-Mivneh, ha-Megammot veha-Tokhen shel Ḥibbur Rav Natan ha-Bavli," in *Tarbut ve-Ḥevrah be-Toledot Yisra'el bi-Yemei ha-Beinayim: Qovets Ma'amarim le-Zikhero shel Ḥayyim Hillel Ben-Sasson*, edited by Robert Bonfil et al. (Jerusalem, 1989), pp. 137–196. Aaron Hyman, *Toledot Tanna'im ve-'Amora'im* (1910; Jerusalem, 1987). Mordecai Margaliot, ed., *Entsiqlopediyyah le-Ḥakhmei ha-Talmud veha-Ge'onim* (Jerusalem, 1946). —MICHAEL CHERNICK

NATAN OF GAZA (c.1644–1690), kabbalist and messianic enthusiast. He met *Shabbetai Tsevi in 1665 and became his prophet and the theologian of his messianic movement. In his tracts and epistles, Natan of Gaza proclaimed Shabbetai Tsevi's Messiahship and the imminence of redemption. Natan traveled extensively on behalf of the Shabbatean movement and remained faithful to Shabbetai Tsevi even after the latter's conversion to Islam, spending his last years in misery and poverty among fellow Shabbateans in Macedonia. His doctrines were based on a new interpretation of Lurianic Kabbalah (see LURIA, YITSḤAQ). Natan of Gaza taught that the soul of the Messiah must first descend to the realm of darkness and impurity in order to redeem the divine sparks imprisoned there, thereby accomplishing the process of restoration (*tiqqun*); only then would the soul of the Messiah be fully revealed in its earthly incarnation. This theory provided an explanation for Shabbetai Tsevi's apostasy and the movement's antinomianism.

• Abraham Elqayam, *Sod ha-'Emunah be-Khitvei Natan ha-'Azzati* (Jerusalem, 1993). Gershom Gerhard Scholem, *Shabbetai Tsevi ve-Natan ha-'Azzati* (Tel Aviv, 1941).

NATHAN (Heb. Natan), prophet ministering during the reigns of David and Solomon. His parable of the ewe lamb brought home to King David the wickedness of his crimes of adultery with Bath-sheba and his instigation of her husband Uriah's death on the battlefield. It was also Nathan who informed David that the Temple would be built by his son and not by himself (*2 Sm*. 7; *1 Chr*. 17) and that his own wives would be publicly defiled and that the sword would not disappear from his house (i.e, his sons would revolt against him; *2 Sm*. 11–12). The prophet's intervention against Adonijah's usurpation of the throne ensured the anointing of Solomon as king of Israel (*1 Kgs*. 1.5–39).

• P. Kyle McCarter, ed. and trans., *II Samuel* (Garden City, N.Y., 1984), pp. 190–231. —SHALOM PAUL

NATHANSON, YOSEF SHA'UL (c.1808–1875), Galician rabbi and halakhic authority. As a young married man, Nathanson was supported by his wealthy in-laws and spent many years in fruitful study and collaboration with his brother-in-law Mordekhai Ze'ev Ettinger. The pair published a number of halakhic and Talmudic works. They eventually came to a parting of the ways and even competed against each other for the post of rabbi of Lwów, to which Nathanson was named in 1857. Independently wealthy, Nathanson received no salary from the community. He was involved in all aspects of communal life, from Jewish education to support for the poor. He opposed both Hasidism and the Haskalah, although he maintained cordial relations with the preachers of the local Reform congregation and with some of the Hasidic leaders of the time, quoting the works of the latter in his own books. Nathanson is famed as a decisor in halakhic matters, and he wrote thousands of *responsa* to questioners around the globe. He participated in the major halakhic controversies of his era, such as those over machine-made *matsot* and *etrogim* from Corfu (both of which he permitted). His voluminous *responsa* appeared under the title *Sho'el u-Meshiv* (6 vols. [1865–1890]). His other works include *Divrei Sha'ul* and commentaries on the Pentateuch and Five Scrolls (1877–1878), on the *aggadot* of the Talmud Bavli (1877), and on the Haggadah of Pesaḥ (1879).

• Avraham Bromberg, *Mi-Gedolei ha-Torah ve-ha-Ḥasidut: Ha-Ga'on Rabbi Yosef Sha'ul Natanson* (Jerusalem, 1981). Abraham Stern, *Melitsei Esh* (New York, 1962), vol. 3. Meir Wunder, *Me'orei Galitsyah* (Jerusalem, 1986), vol. 3. —GERSHON BACON

NATIONALISM, a term coined in the nineteenth century to refer to ideologies and political attitudes that centers on the nation as a supreme value. The Latin word from which the term is derived, however, is ancient and has served, together with analogous nouns (derived from Gr. *ethnos*, Lat. *populus, gens*; the biblical equivalents are *'am, le'om, goy*), to designate groups sharing a sense of collective identity. The Bible considers humanity as a "family of nations" and not as an aggregate of individuals; Israel is a people, albeit a chosen one, among others. The call to humanity to worship God is phrased "Praise the Lord all you nations, extol him all you peoples" (*Ps*. 117.1; see also *Ps*. 67). Called to be a "holy nation," Israel was, according to the prophets, also subject to particularly severe judgment as a collective entity. Rabbinic tradition perpetuated this view, using the number seventy as a symbol for the totality of peoples; persecuted Israel, dispersed among nations, was a "sheep among seventy wolves." Judaism as a religion therefore always had a basic ethnic–national component. The classic expression of the unity of these elements was given by the best-known convert, Ruth the Moabite, ancestress of King David and, by implication, of the Messiah: "your people shall be my people and your God my God" (*Ru*. 1.17). Nineteenth-century *Reform Judaism attempted to eliminate the ethnic–national, and, by implication, also Zion-oriented territorial, elements for the sake of what was held to be a more universalist religious conception but subsequently moved away from this extreme position. In the late nineteenth century, modern nationalism—under the impact of the political environment in Europe—became a strong element in *Jewish identity, expressed in movements such as the socialist Bund and *Zionism. This reached its clearest expression with the establishment of the State of Israel.

• Salo W. Baron, *Modern Nationalism and Religion* (New York, 1960). Yoel Ben-Nun, "Nationalism, Humanity, and Knesset Yisrael," in *The World of Rav Kook's Thought*, edited by Benjamin Ish Shalom and Shalom Rosenberg (Jerusalem, 1991). Arnold Eisen, *Galut* (Bloomington, Ind., 1986). Ben Halpern, *The Idea of the Jewish State*, 2d ed. (Cambridge, Mass., 1969). Jacob Katz, *Le'umiyut Yehudit* (Jerusalem, 1983). Gershom Gerhard Scholem, *The Messianic Idea in Judaism* (New York, 1971).

NATIONS, SEVENTY, a rabbinic term referring to the totality of humankind (*Gn. Rab*. 39.11; compare this to the parallel term *seventy tongues*, *Sot*. 36b). The concept of seventy distinctive ethno-linguistic groups is based on the number of Noah's descendants listed in *Genesis* 10. Each of Noah's three sons branched out into particular areas of the ancient Near East. The tradition of seventy primary descendants is also echoed in Canaanite mythology, referring to the sons of the gods El and Asherah.

• Umberto Cassuto, *A Commentary on the Book of Genesis*, pt. 2, *From Noah to Abraham*, translated by Israel Abrahams (Jerusalem, 1964), pp. 172–225. Ephraim Avigdor Speiser, *Genesis: Introduction, Translation and Notes*, The Anchor Bible, vol. 1 (Garden City, N.Y., 1964), pp. 64–73. —DAVID A. GLATT-GILAD

NATOREI QARTA'. See NETUREI QARTA'.

NATRONA'I BAR HILA'I (9th cent.), ga'on of *Sura, perhaps the most prolific and influential ga'on in the period preceding Sa'adyah ben Yosef Ga'on, during which the literary activity of the ge'onim was restricted to the writing of **responsa*. Over five hundred of the *responsa* of Natrona'i bar Hila'i have survived; particularly noteworthy are his numerous letters dealing with liturgical customs and those devoted to Talmudic exegesis. He was fiercely opposed to the *Karaites but seems to have had little first-hand knowledge of their practices; he attacked a Seder ritual that he thought was of Karaite origin but that in actuality was probably Palestinian. His *responsa* were published in 1994 in two volumes by Robert Brody (*Teshuvot Rav Natrona'i bar Hila'i*).

• Simḥa Assaf, ed., *Teshuvot ha-Ge'onim* (1928; Jerusalem, 1986). Louis Ginzberg, *Geonica* (1909; Jerusalem, 1986). —ROBERT BRODY

NATURAL LAW, the law by which *nature, that is, the cosmic order, operates and the moral law inherent in the natural order, discoverable by contemplation of human nature and that of all things around, even without a special *revelation from God. Whereas the rabbinic doctrine of the seven *Noahic laws does not refer to natural law but rather to an original revelation for all humankind, many other rabbinic dicta suggest a vaguely assumed existence of a natural law. Medieval philosophers stressed that revelation was necessary for such ritual regulations or details as would not occur to human beings, or for such insights and precepts as the human intellect might not arrive at unaided. In order not to leave the formulation of the basic rules of religion and morals to the vicissitudes of human intellectual development, God also revealed laws that actually form part of natural law (e.g., the prohibition against murder, or the duty of honoring one's father and mother). Non-philosophical theologians held that the purpose of the *Torah was to lift Israel above natural law to a supernatural order reflected by the revealed law.

• Markus Bockmuehl, "Natural Law in Second Temple Judaism," *Vetus Testamentum* 45 (1995): 17–44. Ze'ev W. Falk, *Law and Religion: The Jewish Experience* (Jerusalem, 1981). Paul T. Sagal, "Maimonides, Natural Law, and Medieval Jewish Philosophy," *Scottish Journal of Religious Studies* 12 (1991): 29–45. Eckhard J. Schnabel, *Law and Wisdom from Ben Sira to Paul* (Tübingen, 1985). Ruth H. Sohn, "Law and Ethics in the Talmud," rabbinic thesis, Hebrew Union College, 1982.

NATURE. The concept of nature as a system operating according to fixed laws of its own derives from Greek philosophy rather than from the Bible. The biblical writers, while evincing an appreciation of the regular workings of the universe (cf. *Ps.* 104 and 148), are nevertheless primarily concerned with the acts of the Creator and his permanent and direct responsibility for the cosmic order (see also *Ps.* 19). In fact, there is a natural order, but it exists not by itself but is owed to God's covenant with his creation (cf. *Gn.* 8.22 and *Jer.* 31.34, 33.20, 33.25). The rabbis held a similar view: the regularity of natural phenomena was an expression of God's will, just as were *miracles. Some medieval thinkers (e.g., *Baḥya ben Yosef ibn Paquda') held—under the influence of Sufi thought—that admitting the existence of nature and an autonomous natural law was tantamount to denying the sole and exclusive role of God's will and providence. However, most philosophers argued that there was no contradiction between belief in God as the "First Cause" of all things and an established secondary order ("creation") that he had made to function according to a causality of its own. It was generally admitted that the Creator could suspend or "break through" the natural order by miracles. Modern philosophers of nature often require a theological reformulation of the relationship of nature to God. Whereas most traditional systems agreed that God was "outside"—namely, "above"—nature, some modern "naturalistic" (that is, antisupernaturalistic) doctrines take a different view. *Spinoza's pantheism identified God with nature. The ancient rabbis and medieval thinkers insisted that the contemplation of nature led to a recognition of God, and Abraham is said by the Midrash to have become convinced of the existence of God by speculating on the nature and origin of the universe. He therefore possessed a natural religion, arrived at by natural theology, even before God manifested himself to Abraham and introduced him to the order of revealed religion.

• Avigdor Miller, *The Universe Testifies* (New York, 1995). Aubrey Rose, *Judaism and Ecology* (New York, 1992). Marc Swetlitz, *Judaism and Ecology, 1970–1986: A Sourcebook of Readings* (New York, 1989).

NAZARENES. See JEWISH CHRISTIANS.

NAZIR (נָזִיר; Nazirite), tractate consisting of nine chapters in Mishnah order Nashim, with related material in the Tosefta' and both Talmuds, dealing with the rules of the *Nazirite (*Nm.* 6.1–21). *Nazir*'s treatment of this topic largely follows the biblical presentation, discussing in turn the three central prohibitions of the Nazirite: defilement through contact with a corpse; consumption of wine or grape products; and cutting hair (*Naz.* 6.1). *Nazir* devotes much attention to the definition and formulation of the Nazirite vow, examining permutations and variations of standard Nazirite formulae and their ramifications. Opening with a discussion of the Nazirite in the mold of Samson (*Naz.* 1.2) and closing with the Nazirite status of Samuel, *Nazir* alludes to a tension within rabbinic thought between the majestic devotion (Samuel) and the uneasy asceticism (Samson) represented by the figure of the Nazirite.

An English translation of the tractate by B. D. Klien appears in the Soncino Talmud (London, 1936).

• Chanoch Albeck, ed., *Shishah Sidrei Mishnah, Seder Nashim* (Jerusalem, 1954). Philip Blackman, ed. and trans., *Mishnayoth*, vol. 2, *Order Nashim* (Gateshead, 1973). Pinhas Kehati, ed., *Mishnah: A New Translation with a Commentary, Seder Nashim*, vol. 2, *Nedarim, Nazir, Sotah* (Jerusalem, 1992). Hermann Leberecht Strack and Günter Stemberger, *Introduction to the Talmud and Midrash*, rev. and updat. ed., translated by Markus Bockmuehl (Minneapolis, 1992). —AVRAHAM WALFISH

NAZIRITE (Heb. *nazir* [one who abstains]), a man or woman who takes a vow consecrating him- or herself to God by accepting prohibitions beyond those observed by all other Israelites (*Nm.* 6.1–21). These are prohibitions against drinking wine, products of the vine, or other intoxicants; a prohibition against cutting one's hair; and a prohibition against contracting impurity by contact with a corpse, even that of a close relative. Most Nazirites imposed upon themselves such a vow for a designated period, usually a month, but there are also biblical examples of a person becoming a Nazirite for life (*nezir 'olam*), namely, Samuel and Samson, who were dedicated from before birth (*Jgs.* 13.7; *1 Sm.* 1.11, 22, especially as stated in the Qumran text; *Ben Sira* 46.13). The lifelong Nazirite was not subject to the prohibition against corpse contamination (*Jgs.* 13.14). The Nazirite is consecrated (*qadosh*) to the Lord (*Nm.* 6.5, 8), an expression elsewhere used of priests, and the Nazirite's prohibitions resemble those pertaining to a priest. Thus, a male Israelite aspiring to greater sanctity and nearness to God could do so by assuming the priestly severities, even though he could not discharge priestly functions. The unique, distinctive characteristic of the Nazirite is his uncut hair, featuring prominently in the story of Samson (*Jgs.* 16); the term *nazir* is connected with *nezer*, which can also refer to the Nazirite's hair (see *Nm.* 6.6–7, 12, 18; *Jer.* 7.29). Biblical legislation concerning the Nazirite deals primarily with two matters: the unexpected interruption of a Nazirite's vow by sudden contamination from a corpse (*Nm.* 6.9–12) and the sacrificial procedure followed by Nazirites at the end of their terms (*Nm.* 13–20), by which the Nazirites are desacralized. Nazirites in Judaism do not withdraw from community life nor are they celibate. Nonetheless, the rabbis recommended moderation rather than abstention and limited to a minimum the situations in which a Nazirite vow was desirable. The rabbinic laws concerning the Nazirite are contained in the Talmudic tractate **Nazir*.

• Baruch A. Levine, ed., *Numbers 1–20*, The Anchor Bible, vol. 4a (New York, 1993), pp. 218–226, 229–236. Jacob Milgrom, ed., *Numbers*, The JPS Torah Commentary (Philadelphia, 1990), pp. 43–50, 355–358.

–BARUCH J. SCHWARTZ

NECROMANCY, divination through communication with the dead. Necromancy is forbidden in the Bible and is termed "an abomination unto the Lord" (*Dt.* 18.11–12). The detailed vocabulary used in the Bible suggests the existence of different kinds of necromancy, but the only actual account of its practice is Saul's resort to the witch of En-dor to raise the soul of Samuel (*1 Sm.* 28.7–20). Most earlier Jewish authorities regarded the practice as efficacious but forbidden, though the more rationalistically inclined thinkers (Pinḥas ben Ḥofni Ga'on, Maimonides, etc.) denounced it as gross superstition and explained the story of Saul at En-dor as an anguished dream. See also MAGIC.

• Joshua Trachtenberg, *Jewish Magic and Superstition: A Study in Folk Religion* (New York, 1974), pp. 61–68.

–SHIFRA EPSTEIN

NEDARIM (נְדָרִים; Vows), tractate in Mishnah order Nashim, in eleven chapters, with related material in the Tosefta' and in both Talmuds. The tractate deals with *vows and oaths and their annulment (*Nm.* 30.2–17). In biblical as well as rabbinic thought, oaths and vows were both widespread and fraught with danger; hence, the regulation of these forms of speech was a matter of vital importance. Originally a verbal consecration of an object to the Temple, vows were used to prohibit benefit from an object or an action by conferring upon it a quasi-consecrated status. The often ambiguous or unarticulated language of a vow (*Ned.* 1.1) was subjected to canons of interpretation. The laws of *nedarim* seek to strike a balance between the inward intent and the social context of language, enabling the speaker to control his meaning while requiring submissive reverence to the consequences of his utterance.

Biblical laws governing annulment of a woman's vows by her father or husband are rigorously defined. Rabbinic scholars and courts were empowered to annul vows by the creative discovery of ramifications of which the vow's author was unaware.

The tractate in the Talmud Bavli was translated into English by Harry Freedman in the Soncino Talmud (1936).

• Chanoch Albeck, ed., *Shishah Sidrei Mishnah, Seder Nashim* (Jerusalem, 1954). Philip Blackman, ed. and trans., *Mishnayoth*, vol. 2, *Order Nashim* (Gateshead, 1973). Pinhas Kehati, ed., *Mishnah: A New Translation with a Commentary, Seder Nashim*, vol. 2, *Nedarim, Nazir, Sotah* (Jerusalem, 1992). Hermann Leberecht Strack and Günter Stemberger, *Introduction to the Talmud and Midrash*, rev. and updated ed., translated by Markus Bockmuehl (Minneapolis, 1992).

–AVRAHAM WALFISH

NEDAVAH. See FREE-WILL OFFERING; VOWS AND OATHS.

NEDER. See VOWS AND OATHS.

NEDUNYAH. See DOWRY.

NEFILAT APPAYIM. See TAḤANUN.

NEGAʿIM (נְגָעִים; Plagues), tractate in Mishnah order Toharot, in fourteen chapters, with related material in the Tosefta'. It has no *gemara'* in either Talmud. It deals with the laws concerning the disease described in *Leviticus* 13–14, usually translated as *leprosy. *Negaʿim* discusses the symptoms that render persons, clothing, or houses leprous and therefore impure; the regulations governing the impure person or object; and the rituals of purification for afflicted persons or objects that have been cured. A modification of the biblical discussion of *negaʿim* relates to the role of the priest in establishing the presence of leprous *negaʿim*. The biblical priest was assumed to be expert in diagnosing *negaʿim*. In rabbinic times, the actual diagnosis would normally be made by a rabbinic expert, while the role of the priest, who was not presumed to possess halakhic expertise, was to issue a ritual proclamation of the patient's impurity (*Neg.* 3.1; cf. T., *Neg.* 1.1–2).

Because of their intricacy, the laws of *Negaʿim*, together with those of **Ohalot*, were used by the rabbis to symbolize halakhic study of the deepest profundity (*San.* 67b). Accordingly, *Negaʿim* is marked by a high proportion of pericopes that present Midrashic expositions (see especially *Neg.* 12.5–7) or halakhic argumentation (e.g., *Neg.* 10.1–2, 9). Several pericopes refer to the relationship between halakhic reasoning and halakhic traditions (*Neg.* 7.4, 9.3, 11.7). Some rabbis claim (T., *Neg.* 6.1) that portions of the laws of *negaʿim*, the laws of leprous houses, have no applicability to reality and are taught only to derive instruction from them. Based on the assumption that the disease of *negaʿim* is divine punishment for human wickedness (T., *Neg.* 6.7), *Negaʿim* derives from the laws of afflicted houses moral instruction regarding God's consideration for the property even of wicked Jews (*Neg.* 12.5) and regarding the dangers of having wicked neighbors (*Neg.* 12.6).

An English translation of the tractate by I. W. Slotki is in the Soncino Talmud (London, 1948).

• Chanoch Albeck, ed., *Shishah Sidrei Mishnah, Seder Tohorot* (Jerusalem, 1958). Philip Blackman, ed. and trans., *Mishnayoth*, vol. 5, *Order Taharoth* (Gateshead, 1973). Hermann Leberecht Strack and Günter Stemberger, *Introduction to the Talmud and Midrash*, rev. and updat. ed., translated by Markus Bockmuehl (Minneapolis, 1992). Yeḥi'el Avraham Zilber, *Zer Kesef: Nega'im Pereq 1–6* (Bene Beraq, 1959).

—AVRAHAM WALFISH

NEGLIGENCE. Charges of negligence arise when an artisan or laborer performs the work given to him poorly or with disregard for the instructions of the owner or ruins the material entrusted to him by the owner. In these instances full compensation must be made by the artisan or laborer. In addition, the *halakhah* recognizes two other categories of negligence, "negligence that borders upon intention" and "negligence that borders upon accident." In these cases the ordinary penalty for negligence does not apply—in the former instance because the penalty would be too light; in the latter instance because it would be too severe. In the case of movable property given in trust without payment, the bailee (unpaid guardian) is responsible for criminal negligence (*peshi'ah*) only.

• Menachem Elon, *Jewish Law: History, Sources, Principles*, 4 vols. (Philadelphia, 1994).

NEHARDEA, Babylonian *academy situated in a city of that name near the junction of the Euphrates River and the Malka Canal. The city's Jewish origins were traditionally traced back to King Jehoiachin, who was said to have erected a synagogue there for which earth and stone were brought from Jerusalem. The ancient academy at Nehardea reached its zenith under the *amora' *Shemu'el; shortly after his death, the city was destroyed by the Palmyrenes (259 CE). The Nehardean tradition of Jewish scholarship was carried on by the academy of *Pumbedita, which was founded by Shemu'el's pupil *Yehudah bar Yeḥezqe'l. Although many scholars continued to reside in Nehardea after it was rebuilt, the town never regained its former prominence as a center of Jewish learning. In the geonic period, "Nehardea" was an alternative designation for the academy of Pumbedita.

• Solomon Funk, "Die Stadt Nehardea und ihre Hochschule," in *Festschrift zum siebzigsten Geburtstage David Hoffmann's*, edited by Simon Eppenstein, Meier Hildesheimer and Joseph Wohlgemuth (Berlin, 1914). Morduch Judelowitz, *Ḥayyei ha-Yehudim bi-Zeman ha-Talmud: Sefer Neharde'a'* (1906; Jerusalem, 1971). Jacob Neusner, *A History of the Jews in Babylonia* (Leiden, 1969). Aharon Oppenheimer, *Babylonia Judaica in the Talmudic Period* (Weisbaden, 1983). —ROBERT BRODY

NEHEMIAH (Heb. Neḥemyah; 5th cent. BCE), cupbearer to the Persian king Artaxerxes I (465–424) by whom he was appointed governor of Judah. Nehemiah arrived in Jerusalem in the twentieth year of Artaxerxes (444 BCE) for the primary purpose of rebuilding the walls of Jerusalem, but he skillfully established his position as governor in the face of stiff opposition from his two enemies, Sanballat, governor of Samaria, and Tobiah the Ammonite and others as well. Nehemiah's main period of service lasted twelve years (2.1, 13.6), although the bulk of the narrative in *Nehemiah* relates only to the activities of his first year or two. Nehemiah's first and most pressing undertaking was rebuilding the city walls, a project that he directed to successful completion in only fifty-two days (6.15), despite the organized interference mounted by his enemies. The narrative describing the wall-building project gives the image of how the builders were "doing work with one hand while the other held a weapon" (4.11). Next, Nehemiah turned his attention to the socioeconomic ills plaguing the Jewish community, in particular moving to rectify the outrage of children and property being taken by creditors as security deposits (chap. 5). Nehemiah also led the drive to repopulate Jerusalem after the city had been depleted of many of its residents by ordering that one out of ten Jews should take up residence there (7.4, 11.1–2). Finally, Nehemiah is mentioned as the first signatory to the famous *amanah* (pledge, contract) that was drawn up in the wake of *Ezra's public reading of the Torah (10.2). The *amanah* included provisions forbidding mixed marriages and business dealings on the Sabbath, canceling of debts owed by the poor, and aiding the smooth operation of the Temple cult. Nehemiah was personally involved in enforcing these matters (chap. 13), though his precise administrative and chronological relationship to Ezra, who was active in the same areas of concern, is debated among scholars. Nehemiah's vigor and drive and the success of his campaign testify to a character of singular power, zealously devoted to the cause of God and his people. Nehemiah's own memoirs form the basis of the biblical account. Traditionally regarded as a unit, Ezra-Nehemiah (now divided into two separate works) is tenth in the Hagiographa (see EZRA-NEHEMIAH, BOOK OF). The Talmud credits Nehemiah with the completion of the *Book of Chronicles*, started by Ezra (*B. B.* 15a).

• Joseph Blenkinsopp, *Ezra–Nehemiah: A Commentary*, The Old Testament Library (Philadelphia, 1988). Yehezkel Kaufmann, *History of the Religion of Israel: Vol. IV, From the Babylonian Captivity to the End of Prophecy* (New York, 1977), pp. 359–430. Harold Henry Rowley, "Nehemiah's Mission and Its Background," in H. H. Rowley, *Men of God: Studies in Old Testament History and Prophecy* (London and New York, 1963), pp. 211–245. H.G.M. Williamson, *Ezra, Nehemiah*, Word Biblical Commentary, vol. 16 (Waco, Tex., 1985). —DAVID A. GLATT-GILAD

NEHEMIAH, BOOK OF. See EZRA-NEHEMIAH, BOOK OF.

NEHER, ANDRÉ (1913–1988), French historian of Jewish thought. He wrote on diverse subjects, ranging from biblical prophecy (*Amos, contribution à l'étude du prophétisme* [1950]; *L'Éssence du prophétisme* [1955]; *Moïse et la vocation juive* [1956], translated as *Moses and the Vocation of the Jewish People* [1959]; *The Prophetic Existence* [1969]), through Renaissance thought (*David Gans, 1541–1613: Disciple du Maharal* [1974], translated as *Jewish Thought and the Scientific Revolution of the Sixteenth Century* [1986]), and including the Enlightenment and modern thought (*Ils ont refait leur âme* [1979], translated as *They Made Their Souls Anew* [1990]). His *L'Exil de la parole* (1970; translated into English in 1981) addresses the theological questions posed by the Holocaust. A leading figure of the post-Holocaust Jewish community of France, he taught Jewish studies at the

University of Strasbourg until moving to Jerusalem in 1972. He believed that through the *berit* (covenant) the Hebrews, and through them all humanity, entered a historic dialogue with the divine.

• *Mélanges André Neher* (Paris, 1975), in French and English, includes bibliography. —STEVEN BALLABAN

NEḤUNYA' BEN HA-QANAH (1st cent.), tanna' quoted frequently in the Talmud, especially as a halakhist, although only a single *halakhah* has come down in his name (*Pes.* 29a). He was regarded as pious and deeply humane, never seeking his own betterment at the expense of others, always forgiving his neighbor before he went to sleep, and forgoing monetary benefits. He may have lived in Emmaus in Judea for some time. He was the teacher of R. *Yishmaʿeʾl ben Elishaʿ and taught him the exegetical principle of *kelal u-ferat* (deducing from the general to the particular). Neḥunya' ben ha-Qanah was highly regarded by kabbalists, who ascribed to him **Sefer ha-Bahir*, the prayer *Anna' ba-Koaḥ, and other mystical compositions, such as **Sefer ha-Qanah*.

• Gershom Bader, *The Encyclopedia of Talmudic Sages*, translated by Solomon Katz (Northvale, N.J., 1993), pp. 12, 169–171, 237. —DANIEL SPERBER

NEHUSHTAN (from Heb. *naḥash* [snake] and *neḥoshet* [copper/bronze]), name of the bronze serpent destroyed by King *Hezekiah of Judah (*2 Kgs.* 18.4) in his campaign for religious reform. Nehushtan was a sacred symbol within Mosaic traditions. Moses fashioned a bronze serpent as a prophylactic agent for the Israelites bitten by serpents (*Nm.* 21.6–9). By Hezekiah's time (late 8th cent. BCE), it was no longer an acceptable object of worship. Snakes are common in ancient Near Eastern iconography, usually associated with fertility cults. A bronze serpent was found at Midianite Timnah in Sinai, others at Canaanite Gezer, Hazor, and Tel Mevorakh.

• J. Gray, *I and II Kings: A Commentary* (Philadelphia, 1976). Karen Randolph Joines, *Serpent Symbolism in the Old Testament* (Haddonfield, N.J., 1974). Jacob Milgrom, *Numbers*, The JPS Torah Commentary (Philadelphia, 1990), pp. 173–175, 459–460. —NILI SACHER FOX

NEʿILAH (נְעִילָה; Closing [of the Gates]), originally a prayer offered on all public fast days at sunset, when the Temple gates were closed; now recited only on Yom Kippur. It is the last of the five prayers of Yom Kippur, and its recital is concluded at nightfall, when the fast ends. Neʿilah is regarded as the last opportunity to pray for forgiveness for transgressions committed during the previous year and is recited with particular solemnity. The medieval poets interpreted the word *neʿilah* as referring to the closing of the heavenly gates at the sealing of divine judgment on Yom Kippur. This is reflected in the *ʿAmidah, where the text changes from the previous invocation of the High Holy Days, "inscribe us in the Book of Life," to "seal us in the Book of Life." After *Ashrei (*Ps.* 145) and *U-Va' le-Tsiyyon, the ʿAmidah, preceded and followed by *Qaddish, is first said silently by each worshiper and then repeated aloud by the reader. It differs from the other ʿAmidot of Yom Kippur in that it contains only the shorter confession of sins (Viddui) and not the long version, which is replaced by *Attah Noten Yad, a prayer extolling God's mercy in forgiving the repentant sinner. The ark remains open during the reader's repetition of the ʿAmidah. After the ʿAmidah, the petition *Avinu Malkeinu is repeated for the last time (even when Yom Kippur coincides with Shabbat), the first verse of the *Shemaʿ is proclaimed once by the reader and repeated by the congregation, followed by **barukh shem kevod malkhuto le-ʿolam va-ʿed*, said three times, and "the Lord is God" (*1 Kgs.* 18.39), said seven times. After this (if night has fallen), the shofar is sounded with a single long blast, *teqiʿah gedolah*, to indicate the termination of the solemn fast day. The congregation adds **la-shanah ha-ba'ah bi-Yerushalayim*, "next year in Jerusalem." The *tallit* is worn at Neʿilah as at all Yom Kippur services. Neʿilah is followed by Maʿariv and Havdalah.

• Ismar Elbogen, *Jewish Liturgy: A Comprehensive History*, translated by Raymond P. Scheindlin (Philadelphia, 1993). Irving Greenberg, *The Jewish Way: Living the Holidays* (New York, 1988). Lawrence A. Hoffman, *The Canonization of the Synagogue Service* (Notre Dame, 1979). Isaac Klein, *A Guide to Jewish Religious Practice* (New York, 1992). Abraham Millgram, *Jewish Worship* (Philadelphia, 1971). —PETER KNOBEL

NEO-HASIDISM, the application of Hasidic values and teachings to the lives of non-Hasidic, and even non-observant, Jews. Among the first Jews in the West to find inspiration in Hasidism was Martin *Buber, who saw in it, and especially in *Hasidic literature, a great religious creation. Through the influence of Buber and others, attempts were made to bring the spirit of Hasidism to the *kibbuts* movement, to Zionist youth groups, and to various audiences in Europe and America. In eastern Europe Neo-Hasidism was especially the province of Hillel Zeitlin (1872–1943), who sought an authentically Jewish philosophy of life in his rereading of the Hasidic sources. His potentially important contribution was cut off by the Holocaust. Neo-Hasidism has also been important in Jewish literature; many of Jewry's most important writers in the twentieth century (Peretz, Asch, Agnon, Singer, etc.) depicted Ḥasidim or employed Hasidic themes in their writings. The same is true of Jewish music, in which adaptations from Hasidism have been widely influential far beyond Hasidic circles. In North America, a Neo-Hasidic approach to Judaism began to develop in the 1960s, partly in response to the great interest in meditation and spirituality in the general culture. The two persons most responsible for this growth were rabbi–folk singer Shlomo Carlebach (died 1994) and R. Zalman Schachter, a former Ḥabad Ḥasid who founded the Pnai Or Religious Fellowship and has been called the spiritual grandfather of the Jewish counterculture and **ḥavurah* movements.

• Martin Buber, "My Way to Hasidism," in *Hasidism and Modern Man*, edited and translated by Maurice Friedman (New York, 1958). Zalman Schachter, *Fragments of a Future Scroll* (Germantown, Pa., 1975). —ARTHUR GREEN

NEOLOGY, a term borrowed from enlightened Protestant circles in Germany to characterize the Hungarian brand of *Reform Judaism. During the 1840s, Leopold Löw and other rabbis who followed the example of

Aharon ben Kalman *Chorin became dominant in ethnic Hungary and Transylvania. Their pressure for religious change and identification with Magyar nationalism led to a clash with Orthodox Jews, headed by the dynasty of Mosheh Sofer (see SOFER FAMILY) in Slovakia and the Ḥasidim of Galicia. At a rabbinical assembly held in 1865, the traditionalists banned worship in "choir temples" and many other innovations of the Neologists, some of which (e. g., preaching in the vernacular) had already been adopted by the German *Neo-Orthodoxy movement. Two years later, Baron József Eötvös, the architect of Jewish emancipation, who served as minister of religious and educational affairs, helped organize elections to a National Congress of Hungarian Jewry (1868–1869). Held in the Neologist stronghold of Pest, this congress—far from restoring communal harmony—provoked a three-way split between the Neologist majority, Orthodox "Guardians of the Faith," and nonaligned, Status Quo Ante traditionalists.

After Orthodox separatism was recognized by the Hungarian parliament in 1871, leading Neologists feared that their break with the Orthodox might become irreparable. Having thwarted attempts to establish German-style Reform congregations in 1848 and 1884, they sought a modus vivendi with the Orthodox rabbinate by pursuing a discreetly conservative line. Apart from organ accompaniment, Neologist services remained largely traditional, religious observance (e.g., *kashrut*) was upheld, and graduates of the new Budapest Rabbinical Seminary (1877) often were quite like their Neo-Orthodox counterparts in western Europe. Through Hungarian Neology, during and after World War II, many assimilated Jews rediscovered their traditional roots. The postwar Communist regime brought surviving Neologist and Orthodox communities under one umbrella organization, which (since the democratic reforms of the late 1980s) has revitalized Jewish life in Hungary.

• Moshe Carmilly, ed., *The Rabbinical Seminary of Budapest, 1877–1977* (New York, 1986). Yekuti'el Yehudah Greenwald, *Le-Toledot ha-Reformatsyah ha-Datit de-Germanyah uve-Ungaryah* (Columbus, Ohio, 1948). William O. McCagg, Jr., *Jewish Nobles and Geniuses in Modern Hungary* (New York, 1972). Michael A. Meyer, *Response to the Modernity: A History of the Reform Movement in Judaism* (New York, 1988), pp. 194–196, 440.

—GABRIEL A. SIVAN

NEO-ORTHODOXY, term designating the stand taken by "modern" traditionalists against *Reform Judaism in Germany. Their platform combined strict observance of Jewish law with a positive approach to Western society and culture. Architects of Neo-Orthodoxy included Isaac *Bernays (Hamburg), Yaʿaqov *Ettlinger (Altona), Michael Sachs (Berlin), and Shemu'el David *Luzzatto (Italy), as well as Nathan Marcus Adler (Hanover; see ADLER FAMILY), who became England's chief rabbi in 1845. Their enlightened measures ranged from preaching in the vernacular to establishing an Orthodox press (Ettlinger) and one of the first *rabbinical seminaries (Adler).

Samson Raphael *Hirsch, a disciple of Bernays and Ettlinger, created the ideological foundation of Neo-Orthodoxy through his own religious accommodation with modernity and its challenges. Turning the Mishnaic concept of "*Torah im derekh erets*" (*Avot* 2.2, 3.21) into a doctrinal slogan—"Torah Judaism in harmony with secular culture"—he aimed to win over middle-class Jews in Frankfurt and elsewhere who were in the process of abandoning traditional norms. While readily adopting the externals of modernism (educational reform, German patriotism, Western dress, and an improvement in the status of women), Hirsch reemphasized the authority of the **Shulḥan ʿArukh* and the importance of Torah study (albeit in a wider form), and he promoted the development of self-contained Orthodox congregations (see ADASS JISROEL). Hirsch's ideological works and his commentaries on the Bible and prayer book played an especially vital role in this campaign.

Some exponents of Neo-Orthodoxy objected to Hirsch's dogmatic intolerance, his negation of modern scholarly research (*Wissenschaft des Judentums), his lack of interest in the fate of Jews abroad, and his positive view of life in exile (translated into "Israel's universal mission"). From 1876 his advocacy of separatism or secession created a permanent rift not only in the broad communal framework but even within Neo-Orthodoxy itself. Ezriel *Hildesheimer, for example, split with Hirsch over the issues of the Berlin Rabbinical Seminary's establishment, cooperation with the non-Orthodox in matters of general concern, and renewed Jewish settlement in Erets Yisra'el. These divisions would later be reflected in the rift between Orthodox Zionism (Mizrachi) and anti-Zionism (Agudat Israel), also giving rise to the uneasy contemporary coexistence of "modern" (centrist) and "right-wing" (see ḤAREDIM) Orthodox groups. See also ORTHODOXY.

• Hans I. Bach, *The German Jew: A Synthesis of Judaism and Western Civilization, 1730–1930* (Oxford, 1984), pp. 87–91, 97–98. Alexander Carlebach, "The Image of German Orthodoxy," in *Men and Ideas: Selected Writings, 1935–1980* (Jerusalem, 1982), pp. 35–51. Noah H. Rosenbloom, *Tradition in an Age of Reform: The Religious Philosophy of Samson Raphael Hirsch* (Philadelphia, 1976). David Rudavsky, *Modern Jewish Religious Movements: A History of Emancipation and Adjustment*, 3d ed. (New York, 1979), pp. 218–270. Jonathan Sacks, *One People?: Tradition, Modernity, and Jewish Unity* (London/Washington, 1993). Hermann Schwab, *The History of Orthodox Jewry in Germany* (London, 1950).

—GABRIEL A. SIVAN

NEOPLATONISM, a modification of Platonism initiated by Plotinus (3d cent. CE) and his successors, and mediated by Islamic and Christian sources, that made a profound and lasting mark on Jewish thought during the Middle Ages. The philosophical systems of Plato (427–347) proved congenial to many religious minds (for example, *Philo of Alexandria, who sought to reconcile Platonic and Jewish traditions through the use of allegory). The Jewish Neoplatonists identified the Platonic "forms" with the creative thoughts of God, and God was defined as the Good, the First Principle, and "The One," that is, as absolutely singular and self-sufficient. From this ultimate One descended or emanated (see EMANATION; SEFIROT) the world of ideas and the material world. The human soul was a particle from a higher realm of being (the "World Soul" according to Plotinus, the "Throne of Glory" according to the Jewish Neoplatonists) to which it longed to return. Neoplatonism provided a philosophical basis not only for the rational but also for the spiritual and even mystical life. Its aim was to reach the ultimate One lying behind all concrete experience; its method was that of intellectual abstraction (namely, of contemplative ascent), by which it divested experience of all that was specifically human until nothing was left but God. Medieval Neoplatonism received a powerful impetus through the *Liber de causis* (attributed to Aristotle but actually written in the ninth century by a Muslim philosopher and containing extracts from the fifth-century Neoplatonist Proclus) and deeply affected Jewish philosophical and religious thought. Beginning with Yitsḥaq *Israeli (c.850–950), Jewish Neoplatonism reached its height with Shelomoh *ibn Gabirol in the purely philosophical sphere, and with *Baḥya ben Yosef ibn Paquda' and *Yehudah ha-Levi's *Kuzari* in the ascetic and theological sphere. Other representatives of Neoplatonism were Avraham *ibn Ezra and Yosef ben Ya'aqov ibn *Zaddik. While Neoplatonism was soon eclipsed by *Aristotelianism in philosophy, Neoplatonism continued to exert a powerful influence on mystical speculation and, in particular, on the emergent *Kabbalah in the thirteenth century, which adapted its theory of emanation. Some modern critics maintain that Neoplatonism, with its monistic tendency, its exaltation of the abstract above the concrete, and its hostility to the material order of creation, is essentially incompatible with biblical teaching and spirituality.

• Lenn E. Goodman, ed., *Neoplatonism and Jewish Thought* (Albany, 1992). Julius Guttmann, *Philosophies of Judaism* (New York, 1973). Gershom Gerhard Scholem, *Major Trends in Jewish Mysticism* (New York,

NER TAMID (נֵר תָּמִיד; perpetual or eternal lamp), originally, a lamp, prescribed in *Exodus* 27.20–21 and *Leviticus* 24.2 as an essential requirement of the Tabernacle in the wilderness and later in the Temple. The *ner tamid* had to be placed "outside the veil of testimony in the tabernacle of the congregation" and was part of the seven-branched candelabrum. The priests had to see that it was kept continually burning, and only pure olive oil could be used for it. The ever-burning lamp was taken to symbolize, among other things, God's eternal watchfulness over and providence for his people. The account of the origin of *Ḥanukkah given in the Talmud (*Shab.* 21b) centers around the miracle by which a single day's supply of pure oil found in the Temple by the victorious Maccabees burned for eight days as the *ner tamid* until new oil could be prepared. The eternal lamp was the westernmost branch of the candelabrum and was therefore called "the western lamp" (*Tam.* 6.1; *Shab.* 22b). According to the Midrash (*Sifra' Emor* 13), all seven branches of the candelabrum were filled with the same quantity of oil each night, but while all the other wicks in the branches of the candelabrum burned until the morning, the *ner tamid* remained alight until the next evening, at which time it was refilled. Since the *synagogue is called a "minor sanctuary" (*Meg.* 29a), it became customary, but not obligatory, to incorporate a *ner tamid* into its design. At first, there was considerable objection to the practice of suspending the *ner tamid* in front of the ark, on the grounds that this was a gentile custom, and it was felt by some that, as in the Temple, the *ner tamid* should be suspended on the western wall. It was regarded as highly meritorious to provide oil for the *ner tamid*. Those who did so are blessed in the Sabbath morning *Mi she-Berakh prayer. Today the lamp is usually electric.

• Judah David Eisenstein, *Otsar Dinim u-Minhagim* (New York, 1917), pp. 273–274. Carol L. Meyers, *The Tabernacle Menorah: A Synthetic Study of a Symbol from the Biblical Cult* (Missoula, Mont., 1976). Leon Yarden, *The Tree of Light* (London, 1971). —SHMUEL HIMELSTEIN

NESHAMAH YETERAH (נְשָׁמָה יְתֵרָה; additional soul), according to legend, a higher soul given by God to Abraham that dwelt within him and elevated him throughout the Sabbath. This soul is granted to every person for the duration of the Sabbath (*Beits.* 16a), and, according to one source, the custom of smelling *spices during the *Havdalah service at the termination of the Sabbath is meant to comfort individuals for the loss of this extra soul. The kabbalists applied the concept of an additional soul mystically, and in one of the **zemirot* ascribed to Yitsḥaq ben Shelomoh *Luria (Yom Zeh le-Yisra'el), the Sabbath is called "an additional soul for the suffering."

• Abraham Danzig, *Sefer Ḥayyei Adam* (Jerusalem, 1985).
—CHAIM PEARL

NETAN'EL BEIRAV FAYYUMI (died c.1165), leader of Yemenite Jewry. Maimonides lavishes praise upon him in his *Iggeret Teiman*, addressed to Netan'el's son, Ya'aqov. In his apologetic work *Bustan al-'Uqul* (published with an English translation and edited by David Levine [New York, 1908; repr., 1966]), Netan'el presents a Neoplatonic philosophy of Judaism that owes much to Sa'adyah Ga'on, Yehudah ha-Levi, and Baḥya ibn Paquda'. Drawing on the *Ikhwan al-Safa* of the Isma'iliyah, Netan'el maintains that God sends a prophet to every people according to its language and level of spiritual development; hence, Muḥammad was a true prophet and the Qur'an an authentic revelation for the Arabic-speaking peoples. There is some controversy as to whether Fayyumi is a personal or place name, and Netan'el is often referred to as ibn al-Fayyumi.

• Reuben Ahroni, *Yemenite Jewry* (Bloomington, Ind., 1986), pp. 61–65. Colette Sirat, *A History of Jewish Philosophy in the Middle Ages* (Cambridge, 1985), pp. 88–93, 424. —NORMAN SOLOMON

NETHERWORLD. See GEIHINNOM.

NETHINIM, the lowest class of Temple servants from the time of Joshua until Ezra. According to one tradition, they were originally the conquered Canaanites ("hewers of wood and drawers of water") given by David to the Levites to perform menial tasks in the sanctuary along with Gibeonites. Nethinim went into the Babylonian exile and returned with Zerubbabel and Ezra. Though subscribing to the commandments as incorporated into Ezra's covenant, they were still regarded as inferior, and intermarriage with them remained forbidden. They did, however, enjoy a special tax exemption, as did the priests and Levites (*Ezr.* 7.24). They lived in a designated section of Jerusalem (*Neh.* 3.26) and in other cities of Judah; the Nethinim were still known at the time of R. Yehudah ha-Nasi', while in amoraic times mention is made of a village of Nethinim.

• Magen Broshi and Ada Yardeni, "On *Nethinim* and False Prophets," in *Solving Riddles and Untying Knots: Biblical, Epigraphic, and Semitic Studies in Honor of Jonas C. Greenfield*, edited by Ziony Zevit et al. (Winona Lake, Ind., 1995), pp. 29–37. Émile Puech, "The Tell el-Ful Jar Inscription and the Nethinim," *Bulletin of the American Schools of Oriental Research* 261 (1986): 69–72. —SHALOM PAUL

NETILAT YADAYIM. See ABLUTION.

NETSIV. See BERLIN, NAFTALI TSEVI YEHUDAH.

NETUREI QARTA' (Aram.; Guardians of the City), name adopted by a group of Orthodox extremists in Jerusalem who refuse to recognize the existence or the authority of the State of Israel, in view of the secular nature of its creation and orientation. The group first appeared in 1938, splitting off from *Agudat Israel. The name Neturei Qarta' originates from an incident in which R. Yehudah ha-Nasi' sent R. Ḥiyya' and R. Ashi on a pastoral tour of inspection. In one town, they asked to see the "guardians of the city," and the city guard was paraded before them. They said that these were not the guardians of the city but its destroyers, which prompted the citizens to ask who, then, could be considered the guardians. The rabbis answered, "The scribes and the scholars," referring them to *Psalms* 127.1 (Y., *Ḥag.* 76c).

• I. Domb, *The Transformation: The Case of the Neturei Karta* (Brooklyn, 1989). Prime Minister's Office, Overseas Division, *A Study in Fanaticism: The Neturei Karta Extremist Group* (Jerusalem, 1964).

NEVELAH. See CARCASS.

NEW CHRISTIANS. See MARRANOS.

NEW MONTH, ANNOUNCEMENT OF THE. See BIRKAT HA-ḤODESH.

NEW MOON. See RO'SH ḤODESH.

NEW TESTAMENT, name given to the specifically Christian holy scriptures, as distinct from the Hebrew Bible that Christians call the *Old Testament. The term is derived from *Jeremiah* 31.31: "Behold the days come, says the Lord, that I will make a new covenant with the House of Israel and the House of Judah." Christians applied this verse to accord with their belief in the abrogation of the Law through the fulfillment of the messianic prophecies of *Jesus. To Jews, the term is pejorative, implying that the New Testament has replaced the Old.

The earliest sources of the New Testament are the oral traditions transmitted by Jesus' disciples (probably in Aramaic or Mishnaic Hebrew), which were eventually committed to writing and edited (in Greek) as the Gospels. The chronology of the editing of the Gospels is a matter of scholarly controversy, but it is generally agreed that the final versions date from long after the events described, probably from about the end of the first century CE. The earliest canon dates from the middle of the second century CE. Modern scholars are of the view that attitudes of the period of the editing were interjected into the Gospel stories. By the end of the first century, the Christians were in a state of considerable tension with the Jews and were seeking to curry favor with the Roman overlords. This is reflected in the Gospels, especially in the account of the last days of Jesus.

The New Testament has been seen by Jews as a major source of the teaching of contempt, characterizing Christian *antisemitism. Its anti-Jewish polemic has various aspects. One is Christological—the teaching that God can only be seen in terms of Christ. Another is the supersessionist doctrine, which teaches that the new covenant has replaced the ancient covenant between God and the Jews, with all that this entails. The validity of the Old Testament is solely as a preparation for the New. There is also the defamation of Jews, branded as deicides, with their guilt extending to all future generations.

Modern Jewish scholars have made important contributions to the study of the New Testament, and Christian scholarship has become increasingly aware of the polemic elements. The 1985 Vatican document, "The Common Bond," states: "It cannot be ruled out that some references in the New Testament, hostile or less than favorable to the Jews have their historical context in conflicts between the nascent church and the Jewish community. Certain controversies reflect Christian-Jewish relations long after the time of Jesus. To establish this is of capital importance if we wish to bring out the meaning of certain Gospel texts for Christians today."

• Gregory Baum, *Jews and the Gospels* (Westminster, Md., 1961). Norman A. Beck, *Mature Christianity* (London, 1985). David Flusser, *Judaism and the Origins of Christianity* (Jerusalem, 1988). Joseph Klausner, *From Jesus to Paul* (New York, 1943). Joseph Klausner, *Jesus of Nazareth* (New York, 1925). Samuel Tobias Lachs, *A Rabbinic Commentary on the New Testament* (Hoboken, N.J., and New York, 1987). Claude Joseph Goldsmid Montefiore, *Synoptic Gospels* (London, 1909). Samuel Sandmel, *A Jewish Understanding of the New Testament* (New York, 1974).

NEW YEAR. See RO'SH HA-SHANAH.

NEW YEAR FOR TREES. See TU BI-SHEVAT.

NEXT YEAR IN JERUSALEM. See LA-SHANAH HA-BA'AH BI-YERUSHALAYIM.

NEZIQIN (נְזִיקִין; Damages), fourth order of the Mishnah and Tosefta', dealing primarily with monetary subjects and damages that are legally adjudicated. It contains ten tractates: *Bava' Qamma'*, *Bava' Metsi'a'*, *Bava' Batra'* (these three originally constituted a single tractate called *Neziqin*), *Sanhedrin*, *Makkot* (originally the concluding chapters of tractate *Sanhedrin*), *Shevu'ot*, *'Eduyyot*, *'Avodah Zarah*, *Avot*, and *Horayot*. Except for *Avot* and *'Eduyyot*, which have no *gemara'* in either Talmud, all have *gemara'* in both Talmuds.

—AVRAHAM WALFISH

NIDDAH (נִדָּה; Menstruating Woman), tractate in Mishnah order Tohorot, in ten chapters, with related material in the Tosefta', the Talmud Bavli, and partially in the Talmud Yerushalmi. In biblical law, *menstruation renders a woman ritually impure (*Lv*. 15.19–33), as well as halakhically unfit for sexual relations (*Lv*. 18.19). *Niddah* deals almost exclusively with the ritual impurity of a menstruating woman, touching only briefly on the prohibition against sexual relations (*Nid*. 1.7–2.3, 10.8).

The rabbinic discussion of *niddah* focuses on uncertainties regarding the status of a woman's purity. Normally in *halakhah* people are presumed to be pure unless and until they know themselves to have been defiled. Inasmuch as emissions from a woman's genital region are often irregular regarding their timing, their nature, and their source, rabbinic *halakhah* modified this assumption of purity regarding women during their menstruating years. Hence, a menstruating woman is presumed—with respect to the opinion of Shamm'ai (*Nid*. 1.1)—to have defiled food or utensils with which she has come in contact for up to twenty-four hours prior to discovering the menstruation, unless her period is highly regular. The rabbis encouraged women to check themselves regularly and frequently, particularly before conjugal relations or handling sanctified food.

Following the biblical equation of the impurity resulting from childbirth with the impurity of *niddah* (*Lv*. 12.2), *Niddah* discusses the halakhic definition of childbirth, defining the stages of development of the fetus as well as the laws governing the halakhic status of children at various stages of their development. Adult status, for males as well as for females, is defined in terms of the attainment of sexual majority.

An English translation of *Niddah* by I. W. Slotki appears in the Soncino Talmud (London, 1948).

• Chanoch Albeck, ed., *Shishah Sidrei Mishnah, Seder Tohorot* (Jerusalem, 1958). Philip Blackman, ed. and trans., *Mishnayoth*, vol. 5, *Order Taharoth* (Gateshead, 1973). Hermann Leberecht Strack and Günter Stemberger, *Introduction to the Talmud and Midrash*, rev. and updat. ed., translated by Markus Bockmuehl (Minneapolis, 1992).

—AVRAHAM WALFISH

NIDDUI. See EXCOMMUNICATION.

NIETO, DAVID (1654–1728), rabbi of the Spanish-Portuguese community in London from 1701. Born to an ex-*converso* family in Venice, he studied medicine and philosophy in Padua. Until 1701 he served as member of the rabbinical court in Leghorn. Nieto strongly defended traditional Judaism against neo-Karaite and fundamentalistic trends prevailing among his ex-*converso* brethren (*Matteh Dan* [London, 1714]) and vehemently attacked contemporary neo-Shabbatean currents (*Esh dat* [London, 1715]). Following suspicions that he shared deistic views identifying God with nature, he clarified in his work *De la divina providencia* (London, 1705) that his theological view concerning divine providence is in accordance with that of the classical Jewish thinkers and biblical interpreters. Nieto's book is considered a significant contribution to contemporary antideistic doctrines.

• Jakob Josef Petuchowski, *The Theology of Haham David Nieto* (New York, 1954).

—NISSIM YOSHA

NIGGUN (נִגּוּן; Yi. *nign*), one of several words meaning tune; it most commonly denotes one of the wordless melodies first popularized by the Ḥasidim in the eighteenth century. Table melodies, dance tunes, and marches comprise the primary genres; different Hasidic sects favor particular forms of each. Adapting kabbalistic traditions from Safed, Hasidism viewed music as the key to unlock the gates of heaven. Some *niggunim* carry liturgical texts in Hebrew or Yiddish, but the absence of text enables the expression of pure emotion through wordless song. The belief that the expression of joy and religious fervor through music is dearer to God than formalistic prayers contributed to the schism between Ḥasidim and their opponents in the *yeshivah* community.

• Irene Heskes, "The Music of Hasidism: Melodies of Spiritual Ecstasy," in *Passport to Jewish Music: Its History, Traditions and Culture* (Westport, Conn., 1994). Chemjo Vinaver, *Anthology of Hassidic Music*, edited by Eliyyahu Schleifer (Jerusalem, 1985).

—MARSHA BRYAN EDELMAN

NIGHT. See DAY AND NIGHT.

NIGHT OF WATCHING. See LEIL SHIMMURIM.

NIGHT PRAYERS. See QERI'AT SHEMA' ʿAL HA-MITTAH.

NINE DAYS. See BEIN HA-METSARIM.

NINTH OF AV. See TISHʿAH BE-'AV.

NIQQUR (נִקּוּר; porging), the removal of forbidden fat (**ḥelev*) from meat. The fat of those species of animals fit to be brought as sacrifices in the Temple was forbidden for consumption (*Lv*. 7.25) and was burnt on the altar (*Lv*. 3.3–4). Generally the forbidden fats form a separate solid layer that is surrounded by a skin or membrane, which is easily peeled off. There are, however, some threads of forbidden fat that must be porged out with great skill and care. (The rabbis legislate the porging of 51 out of 121 sinews). *Niqqur* may be undertaken only by a *menaqqer* who has received practical training from a recognized expert on the subject. It should be performed as soon as possible after the slaughter of an animal to prevent the fats from hardening. The laws of *niqqur* are found in the *Yoreh Deʿah* section of the *Shulḥan ʿArukh*.

• I. M. Levinger, *Madrikh le-Hilkhot Niqqur* (Jerusalem, 1964). *Matsav ha-Niqqur be-'Arts. ha-B.* (Bene Beraq, 1982).

NISAN (נִיסָן), first month of the religious year, seventh of the civil. It has thirty days, and its zodiac sign is Aries (which the rabbis connected with the paschal lamb). In the earlier biblical books its name is given as Abib (see AVIV), *Nisan* being derived from the Assyrian. According to tradition, Nisan is the month of the creation of the world, the birth of the patriarchs, the Exodus from Egypt, the erection of the Tabernacle, and it will also be the month of redemption. The first day of Nisan was the New Year of Kings, and reigns were reckoned from that date. The fourteenth day of Nisan is the firstborn fast, 15 Nisan is the start of *Pesaḥ (which lasts until 21 Nisan in Israel, until 22 Nisan in the Diaspora), and the ʿOmer period is counted from 16 Nisan. Nisan is a festive month when public mourning is avoided and *Taḥanun omitted from the daily prayers. Yom ha-Sho'ah (Holocaust Memorial Day) is now observed on 27 Nisan (the date is connected to the Warsaw Ghetto Uprising).

• Nathan Bushwick, *Understanding the Jewish Calendar* (New York, 1989). George Zinberg, *Jewish Calendar Mystery Dispelled* (New York, 1963).
—CHAIM PEARL

NISHMAT KOL ḤAI. See BIRKAT HA-SHIR.

NISSIM BEN RE'UVEN GERONDI (c.1315–1375), leading Spanish Talmudist; also known as the Ran. He was probably born in Gerona but lived most of his life in Barcelona, where he headed a *yeshivah* and was also court physician. He issued many *taqqanot* that were applicable to all of Spain, and he sent rulings in response to halakhic queries from places as distant as Erets Yisra'el and Syria. His halakhic writings, for which he was best known, were characterized by their clarity. They included comments and *novellae* on the Talmud (his commentary to the Talmudic tractate *Nedarim* replaces that of Rashi in standard editions), a commentary on the *halakhot* of Yitsḥaq Alfasi, *responsa*, and a book of sermons written in a philosophic style but antiphilosophic in content. Similarly his commentary on the Pentateuch stresses the superiority of Torah and prophecy over philosophy.

• Leon A. Feldman, ed., *Perush ʿal ha-Torah*, by Nissim ben Re'uven Gerondi (Jerusalem, 1968), introduction.

NISSIM BEN YAʿAQOV BEN NISSIM IBN SHAHIN (c.990–1062), North African rabbinic scholar. He lived in Kairouan, where he succeeded his father, Yaʿaqov ben Nissim ibn Shahin (died 1006/7), as head of one of the city's two famous academies. Kairouan was the leading Jewish center in North Africa and was deeply influenced by the traditions of the Babylonian academies. Nissim was in correspondence with *Ha'i Ga'on and was also in close contact with *Shemu'el ha-Nagid in Spain. When his daughter married Shemu'el's son, he visited Granada and taught there for a time. Nissim wrote extensively, and three of his major compositions are known. His major scholarly work, *Sefer Mafteaḥ Manʿulei ha-Talmud* (Vienna, 1847, and in the Vilna [Romm] edition of the Talmud), gives sources for quotations in the Talmud and also provides commentaries on many Talmudic themes. Only part has been preserved. It was written in Arabic and translated into Hebrew. *Megillat ha-Setarim* is a bilingual (Hebrew and Arabic) miscellany covering many subjects of interest to scholars, such as explanations of the biblical text in the contemporary spirit, expositions of sections of the Talmud and Midrash, *responsa*, and customs. The original has not been preserved, but it was widely quoted and a subject index has been found (by S. Assaf, *Tarbiz* 11 [1940]: 229–259). The work for which he is best remembered is *Ḥibbur (Yafeh) min ha-Yeshuʿah* (Ferrara, 1557; Jerusalem, 1969; English translation by William M. Brinner, *An Elegant Composition Concerning Relief After Adversity* [New Haven, 1977]). This anthology of entertaining stories and folktales was a pioneering work of its kind, the first medieval Hebrew prose example of belles-lettres, and basically it had an ethical purpose, directed to the lay reader. It was written in Arabic but was translated into Hebrew and became highly popular.

• Julian Obermann, ed., *Studies in Islam and Judaism: The Arabic Original of Ibn Shahin's Book of Comfort* (New Haven, 1933).
—SHALOM BAR-ASHER

NISSU'IN. See BETROTHAL.

NOAH (Heb. Noaḥ), hero of the biblical story of the Flood; son of Lamech (*Gn*. 5.28–29). Noah was a just and righteous man who "walked with God" (*Gn*. 6.9). He, his family, and representatives of all existing species were saved from the annihilation of all living things by the Flood in an ark (see ARK OF NOAH), which he built at God's command. Noah's first act upon leaving the ark, which had come to rest on mountains of Ararat (in Armenia) as the flood waters had receded, was to make a sacrifice to God. His sacrifice was accepted, and the blessing of fertility and dominion previously vouchsafed to Adam was now bestowed in a covenant upon him (*Gn*. 9.1–17). Unlike the heroes of other ancient accounts of floods, such as the Sumerian Ziusudra or the Babylonian Utnapishtim, for whom escape from the deluge resulted in apotheosis, Noah remained mortal. The biblical tale also stresses the moral dimension of the story; moral corruption caused the eventual annihilation of humankind, and Noah was saved because he was found to be a righteous man (*Gn*. 6.9). Unlike the other Mesopotamian traditions, the biblical Flood story concludes with the making of a covenant between God and humanity. Noah was remembered in later tradition as being one of the three prototypes of righteousness (together with Daniel and Job; *Ez*. 14.14, 20). Talmudic controversy over the proper evaluation of Noah's virtue derived from the passage "Noah was a righteous and wholehearted man in his generation" (*Gn*. 6.9). The rabbis commented that "in his generation" could have either a derogatory or a laudatory implication (*San*. 108a). He is described as a husbandman, but the story of his planting a vineyard and his subsequent intoxication contributed to the division of opinion among the rabbis as to the strength of his character and virtue. Humanity as a whole descended from Noah's three sons, Shem, Ham, and Japheth (*Gn*. 10.1).

• Umberto Cassuto, *A Commentary on the Book of Genesis*, pt. 2, *From Noah to Abraham* (Jerusalem, 1974), pp. 3–249. Nahum M. Sarna, *Genesis*, The JPS Torah Commentary (Philadelphia, 1989), pp. 47–67. Claus Westermann, *Genesis 1–11* (Minneapolis, 1984), pp. 384–494.
—SHALOM PAUL

NOAHIC LAWS, injunctions traditionally given to *Noah and therefore binding upon Jews and gentiles alike. According to the Talmud, there were seven such laws, or rather categories of laws, derived from the early chapters of *Genesis* and consisting of prohibitions against blasphemy, idolatry, sexual immorality (including homosexuality), murder (including abortion), robbery, and eating a portion of a living animal, and an injunction concerning the administration of justice (*Sanh.* 56a). The last of these is interpreted by Nahmanides to include the entire range of social legislation and is also the basis of Maimonides' justification of Simeon and Levi's slaughter of the city of Hamor and Shechem (*Gn.* 34). Another Talmudic source (*Ḥul.* 92a) counts thirty such laws, but they are seen as mere derivations from the basic seven. According to Maimonides a gentile had to acknowledge the divine source of the Noahic laws in order to be regarded as one of the pious of the world. According to the Talmud, gentiles are subject to the death penalty for violating any of the seven Noahic laws, a penalty more severe than that suffered by Jews. There is, however, no evidence that this ruling ever had practical implications. Modern scholars are divided on the date of the conception of the Noahic laws. Louis Finkelstein argued that the laws were formulated to deal with gentiles living under Jewish rule during the Hasmonean period. Ḥayyim Tchernowitz regarded Noahic law as originating in ancient Hittite law. David Novak has argued that, lacking any real evidence for an earlier dating, the Noahic laws should be regarded as having originated in the post-Temple tannaitic period. Throughout Jewish history the Noahic laws were of only theoretical interest to Jews. However, in the 1980s the Lubavitch movement began missionizing to gentiles in an effort to encourage worldwide observance of these laws.

• Louis Finkelstein, *Pharisaism in the Making: Selected Essays* (New York, 1972). Aaron Lichtenstein, *The Seven Laws of Noah* (New York, 1981). David Novak, *The Image of the Non-Jew in Judaism: An Historical and Constructive Study of the Noahide Laws* (New York, 1983). Herbert N. Zulinski, *Noachidische Thoradeutung* (Vienna, 1984).

—MARC SHAPIRO

NOBEL, NEHEMIAH (1871–1922), Orthodox rabbi and Zionist leader in Germany. A Hungarian-born graduate of the Berlin Rabbinical Seminary, he acquired a broad academic education and later studied under Hermann *Cohen in Marburg. After serving the Cologne, Leipzig, and Hamburg communities, Nobel succeeded Marcus Horovitz as communal Orthodox rabbi and *av beit din* in Frankfurt am Main in 1910. Two of his measures, restoring the *ʿeruv* to permit carrying on the Sabbath and granting women a vote in communal affairs, angered Orthodox secessionists. Unlike most German rabbis of his time, Nobel was an outspoken Zionist from 1897 and also chaired the first Mizrachi (Religious Zionist) conference in Pressburg in 1904. His sermons, lectures, and personality influenced Franz *Rosenzweig, Martin *Buber, and other young intellectuals. Nobel was elected president of the Union of German Rabbis in 1919, the only Orthodox Jew to be so honored. A collection of Nobel's addresses and learned articles was published in the volume *Hagut ve-Halakhah* (Jerusalem, 1969), which also includes a biographical study by Yeshayahu Aviʿad.

• Yehudah Leib ha-Kohen Maimon, *Sefer ha-Mizraḥi* (Jerusalem, 1946), pp. 138–139, 141–143, 151. Eugen E. Mayer, "Nehemiah Anton Nobel," in *Guardians of Our Heritage*, edited by Leo Jung (New York, 1958), pp. 565–580. Yizhak Raphael, *Entsiklopedyah shel ha-Tsiyyonut ha-Datit*, vol. 4 (Jerusalem, 1971), cols. 19–27.

—GABRIEL A. SIVAN

NOTARIQON (נוֹטָרִיקוֹן; Gr. *notarikon*; Lat. *notaricum*, from "shorthand writer"), representation of a word or phrase by a single letter, usually the initial; also a method of interpreting a word by considering each letter to be the initial of another word, in contrast to **gimatriyyah*, a form of interpretation based on the numerical value of a word (each Hebrew letter has a numerical value). Interpretation by *notariqon* consists of moral and homiletical lessons derived from the reading of a word as composed of initial letters of other words. Thus a rabbinical *notariqon* explains the word *mizbeaḥ* (altar) as constituting an *abbreviation of *meḥilah, zekhut, berakhah, ḥayyim* (forgiveness, merit, blessing, life). *Notariqon* was also popular among the kabbalists, who, for example, explained the word *tesht* (drink) in *Judges* 13.14 as *tefillat shikor toʿeveh*, "the prayer of a drunkard is an abomination" (*Avqat Rokhel*, last section). Sometimes the words were divided up; thus, the name *Reuben* (*Gn.* 29.32) was explained as *re'u ben*, "see a son" (*Pirqei de-Rabbi Eliʿezer* 36). *Notariqon* was recognized by the rabbis as one of the thirty-two methods of homiletical interpretation of the Bible.

• Matityahu Glazerson, *Letters of the Fire: Mystical Insights into the Hebrew Language* (Jerusalem, 1991).

NOTHINGNESS (Heb. *ʿayin*). The Hebrew term *ʿayin* has had a complex, paradoxical history in Jewish mysticism. *Job* 28.20, "Whence then does wisdom come" (the word *whence* in Hebrew is *me-ʿayin*, which could be interpreted as "from nothingness"), was understood, in kabbalistic terms, to mean that the origin of Ḥokhmah, the second **sefirah*, is from *ʿayin*; because of this, *ʿayin* became a term for the highest *sefirah*, Keter, and the source of all existence. Some kabbalists identified it with the hidden, eternal Godhead itself. *ʿAyin* thus became a term designating true, pure, and eternal existence, unlike the ephemeral and imperfect existence of everything else. In the early Kabbalah, this "nothingness" represents reality. In modern times, the term acquired a central position in the mystical theology of *Ḥabad Hasidism, which postulates that one must turn one's self into nothingness by disregarding worldly phenomena that are meaningless; by negating them and the physical self, union is made with the *ʿayin* in a bond that is the supreme spiritual achievement.

• Joseph Dan, "Paradox of Nothingness in Kabbalah," in *Argumentum e Silentio*, edited by Amy Colin (Berlin and New York, 1987), pp. 359–363. Rachel Elior, *The Paradoxical Ascent to God: The Kabbalistic Theosophy of Habad Hasidism* (Albany, N.Y., 1993). D. Matt, "Ayin: The Concept of Nothingness in Jewish Mysticism," in *The Problem of Pure Consciousness: Mysticism and Philosophy*, edited by Robert K. C. Forman (New York, 1990), pp. 121–150.

—JOSEPH DAN

NOVELLAE. See Ḥiddushim.

NUMBERS. Although numbers play a great role in religious symbolism, there are few numbers with special significance in the Bible. The most prominent number is seven (e.g., seven days of Creation; the Sabbath as the seventh day of the week; the seventh—sabbatical—year; the jubilee year after seven cycles of sabbatical years; the ʿOmer cycle of seven times seven days; the conquest of

Jericho, in which seven priests with seven shofars circled the city for seven days, including seven circuits on the seventh day—*Jos.* 6.1ff.). Other numbers mentioned frequently in the Bible include ten (the smallest number of men who might save Sodom; the ten plagues of Egypt; the Ten Commandments; the tithes) and forty (the Flood, during which it rained for forty days and forty nights; the forty days and nights that Moses spent on Mount Sinai—twice—receiving the Torah; the forty-day period during which the spies spied out the land of Canaan; the forty-year punishment during which the Jews had to remain in the desert; the forty-lash—in practice reduced to thirty-nine—penalty for various offenses; stretches of forty years of quiet in Erets Yisra'el during different eras of the period of the judges). Although the Hebrew numerical system was a decimal one, its method of calculating time was evidently Babylonian, with a twenty-four-hour day and a sixty-minute hour. The attribution of numerical values to letters of the alphabet encouraged mystical exegesis and speculation as well as magical practice. The fact that every Hebrew word has its numerical equivalent gave rise to interpretation by *gimatriyyah*, a method extensively employed in the Midrash for homiletical purposes. *Gimatriyyah* is the twenty-ninth of the thirty-two hermeneutical rules of R. Yosei ha-Galili. Another of R. Yosei's hermeneutical rules that relates to numbers is his twenty-seventh, which states that whenever the same number appears in two different contexts (e.g., the forty days of the Flood and the forty years in the desert), one may draw parallels between the two events. These methods were developed to extremes in Jewish mystical literature (see SEFER YETSIRAH), particularly in the Kabbalah.

• Benjamin Blech, *The Secrets of Hebrew Words* (Northvale, N.J., 1991). Gutman G. Locks, *The Spice of Torah: Gematria* (New York, 1985).

—SHMUEL HIMELSTEIN

NUMBERS, BOOK OF, the fourth book of the Torah. Its traditional name is *Ba-Midbar* (In the Wilderness [of Sinai]), taken from the opening verse; the rabbis also called it *Ḥomesh ha-Pequdim* (The Fifth of [the Torah Concerning] Those Who Were Counted), referring to the censuses of the Israelites the book recounts; this is the origin of the Greek title *Arithmoi*, from which the English name *Numbers* is derived.

Numbers is the direct continuation of *Leviticus*. A month after the erection of the Tabernacle at Mount Sinai, God orders the Israelites to prepare for the journey to Canaan. The preparations include conducting a census of the Israelites (chap. 1) and the Levites (chap. 3), arranging the tribes for the journey (chap. 2), supplying the Tabernacle with sacrificial implements and ingredients (contributed by the chiefs of each tribe; chap. 7), purifying and dedicating the Levites (chap. 8), and manufacturing silver trumpets for use in mustering the tribes (chap. 10.1–10). Interspersed are instructions concerning the duties of each Levitical family in transporting the Tabernacle (chap. 4), the purity of the camp, atonement for false oaths, the Nazirite, the ordeal of jealousy, the Birkat ha-Kohanim (chaps. 5–6), the Menorah (chap. 8.1–4), and Pesaḥ Sheni (chap. 9.1–14).

Following the pillar of cloud and fire (chap. 9.15–23), guided by Hobab, Moses' father-in-law, and with the Ark of the Covenant leading the way (chap. 10.29–36), the Israelites commence their march. They immediately complain about food and water; God provides amply for their needs but punishes them for their faithlessness (chap. 11). Aaron and Miriam are chastised for questioning Moses' privileged position (chap. 12). Arriving at the edge of the Promised Land, the tribes dispatch scouts, who report that the Canaanites are too fierce, and their cities too highly fortified, for Israel to defeat. The people, convinced that the land is too difficult to conquer, wish to return to Egypt; for this sin, God sentences the entire generation to die in the wilderness, decreeing that only their children will enter the Promised Land (chaps. 13–14).

Few of the events of the next thirty-eight years are related; the most significant is the failed insurrection of Korah and his followers (chaps. 16–17). The process of law giving continues: instructions are received concerning sacrifice, fringes on garments (chap. 15), encroachment on the sanctuary, tithes (chap. 18), and purification from contact with the dead (chap. 19). The accounts of the deaths of Miriam and Aaron and the story of Moses' sin, for which he too is condemned to die in the wilderness, mark the end of this tragic period (chap. 20).

The account is resumed in the thirty-ninth year following the Exodus. Approaching the land of Canaan, Israel is forced to fight against Edom and the king of Arad, as well as against Sihon and Og (chaps. 20–21). Finally they encamp on the Plains of Moab across the Jordan from Jericho, where the alarmed Moabites attempt to invoke the curses of *Balaam. The latter is prevented by God from cursing Israel and blesses them instead (chaps. 22–24). The threat of Midianite apostasy leads to all-out war and the utter defeat of Midian (chaps. 25 and 31). A census of the second generation is conducted (chap. 26), and instructions are given for the distribution of the land of Canaan among the tribes, as well as for the allotment of Levitical cities and cities of refuge (chaps. 27 and 34–36). Joshua is appointed as Moses' successor (chap. 27.12–23). Two and a half tribes convince Moses to allow them to settle east of the Jordan, but only after the conquest of Canaan has been completed (chap. 32). More laws are given, including the laws of daily, Sabbath, new moon, and festival offerings, and those concerning vows (chaps. 28–30); the process of law giving finally completed and the itinerary recorded for posterity (chap. 33), the Israelites are ready for their invasion of Canaan.

Bible critics assign most of *Numbers*, including almost all of the laws and the chronology, to the Priestly source, but significant portions of the narrative belongs to the epic sources (J and E). *Numbers* is divided into ten weekly portions, read in the synagogue in early summer, from just before Shavu'ot until shortly before 9 Av.

• Timothy R. Ashley, *The Book of Numbers*, New International Commentary on the Old Testament (Grand Rapids, 1993). Philip J. Budd, *Num-*

bers, Word Biblical Commentary, vol. 5 (Waco, Tex., 1984). Mary Douglas, *In the Wilderness: The Doctrine of Defilement in the Book of Numbers*, Journal for the Study of the Old Testament, Supplement Series 158 (Sheffield, Eng., 1993). Baruch A. Levine, ed., *Numbers 1–20*, The Anchor Bible, vol. 4a (New York, 1993). Jacob Milgrom, *Numbers*, The JPS Torah Commentary (Philadelphia, 1990). Dennis T. Olsen, *The Death of the Old and the Birth of the New: The Framework of the Book of Numbers and the Pentateuch*, Brown Judaic Studies, no. 71 (Chico, Calif., 1985).

–BARUCH J. SCHWARTZ

NUMBERS RABBAH, Midrashic work on the *Book of* **Numbers* in the medieval anthology *Midrash Rabbah, composed of two distinct sections. *Numbers Rabbah I* (chaps. 1–14) is an extensive Midrashic commentary to the annual cycle lections "Ba-Midbar" and "Naso' " (*Nm.* 1–7), which seems to have been edited in the twelfth century CE, probably in Provence. The author-editor made use of both Talmuds Bavli and Yerushalmi, earlier Midrashic works, and, most significantly, the teachings of *Mosheh ha-Darshan. *Numbers Rabbah II* (chaps. 15–23) is essentially the same text as *midrash Tanḥuma'* to the rest of *Numbers* (chaps. 8–36). An English translation of the work by J. J. Slotki appeared in the Soncino Midrash (London, 1939).

• Hananel Mack, "Midrash Be-Midbar Rabbah," Ph.D. dissertation, The Hebrew University of Jerusalem, 1991. Hermann Leberecht Strack, *Introduction to the Talmud and Midrash* (1931; Minneapolis, 1992). Leopold Zunz, *Ha- Derashot be-Yisra'el ve-Hishtalshelutan ha-Historit*, edited by Chanoch Albeck (1892; Jerusalem, 1974).

–MARC BREGMAN

NUSSAḤ (נֻסָּח), a Hebrew term that originally meant "removal" and hence "copying"; it is now used in three different ways, each conveying the idea of "accepted formula": to refer to textual variants (Rashi and the tosafists, however, employed the word *girsa'* to signify different readings); to distinguish the differing liturgical rites of the various communities and groups, also known as **minhag*; and to denote the *nussaḥ ha-tefillah*, the traditional manner in which the prayers are chanted as they have been handed down through the centuries. Sabbaths, festivals, and weekdays have unique melodies that distinguish one occasion from the other. Books such as *Lamentations* and *Esther* have their own melodies. Various communities have also chanted the Torah and *haftarah* readings with unique systems of cantillation. See also MUSIC.

• Ismar Elbogen, *Jewish Liturgy; A Comprehensive History*, translated by Raymond P. Scheindlin (Philadelphia, 1993). Isaac Klein, *A Guide to Jewish Religious Practice* (New York, 1992). Stefan C. Reif, *Judaism and Hebrew Prayer: New Perspectives on Jewish Liturgical History* (Cambridge, 1993).

–PETER KNOBEL

O

OATH. See Vows and Oaths.

OATH MORE JUDAICO, a special oath that Jews had to take when in litigation with non-Jews. As early as the sixth century, Emperor Justinian I legislated that Jews were inadmissible as witnesses against Christians. During the Middle Ages, Jews were permitted to testify under this special oath, which took various forms, very often of a degrading nature. The oath was sometimes accompanied by a humiliating ceremony (for example, standing on the skin of a sow). The model for later legislation was the oath adopted by German courts in 1555, in which the Jewish witness had to call down upon himself all the curses in *Leviticus* 26, *Deuteronomy* 28, and the plagues of Egypt. Moses *Mendelssohn succeeded in persuading the Prussian government to modify the oath, but it remained in force in some countries until the beginning of the twentieth century. The imposition of this oath was based upon the false allegation that by the *Kol Nidrei formula the Jew absolves himself from all oaths.

• Volker Zimmermann, *Die Entwicklung des Judeneids* (Bern, 1973).

OBADIAH (Heb. ʿOvadyah; 6th cent. BCE), prophet in the kingdom of Judah. The *Book of Obadiah*, which provides no information about the prophet, consists of oracles against Edom, describing Edom's actions during the fall of Jerusalem in 586 and foretelling Edom's future downfall. Talmudic tradition identifies the prophet as an Idumean proselyte identical with the Obadiah in *1 Kings* 18 who hid the prophets during the time of Elijah (*San*. 39b).

The *Book of Obadiah* is the fourth book of the Minor Prophets. The shortest book in the entire Bible, it consists of one chapter with twenty-one verses describing the guilt of Edom in connection with the fall of Jerusalem. The Edomites not only rejoiced over the destruction of the city, but intercepted the Judahites when they attempted to flee. In a vivid "Day of the Lord" prophecy, Obadiah predicts that the tables will be turned and that Israel will possess Edom. *Obadiah* shares many affinities with the oracle against Edom in *Jeremiah* 49.7–22. Critical opinion is divided as to whether *Obadiah* is a single work or a composite of two authors (the second part said to consist of the first half of verse 15 and verses 16–21).

• Leslie C. Allen, *The Books of Joel, Obadiah, Jonah, and Micah*, New International Commentary on the Old Testament (Grand Rapids, 1976). Mordechai Cogan, *ʿOvadyah: ʿIm Mavo u-Ferush*; Uriel Simon, *Yonah: ʿIm Mavo u-Ferush*, Mikra le-Yisraʾel (Tel Aviv and Jerusalem, 1992). R. J. Coggins, *Israel Among the Nations: A Commentary on the Books of Nahum and Obadiah*; S. P. Reʾemi, *Esther*, International Theological Commentary (Edinburgh and Grand Rapids, 1985). Douglas K. Stuart, *Hosea–Jonah*, Word Biblical Commentary, vol. 31 (Waco, Tex., 1987). Hans Walter Wolff, *Obadiah and Jonah*, translated by Margaret Kohl (Minneapolis, 1986). —Marvin A. Sweeney

OBLATION. See Meal Offering.

ODEL, daughter of Yisraʾel ben Eliʿezer *Baʿal Shem Tov. Hasidic tradition says that he derived her soul, and so her name, from the Torah, by constructing it out of the initial letters of *Deuteronomy* 33.2: "A fiery law unto them" (*esh dat lamo*). She is known principally from Hasidic legends collected in *Shivḥei ha-Besht* and from letters drawn from a *genizah* of Hasidic forgeries in Kherson. Some sources characterize her as one of her father's disciples, who gave out magical remedies to the sick; other traditions do not portray her as possessing any spiritual ambition. She married Yeḥiʾel Ashkenazi and was the mother of the renowned Hasidic masters R. Mosheh Ḥayyim Efrayim of Sudylkow and R. Barukh of Medzhibozh. Her daughter Feigeh was the mother of Hasidic master Naḥman of Bratslav, who was quoted as having said of Odel: "All the masters knew her to be endowed with divine inspiration; she was a woman of great intellect."

• Ada Rapoport-Albert, "On Women in Hasidism," in *Jewish History: Essays in Honour of Chimen Abramsky*, edited by Ada Rapoport-Albert and Steven Zipperstein (London, 1988), pp. 516–517. Avraham Rubinstein, ed., *Shivḥei ha-Besht* (Jerusalem, 1991), p. 182. —Rachel Elior

OFANNIM (אוֹפַנִּים), class of *angels. The term is derived from Ezekiel's vision of the divine throne-chariot (*Ez*. 1.15ff.) and originally referred to the wheels that bear the throne. In later literature, *ofannim* became the designation of an angelic hierarchy, similar to *cherubim, *seraphim, and *ḥayyot*. The name was also given to a genre of liturgical prayers inserted by Ashkenazim into the *Yotser prayer on Sabbaths and festivals, describing the angelic praise of God and beginning with the words, "The *ofannim* and holy *ḥayyot*."

OFFERINGS. See Sacrifices.

OHALOT (אֳהָלוֹת; Tents), tractate in Mishnah order Toharot, in eighteen chapters, with related material in Toseftaʾ. It has no *gemaraʾ* in either Talmud. It discusses the ritual impurity spread by a corpse, which defiles for seven days anything that touches it, as well as whatever is together with it in one tent (*Nm*. 19.13–20). The tractate's main topic is the delineation of the rules applying to the impurity transmitted by tents. In rabbinic law, this is understood to include any person, utensil, clothing, or food that passes above or below the corpse, as well as persons or susceptible items that are under the same roof as the corpse. Furthermore, the impurity spreads to openings and passages, following the rule that "the manner of impurity is to go out" (*Ohal*. 3.7). Therefore, the impurity of a sealed grave (*Nm*. 19.16) is transmitted to anyone who touches it or passes over it. Places where there is suspicion that corpse parts may be found must be treated as impure.

Ohalot 7 brings together a collection of diverse regulations, ranging from the minimum dimensions of a sealed grave to the conditions for a dead fetus in the womb to contaminate and culminates in the permission to abort the fetus in order to save the life of the mother.

An English translation of the tractate is in Herbert Danby's *The Mishnah* (London, 1933).

• Chanoch Albeck, ed., *Shishah Sidrei Mishnah, Seder Tohorot* (Jerusalem, 1958). Philip Blackman, ed. and trans., *Mishnayoth*, vol. 5, *Order Taharoth* (Gateshead, 1973). Hermann Leberecht Strack and Günter Stemberger, *Introduction to the Talmud and Midrash*, rev. and updat. ed., translated by Markus Bockmuehl (Minneapolis, 1992).

—AVRAHAM WALFISH

OHEL (אֹהֶל; tent). *Numbers* 19.14 states that any human beings or utensils in the same tent with a *corpse contract ritual *impurity for a period of seven days. Because priests are not permitted to contract ritual uncleanness, they must not enter a house where a corpse lies, nor may they enter a cemetery. The term *ohel* is also used for a structure over a tomb and was especially applied to those structures erected over the graves of outstanding Hasidic rabbis.

• Jacob Milgrom, "The Rationale for Biblical Impurity," *Journal of the Ancient Near East Society* 22 (1993): 107–111. Lawrence Schiffman, "The Impurity of the Dead in the Temple Scroll," in *Archaeology and History in the Dead Sea Scrolls*, edited by L. Schiffman (Sheffield, Eng., 1990), pp. 135–156.

OIL, together with grain and wine, is listed as one of the three blessings bestowed by God on Erets Yisraʾel (*Dt.* 11.14). In the Tabernacle and Temple only "pure olive oil beaten for the light to cause the lamp [see CANDLES; MENORAH] to burn always" (*Ex.* 27.20) was permitted for use; among eastern Jews this is still the only oil permitted for the eternal lamp in the synagogue. Rabbi *Tarfon similarly declared that only olive oil could be used for the Sabbath lamps (*Shab.* 26a), but the accepted ruling is that generally any oil may be used (*Shab.* 2). Oil was used for the ceremonial *anointing of high priests and kings and in the purification process after leprosy (*Lv.* 13.45). Candles have largely replaced oil, though many still prefer the use of oil for the Ḥanukkah lamp. Oil also formed part of some sacrificial offerings, for example, in the burnt offering and cereal offerings (*Lv.* 2.4). See also KINDLING OF LIGHTS.

• John J. Castelot, *Anointing in the Old Testament* (Washington, D.C., 1950). Martin Goodman, "Kosher Olive Oil in Antiquity," in *A Tribute to Geza Vermes*, edited by P. Davies and R. White (Sheffield, Eng., 1990), pp. 227–245.

OKHLAH VE-OKHLAH, a work based on the *Masorah, probably composed in Babylonia in the tenth century, that catalogs in 398 lists peculiarities and distinctive features in the spelling of the biblical text. The opening list of the book records pairs of words that occur in the Bible only once with and once without the letter *vav*. The first pair of words is *okhlah* and *ve-okhlah* (*1 Sm.* 1.9 and *Gn.* 27.19, respectively). In its present form the work includes additions by later Sephardi and Ashkenazi scholars.

• S. Frensdorff, *Das Buch Ochlah W'ochlah* (Hannover, 1864; repr. Tel Aviv, 1969). Israel Yeivin, *Introduction to the Tiberian Masorah*, translated and edited by E. J. Revell, Masoretic Studies, no. 5 (Missoula, Mont., 1980).

ʿOLAH. See BURNT OFFERING.

ʿOLAM (עוֹלָם), originally a term with temporal connotation: from unending past to unending future, eternity. *Psalms* 106.48 praises God from *ʿolam* to *ʿolam* (for ever and ever). The word also acquired a spatial meaning: world or universe. In the eschatological terminology of the late Second Temple period, *ʿ*olam ha-zeh* and *ʿolam ha-baʾ* signified, respectively, the present age and the future age (i.e., the messianic dispensation, the kingdom of God, etc.), but the terms later came to mean this world in which we live and, like the English word *hereafter*, a more spatially conceived celestial abode of the soul after death. One of the appellations of God in liturgy and rabbinic literature is *ribbono shel ʿolam* (Lord of the universe). The title *melekh ha-ʿolam* (King of the universe), which occurs in every benediction formula, similarly refers to God as creator, ruler, and master of the universe.

• Ernst S. Jenni, *Wort ʿOlam im Alten Testament* (Berlin, 1953). Mark S. Smith, "Berît am/Berît ôlam: A New Proposal for the Crux of Isa 42:6," *Journal of Biblical Literature* 100 (1981): 241–243. Arthur I. Waskow, "Tikkun Olam: Adornment of the Mystery ('Repair the World')," *Religion and Intellectual Life* 2 (1985): 109–115.

ʿOLAM HA-ZEH AND ʿOLAM HA-BAʾ (עוֹלָם הַזֶּה; עוֹלָם הַבָּא; this world and the world to come), eschatological concepts developed during the Second Temple period and in subsequent rabbinic literature. Originally, the meaning of the word *ʿolam* was temporal (age) rather than spatial (world), and the terms signified, respectively, the present age, with all its shortcomings and miseries, and the future or messianic age (often identified with the *kingdom of heaven). It was believed that a major event, such as the Day of Judgment, would terminate *ʿolam ha-zeh* and usher in *ʿolam ha-baʾ*. The concept of *ʿolam ha-baʾ* is thus different from that of *heaven or *paradise (see EDEN, GARDEN OF), which is the abode of departed souls pending the advent of the "coming age." However, the distinction was not always maintained in later literature, and in many rabbinic sayings the "other world" was understood as referring to the celestial realm of blessed souls. *Berakhot* 17a says, "The world to come is unlike this world. In the world to come there is no eating or drinking or propagation or business or jealousy or hatred or rivalry, but the righteous sit with crowns on their heads, enjoying the radiance of the divine presence." The punishment awaiting certain heretics is deprivation of their "share in the world to come," a state to which every Jew, as well as the righteous gentile, is entitled (*San.* 10.1). The relationship between *ʿolam ha-zeh* and *ʿolam ha-baʾ* is expressed in two Mishnaic statements (*Avot* 4.21–22): "*ʿolam ha-zeh* is like an antechamber to *ʿolam ha-baʾ*. Prepare yourself in the antechamber so that you may enter the palace." Thus, *ʿolam ha-zeh* is regarded as the place for performing good deeds and acquiring merits, which are then rewarded in *ʿolam ha-baʾ*, the place of bliss. The other statement reads, "Better is one hour of repentance and good deeds in *ʿolam ha-zeh* than the whole life of *ʿolam ha-baʾ*; and one hour of bliss in *ʿolam ha-baʾ* is better than the whole life of *ʿolam ha-zeh*." See also AFTERLIFE; ESCHATOLOGY; RESURRECTION.

• Leonard B. Gerwirtz, *Jewish Spirituality* (Hoboken, N.J., 1986). Aryeh Kaplan, *Immortality, Resurrection, and the Age of the Universe* (Hoboken, N.J., 1993). Simcha Paull Raphael, *Jewish Views of the Afterlife* (Northvale, N.J., 1994).

OLD TESTAMENT, the traditional Christian name for the Jewish sacred scriptures (see BIBLE). The word *testament* is one of the terms used to translate the Hebrew word *berit* (covenant), the Bible's designation of the relationship between God and the Israelite people. Jeremiah, who prophesied on the eve of the fall of Judah and the exile to Babylonia, foresaw that the end of Israel's national existence would be followed by its eventual restoration. To express this, the prophet makes use of the concept of *berit*. God, he says (*Jer.* 31.30–33), will soon make a "new covenant" with the Israelites, that is, he will reestablish the relationship that had been terminated by the exile, restoring the Israelites to their land and their national sovereignty. The new covenant will be precisely like the old, the prophet says, except for one feature: the Israelites, by failing to keep God's laws, had broken the earlier one; the new one will be unbreakable. This, Jeremiah says, will be the result of God's inscribing the terms of the new covenant "on their hearts," a metaphoric way of saying that obedience to God will become effortless and natural; thus, it will endure forever.

Christian thinkers reinterpreted Jeremiah's prophecy in accord with their belief in God's rejection of the Jews and in the nullification of the commands of the Torah. They saw the term *new covenant* as an ancient prediction of the Christian promise of salvation through grace (the covenant "in the heart" was reinterpreted to refer to faith rather than practice), thus giving Christian gospel the stamp of prophetic corroboration. Eventually this led to the use of the term *new covenant* to denote Christian scripture, and ultimately to the use of the term *old covenant* to denote the sacred scriptures of the Jews. The English word *testament* (as in last will and testament) tends to emphasize one side of the *berit*: the promises made by God to Israel, whereas the word *covenant* (literally, a pact or agreement) emphasizes the mutual obligations imposed. In recent times, religiously neutral terms, such as Hebrew Bible (or Hebrew Scripture) and Christian Scripture, are favored over Old and New Testament (with the pejorative implication that the new replaces the old).

• Jon D. Levenson, *The Hebrew Bible, the Old Testament, and Historical Criticism: Jews and Christians in Biblical Studies* (Louisville, Ky., 1993).

—BARUCH J. SCHWARTZ

OMEN. See ORACLES.

ʿOMER (עֹמֶר), a sheaf of newly harvested barley. The children of Israel were commanded to bring an *ʿomer* "on the morrow of the Sabbath," and only after offering the *ʿomer* and the appropriate accompanying sacrifice were they permitted to eat the grain of the new harvest (*Lv.* 23.10–14). The *Pharisees maintained that the Sabbath mentioned in this verse refers to the first day of Pesaḥ, which is the subject of the previous paragraph; in other words the *ʿomer* was to be offered on the second day of Pesaḥ (16 Nisan) and was to consist of a tenth of an *ephah* of barley. Seven full weeks were counted from this day, and the fiftieth day was observed as *Shavuʿot. The *Sadducees, and later the *Karaites, interpreted the Sabbath in the verse as meaning the first Sabbath day during Pesaḥ; therefore, Shavuʿot would always fall on a Sunday. To emphasize the importance of cutting the *ʿomer* on 16 Nisan, the rabbis permitted it even when it fell on a Sabbath (*Men.* 10.1). The counting, which is observed to the present day, is called the "counting of the ʿOmer." The announcement of each day is generally incorporated into the Maʿariv service (the *ʿomer* was reaped by night) after the recitation of an appropriate benediction, which is followed by a prayer for the restoration of the Temple service. The wall calendar hung in the synagogue to keep track of the counting of the ʿOmer was sometimes the object of artistic design. The period between the first harvest and the first fruit harvest, which the counting of the ʿOmer commemorates, must originally have been one of joy, but tradition has established it as a period of sadness and semimourning, during which—with the exception of *Lag ba-ʿOmer—merriment, the celebration of marriages (among Sephardim until Lag ba-ʿOmer), the cutting of hair, and the wearing of new clothes are all forbidden. The only basis for these abstinences is a vague statement in the Talmud (*Yev.* 62b) that "12,000 pairs of the disciples of R. Akiva died in one period" and that that period was "between Pesaḥ and Shavuʿot." The passage is taken by most scholars to refer to the Bar Kokhba' Revolt. The ceremonious cutting of the first sheaf of corn on the morrow of the first day of Pesaḥ has been revived in many agricultural settlements in the State of Israel. The Israel chief rabbinate and rabbis in the Diaspora (but not the Ḥaredim) permit *Yom ha-ʿAtsma'ut (Independence Day) celebrations and the recital of sections of the *Hallel prayer on 5 Iyyar during the ʿOmer. Celebrations are also held in Israel on *Yom Yerushalayim (Jerusalem Day; 28 Iyyar).

• Samuel H. Dresner, "A Homily on Counting the Omer," *Conservative Judaism* 41 (Spring 1989): 71–78. Menahem Haran, *Temples and Temple-Service in Ancient Israel* (Winona Lake, Ind., 1985).

ʿOMER, THIRTY-THIRD DAY OF THE. See LAG BA-ʿOMER.

OMNAM KEN (אָמְנָם כֵּן; Indeed It Is So), penitential poem (*seliḥah*) recited in the Ashkenazi during the evening service of Yom Kippur. Begging God to forgive his people for their wrongdoings, each verse concludes *salaḥti*, "I have forgiven." Its author has been identified as R. Yom Tov ben Yitsḥaq of Joigny, who died a martyr's death with the Jews of York, who committed suicide in order to escape massacre in 1190.

• Macy Nulman, *The Encyclopedia of Jewish Prayer* (Northvale, N.J., and London, 1993), p. 260.

ONA'AH. See FRAUD.

ʿONEG SHABBAT (עֹנֶג שַׁבָּת; Sabbath delight), phrase based on *Isaiah* 58.13—"And you shall call the Sabbath a delight"—expressive of the traditional attitude toward the Sabbath. The rabbis approved of everything that would enhance the "Sabbath delight," recommending that additional dishes be served at the Sabbath meal and insisting on a minimum of three meals in honor of the day. Since the *Se'udah Shelishit (third meal) was the specific additional meal of the Sabbath, it became the principal occasion for *'oneg Shabbat* and is marked by the singing of **zemirot* and the delivery of discourses on the biblical lesson of the day. The modern 'Oneg Shabbat, a cultural rather than a strictly religious occasion that attempts to capture the spirit of the Sabbath without necessarily adhering to its ritual forms, was introduced in Tel Aviv by the poet Ḥayyim Naḥman Bialik in the 1920s. It included Bible study, a lecture, and the singing of Sabbath songs. The custom spread throughout Israel and to the Diaspora. In America, the term is often used for a collation after Friday night services.

• Abraham Joshua Heschel, *The Sabbath: Its Meaning for Modern Man* (New York, 1951). Abraham Ezra Millgram, *Sabbath, the Day of Delight* (Philadelphia, 1944). —CHAIM PEARL

ONEN. See ANINUT.

ONES. See DURESS; RAPE.

ONIAS, TEMPLE OF, temple erected in the mid-second century BCE at Leontopolis in Egypt by the deposed high priest Onias III (who had fled to Egypt during persecutions by Antiochus IV Epiphanes in Jerusalem) or possibly by his son Onias IV (see *Men.* 109a–110b). It was built at the site of the shrine of an Egyptian goddess and seems to have served the local Jewish military colony, which may have included members of the priestly family who had fled with Onias. They offered sacrifices there, but it was never a rival to the Temple in Jerusalem. Among the explanations offered for why Onias built a temple and not a synagogue are personal ambition and Egyptian political aspirations. The temple was closed by the Romans in approximately 71 CE.

• Gideon Bohak, "CPJ III, 520: The Egyptian Reaction to Onias' Temple," *Journal for the Study of Judaism* 26 (1995): 32–41. Fausto Parente, "Onias III's Death and the Founding of the Temple of Leontopolis," in *Josephus and the History of the Greco-Roman Period*, edited by F. Parente et al. (Leiden, 1994), pp. 69–98.

ONKELOS, TARGUM. See TARGUM.

OPPENHEIM, DAVID BEN AVRAHAM (1664–1736), rabbinic scholar, halakhist, patron. He was born in Worms and studied in Metz and Landsberg. He served the communities of Nikolsburg and Prague and was named *Landesrabbiner* of Moravia and later of all Bohemia. He came into conflict with Yonatan Eybeschuetz of Prague, and disturbances between their students prompted Emperor Charles VI to intervene in favor of Oppenheim. Oppenheim was responsible for the collection and transfer of all funds raised in Europe for the benefit of Jews in Jerusalem.

In addition to his recognized erudition in rabbinic and halakhic literature, Oppenheim was a mathematician. He was also a collector of rare manuscripts and books, which he amassed using the wealth that he inherited from a variety of sources. A substantial portion of the Hebrew sections of the Bodleian Library in Oxford consists of items from his library. Oppenheim also was a patron of Jewish scholarship, dispensing numerous publication grants to editors of rabbinic works. Moreover, he allowed publishers access to his manuscripts in order to bring the works to the attention of the wider public. Most of Oppenheim's own work remains unpublished, although his *responsa* are preserved in a number of leading rabbinic collections of his day, including the *responsa* of R. Ya'ir Ḥayyim Bacharach and R. Ya'aqov Reischer.

• L. Loewenstein, "David Oppenheim," in *Gedenkbuch zur Erinnerung an David Kauffmann*, edited by Marcus Brann (Breslau, 1900), pp. 538–539. Heimann Michael, *Or ha-Ḥayyim* (Frankfurt am Main, 1891), pp. 314–318. Otto Muneles, *Ketovot mi-Beit he-'Almin ha-Yehudi ha'Atiq be-Prag* (Jerusalem, 1988), pp. 351–352. —EPHRAIM KANARFOGEL

ORACLES. The custom of consulting an oracle in times of crisis is almost universal. In ancient Mesopotamia, many types of natural phenomena as well as human behavior were considered ominous if interpreted properly, and several mechanical devices, such as oil in water, smoke, the flight of birds, or cracks in bones (shoulder blades) heated by fire, were considered signs of divine communication or signals heralding future events. The standard method of oracular inquiry in Mesopotamia was hepatoscopy, that is, liver divination, in which contours, marks, and colors on the liver of a sacrificial sheep were interpreted as ominous by a diviner (cf. *Ez.* 21.6). Biblical narratives mention certain methods of divination practiced by neighboring peoples (*Nm.* 22–24; *1 Sm.* 6; *Ez.* 21.23–28), but their use was prohibited and characterized as an abomination (*Lv.* 19.25, 31; *Dt.* 18.9–13). *Necromancy was prohibited and, according to the biblical account, was suppressed by Saul although it seems to have been considered effective not only by Saul himself but by the biblical author (*1 Sm.* 28). The three acceptable oracular methods in Israel are mentioned in the passage "And when Saul inquired of the Lord, the Lord did not answer him, either by dreams, or by Urim, or by prophets" (*1 Sm.* 28.6). There are many instances of specific inquiries being answered by means of *dreams (*Jgs.* 7.13) or prophets (*1 Kgs.* 14) or other oracular media (*2 Sm.* 5.24); Urim and Thummim was the only method of divination by mechanical devices officially sanctioned by the Bible. When Joshua was appointed to succeed Moses as national leader, he was told that in the future he was to stand before Eleazar, the high priest, who would "ask counsel of him after the Urim," so as to determine the goings out and comings in of Israel (*Nm.* 27.21). It has been assumed that when mention is made of asking divine counsel (e.g., *Jos.* 9.14; *Jgs.* 1.1–2), it was sought through the Urim and Thummim. The precise nature of the terms and mode of operation are unknown apart from the statement that in putting the breastplate (*ḥoshen*) on Aaron, Moses "also put in the breastplate the Urim and Thummim" (*Lv.* 8.8). Some rabbinic sources as well as modern scholars identify the Urim and Thummim with the twelve gemstones decorating the high priest's breastplate, but these objects are unrelated. The Urim and Thummim probably served as a form of divination by lots that were kept in the breastplate of the high priest, and the procedure seems to be related to forms of oracular divination mentioned elsewhere, such as the *ephod (*1 Sm.* 23.9) and *lots (*goral*; *Nm.* 26.55). The Urim and Thummim were used in the preexilic period but are not mentioned after the time of Solomon. *Nehemiah* 7.65 states explicitly that they were no longer available in the postexilic age. The oracular use of the ephod is referred to in *1 Samuel* 23.9, but this, too, may refer to the Urim and Thummim. Scholars have looked for analogies in extra-biblical sources that might provide answers to several of the enigmas of the Urim and Thummim. One such source is an Akkadian text found at Assur prescribing a ritual for psephomancy, divining by stones. This text bears some similarities to aspects of the Urim and Thummim. In this ritual, simple questions requiring a "yes" or "no" answer are posed, and the answer is provided by two stones that seem to be drawn from a garment. Of these, one is called a "stone of request" and the other a "stone of no request." The stones were white (alabaster) and black (hematite). The Akkadian word for alabaster (*gishnugallu*) means "the great light," which may correspond with the Hebrew *urim* (lights), while a popular name for hematite is "stone of truth," which parallels the Hebrew *thummim* (perfection, righteousness).

• Frederick H. Cryer, *Divination in Ancient Israel and Its Near Eastern Environment*, Journal for the Study of the Old Testament, Supplement Series 142 (Sheffield, Eng., 1994). C. van Dam, *The Urim and Thummim: An Old Testament Means of Revelation* (Winona Lake, Ind., 1993). Wayne Horowitz and Victor (A.) Hurowitz, "Urim and Thummim in Light of a Psephomancy Ritual from Assur (LKA 137)," *Journal of the Ancient Near Eastern Society* 21 (1992): 95–115. Victor (A.) Hurowitz, "The Expression *ûqsamîm beyadam* (*Numbers* 22.7) in Light of Divinatory Practices from Mari," *Hebrew Studies* 33 (1992): 5–15. Jacob Milgrom, *Leviticus 1–16: A New Translation with Introduction and Commentary*, The Anchor Bible, vol. 3 (New York, 1991), pp. 507–511.

—VICTOR HUROWITZ

ORAḤ ḤAYYIM. See SHULḤAN ʿARUKH.

ORAL LAW. According to rabbinic tradition, the oral law (*torah she-be-ʿal peh*) was given together with the *written law. The proof text for this tradition is the divine charge to Moses to teach the Torah to the Israelites by "putting it in their mouths" (*Dt.* 31.19), that is, orally.

The standard argument used by medieval authorities to demonstrate the need for the oral law is that in its absence it would be impossible to carry out most of the biblical commandments, since the specific details of their observance are generally missing from the biblical text. Classic examples of this difficulty are the definition of forbidden work on the Sabbath day and the precise nature of the "affliction of the soul" required on Yom Kippur. Dimensions and quantities, which are the lifeblood of *halakhah*, are entirely missing from the written law and rely upon the oral tradition for their existence (see Maimonides, *Introduction to the Mishnah*; Yehudah ha-Levi, *Kuzari* 3.35; R. Mosheh ben Yaʿaqov of Coucy, *Sefer Mitsvot Gadol*, Introduction). The problem of applying biblical laws solely on the basis of their written text is highlighted in scripture itself. Although Moses knew that the penalty for breaking the Sabbath was death, he was unaware of the punishment to be meted out to a person caught gathering sticks on the Sabbath day. God proceeded to inform Moses that the individual concerned was to be put to death, and the precise method of execution was to be "stoning by the whole congregation" (*Nm.* 15.32–35). Moses also experienced practical difficulties in applying the law of inheritance recorded in the Bible to the family of Zelophehad, which consisted of five daughters, until God gave him the necessary instructions regarding female succession (*Nm.* 27.1–11). The necessary interdependence of the written and oral laws is expressed in the Talmudic account of a proselyte who had initially refused to accept the oral law. Hillel converted him and then proceeded to demonstrate that he could not possibly understand the written law without also accepting the oral law. The convert took Hillel's point and gave up his opposition to the oral tradition (*Shab.* 31a). The hermeneutical principles for the development of the written law eventually crystallized into the thirteen *middot* of R. Yishmaʿeʾl ben Elishaʿ, and it is these *middot* that constitute the basis of the legal nexus between the written and the oral laws (see HERMENEUTICS). Although the appellation *oral* is prescriptive as well as descriptive (*Git.* 60b), it is evident from the Talmud itself that halakhic material derived from the written law by the hermeneutical principles, together with rabbinic legislation and rational principles, was written down in scroll form for reference purposes (*Shab.* 6b; Rashi on *Shabbat* 6b, s.v. *megillat setarim; B. M.* 92a). The reasons offered for the prohibition against committing the oral law to writing include the jurisprudential need for flexibility in adapting the Torah to changing conditions (*Sefer ha-ʾIqqarim* 3.23) and the theological claim that the authentic interpretation of scripture is embodied in the oral law, which is the sole possession of Israel, as opposed to the other nations (*Midrash Tanḥuma'*, "Ki Tissa'," no. 34). The Talmud links the permission to commit the oral law to writing in the period of R. Yehudah ha-Nasi' with the impossibility of remembering the vast body of oral *halakhah* that was in existence at that time. In justifying the elimination of the prohibition against the writing down of the oral law, the rabbis cite a verse in *Psalms* 119.126, "It is a time to act for the Lord for they have violated your Torah," interpreting it to mean "when it is time to act for the Lord, your Torah may be violated," that is, "it is better that one letter of the Torah should be uprooted so that the entire Torah will not be forgotten by Israel" (*Git.* 60a; *Tem.* 14b). The classical text of the oral law is the *Mishnah, but there is a scholarly debate as to whether or not it was actually put into writing contemporaneously with its redaction by R. Yehudah ha-Nasi' in the second century CE. The Babylonian and the Jerusalem Talmuds contain the bulk of the oral law, and this body of work has been added to over the ages by innumerable commentators and codifiers. According to the oral tradition, the rabbis have the power to suspend the provisions of the written law itself, albeit on a temporary basis (Maimonides, *Hilkhot Mamrim* 2.4). The Sadducees and the Essenes possessed different systems of oral law during the Second Temple period, but neither one survived the destruction of the Temple. The Karaite sect in the Middle Ages also rejected the oral law and preached a return to pure scriptural Judaism. The oral law was opposed by classical Reform Judaism, but in recent years it has been restored to favor as a result of a quest for Reform *halakhah*.

• Zevi Chajes, *The Student's Guide Through the Talmud* (London, 1952), pp. 1–28. Boaz Cohen, *Law and Tradition in Judaism* (New York, 1959), pp. 39–61. Menachem Elon, *Jewish Law: History, Sources, Principles* (Philadelphia, 1994), pp. 190–227. David Weiss Halivni, *Midrash, Mishnah and Gemara: The Predilection for Justified Law* (Cambridge, Mass., 1986). Susan Handelman, *The Slayers of Moses* (Albany, 1982) pp. 42–50. David Kraemer, *The Mind of the Talmud* (New York, 1990). Jacob Neusner, *How the Talmud Shaped Rabbinic Discourse* (Atlanta, 1991), pp. 1–20. Jacob Neusner, *Uniting the Dual Torah: Sifra and the Problem of the Mishnah* (Cambridge, 1990). Hermann Strack, *Introduction to the Talmud and Midrash*, (New York, 1974). Adin Steinsaltz, *The Essential Talmud*, (New York, 1976), pp. 10–23. —DANIEL SINCLAIR

ORDEAL OF JEALOUSY (Heb. *torat ha-qena'ot*), ritual procedure prescribed in the Bible (*Nm.* 5.11–31) for determining the guilt or innocence of a married woman suspected by her husband of having committed *adultery (*sotah*), so named because of its similarity to the trial by ordeal known in various cultures. In the Bible, unlike some of the other ancient Near Eastern legal compilations, adultery is considered to be a major crime not only against the husband but also against God and therefore could not go unpunished. Yet, because it is unwitnessed, it is normally impossible to prosecute. The Torah, therefore, actually encourages a husband plagued by a "spirit of jealousy," that is, an instinctive suspicion concerning his wife's behavior, to have her undergo the ordeal of jealousy. The primary element of this ordeal, along with a sacrifice of jealousy presented by the woman, is for her to answer amen to a curse administered by the priest, calling for divine punishment if she is guilty. Then the words of the curse, which have been written down, are "wiped off" into a solution of sacred water and earth from the floor of the Tabernacle. The woman then drinks the "water of bitterness that causes the curse" (*may ha-marim hame'arerim*), thus activating the spell. God's involvement is direct: the spell will act only if she is guilty; if she is not, the waters will have no effect. Though those convicted of adultery in court are punished by death (*Lv.* 20.10, *Dt.* 22.22), punishment in this case takes the form of the "swelling of belly and collapse of thigh." When the suspected wife is innocent, "she is cleared and can then conceive" (*Nm.* 5.28). The pertinent laws are discussed in the Talmudic tractate **Sotah*, so named because the Bible refers to the suspected adulteress as one who may have "strayed" (*Nm.* 5.12). According to rabbinic tradition, the ordeal of jealousy was practiced until Second Temple times (*Sot.* 1.5; *'Eduy.* 5.6), when it was abolished by R. Yoḥanan ben Zakk'ai (*Sot.* 9.9). The case of the *sotah* is the only clear example of trial by ordeal to be found in Judaism.

• Tikva Simone Frymer-Kensky, "The Judicial Ordeal in the Ancient Near East," Ph.D. dissertation, Yale University, 1977. Tikva Simone Frymer-Kensky, "The Strange Case of the Suspected Sotah (Numbers V 11–31)," *Vetus Testamentum* 34 (1984): 11–26. Baruch A. Levine, ed., *Numbers 1–20*, The Anchor Bible (New York, 1993), pp. 192–212. Jacob Licht, *Perush 'al Sefer Ba-Midbar* (Jerusalem, 1984–1995), vol. 1, pp. 67–82, 166–169. Jacob Milgrom, ed., *Numbers*, The JPS Torah Commentary (Philadelphia, 1990), pp. 37–43, 350–354. —BARUCH J. SCHWARTZ

ORDINANCE. See TAQQANAH.

ORDINATION, in rabbinical law, the formal transmission of judicial rabbinic authority. It is traditionally believed that the original rabbinic authority was granted by God to Moses. Before his death, Moses asked God to appoint a successor, and Joshua was selected with the words "Take you Joshua the son of Nun . . . and lay your hand [*semikhah*] upon him" (*Nm.* 27.18). Nowhere else in the Bible is there mention of this manner of the transfer of authority, but Jewish tradition accepts that the ordination conferred upon Joshua was in turn transferred by him to his successor, and so on, in an unbroken chain throughout the centuries up to the period of the Second Temple. The Mishnaic statement concerning the transmission of the tradition, "Moses received the Torah from Sinai and handed it down to Joshua, and Joshua to the elders, the elders to the prophets, and the prophets handed it to the Men of the Great Assembly" (*Avot* 1.1), was interpreted as referring to the succession of authority. Only a duly ordained person was empowered in turn to ordain others. During the Hadrianic persecution, which followed the defeat of Bar Kokhba' in 135 CE, the Romans, wanting to destroy Jewish religious authority, decreed capital punishment for those conferring or receiving ordination. One of the *Ten Martyrs, Yehudah ben Bava', was stabbed to death by Roman soldiers who surprised him in the act of ordaining five of his disciples (*San.* 14a). Rabbinic law stated that ordination could be conferred only in Erets Yisra'el, in order to ensure its continuation as the spiritual center of Jewry. Only ordained rabbis could determine the calendar, judge certain cases, or impose fines. After the time of Hillel, the title of rabbi was awarded to those who had been ordained; Babylonian amora'im were given the title of *rav*, rather than rabbi. As a result of the political, spiritual, and economic decline of Erets Yisra'el Jewry in the fourth century, ordination came to an end. Theoretically, once the chain had been broken, it could not be reestablished. Maimonides (*Hilkhot Sanhedrin* 4.2) explicitly ruled that *semikhah* did not imply actual laying on of hands (as is still practiced in Christian churches). He specified that the only literal *semikhah* was when Moses laid his hands on Joshua (cf. *Dt.* 34.9; *Hilkhot Sanhedrin* 4.1). Maimonides suggested the possibility of renewing ordination by the unanimous decision of all the rabbis assembled in Erets Yisra'el, who could invest one of their number with this authority, and he, in turn, would then be able to ordain others (*Hilkhot Sanhedrin* 4.11). It was on the basis of this suggestion that in 1538 Ya'aqov *Berab, motivated by messianic hopes, made an attempt in Safed to reintroduce ordination and had it conferred upon himself. A violent controversy ensued, and the attempt failed because of the determined opposition of R. Levi ibn Ḥaviv, the rabbi of Jerusalem, who had not been consulted and who rallied other scholars to his view that the undertaking was illegitimate.

Modern discussions on the possibility of reestablishing the *Sanhedrin, which depends upon ordination, center around this incident, in which almost all possible arguments for and against had been brought forward and discussed. The ordination conferred upon a rabbi today is not the same as the ancient *semikhah* and does not confer the judicial authority that resides in Talmudic *semikhah* alone. It is rather *hattarat hora'ah* (permission to teach), which replaced the ancient *semikhah*, and which certifies competence to serve as a rabbi. Maimonides (*Hilkhot Sanhedrin* 4.8) lists four different levels of ordination, each dealing with a specific area of rabbinic expertise. Of these, only two are in effect today. These are *yoreh yoreh*, permission to rule in matters dealing with religious practice and *kashrut*, and *yadin yadin*, which involves permission to rule in civil matters, such as torts. *Yoreh yoreh* is generally regarded as a higher level of ordination, and in most cases one who has achieved this level is granted a dual certificate of *yoreh yoreh yadin yadin*. In the United States today, some of the largest rabbinic seminaries require candidates for ordination to have a university degree, often at the master's level. The Reform, Conservative, and Reconstructionist movements now permit women to be ordained. In Israel, the chief rabbinate has formalized the requirements for ordination, and candidates must pass a series of written examinations before being ordained by that body. While Protestant ordination of clergy is done by denominational authorities and Catholic ordination of priests is done by local bishops or heads of orders, rabbis are ordained by a court of three rabbis or, in modern times, by seminaries. In contrast to Christians, who can be stripped of their status as ordinees at any time by the authorities in charge of such matters, once a rabbi is ordained he or she is a rabbi for life, although for reasons of moral, ritual, or institutional impropriety he or she might be denied continuing membership and privileges in the rabbinic organizations of the various movements.

• Simon Greenberg, *The Ordination of Women as Rabbis: Studies and Responsa* (New York, 1988). Eduard Lohse, *Die Ordination im Spatjudentum und im Neuen Testament* (Berlin, 1951). Julius Newman, *Semikhah (Ordination): A Study in Its Origin, History, and Function in Rabbinic Literature* (Manchester, Eng., 1950). —SHMUEL HIMELSTEIN

ORGANS. The Talmud Bavli and other ancient sources provide conflicting and ambiguous descriptions of an organlike instrument called the *magrefah* that was said to have been in use in the Jerusalem Temple (*ʿArakh.* 10b–11). It is considered by most to have been a sort of water-powered organ, identical with the Greek *hydraulis* and capable of producing as many as a hundred sounds of great volume. In the aftermath of the Temple's destruction, however, the rabbis instituted a state of mourning and proscribed the use of the *magrefah* and all other instruments in synagogues. Accordingly, instrumental music was virtually absent from the traditional synagogue service as it developed in the Middle Ages. The suggestion that the modern pipe organ be admitted into this service constituted a main subject of contention between Orthodox and Reform factions in the nineteenth century. In Germany, the organ was first introduced by Israel Jacobson at Seesen in 1810 and Berlin in 1815. Orthodox opponents led by Mosheh Sofer and ʿAqivaʾ Eger objected that its use on the Sabbath would violate halakhic restrictions and that, in any case, its strong identification with Christian worship made its use in the synagogue assimilationist and inappropriate. Nevertheless, the use of the organ became increasingly common in Reform congregations; a Christian organist was engaged by the Hamburg reformers in 1818, and in the United States, an organ was introduced in the Reform temple at Charleston, South Carolina, in 1841. The use of the organ has since become a regular feature in Reform services but occasioned renewed debate when its use was first suggested among Conservative Jews in the United States. Some argued that the presence of an organ in the Jerusalem Temple legitimized its reintroduction to the Jewish service; others pointed to the uncertainty regarding the nature or even existence of a Temple organ and repeated the Orthodox claim that its use represented *ḥuqqat ha-goy*, the inappropriate imitation of a practice associated with non-Jewish worship. The conflict continues, but today organs are often found in Conservative congregations, though their use may be limited to certain services (e.g., Sabbath evening, but not morning). Orthodox congregations continue to forbid the use of the organ, or any other instrument, during worship services.

• Earline Moulder, "Jewish Organ Music of the Twentieth Century: An Annotated Bibliography," D.M.A. thesis, University of Kansas, 1991. Joseph L. Saalschutz, *Geschichte und Wurdigung der Musik bei den Hebraern, im Verhaltnis zur sonstigen Ausbildung dieser Kunst in alter und neuer Zeit, nebst e. Anhang über d. hebraische Orgel* (Niederwalluf b. Wiesbaden, 1970). Alfred Sendrey, *Music in Ancient Israel* (New York, 1969), pp. 394–405. —MARSHA BRYAN EDELMAN

ORḤOT ḤAYYIM, title of an *ethical will first printed in 1544; also called *Tsavva'at Rabbi Eliʿezer*. It begins with a citation from the Talmud Bavli (*San.* 68a) describing the final illness of Eliʿezer ben Hurqanos. In it, he promises that before he dies he will teach his son "the paths of life," from which the title of this work is derived. Opinions are divided as to its date of composition; some maintain that it was written in the eleventh century or even earlier. Others, such as Gershom Scholem, have noted the similarity of the second half of the work (titled *Seder Gan ʿEden*) to the Zohar and argue that it was composed some time after the middle of the fourteenth century. The issue of authorship, too, has not been settled. Some attribute it to Eliʿezer ben Hurqanos, who lived in the first and second centuries CE. Others attribute it to R. Eliʿezer ben Yitsḥaq of Worms (fl. 1050). It was printed in Venice in 1544 and has been reprinted many times since. An English translation appears in *Hebrew Ethical Wills* by Israel Abrahams (Philadelphia, 1926), vol. 2, pp. 31–49.

• Adolph Jellinek, *Beit ha-Midrash* (Leipzig, 1877), vol. 3, pp. 131–140. Gershom Gerhard Scholem in *Yuval Shai: Maʿamarim li-Khevod Shemu'el Yosef ʿAgnon* (Ramat Gan, 1958), pp. 293ff.

—STEVEN BALLABAN

ORḤOT TSADDIQIM, an anonymous work on ethics written in Germany; called *Sefer ha-Middot* by the author. The work contains a reference to the expulsion of the Jews from France in 1394 and may date from a generation or two afterwards. It emphasizes practical behavior and reflects the attitudes of the *Ḥasidei Ashkenaz. The author criticizes the students of his own generation as lazy and given to idleness. A partial Judeo-German version was published in Isny in 1542. The first Hebrew version appeared in 1581 in Prague. It became extremely popular and has been frequently reprinted. An English translation with pointed Hebrew text by Seymour J. Cohen was published in New York in 1969.

• Joseph Dan, *Ḥasidut Ashkenaz be-Toledot ha-Maḥashavah ha-Yehudit* (Tel Aviv, 1990–1991). —STEVEN BALLABAN

ORIENTAL JEWS. See ʿADOT HA-MIZRAḤ.

ʿORLAH (עָרְלָה;), name of the foreskin, an agrarian law, and a Mishnaic tractate.

Foreskin. The *ʿorlah* is the part cut off of the penis during *circumcision. The term was applied metaphorically to the uncircumcised (cf. *Ex.* 6.12, "uncircumcised lips"; *Ez.* 44.7, 44.9, "uncircumcised heart").

Agrarian Law. The term is applied to the fruit of young trees during their first three years of producing; such fruit is forbidden for use. In the fourth year the fruit was to be taken to Jerusalem to be consumed amid praise and thanksgiving. This fruit, called *netaʿ revaʿi* (planting of the fourth year), could, however, be redeemed and used outside Jerusalem, while the money value plus a fifth was to be taken to Jerusalem and spent there. Today *netaʿ revaʿi* is regarded as the same as *ʿorlah*, and the fruit is wholly permitted only from the fifth year on. *ʿOrlah* is one of the few *agrarian laws that apply even outside of Erets Yisra'el.

Tractate. The tractate *ʿOrlah* is in Mishnah order Zeraʿim, in three chapters, with related material in the Tosefta' and the Talmud Yerushalmi. It deals with the laws of *ʿorlah*, according to which the fruit of a newly planted tree or vine is regarded as uncircumcised, hence forbidden for consumption (cf. *Lv.* 19.23–25). Opening with a discussion of the parameters of planting, including questionable cases such as replanting or grafting, *ʿOrlah* proceeds to define the precise nature of the *ʿorlah* prohibition—the parts of the tree that are prohibited, use of the tree for purposes other than food, and so forth. The second chapter contains a discussion of the laws of forbidden foods that have been mixed with other foods. Although *ʿorlah* differs from most other agricultural laws insofar as it applies both inside and outside Erets Yisra'el (*Qid.* 1.9), the opening (*ʿOrl.* 1.2) and closing of the tractate both underscore the special connection of this commandment to Erets Yisra'el (cf. *Qid.* 38b).

An English translation of the tractate is in Herbert Danby's *The Mishnah* (London, 1933).

• Chanoch Albeck, ed., *Shishah Sidrei Mishnah, Seder Zeraʿim* (Jerusalem, 1957). Philip Blackman, ed. and trans., *Mishnayoth*, vol. 1, *Order Zeraim* (Gateshead, 1973). Pinhas Kehati, ed., *Mishnah: A New Translation with a Commentary, Seder Zeraim*, vol. 4, *Maʿaser Sheni, Hallah, Orlah, Bikkurim* (Jerusalem, 1994). Hermann Leberecht Strack and Günter Stemberger, *Introduction to the Talmud and Midrash*, rev. and updat. ed., translated by Markus Bockmuehl (Minneapolis, 1992). David Marchant, *Understanding Shmittoh: Its Sources and Background*, rev. ed. (Jerusalem and New York, 1993). —AVRAHAM WALFISH

ORNSTEIN, YAʿAQOV MESHULLAM (1775–1839), Galician rabbi and author of halakhic works. After serving five years as rabbi of Zólkiew (1801–1805), Ornstein was named rabbi of Lwów, a post he held until his death. Known as one of the great halakhic minds of his generation, he was consulted by rabbis from far and wide on difficult halakhic issues. In Lwów, the independently wealthy Ornstein involved himself in all areas of communal affairs. He came into conflict with the nascent Haskalah presence in the city, even issuing a ban of excommunication against the Maskilim in 1816, which Austrian officials forced him to retract. Ornstein gained fame in rabbinic circles with the publication of his multivolume pilpulistic commentary and analysis of the *Shulḥan ʿArukh* entitled *Yeshuʿot Yaʿaqov* (1809–1835; reprinted 1863, 1960, 1976). He also wrote a commentary on the Pentateuch and *responsa* under the same title.

• Salomon Buber, *Qiryah Nisgavah* (Kraków, 1903). Ḥayyim Nathan Dembitzer, *Sefer Kelilat Yofi* (Kraków, 1888; repr. New York, 1959). Meir Vunder, *Me'orei Galitsiyah* (Jerusalem, 1977), vol. 1. —GERSHON BACON

OROBIO DE CASTRO, ISAAC (1617–1687). Born in Braganza, Spain, of a *converso* family, he studied medicine and theology in the Universities of Osuna and Alcalá de Henares. Accused of Judaizing, he was arrested in 1654 together with his family, tortured, and condemned by the Inquisition in Seville. In 1660 he escaped from Spain and reached Bayonne, France, where he joined his father and other escaping *conversos*. Later he took a position at the University of Toulouse as professor of medicine. In 1662 he decided to return openly to Judaism and, together with his family, became a member of the prosperous Jewish Spanish-Portuguese community of Amsterdam. There, beside his medical career, he was intensively engaged in intellectual and cultural activities. His main contribution to Jewish scholarship was in apologetics. He strongly defended rabbinical Judaism against deistic heretics, such as Juan Prado, an ex-*converso* colleague and student of his in Alcalá de Henares who shared with *Spinoza the fate of being excommunicated by the community of Amsterdam. Like other thinkers of *converso* origin, Orobio challenged the racial theory that considered the *limpieza de sangre* (purity of blood) as a decisive factor in determining the supremacy of the "old Christians" against the "new Christians" of Jewish origin. Instead, he strongly advocated the view that Israel is the chosen people. He maintained close contacts with Calvinist thinkers, particularly with Philip van Limburg. In many of his writings, Orobio zealously propounded what he considered to be the Jewish truths in contrast to the Christian distortions. His deep academic acquaintance with Christian theology gave weight to his apologetic argumentation.

• Yosef Kaplan, *From Christianity to Judaism: The Story of Isaac Orobio de Castro*, translated by Raphael Loewe (Oxford, 1989).

—NISSIM YOSHA

ORPHAN, together with the *widow and the *stranger, in the social and economic system of ancient Israel, a helpless member of society and hence a special object of solicitude in biblical legislation, which emphasized the claims of orphans to justice (*Dt*. 24.17; *Is*. 1.17; *Ps*. 82.3), protection from oppression (*Ex*. 22.22), and charity (*Dt*. 16.11, 14). In their denunciation of evil, the prophets frequently singled out the exploitation and inconsiderate treatment of orphans (*Is*. 1.23, 10.2; *Ez*. 22.7; *Mal*. 3.5). God himself, "the father of orphans" (*Ps*. 68.6), is the guardian of their rights (*Dt*. 10.18); he hears their cries, and his judgment may turn those who oppress them into orphans themselves (*Ex*. 22.22–23). In Talmudic law the general biblical injunctions are elaborated and expanded to grant orphans many legal privileges and concessions. Orphans are exempt from taxation (*B. B.* 8a); they are not required to pay compensation for damage caused by their animals under certain conditions (*B. Q.* 39a); they need no **perozbol* to claim the repayment of loans after the sabbatical year (*Git*. 37a); and their property is regarded as equivalent to sacred property (*B. M.* 56b). Altogether, one should treat orphans with special gentleness and dignity, address them in soft words, and guard their possessions as zealously as one's own. All these regulations apply to rich as well as to poor orphans, and there is no age limit (Maimonides' *Mishneh Torah*, *De'ot* 6.10). It is particularly meritorious to provide a home for orphans, and whoever brings up an orphan is regarded as his parent (*San*. 19b). Upon losing a parent, one is required to observe a full year's mourning and to say *Qaddish for eleven months.

• Louis M. Epstein, *The Jewish Marriage Contract: A Study in the Status of Women in Jewish Law* (New York, 1927). Yaakov K. Reinitz, "Ha-'Apotropos li-Yetomim ba-Mishpat ha-'Ivri: Aḥrayuto, Darkhei ha-Piqquaḥ veha-Biqqoret Alav," Ph.D. dissertation, Hebrew University, 1984.

ORTHODOXY, the modern designation for the traditional section of Jewry that maintains the halakhic way of life based on a divinely ordained Torah. The term itself is borrowed from Christian usage and was first applied in the nineteenth century by Reform Jews to describe, somewhat disparagingly, those who remained rigidly faithful to traditional Judaism. Though Orthodoxy is widely diversified among its many religious groupings and nuances of belief and practice (e.g., Ḥasidim and Mitnaggedim; Jews following Ashkenazi and Sephardi rites, etc.), all Orthodox Jews are united in their belief in the historical event of revelation at Sinai, as described in the Torah; in their acceptance of the divine law, in its written and oral forms, as immutable and binding for all times; in their acknowledgment of the authority of duly qualified rabbis—who themselves recognize the validity of the Talmud, the Shulḥan 'Arukh, and all other traditional sources of the *halakhah*—to interpret and administer Jewish law; and in their adherence to traditional Jewish beliefs.

Unlike Reform and Liberal groups, Orthodoxy rejects the doctrine of progressive revelation, denies the assumptions and conclusions of Higher Criticism, especially with regard to the Pentateuch, and generally opposes radical departures from traditional attitudes and practices. Thus Orthodoxy opposes proselytizing propaganda and objects to organ music and to mixed seating of men and women in synagogue worship. Its halakhic observance does not admit distinction between ethical versus merely ceremonial precepts. Orthodoxy has exhibited a reluctance to cooperate with non-Orthodox groups in religious areas. The relations between Orthodox and non-Orthodox are especially troubled by Orthodox refusal to recognize the marriages, divorces, and conversions carried out by rabbis who do not submit to the authority of traditional Jewish law. To distinguish the "modern" type of Orthodoxy as developed in Germany during the second half of the nineteenth century under the guidance of Samson Raphael Hirsch and Ezriel Hildesheimer (modern dress, use of the vernacular, study of secular sciences, and participation in the general culture) from the early ghetto-type of Orthodoxy, the term *Neo-Orthodoxy* has been used.

Today Orthodox Jews constitute a minority among Jewish religious denominations. Although found in all principal areas of Jewish settlement, they are primarily resident in the United States, Israel, and western Europe. In the United States, where they number about 425,000, the Orthodox are, according to the 1990 National Jewish Population Survey, approximately 7 percent of the Jewish population. Most of these are those called centrist Orthodox, Jews who choose a middle way between wholehearted acculturation to America and insulation from its influences. These are Jews who, although attached to *halakhah*, value and receive a general education in addition to an intensive Jewish one (commonly by means of attendance at a Jewish day school), attend university, and embrace middle-class aspirations of professional career and residence. They share strong feelings for Israel and, more than any other Jewish denomination, entertain the idea of moving there. American centrist Orthodox Jews tend to have just under three children per family, giving them about a 33 percent higher fertility rate than the rest of American Jewry. Located mostly along the northeast corridor of the United States, they are also established in Los Angeles, southern Florida, Cleveland, and Chicago.

In addition to centrists, about 25 percent, or 105,000, of American Orthodox Jews qualify as *Ḥaredim, sometimes called ultra-Orthodox or strictly Orthodox. Most Ḥaredim affiliate with Hasidism—followers of a particular charismatic leader or *rebbi*—but some are instead associated with the Lithuanian-style *yeshivah* world, the Mitnaggedim. While the differences between these two categories of Ḥaredim are significant, when compared with other American Jews, the similarities between them are striking. In general, Ḥaredim—the most noticeable of Orthodox Jews—eschew the values and many of the lifestyles of contemporary secular society and emphasize instead a punctiliousness in religious ritual, a cultural separation from what they view as the corrupting influences of the outside world, and an attachment to the idea of preserving sacred tradition containing venerable truths and practices that may not be abrogated.

In Israel, the numbers of Orthodox Jews are greatest, but the definitions of precisely who is to be included are far more ambiguous. In addition to Ḥaredim, there are those who define themselves as Dati, roughly equivalent to the centrist Orthodox. But there are also those who identify themselves as Masorati (traditional), who abide by some of the religious and ritual restrictions but not others. Many of these Jews support religious political parties but are somewhat more religiously lax in their personal practices and lifestyles. It has been estimated that about 14 percent of the Jewish population in Israel, or 630,000 Jews, can be identified as Dati, Masorati, or Ḥaredi.

Important secondary Orthodox Jewish communities are located in Greater Toronto and Montréal in Canada; Melbourne, Australia; Antwerp, Belgium; and countries of the former Soviet Union. Altogether, there are probably about a hundred thousand Orthodox Jews in these locales.

• Menachem Friedman, "Life Tradition and Book Tradition in the Development of Ultraorthodox Judaism," in *Judaism Viewed from Within and Without: Anthropological Studies*, edited by Harvery E. Goldberg (Albany, 1987). Menachem Friedman and Samuel C. Heilman, "Religious Fundamentalism and Religious Jews: The Case of the 'Haredim,'" in *Fundamentalisms Observed*, edited by Martin Marty and Scott Appleby (Chicago, 1991), pp. 197–264. Samuel C. Heilman, *Defenders of the Faith: Inside Ultra-Orthodox Jewry* (New York, 1992). Samuel C. Heilman, *Portrait of American Jews: The Last Half of the Twentieth Century* (Seattle, 1995). Samuel C. Heilman and Steven M. Cohen, *Cosmopolitans and Parochials: Modern Orthodox Jews in America* (Chicago, 1989). Leo Jung, *What Is Orthodox Judaism?*, The Jewish Library, 2d ser., edited by L. Jung (New York, 1930). Jacob Katz, ed., *Toward Modernity: The European Jewish Model* (New Brunswick, N.J., 1987).

—SAMUEL C. HEILMAN

OSHAʿYAʾ RABBAH. See HOSHAʿYAH RABBAH.

OSSUARIES, containers for the bones of the dead. The Mishnah mentions the custom of gathering up the bones of the dead after decomposition of the flesh (*San.* 6.6) and giving them a second burial in an ossuary (*Pes.* 8.8; *Moʿed Q.* 1.5). Contrary to the accepted opinion that relatives observe that day as one of mourning, R. Meʾir suggests that since the act of giving the dead their final burial is a cause of satisfaction, it may even be performed on the intermediate days of festivals (*Moʿed Q.* 8a). The bones were collected in a sheet and then deposited in stone ossuaries, sometimes with decorations, many examples of which have been found dating from the second and third centuries, with inscriptions in Hebrew, Aramaic, or Greek.

• Eric M. Meyers, *Jewish Ossuaries: Reburial and Rebirth* (Rome, 1971). L. Y. Rahmani, *A Catalogue of Jewish Ossuaries* (Jerusalem, 1994). Hershel Shanks, *In the Temple of Solomon and the Tomb of Caiaphas* (Washington, D.C., 1993).

OUZIEL, BEN-TSIYYON MEʾIR ḤAI (1880–1953), rabbinic scholar; *riʾshon le-Tsiyyon* (Sephardi chief rabbi of Palestine/Israel; see CHIEF RABBINATE) from 1939 to 1953. Born in Jerusalem to a prominent Sephardi family, he was elected chief rabbi of Jaffa and its environs in 1911. For two years, from 1921 to 1923, he served as chief rabbi of Salonika, Greece, and during the British Mandate, from 1923 to 1939, was chief rabbi of Tel Aviv and Jaffa. He was active in the struggles of the Jewish community in Palestine. He was a leader of the Mizrachi movement and a delegate to Zionist congresses. Together with his colleague R. Isaac *Herzog, he sought halakhic solutions to the problems of reconciling Torah and state. Ouziel wrote many books and articles on all areas of *halakhah* and was recognized as a leading authority. His works include *Mishpatei ʿUziʾel* (*responsa*; 7 vols. [Tel Aviv and Jerusalem, 1935–1964]); *Shaʿarei ʿUziʾel* (on the laws of minors, widows, guardianship, and charity; 2 vols. [Jerusalem, 1944–1946]); and *Mikhmanei ʿUziʾel* (sermons [Tel Aviv, 1939]).

• Shabbetai Don-Yaḥia, *Anshei Torah u-Malkhut: Shivah Ishim ve-Divreihem ʿal Medinat Yisraʾel* (Jerusalem, 1966), pp. 97–229. *Entsiqlopedyah shel ha-Tsiyyonut ha-Datit* (Jerusalem, 1971), vol. 4, pp. 173–184.

—ELIAV SHOCHETMAN

ʿOVADYAH OF BERTINORO. See BERTINORO, ʿOVADYAH.

OWNERSHIP. See PROPERTY.

P

PAGANISM. See IDOLATRY.

PAIRS. See ZUGOT.

PALESTINE. See ERETS YISRA'EL; HOLY LAND.

PALESTINIAN TALMUD. See TALMUD.

PALM. See FOUR SPECIES.

PANTHEISM, term used since the eighteenth century to designate the belief that the entire universe or nature is God. Among the various types of pantheism are such individual views as God is everything (theopanism); everything that exists is divine; and God is immanent in everything. A modified version of pantheism holds that, although reality and God are not identical, all reality is in God (panentheism). *Neoplatonism, which holds that all being flows out of God (see EMANATION), is much closer to pantheism than is Aristotelianism. Mysticism, by obliterating the difference between God and the human soul in the ecstasy of mystical union, also tends toward pantheism. All forms of pantheism are opposed to classical theism, which assumes the nonidentity of Creator and creation and thus the nonidentity of God and the human soul. For theism the relationship between God and the soul is not one of ultimate unity, but an I–Thou confrontation. Jewish Orthodoxy has always adhered to the basic pattern of biblical theism, and pantheism was considered heretical. Kabbalistic doctrines often exhibited pantheistic tendencies and were consequently regarded with suspicion. The classical kabbalistic statement of a limited pantheism was formulated by Mosheh ben Yaʿaqov *Cordovero: "God is all reality, but not all reality is God." The formula "Elohim (God) equals *ha-tevaʿ* (nature)" (the numerical value of the two words are identical) does not imply genuine pantheism. See also HASIDISM; KABBALAH; SPINOZA, BARUCH.

• Peter A. Degen, "Einstein's Weltanschauung and Its Spinozistic Elements," in *Science and Religion*, edited by A. Baümer and M. Büttner, 18th International Congress on the History of Science (Bochum, Ger., 1989). Michael P. Levine, *Pantheism: A Non-Theistic Concept of the Deity* (London, 1994).

PAPA' (died c.376), prominent amora'. He was one of the major fifth-generation Babylonian amoraic figures and the most prominent student of Rava'. Throughout his life, Papa' studied with his colleague Huna' ben Yehoshuʿa, who was also his neighbor and business partner. After Rava' died, many students followed Papa' to Naresh, where he established a *yeshivah*. His personal wealth allowed him to support many of his students.

Traditions followed by Papa' appear frequently throughout the Talmud. He seems to have favored a harmonizing approach and suggested observance patterns that would satisfy several differing opinions or ways in which apparent differences among earlier sages might be minimized.

Papa' headed the Naresh academy for nineteen years, until his death.

• Chanoch Albeck, *Mavo' la-Talmudim* (Tel Aviv, 1987). Alfred J. Kolatch, *Who's Who in the Talmud* (New York, 1964). —MICHAEL CHERNICK

PARABLES, a didactic device occasionally found in the Hebrew Bible. The most outstanding example is Nathan's parable of the poor man's lamb (*2 Sm.* 12.1–4). Jehoash's story of the thornbush and cedar (*2 Kgs.* 14.9) might fall into this category, and Isaiah's song of the vineyard (*Is.* 5.1–6) can be regarded as an example of either *allegory or parable. The parable is a frequent ingredient of the rabbinical sermon in aggadic literature, introduced by the standard phrase: *mashal, le-mah ha-davar domeh*, "a parable: to what is the matter to be compared?" However, neither biblical nor Talmudic literature differentiate between allegory, parable, or fable, which are all included under the general term *mashal*. For example, the view was advanced that "Job never existed but was an allegory or parable" (*B. B.* 15a). A knowledge of parables was regarded as a basic rabbinic accomplishment (*Suk.* 28a), part of the universal store of wisdom literature. *Maimonides regarded prophetic visions that could not be taken literally as parables or allegories (*Guide of the Perplexed* 2. 46–47). Parables continued to be used by medieval Jewish preachers and moralists. One of the best-known exponents of this genre was R. Yaʿaqov ben Wolf *Kranz (1741–1804), also known as the Dubno Maggid.

• Ḥayyim Naḥman Bialik and Yehoshuʿa Ḥana Rawnitzki, eds., *The Book of Legends, Sefer ha-Aggadah: Legends from the Talmud and Midrash*, translated by William G. Braude (New York, 1992), pp. 807–810. Herman A. Glatt, *He Spoke in Parables: The Life and Work of the Dubno Maggid* (New York, 1957). —ARYEH NEWMAN

PARADISE (from Gr. *paradeisos* [garden]), common designation for the abode of the blessed after death, based on the Septuagint translation of the biblical garden of *Eden as "paradise." The Hebrew equivalent of *paradise*, **pardes*, occurs three times in the Bible; in the Talmud (*Ḥag.* 14b), the word is applied to the realm of celestial visions and the mystical ascent of the soul. It was thought that the souls of the righteous would enjoy celestial bliss in a heavenly garden of Eden. The Apocrypha and Midrashic literature contain many descriptions of both earthly paradise and the heavenly paradise of souls. The latter is usually described as a place of spiritual delights. See also AFTERLIFE; HEAVEN; ʿOLAM HA-ZEH AND ʿOLAM HA-BAʾ.

• Jean Delumeau, *The History of Paradise: The Garden of Eden in Myth and Tradition*, translated by Matthew O'Connell (New York, 1995). Martha Himmelfarb, *Ascent to Heaven in Jewish and Christian Apocalypses* (New York, 1993).

PARAH (פָּרָה; Cow), tractate in Mishnah order Tohorot, in twelve chapters, with related material in Tosefta'. It has no *gemara'* in either Talmud. The impurity engendered by contact with a corpse is unique in its severity, requiring for its purification the special ceremony of sprinkling water mixed with the ashes of the *red heifer

(*Nm.* 19). *Parah* describes the red heifer ceremony and its regulations, as well as the laws governing purification by means of the red heifer ashes. The burning of the red heifer, in Second Temple times, was a public ceremony carried out with great pomp. Considerable care was taken to ensure that the ceremony be carried out under conditions of optimal purity, leading one rabbi to protest that some of the measures taken were excessive (*Par.* 3.3). Because the Sadducees insisted on absolute purity, the rabbis required that the priest, hitherto protectively isolated from all forms of defilement for seven days (*Par.* 3.1), be defiled and immersed immediately prior to the burning of the heifer, thus firmly demonstrating the authority of Pharisaic *halakhah*.

The paradoxical nature of the red heifer, which "purified the impure . . . [whereas] all who handled it from beginning to end defiled their clothes" (*Pesiqta' de-Rav Kahana'* 4.1; cf. *Par.* 4.4, 8.3), engendered the rabbinic conception of the laws of *parah* as paradigmatic of divine decrees unfathomable to the human mind (*Pesiqta' de-Rav Kahana'* 3).

An English translation of the tractate is to be found in Herbert Danby's *The Mishnah* (London, 1933).

• Chanoch Albeck, ed., *Shishah Sidrei Mishnah, Seder Tohorot* (Jerusalem, 1958). Philip Blackman, ed. and trans., *Mishnayoth*, vol. 5, *Order Taharoth* (Gateshead, 1973). Hermann Leberecht Strack and Günter Stemberger, *Introduction to the Talmud and Midrash*, rev. and updat. ed., translated by Markus Bockmuehl (Minneapolis, 1992).

—AVRAHAM WALFISH

PARAH ADUMMAH. See RED HEIFER.

PARASHAH. See QERI'AT HA-TORAH; SIDRAH.

PARASHIYYOT, FOUR. See SABBATHS, SPECIAL.

PARDES (פַּרְדֵּס; orchard), Hebrew word used as an acronym-mnemonic to suggest four different approaches to understanding the Bible. *P* signifies the word **peshat*, which refers to the plain meaning of the text; *r* signifies *remez* (allusion), connoting some veiled reference in the biblical text that can be discovered by the numerical value of the letters (**gimatriyyah*) or by an acronym (**notariqon*); *d* signifies **derash*, or homiletical interpretation; and *s* signifies *sod* (secret), which suggests a mystical or kabbalistic interpretation. Although these terms all occur in classical rabbinic literature, they were not used to organize biblical commentary systematically until the thirteenth century, in the commentaries of Baḥya ben Asher of Saragossa of Spain. Pardes may suggest some comparisons with the classical Christian "Four-fold senses of Scripture." In an early mystical text found in the Talmud (*Hag.* 14b), the word *pardes* is used for divine wisdom.

• Albert van der Heide, "PARDES: Methodological Reflections on the Theory of the Four Senses," *Journal of Jewish Studies* 34 (1983): 147–159.

—MICHAEL A. SIGNER

PARENTAL BLESSING. See BLESSING OF CHILDREN.

PARENTS. Biblical Hebrew uses no generic word to denote parents but refers to them always as **father* and **mother* (e.g., *Ex.* 20.12; *Lv.* 19.3; *Prv.* 1.9). Later Hebrew adopted the word *horim*, which occurs only once in the Bible (*Gn.* 49.26) and probably means forebears. Respect for parents is enjoined by the Decalogue (see TEN COMMANDMENTS) and was affirmed by the rabbis. Rabbinic law permits only two exceptions to the duty of unquestioning obedience: parents must be disobeyed when they order their children to transgress the Torah (*B. M.* 2.10), and a son may ignore his parents' wishes in choosing a wife (Isserles, *Yoreh De'ah* 250.25). Otherwise the duty of honoring and revering parents knows no bounds. The Talmud specifies "The son should not stand nor sit in his father's place nor contradict him. He must provide for his father's material wants and lead him in and out" (*Qid.* 31b). According to Jewish law, the parent should repay the expenses incurred by the son in caring for the parents' needs, unless the parent is impoverished (*Qid.* 32a; *Shulḥan 'Arukh, Yoreh De'ah* 240.5). The father has the legal duty to support his children up to the age of six; after that his support is regarded as an act of charity (*Ket.* 49b, 65b). The mother is not obliged to maintain her children. Traditionally, a parent's most important obligation to his children is to teach them Torah, but a father must also teach his son a trade (*Qid.* 29a, 30b), and the parents must get the child accustomed to fulfilling the commandments (*Suk.* 42a; *Ḥag.* 4a). The egalitarian approach widespread today extends full obligations to both mothers and daughters. The father is permitted to chastise his children, but only while they are minors (*Mo'ed Q.* 17a). Father and mother are equal in terms of the duties owed to them by the child, and their special status is affirmed in the statement that in every man's life "there are three partners: his father, his mother, and God" (*Qid.* 30b). Respect for parents extends after their death and is expressed ritually in the recitation of *Qaddish and **yortsayt*.

• Gerald Blidstein, *Honor Thy Father and Mother: Filial Responsisbility in Jewish Law and Ethics* (New York, 1976). Steven M. Brown, "Parents as Partners with God: Parenting Young Children," in *Celebration and Renewal*, edited by Rela M. Geffen (Philadelphia, 1993). Hayim Halevy Donin, *To Raise a Jewish Child* (New York, 1977). Allen Glicksman, *The New Jewish Elderly* (New York, 1991). Miriam Levi, *Effective Jewish Parenting* (Jerusalem, 1986). Claude Goldsmid Montefiore and Herbert Loewe, eds. and trans., *A Rabbinic Anthology* (London, 1938), chaps. 22 and 24.

PAREV (Yi.; פּאַרעוו), the term applied to foods classified as neither *milk dishes nor *meat dishes and that may be eaten with either without violating the *dietary laws forbidding the simultaneous consumption of meat and milk or the consumption of milk after meat. Care is taken to keep *parev* utensils separate from either milk or meat utensils, including cleaning them separately.

• Binyomin Forst, *The Laws of Kashrus: A Comprehensive Exposition of Their Underlying Concepts and Applications* (Brooklyn, N.Y., 1993). Isidor Grunfeld, *The Jewish Dietary Laws*, 2 vols. (London and New York,

PARIS, DISPUTATION OF, Jewish–Christian public *disputation, held in 1240. In the course of the 1230s, a Jewish convert to Christianity, Nicholas Donin, began a campaign against Judaism based primarily upon citations from rabbinic literature. Donin prepared a Latin digest of Talmudic material and succeeded in obtaining papal support for an investigation into the allegedly offensive work that lay at the heart of medieval Judaism.

Donin charged that the Talmud was replete with foolishness and theological improprieties, that it discriminated against Christians and urged their murder, and that it blasphemed Jesus and Mary. Even more fundamentally, Donin argued that the classic justification for tolerating Jews as the preservers of the old law was ill-conceived: Jews had replaced the Hebrew Bible with Talmudic law; consequently, they were a people without faith, and should not be tolerated in the Christian world.

In 1240 Donin confronted R. Yeḥi'el of Paris and several other rabbis at a trial of the Talmud. Rabbi Yeḥi'el responded to the wide array of charges with a variety of strategies: he defended the reasonableness of Talmudic passages, demonstrated that scripture itself contained assertions similar to those mocked by Donin, pointed to the willful distortion of the statement that allegedly encouraged the killing of gentiles, maintained the need for a work that would clarify the legal code of the Bible, insisted that the pagans of the Talmud were legally distinct from contemporary Christians, and made the striking claim that the Jesus occasionally denounced by the Talmud lived before the Christian Jesus and consequently had nothing to do with the founder of Christianity.

In the short run, the effort to defend the Talmud failed; cartloads of Jewish books were burned on the streets of Paris a few years after the disputation. In the long run, the Talmud was censored but tolerated by church authorities, who recognized that it could not be outlawed without banning Judaism itself.

• Morris Braude, *Conscience on Trial* (New York, 1952). Robert Chazan, "The Condemnation of the Talmud Reconsidered (1239–1248)," *Proceedings of the American Academy for Jewish Research* 55 (1988): 11–30. Jeremy Cohen, *The Friars and the Jews* (Ithaca, 1982). Chenmelech Merchavia, *Ha-Talmud bi-Re'i ha-Natsrut* (Jerusalem, 1970). Joel Edward Rembaum, "The Talmud and the Popes: Reflections on the Talmud Trials of the 1240's," *Viator* 13 (1982): 203–223.

—DAVID BERGER

PARNAS (פַּרְנָס; provider), generally, a leader or guide of a whole generation; more specifically, a religious and administrative functionary. The word would seem to imply that at first the office involved disbursing funds to the needy. The Talmud describes Moses, Aaron, and Miriam as "three good *parnasim* of Israel" (*Ta'an*. 9a) and applied the term also to David (*Yoma'* 86b). Rabbi Yehoshu'a ben Ḥananyah referred to R. Gamli'el as "the *parnas* of his generation," yet, because of Gamli'el's imperious manner, added, "Woe to the generation whose *parnas* you are!" (*Ber*. 28a). The *parnas* was chosen by the sages, but approval was needed from the public at large (*Ber*. 55a). In the sixteenth century, in most communities the term *parnas* came to mean the lay leader—generally a wealthy individual—of a community or congregation rather than a rabbinic leader. Though supposed to be learned men (cf. "Who is a scholar worthy of being appointed *parnas*? He who is asked about a law from any source—even from the tractate of *Ḥallah*—and is able to answer," *Shab*. 114a), *parnasim* were not necessarily chosen from the aristocracy of learning or because of their exemplary conduct; there are many references in the Talmud and later sources to their autocratic behavior. The heads of the Council of the Four Lands, which guided the Jewish communities of Poland and Lithuania in the sixteenth, seventeenth, and eighteenth centuries, were called *parnasim*; in some communities the office went by monthly rotation. In modern times, the word is used in western Sephardi congregations to refer to members of the governing board of a congregation, headed by a *parnas presidente*. Among Ashkenazim, the *parnas* is usually the president of the synagogue.

• Shlomo Eidelberg, *R. Yuspa, Shammash di-Kehillat Varmaisa: 'Olam Yehudeyah ba-Me'ah ha-17* (Jerusalem, 1991), pp. 20–21.

—SHMUEL HIMELSTEIN

PAROKHET (פָּרֹכֶת; curtain), the curtain of the Sanctuary, made of "blue and purple and scarlet and fine twined linen" (*Ex*. 26.31). It was placed in the Sanctuary to mark the division "between the holy place and the most holy" (*Ex*. 26.33). In the Temple the task of making the Parokhet was entrusted to women (*Ket*. 106b). The Parokhet in the Sanctuary and Temple is the model for the *parokhet* of the Ashkenazi synagogue, which is placed in front of the ark. On the High Holy Days and on *Hosha'na' Rabbah a white *parokhet* is used; otherwise it may be of any color, and there are many magnificent examples of embroidered *parokhot*. The term *parokhet* is used only by Ashkenazi Jews. The Sephardi rite has no *parokhet*, except on Tish'ah be-'Av, when the ark is draped with a black curtain; the Ashkenazi custom is to remove the *parokhet* altogether.

• Sol Cohen, *A Seventeenth-Century Parochet* (London, 1953). Clandia Z. Fechter, *The Loom and the Cloth: An Exhibition of the Fabrics of Jewish Life* (Cleveland, 1988).

PARTITION. See MEḤITSAH.

PARTNERSHIP (Heb. *shutafut*), a relationship established by joint acquisition or inheritance, or joint investment, even if only one of the partners is active. The partnership is effected by means of an act of *acquisition (*qinyan*), and the conditions are usually set down in writing. Unless agreed otherwise, capital gains or losses are shared equally. Each partner can obligate the partnership through his contracts. A partnership may be dissolved by mutual agreement or on the basis of predetermined conditions, involving actual partition or by allowing one partner the option of buying or selling a half share for an agreed sum. The death of a partner immediately voids the partnership.

• David ben Solomon Ibn Abi Zimra, *Yeqar Tiferet* (Jerusalem, 1944).

PASCHAL LAMB (Heb. *qorban pesaḥ* or *zevaḥ pesaḥ*), Pesaḥ sacrifice offered by the Israelites from the time of the *Exodus until the destruction of the Second Temple. Shortly before the Exodus from Egypt, the children of Israel were commanded to take a male lamb in the first year of its life on the tenth day of the month of Nisan and to slaughter it on the eve of the fourteenth. The Israelites were to sprinkle some of the lamb's blood on the two side posts and on the lintel of the doors of their residences. The animal was to be roasted and eaten in haste as the people made ready for the Exodus that night (*Ex.* 12).

Thereafter, and throughout the period of the First and Second Temples, the eating of the paschal lamb was the central feature of the observance of the Pesaḥ festival. The animal was to be wholly roasted (it could not be eaten half-roasted or boiled), and it had to be eaten that night; anything remaining had to be burned. The meat was eaten together with some *matsah* (unleavened bread) and bitter herbs. The entire procedure was interpreted as a reminder of the redemption from the bitter slavery in Egypt through the Exodus. Non-Jews or the uncircumcised could not participate, and since the meat of the paschal lamb was regarded as holy food, it could be eaten only by those who were in a state of ritual purity.

So important was the ritual of the paschal lamb that biblical law gave those who were unable to participate on the correct date, 14 Nisan, a second chance to observe the ceremony one month later, on 14 Iyyar (*Nm.* 9.6–12; see PESAḤ SHENI).

After the destruction of the Temple and the cessation of sacrifices, the laws of the paschal lamb fell into disuse. Because of this, some Jews follow the custom of not eating roasted meat at the *Seder meal (*Shulḥan ʿArukh, Oraḥ Ḥayyim* 469, 476). A reminder of the eating of the paschal lamb as the last meal of the people prior to the Exodus is preserved by the eating of the **afiqoman* following the Seder meal, after which nothing more may be eaten. The roasted bone on the ceremonial Seder plate is a visible symbol of the paschal lamb of Temple days.

*Samaritans still follow the biblical practice of slaughtering a lamb on the eve of Pesaḥ on Mount Gerizim in Samaria. Ethiopian Jews and some descendants of Marrano Jews in Mexico maintain the observance of sprinkling some blood from a slaughtered lamb on the doorposts of their houses. The regulations concerning the killing and consumption of the paschal lamb are found in *Pesaḥim*, chapters 5 through 9.

• Baruch M. Bokser, *The Origins of the Seder: The Passover Rite and Early Rabbinic Judaism* (Berkeley, 1986). Mordechai Breuer, "Pesaḥ Mitsrayim u-Pesaḥ Dorot," *Megadim* 20 (1993): 9–19. —CHAIM PEARL

PASSOVER. See PESAḤ.

PASSOVER, SECOND. See PESAḤ SHENI.

PASSOVER SEDER. See HAGGADAH OF PESAḤ.

PATERNITY. In Jewish law, the offspring of a married woman is always presumed to be the child of her husband since, "for the most part, a woman cohabits with her husband" (*Ḥul.* 11b). This presumption may, however, be vitiated by objective evidence such as a twelve-month period of absence of the husband prior to the birth of the child. The husband's denial is also an effective bar to paternity, provided that there is no evidence, either expressly or by implication, of his having adopted a paternal role with regard to the child. A denial of paternity is effective even if the result is to make the children of the marriage *mamzerim* (see MAMZER). This would not, however, be the case if there were grandchildren, who would also suffer the taint of *mamzerut* as a result of such a denial. In the case of an unmarried woman, a paternity suit would only succeed if it were supported by the admission of the putative father or by objective evidence of paternal conduct. Blood tests are not always recognized in paternity suits before rabbinical courts. It is generally agreed that the father of an artificially inseminated child is the sperm donor.

• Michael Broyde, "The Establishment of Maternity and Paternity in Jewish and American Law," *National Jewish Law Review* 3 (1988): 117–158.
—DANIEL SINCLAIR

PATER SYNAGOGAE (Lat.; father of the synagogue), title conferred in the classical period on an outstanding member of the congregation. The office was probably honorary and involved no active duties, although there is an opposing view that the term was the equivalent of **parnas*. The term *pater synagogae* has been found in the Diaspora (in both Greek and Latin inscriptions) but not in Erets Yisra'el. A parallel title of honor—*mater synagogae* (mother of the synagogue)—was applied on occasion to a leading female member of the congregation.

• Ismar Elbogen, *Jewish Liturgy: A Comprehensive History*, translated by Raymond P. Scheindlin (Philadelphia, New York, and Jerusalem, 1993), p. 369. —SHMUEL HIMELSTEIN

PATRIARCHATE. See NASIʾ.

PATRIARCHS (Heb. *avot*), the founding fathers of the Jewish people, *Abraham, *Isaac, and *Jacob. The patriarchs were divinely elected and were the human parties to God's *covenant. Their descendants, the children of Israel, inherited their blessings, promises, and duties (i.e., the land of Canaan, the Torah, and the obligation to walk in the ways of God). Abraham, the first patriarch, is in his own category, as is reflected in the first paragraph of the ʿAmidah (called Avot [i.e., Patriarchs]), which mentions all three patriarchs by name, but which concludes, "Blessed are you, O God, shield of Abraham." The morning prayer service is traditionally regarded as having been instituted by Abraham, the afternoon prayer service by Isaac, and the evening prayer service by Jacob. The significance of the patriarchs and their enduring merits are constant themes of synagogal poetry. See also MATRIARCHS; ZEKHUT AVOT.

• Hillel Goldberg, *Illuminating the Generations . . . : From the Middos of the Patriarchs and Matriarchs to the Musar Thinkers of Our Time* (Brooklyn, N.Y., 1992). Benjamin Mazar, ed., *Patriarchs* (Tel Aviv, 1970). Claus Westermann, *The Promises to the Fathers: Studies on the Patriarchal Narratives* (Philadelphia, 1980). —SHALOM PAUL

PATRILINEAL DESCENT. Many Israelite men such as Moses and Solomon are recorded as having married foreign women; patrilineal descent seems to have been the rule in biblical times. By marrying an Israelite man, the woman automatically became part of her husband's people, as there was not yet any ritual ceremony of conversion. Moreover, the priesthood also descended by patrilineal consideration. By the Mishnaic period, however, Jewish law established that children's religious identity was determined by the mother (matrilineal descent). The Talmud states "Your son by an Israelite mother is called your son, but your son by a heathen woman is not called your son" (*Qid.* 68b).

Various theories have been offered to account for the development from patrilineal descent to matrilineal descent. Some have pointed to Ezra's crusade against intermarriage as the first evidence of the matrilineal principle. Others regard the adoption of matrilineal descent as an act of pity by the rabbis in the face of the rapes of Jewish women by Roman soldiers in the first and second centuries CE. Shaye J. D. Cohen has identified the influence of Roman law in the transition from patrilineal to matrilineal descent. He has also suggested that the matrilineal principle is parallel to a Mishnaic opinion that classifies mixed breed animals in accordance with the mother's species.

In 1982 the Reform movement decided to recognize patrilineal descent: a person who is born of a Jewish father and a non-Jewish mother is recognized as a Jew if he or she so desires and observes certain Jewish obligations, without having to go through a process of conversion. The decision was accepted the next year by Reconstructionist Jews. However, it proved controversial even in the Reform movement and was accepted only in the United States and Britain and not, for example, in Canada or Israel. In 1984 the issue was debated by the Conservative movement and rejected. Orthodox Judaism unqualifiedly rejects patrilineal descent.

• Shaye J. D. Cohen "The Origins of the Matrilineal Principle in Rabbinic Law," *AJS Review* 10 (1985): 19–54. "The Issue of Patrilineal Descent," *Judaism* 34.1 (Winter 1985), symposium on patrilineal and matrilineal descent. "Who Is a Jew?" *Journal of Reform Judaism* 30 (Winter 1983), theme issue on matrilineal descent.

—MARC SHAPIRO

PAUL, the "apostle to the gentiles," originally a Jew named Saul from Tarsus in Asia Minor. He studied for some time under the patriarch *Gamli'el the Elder (*Acts* 22.3), but his spiritual background was Hellenism rather than Palestinian Judaism. Paul wrote in Greek, and his Bible quotations are drawn from the *Septuagint. At first a zealous adherent of the Pharisaic party and a violent opponent of *Christianity (at that time a Jewish sect), he became an enthusiastic convert as a result of a visionary experience on the road to Damascus, while on a mission to put down the nascent Christian movement in that city. Changing his name from Saul to Paul, he embarked on missionary journeys to Asia Minor, Greece, and Rome. Paul's activity was largely instrumental in bringing about the development of Christianity from a Jewish sect to a world religion. He not only founded the church of the "gentiles" but also evolved the theology of the new dispensation, according to which the Law of Moses and the promises of the prophets had been fulfilled in *Jesus. Thus, in his view Israel and its law were now superseded by the church and faith in Christ. Many of the terms in which Paul elaborated his thought go back to sectarian, non-Pharisaic Jewish sources; for example, the notions of children of light versus children of darkness, flesh versus spirit, election of grace, predestination, and so forth that are prominent in the *Dead Sea Scrolls. Paul's epistles became part of the New Testament and his *Epistle to the Romans* is a crucial statement of his attitude toward the Jews. He discerns great continuities between the church and Israel but finds the effective discontinuity much greater. Hence, his ideas regarding the Torah (he held that the law could not lead to true salvation but only to consciousness of man's innate sinfulness) have decisively influenced Christian attitudes toward Judaism. Modern Christian scholars (K. Stendahl, E. P. Sanders) do not see Paul's position as placing the teaching of Jesus in opposition to Judaism but as showing how Christ fulfilled the Torah.

• Francis H. Agnew, "Paul's Theological Adversary in the Doctrine of Justification by Faith: A Contribution to Jewish–Christian Dialogue," *Journal of Ecumenical Studies* 25.4 (1988): 538–554. John Duncan Martin Derrett, "New Creation: Qumran, Paul, the Church, and Jesus," *Revue de Qumran* 13.1–4 (1988): 597–608. Craig A. Evans and James A. Sanders, eds., *Paul and the Scriptures of Israel* (Sheffield, Eng., 1993). Martin Hengel and Ulrich Heckel, eds., *Paulus und das antike Judentum. Tuebingen-Durham-Symposium im Gedenken an den 50. Todestag Adolf Schlatters* (Tübingen, 1991). Joseph Klausner, *From Jesus to Paul* (New York, 1943). Hyam Maccoby, *The Mythmaker: Paul and the Invention of Christianity* (New York, 1986). Steven N. Paul Mason, "Classical Anti-Jewish Polemic, and the Letter to the Romans," in *Self-Definition and Self-Discovery in Early Christianity: A Study in Changing Horizons, Essays in Appreciation of Ben F. Meyer*, edited by David J. Hawkin and Tom Robinson (Lewiston, N.Y., 1990), pp. 181–223. Ellis Rivkin, "Paul's Jewish Odyssey," *Judaism* 38.2 (1989): 225–234. E. P. Sanders, *Paul and Palestinian Judaism* (London, 1977). Krister Stendahl, *Paul among the Jews and Gentiles* (Philadelphia, 1976). Leonard Swidler et al., *Bursting the Bonds? A Jewish-Christian Dialogue on Jesus and Paul* (New York, 1990).

PAYYETAN (פַּיְטָן), author of sophisticated prayer-poems for the Jewish *liturgy (see PIYYUT). The word *payyetan* comes from the Greek *poietes* (poet), and the *payyetanim* wrote elaborate poetical compositions filled with recondite allusions, intended to supplement the statutory prayers by injecting an element of novelty into the standard devotions. The first known *payyetan* was *Yosei ben Yosei, who may have lived and worked as early as the fifth century CE. The prolific poet *Yann'ai—some eight hundred of his compositions are extant—lived in Palestine around 550 CE. His pupil El'azar *Kallir, also Palestinian, wrote intricate compositions that were frequently criticized for the liberties that he took with Hebrew grammar and for his neologisms. Other *payyetanim* of renown include, for the Ashkenazi rite, Shim'on ben Yitsḥaq ben Abun (11th cent.), and, among the Sephardim, Shelomoh *ibn Gabirol, Mosheh *ibn Ezra, *Yehudah ha-Levi, and Avraham *ibn Ezra.

• Lawrence A. Hoffman, *The Canonization of the Synagogue Service* (Notre Dame, 1979), chap. 4. Abraham Z. Idelsohn, *Jewish Liturgy and Its Development* (New York, 1932), chap. 5.

—A. STANLEY DREYFUS

PEACE (Heb. *shalom*), a term in Biblical Hebrew signifying well-being in the widest sense and the full, undisturbed unfolding of the blessed life. In a narrower sense it means the absence of war and violence. The passion for peace as the *summum bonum* runs throughout Jewish literature and thought. It applies both to the messianic vision of universal peace when "nation shall not lift up sword against nation, neither shall they learn war any more" (*Is.* 2.4; *Mi.* 4.3) and to the more homely sphere of domestic peace between man and his fellow man and between husband and wife (see SHELOM BAYIT). *Shalom* is also considered to be one of the names of God, and punctilious observance prohibits the pronouncement of the word in an unclean place or bathroom. *Aaron is regarded as the prototype of those who "love peace and pursue peace and love all creatures," and every Jew is enjoined to follow his example (*Avot* 1.12). R. Shim'on ben Ḥalafta' said, "God could find no better vessel of blessing for Israel than peace" (*'Uqts*. 3.12). Indeed, peace is the ultimate purpose of the Torah (*Tanḥuma' Shofetim* 18) according to the sages. Every single prayer of importance (e.g., Birkat ha-Kohanim, the Qaddish, the 'Amidah, the Birkat ha-Mazon) ends with a prayer for peace and the hope that the same peace that exists among the heavenly spheres shall also reign on earth. The original, full signification of the term is preserved in the traditional Jewish greeting "peace unto you" (*shalom aleikhem*); the shorter version, *shalom*, is the usual formula of greeting in Modern Hebrew. See also JUSTICE; WAR.

• Avieser Ravitsky, "Peace" in *Contemporary Jewish Religious Thought*, edited by Arthur A. Cohen and Paul Mendes-Flohr (New York, 1987), pp. 685–702. Marcus Wald, *Jewish Teaching on Peace* (New York, 1944).

PEACE OFFERING (Heb. *zevaḥ shelamim*), one of the *sacrifices (*Lv*. 3; 7.11–34). Its distinctive features were that only the blood and the representative fatty portions of the animal were placed on the altar and the prescribed portions of the flesh were eaten by the priests; the sacrifice itself was consumed by the offerer and his invited guests as a festive meal "before the Lord." According to one widespread biblical tradition, no meat could be eaten from the flock or the herd unless it was offered as a *shelamim* sacrifice (*Lv*. 17.3–7). According to *Deuteronomy*, however (12.15ff.), the profane slaughter of sheep, goats, and cattle was permitted, a concession that became operative in Judaism. Peace offerings sacrificed by individuals were of three types: spontaneous offerings of devotion (*nedavah*; see FREE-WILL OFFERING), those made in fulfillment of a vow (*neder*), and those offered in thanksgiving (*todah*; see THANKSGIVING OFFERING); they were never a means of atonement. Peace offerings were thus the natural expression of joy and gladness in ancient Israel; the worshiper celebrated by enjoying the uplifting experience of feasting in the presence of God in acknowledgment of his lovingkindness.

• Gary A. Anderson, *A Time to Mourn, A Time to Dance: The Expression of Grief and Joy in Israelite Religion* (University Park, Pa., 1991). Baruch A. Levine, *In the Presence of the Lord* (Leiden, 1974). Jacob Milgrom, ed., *Leviticus 1–16* (New York, 1991), pp. 202–225.

—BARUCH J. SCHWARTZ

PE'AH (פֵּאָה; Corner), tractate in Mishnah order Zera'im, in eight chapters, with related material in the Tosefta' and the Talmud Yerushalmi. It deals with gifts to the poor, primarily those given from agricultural produce. The owner of a field is biblically enjoined, while harvesting, to allow the poor to gather from *pe'ah*, a corner of the field designated for the poor (*Lv*. 19.9); loose grains dropped by the harvester (*Lv*. 19.9); sheaves forgotten in the field (*Dt*. 24.19); and scattered grapes growing unclustered on the vine (*Lv*. 19.10; see LEQET, SHIKHḤAH, AND PE'AH). These forms of charity allow the poor free access to the field during the time of harvest (cf. *Ru*. 2). *Pe'ah* stresses that these gifts are not to be distributed—unless the poor unanimously agree (*Pe'ah* 4.1)—but are to be left for the poor to pick for themselves, despite the quarreling that may be anticipated (see *Pe'ah* 4.4). The idea that the owners' sovereignty over their fields is not absolute is reflected in the opening pericope of *Pe'ah*, which groups *pe'ah*, as a "matter which has no mandated quantity," together with other commandments—first fruits and pilgrimage offerings—that express divine sovereignty.

The last chapter of *Pe'ah* discusses the poor *tithe, defining the minimum amount that must be distributed to each individual, as well as establishing a definitive poverty line for all the gifts described in *Pe'ah*. *Pe'ah* stresses at its conclusion, as in its opening, the theological significance of the laws of charity. The rabbis regarded *pe'ah* as a unique moral achievement of Jewish ethics (*Lv. Rab*. 29.2) and required prospective converts to be instructed specifically regarding the laws of *pe'ah* (*Yev*. 46a).

An English translation of the tractate is to be found in Herbert Danby's *The Mishnah* (London, 1933).

• Chanoch Albeck, ed., *Shishah Sidrei Mishnah, Seder Zera'im* (Jerusalem, 1957). Philip Blackman, ed. and trans., *Mishnayoth*, vol. 1, *Order Zeraim* (Gateshead, 1973). Jacob David Herzog, ed. and trans., *Mishnah* (Jerusalem, 1945). Pinhas Kehati, ed., *Mishnah: A New Translation with a Commentary, Seder Zeraim*, vol. 1, *Berakhot, Pe'ah* (Jerusalem, 1989). Hermann Leberecht Strack and Günter Stemberger, *Introduction to the Talmud and Midrash*, rev. and updat. ed., translated by Markus Bockmuehl (Minneapolis, 1992).

—AVRAHAM WALFISH

PELI'AH, SEFER. See SEFER HA-QANAH.

PELUGTA'. See CONFLICT OF OPINION.

PENAL LAW. Jewish law contains within it a complete criminal law code governing all areas of criminal law. There are numerous substantive offenses designed to cover the spectrum of human vices (such as murder, incest, gambling), as well as detailed *criminal procedure rules designed to determine whether sufficient substantiation has been adduced to prove commission of a crime. Finally there are *punishments, from death to fines, designed to condemn and deter criminal activity.

Jewish law required that the source of each criminal statute be clearly spelled out, both as to the crime and the punishment. Crimes may not be inferred, even when such inferences would appear logical.

As a general rule, Jewish law required intent to commit crimes, and any action for which the intent could not be shown could not be criminally punished. Thus, there were categories of people who were exempt from criminal punishment: minors, the mentally unstable, and the mentally retarded; so too, certain actions committed under duress were exempt. Perhaps unique was the belief that ignorance of the law was a valid defense to criminal prosecution, and thus a system by which people were warned prior to punishment was followed. Witnesses were required to verify that the person in question actually committed the crime.

A court had exigency jurisdiction to punish criminals in circumstances in which the procedural safeguards allowed those who were repeat violators to escape punishment. All post-Talmudic invocation of criminal law is predicated on this exigency jurisdiction, and punishments meted out were not in accordance with Talmudic legal requirements. Thus, people were punished without warning or based on evidence other than that given by two male witnesses or in other ways not found in Jewish law. Deadly force may be employed to protect one's own life or the life of another when it is illegally threatened. A burglar who robs at night can be preemptively killed when it is clear that the robber is prepared to use deadly force if challenged. In those areas of civil law that govern illicit activity self-help may be used. Thus, one may snatch back items taken from one's possession by a thief and need not resort to the authorities prior to invoking that remedy.

• J. David Bleich, "Jewish Law and the State's Authority to Punish Crime," *Cardozo Law Review* 12 (1991): 829–857. Haim H. Cohn, "Penal Law" and "Extraordinary Remedies," in *Principles of Jewish Law*, edited by Menachem Elon (Jerusalem, 1975), pp. 469–475, 550–554. Arnold N. Enker, "Aspects of Interaction between the Torah Law, the King's Law, and the Noahide Law in Jewish Criminal Law," *Cardozo Law Review* 12 (1991): 1137–1156. Marilyn Finkelman, "Self-Defense and Defense of Others in Jewish Law: The Rodef Defense," *Wayne Law Review* 33 (1987): 1257–1287. Aaron M. Schreiber, "The Jurisprudence of Dealing with Unsatisfactory Fundamental Law: A Comparative Glance at the Different Approaches in Medieval Criminal Law, Jewish Law and the United States Supreme Court," *Pace Law Review* 11 (1991): 535–564.

—MICHAEL BROYDE

PENITENCE. See REPENTANCE.

PENITENCE, TEN DAYS OF. See ʿASERET YEMEI TESHUVAH.

PENITENTIAL PRAYERS. See SELIḤOT.

PENTATEUCH. See TORAH.

PENTECOST. See SHAVUʿOT.

PEOPLE OF ISRAEL (Heb. *ʿam Yisra'el*). This particular term is relatively late, although the perception of Israel as a "people" (*ʿam*) or a "nation" (*le'om*) has always been taken for granted (see NATIONALISM). The most frequent biblical terms are "people of God" and "house of Israel," but "your people Israel" is also found; for example, in David's prayer, "who is like your people Israel, a nation one in the earth" (*2 Sm.* 7.23). The phrase *ʿam Yisra'el ḥay* (the people of Israel live) has become almost a slogan, affirming the eternal life of the people.

• David Novak, *The Image of the Non-Jew in Judaism: An Historical and Constructive Study in the Noahide Laws* (New York, 1983).

PE'OT (פֵּאוֹת; corners), side locks. According to the Bible (*Lv.* 19.27), it was forbidden to remove the hair at the corners of the head, possibly to distinguish Israelite practice from that of certain pagan priests. The rabbis interpret this regulation as meaning that the temples must not be rendered as smooth as the forehead (*Mak.* 20b). The length of the *pe'ot* is not specified, but it is understood to be the length of a line drawn from the top of the forehead to the base of the ear lobe and long enough to be grasped by two fingers. The custom arose among Orthodox Jews (at first in Hungary and Galicia) of allowing the sideburns to grow completely uncut. Yemenite Jews follow a similar custom, but this originated in a decree forbidding Jews to cut their sideburns in order to distinguish them from Muslims. The biblical injunction not to "mat the corners of the beard" (*Lv.* 19.27) has been traditionally interpreted as a prohibition against shaving. Mystics of the Lurianic school found significance in the fact that the **gimatriyyah* (numerical value) of *pe'ot* was eighty-six, the same as Elohim (God). Women are exempt from the regulations of *pe'ot* (*Qid.* 1.7). See also BEARDS.

• Philip Birnbaum, *A Book of Jewish Concepts* (New York, 1964).

PEREQ HA-SHALOM, an aggadic chapter, devoted to the value of peace, which originated as an independent work but was appended to the tractate *Derekh Erets Zuta'*. The sayings in Pereq ha-Shalom, most of which open with "Great is peace . . . ," present peace as a value that finds expression on many levels: peace is one of the pillars on which the world stands; it is the name of God himself; and peace serves as the basis for relationships within the household, within society, and among nations. The chapter was translated into English by Daniel Sperber (Jerusalem, 1976).

• Michael Higger, ed. and trans., *The Treatises Derek Erez* (New York, 1935). Daniel Sperber, *Great Is Peace: Perek ha-Shalom from the Talmudic Tractate Derekh Eretz Zuta* (Jerusalem, 1979). Daniel Sperber, *A Commentary on Derech Erez Zuta* (Jerusalem, 1990). —AVRAHAM WALFISH

PEREQ SHIRAH (פֶּרֶק שִׁירָה; Chapter of Song), a collection of hymns of praise to the Creator as sung by the heavenly bodies, the earth, animals and birds, and vegetation. The idea that all creation praises God is frequently expressed in the Bible (e.g., *Ps.* 148) and seems to have given rise to the selection of appropriate scriptural verses to represent the "hymnal of creation." Pereq Shirah is only indirectly mentioned in the Talmud, but it appears to be an ancient *baraiyta'* known to have existed in the geonic period, although the version extant today is certainly late. Its authorship was variously ascribed to R. Eliʿezer ben Yaʿaqov, to R. Yehudah ha-Nasi', and even to David. It is printed in several editions of the prayer book and is recited by some as a private devotion after the morning service. Several manuscripts show its development in three versions: Askenazi, Sephardi, and ʿAdot ha-Mizraḥ. It was first printed in Venice in 1576 with a commentary by Mosheh ben Yosef di Trani. Its incorporation in the prayer book was inspired by the kabbalists of Safed.

• Malachi Beit-Arié, "Pereq Shirah," Ph.D. dissertation, The Hebrew University of Jerusalem, 1966. Louis Ginzberg, *The Legends of the Jews* (Philadelphia, 1909–1939). —AVRAHAM WALFISH

PERJURY, the violation of an oath (see VOWS AND OATHS), regarded as a great sin (see *Zec.* 5.4) punishable only by God. If a man admitted to committing perjury in a civil transaction, he could atone by means of a special offering (*Lv.* 5). Witnesses are not obligated to take an oath guaranteeing the truth of their *evidence. See also FALSE WITNESS.

• Emanuel B. Quint, *A Restatement of Rabbinic Civil Law*, vol. 1 (Northvale, N.J., 1990).

PEROZBOL (פְּרוֹזְבּוֹל; from Gr. *prosbolē*, meaning "for the court," or "official notice"), a legal instrument annulling the sabbatical release of debts (see SHEMITTAH). All private loans were automatically remitted in the sabbatical year (*Dt.* 15.2); hence, it became difficult to obtain loans immediately before the onset of that year. In order to avoid hardship and encourage lending, *Hillel instituted the *perozbol* (*Shevi'it* 10.3), which is a declaration made before a court of law by the creditor, and signed by witnesses, stating that all debts due to him are given over to the court for collection. Since the remission of loans during the seventh year applies only to individuals but not to public loans, the effect of the *perozbol* is to render the individual's loan public, and it is therefore not nullified (see DISPENSATION). The amora'im criticized the *perozbol* as a circumvention of biblical law, but the authority of Hillel ensured its retention.

• Emanuel B. Quint, *A Restatement of Rabbinic Civil Law*, vols. 1 and 2 (Northvale, N.J., 1994). Yisroel Reisman, *The Laws of Ribbis: The Laws of Interest and Their Application to Everyday Life and Business* (Brooklyn, N.Y., 1995).

PERPETUAL LIGHT. See NER TAMID.

PERPETUAL OFFERING (Heb. *tamid*), the regularly recurring ritual acts performed in the Tabernacle and later in the Temple that make up a systematic method of symbolically paying homage to God, envisaged as enshrined in his earthly abode, at the same time as petitioning him on Israel's behalf. These rituals were the entry of the high priest into the *heikhal* (holy place) each morning and evening, wearing the *priestly vestments, as a representative of the Israelite people "before the Lord"; the lighting of the lamp (see NER TAMID) by the high priest each evening and its refueling each morning; the offering of *incense on the golden altar each morning and evening; and the placement of the *showbread on the table each week. The term *tamid* is also used to refer to the daily *burnt offering (*Ex.* 29.38–42; *Nm.* 28.1–8; see SACRIFICES).

• Menahem Haran, *Temples and Temple-Service in Ancient Israel* (Winona Lake, Ind., 1985), pp. 205–229. —BARUCH J. SCHWARTZ

PERUSHIM (פְּרוּשִׁים; Separatists), name given to the disciples of *Eliyyahu ben Shelomoh Zalman of Vilna, the Vilna Ga'on, in Erets Yisra'el. The first group of the Ga'on's disciples began arriving in 1808. Their leader, Menaḥem Mendel of Shklov (died 1827), established a *yeshivah*, Kolel ha-Perushim, in Safed, where he was joined in 1809 by the Talmudist Yisra'el ben Shemu'el of Shklov (died 1839). Following a plague in Safed in 1812, they relocated to Jerusalem, where they were instrumental in reviving the Ashkenazi community.

• Jaacov Even Chen, *'Aliyyot Eliyyahu: 'Aliyyat Talmidei ha-Gera' le-'Erets Yisra'el* (Tel Aviv, 1986). —MILES KRASSEN

PESAḤ (פֶּסַח; Passover), the first of the *Shalosh Regalim, observed for eight days in the Diaspora (see YOM TOV SHENI SHEL GALUYYOT) and seven days in Erets Yisra'el and by Reform Jews. The festival commemorates the *Exodus of the children of Israel from Egypt; hence, it is also called the Festival of Freedom. The term *pesaḥ*, which indicates the "passing over" or sparing of the houses of the children of Israel during the plague of the killing of the firstborn (*Ex.* 12.13), is used in the Bible solely with respect to the sacrifice of the *paschal lamb, which took place on the eve of the Exodus (14 Nisan). The day before the festival is observed as *Ta'anit Bekhorim. The seven-day festival that follows (15–22 Nisan) is called in the Bible "the festival of unleavened bread" (Ḥag ha-Matsot; cf. *Lv.* 23.5–6: "On the fourteenth day of the first month at even is the Lord's Passover. And on the fifteenth day of the same month is the feast of unleavened bread to the Lord"). The agricultural aspect of the festival is connected with the spring season and the beginning of the barley harvest and was expressed in ancient times by the offering of the *'*omer* in the Temple on the second day of the festival. Both the first and last day (first two days and last two days in the Diaspora) are considered holy days, and all work is prohibited. The intermediate days are **ḥol ha-mo'ed*. The dietary laws require the eating of *matsah* on the first night(s) and prohibit the eating of any *ḥamets* (leaven) throughout the holiday. The rabbis added extra stringency to the first of these regulations by ordaining that, unlike other accidental admixtures of prohibited food that may be disregarded if the quantity is less than a sixtieth of the total, the tiniest amount of leaven in food renders it unfit for use on Pesaḥ. Hence, the most rigid care must be exercised in the preparation of food and utensils for Pesaḥ. The rabbis also ruled that *ḥamets* that has been in the possession of a Jew during Pesaḥ remains forbidden even after the festival, therefore it must be sold beforehand. A pre-Pesaḥ ceremony is performed in the home to ensure that all *ḥamets* has been removed (see BEDIQAT ḤAMETS; BI'UR ḤAMETS). The Pesaḥ Seder (see *HAGGADAH OF PESAḤ), celebrated on the first night(s) of the festival, is one of the most important home ceremonies of the liturgical year. The laws of the festival are discussed in tractate **Pesaḥim*. After the first day(s) of Pesaḥ, only the shorter form of *Hallel is said in the synagogue. A prayer for dew (see TEFILLAT TAL), recited on the first day of the festival, marks the end of the winter season and the beginning of spring. On the intermediate Sabbath of Pesaḥ, **Song of Songs* is recited in Ashkenazi synagogues. Allegorically this book represents the bond established at the Exodus between God and the children of Israel, but the spirit of spring with which it is infused (cf. *Song.* 2.11–13) serves as a reminder of the agricultural aspect of the festival. In Temple times, those unable to observe the festival had another opportunity to offer the paschal sacrifice a month later (see PESAḤ SHENI). The coincidence of Pesaḥ with Easter led, in the Middle Ages, to the linking of the *blood libel with the Pesaḥ festival. Jews of North Africa (and certain other ʿAdot ha-Mizraḥ) celebrate a family festival on the day following the conclusion of Pesaḥ (*Mimunah). It has become a popular holiday among Jews of North African descent in Israel. *Samaritans still sacrifice a paschal lamb at their annual Pesaḥ ceremony in Shechem (Nablus). *Marranos observed the festival a day later so as to avoid suspicion of keeping Jewish holidays. See also FESTIVAL PRAYERS.

• Shimon Finkelman, *Pesach: Passover: Its Observance, Laws, and Significance* (Brooklyn, N.Y., 1994). Theodor Herzl Gaster, *Passover, Its History and Traditions* (Westport, Conn., 1984). Philip Goodman, ed., *The Passover Anthology* (Philadelphia, 1961). Irving Greenberg, *The Jewish Way: Living the Holidays* (New York, 1993), pp. 34–65. Mordell Klein, *Passover* (Philadelphia, 1973). Eliyahu Safran, *Kos Eliyahu: Insights on the Haggadah and Pesach* (Hoboken, N.J., 1993).

PESAḤIM (פְּסָחִים; Paschal Lambs), tractate in Mishnah order Moʿed, in ten chapters, with related material in the Tosefta' and both Talmuds. It deals with the laws of the paschal sacrificial order and the *Pesaḥ festival. The biblical injunctions against eating leavened bread (*Ex.* 12.20, 13.3) during the festival or maintaining it in one's possession (*Ex.* 12.15, 13.7) are defined and expanded. Much of the day preceding Pesaḥ is devoted to the elimination of leavened items, commencing with a meticulous candlelight inspection on the night of 14 Nissan (see BEDIQAT ḤAMETS) and concluding with the burning of the leaven the next morning (see BIʿUR ḤAMETS). Many of these practices stem from Second Temple times; the burning of the leaven, although not required by all authorities (*Pes.* 2.1), seems to have been the normal practice (*Pes.* 1.4). *Pesaḥim* dwells on the similarity between burning leaven and burning sacred foods that have been defiled (*Pes.* 1.5–6) or disqualified due to time lapse (*Pes.* 1.4), suggesting that the symbolic significance of forbidding leaven on Pesaḥ may be related to the prohibition against using leaven in sacrificial offerings (*Lv.* 2.11).

Whereas the paschal blood was smeared on the door posts at the time of the Exodus, the blood of the Second Temple offering described in *Pesaḥim* was poured onto the altar in an impressive communal ceremony. The Second Temple paschal offering was, however, clearly a commemoration, indeed a reenactment (*Pes.* 10.5), of the redemption from Egypt. This is further reinforced by the description in *Pesaḥim* 10 of the festive Pesaḥ-night meal, in which the paschal lamb, along with the foods that accompany it—unleavened bread and bitter herbs—serve as the focal point of the recounting and celebration of the Exodus.

The tractate in Talmud Bavli was translated into English by Harry Freedman in the Soncino Talmud (London, 1938).

• Chanoch Albeck, ed., *Shishah Sidrei Mishnah, Seder Moʿed* (Jerusalem, 1952). Philip Blackman, ed. and trans., *Mishnayoth*, vol. 2, *Order Moed* (Gateshead, 1973). Pinhas Kehati, ed., *Mishnah: A New Translation with a Commentary, Seder Moed*, vol. 3, *Pesahim, Shekalim* (Jerusalem, 1993). Hermann Leberecht Strack and Günter Stemberger, *Introduction to the Talmud and Midrash*, rev. and updat. ed., translated by Markus Bockmuehl (Minneapolis, 1992). —AVRAHAM WALFISH

PESAḤ SHENI (פֶּסַח שֵׁנִי; Second Passover), a celebration introduced for those who, through ritual uncleanness or unavoidable absence from Jerusalem, were unable to sacrifice the paschal lamb on the proper date, 14 Nisan (*Nm.* 9.9–25). A concession was made to enable such persons to offer the sacrifice a month later. The only recorded instance of the celebration of Pesaḥ Sheni was by King *Hezekiah, after consultation with "the princes of the congregation in Israel" (*2 Chr.* 30.2). Pesaḥ Sheni (on 14 Iyar) is marked today by the omission of supplicatory prayers (*Taḥanun) in the synagogue service and in some communities by eating a piece of *matsah*. Some Orthodox Jews put aside three pieces of *matsah* on Pesaḥ and save them to be eaten on Pesaḥ Sheni.

• Emanuel Feldman, "The Second Pesah: Mitzvah as Paradigm," *Tradition* 24.2 (1989): 38–43. Eliyahu Kitov, *The Book of Our Heritage: The Jewish Year and Its Days of Significance*, rev. ed. (Jerusalem and New York, 1978).

PESHAT (פְּשָׁט), simple or literal meaning, associated with the exegesis of biblical texts. In classical rabbinic literature and medieval commentaries, *peshat* is contrasted with the term **derash* in referring to the literal as opposed to the homiletical meaning of the Bible. Many scholars have focused on the Talmudic use of the phrase *ein miqra' yotse' middei peshuto* (*Shab.* 63a; *Yev.* 11b, 24a) as evidence that the rabbis insisted that their derivation of practice should be grounded in the literal meaning. The dialectic of *peshat* and *derash* became especially significant in the biblical commentaries of the Middle Ages, when Rashi and his school as well as R. Avraham ibn Ezra focused their efforts on grounding all interpretation in *peshat*.

• Michael Fishbane, ed., *The Midrashic Imagination: Jewish Exegesis, Thought and History* (Albany, N.Y., 1993). Benjamin J. Gelles, *Peshat and Derash in the Exegesis of Rashi* (Leiden, 1981). David Weiss Halivni, *Peshat and Derash: Plain and Applied Meaning in Rabbinic Exegesis* (New York, 1991). Yeshayahu Maori, "The Approach of Classical Jewish Exegetes to Peshat and Derash and Its Implications for the Teaching of Bible Today," *Tradition* 21 (Fall 1984): 40–53. —MICHAEL A. SIGNER

PESHER (פֵּשֶׁר; interpretation), the technical term for commentary on scripture used in the writings of the Qumran community. Continuous *pesharim* cite successive verses from one biblical book; thematic *pesharim* cite nonconsecutive verses from several biblical books. The bible text is followed by its interpretation. Typically, each interpretation is introduced by a formula featuring the word *pesher*. Exegetical techniques (allegory, puns, *notariqon*, analogy between verses, etc.) are used to apply the prophetic citations to the history and eschatological beliefs of the Qumran community. The interpretations reveal the mysteries of the end of days hidden in biblical prophecy and are held to be the product of divine inspiration granted to a chosen interpreter.

While the term *pesharim* refers primarily to the literary genre described above, it sometimes designates units of similar form and content embedded in other types of compositions.

• George J. Brooke, *Exegesis at Qumran: 4QFlorilegium in Its Jewish Context*, Journal for the Study of the Old Testament, Supplement Series 29 (Sheffield, Eng., 1985). Maurya P. Horgan, *Pesharim: Qumran Interpretations of Biblical Books*, Catholic Biblical Quarterly Monograph Series 8 (Washington, D.C., 1979). Menahem Kister, "Biblical Phrases and Hidden Biblical Interpretations and *Pesharim*," in *The Dead Sea Scrolls: Forty Years of Research*, edited by Devorah Dimant and U. Rappaport (Leiden, 1992) pp. 27–39. Bilha Nitzan, *Megillat Pesher Havaqquq: Mi-Megillot Midbar Yehudah (1QpHab)* (Jerusalem, 1966).

—ESTHER GLICKLER CHAZON

PESHITTA', the Syriac translation of the Bible (including the New Testament), called Peshitta' or Peshitto (simple [translation]) because the Syriac translation was considered natural in contrast to the Syro-Hexapla version (a Syriac version of Origen's Hexapla) which, as a literal Syriac translation of the Greek, had an unnatural flavor in Syriac. The greater part of the translation, which was produced by many translators working at different periods, is of Jewish origin and still retains traces of rabbinical interpretations; it differs occasionally from the Masoretic Text. The Peshitta' may have been initiated in the second or even in the first century CE. Although it was intended for use by Jews, by the third century it had become the Bible of the Syriac-speaking Christians. The translations of *Genesis*, *Isaiah*, the Minor Prophets, and *Psalms* in the Peshitta' accord closely with the Septuagint, while *Ezekiel* and *Proverbs* accord closely with the *Targum. The Peshitta' did not include *Esther*, *Ezra*, *Nehemiah*, *Chronicles*, or books of the Apocrypha; these books were added later.

• P. B. Dirksen, *An Annotated Bibliography of the Peshitta of the Old Testament*, Monographs of the Peshitta Institute, no. 5 (Leiden, 1989). P. B. Dirksen, "The Old Testament Peshitta," in *Mikra: Text, Translation, Reading and Interpretation of the Hebrew Bible in Ancient Judaism and Early Christianity*, edited by M. J. Mulder, Compendia rerum Iudaicarum ad Novum Testamentum, sect. 2, vol. 1 (Assen and Philadelphia, 1988), pp. 255–297. P. B. Dirksen and M. J. Mulder, *The Peshitta: Its Early Text and History* (Leiden, 1988). M. J. Mulder, "The Use of the Peshitta in Textual Criticism," in *La Septuaginta en la investigacion contemporanea*, edited by N. Fernández Marcos, Textos y Estudios "Cardenal Cisneros" 34 (Madrid, 1985), pp. 37–53.

PESIQTA' (Aram.; פְּסִיקְתָּא; section) cycle of Palestinian *midrashim*, so called because it deals only with selected passages from the Pentateuch and the Prophets. Two versions are extant. The first is usually referred to as the *Pesiqta' de-Rav Kahana'* (the opening section begins with his name). Though much of it dates from approximately the fifth century CE, the work as a whole was probably completed in the seventh century. The other version—*Pesiqta' Rabbati*—is still later (after 815 with later glosses from the 13th cent.). It draws upon the *Pesiqta' de-Rav Kahana'* and *Tanḥuma'-Yelammedenu literature. It also includes a section (20–24) called *Midrash Mattan Torah* by medieval authorities, which differs in style and structure from the rest of the work and seems to constitute a separate unit; it reflects the influence of early mystical sources. Earlier scholars confused the two versions of the *Pesiqta'* with each other and with the eleventh-century *midrash* **Leqaḥ Tov*, which was also known as *Pesiqta' Zutarta'*. The *Pesiqta'* follows the cycle of the Jewish calendar, beginning with Ro'sh ha-Shanah and concluding with the Sabbath before Ro'sh ha-Shanah. In addition to *aggadah*, the *Pesiqta'* contains a great deal of important halakhic material. The *Pesiqta' de-Rav Kahana'* was published by Bernard Mandelbaum (New York, 1962). A critical edition of *Pesiqta' Rabbati*, edited by Me'ir Friedman, appeared in 1880 and was translated into English by William G. Braude in 1968.

—DANIEL SPERBER

PESUQEI DE-ZIMRA' (פְּסוּקֵי דְזִמְרָא; Verses of Song or Praise), a collection of biblical hymns recited daily at the beginning of the morning service. Sephardim refer to them as Zemirot (songs). They are preceded and followed by a benediction (Barukh she-'Amar and Yishtabaḥ respectively). The Pesuqei de-Zimra' are not mentioned in the Talmud, though they or a similar selection of hymns were probably already recited then by pious worshipers. The Pesuqei de-Zimra' are found in the ninth-century prayer book of R. *ʿAmram bar Sheshna'. The main components are Psalm 145 through Psalm 150 (see HALLEL) and *Exodus* 15. On Sabbaths and festivals several more psalms are added, and the hymn of praise, Nishmat Kol Ḥai, precedes the opening blessing (see BIRKAT HA-SHIR). The Pesuqei de-Zimra' are followed by the Short *Qaddish and *Barekhu. In the Ashkenazi service, usually worshipers read the Pesuqei de-Zimra' silently, while the reader chants only the opening or concluding verses of each section; in other rites, the Pesuqei de-Zimra' are often recited aloud, either in unison or antiphonally. No **minyan* is required for the recitation of the Pesuqei de-Zimra', and their insertion into the early part of the morning service is in accord with the rabbinic teaching that man should first praise God and then present his own petitions (*Ber.* 32a).

• Ismar Elbogen, *Jewish Liturgy: A Comprehensive History*, translated by Raymond P. Scheindlin (Philadelphia, New York, and Jerusalem, 1993), pp. 72–76.

PETIḤAH (פְּתִיחָה; opening or proem), a formula, found at the beginning of a *parashah* (section) in aggadic *midrashim*. It presents an exposition of a verse (called the *petiḥah* verse), frequently culled from the Hagiographa, unconnected to the biblical passage at hand, ultimately relating it to the first significant verse of the passage (called the *parashah* verse). *Petiḥot* may be attributed to a particular sage. In early aggadic *midrashim* (viz., *Genesis Rabbah*, *Leviticus Rabbah*, *Pesiqta' de-Rav Kahana'*), several *petiḥot* to the same *parashah* verse are found at the beginning of almost every section; in other *midrashim* (notably *Lamentations Rabbah*), a large collection of *petiḥot* introduce the entire work. Many *petiḥot* are enlarged through the insertion of Midrashic material (exegesis, stories, parables, and the like), which may then serve as an artful homiletical bridge leading from the *petiḥah* verse to the *parashah* verse. The origin of the *petiḥah* is still debated; a widely held view is that the form originated in the oral homilies delivered in the synagogue on the Sabbath and holy days, where it served as an introduction to the Torah reading.

• Wilhelm Bacher, *Die Prooemien der alten judischen Homilie* (Leipzig, 1913). Hermann Leberecht Strack and Günter Stemberger, *Introduction to the Talmud and Midrash*, translated by Markus N. A. Bockmuehl (Edinburgh, 1991), pp. 265–268. —PAUL MANDEL

PETUCHOWSKI, JAKOB JOSEF (1925–1991), Reform thinker. Petuchowski was born in Berlin but emigrated from Nazi Germany before World War II. In 1956 he began teaching rabbinics at Hebrew Union College in Cincinnati. He wrote or edited more than thirty books including *Ever since Sinai* (1961), *Zion Reconsidered* (1966), and *Prayer Book Reform in Europe* (1968). Initially critical of secular Zionism, he became more positive after the 1967 Six-Day War. He maintained a belief in the authority of revelation, but as a Reform Jew, he understood both *halakhah* and revelation in the light of evolutionary theory and saw Reform Judaism as merely one stage in the ongoing development of the Jewish tradition. His views influenced several generations of rabbis whom he taught in Cincinnati.

• Kerry M. Olitzky, ed., *Reform Judaism in America* (Westport, Conn., 1993), pp. 161–162. —LAVINIA COHN-SHERBOK

PFEFFERKORN, JOHANNES (1469–c.1521), apostate. A butcher by trade, he converted to Christianity in approximately 1504 and, encouraged by the Dominicans, denounced Jewish literature for containing anti-Christian blasphemies. Emperor Maximilian I empowered him to examine all Jewish books in Germany except the Bible and to destroy any that were anti-Christian. The order was eventually rescinded after a bitter dispute in which several Christians took part; Pfefferkorn's sponsors (the Obscurantists) were opposed by the Humanists led by Johannes Reuchlin.

• Samuel Abraham Hirsch, "Johann Pfefferkorn and the Batttle of the Books," in *A Book of Essays* (London, 1905). Hans-Martin Kirn, *Das Bild vom Juden im Deutschland des frühen 16 Jahrunderts* (Tübingen, 1989).

PHARAOH (Heb. *parʿoh*), Egyptian word meaning literally "great house," referring to the palace of the king, which in time came to be used to designate the king himself. Various pharaohs are mentioned in the Bible. Though in the earlier books of *Genesis* and *Exodus* their personal names are not given, in the later historical sources of *Kings* and *Jeremiah*, the individual pharaohs' names are generally recorded. Most scholars agree that the pharaoh who enslaved the Israelites (*Ex*. 1.8–11) is Ramses II (c.1279–1212), whose inscriptions mention the use of ʿApiru (see HEBREWS) slaves for building projects. His name endures in the name of one of the stone cities, Ramses, built by the Israelites (*Ex*. 1.11). The pharaoh under whom Joseph served would thus be a predecessor of this monarch, but he cannot be identified with any confidence. Ramses II's son and successor, Merneptah (c.1212–1202), left an inscription from his fifth year that mentions for the first time outside of the Bible Israel as a people. Many scholars relate this reference to the period after the Israelites had entered Canaan. Solomon married the daughter of a pharaoh (*1 Kgs*. 3.1), usually identified as Siamun (c.978–959). Other pharaohs mentioned in the Bible include Shishak (*1 Kgs*. 14.25), Necho (*2 Kgs*. 23.29–34), and Hophra (*Jer*. 44.30), all well-known figures from Egyptian sources.

• Alan Henderson Gardiner, *Egypt of the Pharaohs* (London, 1976). K. A. Kitchen, *The Third Intermediate Period in Egypt, 1100–650 B.C.* (Warminster, Eng., 1986). Gary Rendsburg, "The Date of the Exodus and the Conquest/Settlement: The Case for the 1100's," *Vetus Testamentum* 42 (1992): 510–527. Naham M. Sarna, *Exploring Exodus* (New York, 1986). —GARY A. RENDSBURG

PHARISEES (Heb. Perushim [Separatists]), one of the three main Jewish sects in the Second Temple period, said by *Josephus Flavius to have comprised at one point six thousand members and to have been supported by the majority of Jews. Their origins, in the second century BCE, are obscure, although they may be related to the *Hasideans. Josephus writes that the Pharisees were distinguished from other sects by their acceptance of the *oral law, and they were acknowledged to be skillful interpreters of the Torah. According to Josephus, whose account is not completely reliable, the Pharisees differed in their theology from the *Sadducees in maintaining a belief in the immortality of the soul (in actual fact the Pharisees taught the resurrection of the dead), in the existence of angels, and in divine providence. Unlike the *Essenes, who emphasized predetermination, the Pharisees asserted freedom of will. They also differed from the other groups in their halakhic rulings, although not all of these differences can be reconstructed from the extant sources. In rabbinic literature, which views the Pharisees as the predecessors of tannaitic Judaism, they were depicted as punctilious observers of the laws of purity and priestly tithings, separating themselves from the common people who were less strict in their observance of these laws. Josephus reports that the Pharisees were deeply involved in the inner-Jewish disputes of the Hasmonean period (see HASMONEANS), and their views won the largest following among the Jewish masses. However, neither the Pharisees nor other Jewish movements were political parties, and their involvement in politics stemmed mainly from their insistence that the nation, and the high priests in particular, should follow their religious precepts. Thus, they were at odds with several of the Hasmonean rulers, especially Alexander Yannai (r. 103–76), but were influential with other members of that dynasty, such as Yannai's wife and successor, Salome Alexandra (r. 76–67). Given the paucity of sources and their possible tendentiousness (Josephus, for example, claims to have been a Pharisee, and his description of the Pharisees is far from objective), it is not easy to assess the Pharisees' real influence over the wider Jewish population (especially since Josephus is not entirely consistent on this point), but it seems that they had a wider appeal than that of either the Sadducees or the Essenes. Moreover, the Pharisees' central position in the Jewish community of the time is also apparent from other sources, including the *Dead Sea Scrolls (in which "the seekers of smooth things" is probably a pejorative reference to the Pharisees) and the *New Testament, where they are often denounced in the most bitter terms.

This hostile description of the Pharisees in early Christian literature, which is the source of the negative connotation that the term *Pharisee* has acquired in many European languages, may reflect the Pharisees' relative importance at the time when *Jesus' followers were trying to spread their master's message among the Jewish masses. Recent church documents (such as the Vatican's 1985 Notes on the Teaching of Judaism) have been aimed at changing traditional Christian condemnation of the Pharisees.

• Louis Finkelstein, *The Pharisees: The Sociological Background of Their Faith*, 2 vols. (Philadelphia, 1938). Jacob Neusner, *From Politics to Piety: The Emergence of Pharisaic Judaism*, 2d ed. (New York, 1979). Anthony J. Saldarini, *Pharisees, Scribes and Sadducees in Palestinian Society* (Wilmington, Del., 1988). E. P. Sanders, *Judaism: Practice and Belief, 63* BCE–*66* CE (Philadelphia, 1992). Emil Schürer, Geza Vermes, and Fergus Millar, *The History of the Jewish People in the Age of Jesus Christ, 175 B.C.–A.D. 135* (Edinburgh, 1979), vol. 2, pp. 381–414. Seth Schwartz, *Josephus and Judean Politics* (Leiden, 1990). —GIDEON BOHAK

PHILANTHROPY. See CHARITY.

PHILISTINES, people who settled on the southern coast of Canaan in the twelfth century BCE. Their ethnic identification is debated. They originated in the Aegean and were not circumcised (unlike most others in the land of Canaan), which suggests they were not Semitic but may have been Indo-European. Their god, however, was Dagon, an old Semitic deity, and the Bible assumes that Israelites and Philistines could communicate without difficulty, suggesting that their language was a dialect of Canaanite. However, no Philistine texts have been discovered. The first reference to the Philistines occurs in a series of Egyptian historical texts from the reign of Ramses III (c.1182–1151), when the Philistines led an alliance of nations called the Sea Peoples in an attack against Egypt. The Egyptians repulsed the invaders, who then settled in Canaan. The Bible agrees with this picture, as it consistently portrays the Philistines as originating in Caphtor, a name used either for the Aegean in general or for Crete in particular (see, e.g., *Am.* 9.7). The Philistine arrival on the Canaanite coast coincided with the arrival and settlement of the Israelites in the central hill country of Canaan. A short while later, when both groups attempted to expand their territories, tensions arose and they became enemies. Two biblical judges, Shamgar (*Jgs.* 3.31) and Samson (*Jgs.* 14–16), fought against the Philistines in the late twelfth and early eleventh centuries BCE. Major battles occurred later in the eleventh century BCE. In one encounter, the Philistines captured the Ark (*1 Sm.* 4–6). Although they later returned the Ark, this event resulted in the Israelites pressing their leader Samuel to establish a monarchy (*1 Sm.* 8). The first king, Saul, was initially victorious against the Philistines, but in the end he was defeated by them and met his death on the battlefield at Gilboa (*1 Sm.* 31). When David became king of Israel about 1000 BCE, he set out to rid his nation of the Philistine menace. He was successful (*2 Sm.* 5.17–25, 8.1, 21.15–22, 23.9–17), and never again do the Philistines appear in the Bible as a major threat to the Israelites. They eventually came under Assyrian rule in 734 BCE. The Bible also refers to Philistines living in Canaan at the time of the Patriarchs (*Gn.* 20 and 26). These Philistines either belong to an earlier wave that came from the Aegean or it is an anachronism. The Philistines in *Genesis* differ in many ways from the Philistines in *Judges* and *Samuel*: they live in Gerar, not in the five city-states of Gath, Gaza, Ekron, Ashdod, and Ashkelon, called the Pentapolis; they are ruled by a king, not by lords (Heb. *seranim*, probably of Philistine origin); and they make peace with the Israelites instead of appearing as belligerent. Recent excavations at several of the cities of the Pentapolis (Ashdod, Ashkelon, and Ekron), as well as Tel Qasile on the Mediterranean coast at Tel Aviv, have revealed many aspects of the material culture of the Philistines.

• Moshe Dothan and Trude Krakauer Dothan, *People of the Sea: The Search for the Philistines* (New York, 1992). Trude Krakauer Dothan, *The Philistines and Their Material Culture* (New Haven, 1982). N. K. Sandars, *The Sea Peoples: Warriors of the Ancient Mediterranean, 1250–1150 B.C.*, Ancient Peoples and Places (New York, 1985). D. J. Wiseman, ed., *Peoples of Old Testament Times* (Oxford, 1973). —GARY A. RENDSBURG

PHILO (c.20 BCE–50 CE), Alexandrian philosopher and exegete. Little is known about his life beyond the fact that he came from a wealthy and influential family, some of whose members gave up the Jewish way of life, and that he participated in a Jewish embassy to Caligula in Rome between 39 and 40. Fully at home in Greek culture, Philo interpreted the Greek verison of the Torah, the *Septuagint, within the conceptual framework and methodologies of Hellenistic philosophy. He was convinced that the books of Moses were actually the fountainhead of Greek philosophy, and most of his work was in the form of a detailed exegesis of the Torah, which he believed was almost entirely allegorical, aimed at penetrating through the surface narrative and exploring its spiritual depths. Thus, the biblical story of Abraham, Sarah, and Hagar (*Gn.* 16.1ff.) really describes the way to wisdom. The devoted learner (Abraham) must first obtain a basic education (of grammar, rhetoric, music, and so forth), which is the handmaiden (Hagar) of virtue, before possessing virtue (Sarah) itself. While interpreting even the legal sections of the Torah in a like manner, Philo insisted on the necessity of keeping the commandments according to their literal meaning; their deeper, allegorical sense was no substitute for actual observance. Though his biblical interpretation is basically universalistic, he stressed Jewish uniqueness and the significance of the Jewish people as mediators between humanity and the creator God, whose creation is so perfectly embodied in the Torah of Moses. Philo's exegesis contains much numerical speculation, since numbers possess special qualities, the knowledge of which is important for the full understanding of Moses' message, and exhibits an interest in the physical world, which was created by God and fully understood by Moses. Philo nowhere systematically expounds his philosophical system, which is clearly indebted to pre-Neoplatonism and Stoicism. The main tenets of his thought include a belief in one, absolutely perfect God, who operates in the world through a mediating *Logos. God formed the world from primordial matter and breathed his spirit into humans; humanity's goal is to gain release from the shackles of bodily needs and desires by philosophical contemplation, which will enable the soul to soar, in divine ecstasy, into the heavenly realm. While Christian thinkers found some of Philo's ideas (e.g., his emphasis on the allegorical nature of the Bible, and particularly his doctrine of the mediating Logos) particularly congenial, his influence within Judaism was limited. Josephus knew of him and had read some of his works, but he is not referred to in rabbinic literature nor by medieval Jewish philosophers. Philo's impact on modern Jewish thinkers is minimal, perhaps because his allegorical technique, his numerical mysticism, and his repetitive style make him unattractive to modern readers. Nevertheless, his attempt to fuse the Jewish and Greek cultures makes him one of the most intriguing intellectuals of the ancient world.

• F. H. Colson et al., eds and trans., *Philo*, 10 vols. and 2 suppl. vols., Loeb Classical Library, (Cambridge, Mass., 1929–1962), a Greek text with an English translation. Erwin R. Goodenough, *An Introduction to Philo Judaeus* (Oxford, 1962). Wolfgang Haase, ed., *Aufstieg und Niedergang der römischen Welt*, 2.21.1 (Berlin and New York, 1984), an entire volume dedicated to Philo; most of the studies are in English. Emil Schürer, Geza Vermes and F. Millar, *The History of the Jewish People in the Age of Jesus Christ, 175 B.C.–A.D. 135* (Edinburgh, 1987), vol. 3.2, pp. 809–889. Harry A. Wolfson, *Philo: Foundations of Religious Philosophy in Judaism, Christianity, and Islam*, 2 vols. (Cambridge, Mass., 1947). C. D. Yonge, trans., *The Works of Philo* (Peabody, Mass., 1993).

—GIDEON BOHAK

PHILOSOPHY. The *Weltanschauung* of the Bible and the rabbis was to be found scattered through Jewish literature. It was only as a result of external stimulation—Hellenism, Muslim Neoplatonism, Aristotelianism, post-Kantian idealism, and modern existentialism—that a philosophical outlook was systematized. The categories of contemporary philosophies were applied as a means of arriving at a philosophical understanding of Judaism. Indeed it took until the Middle Ages for the first Jewish creedal formulations to appear (see CREED; DOGMA).

The development of philosophical writing in Jewish circles led to deep rifts between a fundamentalist school, which condemned philosophy as a vain exercise of human reason that should be guided solely by *revelation, and a rationalist approach exalting philosophy as the index of the truth or error of religious doctrines. Philosophy has often been called upon to prove, confirm, or buttress religious doctrines or to elucidate their implications and presuppositions in the light of philosophical understanding. Although the Bible is essentially nonphilosophical in character, there are underlying ideas and concepts that lend themselves to philosophic elaboration: God, revelation, transcendence, monotheism, theodicy, creation, the relationship between God and humankind, and so on. The ancient rabbis occasionally raised philosophical problems but in epigrammatic form without philosophic discussion.

The effective beginning of Jewish philosophy came only during the Middle Ages, but it was anticipated in Hellenistic times by *Philo of Alexandria and a number of minor writers of whom little is known. Philo interpreted Judaism in terms of Platonic and Stoic ideas, basing his efforts at reconciliation on an allegorical approach. However, Philo was soon forgotten in Jewish circles, and his main impact was on Christian thought.

Of far greater significance was the medieval revival of Greek philosophy among the Muslims and the use to which it was put by the theological schools of *Islam (*Kalam). The fact that two competing universal religions, both rejecting Judaism, claimed exclusive validity, as well as the rationalist criticism of religion in general, gave an enormous impulse to the theological attempts to prove the validity of religion by rational means. The first major Jewish medieval philosopher, *Saʿadyah ben Yosef Ga'on, depended on the Kalam school, as did David ibn Marwan *Mukammis and many others, both Rabbanites and Karaites. But whereas Mukammis's philosophy remained in the Muʿtazili tradition, rabbinic thought developed under the decisive influence of the two main streams of Greco-Arabic philosophy, Neoplatonism and Aristotelianism. Neoplatonism was the major influence in the thought of Yitsḥaq *Israeli and in Shelomoh *ibn Gabirol's *Meqor Ḥayyim*; its moral theology can also be seen in the *Ḥovot ha-Levavot* of *Baḥya ben Yosef ibn Paquda', in Yosef ben Yaʿaqov ibn *Zaddik's *Sefer ha-ʿOlam ha-Qatan*, and in *Yehudah ha-Levi's *Kuzari* (although Yehudah ha-Levi did not seek to reconcile Judaism with philosophy but to demonstrate the superiority of revelation). Aristotelianism, however, proved the more powerful trend. It appeared in the thinking of Avraham *ibn Daud and reached its peak in Moses *Maimonides' *Guide of the Perplexed*, which offers the most comprehensive justification and reconciliation of philosophy and Judaism along Aristotelian lines. Most subsequent writings either commented on or developed Maimonides' ideas or criticized and combated them. The controversy engendered by Maimonides' writings (see MAIMONIDEAN CONTROVERSY) rent Jewry into two hostile camps, one of the most dramatic examples of the constant tension between those who advocated a philosophic approach and those who were convinced that it threatened Judaism and so forbade or limited its study. The controversy could not in the long run prevent the victory of Maimonides' philosophy. This was exemplified in the works of Yitsḥaq *Albalag and *Levi ben Gershom, who continued to build on the Aristotelian foundations laid by Maimonides and who were further influenced by Arabic sources, notably Averroës. Ḥasda'i ben Avraham *Crescas and his pupil Yosef *Albo were critical of Aristotelianism but wrote within its tradition. Most of the philosophers mentioned lived in or came from Spain, but this ended with the expulsion of 1492, its last representative being the prolific and versatile Yitsḥaq Abravanel (see ABRAVANEL FAMILY). The tradition was cultivated in Italy, where Jews philosophized in a Christian environment at least from the time of *Hillel ben Shemu'el.

There was little further writing of a philosophical nature until the modern period was inaugurated by Moses *Mendelssohn. His object was to bridge the German Enlightenment and traditional Judaism; he taught that Judaism was not a revealed religion but a revealed law. His thought, in many ways typical of the *Haskalah, was soon superseded by the triumph of German idealism, applied to Judaism by Salomon *Formstecher and Samuel Hirsch (see HIRSCH FAMILY). Naḥman *Krochmal in his *Guide of the Perplexed of the Time* used historical research in the service of an ambitious philosophy of history with distinct Hegelian overtones. Salomon Ludwig *Steinheim propounded an antirationalist philosophy of revelation. The end of the twentieth century witnessed a revival of Kantianism, exemplified by Moritz *Lazarus's *Ethik des Judentums* and particularly by the work of Hermann *Cohen. Existentialist trends came to the fore in Franz *Rosenzweig's *Star of Redemption*, and the last decades of German Jewry were marked by the activities of other leading thinkers such as Martin *Buber (whose philosophy of dialogue was influential in Christian circles) and Leo *Baeck. Jewish nationalism was an outgrowth of the Haskalah movement. The outstanding Zionist philosophical essayist was *Aḥad ha-ʿAm, whose doctrine of Zion as a spiritual center was opposed by the historian Simon *Dubnow, whose theories of successive social and cultural centers affirmed life in the Diaspora as a legitimate form of Jewish existence. Jacob *Klatzkin preached a radical "negation of the Diaspora." *Holocaust theology probed the relation between God and Israel. The destruction of German Jewry meant the end of its hegemony in Jewish philosophy. Successors have been found in France (Emmanuel Levinas, André *Neher) but mainly in the United States (Abraham Joshua *Heschel, Yosef Dov Soloveichik [see SOLOVEICHIK FAMILY], Mordecai Menahem *Kaplan, Eugene Borowitz) and Israel (Yeshaʿyahu *Leibowitz). The establishment of the State of Israel led to a greater emphasis on the philosophical problems of statehood and political existence (such as the philosophy of history and individual and collective destiny).

• Arthur A. Cohen and Paul Mendes-Flohr, *Contemporary Jewish Religious Thought* (New York, 1987). Julius Guttmann, *Philosophies of Judaism* (New York, 1973). Isaac Husik, *Mediaeval Jewish Philosophy* (Philadelphia, 1941). Louis Jacobs, *A Jewish Theology* (London, 1973). Steven T. Katz, ed., *Jewish Ideas and Concepts* (New York, 1975). Steven T. Katz, ed., *Jewish Philosophers* (New York, 1975). Nathan Rotenstreich, *Jewish Philosophy in Modern Times* (New York, 1968). Colette Sirat, *A History of Jewish Philosophy in the Middle Ages* (Cambridge and New York, 1985).

PHINEHAS (Heb. Pinḥas), son of Eleazar and grandson of Aaron the high priest. When the Israelites began to offer sacrifices to the Moabite god Baal-peor and engaged in harlotry with the daughters of Moab, Phinehas ran a spear through Zimri, a chief of the tribe of Simeon, who had defiantly entered the encampment at Shittim with a Midianite woman. Phinehas's zeal persuaded God to end the plague that was ravaging Israel in punishment for their infidelity, and Phinehas and his offspring were rewarded with eternal priesthood (*Nm.* 25.10–13). Later, when Moses waged war against the Midianites, Phinehas was entrusted with the sacred utensils and "the trumpets for sounding the blasts" (*Nm.* 31.6). The Zadokites traced their descent to him. Rabbinic *aggadah* identifies Phinehas with the prophet Elijah, both of whose deeds exemplified zealous action in the name of the Lord.

• Jacob Milgrom, *Numbers*, The JPS Torah Commentary (Philadelphia, 1990), pp. 476–480.

—SHALOM PAUL

PHOENICIANS, Greek name for the peoples of the Levant (greater Canaan), especially the coastal region, and used by scholars today to refer to the Canaanites of such major city-states as Byblos, Tyre, and Sidon from c.1200 BCE onward. The Bible portrays the Phoenicians as being on friendly political terms with the Israelites. For example, King Hiram I of Tyre (c.980 BCE) made a treaty with David and Solomon, and the Phoenicians supplied the architects, workmen, and raw materials (cedar of Lebanon, especially) for the construction of David's and Solomon's palaces and for the Temple in Jerusalem (*2 Sm.* 5.11; *1 Kgs.* 5.15–32, 7.13–14). The detailed biblical description of the Temple dovetails with the data from the archeological discovery of various Phoenician temples, clearly demonstrating that Solomon's Temple was built according to the design of a Phoenician–Canaanite prototype. Solomon and Hiram also had joint maritime ventures from the Red Sea port of Ezion-geber (near Elat) to develop trade with regions to the far south and east (perhaps East Africa and India; *1 Kgs.* 9.26–28, 10.11, 10.22). Later, King Ethbaal I of Sidon (c.880 BCE) appears to have entered into a treaty with Omri, marked by the marriage of their children, Ahab, later king of Israel, and Jezebel, the Phoenician princess (*1 Kgs.* 16.31). These alliances, especially the latter, resulted in the introduction of Phoenician worship, especially the cult of Baal (see BAAL WORSHIP), into Israelite circles (*1 Kgs.* 16.31–32) and the subsequent confrontation of *Elijah with the Baal worshipers to preserve the purity of the Israelite religion. The Phoenicians were well known for their extensive trade with and colonization of the entire Mediterranean basin. They developed the linear alphabet, which then was taken over by the Israelites and many others in the Near East. Similarly, the Greeks (and through them all other Europeans) borrowed the use of alphabetic writing from the Phoenicians.

• Donald B. Harden, *The Phoenicians*, Ancient Peoples and Places 26, 2d ed. (New York, 1963). H. Jacob Katzenstein, *The History of Tyre* (Jerusalem, 1973). Sabatino Moscati, *The World of the Phoenicians* (London, 1968). D. J. Wiseman, ed., *Peoples of Old Testament Times* (Oxford, 1973).

—GARY A. RENDSBURG

PHYLACTERIES. See TEFILLIN.

PHYSICIANS. See MEDICINE.

PIDYON HA-BEN. See FIRSTBORN, REDEMPTION OF THE.

PIDYON SHEVUYIM. See RANSOM.

PIETY (Heb. *ḥasidut*), a concept, frequent in Talmudic and Midrashic literature, denoting devotion to worship beyond the demands of *halakhah*. In this sense, it is essentially a legal term, referring to individuals and groups who devote themselves to transcending the demands of the law, which they regard as minimal rather than optimal. Thus the Mishnah refers to a group that practiced spiritual concentration before and after statutory prayers beyond the time required as the Early Pietists (Ḥasidim ha-Ri'shonim). The meaning of the term *ḥasidut* was extended to include the concept of sacrifice: a *ḥasid* is one who dedicates much more to the performance of ritual and ethical precepts than is expected from others. In the Middle Ages, especially in the Rhineland, this term was used almost synonymously with *qadosh* (martyr). Another word used to denote a pious individual is *tsaddiq (righteous); in the Bible, the words *ḥasid* and *tsaddiq* are used almost interchangeably to refer to the faithful, obedient, and righteous servant of God. In later literature, a distinction developed, but there is no systematic definition that separates a *ḥasid* from a *tsaddiq*. In some writings, a *ḥasid* is one who tries; the *tsaddiq* is one who has achieved. However, this distinction has not been consistently maintained throughout Hebrew religious literature. In the writings of Judeo-Arabic spiritual authors the *ḥasid* is very similar to the Sufi ascetic and mystic.

The terms *ḥasidut* and *ḥasid* did not usually designate a movement or an organization, but rather an individual pietist; the cases in which the term has been used to describe movements were exceptions rather than the rule. One biblical example is the *Hasideans (Gr. Asidaioi), who are mentioned in *Maccabees*. As far as the early Ḥasidim are concerned, it is unclear whether they were part of a cohesive movement. In the Middle Ages, there was one movement to which this term was applied—the *Ḥasidei Ashkenaz—which received the name mainly because its leaders were known by this term (R. Shemu'el he-Ḥasid, R. Yehudah he-Ḥasid), as was its central work, the *Sefer Ḥasidim*. On the other hand, the nineteenth-century *Musar (ethics) movement could well be described as pietistic, though it was not referred to by that term. In the context of the modern Hasidic movement, the term *ḥasid* has lost its original meaning; today it means follower or adherent of a *tsaddiq*, rather than an individual pietist. See also HASIDISM.

• Michael D. Oppenheim, "The Meaning of Hasidut: Martin Buber and Gershom Scholem," *Journal of the American Academy of Religion* 49 (1981): 409–423.
—JOSEPH DAN

PIGGUL (פִּגּוּל), term applied to the flesh of a *peace offering, specifically a *free-will offering or votive offering, that was eaten beyond the prescribed two-day period following the sacrifice (*Lv*. 7.18, 19.7–8). The definition of the term *piggul* is unknown; perhaps it means foul, offensive, or otherwise desecrated. Rabbinic usage employed the term to include as well the flesh of the *thanksgiving offering eaten beyond its one-day period. The sacred meal had to be consumed reasonably close in time to the sacrifice itself and not become a separate, thereby secular, occasion; also, only the freshest, that is, the most desirable, meat was acceptable. Eating *piggul* invalidated the sacrifice. In the Bible, this is said to occur retroactively, desecrating what is sacred to the Lord two days after the sacrifice was performed. The rabbis, however, reinterpreted the passage to mean that the sacrificer, already at the time of slaughter, intends ultimately to partake of the flesh beyond its allotted time or outside of its proper place (*Zev*. 2.2–5, 3.6).

• Moshe Greenberg, *Ezekiel 1–20*, The Anchor Bible, vol. 22 (Garden City, N.Y., 1983), p. 107. Jacob Milgrom, *Leviticus 1–16*, The Anchor Bible, vol. 3 (Garden City, N.Y., 1991), pp. 417–423. Baruch J. Schwartz, "Selected Chapters of the Holiness Code," Ph.D. dissertation, Hebrew University, 1987, pp. 131–133. David P. Wright, *The Disposal of Impurity*, Dissertation Series (Society of Biblical Literature) 101 (Atlanta, 1987), pp. 140–143.
—BARUCH J. SCHWARTZ

PIGS, cloven-hoofed quadrupeds that are forbidden as food since they do not chew their cud (*Lv*. 11.7; *Dt*. 14.8). Since they also wallow in dirt, pigs became for Jews a symbol of filth and of all that is unseemly and abominable. The use of pigs in pagan sacrifices, which some pagan rulers attempted to force upon Jews, may also have contributed to the particular abhorrence with which Jews view pigs. Pigs became so repugnant that they were often referred to not by name but as "the other things." One who raises swine is considered accursed (*Men*. 64b), and it was forbidden to trade in or derive benefit from them. Some authorities (for example, Maimonides) interpreted the ban as being based on physical considerations, but others, including the kabbalists, stressed the spiritual aspect of the ban.

• Richard Walther Darre, *Das Schwein als Kriterium für nordische Völker und Semiten* (Munchen, 1933). Claudine Fabre-Vassas, *La Bête singulière: Les Juifs, les chrétiens et le cochon* (Paris, 1994).
—SHMUEL HIMELSTEIN

PILGRIMAGE. The duty to journey to a central shrine "at the place the Lord shall choose" (*Dt*. 16.16) from all parts of Erets Yisra'el and beyond to offer prayer and sacrifice and to participate in a whole gamut of religious activities, "that you may learn to fear the Lord your God" (*Dt*. 14.23; *Is*. 2.3; *B. B*. 21b), was already central in the Mosaic code. This prescribed that every Jewish male "appear before the Lord" on the annual *Shalosh Regalim (*Ex*. 23.17; *Dt*. 16.16). In addition, voluntary sacrifices and obligatory sin, purificatory, thanksgiving, and postparturition offerings had to be brought to the Temple. Major litigation had to be heard at the Temple court (*Dt*. 17.8). The first fruits, second tithes, or their proceeds were only to be enjoyed within the precincts of the central shrine (*Dt*. 14.22–27), subsequently delineated as within the walls of Jerusalem. All this ensured a steady stream of pilgrims—men, women, and children—making their way to the holy city throughout the year. It was promised (*Ex*. 34.24) that no one would covet the land the pilgrim might leave unattended in fulfillment of this duty. In the period of the judges, before the building of the Temple, the people went to Shiloh (*1 Sm*. 1.3). Solomon, in his dedicatory prayer, underlined the role of the Temple as the focus of pilgrimage for Jews and gentiles (*1 Kgs*. 8.41, 8.48). When the northern kingdom of Israel was established, Jeroboam attempted to set up rival shrines to attract pilgrims to Bethel and Dan (*1 Kgs*. 12.26–33).

The most impressive record of mass pilgrimage to Jerusalem was during the Second Temple period, from both the Erets Yisra'el and the Diaspora, and is described in tannaitic literature (e.g., *Bik*. 3.2–4), as well as in Philo (*De specialibus legibus* 1.69–70) and Josephus (*Antiquities of the Jews* 18.9.1; *The Jewish War* 19.11), which emphasizes the crucial unifying, social, religious, and national educational function of pilgrimage. The Mishnah (*Pe'ah* 1.1) includes *re'ayyon*, "appearing" before God, together with the bringing of the first fruits, leaving the corner of the field for the poor, acts of charity, and Torah study as things for which no maximum measure was prescribed. The local population was obliged by religious law (*Yoma'* 12a) to provide free accommodations for the pilgrims in return for the skins of their sacrifices. The prayer for rain in the fall was postponed for fifteen days after Sukkot to enable the pilgrims from the Babylonian Diaspora "to reach the Euphrates" (*Taʿan*. 1.3). Josephus (*The Jewish War* 6.9) reported that on the eve of the Jewish rebellion against the Romans in 66 CE the official census recorded the sacrifice of 255,600 paschal lambs, each of which was partaken of by a whole family and friends (cf. T., *Pes*. 4.3).

The institution of pilgrimage retained its hold even after the destruction of the Temple and the dispersion. Talmudic rulings (*Yev*. 6b) emphasized that the Temple ruins were to be approached with the same reverence as the Temple itself, since the divine presence—"He who gave the commandment 'to revere my holy place' " (*Lv*. 19.30)—continues to reside there. Even during the most difficult periods of persecution and Jewish depopulation, the *Holy Land remained a center of pilgrimage for individuals and groups from all parts of the Diaspora. From the Middle Ages onward, there began a process of marking the graves of prophets and Talmudic sages as Jewish pilgrim sites. In the sixteenth century Yitsḥaq Luria and his followers claimed to have identified many graves of Talmudic rabbis in Galilee, and pious Jews would make pilgrimages to the Holy Land to prostrate themselves on these tombs. Prayers and guide books were composed for the pilgrims. The Safed mystics in the seventeenth century proclaimed nearby Mount Meron, the site of R. *Shimʿon bar Yoḥ'ai's grave (he is regarded as the father of the Kabbalah) a major site of Jewish pilgrimage and feasting on Lag ba-ʿOmer, in spite of rabbinic disapproval (*Responsa Ḥatam Sofer, Yoreh Deʿah* 233), and to this day Mount Meron attracts thousands of Jews, mainly Sephardi and Hasidic. For the latter, fervent and carnival-like festivities at the graves, reputed or real, of distinguished rabbis and biblical figures remains an essential part of their folk culture, and organized groups regularly make pilgrimages to eastern Europe and elsewhere to visit the tombs of their *rebbi*s on the anniversaries of their deaths. In Muslim lands, it often became customary for Jews to make pilgrimages to graves, real or reputed, of biblical figures (such as Ezra and Daniel in Mesopotamia) and rabbis revered as saints, and to special synagogues (in Jerba, Tunisia). Lately, Jews from Muslim lands have begun making annual pilgrimages on 3 Shevat to Netivot to the tomb of Yisra'el Abi-Ḥasira (Baba Sali), a reputed saint of North African origin who died on that date.

Maimonides and subsequent halakhists forbade any feasting at actual gravesides and frowned on organized prayer at cemeteries, except that associated with fasting and mourning to arouse the people to repentance. Subsequently, the surviving *Western Wall of the Temple mount became the focal point of Jewish pilgrimage and has remained so to this day.

• James D. Purvis, *Jerusalem, the Holy City*, vols. 1 and 2 (Metuchen, N.J., 1988, 1991). Samuel Safrai, *Ha-ʿAliyyah le-Regel bi-Yemei Bayyit Sheni* (Jerusalem, 1958). Abraham Yaari, *The Goodly Heritage* (Jerusalem, 1958). Shelomoh Yosef Zevin, *Ha-Mo'adim be-Halakhah*, new rev. ed. (Jerusalem, 1980), vol. 1, pp. 178–180; vol. 2, pp. 360–364.

—ARYEH NEWMAN

PIGRIMAGE FESTIVALS. See SHALOSH REGALIM.

PILLAR OF CLOUD AND FIRE. According to the Bible, the method by which God led the Israelites after their Exodus from Egypt on their way through the desert to Canaan was in the form of a cloud by day and of fire by night (*Ex*. 13.21–22). The Midrash interprets the double description as referring to two separate entities, a fiery pillar rising at night and replacing the setting cloud (*Mekhilta'* "Be-Shallaḥ," p. 82); the biblical text suggests a pillar of cloud containing the divine presence by day and a pillar of fire by night. While the non-Priestly tradition confines the function of the cloud of fire to guidance through the desert, apparently envisioning it as a cloud led by an angel (*Ex*. 14.19), the Priestly source sees it as a means of divine revelation throughout the wilderness wanderings. This account reaches a climax when the cloud of fire, visible to all Israelites, alights on Mount *Sinai and Moses is summoned to enter it (*Ex*. 19.1, 24.15–18). After the construction of the *Tabernacle, the cloud, signifying the divine presence, enters and takes up permanent residence in the Sanctuary (*Ex*. 40.34–35). Thereafter, its periodic ascents and descents indicate to the Israelites when the march is to be resumed or interrupted (*Ex*. 40.36–38; *Nm*. 15–23). Though Moses is said to have met directly with God in the Tabernacle on numerous occasions (*Ex*. 25.22, 29.42–43, 30.6, 30.36, 34.34–35; and esp. *Nm*. 7.89), it was believed to be fatal for ordinary humans to gaze on the deity in its cloud of fire (*Lv*. 16.2, 16.13).

• Umberto Cassuto, *A Commentary on the Book of Exodus*, translated from Hebrew by Israel Abrahams (Jerusalem, 1967), pp. 108, 220. Louis Ginzberg, *The Legends of the Jews*, vol. 2 (Philadelphia, 1913), pp. 374–375. Jacob Milgrom, *Leviticus*, The JPS Torah Commentary (Philadelphia, 1990), pp. 134–139.

—BARUCH J. SCHWARTZ

PILPUL (פִּלְפּוּל), the process of dialectical reasoning applied in the study of the oral law. *Pilpul* can mean the application of hermeneutics to the halakhic parts of the Bible, but more particularly it signifies the logical analysis and argumentation characteristic of legal casuistry. Originally, *pilpul* was considered a legitimate method of Talmudic study, and it was listed in the Talmud as the twelfth of forty-eight methods by which Torah learning is acquired (*Avot* 6.6). The process was occasionally carried to extremes in order to sharpen the acumen of students (*ʿEruv*. 13a), but because of the misuse to which unrestrained dialectic could be put (*Sot*. 47b), the pilpulistic method was eventually condemned by various rabbis. The use of *pilpul* to demonstrate intellectual brilliance for its own sake aroused the disapproval of scholars of all ages. Following the methodology of R. Yaʿaqov *Pollak of Kraków, the pilpulistic approach was highly developed by eastern European *yeshivot*, despite the protests of some leading Talmudists. Eventually, *pilpul* was replaced as the principal avenue of Talmudic study by the logical method of study pioneered by *Eliyyahu ben Shelomoh Zalman of Vilna, the Vilna Ga'on, and spread by his disciples.

• Joseph L. Bloch, *Shiʿurei Halakhah* (Bene Beraq, 1994). Shimon M. Diskin, *Qunteres Poteaḥ Shaʿar* (Jerusalem, 1994). Heinrich Ehrentreu, *Über den 'Pilpul' in den alten Jeschiboth* (Frankfurt, 1905).

—SHMUEL HIMELSTEIN

PINḤAS BEN YA'IR (2d–3d cent.), Palestinian tanna'. The son-in-law of R. Shimʿon bar Yoḥ'ai (according to the Zohar, the father-in-law) and a respected contemporary of R. Yehudah ha-Nasi' (*Ḥul.* 7b), he resided in Lydda and was an ascetic who, while known for his brilliance (*Shab.* 33b), was especially famed for his saintly living (e.g., *Ḥul.* 7b; *Dt. Rab.* 3.3) and miraculous powers. Although he is most frequently mentioned in aggadic contexts, halakhic disputes are preserved in which he leaned towards stringency (cf. T., *Ohal.* 18.18). He spoke of the spiritual decline of the generations after the destruction of the Temple (*Sot.* 9.15), and coined the oft-quoted saying that zeal (for Torah, others, good works) leads to fastidiousness, fastidiousness to cleanness, cleanness to abstinence, to holiness, to modesty, to fear of sin, to piety, to the Holy Spirit, to the resurrection of the dead, which comes through Elijah. This saying took on special significance in the Musar movement. **Midrash Tadshe'* is sometimes incorrectly attributed to him based on his introductory comments to the work.

• Wilhelm Bacher, *Die Agada der Tannaiten* (1903; Berlin, 1965–1966). Israel Konovitz, comp., *Maʿarakhot Tanna'im: Osef Shalem shel Mishnatam u-Ma'amareihem bi-Sifrut ha-Talmudit veha-Midrashit* (Jerusalem, 1967–1969). ʿOfrah Me'ir, "Ḥamurato shel R. Pinḥas ben Ya'ir," in *Studies in Aggadah and Jewish Folklore: Dedicated to Dov Noy on His 60th Birthday*, edited by Issachar Ben-Ami and Joseph Dan, Folklore Research Center Studies, vol. 7 (Jerusalem, 1983). On the end of Sotah 9.15, Peter Schäfer, *Die Vorstellung vom heiligen Geist in der rabbinischen Literatur* (Munich, 1972).

—MICHAEL L. BROWN

PINḤAS OF KORZEC. See SHAPIRO, PINḤAS BEN AVRAHAM, OF KORETS.

PIQQUAḤ NEFESH. See DANGER.

PIRQEI AVOT. See AVOT.

PIRQEI DE-RABBI ELIʿEZER, pseudepigraphous narrative *midrash* written in Hebrew and ascribed to the tanna' *Eliʿezer ben Hurqanos (1st–2d cent.), whose life story is told in the first chapter; in fact, however, the composition of much of the work has been dated to the eighth century. *Pirqei de-Rabbi Eliʿezer* is an aggadic *midrash*, the avowed purpose of which is to "declare the glory of God." Many sections are devoted to the Creation chapters of *Genesis* and the early history of the patriarchs; its sudden conclusion with the punishment of Miriam for slandering Moses indicates that the work was unfinished or that part of it has been lost. Three chapters (chaps. 6–9) are devoted to the calendar, others to topics such as the Sabbath (chap. 18), repentance (chap. 43), and circumcision (chap. 29). The author often relates certain precepts to events in the lives of the patriarchs and draws upon a broad range of rabbinic sources, *midrashim*, the Talmud, the Palestinian *targumim*, and so on. He was also deeply influenced by the apocryphal literature, especially the Enoch cycle. He cites Arabic legends and gives a remarkable description of the Muslim Omayyad dynasty, looking forward to its fall, which he sees as an omen of the end of the exile. *Pirqei de-Rabbi Eliʿezer* cites many halakhic customs current in Erets Yisra'el at the beginning of the geonic period. This proves that the work is Palestinian in origin and dates from the first half of the eighth century CE, just prior to the fall of the Omayyad dynasty but before the rise of the Abbasid dynasty. It was first published in Constantinople in 1514 and translated into English by Gerald Friedlander in 1916.

• Leopold Zunz, *Ha-Derashot be-Yisra'el ve-Hishtalshelutan ha-Historit*, edited by Chanoch Albeck (1892; Jerusalem, 1974).

—DANIEL SPERBER

PIRQOI BEN BABOI (fl. c.800 CE), Babylonian scholar who described himself as a disciple of *Rabba' bar Naḥmani (or *Rava') and *Yehuda'i ben Naḥman Ga'on. He is known only as the author of a polemical tract in Hebrew, large portions of which have been published during the course of the twentieth century by a number of scholars. Pirqoi's epistle, addressed to the Jewish communities of North Africa and Spain, contains an unbridled attack on various Palestinian customs, notably the poetic elaborations of the liturgy that were an extremely important element of Palestinian Jewish tradition (see PIYYUT). According to Pirqoi's one-sided and historically suspect presentation, only Babylonian Jewry had maintained an uninterrupted tradition from the Talmudic period (and earlier), while Palestinian tradition had been totally disrupted as a result of Christian persecutions and could no longer assert a claim to continuity or authority with regard either to customary practice or to literary sources (especially the Talmud Yerushalmi). Pirqoi was a great admirer of Yehuda'i Ga'on, whom he describes as an arch-conservative who prided himself on never asserting a halakhic position unless he could support it both by Talmudic sources and by direct tradition from his teachers. Pirqoi further claims that Yehuda'i preceded him in the struggle against Palestinian customs and had gone so far as to attempt to convince the Palestinian Jews themselves to abandon their traditional practices in favor of Babylonian ones.

• Louis Ginzberg, ed., *Ginze Shekhter*, vol. 2 (New York, 1928–1929). Shalom Spiegel, "Le-Parshat Ha-Pulmus shel Pirqoi ben Baboi," in *Harry Austryn Wolfson Jubilee Volume* (Jerusalem, 1965), pp. 243–274.

—ROBERT BRODY

PITTSBURGH PLATFORM, program adopted by a conference of American Reform rabbis who met in Pittsburgh in 1885. It provided the guidelines for the Reform movement in the United States for fifty years until superseded by the *Columbus platform. The Pittsburgh platform was based on a "Declaration of Principles" formulated by Kaufmann *Kohler, who was the moving spirit in convening the conference. Kohler had been challenged by the traditionalist rabbi Alexander *Kohut to define the principles of Reform Judaism. There had been sharp differences in outlook between the more radical Reform, led by David *Einhorn, and those led by Isaac Mayer *Wise who propounded a more moderate Reform. Wise presided over the conference, which presented a compromise between the two groups, but with Kohler's views predominating.

The Pittsburgh platform consisted of eight paragraphs. While recognizing the significance of other faiths, it held that Judaism taught the highest concept of God; it extolled the Bible as an instrument of moral and religious instruction, while stating that the Bible often reflected the primitive ideas of its own age; it recognized only the moral Mosaic laws and those ceremonies that were elevating, rejecting the dietary laws and regulations concerning priestly purity; it stated that the Jews were not a nation but a religious community, who had no expectation to return to Palestine or to restore the Temple; it affirmed the immortality of the soul but rejected the doctrines of resurrection and reward and punishment in the hereafter; and it asserted that the mission of Israel was to bring the world to a universal morality. The platform was adopted by the *Central Conference of American Rabbis in 1889.

• Sefton D. Temkin, *Isaac Mayer Wise* (Oxford, 1992), pp. 286–294.

PITTUM HA-QETORET (פִּטּוּם הַקְּטֹרֶת; Compound Forming the Incense), *baraiyta'* (*Ker.* 6a; also Y., *Yoma'* 4.5) describing the preparation of incense in the Temple (*Ex.* 30.34–38) recited at the end of the morning service or—among Sephardim and Yemenites—also prior to the afternoon service. The recitation of Pittum ha-Qetoret goes back to the time of R. *ʿAmram bar Sheshna' (9th cent.), when it was recited morning and evening (corresponding to the times when the incense was offered in the Temple). In the Provençal rite, it was said at the end of Sabbath. The mystics attached great significance to its meticulous recitation, and for fear that the worshiper might be negligent in his recital on weekday mornings, they restricted the passage to the liturgy of Sabbaths and festivals, a practice that has remained the Ashkenazi custom in the Diaspora.

• Mervyn D. Fowler, "Excavated Incense Burners: A Case for Identifying a Site as Sacred," *Palestine Exploration Quarterly* 117 (1985): 25–29.

PIYYUT (פִּיּוּט), a poem, especially a liturgical poem inserted into a statutory prayer. The genre originated in Palestine around the fifth century. Subsequently, *piyyutim* were composed to a minor extent in Babylonia, and then again abundantly in Germany, France, Spain, and Italy. Though continuing until the eighteenth century, the writing of such poetry reached its height by the fourteenth, after which, *payyetanim* (composers of *piyyutim*; see PAYYETAN) were less prolific, and their *piyyutim* were rarely incorporated into the *liturgy. By then, readily available mass-printed prayer books had virtually closed off the opportunity for new creations to be admitted into the official liturgical corpus. By 1924 Israel Davidson (*Thesaurus of Medieval Poetry*) had enumerated some 35,000 *piyyutim* and listed nearly 3,000 poets; many more have been discovered since then.

The rise of the genre has been variously explained as a result of either persecution or natural liturgical creativity. *Yehudah ben Barzillai al-Bargeloni (12th-cent. Barcelona) traces poetic composition dealing with Jewish holy day regulations to an unspecified ban on the study of Torah—perhaps a 553 edict of Justinian prohibiting the study of *Deuterosis* (a word taken to mean Judaism's oral law). Samau'al ibn Yaḥya' al-Magribi (known also as Shemu'el ben Yehudah ibn Abbas), a convert to Islam, provides a similar report locating *piyyutim* as a response to Persian persecution—taken by some to mean the Sassanian dynasty of the fifth through the sixth century. The majority opinion today discounts both views as fanciful *ex post facto* etiologies and explains *piyyut* instead as a natural outgrowth of the synagogue service, which had begun as a creative oral art but was assuming greater linguistic fixity by the third and fourth centuries. The *piyyutim* represent an attempt to retain liturgical creativity. The earliest compositions were modest and their authors remain anonymous, but they culminated in a classical Palestinian period (c.5th–7th cent.), represented most prolifically by *Yosei ben Yosei, *Yann'ai, and Elʿazar *Kallir. They reflect a Jewish mosaic of words, akin to the surrounding Byzantine poetry, and a verbal analogue to Byzantine mosaic architecture.

These poets composed epic poems called *qerovot* (later garbled by medieval copyists as *qrovets*; see QEROVAH) for each and every Sabbath, linking the *ʿAmidah prayer to the weekly Torah reading. Since the cycle of readings, to which holiday readings were added, was triennial, the poetic output amounted to some 150 to 200 poems, each of which had many highly formalized stanzas inserted according to complex rules into the various paragraphs (or blessings) of the prayer in question. They also wrote poetry for other liturgical staples, including *yotserot* (see YOTSER) and **maʿaravot* (insertions in the morning and evening Shemaʿ and its blessings, taking their name from the liturgical staples in which they are placed and the time of day of the service). Their *piyyutim* for holy days included *ʿavodot* (for Yom Kippur afternoon; see ʿAVODAH); **seliḥot* (penitential poems for the High Holy Day period); **hoshaʿnot* (poetry recited while circumambulating the synagogue on Sukkot; **azharot* (poetry for Shavuʿot); and *qinot* (elegies for Tishʿah be-'Av; see QINAH). Relatively little of their work was ultimately included in the canonized prayer service, however, because the Babylonian prayer book of Amram Ga'on (9th cent.) became normative throughout the Jewish world, and Babylonian liturgy had frowned on Palestinian practice in general and on Palestinian poetry in particular. After the coming of Islam, *piyyutim* were composed also in Babylonian, especially by *Saʿadyah ben Yosef Ga'on, who, however, hailed from Egypt and the Palestinian cultural orbit. Other Babylonian poets from the ninth to the eleventh century left little overall impact on the genre.

Thereafter, Spanish *payyetanim* dominated. They experimented early on with the application of Arabic meter to Hebrew and produced a galaxy of famous poets notable for their religious and secular output. Among other things, they are known for creating *seliḥot* for the entire month of Elul. Especially noteworthy are Shelomoh *ibn Gabirol and *Yehudah ha-Levi. The parallel Ashkenazi school began in ninth-century Italy, then moved north to Germany, but, lacking the impact of Islamic culture, never achieved the independence from the classic style nor the Hebrew poetic sophistication that marked Spain. With the decline of western European culture and the expulsions of Jews from newly sovereign states (England, 1290; France, 1305; Spain, 1492), poetry moved east to Poland or the eastern Mediterranean countries, especially those under Ottoman control. However, despite some notable exceptions, especially among the sixteenth-century kabbalists of Safed, the service was rapidly being standardized and would soon be fixed by the printing press. New poetry was relegated to extrasynagogue settings, such as Sabbath eve table songs (see ZEMIROT).

Elementary rhythmic patterns can be found already in the earliest anonymous *piyyutim*, but it was the Spanish school that created advanced metrical schemes, such as measuring out a fixed number of syllables per line. Experiments in rhyme dominate the classical Palestinian era, especially with Yann'ai and more spectacularly, with Kallir. The latter also took enormous liberty with inventing or altering words for poetic ends, often to make his poems accord with acrostics that follow the alphabet or spell out the poet's name. Eventually, more and more critics (e.g., Avraham ibn Ezra, commentary to *Ecc*. 5.1) attacked the poets for linguistic obscurity and grammatical obfuscation. Maimonides objected to what he considered theologically objectionable imagery for God. In the eighteenth century, Ya'aqov *Emden summed up negative opinion saying that the *piyyutim* are so prolix that "even the angels do not understand them."

Nonetheless, *piyyutim* became staples of holiday worship in particular, and collections were eventually codified *de facto* by traditional usage and then by printers, who made available standard sets of poems as part of their prayer books. By the nineteenth century, Enlightenment aesthetics and theology intensified objections to poetry that was increasingly seen as hard to understand and serving only to add tedium and length to the worship service. Liturgical reformers streamlined the liturgy by shortening or eliminating all but the most popular offerings, which were retained as often as not only because of their musical features, which attracted people who rarely understood the Hebrew lyrics themselves.

Scholarship, on the other hand, has always found the *piyyutim* attractive. Nineteenth-century founders of modern scholarship saw them as evidence of Jewish culture beyond stereotypical medieval rabbinics, particularly from the Spanish golden age. Rites were classified geographically, according to the particular selection of poems incorporated, and poems were classified not only according to liturgical place and calendrical occasion, but also by style. Commentaries tried valiantly to provide keys to poetic allusions and to decipher word plays. With the discovery of the Cairo Genizah, thousands of new poems came to light, expanding the scope of known Jewish creativity far beyond what anyone had imagined. The poetry that began as a practical means to embellish the liturgy has largely fallen into liturgical ill favor and has instead become the domain of specialized scholarship intent on rounding out knowledge of Jewish creativity over the centuries.

• Israel Davidson, *Thesaurus of Mediaeval Hebrew Poetry*, 4 vols. (1924; repr. New York, 1970). Ismar Elbogen, *Jewish Liturgy: A Comprehensive History*, translated by Raymond P. Scheindlin (Philadelphia, 1993). Ezra Fleischer, *Shirat ha-Qodesh ha-'Ivrit bi-Yemei ha-Beinayim* (Jerusalem, 1975). E. Daniel Goldschmidt, *Maḥazor la-Yamim ha-Nora'im*, vol. 1 (Jerusalem, 1970). E. Daniel Goldschmidt, *Seder ha-Kinot le-Tish'ah be-'Av* (Jerusalem, 1968). E. Daniel Goldschmidt, *Seder ha-Seliḥot ke-Minhag Lita' u-Kehillot ha-Perushim be-'Erets Yisra'el* (Jerusalem, 1965). Abraham M. Habermann, *'Iyyunim ba-Shirah uva-Piyyut shel Yemei ha-Beinayim* (Jerusalem, 1972). Jakob J. Petuchowski, *Theology and Poetry: Studies in the Medieval Piyyut* (London, 1977). Zvi Meir Rabinowitz, *Maḥazor Piyyutei Rabbi Yann'ai la-Torah vela-Mo'adim* (Jerusalem, 1985). Abraham Rosenfeld, *The Authorised Selichot for the Whole Year* (London, 1962). Shalom Spiegel, "On Medieval Hebrew Poetry," in *The Jews: Their History, Culture and Religion*, by Louis Finkelstein, vol. 2 (Philadelphia, 1949). Menahem Zulay, *Ha-'Askolah ha-Paitanit shel Rav Sa'adyah Ga'on* (Jerusalem, 1964).

—LAWRENCE A. HOFFMAN

PLAGUES OF EGYPT (Heb. *'eser ha-makkot*), the series of afflictions brought upon the Egyptians by God in order to coerce Pharaoh into releasing the Israelites from slavery (*Ex*. 3.20, 7.8–11.10, 12.12–13, 29–30). Various traditions seem to have existed regarding the exact number and sequence of plagues (see *Ps*. 78.44–51, 105.28–36, in which the number of plagues is less than ten); the detailed version in *Exodus* mentions ten plagues, arranged in three groups of three plus a final, decisive one. In each of the three groups, the first two plagues were unleashed after a warning by Moses, while the third followed unannounced. In this account all the water in Egypt is transformed into blood, swarms of frogs cover all of Egypt, lice infest the entire land, Egypt is invaded by swarms of insects (others say wild beasts), a pestilence kills off Egypt's livestock, a skin inflammation (boils) afflicts man and beast, hail destroys the crops and surviving livestock, swarms of locusts darken the skies and consume all vegetation, darkness descends and covers the land for three days, and all the firstborn sons of Egypt are struck dead by the Lord himself. In each of the plagues, the Israelites themselves are unharmed. Following several of the plagues, Pharaoh temporarily agrees to release the Israelites, only to change his mind immediately after the plague is terminated; otherwise, he is simply unmoved. Pharaoh's stubborn refusal to set the Israelites free is God's own doing; he hardens Pharaoh's heart, making him incapable of giving in (*Ex*. 4.21, 9.12, 10.1, 20, 11.10). This is in order that God may exert and display his might, thus proclaiming his lordship and providing an object lesson for future generations (*Ex*. 9.15–16, 20.1–2). This is what is meant by the often repeated statement that God redeemed Israel from Egypt "with a strong hand and an outstretched arm" (*Dt.* 4.34 and elsewhere). Later commentators attenuated this by arguing that only after the sixth plague does God harden Pharaoh's heart; before this, his obstinacy is said to be his own doing (compare *Ex.* 8.11, 28 with *Ex.* 9.12, 10.20); Maimonides contended that God's preventing Pharaoh's repentance was the punishment for his initial stubbornness (*Hilkhot Teshuvah* 6.3). (But to inflict suffering on Pharaoh without enabling him to relent is only unfair at first glance; as far as the Bible is concerned, whatever calamities befall the Egyptians are richly deserved. Actually, the notion that the Egyptians might go unpunished for the brutality of the long enslavement would be a far greater injustice.) The Pesaḥ Seder includes the recital of the ten plagues, followed by several Midrashic arguments enlarging their number.

• Moshe Greenberg, *Understanding Exodus* (New York, 1969), vol. 1, pp. 151–192. Samuel E. Loewenstamm, *The Evolution of the Exodus Tradition*, translated by Baruch Schwartz (Jerusalem, 1992), pp. 69–188. Nahum M. Sarna, *Exploring Exodus: The Heritage of Biblical Israel* (New York, 1986), pp. 63–80.

—BARUCH J. SCHWARTZ

PLATONISM. See NEOPLATONISM.

PLEDGES (Heb. *mashkon*), personal property offered as security against the repayment of a debt that may be given when the debt originates or when repayment is due (as a security); it may also be given to the creditor for his use. The pledge may be any object belonging to the borrower. The creditor may not enter the home of the debtor to choose or to take the pledge but must accept whatever pledge the debtor chooses to give him. The debtor's tools of trade (*Dt.* 24.6) or necessary clothes or covering (*Ex.* 22.26) cannot be taken during the time of day or night when they are normally used, nor may the clothing of a widow or vessels required to prepare food be taken as a pledge (*Dt.* 24.10–17). If a debt is not repaid when it falls due, the pledge may be sold, and the proceeds accrue to the creditor. The indiscriminate taking of pledges was severely denounced by the prophets. See also LIEN.

• Yisroel Reisman, *The Laws of Ribbis: The Laws of Interest and Their Application to Everyday Life and Business* (Brooklyn, N.Y., 1995).

PLURALISM, RELIGIOUS, the view that different, or even contradictory, forms of religious belief and behavior could or even should coexist. The problem with religious pluralism arises, when one particular tradition (the mainstream) dominates society, denying the legitimacy of other streams and marginalizing them as sectarian phenomena.

In the latter part of the Second Temple period and in the absence of one dominant orthodoxy, *Sadducees, *Pharisees, and *Essenes existed side by side in Judea, while Hellenized Jews flourished in Alexandria and elsewhere in the Diaspora. When, after the destruction of the Temple, the Pharisaic-rabbinic tradition came to predominate, the internal rabbinic controversies became part of the corpus of rabbinic literature. The Mishnah (*San.* 10.1) presents a first attempt to define those who are excluded from the community: among those who "have no share in the world to come" are those who deny that the Torah enjoins belief in the resurrection of the dead, those who deny that the Torah was divinely revealed, and the "Epicurean" (who presumably denied that there was a divine judge). More important than these exclusions was the basic unity created by the possession and study of the same sacred and authoritative sources (especially the Talmud) and the use of a common prayer book.

Inevitably, considerable liturgical and other divergences developed in the Diaspora (see ASHKENAZIM; SEPHARDIM), but these were never felt to endanger the unity of the Jewish people as a community of faith, although attempts were made from time to time, especially in some of the codes of religious law, to impose more uniformity (see SHULḤAN ʿARUKH). The most disruptive schism was that of the *Karaites, who rejected the authority of the rabbinic tradition and disavowed the Talmud. But even in this case, the separation between Karaites and Rabbanites was not total, and intermarriages between the two groups were frequent. Attempts by some philosophers, such as Maimonides, to define principles of faith that would constitute minimum requirements for religious identity were opposed by other authorities. Kabbalists developed remarkably unorthodox concepts of divinity and ritual, but these in turn became the Orthodox standard. A similar conflict, which almost led to a schism, occurred toward the end of the eighteenth century in eastern Europe, with the spread of the Hasidic movement (see HASIDISM). Rabbinic attempts to excommunicate the new "sect" were of no avail, and in due course the two camps closed ranks against their common enemy: Enlightenment modernism and religious reform.

In nineteenth-century Germany and America, separate denominational tendencies crystallized around the modern view of Torah and tradition as products of historical development and the widely felt need for changes as a result of the political emancipation of Jews and the cultural challenges of modern civilization. The modern emphasis on personal freedom ran counter to a traditional system based on obedience to inherited patterns of thought and action. A main difference between *Reform Judaism on the one hand and *Conservative Judaism and *Orthodoxy on the other was the centrality of *halakhah* in defining correct Jewish practice. Although they consider rabbinic tradition an invaluable resource, Reform (and Reconstructionist) Judaism feels free to reject much of *halakhah* as not binding. Conservative Judaism acknowledges the need for greater flexibility and even innovation in *halakhah* to meet the conditions of modern life, which Orthodox authorities, especially the Ḥaredim, deny. The Orthodox consider the non-Orthodox as deviating from a divinely ordained system of belief and practice; proponents of adaptation and change argue that the very concept of Orthodoxy is a modern construction imposed on a heterogeneous Jewish past and that the Orthodox rejection of religious pluralism should be viewed as a modern rather than traditional position. Especially divisive are the halakhic rules defining who is a Jew, conversion to Judaism, and requirements for a Jewish marriage (see DIVORCE; JEW, WHO IS A?, CONTROVERSY; PATRILINEAL DESCENT; PROSELYTE).

A related set of issues affecting religious pluralism has arisen as a result of modern *Zionism and the establishment of the State of Israel (see SECULARISM). In America, where adherents to the non-Orthodox forms of Judaism are the majority, religious pluralism is a fact, and efforts have been made to define a "civil religion" of American Jews that embraces the wide range of behaviors and beliefs that are considered acceptable by most Jews. In Israel, Orthodox Judaism is politically powerful, although secular Jewish identity is prevalent. There the non-Orthodox religious movements are much smaller and have been denied recognition and support by the Orthodox religious establishments, although their rights (e.g., the validity of their conversions) have often been upheld by the civil courts.

• S. Zalman Abramov, *Perpetual Dilemma: Jewish Religion in the Jewish State* (Rutherford, N.J., 1976). Eugene B. Borowitz, *Renewing the Covenant: A Theology for the Postmodern Jew* (Philadelphia, 1991), pp. 235–253. Jonathan Sacks, *One People?: Tradition, Modernity, and Jewish Unity* (London, 1993). David Vital, *The Future of the Jews* (Cambridge, Mass., 1990). Jack Wertheimer, *A People Divided: Judaism in Contemporary America* (New York, 1993). Jonathan S. Woocher, *Sacred Survival: The Civil Religion of American Jews* (Bloomington, Ind., 1986).

—ROBERT M. SELTZER

POETRY. Biblical literature can be divided into two categories: poetry and prose. The Torah and the Former Prophets are prose except for certain poetic compositions (*Gn.* 49, the Testament of Jacob; *Ex.* 15, the Song of Moses; *Nm.* 23.7–10, 18–24, 24.3–9, 15–24, the Sayings of Balaam; *Dt.* 32, the Song of Moses; *Dt.* 33, the Testament of Moses; *Jgs.* 5, the Song of Deborah; *1 Sm.* 2, the Prayer of Hannah; *2 Sm.* 1, the Elegy of David; and *2 Sm.* 22/*Ps.* 18, the Royal Psalm of Thanksgiving) and smaller units that may be either partial quotations of unpreserved poetic works or *incipits* (e.g., *Gn.* 4.23–24; *Ex.* 15.21; *Nm.* 21.17–18, 27–30; *Jos.* 10.12–13; *1 Sm.* 18.7, 21.12, 29.5; and *1 Kgs.* 8.12–13). In the Latter Prophets most chapters are an admixture of poetry and prose (although some chapters may be purely prose, such as *Jonah* 1, 3, 4, while others may be purely poetic, such as *Jonah* 2.3–10 and *Hb.* 3). In the Hagiographa, the books of *Psalms, Proverbs*, and *Job*, and part of the *Ḥamesh Megillot, are poetry, while the rest are mostly prose. Scholars such as David Noel Freedman have used statistical analysis to distinguish definitively between prose and poetry, but it is clear that poetic units in the Bible are characterized by two main poetic features: some sort of poetic meter or rhythm involving the basic division between two or more stichs; and poetic parallelism between two or more stichs. Both Ugaritic and Biblical Hebrew poetic parallelism can best be defined as the relationship between two or more stichs, whereby the second stich expresses more or less the same concept as the first, usually in different words.

Alphabetical and nominal acrostics were favorite devices in post-biblical poetry and served mnemonic purposes as well, since books were not generally available and the congregation had to pray by heart. During the geonic period, largely under Arabic influence, rhyme became a prominent feature of Hebrew poetry. Dunash ben Labrat (10th cent.) applied Arabic poetic forms to Hebrew poetry, which led to the development of meter. Hebrew sacred poetry flourished from the fifth through the fourteenth century, starting with the period of *payyetanim* (see PAYYETAN), when many of the best known *piyyutim, seliḥot*, and *qinot* were composed. Outstanding poets in medieval Spain included Shelomoh ibn Gabirol (whose Keter Malkhut is a classic of religious poetry); Mosheh ibn Ezra (whose *seliḥot* received wide currency); Yehudah ha-Levi (whose sacred poems were imbued with national sentiments and the love of Zion); and Avraham ibn Ezra. Distinguished religious poets in Italy, France, and Germany carried on the ancient Palestinian tradition. The Crusader massacres inspired many moving dirges, some of which found permanent places in the prayer service. From the thirteenth century, sacred poetry was marked by quantity rather than originality. Among the exceptions were the kabbalist poets of Safed (Yisra'el ben Mosheh Najara, Shelomoh Alkabez) and the Yemenite poet Shalem ben Yosef Shabbazi. Few poetic additions to the liturgy have won a permanent place in recent centuries, although the Reconstructionist prayer book includes poems by modern Hebrew poets.

• William F. Albright, *Yahweh and the Gods of Canaan* (Garden City, N.Y., 1968), pp. 1–52, 265–267. Adele Berlin, *The Dynamics of Biblical Parallelism* (Bloomington, Ind. 1985). Chaim Cohen in *Beer-Sheva* 3 (1988): 91, 106–107, nn. 151–153, in Hebrew. Frank Moore Cross and David N. Freedman, *Studies in Ancient Yahwistic Poetry*, 2d ed. (Missoula, Mont., 1975). Frank Moore Cross, *Canaanite Myth and Hebrew Epic* (Cambridge, Mass., 1973). David N. Freedman in *Directions in Biblical Hebrew Poetry* (Sheffield, Eng., 1987), pp. 11–28. Stephen A. Geller, *Parallelism in Early Biblical Poetry* (Missoula, Mont., 1979), pp. 375–385. Stanley Gevirtz, *Patterns in the Early Poetry of Israel*, 2d ed. (Chicago, 1973). Edward Greenstein, "How Does Parallelism Mean?," in *A Sense of Text*, edited by Stephen Geller et al. (Philadelphia, 1983), pp. 41–70. Jose Krasovec, *Antithetic Structure in Biblical Hebrew Poetry* (Leiden, 1984). James L. Kugel, *The Idea of Biblical Poetry: Parallelism and Its History* (New Haven, 1981). Articles by Landy, Watson, Miller, and Kugel in *Journal for the Study of the Old Testament* 28 (1984): 61–117. Dennis Pardee, *Ugaritic and Hebrew Poetic Parallelism* (Leiden, 1988). David L. Peterson and K. H. Richards, *Interpreting Hebrew Poetry* (Minneapolis, 1992). Meyer Waxman, *A History of Jewish Literature*, 5 vols. (New York, 1960). Wilfred G. E. Watson, *Classical Hebrew Poetry: A Guide to Its Techniques* (Sheffield, Eng., 1984).

—CHAIM COHEN

POLEMICS (from Gr. *polemos* [war]), controversies conducted either verbally or in writing.

Jewish–Christian Polemics. The Jewish–Christian debate can be said to be as old as Christianity; that is, when the first Christians, who were Jews, tried to convince other Jews that Jesus was the Messiah. Most Jews rejected this claim, maintaining that messianic promises continued to be unfulfilled. Christian treatises polemicizing specifically against Judaism go back at least to the second century (most notably Justin Martyr's *Dialogue with Trypho*). Many church fathers, including Tertullian, Origen, and Augustine, wrote anti-Jewish polemical works. Polemics could be conducted on the purely literary level or in personal encounters. In the later Middle Ages, the latter were occasionally staged with pomp and circumstance at the initiative of the aggressively dominant (i.e., Christian) side, held in the presence of the king or other ruling authorities, and imposed on the Jews who were limited in their freedom to respond (see DISPUTATIONS).

The first Jewish compositions aimed at refuting Christianity date only from the ninth century and were written in Muslim countries in Arabic. One of those works was translated into Hebrew as *The Book of Nestor the Priest* and greatly influenced medieval Jewish polemical writings in Christian Europe, including the first such treatises; namely Ya'aqov ben Re'uven's *Milḥamot Adonai* and Yosef Kimḥi's *Sefer ha-Berit* (both 1170).

The Jewish–Christian debate took a decisive turn in the thirteenth century when Christians began using rabbinic literature for polemical purposes. This use was expressed in two ways, either as an attack on the Talmud as nonsensical and blasphemous (as in the Disputation of *Paris of 1240, after which the Talmud was burned), or as part of the claim that rabbinic literature supports the truth of Christianity (as in the Disputation of *Barcelona of 1263 between Nahmanides and the former Jew Pablo Christiani, and in Raymund Martini's *Pugio fidei* [1278]). The employment of the Talmud for polemical purposes was not merely an academic exercise, but part of a larger, intensified anti-Jewish missionary campaign.

The deterioration in Jewish status in late fourteenth- and fifteenth-century Spain saw a flourishing of Jewish polemical works, most notably Profiat Duran's *Al Tehi ka-'Avotekha* (c.1393) and *Kelimat ha-Goyyim* (c.1397), and Ḥasda'i Crescas's *Refutation of the Christian Principles*. These works were marked by both a close knowledge of Christian theology and the use of philosophy to refute it. The last great public disputation was held in *Tortosa, Spain, in 1413 and 1414.

Jewish–Christian polemics continued also after the Protestant Reformation, with Martin *Luther setting the tone. Johann Christoph Wagenseil and Johann Andreas Eisenmenger (*Judaism Revealed* [1700]) wrote notorious examples. Anti-Jewish polemics became "academic" in the nineteenth century; in the latter part of the century, they were joined with modern non-theological *antisemitism. The Jewish response, in the form of theological and philosophical writings, was usually apologetic (see APOLOGETICS) in intent and only rarely aggressive, depending on the readership intended; compare **Toledot Yeshu*, and the *Sefer Nitsaḥon* of Yom Tov Lipmann *Muelhausen, with the first edition of Leo *Baeck's *The Essence of Judaism* (1905), in response to the German theologian A. Harnack. More recently, and especially after the Holocaust, attempts are being made on both sides to substitute dialogue in place of polemics.

Jewish–Muslim Polemics. Muslim polemics against Judaism has its beginnings in the Qur'an and certain Ḥadith traditions. In the eleventh and fourteenth centuries it produced a few major and systematic compositions (Ibn Ḥazm, al-Maghribi), but never became a major preoccupation. Jewish response kept a low profile, and the more important polemical reactions (e.g., *Maimonides' *Epistle to Yemen*) were written for internal consumption. A somewhat special feature was Islam's dogmatic affirmation of earlier prophecy (Moses, Jesus) and revealed scriptures, and hence the special status accorded to the "peoples of the book" (see DHIMMI). Religious polemics have therefore frequently been tripartite (e.g., al-Raqili, but especially Ibn Kammunah's *Critical Enquiry into the Three Faiths* [1280]). This tradition gave birth to the well-known parable of the Three Rings which passed via Boccacio's *Decameron* to G. E. Lessing's *Nathan the Wise*. In the nineteenth century, European antisemitism began to infiltrate Muslim writings and attitudes, mainly from French sources, and in the twentieth century became joined to anti-Zionist and anti-Israeli polemics.

The most frequent and interesting type of religious polemics expresses conflicts, tensions and developments within religious traditions. These can be innovative or "reforming" attacks on established orthodoxies or, conversely, attacks by traditionalists on what they consider as heretical deviations. Intersectarian disputes are often expressed in this idiom (See CONTROVERSIES; KARAITES, MITNAGGEDIM).

• Samau'al al-Maghribi, *Ifḥam al-Yahud: Silencing the Jews*, edited and translated by Moshe Perlmann (New York, 1964). Salo W. Baron, *A Social and Religious History of the Jews*, 2d ed., vol. 5 (New York, 1957), pp. 82–108, with extensive bibliography. David Berger, *The Jewish–Christian Debate in the High Middle Ages: A Critical Edition of the Nizzahon Vetus* (Philadelphia, 1979). Robert Chazan, *Daggers of Faith: Thirteenth-Century Christian Missionizing and Jewish Response* (Berkeley, 1989). Jeremy Cohen, *The Friars and the Jews: The Evolution of Medieval Anti-Judaism* (Ithaca, N.Y., 1982). Ignac Goldziher, in *Gesammelte Schriften*, 3 vols. (Hildesheim, 1967–1970). Yehoshafat Harkabi, *Arab Attitudes to Israel*, translated by Misha Louvish (Jerusalem, 1972). Ali ibn Ḥazm, *Kitab al-fiṣal fi al-milal wa-al-niḥal*, 5 vols. in 2 (Cairo, 1899–1903). Daniel J. Lasker, *Jewish Philosophical Polemics Against Christianity in the Middle Ages* (New York, 1977). Hava Lazarus-Yafeh, *Intertwined Worlds: Medieval Islam and Bible Criticism* (Princeton, 1992). Hyam Maccoby, *Judaism on Trial: Jewish–Christian Disputations in the Middle Ages* (Rutherford, N.J., and London, 1982). Moses Maimonides, *Epistle to Yemen*, edited by Abraham S. Halkin and translated by Boaz Cohen (New York, 1952). Miguel Asín Palacio, "Un Tratado morisco de polémica contra los judios," in *Mélanges Hartwig Derenbourg*, edited by G. Maspero (Paris, 1909), pp. 343–366. Joseph Perles, *R. Salomo ben Abraham ben Adereth: Sein Leben und seine Schriften* (Breslau, 1863). Moshe Perlmann, ed. and trans., *Ibn Kammuna's Examination of the Three Faiths: A Thirteenth-Century Essay in the Comparative Study of Religion* (Berkeley, 1971). Moshe Perlmann, "The Medieval Polemics between Islam and Judaism," in *Religion in a Religious Age*, edited by S. D. Goitein (Cambridge, Mass., 1974). Sa'adyah Ga'on, *The Book of Beliefs and Opinions*, translated by Samuel Rosenblatt (New Haven, 1948). Moritz Steinschneider, *Polemische und apologetische Literatur in arabischer Sprache, zwischen Muslimen, Christen und Juden* (Leipzig, 1877; repr. Hildesheim, 1966). 'Afif 'Abd al-Fattaḥ Tabbarah, *Al-Yahud fi al-Qur'an* (Beirut, 1966). Frank Talmage, *Disputation and Dialogue: Readings in the Jewish–Christian Encounter* (New York, 1975). A. Lukyn Williams, *Adversus Judaeos* (Cambridge, 1935).

—DANIEL J. LASKER

POLGAR, YITSḤAQ (13th–14th cent.), philosopher and polemicist. He is best known as the principal opponent of Abner of Burgos, a Spanish–Jewish philosopher who converted to Christianity and adopted the name Alfonso de Valladolid. Soon after Abner's conversion, Polgar wrote *Iggeret ha-Ḥarifot*, a pamphlet of personal attacks against the apostate. In *'Ezer ha-Dat*, Polgar defended Judaism along Aristotelian–Averroistic lines, emphasized free will, and opposed astrological beliefs. The book was published with an English summary by Gershon Belasco (London, 1906) and in an annotated edition by Ya'aqov Levinger (Tel Aviv, 1984). Polgar also wrote commentaries on *Genesis*, *Ecclesiastes*, and

Psalms, and a book on ethics, none of which has been preserved.

• Jonathan L. Hecht, "The Polemical Exchange between Isaac Pollegar and Abner of Burgos/Alfonso of Valladolid according to Parma MS 2440," Ph.D. dissertation, New York University, 1993.

–FRANCISCO MORENO CARVALHO

POLLAK, YAʿAQOV (died c.1530), Polish rabbi. He completed his studies at the Nuremberg Yeshivah and was then appointed rabbi of Prague and, in the 1490s, rabbi of Kraków. In 1503 he was recognized as chief rabbi by the king of Poland and granted extensive judicial authority. According to Polish-Jewish tradition, he was responsible for the transfer of the traditions of Jewish learning from Ashkenaz to eastern Europe and for establishing Poland as a center of the Jewish religious world. One of the leading rabbinical authorities of his day, he is supposed to have invented the method of *pilpul-ḥilluqim* (precise distinctions), which transformed **pilpul* from a pedagogical tool to a hermeneutic system (for which he was known as *baʿal* [or *avi*, i.e., father of] *ha-ḥilluqim*). He was a controversial figure, and his decision allowing his sister-in-law to divorce at the age of twelve led to a *ḥerem* (ban) being placed on him by a number of prominent rabbis. A dispute within the Kraków community in 1522 seems to have been the cause of his leaving Poland and settling in Jerusalem, apparently the place of his death. None of his writings was published, and only a few of his teachings survive in the works of later rabbis. Among his many students was Shalom ben Yosef *Shakna, one of the leading rabbinic authorities of the mid-sixteenth century.

• Elchanan Reiner, "Temurot bi-Yeshivot Polin ve-Ashkenaz ba-Me'ot ha-16-ha-17 ve-ha-Vikkuaḥ ʿal ha-Pilpul," in *Ke-Minhag Ashkenaz u-Polin: Sefer Yovel le-Ḥonah Shmeruk; Kovets Maʿamarim be-Tarbut Yehudit*, edited by Yisrael Bartal et al. (Jerusalem, 1993), pp. 9–80.

–ADAM TELLER

POLYGAMY. Although the Creation account suggests that monogamy was a biblical ideal (*Gn.* 1.27; 2.18–24), the Bible contains numerous cases of polygamy, including Lamech in *Genesis*, 4.19, and, most notably, Solomon, in *1 Kings* 11.3, and the practice is permitted under biblical law. Polygamy was also recognized by the rabbis as legally valid, though Talmudic society was predominantly monogamous and very few rabbis had more than one wife. The Talmud stipulates that the husband must be capable of fulfilling his marital obligations toward additional wives before he will be permitted to enter into additional marriages. If the first wife's *ketubbah* contains a stipulation against additional wives, then her husband may not ignore it. Moreover, if the local custom is to practice monogamy then all local *ketubbot* will be read as if they contained such a stipulation (*Shulḥan ʿArukh, Even ha-ʿEzer* 76.8; Ḥelqat Meḥoqqeq, *Even ha-ʿEzer* 76.15). A *taqqanah* attributed to R. Gershom in the tenth century officially banned polygamy among Ashkenazi Jews, unless permission to take an additional wife is granted by one hundred rabbis from three different countries or districts (*Shulḥan ʿArukh, Even ha-ʿEzer* 1.10). A breach of this *taqqanah* constitutes grounds for the first wife to request the *beit din* to force her husband to divorce the second wife or, alternatively, to give her a *get* and return her *ketubbah* (*Shulḥan ʿArukh, Even ha-ʿEzer* 154). There was no such *taqqanah* among Sephardi Jews, although the use of a *ketubbah* stipulation banning polygamy became widespread, and the consequences of its breach were similar to those incurred by disregarding R. Gershom's *taqqanah*. The difference between the Ashkenazi and the Sephardi responses to polygamy is clearly a result of the influence of the general cultures in which the two Jewries flourished. The *ḥerem* of Rabbenu Gershom, as the above-mentioned *taqqanah* is known, also banned divorce of a wife against her will, and in order to deal with a situation involving an insane or recalcitrant wife, the release by one hundred rabbis was introduced at the same time. Such a step will, however, only be taken if a full investigation of the facts reveals that the release is fully justified. In 1950 the chief rabbis of Israel enacted that monogamy was binding upon all Jews irrespective of their communal affiliations, and polygamy is an offense under Israeli criminal law. The release of the hundred rabbis is, however, still valid if approved by the two chief rabbis of the state.

• Louis Epstein *The Jewish Marriage Contract: A Study of the Status of the Woman in Jewish Law* (New York, 1927), p. 272. Zeev Falk, *Jewish Matrimonial Law in the Middle Ages* (London, 1966), pp. 1–34. Louis Finkelstein, *Jewish Self-Government in the Middle Ages* (New York, 1924), pp. 20–33, 139–148.

–DANIEL SINCLAIR

POLYTHEISM. See MONOTHEISM.

POOL, DAVID DE SOLA (1885–1970), rabbi, communal leader, and author. Born in London, Pool served as rabbi of Congregation Shearith Israel, known as the Spanish and Portuguese Synagogue of New York City, from 1907 to 1956, and then as rabbi emeritus.

Pool was the foremost spokesman of Sephardi Jewry in North America. He founded the Union of Sephardic Congregations (1928), which later published the prayer book he compiled.

From 1920 through 1921, he served in Palestine as regional director for the American Joint Distribution Committee. He was president of the New York Board of Rabbis (1916–1917), the Synagogue Council of America (1938–1940), and the American Jewish Historical Society (1955–1956). Pool was a prolific author, especially on the subject of American Jewish history. His works include *Portraits Etched in Stone: Early Jewish Settlers, 1682–1831* (New York, 1952) and *An Old Faith in the New World: Portrait of Shearith Israel, 1654–1954* (with Tamar de Sola Pool, New York, 1955).

• Jewish Theological Seminary of America, *Thirteen Americans: Their Spiritual Autobiographies*, edited by Louis Finkelstein (New York, 1953), pp. 201–217.

–MARC D. ANGEL

POOR. See POVERTY.

PORGING. See NIQQUR.

POSEQIM (פּוֹסְקִים; deciders), scholars who rule on questions of Jewish law, in particular when there is no explicit answer in the sources and the scholar is forced to arrive at the law through his own reasoning. Implicit in the term is that these scholars are recognized as authorities by communities or groups of Jews. An individual rabbi who publishes a book on Jewish law, without such acknowledgment, is not regarded as a *poseq*. Although many *poseqim* have written works on Jewish law, this is not essential to the role. Indeed, every Jewish town in premodern times had a *poseq*, usually the town rabbi. He was required to issue rulings on a wide range of questions of Jewish law, in particular concerning the slaughter of meat and fowl. Many generations have a *poseq* who stands above all others, and the most difficult questions are submitted to him.

In order to function as a *poseq*, one must be trained in the classic works of Jewish law, of which Yosef Karo's **Shulḥan ʿArukh* is the most important. Although all acknowledge the need for a *poseq*, some capable scholars throughout history refused to assume this role. This was either because they did not want to shoulder the great responsibility or because they frowned upon practical halakhic decision making as the central focus of study, preferring instead the theoretical elements of Talmudic learning.

• Menachem Elon, *Jewish Law: History, Sources, Principles*, translated by Bernard Auerbach and Melvin J. Sykes (Philadelphia, 1994). David M. Feldman, *Marital Relations, Birth Control, and Abortion and Jewish Law* (New York, 1968), chap. 1. Joel Roth, *The Halakhic Process: A Systemic Analysis* (New York, 1986). —MARC SHAPIRO

POST-MORTEM. See AUTOPSIES.

POVERTY. Biblical and rabbinic writers generally regarded poverty as an unmitigated misfortune. God's blessing upon his people is meant to include material prosperity along with the other felicities of life, but because the Bible recognizes that "the poor shall not cease out of the land," it commands those more fortunate to "open your hand wide unto your brother, to the poor, and to the needy in your land" (*Dt*. 15.11). The prophets repeatedly stress the obligation to succor the poor; failure to do so brings collective punishment. Care and consideration for the poor were not only moral virtues but legal requirements. Although poverty was considered one of the worst afflictions, too much wealth was also regarded as a danger and temptation (cf. *Dt*. 8.11–18, 32.15), and it was thought most desirable to achieve a mean between poverty and wealth. Nevertheless, other views of poverty are in evidence, too; occasionally the rabbis even praise poverty as a positive virtue. On the verse "I test you in the furnace of affliction" (*Is*. 48.10), the Talmud comments, "This teaches that the Holy One, blessed be he, went through all the virtues in order to bestow them upon Israel and found none more becoming than poverty" (*Ḥag*. 9b). This view of poverty as a positive religious value was expressed by ascetic moralists (e.g., *Baḥya ben Yosef ibn Paquda') and mystics (cf. the *Sefer Ḥasidim* and the Zohar) but never became dominant. Throughout Jewish history both the *community and the individual have been obligated to help the poor. See also CHARITY; WEALTH.

• Jonathan Sacks, *Wealth and Poverty: A Jewish Analysis* (London, 1985). —SHMUEL HIMELSTEIN

PRAYER. The Bible contains many individual prayers (e.g., of Moses, *Nm*. 12.13; Hannah, *1 Sm*. 2.1–10; Solomon, *1 Kgs*. 8.15–23; Hezekiah, *2 Kgs*. 19.15–19); in addition, many biblical psalms (see PSALMS, BOOK OF) are, in fact, prayers. The institution of three daily prayer services was legendarily ascribed by the sages to the three *patriarchs, and they attributed the introduction of set formulas for prayer to the Men of the *Keneset ha-Gedolah, although modern scholars question this attribution. Though the Bible makes no statements about the actual nature of prayer, the rabbis found its theological essence expressed in the biblical phrase "serving God with the heart." Whereas **ʿavodah* (divine service) had originally signified sacrificial worship in the Temple, corporate prayer as the principal form of worship developed in the Second Temple period when the *synagogue emerged. After the destruction of Jerusalem by the Romans in 70 CE, the synagogue—whose functions were often merged with that of the house of study (**beit midrash*)—became the center of communal and religious life.

Although occasionally referred to as merely a substitute for the sacrifices of the Temple, prayer has always been considered an essential and major expression of religion. Traditionally prayer has consisted of two essential elements: supplication and petition on the one hand, and praise and thanksgiving on the other. In due course, a fixed pattern emerged, particularly for the preeminent prayer, the *ʿAmidah. The full prayer service included opening *benedictions, the recitation of the *Shemaʿ with its benedictions, the ʿAmidah, and the reading of the Torah. (See also FESTIVAL PRAYERS; MAʿARIV; MINḤAH; MUSAF; NEʿILAH; SABBATH PRAYERS; SHAḤARIT). Prayers of various kinds (see PIYYUT; QINAH; SELIḤOT) continued to be composed throughout the ages and were added to the prayer book (*siddur*). Prayers were regarded as a genuine outpouring of the heart, and even after the introduction of fixed prayers, the rabbis emphasized the need to retain an element of spontaneity. One should pray only in a devout and reverential frame of mind (*Ber*. 5.1), and "he who makes his prayer a fixed, routine exercise, does not make his prayer a supplication" (*Ber*. 4.4). The early pietists spent an hour of devotion in preparation for prayer (*Ber*. 5.1). The Mishnah condemns prayer undertaken as a burden to be discharged or prayer that contains no original thought (*Ber*. 29b). Prayers should be recited "not in a spirit of sorrow, or of idleness, or of laughter or chatter or frivolity or idle talk, but with the joyousness of the performance of a religious act" (*Ber*. 31a). The manner of prayer is equally important: "He who raises his voice in prayer is of little faith" (*Ber*. 24a); rather, one should form the words of the prayer with the lips (*Ber*. 31a). At the same time, however, prayer obligations can be discharged by listening with devotion to the person conducting the prayer service and answering **amen* to his blessings (cf. *Ber*. 52b. and *Shev*. 29a). Although, as a general rule, the person who leads the congregation in prayer (**sheliaḥ tsibbur*) should be of irreproachable moral character and the prayer of the righteous son of a righteous father is more acceptable than that of the righteous son of a sinner (*Yev.* 64a), the rabbis loved to expatiate on incidents illustrating that the prayer of a reprobate who has a single redeeming feature can be more efficacious than that of the most blameless person (cf. Y., *Taʿan.* 1.64). God is said to "listen to prayer," and the rabbis had no doubts as to its efficacy. Rabbi *Ḥanina' ben Dosa', after praying for the sick, could tell whether or not his prayer would be answered (*Ber.* 5.5). Prayer has the effect of averting the evil fate decreed for an individual in the new year (*R. ha-Sh.* 18a), but prayers about past events are considered vain and useless (*Ber.* 9.3).

The rabbis never systematically discussed the theological and philosophical problems inherent in prayer, and in petitionary prayer in particular (e.g., will an all-knowing and all-good God change his designs—which are, by definition, for the good of his creatures—because the persons praying express their own desires? Should prayer consist only of praise and expressions of thanksgiving to the divine will?). For the medieval mystics prayer was an occasion for specific devotions (*kavvanot*); for others it was a spiritual exercise to increase communion with God. In rabbinic tradition, prayer was primarily the fulfillment of a commandment, that is, part of the wider discipline of serving God: God wants the person praying to bring personal fears and wishes to him, as a child would to his or her father. In this view the philosophical objections are not so much answered as irrelevant. In Hasidism, all of life is to be centered around the daily hours of prayer. The Ḥasid strives to "become nothing" in the act of prayer, to empty his mind of all content so that he may be an empty vessel to be filled by the divine presence. This sort of contemplative passivity was taught by R. *Dov Ber of Mezhirech and remained, with some further development, a key part of *Ḥabad experience. Particular forms of prayer, beyond the universally prescribed liturgy, also exist within Hasidism. These include the abstract *hitbonenut* (meditation) of Ḥabad worship, the daily *hitbodedut* (spontaneous verbal outcry) of the Bratslav Ḥasidim, and various original prayer compositions, often in Yiddish, attributed to Hasidic figures ranging from R. *Levi Yitsḥaq of Berdichev to the twentieth-century R. Arele Roth.

Prayer can be private or corporate, statutory or nonstatutory. The most common of the nonstatutory prayers are those for rain in time of drought. Many of the prayers included in the *liturgy for public and statutory worship were originally composed as private prayers. The statutory liturgy should be recited in community (see MINYAN); in private, certain prayers are omitted. When praying, and especially when reciting the ʿAmidah, one turns in the direction of Jerusalem and the Temple mount.

• Ismar Elbogen, *Jewish Liturgy: A Comprehensive History*, translated by Raymond P. Scheindlin (Philadelphia, New York, and Jerusalem, 1993). Arthur Green and Barry W. Holtz, eds., *Your Word Is Fire: The Hasidic Masters on Contemplative Prayer* (Woodstock, Vt., 1993). Moshe Greenberg, *Biblical Prose Prayer as a Window to the Popular Religion of Israel* (Berkeley, 1983). Reuven Hammer, *Entering Jewish Prayer: A Guide to Personal Devotion and the Worship Service* (New York, 1994). Lawrence A. Hoffman, *Beyond the Text: A Holistic Approach to Liturgy* (Bloomington, Ind., 1987). Louis Jacobs, *Hasidic Prayer* (London, 1972). Abraham Millgram, *Jewish Worship* (Philadelphia, 1971). Meyer J. Perath, *Rabbinical Devotion: Prayers of the Jewish Sages* (Assen, 1964). Jakob Josef Petuchowski, ed., *Understanding Jewish Prayer* (New York, 1972). Stefan C. Reif, *Judaism and Hebrew Prayer: New Perspectives on Jewish Liturgical History* (Cambridge, 1993). Raphael Posner et. al, *Jewish Liturgy* (Jerusalem, 1975). Joseph Tabory, *Reshimat Maʿamarim be-ʿInyenei Tefillah u-Moʿadim* (Jerusalem, 1992–1993). Eric Werner, *The Sacred Bridge: Liturgical Parallels in Synagogue and Early Church*, pt. 1 (New York, 1959; 1970 ed.). Tzvee Zahavy, *Studies in Jewish Prayer* (Lanham, Md., 1990).

PRAYER BOOK (Heb. *siddur* [order (of prayer)]). The Hebrew prayer book contains the statutory synagogue and home *liturgy, along with optional devotional material like **zemirot*, and even study material such as *Pirqei *Avot*. Some contain detailed rules (the *halakhot*) of prayer and historical or homiletical commentary for edification. Nowadays, a separate prayer book, normally called a **maḥazor* (Heb. cycle), exists for each festival.

The first known comprehensive prayer book, a combination *siddur* and *maḥazor*, is *Seder Rav Amram*, by Amram Ga'on of Babylonia (c.860). Its appearance reflects the trend toward centralization typical of the surrounding Islamic caliphate. Directed largely against Palestinian liturgical alternatives, it successfully championed Babylonian custom, which was subsequently adopted worldwide as normative Jewish practice. A second *siddur*, by Saʿadyah ben Yosef Ga'on (c.920), exercised secondary influence in certain regions. At first, only the prayer leader used a prayer book, but the invention of printing made prayer books widespread, and altered the very nature of worship by changing what had been an oral exercise into one that was dominated by dependence on a given text.

All prayer books contain the same basic liturgical material, but they differ somewhat according to the rite. After the geonic prototypes, the earliest complete texts (still combined as *siddur* and *maḥazor*) are *Maḥazor Vitry* (11th-cent. France), *Seder Ḥibbur Berakhot* (12th-cent. Italy), and *Sefer Abudarham* (14th-cent. Spain). Also preserved are fragments of the English order of service prior to the expulsion of 1290, as well as early partial prayer manuscripts from Erets Yisra'el and Egypt and vicinity, going back to geonic times. Kabbalistic tradition adopted its own rite, *Minhag Ari*, named for the ideological leader of the kabbalistic tradition in Erets Yisra'el, Yitsḥaq Luria, known also as the Ari. Individual Hasidic communities developed their own variants on that version.

An early attempt to standardize the prayer book emerged in seventeenth-century Poland but failed. To this day, there is no single standardized version that all Jews accept. Instead, movements develop their own books, which reflect ideological and geographical idiosyncrasies and which member congregations may be asked (with greater or lesser success) to use. Privately published versions abound as well, and congregations are free to adopt whatever book they want. The movement approach is rooted in nineteenth-century European and American thought. In Europe, liturgical reform from 1816 onward led to over a hundred fifty new books being published in as many years, each book by a given rabbi who tried to wed tradition and modernity. The earliest and most influential such volume is the 1819 *Hamburg Prayer Book*, which occasioned charges and countercharges, dividing central European Jewry between reformers and traditionalists. Only in 1929 was an attempt made to unify at least the liberal congregations by means of an *Einheitsgebetbuch*, but with limited success.

German immigrants to North America soon demanded new books expressive of their new American identity. By the 1860s, Isaac Mayer *Wise and David *Einhorn, rival liberal rabbis in Cincinnati and Baltimore, respectively, published especially influential volumes. By 1895 the Reform movement had settled on a *Union Prayer Book*, hoping to differentiate its modern style of worship from that of the eastern European immigrants who were importing customs of which the Germans disapproved. These eastern customs were codified as American Conservative Judaism, which adopted its own official prayer book in 1946. American Orthodox congregations have tended to use privately published volumes, especially one by Philip Birnbaum, which appeared only in 1949.

Similar developments occurred in other countries as part of the modernistic trend toward movement identities. England, for instance, produced the *Singer Prayer Book*, an authorized *siddur* for Orthodox Jews, in 1890, while Britain's Reform movement had already adopted the West London Synagogue's *Forms of Prayer* in 1841. Between 1902 and 1912, an alternative Liberal movement emerged with its own set of worship volumes. As Israeli Jewry has developed alternative movements in the 1960s and beyond, it too has begun to experiment with new prayer books.

Western religion has undergone a virtual liturgical renewal since the 1960s, beginning, perhaps, with Vatican II in 1962. Protestants, Catholics, and Jews have revised their liturgies repeatedly since then, with a resulting plethora of new prayer books. An outstanding example is the *Artscroll* series, an Orthodox set of volumes that has largely replaced the Birnbaum prayer book and may supersede the venerable *Singer Prayer Book* in Great Britain. It combines theological ultraconservatism with traditional scholarship, and even restores old liturgical lines once removed by Jewish printers who had either frowned upon certain statements of Jewish faith or feared hostile gentile reaction to them.

Progressive congregations worldwide are in the midst of their own prayer-book revolution, influenced most by the three North American liberal movements, whose recent prayer books feature modern English translations or altogether new creations alongside Hebrew originals; the recapturing of poetry from the gamut of Jewish tradition, especially by Hebrew poets who exemplify a new Jewish cultural consciousness occasioned by Israel's rebirth; creative ritual for the new Jewish holy days of Yom ha-Sho'ah (Holocaust Day) and Yom ha-'Atsma'ut (Israel Independence Day); and an affirmation of gender egalitarianism through gender-inclusive language.

Prayer books have always functioned to express the identity of the worshipers who use them, but their appearance has been dependent on available technology. The original Babylonian book was possible, in part, because of the availability of the codex, rather than scrolls. The printing press served to make volumes available to a mass audience. Inexpensive printing has increasingly multiplied volumes over the last two centuries. The latest development is desk-top publishing, which permits individual congregations to tailor-make a prayer book to their own needs, and then to alter it inexpensively if need be. If the most significant development of the last two hundred years has been movement prayer books, the next development may be their demise, in favor of local and individualized books, reflective of local Jewish identity and custom, a situation perhaps reminiscent of what existed before printing began the long process of standardization.

• Paul F. Bradshaw and Lawrence A. Hoffman, eds., *The Changing Face of Jewish and Christian Worship in North America* (Notre Dame, 1991). Ismar Elbogen, *Jewish Liturgy: A Comprehensive History*, translated by Raymond P. Scheindlin (Philadelphia, 1993). Joseph Heinemann, *Prayer in the Talmud: Forms and Patterns*, translated by Richard Sarason (Berlin, 1977). Lawrence A. Hoffman, *Beyond the Text: A Holistic Approach to Liturgy* (Bloomington, Ind., 1987). Lawrence A. Hoffman, *Canonization of the Synagogue Service* (Notre Dame, Ind., 1979). Lawrence A. Hoffman with Nancy Wiener, "The Liturgical State of the World Union for Progressive Judaism," *European Judaism* 24.1 (1991): 10–22. Jakob J. Petuchowski, *Contributions to the Scientific Study of Jewish Liturgy* (New York, 1970). Jakob J. Petuchowski, *Prayerbook Reform in Europe* (New York, 1969). Stefan C. Reif, *Judaism and Hebrew Prayer: New Perspectives on Jewish Liturgical History* (Cambridge, 1993). Stefan C. Reif, *Shabbetai Sofer and his Prayer-book* (Cambridge, 1979). Lou H. Silberman, "The *Union Prayer Book*: a Study in Liturgical Development," in *Retrospect and Prospect*, edited by Bertram Wallace Korn (New York, 1965). Joseph Tabory, *Reshimat Ma'amarim be-'Inyenei Tefillah u-Mo'adim* (1992–1993).

—LAWRENCE A. HOFFMAN

PRAYER OF MANASSEH, a short, poetic work in Greek, purporting to be the confession of sin and prayer of repentance uttered by Manasseh, king of Judah, during his captivity in Babylon (cf. *2 Chr.* 33.12). Though the composition is undoubtedly of Jewish origin, it has been preserved only in Christian sources. The date of its authorship is uncertain, as is its original language (Hebrew, Aramaic, Syriac, or Greek).

• Bruce M. Metzger, *An Introduction to the Apocrypha* (New York, 1957), pp. 123–128.

PRAYER SHAWL. See TALLIT.

PREACHING. See HOMILETICS.

PRECEDENT. See MA'ASEH.

PRECEPT. See MITSVAH.

PRECEPTS, 613. See COMMANDMENTS, 613.

PREDESTINATION, the doctrine that one's life, and its ultimate destiny (salvation or damnation) in particular, are determined solely by the inscrutable will of God and not by anything that the individual can do. The doctrine is well known from Islam and Christianity (in the latter religion it is associated more particularly with Paul, Augustine, and Calvin) but has generally been held to be alien to the Jewish tradition. The *Dead Sea Scrolls have shown, however, that predestinarian views were held by Jewish sectarians, and it might be from them that Paul inherited his doctrine. See also ASTROLOGY; DETERMINISM; FREE WILL.

• Seymour W. Feldman, "A Debate Concerning Determinism in Late Medieval Jewish Philosophy," *Proceedings of the American Academy for Jewish Research* 51 (1984): 15–54.

PREEXISTENCE, the presence in time of something before the creation of this universe. The notion of preexistence presupposes belief in a higher, spiritual, and possibly, though not necessarily, eternal sphere in which things can preexist. Thus, according to Platonic and Neoplatonic doctrine, individual souls are not created together with the physical body but are preexistent and merely enter the physical body destined for them. This belief was adopted by the ancient rabbis and underlies the doctrine of *transmigration of souls (*gilgul*) adopted later by the kabbalists. According to one rabbinic statement (*Pes*. 54a), seven things were created before the creation of the world: the Torah, repentance, the garden of Eden, Geihinnom, the throne of God's glory, the heavenly temple (of which the Temple in Jerusalem was regarded as an earthly reproduction), and the names of the Messiah. Preexistence does not imply eternity, but that certain things had been created by God before the creation of the world. The most important doctrine, theologically, of preexistence is that of the Torah, which, according to the rabbis, was created by God and then served as a model for creation. This idea was possibly influenced by Platonic notions of the demiurges (creators) using, like an architect, a ground plan. But rabbinic thought (unlike Islamic theology, which holds the Qur'an to be eternal) always considered the Torah, though preexistent, as created.

• David Winston, "Preexistence in Hellenic, Judaic and Mormon Sources," in *Reflections on Mormonism*, edited by T. G. Madsen (Provo, Utah, 1978), pp. 13–35.

PREGNANCY. The Bible refers to the pain of pregnancy as the punishment meted out to Eve for eating of the fruit of the tree of knowledge of good and evil in the garden of Eden (*Gn*. 3.16). The Talmud notes, however, that the process of becoming pregnant is not an unpleasant one and that righteous women are spared Eve's punishment (*Sot*. 12a). The duration of pregnancy according to the Talmud is 271 to 273 days from conception (*Nid*. 38a–b), although the possibility of a twelve-month pregnancy is recognized in the context of the laws of adultery (*Yev*. 80b). A pregnant woman is not a menstruant for the purpose of the laws of *niddah* (*Nid*. 9a), and, according to the Midrash, her menstrual blood is the source of the milk in her breasts (*Lv. Rab*. 14.3). A pregnant woman who is overcome with a desire to break her fast on Yom Kippur may eat, although, initially, she is fed only a small amount. In the final analysis, she is allowed to eat the amount required to restore her health, since a pregnant woman is always considered to be in a dangerous physical state (*Yoma'* 82a). There is no ban on sexual intercourse during pregnancy (*Nid*. 31a). A man may not marry a woman who is carrying another man's child (*Yev*. 36b).

• David M. Feldman, *Marital Relations, Birth Control and Abortion in Jewish Law* (New York, 1974), pp. 180–187. Immanuel Jakobovits, *Jewish Medical Ethics* (New York, 1959; repr. 1975), pp. 84–91. Julius Preuss, *Biblical and Talmudic Medicine*, edited and translated by Fred Rosner (New York, 1993), pp. 381–387. —DANIEL SINCLAIR

PRIESTHOOD, a hereditary class of Jews to whom specific sacred functions are assigned. The essential role of the priest (*kohen*) in Israel was to officiate in Temple rituals, where he served as the "palace servant" in the earthly abode of the divine King. Spoken of in frankly anthropomorphic terms, the basic role of the priest was to approach the Lord's table to serve him his food (*Lv*. 21.6, 17; *Ez*. 44.15–16; see SACRIFICES; TABERNACLE; TEMPLE). Outside of cultic centers, Israelites in ancient times certainly sacrificed without benefit of priest; with the establishment of cultic centers a priesthood became crucial.

According to tradition, priests are only one family of the Levitical tribe (see LEVITES). According to the Torah, they are the descendants of Aaron; in *Ezekiel* they are called the sons of Zadok. As related in *Exodus* 29 and *Leviticus* 8–9, the priesthood was established when the Tabernacle was built. It consisted of Aaron and his four sons (and later, his grandsons). These original priests were consecrated by means of a seven-day ceremony of investiture: the *priestly vestments were placed upon them, they remained in the Tabernacle, and Moses performed sacrifices from which they received their first priestly dues (see PRIESTLY PRIVILEGES). Immediately thereafter, their ranks were severely diminished, when two of Aaron's sons, Nadab and Abihu were put to death for their sin (*Lv*. 10).

Ritual acts of the highest sanctity could be performed only by the *high priest; lesser priests would officiate at less sacred offerings performed at the outer altar located in the Temple court. Slaughter of sacrificial animals was not considered a sacred act and could be performed by anyone; still, the priest's expertise probably best qualified him for slaughtering even private sacrifices on behalf of the worshiper. The priest's sacred duty commenced after the slaughter: receiving the blood; placing the prescribed amount on the altar and draining the remainder; placing upon the altar those parts which were to be offered up to God; and correctly disposing of those that became the possession of the priests, those that were eaten by the worshiper, and those that had to be discarded.

The priests were charged with guard duty at the entrance to the Tabernacle, to prevent encroachment by unauthorized persons (*Nm*. 3.38, 18.1–7), and they took care of the most sacred objects on the journey through the wilderness (*Nm*. 4.5–16). Of course, with the establishment of the permanent Temple, these tasks were no longer necessary.

Unlike other cultures, the priesthood in Israel was exclusively male (though women married to priests and the daughters of priests benefited from priestly privileges). In order to serve, priests needed to be without physical blemish (*Lv.* 21.16–24). They were also to avoid all forms of physical impurity and were strictly cautioned against coming into contact with the dead (except for their closest relatives; the high priest was forbidden to come into contact with the corpses even of these; *Lv.* 21.1–5). They were also limited in their choice of wives; a priest could not marry a divorcee, a harlot (broadly defined by the rabbis to include the convert), or a *ḥalallah* (interpreted by some to mean a woman who had been raped; traditionally taken to mean a woman born of an illicit priestly marriage; *Lv.* 21:7). Celibacy was never a feature of Israelite priesthood.

In addition to their primary, sacrificial role, the priests were expected to pronounce God's blessing upon the people (*Nm.* 6.22–27) and to sound the trumpets on certain occasions (*Nm.* 10.1–10). They were also to instruct the Israelites on all matters of law and ritual, rendering legal decisions and distinguishing between pure and impure objects and conditions, permissible and forbidden foods, and sacred and profane places, times, and objects (*Lv.* 9.10; *Dt.* 17.8–11, 17.18, 19.17, 21.5, 24.8). This role is expressed by the word *torah* in one of its original meanings (ritual instruction). In particular the priest was required to pronounce as clean or unclean persons or houses afflicted with skin disease (see LEPROSY) and to preside over the *ordeal of jealousy. The priests could also give oracular teaching by means of the Urim and Thummim (*Ex.* 28.30; *Nm.* 27.21; *Ezr.* 2.63; see ORACLES). Although the prophets stressed the educational role of the priests (*Jer.* 18.18; *Ez.* 44.23–24; *Mal.* 2.7) study of the priestly literature in the Bible makes it clear that even in ancient times an elaborate system of legal, historical, and theological doctrine developed in priestly circles.

Though a number of priestly families and villages existed, in time the Israelite priesthood was confined to the Zadokites. By Second Temple times, the priesthood had become more institutionalized and was organized into a strict hierarchy divided into twenty-four divisions that served in rotation in the Temple.

With the destruction of the Temple, the priesthood could have become virtually meaningless, had not certain rights and duties been perpetuated. The rabbis held that the obligation to treat the priests as holy is permanent, and priestly families have steadfastly maintained their identity (often detectable in such surnames as Cohen, Katz, and Azulai). In traditional practice today, priests are called first to lead the *Birkat ha-Mazon and to the reading of the Torah in the synagogue; they continue to pronounce the *Birkat ha-Kohanim as part of the prayer service; they receive the monetary redemption of the *firstborn; the marital restrictions imposed on them are considered to be in effect; and they must refrain from contact with the dead, avoiding cemeteries and closed funeral halls. The festival *Musaf prayer beseeches God to restore the priests to their sacrificial tasks. See also PRIESTLY PRIVILEGES.

• Aelred Cody, *A History of the Old Testament Priesthood*, Analecta Biblica, vol. 35 (Rome, 1969). Tikva Simone Frymer-Kensky, *In the Wake of the Goddesses: Women, Culture, and the Biblical Transformation of Pagan Myth* (New York, 1992). Menahem Haran, *Temples and Temple-Service in Ancient Israel* (Winona Lake, Ind., 1985), pp. 58–111. Baruch A. Levine, ed., *Leviticus*, The JPS Torah Commentary, vol. 3 (Philadelphia, 1989). Jacob Milgrom, *Leviticus 1–16*, The Anchor Bible, vol. 3 (New York, 1991), pp. 52–57, 281–284, 491–635 and *passim*. Jacob Milgrom, *Studies in Cultic Theology and Terminology* (Leiden, 1983).

—BARUCH J. SCHWARTZ

PRIESTLY BLESSING. See BIRKAT HA-KOHANIM.

PRIESTLY CODE, term used to refer to the body of laws contained in the Priestly source, which, according to critical biblical scholarship, forms one of the originally separate documents from which the Torah is composed. See also BIBLE; PRIESTHOOD; TORAH.

• Pieter A. H. de Boer, ed., *The Priestly Code and Seven Other Studies* (Leiden, 1969). Mayer Gruber, "Women in the Cult According to the Priestly Code," in *Judaic Perspectives on Ancient Israel*, edited by Jacob Neusner et al. (Philadelphia, 1987). —BARUCH J. SCHWARTZ

PRIESTLY PRIVILEGES (Heb. *mattenot kehunnah*), the livelihood provided for the priests by the Israelites, on whose behalf they performed their sacred duties. The priests of ancient times (see LEVITES; PRIESTHOOD) were given no land of their own; their sole task was to serve in the Temple and perform its rituals. In all their material needs, the priests were thus dependent on those portions of Israel's sacrifices that they received. These were not gifts or a form of charity. Rather, they were the priests' due, in return for their labors (*Nm.* 18.31), and they were precisely assigned to them by law. The Torah stresses that God, not the people, provides the priests' portions: the people offer the sacrifices—both public and private offerings—to God; it is he who then presents the priests with a portion thereof (e.g., *Lv.* 6.10–11, 7.34–35). There are two types of portions: most holy (Heb. *qadshei qadashim*), which may be consumed only by male priests within the holy precincts, and holy portions (*qadashim qallim*), which may be consumed anywhere, by all members of priests' families, including household servants, so long as they are ritually pure. In the former category are the priests' share of the *purification offering, the *reparation offering, and the *meal offering. All other priestly emoluments fall into the latter category. These include the priest's share of the *peace offering in all its variations; the two lambs presented on Shavu'ot; firstlings of pure animals; first fruits, oil, and wine; first shorn wool of the flock; the redemption price of firstborn sons and of asses; and the first of the dough (see ḤALLAH). In addition, a tenth of the tithes of crops given to the Levites was forwarded to the priests. The rabbis set the precise number of priestly privileges at twenty-four; the precise Talmudic enumeration is found in *Bava' Qamma'* 110b and *Ḥullin* 133b, and, in the Talmud Yerushalmi, in *Ḥallah* 60b.

• Joseph Blenkinsopp, *Sage, Priest, Prophet: Religious and Intellectual Leadership in Ancient Israel* (Louisville, Ky., 1995). Aelred Cody, *A History of Old Testament Priesthood*, Analecta Biblica 35 (Rome, 1969). Menahem Haran, *Temples and Temple-Service in Ancient Israel* (Winona Lake, Ind., 1985). —BARUCH J. SCHWARTZ

PRIESTLY SOURCE (P), the largest and most important of the originally separate documents that comprise the Torah in the view of critical biblical scholarship. See also BIBLE; PRIESTHOOD.

• Avi Hurvitz, *A Linguistic Study of the Relationship between the Priestly Source and the Book of Ezekiel* (Paris, 1982). Baruch A. Levine, *Leviticus: The Traditional Hebrew Text* (Philadelphia, 1989). Brian Peckham, *The Composition of the Deuteronomistic History* (Atlanta, 1985). Edward Robertson, *The Priestly Code* (Manchester, 1942).

–BARUCH J. SCHWARTZ

PRIESTLY VESTMENTS, articles of clothing or ceremonial items worn by the priests when performing their ritual functions in the Temple in ancient times. Ordinary priests wore four white linen garments when performing their ritual tasks: the first three, a fringed tunic, a headdress, and an embroidered sash, were explicitly for "majesty and adornment" (*Ex.* 28.39–41); the fourth, a set of breeches worn under the tunic, was required for modesty (in order that the priest's genitals not be visible, presumably to the deity, even from below). In addition to these, the high priest was required to don four symbolic items as components of the daily *tamid* ritual (*Ex.* 28.6–38). The first two items were the *ephod, a sort of apron worn over the priest's robe, with two lapis lazuli stones on the epaulets upon which the names of the tribes of Israel were engraved; and a square *ḥoshen* (breastplate of decision) into which twelve stones were mounted in four rows of three each, one for each of the tribes, engraved with seals bearing their names. These two had basically the same purpose: to serve as a "reminder," that is, a representation, of the Israelite people "before the Lord" (*Ex.* 28.12, 29); by wearing them when he entered the divine abode, the high priest embodied the entire community on whose behalf he came and called God's attention to their needs. The breastplate contained the oracular Urim and Thummim (*Ex.* 28.30; see ORACLES). The other two articles were a pure blue robe, the lower hem of which was encircled with tinkling bells so that the high priest could be heard by the deity when he approached the shrine (*Ex.* 28.35), and a golden diadem set into the high priest's headdress, upon which the words *qodesh le-YHVH* (holy to YHVH) were inscribed. The diadem was said to secure the divine acceptance of Israel's worship and remove their impurities. The priests were consecrated for service by having the vestments placed upon them (*Lv.* 8), and their transferral from Aaron to Eleazar signaled the transfer of high priesthood from father to son. The finest wools, linens, gold, and stones, and the most intricate embroidery work, characterized the high priest's vestments, as they belonged, like the high priest himself, to the innermost sphere of the sacred.

• Johannes Gabriel, *Unterschungen uber das alttestamentliche Hohepriestertum mit besonderer berucksichtigung des hohepriesterlichen ornates* (Vienna, 1933), pp. 25–90. S. Shafer, *Construction of the Holy Tabernacle and Its Vessels and Priestly Garments* (Jerusalem, 1994). Shalom Duber Shtainberg, *The Mishkan and the Holy Garments*, translated by Moshe Miller (Jerusalem, 1992).

–BARUCH J. SCHWARTZ

PRIMOGENITURE. See BIRTHRIGHT; FIRSTBORN; INHERITANCE.

PRIMORDIAL MAN. See ADAM QADMON.

PRINCIPLES OF FAITH. See CREED; THIRTEEN PRINCIPLES OF FAITH.

PROCREATION. The *mitsvah* of procreation is the first commandment in the Bible (*Gn.* 1.28), and its nonfulfillment is tantamount to the diminution of the divine image in the world (*Yev.* 63b). The minimum requirement for the fulfillment of this *mitsvah* is begetting a boy and a girl, who are themselves capable of procreation (*Yev.* 61b), but there is a rabbinic obligation "not to cease being fruitful and multiplying as long as one has the power to do so, because whosoever adds one soul to Israel is considered as if they had built a whole world" (Maimonides, *Hilkhot Ishut* 15.16). Although Talmudic law restricts the *mitsvah* to the male sex (*Yev.* 65b), females receive a share in it by virtue of their vital role in bringing children into the world. The obligation to procreate devolves upon a male in his eighteenth year, and in principle, although not necessarily in practice, he may divorce his wife if she is not capable of conceiving a child and a period of ten years has elapsed since the marriage (*Yev.* 64a). If a woman in such circumstances refuses to accept a *get*, then her husband may be granted permission to take a second wife (*Shulḥan ʿArukh, Even ha-ʿEzer* 1.10). Marriage for the purpose of procreation may be financed by selling a Sefer Torah, but marital relations are suspended during a famine or any other public calamity (*Taʿan.* 11a). The question of the fulfillment of the *mitsvah* of procreation by means of *artificial reproduction techniques is still an open one in Jewish law.

• Jeremy Cohen, *"Be Fertile and Increase, Fill the Earth and Master It:" The Ancient and Medieval Career of a Biblical Text* (Ithaca, N.Y., 1989). Louis M. Epstein, *Sex Laws and Customs in Judaism* (New York, 1967). D. Feldman, *Marital Relations, Birth Control and Abortion in Jewish Law* (New York, 1974), chap. 3. Immanuel Jakobovits, *Jewish Medical Ethics* (1959; repr. New York, 1975), pp. 154–169. D. Shapiro, "Be Fruitful and Multiply," in *Jewish Bioethics*, edited by F. Rosner and J. D. Bleich (New York, 1979), pp. 59–79.

–DANIEL SINCLAIR

PROFANATION (Heb. *ḥillul*), transference from the realm of the sacred to that of the profane or common. The Temple, as the abode of the divine presence, is sacred, as are all its appurtenances: its furnishings, the sacred oil and incense, the priestly garments, animals donated or used for sacrifices and the flesh of such animals, and all monetary and other gifts made to the Temple. Unauthorized profanation is a serious sin. It occurs when something sacred comes into contact with the impure; for instance, when a ministering high priest leaves the Temple precincts or a nonpriest enters them, when a lay person consumes sacred flesh (*Lv.* 22.15), when a sacrifice is consumed after its designated time (*Lv.* 19.8), or when the anointing oil is used for everyday purposes (*Ex.* 30.31–33). Priests are specifically commanded to guard against desecration of sacred offerings, such as by eating them while impure (*Lv.* 22). Deliberate profanation may subject a person to death or a divine penalty; accidental profanation maybe expiated in some cases by repaying the value of the object plus one-fifth. Legitimate profanation is prescribed when it is necessary to remove an object that has become holy from this state. A sacrificial animal found to have a blemish could be "desanctified" (*Lv.* 27), as could other consecrated property, persons, or animals. Sacred persons include: the priests, who are declared to have profaned their seed if they fail to observe the priestly marital restrictions (*Lv.* 21.15) or whose daughters profane them if they engage in prostitution (*Lv.* 21.9); and the *Nazirite, who returns to his previous, profane state by means of the sacrifices he offers at the end of his term (*Nm.* 6.14). The Sabbath and festivals are sacred, performing everyday activities on them profanes them (*Ex.* 31.14; see ḤILLUL SHABBAT). The name of God (YHVH) is also sacred; misusing it in false oath (*Lv.* 19.12) or worshiping *Molech (*Lv.* 18.21) is called "profanation of the name of God" (see ḤILLUL HA-SHEM). Illegitimate profanation is virtually synonymous with the concept of *me'ilah* (see SACRILEGE).

• Menahem Haran, *Temples and Temple-Service in Ancient Israel* (Winona Lake, Ind., 1985), pp. 158–188. Jacob Milgrom, ed., *Leviticus 1–16*, The Anchor Bible, vol. 3 (New York, 1991), pp. 345–363.

—BARUCH J. SCHWARTZ

PROFIAT DURAN. See DURAN, PROFIAT.

PROGRESSIVE JUDAISM. See REFORM JUDAISM.

PROMISCUITY. Illicit sexual activity is strongly condemned in the Bible and is deemed the major cause of "the defilement of the land" and "the vomiting out of its inhabitants" (*Lv.* 18.25, 28). Prostitution is banned on the basis of a biblical verse requiring that "there be no harlot of the daughters of Israel" (*Dt.* 23.18; *San.* 82a). *Adultery is a capital offense, which is mentioned in the Ten Commandments, and constitutes one of the three cardinal offenses, along with homicide and idolatry, which may not be committed, even at the cost of a person's life (*San.* 74a). Although adultery in this context is that involving a married woman, sexual relations between a married man and a single woman are forbidden, and in the late Middle Ages it was accepted that they would constitute grounds for *divorce. Maimonides states that sexual relations between single individuals are forbidden on the grounds of the prohibition on harlotry (*Laws of Marriage* 1.4). Physical contact between the sexes in situations in which forbidden sexual relations may occur is outlawed by the rabbis, as is being alone (**yiḥud*) with such individuals (Maimonides, *Laws of Forbidden Intercourse* 21–22; *Shulḥan ʿArukh, Even ha-ʿEzer* 22). *Yiḥud* with a single woman was specifically outlawed by virtue of a rabbinic decree (*ʿA. Z.* 36b). The rabbis formulated a large number of rules and regulations aimed at the prevention of lewd thoughts and immodest conduct, even between spouses (*Shulḥan ʿArukh, Even ha-ʿEzer* 21–25). Indeed, even in the context of marriage itself, the laws of **niddah* ensure that spouses exercise self-control and abstain from sexual relations for a significant period during every menstrual cycle (see MENSTRUATION). Maimonides remarks that "for most people there is nothing harder in the entire Torah than to abstain from sex and forbidden sexual relations" (*Laws of Forbidden Intercourse* 22.18). Jewish tradition does not regard the sex drive as an inherently negative phenomenon but, rather, as a healthy force that must be properly controlled and diverted. Marriage is deemed the correct framework for sexual relations and within that institution, asceticism is discouraged. The Talmud provides that "a man may do with his wife as he pleases" (*Ned.* 20b), provided that she is a willing partner (Ra'avad, *Baʿalei ha-Nefesh; Shaʿar ha-Qedushah*), and the refusal of a spouse to remove clothing during intercourse, "in the manner of the Persians," is grounds for divorce in Jewish law (*Ket.* 48a).

• Eugene Borowitz, *Choosing a Sex Ethic: A Jewish Inquiry* (New York, 1969). Louis Epstein, *Sex Laws and Customs in Judaism* (New York, 1967). David Feldman, *Marital Relations, Birth Control and Abortion in Jewish Law* (New York, 1974). Robert Gordis, *Love and Sex: A Modern Jewish Perspective* (New York, 1978). Maurice Lamm, *The Jewish Way in Love and Marriage* (San Francisco, 1980).

—DANIEL SINCLAIR

PROMISED LAND. See ERETS YISRA'EL.

PROOF. See EVIDENCE.

PROPERTY. Jewish law distinguishes between two kinds of property: personal, movable property (*mittaltelim*), which may be disposed of at will; and fixed property (real estate [*qarqaʿot*]), which, while it may also be disposed of at will, can never be absolutely alienated in Erets Yisra'el (*Lv.* 25.23). Beside an individual's right to dispose of property, the courts had full power to divest an individual of property (*Git.* 36b). The act of possession, without which no commercial transaction is ultimately binding, is called *qinyan* (see ACQUISITION). Movable property is exchanged by means of the following *qinyanim*: actual grasping of the object (*hagbahah* or *meshikhah*); exchange (*sudar* or *ḥalifin*; see BARTER) or the symbolic transfer of the actual goods (cf. *Ru.* 4.7); the bringing of an object into the territory of the person who has acquired it (*ḥatser* [court]); and the transfer of movable goods together with the *real estate upon which they are situated (*agav*). The laws of transference of property take into account local custom and business practices; handshakes, the handing over of keys, and various other customs are all legally recognized means of acquisition. The forms of *qinyan* prescribed for the transfer of real estate are payment of the purchase price (or part thereof if the seller is agreeable); composing a document containing the words "my field is sold to you"; and seizure (**ḥazaqah*), that is, performance of an action regarded as a declaration of ownership, or unchallenged occupation of a piece of real estate for a specific period of time (usually three years). Verbal promises regarding gifts of property to the Temple or to charitable institutions required no formal *qinyan* but were legally binding.

• Shalom Albeck, *Dinei ha-Mamonot ba-Talmud* (Tel Aviv, 1976).

PROPHECY. The Greek word *prophētēs* means "one who speaks on behalf of [a god]"; this appears to be the meaning of the Hebrew *nabi*, which is derived from the Akkadian verb *nabir* (to proclaim; hence, the proclaimer). *Moses is told that he will be "a god" to Pharaoh, and *Aaron will be his *nabi* (prophet); figuratively speaking, this means that Aaron is Moses' spokesman (*Ex.* 7.1–2). Thus a *nabi* is a spokesman for God: "I will raise up a *nabi* . . . I will put My words in his mouth" (*Dt.* 18.18). The words of the prophets (apart from Moses, who came to be regarded as the greatest of prophets) are preserved in the historical books of the *Bible and in the books of the *prophets.

The essence of biblical prophecy is not the accurate prediction of future events. Israelite prophets readily admitted that God's threats and promises might or might not materialize, depending on human behavior. Rather, prophecy in the Bible is the communication of the divine word to human beings, by means of chosen messengers, in order to influence their thoughts and actions; the form and content of the actual message vary with circumstances.

Ancient Israel admitted that God communicates with humans in various ways: in dreams, by means of the Urim and Thummim (see ORACLES), and through prophets. Prophets are said to have received their messages in dreams, visionary experiences, ecstatic states, and, in the case of Moses, by direct verbal dialogue with the deity. Other words for prophet in the Bible are *ro'eh* (seer; which eventually ceased to be used [*1 Sm.* 9.9]), *ḥozeh* (seer; *2 Sm.* 24.1; *Am.* 7.12–13), and *ish ha-'Elohim* (man of God; *1 Sm.* 9.6; *2 Kgs.* 4.9). These terms express the prophet's clairvoyance and intimate knowledge of information inaccessible to ordinary humans. Still, it is maintained that the prophet has no natural gifts; God alone is the source of his powers and knowledge. Other means of acquiring knowledge of the occult—omens, sorcery, spells—are prohibited and condemned as strictly pagan practices (*Dt.* 18.9–22).

Though Abraham is the first to be called a prophet (*Gn.* 20.7) because of his ability to pray to God on behalf of Abimelech, it is with the career of Moses that prophecy becomes a permanent institution in biblical tradition. Moses is thus referred to in Judaism as the "father of the prophets." His prophecy is said to have been unique in form—only he spoke to God "face to face, as a man speaks to his fellow" (*Ex.* 33.11), not in riddles and dreams (*Nm.* 12.6–8)—and in content—his prophetic message was composed almost entirely of commands, laws, and statutes binding for all time. The Torah account takes for granted that God must have open channels of communication with Israel; thus, when Israel is terrified by the prospect of having God speak to them directly, God agrees to their request to use prophetic mediation (*Ex.* 20.15–18; *Dt.* 5.19–28, 18.15–17).

Delivering the word of God takes place in two stages: the message is delivered by God to the prophet and then by the prophet to the individual or the people. Since the first stage is always private, the question of the prophet's credibility necessarily arises: why should a person who declares "thus said the Lord" be believed? The Torah asserts that this problem was resolved once and for all at Sinai. God revealed himself in order that the people of Israel might overhear him speaking to Moses, as a result of which they would believe in Moses and his prophetic successors forever after (*Ex.* 19.9). The problem of false prophecy never ceased to trouble, however (see PROPHETS, FALSE).

The death of Joshua, Moses' successor, marks the beginning of a long break in prophecy in the biblical view. Though *Deborah is called a prophetess (*Jgs.* 4.4), in general the lawlessness of the period of the judges is seen as a result of this having been a time when God refrained from communicating with man (*1 Sm.* 3.1). This divine silence ends with *Samuel, who inaugurates the age of popular prophecy. Samuel's prophetic career, as well as those of *Gad and *Nathan, is associated with the establishment of the monarchy, just as Moses' is associated with the establishment of the sacrificial cult. Kings of the northern kingdom of Israel were anointed and appointed by prophets. The prophetic role is thus held to be superior to that of priest and king, both of the latter positions having been instituted, at God's behest, by prophets.

This period in Israelite prophecy is characterized primarily by popular, mantic, wonderworking prophets. As intimates of God, they were consulted by ordinary Israelites, by kings, and by the community as a whole, for guidance, military oracles, miraculous healing, and even for help in locating lost property. Notable among these are figures such as Samuel, Nathan, Gad, *Elijah, and *Elisha, who are called by God to transcend their popular roles. They are sent on errands of national importance, to condemn severely moral and religious offenses. Occasionally, the Bible speaks of companies or bands of prophets, characterized by ecstatic behavior accompanied by musical performance; they were thought to be possessed of an unusual dose of the "spirit of God." Saul's election to kingship was marked by his being caught in the ecstasy of such a band. Most of the biblical prophets, however, are individuals who have no previous training and are unable to induce trances or ecstatic states on their own. Rather, they are driven by an irresistible compulsion to deliver the divine word, which burns as a fire within them until it is spoken.

The golden age of Israelite prophecy was the period of the classical or literary prophets, beginning with *Hosea and *Amos in the eighth century BCE and ending with the prophets of the return to Zion in the fifth century. The extent of the social and religious critique they delivered, and the highly developed, elaborate literary and rhetorical form of their messages are unique. The literary prophets dwelled on several recurring themes, none entirely new but each one elevated to a level of importance previously unknown. They regularly condemned the lack of social justice—in particular, the plight of the poor, the weak, the widow and orphan, and the corruption of the wealthy, landowning classes; the pervasive contamination of the cult and worship of YHVH, and the repeated backsliding into idolatry; the mistaken idea that God could be satisfied in the cultic sphere alone (see SACRIFICES), while his people continued to oppress the weak and ignore their suffering; haughty, false reliance on human might and political alliances; and the arrogant notion that, despite Israel's wrongdoing, God would never forsake or destroy his people. Classical prophecy's teaching was thus cataclysmic: it maintained that God would not tolerate Israel's sinfulness and that he would put an end to his covenantal relationship with them. The historical background for this development was the rise of the Assyrian and Babylonian empires, which rendered insignificant the tiny Israelite kingdoms and threatened their continued existence.

The threat of national destruction was usually accompanied by the assurance, implicit or direct, that it could be avoided if Israel would realize the error of its ways and return to God. Thus the prophetic message includes the call to repentance and the promise that repentance will avert disaster. The forecast of impending doom was usually counterbalanced by the promise of a glorious future, if only Israel would walk in the paths of righteousness. This was not always the case, however; occasionally the decree of doom is quite irrevocable, the prophet aims not at preventing it but simply at announcing and justifying its inevitability.

From earliest times, even messages of inescapable doom were followed by the promise of subsequent reconciliation. As the destruction of the kingdom drew nearer, and after it came to pass, the prophets never relinquished their vision of the future. Prophetic words of consolation and oracles of national rehabilitation are particularly characteristic of the period of the return to Zion. Thus was born the idea that Israel would ultimately be reunited; its monarchy restored; peace, prosperity, and security established; the exiles of Israel returned; and the peoples of the world converted to the worship of the God of Israel. This complex of ideas gave birth to Jewish messianism.

The Talmudic rabbis perceptively realized that the prophetic oracles preserved in the Bible are but a fraction of the prophecies actually uttered and reasoned that those prophecies that had permanent relevance, that is, that could be recycled when situations arose similar to those in which they were originally uttered, were preserved for future generations. To this may be added the suggestion that prophets whose credentials were impeccable, who had been shown by experience to be true bearers of the divine word, were likely to have had their speeches written down and passed on, on the assumption that their relevance would eventually become apparent. Thus Judaism's sustained interest in the biblical prophecies required shifting the focus from their original intent to some as yet unknown one. The rabbis realized that prophecy belonged to the past. Though occasional reports of revelations and inspiration persisted well into medieval times, the dominant view is that the last of the biblical prophets, *Haggai, *Zechariah, and *Malachi, marked the final departure of the holy spirit from Israel. Thereafter the word of God was to be sought in the Torah and in the prophecies already delivered, which were to be scrutinized and expounded by the sages.

Medieval philosophers offered two different explanations of the nature of biblical prophecy. Rationalistic philosophers such as Maimonides held that the prophet was naturally endowed with perfect reason, imagination, and moral character, coupled with perfect wisdom and knowledge acquired from learning and from contemplation of a philosophical nature. These faculties are activated by God, causing prophetic illumination to occur. Prophecy is thus essentially a projection of the human intellect. Others, such as Yehudah ha-Levi, insisted that prophecy was entirely supernatural, a gift bestowed by God upon deserving mortals and originating entirely in the metaphysical realm.

• Joseph Blenkinsopp, *A History of Prophecy in Israel* (Philadelphia, 1983). Abraham Joshua Heschel, *The Prophets* (New York, 1962). Yehezkel Kaufmann, *The Religion of Israel: From Its Beginnings to the Babylonian Exile* (Chicago, 1960), pp. 212–216, 262–286, 343–446. Johannes Lindblom, *Prophecy in Ancient Israel* (Philadelphia, 1973). Claus Westermann, *Basic Forms of Prophetic Speech* (Louisville, Ky., 1991). Claus Westermann, *Prophetic Oracles of Salvation in the Old Testament* (Louisville, Ky., 1991). Robert R. Wilson, *Prophecy and Society in Ancient Israel* (Philadelphia, 1980).

–BARUCH J. SCHWARTZ

PROPHETS, BOOKS OF THE (Heb. Nevi'im), the second section of the Bible, preceded by the Pentateuch (Torah) and followed by the Hagiographa (Ketuvim). In Jewish tradition there are eight prophetic books. The first four—*Joshua, Judges, Samuel,* and *Kings* (customarily referred to as the Former Prophets)—are historiographical works, but Jewish tradition assigns them to the prophetic division in order to keep the Pentateuch in a class by itself, and because they provide the historical background for the lives and oracles of the literary prophets; they were believed to have been written by prophets (such as Samuel and Jeremiah), and they contain stories about prophets including Samuel, Nathan, Elijah, and Elisha. The other four prophetic books (called the Latter Prophets)—*Isaiah, Jeremiah, Ezekiel,* and the Twelve (Minor Prophets)—are primarily literary collections of the speeches of the prophets whose names they bear. The division of *Samuel* and *Kings* into two books each is not mentioned in rabbinic sources; it derives from the Septuagint and entered Hebrew Bibles in late medieval times. The twelve minor prophetic collections (*Hosea, Joel, Amos, Obadiah, Jonah, Micah, Nahum, Habakkuk, Zephaniah, Haggai, Zechariah,* and *Malachi*) are traditionally considered to be one book. When all biblical books were written on scrolls, these twelve were written on a single scroll, their combined length comprising a text long enough to fill an average scroll. Prescribed selections from the prophetic books are read in the synagogue on Sabbaths, festivals, and fast days (see HAFTARAH).

• Joseph Blenkinsopp, *A History of Prophecy in Israel* (Louisville, Ky., 1996). Abraham Joshua Heschel, *The Prophets* (New York, 1962). Barry A. Jones, *The Formation of the Book of Twelve: A Study in Text and Canon* (Atlanta, 1995).

–BARUCH J. SCHWARTZ

PROPHETS, FALSE. In Israelite belief, the prophet was God's spokesperson. Prophetic speech and actions, however, could be imitated by anyone. It was therefore a problem to distinguish between the prophet whom God had actually sent and the pretender. The ability to work miracles was no proof; it was readily admitted that even a prophet advocating the worship of foreign gods might successfully produce signs and portents, God himself taking advantage of the opportunity to test Israel's loyalty to him (*Dt.* 13.2–6). According to *Deuteronomy*, a prophet whose words come true is God's faithful messenger; one whose predictions fail to materialize is not (*Dt.* 18.21–22). But even if Israelite prophecy merely had been about predicting the future, which it was not, this would have been insufficient. Questions were raised about how long it was reasonable to wait for the fulfillment of a prophecy and about what if God changed his plans, as he asserts he does constantly in response to human repentance or backsliding (*Jer.* 18.7–10). In Israel, moreover, prophecy was instruction. This turned the matter into a practical issue, since the words of the true prophet were to be heeded on pain of death, while the false prophet had to be shunned and put to death (*Dt.* 18.19–20). Following or rejecting the words of a prophet could also have immediate and far-reaching consequences on the individual and national level. Thus, the law in *Deuteronomy* is inadequate, as it covers only cases in which it is possible to wait and see. Jeremiah's confrontation with the false prophet Hananiah the son of Azzur led to a different formulation (*Jer.* 28.8–9). The prophet who prophesies doom (and, presumably, urges repentance) is to be given the benefit of the doubt, since only a true prophet would be likely to sacrifice his popularity by harshly scolding his listeners. Jeremiah proposes that the true prophet is the one who is willing to entreat God on his people's behalf (*Jer.* 27.18). The real prophet recognizes the impending doom and wishes to prevent it. Still, the problem was not solved, as is shown by Jeremiah's entire prophetic career (see *Jer.* 23). He himself was convicted of false prophecy when he warned that the Temple would be destroyed (*Jer.* 26.11); *Lamentations* blames the destruction and exile on the fact that false prophets misled the people (*Lam.* 2.14). The rabbinic criteria for distinguishing between true and false prophets were codified by Maimonides (*Yesodei ha-Torah* 8–10).

• Joseph Blenkinsopp, *A History of Prophecy in Ancient Israel* (Louisville, Ky., 1996). James E. Brenneman, "Canon(s) in Conflict: Negotiating Texts in True and False Prophecy, Isaiah 2:2–4/Micah 4:1–4 vs. Joel 4:9–12," Ph.D. dissertation, Claremont Graduate School, 1994. Richard J. Coggins, "Prophecy—True and False," in *Of Prophets' Visions and the Wisdom of Sages: Essays in Honour of R. Norman Whybray*, Journal for the Study of the Old Testament, Supplement Series 162 (Sheffield, Eng., 1993).

—BARUCH J. SCHWARTZ

PROSELYTE (from the Septuagint translation [*proselytos*] of the Heb. *ger* [stranger]), person converted to Judaism. The Bible refers to proselytes in *Exodus* 12.48 and elsewhere (cf., *Is.* 56.3, 6) and to actual conversion in *Ruth* 2.12 and *Esther* 8.17. The rabbis distinguished between two types of proselytes. The half proselyte, called *ger toshav* (i.e., settler proselyte [*Lev.* 25.47]) or *ger ha-sha'ar* (the proselyte of the gate [cf., *Ex.* 20.10]), undertook in the presence of three *ḥaverim* (scholars) to observe some of the basic principles (but not the ceremonies) of Judaism, such as the renunciation of idolatry and the keeping of the seven *Noahic laws (*'A. Z.* 64b); Maimonides calls these "the righteous gentiles." The full proselyte, called *ger tsedeq* (righteous proselyte), converts out of love of Judaism and accepts all its laws and ceremonies. Especially blessed in the thirteenth benediction of the 'Amidah, the full proselyte is to be shown every consideration, and even the forebears of such a convert may not be disparaged. He or she is considered like "a new-born child," and all former family ties are regarded as terminated. He or she is now called "son/daughter of Abraham," who is seen as the father of converts, and takes a Hebrew name (Abraham and Ruth—herself seen as the paragon of conversion—are favored). Sincerity of motive is an indispensable prerequisite for conversion, although Maimonides (*Issurei Bi'ah* 13.14) accepts as Jews those who convert for personal reasons. To ensure sincerity, initial efforts are made to dissuade a would-be proselyte. Conversion (*giyyur*) of a full proselyte, but not of a half proselyte, entails a period of study, circumcision (for men), immersion in a ritual bath (for men and women), and (during the existence of the Temple) a sacrifice.

In the early period, active propaganda, though not by professional missionaries, was directed toward gaining proselytes, and according to R. El'azar ben Pedat, this was actually the divine purpose for the dispersion of the Jewish people (*Pes.* 87b). Thus the rabbis interpret "the souls that they had gotten in Haran" (*Gn.* 12.5) as referring to the proselytes made by Abraham (*Sifrei* on *Dt.* 6.5). Hillel's lenient attitude toward intending proselytes, in contrast to the somewhat sterner approach of Shamm'ai (*Shab.* 31a), most probably reflected the dominant view. Immediately before and after the destruction of the Second Temple, many converts were made both among the masses and the upper classes. Josephus states that there was no city anywhere into which Jewish observances had not penetrated (*Against Apion* 2.40), that almost all the women in Damascus were "addicted to the Jewish religion" (*The Jewish War* 2.20.2), and that Queen Helena and her son King Izates of Adiabene were converted to Judaism (*Antiquities of the Jews* 20.2.1–4). Rabbinic literature tells, for example, of many converts in Maḥoza in Babylonia (*Qid.* 73a), while among scholars of note, R. Me'ir, Shema'yah, Avtalyon, R. 'Aqiva', and Onkelos, the author of the Targum on the Pentateuch, were regarded as proselytes or descendants of proselytes. When, however, *Christianity began to gain successes among proselytes and half proselytes, the Jewish attitude to proselytism changed. Josephus (*Against Apion* 2.11) reported that of the many Greek proselytes only some had remained faithful, while others had forsaken Judaism. This may have prompted R. Eli'ezer ben Hurqanos to speak of the unreliability of proselytes (*B. M.* 59b). It was said that spies, under the guise of proselytes, were planted among the Jews by the Romans, which was doubtless a major reason that conversion was difficult "in these days" (*Yev.* 47a, probably referring to the period of the Hadrianic persecutions). Bitter historical experiences led to the statement of R. Ḥelbo (*Qid.* 70b) that proselytes are as grievous to Israel as a scab on the skin. To this inner resistance against proselytes were added the outer restrictions imposed by Christianity, which in the fourth and fifth centuries prohibited conversion to Judaism as a criminal offense, punishable at first by the confiscation of property and later by the death of the proselytizing Jew. During the following centuries, there were comparatively few proselytes, although Dhu Nuwas, the Jewish king of Yemen (6th cent.), and the *Khazars in southern Russia (8th cent.) are important exceptions. In the Middle Ages occasional conversions to Judaism, even by clerics, occurred in Europe. Once formally converted (following a period of instruction in the teachings and practices of Judaism and approval by a **beit din* [religious court]), the proselyte ranks as a full member of the Jewish people; the only halakhic disability is the prohibition on a priest marrying a female proselyte. A proselyte is permitted to marry a **mamzer*.

In modern times, the halakhic rules concerning conversion have been eased by Reform Judaism, which often does not require circumcision and ritual immersion but bases its conversion process on study and a ceremony. Reform actively encourages proselytization especially among non-Jewish partners in mixed marriages. The Orthodox do not recognize Reform conversions in view of its nonhalakhic aspects and also because of what they regard as the unsuitability of Reform rabbis to constitute a *beit din*, and this has been a major source of friction between the Orthodox and non-Orthodox (the Orthodox also reject Conservative conversion, although the Conservatives adhere to halakhic regulations). This has led to major confrontations over the eligibility of non-Orthodox converts to be covered by Israel's *Law of Return (see JEW, WHO IS A?, CONTROVERSY). The Orthodox rabbinate in many places has adopted a particularly stringent attitude and in some countries refuses to convert non-Jews to Judaism. Converts today often refer to themselves as "Jews by choice."

• Lawrence J. Epstein, ed., *Readings on Conversion to Judaism* (Northvale, N.J., 1995). Martin Goodman, *Mission and Conversion: Proselytizing in the Religious History of the Roman Empire* (Oxford, 1994). Walter Jacob and Moshe Zemer, eds., *Conversion to Judaism in Jewish Law: Essays and Responsa* (Tel Aviv and Pittsburgh, 1994), on Reform views. Benzion Netanyahu, *The Origins of the Inquisition in Fifteenth-Century Spain* (New York, 1995), on forced conversions.

PROSTRATION, casting oneself flat on the ground. Like bowing and kneeling, prostration is a gesture of reverence to God and was practiced in the ancient Temple. Four forms of prayer are mentioned in the Talmud: *berikhah*, bending the knee (Y., *Ber*. 1.8); *qidah*, bowing with one's face to the ground; *keri'ah*, kneeling; *hishtaḥavvayah*, prostration with outstretched hands and feet (*Ber*. 34b). Practiced also in biblical times, *hishtaḥavvayah* was performed by the priests and people in the Temple at thirteen different locations (corresponding to the thirteen Temple-court gates; *Sheq*. 6.3; *Mid*. 2.3) when the high priest pronounced the Tetragrammaton during the Yom Kippur service (*Yoma'* 6.2). A form of prostration is still practiced in the Ashkenazi rite during the recital of the Yom Kippur *'Avodah and during the *'Aleinu prayer on Ro'sh ha-Shanah and Yom Kippur. A still more modified form is performed (seated, with the head resting on the arm) when *Taḥanun is said in the presence of a Torah scroll.

• Uri Ehrlich, *Darkhei ha-Tefillah u-Mahma'utan bi-Tequfat ha-Mishnah veha-Talmud* (Jerusalem, 1993). Ismar Elbogen, *Jewish Litergy: A Comprehensive History*, translated by Raymond P. Scheindlin (Philadelphia, 1993), pp. 66f., 354, 379. Herman Kieval, *The High Holy Days* (New York, 1959), pp. 155f.

PROTESTANTISM, a movement begun in the sixteenth century by Martin Luther and other Reformers when they split from the Roman Catholic church. At the beginning of his career as a Reformer, Luther hoped for the conversion of the Jews to his new, reformed version of Christianity. When this did not materialize, he expressed anger and hatred toward the Jews. Theologically, Protestantism followed the traditional Christian claim to be the true Israel and denied the legitimacy of Jewish existence independent of the church. However, some of the smaller, more radical groups of the Reformation did view the Jews as historical Israel. Moreover Protestant theology was free of some of the anti-Jewish teachings of the Catholic church, while its devotion to the Old Testament led to new perspectives on Judaism and the Jewish people that had been closed to Catholics. Pietistic European and British Puritan groups that emerged in the seventeenth century viewed the Jews as the chosen people and the object of biblical prophecies. Influenced by a more literal reading of the Bible, they anticipated the return of the Jews to their land. Such philosemitic notions influenced the decision in the mid-seventeenth century to allow Jews to settle in England. A new wave of Protestant interest in the Jews, based on messianic expectations, took place among pietists and evangelical Protestants in the nineteenth century. It inspired among other things proto-Zionist initiatives and later on support for the developing Zionist movement. The evangelical understanding of the Jews as the true Israel was at the same time the impetus for extensive missionary work among Jews.

A dramatic change in Protestant attitudes toward Jews took place in the decades following World War II. A spirit of interfaith dialogue, as well as a realization that the Nazi persecution of Jews was nourished by Christian antisemitism, caused many Protestant churches to reevaluate their position on the Jewish people. During the 1970s and 1980s, a series of liberal Protestant churches, among them Anglicans, Lutherans, Presbyterians, and Methodists, issued statements in which they rejected the deicide charge and recognized Judaism as a legitimate religion alongside Christianity. Statements by the World Council of Churches reflected changes in liberal Protestant theological thinking. The declarations also expressed regret for Christian harassment of Jews throughout the ages. Liberal churches have given up on missionizing among Jews. Conservative evangelical Christianity did not join in dialogue, insisting that only those persons who accepted Jesus as their personal Savior could be saved. Evangelical Protestantism continues to carry on extensive missionary work among Jews. An important dimension of the Protestant–Jewish encounter since 1948 has been Protestant attitudes toward Israel. Liberal Protestants recognize the right of Israel to exist. However, particularly after 1967, they often adopted a critical position toward Israeli policies. Evangelical Protestants, on the other hand, have rendered enthusiastic support for Israel, believing that its creation was divinely ascribed and indicates that the arrival of the Messiah is near. See also INTERFAITH RELATIONS.

• Yaakov Ariel, *On Behalf of Israel: American Fundamentalist Attitudes toward Jews, Judaism, and Zionism, 1865–1945* (New York, 1991). Allan R. Brockway, ed., *The Theology of the Churches and the Jewish People: Statements by the World Council of Churches* (Geneva, 1988). David Katz, *Philo-Semitism and the Readmission of the Jews to England, 1603–1655* (Oxford, 1982). Yona Malachy, *American Fundamentalism and Israel: The Relation of Fundamentalist Churches to Zionism and to the State of Israel* (Jerusalem, 1978). Louis Israel Newman, *Jewish Influence on Christian Reform Movements* (New York, 1925). Heiko A. Oberman, *The Roots of Anti-Semitism in the Age of Renaissance and Reformation* (Philadelphia, 1984). Johan M. Snoek, *The Grey Book: A Collection of Protests against Anti-Semitism and the Persecution of Jews Issued by Non-Roman Catholic Churches and Church Leaders during Hitler's Rule* (Assen, 1969).

—YAAKOV ARIEL

PROVERBS (Heb. *meshalim*). There are two uses of the term in the Bible. The first refers to didactic sayings, such as those of Balaam concerning Israel's security and military strength (*Nm.* 23–24) and those of Ezekiel concerning the brushland of the Negev (*Ez.* 21.1–5), or such compositions as the parable of Jotham (*Jgs.* 9), as well as pithy aphorisms, such as "like mother, like daughter" (*Ez.* 16.44), or one-line "wisdom sentences" (especially in *Prv.* 10–22, 25–29), such as, "A wise son brings joy to his father, a dull son is his mother's sorrow" (*Prv.* 10.1). The term *mashal* also means a model of derision and is used in respect of nations (e.g., *Dt.* 28.37), people (e.g., *Ps.* 69.12), or even the destroyed Temple (*2 Chr.* 7.20), which exemplify shame for future generations. The noun *mashal* (model, saying) is derived from the Hebrew verb *m sh l* (be like). In Akkadian, the root *mašalu* (be like) occurs several times in the Amarna Letters; for example, "My field without plowing is like (*mashil*) a woman without a husband."

The *Book of Ben Sira*, in the Apocrypha, is a collection of aphorisms, reminiscent of *Proverbs*. The Talmud and the Midrash are replete with maxims relating to the cycle of everyday and religious life. Notable examples appear in *Avot*, *Avot de-Rabbi Natan*, *Derekh Erets Rabbah*, and *Derekh Erets Zuta'*. Among later authors who are noted for their collections of proverbs are Ha'i Ga'on, Shemu'el ha-Nagid, and Mosheh ibn Ezra. Both Yiddish and Ladino literature and folklore are rich in proverbs. Examples from the Yiddish include: "One road leads to heaven but a thousand to hell"; "A man without a wife is like a *lulav* without an *etrog*"; and "Every Jew has his own *Shulḥan ʿArukh*." The Sephardi vernacular has been punctuated with proverbs such as "He who hesitates will never reach Jerusalem" and "Preach, rabbi, only when you have an audience."

• Chaim Cohen, in *ʿIyyunim be-Miqra' Sefer Zikkaron li-Yehoshuʿa Me'ir Grintz* (Tel Aviv, 1982), pp. 315–324, in Hebrew with English summary. Otto Eissfeldt, *The Old Testament: An Introduction* (New York, 1965), pp. 81–87. A. R. Johnson, "Mashal," in *Wisdom in Israel and in the Ancient Near East*, edited by M. Noth and D. W. Thomas, Supplements to Vetus Testamentum, vol. 3 (Leiden, 1969), pp. 162–169. G. M. Landes, in *Israelite Wisdom: Theological and Literary Essays in Honor of Samuel Terrien*, edited by John G. Gammie et al. (Missoula, Mont., 1978), pp. 137–158. William McKane, *Proverbs: A New Approach* (Philadelphia, 1970), pp. 22–33. Gerhard von Rad, *Wisdom in Israel* (London, 1972), pp. 24–34.

PROVERBS, BOOK OF, second book of the Hagiographa. The work belongs to Hebrew *wisdom literature and exhibits many of the characteristics that that genre shares with ancient Near Eastern literature in general. *Proverbs* shows Egyptian influence with parallels to Babylonian literature. Its thirty-one chapters contain collections of aphorisms, generally optimistic in tone, exhorting its readers to be mindful of the dictates of wisdom for their own good. In addition to the utilitarian character of its teachings, the book also emphasizes that true wisdom is associated with fear of God (1.7). Though poetically personified (chap. 8), the idea of wisdom in *Proverbs* is not to be confused with the hypostatized concept of *sophia* in later gnostic writings. The opening verse ascribes its authorship to Solomon, probably due to his reputation for wisdom and composing proverbs (*1 Kgs.* 5.9–14). According to the Talmud, the book received its definitive form at the time of Hezekiah and his scribes (*B. B.* 15a). It teaches that the wise will be duly rewarded and the wicked—in particular, the ignorant—punished. The book consists of praise of wisdom (chaps. 1–9); proverbs of Solomon (10.1–22.16); words of the wise (22.17–24.22); sayings of the wise (24.23–4); proverbs of Solomon that the men of Hezekiah, king of Judah, copied out (25.1–29.27); words of Agur, son of Jakeh (30.1–33); words of King Lemuel's mother (31.1–9); and praise of a virtuous wife (31.10–31; see ESHET ḤAYIL). Critical scholarship admits the possibility that some of the material in *Proverbs* may go as far back as King Solomon's court (cf. *1 Kgs.* 5.12) but holds that the constituent parts of *Proverbs* date from various periods, some even from postexilic times. The final redaction of the compilation in written form is attributed to the period of the Keneset ha-Gedolah.

• Wilfred G. Lambert, *Babylonian Wisdom Literature* (Oxford, 1960). William McKane, *Proverbs*, Old Testament Library (Philadelphia, 1970). Robert B. Y. Scott, *Proverbs; Ecclesiastes*, Anchor Bible (New York, 1982). Crawford H. Toy, *The Book of Proverbs*, International Critical Commentary (New York, 1916). R. N. Whybray, *Proverbs*, New Century Bible Commentary (Grand Rapids, 1994).

PROVERBS, MIDRASH, Midrashic work on the *Book of Proverbs*. It elaborates considerably on the opening chapters of *Proverbs*, less so on the later portions of the book, and includes no *derashot* on chapters three or eighteen. There is no interpretation of *Proverbs* 2.13–4.22 and 17.2–18.24; in chapter seven only verses 25–27 are interpreted briefly and in chapter twenty-nine only verse four. It resembles classical Midrashic literature in its exegetical style, though it contains few proems or introductory words. It employs many of the hermeneutic methods of earlier *midrashim*. Many verses of *Proverbs* are interpreted as referring to the Torah, and Lady Wisdom is construed almost exclusively in this manner. *Midrash Proverbs* utilizes material found in the Talmud Bavli as well as such Palestinian sources as the Mishnah, Tosefta', *Mekhilta'*, *Genesis Rabbah*, and *Pesiqta' de-Rav Kahana'*. It is also familiar with both versions of *Avot de-Rabbi Natan*. *Midrash Proverbs* makes use of Heikhalot literature. Especially noteworthy is chapter 10, which maps out a Heikhalot curriculum of study. *Midrash Proverbs* contains some original narrative material, such as the encounter between King Solomon and the Queen of Sheba, as well as four stories of legendary deaths. A different Midrashic work to the final chapter of *Proverbs* (31; see MIDRASHEI ESHET ḤAYIL) is found as an addition in the printed editions and in some manuscripts of *Midrash Proverbs*. It is quoted in works of the eleventh century, though several indications seem to point to a ninth-century redaction; among them, liturgical customs mentioned in passing that were evidently in practice in the ninth century and an anti-Karaite polemic, including an apparent dialogue with Daniyye'l ben Mosheh al-*Qumisi. There is no conclusive evidence to determine the exact locale of compilation.

• Salomon Buber, ed., *Midrash Mishlei* (Vilna, 1893). Burton Lyle Visotzky, ed., *Midrash Mishlei* (New York, 1990). Burton Lyle Visotzky, ed. and trans., "Midrash Mishlei," Ph.D. dissertation, Jewish Theological Seminary, 1982. Burton Lyle Visotzky, ed. and trans., *The Midrash on Proverbs* (New Haven, 1992). Leopold Zunz, *Ha-Derashot be-Yisra'el ve-Hishtalshelutan ha-Historit*, edited by Chanoch Albeck (1892; Jerusalem, 1974).

—YAEL LEVINE KATZ

PROVIDENCE (Heb. *hashgaḥah*), the power that rules both the world and human destiny, sustaining all and guiding everything in accordance with its purposes. Originating in Stoic philosophy, the term *providence* has been adopted by theistic theologies to designate the fundamental belief that God is "great in counsel and mighty in work" and that his eyes "are open upon all the ways of the sons of men, to give every one according to his ways, and according to the fruits of his doings" (*Jer.* 32.19). Biblical history is a record of God's immediate participation in the affairs of humankind; in fact, "by him actions are weighed . . . The Lord kills and makes alive . . . makes poor and makes rich; he brings low and lifts up" (*2 Sm.* 2.3–9). God's providence extends also to the nonhuman part of creation (cf. *Ps.* 104.21–33, 145.15–16). The ancient rabbis further emphasized these beliefs: "Know what is above you—a seeing eye, and a hearing ear, and all your deeds written in a book" (*Avot* 2.1), and "no one lifts even a finger here below, unless it is ordained above" (*Ḥul.* 7). Belief in a divine providence was confronted by contrary views (scientific, philosophical, or religious) that emphasized the ineluctable rule of necessity in the cosmos. In the Hellenistic period this inflexible cosmic law was identified with the stars, and the rabbis taught that Israel, being under God's immediate providence as his *chosen people, was not subject to the sway of the stars (the *mazzal*). In medieval times, the emergence of the concepts of nature and natural causality also challenged belief in providence. The tightly knit and autonomous causal nexus seemed to leave room for a divine "First Cause" but not for the exercise of immediate and direct providence (such as miracles, answer to prayer). All medieval philosophers (e.g., *Saʿadyah ben Yosef Ga'on , *Baḥya ben Yosef ibn Paquda', *Yehudah ha-Levi, Moses *Maimonides) wrestled with this problem, which was further complicated by considerations of people's *free will in relation to God's—possibly determining—foreknowledge. Some thinkers (e.g., Avraham *ibn Ezra) held that divine providence extended only to general categories and processes (general providence) but not to the fate of individuals. Traditional orthodoxy, however, assumed an "individual providence" (Heb. *hashgaḥah peratit*). The fact that modern definitions of nature, causality, or God differ from their medieval counterparts does not seem essentially to affect the problem of providence as it was stated by the thinkers of the Middle Ages. The Holocaust led later Jewish thinkers to wrestle with the notion of a divine providence for the Jewish people. See also ASTROLOGY; DETERMINISM; HOLOCAUST THEOLOGY; PREDESTINATION.

• Julius Guttman, *Philosophies of Judaism* (New York, 1964). H. Levine, in *Contemporary Jewish Religious Thought*, edited by Arthur A. Cohen and Paul Mendes-Flohr (New York and London, 1987), pp. 735–739. Yosef Hayim Yerushalmi, *Zakhor* (Seattle, 1983).

PSALMODY. The *Book of Psalms* has been described as the hymn book of the Second Temple, and some prayers are largely compilations of *Psalms* verses; for example, *Barukh Adonai le-ʿOlam in the weekday evening service, and Yehi Khavod in the Sabbath morning liturgy. Psalms with special liturgical significance are Psalm 145, which is recited three times daily; and Psalms 146–150, which are recited daily in the morning service, symbolically carrying on an old tradition that the entire Psalter was to be read each day. Other psalms featured in the liturgy are Psalms 113–118 (known as the Egyptian *Hallel), recited on the *Shalosh Regalim and on other joyous occasions, and Psalms 95–99 and 29, which inaugurate the Sabbath. Following the practice of the Second Temple, a different psalm is sung at the conclusion of the morning service every day of the week, each suggesting the events that took place on that particular day of Creation; the cycle culminates with Psalm 92, which bears the superscription, "A Song for the Sabbath Day" (see PSALMS, DAILY). Like the traditional ritual, the Conservative, Reconstructionist, and Reform prayer books make frequent use of *Psalms*.

• Joseph H. Hertz, ed., *The Authorized Daily Prayer Book* (New York, 1948), pp. xxi–xiii. Abraham E. Millgram, *Jewish Worship* (Philadelphia, 1971), pp. 59–63.

—A. STANLEY DREYFUS

PSALMS, BOOK OF, the first book of the Hagiographa, called in Hebrew *Tehillim* (Songs of Praise). The name *Tehillim* is first attested in the *Psalms Scroll* from Qumran (11QPs), in which David is said to have written *Tehillim*. The *Book of Psalms* is a collection of religious poetry in which an individual addresses God and expresses faith in God or longing for nearness to God. God is conceived as a personal God, whose ears are attuned to human needs. God executes justice and protects the weak, the poor, and the oppressed.

The *Book of Psalms* includes one hundred fifty chapters. The Septuagint contains, in addition to the canonical psalms, Psalm 151, not found in the Masoretic Text but known from Qumran 11QPs. This apocryphal psalm tells, in autobiographical terms, of David's youth and election to the kingship. The *Book of Psalms* is divided into five "books," comprising chapters 1–41; chapters 42–72; chapters 73–89; chapters 90–106; and chapters 107–150. Each of the first four books concludes with a doxology, such as "Blessed be the Lord, the God of Israel, from everlasting and to everlasting. Amen and amen" (*Ps.* 41.14; cf. *Ps.* 72.18–19, 89.53, 106.47–48). The psalm concluding the fifth book, Psalm 150, serves as the conclusion of the entire *Book of Psalms*. It appears that the first three "books" were originally separate collections. The division of the last collection into the fourth and fifth "books" by means of a doxology is artificial and was intended to bring about a five-part division of the *Book of Psalms*, analogous to the five books of Moses. The rabbinic sages commented on this analogy: "Moses gave the five books of law to Israel and David gave the five books of Psalms to Israel" (*Midrash Shoḥer Tov* 1.2).

This attribution to David of the authorship of the work is also mentioned in Qumran 11QFs, which states that David composed four thousand fifty psalms. The origin of this tradition is found in the Bible itself, which presents David as a musician and as an inventor of musical instruments (*Am.* 6.5). He is called "the sweet psalmist of Israel" (*2 Sm.* 23.1); the *Book of Chronicles* even represents him as the founder of the cultic singing in the Temple (*2 Chr.* 23.18). These traditions concur with the appearance of David's name in the titles of seventy-three individual psalms. Thirteen of these make the occasion of their composition a particular event in David's life (Psalm 3, 7, 18, 34, 51, 54, 56, 57, 59, 60, 63, 142). The Hebrew title *le-David* is problematic, however, in regard to the original meaning of the preposition *le*, but already in ancient times it was understood to refer to David's authorship of the psalms. The title of Psalm 18 is expounded in the parallel psalm in *2 Samuel* 22: "And David spoke unto the Lord the words of this song." Also, in similar psalm titles it seems that the preposition indicates the psalm's author: "of the sons of Korah" (Psalm 42 et al.), "of Asaph" (Psalm 50 et al.), "of Solomon" (Psalm 72), "of Heman the Ezrahite" (Psalm 88), "of Ethan the Ezrahite" (Psalm 89), and "of Moses" (Psalm 90). The colophon of the second book, "The prayers of David the son of Jesse are ended" (*Ps.* 72.20) also points to David's authorship.

It is difficult to date *Psalms*. The content of some (Psalm 126, 137), or their language (many of the psalms of the fourth and fifth book), testifies to the postexilic period. Nevertheless, many psalms were clearly composed already in the monarchic period (for example, Psalm 2, 24, 45, 74, 110). The *Book of Psalms* in its present form is the result of a long period of development, beginning with the composition of the individual psalms, continuing with the compilation of small collections, which later crystallized into larger compilations, and finally were collected into one book. The most ancient collection is Psalm 3 through Psalm 41 (Psalm 1 and Psalm 2 function as a general introduction to the *Book of Psalms*). All the psalms in this group are attributed to David, except for Psalm 10, which may have originally been the continuation of Psalm 9, and Psalm 33, a late psalm added to the collection. The second book is comprised of psalms attributed to various authors. The recurrence in this book of several psalms from the first (Psalm 53 = Psalm 14; Psalm 70 = Psalm 14 through Psalm 18) testifies to the independent existence of the first two books. The concluding comment, "The prayers of David the son of Jesse are ended" (*Ps.* 72.20), derives from the pen of someone unaware of the fact that certain psalms are attributed to other authors in the second book and that eighteen psalms are attributed to David in the fourth and fifth books. The second and third books (Psalm 42 through Psalm 83) contain what is known as the Elohistic psalms. These psalms are characterized by their clear preference for the divine name "Elohim" over "Yahveh." In the second and third books, eleven psalms are attributed to the Levitical family of psalmists, the sons of Korah, and twelve are attributed to Asaph. The fourth and fifth books have common characteristics that distinguish them from the rest of the psalmic books: most of the psalms here are hymns to nature, and in form, they are the only books containing the exclamation "Hallelujah." These last two books contain traces of several smaller collections such as coronation psalms (Psalm 93 and Psalm 95 through Psalm 100) and the songs of ascent (Psalm 120 through Psalm 134).

Three main types of psalms can be distinguished in the *Book of Psalms*: hymns, songs of God's greatness in nature and in history; complaints, in which the individual or the congregation addresses God and asks for help (cure for illness, deliverance from enemies, victory in war, end of famine or other misfortunes), complaining, rhetorically, against God's anger and typically revealing an absolute faith in God's salvation; and songs of gratitude, which are mostly of an individual nature and contain an exclamation of God's praises out of gratitude for his mercy and answering of the supplicant's prayers. There exist also several secondary types of psalms, such as praises of Zion, royal psalms, and sapiental (wisdom) psalms. Thirteen psalms are characterized as historical, because they contain allusions to historical events mentioned in various places in the Bible: the patriarchs, the Exodus, the parting of the Sea of Reeds, the wandering in the wilderness, the leadership of Moses and Aaron, the conquest, and the period of the judges (Psalm 44, 77, 78, 80, 81, 83, 95, 99, 105, 106, 114, 135, 146). In these psalms, the mention of past history is intended to serve as testimony of God's faithfulness to his people.

Many psalms were used liturgically in the Temple service including a psalm for each day of the week (*Tam.* 7.4; see PSALMS, DAILY). The songs of ascent (see DEGREES, SONG OF) may have been recited while going up into the Temple compound or as part of a Levitical musical rendition on steps inside the Temple (*Suk.* 5.4). The meaning of the heading of some of the psalms is uncertain and may contain musical instructions. By Second Temple times, the book was used in the synagogue where it has continued to form an important part of the *liturgy. The *prayer book contains seventy complete psalms and numerous other excerpts. These include the *Hallel, the daily psalms, the *Pesuqei de-Zimra', and the *Qabbalat Shabbat. In many Jewish communities, a *ḥevrat tehillim* (psalms society) was formed for daily recitation of psalms. Through Christianity, the psalms have had a profound influence on Western culture.

• Yitshak Avishur, *Studies in Hebrew and Ugaritic Psalms* (Jerusalem, 1994). Hermann Gunkel, *The Psalms: A Form-Critical Introduction* (Philadelphia, 1967). Avi Hurvitz, "Wisdom Vocabulary in the Hebrew Psalter: A Contribution to the Study of 'Wisdom Psalms,'" *Vetus Testamentum* 38 (1988): 41–51. Hans-Joachim Kraus, *Psalms: A Continental Commentary*, 2 vols. Minneapolis, 1988–1989). Sigmund Mowinckel, *The Psalms in Israel's Worship*, translated by D. R. Ap-Thomas, 2 vols. (New York, 1962). James A. Sanders, *The Psalms Scroll of Qumran Cave 11 (11QPs)* (Oxford, 1965). Matitiahu Tsevat, *A Study of the Language of the Biblical Psalms* (Philadelphia, 1955). Arthur Weiser, *The Psalms: A Commentary*, Old Testament Library (Philadelphia, 1962). Claus Westermann, *The Praise of God in the Psalms* (Richmond, 1965).

—LEA MAZOR

PSALMS, DAILY, psalms recited at the conclusion of *Shaḥarit, a different one on each day of the week (Sunday—Psalm 24; Monday—48; Tuesday—82; Wednesday—94.1–95.3; Thursday—81; Friday—93; Saturday—92). The same psalms were recited by Levites in the Temple service after the daily sacrifice (*Tam.* 7.4), and the custom was continued following the destruction of the Temple (*Soferim* 18.4). The Talmud finds a connection between the contents of the seven psalms and the seven days of Creation (*R. ha-Sh.* 31a).

• Jacob Mann, *The Bible as Read and Preached in the Old Synagogue: A Study in the Cycles of the Readings from Torah and Prophets, as well as from Psalms, and in the Structure of the Midrashic Homilies* (Cincinnati, 1940).

PSALMS, MIDRASH. See SHOḤER TOV.

PSALMS OF SOLOMON, pseudepigraphous collection of eighteen psalms attributed to King Solomon, extant in Greek and Syriac. Since the psalms refer to the Hasmonean dynasty (see HASMONEANS), to Pompey's conquest of Jerusalem in 63 BCE and the ensuing desecration of the Temple, and to Pompey's death in Egypt in 48 BCE, they probably were composed in the second half of the first century BCE. Originally written in Hebrew, possibly in Jerusalem, the *Psalms of Solomon* stress the unbridgeable gap between the righteous and the impious, call on God to save his righteous servants, and express longing for the day when God will send the Messiah, Son of David, "to purge Jerusalem of gentiles," gather all the Jews, and raise them high above all the other nations. Certain elements of the psalms' piety as well as their rejection of the Hasmoneans have often led scholars to assume a Pharisaic (see PHARISEES) origin for this work, a hypothesis that is plausible but far from certain.

• George W. E. Nickelsburg, *Jewish Literature between the Bible and the Mishnah* (Philadelphia, 1981), pp. 203–212. Robert B. Wright, "Psalms of Solomon," in *The Old Testament Pseudepigrapha*, edited by James H. Charlesworth, vol. 2 (Garden City, N.Y., 1985), pp. 639–670.

—GIDEON BOHAK

PSEUDEPIGRAPHA. See APOCRYPHA AND PSEUDEPIGRAPHA.

PSEUDO-JONATHAN, TARGUM, Aramaic translation of the Prophets that frequently paraphrases the text of the Bible and adds homiletical interpretations. The Talmud (*Meg.* 3a) attributes the *targum* to Yonatan ben 'Uzzi'el, "from the mouths of Haggai, Zechariah, and Malachi," and says that he also intended to translate the Hagiographa but was prevented from doing so by a heavenly voice. Yonatan was a pupil of *Hillel (*B. B.* 134a); nothing else is known about him. Modern scholars—on stylistic and other grounds—doubt that Yonatan composed the *targum*, which is therefore named the Targum Pseudo-Jonathan. Its abbreviated name, Taf-Yud (Targum Yerushalmi), has been incorrectly taken to mean Targum Jonathan. A *targum* of the Pentateuch was also erroneously attributed to Yonatan ben 'Uzzi'el.

• Gerard J. Kuiper, *The Pseudo-Jonathan Targum and Its Relationship to Targum Onkelos* (Rome, 1972).

PSEUDO-MESSIAHS. See MESSIAH.

PSEUDO-PHILO'S BIBLICAL ANTIQUITIES, a Latin work that relates the history of the Jewish people from Adam to David and combines biblical scenes with numerous legendary expansions. The work, translated from a lost Greek text, which probably was translated from a lost Hebrew original, was most likely written in the first century CE, perhaps in Erets Yisra'el, but its author remains unknown. In the manuscripts it is erroneously attributed to *Philo, hence its name.

• Daniel J. Harrington, "Pseudo-Philo," in *The Old Testament Pseudepigrapha*, edited by James H. Charlesworth (Garden City, N.Y., 1985), vol. 2, pp. 297–377. Frederick J. Murphy, *Pseudo-Philo: Rewriting the Bible* (New York, 1993).

—GIDEON BOHAK

PUBERTY. See ADULT.

PUMBEDITA, city in northern Babylonia on the Euphrates River that was the home of an important *academy rivaled only by that of *Sura. The Pumbedita academy was founded by *Yehudah bar Yeḥezqe'l, pupil of *Shemu'el (contemporary of *Rav, the founder of Sura), in approximately 260 CE. The academy continued the traditions of *Nehardea, and the names Nehardea and Pumbedita became virtually synonymous. Yehudah bar Yeḥezqe'l was succeeded by *Rabbah bar Naḥmani, *Yosef ben Ḥiyya', *Abbayei, and *Rava', names that appear throughout the Talmud Bavli and bear witness to the enormous part played by Pumbedita in the formulation of this work. With the death of Rava' in 353, decline set in, and many rabbis from Pumbedita, such as *Papa', founded academies in other cities of Babylonia. From the time of *Ashi, Pumbedita took second place to Sura. In the geonic period, Pumbedita supplied several heads for the academy of Sura, of whom the most famous and influential was *Yehuda'i ben Naḥman Ga'on. Toward the end of the ninth century, the academy at Pumbedita was relocated to Baghdad, but it retained its traditional title. It regained its dominant position in the late tenth and early eleventh centuries, under *Sherira' ben Ḥanina' Ga'on and *Ha'i Ga'on, and closed finally a short time after the latter's death in 1038.

• Morduch Judelowitz, *Ḥayyei ha-Yehudim bi-Zeman ha-Talmud: 'Ir Pumbedita' bi-Yemei ha-'Amora'im* (1939; Jerusalem, 1971). Morduch Judelowitz, *Yeshivat Pumbedita' bi-Yemei ha-'Amora'im* (Tel Aviv, 1935). Jacob Neusner, *A History of the Jews in Babylonia* (Leiden, 1969). Aharon

Oppenheimer, *Babylonia Judaica in the Talmudic Period* (Weisbaden, 1983).
—ROBERT BRODY

PUNCTUATION. See MASORAH; NAQQEDANIM; VOCALIZATION.

PUNISHMENT. Biblical and rabbinic law provide for the following types of punishment: death by stoning, burning, decapitation, or strangulation (see CAPITAL PUNISHMENT); excision (Heb. *karet*), which refers to premature death, according to some, or childlessness (cf. *Lv*. 20.20) according to others; *divine punishment; *banishment; corporal punishment, including *makkat mardut* (*flogging); *fines; servitude (see SLAVERY); *imprisonment; *excommunication (*ḥerem*); or "death at the hand of the zealot" (for example, the death of Zimri at the hands of Phinehas; see *Nm*. 25.6–8 and *San*. 9.6). Capital punishment is described in the Bible as a deterrent ("All Israel shall hear and fear and shall do no more any such wickedness in your midst," *Dt*. 13.12), as a means of rooting out evil elements from the nation (*Dt*. 17.7), and as a means of expiation for wrongdoing (*Nm*. 35.31–33). *Homicide is considered a crime against the sanctity of the land, and "no expiation can be made . . . for the blood shed therein but by the blood of him that sheds it." In practice, capital punishment was discontinued some time before the destruction of the Second Temple. Corporal punishment (derived from *Dt*. 25.1–3) is meted out for transgression of biblical prohibitions. Of 365 biblical prohibitions, 207 are punishable by flogging. Property damage is punishable only by the imposition of a fine, as is personal injury. However, if a male thief is unable to make restitution, he is sold to the person from whom he stole and must work off the value of the stolen property (*Ex*. 22.2). A woman may not be sold into servitude for her theft. A minor is not liable for any punishment. Many of the detailed Talmudic discussions about these subjects date from a period when certain forms of punishment were no longer administered and, therefore, do not necessarily reflect earlier or actual practice. On the other hand, Jewish courts (see BEIT DIN) enjoyed a measure of autonomy throughout the Middle Ages, including the power to impose fines, corporal punishment, and in rare instances death sentences (notably for *denunciation). Already the Talmud had conceded to the courts the power to "administer corporal or other punishment not in accord with biblical law" (*Yev*. 90b) when circumstances warranted it (see TAQQANAH), for example, in the absence of ordained rabbis (see ORDINATION). In modern times, rabbinic courts no longer administer punishment; even excommunication is rare. In Israel the rabbinic courts can refer those who defy its decisions to the civil courts (for example, husbands who refuse to grant a divorce to their wives when ordered by a rabbinic court have been sent to prison by the civil court).

• Simḥah Assaf, *Ha-ʿOnshin Aḥarei Ḥatimat ha-Talmud* (Jerusalem, 1922). Jacob Bazak, *Ha-ʿAnishah ha-Pelilit* (Jerusalem, 1981). Mordechai Frishtik, *ʿAnishah ve-Shiqqum bi-Yahadut* (Jerusalem, 1986). Avraham Mosheh Hevroni, *Mass'at Mosheh* (Jerusalem, 1980–1981). Naftali Hoffner, *Our Faith and Strength* (Spring Valley, N.Y., 1994).

PURIFICATION. See ABLUTION; IMPURITY.

PURIFICATION OFFERING (Heb. *ḥatta't*), one of the sacrifices that figures prominently in the sacrificial system. Because its name is connected with *ḥet'* (sin), it has often been mistakenly translated as sin offering—especially since it was prescribed for inadvertent sinners who upon realizing their guilt desired to make *atonement (*Lv*. 4). In fact, however, its function is purification (Heb. *ḥitte'* [to purge, purify]). It is required not only of those guilty of sin but also of those who have been cleansed of major physical impurities (childbirth, *Lv*. 12; leprosy, *Lv*. 14; abnormal genital flux, *Lv*. 15) and even those who have allowed a minor impurity, such as contact with a corpse, to go uncleansed (*Lv*. 5.2ff.). The purification offering does not cleanse the person: the sinner himself is cleansed by remorse and repentance, and the impure are cleansed by bathing and laundering their garments. The function of the purification offering is to decontaminate the Temple and the sacred objects therein—which are said to have become contaminated by the transgressions and impurities of Israel—thus ensuring the continued presence of God in his earthly abode. The offering was therefore required not only in specific cases of impurity or transgression but also on a regular basis, as part of the regimen of public sacrifice (in particular, on Ro'sh Ḥodesh and during festivals), and on special occasions as well. It was the central ritual of *Yom Kippur. The essence of the purification offering was the sprinkling of its blood—the agent of purification—on the altar (the inner altar, in the case of severe transgressions; the outer altar in normal circumstances) or on Yom Kippur in the Holy of Holies itself. In this basic feature, the purification offering resembles temple cleansing rituals practiced by ancient Israel's neighbors.

• N. Kiuchi, *The Purification Offering in the Priestly Literature: Its Meaning and Function*, Journal for the Study of the Old Testament, Supplement Series 56 (Sheffield, Eng., 1987), pp. 21–66. Alfred Marx, "Sacrifice pur les péchés ou rites de passage? Quelques réflexions sur la fonction du *ḥatta't*," *Revue biblique* 96 (1989): 27–48. Jacob Milgrom, *Leviticus 1–16*, The Anchor Bible, vol. 3 (Garden City, N.Y., 1991), pp. 253–292. Baruch J. Schwartz, "The Bearing of Sin in the Priestly Literature," in *Pomegranates and Golden Bells: Studies in Biblical, Jewish, and Near Eastern Ritual, Law, and Literature in Honor of Jacob Milgrom*, edited by David P. Wright et al. (Winona Lake, Ind., 1995), pp. 3–21.
—BARUCH J. SCHWARTZ

PURIM (פּוּרִים, lots), festival commemorating the deliverance of the Jews of the Persian empire from extermination. The story of Purim is told in the biblical *Book of *Esther*. *Haman, chief minister of *Ahasuerus, plotted to destroy the Jews of the empire. With the king's consent, Haman fixed the date of their doom by lot as 13 Adar. Esther (Hadassah), the king's Jewish wife, encouraged by her cousin *Mordecai, courageously interceded with Ahasuerus; as a result, the king authorized the Jews to defend themselves, and on the appointed day they routed their enemies while Haman himself was hanged. On the next day, the Jews celebrated their victory and called the day Purim, an allusion to the lots Haman had drawn. To commemorate this event, 14 Adar is marked with festivities and rejoicing. In Shushan (Susa), capital of the Persian empire, fighting occurred on 14 Adar as well, and the victory there was celebrated only on 15 Adar. Cities that had already been walled at the time of Joshua (e.g., Jerusalem) observe Purim on that date (Shushan Purim). Ahasuerus is identified with Xerxes I, who ruled Persia from 486 to 465. The first record of the observance of Purim dates from the Hasmonean period.

Many laws and customs as well as a rich folklore are associated with Purim. The regulations for the celebration of Purim are discussed in the tractate *Megillah*. As a minor festival, it is not a day on which refraining from work is mandatory. The most important ceremony is the reading of the *Book of Esther* from a handwritten parchment scroll. Both men and women are obliged to hear the reading of the Megillah (Scroll); children too should hear the story. The Megillah is read both at night and in the morning. Before the reading, three special blessings are pronounced. It is customary to make a din with noisemakers, called **gragers*, at every mention of the name of Haman. ʿAl ha-Nissim is recited in the ʿAmidah and in the Birkat ha-Mazon. The Pentateuchal reading during Shaḥarit recounts the attack of *Amalek (from whom Haman is said to be descended) on the Jews. One is required to send gifts (*mishloaḥ manot*) to friends (usually two kinds of sweetmeats), and to the poor (*mattanot la-'evyonim*) in the form of food or money. An important feature of the celebration is the Purim banquet (*seʿudah*), when inebriation is encouraged. In general a certain amount of levity and popular amusement was permitted on Purim, and masquerades and Purim plays (*Purim-shpil*) became a widespread feature of the celebration in medieval times (possibly under the influence of the Christian carnival). In some European Talmudic academies it was customary to elect one of the students as rabbi for a day (Purim rabbi). In the State of Israel, Purim is a carnival period, especially for children, and the occasion for the *ʿ*adlayada*ʿ procession. In leap years, Purim is observed in the second month of Adar. See also ESTHER, FAST OF; PURIM QATAN; PURIMS, LOCAL.

• Theodor Gaster, *Purim and Hanukkah: In Custom and Tradition* (New York, 1950). Avie Gold, *Purim: Its Observance and Significance* (Brooklyn, N.Y., 1991). Philip Goodman, ed., *The Purim Anthology* (Philadelphia, 1988). Irving Greenberg, *The Jewish Way* (New York, 1993), pp. 224–257.

PURIM QATAN (פּוּרִים קָטָן; minor Purim), the designation during a leap year of the fourteenth (or fifteenth) day of the first month of Adar. In a leap year, there are two months of *Adar, in which case the festival of Purim is celebrated during the second of them, on 14 (or 15) Adar. The corresponding days of the first Adar, Purim Qatan, are not marked by any celebration apart from the fact that supplicatory prayers (*Taḥanun) are omitted from the morning and afternoon services, and fasting and funeral eulogies are forbidden.

• Philip Goodman, ed., *The Purim Anthology* (Philadelphia, 1988).

PURIMS, LOCAL, provincial festivals commemorating a signal deliverance from danger. The custom of celebrating the anniversary of such deliverance—analogous to the festival of *Purim—developed both among individual families and whole communities. The forms of the celebration were often patterned on the original Purim: the particular event would be recorded in a **megillah*, special prayers of thanksgiving recited, a banquet held, and the day observed as a holiday. Examples of local Purims are the Purim of Narbonne (29 Adar, instituted in 1236), of Cairo (28 Adar, instituted in 1524), of Frankfurt am Main (20 Adar, instituted in 1616), and of Leghorn (22 Shevat, instituted in 1743). An example of a familial Purim is that observed by the family of Yom Tov Lipmann *Heller to commemorate his release from prison in Vienna on 1 Adar 1629.

PURIM-SHPIL. See PURIM.

PURITY, RITUAL. See IMPURITY.

PUSHKA. See QUPPAH.

Q

QABBALAH. See KABBALAH.

QABBALAT SHABBAT (קַבָּלַת שַׁבָּת; Reception of the Sabbath), service preceding Maʿariv on Friday nights, which developed in late-sixteenth-century kabbalistic circles in Safed. It is now included, though to varying degrees, in all modern rites. It consists mainly of a selection of psalms (in the Ashkenazi rite, Psalms 95–99; among Sephardim, Psalm 29) and the *piyyut* *Lekhah Dodi. Qabbalat Shabbat became one of the most popular parts of the liturgy.

• Ismar Elbogen, *Jewish Liturgy: A Comprehensive History*, translated by Raymond P. Scheindlin (Philadelphia, 1993), pp. 91–95, 170–176, 292–294. Moshe Hallamisch, "The Influence of the Kabbalah on Jewish Liturgy," in *Prière, mystique et judaisme*, edited by Roland Goetschel (Paris, 1987), pp. 121–131. Elie Munk, *The World of Prayer*, vol. 2 (New York, 1963), pp. 1–20.

—PETER LENHARDT

QADDISH (Aram.; קַדִּישׁ; Sanctification; cognate with Heb. *Qiddush and *Qedushah), Aramaic prayer praising God, recited at the conclusion of each principal section of every service. It was originally not part of the fixed liturgy and, despite the fact that it has become best known as a mourner's recitation, was unrelated to mourning. The Qaddish was an expression of praise to God recited by the preacher at the close of his discourse or after the study of *aggadah*. Its central feature was the congregational response: "May His great name be praised for all eternity" (cf. *Dan*. 2.20 and *Ps*. 113.2). There is no clear evidence as to when the Qaddish was composed. It probably achieved something like its present form by the eighth or ninth century, and there is evidence that it was one of several prayers common in the first or second century. A Hebrew version may have existed (cf. *Ber*. 3a; *Sifrei* to *Dt*. 306). As the Qaddish passed from the school to the synagogue and became part of the liturgy, its text was expanded.

There are five forms of Qaddish: the Short, or Half, Qaddish (Ḥatsi Qaddish), recited by the reader before or after certain sections of the service; the Full Qaddish (Qaddish Shalem), recited at the end of the main part of the service and containing the additional sentence, "May the prayers and entreaties of the whole House of Israel be accepted by its Father in heaven"; the Mourner's Qaddish (Qaddish Yatom); the Rabbinical Qaddish (Qaddish de-Rabbanan or Qaddish Titqabbel), recited after the study of rabbinical literature or after a sermon; and the Qaddish of Renewal, or the Great Qaddish (Ha-Qaddish ha-Gadol), used at the conclusion of the study of a Talmudic tractate and at funerals, where it is recited at the graveside immediately after the burial. In its opening section, the messianic prayer is elaborated, and specific requests for the revival of the dead, the rebuilding of the Temple, and so forth are added. According to Maimonides, this Qaddish should be recited after the study of *aggadah*, a practice followed by some Eastern communities (see ʿADOT HA-MIZRAḤ).

Qaddish is known as a mourner's prayer from an eighth-century Palestinian source, but its recitation became accepted practice only several centuries later. Its appeal is due to its exhortation to sanctify God's name and glorify his sovereign kingdom, and its expression of hope for the speedy advent of the Messiah. It also conveys the idea of the necessity to accept God's judgment though his ways may be inscrutable. Originally, the mourner would recite the Qaddish during the course of the liturgy. Soon, however, it became customary to place the Mourner's Qaddish at the end of the service. The practice of having it recited by the bereaved son did not gain general acceptance until the High Middle Ages, and its recitation on the *yortsayt* dates from about the fifteenth century. According to tradition, the punishment of sinners in *Geihinnom lasts for a full year; so as not to make it appear that the deceased was wicked, Qaddish is recited for eleven months and one day only (although Reform Jews say it for a whole year). When there is no son to recite the Qaddish, it may be said by any adult male member of the immediate family or any male Jew who volunteers. The Qaddish can only be recited when a *minyan* is present. In Conservative, Reconstructionist, Reform, and in a limited number of Orthodox services, it is the practice for female as well as male kin to recite the Qaddish, and it is often recited in unison by the whole congregation.

There are minor differences in wording in various rites. In German liberal congregations, a sentence was added referring to the dead who have departed this world: "For Israel and for the righteous and for all who have departed this world in accord with the will of God, may there be great peace, a good portion in the life of the world to come, and grace and mercy from the Lord of Heaven and earth. And say Amen." The sentence also appears in the Sephardi liturgy in the Hashkavah prayer (see ASHKAVAH) for the dead but not in the Qaddish. It was not accepted in England, but it was included in North American Reform liturgies (*Union Prayer Book*); in fact, this was the only form of Qaddish found in the *Union Prayer Book*. However, in *Gates of Prayer*, the new Reform prayer book, the specific reference to the departed has been deleted and the text as found in the traditional *siddur* has been restored, as well as the Ḥatsi Qaddish in various places.

• Ismar Elbogen, *Jewish Liturgy: A Comprehensive History*, translated by Raymond P. Scheindlin (Philadelphia, 1993). Reuven Hammer, *Entering Jewish Prayer: A Guide to Personal Devotion and the Worship Service* (New York, 1994). Lawrence A. Hoffman, *The Canonization of the Synagogue Service* (Notre Dame, 1979). Isaac Klein, *A Guide to Jewish Religious Practice* (New York, 1992). Abraham Millgram, *Jewish Worship* (Philadelphia, 1971). Jakob Petuchowski, "The Liturgy of the Synagogue: History, Structure, and Contents" in *Approaches to Ancient Judaism*, vol. 4, *Studies in Liturgy, Exegesis, and Talmudic Narrative*, edited by William Scott Green (Chico, Calif., 1983). Stefan C. Reif, *Judaism and Hebrew Prayer* (Cambridge, 1993).

—PETER KNOBEL

QAHAL. See COMMUNITY.

QALONIMOS. See KALONIMOS.

QANAH, SEFER HA-. See SEFER HA-QANAH.

QARA, YOSEF. See KARA, YOSEF.

QARAITES. See KARAITES.

QARO, YOSEF. See KARO, YOSEF.

QEDESHAH (קְדֵשָׁה; she who is set apart [for sexual services]), a prostitute. The semantic affinity between the term *qedeshah* and the adjective *qadosh* (holy) led scholars to assume until recently that the *qedeshah* functioned as a sacred harlot in temple fertility cults. However, the latest research indicates that the evidence for the *qedeshah*'s sexual role in the cult, both within biblical Israel and outside of it, is extremely tenuous. Thus, the biblical references to the *qedeshah* are best understood as being synonymous with *zonah* (prostitute). Such women offered their services either on the highway (*Gn.* 38.15, 21–22) or in the vicinity of the temples, where they could attract a larger number of clients (*Hos.* 4.13–14). The practice was strongly condemned and outlawed as an abomination to the Lord, both in the Pentateuch and by the prophets (cf. *Dt.* 23.18). Reference is also made to male prostitutes (*qadesh*; cf. *1 Kgs.* 15.12).

• Mayer I. Gruber, "Hebrew *Qedesha* and Her Canaanite and Akkadian Cognates," *Ugarit-Forschungen* 18 (1986): 133–148. Edwin M. Yamauchi, "Cultic Prostitution: A Case Study in Cultural Diffusion," in *Orient and Occident: Essays Presented to Cyrus Gordon on the Occasion of His Sixty-fifth Birthday*, edited by Harry A. Hoffner, Alter Orient und Altes Testament, Bd. 22 (Kevelaer and Neukirchen-Vluyen, 1973), pp. 213–222.

—DAVID A. GLATT-GILAD

QEDUSHAH (קְדֻשָּׁה; Sanctification). [*This entry discusses the Qedushah prayers; for a discussion of holiness, see* HOLINESS.] Qedushah is the name given to prayers describing the sanctification of God by the angels in heaven and its imitation on earth. The Qedushah prayers contain the verses *Isaiah* 6.3 ("Holy, Holy, Holy," etc.) and *Ezekiel* 3.12 ("Blessed be the glory of the Lord from his place"). One Qedushah, said while sitting (Qedushah de-Yeshivah or de-Yotser), is interwoven with the *Yotser benediction. Another is known as the Qedushah de-Sidra', contained in the prayer *U-Va' le-Tsiyyon. The main Qedushah (Qedushah de-ʿAmidah) forms part of the third benediction of the ʿAmidah when recited aloud by the reader; the congregational responses are more recent than the prayer and probably originated in the geonic period. It opens by expressing Israel's readiness "to sanctify his name in the world, as the angels sanctify it in the heavens above." In the enlarged form of the Qedushah (the Qedushah Rabbah, used in Musaf), Israel, too, joins the angelic choir by professing "Hear, O Israel," and is answered by God himself, who proclaims "I am the Lord, your God." The Qedushah is of early date and its introduction is usually attributed to the Yordei Merkavah (see MAʿASEH MERKAVAH), a group largely responsible for the creation of the *Heikhalot literature, which seems in its earliest form to date from the tannaitic period. The Talmud ascribes the composition of the Qedushah to the Men of the Keneset ha-Gedolah (*Ber.* 33a). It belongs to the most solemn and exalted portions of the service. The Qedushah as part of the ʿAmidah is recited only when a *minyan* is present. There are differences in formulation between the Ashkenazi and Sephardi versions. Reform prayer books remove all the references to angels. In geonic times, the Qedushah was not a generally accepted practice in the Palestinian rite, except on Sabbaths and festivals; but in the Babylonian rite it became part of the daily liturgy. Many piyyutic compositions elaborated the theme of the Qedushah; some are still in use on Ro'sh ha-Shanah and Yom Kippur. The Qedushah has remained a favorite for synagogue composers, who see it as a particularly apt place to achieve a sense of the transcendent. The basic part of the Qedushah (the Trisagion [Holy, Holy, Holy] and its preface) also became prominent in Christian liturgy.

• Ismar Elbogen, *Jewish Liturgy: A Comprehensive History*, translated by Raymond P. Scheindlin (Philadelphia, 1993). Reuven Hammer, *Entering Jewish Prayer: A Guide to Personal Devotion and the Worship Service* (New York, 1994). Abraham Millgram, *Jewish Worship* (Philadelphia, 1971). Jakob Petuchowski, "The Liturgy of the Synagogue: History, Structure, and Contents," in *Approaches to Ancient Judaism*, vol. 4, *Studies in Liturgy, Exegesis, and Talmudic Narrative*, edited by William Scott Green (Chico, Calif., 1983), pp. 1–64. Michael D. Swartz, *Mystical Prayer in Ancient Judaism: An Analysis of Maase Merkavah* (Tübingen, 1992).

—PETER KNOBEL

QEFITSAT HA-DEREKH (קְפִיצַת הַדֶּרֶךְ; path jumping), common motif in classical rabbinic literature and Jewish magical writings. In *Sanhedrin* 95a–b, a number of biblical figures, including Jacob and Abishai (King David's nephew), experienced a geological miracle in which the ground shrank, and they were instantaneously transported a great distance. In magical literature, beginning with *The Sword of Moses* and continuing in such medieval works as *Berit Menuḥah* and *Shoshan Yesod ʿOlam*, magical recipes are recorded for engineering path jumping. Common motifs include purification rites, acquiring a seven-knotted reed, donning a blindfold, and conjuring special angels (e.g., Kaftsiel [God Jumps]). Abraham Baer Gottlober, a nineteenth-century *maskil*, recounted that in his youth he transcribed a secret amulet and together with a friend accomplished path jumping; however, for many days afterward he was bedridden.

• G. Nigal, *Magic, Mysticism, and Hasidism* (Northvale, N.J., 1994), pp. 33–49. Mark Verman and S. Adler, "Path Jumping in the Jewish Tradition," *Jewish Studies Quarterly* 1:2 (1993–1994): 131–148. Ḥayyim ben Joseph Vital, "Ma'amar Pesiʿotav shel Avraham Avinu" in *Ketavim Ḥadashim* (Jerusalem, 1987–1988).

—MARK VERMAN

QEHILLAH. See COMMUNITY.

QELIPPOT (קְלִפּוֹת, husks or shells), a common name in the Kabbalah for the powers of evil. Following the spread of Lurianic Kabbalah in early modern times, the word was used for everything evil. The origin of the concept is to be found in a short text known as *Sod ha-'Egoz*, which describes a great nut, presented as a metaphor for the world of the holy chariots, surrounded by four *qelippot*: a great cloud, an erupting fire, a tempestuous wind, and a splendid light. The Ḥasidei Ashkenaz wrote several commentaries on this metaphor, and at the same time some Christian writers described Christ using the same images. Early kabbalists developed this concept, and gradually their dualistic conceptions transformed at least the first three *qelippot* into powers of evil, while the fourth, *nogah*, is regarded as an intermediate realm between good and evil. The Zohar and subsequent kabbalists continued to develop this metaphor into one of the central terms for the realm of evil in the Kabbalah.

• Gershom Gerhard Scholem, *Major Trends in Jewish Mysticism* (New York, 1941).

—JOSEPH DAN

QENAS. See FINES.

QERIʿAH. See RENDING OF CLOTHES.

QERI AND KETIV. See MASORAH.

QERI'AT HA-TORAH (קְרִיאַת הַתּוֹרָה; reading of the Torah), the public reading from the Torah, in the presence of a **minyan*, that constitutes part of the synagogue service on Sabbaths, festivals, Ro'sh Ḥodesh (the new moon), Ḥanukkah, Purim, and fast days, as well as on ordinary Mondays and Thursdays. The reading of the Torah takes place at the end of *Shaḥarit; on Sabbaths and fast days the Torah is also read during *Minḥah. Special handwritten parchment scrolls (see SEFER TORAH) must be used; those persons called up to "read" (*ʿaliyyah la-Torah*) recite a benediction (*Birkat ha-Torah) both before and after the reading. The handwritten text has no vowels, punctuation, or *accents and requires considerable skill to read. In most congregations (except the Yemenite), the one "called up" no longer reads the portion; instead, the entire text is chanted by an appointed reader. The number of persons to be called is fixed in accordance with the status of the day: on the morning of the Sabbath, at least seven people are called; on Yom Kippur, six; on festivals, five (all of the above apart from the **maftir*; see HAFTARAH); on Ro'sh Ḥodesh and *ḥol ha-moʿed*, four; on all other occasions, three. The Torah was read as part of the service as far back as Temple times (rabbinic tradition ascribes the institution of the Sabbath, festival, and new moon readings to Moses and the readings on Mondays, Thursdays, and during Sabbath Minḥah to Ezra; *Meg*. 31a; *B. Q*. 82a), but the portions to be read were not definitively marked out. On festivals, portions appropriate to the day were read (cf. *Meg*. 3–4); if too short, they were repeated several times.

On Sabbaths, it was usual to begin where the reading had been terminated the previous Sabbath, and a minimum of twenty-one verses had to be read—three for each person called; but there is no indication that even by the Mishnaic period a definite portion had been allocated to each Sabbath. Every verse was translated orally into Aramaic after it had been read in Hebrew (see TARGUM). In some countries of the Diaspora, the reading took place in the vernacular, such as Greek. Two cycles of the reading of the Torah emerged: a *triennial cycle in Erets Yisra'el, which divided the Torah into over 150 *sedarim*; and an annual cycle in Babylonia, based on a division of 54 *parashiyyot* (some of which are combined in years with less than fifty-four Sabbaths, none of which is also a festival). Eventually the Babylonian cycle prevailed and was adopted by all congregations in the Diaspora and even in Palestine. The annual reading concludes on *Simḥat Torah, whereupon the new cycle is begun. Each Sabbath is known by the name of its portion. For festivals, too, suitable portions were determined, and those are followed by an appropriate passage from *Numbers* 28–29 for the *maftir*. On Sabbath afternoons, Mondays, and Thursdays, the beginning of the *parashah* (portion) of the following Sabbath is read. The scroll is taken out of the ark for *qeri'at ha-Torah* and is then returned with great ceremony while the congregation stands and recites psalms and hymns. When a *kohen* is present, he must be called first, followed by a Levite; often the rabbi or some other distinguished person is called third. The *maftir* is considered a special honor. A boy celebrating his **bar mitsvah* (or a girl celebrating her **bat mitsvah* in a non-Orthodox congregation) is usually called for *maftir* and generally reads this portion himself (herself). Reform congregations generally read selected portions only; some Conservative congregations have reintroduced the ancient Palestinian triennial cycle. In many non-Orthodox congregations, women are now called up to the reading of the Torah. See also MI SHE-BERAKH.

• Ismar Elbogen, *Jewish Liturgy: A Comprehensive History*, translated by Raymond P. Scheindlin (Philadelphia, 1993). Maurice Gellis, *The Glory of Torah Reading* (Monsey, N.Y., 1983). Jacob Mann, *The Bible as Read and Preached in the Old Synagogue*, 2 vols. (Cincinnati, 1940). Samuel Rosenbaum, *A Guide to Torah Reading: A Manual for the Torah Reader* (New York, 1982). Matthew B. Schwartz, "Torah Reading in the Ancient Synagogues," Ph.D. dissertation, Wayne State University, 1975.

QERI'AT SHEMAʿ. See SHEMAʿ.

QERI'AT SHEMAʿ ʿAL HA-MITTAH (קְרִיאַת שְׁמַע עַל הַמִּטָּה; Reading of the *Shemaʿ in Bed), special night prayers (as distinct from *Maʿariv, the statutory evening prayer service), including a prayer for undisturbed repose, the first paragraph of the Shemaʿ, Psalm 91 and Psalm 3, and, in different rites, other verses and texts. The recitation of the Shemaʿ before sleeping is based on a saying of R. Yehoshuʿa ben Levi (*Ber*. 4b) that "all the demons of the night flee from the person who recites the Shemaʿ in bed." Some of the sections now included were added in medieval times. Young children recite a short version.

• Ismar Elbogen, *Jewish Liturgy: A Comprehensive History* (Philadelphia, 1993).

QEROVAH (קְרוֹבָה), a poetic embellishment (**piyyut*) of the *ʿAmidah, recited by the reader. The term is derived from the Aramaic word *qarova'* meaning "near," applied to the **sheliaḥ tsibbur*, who stands close to the ark. The earliest examples go back to Byzantine Erets Yisra'el of the sixth century; new composition in the genre had virtually ceased by the thirteenth century. The aim of the *qerovah* was to increase the praise of God and to connect the statutory prayer with appointed times in the Jewish calendar or community life. There are two major groups. One occurs prior to the *Qedushah in the third blessing of the Shaḥarit ʿAmidah, mainly on Sabbaths and holidays, and therefore called Qedushta'. The other occurs in the Musaf ʿAmidah, when, according to the rite of Erets Yisra'el, no Qedushah was recited; it was called Shiv'ata' or Shiv'ah (seven) because it had seven sections. *Yann'ai wrote a complete cycle of *qerovah* for the Sabbath, according to the cycle of Torah readings. El'azar *Kallir wrote for almost every festive occasion. His work is found in almost all European rites and influenced later authors.

• Ismar Elbogen, *Jewish Liturgy: A Comprehensive History*, translated by Raymond P. Scheindlin (Philadelphia, 1993). Maurice Gellis, *The Glory of Torah Reading* (Monsey, N.Y., 1983). Jacob Mann, *The Bible as Read and Preached in the Old Synagogue*, 2 vols. (Cincinnati, 1940). Samuel Rosenbaum, *A Guide to Torah Reading: A Manual for the Torah Reader* (New York, 1982). Matthew B. Schwartz, "Torah Reading in the Ancient Synagogues," Ph.D. dissertation, Wayne State University, 1975.

—PETER LENHARDT

QES (or *kahen* [priest]), title given to *Beta Israel religious leaders who replaced celibate monks. Among Beta Israel, the priesthood was not hereditary and could be entered by any male from a family whose lineage was not blemished by intermarriage or other faults. The *qes* filled a wide variety of roles: leading prayers; performing sacrifices; hearing confessions; officiating at circumcisions, weddings, and funerals; and mediating disputes. In exchange for these services, he received remuneration from community members. In each region, one priest was recognized as the high priest. Since the immigration of Ethiopian Jews to Israel, their *qessotch* have been denied official recognition.

• Steven H. Kaplan, *Les Falashas* (Turnhout, 1990), pp. 181–188. Kay Kaufman Shelemay, *Music, Ritual, and Falasha History* (East Lansing, Mich., 1986), pp. 78–88.

—STEVEN KAPLAN

QETSATSAH (קְצָצָה; cutting off), term used in the Talmud for a ceremony marking the severance of all connections with a family member who married beneath his rank or sold part of his ancestral estate. The main feature of the *qetsatsah* ceremony was the breaking of a barrel filled with fruit in the town square and a declaration to the effect that the renegade's children would not be allowed to marry into the family (*Ket*. 28b). *Qetsatsah* also served as a form of **qinyan* in early times (Y., *Qid*. 1.5).

• Menachem Elon, ed., *The Principles of Jewish Law* (Jerusalem, 1975), p. 208.

—DANIEL SINCLAIR

QEVER AVOT (קֶבֶר אָבוֹת; ancestral graves), a term relating to periodic visits to the burial place of parents or to the graves of sages and religious leaders. It is a widespread custom to visit the grave of a parent before *Ro'sh ha-Shanah (Isserles on *Oraḥ Ḥayyim* 581.4), from which the practice was extended to visiting the cemetery during the month of Elul. In some communities in America, rabbis organize a public memorial service in the cemetery, after which an individual goes to visit his or her own parents' graves. Sephardim visit a parent's grave after **shiv'ah*, **sheloshim*, and on the **yortsayt*. The custom among Ashkenazim is not to go to the cemetery after burial until *sheloshim*. In addition, the fast day of *Tish'ah be-'Av is regarded as an appropriate day to observe the practice of *qever avot* (*Oraḥ Ḥayyim* 579). One may not visit a cemetery on the Sabbath or festivals, or even on such minor days as *Ro'sh Ḥodesh and *Purim (except in the case of a funeral).

The term *qever avot* also applies to pilgrimages made by the faithful to the graves of the great and the righteous. Jewish folklore describes Caleb praying at the graves of the patriarchs in Hebron, pleading for their intervention to save him from the evil counsel of the other spies (*Sot*. 34b). Legend also tells how, after the destruction of the First Temple, the prophet Jeremiah went to the graves of the patriarchs and Moses to appeal for their help in pleading with God to save the Jewish people. Similar legends are recorded about the prophet Elijah, who visited the *qever avot* at the time that *Haman's plot to destroy the Jews of Persia was authorized by the king. Since the Middle Ages, it has been customary to pray at the graves of the pious in order to seek their intercession in times of distress. Visits to graves of holy sages were regarded as highly meritorious by the kabbalistic school of Yitsḥaq *Luria in Safed, who himself claimed to have identified numerous tombs of Talmudic rabbis in Galilee. In modern times the practice is still continued, particularly in Israel. The Tomb of *Rachel at the approach to Bethlehem is a popular place of pilgrimage on 11 Ḥeshvan, the traditional date of her death; the tomb of *Shim'on ha-Tsaddiq in Jerusalem is visited on *Lag ba-'Omer and 7 Sivan; and the tomb of *Shim'on bar Yoḥ'ai on Mount Meron is the site of mass pilgrimages on Lag ba-'Omer.

Ḥasidim (see HASIDISM) are particularly zealous in following the practice of *qever avot* (to which their opponents, the *Mitnaggedim, strongly objected). Both in Israel and in the United States, Ḥasidim visit the graves of their leaders, light candles, write petitions that they leave by the grave, and offer prayers for their leaders' intercession with God on their behalf. Bratslav Ḥasidim visit the grave of their rabbi *Naḥman of Bratslav in Uman in the Ukraine.

In Muslim lands, the custom of making pilgrimages to tombs connected with biblical figures or revered sages is widespread. Visitors pray at the tombs and light candles. See also PILGRIMAGE.

• Isaac Klein, *A Guide to Jewish Religious Practice* (New York, 1979). Jehiel Michael Tucatzinsky, *Gesher ha-Ḥayyim* (n.p., 1946).

—CHAIM PEARL

QIBBUTS GALUYYOT. See EXILES, INGATHERING OF THE.

QIDDUSH (קִדּוּשׁ; Sanctification), a ceremony and prayer proclaiming the holiness of the Sabbath or a festival as a memorial to Creation and to the Exodus from Egypt. The term is an abbreviation of the Talmudic expression *qiddush ha-yom* (more properly, *qedushat ha-yom* [sanctification of the day]). The Qiddush is recited on the Sabbath or festival eve over a cup of wine immediately before the meal. It is chanted by one person, usually the head of the house, while all present identify themselves with the recitation by answering *amen*. In some homes, it is recited (in unison or separately) by all present. The Talmud specifies that women are obligated to hear or recite the Qiddush (*Ber.* 20b). The reciter takes the cup into his right hand, preferably in the palm, enclosing the cup with his fingers, chants the Qiddush, drinks, and gives all present a sip of the wine. If no wine is available, the Qiddush may be recited over bread. For those who do not wish to consume alcohol, grape juice may be substituted. Even when wine is used, traditional usage holds that there should be on the table two whole loaves of *ḥallah* (covered by a cloth), which symbolize the double portion of manna gathered by the children of Israel each Friday during their forty years in the wilderness. The Qiddush is essentially a home ritual associated with the Sabbath or festival meal, but from early times it has been customary to recite it on these days in the synagogue, at the end of the evening prayer, for the benefit of travelers or the poor who would lodge and eat in the synagogue. When the latter custom fell into disuse, some rites abolished the chanting of the Qiddush in the house of worship, while others retained it as an act of public sanctification of the Sabbath. Scriptural warrant for the Qiddush ceremony is found by the rabbis in *Exodus* 20.8, "Remember the Sabbath day and keep it holy," which the Talmud interprets as meaning "Remember it over wine" (*Pes.* 106a). The Qiddush consists of two benedictions: one for the wine (or bread) and one for the Sabbath or festival. The rabbis of the Mishnah differed as to which should be recited first, but Hillel's view that the blessing over wine takes precedence prevailed. In the Qiddush for Friday evening it is customary to recite the account of the Sabbath of Creation (*Gn.* 2.1–3) before making the blessing. It was formerly omitted in Reform liturgies but has now been widely reintroduced, though generally without the references to the chosen people. On festivals (except for the last days of Pesaḥ), the *She-Heḥeyanu blessing is recited at the conclusion of the evening Qiddush. The Qiddush chanted after the morning service on Sabbaths or festival days is called Qedushah Rabbah (the Great Qiddush), as it may be recited over all kinds of drink and not necessarily wine. It contains no benediction apart from the one recited over wine (or other drink) and is preceded by appropriate Bible passages (on Sabbath, *Ex.* 20.8–11; on the Shalosh Regalim, *Lv.* 23.44; and on Ro'sh ha-Shanah, *Ps.* 81.4–5).

• Ismar Elbogen, *Jewish Liturgy: A Comprehensive History*, translated by Raymond P. Scheindlin (Philadelphia, 1993). Reuven Hammer, *Entering Jewish Prayer: A Guide to Personal Devotion and the Worship Service* (New York, 1994). Lawrence A. Hoffman, *The Canonization of the Synagogue Service* (Notre Dame, 1979). Isaac Klein, *A Guide to Jewish Religious Practice* (New York, 1992). Abraham Millgram, *Jewish Worship* (Philadelphia, 1971). Stefan C. Reif, *Judaism and Hebrew Prayer: New Perspectives on Jewish Liturgical History* (Cambridge, 1993).

—PETER KNOBEL

QIDDUSH HA-SHEM. See MARTYRDOM.

QIDDUSHIN (קִדּוּשִׁין; Betrothal), last tractate of Mishnah order Nashim, consisting of four chapters, with related material in the Tosefta' and both Talmuds. *Betrothal, called *qiddushin* (sanctification) in rabbinic sources, corresponds to the biblical term *erus* (e.g., *Dt.* 22.23) and constitutes the first of the two stages of marriage. Following *qiddushin*, the betrothed woman is consecrated to her husband, and adultery is strictly forbidden; however, she continues to live in her father's household and mutual marital rights do not commence until formalized by the *nissu'in*, which marks the entry of the bride into the home of her husband. Betrothal is formalized by an act of acquisition, which grants the husband exclusive conjugal rights, and betrothal is first among a list of forms of acquisition that formalize a spectrum of relationships ranging from marriage to property transfer to the consecration of holy objects. *Qiddushin* emphasizes the need for honesty and mutual understanding in the act of betrothal, as well as the central role of a stable family structure in ensuring the building of an enduring and sanctified society.

The Talmud Bavli tractate was translated into English by H. Freedman in the Soncino Talmud (London, 1936).

• Chanoch Albeck, ed., *Shishah Sidrei Mishnah, Seder Nashim* (Jerusalem, 1954). Philip Blackman, ed. and trans., *Mishnayoth*, vol. 2, *Order Nashim* (Gateshead, 1973). Pinhas Kehati, ed., *Mishnah: A New Translation with a Commentary, Seder Nashim*, vol. 3, *Gittin, Kiddushin* (Jerusalem, 1989). Hermann Leberecht Strack and Günter Stemberger, *Introduction to the Talmud and Midrash*, rev. and updat. ed., translated by Markus Bockmuehl (Minneapolis, 1992). —AVRAHAM WALFISH

QIDDUSH LEVANAH (קִדּוּשׁ לְבָנָה; Sanctification of the Moon), blessing recited during the period of the moon's waxing following *Ro'sh Ḥodesh (but not before three nights have elapsed). The regular reappearance of the new moon is regarded as one of those benefits for which praise and thanksgiving should be given to God. A Talmudic passage (*San.* 42a) and a *baraiyta'* (*Soferim* 20.1–2) contain the text of the relevant blessing together with the regulations. Differences in custom exist, but the most prevalent tradition is that the Qiddush Levanah is recited by a *minyan* in the synagogue courtyard on the Saturday night prior to the tenth day of the lunar month, providing the crescent is visible. Because of its joyous nature, the blessing is not recited in the month of Tishrei prior to Yom Kippur or in Av before Tish'ah be-'Av. The Talmud (*R. ha-Sh.* 25a) relates that R. *Yehudah ha-Nasi' instructed R. *Ḥiyya' to determine the date of the new moon and to say "David, king of Israel is alive and exists." This phrase, with its undertones of hope for the coming of the Messiah, has therefore been incorporated into the Qiddush Levanah prayers. The benediction (Birkat ha-Levanah) emphasizes renewal in nature, which is symbolic of Israel's renewal and redemption. In prayer books, the text of the ceremony was printed in large letters so that they could be read by moonlight, and large print became known as Qiddush Levanah letters. In some communities the text was affixed to the outer wall of the synagogue.

• Chaim U. Lipschitz, *Kiddush Levono: The Monthly Blessing of the Moon* (Brooklyn, N.Y., 1987).

QIMḤI FAMILY. See KIMḤI FAMILY.

QINAH (קִינָה; lament), elegy recited in biblical and Talmudic times upon the death of an individual (for example, David's *qinah* for Saul and Jonathan, *2 Sm.* 1.17ff.), or upon a national catastrophe (Jeremiah's lament upon the destruction of the First Temple and the deportation of Jews to Babylonia). The *Book of Lamentations* is referred to as *Qinot* in the Talmud (*B. B.* 14b). In geonic times, special **seliḥot* (i.e., prayers of a penitential character) were composed in Babylon for Tish'ah be-'Av, then a day devoted largely to penitence; these resembled the *qinot* of El'azar *Kallir, probably the first poet to use the term *qinot*, which was later applied specifically to the *piyyutim* for Tish'ah be-'Av. Many *qinot* about tragic historical events (for example, the massacres of whole Jewish communities during the Crusades, the persecutions in Spain in 1391, the Chmielnicki massacres of 1648, and the Baghdad pogrom of 1941) were composed by Ashkenazi and Sephardi poets, and some of them found a permanent place in the liturgy. All Yom Kippur rites incorporate the *qinot* on the *Ten Martyrs of the Hadrianic persecutions. The elegies on Zion by *Yehudah ha-Levi represent a special type of *qinah*, known as *Tsiyyoniyyot* after their first word *Tsiyyon* (Zion), which express yearning for Zion and the hope of redemption. Ashkenazi *qinot* were first published in Kraków in 1585; a scientific edition by Daniel Goldschmidt was published in 1968. The *qinot* of the Sephardi Jews and 'Adot ha-Mizraḥ appeared in *Seder Arba' Ta'aniyyot* (Venice, 1590), in the Yemenite prayer book (*Tiklal*), and elsewhere. In modern times, *qinot* have been written in memory of the Holocaust.

• E. Adler, G. Davidson et al., eds., *J. Schirmann's Bibliography of Studies in Hebrew Medieval Poetry 1948–1978* (Beersheba, 1989), pp. 333–338, in Hebrew. E. D. Goldschmidt, *Seder ha-Qinot le-Tish'ah be-'Av* (Jerusalem, 1972). Avraham M. Habermann, *Sefer Gezerot Ashkenaz ve-Tsarfat* (Jerusalem, 1971).

QINNIM (קִנִּים; Birds' Nests), last tractate, consisting of three chapters, in Mishnah order Qodashim; it has no parallel in the Tosefta' and no *gemara'* in either Talmud. Biblical law requires a sacrificial offering of a "nest," consisting of two pigeons or two turtledoves, as a purification offering after childbirth (*Lv.* 12.8) or as atonement by the poor for certain offenses (enumerated in *Lv.* 5) for which they cannot afford the more expensive sin offering (*Lv.* 5.11). *Qinnim* deals with intricate questions arising from cases, many of them highly theoretical, in which birds fly from nest to nest, creating confusion as to the identity and status of the birds residing in any given nest. Due to their complexity, the laws of *Qinnim* were considered a symbol of the highest level of Torah scholarship (*Avot* 3.23).

An English translation of the tractate by Herbert Danby is in *The Mishnah* (Oxford, 1933).

• Chanoch Albeck, ed., *Shishah Sidrei Mishnah, Seder Qodashim* (Jerusalem, 1956). Philip Blackman, ed. and trans., *Mishnayoth*, vol. 5, *Order Kodashim* (Gateshead, 1973). Hermann Leberecht Strack and Günter Stemberger, *Introduction to the Talmud and Midrash*, rev. and updat. ed., translated by Markus Bockmuehl (Minneapolis, 1992).

—AVRAHAM WALFISH

QINYAN. See ACQUISITION.

QIRQISANI, YAQUB (10th cent.), *Karaite scholar and theologian. Very little is known of his life other than that he lived in Iraq. He was familiar with all branches of rabbinic literature and thoroughly acquainted with contemporary Arabic philosophical and scientific writings, and he established personal contacts with scholars of various faiths. His guiding principle was the absolute priority of reason, rational investigation being the key to understanding revelation. The influence of Kalam can be discerned in his writings, as well as that of other contemporary philosophical trends. His two major works are *Kitab al-Anwar wa-al-Maraqib* (edited by Leon Nemoy [1939–1943]), a systematic, erudite, and detailed code of Karaite law, which also contains a valuable survey of Jewish sects from the Samaritans and Sadducees to his time, a treatise on legal theory, discussions of Christianity and Islam, as well as excursuses on various other nonlegal topics; and *Kitab al-Riyad wa-al-Ḥada'iq*, a commentary on the nonlegal sections of the Pentateuch (portions of the introduction on methods of biblical exegesis have been published, and much of the work is preserved in manuscript fragments). These works were completed by 937 or 938. His smaller works, most of which have not survived, include *Tafsir Be-Re'shit*, an extensive philosophical commentary on the story of creation; commentaries on *Job* and *Ecclesiastes*; a tract refuting Muḥammad's claim to prophecy; an essay on translation; and *Kitab al-Tawḥid*, on the principles of faith. His writing is characterized by moderation, and he frequently mentions varying opinions, quoting 'Anan ben David, Binyamin ben Mosheh Nahawendi, and Daniyye'l ben Mosheh al-Qumisi, as well as Rabbanite opponents such as Sa'adyah ben Yosef Ga'on and Yaqub ben Efrayim.

• Haggai Ben-Shammai, "Qirqisani on the Oneness of God," *Jewish Quarterly Review* 73 (1982): 105–111. Haggai Ben-Shammai, "Shitot ha-Masḥavah ha-Datit shel Abu Yusuf Ya'qub al-Qirqisani ve-Yefet ben 'Eli," Ph.D. dissertation, Hebrew University, 1977. Bruno Chiesa, "Dai 'Principii dell'Esegesi Biblica' di Qirqisani," *Jewish Quarterly Review* 73 (1982): 124–137. Bruno Chiesa and Wilfrid Lockwood, eds. and trans., *Ya'qub al-Qirqisani on Jewish Sects and Christianity* (Frankfurt am Main, 1984). Leon Nemoy, *Karaite Anthology: Excerpts from the Early Literature*, Yale Judaica Series 7 (New Haven, 1952), pp. 42–68.

—DAVID E. SKLARE

QODASHIM (קָדָשִׁים; Holy Things), fifth of the six orders of the Mishnah, dealing with sacrifice, ritual slaughter, and Temple procedure. In the Mishnah, Qodashim consists of eleven tractates: **Zevaḥim*, **Menaḥot*, **Ḥullin*, **Bekhorot*, **'Arakhin*, **Temurah*, **Keritot*, **Me'ilah*, **Tamid*, **Middot*, and **Qinnim*. Eight of these have related material in the Tosefta', and nine have *gemara'* in the Talmud Bavli, but none has *gemara'* in the Talmud Yerushalmi. In the late nineteenth century, an alleged Palestinian *gemara'* to Qodashim was discovered but subsequently proved to be a forgery. Much of the material in the Mishnah of Qodashim is believed by scholars to belong to the most ancient strata of Mishnaic redaction, dating back to late Second Temple times.

—AVRAHAM WALFISH

QOHELET. See ECCLESIASTES, BOOK OF.

QOHELET RABBAH. See ECCLESIASTES RABBAH.

QORBANOT (קָרְבָּנוֹת; sacrifices), the *sacrifices offered by the priests (*kohanim*) in the Temple of Jerusalem before its destruction in 70 CE. As a liturgical term, it refers to the second section of the *Shaḥarit (morning) service in the synagogue, in which, through appropriate biblical and rabbinic readings, the ancient rituals practiced in the Temple are reviewed. This is in accordance with a rabbinic teaching (*Ber.* 26b) that whoever studies the biblical and Talmudic passages governing the sacrificial cult is deemed to have actually brought the required offerings. Indeed, the hours fixed for the morning and afternoon services correspond to the time of the daily Temple sacrifices. Prayers enumerating the special sacrifices for Sabbaths and festivals are incorporated into the *Musaf (additional) service for these occasions, with the plea that God speedily restore the Temple so that the sacrifices ordained in the Torah can be reinstated. Reform Judaism has removed all references to the sacrificial cult from its prayer books. The Conservative prayer book has recast the prayers for the restoration of the sacrifices into a recapitulation of ancient practice and substitutes readings on Jewish ethics for the *qorbanot* section of the morning service.

• Ismar Elbogen, *Jewish Liturgy: A Comprehensive History*, translated by Raymond P. Scheindlin (Philadelphia, 1993), pp. 98f., 332. Abraham E. Millgram, *Jewish Worship* (Philadelphia, 1971), pp. 42ff., 51ff.

—A. STANLEY DREYFUS

QUERIDO, YAʿAQOV (c.1650–1690), a radical Shabbatean leader in his native Salonika. The son of R. Yosef Filosof, a respected rabbi and follower of *Shabbetai Tsevi, he became known as Querido (the beloved). His sister was married to Shabbetai Tsevi, and after his death in Albania in 1676 she returned to Salonika, joining her brother. In 1683 Querido, supported by his father, R. Shelomoh Florentin, and others, led a mass apostasy in Salonika. Together with the believers who had apostatized earlier under Shabbetai Tsevi's influence, they formed the nucleus of the *Dönmeh sect. Querido was given the Turkish name Abdullah Yacoub. Because of his despotic leadership several dissensions occurred within the sect. In 1688 he made a pilgrimage to Mecca and died soon after in Egypt. His followers, who were called Jacobites, attributed to him a divine character.

• Abraham Galante, *Nouveaux documents sur Sabbetai Sevi* (İstanbul, 1935), pp. 58–62. Gershom Gerhard Scholem, *The Messianic Idea in Judaism and Other Essays on Jewish Spirituality* (New York, 1971).

—NISSIM YOSHA

QULLA'. See Ḥumra'.

QUMISI, DANIYYE'L BEN MOSHEH AL- (c.840–900), *Karaite scholar. Born in the Persian province of Qumis, by 875 he was living in Jerusalem, where he became a leader of the *Avelei Tsiyyon. Qumisi was the first to formulate the classic Karaite ideology of biblicism. Qumisi opposed the study of foreign (i.e., Greco-Arabic) philosophy, and Yaqub Qirqisani points out the contradiction between his opposition to the use of rational investigation and his own rationalistic tendencies. For example, Qumisi denied the existence of angels and interpreted them in the Bible as expressions of natural forces. His antagonism to theology also seems to be in tension with the Muʿtazili ideas found in his writings. He criticized the Rabbanite "shepherds of the Diaspora," blaming them for the prolongation of the exile, and decried the degeneration of the Jewish people resulting from the pursuit of worldly wealth and pleasures. In a circular letter sent to the Karaite communities in the Diaspora, he proposed, however, a program in which the Diaspora would send and support representatives in Jerusalem to live an ascetic life of mourning and prayer for redemption.

Qumisi wrote a number of biblical commentaries, including those on the Pentateuch, of which a number of fragments have been identified: the Minor Prophets (published as *Pitron Sheneim ʿAsar*, edited by Isaac Markon [1958]), *Psalms*, *Ecclesiastes*, and *Daniel* (fragments of these have also been identified). A number of parallels between his commentaries and the Dead Sea Scrolls have been pointed out, raising questions about possible connections between the Qumran sect and the early Karaites. In addition, he evidently wrote a legal code and possibly a book on the laws of inheritance. While all of the above were written in Hebrew, fragments of an Arabic theological work of his, *Kitab Tafsir al-Tawḥid*, have been found and published (Moshe Zucker, *ʿAl Targum Rasag la-Torah* [1959], pp. 176–182, 481–485), although it is possible that this is a later translation from the Hebrew.

• Zvi Ankori, *Karaites in Byzantium: The Formative Years, 970–1100* (New York, 1959). Haggai Ben-Shammai, "Between Ananites and Karaites: Observations on Early Medieval Jewish Sectarianism," *Studies in Muslim-Jewish Relations* 1 (1993): 19–29. Haggai Ben-Shammai, "Fragments of Daniel al-Qumisi's Commentary on the Book of Daniel as a Historical Source," *Henoch* 13 (1991): 259–281. Haggai Ben-Shammai, "The Karaite Controversy: Scripture and Tradition in Early Karaism," in *Religionsgespräche im Mittelalter*, edited by Bernard Lewis and Friedrich Niewöhner, Wolfenbütteler Mittelalter-Studien 4 (Wiesbaden, 1993), pp. 11–26. Jacob Mann, *Texts and Studies in Jewish History and Literature*, vol. 2 (Cincinnati, 1935). Naphtali Wieder, *The Judean Scrolls and Karaism* (London, 1962).

—DAVID E. SKLARE

QUMRAN, site on the western shore of the Dead Sea approximately nine miles south of Jericho and thirteen miles east of Jerusalem. Ruins on the marl terrace adjacent to the Wadi Qumran were first excavated by Roland de Vaux. He found five main phases of occupation: an Iron II Israelite phase, identified with the biblical "City of Salt" (*Jos.* 15.61–62); three phases of occupation, Periods 1a, 1b, and 2, beginning in the mid-second century BCE and ending in the mid-first century CE, the remains of which included communal buildings of a self-contained Jewish group numbering between 150 and 200 (the adjacent cemeteries from the same periods contain about a thousand graves); and the final phase, a temporary Roman army camp from the time of the Jewish Revolt (66–70). The main phases of occupation show an extensive water system, an industrial complex including a pottery kiln and stables, communal rooms, a watchtower, and a wall surrounding the complex. There was a satellite farming community at the oasis of ʿEin Feshka, two miles to the south. Most scholars accept that the scrolls found in eleven caves in the vicinity of Qumran (see Dead Sea Scrolls) belonged to the inhabitants of the site, although doubts have been raised. The latest interpretations of the material evidence suggest several new possibilities: that Period 1a was a "rustic villa," succeeded by the communal settlement; that the site was a "rustic villa" with no connection to the scrolls; or that it was a commercial way station between the Dead Sea and Jerusalem, again with no connection to the scrolls.

• Magen Broshi, "The Archeology of Qumran—A Reconsideration" in *The Dead Sea Scrolls: Forty Years of Research*, edited by Devorah Dimant and Uriel Rappaport (Leiden and Jerusalem, 1992), pp. 103–115. Philip R. Davies, *Qumran* (Grand Rapids, 1982). Robert Donceel, "Reprise des travaux de publication des fouilles au Khirbet Qumrân" *Revue biblique* 99.3 (1992): 557–573. Ernest Marie Laperrousaz, *Qoumrân, l'établissement essésien des bords de la Mer Morte, histoire et archéologie du site* (Paris, 1976). *Scrolls from the Dead Sea: An Exhibition of Scrolls and Archaeological Artifacts from the Collections of the Israel Antiquities Authority*, edited by Ayala Sussmann and Ruth Peled (New York, 1993). Roland de Vaux, *Archaeology and the Dead Sea Scrolls*, The Schweich Lectures, 1959 (London, 1973).

—SIDNIE WHITE CRAWFORD

QUMRAN COMMUNITY, a group living at the site of Khirbat *Qumran, on the western shore of the Dead Sea, between approximately 150 BCE and 68 CE, when the site was destroyed by the Romans during the Great Revolt. The site is connected with the caches of scrolls discovered in the Judean wilderness beginning in 1947 known as the *Dead Sea Scrolls. It has been generally accepted that the group living at Qumran owned the scrolls found in caves 1 through 11 and that they may have written or copied many of them.

Three texts from the Dead Sea Scrolls are pivotal for determining the identity of the community: the **Rule of the Community*, the **Damascus Document*, and 4Q **Miqtsat Maʿasei ha-Torah*. The *Rule of the Community*, written between approximately 150 and 100 BCE, prescribes, for the leaders of the group, the regulations for a distinct community of Jews. These regulations involve a three-year period of probation for the new member, a zealous concern for purity, a strict hierarchy of membership led by *Zadokite priests, participation in communal meals, continual communal study and prayer, and property held in common. The aim of these statutes was the separation of the members of the community from "the men of iniquity" around them, so that the community would become the true people of Israel, prepared for the coming end of days. The *Damascus Document*, originally discovered in the Cairo Genizah in the nineteenth century and later found in multiple copies in Cave 4, contains an exhortation (probably by a leader of the community) that gives the history and purpose of the community, followed by a list of statutes. While the *Damascus Document* differs in some particulars from the *Rule of the Community*, it also envisages self-contained communities living in camps throughout Judea. There is a distinct concern with purity and the correct observation of biblical commandments (e.g., the Sabbath). The exact relationship between the two documents is still unclear, although it seems probable that they are describing two different types of settlement, but belonging to the same general movement, particularly since the Cave 4 fragments of the *Damascus Document* contain a form of the ritual for the Feast of the Renewal of the Covenant, which is closely connected with the initiation ritual of the *Rule of the Community*. The Qumran community, with its satellite settlement at ʿEin Feshka, was probably largely self-contained and isolated. This evidence has led to the major hypothesis that the Qumran community was a settlement of *Essenes, one of the three major groups of Jews in the Second Temple period, as described by Josephus, Philo, and the Roman historian Pliny the Elder. Josephus describes the Essenes as a sect that held their goods in common, kept strict rules of purity, required a period of probation for new members, and spent much time in study and prayer. Josephus also claims that the Essenes worshiped the sun; the Qumran scrolls make it clear that the community followed a solar calendar. Philo's description of the Essenes agrees in most points with Josephus. Pliny describes a community of Essenes that is located at a place that fits the physical description of Khirbat Qumran remarkably well. Although there are areas of disagreement between the ancient writers and the scrolls, a good example being the question of celibacy, the agreements are far-reaching enough to make the identity of the Qumran community as Essene very plausible.

Although the general consensus of scholarly opinion has accepted the Essene hypothesis, new evidence has come to light that suggests that the Qumran group were proto-*Sadducees. This is based on the fact that several of the legal interpretations espoused in 4Q *Miqtsat Maʿasei ha-Torah*, a text found in multiple copies in Cave 4, resemble positions described as Sadducean in the Mishnah, while the description of the opinions of the opposition group resembles that of the Pharisees. Further evidence for this position is adduced from the fact that the community's favorite name for itself is "sons of Zadok," the name from which the later term *Sadducee* is derived. However, 4Q *Miqtsat Maʿasei ha-Torah*, like other Qumran documents, also contains a solar calendar, which makes the link to the Jerusalem Sadducees, the opponents of the Pharisees in the Mishnah, questionable, since the Jerusalem hierarchy followed a lunar calendar. Earlier identification theories of the inhabitants of Qumran as Zealots or Christians have subsequently been rejected.

Others would question the identification of the inhabitants of Qumran as sectarian at all. Recent reassessments of the archeological evidence have led some to the conclusion that the site of Qumran was not an isolated communal settlement but a rustic villa or a commercial way station, with no particular connection to the scrolls found in the surrounding caves. However, this position ignores the peculiar aspects of the site of Qumran, such as the extremely large cemetery (over 1,000 graves) and the ritually buried animal bones scattered throughout the site, as well as the fact that the major scroll cave, Cave 4, lies within hundreds of feet of the site.

• Magen Broshi, ed., *The Damascus Document Reconsidered* (Jerusalem, 1992). Millar Burrows, John C. Trever, and William H. Brownlee, *The Dead Sea Scrolls of St. Mark's Monastery*, 2 vols. (New Haven, 1950–1951). Edward M. Cook, *Solving the Mysteries of the Dead Sea Scrolls* (Grand Rapids, 1994). Frank M. Cross, *The Ancient Library of Qumran and Modern Biblical Studies*, 3d ed. (Minneapolis, 1995). Philip R. Davies, *The Damascus Covenant* (Sheffield, Eng., 1982). Devorah Dimant, "Qumran Sectarian Literature" in *Jewish Writings of the Second Temple Period*, edited by Michael E. Stone (Assen and Philadelphia, 1984). Jacob Licht, *Megillat ha-Serakhim* (Jerusalem, 1965). Jozef T. Milik, *Ten Years of Discovery in the Wilderness of Judea* (Naperville, Ill., 1959). Elisha Qimron and John Strugnell, "Miqsat Maʿase ha-Torah," in *Discoveries in the Judaean Desert*, vol. X (Oxford, 1994). Solomon Schechter, *Documents of Jewish Sectaries* (Cambridge, 1910). Lawrence Schiffman, *Reclaiming the Dead Sea Scrolls: The History of Judaism, the Background of*

Christianity and the Lost Library of Qumran (Philadelphia, 1994). James C. VanderKam, *The Dead Sea Scrolls Today* (Grand Rapids, 1994). Roland de Vaux, *The Archaeology of the Dead Sea Scrolls* (London, 1973). Geza Vermes, *The Dead Sea Scrolls in English*, 4th ed. (Sheffield, Eng., 1987). Geza Vermes, *The Dead Sea Scrolls: Qumran in Perspective*, 3d ed. (London, 1994).

—SIDNIE WHITE CRAWFORD

QUNTERES, term of uncertain etymology used in medieval sources for a register or notebook. Its most common application is by the tosafists, who invariably refer to *Rashi's commentary on the Talmud by that name. Consequently Leopold *Zunz inferred that Rashi's commentary was in the form of "lecture notebooks."

QUORUM. See MINYAN.

QUPPAH (קֻפָּה; poor box), box to which contributions were made on joyful as well as solemn occasions and at weekday prayer services. The distribution of the money—generally made on Fridays—was supervised by a group of overseers. The word *quppah* came to refer to general relief, whereas its companion word in the Talmud, *tamḥui* (dish) referred to aid offered in the form of prepared food, a type of soup kitchen. The overseers fixed the amount to be raised by the community, and each member—man, woman, and child—was expected to contribute according to his or her means. Even the poor themselves were taxed, as they, too, were obligated to fulfill the commandment of charity. A dignified method of disbursing charity to those during the week of mourning was used in Frankfurt, where a *quppah* filled with money would be left at the mourner's home. Those visiting the mourner who needed money for that week were free to take whatever they needed, while those who did not need such aid would leave money in the *quppah*. Among Ashkenazi Jews the *quppah* is known by the Yiddish term *pushka*.

• David Hartman et al., *The Dynamics of Tzedakah*, 2 vols. (Jerusalem, 1985).

—SHMUEL HIMELSTEIN

QUR'AN (Arab.; Reading), the holy scripture of *Islam. The Qur'an consists of the utterances of *Muḥammad; a standard version of the text was edited on the authority of ʿUthman ibn ʿAffan, third Muslim caliph, in the mid-seventh century, approximately nineteen years after the prophet Muḥammad's death. According to Muslim belief, the Qur'an, as divinely revealed to Muḥammad, is an exact replica of a heavenly prototype; other holy books, revealed by earlier prophets (e.g., Moses and Jesus), carried essentially the same message as the Qur'an, but their text and teaching had been corrupted. Nevertheless, people possessing such scriptures (peoples of the book) were to be treated differently from pagans. Muslims consider Muḥammad to be the last in a series of prophets sent by God, and he supersedes them all. The Qur'an is divided into 114 suras or chapters, arranged according to their length (from 286 to 3 sentences), with the exception of the first sura, which stands alone. Muslim veneration of the Qur'an and the practice of reading it at Friday assemblies and other religious holidays is similar to Jewish practice. In Muslim theology, the Qur'an is one of two sources of authority; it represents the written law but is supplemented by tradition (*ḥadith*), that is, reliable testimonies of what Muḥammad said or did on certain occasions. The Qur'an contains much biblical and aggadic material, frequently in garbled form because of misunderstandings and errors on the part of either Muḥammad or his informants. Sarcastic criticism of his errors contributed much to Muḥammad's increasing hostility toward Jews. Many biblical heroes figure prominently in the Qur'an, including Adam, Noah, Abraham, Ishmael, Lot, Joseph, Saul, David, Solomon, Elijah, Job, and Jonah. Moses' name appears in thirty-four suras. Modern scholars have made detailed studies tracing some of the Quranic references back to their Jewish sources. Some formulations in Maimonides' *Thirteen Principles of Faith (e.g., that Moses is the greatest of all prophets, and that the Torah as extant is the one given to Moses and that it will never be superseded) are said to have been directed against Muslim claims regarding the Qur'an.

• Muhammad M. Al-Akili, trans., *Quran: Selected Commentaries* (Philadelphia, 1993). Kenneth Cragg, *The Call of the Minaret* (London, 1986). Abraham I. Katsh, *Judaism and the Koran* (New York, 1962). Mohammad Pickthall, trans., *The Glorious Quran: Arabic Text and English Rendering*, 10th rev. ed. (Des Plaines, Ill., 1994).

R

RAʿAYA' MEHEIMANA' (Aram.; רַעְיָא מְהֵימְנָא; faithful shepherd), the appellation of Moses in kabbalistic literature, especially in the Zohar, based on a Midrashic legend according to which Moses' devotion to his flock of sheep (cf. *Ex.* 3.1) made him God's choice for the shepherd of Israel. The term is also used as the title of a mystical work by an anonymous Spanish kabbalist written toward the end of the thirteenth century and subsequently incorporated into the Zohar. The work is in the form of a conversation between Moses, the prophet Elijah, and Shimʿon bar Yoḥ'ai.

• Louis Ginzberg, *Legends of the Jews* (Philadelphia, 1954). Isaiah Tishby et al., *The Wisdom of the Zohar: An Anthology of Texts*, 3 vols. (London, 1991).

RABAD. See Avraham ben David of Posquières; Ibn Daud, Avraham.

RABBAH BAR NAḤMANI (died c.321), Babylonian *amora'; head of the *Pumbedita academy for twenty-two years. Under his direction the academy flourished, reaching a steady student population of four hundred (*Ket.* 106a); this number did not include the hundreds of additional students who came on special occasions (*B. M.* 86a). Although his legal interpretations tended to be severe, he was, nonetheless, a popular teacher and attracted many pupils (including *Abbayei and *Rava'). His halakhic views are often quoted in the Talmud, as are his legal disputes with his colleague R. *Yosef ben Ḥiyya'. Rabbah bar Naḥmani was a poor man who lived a life of great piety. Legend has it that at the time of his death, at about age forty, he was discussing a certain issue and ruled, "Pure, pure," at which time a heavenly voice announced, "Blessed are you Rabbah bar Naḥmani whose body is pure and . . . [whose] soul departs in purity" (*B. M.* 86a).

• Elyakim Veisberg, "Ketiv ha-Shemot Rabba' ve-Rava': Shitat Rav Hai Ga'on ve-Shitot Holkot," *Mehkarim be-Lashon* 5–6 (1992): 181–214.

—DANIEL SPERBER

RABBAN (רַבָּן; our master), title of honor. No titles of this nature were used in ancient times (thus, great sages such as Hillel and Shamm'ai were never given any such appellation), but in the Mishnaic period, *rabban*, which is a variant form of the more common *rabbi*, was applied honorifically to leading scholars and more particularly to presidents of the Sanhedrin. The first person to be given this title was Rabban *Gamli'el the Elder.

—SHMUEL HIMELSTEIN

RABBANITES, followers of the rabbinical tradition. The term was first applied to adherents of the oral law and rabbinic Judaism in the tenth century by the *Karaites, who employed the term in a contemptuous sense to designate the partisans of rabbinic tradition as opposed to a purely scripture-based Judaism.

—DAVID E. SKLARE

RABBENU MESHULLAM. See Meshullam ben Yaʿaqov of Lunel.

RABBENU TAM. See Yaʿaqov ben Me'ir Tam.

RABBENU YERUḤAM. See Yeruḥam ben Meshullam.

RABBI. See Yehudah ha-Nasi'.

RABBI AND RABBINATE. *Rabbi* (my master) is an honorific term that was originally used in Erets Yisra'el to address sages, but it has gradually developed into a title for any person qualified to render decisions on Jewish law. The word *rav, from which rabbi is derived, means great or distinguished in Biblical Hebrew and was later used to mean master. The conferring of *ordination was restricted to Erets Yisra'el, where it was curtailed in the fourth century, but a limited authorization (*hattarat hora'ah* [permission to teach]) was subsequently introduced (*San.* 5a; *Ket.* 79a). At a later period, it was decreed that a candidate for the office of rabbi must sit for an examination in Talmud and codes. The formal conferment of a *morenu diploma was first introduced in Germany in the fourteenth century; it entitled the recipient to act as a rabbinical *dayyan (judge). Only men steeped in Talmud and rabbinic literature after many years of intensive study were admitted to full rabbinic honors. The examination of candidates for the rabbinate was administered by *yeshivot* (see Yeshivah) or by individual rabbis of repute and could bear on any subject in the Talmud and codes. In the nineteenth century, *rabbinical seminaries and special theological institutions for the training of rabbis were founded in western Europe and America. Many of these added a body of secular studies to the traditional rabbinical requirements.

Until medieval times, rabbis received no salary from their congregations, in accordance with the Mishnaic law that prohibits deriving any income or benefits from the Torah. Thus, rabbis always had private occupations—artisan, doctor, farmer, or even laborer. As the demands on rabbis' time increased, they were permitted to obtain financial remuneration in lieu of the money they might have earned had they had the time to engage in a different occupation. This was referred to as *sekhar battalah* (wages for being idled [from another occupation]). This situation changed during the Middle Ages, especially after the persecutions in Spain (14th–15th cent.); the refugee rabbis who fled to countries of asylum found little opportunity for making an outside living, and at the same time, new communities of exiles needed full-time professional rabbis to minister to them. Some rabbis achieved international reputation and authority beyond the limits of their own communities. The *responsa that they sent to correspondents often formed a link between the scattered communities of Jews in many parts of the world, and unity was also strengthened by rabbinic codifications of Jewish law and custom. Rabbinical synods established unified norms on many important problems, such as monogamy, inheritance, and marriage and divorce, and promulgated laws against informers. In matters such as the administration of communities (see COMMUNITY) and their relations with the civil authorities, the rabbinate acted in concert with (and was to some extent subject to) the lay leadership. Often the election of a rabbi was subject to confirmation by the civil authorities. In Poland, during the reign of King Sigismund I (r. 1506–1548), the rabbi was confirmed by the king and was, in a sense, an agent of the crown, collecting the poll tax and enjoying large powers of civil and criminal jurisdiction. Outside interference, however, was strongly resented (for example, Shim'on ben Tsemaḥ Duran [see DURAN FAMILY] was elected rabbi in Algiers on the express condition that he forgo the custom of seeking ratification of his appointment from the government). In spite of external influence, the internal management of Jewish communities was largely left to the Jews themselves. Very often the rabbinic courts were permitted to try even criminal cases in which only Jews were involved. The main duties of a rabbi lay in deciding Jewish legal questions, acting as judge in civil and criminal cases, forming a *beit din* (rabbinical court), and supervising religious institutions such as ritual slaughter and ritual baths. Some rabbis also acted as the head of local Talmudic academies. Until the nineteenth century, preaching was of secondary importance; the rabbi usually preached only on Shabbat ha-Gadol (the Sabbath before Pesaḥ), Shabbat Shuvah (the Sabbath before Yom Kippur), and during the months of Elul and Adar. In certain Middle Eastern countries, the rabbi was known as **marbits Torah* or **ḥakham*. The Hasidic master (*tsaddiq*) was often referred to as *rebbi* (Yi. of rabbi) even if he did not have formal rabbinic ordination. His rabbinate consisted of charismatic leadership of his community, exemplary personal piety, spiritual teaching, and a special concern for healing.

In modern times, rabbinical emphasis has changed. The rabbi is a communal official whose duties include not only religious activities (in which preaching and public speaking play an important part) but also embrace educational, pastoral, social, and interfaith activities; not all modern rabbis are trained as *dayyanim*, that is, able to render decisions in matters of rabbinical law. It has been argued that the modern rabbi, especially outside of Orthodoxy, owes more to the model of Hasidic *rebbi* than to that of the classical *rav*. Particularly in North America, it is spiritual leadership and traits of personality that define the rabbinate rather than the legal authority that derives from Talmudic learning. In imitation of Protestant practice, preaching (hitherto the task not of the rabbi but of the **maggid*) became more central, as evidenced by the American use of the word *pulpit* for rabbinical office. In the British Commonwealth, the term *minister* is used for a person who is allowed to carry out the traditional functions of a rabbi. Since the Middle Ages, chief rabbis (see CHIEF RABBINATE) have been appointed with jurisdiction over countries or regions. In czarist Russia, the government appointed government rabbis (**kazyonny ravvin*), individuals with little or no rabbinical knowledge, to regulate communal life. The training and manner of ordination of rabbis vary according to the character (rabbinical seminary, *yeshivah*) and affiliation (Orthodox, Conservative, Reform, Reconstructionist) of the institution of study. Judaism does not in any way regard the rabbi as being a Jew's intermediary or surrogate between him- or herself and God. Jewish law demands no less of the layperson than it demands of the rabbi. While the title of rabbi has throughout the ages been reserved for males, the Conservative, Reform, and Reconstructionist bodies now ordain *women as rabbis. In Israel, Orthodox rabbis are salaried by the state for their official duties, such as serving as marriage registrars and *kashrut* supervisors.

• Simon Schwarzfuchs, *A Concise History of the Rabbinate* (Oxford and Cambridge, 1993).

—SHMUEL HIMELSTEIN

RABBINICAL ALLIANCE OF AMERICA (Igud Horabbonim), an organization of Orthodox rabbis. The Rabbinical Alliance abides by the "Das Torah" pronouncements and guidance of the Gedolei Torah, many of whom are official members. Igud Horabbonim was founded in 1942 in New York City and is dedicated to furthering the study of Torah and fostering the observance of strict Torah Judaism. Membership in the Rabbinical Alliance (now numbering approx. 600) is available to any rabbi of good standing who has been ordained with traditional *semikhah* from a recognized *yeshivah* or Orthodox synagogue, or one who is involved in a kindred field of Jewish education or other allied field of endeavor.

RABBINICAL ASSEMBLY, the rabbinical arm of the Conservative movement (see CONSERVATIVE JUDAISM). Organized in 1901, it has approximately twelve hundred members, about two-thirds of whom are graduates of the *Jewish Theological Seminary of America. Women have been admitted since 1985, and there are more than fifty women rabbis in the assembly today. The assembly is responsible for placing rabbis in suitable congregations. Various committees of the Rabbinical Assembly deal with such matters as social action, education, prayer and worship, and family ethics; its law committee serves in an advisory capacity to assembly members on issues of Jewish law and synagogue practice; and its Commission on Human Sexuality issued a pastoral letter on intimate relations dealing with heterosexual and homosexual relations. The assembly publishes the quarterly *Conservative Judaism* and other educational and scholarly materials, as well as prayer books (such as *Siddur Sim Shalom* [1989]).

• Pamela S. Nadell, *Conservative Judaism in America: A Biographical Dictionary and Sourcebook* (New York, 1988).

RABBINICAL CONFERENCES. With the establishment of *Reform Judaism during the first half of the nineteenth century in Germany, its advocates felt the need to lay down the principles of the new movement and to establish a uniform policy with regard to departures from the accepted norms. The first of the Reform rabbinical conferences (which differed from medieval synods in that they were confined solely to rabbis) was the Brunswick Conference held in 1844; it concerned itself mainly with matters that might impair Jewish–Christian relations, for example, the *Kol Nidrei prayer, the Jewish oath (see VOWS AND OATHS), and the prohibition against *intermarriage. The rabbis agreed to permit intermarriage, providing any resulting children were raised as Jews. This conference was followed by one in Frankfurt am Main the following year (at which such radical innovations as the use of *organs, the introduction of the vernacular into the service, the abolition of any mention in prayers of the restoration of a Jewish state, and the triennial cycle of scriptural readings were adopted) and the Breslau conference in 1846 (which authorized congregations to abolish the second day of every festival except Ro'sh ha-Shanah and the traditional signs of *mourning, which were said to be "repulsive to religious feeling"). The first conferences of American Reform rabbis were held in Philadelphia in 1869 and Pittsburgh in 1885. It was at the Philadelphia conference that the traditional belief in the restoration of a Jewish state was formally renounced; the principle was affirmed that the Diaspora, far from being a punishment for sin, was in accordance with the divine will and essential to the "Jewish mission"; and all the laws applying to *priesthood were abolished. The *Pittsburgh platform, while reiterating many points of the Philadelphia conference, also permitted the holding of weekly services on Sunday rather than on Saturday, when "the necessity for such services appears or is felt." In 1937 at the Columbus conference (see COLUMBUS PLATFORM), the Reform rabbinate reversed itself on a number of points, such as the use of Hebrew in services, and came out in support of *Zionism. Since the beginning of the twentieth century, the different religious groups in the United States—Orthodox, Conservative, and Reform—have convened annual rabbinic conferences; Reconstructionst rabbis have followed suit. In recent years, at the initiative of the chief rabbi of Great Britain, several conferences of Orthodox European chief rabbis have been convened. See also COUNCILS AND SYNODS.

• Raphael Kirchheim, *Sendschreiben eines Rabbiner's an die Rabbiner-Versammlung zu Frankfurt am Main* (Frankfurt am Main, 1983). Michael A. Meyer, *Veidot ha-Rabbanim be-Germanyah ba-Shanim 1844–1846* (Jerusalem, 1986).

—SHMUEL HIMELSTEIN

RABBINICAL COUNCIL OF AMERICA, a professional organization founded in 1936 in New York City and serving about one thousand Orthodox rabbis in the United States, Canada, Israel, and elsewhere. Membership is comprised of ordained rabbis who serve as congregational rabbis, Jewish educators, chaplains, and other allied positions within the Jewish community. While many members received their ordination from New York's Rabbi Isaac Elchanan Theological Seminary (affiliated with *Yeshiva University) and Bet Midrash Letorah (affiliated with *Hebrew Theological College), a large number were ordained by other major *yeshivot* and by recognized rabbinic authorities.

The Rabbinical Council of America is a voice for Orthodoxy on the national and international level. It sponsors conferences and disseminates information on various issues, as well as working to protect the interests of the Orthodox community. One of its primary goals is to generate Jewish continuity, learning, and life by promoting widespread knowledge and study of Torah and by encouraging observance of Torah Judaism. The Rabbinical Council serves as the rabbinic authority of the Joint Kashrut Commission together with the *Union of Orthodox Jewish Congregations. Its affiliate, the Beth Din of America, services the membership and the community by both administering and processing Jewish divorce and other documents of personal status, and by adjudicating and arbitrating civil litigation, as well as offering legal guidance. The Rabbinical Council maintains a Vaad Halakha which guides the organization and its members on halakhic issues. The Rabbinical Council also publishes *Tradition*, an academic journal of Orthodox Jewish thought in English, and *Hadarom*, a Hebrew halakhic periodical. The Rabbinical Council of America is committed to the ideals of *Religious Zionism and supports two institutions of study in Israel: Yeshivat Hadarom in Rehovot and Yeshivat Aḥuzat Yaʿakov in Gan Yavneh. It also sponsors programs and study groups for Israeli soldiers.

RABBINICAL COURTS. See BEIT DIN.

RABBINICAL SEMINARIES, institutions for training rabbis that combine traditional education with modern scholarly methodology (see WISSENSCHAFT DES JUDENTUMS). *Yeshivot* (see YESHIVAH) granted rabbinical *ordination after an intensive course solely of Talmudic and halakhic study. However, by the 1820s, a combination of circumstances—notably Jewish *emancipation and the *Haskalah—had changed attitudes toward the rabbinate's function in modern society in central and western Europe. Worshipers, even many of the devoutly observant, now sought a more broadly educated type of rabbi, who could preach in the vernacular and tackle the growing drift away from Judaism. They felt that a *yeshivah* education was no longer sufficient and therefore began to develop the rabbinical seminary, in which graduates could acquire a university degree as well as a rabbinical diploma. This move aroused bitter opposition among traditionalists in central and eastern Europe.

Elsewhere, however, the charge that these seminaries promoted heresy and assimilation was at first harder to justify. Italy's *Collegio Rabbinico Italiano, founded in 1829, and the *Séminaire Israélite de France were traditionalist. *Jews' College, established in 1855 in London by Nathan Marcus Adler (see ADLER FAMILY), reflected *Neo-Orthodoxy. The *Breslau Rabbinical Seminary, opened in 1854 and headed by Zacharias *Frankel, steered a course between Orthodox and *Reform Judaism, imbuing its students with a positive–historical approach to Jewish tradition. The leaders of Germany's two opposing camps, Samson Raphael *Hirsch (Neo-Orthodox) and Abraham *Geiger (Reform), each criticized Frankel's moderation. Thus, when Geiger's campaign led to the establishment of the *Hochschule für die Wissenschaft des Judentums in Berlin in 1872, Ezriel *Hildesheimer promptly founded his *Berlin Rabbinical Seminary in 1873. There were also vehement objections to the *Budapest Rabbinical Seminary, founded by exponents of Hungarian *Neology in 1877, although it soon proved much more conservative than the Berlin Hochschule. Vienna's *Israelitisch-Theologische Lehranstalt, began in 1893, followed the traditionally moderate Austrian line.

Established in 1875 before Orthodox Jews from eastern Europe brought the first *yeshivot* to America, Hebrew Union College (HUC, see HEBREW UNION COLLEGE–JEWISH INSTITUTE OF RELIGION) in Cincinnati was planned by Isaac Mayer *Wise to train all rabbis in the United States, but it became a radical Reform institution. Opponents founded the *Jewish Theological Seminary of America (JTS) in New York in 1887, which Solomon *Schechter reorganized and turned into a bulwark of *Conservative Judaism on the Breslau pattern. Orthodox Jews later founded the Rabbi Isaac Elchanan Theological Seminary in 1897, out of which New York's *Yeshiva University (YU) later emerged. The twentieth century brought two new foundations in Warsaw, the Orthodox Taḥkemoni Rabbinical Seminary in 1920 and the Conservative Makhon le-Madda'ei ha-Yahadut in 1928. Apart from Jews' College, however, only the Paris, Rome, and Budapest seminaries in Europe outlived Hitlerism.

Other rabbinical seminaries include the Orthodox *Hebrew Theological College of Skokie, Illinois, founded in 1922; the Jewish Institute of Religion in New York, begun in 1922 and combined with HUC in 1950; the Progressive (Liberal–Reform) *Leo Baeck College in London established in 1956; the Conservative *Seminario Rabínico Latinoamericano of Buenos Aires opened in 1962; and the *Reconstructionist Rabbinical College in Philadelphia founded in 1968. There are branches of all three major American seminaries (HUC-JIR, JTS [see UNIVERSITY OF JUDAISM], YU) in Los Angeles and Jerusalem. Breaking with JTS a group also established the Institute for Traditional Judaism in Mount Vernon, New York, in 1990.

Many of the world's leading Jewish scholars and periodicals have been associated with rabbinical seminaries.

• Samuel K. Mirsky, ed., *Mosedot Torah be-'Eiropah be-Vinyanam uve-Ḥurbanam* (New York, 1956), pp. 561–730. —GABRIEL A. SIVAN

RABBINITES. See RABBANITES.

RAB DE LA CORTE (Span.; court rabbi), title given to an official appointed by the crown in the Spanish provinces of Navarre and Castile. This position existed from the mid-thirteenth century to the expulsion of Jews from Spain in 1492. The position itself was, to a great extent, administrative, involving supervision of tax collection and tax distribution, although the *rab de la corte* also served as a type of "court of appeal" for Jews who had been involved in litigation before the rabbinic courts. The appointees were generally individuals who, due to their talents in fields such as medicine or art, were close to the monarchs; many of those appointed were men of little Jewish learning. The position of **arraby moor* in Portugal was largely analogous to that of *rab de la corte*.

—SHMUEL HIMELSTEIN

RABINOWITZ, REFA'EL NATAN (1835–1888), rabbinic scholar and bibliographer. Born in Novo-Zhagory, Lithuania, Rabinowitz spent many years in Munich, where he published fifteen volumes of a valuable, though incomplete, study of the Talmud, *Diqduqei Soferim*. Using an uncensored manuscript of the Talmud from 1342—the Hebrew Munich Codex 95 (Codex Hebraicus)—he studied the accuracy of printed editions of the Talmud and other manuscripts, listing existing discrepancies. An extensive introduction to this work, *Ma'amar 'al Hadpasat ha-Talmud* (Munich, 1877), describes various editions of the Talmud Bavli since the fifteenth century. In addition, Rabinowitz published numerous critical editions of older rabbinic works.

• Marvin J. Heller, *Printing the Talmud* (Brooklyn, N.Y., 1992), pp. 13–14. —DIDIER Y. REISS

RABINOWITZ-TEOMIM, ELIYYAHU DAVID (c.1843–1905), Ashkenazi chief rabbi of Jerusalem, known by the acronym Aderet. He was appointed rabbi of Ponevezh in 1874, of Mir in 1893, and of the Ashkenazi community of Jerusalem in 1901 as successor to Shemu'el Salant. An erudite scholar and prolific author of over one hundred works and contributor to numerous periodicals, Rabinowitz-Teomim was an activist communal leader, who united the fragmented Ashkenazi community, systematized its communal regulations, and established a single organization for *sheḥitah* (ritual slaughter). He was the father-in-law and mentor of Avraham Yitsḥaq Kook (see KOOK FAMILY). His autobiography, *Seder Eliyyahu*, appeared in Jerusalem in 1983.

• Abraham I. Kook, *'Eder ha-Yaqar* (Jerusalem, 1906).

—JUDITH BLEICH

RACHEL (Heb. Raḥel), the younger daughter of Rebekah's brother, Laban, and the co-wife (with Leah) of *Jacob; Rachel is regarded as the fourth *matriarch of the Jewish people. She was "of beautiful form and fair to look upon" (*Gn*. 29.17), and Jacob agreed to labor seven years for Laban to obtain her as a wife. However, by substituting Rachel's less comely sister, Leah, on the long-awaited wedding night, Laban was able to extort seven additional years of service from Jacob for Rachel's bride-price (*Gn*. 29.15–30). Though initially able to provide children (Dan and Naphtali) for Jacob only by means of her servant girl, Bilhah (*Gn*. 30.3–8), she eventually bore a son of her own, *Joseph (*Gn.* 30.22–24). When fleeing with her husband from Laban, she stole her father's household gods (**teraphim*) and avoided detection by sitting on them and claiming to be having her period (*Gn.* 31.34–35). Rachel died giving birth to her second son, whom she named Ben-oni (Son of My Trouble), but who was renamed *Benjamin by his father. She was buried on the way to Bethlehem and her tomb marked with a pillar (*Gn.* 35.16–20). Jeremiah refers to her poetically as the anguished mother weeping for her sons who refuses to be comforted (*Jer.* 31.15). In the blessing bestowed on brides, she is named first before her elder sister (*Ru.* 4.11). A tomb near Bethlehem was mentioned in early Christian sources as that of Rachel. The first Jewish references date from the Middle Ages. The domed structure built over the tomb in the late eighteenth century became a favorite theme in Jewish artistic depictions of Jerusalem. It became an object of pilgrimage, and infertile women came to pray there in the hope that, like Rachel, they would eventually bear children.

• Robert Alter, *The Art of Biblical Narrative* (New York, 1981). Sharon Pace Jeansonne, *The Women of Genesis* (Minneapolis, 1990). Zev Vilnay, *Matsevot Qodesh be-Erets Yisra'el*, 3d ed., vol. 1 (Jerusalem, 1985), pp. 147–166. Claus Westermann, *Genesis 12–36*, translated by John J. Scullion, A Continental Commentary (Minneapolis, 1995).

—MICHAEL JAMES WILLIAMS

RADAQ. See KIMḤI FAMILY.

RADBAZ. See DAVID BEN SHELOMOH IBN AVI ZIMRA.

RAIN. In Erets Yisra'el rain is seasonal; the early rains (*yoreh*) fall in Ḥeshvan (around October), and the late rains (*malqosh*) come to an end during Nisan (around April). Rain that falls out of season or with undue force is considered harmful (*Ez.* 13.13), while that which falls in good quantity and at the expected time is called a blessing (*Ez.* 34.26). An abundance or, conversely, a lack of rain is considered to be a divine means of reward or punishment for the people of Israel, because the "keys of rain" have been retained by the Almighty to chasten man and cause him to repent (*Dt.* 28.12). Both unseasonal rain (*1 Sm.* 12.18ff.) and drought (*1 Kgs.* 17) are invoked by the prophets as signs of God's displeasure. The formula *Mashiv ha-Ruaḥ u-Morid ha-Geshem, a supplication for the blessing of rain and recognition of God's instrumentality in the bestowal of this blessing, is included in the daily service during the winter months. The festival of Sukkot and its practices are particularly associated with rain and *water (see SIMḤAT BEIT HA- SHO'EVAH), and the additional service for *Shemini ʿAtseret, called Geshem (rain), opens with a petition for rain that is timed in accordance with the seasons of Erets Yisra'el (see TEFILLAT GESHEM). A series of special services and fasts, varying in intensity with the progression of a drought, are inaugurated if the rains fail to arrive in due season. The Talmudic tractate **Taʿanit* is devoted to the description of these services and the regulations governing the fasts.

• Philipe Reymond, *L'Eau, sa vie, et sa Philippe signification dans l'Ancien Testament* (Leiden, 1958), pp. 9–53.

RAIN, PRAYERS FOR. See TEFILLAT GESHEM.

RAINBOW. According to *Genesis* 9.12–17, the arc containing the colors of the spectrum that appeared after the *Flood was placed there by God as a sign of his covenant, that is, his promise, never again to destroy mankind. Every rainbow thereafter would serve to remind God of this pledge. The Bible calls the arc God's "bow." The arc resembles a warrior's bow; by "hanging up" his bow, God undertakes never again to "make war" against mankind. Later interpreters, uncomfortable with the idea that God needed reminders, preferred to view the rainbow as a sign for humanity of God's resolve to ensure the survival of his creations. Upon seeing a rainbow, a Jew recites a blessing praising God ". . . who remembers his covenant, is faithful to his covenant, and keeps his promise."

• Avigdor Miller, *The Beginning: Comments and Notes on Breshis* (New York, 1987), pp. 174–175.

—BARUCH J. SCHWARTZ

RALBAG. See LEVI BEN GERSHOM.

RAMAQ. See CORDOVERO, MOSHEH BEN YAʿAQOV.

RAMBAM. See MAIMONIDES, MOSES.

RAMBAN. See NAHMANIDES, MOSES.

RAMḤAL. See LUZZATTO, MOSHEH ḤAYYIM.

RAM'S HORN. See SHOFAR.

RAN. See NISSIM BEN RE'UVEN GERONDI.

RANSOM (Heb. *kofer, pidyon*). The Bible explicitly prohibits the taking of ransom (blood money) in the case of murder (*Nm.* 35.31–32), and the only trace of the ancient legal institution of ransom in Jewish law is the indemnification paid by the owner of an ox that has killed a man by goring (*Ex.* 21.30). At the taking of the *census, each individual was to give "a ransom for his soul unto the Lord . . . a half shekel" (*Ex.* 30.12). The ransoming of *captives (*pidyon shevuyyim*) played an important part in Jewish history both in Talmudic times and during the Middle Ages and was considered a supreme duty of charity. Almost every Jewish community had a fund for ransoming captives. The term *pidyon* is also used for the "redeeming" of the firstborn (see FIRSTBORN, REDEMPTION OF THE).

• Philip Birnbaum, *A Book of Jewish Concepts* (New York, 1964).

RAPE, nonconsensual sexual intercourse with a woman. When it occurs in a secluded place where screams for help would not normally be answered, no additional evidence is needed to prove the woman's innocence. If the sexual activity occurred in a public place where the woman's cries for help would normally be answered, and she did not cry out, it is assumed that she too is culpable for the sexual activity (*Dt*. 22.25) and that no rape occurred. According to Talmudic law, a woman who is asleep when the act takes place is presumed to have been violated. Furthermore, if intercourse began forcibly but became consensual, it is still regarded as a violation. According to biblical law, a man who rapes a woman who is not betrothed is obligated to pay a fine of fifty shekels as well as marry her without the possibility of divorce (had the woman been betrothed, the perpetrator would be subject to death; *Dt*. 22.25–29). The rabbis explain that the woman need not marry the man if she, or her father, does not desire the marriage. However, even in such a case the perpetrator is obligated to pay the fine. According to the majority rabbinic opinion, the Deuteronomic law only refers to a girl under the age of twelve and a half. Older women who have been raped are compensated for humiliation and physical and mental anguish. A married woman who is raped is not prohibited to her husband unless he is a *kohen*, in which case he must divorce her.

• Lyn M. Bechtel, "What If Dinah Is Not Raped (Genesis 34)?" *Journal for the Study of the Old Testament* 62 (1994): 19–36. Fokkelien van Dijk-Hemmes, "Tamar and the Limits of Patriarchy: Between Rape and Seduction (2 Samuel 13 and Genesis 38)," in *Anti-Covenant: Counter-Reading Women's Lives*, edited by Mieke Bal (Sheffield, Eng., 1989), pp. 135–156. Louis Epstein, *Sex Laws and Customs in Judaism* (New York, 1968). Leon R. Kass, "Regarding Daughters: The Rape of Dinah," *Commentary* 93 (April 1992): 29–38. Susan B. Thistlethwaite, " 'May You Enjoy the Spoil of Your Enemies': Rape as a Biblical Metaphor," *Semeia* 61 (1993): 59–75.

—MARC SHAPIRO

RAPHAEL, archangel. Unlike *Michael, and Gabriel, Raphael is not mentioned in the Bible, but he figures prominently in both the Apocrypha (e.g., *Tb*. 12.11) and in kabbalistic literature. Together, Michael, Gabriel, *Uriel, and Raphael fulfill such functions as taking command of the four points of the camp of Israel and the four points of the compass, or standing to the right and left, above and below the heavenly choir, which sings the praises of God. More particularly, Raphael is the angel of healing (*rafa'* [healed] and El [God]) and was therefore identified by legend as one of the three angels who visited Abraham after he had circumcised himself (*Yoma'* 37a). See also ANGELS.

• Gustav Davidson, *A Dictionary of Angels: Including the Fallen Angels* (New York, 1967).

RAPOPORT, ḤAYYIM HA-KOHEN (c.1700–1771), Polish rabbi and disputant. He was rabbi of Sluck and from 1740 of Lemberg (Lwów), where he served until his death. He engaged for many years in a dispute over his right to the income from the regional chief rabbinate of Lwów, in which, despite the support of the local authorities, he was unsuccessful. In 1759 he was the head of the Jewish delegation in the disputation with the Frankists (see FRANK, YAʿAQOV) in Lwów cathedral. Though able to understand and read Polish, he engaged the services of Dov Ber from Bolechów, the Jewish memoir writer, as his scribe. His speech in refutation of the Frankists' seventh point, that Jews use human blood in the baking of *matsot*, has been preserved. In addition to exposing the Frankists' misrepresentation of Talmudic and other Jewish sources, he also quoted Christian authorities who denied the truth of such charges. *Zekher Ḥayyim*, a collection of his *responsa*, was published in Lemberg in 1865.

• Majer Balaban, *Le-Toledot ha-Tenuʿah ha-Frankit* (Tel Aviv, 1934–1935). Hayyim Nathan Dembitzer, *Sefer Qelilat Yofi* (New York, 1959–1960). Mark Wischnitzer, ed., *The Memoirs of Ber of Bolechów, 1723–1805* (London and New York, 1922).

—ADAM TELLER

RAPOPORT, SHELOMOH YEHUDAH LEIB (1790–1867), known by the acronym Shir; one of the founders of modern Jewish studies (Wissenschaft des Judentums); rabbi in Tarnopol in 1837 but, owing to the opposition of the Ḥasidim, left after a year for Prague, where he became chief rabbi in 1840. Rapoport was a pioneer in applying the methods of modern scholarship to Jewish cultural history; his works include monographs on Jewish personalities (e.g., *Saʿadyah ben Yosef Ga'on, *Ha'i Ga'on, Elʿazar *Kallir) and the first (and only) volume of a projected Talmudic encyclopedia, *ʿErekh Millin*. Rapoport insisted on freedom of inquiry (thus arousing the bitter enmity of the ultra-Orthodox and the Ḥasidim) but opposed Reform Judaism and severely attacked the views of Abraham *Geiger.

• Isaac E. Barzilay, *Shlomo Yehudah Rapoport (1790–1867) and His Contemporaries* (Ramat Gan, 1969). Simon Bernfeld, *Toledot Shir* (Berlin, 1899). Meyer Waxman, *History of Jewish Literature*, vol. 3 (New York, 1961), pp. 384–389, 443–451.

RASHBA'. See ADRET, SHELOMOH BEN AVRAHAM.

RASHBAM. See SHEMU'EL BEN ME'IR.

RASHBASH. See DURAN FAMILY.

RASHBATS. See DURAN FAMILY.

RASHI (1040–1105), acronym for R. Shelomoh Yitsḥaqi (son of Isaac); the outstanding commentator on the Bible and Talmud. Rashi was born in Troyes in northern France. Factually, little is known of his early years, but legends abound.

Rashi grew up in an environment where Bible commentary and study of the Talmud were the chief subjects on the curriculum of Jewish scholars. After his early years of study in Troyes, Rashi became a traveling scholar, moving from one place to another to find the most distinguished teachers available. For some years he lived in Worms, where he studied and taught, and his reputation as a brilliant young teacher soon attracted disciples from all over Lorraine. Finally he moved back to Troyes, where he established his own academy. He served the community as a rabbinic judge, while devoting as much time as possible to teaching and writing. He supported himself by growing grapes and making wine.

Rashi wrote his commentary on the entire Bible, with the exception of the *Book of Chronicles*. Some have doubted his authorship of the commentaries on parts of the *Book of Job*, *Ezra*, and *Nehemiah*. His commentary is distinctive in a number of significant features. Generally, rabbinic commentaries on the Bible fall into two main classes: *peshat* (the plain meaning of the text) and *derash* (expounding the inner meanings, including mystical, ethical, and homiletical ones). Rashi stressed the *peshat* and provided meanings for all difficult words and phrases in the text. Rather than suggest forced interpretation, he occasionally admitted that he had no explanation. However, he also used *derash*, quoting rabbinic teachings from the Talmud and Midrash to enliven the biblical text. He explained that he used *derash* only when the *peshat* on its own failed to give a satisfactory meaning to the Bible (see his comment on *Gn*. 3.8), but in fact he often introduced *derash* even when the *peshat* alone was sufficient to make the biblical word or phrase perfectly intelligible. His work was criticized because of this use of *derash*. Even his grandson, *Shemu'el ben Me'ir (Rashbam) raised the point with his grandfather and says that Rashi acknowledged the justice of such criticism, observing that if he only had the time he would have written a different kind of commentary, concentrating only on the *peshat* (Rashbam's commentary on *Gn*. 37.2). However, much of Rashi's popularity over the ages can be attributed to the *derash*.

Rashi's Bible commentary has a unique blend of brevity and clarity. He only adds a comment when there is a question as to the meaning of the text and used the equivalent French translation for a difficult Hebrew word. These French words (1,000 in the Bible and 2,000 in the Talmud) are known as *lo'azim* (see LA'AZ) and have proved important for the study of Medieval French and its pronunciation.

Rashi was frequently referred to as the *parshandata'*, that is, "the commentator" par excellence. His influence on the Jewish masses was, and still is, significant. The first Hebrew book to be printed was Rashi's commentary on the Pentateuch (without the Bible text) in Reggio de Calabria, Italy, in 1475. Afterward, the Pentateuch with his commentary became the first classical text in Jewish education. Over a hundred supercommentaries on Rashi's work have appeared in print. Rashi's influence even extended to Christian scholars, who frequently relied heavily on his explanations of biblical texts. Foremost among these was the Franciscan monk Nicholas de Lyra, who acknowledged his debt to Rashi and whose works influenced Martin Luther's scriptural translations as well as the leaders of the Reformation. An English translation of Rashi's commentary on the Pentateuch was published by M. Rosenbaum and A. N. Silbermann (5 vols. [1938]).

Rashi's commentary on the Talmud Bavli covered the entire work, with the exception of parts of two tractates (*Makkot* and *Bava' Batra'*). As the Talmud is written in Aramaic, it was difficult for average students to read it, and the meaning of words and rabbinic phrases was often beyond their understanding; Rashi's commentary opened up this vast literature to them. Indeed, the fact that no similar commentary was written on the Talmud Yerushalmi meant that this work remained virtually unstudied for centuries. Unlike in his commentary on the Bible, Rashi saw no need to introduce *derash* into his Talmud commentary, and he concentrated entirely on exposing the plain meaning of the Talmudic text.

As in the case of his Bible commentary, Rashi's Talmud commentary also drew later scholars to interpret his explanations and conclusions. The first such scholars are known as tosafists (supplementary commentators), and their writings are therefore known as **tosafot*. The first tosafist was Rashi's grandson *Ya'aqov ben Me'ir Tam. All of Rashi's grandsons were scholars, and their children were among the leading tosafists.

Rashi also wrote a number of **responsa* on questions of religious law submitted to him by individuals and communities. It was due to the influence of Rashi and his school that Franco-Germany became a focus of Bible and Talmud study.

• American Academy of Jewish Research, *Rashi Anniversary Volume*, edited by H. L. Ginsberg (New York, 1941). Abraham Berliner, *Kuntres habe-Laazin* (Kraków, 1905), in Hebrew and German. Samuel Blumenfeld, *Master of Troyes* (New York, 1946). Avraham Grossman, *Ḥakhemei Tsarfat ha-Ri'shonim* (Jerusalem, 1995). Herman Hailperin, *Rashi and the Christian Scholars* (Pittsburgh, 1963). Maurice Liber, *Rashi* (Philadelphia, 1948). Chaim Pearl, *Rashi* (New York, 1988). Esra Shereshevsky, *Rashi, The Man and His World* (New York, 1982). —CHAIM PEARL

RASHI SCRIPT, the cursive script of Spanish Jews, a modification of the usual square Assyrian script designed to expedite writing. The *ḥet*, *gimel*, and *shin*, for instance, are reduced by this script from two or three strokes to one each. When the first Hebrew book was printed—a Bible with *Rashi's commentary (Reggio de Calabria, 1475)—this script was selected as the model for the typeface used for the commentary, hence the name "Rashi script" (i.e., the script in which Rashi was first printed, not, as is commonly supposed, the script in which he wrote). It was frequently used in printing rabbinical works.

• Salomo A. Birnbaum, *The Hebrew Scripts*, 2 vols. (London, 1954–1971).

RATIONALISM, the view that reason, however defined, is the ultimate foundation of knowledge. Faith and reason were viewed as antithetical, and rationalism became synonymous with criticism of certain religious beliefs (e.g., revelation, miracles, the sacred character of scripture). Apologetics usually attempted to demonstrate by rational argument the reasonableness of religious doctrines if properly understood, or at least to deny that they contained anything inherently unreasonable. Medieval philosophy, in both its Neoplatonic and Aristotelian forms, held that the intellect (*sekhel*) was a human being's noblest faculty, the divine soul that made people the image of God and the means by which they could commune with God. This tradition maintained itself, at least terminologically, in mystical literature. In Medieval Hebrew, the biblical noun *maskil* (wise) could mean "philosopher" or "kabbalist," depending upon who used the term. In the great *Maimonidean Controversy (13th cent.), philosophical rationalism was said to lead to unbelief and even heresy. Rationalism was the watchword of eighteenth-century Enlightenment (rendered since c.1800 into the Hebrew word *Haskalah) as opposed to "obscurantism." According to twentieth-century German philosopher Hermann *Cohen, Judaism was the prototype of the "Religion of Reason," the assumed superiority of which was only challenged by the growing influence of existentialist trends.

• Eugene Borowitz, "Reason," in *Contemporary Jewish Religious Thought*, edited by Arthur A. Cohen and Paul Mendes-Flohr (New York, 1987). Joseph Sarachek, *Faith and Reason* (New York, 1970).

RAV (רַב; great), a term used in Babylonia for those qualified for the office of rabbi. The term *rabbi* (my *rav*) was conferred only in Erets Yisra'el upon those who received *ordination and were authorized to judge penal cases. The title *rav* is still used in communities where Hebrew or Yiddish is spoken. —SHMUEL HIMELSTEIN

RAV (died c.248), the first Babylonian amora'; his full name was Abba' bar Aivu, and he was also called Abba' Arikha' (Abba' the Tall). He studied for many years with R. *Yehudah ha-Nasi' in Palestine, after which, in the year 219, he returned to Babylonia. His period of scholarly activity spanned the last generation of the tanna'im and the first generation of amora'im, and his status is sometimes considered to be equal to that of a tanna'. Some time after his return to Babylonia, he left *Nehardea, seat of his colleague *Shemu'el, to found the *academy at *Sura; it was the authority of the two men that ensured the independent status and prestige of the Babylonian academies. The Talmud reports many of the discussions of Rav and Shemu'el and ruled that in matters of ritual law Rav's opinion was to be followed. He also empowered the *beit din* to excommunicate any person refusing to answer its summons. Rav was a noted aggadist, many of whose homilies dealt with ethical questions. Several prayers composed by him (e.g., *ʿAleinu; Teqiʿata' de-Vei Rav, in the Ro'sh ha-Shanah Musaf service; and, together with Shemu'el, Va-Todiʿenu) were included in the liturgy. He also expressed views on esoteric subjects, such as the names of God and *Maʿaseh Be-Re'shit. Rav has been called the father of Jewish learning in Babylonia. He was a person of great piety, but he did not advocate asceticism (*ʿEruv*. 54a). One of his memorable sayings is, "A person will be answerable to heaven for everything his eye saw that he did not eat [i.e., benefit from]" (*Qid*. end). Another of his famous aphorisms is, "The *mitsvot* were given to man to refine his soul" (*Gn. Rab*. 44a).

• Gershon Bader, *Encyclopedia of Talmud Sages* (Northvale, N.J., 1988). Joseph Umanski, *Ḥakhmei ha-Talmud: Sefer Rav* (Tarnow, 1931). —DANIEL SPERBER

RAVA' (4th cent.), Babylonian amora' whose full name was Rava' (Rabbi Abba') ben Rabbi Yosef bar Ḥama'. He studied with Naḥman bar Yaʿaqov, R. Ḥisda' (whose daughter he married), and R. Yosef ben Ḥiyya'. Almost every page of the Talmud reports discussions between Rava' and his colleague *Abbayei, based on their profound knowledge of the oral law and great analytical powers. With six exceptions, the decision in each case is in accordance with the views of Rava'. He stressed the importance of study and also emphasized ethical conduct. He headed the academy at Maḥoza; after the death of Abbayei (in 340) the academy of Pumbedita merged with the academy at Maḥoza, and Rava' became the undisputed Talmudic authority in Babylonia until his death in 354. He placed great emphasis on learning the Torah, asserting that he who is engaged in Torah needs no burnt offering, no sin offering, and no guilt offering (*Men*. 110b) for the Torah will protect him from sin (*B. B*. 16a) and is like the elixir of life (*Shab*. 88b). He stressed the great need for intellectual honesty (*Yoma'* 72b) and was one of the leading Babylonian aggadists.

• Gershom Bader, *The Encyclopedia of Talmudic Sages*, translated from the Yiddish by Solomon Katz (Northvale, N.J., and London, 1988). Aaron Hyman, *Toledot Tanna'im ve-'Amora'im* (1910; Jerusalem, 1987). Mordecai Margaliot, ed., *Entsiqlopediyyah le-Ḥakhmei ha-Talmud veha-Ge'onim* (Jerusalem, 1946). —DANIEL SPERBER

RAV KAHANA', PESIQTA' OF. See PESIQTA'.

RAV MI-TAʿAM. See KAZYONNY RAVVIN.

RAV RA'SHI. See CHIEF RABBINATE.

RAZA' RABBA', a secret book from the geonic period, known by both its Aramaic title, *Raza' Rabba'* (Great Secret), and its equivalent Hebrew title *Sod ha-Gadol*. It is mentioned in lists of mystical and magical works by the ge'onim, and it is probably the work mentioned by Petrus Alfonsi in the eleventh century as a Hebrew work on the Tetragammaton, the *Secreta secretorum* (see GOD, NAMES OF). Many quotations from *Raza' Rabba'* are included in the commentary on the **Shiʿur Qomah* by R. Mosheh ben Eliʿezer ha-Darshan, an Ashkenazi Hasidic writer, who was familiar with the Kabbalah and wrote at the end of the thirteenth century. Gershom Scholem, who discovered and analyzed these quotations, demonstrated that the *Raza' Rabba'* was one of the main sources of the **Sefer ha-Bahir*, the earliest work of the Kabbalah. The work appears to have contained speculations concerning the structure of the Tetragrammaton, the names of archangels, and some magical material. The work may have been used by the thirteenth-century esoteric writer R. Elḥanan ben Yaqar of London, in his treatise *Sod ha-Sodot*.

• Joseph Dan, "Jewish Gnosticism?" *Jewish Studies Quarterly* 2 (1995): 309–328. Gershom Gerhard Scholem, *Origins of the Kabbalah* (Philadelphia, 1987), pp. 106–123. —JOSEPH DAN

RAZIEL, the *angel entrusted with guarding or transmitting divine secrets. The name occurs in the Slavonic *Apocalypse of Enoch*, the Targum of *Ecclesiastes* 10.20, and the later pseudepigrapha, but is far less prominent than that of the archangels. Nevertheless, the book ascribed to Raziel (see SEFER RAZI'EL) played an important role in folklore and magic.

• Gustav Davidson, *A Dictionary of Angels: Including the Fallen Angels* (New York, 1967).

RAZI'EL, SEFER. See SEFER RAZI'EL.

RAZIM, SEFER HA-. See SEFER HA-RAZIM.

READING OF THE TORAH. See QERI'AT HA-TORAH.

REAL ESTATE. Fixed property may be acquired by three means: purchase, presumptive right, or deed (see ACQUISITION). If intention is present, all movable property within the area of the real estate being transferred is automatically transferred at the same time without a separate *qinyan*; this is called *agav*. Real estate serves as security for a loan contracted by deed but not for one contracted verbally. No oath is taken on claims involving real estate, nor do the laws of the bailee apply to it. Unless the purchase price exceeds the value of the land by more than half, no claim of overcharging may be brought against the seller. Real estate cannot be stolen; hence, no matter how many times it may have been resold without permission of the owner and regardless of any improvements that have been made on it, it always reverts to the original owner. The "thief" is not reimbursed for such improvements, and he must indemnify the owner for any usufruct enjoyed. Land, or anything joined to it, cannot contract ritual impurity.

• Yisroel Reisman, *The Laws of Ribbis: The Laws of Interest and Their Application to Everyday Life and Business* (Brooklyn, N.Y., 1995).

REBBI (Yi.; רֶבִּי; rabbi), a title used for Hasidic leaders and spiritual guides. The *rebbi* or **tsaddiq* is not necessarily a halakhic scholar or teacher—the position, in most cases, being hereditary—but guides his followers by the spiritual power and holiness thought to be inherent in him. The term is also used in *yeshivot* to denote those who teach the Talmud. —SHMUEL HIMELSTEIN

REBEKAH (Heb. Rivqah), wife of *Isaac, daughter of Bethuel (*Gn.* 22.23). Abraham's servant journeyed to Haran, where Abraham's family lived, and selected her as Isaac's bride (*Gn.* 24). After a difficult pregnancy and her husband's prayer, she gave birth to twins: Jacob and Esau (*Gn.* 25). Each of the parents had a favorite: Rebekah's was Jacob, Isaac's was Esau. Sibling rivalry was inevitable, as already predicted to Rebekah in a prenatal prophecy (*Gn.* 25.23). Rebekah helped Jacob extract the paternal blessing for the firstborn through a deception of the blind Isaac (*Gn.* 27), then helped Jacob escape to Haran (*Gn.* 28). Rebekah was also involved in one version of the wife–sister ploy (see SARAH), when she was introduced to a foreign king as her husband's sister, but she eventually escaped unharmed (*Gn.* 26). Upon her death, she was buried in the cave of *Machpelah in Hebron (*Gn.* 49.31). In all the stories about her, Rebekah is presented as independent, strong-willed, and a worthy *matriarch.

• Christine G. Allen, "Who Was Rebekah? 'On Me Be the Curse, My Son,' " in *Beyond Androcentrism: New Essays on Women and Religion*, edited by Rita M. Gross (Missoula, Mont., 1977), pp., 183–216. Esther Fuchs, "Structure, Ideology and Politics in the Biblical Betrothal Type-Scene," in *A Feminist Companion to Genesis*, edited by Athalya Brenner (Sheffield, Eng., 1993), pp. 273–281. Nahum M. Sarna, *Understanding Genesis* (New York, 1966). —ATHALYA BRENNER

REBELLIOUS ELDER. See ZAQEN MAMRE'.

REBELLIOUS SON. See BEN SORER U-MOREH.

RECHABITES, a clan headed by Jehonadab, son of Rechab (c.841 BCE), claiming descent from *Jethro and the Kenites. The Rechabites resided among the Israelites, leading a pastoral existence, and abstaining from intoxicating drink. Zealous anti-Baalists, they cooperated with Jehu in extirpating the household of Ahab (*2 Kgs.* 10.15–27). They still existed in the time of Jeremiah, who held them up to the recalcitrant Judeans as an example of fidelity and self-discipline (*Jer.* 35).

• S. Abramsky, "Beit ha-Rechabim," *Eretz-Israel* 8 (1967): 255–264. Aaron Demsky, "The Clans of Ephrath: Their Territory and History," *Tel Aviv* 13–14 (1986–1987): 46–59. —AARON DEMSKY

RECONSTRUCTIONISM, religious movement initiated in the United States by Mordecai Menahem *Kaplan with the founding of the Society for the Advancement of Judiasm in 1922. It attempts to integrate Western democratic values and social scientific scholarship into a reconstruction of Judaism. The Jewish Reconstructionist Federation, founded in 1955, has grown since 1980, as a result of the leadership provided by the rabbis ordained by the *Reconstructionist Rabbinical College. Reconstructionism views Judaism as the evolving religious civilization of the Jewish people and seeks to adapt inherited Jewish beliefs and practices to the needs of the contemporary world. Embracing the perspective of the historian, this view rejects the traditional claim that the Torah was revealed at Mount Sinai. Rather, it sees Judaism as having undergone a process of continuous adaptation by successive generations to ever changing social and cultural circumstances. Jewish traditions are to be treasured because they represent the most lasting and compelling insights reached by preceding generations about the ultimate meaning and sanctity of life. It is, however, the responsibility of each generation to continue the process of evolution. The constant factor throughout the process has been the Jewish people. The emphasis on peoplehood has led Reconstructionists to stress the importance of Jewish community as the primary vehicle for the transmission of Jewish life. In contrast to the value Western culture places on personal autonomy and choice, Reconstructionists have sought to create communities in which individuals are closely interconnected and decisions are made collectively, with individuals following the communal will. Communal decisions are made through serious study and discussion by everyone, rather than by the rabbi alone. The emphasis on Judaism as a civilization has entailed a close connection to the Hebrew language, in prayer and elsewhere, and to traditional ritual practices. The movement has from its beginnings been a strong advocate of Zionism, believing that it is in Israel that Jews can live most fully in a Jewish civilization. Theologically, Reconstructionists reject belief in a supernaturalist God who intervenes miraculously in human affairs but affirm a serious belief in spiritual practice. God is generally understood as a process rather than as a person, and divine communication through the ages is valued as the record of the human experience of God rather than as literal divine word. The Jewish people is not believed to be exclusively chosen by God; rather, all peoples have the ability to express the divine will. Rituals are practiced and classical texts studied by Reconstructionists because they convey the sacred insights, values, and worldview of previous generations. The new Reconstructionist series of prayer books, *Kol Haneshamah* (edited by A. Teutsch [1989, 1991, 1994, 1996]), represents an ongoing commitment to the traditional words of the liturgy, while reflecting feminist and other ethical considerations. The movement considers itself post-halakhic because it views the *mitsvot* not as commandments from God but as treasured expressions of the past that reflect the specific historical contexts of the generations in which they originated. They are therefore subject to cautious change on ethical grounds. The movement has pioneered in the area of gender equality, initiating the *bat mitsvah* ceremony for girls in 1922, according women full ritual equality in the 1940s, ordaining women as rabbis beginning in 1968, developing women-initiated *gittin* divorces in 1978, and experimenting with nonmasculine God-language in prayer.

• Rebecca T. Alpert and Jacob J. Staub, *Exploring Judaism: A Reconstructionist Approach* (New York, 1985). Ira Eisenstein, *Reconstructing Judaism: An Autobiography* (New York, 1987). Emanuel S. Goldsmith and Mel Scult, eds., *Dynamic Judaism: The Essential Writings of Mordecai M. Kaplan* (New York, 1985). Mordecai M. Kaplan, *Judaism as a Civilization: Toward a Reconstruction of American-Jewish Life* (New York, 1934). *The Reconstructionist* (New York, 1935–present), originally edited by Kaplan, this journal has been the voice of the movement for over sixty years. Jeffrey L. Schein and Jacob J. Staub, eds., *Creative Jewish Education: A Reconstructionist Perspective* (Chappaqua, N.Y., 1985).

—JACOB J. STAUB

RECONSTRUCTIONIST RABBINICAL COLLEGE, educational institution in Wyncote, Pennsylvania, founded in 1968 by R. Ira Eisenstein to train the leaders of Reconstructionism. Its curriculum is based on the definition of Judaism as the "evolving religious civilization of the Jewish people" and emphasizes the study of the Jewish past in its historical context. With a strong accent on professional training, its graduates are prepared to pursue careers as educators, chaplains, communal executives, and campus directors, as well as congregational rabbis. Its Center for Jewish Ethics and its Center for Outreach develop programs and study materials for broader use. Nearly two hundred rabbis had been ordained by 1995 and belong to the Reconstructionist Rabbinical Association.

• Rebecca T. Alpert, "Reconstructionist Rabbis," *Encyclopedia Judaica Yearbook 1983–1985* (Jerusalem, 1985), pp. 101–105. Jacob J. Staub, "The Rabbi: Past Images, Future Visions," *Reconstructionist* 55.4 (March 1990): 9–12. Jacob J. Staub, "Training Rabbis for the Future: A Response," *Reconstructionist* 56.4 (Summer 1991): 12–15. Jack Wertheimer, "Reconstructionism: Building a Fourth Movement," *American Jewish Yearbook* 89 (1989): 139–144.

—JACOB J. STAUB

REDEMPTION (Heb. *ge'ullah*). The religious and theological meanings of redemption are derived from ancient Israelite law and social custom. To "redeem" meant to fulfill the duty of next of kin ("redeemer") in certain specific situations (cf. *Ru.* 3.9–4.9) by ransoming a kinsman who had sold himself into slavery or by exercising the option to buy back family property that had been alienated. The next of kin who acts as a *blood avenger is called a *go'el*. God is also described as a *go'el* (cf. *Jb.* 19.25, "I know that my redeemer lives"). In saving his people (cf. *Is.* 11.11; *Jer.* 31.10), he acts the part of the kinsman in ancient law. Liturgical reference to God as Israel's redeemer (cf. *Is.* 59.20) is made daily in the benediction following the *Shema' and in the seventh benediction of the weekday 'Amidah. The idea of redemption operates on a variety of levels: as social and political liberation (the prototype being the *Exodus from Egypt), as freedom from sin, and as a general cosmic transformation. Only in later usage was the term applied to the expected Davidic Messiah. The Kabbalah, in particular, developed the notion of a redemption (**tiqqun*) in which God himself shares, since he, too (in the aspect of the Godhead called the *Shekhinah), was involved in the suffering of a disarranged and "fallen" world. It has been suggested that modern Zionism is merely the national and secularized reinterpretation of the ancient Jewish striving for redemption; in Zionist terminology "redemption of the land" means buying land in Erets Yisra'el for Jewish ownership. The term *redemption* is generally used in a concrete collective or individual (e.g., salvation from illness, oppression, suffering) sense but not in the sense of a change in spiritual state, where a different terminology (atonement, sanctification) applies.

• Arthur A. Cohen, "Redemption," in *Contemporary Jewish Religious Thought*, edited by Arthur A. Cohen and Paul Mendes-Flohr (New York, 1987), pp. 761–765.

REDEMPTION OF FIRSTBORN. See FIRSTBORN, REDEMPTION OF THE.

RED HEIFER (Heb. *parah adummah*), animal whose ashes are used in preparing the "waters of purification," by which a person who had come into contact with a human corpse was decontaminated. The ritual (*Nm.* 19) is modeled after the *purification offering and is even called a *ḥatta't* (*Nm.* 8.7, 19.9, 17). The flesh of a cow is completely incinerated, so that whenever necessary a small amount of its ashes may be mixed with water and sprinkled on an impure person. This is to be done on the third and seventh days of his defilement, after which he is pure once again. The requirement that the sacrificial animal be red (*adummah*—actually earth-colored or brown) and that its blood be incinerated along with its flesh, together with cedar wood and crimson yarn (and hyssop, a symbol of purification), is not merely in order to obtain the greatest possible quantity of ash. The mixture of the ash with water symbolizes actual blood, as employed in the purification offering; the ash is a sort of instant blood, kept for use as needed. In biblical thought, death in all of its manifestations is defiling; the ritual purification of humans from corpse contamination is essential, lest the spread of defilement cause the pollution of the Temple, God's abode, and drive him from there (*Nm.* 19.13, 20). In post-biblical thought, the original significance of the procedure was no longer acknowledged, and it was reinterpreted by the rabbis as a rite designed to atone for the sin of the golden calf. Following the teaching of R. Yoḥanan ben Zakk'ai (*Pesiqta' de-*

Rav Kahana' 4.7), the seemingly illogical ritual of the red heifer has become the archetype of the *ḥuqqim*: commands that require compliance though they are incomprehensible and that are considered sublime expressions of the inscrutable divine will. Since those involved in the preparation and sprinkling of the ash are defiled, the red heifer presents the classic halakhic paradox: though it purifies the impure, it contaminates the pure.

Corpse contamination, one of the most frequent types of defilement, prevented one from participating in sacrifice. Thus, it was necessary for all to be reminded of the need to undergo purification before the annual Pesaḥ offering, in which everyone was required to participate. For this reason the rabbis enjoined the public reading of the law of the red heifer from the Torah on one of the Sabbaths preceding Pesaḥ, called Shabbat Parah (*Meg.* 3.4).

• Baruch A. Levine, *Numbers 1–20*, The Anchor Bible, vol. 4A (New York, 1993), pp. 457–479. Jacob Milgrom, *Numbers*, The JPS Torah Commentary (Philadelphia, 1990), pp. 158–163, 437–447.

—BARUCH J. SCHWARTZ

REFORM JUDAISM, a religious movement advocating the modification of Orthodox tradition in conforming with the exigencies of contemporary life and thought. In some places it is called Liberal or Progressive Judaism. The essential difference between Orthodox and Reform revolves around the authority of the *halakhah*; whereas Orthodoxy maintains the divine authority of the *halakhah* in both its biblical and rabbinic expressions, Reform Judaism subjects religious law and customs to human judgment. While granting the elements of divine inspiration in the Bible and Jewish tradition, it attempts to differentiate between those elements of the Torah that are eternal and the legal forms and customs that it believes are the products of a particular age. It thus maintains its right to adapt and change Jewish traditions to make them more relevant to each generation. Its historic origins were motivated less by theological or ideological attitudes than by a desire for a more attractive form of service that would appeal to Jews who were in danger of dropping out of Judaism completely.

The seeds of the movement were sown when a prominent German Jew, Israel *Jacobson, organized a progressive Jewish school and then a synagogue in Seesen in the early years of the nineteenth century. He later moved to Berlin, where religious services along the lines he had initiated were organized in private homes (under Orthodox pressure, the government prohibited the establishment of Reform places of worship). Jews in Hamburg built a synagogue in 1818 that they called a temple. The organizers of these early Reform services conducted some of the prayers in the vernacular, shortened the service, eliminated some ideas that they felt were outdated, used musical accompaniment (see ORGANS), and delivered sermons in German. Jacobson also introduced the *confirmation ceremony into the religious calendar of the new community. Reform leaders relinquished the belief in a personal Messiah who would lead the Jews back to the Land of Israel. They insisted that Jews look upon the lands of their residence as their permanent homes and not places of temporary exile. Covering the head during prayer, dietary restrictions, the donning of *tefillin*, and other traditional customs and laws were regarded by some early reformers as outmoded. They looked to the prophetic and ethical elements of biblical Judaism rather than to the ritual elements for inspiration. The negation of ritual also divided the emergent Reform movement. At a series of conferences (synods) in Germany at Brunswick in 1844, Frankfurt in 1845, and Breslau in 1846, the new movement split into a radical faction (Samuel *Holdheim) and a moderate faction (Zacharias *Frankel). Abraham *Geiger and others tried to occupy a middle position and worked for a platform of religious principles and order of prayers acceptable to all groups. Reform Judaism in Germany achieved only modest growth; it organized a seminary and a number of congregations. In France and England, too, it made slow organizational headway. In 1903 the Union Israélite Liberale was formed in France and built its own temple in Paris. In England, where the movement became known as Liberal Judaism, a moderate Reform synagogue was established in 1842 and the Jewish Religious Union in 1902.

A small movement in North America developed concurrently, first evidenced in the Reformed Society of the Israelites in Charleston, South Carolina (1825–1833), led by Isaac Harby. With the arrival of central European immigrants, new Reform groups formed in Baltimore (Har Sinai Verein, 1842) and in New York (Temple Emanu-El, 1846). However, the North American Reform movement took on a momentum of its own and became the first branch of American Judaism to organize itself on a denominational basis when Isaac Mayer *Wise founded an organization of synagogues, the *Union of American Hebrew Congregations (UAHC), in 1873, Hebrew Union College (see HEBREW UNION COLLEGE–JEWISH INSTITUTE OF RELIGION [HUC-JIR]) in 1875, and a professional association of rabbis, the *Central Conference of American Rabbis (CCAR), in 1889. Wise also worked toward the acceptance of a uniform prayer book. Released as the *Union Prayer Book*, it was modeled after David *Einhorn's *'Olat Tamid* rather than Wise's own *Minhag America*. While Wise became the undisputed organizational leader of the movement, Einhorn significantly influenced Reform Judaism with his more radical approach to theology and liturgy, particularly during the incipient stages of its growth in North America. His theology reflected a Hegelian understanding of "progressive or evolving revelation," which continues through our day (rather than one bound by Sinai in time and space and later fixed by the rabbis as oral law); ethical monotheism; and the "mission of Israel" (a universalistic interpretation of the "election of Israel" as a chosen people), which implies the moral responsibility of Jews to be a "light to the nations." Reform rabbis attempted to articulate this theological outlook in two official platforms: the *Pittsburgh platform of 1885, prepared by *Kaufmann Kohler; and the *Columbus platform of 1937, prepared by Samuel Cohon. In 1976 theologian Eugene B.

Borowitz wrote, on behalf of the movement, a centenary perspective in order to describe the pluralistic approach to Judaism that marked the Reform movement in the last quarter of the twentieth century. This document summarized, among other things, these pioneering contributions of Reform Judaism: "that our tradition should interact with modern culture; that its form ought to reflect a contemporary esthetics; that its scholarship needs to be conducted by modern, critical methods; and that change has been and must continue to be a fundamental reality in Jewish life." When the CCAR originally rejected a proposal to establish under its auspices a synod for all American Jews, it opted instead to establish a standing *responsa* committee in 1907. While eventually more accepting of traditional liturgical practices, North American Reform Judaism generally takes a more radical approach to Judaism than did its European counterpart, arguing for personal autonomy and spirituality.

The influx of eastern European Jews to the United States both threatened and influenced the elitist German Jewish approach to Reform in the late nineteenth century. Classical Reform reached the extent of its strength with a denunciation of Zionism following the First Zionist Congress in Basel in 1897. It later abandoned this posture (except among the small minority who formed the anti-Zionist American Council for Judaism in 1942). The significant reorientation toward Zionism (evidenced in the Columbus platform) was fostered by leaders like R. *Stephen Samuel Wise, who founded the Jewish Institute of Religion in New York in 1922, and R. Abba Hillel Silver. The Reform movement later more fully embraced Zionism with the move of the international headquarters of the *World Union for Progressive Judaism to Jerusalem and the establishment of Reform synagogues, schools, and kibbutzim in Israel, as well as the building of an HUC-JIR campus in Jerusalem. The Association of Reform Zionists of America (ARZA), founded in 1977, has become a major force in Zionist politics. Reform communities now exist in twenty-five countries and since 1989 have been founded in many republics of the former Soviet Union.

The Reform movement's stress on social justice led to the establishment of the Religious Action Center in Washington, D.C., in 1961. While the CCAR rejected two early resolutions in support of women's suffrage, it finally passed a resolution of support in 1917. As a manifestation of its principle of equality (removing all class distinctions and the vestige of priestly lineage in the synagogue from the outset), Reform Judaism eventually gave women full equality in synagogue ritual and government. In 1972 HUC-JIR became the first seminary in North America to ordain a woman as rabbi (Sally J. Priesand).

In the latter part of the twentieth century, the Reform movement in the United States has taken steps that have stirred controversy in the Jewish world; these include seeking to influence non-Jews married to Jews through its outreach program, adopting patrilineal descent (in contradistinction to the traditional notion of matrilineal descent) in matters of personal status, and affirming the sexual orientation of gays and lesbians, including their ordination as rabbis.

By the 1990s, the Reform movement claimed to be the largest of the Jewish religious movements in North America.

• Eugene B. Borowitz, *Liberal Judaism* (New York, 1984). Eugene B. Borowitz, *Reform Judaism Today* (New York, 1977). Leonard Fein, *Reform Is a Verb: Notes on Reform and Reforming Jews* (New York, 1972). Solomon B. Freehof, *Reform Responsa* (New York, 1973). Joseph Glaser, *Tanu Rabbanan: Our Rabbis Taught: Essays on the Occasion of the Centennial of the Central Conference of American Rabbis* (New York, 1990). Walter Jacob, *Questions and Reform Jewish Answers: New American Reform Responsa* (New York, 1992). Samuel E. Karff, ed., *Hebrew Union College–Jewish Institute of Religion At One Hundred Years: 1875–1975* (Cincinnati, 1976). Bertram Korn, ed., *Retrospect and Prospect: Essays in Commemoration of the Seventy-fifth Anniversary of the Founding of the Central Conference of American Rabbis: 1889–1964* (New York, 1965). Michael A. Meyer, *Response to Modernity: A History of the Reform Movement in Judaism* (Detroit, 1988). Kerry M. Olitzky, Lance Sussman, and Malcolm Stern, *Reform Judaism in America: A Biographical Dictionary and Source Book* (Westport, Conn., 1993). Jakob J. Petuchowski, *Prayerbook Reform in Europe: The Liturgy of European Liberal and Reform Judaism* (New York, 1968). David Philipson, *The Reform Movement in Judaism*, rev. ed. (New York, 1931). W. Gunther Plaut, *The Growth of Reform Judaism: American and European Sources until 1948* (New York, 1965). W. Gunther Plaut, *The Rise of Reform Judaism: A Sourcebook of Its European Origins* (New York, 1969). David Polish, *Renew Our Days: The Zionist Issue in Reform Judiasm* (Jerusalem, 1976). *Reform Judaism: Essays by Hebrew Union College Alumni* (Cincinnati, 1949).

—KERRY M. OLITZKY

REFUGE. See ASYLUM.

REFUGE, CITIES OF. See ASYLUM.

REINES, YITSḤAQ YA'AQOV (1839–1915), Lithuanian rabbi, Zionist, and Talmudist, founder and first president of Mizrachi, the Religious Zionist movement. In the face of the vehement opposition of his rabbinic colleagues, he pioneered the introduction of secular studies into the *yeshivah* curriculum as a response to the tide of assimilation and secularism that was sweeping eastern European Jewry. After a short-lived experiment in 1884 in Sventsyany (Svencionys, Lithuania), he eventually established a similar *yeshivah* incorporating a secular study program in Lida (1905), the seat of his rabbinate, which functioned until his death. He also formulated an innovative theoretical framework of Talmudic logic (*ḥotam tokhnit*). He joined the Ḥibbat Zion (Lovers of Zion), a precursor to the Zionist movement, and later joined forces with the Zionist leader Theodor Herzl, becoming a leading figure at the Zionist congresses from 1902. As a counterbalance to the secular national educational program adopted by the Zionist movement, he founded the Mizrachi movement in Vilna (1902), focusing on establishing a school system in Erets Yisra'el that would combine Orthodoxy and Religious Zionism with secular studies. His major published works include *'Edut be-Ya'aqov* (Vilna, 1871; Jerusalem, 1951), *responsa* on the laws of evidence; *Ḥotam Tokhnit—Derekh ba-Yam* (Mainz, 1880; Pressburg, 1881; Jerusalem, 1934), Talmudic logic; *No'd shel Dema'ot* (Vilna, 1891; Jerusalem, 1951), homiletic interpretation; *Or Ḥadash 'al Tsiyyon* (Vilna, 1902; New York, 1946), a Religious Zionist ideological statement; and *Mishkenot Ya'aqov*, program of the Lida Yeshivah.

• Leo Jung, ed., *Jewish Leaders 1750–1940* (New York, 1953), pp. 273–293. Monty Noam Penkower, *The Emergence of Zionist Thought* (New York, 1986). Joseph Wanefsky, *Rabbi Jacob Reines: His Life and Thought* (New York, 1970). —ARYEH NEWMAN

REISH GALUTA'. See EXILARCH.

REISH KALLAH (רֵישׁ כַּלָּה; head of a row), a term that refers to a sage who delivered discourses during *kallot* (see KALLAH MONTHS); the title appears a few times in the Talmud Bavli (e.g., *B. B.* 22a), however, it is much more widely attested in the geonic period. In geonic literature, it primarily signifies a leading member of one of the Babylonian *academies, who is responsible (in some undetermined fashion) for ten scholars, comprising one of the seven rows into which the permanent core of the academy was divided. *Reish kallah* was also an honorary title given to distinguished correspondents or supporters of the academy. A related and probably synonymous title, in the geonic period, was *aluf*.

• Isaiah Gafni, *Yehudei Bavel bi-Tequfat ha-Talmud* (Jerusalem, 1990). David Mordecai Goodblatt, *Rabbinic Instruction in Sasanian Babylonia* (Leiden, 1975). Samuel Abraham Poznanski, *ʿInyanim Shonim ha-Nogʿim li-Tequfat ha-Ge'onim* (Warsaw, 1909). —ROBERT BRODY

REISH LAQISH. See SHIMʿON BEN LAQISH.

REJOICING OF THE LAW. See SIMḤAT TORAH.

RELEASE, YEAR OF. See SHEMITTAH.

RELIGIOUS PARTIES IN ISRAEL. The World Zionist Organization (WZO), established in 1897, was not welcomed by Orthodox Jews in central and eastern Europe, who believed that the redemption of the Jewish people would come about solely as a result of divine intervention and a messianic process rather than through political activism. However, a number of Orthodox Jews, headed by R. Yitsḥaq Yaʿaqov *Reines of Lithuania, joined the Zionist movement and founded in 1902 a Religious Zionist party, Mizrachi, whose slogan was: "The Land of Israel to the People of Israel according to the Torah of Israel" (see RELIGIOUS ZIONISM). Before long, the party's popularity spread throughout the world, and it became a significant factor in the WZO. It represented a synthesis of the religious and national components in Judaism. From its early beginnings, it was in constant confrontation with the ultra-Orthodox *Agudat Israel, which rejected the nationalist component and fought cooperation with the secularists.

Between 1920 and 1948, Mizrachi was active building up the Jewish national home in Palestine. Following the establishment of the State of Israel, membership in Mizrachi and its labor wing, Ha-Poʿel ha-Mizrachi, broadened as a result of mass immigration. In 1956 the two organizations united to form Mafdal, the National Religious Party (NRP), as the Israeli branch of the World Mizrachi Organization. While the NRP viewed the rise of a Jewish state as "the beginning of Redemption," Agudat Israel denied religious legitimacy to the state. Until 1992 the NRP participated in all coalition governments, while Agudat Israel usually stayed out because of its opposition to women serving in the army.

In the 1984 elections, a third religious party appeared, Shas, founded by ultra-Orthodox elements in the *ʿAdot ha-Mizraḥ.

The NRP is organized on a democratic basis, unlike the two ultra-Orthodox parties. The supreme authority of Agudat Israel is the Council of Torah Sages, while Shas is headed by the Council of Rabbis. All decisions of these parties are referred to their respective council of rabbinical authorities for consideration and approval.

In Knesset elections, religious parties have received, on average, between 11 and 13 percent of the total vote, but they have wielded political power far beyond their numerical strength. In exchange for their support of the major political parties in Israel, the religious parties have secured legislation in matters of Sabbath observance, *kashrut*, support for the several religious schools systems, as well as support for *yeshivot* and their students.

As regards foreign policy, Agudat Israel holds moderate views, while Shas's attitude has been conditioned by coalition considerations. After the 1967 Six-Day War, NRP underwent a reorientation, advocating the principle of *shelemut ha-'arets*, that is, Israel in its historical boundaries. It has actively supported the establishment of settlements in Judea and Samaria, and Gush Emunim, the movement for settling the West Bank, became the dominant force in the NRP. Subsequently the NRP's power declined, thousands defected from its ranks, and it lost its hold over the rabbinic establishment. Following the 1977 elections, the NRP held twelve seats in the Knesset; following the elections of 1992, the NRP held six seats, and Shas became the largest religious party. The 1996 elections saw a substantial increase in support for the religious parties, which received a record twenty-two seats in the hundred-twenty-seat Knesset and considerable power in the coalition government.

• S. Zalman Abramov, *Perpetual Dilemma: Jewish Religion in the Jewish State* (Rutherford, N.J., 1976). *Encyclopedia of Religious Zionism* (Jerusalem, 1965). Yeshayahu Leibowitz, *Yahadut, ʿAm Yehudi u-Medinat Yisra'el* (Jerusalem, 1975). Yosef Salmon, *Dat ve-Tsiyyonut* (Jerusalem, 1990). Mosheh Unna, *Separate Ways: In the Religious Parties' Confrontation of Renascent Israel* (Jerusalem, 1987). —S. ZALMAN ABRAMOV

RELIGIOUS PLURALISM. See PLURALISM, RELIGIOUS.

RELIGIOUS ZIONISM, conceived in the mid-nineteenth century as a modernizing response of Orthodox Judaism to *emancipation. Religious Zionism aimed to preserve the continuity of Torah as a national religious culture within a modern independent Jewish society.

A major source of Religious Zionistic ideology is the traditional messianic motif of the return to and settlement of Erets Yisra'el. The movement's fathers, Tsevi Hirsch *Kalischer and Yehudah Shelomoh Ḥai *Alkalai, departed from the accepted religious view that the Jewish people must passively await the coming of the Messiah by distinguishing between a natural or rational first stage in the messianic process, and a second, supernatural stage, of which the former is a necessary precondition. This provided religious justification for the idea that Jews could shape their own future.

Religious Zionists were further motivated by concerns first articulated in the 1870s about rising assimilation and rising antisemitism. Affirming the religious value of national existence, Religious Zionism championed a modern sovereign Jewish polity. Religious Zionists cooperated with secular Zionists to attain common goals.

Religious Zionism developed in three phases. The Mizrachi party was founded in 1902 in Vilna. In 1909 it created a network of schools in Palestine, for boys and girls, the curriculum of which combined secular and sacred studies. (In 1947 Mizrachi schools educated about 25 percent of all the children in the Zionist educational system.) Mizrachi also supported women's suffrage.

The second phase of the development of Religious Zionism was initiated by Ha-Poʿel ha-Mizrachi (the Mizrachi Worker). This labor organization, founded in Palestine in 1922, also constituted a political party and under the slogan of "Torah and Labor" promoted the integration of Orthodox youth into the larger society. Of particular import was the cooperative settlement movement sponsored by Ha-Poʿel ha-Mizrachi; in 1990 it comprised eighty *moshavim* (smallholder agricultural communities) and seventeen kibbutzim, organized as Ha-Kibbutz ha-Dati. In 1929 Ha-Poʿel ha-Mizrachi founded its own youth movement, Benei Akiva, active both in Palestine (later Israel) and the Diaspora. In 1956 Ha-Poʿel ha-Mizrachi and Mizrachi merged into Mafdal (the National Religious Party [NRP]), but Ha-Poʿel ha-Mizrachi continues to exist independently as a labor organization.

The third phase in the development of Religious Zionism centered around Gush Emunim. Created by graduates of Benei Akiva after the Six-Day War (1967), Gush Emunim initiated the establishment of scores of Jewish settlements in the West Bank and Gaza Strip, viewing Jewish political possession of all of Erets Yisra'el as a great milestone in the messianic process. Gush Emunim, however, did not enjoy the support of the entire Religious Zionist movement. See also ISRAEL, STATE OF, JEWISH RELIGIOUS LIFE IN; RELIGIOUS PARTIES IN ISRAEL; ZIONISM.

• Janet O'Dea Aviad, "The Messianism of Gush Emunim," in *Studies in Contemporary Jewry* VII (1991): 197–213. Shlomo Avineri, *The Making of Modern Zionism: The Intellectual Origins of the Jewish State* (New York, 1981), pp. 398–439. Pinkhos Churgin, ed., *Mizraḥi: Kovets Yovel li-Melot 25 Shanah le-Kiyumah shel Histadrut ha-Mizraḥi ba-'Amerikah* (New York, 1936). Aryei Fishman, *Judaism and Modernization on the Religious Kibbutz* (Cambridge, 1992). Aryei Fishman, "Modern Orthodox Judiasm: A Study in Ambivalence," *Social Compass* (March 1995): 89–95. Aryei Fishman, "Torah and Labor: The Radicalization of Religion within a National Framework," *Studies in Zionism* 6 (1982): 255–271. Arthur Hertzberg, ed., *The Zionist Idea* (New York, 1972), pp. 398–439. Jacob Katz, *Le'umiyyut Yehudit* (Jerusalem, 1979), pp. 287–341. Charles S. Liebman and Eliezer Don-Yehiya, *Religion and Politics in Israel* (Bloomington, Ind., 1984). Ehud Luz, *Parallels Meet: Religion and Nationalism in the Early Zionist Movement*, translated by Lenn J. Schramm (Philadelphia, 1988). Yosef Salmon, *Dat ve-Tsiyyonut: 'Imutim Ri'shonim* (Jerusalem, 1990). Gary S. Schiff, *Tradition and Politics; the Religious Parties of Israel* (Detroit, 1977). Yosef Tirosh, ed., *Religious Zionism: An Anthology* (Jerusalem, 1975). Mosheh Unna, *Separate Ways in the Religious Parties' Confrontation of Renascent Israel* (Jerusalem, 1987); English version by Barry Mindel.

—ARYEI FISHMAN

REMA'. See ISSERLES, MOSHEH.

REMAQ. See KIMḤI FAMILY.

REMEZ. See PARDES.

REMNANT OF ISRAEL (Heb. *she'erit Yisra'el*), a doctrine expressing the belief that despite the catastrophes and dire punishments visited upon the sinful people of Israel, either directly by God or at the hands of other nations before the Day of Judgment, the people will not be utterly destroyed; a repentant and righteous remnant will survive, return to its land, and ultimately constitute the kingdom of God. The idea of the remnant of Israel is expressed by nearly all the prophets. This teaching, hinted at in *Leviticus* 26.44–45, is clearly enunciated by Isaiah, who thought of the remnant as a small minority ("a tenth part") of the people (*Is.* 6.13) and who gave one of his children the symbolic name Shear-jashub (the Remnant Will Return) in token of this belief (*Is.* 7:3). Jeremiah elaborated upon the theme: "I will gather the remnant of my flock out of all the countries to which I have driven them and bring them again to their folds" (*Jer.* 23:3). Ezekiel also accepted the doctrine to the extent that he designated the Babylonian exiles as "the remnant of Israel" (cf. *Ez.* 9.8, 11.13). Persecutions and massacres kept the idea of the remnant of Israel alive in liturgy and historical consciousness, and those who were not killed in the Holocaust were known as "the surviving remnant."

• Nahum M. Glatzer, "Remnant of Israel," in *Contemporary Jewish Religious Thought*, edited by Arthur A. Cohen and Paul Mendes-Flohr (New York, 1987).

RENDING OF CLOTHES (Heb. *qeriʿah*). The practice of rending one's garments is found in the Bible as a sign of mourning (*Gn.* 37.34) and of national (*Jos.* 7.6) and personal (*Gn.* 37.29) distress. Jewish mourners, male and female, rend their garments upon the demise of any one of the following seven close relatives: father, mother, brother, sister, son, daughter, spouse (*Shab.* 105b). The Talmud (*Moʿed Q.* 25a) says it should be done immediately after death, but the custom is to perform it before or after the burial service. The mourner stands during the rending. While doing so he or she recites the blessing *Barukh Dayyan Emet (Blessed Is the True Judge). The rent is made on the left side over the heart in the case of parents; on the right side for other relatives. For parents all garments are rent and the tear is left permanently; in the case of other relatives, only the upper garment is rent and crudely sewn together again after the week of mourning (women may sew it up immediately). Other occasions upon which Orthodox Jews rend their garments are: when beholding the Temple site for the first time; for a Sefer Torah that has been burned; and upon receiving news of a communal or national Jewish calamity. Today some mourners wear a torn black ribbon to symbolize the rending of clothes.

• Jack Riemer, *Jewish Insights on Death and Mourning* (New York, 1996).

REPARATION OFFERING (Heb. *asham*), one of the types of *sacrifices of expiation. Though its procedure resembled that of the *purification offering (*ḥatta't*), it was mandated for the individual in specific circumstances: desecration of sacred objects, suspected sacrilege, false oath in property offenses (*Lv*. 5.14–26; *Nm*. 5.5–10), purification from *leprosy (*Lv*. 14.10–14), as a penalty for ravishing a betrothed slave (*Lv*. 19.21–22), and for a *Nazarite following contamination by a corpse (*Nm*. 6.12). The basic purpose of the reparation offering was to fine the individual offender for mistreatment of things sacred (beyond the material restitution he was required to make in the case of actual misappropriation of property). For this reason, and since Hebrew *asham* primarily means payment of a fine, the English translation "reparation offering" is preferable to the traditional translations "guilt offering" or "trespass offering." No reparation offerings figure in the public cult at all. The three most significant features of the reparation offering were that it was usually commutable into silver since it was essentially a fine; that it was required even when nonspecific pangs of conscience moved the individual merely to suspect that he may have been guilty of sacrilege; and that it explicitly required confession of wrongdoing along with the sacrificial procedure itself.

• Baruch A. Levine, *Leviticus: The Traditional Hebrew Text* (Philadelphia, 1989), pp. 30–34. Jacob Milgrom, *Cult and Conscience: The Asham and the Priestly Doctrine of Repentance* (Leiden, 1976). Jacob Milgrom, *Leviticus 1–16*, The Anchor Bible, vol. 3 (Garden City, N.Y., 1991), pp. 319–378. Baruch J. Schwartz, "A Literary Study of the Slave-girl Pericope," in *Studies in the Bible*, edited by Sara Japhet, Scripta Hierosolymitana, vol. 31 (Jerusalem, 1986), pp. 241–255. —BARUCH J. SCHWARTZ

REPENTANCE. The Hebrew word for repentance is *teshuvah* (return), which clearly indicates that the Jewish concept of repentance means a return to God and to the right path (cf. *Hos*. 14.2; *2 Kgs*. 17.13; *Jer*. 13.14, 18.11; *Jl*. 2.12–13, etc.). Repentance in the narrow sense of regret for past transgressions is called *ḥaratah* and is held to be a precondition of genuine *teshuvah*. According to rabbinic teaching, human beings were created with an evil inclination—a tendency to sin—and sin can only be exculpated by repentance. It is within each person's power to redeem himself or herself from sin by sincerely changing behavior and returning to God. The rabbis frequently extol the merits and significance of repentance, for example, "Great is repentance, for it brings healing to the world. Great is repentance, for it reaches to the throne of God. Great is repentance, for it brings redemption near. Great is repentance, for it lengthens a man's life" (*Yoma'* 86a); and "Where penitents stand, the perfectly righteous cannot stand" (*Ber*. 34b). The fundamental text quoted and emphasized in the liturgy of Yom Kippur (*Ez*. 33.11) states that God delights not in the death of the wicked but that the individual turn away from evil and live. Repentance is the central theme of the biblical *Book of Jonah*, which is read as a prophetic lesson (*haftarah*) on Yom Kippur. The importance of repentance as a moral act became stressed all the more after the destruction of the Temple and the cessation of atonement offerings. Particular importance was attached to the penitential season—the *ʿAseret Yemei Teshuvah (as well as the preparatory month of *Elul). Penitence is also prominent in the liturgy, being the subject of the fifth blessing of the ʿAmidah and the *Taḥanun and *Seliḥot prayers. Strictly Orthodox Jews devote the day before the new moon to repentance (see YOM KIPPUR QATAN). The exhortation of the rabbis "repent one day before you die" implies daily repentance as one never knows when one will die (*Avot* 2.10). A distinction is made between repentance for sins committed against God and those committed against one's fellow human beings. Whereas the former demands only regret, confession, and abnegation of the offense, the latter involves complete restitution for the wrong committed or, in the case of a nonmaterial offense, reconciliation and forgiveness. Repentance is regarded as so fundamental that it is enumerated in the Talmud as one of the seven things created by God before he created the world (*Pes*. 54a; see PREEXISTENCE). A penitent should not be reminded of past sins. Providing it is sincere, repentance has the power of completely erasing all of one's previous transgressions. Repentance is a major theme in the ethical, devotional, spiritual, and ascetic writings of the medieval philosophers (e.g., Maimonides, Baḥya ben Yosef ibn Paquda'), kabbalists (e.g., Yitsḥaq Luria), and moralists and later of the *Musar movement. See also ATONEMENT; CONFESSION.

• Benjamin Beit-Hallahmi, "Back to the Fold: The Return to Judaism," in *Tradition, Innovation and Conflict: Jewishness and Judaism in Contemporary Israel*, edited by Zvi Sobel and Benjamin Beit-Hallahmi (Albany, 1991), pp. 153–172. Joseph Dan, "Le-Toledot Torat ha-Teshuvah shel Ḥasidei Ashkenaz," *Yovel Orot*, edited by Binyamin Ish-Shalom and Shalom Rosenberg (Jerusalem, 1987). Alan T. Levenson, "Reclaiming the *Baʿal Teshuvah* Movement: A Liberal Critique," *CCAR Journal* 40 (1993): 23–33. Leonard Rosenfeld, "Two-Tier Teshuva," *Reverence, Righteousness and Rahamanut: Essays in Memory of Leo Jung*, edited by Jacob Schachter (Northvale, N.J., 1992), pp. 229–249.

REPENTANCE, TEN DAYS OF. See ʿASERET YEMEI TESHUVAH.

RESHUT (רְשׁוּת; permission), a *piyyut* in which the prayer leader (**sheliaḥ tsibbur*) asks permission of the congregation to serve as their representative to God, especially on the High Holy Days, when many of the congregants, unfamiliar with the difficult Hebrew, cannot pray properly on their own behalf. Various forms of the *reshut* occur in the traditional liturgy. Among the best known are Mi-Sod Ḥakhamim, before the *piyyutim* that are inserted into the *ʿAmidah; Yar'eiti bi-Fetsoti (by R. Yekuti'el ben Mosheh of Speyer, 11th cent.); and Oḥilah la-'El, introducing the blowing of the shofar in the *Musaf service for *Ro'sh ha-Shanah. On Simḥat Torah a *reshut* by R. Menaḥem ben Makhir (11th cent., Germany) precedes the reading of the final verses of *Deuteronomy* and the beginning of the *Book of Genesis*.

• Max Arzt, *Justice and Mercy: Commentary on the Liturgy of the New Year and the Day of Atonement* (New York, 1963), pp. 82f., 89, 179. Ismar Elbogen, *Jewish Liturgy: A Comprehensive History*, translated by Raymond P. Scheindlin (Philadelphia, 1993), pp. 168–173. —A. STANLEY DREYFUS

RESHUT HA-YAḤID. See DOMAIN.

RESPONSA (Heb. *she'elot u-teshuvot* [questions and answers]), answers to questions of Jewish law and observance written by halakhic scholars in reply to inquiries addressed to them; the role of *responsa* is similar to that of case law. Mentioned in the Talmud, *responsa* emerged as a distinct branch of Jewish legal literature during the geonic period and became especially important after the Muslim conquest. The unquestioned spiritual authority of the ge'onim—the heads of the Babylonian academies—led far-flung communities throughout the Islamic world to send their questions about disputed or unknown points of Jewish law or procedure to the ge'onim for solution. Generally, questions were composed by representatives of the Babylonian academies in distant lands and delivered to the ge'onim, together with donations for the academies, by travelers along the caravan routes. Before answering an inquiry, the ga'on allowed the students in the academy to discuss the pertinent legal issues, and only after considering the issues that they had raised did he come to a conclusion. *Responsa*, thousands of which are still extant in Hebrew, Aramaic, and Arabic (those of *Ha'i Ga'on alone number over a thousand), were typically couched in the briefest of terms and consisted of a single sentence or even a word ("forbidden" or "permitted"), although monographs that dealt extensively with the subject at hand were not unknown, particularly as the geonic period progressed. The decisions of the ge'onim were viewed by contemporaries as binding. Correspondents also wrote to the ge'onim for clarification of matters of Jewish belief and textual problems in the Bible, Talmud, and liturgy. Many of the extant copies of the responses of the ge'onim have been found in the Cairo *Genizah.

The first prayer book was contained in a *responsum* sent to the Jewish community of Lucena by *ʿAmram bar Sheshna' in answer to a query about the correct liturgy. The only connected history of the geonic period, by Sherira' Ga'on, was a *responsum* to a letter written to him from the community of Kairouan, while most of what is known about the mysterious *Eldad ha-Dani, who appeared in Kairouan in the ninth century, is contained in a query sent by that community to the ga'on Cohen Tsedeq.

Toward the end of the tenth century, new centers of Jewish scholarship emerged in Europe and North Africa, and communities in these regions began to turn to local halakhic scholars such as R. *Mosheh ben Ḥanokh of Cordova, R. *Ḥanan'el ben Ḥushi'el of Kairouan, and R. Kalonimos of Lucca. These authorities and their successors were asked to clarify issues regarding religious custom as well as to define the parameters of communal authority. Questions arising from situations that were without clear precedent in Jewish law, whether ritual or economic, or even problems stemming from climatic conditions (for example, could Jews ask non-Jews to light a fire so that they could remain warm during the cold winter Sabbaths of northern Europe), continued to characterize this legal genre. Issues of personal status (e.g., divorce, *ʿagunah*) were particularly complex and were also often the subject of queries. While *responsa* from the Muslim world considered geonic precedents, legists in Christian countries, who had been all but cut off from geonic authority for centuries, were generally free from this restraint. *Responsa* from the period of the **ri'shonim*, which were almost entirely written in Hebrew and generally dealt only with legal problems, typically sought paradigmatic cases in the Talmud that could serve as precedents for contemporary problems. Talmudic methods, such as casuistry, were brought to bear on practical halakhic discussions as respondents attempted to explain and justify their conclusions. As in Talmudic times, public practice was not ignored as a source of legal authority. Major collections of *responsa* by *ri'shonim* include the works of R. *Me'ir ben Barukh of Rothenburg, R. *Asher ben Yeḥi'el, R. Shelomoh ben Avraham *Adret, R. *Yitsḥaq ben Sheshet Perfet, and R. Shimʿon ben Tsemaḥ Duran (see DURAN FAMILY).

Authorities from the fifteenth century onward tended to show less judicial independence and gave great weight to the precedents of earlier authorities in their decisions (see AḤARONIM). Beginning in the sixteenth century, *responsa* became more complex, accessible only to the well-educated. The best-known *responsa* collections of recent centuries include the works of R. Yeḥezqe'l *Landau of Prague, R. Mosheh Sofer of Pressburg (see SOFER FAMILY), R. Yitsḥaq Elḥanan *Spektor of Kovno, and R. Mosheh *Feinstein of New York. In addition to traditional concerns, contemporary *responsa* have tried to deal with the halakhic problems raised by the disintegration of the traditional Jewish community (for example, does *halakhah* recognize Reform marriages) and the advent of new technology (for example, the abortion of fetuses with Tay Sachs disease).

The authority of a **poseq*, an arbiter of Jewish law, was dependent on how his decisions were received. Someone whose legal positions were not in keeping with publicly accepted values was unlikely to continue to receive questions. Collections of *responsa*, which were often edited not by the author but by his disciples or descendants, were generally not systematically organized. However, with the widespread acceptance of R. Yosef *Karo's *Shulḥan ʿArukh* and the accompanying glosses of R. Mosheh *Isserles in the seventeenth century, *responsa* began to be loosely organized along the lines of Karo's work.

Responsa have almost always dealt with concrete problems. R. Yisra'el ben Petaḥyah *Isserlein (15th-cent. Germany) did, however, use the question and answer format of *responsa* to discuss hypothetical halakhic issues as well as practical problems. A limited number of rabbis have followed in his path. *Responsa* continue to be used as a means of clarifying contemporary halakhic issues, not only by Orthodox Jews but by Reform and Conservative rabbis as well, who often write their *responsa* in English. Since rabbinic *responsa* reflect on daily life, they have become a useful tool for uncovering the social, economic, and religious histories of both Jewish and non-Jewish communities.

Large-scale programs to compile and classify *responsa* literature have been undertaken in Israel at Hebrew University of Jerusalem and Bar-Ilan University.

• Boaz Cohen, *Qunteres ha-Teshuvot* (Farnborough, Eng., 1970), an annotated bibliography of *responsa* of the Middle Ages. Menachem Elon, *Jewish Law: History, Sources, Principles*, translated from the Hebrew by Bernard Auerbach and Melvin J. Sykes (Philadelphia, 1994). Solomon

Bennett Freehof, *The Responsa Literature* (Philadelphia, 1955). Solomon Bennett Freehof, *Reform Responsa* (Cincinnati, 1960). Solomon Bennett Freehof, *A Treasury of Responsa* (Philadelphia, 1962). Solomon Bennett Freehof, *Recent Reform Responsa* (Cincinnati, 1963). Solomon Bennett Freehof, *Current Reform Responsa* (Cincinnati, 1969). Solomon Bennett Freehof, *Modern Reform Responsa* (Cincinnati, 1971). Solomon Bennett Freehof, *Contemporary Reform Responsa* (Cincinnati, 1974). Solomon Bennett Freehof, *Reform Responsa for Our Time* (Cincinnati, 1977), Solomon Bennett Freehof, *New Reform Responsa* (Cincinnati, 1980). Samuel Morell, *Precedent and Judicial Discretion* (Atlanta, 1991). Haym Soloveitchik, *She'elot u-Teshuvot ke-Meqor Histori* (Jerusalem, 1990).

—EDWARD FRAM

RESPONSES, LITURGICAL, a phrase or word spoken or chanted antiphonally after the prayer leader by the congregation at set parts of the liturgy. The most frequently used responses are **amen*, **Barukh hu' u-varukh shemo* ("Blessed be he and blessed be his name"), *Barukh Adonai ha-mevorakh le-ʿolam va-ʿed* ("Blessed is the Lord who is to be blessed forever and ever"), *Yehe' shemeh rabba' mevorakh le-ʿolam u-le-ʿolmei ʿolmayya'* ("Let his great name be blessed forever and to all eternity" [*Shab.* 119a; cf. *Ps.* 113.2]), and *Berikh hu'* ("Blessed be he").

The antiphonal form of liturgical response probably originated in the Temple service when congregational responses accompanied the Levitical choirs.

• Ismar Elbogen, *Jewish Liturgy: A Comprehensive History*, translated by Raymond P. Scheindlin (Philadelphia, New York, and Jerusalem, 1993), pp. 376–377. Eric Werner, *The Sacred Bridge* (New York, 1970).

—CHAIM PEARL

RESURRECTION (Heb. *teḥiyyat ha-metim*). The doctrine of resurrection teaches that the bodies of the dead will arise from their graves before the Day of Judgment (see YOM HA-DIN). Belief in resurrection began to develop toward the end of the biblical period, possibly under Persian influence, and is referred to in the *Book of Daniel* (12.2). By the end of the Second Temple period, resurrection had developed into a fundamental dogma of the Pharisees, who declared it heresy to deny, as did the Sadducees (Josephus, *Antiquities of the Jews* 18.1.4; *San.* 90b), that the doctrine possessed Mosaic authority (*San.* 10.1). Resurrection is referred to in the liturgy, where it is the subject of the second paragraph of the *ʿAmidah, and is commonly associated with the "world to come" (*ʿolam ha-ba'*) rather than the messianic era (see ESCHATOLOGY). Maimonides states it as the last of his *Thirteen Principles of Faith. However, the doctrine proved a stumbling block to those thinkers to whom the heavenly bliss of the soul seemed a more worthy possibility than continued life in a material body. Maimonides himself seems to have identified resurrection with immortality of the soul and later composed a special "Treatise on Resurrection," in which he argued that a spiritual view of immortality was not in conflict with the doctrine of the return of the soul to the body. Some thinkers believed that all mankind would be resurrected (Manasseh ben Israel), others that the doctrine applied only to the Jewish people (Yitsḥaq Abravanel), and still others that it applied only to the righteous (Moses Maimonides and Ḥasda'i ben Avraham Crescas). Reform Judaism denies the concept of bodily resurrection (and has revised the liturgy accordingly) and has asserted that the belief is a foreign import into Jewish thought that should be rejected. It is not accepted by Reconstructionists either. Moderate Reform and Conservative Jews tend to identify resurrection with the doctrine of the immortality of the soul. (See also AFTERLIFE).

• Arthur A. Cohen, "Resurrection of the Dead," in *Contemporary Jewish Religious Thought*, edited by Arthur A. Cohen and Paul Mendes-Flohr (New York, 1987) pp. 807–813. Joshua Finkel, "Maimonides' Treatise on Resurrection: A Comparative Study," in *Essays on Maimonides*, edited by Salo Wittmayer Baron (New York, 1941).

—MARTHA HIMMELFARB

RETALIATION. See JUS TALIONIS.

RETRIBUTION, DIVINE. See REWARD AND PUNISHMENT.

RETSEH (רְצֵה; Be Pleased), the seventeenth of the nineteen benedictions of the *ʿAmidah for the three daily services on weekdays, and the fifth benediction of the seven in the ʿAmidah for Sabbaths and festivals. Dating to Temple times, this was originally a supplication for the acceptance of the sacrifices. After the destruction of the Temple in 70 CE, it was modified into a supplication for the reestablishment of the sacrificial cult. God is implored to restore his presence to Zion, and to receive the Jew's worship favorably. The Reconstructionist prayer book, *Kol ha-Neshamah*, invokes God to accept Israel's "passionate prayers." In a paraphrase of the traditional text, the Reform *Gates of Prayer* declares that God is responsive to all who seek him in sincerity, whether in Israel or in other lands.

• Philip Birnbaum, ed., *Daily Prayer Book* (New York, 1949), pp. 89f. Lawrence A. Hoffman, ed., *Shaarei Binah: Gates of Understanding: A Companion Volume to Shaarei Tefillah* (New York, 1977), pp. 191f.

—A. STANLEY DREYFUS

RETURN TO ZION. See ZION; ZIONISM.

REUBEN (Heb. Re'uven), Jacob's eldest child. The name, which means "Look! A son!," was chosen by his mother, Leah, who hoped that Jacob would now love her for bearing him his first son (*Gn.* 29.32). Reuben regularly played a role in Leah's struggle to wrest Jacob's love from Rachel. He brought Leah mandrakes, which indirectly led to her bearing three more sons and a daughter (*Gn.* 30.14–21). After Rachel's death, he slept with Bilhah, Rachel's maidservant and one of Jacob's concubines (*Gn.* 35.22), which ultimately earned him Jacob's severe rebuke (*Gn.* 49.4). Nevertheless, Reuben attempted to save Rachel's son Joseph from the other jealous brothers, and, thinking he had failed, mourned for him (*Gn.* 37.1–30). He blamed the brothers for Joseph's death (*Gn.* 42.22), and when he attempted to persuade Jacob to allow them to take Benjamin, Rachel's other son, to Egypt, he offered the lives of his own two sons as surety (*Gn.* 42.37). In their final blessings, Jacob revoked Reuben's leadership position among the brothers (*Gn.* 49.3) while Moses prayed for the survival of Reuben's tribe (*Dt.* 33.6). The tribe of Reuben received its inheritance in Transjordan, where in time it was largely absorbed by its stronger neighbor, the tribe of Gad.

• James Stokes Ackerman, "Joseph, Judah, and Jacob," in *Literary Interpretations of Biblical Narratives*, vol. 2, edited by Kenneth R. R. Gros Louis with James Stokes Ackerman and Thayer S. Warshaw (Nashville, 1982), pp. 98–102. Nahum M. Sarna, ed., *Genesis*, The JPS Torah Commentary (Philadelphia, 1989), pp. 206, 209–210, 244–245, 259, 261–262, 295, 297, 332–333. –SIMEON B. CHAVEL

RE'UVENI, DAVID (died c.1538), a mysterious messianic activist who appeared in the Middle East and Europe in 1517, presenting himself as a representative of the ten lost tribes, and as the brother of Joseph, the king of the tribes of Reuben, Gad, and half of Manasseh. He tried to mobilize both Jewish communities and non-Jewish powers to a concerted effort to bring about the redemption. Most of the information concerning his enterprise is derived from a detailed diary which he kept, describing his travels, his meetings and his ambitions, and from evidence found in letters of contemporary writers concerning their meetings with him. His origin is unknown; it has been suggested that he was a Jew from Ethiopia, but no proof of that has been found. His messianism was intensely political and military in character: he envisaged a coalition between the Christian European powers and the Catholic church with the vast army of the lost tribes, whose commander he claimed to be; they were to fight against the Ottoman empire and redeem Erets Yisra'el. It is not clear whether the existing text of his diary was written by his hand or was edited by someone else. Much of the material in his diary concerning his early travels is fictional, modeled, to some extent, on the legends of *Eldad ha-Dani, the early medieval traveler who also claimed to have come from the lost tribes. Re'uveni also included descriptions of some miracles that had happened to him, but mostly his account is mundane, including discussion of his financial difficulties. He visited Jerusalem, Damascus, and Alexandria, and reached Italy—mainly Venice and Rome—in 1523. He received from the pope, Clement VII, letters of introduction to the king of Portugal and to the legendary Christian ruler Prester John. Among the people he met was the Hebraist and Christian kabbalist Egidio da Viterbo. He went to Portugal in 1525, where he was received warmly by the *converso* community; he made a great impression on the young Diego Pieres, who returned to Judaism in Portugal, assumed the name Shelomoh *Molkho, and was subsequently burned at the stake by the inquisition. Re'uveni was imprisoned because of his effect on the New Christians in Portugal, but the details of his long imprisonment, and his death (probably in 1538) are unknown.

• Aaron Z. Aescoly, *Sippur David ha-Re'uveni*, 2d ed. (Jerusalem, 1993). Julius Voos, *David Reubeni und Salomo Molcho: Ein Beitrag zur Geschichte der messianischen Bewegung in Judentum in der ersten Halfte des 16 Jahrhunderts* (Berlin, 1933). –JOSEPH DAN

REVEL, BERNARD (1885–1940), Orthodox rabbi who molded twentieth-century Orthodox educational institutions in the United States. He was born in Pren, Lithuania, and studied in *yeshivot* in Tels and Kovno. Upon arrival in the United States in 1905, Revel, who believed in the compatibility of Torah learning with secular knowledge, studied at New York and Temple universities and earned a doctorate at Dropsie College in 1911.

Revel's commitment to synthesizing traditional learning and modern culture found expression in the Rabbi Isaac Elchanan Theological Seminary, which under his presidency beginning in 1915 became America's first modern Orthodox *yeshivah*. The Talmudical Academy, also founded in 1915, and Yeshiva College, established in 1929, likewise embodied Revel's core beliefs (see YESHIVA UNIVERSITY).

• Jeffrey S. Gurock, *The Men and Women of Yeshiva: Higher Education, Orthodoxy and American Judaism* (New York, 1988). Aaron Rakefet-Rothkoff, *Bernard Revel: Builder of American Jewish Orthodoxy* (Philadelphia, 1972). –JEFFREY S. GUROCK

REVELATION, the act by which God manifests himself (his saving presence, his will, his commandments) to humans. Biblical and rabbinic Hebrew have no specific term corresponding to revelation. The great theophany on Mount Sinai is traditionally referred to as the "giving of the Torah" (*mattan Torah*). God is said to "appear" to the patriarchs and prophets, and the appearances are described in varying degrees of *anthropomorphism and concrete imagery (cf. *Gn*. 3.8, 18.1, 38; *Ex*. 19.20). Sometimes the divine manifestation takes place "in a *vision" or "in a *dream" (*Gn*. 31.13ff.; *Nm*. 12.6) or by means of an *angel. At the same time, the Bible emphasizes that no direct, sensory perception of God is possible, and hence various circumscriptions were used when describing divine manifestations, for example, *kavod* (glory; see *Ex*. 33.18–23) and, in later rabbinic usage, **shekhinah* (e.g., *gilluy shekhinah* [divine manifestation]). Sometimes the agent of revelation is described as the "word" (*davar*; see LOGOS) or as the "spirit" (see RUAḤ HA-QODESH). Although any event in which the divine majesty or presence becomes immediately manifest (e.g., theophany; see MIRACLE) is called revelation, the term has come to be applied more particularly to the communications of the divine will as revealed to God's messengers. According to the traditional view, the highest type of revelation was that granted to Moses, and the Pentateuch (the Five Books of Moses) is the highest expression of revelation (see ORAL LAW; TORAH; WRITTEN LAW). The prophets experienced lesser degrees of revelation, whereas for other parts of scripture, the term *inspiration rather than revelation would be appropriate. Rabbinic theology correlates the different divine names (see GOD, NAMES OF) with different manifestations of the Divine (see also GOD, ATTRIBUTES OF). In the Talmudic period a celestial voice (**bat qol*) is reported to have sometimes communicated divine approval or disapproval. For medieval thinkers, revelation was identical with prophecy, and they considered such problems as the degrees of prophetic revelation, the relationship between suprarational revelation and reason, and the role of human faculties in revelation. *Yehudah ha-Levi held revelation to be essentially different from and superior to rational knowledge, but others (e.g., *Sa'adyah ben Yosef Ga'on, Moses *Maimonides) held prophecy to be the perfection of the intellect itself and supernaturally revealed laws to be anticipations of subsequent rational insight. The view that revelation was essentially the manifestation of divine law, since reason itself was sufficient for insight into the principles of religious truth and ethics, was still held by Moses *Mendelssohn in the eighteenth century. In the nineteenth century, Solomon Ludwig *Steinheim was exceptional in formulating a radical philosophy of revelation, maintaining that reason had to abdicate in the face of revelation. The antisupernaturalist and rationalist character of modernism in general and biblical criticism in particular challenged the traditional conceptions of revelation, revealed laws, and revealed scriptures. Liberal and Reform theologians spoke of revelation as a subjective mode of experience or as a growing (and increasingly refined) perception of the divine creative power and of moral values in human history. Hence the notion of a "progressive revelation" rather than that of revelation as a distinct, objective, and supranatural event. In the philosophy of Franz *Rosenzweig, revelation is the term for the specific mode of relationship between God and humans (i.e., the individual man not humanity as a collective). Charismatic revelatory experiences, often defined as lower forms of revelation (e.g., illuminations, visions, infusions of holy spirit, etc.), played a considerable role in the history of Jewish *mysticism.

• Isidore Epstein, *The Faith of Judiasm* (London, 1954), pp. 99–133. Abraham Joshua Heschel, *Torah min ha-Shamayim ba-'Aspaklaryah shel ha-Dorot*, 3 vols. (London and New York, 1962–1990). Louis Jacobs, *God, Torah, Israel* (Cincinnati, 1990). Shalom Rosenberg, "Revelation," in *Contemporary Jewish Religious Thought*, edited by Arthur A. Cohen and Paul Mendes-Flohr (New York, 1987).

REVENGE. See Blood Avenger; Vengeance.

REWARD AND PUNISHMENT, the belief that God rewards those who keep his commandments and punishes transgressors. In any monotheistic theology, the belief that God is good and just, as well as omnipotent, is in seeming contradiction to a world in which the righteous suffer and evil doers flourish. This finds its classical biblical expression in the anguished outcry of the prophet Habakkuk (*Hb.* 1.3–4). The Pentateuch, especially the *Book of Deuteronomy*, assumes that well-being and blessing result from faithful adherence to the covenant, whereas dire punishment and disaster are the wages of sin (e.g., *Lv.* 26; *Dt.* 11.13–15, 28). The same view, transposed from the national collective to the individual, is presupposed in many psalms. The *Book of Job* apparently protests against this simplistic view but leaves the problem unsolved. Ezekiel (*Ez.* 18) repudiated the concept that descendants can be punished for their ancestors' sins. The rabbinical exhortation to serve God without thought of a reward (*Avot* 1.3) is an exalted maxim but could not suffice as the basis for religious *ethics. Justice implies a measure-for-measure dispensation, though its demands may be mitigated by genuine *repentance. During the Second Temple period, two major solutions emerged, which were further developed in rabbinic, Midrashic, and later medieval literature. These were the doctrines of immortality and *resurrection, both of which assumed some form of *afterlife in which justice would prevail through a system of reward and punishment. Nevertheless R. Yann'ai stated "It is not in our power to explain either the prosperity of the wicked or the sufferings of the righteous" (*Avot* 4.19). Maimonides enumerates the doctrine of reward and punishment (retribution) as the eleventh of his *Thirteen Principles of Faith, and Yosef *Albo, whose *'Iqqarim* is a critique of these principles, nevertheless accepts the doctrine of reward and punishment as one of the three basic tenets of Judaism. In the late Middle Ages, the kabbalists also adopted the belief in *transmigration of souls as a solution. The problem of theodicy remains one of the major challenges to theological thinking on the level of both individual consciousness and historical experience. It became particularly acute in the aftermath of the Holocaust (see Holocaust Theology). Many liberal thinkers have denied the possibility of divine reward and punishment or endeavored to rationalize it in terms of historical processes.

• Ḥayyim N. Bialik and Yehoshua Rawnizky, *The Book of Legends: Sefer ha-Aggadah, Legends from the Talmud and Midrash*, translated by William G. Braude (New York, 1992), pp. 561–568. Emil L. Fackenheim, *God's Presence in History: Jewish Affirmations and Philosophical Reflections* (New York, 1970). Julius Guttmann, *Philosophies of Judaism* (Garden City, N.Y., 1964). Louis Jacobs, *Principles of the Jewish Faith* (Northvale, N.J., 1988), pp. 350–367. Kaufmann Kohler, *Jewish Theology: Systematically and Historically Considered* (New York, 1918), pp. 107–111. Arthur Marmorstein, *The Doctrine of Merits in Old Rabbinical Literature* (New York, 1968). Claude G. Montefiore and Herbert Loewe, *A Rabbinic Anthology* (Philadelphia, 1960). Ephraim Rottenberg, in *Contemporary Jewish Religious Thought*, edited by Arthur A. Cohen and Paul Mendes-Flohr (New York, 1987), pp. 827–832. Solomon Schechter, *Studies in Judaism*, 1st ser. (Philadelphia, 1938), pp. 213–232.

RIBA'. See Yitsḥaq ben Asher.

RIBASH. See Yitsḥaq ben Sheshet Perfet.

RICCHI, REFA'EL 'IMMANU'EL (1688–1743), rabbi and kabbalist born in Ferrara, Italy, who wandered throughout the Mediterranean area, including the Holy Land. For twelve years he served as rabbi in Florence and lived for three years in Leghorn, where he published various legal and mystical writings. He was murdered by robbers near Cento, not far from Leghorn.

His two important kabbalistic writings are *Mishnat Ḥasidim*, a systematic review of Lurianic Kabbalah divided into six parts (like the Mishnah), and *Yotser Levav*, written in Jerusalem, which treats Lurianic aspects of theosophy. Unlike kabbalists such as Avraham *Cohen de Herrera, Menaḥem 'Azaryah da *Fano, and Yosef Shelomoh *Del-Medigo, who advocated a metaphorical interpretation of the doctrine of **tsimtsum*, Ricchi considered this contraction as a real occurrence in the *Ein Sof, the highest aspect of the Godhead. Ricchi argued that the logical consequence of the opposite position would be the inconceivable doctrine of the total immanence of God in the created material world and attacked kabbalists, such as his contemporary, Yosef Ergas, who defended it.

• Efrayim Ghirondi and Hananel Neppi, *Toledot Gedolei Yisra'el: U-Ge'onei Italyah* (Trieste, 1853), p. 289. Roland Götschel, "Le Problème de la Kawanah dans le 'Yoser Lebab' d'Emmanuel Hay Ricchi," in *Prière mystique et judaïsme* (Paris, 1987), pp. 207–223. Roland Götschel, "L'Interprétations du Simsum dans le 'Yoser Lebab' d'Emmanuel Hay

Ricchi," in *Dutch Jewish History*, edited by Jozeph Michman (Jerusalem, 1984), pp. 87–110. –NISSIM YOSHA

RICE, ABRAHAM (1802–1862), Orthodox rabbi in the United States. Rice was born in Gochsheim, Bavaria, and was a student of R. Wolf Hamburger and R. Abraham Bing. After heading a *yeshivah* in Zelle, Rice was sent by the rabbis of Bavaria to the United States. Soon after his arrival, Rice became rabbi of Baltimore's Nidche Israel—also known as the Baltimore Hebrew Congregation—where he served initially from 1840 to 1849. He was the first ordained rabbi to serve in the United States. He attempted, largely unsuccessfully, to strengthen his congregants' commitment to Orthodox teachings through severe measures, such as denying *ʿaliyyot* to public Sabbath transgressors. Rice left the congregation for a smaller pulpit, Sherith Israel, where he officiated from 1850 to 1861, only to return to the Baltimore Hebrew Congregation in 1862, shortly before his death. Rice was an outspoken opponent of Reform Judaism in America, expressing his views in the *Occident*, published in Philadelphia and edited by Isaac *Leeser.

• Moshe Davis, ed., "Abraham I. Rice: Pioneer of Orthodoxy in America," in *With Eyes Toward Zion* IV (Westport, Conn., 1995): 97–110. Moshe Davis, *The Emergence of Conservative Judaism* (Philadelphia, 1963). Isaac M. Fein, *The Making of an American Jewish Community* (Philadelphia, 1971). I. Harold Sharfman, *The First Rabbi: Origins of Conflict between Orthodoxy and Reform: Jewish Polemic Warfare in pre-Civil War America*, (Malibu, Calif., 1988). –JEFFREY S. GUROCK

RIF. See ALFASI, YITSḤAQ.

RIGHTEOUS GENTILES. See ḤASIDEI UMMOT HA-ʿOLAM.

RIGHTEOUSNESS (Heb. *tsedeq*, *tsedaqah*). The keynote of biblical legislation and prophetic preaching, and a divine attribute, righteousness—meaning uprightness, honesty, and *justice, freedom from wickedness, sin, and deceit—is seen as the totality of morality. Noah was saved because he was righteous (*Gn*. 6.9), and had there been ten righteous men in Sodom, the city would have been saved (*Gn*. 18.32). Abraham was admitted to God's covenant in order that he and his seed might "keep the way of the Lord, to do righteousness and justice" (*Gn*. 18.19), and in *Deuteronomy* 16.20 Israel is exhorted "that which is wholly righteous you shall follow, that you may live and inherit the land." Books such as *Proverbs* and *Ecclesiastes* contrast the righteous with the wicked, implying that the righteous will ultimately be rewarded and the wicked punished (see REWARD AND PUNISHMENT). *Habakkuk* 2.4 states that "The righteous man is rewarded with life for his fidelity," which, mistranslated as "the righteous shall live by his faith," played an important role in Christian theology. Paul's distinction between a righteousness of faith and of works (*Rom*. 4) did not find a place in Judaism. It is assumed that no perfectly righteous man exists (cf. "There is not a righteous man on earth who does good and does not sin," *Eccl*. 7.16), but that a man's status depends on the balance of his deeds. Legend, however, holds that there are thirty-six (*lamed vav*) perfectly righteous men through whose righteousness the world exists. References to a *Teacher of Righteousness figure prominently in the writings of the *Qumran community, of which he was possibly the founder. According to *Tanḥuma'* (*Pequdei*, *Ex*. 38.21–40.38) poverty and wealth, health and sickness are predetermined; whether a person will be righteous or wicked is left undetermined and depends on the human exercise of *free will. The minimum ideal of righteousness is conformity to the requirements of the law. The higher ideal of boundless devotion to God is exemplified by the **ḥasid* (pious man). Righteousness is not limited to Jews, and the righteous among the gentiles (**ḥasidei ummot ha-ʿolam*) will also have a place in the world to come. In Rabbinic and Medieval Hebrew, the word *tsedaqah* came to denote only one aspect of righteousness, that of almsgiving and *charity. A **tsaddiq* (righteous man) is one who lives righteously by adhering to the divine law, a person in whom no fault or transgression is to be found. Ḥasidim identified righteousness and holiness with their leaders, the *tsadiqqim*, who mediated between man and God.

• Martin Buber, *Between Man and Man* (Boston, 1955). Joshua O. Huberman, "Righteousness," in *Contemporary Jewish Religious Thought*, edited by Arthur A. Cohen and Paul Mendes-Flohr (New York, 1987), pp. 833–839. –SHMUEL HIMELSTEIN

RIMMONIM. See TORAH ORNAMENTS.

RI'SHONIM (רִאשׁוֹנִים; first ones), in Talmudic literature a term referring to rabbinic scholars of earlier generations who, because they were chronologically closer to the revelation at Mount Sinai, were deemed by subsequent generations to be more pious and greater authorities in the tradition. Now the term refers to rabbinic scholars during the period between the emergence of independent rabbinic scholarship in Europe and North Africa (late 10th cent.) and approximately the fifteenth or sixteenth century. Subsequent halakhists and Talmudists, known as **aḥaronim*, generally held the opinions of authorities from this period in high esteem and were often reluctant to disagree with them. Sometimes a regional distinction is made between the *ri'shonim* of Ashkenaz, Spain, France, North Africa, and so on. The literature of the *ri'shonim* comprises two genres: commentaries on the Talmud and on the code of Yitsḥaq *Alfasi, and **ḥiddushim* (*novellae*), often reached through critical study of the texts. Many of these works remain in manuscript, but a considerable number have been published in recent decades.

• Israel Jacob Yuval, "Ri'shonim ve-'Aḥaronim, Antiki et Moderni," *Zion* 57.4 (1992): 369–394 (with English summary). –EDWARD FRAM

RI'SHON LE-TSIYYON. See CHIEF RABBINATE.

RITES. See LITURGY; MINHAG; NUSSAḤ.

RITUAL BATH. See MIQVEH.

RITUAL LAW. See ISSUR VE-HETTER.

RITUAL MURDER ACCUSATION. See BLOOD LIBEL.

RITUAL PURITY. See IMPURITY.

RITUAL SLAUGHTER (Heb. *sheḥitah*), the act of butchering an animal or bird that is fit for consumption (*kasher*; see DIETARY LAWS) according to Jewish law (derived from *Dt*. 12.20–21), which consists of cutting through both the windpipe and the gullet by means of a sharp implement. Fish and those species of locust permitted as food (*Lv*. 11) do not require *sheḥitah*. The ritual slaughterer (**shoḥet*) must examine both windpipe and gullet after *sheḥitah* in order to ascertain that at least the major portion of both (or, in the case of fowl, of one) has been cut through. A knife or any sharp instrument may be used for *sheḥitah*, but the implement (*ḥallaf*) must be so sharp that the slit is effected by the keenness of the knife, without requiring downward pressure from the *shoḥet*. The cutting edge must be free from even the slightest imperfection (*pegimah*) and the sides of the cutting edge must be perfectly smooth. The implement is examined both before and after the *sheḥitah*. This examination is made by drawing the cutting edge and sides forward and backward slowly and carefully over the tip of the finger and nail in order to feel for any imperfection, by holding the edge against the light so that an imperfection would cast a shadow, or by drawing the knife across the surface of still water, in which case an imperfection in the cutting edge would leave a ripple. Five factors render *sheḥitah* invalid: *shehiyyah*, that is, if after commencing to slaughter the *shoḥet* interrupts or stays the progress of the knife; *derasah*, that is, if the knife is pressed downward instead of being drawn across the throat; *haḥladah*, that is, if the gullet and/or the windpipe are cut from the inside; *hagramah*, that is, if the cut is made too close to the head or body of the animal, thus going beyond the bounds of what is legally considered the neck; or *ʿiqqur*, that is, if the implement used is notched or otherwise unfit and the tissues are torn, not cut. *Sheḥitah* is supposed to be preceded by a special blessing, but the *sheḥitah* is not invalidated if the blessing is not recited. *Sheḥitah* has been both attacked and defended on humanitarian grounds; it is clear, however, that an animal loses consciousness almost immediately after the jugular vein has been severed. Most of the laws of *sheḥitah* can be found in Talmud tractate *Ḥullin* and in the *Yoreh Deʿah* section of the *Shulḥan ʿArukh*.

• Michael L. Munk, Eli Munk, and Yisra'el Me'ir Levinger, eds., *ʿEdut Ne'emanah*, 2 vols. (Brooklyn, N.Y., 1974–1976). Solomon David Sasson, *A Critical Study of Electrical Stunning and the Jewish Method of Slaughter (Shechita)*, 3d ed. (Letchworth, Eng., 1955). Ḥayyim Yosef Valdman, ed., *Torat ha-Sheḥitah* (Jerusalem, 1991).

RIZHIN. See RUZHIN, YISRA'EL OF.

ROBBERY, the open and forcible appropriation of another's goods (as opposed to *theft, which is carried out secretly). Withholding another's property, even though it has come legitimately into one's possession, is considered "oppression" (*Lv*. 19.13) and is included in the prohibition against robbery, as is the misappropriation of funds entrusted to one's care. The forcible taking of a pledge and borrowing without permission also fall under this prohibition. A robber (*Lv*. 19.13) is not subject to corporal punishment since his felony can be rectified by restoring the stolen property. If the stolen goods have undergone a change, for example, a beam that has been used in constructing a building, monetary restitution may be made (*Git*. 55a). The penalty for falsely denying a robbery while under oath is an additional quarter of the value of the stolen property. The prohibition against robbery is one of the seven *Noahic laws. See also BURGLARY.

• Emanuel B. Quint, *A Restatement of Rabbinic Civil Law*, vol. 1 (Northvale, N.J., 1990).

ROGACHOVER. See ROZIN, YOSEF.

ROMAN CATHOLIC CHURCH. Classic Christian attitudes and ecclesiastical policies toward the Jews crystallized mainly within the framework of Roman Catholicism, which, until the Reformation, was the standard form of Western *Christianity and which preserved the Adversus Iudaeos traditions of the *church fathers and sought to govern Jewish life in Christendom in accordance with them, while never entirely forsaking the tradition of the Roman empire, where Jews were a legally recognized religious minority.

From Late Antiquity to the Early Middle Ages. Though Christianity borrowed many essentials from Judaism, it viewed the continued existence of the latter as threatening or at least offensive. This ambivalence characterized the historic stance of Catholicism vis-à-vis the Jews, both theologically and in the efforts of Catholic leaders to translate doctrinal principles into legislation and public policy. Throughout the late ancient and medieval periods, councils of Catholic bishops struggled to assert the superiority of Christianity and to minimize the influence of Jews over Christians. The conversion of the Roman emperor Constantine, who proclaimed religious freedom for Christians in 313 and presided over the Nicene Council in 325, signaled an opportunity to implement such ecclesiastical demands, particularly enforced after Theodosius I (r. 379–395) proclaimed Catholicism the official religion of the empire. Yet the Christian emperors of Rome, as reflected in the Theodosian Code (438), wavered in their willingness to abandon their traditional toleration of the Jews, and their legislation, in its rhetoric and its substance, ranged from discriminatory to permissive. After the fall of the empire in the west, the treatment of the Jews by Catholic rulers continued to vary widely. Influenced by patristic teachings and Roman legal tradition alike, Pope Gregory the Great (r. 590–604) preached a policy that balanced restriction, especially against Jewish ownership of Christian slaves, and protection; in the precedent-setting bull of *Sicut Judaeis* (598), he decreed that just as one ought not to grant anything to the Jews beyond that allowed by law, so, too, they ought not to be deprived of what is rightfully theirs. The Catholic kings of the Visigoths, however, banned the Jews from Spain, outlawed the practice of Judaism, and even persecuted baptized Jews. In the ninth-century, on the other hand, Louis the Pious granted broad privileges to the Jews, provoking the protests and bitter anti-Jewish polemic of Archbishop Agobard of Lyons.

From the Crusades to the Catholic Reformation. The First Crusade in 1096 ushered the Catholic church into a period of unprecedented power, and the massacres of Jews by the Crusaders in the Rhineland underscored the need to define the place of the Jew in a properly ordered Christian society. The burgeoning of Christian scholarship in the twelfth and thirteenth centuries prompted the study of hitherto neglected Jewish texts, and the plenitude of papal power claimed by contemporary popes included jurisdiction over Jewish and Muslim infidels. Collections of canon law, notably the *Decretum Gratiani* (1140) and the decretals of Pope Gregory IX in 1234, codified old and new decrees concerning the proper status and behavior of Jews. Ecumenical councils convened by the papacy included the Jewish question in their agenda. Pope Innocent III (r. 1198–1216) complained bitterly of Jewish insubordination and endeavored to restrict the Jews to their divinely ordained servitude; under Innocent's direction, the Fourth Lateran Council of 1215 legislated against Jewish moneylending and ordered Jews under Christian rule to wear distinguishing marks on their clothing. Papal initiative subsequently led to condemnations and burnings of the Talmud (see BOOKS, BURNING OF) increased missionary activity among the Jews, and inquisitorial harassment of entire Jewish communities. Critical to these efforts were the mendicant friars of the Dominican and Franciscan orders. Spearheading the church's confrontation with the Jews, many friars believed that the Jews had abandoned their biblical religion for a satanic, Talmudic heresy and had accordingly forfeited their rights to toleration in Christendom. As the Middle Ages wore on, this outlook nourished popular conceptions of the Jew as an agent of Satan and the Antichrist. Jews were depicted as anatomically disfigured sexual perverts with offensive bodily odor and as the perpetrators of heinous crimes, including the desecration of the host, the ritual murder of innocent Christians (see BLOOD LIBEL), and the poisoning of wells. For the Jews of central Italy and Avignon, the Counter-Reformation heralded a new series of oppressive measures: the establishment (at Jewish expense) of a house of converts in Rome, renewed burning of the Talmud, Pope Paul IV's restriction of the Jews to ghettos and the most menial occupations in 1555, and Pope Pius V's expulsion of the Jews from all papal territory except Rome and Ancona in 1569.

From the Reformation to the Twentieth Century. Catholic attitudes toward the Jews underwent little substantive change prior to the twentieth century. While the church lost much of its influence in western Europe during the centuries following the Reformation, Catholic clergy continued to promote the persecution of Jews in many lands. Only in the twentieth century has the Catholic church begun to disavow the blatant antisemitism of its past. The record of the church during the Holocaust continues to evoke debate; Pope Pius XII refused to condemn Hitler's Final Solution publicly, but members of the church did exert themselves on behalf of Jews in some communities. Guided by Pope John XXIII, the Second Vatican Council issued its decree on non-Christian religions, *Nostra aetate* (1965), which absolved the Jewish people of blanket, collective responsibility for the crucifixion of Jesus and instigated Catholic–Jewish dialogue. Subsequent Catholic leaders have made additional gestures of rapprochement, and John Paul II displayed concern with the Holocaust, its implications for Christians, and its significance for contemporary Jews. He also spoke of the continuing validity of God's covenant with the Jews, traditionally denied in Catholic teaching. Opening a new era in Catholic–Jewish relations, and departing from established patristic teachings that the Jews lost their homeland as punishment for rejecting Christianity, the Holy See established formal diplomatic relations with the State of Israel in 1994.

Jewish Attitudes toward the Catholic Church. While Jews and Judaism have always figured prominently in Christian doctrine, Christianity, after having severed its links with the Jewish community to become a distinct gentile religion, mattered relatively little to Jewish theologians. Yet the exigencies of history, particularly in the wake of the Christianization of the Roman empire, assured the church a prominent place in Jewish life and thought, characterized by negative attitudes or, at best, by ambivalence. On the one hand, Jews perceived the Catholic church as the great oppressor, responsible for much of their misery and persecution throughout history. They strove to respond in kind to the polemical attacks of Catholics, and in theological typology Latin Christendom was identified with Edom, destined to bring Jewish suffering to its eschatological climax. On the other hand, Jews of western Europe realized the value of papal protection, and they habitually petitioned the Holy See for guarantees and privileges; medieval liturgies for papal coronation ceremonies indicate that Roman Jews presented a gift of a Torah scroll to newly elected popes, who then affirmed the linkage between Judaism and Christianity that rationalized continued Jewish existence in a Christian world. More recently, many Jews, particularly in non-Orthodox circles, have responded positively to the new Catholic openness to religious dialogue. See also INTERFAITH RELATIONS.

• **Collections of Documents:** David Berger, ed., *The Jewish–Christian Debate in the High Middle Ages: A Critical Edition of the Nizzahon Vetus* (Philadelphia, 1979). Robert Chazan, ed., *Church, State, and Jew in the Middle Ages* (New York, 1980). Solomon Grayzel, *The Church and the Jews in the XIIIth Century*, 2 vols. (New York, 1966–1989). Amnon Linder, ed., *The Jews in Roman Imperial Legislation* (Detroit, 1987). Hyam Maccoby, *Judaism on Trial: Jewish–Christian Disputations in the Middle Ages* (London, 1993). Shlomo Simonsohn, *The Apostolic See and the Jews*, 8 vols. (Toronto, 1988–1991). **Secondary Sources:** Jeremy Cohen, ed., *Essential Papers on Judaism and Christianity in Conflict* (New York, 1991). Charlotte Klein, *Anti-Judaism in Christian Theology* (Philadelphia, 1978). Guenter Lewy, *The Catholic Church and Nazi Germany* (New York, 1964). Walter Pakter, *Medieval Canon Law and the Jews* (Ebelsbach, 1988). James Parkes, *The Conflict of the Church and the Synagogue* (London, 1934). Rosemary Ruether, *Faith and Fratricide: The Theological*

Roots of Anti-Semitism (New York, 1974). Kenneth R. Stow, *Catholic Thought and Papal Jewry Policy, 1555–1593* (New York, 1976). Wolfgang Seiferth, *Synagogue and Church in the Middle Ages: Two Symbols in Art and Literature* (New York, 1970). Edward A. Synan, *The Popes and the Jews in the Middle Ages* (New York, 1965). Joshua Trachtenberg, *The Devil and the Jews* (New Haven, 1943). Diana Wood, ed., *Christianity and Judaism*, Studies in Church History 29 (Oxford, 1992).

—JEREMY COHEN

ROMANIOT RITE, liturgical rite originally followed by the Jews of the Byzantine empire, the Balkans, and Asia Minor. It was based chiefly upon the liturgy established by the authorities of the late gaonic period (latter half of the 10th and early 11th cents.), although it was also influenced by the Palestinian and Italian rituals. By the beginning of the twentieth century, it still survived among a few congregations on the island of Corfu though it had been almost completely abandoned elsewhere. The Romaniots spoke a Judeo-Greek dialect, and their prayer book included a prayer for the new moon in that language. On Yom Kippur, they read the *Book of Jonah* in both Hebrew and Greek, and they chanted *Kol Nidrei in Hebrew rather than Aramaic, as is the common practice.

• Stefan C. Reif, *Judaism and Hebrew Prayer: New Perspectives on Jewish Liturgical History* (Cambridge, 1993), pp. 133, 111, 227, 372.

—A. STANLEY DREYFUS

ROQEAḤ, ELʿAZAR. See ELʿAZAR BEN YEHUDAH OF WORMS.

ROSEN, YOSEF (died 1885), rabbi and scholar. Born in the Belorussian city of Gorodok, Rosen held rabbinic posts in *Tels and Slonim. In Slonim he came into conflict with both Ḥasidim and the growing community of Maskilim. Rosen's conciliatory nature and temperate character enabled him to retain authority and recognition in this complex situation. Rosen's writings, *ʿEdut bi-Yosef*, *Porat Yosef*, and *She'erit Yosef*, offer *responsa*, *novellae*, and legal analyses stemming from the *Yoreh Deʿah* and *Ḥoshen Mishpat* sections of the *Shulḥan ʿArukh*.

• Yohanan Lederman, *Sefer Megillat Razin: Le-Yovlo shel . . . Yosef Rosen . . .* (Jerusalem, 1986).

—JACOB MESKIN

ROSENBLATT, JOSEF (1882–1933), Russian-born cantor and composer. After conducting services throughout eastern Europe as a child prodigy, Rosenblatt served as *ḥazzan* in Mukachevo, Bratislava, and Hamburg before immigrating to the United States in 1912. Concert tours of Europe and the United States brought him great fame. Nevertheless, Rosenblatt maintained a scrupulous adherence to Jewish law and refused lucrative offers to appear in operatic roles and secular films. He did, however, allow his voice to be heard in *The Jazz Singer* (1927), and at the time of his sudden death, he was working in Jerusalem on a Yiddish film that would feature landscapes of Israel as a background to his own compositions.

Rosenblatt possessed a brilliant tenor voice with an impressive coloratura and an extensive range of two and a half octaves. Some of his best-known works were included in the 1907 collection *Tefillot Yosef*. He was among the leading performers and recording artists during the golden age of eastern European *ḥazzanut* (see CANTORIAL MUSIC), and several of his melodies retain a place in the synagogue repertoire.

• Henry Rosenblatt, *The Music of Yossele Rosenblatt* (Cedarhurst, N.Y., 1989), music score. Samuel Rosenblatt, *Yossele Rosenblatt: The Story of His Life as Told by His Son* (New York, 1954).

—MARSHA BRYAN EDELMAN

ROSENZWEIG, FRANZ (1886–1929), German religious philosopher. His path to Judaism was marked by a dramatic turn from assimilation and philosophical relativism to a religious faith that took him at first, to the threshold of conversion to Christianity. His affirmation of religious faith, and eventually traditional Judaism (although his stance was hardly Orthodox) as a framework to realize this faith, was prompted by his adoption of a belief in revelation as a historical and existential reality. Such a belief must be the matrix of any genuine theology, he contended, otherwise one embraces an atheistic theology. Theology must proceed from the theocentric fact of divine revelation, of God's address to human beings. Rosenzweig developed his understanding of this address on the basis of a radical critique of philosophical idealism, with its quest for universal and thus timeless abstract truths. In contrast, revelation is in time; it is an occurrence whereby God establishes a relation with specific time-bound individuals. God addresses individuals in their finite existence calling them, as it were, by their "first and last names" which distinguish them existentially from all others. This relation is one of love, the divine utterance of Thou to the temporally contingent I of the individual. In revelation, the individual, in finite existence, is thus confirmed by divine love and blessed with an encounter with eternity.

This affirmation of revelation allowed Rosenzweig to discern in Judaism what many of his generation of assimilated German Jews had denied, namely, that Judaism was a faith of enduring existential significance. He elaborated his conception of faith and of Judaism in *Der Stern der Erlösung* (1921; English trans., *The Star of Redemption* by W. Hallo [New York, 1970; Notre Dame, 1985]). In this work, Rosenzweig focuses on the spiritual life of the Jews as structured by their ancient liturgical calendar. As a community of prayer, he argues, the Jews experience time not only as sacred but as cyclical: the pattern of prayer that guides the Jews' passion and spiritual imagination is set in a recurring yearly cycle. Hence, in prayer Jews do not experience the "growth" of time moving from year to year, but rather as spinning upon itself, in a recurring pattern of liturgical celebration. The linear, ever unfolding time of the mundane world, thus, hardly affects the spiritual reality of the Jews. The Jewish people, Rosenzweig concludes, is a community apart from history. But although insulated from history, or, rather, from the conceits and follies of a nation that lives in history, the Jews are not, as is often charged by Christian critics, a-historical; rather, they are meta-historical. Standing apart from history, they anticipate the spiritual reality of redemption, and thus, as the existential embodiment of the eschatological promise, they serve to inspire and prod the church (which, because of its divinely appointed mission to the gentiles, must perforce act through history) to lead humanity to the goal of a world beyond history; that is, a world that has overcome division, strife and war. For Rosenzweig, the Synagogue, as he preferred to call Jewry as a liturgical community, and the church are complementary covenants; the former being the sustaining "fire," the latter the luminous "flame" of God's saving light.

Subsequent to writing the *Star*, Rosenzweig devoted himself to adult Jewish education (see his *On Jewish Learning*, edited by N. N. Glatzer [New York, 1955]), founding the Freies Jüdisches Lehrhaus in Frankfurt. Guided by a unique dialogical approach to study of the classical sources of Judaism, the Lehrhaus became the fulcrum for a veritable spiritual renaissance of German Jewry. Although bedridden for the last seven years of his life by an almost total paralysis, he continued his religious quest. In particular, he explored the extra-liturgical expressions of Jewish piety, such as the commandments (*mitsvot*), which, when observed not as law but as a sacramental calling, he regarded as facilitating one's relation to the living God. Rosenzweig collaborated with Martin *Buber in translating the Bible into German.

• Luc Anckaert and Bernhard Casper, eds., *Franz Rosenzweig: A Primary and Secondary Bibliography* (Louvain, 1990). Nahum N. Glatzer, *Franz Rosenzweig: His Life and Thought*, 2d ed. (New York, 1961). Paul Mendes-Flohr, ed., *The Philosophy of Franz Rosenzweig* (Hanover, N.H., 1988). Stéphane Mosès, *System and Revelation: The Philosophy of Franz Rosenzweig*, translated by Catherine Tihanyi (Detroit, 1992).

—PAUL MENDES-FLOHR

RO'SH. See ASHER BEN YEHI'EL.

RO'SH HA-SHANAH (רֹאשׁ הַשָּׁנָה; New Year), name of a festival and of a Mishnaic tractate.

Festival. Four days of the year are regarded as the New Year for different and specific purposes. They are enumerated in the first *mishnah* of tractate *Ro'sh ha-Shanah*. The first day of Nisan marked the New Year for dating the reigns of Jewish kings and the order of months for religious purposes, including the festivals. In Temple times, 1 Elul marked the New Year for cattle tithes, when tithes had to be given for cattle born during the previous year. The first day of Tishrei is the New Year for civil calendrical purposes and for **shemittah* and **yovel*. The fifteenth day of Shevat (or 1 Shevat, according to Beit Shamm'ai) is the New Year for trees (see TU BI-SHEVAT).

Of the four New Years, only 1 Tishrei is celebrated as a religious New Year festival (Ro'sh ha-Shanah), since on that day "all who have entered into the world pass before him [in judgment] like a flock of sheep" (*R. ha-Sh.* 1.2) and also because the first day of Tishrei is the only one of the four New Years to be specified in the Bible as a festival—"A Sabbath, a memorial of the sounding of the *shofar" (*Lv.* 23.23–24)—and "A day of sounding of the shofar (*Nm.* 29.1–6)—although no mention is made of it there as the New Year. The sounding of the shofar is one of the distinctive features of the religious celebration of the festival and has largely determined the character of the liturgy of the day, particularly the *Musaf service (see FESTIVAL PRAYERS). In the Ashkenazi rite, worshipers wear white as a symbol of purity, which traditionally is the color of the synagogue ark cover and Torah scroll cover on this day. Three groups of prayers, each consisting of ten scriptural verses selected from all three sections of the Bible, are inserted into the Musaf service, each with an introduction and closing paragraph compiled by Rav in the third century. The first section consists of verses describing the sovereignty of God (hence, called *Malkhuyyot), the second speaks of God's remembrance of his creatures (*Zikhronot), and the third is related to the sounding of the shofar (*Shofarot). After each section the shofar is sounded according to a fixed pattern (with minor differences between the Sephardi and Ashkenazi rites). The solemn liturgy for the day includes special *piyyutim*, *Avinu Malkenu, and in the Ashkenazi rite *U-Netanneh Toqef (culminating in the declaration that penitence, prayer, and charity can annul a negative divine judgment), while during the recitation of *ʿAleinu in the repetition of Musaf, it is customary among Ashkenazim in Orthodox and some Conservative and Reform synagogues for the reader (and congregants) to prostrate themselves and kneel. Ro'sh ha-Shanah takes on additional significance since it marks the beginning of ten days of penitence (see ʿASERET YEMEI TESHUVAH), which culminate in *Yom Kippur. Ro'sh ha-Shanah does not commemorate any historical event in Jewish history but rather the creation of the world. It has been since rabbinic times a period of self-examination and divine judgment, a judgment in this case universal. On this day God judges mankind for the forthcoming year, a judgment finally sealed on Yom Kippur. The liturgy stresses people's yearning for the establishment of God's sovereignty over the entire world and the ushering in of the millennium. Ro'sh ha-Shanah, observed for one day in biblical times, is now observed for two days, even in Erets Yisra'el (1–2 Tishrei; see YOM TOV SHENI SHEL GALUYYOT). However, many Reform congregations follow the biblical custom of one day. Various customs are connected with its celebration. On the first night, dishes are prepared that are meant to augur well for the new year; for example, apples dipped in honey are eaten while a prayer is recited for a "good and sweet year." On the second night, new fruit is eaten in order to be able to say the *She-Heheyanu blessing. It is also customary to go to a river or pond to recite *Tashlikh. The sages also called the festival Yom ha-Din (Day of Judgment) and Yom ha-Zikkaron (Day of Remembrance, i.e., a day on which God remembers humankind). The traditional greeting on the holiday is "may you be inscribed [in the Book of Life] for a good year."

• Shmuel Yosef Agnon, *Days of Awe: Being a Treasury of Traditions, Legends, and Learned Commentaries . . .* (New York, 1965). Max Arzt, *Justice and Mercy: Commentary on the Liturgy of the New Year and the Day of*

Atonement (New York, 1963). Philip Goodman, ed., *The Rosh Hashanah Anthology*, with a new introduction by Ellen Frankel (Philadelphia, 1992). Devorah HaKohen and Menaḥem HaKohen, *Ḥaggim u-Moʿadim Ro'sh ha-Shanah . . .* (Jerusalem, 1978).

Tractate. The tractate *Ro'sh ha-Shanah* is in Mishnah order Moʿed, in four chapters, with related material in the Tosefta' and in both Talmuds. Its four chapters are evenly divided between two topics: the laws governing the sanctification of the new moon and the laws of Ro'sh ha-Shanah, especially the sounding of the shofar and the liturgy.

The sanctification of the new moon (see RO'SH ḤODESH) was charged with great significance for several reasons, including the establishment of the date of the festivals and the existence, during Second Temple times, of competing sectarian calendars (Boethusians, Samaritans, Qumran community). The sanctification was a dramatic public event that reinforced the connection between the high court in Jerusalem (later in Yavneh, see *R. ha-Sh.* 2.9) and the people (*R. ha-Sh.* 2.3–4). Although the festivals were sanctified by God (*R. ha-Sh.* 2.2), the authorization granted the court to determine the time when the festivals would occur symbolized the autonomy conferred by God upon human authority.

The central rule of the Ro'sh ha-Shanah festival is the sounding of the shofar. Although the scriptural sources for this ritual (*Lv.* 23.24; *Nm.* 29.1) do not define the instrument to be used, *Ro'sh ha-Shanah* specifies the use of animal horns, examining the symbolic meaning of the horns of various animals.

The tractate in Talmud Bavli was translated into English by Maurice Simon in the Soncino Talmud (London, 1938).

• Chanoch Albeck, ed., *Shishah Sidrei Mishnah, Seder Moʿed* (Jerusalem, 1952). Philip Blackman, ed. and trans., *Mishnayoth*, vol. 2, *Order Moed* (Gateshead, 1973). Pinhas Kehati, ed., *Mishnah: A New Translation with a Commentary, Seder Moed*, vol. 4, *Yoma, Sukkah, Betzah, Rosh Hashanah* (Jerusalem, 1990). Hermann Leberecht Strack and Günter Stemberger, *Introduction to the Talmud and Midrash*, rev. and updat. ed., translated by Markus Bockmuehl (Minneapolis, 1992).

—AVRAHAM WALFISH

RO'SH HA-SHANAH LA-'ILANOT. See TU BI-SHEVAT.

RO'SH ḤODESH (רֹאשׁ חֹדֶשׁ; New Moon), the beginning of the Hebrew month. During the period of the First Temple, Ro'sh Ḥodesh was regarded as a semi-festival (possibly the continuation of an ancient moon-festival tradition) when the people abstained from business (*Am.* 8.5), thronged the Temple (*Is.* 1.13–14, 66.23), held family feasts (*1 Sm.* 20.5), and visited the prophet (*2 Kgs.* 4.23). The festive character of the day was equally signified by its special sacrifice (*Nm.* 28.11–15) and by the blowing of the trumpet (*Nm.* 10.10). The festivities surrounding the new moon disappeared during the Second Temple period, except for the custom granting freedom from work on that day. According to rabbinic legend, when the Israelites were at Mount Sinai, women refused to join their husbands in building the golden calf. As a reward, God made Ro'sh Ḥodesh a special day for women (*Pirqei de-Rabbi Eliʿezer*). Considerable attention was paid to the determination of the new moon by the Sanhedrin through the testimony of two eye witnesses (see CALENDAR), and the liturgy of the day reflects its ancient importance. The dates of Ro'sh Ḥodesh were finally fixed in 358 CE under *Hillel II, whose calendar was based on astronomic calculation. When in the third century Rav, on a visit to Babylon from Palestine, heard a community reciting the half *Hallel on that day, for which there was no apparent authority, he decided to retain the custom—it was obviously based on an old tradition; recitation of the half Hallel has since become universal. The festive nature of Ro'sh Ḥodesh is further stressed by the scriptural reading, the recitation of *Yaʿaleh ve-Yavo', and the removal of the *tefillin* before the recitation of *Musaf. Fasting and mourning are forbidden on Ro'sh Ḥodesh, which is observed for two days, the last day of the old month and the first of the new, when the preceding month has thirty days. If the preceding month has twenty-nine days, Ro'sh Ḥodesh is observed for only one day. The blessing recited on the Sabbath preceding the new moon (Shabbat Mevarekhim) is a relic of a custom in the synagogue, antedating the fixing of the calendar, to establish the new moon on the evidence of eyewitnesses. Since the early 1970s, growing numbers of Jewish women, particularly in the United States, have rediscovered the new moon's special significance. Orthodox women's prayer groups often meet on Ro'sh Ḥodesh, naming ceremonies for baby daughters are frequently held then, and communities of women, in synagogue and private settings, participate in rituals celebrating the rebirth and renewal of women and the moon. See also BIRKAT HA-ḤODESH; SABBATHS, SPECIAL; YOM KIPPUR QATAN.

• Susan Berrin, ed., *Celebrating the New Moon: A Rosh Chodesh Anthology* (Northvale, N.J., 1996). Judith Y. Solomon, *The Rosh Hodesh Table* (New York, 1995).

RO'SH YESHIVAH (רֹאשׁ יְשִׁיבָה; head of the *yeshivah*), the head of an institution for the study of the Talmud. In the *Yequm Purqan prayer, the phrase occurs in the Aramaic plural as *reishei metivata'*; in that passage, the heads of *yeshivot* rank after the ge'onim and exilarchs but take precedence over "judges in the gates." Now, the title is also applied in some *yeshivot* not only to the head of the *yeshivah* but also to the permanent members of the teaching staff. In the national religious *yeshivot* in Israel, the term is reserved for the head of the institution, while the other lecturers are known as *ramim* (the plural of *ram*, an abbreviation of the phrase *ro'sh metivta'*). In eastern Europe the *ro'sh yeshivah* traditionally deferred to the town rabbi in questions of Jewish law. Currently, however, particularly among the Ḥaredim, it is the *ro'sh yeshivah* who is the final arbiter in matters of Jewish law.

—SHMUEL HIMELSTEIN

ROSSI, ʿAZARYAH BEN MOSHEH DEI (c.1511–1577), Italian scholar. Born in Mantua into a prominent Italian-Jewish family, Rossi studied medicine as well as archaeology and history, and he was familiar with Hebrew, Latin, and Italian literature. He lived in various towns in Italy, notably Ferrara and Mantua. The first section of Rossi's major work, *Me'or ʿEinayim* (Mantua, 1573–1575), compared Jewish and non-Jewish classical and medieval theories of earthquakes. The second section consisted of the first Hebrew translation of the **Letter of Aristeas*. In the final section, Rossi critically examined the veracity of Jewish sources (but not the Bible) in light of contradictory non-Jewish sources, including the writings of the church fathers. The effect was to reconfigure Jewish history and chronology. Rossi challenged the accuracy and origin of the traditional Jewish calendar and concluded that the Persian period of Jewish history was longer and more important than acknowledged. He further proved that *Sefer Yosippon*, considered an authoritative source of ancient Jewish history, was a medieval forgery. As the first Jewish scholar to use Greek-Jewish literature in his reconstruction of Jewish history, literature, religion, and culture, Rossi was largely responsible for reviving interest in the works of *Philo. Though contemporary religious scholars never doubted Rossi's personal piety, his work was found objectionable and banned. Some historians view Rossi's book as the first modern work of Jewish history.

• Salo W. Baron, *History and Jewish Historians* (Philadelphia, 1964). David Ruderman, ed., *Essential Papers on Jewish Culture in Renaissance and Baroque Italy* (New York, 1992). Lester Segal, *Historical Consciousness and Religious Tradition in Azariah de' Rossi's Meor Einayim* (Philadelphia, 1989). Giuseppe Veltri, "The Humanist Sense of History and the Jewish Idea of Tradition: Azariah de' Rossi's Critique of Philo Alexandrinus," *Jewish Studies Quarterly* 2 (1995): 372–393. Yosef Yerushalmi, *Zakhor: Jewish History and Jewish Memory* (New York, 1989).

—DIDIER Y. REISS

ROSSI, SALAMONE (c.1570–1628), first composer of music for the synagogue. Born in Mantua, Italy, Rossi entered the service of the Gonzagan court of Mantua as a singer and violist in 1587. He also conducted an instrumental ensemble comprised largely of Jewish musicians and is credited as the originator of the "trio sonata." Relying upon a 1605 *responsum* by R. Leone *Modena permitting choral music in the synagogue, Rossi published a group of thirty-three settings of Hebrew psalms and other liturgical texts for varying combinations of three to eight voices, *Ha-Shirim Asher li-Shelomoh* (1622–1623). The limited musical vocabulary of Rossi's time required him to employ the Western harmonic techniques of the seventeenth century and to largely abandon the Eastern flavored traditional melodies of the Italian synagogue. Rossi took great care in selecting his texts, however, often displaying uniquely Jewish sensitivities in settings including Barekhu and Psalm 137.

Although his ducal patrons absolved him of the requirement to wear a yellow patch identifying him as a Jew and restricting his movement throughout the duchy, Rossi remained a proud Jew, adding the name Ebreo (the Hebrew) to his signature. Nothing is known about him after the Austrian invasion of Mantua (1628–1630), but the nineteenth-century recovery of his scores (in the attic of a Paris synagogue) brought to light his contribution to synagogue music history.

• Irene Heskes, "Reflections on Creativity and Heritage: Salomone Rossi and His Era," in *Passport to Jewish Music: Its History, Traditions and Culture* (Westport, Conn., 1994).

—MARSHA BRYAN EDELMAN

ROZIN, YOSEF (1858–1936), one of the outstanding Talmudists of the nineteenth and twentieth centuries; known as the Rogachover, after his birthplace, Rogachov, Poland. From 1889 he served as rabbi to the Hasidic community of Dvinsk (Daugavpils, Latvia). Rozin knew a great deal of rabbinic literature, including both Talmuds, by heart and was a prolific author. Unlike his clear verbal expositions, his writings are obscure and contain many arguments that are made by referring to unspecified sources. His entire literary body of work is known as *Tsofnat Paʿneaḥ* Many of his *responsa* as well as his commentary on Maimonides' *Mishneh Torah* (1903–1908) have been published.

• Moshe Grosberg, *Tsefunot ha-Rogachovi* (Jerusalem, 1976). H. Sapir and M. S. Kasher, *Ha-Ga'on ha-Rogachovi ve-Talmudo* (Jerusalem, 1958).

RUAḤ HA-QODESH (רוּחַ הַקֹּדֶשׁ; holy spirit), divine spirit; spirit emanating from *God. The expression occurs only three times in the Bible, where it is synonymous with God (*Is*. 63.10) or else signifies his sustaining and inspiring presence (*Is*. 63.11; *Ps*. 51.13). Elsewhere biblical usage prefers "spirit of God" (Ruaḥ Elohim, Ruaḥ YHVH, or Ruaḥ El) to denote the creative action of God (*Gn*. 1.2; *Ps*. 129.7; *Job* 33.4), as well as the powers of superior wisdom, statesmanship, and valor that he imparts to human beings (e.g., *Jgs*. 13.25; *Is*. 11.2), more particularly the gift of inspired speech (*2 Sm*. 23.2). It is the latter sense that became especially associated with the later usage of the expression. According to the Talmud (*Sot*. 48b) the holy spirit departed from Israel with the death of the last prophets, although a minor form of celestial communication still existed in the **bat qol*. Hence, in some apocryphal writings "holy spirit" refers either to the age of biblical *prophecy or to the prophetic revival in the messianic age (cf. *Jl*. 2.28–29); in others, the term is made to approximate the concept of an ever-present divine *wisdom. The *Targum often renders the "spirit of God" as the "spirit of prophecy" and in this sense the term "holy spirit" is often akin to the concept of **shekhinah*. Rabbinic and medieval philosophical writers distinguished higher and lower forms of *inspiration and degrees of action attributed to the holy spirit, for example, the direct inspiration of the Pentateuch, the "prophetic spirit" in the prophetic books proper, and the holy spirit informing the *Hagiographa. Following R. Pinḥas ben Ya'ir's dictum (*Sot*. 9.15), "piety leads to the holy spirit," it has been generally held—with many variations of form and emphasis—that the holy spirit as a degree of spiritual perfection (viz., communion with God, **devequt*, and even illumination) can be attained by earnest striving, religious observance, ascetic discipline, and moral and intellectual perfection.

• Joshua Abelson, *The Immanence of God in Rabbinical Literature* (New York, 1969). Abraham Joshua Heschel, *Between God and Man* (New York, 1975).

RULE OF THE COMMUNITY, a work among several others found in the *Dead Sea Scrolls containing regulations for the sectarian *Qumran community. The *Rule* *of the Community* (*Serekh ha-Yaḥad*) deals with admission of new members, the annual covenant ceremony, communal organization and meetings, and the penal code. It incorporates a manifesto of the community's aims, a treatise on the "Two Spirits," and a concluding hymn. Appended to one manuscript (1QS) are rules for the eschatological community (the Rule of the Congregation and the Rule of Benedictions). The numerous copies of *Rule of the Community* reflect the importance of these rules for the Qumran sect.

• J. H. Charlesworth et al., eds., *The Dead Sea Scrolls: Hebrew, Aramaic, and Greek Texts with English Translations*, vol. 1, *Rule of the Community and Related Documents* (Tübingen and Louisville, 1994). Sarianna Metso, "The Preliminary Results of the Reconstruction of 4QS[e]," *Journal of Jewish Studies* 44 (1993): 303–308. —ESTHER GLICKLER CHAZON

RUTH, book in the Hagiographa section of the Bible, one of the Five Scrolls (see ḤAMESH MEGILLOT). The story, which is set in the time of the judges, tells of Naomi, wife of Elimelech of the tribe of Judah, who moved to Moab to escape a famine. After a ten-year sojourn in Moab, during which her husband and two sons die, Naomi returns impoverished to Bethlehem. Her Moabite daughter-in-law Ruth insists on following her, and Naomi fails in her attempt to dissuade her. While gleaning in the fields, in her concern for Naomi's survival, Ruth meets a wealthy landowner, Boaz, whom she discovers to be a kinsman of Naomi. Boaz has heard of Ruth's selfless devotion to Naomi and treats her deferentially. At the end of the harvest, Ruth, acting on Naomi's advice, seeks out Boaz by night on the threshing floor and entreats him to assume the responsibilities of the next of kin and redeem the fortunes of the family. Boaz agrees but does not compromise Ruth's honor. Only after dutifully ascertaining that another, closer kinsman has forfeited his rights does Boaz make Ruth his lawfully wedded wife. She bears him a son, who is declared to be Naomi's child and is reared by Naomi. The son, Obed, is the grandfather of King David. Rabbinic tradition ascribes the book to Samuel (*B. B.* 14b), but linguistic and other evidence indicate that it was probably written in postexilic times. The basic aim of the book, which is divided into four chapters, is to provide a genealogy for David, missing in the *Book of Samuel*. Many commentators assume that the book, by arguing that a non-Israelite can be worthy of producing royal progeny, opposes the measures taken by Ezra to combat intermarriage. Others claim the opposite: that Ruth is an atypical non-Israelite, and that by stressing that Obed is legally Naomi's child and not Ruth's, the book merely acknowledges a Moabite strain in David's lineage but minimizes its importance. The *Book of Ruth* is read in the synagogue on the festival of Shavuʿot because of its connection with the harvest and with King David, traditionally believed to have been born on Shavuʿot.

• Edward F. Campbell, Jr., *Ruth*, The Anchor Bible, 2d ed. (Garden City, N.Y., 1975). Jack M. Sasson, *Ruth: A New Translation with a Philological Commentary and a Formalist–Folklorist Interpretation* (Baltimore, 1979). Yair Zakovitch, *Rut: 'Im Mavo' u-Ferush* (Jerusalem, 1990). —BARUCH J. SCHWARTZ

RUTH RABBAH, Midrashic work on the biblical book of *Ruth* contained in the medieval anthology *Midrash Rabbah; probably compiled in Palestine about 500 CE. It was first published in Pesaro in 1519. There is an English translation by Louis Isaac Rabinowitz in the Soncino edition of *Midrash Rabbah* (1951) and another by Jacob Neusner entitled *Ruth Rabbah: An Analytical Translation* (1989).

• Myron Bialik Lerner, "Aggadat Rut u-Midrash Rut Rabbah," Ph.D. dissertation, The Hebrew University of Jerusalem, 1971. Hermann Leberecht Strack and Günter Stemberger, *Introduction to the Talmud and Midrash*, rev. and updat. ed., translated by Markus Bockmuehl (Minneapolis, 1992). —MARC BREGMAN

RUZHIN, YISRA'EL OF (1796–1850), great-grandson of R. *Dov Ber of Mezhirech; one of the most controversial figures in the history of Hasidism. Rabbi Yisra'el Friedmann is known for the great luxury and splendor with which he surrounded himself. He was revered as a powerful holy man by thousands of followers, and his blessing was thought to have great impact. In 1838 he was accused (probably accurately) of collusion in the murder of two Jews who were informers for the Russian government. His imprisonment, which lasted nearly two years, caused great consternation among his faithful. Even after he was released for lack of evidence, the government continued to watch him, suspecting that he wanted to establish political hegemony for himself in the Jewish community. He fled Russia, first to Kishinev in Bessarabia, then to Jassy, in Moldavia, and in 1845 he settled in Sadagora, just outside Chernovtsy, Bukovina, then under Austrian rule. There he reestablished his court in undiminished glory. His sons succeeded him in Sadagora, Chortkov, and also in various towns of Romania. In 1869 his son Dov of Leova caused great scandal by leaving his Ḥasidim, moving to the home of a supporter of the Haskalah in Chernovtsy, and denouncing Hasidism as a sham. While he soon recanted, perhaps forced by his brothers, the incident was not forgotten. Rabbi Ḥayyim *Halberstam claimed that his apostasy had been punishment for the opulent life-style of the Friedmanns, and a long controversy ensued. Later generations of the Ruzhin dynasty were scattered throughout the Galician-Romanian border areas. Many perished during the Holocaust.

• David Assaf, "R. Yisra'el mi-Ruz'in u-Meqomo be-Toledot ha-Ḥasidut ba-Maḥatsit ha-Ri'shonah shel ha-Me'ah ha-Teshaʿ-'Esreh," Ph.D. dissertation, Hebrew University, 1992. —ARTHUR GREEN

RYMANOWER, MENAḤEM MENDEL. See MENAḤEM MENDEL BEN YOSEF OF RYMANÓW.

S

SAʿADYAH BEN YOSEF GA'ON (882–942), scholar and ga'on in Babylonia. Saʿadyah was born in the Fayum district of Egypt and wandered through Palestine and other lands before settling in Babylonia. After playing a leading role in the controversy between Palestine and Babylonia concerning the fixing of the calendar (921–922), he was appointed ga'on of Sura in 928, in spite of his unconventional background (ge'onim usually belonged to one of a small number of Babylonian families intimately associated with a given academy and spent their entire careers within that setting) and reservations concerning his uncompromising personality. These misgivings were not entirely unfounded. Shortly after his appointment, Saʿadyah became embroiled in a bitter conflict with the exilarch David ben Zakk'ai, who had secured his appointment; each declared the other to be deposed and appointed a sucessor. Years passed before the two men were reconciled, by dint of the efforts of leading members of the Jewish community of Baghdad.

Saʿadyah's background and personality led to a profound revolution in the nature of geonic intellectual and literary activity. Prior to his period of office, the intellectual elite of Babylonian Jewry concerned itself almost exclusively with the transmission, explication, and practical application of the Talmud Bavli, the literary vehicle for these endeavors being **responsa*. Saʿadyah expanded the canonical library to include the Talmud Yerushalmi, and probably other works of post-tannaitic Palestinian rabbinic literature, such as various *midrashim*. Another innovation was the composition of systematic treatises on selected halakhic topics. These were modeled on similar works in the field of Islamic law (*fiqh*); a striking indication of this dependence is that they were invariably written in Judeo-Arabic. These works represented a radical departure in rabbinic literature, which had previously been dominated by collective and largely anonymous works (e.g., the two Talmuds), and served as a precedent for later rabbinic authors.

Particularly noteworthy is Saʿadyah's *siddur* (prayer book; *Siddur Rav Saʿadyah Ga'on*, edited by. S. Assaf, I. Davidson, and B. I. Joel [1941]), which combines liturgical texts with halakhic instructions, not all of them concerned with liturgical matters. In contrast to his other halakhic monographs, Saʿadyah dispensed with Talmudic proof texts in his *siddur*, on the ground that it was intended to be a practical manual rather than an academic text. A large part of the prayer book is devoted to describing and analyzing various local customs that Saʿadyah had encountered in the course of his travels. Numerous liturgical poems (*piyyutim*) are also included, as are two prose petitions (*baqqashot*) that he composed.

Although apparently not the first, Saʿadyah's Judeo-Arabic translation of the Torah and several other biblical books achieved great popularity and influence among Arabic-speaking Jews. He also wrote innovative commentaries on a number of biblical books, including at least half of the Torah. These had a profound impact on later Jewish biblical commentators (especially, though not exclusively, on those writing in Arabic) and emphasized philological, philosophical, and polemical themes.

In the field of *piyyut*, Saʿadyah was one of the earliest leading poets to reside in Babylonia. Much of his poetry is characterized by linguistic innovations, in keeping with his belief that any morphological form attested in Biblical Hebrew might legitimately be applied to any Biblical Hebrew root. Closely related to his work in the biblical and poetic fields are a number of grammatical and lexicographical writings, including the *Egron*, a dictionary of which one half was arranged in alphabetical order and the other half as a rhyming dictionary to assist poets (edited by N. Allony [1969]).

Saʿadyah's *Book of Beliefs and Opinions*, known in Hebrew under the title *Emunot ve-Deʿot*, is the first great medieval Jewish philosophical classic. This work is indebted to Aristotelianism and Platonism and clearly states the view held by most medieval philosophers that there was a distinction but no contradiction between reason and revealed religion. Intellectual speculation only confirms the truths of Judaism. The Torah provides a philosophical system. Creation is *ex nihilo* and within time, and proof of God's existence can be inferred from creation. The object of creation was to bring happiness within the reach of all creatures; for the individual, this is attained through the commandments, which fall into two categories: ethical commandments, which conform to reason and would be observed even without revelation; and ceremonial commandments, which have the authority of revelation alone. The Torah is revealed reason. Saʿadyah's definitions of God and his attributes influenced philosophers and mystics (e.g., the Ḥasidei Ashkenaz). His philosophical approach owes much to Islamic writers of the Kalam school, who had grappled with similar issues after becoming acquainted with the works of classical philosophers. *Emunot ve-Deʿot*, written in Judeo-Arabic, was translated into and paraphrased in Hebrew several times during the Middle Ages and represents an important milestone in the history of Jewish philosophy, although it was harshly criticized by later authors, including Maimonides.

An important number of Saʿadyah's writings are explicitly polemical and directed mainly at the Karaites and other sectarians or heretics (notably against Ḥivi al-Balkhi, published by Israel Davidson [1915]) but also at opponents within the world of rabbinic Judaism, such as David ben Zakk'ai. Implicit polemics also occur in many of Saʿadyah's works in other fields.

Most of Saʿadyah's halakhic works remain in manuscript. A number were published by J. Müller (Paris, 1897). The first Hebrew edition of *The Book of Beliefs and Opinions* appeared in Constantinople in 1562; the Arabic original, edited by S. Landauer, in 1880; and an English translation by S. Rosenblatt in 1948. Yosef Kafaḥ published a Hebrew translation with the Arabic original in 1970. Saʿadyah's Bible commentary on *Genesis* appeared in 1980, edited by M. Zucker, and an English translation of the commentary on *Job*, by L. E. Goodman (*The Book of Theodicy*), in 1988. A five-volume edition, *Saadia ben Joseph al-Fayyumi: Oeuvres completes*, edited by J. Derenbourg, H. Derenbourg, and M. Lambert, was issued between 1893 and 1899.

• Louis Finkelstein, ed., *Rav Saadia Gaon: Studies in His Honor* (New York, 1944). H. Malter, *Saadia Gaon: His Life and Works* (Philadelphia, 1942). Erwin I. J. Rosenthal, ed., *Saadya Studies* (Manchester, 1943). Solomon L. Skoss, *Saadia Gaon, The Earliest Hebrew Grammarian* (Philadelphia, 1955). M. Ventura, *La Philosophie de Saadia Gaon* (Paris, 1934). Moshe Zucker, *ʿAl Targum Rasag la-Torah* (New York, 1959), with English summary. Menahem Zulai, *Ha-'Askolah Ha-Paytanit shel Rav Saʿadyah Ga'on* (Jerusalem, 1964).

—ROBERT BRODY

SABA, AVRAHAM BEN YAʿAQOV (15th–16th cent.), Bible commentator and kabbalist. When the Jews were expelled from his native Spain, he moved to Oporto in Portugal. There his wife and children were subjected to forced baptism; he was imprisoned but managed to escape to Morocco and settled in Fez. He had had to leave his writings behind but rewrote them from memory. Later he moved to Tlemcen in Algeria and possibly from there to Italy and Adrianople.

His major work, *Tseror ha-Mor* (Venice, 1522; repr. under the title *Ḥibbur Qadosh ve-Nora'* [Warsaw, 1880]; edited by B. Wichleder [Bene Beraq, 1990]), is a commentary on the Torah containing many topical messages for his contemporaries, among them the importance of observing the Sabbath and not taking non-Jewish wives. He identifies with the biblical stories, seeing Mordecai and Esther as precursors of the Marranos, and criticizes Esther for entering the palace of Ahasuerus, compared to Ruth, who clung to the God of Israel. Saba sharply criticized Spain and Portugal and did not spare the Muslim lands on account of the sufferings of Jews in North Africa (in his *Eshkol ha-Kofer*, commentaries on the Five Scrolls, of which his commentaries on *Ruth* and *Esther* were published by A. Segal [Breslau–Drogobych, 1904–1908]).

• Shalom Bar-Asher in *Gerushei Sefarad u-Shemad Portugal: Hishtaqqefutam be-Ve'urei R. Avraham Saba . . .* , by Zebulun Buaron (Jerusalem, 1993), pp. 1–2. Abraham Gross, "The World of R. Abraham Saba," Ph.D. dissertation, Harvard University, 1982. Nehemiah S. Leibowitz, *Rabbi Avraham Saba' u-Sefarav* (Brooklyn, N.Y., 1936).

—SHALOM BAR-ASHER

SABBATAI TSEVI. See SHABBETAI TSEVI.

SABBATH, the weekly day of rest observed from sunset on Friday until nightfall on Saturday (a period of approximately twenty-five hours). It has been suggested that the biblical Sabbath displays certain similarities to the Babylonian *shappatu*, but the connection is dubious. The Sabbath is central to the Bible. God created the world in six days and rested on the seventh. Moreover, it is written, "and God blessed the seventh day and declared it holy" (*Gn*. 2.3). The Sabbath is the only festival mentioned in the Ten Commandments (*Ex*. 20.8–11), and it is especially emphasized in God's words to Moses in *Exodus* 31.12–17. Both of these passages refer to God's rest from the work of creation; from this principle is derived the ban on all work by humans (with special mention of all slaves) and animals on the Sabbath day. In the repetition of the Decalogue (*Dt*. 5.15), the Sabbath is also linked to the Exodus and the miraculous deliverance from slavery to freedom that that narrative expresses. The Sabbath is referred to as a symbol of the *covenant between God and Israel (*Ex*. 31.16–17). Therefore, in rabbinic law, **tefillin*, which are also a symbol of the divine covenant, do not have to be worn on the Sabbath. Even before the revelation at Sinai, the Israelites were forbidden to gather manna on the Sabbath because it was "a day of rest, a holy Sabbath to the Lord" (*Ex*. 16.23). Public desecration of the Sabbath was punishable by death according to biblical law (see *Nm*. 15.32–36); the rabbis, in fact, considered the public desecration of the Sabbath a sin equal to idolatry. During the First Temple period, observance of the Sabbath was taken for granted, and there are few biblical references to it, but in the early Second Temple period, Nehemiah enforced the suspension of all trade and business activities on the Sabbath (*Neh*. 13.14–22). At the time of the Maccabean Revolt, Sabbath observance was so strict that Jewish warriors preferred to be killed rather than offer resistance on that day. In response, a ruling was promulgated saying that the preservation of life overrides the observance of the Sabbath, and the warriors were allowed to fight in their own defense (*1 Mc*. 2.40–41). *Exodus* 31.14 is considered the scriptural reference for this *halakhah*: "for it [the Sabbath] is holy unto you," implying that "the Sabbath is given unto you; you are not to be delivered to the Sabbath" (*Yoma'* 85b).

The Mishnaic sages enumerated thirty-nine principal categories of work (*mal'akhah*) forbidden on the Sabbath, each of which is further subdivided. These included sowing, plowing, reaping, binding sheaves, threshing, winnowing, cleansing crops, grinding, sifting, kneading, baking, shearing wool, washing wool, spinning, weaving, making two loops, weaving two threads, separating two threads, tying a knot, loosening a knot, sewing two stitches, tearing, hunting, slaughtering or salting or curing the skin of an animal, cutting up an animal, writing two letters of the alphabet, erasing, building, demolishing, putting out a fire, lighting a fire, striking with a hammer, or carrying from one domain to another. In addition, the rabbis added further restrictions (see SEYAG LA-TORAH) so that there would be no danger of infringing the categories. For example, the rabbis forbade even the handling of certain objects associated with work (see MUQTSEH). At the same time, a number of laws and legal fictions were introduced to offer ways around certain restrictions (see, for example, ʿERUV). In certain emergencies, the laws of the Sabbath could be overruled, especially if their observance posed a *danger to life. Jews often employed non-Jews to perform some of these labors for them; in eastern Europe such an employee was known as a *shabbes goy*.

Essentially, the Sabbath is a day of physical rest and spiritual joy, centered around the twin poles of home and synagogue (for the distinctive liturgy, see SABBATH PRAYERS). As the men leave for synagogue for the evening service (*Qabbalat Shabbat), the women recite a special blessing over the Sabbath candles (see KINDLING OF LIGHTS). Upon his return, the husband blesses his wife (see ESHET ḤAYIL) and the children (see BLESSING OF CHILDREN). Then the *Qiddush prayer, sanctifying the Sabbath day, is recited over wine and the *Birkat ha-Motsi' is recited over two loaves of bread (*ḥallah*), which recall the two portions of manna gathered by the Israelites on the Sabbath eve. The festive meal is punctuated with the singing of Sabbath **zemirot*. At the conclusion of the meal, the *Birkat ha-Mazon is said. In non-Orthodox homes, the Sabbath meal may be eaten before the family goes to a late synagogue service. It is a widespread custom to invite guests to the Sabbath meals. Marital intercourse is regarded as especially meritorious on the Sabbath eve. In general, the Sabbath should be a "day of delight" (see ʿONEG SHABBAT).

After Sabbath morning services, another festive meal is eaten, also preceded by Qiddush, and the afternoon is spent in study or rest. In ancient times it was customary to eat two meals a day, but the rabbis decreed that on the Sabbath there should be a third meal (*Seʿudah Shelishit). This is enjoyed in the late afternoon, and participants sing *zemirot* and expound Torah. Under the influence of the kabbalists and Hasidism, this meal may be prolonged as long as possible, to retain the Sabbath spirit, and is called *Melavveh Malkah (Escorting the Queen, from the concept of the Sabbath as a queen). Sabbath ends with the evening service, which is held after three stars appear in the sky. *Havdalah, which marks the separation between the holy and the secular, is recited in the synagogue (in certain communities) and the home.

In the nineteenth century, some Reform congregations celebrated a "second Sabbath," by holding Sabbath services on Sunday mornings for those who had to work on Saturdays, but this practice was rejected by the moderate Reform as a step too far in the direction of Christianity. In the course of time, the entire Reform movement accepted the traditional Sabbath day. In the Mishnah and Talmud, tractate **Shabbat* is devoted to the laws of the Sabbath.

The idea of the weekly Sabbath passed into the other monotheistic religions, although the Christian Sunday originally had a different emphasis and only later became a "day of rest"; the Muslim Friday is not a day of rest at all but a day of communal prayer. A number of Christian sects, however, observe Saturday as their Sabbath.

• Stephen Garfinkel, ed., *Slow Down and Live: A Guide to Shabbat Observance and Enjoyment*, rev. ed. (New York, 1986). Elliot K. Ginsburg, *The Sabbath in the Classical Kabbalah* (Albany, N.Y., 1989). Irving Greenberg, *Guide to Shabbat* (New York, 1981). Abraham Joshua Heschel, *The Sabbath: Its Meaning for Modern Man* (New York, 1951). Aryeh Kaplan, *Sabbath: Day of Eternity* (New York, 1982). Simeon J. Maslin, *Gates of Mitzvah* (New York, 1979). Abraham Ezra Millgram, *Sabbath, the Day of Delight* (Philadelphia, 1944). Mark Dov Shapiro, *Gates of Shabbat* (New York, 1991).

—CHAIM PEARL

SABBATH, GREAT. See SABBATHS, SPECIAL.

SABBATH EVE. See QABBALAT SHABBAT.

SABBATH LIGHTS. See KINDLING OF LIGHTS.

SABBATH PRAYERS. As far as their basic structure is concerned, the prayers recited on Sabbath do not differ from those of other days, except that the ʿAmidah consists of only seven benedictions (*Ber*. 3.12), and that in addition to the three regular daily prayers a fourth—*Musaf—is added, as on festivals. Reform Judaism eliminated the Musaf service and the most recent Conservative and Reconstructionist *siddurim* have modified it extensively. The Sabbath ʿAmidah does not contain the series of petitions prescribed for weekdays. The intermediate benediction of the ʿAmidah, which is devoted to the sanctification of the day (Qedushat ha-Yom), opens differently in each Sabbath service, though the conclusion is always the same ("Blessed . . . who sanctifies the Sabbath"). During *Maʿariv, the opening *Attah qiddashta*, "You have sanctified," followed by *Genesis* 2.1–3, emphasizes the Sabbath of Creation. In Shaḥarit, the opening *Yismaḥ Mosheh*, "Moses rejoiced," followed by *Exodus* 31.16–17, refers to the revelation at Sinai; in *Minḥah, the opening *Attah eḥad*, "You are One," evokes the "perfect rest and peace" of messianic redemption. Taken together, these three openings express three different aspects of the Sabbath—as a commemoration of Creation and of revelation, and as a symbol of future redemption. In the Musaf prayer the intermediate benediction of the Ashkenazi rite opens with *Tiqqanta Shabbat*, "You have instituted the Sabbath," a paragraph whose words are arranged in reverse alphabetical order.

On Friday evenings, Maʿariv is preceded by *Qabbalat Shabbat, a ceremony that consists in most rites of a number of psalms (among them Psalm 92, the "Sabbath psalm") and the hymn *Lekhah Dodi, which was introduced by the kabbalists in Safed at the end of the sixteenth century. The benedictions before and after the Shemaʿ are in most rites today the same as on weekdays, except for a different conclusion to *Hashkivenu and the addition of *Exodus* 31.16–17, *Ve-Shameru. This is followed by the ʿAmidah and the recital of *Genesis* 2.1–3. The reader then repeats aloud a summary of the ʿAmidah (*Magen Avot) in a single benediction. It is customary to read the second chapter of Mishnah *Shabbat* (*Ba-Meh Madliqin), and in many congregations *Qiddush is also recited by the reader. At home, prior to sunset (or, among many non-Orthodox Jews, when the family gathers for dinner), candles are lit to welcome the Sabbath, then Qiddush is recited, followed by the meal, which is accompanied by the singing of **zemirot*. At the end of the meal, *Birkat ha-Mazon is recited, with special additions for the Sabbath. During Shaḥarit, the *Pesuqei de-Zimra' are said in extended form and are followed by Nishmat Kol Ḥai. *Yotser is enlarged by *piyyutim*, which combine the Sabbath motif with the prayer text. The ʿAmidah is followed by the reading of the law (see QERI'AT HA-TORAH) and **haftarah*. The Torah scroll is taken out and returned to the ark with great ceremony, including various prayers not used on weekdays. Before the morning meal, Qiddush (differing significantly from the evening version) is again recited. For

Minḥah there is again a short reading of the law from the *sidrah of the following week. It is customary after Minḥah to read, in the summer, one of the chapters of Mishnah *Avot, and in the winter, a collection of psalms (Psalm 104 and the Song of Degrees, Psalm 120, through Psalm 134). Upon the termination of the Sabbath, Ma'ariv is recited, as on weekdays, and is followed by *Havdalah. The Sabbath has a distinct beginning and a distinct end. It is sanctified at the beginning with light and wine and is concluded with light and wine.

• Ismar Elbogen, *Jewish Liturgy: A Comprehensive History*, translated by Raymond P. Scheindlin (Philadelphia, 1993). Reuven Hammer, *Entering Jewish Prayer: A Guide to Personal Devotion and the Worship Service* (New York, 1994). Lawrence A. Hoffman, *The Canonization of the Synagogue Service* (Notre Dame 1979). Isaac Klein, *A Guide to Jewish Religious Practice* (New York, 1979). Abraham Millgram, *Jewish Worship* (Philadelphia, 1971).

—PETER KNOBEL

SABBATHS, SPECIAL, so designated because of their place in the calendrical year or because of the particular scriptural readings on them.

Shabbat Shuvah (שַׁבָּת שׁוּבָה; Sabbath of Return), the name given to the Sabbath that falls during the ten days of penitence (see 'ASERET YEMEI TESHUVAH) between *Ro'sh ha-Shanah and *Yom Kippur, which is derived from the first word of the **haftarah* designated for that day, *Shuvah Yisra'el 'ad Adonai Elohekha*, "Return, O Israel, unto the Lord your God" (*Hos.* 14.2). It is customary on this Sabbath for the rabbi to deliver a sermon on the theme of repentance. The day is also referred to as Shabbat Teshuvah (Sabbath of Repentance).

Shabbat be-Re'shit (שַׁבָּת בְּרֵאשִׁית; Sabbath of the Beginning [also, of Genesis]), the first Sabbath after *Simḥat Torah, when the annual cycle of weekly Torah readings begins anew with the portion *Genesis* 1–6.8 (*parashah* or *sidrah*). Shabbat be-Re'shit retains a little of the festive atmosphere of Simḥat Torah, and in many communities, it is customary for the *ḥatan Be-Re'shit* (see ḤATAN TORAH AND ḤATAN BE-RE'SHIT) to host a Qiddush reception for the congregation after services.

Shabbat Shirah (שַׁבָּת שִׁירָה; Sabbath of Song), the Sabbath when the *parashah* Be-Shalaḥ (*Ex.* 13.17–17.6) is read, which contains Shirat ha-Yam (Song of the Sea; a hymn of praise), which Moses and the children of Israel sang after their deliverance at the Red Sea. All communities—Ashkenazi, Sephardi, and Oriental—have their own special melodies to which the song is chanted. In Ashkenazi communities, the congregation stands during the song's recitation. Special *piyyutim* (see PIYYUT) are recited in some rites.

Shabbat Sheqalim (שַׁבָּת שְׁקָלִים; Sabbath of the Shekels), the Sabbath before the first of Adar (or on the first of Adar if it falls on the Sabbath; in a leap year, the second month of Adar); the first of four (Arba' Parashiyyot) leading up to Pesaḥ. A second Torah scroll is removed from the synagogue ark for the reading of a special **maftir* (*Ex.* 30.11–16). The *haftarah* is *2 Kings* 12.1–17 for Ashkenazim, *2 Kings* 11.17–12.17 for Sephardim. The *maftir* contains the law of the half-shekel tax that was paid by every adult male over the age of twenty and is described as "a ransom for the soul." The money collected went to finance the sacred service. The tax was announced on the first day of Adar and was payable during that month. Shabbat Sheqalim was instituted after the Temple period as a reminder of the tax. Special *piyyutim* were composed for recitation on this Sabbath.

Shabbat Zakhor (שַׁבָּת זָכוֹר; Sabbath of Remembering), the name given to the Sabbath before the festival of *Purim, on which a special *maftir* (*Dt.* 25.17–19), which begins with the word *zakhor* (remember), is read in the synagogue from a second Torah scroll. These biblical verses contain an exhortation to remember the vicious cruelty of the *Amalekites, who attacked the Israelites soon after the *Exodus from Egypt. According to tradition, *Haman, the archvillain of the Purim story, was a descendant of the Amalekite tribe. The special *haftarah*, which deals with the execution of the king of the Amalekites, is from *1 Samuel* 15.1–34. Special *piyyutim* were written to be recited on this Sabbath.

Shabbat Parah (שַׁבָּת פָּרָה; Sabbath of the [Red] Heifer), the Sabbath preceding Shabbat ha-Ḥodesh (see below) when a special *maftir* about the *red heifer and a special *haftarah* about ritual purity (from *Ez.* 36) are read. During the Temple period, anyone in a state of ritual impurity was prohibited from participating in the ritual of the paschal sacrifice (see PESAḤ). One could be cleansed only with the ashes of the red heifer mixed with water. In some rites, special *piyyutim* are recited.

Shabbat ha-Ḥodesh (שַׁבָּת הַחֹדֶשׁ; Sabbath of the Month), the title given to the Sabbath before the first of the month of Nisan (or the first of Nisan if that day falls on a Sabbath), which signifies the arrival of the month of Nisan, in which the Israelites were delivered from Egyptian bondage. A second Torah scroll is removed from the synagogue ark, and a special *maftir*, *Exodus* 12.1–20, on the laws of the paschal lamb, is recited. The *haftarah* is *Ezekiel* 45.16–46.18. If Shabbat ha-Ḥodesh coincides with *Ro'sh Ḥodesh (the New Moon) Nisan, the regular weekly portion is read from the first scroll, the designated reading for Ro'sh Ḥodesh is read from a second scroll, and a third scroll is used for the reading of the *maftir* for Shabbat ha-Ḥodesh.

Shabbat ha-Gadol (שַׁבָּת הַגָּדוֹל; Great Sabbath), the Sabbath before Pesaḥ. Various reasons have been suggested for this Sabbath's designation. First, the Exodus from Egypt took place on 15 Nisan, which was a Thursday. On the tenth of the month (a Sabbath) the children of Israel were commanded to slaughter a lamb. In view of the sacredness of the lamb to the Egyptians, the Israelites showed great courage and faith in obeying the command; hence, the name Great Sabbath. Second, the Sabbath before Pesaḥ may also take its special title from the *haftarah* for that day, which concludes, "Behold I will send you Elijah the prophet before the coming of the great and terrible day of the Lord" (*Mal.* 3.24). The reference to *Elijah, who features in the Pesaḥ *Seder, and to the "the great . . . day" give this Sabbath its distinctive name. Finally, on this Sabbath, it is customary for the rabbi to review all the laws of Pesaḥ with the congregation. In earlier times, his lesson was so lengthy that the congregation, feeling they had spent most of the day in the synagogue, began calling that Sabbath "the great [i.e., long] Sabbath." There is no special *maftir* for this Sabbath, but there is a special *haftarah*, *Malachi* 3.4–24. It is customary to read the first narrative section of the *Haggadah of Pesaḥ after the *Minḥah service. In certain Sephardi communities (e.g., Salonika), Jewish schoolchildren received new garments on this day, which was known as Ḥag ha-Halbashah (the Feast of Putting on [New] Garments).

Shabbat Ḥazon (שַׁבָּת חֲזוֹן; Sabbath of Vision), the Sabbath immediately preceding the fast of *Tish'ah be-'Av, so called because the *haftarah* for that Sabbath, *Isaiah* 1.1–27, begins with the words *Ḥazon Yesha'yahu ben Amots*, "The vision of Isaiah the son of Amoz." This is the last of the three prophetic readings of "rebuke" (Sheloshah de-Puranata') read on the three Sabbaths during the three-week mourning period that culminates with Tish'ah be-'Av. In this *haftarah*, the prophet castigates the people of Judah for their serious religious sins and social crimes and warns them of the impending destruction of the land and the downfall of the people. In Ashkenazi synagogues, the chapter is traditionally chanted to the tune used for reading the *Book of *Lamentations*. The *Lekhah Dodi hymn recited at the preceding Friday-evening service is also chanted to the mournful melody of *Eli Tsiyyon. In geonic times, Shabbat Ḥazon was called Shabbat Sheḥorah (Black Sabbath), and the ark was covered with a black curtain. In some communities, it was not unusual for people to wear regular weekday clothes instead of their festive Sabbath attire. Yemenite Jews read *Isaiah* 1.21–27 for the *haftarah* and call the day Shabbat Eikhah (*Eikhah* being the Hebrew name for the *Book of Lamentations*).

Shabbat Naḥamu (שַׁבָּת נַחֲמוּ; Sabbath of Comfort), the Sabbath immediately following the fast of Tish'ah be-'Av. The *haftarah*, from *Isaiah* 40, begins with the words *Naḥamu naḥamu 'ami*, "Comfort ye, comfort ye, my people." In it, the prophet offers a message of encouragement and hope for the return of the Jewish exiles and for the physical and spiritual rebuilding of the destroyed Jerusalem and the Holy Land. Shabbat Naḥamu is the first of the seven *haftarot* of "consolation" (Sheva' de-Neḥemta') that are read on the seven Sabbaths between Tish'ah be-'Av and Ro'sh ha-Shanah.

Shabbat Mevarekhim (שַׁבָּת מְבָרְכִים; Sabbath of Blessing), the Sabbath before Ro'sh Ḥodesh (the new moon), on which a special prayer is recited before the *Musaf service invoking God to make the coming month one of spiritual fulfillment and material prosperity. As part of the ceremony, the name of the new month is formally announced, as well as the day or days upon which Ro'sh Ḥodesh falls. The ritual was introduced in the fourth century, when *Hillel II determined the calendar, and became particularly important in the eighth century, when the rabbinic method of calculation was challenged by the *Karaites. A private prayer composed by third-century scholar *Rav for recitation after the 'Amidah was added at a late date (c.18th cent.). The Sephardi version of this prayer (beginning *Yehi ratson*, "May it be your will") is longer than the Ashkenazi version. The ritual is omitted on the Sabbath before the month of Tishrei, since 1 Tishrei is also Ro'sh ha-Shanah, and it is assumed that everyone is aware of that date.

Shabbat Ro'sh Ḥodesh (שַׁבָּת רֹאשׁ חֹדֶשׁ; Sabbath of the New Moon), a Sabbath that coincides with Ro'sh Ḥodesh. Two scrolls of the Torah are removed from the ark; the regular weekly portion is read from the first, and a special Ro'sh Ḥodesh *maftir*, *Nm*. 25.9–15, is read from the second. There is also a special *haftarah*, *Isaiah* 66. There are a number of additions and changes in the liturgy on Shabbat Ro'sh Ḥodesh, including the introduction of *Hallel before the Torah reading and changes in the Musaf service to make it more appropriate for Ro'sh Ḥodesh.

Shabbat Maḥar Ḥodesh (שַׁבָּת מָחָר חֹדֶשׁ; Sabbath [of the] Month [That Comes] Tomorrow), designation of a Sabbath when Ro'sh Ḥodesh falls on the next day, Sunday. The title derives from the opening words of the special *haftarah* read on this occasion (*1 Sm*. 20.18–42), "and Jonathan said unto [David]: 'Tomorrow is the new moon [*maḥar ḥodesh*].'" Other than the specially selected *haftarah* there are no liturgical additions to mark this day.

• Judah David Eisenstein, *Otsar Dinim u-Minhagim* (Tel Aviv, 1975), pp. 401–403. Yom-Tov Levinsky, *Havaii u-Masoret ba-Yahadut* (Tel Aviv, 1975). Abraham Ezra Millgram, *Jewish Worship* (Philadelphia, 1971), pp. 264–266. *Min ha-Massad* (Jerusalem, 1986), pp. 546–549.

—CHAIM PEARL

SABBATH SOUL. See NESHAMAH YETERAH.

SABBATIANISM. See DÖNMEH; SHABBETAI TSEVI.

SABBATICAL YEAR. See SHEMITTAH.

SACRIFICE OF ISAAC. See 'AQEDAH.

SACRIFICES, the primary form of worship in Judaism from biblical times until the destruction of the Second Temple. Sacrifice was the dominant way of serving the gods throughout the ancient Near East and was embraced by the Israelites as the means by which the people of YHVH could pay homage to the one God. The word *sacrifice* corresponds to the Hebrew *qodashim* (consecrated things; *Lv*. 22.2–3); other Hebrew terms are *qorban* (that which is brought near, an offering; *Lv*. 1.2), *minḥah* (tribute; *Gn*. 4.3), and *isheh* (formerly thought to mean "fire offering" [from *esh* (fire)] but now known to mean "gift"; *Lv*. 1.9). These terms demonstrate the idea that the individual and the community were expected to express physically and tangibly their love of God, their dependence upon him, their gratitude and subservience to him, and their desire to continue to enjoy his blessings by offering to him a portion of the bounty he had given them.

Though Israelite sacrifice was somewhat similar in form to its Near Eastern parallels, it was thoroughly adapted to Israel's monotheistic faith. Obviously, sacrifices in Israel could be made to YHVH alone; the frequent prohibition against worshipping other gods refers precisely to this (e.g., *Ex*. 20.5). Sacrifice to spirits, such as those of dead ancestors, was also strictly forbidden (*Dt.* 26.14). Because of Israel's belief that man is created in God's image, human sacrifice was strictly outlawed; in fact, it was the outstanding example of foreign practices that were not to be copied (*Dt.* 12.31; see MOLECH).

Israelite sacrifice was cleansed of all theurgic elements: it was not believed to activate supernatural forces or to have a magical influence on the deity or on nature; nor was sacrifice used, as in Mesopotamia, for divination. By insisting that all the details of sacrificial procedure were ordained by God, Israel rejected the pagan idea that sacrifice was the product of human cleverness, a method of manipulating the forces of the universe to secure or predict a desired outcome. Israelite sacrifice attached no intrinsic role to the taking of life; the actual slaughter of the animal was not an act of worship. God was not pictured as desirous of the animal's death but rather of the offering made of its flesh and the use of its blood for purification; slaughter was simply a necessary step in the process.

Sacrifice in Israel was organized around the idea of the divine abode (see TABERNACLE; TEMPLE) and the metaphor of God as King (see GOD). As Israel's only true sovereign God was conceived of as actually residing in his earthly palace. There, much as an earthly ruler, he received his royal tribute, primarily in the form of food gifts presented on behalf of the Israelite people by the palace servants—the priests—in an uninterrupted pageant proclaiming his sovereignty and nearness. The Bible unabashedly speaks of the sacrifice as God's "food" (*Lv.* 21.6, 8; *Nm.* 28.2) and of the *altar as God's "table" (*Ez.* 41.22, 44.16; *Mal.* 1.7, 12). Still, it is clear that in biblical thought God is not believed to need sacrifices for his sustenance (as in Mesopotamian belief) but rather to desire them and be pleased by them. The idea that God eats is rejected outright (*Ps.* 50.8–13); the *showbread was simply displayed in his presence, and the sacrificial flesh of animals was turned into smoke upon an altar in order that its aroma be pleasing (e.g., *Lv.* 1.9). Israelite sacrifice, for all its anthropomorphic detail, was a huge, elaborate symbol, a sacred drama rather than a method of satisfying any physical needs of the deity.

Animal sacrifices were "from the herd and from the flock" (*Lv.* 1.2): oxen, cattle, calves, sheep, and goats. In some cases fowl—turtledoves and pigeons—were acceptable or even prescribed (*Lv.* 1.14–17, 5.7, 12.6). The meal offering was made of semolina and oil. Wines, oils, and incense also had their roles in the sacrificial system, as did silver and gold (used primarily for beautifying the Temple and for purchasing the sacrificial animals).

There were two classes of sacrifice: offerings on behalf of the community and those presented by an individual. Sacrifices might be required or voluntary. Most public sacrifices were of the former type, meaning they had to be offered on particular, recurring occasions (see TAMID); these include the daily, Sabbath, new moon, and festival offerings (see BURNT OFFERING). Private offerings might be required—such as those made in fulfillment of a vow, the Pesaḥ offering, or sacrifices upon making a festival pilgrimage—or they might be spontaneous expressions of an individual's gratitude or piety. Private sacrifices of *atonement (*purification and *reparation offerings) were necessitated by circumstances. Their purpose was to make reparation for sacrilege and to purge the divine abode of impurities and sins. Failing to offer them was held to be criminal. Public atonement sacrifices belonged to the yearly cycle of required offerings.

An essential part of the procedure was the sprinkling, daubing, or pouring—as specifically prescribed in each case—of the animal's blood on or around the altar. The burning of the suet and other portions of the animal on the altar was the way in which the deity was given his "share." The burnt offering was entirely consumed on the altar; the meal offering was eaten by the priests, but a token portion was burned on the altar; the peace offering was essentially a sacred meal. Most of the flesh was enjoyed by the worshiper and his family, with only certain choice portions being placed on the altar and others given to the priests.

Biblical tradition differs on when sacrifice began. The priestly view is that it was instituted after the Exodus from Egypt with the building of the Tabernacle (*Lv.* 1.1ff.); non-Priestly texts hold that Cain and Abel, Noah, and the patriarchs all offered sacrifices, though at private altars, without a Temple (e.g., *Gn.* 4.3–4, 8.20–21, 12.8). The Pentateuch demands the centralization of all sacrifice at one single shrine (*Lv.* 17.8–9; *Dt.* 12), but the historical books attest to the existence of local shrines, both legitimate and illegitimate, and a gradual process of centralization that was only completed toward the end of the First Temple period, under the reign of Josiah (see HIGH PLACE).

The laws of sacrifice are found in the second half of *Exodus*, in much of *Leviticus*, and in a few chapters of *Numbers*. Outside the Pentateuch, too, it is clear that sacrificial ritual was the central feature of worship in biblical times. Occasionally, prophets harshly denounced the offering of sacrifices (*Is.* 1.11–14; *Am.* 5.21–23; *Jer.* 7.21–22; *Mi.* 6.6–9). In all these cases, the intent is not to negate sacrifice itself but to decry piety divorced from morality; God rejects the tokens of Israel's affection when his people are incorrigible wrongdoers. When, however, Israel was neglectful of its sacrificial duties, prophets also rebuked them (*Mal.* 1.6ff).

By the time sacrifice ceased (with the destruction of the Second Temple in 70 CE), statutory *prayer, which had formed a part of the Temple service, had already begun to become institutionalized. Its meticulous, daily observance by all Jews eventually became the substitute for sacrifice as the required, regular service of God. Still, as the rabbis stated, sacrificial worship was deemed to be one of the pillars upon which the earth's very existence rests (*Avot* 1.2). Thus, traditional Jewish thought does not admit that sacrifice has actually been abolished. Rather, it holds that the destruction of the Temple has made sacrifice temporarily impossible, and the traditional Jew continues to pray for the rebuilding of the Temple and the resumption of the sacrificial system.

Non-Orthodox prayer books have eliminated most prayers for the restoration of sacrifice; many of those who retain them interpret them symbolically rather than literally.

Talmud order Qodashim deals extensively with all the laws of sacrifice, particularly tractates *Zevaḥim and *Menaḥot. The rabbis' attitude toward sacrifice indicates a gradual de-emphasis on the anthropomorphic element, placing stress upon the humanistic value of sacrifice. Discomfort with this seemingly primitive element in Judaism reaches its peak in the opinion of Maimonides, who believed that sacrifice was instituted as a necessary evil, to wean the Israelites gradually away from paganism, as they could not have grasped the idea of a religion without sacrifice (*Guide of the Perplexed* 3.32, 46). He was severely criticized by Nahmanides, who insisted that such a view was totally inconsistent with the biblical text, according to which sacrificial ritual is divinely ordained and the noblest form of serving God (commentary on *Lv.* 1.9). See also FREE-WILL OFFERING; INCENSE; PIGGUL; PRIESTHOOD; PRIESTLY PRIVILEGES; RED HEIFER; TERUMAH; THANKSGIVING OFFERING; WAVE OFFERING.

• Gary A. Anderson, *Sacrifices and Offerings in Ancient Israel: Studies in Their Social and Political Importance* (Atlanta, 1987). Menahem Haran, *Temples and Temple-Service in Ancient Israel* (Winona Lake, Ind., 1985). Moshe Moskowitz, "Towards a Rehumanization of the Akedah and Other Sacrifices," *Judaism* 37 (1988): 288–294. Marcel Neusch, ed., *Le Sacrifice dans les religions* (Paris, 1994), comparative studies. Jan Quaegebeur, ed., *Ritual and Sacrifice in the Ancient Near East* (Louvain, 1993).

–BARUCH J. SCHWARTZ

SACRILEGE (Heb. *ma'al; me'ilah*), strictly speaking, the misappropriation of sacred property, such as sacrificial animals. When the offender realized the misdeed, a *reparation offering was required (see *Lv.* 5.14–16). In its wider usage, the concept is virtually identical to the illicit type of *profanation. King Uzziah's crime of entering the Temple and offering incense (both forbidden to a non-priest), King Ahaz's disregard for Temple sanctums, and the general sin of contaminating the Temple are all called *ma'al* (*2 Chr.* 26.16, 28.19, 36.14), as is Achan's misappropriation of the spoils of Jericho (*Jos.* 7.1ff.), which were dedicated to the Lord. *Sacrilege* can refer to any misuse of sacred objects, treated in the Talmudic tractate *Me'ilah*, and in later times to the prohibited disrespect for Torah scrolls, holy books, *tsitsit*, *tefillin*, and so forth.

• Jacob Milgrom, *Studies in Levitical Terminology*, vol. 1, *The Encroacher and the Levite: The Term 'Aboda* (Berkeley, 1970).

–BARUCH J. SCHWARTZ

SADDUCEES (Heb. Tseduqim), one of the three main Jewish sects that flourished during the last two centuries of the Second Temple period. The origin of the name is uncertain, but it is probably derived from *Zadok, whose descendants had held the Jerusalem high priesthood since Solomon's time. *Josephus Flavius (and other sources) described the Sadducees as wealthy, especially the priestly aristocracy. Their origins as well as those of the other Jewish sects, are obscure, and the Sadducees first appear in Josephus's accounts of the internal Jewish feuds of the *Hasmonean period. From these accounts, the Sadducees emerge as the more conservative element of the Jewish population, refusing to acknowledge such Pharisaic innovations as the belief in angels, in resurrection, and in the immortality of the soul. Moreover, they refused to accept the Pharisaic concept of a binding oral law and adhered only to those laws that were written in the Torah. Knowledge of Sadducean beliefs and halakhic rulings is incomplete and is mostly derived from sources that do not view them favorably—Josephus (who describes himself as a Pharisee), the *New Testament (in which *Jesus is depicted as arguing not only with Pharisees but with Sadducees as well), and rabbinic literature (the rabbis claim to be the spiritual heirs of the Pharisees)—and therefore it is hard to reconstruct the Sadducees' worldview, beyond enumerating those areas in which they differed from the Pharisees.

The Sadducees maintained that *Shavu'ot always had to fall on a Sunday, insisted that the high priest enter the Holy of Holies in the Temple on Yom Kippur with the incense burning in a censer (rather than placing it in the censer after entering the Holy of Holies), allowed individuals to finance the daily public sacrifices (rather than financing such sacrifices only from the public coffers), and held slaveholders responsible for crimes committed by their slaves. In a recently published halakhic letter (known as 4Q*MMT*) found among the *Dead Sea Scrolls, the Qumran sectarians espouse some halakhic views known from rabbinic sources as typically Sadducean: that an unbroken column of liquid (*nizzoq*) can transmit ritual impurity and that the priests who burned the red heifer had to immerse themselves and wait until after sunset before performing the purification ceremony. These similarities, as well as the affinities between the halakhic injunctions of the previously published Temple Scroll and the *halakhot* attributed to the Sadducees, point to some affinity between the Sadducees and the *Essenes. It has been suggested that the two groups shared a common origin. With the destruction of the Temple in 70 CE, the Sadducees lost their social and ideological center and no more is heard of them.

• Jacob Neusner, *From Politics to Piety: The Emergence of Pharisaic Judaism* (Englewood Cliffs, N.J., 1973). Elisha Qimron and John Strugnell, eds., *Qumran Cave 4.V: Miqsat Ma'ase ha-Torah*, Discoveries in the Judaean Desert, vol. 10 (Oxford, 1994). Anthony J. Saldarini, *Pharisees, Scribes and Sadducees in Palestinian Society* (Wilmington, Del., 1988). E. P. Sanders, *Judaism: Practice and Belief, 63* BCE–66 CE (Philadelphia, 1992). Lawrence H. Schiffman, *Reclaiming the Dead Sea Scrolls* (Philadelphia, 1994). Emil Schürer, Geza Vermes, and Fergus Millar, *The History of the Jewish People in the Age of Jesus Christ, 175 B.C.–A.D. 135* (Edinburgh, 1979), vol. 2, pp. 381–414.

–GIDEON BOHAK

SAFED, a town in Galilee which became the center of concentrated literary and spiritual activity in the sixteenth century; regarded later as one of the four *holy cities. Early evidence of Jewish presence is sketchy; Safed is not mentioned in the Bible. The name *Safed* is related to the Hebrew root meaning "looking over," and in the Talmud Yerushalmi (*R. ha-Sh.* 2.1) it is noted as one of the mountain tops on which a signal fire was lit to announce the arrival of *Ro'sh Ḥodesh. A stable community is known from the thirteenth century on. It became the center of remarkable literary and spiritual activity in the sixteenth century when it attracted scholars who were refugees from Spain. Many outstanding Talmudists and kabbalists, such as Mosheh *Cordovero, Yosef *Karo, and especially Yitsḥaq *Luria and his school lived in Safed. Luria claimed that he had identified many ancient graves in the vicinity of Safed as tombs of ancient rabbinical authorities, and the area became widely visited by pilgrims coming to worship at these tombs. Safed was also the site of the attempt by Ya'aqov *Berab to renew rabbinic *ordination.

• Itzhak Ben-Zvi and Meir Benayahu, eds., *Sefer Tsefat*, 2 vols. (Jerusalem, 1962–1963), with bibliography. Dov Silverman, *Legends of Safed* (Jerusalem, 1984). Aryeh Wineman, *Beyond Appearances: Stories from the Kabbalistic Ethical Writings* (Philadelphia, 1988). —FERN SECKBACH

SAGES. See Ḥazal; Talmid Ḥakham.

SAHL BEN MATSLIAḤ (10th cent.), *Karaite scholar, exegete, and propagandist; known in Arabic as Abu al-Sarri. He was highly regarded as a scholar by Karaites of his generation and accepted as a major authority on religious law by later Karaites. He was a resident of Jerusalem but traveled abroad seeking to convert Rabbanites to Karaism. On one such journey, he came into conflict with Ya'aqov ben Shemu'el, an ardent follower of Sa'adyah Ga'on. As a result of this, Sahl wrote a long missionizing epistle in Hebrew (published by Simḥah Pinsker, *Liqqutei Qadmoniyyot* [1860], appendix) responding to Ya'aqov ben Shemu'el's attack and addressing the Rabbanite community, appealing to them to cast off the yoke of their greedy and insincere leaders and return to the original and pure biblical faith. He accuses the Rabbanite leaders of persecuting the Karaites, laxity in observance, and superstition. In addition, Sahl wrote *Sefer Mitsvot*, an Arabic code of ceremonial law (the Hebrew introduction has been published by A. Harkavy, *Me'assef Niddaḥim I*, no. 13); *Sefer Dinim*, an Arabic work on civil and criminal law; a commentary on the Pentateuch; a commentary on *Isaiah*; a work on grammar; and a polemic against Sa'adyah Ga'on. (Manuscript fragments of the first four of the above works have been preserved; manuscripts of the rest have not been identified.)

• Samuel Poznanski, *Karaite Literary Opponents of Saadiah Gaon* (London, 1908), no. 13. —DAVID E. SKLARE

SALANTER, YISRA'EL (1810–1883), founder of the *Musar movement. Born Yisra'el Lipkin in Zhagare, Lithuania, at age twelve he entered the *yeshivah* of Tsevi Hirsch Broda in Salant, where he became renowned for his brilliance. Inspired by the example of R. Zundel of Salant, an unusually saintly and humble scholar in the Mitnaggedic tradition, Salanter decided to devote his life to disseminating R. Zundel's personal ethical principles by establishing a general movement to promote the deliberate pursuit of pietism, adopting innovative educational and psychological techniques. Beginning in Vilna as a *mashgiaḥ* and *ro'sh yeshivah*, Salanter established a reputation as a powerful orator, delivering sermons that drew huge audiences. These sermons, specially calculated to appeal to both scholars and laymen, introduced *musar* insights in the form of learned homilies. Salanter also founded groups for the study of *musar* (ethics) and established a special institution called a *musar-shtibl*, in which he delivered his discourses.

Much to his chagrin, R. Yisra'el's activities also gained approval in Haskalah circles. Proponents of the Haskalah discerned in them a new sense of social responsibility for the needs of the unlearned and downtrodden and a welcome extension of the parameters of Jewish spirituality. The boldness of leadership that Salanter projected, reinforced by his dramatic behavior during the cholera epidemic that swept Vilna in 1848, when he ordered the congregation to break their Yom Kippur fast, led to government pressure upon him to head the rabbinical seminary of Vilna. Salanter moved to Kovno, where he founded his own Musar *yeshivah*, producing an important second generation of Musar leaders and disciples.

In 1857 Salanter moved to Germany, where he lectured to university students on Judaism, published a Torah journal (*Tevunah*), and corresponded with his Kovno disciples. After two years of similar activity in Paris, he returned to Königsberg, where he died. A few articles that he published were collected in a volume entitled *Imrei Binah* (1878), some of his letters were published by his pupil Yitsḥaq Blaser in *Or Yisra'el* (1900), and a collection of his discourses recorded by his pupils was published under the title *Even Yisra'el* (1883). Many of his works, edited by Mordechai Pachter, appeared in *Kitvei Rav Yisra'el Salanter* (Jerusalem, 1972).

• I. Etkes, *Rabbi Israel Salanter and the Musar Movement: Seeking the Torah of Truth* (Philadelphia, 1993), contains extensive bibliographic resources. Louis Ginzberg, *Students, Scholars, and Saints* (Philadelphia, 1928; repr. Lanham, Md., 1985), pp. 145–194. Hillel Goldberg, *Israel Salanter: Text, Structure, Idea: The Ethics and Theology of an Early Psychologist of the Unconscious* (New York, 1982), contains extensive bibliographical resources. Tamar Ross, "Pitronotav shel R. Yisra'el Salanter le-Ve'ayat Ḥulshat ha-Ratson," *Meḥqarei Yerushalayim be-Maḥ-shevet Yisra'el* 11 (1993): 139–185. —TAMAR ROSS

SALE. To become legally binding, any sale or purchase requires an act called *qinyan* (see Acquisition; Property), with which ownership is immediately transferred. An oral agreement to buy or sell an article is not binding, and either party may withdraw. If the vendee pays money to the vendor after an agreement for the sale of movable property has been reached, the vendor still has the legal right to void the sale if the formal *qinyan* has not yet taken place; however, it is considered morally dishonest to retract an agreement under such circumstances. A sale is effected in cases of immovable property by payment of the full price or by writing and signing the deed of sale; for movable property, an action of ownership (e.g., pulling or raising the object) is required.

• Yosef Karo, *The Traditional Jewish Law of Sale: Shulḥan 'Arukh, Ḥoshen Mishpat, Chapters 189–240*, translated and annotated by Stephen M. Passamaneck (Cincinnati, 1983). Binyamin Rabinovitz Te'omim, *Sefer Ḥuqqat Mishpat* (Jerusalem, 1956–1957).

SALIḤ, YAḤYA BEN YOSEF (1665–1749), Yemenite rabbi, also known as Maharits. He was the head of the *beit din* in Sanaa and the undisputed leader of the community during the first half of the eighteenth century.

He mediated a bitter dispute between those who viewed the *Shulḥan ʿArukh* as the supreme authority in all halakhic matters and the more conservative, who championed Maimonides. Saliḥ's writings were aimed at summarizing Yemenite Jewish traditions from their earliest appearance to his own day. This was of special importance since printed prayer books were arriving from Erets Yisra'el and being used by the community, as a result of which the unique Yemenite traditions were being overlooked. He gathered the *responsa* of Yemenite rabbis in *Peʿullat Tsaddiq* (3 vols. [1946–1965]) and wrote a commentary, *Ets Ḥayyim* (1894), on the Yemenite prayer book. Both of these works were the subject of commentaries by later scholars. He also wrote commentaries on the Torah and the Five Scrolls, in addition to writing *Megillat Teiman* (Jerusalem, 1986), a short history of Yemenite tradition.

• Joseph Tobi, *ʿIyyunim be-Megillat Teiman* (Jerusalem 1986). Joseph Tobi in *Toledot ha-Yehudim be-'Artsot ha-'Islam*, edited by Samuel Ettinger (Jerusalem, 1981), pp. 3–23. Yisra'el Yeshayahu and Shimʿon Gridi, eds., *Mi-Teiman le-Tsiyyon* (Tel Aviv 1938), pp. 106–138.

—SHALOM BAR-ASHER

SALMON BEN YERUḤIM (10th cent.), *Karaite polemicist and exegete. He was born either in Iraq or Erets Yisra'el and was active as a member of the Karaite community of *Avelei Tsiyyon in Jerusalem during the 940s and 950s. According to Karaite tradition, he taught Saʿadyah Ga'on, and Saʿadyah mourned him in Aleppo, where he was buried. This, however, is impossible since Salmon was much younger than Saʿadyah; but it may reflect an actual confrontation between the two. In what is evidently a work of his youth, Salmon wrote a violent polemic against the Rabbanites and Saʿadyah in particular (published as *Milḥamot Adonai* by I. Davidson [New York, 1934]). It was written in rhymed Hebrew, using exceptionally abusive language. An anonymous student of Saʿadyah, writing in Arabic, responded to this polemic, and fragments of Salmon's Arabic rejoinder have been preserved. Salmon wrote Arabic commentaries on a number of biblical books, including the Torah, *Isaiah, Psalms* (chaps. 42–72; edited by L. Marwick [Philadelphia, 1956]), *Proverbs, Job, Song of Songs, Lamentations* (partially edited by Feuerstein [Kraków, 1898]), *Ecclesiastes* (edited by M. Riese, Ph.D. dissertation, Yeshiva University, 1973), *Esther*, and *Daniel*. His commentary on *Lamentations* was actually a text used for ritual recitations by the Avelei Tsiyyon. In addition, he wrote *Kitab Aḥruf al-Ibdal*, a work on grammar; *Kitab Intisar lil-Ḥaq*, evidently a polemical work; and a work on the virtues of the priests. In his writings Salmon condemned the study of foreign philosophy and the Arabic language.

• Haggai Ben-Shammai in *Keneset 'Ezra': Sifrut ve-Ḥayyim be-Veit ha-Keneset: Asupat Ma'amarim Mugeshet le 'Ezra' Flaisher* (Jerusalem, 1994), pp. 191–234. Leon Nemoy, *Karaite Anthology* (New Haven, 1952), pp. 69–82. Samuel Poznanski, *Karaite Literary Opponents of Saʿadyah Ga'on* (London, 1908), no. 5. Georges Vajda, *Deux commentaries karaites sur l'Ecclesiaste* (Leiden, 1971).

—DAVID E. SKLARE

SALT is first mentioned in the Bible in reference to Lot's wife, who was turned into a pillar of salt (*Gn.* 19.26) in the vicinity of the Dead Sea (which in Hebrew is called the Salt Sea). As a preservative, salt was a symbol of the eternal covenant between God and his people (*Nm.* 18.19; *2 Chr.* 13.5). All sacrifices and meal offerings had to be salted prior to being placed on the altar (*Lv.* 2.13; *Men.* 20a); the salt used for this purpose was stored in a special place known as the salt chamber on the north side of the Temple court (*Mid.* 5.3). After the Temple period, a table at which meals were taken came to symbolize the altar, and it therefore became customary to place salt on the table at each meal and to dip the bread into salt after reciting the *Birkat ha-Motsi'. According to Jewish *dietary laws, all *meat must be thoroughly salted and sit for an hour after having been soaked for a half hour in water to drain the blood and make it permissible for consumption.

• Immanuel Löw, "Das Salz," in *Fauna und Mineralien der Juden* (Hildesheim, 1935; repr. 1969), pp. 137–170.

SALVATION (Heb. *yeshuʿah*, also *teshuʿah*), acts whereby God delivers his people from distress. The term occurs frequently in biblical and liturgical texts (cf. *Gn.* 49.18; *Ex.* 14.13, 14.30) and in the prophetic books, particularly in *Isaiah* (cf. *Is.* 45.17, "Israel is saved by the Lord with an everlasting salvation"), and in *Psalms*, but almost always refers to deliverance from concrete and specific sufferings, such as oppression and exile. It is not used in connection with the remission of sin, atonement, and the like. The noun *moshiʿa* (savior) is occasionally used for the leaders sent by God to succor the people in times of distress (cf. *Jgs.*) but is generally applied only to God (Prophets; *Ps.*). A favorite image is that of the sprouting or flourishing of salvation (cf. the second and fifteenth benedictions of the *ʿAmidah, "who causes the horn of salvation to flourish"), which is connected with the idea of the messianic sprouting of the "shoot of David." Salvation played an important role in the thought of Mordecai Menahem *Kaplan, who conceived it as a striving for the fulfillment of human destiny, while God was the source of the human will to salvation. See also REDEMPTION.

• Ecumenical Institute for Advanced Theological Studies, *Concepts of Salvation in Living Faiths* (Jerusalem, 1979). Paul Garnet, *Salvation and Atonement in the Qumran Scrolls* (Tübingen, 1977). Jacob Neusner, *Scriptures of the Oral Torah: Sanctification and Salvation in the Sacred Books of Judaism* (Atlanta, 1990). Claus Westermann, *Prophetic Oracles of Salvation in the Old Testament* (Louisville, 1991). R. J. Zwi Werblowsky and C. J. Bleeker, eds., *Types of Redemption* (Leiden, 1970).

SAMAEL, the prince of demons in Jewish folklore; identical with *Satan. The name occurs in the Slavonic *Apocalypse of Enoch*, and, together with his wife *Lilith, he plays an important role in popular legend and kabbalistic literature, acting as seducer, accuser, and destroyer of the Jews as well as guardian angel of the gentiles. His antagonist is the archangel *Michael, the guardian angel of Israel. *Pirqei de-Rabbi Eliʿezer* describes Samael's initiative in planning Adam's fall, his descent from heaven, and his use of the serpent to seduce Eve. He acted as the accuser against the children of Israel to persuade God not to redeem them from the bondage of Egypt (*Ex. Rab.* 21.7), and it was he who was sent by God to take the soul of Moses (*Dt. Rab.* end).

According to Jewish folklore, he continues throughout history to act as the accuser of Israel, except on Yom Kippur, when he is powerless. See also DEMONS.

• Bernard Jacob Bamberger, *Fallen Angels* (Philadelphia, 1952). Gustav Davidson, *A Dictionary of Angels: Including the Fallen Angels* (New York, 1967). Joshua Trachtenberg, *The Devil and the Jews* (New Haven, 1943).

SAMARIA (Heb. Shomron), capital of the northern kingdom of Israel, identified with modern Sebastia (about 10 km [7 miles] northwest of Nablus [Shechem]). It was founded by King Omri (c.876 BCE), who bought the site from Shemer (*1 Kgs*.16.24) and moved his capital there from Tirzah. His son Ahab expanded the city and imported Phoenician luxury items. Ivories found in the palace remains are evidence of Ahab's "house of ivory" (*1 Kgs*. 22.39). During his reign, under the influence of his Phoenician wife Jezebel, shrines were erected to Baal and Asherah. An inscription from the eighth century BCE found in northern Sinai, dedicated to Yahveh of Samaria and his Asherah, emphasizes the religious significance of the site. Corruption and excessive luxuries were the subjects of rebuke of such prophets as Amos when Samaria reached the zenith of its prosperity and expansion during the reign of Jeroboam II (784–748). A collection of sixty-three ostraca (which are inscriptions on potsherds) dated to this period records shipments of wine and oil to officials at Samaria.

After the Assyrian conquest of the West under Tiglath-pileser III (734–732), most of the territory of the northern kingdom of Israel was annexed by Assyria, and the people were exiled. Only Samaria and its surroundings remained; its king, Hoshea, became an Assyrian vassal. He soon conspired against Assyria (*2 Kgs*. 17), and Samaria was finally conquered by Shalmaneser V in 722 BCE. Shalmaneser's successor, Sargon II, exiled the Israelites, resettled foreigners in Samaria (*Samaritans) and made it an Assyrian provincial administrative center. Samaria was subsequently captured by the Babylonians and Persians. Under Alexander the Great, who first destroyed it after a rebellion in 331 BCE, it became a Hellenistic city, but it, too, was destroyed in the late Hellenistic period by John Hyrcanus in 107 BCE. Roman Samaria was rebuilt by Herod the Great, who renamed it Sebaste and erected a temple there to Augustus in 30 CE.

• Bob Becking, *The Fall of Samaria: An Historical and Archaeological Study*, Studies in the History of the Ancient Near East, vol. 2 (Leiden, 1992). Mordechai Cogan and Hayim Tadmor, *II Kings*, The Anchor Bible, vol. 11 (Garden City, N.Y., 1988). John Winter Crowfoot, Kathleen Mary Kenyon, and Eleazar Sukenik, *The Buildings at Samaria* (London, 1966). Kathleen Mary Kenyon, *Royal Cities of the Old Testament* (London, 1971). Ephraim Stern, ed., *The New Encyclopedia of Archaeological Excavations in the Holy Land*, vol. 4 (New York, 1993). Ron E. Tappy, *The Archaeology of Israelite Samaria*, Harvard Semitic Studies, vol. 1 (Atlanta, 1992).

—NILI SACHER FOX

SAMARITAN PENTATEUCH, a recension of the Hebrew text of the Pentateuch used by the *Samaritans. It is written in an archaic script evolved from Old Hebrew (Phoenician) writing. Its antiquity is attested, among other things, by the shape of the letters, as well as by the fact that a dot is placed after each word. Possibly the Samaritan Pentateuch dates back in its primary form to the time of Josiah, but it has been much altered in the course of the generations, and the best known surviving manuscripts belong to the twelfth century. It nevertheless constitutes the earliest external witness to the Hebrew text. Although independent of Jewish tradition from the time of *Nehemiah (cf. *Neh*. 13.23–31), it substantially corroborates the Masoretic recension, while containing some six thousand variant readings. Most of the divergences are due to scribal errors, ignorance, or a desire to facilitate the comprehension of difficult texts and to harmonize related passages. Doctrinal reasons account for other emendations (e.g., the substitution of Gerizim for Ebal in *Dt*. 27.4). A residual number of variants are of critical value, especially where these agree with the Septuagint. There exist Aramaic and Arabic translations of the Samaritan Pentateuch; but a Greek version (the Samareitikon) is known chiefly from patristic references. The first printed edition was in the Paris Polyglot Bible (1629–1665), and the editions of August Freiherr von Gall (Giessen, 1918) utilized many manuscripts.

• Jean-Pierre Rothschild and Guy D. Sixdenier, eds., *Études samaritains: Pentateuch et Targum, exégèse et philologie, chroniques* (Louvain, 1988). Emanuel Tov, *Textual Criticism of the Hebrew Bible* (Minneapolis and Assen, 1992).

SAMARITANS, the population of *Samaria after the destruction of the northern kingdom of Israel in 721 BCE. Known in Hebrew as Shomronim (cf. *2 Kgs*. 17.29), or, in the Talmud, as Kutim (Cutheans), they call themselves Benei Yisra'el (Children of Israel) or Shomerim (Observant Ones). According to their own tradition, the Samaritans are the descendants of that part of the Israelite population that remained in the country after the deportation of the ten *tribes of Israel by Sargon II of Assyria. The biblical account describes them as descendants of the heathen colonists from various parts of Mesopotamia, especially Cuthah, whom Sargon II settled in the depopulated Samaria. The heterogeneous ethnic character of the new population (*2 Kgs*. 17.24) also produced a heterogeneous syncretistic religion, which provided fertile soil for friction, both political and religious, with the Judean exiles returning from Babylonia. According to the biblical account (*Neh*. 6), the Samaritans wished to participate in the rebuilding of the Temple but were rebuffed by the Jewish leadership. The resulting breach between the two groups developed into a permanent schism after Nehemiah expelled the son-in-law of Sanballat, governor of Samaria, who was a priest in Jerusalem, for marrying the daughter of a Samaritan (*Neh*. 13.28; Josephus, *Antiquities of the Jews* 11.8). In the fourth century BCE, by permission of Alexander the Great, the Samaritans built a temple on Mount *Gerizim; it was destroyed by John Hyrcanus (c.129 BCE). A second Samaritan temple was destroyed by Emperor Zeno in 486 CE.

The Samaritan religion has its origin in the Israelite traditions of the northern kingdom and resembles Sadducean Judaism (see SADDUCEES) in many respects; hence, also its resemblance to Karaism (see KARAITES), which likewise exhibits certain Sadducean features. The

Samaritans believe in God, who is unique; Moses, the only prophet; the Torah; the sanctity of Mount Gerizim; and future reward and punishment, a concept linked with the advent of the messianic restorer (*taheb*), who will end the period of *fanuta* (God's displeasure) and introduce that of *rahuta* (divine favor). Their Decalogue begins with the Second Commandment in the Jewish tradition ("You shall have no other gods before me") and adds a new tenth commandment prescribing the building of an altar on Mount Gerizim. The Samaritans observe seven biblical festivals—Pesaḥ, Matsot, Shavuʿot, Yom Teruʿah, Yom Kippur, Sukkot, and Moʿed Shemini—and two minor feasts—Tsimmut (conjunction of) Pesaḥ (15 Shevat) and Tsimmut Sukkot (15 Av). However, their calendar differs from the Jewish one in the determination of leap months; consequently there are numerous discrepancies in dates.

In some respects, the rabbis regarded the Samaritans as Jews (e.g., *Ber*. 7.1) and held that "when the Samaritans adopt a commandment they observe it more scrupulously than do the Jews" (*Ḥul*. 4a). However, with respect to marriage and other laws, they are treated like non-Jews. Talmudic law with regard to the Samaritans is summarized in the minor tractate **Kutim*. The Samaritans recognize as holy scripture only the Pentateuch, which they have preserved in a pre-Masoretic Hebrew recension, written in archaic script developed from Phoenician writing (see SAMARITAN PENTATEUCH). The addition, at the end of the Ten Commandments (*Ex*. 20.17; *Dt*. 5.21), of a commandment to build an altar and to sacrifice on Mount Gerizim (cf. *Dt*. 27.6ff.) and the substitution of Gerizim for Ebal in *Deuteronomy* 27.4 are obvious interpolations. To this day, Samaritans sacrifice the paschal lamb on Mount Gerizim before Pesaḥ. There is also a **targum* (4th cent.) to the Pentateuch composed in the original Samaritan tongue, a dialect of western Aramaic. Some of the early Samaritan liturgical compositions (*defter*) and Midrashic writings (e.g., the *Memar Markah*) are likewise in Aramaic. After the Muslim conquest of Palestine in 632, the Samaritans gradually adopted Arabic as their vernacular (except for prayers, for which they continued to use Hebrew), translating the Bible into Arabic (11th–12th cent.) and producing a considerable body of literature, mainly religious, in that language. The history of the Samaritans under Muslim rule is one of persecution and decline.

There are now over five hundred Samaritan adherents in Nablus (adjoining Mount Gerizim) and Ḥolon (near Tel Aviv). The Samaritans are recognized as citizens of the State of Israel under the *Law of Return. They continue to conduct their traditional rites on Mount Gerizim, and in 1963 the first Samaritan synagogue was dedicated in Nablus. According to their law, Samaritans may intermarry with Jews, provided that the Jewish partner fully observes the Samaritan customs. These marriages are recognized by the Israeli Ministry of the Interior but not by the Israeli chief rabbinate. The supreme Samaritan religious leader is the hereditary high priest. Until 1624, he was reputedly the direct descendant of Aaron, brother of Moses. With the death of Shalmiaḥ ben Pinḥas (1613–1624) the line died out, and the position was then held by the traditional descendants of Uzziel, uncle of Aaron. When a high priest dies, he is succeeded by the most senior of the Levites.

• Arthur Ernest Cowley, *The Samaritan Liturgy* (Oxford, 1909). Alan D. Crown, *A Bibliography of the Samaritans* (Metuchen and London, 1984). Alan D. Crown, *The Samaritans* (Tübingen, 1989). John Macdonald, *The Theology of the Samaritans* (London, 1964). James Alan Montgomery, *The Samaritans* (New York, 1968). Reinhard Pummer, *The Samaritans* (Leiden, 1987). Abraham Tal, *Proceedings of the First International Congress of the Société d'études Samaritaines* (Tel Aviv, 1991).

SAMBARI, YOSEF BEN YITSḤAQ (1640–1703), known also as Qataya; Egyptian Jewish historian. Almost nothing is known of his life. His major work, *Divrei Yosef* (Jerusalem, 1994; much of it in A. Neubauer, *Medieval Jewish Chronicles* [1887], vol. 1, pp. 115–162; repr., 1965) shows his developed sense of history. It is possible that the disillusionment following the collapse in 1666 of Shabbateanism (which he bitterly opposed) moved him to complete his work in 1673. It begins in the sixth century and continues until his own time (a first part covering up to the sixth century is lost) and deals mainly with the Egyptian community in the Mamluke and Ottoman periods. He pays particular attention to leading Egyptian Jews and the role of the *nagid*, especially the descendants of Maimonides. His book is valuable for its information on the Jewish scholars of Spain, North Africa, and the Middle East from the fifteenth through the seventeenth century. His *Porat Yosef* on the Torah text, which reflects the insistence of Egyptian scholars on accuracy in the reading and writing of the Torah, was printed with *Divrei Yosef*. Sambari had a positive attitude toward Kabbalah, which he studied with Shemu'el Vital (see VITAL FAMILY), and his works betray a strong mystic influence.

• Jacob Mann, *The Jews in Egypt and Palestine under the Fatimid Caliphs* (Oxford, 1920), pp. 251–257. Shimon Shtober, "Muhammad and the Beginning of Islam in the Chronicle 'Sefer Divrey Yosef,' " *Ayalon* (1986): 319–352.

—SHALOM BAR-ASHER

SAMBATYON, legendary river beyond which the ten lost *tribes of Israel were supposedly condemned to live in exile. On weekdays, the river was impassable because of the rocks and debris it churned up; on Sabbaths, when it lay at rest, Jewish law prevented the exiles from crossing its banks. Targum Jonathan (*Ex*. 34.10) identifies it with the river Gozan of Israel's captivity (*2 Kgs*. 17.6, 18.11; cf. Y., *San*. 10.6; *Gn. Rab*. 73.5). The legend was current in Second Temple times and is found in accounts by Pliny the Elder (*Natural History* 31.24) as well as by Josephus, who claimed that the river flowed only on Sabbaths (*The Jewish War* 7.5.1). Rabbi *ʿAqiva' ben Yosef also referred to the mysterious Sambatyon (*San*. 65b; *Gn. Rab*. 11.6). Widespread interest was later aroused by the tales of the ninth-century adventurer *Eldad ha-Dani, and Jews became convinced that the Sambatyon had a definite location in Asia or Ethiopia. This belief can be traced through the *Book of Yosippon* (953 CE), the bible commentary of Moses *Nahmanides (on

Dt. 32.26), the journeys undertaken by Avraham ben Shemu'el Abulafia in 1260 and ʿOvadyah Bertinoro in 1489, and the travel tales of Gershom ben Eliʿezer ha-Levi (*Gelilot Erets Yisra'el* [1634]). Avraham Farissol, in his cosmography (*Iggeret Orḥot ʿOlam* [1524]), provided an exact location for the Sambatyon on a map of the New Indies. In his *Miqveh Yisra'el* (1650), written at a time when messianic speculation had reached new heights, *Manasseh ben Israel placed the lost tribes and the Sambatyon in America.

• Elkan N. Adler, *Jewish Travellers* (London, 1930). Nathan Ausubel, *A Treasury of Jewish Folklore* (New York, 1948), pp. 515–529. Yehudah David Eisenstein, *Otsar Massaʿot* (New York, 1926), pp. 122, 184–185. Avraham Epstein, *Eldad ha-Dani* (Pressburg, 1891), pp. 13–16. André Neher, *Jewish Thought and the Scientific Revolution of the Sixteenth Century: David Gans (1541–1613) and His Times* (Oxford, 1986), pp. 119ff., 126–127, 132–133, 136–137, 140ff. —GABRIEL A. SIVAN

SAMSON (Heb. Shimshon), the twelfth and last of the judges (see JUDGE), from the tribe of Dan, whose twenty years of adventurous exploits are recounted in *Judges* 13–16. Samson, whose birth was predicted by an angel to his barren mother (a familiar biblical motif), was a *Nazirite from birth. He became the hero of a cycle of tales relating to his vengeful encounter with the Philistines that all took place between the borders of the tribes of Dan and Judah. Possessed of enormous strength, which resided in his uncut hair—the only one of the Nazirite vows which he fulfilled—he ripped a lion apart with his bare hands; killed thirty Philistines in Ashkelon; tied blazing torches to the entwined tails of three hundred foxes, incinerating Philistine fields; slew another thousand Philistines with the jawbone of an ass; uprooted the city gates of Gaza, carrying them all the way to Hebron; and eventually met his tragic end after toppling the pillars of the Philistine temple of Dagon in Gaza, where he was held captive. He also courted Philistine women, who tricked and betrayed him. One of them, Delilah, seductively coaxed out of him the source of his superhuman strength, which eventually led to the successive loss of his hair, power, eyes, and life. His final words, reflecting his personal vendetta, were "Let me die with the Philistines" (*Jgs*. 16.30).

• James L. Crenshaw, *Samson: A Secret Betrayed, A Vow Ignored* (Macon, Ga., 1978). J. Cheryl Exum, "Aspects of Symmetry and Balance in the Samson Saga," *Journal for the Study of the Old Testament* 19 (1981): 3–29. J. Cheryl Exum, "The Theological Dimension of the Samson Saga," *Vetus Testamentum* 33 (1983): 30–45. Edward L. Greenstein, "The Riddle of Samson," *Prooftexts* 1 (1981): 237–260. —SHALOM PAUL

SAMUEL (Heb. Shemu'el; 11th cent. BCE), prophet and the last Israelite *judge. Born to Elkanah and *Hannah after many years of childlessness and in answer to fervent prayer, he was dedicated by his mother to serve in the sanctuary as a *Nazirite. Samuel was therefore brought up at Shiloh by the high priest *Eli. As a child, Samuel received his first prophetic revelation, which foretold the destruction of the family of Eli. After the Philistine victory at Aphek (where the Ark of the Covenant was captured) and the death of Eli and his sons, Samuel became a leading national figure, acknowledged "from Dan to Beersheba" (*1 Sm*. 10) as a seer, judge, and military leader (*1 Sm*. 7.13–15). Residing in Ramah, he tried to restore traditional religious worship and judged cases in Israel on his regular circuit of the sacred towns of Bethel, Gilgal, and Mizpah. The need for greater national unity, in view of the growing Philistine pressure, resulted, in Samuel's old age, in the popular demand for a king. Samuel considered the institution of monarchy to be a breach of the original covenant, according to which Israel was to have no king but God. In obedience to God's word, however, he anointed Saul as the first king of Israel (*1 Sm*. 10). Relations with Saul deteriorated over the years and ended in a complete break when Saul showed leniency toward Agag, king of the Amalekites (*1 Sm*. 15.1–23). Thereupon Samuel anointed *David as Saul's successor (*1 Sm*. 16.3–13). After Samuel died, Saul requested the sorceress of En-dor to bring up his spirit from the nether world in order to discover the outcome of his forthcoming battle with the Philistines (*1 Sm*. 28).

The *Book of Samuel* (originally third in the section of the Bible known as the Former Prophets) was divided into two books (*1 Samuel* and *2 Samuel*) in the printed Hebrew Bible of 1516–1517, based on the Septuagint and Vulgate. It contains an account of Israel's history from the end of the period of the judges until David's old age. At the center of this formative period are the personalities of Samuel (whose death is related in *1 Sm*. 28.3), Saul, and David. The chief purpose of the book(s) is to describe the factors that led to the rise of the monarchy, to show the divine roots of this institution, and to emphasize that the king, no less than his people, is bound by the terms of the divine covenant and is subject to God's will. The content of the book(s) may be divided as follows: the birth and dedication of Samuel, the capture of the Ark of the Covenant and its return, and Samuel's functioning as a judge (*1 Sm*. 1.1–7.17); the selection of Saul as king and his victory over the Ammonites, Samuel's farewell address, and Saul's military excursions against the Philistines and Amalekites (*1 Sm*. 8.1–15.35); the anointing of David, David's battle with Goliath, his stay at court and his outlaw activities, the sorceress of En-dor, David's sojourn with Achish and his battle against the Amalekites, Saul and Jonathan's deaths at the battle of Mount Gilboa, and David's lament over them (*1 Sm*. 16.1–*2 Sm*. 1.24); David becoming king first in Hebron and then over all Israel, his capture of Jerusalem, which he makes his political capital and resting place of the Ark of the Covenant, and Nathan's prophecy forbidding David to build a Temple for the Ark (*2 Sm*. 2.1–8.18); David's battles against the Ammonites and Arameans, the Bath-sheba affair, and the rebellion of his son Absalom and that of Sheba (*2 Sm*. 9.1–20; 26); a final appendix comprising the burial of Saul, a list of David's military heroes, a psalm of David, and his last words, followed by a census of the Israelites (*2 Sm*. 21.1–24.25). According to one Talmudic view, *Samuel* (as well as *Judges* and *Ruth*) was written by Samuel himself. Modern scholars distinguish two or more historical sources, worked over by Deuteronomistic redactors.

• William Foxwell Albright, *Samuel and the Beginning of the Prophetic Movement* (Cincinnati, 1961). J. P. Fokkelman, *Narrative Art and Poetry in the Books of Samuel* (Assen, 1981). P. Kyle McCarter, Jr., *I Samuel: A New Translation* (New York, 1980). —SHALOM PAUL

SAMUEL, MIDRASH, late *midrash* on the *Book of Samuel*, first quoted by Rashi in the eleventh century in his commentary to *1 Samuel* 2.30. The work consists of aggadic commentaries taken from earlier Midrashic compilations and arranged in sequence by the collator. Primarily homiletic, it contains both early and late tannaitic and amoraic exegetical material. It is of Palestinian origin, but the author is unknown. It was first published in Constantinople in 1517, and a modern critical edition by Solomon Buber appeared in Kraków in 1893. A book by the same name, by Shemu'el Uzeda, a disciple of Yitsḥaq Luria, is a commentary on the tractate *Avot*.

• Leopold Zunz, *Ha-Derashot be-Yisra'el ve-Hishtalshelutan ha-Historit*, edited by Chanoch Albeck (1892; Jerusalem, 1974).

—DANIEL SPERBER

SANCTIFICATION (Heb. *qiddush*) refers to the religious discipline or the process of spiritual growth by which a person increases in *holiness; the consecration, usually by a vow, of objects, persons, or specific times, which are thereby set apart and made subject to special ritual rules; or the formal acknowledgment of the character of sanctity attaching to persons or times. Religious practice from early rabbinic times established statutory acts of sanctification to mark the setting aside of holy days and times as separate (*qadosh*) and distinct from the ordinary (*ḥol*) and profane. Thus, at the beginning of the Sabbath and festivals the *Qiddush is recited, which declares the holy days as divinely set aside. The setting aside and lifting of the relationship of marriage into the dimension of the sacred is expressed in the act of *qiddushin*, marked by a public declaration that creates the marriage bond: *Harei at mequddeshet li* . . . , "Behold you are sanctified unto me . . . ."

A focal prayer in the recitation of the morning and afternoon *ʿAmidah is called the *Qedushah, which affirms the source of all sanctity in God. Its opening declaration is the celebrated quotation from the divine call to Isaiah (*Is*. 6.3), "Holy, holy, holy is the God of hosts, the whole earth is the fullness of God's glory." The *Qaddish (Aram.) is a doxology encouraging affirmation of the kingdom of God. Recited from late antiquity at the end of worship services or following Torah lectures, the Qaddish also became a memorial prayer for the dead.

Examples of sanctification by consecration are the *dedication of an animal or inanimate object to the Temple, or the consecration of something for religious use whereby it ceases to be profane and is reserved for a sacred purpose. In some cases a consecrated object can revert to its previous state by redemption. The legal and practical corollaries of sanctification are illustrated by the laws of priesthood. The priest is invested with an inherent sanctity as a result of his priestly descent ("They shall be holy unto the Lord their God," *Lv*. 21.6) and has the duty to preserve this sanctity ("and they shall not profane the name of their God," loc. cit.). For this reason priests are forbidden to contaminate themselves with the dead. It is solely on account of this duty to preserve their state of sanctity and transmit it to their descendants that a priest is forbidden to marry a divorcee or a convert; the offspring of such a union would be profane, that is, disqualified from the priesthood.

• Ismar Elbogen, *Jewish Liturgy: A Comprehensive History*, translated by Raymond P. Scheindlin (Philadelphia, 1993). Kaufmann Kohler, *Studies, Addresses, and Personal Papers* (New York, 1931). Simeon Singer, *Authorized Daily Prayer Book*, annotated ed. (London, 1904), pp. xxxix–xli, xlvii–xlviii, lx–lxi, lxxxiii–lxxxix. —HERBERT BRONSTEIN

SANCTIFICATION OF THE MONTH. See BIRKAT HA-ḤODESH; RO'SH ḤODESH.

SANCTIFICATION OF THE NAME. See MARTYRDOM.

SANCTUARY. See ASYLUM; TABERNACLE; TEMPLE.

SANDALFON, an angel who figures prominently in the ancient divine-chariot mysticism (*Maʿaseh Merkavah), where he is identified as the *ʿofan* (wheel) of *Ezekiel* 1.15 and is said to stand "on earth but his head reaches to the heavens, being higher than his fellow angels by a distance of 500 years' journey." According to the Talmud, Sandalfon stands behind the divine chariot weaving crowns of prayer for his creator (*Ḥag*. 13b). The name Sandalfon is Greek and means "co-brother," but it does not occur in non-Jewish sources. It may refer to his identification as a brother of *Metatron. Sandalfon figures prominently in kabbalistic *amulets. See also ANGELS.

• Gustav Davidson, *A Dictionary of Angels: Including the Fallen Angels* (New York, 1967), p. 257. Joshua Trachtenberg, *Jewish Magic and Superstition: A Study in Folk Religion* (New York, 1974), pp. 68–78.

—SHIFRA EPSTEIN

SANDAQ (סַנְדָּק; godfather), the person given the honor of holding the child on his knees during the *circumcision ceremony. The word is probably derived from the Greek *sunteknos* (companion to the child) and is found in the Talmud. Traditionally it was regarded as a great *mitsvah* to be a *sandaq*, and the honor was often given to a grandfather or to a man of outstanding piety. In some communities the woman who brings the child into the ceremony is called the *sandaqit*.

• Paysach J. Krohn, *Bris Milah: Circumcision, the Covenant of Abraham: A Compendium* (Brooklyn, N.Y., 1985).

SANHEDRIN (סַנְהֶדְרִין; High Court), name of a Jewish court and of a Mishnaic tractate.

Jewish Court. The Sanhedrin, a term derived from Greek, was the Jewish court that held supreme religious, political, judicial, and legislative authority in Palestine during the Roman and Byzantine periods. Hellenistic sources depict the Sanhedrin as a political and judicial body headed by the ruler or high priest. Josephus writes of the Sanhedrin primarily in its capacity as a court: Hyrcanus, the governor of Judea, presided over the Sanhedrin trying Herod for murder (*Antiquities of the Jews* 14.168–170); Herod later had the Sanhedrin condemn Hyrcanus (*Antiquities of the Jews* 15.173); Augustus convened a Sanhedrin of Roman officials to try political rebels (*Antiquities of the Jews* 16.365); Ananus, a Sadducean high priest, convened the Sanhedrin to try James, the brother of Jesus (*Antiquities of the Jews* 20.200); and Herod Agrippa II had a Pharisaic Sanhedrin rule on a cultic matter (*Antiquities of the Jews* 20.216–218). In the New Testament, in the trial of Jesus, the interrogation of Peter and John Zebedee (*Acts* 4.3–6), and the trial of Paul (*Acts* 22.25–30), the Sanhedrin appears as a court presided over by the high priest. According to the New Testament, the Sanhedrin conducted its business on festivals and in the evening. *Acts* describes the Sanhedrin as "one part Sadducees and the other Pharisees."

By contrast, the Sanhedrin appears in rabbinic sources as an assembly of sages headed by Pharisaic scholars—the **nasi'* and the **av beit din*. Also referred to as the Great Beit Din, the Sanhedrin, consisting of seventy-one members, met in the Chamber of the Hewn Stone in the Temple and appointed small Sanhedrins of twenty-three members to function in every city or region. It is depicted as primarily a judicial body that dealt with religious matters, although it possessed some legislative and national–political functions, and it conducted its business during daylight hours and never at night or on Sabbaths and festivals. Only the Great Sanhedrin could try a whole tribe, a false prophet, or national figures, such as the king and the high priest. Only the Sanhedrin could appoint a king or high priest. Offensive wars required the sanction of the Sanhedrin, and additions to the city of Jerusalem and the Temple courts required its approval. As the final court of appeal and ultimate halakhic authority, the Sanhedrin could impose the death penalty on a scholar who defied its rulings. Finally, certain cultic procedures were performed under the supervision of the Great Sanhedrin.

Various resolutions of the conflicting data provided by rabbinic and Hellenistic sources have been proposed. Some scholars (e.g., Abraham Geiger) posit the existence of three twenty-three-member Sanhedrins in Jerusalem with distinct functions: a priestly Sanhedrin, a Pharisaic Sanhedrin, and an aristocratic Sanhedrin. Together the three smaller bodies constituted the Great Sanhedrin, which was headed by a *nasi'* and an *av beit din*. Other scholars contend that there were two councils in Jerusalem, one political and one religious. Solomon Zeitlin would date this division to Hasmonean times, while Adolf Büchler maintains that the religious Sanhedrin described in tannaitic sources was merely the ideal. Finally, those scholars who argue for a single Sanhedrin generally must give greater weight to one or the other set of sources. David Hoffman accepts the rabbinic description of a body headed by a Pharisaic *nasi'*, who was ousted on occasion by the secular ruler. Emil Schürer simply dismisses the rabbinic sources and asserts that the Sanhedrin was a court headed by the high priest. According to other theories, the high priest and a Pharisaic sage filled the positions of *nasi'* and *av beit din*, respectively. The conflicting data should probably be explained by the specific purpose of each source. Josephus, as a political historian, focused on the political role of the Sanhedrin; the New Testament, concerned with the trials of Jesus and his followers, depicted the Sanhedrin's activity as a court; and the tannaitic sources describe its legislative and judicial functions.

The Sanhedrin was probably at the peak of its power in the later Second Temple period. Alon maintains that Pharisees and Sadducees dominated the body in turns. John Hyrcanus (ruled 134–104) broke with the Pharisees, expelled them from the Sanhedrin, and annulled their religious rulings. They were reinstated by Salome Alexandra (ruled 76–67). Under Herod, the authority of the Sanhedrin was drastically reduced. After the destruction of Jerusalem in 70 CE, the term Sanhedrin designated the assemblies of Jewish scholars that functioned first as a religious body and then increasingly as a political body in Yavneh (in Judea) and, after the Bar Kokhba' Revolt, in Usha', Shefaram, Beit She'arim (under R. Yehudah ha-Nasi'), Sepphoris, and Tiberias (in Galilee). Outside Palestine, the authority of the Sanhedrin depended on voluntary acceptance by the people; the Sanhedrin issued *gezerot* (decrees) and *taqqanot* (ordinances) according to the needs of the times. The Sanhedrin was apparently abolished with the patriarchate in 425 CE.

• Gedalia Alon, *The Jews in Their Land in the Talmudic Age*, translated by Gershon Levi (Jerusalem, 1980–1984), vol. 1, pp. 43–45, 185–252, 308–322; vol 2, pp. 461–468, 625–628, 663–673, 705–737. Adolf Büchler, *Das Synedrion in Jerusalem und das Grosse Beth-din in der Quaderkammer des Jerusalemischen Temples* (Vienna, 1902). Abraham Geiger, *Urschrift und Übersetzungen der Bibel in ihrer Abhangigkeit von der Innernentwickelung des Judentums* (Breslau, 1857). Sidney Benjamin Hoenig, *The Great Sanhedrin* (Philadelphia, 1953). David Hoffman, *Der oberste Gerichtshof in der Stadt des Heiligtums* (New York, 1977). Hugo Mantel, *Studies in the History of the Sanhedrin* (Cambridge, 1961). Shemuel Safrai, "Jewish Self Government," in *The Jewish People in the First Century*, edited by Shemuel Safrai and Menahem Stern (Assen, 1976), pp. 377–392. Emil Schürer, *Geschichte des jüdischen Volkes im Zeitalter Jesu Christi*, vol. 2 (Leipzig, 1886). Solomon Zeitlin, *The Rise and Fall of the Judaean State*, 3 vols. (Philadelphia, 1962–1978).

–CHRISTINE E. HAYES

Tractate. The tractate *Sanhedrin* is in Mishnah order Neziqin, in eleven chapters, with related material in the Tosefta' and in both Talmuds. It deals with the rules and procedures of law courts. *Sanhedrin* lists several types of law courts, the functions of which include civil and criminal law as well as a variety of ritual and political responsibilities. The types of law courts are hierarchically arranged from the three-member courts of civil law, through the twenty-three-member courts of capital crimes, to the seventy-one-member high court, which deals with matters affecting the Temple and other issues of national importance.

Much of the tractate is concerned with the procedures for the two main areas of jurisprudence: monetary law and capital offenses. While the rules of evidence are similar in both areas, requiring at least two witnesses who are subjected to interrogation by the judges, there are significant differences between them, focusing mainly on the different orientations of the two kinds of courts. Whereas the monetary court strives for complete impartiality, the procedures of the capital offense court are weighted heavily in favor of acquittal (see MAKKOT). The ambivalence of Jewish law regarding the proper attitude toward criminals is poignantly expressed in *Sanhedrin* by several aggadic statements, which counterpoise the joy of ridding the world of wickedness (*San*. 4.5, 10.6) to the divine sorrow of losing one's child, wicked though he may be (*San*. 6.5). An additional aggadic digression (*San*. 1) promises all of Israel a portion in "the world to come," with several exceptions, notably proponents of heresies that were regarded by the rabbis as particularly dangerous. The lengthy Talmudic expatiation on this section is one of the most important sources of rabbinic eschatology. Tractate *Makkot* originally was included in *Sanhedrin*.

The Babylonian tractate was translated into English by Jacob Schachter and Harry Freedman in the Soncino Talmud (London, 1935).

• Chanoch Albeck, ed., *Shishah Sidrei Mishnah, Seder Nezikin*, 2d ed. (Jerusalem, 1956). Philip Blackman, ed. and trans., *Mishnayoth*, vol. 4, *Order Nezikin* (Gateshead, 1973). Pinhas Kehati, ed., *Mishnah: A New Translation with a Commentary, Seder Nezikin*, vol. 2, *Bava Batra, Sanhedrin* (Jerusalem, 1988). Hermann Leberecht Strack and Günter Stemberger, *Introduction to the Talmud and Midrash*, rev. and updat. ed., translated by Markus Bockmuehl (Minneapolis, 1992).

—AVRAHAM WALFISH

SANHEDRIN, FRENCH, the seventy-one-member, largely rabbinical, authority convened in Paris by Napoléon Bonaparte (4 February–9 March 1807) to translate the "secular" resolutions passed by the *Assembly of Jewish Notables into "religious" imperatives. This caricature of the ancient, autonomous *Sanhedrin was headed by Joseph David Sinzheim (*nasi'*), two assessors (the *av beit din* and the *ḥakham*), and Abraham Furtado, lay president of the assembly. In accordance with Napoléon's directives, they first separated the "immutable" (religious) from the "defunct" (civil and political) laws of Judaism and then made it obligatory for Jews to contract or dissolve a marriage after civil procedures; to make a religious virtue of patriotism and army service; and to abandon their "discreditable" occupations. Ignoring the emperor's urge to "dilute Jewish blood," however, they refused to declare mixed marriages religiously valid.

As though empowered by his "Grand Sanhedrin," Napoléon exploited its new "precepts" in his discriminatory legislation of 17 March 1808. Consistories (see CONSISTOIRE) on the French Protestant model were established to regulate Jewish life, tax congregants, and even enforce conscription. The "Infamous Decree" suspended repayment of debts to Jews for ten years, restricted their immigration and freedom of movement, and often drove them into bankruptcy. Realizing that he and his fellow "notables" had been duped, Furtado made unsuccessful protests at the highest level. French Jewry's plight was alleviated with the Bourbon restoration in 1815, but substantial religious equality—including state support for rabbis and consistories—was only attained under King Louis-Philippe (1830). By compelling the Jews to pay a high price for their emancipation, Napoléon encouraged apostasy and assimilation.

• Robert Anchel, *Napoléon et les juifs* (Paris, 1928). Jacob Katz, *Exclusiveness and Tolerance* (London, 1961), pp., 182–196. Barukh Mevorakh, ed., *Na'polei'on u-Tequfato* (Jerusalem, 1968), pp. 77–132. François J. Pietri, *Napoléon et les Israélites* (Paris, 1965), pp. 84–115. Simon Schwarzfuchs, *Napoleon, the Jews and the Sanhedrin* (London, 1979). Zosa Szajkowski, "Judaica-Napoleonica," in *Studies in Bibliography and Booklore* 2 (1956), pp. 107–152, republished in *Jews and the French Revolutions of 1789, 1830 and 1848* (New York, 1970), pp., 971–1016. Diogene Tama, *Collection des procès-verbaux et décisions du Grand Sanhedrin* (Paris, 1807), translated by F. D. Kirwan in *Transactions of the Parisian Sanhedrim* (London, 1807).

—GABRIEL A. SIVAN

SARAH, Abraham's wife and Isaac's mother (*Gn*. 11.29–31, 12, 16–21, 23–25; also mentioned in 49.31; *Is*. 51.2; *Rom*. 4.19, 9.9; *Heb*. 11.11; *1 Pt*. 3.6). Her original name, Sarai, was changed to Sarah (*Gn*. 17.15); both names mean princess. Sarah is portrayed as a very beautiful woman (see GENESIS APOCRYPHON) who inspired lust in foreign rulers, which led to the wife-sister stories of *Genesis* 12 and 20. Like other *matriarchs, she was at first barren, which led Abraham to take Hagar in order to bear a son (Ishmael) to be his heir (*Gn*. 16). Upon being informed by an angel that she would give birth, Sarah broke out in laughter because of her and her husband's advanced ages; hence, her child's name *Isaac, which is derived from the Hebrew verb meaning "to laugh" (*Gn*. 18). After Sarah gave birth to Isaac (*Gn*. 21), she had Hagar and Ishmael exiled. Sarah lived to be 127 years old and upon her death was buried in the cave of *Machpelah in Hebron (*Gn*. 22.19).

• Katheryn F. Darr, *Far More Precious Than Jewels: Perspectives on Biblical Women* (Louisville, Ky., 1991), pp. 85–131. Susan Niditch, "The Three Wife-Sister Tales of Genesis," in *Underdogs and Tricksters: A Prelude to Biblical Folklore* (San Francisco, 1987), pp. 23–69. Nahum M. Sarna, *Understanding Genesis* (New York, 1966). Claus Westermann, *Genesis 12–36: A Commentary*, translated by John J. Scullion (Minneapolis, 1985).

—ATHALYA BRENNER

SARUG, YISRA'EL (c.1560–1610), kabbalist and propagandist of Lurianic Kabbalah. He was born and educated in Egypt, where he became familiar with Yitsḥaq *Luria and his early kabbalistic doctrines. Sarug later claimed to have been Luria's personal disciple and was recognized as such by his contemporaries, although this has been disputed by modern scholarship. Between 1594 and 1600, he taught Lurianic Kabbalah in Italy, adding to it speculations of his own. Later, he taught Avraham *Cohen de Herrera in Ragusa, Illyria, and spent short periods in Salonika and Poland, where according to legend he taught Shelomoh Luria of Kraków. The main writings attributed to Sarug, such as *Limmudei Atsilut* and the commentary on *Sifra' di-Tseniʿuta'* (part of the Zohar), were published erroneously in 1897 under the name of Ḥayyim Vital (see VITAL FAMILY). Sarug's exposition of Luria's doctrine of the **tsimtsum* was articulated in terms of the tenets of the *malbush* (garment) and *shiʿashuʿa* (enjoyment). According to Leone Modena, and later to Gershom Scholem, Sarug's teachings were strongly infused with Platonic ideas, whereas other scholars find gnostic or atomist elements in his writings. It is evident, however, that his main disciples, Menaḥem ʿAzaryah da *Fano and Cohen de Herrera, did not attribute to him any philosophic background, nor did they mention any philosophic school with which he was affiliated. Sarug died in Poland.

• Samuel A. Horodezky, *Torat ha-Qabbalah shel Rabbi Yitsḥaq Ashkenazi* (Jerusalem, 1984), pp. 79–82. Moshe Idel, "Differing Conceptions of Kabbalah in the Early 17th Century," in *Jewish Thought in the Seventeenth Century*, edited by Isadore Twersky and Bernard Septimus (Cambridge, Mass., 1987), pp. 137–200. Ronit Meroz, "Rabbi Israel Sarug Talmid ha-'Ari: 'Iyyun Meḥuddash ba-Sugya'," *Da'at* 28 (1992): 41–50.

—NISSIM YOSHA

SASPORTAS, JACOB (1610–1698), rabbinic scholar and anti-Shabbatean controversialist. Raised and educated in Oran, Algeria, Sasportas subsequently served as rabbi of Tlemcen and neighboring towns. After being dismissed by the government, he moved to western Europe, where he held rabbinic positions in London, Hamburg, and Amsterdam. Sasportas was the most persistent and vigorous opponent of Shabbetai Tsevi at the height of the messianic movement in 1666. At a time when most rabbis and lay leaders, impressed by the waves of repentance that they considered a very positive phenomenon, suppressed their hesitations concerning the messianic outburst, Sasportas persistently warned of its dangers. In his view, the movement ran counter to traditional teachings concerning the messianic era, contradicted rabbinic authority on many points, and, like early Christianity, contained the seeds of antinomian sectarianism. He continued to combat the movement after its failure and collected his correspondence concerning it, as well as letters and pamphlets issued by followers of Shabbetai Tsevi, in his *Tsitsat Novel Tsevi* (shortened version [Amsterdam, 1737]; full version [Jerusalem, 1954]), by all accounts a primary source for knowledge of the history of Shabbateanism. A comparison of the original documents with the edited final version, however, shows that Sasportas, to some extent, doctored his sources, hiding his moments of sympathy and near belief and depicting himself as the persistent, relentless, and unwavering opponent of the movement. His *responsa, Ohel Yaʿaqov*, appeared in Amsterdam in 1737.

• Gershom Gerhard Scholem, *Sabbatai Sevi: The Mystical Messiah, 1626–1676* (Princeton, 1975), *passim*. —ELISHEVA CARLEBACH

SATAN (שָׂטָן; adversary), word occurring in most of the Bible as a common noun and referring to human antagonists (e.g., *1 Sm.* 29.4; *1 Kgs.* 5.18). There are, however, intimations, even in preexilic biblical literature, of a malign influence, variously described, that seeks to mislead human beings (e.g., *1 Kgs.* 22.22). Only in three passages, all of them late, is Satan depicted as an individualized superhuman being: in *Zechariah* 3.1–2 he appears as accuser; in *Job* 2.1 he is the heavenly persecutor (included among "the sons of God") who tests Job's piety on the rack of affliction; and in *1 Chronicles* 21.1 he functions as seducer. In all these passages Satan, though hostile to humans, remains obedient to God (cf. *Is.* 45.6–7). In apocryphal and apocalyptic literature, however, and to an even greater degree in the New Testament, the concept of Satan evolved, probably under Persian influence, as the incarnation of evil and the supreme antagonist of God. Satan rules countless demons, and his kingdom extends throughout the world. He is cast out from heaven (a misinterpretation of *Is.* 14.12) but continues with other fallen angels (cf. *Gn.* 6.1–4) to work evil upon earth. In tannaitic literature, Satan is rarely mentioned. It is the later, chiefly Babylonian, *aggadah* that enlarges the scope of his influence and activities. He is identified—among others—with *Asmodeus, *Samael (prince of the demons), the evil inclination, and the angel of death. He first tempts, then accuses and slays. Kabbalah gives even greater prominence to the concept of evil and uses a variety of synonyms for Satan (e.g., *qelippah* [shell of evil]). Jewish tradition has circumscribed his powers: it is said that on Ro'sh ha-Shanah Satan is confused by the shofar, and on Yom Kippur his authority is annulled. Ultimately he will be vanquished by the Messiah. There are occasional allusions to Satan in liturgy, but these have the general connotation of "corrupting desires" and possess no doctrinal significance. See also DEMONS.

• Bernard Jacob Bamberger, *Fallen Angels* (Philadelphia, 1952). Peggy Lynne Day, *An Adversary in Heaven* (Atlanta, 1988). Joshua Trachtenberg, *The Devil and the Jews* (New Haven, 1943).

SATMAR, Hasidic dynasty originating in Satu-Mare, Hungary (now Romania). It is now one of the largest Hasidic groups in the United States. The dynasty began with Mosheh Teitelbaum (1759–1841), an early Hasidic rabbi in Hungary. But it was Yo'el Teitelbaum (1888–1979) who, as rabbi of Satu-Mare from 1928, molded the sect's anti-Zionism and isolationism. He served as its charismatic *rebbi* until his death. Escaping from Europe in 1944, Yo'el settled in Williamsburg in Brooklyn, New York, in 1947. His congregation has its own welfare organizations and the world's largest *yeshivah*. He was succeeded by his nephew, Mosheh Teitelbaum. The Satmar Ḥasidim participate in New York's economic life but are unassimilated. Satellite communities exist in Kiryas Joel (Monroe, New York) and internationally. They consider modern Zionism and the existence of the State of Israel a violation of *halakhah* and believe its existence is responsible for delaying the coming of the Messiah and for all Jewish misery in the twentieth century, including the Holocaust. Rabbi Yo'el permitted his followers to live in Israel, but not to make mass *ʿaliyyah*, and forbade them to visit the Western Wall. They oppose the use of spoken Hebrew.

• Jerome R. Mintz, *Hasidic People: A Place in the New World* (Cambridge, Mass., 1992). Israel Rubin, *Satmar: An Island in the City* (Chicago, 1972). Joel Teitelbaum, *Safer mi-Torato shel Rabbenu*, 4 vols. (Brooklyn, N.Y. 1984). —DENNIS M. DREYFUS

SAUL, the first king of Israel. His story is found in *1 Samuel* 9 to *2 Samuel* 1. Saul was a member of the tribe of Benjamin. The genealogies in *1 Chronicles* 8.29–40 and 9.35–44 indicate that his family lived near Gibeon and may have continued to inhabit the area at least until the end of the First Temple period. The Bible relates that Saul was anointed privately by the prophet Samuel at Ramah. Upon reaching home, Saul was imbued by a divine spirit and behaved like an ecstatic prophet. Samuel called for the choice of the king by lot at a public convocation at Mizpah, at which time Saul was chosen, while hiding among the baggage. In the face of opposition to his election, Saul proved himself by rescuing the Gileadites of Jabesh from the harsh conditions of a treaty imposed by Nahash the Ammonite (*1 Sm.* 11.1–11).

Saul laid the groundwork for a centralized monarchy by first creating a royal court at the uninhabited Tel el-Ful, formerly Gibeah (*Jgs.* 19–21), which he renamed for himself: Gibeath-saul. Saul established the rudiments of an administration and a standing army, based on personal loyalty to the king, as well as a high court for judging the people. He supported the local cultic centers and the priestly community at Nob. His officials included his paternal uncle, Abner ben Ner, as commander-in-chief; Ahimelech the great-grandson of Eli, as high priest; and Doeg, the Edomite, in charge of the royal flocks. Saul followed a defensive military policy, securing the borders from the attacks of Israel's neighbors. He secured the eastern Transjordanian frontier from the Ammonites and the desert-dwelling Hagarites (*1 Chr.* 5.10), the northern border from Aramean incursions, and, on the southern side, he delivered the death-blow to the Amalekites (*1 Sm.* 15). However, the major enemy of the Israelites were the Philistines, whom Saul engaged several times. Saul died in the course of a battle with the Philistines; three of his sons were killed as well. He was survived by his son, Esh-baal, who was briefly king of a reduced territory (*2 Sm.* 2.9), and by his grandson, Merib-baal, the son of Jonathan, who became the father of a long line of descendants recorded in *1 Chronicles* 8.34–40.

• Joseph Blenkinsopp, "The Quest for the Historical Saul," in *No Famine in the Land*, edited by James W. Flanagan and Anita Weisbrod Robinson (Missoula, Mont., 1975), pp. 75–99. J. P. Fokkelman, *Narrative Art and Poetry in the Books of Samuel*, vol. 2, *The Crossing Fates, 1 Sam. 13–31 and 2 Sam. 1* (Assen, 1986). James B. Pritchard, *Gibeon, Where the Sun Stood Still: The Discovery of a Biblical City* (Princeton, 1962).

—AARON DEMSKY

SAVIOR. See MESSIAH.

SAVORA' (סָבוֹרָא; expositor), title given to scholars and heads of the Babylonian *academies in the period (6th cent.) following that of the amora'im and preceding that of the ge'onim. The title, first found in geonic sources, is based on the word *savora'* in the Talmud Yerushalmi, *Qiddushin* 2 and 63d, where it means a scholar competent to render decisions, implying that the scholar made private subjective decisions rather than authoritative ones. While the amora'im were the authors of the **gemara'*, interpreting the Mishnah and handing down decisions on practical law, it would seem that the savora'im merely expounded certain obscure passages in the Talmud and added their explanatory notes to the text of the Talmud Bavli. They were also responsible for the final editing of the amoraic redaction of the Talmud Bavli. However, there is a wide divergence of scholarly opinion as to the extent of their editorial activity. Only a few major personalities have been identified as savora'im, such as Abba' Yosef, Aḥa'i ben Huna', Aḥa' of Ḥattim, Geviha of Argiza, Mordekhai Pappias, Rabbah of Rov, and Shemu'el ben Abbahu.

• Salo Wittmayer Baron, *A Social and Religious History of the Jews*, 2d ed., vols. 2 and 6 (New York, 1952–1983). Jacob E. Ephrathi, *Tequfat ha-Savora'im ve-Sifrutah be-Bavel uve-Erets Yisra'el, 500–689* (Petaḥ Tiqvah, 1973). Morduch Judelowitz, *Yeshivat Pumbedita' bi-Yemei ha-'Amora'im* (Tel Aviv, 1935). Benjamin Manasseh Lewin, *Rabanan Savora'i ve-Talmudam* (Jerusalem, 1937). Abraham-Weiss, *Ha-Yetsirah shel ha-Savora'im* (Jerusalem, 1952).

—DANIEL SPERBER

SAYINGS OF THE FATHERS. See AVOT.

SCAPEGOAT. See AZAZEL.

SCHECHTER, SOLOMON (1848–1915), scholar, theologian, and architect of *Conservative Judaism. Born in Romania, he taught in Cambridge (to where he brought the bulk of the Cairo *Genizah from 1890 to 1902) and thereafter in New York, where he headed the *Jewish Theological Seminary of America and laid the groundwork for the Conservative movement. He attracted a faculty of outstanding European scholars, presided over the movement's growth, and in 1913 created the United Synagogue of America (later *United Synagogue of Conservative Judaism). Schechter avoided broad programmatic statements, but the philosophy implicit in his writings still provides a major part of the ideological foundation of Conservative Judaism. His theology reflects a shift of emphasis from God, as a philosophical concept, to Israel as a historical entity. According to Schechter revelation is manifest in tradition: the scriptures reveal history, and it is in the history of the Jewish people that the raw material for any Jewish theology has to be found. Schechter's most influential contribution to American Jewish life was his popularization of the concept of a "catholic (i.e., all-embracing as opposed to denominational) Israel." This was meant to provide a theoretical basis for the continuation of the *Historical movement's search for Jewish unity. He stressed the "secondary meaning of the Bible" (i.e., the Bible as interpreted by Jewish tradition) over the Bible as a textbook of dogmatic theology, the authority of which was vested in "the collective conscience of catholic Israel as embodied in the universal synagogue." Judaism was a living organism that had developed through the ages within the framework of rabbinic tradition. Schechter saw Jewish nationalism as part of the essence of Judaism and supported Zionism. He maintained contact with Reform leaders, although he continued to criticize them. His writings include editions of ancient texts (*Avot de-Rabbi Natan* [London, 1887]; the Hebrew text of *Ben Sira; Documents of Jewish Sectaries* [Cambridge, 1910], the first publication of the **Damascus Document*) and theological studies, including three volumes of *Studies in Judaism* (Philadelphia, 1896, 1908, 1924).

• Norman Bentwich, *Solomon Schechter: A Biography* (Cambridge, 1938). Louis Ginzberg, "Solomon Schechter," in *Students, Scholars, and Saints* (Philadelphia, 1943). Alexander Marx, "Solomon Schechter," in *Essays in Jewish Biography* (Philadelphia, 1947).

SCHENIRER, SARAH (1883–1935), founder of the *Beth Jacob schools for Orthodox girls. Born in Kraków to a Hasidic family, she was a self-educated woman who never attended high school. Beginning with a handful of girls, Schenirer, a dynamic educator, opened a school in her home in 1917 in Kraków and worked hard to convince Orthodox leaders of the need to respond to the sweeping forces of modernism and start a school system for girls. Formal religious education had been strictly reserved for males until that time. When enrollment reached 280 students, Schenirer was pressured by other communities to open additional schools, and she founded a teachers' seminary. Many of her graduates went on to open Beth Jacob schools in other cities or to serve as teachers in these schools. Schenirer's collected writings, translated into Hebrew from the original Yiddish, were published in Tel Aviv (1955–1960).

• Judith Grunfeld-Rosenbaum, *Sara Scheneirer* (New York, 1968). D. Weissmann in *The Jewish Woman: New Perspectives*, edited by Elizabeth Koltun (New York, 1976). —SHMUEL HIMELSTEIN

SCHICK, MOSHEH BEN YOSEF (1807–1879), rabbinic scholar; the intellectual and spiritual heir to Mosheh Sofer (see SOFER FAMILY), the German-born rabbinic leader of Hungarian Orthodoxy in the first half of the nineteenth century. Schick was born in Brezove, Slovakia. At the age of fourteen, he entered Sofer's *yeshivah* in Pressburg (Bratislava). In 1861 he became the rabbi of Hust, where he established his own *yeshivah*, which speedily won renown. He was considered the most prominent halakhist of his time in Hungary and received queries from the entire Jewish world.

Schick fought vociferously against *Neology. In the wake of the Hungarian Jewish Congress of 1869–1870, he advocated official separation from the non-Orthodox communities. This included those Jews, called the *Status Quo Ante, who continued to abide by the *halakhah* but did not share the views of the Orthodox establishment regarding communal issues. Despite this fact, in the context of Hungarian Orthodoxy, where extremes reigned, his was considered a middle position. For example, he refused to sign the Michalovic Declaration of 1865, which forbade entering a synagogue in which the rabbi preached in the vernacular. Similarly, Schick did not concur with Ḥatam Sofer's opposition to Mendelssohn's *Bi'ur*.

Schick's *responsa* were collected by his son as *She'elot u-Teshuvot Maharam Schick* (Munkács and Lwów [Lemberg], 1880–1884).

• Leopold Greenwald, *Le-Toledot ha-Reformatsyon ha-Datit be-Germanyah uve-Hungaryah* (Columbus, Ohio, 1948). Jacob Katz, "Nineteenth-Century Russia and Poland," in *The "Shabbes Goy": A Study in Halakhic Flexibility*, translated by Yoel Lerner (Philadelphia, 1989), pp. 181–216. Shnayer Z. Leiman, "R. Moses Schick: The Ḥatam Sofer's Attitude toward Mendelsohn's *Biur*," *Tradition* 24.3 (1989): 83–86. Alex Schick, "Moses Schick," in *Men of the Spirit*, edited by Leo Jung (New York, 1964), pp. 301–326. Michael K. Silber, "The Emergence of Ultra-Orthodoxy: The Invention of a Tradition," in *The Uses of Tradition: Jewish Continuity in the Modern Era*, edited by Jack Wertheimer (Cambridge, Mass., 1992), pp. 23–82. —ADAM S. FERZIGER

SCHIFF, ME'IR BEN YAʿAQOV (1605–1641), German Talmudist; known as Maharam Schiff. Renowned as a youth for his Talmudic brilliance, Schiff was appointed in 1622 to the rabbinate of Fulda, where he developed a reputation as a talented preacher and a vigorous opponent of the use of *pilpul* in the study of Talmud. He wrote Talmudic commentaries under the title *Ḥiddushei Halakhot*. The commentaries to ten tractates were published in 1737 and 1741, achieved wide popularity, and are included today in most editions of the Talmud.

• Samuel Horodezky, *Le-Qorot ha-Rabbanut* (Warsaw, 1910). Marcus Horovitz, *Frankfurter Rabbinen: Ein Beitrage zur Geschichte der israelitischen Gemeinde in Frankfurt a. M.* (Hildesheim, 1972), pp. 75–78.
—MARK WASHOFSKY

SCHISMS. See CONTROVERSIES; MINIM.

SCHLETTSTADT, SHEMU'EL BEN AHARON (14th cent.), rabbinic scholar, academy head, and Talmudic commentator. One of the few details known about his life is an incident in which he passed a death sentence on two Jews from Strasbourg, who were involved in a conspiracy with local knights to take economic advantage of other Jews. One of the Jews was put to death, but the other managed to escape and alert the knights, who then went to war against Strasbourg. Shemu'el was forced to flee Strasbourg, concealing himself with students of his *yeshivah* for a period of several years (1370–1376). Members of the Jewish community failed to appease the knights during that period. In 1376 Shemu'el traveled to the East, where he received a writ from the Babylonian authorities, and confirmation of this from a number of Jerusalem rabbis, instructing the Strasbourg community to reinstate him.

Rabbi Shemu'el's best-known work is his *Ha-Mordekhai ha-Qatan* or *Ha-Qatsar*, an abridgment (with addenda from subsequent halakhic authorities) of Mordekhai ben Hillel's *Sefer Mordekhai*. The work has never been published, although it is found in many manuscripts. Shemu'el also wrote a number of *responsa*.

• Avraham Halperin, *Sefer ha-Mordekhai ha-Shalem: Massekhet Bava' Qamma'* (Jerusalem, 1978). Israel Yuval, *Ḥakhamim be-Doram: Ha-Manhigut ha-Ruḥanit shel Yehudei Germanyah be-Shilhei Yemei ha-Beinayim* (Jerusalem, 1988). —EPHRAIM KANARFOGEL

SCHNEERSOHN FAMILY, foremost family of *Ḥabad Hasidic masters for the past two hundred years. R. *Shneur Zalman established Ḥabad Hasidism in Lyady in Belorussia. The dynasty includes seven masters; among them are Shneur Zalman's son R. Dov Ber (1773–1827), the Mittler Rebbi, who instituted the Ḥabad center in *Lubavich; Shneur Zalman's grandson R. Menaḥem Mendel, ha-Tsemaḥ Tsedeq (1789–1866), who expanded the movement; the sixth rabbi, R. Yosef Yitsḥaq (1880–1950), who emigrated from Russia to America in 1940 and established the Lubavitch center in Brooklyn, New York; and the seventh rabbi, R. Menaḥem Mendel Schneerson (1902–1994), one of the principal Jewish religious leaders of the twentieth century. He studied with his father, Levi Yitsḥaq, in the Ukrainian town of Ekaterinoslav and later studied engineering in Europe between 1928 and 1940. In 1941 he settled in America and assisted his father-in-law, R. Yosef Yitsḥaq, the sixth Lubavitcher *rebbi*. Schneerson (the spelling had been changed in the United States) succeeded to the Lubavitch leadership in 1950 and led the movement until his death. His unique position among modern Jewish leaders rested on his perception of spiritual responsibility to the entire Jewish community, as well as on his comprehension of Torah and religious law, his organizational skills, and his scientific background, which enabled him to utilize modern innovation in mass communication. He founded the Ḥabad International Education Network, which dispatched personal envoys and assured religious instruction for all Jewish communities, concentrating on remote areas and those countries isolated from contact with Judaism. He established the custom of weekly assemblies, which were attended by multitudes of Ḥabad adherents as well as observant and secular Jews who all sought his advice and blessing. In his later days, Schneerson stood at the center of a clamorous controversy concerning messianic claims for him held by many of his followers.

• Levi Itzhak Ginzburg, *Le-Havi' li-Yemot ha-Mashiaḥ: Shi'urim* (Jerusalem, 1994). Abraham Chanoch Glitzenstein, *Sefer ha-Toledot: Rabbi Shne'or Zalman mi-Li'adi* (Brooklyn, N.Y., 1975). Ḥayyim Me'ir Heilman, *Sefer Beit Rabbi* (Varsha, 1900). Joseph Isaac Schneersohn, *Lubavitcher Rabbi's Memoirs*, 2 vols. (Brooklyn, N.Y., 1956). —RACHEL ELIOR

SCHOLARSHIP. See EDUCATION; JEWISH STUDIES; STUDY; WISSENSCHAFT DES JUDENTUMS.

SCHOLEM, GERSHOM GERHARD (1897–1982), the founder of the modern study of Jewish *mysticism. Raised in an assimilated family in Berlin, he was drawn to Zionism and studied Hebrew and the Talmud. He chose the *Kabbalah as the subject of his doctorate, writing a study of **Sefer ha-Bahir*, which he translated into German. In 1923 he moved to Jerusalem, where he was the Judaica librarian at the National Library. He served as a professor at Hebrew University for forty years and was highly influential in shaping its academic development.

Until 1937, he published scores of studies and several books dealing with the history and development of kabbalistic literature, the biographies of some major figures, and works published from manuscripts, including a detailed catalog of kabbalistic manuscripts in the National Library. In 1937, his essay *Redemption through Sin* revolutionized the study of the Shabbatean movement and the concepts of Jewish medieval and early modern Jewish history. In 1941 he published his first great synthesis, *Major Trends in Jewish Mysticism* (rev. ed. 1954), which immediately was established as the standard textbook on Jewish mysticism.

In his lifetime, Scholem published about forty books and nearly seven hundred studies, almost all of them dealing with various aspects of Jewish mysticism, messianism, Hasidism, magic, and related subjects. Particularly noteworthy are his study *Origins of the Kabbalah* (Hebrew, 1948; German, 1962; and English, 1987) and *Sabbatai Tsevi: The Mystical Messiah* (Hebrew, 1957; English, 1978). He demonstrated in detail the role played by Jewish mysticism in Jewish religious culture, planting it firmly in the Jewish cultural mainstream and not considering it an aberration, as many had previously contended.

Scholem's studies, and a handful of nonscholarly essays dealing with essential problems facing contemporary Judaism, established his place as one of the most penetrating voices of Zionism and of the renewed cultural center in Jerusalem. He presented the Jewish past as vibrant and dynamic and described the intense spiritual forces that worked, in conflicting ways, throughout Jewish history. He denied the messianic nature of Zionism, insisting on its political, realistic approach to solving Judaism's contemporary problems.

After his death, many of his unpublished books were printed, including his annotated text of the *Zohar and a memoir, *From Berlin to Jerusalem*. Bibliographies of his writings are in *Studies in Mysticism and Religion* (1967) and *Bibliography of the Writings of Gershom Scholem* (1978).

• David Biale, *Gershom Scholem and Counter-History* (Cambridge, Mass., 1979). Joseph Dan, *Gershom Scholem and the Mystical Dimension in Jewish History* (New York, 1987). —JOSEPH DAN

SCHOOL. See EDUCATION.

SCHREIBER, MOSHEH. See SOFER FAMILY.

SCIENCE, systematic knowledge arrived at by observation, experiment, induction, logical deduction, and so on. Different branches of science recognize varying premises and require the use of different methods—hence also the usage that restricts the term science to the natural and so-called exact sciences. Science and religion have clashed in modern times, but the conflict is merely a modern variation of medieval conflict between the spirit of rational enquiry and that of mute acceptance of traditional dogma. The conflict arises whenever contradictions are discovered between the findings or claims of science and the real or alleged teachings of religion. Sometimes not only specific religious doctrines (e.g., the account of Creation, the manner of the composition of Bible, etc.) are contested in the name of natural or historical science, but religion itself is turned into an object of rational enquiry (e.g., by psychology or sociology). Attempts to resolve the ensuing conflicts usually take the form of: limiting the sphere of competence of science, for example, by pointing out the *a priori* character of its axiomatic assumptions or by showing that some of its claims are not scientific at all but philosophical; limiting and defining the proper sphere of religious teaching, for instance, by distinguishing between what is held to be genuinely and essentially religious doctrine and what is outmoded science falsely claiming religious authority; and reinterpreting, by various methods of exegesis, the meaning of traditional statements and of biblical and other authoritative texts, so as to make them appear consonant with scientific views (e.g., when the six days of Creation are said to correspond to geological ages). Whereas Reform and Liberal Judaism generally accept the authority of the sciences in their respective spheres, Orthodoxy tends to be more fundamentalist and to insist on the literal acceptance of biblical and even rabbinic statements. Thus biblical criticism, theories of *evolution, and other scientific or critical views are still considered heretical in certain Orthodox circles.

• Aryeh Carmel and Cyril Domb, eds., *Challenge: Torah Views on Science and Its Problems* (New York, 1976). Hillel Levine, "Science," in *Contemporary Jewish Religious Thought*, edited by Arthur A. Cohen and Paul Mendes-Flohr (New York, 1987).

SCIENCE OF JUDAISM. See WISSENSCHAFT DES JUDENTUMS.

SCRIBES. See SOFERIM.

SCRIPT, HEBREW. The ancient Hebrew script, as it is found on coins, seals, and other inscriptions from the First Temple period, was similar to neighboring Semitic (Phoenician, Canaanite) scripts but was replaced after the Babylonian exile by the square script currently in use. The Talmud refers to the former as *ketav 'Ivri* (Hebrew script) and to the latter as *ketav Ashuri* (Assyrian script—although in *San.* 21b the Talmud explains the latter term as meaning "upright, square script"). Most Talmudic rabbis hold that scripture was originally written in the ancient script but was rewritten by *Ezra in accordance with the injunction of "a prophet who came up from Babylon" (*San.* 21b). A different view, found in the Talmud and accepted by 'Azaryah ben Mosheh dei *Rossi in the sixteenth century, claims priority for the square script and maintains that the Bible was originally written (by Moses) in the Assyrian script and then changed to the Hebrew script, after which the Assyrian script was reintroduced. Detailed regulations are laid down as to the ink and parchment or hide that may be used for sacred scrolls, as well as the manner of writing to be employed (see SEFER TORAH; SOFER SETAM). From the standard square script, various types of cursive scripts have developed (see RASHI SCRIPT). The ancient Hebrew script is still used by the *Samaritans.

• Malachi Beit-Arie, *Hebrew Codicology: Tentative Typology of Technical Practices Employed in Hebrew Dated Medieval Manuscripts* (Jerusalem, 1981). Peter T. Daniels and William Bright, eds., *The World's Writing Systems* (New York, 1996), pp. 727–742, 782, 800, 883. Joseph Naveh, *Origins of the Alphabet* (Herzlia, 1994). Ada Yardeni, *Sefer ha-Ketav ha-'Ivri: Toledot, Yesodot, Signonot, 'Itsuv* (Jerusalem, 1991).

SCRIPTURE. See BIBLE.

SCROLL OF ANTIOCHUS, also known as the *Scroll of the Hasmoneans*; pseudepigraphous work written in Aramaic in the sixth or seventh century CE, extant also in Hebrew and Arabic translations. It describes various events of the Hasmonean Revolt and is entirely legendary in its character, even though its author was familiar with at least some of the historical accounts of *1 Maccabees* (see MACCABEES, BOOKS OF THE). A number of its traditions—such as the miracle of the oil—are well-known from other rabbinic sources, while others—for example, the story of how Judah killed Nicanor—were probably invented for etiological purposes, to explain the origins of the festival known as Nicanor Day to an audience ignorant of *1* and *2 Maccabees*.

• Leon Nemoy, *The Scroll of Antiochus* (New Haven, 1952), facsimile of a 1558 Hebrew codex, includes a bibliographic preface.

—GIDEON BOHAK

SCROLL OF ESTHER. See ESTHER; ḤAMESH MEGILLOT.

SCROLL OF THE TORAH. See SEFER TORAH.

SCROLLS (Heb. *megillot*). In ancient times, all biblical books were written on scrolls. Even after the introduction of bound leaves (codices), the scroll form was maintained for religious purposes, primarily the public reading of the Bible in the synagogue. The writing materials used and the length of the scrolls that were produced developed and changed over time; the regulations concerning these are dealt with at length by rabbis in their halakhic writings. The Torah scroll (see SEFER TORAH) used in the synagogue today dates from Talmudic times; prior to this, the individual books (see ḤUMMASH) were written on separate scrolls. In time, however, the manufacture of biblical scrolls became virtually limited to those books that were actually read in the synagogue: primarily, Torah scrolls and the *Ḥamesh Megillot, the Five Scrolls of the Hagiographa. Some synagogues employ parchment scrolls of the books of the prophets, from which the **haftarah* is read. See also MEGILLAH.

• Menahem Haran, "Bible Scrolls in Eastern and Western Jewish Communities from Qumran to the High Middle Ages," *Hebrew Union College Annual* 56 (1985): 21–62. Menahem Haran, "Book-Scrolls in Israel in Pre-Exilic Times," *Journal of Jewish Studies* 33 (1982): 161–173; 35 (1984): 84–85. Menahem Haran, "Book-Scrolls at the Beginning of the Second Temple Period: The Transition from Papyrus to Skins," *Hebrew Union College Annual* 54 (1983): 111–122. Menahem Haran, "Technological Heritage in the Preparation of Skins for Biblical Texts in Medieval Oriental Jewry," in *Pergament: Geschichte, Struktur Restaurierung, Herstellung*, edited by Peter Ruck (Sigmaringen, 1991), pp. 35–43.

—BARUCH J. SCHWARTZ

SCROLLS, FIVE. See ḤAMESH MEGILLOT.

SEA, BRAZEN. See BRAZEN SEA.

SEA OF THE TALMUD, a metaphoric phrase expressing the great breadth and unfathomable depth of Talmudic literature. It appears frequently in rabbinic sources from the eighteenth century onwards, in phrases such as "he knows to swim in the great sea of the Talmud," "the sea of the Talmud is great and broad encompassing numberless subjects of untold depths" (Ben Yehuda, *Dictionary* 4, 2056). —DANIEL SPERBER

SEARCH FOR LEAVEN. See BEDIQAT ḤAMETS.

SEAT OF MOSES. See MOSES, SEAT OF.

SECOND DAY OF FESTIVALS. See YOM TOV SHENI SHEL GALUYYOT.

SECOND PASSOVER. See PESAḤ SHENI.

SECOND TEMPLE. See TEMPLE.

SECTS. See CONTROVERSIES; MINIM.

SECULARISM, a term that literally means "of this world" (the social, political, and cultural spheres as distinct from the religious sphere), has often taken on the meaning of "antireligious." The notion of "secular" came late to Judaism; traditional Hebrew has no word for "secular" because both *qodesh* (the holy) and *ḥol* (the profane) were ritual terms.

Since the early nineteenth century, the authority of religious establishments and of religious law has been narrowed. After the Emancipation, Jews could increasingly define themselves as such without having to belong to the religious community. Activities formerly in the hands of religious bodies (education, charity, the administration of justice, punishment) have been taken over by secular agencies, which provide such services as social welfare, health care, and education. Most Jews send their children to state schools and participate in the secular cultural and political process. In Jewish communal life, many Jewish organizations, such as philanthropic federations, Zionist groups, and the like, function independently of religious direction.

The word *secular* (i.e., concern with this world as opposed to the realm of religion) should be distinguished from the word *secularist* (i.e., adherence to any ideology, such as Marxism, which rejects religion per se as illusory, escapist, or obscurantist). One of the strongest Jewish movements in eastern Europe in the first third of the twentieth century, the Bund, was outspokenly secular and antireligious. The Zionist movement, which emerged at the end of the nineteenth century, although having a religious component, was secular in leadership and goals, thus leading to the anti-Zionism of the ultra-Orthodox, who believed that the return to Zion could only be achieved through divine intervention. Soviet Russia was officially atheistic, and its ban on religious education meant that almost all Soviet Jews came to regard themselves as secular Jews.

Once the possibility of a secular Jewish identity came to be recognized, the Hebrew term *ḥiloni* (a secular person) was coined. While the Orthodox movement deplored the rejection of *halakhah* by secularists, it recognized that they were still Jews, if born of a Jewish mother. Secular Jews prefer either to identify Judaism with humanist values or to define Jewishness as an ethnic bond.

In Israel, the Knesset, a secular legislature, conferred many rights on the religious establishment and its law courts, but the Israeli rabbinate remains subject to the authority, in important legal matters, of the secular Supreme Court. Powers entrusted to the rabbinical authorities (all matters of personal status) have meant that there is no clear-cut wall of separation in Israel between state and religion, resulting in tensions between the secular and religious segments of the population. Since there are other forms of modern Jewish religiosity apart from Orthodoxy, secular Jews, properly so-called, are those who have no religious affiliation, especially in the Diaspora, but who adhere to an ethnic, cultural, or national Jewish identity. See also HUMANISTIC JUDAISM; ISRAEL, STATE OF, JEWISH RELIGIOUS LIFE IN; KIBBUTZ FESTIVALS; PLURALISM, RELIGIOUS.

• Arnold M. Eisen, "Secularization, 'Spirit,' and the Strategies of Modern Jewish Faith," in *Jewish Spirituality*, edited by Arthur Green, vol. 2 (New York, 1987) pp. 283–316. Ben Halpern, "Secularism," in *Contemporary Jewish Religious Thought*, edited by Arthur A. Cohen and Paul Mendes-Flohr (New York, 1987). Jacob Katz, *Out of the Ghetto: The Social Background of Jewish Emancipation* (Cambridge, Mass., 1973). Jehuda Reinharz, *Fatherland or Promised Land: The Dilemma of the German Jew 1893–1914* (Ann Arbor, Mich., 1975).

SECULAR JUDAISM. See HUMANISTIC JUDAISM.

SEDER (סֵדֶר; arrangement), a term most commonly used for the home service on the first night (two nights in the Diaspora) of Pesaḥ (see HAGGADAH OF PESAḤ). The term also refers to instructions for conduct; small books containing prayers, laws, or customs (for example, *Seder Zemanim*, a calendar; *Seder Meliḥah*, a book with laws about salting meat); the division of the Torah according to the *triennial cycle (also applied to the weekly reading of the annual cycle; see SIDRAH); the order of the *Mishnah; or the order of prayers (usually called *siddur* [*prayer book]).

SEDER ELIYYAHU, Midrashic work, also known as *Tanna' de-Vei Eliyyahu*. The book consists of homilies concerned with the reasons for the commandments, love of and study of Torah, and other religious and ethical teachings. The work was written between the third century and the tenth century CE, probably by one author, who claims to have lived in Jerusalem and Babylon.

• Victor Aptowitzer, in *Jewish Studies in Memory of George A. Kohut*, edited by Salo W. Baron and Alexander Marx (New York, 1935). Max Kadushin, *The Theology of Seder Eliahu* (New York, 1932).

SEDER ʻOLAM, name given to an early historical work (also known as the *Seder ʻOlam Rabbah*) that summarizes the history of the world and, in particular, of the Jews up to the second century CE. It was edited by the tanna' R. Yosei ben Ḥalafta' and his school.

• Chaim Milikowsky, "*Kima* and the Flood in *Seder ʻOlam* and B. T. Rosh-Ha Shana: Stellar Time-Reckoning and Uranography in Rabbinic Literature," *Proceedings of the American Academy for Jewish Research* 50 (1983): 105–132. Chaim Milikowsky, "*Seder ʻOlam* and Jewish Chronography in the Hellenistic and Roman Periods," *Proceedings of the American Academy for Jewish Research* 52 (1985): 115–139.

—CHAIM MILIKOWSKY

SEDER ʻOLAM ZUTA', a short historiographical work, so-called because of a superficial resemblance to the much earlier text **Seder ʻOlam*. This anonymous work presumably dates from the late geonic period, although in its present form it includes later additions. It begins with the reign of King David and attempts to demonstrate that the exilarchs of Babylonia were his direct descendants and continued the royal line, thus maintaining a sort of quasi-sovereignty after the end of the monarchy. Much of the text is devoted to a list of exilarchs of the Talmudic period and sages said to have been associated with them. There is a detailed account, at least partly legendary, of the career of Mar Zutra', who is said to have been executed after rebelling against Sassanian authority. His son, also called Mar Zutra', is reported to have gone to Erets Yisra'el in the early sixth century and achieved high rank there.

• Moshe Beer, *Ra'shut ha-Golah be-Bavel bi-Yemei ha-Mishnah veha-Talmud* (Tel Aviv, 1970). Adolf Neubauer, *Mediaeval Jewish Chronicles and Chronological Notes* (1887–1895; Jerusalem, 1967).

—ROBERT BRODY

SEDER TANNA'IM VE-'AMORA'IM, a short anonymous work of the geonic period of which at least part dates from the end of the ninth century CE. It contains two major sections, one historical and the other methodological. The historical section, although beginning with Moses, is devoted primarily to Talmudic Babylonia and gives the dates of death of leading amora'im. The methodological section represents the first large-scale attempt to catalog rules concerning the interpretation of Talmudic sources and, more particularly, rules for adjudicating disputes between Talmudic authorities. This section may be further divided into a portion concerning the tannaitic period and another concerning amoraic sources. There are substantial differences in style and organization between the various sections of the work (and even within some of these sections), and it is doubtful whether the book as known is the work of a single author. The work, edited by K. Kahana, was published in Frankfurt in 1935.

• Shraga Abramson, "Le-Toledot Nusaḥ Seder Tanna'im ve-'Amora'im," in *'Iyyunim be-Sifrut Ḥazal be-Mikra' uve-Toledot Yisra'el Muqdash le-Profesor 'Ezra' Tsion Melammed*, edited by Y. D. Gilat et al. (Ramat Gan, 1982). —ROBERT BRODY

SEER (Heb. *ro'eh*; *ḥozeh*), an early designation for prophet, indicative of the visionary aspect of *prophecy (cf. *Nm*. 12.6ff.). *Ro'eh* was the popular title for a man of God prior to the time of Samuel (*1 Sm*. 9.8) and probably referred to his function as a clairvoyant diviner who would be consulted for practical ends (e.g., Saul and his servant turned to Samuel in order to find the lost she-asses; *1 Sm*. 9.6ff.). In the Akkadian prophetic texts from Mari, on the left bank of the Euphrates River, there are multiple references to a similar diviner called the *barum*, who interpreted the liver and other entrails of slaughtered animals. The term *ro'eh* fell into disuse with the development of the vocation of prophet from seer, diviner, and predictor to the recipient of the word of God, the message of whom was to be transmitted to the people and its rulers. The Ḥasidim bestowed the title of seer upon R. *Ya'aqov Yitsḥaq, ha-Ḥozeh mi-Lublin, who was reputed to possess the gift of second sight.

• Abraham Malamat, *Mari and the Early Israelite Experience* (Oxford, 1989), pp. 79–96. Jacob Milgrom, ed., *Numbers*, The JPS Torah Commentary (Philadelphia, 1990), pp. 380–384. —SHALOM PAUL

SEER OF LUBLIN. See YA'AQOV YITSḤAQ, HA-ḤOZEH MI-LUBLIN.

SEFARDIM. See SEPHARDIM.

SEFER HA-BAHIR, earliest work of kabbalistic literature, written by an unknown author in northern Spain or Provence at the end of the twelfth century. This is the first work formulating the kabbalistic symbolism of the ten emanated "attributes" (called *sefirot* by later kabbalists) that constitute the divine *pleroma* and the concept that there is a feminine aspect in the divine realm. The dating of the book is based on the presence of terminology derived from the works of *Avraham bar Ḥayya' (mid-12th cent.), probably from Avraham *ibn Ezra (died 1167), and possibly from the translations of Yehudah ibn Tibbon (1170s; see IBN TIBBON FAMILY). Its teachings are quoted by the Gerona kabbalists in the beginning of the thirteenth century, when it became the standard kabbalistic text and had an impact on the Zoharic system of symbols.

The book was written in the form of a *midrash*. The first paragraph is attributed to *Neḥunya' ben ha-Qanah, who has a minor role in Mishnaic tradition but is presented as the leader of the *Heikhalot mystics in *Heikhalot Rabbati*. Others in the book include R. *'Aqiva', but the main characters are the fictional R. Reḥum'ai and the impossibly named "Rabbi Amora'," this being a generic term and not a personal name. In several paragraphs, a discussion between the speaker and a group of disciples is indicated. The main sources of the book are Talmudic sayings, Heikhalot traditions, and the **Sefer Yetsirah*, but use of these sources is creative; in almost every case the original meaning is obscured and a new one presented. The last section of the book is based on chapter thirteen in **Pirqei de-Rabbi Eli'ezer*, a description of the sins of Adam and Eve and the actions of Samael in the garden of Eden. The author develops a unique style in presenting his teachings through parables, many of them including the figures of a king, queen, or princess, in reference to the divine world.

The divine *pleroma* is presented as a divine tree (*ilan*; only later kabbalists combined the divine *ilan* with the tree [*'ets*] of life) that is upside-down, its root reflecting the Hebrew letter *shin*. In the last third of the work, the *pleroma* is described as a sequence of ten divine utterances, the first being the supreme crown; the second, divine wisdom; and so on. This sequence served as a basis for later kabbalistic descriptions of the ten *sefirot*.

The femininity of the *Shekhinah is one of the most important innovative symbols of this work, but the intense erotic character of the dynamism within the divine world was developed only by later kabbalists; it is hardly hinted at in the book. Many paragraphs depict the powers of evil, but they do not acquire an independent status; the evil elements are described as the fingers of the left hand of God. This is the first Jewish work that accepts the concept of *transmigration of souls, long known but rejected by Jewish thinkers.

Gershom Scholem described *Sefer ha-Bahir* as "a renewed explosion of the mythical within the heart of rabbinic Judaism." He did not determine whether these mythical elements, many of them having distinct gnostic character, were derived from Jewish sources or from non-Jewish gnostic traditions. About eighty manuscripts of the book are extant. It was printed several times and translated into German by Scholem and appeared in several English editions.

• Joseph Dan, "The Emergence of Jewish Mysticism in Medieval Europe," in *Mystics of the Book*, edited by P. Herrera (New York, 1993). Marianne Wallach-Fahler, "Die judische feministische Theologie auf der Suche nach einem weiblicheren Gottesbild: Weiblich Aspekte Gottes im Buch Bahir," in *Aus Zweier Zeugen Mund: Festschrift für Pnina Nave Levinson und Nathan Peter Levinson*, edited by Julius H. Schoeps (Gerlingen, 1992), pp. 236–245. —JOSEPH DAN

SEFER HA-ḤINNUKH, one of the most popular books on the reasons for the commandments (see COMMANDMENTS, REASONS FOR) written in the thirteenth century. Some believe that the book was composed by R. Pinḥas ha-Levi of Barcelona, a colleague and contemporary of Nahmanides, while others have ascribed it to his nephew, R. Aharon ha-Levi of Barcelona, a pupil of Shelomoh ben Avraham Adret. It is directed to students ages eighteen through twenty and is a précis of Moses *Maimonides' work on the rational nature of the commandments. *Sefer ha-Ḥinnukh* stresses observance of the commandments and says that performance should precede intention. A person must not try to calculate the reward for the fulfillment of a commandment but may consider its reasons. The author recommends that students read the book on Sabbath eves so that they will not run wild in the streets and states that the book is also of value to adults as a source for the study of *halakhah*. There have been many editions since its first publication (Venice, 1513); most recently in Jerusalem in 1991.

• D. Metzger, "Sefer Ḥinnukh u-Meḥabbero," in *Sefer ha-Ḥinnukh* (Jerusalem, 1991), pp. 7–20. Y. Ta-Shema, "Meḥabbero ha-'Amiti shel Sefer ha-Ḥinnukh," *Kiryat Sefer* 55 (1980): 787–790. –SHALOM BAR-ASHER

SEFER HA-QANAH, kabbalistic work by the anonymous author of *Sefer Peli'ah*, who seems to have written early in the fifteenth century in a Greek–Jewish rather than Spanish environment. Both works are in the form of dialogues between the wonder child Naḥum, who received heavenly revelations at the age of five, and his father Qanah. The books contain, in the main, material from earlier mystical writings but are sharply critical of purely exoteric halakhic observance unaccompanied by mystical intentions. Some of the ideas in *Sefer ha-Qanah* and *Sefer Peli'ah* seem to have influenced *Shabbetai Tsevi. The first complete edition of *Sefer ha-Qanah* appeared in Poritsk in 1786; the first complete edition of *Sefer Peli'ah* appeared in Korets in 1784.

• Avigdor ben Isaac, *Sefer Peli'ah* (Tel Aviv, 1977–1978).

SEFER HA-RAZIM, ancient Hebrew work of magic and angelology, probably originating from the fourth century CE. Many sections of this work were known in a fragmentary form scattered in Ashkenazi Hasidic and kabbalistic collections (like the *Sefer Razi'el*). Mordechai Margulies found several parts of this work among the Cairo Genizah fragments and successfully re-created its text and structure in his edition of the book (1966). The treatise is divided into seven chapters, each describing the celestial powers in charge of the various aspects of one of the seven firmaments, starting with the lowest and ascending to the seventh. The description of the lower spheres includes detailed magical formulas by means of which these celestial powers can be utilized. This is one of the largest collections of Jewish spells and magical incantations for protection against thieves and enemies, the concoction of love-potions, and the securing of other worldly needs. The book abounds with Greek terms, including incantations based on pagan prayers, indicating the close ties between Jewish and Greek *magic during this period.

• Michael Morgan, trans., *Sepher ha-Razim, the Book of Mysteries* (Chico, Calif., 1983). –JOSEPH DAN

SEFER ḤASIDIM, the most extensive work in the field of Jewish *ethics written in the Middle Ages. Its author was R.*Yehudah ben Shemu'el he-Ḥasid of Regensburg (died 1217), one of the great teachers among the Ḥasidei Ashkenaz. Rabbi Yehudah dedicated many years to this work, and his son, R. Mosheh Zaltman, testifies that, in the last week of his life, he wrote two folios of the book. The work has not been preserved in its original form; two editions are extant, one—shorter and probably later—was published in Bologna in 1538, and the second—more extensive and probably earlier—was preserved in a Parma manuscript and published by J. Wistinezki (1896) and again, later, with a detailed introduction by J. Freimann (Frankfurt am Main, 1924). A facsimile edition of the Parma manuscript was published by I. Marcus (Jerusalem, 1986). Several early quotations from this work are not found in these two editions, suggesting that the original work may have been larger than the ones we have. It is probable that the first part of the Parma manuscript, dealing with the fear of God and repentance, was written by R Shemu'el ben Kalonimos, R. Yehudah's father (see KALONIMOS FAMILY).

The book is made up of sections, some of them paragraph-length, and some extending to several pages (1,200 in the Bologna edition; 2,000 in the Parma ms.). Parts of the book are organized in chapters, each dedicated to a specific subject. Many of the sections are homiletical and present basic norms of Jewish ethics. Most of them deal with practical, everyday problems of conduct in ritual and ethical matters, as well as conduct for the teaching and studying of the Torah, social and family norms, attitudes toward gentiles, and the dangers of demons and witches. The work includes many stories, most of them exempla demonstrating correct behavior; others describe miracles, demonological phenomena, and historical events. The narratives in the work often reflect popular beliefs current in Germany in the twelfth century.

• Tamar Alexander-Frizer, *The Pious Sinner: Ethics and Aesthetics in the Medieval Hasidic Narrative*, Texts and Studies in Medieval and Modern Judaism 5 (Tübingen, 1991). Joseph Dan, *Ḥasidut Ashkenaz be-Toledot ha-Maḥashavah ha-Yehudit* (Tel Aviv, 1990–1991). Gershom Gerhard Scholem, *Major Trends in Jewish Mysticism* (New York, 1941), pp. 80–118. –JOSEPH DAN

SEFER MITSVOT GADOL. See MOSHEH BEN YA'AQOV OF COUCY.

SEFER MITSVOT QATAN. See YITSḤAQ BEN YOSEF OF CORBEIL.

SEFER PELI'AH. See SEFER HA-QANAH.

SEFER RAZI'EL, a mystical book ascribed to the angel *Raziel. According to its author, its secrets were imparted by Raziel to Adam when he was driven from the garden of Eden, and to Noah before he entered the ark, and ultimately came into the possession of Solomon.

The work contains much ancient magical and cosmological material as well as texts connected with the Merkavah (see Ma'aseh Merkavah) and *Heikhalot literature. *Sefer Razi'el*, compiled in its present form probably in the seventeenth century, had an unusually large circulation in eastern Europe, owing to the belief that its presence in a house ensured protection against fire and other dangers.

• Bernard Jacob Bamberger, *Fallen Angels* (Philadelphia, 1952). Gustav Davidson, *A Dictionary of Angels: Including the Fallen Angels* (New York, 1967).

SEFER TORAH (סֵפֶר תּוֹרָה; Torah scroll), a scroll that contains the first five books of the Bible—the Torah or Pentateuch. The Sefer Torah is used for synagogue readings on Mondays, Thursdays, Sabbaths, and holy days. The entire scroll is written by a scribe (see Sofer Setam) on strips of vellum or parchment that have been specially treated to be durable. Their source must be leather from a kosher species of animal, although the particular animal need not have been slaughtered ritually. Originally the use of a reed pen was considered obligatory, but later a quill was permitted. The strips of parchment are sewn together with threads made from the tendons of ritually clean beasts to form a long roll, both ends of which are wound around wooden staves (*'atsei ḥayyim*). In Ashkenazi and western Sephardi synagogues, the scroll is tied with a sash—sometimes decorated—then covered with an embroidered mantle (*me'il*). A decorative silver breastplate (*ḥoshen*) and pointer (*yad*)—the latter used to indicate the place during the Torah reading—are often suspended from the staves. The staves are frequently surmounted by either two silver finials (*rimmonim*) or a silver crown (*keter Torah*). In eastern Sephardi synagogues, the Sefer Torah is placed inside a wooden or metal cylindrical chest (*tiq*), and a cloth is draped on the outside of the chest. Jewish law forbids direct touching of the parchment; when necessary the parchment is handled by means of such a cloth.

When a scroll is being written, the scribe must maintain a devout frame of mind and utter each word aloud before writing it. He must copy the Torah scroll from another and may not write from memory. There are scribes who immerse themselves in a *miqveh* prior to each writing of the divine name. Each letter in the scroll must be separated from the next by a space. In the event of a mistake, the scribe may erase a letter, unless this occurs during the writing of the divine name, in which case the scribe can either cut out the word and patch the parchment or elect to discard the entire strip and replace it with a new strip. If a mistake is found in a Torah scroll, it must be corrected before the scroll may be used again for the Torah reading. If three or more mistakes are found, the Torah scroll may not be used again until the corrections have been made and the entire Torah scroll has been checked for accuracy. The text is written without vocalization or accentuation. Decorative titles (*tagin*) are appended to the tops of thirteen specific letters of the alphabet. There is no punctuation or verse division, but sections are indicated either by leaving a space equivalent to the width of at least nine letters within a line (*setumah* [closed section]) or by leaving the rest of the line blank (*petuḥah* [open section]). The location of each *setumah* or *petuḥah* has been handed down by tradition, and their placement is not at the scribe's discretion. Since the advent of printed guides for scribes, most Torah scrolls written in the past century have followed one of two standard patterns in terms of number of lines per page, number of words on each line, and so on. Most Torah scrolls today have either 245 or 248 columns. A column has no fewer than forty-two but not more than sixty lines. It is customary for six specific columns to begin with six specific letters, which together spell out, in Hebrew, the phrase "in God's name." In the case of one of the two models generally used for writing Torah scrolls today, all the columns, with the exception of the six mentioned previously, begin with the letter *vav*. The conclusion (**siyyum*) of the writing of a Sefer Torah is an occasion for celebration; each member of the congregation writes one of the last letters. In most cases the scribe will outline the last letters, and participants will then fill in the outline.

The Sefer Torah is the central object of veneration in the *synagogue. When the Torah is carried, the congregation stands, and those nearest to it kiss the mantle as the Torah passes them. Should a scroll be dropped, the entire congregation is under obligation to fast. In early times, the rabbis would not allow any worshiper to leave the synagogue until after the Sefer Torah had been replaced in the ark following the reading of the Torah. The Sefer Torah is kept in the ark (*aron* or *heikhal*), which is located on the synagogue wall facing Jerusalem. One Sefer Torah may be placed on another, but a Sefer Torah may not lie under a scroll of the Prophets, the latter considered less holy. The open scroll is displayed to the congregation before (in Sephardi practice) or after (in Ashkenazi practice) the reading of the portion of the Torah. Usually, all readings are taken from a single scroll; however, on special days they may be taken from two or even three scrolls. On Simḥat Torah (in Israel, on *Shemini 'Atseret) all available scrolls are taken from the ark and carried in procession seven times around the synagogue. It is the custom of Ḥasidim outside Israel to carry the Torah scrolls in procession both on Shemini 'Atseret and on Simḥat Torah. If a synagogue is in danger, the scrolls must be rescued first. A Sefer Torah that is worn out or disqualified for other reasons is not destroyed but either placed in a special storeroom (**genizah*) or ceremoniously buried. Should a Sefer Torah have been burned, its ashes, too, are ceremoniously buried. During the Second Temple period, a Sefer Torah was deposited in the Temple sanctuary and taken out on solemn occasions when the high priest or king would read portions to the public. The last of the 613 Torah commandments states that each male is obligated to write a Torah scroll; many rabbinic authorities rule that this commandment can be fulfilled by the purchase of a completed Torah scroll. In ancient times, Jewish kings were commanded to write two Torah scrolls and to keep one with them wherever they went. Laws regarding the Torah scroll are codified in the *Shulḥan ʿArukh, Yoreh Deʿah* 270–284.

• J. Simcha Cohen, *The 613th Commandment: An Analysis of the Mizvah to Write a Sefer Torah (Derush vechiddush)* (New York, 1983). Jacob Neusner, *Torah: From Scroll to Symbol in Formative Judaism* (Philadelphia, 1985). Jonathan P. Siegel, "The Scribes of Qumran: Studies in the Early History of Jewish Scribal Customs . . . ," Ph.D. dissertation, Brandeis University, 1971. Colette Sirat, *Du Scribe un livre: Les Manuscrits hébreux au moyen âge* (Paris, 1994). —SHMUEL HIMELSTEIN

SEFER YETSIRAH, ancient Hebrew treatise on cosmogony and cosmology dating from the third or fourth century CE; one of the most influential works of Jewish science, philosophy, and, because of the kabbalistic commentaries written on it, mysticism. It presents, in brief and enigmatic sentences, a systematic view of the principles of the process of creation and the laws governing nature and humans. It states that the world was created by "thirty two paths of [divine] wisdom," which are the first ten numbers and the twenty-two letters of the Hebrew *alphabet. The basic concept follows the Mishnaic statement that the world was created by ten divine utterances (*Avot* 5.1) and the Talmudic view that the world was created by the letters of the alphabet (e.g., *Men.* 29b). *Sefer Yetsirah* systematized these concepts and presented a picture of the process of creation largely independent of the description in *Genesis* 1. The ten numbers (**sefirot*) are the ten directions or five dimensions of the universe: north, south, east, west, up, down (space), beginning, end (time), good, and evil. They also express the evolvement of the three elements, air, water, and fire. Each letter of the alphabet is in charge of three realms, one in the universe (the stars), one in time (month, week, day), and one in humans (an organ or a sense). The author invented a system of Hebrew grammar, seeing in the rules of language the source of the laws of nature. The grammatical distinction between masculine and feminine governs all existence. He viewed the difference between good and evil as a grammatical one, and as such they are present in the universe and in individuals. The work does not deal with religious or ethical subjects, such as the commandments, the people of Israel, the human soul, or prayer. There is at the end of the book an indication that the understanding of these scientific laws brought Abraham into a religious union with God, and everyone following him in this may achieve the same goal.

The concept of the Hebrew alphabet in *Sefer Yetsirah* is more limited than that of the Midrash; no use is made of *gimatriyyah*, *notariqon*, or other methods. The one context in which the permutation of letters is mentioned is in connection with good and evil; evil is created by a minute change in the order of the letters in a "good" word. The author describes in great detail how the universe evolved and is governed by individual letters and their groupings. The most extensive description in this work is that of God "crowning" each letter and empowering it to "govern" an aspect of the universe. These "aspects" are portrayed as having three layers: universal, temporal, and anthropological. Each of the twelve "simple" letters, for instance, rules over one constellation of stars, one month in the year, and one human limb. Each of the seven "double" letters, after being "crowned," is in charge of a planet, a day of the week, and a human characteristic. At the top of the pyramid of the alphabet are the "mothers," the three principal letters *alef*, *mem*, and *shin*, which govern, respectively, the three elements of air, water, and fire (the author of *Sefer Yetsirah* does not recognize earth as an element); the three seasons of the year; and the three principal parts of the human figure.

While thus formulating a theory of divine creation and providence by means of the alphabet, the author also developed a theory of language; words are derived from roots, each of which is comprised of two letters. The 231 possible combinations of two letters are the source of all words. He describes the alphabet as two revolving wheels meeting at each point to create a root. The groupings of the letters indicate the first formulation of Hebrew grammar, centuries before Hebrew adopted its current grammar from Arabic examples. This highly sophisticated concept of the alphabet does not follow Midrashic concepts: there is no discussion of the shapes of the letters, their numerical value, transmutations, or their adornments.

Sefer Yetsirah is not mentioned in ancient Hebrew literature, and its terminology is original and unique. It was discovered by Jewish rationalists and scientists in the tenth century; *Saʿadyah ben Yosef Ga'on wrote a detailed commentary in Arabic, and Shabbetai *Donnolo, in Hebrew. Many rationalistic scientific commentaries followed until the twelfth century, the most detailed by *Yehudah ben Barzillai al-Bargeloni. Late in the twelfth century the treatise became a major source for Jewish mystics in Europe, kabbalists and non-kabbalists, many of whom derived their terminology from it; since then it has been regarded as an ancient expression of Jewish mysticism.

It first appeared in Latin translation in Paris in 1552 and then in Hebrew in Mantua in 1562. The best-known edition appeared in Warsaw in 1884. Various English translations have been published, including that of Knut Stenring and Akiva ben Joseph (1970).

• Joseph Dan, "The Emergence of Jewish Mysticism in Medieval Europe," in *Mystics of the Book*, edited by R. A. Herrera (New York, 1993). Gershom Gerhard Scholem, *Origins of the Kabbalah*, edited by R. J. Zwi Werblowsky, translated by Allan Arkush, 1st English ed. (Philadelphia and Princeton, 1987), pp. 24–35. —JOSEPH DAN

SEFIRAT HA-ʿOMER. See ʿOMER.

SEFIROT (סְפִירוֹת; numbers), a term probably originating in the **Sefer Yetsirah*, where it refers to the primordial numbers. In later kabbalistic writings under Neoplatonic and gnostic influence, *sefirot* refers to the *emanations and manifestations of the Godhead. Early kabbalistic literature has a variety of names for these ten *sefirot*. The usual designation and order is in the form of a kabbalistic "tree" in the following order: Keter Elyon, the "supreme" crown of God; Ḥokhmah, the "wisdom" or primordial idea of God; and Binah, the "understanding" of God—these form the first triad. Forming a second triad are: Ḥesed, "love" of mercy of God; Gevurah or Din, his "power," in particular the power of stern judgment; and Tiferet or Raḥamim, the "beauty" or "compassion" of God. The last of the *sefirot* is Netsaḥ, the "lasting endurance" of God, identified with the *Shekhinah and with Keneset Yisra'el (the mystical archetype of Israel), which functions as the recipient of the divine life that flows into it from all the others. (The names of the seven lower *sefirot* are based on *1 Chr.* 29.11). A large part of kabbalistic speculation is concerned with describing the nature of the *sefirot*, their relationship with each other, as well as with their fountainhead, which is the unfathomable Godhead or *Ein Sof, and with the lower worlds. In terms of practical mystical life, this means that every religious commandment and observance is related to a specific *sefirah*, as are the accompanying mystical meditations.

• Moshe Halamish, *Mavo' la-Qabbalah* (Jerusalem, 1991), pp. 97–133. Moshe Idel, *Kabbalah: New Perspectives* (New Haven, 1988). Gershom Gerhard Scholem, *On the Kabbalah and Its Symbolism* (New York, 1972).

SELAH (סֶלָה), a word of uncertain etymology and meaning that appears seventy-one times in the *Book of Psalms*, three times in *Habakkuk* (chap. 3), and in the third and eighteenth benedictions of the ʿAmidah. It has been variously interpreted as meaning "forever" (Targum), "eternally, without interruption" (*ʿEruv.* 54a), or "it is so" (Avraham ibn Ezra on *Ps.* 3.3); as a musical instruction for a change in rhythm or tune, fortissimo ("lift up" your voices), an interlude during which musical instruments are played while the singers are silent, or a pause whose significance was concealed from those not engaged in the Temple service; or as a liturgical response by worshipers ("lift up" your benediction).

SELF-DEFENSE. See Homicide.

SELIḤOT (סְלִיחוֹת), non-statutory additional prayers originally composed for Yom Kippur and fast days but later extended to other services. The kernel of all *seliḥot* consists of the recitation of *Exodus* 34.6–7, with its enumeration of the thirteen divine attributes: "The Lord! the Lord! a God compassionate and gracious, slow to anger, abounding in kindness and faithfulness, extending kindness to the thousandth generation, forgiving iniquity, transgression, and sin; yet he does not remit all punishment, but visits the iniquity of parents upon children and children's children, upon the third and fourth generations." The *seliḥot* were incorporated within the framework of the *ʿAmidah, though early Palestinian *payyetanim* (see Payyetan) connected them with the **qerovah*, as is still to be found in certain fast-day rites. In the Middle Ages, an amplified version of *seliḥot* came to be used on Ro'sh ha-Shanah and the intermediate days between Ro'sh ha-Shanah and Yom Kippur (the ʿAseret Yemei Teshuvah), and then during the whole period preceding Ro'sh ha-Shanah—from 1 Elul among Sephardim and among Ashkenazim from the Sunday before Ro'sh ha-Shanah (or from two previous Sundays when Ro'sh ha-Shanah falls on a Monday or Tuesday). *Seliḥot* are divided into several categories, according to their subject: **tokhaḥah* (admonition), in which the worshiper is called upon to consider his ultimate destiny; **baqqashah* (petition), not always poetical, which address the suffering of Israel and contain a request for God's mercy; **gezerah* (evil decree), which describe various persecutions and sufferings, particularly those of the Crusades in the eleventh century; **ʿaqedah* (the binding of Isaac), which address martyrdom; **teḥinnah* (supplication), on the theme of the relationship between God and Israel; *viddui* (confession), in prose; and *ḥata'nu*, which address Jewish martyrdom, especially that of the *Ten Martyrs (e.g., *Elleh Ezkerah, recited during the Musaf service on Yom Kippur). The poetical forms of *seliḥot* include *sheniyyah; shelishiyyah; motsejab*; and *pizmon*, a *seliḥah* consisting of strophes of more than four lines, with a refrain. The earliest known writer of *seliḥot* is *Yosei ben Yosei (5th cent.), one of whose compositions, Omnam Ashameinu, is included in the evening service of Yom Kippur. In the Italian rite, the Seliḥot service is called Taḥanunim (Supplications). The practice of having a minimum of four days before Ro'sh ha-Shanah when *seliḥot* are recited is connected to the Temple practice of examining the sacrificial offering for four days to ensure that it had no defects or blemishes; therefore, the need for four days of self-examination prior to repentance. In North America, it has become customary to hold a late night Seliḥot service on the Saturday night preceding Ro'sh ha-Shanah. *Seliḥot* have also served as an opportunity for liturgical creativity in the modern period; some have been inspired by the Holocaust. Seliḥot was re-introduced into the Reform movement by R. David Polish, and in recent years the Reform movement in North America produced a Seliḥot service entitled *Gates of Forgiveness*. Among its liturgical innovations is the use of feminine imagery to refer to God.

• Ismar Elbogen, *Jewish Liturgy: A Comprehensive History*, translated by Raymond P. Scheindlin (Philadelphia, 1993). Irving Greenberg, *The Jewish Way: Living the Holidays* (New York, 1988). Lawrence A. Hoffman, *The Canonization of the Synagogue Service* (Notre Dame, 1979). Isaac Klein, *A Guide to Jewish Religious Practice* (New York, 1979). Abraham Millgram, *Jewish Worship* (Philadelphia, 1971). Stefan C. Reif, *Judaism and Hebrew Prayer* (Cambridge, 1993). —Peter Knobel

SEMAḤOT. See Evel Rabbati.

SEMIKHAH (סְמִיכָה, laying on of hands), originally, the laying of hands on *sacrifices prior to their being slaughtered, as mandated by the Torah (*Lv.* 1.4). *Semikhah* was required of all sacrifices brought by individuals but not those offered by the community. The sacrificer placed his hands between the horns of the animal and, where required, made his confession. The term was also used to denote the passing on of permission to rule on questions of Jewish law, which was originally performed by a laying on of the hands (see Ordination).

• Lawrence A. Hoffman, "The Origins of Ordination," in *Rabbinic Authority*, edited by Elliot Stevens (New York, 1982), pp. 71–94. Simon

Schwarzfuchs, *A Concise History of the Rabbinate* (Oxford, 1993), pp. 27–37. —SHMUEL HIMELSTEIN

SÉMINAIRE ISRAÉLITE DE FRANCE, French rabbinical college, also known as École Rabbinique, that was founded as a *yeshivah* in 1704 in Metz. In 1859 the college moved to Paris and was supervised by the central *consistoire*. Rabbis are graduated after a five-year course of study; the college also trains cantors and teachers in a spirit of modern Orthodoxy.

SEMINARIES, RABBINICAL. See RABBINICAL SEMINARIES.

SEMINARIO RABÍNICO LATINOAMERICANO, Conservative rabbinical seminary founded in 1962 in Buenos Aires, Argentina, by Jewish Theological Seminary of America graduate R. Marshall T. Meyer. The school was modeled after pre–World War II modern rabbinical seminaries in western Europe and the United States and was the first of its kind in Latin America.

Seminary functions include publication of new Spanish translations of major Jewish works and a journal (*Majshavot*), Jewish teacher training, and synagogue outreach as a *beit din*. The school also sponsors a professional rabbinic association.

In 1984 R. Meyer returned to the United States but remained active at the seminary until his death in 1993. The seminary is administered by graduates of its programs. Over forty rabbis and hundreds of Jewish educators have graduated from the seminary since 1962 and serve over eighty-five congregations in Latin and North America.

• Richard A. Freund, "The First Thirty Years of the Seminario Rabínico Latinoamericano," *Conservative Judaism*, vol. 44.2 (1992): 67–78. Richard A. Freund, "Somos Testigos–We Are Witnesses: The Theology of Liberation of Rabbi Marshall T. Meyer," *Conservative Judaism*, vol. 47.1 (1994): 27–38. —RICHARD A. FREUND

SEMITES, a term deriving from the list of the descendants of Shem, son of Noah, found in *Genesis* 10.21–31, which is used to designate the speakers of a family of related languages. Thus, the term is properly a linguistic and not an ethnic classification, with the adjective *Semitic*, first introduced by the German historian A. L. Schlözer in 1781, describing the languages spoken by these peoples. Remnants of the primitive Semitic religion can be discerned in aspects of Judaism, Christianity, and Islam. The languages classifiable under the general heading of Semitic may be broken down into Northeast Semitic (Mesopotamia), Northwest Semitic (Syria-Palestine), and Southwest Semitic (Arabia and Ethiopia). Northeast Semitic is represented by Akkadian (Assyrian and Babylonian). The Northwest Semitic language group includes Ugaritic, *Aramaic (western Aramaic: Nabatean, Palmyrene, Samaritan Aramaic, Jewish Palestinian Aramaic, and Christian Palestinian Aramaic; eastern Aramaic: Syriac, Babylonian Aramaic, and Mandean), and Canaanite (the *Hebrew language, Phoenician, Punic, also related to Edomite, Ammonite, and Moabite). Arabic and Ethiopic constitute the Southwest Semitic language group. These various Semitic languages have in common a basic lexical stock, with the majority of words having a triconsonantal root to which various morphemes are affixed in order to modify the root meaning. Semitic languages are usually graphically consonantal, although most later added vowel signs. Semitic languages also have similar syntax, no neuter gender, and are all written from right to left with the exception of Akkadian and Ethiopic.

The term **antisemitism* was first used in late nineteenth-century Germany to describe hatred of Jews and is therefore a misnomer as it does not relate to other Semitic peoples.

• J. H. Hospers, *A Basic Bibliography for the Study of the Semitic Languages*, 2 vols. (Leiden, 1973–1974). Julian Morgenstern, *The Rites of Birth, Marriage, Death, and Kindred Occasions among the Semites* (Cincinnati, 1966; repr. New York, 1974). Sabatino Moscati, ed., *An Introduction to the Comparative Grammar of the Semitic Languages* (Wiesbaden, 1980). W. Robertson Smith, *The Religion of the Semites* (1894; repr. New York, 1972). —MICHAEL JAMES WILLIAMS

SEPHARDIM, form of the place name Sepharad, which appears in *Obadiah* 1.20 and which originally referred to the kingdom of Lydia in Asia Minor but was early identified by commentators with the country of Spain (the name Zarephath in the same verse was identified with France). As a result, the Jews of the Iberian Peninsula and their descendants came to be known as Sephardim, in distinction to the Jews of the Franco-German tradition, who are known as *Ashkenazim (Ashkenaz in *Gn*. 10.3 having been identified with Germany). It has been suggested that in ritual and liturgical matters, Sephardi Jewry represents a continuation of the Babylonian tradition, since all the Mediterranean countries came under the influence of the Babylonian ge'onim during the period of Muslim rule, while Ashkenazi Jewry largely followed the tradition of the Palestinian scholars, but the clear origin and demarcation of the two liturgies is still a matter of discussion. The Jews in medieval Spain created a rich and varied culture, and it was there that the Kabbalah saw its first flowering in the thirteenth and fourteenth centuries. The Sephardim differ from the Ashkenazim in their Hebrew pronunciation (see HEBREW LANGUAGE; the modern State of Israel—and in its wake, many Ashkenazi communities—has adopted the Sephardi pronunciation), aspects of their prayer rites (although the basis is identical), and many customs and traditions. After the expulsion of the Jews from Spain in 1492, Sephardim imposed their culture and traditions upon the Jewish communities of North Africa, the Balkans, and the Middle East. Subsequently *Marranos escaping from the Iberian Peninsula founded communities in western Europe and the Americas. Currently, Sephardim constitute some 20 percent of worldwide Jewry; some 50 percent of the Jewish population in Israel. Israel has both a Sephardi and Ashkenazi *chief rabbinate. See also JUDEO-SPANISH.

• Michel Abitbol, *Ha-Pezurah ha-Yehudit ha-Sefaradit aḥarei ha-Gerush* (Jerusalem, 1992). Marc Angel, *The Rhythms of Jewish Living: A Sephardic Approach* (New York, 1986). Solomon Gaon, *Sephardim and the Holocaust* (New York, 1987). Jane S. Gerber, *The Jews of Spain* (New York, 1992). Lucien Gubbay, *The Sephardim* (London, 1992). José Luis Lacave,

Sefarad, Sefarad: La España judía (Madrid, 1987). Henry Méchoulan, ed., *Les Juifs d'Espangne: Histoire d'une diaspora, 1492–1992* (Paris, 1992). Chaim Raphael, *The Sephardi Story* (London, 1991). Norman A. Stillman, *Sephardi Religious Responses to Modernity* (Buffalo, 1995).

SEPTUAGINT, oldest Greek version of the Bible. The name (*septuaginta* in Latin means seventy) is derived from a legend (*Letter of Aristeas*; *Meg.* 9a; minor tractate *Soferim* 1.8) according to which Eleazar, the high priest, at the command of the Egyptian ruler Ptolemy Philadelphus (c.288–247) sent seventy-two scholars from Jerusalem to Alexandria to render the Torah into Greek for the royal library. Each translator worked in his own cell, yet guided by divine inspiration, they finished simultaneously, and all the translations were identical. According to the church fathers, the seventy sages translated not only the Pentateuch but the whole Hebrew Bible. The Septuagint owes its existence to the fact that the growing Jewish population of Egypt had become sufficiently Hellenized to need a Greek translation of the Hebrew Scriptures, especially for liturgical purposes in the synagogue. The first Greek translations were probably oral and accompanied the public reading of the Hebrew text; later a written translation emerged, and in time the Greek version often took the place of the original. The legend appears to contain a core of fact: the Pentateuch was probably translated in the third century, possibly with the encouragement of Ptolemy Philadelphus II. The first translators may have been born in Palestine or else received guidance from Palestinian scholars; but the translation was made in Egypt. The Prophets and part of the Hagiographa were rendered in the second century BCE. In the Septuagint, the canonical books are arranged in a different order (law, history, poetry, prophecy) from that of the Masoretic Text (see BIBLE TEXT). In addition, the collection of Greek sacred writings also contains translations of a number of additional compositions known as the Apocrypha (see APOCRYPHA AND PSEUDEPIGRAPHA).

The Greek translation is a composite and uneven work; at times it is literal to the point of unintelligibility; at times it is paraphrastic. The translators' knowledge of Hebrew often seems to have been inadequate, but in general their understanding of the language and subject matter is excellent (see BIBLE TRANSLATIONS). Based on a Hebrew text that differed in many respects from the Masoretic Text and other Hebrew texts found at Qumran, the Septuagint is of utmost importance for biblical criticism. The various manuscripts of the Septuagint (Vaticanus, Sinaiticus, and Alexandrinus, as well as early papyrus fragments) differ from one another, but they probably originate from a single translation. At first the Septuagint was viewed with favor by the Palestinian rabbis (*Meg.* 9b; *Soferim* 1.8; cf. *Meg.* 1.8). Hellenistic Jewry revered it and even instituted an annual celebration in its honor (Philo, *Life of Moses* 2.7). But the growing recognition of divergences between the text of the Hebrew Bible and that of the Greek, and at a later stage its acceptance as the official Christian Bible, produced a hostile reaction in rabbinic circles. The day on which the Septuagint was completed was likened to the day on which the golden calf was made (*Soferim* 1.7), and study of the Greek language, once highly esteemed, was frowned upon (*Sot.* 9.14, 49b). Thus, the Septuagint ultimately became a barrier between Jewish and Greek cultures and the instrument for the propagation of a rival religion. New Greek translations became necessary for Hellenistic Jewry, each of which revised the Septuagint. The best known of these are the translations of *Aquila, *Symmachus, and *Theodotion.

• Sebastian P. Brock et al., *A Classified Bibliography of the Septuagint* (Leiden, 1973). Sidney Jellicoe, *The Septuagint and Modern Study* (Oxford, 1968). Henry Barclay Swete, *An Introduction to the Old Testament in Greek*, 2d ed. (Cambridge, 1914). Emanuel Tov, *The Text-Critical Use of the Septuagint in Biblical Research*, Jerusalem Biblical Studies 3 (Jerusalem, 1981).

SERAPHIM, heavenly beings mentioned only once in the Bible, in *Isaiah* 6.2, where they are described as six-winged creatures who sing God's praise ("holy, holy, holy"). In the apocryphal *Book of Enoch*, the seraphim are identified with the "burning serpents" (*neḥashim seraphim*) of *Numbers* 21.6. They are also mentioned in the liturgical elaboration of the *Qedushah in the daily morning service. See also ANGELS.

• Gustav Davidson, *A Dictionary of Angels: Including the Fallen Angels* (New York, 1967), p. 267. —SHIFRA EPSTEIN

SERKES, YO'EL BEN SHEMU'EL. See SIRKES, YO'EL BEN SHEMU'EL.

SERMONS. See HOMILETICS.

SERPENT. There are several terms referring to the serpent in Biblical Hebrew, and they often appear in different combinations in poetic parallelism. The two more prevalent contextual themes occurring in these verses have to do with snake venom (e.g., *Dt.* 32.33; *Ps.* 58.5, 140.4; *Jb.* 20.14, 16) and snake bites (e.g., *Gn.* 49.17; *Nm.* 21.6, 8; *Jer.* 8.17; *Prv.* 23.32). Other snake themes include procreation through the hatching of eggs (*Is.* 59.5); dwelling in holes in the ground and dens (*Is.* 11.8); hiding in walls and stone fences (*Am.* 5.19; *Eccl.* 10.8); eating dust (*Is.* 65.25); the lethal "tongue" (*Ps.* 140.4; *Jb.* 20.16); and snake charmers who chant magical spells against snakebites (*Ps.* 58.5–6; *Jer.* 8.17; *Eccl.* 10.11). All of these themes have parallels in ancient Near Eastern literature, especially in Akkadian and Ugaritic. In both Akkadian and Sumerian, a term for *snake* is used that literally means "fire-snake," paralleling the biblical term *saraf*, which, in light of this precedent, may be seen to derive from the Hebrew verb *s r f* (burn).

In the Bible the serpent was regarded as a symbol of evil, and as such figures as the tempter in the story of the garden of *Eden (*Gn.* 3). Its negative association with the tree of life stands in contrast to Babylonian myth, in which the serpent appears on a tree as one who bestows life. As proof of Moses' divine mission to Pharaoh, his staff turned into a serpent (*Ex* 4.2–4). A brazen serpent (*Nehushtan) served to cure the stricken Israelites in the wilderness (*Nm.* 21); the representation was kept in the Temple and must have constituted an object of superstitious worship until destroyed by Hezekiah

(*2 Kgs*. 18.4). The rabbis counted among the wonders of the Temple in Jerusalem the fact that serpents never caused any harm within its precincts (*Avot* 5.9).

• Friedrich S. Bodenheimer, *Animal and Man in Bible Lands* (Leiden, 1960), pp. 65–68, 106–108, 111–112, 200. Chaim Cohen in *Sefer H. M. Y. Gevaryahu*, vol. 2 (Jerusalem, 1989), pp. 74–81, in Hebrew. Benno Landsberger, *Die Fauna des alten Mesopotamien* (Leipzig, 1934), pp. 2–5, 32–33, 45–66. R. M. Whiting in *Journal of Cuneiform Studies* 36.2 (1984): 206–210. —CHAIM COHEN

SERPENT, BRAZEN. See NEHUSHTAN.

SERVANT OF THE LORD. The concept of a servant of God, through whose suffering light and salvation will come to the world, is found in the second part of the *Book of Isaiah* (42.1–7, 49.1–9, 50.4–9, 52.13–53.12). The servant of the Lord is described as proclaiming justice and truth to the people through the divine spirit, but his path is strewn with obstacles: his own people do not recognize him, he is smitten by his adversaries, and he submits silently to suffering for the sins of others. God, however, will ultimately raise him up, and his message will triumph throughout the world. The interpretation of these somewhat obscure prophecies has been complicated by the early Christian identification of Jesus with the suffering servant (*Acts* 3.13, 3.26, 4.27, 4.30). Commentators disagree about whether the symbol of the servant refers to an individual (the prophet or a future messianic figure) or to a group (Israel as a whole or the righteous and loyal minority of the people). Jewish exegetes have, as a rule, favored the collective interpretation.

• Yehezkel Kaufmann, *History of the Religion of Israel*, vol. 4, *The Babylonian Captivity to the End of Prophecy*, translated from Hebrew by C. W. Efroymson (New York, 1977). Christopher R. North, *The Suffering Servant in Deutero-Isaiah*, 2d ed. (Oxford, 1969). —SHALOM PAUL

SEʿUDAH (סְעוּדָה; meal), a festive meal on the occasion of the observance of a particular **mitsvah* or on a special day. Such meals include those partaken of on Sabbaths and festivals (which in biblical times included Ro'sh Ḥodesh). A Seʿudat Mitsvah (Meal of a Commandment) is a meal that is connected with a religious ceremony or celebration, such as a circumcision, *bar* or *bat mitsvah*, betrothal, or wedding. The rabbis held the completion of the study of a Talmudic tractate (**siyyum*) to be an occasion for such a festive gathering (*Shab*. 118b). Such a *seʿudah* is often arranged to fall on the day before Pesaḥ; participation in it by firstborn males supersedes their obligation to fast on that day (see TAʿANIT BEKHORIM,).

On festivals, the obligation is to consume two festive meals, but on the Sabbath a third meal is added in the afternoon—the Seʿudah Shelishit (Third Meal). Eating three meals on the Sabbath became synonymous with giving the day full honor; hence, the Talmud says, "May my portion be with those who eat three meals on the Sabbath" and "He who observes the three meals on the Sabbath is delivered from three evils" (*Shab*.118a). Although this meal has no Qiddush, in the course of time a special sanctity was attached to it, particularly under kabbalistic influence. Among the Polish Ḥasidim, the Seʿudah Shelishit became a major feature of religious and social life. Gathering at the table of the **tsaddiq*, Ḥasidim would spend hours at the sacred meal, until well after the end of the Sabbath, listening to their master's mystical discourse and singing hymns or wordless tunes that produced both ecstatic enthusiasm and quiet meditation. This inspired the custom of the *ʿOneg Shabbat.

The meal provided for mourners by their friends on their return from the funeral is known as Seʿudat Havra'ah (Meal of Recovery). Tradition requires that it include round foods (such as eggs and rolls) to symbolize the recurring cycle of life and death. An appropriate addition is made to the *Birkat ha-Mazon on this occasion. The meal eaten prior to the fasts of Yom Kippur and Tishʿah be-'Av is called the Seʿudah Mafseqet. In the former case, it has a festive character, but the Seʿudah Mafseqet on 8 Av expresses the mournful nature of the occasion: one course only (no meat or wine) is served. According to one tradition, the meal consisted of simply a piece of bread and an egg dipped in ashes.

• Yitzhak Buxbaum, *Jewish Spiritual Practices* (Northvale, N.J., 1990), pp. 225–279. Moshe Aleksander Zusha Kinstlikher, *Taʿanit Bekhorim u-Seʿudot Mitsvah be-ʿErev Pesaḥ* (Bene Beraq, 1980–1981). Aharon Verthaim, *Law and Custom in Hasidism*, translated by Shmuel Himelstein (Hoboken, N.J., 1992). Shelomoh Yosef Zevin, *The Festivals in Halachah*, translated by Shlomo Fox-Ashrei (New York, 1981).

SEʿUDAT RABBI ḤIDQA'. Rabbi Ḥidqa' (2d cent. CE) held that the Sabbath should be honored by four meals instead of the customary three (*Shab*. 117b). Hence, certain Orthodox Jews partake of a fourth Sabbath meal, usually after the Sabbath morning Qiddush, called "the meal of Rabbi Ḥidqa'."

SEVARAH (סְבָרָה; logical argument). Reason is one of the normative sources of Jewish law, and laws derived on the basis of *sevarah* are generally endowed with the status of biblical law. The rule that a person must allow himself or herself to be killed rather than shed the blood of an innocent individual is derived from an argument that asks, "Who says that your blood is redder? Perhaps the blood of the other person is redder?" (*San*. 74a). In the area of civil law, the rule that the burden of proof is upon the plaintiff is expressed in terms of the argument that just as a sick person who goes to the doctor must explain symptoms, so the plaintiff must prove that there is a case against the defendant (*B. Q*. 46b). Legal presumptions throughout the *halakhah* are based upon *sevarah*. The use of *sevarah* was particularly prevalent in the amoraic period, and the Talmud frequently reacts to the question of how to establish the source of a particular law with the remark that its origin may lie "either in Scripture or in *sevarah*" (*San*. 30a; *Yev*. 35b). The fundamentally rational approach characteristic of the Talmud makes *sevarah* into an almost meta-legal source of *halakhah*, and it is in this respect that later authorities observe that monetary matters, which are to a great extent *sevarah*-based, constitute the highest form of Torah study (*B. B*. 10.8).

• Zevi H. Chajes, *The Student's Guide Through the Talmud* (London, 1952), pp. 29–31. Menachem Elon, *Jewish Law: History, Sources, Prin-*

ciples, 4 vols. (Philadelphia, 1994), pp. 987–1014. Abraham Rabinowitz, *The Jewish Mind, in Its Halakhic Talmudic Expression* (Jerusalem, 1978), pp. 149–165.
–DANIEL SINCLAIR

SEVEN BENEDICTIONS. See SHEVAʿ BERAKHOT.

SEVEN SPECIES, foods mentioned in *Deuteronomy* 8.7–8 as characterizing the promised land of Canaan: "For the Lord your God is bringing you into a good land, . . . a land of wheat and barley, of vines and fig trees and pomegranates, a land of olive trees and honey." The eating of these foods or their products is preceded by a special blessing and followed by a special, shortened form of *Birkat ha-Mazon.

• Hayim Halevy Donin, *To Be a Jew: A Guide to Jewish Observance in Contemporary Life* (New York, 1972). Isaac Klein, *A Guide to Jewish Religious Practice* (New York, 1979).
–PETER KNOBEL

SEX. Sexual relations play a central role in Jewish theology and law. Unlike Christianity, but like Islam, Judaism does not value celibacy, legislating instead that all men must marry and procreate. Rabbinic law also legislates a woman's conjugal rights (*ʿonah*; see *Ket*. 5.6 and *Ket*. 62b).

The Bible is repeatedly concerned with problems of fertility, and the creation of man and woman is accompanied by the divine blessing to "be fruitful and multiply" (*Gn*. 1.28). Strict laws defined the borders between legitimate and illegitimate sexual practices (*Lv*. 19–20). Incest, adultery, sodomy (i.e., male homosexual relations), bestiality, and sex with a menstruating woman are all forbidden. These laws may have been motivated in part by the belief that these practices either diminished fertility or confused genealogical lines. The prophets used sexual metaphors to describe Israel's relationship with God and condemned idolatry as adultery against God (see *Hos*. 1–2 and *Ez*. 16).

The rabbis of late antiquity, possibly under the influence of the Hellenistic concept of the passions, regarded the sexual drive as problematic. The rabbis termed it the *yetser ha-raʿ* (evil inclination). Yet, properly channeled, this evil inclination was the necessary source for much that is positive in the world: "were it not for the evil inclination, no man would build a home, marry a wife, or have children" (*Gn. Rab*. 9.7). The rabbis ruled that men (although not women) were required to procreate (*Yev*. 63b–65b). This may have been designed to counter tendencies toward celibacy among the rabbinic elite, since the Talmud contains stories of rabbis who absented themselves from home for long periods for the purpose of studying (*Ket*. 62b–63a).

Medieval Jewish philosophers, influenced by medieval Neoplatonism and Aristotelianism, tended to devalue the material world and to create a hierarchy between soul and body. Moses Maimonides, for example, held that sexual intercourse should be undertaken solely for the purpose of procreation and the pleasures of the body minimized. He argued that circumcision was designed to curb the desire for sex both physiologically and psychologically (*Guide of the Perplexed* 3.49). Medieval mystics shared the philosophers' ambivalence toward the body but believed that proper sexual relations between husband and wife caused the male and female emanations of God (*sefirot*) to come together in a kind of spiritual union. Proper sexual relations required adherence to the law; even one's thoughts during intercourse, said the mystics, should be directed toward the divine and away from physical pleasure. The kabbalists celebrated eroticism through their erotic theology but also tended toward asceticism in their suspicion of male physical pleasure. Thus, the thirteenth-century Zohar, the classic text of Kabbalah, and the sixteenth-century teachings of Yitsḥaq Luria (the leading kabbalist of the Safed school) were both replete with powerful erotic images. The Zohar, however, considered minor sexual infractions, such as nocturnal emissions, great sins. Among eighteenth-century Ḥasidim, stories circulated about wonder-working rabbis who took vows of celibacy even within marriage.

Mainstream rabbinic culture in the Middle Ages viewed a healthy sexual relationship between husband and wife as the primary protection against illicit relations and fantasies. Jewish popular culture and folklore also contain rich speculations about erotic matters. At times, popular culture developed practices at variance with rabbinic law.

• David Biale, *Eros and the Jews: From Biblical Israel to Contemporary America* (New York, 1992). Rachel Biale, *Women and Jewish Law: An Exploration of Women's Issues in Halakhic Sources* (New York, 1984). Daniel Boyarin, *Carnal Israel: Reading Sex in the Talmud* (Berkeley, 1993). Jeremy Cohen, *Be Fertile and Increase, Fill the Earth and Master It: The Ancient and Medieval Career of a Biblical Text* (Ithaca, N.Y., 1989). Louis Epstein, *Sex Laws and Customs in Judaism* (New York, 1948). David Feldman, *Marital Relations, Birth Control and Abortion in Jewish Law* (New York, 1968). Jacob Katz, *Tradition and Crisis: Jewish Society at the End of the Middle Ages* (New York, 1961).
–DAVID BIALE

SEXTON. See SHAMMASH.

SEXUAL OFFENSES. In addition to *adultery and *incest, there are a number of biblical and rabbinic offenses of a sexual nature. Sodomy and *homosexuality are capital offenses under biblical law, as is the act of having carnal relations with a beast (*Lv*. 18.22–23, 20.13–16). A betrothed woman and her lover are both liable to the death penalty unless the former was raped, in which case the rapist alone is liable to execution (*Dt*. 22.20–27). The *rape of an unmarried, unbetrothed woman carries a financial penalty under biblical law (*Dt*. 22.28–29), and the Talmud specifies that compensation must also be paid for any physical or psychological damage sustained by the rape victim (*Ket*. 42a–43b). The penalty for sexual intercourse with a menstruant is *divine punishment (*Lv*. 18.19, 20.18). Lesser sexual offenses, the punishment for which is flogging rather than death, include intercourse with non-Jews and *mamzerim*, and relations between priests and women belonging to classes into which they are forbidden to marry. The Bible prohibits marrying a person whose testes are crushed or whose member is cut off (*Dt*. 23.2). It is also illegal to castrate (see CASTRATION) a man or a male animal (Maimonides, *Laws of Forbidden Intercourse* 16.10–

12). Sexual acts falling short of intercourse are prohibited between those individuals who are forbidden to marry one another (*Lv.* 18.6), and are expected to be punished by divine hand (see DIVINE PUNISHMENT). Behavior such as lesbianism, marital intercourse in public, and being secluded with a woman with whom intercourse is prohibited are offenses for which there is no positive sanction. Coercive sexual relations between a husband and a wife are forbidden by Jewish law and marital rape is recognized as a crime under Israeli law on that basis.

• David Biale, *Eros and the Jews: From Biblical Israel to Contemporary America* (New York, 1992). Menachem Elon, *Jewish Law: History, Sources, Principles*, 4 vols. (Philadelphia, 1994), pp. 339–340, 1030–1031. Louis Epstein, *Sex Laws and Customs in Judaism* (New York, 1968).
—DANIEL SINCLAIR

SEYAG LA-TORAH (סְיָג לַתּוֹרָה; fence around the law), preventive rabbinic injunction enacted to safeguard the observance of biblical commandments. The injunction to erect such safeguards is found in *Avot* 1.1, where it is given as one of the three precepts of the Men of the Keneset ha-Gedolah. The "fence" consisted of a stringent intensification of the law to safeguard the original commandments. An example of such a fence around the law, given in tannaitic sources, is the prohibition against eating the paschal sacrifice and other sacrifices after midnight, although according to biblical law they may be eaten until morning.

• Siegfried Stein, "The Concept of the 'Fence': Observations on Its Origins and Development," in *Studies in Jewish Religious and Intellectual History: Presented to Alexander Altmann*, edited by Siegfried Stein and R. Loewe (University, Ala., and London, 1979), pp. 301–329.

SFORNO, ʿOVADYAH BEN YAʿAQOV (1475–1550), Italian philosopher, Bible commentator, and physician. He studied medicine in Rome and also taught Hebrew to the famous humanist Johannes Reuchlin. From 1525 Sforno lived in Bologna. His commentaries on the Torah and other biblical books are concerned mainly with the plain meaning of the text (*peshat*), although they reflect his philosophical propensities. Sforno rejected the then prevalent kabbalistic doctrines and also paid little attention to philological questions. Among his works are *Or ʿAmmim*, a polemic (which he himself translated into Latin) against Aristotelian theories on the eternity of matter, divine omniscience, and the nature of the soul; a philosophical commentary on *Avot*; a Hebrew grammar; *responsa*; and a translation of Euclid.

• S. Daniel Breslauer, "The Theology of Ovadya ben Yaakov S'forno as Reflected in His Commentary on the Torah," rabbinic thesis, Hebrew Union College, 1969. Ralph Pelcovitz, *Sforno: Commentary on the Torah* (New York, 1987).
—FRANCISCO MORENO CARVALHO

SHAʿATNEZ. See KIL'AYIM.

SHABBAT (שַׁבָּת; Sabbath), tractate in Mishnah order Moʿed, in twenty-four chapters, with related material in the Tosefta' and in both Talmuds. Despite frequent references to the *Sabbath and its observance in the Bible (*Gn.* 2.1–3; *Ex.* 16.22–30, 20.8–11; *Lv.* 19.3, 23.3; *Nm.* 15.32–36; *Is.* 58.13–14; etc.), the laws of the Sabbath are not elaborated in biblical sources and are regarded by the rabbis as a striking example of "mountains hanging by a hair, in which there is scant scriptural evidence but many oral laws" (*Ḥag.* 1.8). *Shabbat* divides the kinds of prohibited work on the Sabbath into thirty-nine categories, including activities relating to agriculture and the preparation of bread, making clothing, writing, building, and transferring items from private to public domains. All other forms of prohibited work on the Sabbath are classified as "offspring" of these thirty-nine categories.

The opening chapters of *Shabbat* focus on preparations for the Sabbath, specifically the need to ensure that work begun on Friday not be continued after nightfall. Much of the tractate is devoted to defining the laws governing transfer of items from private to public domains, including a discussion of the status of various articles worn by men, women, or animals. The last chapters of *Shabbat* primarily deal with care for animals or for the human body on the Sabbath, addressing such issues as childbirth, circumcision, medical practices, and treatment of corpses.

The tractate in the Talmud Bavli was translated into English by Harry Freedman in the Soncino Talmud (London, 1938).

• Chanoch Albeck, ed., *Shishah Sidrei Mishnah, Seder Moʿed* (Jerusalem, 1952). Philip Blackman, ed. and trans., *Mishnayoth*, vol. 2, *Order Moed* (Gateshead, 1973). Pinhas Kehati, ed., *Mishnah: A New Translation with a Commentary, Seder Moed*, vol. 1, *Shabbat, Eruvin* (Jerusalem, 1990). Hermann Leberecht Strack and Günter Stemberger, *Introduction to the Talmud and Midrash*, rev. and updat. ed., translated by Markus Bockmuehl (Minneapolis, 1992).
—AVRAHAM WALFISH

SHABBAT BE-RE'SHIT. See SABBATHS, SPECIAL.

SHABBAT HA-GADOL. See SABBATHS, SPECIAL.

SHABBAT ḤAZON. See SABBATHS, SPECIAL.

SHABBAT MEVAREKHIM, MAḤAR ḤODESH, RO'SH ḤODESH. See SABBATHS, SPECIAL.

SHABBAT NAḤAMU. See SABBATHS, SPECIAL.

SHABBAT SHEQALIM, ZAKHOR, PARAH, HA-ḤODESH. See SABBATHS, SPECIAL.

SHABBAT SHIRAH. See SABBATHS, SPECIAL.

SHABBAT SHUVAH. See SABBATHS, SPECIAL.

SHABBAZI, SHALEM BEN YOSEF (c.1619–1680), the most outstanding Jewish religious poet of Yemen. He was born in Shabbaz and was apparently a weaver who lived a life of poverty. He was acquainted with Talmud and rabbinical writers, Kabbalah and philosophy, as well as Islamic literature. Shabbazi gave faithful expression to both the tribulations and the yearnings of his contemporaries in a difficult era. Many of his poems were written in reaction to the period of extreme communal suffering, culminating in the exile of all Yemenite Jewry, including Shabbazi, to the town of Mawza on the shores of the Red Sea (1679–1680) by the fanatical Imam Aḥmed. Shalem ben Yosef Shabbazi's favorite theme, redemption, struck a responsive chord among his fellow Jews.

He wrote poems for Sabbaths and festivals, weddings and circumcisions, about Torah and the world to come. Some of his poems were incorporated into the Yemenite liturgy, and some, such as "Ahavat Hadassah," have become part of modern Israeli religious poetry. His five hundred fifty known poems (all of which incorporate an acrostic of his name) were written in Hebrew, Aramaic, and Arabic. His songs of Zion, like his other poetry, betray the kabbalistic influences of his time. His tomb in Ta'izz was a focus of pilgrimage by both Jews and Muslims, among both of whom he had a reputation as a wonder worker. He only became known beyond Yemen in the nineteenth century.

• Avner Afag'in, *Aba Shalom Shabbazi Ne'im Zemirot Yisra'el* (Rosh ha-'Ayin, 1994). Saadyah Ḥozeh, *Toledot ha-Rav Shalom Shabbazi . . . u-Minhagei Yahadut Sharab he-Teman, ve-Sefer Galut Teman, Qorei ha-Dorot* (Jerusalem, 1973).

SHABBETAI BEN ME'IR HA-KOHEN (1621–1662), known as the Shakh from the initials of his best-known work; Lithuanian halakhist and rabbi. Shabbetai ben Me'ir ha-Kohen settled in Vilna, where he became *dayyan* (judge) and married the great-granddaughter of Mosheh *Isserles. In 1655 during the Polish wars, he fled to Lublin, later leaving Poland for Bohemia and Moravia and becoming rabbi of Holesov, where he died.

His most famous work, published in Kraków in 1646, is *Siftei Kohen*, an incisive commentary on the **Shulḥan 'Arukh* aimed at clarifying its rulings (including those added by Mosheh Isserles). His work paved the way for Polish rabbis to accept the *Shulḥan 'Arukh* after three generations of opposition; his commentary is commonly printed together with the *Shulḥan 'Arukh* and his rulings accepted as standard. He engaged in a dispute with *David ben Shemu'el ha-Levi, whose parallel commentary, *Turei Zahav*, was published in the same year. Shabbetai ben Me'ir ha-Kohen's criticism of *Turei Zahav*, *Nequdot ha-Qesef*, was posthumously published (Frankfurt an der Oder, 1677). His other halakhic works include *Toqfo Kohen* on the laws of possession (Frankfurt an der Oder, 1677), *Gevurat Anashim* on chapter 154 of the *Shulḥan 'Arukh* (Dessau, 1697), *Po'el Tsedeq* on the 613 commandments (Jesenice, 1720), and *He-'Arukh* on the *Arba'ah Turim* (Berlin, 1767). He gave an important account of the Chmielnicki uprising, *Megillat 'Eifah* (Amsterdam, 1651), and composed penitentiary prayers to be recited by eastern European Jewry (Amsterdam, 1651).

• Ben-Zion Katz, *Rabbanut, Hasidut, Haskalah*, vol. 1 (Tel Aviv, 1956–1958), pp. 108–111. Moses A. Shulvass, "Ha-Torah ve-Limmudah be-Polin u-Lita'," in *Beit Yisra'el be-Polin*, edited by Israel Halpern, vol. 2 (Jerusalem, 1953), pp. 13–35; English translation, "Torah Study in Eastern Europe," in *Between the Rhine and the Bosphorus*, by Moses A. Shulvass.

—ADAM TELLER

SHABBETAI TSEVI (1626–1676), messianic pretender. Born in Smyrna, he dedicated himself to Talmudic and kabbalistic studies and devoted himself to ascetic practices. He was surrounded by a circle of companions and disciples to whom, at the early age of twenty-two, he confided mystical revelations, possibly containing hints of his messianic calling. The fact that he was said by his followers to have been born on 9 Av, the traditional date of the birth of the Messiah, bolstered his claim. His not infrequent fits of strange and objectionable behavior, including uttering the Tetragrammaton in public, however, caused scandal, and he was forced to leave his hometown. Wherever he went (Salonika, Constantinople, Jerusalem), his behavior caused uproar and frequently led to his expulsion from the community. In Cairo he married Sarah, an orphan of the Chmielnicki massacres; the marriage was given mystic import by Shabbetai and his followers. Of decisive importance was his meeting (in the summer of 1665) with *Natan of Gaza, who recognized Shabbetai Tsevi as the Messiah and became his prophet. In December 1665 he publicly proclaimed himself king and Messiah in the synagogue at Smyrna. Practically the entire Jewish world was seized with the delirium of messianic fever. Prayers were offered up for Shabbetai Tsevi, and families even sold their houses in sure hope of imminent and miraculous transport to Erets Yisra'el. In 1666 Shabbetai Tsevi proceeded to Constantinople, where, immediately upon his arrival, he was arrested. After two months of imprisonment in the capital, he was incarcerated at Abydos. Since he was allowed considerable freedom, his imprisonment did nothing to diminish the messianic fervor. His followers referred to Abydos as Migdal 'Oz (Tower of Strength), and on Pesaḥ, Shabbetai Tsevi, himself, sacrificed a paschal lamb there. Then, denounced by a certain Neḥemyah ha-Kohen, he was summoned before the Sultan's privy council, and following the advice of the sultan's physician, a Jewish apostate, Shabbetai Tsevi adopted Islam to save his life. His apostasy led to confusion and shame, except among his most fervent followers (the Shabbateans), who clung to their belief that his sham conversion was part of a divine plan (a belief retained by the *Dönmeh). Ultimately banished to a small village in Albania, Shabbetai died in obscurity. Shabbateanism was the last major messianic movement in Jewish history and left a long and bitter legacy. It has been suggested that the Hasidic movement in eighteenth-century Poland (see HASIDISM) was influenced by the Shabbatean movement, but that by "neutralizing" the messianic element, they remained a mystico-pietistic sect within traditional Judaism. The view has also been advanced that the radical Shabbateans, having burned behind them all bridges to the past, were particularly receptive to the ideas of the Enlightenment. See also EYBESCHUETZ, YONATAN; FRANK, YA'AQOV.

• Josef Kastein, *Shabbatai Zewi* (Berlin, 1930). Leib ben Ozer, *Sippur Ma'asei Tsevi* (Jerusalem, 1978). Gershom Gerhard Scholem, *Sabbatai Sevi: The Mystical Messiah, 1626–1676*, translated by R. J. Zwi Werblowsky (Princeton, 1973).

SHADAL. See LUZZATTO, SHEMU'EL DAVID.

SHADAR. See MESHULLAḤ; SHALIAḤ.

SHADDAI. See GOD, NAMES OF.

SHADDEKHAN (שַׁדְּכָן; marriage broker), a professional intermediary who fulfilled an important social function in the traditional Jewish community, where it was considered unseemly for young people to do their own courting. The verb from which the term is derived is found in the Talmud (*Shab*. 150a), where it signifies "to arrange a marriage," a transaction permitted even on the Sabbath. The *shaddekhan* was indispensable in the medieval period, when Jews lived in small and scattered groups. Jews regarded matchmaking as a highly praiseworthy and honorable occupation, and famous rabbis were proud to engage in it. It was even fancifully said that matchmaking was one of God's main functions (*Pesiqta' de-Rav Kahana'* 2). Brokerage (usually a percentage of the dowry) was regulated by custom, and litigation on the subject (particularly when the marriage did not take place) is occasionally mentioned in rabbinic *responsa*. Women also worked as matchmakers, notably in eastern Europe and Muslim lands. In Jewish folklore and humor, the *shaddekhan* and his profession have become the subject of many jokes. The *shaddekhan* is still an institution in some Orthodox circles.

• Philip Goodman and Hanna Goodman, eds., *The Jewish Marriage Anthology* (Philadelphia, 1965). Israel J. Zevin, *The Marriage Broker: Based on the Stories of Sholem the Shadchen* (New York, 1960).

SHAḤARIT (שַׁחֲרִית; morning), the morning prayer service, recited daily before the first quarter of the day has passed. The Talmud (*Ber*. 26b) ascribes the institution of this prayer to the patriarch Abraham (on the basis of *Gn*. 19.27); it corresponds to the daily dawn sacrifice (**tamid*) in the Temple. In its present form Shaḥarit is the most extensive of the daily services. First, various *benedictions of thanks and praise (*Birkot ha-Shaḥar) are recited (though these were originally intended to be spoken by each individual upon arising), followed by various private prayers and Bible passages (not obligatory). Then comes *Pesuqei de-Zimra' (for which no **minyan* is required). The synagogue service proper begins with *Barekhu, followed by the *Shemaʿ and its benedictions (*Yotser, *Ahavah Rabbah). After the last of these—*Ge'ullah—the ʿAmidah follows without interruption, thus welding the Shemaʿ and the ʿAmidah into a single, continuous entity. In Jerusalem, the *Birkat ha-Kohanim is recited daily in the course of the Shaḥarit ʿAmidah. After the ʿAmidah (which is repeated by the reader, with the inclusion of the *Qedushah) on ordinary weekdays there follow *Taḥanun, and the Half *Qaddish, *Ashrei and *U-Va' le-Tsiyyon, the Full Qaddish, *ʿAleinu, the daily *psalm(s), and the Mourner's Qaddish. On Mondays and Thursdays, a section from the week's Torah portion is read from the Sefer Torah (see QERI'AT HA-TORAH) after Taḥanun. Further additions are customary in some congregations. On *Ro'sh Ḥodesh and most festivals, *Hallel is read immediately after the ʿAmidah, followed by the Full Qaddish, then the reading of the Torah; on the Sabbath, too, the latter two follow the conclusion of the ʿAmidah. On Sabbaths and festivals, it is usual to recite *Musaf immediately after the Torah reading. For Shaḥarit, male worshipers clothe themselves in the **tallit* and on weekdays also put on **tefillin* (in recent years, some women have begun to put on *tallit* and *tefillin*). The *tefillin* are not worn on Sabbaths and festivals, while on Tishʿah be-'Av, they are worn at the afternoon service. On festivals, especially Ro'sh ha-Shanah and Yom Kippur, Shaḥarit is extended considerably by the addition of *piyyutim*.

• Ismar Elbogen, *Jewish Liturgy: A Comprehensive History* (Philadelphia, 1993). Joseph Heinemann, *Prayer in the Talmud: Forms and Patterns* (Berlin, 1977).

SHAKH. See SHABBETAI BEN ME'IR HA-KOHEN.

SHAKNA, SHALOM BEN YOSEF (died 1558), Polish rabbi. A student of Yaʿaqov Pollak, he was appointed rabbi of Lublin by the king of Poland in 1541. In 1551 Shalom ben Yosef Shakna received royal appointment as one of two regional chief rabbis in southern Poland. He was one of the outstanding rabbinic authorities of his day and groomed many distinguished disciples (R. Mosheh *Isserles was his son-in-law), but he refused to permit any of his teachings to be published in order to allow future generations independence of thought. His use of *pilpul* in halakhic decision making was widely criticized. An autocratic figure, he was involved in many bitter disputes both within Poland and abroad.

• Majer Balaban, *Die Judenstadt von Lublin* (Berlin, 1919), pp. 17–19. Tovia Preschel, "Rabbi Shalom Shakhna' mi-Lublin," *Sinai* 100 (1987): 682–700.
—ADAM TELLER

SHALIAḤ (שָׁלִיחַ; messenger), a term with both legal and religious denotations. A *shaliaḥ* can be either an *agent appointed by and empowered to act on behalf of his principal or an emissary appointed to fulfill religious functions (*sheliaḥ mitsvah*), who, the Talmud says, is divinely protected from harm while he is carrying out his duties (*Pes*. 8a). The *sheliaḥ mitsvah* can belong to one of two categories—one who leads worshipers in prayer (a **sheliaḥ tsibbur*) and one who collects money on behalf of an institution (also known as a *shadar*; see MESHULLAḤ). An emissary who collects money for an institution in Erets Yisra'el is sometimes referred to as a *sheliaḥ Tsiyyon* (cf. *Beits*. 25b).

SHALOM ʿALEIKHEM (שָׁלוֹם עֲלֵיכֶם; "Peace be upon you"), opening words of hymn welcoming the Sabbath angels to the home. Shalom ʿAleikhem is sung on the eve of the Sabbath, in some places at the end of the synagogue service, and in homes before the Qiddush or around the table. The hymn is of late composition; it is associated with the Talmudic statement (*Shab*. 119b) that on Sabbath eve two ministering angels accompany the Jew going home from the synagogue. The phrase is also used as a greeting (see GREETINGS AND CONGRATULATIONS).

• Israel Davidson, *Thesaurus of Medieval Jewish Poetry*, 4 vols. (New York, 1970), pp. 1268. Macy Nulman, *The Encyclopedia of Jewish Prayer* (Northvale, N.J., and London, 1993), pp. 290–291.

SHALOM BAYIT. See SHELOM BAYIT.

SHALOM ZAKHAR (שָׁלוֹם זָכָר; peace to the male child), a gathering hosted by the parents of a newborn baby boy on the Sabbath eve before the circumcision or on the evening before the circumcision. Among the refreshments served to the guests, it is customary to offer lentils and peas. Lentils are traditionally the food of mourners, but in this case the "mourning" is related to the belief that the baby had knowledge of the entire Torah but that an angel made it forget at the moment of birth. Peas are eaten because of the association of the Yiddish word *arbes* with the divine promise to Abraham, *harbeh arbeh et zarʿakha,* "I will multiply your seed" (*Gn.* 22.17). In Eastern communities, the gathering is called a *shasha* or *blada* and includes special prayers and readings in honor of the prophet Elijah who is welcomed at every circumcision. Some Sephardi and Eastern communities do not observe the ceremony but hold a festive gathering marked by readings from the Bible and Talmud on the eve of the circumcision.

• Yosef David Weisberg, *Otsar ha-Berit* (Jerusalem, 1985), pp. 87–91. H. J. Zimmels, *Ashkenazim and Sephardim: Their Relations, Differences, and Problems as Reflected in the Rabbinical Responsa*, Jews' College Publications, no. 2 (London, 1958), pp. 164–165. —CHAIM PEARL

SHALOSH REGALIM (שָׁלוֹשׁ רְגָלִים; three pilgrimages), the three annual festivals when pilgrimages were made on foot to Jerusalem. Every male Israelite was enjoined to make the pilgrimage to "the place the Lord your God will choose" (later defined as Jerusalem) three times a year, on the festivals of *Pesaḥ, *Shavuʿot, and *Sukkot (*Ex.* 23.17; *Dt.* 16.16), which were therefore termed the Shalosh Regalim (cf. *Ex.* 23.14). The pilgrim had to offer a sacrifice, the minimum value of which was specified in the Mishnah as three pieces of silver (*Ḥag.* 1.1–2). The pilgrims also brought with them the second *tithe of their produce, which had to be consumed in Jerusalem. The three festivals had agricultural origins (Pesaḥ, the barley harvest; Shavuʿot, the end of the barley harvest and the beginning of the wheat harvest and the first ripe fruits; and Sukkot, the final ingathering of crops), as well as historical associations (Pesaḥ, the Exodus; Shavuʿot, the giving of the Torah; Sukkot, the sojourn in the wilderness). In the Diaspora the historical aspects predominated, but the agricultural significance was revived over the past century with the return to living in Erets Yisra'el. In the synagogue *festival prayers, including the *Hallel, are recited on the pilgrimage festivals. These special statutory prayers vary from one festival to another only by the mention of the specific festival and its sacrifice and in the relevant scriptural readings. In addition, each festival has its specific liturgical features, ceremonies, and customs, such as the recitation of *Aqdamut Millin on Shavuʿot (among Ashkenazim), and the waving and procession of the *four species on Sukkot. *Song of Songs* is read on Pesaḥ; *Ruth* on Shavuʿot; and *Ecclesiastes* on Sukkot. Doubt is expressed in the Talmud as to whether *Shemini ʿAtseret is to be regarded as the final day of Sukkot or as an independent festival. See also YOM TOV SHENI SHEL GALUYYOT.

• Ismar Elbogen, *Jewish Liturgy: A Comprehensive History*, translated by Raymond P. Scheindlin (Philadelphia, 1993). Menahem Haran, *Temples and Temple-Service in Ancient Israel* (Winona Lake, Ind., 1985). *Maḥazor Kol Bo: ʿIm Perush ʿIvri Taitsh be-Shem Bat Yisra'el ve-Yalqut Peninim Yeqarim u-Maʿaseh Alfas, Nusaḥ Sefarad* (New York, 1946). Hayim Shoys, *Guide to Jewish Holy Days: History and Observance*, translated by Samuel Jaffe (New York, 1962). Nosson Scherman, ed., *Siddur Kol Yaacov: The Complete Art Scroll Siddur: Ḥol Shabbat, Shalosh Regalim, Nusaḥ Ashkenaz* (Brooklyn, N.Y., 1984).

SHALOSH SEʿUDOT. See SEʿUDAH.

SHAMM'AI (c.50 BCE–30 CE), tanna'. A colleague of *Hillel (together they form the last of the **zugot* [pairs]), he was vice president of the Sanhedrin, succeeding Menaḥem the Essene (*Ḥag.* 2.2) in the first decades of the Common Era. Shamm'ai has been identified by some scholars with Samaias, the Pharisee leader during Herod's rule and mentioned in Josephus's works, but other scholars have rejected this identification (see SHEMAʿYAH). Shamm'ai's severe character is often presented in contrast to the gentle personality of Hillel, who tended toward a liberal and progressive interpretation of the *halakhah* while Shamm'ai favored a strict and conservative interpretation. However, Shamm'ai's favorite maxim concludes, "Receive every man with a cheerful countenance" (*Avot* 1.15). Both Hillel and Shamm'ai established schools, known, respectively, as *Beit Hillel and Beit Shamm'ai, the members of which continued the traditions of their founders. A possible key to understanding Shamm'ai's legal approach, versus that of Hillel's, is that Shamm'ai considered the act more significant than the intention. The later authority *Eliʿezer ben Hurqanos followed Shamm'ai in this regard.

• Israel Ben-Shalom, *The School of Shammai and the Zealots' Struggle against Rome* (Jerusalem, 1993). Israel Konovitz, *Beth Shammai–Beth Hillel: Collected Sayings in Halakah and Aggadah in the Talmudic and Midrashic Literature* (Jerusalem, 1965). —DANIEL SPERBER

SHAMMASH (שַׁמָּשׁ; servant), the sexton of a synagogue or a *beit din*. During the Middle Ages the *shammash* fulfilled a number of extrasynagogal functions, such as acting as the public crier, calling worshipers to prayer, making communal announcements, summoning the local residents to a town meeting, or inviting local residents to a celebration of some joyous event. Subsequently his duties became confined to matters pertaining to the synagogue. In large towns, the *beit din* would have its own *shammash*, whose duties included summoning people to appear before the court.

By extension of the meaning "servant," the term *shammash* is also used to identify the additional (ninth) light used to kindle the *Ḥanukkah lamp.

• Shlomo Eidelberg, *R. Juspa, Shammash of Warmaisa (Worms): Jewish Life in 17th Century Worms* (Jerusalem, 1991), in English and Hebrew.
–SHMUEL HIMELSTEIN

SHAPIRA', ME'IR (1887–1934), Orthodox rabbi, leader, and educator in Poland. He was elected to the Polish parliament, the Sejm, in 1922, representing the Agudat Israel party, but resigned in 1924 in order to devote himself to education. In 1930 he opened the Yeshivat Ḥakhmei Lublin (the *yeshivah* of the Lublin sages). Unlike the other Polish *yeshivot*, which were centered around a particular dynamic individual—often a Hasidic rabbi— or were located within the confines of a local synagogue or *beit midrash*, this *yeshivah* was founded as an educational institution in its own right, with its own facilities, including a large Talmudic library, dormitories, and lecture halls. It served as a model for *yeshivot* throughout the world. It was closed by the Germans in 1939. The other major venture of Shapira', which still flourishes, is the **daf yomi* cycle for the daily study of the Talmud.

• Yehoshu'a Boimel, *A Blaze in the Darkening Gloom: The Life of Rav Meir Shapiro* (Spring Valley, N.Y., 1994). David Avraham Mandelbom, *Yeshivat Ḥakhmei Lublin: Ha-Yeshivah u-Meyasdah Maharam Shapira* (Jerusalem and Tel Aviv, 1993). –SHMUEL HIMELSTEIN

SHAPIRO, PINḤAS BEN AVRAHAM, OF KORETS (1726–1791), Hasidic master. An associate of Yisra'el ben Eli'ezer *Ba'al Shem Tov, R. Pinḥas developed Hasidic teachings and practices that were somewhat independent of the emerging Hasidic movement. He did not accept the authority of *Dov Ber of Mezhirech; instead R. Pinḥas had a somewhat more worldly sense of the Hasidic message, one concerned with moral self-improvement and the struggle against temptation and evil. Though he was an avid student of the Zohar, he did not like the ready turn toward mystical otherworldliness that characterized some members of the Mezhirech school. His teachings, often preserved in the form of brief aphorisms rather than homilies, are found in several collections (notably *Imrei Pinḥas ha-Shalem* [Ramat Gan, 1988], some of which are still in manuscript. Rabbi Pinḥas took an interest in worldly affairs and avidly supported the Poles in their struggle both against the Haidamaks in 1768 and against the Russians.

• Martin Buber, *Tales of the Hasidim: Early Masters* (New York, 1961). Abraham Joshua Heschel, *The Circle of the Ba'al Shem Tov: Studies in Hasidism*, edited by Samuel H. Dresner (Chicago, 1985), pp. 1–43.
–ARTHUR GREEN

SHARABI, SHALOM (1720–1777), Jerusalem kabbalist. He was born in San'a, Yemen. Around 1740, he went to Jerusalem, where, in 1751, he became head of the *yeshivah* of the Beth-El kabbalists. Sharabi was one of the most renowned figures of the Lurianic school of Kabbalah. His prayer book, *Nehar Shalom* (Salonika, 1806), became a basic liturgical exposition of the annual cycle according to Lurianic Kabbalah, and was a standard prayer book in Erets Yisra'el, North Africa, Iraq, Persia, and Bukhara. It was an important vehicle in ensuring the predominance of prayers and rites inspired by kabbalah—especially in Safed—over previous liturgical usages. Sharabi was greatly revered. His life became embellished with legends, and his grave on the Mount of Olives was a place of pilgrimage.

• Serayah Dablitski, *Petaḥ Einayyim he-Ḥadash* (Bene Beraq, 1975). Yaakov Hasid, *Ve-'Arakh ha-Kohen* (Jerusalem, 1987). Aharon Haiby, *Anaq ha-Ruaḥ: Ha-Sar Rabbi Shalom Shar'abi* (Jerusalem, 1987).
–SHALOM BAR-ASHER

SHAS (ש״ס), word made of the initial letters of *shishah sedarim*, the "six orders" into which R. Yehudah ha-Nasi' divided the *Mishnah. The word came to be applied universally to the *Talmud as a whole and was widely used after Catholic censorship forbade the use of the word *Talmud* in the sixteenth century.

SHATS. See SHELIAḤ TSIBBUR.

SHAVING. See BEARDS.

SHAVU'OT (שָׁבוּעוֹת), the second of the *Shalosh Regalim (pilgrim festivals), known as the Feast of Weeks, Pentecost, Ḥag ha-Qatsir (see HARVEST FESTIVALS), Yom ha-Biqqurim (Day of the *First Fruits), and Zeman Mattan Toratenu (Season of the Giving of Our Torah). It is observed only on 6 Sivan in Israel and by Reform Jews (though some Reform congregations have chosen to observe it for two days); elsewhere it is observed on 6 and 7 Sivan. It is called the Feast of Weeks because it occurs seven full weeks after the "morrow of the Sabbath," when the "sheaf of the wave offering" of barley was offered up (*Lv*. 23.15; hence, the name Pentecost [fiftieth], i.e., the fiftieth day after Pesaḥ). These seven weeks, which begin on the second day of Pesaḥ, are marked by the counting of the *'Omer (hence, the name 'Atseret [termination], given to the festival in the Mishnah). The interpretation of the words "on the morrow of the Sabbath" was a subject of controversy between the Pharisees and the Sadducees. The former maintained that the word Sabbath in this context referred to the first day of Pesaḥ (with the result that the Feast of Weeks always fell on the same day of the week as the second day of Pesaḥ); while the Sadducees (as well as the Samaritans and later the Karaites) maintained that the reference was to the first Sunday after the first day of Pesaḥ (according to which the Feast of Weeks would always fall on a Sunday). The *Beta Israel interpreted the expression to mean the morrow of Pesaḥ (i.e., after the festival was over) and observed the Feast of Weeks on 12 Sivan. The Pharisaic interpretation was accepted as normative. As in the case of the other two pilgrim festivals (Pesaḥ and Sukkot), Shavu'ot has agricultural significance—it is the festival celebrating the conclusion of the grain harvest—and the Mishnah gives a vivid account of the bringing of the first fruits to the Temple on this festival (*Bik*. 3). Subsequently, however, the day also became associated with the commemoration of the revelation on Mount Sinai. Nowhere in the Bible is the date of revelation explicitly given, but the Talmud deduced it from the narrative in *Exodus* 19.1–16; the difference of opinion about whether the Sinaitic revelation took place on 6 or 7 Sivan was resolved in favor of the former date (*Shab*. 86b). The three days preceding the festival are known as *Sheloshet Yemei Hagbalah. The liturgy follows the same pattern as that of the other two pilgrim festivals (see FESTIVAL PRAYERS). The scriptural reading, which is preceded in the Ashkenazi tradition by the recitation of *Aqdamut Millin, includes the Decalogue. The *Book of *Ruth* is read in the synagogue because it mentions the barley and wheat harvests and also because its heroine is a proselyte who accepted the Torah; another explanation is that Ruth's great grandchild, King David, was born and died on Shavu'ot. A type of *piyyut* called **azharot*, which enumerates the 613 commandments, also forms part of the traditional readings on the festival in many congregations. The synagogue is decorated with plants and greenery and dairy food is consumed instead of meat to stress the agricultural aspect of the festival. Under the influence of the Kabbalah, it became customary to spend the (first) night studying the Bible and rabbinic texts (**tiqqun*). Among Conservative Jews in the Diaspora, it is customary to hold consecration ceremonies for first graders and/or *confirmation ceremonies for teenagers who have completed a prescribed course of study on Shavu'ot. Reform congregations generally hold confirmation services on Shavu'ot as well.

• Philip Goodman, ed., *The Shavuot Anthology* (Philadelphia, 1992). Irving Greenberg, *The Jewish Way* (New York, 1993), pp. 66–93.

SHEDIM. See DEMONS.

SHE'ELOT U-TESHUVOT. See RESPONSA.

SHE-HEḤEYANU (שֶׁהֶחֱיָנוּ; Who Has Kept Us in Life), name given to the benediction of time, of which *sheheḥeyanu* is the first distinctive word. It is recited as a blessing of thanksgiving for certain things when they are enjoyed for the first time. The occasions may be general, such as the acquisition of new property or clothes ("He who acquires a new house or purchases new vessels" [*Ber*. 9.1]), or seasonal, as on eating the fruit of a new season or on the advent of festivals. The wording of the benediction is "Blessed are you, . . . who has kept us in life, and preserved us, and enabled us to reach this season."

• Henry Sosland, "Some Thoughts About the Sheheḥeyanu Blessing," *Proceedings of the Rabbinical Assembly* 46 (1984): 114–118. Ephraim Judah Wiesenberg, "Ha-Nusḥa'ot shel Birkat ha-Zeman," *Birkhatah de-'Eliyyahu . . . Eliyyahu Munk* (London, 1982), pp. 57–96.

SHEḤITAH. See RITUAL SLAUGHTER.

SHE'ILTOT. See AḤA' OF SHABḤA.

SHEITL. See WIGS.

SHEKEL, the most basic monetary weight, containing twenty *gerah* (*Nm*. 3.47). Abraham bought the cave of Machpelah for four hundred shekels of silver (*Gn*. 23.15). Originally a standard weight of silver (about fourteen grams), the shekel became a current coin in Maccabean times. A half-shekel, called *beqa'* (*Gn*. 24.22; *Ex*. 38.26), was paid into the treasury by all participants in the national census (*Ex*. 30.13–15). A per capita tax of one-third shekel was imposed to cover the cost of work connected with the restoration of the Second Temple (*Neh*. 10.33–34). During the Second Temple period, Jews everywhere paid an annual levy of a half-shekel for the maintenance of the Sanctuary. The Mishnah tractate **Sheqalim* describes regulations concerning this levy, which is still commemorated in the symbolic "ceremony of the half-shekel," which takes place in many synagogues on the eve of Purim before the reading of *Esther*. The Zionist movement revived the idea of the shekel by giving the name to the small annual contribution that entitled members to participate in elections, and in 1980 the shekel was introduced as the basic currency in Israel.

• Shalom M. Paul and William G. Dever, eds., *Biblical Archaeology* (Jerusalem, 1973), pp. 176–183. —SHALOM PAUL

SHEKHINAH (שְׁכִינָה; divine presence), the term, derived from biblical verses (e.g., *Ex*. 25.8; *Lv*. 16.16), speaks of God's "dwelling"—that is, presence—in the midst of Israel. At first sight, *shekhinah* might be regarded as one of the many circumlocutions employed by the Talmud to avoid mentioning the name of God directly. Closer analysis, however, shows that the rabbis used the term in the more specific sense of the manifestation of the divine presence in the life of man or to express the principle of divine immanence in creation. According to aggadic teaching, the *shekhinah* dwells only among Israel (*Ber*. 8a), and probably for this reason conversion to Judaism is called "being brought under the wings of the *shekhinah*." The *shekhinah* dwells among the children of Israel "even in their impurity," that is, sin (*Yoma'* 56b, based on *Lv*. 16.16). The *shekhinah* may also rest upon individuals: "The *shekhinah* rests upon man not through gloom, indolence, frivolity, or idle chatter, but only through the joy experienced in fulfilling divine commandments" (*Shab*. 30a). The *shekhinah* is present in every home where there is domestic peace and blesses that home (*Sot*. 17a). Study (*Avot* 3.7) and congregational prayer (*Ber*. 6a) call forth the presence of the *shekhinah*, whereas sin (*Sot*. 3b) and injustice (*San*. 7a) drive it away. When Israel goes into exile, the *shekhinah* accompanies the Jews, as it will accompany them on their return (*Meg*. 29a). The beatific vision of the future world is expressed in the words, "there the righteous sit and enjoy the splendor of the *shekhinah*" (*Ber*. 17a). In many cases the term *shekhinah* is synonymous with God. In the teachings of the Ḥasidei Ashkenaz, the *shekhinah* was equated with *kavod* (the created "divine splendor"), a notion derived from Sa'adyah Ga'on. In the kabbalistic doctrine of **sefirot*, the Shekhinah plays a key role as the tenth and last *sefirah*, marking the point of contact between the divine and the lower spheres ("Gate of Heaven"), and representing the feminine aspect of the deity, the holy union of which with the male aspect constitutes the fullness of the life divine. Contemporary feminists frequently use the word *shekhinah*, a feminine noun, for God.

• Joshua Abelson, *Jewish Mysticism* (London, 1913). Gershom Gerhard Scholem, *Major Trends in Jewish Mysticism* (Jerusalem, 1941). Gershom Gerhard Scholem, *Zohar, the Book of Splendor* (New York, 1963). Isaiah

Tishby, *The Wisdom of the Zohar: An Anthology of Texts*, translated by David Goldstein (Oxford, 1989).

SHELAH. See Horowitz Family.

SHELIAḤ TSIBBUR (שְׁלִיחַ צִיבּוּר; representative of the community), designation for the leader of prayer in the *synagogue. First mentioned in the Mishnah (*R. ha-Sh.* 4.9), the *sheliaḥ tsibbur* is often referred to by the acronym *shats*. Based on the rabbinical ruling that "one who hears the recitation is considered as if he himself had recited it" (T. *Ber.* 21b), the office of *sheliaḥ tsibbur* was introduced in the synagogue to fulfill the obligations of those who were unable to recite the prayers themselves—especially the ʿAmidah. The Talmud (*Taʿan.* 16a) recommends that the *sheliaḥ tsibbur* be, among other things, a man with many children, whom he is unable to support; hence, he will pour his whole soul into the prayer. See also Baʿal Tefillah; Cantor; Reshut.

• Ismar Elbogen, *Jewish Liturgy: A Comprehensive History*, translated by Raymond P. Scheindlin (New York, 1993), pp. 372–381. Judith Hauptman, "Women as Cantors," *Journal of Synagogue Music* 17.1 (1987): 4–8. Joseph Heinemann, *Prayer in the Talmud: Forms and Patterns* (Berlin, 1977). Leo Landman, *The Cantor: An Historical Perspective, a Study of the Origin, Communal Position and Function of the Hazzan* (New York, 1972).

—SHMUEL HIMELSTEIN

SHELOM BAYIT (שְׁלוֹם בַּיִת; peace in the house), domestic harmony between husband and wife and within the family. Many rabbinic regulations are said to have been made in order to promote *shelom bayit* and to protect the home from disturbance. "Where there is peace between husband and wife the divine presence dwells with them" (*Sot.* 17a). The kindling of the Sabbath lights is regarded as the outstanding symbol of *shelom bayit* (*Shab.* 23b). Where the Ashkenazi prayer book quotes as one of the supreme virtues "making peace between man and his fellow" (based on *Pe'ah* 1.1), the Sephardi prayer book adds "and between man and wife." See also Family; Matrimony.

• Tsevi Koyfman, *Sefer Shelom Bayit* (Brooklyn, N.Y., 1988). Aharon Zakai, *Shelom Bayit: Halakhot ve-Hanhagot be-Musar uve-'Aggadah* (Jerusalem, 1991).

SHELOSHET YEMEI HAGBALAH (שְׁלֹשֶׁת יְמֵי הַגְבָּלָה; Three Days of Restriction), the three days prior to the festival of Shavuʿot (3 through 5 Sivan). The name is derived from *Exodus* 19.12, "You shall set bounds [*ve-higbalta*] for the people." They correspond to the three days of preparation prescribed for the Israelites before the giving of the Torah at Sinai. On these days the special supplication Taḥanun is not recited in the synagogue service.

• Isaac Klein, *A Guide to Jewish Religious Practice* (New York, 1992).

—PETER KNOBEL

SHELOSHIM (שְׁלוֹשִׁים, thirty), the thirty days of *mourning following the death of a close relative (parent, spouse, sibling, child). The entire mourning period lasts for a year, of which the first week (**shivʿah*) is a period of intense mourning; some of the most stringent rules of mourning are relaxed during the rest of the first month, which is reckoned from the day of the funeral, while during the remainder of the year the main expression of mourning is the recital of the *Qaddish. Traditionally the obligation to recite Qaddish was restricted to a male mourner. Today, in Reform, Conservative, and Reconstructionist Judaism, the obligation falls equally on men and women. After the conclusion of the *shivʿah*, the mourner is permitted to leave the house and return to work and a normal routine, but law and custom still restrict some activities during the *sheloshim*. The mourner may not attend weddings or any parties or go to a place of entertainment (this restriction applies for the full year when mourning a parent). Many mourners will not shave or cut their hair during this period, although some halakhic authorities would seem to be more lenient in this respect (*Kol Bo ʿal Aveilut* 352). If a festival (other than Ḥanukkah or Purim) falls during the *sheloshim*, and the *shivʿah* has been concluded, the restrictions of the thirty days are canceled (except when mourning a parent). The origin of the *sheloshim* is traced to the Bible, where Aaron (*Nm.* 20.29) and Moses (*Dt.* 34.8) were mourned for thirty days, while R. *Yehudah ha-Nasi' left instructions that the assembly for study should be reconstituted thirty days after his death (*Ket.* 103b).

• Chaim Binyamin Goldberg, *Mourning in Halachah: The Laws and Customs of the Year of Mourning*, translated by Shlomo Fox-Ashrei, edited by Meir Zlotowitz (Brooklyn, N.Y., 1991). Leopold Greenwald, *Kol Bo ʿal Aveilut* (New York, 1947). Maurice Lamm, *The Jewish Way in Death and Mourning* (New York, 1969). Harry Rabinowicz, *A Guide to Life* (London, 1964), pp. 92–99.

—CHAIM PEARL

SHEMAʿ (שְׁמַע; Hear), the first word of *Deuteronomy* 6.4, "Hear, O Israel, the Lord is our God, the Lord is One"; the name given to three Bible passages (*Dt.* 6.4–9, 11.13–21; *Nm.* 15.37–41) that must be read (hence, *qeri'at Shemaʿ* [the reading of the Shemaʿ]) every morning and evening. The Reform prayer book in North America eliminates the reference to divine retribution and to **tsitsit*. The custom of *qeri'at Shemaʿ* was part of the Temple service (*Tam.* 5.1) and was continued in the synagogue. In the Jerusalem Temple, *Deuteronomy* 6.4–9 was preceded by the recitation of the Decalogue, which was later eliminated because of heretics who argued that only the Ten Commandments were revealed by God to Moses. The recitation of the Shemaʿ is considered an obligation prescribed by the Bible itself on the basis of the verse: "and you shall speak of them . . . when you lie down and when you rise up" (*Dt.* 6.7). While there is much discussion in the Mishnah and Talmud about when the Shemaʿ should be recited, the obligation is taken for granted. In the morning, the Shemaʿ should be recited before the first quarter of the day has passed; in the evening, before midnight, although if this is impossible it may be read any time during the night. The Shemaʿ is not, strictly speaking, a prayer so much as a proclamation. It is the basic theological statement of Judaism—the Jewish "confession of faith." It is a vital part of the liturgy an integral part of the morning and evening services and benedictions must be recited before and after it.

After the Shemaʿ, the ʿAmidah should follow immediately, without interruption. No *minyan* is required for the recitation of the Shemaʿ or its benedictions; a *min-*

yan is required, however, for the recital of *Barekhu, which precedes the benedictions and is a call to communal worship. In olden times, the Shemaʿ was recited antiphonally, with the reader saying one verse, the congregation the next, and so on. In Ashkenazi communities today, the Shemaʿ is recited silently by the entire congregation; among the *ʿAdot ha-Mizraḥ, it is customary to read it aloud in unison. Its recitation is immediately preceded by the phrase, **El melekh ne'eman*. After the first verse a doxology is added silently: **Barukh shem kevod malkhuto le-ʿolam va-ʿed*, "Blessed be the name of the glory of his kingdom for ever and ever"; on Yom Kippur this doxology is recited aloud. Apart from the twice-daily reading of the Shemaʿ with its benedictions, the first passage is read by the individual before retiring at night (see QERIʿAT SHEMAʿ ʿAL HA-MITTAH), and the first verse is also recited when the Torah scrolls are taken out of the ark, as part of the *Qedushah of Musaf, and at the conclusion of *Neʿilah on Yom Kippur. Traditionally, the Shemaʿ is uttered by a Jew on the deathbed. Its recitation has also figured prominently in Jewish martyrology.

• Ismar Elbogen, *Jewish Liturgy: A Comprehensive History*, translated by Raymond P. Scheindlin (Philadelphia, 1993). Reuven Hammer, *Entering Jewish Prayer: A Guide to Personal Devotion and the Worship Service* (New York, 1994). Lawrence A. Hoffman, *The Canonization of the Synagogue Service* (Notre Dame, 1979). Isaac Klein, *A Guide to Jewish Religious Practice* (New York, 1992). Abraham Millgram, *Jewish Worship* (Philadelphia, 1971). Jakob Petuchowski, "The Liturgy of the Synagogue: History, Structure, and Contents," in *Approaches to Ancient Judaism*, vol. 4, *Studies in Liturgy, Exegesis, and Talmudic Narrative*, edited by William Scott Green (Chico, Calif., 1983), pp.1–64. Stefan C. Reif, *Judaism and Hebrew Prayer* (Cambridge, 1993).

—PETER KNOBEL

SHEMAʿ QOLI (שְׁמַע קוֹלִי; Hear My Voice), rhymed hymn recited in the Sephardi ritual on the eve of Yom Kippur, preceding the *Kol Nidrei prayer. It has been ascribed to R. *Ha'i Ga'on.

• Israel Davidson, *Thesaurus of Medieval Jewish Poetry*, 4 vols. (New York, 1970). Macy Nulman, *The Encyclopedia of Jewish Prayer* (Northvale, N.J., and London, 1993), p. 300.

SHEMAʿYAH (1st cent. BCE), president (**nasi'*) of the Sanhedrin, who taught in the same *beit midrash* as *Avtalyon (*Yoma'* 35b); together they constituted the fourth of the **zugot* (pairs). Traditionally (see *Git.* 57b) both Shemaʿyah and Avtalyon were said to be converts (or sons of converts). The most famous disciple of their *beit midrash* was the renowned *Hillel. Some scholars have identified them with Samaias and Pollio, Pharisee leaders in the time of Herod mentioned in the work of Josephus, but the identification remains uncertain (see SHAMM'AI). Shemaʿyah was widely admired and respected as an authority, although no *halakhot* are directly quoted in his name. *Avot* quotes this maxim of Shemaʿyah: "Love labor, shun power, and do not become close with the ruling authorities" (1.10).

• Sidney Benjamin Hoenig, *The Great Sanhedrin* (Philadelphia, 1953). Hugo Mantel, *Studies in the History of the Sanhedrin* (Cambridge, 1961).

—DANIEL SPERBER

SHEM HA-MEFORASH. See GOD, NAMES OF.

SHEMINI ʿATSERET (שְׁמִינִי עֲצֶרֶת; the eighth day of the assembly; cf. *Nm.* 29.35), last day of *Sukkot (22 Tishrei) in Erets Yisra'el; elsewhere Orthodox and Conservative Jews celebrate it as two days (22–23 Tishrei), and Reform Jews as one day. The Talmud (*Suk.* 47a) discusses whether Shemini ʿAtseret should be considered an independent festival immediately following Tabernacles or whether it is actually the concluding day of that festival, comparable to the last day of Pesaḥ (cf. *Nm.* 28.16, 25). The solution reached by the rabbis regards Shemini ʿAtseret as an independent festival in certain respects (one of which is its name), but otherwise treats it as a continuation of Sukkot. The holiday is not linked to any specific historical event. The *lulav* and *etrog*, which are basic to the Sukkot ritual, do not figure in the service for the day, and the **sukkah* is no longer an integral part of the holiday, although traditions vary in that area, from not using it at all to reciting the Qiddush and eating the midday meal there. Syrian Jews, for example, recite a prayer of farewell to the *sukkah* after eating there. The striking difference between the number of sacrifices offered during the previous seven days, which total seventy in all (*Nm.* 29.12–32) and the solitary "one ram, one bullock" of this festival (*Nm.* 36), is the basis of a *midrash* to the effect that the seventy sacrifices correspond to the "seventy nations" (i.e., humankind), while Shemini ʿAtseret symbolizes the special relationship between God and Israel. In the Diaspora, where the biblical festivals are extended to two days, the conclusion of the Torah is read in the synagogue on the second day, which is called *Simḥat Torah (though in the liturgy, the name Shemini ʿAtseret is retained); in Erets Yisra'el the one day of Shemini ʿAtseret is also Simḥat Torah. The distinctive liturgical feature of this holiday is the prayer for rain (see TEFILLAT GESHEM), recited in the Musaf service, with the cantor, in traditional Ashkenazi synagogues, wearing a white robe as on the High Holy Days. In Ashkenazi synagogues, the *Yizkor prayer is recited in the Shaḥarit service. If there has been no intermediate Sabbath during Sukkot, the *Book of Ecclesiastes* is read in the synagogue on Shemini ʿAtseret.

• Herbert C. Dobrinsky, *A Treasury of Sephardic Laws and Customs* (Hoboken, N.J., and New York, 1986), contains extensive bibliography. Stephen J. Einstein and Lydia Kukoff, *Every Person's Guide to Judaism* (New York, 1989). Isaac N. Fabricant, *A Guide To Succoth* (London, 1958). Philip Goodman, ed., *A Sukkot and Simhat Torah Anthology* (Philadelphia, 1973), with bibliography. Isaac Klein, *A Guide to Jewish Religious Practice*, 2d ed. (New York, 1992), pp. 155–173. Peter Knobel, ed., *Gates of the Seasons: A Guide to the Jewish Year* (New York, 1983). Hayim Shoys, *The Jewish Festivals: From Their Beginnings to Our Own Day*, translated by Samuel Jaffe (Cincinnati, 1938). Arthur Waskow, *Seasons of Our Joy: A Modern Guide to the Jewish Holidays* (Boston, 1990).

SHEMITTAH (שְׁמִטָּה; let fall, let rest), a sabbatical year. Every seventh year "the land must keep Sabbath unto the Lord" (*Lv.* 25.2). During this year, land must lie fallow; whatever grows on it is designated ownerless property (**hefqer*), to which all enjoy equal rights with the owner. The Bible (*Lv.* 25.22) promises a threefold crop in the sixth year to tide the farmer and the consumer over during the seventh year. It is forbidden to trade with produce of the *shemittah* year, which, in its ownerless state, is also free from *tithes. At the end of the year all debts are forgiven (*Lv.* 25; *Ex.* 23.10–11; *Dt.* 15.1–3). The precept of the sabbatical year is meant to emphasize the conditional nature of the possession of the

Holy Land by the Jewish people ("for the land is mine . . . you are strangers and sojourners with me," *Lv*. 26.34; *Shab*. 33a). The laws of the sabbatical year are discussed in the Talmudic tractate **Sheviʿit* and in later rabbinic literature. *Shemittah* constitutes a problem for Orthodox Jews in the State of Israel; the Israeli rabbinate permits the land to be temporarily sold to non-Jews and worked during the *shemittah* year, but this is not accepted by all Orthodox. The actual yearly reckoning of the sabbatical year is no longer certain, but according to the system in place, a sabbatical year will be observed, for instance, in 5761 (2000–2001), counting from one Ro'sh ha-Shanah to the next. See also DISPENSATION; PEROZBOL; YOVEL.

• Dovid Marchant, *Understanding Shmittoh: Its Sources and Background*, rev. ed. (Jerusalem and New York, 1993).

SHEMONEH ʿESREH. See ʿAMIDAH.

SHEMOT. See EXODUS, BOOK OF.

SHEMOT RABBAH. See EXODUS RABBAH.

SHEMU'EL (died c.254), Babylonian *amora'; younger contemporary of *Rav. He was already established as a religious judge (*dayyan*) in *Nehardea when Rav returned from Palestine. The Talmud rules that in matters of civil law Shemu'el's opinion is to be followed; his dictum "The law of the land is binding on Jews who live there" (*Git*. 10b) became of far-reaching importance for Jews living in the Diaspora. Shemu'el had a broad education. He was a famous eye doctor who produced a widely used eye ointment, (*B. M.* 85b), and he was known for his medical theories relating health to climate (*B. M.* 107b). However, it was as an astronomer that he acheived his greatest renown, creating a fixed *calendar, although out of respect for the Palestinian gaonate he refrained from circulating it. He once said that "the paths of heaven are as familiar to me as the paths of Nehardea" (*Ber*. 58b). His discussions with Rav laid the foundation for the *Talmud Bavli. Shemu'el was a distinguished judge, who exercised the greatest personal integrity, refusing to adjudicate for anyone from whom he had received even the slightest benefit (*Ket*. 105b). He devoted his life to the community, especially to the underprivileged and particularly orphans. Even though lending money with interest was forbidden by biblical law, he permitted the lending of orphans' monies with interest for their benefit (*B. M.* 20a). He also controlled market practices, attempting in all ways to keep prices down (*B. B.* 90b; *Suk*. 34b; *Pes*. 30a). He was a person of humility, effacing himself before Rav (*ʿEruv*. 90b), but he opposed asceticism (*Taʿan*. 11a), holding that the good things of the world were to be enjoyed—as long as the relevant blessings were recited (*Ber*. 35a). He summed up his attitude to messianism in his famous statement, "There is no difference between this world and the next except the subjugation of the kingdoms," that is, the absence of subjugation by foreign kingdoms (*Ber*. 34b). He was called Mar Shemu'el as a sign of special respect.

• Baruch M. Bokser, *Post Mishnaic Judaism in Transition: Samuel on Berakhot and the Beginnings of Gemara*, Studies in Judaism in Late Antiquity (Leiden, 1975). Baruch M. Bokser, *Samuel's Commentary on the Mishnah: Its Nature, Forms, and Content, Part One: Mishnayot in the Order of Zera'im* (Leiden, 1975). Baruch M. Bokser, "Two Traditions of Samuel: Evaluating Alternative Traditions," in *Christianity, Judaism and Other Greco-Roman Cults: Studies for Morton Smith at 60*, edited by Jacob Neusner, vol. 4 (Leiden, 1975), pp. 46–55. Richard Kalmin, "Changing Amoraic Attitudes toward the Authority of Rav and Shmuel: A Study of the Talmud as a Historical Source," *Hebrew Union College Annual* 63 (1993): 83–106.

—DANIEL SPERBER

SHEMU'EL BEN ʿALI (12th cent.), the best known of the heads of the academy in Baghdad (see PUMBEDITA) during the period in which the Babylonian academies had lost their central role in the Jewish world. Several of Shemu'el's *responsa* have survived (a collection was published by S. Assaf in 1930), as have a larger number of his letters, which shed light on the nature and standing of the Baghdad academy. Shemu'el was involved in controversy both with the *exilarchs and with his contemporary Moses *Maimonides, who wrote disparagingly of Shemu'el's pretensions and contentiousness.

• Samuel Abraham Poznanski, *Babylonische Geonim im nachgaonäischen Zeitalter* (Berlin, 1914).

—ROBERT BRODY

SHEMU'EL BEN ḤOFNI (died 1013), ga'on of *Sura from approximately 997 and father-in-law of *Ha'i Ga'on of Pumbedita. In addition to writing **responsa*, as was usual for Babylonian ge'onim, Shemu'el followed the example of his illustrious predecessor, *Saʿadyah ben Yosef Ga'on, and produced a number of works in less traditional genres, all written in Judeo-Arabic, including a translation of and commentary on at least half of the Pentateuch, dozens of monographs on halakhic topics, and several works of religious philosophy. Most of these works have survived only in fragmentary form and have yet to be published, although his commentary on the Pentateuch was published in 1979, and sections from his introduction to the Talmud were published in 1990.

• Abraham Elijah Harkavy, *Me'assef Nidaḥim* (1878; Jerusalem, 1970). David Eric Sklare, "The Religious and Legal Thought of Samuel ben Hofni Gaon," Ph.D. disseration, Harvard University, 1992.

—ROBERT BRODY

SHEMU'EL BEN ME'IR (c.1080–1160), rabbinic scholar and biblical and Talmudic commentator; known by the acronym Rashbam. He was the eldest son of R. Me'ir ben Shemu'el and Rashi's daughter Yokheved. He studied under his father in Ramerupt and with Rashi in Troyes, noting that Rashi accepted some of his suggestions with regard to biblical interpretations. Shemu'el earned his livelihood by raising livestock and from viticulture. He lived mainly in Ramerupt but also in Caen and Paris. He was involved in disputations with Christians and attacked their Christological scriptural interpretations.

He apparently commented on all the books of the Bible. His commentary on the Torah has survived almost in its entirety. Fragments of other books have also survived, including his commentaries to most of the Five Scrolls. The commentary on *Ecclesiastes* edited by Sara Japhet and Robert B. Salters (1985) has been judged by most scholars to be that of Rashbam.

Shemu'el's biblical commentaries stress the literal meaning in its most profound sense. He cites or utilizes Midrashic material if it follows closely the literal (*peshat*) meaning. He makes it clear, in several programmatic introductory statements, that the rabbinic interpretation of each verse is the most important one. Since there is a rabbinic dictum, however, that every verse can also be interpreted according to *peshuto shel miqra'* (its simple meaning), he aims to fill this gap without competing with rabbinic interpretations.

He was most interested in the study of biblical grammar and syntax. He explains certain conventions and phrases in biblical verses as *derekh erets*, based upon realia, rather than attempting to interpret the scriptural details. Like Rashi, he often uses Targum Onkelos. His desire to refute Christological explanations occasionally leads him to suggest that a particular interpretation is both "according to the literal meaning of the text and in response to heretics." S. Z. Ashkenazi wrote a supercommentary, *Kerem Shemu'el*, to Shemu'el's commentary on the Pentateuch (Frankfurt an der Oder, 1727).

Shemu'el supplemented Rashi's Talmudic commentary to the tenth chapter of *Pesaḥim* and his commentary to *Bava' Batra'* (from folio 29a). Although his commentary in these sections is similar in format to Rashi's running commentary, he raises and answers difficulties and proposes and weighs alternative explanations. He also wrote *tosafot* to a number of tractates. The anonymous commentary to *Avot* found in *Maḥazor Vitry* contains large segments of Shemu'el's commentary to that tractate.

Shemu'el was the first rabbinic scholar in northern France to use R. Yitsḥaq Alfasi's legal compendium. He also wrote commentaries to a number of *piyyutim* and composed a grammatical work entitled *Sefer Daiqut*. Although familiar with mystical works and concepts, Shemu'el downplays the need for esoteric wisdom in his commentary about the Creation and in his commentary to *Ecclesiastes*. He hoped, perhaps, to eliminate this aspect of early rabbinic culture in Ashkenaz.

• Sara Japhet and Robert B. Salters, *Perush Rabbi Shemu'el ben Meir (Rashbam) le-Qohelet* (Jerusalem, 1985). Sarah Kamin, "Rashbam's Conception of the Creation in Light of the Intellectual Currents of His Time," *Scripta Hierosolymitana* 31 (1986): 91–131. Martin I. Lockshin, *Rabbi Samuel ben Meir's Commentary on Genesis: An Annotated Translation* (Lewiston, N.Y., 1989). David Rosin, ed., *Perush ha-Torah* (New York, 1881).

—EPHRAIM KANARFOGEL

SHEMU'EL HA-NAGID (993–1056), rabbinic scholar, Hebrew poet and grammarian, and highly skilled court secretary who rose through the ranks of state chancery in Muslim Granada to achieve prominence in the caliph's court. As a consequence of the unique range of his literary and scholarly activities and his political acumen, Shemu'el ha-Nagid was widely respected in both the Muslim civic sphere and the Jewish social and cultural milieu. He assumed the role of *nagid* (c.1027), unofficial head of the Jews of Spain (*nagid* means head of the community), and functioned as the highest financial and administrative official of Granada from 1038 until his death in 1056. He may also have served his ruler in some military capacity, although the nature and extent of this involvement are uncertain.

The first virtuoso poet of the "golden age" of Jewish culture in Spain, Shemu'el ha-Nagid extended the prosodic possibilities and thematic range of Hebrew verse by drawing creatively upon the forms and conventions of Arabic poetry. He composed one of the earliest strophic songs in Hebrew and employed a greater variety of poetic meters than earlier generations of Spanish-Hebrew poets. His love lyrics, drinking songs, laments, gnomic verse, and poems imitate Biblical Hebrew. He was the author of commentaries on books of the Bible (which have not survived); a treatise attacking the Qur'an and describing its contradictions; a major halakhic work *Sefer Hilkhata' Gevarata'* (existing fragments of which were published by M. Margaliot in 1962 as *Hilkhot ha-Nagid*); and a Talmudic compendium based on both the Talmud Bavli and Talmud Yerushalmi, as well as on geonic *responsa*. Shemu'el ha-Nagid is considered one of the most significant representatives of Judeo-Muslim culture in eleventh-century Spain.

• Eliyahu Ashtor, *The Jews of Moslem Spain*, 3 vols., translated by Aaron Klein and Jenny Machlowitz Klein, with an introduction by David J. Wasserstein (Philadelphia, 1992). Ross Brann, *The Compunctious Poet: Cultural Ambiguity and Hebrew Poetry in Muslim Spain* (Baltimore, 1991). Abraham ben David ibn Daud ha-Levi, *A Critical Edition with a Translation and Notes of The Book of Tradition (Sefer ha-Qabbalah)*, edited by Gerson D. Cohen (Philadelphia, 1967). Samuel ha-Nagid, *Jewish Prince in Moslem Spain: Selected Poems of Samuel ibn Nagrela*, introduction, translation and notes by Leon J. Weinberger (University, Ala., 1973). Raymond P. Scheindlin, compiler, *Wine, Women and Death: Medieval Hebrew Poems on the Good Life* (Philadelphia, 1986). David Wasserstein, "Samuel ibn Naghrila ha-Nagid and Islamic Historiography in al-Andalus," *al-Qantara* xiv (1993): 109–125.

—ROSS BRANN

SHEMU'EL HA-QATAN (1st–2d cent.), tanna'. None of his *halakhot* is recorded, but he was well known for his gentleness, humility, and pacifism. At the request of the patriarch *Gamli'el, he composed (probably c.80–90) the *Birkat ha-Minim, which was inserted as the nineteenth benediction of the *ʿAmidah (*Ber.* 28b). It has been suggested that the original version of this prayer, which was directed against heretics (*minim*) in general, was subsequently worded specifically so that Judeo-Christians, who at that time still worshiped in synagogues, would henceforth be unable to participate in the prayer service. This practical expulsion of Christians from the synagogue contributed to the final separation between Judaism and Christianity.

An apocryphal tractate dealing with astronomy, *Baraiyta' de-Shemu'el ha-Qatan*, has been mistakenly attributed to him. It probably dates from the eighth or ninth century.

• Naomi Cohen, "Mah Ḥiddesh Shemu'el ha-Qatan be-'Virkhat ha-Minnim'?," *Sinai* 94 (1984): 57–70. Reuven Kimelman, "Birkat ha-Minim and the Lack of Evidence for an Anti-Christian Jewish Prayer in Late Antiquity," in *Jewish and Christian Self-Definition*, vol. 2, *Aspects of Judaism in the Graeco-Roman Period*, edited by E. P. Sanders et al. (Philadelphia, 1981), pp. 229–244, 391–403.

—DANIEL SPERBER

SHEMURAH MATSAH. See MATSAH.

SHENI VA-ḤAMISHI (שֵׁנִי וַחֲמִישִׁי; Monday and Thursday), two weekdays characterized liturgically by the reading of the Torah (the first section of the Pentateuch portion for the following Sabbath), to which three people are called, and the recitation of additional penitential and supplicatory prayers at the morning service. They are also the preferred days for voluntary fasts. In ancient times, villagers went to town on Mondays and Thursdays to attend the markets and the law courts, and the Talmud credits *Ezra with instituting instruction in the law on those days (*Meg*. 31b). The three voluntary fasts known as Behab, an abbreviation for Monday-Thursday-Monday, and observed shortly after Pesaḥ and Sukkot, are meant to atone for unintentional sins and levity during the festive season, after the example of Job (*Jb*. 1.5).

• Ismar Elbogen, *Jewish Liturgy: A Comprehensive History*, translated by Raymond P. Scheindlin (Philadelphia, New York, and Jerusalem, 1993), pp. 68–69, 106–107, 163. Yom Tov Lewinsky, ed., *Sefer ha-Mo'adim*, vol. 7 (Tel Aviv, 1978), pp. 43–49. Israel Schepansky, *The Takkanot of Israel*, vol. 1 (Jerusalem, 1991), pp. 190–194.

SHEOL. See GEIHINNOM.

SHEQALIM (שְׁקָלִים; Shekels), tractate in Mishnah order Mo'ed, in eight chapters, with related material in the Tosefta' and the Talmud Yerushalmi. It deals with the half-shekel tax that was used for purchasing communal sacrifices during the Second Temple period, which was based on the half-shekel tax that was levied for the construction of the Israelites' desert sanctuary (*Ex*. 30.11–16). Many of the laws in *Sheqalim* reflect the Pharisaic insistence, against Sadducean opposition (see *Men*. 65a), that communal sacrifices had to be brought from communal property. Hence, the laws of *Sheqalim* help to define the rabbinic conception of community, as opposed to corporate partnership.

Sheqalim describes in detail the financial management of the Temple and its service, including a list naming Temple officials, which is of great historical interest. A hortatory pericope (*Sheq*. 3.2) admonishes the priest who draws money from the communal chest in the Temple not to wear garments with wide sleeves or flowing hems, lest he be suspected of misappropriating some of the funds, thus violating the command to "be blameless before God and before Israel" (*Nm*. 32.22).

An English translation of the tractate is in Herbert Danby's *The Mishnah* (London, 1933).

• Chanoch Albeck, ed., *Shishah Sidrei Mishnah, Seder Mo'ed* (Jerusalem, 1952). Philip Blackman, ed. and trans., *Mishnayoth*, vol. 2, *Order Moed* (Gateshead, 1973). Pinhas Kehati, ed., *Mishnah: A New Translation with a Commentary, Seder Moed*, vol. 3, *Pesahim, Shekalim* (Jerusalem, 1993). Hermann Leberecht Strack and Günter Stemberger, *Introduction to the Talmud and Midrash*, rev. and updat. ed., translated by Markus Bockmuehl (Minneapolis, 1992). —AVRAHAM WALFISH

SHERIRA' BEN ḤANINA' GA'ON (10th cent.), ga'on of *Pumbedita. He succeeded to the gaonate when he was about seventy years old and restored the declining prestige of the Pumbedita academy. Toward the end of his long life, his son *Ha'i Ga'on was appointed as his assistant (*av beit din*); in a departure from tradition, father and son served jointly as heads of the academy for about a dozen years until Sherira' retired. Sherira' left a number of *responsa*, of which the most famous and important is his **Iggeret Rav Sherira' Ga'on*, written in 986. This is a response to a number of questions raised by scholars of Kairouan, North Africa, concerning the nature of rabbinic tradition and literature. Sherira' provided an overview of the ways in which rabbinic literature developed from oral tradition and discussed such topics as the role of the individual teacher or editor within the context of collective transmission. In addition, he provided an annotated list of Babylonian *amora'im, *savora'im, and *ge'onim that constitutes the chief source for the chronology—and, to some extent, for the history—of the Babylonian center from the third to the tenth century. The epistle was translated into Hebrew (from Aramaic) and published by Aaron Hyman (London, 1910), and an English translation with commentary by N. D. Rabinovich appeared in 1988. The original was published by B. M. Lewin in 1921.

• Isaiah Gafni, "Le-Ḥeqer ha-Kronologiah ha-Talmudit be-'Iggeret Rav Sherira' Ga'on," *Zion* 52 (1987): 1–24. —ROBERT BRODY

SHESHET (3d–4th cent.), Babylonian amora'. A wealthy clothing dealer by profession, he was famed for both his piety (cf. *Shab*. 118b) and his learning. He was known to have committed to memory an exceptionally large amount of traditional material, necessitated by the fact that he was blind and required his lessons to be read to him (*San*. 86a; *'Eruv*. 67a; *Shab*. 41b); it was his habit to review his studies every thirty days (*Pes*. 68b). He studied with R. Yirmiyahu ben Abba' and R. Huna', and there are numerous scholars who transmit in his name. He taught in Nehardea before moving to Maḥoza, and then to Shilḥe on the Tigris, where, according to the *Iggeret Rav Sherira' Ga'on*, he founded an academy. He made constant appeal to the tannaitic sources extant in his day, thus leaning heavily on the weight of precedent (*Zev*. 96b), and he disdained the more dialectical approach of the Pumbedita scholars (cf. *B. M*. 38b). Although some of his Midrashic comments are preserved (e.g., *Shab*. 63a to *Prv*. 3.16), he busied himself primarily with *halakhah* (cf. *Suk*. 52b), and the Talmud records many of his debates with R. Naḥman. His most famous adage is "The borrower is servant of the lender" (*Git*. 14a).

• Wilhelm Bacher, *Die Agada der babylonischen Amoräer* (1913; Hildesheim, 1967). Gershom Bader, *The Encyclopedia of Talmudic Sages*, translated from the Yiddish by Solomon Katz (Northvale, N.J., and London, 1988). Aaron Hyman, *Toledot Tanna'im ve-'Amora'im* (1910; Jerusalem, 1987). —MICHAEL L. BROWN

SHETAR. See DEED.

SHEVA' BERAKHOT (שֶׁבַע בְּרָכוֹת; Seven Blessings), the seven benedictions recited at the wedding ceremony. They are of ancient origin and are quoted in the Talmud (*Ket*. 8a). The first benediction is recited over the wine, and the following three praise God who has created all things for his glory, formed humankind, and created male and female in his image. The fifth benediction refers to the joy of the restoration of Zion, and the sixth evokes the joy of the first couple in Paradise. The seventh blessing gives thanks to God for having created "joy and gladness, bride and bridegroom" and concludes "Blessed

. . . who makes the bridegroom rejoice with the bride." During the seven days following the marriage, the Sheva' Berakhot are recited during *Birkat ha-Mazon after every meal at which a *minyan is available (the *minyan* must include some new guests on each occasion).

• Philip Goodman and Hanna Goodman, eds., *The Jewish Marriage Anthology* (Philadelphia, 1965). Eliyahu S. Vind, *Ohel Ester: Halakhot u-Minhagim la-Kallah* (Jerusalem, 1989).

SHEVARIM. See SHOFAR.

SHEVAT (שְׁבָט), fifth month of the civil year, eleventh month of the religious year; its zodiac sign is Aquarius. The word *shevat* is Akkadian/Babylonian in origin; it appears only once in the Bible (*Zec.* 1.7), but it is the "eleventh month" referred to in *Deuteronomy* 1.3 when Moses began to read the *Book of Deuteronomy* to the people. Shevat always has thirty days, and *Tu bi-Shevat (New Year for Trees) falls, following the tradition of Beit Hillel, on 15 Shevat (the Beit Shamm'ai date—1 Shevat—did not gain acceptance).

• Nathan Bushwick, *Understanding the Jewish Calendar* (New York, 1989). George Zinberg, *Jewish Calendar Mystery Dispelled* (New York, 1963). —CHAIM PEARL

SHEVAT, FIFTEENTH DAY OF. See TU BI-SHEVAT.

SHEVI'IT (שְׁבִיעִית; Seventh Year), tractate in Mishnah order Zera'im, in ten chapters, with related material in Tosefta' and in the Talmud Bavli. It deals with the laws pertaining to the *shemittah* (sabbatical), the seventh year, when Israel is commanded to let the land lie fallow (*Ex.* 23.10–11; *Lv.* 25.1–7) and to release debts (*Dt.* 15.1–3). The laws of *shemittah* are arranged in roughly chronological order, opening with a rabbinic interdiction against preparing the ground during the sixth year for agricultural work and concluding with laws governing the release of debts at the conclusion of the seventh year. In between, *Shevi'it* discusses in detail forbidden and permitted forms of agricultural activity during the seventh year and the laws governing the consumption of *shevi'it* produce.

According to the rabbis, not only was the owner of a field required to leave his produce to be taken and consumed by anyone who so desired (*Lv.* 25.6), but Beit Shamm'ai even forbade requesting permission of the owner to enter the field and pick fruit. This requirement gave concrete expression to the ideas of social equality (*Lv.* 25.6) and of divine sovereignty (*Lv.* 25.2, cf. 25.23) associated with *shevi'it*. However, many Jews were unwilling to abide by the laws; hence, a sizable portion of the tractate outlines laws designed to render the deceitful flouting of *shevi'it* more difficult, while maintaining cordial relations between *shevi'it* observers and nonobservers. The law of releasing debts was also widely disregarded, leading Hillel to institute the *perozbol*, a legal fiction that legitimated the collection of debts after the date of release had passed.

An English translation of *Shevi'it* appears in *The Mishnah* by Herbert Danby (London, 1933).

• Chanoch Albeck, ed., *Shishah Sidrei Mishnah, Seder Zera'im* (Jerusalem, 1957). Philip Blackman, ed. and trans., *Mishnayoth*, vol. 1, *Order Zeraim* (Gateshead, 1973). Pinhas Kehati, ed., *Mishnah: A New Translation with a Commentary, Seder Zeraim*, vol. 2, *Demai, Kilayim, Shevi'it* (Jerusalem, 1992). Hermann Leberecht Strack and Günter Stemberger, *Introduction to the Talmud and Midrash*, rev. and updat. ed., translated by Markus Bockmuehl (Minneapolis, 1992). —AVRAHAM WALFISH

SHEVU'OT (שְׁבוּעוֹת; Oaths), tractate in Mishnah order Neziqin, in eight chapters, with related material in the Tosefta' and commentary in both Talmuds. The biblical oath, invoking the name of God to bolster a statement or commitment (e.g., *Dt.* 6.13; *Lv.* 19.12), was closely associated with the invocation of a divine curse (e.g., *Nm.* 5.21; *Neh.* 10.30), and violation of an oath was considered a desecration of the name of God (*Lv.* 19.12). *Shevu'ot* follows biblical law in differentiating between various categories of oaths.

The false "oath of utterance," defined in the Bible (*Lv.* 5.4) as the inadvertent violation of a commitment to deny or grant oneself a benefit, is expanded by R. 'Aqiva' (*Shev.* 3.5, *pace* R. Yishma'e'l) to include oaths affirming or denying events in the past. *Shevu'ot* opens with a formulaic encapsulation of the position of R. 'Aqiva': "Oaths are of two kinds [i.e., affirmative and negative], which divide into four [i.e., future and present]." *Shevu'ot* dwells at great length on defilement, by impurity, of the Temple or of sacred foods. In rabbinic as in biblical law, oaths played an important part in judicial proceedings, as attested to by the five chapters of *Shevu'ot* (chaps. 3–8) devoted to the laws of various forms of oaths arising out of monetary disputes.

An English translation of the tractate by A. E. Silverstone is in the Soncino Talmud (1935).

• Chanoch Albeck, ed., *Shishah Sidrei Mishnah, Seder Nezikin* 2d ed. (Jerusalem, 1956). Philip Blackman, ed. and trans., *Mishnayoth*, vol. 4, *Order Nezikin* (Gateshead, 1973). Pinhas Kehati, ed., *Mishnah: A New Translation with a Commentary, Seder Nezikin*, vol. 3, *Makkot, Shevuot, Eduyot* (Jerusalem, 1988). Hermann Leberecht Strack and Günter Stemberger, *Introduction to the Talmud and Midrash*, rev. and updat. ed., translated by Markus Bockmuehl (Minneapolis, 1992). —AVRAHAM WALFISH

SHEW BREAD. See SHOWBREAD.

SHIDDUKH. See BETROTHAL.

SHIELD OF DAVID. See MAGEN DAVID.

SHIKHHAH. See LEQET, SHIKHHAH, AND PE'AH.

SHILOH, an important cultic center of premonarchic Israel, identified with Khirbet Seilun in the hill country of Ephraim. The *Book of Joshua* identifies Shiloh as the site that first housed the Tent of Meeting and from where Joshua apportioned the tribal allotments (*Jos.* 18.1–10). Other sources allude to an actual temple structure at Shiloh, where the prophet Samuel came of age (*1 Sm.* 1; cf. *Jgs.* 18.31). Archaeological evidence indicates that this temple was destroyed in the mid-eleventh century BCE (cf. *Jer.* 7.12; *Ps.* 78.60–64).

• Menahem Haran, *Temples and Temple-Service in Ancient Israel* (Winona Lake, Ind., 1985). Donald G. Schley, *Shiloh: A Biblical City in Tradition and History*, Journal for the Study of the Old Testament, Supplement Series 63 (Sheffield, Eng., 1989). —DAVID A. GLATT-GILAD

SHIM'ON BAR YOḤ'AI (2d cent.), tanna'; pupil of R. *'Aqiva' ben Yosef. He conducted his school at Tekoa in Upper Galilee, where his pupils included R. *Yehudah ha-Nasi'. The halakhic *midrashim* **Sifrei* and **Mekhilta' de-Rabbi Shim'on bar Yoḥ'ai* evolved from the teachings of his academy, which was noted for systematic classification of *halakhot* and attempts to adduce a rational basis for the law. Shim'on, who is frequently quoted in the Mishnah and other tannaitic sources as R. Shim'on, also had a reputation as a miracle worker. For speaking against the Romans he was condemned to death, and he and his son El'azar ben Shim'on consequently had to go into hiding—they are said to have spent twelve or thirteen years in a cave until the death sentence was annulled. After the Bar Kokhba' Revolt (see BAR KOKHBA', SHIM'ON) and subsequent persecution, Shim'on feared for the continuation of Torah studies and developed an ideology that gave ultimate priority to the learning of the law above all other activities. Many legends were woven around him, and kabbalists subsequently claimed that the *Zohar expressed the mystical doctrines revealed by Shim'on during his sojourn in the cave. At the reputed site of his grave in Meron in Lower Galilee, bonfires are lit and special poems composed in his honor are sung on *Lag ba-'Omer, the date of his death.

• Israel Konovitz, *Rabbi Simeon Bar Yohai: Collected Sayings in Halakah and Aggadah in the Talmudic and Midrashic Literature* (Jerusalem, 1966). Gershom Gerhard Scholem, *Kabbalah*, Library of Jewish Knowledge (New York, 1974). Gershom Gerhard Scholem, *Major Trends in Jewish Mysticism*, Hilda Stich Strook Lectures, 1938 (Jerusalem, 1941).

—DANIEL SPERBER

SHIM'ON BEN 'AZZAI (2d cent.), one of the great tannaitic scholars of his generation, he died in his prime before being formally ordained; hence, his name is not preceded by the title "rabbi." He remained unmarried—contrary to the requirements of rabbinic law—in order to devote his time exclusively to study. Tradition connects him with a circle of mystics and attributes his premature death to a mystical experience (against the danger of which the rabbis frequently warned; cf. *Ḥag*. 14a–b). This tradition is further elaborated on in the mystical *Heikhalot literature that Gershom Gerhard *Scholem has shown dates back to the Talmudic period. Few halakhic statements have come down in his name, and his aggadic sayings reflect his great piety (*Avot* 4.2).

• Gershom Gerhard Scholem, *Jewish Gnosticism, Merkabah Mysticism and Talmudic Tradition* (New York, 1960), pp. 14ff.

—DANIEL SPERBER

SHIM'ON BEN GAMLI'EL (1st cent.), tanna'; son of *Gamli'el the Elder, whom he succeeded as **nasi'* of the Sanhedrin in the years immediately preceding the destruction of the Second Temple (Yoḥanan ben Zakk'ai was *av beit din*). He was a forceful and charismatic leader (*Ker*. 1.7), who belittled intellectual argument and pedagogic activity (he himself had no disciples) saying, "Not the study but the practice of the Torah is essential" (*Avot* 1.17). He served as a leader in the early stages of the rebellion against Rome, though later his views became more moderate. According to tradition, he was one of the *Ten Martyrs executed by the Romans, but it is possible that he was put to death by the Zealots during the last year of the war.

—DANIEL SPERBER

SHIM'ON BEN GAMLI'EL (2d cent.), tanna'; son of *Gamli'el and *nasi'* of the Sanhedrin at Usha' in the generation after the Bar Kokhba' Revolt (see BAR KOKHBA', SHIM'ON). Under his statesmanship, the position of *nasi'* and the status of the Sanhedrin recovered much of its significance. Shim'on was noted for his humility (*B. M.* 84a) and leniency but was firm and decisive in his judgments when necessary (*Mak*. 1.10). Many *halakhot* are quoted in his name, and in a later generation, R. Yoḥanan bar Nappaḥa' (died 279) ruled that, with the exception of three cases, whenever R. Shim'on ben Gamli'el's view is cited in the Mishnah, it is to be followed. Shim'on coined the phrase, "The world rests on three things: judgment, truth, and peace" (*Avot* 1.18).

• Jacob Neusner, *A History of the Jews in Babylonia* (Leiden, 1969).

—DANIEL SPERBER

SHIM'ON BEN LAQISH (died c.275), Palestinian *amora' also known as Reish Laqish. Originally a gladiator, he was influenced by *Yoḥanan bar Nappaḥa' to turn to sacred studies. Shim'on became an outstanding and independent scholar and noted aggadist; he was deputy to (and brother-in-law of) R. Yoḥanan, and their legal discussions constitute one of the main elements of the Talmud Yerushalmi. Shim'on was famed for his scrupulous honesty (*Yoma'* 9b), his saintly goodness, and his willingness to endanger himself to help others (Y., *Ter*. 8ff.). He was greatly respected but refused to gain personal benefit from the esteem in which he was held (*Meg*. 28b). Deeply aware of man's inner conflicts, he taught that, but for the help of God, man's evil inclinations would overcome him every day (*Suk*. 52b), though ultimately bad deeds were due to a "spirit of foolishness" (*Sot*. 3a). One of God's great gifts to man is repentance, which could turn the evil deeds of the past to positive merits (*Yoma'* 86b).

• Israel Konovitz, *Ma'arkhot ha-'Amora'im: Ma'amreihem shel ha-'Amora'im be-Halakhah uve-'Aggadah Mesudarim lefi Nos'im*, vol. 1 (Jerusalem, 1973).

—DANIEL SPERBER

SHIM'ON BEN SHETAḤ (1st cent. BCE), scholar and president (*nasi'*) of the *Sanhedrin. A Pharisaic leader during the reign of Alexander Yannai and his widow Salome Alexandra (Shim'on's sister), Shim'on was renowned for his integrity. He and Salome Alexandra transformed the Sanhedrin from a Sadducean to a Pharisaic body (possibly by introducing scribes [**soferim*] into its ranks, which hitherto had been composed of priests and lay aristocracy). He was forced to hide from the persecutions of the pro-Sadducee Alexander Yannai until the latter was pressured to reinstate him. Shim'on then recalled *Yehudah ben Tabb'ai from exile in Alexandria; together they constituted one of the **zugot*. Shim'on initiated several important legal and religious ordinances, for example, the institution of the marriage contract (**ketubbah*) and the requirement that a court must pass judgment on the basis of the testimony of two witnesses and not on circumstantial evidence. He also laid the foundation for the elementary education of children. He vigorously strove to eradicate witchcraft, and legend has it that he hanged eighty witches in Ashkelon. Their relatives took revenge by fabricating evidence implicating his son in murder, thus forcing Shim'on to execute his own son, knowing that he was innocent.

• Gershon Bader, *Encyclopedia of Torah Sages* (Northvale, N.J., 1988). Amihai Yisreeli, *'Olamam shel Ḥakhamim* (Tel Aviv, 1977–1978).
—DANIEL SPERBER

SHIM'ON BEN ZOMA' (1st–2d cent.), Palestinian tanna'. He was the colleague of Shim'on ben 'Azzai, both of whom were highly regarded, although neither was ordained (cf. *San.* 17b; occasionally, however, each is called rabbi; cf. *Ber.* 6b). It was said that whoever saw Ben Zoma' in a dream could expect an increase in wisdom (*Ber.* 57b). He was given to mystical studies (particularly on creation and the divine chariot) and was one of the four sages who entered "the garden" (i.e., esoteric mysticism; according to others, heaven), going mad as a result ("he looked and became demented," T., *Ḥag.* 2.3; *Prv.* 25.16 is applied to him there). Shortly before Ben Zoma' died, his original teacher, R. Yehoshu'a ben Ḥananyah, found him absorbed in speculation on the upper and lower waters of the firmament and deemed him still deluded (T., *Ḥag.* 2.5). With his death, it was said that expounders of Torah (*darshanim*) ceased (*Sot.* 9.15). His aphorism on the nature of true wisdom, might, riches, happiness, and honor is found in *Avot* 4.1. His exposition of *Deuteronomy* 16.3 (*Ber.* 1.5), namely that the words "all the days of your life" include the nights, is preserved in the Haggadah of Pesaḥ.

• Gershom Bader, *The Encyclopedia of Talmudic Sages*, translated from the Yiddish by Solomon Katz (Northvale, N.J., and London, 1988). Henry A. Fischel, *Rabbinic Literature and Greco-Roman Philosophy: A Study of Epicurea and Rhetorica in Early Midrashic Writings* (Leiden, 1973). Israel Konovitz, comp., *Ma'arakhot Tanna'im: Osef Shalem shel Mishnatam u-Ma'amreihem bi-Sifrut ha-Talmudit veha-Midrashit* (Jerusalem, 1967–1969).
—MICHAEL L. BROWN

SHIM'ON HA-TSADDIQ (fl. 200 BCE), high priest. According to Josephus (*Antiquities of the Jews* 12.43), he is Shim'on I (4th–3d cent.), called "ha-Tsaddiq" (the Just) because of his benevolence and fear of heaven. However, Talmudic sources and Ben Sira (*Ben Sira* 50.1–6) indicate that he was Shim'on II (fl. 200 BCE), thought by scholars to have been head of the pro-Seleucid party. In rabbinic historiography Shim'on ha-Tsaddiq is referred to as "one of the survivors of the Great Assembly"; his influence is said to have spanned the period of the Great Assembly and the period of the paired authorities (*zugot*) that preceded the earliest tanna'im (rabbinic scholars). Ben Sira refers to Shim'on's communal activities in the aftermath of Antiochus III's conquest of Judea and to his Temple renovations. Shim'on is traditionally credited with formulating the liturgy and establishing the central role of study in Judaism, though there is little concrete historical evidence for these and other accomplishments attributed to him.

• Chanoch Albeck, *Mavo' la-Mishnah* (Jerusalem, 1967). George Foot Moore, *Judaism in the First Centuries of the Christian Era, the Age of the Tannaim*, vol. 1 (Cambridge, Mass., 1927), pp. 34–36. Avigdor Tcherikover, *Hellenistic Civilization and the Jews* (Philadelphia, 1959), pp. 80–81, 156–158.
—CHRISTINE E. HAYES

SHIMSHON BEN AVRAHAM OF SENS (died 1214), rabbinic scholar, tosafist, legal authority. Rabbi Shimshon was known as Rash (or ha-Sar) of Sens. In his youth, R. Shimshon studied with his brother-in-law, R. Ya'aqov ben Me'ir Tam, and with R. Ḥayyim ha-Kohen, but his most important teacher was R. Yitsḥaq ben Shemu'el of Dampierre. Rabbi Shimshon composed or dictated *tosafot*, known as *Tosafot Sens*, on almost the entire Talmud, and some were printed in standard editions of the Talmud. He also wrote a commentary to the Mishnah orders of Zera'im and Tohorot. Several of his Talmudic commentaries are not extant, and others are attributed incorrectly to him. He wrote numerous *responsa* that are scattered throughout medieval rabbinic literature. A collection of his legal decisions has been lost.

He was consulted by R. Me'ir Abulafia and others at the beginning of the *Maimonidean Controversy. He was opposed to Maimonides' views on resurrection and to other aspects of the *Mishneh Torah*, but he also recognized Maimonides as a great Torah scholar. Shimshon's own lack of philosophical training caused him to judge Maimonides' work solely as a rabbinic composition, a posture that did not satisfy the anti-Maimonists.

Rabbi Shimshon led a group of tosafists who emigrated to Erets Yisra'el around 1210. He died in Acre and was buried at the foot of Mount Carmel, the site of the famous contest between Elijah and the priests of Baal. He is referred to occasionally in tosafistic literature as R. Shimshon of Erets Yisra'el or of Jerusalem, where he apparently had also settled for a time.

• Ephraim Kanarfogel, "The 'Aliyah of 'Three Hundred Rabbis' in 1211: Tosafist Attitudes Toward Settling in the Land of Israel," *Jewish Quarterly Review* 76 (1986): 191–215. Israel Ta-Shema, "Qeroniqah Ḥadashah li-Tequfat Ba'alei ha-Tosafot me-Ḥugo shel Ri ha-Zaqen," *Shalem* 3 (1981): 319–324. Efraim E. Urbach, *Ba'alei ha-Tosafot* (Jerusalem, 1980), vol. 1, pp. 271–318, and index.
—EPHRAIM KANARFOGEL

SHIRAYIM. See TISH.

SHIR HA-KAVOD (שִׁיר הַכָּבוֹד; Hymn of Glory; also known after its opening words as An'im Zemirot [I Shall Sing Songs]), alphabetic acrostic recited responsively by Ashkenazim at the end of the morning service (in some rites restricted to the conclusion of the Sabbath additional service, in Israel sometimes recited before the reading of the Torah, in other places omitted entirely). Shir ha-Kavod is often recited by a boy (or girl in non-Orthodox congregations) under the age of thirteen, with the congregation reading the responses. In certain rites Shir ha-Kavod is also sung on the eve of Yom Kippur. The composition of the hymn, a doxology that does not shun anthropomorphisms, has been attributed to R. *Yehudah ben Shemu'el he-Ḥasid.

• Abraham M. Habermann, *Shirei ha-Yiḥud veha-Kavod* (Jerusalem, 1948). M. H. Levine, "Redemption in the Hymn of Glory," *Conservative Judaism* 37.4 (1984): 83–85. Ismar Schorsch, "Poetry and Pietism: The 'Hymn of Glory,'" *Judaism* 37.1 (1988): 67–72.

SHIR HA-MAʿALOT. See DEGREES, SONG OF.

SHIR HA-SHIRIM. See SONG OF SONGS, BOOK OF.

SHIR HA-SHIRIM RABBAH. See SONG OF SONGS RABBAH.

SHIR HA-YIḤUD (שִׁיר הַיִּחוּד; Song of [God's] Unity), hymn divided into seven sections, one of which is read (by Ashkenazim) at the end of *Shaḥarit on each day of the week, although in practice only the Sabbath section is recited in many congregations. The hymn, praising God by glorifying his attributes, seems to have been partly inspired by Shelomoh *ibn Gabirol's *Keter Malkhut*. It has also been suggested that the hymn is a poetic presentation of the philosophy of Saʿadyah ben Yosef Ga'on, intermingled with the mysticism of the Ḥasidei Ashkenaz. Shir ha-Yiḥud is attributed to R.Yehudah he-Ḥasid (d.1217) or to his father, R. Shemu'el ben Kalonimos (b.1115). An English translation of the entire hymn, by Nina Salamon, Elsie Davis, and H. M. Adler, is given in Davis and Adler's *Service of the Synagogue* (London, 1908), pages 60–72.

• Abraham Meir Habermann, *Shirei ha-Yiḥud veha-Kavod* (Jerusalem, 1948). Macy Nulman, *The Encyclopedia of Jewish Prayer* (Northvale, N.J., and London, 1993), pp. 306–307. —A. STANLEY DREYFUS

SHIROT ʿOLAT HA-SHABBAT. See SONGS OF THE SABBATH SACRIFICE.

SHIʿUR QOMAH, mystical work dating from the geonic period, possibly earlier (in the light of its similarities to Maʿaseh Merkavah mysticism). It attempts to convey the greatness and majesty of God by attributing to him colossal dimensions of stupendous magnitude; for instance, "the soles of his feet cover the whole universe; the height of his soles is 30,000 thousand parasangs; from the sole to the heel 1,000 times 1,000 plus 500 parasangs; his square beard is 11,500 parasangs. Each parasang is 3 miles and each mile 10,000 cubits." Many authorities denounced the work as spurious, grossly anthropomorphic, and heretical, and Maimonides declared that it ought to be burned. Defenders of the *Shiʿur Qomah* claimed that it was esoteric, not meant to be taken literally, and that the fantastic numbers were meant to convey a sense of God's infinite greatness.

• Martin Samuel Cohen, *The Shiur Qomah: Texts and Recensions*, Texte und Studien zum antiken Judentum 9 (Tübingen, 1985).

SHIVʿAH (שִׁבְעָה; seven), the seven days of mourning following the death of one's close relative: a father, mother, son, daughter, brother, sister, husband, or wife. The period of the *shivʿah* begins immediately after the burial and ends on the morning of the seventh day. On the seventh day, the mourners sit only briefly after morning prayers and then visit the cemetery to mark the conclusion of the *shivʿah*. The first three days are regarded as the days of deepest mourning. Biblical authority for the custom is found, for example, in the account of the seven days of mourning that Joseph observed for his father, Jacob (*Gn*. 50.10); other rabbis ascribe its origin to Moses (Y., *Ket*. 1). The rules and customs for the week of *shivʿah* provide the mourners with time away from their normal daily pursuits in order to give expression to their grief and to afford friends the opportunity of showing their respect to the deceased and offering their condolences to the bereaved family, traditionally comforting them with the phrase, "May the Almighty comfort you together with those who mourn for Zion and Jerusalem." The mourners are prohibited to greet others, though on the third day they may respond if greeted first. *Shivʿah* commences on returning from the cemetery; it is customary for a light meal to be prepared by neighbors and served to the mourners. This meal is called Seʿudat Havra'ah (Meal of Condolence) and consists, traditionally, of eggs and lentils. All mirrors in the home of mourning are kept covered during the *shivʿah*, a late medieval custom probably stemming from folk beliefs. A *memorial light remains lit throughout the week. Mourners sit on the floor or on low stools, and since leather was considered a luxury, they wear cloth slippers instead of leather shoes.

The *shivʿah* week is usually observed in the home of the deceased, where the three daily prayer services are held. It is forbidden to study the Torah, except for *Job*, *Lamentations*, and the laws of mourning. Shaving is prohibited during *shivʿah*; bathing is permitted for hygienic reasons but not for pleasure (*Shulḥan ʿArukh, Yoreh Deʿah* 381.1–2). Marital relations are also prohibited during the week. Mourners do not work during the *shivʿah*, though, if absolutely essential, some work may be performed after the third day. If essential, a doctor is allowed to see patients during his *shivʿah*.

On the Sabbath, there is no *shivʿah* or mourning in public, and mourners may leave the house and attend services in the synagogue. The *shivʿah* is resumed after the Sabbath. If the funeral takes place before one of the major festivals (not Ḥanukkah or Purim), the onset of the festival cancels the *shivʿah*. If, however, the funeral took place during the intermediate days of a festival (see ḤOL HA-MOʿED), the *shivʿah* starts at the conclusion of the festival.

If news of a death and burial reach a close relative within three days of the commencement of the *shivʿah*, the mourner observes the rest of the *shivʿah* week and finishes at the same time as the rest of the family. If one receives the news after the third day, then the full seven days after that are to be observed privately. If the news comes after thirty days (**sheloshim*), *shivʿah* is not observed, except symbolically for one hour.

• Chaim Binyamin Goldberg, *Mourning in Halachah: The Laws and Customs of the Year of Mourning*, translated by Shlomo Fox-Ashrei, edited by Meir Zlotowitz (Brooklyn, N.Y., 1991). Leopold Greenwald, *Kol Bo ʿal Avelut* (New York, 1947). Maurice Lamm, *The Jewish Way in Death and Mourning* (New York, 1969). Harry Rabinowicz, *A Guide to Life* (London, 1964), pp. 92–99. —CHAIM PEARL

SHIVʿAH ʿASAR BE-TAMMUZ (שִׁבְעָה עָשָׂר בְּתַמּוּז; 17 Tammuz), the fast of the fourth month mentioned in *Zechariah* 8.19, commemorating the breach of the walls of Jerusalem three weeks before the complete fall of the city and the destruction of the Temple. According to *Jeremiah* 39.2, the breach of the walls by the Babylonians under Nebuchadnezzar in 586 BCE took place on 9 Tammuz, and the fast was presumably observed on that date until the building of the Second Temple, when minor fasts were abolished. When the break into Jerusalem made by Titus in 70 CE fell on 17 Tammuz, the latter date was chosen for the fast to commemorate both tragedies (*Ta'an.* 26a). The Mishnah (*Ta'an.* 4.6) adds other mournful anniversaries that occurred on this date, including the breaking by Moses of the tablets of the Law, the cessation of the daily sacrifice in 70 CE, and the burning of the scrolls of the Law by an otherwise unknown Apostomos, who also erected an idol in the sanctuary. The seventeenth of Tammuz marks the start of *Bein ha-Metsarim (the Three Weeks of Mourning), which culminates in Tish'ah be-'Av. Shiv'ah 'Asar be-Tammuz is observed from sunrise to sundown, and special Torah readings are inserted in *Shaḥarit and *Minḥah, **seliḥot* are read, and an addition is made to the 'Amidah. See also FASTS.

• Dudley Weinberg, "A Study of the Seventeenth of Tammuz, the Month of Ab and the Intervening Period," rabbinic thesis, Hebrew Union College, 1941.

SHIVAT TSIYYON. See ZIONISM.

SHIVḤEI HA-BESHT, the mythical biography of Yisra'el ben Eli'ezer *Ba'al Shem Tov, the founder of *Hasidism, first published in Kopyś, Belorussia, in 1814, fifty-four years after his death. This compilation of fanciful tales and typologically prescribed stories purports to relate the events of his life. During the second half of the eighteenth century, when first recounted, these tales were a meaningful relation of events, but through transmission they underwent embellishment and exaggeration. Nevertheless, close scrutiny reveals several levels of authenticity, and valuable historical data can be determined alongside obvious legendary narration.

• Dan Ben-Amos and Jerome R Mintz, *In Praise of the Ba'al Shem Tov: The Earliest Collection of Legends about the Founder of Hasidism* (Bloomington, 1972). Rachel Elior, *Israel Ba'al Shem Tov, Between Magic and Mysticism* (Jerusalem, 1996). Joshua Mondshein, ed., *Shivḥei ha-Besht* (Jerusalem, 1981). Ada Rapoport-Albert, "Hagiography with Footnotes: Edifying Tales and the Writing of History in Hasidism," in *Essays in Jewish Historiography* (Middletown, Conn., 1988), pp. 119–159.

—RACHEL ELIOR

SHIVVITI (שִׁוִּיתִי), plaque or paper inscribed with the verse, "I have set the Lord always before me" (*Ps.* 16.8). The name *shivviti* is derived from the first Hebrew word of this biblical verse. These decorative plaques are hung on the synagogue wall next to the cantor's podium or in the interior of a private home and are intended to serve as a constant reminder of God's presence. *Shivvitis* may also contain a variety of other biblical and Talmudic passages. Many feature the names of protective angels or magical formulas and function as amulets. They are commonly decorated with images of the seven-branched Menorah, the holy sites of Israel, animals, and flowers. Many *shivvitis* were created in eastern Europe during the nineteenth century; additional examples were produced in North Africa.

• Joseph and Yehudit Shadur, *Jewish Papercuts: A History and Guide* (Jerusalem, 1994). Joy Ungerleider-Mayerson, *Jewish Folk Art: From Biblical Days to Modern Times* (New York, 1986).

—SHARON LIBERMAN MINTZ

SHMUEL BUKH, a major Yiddish poetic work setting ancient Jewish content in a European form. Thought to be of fifteen century origin, it is attributed to Moyshe 'Esrim ve-Arba', a late fifteenth-century German-born rabbi who became an emissary of the Jerusalem community. The narrative features stories drawn from *1* and *2 Samuel* and emphasizes the glory and tragedy of King David. The work is cast in the Germanic *Nibelungen* (Hildebrand) stanza form. The first printed edition is from Augsburg in 1544.

• Max Erik, *Di geshikhte fun der yidisher literatur: fun di eltste tsaytn biz der haskalah-tekufah* (Warsaw, 1928; repr. New York, 1979), pp. 79–81, 112–121, 221–222. Felix Falk and Lajb Fuks, eds., *Das Schemuelbuch des Mosche Esrim Wearba, ein biblisches Epos aus dem 15. Jahrhundert*, 2 vols. (Assen, 1961). Chone Shmeruk, *Prokim fun der yidisher literatur-geshikhte* (Tel Aviv, 1988), pp. 114–116, 192–198.

—DOVID KATZ

SHNEERSON FAMILY. See SCHNEERSOHN FAMILY.

SHNEUR ZALMAN OF LYADY (1745–1813), Hasidic master and founder of *Ḥabad *Hasidism, that is, the school of Hasidic thought and the organization that later became known as the Lubavitch movement. Shneur was born in Lithuania and achieved a reputation as a brilliant Talmudic scholar. He studied further in Mezhirech, in Volhynia, under the renowned Hasidic master R. *Dov Ber of Mezhirech, who recognized his exceptional talents and encouraged him to compose a revised version of the **Shulḥan 'Arukh*. Shneur completed this prodigious task at the age of twenty-five. Dov Ber then assigned to him and to R. Menaḥem Mendel of Vitebsk the task of proclaiming Hasidic ideology in Lithuania, the stronghold of the *Mitnaggedim (as the opponents of Hasidism were termed). After Menaḥem Mendel left for Palestine in 1777, Shneur became one of the foremost leaders of Hasidism in the northeastern provinces of Russia. He owed his prominence to great erudition in **halakhah* and *Kabbalah, as well as to great mystical inspiration and to his charismatic personality. In Lithuania, he attempted to meet *Eliyyahu ben Shelomoh Zalman of Vilna, the Vilna Ga'on, leader of the anti-Hasidic opposition, in order to bring about a reconciliation, but the latter refused to confront him. Shneur was twice imprisoned by the Russian authorities as a result of false accusations by the Mitnaggedim. His disciples and adherents of the Ḥabad movement observe the date of his release, 19 Kislev, as a festival to this day. Shneur developed his system of mystical theology in several important works, the best known of which, entitled *Liqqutei Amarim* (or *Tanya'* [Slawita, 1796]; English trans. Nissan Mindel [Brooklyn, N.Y., 1962]), is regarded within the Lubavitch movement as the fundamental text of Hasidic spirituality. Shneur offered a comprehensive conception of both the spiritual and pragmatic demands of life according to a dialectic principle embodied simultaneously in the relationship to God, to the world, and to fellow humans. Though deemed by his followers to be a *tsaddiq*, he denied the possession of miraculous faculties, stressing the need for mutual support and cooperation between the Ḥasid and his *rebbi*. His other works include *Torah Or* (Kopyś, 1837) and *Liqqutei Torah* (Zhitomir, 1948).

• Rachel Elior, "The Contemplative Ascent to God," in *Jewish Spirituality: From the Sixteenth Century Revival to the Present*, edited by Arthur Green, World Spirituality, vol. 14 (New York, 1987), pp. 157–205. Rachel Elior, *The Paradoxical Ascent to God: The Kabbalistic Theosophy of Habad Hasidism* (Albany, 1993). Roman Foxbruner, *Habad: The Hasidism of R. Shneour Zalman of Lyady* (Tuscaloosa, Ala., 1992). Hayim Me'ir Heilman, *Sefer Beit Rabbi* (Varsha, 1900). David Tsevi Hilman, *Iggerot Ba'al ha-Tanya' u-Venei Doro* (Jerusalem, 1953). Naftali Loewenthal, *Communicating the Infinite: The Emergence of the Habad School* (Chicago, 1990).
—RACHEL ELIOR

SHO'AH. See HOLOCAUST, RELIGIOUS RESPONSES DURING THE; HOLOCAUST THEOLOGY.

SHOFAR (שׁוֹפָר), a ram's horn sounded on ceremonial occasions, including the proclamation of the jubilee year (*Lv*. 25.9), the anointing of a new king (e.g., *1 Kgs*. 1.34), or as a summons to war; today the sounding of the shofar is almost entirely confined to the synagogue, during the High Holy Days. Although Ashkenazi custom is to sound the shofar daily during the month of Elul (except on Sabbaths and the day before *Ro'sh ha-Shanah), Western Sephardim sound it on Hoshʿana' Rabbah, and it is sounded in all rites at the close of the service on Yom Kippur. The shofar is first mentioned at the Sinaitic revelation (*Ex*. 19.16, 19); however, it is enjoined in the Bible only for Ro'sh ha-Shanah (which is called a *yom teruʿah*, "a day of sounding [the shofar]"), with the phrase "it shall be a day of sounding to you" (*Nm*. 29.1). The phrase "A memorial of sounding" (*Lv*. 23.24) serves as an injunction against sounding the shofar on the Sabbath, although the shofar was sounded on Sabbaths in the Temple. A shofar may be made from the horn of any animal that is ritually pure (except a cow, excluded because of the incident of the *golden calf); the custom of using a ram's horn was influenced by the story of the *ʿ*aqedah* (the binding of Isaac; *R. ha-Sh*. 26b). The rabbis evolved an elaborate order of sounding the shofar: broken notes resembling sobbing (the *shevarim* sound) and wailing (the *teruʿah* sound), which are both preceded and followed by a long unbroken sound (*teqiʿah*); this order is repeated three times after the recital of each of the three sections of the ʿAmidah of the Musaf service. In many places the tradition is that one hundred notes be sounded on each day of Ro'sh ha-Shanah. Saʿadyah Ga'on adduced ten reasons for the sounding of the shofar (for example, to proclaim God's sovereignty and as a symbol of the ingathering of the exiles). Maimonides gives as its message (*Hilkhot Teshuvah* 3.4), "Awake you sleepers from your sleep, and you that are in slumber, rouse yourselves. Consider your ways, remember God, turn unto him." The shofar was sounded on various solemn occasions including the imposition of an *excommunication. The use of the shofar on official occasions has been reintroduced in the State of Israel for the swearing in of the president. It is also sounded in Orthodox residential neighborhoods to herald the advent of the Sabbath. See also BAʿAL TEQIʿAH.

• Tsiyyon Lahat, *Be-Ḥatsotsrot ve-Qol Shofar* (Israel, 1990). Yoel ben Aharon Shvarts, *Zikhron Teruʿah* (Jerusalem, 1985–1986).

SHOFAROT (שׁוֹפָרוֹת), name given to the section of the ʿAmidah including ten biblical verses that mention the sounding of the *shofar recited during the additional service on Ro'sh ha-Shanah (following the *Malkhuyyot and the *Zikhronot) and after which the shofar is sounded. The biblical selection is made up of three verses from each of the three portions of the Bible, the tenth verse being taken from the Pentateuch.

SHOFETIM. See JUDGES, BOOK OF.

SHOḤER TOV, *midrash* on *Psalms* (also called *Midrash Tehillim*), named after its opening words (cf. *Prv*. 11.27). It contains homilies and interpretations, collated from many aggadic sources, of 143 psalms. The work is not uniform and is divided into two sections, homilies on Psalms 1–118 and homilies on Psalms 119–150, with the exception of Psalm 123 and Psalm 131 (much of the latter is drawn from *Yalqut Shimʿoni*). The date of the work is uncertain, and it may have been edited over a period of some centuries, beginning during the time of the ge'onim. It was certainly widely known by the eleventh century. It has been suggested that it was composed in southern Italy. It has also been suggested that this *midrash* reflects a *triennial cycle of reciting the *Book of Psalms*, parallel to that of the Torah (in Erets Yisra'el), and that this is the key to a deeper understanding of the homilies. However, this contention has not been proved conclusively. *Shoḥer Tov* was first published in Constantinople in 1512; Solomon Buber edited an edition in 1891 (Vilna) based on eight manuscripts. William G. Braude translated the work into English in 1959. The name *Shoḥer Tov* has been erroneously applied to *Midrash Proverbs* and *Midrash Samuel*.

• Leopold Zunz, *Ha-Derashot be-Yisra'el ve-Hishtalshelutan ha-Historit*, edited by Chanoch Albeck (1892; Jerusalem, 1974).

SHOḤET (שׁוֹחֵט; slaughterer), one trained to perform *sheḥitah* (*ritual slaughter). In order to receive his diploma (*qabbalah*), a *shoḥet* must not only know the laws and theory of *sheḥitah* but must also have had practical experience under the guidance of experts. In awarding the diploma, the personal habits and character of the candidate are fully considered; a person who is not punctiliously observant or God-fearing, or who rejects rabbinic tradition (e.g., a Karaite), is not to receive the *qabbalah*. According to custom, the person ordained must be at least eighteen years of age; he cannot be prone to drunkenness; and his fingers cannot have lost their delicacy of touch. Women, although permitted to perform *sheḥitah*, are not in fact so ordained. A non-Jew may not act as a *shoḥet*. While there were historical eras in which many men received a *qabbalah* to perform ritual slaughter, the modern trend is that very few people are so trained, and those that are engage in the activity as a profession.

• Charles Duschinsky, "May a Woman Act as a Shoḥeteth?" in *Occident and Orient: Being Studies in Semitic Philology . . . in Honor of Haham Dr. Moses Gaster's 80th Birthday* (London, (1936), pp. 96–106. Michael L. Munk et al., *Shechita: Religious and Historical Research on the Jewish Method of Slaughter* (Brooklyn, N.Y., 1976). —MICHAEL BROYDE

SHOLEM ZOKHER. See SHALOM ZAKHAR.

SHOMERIM (שׁוֹמְרִים; bailees), people to whom property is delivered under contract of bailment. A bailment arises when one person (the bailee) is lawfully entrusted with the goods of another (the bailor) with the understanding that the goods will be returned. The law of bailment deals with the duty of the bailee to return the articles in good condition. In assessing the responsibility and liability of the bailee, Jewish law recognizes four categories of *shomerim*: the unpaid bailee (*shomer ḥinnam*); the borrower (*sho'el*); the paid bailee (*nosei sakhar* or *shomer sakhar*); and the hirer (*sokher*) (*Ex.* 22.6–14; *B. M.* 7ab). The Talmudic discussion of the subject is contained in the treatise *Bava' Metsi'a'*. The Israeli bailment law, adopted in 1967, closely follows Jewish law. See also BREACH OF TRUST.

SHOMER YISRA'EL (שׁוֹמֵר יִשְׂרָאֵל; Guardian of Israel), a late *piyyut* of unknown date and authorship, first found among the *seliḥot* (penitential poetry) for the fast day of *'Asarah be-Tevet in a thirteenth-century manuscript. Shomer Yisra'el was originally recited on fast days but later (apparently only in the 19th cent.) was incorporated into *Taḥanun in the Ashkenazi and Hasidic rituals, while in other rites it is still reserved for fast days and also, with an additional stanza, for the ten days of penitence. The version given in the prayer book is greatly shortened, and further stanzas are found in some manuscripts. The title Shomer Yisra'el is derived from Psalm 121, verse 4.

• Israel Davidson, *Thesaurus of Medieval Jewish Poetry*, 4 vols. (New York, 1970). Macy Nulman, *The Encyclopedia of Jewish Prayer* (Northvale, N.J., and London, 1993), pp. 310–311.

SHOSHANNAT YA'AQOV (שׁוֹשַׁנַּת יַעֲקֹב; Lily of Jacob), the concluding section of *piyyut* Asher Heni' ("who brought the counsel of the heathen to nought"), which is recited on Purim after the reading of the *Book of Esther* both in the evening and in the morning. While Asher Heni' dates from the geonic period, Shoshannat Ya'aqov is a later addition, consisting of two parts, the first of which is not contained in the Sephardi ritual.

• Macy Nulman, *The Encyclopedia of Jewish Prayer* (Northvale, N.J., and London, 1993), pp. 311.

SHOVAVIM TAT (שׁוֹבָבִי"ם תַּ"ת), Hebrew acrostic for the first eight weekly portions in *Exodus*. These are Shemot, Va-'Er'a, Bo', Be-Shelaḥ, Yitro, Mishpatim, Terumah, and Tetsavveh. A medieval custom, prevalent among the kabbalists, was to fast during the weeks when those portions were read. Opinions differ as to the reason for such an observance. The most prevalent view holds that the first word of the acrostic, *shovavim*, suggests the theme of repentance and return, on the basis of the text *shuvu banim shovavim*, "Return you backsliding children" (*Jer.* 3.22). The second word of the acrostic, *tat*, can stand for *talmud Torah* (study of the Torah), *Torah tefillah* (Torah and prayer), *teshuvah tefillah* (repentance and prayer), or other similar sets of religious values beginning with those Hebrew letters. Another view holds that the fasts and the accompanying penitential prayers were instituted during those two months of the winter when those portions of the Torah were being read because epidemics and serious illnesses were prevalent, especially among children. Others find a folkloric origin in the kabbalistic custom of instituting fasts to protect against evil spirits (*shovavim*).

The degree of fasting varied from place to place and even from individual to individual. One custom was to fast only during the day. Another custom was to fast only during the first and last weeks of the period. Yet another practice restricted the fasting to Mondays and Thursdays during a leap year, since it was thought that a leap year called for more serious repentance. A special service of *seliḥot was recited in synagogues on Mondays and Thursdays during this period. The observance of Shovavim Tat has virtually dropped out of Jewish practice in modern times.

• Judah David Eisenstein, *Otsar Dinim u-Minhagim* (New York, 1917). Eliyahu Kitov, *The Book of Our Heritage: The Jewish Year and Its Days of Significance*, rev. ed. (Jerusalem and New York, 1978), pp. 337–338. R. J. Zwi Werblowsky, *Joseph Karo: Lawyer and Mystic*, Scripta Judaica 4 (London, 1962). —CHAIM PEARL

SHOWBREAD (Heb. *leḥem ha-panim* [bread of the countenance]), twelve loaves of unleavened bread, baked of fine flour and sprinkled with frankincense, placed on the table in the Tabernacle and in the Temple (*Ex.* 25.30, 40.22–23; *Lv.* 24.5–9). The loaves were not sacrificed on the altar but were rather arrayed in two rows (or perhaps piles; in later times on six parallel golden-shelved trays) of six on display "before the Lord." Their location and the number twelve indicate that they were a regular, representative gift made on behalf of the twelve tribes of Israel. Each Sabbath day the high priest replaced the week-old loaves with twelve fresh ones, after which the previous week's loaves were eaten by the priests (in *Nm.* 4.7 they are called *leḥem ha-tamid* [the regular bread]). Thus, the bread was considered an offering to God, and when eaten, it was as though the priests were given a share in the deity's sacred gifts. The showbread is mentioned occasionally outside of the Torah; David and his men were permitted by the priest at the Nob sanctuary to eat of the sacred loaves (since no other bread was available) once it was determined that they had avoided physical impurity (*1 Sm.* 21.1–7). In ancient Mesopotamia, Egypt, and among the Hittites, loaves of bread were placed daily before the statues of the gods, who were believed to consume them.

• Roy Gane, "'Bread of the Presence' and Creator-in-Residence," *Vetus Testamentum* 42 (1992): 179–203. Menahem Haran, *Temples and Temple-Service in Ancient Israel* (Oxford, 1978), pp. 205–229. Baruch A. Levine, *Leviticus*, The JPS Torah Commentary (Philadelphia, 1989), pp. 165–166. —BARUCH J. SCHWARTZ

SHROUDS. See BURIAL.

SHTIBL (Yi.; שטיבל; little room), room used for prayer gatherings as distinct from a regularly consecrated synagogue. In the eighteenth century, adherents of the emerging Hasidism used such temporary prayer rooms for their services after having been forbidden, due to changes they had introduced into the prayer text, to lead prayer services in the local synagogues. As a result, the *shtibl* became the characteristic prayer house of the Ḥasidim. Partly due to Hasidic influence, partly to the desire of various groups to maintain their specific liturgical customs, and partly for economic reasons, the *shtibl* is more widespread in the State of Israel than is the formal synagogue.

• Aharon Verthaim, *Law and Custom in Hasidism*, translated by Shmuel Himelstein (Hoboken, N.J., 1992). —SHMUEL HIMELSTEIN

SHTREIML. See COSTUME.

SHUL (Yi.; שול; school), term employed by Ashkenazi Jews to refer to the *synagogue. The origin of the term lies in non-Jewish sources: Romans, well aware of the great amount of study that took place in the synagogue, dubbed it a *schola*—a school. Later, in Germany, the name became *Judenschule* (Jewish school). Finally the name was transformed to *shul* in eastern Europe, where it was used by Mitnaggedim to describe their synagogue, whereas the Ḥasidim referred to their synagogue as a **shtibl*.

• Brian De Breffny, *The Synagogue* (Jerusalem, 1978). Uri Kaploun, *The Synagogue* (Philadelphia, 1973). —SHMUEL HIMELSTEIN

SHULḤAN ʿARUKH, the standard code of Jewish law and practice compiled by Yosef *Karo of Safed and first published in 1565. Karo wrote the *Shulḥan ʿArukh* as a key to and synopsis of his larger work *Beit Yosef*, which was based in turn on the *Arbaʿah Turim* of *Yaʿaqov ben Asher. Following the pattern of the *Turim*, the *Shulḥan ʿArukh* is divided into four parts: *Oraḥ Ḥayyim*, dealing with the ritual obligations of daily life from waking to sundown and covering blessings, prayers, Sabbaths, and festivals; *Yoreh Deʿah*, dealing mainly with dietary and ritual laws including mourning, vows, respect to parents, and charity; *Even ha-ʿEzer*, on personal status, marriage, and divorce; and *Ḥoshen Mishpat*, which embraces the entire body of Jewish civil law as far as it is applicable in Diaspora conditions.

There was no reason to assume that the *Shulḥan ʿArukh* would be more successful than the codes that preceded it. This was especially so since it only reflected Sephardi practice. However, Karo's contemporary, Mosheh *Isserles of Kraków, who was working on his own code when Karo's was published, abandoned his original plan and instead added notes to Karo's laws, covering Ashkenazi practice; these notes were called *Mappah*. The *Shulḥan ʿArukh*, which was now understood in the larger sense as comprising the opinions of both Karo and Isserles, provided a normative framework and guide for Jewish practice.

From the time of the *Shulḥan ʿArukh* on, the genre of codes of Jewish law lost popularity (see CODIFICATION OF LAW). The success of the *Shulḥan ʿArukh* ensured that alternative codes would be ignored, and the way for scholars to register their disagreement with it was through the medium of commentary. The commentaries that are printed on the page of the standard edition of the *Shulḥan ʿArukh* have assumed a special authority and are themselves often considered part of the *Shulḥan ʿArukh*. Contemporary scholars are almost always reluctant to rule against Karo and Isserles without having the support of one of these commentaries. With all of the commentaries on the *Shulḥan ʿArukh*, it was no longer a book that laymen could use, as was its author's intention. Therefore, a series of abridgments of the *Shulḥan ʿArukh* have been published with a popular audience in mind. The most significant such works are Avraham Danzig's *Ḥayyei Adam* and Shelomoh Ganzfried's *Kitsur Shulḥan ʿArukh*, both written for Ashkenazi Jewry, and *Kaf ha-Ḥayyim* by Yaʿaqov Ḥayyim Sofer, which was written for the Sephardi community.

• *Asupot* 3 (1989), a series of important articles on the *Shulḥan ʿArukh*. Boaz Cohen, *The Shulhan Aruk as a Guide for Religious Practice Today* (New York, 1983). Mosheh S. Eisenbach, *Massa Halacha: Questions and Answers on Halacha Based on the Shulhan Arukh* (Jerusalem, 1977). Menachem Elon, *Jewish Law: History, Sources, Principles*, translated by Bernard Auerbach and Melvin J. Sykes (Philadelphia, 1994). Chaim Tchernowitz, *Toledot ha-Poseqim*, vol. 3 (New York, 1946). R. J. Zwi Werblowsky, *Joseph Karo: Lawyer and Mystic* (London, 1962). Makhon Yerushalayim, ed., *Shulḥan ʿArukh* (Jerusalem, 1994), introduction. —MARC SHAPIRO

SHUL KLAPPER (Yi.; שול קלאַפּער; synagogue knocker), name given to the synagogue official whose duty was to make the rounds of the houses in villages in eastern Europe and call the men to prayer, usually for the morning service and for **seliḥot*, which were recited in the very early hours of the morning. The *shul klapper* would knock on bedroom windows and announce in a plaintive chant, "Arise for the service of the Creator."

• Shlomo Eidelberg, *R. Yuzpa, Shammash di-Keḥillat Varmaisa: ʿOlam Yehudeyah ba-Me'ah ha-17* (Jerusalem, 1991), pp. 17–18. Ismar Elbogen *Jewish Liturgy: A Comprehensive History*, translated by Raymond P. Scheindlin (Philadelphia, New York, and Jerusalem, 1993), p. 371. Macy Nulman, *The Concise Encyclopedia of Jewish Music* (New York, 1975), pp. 215–217. Herman Pollack, *Jewish Folkways in Germanic Lands (1648–1806): Studies in Aspects of Daily Life* (Cambridge, Mass., 1971), p. 314, n. 5. —SHMUEL HIMELSTEIN

SHUSHAN PURIM. See PURIM.

SIBYLLINE ORACLES, a series of quasi-prophetic books written in Greek hexameters under the pseudonym of the Sibyl (pagan priestess) and dating from the second century BCE to the seventh century CE. Redacted in the early Byzantine period, these composite texts stem from Jewish, pagan, and Christian circles, with the Jewish passages concentrated mainly in the Third, Fourth and Fifth Sibylline Oracles. The earliest Jewish sections, in the Third Sibylline Oracle, come from second-century BCE Egypt, perhaps from circles connected with the Temple of *Onias, and foretell the prosperity of the Jews under the seventh Ptolemaic king. In this oracle, the Sibyl often calls upon all the gentiles to repent their idolatry and turn to the one true God and presents herself as the daughter-in-law of Noah, sent to the Greeks to foretell the future. The Fourth Sibylline Oracle, whose geographical provenance is unknown, foretells, among other events, the eruption of Vesuvius (79 CE), which is interpreted as God's punishment of the Romans for the destruction of the Jerusalem Temple in 70 CE. The Fifth Sibylline Oracle, most of which was probably written in Egypt, also foretells the destruction of the Jerusalem Temple and may even refer to the closing of the Temple of Onias by the Romans in approximately 71 CE.

• John J. Collins, "Sibylline Oracles," in *The Old Testament Pseudepigrapha*, edited by James H. Charlesworth, vol. 1 (Garden City, N.Y., 1983), pp. 317–472. John J. Collins, *The Sibylline Oracles of Egyptian Judaism*, Society of Biblical Literature, Dissertation Series 13 (Missoula, Mont., 1974). Herbert William Parke, *Sibyls and Sibylline Prophecy in Classical Antiquity* (London, 1988). —GIDEON BOHAK

SICK, PRAYER FOR THE. See MI SHE-BERAKH LE-ḤOLIM.

SICK, VISITING THE (Heb. *biqqur ḥolim*). The duty of visiting the sick ranks among the major acts of charity. When the rabbis wished to emphasize the special value of a moral act, they would describe God performing it himself. Thus, God appeared to Abraham after Abraham had undergone circumcision (*Gn.* 18.1) in order to fulfill the duty of visiting the sick (*Sot.* 14a). According to the rabbis, "whosoever visits the sick reduces their ailment by one-sixtieth" (*Ned.* 39b), and "visiting the sick can hasten recovery, just as refraining from doing so can hasten the death of the patient" (*Ned.* 40a). Visiting is only part of the obligation; the patient is to be assisted and his needs provided for. The schools of Shamm'ai and Hillel differed on the obligation to visit the sick on the Sabbath; because the Sabbath should be a day of unimpaired joy (*Shab.* 12a), the school of Shamm'ai forbade it. Societies for visiting the sick have been a prominent feature of Jewish social services throughout the ages. The visitor recites a special prayer for the patient's recovery (see MI SHE-BERAKH LE-ḤOLIM). The rules for the fulfillment of this commandment are formulated in the **Shulḥan ʿArukh, Yoreh Deʿah* 335.

• Jacob Rader Marcus, *Communal Sick Care in the German Ghetto* (Cincinnati, 1947). Nahum M. Waldman, "Bikkur Holim," in *Celebration and Renewal*, edited by Rela M. Geffen (Philadelphia, 1993).

SIDDUR. See PRAYER BOOK.

SIDELOCKS. See PE'OT.

SIDRAH (סִדְרָה; arrangement), the weekly portion of the Pentateuch read publicly in the synagogues on Sabbaths (the first section of which is read on Sabbath afternoons and Monday and Thursday mornings). The term is found in Talmudic times (*Shab.* 116b; *Yoma'* 87a). Sephardim use the term *parashah*, which was the old Palestinian term (and is used by Ashkenazim for a section of the *sidrah*). The fifty-four *sidrot* are so arranged (two are sometimes joined together) that the public reading of the Pentateuch commences on the first Sabbath after Simḥat Torah (Shabbat Be-Re'shit) and concludes annually on Simḥat Torah. This follows ancient custom and is in contrast to the Palestinian custom whereby the Pentateuch, variously divided into 154 (the Masoretic total of *sedarim*), 167 (Yemenite scrolls), or 175 (*Sof.* 16.10) *sidrot*, was read once in approximately three years (the *triennial cycle). Each *sidrah* is named after one of its initial words. See also QERI'AT HA-TORAH.

• Ismar Elbogen, *Jewish Liturgy: A Comprehensive History*, translated by Raymond P. Scheindlin (Philadelphia, New York, and Jerusalem, 1993), pp. 132–134.

SIFRA' (Aram.), a tannaitic *midrash* on *Leviticus* produced by the school of R. ʿAqiva', also known as *Torat Kohanim* or *Sifra' de-Vei Rav*. Current editions of *Sifra'* include later additions from the school of R. Yishmaʿe'l ben Elishaʿ, which were not originally part of *Sifra'*. *Sifra'* presents a verse-by-verse halakhic explication of *Leviticus*, with only relatively small amounts of aggadic material.

Many of the *baraiytot* in *Sifra'*, which is written in Mishnaic Hebrew, have close parallels in the Talmuds, particularly the Talmud Yerushalmi. The Talmud Bavli explicitly mentions *Sifra'* and *Sifra' de-Vei Rav*, although these works are apparently not identical with the existing *Sifra'*. The exact identity of the redactor of *Sifra'* (variously identified by previous scholars as Rav or R. Ḥiyya') remains unclear.

• Jacob Nahum Epstein, *Mevo'ot le-Sifrut ha-Tanna'im* (Jerusalem, 1957). Louis Finkelstein, ed., *Sifra' de-Vei Rav* (New York, 1983–1992). Hermann Leberecht Strack and Günter Stemberger, *Introduction to the Talmud and Midrash*, rev. and updat. ed., translated by Markus Bockmuehl (Minneapolis, 1992). —LEIB MOSCOVITZ

SIFREI (Aram.), tannaitic *midrashim* on *Numbers* and *Deuteronomy*. These *midrashim* are distinct works and stem from different schools: *Sifrei Numbers* from the school of R. Yishmaʿe'l ben Elishaʿ, and the majority of *Sifrei Deuteronomy* (except for most of pericopes 1–54) from the school of R. ʿAqiva'. Both works, however, offer verse-by-verse exegesis, in Midrashic Hebrew, of the biblical books in question. Both *midrashim* are primarily halakhic in nature, although both also contain significant amounts of aggadic material. Both books were evidently redacted no later than the third century CE and have parallels in the Talmuds.

Both *Sifrei Numbers* and *Sifrei Deuteronomy* have Midrashic counterparts produced by the rival exegetical school: *Sifrei Numbers* is paralleled by **Sifrei Zuta'*; *Sifrei Deuteronomy*, by **Mekhilta' de-Rabbi Shimʿon bar Yoḥ'ai* on *Deuteronomy*, a fragmentary *midrash* that very closely resembles *Sifrei Deuteronomy*.

• Jacob Nahum Epstein, *Mevo'ot le-Sifrut ha-Tanna'im* (Jerusalem, 1957). Menaḥem Kahana, "Aqdamot le-Hotsa'ah Ḥadashah shel Sifrei Be-Midbar," Ph.D. disseration, Hebrew University of Jerusalem, 1982. Hermann Leberecht Strack and Günter Stemberger, *Introduction to the Talmud and Midrash*, rev. and updat. ed., translated by Markus Bockmuehl (Minneapolis, 1992). —LEIB MOSCOVITZ

SIFREI ZUTA' (Aram.), tannaitic *midrash* on *Numbers*, produced by the school of R. ʿAqiva'. *Sifrei Zuta'* has been preserved in fragmentary form and is attested in citations in medieval *midrashim*, medieval commentaries, and *genizah* fragments, although the original *mid-*

rash presumably included additional material. A similar *midrash* was apparently composed on *Deuteronomy*.

Sifrei Zuta' is distinguished from other tannaitic *midrashim* by its unique language, style, terminology, and *halakhah*, as well as by the tanna'im cited therein. The work is written in Rabbinic Hebrew and deals primarily with halakhic matters.

It is not clear where *Sifrei Zuta'* was redacted or by whom, although it is frequently at odds with the Mishnah, never citing R. Yehudah ha-Nasi', and apparently stems from different circles. The teachings of R. Eli'ezer ben Ya'aqov figure prominently in *Sifrei Zuta'*. It has been suggested by Saul Lieberman that the work was redacted in Lydda by *Bar Qappara'.

• Jacob Nahum Epstein, *Mevo'ot le-Sifrut ha-Tanna'im* (Jerusalem, 1957). Menaḥem Kahana, "Mevo'ot mi-Midrash Tanna'i Ḥadash le-Sefer Devarim ve-Yaḥasan le-Sifrei Zuta'," *World Congress of Jewish Studies* 11C1 (1994). Saul Lieberman, ed., *Sifrei Zuta'* (New York, 1968). Hermann Leberecht Strack and Günter Stemberger, *Introduction to the Talmud and Midrash*, rev. and updat. ed., translated by Markus Bockmuehl (Minneapolis, 1992). —LEIB MOSCOVITZ

SIGD, pilgrimage festival and partial fast observed by the *Beta Israel on the twenty-ninth day of the eighth month, forty-nine days after Yom Kippur. The name derives from the Ethiopic root *sagada* and means to bow or prostrate oneself. According to the Beta Israel, Sigd commemorated the renewal of the covenant of God and Israel in the time of Ezra and Nehemiah. On the day of the festival, the Beta Israel fasted and ascended a hilltop, uncontaminated by waste matter or graves, carrying rocks on their heads as a sign of submission. The Ten Commandments and passages from the books of *Ezra* and *Nehemiah* were read. When they descended, a festive meal was consumed. Ethiopian Jews in Israel have continued to observe Sigd at several sites.

• Shoshanah Ben-Dor, "The Sigd of Beta Israel: Testimony to a Community in Transition," in *Ethiopian Jews and Israel*, edited by Michael Ashkenazi and Alex Weingrod (New Brunswick, N.J., 1987), pp. 140–159. Kay Kaufman Shelemay, "Seged: A Falasha Pilgrimage Festival," *Musica Judaica* 3.1 (1980–1981): 43–62. —STEVEN KAPLAN

SILENT PRAYER seems to have been unknown in ancient times, when worshipers called on God with a loud voice or at least moved their lips (cf. *1 Sm*. 1.13). Originally silent prayer was a category of synagogue worship, connected with the *'Amidah but not identical to it. Silent prayer was composed by each worshiper (a practice that has been revived in certain Reform congregations). In rabbinic usage silent prayer came to mean the formulated prayer recited silently by the individual during the recitation of the 'Amidah, during the *sheliaḥ tsibbur*'s repetitions of the 'Amidah, and in some other parts of congregational service. In many cases formulations of silent prayer by rabbis or readers became incorporated as part of private (e.g., Elohai Netsor at the end of the 'Amidah) and even congregational prayer (see RESHUT).

• Moshe Greenberg, *Biblical Prose Prayer: As a Window to the Popular Religion of Ancient Israel* (Berkeley, 1983). Joseph Heinemann, *Prayer in the Talmud: Forms and Patterns* (Berlin and New York, 1977), pp. 156–192.

SILVA, ḤIZQIYYAHU DE (1659–1695), rabbinical authority in Jerusalem. Born in Leghorn, he was the brother-in-law of Mosheh Ḥagiz (see ḤAGIZ FAMILY). He went to Jerusalem before 1679 and studied with Mosheh Galante (see GALANTE FAMILY), who sent him in 1688 as an emissary to central and western Europe. In Amsterdam (where he turned down an offer to become rabbi), he influenced the wealthy Jacob Pereira to found the Midrash Beit Ya'aqov in Jerusalem, which he headed from 1692.

He is best known for his *Peri Ḥadash* (Amsterdam, 1692, 1706, 1730) on sections of the *Shulḥan 'Arukh*, which strongly criticizes Yosef *Karo and other codifiers, with the exception of Maimonides, whom Ḥizqiyyahu greatly admired. His independent approach is shown in his ruling on drinks prepared by a non-Jew. He held that while it was forbidden to partake of strong liquor in the house of a non-Jew, coffee may be drunk. He also permitted drinking milk in the house of a non-Jew, even without Jewish supervision. His book was popular in Europe but was banned by the Egyptian rabbis. A somewhat toned-down version was published in editions of the *Shulḥan 'Arukh*.

• Chaim Tchernowitz, *Toledot ha-Poseqim* (New York, 1947), pp. 175–184. Isaiah Tishby, *Netivei Emunah u-Minut* (Tel Aviv, 1964), pp. 145–158. —SHALOM BAR-ASHER

SIMEON (Heb. Shim'on), the second son of Jacob and Leah and the eponymous ancestor of the tribe and territory of that name. Simeon, along with his brother Levi, plays a central role in avenging the rape of their sister Dinah (*Gn*. 34), by killing all the males of Shechem. Simeon is the one brother singled out by Joseph to be held hostage until the brothers return to him with Benjamin (*Gn*. 42.24). In Jacob's last testament, Simeon and Levi are chastised for their uncontrolled violence, for which they will be punished by being scattered among the tribes of Israel (*Gn*. 49.5–7). In *Joshua* 19.1–9 and *1 Chronicles* 4.24–32, the territory of Simeon overlaps the southwestern limits of Judah. When this area was overrun by Shishak I (c.924 BCE), some of the tribe might have been taken into Egyptian captivity. Members of the tribe were counted in the census taken by King Hezekiah (*1 Chr*. 4.41). Some of their number moved eastward to Seir (*1 Chr*. 4.42). The heroine of the *Book of Judith* and her husband's family, living in Jibleam near the Dothan valley and Jenin, are given Simeonite ancestry.

• Yohanan Aharoni, *The Land of the Bible: A Historical Geography* (Philadelphia, 1979). Jehoshua M. Grintz, *Sefer Yehudit* (Jerusalem, 1957), pp. 29ff. Ephraim A. Speiser, *Genesis*, The Anchor Bible (Garden City, N.Y., 1964). —AARON DEMSKY

SIMḤAH BEN SHEMU'EL OF VITRY (died 1105), French scholar; pupil of *Rashi. Simḥah ben Shemu'el compiled the *Maḥazor Vitry*, which, in its complete version, is an encyclopedic work including Midrashic excerpts, *responsa*, a commentary on *Avot*, a treatise on the calendar, and the complete annual cycle of prayers, together with a codification of laws related to the liturgy and the synagogue service. *Maḥazor Vitry* reflects the ancient French rite, which is closely related to the more widespread German (Ashkenazi) rite, and has been a valuable sourcebook for students of liturgy and *piyyut*. It was published by Shimʿon Hurwitz in 1893.

• Simha Emanuel, "Le-ʿInyano shel Maḥzor Vitry," *Alei Sefer* 12 (1986): 129–130. Stefan C. Reif, *Judaism and Hebrew Prayer: New Perspectives on Jewish Liturgical History* (Cambridge, 1993).

SIMḤAH BUNEM OF PRZYSUCHA (1765–1827), Hasidic master. He was the successor of Yaʿaqov Yitsḥaq, the "Holy Jew," who founded the Przysucha school of Hasidism in Poland. In his youth, he received a Talmudic education at the *yeshivot* of Mattersdorf and Nikolsburg. He later came under the influence of Hasidism in Poland through associations with Yisra'el of Kozienice, Mosheh Leib of Sasov, and David of Lelów. However, it was while at the court of Yaʿaqov Yitsḥaq, the Seer of Lublin, that he met his master, the "Holy Jew." His early experience was unusually worldly for a Hasidic master. He shunned Hasidic dress, indulged in secular entertainments, and was a licensed pharmacist. This early disregard for Hasidic convention would later color his teachings as a *rebbi*. After the death of his master in 1814, most of the Przysucha Ḥasidim chose Simḥah Bunem as successor. He continued his teacher's highly revolutionary approach, downplaying mystical sources and emphasizing study of the Talmud and the works of Yehudah Liva' ben Betsal'el of Prague (Maharal). His fundamental concern was for an uncompromisingly sincere, inner spiritual development and the eradication of all vestiges of conceit. This manifested in his disciples' efforts to conceal their spiritual accomplishments and virtues, sometimes to the extreme of feigning boorishness. His principal disciples included Menaḥem Mendel of Kotsk, Yitsḥaq Me'ir of Gora Kalwaria (Ger), Mordekhai Yosef of Izbica, and Ḥanokh of Aleksandrów. His *Qol Simḥah* was published in Bene Beraq in 1987.

• Martin Buber, *Tales of the Hasidim* (New York, 1947). Morris M. Faierstein, *All Is in the Hands of Heaven: The Teachings of Rabbi Mordecai Leiner of Izbica* (New York, 1989). —MILES KRASSEN

SIMḤAT BEIT HA-SHO'EVAH (שִׂמְחַת בֵּית הַשּׁוֹאֵבָה), the ceremony of the water *libation that took place in the Temple amid great popular rejoicing on the last six days of the festival of *Sukkot (except on the eve of the Sabbath and the eve of *Shemini ʿAtseret). Prayers were offered for rain during the forthcoming winter, and huge bonfires were lit in the outer court of the Temple and by every household (*Suk.* 51a) so that the whole of Jerusalem was ablaze with light. The men danced and sang to the accompaniment of Levitical musicians, and even the leading sages took part in the public rejoicing. The cryptic reference in *Isaiah* 12.3 ("you shall joyfully draw water from the fountains of salvation") has been taken as indicating the ancient origin of the celebration. The *Pharisees considered it a Mosaic tradition, but this view was opposed by the *Sadducees. The popularity of the feast is reflected in the statement that whoever had not seen it did not know the meaning of joy (*Suk.* 53a). When the Sadducean king Alexander Yannai contemptuously threw the water on his feet, he was pelted with *etrogim* by the outraged crowd at the Temple (*Suk.* 34a). The rite ceased with the Temple's destruction.

• Menahem Zvi Fuks, "Simḥat Beit ha-Sho'evah," *Tarbiz* 55 (1986): 173–216. Solomon Zeitlin, *Studies in the Early History of Judaism* (New York, 1973), pp. 176–182.

SIMḤAT TORAH (שִׂמְחַת תּוֹרָה; rejoicing of the Torah), name given in the Diaspora to the second day of *Shemini ʿAtseret (see YOM TOV SHENI SHEL GALUYYOT); in Israel, it is an additional name of the latter festival. Simḥat Torah is an outstanding example of a comparatively late custom becoming entrenched so firmly in the affections of the people that it came to rank as a major celebration. The Talmud knows nothing of it; during the geonic period there are only the vaguest intimations of this day having any special character. The name, Simḥat Torah, is found first in post-geonic literature and in the Zohar. Its emergence followed the abolition of the Palestinian custom of completing the synagogal cycle of Pentateuch reading every three years (*Meg.* 29b) and the universal adoption of the Babylonian custom of finishing the reading of the Torah each year. In the fourteenth century, Yaʿaqov ben Asher codified the custom of immediately recommencing the reading of the Torah after its completion on Simḥat Torah "in order that Satan shall have no opportunity of accusing the Jews of having finished with the Torah." In the sixteenth century, Mosheh Isserles mentioned the Ashkenazi customs of taking all the scrolls out of the ark and making seven circuits of the synagogue with them on the analogy of the seven circuits (see HAQQAFOT) with the four species on Hoshʿana' Rabbah; of calling up an indefinite number of worshipers to the reading of the Torah; of calling children up to the reading in a group; and of celebrating the occasion with feasting. Other customs include reading from the Torah, on Simḥat Torah night, at whatever point at which the scroll is opened, calling up adults to the Torah in groups, and having children join the circuits with special Simḥat Torah flags. Later came the custom of appointing a **ḥatan Torah* and *ḥatan Be-Re'shit* for the honor of reading the concluding and the beginning portions of the Pentateuch respectively. In recent years among non-Orthodox congregations, women, in addition to being called up for Torah readings, have been included in this custom, as *kallat Torah* and *kallah Be-Re'shit*. All these customs have now become "statutory law," and the celebrations are accompanied by singing, dancing, and merrymaking in the synagogue. The focal point of this holiday is the synagogue, rather than the home. The *haqqafot* and accompanying celebration is observed both at the evening service and again the following morning. In Israel, it has become the custom to have a further *haqqafot* on the evening following Simḥat Torah, often held outdoors with musical accompaniment. In the former Soviet Union, beginning in the 1960s, Jews evolved the custom of gathering together at synagogues on Simḥat Torah as an open expression of their Jewish identity.

• Herbert C. Dobrinsky, *A Treasury of Sephardic Laws and Customs* (Hoboken, N.J., and New York, 1986), contains extensive bibliography. Stephen J. Einstein and Lydia Kukoff, *Every Person's Guide to Judaism* (New York, 1989). Isaac N. Fabricant, *A Guide to Succoth* (London, 1958). Philip Goodman, ed., *A Sukkot and Simhat Torah Anthology* (Philadelphia, 1973), includes extensive bibliography. Isaac Klein, *A Guide to Jewish Religious Practice*, 2d ed. (New York, 1992), pp. 155–173. Peter Knobel, ed., *Gates of the Seasons: A Guide to the Jewish Year* (New York, 1983). Hayim Shoys, *The Jewish Festivals: From Their Beginnings to Our Own Day*, translated by Samuel Jaffe (Cincinnati, 1938). Arthur Waskow, *Seasons of Our Joy: A Modern Guide to the Jewish Holidays* (Boston, 1990).

SIN, any departure from the right path enjoined on man by God; in more formally legal terms, any transgression of the divine commandments as stipulated in covenantal law. In Biblical Hebrew the most frequently used term for sin is *ḥet'* (miss the mark). A general term for sin in Rabbinic Hebrew is *'averah* (crossing over [the line of right conduct]). *'Averot*, like *mitsvot*, are divided into two main classes: those committed by man against his fellow man, and those committed by man against God. Only for the latter is *Yom Kippur effective; the former are not atoned for (see ATONEMENT) "until his fellow be appeased" (*Yoma'* 85b). The three cardinal *'averot* are the shedding of innocent blood, adultery, and idolatry—rather than transgress these, a man must sacrifice his life; all other *'averot* may be transgressed if human life is at stake (*San*. 74a). In Jewish law, a man may not engage another person to commit a transgression on his behalf (*San*. 42b). Jewish moralists generally assume that *'averot* are committed not because of inherent wickedness but on account of spiritual lethargy and lack of awareness. A popular saying is that one transgression generates another (*Avot* 4.2).

In addition to the eloquent imagery of the expressions "transgression" and "departing from the way," biblical, Talmudic, and liturgical literature employ a great number of terms to signify and categorize sin. The most important of these are *ḥet'*, *'avon*, and *pesha'* (cf. the high priest's confession of sin in behalf of the people [*Lv*. 16.21])—usually interpreted as unwillful sin, knowledgeable sin, and rebellious sin. The rabbis distinguish between additional categories of sin; for example, lighter and more serious sins (according to the punishment decreed by biblical law). However, a man should "not consider the gravity or lightness of the sin, but the greatness of him who has given the commandment." Though rabbinic (as distinct from kabbalistic) theology has no formal doctrine of original sin, it is assumed that no man is completely free of sin (*1 Kgs*. 8.46). No sin is unpardonable, however, since "man's power to sin cannot be greater than God's power to forgive" (Yosef *Albo). Medieval ascetic manuals gave detailed penitential prescriptions for specific sins, and some of these go to extreme lengths in prescribing fasts and ascetic exercises to atone for sins. See also YETSER HA-RA' AND YETSER HA-TOV.

• David Noel Freedman, "The Nine Commandments: The Secret Progress of Israel's Sins," *Bible Review* 5.6 (1989): 28–37, 42. Reuven Hammer, "The Biblical Perception of the Origin of Evil," *Judaism* 39 (1990): 318–325. Israel Knohl, "The Sin Offering Law in the 'Holiness School' (Numbers 15.22–31)," in *Priesthood and Cult in Ancient Israel*, edited by Gary A. Anderson (Sheffield, Eng., 1991), pp. 192–203. Jacob Milgrom, "The 'Hatta't': A Rite of Passage?," *Revue biblique* 98 (1991): 120–124. Ernest Neufeld, "On the Trail of Original Sin," *Midstream* 38 (1992): 29–31. Karel van der Toorn, *Sin and Sanction in Israel and Mesopotamia: A Comparative Study* (Assen/Maastricht, 1985). Michael Wyschogrod, "Sin and Atonement in Judaism," in *The Human Condition in the Jewish and Christian Traditions*, edited by Frederick E. Greenspahn (Hoboken, N.J., 1986), pp. 103–128.

SINAI, MOUNT, mountain located in the Sinai Peninsula, variously called Sinai (e.g., *Ex*. 19.11), Horeb (e.g., *Dt*. 4.10), or simply "the mountain of the Lord" (e.g., *Nm*. 10.33) or "the mountain of God" (*Ex*. 18.5). In biblical tradition, Moses first encountered God there at the *burning bush (*Ex*. 3), having chanced upon the mountain upon which God was residing. He was told that after leaving Egypt, the Israelites would worship God at the same mountain. The Israelites encamped at Sinai shortly after the Exodus (*Ex*. 19.1), remaining there for just under a year (*Nm*. 10.11). Their stay at Sinai had two interconnected purposes: the *giving of the Torah and the building of the portable *Tabernacle, which accompanied them on the journey through the wilderness. Once they left Sinai, however, the site was virtually forgotten. It never became a cultic or commemorative location. God's presence was said to have come from Sinai (*Dt*. 33.2) to abide among the Israelites and not to continue to reside there. Only one other biblical story refers to Horeb: the account of Elijah's flight from King Ahab (*1 Kgs*. 19.8). Several locations have been proffered as the exact site of Mount Sinai. The most popular choice is Gebel Musa, near Saint Catherine's Monastery in the southern Sinai desert. However, this identification is very late, stemming from Byzantine monks in the fourth century, and there is no evidence to support it. The geographic location of Mount Sinai played no role in Jewish consciousness, and no attempt was made to establish a holy site there, although in Jewish thought, Sinai is one of two sacred mountains (the other being Mount Zion/Mount *Moriah). See also HALAKHAH LE-MOSHEH MI-SINAI; MI-SINAI.

• Thomas B. Dozeman, *God on the Mountain: A Study of Redaction, Theology, and Canon in Exodus 19–24*, Monograph Series (Society of Biblical Literature), no. 37 (Atlanta, 1989). Jŏn Douglas Levenson, *Sinai and Zion* (San Francisco, 1987). R.W.L. Moberly, *At the Mountain of God: Story and Theology in Exodus 32–34*, Journal for the Study of the Old Testament, Supplement Series 22 (Sheffield, Eng., 1983).

—BARUCH J. SCHWARTZ

SIN OFFERING. See PURIFICATION OFFERING.

SIRACH, WISDOM OF. See WISDOM OF BEN SIRA.

SIRKES, YO'EL BEN SHEMU'EL (c.1561–1640), Polish Talmudist and legal commentator; known as Baḥ from the initials of his best-known work, *Bayit Ḥadash*. Born in Lublin, Sirkes primarily served the Jewish communities in Brest Litovsk, and, after 1619, in Kraków, where he remained until his death. His principal disciples include his son-in-law, *David ben Shemu'el ha-Levi (Taz), Menaḥem Mendel Krochmal, and Gershon Ashkenazi.

Sirkes's writings include glosses on the Talmud, several hundred *responsa*, and *Meshiv Nefesh* (Koretz,

1787), a commentary on the *Book of Ruth*; his *Bayit Ḥadash* (Kraków 1631–1639) is a comprehensive commentary on Yaʿaqov ben Asher's *Arbaʿah Turim* (found in standard editions of that work) analyzing Talmudic sources and post-Talmudic legal interpretations. On a number of occasions, Sirkes rejected the legal rulings of Yosef *Karo's commentary *Beit Yosef* and declared that "those who determine laws according to the *Shulḥan ʿArukh* [Karo's legal code] are not teaching according to *halakhah*" (*Bayit Ḥadash*, no. 80). Sirkes rendered several controversial legal decisions, including permitting the consumption of **ḥadash* (grain of the new harvest, grown by non-Jews in the Diaspora) and the selling of *ḥamets* prior to Pesaḥ without removing it from the premises. He also sanctioned rabbis' acceptance of remuneration for their services. His *responsa* vividly reflect Jewish communal, social, political, and economic life in seventeenth-century Lithuania and Poland; several of his *responsa* portraying tensions in relationships between Jews and gentiles were censored, the remainder were published after his death as *She'elot u-Teshuvot ha-Bayit ha-Ḥadash* (Frankfurt, 1697) and *She'elot u-Teshuvot ha-Bayit ha-Ḥadash ha-Ḥadashot* (Koretz, 1785).

• Haim Hillel Ben-Sasson, *Hagut ve-Hanhagah* (Jerusalem, 1959), pp. 211–221 and *passim*. Elijah Judah Schochet, *Rabbi Joel Sirkes: His Life, Works, and Themes* (Jerusalem, 1971). —ELIJAH J. SCHOCHET

SITRA' AḤRA' (סִטְרָא אַחֲרָא; the other [i.e., left] side), kabbalistic term used in the Zohar and subsequent literature to designate the realms of the powers of evil. The author of the Zohar coined this term following the structure of the divine worlds described in *Ma'amar ʿal ha-'Atsilut ha-Sema'lit* (Treatise on the Emanations of the Left) by R. Yitsḥaq ben Yaʿakov of Castile in the second half of the thirteenth century. Rabbi Yitsḥaq was the first kabbalist to suggest that the powers of evil existed as a countersystem to the divine emanations; Samael and Lilith represented its male and female elements, respectively. In the Zohar this notion was developed into a full-blown demonic mythology in which the *sitra' aḥra'* attempts, sometimes successfully, to captivate the *Shekhinah and separate her from her husband, the *sitra' di-qedusha'* (the side of holiness, i.e., the right side). Later *sitra' aḥra'* was used to indicate any satanic or evil entity. In the Zohar it is the tree of death, because in its form of the primeval serpent in the garden of Eden, it succeeded in turning the tree of knowledge into a tree of death.

• Joseph Dan and Ronald Kiener, *The Early Kabbalah* (New York, 1986), pp. 165–182. Gershom Gerhard Scholem, *Kabbalah*, Library of Jewish Knowledge (New York, 1974). Isaiah Tishby, *The Wisdom of the Zohar*, vol. 2 (Oxford, 1989). —JOSEPH DAN

SIVAN (סִיוָן), ninth month of the civil year, third month of the religious year; its zodiac sign is Gemini. The word *sivan*, of Akkadian/Babylonian origin, is mentioned in the Bible (*Est.* 8.9). Sivan always has thirty days. *Shavuʿot, which marks the anniversary of the giving of the Torah (and also the traditional date of the death of King David), falls on 6 and 7 Sivan (in Erets Yisra'el on 6 Sivan). In addition, 3, 4, and 5 Sivan are known as Sheloshet Yemei Hagbalah, (Three Days of Restriction; *Ex.* 19.10–15), when, according to the Bible, the Israelites undertook strict physical and spiritual preparations for the Revelation at Mount Sinai on 6 Sivan. With the new moon of Sivan, the days of semimourning of the *ʿOmer period come to an end (Sephardim terminate the mourning period much earlier, on Lag ba-ʿOmer). According to **Megillat Taʿanit*, God performed miracles for the Jews during the Hasmonean period on 15, 16, and 25 Sivan, and fasting was therefore forbidden on those days. In eastern Europe a fast was observed on 20 Sivan in commemoration of the Chmielnicki massacres of 1648 and 1649.

• Nathan Bushwick, *Understanding the Jewish Calendar* (New York, 1989). George Zinberg, *Jewish Calendar Mystery Dispelled* (New York, 1963). —CHAIM PEARL

613 PRECEPTS. See COMMANDMENTS, 613.

SIYYUM (סִיּוּם; end), celebration held at the conclusion of the study of a tractate of the Talmud. The occasion is considered a Seʿudat Mitsvah (see SEʿUDAH) and is usually accompanied by a *hadran*, a halakhic discourse relating to the tractate just studied. Individuals or study groups about to finish a tractate usually leave the last few lines for completion at the *siyyum*. These are followed by the recital of a special *Qaddish and a prayer expressing the hope that the person completing this tractate will be granted the opportunity to continue to study other tractates and that his offspring will likewise remain committed to the study of Torah. This prayer also expresses the hope that the Talmudic authorities mentioned in the tractate will serve as positive referees before the divine court at the judgment after death. The *hadran* itself is a special genre of homily that seeks to relate the conclusion of one tractate to the following one to be learned. It is followed by a brief reading of the first few lines of the next tractate to be studied. It is customary to arrange for a *siyyum* to be held on 14 Nisan (*Taʿanit Bekhorim) so as to exempt the participating firstborn from the obligation of fasting. Another type of *siyyum* is held upon the completion of the writing of a scroll of the Torah. Each man present writes one of the final letters (generally a letter contained in his own name), and the ceremony is followed by a festive celebration.

SKEPTICISM. See AGNOSTICISM.

SLANDER. The verse "You shall not take up a false report" (*Ex.* 23.1) forbids one from either originating a calumny or encouraging its propagation. Injury to another person's reputation caused by the spreading of falsehood, slander, or careless gossip is often mentioned in the Bible ("you shall not curse the deaf" [*Lv.* 19.14] is interpreted by the rabbis to apply to all kinds of slander about those absent or dead) and severely denounced by the rabbis. The Talmud says, "Calumny kills three—the slanderer himself, the one who listens, and the person spoken of." In certain cases, rabbinic law provides for monetary fines or even excommunication until the slander is retracted. Strictly speaking, the term often used for slander, *lashon ha-ra'* (evil tongue), applies specifically to talebearing (i.e., where the information transmitted is true), whereas the term *motsi' shem ra'* (causing a bad name) applies to one who tells untruths about another. Both are totally forbidden by Jewish law, even if the tellers had no intention of harming the people about whom they spoke. Jewish law permits—even requires—one, under scrupulously defined limits, to relate disparaging material about another if failure to do so can cause damage to a third party, such as when a person is consulted about the character of an individual who is being considered as a potential marriage or business partner.

• Israel Meir ha-Kohen, *Sefer Ḥafets Ḥayyim* (Vilna, 1873; repr. Brooklyn, N.Y., 1993). Israel Meir ha-Kohen, *Sefer Shemirat ha-Lashon* (Jerusalem, 1965). Zelig Pliskin, *Guard Your Tongue* (Jerusalem, 1975). Zelig Pliskin, *The Power of Words* (Brooklyn, N.Y., 1988). –SHMUEL HIMELSTEIN

SLAUGHTER, RITUAL. See RITUAL SLAUGHTER.

SLAVERY. The institution of slavery, whereby a person forfeits individual liberty and becomes bonded to an owner, is accepted by the Bible and Talmud as a normal feature of the economic and social system. Both the Bible and Talmud endeavored, however, to ensure humane and considerate treatment of slaves. There was a considerable difference between the status of the Hebrew male slave and the non-Hebrew (Canaanite) male slave (cf. *Gn*. 9.25). The Hebrew could become a slave only through being sold by the *beit din* in payment of debt (*Ex*. 21) or by voluntarily selling himself on account of poverty (*Lv*. 25.39). He had to be released after six years of service or before that if he paid off the outstanding balance of his debt. Upon his release, he was given a generous gift (*Dt*. 15.13–15). However, if he so chose, his ear would be pierced with an awl (*Ex*. 21.5–7), and he would remain a slave until the jubilee year (see YOVEL), when all slaves were freed. A Jew could not be sold as a slave to a non-Jew. Special regulations applied to the Hebrew female slave (*Ex*. 21.7–11). So liberal was the interpretation of the injunction not to treat the slave harshly that the Talmud declares, "One who acquires a slave acquires a master" (*Qid*. 20a).

The position with regard to the Canaanite bondman was very different. He was regarded as the property of his master and could be bequeathed to his master's heirs together with the other possessions of the legator (*Lv*. 25.46). He could be freed in return for payment, if his master wrote a document freeing him, or as a consequence of any ill-treatment resulting in the loss of an eye or a tooth (*Ex*. 21.26–27). If the slave was circumcised, he was regarded as a member of the community and bound to perform certain religious duties. In addition, if he became a full Jew, every encouragement was given for his manumission. The Bible bases its compassionate legislation for slaves on the recollection of the Israelite slavery in Egypt (*Dt*. 15.15).

• Gregory Chirichigno, *Debt-slavery in Israel and the Ancient Near East*, Journal for the Study of the Old Testament, Supplement Series 141 (Sheffield, Eng., 1993). Paul V. M. Flesher, *Oxen, Women, or Citizens? Slaves in the System of the Mishnah*, Brown Judaic Studies, no. 143 (Atlanta, 1988). Zadoc Kahn, *Ha-'Avdut 'al pi ha-Torah veha-Talmud* (Kraków, 1892). Isaac Mendelsohn, *Slavery in the Ancient Near East* (New York, 1949; repr. Westport, Conn., 1978). Ephraim E. Urbach, *The Laws Regarding Slavery* (New York, 1979).

SLOBODKA, suburb of Kovno (Kaunas) in Lithuania and seat of a famous *yeshivah*. In 1892 the *Volozhin Yeshivah was closed by Russian authorities for failing to introduce secular studies; its pupils flocked to the Slobodka Yeshivah, the enrollment of which by 1897 numbered some two hundred students. Its curriculum was influenced by the *Musar movement. After World War I, the *yeshivah* was divided into three sections based upon student age, since younger students often felt inferior in the presence of older, more learned students. In 1925 some of the *yeshivah*'s students emigrated to Palestine and established a branch of the *yeshivah* in Hebron. After the 1929 Arab riots, the *yeshivah* moved to Jerusalem, where it was called the Hebron Yeshivah. It continues to carry on the traditions of Slobodka. Most of the students in the original Slobodka Yeshivah perished at the hands of the Nazis in 1941. A Slobodka Yeshivah has also been established in Bene Beraq, Israel.

–SHMUEL HIMELSTEIN

SLONIK, BINYAMIN AHARON (c.1550–1619), eastern European Talmudist and rabbi. A disciple of Natan Nata' Spiro, Shelomoh *Luria, and Mosheh *Isserles and an associate of Yehoshu'a ben Aleksander ha-Kohen *Falk, Mordekhai ben Avraham *Jaffe, and *Me'ir ben Gedalyah of Lublin, Slonik was a fine stylist and lucid writer. He wrote a volume of 112 *responsa*, *Masat Binyamin* (Kraków, 1633), and composed a guide for women, *Seder Mitsvot Nashim, Eyn Schön Frauenbuechlein* (Kraków, 1577), detailing the three halakhic areas of greatest concern for women: the laws of menstruation, the separation of *ḥallah*, and the kindling of the Sabbath lights. The latter volume, in Yiddish, proved to be exceedingly popular; it was reprinted three times during Slonik's lifetime and was translated into Italian (Padua, 1625).

Slonik's *responsa* reflect the turbulence of his era. A number of cases deal with the killing of Jewish merchants en route to trade and the problems of *'*agunot* (women whose husbands were missing but whose deaths have not been verified). Slonik sought to free *'agunot* so that they might remarry.

Little is known of Slonik's rabbinic tenure. In his younger years he resided in Kraków and later served as rabbi in Silesia and Podhajce; in his later years he described himself as ailing, nearly blind, and destitute.

• Nisson E. Shulman, *Authority and Community: Polish Jewry in the Sixteenth Century* (Hoboken, N.J., 1986). –ELIJAH J. SCHOCHET

SOCIAL JUSTICE. The concept of social justice is a major component of biblical *ethics, in both Mosaic legislation and prophetic pronouncements, and has characterized Jewish thinking through the ages. The biblical ideal of social justice has also deeply influenced the ideas and behavior of Western civilization. From its earliest sources in the Pentateuch, the law takes into account the needs of the less fortunate in society. The injunction to care for the "stranger, the orphan, and the widow" appears seventeen times in the Bible, eleven of these in the Torah. Provision is made in biblical law for the poor to have access to gleanings, to grain forgotten in the field, and to a corner of each field (see AGRARIAN LAWS). Furthermore, no land could be sold in perpetuity, and all land bought had to be returned to its original family (as determined in the original land division by tribe and clan after the Israelite occupation of Canaan) in the *yovel (jubilee) year. In an agricultural society, where land was the key to self-sufficiency, this provision served to prevent the development of a permanent indentured class. No Jew could be sold into slavery forever, and one who had sold himself into slavery had to be freed automatically in the jubilee year. Furthermore, in order to prevent people from sinking permanently into the morass of debt, the Torah legislates that each *shemittah year all debts be canceled. The Torah cautions lenders that failure to lend money for fear that it might not be repaid "will be a sin to you" (*Dt.* 15.9). The prophets preached social justice as a natural and logical complement to ritual observance (see, for example, *Is.* 1.13–14). The failure to pay wages on time (*Lv.* 19.13) is a biblical offense (see LABOR). An employer does not have the right to force workers to put in a workday that is longer than customary for that locale (*B. M.* 7.1). Furthermore, workers have the right at any time to resign from their jobs—no person save a slave can be forced to work unwillingly—and the most they can be liable for is any damages their employer might sustain. The sages went beyond the letter of the law in order to secure justice for the weak, and rabbinic literature is replete with instances of such legislation and practice. See also JUSTICE.

• Simon Federbusch, *The Jewish Concept of Labor* (New York, 1956). Richard G. Hirsch, *The Way of the Upright: A Jewish View of Economic Justice* (New York, 1973). Moshe Prager, ed., *Le'or ha-Netsakh: Be'ayot ha-Yahadut bi-Zemanenu ba-'Aspaklaryat ha-Maḥashavah ha-Datit* (New York, 1962), section 4.

—SHMUEL HIMELSTEIN

SOFER (סוֹפֵר; scribe), a term used in the Bible to signify a high administrative official; in the early Second Temple period, it came to mean a literate man engaged in the interpretation of the Torah and the transmission of the *oral law. *Soferim* are generally considered the precursors to the *Pharisees and the initiators of the Jewish, as distinct from the Israelite, period of history. From their ranks came the Men of the Keneset ha-Gedolah, who were active in the two centuries after *Ezra (known as Ezra the Scribe). Information as to their activities is meager, but there are many Talmudic references to *divrei soferim* (words of the scribes, i.e., ancient post-biblical regulations), *diqduqei soferim* (legal minutiae), and *taqqanot soferim* (enactments not derived from the Torah). Many of their ordinances were said to have formed a fence around the Law (see SEYAG LA-TORAH). The Talmud ascribes to them regulations relating to prayer, *tefillin*, *tsitsit*, ritual slaughter, the blowing of the shofar, the institution of Ḥanukkah and Purim, and the introduction of eighteen emendations into the biblical text (see TIQQUN SOFERIM). Subsequently the term underwent another change of meaning to denote one who taught the Bible to children (in later Talmudic usage, the term *local scribe* is used for elementary teacher). The sages and rabbis of the tannaitic period were never called scribes. In the New Testament, the words *scribes* and *Pharisees* are used pejoratively to connote hypocrisy. Eventually the meaning of the term was limited to a penman (known as a **sofer setam*) occupied in the writing of Torah scrolls, *mezuzot*, and *tefillin*, as well as documents that are valid only if written by hand, such as bills of divorce. Minor tractate **Soferim*, appended to the Talmud Bavli, contains the meticulous laws that such scribes have to observe.

• Morris Lutzki, "The History and Principles of the Hebrew Professional Scribes (Soferim)," Ph.D. disseration, Oxford University, 1935. Malachi Martin, *The Scribal Character of the Dead Sea Scrolls*, 2 vols. (Louvain, 1958). *Of Scribes and Scrolls: Studies on the Hebrew Bible, Intertestamental Judaism, and Christian Origins: Presented to John Strugnell on the Occasion of His Sixtieth Birthday* (Lanham, Md., 1990). Shmuel Safrai, ed., *The Literature of the Sages*, pt. 1, *Oral Tora, Halakha, Mishna, Tosefta, Talmud, External Tractates* (Van Gorcum, 1987), pp. 144–153. Anthony J. Saldarini, *Pharisees, Scribes and Sadducees in Palestinian Society* (Wilmington, Del., 1988).

SOFER FAMILY, leading Orthodox family.

Mosheh Sofer (1762–1839), or the Ḥatam Sofer, as he is known in Orthodox circles, was the preeminent rabbinical figure in Hungary in the first half of the nineteenth century. His ideology, embodied in the slogan *ḥadash asur min ha-Torah* (all that is new is biblically forbidden), inspired the antimodernist, separationist Orthodoxy that developed there. Born in Frankfurt, at age nineteen he followed his teacher R. Natan Adler to Moravia. Twelve years later he began his formal rabbinic career in the town of Dresnitz (Moravia). In 1806 he was appointed to the prestigious post of rabbi of Pressburg (Bratislava). Sofer was an innovative scholar and educator. His reputation as a skillful halakhist provided the backing for the campaign against Emancipation, Haskalah, and the Reform movement. Through his legal rulings, he sought to enhance the sanctity of all aspects of traditional life by proving its halakhic authenticity. Moreover, the *yeshivah* that he founded was considered the largest in the world at the time and served as a training ground for communal rabbis who popularized the ideas of their teacher. Sofer's legacy as a halakhist and ideologue is found in his posthumously published *responsa* (7 vols. [1855–1912]) and sermons (2 vols. [1829]). Among the issues discussed in these volumes is his strong attachment to Erets Yisra'el. In 1812 Sofer married the daughter of R. ʿAqiva' *Eger, the famed Talmudist and rabbi of Posen. Two of their sons made particular marks.

Avraham Shemu'el Binyamin Wolf Sofer (1815–1871), the oldest son of Mosheh, inherited the Pressburg rabbinic post as well as the directorship of the *yeshivah*. Although only twenty-four years old at the time of his father's death, he established himself as a scholar and leader of the Orthodox community. His approach to issues such as secular education was more pragmatic and less doctrinaire than his father's. Yet, he ultimately confirmed his identification with his father's ideology through his guidance of the Orthodox community in the fierce internal battles that erupted during the Hungarian Jewish Congress of 1869 and 1870. His erudition and his keen awareness of the changes that Jewish society was undergoing are reflected in the *responsa* collection *Ketav Sofer* (1873–1938).

Shim'on Sofer (1820–1883), Mosheh Sofer's second son, was rabbi of Kraków, where he fought with the modernists who had made inroads into this Hasidic stronghold. He gained membership in the parliament in Vienna in 1878, a position he sought in order to advance the cause of tradition. The descendants of Mosheh Sofer continued to lead the Pressburg community and *yeshivah* until World War II. After the war, the *yeshivah* was reestablished in Jerusalem under the guidance of Mosheh's great-grandson, 'Aqiva' Sofer (1878–1959).

• **General References on the Sofer Family:** Armin H. Friedman, "Major Aspects of Yeshivah Education in Hungary, 1848–1948, with Special Emphasis on the Role of the Yeshivah of Pressburg," Ph.D. dissertation, Yeshiva University, 1971. Samuel Heilman, "The Many Faces of Orthodoxy (part I)," *Modern Judaism* 2 (1982): 23–52. Jacob Katz, "Conservatives in a Quandry," in *Out of the Ghetto: The Social Background of Jewish Emancipation, 1770–1870* (Cambridge, Mass., 1973), pp. 142–160. Joseph H. Schreiber, *Toledot Soferim: A Biography of Joachim Schreiber (R. Chajim Sofer) from Pressburg, Chief-Rabbi of Budapest and His Family* (n.p., 1965). Shelomoh Sofer, *Sefer Ha-Ḥut ha-Meshullash* (Mukachevo, 1893). **Mosheh Sofer:** S. Ehrmann, "Hatam Sofer," in *Jewish Leaders*, edited by Leo Jung (New York, 1953). J. Katz, "Contributions Towards a Biography of the Hatam Sofer," in *From East and West: Jews in a Changing Europe, 1750–1870*, edited by Frances Malino and David Sorkin (Oxford, 1990), pp. 223–266. Leon Katz, *Ha-Ḥatam Sofer: Rabbi Mosheh Sofer Ḥayyav vi-Yetsirato* (Jerusalem, 1959). M. Samet, "Ma'avaqo shel ha-Ḥatam Sofer ba-Ḥadshanim," in *Yehudei Hungaryah*, edited by Moshe E. Gonda et al. (Tel Aviv, 1980), pp. 92–103. **Shim'on Sofer:** Isaac Kunstadt, *Trauerrede sr. Hochwurden R. Simon Schreiber, Oberrabbiner zu Krakau* (Grosswardein, 1883). Mordechai Rubinstein, *Aryeh Sofer* (Kraków, 1884), funeral sermon. Isaac Loeb Sofer, *Shem mi-Shim'on: Derush Hesped 'al ha-Rav Shim'on Sofer* (Drogobych, 1883).

—ADAM S. FERZIGER

SOFERIM, minor tractate, printed in standard editions of the Talmud Bavli at the end of tractate *'Avodah Zarah*, dealing with the laws pertaining to the writing and public reading of scriptural texts. *Soferim* was probably compiled during the geonic period, even though some of its material appears to date from an earlier time. For the most part, *Soferim* reflects Palestinian practices and is based largely on the Talmud Yerushalmi; however, since there are several passages that would seem to indicate Babylonian provenance, not all scholars accept the prevailing opinion that *Soferim* was composed in Erets Yisra'el. *Soferim* served as an important source for many liturgical customs and practices. It was edited by Michael Higger (Jerusalem, 1970). —AVRAHAM WALFISH

SOFER SETAM (סוֹפֵר סְתָ"ם; scribe of *stam* [an acronym for *sefarim* (Torah scrolls), *tefillin*, *mezuzot*]), one specially trained in the scribal arts. Jewish law requires that Torah (see SEFER TORAH), *tefillin*, and *mezuzot* parchments be written by hand, and there are numerous regulations concerning the shape of each letter and the writing of each word (enumerated in the minor Talmudic tractate *Soferim*). Scribes are supposed to be particularly God-fearing; a Torah scroll, the holiest of objects, written by a heretic, must be burned and cannot be used even if it is letter-perfect. So important is the position of the *sofer setam* (often simply referred to as *sofer*) that the Talmud (*San*. 17b) advises scholars not to live in a town that does not have a resident *sofer*. Yehoshu'a ben Levi reported that the Men of the Keneset ha-Gedolah fasted for twenty-four days, praying God not to allow *soferim* to become wealthy, for if they did, they might cease to practice their craft, indispensable to Jewish life.

• Ze'ev Grinvald, ed., *Tefillin u-Mezuzot ke-Hilkhatan* (Kefar Hasidim, Israel, 1989). Israel Meir, ha-Kohen, *Mishnas Sofrim: A Translation of the Mishna Berura Dealing with the Laws of Writing the Ashuris Script* (Monsey, N.Y., 1984).

—SHMUEL HIMELSTEIN

SOLOMON (Heb. Shelomoh; 10th cent. BCE), son of *David and Bath-sheba, third king of Israel. His forty-year reign was characterized by peace, prosperity, and international political and economic ties. He had relations with Sheba in southern Arabia (*1 Kgs*. 10) and with Tyre in Phoenicia (*1 Kgs*. 9.26–28). With Phoenician aid he built a naval fleet that reached distant Ophir (*1 Kgs*. 10.11–12), and, most significantly, over a seven-year period, he constructed the *Temple with cedars of Lebanon and the help of Phoenician craftsmen (*1 Kgs*. 6–7). Solomon also dedicated thirteen years to building his palace (*1 Kgs*. 7.1–12), fortified the three key cities of Hazor, Megiddo, and Gezer, and strengthened and modernized his army with the introduction of cavalry and chariots, for which he constructed extensive stables. Since he was so renowned for his wisdom (*1 Kgs*. 5.9–14; he was said to have written 3,000 proverbs and 1,000 songs), *Proverbs*, *Ecclesiastes*, and *Song of Songs* were attributed to his authorship. Resentment of Solomon's heavy taxation and multiple political marriages (700 wives and 300 concubines; *1 Kgs*. 11.3) led to the division of his kingdom after his death.

• John Bright, *A History of Israel*, 2d ed. (Philadelphia, 1975), pp. 206–224. John Gray, *I and II Kings* (Philadelphia, 1963), pp. 114–277. Gary N. Knoppers, *Two Nations Under God: The Deuteronomistic History of Solomon and the Dual Monarchies*, 2 vols. (Atlanta, 1993–1994). Eugene M. Maly, *The World of David and Solomon* (Englewood Cliffs, N.J., 1966).

—SHALOM PAUL

SOLOMON, PROVERBS OF. See PROVERBS, BOOK OF.

SOLOMON, PSALMS OF. See PSALMS OF SOLOMON.

SOLOMON, SONG OF. See SONG OF SONGS, BOOK OF.

SOLOMON, TEMPLE OF. See TEMPLE.

SOLOMON, TESTAMENT OF. See TESTAMENT OF SOLOMON.

SOLOMON, WISDOM OF. See WISDOM OF SOLOMON.

SOLOVEICHIK FAMILY, Lithuanian rabbinical family whose members have been among the leading Talmud scholars and heads of *yeshivot* since the mid-nineteenth century.

Yosef Baer Soloveichik of Volozhin (1820–1892), a direct descendant of R. Ḥayyim *Volozhiner, served as joint head of the Volozhin Yeshivah (1854–1865) together with R. Naftali Tsevi Yehudah *Berlin. Because of tensions between the two heads, R. Yosef Baer left the *yeshivah* to become rabbi of Slutsk (1865–1875). He left Slutsk in 1875, primarily as a result of communal conflicts, and in 1878 became the rabbi of Brest Litovsk (Brisk), where he died. An exceptionally sharp-witted individual, known more for his acumen than his erudition, R. Yosef Baer's published writings, entitled *Beit ha-Levi* (1863–1891), include Talmudic *novellae*, sermons, and a homiletical commentary on *Genesis* and *Exodus*. The latter work is noted for its skillful combination of topicality and homiletic creativity.

Ḥayyim Soloveichik (1853–1918), son of Yosef Baer, became a member of the faculty of the Volozhin Yeshivah in 1880, retaining his position until the forced closure of the *yeshivah* by the czarist government in 1892. After his father's death in the same year, he succeeded him as communal rabbi of Brisk. R. Ḥayyim was recognized as the leading Talmudist of his day, and he brought a new method of rigorous, highly abstract, conceptual analysis to the study of Talmud. An exceptionally influential teacher, many of R. Ḥayyim's students went on to become the leading *yeshivah* heads of the next generation, carrying his method with them. The popularity of this "Brisker method," according to some, was due to its encouragement of intellectual creativity on the part of students, to its modern flavor, and to the sense that the method could serve as a protection against the intellectual lure of secular enlightenment. As a communal rabbi, R. Ḥayyim was known for his care and concern for the poor and needy. He was a staunch opponent of all attempts to modernize Jewish life, whether that meant Zionism or introducing secular studies into the *yeshivot*. A perfectionist, he published nothing in his lifetime. His *novellae* on Maimonides, published by his sons in 1936, is viewed as one of the classics of twentieth century rabbinic literature and the finest exemplar of R. Ḥayyim's own method.

Mosheh Soloveichik (1876–1941), the eldest son of R. Ḥayyim, studied under his father and served first as rabbi of Rasseyn, a Lithuanian town near Kovno, and later as rabbi of Khislavichi in White Russia. After World War I, he headed the Department of Talmud of the recently founded Taḥkemoni Rabbinical Seminary in Warsaw. As a result of conflicts with the noted historian and head of Taḥkemoni's secular department, Me'ir Balaban, R. Mosheh left Taḥkemoni in 1929 to become the head of the Rabbi Isaac Elchanan Theological Seminary of New York's Yeshiva College. His lectures greatly raised the standard of Talmudic education in the American Orthodox community and helped spread his father's methodology within it. Some volumes of his Talmudic *novellae* have recently been published.

Yitsḥaq Ze'ev Soloveichik (1888–1962), the youngest son of R. Ḥayyim, also studied under his father, whom he succeeded as rabbi of Brisk. Rabbi Velvel, as he was popularly known, was viewed as his father's spiritual heir, and continued his father's tradition of Talmudic study as well as his tradition of opposition to secular studies and Zionism. He established a private *beit midrash* in Brisk, to which admission was eagerly sought by the finest *yeshivah* graduates in Europe. With the outbreak of war in 1939 he managed to escape from Europe and resettled in Jerusalem in 1941, where he established a private *kolel*, but refused to accept any public position. While he did not issue legal rulings, he did speak out in cases where he saw a danger to the foundations of faith. After the death, in 1953, of Avraham Yesha'yahu *Karelitz, the Ḥazon Ish, he was generally viewed as the leading rabbinic figure of the Ḥaredi community in Israel. His published writings and lecture notes further develop his father's Talmudic methodology and are studied widely. Several of R. Yitsḥaq Ze'ev's sons became noted heads of *yeshivot*.

Yosef Dov Soloveichik (1903–1993), the eldest son of R. Mosheh, was born in Pruzana, Belorussia. A child prodigy, Yosef Dov mastered his grandfather's "Brisker method" under the guidance of his father. At the same time, under the influence of his mother, he acquired a strong interest in secular education. He studied political science at the Free Polish University in 1924, and in 1926 went to the University of Berlin to study philosophy, receiving his doctorate in 1932 for a thesis on the epistemology and ontology of Hermann *Cohen. That same year he went to the United States, where he became rabbi in Boston, which remained his home. In the 1930s, R. Yosef Dov headed a private Talmudic institute for advanced students, but this was disbanded when, in 1941, he succeeded his father as the head of the Talmud faculty of the Rabbi Isaac Elchanan Theological Seminary; he also went on to teach Jewish philosophy at Yeshiva University's graduate school of Jewish studies. In the 1950s, R. Yosef Dov emerged as the leading rabbinic figure of American modern Orthodoxy, and became the honorary president of the Religious Council of Zionists of America and chairman of the *halakhah* commission of the Rabbinical Council of America. An outstanding teacher and a fine orator in both English and Yiddish, he lectured widely to the most varied audiences. Perhaps more than any other single individual, he molded the spiritual profile of the American Orthodox community in the last half of the twentieth century.

His unique authority stems from the fact that he was the only major halakhic scholar of modern times who also was a creative theologian and philosopher, having mastered the entire Western tradition of scientific and philosophic thought. His goal was an interaction of philosophy and *halakhah*. He sought to show how the *ish ha-halakhah*, "the man of *halakhah*" (a term he coined), combines the cognitive drive and this-worldly orientation of scientific man with the religious pathos and yearning for the divine presence of *homo religiosus*, how through the study and practice of *halakhah* the contradictions between rational consciousness and the revealed religion can be overcome, and how a combined halakhic-phenomenological analysis reveals that exteriority of deed and interiority of experience are built into the very fabric of such central commandments as prayer, repentance, mourning, and rejoicing on holidays. He used his great powers of poetic description, and of philosophic and halakhic analysis, to depict the life of *halakhah*, particularly as expressed in the central commandments of Torah study and repentance, as one of freedom, autonomy, intellectual creativity, and self-creation. At the same time, he highlighted the importance that the *halakhah* accords to submission to the inscrutable divine will, a submission which, he argued, is both cathartic and redemptive.

Soloveichik departed from the position of most *yeshivah* heads and from the tradition of his own family by affirming the value of secular studies and Western civilization and by urging that Orthodox Jews both participate in and contribute to that civilization. In a similar break, he became an adherent of and an eloquent spokesman for Religious Zionism, adopting a positive attitude to the State of Israel, despite the generally secular character of Israeli society. For Soloveichik, the establishment and flourishing of the state is God's great act of loving-kindness in our time, a reaffirmation of the divine covenant of fate, a particularist Jewish expression of the majesty and dignity of Western civilization. He also stated that faith in the ultimate redemption is dependent upon prior faith in the spiritual capabilities of the Jewish people.

His works include *Ish ha-Halakhah: Galui ve-Nistar* (1979); *Shiʿurim le-Zekher Abba' Mari* (1982–1985); *Halakhic Man* (1983); *The Halakhic Mind: An Essay on Jewish Tradition and Modern Thought* (1986); *The Lonely Man of Faith* (1992); and *On Repentance: In the Thought and Oral Discourses of Rabbi Joseph D. Soloveitchik* (1980).

• **Soloveichik family:** Shulamith Soloveitchik Meiselman, *The Soloveitchik Heritage: A Daughter's Memoir* (Hoboken, N.J., 1995). **Ḥayyim Soloveichik:** Norman Solomon, *The Analytic Movement: Hayyim Soloveitchik and His Circle* (Atlanta, 1993). **Yosef Dov Soloveichik:** Gerald Blidstein, "On the Jewish People in the Writings of Rabbi Joseph Soloveitchik," *Tradition* 24:3 (1989): 21–43. Lawrence Kaplan, "Rabbi Joseph Soloveitchik's Philosophy of Halakhah," *Jewish Law Annual* 7 (1987): 139–197. Mordechai Gafni, "The Writings of Rabbi Soloveitchik," *Daat* 31 (Summer, 1993): 105–115, includes a comprehensive bibliography. Allan Nadler, "Soloveitchik's Halakhic Man: Not a *Mithnagged*," *Modern Judaism* 13:2 (1993): 119–147. Pinḥas Peli, ed., *Be-Sod ha-Yaḥid veha-Yaḥad* (Jerusalem, 1976). Aviezer Ravitsky, "Rabbi J. B. Soloveitchik on Human Knowledge: Between Maimonidean and Neo-Kantian Philosophy," *Modern Judaism* 6.2 (1986): 157–188. Hershel Schachter, *Nefesh ha-Rav* (Jerusalem, 1994). David Singer and Moshe Sokol, "Joseph Soloveitchik: Lonely Man of Faith," *Modern Judaism* 23 (1982): 227–272.

—LAWRENCE J. KAPLAN

SONG OF ASCENSION. See DEGREES, SONG OF.

SONG OF MOSES. See MOSES, SONG OF.

SONG OF SONGS, BOOK OF (Heb. *Shir ha-Shirim*), also known as *Canticles* and as the *Song of Solomon*; fourth book in the Hagiographa section of the Bible, and first of the Five Scrolls. Its eight chapters consist of a series of lyric love songs and poetic dialogues and monologues. The two lovers give rapturous expression of their yearnings; their lavish praise of each other's physical beauty is expressed in language that is at times delicate and at other times frankly erotic. The beautifully simple descriptions of scenery are permeated with a love of nature and the land. From a literary standpoint the *Song of Songs* includes some of the most notable poetry in the Bible.

The work has much in common with other ancient Near Eastern love poetry, especially compositions from Egypt. As a result of its manifest secular character, its canonization was opposed by some. Its acceptance into the canon was effected only in the second century CE (see *Yad.* 3.5) on the basis of the allegorical interpretation of R. ʿAqiva', who declared that "All the writings are holy, but the *Song of Songs* is the Holy of Holies" and who identified the protagonists not as human lovers but as God, the groom, and Israel, the bride. The love expressed between the two was thus viewed as symbolic of the covenant of God and Israel. The Targum and the Midrash Rabbah go further and create an expansive text that understands the *Song of Songs* as a complete record of Israel's history in biblical times (Exodus, Sinai, entrance into Canaan, etc.). The tradition of allegorical interpretation was inherited by Christian exegetes, for whom Jesus became the bridegroom, and the church, the bride. Gershom Scholem, supported by Saul Lieberman, has argued that the symbolic interpretation of the *Song of Songs* in terms of ancient Merkavah mysticism (see MAʿASEH MERKAVAH) goes back to the tannaitic period. In late medieval exegesis, both Jewish and Christian, the allegorical understanding gave way to an individual-mystical one; the bride and groom symbolized the human soul and its divine beloved respectively. Traditionally, Jews have understood the work to be of Solomonic authorship, but the superscription in *Song of Songs* 1.1 is subject to various interpretations (e.g., by Solomon, concerning Solomon, etc.). The Talmud (*B. B.* 15a) assigned it to King Hezekiah and his contemporaries. Most modern scholars assign it a postexilic date on linguistic grounds, based on the presence of one Persian loanword, *pardes* (garden), and many Aramaic ones, for example, *kotel* (wall), but scholars have not reached a consensus on whether it is a unified composition or a collection of individual love poems. The book, redolent of spring, is read on Pesaḥ in the synagogue and at the end of the Pesaḥ Seder among Sephardim. In addition, in some communities (mainly Sephardi) the *Song of Songs* is recited every Friday evening, based on the view that casts the Sabbath as the beloved bride.

• Michael V. Fox, *The Song of Songs and the Ancient Egyptian Love Songs* (Madison, Wis., 1985). Robert Gordis, *The Song of Songs and Lamentations* (New York, 1974). Marvin H. Pope, *Song of Songs: A New Translation with Introduction and Commentary* (Garden City, N.Y., 1977). Gershom Gerhard Scholem, *Jewish Gnosticism, Merkabah Mysticism and Talmudic Tradition*, 2d improved ed. (New York, 1965).

—GARY A. RENDSBURG

SONG OF SONGS RABBAH, aggadic *midrash* on the *Song of Songs*. This *midrash*, called *Shir ha-Shirim*

Ḥazita' or *Aggadat Ḥazita'* by medieval authorities because of the opening scriptural quote (*Prv*. 22.29) of the first proem, or simply *Midrash Shir ha-Shirim* or *Midrash Ḥazita'*, was composed in Erets Yisra'el probably in the sixth century CE. It draws on classical amoraic *midrashim* and on the Talmud Yerushalmi. The *midrash*, written in Galilean Aramaic and Rabbinic Hebrew, is rich in Greek loanwords. In the manuscripts, the *midrash* is divided into two uneven sections (*sedarim*), whereas it is divided into eight chapters in later printed editions.

Song of Songs Rabbah begins with five proems that include a Midrashic biography of Solomon and varied hermeneutic approaches to the *Song of Songs*, which are grouped at the end of the *midrash* on *Song of Songs* 1.1 and the beginning of 1.2. Scholars disagree about whether the king in the *Song of Songs* is emblematic of God or of Israel, about whether the *Song of Songs* was sung by God or by the angels, and about whether it originally was sung at the Red Sea, at Sinai, in the Tabernacle, or in the Temple. *Song of Songs Rabbah* was first published in Pesaro in 1519. An English translation by Maurice Simon appears in the Soncino Midrash (1939).

• Reuven Kimelman, "Rabbi Yoḥanan and Origen on the Song of Songs: A Third Century Jewish-Christian Disputation," *Harvard Theological Review* 73 (1980): 567–595. —MARC HIRSHMAN

SONG OF SONGS ZUTA', small aggadic *midrash* on the **Song of Songs*. First published by Solomon Schechter (*Jewish Quarterly Review* [1894]) and Solomon Buber (Lwów, 1895) independently, on the basis of the same Parma manuscript, the date of origin of this unusual *midrash* has not been satisfactorily established. Schechter believed it dated from the ninth century, Zvi Meir Rabinovitz suggested that the terminology, the sages mentioned, the theomorphic ha-Maqom, and some of the historical allusions indicated a tannaitic origin. *Song of Songs Zuta'* contains numerous allusions to the **kavod* (celestial visions) and messianic apocalypse, giving the work a more mystical bent than that of **Song of Songs Rabbah*.

• Zvi Meir Rabinowitz, *Ginzei Midrash* (Tel Aviv, 1976). Solomon Schechter, ed., *Aggadat Shir ha-Shirim* (1896; Jerusalem, 1967). Hermann Leberecht Strack and Günter Stemberger, *Introduction to the Talmud and Midrash*, rev. and updat. ed., translated by Markus Bockmuehl (Minneapolis, 1992). —MARC HIRSHMAN

SONG OF THE THREE CHILDREN. See DANIEL, ADDITIONS TO BOOK OF.

SONGS OF THE SABBATH SACRIFICE, a series of hymns, manuscripts of which were discovered in Qumran and Masada. The collection is made up of songs for the first thirteen Sabbaths of the year (e.g., Song of the Sacrifice of the First Sabbath on the Fourth of the First Month). The cycle presumes a solar calendar of three hundred sixty-four days.

This earthly liturgy invites the angels to praise God and describes their worship in the heavenly Temple. Climaxes are the sevenfold calls to praise (Song 7), the description of the divine chariot throne (*merkavah*) with its attendant angels (Song 12), and the depiction of the angelic priests offering sacrifices (Song 13). It has been suggested that the songs were a liturgical accompaniment to the heavenly cult or a catalyst for the experience of being present in the heavenly Temple.

Nine manuscripts from Qumran indicate this liturgy's importance in the Qumran community; however, the Masada manuscript suggests a nonsectarian origin or use.

• Carol Ann Newsom, *Songs of the Sabbath Sacrifice*, Harvard Semitic Studies 27 (Atlanta, 1985). —ESTHER GLICKLER CHAZON

SONNENFELD, YOSEF (1849–1932), rabbinic authority. Born in Slovakia, he studied in various Hungarian *yeshivot* before settling in Jerusalem in 1873. There he helped to found schools, an orphanage, and a religious quarter (Batei Ungarn). Sonnenfeld vehemently opposed secular education, Zionism, and the establishment of a chief rabbinate in 1920. In protest, he founded a separatist community in Jerusalem ('Edah Ḥaredit), serving as its rabbi until his death.

• Shelomo Zalman Sonnenfeld, *Guardian of Jerusalem* (Brooklyn, N.Y., 1983), adapted by Hillel Danziger from the biography *Ha-'Ish 'al ha-Ḥomah*, 3 vols. (Jerusalem, 1971).

SON OF GOD, term occasionally found in Jewish literature, biblical and post-biblical, but nowhere implying physical descent from the Godhead. In general terms, the Jewish people are referred to as "the children of the Lord your God" (*Dt*. 14.1; cf. *Ex*. 4.22 and *Hos*. 11.1), in relation to the concept of the fatherhood of God. *Genesis* 6.2 mentions the "sons of God" who intermarried with the daughters of man; the phrase is generally taken to refer to angels (also in *Ps*. 82.6) and is used in this sense in the Berikh Shemei prayer (in its Aramaic form) from the *Zohar, which is recited in some rites at the opening of the ark of the covenant in the synagogue. The application of the term to Jesus by the early Christian church was probably a combination of the metaphorical use of the term in Jewish apocryphal literature (e.g., *Wisdom of Solomon*. 2.18) with the literal conception of the term in pagan tradition. When used by the rabbis, the reference was to Israel or to human beings in general.

• Brendan Byrne, *Sons of God, Seed of Abraham: A Study of the Idea of the Sonship of God of All Christians in Paul Against the Jewish Background* (Rome, 1979). Martin Hengel, *The Son of God: The Origin of Christology and the History of Jewish-Hellenistic Religion*, translated by John Bowden (Philadelphia, 1976). Albert Schweitzer, *The Quest of the Historical Jesus* (New York, 1960).

SON OF MAN. With one exception, the phrase is used in the Hebrew Bible to convey the idea of an ordinary man, a mortal: "God is not a man that he should lie, neither the son of man that he should repent" (*Nm*. 23.19). The phrase is found most extensively (some 93 times) in *Ezekiel*, referring to the prophet himself. Ezekiel insisted that he possessed no special gift but rather was chosen by God as one of the people and to be a watchman (*Ez*. chap. 33). The term, which also occurs in an apocalyptic context in the *Book of Daniel*, "Behold, one like the son of man came with the clouds of heaven, and came to the Ancient of Days" (*Dn*. 7.13), has been interpreted to mean an exalted human being (a collective symbol for the Jewish people) or a heavenly angelic being, perhaps the archangel Michael. It eventually passed into eschatological terminology as a messianic title. As such, it played a great role in Christian phraseology, occuring frequently in the Gospels. The rabbinic view is evident in R. Abbahu's comment in an anti-Christian polemic on *Numbers* 23.19: "If a man says 'I am the Lord,' he lies; if he says 'I am the son of man' he will repent" (Y., *Ta'an*. 2.65).

• John J. Collins, *The Apocalyptic Vision of the Book of Daniel* (Missoula, Mont., 1977), pp. 144–146. John J. Collins, *Daniel*, Hermeneia (Minneapolis, 1993), pp. 304–310. —SHALOM PAUL

SONS OF LIGHT AND DARKNESS, SCROLL OF THE. See WAR SCROLL.

SORCERY. See WITCHCRAFT.

SOTAH (סוֹטָה; Woman Suspected of Adultery), tractate in Mishnah order Nashim, containing nine chapters, with related material in the Tosefta' and in both Talmuds. It expands and interprets the laws governing the *sotah* (*Nm*. 5.11–31). The rabbis held that a husband's jealousy, which initiates the *sotah*'s trial by ordeal (*Nm*. 5.14), is not a baseless fit of passion but a legalistic procedure that serves, together with circumstantial testimony of immodest behavior, as grounds for suspicion of adultery. According to *Sotah*, a woman may forego the *ordeal of jealousy by agreeing to a divorce and the forfeiture of her **ketubbah* payment. Further, the majority opinion in the Mishnah (*pace* R. Shim'on; *Sot*. 3.5) tempers the supernatural component of the ordeal of jealousy by the moral observation that good deeds done by the *sotah* may suspend the carrying out of divine justice. This observation leads to a dispute between two leading sages about whether study of Torah by women is meritorious or ought rather to be discouraged.

The fate of the *sotah*, both her humiliation by the hand of man and her divine punishment, is seen as a prominent example of justice "measure for measure," which is further illustrated in the Mishnah by examples that highlight the centrality of sexual impropriety (Samson) and of family commitment (Miriam and Moses). Another central theme of *Sotah* is the use in the *sotah* procedure of the divine name, both in the oath taken by the *sotah* and in the erasure of the *sotah* scroll into the bitter waters. Rabbi Yishma'e'l believed this exemplified the value of domestic peace, for the sake of which God allows his holy name to be erased (*Shab*. 116a and parallels).

Chapter 7 opens with a ruling permitting the *sotah* oath to be recited in any language, occasioning a lengthy digression regarding which liturgical recitations may be made in other languages and which must be performed in the holy tongue. Into the latter category falls the recitation associated with breaking the neck of the heifer, performed in cases of homicide where the murderer is unknown, a procedure with striking legal and conceptual similarities to the *sotah* ordeal. *Sotah* concludes with the abolition, prior to the destruction of the Second Temple, of the breaking of the neck of the cow and of the *sotah* procedures, occasioning a further digression that outlines the moral decline that accompanied the destruction and continued for several generations afterwards, as well as the moral turpitude that will signal the coming of the Messiah.

An English translation of the Talmud Bavli tractate is in the Soncino Talmud (1936).

• Chanoch Albeck, ed., *Shishah Sidrei Mishnah, Seder Nashim* (Jerusalem, 1954). Philip Blackman, ed. and trans., *Mishnayoth*, vol. 2, *Order Nashim* (Gateshead, 1973). David Yechiel Ebner, "The Composition and Structure of Mishnah 'Sotah,'" Ph.D. dissertation, Yeshiva University, 1980. Pinhas Kehati, ed., *Mishnah: A New Translation with a Commentary, Seder Nashim*, vol. 2, *Nedarim, Nazir, Sotah* (Jerusalem, 1992). Hermann Leberecht Strack and Günter Stemberger, *Introduction to the Talmud and Midrash*, rev. and updated ed., translated by Markus Bockmuehl (Minneapolis, 1992). —AVRAHAM WALFISH

SOUL. The belief that "something" in human beings survives physical death was current in biblical times, although the notion of a soul as an independent spiritual entity had not yet emerged. Life was not so much the presence of a soul as the animation of a body, and the original meanings of the biblical terms for soul are "breath" or "wind" (cf. *Gn*. 2.7). The seat of life was believed to be *blood. After death, the individual was thought to lead a "lifeless," shadowy existence in a Hades-like underworld (*sheol*); when Saul seeks to call upon the spirit of the deceased Samuel, the spirit emerges from below rather than from above (*1 Sm*. 28). During the latter half of the Second Temple period, the notion of a distinct soul-substance, joined to the body at birth and leaving it again at death, began to gain some ground. In accord with the Platonic tradition, the soul was held by the rabbis to be preexistent (see PREEXISTENCE) and of heavenly origin. According to the medieval thinkers it was "hewn from the throne of glory"; by being sent down into a body it is contaminated, or at least exposed to the danger of contamination through sin. Rabbinic thought generally steered clear of the radical Hellenistic *dualism, exemplified by *Philo, which equated spirit, soul, and good on the one hand, and matter, the body, and evil on the other. The traditional view on the subject is summarized in the daily morning prayer: "O my God, the soul that you gave me is pure; you did create it, you did form it, you did breathe it into me . . . and you will take it from me, but will restore it to me in the future" (see AFTERLIFE; RESURRECTION). The Platonic and Neoplatonic assumption of a spiritual and preexistent soul-substance also underlies the doctrine of the *transmigration of souls, elaborated by the medieval kabbalists. The Aristotelian thinkers, such as Maimonides, who defined the soul as the "form" of a living organism, had greater difficulty than the Platonists in giving a philosophical account and justification of the doctrine of immortality, which, they held, extended only to that part of the mind that humans acquired by intellectual effort and insight (the "acquired *intellect"). The development by philosophers of an increasingly complex doctrine of the soul also led to an increasingly differentiated terminology. In addition to the biblical words *ruaḥ*, *nefesh*, and *neshamah*, the terms *ḥayyah* and *yeḥidah* were added. The usual view was that after death the soul was punished for sins committed during its life on earth (see GEIHINNOM), for a maximum of twelve months, before being admitted to celestial bliss (see PARADISE). In the late Middle Ages, various rites were developed, intended to improve the lot of departed souls in the hereafter; some of these have become permanent features of the synagogue service (see ASHKAVAH; QADDISH; YIZKOR).

• Philip David Bookstaber, *The Idea of the Development of the Soul in Medieval Jewish Philosophy* (Philadelphia, 1950). Ellis R. Brotzman, "The Plurality of 'Soul' in the Old Testament with Special Attention Given to the Use of 'Nepes,' " Ph.D. dissertation, New York University, 1987. Herbert Davidson, "Saadia's List of Theories of the Soul," in *Jewish Medieval and Renaissance Studies*, edited by Alexander Altmann (Cambridge, Mass., 1967), pp. 75–94. Rachel Elior in *Contemporary Jewish Religious Thought*, edited by Arthur A. Cohen and Paul Mendes-Flohr (New York, 1987), pp. 887–896. Kaufmann Kohler, "The Immortal Soul of Man," in *Jewish Theology, Systematically and Historically Considered* (Cincinnati, 1943). George W. E. Nickelsburg, *Resurrection, Immortality, and Eternal Life in Intertestamental Judaism* (Cambridge, Mass., 1972). Simcha Paull Raphael, *Jewish Views of the Afterlife* (Northvale, N.J., 1994). Efraim Elimelech Urbach, *The Sages, Their Concepts and Beliefs* (Jerusalem, 1979). Gershon Winkler, *The Soul of Matter* (New York, 1982).

SPEKTOR, YITSḤAQ ELḤANAN (1817–1896), Lithuanian rabbi and halakhic authority. After serving as rabbi in several smaller communities, Spektor was named rabbi of Kovno, a post he held for over three decades. From this communal base, he built an international reputation as a halakhic expert and as an intercessor on behalf of Russian Jewry in times of distress. Together with R. Yisra'el *Salanter, Spektor established an advanced Talmudic study institute in Kovno for married students. He maintained good relations with the Jewish plutocracy of Saint Petersburg and Moscow and participated in conferences held to discuss the plight of Russian Jewry. An underground information service organized by Spektor smuggled out of Russia details about the pogroms of 1881 and 1882, revelations that led to protest meetings in the West against Russia's Jewish policies. Spektor fought attempts to alter the nature of traditional Jewish education, defended Jewish tradition against its attackers, and helped provide for the needs of Jewish soldiers and communities threatened by plagues. He was often called upon to arbitrate communal disputes, both in Russia and abroad. He devoted much of his halakhic writing to freeing *'agunot* (see 'AGUNAH) to remarry, a weighty responsibility few rabbis took upon themselves. Spektor gave his assent to the arrangement of selling Jewish-owned land in Erets Yisra'el to gentiles for the duration of the sabbatical year, a halakhic solution that was deemed crucial for the survival of the then struggling Jewish agricultural settlements (1889). Included among his written works are collections of *responsa* entitled *Be'er Yitsḥaq* (1858) and *'Ein Yitsḥaq* (1889 –1895).

• Ephraim Shimoff, *Rabbi Isaac Elchanan Spektor: His Life and Letters* (Jerusalem and New York, 1959). G. Yaakovi, *Rabbenu Yitsḥaq Elḥanan: Sippur Ḥayav, Hanahgotav u-Fe'alav shel Ro'sh Benei ha-Golah* (Jerusalem, 1990).

–GERSHON BACON

SPICES (Heb. *besamim*). The use of spices both as condiments and for perfume was widespread in ancient times. The maiden in *Song of Songs* was perfumed with "myrrh and frankincense and with all the powders of the merchant" (3.6), and the maidens brought before Ahasuerus were prepared "six months with oil of myrrh and six months with sweet odors" (*Est.* 2.12). According to the Midrash, only women perfumed themselves (*Gn. Rab.* 17.13), and it was regarded as unseemly for a scholar to do so (*Ber.* 43b). It was customary to burn spices after a meal (*Ber.* 42b), and a blessing was to be said before smelling them. This is probably the origin of the one instance of this ritual used today—in the *Havdalah service marking the conclusion of the Sabbath, which includes the smelling of spices and an accompanying blessing. Just as specific blessings are recited upon eating or drinking, blessings are also recited upon smelling fragrances. The blessing over spices derived from trees is "Blessed are you, O Lord . . . who creates spice trees"; and over herbal spices, "Blessed are you . . . who creates herbal spices." For the use of spices in the Temple, see INCENSE.

• Yehudah Feliks, *'Olam ha-Tsomeaḥ ha-Miqra'i* (Ramat Gan, 1968), pp. 176–185. Mordecai Narkiss, "Origin of the Spice Box Known as the 'Hadass,' " *Eretz-Israel* 6 (1980): 189–198, Hebrew with English summary, p. 40.

SPINOZA, BARUCH (1632–1677), Dutch philosopher of a Portuguese *Marrano family that had escaped to Amsterdam; also known as Benedictus Spinoza. Spinoza had a traditional Jewish education and a good knowledge of the medieval Jewish philosophers, possibly also of kabbalistic teachings, but his own philosophic development, greatly influenced by Descartes, led him away from traditional Orthodoxy. His profound and elaborate monistic metaphysics, his radical demand for unfettered freedom of inquiry, and his moral stature have made him one of the great figures in modern European philosophy. His place, however, is in the history of Western thought rather than Jewish philosophy. His unorthodox views, which came close to "atheism" as understood by the Calvinist authorities in Amsterdam, led to his excommunication by the Sephardi community in 1656. For many eighteenth- and early nineteenth-century thinkers, Spinozism, or the mere suspicion of it, was held to be tantamount to atheism. Enlightenment philosophers and many Romantics sympathized, however, with Spinozism as the way to true religion. Spinoza's views on the Bible were contained in his *Tractatus theologico-politicus*. He denied traditional ascriptions of authorship and laid the groundwork for subsequent textual criticism by asserting that generations of scribes had introduced errors into the text. The text, while containing universal teachings, is of human, not divine, origin. Biblical laws retain their validity only when Jews have a polity. Bible stories are not to be taken literally but are intended to convey abstract value.

• Genevieve Brykman, *Ha-Yehudiyyut shel Shpinozah* (Jerusalem, 1994). Zeev Levy, *Baruch or Benedict: On Some Jewish Aspects of Spinoza's Philosophy* (New York, 1989). Richard H. Popkin, *The History of Scepticism from Erasmus to Spinoza* (Berkeley, 1979). Leon Roth, *Spinoza, Descartes and Maimonides* (Oxford, 1924). Leo Strauss, *Persecution and the Art of Writing* (Glencoe, Ill., 1952). Harry Austryn Wolfson, *The Philosophy of Spinoza* (New York, 1969). Yirmiahu Yovel, *Spinoza and Other Heretics*, vol. 2, *The Adventures of Immanence* (Princeton, 1989).

STAR OF DAVID. See MAGEN DAVID.

STATUS QUO ANTE, name given to those communities that, though traditionalist, remained nonaligned after the Hungarian National Jewish Congress of 1868 and 1869 and provoked a split between adherents of *Neology and traditional Orthodoxy. The Status Quo Ante group controlled Debrecen and a few other centers, but in 1930, two years after receiving governmental recognition, its total membership (17,440) was vastly outnumbered by the Neologist (292,159) and Orthodox (134,972) congregants within Hungarian Jewry. Following the Habsburg empire's collapse in 1918, Orthodoxy retained its hold on the Jews of Slovakia, where there were fewer Neologist than Status Quo Ante communities. These two smaller groups joined together in 1926 to establish a Union of Jewish Religious Communities (Yeshurun). After World War II, the competing trends were unified in Slovakia, and, when centralization was imposed in communist Hungary in 1950, the Status Quo Ante group disappeared.

• Robert Buchler et al., eds., *Museum of Jewish Culture in Slovakia: Catalogue to Permanent Exhibition* (Bratislava, 1993), pp. 11–13.
–GABRIEL A. SIVAN

STATUTE OF LIMITATIONS. See LIMITATION OF ACTIONS.

STEINBERG, MILTON (1903–1950), U.S. Conservative rabbi. He served Congregation Beth-El Zedeck in Indianapolis and the Park Avenue Synagogue in New York City. A student of Morris Raphael Cohen and Mordecai Menahem *Kaplan, he emerged as a leading writer of philosophical theology. At first a leader of *Reconstructionism, he later criticized it for its lack of poetry and philosophical rigor. His writings deal with the range of issues of Jewish belief: faith and reason, the nature of God, and the meaning of Jewish history. His novel *As a Driven Leaf* (1939) was a rendering of the life of the Talmudic heretic Elisha' ben Avuyah. He also wrote *Basic Judaism* (1947); *The Making of the Modern Jew* (1934); *A Partisan Guide to the Jewish Problem* (1945); and *Anatomy of Faith* (1960).

• Simon Noveck, *Milton Steinberg: Portrait of a Rabbi* (New York, 1978).
–JACOB J. STAUB

STEINHEIM, SALOMON LUDWIG (1789–1866), philosopher of religion and German poet who was born in Bruchhausen, Westphalia, and practiced as a physician in Altona. From 1846, his main residence was in Rome. Besides works on medicine, he wrote several books of poetry and on theology. In his most important book, the four-volume *Die Offenbarung nach dem Lehrbegriffe der Synagoge* (1835–1865), he inveighed both against Christianity and against the rationalism of the school of Moses *Mendelssohn. He contrasted the speculations of philosophers that led to belief in a dualistic system of good and evil with the biblical revelation of creation out of nothing and the absolute oneness of God. Although he insisted that the insights of revelation were derived independently from those of natural reason, he nonetheless maintained that the truths of revelation must inevitably be confirmed by philosophy. Steinheim's ideas were rejected by the Reform community as being too supranaturalist and by the Orthodox as too rational. In particular, he did not accept the absolute sanctity of the written and oral law. He also attacked the writings of Hegel and Schelling but made little lasting impression on his contemporaries. Nonetheless his system, with its stress on personal experience rather than theory, was subsequently used by the German thinker Hans-Joachim Schoeps as a foundation for his own existentialism. Steinheim's view of religion as an element of human experience and as subject to the same tests of certainty as empirical experience is seen by some as prefiguring the methods of modern scientific investigation.

• Julius Guttman, *Philosophies of Judaism* (New York, 1964), pp. 344–349. Walter Jacob, *Christianity through Jewish Eyes* (New York, 1974), pp. 61–66. Nathan Rotenstreich, *Jewish Philosophy in Modern Times* (New York, 1968).
–LAVINIA COHN-SHERBOK

STERILITY. See BARRENNESS.

STERILIZATION. The Bible specifically disqualifies a castrated priest from serving in the Temple (*Lv.* 21:20) and a castrated animal from serving as a sacrifice on the altar (*Lv.* 22.24; see CASTRATION). The Talmud extends these prohibitions into a general ban on all forms of surgical sterilization of men, women, animals, and fowl (*Shab.* 110b). There is also a biblical prohibition against marrying a man with "crushed or maimed genitals" (*Dt.* 23.2), which, it is generally accepted, is limited to deliberate mutilations of a nontherapeutic nature. The prohibition against surgical sterilization does not apply if danger to life is involved; hence, it is permitted to remove a diseased prostate gland by surgical means if no other method is available. Indirect sterilization such as freezing the sexual organs or drinking a potion known in the Talmud as a "cup of sterility" (*Yev.* 65b) is forbidden to males but is permitted to females. A woman, therefore, is allowed to drink such a potion for medical reasons or to avoid extreme pain during childbirth. The Talmud extends the disqualification of castrated priests to judges and to those who lead the community in prayer (*San.* 36b; minor tractate *Soferim* 14.17).

• J. David Bleich, "Prostate Surgery," in *Contemporary Halakhic Problems*, vol. 3, The Library of Jewish Law and Ethics (New York, 1989), pp. 141–159. Immanuel Jakobovits, *Jewish Medical Ethics* (New York, 1959), pp. 159–169.
–DANIEL SINCLAIR

STOICISM, philosophical school (founded c.300 BCE in Athens) that flourished in the Greco-Roman era. Its main emphasis was on ethics, and it stressed the ideal of the wise person whose virtue consists in becoming liberated from the sway of the passions and living in conformity with nature and the cosmic law. This cosmic law was conceived by the Stoics as an immanent divine principle (cosmic reason; see LOGOS); life in accordance with it was of the highest felicity. In spite of its pantheistic character (see PANTHEISM) and pagan origin, Stoicism, particularly its stern morality, its belief in a universal governing principle, and its conception of the divine principle active in the cosmos as reason, profoundly influenced Jewish thought (notably *Philo and the Mishnaic, Talmudic, and Midrashic teachers) and religious ethics. To the extent that Stoic elements became part of Greek philosophical tradition, the influence of Stoicism is evident throughout medieval Jewish philosophy.

• Henry Fischel, ed., *Essays in Greco-Roman and Related Talmudic Literature* (New York, 1977). Julius Guttmann, *Philosophies of Judaism* (New York, 1973). Harry A. Wolfson, *Philo: Foundations of Religious Philosophy in Judaism, Christianity, and Islam* (Cambridge, Mass., 1947).

STONING. See CAPITAL PUNISHMENT.

STRANGER. In ancient times strangers (i.e., those who were not members of the ethnic or tribal group) were normally without legal or other protection. For this reason they are often mentioned alongside widows, orphans, and the poor, who are in need of assistance (*Dt.* 24.17–21). Hence, the insistence of the Bible on the duty of showing every consideration to the "stranger within your gates" and treating the stranger like the native Israelite, since the Israelites themselves were once strangers in Egypt (*Ex.* 22.21, 23.9). God "loves the stranger in giving him food and raiment" (*Dt.* 10.18) and has commanded humans to love the stranger (*Dt.* 10.19), for "the stranger who dwells with you shall be unto you as one born among you" (*Lv.* 19.33–34). According to Yehezkel Kaufmann, the idea of the resident alien evolved from an ethnic concept into a religious attitude, based on a rejection of idolatry. In the rabbinic view, the stranger, in order to qualify for the protection provided by Jewish law, was expected to adhere to the seven *Noahic laws. The word **ger*, which in the Bible almost without exception refers to a resident alien (*ger toshav*, e.g., *Gn.* 23.4), is used in the Talmud to mean *proselyte (*ger tsedeq*).

The thinkers of the Emancipation period stressed the liberalism of the biblical attitude to back their own claims to civil rights. Thus, Hermann Cohen stressed the ideal of civil equality found in ancient legislation (*Religion of Reason out of the Sources of Judaism*), while Shemu'el David *Luzzatto called his son Philxene (Love of the Stranger). In the State of Israel, the chief rabbi Yitsḥaq Herzog ruled that the country's minorities should be treated as the ancient *ger toshav* (even without the obligation to abstain from idol worship).

• Leo Baeck, *The Essence of Judaism*, translated by Victor Grubwieser (New York, 1961), pp. 190ff. Isaac Herzog, "Zekhuyyot ha-Miyyutim le-Fi ha-Halakhah," *Teḥumin* 2 (1981): 169–179. Jacob Katz, *Exclusiveness and Tolerance: Studies in Jewish–Gentile Relations in Medieval and Modern Times*, Scripta Judaica, vol. 3 (Westport, Conn., 1980). Yehezkel Kaufmann, *Golah ve-Nekhar* (Tel Aviv, 1932), pt. 4, pp. 209–256. Joseph Levi, "Stranger," in *Contemporary Jewish Religious Thought*, edited by Arthur A. Cohen and Paul Mendes-Flohr (New York, 1987), pp. 917–930. Saul Lieberman, "Gentiles and Semi-Proselytes," in *The Greek in Jewish Palestine* (New York, 1942). Roland de Vaux, *Ancient Israel: Its Life and Institutions*, translated by John McHugh (New York, 1961), pp. 74–76, 80–82.

—SHALOM PAUL

STRANGULATION. See CAPITAL PUNISHMENT.

STRASHUN, SHEMU'EL BEN YOSEF (1794–1872), Lithuanian Talmudist. Strashun studied under R. Avraham Danzig in Vilna, where he later settled. He is best known for his many annotations on the Talmud, which are included in the back of the Vilna (Romm) editions. These notes are usually short and incisive, often offering new interpretations in a few words. They also reveal his great knowledge of history and languages. Although not trained in modern scholarly methods, Strashun approached Talmudic texts with a critical mind, leading him to correct many textual errors. He also wrote glosses and *novellae* to the Midrash Rabbah, *Sifrei*, Maimonides' *Mishneh Torah*, and portions of the *Shulḥan ʿArukh*.

• Tsevi Harkavi, *Le-Ḥeqer Mishpaḥot* (Jerusalem, 1953), pp. 44–48. Tsevi Harkavi, ed., *Meqorei ha-Rambam le-Rashash* (Jerusalem, 1957), pp. 53–64, includes biographical appendix.

—MARC SHAPIRO

STUDY. The study of the Torah (*talmud Torah*) is one of the most highly esteemed duties. Among the first benedictions in the daily morning prayer service is one blessing God for the commandment "to engage in the study of the Torah." In the list of meritorious activities enumerated in the Mishnah in *Pe'ah* 1.1, the study of Torah is said to surpass all others. The blessing preceding the reading of the Shemaʿ in both the morning and evening services asks for the grace to be enabled to study the Torah. The divine presence dwells among those who study the Torah. According to *Avot* 1.15, study should be a regular habit. The earlier injunction to devote one-third of one's free time to the study of Torah, one third to Mishnah, and one third to Talmud (*Qid*. 30a) was later modified in favor of the Talmud, for, according to Rabbenu Tam, this contains all the others. According to Maimonides (*Hilkhot Talmud Torah* 1.12), the ideal division of time should be nine hours of study and three hours of pursuing one's occupation each day. The relative value of the study of Torah as compared with religious observance is expressed in the paradoxical summing up of a famous debate on the subject: "Study is the more important since it leads to observance" (*Qid*. 40b). The commandment to study Torah applies both during the day and at night (Y., *Ber*. 25b). Although it is not a time-related precept, women are exempt from Torah study (*ʿEruv*. 27a); however, women studied the Bible and those sections of the oral law that applied to them. The high value placed on *talmud Torah* also implies honoring those who teach and study. Study of Torah has at all times been a central value and the student its incarnation. It became accepted in many places for the wife to earn the family's livelihood so as to enable the husband to devote himself to study. The emphasis on intellectual achievement occasionally led to counteractions stressing the more inward (i.e., devotional and moral) values of Judaism (see ḤASIDEI ASHKENAZ; HASIDISM; MUSAR MOVEMENT). In modern times, the duty of study has been extended to *women, even in very Orthodox circles (although there boys and girls study separately). According to the *aggadah*, God himself studies, and the reward of the righteous will be to study with him in the world to come.

• Shalom Carmy, *Modern Scholarship in the Study of Torah: Contributions and Limitations* (Northvale, N.J., 1995). Shalom Freedman, *In the Service of God: Conversations with Teachers of Torah in Jerusalem* (Northvale, N.J., 1995). Leo Levi, *Torah Study: A Survey of Classic Sources on Timely Issues* (New York, 1990). Jacob Neusner, *History and Torah: Essays on Jewish Learning* (London, 1965). —SHMUEL HIMELSTEIN

SUBBOTNIKI (Rus.; Sabbath Observers), name given to a Judaizing sect in Russia that first emerged at the end of the eighteenth century. Their main characteristic was observance of the Jewish Sabbath, but they also adopted various other biblical and Jewish customs, such as circumcision, abstention from unclean animals, rejection of the New Testament, and a strict monotheism. Subjected to cruel persecution by the Russian authorities at the beginning of the nineteenth century, the Subbotniki were exiled to Siberia in 1826. They obtained religious freedom only at the beginning of the twentieth century. A number of their descendants adopted Judaism and settled in Palestine. See also JUDAIZING SECTS.

• Willard B. Moore, *Molokan Oral Traditions: Legends and Memories of an Ethnic Sect* (Berkeley, 1973). Louis I. Newman, *Jewish Influence on Christian Reform Movements* (New York, 1925). Marcel Simon, *Recherches d'histoire judeo-chrétienne* (Paris, 1962).

SUFFERING becomes a theological problem if one maintains religious belief in a just God who rewards virtue and goodness, in which case suffering must be conceived as divine punishment for sin. This simple theological scheme, however, is not always confirmed by reality, and the problem of suffering occupies a prominent place in both the Bible and Talmud. It is the subject of the *Book of Job*, whose theme is that the righteous man can be made to undergo suffering in order to prove that he is capable of selfless piety. Other books of the Bible seem to assume a direct relation between suffering and sin. There is a distinct ambivalence in the approach of the rabbis to the problem. Although they lay down that suffering is the result of sin (*Shab*. 55a) and that it acts as an expiation for sin (*Yoma'* 86a), they concede that suffering can come on an innocent person and that, in fact, it is the fate of the righteous in this world. According to a rabbinic legend, Moses protested against the agony of the martyrdom and torture of R. *ʿAqiva' ben Yosef, which he beheld in a vision, but God's reply was "Be silent! Such is my decree" (*Men*. 29b). Both views are combined in the passage: "If a person is visited by suffering let him examine his actions. Should he find them blameless let him attribute it to neglect of the study of Torah. If he still finds no cause, let him accept that they are the chastenings of love, as it is said [*Ps*. 94.12] 'For whom the Lord loves he chastens' " (*Ber*. 5a). The usual explanation of suffering resorts to *eschatology and to the doctrine of retribution (see REWARD AND PUNISHMENT) in the world to come. The common rabbinic view is that the righteous person expiates his few sins on this earth in order to enjoy the full reward for his righteousness in the world to come (cf. *Qid*. 40b) or that the righteous atone by their sufferings for the sins of the world. Ultimately the question is considered a divine mystery beyond human understanding. The sufferings, persecutions, and exile of the people of Israel, culminating in the Holocaust, have exercised Jewish thinkers throughout the ages. See also GOOD AND EVIL; HOLOCAUST THEOLOGY.

• Adolf Büchler, *Studies in Sin and Atonement in the Rabbinic Literature of the First Century*, The Library of Biblical Studies (New York, 1967), pp. 119–211. David Hartman, "Suffering," in *Contemporary Jewish Religious Thought*, edited by Arthur A. Cohen and Paul Mendes-Flohr (New York, 1987), pp. 939–946. Efraim Elimelech Urbach, *The Sages, Their Concepts and Beliefs*, translated by Israel Abrahams, Publications of the Perry Foundation in the Hebrew University of Jerusalem (Jerusalem, 1975), pp. 420–523.

SUFISM, the traditional designation for Muslim mysticism (from *suf*, the coarse woolen cloth worn by early Muslim ascetics). The ultimate aim of the Sufis was to achieve a mystical union with God by passing through the stages of abstinence, renunciation, poverty, trust, purity of will and mind, and love of God. The teachings of Sufism were greatly influenced by the philosophy of *Neoplatonism and, in some branches at least, exhibited gnostic traits. Long suspected of being heretical and opposed by orthodox theologians, Sufism was finally reconciled with orthodox thought in the twelfth century. Sufism also exerted considerable influence on medieval Jewish piety and ascetic theology, notably on Baḥya ben Yosef ibn Paquda', whose *Ḥovot ha-Levavot* contains Sufi terminology, ideas, and quotations. Another Jewish thinker who was deeply influenced by Sufism was *Avraham ben Mosheh ben Maimon.

• Henry Corbin, *The Man of Light in Iranian Sufism* (Boulder, Colo., 1978). Annemarie Schimmel, *Mystical Dimensions of Islam* (Chapel Hill, N.C., 1990). Margaret Smith, *Studies in Early Mysticism in the Near and Middle East* (Oxford, 1995).

SUICIDE. Since an individual is not considered to be the owner or master of his own life, suicide, which amounts in rabbinic thought to *homicide, is strictly forbidden. "For your own lifeblood, I will require a reckoning" (*Gn*. 9.5) is considered a biblical prohibition against suicide. A man is permitted to sacrifice his life only to avoid committing one of three cardinal sins—murder, adultery, idolatry; indeed, many authorities hold that a man is to allow himself to be killed rather than violate these sins but that he must not actively destroy himself. Many examples of individual and collective suicide to escape the hand of the enemy and the threat of slavery or apostasy are recorded in Jewish history: King Saul (*1 Sm*. 31.4–5); Ahithophel (*2 Sm*. 17.23); the fighters at Masada (71 CE); the martyrs of York (1190). That suicides have no share in the world to come is recorded as a Jewish doctrine by Josephus but does not appear in the Talmud. A suicide is to be buried in a separate part of the cemetery. However, today rabbis tend to consider those who commit suicide as being of unsound mind, and therefore they are not restricted to a separate area of the cemetery. The minor tractate **Evel Rabbati* discusses laws concerning suicides (2.1–5).

• Arthur J. Droge and James Tabor, *A Noble Death: Suicide and Martyrdom among Christians and Jews in Antiquity* (San Francisco, 1992), includes texts and bibliography. Sidney Goldstein, *Suicide in Rabbinic Literature* (Hoboken, N.J., 1989). Yechezkel Lichtenshtein, "Isur Hit'abedut: 'Iyyun Halakhti, Histori le-Hishtalsheluto shel Isur Hit'abedut be-Mahalakh ha-Dorot," master's thesis, Bar Ilan University, 1991, with English abstract.

SUKKAH (סוּכָּה), name of a booth and of a Mishnaic tractate.

Booth. A *sukkah* is a booth or tabernacle (hut) in which the children of Israel were enjoined to dwell for seven days "in order that your generations may know that I caused the children of Israel to dwell in tabernacles when I brought them out of the land of Egypt" (*Lv.* 23.42–43) and from which the festival of *Sukkot derives its name. Booths probably played a part in the ancient *harvest festivals; hence, their association with Sukkot, which is also called the "harvest festival" in the Bible. The *sukkah* must be a temporary structure, its roof covered with cut vegetation and open to the sun, though it must give "more shade than light." An Orthodox tradition is to start building the *sukkah* shortly after the conclusion of Yom Kippur. Orthodox Jews take their meals in the *sukkah* (where a special blessing is recited), and many also sleep there during the seven days of the festival. In Western communities a *sukkah* is built adjacent to the synagogue and visited by the congregation for light refreshments after the services on the festival. Although the rite of the *four species is considered independent of that of the *sukkah* (*Lv.* 23.40), it appears that *Nehemiah (*Neh.* 8.15) regarded the four species as the materials from which the *sukkah* was to be constructed; a similar opinion voiced in the Talmud by R. Yehudah (*Suk.* 37a) was overruled. A *sukkah* must have a minimum of three walls and stand not more than twenty cubits (approximately 30 feet) high. Inclement weather absolves one from the duty of dwelling in the *sukkah*. Women are exempt from the obligation to dwell in the *sukkah* (as they are from all commandments that depend upon a fixed time for their performance), but they may do so if they wish. The kabbalistic custom of welcoming Abraham, Isaac, Jacob, Joseph, Moses, Aaron, and David to the *sukkah*, each one on a different day of the festival, is called **ushpizin* (guests), and an appropriate invocation is recited. The halakhic regulations regarding the *sukkah* and Sukkot are expounded in the Mishnah and both Talmuds.

Tractate. The tractate *Sukkah* is in Mishnah order Mo'ed, in five chapters, with related material in the Tosefta' and in both Talmuds. It discusses the laws of the festival of *Sukkot, described in the Bible as a fall harvest festival (*Ex.* 23.15, 34.22; *Lv.* 23.27ff.; *Nm.* 29.12ff.; *Dt.* 16.13ff.), marked by the requirements of the taking of the branches and fruit of *four species of trees (*Lv.* 23.40) and of dwelling in booths for seven days (*Lv.* 23.42).

Sukkah requires the four species to be free of blemishes, physical as well as moral (such as items that had been stolen or used for idolatry), rendering them fit for divine service. They were used in the Temple as part of a multifaceted ceremony, in which a water libation and the symbolic planting of willow branches near the altar were performed, expressing thanksgiving for the previous year's harvest as well as offering a petition for abundant rainfall in the coming year. After the destruction of the Temple, the waving of the four species before God was incorporated into the festive recitation of Hallel. During the Sukkot festival an ongoing water-drawing celebration took place in the Temple (see SIMḤAT BEIT HA-SHO'EVAH), marked by festive candelabra and music, as well as dancing and juggling led by distinguished scholars and pious men. The great joyousness of these festivities led the sages to erect a partition in the women's courtyard to prevent immodest mingling of men and women and prompted the remark that "whoever has not seen the rejoicing of the drawing of the water has never in his life seen rejoicing" (*Suk.* 5.1).

The tractate in the Talmud Bavli was translated into English by I. W. Slotki in the Soncino Talmud (1938).

• Chanoch Albeck, ed., *Shishah Sidrei Mishnah, Seder Mo'ed* (Jerusalem, 1952). Philip Blackman, ed. and trans., *Mishnayoth*, vol. 2, *Order Moed* (Gateshead, 1973). Pinhas Kehati, ed., *Mishnah: A New Translation with a Commentary, Seder Moed*, vol. 4, *Yoma, Sukkah, Betzah, Rosh Hashanah* (Jerusalem, 1990). Hermann Leberecht Strack and Günter Stemberger, *Introduction to the Talmud and Midrash*, rev. and updat. ed., translated by Markus Bockmuehl (Minneapolis, 1992).

—AVRAHAM WALFISH

SUKKOT (סֻכּוֹת; Tabernacles), the third of the pilgrim festivals (see SHALOSH REGALIM). The Hebrew name derives from the main aspect of the festival, which involves the celebrant's dwelling in a **sukkah* (booth). Originally one of the *harvest festivals (*Ex.* 23.16; *Dt.* 16.13), Ḥag ha-'Asif (Festival of the Ingathering [of the Crops]), it was given added historical significance as a commemoration of the forty years of wandering in the wilderness (*Lv.* 23.43). The festival became so popular that in Mishnaic times it was known simply as Ḥag, that is, the festival par excellence. Liturgically, it is described as *zeman simḥatenu* (the time of our rejoicing) following the biblical injunction to be completely joyous on this festival (*Dt.* 16.15). The Bible enjoins Jews to dwell in the *sukkah* and to take the *four species. A circuit of the synagogue with the four species in hand is made daily to the accompaniment of chanted Hosha'not, and the four species are waved in prescribed fashion during the recitation of the *Hallel. During the festival, religious Jews take their meals and spend the day in the temporary *sukkah* structure, and many synagogues also construct an adjoining *sukkah*. The symbolic welcoming of biblical guests (see USHPIZIN), a custom of sixteenth-century kabbalistic origin, is also observed during Sukkot. On the seventh day of the festival, which has been given the name *Hosha'na' Rabbah, a sevenfold circuit of the synagogue is made with the four species (see HAQQAFOT). Most of these ceremonies originated in ancient Temple custom. During the intermediate days of the festival, the Feast of Water-Drawing (see SIMḤAT BEIT HA-SHO'EVAH), of which a vivid description is given in the Talmud (*Suk.* 53a), was celebrated in the Temple as the most joyous occasion of the year. Sukkot begins on 15 Tishrei and lasts seven days; the eighth day (according to some, a separate festival) is *Shemini ʿAtseret, on which a prayer for rain is recited (see TEFILLAT GESHEM). In the Diaspora, a ninth day is added for *Simḥat Torah (in Erets Yisra'el, this is combined with Shemini ʿAtseret), when the annual cycle of the reading of the Torah (see QERI'AT HA-TORAH) is concluded and a new one begun. The ancient ceremony of *Haqhel during Sukkot has been revived in modern Israel. Work is prohibited only on the first and last days of the holiday (in the Diaspora, the first two and last two); the intermediate days are *ḥol ha-moʿed*. Hallel and the Musaf service are recited each day (see FESTIVAL PRAYERS). In addition, the *Book of *Ecclesiastes* is read in the synagogue. The unusual order of the *sacrifices offered during the festival in Temple times (thirteen bullocks were offered on the first day, and the number was progressively reduced by one daily until on the seventh day only seven were offered, making a total of seventy; *Nm.* 29.12–32) has given rise to the tradition that these sacrifices represent the offerings made by Israel on behalf of the seventy nations that traditionally inhabit the earth. One of the festival's prophetical readings is from *Zechariah* 14.16–19, which states that all nations will go to Jerusalem to keep the feast of Sukkot. There is evidence that in Second Temple times greater numbers of people made the pilgrimage to Jerusalem on this festival than on the other pilgrim festivals, since at this time the harvest had been fully gathered, and farmers were free to leave their fields. The laws concerning the festival are in Talmud tractate *Sukkah*.

• Hersh Goldwurm, ed., *Succos: Its Significance, Laws, and Prayers* (Brooklyn, N.Y., 1989). Philip Goodman, ed., *The Sukkot and Simhat Torah Anthology* (Philadelphia, 1973). Jeffrey L. Rubenstein, *The History of Sukkot in the Second Temple and Rabbinic Periods* (Atlanta, 1995). William R. Scott, "The Booths of Ancient Israel's Autumn Festival," Ph.D. dissertation, Johns Hopkins University, 1993.

SULZER, SALOMON (1804–1890), Viennese cantor and composer. From the age of sixteen, he served as an itinerant cantor in Germany, Switzerland, and France. In 1826 he was named cantor of the Stadttempel in Vienna, a post he held for fifty-five years. A student of Ignaz von Seyfried, Sulzer was one of the first modern cantors to receive classical musical training, which he employed in his efforts to reconstruct traditional synagogue music to suit the modern era. Sulzer's monumental *Shir Tsiyyon* (with volumes published in 1840 and 1866) included cantorial recitatives, congregational responses, and choral settings for the entire liturgical year. Sulzer's strength of personality and impressive voice earned him the admiration of Franz Schubert and Franz Liszt, as well as the other cantors of his day, whose eagerness to emulate him assured the acceptance of his compositions. Sulzer is often regarded as the father of the modern cantorate and is considered an important reformer of synagogue song; his published work represented a compromise between synagogue traditions and the prevailing musical style. His accomplishments won him widespread renown well beyond the Jewish community, but he was reviled for his reforms by more traditional elements from eastern Europe. Nevertheless, Sulzer's music continues to be sung throughout the Ashkenazi world.

• Abraham Z. Idelsohn, *Jewish Music in Its Historical Development* (New York, 1929; repr. 1967; Westport, Conn., 1981).

—MARSHA BRYAN EDELMAN

SUMPTUARY LAWS, laws issued by Jewish communities directed against ostentation and public displays of luxury. The reasons for such restrictions were to prevent people from constantly outspending one another, with the less affluent often going into debt by trying to emulate the more fortunate, or to keep individual Jews from flaunting their wealth before their non-Jewish neighbors. Often such laws were also enacted by local rulers prohibiting Jews in their realms from appearing in costly attire. One example of a sumptuary law is found in the Talmudic statement (*Moʿed Q.* 27a–b) that "formerly, [the body of] the rich was brought [for burial] in an ornate litter and that of the poor in a plain box and the poor felt ashamed; they [the rabbis] therefore instituted that all should be brought in a plain box." Sumptuary laws restricted the number of guests who might be invited to a wedding, the weight of silver goblets, and the number of rings it was permissible to wear. In actual fact, sumptuary laws were often ignored, and community minutes frequently refer to the need to find ways to force people to comply.

• David Fichman, "Sumptuary Laws of the Jews from the Fifteenth to the Eighteenth Centuries," Rabbinic thesis, Hebrew Union College, 1913. Diane Owen Hughes, "Regulating Women's Fashion," in *A History of Women in the West*, vol. 2, *Silences of the Middle Ages*, edited by C. Kapisch-Zuber (Cambridge, Mass., 1992), pp. 136–158.

SUN. The sun was created on the fourth day "to rule the day" (*Gn.* 1.16). In the Bible, it is a symbol of joy, light, and blessing (cf. *Ps.* 19.5–7; *Mal.* 3.20), while an eclipse of the sun presages impending judgment and doom (cf. *Is.* 13.10; *Am.* 8.9; *Mi.* 3.6). The movement of the sun can be arrested by divine intervention; for example, when it stood still to enable the Israelites to defeat the Amorites (*Jos.* 10.12–14). Sun worship was common in the ancient Near East, and the fact that King Josiah's monotheistic reforms abolished all worship of "sun, moon, and stars" (*2 Kgs.* 23.5) indicates that it was practiced to some extent in Israel. A rabbinic legend relates that God originally intended the sun to be the sole luminary, but to avoid it becoming an object of worship, he also created the moon (*Gn. Rab.* 6.1). Similarly, it is said of Abraham that he was tempted to regard the sun as God, but when night fell, and it was replaced by the moon, he realized that there must be a higher power. Calendrical needs, both for the purpose of establishing the solar year and its solstices and for accurately determining the beginning and conclusion of the Sabbath and the festivals and the times of prayers and sacrifices, stimulated close study of the sun by the rabbis. The length of the year and the exact determination of sunset, sunrise, and the onset of *twilight were all exhaustively debated and finally determined. See also BIRKAT HA-ḤAMMAH; CALENDAR; MOON.

• Louis Ginzberg, *Legends of the Jews* (Philadelphia, 1909–1938), index. Nahum M. Sarna, "Psalm XIX and the Near Eastern Sun-God Literature," *Fourth World Congress of Jewish Studies*, vol. 1 (1967), pp. 171–175.
—CHAIM PEARL

SUN, BLESSING OF THE. See BIRKAT HA-ḤAMMAH.

SUPPLICATION. See BAQQASHAH.

SURA, city in southern Babylonia where *Rav founded (c.219 CE) a famous *academy that flourished for eight centuries. Prominent leaders of the academy during the third and fourth centuries included Ḥisda' and Huna'. In the fifth century, it was headed by *Ashi, one of the chief editors of the Talmud Bavli. During the geonic period (see GA'ON), the academy of Sura maintained closer ties with the court of the *exilarch than did its sister academy of *Pumbedita. Another institution closely associated with Sura was the ancient synagogue known as Beit Rabbenu shebe-Bavel, believed to have been founded by Rav, the customs of which are frequently cited. Other outstanding heads of the academy include: *Yehuda'i ben Naḥman Ga'on in the mid-eighth century (although he received his training in Pumbedita); Mosheh Ga'on, and *Natrona'i bar Hila'i in the ninth century.

In the tenth century, the position of the Sura academy became increasingly tenuous, and the school was transferred to Baghdad, though retaining its name. It was on the verge of closure until the appointment in 928 of the dynamic but controversial *Saʿadyah ben Yosef Ga'on gave it a new lease on life. After his death, the academy closed for almost half a century; it was reopened toward the end of the tenth century. The most important figure associated with Sura in this period was *Shemu'el ben Ḥofni.

• Jacob Neusner, *A History of the Jews in Babylonia* (Leiden, 1969). Aharon Oppenheimer, *Babylonia Judaica in the Talmudic Period* (Weisbaden, 1983).
—ROBERT BRODY

SURETY (Heb. *ʿarevut*), a person who guarantees the financial obligations of another. Such guaranties are valid, even if given orally, whether at the time of the loan or later, although guaranties of repayment provided after the loan was made must be effectuated with a *qinyan* (see ACQUISITION). There are two different types of guarantors. The first, an *ʿarev*, is only obligated to pay when the debtor cannot. The second, an *ʿarev qablan*, agrees to pay whether the debtor has defaulted or not. In cases where the debtor fails to pay and the surety pays, the surety has the right to recourse from the debtor for all of his expenses. In situations where the debt has been canceled for any reason, the surety is also canceled.

• Arnold Cohen, *An Introduction to Jewish Civil Law* (Jerusalem and New York, 1991). Menachem Elon, "Surety," in *Principles of Jewish Law* (Jerusalem, 1975), pp. 281–287.
—MICHAEL BROYDE

SURROGACY. It is a general principle of Jewish law that maternity, like paternity, is established by nature and not by law. According to one view, the birth mother is the mother for all halakhic purposes. This view is based upon various Talmudic passages regarding the conversion to Judaism of pregnant women (*Yev.* 78a–b, 97b). The common theme underlying these passages is that the child born after the mother's conversion is Jewish. There is, however, another view, according to which maternity is established at conception rather than birth, and Talmudic support is also available for this (*Nid.* 31a; *San.* 91b). A third approach suggests that the genetic mother is sometimes the legal mother, depending upon the time that elapses between conception and implantation in the surrogate. It has also been suggested that the product of a surrogate birth might have two legal mothers, that is, the birth mother and the genetic mother. The establishment of maternity is particularly significant from a halakhic perspective, since it is the mother who determines the Jewish identity of the child. Other problems related to surrogacy are the possibilities of incest or adultery. In light of these, surrogacy is generally frowned upon by contemporary halakhists. In 1995 the Israel Supreme Court ruled that surrogate motherhood be permitted; some rabbinical authorities concurred, with the proviso that the requirements of Jewish law be met. See also ARTIFICIAL REPRODUCTION TECHNIQUES.

• Ezra Bick, "Ovum Donations: A Rabbinic Conceptual Model of Maternity," *Tradition* 28.1 (1993): 28–45. J. David Bleich, "In Vitro Fertilization: Questions of Maternal Identity and Conversion," *Tradition* 25.4 (1991): 82–102.
—DANIEL SINCLAIR

SUSANNA AND THE ELDERS. See DANIEL, ADDITIONS TO BOOK OF.

SWINE. See PIGS.

SYMBOLISM. A distinct vocabulary of visual symbols has been used by Jews from antiquity until today to signify community and convey religious concepts. Often they indicate that particular sites, buildings, art, or artifacts are Jewish. Depictions of the Temple façade are common, as are depictions of Temple implements such as the *Menorah, priestly garb, and Ark of the Covenant, which are frequently represented in Spanish medieval Bible manuscripts, on Italian ritual silver, or on central European *aron ha-qodesh* valances. Representations of the Temple and implements reflect shared remembrance of the destroyed First and Second Temples and messianic longings for the construction of the Third. The Menorah, the seven-branched candelabrum, that is described in *Exodus* 25.31–40 and 37.17–24, is the most commonly represented Temple implement. It frequently appears in art of the Second Temple and Talmudic periods. It became symbolic not only of the Temple service, but of Jews and Judaism as a whole. Also common in Jewish art from antiquity through modernity are items used in Jewish ritual, such as the *lulav*, *etrog*, or shofar, symbolizing ritual practice and frequently signifying particular festivals (for example, a shofar signifies Ro'sh ha-Shanah). *Zodiac symbols frequently decorate the mosaic floors of ancient synagogues; such images were used throughout the centuries as symbols of the Jewish calendar. Animals appear frequently in Jewish art. Birds flank images of the Torah shrine in ancient synagogue mosaics and adorn the earliest extant decorated medieval *ketubbah* (Tudela, 1300). Eagles and lions often appear on Torah ornaments, symbols of majesty and strength. Animal motifs are very common in eastern European Jewish folk art. Depictions of animals are often associated with the text, "be as strong as a leopard, as light as an eagle, as swift as a deer, as brave as a lion to do the will of your Father in heaven" (*Avot* 5.20). Images of the Aron ha-Qodesh stress the centrality of the Torah in Jewish life. The two tablets of the Law, often with abbreviated text, are commonly used as a symbol of the Mosaic faith and became the preferred symbol in Reform synagogues, although their use precedes the Reform movement. Images of Torah scrolls are used similarly. The tree of life symbolizes the Torah (*Prv*. 3.18) or refers to the garden of Eden or messianic times. Portals, frequently flanked by columns or figures, represent entrances to forgiveness, learning, or righteousness and frequently appear on frontispieces and Torah ark curtains, often associated with the text "This is the gateway of the Lord" (*Ps*. 118.20). Two flanking columns are also associated with Jachin and Boaz, the two pillars at the front of Solomon's Temple. Crown forms symbolize the majesty and strength of God or the Torah, or are associated with the text "there are three crowns: the crown of Torah, the crown of priesthood, and the royal crown, but the crown of a good name surpasses them all" (*Avot* 4.13). Apotropaic symbols are used on amulets and other objects to ward off evil spirits and include formulary representations of angels and the *ḥamsa* (hand). On tombstones, hands raised in the pose of priestly blessing are used as a symbol of a *kohen*; a pouring jug of water is a symbol of a Levite. The six-pointed Star of David (see MAGEN DAVID) has only been used exclusively as a Jewish symbol in recent centuries. In the seventeenth and eighteenth centuries in central Europe, most frequently in Prague, the star was first widely used in a Jewish context. In the nineteenth century the star became widely accepted as the central symbol of Jews and Judaism and was adopted for use by the Zionist movement and the State of Israel. See also ART.

• Ellen Frankel and Betsy Platkin Teutsch, *The Encyclopedia of Jewish Symbols* (Northvale, N.J., 1992). Erwin R. Goodenough, *Jewish Symbols in the Greco-Roman Period*, 13 vols. (New York, 1953–1968). Abram Kanof, *Jewish Symbolic Art* (Jerusalem, 1990). Shalom Sabar, *Mazal Tov: Illuminated Jewish Marriage Contracts from the Israel Museum Collection* (Jerusalem, 1993). Gershom Gerhard Scholem, "The Star of David: History of a Symbol," in *The Messianic Idea in Judaism and Other Essays in Jewish Spirituality* (New York, 1971).

—GABRIEL M. GOLDSTEIN

SYMMACHUS (c.2d–3d cent.), translator of the Bible into Greek. Various conjectures have been made about his identity; for example, that he may have been a member of the *Ebionites, a Samaritan convert to Judaism, or a Jewish disciple of R. Me'ir. Symmachus's translation, which was included in Origen's Hexapla, was transmitted as part of the Hexapla. On the whole, although he often represented the sense of the words rather than their literal meaning, Symmachus's translation was very precise; however, very little of his translation has been preserved.

• Dominique Barthélemy, *Les Devanciers d'Aquila*, Supplements to Vetus Testamentum, vol. 10 (Leiden, 1963). Alison Salvesen, *Symmachus in the Pentateuch*, Journal of Semitic Studies, Monograph no. 15 (Manchester, 1991).

SYNAGOGUE, a term from the Greek meaning "assembly"; in Hebrew *beit ha-keneset* (house of meeting). The exact origin of the synagogue is unknown. Although prayer was an integral part of the sacrificial service from early times, there is no record of special prayer houses. The synagogue may have originated during the period of Babylonian captivity, although some scholars trace its beginnings to the period of the monarchy. The first Babylonian exiles (597 BCE) seem to have met for the purpose of exposition of the scriptures and public worship on Sabbaths and festivals; when the bulk of the people were exiled to Babylonia (586), the institution of meeting for prayer and instruction already was in existence. Such gatherings are recorded in the *Book of Ezekiel*, and the reference in *Ezekiel* 11.16 possibly reflects the emergence of the synagogue in the Babylonian exile. To the allegation of the inhabitants of Jerusalem that the exiles, being far removed from the Temple, had forfeited the presence and protection of God, the prophet replied with the divine message that God himself would be a *miqdash me'at* (little sanctuary) to Israel in exile (*Ez*. 11.15–16). This was interpreted by the rabbis to refer to the "houses of worship and houses of learning." No definite reference to the existence of the synagogue is known until long after the return from the Babylonian exile. By the time Ezra instituted the reading of the Torah on Sabbath afternoons and on Mondays and Thursdays (*B. Q*. 82a), as well as statutory daily prayers (*Ber*. 33a; *Meg*. 17b), assemblies for worship were possibly already in existence throughout the land. The first archeological evidence comes from Schedia, near Alexandria, Egypt, from the third century BCE. By the end of the Second Temple era the synagogue was a well-established institution both in Erets Yisra'el and in the Diaspora. Matter-of-course references in the New Testament speak of Jesus' preaching in the synagogues in Galilee, and pre-70 CE synagogues have been excavated in Masada, Herodion, and Gamla. A synagogue existed even in the precincts of the Temple (*Yoma'* 7.1; *Suk*. 4.3), but the date of its establishment is unknown. Until the destruction of the Temple, synagogues were places for reading the Bible and for sermons, and there is no evidence that they were used for communal prayer. According to the Talmud (*Ket*. 105), when Titus took Jerusalem in 70 CE, he destroyed 394 synagogues in the city. The Talmud relates (*Suk*. 51b) that the great synagogue of Alexandria was so large that it was impossible for those far removed from the center to hear the reader, and a man was appointed to stand and wave a scarf at the times when the congregation had to utter "amen" to the prayers. The epistles of Paul attest to the centrality of the synagogue in Diaspora life; thirteen synagogues flourished in Rome. The synagogue had so much become the focus of religious life that the destruction of the Second Temple left much less of a vacuum than had the destruction of the First Temple. The rabbis adopted the *liturgy as a substitute for and a reminder of the Temple ritual.

About a hundred synagogues, dating up to the eighth century, have been excavated in Israel, most of them conforming to the rabbinical teaching that synagogues should be built on hills, so that other buildings would not rise above them, or near bodies of water. The rabbis taught that a synagogue should be constructed wherever a Jewish community exists, and, after 70 CE, the synagogue became the focus of spiritual and communal life in its triple role of prayer house, place of study and religious instruction, and center of communal assembly. From earliest times, synagogues were oriented toward Jerusalem (inside Jerusalem, toward the Temple mount). There was no prescribed form, and the buildings were at all times heavily influenced by the architecture of their environment (and indeed, for the most part, the architects were non-Jews). In the classical period, they reflected Greco-Roman public buildings. At different times and in different places the attitude toward artistic decoration varied (see ART). Sometimes it was austere, and no human forms were depicted; at other times, the attitude was liberal, and human figures in biblical scenes were depicted, and even the hand of God (as in the third-century synagogue at Dura-Europos in Syria and the sixth-century synagogue at Beth Alpha in Israel). In Babylonia, synagogues were often situated outside towns, as the rabbis considered the cities to be filled with unclean things. Although reverence for the synagogue is enjoined, the atmosphere often tended to be informal and decorum not too stringent, with the congregants feeling very much at home. Architecturally, the central feature is the ark (*aron ha-qodesh*) on the wall facing Jerusalem, which contains the *scrolls of the Torah (see SEFER TORAH). In ancient times the ark was portable; it was brought into the prayer hall only for services and placed in a special niche. In front of the ark burns the **ner tamid*, reminiscent of the perpetual light in the Temple (*Nm.* 8.1–4). The seats along the wall where the ark is situated are regarded as especially privileged. The medieval period saw various architectural changes. Special arrangements were made for the separate seating of *women, in balconies, annexes (see 'EZRAT NASHIM), or behind partitions (**meḥitsah*), which were unknown in the ancient and classical periods. Hostile Christian and Muslim restrictions limited the height of buildings and sometimes prohibited the erection of new synagogues. To compensate for the lack of external height, synagogues were often built below the street level (the rabbis interpreted this as a fulfillment of *Ps.* 130.1, "From out of the depths I call on you, O Lord"). Apart from the ark, the other main feature was the reader's platform (**bimah*), which was usually in the center of the prayer hall but was also sometimes to be found against the western wall.

No priest or ordained official was required to conduct the service; any competent member of the congregation could lead the prayers, although later, paid *cantors, chosen for their vocal accomplishment rather than learning, were employed. The synagogue was the hub of communal life and the venue for all its activities. Its original role as a gathering place for congregational worship profoundly influenced Christian and Muslim forms of worship.

When the Italian Jews were forced into *ghettos, they were only allowed a single synagogue building; in Rome this housed a number of prayer halls, while in Venice the synagogues were constructed in the top stories of existing buildings, inconspicuous from the outside but with interiors rich with examples of Renaissance art. In eastern Europe, wooden synagogues were popular, reflecting the architecture of the region (almost all of the last surviving examples were destroyed by the Germans in World War II). Some synagogues were built as fortresses so that the Jews could protect themselves in the event of attack. Characteristic of many eastern European synagogues were the four pillars supporting the building and surrounding the reader's platform. In Muslim lands, Jewish worshipers replicated certain Islamic customs and often removed their shoes for worship or sat on the floor. Muslim rulers sometimes enacted harsh laws forbidding the construction of synagogue buildings, but ways were found to circumvent such decrees, and prayer rooms could also be found in private homes. In India, the *Bene Israel, when first discovered in the eighteenth century, had no synagogues; they were only introduced when the people moved to the large towns. The Chinese Jews of K'ai-feng had a notable synagogue, including a hall of ancestors, but this was destroyed in the nineteenth century. In Ethiopia, the synagogues were divided into three sections, admission to each regulated by Levitical law. The eastern entrance was reserved for the monks of the community.

The era of *Emancipation brought revolutionary changes to the European synagogue. Jews sought to proclaim their status as equal citizens by building imposing and monumental edifices in prominent places, but at the same time indicated their difference by preferring an Oriental-style architecture. Internal changes introduced by the Reform movement included family seating, the abolition of the separate platform for the reader, which was now situated in front of the ark, and places for organ and choir. Reform Judaism also preferred the term **temple* to *synagogue.* Most of the monumental synagogues in central Europe were destroyed by the Nazis on Kristallnacht (9–10 Nov. 1938).

Since World War II, the most imaginative building manifesting new aesthetic standards has taken place in the United States. Leading architects, sculptors, painters, and other artists have participated in the building and decoration of synagogues. The synagogue has resumed its role as a community center, providing educational, social, and athletic activities in addition to its religious functions. In the Soviet Union, where religious expression was suppressed, few synagogues remained by the 1980s, but to the extent that Jews began openly to display their national identity from the late 1960s, the synagogue and its vicinity was the focus. In Israel, where there are many other avenues for Jewish self-expression, the synagogue is primarily a place of prayer.

• Marilyn Joyce Segal Chiat, *A Handbook of Synagogue Architecture* (Chico, Calif., 1982). Brian de Breffny, *The Synagogue* (New York, 1978). Azriel Louis Eisenberg, *The Synagogue Through the Ages* (New York, 1974). Ismar Elbogen, *Jewish Liturgy: A Comprehensive History*, translated by Raymond P. Scheindlin (Philadelphia, New York, and Jerusalem, 1993), pp. 337–368. Joseph Gutmann, ed., *Ancient Synagogues: The State of Research* (Chico, Calif., 1981). Joseph Gutmann, ed., *The Synagogue: Studies in Origins, Archaeology, and Architecture* (New York, 1975). Zvi Ilan, *Batei Keneset Qedumim be-Erets Yisra'el* (Tel Aviv, 1991). Avram Kampf, *Contemporary Synagogue Art* (Philadelphia, 1966). Uri Kaploun, *The Synagogue* (Philadelphia, 1973). Carol Herselle Krinsky, *Synagogues of Europe* (Cambridge, Mass., and New York, 1985). Isaac Levy, *The Synagogue: Its History and Function* (London, 1963). Maria and Kazimierz Piechotka, *Wooden Synagogues* (Warsaw, 1959). J. B. Soloveichik, "The Synagogue as an Institution and as an Idea," in *Rabbi Joseph H. Lookstein Memorial Volume*, edited by Leo Landman (New York, 1980), pp. 321–339. Geoffrey Wigoder, *The Story of the Synagogue: A Diaspora Museum Book* (San Francisco, 1986). Rachel Wischnitzer, *The Architecture of the European Synagogue* (Philadelphia, 1964). Rachel Wischnitzer, *Synagogue Architecture in the United States* (Philadephia, 1955).

–SHMUEL HIMELSTEIN

SYNAGOGUE, GREAT. See KENESET HA-GEDOLAH.

SYNCRETISM, the act or system of blending or reconciling heterogeneous elements. In the history of religion it signifies the mixing of beliefs and practices of different—and at times conflicting—character and origins. Syncretism (originally a pejorative term of abuse) occurs wherever different cultures meet. The biblical record contains indications of much popular syncretism between Israelite and Canaanite religion, an amalgamation that the prophets had continually to combat. An example of conscious theological syncretism can be found in *Genesis* 14.22, where Abram (see ABRAHAM) identifies his God with Melchizedek's El Elyon. In a narrower sense, syncretism refers to the blending of Greek and Oriental religions in the Hellenistic period; from the point of view of Jewish monotheism this was merely another form of paganism (see HASMONEANS).

SYNOD. See COUNCILS AND SYNODS.

T

TA'AMEI HA-MIQRA'. See ACCENTS; CANTORIAL MUSIC; TROP.

TA'AMEI HA-MITSVOT. See COMMANDMENTS, REASONS FOR.

TA'ANIT (תַּעֲנִית; Fast), tractate in Mishnah order Mo'ed, in four chapters, with related material in the Tosefta' and in both Talmuds. It deals with laws related to various forms of fast days (see FASTS), primarily with fasting in times of drought. *Ta'anit* opens with the chronology of the yearly prayers for rain, outlining a sequence of liturgical acts and prayers in which the inhabitants of Erets Yisra'el anticipate the rainy season by various modes of addressing God who grants rain. The fast days, which begin shortly after the earliest signs of delay in the falling of rain and increase in intensity, are presented in *Ta'anit* as a response to the rejection of Israel's prayers, as well as to the imminent danger of drought. The later, more intense fast days are observed by a cessation of work, as the community assembles in a public square for a ceremony that includes signs of mourning and humiliation and a call by prominent leaders of the community to repent their evil actions. Special prayers are recited, highlighting God's responsiveness to his people in previous times of distress, accompanied in the Temple by the sounding of trumpets.

Similar fast days are mandated for other occasions of communal distress and danger, such as plague, locusts, and war. The fourth chapter of *Ta'anit* focuses on various elements of the Temple service incidentally related to fasting and concludes with two fast days (Shiv'ah 'Asar be-Tammuz and Tish'ah be-'Av) that commemorate historical tragedies, national as well as spiritual, which befell the Jewish people. Prominently featured among these tragedies are events connected to the destruction of the two Temples, underscoring the central role of the Temple both as a national and as a spiritual center. These two historically oriented fast days are counterbalanced by two days of rejoicing, Tu be-'Av and Yom Kippur, on which daughters of Jerusalem, clothed in white, dance in the vineyards, and sons of Jerusalem select their mates. The rather paradoxical characterization of Yom Kippur as a uniquely festive day underscores the dialectical interrelationship of fasting and feasting that underlies many of the laws and features of *Ta'anit*.

A critical edition and an English translation were published by Henry Malter (New York, 1930).

• Chanoch Albeck, ed., *Shishah Sidrei Mishnah, Seder Mo'ed* (Jerusalem, 1952). Philip Blackman, ed. and trans., *Mishnayoth*, vol. 2, *Order Moed* (Gateshead, 1973). Pinhas Kehati, ed., *Mishnah: A New Translation with a Commentary, Seder Moed*, vol. 5, *Ta'anit, Megillah, Moed Katan, Haggigah* (Jerusalem, 1991). Henry Malter, ed. and trans., *The Treatise Ta'anit of the Babylonian Talmud* (1930; Philadelphia, 1978). Hermann Leberecht Strack and Günter Stemberger, *Introduction to the Talmud and Midrash*, rev. and updat. ed., translated by Markus Bockmuehl (Minneapolis, 1992).
—AVRAHAM WALFISH

TA'ANIT BEKHORIM (תַּעֲנִית בְּכוֹרִים), fast traditionally observed by male firstborns (whether on the father's or mother's side) during all or part of the day preceding the Pesaḥ festival (14 Nisan) in memory of the saving of the Israelite firstborns when the Egyptian firstborns were killed (*Ex.* 12–13). Until a firstborn reaches maturity, his father fasts on his behalf. The fast is mentioned in minor tractate *Soferim* 21.3 and was instituted in the geonic period. Later it became customary to conclude the study of a Talmudic tractate on that day, thereby permitting the breaking of the fast with a festive Se'udat Mitsvah (see SE'UDAH). According to some authorities, the rabbis thus bent the rules on this occasion to avoid any comparison to the Christian practice of fasting in the pre-Easter period, often on the same date. If the fast falls on a Sabbath, it is observed on the preceding Thursday.

• Daniel Goldschmidt, "'Al Ta'anit Bekhorot," in *Meḥqerei Tefillah u-Fiyyut* (Jerusalem, 1978), pp. 384–386. Philip Goodman, ed., *The Passover Anthology* (Philadelphia, 1993). Mosheh Alexander Kinstlicher, *Ta'anit Bekhorim u-Se'udot Mitsvah be-'Erev Pesaḥ . . .* (Bene Beraq, 1981). Eliyahu Ki Tov, *The Book of Our Heritage* (Jerusalem, 1968), pp. 205–207.
—CHAIM PEARL

TA'ANIT ESTER (תַּעֲנִית אֶסְתֵּר), fast day observed on 13 Adar, the day preceding *Purim; if this should fall on a Sabbath, the fast (from sunrise to sunset) is observed on the preceding Thursday. While this has become linked with the fast ordered by the biblical Esther (*Est.* 4.16), it is in fact unconnected to that fast, which occurred in the month of Nisan (cf. *Est.* 3.12); (there was an ancient custom to observe three "fasts of Esther" during the month of Nisan [*Massekhet Soferim* 21.1]). From the time of *Judah the Maccabee, 13 Adar was a day of celebration—Nicanor Day (see *1 Mac.* 7.43–50), commemorating Judah's victory over the Syrian general Nicanor—when fasting was specifically prohibited (cf. **Megillat Ta'anit*). This celebration, however, fell into disuse after the destruction of the Temple. As fasting became forbidden during the joyous month of Nisan, the fasts of Esther were transferred to Adar. The custom of fasting on 13 Adar is first mentioned in the eighth century CE (in the *She'iltot* of R. Aḥa' of Shabḥa). As it is of late origin, its observance is less strictly enforced than other fasts, although it was kept with particular stringency by Persian Jews. Special penitential prayers are said in the Orthodox synagogue service on this day.

• Alter Hilawitz, "Ta'anit Ester," in *Ḥiqrei Zemanim* (Jerusalem, 1976), pp. 347–376. Chaim Pearl, *A Guide to the Minor Festivals and Fasts* (London, 1963), pp. 73–76. A. Schwarz, "Taanith Esther," in *Festskrift i anledning af Professor David Simonsens*, by David Jacob Simonsen (Copenhagen, 1923), pp. 188–205.

TA'ANIT SCROLL. See MEGILLAT TA'ANIT.

TABERNACLE (Heb. Mishkan [Dwelling Place, Abode], the portable shrine erected by the Israelites in the wilderness (*Ex.* 25.9, 26.1). It is also referred to as the Miqdash (Sanctuary; *Ex.* 25.8; *Nm.* 10.21) and as the Ohel Mo'ed (Tent of Meeting; *Ex.* 29.10, 30.16; see also

Ex. 39.3, 40.2). These names express the Tabernacle's three functions, respectively: an earthly abode for the enshrined deity (*Ex.* 25.8, 29.45); a sacred domain for sacrificial worship; and the place where Moses was to meet with God in order to receive the laws (*Ex.* 25.22, 29.42–43). The Tabernacle is also referred to as Mishkan ha-ʿEdut or Ohel ha-ʿEdut (Abode or Tent of the Testimony; *Ex.* 38.21; *Nm.* 1.50, 17.23, 18.2; see ARK OF THE COVENANT).

According to the biblical account (*Ex.* 25–31, 35–40), when Moses ascended Mount Sinai to receive the tablets of the Law, he was first given detailed instructions for the building of the Tabernacle. In order for Moses to carry out these instructions properly, God also displayed to him a heavenly image of the Tabernacle (*Ex.* 25.9, 40; 26.30, 27.8). The orders were then delivered to the people, who willingly contributed all the necessary materials and participated enthusiastically in the construction under the divinely inspired direction of Bezalel and Oholiab (*Ex.* 35.20–36.7). By the start of the next year, the entire project was completed, after which the majestic presence of God (*kevod* YHVH), in the form of a fiery cloud, took up residence (*Ex.* 40). In a series of meetings with Moses, with the voice of God emanating from the inner sanctum, the laws of sacrifice were given (*Lv.* 1–7); then the Tabernacle and its priesthood were consecrated (*Lv.* 8–9), and the sacrificial worship of God commenced. Following this, the remainder of the laws were given. When the Israelites departed from Sinai to begin their wanderings in the wilderness (*Nm.* 10.11–28), the shrine was dismantled and transported by the priests and Levites (*Nm.* 3.14–4.20). At each new location it was reassembled, and on each new journey it was taken apart again. The Israelites brought the Tabernacle with them into Canaan, where it was erected for the last time at Shiloh (*Jos.* 18.1). There it remained and eventually became a fixed sanctuary (*1 Sm.* 1).

The tabernacle is described as a rectangular structure of 30 × 10 cubits (45 × 15 ft.). On three sides (north, west, and south) were walls consisting of upright wooden planks inserted in sockets and held together by bars and bolts. Stretched over the top of the Tabernacle, forming its roof, and draped down over the three sides was a set of curtains of fine fabrics with the cherub motif embroidered onto them; over these was draped a set of goat-hair curtains; and these, in turn, were draped with skins. The fabric coverings and the absence of any other roof made the Tabernacle a tent. The fourth side, to the east, was a woven screen of fine fabrics suspended on five pillars, which formed the entrance. Another screen of fabric embroidered with the cherub motif, called the Parokhet (Veil), divided the inside of the Tabernacle into two parts. At the western end was the smaller, inner sanctum (10 × 10 cubits), the Holy of Holies (Qodesh ha-Qodashim). The eastern end (10 × 20 cubits) was the outer sanctum or Holy Place (Qodesh). In the pitch-black inner sanctum, containing only the Ark, the deity was said to reside in isolation, enthroned on the cherubim. The outer sanctum contained three golden furnishings: the lamp stand (see MENORAH), the table (see SHOWBREAD), and the incense *altar. These featured in the twice-daily **tamid* ritual. Entry into the inner sanctum was confined to the annual purification ritual performed by the high priest on Yom Kippur. The gold, silver, bronze, fine wool and linen, skins, and expensive woods said to have been used to make the Tabernacle and its furnishings gave the Tabernacle its majestic splendor. These materials were arranged in graded fashion; the nearer one got to the inner sanctum, the more expensive the materials and the more intricate the workmanship. An inseparable part of the Tabernacle was its courtyard (100 × 50 cubits), enclosed by hanging screens, delineating the sacred precincts. In the center of the eastern court, opposite the entrance to the Tabernacle, stood the sacrificial altar; this is where the main sacrificial rituals took place "in the presence of the Lord." The Tabernacle was thus the forerunner of the Jerusalem *Temple, its design, proportions, and ritual functions making it a miniature, portable version of the future, permanent abode of Israel's God.

Modern scholars find that the Tabernacle belongs exclusively to the Priestly source of the Pentateuch; the non-Priestly sources make no mention of it. Some scholars describe the story as an idealized, retroactive account of the origins of Israel's institutions of worship, written in light of later developments and greatly embellished. It is possible, however, that the historical kernel is to be sought in the sanctuary at Shiloh, which, according to Priestly tradition, had its origin in the wilderness period.

• Menahem Haran, *Temples and Temple-Service in Ancient Israel* (Oxford, 1978), pp. 149–204. Victor Hurowitz, "The Priestly Account of Building the Tabernacle," *Journal of the American Oriental Society* 105 (1985): 21–30. Craig R. Koester, *The Dwelling of God: The Tabernacle in the Old Testament, Intertestamental Jewish Literature, and the New Testament*, Catholic Biblical Quarterly Monograph Series 22 (Washington, 1989). Moshe Levine, *The Tabernacle: Its Structure and Utensils* (London and New York, 1969).

—BARUCH J. SCHWARTZ

TABERNACLES, FEAST OF. See SUKKOT.

TABLE SONGS. See ZEMIROT.

TABLETS OF THE LAW (Heb. *luḥot ha-berit* or *luḥot ha-ʿedut*), two tablets of stone received by Moses from God at Mount *Sinai (*Ex.* 24.12–18, 31.18, 32.15; *Dt.* 9.9–11). As the written record of the revelation at Sinai, they functioned as physical evidence of the divine covenant with Israel. In the biblical tradition, the original divine tablets were engraved "by the finger of God" (*Ex.* 31.18), and the writing miraculously covered both sides (*Ex.* 32.15). Moses, however, smashed these to bits when he discovered the Israelites worshiping the *golden calf, and he was instructed to make a new set to replace them. After Moses returned to the top of Mount Sinai with a new set of tablets, God wrote upon them precisely what had been on the original tablets, the Ten Words (*Ex.* 34.28; *Dt.* 10.1–4; see TEN COMMANDMENTS). The tablets were placed in the Ark (in rabbinic legend, along with the fragments of the original set), which was thus known as the *Ark of the Covenant. According to *1 Kings* 8.9, these tablets were still in the Ark at the inauguration of Solomon's Temple in Jerusalem. Rabbinic tradition holds that the size of the tablets was 6 × 3 × 6 cubits (*B. B.* 14a), and the Ten Words were arranged in two parallel groups, five on each tablet. Legend deals copiously with the substance of the tablets, the wondrous nature of the script, and the circumstances of their transmission. The later fate of the tablets is not known; according to one legend they were hidden by Josiah; another says that they were taken into the Babylonian exile when the first Temple was destroyed in 586 BCE. By Second Temple times, the tablets had disappeared. The later artistic use of the tablets as a symbol of Judaism was probably inspired by Christian art, which depicted the tablets as a vertical rectangle rounded at the top to symbolize the meeting between heaven and earth. In medieval sculptures of "church and synagogue" on cathedrals, the synagogue was often pictured with the tablets upside down to hint that Judaism did not understand the implication of their teaching. In Jewish art, the earliest depictions of the tablets date from the fifteenth or sixteenth century and were placed as decoration over the ark in the synagogue. The use of the motif became widespread in the nineteenth century, especially in central Europe, where designers of Reform temples found them a more universal symbol than the particularistic *menorah*. Mosaic law was stressed as the antithesis of Talmudic tradition. Today, tablets are frequently found not only in synagogues of all kinds but also on ceremonial objects and on items possessing religious associations.

• Ida Huberman, *Living Symbols: Symbols in Jewish Art and Tradition* (Tel Aviv, 1988), pp. 65–68. —BARUCH J. SCHWARTZ

TADSHE'. See MIDRASH TADSHE'.

TAGIN (Aram.; תָּגִין; crowns), decorative crownlike flourishes that are added to the tops of certain letters of Torah scrolls. Their origin is traditionally ascribed to Sinaitic revelation, and Talmudic and Midrashic sources assign them a mystical significance. A work called *Sefer Tagin* (copied by Simḥah ben Shemu'el of Vitry in his *Maḥazor Vitry* [edited by Shim'on Hurwitz (1923)]) sets out the rules for their correct application. *Tagin* also appear on the **mezuzah* and **tefillin* but not in printed texts of the Bible.

TAḤANUN (תַּחֲנוּן; Supplication), petition for grace and forgiveness (the name is derived from the original introduction: " . . . and receive my supplications [*taḥanunai*]") said daily, except on Sabbaths, festivals, days of joy (e.g., in the presence of a bridegroom), on Tish'ah be-'Av, and in houses of a mourner during the week of mourning after the morning and afternoon 'Amidah. The liturgical Taḥanun replaced the earlier, silent, personal petitions for mercy. Taḥanun is also called Nefilat Appayim (Falling on the Face) from the attitude in which it was originally recited. Today worshipers lean their heads on their left arms (or on their right arms when *tefillin* are on the left). *Sa'adyah ben Yosef Ga'on described the worshiper as "half sitting and half kneeling" during Taḥanun, but the Western tradition is to sit. Since the eighteenth century, the prayer has been introduced with the verse "And David said . . . 'I am in a great strait; let us fall now into the hand of the Lord' " (*2 Sm.* 24.14), which is followed by Psalm 6 and the *piyyut* *Shomer Yisra'el (Guardian of Israel). The prayer concludes with the paragraph, "As for us, we know not what to do." The Sephardi ritual (followed by most Israeli Ashkenazim) omits Psalm 6 and substitutes Psalm 25. In the Israeli Sephardi and Hasidic rites, Taḥanun commences with the confession of sins (Viddui) and the thirteen divine attributes; in the Diaspora, in the Sephardi rite, these are recited only on Mondays and Thursdays. Kabbalistic interpretations of Taḥanun include a view of it as ritual death or as spiritual "fall," following the supreme elevation of the worshiper during the 'Amidah. See also VE-HU' RAḤUM.

• Ismar Elbogen, *Jewish Liturgy: A Comprehensive History*, translated by Raymond P. Scheindlin (Philadelphia, New York, and Jerusalem, 1993), pp. 68–69. Kurt Hruby, "Quelques notes sur le Tahanun et la place de la prayer individuelle dans la liturgie synagogale," in *Littera Judaica in Memoriam Edwin Guggenheim* (Frankfurt am Main, 1964), pp. 76–104. Isaiah Tishby, *Wisdom of the Zohar* (Oxford, 1989), vol. 3, pp. 969–971, 1,033–1,036.

TAHARAH. See TOHORAH.

TAHARAT HA-MISHPAḤAH (טַהֲרַת הַמִּשְׁפָּחָה; family purity), term popularly used to denote the observance of the laws of *niddah* (see MENSTRUATION). The use of the word purity indicates that lack of observance in this area serves to render the family impure and subjects its offspring to a certain taint and stigma. Indeed, the Talmud records the opinion of R. 'Aqiva' that the son of a *niddah* is a *mamzer* (*Yev.* 29). This opinion is not normative *halakhah*. The title "son of a *niddah*" is, nevertheless, a pejorative one and the Talmud attributes improper conduct among children, *inter alia*, to the fact of their being the offspring of a *niddah* (cf. *Massekhet Kallah*). The major thrust of the concept of *taharat ha-mishpaḥah* is, however, a positive one, and it has traditionally been understood to refer to the effect of the practice of the laws of *niddah* in reducing sexual tension in a marriage during a period in which the wife may not be inclined to respond to her husband's physical desires. In addition to the shift in focus from the sexual to other forms of communication between spouses, the practice of the laws of *niddah* may also aid in maintaining sexual excitement in a marriage. According to R. Me'ir, the reason for the seven-day waiting period of a menstruant is "in order that she shall be beloved by her husband at the time of her first entry into the bridal chamber" (*Nid.* 31b). The observance of these laws was widespread among Jewish communities in the past, and continues to be so among Sephardi and Ḥaredi communities.

• Norman Lamm, *A Hedge of Roses: Jewish Insights into Marriage and Married Life* (New York, 1966). Mendell Lewittes, *Jewish Marriage: Rabbinic Law, Legend, and Custom* (Northvale, N.J., 1994), pp. 121–128. —DANIEL SINCLAIR

TAHAROT. See TOHOROT.

TAITAZAK, YOSEF (died before 1545), exegete, halakhic scholar, and kabbalist in Salonika. Taitazak went from Spain to Salonika with his father and soon earned a reputation as one of the leading rabbinic authorities there. His students included R. Yitsḥaq Adarbi, who continued his teacher's exegetical tradition and cited teachings from Taitazak in his works; R. Shemu'el de *Medina; and R. Shelomoh *Alkabez. His circle was known for its Talmudic scholarship as well as for its intense kabbalistic pursuits. It was, in fact, the latter which attracted the young ex-Marrano Shelomoh *Molkho, after his escape from Portugal, to Salonika. Taitazak left no kabbalistic writings. His non-halakhic writings are evidently based on Midrashic and Jewish philosophic texts, including the works of *Mosheh ben Yehoshu'a of Narbonne and Ḥasda'i ben Avraham *Crescas. They also display a deep knowledge of scholastic literature, such as the works of Thomas Aquinas and Aegidius Romanus. Major themes of his philosophical thought include the infinite character of the divine, the nature of the divine light, God as the paradigm of all existence, and the soul as divine in origin. His works include a commentary to *Ecclesiastes*, entitled *Porat Yosef* (Venice, 1576); a commentary to *Daniel* and the Five Scrolls, *Leḥem Setarim* (Venice, 1608); and various other works still in manuscript. Taitazak's legal decisions appear in printed *responsa* literature of his period, such as *She'erit Yehudah* of his brother Yehudah and *Avqat Rokhel* by Yosef *Karo.

• Bracha Sack, in *Meḥqerei Yerushalayim be-Maḥashevet Yisra'el* 7 (1988): 341–356. R. J. Zwi Werblowsky, *Joseph Karo: Lawyer and Mystic* (London, 1962), index. —BRACHA SACK AND DANIEL ABRAMS

TAL. See Tefillat Tal.

TALLIT (טַלִּית), four-cornered cloth with fringes (cf. *Nm.* 15.38), worn as a prayer shawl during the Shaḥarit and Musaf services. It is called *tallit gadol* (large *tallit*) to distinguish it from the *tallit qatan* (small *tallit*), or *tsitsit, worn beneath the outer garments. The *tallit* is donned before the *tefillin* are put on (on those days when *tefillin* are worn). After the recitation of a special blessing, the *tallit* is wrapped around the head and then dropped to the shoulders. The *tallit* must be at least large enough to cover the head and upper body of a youngster. In some areas, particularly in eastern Europe, only married men wore the *tallit*. Sephardim wear it from the age of *bar mitsvah*, as do Jews of German descent, and this has become a widespread practice. The *tallit* should be made of wool with wool fringes attached, but it may be made of other fabrics, in which case the fringes must be made of the same fabric. Today, prayer shawls are often made from silk. Unless an alternative is unavailable, a linen *tallit* should not be used. "To glorify the *mitsvah*," some prayer shawls have a band (*'atarah*) across the top. At the Minḥah and Ma'ariv services, only the officiant wears a *tallit*; on Yom Kippur, worshipers wear their prayer shawls at all five services; and on Tish'ah be-'Av, the *tallit* is worn at the Minḥah service instead of at the Shaḥarit service. Priests called to give the *Birkat ha-Kohanim cover their heads and hands with their *tallit*. Women are exempt from wearing the *tallit* because the commandment is related to a specific time, but in recent years, it has become the practice for many non-Orthodox women to wear a *tallit*. The biblical prescription ordains that a blue thread be added to the fringes, but although some Hasidic sects still attach a blue thread, most Orthodox Jews do not, since the proper process for making the blue dye (**tekhelet*) is still unclear. The *tallit* is usually decorated by several stripes running from top to bottom near the ends. This design and the blue color of the thread inspired the pattern of the Zionist banner, which was later adopted as the flag of the State of Israel.

• Naftali Hoffner, *Dinei Teḥilat Yom* (Tel Aviv, 1974). Abraham Israel Kon, *Prayer*, translated by the author from his book *Si'aḥ Tefillah* (London, 1971). Zeev Meller, "Tallit shel Tefillah," master's thesis, Bar-Ilan University, 1986. —PETER LENHARDT

TALLIT QATAN. See Tsitsit.

TALMID ḤAKHAM (תַּלְמִיד חָכָם; disciple of the wise), the favorite term in rabbinic literature for a scholar, implying that the true scholar is always a student and that the study of the Torah is never ending. His learning must cover all fields, and no matter what question he is asked in any realm of Jewish law, he should be able to answer immediately (*Shab*. 114a). He is the embodiment of a religious ideal, and, according to the Talmud (*Hor*. 13a), "a **mamzer* who is a *talmid ḥakham* takes precedence over a high priest who is an ignoramus." Scholarship must, however, be combined with moral qualities, and a scholar "whose inside is not like his outside is not a real *talmid ḥakham*" (*Yoma'* 72b). The rabbis are exacting in the standards of personal conduct they demand from the *talmid ḥakham*; actions considered normal for others would be a "profanation of God's name" (**ḥillul ha-Shem*) in a Torah scholar, even as regards outward appearance. Thus it is said with deliberate hyperbole (*Shab*. 114a) that a *talmid ḥakham* who has a stain on his garment is worthy of the death penalty. Rabbinic law provides certain privileges (e.g., exemption from taxes) for the *talmid ḥakham*.

• Efraim E. Urbach, *The Sages, Their Concepts and Beliefs*, 2 vols. (Jerusalem, 1987). —SHMUEL HIMELSTEIN

TALMUD (תַּלְמוּד; Teaching), name applied to each of two great compilations, distinguished respectively as the Talmud Yerushalmi (Palestinian Talmud) and the Talmud Bavli (Babylonian Talmud), in which are collected the teachings of the major Jewish scholars (amora'im) who flourished between 200 and 500 CE, the classic period of rabbinic Judaism.

After the *Mishnah was edited in approximately 200 CE, the sages studied and interpreted it with intense scrutiny during the amoraic period in their two major centers of Palestine and Babylonia, often yielding conflicting opinions that were themselves subject to debate and clarification. The Mishnah's laws were extended into general legal principles and, at the same time, were applied to specific new cases. This material forms the basis of the Talmuds, which, however, include additional genres corresponding to the wide range of intellectual activity carried on by the amora'im, among which are new legal enactments, biblical interpretation, and the recording of the sacred history of their society. Neither Talmud covers the entire span of the Mishnah's six orders. Despite this fact, a popular term for the Talmud is the Shas (an acronym for *shishah sedarim*, "six orders [of the Mishnah]"). However, the central orders Mo'ed, Nashim, and Neziqin are largely included in both. The Talmuds have correctly been described as dealing with religion and ethics, exegesis and homiletics, jurisprudence and ceremonial law, ritual and liturgy, philosophy and science, medicine and magic, astronomy and astrology, history and geography, commerce and trade, politics and social problems. Thus the Talmuds serve as prime source material for knowledge of the real and intellectual world of late antiquity in general, and of classical Jewish law and doctrine in particular.

The two Talmuds are separate works in their final form but in their earlier stages can be viewed as individual records of the same intellectual activity. The two centers were in constant communication; traveling sages (**naḥotei*) reported the opinions of the Palestinian sages in Babylonia and vice versa.

Materials contained in the Talmudic passages (also called **gemara'*) are of three types: pericopes of tannaitic material (see TANNA'); dictums of individual amora'im quoted by name; and later anonymous connective and discursive constructions. Identical or similar passages of tannaitic or amoraic material are often recorded in both Talmuds, with the Talmud Bavli exhibiting a greater tendency to editorial reworking; the anonymous framework (*setam ha-Talmud*) is likewise more extensive in the Talmud Bavli than in the Yerushalmi. The tannaitic material largely parallels passages in existing tannaitic works, but its Hebrew is influenced by later linguistic forms. The amoraic dictums are in amoraic Hebrew or Aramaic, but rarely a mix of the two. The anonymous dialectical framework is essentially in Aramaic. A given textual unit of *gemara'* is called a *sugya'* and usually contains materials of each of the three types.

The Talmuds are the outgrowth of the intense scholarly activity of generations of sages and their institutions of learning, of which they represent only a partial distillation. The literary expressions of this activity were transmitted orally, compiled and edited, and eventually committed to writing. The compilation of the Talmud Yerushalmi (c.400 CE) preceded that of the Talmud Bavli by about one hundred years. As a result, the Yerushalmi often preserves more pristine and accurate versions of material; the more developed Bavli achieved a greater sophistication of juristic abstraction and dialectic analysis. Disseminated throughout the entire Jewish world (including Palestine) under the aegis of the Babylonian gaonate, the Talmud Bavli became the source of all legal authority for subsequent Jewish law and has been subjected to extended and diverse scholastic treatment over the last fifteen hundred years.

The Talmud Bavli. The *sugya'* is the basic literary unit of the Talmud Bavli; one or more can appear for any specific *mishnah*. The *sugya'* is presented dialectically, with all material appearing in a connected succession of questions and answers. A linear reading of Talmud Bavli *sugyot* leads to a perception of them as a flowing record of live debate in the amoraic academies. Actually they are careful literary constructions. In their earlier stages they often contained unconnected tannaitic and amoraic dictums around which was woven the anonymous framework connecting the parts into a whole, sometimes through an adaptation of their basic meaning. A monolithic reading of a *sugya'* yields an extended inquiry of dogmatic quality; a critical reading reveals a skillful composition of independent components with precise literary shape and a dual level of meaning.

The Talmud Bavli is based on diverse literary sources. Dictums of Babylonian amora'im are the main building blocks, with an amoraic statement or dispute often serving as the point of departure for a *sugya'* in place of a *mishnah* or *baraiyta'*. The use of Palestinian literary sources is evident, whether in a single tannaitic pericope (*baraiyta'*) or amoraic dictum, or in longer units such as entire Palestinian *sugyot*, collections of statements by a given authority, or a complex aggadic composition artistically rewoven into the Talmud Bavli *sugya'*.

The amora'im were a society of masters and their disciples, whose activity extended over more than five generations in several centers. In the first generation (early 3d cent. CE), *Shemu'el was the outstanding authority in the academy of *Nehardea, and *Rav emigrated from Palestine and established a center of learning in *Sura. In the fourth generation under *Abbayei at *Pumbedita, and afterwards under *Rava' in Maḥoza, amoraic activity reached its acme. Fifth-generation *rav* *Ashi is considered the editor of the Talmud Bavli in traditional writings. While earlier amora'im concentrated more upon the detailed legal exegesis of the Mishnah, later generations developed sophisticated juristic principles. The Talmud Bavli might be considered the most developed work of legal conceptualization of antiquity.

The final literary touches to the Talmud were the work of the savora'im (see SAVORA'). Concepts in the Talmud Bavli were extended to logical completeness and harmony, more so than in the Talmud Yerushalmi. Legal positions in the Talmud Bavli were attributed to individual tanna'im in quasi-quotations (*de-amar*, "who said," has the force of "who held") more encompassing and balanced than actual quotations. Harmonizations were suggested for uneven juxtapositions in the Mishnah. Savoraic *sugyot* used hermeneutic methods (see HERMENEUTICS) in explicating the language of the Mishnah. Precise language and technical terminology were gradually developed.

The Talmud Bavli contains rich aggadic passages (see AGGADAH) that often exhibit unbridled imaginative embellishments when compared to their Yerushalmi parallels. The *Aramaic used in the Talmud has affinities with Syriac, Mandaic, and other eastern dialects.

The compilation or editing of the Talmud Bavli was not performed in a uniform manner; thus *Nedarim, Nazir*, and *Keritot, Me'ilah*, and *Tamid* can be distinguished from the rest of the tractates largely by the different technical terminology that appears in them. This group of tractates contains early amoraic strata, on the one hand, and, on the other, an anonymous editorial stratum composed later than the rest of the Talmud. Several middle stages of development are apparently missing. Both chronological and geographic factors have been considered by scholars in explaining the uniqueness of this group of tractates.

In addition to printed editions of the Talmud Bavli (the first published in Venice, 1520–1523), about two hundred codices of one or several tractates have been preserved (c.11th–15th cent.) as have many manuscript fragments, perhaps from as early as the eighth or ninth century. It was too difficult to produce the entire Talmud in one codex or even a coordinated set of codices; the Munich Codex must be considered a carefully planned exception in this regard. The textual variants that can be culled from this corpus and from quotations in medieval literature are significant for scholarly research. Some scholars had suggested that these variants derived from the oral transmission of the Talmud after its editing, which did not produce a fixed text but only fixed contents. More recent research has indicated that a relatively fixed text of the tractates existed after their editing, but the transmission of the text was sometimes in the hands of conservative tradents and at other times handled in a liberal manner, allowing some early tradents to update vocabulary and terminology and perform other editorial functions. Basic reworking was extremely rare; however, a manuscript text of *Moʿed Qatan* with far-reaching variants has recently been brought to scholarly attention.

Various works entitled *Introduction to the Palestinian Talmud*, in which the Talmud Bavli is used as a point of comparison for the Talmud Yerushalmi, contain much of the scholarly enterprise describing literary aspects of the Talmud Bavli. Abraham Weiss has written extensively on the Talmud Bavli. Several English translations of the Talmud are available, notably the Soncino Talmud (London, 1935–1952), as is a dictionary devoted exclusively to Babylonian Aramaic. Scholars are at work on the first modern edition of the Talmud Bavli with a critical commentary.

The Talmud Yerushalmi. Also called the Jerusalem Talmud, the Talmud Yerushalmi is the commentary on the Mishnah produced in Palestine during the third and fourth centuries CE. Some medieval scholars termed this work *Talmud ha-Maʿarav* or *Talmuda' di-Venei Maʿarava'*, although Talmud Yerushalmi, which is actually a misnomer since it was produced in Galilee and not in Jerusalem, is more commonly used.

The Talmud Yerushalmi includes the orders Zeraʿim, Moʿed, Nashim, and Neziqin (except for tractates *ʿEduyyot* and *Avot*), and part of tractate *Niddah*. The final chapters of tractates *Shabbat* (chaps. 20–24), *Makkot* (chap. 3), and *Niddah* (chaps. 4ff.) are no longer extant and were apparently lost during the early medieval period. By contrast, there is no conclusive evidence that the Talmud Yerushalmi ever contained Qodashim and Tohorot, although Palestinian amora'im clearly studied these orders of the Mishnah.

The Talmud Yerushalmi includes the dictums of hundreds of amora'im. Five generations of Palestinian amora'im and perhaps a few sixth-generation scholars are cited. Likewise, Babylonian amora'im from the first three generations are cited, although there is hardly any mention of later Babylonian scholars. No explicit information about the Talmud Yerushalmi's redaction or chronology has been preserved in its pages or in the works of reliable post-Talmudic chroniclers; hence, the identity and date of the work's redactor(s) cannot be determined with certainty. However, it would appear that the bulk of the redaction took place in Tiberias, although material from other academies (e.g., Sepphoris and Caesarea) is also cited frequently. Since the latest named scholars flourished at the end of the fourth century, it reasonably may be assumed that the work was redacted at that time, although it is possible that some activity took place later. Some scholars have suggested, on the basis of its unpolished style, that the work was concluded in haste and never adequately edited due to the difficulties prevailing in fourth-century Palestine. Conscious stylistic decisions, however, also may have played a part.

The Talmud Yerushalmi contains numerous *baraiytot*, many of which bear a strong resemblance to the *baraiytot* in the *Tosefta', although it is clear that the *baraiytot* in the Yerushalmi as a whole were not derived from the Tosefta'. Likewise, the Talmud Yerushalmi cites many halakhic *midrashim* as well as several hundred aggadic passages, both isolated dictums and complete pericopes, many of which closely resemble classic Palestinian aggadic *midrashim* (*Genesis Rabbah, Leviticus Rabbah*, etc.). These nonlegal passages occur in virtually all of the tractates. The *aggadah* is both tannaitic (much of it paralleling the *aggadah* in the Tosefta') and amoraic. Virtually all aggadic genres are represented in the work: biblical exegesis, homiletics and hermeneutics, history (as seen through rabbinic eyes), exempla, and other tales.

The nonlegal material serves diverse functions: illustrating (and occasionally even contradicting) halakhic rulings cited in the legal portions of the Talmud; supplementing and explaining aggadic passages in the Mishnah; and expanding the purview of the primary discussion with tangential material. Some of the *aggadot* were ostensibly taken en bloc from ancient aggadic compendiums, and certain passages were apparently introduced by ancient copyists, although most of the nonlegal material was presumably included there by the work's authors or redactors.

The *aggadah* in the Talmud Yerushalmi generally lacks a clear-cut ideological or theological orientation. In addition, it is generally devoid of the literary embellishments characteristic of the nonlegal material in the Talmud Bavli and is often considered more historically reliable than its Babylonian counterpart.

The Talmud Yerushalmi's principal concern is explication of the Mishnah, usually interpreted in accordance with the plain sense of the text. The complex dialectic characteristic of the Talmud Bavli is rarely found in its Palestinian counterpart. The give and take in the Talmud Yerushalmi is generally shorter and more straightforward than in the Bavli.

One of the most prominent features of the Talmud Yerushalmi is the frequent citation of identical pericopes in different places. These pericopes were presumably copied by scribes, who sought to enlarge the scope of the work by duplicating relevant material wherever feasible. However, some of these parallel pericopes were apparently duplicated or briefly alluded to by the authors and editors and later filled in by copyists.

The language of the Talmud Yerushalmi is a mixture of Galilean Aramaic and Hebrew. The work is formulated in a terse, allusive, and often cryptic style, as a result of which the meaning of numerous passages remains obscure, despite the best efforts of exegetes.

The numerous dictums of Babylonia amora'im cited in the Talmud Yerushalmi frequently differ in form and content from their parallels in the Talmud Bavli. (The same holds true for the dictums of Palestinian scholars that appear in the Bavli.) Very few complete *sugyot* of Babylonian provenience are found in the Yerushalmi. Thus, while its scholars were clearly acquainted with many Babylonian teachings, they apparently were not familiar with the Talmud Bavli as such. Similarly, the Talmud Yerushalmi, as it now stands, was apparently unknown to the scholars of the Talmud Bavli, although they were clearly familiar with many of the teachings of their Palestinian counterparts.

The text of the Talmud Yerushalmi is relatively corrupt. Few text witnesses are extant, and these witnesses apparently derive from a common ancestor as evidenced by the presence of similar discriminative errors. Only one manuscript of all of the Talmud Yerushalmi is extant (MS Leiden, Scaliger 3, 13th cent.). Other manuscripts include MS Vatican 133 (highly corrupt, on Zera'im and tractate *Sotah*), MS Escorial (Neziqin), and Cairo Genizah fragments. Superior readings are frequently found in medieval testimonia.

The Talmud Yerushalmi was first printed (without commentaries) in Venice in 1523 and 1524 by Daniel Bomberg from a corrected version of MS Leiden (although these corrections are often unfounded). The most important later editions, all of which are based on the Venice edition, were published in Krotoszyn in 1866 (without commentaries); in Zhitomir between 1860 and 1867; in Piotrków between 1899 and 1901; and in Vilna in 1922 (a photographic reproduction of the Piotrków edition, with additional commentaries).

Hardly any medieval commentaries on the Talmud Yerushalmi are extant, although medieval commentators on the Talmud Bavli frequently cite and discuss individual passages. The first extant commentary on a major portion of the Yerushalmi was written in the sixteenth century by R. Shelomoh Sirillio (on Zera'im and tractate *Sheqalim*). The only commentary on the complete work is *Penei Mosheh*, by R. Mosheh *Margalit, who also composed a more in-depth commentary on select sections (*Mar'eh ha-Panim*). Other important commentators include R. Eliyyahu of Fulda (17th–18th cent.), R. David *Franckel (18th cent.), and R. *Eliyyahu ben Shelomoh Zalman of Vilna (the Vilna Ga'on), whose comments on the Yerushalmi were recorded by his students. Modern scholars, particularly Louis *Ginzberg, Jacob Nahum *Epstein, and Saul *Lieberman, have significantly advanced the understanding of the Talmud Yerushalmi, although there is still no comprehensive commentary or critical edition.

Medieval halakhists generally considered the Talmud Yerushalmi less authoritative than its Babylonian counterpart, although their views about the extent of its authority vary considerably. Some scholars disregarded the work almost entirely (including most ge'onim), while others accorded it a position of prominence in deciding halakhic issues (e.g., Maimonides).

• Chanoch Albeck, *Mavo' la-Talmudim* (Tel Aviv, 1987). Baruch M. Bokser, "An Annotated Bibliographical Guide to the Study of the Palestinian Talmud," in Jacob Neusner, ed., *The Study of Ancient Judaism II* (New York, 1981), pp. 1–119. Baruch M. Bokser, "Talmudic Studies," in *The State of Jewish Studies*, edited by Shaye J. D. Cohen and Edward L. Greenstein (Detroit, 1990), pp. 80–112. Robert Brody, "Sifrut ha-Ge'onim veha-Teqst ha-Talmudi," in *Meḥqerei Talmud*, edited by Ya'aqov Sussman and David Rosenthal (Jerusalem, 1990), vol. 1, pp. 237–303. Jacob Nahum Epstein, *Mevo'ot le-Sifrut ha-'Amora'im* (Jerusalem, 1962). Shamma Friedman, "Introduction," *Talmud 'Arukh: Pereq ha-Sokher et ha-Omanin Bavli Bava' Metsi'a', Text Volume* (Jerusalem, 1996). Shamma Friedman, "Literary Development and Historicity in the Aggadic Narrative of the Babylonian Talmud," in *Community and Culture: Essays in Jewish Studies in Honor of the Ninetieth Anniversary of the Founding of Gratz College, 1895–1985*, edited by Nahum M. Waldman (Philadelphia, 1987), pp. 67–80. Shamma Friedman, "The Manuscripts of the Babylonian Talmud: A Typology according to Orthography," in *Studies in Hebrew and Jewish Languages: Presented to Shlomo Morag*, edited by Moshe Bar-Asher (Jerusalem, 1996), in Hebrew with English summary. Shamma Friedman, "On the Origin of Textual Variants in the Babylonian Talmud," *Sidra* 7 (1991): vi–vii, 67–102, in Hebrew with English summary. Louis Ginzberg, "The Palestinian Talmud," in *A Commentary on the Palestinian Talmud* vol. 1, pp. xiii–l (New York, 1941). Abraham Goldberg, "The Babylonian Talmud," in *The Literature of the Sages*, edited by Shmuel Safrai (Assen and Philadelphia, 1987), pt. 1, pp. 323–345. D. Goodblatt, "The Babylonian Talmud," in *Aufstieg und Niedergang der romischen Welt: Geschichte und Kultur Roms im Spiegel der neueren Forschungen*, edited by Hildegard Temporini (Berlin and New York, 1979); appeared also in *The Study of Ancient Judaism*, edited by Jacob Neusner (New York, 1981). David Weiss Halivni, *Midrash, Mishnah, and Gemara: The Jewish Predilection for Justified Law* (Cambridge, Mass., 1986). Judith Hauptman, *Development of the Talmudic Sugya: Relationship between Tannaitic and Amoraic Sources* (Lanham, Md., 1988). Marvin J. Heller, *Printing the Talmud: A History of the Earliest Printed Editions of the Talmud* (Brooklyn, N.Y., 1992). Louis Jacobs, *Structure and Form in the Babylonian Talmud* (Cambridge, 1991). Richard L. Kalmin, *The Redaction of the Babylonian Talmud: Amoraic or Saboraic?* (Cincinnati, 1989). Richard L. Kalmin, *Sages, Stories, Authors, and Editors in Rabbinic Babylonia* (Atlanta, 1994). Julius Kaplan, *The Redaction of the Babylonian Talmud* (New York, 1933). Saul Lieberman, *'Al ha-Yerushalmi* (Jerusalem, 1929). Saul Lieberman, *Meḥqarim be-Torat Erets Yisra'el*, edited by David Rosenthal (Jerusalem, 1991), pp. 165–328. Eli'ezer S. Rosenthal, "The History of the Text and Problems of Redaction in the Study of the Babylonian Talmud," *Tarbiz* 57 (1987): i–ii, 1–36, in Hebrew with English summary. Yo'av Rosenthal, "'Iqarav've-'Anafav' shel Bavli Shevu'ot 42a–b," in *Meḥqerei Talmud: Qovets . . . le-Zikhro shel Prof. Eli'ezer Shimshon Rosenthal*, edited by Moshe Bar-Asher and David Rosenthal (Jerusalem, 1993), vol. 2, pp. 517–525. 'Adi'el Schremer, "Between Text Transmission and Text Redaction: Fragments of a Different Recension of TB Mo'ed-Qatan from the Genizah," *Tarbiz* 61 (1992): ii–iii, 375–399, in Hebrew with English summary. 'Adi'el Schremer, "Fragments of Lishana Aharina of Bavli Moed Qatan from the Geniza," *Sidra* 9 (1993): viii–ix, 117–161, in Hebrew with English summary. Jacob S. Spiegel, "Comments and Late Additions in the Babylonian Talmud," in *Meḥqarim be-Sifrut ha-Talmud, be-lashon Ḥazal, uvi-Parshanut ha-Miqra'*, edited by Mordecai Akiba Friedman, Abraham Tal, and Gerson Brinn Te'udah, vol. 3 (Tel Aviv, 1983), in Hebrew with English summary. Hermann Leberecht Strack, *Introduction to the Talmud and Midrash* (New York, 1959), pp. 1–198, 237–327. Hermann Leberecht Strack and Günter Stemberger, *Introduction to the Talmud and Midrash*, rev. and updated ed., translated by Markus Bockmuehl (Minneapolis,

1992), pp. 208–244. Ya'aqov Sussman, "Ve-Shuv li-Yerushalmi Neziqin," in *Meḥqerei Talmud*, edited by Ya'aqov Sussman and David Rosenthal (Jerusalem, 1990), vol. 1, pp. 55–133. Abraham Weiss, *'Al ha-Yetsirah ha-Sifrutit shel ha-'Amora'im* (New York, 1962).

—SHAMMA FRIEDMAN AND LEIB MOSCOVITZ

TALMUD, BURNING OF THE. In the year 1240, the apostate Nicholas Donin laid a charge before the authorities in northern France that the *Talmud contained blasphemies against Jesus. The Jews were compelled to surrender their copies of the Talmud pending clarification of the charge; this took the form of the Disputation of *Paris, at the end of which Louis IX ordered that all copies of the Talmud be confiscated and burned. Twenty-four cartloads were consigned to the flames in 1242. The occasion was commemorated in R. *Me'ir ben Barukh of Rothenburg's dirge Sha'ali Serufah be-'Esh, which was subsequently included in the dirge of the Ashkenazi rite recited on 9 Av. The precedent of 1242 was followed in later centuries; instances of Talmud burnings are recorded in Italy, Poland, and elsewhere. After 1242 the popes continued to advocate burning the Talmud. In general, although censored, the Talmud was not burned on a large scale until a renewed order in 1552 by Pope Julius III led to a big bonfire in Rome (commemorated thereafter by an annual fast among the Jews of Rome), followed by many others in Italy under the instructions of the *Inquisition. It was reported that in Venice over a thousand copies of the Talmud and other sacred literature were burned. The last such public burning was held in Kamieniec-Podolski in Poland in 1757, when a thousand copies were put into a pit and burned following a *disputation between the Jews and the Frankists (see FRANK, YA'AQOV), who played a leading role in hunting down copies of the Talmud for incineration.

• Salo W. Baron, "The Burning of the Talmud in 1553, in Light of Sixteenth-Century Catholic Attitudes toward the Talmud," in *Essential Papers on Judaism and Christianity in Conflict: From Late Antiquity to the Reformation* (New York, 1991). Solomon Grayzel, *The Church and the Jews in the XIIIth Century* (New York, 1966).

TALMUD COMMENTARIES. The first Talmud commentaries covering full tractates appeared at the beginning of the eleventh century CE in Kairouan, the North African center of Jewish learning. Rabbi *Ḥanan'el ben Ḥushi'el wrote a commentary that summarized the basic Talmudic argument and clarified difficult sections. His short elucidations became the model for later Talmud commentators. Ḥanan'el's contemporary, R. *Nissim ben Ya'aqov ben Nissim ibn Shahin, wrote a work called *Sefer Mafteaḥ Man'ulei ha-Talmud* in which he defined difficult terms and explained complex concepts by comparing their uses in different sections of the Talmud and other rabbinic works. Though his commentary is wide-ranging, it, too, did not cover the Talmud's argument in a line-by-line fashion. Only fragments of these commentaries have survived.

The most famous commentary on the Talmud was written by *Rashi. It covers nearly the entire Talmud and is the first line-by-line Talmudic commentary. Rashi's extremely concise comments help connect one point to another, clarify difficult terms, and fill in the lacunae that the Talmud's terseness often generates. To this day, all traditional editions of the Talmud include Rashi's indispensable aid to Talmud study.

Despite its general excellence, Rashi's commentary occasionally exhibited contradictions. Sometimes a wider reading of the Talmud itself indicated that Rashi's commentary was not as cogent as it could be. This led to the **tosafot* (additions), whose authors, the tosafists, sought to correct and improve Rashi's work. Once, however, the work of uncovering and correcting flaws and contradictions in Rashi's commentary began, the tosafists recognized that the Talmud often contradicted itself. Given their view that the Talmud was a well-edited, authoritative statement of the Jewish tradition, they turned to harmonizing discrepancies between Talmudic passages. They often claimed that contradictory passages, for all their similarities, in fact discussed different cases. Thus, they created or recognized subtle distinctions between Talmudic sources that broadened the scope of Jewish legal rubrics and concepts. This movement began in the twelfth century and continued until the late fourteenth century, spreading from Germany and France to Spain.

Between the fifteenth and eighteenth centuries, the tosafists' successors commented less on the Talmud than on Rashi and *tosafot*. The most famous of their super-commentaries are those by Shemu'el Eli'ezer *Edels, *Me'ir ben Gedalyah of Lublin, and Shelomoh *Luria. In the eighteenth century, however, interest in the neglected Talmud Yerushalmi began to flourish, and two major commentaries were written on it: *Penei Mosheh*, by Mosheh *Margalit; and *Qorban ha-'Edah*, by David *Franckel. Both are line-by-line commentaries on the Talmud Yerushalmi modeled on Rashi's work.

With the birth of modern critical-historical Talmudic studies in the nineteenth and twentieth centuries, scholars have distinguished between the Talmud's attributed dictums and its unattributed editorial comments and connectives. Two modern scholars have written Talmud commentaries to individual tractates, trying to solve textual problems and difficulties in content by using this distinction as the basis of their commentaries; they are David Weiss Halivni (*Meqorot u-Mesorot*) and Shamma Y. Friedman (*Ha-'Ishah Rabbah* and *Talmud 'Arukh*). Their commentaries take up problems generated by Talmudic passages rather than individual lines. Adin Steinsaltz has returned to Rashi's style of leading the student through the Talmud's arguments step by step. His work on several tractates has appeared in Modern Hebrew and English.

• Ḥayyim Yosef David Azulai, *Sifrei Shem ha-Gedolim*, 2 vols. (repr. Jerusalem, 1980). Baruch M. Bokser, "An Annotated Bibliographical Guide to the Study of the Palestinian Talmud," *Aufstieg und Niedergang der römischen Welt II*, vol. 19.2 (Berlin, 1979), pp. 139–256. David Goodblatt, "The Babylonian Talmud," *Aufstieg und Niedergang der römischen Welt II*, vol. 19.2 (Berlin, 1979), pp. 257–336. Ezra Z. Melamed, *Pirqei Mavo' le-Sifrut ha-Talmud* (Jerusalem, 1973), contains a description of commentaries on the Talmud Yerushalmi. Adin Steinsaltz, *The Talmud: The Steinsaltz Edition: A Reference Guide* (New York, 1989). Efraim E. Urbach, *Ba'alei ha-Tosafot* (Jerusalem, 1955). Shelomoh Yosef Zevin, *Ishim ve-Shitot* (Tel Aviv, 1958).

—MICHAEL CHERNICK

TALMUD TORAH (תַּלְמוּד תּוֹרָה; study of the Torah), a term that refers both to Torah *study and to the place in which education, particularly of an elementary nature, is provided. From the Middle Ages up to the threshold of the modern period in eastern Europe, elementary Jewish education was provided privately in the *ḥeder or through community-supported *talmud Torah*s. Unlike the *ḥeder*, which was the equivalent of a one-room schoolhouse—often in the teacher's home—the *talmud Torah* would customarily have a number of classes. Although the famous *talmud Torah* established in Amsterdam in the sixteenth century served rich and poor alike, the typical eastern European *talmud Torah* was for poor and orphaned children only. *Talmud Torah* classes were in session throughout the day and into the night. The curriculum consisted entirely of religious subjects, the *talmud Torah* being regarded as a preparatory school for the **yeshivah*. Only a select few *talmud Torah* pupils, however, actually entered *yeshivot*; the vast majority went out to work shortly after their *bar mitsvahs*. Under the influence of the *Haskalah, modernized *talmud Torah*s, with more up-to-date methods of instruction, were set up, particularly in Russia. Old-time *talmud Torah*s still exist, especially in more Orthodox communities, and the instruction in these schools incorporates a considerable degree of rote learning, especially in classes for younger students. Much of this involves the recitation of the Torah verse by verse, first in Hebrew and then in Yiddish translation. In the Diaspora, many religious day schools or afternoon Hebrew schools call themselves *talmud Torah*s. See also EDUCATION.

• Glenda Abramson and T. Parfit, eds., *Jewish Education and Learning: Published in Honour of Dr. David Patterson* (Chur, Switzerland, 1994). Ephraim Kanarfogel, *Jewish Education and Society in the High Middle Ages* (Detroit, 1992). —SHMUEL HIMELSTEIN

TAM, YAʿAQOV BEN ME'IR. See YAʿAQOV BEN ME'IR TAM.

TAMḤUI. See QUPPAH.

TAMID (תָּמִיד; Perpetual Burnt Offering), tractate in Mishnah order Qodashim. There is no parallel Tosefta', and there is *gemara'* in the Talmud Bavli only to the first four chapters. *Tamid* has six chapters, according to reliable manuscript versions, whereas printed editions of *Tamid* divide the sixth chapter into two, yielding seven chapters. *Tamid* describes the daily Temple service, focusing on the *tamid* sacrifice (see PERPETUAL OFFERING) that was offered twice daily, in the morning and toward evening (*Ex.* 29.38ff.; *Nm.* 28.1ff.). A central theme of *Tamid* is the division of labor and organization of the priests. The daily tasks were apportioned by a system of lotteries, and *Tamid* portrays the close coordination among the selected functionaries, together with the entire body of priests. The sacrificial service included recitation of central scriptural passages and benedictions, as well as the Birkat ha-Kohanim.

An English translation by Maurice Simon appears in the Soncino Talmud (London, 1948).

• Chanoch Albeck, ed., *Shishah Sidrei Mishnah, Seder Qodashim* (Jerusalem, 1956). Philip Blackman, ed. and trans., *Mishnayoth*, vol. 5, *Order Kodashim* (Gateshead, 1973). Louis Ginzberg, "Massekhet Tamid," in *ʿAl Halakhah ve-'Aggadah* (Tel Aviv, 1960). Hermann Leberecht Strack and Günter Stemberger, *Introduction to the Talmud and Midrash* rev. and updat. ed., translated by Markus Bockmuehl (Minneapolis, 1992). —AVRAHAM WALFISH

TAMMUZ (תַּמּוּז), tenth month of the civil year, fourth month of the religious year; its zodiac sign is Cancer. The word *Tammuz* is of Babylonian origin, Tammuz being the name of a god who figured prominently in the Sumerian and Babylonian pantheon. While the Bible refers several times to the "fourth month," the word *Tammuz* is only used to refer to the Babylonian god (*Ez.* 8.14). Tammuz always has twenty-nine days. On 17 Tammuz (*Shivʿah ʿAsar be-Tammuz) the breachings of the walls of Jerusalem by Nebuchadnezzar in 586 BCE and by Titus in 70 CE are commemorated. The Talmud also associates this date with several additional sad and memorable events; namely, the day Moses smashed the first tablets of the Law, the day daily sacrifices in the Second Temple came to an end, and the day Romans set up an idol in the Temple. This date marks the commencement of the annual three weeks of mourning (see BEIN HA-METSARIM) culminating in the fast of Tishʿah be-'Av.

• Nathan Bushwick, *Understanding the Jewish Calendar* (New York, 1989). George Zinberg, *Jewish Calendar Mystery Dispelled* (New York, 1963). —CHAIM PEARL

TAMMUZ, SEVENTEENTH OF. See SHIVʿAH ʿASAR BE-TAMMUZ.

TANAKH, Hebrew acronym from Torah, Nevi'im (Prophets), and Ketuvim ([sacred] Writings); one of the names for the collection of biblical books. See also BIBLE. —BARUCH J. SCHWARTZ

TANḤUMA'. See TANḤUMA'-YELAMMEDENU.

TANḤUMA' BEN ABBA' (4th cent.), Palestinian amora'. A student of R. Huna' ha-Kohen and the last of the great Palestinian aggadists, he devoted himself to the systematic collection of aggadic materials (cf. the reference to the *masoret aggadah*—the chain of aggadic tradition—in Y., *B. B.* 6.2, 15c). His homiletical compilations are commonly believed to form the basis for *Pesiqta' de-Rav Kahana'*, *Pesiqta' Rabbati*, and the Tanḥuma'-Yelammedenu *midrashim*, all of which frequently cite teachings in his name and often bear his trademark proems, which begin with the citation of a biblical verse followed by, "[With this verse] R. Tanḥuma' began his discourse" (cf. *Midrash Tanḥuma'*, *Lekh Lekhah* sec. 5). While little is known about his personal life and background, the Talmud recounts his polemics with non-Jews regarding Judaism, claiming that, as the result of besting the emperor in personal debate, he was thrown to the wild beasts (*San.* 39a).

• Chanoch Albeck, *Mavo' la-Talmudim* (Tel Aviv, 1987). Wilhelm Bacher, *Die Agada der palästinensischen Amoräer* (1892–1899; Hildesheim, 1965). —MICHAEL L. BROWN

TANḤUMA'-YELAMMEDENU, category of *Midrashic literature, including the following works: *Tanḥuma'* (to the entire Pentateuch), extensive parts of **Exodus Rabbah*, **Numbers Rabbah*, **Deuteronomy Rabbah*, and *Pesiqta' Rabbati* (see PESIQTA'). Many medieval quotations (often citing "Tanḥuma'" or "Yelammedenu") and fragmentary manuscripts (many from the Cairo Genizah) of other partially preserved versions testify to the diversity and popularity of this type of Midrashic work.

Tanḥuma'-Yelammedenu consists primarily of literary homilies based on the triennial cycle of weekly biblical lections. Unlike structurally similar works such as *Leviticus Rabbah* and *Pesiqta' de-Rav Kahana'*, it contains relatively little Aramaic, having been written in late Rabbinic Hebrew, although it still employs many Greek and Latin loan words. Another distinguishing feature is the special halakhic proem (often beginning with the expression *Yelammedenu rabbenu*, "Let our master teach us") that precedes the series of proems, each beginning with a different verse, with which each composite homily normally begins. Many passages are attributed to the homilist R.*Tanḥuma' ben Abba' who was active during the second half of the fourth century in Palestine.

Earlier scholars made conflicting claims about the date and identity of the "early" Tanḥuma' or Yelammedenu, which was thought to be the original source of all the surviving works of this type. Recent research has allowed scholars to distinguish relatively early traditions and sources within early, middle, and late redactional strata running through the various works. Tanḥuma'-Yelammedenu literature is best regarded as a particular Midrashic genre that began to crystallize toward the end of the Byzantine period in Palestine (5–7th cent.) but continued to evolve and spread throughout the Diaspora well into the Middle Ages. For example, *Tanḥuma'* (the first printed version was published in Constantinople [1520–1522]) seems to have undergone final redaction in geonic Babylonia, while *Tanḥuma' Buber* (first published by Solomon Buber in Vilna [1875]), whose books of *Genesis* and *Exodus* differ considerably, seems to be a European (Italian-Ashkenazi) recension of similar Midrashic material. An English translation of *Tanḥuma' Buber* on *Genesis* by J. T. Townsend was published in 1989 (Hoboken, N.J.).

• Marc Bregman, "Divrei Yetsirah ve-ʿArikhah be-Midreshei Tanḥuma'-Yelammedenu," *World Congress of Jewish Studies* 10C1 (1990). Marc Bregman, "Mesorot u-Meqorot Qedumim be-Sifrut Tanḥuma'-Yelammedenu," *Tarbiz* 60.2 (1991): 269–274. Marc Bregman, "Sifrut Tanḥuma'-Yelammedenu," Ph.D. diss., Hebrew University of Jerusalem, 1991. Hermann Leberecht Strack and Günter Stemberger, *Introduction to the Talmud and Midrash*, rev. and updat. ed., translated by Markus Bockmuehl (Minneapolis, 1992).

—MARC BREGMAN

TANḤUM BEN YOSEF OF JERUSALEM (died 1291), biblical exegete and grammarian from Fostat, Egypt. He wrote his biblical commentaries in Judeo-Arabic and also wrote a dictionary to the *Mishneh Torah* of Maimonides. He was acquainted with a broad spectrum of knowledge in medicine, geography, astronomy and physics. He wrote commentaries on many biblical books: *Joshua, Judges, Samuel, Kings*, the Major Prophets (except for *Isaiah*), the twelve Minor Prophets, and the Five Scrolls. While most of these commentaries await modern editions, his dictionary on the *Mishneh Torah* had two recensions and has been found in community libraries throughout the Middle East. Tanḥum ben Yosef also wrote a general introduction to biblical exegesis which he referred to in all of his subsequent commentaries. The introduction provides material on Hebrew grammar, a method of interpreting passages in the Bible which appear to contradict the Pentateuch, and a guide to those biblical characters who are given different names in different parts of the Bible. His primary goal was to provide the plain meaning of scripture, but he did not hesitate to suggest philosophical explanations, which he derived primarily from Maimonides. In addition, he incorporated details of Muslim history, culture and customs, which helped to explain details in the Bible. His commentary on *Jonah* provides a Neoplatonic allegory of the journey of the soul. In contrast with many other Jewish scholars, he maintained a positive attitude toward the Arabic language.

• Wilhelm Bacher, *Aus dem Wörterbuche Tanchum Jeruschalmi's* (Budapest, 1903). Hans-Georg von Mutius, *Der Josua-Kommentar des Tanchum ben Josef ha-Jeruschalmi* (Hildesheim, 1983). Hadassa Shy, *Perush Tanḥum ben Yosef ha-Yerushalmi li-Terei-ʿAsar* (Jerusalem, 1991).

—MICHAEL A. SIGNER

TANNA' (Aram.; תַּנָּא; one who studies, teaches, or repeats traditions), a teacher mentioned in the *Mishnah or **baraiyta'*. The classical period of the tanna'im began after Hillel and Shamm'ai (although there are sources in the Mishnah attributed to even earlier teachers) and ended after R. Yehudah ha-Nasi' in the early third century CE. Most of the best-known tanna'im lived after the destruction of the Second Temple in 70 CE.

The teachings of the tanna'im take two forms, *mishnah*-form and *midrash*-form. *Mishnah*-form is a brief statement of a legal norm or ethical teaching, usually without biblical support or citations. *Midrash*-form connects the teachings of the tanna'im to a biblical verse, mostly, but not exclusively, from the Torah. The large collections of tannaitic *midrash*-form works cover the Torah from *Exodus* to *Deuteronomy* and include both legal and nonlegal materials.

Mishnah-form teachings are collected in the Mishnah and in the *Tosefta'. One of the earliest *tosafot* (*San.* 86a) appears to be a tannaitic commentary to the Mishnah rather than a separate, Mishnah-like work, which is what the Tosefta' is.

Among the best-known tanna'im are the Houses of Hillel and Shamm'ai, Rabban Gamli'el, R. Eliʿezer ben Hurqanos and R. Yehoshuʿa ben Ḥananyah, R. ʿAqiva' and R. Yishmaʿe'l ben Elishaʿ, and R. Yehudah ha-Nasi'. The last is credited with the Mishnah's redaction. Maimonides enumerates one hundred twenty-eight tanna'im mentioned in the Mishnah at the end of his introduction to Zeraʿim.

In the post-tannaitic period, the term *tanna'* was also applied to reciters or repeaters of the Mishnah and other tannaitic texts. They excelled in memorizing these texts and provided ready references for major amora'im, who used their citations as the basis for exegesis, extension of tannaitic laws, and support for their views.

• Chanoch Albeck, *Mavo' la-Mishnah* (Jerusalem, 1959). Philip Blackman, ed. and trans., *Mishnayoth* (Gateshead, 1973). Jacob Nahum Epstein, *Mevo'ot li-Sifrut ha-Tanna'im* (Jerusalem, 1957). Jacob Neusner, ed., *The Modern Study of the Mishnah* (Leiden, 1973).

—MICHAEL CHERNICK

TANNA' DE-VEI ELIYYAHU. See SEDER ELIYYAHU.

TANYA'. See SHNEUR ZALMAN OF LYADY.

TAQQANAH (תַּקָּנָה; regulation), a regulation or an ordinance promulgated for the public welfare or for the purpose of strengthening religious and moral life and supplementing the law of the Torah. Rabbinical authorities have introduced *taqqanot* throughout the ages, usually to accommodate traditional law to new situations, but those ordinances enacted after the Talmudic period were regarded as binding only on the country or community directly under the jurisdiction of the promulgating authority. The Talmud attributes to Moses himself the *taqqanah* of reading excerpts from the Torah on Sabbaths, Ro'sh Ḥodesh (the New Moon), festivals, and on the intermediate days of festivals (Y., *Meg*. 4.1). The *taqqanah* to recite the *ʿAmidah is traditionally considered to have been issued by the Men of the Keneset ha-Gedolah. Among tannaitic *taqqanot* are included provisions that a wife's marriage settlement (*ketubbah*) be considered a general lien on the whole of the husband's property (issued by *Shimʿon ben Shetaḥ), that communities must appoint elementary school teachers (by Yehoshuʿa ben Gamla'), that a father must support his minor children (by the Sanhedrin at Usha'), and that compulsory education be provided for children from the age of six (*B. B.* 21a). Among the first *taqqanot* introduced by rabbinical authorities in Christian Europe are those of *Gershom ben Yehudah (11th cent.). His twenty-five ordinances (including those prohibiting polygamy and opening letters addressed to others) were accepted as binding on Ashkenazim. An ordinance enacted by a *beit din* for a particular reason is not invalidated, even if that reason no longer exists, and only a *beit din* of greater authority can annul it. Nevertheless, many *taqqanot*, particularly those of a local or communal nature, fell out of use. **Taqqanot ha-qahal* (community ordinances) were a special type of *taqqanot* enacted by community leaders (as opposed to rabbinic authorities) that governed the internal life of communities and congregations. In Sephardi communities, congregational *taqqanot* were called *ascamot*. See also GEZERAH; HORA'AT SHAʿAH.

TAQQANOT HA-QAHAL (תַּקָּנוֹת הַקָּהָל; communal enactments). The Talmud recognizes the power of communal leaders to enact legislation in matters relating to public welfare and social administration. It also empowers associations of artisans and traders to regulate their own affairs and to take action against recalcitrant members (*B. B.* 8b). Communal legislation became a significant element, however, only with the rise of the autonomous medieval Jewish community in the tenth century. The appointed or elected representatives of these communities eventually enjoyed powers similar to those of a *beit din* in the financial sphere, although in ritual matters they enjoyed no such status (*Resp. Rashba'* 4, no. 142; 3, no. 411; *Resp. Ribash*, no. 399, 305). Issues such as the power of the majority and its representatives to bind the minority and the judicial review of communal enactments by halakhists are widely discussed in the medieval *responsa* literature. Rabbinic authorities generally acted as the guardians of minority rights in the many communal disputes that they were required to adjudicate. In matters affecting the smooth running of public affairs, *taqqanot ha-qahal* were often passed to suspend the formalities of the *halakhah*; for example, the signature of the town clerk was treated as that of two valid witnesses, and testimony was accepted from individuals who had an interest in the case in question (*Shulḥan ʿArukh, Ḥoshen Mishpat* 7.12, 37.22). Because of the ability of the *taqqanot ha-qahal* to bridge halakhic and lay interests, it has been adopted by some scholars as a model for absorbing Israeli Knesset legislation into Jewish law.

• Salo W. Baron, *The Jewish Community: Its History and Structure to the American Revolution* (Philadelphia, 1945), vol. 2. Menachem Elon, *Jewish Law: History, Sources, Principles* (Philadelphia, 1994), pp. 678–779, 1906–1914. Louis Finkelstein, *Jewish Self-Government in the Middle Ages* (New York, 1964).

—DANIEL SINCLAIR

TARFON (1st–2d cent.), *tanna'; teacher of R. ʿAqiva', with whom he differed on a number of halakhic issues. Tarfon was an advocate of the abolition of the death penalty (*Mak*. 1.10). In a year of famine, Tarfon, who was a priest, underwent a formal ceremony of betrothal with three hundred women so that they might share in his priestly emoluments (T., *Ket*. 5.1). After the destruction of the Temple, he became a leading authority in *Yavneh and was called "the teacher of all Israel." Tarfon was one of the most vigorous opponents of the *Jewish Christians, declaring that he would unhesitatingly burn their books even though they contained the name of God (*Shab*. 116b), and said that a person being pursued by a snake should sooner take refuge in a house of pagan idolatry than in a church, for one could more easily recognize the dangers of idolatry than those of Christianity. Some scholars have identified him with the Jew Tryphon in the dialogue of the early church father Justin, but this identification has little basis. Tarfon's best-known saying is "The day is short and the work is great . . . the workmen are lazy and the Master is demanding. It is not for you to complete the work, but neither are you free to desist from it" (*Avot* 2.20–21).

• Joel David Gereboff, *Rabbi Tarfon: The Tradition, the Man and Early Rabbinic Judaism*, Brown Judaic Studies 7 (Missoula, Mont., 1979).

—DANIEL SPERBER

TARFUT. See TEREFAH.

TARGUM, Aramaic translation of the Bible. After the Babylonian exile, Aramaic became the language commonly spoken by Jews in Erets Yisra'el as well as in Babylonia, and it became necessary to translate the biblical portions read in the synagogue into the vernacular (see *Neh*. 8.8; *Meg*. 3a), at first in an oral version. Each Hebrew verse of the Pentateuchal reading was consecutively translated aloud, and to some extent interpreted, by the **meturgeman* (translator). The need for such translations became particularly pressing with the spread of Christianity, when proponents of the new religion began to interpret certain passages to accord with their own doctrines. According to the Talmud, two translations of the Pentateuch were then made: one by Akylas (*Aquila) the proselyte into Greek (2d cent.), and one by Onkelos the proselyte into Aramaic, both at the dictation of R. Eli'ezer ben Hurqanos and R. Yehoshu'a ben Ḥananyah (Y., *Meg.* 1.11). Modern scholars doubt the reliability of this tradition, which, they think, arose from a confusion of the name Onkelos (who probably was no translator at all) with Aquila. The Targum Onkelos, some argue, reflects Babylonian and not Palestinian Aramaic. Some scholars think that the anonymous second-century Aramaic translator used Aquila's Greek version, and his Targum was hence called Targum Onkelos by the Babylonian Jews. Targum Onkelos came to be accepted as the official and authorized translation of the Torah, and it was obligatory to read it in conjunction with the Hebrew text of the weekly portion; the custom in public worship was to read the Hebrew twice and the Targum once (*Ber.* 8a). Targum Onkelos gives the plain meaning of the Hebrew text, except for a few instances in which it translates according to halakhic interpretation and except for the poetical sections that contain many exegetical elements. Whether composed in Palestine or Babylonia, Targum Onkelos was subsequently adopted by the Babylonian Jews and was referred to as the Babylonian Targum by the tosafists. Several Palestinian Targums are known. One is the Targum Yerushalmi, a translation of the Torah (also known as Targum *Pseudo-Jonathan). Targum Jonathan (attributed to Yonatan ben 'Uzzi'el; *Meg.* 3a) extends to the Prophets and part of the Hagiographa. A Targum known from a single manuscript, Vatican Neophyti 1, discovered in 1956, contains a Palestinian Targum to the Torah. Finally, the so-called fragmentary Targum is known from some manuscripts and printed editions. There are also Targums to the Five Scrolls, Targum Sheni on *Esther*, and a sizable fragment of a Targum on *Job* (1st cent. CE) found in Qumran. Most Palestinian Targums are paraphrastic, and some Targums include homiletical interpretations. The *Job* Targum from Qumran contains a literal translation, however. Though all the Targums originated earlier, several of them were not put into final form until the fourth or fifth century CE. All the known Targums, with the exception of the *Job* Targum from Qumran, reflect a Hebrew text that is almost identical with the Masoretic Text. Common to the Aramaic versions are their fidelity to rabbinic exegesis and their avoidance of anthropomorphic and anthropopathic expressions found in the Bible.

• P. S. Alexander, "Jewish Aramaic Translations of Hebrew Scriptures," in *Mikra, Text, Translation, Reading and Interpretation of the Hebrew Bible in Ancient Judaism and Early Christianity*, edited by M. J. Mulder, Compendia rerum Iudaicarum ad Novum Testamentum, sect. 2, vol. 1 (Assen-Maastricht and Philadelphia, 1988), pp. 217–253. Derek Robert George Beattie and M. J. McNamara, eds., *The Aramaic Bible: Targums in Their Historic Context*, The First International Conference on the Aramaic Bible Held at the Royal Irish Academy, Dublin, 1992, Journal for the Study of the Old Testament, Supplement Series 166 (Sheffield, Eng., 1994). Bernard Grossfeld, *A Bibliography of Targum Literature*, vols. 1–2 (Cincinnati and New York, 1972–1977). Bernard Grossfeld, *The Targum Onqelos to Genesis–Deuteronomy*, The Aramaic Bible, The Targums, vols. 6–9 (Wilmington, Del., 1988). Yehuda Komlosh, *Ha-Miqra' be-'Or ha-Targum* (Tel Aviv, 1973).

TARGUM SHENI, a collection of homilies in Aramaic (but containing many Greek words) on the *Book of Esther*. It is probably Palestinian in origin, dating to the late seventh or early eighth century, and makes extensive use of earlier Midrashic sources, such as Targum Onkelos, Targum Yerushalmi to the Prophets, and *aggadot* from the Talmud, which have been incorporated into the work, adapted, embellished, and paraphrased in a free fashion. The author was fond of long speeches and included lengthy prayers in a poetic style. Targum Sheni contains an important passage listing Haman's accusation against the Jews, an early antisemitic tract that contains many interesting details on otherwise unknown Jewish religious customs.

• Bernard Grossfeld, *The Targum Sheni to the Book of Esther* (Brooklyn, N.Y., 1994).

–DANIEL SPERBER

TARYAG MITSVOT. See COMMANDMENTS, 613.

TASHBETS. See DURAN FAMILY.

TASHLIKH (תַּשְׁלִיךְ), the custom on the first afternoon of *Ro'sh ha-Shanah (or on the second day, if the first falls on a Sabbath), after the Minḥah service, to visit a river, the seashore, or some other place where water is found, and to recite verses from Scripture concerning repentance and the forgiveness of sins. These verses include: "He will again have compassion upon us; he will subdue our iniquities; and you will cast all their sins into the depths of the sea" (*Mi.* 7.19). The custom, which apparently originated in the late Middle Ages (it is first mentioned in *Sefer Maharil* [Warsaw, 1834], 38a, by R. Ya'aqov ben Mosheh ha-Levi *Molin), possibly influenced by non-Jewish folk practices, symbolizes "the casting out of the sins into the sea"; some even turn out the pockets of their garments and let crumbs fall into the water. Different communities introduced variations in the ritual, and many kabbalistic additions were made, especially among Eastern Jews.

• Avrohom C. Feuer and N. Scherman, *Tashlich: Tashlich and the Thirteen Attributes, a New Translation and Commentary* (Brooklyn, N.Y., 1980).

TASHMISHEI QEDUSHAH (תַּשְׁמִישֵׁי קְדֻשָּׁה; appurtenances of holiness), ritual objects (e.g., the shofar, spice box, *menorah*, Seder plate) or items used to decorate ritual objects (e.g., the *keter Torah* or *rimmonim* ornaments for the embroidered *parokhet* [curtain] that covers the synagogue ark). The verse, "This is my God and I will glorify Him" (*Ex.* 15.2) is interpreted by the rabbis as "I will adorn him," and the rabbis emphasized the need to beautify the various ritual objects (*Shab.* 133b). *Tashmishei qedushah* must be treated with reverence and not put to secular use, although the regulations concerning sacrilege (*me'ilah*) do not, in the strict sense, apply to them. See also CEREMONIAL OBJECTS; TORAH ORNAMENTS.

• Joseph Guttmann, *Jewish Ceremonial Art* (New York, 1964). Joseph Guttmann, "Jewish Ceremonial Art: A Basic Bibliography," in *Studies in Jewish Bibliography, History, and Literature in Honor of I. Edward Kiev* (New York, 1971), pp. 161–165. Joseph Tabory, *Jewish Prayer and the Yearly Cycle: A List of Articles* (Jerusalem, 1992–1993), pp. 58–60.

–SHMUEL HIMELSTEIN

TAXATION. Talmudic law refers to two basic types of taxation: municipal, imposed by local authorities; and national, imposed by a central authority or sovereign. The sages recognized the validity and necessity of municipal taxes levied to cover all legitimate expenditures for the benefit of the general public—for example, city defenses (walls, doors, gates, and guards), water and sewage, communal religious facilities and ritual objects, and support of the poor. Twelve months were generally considered to be the minimum term of residence for local tax liability, unless a home was purchased, in which case liability was immediate. Taxes were to be imposed at graduated rates, depending on the taxpayer's means, as well as the relative benefit enjoyed vis-à-vis other citizens unless local custom relied on other yardsticks.

Because of the loss of Jewish independence and sovereignty in Erets Yisra'el, national taxation imposed by Jewish central authorities was not a relevant issue in the development of Jewish law, although various taxes are imposed in the Bible, including *mekhes* paid to the priests (*Nm.* 31.28) and the king's tax levies (*1 Sm.* 8.11–17). The legal issue generally addressed in this context was, therefore, the degree to which taxes imposed by the non-Jewish central government, in Erets Yisra'el or in the Diaspora, were binding on Jews as a matter of Jewish law; the discussion was guided by the Talmudic legal principle, **dina' de-malkhuta' dina'* (the law of the kingdom is law). Initially, a distinction was made between the applicability of this rule in the Babylonian Diaspora, which dictated compliance with the tax laws of the central government, and Erets Yisra'el, where noncompliance was recognized as a legitimate expression of resistance to Roman rule. As rebellion waned, so did the perceived legitimacy of tax resistance, to the point where Maimonides and other codifiers declared an absolute prohibition against tax evasion, whether the sovereign be Jewish or gentile. Ultimately, tax evasion came to be regarded with particular severity, the sages describing it not merely as *gezel* (theft), but as *gezel ha-rabbim* (theft of the public), since tax not paid by any one individual effectively increased the burden on the remaining members of the community.

In the post-Talmudic period, tax was typically imposed by the central authorities on each Jewish community as a whole, leaving to the organized community the burden and responsibility of individual assessment and collection. Such autonomy provided a significant impetus for the development of legal principles for community government and for the fiscal relationships between the local authorities and the citizenry. The burdens of taxation contributed greatly to the refinement of the laws of partnership, which initially provided the theoretical framework for the legal notion of community. Ultimately, this approach was found to be inadequate, and the legal system came to rely instead upon the more flexible tools of **taqqanot ha-qahal* (communal legislation) and **minhag* (custom) in order to address, at the local level, the increasingly complex problems of community tax administration.

• Menachem Elon, ed., *The Principles of Jewish Law* (Jerusalem, 1975), pp. 662–701. Louis Finkelstein, *Jewish Self-Government in the Middle Ages* (New York, 1964). Aaron Levine, *Free Enterprise and Jewish Law: Aspects of Jewish Business Ethics* (New York, 1980), pp. 136–150, 155–160. Aharon Nahlon, "Local Legislation and Independent Local Leadership According to Maimonides," in *Maimonides as Codifier of Jewish Law*, edited by Nahum Rakover (Jerusalem, 1987), pp. 165–174. Nahum Rakover, *Modern Applications of Jewish Law: Resolution of Contemporary Problems According to Jewish Sources in Israeli Courts* (Jerusalem, 1992), pp. 238–239, 824, 834.

—BEN TZION GREENBERGER

TAZ. See DAVID BEN SHEMU'EL HA-LEVI.

TEACHER OF RIGHTEOUSNESS, a personality mentioned in the *Dead Sea Scrolls. Although no historical figure has been definitely identified as the Teacher of Righteousness, it is generally believed that he was the founder and most important leader of the *Qumran community. He was their teacher par excellence, who saw the fulfillment of biblical prophecies in the contemporary situation. His teachings were authoritative and centered on the correct interpretation of the law, over which he publicly disputed with an opposing leader described as the Liar. The Teacher of Righteousness was a priest and prophet, whose other main antagonist was the Wicked Priest, a figure often identified with Jonathan or Simon the Maccabee (c.150–134), and he may have been the originator of the so-called **pesher* form of biblical exegesis and may also have composed several hymns.

• Jean Carmignac, *Christ and the Teacher of Righteousness: The Evidence of the Dead Sea Scrolls*, translated by Katherine Greenleaf Pedley (Baltimore, 1962). Gert Jeremias, *Der Lehrer der Gerechtigkeit*, Studien zur Umwelt des Neuen Testaments, Bd. 2 (Göttingen, 1963). Hartmut Stegemann, "The 'Teacher of Righteousness' and Jesus: Two Types of Religious Leadership in Judaism at the Turn of the Era" in *Jewish Civilization in the Hellenistic-Roman Period*, edited by Shemaryahu Talmon (Sheffield, Eng., 1991), pp. 196–213.

—TIMOTHY H. LIM

TECHNOLOGY AND HALAKHAH. The interaction between modern technology and Jewish law is a complex issue that covers at least three distinct activities: the legal responses to changes in technology; the scientific responses to some unique legal problems that can be realized through technological advances; and the challenges posed to the underpinnings of Jewish law, philosophy, and ethics by certain modern scientific advances.

Legal Responses to Technology. Jewish law directs its adherents' conduct on a wide variety of issues, and advances in technology change the nature of many of the questions asked. Advances in biomedical technology have created a field—Jewish bioethics—devoted exclusively to addressing the legal response to modern biological problems. The same is true in the area of ritual law. Modern technological advances have made Sabbath observance both easier and harder in comparison to a century ago, and whole new areas of ritual law analysis have been created to respond to them. For example, the exact parameters for the use of electricity on Jewish holidays remains an area of considerable debate. From surrogate motherhood to Sabbath observance, significant efforts have been made to understand advances in technology and to develop suitable responses to them.

Responses to technological advances are by no means limited to ritual law. Financial law is as much an area of research as any other. There is a body of literature that discusses whether electronic money transfers are a form of payment or money according to Jewish law and whether video testimony is a valid form of witnessing. The application of modern principles of agriculture to law has created a literature addressing problems of hydroponics.

The process used to respond to new advances varies significantly from decisor to decisor, and perhaps by era as well. Decisors of the last century were much more inclined to use analogical methods of discourse that were not always predicated upon a full understanding of how the technology functioned. Starting with the classical work *Me'orai Esh* by R. Shelomoh Zalman Auerbach (1938), concrete attempts have been made by a number of decisors and modern law institutes to ensure that rules addressing technology are firmly grounded in the analytic principles of Jewish law and a modern understanding of technology. Among the other leaders of this approach are R. Yitsḥaq Halprin and Professor Ze'ev Lev.

Technological Responses to the Mandates of Jewish Law. Many detailed rules governing daily life address the mechanisms of actions and not the desirability of the underlying activity itself. Thus, for example, Jewish law is generally understood to prohibit the intentional, direct engagement of electricity on the Sabbath. With that in mind, timers that automatically turn appliances on and off are used to reach a desired effect (i.e., turn on a light at a specific time) and yet avoid a religious prohibition. These issues have become more numerous and pressing in the last quarter century, as technological advances invade many more areas of life. Technological solutions to technical problems are recognized as desirable, particularly in areas of ritual law. Thus, there are institutes that design electric wheelchairs with capacitors for use on the Sabbath, wind-operated microphones for use on the holidays, and blast furnaces that need not be operated on the Sabbath. There is also consideration of other areas, for example, family law, with its significant issues of family planning.

Modern Scientific Advances and Jewish Thought. Perhaps the greatest impact of technological advance is in the area of Jewish thought. The scientific revolution, both in terms of methodology and in terms of believable data, has challenged contemporary thought on a number of different fronts. Essentially, the scientific truths are not always fully consistent with classical teachings on many different matters. Three responses to scientific advances have come forward that are consistent with classical law. There are those who deny the validity of scientific progress and maintain that not one iota of the historical Jewish tradition should be abandoned because of scientific or historical data. Others maintain that the tradition should follow the Maimonidean motto to accept truth from whoever speaks it and that Torah concepts are fully compatible with modern scientific truth because they have to be. Finally there are those who seek to bridge this chasm and minimize the conflicts through selective reading of both scientific data and Torah traditions. See also MEDICAL ETHICS.

• Shelomoh Zalman Auerbach, *Qovets Ma'amarim be-'Inyanei Ḥashmal be-Shabbat* (Jerusalem, 1978), chaps. 9–13. Michael Broyde, "The Establishment of Maternity and Paternity in Jewish and American Law," *National Jewish Law Review* 3 (1988): 117–158. Michael Broyde and Howard Jachter, "The Use of Electricity on Sabbath and Yom Tov," *Journal of Halacha and Contemporary Society* 21 (1991): 4–47. Aryeh Carmell and Cyril Domb, eds., *Challenge: Torah Views on Science and Its Problems* (London and New York, 1976). L. Yitsḥaq Halperin, *Ma'aliyyot be-Shabbat* (Jerusalem, 1983). Judah Landa, *Torah and Science* (Hoboken, N.J., 1991). Leo Levi, *Torah and Science: Their Interplay in the World Scheme* (New York and Jerusalem, 1983). Fred Rosner and J. David Bleich, eds., *Jewish Bioethics* (New York, 1979). Baruch Sterman, "Judaism and Darwinian Evolution," *Tradition* 29.1 (1994): 48–75.

—MICHAEL BROYDE

TEFILLAH (תְּפִלָּה), a prayer; applied specifically to the *'Amidah, as the prayer surpassing all others. Among Sephardim, the word is used for a prayer book.

TEFILLAH LI-SHELOM HA-MEDINAH (תְּפִלָּה לִשְׁלוֹם הַמְּדִינָה; Prayer for the Welfare of the State [of Israel]), a prayer introduced by Israel's chief rabbis Isaac *Herzog and Ben-Tsiyyon Me'ir Ḥai *Ouziel; it is recited in most Israeli synagogues during the Sabbath service and on state occasions. In many Diaspora synagogues it is added after the prayer for the welfare of the country and its rulers. The prayer describes the Jewish state as "the beginning of the burgeoning of our redemption" and contains petitions for the victory of its defenders, the ingathering of all the Diaspora, and peace for the land and the kingdom of God on earth. It is not recited in some Orthodox synagogues, and the chief rabbinate of the British Commonwealth has substituted a version that omits the redemptive, military, and ingathering references that are included in the authorized daily prayer book of its United Hebrew congregations.

• Aryeh Newman, ed., *Acknowledge the Miracle: Yom ha-'Atsma'ut, Israel Independence Day in the Perspectives of Judaism* (Jerusalem, 1957), p. 28.

—ARYEH NEWMAN

TEFILLAH QETSARAH (תְּפִלָּה קְצָרָה; Short Prayer), a prayer that in extreme emergency is substituted for the 'Amidah, the central prayer of the liturgy. When the worshiper reaches the security of his home, he is expected to pray the 'Amidah in full. Five versions of the prayer are given in the Talmud (*Ber.* 29b). For occasions of lesser urgency, an abridgment of the thirteen intermediate benedictions of the 'Amidah is provided. This prayer, Havinenu, is inserted between the first three and final three benedictions of the 'Amidah.

• Jules Harlow, ed., *Siddur Sim Shalom* (New York, 1985), pp. 229ff. Abraham E. Millgram, *Jewish Worship* (Philadelphia, 1971), p. 140.

—A. STANLEY DREYFUS

TEFILLAT GESHEM (תְּפִלַּת גֶּשֶׁם), prayer for rain (in the Sephardi rite, Tiqqun ha-Geshem) said in anticipation of the winter rains in Erets Yisra'el. It is recited on *Shemini 'Atseret in the Musaf service, and its concluding phrase **mashiv ha-ruaḥ u-morid ha-geshem* is incorporated in every 'Amidah thereafter until Pesaḥ. Tefillat Geshem is recited before an open ark, and in Ashkenazi custom the reader wears a white *kitel. The prayer consists of *piyyutim* that mention the merits of the patriarchs, Moses, Aaron, and the twelve tribes. The rabbis say that on Sukkot "the world is judged for water" (*R. ha-Sh.* 1.2), but the prayer was delayed until Shemini 'Atseret so that rain would not spoil the festival rejoicing.

The Reform liturgy incorporates an abbreviated form of the prayer. In Temple times, the prayer was accompanied by a water *libation.

• Adolf Buechler, "Honi the Hasid and His Prayer for Rain," in *Types of Jewish–Palestinian Piety from 70 B.C.E. to 70 C.E.* (London, 1922). Ismar Elbogen, *Jewish Liturgy: A Comprehensive History*, translated by Raymond P. Scheindlin (Philadelphia, 1993).

TEFILLAT HA-DEREKH (תְּפִלַּת הַדֶּרֶךְ), prayer recited on setting out on a journey. It is enjoined in the Talmud (*Ber.* 29b), from which its form (with additions from *Derekh Erets Rabbah* 11 and of appropriate biblical verses) has entered the rites of both Ashkenazim and Sephardim. Different versions exist for land, sea, and air voyages. The Sephardi rite has the prayer in the first person singular; the Ashkenazi version, in the first person plural, following the view (*Ber.* 29b–30a) that all travelers should be included in the prayer. Recited on reaching a spot about a hundred yards from the outskirts of the place of departure, the prayer is for a minimum journey of about three miles, or for a shorter one if dangerous. *Nahmanides, on sailing for the Holy Land, composed a special version for a sea voyage.

• Macy Nulman, *The Encyclopedia of Jewish Prayer* (Northvale, N.J., and London, 1993), pp. 318–319. Aryeh Weill, "The Wayfarer's Prayer," *Tradition* 24 (1988): 38–49.

TEFILLAT TAL (תְּפִלַּת טַל), a special *piyyut* for dew recited in all rites in the Musaf service on the first day of Pesaḥ. During the winter months a prayer for rain and a prayer for dew ("Give dew and rain for a blessing upon the face of the earth") is inserted into the ninth blessing of the ʿAmidah (Blessing of the Years). The prayer is recited from the sixtieth day after the autumnal equinox (3 or 4 December, or, in leap years, 5 December; in Israel, from 7 Ḥeshvan) until the first day of Pesaḥ. An alternative benediction is recited by Sephardim during the same period. Some rabbis suggested that the prayer should be offered during the appropriate season in one's individual country of residence, but, on the grounds of safeguarding Jewish unity, the suggestion was rejected. In the summer months a prayer for dew is included by Sephardim and by worshipers in the State of Israel in the second of the ʿAmidah blessings. According to the *aggadah*, God will send the "dew of resurrection" when the dead are about to be resurrected. See also TEFILLAT GESHEM.

• Ismar Elbogen, *Jewish Liturgy: A Comprehensive History*, translated by Raymond P. Scheindlin (Philadelphia, 1993), pp. 39–40, 44, 115, 172, 230. Monford Harris, "The Jewish Prayer for Rain," *Conservative Judaism* 37.4 (1984): 79–82. Joseph Heinemann and Jakob J. Petuchowski, *Literature of the Synagogue* (New York, 1975), pp. 237–240. Arnold Lasker and Daniel Lasker, "The Jewish Prayer for Rain in Babylonia," *Journal for the Study of Judaism* 15 (1984): 123–144.

TEFILLIN (תְּפִלִּין; phylacteries), two specially made cubical black leather boxes traditionally worn by adult males during the weekday morning service (originally worn during the afternoon and evening services as well). These boxes, which are bound by black leather straps to the left hand (or to the right hand for a person who is left-handed) and to the head, contain four scriptural passages. These passages (*Ex.* 13.1–10, 13.11–16; *Dt.* 6.4–9, 11.13–21), which include the injunction to wear *tefillin*, are written twice on parchment. In the *tefillah* worn on the head (*shel ro'sh* [of the head]), these four passages are written on four separate pieces of parchment that are inserted into the four compartments of the leather box. In the *tefillah* for the hand (*shel yad* [of the hand]), the four passages are written on one piece of parchment and inserted in one compartment in the leather box. The *shel ro'sh* is placed on the head so that the front edge of the box lies just above the spot where the hair begins to grow and directly above the space between the eyes. It is held in position by a strap (*retsuʿah*) that circles the head and is fastened by a knot at the nape of the neck. The knot is made to resemble the Hebrew letter *dalet*. The *shel yad* is placed on the muscle of the inner side of the left forearm so that the section through which the strap passes is toward the shoulder. A strap knotted in the form of the Hebrew letter *yud* secures it and is then wound seven times around the arm and three times around the middle finger. The remainder of the strap is passed under the palm and wound around it, thus forming the Hebrew letter *shin*; these three Hebrew letters form the word *Shaddai* (Almighty), one of the biblical divine names. This procedure is kabbalistic in origin.

Tefillin are put on at the commencement of the morning service. A special benediction is recited before the fastening of the *shel yad* to the forearm, and a separate benediction is recited before the placing of the *shel ro'sh* on the head. At the completion of the service the *shel ro'sh* is removed first and then the *shel yad*. The object of wearing *tefillin* is to direct the thoughts of the wearer to God and to the teaching contained in the four paragraphs. According to one tannaitic text, God said to Israel, "Observe the commandment of *tefillin* and I shall account it to you as though you were engaged in the study of the Torah day and night." Maimonides (*Mishnah Torah, Hilkhot Tefillin* 4) expresses this as follows: "The holiness of *tefillin* is great, for as long as the *tefillin* are on the head and the arm of a man, he is humble and God-fearing, he eschews levity and idle talk and does not conceive evil thoughts but turns his heart exclusively to words of truth and justice." *Rashi and Rabbenu Tam (see YAʿAQOV BEN ME'IR TAM), renewing an ancient dispute (illustrated by variant *tefillin* from the late Second Temple period found in the caves of Qumran near the Dead Sea), differed in their opinions as to the order of the texts on the four parchments; some pious Jews, particularly Ḥasidim, put on two pairs of *tefillin*. *Tefillin* are not worn on the Sabbath or festivals (since the observances of these days are regarded as sufficient reminders of the events and concepts that the *tefillin* are also worn to recall). Custom differs as to the wearing of *tefillin* on the intermediate days of festivals (in Erets Yisra'el they are not worn). *Tefillin* are not worn by a mourner on the first day of mourning, by a groom on his wedding day, by a leper, or by one who has been excommunicated; on Tishʿah be-'Av, *tefillin* are put on at the afternoon service instead of the morning service. It is customary to have one's *tefillin* examined by a scribe once every seven years. The Reform movement dropped the tradition of wearing *tefillin*. Abraham *Geiger maintained that they were originally pagan amulets; Leopold *Zunz advocated their retention. However, the wearing of *tefillin* has been reinstated in recent Reform usage. Conservative Jews have always worn them. A Talmudic passage (*'Eruv*. 96a) indicates that in those times they were worn by women, too, and this has been renewed in contemporary feminist circles.

• Judah David Eisenstein, *Otsar Dinim u-Minhagim* (Tel Aviv, 1975), pp. 443–446. Shlomo Goren, *Torat ha-Mo'adim* (Tel Aviv, 1964), pp. 496–510. Michael Levi Rodkinson, *History of Amulets, Charms and Talismans* (New York, 1893). Yigael Yadin, *Tefillin from Qumran* (Jerusalem, 1969).

–YAAKOV GARTNER

TEHILLIM. See PSALMS, BOOK OF.

TEḤINNAH. See DEVOTIONAL LITERATURE; TḤINNUS.

TEITELBAUM FAMILY. See SATMAR.

TEKHELET (תְּכֵלֶת), a blue dyestuff mentioned in the Bible as used in making the curtains of the Tabernacle (*Ex*. 26.1), the veil barring entrance into the Holy of Holies (*Ex*. 26.31), and the ephod (*Ex*. 28.6). *Numbers* 15.38 requires that a thread of *tekhelet* be included in the fringes (**tsitsit*). The Talmud (*Men*. 44a) relates that *tekhelet* is extracted from the blood of the **ḥillazon*. The *tekhelet*, which was expensive, apparently was not in common use by late Talmudic times. *Tekhelet* thread is no longer part of the fringes.

• Menaḥem Burshtin, *Ha-Tekhelet* (Jerusalem, 1987). Isaac Herzog, *The Royal Purple and the Biblical Blue: Argaman and Tekhelet*, edited by Ehud Spanier (Jerusalem, 1987). Samuel Krauss, *Talmudische Archäologie*, vol. 1 (Leipzig, 1910; repr. Hildesheim, 1966), pp. 146–147.

–YAAQOV GARTNER

TELS, town in Lithuania (today Telšiai); seat of a famous *yeshivah* established in 1875 that rose to renown under R. Eli'ezer *Gordon, who was appointed rabbi of Tels in 1882 and brought his disciples with him from Kelme. He was succeeded by his son-in-law R. Yosef Leib Bloch, who headed the *yeshivah* from 1910 to 1930 and in many ways pioneered its educational structure. The student body was divided into four classes, based on achievement. Brighter students advanced rapidly from one class to the next, while slower students remained in the same class for longer periods of time. Class participation was the gauge of a student's performance. During the period between World Wars I and II, the *yeshivah* added elementary schools for boys and girls, a girls' high school, a boys' preparatory school, a women's teachers seminary, and a **kolel*. In 1940 a branch of the *yeshivah* was established in Cleveland. Most of the rabbis and students of the *yeshivah* in Europe were killed by the Nazis. In Cleveland, the *yeshivah* branched out into various other educational enterprises. In the 1970s, a branch of the *yeshivah* was established near Jerusalem, in the Telshe-Stone community.

• Julius Jung, "Ha-Gaon Rabbi Eliezer Gordon of Tels," in *Champions of Orthodoxy* (London, 1974). Shaul Stampfer, "Shalosh Yeshivot Lita'iyyot be-Me'ah ha-Tesha'-'Esreh," Ph.D. dissertation, Hebrew University, 1981.

–SHMUEL HIMELSTEIN

TEMPLE (Heb. Beit Elohim [House of God] or Beit YHVH [House of YHVH]), in biblical times, considered to be a place where God resided. Over a dozen Israelite temples were located in such places as Jerusalem, Shiloh, Bethel, Dan, Gilgal, and Mizpah.

The temple par excellence (Heb. Beit ha-Miqdash [the Home of the Sanctuary]; *2 Chr*. 36.17) was built by *Solomon in Jerusalem on the traditional site of Mount *Moriah and was dedicated in approximately 964 BCE. The Solomonic Temple is portrayed as the legitimate heir of the premonarchal temple at Shiloh, from which it received the holy *Ark of the Covenant as well as the Divine Majesty. From the time of King Hezekiah of Judah, this Temple came to be recognized as the only legitimate place of sacrificial worship to the God of Israel. Centralization of Israelite worship in the Jerusalem Temple was reemphasized again under King Josiah. Nonetheless, archaeological and written evidence indicates that temples were built both inside Erets Yisra'el and outside (e.g., at Elephantine and Heliopolis in Egypt even after the time of Hezekiah). While the prophets frequently condemned sacrifices and prayers as mechanical performances, they never spoke disparagingly of the Temple itself. The Jerusalem Temple was destroyed by the Babylonians in Av 586 BCE (*2 Kgs*. 25; *Jer*. 52). During the Babylonian exile, its rebuilding was foretold and described in detail by the prophet Ezekiel. It was restored some seventy years after its destruction by those who returned from the Babylonian exile (*Ezr*. 1–6) and was known as the Second Temple. The Temple was looted and desecrated by the Syrian Antiochus IV Epiphanes between 169 and 167 BCE and reconsecrated in 165 by Judah the Maccabee. King Herod completely rebuilt the Temple, turning it into one of the most beautiful buildings in the Roman empire. It was destroyed by the Roman general Titus in 70 CE. The fast of *Tish'ah be-'Av commemorates the destruction of both Temples. The site of the Temple (see *TEMPLE MOUNT) has been occupied since approximately 700 CE by the Muslim Dome of the Rock, popularly called the Mosque of Omar. Beginning in the Middle Ages, the *Western Wall of the Herodian Temple complex became a site of Jewish worship. Excavations in Jerusalem since 1967 have uncovered further remains around the Herodian Temple complex.

The Temples were originally conceived as God's dwelling place (*mishkan*) on earth. This concept is also reflected in the oldest portion of the dedication prayer ascribed to Solomon: "I have now built for you [God] a stately house, a place where you may dwell forever" (*1 Kgs*. 8.13). The Ark, which was placed in the Holy of Holies, had always been the symbol of God's presence, serving as his mobile throne or chariot. This corporeal concept of the house of the Lord was replaced no later than the seventh century BCE by the notion that although God dwelled in heaven, the Temple served as the place of his "name" (*Dt*. 26.15; *1 Kgs*. 8.26–53).

1 Kings 6 describes the Temple built by Solomon as a two-room building with a porch in front, surrounded by two courtyards. The western, innermost room, or Holy of Holies (Qodesh ha-Qodashim or Devir), was entered only once a year by the *high priest on Yom Kippur. Inside stood two immense olive-wood cherubim, under which was placed the Ark containing the *tablets of the Law. The outer room, or *heikhal*, contained ten lamp stands, a gold-plated altar for incense, and an offering table. In front of the Temple was a porch or forecourt (*ulam*), in which stood two free-standing bronze columns named Jachin and Boaz. In the courtyard stood ten large bronze wagons, each supporting a basin, as well as a larger basin called the Brazen Sea on the backs of twelve bronze bulls. The courtyard objects provided water for priestly ablutions and washing sacrifices.

The Bible contains no explicit account of the regular, daily order of service in the Temple. However, at least toward the end of the First Temple period, it apparently was similar if not totally identical to that prescribed for the Tabernacle. Regular public worship was almost exclusively sacrificial (see SACRIFICES). The sacrifices were performed by all members of the priestly caste. The rituals performed within the Temple were carried out only by the high priest. *Chronicles* relates details of the cultic music instituted by David and performed by *Levites. Numerous psalms seem to have been composed to accompany individual sacrifices of petition or thanksgiving and were accompanied in their recitation by instrumental *music.

The biblical prescription for the Tabernacle cult also served as the model for Second Temple practices as reflected in rabbinic literature. Certain changes were introduced, some procedures were elaborated upon, and numerous prayers were added.

In the Second Temple period the institution of *maʿamadot* was established. The priests and Levites had previously been divided into twenty-four *mishmarot* (courses), each *mishmeret* performing the Temple services during its allotted week, twice a year. Israelites throughout the country were now also divided into twenty-four *maʿamadot*, each representing a section of the country, and every week at least five men from each *maʿamad* went to Jerusalem to witness the offering of the *tamid* (public sacrifice). In this way every Jew had a share in the daily offering.

In the later Second Temple period, the *Sanhedrin had its seat inside the inner forecourt of the Temple mount. There is also reference to a *synagogue within the Temple premises (*Sot*. 7.7–8). A detailed description of the Second Temple is found in Mishnah tractate **Middot*.

The prayer service constructed after the destruction of the Second Temple was modeled on the sacrificial service offered in the Temple, while mourning over the destruction gave rise to numerous ceremonial customs. Restoration of the Temple and its sacrificial worship have been a major theme of Jewish prayer. The third benediction in the *Birkat ha-Mazon includes a prayer for "the great and holy house over which your name has been called." In Temple days, the prayer was for the continuation of the existence of the Temple, but after the destruction the prayer was for its rebuilding. After each recital of the *ʿAmidah, a petition is added: "May it be your will that the Temple be rebuilt soon in our days." The same petition is offered after the counting of the *ʿOmer. The Musaf service on Sabbaths and festivals contains a prayer that "You may have mercy on your Temple and rebuild it soon." Wherever a Jew prays, he faces in the direction of the Temple in Jerusalem. There is hardly a traditional occasion or a prayer in which reference is not made to the destruction of the Temple; the ancient custom of having the groom break a glass at the wedding has been interpreted as a commemoration of the destruction of the Temple. According to *halakhah*, a Jew should leave a square cubit of a wall unwhitewashed in memory of the destruction of the Temple. Some pious Jews, sitting on a low stool in the manner of mourners, recite prayers known as Ḥatsot (Midnight) each midnight for the rebuilding of the Temple. Most Talmudic authorities held that the site of the Temple remained sacred even after the destruction. Maimonides wrote of the Temple that would be built in the future (*Mishnah Torah*, 8.1.i,4). Reform and Conservative prayer books have deleted wishes for restoration of sacrifices and refer to them only as past history.

• R. E. Clements, *God and Temple* (Oxford, 1965). Michael Fox, ed., *Temple in Society* (Winona Lake, Ind., 1988). Menahem Haran, *Temples and Temple-Service in Ancient Israel (Winona Lake, Ind., 1985)*. Victor A. Hurowitz, *I Have Built You an Exalted House: Temple Building in the Bible in Light of Mesopotamian and Northwest Semitic Writings*, Journal for the Study of the Old Testament, Supplement Series 115, JSOT/ASOR Monograph 5 (Sheffield, Eng., 1992). Victor A. Hurowitz, "Inside Solomon's Temple," *Bible Review* 10 (April 1994): 24–37, 50. Mendell Lewittes, trans., *The Code of Maimonides: Book Eight: The Book of Temple Service*, Yale Judaica Series 12 (New Haven, 1957). Carol L. Meyers, "The Elusive Temple," *Biblical Archaeologist* 45 (1981): 33–41. André Parrot, *The Temple of Jerusalem* (New York, 1955).

—VICTOR HUROWITZ

*Reform Judaism adopted the term *temple* in place of **synagogue*. It was first applied to the Hamburg Temple (1818) and expressed the Reform viewpoint that the synagogue had replaced the ancient Temple, in opposition to the Orthodox belief that the Jerusalem Temple would ultimately be restored. Isaac Mayer *Wise claimed that "worship in a temple is conducted in gladness, not in perpetual mourning as in the synagogue" and that a further object of the temple was to proclaim the universal religion of the future, which would be patterned after the faith of Israel. The term has lost any negative connotation and is often used in the United States in the names of Reform, and occasionally Conservative, congregations.

• Eduard Kley, *Predigten in dem neuen israelitischen Tempel* (Hamburg, 1826).

—SHMUEL HIMELSTEIN

TEMPLE MOUNT, the elevated and walled rectangular area in *Jerusalem on which stood the first and second *Temples. It is the most holy place in Judaism and is also regarded as the site of the **ʿaqedah* (*Gn*. 22.2, 14) and the place where Jacob rested his head (*Gn*. 28.10, 17, 22). A *mishnah* (*Kel*. 1.8) outlines the varying degrees of sanctity of the Temple mount, from the Holy of Holies, which only the high priest was permitted to enter once a year on Yom Kippur, to the outside area of the mount, where the people could worship after purification. The Temple mount proper, to which the biblical and Talmudic restrictions of entry applied, was probably situated between the present Dome of the Rock on the north side and the El Aqsa mosque to the south, constituting somewhat less than half of the present area, which was walled in and extended by Herod (first century BCE). After the destruction of the Temple, most rabbinic authorities maintained that the sanctity of the mount remained unchanged. The Temple mount has been in Muslim possession since the seventh century (with the exception of the Crusader period). This meant that entrance was halakhically forbidden to Jews, because all Jews were regarded as ritually impure, and purification was impossible since the lapse of the ceremony of the ashes of the *red heifer (cf. *Num.* 19). When Jews regained access to the area after the Six-Day War, the Israeli rabbinate posted a notice at the gate leading from the *Western Wall site of Jewish pilgrimage to the Temple mount, prohibiting entry to Jews, since it had become impossible to determine the actual boundaries of the sanctified area. This has remained a matter of controversy, with former chief rabbi Shelomoh Goren issuing a minority view specifying those areas of the Temple mount that can be entered after performing the statutory ablution and removing the shoes. The Israeli government, in pursuant of its policy of maintaining the status quo of holy places of all faiths, has left the Temple mount under Muslim control and prevented Jews from attempting to pray there.

• "Har ha-Bayit," in *Entsiqlopediyyah Talmudit*, vol. 10 (Jerusalem, 1961), pp. 575–592. Benjamin Mazar, *The Mountain of the Lord* (Garden City, N.Y., 1975). James Purvis, *Jerusalem, the Holy City: A Bibliography*, vols. 1 and 2, (New Jersey and London, 1988, 1991). Leon Ritmeyer, "The Ark of the Covenant: Where It Stood in Solomon's Temple," *Biblical Archaeology Review* 22 (January–February 1996): 46–55, 70–73. Schaul Schaffer, *Har ha-Bayit* (Jerusalem, 1981). –ARYEH NEWMAN

TEMPLE OF ONIAS. See ONIAS, TEMPLE OF.

TEMPLE SCROLL, the longest complete scroll (11Q19, *Temple Scroll*[a]) found at *Qumran (Cave 11, 1956). The scroll, which consists of nineteen sheets of leather preserving sixty-seven columns of text, is written in Hebrew. The handwriting on the scroll has been dated to the Herodian period (late lst cent. BCE). In addition to the large scroll from Cave 11, one or possibly two other copies were found in the same cave (11Q20, *Temple Scroll*[b]; [c]?); further, fragments that overlap with portions of the *Temple Scroll* were found in Cave 4 (e.g., 4Q365a?).

The *Temple Scroll* presents itself as a direct revelation from God (speaking in the first person) to Moses. The text, classified as "rewritten Bible," is a collection of laws concerning the Temple buildings, festivals, purity, and king, heavily dependent on *Exodus*, *Leviticus*, and especially *Deuteronomy*. However, in many cases the *Temple Scroll* presents a thoroughgoing rewriting of large passages of the Pentateuch, often with additions of its own to make its halakhic position clear. The *Temple Scroll* contains no overtly sectarian language, as is found in other Qumran documents, although it has much in common with some Qumran sectarian texts, such as the **Damascus Document*. Therefore, the *Temple Scroll*, while not a strictly sectarian composition, may be part of an older body of material inherited and used by the Qumran community. The work was originally published by Yigael Yadin (3 vols. [Jerusalem, 1977; English ed. Jerusalem, 1983]).

• Johann Maier, *The Temple Scroll*, Journal for the Study of the Old Testament, Supplement Series, 34 (Sheffield, Eng., 1985). Lawrence H. Schiffman, "The *Temple Scroll* and the Nature of Its Law: The Status of Question," in *The Community of the Renewed Covenant*, The Notre Dame Symposium on the Dead Sea Scrolls, edited by Eugene Ulrich and James VanderKam, Christianity and Judaism in Antiquity Series, vol. 10 (Notre Dame, 1994), pp. 37–55. Ben Zion Wacholder, *The Dawn of Qumran* (Cincinnati, 1983). Michael Owen Wise, *A Critical Study of the Temple Scroll from Qumran Cave 11* (Chicago, 1990). –SIDNIE WHITE CRAWFORD

TEMPLE VESSELS, cultic implements utilized in the Jerusalem *Temple. In the courtyard stood a large bronze *altar for sacrifice (*1 Kgs*. 8.64). Smaller accessories necessary for sacrificing on the altar included pots (*sirot*) and shovels (*ya'im*) for cleaning ashes from the altar and bowls for receiving and pouring out sacrificial blood (*mizraqot*). There was also a large basin (*yam*) that stood upon twelve bronze bulls (see BRAZEN SEA), as well as ten large bronze wagons (*mekhonot*), each of which carried a smaller basin (*kiyyor*). The water in the smaller basins was used for washing sacrifices, while that in the *yam* was for priestly ablutions (*2 Chr*. 4.6). These water vessels may have symbolized the cosmic sea upon which the world was founded and the rivers flowing from the divine garden. On the porch (*ulam*) at the entrance to the Temple were two free-standing bronze columns named *Jachin and Boaz. In the outer sanctum (*heikhal*) stood three gold-covered furnishings, including an altar for incense, a table for presenting bread and drink, and ten lamp stands. The lamp stands were outfitted with lamps (*nerot*) and tongs (*melqaḥayyim*); the table was set with bowls (*sippot*), jars (*mizraqot*), and musical instruments (*mezammerot*); while the incense altar was provided with incense spoons (*kappot*) and pans for handling coals (*maḥtot*). There were also keys (*potot*) to the outer and inner doors of the Temple (*1 Kgs*. 7.48–50). In the inner sanctum, two large cherubim made of olive wood and plated with gold stood on the *Ark of the Covenant, which contained the tablets of the Law. All these items were associated with the regular, fixed Temple ritual. In addition, the Temple treasuries stored numerous vessels that had been presented either by the king or private individuals. Other vessels came into the Temple as spoils of war. The Temple vessels themselves were occasionally handed over to foreign kings as tribute or were plundered as spoils of war (*1 Kgs*. 14.27; *2 Kgs*. 12.19, 16.17, 24.13, 25.13–17; *Jer*. 27.16–22, 52.17–23). When vessels were replaced, the new ones may have been made of less valuable materials than the ones lost. The exiles returning from Babylonia brought with them numerous Temple vessels that were restored to them by the king of Persia (*Ezr*. 1.7–11). These vessels had been stored in the temple of Nebuchadnezzar's gods. Their restoration symbolized the ultimate victory of the God of Israel over the gods of Babylon. According to *Daniel* 5, King Belshazzar and his court drank from the Temple vessels at an idolatrous banquet, provoking the "handwriting on the wall" predicting the king's imminent demise. According to the rabbis, Ahasuerus used the Temple vessels at the great banquet described in *Esther* 1. In reading the scroll of *Esther* at Purim, it is customary to chant the words "and all sorts of vessels" (*Est.* 1.7) to the melody of the *Book of Lamentations* in commemoration of the destroyed Temple. Although synagogues bear certain resemblance to the Temple, it is forbidden to furnish synagogues with implements identical with the Temple vessels. For example, it became customary for synagogue candelabra to have either six or eight rather than seven branches, as would have been found in the Tabernacle and the Temple.

• P. R. Ackroyd, *The Temple Vessels: A Continuity Theme*, Supplements to Vetus Testamentum, vol. 23 (Leiden, 1972), pp. 166–181. Victor A. Hurowitz, "Solomon's Golden Vessels (1 Kings 7:48–50) and the Cult of the First Temple," in *Pomegranates and Golden Bells: Studies in Biblical, Jewish and Near Eastern Ritual, Law, and Literature in Honor of Jacob Milgrom*, edited by D. P. Wright and D. N. Freedman (Winona Lake, Ind., 1995), pp. 151–164. Lawrence H. Schiffman, "The Furnishings of the Temple According to the *Temple Scroll*," in *The Madrid Qumran Congress: Proceedings of the International Congress on the Dead Sea Scrolls, Madrid, 18–21 March 1991*, edited by J. Trebolle Barrera and L. Vegas Montaner (Leiden, 1992), vol. 2, pp. 621–634.

—VICTOR HUROWITZ

TEMURAH (תְּמוּרָה; Exchange), tractate in Mishnah order Qodashim, containing seven chapters, with related material in Tosefta' and in the Talmud Bavli. It deals with the transfer of sanctity from a sacrificial animal to an unsanctified animal. Biblical law, while forbidding such an exchange, considers as sanctified both the original sanctified animal and the animal for which it was "exchanged" (*Lv.* 27.10, 33). Opening with an elaboration of the laws defining such exchanges, *Temurah* broadens the discussion to include a far-ranging treatment of the conditions under which various forms of sanctity may be transmitted, removed, or transformed. The main determinant of these conditions is the purpose of the animal's or object's sanctification. Animals or objects may be sanctified as designated sacrifices or as gifts to be utilized for the maintenance of the Temple. A second determinant of a broad range of questions affecting the status of animals designated as sacrifices is the distinction between public and private ownership of the sacrifice. The concept of sanctity is revealed, within *Temurah*, as an outgrowth of the concept of ownership. Only an owner may confer sanctity, and sanctity may be defined as a form of ownership by the Temple. *Temurah* investigates the similarities, differences, and interactions between the concepts of ownership and sanctity.

An English translation by L. Miller appears in the Soncino Talmud (London, 1948).

• Chanoch Albeck, ed., *Shishah Sidrei Mishnah, Seder Qodashim* (Jerusalem, 1956). Philip Blackman, ed. and trans., *Mishnayoth*, vol. 5, *Order Kodashim* (Gateshead, 1973). Hermann Leberecht Strack and Günter Stemberger, *Introduction to the Talmud and Midrash*, rev. and updat. ed., translated by Markus Bockmuehl (Minneapolis, 1992).

—AVRAHAM WALFISH

TENA'IM. See BETROTHAL; KETTUBAH.

TENANCY. The Mosaic code contains no legislation regarding the duties and obligations of the tenant, except for provisions relating to the **shemittah*. In rabbinic law, the conditions of tenancy are subject to both contract and local custom and can be changed only by common agreement between the parties. The presumptive rights of the person in occupancy are of great force in *halakhah* and render summary eviction extremely difficult. Rabbinic legislation distinguishes between a tenant who pays rent proportionate to his produce (*aris*) and one who pays a fixed rent (*ḥokher* or *sokher*). During the Middle Ages, special **taqqanot* dealing with tenant rights were enacted in order to ensure equitable regulation of the crowded ghetto tenements in which Jews were forced to live. See also HIRING.

• Yosef Karo, *Shulḥan ʿArukh* (Jerusalem, 1995).

TEN COMMANDMENTS, also called the Decalogue (Gr.; Ten Words), spoken by God at Mount Sinai (*Ex.* 20; *Dt.* 5). According to *Exodus*, the giving of the Law at Sinai began with a public theophany, at which God spoke to the entire people (after this event, additional laws were communicated privately to Moses), which was preceded by the appearance of the divine fire cloud; three days of preparation; and manifestations of fire, thunder, and lightning; and accompanied by the sounding of the horn. God's speech was designed to convey to the Israelites a representative sampling of the laws to be given subsequently but was in no sense to be a summary of them, much less an act of legislation in its own right. Thus it contains some of each of the two main types of religious law: those pertaining to the individual's obligations toward God and those pertaining to his relations with other people. It also contains both forms of command, positive and prohibitive. The Ten Commandments were said to be the quintessence of the Law, somehow containing or alluding to all six hundred and thirteen commandments therein (Y., *Sheq.* 6.1).

The account of the giving of the Ten Commandments in *Deuteronomy* (4.9–14, 5.1–28) essentially follows that in *Exodus* 20. The main difference is that *Deuteronomy* describes the promulgation of the Ten Commandments as a covenant in its own right and the subsequent giving of the laws as a second, complementary covenant. *Deuteronomy* explains that the full body of laws was communicated privately to Moses as the result of the people's fear of direct confrontation with God, a motif already adumbrated in *Exodus*. In both accounts, the "Ten Words" were inscribed by God on the first set of tablets given to Moses. When, after the worship of the *golden calf, Moses smashed the original tablets, he was required to hew a new set, upon which God wrote the same text. These were deposited in the *Ark of the Covenant (along with the fragments of the first set, according to the rabbis) for safekeeping and for reference but primarily as physical evidence of the encounter with God and the hearing of his word. The primary revelation of the Ten Commandments, however, was the oral one.

The Bible nowhere refers to the Decalogue as ten commandments. The text of the Decalogue does not even divide naturally into pronouncements; the number of commands (positive and negative) is more than ten, whereas the number of topics is nine: forbidden forms of worship, swearing falsely, observance of the Sabbath, respect for parents, and the prohibitions against murder, adultery, theft, false testimony, and covetousness. Yet the Bible refers to it as "the ten words" (*Ex.* 34.28; *Dt.* 10.4), apparently using this round number as an expression of totality, as is found in other places in biblical and Talmudic literature. Various methods arose for dividing the passage into ten commandments. One ancient rabbinic tradition was to count "I am the Lord" and "You shall have no other gods" as one pronouncement, separating the prohibition of foreign gods from that of idolatry in order to arrive at ten. Traces of this tradition may be found in the Middle Ages, as well as in Christian divisions of the Ten Commandments. Another rabbinic tradition became the normative one: "I am the Lord" was considered a separate pronouncement, interpreted as a command to believe in God, and each of the nine topics enumerated above was counted as one commandment. This method led to the tradition of dividing the Ten Commandments into two parallel groups of five each (on the supposition that God inscribed five on each tablet), which were then interpreted in Talmudic literature as being interrelated: the pronouncement "I am the Lord" corresponding to "you shall not murder" (man being created in God's image); "you shall have no other gods beside me" corresponding to "you shall not commit adultery" (both being types of unfaithfulness); "you shall not swear falsely in the name of the Lord your God" paralleling "you shall not steal" (since theft leads to false oaths); "remember the Sabbath" corresponding to "you shall not bear false testimony" (since the Sabbath is testimony that God created the world in six days); and "honor your mother and your father" corresponding to "you shall not covet . . . your neighbor's wife" (because the latter leads to the deterioration of family life). In light of the style of Near Eastern treaties, which commence with a self-identification clause introducing the king, in which he recounts his former beneficent acts to the vassal with whom he is making the pact, scholars now interpret the first statement, "I the Lord am your God who brought you out of the land of Egypt," as the prologue to the ensuing series of commandments.

The two versions of the Decalogue (in *Ex.* and *Dt.*) differ in several particulars, all of which are stylistic and not substantive in nature. The simplest explanation for this is the special rhetorical style of *Deuteronomy*, in which Moses recapitulates the words of God. Thus the phrase "as the Lord your God commanded you" is added twice. "Observe the Sabbath day" replaces "Remember the Sabbath day," which reminds Jews of the redemption from Egypt and is an imperative to provide rest for all—a humanistic interpretation of the commandment that is characteristic of Deuteronomic legislation, rather than the creation of the world by God, as is found in *Exodus*. In the last portion of the last commandment, the verb *crave* replaces *covet*, both virtually synonymous in their contexts. Midrashic interpretation, however, took literally Moses' statement (*Dt.* 5.19) that "these words" precisely were spoken by God and written on the tablets. It thus dealt with the differences by postulating that both versions of the Decalogue were spoken by God simultaneously. This was one of a number of Midrashic statements designed to express the rabbinic concept of the miraculous nature of divine speech. God is said to be capable of conveying multiple senses and multiple versions of the same statement, and even conflicting statements, in one utterance.

The Talmudic sages differed on the question of how much of the Decalogue the Israelites actually heard directly from God. In one view, closer to the biblical text, the people listened to the divine voice until it ceased. According to another interpretation, after the words "I am the Lord . . . you shall have no other gods" were spoken the people withdrew in terror, and the remainder of the Decalogue was transmitted by Moses. This version emphasized the overpowering nature of divine speech.

The tradition of reading the Decalogue as part of the daily liturgy, first in the Temple and then during Talmudic times, was ultimately discarded, probably in order to combat the mistaken view propounded by sectarians that the Ten Commandments alone were valid (*Ber.* 12a) or that they were more important than the remaining ones. Representations of the Decalogue are, however, prominently displayed in synagogues (see TABLETS OF THE LAW), and the biblical festival of Shavu'ot became, in rabbinic tradition, a commemoration of the day on which the Decalogue was heard. When the Ten Commandments are recited in the course of the Torah reading, the congregation rises to its feet.

Two sets of cantillation notations are used to divide the text of the Decalogue. One divides it into verses of normal length; the other views each of the ten pronouncements as one verse, regardless of length; and it is these notations that are used today for the public reading of the Decalogue from the Torah (in some congregations, only on Shavu'ot). According to rabbinic legend, which suggests the universality of the Decalogue, the tablets were made prior to the creation of the universe (*Pes.* 54a). It is also said that they were offered to other peoples, who turned them down, before they were brought to the Israelites, who accepted them (*Sifrei* on *Dt.* 33.2). However, when they were issued, all the peoples of the world heard them in their own languages (*Shab.* 88b).

• Solomon Goldman, *The Ten Commandments* (Chicago, 1956). Moshe Weinfeld, "The Decalogue: Its Significance, Uniqueness, and Place in Israel's Tradition," in *Religion and Law: Biblical–Judaic and Islamic Perspectives*, edited by E. R. Firmage, B. G. Weiss, and J. W. Welch (Winona Lake, Ind., 1990), pp. 3–47, with extensive bibliography. Moshe Weinfeld, "What Makes the Ten Commandments Different?" *Bible Review* 7.2 (1991): 35–41. Ronald Youngblood, "Counting the Ten Commandments," *Bible Review* 10.6 (1994): 30–35, 50, 52.

—BARUCH J. SCHWARTZ

TEN DAYS OF PENITENCE. See 'ASERET YEMEI TESHUVAH.

TEN LOST TRIBES. See TRIBES OF ISRAEL.

TEN MARTYRS (Heb. *ʿasarah harugei malkhut*). During the Hadrianic persecution following the defeat of Shimʿon *Bar Kokhba' in 135 CE, many tanna'im suffered martyrdom at the hands of the Romans. They were charged with various offenses and executed at different times; for example, the offense of R. Ḥanina' ben Teradyon was the public teaching of the Law and that of Yehudah ben Bava' was the conferring of the prohibited *ordination (*semikhah*) on five of his disciples. This gave rise to the legend of the Ten Martyrs (as found for example, in the *Midrash of the Ten Martyrs*, varying versions of which have been preserved) that turned these individual cases into a tale of a single collective martyrdom. This *midrash* occurs in two poetic versions: Elleh Ezkerah, incorporated in the penitential prayers of Yom Kippur; and Arzei Levanon, in the elegies for 9 Av. The latter only enumerates seven martyrs by name; the former, in addition to the two mentioned above, lists ʿAqiva' ben Yosef, Yishmaʿe'l ben Elishaʿ, Ḥutzpit the Interpreter, Yeshevav the Scribe of the Sanhedrin, Elʿazar ben Shammuʿa, Ḥananiah ben Ḥakhin'ai, Shimʿon ben Gamli'el, and Elʿazar ben Dama'. The legend of the Ten Martyrs became one of the outstanding examples of Jewish martyrology.

• Louis Finkelstein, "The Ten Martyrs," in *Essays and Studies in Memory of Linda R. Miller*, edited by Israel Davidson (New York, 1938). Nelson Glueck, "The Story of the Ten Martyrs," rabbinic thesis, Hebrew Union College, 1923. Arnold Goldberg, "Das Martyrium des Rabbi Aqiva: Zur Komposition einer Märtyrerzählung (bBer 61b)," *Frankfurter Judaistische Beitrage* 12 (1984): 1–82. Gottfried Reeg, *Die Geschichte von den Zehn Martyrern* (Tübingen, 1985), reviewed by M. B. Lerner, *Jewish Quarterly Review* 80 (1990): 391–395. —DANIEL SPERBER

TEN PLAGUES. See PLAGUES OF EGYPT.

TENT OF MEETING (Heb. Ohel Moʿed), one of the names used in the Torah for the elaborate portable shrine and divine abode that accompanied the Israelites in the wilderness (see TABERNACLE). In a number of passages, however, the Tent of Meeting appears as a simple tent pitched by Moses outside of the camp, which could only be reached by leaving the camp. Joshua, as Moses' prophetic apprentice, was said to remain in the tent at all times, while Moses (and others) visited it as necessary to seek an audience with God (*Ex*. 33.7–11; *Nm*. 11.16–29, 12.4–10; *Dt*. 31.14–15). In these passages, God does not reside in the tent; rather, he arrives when summoned, descending from heaven in the form of a cloud, and meets with the prophet at the entrance to the tent—the prophet on the inside, God on the outside. The meetings take place not in order for God to give legislation but rather to provide instruction as needed. No reference is made in these narratives to worship or ritual, nor to an ark or other sacred objects. The stark contrast between this tent and the Tabernacle led some medieval commentators to suppose that there were two separate tents. However, since the two tents appear in distinct literary contexts, each making no mention of the other, modern scholars tend to view this as evidence for separate traditions: "Tent of Meeting" being used as a name for the Tabernacle in sections belonging to the *Priestly source; while the simple Tent of Meeting, representing non-Priestly tradition, is preserved in the *Yahvist source, the *Elohist source, and the *Deuteronomic source.

• Menahem Haran, *Temples and Temple-Service in Ancient Israel* (Oxford, 1978), pp. 260–275. Moshe Levine, *The Tabernacle: Its Structure and Utensils* (New York, 1969). Julian Morgenstern, *The Ark, the Ephod, and the "Tent of Meeting"* (Cincinnati, 1945). Gerhard von Rad, *The Problem of the Hexateuch and Other Essays* (New York, 1966). —BARUCH J. SCHWARTZ

TEOMIM, YOSEF BEN ME'IR (1727–1813), rabbinic authority. He studied with his father in Lemberg (Lwów) and in Berlin. In 1774 he succeeded his father as *dayyan* in Lemberg and in 1781 became the rabbi of Frankfurt an der Oder. His outstanding work is *Peri Megadim* (Berlin, 1771–1772; and subsequently in major editions of the *Shulḥan ʿArukh*), a commentary on the **Shulḥan ʿArukh*. Teomim is often referred to by the name of this book. He extended the earlier commentaries on the Shulḥan ʿArukh—*Turei Zahav* of *David ben Shemu'el ha-Levi and *Siftei Kohen* of *Shabbetai ben Me'ir ha-Kohen—and added laws they had omitted, while subjecting their statements to a through Talmudic and halakhic analysis. Teomim's work is especially valuable because he brings together the codifications of various earlier works.

• Menachem Elon, *Jewish Law: History, Sources, Principles* (Jerusalem, 1994), vol. 3, p. 1432. Mendell Lewittes, *Ha-Halakhah* (Jerusalem, 1989), pp. 126–129. Chaim Tchernowitz, *Toledot ha-Poseqim* (New York, 1946–1947), vol. 3, pp. 193–201. —SHALOM BAR-ASHER

TEQIʿAH. See SHOFAR.

TEQIʿATA' (Aram.; תְּקִיעָתָא; sounding of the shofar), three series of biblical verses added to the Musaf service on Ro'sh ha-Shanah when the *shofar is sounded. They are known as *Malkhuyyot, *Zikhronot, and *Shofarot, which refer, respectively, to the affirmation of God's sovereignty, to remembering the covenant, and to the triumphal blast of the shofar at the time of redemption. The Mishnah (*R. ha-Sh*. 4.5–6) discusses the basic structure of each series and the varying views of the rabbis. Today each series consists of ten verses, three each from the Pentateuch, the Prophets, and the Writings, with a concluding verse from the Pentateuch. Each section concludes with a blessing: "Praised are you . . . king of the whole earth . . . who remembers the covenant . . . who hears the sound of the shofar of his people Israel."

• Ismar Elbogen, *Jewish Liturgy: A Comprehensive History*, translated by Raymond P. Scheindlin (Philadelphia, 1993). Abraham Z. Idelsohn, *Jewish Liturgy and Its Development* (New York, 1932). —PETER KNOBEL

TERAPHIM, human images used as household gods and consulted for purposes of divination. Rachel stole Laban's teraphim (*Gn*. 31.19), in order that they would protect her and her family on their way back to Canaan and also probably as insurance that her husband, Jacob, would become heir to the family estate, a legal custom alluded to in several of the cuneiform texts from that period. Samuel denounced the teraphim as witchcraft (*1 Sm*. 15.23), and their banishment from Israel was part of Josiah's drive for religious reform; they retained their popularity until the Babylonian exile. The prevalence of household teraphim is attested by the story of David's wife, Michal (*1 Sm*. 19.11–16).

The function of the teraphim originally referred to an active, protective spirit of the individual, but the term is used in the Bible only passively, meaning "household idols" (*Gn*. 31.19; cf. *Gn*. 31.30, 32, 35.2–4; *Jgs*. 18.17–18; cf. *Jgs*. 18.24), with emphasis on the imagistic (*Gn*. 31.19, 34, 35; *1 Sm*. 19.13, 16) and fetishistic (*Jgs*. 17.5, 18.14, 17, 18, 20) aspects. Some scholars suggest that teraphim were actually figurines of deceased family members.

• Victor P. Hamilton, *The Book of Genesis: Chapters 18–50* (Grand Rapids, 1995), pp. 292–295. A. Leo Oppenheim and Erica Reiner, *Ancient Mesopotamia: Portrait of a Dead Civilization*, 2d ed (Chicago, 1977), pp. 199–201. Karel van der Toorn, "The Nature of the Biblical Teraphim in the Light of Cuneiform Evidence," *Catholic Biblical Quarterly* 52 (1990): 203–222. –CHAIM COHEN

TEREFAH (טְרֵפָה; among Sephardim, *taref*), a term that originally referred to the tearing or mauling of an animal by a wild beast (*Gn*. 31.39) but now a generic term for any defect that renders an animal unfit for food or any food prepared contrary to the *dietary laws. Early tradition lists a number of defects that render an animal *terefah*. These were expanded by the Mishnah to eighteen (*Ḥul*. 3.11) and by Maimonides to seventy (*Hilkhot Sheḥitah* 10.9–13). The eighteen *terefot* are a pierced gullet, a torn windpipe, a pierced brain membrane, a pierced heart, a broken spine, a severed spinal chord, a missing liver, a pierced lung, a pierced maw, a pierced gall bladder, pierced intestines, a pierced inner stomach, a heavily torn outer coating, a pierced second stomach, a pierced third stomach, a beast that has fallen from a height, a beast with several broken ribs, and a beast that has been mauled. Any animal suffering from an illness or injury and unlikely to live for a full year is also considered *terefah* (*Ḥul*. 42a). *Terefah* may not be eaten, but other benefit (e.g., sale to a non-Jew) may be derived from it (*Ex*. 22.30). The use of the term was broadened in the course of time and is now applied to all nonkosher food. The term was even applied by the Orthodox to followers of the *Haskalah.

• Jacob Cohn, *The Royal Table: An Outline of the Dietary Laws of Israel* (Jerusalem, 1973). Joseph Karo, *The Kosher Code of the Orthodox Jew*, translated by S. I. Levin and Edward A. Boyden (New York, 1969), selections from the *Shulḥan ʿArukh*. Yacov Lipschutz, *Kashruth: A Comprehensive Background and Reference Guide to the Principles of Kashruth* (Brooklyn, N.Y., 1988). Irving Welfeld, *Why Kosher? An Anthology of Answers* (Northvale, N.J., 1996).

TERUʿAH. See SHOFAR.

TERUMAH (תְּרוּמָה; from Heb. *ḥerim min* [lift up from]), heave offering. According to the Torah, a number of sacred gifts are said to be lifted, that is, separated or set apart for God. These are the breast and right thigh of the *peace offering, first given to the priests at their consecration and then ordained to be their portion forever (*Ex*. 29.27–28; *Lv*. 7.32–34; see also WAVE OFFERING); the cakes of the *thanksgiving offering (*Lv*. 7.12–14); the first yield of baked bread (*Nm*. 15.19–20; see ḤALLAH); and the *tithes and their tithes (*Nm*. 18.24–29). According to rabbinic interpretation, these gifts required an actual "lifting up" ritual (*Men*. 5.6). Apparently the word *terumah* could also indicate any offering made by selecting a gift out of one's property; thus, the materials for the building of the Tabernacle (*Ex*. 25.2–3, 35.5), the census silver (*Ex*. 30.13–15), the dedicated spoils of the Midianite war (*Nm*. 31.29ff.), as well as sacred gifts in general (*Nm*. 5.9, 18.8ff.; *Lv*. 22.12, 15) are all called *terumah*. In rabbinic law, *terumah* came to refer primarily to the tithe given to the priest.

• Jacob Milgrom, *Numbers*, The JPS Torah Commentary (Philadelphia, 1990), pp. 426–427. Jacob Milgrom, *Studies in Cultic Theology and Terminology* (Leiden, 1983). –BARUCH J. SCHWARTZ

TERUMOT (תְּרוּמוֹת; Heave Offerings), tractate in Mishnah order Zeraʿim, containing eleven chapters, with related material in Tosefta' and in the Talmud Yerushalmi. It deals with the laws governing the heave offerings that Israelites and Levites were required to bring to the priests (*Nm*. 18.8ff., 25ff.). The biblical discussion of *terumot* focuses on the special privilege of the priests, who have no portion in the land inasmuch as God "is their portion and heritage" (*Nm*. 18.20). *Terumot* focuses on such questions as who may designate *terumot*; under which conditions may *terumot* be designated; what is the nature of the consecrated status of *terumot*; what is the status of *terumot* that have been intermingled with secular produce or that have been planted; and in what manner may *terumot* be consumed by the priest. Post-Temple rabbinic discussions focus on the inherent requirement of produce to be tithed and on the status of the designated *terumot* as consecrated food. A common rabbinic theme stressed in several pericopes in *Terumot* is the importance of intention or human calculation in the designation of *terumot*. This may be seen especially in the latitude given to the owner to determine the percentage of the *terumot* tithe (*Ter*. 4.3, 5), as well as the requirement of tithing on the basis of an estimate rather than on the basis of measurements (*Ter*. 1.7; contrast 4.6).

An English translation of the tractate is in Herbert Danby's *The Mishnah* (London, 1933).

• Chanoch Albeck, ed., *Shishah Sidrei Mishnah, Seder Zeraʿim* (Jerusalem, 1957). Philip Blackman, ed. and trans., *Mishnayoth*, vol. 1, *Order Zeraim* (Gateshead, 1973). Pinhas Kehati, ed., *Mishnah: A New Translation with a Commentary, Seder Zeraim*, vol. 3, *Terumot, Maʿasrot* (Jerusalem, 1993). Hermann Leberecht Strack and Günter Stemberger, *Introduction to the Talmud and Midrash*, rev. and updat. ed., translated by Markus Bockmuehl (Minneapolis, 1992). –AVRAHAM WALFISH

TESHUVAH. See REPENTANCE.

TESHUVOT. See RESPONSA.

TESTAMENT LITERATURE, a genre of literature, popular in Hellenistic times, that contained the deathbed instructions and predictions of famous biblical figures. These deathbed scenes were already found in the Bible, for example *Genesis* 49 (Jacob) and *Deuteronomy*

33 (Moses), and were expanded in the Hellenistic period into full-length literary works, in which the patriarch is usually found on his deathbed, surrounded by his family, to whom he delivers his final discourse. The most complete example of a testament is the **Testaments of the Twelve Patriarchs*, a series of twelve self-contained pieces, each purporting to be the deathbed instructions of one of the twelve sons of Jacob. A consistent pattern is present in each of the testaments: a historical retrospective, ethical instructions, and future predictions. The present form of the text is Christian, but with clear Jewish roots. Certain texts from Qumran may contain the antecedents of the *Testaments of the Twelve Patriarchs*, for example, the Testaments of Naphtali, Judah, Joseph, and the Aramaic Levi document, all found in Cave 4. Other examples of Jewish testaments include the *Testament of Moses* and the *Testament of Job*. The *Testament of Abraham* falls outside the genre, since it does not contain a farewell discourse by Abraham.

• James H. Charlesworth, ed., *The Old Testament Pseudepigrapha: Apocalyptic Literature and Testaments*, vol. 1 (Garden City, N.Y., 1983). John J. Collins, "Testaments," in *Jewish Writings of the Second Temple Period*, edited by Michael E. Stone, Compendia Rerum Iudaicarum and Novum Testamentum, section 2 (Assen and Philadelphia, 1984), pp. 325–356. Florentino García Martínez, *The Dead Sea Scrolls Translated: The Qumran Texts in English* (Leiden, 1994). —SIDNIE WHITE CRAWFORD

TESTAMENT OF ABRAHAM, pseudepigraphous work extant in two Greek recensions and probably composed in that language. It is also extant in Slavonic, Coptic, Arabic, Ethiopic, and Romanian. Its date and place of composition are hard to determine, and although its author may have been an Egyptian Jew living between the first century BCE and the second century CE, the author may have been a Christian. It recounts how God sends the archangel Michael to bring Abraham's soul to heaven, but Abraham refuses to die. Upon his request, he is taken on a heavenly tour, during which he sees the whole world and the judgment of the souls. Still refusing to die, he is tricked by the angel of death into submission, and his soul is taken to paradise.

• M. Delcor, *Le Testament d'Abraham*, Studia in Veteris Testamenti pseudepigrapha, vol. 2 (Leiden, 1973). George W. E. Nickelsburg, ed., *Studies on the Testament of Abraham*, rev. ed., Septuagint and Cognate Studies, vol. 6 (Missoula, Mont., 1976). E. P. Sanders, "Testament of Abraham," in *The Old Testament Pseudepigrapha*, edited by James H. Charlesworth, vol. 1 (Garden City, N.Y., 1983), pp. 871–902. Francis Schmidt, *Le Testament grec D'Abraham*, Texte und Studien zum Antiken Judentum 11 (Tübingen, 1986). —GIDEON BOHAK

TESTAMENT OF JOB, pseudepigraphous work written in Greek and extant in Greek, Slavonic, and Coptic. It probably is a Jewish work, written in the first century BCE or CE, but a second-century CE Christian origin cannot be ruled out. It recounts how Job, about to die, collected his sons and daughters and told them his life story. He describes his righteous behavior and his destruction of a pagan shrine, which provoked Satan to destroy his wealth, kill his children, and afflict him with a severe plague. Next, Job spoke of the three kings who came to see him, of his wife's death, and of his vindication and restoration by God. Having ended his discourse, Job divided his property among his male children and gave his daughters mysterious cords that endowed them with the gift of prophecy. The work ends with Job's death and burial and the ascent of his soul, flying to the east. The *Testament of Job* was excluded from the Apocrypha in the fifth century and only rediscovered in the nineteenth century.

• Michael A. Knibb and Pieter Willem van der Horst, eds., *Studies on the Testament of Job*, Monograph Series (Society for New Testament Studies) vol. 66 (New York, 1989). Russell P. Spittler, "Testament of Job," in *The Old Testament Pseudepigrapha*, edited by James H. Charlesworth, vol. 1 (Garden City, N.Y., 1983), pp. 829–868. —GIDEON BOHAK

TESTAMENT OF MOSES. See ASSUMPTION OF MOSES.

TESTAMENT OF SOLOMON, pseudepigraphous work written in Greek and extant in several Greek recensions as well as an Arabic version. In its current form(s) it stems from Christian circles of the third or fourth century CE, but it is possible that behind it lies a lost Jewish book that was reworked by a Christian redactor. Its geographical provenance is unknown. The work consists of Solomon's account of how the archangel Michael provided him with a potent ring with which to control demons. Solomon relates how he used this ring to summon numerous demons, individually or in groups, and interrogate each of them as to his or her name, destructive powers, and the name of the angel who has power to thwart him or her. Some of the demons also prophesied events in the distant future, including the arrival of *Jesus, while others were forced to assist Solomon in building his Temple or were simply locked up in a safe place.

• Dennis C. Duling, "Testament of Solomon," in *The Old Testament Pseudepigrapha*, edited by James H. Charlesworth, vol. 1 (Garden City, N.Y., 1983), pp. 935–987. Chester Charlton McCown, ed., *The Testament of Solomon: Edited from Manuscripts . . .* (Leipzig, 1922). —GIDEON BOHAK

TESTAMENTS OF THE TWELVE PATRIARCHS, pseudepigraphous work, purporting to record the parting words of the sons of Jacob to their children, made up of twelve separate testaments, most of which include the patriarch's account of his life, his exhortations to his offspring, and his predictions of the distant future. Thus, in the Testament of Judah, Judah lists the many brave deeds of his youth, both his battles with wild beasts and those with Israel's sworn enemies, the Canaanites, the Shechemites, the sons of Esau, and so on. He then briefly recounts his embarrassing encounter with Tamar and mentions some of his other transgressions, exhorting his children to lead better lives. He warns them against drunkenness, promiscuity, cupidity, and other vices. He also encourages them to pay special respect to Levi and his priestly descendants, foretells the future trouble that will befall the Jewish people, which will ultimately end with the arrival of the Messiah and the final salvation. The testaments are extant in Greek, Armenian, and Slavonic, and contain several obviously Christian passages. Thus, it is not easy to determine whether they are a Jewish composition interpolated by its Christian transmittors or an original Christian composition of the late second or early third century CE. Moreover, various Hebrew and Aramaic fragments of the testaments, or of related materials, are known. Some of these are found in medieval Hebrew texts and probably represent a medieval translation from the Greek. The Aramaic fragments, however, were found both in the Cairo *Genizah and among the *Dead Sea Scrolls, and while their exact relationship with the Greek testaments cannot always be determined, they do suggest that much of the material contained in the testaments was written in Erets Yisra'el, in Aramaic, and perhaps partly in Hebrew, in the second century BCE.

• Marinus de Jonge, *The Testaments of the Twelve Patriarchs: A Study of Their Text, Composition and Origin*, 2d ed. (Assen, 1975). Howard Clark Kee, "Testaments of the Twelve Patriarchs," in *The Old Testament Pseudepigrapha*, edited by James H. Charlesworth (Garden City, N.Y., 1983), vol. 1, pp. 775–828. George W. E. Nickelsburg, *Jewish Literature between the Bible and the Mishnah: A Historical and Literary Introduction* (Philadelphia, 1981), pp. 231–241. Emil Schürer, Geza Vermes, and Fergus Millar, *The History of the Jewish People in the Age of Jesus Christ, 175 B.C.–A.D. 135* (Edinburgh, 1987), vol. 3.2, pp. 767–781. H. Dixon Slingerland, *The Testaments of the Twelve Patriarchs: A Critical History of Research*, Society of Biblical Literature, Monograph Series 21 (Missoula, Mont., 1977).

—GIDEON BOHAK

TETRAGRAMMATON. See GOD, NAMES OF.

TEVAH. See BIMAH.

TEVEL (טֶבֶל), agricultural produce that has not yet been tithed and is therefore forbidden for profane use. The rabbis ruled on the basis of *Deuteronomy* 26.13 that liability for *tithes commenced only "when it [the crop] has seen the front of the house," that is, when the crop is gathered in, thus permitting *tevel* to be eaten by the agricultural worker in the field (*Ber*. 35b; *B. M*. 87a). The Talmud reports that this rule was often abused; people would bring in their produce through the roof, so that it would not have "seen the front of the house." If there is doubt about whether the tithe has been taken, the produce is called **dema'i*.

• Yosef Karo, *Shulḥan 'Arukh* (Jerusalem, 1995). Dale Patrick, *Old Testament Law* (Atlanta, 1985).

TEVET (טֵבֵת), fourth month of the civil year, tenth of the religious year; its zodiac sign is Capricorn. The word *Tevet* is of Akkadian/Babylonian origin, and the month always has twenty-nine days. Tevet is mentioned by name in the Bible only in the *Book of Esther* (2.16), although there are references elsewhere in the Bible to the "fourth month." The new moon of Tevet occurs during Ḥanukkah. The tenth day of Tevet ('Asarah be-Tevet) is a fast day in commemoration of the commencement of the siege of Jerusalem by Nebuchadnezzar (*2 Kgs*. 25.1). The Israel chief rabbinate has named 10 Tevet as General Qaddish Day (Yom ha-Qaddish ha-Kelali) in memory of the millions of Jewish victims of the Holocaust whose exact date of death is unknown. According to tradition, 9 Tevet is the anniversary of the death of Ezra and 20 Tevet the anniversary of the death of Maimonides. In ancient times, a fast day was observed on 8 Tevet to mark the completion of the *Septuagint translation (minor tractate *Soferim* 1).

• Nathan Bushwick, *Understanding the Jewish Calendar* (New York, 1989). George Zinberg, *Jewish Calendar Mystery Dispelled* (New York, 1963).

—CHAIM PEARL

TEVET, TENTH OF. See 'ASARAH BE-TEVET.

TEVILAH. See ABLUTION; BAPTISM; MIQVEH.

TEVUL YOM (טְבוּל יוֹם; He Who Immersed Himself That Day) tractate in Mishnah order Tohorot, in four chapters, with related material in Tosefta'. There is no *gemara'* in either Talmud. In biblical law, ritual impurity persists, even after ritual immersion, until sundown (*Lv*. 11.32, 22.6–7). The sages remark (*Tev. Y*. 3.6) that "the *tevul yom* is not regarded as impure," even though he is not yet regarded as entirely pure. The tractate's analysis of the nature of the residual impurity of a *tevul yom* is roughly equivalent to a secondary impurity, one that disqualifies rather than defiles priestly foods (i.e., the sacred food is rendered unfit, but does not transmit impurity further), such as *terumah* and *ḥallah*. The tractate also discusses some of the intricacies of the laws of impurities, most prominently the laws concerning the conjoining of foods contiguous to one another.

An English translation of the tractate is in Herbert Danby's *The Mishnah* (London, 1933).

• Chanoch Albeck, ed., *Shishah Sidrei Mishnah, Seder Tohorot* (Jerusalem, 1958). Philip Blackman, ed. and trans., *Mishnayoth*, vol. 5, *Order Taharoth* (Gateshead, 1973). Hermann Leberecht Strack and Günter Stemberger, *Introduction to the Talmud and Midrash*, rev. and updat. ed., translated by Markus Bockmuehl (Minneapolis, 1992).

—AVRAHAM WALFISH

TEXTUAL CRITICISM. See BIBLE.

THANKSGIVING. In the biblical era, *thanksgiving offerings were brought by individuals to the Temple in Jerusalem as an expression of their gratitude to God. Biblical expressions of thanksgiving frequently begin with **barukh* (blessed be; e.g., *Gn*. 24.27; *Ex*. 18.10; *2 Sm*. 18.28; *Is*. 28.6); hence the statutory opening formula ("Blessed are You, O Lord, our God, king of the universe . . . ") of *benedictions uttered before enjoying anything in this world (*Ber*. 35a). Thanksgiving is the theme of many *psalms which have, for this reason, been included in the liturgy (e.g., the *Hallel). Psalms of thanksgiving have been discovered among the *Dead Sea Scrolls. The introductory part of the daily Shaḥarit service, known among the Ashkenazim as *Pesuqei de-Zimra' (passages of song), and among the Sephardim as *Zemirot, includes the thanksgiving of David (*hodu* [give thanks unto the Lord]; *1 Chr*. 16.8–36). The eighteenth benediction of the *'Amidah is referred to in the Mishnah as Hodayah (Thanksgiving); its shorter form, recited by the congregation during the reader's repetition, is known as the Modim de-Rabbanan (Thanksgiving of the Rabbis) because the passage is compounded of several rabbinic prayers. The special thanksgiving additions for Purim and Ḥanukkah (*'Al ha-Nissim) are inserted at this point to commemorate the deliverance granted on these days. In the second and third paragraphs of the

*Birkat ha-Mazon (*nodeh* [we thank thee] and *ve-ʿal ha-kol* [for all this . . . we thank . . . you]), thanksgiving is offered for the land God has given his people, for his covenant, and for his Torah (*Ber.* 48b–49a). A rabbinic statement (*Lv. Rab.* 9:7) declares that, in messianic times, all sacrifices and prayers will be abolished, except the thanksgiving offering and the prayer of thanksgiving to God, because individuals will always want to express gratitude to the source of all blessings.

• Seligmann Baer, ed., *Sefer ʿAvodat Yisrael* (Jerusalem, 1945), p. 36. Joseph H. Hertz, ed., *Authorized Daily Prayer Book* (New York, 1948), pp. 9, 756f., 984. Louis Jacobs, *Jewish Prayer* (London, 1962), pp. 27–32. Abraham E. Millgram, *Jewish Worship* (Philadelphia, 1971), pp. 13ff. Chaim Stern, ed., *Shaarei Tefillah: Gates of Prayer: The New Union Prayer Book* (New York, 1975), pp. 186f., 200, 233, 272.

—A. STANLEY DREYFUS

THANKSGIVING OFFERING (Heb. *zevaḥ todah*), one of three types of *peace offerings (or well-being offerings). The thanksgiving offering belonged to the category of sacred meals; after the prescribed portions of the animal had been offered on the altar (blood and fat) and to the priest (thigh and breast), the flesh accompanied by unleavened loaves and cakes was eaten by the worshiper and his guests. A thanksgiving offering would be made by an individual who had recovered from an illness, been rescued from danger, or survived a journey (*Lv.* 7.11–18; *Ps.* 107) and was typically accompanied by prayers of thanksgiving, proclaiming to all present the beneficence of God enjoyed by the offerer. It would seem that the paschal sacrifice was a special type of thanksgiving offering. In later times, the thanksgiving sacrifice was replaced by the *Birkat ha-Gomel pronounced by the worshiper in public on similar occasions. See also SACRIFICES.

• Gary Anderson, *A Time to Mourn, a Time to Dance: The Expression of Grief and Joy in Israelite Religion* (University Park, Pa., 1991). Dale Patrick, *Old Testament Law* (Atlanta, 1985). —BARUCH J. SCHWARTZ

THANKSGIVING PSALMS, a series of hymns, discovered in Qumran, in which the formula "I thank you, Lord" appears. The speaker thanks God for his election and endowment with the gift of knowledge. The highly personal Hymns of the Teacher are distinguished from the Hymns of the Community, which introduce "we" language and discuss the human condition, communal affiliation, and congregational praise.

Hymns of the Teacher appear en bloc in the middle of 1Q*Hodayot*. The Cave 4 manuscripts indicate several different collections of Thanksgiving Psalms circulated at Qumran and shed light on the question of their function—private devotion or public liturgy. See also DEAD SEA SCROLLS; QUMRAN COMMUNITY.

• Svend Holm-Nielsen, *Hodayot: Psalms from Qumran*, Acta Theologica Danica 2 (Aarhus, Denmark, 1960). Jacob Licht, *The Thanksgiving Scroll* (Jerusalem, 1957). Eileen Schuller, "The Cave 4 Hodayot Manuscripts: A Preliminary Description," *Qumran Studies* (special issue of *Jewish Quarterly Review*) 85.1–2 (1995): 137–150.

—ESTHER GLICKLER CHAZON

THANKSGIVING SCROLL, one of the original seven *Dead Sea Scrolls found in Cave 1, in Qumran, which takes its name (*Hodayot*) from the verb that regularly introduces the hymns contained in the text: "I thank you [O Lord]." The text, written in Hebrew, exists in two copies from Cave 1 and seven from Cave 4, which were written at various times in the first century BCE. The most complete text, 1QH, contains approximately twenty-five poetic compositions. These hymns are individual rather than communal and are usually considered sectarian, unique to the community at Qumran, rather than an outside composition. The hymns are most often divided into two groups. In the first, which is written in first person, the speaker talks about his divine mission, his role as a leader of a community, and his struggles against opposition. This group is often attributed to the *Teacher of Righteousness himself, the putative founder of the Qumran community. The second group of hymns refers to the more general experiences of a member of the community, for example, the struggle of the righteous against the wicked, and contains praise for God, who creates all things and will guarantee the triumph of the righteous. An English translation is in Theodor H. Gaster's *The Dead Sea Scriptures* (New York, 1956), pages 111–228.

• Devorah Dimant, "Qumran Sectarian Literature," in *Jewish Writings of the Second Temple Period*, edited by Michael E. Stone, Compendia Rerum Iudaicarum ad Novum Testamentum, section 2 (Assen, 1984), pp. 483–550. Bonnie Pedrotti Kittel, *The Hymns of Qumran*, Society of Biblical Literature, Dissertation Series 50 (Atlanta, 1981). Eleazar Lipa Sukenik, *The Dead Sea Scrolls of the Hebrew University* (Jerusalem, 1955).

—SIDNIE WHITE CRAWFORD

THEFT. A thief is one who purloins without the knowledge of the owner, as opposed to the robber, who openly and forcibly appropriates another's goods (see ROBBERY; *B. Q.* 79b). The prohibition "You shall not steal" (*Ex.* 20.13; *Lv.* 19.11) carries no corporal punishment with it, since the crime of theft may be rectified by restoration of the stolen goods. The thief who admits his theft of his own free will must restore the goods or their value and is free from further punishment. If, however, he is convicted by a court, or the goods are traced to him by the authorities, he is fined and must restore double their value to the owner (*Ex.* 22.3); for the theft of an animal followed by its sale or slaughter, four- or five-fold restitution must be made (*Ex.* 21.37). If the owner despairs of receiving back the stolen property, ownership passes to the thief, who has only to pay the owner the value at the time of the theft (*B. Q.* 114a–b). Theft of sacred property (*heqdesh*), or from another who had stolen such, does not carry a double fine. If a thief is unable to repay the amount he stole (but not if he is unable only to pay the additional fine), he may be sold into the service of the owner of the property (*Ex.* 22.2). A woman is not sold into service even if she is unable to repay the value of the stolen goods. Other punishments were imposed in Talmudic times. Maimonides summarized the general law: "Anyone who steals an object worth a penny or more trespasses a negative prohibition." This applies to thefts from Jews or non-Jews, whether the theft is great or small. One must not steal even in fun or with the intention of returning the object (*Mishneh Torah, Hilkhot Genevah* 1). It is forbidden to receive or deal in stolen goods, and one who receives such goods from a known thief is obliged to restore them to the original owner without receiving compensation from him. See also BURGLARY; KIDNAPPING.

• Bernard S. Jackson, *Essays in Jewish and Comparative Legal History*, Studies in Judaism in Late Antiquity 10 (Leiden, 1975).

THEISM. See MONOTHEISM.

THEOCRACY, term used by *Josephus Flavius to describe the constitution of the postexilic Jewish commonwealth (*Against Apion* 2.165). Since then the term has come to mean any system of government where power is vested in the spiritual leadership wielding its authority in the name of God. The concept has often, although incorrectly, been identified with the biblical idea of "kingdom of priests and a holy nation" (*Ex*. 19.6) and the prophetic vision of the kingdom of God on earth. The Jewish concept of God is frequently expressed in terms of kingship, to which the liturgy constantly refers.

The opposition of the prophet *Samuel to the people's demand for a king was made explicitly on the grounds that they wished to substitute a human monarchy for the kingship of God (*1 Sm*. 8.7). Thereafter the king was seen as responsible before God for the people's observance of his commandments. He was subject to God's authority, and God's messengers, the prophets, castigated him harshly if he and the people went astray. A sacerdotal theocracy developed in early Second Temple times under Persian domination. According to Josephus, the motives of the *Zealot rebellion were less political than religious, in their insistence that God should rule over them (*The Jewish War* 2.8.1; *Antiquities of the Jews* 18.1.1–6). During the Middle Ages and until the period of the Emancipation, Jewish life was, in a sense, theocratically governed, since it was dominated by the rabbinate that exercised legislative functions based on the *halakhah*, especially in the frequent instances where Jewish communities enjoyed internal autonomy. According to *Maimonides the messianic rule is theocratic, since it is characterized by the messianic being enforcing obedience to and conformity with the *halakhah*.

In the State of Israel, the term *theocracy* is occasionally used in discussions regarding the demand of religious groups that the state be subject to religious *halakhah* as administered by the rabbinate. Secularists claim that the Orthodox rabbinic authorities are already given too much power by the secular legislative body, for example, in entrusting laws of personal status entirely to ecclesiastical auspices. In this debate *theocracy* is used as a slogan rather than as an exact term. Ultra-Orthodox Jews, including those who reject the State of Israel, anticipate a messianic era in which God will rule the Jewish state and, indeed, the entire world.

• Ella Belfer, *The Jewish People and the Kingdom of Heaven: A Study of Jewish Theocracy* (Ramat Gan, 1986). Margaret H. E. Brown, "The One Whom the Lord Has Chosen: Monarchy in Theocracy, I Samuel 8:1–16:13," Ph.D. dissertation, Marquette University, 1985. Gershon Weiler, *Jewish Theocracy* (Leiden, 1988).

THEODICY. See REWARD AND PUNISHMENT.

THEODOTION (c.2d cent.), translator of the Hebrew Bible into Greek who revised the earlier Greek translation of the *Septuagint. It is not known how much of his translation was actually written by him, since an anonymous earlier translation (c.1st cent. BCE), named by scholars Kaige-Theodotion, was ascribed to Theodotion in antiquity. His version was one of the first Jewish revisions of the Septuagint and formed the basis for later revisions by *Aquila and *Symmachus. Theodotion's translation is literal and follows some of the rabbinic hermeneutical rules. Theodotion's version was included in Origen's Hexapla and was transmitted as part of the Hexapla, but on the whole, very little of Theodotion's translation has been preserved. The best-known section is the *Book of Daniel*, which has been completely preserved, together with the apocryphal sections of that book, since this version replaced the old Greek translation in the manuscripts of the Septuagint.

• Dominique Barthélemy, *Les Devanciers d'Aquila*, Supplements to Vetus Testamentum, vol. 10 (Leiden, 1963). P. M. Bogaert, "Septante et versions grecques," *Dictionnaire de la Bible: Supplément*, vol. XII (Paris, 1993), pp. 536–692. Leonard J. Greenspoon, "Biblical Translation in Antiquity and in the Modern World: A Comparative Study," *Hebrew Union College Annual* 60 (1989): 91–113.

THEOLOGY, the science of subjects pertaining to God, his nature, and his acts. The term, derived from the Greek words *theos* and *logos*, has acquired a distinct Christian flavor as a result of the history of its usage, but is nevertheless applied in current Jewish discourse. In Medieval Hebrew the noun and adjective *elohi* was often used in a sense similar to the English *divinity* and *divine*, referring to theological learning and its specialists. Systematic Jewish teaching being primarily concerned with the normative determination of **halakhah*, theological matters were left in a more fluid and less rigidly defined state (see AGGADAH). In the words of Leo *Baeck, the theology of Judaism is one of teachers and not of a supreme ecclesiastical authority. The authoritative character of the various sources (Bible, Talmud, kabbalistic writings) and of the commentarial traditions is viewed differently by different schools. In the Middle Ages, *philosophy was the major vehicle of theological thinking, and there is practically no distinction between philosophical theology and theological philosophy. This situation has occasionally prompted exaggerated statements to the effect that Judaism has no theology, when the intention was to say that there was no systematically elaborated, official, dogmatic theology of the type developed by the church. Contemporary theological thinking is overshadowed by the experience of the Holocaust (see HOLOCAUST THEOLOGY).

• Eugene Borowitz, *A New Jewish Theology in the Making* (Philadelphia, 1968). Samuel S. Cohen, *Jewish Theology* (Assen, 1971). Louis Jacobs, *A Jewish Theology* (London, 1973). Kaufmann Kohler, *Jewish Theology* (1918; repub. New York, 1968).

THEOPHANY. See REVELATION.

THERAPEUTAE (Gr.; Healers), an ancient sect of Jewish ascetics who lived near Lake Mareotis, not far from Alexandria, Egypt. The existence of this sect is attested solely in one of the writings of *Philo (*De vita contemplativa*). The Therapeutae, men and women alike, lived in individual chambers apart from society and devoted themselves to solitude, prayer, and the study of the scriptures, which they interpreted by way of allegory. On the Sabbath, they assembled for communal study followed by a communal meal that consisted of bread with salt, herbs, and spring water. Most of the Therapeutae ate only twice a week, while others fasted from one Sabbath to the next. In many aspects, the Therapeutae bear a marked resemblance to the *Essenes, and it has often been suggested that the two groups may have been connected.

• Philo, *On the Contemplative Life*, in *Philo*, translated by F. H. Colson, Loeb Classical Library, 10 vols. and 2 suppl. vols. (Cambridge, Mass., 1941), vol. 9, pp. 104–170. Emil Schürer, Geza Vermes, and F. Millar, *The History of the Jewish People in the Age of Jesus Christ* (Edinburgh, 1979), vol. 2, pp. 591–597. David Winston, *Philo of Alexandria: The Contemplative Life, the Giants, and Selections*, The Classics of Western Spirituality (New York, 1981), pp. 41–57, 315–321. —GIDEON BOHAK

THINNUS (תְּחִינּוֹת; supplications), Yiddish word (derived from the Hebrew *teḥinnah*) for prayers written primarily to be recited by women. *Tḥinnus* are voluntary and are often said privately. These prayers first began to appear in print in the late sixteenth century; the rise of *tḥinnus* as a genre was stimulated by the growing pietism stemming from the popularization of Jewish mysticism. Early *tḥinnus* were often derived from voluntary Hebrew devotions for men originating in works such as Natan Netaʿ Hannover's *Shaʿarei Tsiyyon*. Other early *tḥinnus* addressed the specific religious concerns of women, including the three "women's *mitsvot*" (lighting Sabbath candles; taking a portion of dough for *ḥallah*; and observing *niddah*, the menstrual restrictions and purification), pregnancy and childbirth, and visiting the cemetery. While most of the seventeenth-century anthologies of *tḥinnus* published in western Europe (such as *Tkhines* [Amsterdam, 1648]) were anonymous, the eighteenth-century *tḥinnus* published in eastern Europe were often attributed to individual authors. One such author, Mattityahu Sobotki of Prague, was male; most others were female: Sarah Rivqah Rakhel Le'ah (c.1710–1790), daughter of Yaʿaqov Yukl Horowitz, rabbi of Bolekhov and later Brody; Serl (fl. 1760 in Volhynia), daughter of Yaʿaqov ben Wolf Kranz, the Maggid of Dubno; and Sarah bas Tovim (fl. 1740 in Podolia). Popular topics of *tḥinnus* included the Yamim Nora'im, the Sabbath, the announcement of the new moon, and the making of candles for the synagogue. In the mid-nineteenth century, some men, influenced by the Enlightenment, began to write *tḥinnus* pseudonymously, attributing them to fictitious women; this practice gave rise to the erroneous impression that all *tḥinnus* attributed to female authors were actually written by men. Many *tḥinnus* had Reformist content. They stressed the importance of home hygiene and certain sorts of emotional relations within the family, showing the influence of rising bourgeois sensibilities. *Tḥinnus* are still being published in Yiddish in small Yiddish-speaking communities in New York and Israel. The genre has recently aroused interest as a possible model for the prayers of contemporary Jewish women (see WOMEN'S PRAYERS).

• Tracy Guren Klirs and Ida Cohen Selavan, comps., *The Merit of Our Mothers: A Bilingual Anthology of Jewish Women's Prayers* (Cincinnati, 1992). Chava Weissler, "Prayers in Yiddish and the Religious World of Ashkenazic Women," in *Jewish Women in Historical Perspective*, edited by Judith Baskin (Detroit, 1991), pp. 159–181. —CHAVA WEISSLER

THIRTEEN ATTRIBUTES. Based on *Exodus* 34.6–7, rabbinic tradition frequently refers to God's thirteen attributes (*middot*) of mercy. There is no unanimity among the commentators as to the precise nature of these attributes and the distinctions between them, as well as to their correlation to the words of the biblical text. The divisions of the scriptural verses are artificial; for example, the Lord, the Lord, God, merciful, gracious, long-suffering, abundant in lovingkindness, truth, keeping mercy unto the thousandth generation, forgiving iniquity, forgiving transgression, forgiving sin, and clearing (the guilty). There are alternative enumerations, some of which include only one mention of the divine name, some none, but always the words are divided so as to make a total of thirteen. The tradition associating this particular verse with God's attribute of mercy, as well as the number thirteen, seem to be ancient, although other numerical traditions also appear to have existed. Some of these are preserved by the *Karaites, who list nine to eleven attributes. The Talmud quotes R. Yoḥanan as stating that the Almighty said to Moses, "Whenever Israel sins, let them recite these *middot* before me and I will forgive them," while R. Yehudah states, "A covenant has been made with the thirteen *middot*—when the children of Israel recite them they will not be turned away empty-handed" (*R. ha-Sh.* 17b). As a result, they form the central motif of supplicatory prayers on all special occasions. The chapter in which the passage occurs is read as the Pentateuchal lesson on all public fasts, and the verses of the thirteen attributes are recited by the whole congregation before being repeated by the reader. In some rites they are solemnly recited on festivals (but not if these occur on the Sabbath) when the synagogue ark is opened, and they form the most important element of the *seliḥot prayers. During the concluding service (Neʿilah) on Yom Kippur, they form the refrain of a composite *seliḥah*. The kabbalists correlated the thirteen attributes with the ten *sefirot (also called *middot*) of their system, and the problem of how to accommodate the additional three *middot* is much debated in kabbalistic literature.

• A. Feuer, ed., *Taschlich and the Thirteen Attributes: A New Translation with a Commentary Anthologized from Talmudic, Midrashic, and Rabbinic Sources* (New York, 1979). Moses Maimonides, *Guide of the Perplexed*, translated by Shlomo Pines, vol. 1 (Chicago, 1963), pp. 50–60. Gary G. Porton, "Rabbi Ishmael and His Thirteen Middot," in *Religion, Literature, and Society in Ancient Israel*, edited by Jacob Neusner et al. (Lanham, Md., 1987), pp. 1–18.

THIRTEEN PRINCIPLES OF FAITH, customary designation for Moses *Maimonides' formulation of the basic principles underlying Judaism. The first *mishnah* of the tenth chapter of tractate *Sanhedrin* reads, "All Israelites have a share in the world to come . . . and these are they that have no share in the world to come. . . ."

Maimonides took the last clause to mean that those denying the beliefs enumerated there were heretics. In his otherwise succinct commentary to the Mishnah, he expands his explanation of this particular statement into a long and detailed examination of the principles of Judaism: The existence of God, Creator of all things; his absolute unity; his incorporeality; his eternity; the obligation to serve and worship him alone; the authenticity of prophecy; the superiority of Moses above all other prophets; the Torah as God's revelation to Moses; the immutability of the Torah; God's omniscience and foreknowledge; divine retribution; the advent of the Messiah; and the resurrection of the dead. Many philosophers disputed the number of formulations or the formulations themselves. Others disputed the very concept of formal dogmas. Although they were never formally adopted, Maimonides' Thirteen Principles of Faith found their way into the prayer book in two versions: a prose version in which each principle is introduced with "I believe with perfect faith" (*ani ma'amin*), and a rhymed version known as *Yigdal. See also CREED; DOGMA.

• David R. Blumenthal, "The Commentary of R. Hoter Ben Shelomo to the Thirteen Principles of Maimonides," Ph.D. dissertation, Columbia University, 1972. Natan Gurary, *The Thirteen Principles of Faith: A Chasidic Viewpoint* (Northvale, N.J., 1996). Mosheh Max, *I Believe: An Exposition of Maimonides' Thirteen Principles of Faith and Their Implementation in Jewish Life* (Jerusalem, 1973).

THIRTY-SIX SAINTS. See LAMED VAV.

THIRTY-TWO PATHS OF WISDOM, a mystical concept, introduced in the *Sefer Yetsirah*, that refers to the twenty-two letters of the Hebrew alphabet, which, with the numbers one through ten, constitute the elements of creation (an interpretation given also by *Sa'adyah ben Yosef Ga'on and *Yehudah ha-Levi). In kabbalistic literature, the notion of the thirty-two paths was reinterpreted in terms of the doctrine of *sefirot*. The highest *sefirah* (disregarding the almost utterly transcendent first *sefirah*, Crown) is Wisdom, the first recognizable flash of the divine reality manifesting itself. This flash then assumes form and structure and emanates or descends into the lower *sefirot* through thirty-two paths or channels. These paths reflect the manner in which the various *sefirot* unite with each other in order to draw the divine flow into the world.

• Gershom Gerhard Scholem, *Major Trends in Jewish Mysticism* (New York, 1961). Gershom Gerhard Scholem, *On the Kabbalah and Its Symbolism* (New York, 1992).

THREE WEEKS. See BEIN HA-METSARIM.

THRONE OF GOD, an ancient image associated with the idea of divine majesty. In *1 Kings* 22.19, Micaiah the prophet says to the king, Jehoshaphat, "I saw the Lord seated upon his throne, with all the host of heaven standing in attendance to the right and left of him." The call of God came to Isaiah, who "beheld my Lord seated on a high and lofty throne" (*Is*. 6.1). A vivid vision of the divine throne was reported by Ezekiel, in which it appears as a chariot accompanied by strange creatures (*Ez*. 1). This passage became the basis of an important aspect of early Jewish mystical thought (see MA'ASEH MERKAVAH). The divine throne is mentioned in *Daniel* 7.9–11 and by the author of the Ethiopic *Apocalypse of Enoch* (*1 En*. 14.18–19). Early rabbinic literature is replete with references to the celestial throne. The Ark of the Covenant is described as being an image of the throne. When it was carried on the march in the wilderness, it was covered with a blue cloth similar to the color of the throne. The throne is said to be one of the seven objects fashioned prior to the creation of the heaven and the earth (*Shab*. 152b). Some texts speak of two thrones, the throne of mercy and the throne of justice (e.g., *'A. Z.* 3b). The throne of glory is frequently mentioned in the Talmud (e.g. *Yoma'* 86b; *'A. Z.* 3b). The earliest Jewish mystics, using the imagery of Ezekiel, described their experience as an ascent of the soul to the celestial throne to view the majesty of God. The throne and its dimensions are described in detail (*Ḥag*. 13a). The idea of the throne of God was also connected with that of **kavod*, the visible manifestation of the incorporeal God. All of this had an influence on the liturgy of the synagogue and on Kabbalah, in which the throne was linked with one of the **sefirot*. The medieval philosophers accepted the concept but often interpreted it allegorically (cf. Maimonides' *Guide of the Perplexed* 9).

• Louis Ginzberg, *The Legends of the Jews* (Philadelphia, 1909–1938). Bo Reicke et al., *Biblisch-Historisches Handwörterbuch* (Göttingen, 1966), vol. 3, pp. 1976–1981. Gershom Gerhard Scholem, *Kabbalah* (New York, 1974). Gershom Gerhard Scholem, *Major Trends in Jewish Mysticism* (New York, 1941). —LOU H. SILBERMAN

TIBBON. See IBN TIBBON FAMILY.

TIBERIAS (Heb. Teveryah), town in Erets Yisra'el, established between 14 and 18 CE on the western shore of the Sea of Galilee by Herod Antipas; in recent centuries Tiberias has come to be regarded as one of the four *holy cities. In Mishnaic times, leading tanna'im lived in Tiberias as did R. Yehudah II (3d cent.) and members of his Sanhedrin, making it the center of Palestinian Jewry's political and religious leadership until the Arab conquest in the seventh century. Around 400, the *Talmud Yerushalmi was edited there; it was also home to many *batei midrash* and synagogues. In the seventh century, Tiberian Masoretes developed a system of Hebrew *vocalization; and *payyetanim*, including *Yann'ai, composed *piyyutim*. Moses *Maimonides was buried there in 1206 and his grave is still visited; the grave of Yesha'yahu Horowitz (see HOROWITZ FAMILY) is located nearby. After centuries of sporadic settlement, the Jewish community was reestablished in 1777 by a group of Ḥasidim.

• Oded Avissar, *Sefer Teveryah* (Jerusalem, 1973). Helga Dudman and Elisheva Ballhorn, *Tiberias* (Jerusalem, 1988). Yizhar Hirschfeld, *A Guide to Antiquity Sites in Tiberias* (Jerusalem, 1992). Eleanor K. Vogel and Brooks Holtzclaw, "Bibliography of Holy Land Sites, Part II," *Hebrew Union College Annual* 52 (1981): 87–88. —FERN SECKBACH

TIQ (תִּיק; case, sheath), term used in the Mishnah to designate two types of containers: (1) the square black leather *tefillin* box or, according to an alternate interpretation, the bag in which the *tefillin* boxes are stored (*Shab.* 16.1) and (2) a case in which the Torah scroll is contained (*Meg.* 26b). Sephardi communities apply the word to the casing of wood or silver in which the Torah scroll is rolled up and that is placed upright on the reader's desk, the scroll being read in this vertical position (see TORAH ORNAMENTS). –SHMUEL HIMELSTEIN

TIQQUN (תִּקּוּן), order of service for certain occasions, mostly recited at night. Tiqqun Ḥatsot (Midnight Tiqqun) are prayers—generally consisting of Psalm 79, Psalm 102, Psalm 137, the Viddui (confessional), the thirteen divine attributes, and dirges (*qinot*)—recited at midnight by individuals or small groups, sitting on the ground, in mourning over the destruction of the Temple. Instituted in the sixteenth century by kabbalistic circles in Safed, the custom of Tiqqun Ḥatsot spread quickly and became very popular in the seventeenth and eighteenth centuries. Tiqqun Shomerim la-Boqer (Tiqqun of Watchmen for the Morning; cf. *Ps.* 130.6) is similar to Tiqqun Ḥatsot but is said shortly before sunrise. Tiqqun Leil Hosha'na' Rabbah (Tiqqun for the Eve of Hosha'na' Rabbah) includes the reading of *Deuteronomy, Psalms*, and passages from the Talmud, Midrash, and Zohar. This Tiqqun continues through the night, a custom originating in the fourteenth century when the Pentateuch was read during this night. Tiqqun Leil Shavu'ot (Tiqqun for the Eve of Shavu'ot) was introduced by Shelomoh Alkabez and his circle of sixteenth-century kabbalists in Salonika. It includes extracts from the Bible, Mishnah, Talmud, Midrash, and Zohar, as well as prayers and *azharot* on the 613 commandments; it is recited throughout the night. The practice has now been taken up in creative ways by Reform, Reconstructionist, and Conservative Jews. Tiqqun Shabbat (Sabbath Tiqqun) is a collection of *piyyutim*, excerpts from Mishnah *Shabbat*, and so on. Its composition is attributed to the kabbalist Yitsḥaq Luria and it is recited on Friday evenings and Sabbaths. Some rites observed *tiqqunim* on various other occasions, such as on the traditional anniversary of the death of Moses (7 Adar) and of the death of Yitsḥaq Luria (5 Av). See also TIQQUN 'OLAM.

• Ismar Elbogen, *Jewish Liturgy: A Comprehensive History*, translated by Raymond P. Scheindlin (Philadelphia, 1993). Irving Greenberg, *The Jewish Way: Living the Holidays* (New York, 1988). Peter Knobel, ed., *Gates of the Seasons: A Guide to the Jewish Year* (New York, 1983). Abraham Millgram, *Jewish Worship* (Philadelphia, 1971). Stefan C. Reif, *Judaism and Hebrew Prayer* (Cambridge, 1993). –PETER KNOBEL

TIQQUN 'OLAM (תִּקּוּן עוֹלָם). The verb *t q n* (set straight, put in order) occurs in no biblical book except *Ecclesiastes*. The Mishnah (e.g., *Git*. 4.1) already uses the combination in the sense of a proper ordering of the world (*'olam*), thus justifying rabbinic ordinances designed to improve social and legal arrangements. In the liturgy, the term is used in a more eschatological sense: the perfection of the world by the establishment in it of God's kingdom. In Lurianic Kabbalah, the term refers to the mystical process of repairing the primordial catastrophe of the *breaking of the vessels, by which the fallen world of chaos ultimately becomes the redeemed *'olam ha-tiqqun*. See also LURIA, YITSḤAQ.

• Gerald J. Blidstein, "Tikkun 'Olam," *Tradition* 29 (Winter 1995): 5–43. Arthur I. Waskow, "Tikkun 'Olam: Adornment of the Mystery," *Religion and Intellectual Life* 2.3 (Spring 1985): 109–115.

TIQQUN SOFERIM (תִּקּוּן סוֹפְרִים; correction of the scribes), corrections of the biblical text (mostly changes in pronominal suffixes) traditionally ascribed to the Men of the *Keneset ha-Gedolah (see SOFERIM). There are—according to various opinions expressed in Talmudic literature—eight, eleven, or eighteen such changes, intended to avoid anthropomorphism (e.g., *Gn*. 18.22—"but Abraham stood yet before the Lord," instead of a presumed original "but the Lord stood yet before Abraham") or to eliminate offensive terms by a resort to euphemism (e.g., *Jb*. 2.9, where Job is counseled to "bless God and die," meaning "to curse God"). For these verses, the rabbis use two main terms, namely *kinnah ha-katuv* (the verse uses a euphemism) in the early sources, and *tiqqun* (correction) in the later lists. *Tiqqun soferim* is also the colloquial term for an unpointed printed text of the Torah used in preparation for the reading of the Torah (see QERI'AT HA-TORAH).

• Christian D. Ginsburg, *Introduction to the Massoretico-Critical Edition of the Hebrew Bible* (London, 1897; repr. New York, 1966), pp. 347–367. Carmel McCarthy, *The Tiqqune Sopherim and Other Theological Corrections in the Masoretic Text of the Old Testament*, Oris Biblicus et Orientalis 36 (Freiburg and Göttingen, 1981).

TISH (Yi.; טיש; table), name for a Hasidic gathering around the table of a *rebbi*, usually for one of the Sabbath or festival meals, especially on Friday night or for the third Sabbath meal on Saturday. The *rebbi*'s followers assemble while the *rebbi* blesses and partakes of the food; in some courts, portions of the food (*shirayim*) are distributed. The meal is accompanied by the singing of special melodies and features a discourse by the *rebbi*.

• Aharon Vertheim, *Law and Custom in Hasidism* (Hoboken, N.J., 1992).
–MILES KRASSEN

TISH'AH BE-'AV (תִּשְׁעָה בְּאָב; 9 Av), day of mourning in commemoration of the destruction of the two Temples; the culmination of the semi-mourning periods of the Three Weeks and the Nine Days (see BEIN HA-METSARIM). In the words of the Talmud, "disasters recurred again and again to the Jewish people [on that date]"; in point of fact, only the fall of Betar, the last stronghold of Bar Kokhba' (see BAR KOKHBA', SHIM'ON), captured by the Romans in 135 CE, possibly occurred on that day. According to *2 Kings* 25.8–9, the First Temple was burned on 7 Av; according to *Jeremiah* 52.12, the date was 10 Av; however, the Talmud (*Ta'an*. 29a, possibly influenced by the fall of Betar) explained that the destruction of the Temple took place on 9 Av, and all subsequent major catastrophes that happened around that time were ascribed to that sad day. The Second

Temple was destroyed on 10 Av, but by tradition, this date was set back to 9 Av. The Karaites, however, observe the fast on 10 Av. The Mishnah (*Ta'an.* 4.6) adds to the list of tragic events of 9 Av God's decree against the entrance of the children of Israel into the Holy Land after the incident of the twelve spies and the plowing up of Jerusalem in 136 CE. Yitsḥaq Abravanel repeatedly maintains that the expulsion of the Jews from Spain in 1492 (he, himself, was one of the exiles) took place on 9 Av, though the actual date, the last day of July, was a few days earlier. The 9th of Av is observed as a fast, the only fast day, except for the biblical fast of Yom Kippur, to start at sunset and last for twenty-four hours. There is a ban on bathing, shaving, and wearing leather shoes. It is customary not to work or sit on ordinary chairs before midday. The essential features of the special liturgy for the observance are the reading of the *Book of Lamentations* (at the evening service, and in some congregations again the following morning) and the recital of *qinot* (dirges) composed not only in commemoration of the events of 9 Av but in commemoration of all the tragic occasions of Jewish history. In many synagogues, congregants sit on the floor or on low benches and read the *qinot* by dim candlelight as signs of mourning. In some synagogues, the curtain over the ark is removed; and among some Sephardi congregations, a black curtain is placed over the ark. A unique feature of the commemoration is that prayer shawls and phylacteries are donned not in the morning but at the afternoon service (except among Yemenite Jews), which also includes a moving prayer for the occasion. If 9 Av falls on a Sabbath, the observance of the fast day is postponed until the next day. The Midrash (*Lam. Rab.* 1) states that "The Messiah, the Savior, was born on the day that the Temple was destroyed," and Jews have traditionally believed that the Messiah would be born on 9 Av; consequently in certain eastern communities, the women anoint themselves with oil after midday of the fast. It is a custom to visit the cemetery on Tish'ah be-'Av. In Erets Yisra'el, pilgrimages are made to the *Western Wall, and places of entertainment are closed. Reform Jews do not observe 9 Av as a fast day but in recent years have developed alternative ways to mark the day. *Shabbetai Tsevi was said to have been born on Tish'ah be-'Av, and his followers observed it as a feast day to mark the beginning of the messianic age.

• Eric L. Friedland, "Tish'ah Be-Av: A Modest Proposal," *Conservative Judaism* 44 (1992): 56–61. Irving Greenberg, "Some Thoughts on the Meaning of the Restoration of Israel and Jerusalem for Days of Commemoration," in *Jerusalem: City of the Ages*, edited by A. Eckardt (Lanham, Md., 1987). Naomi Seidman, "Burning the Book of Lamentations," *Tikkun* 8 (July–August 1993): 59–62, 91–92.

TISHREI (תִּשְׁרֵי), seventh month in the religious calendar and the first month in the civil and chronological calendar. Tishrei always has thirty days. The name does not occur in the Bible, in which the seventh month is referred to as Ethanim (*1 Kgs.* 8.2). The word *Tishrei* derives from the Akkadian (Tashritu) or from the Aramaic *sherei*, meaning "to begin." Its zodiac sign is Libra, which was related homiletically to the penitential season at the beginning of the month. This period covers the first ten days of the month, known as the Ten Days of Repentance (see 'ASERET YEMEI TESHUVAH), which begins with *Ro'sh ha-Shanah and concludes with *Yom Kippur. According to the **aggadah*, during the month of Tishrei the world was created, the *patriarchs were born, and *Moses descended for the second time from Mount Sinai. Notable days during the month are 1–2 Tishrei, Ro'sh ha-Shanah; 3, *Tsom Gedalyah; 10, Yom Kippur; 15, first day of *Sukkot; 16, second day of Sukkot, observed as a holiday in the Diaspora; 16–21, **ḥol ha-mo'ed* Sukkot in Israel (17–21 in the Diaspora); 21, *Hosha'na' Rabbah; 22, *Shemini 'Atseret (together with *Simḥat Torah in Israel); 23, Simḥat Torah in the Diaspora.

• Nathan Bushwick, *Understanding the Jewish Calendar* (New York, 1989). Eliyyahu Ki Tov, *Sefer ha-Toda'ah* (Jerusalem, 1976), pp. 7–148. George Zinberg, *Jewish Calendar Mystery Dispelled* (New York, 1963).

—CHAIM PEARL

TITHES, the tenth part of one's annual income, set aside for a specific purpose. During the biblical period, detailed laws were promulgated concerning the tithing of agricultural produce and livestock. The earliest biblical reference to the practice concerns Abraham's tithe to Melchizedek (*Gn.* 14.18–20). All produce, fruits, and vegetables, are liable to be tithed. Untithed produce is called **tevel*, and may not be eaten except incidentally while it is still in the field. In addition to the heave offering (see TERUMAH), the first tithe (*ma'aser ri'shon*), second tithe (*ma'aser sheni*), and poor tithe (*ma'aser 'ani*) must be separated. For the purposes of tithing, the calendar is divided into seven-year cycles. The first tithe is to be separated in each of the first six years; the second tithe in the first, second, fourth, and fifth years; the poor tithe in the third and sixth years. Produce of the seventh year (**shemittah*), produce of the **heqdesh*, ownerless property (**hefqer*), gleanings (see LEQET, SHIKHḤAH, AND PE'AH), and corners of fields left for the poor are not liable to be tithed. The first tithe (*Nm.* 18.24) is given to the *Levites, who could own no land themselves, and who, in turn, must give one-tenth of what they receive (that is, one-hundredth of the total produce, called *terumat ma'aser* [the heave offering of the tithe]), to the priest (*Nm.* 18.26). The Levites may then use the remainder as they wish. The second tithe (*Lv.* 27.30–31; *Dt.* 14.22–26) must be taken to Jerusalem and consumed there (according to the rabbis, animal tithes were also brought to the Temple). The second tithe may, however, be exchanged for money, and this amount, together with an additional fifth, must be taken to Jerusalem and spent there. The poor tithe (*Dt.* 14.28–29, 26.12), or its cash equivalent, is distributed to the needy anywhere. Produce untithed at its source is liable to tithing by whoever possesses it. One may not substitute tithes from one type of produce for another, nor from bad produce for good produce, nor produce grown in one location for produce from another. Twice during the seven-year cycle, in the fourth and seventh years, before Pesaḥ, all tithing obligations must be brought up to date, the tithes removed (*bi'ur*; cf. *Dt.* 26.12 ff.; *Ma'as. Sh.* 5), and a relevant confession recited. Tithing was obligatory only in Erets Yisra'el, but the custom arose among some Jews of allocating a tenth of their income to charity. A symbolic tithing ceremony has been developed in modern Israel. Rabbinical discussion of the subject can be found in the Talmudic tractates **Terumot*, **Ma'asrot*, and **Ma'aser Sheni*.

• Joseph M. Baumgarten, "The First and Second Tithes in the Temple Scroll," in *Biblical and Related Studies*, edited by A. Kort and S. Morschanser (Winona Lake, Ind., 1985), pp. 5–15. Martin S. Jaffee, "The Mishnah in Talmudic Exegesis: Observations on Tractate Maaserot of the Talmud Yerushalmi," in *Approaches to Ancient Judaism*, vol. 4, edited by W. Green (Chico, Calif., 1983), pp. 137–157. H. Jagersma, "The Tithes in the Old Testament," in *Remembering All the Way*, edited by B. Albrektson (Leiden, 1981). Richard S. Sarason, *A History of the Mishnaic Law of Agriculture*, sect. 3, *A Study of Tractate Demai*, Studies in Judaism of Late Antiquity 27 (Leiden, 1979).

TOBIT, an apocryphal work of unknown authorship that dates from approximately the third century BCE. Probably written in Aramaic, it is extant in its entirety only in Greek translation and later translations based upon the Greek, but Aramaic and Hebrew fragments of the work were discovered among the *Dead Sea Scrolls. The *Book of Tobit* consists of a first-person account of the righteous Tobit, of the tribe of Naphtali, who was exiled to Assyria in the days of Shalmaneser. Tobit describes how, upon suddenly becoming blind, he sent his son, Tobias, to Media to collect an old debt. Tobias, accompanied by the angel Raphael, goes to Ecbatana and meets Sarah, whose seven husbands had all been killed by the evil spirit *Asmodeus on their wedding night. Tobias marries Sarah and drives Asmodeus away with a secret recipe given to him by Raphael. Upon returning to Nineveh, Tobias uses a similar recipe to restore Tobit's eyesight. The *Book of Tobit* ends with Tobit's final words to Tobias, in which he foretells the restoration of Jerusalem, the ingathering of the exiles, and the coming of the gentiles. English translations can be found in standard versions of the Apocrypha.

• J. C. Dancy, *The Shorter Books of the Apocrypha* (Cambridge, 1972), pp. 1–66. Paul Deselaers, *Das Buch Tobit: Studien zu seiner Entstehung, Komposition und Theologie*, Orbis Biblicus et Orientalis 43 (Göttingen, 1982). Emil Schürer, Geza Vermes, and F. Millar, *The History of the Jewish People in the Age of Jesus Christ* (Edinburgh, 1986), vol. 3, pt. 1, pp. 222–232. Frank Zimmermann, *The Book of Tobit: An English Translation with Introduction and Commentary* (New York, 1958).

–GIDEON BOHAK

TODAH. See THANKSGIVING OFFERING.

TOHORAH (טָהֳרָה; purification), the preparation of a corpse prior to *burial. The rite, which is performed by the **ḥevrah qaddisha'* (burial society), involves the careful washing of the entire body, including the orifices and between the fingers and toes, with warm water, while certain biblical verses and prayers are recited. The body is then dried and wrapped in a plain linen shroud. Women members of the *ḥevrah qaddisha'* attend to women, and men attend to men. The practice is of postbiblical origin. It is not performed in Reform Judaism.

• Isaac Klein, *A Guide to Jewish Religious Practice* (New York, 1979). Maurice Lamm, *The Jewish Way in Death and Mourning* (New York, 1969).

–PETER KNOBEL

TOHOROT (טָהֳרוֹת; Purities), sixth and last order of the Mishnah, dealing with the laws governing ritual impurity and rites of purification. It has twelve tractates: **Kelim*, **Ohalot*, **Nega'im*, **Parah*, **Tohorot*, **Miqva'ot*, **Niddah*, **Makhshirin*, **Zavim*, **Tevul Yom*, **Yadayim*, and **'Uqtsin*. All appear as well in the Tosefta', but only one, *Niddah*, has *gemara'*, in both Talmuds. Tohorot is the largest of the six orders of the Mishnah, indicating its continuing centrality in the religious consciousness of rabbinic Judaism even after the destruction of the Temple.

–AVRAHAM WALFISH

TOKHAḤAH (תּוֹכָחָה; Rebuke), the name given to two sections of the Pentateuch (*Lv*. 26 and *Dt*. 28) that prophesy a series of drastic punishments to be visited upon the Israelites should they forsake the Torah. When these sections are read as part of the weekly portion in the synagogue, it is customary in many places for the reader himself to be called to this portion of the Torah and to read it in an undertone and without a break.

• Boaz Cohen, *Law and Tradition in Judaism* (New York, 1959).

TOLEDOT YESHU, a work about the life of *Jesus that circulated among Jews during the Middle Ages. It dates from the tenth century or later but was compiled from earlier sources. Various versions circulated, and Samuel *Krauss published nine of these. The work gives ignoble interpretations of many details of Jesus' life. In some versions, he was said to have been the illegitimate son of Mary fathered by a Roman soldier named Panthera (as first stated by Celsus in the second century); in others, Mary was said to have been raped by a neighbor. Jesus' powers were purportedly derived from black magic or from stealing a holy name from the Temple. The dates given do not correspond to the historical Jesus, and the work is an expression of vulgar polemics written in reaction to the no less vulgar attacks on Judaism in popular Christian teaching and writing.

• Joseph Jacobs, *Jesus as Others Saw Him* (New York, 1925). Samuel Krauss, *Das Leben Jesu nach jüdischen Quellen* (Berlin, 1902).

TOMB OF RACHEL. See RACHEL.

TOMBS. In the Bible, the Hebrew word *qavar* (bury) is used both for burial in the earth and for interment in tombs, *burial being the only permitted method for the reverential disposal of the dead. In Talmudic times, however, the word *qavar* was confined to a grave in the soil, while the word *kukh* was used for the rock-hewn tombs that were a prominent feature of the hill country of Judah and Galilee. The traditional tombs of the members of the Sanhedrin in Jerusalem and the discovery in recent years of the extensive burial place at Beit She'arim in Galilee are outstanding examples of these tombs. The Bible makes occasional mention of a *matsevah*, that is, some kind of monument or pillar placed over a tomb (for example, that placed by Jacob over the tomb of Rachel, *Gn*. 35.20; the one Absalom prepared for himself, *2 Sm*. 18.18), but the custom of erecting tombstones over graves is of comparatively recent origin among Jews (as late as the sixteenth century Yosef Karo declared that it was not obligatory; *Shulḥan ʿArukh, Yoreh Deʿah* 364). It is extremely common in North America, where the tombstone is unveiled (a cloth covering is removed as part of the ceremony) usually a month or a year after the death. Among Sephardim and among Ashkenazim in Israel the tombstones are laid flat; elsewhere it is the Ashkenazi custom to place tombstones in an upright position. Few inscriptions on Jewish tombs have been found from before the first century BCE, but from that period on, they are a regular feature of Jewish tombs. The epitaphs, though mostly in Hebrew, appear in the classical period in other languages as well, especially in Greek, and the tombs are frequently decorated with typical Jewish symbols (*menorah, etrog, lulav*, etc.). In the Middle Ages, inscriptions were entirely in Hebrew, but in recent centuries the vernacular has again appeared on tombstones, with or without Hebrew. On the tombstones of priests, it is customary to portray two hands in the traditional gesture of the *Birkat ha-Kohanim, and on the tombstones of Levites, it is customary to carve a ewer above the inscription, symbolic of the Levitical function in the ancient Temple. In some communities it became customary for visitors to place a stone on the grave.

• Isaac Klein, *A Guide to Jewish Religious Practice* (New York, 1979). Maurice Lamm, *The Jewish Way in Death and Mourning* (New York, 1969).

–PETER KNOBEL

TOPHETH, designation of cultic installations built in Gei Ben Hinnom, west of Jerusalem, in the time of Jeremiah, just prior to the destruction of Jerusalem by the Babylonians (*2 Kgs*. 23.10; *Jer*. 7.31–32). These shrines were dedicated to the worship of the Canaanite deity *Molech, which consisted of child sacrifice—a practice abhorrent to Israelite law (*Lv*. 18.21; *Dt*. 12.30–31, 18.10) and condemned by Israel's prophets (*Jer*. 19.5–6, 32.35; *Ez*. 16.21, 23.37). The word *topheth* refers to the stand over the fire or the whole hearth on which the victim was burned; in later usage it became synonymous with unspeakable horror and eventually, along with Gei Ben Hinnom (see GEIHINNOM), with hell.

• Mordechai Cogan and Hayim Tadmor, *2 Kings*, The Anchor Bible (Garden City, N.Y., 1988), pp. 287–288. George C. Heider, *The Cult of Molek: A Reassessment*, Journal for the Study for the Old Testament, Supplement Series 43 (Sheffield, Eng., 1985), pp. 336–365. William McKane, *Jeremiah*, International Critical Commentary (Edinburgh, 1886), pp. 178–180. Baruch J. Schwartz, "Selected Chapters in the Holiness Code," Ph.D. dissertation, Hebrew University, 1987, pp. 81–82.

–BARUCH J. SCHWARTZ

TORAH (תּוֹרָה), a term applied both to the entire corpus of sacred literature and to the first section of the Hebrew Bible.

Corpus of Sacred Literature. The word *torah* (instruction, teaching, or guidance) is probably derived from *yarah* (throw [lots for divine guidance by oracle]). In biblical usage, the word has no particular prominence and appears together with similar terms and in the plural form *torot* (commandments, laws, ordinances). The first more specific use of the term, in the singular, seems to be in *Malachi* 3.22, "Remember the Torah of Moses my servant." Only in the Second Temple period, under the influence of Hellenistic usage that considered every religion as a *nomos* (law) and the founder of a religion as a *nomothetēs* (lawgiver), did *torah* (translated in the *Septuagint as *nomos*) come to mean "law" in the more specific sense. This Hellenistic usage is also common in the Greek New Testament (and especially in the Pauline Epistles) and has contributed decisively to the negative Christian stereotype of Judaism, according to which Christianity is a religion (defined as a religion of love) whereas the Jews only have a "law." In rabbinic literature, *torah* is used in a variety of senses, all based on the general understanding of *torah* as the guidance and teaching imparted to Israel by divine *revelation. Thus, Torah designates the Pentateuch as distinct from the other two main sections of the Hebrew Bible—the Prophets and the Hagiographa (see BIBLE)—but in a wider sense also applies to scripture as a whole and to biblical legislation in contradistinction to rabbinical enactments. Scripture, however, is only the *torah she-bi-khetav*, the *written law, which is supplemented by the equally divine *torah she-be-ʿal peh*, the *oral law. Both of these together constitute "the Torah" in its most comprehensive sense. In the Bible, the term is often applied to specific laws and regulations, for example, the law (*torah*) of various offerings (*Lv*. 6–7) or "the law [*torah*] of the leper" (*Lv*. 14.2), where rabbinic writing would have used *din* or **halakhah*. The concept of *torah* is wider than that of *halakhah*, which is only part of Torah. The study of Torah was considered by the rabbis a major religious duty (see EDUCATION; STUDY; TALMUD TORAH) and its fulfillment the highest goal of piety and virtue. Unlike *wisdom, which is shared by all nations, Torah is the exclusive possession of the Jewish people: "If one shall say to you that there is wisdom in Edom, believe it; if he says there is Torah in Edom, believe it not" (*Lam. Rab*. 2). The divine injunction to Joshua (*Jos*. 1.8) "this book of the Torah shall not depart from your mouth, but you shall meditate on it day and night" was interpreted as an exhortation to devote the whole of one's time to the study of the Torah. The daily prayers include a blessing to God for the commandment to occupy oneself with the study of the Torah, while the blessing immediately preceding the reading of the *Shemaʿ, both in the morning and the evening (known as *Ahavah Rabbah and Ahavat ʿOlam), is one of praise to God for giving the Torah and of prayer for divine grace in its acquisition. The rabbinic passage enumerating those things the fruit of which man enjoys in this world, while the main reward is reserved for the world to come, concludes "but the study of the Torah is equivalent to them all" (*Peʾah* 1.1). The idea that the Torah is the source of life of the Jewish people is expressed in many rabbinic parables and homilies, but particularly in the liturgical blessings (see BIRKAT HA-TORAH) recited by the person called to the synagogal reading and in the daily morning prayer: "Blessed is our God, who has created us for his glory and has separated us from them that go astray, and has given us the Torah and thus planted everlasting life in our midst. May he open our heart unto his Torah."

• Shalom Carmy, ed., *Modern Scholarship in the Study of Torah: Contributions and Limitations* (Northvale, N.J., 1995). F. C. Holmgren, "The Way of Torah: Escape from Egypt," in *Preaching Biblical Texts: Expositions by Jewish and Christian Scholars*, edited by F. Holmgren and H. Schaalman (Grand Rapids, 1995). Nehama Leibowitz, *Torah Insights* (Jerusalem, 1995). Isaac Sender, *The Commentators' Gift of Torah: Exploring the Treasures of the Oral and Written Torah* (Chicago, 1993). Jacob Neusner, *Revelation: The Torah and the Bible* (Valley Forge, Pa., 1995).

First Section of the Hebrew Bible. The Torah is subdivided into five sections (see ḤUMMASH), also referred to as "books": *Genesis, *Exodus, *Leviticus, *Numbers, and *Deuteronomy. Christians thus refer to the Torah as the "five books of Moses." This, as well as the common term *Pentateuch* (Gr. *pentateuchos* [five-volumed work]), are really misnomers. Jewish tradition, as well as modern scholarship, sees the entire Torah as a single book, a continuous literary work that was divided into five parts after it was completed, since in ancient times there were not scrolls large enough to contain such a long work. Nowhere in the Bible is the biblical book known in Judaism as the Torah called by this name; this is a post-biblical tradition.

Literarily, the Torah is a unique combination of narrative and law. It is a continuous story, but more than half consists of laws and commandments, which are encased in the story's framework. The story divides into two unequal parts. The first, the introductory "universal history" traces the history of mankind from Creation, until, by gradually narrowing its focus, it centers on one family: that of Terah, father of Abram (*Gn.* 1–11). The second portion, the main body of the narrative (*Gn.* 12–*Dt.* 34), recounts the saga of the family of Abraham, which, through the line of Isaac and Jacob, becomes the Israelite people. The account begins with the patriarchs' wanderings in Canaan, during which time God promises them that this land will eventually become their national territory and that their numerous progeny will fill it and even expand beyond its borders. At the end of the patriarchal period, however, this two-part promise (see COVENANT) seems quite unrealizable: Jacob's descendants are few, and they leave Canaan to settle in Egypt, where they are ultimately enslaved and threatened with extermination. The remainder of the narrative recounts how their fortunes are reversed and how the divine promise is fulfilled. Despite bondage, the Israelites increase vastly in number, after which, under the divinely appointed leadership of Moses, they are delivered by God from slavery and led through the wilderness to the frontier of the Promised Land, which they have but to enter and conquer.

The bulk of the Torah—from *Exodus* 19 through *Numbers* 10—is taken up by the Sinai section. At Sinai, Israel receives God's laws, and the covenant with God becomes conditional on their faithful fulfillment. All the institutions of Israelite society and religion are established. Yet the narrative itself is scant, relating only how the Israelites arrived at Sinai and experienced the revelation of God there; most of the text records the actual laws and statutes. The wilderness section (*Nm.* 11–*Dt.* 34) also contains the laws and teachings given in the wilderness and in the Plains of Moab. Thus, most of the work is comprised of the law codes themselves; the purpose of the narrative is to explain how Israel received them and pledged to follow them, why they are obligated to do so, and what rewards and punishments are in store for them if they comply with the laws or fail to do so.

The story is told by an anonymous, omniscient, third-person narrator, who stands at some distance from the events (*Gn.* 12.10) and is located on the western side of the Jordan, that is, in Canaan (*Dt.* 1.5). Moses is introduced only when the story line arrives at his birth (*Ex.* 2), and his death is recounted by the narrator (*Dt.* 34.1–12). Moreover, the audience addressed is composed of Israelites already living in their land, after the establishment of the monarchy (*Gn.* 36.31) and before the exile to Babylon. Many biblical scholars thus date the Torah to the middle First Temple period. Despite the overall unity, the text is often discontinuous, contradictory, stylistically and theologically diverse, and illogically repetitious. In particular, the several law codes occasionally duplicate and contradict each other and show no awareness of each other's existence. Thus, scholarship detects a multiplicity of traditions, several periods of creativity, various separate authors, and distinct developmental stages in the composition of the work. Some scholars have suggested that the book of *Joshua was originally part of the same unit that they call the Hexateuch.

Tradition, on the other hand, ascribes to Moses the writing of the Torah as a whole, presuming it to have been verbally dictated to him by God, including the accounts of his own birth and death and what preceded and followed them. Maimonides wrote in his *Thirteen Principles of Faith, "the entire Torah in our hands was given to our master, Moses." There are differing views on whether this was done all at once or in stages. Several mediating positions between the scholarly and the traditional views have been proposed by commentators and theologians.

The belief in divine authorship gave rise to the method of *midrash*, by which all of the text's unusual and stylistic features were taken as expressive of additional meaning, since divine language, unlike that of humans, is omnisignificant. In order for the laws to be implemented to the fullest, in an internally consistent fashion, considerable supplementation and harmonization was indispensable. The authoritative body of such creative exegesis, as found throughout Talmudic literature, eventually came to be given divine status as well.

The text is read in the synagogue by a trained reader from a parchment scroll (see SEFER TORAH), written with meticulous care by an authorized, pious scribe (see SOFER SETAM). This constitutes a central part of the synagogue service (see ACCENTS; QERI'AT HA-TORAH). Its purpose is twofold: to instill a thorough knowledge of the Torah in every Jew, reinforced throughout his entire life, and to reenact symbolically the giving of the law at Mount Sinai, reaffirming the Jewish people's commitment to follow the Torah. Sermons in the synagogue on the Sabbath are generally based on the weekly reading from the Torah, a practice that was instituted in rabbinic times.

• Joseph Blenkinsopp, *The Pentateuch: An Introduction to the First Five Books of the Bible*, The Anchor Bible Reference Library (New York, 1992). Richard E. Friedman, *Who Wrote the Bible?* (New York, 1987). Thomas W. Mann, *The Book of the Torah: The Narrative Integrity of the Pentateuch* (Atlanta, 1988). M. H. Segal, *The Pentateuch: Its Composition and Its Authorship and Other Biblical Studies* (Jerusalem, 1967). Roger Norman Whybray, *The Making of the Pentateuch: A Methodological Study*, Journal for the Study of the Old Testament, Supplement Series 53 (Sheffield, Eng., 1987).

–BARUCH J. SCHWARTZ

TORAH, READING OF THE. See QERI'AT HA-TORAH.

TORAH ORNAMENTS. The *Sefer Torah is known to have been ornamented and protected with appurtenances from early sources. The Mishnah discusses "figured" wrappers that covered Torah scrolls (*Kel.* 28.4). Today, most Sephardi and ʿAdot ha-Mizraḥ communities both house and read the scroll upright within a *tiq*, a rigid, hinged, cylindrical case. A *tiq* is mentioned in a document, dated from 1075, found in the Cairo Genizah and is first depicted in early fourteenth-century Spanish Haggadot. A *tiq* is generally crafted of wood or metal and is cylindrical or polygonal, often twelve sided to symbolize the twelve tribes. Many examples feature ornamentation typical of Islamic metalwork; lavish carved and gilded wood examples from Italy or Tunisia are also known. Finials ornament the top or sides of the *tiq*, and scarves are often draped on the *tiq* and used to cover the open scroll before it is read. The reader often uses a pointer (*yad*) to follow the text and to avoid directly touching the Torah scroll. Scrolls in both Ashkenazi and Sephardi congregations are generally attached to carved or inlaid Torah staves (*ʿatsei ḥayyim* [trees of life]), and lengths of fabric are used as binders (*wimpels*) to hold the two sides of the scroll together. Binders were generally crafted of beautiful fabrics. In Italy they were often made and dedicated by women. The Roman liturgy includes a prayer for "every daughter of Israel who makes a mantle or cover in honor of the Torah." It was customary among many German Jews to create Torah binders from the swaddling clothes that wrapped an infant at his circumcision. The *wimpel* has been understood as a physical link between the covenantal relationship established through circumcision and the Torah. The swaddling clothes were cut into strips, sewn together, and embroidered or painted with an inscription specifying the child's name, birth date, and a blessing for his future cited from the circumcision liturgy. The *wimpel* was often presented when the boy was first brought to the synagogue. In many communities a length of fabric, known as a **mappah* in Italy, is rolled with the Torah to cover the outside of the area opened for reading. A textile cover may also be placed over an open scroll. A closed scroll is covered with a fabric mantle (*meʿil*), generally of velvet or fine silks. Extant full-skirted mantles from the seventeenth century on, featuring soft or rigid circular or oval tops with two holes for insertion of the staves, are known from Sephardi communities in western Europe, the Ottoman empire, and America. This form is portrayed in the Sarajevo Haggadah (Spain, 13th cent.). Early Ashkenazi mantles were flat, joined segments of fabric, resembling pillow cases, with spaces at the top for staves. A 1592 example of this type is found in Prague, and similar mantles appear in the Ulm *maḥazor* (Germany, 14th cent.). Most Ashkenazi mantles feature a rigid oval top and a tight, straight skirt, often decorated with dedicatory inscriptions and symbols (e.g., crowns, lions, the Decalogue).

Other Torah ornaments, generally crafted of metal, usually silver, are also frequently used. The Torah staves are topped with a crown (**keter*) or a pair of finials, used simultaneously in many communities. Torah crowns made out of jewelry to be used on Simḥat Torah are discussed in a *responsum* by Ha'i Ga'on (939–1038); the earliest extant crowns are sixteenth-century Italian examples. In some communities, Torah finials are known as *rimmonim* (pomegranates) or *tappuḥim* (apples), suggesting their fruit shapes; in the Spanish and Portuguese communities of England and America they are also known as bells because of the bells attached to most examples. Other finials resemble towers, corresponding to the vertical form of the staves and often reflecting local architectural traditions. Crown-shaped finials are also known. First mentioned in twelfth-century texts, the earliest extant examples of Torah finials are a late fifteenth-century pair now in the cathedral of Palma de Mallorca. A shield (*tas*) is suspended on a chain over the staves in front of the mantle. Torah shields were originally used to label the reading to which a scroll was turned but were later used for purely decorative purposes. Pointers are usually suspended on a chain over one stave. Often made of silver, carved ivory or wood examples of pointers are also known; they generally terminate in a hand shape, often with an extended finger. See also ART; CEREMONIAL OBJECTS.

• Bernard Bernstein, "The Ornamentation of the Torah," Ed.D. thesis, New York University, 1971. Rafi Grafman, *Crowning Glory: Silver Torah Ornaments of the Jewish Museum* (New York, 1996). Joseph Gutmann, *Beauty in Holiness: Studies in Jewish Customs and Ceremonial Art* (New York, 1970). Abram Kanof, *Jewish Symbolic Art* (Jerusalem, 1990). Barbara Kirschenblatt-Gimblett and Cissy Grossman, *Fabric of Jewish Life: Textiles from the Jewish Museum Collection* (New York, 1977). Shlomo U. Nahon, *ʿItturim le-Sefer Torah* (Jerusalem, 1966).

–GABRIEL M. GOLDSTEIN

TORTOSA, DISPUTATION OF, one of the Jewish–Christian *disputations, held in Tortosa, Spain, between 1413 and 1414. From the mid-thirteenth century on, the Roman Catholic church was deeply committed to missionizing among the Jews of western Christendom. It was predominantly on the Iberian Peninsula that this commitment was most fully manifested. With the cooperation of the secular authorities, Jews were regularly forced to present themselves for proselytizing sermons. A variant of the proselytizing sermon was the forced disputation, in which a Christian spokesman would make his case publicly against a major Jewish protagonist or set of protagonists.

The Disputation of Tortosa was one of the most public, protracted, and damaging of these missionizing efforts. It took place under the auspices of Antipope Benedict XIII. Aragonese Jewry, still reeling from the violent attacks of 1391, was forced to send representatives to respond to the claims advanced by the former Jew Yehoshuʿa ha-Lorki, who had been baptized as Hieronymus de Sancta Fide. The twenty-two Jewish representatives included R. *Zeraḥyah ben Yitsḥaq ha-Levi Gerondi and the philosopher Yosef *Albo. The arguments presented by Hieronymus were hardly new. They derived from the thirteenth-century initiative of another former Jew, Friar Paul Christian, who had pioneered in the utilization of rabbinic sources as proof texts for the truth of Christianity (see BARCELONA, DISPUTATION OF). The Tortosa confrontation was distinguished from its predecessors by the intensity of the proselytizing, the protracted nature of the deliberations, which extended from January 1413 through April of 1414, and the significant number of Jews who were moved by the spectacle to renounce Judaism and embrace Christianity.

• Yitzhak Baer, *A History of the Jews in Christian Spain* (Philadelphia, 1961–1966), vol. 2, pp. 170–243. Antonio Pacios Lopez, *La Disputa de Tortosa*, 2 vols. (Madrid, 1957). Frank Talmage, "Trauma at Tortosa: Testimony of Abraham Rimoch," *Mediaeval Studies* 47 (1985): 379–415.

—ROBERT CHAZAN

TORTS (Heb. *neziqin*), acts that cause injury or damage to a person or property, for which compensation is required (see *Ex.* 21). Default on a contract falls into the category of torts as well. As a general rule, the Mishnah states that "a man is always considered forewarned (and therefore liable for any tort caused by him), whether the damage is done in error or wantonly, awake or asleep" (*B. Q.* 2.6). The rabbis enumerated five types of compensation that must be made: compensation for damage to property, pain, medical expenses, loss of income due to injury, and shame. In cases of error, however, one is liable only for damage done but not for pain or shame. An owner is responsible for torts caused by his property on the grounds that he is responsible for guarding his property and taking reasonable precautions to see that no damage occurs through his negligence. In cases where the owner could not reasonably have prevented the tort, he incurs payment of only half of the damage. The major types of torts caused by property (*avot neziqin*) are classified under the following headings: ox (*shor*), damage done directly by an animal; pit (*bor*), damage caused by a stationary obstacle placed in a public thoroughfare; grazing (*mavʿeh*), damage in which advantage accrues to the animal; fire (*havʿer*), inanimate property that travels to do damage. Slander, insult, and betrayal are torts in law. The subject is fully treated in Talmud order *Neziqin and in the *Ḥoshen Mishpat* section of the **Shulḥan ʿArukh*.

• Catherine Hezser, *Form, Function, and Historical Significance of the Rabbinic Story in Yerushalmi Neziqin*, Texte und Studien zum antiken Judentum 37 (Tübingen, 1993). Eliezer Segal, *Case Citation in the Babylonian Talmud: The Evidence of Tractate Neziqin*, Brown Judaic Studies 210 (Atlanta, 1990).

TOSAFISTS. See TOSAFOT.

TOSAFOT (תּוֹסָפוֹת; additions), *novellae* (see ḤIDDUSHIM) to the Talmud written between the twelfth and fourteenth centuries in France and Germany. They are printed on the outer columns of Talmud pages and complement the work of *Rashi. While Rashi provided a line-by-line commentary to the Talmudic text, the tosafists (authors of the *tosafot*) undertook a consideration of the Talmud in its entirety. The Talmudic discussion is reexamined, contradictory passages—even if they originate in different tractates—are harmonized or distinguished, and new interpretations are suggested. Thus the *tosafot* are both additions to Rashi and a continuation of the dialectics of the Talmudic process itself. Rabbi Shelomoh *Luria said "they treated the Talmud as a ball . . . rolling it from place to place . . . though the different pericopes seem to us contradictory."

The tosafists generally are considered to have originated in twelfth-century northern France among the grandchildren of Rashi, on whose work they build. Most *tosafot* begin by citing Rashi and pointing to the difficulties in his interpretation before presenting an alternate perspective. In his work, A. Grossman has argued that the salient intellectual characteristics of the movement are found in late eleventh-century Germany, in Worms and Mainz; the tosafists' major focus is their critique and synthesis of varied Talmudic texts. The tosafists' interest also lies in the practical decision implied by these texts. The influence of Christian glossators and canonists has been detected in tosafist terminology and dialectic, as has the influence of twelfth-century cathedral schools on the organization of the nascent tosafist academies. However, no concrete evidence for these dependencies has surfaced.

Tosafist method quickly spread beyond France and Germany. Some scholars believe that the great Spanish Talmudists of the twelfth and thirteenth centuries, Moses *Nahmanides and Shelomoh ben Avraham *Adret (and their pupils), adopted the tosafist view of the Talmud and mode of argumentation, fusing these with native Spanish traditions and earlier geonic interpretation.

The *tosafot* printed in the Talmud, a staple of Talmudic study, reflect a number of different collections. Independent works of individual tosafists (such as the *Or Zaruʿa* of R. Yitsḥaq ben Mosheh of Vienna or the *Sefer Ra'abiyyah* of R. Eliʿezer ben Yo'el ha-Levi of Bonn) have also appeared in print in the last one hundred fifty years. Of the three hundred tosafists, R. *Yaʿaqov ben Me'ir Tam, *Shemu'el ben Me'ir, *Shimshon ben Avraham of Sens, Yehudah ben Yitsḥaq of Paris, and Shemu'el (Sir Morel) of Falaise are among the best known. The printed *tosafot* cover thirty-eight tractates of the Talmud.

• Irving Agus, *R. Meir of Rothenburg*, 2 vols. (New York, 1970). Zechariah Fendel, *Masters of the Mesorah: Later Rishonim: A History of Torah Transmission with World Backgrounds, from Early Tosafists through the Shulhan Aruch* (New York, 1990). A. Grossman, "Re'shitan shel ha-Tosafot," in *Rashi: ʿIyyunim be-Yetsirato*, edited by Z. Steinfeld (Ramat Gan, 1993), pp. 57–68. Ephraim Kanarfogel, *Jewish Education and Society in the High Middle Ages* (Detroit, 1992). Haim Perlmutter, *Tools for Tosafos* (Southfield, Mich., 1996). Chaim Tchernowitz, *Toledot ha-Poseqim*, vol. 3 (New York, 1946), pp. 20–76. Efraim E. Urbach, *Baʿalei ha-Tosafot*, 4th ed. (Jerusalem, 1980).

—GERALD J. BLIDSTEIN

TOSEFTA' (Aram.; תּוֹסֶפְתָּא; Addition), compilation of oral law designed to serve as a supplementary volume to the *Mishnah. It generally follows the same arrangement as the Mishnah and is divided, like the Mishnah, into six orders, containing tractates, which are subdivided into chapters and *halakhot*. Most halakhic Mishnah tractates have corresponding Tosefta' tractates, with the exception of three tractates from the order Qodashim (*Tamid, Middot*, and *Qinnim*). The aggadic Mishnah tractate *Avot* has no corresponding Tosefta' tractate, but *Avot de-Rabbi Natan*, one of the *minor tractates, serves as a kind of supplement to tractate *Avot*.

While the bulk of the Tosefta' consists of tannaitic material, there is some question regarding the date of its redaction and the relationship between the material in the Tosefta' and Mishnaic material. On occasion the Tosefta' refers to R. Yehudah ha-Nasi', redactor of the Mishnah, as well as to other scholars of his generation and the following generation, and there are passages of the Tosefta' that can only be understood as glosses on the Mishnah. The Talmud refers to *toseftot* (*Yoma'* 70a; *Meg.* 28b; *Qid.* 49b) or *tosafot* (Y., *Pe'ah* 2.6, 17a; Y., *Hor.* 3.9, 48c), some of which are attributed to scholars who preceded the redaction of the Mishnah (see *San.* 86a). Clearly, "our" Tosefta' cannot antedate the redaction of the Mishnah. However, the question of whether it is related to the Tosefta' known to the amora'im remains the subject of considerable scholarly dispute.

Traditional sources, such as *Iggeret Rav Sherira' Ga'on*, have identified the redactor of the Tosefta' as R. Ḥiyya', a leading disciple of R. Yehudah ha-Nasi'. Some scholars, such as Ḥanokh Albeck, have argued for a late dating of the Tosefta', citing Talmudic passages that make no mention of relevant material in the Tosefta' as evidence that the Tosefta' was not compiled until after the redaction of the Talmud Bavli. Other scholars hold that the redaction of the Tosefta' took place within a generation or two after the redaction of the Mishnah, although some of them believe that subsequent to the original redaction of the Tosefta' additional material was added.

Normally the language and formulations of the Tosefta' correspond more closely to *baraiytot* (tannaitic material not incorporated into the Mishnah) cited in the Talmud Yerushalmi than to those cited in the Talmud Bavli, indicating a Palestinian provenance for the redaction of the Tosefta'. However, Saul Lieberman has argued that the Tosefta' has incorporated collections of Babylonian *baraiytot* as well.

In many places the Tosefta' serves as a commentary on the Mishnah, explaining or expanding upon laconic Mishnaic formulations. In other places the Tosefta' supplements the Mishnah by noting variant opinions or citing variant formulations, as well as by including expanded treatment of subjects briefly touched upon in the Mishnah. Abraham Goldberg has noted that the Mishnah itself already contains Tosefta'-like material, in which earlier strata of Mishnaic redaction are explained, expanded, or supplemented by later strata. In his view, the redaction of the Tosefta' follows the same patterns as the redaction of the later strata of the Mishnah, with the difference that, following the closure of the Mishnaic corpus, commentarial and supplemental material could no longer be included in the Mishnah and needed to be incorporated in a separate text.

However, in many places the Tosefta' seems to operate independently of the Mishnah, treating topics not discussed in the Mishnah or treating them in a different order from that of the Mishnah. This has led some scholars, such as J. N. Epstein, to argue that the Tosefta' often reflects an earlier recension of the Mishnah. Some scholars argue further that there are instances in which the Mishnah seems to be a gloss or variation on Tosefta' material. It seems clear that the Tosefta''s redaction is uneven in character. In some places it follows the Mishnah closely, and in others it does not. In some places it displays a tight structure, and in others it does not.

Keen scholarly interest in the Tosefta' in recent years may be attributed to the uneven character of the redaction of the Tosefta', as well as to the insight that deeper understanding of the nature of the Tosefta' may afford regarding the nature and history of the Mishnah's growth and redaction.

Two complete manuscripts of the Tosefta' exist, MS Vienna and MS Erfurt. The complete critical edition of the Tosefta', edited by M. S. Zuckermandel, follows MS Erfurt. The leading Tosefta' scholar, Saul Lieberman, followed MS Vienna in his critical edition of Tosefta' orders Zeraʿim, Moʿed, and Nashim, and of tractate *Neziqin* (*Bavot*). The most important Tosefta' commentaries include R. David Pardo's *Ḥasdei David* and Saul Lieberman's *Tosefet Ri'shonim* and *Tosefta' ki-Feshutah*. Jacob Neusner has produced an English translation of the Tosefta'.

• Chanoch Albeck, *Mavo' la-Talmudim* (Tel Aviv, 1987). Jack Yaakov Elman, *Authority and Tradition: Toseftan Baraitot in Talmudic Babylonia* (New York, 1994). Jacob Nahum Epstein, *Mevo'ot le-Sifrut ha-Tanna'im* (Jerusalem, 1957). Abraham Goldberg, "The Tosefta: Companion to the Mishna," in *The Literature of the Sages*, edited by Shemuel Safrai (Assen and Philadelphia, 1987), pt. 1, pp. 283–302. Hermann Leberecht Strack and Günter Stemberger, *Introduction to the Talmud and Midrash*, rev. and updated ed., translated by Markus Bockmuehl (Minneapolis, 1992).

—AVRAHAM WALFISH

TOVAT HANA'AH (טוֹבַת הֲנָאָה; a benefit), term referring to the freedom of choice for a person who has set aside the appropriate tithes, charity funds, and other gifts, which are required by law to be given to the priests, the Levites, and the indigent, to decide which specific recipient shall receive these gifts. Thus, for example, if a priest or Levite requests that he be given such gifts, the donor may refuse to comply, and choose to grant the gifts to some other qualifying recipient as he sees fit. The Talmud and the post-Talmudic literature record several significant disagreements regarding the scope of *tovat hana'ah*, in light of the biblical passage, "and each man's consecrated property shall be for him" (*Nm.* 5.10), since "for him" does not convey a clear notion of the extent to which the donor may benefit, even indirectly, from his reserved right to choose the recipient of his gifts. Thus, there are different opinions as to whether the donor may validly receive any monetary remuneration in exchange for his selection of a particular recipient, and, similarly, whether or not this reserved freedom of choice may be deemed a pecuniary right of substance (*tovat hana'ah mammon*), which can be conveyed to others by transfer or inheritance. The consensus was that this right is not pecuniary, and the donor therefore cannot receive remuneration or transfer this right to another.

• Nahum Rakover, *Modern Applications of Jewish Law: Resolution of Contemporary Problems According to Jewish Sources in Israeli Courts* (Jerusalem, 1992), p. 728. Shlomo Yosef Zevin, ed., *Entsiqlopedyah Talmudit* (Jerusalem, 1981), vol. 19, pp. 99–148. —BEN TZION GREENBERGER

TOVIYYAH BEN ELIʿEZER (11th cent.), biblical exegete who lived in Castoria, Bulgaria. Toviyyah was the author of a commentary on the Pentateuch and the Five Scrolls called *Leqaḥ Tov*, which was published in an edition by Solomon Buber, entitled *Midrash Leqaḥ Tov* (Lyck, 1884). *Leqaḥ Tov* adapts the Midrashic form, utilizing halakhic *midrashim* and other Midrashic works that have not been preserved, as well as material from the Talmud Bavli. It does not simply repeat the earlier material, but translates the Aramaic passages, as well as Greek and Latin words, into Hebrew. In addition, Toviyyah provides his own interpretations, focusing on the plain meaning of the verses, giving attention to the Masoretic notes and to grammar. He explains anthropomorphic passages as parables, citing the rabbinic dictum, "The Torah speaks in human language." *Leqaḥ Tov* contains allusions to contemporary historical events, such as the martyrdom of Jewish communities during the First Crusade (1096).

• Leopold Zunz, *Ha-Derashot be-Yisra'el: Hishtalshelutan ha-Historit* (Jerusalem, 1964), pp. 145ff., 441–443. —MICHAEL A. SIGNER

TOVIYYAH BEN MOSHEH (11th cent.), *Karaite scholar known as ha-'Avel (the Mourner) or as ha-Maʿatiq (the Translator). He traveled from Constantinople to Jerusalem in the 1030s to join the *Avelei Tsiyyon and studied there with Yosef Basir and Yeshuʿa ben Yehudah. Toviyyah played a central role in the transmission of the teachings of the Jerusalem Karaite school, written in Arabic, to the Byzantine empire through his translations into Hebrew and his own compilations of material from the Jerusalem scholars. By 1048, he had returned to Byzantium to become the leader of the Karaite community there. In this capacity, he traveled to Egypt (some of his letters were preserved in the Cairo Genizah) and maintained a correspondence with the scholars of Jerusalem.

His translations from Arabic into Hebrew include the works of Yosef Basir: *Kitab al-Muḥtawi* (translated as *Sefer Neʿimot*); *Kitab al-Tamyiz* (translated as *Makhkimat Peti*); and *Sefer ha-Moʿadim*, a section from *Kitab al-Istibsar*. Among Toviyyah's compilations are the philosophical work *Meshivat Nefesh* and *Otsar Neḥmad*, a legal commentary on the Bible (only the part on *Lv*. 1–10 has survived). These works provided a literary basis for the Byzantine Karaite community. He also introduced into Byzantine Karaism the concept of *haʿtaqah* (tradition) which paved the way for the establishment of new customs and reforms of Karaite law.

• Zvi Ankori in *Essays on Jewish Life and Thought*, edited by Joseph L. Blau (New York, 1959), pp. 1–38. Zvi Ankori, *Karaites in Byzantium: The Formative Years, 970–1100* (New York, 1959). Jacob Mann, *Texts and Studies in Jewish History and Literature*, vol. 2 (Cincinnati, 1935). —DAVID E. SKLARE

TOWER OF BABEL, a structure erected after the *Flood by the inhabitants of Sinar (Babylonia) for the purpose of reaching heaven (*Gn*. 11.1–9). Looking down upon the builders and finding their purpose ill-conceived, God is said to have confounded their speech and scattered them over the earth. The object of the story is to show that the cradle of humanity was also the provenance of the first rebellion against God, which in turn resulted in human estrangement from one another. God's omnipotent rule was, however, beyond the challenge of humankind. While the exact etymological origin of the term *Babel* is unknown (see BABYLONIA), the Bible derives it by popular etymology from the Hebrew root *balal* (confuse). The story was probably inspired by the high temple towers (*ziggurat*) in Babylonia. The origin of the literary motif of the confusion of tongues and the subsequent division and dispersal of humankind into nations all over the earth (*Gn*. 11.1, 6–9) and its connection in the Bible with the building of a Mesopotamian *ziggurat* (*Gn*. 11.2–5) may now be understood in the light of a new fragment of the Sumerian epic "Enmerkar and the Lord of Aratta." This was first published by S. N. Kramer (*JAOS* 88 [1968]: 108–111), who pointed out that the central motif of the "confounding" of tongues as a result of rivalry was the same in both versions, but that in the Hebrew version the rivalry was between God and humans, rather than god and god (as in the Sumerian). Biblical tradition succeeded in demythologizing this popular ancient Mesopotamian cosmological motif, and at the same time provided it with new didactic and moral dimensions. Talmudic comment ascribes a variety of motives to the builders of the Tower, dwelling upon the arrogance and heartlessness of the people it brands as *dor ha-pelagah* (the generation of secession).

• Martinus A. Beek, *Atlas of Mesopotamia* (London, 1962), pp. 141–144, 151. Chaim Cohen and A. Altman, "Va-Yehi Kol ha-'Erets Safah Eḥat," in *ʿOlam ha-Tanakh: Be-Re'shit* (Tel Aviv, 1982), p. 84. J. Klein, "The Mesopotamian Background of the Tower of Babel Story," in *ʿOlam ha-Tanakh: Be-Re'shit* (Tel Aviv, 1982), pp. 83–84, in Hebrew. Frank A. Spina, "Babel," in *The Anchor Bible Dictionary*, vol. 1 (New York, 1992), pp. 561–563. Moshe Weinfeld, *Sefer Be-Re'shit* (Tel Aviv, 1975), pp. 53–54. Gordon Wenham, *Genesis 1–15*, Word Biblical Commentary (Waco, Tex., 1987), pp. 236–238. —CHAIM COHEN

TRABOT FAMILY. Family of scholars in Italy from the fourteenth to the seventeenth century. The family's origin was in France.

Perets Trabot (14th–15th cent.), also known as Tsarfati or Catalani; author of *Maqrei Dardeqei*, which was a Hebrew-French and Hebrew-Catalan dictionary.

Yehi'el Trabot (15th–16th cent.), rabbi of Pesaro and grandson of Yosef *Colon; author of *responsa*, as was his son Azri'el Trabot (died 1569), and rabbi in Florence and Ascoli.

Netan'el ben Binyamin Trabot (1576–1673), rabbi in Modena; author of *responsa*, including one on the reform of synagogue music.

• Shlomo Simonsohn, *Toledot ha-Yehudim ba-Dukkasut Mantovah* (Jerusalem, 1962).

TRACTATE. See MASSEKHET.

TRADITION, a doctrine or rule handed down from generation to generation by word of mouth. The technical terms for tradition in Hebrew are *kabbalah* (that which is received) and *masoret* (that which is passed on); traditional custom is known as **minhag*. The terms can refer to historical traditions, such as the one claiming that Amoz, father of Isaiah, and Amaziah, king of Judah, were brothers (*Sot.* 10b), or to traditions handed down by a teacher, as in the phrase "I have received a tradition from the mouth of Shemaʿyah and Avtalyon" (*Pes.* 66a). The most common use of the word *tradition*, however, refers to those ordinances of the *oral law for which no proof can be adduced from the Bible but which are regarded as of equal authority with biblical laws. These are called "*halakhot* of Moses from Mount Sinai" (see HALAKHAH LE-MOSHEH MI-SINAI). Thus, Eliʿezer ben Hyrcanus told R. Yosei to ignore a vote taken on a certain occasion since "I have a *kabbalah* from R. Yoḥanan ben Zakk'ai, who heard it from his teacher, and his teacher from his teacher, that it is a *halakhah* of Moses from Mount Sinai that in Ammon and Moab the poor man's tithe is given in the seventh year" (*Yad.* 4.3; *Ḥag.* 3b). Again, finding no biblical authority for the Jewish method of animal slaughter for food, the Talmud declares it to be a tradition (*Ḥul.* 28a). For the rabbis, tradition had the force of law. The phrase "*halakhah* of Moses from Mount Sinai" is not always to be taken literally but is used for any tradition of immemorial antiquity. The Mishnaic statement "Tradition is a fence around the Law" (*Avot* 3.17) refers to observances beyond the requirements of the letter of the Law that act as safeguards against infringing upon biblical law. According to Moses *Maimonides, all laws and enactments that have no biblical authority but are accepted in the Talmud without dissent belong to this class of traditional teaching.

• Boaz Cohen, *Law and Tradition in Judaism* (New York, 1959). Norbert H. Samuelson, "Tradition from a Jewish Perspective," *Toronto Journal of Theology* 9 (1993): 27–50.

TRANI FAMILY, family of scholars originating in Spain, who settled in Trani, Italy, from where they derived their name.

Mosheh ben Yosef di Trani (1500–1580), rabbinic authority in Erets Yisra'el; known by the acronym ha-Mabbit. He was born in Salonika and educated in Adrianople and Safed, where he settled in 1518. At the age of twenty-one, he was recognized as a leading authority on matters relating to the sanctity of the Holy Land. He was one of the four scholars ordained by Yaʿaqov *Berab in his attempt to revive *ordination. Mosheh served for fifty-four years as a member of the Safed *beit din*, headed a *yeshivah*, and sent *responsa* to many parts of the Jewish world. He paid particular attention to the agricultural laws in Erets Yisra'el and was inclined to take lenient positions, for example, regarding the laws of the sabbatical year. His bold decisions led him to a confrontation with Yosef *Karo, who issued a ban against those who followed Mosheh's rulings. Mosheh strongly criticized those authorities who ruled that it was not necessary to settle immediately in the land of Israel. After Karo's death, Mosheh became the religious leader of Safed Jewry. His writings include *Iggeret Derekh ha-Shem*, a work on ethics (Venice, 1553); *Beit Elohim*, a philosophical work (Venice, 1576); *Qiryat Sefer*, on Maimonides, distinguishing his sources between the written and the oral Law (Venice, 1551); and hundreds of *responsa* (Venice, 1629–1630).

Yosef ben Mosheh di Trani (1568–1639), known as Maharit; son of Mosheh ben Yosef. He was born in Safed and studied in Egypt and Safed, where he became head of the community and was sent to Constantinople as its emissary. He settled there and was appointed chief rabbi of Turkey, enacting many *taqqanot*. He established a *yeshivah* at which distinguished scholars received their training. Most of his works have been lost, but his *novellae* on the Talmud and his sermons on the Pentateuch were printed. Citations from his *Tsurat ha-Bayit*, a work on the structure of the Temple, have been preserved.

• Meir Benayahu, *Yosef Behiri* (Jerusalem, 1990), pp. 7–149, in Hebrew. "Ecrivains émigrés d'Espagne en Turquie," in Moise Franco, *Essai sur l'histoire des Israélites de l'Empire Ottoman* (Paris, 1981), pp. 74–80. Solomon Schechter, *Studies in Judaism*, 2d ser. (Philadelphia, 1908), pp. 235–237, 250, 283, 285. Israel Schepansky, *Erets Yisra'el be-Sifrut ha-Teshuvot*, 2 vols. (Jerusalem, 1966, 1969). —SHALOM BAR-ASHER

TRANSGRESSION. See SIN.

TRANSLATIONS OF THE BIBLE. See BIBLE TRANSLATIONS.

TRANSMIGRATION OF SOULS, the belief that after death the *soul enters into a new body; though known in Eastern religions, it is never encountered in biblical or Talmudic Judaism. It is mentioned for the first time in the tenth century by *Saʿadyah ben Yosef Ga'on, who reports that some "foolish" Jews held the belief. The theory reappears as an esoteric Jewish doctrine in the twelfth-century kabbalistic book *Sefer ha-Bahir*, which may have drawn upon earlier Jewish sources or possibly the Catharist heresy that flourished in Provence at that time. Various expressions were used in early kabbalistic literature for the concept of transmigration, but ultimately the term *gilgul* (revolving) became generally accepted. For the early kabbalists and for the author of the *Zohar, the transmigration of the soul, or reincarnation, was a punishment inflicted on individuals who had committed certain sins or failed to fulfill certain commandments, particularly the commandment of procreation. By assuming a new bodily existence, they would have another opportunity to make good where they had failed and to fulfill their destiny. As time went on, the concept of transmigration was extended, and three transmigrations were held to be the minimum for every individual soul. In sixteenth century *Kabbalah and later, the doctrine of transmigration assumed a prominent position. Yitsḥaq *Luria and his disciples in Safed associated the doctrine of transmigration with the fate of Adam's soul after its "fall." Adam's soul contains within itself the souls of all, and its fall expresses its state of alienation—and of all humankind's alienation—from God. Each soul endures its own individual "exile" brought about by its own sins. Its misdeeds on earth may even bring about the reincarnation of a soul in a lower form of life, and it must continue on its transmigration until it achieves its *tiqqun*, that is, its restoration to its proper place in the soul of Adam. The determining of one's previous existences and the search for the proper *tiqqun* became an important element of folk religion in eastern Europe, especially within the Hasidic movement. A soul that is not reborn with a new body but enters and "possesses" another human being is known as a *dybbuk.

• Gershom Gerhard Scholem, "Gilgul: Transmigration of Souls," in *On the Mystical Shape of the Godhead: Basic Concepts in the Kabbalah* (New York, 1991). Gershom Gerhard Scholem, *Origins of the Kabbalah*, translated by Allan Arkush, edited by R. J. Zwi Werblowsky (1962; Philadelphia, 1987), pp. 89–91, 188–198, 234–238, 456–460.

TRANSPLANTS. The halakhic permissibility of live, nonregenerative, organ donations turns on the amount of risk posed to the donor's life. In the absence of any such risk, there would not appear to be any halakhic bar to organ donation provided that the donor's consent is freely obtained. In cases where there is a small risk involved in transplantation, the donor may very well have a choice as to whether or not to donate his or her organ. Cadaver donations are approved if the purpose is the direct and immediate saving of the recipient's life, in accordance with the principle stated by R. Yeḥezqe'l Landau in his seminal *responsum* on autopsies in Jewish law. Modern authorities permit corneal transplants on the grounds that loss of sight constitutes a threat to human life, since a blind person may fall down a flight of stairs or into a ditch and be killed. Heart transplants present a problem in Jewish law, which defines death as the cessation of heartbeat. Since only a still-beating heart will save a recipient's life, heart transplant would be tantamount to killing the donor. In 1987 the Israeli chief rabbinate adopted the view that irreversible cessation of respiration, that is, brain-stem death, is the definitive halakhic definition of death; therefore, heart transplants are permitted in Israeli hospitals. Live donation of regenerative tissue, for example, blood and bone marrow, is permitted, and fetal transplants from spontaneously or legally aborted fetuses would also seem to be permitted under Jewish law.

• Mordechai Halperin, "Organ Transplants from Living Donors," *Israel Law Review* 27.4 (1993): 566–587. Yoel Jakobovits, "Brain Death and Heart Transplants: The Israeli Chief Rabbinate's Directives," *Tradition* 24.4 (1989): 1–14. Fred Rosner, "Organ Transplantation in Jewish Law," in *Jewish Bioethics*, edited by Fred Rosner and J. David Bleich (New York, 1979), pp. 358–374. —DANIEL SINCLAIR

TRAVEL, PRAYER FOR. See TEFILLAT HA-DEREKH.

TREASON. The Bible does not mention any instances of the betrayal of one's country, but it contains many instances of rebellion and regicide (e.g., *2 Sm*. 18.14; *2 Kgs*. 11.1). The penalty of death for disobedience to the king is based (*San*. 49a) upon the declaration made by the people to Joshua: "whosoever rebels against your word shall be put to death" (*Jos*. 1.18). Any disobedience toward the royal command is considered rebellion; the king may punish the offender in any manner considered fit, but he may not confiscate his property. Rabbinic law has transferred to the state the rights previously enjoyed by the king. In the State of Israel, wartime treason is one of the two instances in which the death penalty is applicable.

• Yosef Karo, *Shulḥan 'Arukh* (Jerusalem, 1995).

TREE OF KNOWLEDGE OF GOOD AND EVIL, one of the two trees mentioned by name, along with the tree of life, in the garden of Eden, in *Genesis* 2–3. According to the narrative, Adam was given permission to eat of the fruit of all the trees in the garden, excluding only the tree of knowledge of good and evil, the penalty for which was death (*Gn*. 2.17). The serpent, however, duped Eve into eating the fruit of the tree of knowledge, and she, in turn, gave it to Adam, who ate as well. For transgressing this divine commandment, Adam and Eve (along with the snake) were punished and expelled from the garden.

Since the tree of knowledge is unparalleled in all other biblical and extra-biblical tales and since the narrative does not define the specific nature of the knowledge obtained by the eating of its fruit, several different explanations have been suggested. One theory offers that what is meant by knowledge is moral discernment, the ability to distinguish between what is right and wrong. Others, as early as the medieval Jewish exegete Avraham *ibn Ezra, believe that knowledge refers to sexual awareness, since the first experience after eating the fruit was a consciousness of nudity and shame, followed by Adam's "knowing" Eve, that is, having sexual relations with her (*Gn*. 4.1). This line of thought is supported by another passage of "knowing good and evil" within a similar framework (*2 Sm*. 19.36). However, most scholars today interpret the verse as relating to overall knowledge (cf. *2 Sm*. 14.17), which children do not have (*Dt*. 1.39; *Is*. 7.15) and the possession of which distinguishes childhood from maturity. Thus, the eating of the fruit symbolizes a rite of passage leading to a mature apperception of the world.

• Howard N. Wallace, *The Eden Narrative*, Harvard Semitic Monographs 32 (Atlanta, 1985), pp. 115–132. Claus Westermann, *Genesis 1–11* (Minneapolis, 1984), pp. 240–245. —SHALOM PAUL

TREE OF LIFE, a tree whose fruit gives immortal life to those who partake of it; a frequent mythological symbol found in Semitic and other cultures (e.g., Mesopotamian, Greek, Persian, and Indian). In the ancient Near East, the idea of a tree of life (or the bread, water, or plant of life) is quite common, appearing in the tales of the descent of Inanna to the nether world, Adapa, and Gilgamesh (where the plant of rejuvenation is ultimately stolen from the hero by a serpent). The motif is used in the biblical account of the garden of Eden, where the tree of life is mentioned alongside the tree of knowledge (*Gn*. 2.9). Adam's expulsion from the garden of Eden (*Gn*. 3.23–24) after eating from the tree of knowledge is motivated (*Gn*. 3.22) by the concern that he might also partake of the tree of life and thus gain immortality. In *Proverbs*, the tree is a metaphor for *wisdom (*Prv*. 3.18).

There is much difference of opinion among commentators as to the precise meaning and relationship of the two trees in the paradise story. Apocalyptic literature promises the righteous that they will partake of the tree of life after the final judgment (e.g., *1 En*. 24.4, 25.4–6; *2 Esd*. 8.52). In kabbalistic literature, the symbolism of the two trees, and of the tree of life in particular, is developed in mystical fashion.

• Umberto Cassuto, *A Commentary on the Book of Genesis: From Adam to Noah* (Jerusalem, 1989). Howard N. Wallace, *The Eden Narrative*, Harvard Semitic Monographs 32 (Atlanta, 1985), pp. 115–132. Claus Westermann, *Genesis 1–11* (Minneapolis, 1984), pp. 211–214.

–SHALOM PAUL

TREES, NEW YEAR FOR. See TU BI-SHEVAT.

TRESPASS. The English term *trespass* applies to a variety of acts, which are expressed in Hebrew by different words. The most important of these are offenses against another person's rights or property (*nezeq*; see HASSAGAT GEVUL; TORTS); transgressions against divine law in general (see SIN); and certain offenses for which a special kind of sacrifice is required in order to make atonement (see REPARATION OFFERING).

TRESPASS OFFERING. See REPARATION OFFERING.

TRIAL. See CRIMINAL PROCEDURE.

TRIBES OF ISRAEL, traditionally the descendants of the twelve sons of Jacob (cf. *Gn*. 46.8–27; *Ex*. 1.1–7) by his wives, Leah and Rachel, and concubines, Bilhah and Zilpah. This is based on the popular concept of the common lineage of the tribes and nations. Modern biblical research based on anthropology and the critical approach to the biblical traditions proposes another picture.

The scheme of the twelve tribes of Israel is an artificial one, in which the number is fixed while the components might vary. Its artificiality can be deduced from the fact that the Bible also organizes other tribal groups according to twelve participant units; for example, the Arameans (*Gn*. 22.21–24) and Ishmaelites (*Gn*. 25.13–16). In Israel, the change of the status of Levi caused the split of the house of Joseph into two tribes, Ephraim and Manasseh, in order to retain the number twelve.

The study of tribal units has demonstrated that while smaller units are lineage groups, larger ones are bound together on the basis of common geographical backgrounds and interests. In ancient Israel, this can be discerned in the cases of Benjamin and Ephraim. The name Benjamin means Son of the Right (Side), the south. Benjamin was the southernmost tribe of the confederation of the sons of Rachel. The name Ephraim is unique among West Semitic proper names, but its construction is also typical of geographical names. The tribe of Gilead mentioned in the Song of Deborah (*Jgs*. 5.17) is likewise a geographical name.

In premonarchical Israel, the twelve tribes of Israel never acted in unison. The Pentateuchal descriptions of the twelve tribes, as well as those of the *Book of Joshua*, and the description of the war of the confederation of all Israel against Benjamin in the last chapters of the *Book of Judges* (19–20) are retrospective descriptions. The most that one could say is that some tribes joined together in times of stress, but never all of them.

It is only with the establishment of the united monarchy under King David that Israel and Judah came together under one government and were united. Israel was organized into twelve units, rooted in tribal lines, each one being responsible for the maintenance of the state revenues for one month a year. This system was reformed by King Solomon, who divided the kingdom into twelve provinces that did not always coincide with the former tribal units (*1 Kgs*. 4). The twelve tribes disbanded after the dissolution of the united monarchy, soon after the death of Solomon.

The schism that followed the death of Solomon ended in the secession of ten tribes (Reuben, Simeon, Dan, Naphtali, Gad, Asher, Issachar, Zebulun, Ephraim, and Manasseh), who under Jeroboam I formed the northern kingdom of Israel. Only two tribes, Judah and Benjamin (Simeon was already integrated into Judah), remained in the south. The northern kingdom lasted approximately two hundred years; it fell to the Assyrians in 721 BCE, when the majority of the Israelites were deported to Assyria (*2 Kgs*. 17.6). Unlike the Judeans of the southern kingdom, who survived a similar fate 135 years later, they soon assimilated. Those remaining in Israel commingled with foreign colonists and subsequently became known as *Samaritans. The loss of the ten tribes was never accepted as final by the Jews. From the time of Jeremiah, who prophesied their return (*Jer*. 31.4ff.), and Ezekiel, who connected their eventual return with the era of redemption (*Ez*. 37.16; the concept was also developed in apocalyptic literature), hope of their eventual restoration was never relinquished, although R. ʿAqiva' said they would never return (*San*. 10.3). Belief in their continued existence was nurtured in apocryphal books (*Tobit* [of the tribe of Naphtali]; *2 Esdras* 13.39–50). Different sites are mentioned in the Midrash as their dwelling place (e.g., across the river *Sambatyon, under a blanket of clouds, or within the walls of Antioch), and fantastic reports regarding the lost tribes were a frequent feature of Jewish legend and folklore, particularly in periods of messianic ferment. A vivid description purporting to be of the lost tribes was given by the ninth century Jewish traveler *Eldad ha-Dani.

• C. H. J. de Geus, *The Tribes of Israel* (Assen, 1976). Cyrus Gordon, "The Ten Lost Tribes," in *Hebrew and the Bible in America: The First Two Centuries*, edited by Shalom Goldman (Hanover, N.H., 1993), a learned but unconventional approach. Abraham Gross, "The Expulsion and the Search for the Ten Tribes," *Judaism* 41 (Spring 1992): 130–147. Martin Noth, *History of Israel* (London, 1958), pp. 85–108. Roland de Vaux, *Ancient Israel: Its Life and Institutions*, 2d ed. (London, 1965), vol. 1, pp. 4–13. Roland de Vaux, *The Early History of Israel*, 2 vols. (London, 1978), pp. 695–749.

–SHMUEL AHITUV AND SHALOM PAUL

TRIBUNALS. See BEIT DIN.

TRIENNIAL CYCLE, division of the weekly synagogue reading of the Torah (see QERI'AT HA-TORAH) into a three-year cycle, which was the ancient Palestinian practice. The Babylonian custom of an annual cycle became the general tradition, although evidence of the triennial cycle being followed in Erets Yisra'el and Egypt exists until the twelfth century. A number of *midrashim* are based on a division that follows a three-year cycle. In modern times, Reform Judaism (and some Conservative synagogues) adopted a three-year cycle in order to shorten the weekly Hebrew reading. However, instead of reading the entire Torah consecutively, it divided each weekly portion into three, reading the first third one year, the second third the next year, and the third in the third year, thus maintaining a correspondence to the annual reading and to the celebration of *Simḥat Torah.

• Jacob Mann, *The Bible as Read and Preached in the Old Synagogue*, 2 vols. (Cincinnati, 1940).

TROKI, YITSḤAQ BEN AVRAHAM (c.1533–1594), *Karaite scholar. Born in Troki, the oldest and most important Karaite community in Lithuania, and a physician by profession, he was the most prominent of the Karaite scholars of Troki during the sixteenth century. Yitsḥaq knew Latin and Polish and acquired an extensive knowledge of Christian literature, including contemporary Polish sectarian writings. This enabled him to hold theological discussions with Christian scholars from the variety of denominations and sects active in Poland at that time: Roman Catholic, Eastern Orthodox, Calvinist, Lutheran, Socinian, Arian, and so forth. Out of these came his famous apology for Judaism and critique of Christianity, *Ḥizzuq Emunah*, written at the end of his life.

The book's careful and in-depth examination of the weaknesses of Christian dogma and the inner contradictions of the New Testament, as well as its reasonable defense of Judaism, made it very popular, and it quickly circulated in manuscript form. It was first published by Johann Christoph Wagenseil with a Latin translation and extensive refutation in his *Tela ignea Satanae* (Altdorf, 1681). An English translation by Moses Mocatta appeared in London in 1851 (repr. New York, 1970). In the eighteenth century, *Ḥizzuq Emunah* was used by freethinkers and praised by Voltaire, but also criticized by a number of Christian authors. It has no openly Karaite characteristics, and for many years its author was mistakenly thought to be a Rabbanite.

In addition to *Ḥizzuq Emunah*, Yitsḥaq wrote a refutation of the Rabbanites, a work on the ten principles of faith, a commentary on the section on the laws of impurity in Eliyyahu Bashyazi's *Adderet Eliyyahu* (all of which remain in manuscript), as well as a number of religious hymns that entered into the Karaite prayer book.

• Robert Dan in *Occident and Orient: A Tribute to the Memory of Alexander Scheiber*, edited by Sandor Scheiber and Robert Dan (Budapest and Leiden, 1988), pp. 69–82. Abraham Geiger, *Isaak Troki: ein Apologet des Judenthums am Ende des sechzehnten Jahrhunderts* (Breslau, 1853). Jacob Mann, *Texts and Studies in Jewish History and Literature*, vol. 2 (Cincinnati, 1935). —DAVID E. SKLARE

TROP (from Gr. *tropos* [turn, manner, or mode]), a term that refers to the musical motives associated with graphic signs used in biblical cantillation. While these twenty-eight symbols (also known as *accents or *ta'amei ha-miqra'*) serve a primarily grammatical and syntactical function, a series of musical systems has evolved to distinguish the chanting of various scriptural passages. Indeed, the Talmud asserts that one who merely recites the biblical text without its accompanying *trop* shows a disregard for the law (*Meg.* 32a). Different melodies or *trops* are utilized for Pentateuchal readings (Torah); Prophetic readings (*haftarot*); the *Book of Esther*; the *megillot* read on the three festivals (*Song of Songs* on Pesaḥ, *Ruth* on Shavu'ot, *Ecclesiastes* on Sukkot); the *Book of Lamentations*; and the Pentateuchal passages read at the morning services on Ro'sh ha-Shanah and Yom Kippur. Totally different *trops* are utilized by Sephardi Jews and 'Adot ha-Mizraḥ for chanting these same books. Among some of the latter, *Psalms* and the *Book of Job* are also chanted according to particular *trops*.

• Abraham W. Binder, *Biblical Chant* (New York, 1959 and 1963). Johanna Spector, "Chant and Cantillation," in *Musica Judaica* 9.1 (1988): 1–21. —MARSHA BRYAN EDELMAN

TRUTHFULNESS (Heb. *emet*). In biblical and rabbinic language the term does not so much signify scientific or theological truth as it does honesty, sincerity, loyalty, or integrity. When referring to actions and judgments, it can also mean "right" and "just" (cf. *Zec.* 8.16); in connection with facts, it indicates that they have been authenticated or substantiated. Truthfulness is thus a practical rather than a logical concept. God is true, that is, ever faithful (cf. *Jer.* 10.10; *Ps.* 31.6), and his word, law, and precepts are true (*Ps.* 19.10, 119.43, 142). Truth, one of the *thirteen attributes of God (*Ex.* 34.6; *Ps.* 117.2), is stressed both in the Bible and Talmud as one of the greatest virtues. Only he "who speaks truth in his heart" shall "abide in your tabernacle and dwell in your holy mountain" (*Ps.* 15.2), and the daily morning prayer exhorts: "at all times let a man fear God secretly as well as publicly, acknowledge the truth, and speak the truth in his heart." The Talmudic description of a hypocrite and a liar is a person who has "one thing in his heart and another on his lips" (*Pes.* 113b). Rabbi Shim'on ben Gamli'el enumerates truth as the first of the three pillars upon which the continued existence of the world depends (*Avot* 1.1). "Truth is the seal of the Holy One, blessed be He" (*Yoma'* 69b). Truth will ultimately triumph while falsehood will not endure (*Shab.* 104a), and liars are one of the four groups with whom the divine presence does not abide (*Sot.* 42a). Parents are bid never to break a promise to a child, lest they encourage untruthfulness in the child (*Suk.* 46b). The reinforcement of a statement by an oath, though at times required by law, was discouraged by the rabbis, since it tended to create a double standard of truth. In spite of the command to speak truth and the prohibition against *lying (*Ex.* 23.7), certain situations may present overriding demands (*Yev.* 65b). Thus, the Midrash adduces the difference in wording between *Genesis* 18.12 ("my husband is old") and verse 13 ("I am old"; which is how God repeats Sarah's statement to Abraham) as proof of the propriety of modifying a statement for the sake of domestic harmony. The rabbis in extolling *Aaron as a lover of peace explain that he was not averse to telling a white lie if peace could thereby be established or restored. The use of *emet* in a logical sense (e.g. "necessary truth," "eternal truth," "eternal truth," "revealed truthfulness") only appears in medieval philosophical literature.

• Menachem Elon, "The Essence of Truth," *Studies in Halakha and Jewish Thought Presented to Rabbi Prof. Menachem Emanuel Rackman on His 80th Anniversary*, edited by Moshe Beer (Ramat Gan, 1994), pp. 17–22. Richard A. Freund, "Lying and Deception in the Biblical and Post-Biblical Judaic Tradition," *Scandinavian Journal of the Old Testament* 1 (1991): 45–61. Abraham Joshua Heschel, *A Passion for Truth* (Woodstock, Vt., 1995). C. G. Montefiore, *Truth in Religion and Other Sermons* (London, 1906).

TSAʿAR BAʿALEI ḤAYYIM. See ANIMALS, TREATMENT OF.

TSADDIQ (צַדִּיק; righteous man), a term with a variety of definitions, in legal, kabbalistic, and Hasidic contexts; it is also sometimes applied to God who is "just and righteous." In legal usage it refers to one who has been found innocent in court or who is right in a dispute. In kabbalistic terminology *tsaddiq* is the designation of one of the ten **sefirot*. A prominent folk belief was the notion of thirty-six hidden and unknown *tsaddiqim* (see LAMED VAV), whose humble and anonymous piety sustains the world in every generation. Whereas the Talmud uses the word **ḥasid* for a man whose piety goes beyond that of the *tsaddiq*, the significance of the term was reversed in later usage. In the language of the Hasidic movement (see HASIDISM), the *ḥasid* was the devout and devoted follower of the *tsaddiq* (or **rebbi*), the leader held to be endowed with a special charisma. The *tsaddiq* was not merely a spiritual guide but a mediator between the believers and God, one who it was felt possessed supernatural qualities, including the power of prayer and the ability to work miracles. Many Hasidic masters became founders of dynasties; their charisma was thought to be transmitted by inheritance. Opponents of Hasidism, as well as some scholars, ascribe the decay of the movement in the nineteenth century to the institutionalization of hereditary tsaddiqism.

• Samuel H. Dresner, *The Zaddik: The Doctrine of the Zaddik according to the Writings of Rabbi Yaacov Yosef of Polnoy* (New York, 1974). Arthur Green, "Typologies of Leadership and the Hasidic Zaddik," in *Jewish Spirituality: From the Sixteenth Century Revival to the Present*, edited by Arthur Green, vol. 2 (New York, 1987), pp. 127–156.

TSADDIQ, YOSEF IBN. See ZADDIK, YOSEF BEN YAʿAQOV IBN.

TSADOQ HA-KOHEN OF LUBLIN (1823–1900), Hasidic master and author. Educated in anti-Hasidic, Lithuanian *yeshivot*, he later became an adherent of Hasidism and one of the most profound Hasidic authors of the late nineteenth century. His first *rebbi* was the radically innovative Mordekhai Yosef Leiner of Izbica Lubelski, a leading disciple of Menaḥem Mendel of Kotsk. Later, he became a disciple of Yehudah Leib Eger of Lublin, before becoming a master in his own right. He stands out among Hasidic authors for the range and depth of his prolific teachings. His works reveal a mastery of Talmudic, kabbalistic, and Hasidic literature. He wrote *Peri Tsaddiq* (5 vols. [New York, 1901–1934]).

• Alan Brill, "The Intellectual Mysticism of Rabbi Zadok HaKohen of Lublin," Ph.D. dissertation, Fordham University, 1994. Samuel Unger, *Toledot ha-Kohen mi-Lublin* (Jerusalem, 1965). —MILES KRASSEN

TSEDAQAH. See CHARITY; RIGHTEOUSNESS.

TSE'ENAH U-RE'ENAH, popular Yiddish miscellany written in the 1590s by Yaʿaqov ben Yitsḥaq Ashkenazi of Janów Lubelski, Poland, who took the title from *Song of Songs* 3.11. His work is a paraphrase of the weekly Torah readings, *haftarot*, and the Five Scrolls, woven together with selections from the commentaries of Rashi and Baḥya ben Asher, Midrashic legend, homilies, and other sources. Though meant for anyone unschooled in Hebrew, the work was destined to become staple reading for Jewish women in eastern Europe, familiarizing them with the Bible. The oldest surviving edition was printed in 1622; over two hundred reprints, adaptations, and translations have appeared since then.

• Milly Heyd, "Illustrations in Early Editions of the Tsene-U'Rene," *Journal of Jewish Art* 10 (1984): 64–86. Dorothy Seidman Bilik, "Tsene-rene: A Yiddish Literary Success," *Jewish Book Annual* 51 (1993): 96–111. Khone Shmeruk, "Ha-Nusḥa'ot ha-Mizraḥ Eropiyyot shel ha-Tse'enah u-Re'enah, 1786–1850," in *Sifrut Yidish be-Polin* (Jerusalem, 1981), pp. 147–164. Israel Zinberg, *History of Jewish Literature*, vol. 7, *Old Yiddish Literature From Its Origins to the Haskalah Period*, translated by Bernard Martin (New York, 1975), pp. 129–139. —GABRIEL A. SIVAN

TSHOLNT (Yi.; טשאָלנט), a bean-based dish traditionally eaten by Ashkenazim for Sabbath lunch. Since cooking on the Sabbath is forbidden, the *tsholnt* is prepared on Friday afternoon and placed in the oven to bake overnight or on a metal plate on the stove top, below which a flame is kept burning throughout the Sabbath. Various etymologies have been suggested for the word, most popularly the French *chaud lent* (warming, cooking slowly). Sephardim prepare a similar hot dish for the Sabbath called *ḥamin*; in North Africa the dish is called *dafina*.

• John Cooper, *Eat and Be Satisfied: A Social History of Jewish Food* (Northvale, N.J., 1993). Herman Pollack, *Jewish Folkways in Germanic Lands (1648–1806): Studies in Aspects of Daily Life* (Cambridge, Mass., 1971), p. 100. —CHAIM PEARL

TSIDDUQ HA-DIN (צִדּוּק הַדִּין, Justification of the Judgment), the prayer that is recited at a funeral, signifying, in particular, resigned submission to God's justice in the face of a person's death. The basis of this prayer is found in *ʿAvodah Zarah* 18a; R. Ḥanina' ben Teradyon and his wife were sentenced to death by the Romans and their daughter committed to a brothel. On hearing the sentence, R. Ḥanina' quoted, in acceptance of the divine will, the first half of *Deuteronomy* 32.4, his wife completed the verse, and the daughter quoted *Jeremiah* 32.19. These verses are included in the Tsidduq ha-Din prayer, which originated in Talmudic times and received its final form in the geonic period. In some rites, it is recited after the coffin has been lowered into the grave.

• Joshua S. Sperka, *Eternal Life: A Digest of All Jewish Laws of Mourning* (New York, 1961).

TSIMTSUM (צִמְצוּם; contraction), in Lurianic Kabbalah (see LURIA, YITSḤAQ), the process whereby God, who is all, withdraws or contracts himself sideways so as to leave a kind of primordial space or nondivine vacuum within which creation can take place. The doctrine of *tsimtsum* was meant to account for the possibility of creation, since the infinite being of God does not leave room for the existence of anything else. Yet even the space vacated by God during the act of *tsimstsum* is not devoid of the divine light. An impression of the divine remains "as the fragrance which lingers in the vial after it has been emptied of its perfume." In Lurianic Kabbalah, the notion of *tsimtsum* also served as an explanation for the origin of evil, as well as a theistic qualification of the pantheism inherent in the thought that all creation is included within God. See also BREAKING OF THE VESSELS.

• Maureena Fritz, "A Midrash: The Self-Limitation of God," *Journal of Ecumenical Studies* 22 (1985): 703–714. Roland Goetschel, "La Notion de simsum dans le Somer 'Emunim de Joseph Ergaz," in *Hommage à Georges Vajda*, edited by G. Nahon and C. Touati (Louvain, 1980), pp. 385–396. Gershom Gerhard Scholem, *Major Trends in Jewish Mysticism* (New York, 1995).

TSITSIT (צִיצִית), fringes attached to the four corners of garments. *Numbers* 15.37–41 commands that a blue thread be added to the *tsitsit* at the four corners to remind the Israelites of the commandments and prevent them from going astray. The mnemonic and preventative roles have been a matter of speculation. Some modern scholars have suggested that the law in *Numbers* evolved as the theological rationalization of an originally common ornamentation. The fringes have also been explained as a sign of rank or dignity, an emblem of Israel's status as a holy nation and a kingdom of priests. Ancient Near Eastern art shows figures with fringes decorating corners or ends of seams of garments. Mesopotamian documents reveal that fringes (Akk. *sissiktu*) on garments were considered extensions of the person and could represent him in legal acts and magical rituals. Since modern dress rarely includes four-cornered garments, a special one (known as *tsitsit*, *arba' kanfot* [four corners], or *tallit qatan* [small *tallit]) is worn during the day by observant male Jews (including boys) beneath the outer clothing. In Ḥaredi circles, the custom of wearing the *tsitsit* over the outer clothing is gaining ground. The fringes are attached to this four-cornered garment with a hole in the middle, through which the head is placed. A blessing is recited when putting on the *tsitsit*. The *tsitsit* consists of four long strands drawn through a small hole about one-and-a-half inches from the corner. The two parts of the strands are tied together by a double knot. The longest strand (*shammash*) is then wound seven, eight, eleven, and thirteen times around the other seven halves of the four threads. A double knot is made after each set of windings. The total length of the *tsitsit* should be not less than eleven-and-one-half inches.

• Jacob Milgrom, "Of Hems and Tassels," *Biblical Archaeology Review* 9.3 (1983): 61–65. Eliyyahu Tebager, *Kelil ha-Tekhelet: Be'urim, Ḥiddushim . . . be-'Inyenei Mitsvat Tsitsit* (Jerusalem, 1992–1993). Yigael Yadin, *Bar Kokhba* (London, 1971), on tassels from the second century CE found in caves near the Dead Sea. —VICTOR HUROWITZ

TSOM. See FASTS.

TSOM GEDALYAH (צוֹם גְּדַלְיָה), fast day commemorating the assassination of Gedaliah on 3 Tishrei, the day after Ro'sh ha-Shanah (*R. ha-Sh.* 18b). Gedaliah ben Ahikam, a member of the Shaphan family, which had supported the prophet *Jeremiah, was appointed governor of Judah by Nebuchadnezzar after the destruction of the First Temple. Following Gedaliah's murder at the hands of Ishmael son of Nethaniah, of the royal family, the remaining Jews fled to Egypt, and the last vestige of Jewish self-government in Judah came to an end (*2 Kgs.* 25.25; *Jer.* 40–1). The Bible states that the murder took place in the month of Tishrei, and later tradition dated it to the third day of that month; some authorities suggested that it took place on Ro'sh ha-Shanah but that the commemoration was postponed until after the holiday. The fast of Gedaliah is already mentioned by the prophet Zechariah (*Zec.* 7.5, 8.19). When Ro'sh ha-Shanah falls on Thursday and Friday, the fast is postponed to the following Sunday, 4 Tishrei. Fasting is from sunrise to sunset, and in the synagogue **seliḥot* are read during the Shaḥarit service (as well as before the service in some rites).

• Pierre M. Bogaert, "La Libération de Jérémie et le meurtre de Godolias: Le Texte court (LXX) et la rédaction longue (TM)," in *Studien zur Septuaginta*, edited by D. Fraenkel et al. (Göttinger, 1990), pp. 312–322. Ismar Elbogen, *Jewish Liturgy: A Comprehensive History* (Philadelphia, 1993).

TSOREF, YEHOSHU'A HESHEL (1633–c.1700), pietist, mystic, and a leader of the Shabbatean movement in Poland and Lithuania. Born in Vilna, he lived most of his life there but spent some time in Amsterdam and died in Kraków. He was in close contact with Shabbatean leaders in eastern Europe and in the Middle East and assembled around him a group of devoted disciples. A strict ascetic, he had frequent visions, which he recorded in his unpublished *Sefer ha-Tsoref* (parts are extant in manuscript). His life and work were marked by intense messianic devotion; he regarded himself as the Messiah, Son of Joseph, serving the Messiah, Son of David (Shabbetai Tsevi), whose second coming, Tsoref believed, was imminent. Tsoref's writings were based on *gimatriyyah* and numerological speculations, often revolving around his and Shabbetai Tsevi's names and the date of redemption.

Gershom Gerhard ^Scholem suggested that Tsoref's figure and writings represent the historical element in the evolvement of the legend of R. Adam Ba'al Shem, whose writings are described in Hasidic hagiography as a source of inspiration for R. Yisra'el ben Eli'ezer Ba'al Shem Tov, the founder of the Hasidic movement. This suggestion has not been proven, and many scholars doubt it. However, Tsoref's behavior, the manner of organization of his disciples, as well as the hagiographic stories told about him, contributed to the shaping of the early Hasidic movement.

• Moshe Hillel, *Ba'alei Shem* (Jerusalem, 1993). Gershom Gerhard Scholem, *Kabbalah* (Jerusalem, 1974), pp. 452–453. —JOSEPH DAN

TSUR MI-SHELLO (צוּר מִשֶּׁלּוֹ; Rock from Whose Store [We Have Eaten]), hymn sung at the Sabbath table, though it contains no specific reference to the Sabbath. Tsur mi-Shello is of unknown authorship but dates from about the sixteenth century, its four stanzas corresponding to the first four paragraphs of the *Birkat ha-Mazon and, hence, usually sung immediately before it. The refrain of Tsur mi-Shello is based partly on *2 Kings* 4.44.

• Israel Davidson, *Thesaurus of Medieval Jewish Poetry*, 4 vols. (New York, 1970). Macy Nulman, *The Encyclopedia of Jewish Prayer* (Northvale, N.J., and London, 1993), p. 329.

TU BE-'AV (ט״ו בְּאָב; or Ḥamishah ʿAsar be-'Av [15 Av]), popular festival in Second Temple times. According to the Talmud, on this day eligible maidens went out in borrowed white garments (so that the poorer ones among them would not be shamed) and danced in the vineyards, and the young men present would select their wives from among them (*Taʿan*. 4.8). The day was probably originally a nature festival; as it was regarded as the climax of the period of solar heat, it was also the festival of the wood offering—the last day for bringing wood to the Temple altar; after this date the trees were no longer dry enough and wood hewing ceased until the spring sap began to rise six months later on *Tu bi-Shevat. The Talmud gives various other traditions for Tu be-'Av, including the anniversary of the date when the tribes were first permitted to intermarry or when the dead of Betar could be buried after the *Bar Kokhba' Revolt (*Taʿan*. 30b–31a). Fasting and funeral eulogies are forbidden on this day, and *Taḥanun is not recited in the synagogue.

• Yigael Yadin, ed., *The Temple Scroll*, 3 vols. (Jerusalem, 1989), includes discussion of a Dead Sea Scroll with new references to wood offering festivals, with bibliography.

TU BI-SHEVAT (ט״ו בִּשְׁבָט; 15 Shevat), also known as Ro'sh ha-Shanah la-'Ilanot (New Year for Trees), originally had no religious significance, except that according to the school of Hillel, the age of a tree for purposes of tithes and similar laws (e.g., *ʿ*orlah*) is reckoned from 15 *Shevat, when with the approaching end of winter the sap begins to shoot up in the trees. According to the school of Shamm'ai the date is 1 Shevat. The Talmud gives no indication of any celebration or liturgical observance connected with 15 Shevat, though certain penitential prayers are omitted and fasting is forbidden. Since the seventeenth century, partly under the influence of the kabbalists of Safed, who saw profound esoteric meaning in the verse "For man is like the tree of the field" (*Dt*. 20.19), a special ceremonial evolved. Among Ashkenazim, it consisted merely of eating fruit from Erets Yisra'el, but Eastern Jews observed an elaborate ritual in which fifteen different fruits were eaten to the accompaniment of appropriate readings from the Bible, Talmud, and Zohar. This was modeled on the Pesaḥ Seder and was published in *Peri ʿEts Hadar* (Salonika, 1753). In the State of Israel, Tu bi-Shevat has become an arbor day marked by the ceremonial planting of trees by schoolchildren, while the occasion is also marked in Jewish schools in the Diaspora.

• R. Goetschel, "La Cèlèbration du nouvel an de l'arbre analyse d'un rituel kabbalistique du 18e siècle," *Daat* 10 (1983): 39–49. Y. Goldreich, "The Dispute Concerning the Date of the New Year for Trees: A Climatic Point of View," *Jewish Quarterly Review* 74 (1983): 80–87.

TUM'AH. See IMPURITY.

TURIM. See YAʿAQOV BEN ASHER.

TWERSKY FAMILY, Hasidic dynasty. The Twerskys were one of the two (along with the Friedmanns of Ruzhin; see RUZHIN, YISRA'EL OF) leading families of Hasidic masters in the original Hasidic heartland of western Ukraine. Rabbi Mordekhai Twersky (1770–1837) inherited the modest position of his father, R. *Naḥum of Chernobyl; there he established a major Hasidic court along the lines of R. *Barukh of Medzhibozh. His eight sons all became Hasidic masters, establishing themselves in Chernobyl, Korostyshev, Cherkassy, Makarov, Trisk, Tal'noye, Skvira, and Rotmistrovka. From these places they branched out to many more towns throughout the region, though the followings of most descendants were rather small. Many of the Twerskys suffered severe persecution with the establishment of the Soviet regime, and most fled the region. Several members of the Twersky family were among the first Hasidic leaders to immigrate to North America, settling in the 1920s and 1930s in New York, Boston, Philadelphia, and Milwaukee. The descendants of the Skvira branch have established a village in New Square ("New Skvira"), New York.

• Samuel A. Horodezky, *Ha-Ḥasidut veha-Ḥasidim* (Tel Aviv, 1953), vol. 3, pp. 83–96. Aaron D. Twerski, *Sefer ha-Yaḥas mi-Tshernobil ve-Rozin* (Jerusalem, 1966).

—ARTHUR GREEN

TWILIGHT. Rabbi Yosei said, "twilight is as the twinkling of the eye" (*Shab*. 34b); that is, that though it exists it cannot be measured. The accepted view is that twilight is the period between sunset and darkness; however, opinions differ as to whether twilight is determined by the appearance of the sky or by an amount of time. For halakhic purposes, as long as only two stars of medium magnitude are visible in the sky, it is considered twilight; the appearance of a third star marks the onset of night. The time period differs according to the latitude and the season of the year. See also DAY AND NIGHT.

—CHAIM PEARL

U

UGARIT, a Canaanite city-state that grew to be the principal commercial center of northern Syria during the Late Bronze Age, located near the Mediterranean coast on the site of the present Ras Shamra, uncovered in 1929. The discovery there of a large quantity of clay tablets, most written in a thirty-letter cuneiform alphabet, has revolutionized the study of Canaanite mythology and its bearing upon biblical scholarship. The inscriptions, dating from the fifteenth to the thirteenth century, are written in a language belonging to the family of Northwest Semitic, closely resembling Aramaic and Hebrew, and have thrown light on the literary and cultural background of the Bible in general, as well as on many phrases, linguistic features, poetic structures, and mythological allusions found in biblical literature. Mythological figures with biblical associations include the god El (the chief god in the Ugaritic pantheon) and his consort Asherah (sometimes identified with Astarte), their son Baal, Anath (Baal's consort and cofighter), Yam-Nahar, Mot, and others. There are three main cycles in Canaanite mythology. The first is the Baal–Anath cycle, which contains the deeds, conflicts, and final ascendancy of the storm god Baal, son of Dagon, over his enemies, including his battle against the sea god, Yam, alluded to many times in the Bible (e.g., *Is.* 51.9–10). Baal's palace is on Mount Zaphon. The second cycle is the Legend of King Keret, relating the king's quest for an heir, his illness and recovery, and the revolt of his son. The last cycle is the Legend of Aqhat, who was son of the righteous king Dan'el (cf. *Ez.* 14.14, 14.20, 28.3), which covers his conception to his death and its ultimate consequences.

Like El, the God of Israel is regarded as the "most high" (cf. *Ps.* 47.3), presiding over a divine council (cf. *Ps.* 82). Like Baal, Israel's God is portrayed at times as a storm god and warrior who fights enemy forces. One of the minor deities in Ugarit called Shalem is the eventual origin of the name Jerusalem, literally, "the foundation of [the god] Shalem."

• William F. Albright, *Yahweh and the Gods of Canaan*, 2d repr. (Winona Lake, Ind., 1990). A. Caquot, M. Sznycer, and A. Herdner, *Textes ougaritiques, Tome I: Mythes et légendes* (Paris, 1974). Frank M. Cross, *Canaanite Myth and Hebrew Epic: Essays in the History of the Religion of Israel* (Cambridge, Mass., 1973). Harold L. Ginsberg, "Ugaritic Myths, Epics and legends," in *Ancient Near Eastern Texts Relating to the Old Testament*, edited by James B. Pritchard, 3d ed. with supplement (Princeton, 1969). Cyrus H. Gordon, *Ugaritic Textbook*, Analecta Orientalia 38 (Rome, 1965), grammar, texts in transliteration, cuneiform selections, glossary, and indices. Gordon D. Young, *Ugarit in Retrospect: Fifty Years of Ugarit and Ugaritic* (Winona Lake, Ind., 1981), extensive bibliography. —MICHAEL JAMES WILLIAMS

UNCLEANNESS. See IMPURITY.

U-NETANNEH TOQEF (וּנְתַנֶּה תֹּקֶף; Let Us Evoke the Solemn Holiness of This Day), name and opening words of a *piyyut* recited during the repetition of the Musaf ʿAmidah on the *Yamim Nora'im. Its central motifs are the day of judgment, when "the great shofar is sounded" and the fate of all of God's creatures is decreed each year in heaven, and the proclamation that "repentance, prayer, and charity" can mitigate an ordained punishment. Jewish folk tradition associated U-Netanneh Toqef with the *payyetan* Kalonimos and legendary martyr Amnon of Mainz, and with the horrors of the Crusades. Documentary evidence, however, points to a much earlier composition date, during the Byzantine period by a Jewish contemporary of the emperor Romulus. It was adopted by the Ashkenazi and Italian rites. The prayer, which describes a day of awe and terror, in which God decides "who shall live and who shall die . . . who shall perish by fire, who by water, who by the sword and who by wild beasts . . . ," was regarded with ambivalence in many modern non-Orthodox congregations, some of which omitted it.

• Max Arzt, *Justice and Mercy: Commentary on the Liturgy of the New Year and the Day of Atonement* (New York, 1963), pp. 166–171. Ismar Elbogen, *Jewish Liturgy: A Comprehensive History*, translated by Raymond P. Scheindlin (Philadelphia, 1993). Macy Nulman, *The Encyclopedia of Jewish Prayer* (Northvale, N.J., and London, 1993). —GABRIEL A. SIVAN

UNION FOR TRADITIONAL JUDAISM. See CONSERVATIVE JUDAISM.

UNION OF AMERICAN HEBREW CONGREGATIONS (UAHC), a religious and educational organization dedicated to the principles of *Reform Judaism. The UAHC was founded in Cincinnati in 1873 by Isaac Mayer *Wise with an initial membership of thirty-four congregations from twenty-eight cities. Its purpose, as stated in its constitution and bylaws, is "to encourage and aid the organization and development of Jewish congregations; to promote Jewish education and enrich and intensify Jewish life; to maintain the Hebrew Union College [and] foster other activities for the perpetuation and advancement of Judaism."

The UAHC is the oldest institution of its kind in North America and represents the lay community of North American Reform Judaism. It supports the World Union for Progressive Judaism and the Association of Reform Zionists of America and Arza Canada, and participates in many communal Jewish organizations, including the Synagogue Council of America, the Conference of Presidents of Major American Jewish Organizations, the National Jewish Community Relations Advisory Council, and the Canadian Jewish Congress. It is the patron body of the *Hebrew Union College–Jewish Institute of Religion.

The UAHC's major programmatic areas include Jewish education, synagogue management, social action, youth and camping, interreligious affairs, small congregations, outreach to the unaffiliated, and outreach to non-Jewish partners in interfaith marriages. Its headquarters is in New York City.

• *Annual Report of the Union of American Hebrew Congregations* (published annually by the Union of American Hebrew Congregations, New York and Cincinnati). Simeon J. Maslin, *What We Believe . . . What We Do: A Pocket Guide for Reform Jews* (New York, 1993). Michael Meyer, *Response to Modernity: A History of the Reform Movement in Judaism* (Detroit, 1995). Avi Schulman, *Like a Raging Fire: A Biography of Maurice*

N. Eisendrath (New York, 1993). Al Vorspan and David Saperstein, *Tough Choices: Jewish Perspectives on Social Issues* (New York, 1993).
—GARY M. BRETTON-GRANATOOR

UNION OF ORTHODOX JEWISH CONGREGATIONS OF AMERICA, body serving the North American Orthodox community in the fields of education, outreach, and social service. It was founded in 1898 and has served as a central coordinating agency for American and Canadian Orthodox congregations. The affiliated organizations include the National Conference of Synagogue Youth (NCSY), a youth movement that maintains regional centers; ®Kashruth Certification Service, which administers a staff of over eight hundred rabbinic coordinators, *kashrut* supervisors, food chemists, and support personnel in certifying eighty thousand brand names, hotels, restaurants, and so on; a publishing division, producing books, journals, tapes, and videos; synagogue services, providing linkage and services to one thousand synagogues, in addition to retreats, seminars, conferences, and outreach programs; and a large number of additional services for the Jewish community in the United States, Israel, and around the world.

UNION OF ORTHODOX RABBIS OF THE UNITED STATES AND CANADA, also known as Agudath Harabonim. A rabbinical association founded in 1902 for the purpose of protecting the interests of religious Jewry and strengthening Orthodox Jewish culture in America and elsewhere. The activities of the Union include founding the Central Relief Committee for the rescue and rehabilitation of Jewry in Europe and Erets Yisra'el from 1914 through 1919, and for the restoration and preservation of *yeshivot* in Europe and in Erets Yisra'el. In 1915 Ezras Torah was founded to assist needy Torah scholars and their families. After World War I, the Union published and distributed an edition of the Talmud Bavli. It worked to set up and assist *yeshivot* in New York and in the United States at large. During World War II, it founded Vaad Hatzala, a rescue and rehabilitation agency to rescue Jews from the Holocaust. Over the years, it has consistently worked on behalf of Erets Yisra'el and Orthodox Jewry.

UNION OF SEPHARDIC CONGREGATIONS, an organization founded in 1929 in conjunction with Congregation Shearith Israel in New York, to serve the interests of the Sephardi Jewish community. The union prepares prayer books (both for daily and festival use) for Sephardi congregations, providing accurate English translations for the growing numbers of Sephardi Jews in English-speaking countries. The union also assists in finding jobs for rabbis and Hebrew teachers within the Sephardi community.

UNITED SYNAGOGUE, Orthodox synagogue organization in England, constituted by an act of Parliament in 1870. The United Synagogue (US) embraces synagogues in Greater London and certain provincial towns; these are divided into constituent, district, and associated synagogues. It is administered by a council, and according to its constitution, the British chief rabbi is its sole recognized religious authority. It maintains the London *beit din* and a body that supervises *kashrut* throughout the country. Rabbi Jonathan Sacks, as chief rabbi in 1991, initiated a revitalization of the US at the same time as its lay leaders issued a thorough study and strategic plan entitled *A Time for Change*.

• Aubrey Newman, *The United Synagogue 1870–1970* (London, 1976). Jonathan Sacks, ed., *Orthodoxy Confronts Modernity* (Hoboken, N.J., and London, 1991).
—RELA MINTZ GEFFEN

UNITED SYNAGOGUE OF CONSERVATIVE JUDAISM, an association (formerly United Synagogue of America) of over 830 Conservative congregations in the United States and Canada. Founded in 1913 by Solomon *Schechter, it has grown steadily and was responsible for the establishment in 1957 of the *World Council of Synagogues with affiliates in Israel and several South American and European countries. The United Synagogue coordinates its programs with the *Jewish Theological Seminary of America and is a constituent member of the World Council of Synagogues. Essentially a lay body, it endeavors to secure greater participation by the laity in the conduct of Conservative Jewish education and ritual practice.

• United Synagogue of Conservative Judaism, *Tiku Shofar: A Mahzor and Sourcebook for Students and Families* (New York, 1993). United Synagogue of Conservative Judaism, *United Synagogue of Conservative Judaism Bylaws* (New York, 1995).
—ELLIOT NELSON DORFF

UNITY OF GOD. See MONOTHEISM.

UNIVERSE. See ʿOLAM.

UNIVERSITY OF JUDAISM, the Los Angeles school of higher education that serves as the center for *Conservative Judaism in the West. Founded in 1947 through the efforts of the Los Angeles Bureau of Jewish Education and the *Jewish Theological Seminary of America, it includes an undergraduate college; graduate and professional programs (including rabbinic, education, and communal management); a library; a documentation center on Contemporary Jewish Life; an Educational Resources Center; institutes focusing on preparation for marriage, human services, and Jewish family education; Camp Ramah; a Center for the Arts in Jewish Life; and a continuing education program. Originally conceived by Mordecai Menahem *Kaplan, the university, in keeping with his outlook, provides education and creative programs not only in classical and contemporary Jewish studies but also in contemporary Jewish life and culture.

• Arthur Hoffnung, *The University of Judaism at Forty: A Historical Memoir* (Los Angeles, 1991). Mordecai M. Kaplan, "A University of Judaism," in *The Future of the American Jew* (New York, 1948), pp. 523–535.
—ELLIOTT NELSON DORFF

UNLEAVENED BREAD. See MATSAH.

UNTERFIRER (Yi.; אונטערפֿירער), the man who leads the bride or bridegroom "under the wedding canopy."

The bride and bridegroom are usually led by their parents or, in their absence, by married couples, preferably closely related to them.

ʿUQTSIN (עוּקְצִין; Stalks), tractate in Mishnah order Tohorot, with related material in Tosefta'. There is no *gemara'* in either Talmud. The first two of the tractate's three chapters discuss the conditions under which contact with impure parts of a plant, such as stalks, roots, pits, husks, or leaves, conveys impurity to the rest of the plant. The third chapter contains a collection of diverse laws dealing with impurities associated with plant and animal derivatives.

The laws of *ʿuqtsin* were considered a recondite field of knowledge, as evidenced by R. Me'ir and R. Natan, who plotted to replace R. Shimʿon ben Gamli'el as *nasi'* by exposing his ignorance of *ʿuqtsin*. Another sage, aware of the plot, saved R. Shimʿon embarrassment by loudly reviewing the laws of *ʿuqtsin* in his presence, signaling R. Shimʿon of the need to pay attention and fill in this gap in his knowledge (*Hor.* 13b). Some medieval and contemporary scholars deduce from this story that tractate *ʿUqtsin* was redacted more than a generation earlier than the redaction of the Mishnaic corpus.

An English translation of the tractate is in Herbert Danby's *The Mishnah* (London, 1933).

• Chanoch Albeck, ed., *Shishah Sidrei Mishnah, Seder Tohorot* (Jerusalem, 1958). Philip Blackman, ed. and trans., *Mishnayoth*, vol. 5, *Order Taharoth* (Gateshead, 1973). Hermann Leberecht Strack and Günter Stemberger, *Introduction to the Talmud and Midrash*, rev. and updat. ed., translated by Markus Bockmuehl (Minneapolis, 1992).

—AVRAHAM WALFISH

URBACH, EFRAIM ELIMELECH (1912–1991), Talmud and rabbinics scholar. Born in Włocławek, Poland, Urbach was ordained at the Breslau Rabbinical Seminary in 1934 and also studied at the University of Rome. In 1938 he migrated to Palestine and during World War II served as an army chaplain. From 1953 he taught *aggadah* and rabbinic literature at the Hebrew University of Jerusalem, where he became a professor in 1958, and published books and articles that dealt with many aspects of rabbinic literature. His most significant works are *Baʿalei ha-Tosafot* (1956), which traces the history of the tosafists, and *Ḥazal: Pirqei Emunot ve-Deʿot* (1969; Eng. trans. *The Sages: Their Concepts and Beliefs* [1975]), which traces the rise to leadership of the early rabbis and the development of their thought. Urbach edited the Hebrew journal *Tarbiz* from 1970 and served as president of the Israel Academy of Sciences and Humanities.

• Joseph Dan, "A Tribute to E. E. Urbach," *Judaism* 42.3 (1993): 262–266. "Efraim Elimelech Urbach, 1912–1991," *Israel Exploration Journal* 41 (1991): 295–296. World Union of Jewish Studies, *Efrayim Elimelekh Urbakh: Biyo-Bibliyografyah Meḥqarit* (Jerusalem, 1993).

—DIDIER Y. REISS

URIEL, the fourth of the four archangels (the others being Gabriel, *Michael, and *Raphael) who preside over the four quarters of the globe. Uriel presides over the North. Unlike the other three archangels, he is not mentioned in rabbinic literature but is frequently referred to in the Apocrypha and pseudepigrapha, from which he entered into medieval mystical literature, where he also figures as the angel of fire (*ur*). See also ANGELS.

• James H. Charlesworth, ed., *The Old Testament Pseudepigrapha*, 2 vols. (Garden City, N.Y., 1983–1985), cf. index.

URIM AND THUMMIM. See ORACLES.

USHA', SYNOD OF, early rabbinic synod held in a town in Lower Galilee, mentioned in the annals of Sennacherib. The place became famous during the period of the Mishnah and Talmud, most especially after the Bar Kokhba' defeat, when a group of surviving scholars gathered there (c.140 CE) to reestablish the *Sanhedrin and institute regulations known as the Enactment of Usha' (*Sg. Rab.* 2.5, no. 3). The main authorities at this synod were Rabbis Yehudah bar Il'ai, Neḥemyah, Me'ir, Yosei ben Ḥalafta', Shimʿon bar Yoḥ'ai, Eliʿezer ben Yosei ha-Galili, and Eliʿezer ben Yaʿaqov. The office of **nasi'* was revived, and Shimʿon ben Gamli'el was appointed to the post. Rabbi Natan ha-Bavli headed the *beit din* (rabbinic court), and R. Me'ir acted as a senior advisor (*ḥakham*). The scholars of Usha' applied themselves particularly to the laws of ritual purity; some of them probably adopted the principles of the *Hasideans, which included eating all foods in a state of purity. Some of the enactments of the rabbis of Usha' reflected the economic situation of the period, such as the ruling that "a man must support his young children" (Y., *Ket.* 4.8), not an easy task in a time of poverty and hardship. A further enactment, which strengthened the position of the sages, was that "one may not excommunicate an elder" (Y., *Moʿed Q.* 3.1). Some scholars believe that a number of these enactments are of a later date; namely, the end of the Severan dynasty, around 230 CE. Usha' has been identified with present-day Hushah, where remains of a splendid building, possibly a synagogue, have been uncovered.

• Adolf Buechler, *Studies in Jewish History* (London, 1956). Hugo Mantel, *Studies in the History of the Sanhedrin* (Cambridge, Mass., 1961).

—DANIEL SPERBER

USHPIZIN (Aram.; אֻשְׁפִּיזִין; from Lat. *hospites* [guests]), the custom of welcoming one of seven patriarchs or heroes of biblical history (Abraham, Isaac, Jacob, Joseph, Moses, Aaron, and David) as a spiritual guest to the **sukkah* on each of the seven days of Sukkot. The notion is first mentioned in the Zohar (*Emor* 103b–104a), the seven names serving as symbols of seven of the ten **sefirot* (manifestations of God). The formula of greeting was composed in Safed in the sixteenth century by Yitsḥaq *Luria. Originally practiced only by the kabbalists, the custom of reciting Ushpizin became widespread in Orthodox circles, and its formula (in Aramaic) is found in many festival prayer books. It also became a custom to invite poor students to the *sukkah* as a symbol of the spiritual visitors.

• Yonah Blikshtain, *Sefer ha-'Ushpizin bi-Re'i ha-Meqorot* (Rehovot, 1988).

USUCAPION. See ḤAZAQAH.

USURY. See LOANS; MONEYLENDING.

U-VA' LE-TSIYYON (וּבָא לְצִיּוֹן; "And a redeemer shall come unto Zion"), the opening phrase of one of the concluding prayers in the Shaḥarit service. It consists of *Isaiah* 59.20–21 and *Qedushah de-Sidra', the recitation of *Isaiah* 6.3 in Hebrew and Aramaic. In general parlance the Qedushah de-Sidra' came to be identified with U-Va' le-Tsiyyon. The practice of the Qedushah de-Sidra' is first mentioned in the Talmud, in tractate *Sotah* 49a. According to Ismar Elbogen, following a *responsum* of R. Natrona'i Ga'on, the origin of the Qedushah de-Sidra' is as follows: "Early in the morning, immediately after the service, Torah lessons were held. At the end of the lesson several verses from the Prophets were recited, ending with the verses of the Qedushah; as was customary in these sermons, the verses were translated into Aramaic. As the struggle for survival became increasingly harder and there was no long time for study, the lesson was reduced and eventually eliminated altogether, but the verses remained standing at the end of the morning service." The remainder of U-Va' le-Tsiyyon includes a prayer, based on verses from *1 Chronicles*, *Psalms*, and *Micah*, thanking God for his continuing mercies, and a prayer for enlightenment in the Torah, made up of citations from *Psalms*, *Jeremiah*, and *Isaiah*. On Sabbaths and festivals, U-Va' le-Tsiyyon is recited in the Minḥah service; on Yom Kippur, in the Neʿilah service. With the exception of the first section, the prayer is also incorporated in the Saturday evening service.

• Ismar Elbogen, *Jewish Liturgy: A Comprehensive History*, translated by Raymond P. Scheindlin (Philadelphia, 1993). Isaac Klein, *A Guide to Jewish Religious Practice* (New York, 1979).

—PETER KNOBEL

V

VAKHNAKHT (Yi.; װאַכנאַכט; watch-night), the night before the circumcision, when relatives of the baby gather in its home to recite psalms in order to ward away *Lilith and other evil spirits. In certain communities, it is customary to give the guests a feast, including bread so that the Birkat ha-Mazon could be recited, though in other communities only wine and fruit are eaten. There is a difference of opinion as to whether this meal is to be recognized as a Se'udat Mitsvah (see SE'UDAH). In the time of R. Yitsḥaq Luria, the custom acquired a mystic significance. R. Ya'aqov Emden composed a special book of study for reading throughout the entire night. The custom is mentioned in the Talmud (*San.* 32b). Among Sephardi Jews, the night is called Midrash because a homily on the Bible portion of the week is given by a scholar. Various customs were observed in different communities; in Salonika, for example, the mother stayed awake all night.

• Avrohom Y. Bloch, *The Origin of Jewish Customs: The Jewish Child* (Brooklyn, N.Y., 1980).

VA-YEKHULLU (וַיְכֻלּוּ; And They Were Finished), opening word, serving also as the name, of the concluding paragraph of the Creation account in *Genesis* (2.1–3, "And the heaven and the earth were finished"). The verses are recited three times on Friday evenings: during the 'Amidah; after the 'Amidah; and in the *Qiddush at home. According to the Talmud, everyone who pronounces Va-Yekhullu on the Sabbath thereby becomes God's partner in creation (*Shab.* 119b).

• Macy Nulman, *The Encyclopedia of Jewish Prayer* (Northvale, N.J., and London, 1993), pp. 342–343.

VA-YIQRA'. See LEVITICUS, BOOK OF.

VA-YIQRA' RABBAH. See LEVITICUS RABBAH.

VEGETARIANISM. Although abstention from animal flesh was occasionally suggested for ascetic reasons, vegetarianism as a religious principle was never encouraged in the history of Judaism. Indeed, most of the *dietary laws deal with the specifications of permitted meats and their preparation, and the consumption of meat is considered one of the essential delights of the Sabbath and festivals. The very institution of sacrifice as the main element of cult and its connection with the consumption of meat imply a nonvegetarian culture. The biblical account (*Gn.* 1, 9), however, clearly implies that at the time of Creation humankind was vegetarian. Although humans were given dominion over the animal kingdom, only "every herb bearing seed . . . and every tree in which there is fruit" (*Gn.* 1.30) was granted to them for food. After the Deluge, the covenant with the second father of humanity, Noah, permitted "every moving thing that liveth . . . even as the green herb" (*Gn.* 9.3) while strictly prohibiting the consumption of *blood (*Gn.* 9.4). The ancient rabbis clearly regarded the killing of animals for human consumption as a privilege granted only because of our superior moral and intellectual faculties. This is expressed by the teaching of R. *Yehudah ha-Nasi' that "an *'am ha-'arets* [an ignoramus] should not eat meat" (*Pes.* 49a) and by the rabbis' definition of a "glutton" as one who eats an inordinate measure of meat (*San.* 70a). "Since there is no joy without meat" (*Pes.* 109a), its consumption is to be avoided in times of distress or mourning. Thus, meat should not be eaten following the death of a close relative until after the funeral and customarily should also be avoided during the nine-day period of national mourning culminating in Tish'ah be-'Av; the prohibition, however, does not extend to fish. It is also customary to eat dairy foods on Shavu'ot. Isaiah's prophecy that in messianic times "the lion shall eat straw like the ox" (*Is.* 11.7, 65.25) has been interpreted by some commentators as meaning that even the carnivorous animals would become vegetarians; others simply understand the prophecy as a metaphor for universal peace. See also ANIMALS, TREATMENT OF.

• Louis Arthur Berman, *Vegetarianism in the Jewish Tradition* (New York, 1982). Roberta Kalechofsky, *Rabbis and Vegetarianism: An Evolving Tradition* (Marblehead, Mass., 1995).

VE-HU' RAḤUM (וְהוּא רַחוּם; "And he, being merciful"), the opening words of *Psalms* 78.38 and a verse that occurs in the prayer book in two locations. It appears as the introduction to the weekday Ma'ariv service, dating from the late geonic period, where it is meant as a plea for forgiveness for sins committed during the day. It is also the opening of one of the *seliḥot*, known as the long version of Ve-Hu' Raḥum, recited before *Taḥanun on Mondays and Thursdays (see SHENI VA-ḤAMISHI), which is composed mainly of biblical verses.

VENGEANCE. Different attitudes toward vengeance are expressed in various biblical, rabbinic, moral, and legal texts; any particular attitude depends partly upon historical circumstances and partly upon whether vengeance appears as a divine or a human attribute. Such verses as "Vengeance is mine and I will repay" (*Dt.* 32.35) and "He will avenge the blood of his servants and will render vengeance unto his adversaries" (*Dt.* 44) show that vengeance is regarded as a divine prerogative and is part of the system of divine retribution whereby human injustice is corrected by divine justice. As a human act, vengeance is explicitly restricted. A Torah scholar is required to wreak vengeance in order to defend the honor of heaven (*Yoma'* 23a); however, "you shall not avenge, nor bear any grudge against the children of your people" (*Lv.* 19.18). The only exception to this rule was the law of the *blood avenger, the close relative of a person who had been killed through another's negligence. Even this type of vengeance was restricted by the provision of cities of refuge where the killer could live unharmed (see ASYLUM). The difference between inflicting vengeance and bearing a grudge is explained by the Talmud: If a man asks his neighbor to lend him an article and is refused, and on the next day that neighbor asks something of him, he should not say, "As you refused me yesterday, so I refuse you today," since that would constitute vengeance. If he says, "though you refused me a favor, I will not do likewise," he is bearing a grudge (*Yoma'* 23a). The virtue of the *ma'avir 'al middotav*, that is, one who forbears and suppresses natural emotions of wrath and vindictiveness, is highly praised. The Bible contains many examples of forbearance and abstention from vengeance as well as of savage revenge, one of the most well-known instances of the latter being the massacre of the inhabitants of Shechem by Simeon and Levi, an act that was denounced by Jacob both at the time (*Gn*. 34.30) and on his deathbed (*Gn*. 49.5–7).

• Yosef Karo, *Shulḥan 'Arukh* (Jerusalem, 1995). Dale Patrick, *Old Testament Law* (Atlanta, 1985). Hendrik George Peels, The Vengeance of God: The Meaning of the Root NQM and the Function of the NQM-Texts in the Context of Divine Revelation in the Old Testament (Leiden, 1995).

—SHMUEL HIMELSTEIN

VE-SHAMERU (וְשָׁמְרוּ; "And they shall keep"), first words of the verses (*Ex*. 31.16–17) recited before the 'Amidah in the Friday evening service and on Sabbaths during the morning service 'Amidah as well as in the Sabbath morning Qiddush. The passage describes the Sabbath as an eternal sign between God and Israel.

• Macy Nulman, *The Encyclopedia of Jewish Prayer* (Northvale, N.J., and London, 1993), pp. 355–356.

VESSELS, TEMPLE. See TEMPLE VESSELS.

VIDAL HA-TSAREFATI (c.1540–1617), rabbinic judge and author. He was born in Fez, where he served as head of the rabbinic court. His published works include a sermon book, *Tsuf Devash*; commentaries on *Esther, Ruth*, and *Psalms* called, respectively, *Megillat Setarim, Hatsa'at Rut*, and *Otsar Neḥmad*; and a commentary on *Sifra'* titled *Derekh ha-Qodesh*. Some of his work survives only in manuscript.

• Ḥayyim Yosef David Azulai, *Shem ha-Gedolim*, 2 vols. (repr. Brooklyn, N.Y., 1979). Jacob Toledano, *Sefer Ner ha-Ma'arav: Toledot 'Am Yisra'el be-Maroko* (Jerusalem, 1911; repr. Jerusalem, 1989).

—MICHAEL CHERNICK

VIDDUI. See 'AL ḤET'; ASHAMNU; CONFESSION.

VILNA GA'ON. See ELIYYAHU BEN SHELOMOH ZALMAN OF VILNA.

VIMPEL. See TORAH ORNAMENTS.

VIOLENCE. Jewish law recognizes that violence is a human instinct and seeks to control it. In the third and fourth centuries some rabbis opposed violence even to safeguard Jewish survival, but this was a minority view. The *halakhah* concentrates on limiting those circumstances that would justify violence. It condemned unwarranted forms of violence, including war for war's sake, sadism, masochism, fighting duels, or acts of vengeance. However, violence against an attacker (*rodef*) or informer (*moser*) is permitted, but the life of the *rodef* may not be taken if there is another way to save the person attacked (*San*. 74a). See also HOMICIDE; PEACE; WAR.

• Hannah Arendt, *On Violence* (New York, 1970). Salo Wittmayer Baron and George S. Wise et al., eds., *Violence and Defense in the Jewish Experience* (Philadelphia, 1977). Yeshayahu Leibowitz, *Judaism, Human Values, and the Jewish State*, edited by Eliezer Goldman (Cambridge, Mass., 1992).

VIRGINITY. In the Bible, virginity is an important element in marriage and a groom's accusation that his bride is not a virgin entails serious consequences of both a financial and a legal nature (*Dt*. 22.13–22). The seduction or rape of a virgin carries a monetary penalty, equal in value to the "bride price" (*Ex*. 22.15–16), and the man is required to marry the woman he deflowered. In the case of *rape, he also forfeits his right of divorce (*Dt*. 22.28–29). A *high priest is required to marry a virgin (*Lv*. 21.13) and the Talmudic discussion of whether or not a pregnant virgin is permitted to him (*Ḥag*. 14b) provides the basis for the modern halakhic discussion of artificial insemination by a donor. Under Talmudic law, only a virgin is entitled to the full *ketubbah* sum of two hundred *zuzim*. In the Talmudic period, weddings took place on Wednesday so that a groom who discovered that his bride had lost her virginity prior to the wedding could make his claim before the *beit din* on Thursday morning (*Ket*. 1.1). The Talmud recognizes that virginity may be lost by injury (*Ket*. 1.7). Women taken into captivity and bondswomen are assumed to have lost their virginity, as are all widows and divorcees. In such cases, the *ketubbah* sum is only a hundred *zuzim*.

• Menachem Elon, ed., *The Principles of Jewish Law* (Jerusalem, 1975), pp. 388ff. Louis Epstein, *Marriage Laws in the Bible and Talmud* (Cambridge, Mass., 1924). Ephraim Neufeld, *Ancient Hebrew Marriage Laws* (London, 1944), pp. 95–117.

—DANIEL SINCLAIR

VISIONS. The experience of beholding something with the "eyes of the spirit" may be sought or induced by mystical practices or be spontaneous and unexpected. Its contents may be terrestrial events removed in space (second sight) or time (foresight, prophecy) or spiritual realities and symbols. On the highest religious level, visions are experienced as God's *revelation to the prophets. Different categories of vision are implied in *Numbers* 12.6–8, where a distinction is made between the manner in which God revealed himself to Moses, speaking to him "mouth to mouth, plainly and not in riddles, and he beholds the likeness of the Lord," and his appearance to other prophets to whom he was to make himself known "in a vision, I speak with him in a dream." This may mean that the message of God came to other prophets in *dreams or trancelike states, whereas Moses was in full possession of normal cognitive faculties. The Bible often records visions, many of them theophanies; with some prophets (e.g., Ezekiel, Zechariah) they are more frequent than with others. The identification of visions with prophetic experiences seems to be implied by *1 Samuel* 3.1. Often the prophet received his calling in an initiatory vision (e.g., *Is*. 6). Visionary accounts, which often describe journeys to heaven by biblical personalities, abound in apocalyptic literature (see APOCALYPSE). According to the Talmud, most prophets beheld their visions "as in a cloudy mirror," thus accounting for a certain lack of clarity that often required verbal interpretation. Talmudic literature discusses prophetic vision but does not itself record visions. Visionary experiences were cultivated in mystical circles among the ancient rabbis, while the earliest mystical literature—*Heikhalot and Merkavah (see MAʿASEH MERKAVAH)—is devoted largely to visions of ascents to heaven and the celestial world. Many medieval writings discuss the nature of visions, although some more rationalist philosophers explained them as products of the imagination. Folkloric evidence suggests the widespread occurrence of and belief in visions (for example, in *Sefer Ḥasidim* and other works of the Ḥasidei Ashkenaz). Visions are frequently reported, at times in great detail, in the Zohar and subsequent kabbalistic literature. Somewhat different from visions were auditions, namely, inspired speech, when a celestial voice spoke through the human mouth (as in the cases of Yosef *Karo and Mosheh Ḥayyim *Luzzatto). Many Hasidic tales, some relating to the Baʿal Shem Tov, take visionary experiences for granted.

• Shoshanah Finkelshtain, *Ḥezyonot Tanakhiyyim* (Tel Aviv, 1981). Michael Lieb, *The Visionary Mode: Biblical Prophecy, Hermeneutics, and Cultural Change* (Ithaca, N.Y., 1991). Susan Niditch, *The Symbolic Vision in Biblical Tradition*, Harvard Semitic Monographs (Chico, Calif., 1983). Benedikt Otzen, "Heavenly Visions in Early Judaism," *Ahlstroem* (1984): 199–215. Rebecca Toueg, *Dreams and Visions in the Bible* (Tel Aviv, 1992).

VISITING THE SICK. See SICK, VISITING THE.

VITAL FAMILY, kabbalistic rabbis.

Ḥayyim Vital (1542–1620), the main disciple of R. Yitsḥaq *Luria in Safed. He probably was born in Safed and died in Damascus, where he spent his last years. He was ordained by his teacher Mosheh Alshekh following the reinstitution of the process of *ordination in Safed by R. Yaʿaqov Berab earlier in the century. When Luria came to Safed, Vital became his closest disciple, and after Luria's death, Vital made all the other members of Luria's group sign a contract forbidding them to study and write down Luria's teachings without his presence and supervision. He dedicated his life to the writing of Luria's Kabbalah in several editions, one of the most important ones being *ʿEts Ḥayyim* (Warsaw, 1890; Tel Aviv, 1960). Vital opposed the publication of this material, and, according to tradition, some manuscripts were stolen from his home and copied when he was sick. His writings, especially *ʿEts Ḥayyim*, served as the main text of kabbalistic studies for several centuries.

He regarded himself as the Messiah, even before Luria came to Safed. For several decades, he wrote a detailed diary, collecting material that would prove his messianic destiny. The diary, published as *Sefer ha-Ḥezyonot* (Jerusalem, 1954), was known in an abbreviated form as *Shivḥei ha-Raḥu* and was printed in several editions (Ostróg, 1826; Jerusalem, 1866). It includes the author's dreams concerning his destiny, dreams that others dreamed about him, revelations by sorcerers (including Muslims) about him, but mainly the information he received from Luria concerning the history of the various parts of his soul and their transmigration from the Creation until they reached him as the soul of the Messiah.

Shemu'el ben Ḥayyim Vital (1598–c.1678), youngest son of Ḥayyim. Born in Safed, he was brought up in Damascus, where he became an authority in Talmudic studies. His main literary contribution to Lurianic Kabbalah was the reediting of his father's *ʿEts Ḥayyim*, dividing it into eight parts and adding his own annotations. In 1664 he settled in Cairo, maintaining close contacts with the wealthy head of the Jewish community, the *chelebi*, Refa'el Yosef. In 1666, at the onset of Shabbateanism, Vital played an active role in organizing the repentance movement led by *Natan of Gaza. Shemu'el's writings on Talmudic and kabbalistic subjects are still in manuscript.

• **Ḥayyim Vital:** Lawrence B. Fine, "Techniques of Mystical Meditation for Achieving Prophecy and the Holy Spirit in the Teachings of Isaac Luria and Hayyim Vital," Ph.D. dissertation, Brandeis University, 1975. Ronit Meroz, "Faithful Transmission Versus Innovation: Luria and His Disciples," in *Gershom Scholem's Major Trends in Jewish Mysticism Fifty Years After*, edited by Peter Schäfer and Joseph Dan (Tübingen, 1993), pp. 257–274. Gershom Gerhard Scholem, *Kabbalah* (Jerusalem, 1974), pp. 443–448. **Shemu'el ben Ḥayyim Vital:** J. Avivi, "Kitvei Rabbi Ḥayyim Vital be-Qabbalat ha-'Ari," *Moriah* 10.7–8 (1981): 77–91. Gershom Gerhard Scholem, *Sabbatai Sevi: The Mystical Messiah, 1626–1676* (Princeton, 1973), *passim*. —JOSEPH DAN AND NISSIM YOSHA

VIZHNITZ, Hasidic dynasty established by R. Menaḥem Mendel of Kosov, the son of a disciple of the Baʿal Shem Tov. The name derives from the town of Vizhnitz, in the Ukraine, which served as the home of the rabbis of the dynasty. Due to ideological differences, the dynasty is divided between two grand rabbis, one in Israel and the other in Monsey, New York. Grand Rabbi Mosheh Yehoshuʿa Hagar resides in Qiryat Vizhnitz, Israel, a virtually self-sufficient town south of Bene Beraq. A smaller segment of Vizhnitz Ḥasidim owes its allegiance to Grand Rabbi Mordkhe Hagar, who resides in the New York City area. Vizhnitz has established institutions throughout Israel and, besides New York, has a presence in London, Manchester, Antwerp, Vienna, Zurich, and Montreal.

• Janet Belcove-Shalin, ed., *New World Hasidim: Ethnographic Studies of Hasidic Jews in North America* (Albany, N.Y., 1995). Tzvi M. Rabinowicz, *Hasidism: The Movement and Its Masters* (Northvale, N.J., 1988). —WILLIAM SHAFFIR

VOCALIZATION. The Hebrew *alphabet, like other Semitic alphabets, is entirely consonantal, and for the traditional pronunciation of a biblical word it is necessary to rely on its vowel points as recorded at a rather late date by the Masoretes (see MASORAH). Early sources of the biblical text, such as the Qumran texts, are not vocalized. The main function of the vocalization was to remove doubts regarding the reading of the text when this allowed for more than one interpretation. It was also a necessary component of the Masoretic Text, since this text was sparing in its use of *matres lectionis*. In texts that made abundant use of *matres lectionis*, such as some of the Qumran scrolls, there was less need for vocalization. The earliest method used to indicate vocalization was the insertion of vowel letters in the consonantal text. This method was superseded by a full system of vocalization through punctuation. Although both Jewish and Christian traditions believed in the divine origin of vocalization, it was first introduced after the conclusion of the Talmudic period; Saʿadyah ben Yosef Ga'on (882–942) is the first to mention it. Three main systems of vocalization were developed, sometime between 500 and 700. These are the Tiberian vocalization, with vowel points mainly below the letters, and Palestinian and Babylonian vocalization, with vowel signs above the consonants. In the course of time, one subgroup of the Tiberian system, that of Aharon ben Mosheh ben Asher (see BEN ASHER FAMILY), came to be generally accepted. As a result, this system became the basis for most manuscripts and subsequently all Bible editions, although manuscripts written in the Babylonian and Palestinian supralinear systems were also prevalent for a time in the Middle Ages. In general, Hebrew manuscripts and books are not vocalized, except for certain texts for beginners.

• Paul Kahle, *The Cairo Geniza*, 2d ed. (Oxford, 1959). Shelomo Morag, *Vocalized Talmud Manuscripts in the Cambridge Genizah Collections*, vol. 1 (Cambridge, 1988). Ziony Zevit, *Matres Lectionis in Ancient Hebrew Epigraphs* (Cambridge, Mass., 1980).

VOLOZHIN, town in Lithuania, seat of a famous **yeshivah* established in 1803 by R. Ḥayyim ben Yitsḥaq *Volozhiner, disciple of *Eliyyahu ben Shelomoh Zalman of Vilna, the Vilna Ga'on. This was a time of bitter strife between the Ḥasidim and the Mitnaggedim. The Ḥasidim appeared to be gaining the upper hand among *yeshivah* students, largely as a reaction to the unpopular **pilpul* method then in use. To replace this method, the Volozhin Yeshivah insisted on stressing the study of the text itself and ascertaining its true meaning. Rabbi Ḥayyim was succeeded by his son, Yitsḥaq, who, in turn, was succeeded by his son-in-law, R. Naftali Tsevi Yehudah *Berlin, under whose leadership the *yeshivah* rose to its greatest fame, with four hundred students. The Volozhin Yeshivah was the spiritual forerunner of the entire Lithuanian *yeshivah* movement, and many of its students were later involved in founding and staffing some of the other *yeshivot* in that country. The Russian authorities made efforts over the years to force the Volozhin Yeshivah to close, but in most cases, such closure orders were simply ignored, and the *yeshivah* continued to function. It was closed by the czarist government in 1879; it reopened in 1881, but was closed again in 1892, partially due to pressure upon the Russian authorities by some of the *yeshivah* students who had been influenced by the *Haskalah and wished to force the *yeshivah* to change its educational system. The ultimate reason for the closure was the *yeshivah*'s refusal to introduce secular studies. It was reopened in 1899 but did not reattain its position of eminence. It was destroyed by the Germans in World War II, when all sixty-four of its students were killed.

• Elieser Leoni, ed., *Volozin: Sifrah shel ha-ʿIr ve-shel Yeshivat "'Ets Ḥayyim"* (Tel Aviv, 1970). Moshe Z. Neriah, *Pirqei Volozin* (Jerusalem, 1964). Yonason Rosenblum, *Reb Chaim of Volozhin: The Life and Ideals of the Visionary "Father of Yeshivos"* (Brooklyn, N.Y., 1993).

—SHMUEL HIMELSTEIN

VOLOZHINER, ḤAYYIM BEN YITSḤAQ (1749–1821), rabbi and educator. At age twenty-five he became the disciple of *Eliyyahu ben Shelomoh Zalman, the Vilna Ga'on, whom he eventually succeeded as spiritual leader of the *Mitnaggedim in eastern Europe. In 1773 he was appointed rabbi of Volozhin, Lithuania. Sharing the Vilna Ga'on's sentiments against Hasidism and against the technique of argumentation popular in *yeshivot*, R. Ḥayyim founded the *Volozhin Yeshivah, in 1803, in which he stressed the examination of the plain meaning of the Talmud and introduced secular subjects. The archetype for future Talmudic academies, it was later named ʿEts Ḥayyim in his honor. *Nefesh ha-Ḥayyim* (1824), his most important work, challenges Hasidism and emphasizes *Torah li-shemah*, "Torah study for its own sake."

• Norman Lamm, *Torah li-Shemah: Torah for Torah's Sake in the Works of Rabbi Hayyim of Volozhin and His Contemporaries* (Hoboken, N.J., 1989). Yonason Rosenblum, *Reb Chaim of Volozhin* (Brooklyn, N.Y., 1993).

—DENNIS M. DREYFUS

VOWS AND OATHS, solemn affirmations (oaths) and promises to perform, or abstain from, specific actions (vows). The line separating oaths and vows in Jewish law is not always clearly drawn (cf. the opening of *Kol Nidrei: "All vows, bonds, oaths, anathemas, excommunications," etc.), particularly since swearing to do a certain thing is tantamount to a vow.

Vows (*nedarim*) may be divided into two categories, positive and negative. The former is a solemn undertaking or pledge to consecrate something to God or to do something in his honor; the latter, called an *issar*, is the voluntary abstention from an otherwise legitimate activity or enjoyment. *Nedavah* is the pledging or consecration of a designated gift to God; the destruction or theft of the article or the death of the consecrated animal nullifies the vow. The vow, which must be made voluntarily and in full consideration of its implications, becomes effective upon utterance, and its violation constitutes a transgression of the prohibition "he shall not profane his word" (*Nm.* 30.33). A *neder* or *nedavah* must be fulfilled before the *Shalosh Regalim have passed, lest the prohibition against laxity in the fulfillment of vows be infringed (*Dt.* 23.22). Vows were usually made in times of distress, as in the case of Jacob (*Gn.* 28.20–22), or as an expression of thanksgiving for favors and kindnesses received (cf. *Ps.* 116.16–18). Vows were also undertaken as a sign of penitence or to free oneself from severe temptation (*Avot* 3.17). In matters affecting the physical wellbeing of one's wife or the relationship between husband and wife, a husband may void the vows of his wife on the day he hears them (*hafarah*); he may also void the vows of his unmarried daughters (*Nm.* 30ff.). After careful examination of the circumstances surrounding the making of a vow, a competent *beit din* may nullify it and absolve the vower (*hattarah*). There must exist, however, reasonable grounds for such nullification. It is customary to nullify vows (except those contracted between man and man) before the advent of the High Holy Days. The Talmud's attitude toward the making of vows is generally negative: "He who makes a vow, though he fulfills it, is called wicked" (*Ned.* 22a) or "For sins arising from unfulfilled vows, children die" (*Shab.* 32b). Vows are the subject of tractate **Nedarim*.

An oath taken in vain, forbidden by the Ten Commandments ("You shall not swear by my name falsely" [*Lv.* 19.12]), is one which attempts to deny a self-evident fact or attempts to affirm a self-evident fact or involves one in undertaking the impossible or is directed against the fulfillment of a religious precept. In each of these instances, the oath, which has no validity or effect, is punishable upon utterance. One must also bring a guilt offering, "for the Lord will not hold him guiltless who takes his name in vain" (*Ex.* 20.7). Taking God's name in vain is the greatest sacrilege, since the basic notion of an oath is the total submission of one's words, thoughts, deeds, in fact one's entire personality, to the judgment of God. An oath is only administered in a court of law when other evidence has proved inadequate. An oath, to be valid, may be uttered in any language, and no mention of any of the names of God need be made. An oath may, in certain circumstances, be undertaken for the purpose of strengthening one's moral character and observance or to rid one's self of bad habits, but the taking of oaths, like that of vows, is discouraged in Judaism. An exception is the practice of vowing to make a contribution to a synagogue on the occasion of being called to the reading of the Torah. This is publicly announced with a blessing for the person who has vowed (*she-nadar*); in Yiddish the practice became known as *shnodder*.

• Tony W. Cartledge, *Vows in the Hebrew Bible and the Ancient Near East* (Sheffield, Eng., 1992). Yosef Karo, *Shulḥan ʿArukh* (Jerusalem, 1995). Dale Patrick, *Old Testament Law* (Atlanta, 1985). Lawrence H. Schiffman, "Laws of Vows and Oaths in the Zadokite Fragments and the Temple Scroll," *Revue de Qumran* 15 (1991–1992): 199–214.

VULGATE. See Bible Translations.

W

WAGES, the fee paid for *labor or service. In the Bible, the employer is strictly enjoined to pay such fees without delay upon completion of the labor or service: "The wages of a hired man shall not abide with you all night until morning" (*Lv.* 19.13). The Talmud explains that one hired for the day is to be paid not later than the next morning; one hired for the night, by the following evening (see *Dt.* 24.15). One who withholds such wages transgresses several biblical prohibitions. Crediting the laborer at a shop or bank is considered due payment, but, in order to protect the laborer against possible exploitation in the form of inferior merchandise at inflated prices, payment in kind is strictly forbidden. The terms of hire do not require witnesses or a *qinyan* (see ACQUISITION) in order to bind the parties. When doubt arises concerning the terms, the custom of the place and trade is to be followed. Payment of substandard wages is forbidden as part of the prohibition against oppressing the hired man (*Dt.* 24.14). Workers drafted by the government in times of emergency or war are to be paid fair wages, and even prisoners of war are to receive due compensation if made to work. The coming of the **shemittah* (in which all debts are cancelled) does not affect wages due.

• Yosef Karo, *Shulḥan 'Arukh* (Jerusalem, 1995). Dale Patrick, *Old Testament Law* (Atlanta, 1985). Edward Zipperstein, *Business Ethics in Jewish Law* (New York, 1983).

WAILING WALL. See WESTERN WALL.

WALDENBERG, ELI'EZER YEHUDAH (1917-), rabbinic scholar; *dayyan* at the rabbinical court in Jerusalem and later at the High Rabbinical Court of Appeal. He has written numerous books and articles in all fields of *halakhah*, though he is probably best known for his decisions on controversial medical issues, for example, questions of men's and women's fertility, abortion, transplanting organs, euthanasia, autopsies, and medical experimentation. In addition to his halakhic work *Hilkhot Medinah* (3 vols. [1952–1955]), his writings include *novellae, Divrei Eli'ezer* (1935), and *responsa, Tsits Eli'ezer* (20 vols. [1945–1994]).

• Avraham Steinberg, ed. and comp., *Jewish Medical Law*, translated by David B. Simons (Jerusalem, 1980). —ELIAV SHOCHETMAN

WANDERING JEW, one of the most popular themes in Christian folklore. It is expressed in numerous forms, including prose and poetry, plays, visual art, music, folktales, linguistic idioms, and even in the names of plants and birds. The theme is based on the legend of a cobbler in Jerusalem who refused Jesus a moment of rest next to the wall of his house along the road to the Crucifixion. Because of this, the cobbler was cursed with eternal wandering until Jesus' Second Coming. This oral legend was first published in 1602, in Germany, in a popular pamphlet written by an unknown author from Martin Luther's circle and entitled *Kurtze Beschreibung und Erzehlung von einem Juden mit Namen Ahasverus*. The legend developed from two sources in the New Testament (*Jn.* 18.22 and 20.22–23; see also *Mt.* 16.28). The Wandering Jew appears in different forms in different European traditions, ranging from a poor wanderer asking for water, whose visit means blessing; to a romantic rebel; to a demonic, inhuman figure, who causes disaster and death wherever he goes. As a symbol of the Jewish people, the Wandering Jew was the basis for antisemitic conceptions, including Nazi propaganda.

• George K. Anderson, *The Legend of the Wandering Jew* (Hanover, N.H., 1965). Roland Auguet, *Le Juif errant: Genèse d'une légende* (Paris, 1977). Joseph Gaer, *The Legend of the Wandering Jew* (New York, 1961). Galit Hasan-Rokem and Alan Dundes, eds., *The Wandering Jew: Essays in the Interpretation of a Christian Legend* (Bloomington, Ind., 1986). —TAMAR ALEXANDER

WAR. In biblical times, nations believed that their armies were led by their gods, and the Israelites, too, conceived of God as a man of war (*Ex.* 5.3; *Is.* 42.13) who led their battalions (*Ps.* 68.8). To symbolize the divine presence, the *Ark of the Covenant was carried onto the battlefield (*Nm.* 10.35–36; *1 Sm.* 14.18). Because God could not be conquered, any defeat was ascribed to the faithlessness of the Israelites. The laws of war presented in *Deuteronomy* 20.1–21 were further developed by rabbinic exegesis (*Sot.* 8), the authors of which had no practical experience of warfare. Different categories of war are distinguished: *milḥemet ḥovah* (obligatory war), regarded by some authorities as identical with *milḥemet mitsvah* (war commanded by God); and *milḥemet reshut* (permitted war). To the former category belong the wars of the extermination of the seven Canaanite nations and wars to defend the territorial integrity of Erets Yisra'el. A *milḥemet mitsvah* could be declared by the king alone, and the various exemptions detailed in *Deuteronomy* 20.5–8 are suspended. To wage such a war, one could take "even the bridegroom from his chamber and the bride from her bridal canopy" (*Sot.* 8.7; the phrase is from *Jl.* 2.16 and may be hyperbolic—there is no reference in Jewish literature to women soldiers). A permitted war could be declared only by the Sanhedrin and was subject to the application of the exemptions from conscription detailed in the Torah. Various concessions, such as permission to make free use of fuel, to disregard the dietary laws, and to eat doubtfully tithed produce, were made to soldiers. A vivid account of an apocalyptic war, probably based on contemporary military experience, is contained in one of the Dead Sea Scrolls, the **War Scroll*. The biblical and rabbinic laws of warfare are systematically presented in Maimonides' *Hilkhot Melakhim* 6–8.

In modern times, scholars debated whether Jews could serve in non-Jewish armies in wars that did not directly affect Jews. The majority decided that the principle of **dina' de-malkhuta' dina'* (the laws of the country are to be observed) implied the obligation of Jews to serve in the armies of the countries of which they were citizens.

In the State of Israel, a military rabbinate issues halakhic directives concerning the religious obligations of soldiers.

• David R. Elcott, *Power, War and Peace in Jewish Tradition* (New York, 1991). Yigael Yadin, *The Art of Warfare in Biblical Lands in the Light of Archaeological Study*, 2 vols. (Jerusalem, 1963). Yigael Yadin, *The Scroll of the War of the Sons of Light against the Sons of Darkness* (Oxford, 1962).

WARD. See GUARDIAN.

WARNING. According to Talmudic law, a man could not be sentenced to capital or corporal punishment for a crime unless he had received a specific warning (*hatra'ah*) beforehand not to commit that crime. The object of this legislation was to ensure that a person sentenced to extreme penalties was being punished for a misdeed committed willfully and not accidentally or in ignorance. Should the judges in such cases consider that the deed had been done willfully but no special caution had been issued, the sentence was generally reduced to one of imprisonment.

• Yosef Karo, *Shulḥan ʿArukh* (Jerusalem, 1995).

WAR SCROLL, an eschatological text of the *Dead Sea Scrolls describing the battle between the armies of God and Belial. The first manuscript, 1QM (Cave 1, 1947), which is the most complete, consists of nineteen badly mutilated columns, while six other fragmentary manuscripts were found in Cave 4 in 1951. The manuscripts range in date from the first half of the first century BCE to the middle of the first century CE. The suggested date of composition ranges from the Hasmonean to the late Herodian periods (the latter appears impossible).

The *War Scroll* describes the final battle at the End of Days that will take place between the Sons of Light, including an army of angels led by Michael and the Qumran sect itself, and the Sons of Darkness, headed by Belial and including apostate Jews, the nations of the world as listed in *Genesis* 10, and the Kittim of Asshur. It is a composite document, with column 1, verses 15–19, describing the war against the Kittim, columns 2 through 9 describing a war forty years in length, and columns 10 through 14 containing miscellaneous hymns and prayers. The scroll is particularly concerned with the correct conduct of the army and the purity of the camp, leading to some definite impracticalities in conducting a war. For example, warriors are said to be between forty and fifty years of age, while baggage handlers are said to be between twenty-five and thirty. The scroll was published by Yigael Yadin in *The Scroll of the War of the Sons of Light Against the Sons of Darkness* (English ed. [Oxford, 1962]).

• Maurice Baillet, *Qûmran Grotte 4, III*, Discoveries in the Judaean Desert, vol. 7 (Oxford, 1982), pp. 12–72. Philip Davies, *1QM, The War Scroll from Qumran: Its Structure and History*, Biblica et Orientalia 32 (Rome, 1977). Jean Duhaime, "The 'War Scroll' from Qumran and the Greco-Roman Tactical Treatises," *Revue de Qûmran* 12.1–4 (1988): 133–151.

–SIDNIE WHITE CRAWFORD

WARS OF THE LORD, BOOK OF THE. See BOOK OF THE WARS OF THE LORD.

WASHING. See ABLUTION.

WATER plays an important role in biblical cosmogony and history, while the cleansing and refreshing properties of water guarantee it a prominent place both in the symbolism and in the rituals of religion. It was on the second day of Creation that God made a firmament dividing the waters above from the waters below, which he gathered into the seas and separated from the dry land, the Earth (*Gn.* 1.6–11). Water rights led to a conflict between Abraham and Abimelech (*Gn.* 21.25), while lack of water in the Sinai wilderness led the Israelites to speak against Moses (*Ex.* 15.22–25, 17.1–7; *Nm.* 20.1–13). Biblical and rabbinic law prescribe *ablutions and immersions for various occasions (see MIQVEH), for example, the washing of one's hands before (and after) meals and the ritual bath taken by married women (see NIDDAH). On the other hand, the *halakhah* (based on *Lv.* 11.38) rules that plants are not susceptible to ritual contamination until they come into contact with water. The most spectacular ceremonial use of water was at the annual rite of water *libation, preceded by the solemn drawing of the water that was held on *Sukkot against the opposition of the Sadducees, who maintained that there was no scriptural authority for the ritual (see SIMḤAT BEIT HA-SHO'EVAH). In the *aggadah*, water is regarded as a symbol of the Torah (e.g., *Taʿan.* 7a, based on *Is.* 55.1).

• Raphael Patai, *Ha-Mayim* (Tel Aviv, 1936). Philippe Reymond, *L'Eau, sa vie et sa signification dans l'Ancien Testament* (Leiden, 1958).

WATER DRAWING, REJOICING OF. See SIMḤAT BEIT HA-SHO'EVAH.

WAVE OFFERING (Heb. *tenufah* [elevation]). According to the Torah, a number of sacrificial offerings were required to be presented to God by means of a ritual symbolizing the transfer of ownership from the offerer to the deity. Rabbinic authorities understood the presentation ritual to consist of waving the offering back and forth (see *Men.* 5.6), and this became normative Jewish practice. However, the term *elevation*, also known from ancient times as well as from the depiction of the rite in an ancient Egyptian relief, would seem closer to the biblical usage. The most familiar such offering is the annual *ʿ*omer* barley sheaf offered on 16 Nisan (*Lv.* 23.11–14); the others are the breast of the *peace offering, given to the priest (*Lv.* 7.30); the *reparation offering and purification oil of the healed leper (*Lv.* 14.12–14); the *meal offering of the suspected adulteress (*Nm.* 5.25; see ORDEAL OF JEALOUSY); and certain portions of the offering of the *Nazirite (*Nm.* 6.20). During the Israelites' wilderness period, the metals for the building of the Tabernacle (*Ex.* 35.22) and a portion of the priestly consecration offering (*Lv.* 8.25–29) were reported to have been similarly dedicated. It is also related that the Levites were dedicated to the service of the Tabernacle as a human *tenufah* (*Nm.* 8.11ff.); presumably in this case the ritual was performed symbolically. See also TERUMAH.

• Baruch Levine, *Numbers 1–20*, The Anchor Bible (New York, 1993), pp. 273–279. Jacob Milgrom, *Numbers*, The JPS Torah Commentary (Philadelphia, 1990), pp. 425–426. Jacob Milgrom, "The Tenufah," in *Studies in Cultic Theology Terminology* (Leiden, 1983), pp. 138–158.
—BARUCH J. SCHWARTZ

WEALTH. Differences in wealth and the existence of *poverty are assumed already in the Bible as social realities that need to be mitigated by appropriate legislation and the application of social ethics. The acquisition of wealth by unjust means is among the main themes of prophetic denunciation. Wealth is a blessing from God but also a moral danger (cf. *Jer*. 9.22, "let not the rich man glory in his riches"), though the author of *Proverbs* 14.20 was realistic enough to note "the poor is hated even of his neighbor; but the rich have many friends." The rabbis did not glorify wealth. In their moral teachings they defined as rich he "who is happy with what he has" (*Avot* 4.1).

• Leo Jung, *Business Ethics in Jewish Law* (New York, 1987). Joel Soffin, "The Rabbinic View of Wealth and Poverty," rabbinic thesis, Hebrew Union College, 1976. Meir Tamari, *The Challenge of Wealth: A Jewish Perspective on Earning and Spending Money* (Northvale, N.J., 1995). Harold C. Washington, *Wealth and Poverty in the Instruction of Amenemope and the Hebrew Proverbs* (Atlanta, 1994). Max Weber, *Ancient Judaism*, edited and translated by Hans H. Gerth and Don Martindale (New York, 1967).

WEDDING. See BETROTHAL.

WEEKS, FESTIVAL OF. See SHAVU'OT.

WEIL, YA'AQOV BEN YEHUDAH (died c.1456), German rabbi. A student of R. Ya'aqov ben Mosheh ha-Levi Molin, Weil was one of the leading halakhic authorities of his generation. He served as rabbi in Nürnberg, Augsburg, Bamberg, and Erfurt. His literary works include his volume of *responsa* (Venice, 1523), which he edited himself, and *Hilkhot Sheḥitah u-Vediqah* (Venice, 1549), a summary of some of the more important laws surrounding ritual slaughter, along with a brief but substantive commentary. Its selection of topics and its comparative brevity suggest that the latter volume was intended as a practical guide for the *shoḥet* rather than as a theoretical work for legal scholars.

• Yedidya Dinari, *Ḥakhmei Ashkenaz be-Shelhei Yemei ha-Beinayim* (Jerusalem, 1984).
—MARK WASHOFSKY

WEINBERG, YEḤI'EL YA'AQOV (1885–1966), rabbi and halakhic authority. He was born in Lithuania, studied at the *yeshivot* of Mir and Slobodka, and was appointed rabbi of Pilwishki in 1907. He later moved to Germany and obtained his doctorate at the University of Giessen. He taught Talmud and became head of the Berlin Rabbinical Seminary. During the Holocaust, he was interned in several concentration camps. After the war, he settled in Montreux, Switzerland.

Weinberg became internationally known as a halakhic authority whose *responsa*, collected in *Seridei Esh* (4 vols. [1961–1969]), were highly influential among Orthodox Jews. He was particularly known for his analysis of contemporary issues in *halakhah*. He also published collections of his essays, in Hebrew and German, and studies in Talmudic literature.

• *Sefer ha-Zikkaron le-Morenu . . . Yeḥiel Ya'aqov Vainberg, Rosh Beit ha-Midrash le-Rabbanim be-Berlin* (Jerusalem, 1969). A. Soreski in *Et Aḥai Anokhi Mevaqqesh*, edited by Yeḥi'el Weinberg (Bene Beraq, 1966), pp. 17–42.
—IRA ROBINSON

WEISS, ISAAC HIRSCH (1815–1905), Talmudic scholar and historian. Born in Moravia, he settled in 1861 in Vienna, where from 1864 he taught at the Vienna Rabbinical Seminary. While opposing extreme Orthodoxy and Reform, he sought to combine thorough Talmudic scholarship with scientific methodology. Weiss published *Sifra'* (1862) and *Mekhilta'* (1865), and his outstanding *Dor Dor ve-Dorshav* (1871–1891), a five volume history of oral tradition from earliest times until after the Spanish expulsion of 1492, incorporates biographies of the main rabbis of the Talmudic period. This was a pioneering work in the critical analysis of rabbinic sources and dealt with the development of both the *halakhah* and *aggadah*. The book was frequently reprinted and was widely read, especially in eastern Europe.

• Louis Ginzberg, *Students, Scholars, and Saints* (New York, 1958), pp. 217–240. Solomon Schechter, *Studies in Judaism*, 1st ser. (Philadelphia, 1911), pp. 182–212.

WERBERMACHER, HANNAH RAKHEL (1815–c.1895), Hasidic master. Born in Vladimir, she became noted as, perhaps, the only woman to found her own Hasidic group. Possessed of an unusually refined spiritual nature, given over to ecstatic worship, she acquired a traditional rabbinic education. A mystical experience at her mother's grave left Werbermacher, after a protracted illness, spiritually transformed. She subsequently built her own *beit midrash* in Ludomir. Secluded in a private room, she would offer teachings and blessings to her followers from behind the closed door. She also, it seems, occasionally traveled to other towns to preach, in some cases, especially for women. Her success as a *rebbi* was not well received by male *tsaddiqim*. Mordekhai of Chernobyl expressed the view that a famous male *tsaddiq*'s soul must have transmigrated into her. He felt that the appropriate remedy was marriage. Although she tried marriage several times, none was consummated. Nevertheless, as a married woman, her Hasidic following diminished. She spent the last years of her life in Erets Yisra'el, involved in kabbalistic endeavors.

• Ada Rapoport-Albert, "On Women and Hasidism: S. A. Horodecky and the Maid of Ludmir Tradition," in *Jewish History: Essays in Honour of Chimen Abramsky*, edited by Ada Rapoport-Albert and S. Zipperstein (London, 1988). Samuel A. Horodezky, *Leaders of Hassidism* (London, 1928).
—MILES KRASSEN

WESTERN WALL (Heb. Kotel Ma'aravi), the western side of the supporting wall of the Temple mount constructed by Herod and in recent centuries the main site of Jewish *pilgrimage; known in the writings of Christian travelers as the Wailing Wall. The earliest layers, consisting of large blocks measuring five feet in length by one foot high (some weighing over one hundred tons), date from Herod's reconstruction of the Second Temple in the first century BCE. On top of them is a layer built during the reign of Hadrian (2d cent. CE), and above it, Arab masonry. As a surviving remnant of the Temple, the wall is mentioned in *midrashim* of the amoraic period; it was not destroyed and never will be because the divine presence rests there (*Ex. Rab.* 2.2; *Lam. Rab.* 1.31). It is mentioned in medieval accounts by travelers who, however, ascribed no special sanctity to it. It became a focus of prayer in the sixteenth century, and feeling for the wall deepened in the early nineteenth century when it became part of the growing national consciousness and featured in literature and art. It began to play a major role in religion and folklore starting in the early twentieth century: worshipers lit candles there and placed petitions in the cracks of the wall. The proximity of the wall to the Muslim holy site of the Ḥaram al-Sharif led to outbursts of friction between Jews and Muslims. During the period of Jordanian rule (1948–1967), Israelis were not allowed to visit the wall and few Jews reached it. After it came under Israeli control in the 1967 Six-Day War, the Israelis expanded the narrow strip in front of the Wall, where Jews had until then been allowed to pray, into a large plaza. The area became the site of mass pilgrimages and prayers. The Orthodox rabbinate put up a fence separating men and women. The site became a favorite place for *bar mitsvah* celebrations of boys from both Israel and the Diaspora, army swearing-in ceremonies, and other national and religious gatherings. Since 1967 intensive excavations have been conducted along the entire length of the wall and have exposed many (now subterranean) structures. See also HOLY PLACE; TEMPLE MOUNT.

• M. Ben-Dov, *The Western Wall* (New York, 1983). Moshe A. Druck, ed., *Western Wall*, 3d ed. (Tel Aviv, 1972). Menahem Kasher, *The Western Wall: Its Meaning in the Thought of the Sages* (New York, 1972). Abraham M. Luncz, *Netivot Tsiyyon vi-Yerushalayim: Ha-Kotel ha-Maʿaravi* (Jerusalem, 1979).

WHOLE OFFERING. See BURNT OFFERING.

WIDOW. The obligation to support the widow (often classified together with the *orphan) is a pervasive biblical theme, and the punishment of one who mistreats a widow is dire in the extreme (*Ex.* 22.21). A widow is permitted to marry anyone except a high priest (*Lv.* 21.12), provided that she does not require *ḥalitsah* from her brother-in-law (see LEVIRATE MARRIAGE) and is not in breach of the prohibited relationships imposed upon her by virtue of her previous marriage. While she does not inherit from her husband, she may claim her **ketubbah*, which must be paid out of his estate (*Ket.* 68b). A widow's right to the *ketubbah* lies against all her husband's assets, both movable and immovable, and also against immovable property transferred to third parties (*Ket.* 51a). It has been customary, since the time of Maimonides, to include a clause to this effect in the *ketubbah* (*Laws of Marriage* 16.8). The widow may, however, choose to be maintained out of her husband's estate and maintenance includes the right to occupy the matrimonial home. The heirs are entitled to receive any earnings gained by the widow, in lieu of the maintenance (*Shulḥan ʿArukh, Even ha-ʿEzer* 95.1). The widow's right to maintenance ceases upon payment of the *ketubbah* or upon remarriage (*Ket.* 54a). The Talmud records diverse customs with regard to whether or not the heirs can unilaterally decide to pay the widow her *ketubbah* and thereby relieve themselves of the burden of her maintenance (*Ket.* 52b, 54a). The *halakhah* was decided in favor of the widow, although it is possible to make a *taqqanah* for the purpose of limiting her choice in circumstances in which not to do so would give rise to an injustice (*Shulḥan ʿArukh, Even ha-ʿEzer*, no. 118). In this respect there is a difference between the Sephardi and Ashkenazi communities in Erets Yisra'el. The former follow the Talmudic position and give the widow the right to choose between *ketubbah* and maintenance. The latter allow the heirs to pay her the *ketubbah* even if she would prefer to be maintained.

• Judah D. Eisenstein, ed., *Otsar Yisra'el* (Jerusalem, 1951), vol. 2, pp. 50–51. Menachem Elon, *Jewish Law: History, Sources, Principles*, 4 vols. (Philadelphia, 1994), pp. 296–297, 1679–1680. Menachem Elon, ed., *The Principles of Jewish Law* (Jerusalem, 1975), pp. 399–403.

—DANIEL SINCLAIR

WIFE. See MATRIMONY.

WIGS (Yi. *sheitlakh*; sing. *sheitl*). In Talmudic times, wigs were worn by women for adornment or to hide a lack of hair. The Talmud forbids the exposure of loose hair in the street by married women (even citing this as grounds for divorce), saying "the hair of a woman is unchaste" (*Ber.* 24a), but the rigid development of this regulation—whereby a woman shaves off her hair at marriage and thereafter never appears in public without a wig—dates only from the fifteenth century. In some Orthodox circles, married women cover their hair with wigs. See also COVERING OF THE HEAD.

• Louis M. Epstein, *Sex Laws and Customs in Judaism* (New York, 1948), pp. 46–55. S. Krauss, "The Jewish Rite of Covering the Head," in *Beauty in Holiness: Studies in Jewish Customs and Ceremonial Art*, compiled by Joseph Gutmann (New York, 1970). Ruth Whitman, "Cutting the Jewish Bride's Hair," in *Images of Women in Literature*, edited by Mary Anne Ferguson (Boston, 1991).

WILL, FREE. See FREE WILL.

WILLOW (Heb. *ʿaravah* [*Is.* 15.7; *Ps.* 137.2] or *ʿarvei naḥal* [*Lv.* 23.40; *Jb.* 40.32]), *salix*, which grows abundantly in Erets Yisra'el. Willows of the brook were required on *Sukkot for the *four species. Willows growing in the vicinity of Jerusalem (at Motsa') were picked for the adornment of the altar on the feast day, and branches were carried at the **haqqafot* circuits. They were called **hoshaʿnot* after the responsive refrain of the ceremony. The shaking of willow twigs and shower of leaves (*ḥibbut ʿaravah*) on *Hoshaʿna' Rabbah give a symbolic expression to the prayer for rain (see TEFILLAT GESHEM).

• Jehuda Feliks, *'Olam ha-Tsomeaḥ ha-Miqra'i* (n.p., 1968): 113–115. Immanuel Loew, *Die Flora der Juden*, vol. 3 (Vienna, 1924–1934), pp. 323–337. Hayim Shoys, *Guide to Jewish Holy Days* (New York, 1938). Yehiel M. Stern, *Kashrut Arba'at ha-Minim* (Jerusalem, 1992), pp. 107–133. Eliyahu Weisfisch, *Sefer Arba'at ha-Minim ha-Shalem* (Jerusalem, 1975), pp. 39–49. Michael Zohary, *Plants of the Bible* (Cambridge, 1982), p. 131.

–CHAIM PEARL

WILLS. See INHERITANCE.

WILLS, ETHICAL. See ETHICAL WILLS.

WILOWSKY, YA'AQOV DAVID, (1845–1913), rabbi, Talmudic commentator, and educator; known by the acronym Ridbaz. Born in Kobrin, Russia, Wilowsky held rabbinic posts in Izballin (1869), Bobruisk (1876), Polotsk, Vilkomir, and Slutsk, where he established a noted *yeshivah*. From 1903 to 1905, Wilowsky was in the United States. In 1905 he moved to Safed, where he established a *yeshivah*, Torat Erets Yisra'el, and entered into controversy with R. Avraham Yitsḥaq Kook (see KOOK FAMILY) over the proper observance of the sabbatical year. Wilowsky wrote both *responsa* and works of Talmudic interpretation, notably two commentaries on the Talmud Yerushalmi. The first, modeled on Rashi's commentaries, explained the literal meaning of the text under consideration, while the second, modeled on the **tosafot*, compared and contrasted the significance of the text in question with other Talmudic and halakhic texts. The commentaries were published with the text of the Jerusalem Talmud from 1898 to 1900. His other works include *Migdal David* (1874) and *Ḥanah David* (1876), commentary and *responsa* on both Talmuds; and *Nimmuqei Ridbaz* (1904), a commentary on the Pentateuch.

• Wolf Kaplan, *'Edut be-Ya'aqov: Le-Toledot . . . Rabbi Ya'aqov Vilovski* (Warsaw, 1904). Abraham J. Karp, "The Ridwas, Rabbi Jacob David Wilowsky, 1845–1913," in *Perspectives on Jews and Judaism: Essays in Honor of Wolfe Kelman*, edited by Arthur A. Chiel (New York, 1978), pp. 215–237. Oscar Z. Rand, ed., *Toledot Anshei Shem* (New York, 1950), pp. 44.

–JACOB MESKIN

WIMPEL. See TORAH ORNAMENTS.

WINE (Heb. *yayin*). Despite the fact that the first references to wine in the Bible are connected with the drunkenness of Noah (*Gn*. 9.20–27) and the account of the incest committed by the two daughters of Lot with their father (*Gn*. 19.31–38), wine is generally praised in Jewish tradition for its wholesome qualities and its capacity to "gladden the heart of man" (*Ps*. 104.15). Wine was regularly used as a *libation in the sacrificial services (*Nm*. 28–29). Rabbinic law further amplified and expanded its ritual use. As the symbol of *joy, wine was an essential element of all festivities, for example, the *Qiddush, *Havdalah, the Seder (see FOUR CUPS), weddings, and circumcisions. In Talmudic times, it was customary to bring mourners a gift of wine, and it was said that wine was only created to comfort mourners (*'Eruv*. 65a). Wine was granted a special blessing distinct from that of all other agricultural produce ("Blessed are you . . . who created the fruit of the vine"), and it is almost the only item of a meal which is not covered by the grace before meals (see BIRKAT HA-MOTSI') but requires a separate benediction. Where the written law is compared to water, the oral law is compared to wine; this comparison extends to everything that is praiseworthy—Jerusalem, Israel, the Messiah, and the righteous. According to one rabbinic statement, the *Nazirite is regarded as a sinner for depriving himself of the legitimate pleasure of wine (*Naz*. 19a). Excessive drinking was encouraged on *Purim and in greater moderation on *Simḥat Torah. Only overindulgence is condemned, although the rabbis taught that a teacher who drinks even a small quantity of wine must not render legal decisions because his mind is clouded (*Ket*. 10b). The tradition of moderation was so firmly entrenched that alcoholism was not a social problem among Jews.

Anything used in connection with pagan worship was forbidden as food, drink, or for any other purpose, nor was benefit to be derived from it. As a result of the ancient link between wine and idolatrous ritual, a strict prohibition was enforced against partaking of wine prepared by gentiles (*yein nesekh* [wine of libation]). The ban on drinking gentile wine, one of several prohibitions ascribed to the *Keneset ha-Gedolah and intended to limit social contact and conviviality with non-Jews (*Shab*. 17b), is still considered binding in rabbinic law. Although such wine may not be drunk, benefit from it (e.g., selling it) is permitted. The prohibition against *yein nesekh* also extends to unbottled wine that has been merely touched by a gentile, but does not include liquids not made from grapes. Kosher wine signifies wine guaranteed not to have been touched by a gentile before the bottle has been sealed. These laws have been abandoned in Conservative Judaism and were never accepted by Reform Jews.

• Erwin Goodenough, *Jewish Symbols in the Greco-Roman Period*, Bollingen Series 37, vols. 5–6 (New York, 1956). Moses Stark, *Der Wein im judischen Schrifttum und Cultus* (Vienna, 1902).

WISDOM (Heb. *ḥokhmah*). In biblical usage wisdom is conceived of as a human characteristic, partly the result of experience and learning, but mainly a gift of God. The personification and praise of wisdom in some texts (see WISDOM LITERATURE) and its description as God's first creation, even prior to the creation of the world (cf. *Prv*. 8.22–32), led to its subsequent identification with the concept of *Torah. Since the Torah was conceived of as a primordial manifestation of divine wisdom, the rabbis could use the words spoken by wisdom (*Prv*. 8.22), "the Lord possessed me in the beginning of his way, before the works of old," as a proof text for the doctrine of the *preexistence of the Torah (*Pes*. 54a). Elsewhere the rabbis identify wisdom with practical intelligence and secular knowledge, for example, in the Midrashic statement (*Lam. Rab*. 2.17) "If a person says to you that there is wisdom among the nations, believe him; if he says there is Torah among the nations, do not believe him." The blessing to be recited upon seeing a gentile sage (extended to one whose wisdom is in the secular sphere) is "Blessed be he who has imparted his wisdom to flesh and blood" (*Ber.* 58b), while the blessing for seeing a Torah sage is ". . . who has granted from his wisdom to those who fear him." The wise man must be God-fearing ("the fear of the Lord is the beginning of wisdom," *Prv.* 9.10), and the Mishnah (*Avot* 3.11) warns "He whose fear of sin exceeds his wisdom—his wisdom will endure, but he whose wisdom is greater than his fear of sin—his wisdom will not endure." *Rashi (in his commentary on *Ex.* 31.3 and elsewhere) differentiated between *ḥokhmah* and *binah* (understanding), the former referring to the acquisition of facts, the latter to the knowledge that is deduced from these facts by the use of the intellect. In medieval thought wisdom was considered one of the divine attributes, and in Kabbalah Ḥokhmah was one of the ten manifestations, or **sefirot*, of the Godhead. The term also figures in the triad—wisdom, understanding, and knowledge—of *Ḥabad Ḥasidism. The wise scholar (**talmid ḥakham*) or sage (**ḥakham*), titles which are still used in some communities synonymously with the title *rabbi*, is the ideal of Jewish education.

• Shmuel Boteach, *Wisdom, Understanding and Knowledge: Basic Concepts of Hasidic Thought* (Northvale, N.J., 1996). Daniel J. Harrington, ed., *Wisdom Texts from Qumran* (New York, 1996). Helmer Ringgren, *Word and Wisdom: Studies in the Hypostatization of Divine Qualities and Functions in the Ancient Near East* (Lund, 1947). Robert Wilken, ed., *Aspects of Wisdom in Judaism and Early Christianity* (Notre Dame, 1987).

WISDOM LITERATURE, literature based on the praise of *wisdom as the quintessence of human perfection and virtue. One trend in wisdom literature personified wisdom as a near-divine entity, a development that linked the concept of wisdom with that of *Logos. Wisdom literature, which flourished in the ancient Orient (e.g., Egypt, Mesopotamia), is represented in the Bible by the books of **Proverbs*, **Job*, and **Ecclesiastes* (as well as certain psalms). They contain counsel based upon the rational insight and practical experience of sages, as distinct from the absolute demands based on prophetic experience. Often the words of instruction are addressed to the young and couched in pragmatic terms, the main stress being on practical conduct and personal sagacity. However, in spite of its utilitarian morality, biblical wisdom literature leaves no doubt that piety and the fear of the Lord are the beginning of all wisdom (*Ps.* 111.10). Another outstanding feature of wisdom literature is its universalism. There is no mention of specific Jewish rituals or national interest in *Proverbs, Job*, or *Ecclesiastes*. The lessons, moreover, are addressed to the individual and not to society. The same pragmatic and humanistic tendencies combined with biblical piety are characteristic of post-biblical wisdom literature, for example, the apocryphal **Wisdom of Ben Sira* and the pseudepigraphous **Wisdom of Solomon*. Certain elements and literary forms of wisdom literature were developed by the exponents of the oral law in such works as **Avot* and **Avot de-Rabbi Natan*. All these works were written in the "wisdom tradition," which deals somewhat critically and empirically with such practical issues as the world order, the importance of learning from previous experience, the doctrine of individual retribution, and the significance of the life cycle. The three biblical books may be divided into two subgenres: didactic wisdom (*Proverbs*) and speculative wisdom (*Job* and *Ecclesiastes*). *Proverbs* includes practical instructions and wise sayings; *Job* is mainly a protest against the accepted "orthodox" view that the righteous and the wicked always get their just rewards; and *Ecclesiastes* is a much broader protest against all accepted views concerning how individuals should order their lives to make them worth living. *Psalms* 37.25 states, "I have been young and am now old, but I have never seen a righteous man abandoned, or his children seeking bread." Such a tenet is unacceptable to speculative wisdom because of the clear implication that all forlorn and destitute individuals must be considered sinners while all the wealthy must be deemed righteous. Such passages as *Job* 9.21–24 and *Ecclesiastes* 7.15–18 make it clear that speculative wisdom empirically rejects such an approach and considers the doctrine of individual retribution as no more than partially applicable, with many unexplainable exceptions to the rule.

• James L. Crenshaw, *Old-Testament—An Introduction* (Atlanta, 1981). James L. Crenshaw, ed., *Studies in Ancient Israelite Wisdom* (New York, 1976). John G. Gammie et al., eds., *The Sage in Israel and the Ancient Near East* (Winona Lake, Ind., 1990). Avi Hurvitz, *Shekie Ḥokhmah be-Sefer Tehillim* (Jerusalem, 1991), in Hebrew. Yehezkel Kaufmann, *The Religion of Israel: From Its Beginnings to the Babylonian Exile* (Chicago, 1960), pp. 316–340. Samuel E. Loewenstamm, *Comparative Studies in Biblical and Ancient Oriental Literatures* (Neukirchen-Vluyn, 1980), pp. 146–153, 171–172. Roland E. Murphy, *The Tree of Life: An Exploration of Biblical Wisdom Literature* (New York, 1990). Roland E. Murphy, "Wisdom in the OT," *The Anchor Bible Dictionary*, vol. 6 (New York, 1992), pp. 920–931. James B. Pritchard, ed., *Ancient Near Eastern Texts Relating to the Old Testament*, 3d ed. (Princeton, 1969), pp. 405–407, 412–425, 427–430, 589–591, 593–604. Gerhard von Rad, *Wisdom in Israel* (London, 1972). Jack Sasson, ed., "Oriental Wisdom," *Journal of the American Oriental Society* 101 (1981): 1–131. John H. Walton, *Ancient Israelite Literature in Its Cultural Context* (Grand Rapids, 1989), pp. 169–200.

–CHAIM COHEN

WISDOM OF BEN SIRA, also known as *Ecclesiasticus*; an apocryphal work, written by the Jerusalemite sage and teacher whose name is given as Jesus (i.e., Joshua) the son of Sirach in the Greek texts of the *Wisdom of Ben Sira* but as Simeon the son of Jesus, the son of Eleazar, the son of Sira, in the Hebrew ones. Its author, who wrote between c.190 and 175 BCE, emerges as a well-to-do, self-confident man, closely connected with Jerusalem's high priestly circles and proudly loyal to his nation's ancestral traditions. His work is a book of proverbs, practical and moral maxims and counsels, and exhortations to love wisdom, similar in style and outlook to the biblical *Book of Proverbs*. The *Wisdom of Ben Sira* also contains liturgical texts, prayers, and psalm-like poems and hymns and ends with a long exposition on past leaders, from Enoch to the recently deceased high priest Simon II (*Shimʿon ha-Tsaddiq). The *Wisdom of Ben Sira* identifies divine wisdom with the Torah and exhorts its readers to observe all of the Torah's precepts. It stresses the importance of just and prudent behavior, of charity, moderation, obedience to one's superiors, and fear of God. Although not included in the canon of the Hebrew Bible, it was well-known to the rabbis and is often quoted in the Talmud and in medieval Jewish literature. For many centuries the book was known only through the Greek translation, made by the author's grandson in 132 BCE, which was incorporated into the Septuagint, and through the sections quoted in rabbinic literature. However, large sections of the Hebrew text were discovered at the end of the nineteenth century in the Cairo Genizah, and fragments were discovered in the mid-twentieth century at Qumran and at Masada. English translations are to be found in all English editions of the Apocrypha.

• Alexander A. Di Lella, *The Hebrew Text of Sirach: A Text-Critical and Historical Study*, Studies in Classical Literature 1 (The Hague, 1966). Burton L. Mack, *Wisdom and the Hebrew Epic: Ben Sira's Hymn in Praise of the Fathers* (Chicago, 1985). M. H. Segal, *Sefer Ben Sira' ha-Shalem*, 2d ed. (Jerusalem, 1958). Patrick W. Skehan and Alexander A. Di Lella, *The Wisdom of Ben Sira: A New Translation with Notes*, The Anchor Bible, vol. 39 (New York, 1987).

–GIDEON BOHAK

WISDOM OF SOLOMON, one of the books of the Apocrypha, supposedly written by Solomon—who is never named explicitly, but whose identity is implied in several places—but, in fact, written in Greek by a philosophically minded Jew, perhaps living in Alexandria in the first century BCE or the first century CE. The work contrasts the bliss of piety with the short-lived happiness of the godless and discusses the problem of divine rewards and retribution. It also elaborates upon the nature of wisdom (personified as a woman) and describes, in the first person, the king's (i.e., Solomon's) quest for her. The *Wisdom of Solomon* reviews several events of the Jewish past, especially the Exodus, in order to interpret their meaning and emphasize their didactic nature. It concludes with a strongly worded attack against idolatry, especially in its Egyptian forms, including animal worship. The *Wisdom of Solomon* combines biblical poetry and wisdom literature with elements of popular Greek philosophy; the work as a whole reflects a fusion of the Jewish and Greek cultures in antiquity. English translations are to be found in standard versions of the Apocrypha.

• Ernest G. Clarke, *The Wisdom of Solomon*, The Cambridge Bible Commentary (Cambridge, 1973), translation and notes. David Winston, *The Wisdom of Solomon: A New Translation with Introduction and Commentary*, The Anchor Bible 43 (Garden City, N.Y., 1979), a thorough discussion, with much further bibliography.

–GIDEON BOHAK

WISE, ISAAC MAYER (1819–1900), American Reform leader. After immigrating to the United States from Bohemia in 1846, he officiated for eight years as a Reform rabbi in Albany and then moved to the key Reform congregation, K. K. B'nai Yeshurun, in Cincinnati, where he remained for the rest of his life. Wise was responsible for organizing the main instruments of the Reform movement, namely, the *Union of American Hebrew Congregations (1873); Hebrew Union College (1875; see HEBREW UNION COLLEGE–JEWISH INSTITUTE OF RELIGION), of which he was the first president; and the *Central Conference of American Rabbis (1889). The driving motivation behind his programs was the desire for unity in an anarchic situation. He sought to bring to American Jewry the concept of "community," embracing all sectors, and he propounded his ideas in the two weekly journals that he edited—the English-language *Israelite* and the German-language *Deborah*. He compiled the Reform prayer book *Minhag America* (1857; replaced in 1896 by the *Union Prayer Book*) and advocated shorter services, the use of English (alongside Hebrew) and the organ in the synagogue, and the Friday evening lecture service. Convinced of the profound harmony between American and Jewish ideals, he stressed the Ten Commandments under the slogan "Back to Mosaism." He envisioned the creation of a universal faith to be pioneered by Judaism, based upon monotheism, the concept that humans are created in the image of God and are accountable to him, and the idea that Israel has been divinely chosen to convey these truths to the world. He hoped (unsuccessfully) to attract the Orthodox; this was a goal that was not unfeasible in view of his insistence that authority must be based in the Talmud as well as the Bible. His chief opponent in the Reform movement, David *Einhorn, propounded a far more radical Reform without regard to the concept of unity and was scornful of Wise's loyalty to the Talmud. However, the two men contributed to the *Pittsburgh platform, which formulated basic Reform Judaism. Wise's book *Reminiscences* was published in Cincinnati in 1901.

• James G. Heller, *Isaac M. Wise: His Life, Work and Thought* (New York, 1965). Sefton Temkin, *Isaac Mayer Wise: Shaping American Judaism* (Oxford, 1992).

WISE, STEPHEN SAMUEL (1874–1949), American Reform rabbi, communal and Zionist leader. After studies in New York, he became rabbi of B'nai Jeshurun in 1893, and from 1900 to 1906 he served in Portland, Oregon. In 1907 he founded the Free Synagogue in New York, which allowed free speech from the pulpit, as well as free, unassigned seating to the congregation. A noted orator, Wise advocated universalist ideas and was a devoted crusader for social justice and reform, liberalism, and racial equality. At a time when the Reform movement was strongly anti-Zionist, Wise took a strong pro-Zionist stand and held office in many Zionist bodies, both in the United States and internationally. In 1922 he founded the Jewish Institute of Religion for the training of rabbis. He was its head until his death, after which it merged with the Hebrew Union College (see HEBREW UNION COLLEGE–JEWISH INSTITUTE OF RELIGION). His autobiography, *Challenging Years*, was published in New York in 1949.

• Justine Wise Polier and James Waterman Wise, eds., *The Personal Papers of Stephen Wise* (Boston, 1956). Melvin I. Urofsky, *The Voice That Spoke for Justice: The Life and Times of Stephen S. Wise* (Albany, 1982). Carl Hermann Voss, *Rabbi and Minister: The Friendship of Stephen S. Wise and John Haynes Holmes* (Cleveland, 1964). Carl Hermann Voss, *Stephen S. Wise: Servant of the People* (Philadelphia, 1969).

WISSENSCHAFT DES JUDENTUMS (Ger.; Science of Judaism), a movement of critical Jewish scholarship that emerged in Germany in the early nineteenth century, which created the intellectual and institutional foundation for critical Jewish research throughout the world in subsequent generations. The first circle of university-trained Jewish scholars in Germany organized themselves in 1819 as the Verein für Kultur und Wissenschaft der Juden (Society for the Culture and Science of the Jews). This group was animated by the desire to study scientifically classical Jewish sources, uninfluenced by either traditionalist rabbis or Christian scholars. According to Verein members, the former lacked critical detachment from the sources, whereas the latter were intent on asserting the superiority of Christianity over Judaism. The efforts of Verein members to reclaim Jewish sources and to create a new scientific standard for evaluating Jewish literature and history was motivated by the question of whether, and in what form, Judaism would be viable in the modern age. Facing the challenges of their day—the struggle for civic emancipation and social integration on the one hand, and the resurgence of antisemitism on the other—the first practitioners of Wissenschaft des Judentums saw critical academic scholarship as an instrument through which the contours of Judaism could be clarified both historically and in contemporary terms.

In this formative phase, the scope of intellectual labor was vast. Isaak Markus Jost undertook a nine-volume history of the Jews from antiquity to the modern age. Leopold *Zunz, who became one of the towering figures of modern Jewish scholarship, researched Jewish literature, focusing especially on the homiletic and liturgical genres central to synagogue life. For some of Zunz's colleagues, the social pressure and anxiety proved too much to bear. Eduard Gans, a brilliant legal historian who served as president of the Verein, converted to Protestantism in order to receive a university appointment, a prospect otherwise denied to Jews. The refusal of universities to recognize Jewish studies as a legitimate academic field caused the scholars of Wissenschaft des Judentums to seek an alternative and more stable institutional home for their activities. This need gave rise to the new *rabbinical seminaries that developed in Germany, which also reflected the diverse interpretations of Judaism in nineteenth-century Germany: the conservative *Hochschule für die Wissenschaft des Judentums in Berlin in 1872 and the Orthodox *Berlin Rabbinical Seminary founded by Ezriel *Hildesheimer in 1873. The founding director of the *Breslau Rabbinical Seminary was Zacharias *Frankel, whose seminal *Darkhei ha-Mishnah* explored the historical development of the oral law. Frankel's colleague in Breslau, Heinrich *Graetz, was perhaps the most significant Jewish scholar in Germany during the nineteenth century; beginning in 1854, he commenced publication of his monumental eleven-volume history of the Jews. Frankel and Graetz combined traditional reverence and a new critical spirit in forging a positive–historical Judaism, which stood in opposition to emerging *Reform Judaism, whose most important representative was the rabbi and scholar Abraham *Geiger. Geiger, who spent the last years of his life teaching at the Hochschule in Berlin, was a prolific author, whose historical inquiries into ancient and medieval Jewish history and literature gave shape to the view that Judaism was constantly evolving. Meanwhile, at the Berlin Rabbinical Seminary, Orthodox scholars such as David Tsevi *Hoffmann and Abraham *Berliner sought to effect their own balance of critical scholarship and traditional belief.

The use of modern scholarly tools to articulate or refine Jewish identity was not confined to Germany. The most prominent current of non-German scholars was dispersed throughout Italy, Galicia, and Russia but was united by an attachment to Hebrew as a scholarly language. These scholars of Ḥokhmat Yisra'el (Hebrew for Wissenschaft des Judentums), including Shemu'el David *Luzzatto, Naḥman *Krochmal, and Shelomoh Yehudah Leib *Rapoport, engaged in a wide range of philological, historical, and philosophical work. They did not face the same partisan battles over denominational affiliation as their German colleagues. However, they constantly negotiated between the demands of tradition and their critical scholarly sensibilities. During the nineteenth century, other circles of critical Jewish scholars, supported by learned societies and journals, emerged in France, England, and Hungary. See also *JEWISH STUDIES.

• Nahum Glatzer, *Essays in Jewish Thought* (University, Ala., 1978). Heinrich Graetz, *The Structure of Jewish History and Other Essays*, translated and edited by Ismar Schorsch (New York, 1975). Jay M. Harris, *How Do We Know This? Midrash and the Fragmentation of Modern Judaism* (Albany, 1994). Michael A. Meyer, *The Origins of the Modern Jew* (Detroit, 1967). Michael A. Meyer, *Response to Modernity: A History of the Reform Movement in Judaism* (New York, 1988). David N. Myers, *Re-Inventing the Jewish Past: European Jewish Intellectuals and the Zionist Return to History* (New York, 1995). Ismar Schorsch, *From Text to Context: The Turn to History in Modern Judaism* (Hanover, N.H., 1994). Max Wiener, ed., *Abraham Geiger and Liberal Judaism: The Challenge of the Nineteenth Century* (Philadelphia, 1962). Yosef H. Yerushalmi, *Zakhor: Jewish History and Jewish Memory* (Seattle, 1982). —DAVID N. MYERS

WITCHCRAFT. Different kinds of witchcraft were practiced among the ancient Israelites and their neighbors; the variety is reflected by the biblical vocabulary, which mentions diviners, soothsayers, enchanters, charmers, consulters of ghosts, and necromancers (*Dt.* 18.10–11). All contact with witchcraft and its practitioners was forbidden by the Bible, which demands man's wholehearted allegiance to God (*Dt.* 18.13): "You shall not suffer a witch to live" (*Ex.* 22.17). The verse is preceded by the enumeration of the penalties for sexual offenses (*Ex.* 22.15) and followed by the denunciation of unnatural vice and idolatry (*Ex.* 22.18–19). Saul is reported to have exterminated all witches, though in his hour of despair, he consulted one (*1 Sm.* 28.7). An inclination to witchcraft is ascribed to women in numerous Talmudic passages, and according to one tradition, *Shim'on ben Shetaḥ hanged eighty alleged witches in one day in Ascalon (*San.* 6.4). The use of certain magic formulas for healing the sick was considered acceptable by the rabbis. Medieval authorities were divided in their views on witchcraft: some believed it was illusion; others believed in its use and in its connection with the demonic powers. See also AMULETS; DEMONS; MAGIC.

• Meir Bar-Ilan, "Witches in the Bible and in the Talmud," and Simcha Fishbane, "Most Women Engage in Sorcery: An Analysis of Female Sorceresses in the Babylonian Talmud," in *Approaches to Ancient Judaism*, new series vol. 5, *Historical, Literary, and Religious Studies*, edited by H. Basser et al. (Atlanta, 1993), pp. 7–32, 143–165. Graham Harvey, "The Suffering of Witches and Children: Uses of the Witchcraft Passages in the Bible," in *Words Remembered, Texts Renewed: Essays in Honour of*

John F. A. Sawyer, edited by Jon Davies (Sheffield, Eng., 1995). R. J. Zwi Werblowsky, "Commerce with the Supernaturals," *Numen* 31 (1984): 129–135.

WITNESS. Each individual enjoys a presumption of trustworthiness, and his *evidence, therefore, is acceptable without substantiation by oath. Two witnesses were necessary for a conviction (*Dt*. 19.15), although there were a number of exceptions. Every man is obliged to appear before the court and deliver any relevant testimony in his knowledge. A witness who has given false testimony becomes a *rasha*ʿ (wicked one) and forfeits his trustworthiness as a witness in future cases until such time as his veracity is reestablished. The law that a *rasha*ʿ is ineligible as a witness (*San*. 27a) is derived from the verse "put not your hand with the wicked to be an unrighteous witness" (*Ex*. 23.1). The *rasha*ʿ is further defined as one who intentionally violates a prohibition punishable by lashes or one who unlawfully takes money or property belonging to another; the violator may be reinstated after repentance, the thief after the restoration of the unlawfully acquired property to its owner. A general reservation on grounds akin to the second instance disqualifies those engaged in certain disreputable occupations, such as the professional gambler. Traditional law disqualifies the following (with certain exceptions) from acting as witnesses: women, slaves, relatives, minors, the insane, the deaf, and the blind (Maimonides, *Hilkhot ʿEduyyot* 9.1). No one can testify against himself. See also ʿEDUYYOT; FALSE WITNESS.

• David Daube, *Witnesses in Bible and Talmud*, Oxford Center Papers (Oxford, 1986). Mekhon Hari Fishel, *Laws of Evidence with Halacha Pesuka and Berur Halacha* (Jerusalem, 1993).

WOLFSON, HARRY AUSTRYN (1887–1974), historian of philosophy. Born in Belorussia, Wolfson attended the Slobodka Yeshivah before immigrating to the United States in 1903. He studied at Harvard and was appointed in 1915 to the Harvard faculty, becoming professor of Hebrew literature and philosophy in 1925. His first book was a penetrating study of the thought of Ḥasda'i ben Avraham *Crescas, *Crescas' Critique of Aristotle* (1929), which incorporated an English translation of Crescas's *Or Adonai*. Wolfson's *The Philosophy of Spinoza* (2 vols. [1934]) analyzed the thought of Baruch *Spinoza and its roots, which brought him to the influence of *Philo on Spinoza. In *Philo: Foundations of Religious Philosophy in Judaism, Christianity, and Islam* (2 vols. [1947]), Wolfson resuscitated Philo's role as the founder of religious philosophy in Judaism with a major impact on Christianity and Islam. Wolfson unified Philo's thought into a philosophical system, which, he argued, was the basis of dominant philosophy in European thought until Spinoza.

• *Harry Austryn Wolfson Jubilee Volume*, 2 vols. (Jerusalem, 1965), includes bibliography. Leo W. Schwarz, *Wolfson of Harvard: Portrait of a Scholar* (Philadelphia, 1978). —EUGENE R. SHEPPARD

WOMEN. Two differing versions of the *creation of humanity reflect the dialectical position regarding women, not only in the Bible but throughout the tradition, in law, narrative, and the community. These are: "And God created Adam (humankind) in his image . . . male and female he created them" (*Gn*. 1.27); "And God caused consciousness to fall upon the man . . . and from one of the ribs that he had taken from the man, he formed a woman . . . and the man spoke [saying] . . . this one shall be called woman [*ishah*] for out of man [*ish*] she was taken" (*Gn*. 2.21–23). On the one hand, women are considered equal to men in their very essence; on the other hand, women are derivative, the very power of naming woman vested in man.

In biblical understanding, woman was created to serve as a helpmeet to her husband (*Gn*. 2.20). Yet the Bible offers a romantic version of marriage—"Therefore shall a man leave his father and mother and cling to his wife and they shall become as one flesh" (*Gn*. 1.24)—reverberating with themes of intimacy, fidelity, interdependence, and eternal love. Great value was placed on the Jewish wife. Her virtues were extolled in the classic paean of praise, the *Eshet Ḥayil (*Prv* 31.10–31), and the Talmud states, "Whoever lives without a wife lives without well-being, blessing, a home, Torah, protection and security, without peace" (*Yev*. 62b). A man was enjoined by the rabbis "to love his wife as himself and honor her more than himself." On the verse "All that Sarah tells you listen to her voice" (*Gn*. 21.12), the rabbis of the Talmud comment, "If your wife is small, bend down and whisper in her ear," which is interpreted as take counsel with her in all matters and follow her advice (*B. M*. 59a).

Though polygyny was permitted, monogamous marriages seem to have been the ideal relationship (see *MONOGAMY), as the stories of fractious relations between multiple wives attest (Sarah and Hagar [*Gn*. 21], Rachel and Leah [*Gn*. 29–30], Hannah and Peninnah [*1 Sm*. 1]). The law of *levirate marriage (*Dt*. 25.5–10), which obligated an unmarried man to marry his deceased brother's childless widow, ensured continuity of the line of the dead brother, but it also offered a childless widow a chance at motherhood (*Gn*. 38, Tamar and Judah). Though there is hardly any record of polygyny in Talmudic times, it nevertheless was not formally banned until the tenth century, when R. Gershom ben Yehudah issued a *taqqanah*. As in many other areas, Jewish laws of marriage were influenced by the surrounding culture. The ban against polygyny was operative among Jews who lived in Christian Europe, where celibacy was the ideal, but not among Sephardi Jews, whose Islamic neighbors counted multiple wives as a sign of affluence. Polygyny was finally universally outlawed in 1951 by the Israeli rabbinate. Bearing children was the measure of success for a woman; failure to do so was traumatic (*Gn*. 16; *Gn*. 30; *1 Sm*. 1). In fact, barrenness into ten years of marriage constituted valid reason for divorce.

Women were considered passive in the construction and dissolution of a *marriage. The Torah tradition interchangeably used the words *acquire* and *sanctified* when speaking of marriage. (The traditional marriage and divorce ceremonies reflect this male initiative, with the man reciting the formula and the woman remaining silent.) Yet, it was clearly not a matter of acquiring or discarding property at will. Even a bondswoman (one given in marriage in lieu of her father's debt) was accorded the full rights of a free woman in marriage. If her husband/master tired of her, he could not pass her along to another man but rather was obliged to set her free, with full cancellation of the debt she represented (*Ex.* 21). Moreover, as the story of Rebekah indicates, women were given considerable latitude in determining whom they wished to marry and whether they wanted to leave their parents' home for that of a stranger. Indeed, building on the Rebekah text, the rabbis rule that a young girl may not be given in marriage until she grows up and says "I want to marry this one."

The *divorce laws of the Torah and Talmud exemplify the dialectic. A man could divorce a woman if he found something unseemly (*ʿervat davar*) in her (*Dt.* 24.1), and the rabbinic debate on what constitutes *ʿervat davar* gives him wide latitude (*Git.* 9.10). She, on the other hand, can sue for divorce in the rabbinic courts, but she cannot grant the divorce (*Git* 20a; *B. B.* 168a). If the husband is unwilling or unable to grant her a divorce, she can be rendered an *ʿ*agunah*, a woman chained to an absentee or recalcitrant husband.

Within this hierarchical framework, many protections were built in for the wife: in contrast to the irrevocable oral divorce extant in the ancient Near East, the Torah required a writ of divorce, which served as a delaying tactic and offered a measure of communal oversight. Moreover, the woman was entitled to alimony. The **ketubbah* (marriage contract), a creation of the Second Temple period, protected her during the marriage and after its demise (*Ket.* 4.4, 51a). The *get* process (writ of divorce) became more exacting and was virtually taken over by the rabbinic courts. Though women were otherwise not entitled to serve as witnesses in the religious courts of law, the rabbis allowed a woman to testify regarding the death of her husband, so as not to render her an *ʿagunah* (*Yev.* 93b, 114b–116).

Additionally, women's grounds for divorce were expanded. Ancient Judaism recognized a woman's sexual needs (*ʿonah*) and made her conjugal rights a fixed obligation of her husband, along with food and clothing (*Ex. 21.7–11*). The frequency of a husband's obligation to his wife was stipulated in the Talmud, based on his profession and the amount of time it required him to be away (*Ket.* 61b–62b). Failure to meet her needs for sexual satisfaction entitled her to sue for divorce. Impotence was a legitimate ground, and burden of proof rested upon the husband (*Yev.* 65a–b).

Still, divorce was considered a man's prerogative. Until the tenth century, when forcible divorce was formally outlawed by Rabbenu Gershom, a woman could be divorced against her will. The theory is that the husband is the one who created the bond, and therefore he must be the one to sever it (*Qid.* 56.9b). The principle that a man may not be coerced into giving a *get* still obtains in Jewish law.

In ancient Israel, women were markedly underrepresented in leadership roles, and in the extensive biblical genealogies, daughters are hardly mentioned. The few biblical women who did reach great heights are praised and are even attributed in later rabbinic tradition with special powers of prophecy despite their differing roles as judges, queens, and matriarchs. The term *nevi'ah* (prophetess) is applied to five women in the Bible—Miriam, Deborah, the wife of Isaiah, Huldah, and Noadiah. Additionally, Hannah is considered a prophetess, as are Sarah, Abigail, and Esther. A total of twenty-three prophetesses are listed by the sages (*Midrash Tadshe'* 21).

The language of the Torah is addressed to men. However, the lessons and laws of the Torah clearly included women: with a handful of exceptions, all negative commandments (you shall not) and most affirmative ones were binding upon women. Women were called to the revelation at Sinai and were included in the *mitsvah* of *Haqhel, the public reading and reacceptance of the Torah every seven years. Jewish women entered the covenantal community at birth and entered Jewish maturity at age twelve, but in both instances, without benefit of formal communal ceremony parallel to those created for men (circumcision and *bar mitsvah*).

Women could take vows, although under certain conditions a father or husband could annul these vows (*Nm.* 30.4–9). Women could bring sacrifices to the Temple, which they did for special occasions of gratitude or supplication. Women often accompanied their husbands to Jerusalem for the pilgrimage festivals. A special area was set aside for women in the Temple courtyard.

As tradition developed, certain *mitsvot*, such as the study of Torah and community prayer, became institutionalized, leading to women's exemption if not exclusion from two central aspects of Jewish life. The Talmud rules that women were not obligated in the daily study of Torah (*Qid.* 29b). The famous dictum of R. Eliʿezer, "He who teaches his daughter Torah, it is as if he has taught her trivial things" (*Sot.* 20a), was accepted as the standard rather than the more inclusive statement of Ben ʿAzzai, "A man must teach his daughter Torah." Some exceptional women did study, particularly *Beruryah, who achieved great reputation as a scholar and teacher. During medieval and early modern times, women in Europe studied Torah from the **Tse'enah u-Re'enah*, a work of commentary and homilies in the Yiddish language.

Women's liturgical lives were shaped by the Talmudic principle of exemption from time-bound positive commandments (*Qid.* 1.7). In truth, the principle was characterized by far more exceptions to the rule than inclusions—that is, women were obligated to many of the time-bound positive commandments, but the very principle tended to diminish women's participation even in areas where the obligation did exist, such as daily prayer. On the other hand, certain women excelled in prayer. The rabbis state that Hannah's prayer (*1 Sm.* 1) became the model for the ʿAmidah, the focal point of the daily prayer service. Women in medieval and early times recited special **tḥinnus*, some of which they composed themselves.

Financially, women enjoyed full protection and rights

under the law, with the exception of *inheritance. Women could acquire and sell property, enter into contracts, be litigants or dependents. The statement "Nowadays it is commonplace for women to engage in business" appears in many *responsa* of the medieval period. A woman could go to work and keep her own earnings if she wished, trading that for the reimbursement to her husband for food. Still, the husband was obliged to pay for clothing, shelter, household help, and child care.

The inheritance laws reflect the hierarchy, though in reality certain adjustments often were made in favor of wives and daughters. The Torah enjoins the community to take care of orphans and widows (*Ex.* 22.21). The Biblical protest of the daughters of *Zelophehad established the principle of direct inheritance to daughters in the event that there were no male heirs (*Nm.* 27). Talmudic law legislated that "if the inheritance was too small to maintain both sons and daughters, the daughters would inherit the whole estate and the sons must go begging from door to door" (*B. B.* 139 b). Wives and daughters functioned as creditors to the estate and had prior claim over heirs. Moreover, men were enjoined to "grant sufficient gifts to one's children, especially to one's daughter" (*B. B.* 141 a). Technically, a wife could be assigned an estate as a "gift" rather than an inheritance. Medieval Jewish law further extended inheritance rights to women. Still, inheritance law often worked to the disadvantage of females and was based on the presumption that women were dependent on men.

As the revenge of the *rape of Dinah testifies, the honor of the Jewish woman was carefully guarded (*Gn.* 34). Yet some aspects of the laws reflect the notion that a woman's sexuality was the property of her husband. Rape was a punishable crime, but the penalty was much stiffer if the victim was a married woman (*Dt.* 22.23–29). As the tradition developed, penalties against rape were intensified and included psychological pain as well. Progressively striking the cruel notion of victim complicity, the Talmud taught that a woman's subjective testimony was sufficient to incriminate the offender (*Ket.* 51b; Y., *Sot*).

High value was placed upon the female virtues of modesty, chastity, virginity, and purity. The standard *ketubbah* allowed for alimony payments twice as large for virgins as for nonvirgins. Protective confinement in the family home, particularly for unmarried women, was considered desirable, as the psalmist's phrase cogently suggests: "the honor of the king's daughter is within" (*Ps.* 45.14). Not surprisingly, that very phrase accompanied many of the laws exempting women from roles in the public sector, such as the courts, the synagogue, and the house of study.

Chastity in marriage and purity of family relations were also of great importance. One of the three "women's *mitsvot*" is **niddah* (the other two being *nerot* [candle lighting] and *ḥallah* [separation and consecration of a piece of dough during baking]). During a woman's menses and for seven days thereafter, no marital relations were permitted. Though abstinence fell equally upon men and women, it was a woman's primary responsibility to mark the time and to immerse herself in the ritual bath at the conclusion of the *niddah* period (see MENSTRUATION).

There are statements in Jewish literature both of contempt for women, such as "Women are greedy, eavesdroppers, lazy and envious" (*Ned.* 31b) or " . . . lightminded" (*Shab.* 33b), and of praise, such as "The Holy One granted women greater understanding than men" (*Nid.* 45b) and "The continued existence of the world depends more on women than on men" (*Pesiqta' de-Rav Kahana'* 9.1). As one would expect, these strong statements are used selectively by defenders or critics of the tradition.

As Judaism entered the modern period, the community organized itself along denominational lines. The tradition underwent reinterpretation in many areas, particularly by the liberal communities. One hundred and fifty years ago, Reform Judaism created religious schools in which boys and girls studied in mixed classes and, through the ceremony of confirmation, celebrated graduation together. Reform replaced separate seating for men and women in the synagogue, long a feature of Jewish life, with mixed seating, enabling families to sit together. Early in the twentieth century, the Conservative movement established throughout the United States a network of day schools, youth groups, and summer camps that offered new educational and religious opportunities for girls, while in 1922 Mordecai Kaplan, a Conservative rabbi who later founded Reconstructionist Judaism, instituted the public, religious celebration of a young girl's reaching her religious majority, thus becoming a *bat mitsvah*. In the Orthodox community, radical new institutions of Torah study for women were created, such as the *Beth Jacob schools in Poland in the early 1900s and the coeducational elementary day schools of the Neo-Orthodox. By the 1950s, numerous Jewish educational institutions offered training programs, and female Hebrew teachers were no longer the exception. Also in the 1950s, the rabbinic law arm of the Conservative movement concluded that women could be called up for honors associated with the reading of the Torah.

By the late nineteenth and early twentieth centuries, Jewish women found a new voice and presence in synagogue and communal settings. In the United States, synagogue sisterhoods, established in Reform and Conservative congregations and later coordinated on a national level, engaged women in educational, religious, and philanthropic activities, while the National Council for Jewish Women, founded in 1893, sought to unite Jewish women of different social and religious backgrounds through similar endeavors. Hadassah, the women's Zionist organization co-founded and led by Henrietta Szold in 1912, Jewish Ladies' Aid societies established throughout England and the United States, and Bertha Pappenheim's Jewish feminist organization, the Judischer Frauenbund, created in 1904 to seek greater political, economic, and social rights for Jewish women in Germany and in the Jewish community, were only three of the organizations that successfully enabled Jewish women to work together for practical change.

Yet even greater changes regarding women in Judaism

came as a result of the broad social movement of *feminism. In the mid-1960s, a group of young women from the Conservative movement called themselves Ezrat Nashim (Women's Gallery) and presented an agenda to the Conservative leadership. Within a decade, all of the items were in place. Women were accorded full ritual participation in areas heretofore closed to them, providing their communities sanctioned it. In 1972 Reform Judaism ordained the first woman, R. Sally J. Preisand, after seriously considering the issue of women's ordination for more than fifty years; within a decade, Conservative and Reconstructionist Judaism followed suit. By 1990 the number of female applicants to non-Orthodox rabbinic schools was equal to that of men. Women were also accepted to cantorial schools and hired by congregations.

Increasingly in ritual life, women participate in areas from which they were exempt for centuries. By the mid-1990s, some women, Orthodox among them, where donning *tallit* and *tefillin*, reciting the Mourner's Qaddish, and reading from the Torah. The phenomenon of *bat mitsvah*, revolutionary in the 1920s, was now common practice, even in the Orthodox community (albeit not patterned there directly after the *bar mitsvah*). In the liberal denominations, the adult *bat mitsvah* is becoming ever more popular, as are women's Seders and new moon celebrations. New ceremonies and blessings are being created to celebrate women's life-cycle events. Healing rituals are being formulated for conditions or events such as infertility, miscarriage, or rape. Prayer books are being reissued with attention to gender-inclusive language.

In Orthodoxy, the pattern has been to proceed with caution, lest any aspect of *halakhah* be violated. Still, much is happening: women's *tefillah* (prayer) groups meet, in which women lead the service and read from the Torah, with minimal differentiation from the traditional service. Activist groups on behalf of the *ʿagunah* have grown in influence. Birth ceremonies are being developed, and female participation in wedding ceremonies is growing. There has been a virtual explosion of women's study groups, especially for Talmud study, which was closed to women for almost two millennia. The creation of institutions of higher learning to support women's new sacred yearnings has grown apace.

None of the modernizing tendencies made inroads on Jewish communities in Muslim lands. However, in Israel, a new openness has begun to appear in certain ʿAdot ha-Mizraḥ circles, especially among the younger generations.

• Menachem Brayer, *The Jewish Woman in Rabbinic Literature*, 2 vols. (Hoboken, N.J., 1986). Yael Azmon and Israeli Dafna, eds., *Women in Israel*, Studies of Israeli Society, vol. 6 (New Brunswick, N.J., 1993). Judith R. Baskin, ed., *Jewish Women in Historical Perspective*. (Detroit, 1991). Rachel Biale, *Women and Jewish Law: The Essential Texts, Their History, and Their Relevance for Today* (New York, 1995). Aviva Cantor, *Jewish Women/Jewish Men: The Legacy of Patriarchy in Jewish Life* (San Francisco, 1995). Blu Greenberg, *On Women and Judaism: A View from Tradition* (Philadelphia, 1981). Susan Grossman and Rivka Haut, eds., *Daughters of the King: Women and the Synagogue* (Philadelphia, 1992). Sondra Henry and Emily Taitz, *Written out of History: Our Jewish Foremothers*, rev. ed. (New York, 1983). Michael Kaufman, *The Woman in Jewish Law and Tradition* (Northvale, N.J., 1993). Elizabeth Koltun, ed., *The Jewish Woman: New Perspectives* (Northvale, N.J., 1993). Debra Orenstein, ed., *Lifecycles: Jewish Women on Life Passages and Personal Milestones* (Woodstock, Vt, 1994). Judith Plaskow, *Standing Again at Sinai: Judaism from a Feminist Perspective* (San Francisco, 1990). Jack Nusan Porter, ed., *Women in Chains: A Sourcebook on the Aguna* (Northvale, N.J., 1995). Tamar Rudavsky, ed., *Gender and Judaism: The Transformation of Tradition* (New York, 1995). Susan Weidman Schneider, *Jewish and Female: Choices and Changes in Our Lives Today* (New York, 1984). Ellen Umansky and Diane Ashton, eds., *Four Centuries of Jewish Women's Spirituality: A Sourcebook* (Boston, 1992). Judith Romney Wegner, *Chattel or Person? The Status of Women in the Mishnah* (New York and Oxford, 1990). Avraham Weiss, *Women at Prayer: A Halakhic Analysis of Women's Prayer Groups* (Hoboken, N.J., 1990).

–BLU GREENBERG

WOMEN'S PRAYERS. According to *halakhah*, women are obligated to pray but not to recite all of the same time-bound liturgical prayers as men (*Ber.* 20a–b; *Shulḥan ʿArukh, Oraḥ Ḥayyim* 106.2). This differentiation in level of obligation meant that, in traditional Judaism, women did not count as one of a **minyan* for congregational prayer and could not lead worship. When they did attend congregational services, women sat in a separate section of the synagogue. Thus, women's prayer came to be understood as essentially private. Nonetheless, in Ashkenazi congregations from the Middle Ages forward, a relatively learned woman would sometimes act as precentor (**zogerqa*), leading the other women in prayer. In addition, women recited and sometimes composed private prayers in the vernacular languages, such as Yiddish and Ladino; such prayers were transmitted orally or were written down (see TSE'ENAH U-RE'ENAH) or published.

In the latter half of the twentieth century, the restrictions on women's participation in congregational prayer have been challenged and gradually lifted. Even among Orthodox Jews there are groups of women who meet separately for prayer, although not constituting themselves fully as a *minyan*. Since 1973, Conservative congregations have been permitted to count women in the *minyan*, although not all of them do so. Women are counted in the *minyan* and may lead public prayer in Reform and Reconstructionist congregations. There has been little parallel to these developments among Sephardim and ʿAdot ha-Mizraḥ.

Current issues with regard to women's prayer include the degree to which women's experiences and religious concerns should shape the reformulation of the liturgy; the use of female God-language and imagery in prayer; and the creation of new prayers and rituals specifically for women either for private or public use. See also BAT MITSVAH; TḤINNUS.

• Rachel Biale, *Women and Jewish Law: An Exploration of Women's Issues in Halakhic Sources* (New York, 1984). Nina Cardin, *Out of the Depths I call to You: A Book of Prayers for the Jewish Married Woman* (Northvale, N.J., 1992). Tikva Frymer-Kensky, *Motherprayer: The Pregnant Woman's Spiritual Companion* (New York, 1995).

–CHAVA WEISSLER

WOOD OFFERING. According to *Leviticus* 9.24, the fire on the sacrificial altar in the Tabernacle, which was first ignited by divine fire, was to be kept burning at all times and never to be extinguished. For this to occur, the priest was commanded to feed wood to the fire every morning (*Lv.* 6.5). No details are given as to how this wood was to be provided, and no information exists concerning the wood supply in First Temple times; it may have been a royal responsibility. The *Book of Nehemiah* (10.35, 13.31) first refers to a regular *qurban ha-ʿetsim* (wood offering), which was to be supplied by the priests, Levites, and families at appointed times as determined by lot. As reflected in rabbinic law, in Second Temple times the wood offering became a sacrifice in its own right, performed with elaborate ritual and commemorated, even after the destruction of the Temple, by each family on the date on which it had previously contributed wood for the altar. Tu be-'Av was designated as the day on which the public at large supplied the wood offering (*Taʿan*. 4.5; *Tam*. 2.3; T., *Taʿan*. 3.5, 4.7–8; *Taʿan* 12a, 28a; *Men*. 20b). The wood offering is also known from the practices of the Qumran community (*Temple Scroll* 23–25).

• Jacob Milgrom, *Leviticus 1–16*, The Anchor Bible, vol. 3a (New York, 1981), pp. 387–388. Jacob M. Myers, *Ezra–Nehemiah*, The Anchor Bible, vol. 14 (Garden City, N.Y., 1965), pp. 179–180.

–BARUCH J. SCHWARTZ

WORD OF GOD. See LOGOS.

WORK. See LABOR.

WORLD. See ʿOLAM.

WORLD COUNCIL OF SYNAGOGUES, the international organization of congregations and institutions affiliated with the *Conservative/Masorti movement throughout the world. The World Council of Synagogues was founded in 1957 by lay and professional leaders of the United Synagogue of Conservative Judaism. Its mission was to extend the North American–based Conservative movement around the world and to develop and support new congregations and institutions. The institution has close ties to Seminario Rabínico Latinoamericano in Buenos Aires and its over eighty congregations throughout Latin America. In England, the World Council of Synagogues helped to form the Assembly of Masorti Synagogues, with its seven congregations. There are also congregations in Israel, France, Sweden, and South Africa, and a Teachers' Institute in Hungary affiliated with the World Council of Synagogues.

• Neil Gillman, *Conservative Judaism: The New Century* (West Orange, N.J., 1993).

–RELA MINTZ GEFFEN

WORLD TO COME. See ʿOLAM HA-ZEH AND ʿOLAM HA-BAʾ.

WORLD UNION FOR PROGRESSIVE JUDAISM, founded in London in 1926 as the international body of Reform, Liberal, Progressive, and Reconstructionist Jews; since 1973 its international headquarters has been in Jerusalem. The World Union membership encompasses over one and a half million Jews in more than thirty countries. In Israel, the World Union for Progressive Judaism has established synagogue–community centers, settlements, schools, and a World Education Center in Jerusalem. The newest centers of activity are in eastern and central Europe. In the former Soviet Union, many new congregations and leadership training programs have been established. The World Union publishes prayer books and liturgical and educational materials in various languages, helps recruit rabbinic and professional leaders, and assists new congregations throughout the world.

• Nissim Eliad, "The Work of the World Union for Progressive Judaism," *Judaism* 31 (1982): 405–409.

–RICHARD G. HIRSCH

WORSHIP. See PRAYER; SACRIFICES.

WRITINGS. See HAGIOGRAPHA.

WRITTEN LAW. The primary source of **halakhah* is the *Torah, which consists of the written law (*Torah she-bi-khetav*) and the *oral law (*Torah she-be-ʿal peh*). The written law, which is basically the Pentateuch, is also known as *de-orayta'* (Aram; from the Torah) law, a term which denotes the highest normative legal category in the halakhic hierarchy. Law which is not in the *de-orayta'* category is termed *de-rabbanan*, that is, rabbinic law, and is of a less binding nature. The superior position of *de-orayta'* law emerges in cases which will be resolved strictly only if the law at stake is *de-orayta'*. If the law involved is merely *de-rabbanan*, then it will be decided leniently. Another issue in which the superiority of *de-orayta'* is manifest is the priority of a *de-orayta'* lien on an estate over a *de-rabbanan* charge (Y., *Git*. 5.1). It is generally accepted that the *de-orayta'* category includes many more laws than those specifically stated in the Pentateuch, but the precise definition of this category is a matter of dispute. According to Maimonides, only those laws which are either mentioned in scripture, or are specifically designated by the Talmud as *de-orayta'*, even if they are derived from scripture on the basis of rabbinic interpretation, are to be included in this category (*Sefer ha-Mitsvot*, Second Principle). Nahmanides, however, argues that all laws derived by virtue of the application of the traditional hermeneutical principles (see HERMENEUTICS) possess *de-orayta'* status, unless the Talmud specifically relegates them to the category of *de-rabbanan* (Hassagot ha-Ramban, *Sefer ha-Mitsvot*, Second Principle). Regardless of the outcome of this debate, the combination of *de-orayta'* law with a restrictive approach to its definition constitutes one of the most potent halakhic instruments for ensuring the continual development of the law and its adaptation to changing circumstances.

• Isaac Herzog, *The Main Institutions of Jewish Law*, 2d ed., vol. 1 (London, 1965), pp. 1–8. Daniel Sinclair, "Legal Reasoning in Maimonidean Jurisprudence," in *Jewish Law and Legal Theory*, edited by Martin Golding (Aldershot, 1994), pp. 369–377.

–DANIEL SINCLAIR

Y

YAʿALEH (יַעֲלֶה; Let [Our Prayer] Ascend), *piyyut* recited in the Ashkenazi and Italian rites after the ʿAmidah in the *Yom Kippur evening service. Of unknown authorship, Yaʿaleh consists of eight three-line stanzas, each having three words to a line, the middle word forming a reverse alphabetical acrostic, with *alef* repeated three times; each line in each stanza commences with *yaʿaleh* (may it ascend), *ve-yavo'* (and may it come), and *ve-yera'eh* (and may it appear), respectively. The three verbs are taken from the *Yaʿaleh ve-Yavo' prayers. Yaʿaleh is a plea to God to accept the congregation's Yom Kippur supplications.

YAʿALEH VE-YAVO' (יַעֲלֶה וְיָבוֹא; May [Remembrance] Rise and Come [Before You]), a prayer recited in each ʿAmidah on new moons and festivals and in the Birkat ha-Mazon on those occasions. In ancient times it was also recited in the Musaf service, but this is no longer the case. Specific mention is made of the festival, a practice that dates from tannaitic times, and the prayer asks God to remember the Jewish people and grant them redemption on his special holy days.

• Ismar Elbogen, *Jewish Liturgy: A Comprehensive History*, translated by Raymond P. Scheindlin (Philadelphia, New York, and Jerusalem, 1993). Macy Nulman, *The Encyclopedia of Jewish Prayer* (Northvale, N.J., and London, 1993), pp. 361–362.

YAʿAQOV BEN ASHER (c.1270–1340), codifier; author of the *Arbaʿah Turim*; known as Baʿal ha-Turim. Born in Germany, he immigrated to Toledo, Spain, together with his father, *Asher ben Yeḥi'el, and his brothers in 1303. A pietist who refused to accept an appointment as rabbi, Yaʿaqov remained in dire poverty throughout his life. His great code, the *Arbaʿah Turim* (the first complete edition of which was published in Piove di Sacco in 1475), was directed toward bridging the gulf between the Franco-German and Spanish schools of Jewish law. His sources include the two Talmuds, geonic literature, and later commentators and codifiers, especially his father. Unlike Maimonides in the *Mishneh Torah*, Yaʿaqov quotes all his sources and cites the opinions upon which his decisions (generally following those of his father) are based. Omitting those branches of *halakhah* that had become obsolete with the destruction of the Temple, the work follows an original arrangement that subsequently became classic. The four *Turim* (rows or parts) are *Oraḥ Ḥayyim*, dealing with the daily duties of man, including blessings, prayers, the Sabbath, and festivals; *Yoreh Deʿah*, embracing ritual law, including dietary regulations, vows, and mourning; *Even ha-ʿEzer*, dealing with family laws, marriage, and divorce; and *Ḥoshen Mishpat*, on civil law. This work rapidly became the standard code of Jewish law and was the basis for Yosef Karo's **Shulḥan ʿArukh*. Yaʿaqov also wrote a lengthy commentary to the Pentateuch, only a small section of which was printed (Zólkiew, 1806).

• Simon M. Chones, *Toledot ha-Poseqim* (New York, 1945). Jeffrey R. Portman, "Introduction to Jacob Ben Asher's Commentary on the Torah," rabbinic thesis, Hebrew Union College, 1973. Chaim Tchernowitz, *Toledot ha-Poseqim*, 3 vols. (New York, 1946–1947), vol. 2, pp. 199–220.

YAʿAQOV BEN ME'IR TAM (1100–1171), Talmudic commentator, rabbinic authority, and communal leader; referred to as Rabbenu (Our Master) Tam. He was born in Ramerupt, France, where his father, Me'ir ben Shemu'el, Rashi's son-in-law, and his brother, Shemu'el ben Me'ir, were his primary teachers.

Rabbenu Tam was one of the founders of the tosafistic school of Talmud commentary (see TOSAFOT), which harmonized contradictions in the Talmud, criticized and improved upon Rashi's Talmud commentary, and continued Rashi's work of providing short explanations of Talmudic terms and passages. Rabbenu Tam's incisive questions and answers about Talmudic textual problems and law appear regularly in *tosafot* to the Talmud Bavli.

His reputation as a legal scholar traveled far beyond France. Avraham *ibn Daud, the Spanish chronicler of the sages, mentioned Rabbenu Tam in his *Sefer ha-Qabbalah*, but not Rashi. Rabbenu Tam's work is also cited by R. Zeraḥyah ha-Levi, a Provençal critic. He also received questions from students throughout France and from the Italian communities of Bari and Otranto.

Rabbenu Tam was an extremely independent individual with an interest in commanding Jewish communal affairs. He arrogated to his *beit din* the title of "the generation's [most] significant court," and he is known for communal enactments improving Jewish family life, education, and women's status. His sharp criticism of opponents exhibited itself in his controversies with Meshullam of Melun and Efrayim of Regensburg.

Tam's best-known work is *Sefer ha-Yashar* (Vienna, 1811). It contained both *novellae* and *responsa*, and its main purpose was to resolve Talmudic textual problems without resorting to emendations of the received text. Even the best editions show considerable corruption of Rabbenu Tam's original work, and all present editions of *Sefer ha-Yashar* are fragments collected from it.

• Menachem Elon, *Jewish Law: History, Sources, Principles*, 4 vols. (Philadelphia, 1994). Chaim Tchernowitz, *Toledot ha-Poseqim*, 3 vols. (New York, 1946–1947). Efraim E. Urbach, *Baʿalei ha-Tosafot* (Jerusalem, 1955).

–MICHAEL CHERNICK

YAʿAQOV BEN MOSHEH HA-LEVI MOLIN. See MOLIN, YAʿAQOV BEN MOSHEH HA-LEVI.

YAʿAQOV BEN TSUR. See IBN ZUR, YAʿAQOV.

YAʿAQOV BEN WOLF KRANZ. See KRANZ, YAʿAQOV BEN WOLF.

YAʿAQOV BEN YAʿAQOV MOSHEH OF LISSA (c.1760–1832), Polish halakhist. Before traveling to Lissa (Leszno), he served as rabbi of a few other Polish communities. While in Lissa, his renown as a great scholar continued to spread, and many talented students traveled there to study under him. He is best known for his halakhic works, in particular *Ḥavvat Daʿat* and *Netivot ha-Mishpat*. The latter, which in large measure is directed against R. Aryeh Leib ha-Kohen's *Ketsot ha-Ḥoshen*, is one of the classic commentaries on *Ḥoshen Mishpat*, the fourth order of the *Shulḥan ʿArukh*. Yaʿaqov also published Talmudic *novellae*, biblical commentaries, and *responsa*.

• Isaac Lewin, "Le-Toledot ha-Ga'on Baʿal 'Ḥavot Daʿat,' " in *Leo Jung Jubilee Volume*, edited by Menahem Kasher et al. (New York, 1962), pp. 167–185. Chaim Tchernowitz, *Toledot ha-Poseqim*, vol. 3 (New York, 1946), pp. 252–258. —MARC SHAPIRO

YAʿAQOV OF DUBNO. See KRANZ, YAʿAQOV BEN WOLF.

YAʿAQOV YITSḤAQ, HA-ḤOZEH MI-LUBLIN (1745–1815), renowned Hasidic master, who was among the founders of the Polish Hasidic movement; known as the Seer of Lublin. He formulated the spiritual and social innovations of Polish Hasidism. His teachings consolidated the dual nature of the **tsaddiq*, defining imperative religious and mystical personal characteristics alongside the existential material demands of his congregation. His major works, *Zikkaron Zot* (Warsaw, 1869) and *Zot Zikkaron* (Lwów, 1851), depict the two principal dialectical components in religious life: tradition and innovation, or law and ecstasy. Law relates to normative traditional order, while ecstasy relates to new introspective mystical interpretation. Together these elements form the concealed and revealed realities of all existence and the dual fundamentals of religious worship. He wrote *Divrei Emet* (Zólkiew, 1830). See also YAʿAQOV YITSḤAQ OF PRZYSUCHA.

• Rachel Elior, "Between Yesh and Ayin: The Doctrine of the Tsaddiq in the Works of Jacob Isaac, the Seer of Lublin," in *Jewish History, Essays in Honour of Chimen Abramsky*, edited by Ada Rapoport-Albert and Steven Zipperstein (London, 1988), pp. 393–455. Rachel Elior, *Tarbiz* 62 (1993): 381–432. —RACHEL ELIOR

YAʿAQOV YITSḤAQ OF PRZYSUCHA (1766–1814), Hasidic master, known as ha-Yehudi ha-Qadosh (the Holy Jew). A spiritual perfectionist from his youth, he studied with Aryeh Leib Ḥarif in Przedbórz and Opatów and later under David Tevele at the *yeshivah* of Leszno. He was attracted to Hasidism by two *tsaddiqim*, Mosheh Leib of Sasov and David of Lelów. However, his most important master was Yaʿaqov Yitsḥaq, ha-Ḥozeh mi-Lublin. He became the Seer's closest disciple and served as a spiritual guide in the Seer's court, at that time the most prominent Hasidic center in Poland. Toward the end of his life, he grew disenchanted with the Seer's emphasis on magic and concern for the material well-being of the masses, which was then typical of Polish Hasidism. He broke away from his master and founded his own school of Hasidism in Przysucha, which was strongly opposed by the Seer and his remaining followers. The "Pshishkah" school emphasized an individualistic quest for spiritual perfection. It served the needs of an elite rather than the masses. Study of Talmud and scholarship received renewed emphasis. Sincerity in worship was more highly valued than external conformance to *halakhah*—the rules governing times for prayer were often breached in the interest of spiritual readiness. His leading disciple and successor was *Simḥah Bunem of Przysucha; other major disciples included Menaḥem Mendel of Kotsk, Ḥanokh of Aleksandrów, Yitsḥaq of Warka, and Yissakhar Ber of Radoszyce.

• Martin Buber, *For the Sake of Heaven: A Chronicle* (New York, 1969). Martin Buber, *Tales of the Hasidim* (New York, 1947). Morris M. Faierstein, *All Is in the Hands of Heaven: The Teachings of Rabbi Mordechai Joseph Leiner of Izbica* (Hoboken, N.J., 1989). —MILES KRASSEN

YAʿAQOV YOSEF HA-KOHEN OF POLONNOYE (died c.1782), Hasidic author. A noted rabbi and preacher, R. Yaʿaqov Yosef was the chief literary disciple of Yisra'el ben Eliʿezer *Baʿal Shem Tov and a key theoretician of early Hasidism. He served as rabbi in Shargorod, Raszków, Nemirov, and finally in Polonnoye. His works which show great erudition and interpretive skill, include *Toledot Yaʿaqov Yosef* (Korets, 1780; the first printed Hasidic book), *Ben Porat Yosef* (Korets, 1781), *Tsofnat Pa'neaḥ* (Korets, 1782), and *Ketonet Passim* (Lwów, 1866). In the course of these homilies, he frequently quotes the Baʿal Shem Tov, often referring to him simply as "my teacher." His writings provide several hundred such quotations from the Baʿal Shem Tov and are the major source for his teachings. Rabbi Yaʿaqov Yosef was an active social critic; many of his homilies are directed against the wealthy and the learned elite. Sometimes he also accused the populace of leading their teachers astray. In contrast to these negative examples, he proposed a link between the **tsaddiq*—sometimes also called **talmid ḥakham*—with the masses, for a new type of spiritually dominated Jewish community. Rabbi Yaʿaqov Yosef was known as a stern and demanding teacher, who did not attract disciples. He opposed the selection of R. *Dov Ber of Mezhirech as successor to his teacher, perhaps having hoped to fill that role himself.

• Samuel H. Dresner, *The Zaddik* (London and New York, 1960). —ARTHUR GREEN

YAD. See TORAH ORNAMENTS.

YADAYIM (יָדַיִם; Hands), tractate in Mishnah order Tohorot, with related material in Tosefta'. There is no *gemara'* in either Talmud. In biblical law a person, unlike food, for example, may contract impurity only through contact with a primary source of defilement, in which case impurity of the "first derivative" devolves upon the entire person. An early rabbinic enactment, attributed by the Talmud to King Solomon (*ʿEruv.* 21b), created a state of impurity applying to the hands alone, when they come into contact with a "first derivative" of impurity. Accordingly the rabbis also created a special form of purification for hands—the ritual washing of the hands. *Yadayim* discusses the laws pertaining to this special form of purity and impurity. According to the Talmud (*Ḥul.* 106a), these laws, applying mostly to priests, whose staple diet consisted of sanctified foods, served as a model for the practice of washing one's hands before any meal containing bread.

Paradoxically, the rabbis ruled that hands that had come into contact with scrolls of sacred biblical texts were defiled. *Yadayim*'s treatment of the laws relating to this enactment includes discussion of central themes in rabbinic law, such as the nature of the legal thinking associated with rabbinic enactments and the canonical status of certain problematic biblical books, such as *Ecclesiastes* and *Song of Songs*. The Sadducees objected to regarding contact with biblical scrolls as defiling the hands, believing it absurd that "the books of Holy Writ defile the hands, while the books of Homer do not defile the hands" (*Yad.* 4.6). Yoḥanan ben Zakk'ai offered the Pharisaic response: "the greater the degree to which something is cherished, the greater its connection to impurity" (*Yad.* 4.6).

An English translation of the tractate appears in Herbert Danby's *The Mishnah* (London, 1933).

• Chanoch Albeck, ed., *Shishah Sidrei Mishnah, Seder Tohorot* (Jerusalem, 1958). Philip Blackman, ed. and trans., *Mishnayoth*, vol. 5, *Order Taharoth* (Gateshead, 1973). Hermann Leberecht Strack and Günter Stemberger, *Introduction to the Talmud and Midrash* rev. and updat. ed., translated by Markus Bockmuehl (Minneapolis, 1992).

–AVRAHAM WALFISH

YAD HA-ḤAZAQAH. See MAIMONIDES, MOSES.

YAH. See GOD, NAMES OF.

YAḤAD. See QUMRAN COMMUNITY.

YAḤID VE-RABBIM (יָחִיד וְרַבִּים; the individual and the many), a fundamental principle of community government, which states that legislation enacted by majority decision is legally binding on all members of the community, including those in the minority who were opposed to it. Although the Talmudic sources that serve as a basis for communal legislative authority contain no reference to this issue, the sages readily accepted the principle of majority rule as a necessary corollary to the authority of the community to legislate, since the alternative doctrine of unanimous consent, espoused by R. Ya'aqov ben Me'ir *Tam (12th cent.), would in effect have made community government a practical impossibility. The question thus arose whether majority decisions would be binding upon the minority even where the minority was absent during the deliberations leading up to the vote, in light of the principle of judicial procedure that the majority decision would not be binding in such a case. The rule ultimately established was that majority legislation would be binding in any event, since to hold otherwise would effectively grant the minority a veto through the simple expedient of absenting themselves from the deliberations.

• Menachem Elon, *Ha-Mishpat Ha-'Ivri* (Jerusalem, 1973), vol. 2, pp. 580–587. Menachem Elon, ed., *The Principles of Jewish Law* (Jerusalem, 1975), pp. 163–165. Louis Finkelstein, *Jewish Self-Government in the Middle Ages* (New York, 1974), pp. 49–55.

–BEN TZION GREENBERGER

YAH RIBBON 'OLAM (Aram.; יָהּ רִבּוֹן עָלַם; God, Master of the Universe), Aramaic hymn composed by the kabbalist poet Yisra'el ben Mosheh *Najara, whose first name forms the acrostic. It is generally sung as a table hymn accompanying the Sabbath meals. Its composition is dated much earlier than the melodies now associated with it.

• Israel Davidson, *Thesaurus of Medieval Jewish Poetry*, 4 vols. (New York, 1970).

YAHRZEIT. See YORTSAYT.

YAHVEH. See GOD, NAMES OF.

YAHVIST SOURCE (J), one of the originally separate documents from which the Torah was composed in the view of critical biblical scholarship. It is so called because it uses YHVH as the name of God. See also BIBLE.

• Harold Bloom, *The Book of J* (New York, 1991), a controversial interpretation. Richard E. Friedman, *Who Wrote the Bible?* (New York, 1989).

–BARUCH J. SCHWARTZ

YALQUT (יַלְקוּט; compilation), title given to several Midrashic compilations. The most well-known are *Yalqut Shim'oni* (13th cent.), *Yalqut Makhiri* (date and identity of author not established), and *Yalqut Re'uveni* (17th cent.).

–DANIEL SPERBER

YALQUT MAKHIRI, one of several medieval Midrashic anthologies arranged in biblical verse order. The following extant portions of this particular *yalqut* (anthology) have been published: *Isaiah* (J. Z. Kahana-Spira, 1893), Minor Prophets (A. J. Greenup, 1909–1913, 1924–1925; J. Z. Lauterbach, 1936), *Psalms* (S. Buber, 1899), and *Proverbs* (L. Grünhut, 1902; Y. S. Spiegel, 1985). *Yalqut Makhiri* was compiled by Makhir ben Abba' Mari, probably in Spain in the fourteenth century. Makhir often quoted his sources by name, some of which are no longer extant elsewhere. He appears not to have modified them in his quotations. Thus, Makhir's introductions at the beginning of his *yalqut* to *Isaiah* and *Psalms* and the fact that the *Yalqut Makhiri* seems to preserve relatively rare Sephardi versions of the texts quoted make this work valuable for reconstructing the evolution and dispersion of rabbinic, particularly aggadic, traditions and for text criticism of earlier Midrashic literature.

• Menachem Mendel Kasher and Jacob Ber Mandelbaum, eds. and trans., *Sarei ha-'Elef*, rev. and corr. ed. (Jerusalem, 1978). Hermann Leberecht Strack and Günter Stemberger, *Introduction to the Talmud and Midrash*, rev. and updat. ed., translated by Markus Bockmuehl (Minneapolis, 1992).

–MARC BREGMAN

YALQUT RE'UVENI, an anthology of homiletic and mystical commentaries to the Torah arranged in order of the weekly portions and modeled after the earlier Midrashic anthology, the *Yalqut Shim'oni*. Its author was the seventeenth-century kabbalist, Re'uven ben Hoschke. The work is particularly valuable for its quotations from kabbalistic compositions over the preceding five hundred years, many of which are no longer extant. It was published in two parts: part one, arranged in alphabetical order (Prague, 1660); and part two, following the order of the Torah (Wilmersdorf, 1681).

YALQUT SHIM'ONI, Midrashic thesaurus to the Bible, in which halakhic and aggadic passages of the Talmud and Midrashic works—over ten thousand in number—are arranged in biblical order. The first part of the anthology relates to the Pentateuch, the other to the remaining biblical books. Besides serving as a useful handbook for homiletic purposes, the *Yalqut Shim'oni* has considerably aided comparative and critical evaluation of Midrashic material. Of the fifty sources quoted and attributed, several are no longer extant, such as *Sifrei Zuta', Midrash Esfah, Midrash Avkir, Midrash Tadshe'*, and *Devarim Zuta'*. The work is attributed to R. Shim'on ha-Darshan of Frankfurt (c.13th cent.), about whose identity there are conflicting views. The first edition of the section on the Pentateuch (Salonika, 1526) contains an important addendum, *Qunteres Aḥaron*, which includes numerous aggadic passages from the Talmud Yerushalmi.

• Arthur B. Hyman and Yitsḥak Shiloni, eds., *Yalqut Shim'oni* (Jerusalem, 1973–1992). Arthur B. Hyman, ed., *Meqorot Yalqut Shim'oni* (Jerusalem, 1965–1974). —DANIEL SPERBER

YAMIM NORA'IM (יָמִים נוֹרָאִים; Days of Awe), the Ten Days of Repentance (see 'ASERET YEMEI TESHUVAH). The Bible does not connect the festival of the first day of the seventh month (*Ro'sh ha-Shanah) with the solemn fast of *Yom Kippur, which is observed on the tenth. The Talmud, however, regards Ro'sh ha-Shanah as the beginning and Yom Kippur as the end of a period of self-examination and judgment. The term Yamim Nora'im is first found in *Sefer Maharil* by Ya'aqov ben Mosheh ha-Levi *Molin (14th cent.).

YANN'AI (3d cent.), Palestinian amora'. He was known as Rabbah (the Great) or Sabba' (the Elder) to distinguish him from his grandson, dubbed R. Yann'ai Ze'ira' (the Lesser). It is not always possible to distinguish R. Yann'ai Rabbah from later amora'im called Yann'ai without a patronymic. He studied with R. Ḥiyya', who foresaw his future prominence as a leader (Y., *Dem*. 7.1, 26a). As a first generation amora', he was an important student of R. Yehudah ha-Nasi'. His own most prominent students were R. Yoḥanan and Reish Laqish. While it seems that he resided for a time in Sepphoris, he eventually established an academy in Akbara in Upper Galilee (*'A. Z.* 30a). A prosperous vineyard and orchard owner, his generosity exceeded his wealth (*Mo'ed. Q.* 12b), and during a time of oppressive taxation, he permitted farmers to sow their fields during the *shemittah* year (*San*. 26a). Among his best-known teachings are the following: a person should not put himself in danger and depend on miraculous intervention (*Shab*. 32a); and he who studies without the fear of God is like someone who makes a door before constructing the building (*Shab*. 31b).

• Wilhelm Bacher, *Die Agada der palästinensischen Amoräer* (repr. Hildesheim, 1965), vol. 1, pp. 35–47. Aaron Oppenheimer, "Those of the School of Rabbi Yann'ai," in *Studies in the History of the Jewish People and the Land of Israel*, edited by U. Rappaport (Haifa, 1978), vol. 4, pp. x–xi, 137–145, in Heb. with Eng. summary. —MICHAEL L. BROWN

YANN'AI (6th cent.), **payyetan* in Erets Yisra'el. He is considered the earliest author of synagogal poetry to sign his name in his compositions acrostically (see ACROSTICS), an arrangement found earlier in Christian and Samaritan liturgy. He wrote *Maḥazor Yann'ai*, a cycle of some 167 poetic embellishments for the *'Amidah, connecting the most important prayer of the Sabbath Shaḥarit service with the content of the weekly Torah reading (see QERI'AT HA-TORAH) and its treatment in Midrashic tradition, following the *triennial cycle common in Byzantine Erets Yisra'el. *Maḥazor Yann'ai* and some of Yann'ai's compositions for other occasions were highly esteemed and copied for centuries for liturgical use; numerous copies were found in the Cairo Genizah. However, they were almost lost when the Babylonian Torah-reading cycle replaced the triennial cycle, and payyetanic creativity was applied elsewhere. The literary heritage of Yann'ai is a major source for knowledge of the concepts, beliefs, and literature of the sixth-century synagogue.

• Israel Davidson, ed. and trans., *Maḥzor Yann'ai: A Liturgical Work of the VIIth Century* (New York, 1919). Zvi Meir Rabinowitz, ed., *Maḥazor Piyyutei Rabbi Yann'ai la-Torah vela-Mo'adim*, 2 vols. (Jerusalem, 1985–1987). Joseph Yahalom, ed., *Qeta'i ha-Genizah shel Piyyutei Yann'ai* (Jerusalem, 1978). —PETER LENHARDT

YAQNEHAZ (יַקְנְהָ״ז), acrostic abbreviation of the words *yayin* (wine), *Qiddush (Sanctification), *ner* (light), *Havdalah (Separation), and *zeman* (time; namely, the *She-Heḥeyanu blessing, referred to in rabbinic parlance as Birkat ha-Zeman). The abbreviation served as a mnemonic aid for the correct sequence of benedictions in the Qiddush recited on the eve of a festival that coincides with the conclusion of the Sabbath. The word *yaqnehaz* sounds similar to the German *jagt den Has* (hunt the hare), and the fanciful suggestion has been made that this may be the origin of the hare-hunting scenes—a well-known folkloristic motif—that appear in many illustrated Pesaḥ Haggadot.

YARMELKE. See KIPPAH.

YAVNEH, town in Erets Yisra'el near Ashdod; the first significant Jewish settlement there dates from the reign of Alexander Yannai (103–76 BCE). The Romans, during the First Jewish Revolt (66–70 CE), established a refugee camp in Yavneh. Since it was a predominantly pagan town, the Romans' hope may have been that the Jews would assimilate with the local population. Around the year 68 CE, R. *Yoḥanan ben Zakk'ai interceded with Vespasian for permission to go to Yavneh and organize an academy there. This request was granted, and Yoḥanan was able to receive the scholars who subsequently fled from Jerusalem in 70. At a meeting held in a vineyard, he declared the Yavneh academy the successor to the Jerusalem *Sanhedrin, and the academy became known as the Vineyard of Yavneh (Kerem be-Yavneh). In the course of the next six decades, following the destruction of the Temple, the sages at Yavneh evolved the model of Judaism that came to be accepted as normative. At Yavneh, the canon of the Bible was finally determined. In 132 under Hadrian's rule, the Roman governor—fearing the authority established by the academy at Yavneh—moved the school to Lydda. After the Bar Kokhba' Revolt, attempts to return the Sanhedrin to Yavneh failed.

• Peter Schafer, "Die sogenante Synode von Jabne," in *Studien zur Geschichte und Theologie des rabbinischen Judentums* (Leiden, 1978), pp. 45–55.

—DANIEL SPERBER

YEAR. See CALENDAR.

YEAR OF RELEASE. See SHEMITTAH.

YEB (Gr. Elephantine), an island in the Nile, opposite Aswan in Upper Egypt. During the Persian period (after 525 BCE) it was the southern frontier fortress of the empire (*Est.* 1.1), and Yeb and Swen (Aswan) became the military and administrative centers of regiments made up of different ethnic groups under senior Persian or Babylonian officers. Among these groups was a Jewish community that traced its origins to before the Persian conquest.

During the 1890s, documents later known as the Elephantine papyri were discovered. Written in Aramaic, they were published by A. E. Cowley in 1923 and a second collection edited by E. G. Kraeling appeared in 1953. Recently, B. Porten and A. Yardeni have produced an updated publication. The contents of the papyri afford an insight into the social structure, legal customs and religious beliefs of this early Jewish Diaspora. The Jewish garrison maintained its own temple, with its altar, sacrificial system, and priesthood, while remaining in communication with the religious authorities in Jerusalem. Of particular interest among its documents are the Aramaic versions of the "Wisdom of Aḥiqar" and the Behistun inscription of Darius I. Of importance for Jewish history are three archives: The Woman Mibtahiah (451–410), with personal papers tracing three generations through deeds of gifts in property, marriage and inheritance that offer insight into the legal status of Jewish women in this community; The Temple Servitor Ananiah (451–402), with eleven documents reflecting the status, property and family of this functionary of the local Temple; and The Community Leader Jedaniah (419–406), which includes a letter encouraging the Jews to observe Pesaḥ according to the Torah, reports of the antagonism of the Egyptian priests of Khnub leading to the destruction of the Jewish Temple, and copies of petitions to the leaders of the Jewish community in Jerusalem, dated 407 BCE, asking for help in reconstructing the Temple. The last texts, which mention Johanan the high priest of the Jerusalem Temple and the sons of Sanballat, governor of Samaria, are important for the reconstruction of the chronology of the period of Ezra and Nehemiah a generation earlier.

• Aaron Demsky, "Who Came First, Ezra or Nehemiah?: The Synchronistic Approach," *Hebrew Union College Annual* 65 (1994): 1–19. Yochanan Muffs, *Studies in the Aramaic Legal Papyri from Elephantine: The Life of an Ancient Jewish Military Colony* (Leiden, 1969). Bezalel Porten, *Archives from Elephantine* (Berkeley, 1968). Bezalel Porten and Ada Yardeni, *Textbook of Aramaic Documents from Ancient Egypt*, vols. 1–3 (Jerusalem and Winona Lake, Ind., 1986–1993). Reuven Yaron, *Introduction to the Law of the Aramaic Papyri* (Oxford, 1961).

—AARON DEMSKY

YEDID NEFESH (יְדִיד נֶפֶשׁ; Devoted Friend), liturgical poem by the Safed kabbalist El'azar ben Mosheh *Azikri, published in his *Sefer Ḥaredim* (1601). Teachings of the Lurianic Kabbalah are reflected in this *piyyut*'s yearning for God, the initial letters of the four stanzas making up the Tetragrammaton (see GOD, NAMES OF). Yedid Nefesh is often sung before *Qabbalat Shabbat and at the Sabbath afternoon *Se'udah Shelishit (see ZEMIROT). Various textual errors have been corrected in recent traditional prayer books.

• Shlomo Tal, *Ha-Siddur be-Hishtalsheluto* (Jerusalem, 1985), pp. 66–68.

—GABRIEL A. SIVAN

YEFET BEN 'ALI (10th cent.), *Karaite scholar and exegete; known in Arabic as Abu 'Ali Ḥasan ibn 'Ali al-Lawi al-Basri. He was born in Basra, Iraq, but emigrated to Jerusalem to join the *Avelei Tsiyyon. Few details are known of his life, but he was quickly recognized as a scholar and authority because of his writings, particularly his Bible commentaries, which cover the entire Bible and provide, for the most part, a literalist explication of the text, as well as a translation into Arabic. He often made use of the work of his Karaite predecessors but also added original interpretations of his own. In his commentaries, he vigorously attacked Sa'adyah Ga'on, often quoting Sa'adyah's works word for word. Some of Yefet's commentaries were translated into Hebrew, making them available to Karaites outside the Arabic world. His commentaries were used by Rabbanite commentators, such as Avraham ibn Ezra. Yefet's commentaries on *Hosea, Nahum, Song of Songs, Ruth*, and *Daniel* have been published (as well as individual chapters of other books), while the rest remain in manuscript. In addition, Yefet wrote a code of Karaite law, *Sefer ha-Mitsvot*, manuscripts of which have been recently identified. Sahl ben Matsliaḥ mentions a polemic against Sa'adyah Ga'on written by Yefet, but this may be a reference to the polemical section in his *Sefer ha-Mitsvot*. Yefet also wrote polemics against Christianity and Islam.

• Haggai Ben-Shammai, "Shitot ha-Maḥshavah ha-Datit shel Abu Yosef Ya'aqov al-Qirqesani vi-Yefet ben 'Eli," Ph.D. dissertation, Hebrew University, 1977. Jacob Mann, *Texts and Studies in Jewish History and Literature*, vol. 2 (Cincinnati, 1935), pp. 30–33 and s.v. index. Leon Nemoy, *Karaite Anthology* (New Haven, 1952), pp. 83–102. Samuel Poznanski, *Karaite Literary Opponents of Sa'adyah Ga'on* (London, 1908), no. 12. Uriel Simon, *Four Approaches to the Book of Psalms* (Albany, 1991), chap. 2.

—DAVID E. SKLARE

YEHAREG VE-'AL YA'AVOR (יֵהָרֵג וְאַל יַעֲבֹר), areas of law where one should sacrifice one's life rather than violate the provisions of law. This principle applies to idol worship, sexual violations, and murder (*San.* 74a). The general rule is found in the *Shulḥan 'Arukh* (*Yoreh De'ah* 157.1). With the three exceptions of idolatry, sexual violations, and murder, if one is told to violate a commandment of the Torah or be killed, and the violation is in private, the commandment can be violated. A person may choose *martyrdom if the coercer intends to destroy the Jewish faith. If the action occurs in public, one must lose one's life rather than violate any Jewish law, but only if the coercer intends to destroy the faith. If it is a time of intense anti-Jewish feeling, one should not even transgress in matters of Jewish custom, but should rather die. Some authorities maintain that one may violate commandments if doing so occurs through inaction rather than action (such as in the case of rape); others disagree. Some authorities rule that in any situation where one need not lose one's life, one must not. Others rule that martyrdom is sometimes permissible but not mandatory. According to nearly all authorities, one need not ever sacrifice one's life to fulfill positive commandments; thus, *yehareg ve-'al yaʿavor* is limited to violating negative commandments.

• Arthur J. Drodge and James Tabor, *A Noble Death: Suicide and Martyrdom Among Christians and Jews in Antiquity* (San Fransisco, 1992). Menachem Elon, *Jewish Law: History, Sources, Principles* (Philadelphia, 1994). —MICHAEL BROYDE

YEḤI'EL BEN YOSEF OF PARIS (died 1268), Talmudic commentator, rabbinic authority, and communal leader. He was born in Meaux. His primary teacher was R. Yehudah ben Yitsḥaq upon whose death, he became head of the Paris Talmudic academy. While no separate collection of Yeḥi'el's **tosafot* exists, they are cited by other commentators, especially his students. His contemporary, Yitsḥaq ben Mosheh of Vienna, the codifier, sought and received his responses on Jewish legal questions. It appears Yeḥi'el also wrote a tract on Jewish law (no longer extant).

Yeḥi'el of Paris was a major participant in the Disputation of *Paris, in which he defended the Talmud against papal claims that it contained anti-Christian views and contradicted the Bible. However, he and his colleagues failed to rescue the Talmud; manuscripts of it were burned in Paris in 1242.

Yeḥi'el of Paris and many of his students left Paris in the face of anti-Jewish pressure and established an academy in Erets Yisra'el, in Acre (c.1259), where he died.

• Efraim E. Urbach, *Baʿalei ha-Tosafot* (Jerusalem, 1955). —MICHAEL CHERNICK

YEḤI'EL MIKHA'EL OF ZLOCZÓW (c.1726–1781), early Hasidic master in Galicia. The son of Yitsḥaq of Drogobych, a member of the rabbinical court in Brody, Yeḥi'el Mikha'el was a disciple of the Baʿal Shem Tov and later accepted the authority of Dov Ber of Mezhirech. One of the most prominent Hasidic leaders in the Brody region, Yeḥi'el Mikha'el was the target of anti-Hasidic protests. Although he did not produce any works, he had many outstanding disciples, including Yaʿaqov Yitsḥaq, ha-Ḥozeh mi-Lublin (the Seer of Lublin), Avraham Yehoshuʿa Heschel of Opatów, Meshullam Feibush of Zbarazh, Mordekhai of Neskhiz, and Ḥayyim Tirer of Czernowitz. All of Yeḥi'el Mikha'el's five sons were Hasidic masters, the most famous being Ze'ev Wolf of Zbarazh and Yitsḥaq of Radziwillów. A collection of Yeḥi'el Mikha'el's teachings appeared posthumously as *Mayim Rabbim* (Warsaw, 1899; repr. as *Sheloshah Sefarim Niftalim: Mayim Rabbim* [Brooklyn, N.Y., 1979]). Famous for his extreme dedication to spiritual life, he taught a rigorous asceticism that required abstaining from sensual desires. The goal was directly to cleave to and ultimately become indistinguishable from the Ein Sof, the most ineffable essence of God. According to Hasidic accounts, Yeḥi'el Mikha'el died in a state of ecstatic union on a Shabbat afternoon.

• Martin Buber, *Tales of the Hasidim* (New York, 1947). Abraham J. Heschel, *The Circle of the Baʿal Shem Tov: Studies in Hasidism* (Chicago, 1985). Miles Krassen, " 'Devequt' and Faith in Zaddiqim: The Religious Tracts of Meshullam Feibush Heller of Zbarazh," Ph.D. dissertation, University of Pennsylvania, 1990. —MILES KRASSEN

YEHONATAN BEN DAVID HA-KOHEN OF LUNEL (c.1135–1210), Provençal rabbi and leading scholar of Lunel following the death of R. Meshullam ben Yaʿaqov of Lunel. He was a student of R. Avraham ben David of Posquières and wrote the first commentary to the Alfasi code (see ALFASI, YITSḤAQ), including a comprehensive explication of the Mishnah in which he abridged Rashi's commentary to the Talmud and added Provençal interpretations. His correspondence with Moses *Maimonides, among the most poignant in Hebrew literature, resulted in strong bonds of friendship and mutual admiration between the two scholars; Maimonides sent him and his colleagues copies of his *Mishneh Torah* and *Guide of the Perplexed*. Through the offices of Aharon ben Meshullam of Lunel, Yehonatan defended Maimonides' position on the resurrection against Me'ir Abulafia. Yehonatan was among the leaders of the three hundred French and English rabbis who emigrated in 1210 to Erets Yisra'el, where he died.

• Shamma Friedman, ed., *Perush R. Yehonatan ha-Kohen mi-Lunel ʿal ha-Mishnah veha-Rif Massekhet Bava' Qamma'* (New York, 1968), introduction, pp. 1–62. Heinrich Gross, *Gallia judaica: Dictionnaire géographique de la France d'après les sources rabbiniques*, with a supplement by S. Schwarzfuchs (Paris, 1897; repr. Amsterdam, 1969). Israel Ta-Shema, *Rabbi Zeraḥyah ha-Levi—Baʿal ha-Ma'or u-Venei Ḥugo: Le-Toledot ha-Sifrut ha-Rabbanit be-Provence* (Jerusalem, 1992). Isadore Twersky, *Rabad of Posquières: A Twelfth-Century Talmudist* (Philadelphia, 1980). —SHLOMO H. PICK

YEHOSHUʿA BEN ḤANANYAH (1st–2d cent.), tanna'; one of the five pupils of R. *Yoḥanan ben Zakk'ai, by whom he was ordained. From his teacher, Yehoshuʿa ben Ḥananyah learned Merkavah mysticism (*Ḥag.* 14b) (see MAʿASEH MERKAVAH). He served in the Levitical choir in the Temple before its destruction in 70 CE and must have been at least thirty years old to fill that office. Together with R. *Eliʿezer ben Hurqanos he smuggled R. Yoḥanan ben Zakk'ai out of the besieged Jerusalem in a coffin to the Roman camp (*Git.* 56a). Following the fall of Jerusalem, Yehoshuʿa founded and headed a *beit din* in Peqiʿin, north of *Yavneh, but after the death of Yoḥanan ben Zakk'ai served as **av beit din* in the court of Rabbi Gamli'el in Yavneh. Yehoshuʿa knew many languages and was renowned for his wisdom. He is said to have accompanied Gamli'el on a mission to Rome, where he discussed religious questions with leading non-Jews, reputedly including the emperor Hadrian. A lover of peace, Yehoshuʿa accepted a fundamental ruling of R. Gamli'el on the dating of Yom Kippur, despite his profound disagreement, but when Gamli'el publicly humiliated him in the Sanhedrin, Gamli'el was deposed for his arrogance. When the two men were eventually reconciled, Yehoshuʿa insisted upon R. Gamli'el's reinstatement (*Ber.* 28a). Yehoshuʿa lived to an old age and was still alive when Hadrian visited Palestine in 130. According to the Midrash, Yehoshuʿa once restrained the people from rebelling against Rome after the emperor refused to honor his pledge to rebuild the Temple (*Gn. Rab.* 64). Yehoshuʿa's halakhic views are often quoted in the Talmud. He tended toward leniency, permitting, for example, the conversion of Ammonites, and objected to excessive asceticism and mourning over the destruction of the Temple (*B. B.* 60b). One of his best-known aphorisms was "The evil eye, the evil inclination, and hatred of mankind drive a man out of the world" (*Avot* 2.16).

• William Scott Green, *The Traditions of Joshua Ben Hananiah*, Studies in Judaism in Late Antiquity, vol. 29 (Leiden, 1981).

—DANIEL SPERBER

YEHOSHUʿA BEN LEVI (3d cent.), amora'; head of the Lydda academy and leader of the Jewish community in Palestine. He engaged in halakhic discussions with R. *Yoḥanan bar Nappaḥa' and *Shimʿon ben Laqish, and many of Yehoshuʿa ben Levi's decisions were accepted as *halakhah*. He also instituted many rules regulating the synagogue service. Yehoshuʿa was an outstanding aggadist and was himself the subject of miraculous tales (some depicting him as the companion of Elijah). Legend has it that Yehoshuʿa did not actually die but entered paradise during his lifetime (*Ket.* 77b), after a struggle with the angel of death (*Maʿaseh de-Rabbi Yehoshuʿa ben Levi* and *Seder Gan ʿEden*). Yehoshuʿa believed that the study of the Torah not only transforms the spirit but also protects the body (*ʿEruv.* 54a), and therefore he was not afraid to mingle with people who had contagious diseases (*Ket.* 77b). He stressed ethical behavior and, above all, humility (*ʿA. Z.* 20b).

• Gershom Bader, *The Encyclopedia of Talmudic Sages*, translated from the Yiddish by Solomon Katz (Northvale, N.J., and London, 1988). Aaron Hyman, *Toledot Tanna'im ve-'Amora'im* (1910; Jerusalem, 1987). Mordecai Margaliot, ed., *Entsiqlopediyyah le-Ḥakhmei ha-Talmud veha-Ge'onim* (Jerusalem, 1946).

—DANIEL SPERBER

YEHOSHUʿA BEN PERAḤYAH (1st cent.), tanna'; **nasi'* of the Sanhedrin. Together with Nitt'ai the Arbelite, he constituted one of the **zugot* (pairs) who transmitted the *oral law. Only one *halakhah* is quoted in his name. According to a legend reported in *Sotah* 47a, Yehoshuʿa had a disciple who went astray. Yehoshuʿa rejected him completely, casting him out with his own two hands, and this disciple then became an active heretic. According to some ancient readings, this disciple was Jesus, but chronologically this is extremely unlikely, since Yehoshuʿa lived some two generations before the time of Jesus. Yehoshuʿa's favorite maxim was "Provide yourself a teacher; get a companion [for study] and judge all men on the scale of merit" (*Avot* 1.6).

• Jacob Neusner, *The Rabbinic Traditions about the Pharisees before 70*, 3 vols. (Leiden, 1971).

—DANIEL SPERBER

YEHUDAH BAR IL'AI (2d cent.), tanna' generally referred to simply as R. Yehudah; one of the five most renowned disciples of R. ʿAqiva'. He was the teacher of R. *Yehudah ha-Nasi', who later incorporated in the Mishnah many of the traditions he had received from Yehudah. After the Hadrianic persecutions following the failure of the Bar Kokhba' Revolt (see BAR KOKHBA', SHIMʿON), Yehudah, who had been ordained by R. *Yehudah ben Bava', helped to establish the *academy at Usha' in Lower Galilee (his birthplace). Yehudah taught halakhic *Midrash. The **Sifra'* is based on his teachings and follows the tradition of R. ʿAqiva' (*San.* 6a). In conflicts of opinion between himself and his colleagues, R. Me'ir and R. Shimʿon bar Yoḥai, Yehudah's decisions were followed. He became a leading spokesman for the Jewish community (*Shab.* 33b) and was greatly revered for his humility and saintliness. He also was respected by the Roman authorities. More than six hundred of his rulings have been incorporated into the Mishnah, and with the exception of *Qinnim*, there is not a tractate in which his name does not appear. He was an active aggadist, working in partnership but not necessarily in agreement with R. Neḥemyah; **Genesis Rabbah* alone mentions about two hundred homiletical disagreements between them. While he greatly encouraged the study of Torah, Yehudah also advocated working for one's livelihood (*Ned.* 49b), insisting that parents teach their children a trade (*Qid.* 29a), though one's occupation should always be secondary to Torah studies (*Ber.* 35b).

• Israel Konovitz, *Rabbi Judah Bar Il'a'i: Collected Sayings in Halakah and Aggadah in the Talmudic and Midrashic Literature* (Jerusalem, 1965).

—DANIEL SPERBER

YEHUDAH BAR YEḤEZQE'L (died 291), Babylonian amora'. A pupil of *Rav and *Shemu'el, he meticulously preserved their teachings, and hundreds of their *halakhot* are quoted in the Talmud in his name. Yehudah founded the academy at *Pumbedita, which functioned for almost eight hundred years. The type of Talmudic dialectics that he developed in Pumbedita became standard. His prayer was a combination of careful preparation, deep devotion, and spontaneity (*R. ha-Sh.* 35a) and his piety and devotion (*Shab.* 118b) were such that his petitions were always answered (*Taʿan.* 24b). One of his most famous sayings is that "The Lord only created the world so that people should fear him" (*Shab.* 31b).

• Gershom Bader, *The Encyclopedia of Talmudic Sages*, translated from the Yiddish by Solomon Katz (Northvale, N.J., and London, 1988). Aaron Hyman, *Toledot Tanna'im ve-'Amora'im* (1910; Jerusalem, 1987). Mordecai Margaliot, ed., *Entsiqlopediyyah le-Ḥakhmei ha-Talmud veha-Ge'onim* (Jerusalem, 1946).

—DANIEL SPERBER

YEHUDAH BEN BARZILLAI AL-BARGELONI (12th cent.), leading Spanish halakhist; author of numerous halakhic treatises, including *Sefer ha-ʿIttim*, on the laws of the Sabbath and festivals. He followed the tradition of R. Shemu'el ha-Nagid, often quoting his last great work, *Hilkhata' Gavruta'*. Besides his halakhic work, Yehudah wrote the most extensive commentary on *Sefer Yetsirah* (Berlin, 1885) in the Middle Ages. In fact, his is a supercommentary on Saʿadyah Ga'on's commentary on the ancient treatise, comparing it to other early commentaries and to the Talmudic and Midrashic traditions concerning creation. The author's main purpose was to resolve the differences between the account of creation in *Sefer Yetsirah* and those found in Talmudic traditions, and to prove that Saʿadyah's philosophical and scientific views expressed in his commentary were in conformity with rabbinic tradition. This was especially difficult in regard to Saʿadyah's views on revelation; Saʿadyah denied any possibility of revelation of a divine entity and insisted that what the prophets had seen was a created angel, the *kavod* or *shekhinah*, that serves as a sign that verifies the divine content of the prophetic message. Yehudah supported this view and tried to confirm it by a detailed exegesis of rabbinic statements concerning revelation. He quotes dozens of treatises from late antiquity and the early Middle Ages, some of them unknown from any other source. He used the old translation of Saʿadyah's philosophical works that originated in Byzantium in the late eleventh century; his quotations were very often the only source for this work for medieval authors.

• Joseph Dan in *Massuot: Meḥqarim be-Sifrut ha-Qabbalah uve-Maḥashevet Yisra'el*, edited by Michal Kushir-Oron and Amos Goldreich (Jerusalem, 1994), pp. 99–119. S. J. Halberstam, ed., *Perush Sefer Yetsirah* (Berlin, 1885). —JOSEPH DAN

YEHUDAH BEN BAVA' (2d cent.), tanna'; one of the *Ten Martyrs. He disputed many halakhic subjects with R. *ʿAqiva' ben Yosef. The most noteworthy *halakhah* of Yehudah ben Bava' was the decision that only one witness was required to testify to a man's death in order to permit his widow to remarry. He was famed for his piety, and according to the rabbis, wherever it said "it happened that a certain *ḥasid* [pious man] . . ." did so and so, this referred to Yehudah (*B. Q.* 103b). During the Hadrianic persecutions (late 130s), when the Romans forbade the teaching of the Torah, Yehudah ordained several outstanding pupils of R. ʿAqiva' (including R. *Me'ir and R. *Shimʿon bar Yoḥ'ai), thereby ensuring the continuity of tradition. Caught by the Romans in the act of ordaining students, he bid his disciples to escape and himself suffered martyrdom.

• Wilhelm Bacher, *Die Agada der Tannaiten*, 2 vols. (Strassburg, 1884–1890). Gershon Bader, *Encyclopedia of the Talmud Sages* (Northvale, N.J., 1988). —DANIEL SPERBER

YEHUDAH BEN KALONIMOS OF SPEYER (died c.1199), German halakhist and member of the *beit din* (rabbinic court) of Speyer. His major literary work is the Talmudic lexicon *Yiḥusei Tanna'im ve-'Amora'im*, which, because of its great length, did not achieve widespread circulation and has survived only in manuscript fragments. The book is a compilation of the sayings of every Talmudic sage, along with a commentary that critically analyzes textual variants and explains difficult terminology and halakhic subject matter. Yehudah's remarks on the aggadic passages of the Talmud indicate that he was heavily influenced by the spirit of martyrology that permeated the teachings of the Ḥasidei Ashkenaz.

• Efraim E. Urbach, *Baʿalei ha-Tosafot* (Jerusalem, 1980), pp. 361–378. —MARK WASHOFSKY

YEHUDAH BEN SHEMU'EL HE-ḤASID (died 1217), Talmudic scholar and mystic and one of the leading personalities in the movement known as the *Ḥasidei Ashkenaz. His reputation for asceticism and saintliness made him the subject of many legends. The ethical work *Sefer Ḥasidim* has been ascribed to him; in fact it is a composite work, containing writings of Yehudah, his father Shemu'el, and his pupil *Elʿazar ben Yehudah of Worms. Yehudah is also credited with the authorship of *Shir ha-Kavod. Although his mystical teachings were primarily ethical and devotional, they also contained theosophical doctrines as well as elements of folk religion. His stress on Bible study and devout prayer rather than Talmudic scholarship had popular appeal, and he advised those who knew no Hebrew to pray in any language they understood.

• Jacob Freimann, *Sefer Ḥasidim* (Frankfurt, 1924), pp. 1–15. Gershom Gerhard Scholem, *Major Trends in Jewish Mysticism* (New York, 1961).

YEHUDAH BEN TABB'AI (1st cent. BCE), tanna'; *av bet din* of the Sanhedrin and—together with *Shimʿon ben Shetaḥ—one of the *zugot* (pairs) responsible for transmitting the oral tradition. During the persecution of the Pharisees by King Alexander Yannai, Yehudah fled to Alexandria, where he remained until Shimʿon ben Shetaḥ brought him back to Jerusalem. He may have served as *nasi'* for a time, until he resigned following an error in one of his judgments, part of his running battle against the *Sadducees.

• Jacob Neusner, *The Rabbinic Traditions about the Pharisees before 70*, 3 vols. (Leiden, 1971). —DANIEL SPERBER

YEHUDAH BEN YEḤI'EL. See MESSER LEON FAMILY.

YEHUDAH BEN YITSḤAQ (1166–1224), French Talmudist who headed the noted Paris Yeshivah following the return of the Jews to that city in 1198; also known as Yehudah Sir Leon. He wrote *tosafot* that transmit much of the teachings of his master, R. Yitsḥaq ben Shemu'el of Dampierre, and he was the first tosafist to cite Maimonides' *Mishneh Torah*. His students include R. Yitsḥaq ben Mosheh of Vienna and R. Mosheh ben Yaʿaqov of Coucy.

• Efraim E. Urbach, *Baʿalei ha-Tosafot* (Jerusalem, 1980), pp. 320–335. —MARK WASHOFSKY

YEHUDAH HA-KOHEN (c.975–1050), rabbinic scholar, legal authority. He lived in Mainz and studied at the academy of R. Gershom ben Yehudah, eventually becoming one of its heads. He should not be confused with R. Yehudah ben Me'ir ha-Kohen, a teacher of R. Gershom, who was better known as R. Leontin. Rabbi Yehudah had three sons, all of whom were involved in aspects of Talmudic study or the composition of liturgical poetry. He himself was associated with the study of mystical teachings in chains of tradition preserved by the Ḥasidei Askhenaz.

Rabbi Yehudah issued his halakhic rulings with confidence, disagreeing on occasion with his colleagues in Mainz. He is one of two signatories to a well-known *responsum* to the community of Troyes, which formulated the prerogative of the majority in matters of communal government. His major (and only extant) work is *Sefer ha-Dinim*, a collection of his *responsa* on a variety of topics, both practical and theoretical. Rabbi Yehudah also collected a number of his predecessors' *responsa*. A unified text of *Sefer ha-Dinim* has not been preserved, but it is possible to reconstruct much of the work from citations found in the writings of subsequent Ashkenazi halakhists and from manuscript passages.

• Irving A. Agus, *Urban Civilization in Pre-Crusade Europe* (Leiden, 1965), vol. 1, pp. 43–45. Avraham Grossman, *Ḥakhmei Ashkenaz ha-Ri'shonim* (Jerusalem, 1981), pp. 175–210, and index. Avraham Grossman, ed., *Sefer ha-Dinim* (Jerusalem, 1977). —EPHRAIM KANARFOGEL

YEHUDAH HA-LEVI (c.1075–1141), Spanish poet and religious thinker. A physician by profession, he is known for his Hebrew poetry and his theological prose work the *Kuzari*, written in Arabic (first Hebrew edition, Fano, 1506). Upon completion of this last work he set out for the Holy Land, spending some time in Alexandria and visiting Tyre and Damascus en route. According to legend he was killed by an Arab horseman while reciting his famous "Elegy for Zion" before the gates of Jerusalem, but documents discovered in the Cairo *Genizah indicate that he died in Egypt and never reached Erets Yisra'el.

Yehudah ha-Levi was one of the leading Hebrew poets of the Middle Ages. Like his friend Mosheh *ibn Ezra, he applied the forms and conventions of Arabic poetry, such as rhyme and meter, to classical Hebrew. The body of his poetry falls under three main headings: secular (including songs of love, wine, and friendship), religious, and national. Much of his religious verse, marked by an intense and at times mystical love of God, has found its way into Jewish liturgy, as have some of his national poems. The profound yearning for Zion that characterizes his national poetry is based on his belief that life in exile is by definition incomplete and that only in Zion can full communion with God be achieved. The *Kuzari*—the only major Jewish classic written in Platonic dialogue form—uses as its setting the historical conversion to Judaism of the king of the *Khazars and is cast in the form of a conversation between that king and a rabbi. Unlike other medieval Jewish philosophers, Yehudah aimed not to reconcile Judaism with current philosophical thought, but rather to demonstrate the intrinsic inadequacy of philosophy and the superiority of revelation. His attack on philosophy, however, itself makes use of philosophical arguments, and he is concerned with showing that faith can be expounded philosophically. Rational proofs can be misleading and revelation is a source of higher and surer truth than can be attained rationally; yet there is, he maintains, nothing in the Bible that contradicts reason. The Jewish religion is therefore not irrational but suprarational. The existence of God cannot be proved philosophically; neither does it require such proof. God is known through his revelation and through his manifestation in Jewish history, and long before Pascal, he emphasized the difference between the "God of Abraham" (i.e., of living experience and history) and the "God of Aristotle" (i.e., an abstract philosophical principle, such as a first cause). His philosophy of history and of the contact between God and man culminates in his doctrine of prophecy. Prophecy is both the mission and the ground of the spiritual superiority of Israel, which is conceived as "the heart of the nations"—the intermediary between God and the world. The prophet is the highest type of human being and receives his inspiration directly from God, while the prophetic gift is given only to the Jewish people, and only in Erets Yisra'el. Ha-Levi's view of the Jewish people as a spiritually superior race was not shared by other philosophers. However, he showed more concern for the historical and national character of Jewish existence than any other medieval philosopher.

• David Druck, *Yehuda Halevi: His Life and Works*, translated by M. Z. R. Frank (New York, 1941). Isaak Heinemann, ed., *Kuzari: The Book of Proof and Argument* (Oxford, 1947). Hartwig Hirshfeld, trans., *The Book of Kuzari by Judah Hallevi* (New York, 1946). Jefim Schirmann, *Ha-Shirah ha-ʿIvrit bi-Sefarad uve-Provans* (Jerusalem, 1956–1959). Yochanan Silman, *Philosopher and Prophet: Judah Halevi, the Kuzari, and the Evolution of his Thought*, translated by Lenn F. Schramm (Albany, N.Y., 1995).

YEHUDAH HA-NASI' (c.135–220), patriarch (*nasi') of Palestinian Jewry. Descendant of *Hillel and son and successor of *Shimʿon ben Gamli'el, Yehudah ha-Nasi' belonged to the most distinguished family of his time. He lived most of his life in Galilee and was in office for fifty years, presiding over his Sanhedrin in *Beit Sheʿarim and later in Sepphoris. A towering personality, he combined wisdom, learning, dignity, statesmanship, and wealth. His crowning achievement was the redaction of the *Mishnah, and though scholars differ as to the precise principles according to which he organized this codex, it undoubtedly served both as a textbook for the study of the *oral law and as the first comprehensive code of rabbinic law (*halakhah). Previous attempts at compilation had been made by R. ʿAqiva', R. Me'ir, and R. Natan, among others, but they were uncoordinated and contained great diversities and lacunae. Yehudah's objective was a unified compilation that would serve as the central legal instrument for Judaism and take the place of the academy, which could no longer coordinate all the scattered Jewries. He secured the cooperation of all scholars and determined a unified text, to which finishing touches were applied by his son and successor, Gamli'el III. Yehudah decided which traditions were worthy of preservation; his views were accepted, even when they differed from those of his colleagues. According to one tradition (*Qid*. 72b), Yehudah was born on the day R. ʿAqiva' died; this is not merely a chronological speculation but also implies that the tremendous task of systematizing the oral law to which ʿAqiva' had devoted his life was continued and completed by Yehudah. Yehudah was the last of the *tanna'im; his successors, the amora'im, used his compilation as the basis for their studies, out of which eventually emerged the two *Talmuds. He appears to have had a close relationship with the Roman authorities and most especially with a prominent official called Antoninus (whose exact identity has not been determined), which stood him in good stead as the leading representative of the Palestinian Jewish community. During his period of office, the country enjoyed comparative tranquility, and he worked for the religious and economic welfare of the Jewish community.

• Yisra'el Konovits, *Rabbi Yehudah ha-Nasi' (Rabbi): Osef Shalem Divrei Rabbi ba-Sifrut ha-Talmudit veha-Midrashit* (Jerusalem, 1965). Ofrah Meir, "Sippur Petirato shel Rabbi: 'Iyyun be-Darkhei 'Arikhato shel Mesorot," *Meḥqarei Yerushalayim be-Sifrut 'Ivrit* 12 (1990): 147–177.

—DANIEL SPERBER

YEHUDAH ḤASID HA-LEVI (1660–1701), kabbalist and messianic enthusiast in Poland, where he was close to Shabbatean circles. A popular preacher whose homilies stressed the importance of repentance and good deeds, he founded a holy society called the Ḥasidim (the Pious) that devoted itself to prayer and penitence in the hope of hastening the messianic redemption. Believing that this event was imminent and that *Shabbetai Tsevi would reappear in 1706, Yehudah and his followers (purported to number 1,300, of whom 500 died en route) set out for Erets Yisra'el, arriving in 1700 after an adventurous journey. They bought land in Jerusalem, where the Ḥurvah synagogue in the name of Yehudah Ḥasid was built 150 years later. Yehudah died a few days after arriving in Jerusalem, and the group—persecuted by local Jews who, correctly, suspected their messianic fervor to be of Shabbatean inspiration—soon broke up, many of its members returning to Europe and some converting to Christianity and Islam.

• Elisheva Carlebach, *The Pursuit of Heresy: Rabbi Moses Hagiz and the Sabbatian Controversies* (New York, 1990).

YEHUDAH LIVA' BEN BETSAL'EL (c.1520–1609), also known as Maharal of Prague; legal authority, mystic, communal leader, and legendary creator of the *golem. It is likely that Yehudah Liva' (Löw) was an autodidact, as he never identifies his teachers. He served as chief rabbi of Moravia; of Poznań, Poland, his birthplace; and of Prague. In legend, he is known as the creator of the *golem, a man-like creature brought into existence through the employment of magical techniques. Few Jewish legends have had as strong an influence on Western culture as the legend of the golem. The grave of Yehudah Liva' in Prague continues today to be a major tourist attraction.

Yehudah Liva' was one of the most prolific and profound Ashkenazi authors. His voluminous writings cover almost two thousand printed pages. Besides a lengthy commentary to the Pentateuch, an extensive commentary to sections of the Talmud, and legal *responsa*, he also composed a never-completed series of volumes on the theological meaning of the Jewish holy days. Some of his writings have been lost.

Yehudah Liva' is often correctly credited with "revealing the concealed" that is, making Jewish mystical teachings available to the nonspecialist. Though not presented systematically, his writings nonetheless offer a complete and pervasive theological system. He deals with virtually every major theological issue, and emphasizes the metaphysical and the social distinctiveness of the Jewish people. His theological views serve as a conceptual foundation both for his understanding of Jewish law and for his program for the spiritual, social, and intellectual reformation of Jewish life. This plan was predicated upon his harsh critique of many aspects of contemporary life, but especially that of the rabbinic leadership, and the goals and curricula of Jewish education. Yehudah Liva' was a vocal opponent of the tendency, current in his times, to codify Jewish law. He also attacked those of his contemporaries who, in his view, attempted to introduce "foreign"—especially philosophical and historiographical—elements into faith. His writings offer a creative and constructive alternative to the "abuses" that he identified. While largely rejected during his lifetime, his theological approach, and his program for social and religious reform, found considerable resonance in future generations, especially within Hasidism in nineteenth-century Poland. His works can be found in *Gur Aryeh* (commentary on the Pentateuch), five volumes (Bene Beraq, 1972), and *Kol Sifrei ha-Maharal mi-Prag* (collected writings), twelve volumes (New York, 1969).

• Aaron Fritz Kleinberger, *Ha-Maḥashavah ha-Pedagogit shel ha-Maharal mi-Prag* (Jerusalem, 1962). André Neher, *Le Puits de l'exil: La Theologie dialectique du Maharal de Prague, 1512–1609* (Paris, 1966). Byron L. Sherwin, *Mystical Theology and Social Dissent: The Life and Works of Judah Loew of Prague* (Rutherford, N.J., and London, 1982).

—BYRON L. SHERWIN

YEHUDA'I BEN NAḤMAN GA'ON, most influential head of the *academy of *Sura from 757 to 760; he trained in the academy of *Pumbedita. He is the earliest *ga'on whose *responsa* have been transmitted in significant numbers (several dozen) and is considered to have been a landmark figure, although the reasons are somewhat obscure (see PIRQOI BEN BABOI). A number of anonymous halakhic codes (including **Halakhot Gedolot* and **Halakhot Qetsuvot*) were attributed to him in the medieval period; an earlier code known as **Halakhot Pesuqot* was attributed to him during the geonic period, but this attribution, and others, is questionable. Some medieval authors attributed to him Talmudic passages that they believed to be interpolated, but there is no evidence to support the theory that he emended the Talmudic text.

• Neil Danzig, *Mavo' le-Sefer Halakhot Pesuqot* (Jerusalem, 1993).

—ROBERT BRODY

YEIN NESEKH. See WINE.

YELAMMEDENU (יְלַמְּדֵנוּ), abbreviated form of the expression *yelammedenu rabbenu*, "let our master teach us," normally used to introduce the opening question of the halakhic proem typical of Tanḥuma'-Yelammedenu *midrashim*. Since this expression is usually found at the beginning of the composite homilies that make up this kind of Midrashic literature, *yelammedenu* was used, particularly in medieval quotations, as one of the names for Midrashic works of this type. This led some scholars to search for a supposedly lost, early work by this name. See TANḤUMA'-YELAMMEDENU.

• Marc Bregman, "Sifrut Tanḥuma'-Yelammedenu," Ph.D. dissertation, The Hebrew University of Jerusalem, 1991. Hermann Leberecht Strack and Günter Stemberger, *Introduction to the Talmud and Midrash*, rev. and updat. ed., translated by Markus Bockmuehl (Minneapolis, 1992).
—MARC BREGMAN

YEQUM PURQAN (Aram; יְקוּם פֻּרְקָן; May Salvation Be Granted), name of two Aramaic prayers recited in the Ashkenazi ritual on Sabbaths after the reading of the Torah. One prayer is in behalf of rabbis and teachers in Erets Yisra'el and Babylonia and dates from the geonic period; the other prayer is in behalf of the congregation. Only the second prayer is in the Conservative prayer book, and both have been removed from the Reform prayer book.

• S. D. Goitein, "Prayers from the Geniza for Fatimid Caliphs, the Head of the Jerusalem Yeshiva, the Jewish Community and the Local Congregations," in *Studies in Judaica, Karaitica and Islamica*, edited by William G. Braude et al. (Ramat Gan, 1982), pp. 47–57.

YERUḤAM BEN MESHULLAM (c.1290–1350), Talmudist and legal authority. He was born in Provence, but following the expulsion of Jews from many regions of France in 1306, he wandered through various locales, ultimately settling in Toledo, Spain, where he studied with R. Asher ben Yeḥi'el. Yeruḥam gathered material for his first work, *Sefer Mesharim*, on matters of financial and commercial law, from various sections of the Talmud, Maimonides, and elsewhere. As the result of a request by his colleagues that he do the same for those areas of Jewish law that are applicable to daily life, he composed a second work, *Toledot Adam ve-Ḥavvah* (Constantinople, 1517), which was arranged according to the life cycle and divided into two parts: "Adam," from birth to marriage; and "Eve," from marriage to death. Yeruḥam cites the opinions of scholars in northern France, Provence, and Spain, and in many cases preserved material that was otherwise lost.

Yeruḥam's work was eclipsed to a large degree by the *Arba'ah Turim* of his contemporary, R. Ya'aqov ben Asher. Yosef Karo cites Yeruḥam extensively, however, in his *Beit Yosef*.

• Binyamin Z. Benedikt, *Merkaz ha-Torah bi-Provans: Asupat Ma'amarim* (Jerusalem, 1985). —EPHRAIM KANARFOGEL

YERUSHALMI. See TALMUD.

YESHIVAH (יְשִׁיבָה; sitting), the oldest institution for higher learning in Judaism, primarily devoted to study of the Talmud. The first *yeshivot* outside Erets Yisra'el and Babylonia (see ACADEMIES) were founded in the geonic period, notably in North Africa, where there were centers of learning from the eighth century in Fez, Tlemcen, and Kairouan. There were also important *yeshivot* in Damascus and Aleppo in the eleventh and twelfth centuries. A *yeshivah* in Lucena, Spain, is mentioned in the ninth century, with concrete information from Spain from the tenth century. *Yeshivot* were widespread throughout the country, and in the fifteenth century every community rabbi was obligated to establish one. In southern France, *yeshivot* were first founded about the tenth century (in Narbonne), and soon there were many others. Unlike the Babylonian *yeshivot*, which were considered final arbiters in matters of *halakhah*, the later *yeshivot* enjoyed little such authority and concentrated on study. In the twelfth century, *yeshivot* proliferated in northern France, largely under the guidance of Rashi, his pupils, and his descendants and spread from there to the Rhineland communities and then throughout Germany. After the destruction of the Rhineland communities, in 1348, Austria became an important center, in particular the *yeshivah* in Vienna. Ya'aqov *Pollak (15th–16th cent.), who studied in Nuremberg, was responsible for introducing *yeshivot* to eastern Europe, founding one in Kraków where he introduced the **pilpul* system. The *yeshivot* in Prague and Bohemia flourished from the end of the fifteenth century.

After the expulsion from Spain in 1492, important *yeshivot* were established in the new Sephardi centers. They were initially supported by local philanthropists but later taken over by the communities. The best known were founded in Erets Yisra'el (Jerusalem and Safed, later Hebron), Constantinople, and Salonika.

In the sixteenth and seventeenth centuries, eastern Europe was the great *yeshivah* center. The *yeshivah* heads were at the center of communal life and the *yeshivah* itself was the main institution in the community, which supported the students. At first the *yeshivot* in eastern Europe often consisted of no more than a select number of students. The first large-scale modern *yeshivah*, in *Volozhin, opened its doors in 1803. This was followed by various noted *yeshivot* throughout eastern and central Europe, especially in Lithuania. Among the best known were those in *Slobodka, *Tels, *Mir, and Pressburg in Hungary. They were characterized by an intensive program that was dedicated almost exclusively to the study of Talmud and its commentators, with an emphasis on conceptual analysis and a search for underlying legal principles. The *yeshivot* were not involved in reaching decisions in matters of Jewish law, and the study was highly theoretical. In the latter part of the nineteenth century some *yeshivot* also stressed the development of the highest standards of personal morality and the study of ethical texts (see MUSAR MOVEMENT). Not until shortly before World War II was a major *yeshivah*, *Yeshivat Ḥakhmei Lublin, opened in Poland. The European *yeshivot* were all destroyed in the Holocaust, although survivors reestablished some of them in the United States and Israel.

Today *yeshivot* are found in various countries. The State of Israel has tens of thousands of students in its *yeshivot* (including its high-school *yeshivot*)—the highest such population in history. Most of the *yeshivot* are in Jerusalem and Bene Beraq. The Israeli *yeshivot* can be divided into three broad categories: the Lithuanian, which are direct descendants of the east European *yeshivot* and include the Hebron, Ponevezh, Slobodka, Mir, and Brisk *yeshivot*; the Hasidic *yeshivot*, which are generally linked to specific dynasties; and the Religious-Zionist, of which the best known is the Merkaz ha-Rav in Jerusalem. The last include the *hesder yeshivot*, which combine broad religious studies, including Bible and Jewish thought in addition to Talmud, with terms of service in the Israeli army. Leading American *yeshivot* include: *Yeshiva University in New York, which combines a university education with a comprehensive religious studies curriculum; the Ner Israel Rabbinical College of Baltimore; Yeshivah Torah Vodaath of New York; the Telshe Yeshivah of Cleveland; and the Rabbi Aaron Kotler Institute for Advanced Studies in Lakewood, New Jersey. See also EDUCATION.

• William B. Helmreich, *The World of the Yeshiva* (New York, 1982).
–SHMUEL HIMELSTEIN

YESHIVAH SHEL MAʿLAH. See ACADEMY ON HIGH.

YESHIVAT ḤAKHMEI LUBLIN, *yeshivah* founded by R. Me'ir *Shapira' in Lublin, Poland, in 1930. Unlike the other Polish *yeshivot*, which were often centered upon a particular dynamic individual or were located within the confines of a local synagogue or *beit midrash*, this *yeshivah* was founded as an educational institution in its own right, with its own premises, constructed specifically to house the *yeshivah*. With its large Talmudic library, dormitories, dining facilities, and lecture halls, it served as a model for *yeshivot* throughout the world and soon assumed the status of the paramount Torah institution in all of Poland. It came to an end in 1939 during the German invasion of Poland. The building currently houses a hospital.

• David Halaḥmi, *Yeshivat Ḥakhmei Lublin u-Meholelo Mori ve-Rabbi Maharam Shapira' Zatsal* (Bene Beraq, 1995). Andrzej Trzcinski, *A Guide to Jewish Lublin and Surroundings* (Lublin and Warsaw, 1991).
–SHMUEL HIMELSTEIN

YESHIVA UNIVERSITY, educational institution located in New York City. Founded in 1886, it has grown from a small school for boys on Manhattan's Lower East Side to a multifaceted university. Today it comprises seventeen schools, divisions, and affiliates located on three campuses in Manhattan and one in the Bronx.

Yeshiva University offers undergraduate programs in liberal arts and sciences, business, and Jewish studies; and graduate and professional programs in medicine and biomedical science, law, social work, psychology, Jewish studies, and Jewish education and administration. The total university enrollment is approximately 5,200, with roughly equal numbers of men and women. One thousand additional students attend the affiliated Rabbi Isaac Elchanan Theological Seminary and its associated branches.

Yeshiva University is an independent institution chartered by the state of New York and accredited by the Commission on Higher Education of the Middle States Association of Colleges and Schools and by various specialized professional organizations.

YESHUʿA BEN YEHUDAH (11th cent.), *Karaite scholar and exegete; known in Arabic as Abu al-Faraj Furqan ibn Asad. He lived in Jerusalem and was the last renowned and influential scholar of the Karaite golden age there. He studied with Levi ben Yefet and Yosef ben Avraham Basir and, like them, adopted the highly rationalistic Kalam theology. After Basir's death, Yeshuʿa assumed a central teaching and leadership role in the community and had extensive relationships with the Karaite community in Egypt and with Rabbanites.

Yeshuʿa's major work was his "long" commentary on the *Book of Leviticus* and the Ten Commandments. This is a very large work, the extent of which is still not clear due to the state of the manuscripts. It treats a wide variety of legal and exegetical topics in an exhaustive manner, and in it Yeshuʿa quotes extensively from his Karaite predecessors and rabbinic literature. A wealthy Egyptian Karaite convinced Yeshuʿa to write a shorter commentary on the entire Torah for his son's education. In 1054 Yeshuʿa began to compose this "short" commentary, also quite a lengthy work, which includes a translation of the Torah and a commentary on grammatical, theological, ethical, and legal matters. His other works include *Kitab al-Tawriah*, a work on legal theory and polemical topics, such as the eternal nature of the Torah and the impossibility of its abrogation; and a work on forbidden sexual relationships, translated into Hebrew as *Sefer ha-Yashar* (edited by I. Markon [Saint Petersburg, 1908]). In this work he opposed the then accepted catenary theory of forbidden marriage, which greatly restricted the number of possible marriage partners in the small Karaite community. His position eventually became the accepted one. He also wrote *Be-Re'shit Rabbah*, a Hebrew translation of a philosophical commentary on the first two sections of *Genesis*.

• Haggai Ben-Shammai, *Pe'amim* 32 (1987): 3–20. Jacob Mann, *Texts and Studies in Jewish History and Literature*, vol. 2 (Cincinnati, 1935), pp. 34–39, and index. Samuel Poznanski, *The Karaite Literary Opponents of Saʿadyah Ga'on* (London, 1908), no. 17. Martin Schreiner, *Studien über Jeschua ben Jehuda* (Berlin, 1900).
–DAVID E. SKLARE

YETSER HA-RAʿ AND YETSER HA-TOV (יֵצֶר הָרָע; יֵצֶר הַטּוֹב; the evil inclination and the good inclination), man's impulse to do evil and his impulse to do good, often depicted as being in conflict with each other. The Bible refers to the "inclination of man's heart, which is evil from his youth" (*Gn.* 8.21; cf. *Gn.* 6.5), but the Talmud complements this by positing the existence of an opposing instinct within man that draws him toward the good. The rabbis taught that the evil inclination could be disciplined and pressed into the service of God and interpreted the commandment to love God "with all your heart" (*Dt.* 6.5) as meaning with both the good and evil inclinations (*Sifrei* on *Dt.* 32). According to another rabbinic statement, God created both the evil inclination (i.e., human nature with its desires and passions) and the Torah, which contains the antidote to master the evil inclination (*Qid.* 30b). The identification of the good inclination with Torah resulted in the view that the evil inclination was with man from his birth, whereas the good inclination came to him at *bar mitsvah*, that is, with his full acceptance of Torah. The rabbinic doctrine of the two inclinations was clearly intended to substitute a psychological *dualism, the inner struggle between good and evil, for the cosmic dualism of other systems, in which the forces of light battle the forces of darkness. The more radically dualistic view, in which the *yetser ha-ra*ʿ is identified with *Satan or with demonic forces in general, came to the fore in the *Kabbalah. See also Good and Evil.

• Reuven Bulka, "To Be Good or Evil: Which Is More Natural?" *Journal of Psychology and Judaism* 14 (1990): 53–71. Michael A. Fishbane, *The Kiss of God: Spiritual and Mystical Death in Judaism* (Seattle, 1994). H. Lichtenberger, "Zu Vorkommen und Bedeutung von yetser im Jubiläenbuch," *Journal for the Study of Judaism* 14 (1983): 1–10. Shalom Rosenberg, *Good and Evil in Jewish Thought*, translated by John Glucker (Tel Aviv, 1989). G. H. Cohen Stuart, *The Struggle in Man Between Good and Evil: An Inquiry into the Origin and Rabbinic Concept of Yeser Hara* (Kampen, Netherlands, 1984). Naftali T. Vizner, *In His Own Image: A Study of the Human Soul and the Personal Struggle between Good and Evil* (Brooklyn, N.Y., 1992).

YETSIRAH, SEFER. See Sefer Yetsirah.

YETSIV PITGAM (יְצִיב פִּתְגָם; Firm Stands the Word [of God]), Aramaic hymn chanted in some Ashkenazi congregations outside Israel after the first verse of the **haftarah* on the second day of *Shavuʿot. It is a short poem of fifteen lines, the initial letters giving the name of the author as Yaʿaqov ben Me'ir ha-Levi, who has been identified by some scholars with R. *Yaʿaqov ben Me'ir Tam (1100–1171). A tradition holds that Crusaders broke into his house on the second day of Shavuʿot and he was nearly killed.

There is no reference to Shavuʿot in the hymn, but it is in the form of a *reshut* (introductory prayer), depicting the Sinaitic revelation (commemorated on Shavuʿot) and praying for the welfare of the Jewish people.

• Macy Nulman, *The Encyclopedia of Jewish Prayer* (Northvale, N.J., and London, 1993), p. 375. Chaim Pearl, *A Guide to Shavuot* (London, 1958).
—CHAIM PEARL

YEVAMAH. See Levirate Marriage.

YEVAMOT (יְבָמוֹת; Levirates), tractate in Mishnah order Nashim, containing sixteen chapters, with related material in Tosefta' and in both Talmuds. It deals with the laws of levirate marriage (*Dt.* 25.5ff.), in which the brother of a man who dies childless is required to marry his widow in order to provide an heir for him. *Yevamot* examines in detail the status of levirate marriages in cases where the widow is a relative of the levirate brother, or is otherwise prohibited from marrying him. The tractate opens with a list of fifteen close relatives, which were the subject of a dispute between Beit Hillel and Beit Shamm'ai. If the brother and widow are related to each other—independently of the marriage to the late brother—through one of these relationships (e.g., daughter, granddaughter, maternal aunt), which would prohibit their marriage to one another for reasons of incest, Beit Hillel sees the levirate relationship as being automatically nullified and extends the nullification even to other widows of the deceased brother. Beit Shamm'ai demurs, regarding all nonrelated wives as subject to the levirate marriage. The Mishnah notes that Beit Hillel and Beit Shamm'ai sought arrangements whereby these disputes would not prevent the followers of each school from intermingling and intermarrying with each other (*Yev.* 1.4).

Many of the laws discussed in *Yevamot* stem from the rabbinic understanding of the unique status of a levirate marriage. Even prior to the formal entry into a levirate marriage, the brother and widow have a quasi-marital relationship that has several legal ramifications. Accordingly, biblical law did not require any ceremonial act of betrothal prior to consummation of the marriage. However the rabbis instituted an act of betrothal, the ramifications of which are discussed in detail in *Yevamot*. The laws of levirate marriages in *Yevamot* serve as a backdrop for discussion of many basic laws related to marriage, such as prohibited marriage partners and their legal status; the legal effects of permitted and prohibited marriages, including property rights, the laws of inheritance, and the right of a priest's wife to eat *terumah* (heave offering); and marriage to a minor or a deaf-mute. A central topic of *Yevamot* is the problematic case of a woman whose husband went abroad and never returned. The rabbis sought to be lenient in such cases, suspending many of the normal rules of evidence in order to enable such a woman to remarry.

The Babylonian tractate was translated into English by I. W. Slotki in the Soncino Talmud (London, 1936).

• Chanoch Albeck, ed., *Shishah Sidrei Mishnah, Seder Nashim* (Jerusalem, 1954). Philip Blackman, ed. and trans., *Mishnayoth*, vol. 2, *Order Nashim* (Gateshead, 1973). Pinhas Kehati, ed., *Mishnah: A New Translation with a Commentary, Seder Nashim*, vol. 1, *Yevamot, Ketubot* (Jerusalem, 1992). Hermann Leberecht Strack and Günter Stemberger, *Introduction to the Talmud and Midrash*, rev. and updat. ed., translated by Markus Bockmuehl (Minneapolis, 1992).
—AVRAHAM WALFISH

YHVH. See God, Names of.

YIBBUM. See Levirate Marriage.

YIDDISH, the language of Ashkenazi Jewry (see Ashkenazim). Yiddish originated about a thousand years ago in the Rhine and Danube basins, in a process of fusion between a majority Germanic component (from East Central German and Bavarian city dialects) and a minority Semitic component (from post-Biblical Hebrew and Aramaic). Migrations eastward, spurred by the *Crusades and other violence in central Europe, and encouraged by benevolent Lithuanian and Polish kings, resulted in the rise of Eastern Yiddish in the Slavic and Baltic lands. The older Western Yiddish (in Germany, Alsace, Holland, and adjacent areas) became the basis of the literary standard that accompanied the initiation of Yiddish printing in the sixteenth century. By the end of the eighteenth century, the western dialects were in decline, as a consequence of creeping Germanization and the anti-Yiddish campaign of Moses *Mendelssohn's "Berlin Enlightenment." In nineteenth-century eastern Europe, in contrast, the proponents of modernization ultimately contributed to the rise of modern Yiddish literature. In the twentieth century, Yiddish literature had major centers in interwar Poland, the Soviet Union, and New York City. Nearly all the leading authors grew up in a religious environment and broke away to join one of the secularist or revolutionary movements.

Yiddish suffered the devastating blow of the Holocaust, whose six million Jewish victims were nearly all native Yiddish speakers. Stalin's repression of Yiddish culture in the Soviet Union, the dominance of Hebrew in Palestine/Israel, and massive voluntary linguistic assimilation in western countries, have drastically reduced the number of Yiddish speakers. Yiddish continues to thrive among many Hasidic groups, however. In addition, there are small groups of nonreligious adherents of the language, who pursue it as a spoken language and as a focus of literary, cultural or scholarly activity.

Prior to the Haskalah, Yiddish was the language of religious Jews, and reflected the worldview and lifestyle of traditional Ashkenazi Jewry. It stood in a harmonious, complementary relationship with two nonspoken languages inherited from the ancient Near East: *Hebrew and *Aramaic. A special Yiddish translation language, used for sacred texts, was known as *'Ivri taytsh*. The oldest (known) Yiddish sentence was penned in 1272, in a festival *prayer book. From then until the end of the sixteenth century, Yiddish often filled the secular gap left by Hebrew and Aramaic; Old Yiddish literature fused ancient Jewish motifs with European genres (see MLOKHIM BUKH; SHMUEL BUKH) and adapted European works (such as the King Arthur cycle and Ducus Horant). From around 1600 onward, works steeped in Jewish religious and moral values, intended for the masses, prevailed. Among the most successful were the *Mayse Bukh* (Basel, 1602), collections of pietistic mini-tales (see MA'ASEH BOOK), and the **Tse'enah u-Re'enah* (apparently first published in the 1590s), an interweaving of the Pentateuch and weekly readings from the Prophets with traditional homiletic and moralistic interpretation; the latter has gone through hundreds of editions and lives on in Ḥasidic communities. The movement for the sanctity of Yiddish includes the pro-Yiddish pronouncements of kabbalist Yeḥi'el Mikhal *Epstein (died 1706); the hundred-year saga of the Zohar in Yiddish (finally published in 1711); and the traditionalist campaign of the Ḥatam Sofer (see SOFER FAMILY) whose influence on many Ḥasidic groups remains strong. The classic Hasidic movement itself, from the eighteenth century onward, raised Yiddish to a level of explicit sanctity as a corollary of its emphasis on direct communication with God and the exalted role of ordinary individuals. Since the Holocaust, those who maintain the sanctity of Yiddish see it as *loshn ha-kdoyshim* (language of the martyrs).

• Solomon A. Birnbaum, *Yiddish, A Survey and a Grammar* (Manchester and Toronto, 1979), with an extensive bibliography. Joshua A. Fishman, ed., *Never Say Die! A Thousand Years of Yiddish in Jewish Life and Letters* (The Hague, 1981), with an extensive bibliography. Dovid Katz, ed., *Origins of the Yiddish Language* (Oxford, 1987), with an extensive bibliography. Shlomo Noble, *Ḥumesh-taytsh: An oysforshung vegn der traditsye fun taytshn ḥumesh in di ḥadorim* (New York, 1943). Max Weinreich, *History of the Yiddish Language*, translated by Shlomo Noble with the assistance of Joshua A. Fishman (Chicago, 1980), a partial translation of the original Yiddish edition, *Geshikhte fun der yidisher shprakh*, 4 vols. (New York, 1973).

—DOVID KATZ

YIGDAL (יִגְדַּל; Magnified and Praised Be the Living God), hymn sung at the conclusion of Sabbath and festival evening services; among Ashkenazim, it is also recited before the daily morning service. It is based on Maimonides' *Thirteen Principles of Faith (each line treating one of the principles). The Sephardi and Eastern version has a fourteenth, concluding line (a later addition), which reads: "These are the Thirteen Principles . . . ." It was not accepted by Yitsḥaq *Luria and the Safed kabbalists who were dissatisfied with the formulation of the Thirteen Principles, and it is not found in the Hasidic prayer book. The authorship of Yigdal has been assigned to Daniyye'l ben Yehudah of Rome (14th cent.).

• Macy Nulman, *The Encyclopedia of Jewish Prayer* (Northvale, N.J., and London, 1993), pp. 375–376. Frank Talmage, "Angels, Anthems, and Anathemas: Aspects of Popular Religion in Fourteenth-Century Bohemian Judaism," *Jewish History* 6.1–2 (1992): 13–20.

YIḤUD (יִחוּד; seclusion [with a woman]). A man and a strange woman are not to be alone together in a secluded place (*Shulḥan 'Arukh, Even ha-'Ezer*, no. 22). Seclusion is defined as the absence of any possibility of disturbance by other people; if such a possibility does exist then the prohibition does not apply. *Yiḥud* is suspended in the case of a man, if his wife is at home, and in the case of a woman, if her husband is in town. The presence of a child also suspends the prohibition. Different rules are applicable by night and in situations in which the moral standards of the residents of a particular dwelling are lax. *Yiḥud* between a bride and groom is an important element of the marriage ceremony and takes place after the ceremony in a room specifically designated as "the *yiḥud* room" (Rema', *Even ha-'Ezer* 55.1).

• Getsel Ellinson, *Hatsne'a Lekhet: Meqorot Halakhatiyim Mevo'arim* (Jerusalem, 1981). Alan Unterman, *Dictionary of Jewish Law and Legend* (London, 1991), p. 128.

—DANIEL SINCLAIR

YIḤUS. See YUḤASIN.

YIMMAḤ SHEMO (יִמַּח שְׁמוֹ; "May his name be blotted out"), an execratory appellation added to the mention of the name of an inveterate enemy of the Jewish people. Its origin is attributed to the commandment in *Deuteronomy* 25.19 to "blot out the memory of Amalek" (see AMALEKITES), and the phrase is sometimes therefore extended to *yimmaḥ shemo ve-zikhro*, "May his name and memory be blotted out." A *Purim custom was to write the name of *Haman (traditionally descended from the Amalekites) on a stone or piece of wood and then hit it until the name was defaced. In the Middle Ages, Christian anti-Jewish polemicists alleged that the imprecation applied to Jesus because the initials of the fuller version spelled *yeshu* (Heb. for Jesus).

YIRMIYAHU BEN ABBA' (4th cent.), Palestinian amora', often simply called Yirmiyahu. He is to be distinguished from the earlier Babylonian amora' of the same name who is often referred to as Yirmiyahu, without patronymic, in the Talmud Yerushalmi. While still a young man he emigrated from Babylonia to Tiberias, in Erets Yisra'el, where he studied with R. Zeʿira' I, himself a Babylonian emigré (e.g., *Taʿan*. 7a; *Shab*. 10a). He eventually succeeded R. Zeʿira' as head of the Tiberias academy. Known for both his spiritual devotion (e.g., Y., *Ber*. 1.8, 3d) and academic precision (cf. *B. B*. 23b), he became one of the leading sages of his generation, influential also in community affairs. He is mentioned frequently in both halakhic and aggadic contexts in both Talmuds, although his primary work was in *halakhah* (cf. Y., *Maʿas*. 3.10, 51a; *Shab*. 63a). His teachings were transmitted to Babylonia by the **naḥotei* (*Pes*. 60b) and were highly regarded there, although the fact that he did not think highly of the Babylonian sages (cf. *Men*. 52a; *San*. 24a) was known to them (*Ket*. 75a). Among his Midrashic teachings are: "a gentile who observes the Torah is like a high priest" (*B. Q*. 38a, with ref. to *2 Sm*. 7.19; *Is*. 26.2; *Ps*. 118.20, 33.1, 125.4); and "physical labor is more precious than the merits of the fathers" (*Gn. Rab*. 74.10, to *Gn*. 31.42). His dying request was to be placed on his side by the road, clothed and with a staff in hand, that he might be ready when the Messiah came (Y., *Kil*. 9.3, 32b; *Gn. Rab*. 100.2).

• Wilhelm Bacher, *Die Agada der palästinensischen Amoräer* (1892–1899; Hildesheim, 1965). Isaak Halevy, *Dorot ha-Ri'shonim* (Jerusalem, 1979).

—MICHAEL L. BROWN

YISHMAʿE'L BEN ELISHAʿ (2d cent.), tanna' who lived in Kefar ʿAziz in southern Judea (*Kil*. 6.4). Prominent in both halakhic and aggadic Midrash, he is responsible for the **Mekhilta' de-Rabbi Yishmaʿe'l* to *Exodus*, parts of **Sifrei* to *Numbers* and *Deuteronomy*, and for the famous school of *halakhah* that bore his name, *De-Vei Rabbi Yishmaʿe'l*. He formulated the thirteen hermeneutical rules (see HERMENEUTICS) "by means of which the Torah is to be expounded," but these are, in fact, an amplification of the seven rules previously promulgated by *Hillel and known as the *Baraiyta' shel Rabbi Yishmaʿe'l* or *Baraiyta' shel Shelosh ʿEsreh Middot*, which opens the **Sifra'* and was incorporated into the readings in the first part of Shaḥarit. Yishmaʿe'l's work was largely devoted to the formulation of categories, classifications, and rules in connection with both biblical exposition and the oral law. Yishmaʿe'l formulated the principles that "the Bible speaks in ordinary language" (*Ker*. 11a) and that the order of biblical passages is not necessarily chronological. His approach was rational and avoided extremes in the interpretation of biblical verses. Although his name is listed among the *Ten Martyrs killed after the Bar Kokhba' Revolt (see BAR KOKHBA', SHIMʿON), it is unlikely that he lived until that time. Many mystical compositions were anachronistically ascribed to him.

• Gershom Bader, *The Encyclopedia of Talmudic Sages*, translated from the Yiddish by Solomon Katz (Northvale, N.J., and London, 1988). Aaron Hyman, *Toledot Tanna'im ve-'Amora'im* (1910; Jerusalem, 1987). Mordecai Margaliot, ed., *Entsiqlopediyyah le-Ḥakhmei ha-Talmud veha-Ge'onim* (Jerusalem, 1946).

—DANIEL SPERBER

YISHTABBAḤ. See PESUQEI DE-ZIMRA'.

YISRA'EL BEN ELIʿEZER. See BAʿAL SHEM TOV, YISRA'EL BEN ELIʿEZER.

YISRA'EL BEN SHABBETAI HAPSTEIN KOZIENICE (1733–1814), Hasidic master, author, and preacher. Along with Yaʿaqov Yitsḥaq, ha-Ḥozeh mi-Lublin, Yisra'el, the Maggid of Kozienice, was one of the first highly influential Hasidic leaders in Poland. His teachers, Shemu'el Shmelke Horowitz of Nikolsburg, Elimelekh of Lyzhansk, and Levi Yitsḥaq of Berdichev, were disciples of Dov Ber of Mezhirech. A prolific author, Yisra'el's writings deal with *halakhah* (*Beit Yisra'el*), Kabbalah (*Or Yisra'el*), as well as Hasidism (*ʿAvodat Yisra'el* [Jerusalem, 1988]). He was also a popular *tsaddiq*, revered for his ecstatic worship and therapeutic amulets. He represented the Jews before the Polish nobility in Warsaw.

• Martin Buber, *Tales of the Hasidim* (New York, 1947). Rivka Schatz Uffenheimer, *Hasidism as Mysticism* (Princeton, 1993).

—MILES KRASSEN

YISRA'EL BEN SHEMU'EL ASHKENAZI OF SHKLOV (c.1770–1839), Talmudist. A pupil of Eliyyahu ben Shelomoh Zalman (the Vilna Ga'on), he was the preacher in Shklov (Belorussia) for twelve years and co-editor of the Ga'on's glosses on the *Shulḥan ʿArukh*. In 1809 Yisra'el went to Erets Yisra'el and settled in Safed, where he founded a *yeshivah* and headed the community of *perushim* (separatists; so called because they did not belong to the Hasidic community in Safed, which had been extant since 1757). He led the community through many difficult crises (plagues, Arab attacks, earthquakes) and in 1837 went to Jerusalem and founded another congregation of *perushim*. His major work is *Pe'at ha-Shulḥan* (Safed, 1836), a codification of the rabbinic laws dealing with residence in the Holy Land (which had been omitted by Yosef *Karo in his code).

• David E. Fishman, *Russia's First Modern Jews: The Jews of Shklov* (New York, 1995).

YISRA'EL ME'IR HA-KOHEN (1838–1933), rabbi and author; known after the title of his first book as the Ḥafets Ḥayyim. He was born in Lithuania, studied in Vilna, and settled, upon his marriage, in the town of Raduń, where he lived for the rest of his life and whose *yeshivah* he supported both materially and spiritually.

Though he never possessed any official rabbinical title or position, the Ḥafets Ḥayyim was one of the most important and influential figures in Orthodox Judaism of the nineteenth century. His first book, *Ḥafets Ḥayyim* (Vilna, 1873), is devoted to the centrality of the Torah's laws concerning the prohibition against *lashon ha-ra'* (slander) for Jewish life. It was a theme he returned to continually throughout his life. His greatest work, entitled *Mishnah Berurah* (6 vols. [1894–1907]), is an extensive commentary on Yosef Karo's *Shulḥan ʿArukh, Oraḥ Ḥayyim*, dealing with the laws of everyday Jewish life. *Mishnah Berurah* became an extraordinarily successful and authoritative guide to halakhic life for many Orthodox Jews.

His other major works include *Maḥaneh Yisra'el* (1881), on the halakhic and ethical problems faced by Jews serving in the army; *Ahavat Ḥesed* (1888), on charity; and *Niddeḥei Yisra'el* (1894), a halakhic guide and moral exhortation to Jews emigrating from eastern Europe to the West not to abandon Jewish tradition.

He was a founder and great supporter of the Orthodox Jewish organization Agudat Israel, both in Poland and on the international scene. He was also instrumental in raising funds for the *yeshivot* of Poland between World Wars I and II.

• Simcha Fishbane, *The Method and Meaning of the Mishnah Berurah* (Hoboken, N.J., 1991). Mosheh M. Yashar, *Saint and Sage: Hafetz Hayim* (New York, 1937). —IRA ROBINSON

YISRA'EL OF RUZHIN. See RUZHIN, YISRA'EL OF.

YITSḤAQ BEN ABBA' MARI (c.1120–1190), Provençal scholar. He studied under his father and at age seventeen composed a work on the dietary laws. While visiting Barcelona, he wrote a commentary to chapter four of tractate *Menaḥot*, which deals with the laws of *tsitsit*, *mezuzah*, and *tefillin*. His major work is the encyclopedic *Sefer ha-ʿIttur*. The first part deals with various laws for composing legal documents and offers examples of each one; Marseilles was an international port and these documents were useful among Jewish traders. The second part deals with ritual law. He extensively utilized geonic sources together with later Spanish and Franco-German ones. He corresponded with his relative Avraham ben David of Posquières and Yaʿaqov ben Me'ir Tam. He also wrote a short treatise on the Alfasi code entitled *Me'ah Sheʿarim*.

• Mordechai Glatzer, *ʿIttur Soferim (Sefer Ha-ʿIttur) le-Rav Yitsḥaq ben Rav Abba' Mari*, 2 vols. (Jerusalem, 1985). Heinrich Gross, *Gallia judaica: Dictionaire géographique de la France d'après les sources rabbiniques*, with a supplement by S. Schwarzfuchs (Paris, 1897; repr. Amsterdam, 1969). —SHLOMO H. PICK

YITSḤAQ BEN ASHER (died c.1133), Talmudist and student of Rashi; considered the first of the German tosafists; known as Riva of Speyer. His *tosafot* are cited by later scholars such as R. Yehudah ben Kalonimos of Speyer, R. Yitsḥaq ben Mosheh of Vienna, and R. Mordekhai ben Hillel. A respected legal authority whose opinion was sought from far and near, he was confident in his judgments and did not shrink from defending them before such critics as R. Yaʿaqov ben Me'ir Tam. His students include the prominent tosafists R. Eliʿezer ben Natan of Mainz, R. Yitsḥaq ben Mordekhai, and R. Efrayim of Regensburg.

• Victor Aptowitzer, *Mavo' le-Sefer ha-Rabiyah* (Jerusalem, 1938), pp. 369–370. Efraim E. Urbach, *Baʿalei ha-Tosafot* (Jerusalem, 1980), pp. 165–173. —MARK WASHOFSKY

YITSḤAQ BEN ASHER HA-LEVI (11th–12th cent.), rabbinic scholar, tosafist, legal authority; known by the acronym Riba. He studied with Rashi and lived in Speyer. He was the first German tosafist, compiling *tosafot* to most tractates of the Talmud. Only portions have survived, however, in later *tosafot* collections. His *tosafot* reached Rabbenu Tam in Ramerupt, through their mutual student, R. Yitsḥaq ben Mordekhai (Ribam); he also composed treatises on usury and on several Talmudic tractates.

He was referred to as ha-Qadosh (the Holy One, or the Martyr), perhaps reflecting his overall piety as well as the manner of his death. According to a later Italian rabbinic text (*Sefer Recanati*), Riba died after fasting on Yom Kippur against the advice of his physicians. According to the commentary on *Sefer Yetsirah* attributed to R. Saʿadyah Ga'on (but actually composed in northern France in the 12th cent.), Yitsḥaq and his students attempted to create a *golem.

• Moshe Idel, *Golem: Jewish Magical and Mystical Traditions on the Artificial Anthropoid* (Albany, N.Y., 1990), pp. 91–92. Y. Lifshits, ed., *Sanhedrei Gedolah ʿal Massekhet Sanhedrin*, vol. 1, *Liqutei Tosafot ha-Riva* (Jerusalem, 1968). Efraim E. Urbach, *Baʿalei ha-Tosafot* (Jerusalem, 1980), vol. 1, pp. 165–173, 366–367, and index. —EPHRAIM KANARFOGEL

YITSḤAQ BEN AVRAHAM OF TROKI. See TROKI, YITSḤAQ BEN AVRAHAM.

YITSḤAQ BEN MOSHEH OF VIENNA (c.1180–1250), halakhic authority; known as Or Zaruʿa after his major work. In his youth, he traveled widely and studied with such scholars as R. Eliʿezer ben Yo'el ha-Levi of Bonn, R. Yehudah ben Yitsḥaq of Paris, and R. Yehudah ben Shemu'el he-Ḥasid of Regensburg. R. Me'ir ben Barukh of Rothenburg was his student. Yitsḥaq incorporated the halakhic teachings of his French and German masters into his work, *Or Zaruʿa*. It is a valuable collection of halakhic material, historical data, and information concerning Jewish religious customs and observance. The compendium remained very much a work in progress; Yitsḥaq himself continued to add supplements to it, and his son, Ḥayyim ben Yitsḥaq of Vienna, and students carried on this process after his death. Ḥayyim also wrote an abbreviated version of the *Or Zaruʿa*, which is frequently cited by R. Yisra'el of Krems in his notes to the work of R. Asher ben Yeḥi'el.

• Menachem Elon, *Jewish Law: History, Sources, Principles* (Philadelphia, 1994), p. 1241. Efraim E. Urbach, *Baʿalei ha-Tosafot* (Jerusalem, 1980), pp. 436–447. —MARK WASHOFSKY

YITSḤAQ BEN SHEMU'EL OF ACRE (c.1250–1340), kabbalist. Several of his works, both on theoretical Kabbalah and on mystical, prophetic, and trance-like experiences, have been preserved and contain valuable references to otherwise unknown kabbalistic writings and authors. He journeyed from Palestine via Italy to Spain, where he met many of the leading kabbalists. He also investigated the authenticity of the Zohar and questioned the son of *Mosheh de León on the subject. Yitsḥaq was an outstanding exponent of mystical thought and contemplative practice, and his works are an important source for modern research on Kabbalah.

• Amos Goldreich, "Sefer Me'irat ʿEinayyim by R. Isaac of Acre," Ph.D. dissertation, Hebrew University, 1983.

YITSḤAQ BEN SHEMU'EL OF DAMPIERRE (died c.1185), rabbinic scholar, tosafist, legal authority; known by his acronym as Ri, Ri ha-Zaqen, or Ri of Dampierre. He and his uncle and teacher, *Ya'aqov ben Me'ir Tam (Rabbenu Tam), formed the core of the northern French tosafists, and Ri's name appears constantly in **tosafot* collections, although few, if any, of his original *tosafot* have survived. (The *tosafot* printed in tractate *Qiddushin* under the name *Perush Ri ha-Zaqen* were written not by Yitsḥaq but by the Provençal scholar Avraham ben Yitsḥaq of Montpellier.) An account in the introduction to R. Menaḥem ben Aharon ben Zeraḥ's *Tsedah la-Derekh*, which suggests that sixty students studied with Yitsḥaq at one time and that each was responsible for a particular tractate, cannot be verified and is, in all likelihood, an exaggeration. It does, however, reflect the centrality of both Yitsḥaq and Rabbenu Tam (who is described similarly in the introduction to R. Shelomoh Luria's *Yam shel Shelomoh*) to the compilation of the *tosafot*. Yitsḥaq was known for his piety, and there is evidence of his involvement in mystical studies.

• Victor Aptowitzer, *Mavo' le-Sefer Rabiyah* (Jerusalem, 1938), pp. 379–381. Simha Assaf, "Sefer Pesaqim le-Ri ha-Zaqen, Rabbenu Tam u-She-'ar Ba'alei ha-Tosafot," in *Sefer ha-Yovel li-Khevod Alexander Marx* (New York, 1950), pp. 9–22. Efraim E. Urbach, *Ba'alei ha-Tosafot* (Jerusalem, 1980), vol. 1, pp. 220–260, and index. —EPHRAIM KANARFOGEL

YITSḤAQ BEN SHESHET PERFET (1326–1408), Spanish halakhic authority who spent his last years in Algiers; known by the acronym Ribash. He lived in Barcelona, Saragossa, and Valencia, before fleeing Spain as a result of the 1391 anti-Jewish riots. In Algiers he was appointed **dayyan*. Many queries were addressed to him, and his *responsa* (Constantinople, 1546) were noted for their clarity and erudition. A strict legalist, he warned against the study of philosophy and, even more, Kabbalah. He was also the author of Talmudic commentaries and *piyyutim*. His tomb near Algiers became a center of pilgrimage for North African Jews.

• Abraham Moses Hershman, *Rabbi Isaac bar Sheshet Perfet and His Times* (New York, 1943). Roger Kohn, "Royal Power and Rabbinic Authority in Fourteenth Century France," in *Approaches to Judaism in Medieval Times*, edited by David Blumenthal, vol. 2 (Chico, Calif., 1985), pp. 133–148.

YITSḤAQ BEN YA'AQOV OF CASTILE (13th cent.), Spanish kabbalist. Following in the footsteps of their father, Ya'aqov ha-Kohen, Yitsḥaq, together with his brother Ya'aqov, formed one of the most important schools of kabbalists in thirteenth-century Spain. His treatises influenced R. Mosheh de León, author of the Zohar, who derived from them some of the central ideas of the Zohar, especially concerning the nature of evil and the messianic redemption. Rabbi Yitsḥaq's most important work is the treatise *Ma'amar 'al ha-'Atsilut ha-Sema'lit*, written about 1260, which is the earliest statement of a dualistic concept of the celestial realm in kabbalistic literature. According to the author, before the Creation there existed a Satanic realm that caused previous attempts by God to create the world to fail; in this world there is a constant struggle between the powers of goodness, which are on the right side, and the Satanic powers, led by Samael and Lilith, on the left side. The divine emanation on the right has a parallel in the evil system of spiritual powers on the left, which is responsible for all evil, including leprosy and other earthly maladies, and all demons are subservient to it. The concluding part of the treatise is dedicated to an apocalyptic description of the last battle between the powers of evil and the Messiah, presenting for the first time a kabbalistic concept of messianic redemption. Rabbi Yitsḥaq's work on this subject was followed by a treatise by his disciple R. Mosheh of Burgos, *'Amud ha-Sema'li*, which presents a similar system of diabolic powers.

• Joseph Dan, "Samael, Lilith and the Concept of Evil in Early Kabbalah," *AJS Review* 5 (1980): 17–40. Joseph Dan and Ronald Kiener, eds. and trans., *The Early Kabbalah* (New York, 1986). —JOSEPH DAN

YITSḤAQ BEN YOSEF OF CORBEIL (died 1280), rabbinic scholar, tosafist, and codifer; known as Semaq, the initials of his main work, *Sefer Mitsvot Qatan*. He was the son-in-law of R. Yeḥi'el ben Yosef of Paris. His halakhic compendium, *Sefer Mitsvot Qatan* (Constantinople, 1510) achieved wide popularity and was praised by French and German scholars, such as R. Me'ir ben Barukh of Rothenburg. *Sefer Mitsvot Qatan* was based on R. *Mosheh ben Ya'aqov of Coucy's *Sefer Mitsvot Gadol* but was written in much briefer form. Rabbi Yitsḥaq divided his work into seven pillars, which corresponded to the seven days of the week, creating a format so that people could review it weekly. *Sefer Mitsvot Qatan* became an important source for subsequent decisors and was used heavily in Aharon ben Ya'aqov ha-Kohen of Lunel's *Oreḥot Ḥayyim* and the parallel *Kol Bo*. A number of glosses were added to *Sefer Mitsvot Qatan*, including those by R. Perets of Corbeil and R. Mosheh of Zurich, which contained selections from a number of French and German works. Rabbi Yitsḥaq was known for his great piety and is referred to in a number of texts as He-Ḥasid. Rabbi Yitsḥaq also authored a series of legal decisions (*pesaqim*), some of which are still in manuscript.

• Ephraim Kanarfogel, "Rabbinic Figures in Castilian Kabbalistic Pseudepigraphy: R. Yehudah he-Ḥasid and R. Elḥanan of Corbeil," *Journal of Jewish Thought and Philosophy* 3 (1993): 77–109. Efraim E. Urbach, *Ba'alei ha-Tosafot* (Jerusalem, 1980), pp. 571–578.
—EPHRAIM KANARFOGEL

YITSḤAQ ELḤANAN. See SPEKTOR, YITSḤAQ ELḤANAN.

YITSḤAQ NAPPAḤA' (c.250–300), Palestinian amora', possibly a grandson of the tanna' of the same name (c.140–180). He was a member of R. Yoḥanan's academy and a colleague of R. Yoḥanan's great disciples R. 'Ammi and R. Assi. Probably toward the end of the third century, he went to Babylonia, where he is mentioned in the company of its leading authorities, such as R. Naḥman bar Ya'aqov. He was expert in both **halakhah* (law) and **aggadah* (homiletics) (*B. Q.* 50b), but felt that in his time, which was one of great hardship, poverty, and privation in Palestine, people had more need of homiletic comfort than legalistic education (*Soferim* 16.4). One of his famous aphorisms is "If a person tells you: 'I have toiled in search and have not found,' believe him not; 'I have not toiled in search and have found,' believe him" (*Meg.* 6b). He expressed himself strongly against asceticism, saying, "Is not that which the Torah has forbidden sufficient, yet you wish to forbid yet more upon yourself" (Y., *Ned.* 9.1). —DANIEL SPERBER

YITSḤAQ OF ACRE. See YITSḤAQ BEN SHEMU'EL OF ACRE.

YITSḤAQ SAGGI NAHOR (c.1160–1235), kabbalist, known as "the Pious" (he-Ḥasid); son of R. *Avraham ben David of Posquières. Many sayings by him or attributed to him are found in early kabbalistic works in Provence and especially in the writings of the kabbalists of Gerona. According to traditions preserved by the kabbalists, he was born blind (the term *saggi nahor* [much light] is a euphemism for blind), yet his writings include intense color symbolism. The one treatise of his to have survived, probably in the original form, is his commentary on the **Sefer Yetsirah*, a detailed study of the process of creation, presented as the emanation of the **sefirot* from their hidden source within the Godhead. The symbolism used by R. Yitsḥaq to describe the *sefirot* became the standard terminology of the Kabbalah for several centuries, and many of the central ideas that characterize the Kabbalah are first found in this treatise. Rabbi Yitsḥaq probably wrote at a later date than the composition of **Sefer ha-Bahir*, the earliest kabbalistic work known, yet his symbolism is not dependent on that work. However, despite some similarities, it cannot be established that the terminology used by R. Yitsḥaq is based on the *Sefer ha-Bahir*. Rabbi Yitsḥaq insisted that the Kabbalah be taught in secret and that books of kabbalistic speculation should not be committed to writing. When he heard that scholars in Gerona (probably R. Ezra and R. ʿAzri'el) were writing books of Kabbalah, he sent an angry letter to the scholars of Gerona, addressed to R. Yonah ben Avraham Gerondi and R. Moses Nahmanides, demanding that such activity be discontinued. He sent his nephew, R. Asher ben David, to Gerona as his personal emissary to teach and direct the activities of the kabbalists in that city.

• Gershom Gerhard Scholem, *Origins of the Kabbalah* (Philadelphia, 1990), pp. 248–309. Gershom Gerhard Scholem, *Ha-Qabbalah bi-Provans: Ḥug ha-Rabbi Avraham ben David u-Veno Rabbi Yitsḥaq Sagi Nahor* (Jerusalem, 1963). —JOSEPH DAN

YITSḤAQ YISRA'ELI. See ISRAELI, YITSḤAQ.

YIZKOR (יִזְכּוֹר; May [God] Remember), synagogue service in which prayers are offered in memory of the dead and for their repose. It is customarily conducted in the Ashkenazi rite on the last days of the *Shalosh Regalim and *Yom Kippur. The traditional service consists of brief prayers in which the names of the deceased are mentioned, martyrs are remembered, and *El Male' Raḥamim, a supplication on behalf of the departed, is solemnly chanted. It is now usual to recall Holocaust victims and deceased members of the congregation. In Israel, mention is made of fallen soldiers. Traditionally, Yizkor follows the reading of the Torah, before the scrolls are returned to the ark. In some synagogues, the Yom Kippur memorial service may be held in the afternoon, and it may be augmented by meditations, appropriate prayers, and a sermon. A formal memorial service is seldom conducted in Sephardi communities, although Congregation Shearith Israel of New York holds one after Kol Nidrei on the eve of Yom Kippur. It has become a custom, probably of superstitious origin, for those who have not lost a close relative to leave the synagogue during the recitation of Yizkor. This, however, is now discouraged by many rabbis.

• Abraham Z. Idelsohn, *Jewish Liturgy and Its Development* (New York, 1967), pp. 230f., 293. Jakob J. Petuchowski, *Prayerbook Reform in Europe: The Liturgy of European Liberal and Reform Judaism* (New York, 1968), pp. 323ff. —A. STANLEY DREYFUS

YOḤANAN BAR NAPPAḤA' (fl. c.240–279), generally known just as R. Yoḥanan; the most outstanding of the Palestinian amora'im. His life was fraught with hardships. Born into a well-to-do family, he had to sell his various estates to support himself so that he could study the Torah. Legend has it that he had ten sons, all of whom died in tragic circumstances during his lifetime. Nonetheless, his courage and persistence enabled him to become a brilliant halakhist and aggadist, who taught in his native Sepphoris and later in Tiberias, where his pupils included distinguished rabbis who laid the foundation for the Talmud Yerushalmi. Yoḥanan was involved in many halakhic discussions with his brother-in-law *Shimʿon ben Laqish, and the two profoundly analyzed the Mishnah. After the death of *Rav and *Shemu'el, Yoḥanan was regarded as the outstanding rabbinical authority; his decisions and views were respected in Babylonia, and he was frequently quoted in the Talmud Bavli. He placed personal integrity above brilliance and knowledge and ruled that one may not study under a great scholar who was morally flawed (*Ḥag.* 15b). He believed that true understanding of the Torah was to be found among the humble and righteous (*Sot.* 21b; *Shab.* 114a), and in opposition to some of his scholarly colleagues, he held prayer to be of equal importance with Torah studies (*Ber.* 21a).

• Israel Konovitz, *Maʿarekhot ha-'Amora'im: Ma'amreihem shel ha-'Amora'im be-Halakhah uve-'Aggadah Mesuddarim Lefi Nos'im*, vol. 1 (Jerusalem, 1973). —DANIEL SPERBER

YOḤANAN BEN ZAKK'AI (1st cent.), tanna' from Erets Yisra'el, responsible for reconstituting Jewish religious authority after the destruction of the Temple in 70 CE, and first of the Mishnaic scholars following the period of the pairs (**zugot*), named in *Avot* 1. He is described in *Avot* 2.8 as a student of both Hillel and Shamm'ai; other sources relate that "Hillel had eighty pairs of disciples . . . the youngest (or least) among them was Yoḥanan ben Zakk'ai" (*Suk.* 28a). Some sources imply that he was a *kohen*, though, unlike most of the priestly class, he was not a supporter of zealotry. He was both a teacher (*Avot* 2.8 mentions five outstanding disciples whom he taught) and a leader of the Pharisaic party, representing the Pharisees in various debates with the Sadducees over the authority of the oral law and particulars of *halakhah*.

The most famous stories about Yoḥanan relate how he managed to escape from Jerusalem during the Roman siege (68–70) in a coffin carried by his disciples (according to the best-known version in *Git*. 56ab) in order to meet with Vespasian, the Roman commander. He is said to have foretold to Vespasian that he would become emperor; when this indeed happened, Vespasian offered to grant him a request, and Yoḥanan asked that Vespasian spare *Yavneh and its scholars. This request was granted, enabling him after the destruction of the Temple to establish a center of learning and spiritual leadership in Yavneh (near present-day Ashdod), which passed regulations (*taqqanot*) and helped define Judaism apart from a Temple. Under Yoḥanan's leadership, key decisions were made regarding the adaptation of the synagogue and its liturgy to incorporate elements of the cult previously confined to Jerusalem; the hegemony of the rabbis—heirs, as it were, to the Pharisees—was greatly strengthened. After R. Gamli'el was appointed *nasi'* at Yavneh, Yoḥanan moved to Beror Ḥayil in southern Israel, where he remained until his death.

• Jacob Neusner, *The Development of a Legend: Studies on the Traditions Concerning Yohanan ben Zakkai* (Leiden, 1970). Jacob Neusner, *A Life of Rabban Yohanan ben Zakkai* (Leiden, 1962). —ISAAC B. GOTTLIEB

YOḤANAN HA-SANDELAR (2d cent.), Palestinian tanna'. Along with R. *El'azar ben Shammu'a, he was among the last five disciples of R. 'Aqiva' (*Yev*., 62b; *Gn. Rab*. 61.3). When R. 'Aqiva' was imprisoned by the Romans, R. Yoḥanan was sent by the sages to consult with him on a halakhic question, which he did under the guise of a peddler, subtly posing his question, to which R. 'Aqiva' responded as Yoḥanan stood outside the prison (*Yev*. 104b; Y., *Yev*. 12.5, 12d). The epithet ha-Sandelar refers either to his profession (cobbler, although according to others he was a stonecutter, from *sandalkhonin* [gems]) or to his Alexandrian origins. He is listed among the sages who gathered in Beit Rimmon after the Hadrianic persecutions subsided (Y., *Ḥag*. 3.1, 78d) and is mentioned in halakhic discussions in the Mishnah and *baraiytot*. His adage on the permanence of only those assemblies that are for the sake of heaven is found in *Avot* 4.11. He also said that "dwelling in Erets Yisra'el is equivalent to keeping all the commandments of the Torah" (*Sifrei* on *Dt*. 80).

• Wilhelm Bacher, *Die Agada der Tannaiten* (1903; Berlin, 1965–1966). Israel Konovitz, comp., *Ma'arakhot Tanna'im: Osef Shalem shel Mishnatam u-Ma'amreihem be-Sifrut ha-Talmudit veha-Midrashit* (Jerusalem, 1967–1969). Jacob Neusner, *A History of the Jews in Babylonia* (Leiden, 1969). —MICHAEL L. BROWN

YOLEDET (יוֹלֶדֶת; woman who has given birth). The Bible specifies that a *yoledet* is treated as a *niddah* (see MENSTRUATION), but the period of impurity varies in accordance with the sex of her offspring (*Lv*. 12.1–8). It lasts for seven days after the birth of a boy but fourteen days after the birth of a girl. Under biblical law, a further period of "pure blood" of thirty-three days applies in the case of a male child and sixty-six in that of a female. During this period, a woman is permitted to her husband but may not enter the Temple. In the geonic period, it became the custom for all women after childbirth to treat any discharge during the period of "pure blood" as regular menstrual blood and to fulfill all the requirements of the laws of *niddah* prior to engaging in sexual relations with their husbands (Maimonides, *Laws of Forbidden Relations* 11.6–7). A more stringent custom is found in the *Baraiyta' de-Niddah*, a work attributed to the tannaitic period but probably of a much later date and of a distinctly ascetic and, in some instances, almost heretical character. According to this work, a woman is to be treated as a *niddah* for forty days after the birth of a boy and eighty days after that of a girl. Maimonides is highly critical of this custom and regards it as the "way of heretics" (*Laws of Forbidden Relations* 11.15). It is to be found in Karaite works ('Anan, *Sefer ha-Mitsvot*, no. 19). Maimonides' criticism was echoed in the eighteenth century by R. Yeḥezqe'l Landau, who felt that its observance could lead to the commission of serious halakhic offenses as a result of the overlong period of abstinence involved (*Resp. Noda' bi-Yehudah, Yoreh De'ah*, no. 54). The commentators on the *Shulḥan 'Arukh*, however, maintain that a person who wishes to follow this custom may do so provided that no claim is made that it has any basis in *halakhah* (Turei Zahav, *Yoreh De'ah* 194.3; Siftei Kohen, *Yoreh De'ah* 194.1). It is customary for a woman after childbirth to say the *Birkat ha-Gomel blessing in the presence of a *minyan*. The focus of classical Jewish *abortion law is the woman in labor whose life is threatened by complications in the birth process (*Ohal*. 7.6).

• Rachel Biale, *Women and Jewish Law: An Exploration of Women's Issues in Halakhic Sources* (New York, 1984), pp. 151–153. Judah D. Eisenstein, ed., *Otsar Yisra'el* (Jerusalem, 1951), vol. 5, pp. 108–109. —DANIEL SINCLAIR

YOMA' (Aram.; יוֹמָא; The Day [of Atonement]), tractate in Mishnah order Mo'ed, originally known as *Kippurim*, with related material in Tosefta' and in both Talmuds. Seven of its eight chapters deal with laws concerning Yom Kippur, focusing primarily on elaborating the sacrificial service for the day outlined in *Leviticus* 16. The entire service on this day was performed by the high priest, who was sequestered in a special chamber within the Temple for seven days preceding Yom Kippur, in order to prepare himself for the solemn and uplifting responsibility that awaited him. The service itself centered on the high priest's entry into the Holy of Holies, forbidden every other day of the year, with the blood of two sin offerings, one that purified the Temple of the sins of the high priest and his family, and one that purified the Temple of the sins of the people. The entry into the Holy of Holies required an incense offering, occasioning a dispute between the Pharisees and the Sadducees about whether the incense needed to be placed on the fire before entering or after.

Another unique feature of the Yom Kippur service was the scapegoat, which was sent to the wilderness, where it was pushed off a cliff to atone for the sins of Israel. The eighth chapter of *Yoma'* discusses the laws of fasting and repentance connected with Yom Kippur. Despite the solemn character of most of the laws associated with the holiday, it was regarded as a festive day (*Taʿan.* 4.8) due to the joy resulting from the forgiveness of sins. The pericope that concludes the description of the sacrificial service (*Yoma'* 7.4) describes the celebration that the high priest made for his friends when he emerged safely from the Holy of Holies. In the concluding pericope of the tractate, R. ʿAqiva' exults: "Happy are you, Israel. Before whom are you purified and who purifies you? Your Father in Heaven!"

The Babylonian tractate was translated into English by Isidore Epstein in the Soncino Talmud (London, 1938).

• Chanoch Albeck, ed., *Shishah Sidrei Mishnah, Seder Moʿed* (Jerusalem, 1952). Philip Blackman, ed. and trans., *Mishnayoth*, vol. 2, *Order Moed* (Gateshead, 1973). Pinhas Kehati, ed., *Mishnah: A New Translation with a Commentary, Seder Moed*, vol. 4, *Yoma, Sukkah, Betzah, Rosh Hashanah* (Jerusalem, 1990). Hermann Leberecht Strack and Günter Stemberger, *Introduction to the Talmud and Midrash*, rev. and updat. ed., translated by Markus Bockmuehl (Minneapolis, 1992).

—AVRAHAM WALFISH

YOM HA-ʿATSMA'UT (יוֹם הָעַצְמָאוּת; [Israel] Independence Day), the anniversary of the proclamation of Israel's independence on 5 Iyyar 5708 (1948). It was declared a religious holiday by the chief rabbinate, which formulated a special order of prayer for the evening and morning services, now incorporated in many Israeli and Diaspora prayer books. Separate Yom ha-ʿAtsma'ut prayer books have also been produced, similar to those in use for the biblical festivals. The Yom ha-ʿAtsma'ut service includes *Hallel and a special *haftarah* (*Is.* 10.32–11.12) but deliberately excludes the accompanying benedictions and the She-Heḥeyanu blessing, which would have elevated Independence Day to the status of the post-Pentateuchal festivals of Ḥanukkah and Purim. The chief rabbinate suspended such post-Talmudic customs as the mourning restrictions of the *ʿOmer period, as well as the Monday and Thursday fasts (see SHENI VE-ḤAMISHI) following Pesaḥ, if one of them falls on that day. The halakhic reasoning was that while there was no doubt as to the religious obligation to celebrate the occasion, the recital of Talmudically ordained benedictions would constitute "an innovation after a lapse of two thousand years requiring an Orthodox rabbinic consensus," which was not forthcoming. However, the religious kibbutz movement and individual rabbis who share the Religious Zionist theology of R. Avraham Yitsḥaq Kook (see KOOK FAMILY), more intensely advocated on the emergence of the State of Israel by his son R. Tsevi Yehudah Kook, demonstratively recite these benedictions. Ḥaredim, represented in Israel by *Agudat Israel, regard Yom ha-ʿAtsma'ut as a purely secular holiday, raising the flag of the state of Israel on their public institutions as prescribed by law, but carefully refraining from giving it any religious expression. The *Neturei Qarta', for whom the establishment of a "heretical" Jewish state represented a blasphemous anticipation of the divinely operated messianic redemption, proclaim Yom ha-ʿAtsma'ut a day of mourning and lamentation and display black flags outside their homes. By Knesset statute, if the holiday falls on Friday or Saturday, the celebration is moved to the preceding Thursday to avoid desecration of the Sabbath. The day before Yom ha-ʿAtsma'ut is Yom ha-Zikkaron (Memorial Day), which is marked by prayers for those who died defending Israel, and services are held at military cemeteries.

• Menachem Elon, *Ḥaqiqah Datit* (Tel Aviv, 1968), p. 15. Moses Friedlander, ed. and trans., *Order of Service and Customs for the Synagogue and Home for Israel Independence Day* (London, 1964). Aryeh Newman, *Acknowledge the Miracle, Yom ha-Atsma'ut: Israel Independence Day in the Perspectives of Judaism* (Jerusalem, 1957), an anthology of readings, prayers and *responsa*. Aryeh Newman, ed., *Selected Articles on the Teaching of the Theme of Yom Haatzmaut, the Festival of Israel's Independence* (Jerusalem, 1967). *Seder Tefillot le-Yom ha-ʿAtsma'ut ke-Minhag Kehillot ha-Qibbuts ha-Dati* (Tel Aviv, 1968).

—ARYEH NEWMAN

YOM HA-DIN (יוֹם הַדִּין), day on which mankind will be judged by God (or one of his appointed) at the end of days (*aḥarit ha-yamim*). The biblical idea of *reward and punishment in this world was paralleled by the concept of the *Day of the Lord, the day upon which Israel would be exalted and her foes delivered up to divine justice. This predominantly nationalistic idea was transformed by the prophets (particularly *Amos), who proclaimed that on Yom ha-Din all evildoers would be judged, including those among the people of Israel, whose punishment would be exile. Once the nation was purged of its sinful dross, the *remnant of Israel, the upright and righteous, would return to the land (ingathering of the *exiles) and enjoy a long and prosperous life. These hopes of return are emphatically expressed by the post-exilic prophets, particularly Haggai and Zechariah, who believed that the reestablishment of the Jewish community in Jerusalem and the rebuilding of the Temple heralded the dawn of the messianic era. When this hope was not fulfilled, the notion of the final Yom ha-Din was transformed—it had not yet occurred but would happen only at the end of days.

Yom ha-Din became a major feature of apocalyptic literature. Not only would it witness the judgment of Israel, but the judgment of mankind and the cosmos as a whole; even the wicked angels would be called to account. Later apocalyptic literature assumed that the *resurrection of the dead would occur before Yom ha-Din, so that the dead might also be judged. There is a wide divergence of views regarding Yom ha-Din in pseudepigraphous and tannaitic literature. On that great and terrible day, either God himself or his anointed *Messiah will judge the entire world and declare its fate. In earlier apocalyptic literature, the eschatological Yom ha-Din was identified with "messianic woes," the period of trial and tribulation preceding the advent of the Messiah. In later apocalyptic works (Syriac *Apocalypse of Baruch*, the *Fourth Book of Esdras*), the view is expressed that the messianic age is merely a transitional period between this world and a new era, described as the "world to come" (see ʿOLAM HA-ZEH AND ʿOLAM HA-BAʾ). The distinction between the messianic age and the world to come is also made in tannaitic and later rabbinic literature (see ESCHATOLOGY).

Yom ha-Din is also a name for *Ro'sh ha-Shanah, the day on which, according to tradition (*R. ha-Sh.* 1.2; T., *R. ha-Sh.* 1.13), all humankind is judged by God. The decisions about each person's fate are sealed on Yom Kippur.

• David Novak and Norbert Samuelson, eds., *Creation and the End of Days: Judaism and Scientific Cosmology, Proceedings of the 1984 Meeting of the Academy for Jewish Philosophy* (London, 1987). D. S. Russell, *Di-*

vine Disclosure: An Introduction to Jewish Apocalyptic (London, 1992). Gershom Gerhard Scholem, *The Messianic Idea in Judaism and Other Essays on Jewish Spirituality* (New York, 1995). Shemaryahu Talmon, *Eschatology and History in Biblical Judaism* (Jerusalem, 1986).

YOM KIPPUR (יוֹם כִּפּוּר; Day of Atonement), the most solemn occasion of the Jewish calendar, falling on 10 Tishrei; the only fast day never postponed, even if it falls on a Sabbath. Although strictly observed from sunset as a twenty-five-hour fast (see FASTS) in accordance with the biblical injunction "and you shall afflict yourselves," it formally belongs to the category of festivals (see ḤAGGIM). The biblical commandment regulating its observance (*Lv*. 23.26–32) indicates no link with the holiday observed a few days earlier on 1 Tishrei (*Ro'sh ha-Shanah), but at an early period the two were linked in the framework of the *ʿAseret Yemei Teshuvah. The concept was that on Ro'sh ha-Shanah the fate of every individual for the coming year is decreed, and on Yom Kippur it is sealed. An unfavorable decree can be averted by repentance, prayer, and charity. The rabbis insist that a worshiper's contrite behavior on Yom Kippur itself will not effect forgiveness unless it is accompanied by sincere *repentance (*Yoma'* 8.8–9; tractate *Yoma'* is entirely devoted to Yom Kippur). During Temple times, Yom Kippur was the occasion for an elaborate sacrificial ceremony based on *Leviticus* 16. This consisted of two parts. The first was the sacrificial service in the Temple, at which the *high priest pronounced the threefold confession of sins on behalf of himself, the priests, and all Israel. The climax came when, clothed in white linen, he entered the Holy of Holies (the one occasion during the year when this was permitted) to sprinkle the blood of the sacrifice there and to offer incense. The second part of the ceremony consisted of hurling the scapegoat that "shall bear upon him all their iniquities"—that is, to which the sins of the community had been symbolically transferred—to its death in the wilderness (see AZAZEL). There is no historical source material concerning the observance of Yom Kippur in First Temple times, but there is much material depicting celebration of the day during the Second Temple period (e.g., *Ben Sira* 50, which describes the celebration during the high priesthood of Shimʿon, son of Onias, c.200 BCE; and the Mishnah tractate *Yoma'*). A Mishnaic statement that Yom Kippur was one of the happiest days in Israel, when maidens danced in the vineyards, has been found puzzling in view of the solemn nature of the day; one suggestion is that the celebration of the young people was connected with the feast that the high priest made for his friends when he emerged safely from the Holy of Holies (*Yoma'* 7.4). Today the ancient sacrifice is commemorated by the *ʿAvodah service, an elaborate poetical description of the Temple ceremony included in the Musaf service. **Kapparot* was once widespread and is still practiced in certain communities. At one time, in some communities, male congregants would submit to a whipping in the synagogue as a symbolic punishment for their sins. The rabbis insist that while one's proper observance of Yom Kippur can serve to atone for transgressions against God, sins committed against others require their forgiveness prior to the day. The *festival prayer is divided into five services, the first of which is the evening service (Maʿariv), preceded in most rites by the recitation of *Kol Nidrei; hence, Yom Kippur eve has come to be known as Kol Nidrei. The services on the day itself include the morning (Shaḥarit), the additional (Musaf), the afternoon (Minḥah), and the concluding service (*Neʿilah). Five mortifications are prescribed for the day: abstention from food, drink, marital intercourse, anointing with oil, and wearing leather shoes. All Sabbath work prohibitions are in effect on Yom Kippur. The prayers of the day stress confession of sins and supplications for forgiveness. Like all congregational prayers, they are couched in the plural, confession and forgiveness being sought on behalf of "the whole congregation of Israel" (*Nm*. 25.26). The formulas of confession include one that is composed of alphabetically arranged synonyms for transgression (*Ashamnu) and a longer alphabetical list enumerating a comprehensive catalog of sins (*ʿAl Ḥet'). With one possible exception, all of the sins listed appertain to the moral and ethical aspects of Judaism and not to Jewish observance.

Many worshipers remain in the synagogue for the entire day (some Orthodox Jews for the entire twenty-five hours), and the four services, with their many additional hymns, litanies, and confessions, are designed so that prayer should continue throughout the day. The morning Torah reading relates to the sacrificial rituals of Yom Kippur in the ancient Temple (*Lv*. 16; *Nm*. 29.7–11), while the *haftarah* (*Is*. 57.14–58.14) emphasizes the spirit of devotion and penitence without which the ritual is worthless. The Torah is read again at the afternoon service (*Lv*. 18, devoted to forbidden marriages), followed by the recitation of the *Book of Jonah*, with its message of divine forgiveness for genuine repentance. Some Reform congregations have chosen alternative readings for Yom Kippur. The dominating theme of the Neʿilah service is that the Day of Judgment is coming to an end and the divine verdict is about to be sealed. Neʿilah concludes with the declaration of God's unity, the sounding of the *shofar, and the prayer La-Shanah ha-Ba'ah bi-Yerushalayim (in Israel, Jerusalem Rebuilt). The *tallit* is worn during all five services. In many Ashkenazi congregations it was customary for a man to wear a **kitel* during services; this custom is no longer extensively practiced, although white is the predominant color in the synagogue. The traditional greeting on Yom Kippur is *gemar ḥatimah tovah*, "A propitious final sealing [of the divine judgment]."

• Shmuel Yosef Agnon, ed., *Days of Awe* (New York, 1965). Estelle Frankel, "Yom Kippur, Teshuvah, and Psychotherapy," *Tikkun* (September–October 1994): 23–24, 104–105. Theodor H. Gaster, *Festivals of the Jewish Year* (New York, 1953). Philip Goodman, *The Yom Kippur Anthology* (Philadelphia, 1974).

YOM KIPPUR QATAN (יוֹם כִּפּוּר קָטָן; Minor Day of Atonement), observance of the day preceding the new moon as a period of atonement and fasting. Tiqqun Yom Kippur Qatan, a special order of service (including *seliḥot* and *Psalms*), was drawn up to be recited at midnight and at the afternoon service (first printed in Natan Nataʿ Hannover's *Shaʿarei Tsiyyon* [1662]). The custom, which originated with the sixteenth-century kabbalists in Safed (which they related to the *aggadah* that Israel had to make atonement to God for making the moon smaller [*Ḥul.* 60b]), is now not widely observed.

• Joseph Apfel, "The Service for Yom Kippur Kattan," *L'Eylah* 24 (1987): 34–36. Ismar Elbogen, *Jewish Liturgy: A Comprehensive History*, translated by Raymond P. Scheindlin (Philadelphia, New York, and Jerusalem, 1993), pp. 104–106. Gershom Gerhard Scholem, *On the Kabbalah and Its Symbolism* (New York, 1965), pp. 151–153.

YOM TOV. See BEITSAH; ḤAGGIM.

YOM TOV BEN AVRAHAM ISHBILI (13th–14th cent.), Spanish Talmudic scholar; also known as Ritba'. He was noted for his learning while still a youth and became regarded as the outstanding rabbinical authority in Spain. He lived in Saragossa. In addition to his rabbinic expertise, he studied philosophy and logic. He is best known for *Ḥiddushei ha-Ritba', novellae* on most Talmudic tractates; commentaries on the Haggadah of Pesaḥ and the halakhic compendium of Yitsḥaq Alfasi; and a philosophic treatise, *Sefer ha-Zikkaron*, in which he attacked Nahmanides' strictures on Maimonides' theology.

• M. Y. Blau, ed., *Ḥiddushei ha-Ritba' al Massekhet Bava' Batra'* (New York, 1952), introduction. Kalman Kahana, ed., *Sefer ha-Zikkaron* (Jerusalem, 1956), introduction.

YOM TOV LIPMANN. See MUELHAUSEN, YOM TOV LIPMANN.

YOM TOV SHENI SHEL GALUYYOT (יוֹם טוֹב שֵׁנִי שֶׁל גָּלֻיּוֹת), term used for the additional day of festivals celebrated outside Erets Yisra'el. The fixing of the *calendar originally depended on the verbal testimony of witnesses who came to the *Sanhedrin in Jerusalem to assert that they had seen the new moon. Messengers were then sent out to announce the fact, but as they could not reach the Diaspora communities speedily, these communities were in doubt as to which of two days was the first of the month, and consequently as to which day marked the actual beginning of the festival in question. As a precaution, two days were observed at the beginning and end of Pesaḥ and Sukkot and on Shavu'ot. A second Seder was kept at the beginning of Pesaḥ, while at the end of Sukkot the extra (ninth) day was also observed as Simḥat Torah. Since Ro'sh ha-Shanah falls on the first day of the month, this information could not be passed on in time even in Erets Yisra'el, and this festival alone was, and still is, celebrated for two days there also. Strictly speaking, Yom Kippur also should be observed for two days, but this custom was dispensed with; nevertheless, some pietists in the Middle Ages observed a two-day fast, despite rabbinical disapproval of the custom as being injurious to health. Doubt regarding the second day was ignored with respect to the counting of the 'Omer. By the fourth century the question was raised as to why the observance of a second day of festivals should be continued since the calendar had already been fixed by astronomical calculation; the answer was that established custom and tradition should not be lightly discarded (*Beits.* 4b), and this ruling was sent to Babylonia by the authorities of Erets Yisra'el. Reform Judaism has abolished second day observances in the Diaspora, but some Reform congregations maintain two-day celebrations nevertheless. The Conservative movement has left the decision to each individual congregation.

• Solomon Zeitlin, *Studies in the Early History of Judaism* (New York, 1973), pp. 223–233. Hirsch Jacob Zimmels, "The Controversy about the Second Day of the Festival," in *The Abraham Weiss Jubilee Volume* (New York, 1964), pp. 138–168.

YOM YERUSHALAYIM (יוֹם יְרוּשָׁלַיִם; Jerusalem Day), the anniversary of the Israeli capture of the Old City of Jerusalem in the 1967 Six-Day War, which falls on 28 Iyyar. Officially recognized as an optional public holiday (*yom beḥirah*), the Israeli chief rabbinate ruled that, unlike on *Yom ha-'Atsma'ut, the whole Hallel be recited with the accompanying benediction to mark the regaining of access to Israel's holiest shrine, the *Western Wall. The central event is a mass thanksgiving assembly at the Western Wall, which resumed its status as the major pilgrimage site for Jews, including many *Ḥaredim.

• Shlomo Goren, *Torat ha-Shabbat veha-Mo'ed* (Jerusalem, 1981), pp. 432–446.

—ARYEH NEWMAN

YONAH (4th cent.), Palestinian amora'. His name is intimately associated with that of his colleague R. Yosei, his business associate in the production of wine and close friend, with whom he visited the sick and attended weddings and funerals. After R. 'Ammi moved his academy to Caesarea (c.350), the two became co-leaders of the Tiberias academy and "Sanhedrin" (R. Yonah was succeeded by his son Mani II). Their halakhic discussions are found in every tractate of the Talmud Yerushalmi, while the Talmud Bavli singles out R. Yonah as a praiseworthy and saintly Palestinian sage (*Ta'an.* 23b; for the most famous example of his charity, see Y., *Pe'ah* 8.9, 21b). Rabbi Yonah studied with R. Yirmiyahu, R. Ze'ira', and R. Il'ai and was responsible for the development and fixing of basic principles of Talmudic interpretation (cf., Y., *Pe'ah* 1.1, 15a). In contrast to R. Yosei, R. Yonah's treatment of tannaitic sources often preferred the text of the Tosefta' to that of the Mishnah.

• Wilhelm Bacher, *Die Agada der palästinensischen Amoräer* (1892–1899; Hildesheim, 1965). Jacob Nahum Epstein, *Mavo' le-Nusaḥ ha-Mishnah*, 2d ed. (Tel Aviv, 1964).

—MICHAEL L. BROWN

YONAH BEN AVRAHAM GERONDI (c.1200–1263) Spanish halakhist and ethicist; also known as Yonah the Pious. A relative of Nahmanides, Yonah remained in close contact with Nahmanides all of his life. He studied in France, where he became a zealous partisan in the campaign against the works of Maimonides. However, he later repented and, according to a popular but unlikely tradition, planned a pilgrimage to Maimonides' tomb. Yonah returned to Gerona and lived there and in Barcelona. He then set out for Erets Yisra'el but on passing through Toledo acceded to the request of the community to remain there and establish a rabbinic academy, which he headed until his death. He was noted for his ascetic and moralistic tracts with their stress on social ethics, and he condemned the widespread custom of concubinage. Many of his works display his halakhic skills. These include Bible, Mishnah, and Talmud commentaries and a commentary on Yitsḥaq Alfasi's digest of tractate *Berakhot*.

• Abe T. Shrock, *Rabbi Jonah ben Abraham of Gerona: His Life and Ethical Works* (London, 1948).

YONATAN BEN ʿUZZIʾEL (1st cent.), tanna' known as the most outstanding of *Hillel's eighty pupils. Although no *halakhot* have been preserved in his name, many of his opinions probably formed the basis for the rulings of Beit Hillel (see BEIT HILLEL AND BEIT SHAMMʾAI). The Talmud attributes to him a **targum* of the Prophets, but the one commonly known by his name dates in its present form from much later (4th–5th cent. Babylonia). A *targum* on the Pentateuch (named by scholars Targum *Pseudo-Jonathan) has also been attributed to Yonatan, but it dates from the third or fourth century, and the ascription appears erroneous. See also BIBLE TRANSLATIONS.

• M. Klein, "Introductory Poems R'shuyot to the Targum of the Haftarah in Praise of Jonathan ben Uzziel," in *Bits of Honey: Essays for Samson H. Levey*, edited by S. F. Chyet and D. Ellenson (Atlanta, 1993), pp. 43–56. —DANIEL SPERBER

YOREH DEʿAH. See SHULḤAN ʿARUKH.

YORTSAYT (Yi; יאָרצײַט; anniversary), the anniversary (based on the Hebrew calendar) of the death of a relative for whom *mourning is enjoined. During the Talmudic period, this anniversary was commemorated by a voluntary fast (*Ned*. 12a). In addition it was customary to visit the grave on that day (Rashi on *Yev*. 122a). In the course of time, and especially during the late Middle Ages, customs appertaining to the *yortsayt* were regulated. Fasting on the *yortsayt* has fallen largely into abeyance. The mourner observes the day by lighting a candle to burn for the full twenty-four hours (adduced from the verse "the soul of man is the lamp of the Lord"; *Prv*. 20.27) and by reciting *Qaddish at the daily services. Ḥasidim regard the *yortsayt* of their great rabbis not as an occasion for sorrow but as an occasion for celebration, since it marks the anniversary of the translation of the soul to higher spheres to receive its reward; it is celebrated by the omission of supplicatory prayers, as on all semifestivals, and even by dancing. This custom is frowned upon by the Mitnaggedim. However the traditional anniversary of the death of R. *Shimʿon bar Yoḥ'ai on *Lag ba-ʿOmer has been celebrated since the sixteenth century as a popular festival, particularly at his tomb in Meron. It is also customary to permit a person observing *yortsayt* to lead the congregational prayer and to be called to the reading of the Torah. Sephardim in particular attach great value to reading the **haftarah* on the Sabbath preceding the *yortsayt* for one's parents. The term *yortsayt* was first used by the fifteenth century rabbi Moshe *Mintz. Among Sephardim the *yortsayt* is called *naḥalah, meldado*, or *annos*.

• Maurice Lamm, *The Jewish Way in Death and Mourning* (New York, 1988). Steven L. Silver, "An Investigation into the Origins of Jahrzeit Practices," rabbinic thesis, Hebrew Union College, 1984. Jack Riemer, *Jewish Insights on Death and Mourning* (New York, 1996).

YOSEF BEN AVRAHAM HA-KOHEN. See BASIR, YOSEF BEN AVRAHAM.

YOSEF BEN ḤIYYA' (died 333), Babylonian amora'. He was given the title of "Sinai" (*Hor*. 13b) because of his encyclopedic knowledge of traditional law. He headed the Pumbedita academy after the death of his colleague Rabbah, with whom he frequently engaged in halakhic debates, recorded hundreds of times in the Talmuds; in *Sanhedrin* 17b the two are called "the amora'im of Pumbedita." He was known for both his aggadic and halakhic acumen, and specialized in biblical interpretation and translation; the *Targum to *Chronicles*, called the Targum of Rabbi Yosef, is traditionally attributed to him. Known for his great humility (*Ber*. 64a; *Pes*. 113b) and careful piety (*Pes*. 107a), the Talmud recounts that he became blind and forgot all his Torah learning, both, apparently, due to a severe illness, but Abbayei and Rava', his principal students, retaught him (*ʿEruv*. 10a; *Men*. 99b). It is said that when he died, so many mourners came to attend his funeral that the bridge over the Euphrates cracked (*Moʿed Q*. 25b). He taught that he who scorned the sages was a heretic (*San*. 99b) and that it was of greater merit to engage in Torah study than to perform *mitsvot* (*Sot*. 21a). He played a role in the development of Merkavah mysticism (*Ḥag*. 13a). For some of his proverbial sayings, see *Ketubbot* 104a and *Gittin* 45a.

• Wilhelm Bacher, *Die Agada der babylonischen Amoräer* (1913; Hildesheim, 1967). Aaron Hyman, *Toledot Tanna'im ve-'Amora'im* (1910; Jerusalem, 1987). —MICHAEL L. BROWN

YOSEF BEN YITSḤAQ BEKHOR SHOR (12th cent.), biblical commentator whose name, Bekhor Shor (Firstborn Bull) is derived from the description of the biblical Joseph in *Deuteronomy* 33.17. The author of liturgical poems (*piyyutim*) and of legal questions addressed to *Yaʿaqov ben Me'ir Tam, Bekhor Shor is best known for his commentaries on the Torah and on *Psalms*. His commentaries on other biblical books seem to have been lost. Following in the footsteps of R. Shemu'el ben Me'ir (Rashbam), Bekhor Shor endeavored to delineate large literary units within the scriptures, to explain the contextual meaning of many legal texts not in accordance with their treatment in rabbinical literature, and to show that the primary meaning of various biblical verses undermines the Christological interpretations imposed upon them by Christian theologians. The implication is that the scientific study of Hebrew scriptures proves that the natural and logical continuation of them is Judaism and not Christianity. Other characteristic features of Bekhor Shor's exegesis are his examination of the motives of characters in biblical narrative, his attempt to provide a rational basis for the divine commandments, his attack upon the allegorization of the commandments, and his extensive discussion of the legal implications of various biblical laws.

• Sarah Kamin, "The Polemic against Allegory in the Commentary of Rabbi Joseph Bekhor Shor," in *Jews and Christians Interpret the Bible*, edited by Sarah Kamin (Jerusalem, 1991), pp. 73–98. Nathan Porges, *Joseph Bechor Shor* (Leipzig, 1908). Yosefa Rachman, "The Process of

Speculation in Bekhor Shor's Commentary on the Torah," *Tarbiz* 53 (1984): 615–618. Gotthilf Walter, *Joseph Bechor Shor* (Breslau, 1890).
—MAYER I. GRUBER

YOSEF DELLA REINA. See DELLA REINA, YOSEF.

YOSEF ḤAYYIM BEN ELIYYAHU AL-ḤAKHAM (1833–1909), rabbinical authority in Baghdad. He was a popular and influential preacher at a time when the Baghdad community was reattaining a position of influence, which had lapsed in the geonic period. His comprehensive literary output consisted of seventy books ranging from the five-volume *Ben Yehoiada'* (1898–1904) on Talmudic *aggadah* to *Ḥuggei Nashim* on Jewish law concerning women, and he was the first Jewish religious leader to assert that a girl should celebrate a **bat mitsvah*. His *responsa*, *Rav Pe'alim* (1901–1912), reflected the struggle within the Baghdad community between the sages and the wealthy leadership. His volume of homilies, *Ben Ish Ḥai* (1898; Jerusalem, 1957), is still studied, and some of the two hundred *piyyutim* that he composed entered the Baghdad liturgy.

• Abraham Ben-Jacob, *Ha-Rav Yosef Ḥayyim: Mi-Gedolei Rabbanei Bavel* (Jerusalem, 1971). Abraham Ben-Jacob, *Rav Yosef Ḥayyim mi-Baghdad: Toledot Ḥayav u-Reshimat Ketavav* (Or Yehudah, 1984).
—SHALOM BAR-ASHER

YOSEI BEN ḤALAFTA' (2d cent.), called Rabbi Yosei in the Mishnah and *baraiytot*; Palestinian tanna'; one of the five famous pupils of R. *'Aqiva' ben Yosef. He was forced to flee during the Hadrianic persecutions but eventually settled at Sepphoris in Lower Galilee, where he headed the academy. His halakhic preeminence and the respect in which he was held by R. *Yehudah ha-Nasi' and R. *Shim'on ben Gamli'el led to his views being accepted in legal disputations (*'Eruv*. 46b), and, indeed, he is mentioned more than three hundred times in the Mishnah and *Tosefta'. He is the first scholar of whom it is said that he was privileged to have *Elijah the Prophet reveal himself to him (*San*. 113a). He frequently engaged in polemics on matters of belief with non-Jews. His original philosophical beliefs included his view that God bears no relationship to space or time: "God is the place of the world and the world is not his place" (*Gn. Rab*. 68.9). He opposed the view that men were judged on *Ro'sh ha-Shanah, stating that men are judged daily (T., *R. ha-Sh*. 1.13). He further thought that the **shekhinah*, the divine countenance, thrice daily mourns the destruction of the Temple but takes comfort in the prayers and praises of the synagogue (*Ber*. 3a).

• Israel Konovitz, *Rabbi Jose Ben Halafta: Collected Sayings in Halakah and Aggadah in the Talmudic and Midrashic Literature* (Jerusalem, 1966).
—DANIEL SPERBER

YOSEI BEN YO'EZER (2d cent. BCE), scholar from Zeredah in southern Samaria; president of the *Sanhedrin; disciple of Antigonus of Sokho. Together with Yosei ben Yoḥanan, he constituted the first of the five "pairs" (**zugot*). He was a *kohen* (priest), belonged to the party of the *Hasideans, and strongly opposed the Hellenists. Rabbinic tradition has it that in his time the first halakhic controversy arose, as to whether or not one places one's hands on an animal sacrificed during a festival, a controversy that continued for many generations. Regarding the laws of purity and *impurity, Yosei ben Yo'ezer tended to be lenient. According to legend, his nephew was the Hellenized high priest Alcimus, who persecuted the Hasideans and executed Yosei ben Yo'ezer in a cruel manner.

• R. Travers Herford, *Pirke Aboth: The Ethics of the Talmud, Saying of the Fathers* (New York, 1971).
—DANIEL SPERBER

YOSEI BEN YOḤANAN. See YOSEI BEN YO'EZER.

YOSEI BEN YOSEI (4th or 5th cent.), the first well-known liturgical poet (*payyetan*) of Erets Yisra'el. Nothing is known of his life. Some of his *piyyutim* (see PIYYUT) have been incorporated into the Sephardi liturgy for Yom Kippur (e.g., Azkir Gevurot—a picturesque portrayal of the Temple ritual of that day) and Ro'sh ha-Shanah (Ahalelah Elohai Ashirah 'Uzzo—about the majesty of the Creator). His compositions are alphabetic, with rhythmic pattern and occasional alliteration, but lack rhyme or meter.

• Ismar Elbogen, *Jewish Liturgy: A Comprehensive History*, translated by Raymond P. Scheindlin (Philadelphia, New York, and Jerusalem, 1993), pp. 238–239 et *passim*. Aharon Mirsky, *Yosse ben Yosse: Poems* (Jerusalem, 1977).

YOTSER (יוֹצֵר), the first of the two *benedictions preceding the *Shema' in the morning service, so called because it opens with the words "Blessed . . . who forms [*yotser*] light and creates darkness. . . . " Its theme is praise to God for creation and for renewing it and restoring light to the earth every morning. The quotation from *Isaiah* 45.7, with its mention of creation and also of God's power to bring darkness, was meant as a polemical rejection of dualistic beliefs in two separate deities of light and darkness (*Ber*. 11b). In its present form, Yotser contains the alphabetic hymn probably originating in early mystic circles, El Barukh, a poetic description of the angelic praise of God, "Holy, holy, holy is the Lord . . ." (see QEDUSHAH). Brief *piyyutim* are inserted into Yotser, especially on the Sabbath (e.g., El Adon) and festivals; these are generally known as *yotserot*. Before the conclusion of the blessing, some rites (but not the Sephardi) insert a messianic petition: "Cause a new light to shine upon Zion"; however, some authorities in geonic times opposed this on the grounds that the subject of the benediction is the physical light of creation and not the spiritual light of redemption. The term *yotser* is loosely applied to all the extra hymns that were introduced into the morning service (the general tendency in recent times is to omit these accretions).

• Ezra Fleischer, *The Yozer: Its Emergence and Development* (Jerusalem, 1984). Reuven Hammer, "What Did They Bless? A Study of Mishnah Tamid 5.1," *Jewish Quarterly Review* 81 (1991): 305–324. L. J. Liebreich, "The Benediction Immediately Preceding and the One Following the Recital of the Shema," *Revue des études juives* 125 (1966): 151–165. Macy Nulman, *The Encyclopedia of Jewish Prayer* (Northvale, N.J., and London, 1993), p. 386. J. Vellian, "The Anaphoral Structure of Addai and Mari Compared to the Berakoth Preceding the Shema in the Synagogue Morning Service," *Le Muséon* 85 (1972): 201–223.

YOVEL (יוֹבֵל; jubilee), the year of release that occurs at the end of the cycle of seven sabbatical years (see SHEMITTAH) once every fifty years. The laws concerning cultivation of the land and produce during the sabbatical year apply to the jubilee as well, but the main function of the jubilee is to complement the laws of redemption, which stipulate that Israelites who have been reduced to servitude must be permitted to buy back their freedom and that those who have been forced to sell their property must be given ample opportunity to regain possession of it; further, that one whose kinsman has been forced into such straits must assist him to extricate himself. The jubilee provides the ultimate remedy: every fifty years all land that has not yet been redeemed reverts to its original owners, and any slaves who have not yet earned their freedom become free. The jubilee and all of the provisions pertaining to it are found in *Leviticus* 25. The jubilee began on Ro'sh ha-Shanah and its arrival was proclaimed by the sounding of horns on Yom Kippur. The English word *jubilee* is derived from the Hebrew word *yovel*, which may mean ram (*R. ha-Sh.* 26a). The land release preserves the ancient, tribal division of the land of Canaan among the Israelites. The aim seems to have been to prevent a few individuals, families, or tribes from accumulating large portions of land, thereby depriving many of an independent means of livelihood. The Bible provides a theological rationale: Erets Yisra'el is God's possession; the Israelites are merely his tenants and cannot conduct permanent real estate transactions on his property (*Lv.* 25.23). The release of Israelite slaves is similarly explained: "For it is to me that the Israelites are slaves; they are my servants, whom I freed from the land of Egypt" (*Lv.* 25.55); thus they cannot become permanent slaves of each other. The practical implications are spelled out clearly. The price paid, either for a piece of land or an Israelite slave, was to be calculated in accord with the number of years remaining until the next jubilee.

According to the law in *Leviticus* 25.8–10, the jubilee is the fiftieth year, which means it follows the seventh sabbatical year rather than coinciding with it; rabbinic opinion, however, was divided on this question (*Ned.* 61a). It is not known whether the jubilee was ever observed in actual practice, although some similar institutions did exist in the ancient Near East. In particular, the biblical injunction "you shall proclaim freedom [*deror*] throughout the land" (*Lv.* 25.10) recalls the release of slaves in Mesopotamia, called *anduraru*. There is no mention of the jubilee in biblical history during First Temple times, and according to the rabbis it was not observed in the Second Temple period at all (*'Arakh.* 32b). There are, however, indications that a fifty-year cycle was employed in the calendar in ancient times; traditions of calculating the jubilees survived beyond the biblical period.

• Jeffrey A. Fager, *Land Tenure and the Biblical Jubilee*, Journal for the Study of the Old Testament, Supplement Series 155 (Sheffield, Eng., 1993). Baruch Levine, *Leviticus*, The JPS Torah Commentary (Philadelphia, 1989), pp. 168–181, 270–274. James C. VanderKam, ed., *The Book of Jubilees: A Critical Text*, 2 vols. (Leuven, Belgium, 1989).

—BARUCH J. SCHWARTZ

YUDGHAN. See MESSIAH.

YUḤASIN (יוּחֲסִין; pedigrees), the legal consequence of a person's lineage relating, in particular, to marital status. The child of a regular married couple is permitted to marry any Jew (*Qid.* 69a). In such cases, status is determined by paternity; thus, the son of a priest and an Israelite will be a priest, and one born to a priest's daughter and an Israelite will be an Israelite (*Nm.* 1.2, 18; *Shulḥan 'Arukh, Even ha-'Ezer* 8.1). In the case of a valid prohibited marriage, status is determined by the "tainted" parent. Hence, the child of a *mamzer* and a regular Jew will be a *mamzer* (*Qid.* 66b) and the child of a priest and a divorcee will be a *ḥalal*, that is, unfit to serve as a priest (*Qid.* 66b, 77a). A female *ḥalal* is not permitted to be married to a priest (*Qid.* 77a). Children born out of wedlock suffer no legal impediments under Jewish law and the only legal issue of significance is the establishment of their paternity. Upon the establishment of paternity, the normal rules of *yuḥasin* apply. Where only one parent is Jewish, the *halakhah* is that the child's status is determined in accordance with the matrilineal principle. Hence, the child of a Jewish mother and a non-Jewish father is a Jew with the sole proviso that a female may not marry a priest. The offspring of a Jewish father and a non-Jewish mother is non-Jewish and may only enter the community of Israel by means of conversion to Judaism. Reform Judaism in the United States, however, now accepts such a child as a Jew if raised as a Jew.

• Menachem Elon, *Jewish Law: History, Sources, Principles*, 4 vols. (Philadelphia, 1994), pp. 1652–1690, 1753–1784. Isaac Klein, "The Marriage of a *Cohen* to a *Giyyoret*," in *Responsa and Halakhic Studies* (New York, 1975), pp. 22–26.

—DANIEL SINCLAIR

Z

ZACUTO, MOSHEH (c.1610–1697), kabbalist and poet. He studied in his native Amsterdam and in Posen (Poland), and later he moved to Verona and Venice, where he edited kabbalistic books, including *Zohar Ḥadash* (1658). In 1666 he supported the messianic claims of *Shabbetai Tsevi. While he favored the Shabbatean emphasis on repentance, he strongly opposed the liturgical reforms practiced by the Shabbateans. Although some of his favorite disciples, such as Benyamin ha-Kohen and Avraham Rovigo, remained loyal Shabbatean believers, Zacuto turned his back on Shabbateanism after Shabbetai Tsevi's apostasy. In 1673 he became rabbi in Mantua; he never realized his desire to settle in the Holy Land. Besides his literary activities as a poet and a kabbalist, his main contribution was the introduction of Lurianic liturgical practices into Italian synagogues. He wrote the first biblical drama in Hebrew literature, *Yesod ʿOlam* (1874).

• A. Apfelbaum, *Mosheh Zakuth* (Lemberg, 1926). Meir Benayahu, *Dor Eḥad ba-'Arets: ʿIggerot Rabbi Shemu'el Abuhav ve-Rabbi Mosheh Zakut be-ʿInyenei Erets Yisra'el 399–426* (Jerusalem, 1988). J. Melkman, "Moses Zakuto en Zijn familie," in *Studia Rosenthaliana*, vol. 3 (Assen, 1969), pp. 145–155. Yohanan Twersky, ed., *Dor Dor ve-Sofrav: Antologyah Sifrutit le-Talmidim vela-ʿAm* (Tel Aviv, 1950). —NISSIM YOSHA

ZADDIK, YOSEF BEN YAʿAQOV IBN (c.1070–1149), Spanish poet, philosopher, and Talmudist. In 1138 he was appointed *dayyan* of Cordova, along with Maimon ben Yosef. He composed several liturgical poems and a work on ethics. He is best known for his introduction to philosophy, *Sefer ha-ʿOlam ha-Qatan* (edited by A. Jellinek, 1854; edited by S. Horowitz, 1903). Written in Arabic in answer to a student's questions concerning the meaning of certain philosophical terms, it was later translated into Hebrew, possibly by Naḥum ha-Maʿarabi. His central thesis is that the human being is a *microcosm (*ʿolam qatan*) of the universe—both physical and metaphysical—and the study of human beings will yield the truths of cosmology and theology. Zaddik's approach is Neoplatonic, with some Muʿtazili (see KALAM) and Aristotelian elements. The work is composed of four parts. The first is a presentation of Aristotelian physics and deals with definitions. The second is a study of human beings, based on the concept of the microcosm. The third examines theology, notably God's unity and his attributes, in the manner of the Kalam *Bab al-Tawḥid*. The fourth division is a vindication of God's justice in the manner of the Kalam *Bab al-Adl*.

• Max Doctor, *Die Philosophie des Joseph (ibn) Zaddik* (Munster, 1973). Julius Guttmann, *Philosophies of Judaism* (New York, 1964), pp. 144–148. Isaac Husik, *A History of Mediaeval Jewish Philosophy* (New York, 1960), pp. 125–149. H. Schirmann, "The Poets Contemporary with Moses ibn Ezra and Judah Halevi," in *Mitteilungen des Forschungsinstitutus für Hebräische Dichtung*, vol. 2 (Berlin, 1936), pp. 163–174. —STEVEN BALLABAN

ZADOK (Heb. Tsadoq), priest; descendant of Eleazar, son of Aaron (*1 Chr.* 5.30–34). He sided with David against Absalom (*2 Sm.* 19.12) and anointed Solomon as king against his rival Adonijah, who was banished (*1 Kgs.* 1.32–40). The descendants of Zadok ruled as *high priests until the time of the Hasmoneans. The sons of Zadok are also mentioned in the Dead Sea Scrolls (Zadokite fragments), where the reference is to the ancient priestly family. It has been suggested that the name *Sadducees is derived from Zadok.

• Johann Maier, "Von Eleazar bis Zadok: CD V, 2–5," *Revue de Qumran* 15 (1991–1992): 231–241. Saul Olyan, "Zadok's Origins and the Tribal Politics of David," *Journal of Biblical Literature* 101 (1982): 177–193. James C. VanderKam, "Zadok and the *spr htwrh hhwtm* in Dam Doc 5: 2–5," *Revue de Qumran* 11 (1984): 561–570. —SHALOM PAUL

ZADOKITES, descendants of *Zadok, one of David's high priests in Jerusalem (*2 Sm.* 15.24–37), who remained the dominant priestly family in Jerusalem until the Babylonian exile (586 BCE). After the return from exile, the Zadokites regained control of the high priesthood and retained that office until the deposition and murder of Onias III in the early second century BCE (*2 Mc.* 4.33–34).

In Ezekiel's program for the restoration of the Temple, the Zadokites are considered the only legitimate priests (*Ez.* 44.15–31). In postexilic literature, the Zadokites appear most prominently in the sectarian texts of the *Dead Sea Scrolls. For example, in the **Rule of the Community*, authority in the community is given to "the priests, the sons of Zadok" (5.2b–3a). This emphasis on priestly authority and particularly the importance of the Zadokite priests indicates a possible area of dissension between the Qumran group and the Temple authorities, led by the non-Zadokite Hasmoneans.

• Frank Moore Cross, *The Ancient Library of Qumran* (Garden City, N.Y., 1961). Lawrence H. Schiffman, *The Halakhah at Qumran*, Studies in Judaism in Late Antiquity, vol. 16 (Leiden, 1975), pp. 72–75. —SIDNIE WHITE CRAWFORD

ZADON. See INTENT.

ZAKHUR LA-TOV. See ZIKHRONO LI-VERAKHAH.

ZAQEN MAMRE' (זָקֵן מַמְרֵא, elder rebel), a member of the Sanhedrin who refused to concede the correctness of the majority opinion and continued to rule that his own approach—a minority opinion—was correct and should be followed. He was liable for the death penalty for that conduct. However, the elder rebel was not liable for the death penalty if he merely affirmed the correctness of his own opinion on an intellectual basis but declined to seek that it be considered normative and be practiced. There is a dispute as to whether such conduct is completely permissible or merely not liable to the death penalty.

• Menachem Elon, *Jewish Law: History, Sources, Principles* (Philadelphia, 1994). Hugo Mantel, *Studies in the History of the Sanhedrin* (Cambridge, Mass., 1965). —MICHAEL BROYDE

ZAVIM (זָבִים; Persons with Impure Discharge), tractate in Mishnah order Tohorot, with related material in Tosefta'. There is no *gemara'* in either Talmud. Its five chapters deal with the laws concerning men and women who are rendered impure due to genital discharge (*Lv.* 15). Both normal, healthy discharges and abnormal, unhealthy discharges render one impure, but normal discharges, namely male seminal emissions and female menstruation, create less severe types of impurity than abnormal discharges. *Zavim* elaborates the differences among these forms of impurity and their ramifications. With the exception of a man with normal seminal emissions, furniture or implements designed for sitting on or reclining in become primary sources of impurity (i.e., possessing the power to defile others) when a *zav* has sat on or reclined in them. This law renders the issue of social intercourse and contact between a *zav* and an undefiled person highly problematic, a matter that is discussed quite extensively in *Zavim*. The tractate concludes with a presentation of the stages of transmission of various forms of defilement.

An English translation of the tractate is in Herbert Danby's *The Mishnah* (London, 1933).

• Chanoch Albeck, ed., *Shishah Sidrei Mishnah, Seder Tohorot* (Jerusalem, 1958). Philip Blackman, ed. and trans., *Mishnayoth*, vol. 5, *Order Taharoth* (Gateshead, 1973). Hermann Leberecht Strack and Günter Stemberger, *Introduction to the Talmud and Midrash*, rev. and updat. ed., translated by Markus Bockmuehl (Minneapolis, 1992).

—AVRAHAM WAFISH

ZAYIN BA-'ADAR (7 Adar), the traditional date of *Moses' birth and death (*Qid.* 38a; *Meg.* 13b). In earlier generations 7 Adar was observed as a solemn day of fasting and prayer. The following day was a day of celebration, which, in medieval Egypt, even took on the character of a carnival day. A special *tiqqun* (anthology of readings) for the day was compiled in 1654 by R. Shemu'el Aboab of Venice, comprising selections from the Bible, Mishnah, Midrash, and Zohar.

In recent times the **ḥevrah qaddisha'* (burial society) in each community observes the date by using the first part of the day as a time for fasting, reflection, and self-examination. Visits are made to cemeteries, where petitions are offered for forgiveness from the deceased in case proper respect was not shown at the time of their burial. In the evening there is a festive meal, with appropriate Torah lessons. The occasion is also used for admitting new members to the *ḥevrah qaddisha'*. The silver cups used by the burial societies for the 7 Adar banquet are often outstanding examples of ritual art.

In modern Israel, 7 Adar is designated as a memorial day for Israeli soldiers killed in war and whose last resting place is unknown.

• Judah D. Eisenstein, *Otsar Dinim u-Minhagim* (Tel Aviv, 1975), p. 8. Mordekhai ha-Kohen, *Seder Zayin Adar, Meqorot, Minhagot, Seliḥot u-Tefillot* (Jerusalem, 1961). Eliyahu Ki Tov, *The Book of Our Heritage* (Jerusalem, 1968), pp. 12–28. Yom-Tov Lewinsky, *Entsiqlopedyah shel Havai u-Masoret ba-Yahadut*, vol. 1 (Tel Aviv, 1975), p. 166.

—CHAIM PEARL

ZEALOTS, a term applied to a sect that existed during the last decades of the Second Temple period, who rejected the Roman dominion without compromise. *Josephus, the main source for Jewish history of this period, states that a *census the Romans conducted in Judea in 6 CE generated strong opposition from some Jewish circles, led by Judah of Gamala and Zadok the Pharisee, who, partly for religious reasons (cf. *2 Sm.* 24), objected to this attempt to count the Jewish population. Their opposition led to the creation of a "fourth philosophy" (in addition to the *Pharisees, *Sadducees, and *Essenes), whose followers are described by Josephus as similar in everything to the Pharisees, except for their invincible passion for liberty and their insistence that God alone was their leader and master. This movement, whose adherents combined a violent anti-Roman stance with strong messianic expectations, seems to have split into several subgroups, among which Josephus names the Zealots (the Greek equivalent of the Hebrew *qanna'im*, "the ones zealous [for God]") and the Sicarii (from *sica*, the Latin word for dagger, their favorite weapon). Their activities ranged from guerrilla warfare against Roman soldiers and officials to political assassinations of their Jewish opponents. The various groups of Zealots were deeply involved in the Great Revolt of 66–73 and perished, in Jerusalem and on Masada, when the messianic salvation they were hoping for failed to materialize.

The concept of zeal for the Torah was a rabbinical ideal exemplified by Phinehas (*Nm.* 25.6–13), who was praised as "zealot, son of a zealot."

• Martin Hengel, *The Zealots*, translated by David Smith from *Die Zeloten* (Leiden, 1961; Edinburgh, 1989). David M. Rhoads, *Israel in Revolution: 6–74 C.E.: A Political History Based on the Writings of Josephus* (Philadelphia, 1976). E. Mary Smallwood, *The Jews under Roman Rule: From Pompey to Diocletian*, Studies in Judaism and Late Antiquity 20 (Leiden, 1976).

—GIDEON BOHAK

ZEBULUN (Heb. Zevulun), the sixth son born to Leah and Jacob and the eponymous ancestor of the tribe whose territory was located in southern Galilee and the Jezreel Valley. In giving Zebulun his name, Leah played on the assonance of the roots *z b d* (gift) and *z b l* (dwell), saying, "God has given me a choice gift (*zebadni . . . zebed*); this time my husband will dwell with me" (*Gn.* 30.19–20). The tribe of Zebulun extended from the Mediterranean Sea to Mount Tabor in the east, and included such prominent sites as Jokneam, Nahalal, Shimron, Hannathon and Bethlehem of Galilee (*Jos.* 19.10–16). The tribe answered Deborah's call to arms against Sisera (*Jgs.* 5.14, 15.18) and supported Gideon in his war against the Midianites (*Jgs.* 6:35). Two minor judges—Ibzan from Bethlehem and Elon the Zebulunite—came from this tribe (*Jgs.* 12:8–12). From the reference in Jacob's blessing (*Gn.* 49.13), "Zebulun shall dwell by the seashore; he shall be a haven for ships and his flank shall rest on Sidon," it may be concluded that the tribal territory extended to the Mediterranean, perhaps along the Kishon River bordering the Sidonian colony at Acco, and included a subjugated Canaanite populace (*Jgs.* 1.30–31). In the second and third centuries, the main Torah academies of *Beit She'arim and Sepphoris were in the former territory of Zebulun. The later *aggadah* emphasizes the close relationship between Zebulun and his brother and neighbor *Issachar, a paradigm of the wealthy merchant brother supporting the scholarly brother in pursuing his studies undisturbed by the demands of making a living.

• Yohanan Aharoni, *The Land of the Bible: A Historical Geography*, 2d ed. (Philadelphia, 1979). Louis Ginzberg, *Legends of the Jews* (Philadelphia, 1954). Samuel Klein, *Erets ha-Galil* (Jerusalem, 1967), pp. 1–8.

—AARON DEMSKY

ZECHARIAH (Heb. Zekharyah; 6th cent. BCE), prophet and priest in the kingdom of Judah; son of Berechiah and grandson of Iddo. Like his contemporary, the prophet *Haggai, Zechariah called upon the postexilic Jewish community to rebuild the Temple in Jerusalem (cf. *Ezr.* 5.1). He proclaimed that the Temple of Solomon was destroyed because of the evil deeds of past generations but that repentance would help future generations avoid similar catastrophes. The core of his message appears in a series of eight visions. These emphasize the dual leadership of the community: the royal figure *Zerubbabel, son of Shealtiel, and the high priest Joshua, son of Jehozadak. Zechariah projects a future day when all nations will recognize the sanctity of God, Jerusalem, and the Jewish people.

The *Book of Zechariah* is the eleventh book of the Minor Prophets. Traditionally Zechariah is considered to be the author of the *Book of Zechariah*, but many modern scholars attribute to him only the first eight chapters, which can be dated to 520–518 BCE. Basing their views upon differences in form and references to the Greeks in later parts of the book, these scholars suggest *Zechariah* contains the work of at least two and possibly three prophets. The visions of Zechariah in chapters 1–8 are an example of early apocalyptic literature, in which God reveals to Zechariah his purposes in the building of the Second Temple. The second part of *Zechariah* (chaps. 9–14) is written in a totally different and obscure style, with strong eschatological content. The portrayal of the king of Jerusalem and the downfall of Israel's enemies in *Zechariah* 9–11 is identified as the work of a second prophet, often called Deutero-Zechariah. The work of this prophet is often dated to the late Persian or Hellenistic period (4th cent. BCE) because of its references to the Greeks and a possible depiction of Alexander the Great's advance through the Phoenician-Israelite region. Deutero-Zechariah speaks of the punishment of neighboring peoples and the eventual redemption of Israel. The description of the final apocalyptic battle on "the Day of the Lord" in *Zechariah* 12–14 is attributed to a third prophet called Trito-Zechariah. Chapters 12–14 are dated to the Hellenistic period and portray an apocalyptic scenario of judgment against the nations and the restoration of Jerusalem.

• Mike Butterworth, *Structure and the Book of Zechariah*, Journal for the Study of the Old Testament, Supplement Series 130 (Sheffield, Eng., 1992). R. J. Coggins, *Haggai, Zechariah, Malachi*, Old Testament Guides, (Sheffield, Eng., 1987). Carol L. Meyers and Eric M. Meyers, *Haggai, Zechariah 1–8* and *Zechariah 9–14*, The Anchor Bible, vols. 25B and 25C (New York, 1987, 1993). David L. Petersen, *Haggai and Zechariah 1–8*, The Old Testament Library (London, 1984). Ralph L. Smith, *Micah–Malachi*, World Biblical Commentary, vol. 32 (Waco, Tex., 1984).

—MARVIN A. SWEENEY

ZE'IRA', the name of two scholars (referred to in Babylonian sources as Zera') born in Babylonia, who studied in Babylonian academies and then immigrated to Palestine, where they spent the latter part of their lives. On occasion, the two scholars are described as arguing with one another (e.g., *Men.* 40b).

The earlier Ze'ira' was a rabbi who went to Palestine within the lifetime of R. Yoḥanan bar Nappaḥa' (died 279) and probably died around 300 CE. The more famous of the two, he was primarily a man of *halakhah*. He belittled the importance of Midrash and referred to works of *aggadah* as "books of magic" (*sifrei qosemim*). He was well known for his piety (*Ḥul.* 122a) and his asceticism, and often fasted to protect himself from the fires of hell (*B. M.* 85a).

The latter Ze'ira' was a rabbi who lived in the first half of the fourth century CE and was a candidate to head the academy in Pumbedita. However, Abbayei, his colleague, received the position.

• Aaron Hyman, *Toledot Tanna'im ve-'Amora'im* (1910; Jerusalem, 1987). Mordecai Margaliot, ed., *Entsiqlopediyyah le-Ḥakhmei ha-Talmud veha-Ge'onim* (Jerusalem, 1946).

—DANIEL SPERBER

ZEKHER LA-ḤURBAN (זֵכֶר לַחֻרְבָּן; a reminder of the destruction [of the Second Temple]), customs and regulations that entered Jewish usage intended to serve as reminders of the tragedy of the Temple's destruction. These were instituted for a number of reasons: to perpetuate the sorrow of the tragedy; to keep mourning within bounds and prevent its excess; to moderate expressions of joy at a time when the Temple lay in ruins and the people were scattered in exile; and to keep alive the memory of the Temple and its service. After the destruction of the First Temple, four fasts were instituted to commemorate the event and the events leading up to it (see FASTS); observance of the fasts was strengthened after the destruction of the Second Temple. As a sign of mourning for the Second Temple, the custom arose of reciting Psalm 137 ("By the waters of Babylon . . .") before the Birkat ha-Mazon on weekdays, and appropriate references to the destruction of the Temple were introduced into prayers. Instrumental music and singing were forbidden on joyful occasions. The rabbis decreed that Jews should leave one square cubit of one wall unpainted in their homes. When preparing a festive meal, one item was to be omitted in order to make the feast incomplete. Similarly, when adorning herself with her jewelry, a woman was to leave off one piece as a symbol of the national sorrow (*B. B.* 60b). While most of these customs have lapsed, a bridegroom occasionally will place a small quantity of ash under his hat during the wedding ceremony as a reminder that even in a moment of personal joy he is to recall his people's sorrow. For the same reason, it is customary for a groom to break a glass underfoot at the end of the wedding ceremony.

• Judah D. Eisenstein, *Otsar Dinim u-Minhagim* (Tel Aviv, 1975). *Entsiqlopedyah Talmudit*, vol. 12 (Jerusalem, 1967), pp. 226–236.

—CHAIM PEARL

ZEKHER LI-YETSI'AT MITSRAYIM (זֵכֶר לִיצִיאַת מִצְרָיִם; a memorial of the Exodus from Egypt), ordinances and customs connected to the memory of the *Exodus from Egypt. The Bible links many of its laws to the Exodus (*Lv.* 19.34, 25.38, 26.13; *Nm.* 15.41). The first of the Ten Commandments lays down the basis for all the other laws with its proclamation, "I am the Lord your God who brought you out of the land of Egypt" (*Ex.* 20.2). The liturgy explicitly designates the Sabbath and every festival as "a memorial of the Exodus from Egypt," and the rabbis taught that the Exodus is to be remembered for all time—even to the days of the Messiah (*Ber.* 1.5). The Exodus was seen as the pivotal event in Jewish history, and all that followed—the revelation at Sinai, the giving of the commandments, and the possession of the Promised Land—ensued from the Exodus. The Pesaḥ eve service (the Seder) is devoted to the recollection of the wonders of the event, and the commandment to relate it to one's children is emphasized with the statement, "whoever amplifies the description of the Exodus is praiseworthy."

• Judah D. Eisenstein, *Otsar Dinim u-Minhagim*, (Tel Aviv, 1975). *Entsiqlopedyah Talmudit*, vol. 12 (Jerusalem, 1967), pp. 199–212.

—CHAIM PEARL

ZEKHOR BERIT (זְכוֹר בְּרִית; "Remember the covenant"), opening words of a number of poems but mainly refers to a penitential hymn composed by R. *Gershom ben Yehudah (960–1028) and recited in the Ashkenazi ritual *Seliḥot on the day before Ro'sh ha-Shanah. It is recited with the ark open and is so highly regarded that the Seliḥot service of that day is commonly referred to as Zekhor Berit. It is also recited in the Ashkenazi rite during the concluding service on Yom Kippur.

• Israel Davidson, *Thesaurus of Medieval Hebrew Poetry* (New York, 1970). Ernst Daniel Goldschmidt, *Maḥazor la-Yamim ha-Nora'im* (Jerusalem, 1970), p. 766.

ZEKHUT AVOT (זְכוּת אָבוֹת; merits of the fathers). The traditional doctrine of *merits emphasizes that the pious deeds of parents secure blessings for their descendants as well. This receives expression in the *Ten Commandments, in which God "shows kindness to the thousandth generation of those who love me and keep my commandments" (*Ex.* 20.6). Rabbinic *aggadah* and liturgical texts accord a unique place in this respect to the lasting merit of the *patriarchs Abraham, Isaac, and Jacob (recalled by Moses in pleading with God after the sin of the *golden calf [*Ex.* 32.13]), although the view was also expressed that even their merits were not limitless (*Shab.* 55a). Rabbenu *Ya'aqov ben Me'ir Tam held that even if the merits of the patriarchs could be exhausted, God's covenant with them was unbounded. Judaism thus insists on "original merit" rather than original sin. In the Middle Ages, the notion developed that the merits of children (a pious life, prayer) can also benefit their departed parents.

• Moshe Greenberg, "The Decalogue Tradition Critically Examined," in *Ten Commandments in History and Tradition*, edited by Ben Zion Segal (Jerusalem, 1990), pp. 83–119. Arthur Marmorstein, *The Doctrine of Merits in Old Rabbinical Literature* (London, 1920).

ZELOPHEHAD, DAUGHTERS OF. Zelophehad was an Israelite of the tribe of Manasseh in the time of Moses. He died in the desert, leaving no male offspring, but five daughters: Mahlah, Noah, Hoglah, Milcah, and Tirzah. The daughters presented their case before Moses and the elders for the right to inherit their father's portion (*Nm.* 27). The divine decision was that "The plea of Zelophehad's daughters is just," and they were granted a hereditary holding among their father's kinsmen. When the decision was challenged by the kinsmen (*Nm.* 36), Moses clarified the intent of God's decision in that the daughters had to marry within the tribe of Manasseh. These decisions became legal precedents in the laws of inheritance of territory.

The Samaria ostraca, discovered in 1908–1910 and dating from the early eighth century BCE, indicates that certain Manassite clans, residing north of Shechem, were called by matronymics referring to the daughters Noah and Hoglah.

• Zafrira Ben-Barak, "Inheritance by Daughters in the Ancient Near East," *Journal of Semitic Studies* 25 (1980): 22–33. Aaron Demsky, "The Genealogies of Manasseh and the Location of the Territory of Milkah the Daughter of Zelophehad," *Eretz-Israel* 16 (1982): 70–75. Michael Fishbane, *Biblical Interpretation in Ancient Israel* (Oxford, 1985), pp. 103ff.

—AARON DEMSKY

ZEMIROT (זְמִירוֹת; songs), the term used by Sephardi-Eastern and Italian Jews to denote the passages of song that introduce the morning prayers, which are equivalent to the *Pesuqei de-Zimra' of the Ashkenazi prayer book; in the Ashkenazi tradition, the term that refers to the two dozen or more joyous table hymns that may be sung during or after the Sabbath meals. The singing of *zemirot*, a familiar custom by 1105 (*Siddur Rashi; Maḥazor Vitry*), was influenced by Lurianic Kabbalah and Hasidism. As their Hebrew or Aramaic titles indicate, these *zemirot* emphasize the rewards of Sabbath observance, give praise to God, and create a sense of well-being at the family table. Some are by famous poets; others by unknown authors. Included in the group for Sabbath eve are Kol Meqaddesh, Shevi'i, Menuḥah ve-Simḥah, Mah Yedidut Menuḥatekh, *Yah Ribbon 'Olam (by *Yisra'el ben Mosheh Najara), Yom Zeh le-Yisra'el (by *Yitsḥaq Luria), and *Tsur mi-Shello (prelude to *Birkat ha-Mazon). Two additional *zemirot* are Tsame'aḥ Nafshi (by Avraham *ibn Ezra) and Shalom Lekha Yom ha-Shevi'i (by *Yehudah ha-Levi). A second group, for the Sabbath midday meal, includes Barukh El 'Elyon, Yom Zeh Mekhubbad, Yom Shabbaton (by Yehudah ha-Levi), Shimru Shabbetotai, Ki Eshmerah Shabbat (by Avraham ibn Ezra), and Deror Yiqra' (by Dunash ben Labrat). Mizmor le-David (*Ps.* 23) and *Yedid Nefesh (by El'azar ben Mosheh Azikri) usually accompany *Se'udah Shelishit). Finally, at the Sabbath's termination, *Ha-Mavdil, Eliyyahu ha-Navi' (linking the prophet Elijah with Israel's messianic redemption), and Amar Adonai le-Ya'aqov are widely sung. Ashkenazim have a particularly wide range of tunes for their *zemirot*. Not all of these hymns figure in the more voluminous Sephardi-Eastern repertoire, which also has *zemirot* in the vernacular, such as Arabic and Persian. Special booklets (*birkonim*) have been published containing the best-known examples of *zemirot*.

• Naftali Ben-Menaḥem, *Zemirot shel Shabbat* (Jerusalem, 1949). Menaḥem Ha-Kohen and Benny Don-Yechiya, *Shalom le-Vo Shabbat* (Tel Aviv, 1977). Abraham Z. Idelsohn, *Jewish Liturgy and Its Development* (New York, 1932), pp. 80–83, 151–157. Abraham E. Millgram, *Sabbath: The Day of Delight* (Philadelphia, 1944), pp. 37–49, 73–82, 92–95, 302–308, 418–437. Arno Nadel, *Zemirot Shabat: Die häuslichen Sabbatgesänge* (Berlin, 1937). Nosson Scherman, *Zemiroth: Sabbath Songs with Additional Sephardic Zemiroth* (Brooklyn, N.Y., 1979). —GABRIEL A. SIVAN

ZEPHANIAH (Heb. Tsefanyah; 7th cent. BCE), prophet in the kingdom of Judah during the reign of King *Josiah (639–609); son of Cushi, grandson of Gedaliah, great-grandson of Amariah, and great-great-grandson of Hezekiah (possibly the king of that name). Zephaniah supported Josiah's (to whom he may have been related) program of religious reform and national restoration, condemned those who identified with pagan perspectives, and called for judgment against Josiah's enemies. These included Assyria and Cush (Egypt), the major powers who opposed Josiah, and Philistia and Moab, countries into which Josiah hoped to expand.

The *Book of Zephaniah* is the ninth book of the Minor Prophets. It is cast in the form of an exhortation to the people to support the king's reforms and has two basic parts. The first oracle (1.2–18) announces the coming of the "Day of the Lord," which will bring a cataclysm upon the people of Judah for their religious syncretism. Zephaniah's description of this judgment day is one of the most detailed in the entire Bible. The second oracle (chaps. 2–3) is an exhortation to seek the Lord, calling on heathen nations to repent for opposing Josiah, together with a scenario of judgment and restoration for Jerusalem and Israel. Zephaniah was greatly influenced by the prophecies of Isaiah. Fragments from the *Book of Zephaniah* have been found at Qumran.

• Ivan J. Ball, *A Rhetorical Study of Zephaniah* (Berkeley, 1988). Ehud Ben Zvi, *A Historical–Critical Study of the Book of Zephaniah*, Beihefte zur Zeitschrift für die alttestamentliche Wissenschaft 198 (Berlin and New York, 1991). Duane L. Christensen, "Zephaniah 2.4–15: A Theological Basis for Josiah's Program of Political Expansion," *Catholic Biblical Quarterly* 46 (1984): 669–682. Arvid Schou Kapelrud, *The Message of the Prophet Zephaniah: Morphology and Ideas* (Oslo, 1975). J.J.M. Roberts, *Nahum, Habakkuk, Zephaniah: A Commentary*, The Old Testament Library (Philadelphia, 1991). Ralph L. Smith, *Micah–Malachi*, Word Biblical Commentary, vol. 32 (Waco, Tex., 1984). Marvin A. Sweeney, "A Form-Critical Reassessment of the Book of Zephaniah," *Catholic Biblical Quarterly* 53 (1991): 388–408.

—MARVIN A. SWEENEY

ZERAḤYAH BEN YITSḤAQ HA-LEVI GERONDI (c.1115–1186), rabbinical scholar. He was born in Gerona, Spain, and immigrated to Narbonne, in southern France. There he studied under R. Mosheh ben Yosef and R. Avraham ben Yitsḥaq of Narbonne. Afterwards he moved to Lunel to study under the patronage of R. Meshullam ben Yaʿaqov of Lunel. He engaged in a lifelong controversy with *Avraham ben David of Posquières. Their literary quarrels stemmed from basic differences in personality, cultural background, and approaches to source material. Zeraḥyah wrote a commentary to Mishnah tractate *Qinnim*, which included a critique of Avraham ben David's commentary; *Selaʿ ha-Maḥloqet*, a critique of Avraham ben David's *Baʿalei Nefesh*; and *Divrei Rivot*, which recorded the exchange of letters between himself and Avraham ben David over the interpretation of a Talmudic passage. His *Sefer ha-Ma'or*, completed in the 1180s, was a synthesis of *novellae* to the Talmud and a criticism of Yitsḥaq *Alfasi's code (published in 1552 in the Venice edition of the Talmud). His critique of the Alfasi code was comprehensive and systematic and offered alternative interpretations to Talmudic passages. In his commentaries to the Talmud, Zeraḥyah introduced the *tosafot* system, betraying the strong influence of R. Yaʿaqov ben Me'ir Tam. He also wrote a short treatise on the laws of ritual slaughter; *responsa*; religious poems (collected and published under the title *Shirat ha-Ma'or*, Jerusalem, 1984); and *Sefer ha-Tsava'*, describing the methodology of the Talmud and the exact definitions of its terms.

• Binjamin Ze'ev Benedikt, *Merkaz ha-Torah bi-Provans* (Jerusalem, 1985). Isaac Meiseles, ed., *Shirat ha-Ma'or: Piyyutei Zeraḥyah ha-Levi* (Jerusalem, 1984). Israel Ta-Shema, *Rabbi Zeraḥyah ha-Levi—Baʿal ha-Ma'or u-Venei Ḥugo: Le-Toledot ha-Sifrut ha-Rabbanit be-Provans* (Jerusalem, 1992). Isadore Twersky, *Rabad of Posquières: A Twelfth-Century Talmudist*, rev. ed. (Philadelphia, 1980).

—SHLOMO H. PICK

ZERAḤYAH ḤEN. See GRACIAN, ZERAḤYAH.

ZERAʿIM (זְרָעִים; Seeds), first order of the Mishnah, ten of whose eleven tractates deal with laws governing agricultural work and produce. These are *Pe'ah*, *Dema'i*, *Kil'ayim*, *Sheviʿit*, *Terumot*, *Maʿasrot*, *Maʿaser Sheni*, *Ḥallah*, *ʿOrlah*, and *Bikkurim*. Its first tractate, *Berakhot*, deals with benedictions and prayers. The Talmud Yerushalmi contains *gemara'* on the entire order, but the Talmud Bavli contains *gemara'* only to tractate *Berakhot*.

—AVRAHAM WALFISH

ZERUBBABEL, a scion of the Davidic line who served as governor of Judah under the Persian ruler Darius I for at least the years 521–516 BCE. Apparently, in the second year of the reign of Darius I, Zerubbabel was appointed governor of the small province of Yehud (Judah). Along with Joshua ben Jozadak (the grandson of the last high priest of the First Temple) and the prophets *Haggai and *Zechariah, Zerubbabel led a multitude of exiles, numbering about forty-four thousand people, back to Judah (*Ezr.* 2). Encouraged by the prophets, Zerubbabel was able to overcome the economic and political obstacles, as well as the popular apathy, facing the project of restoring the Temple; the restoration was completed by Pesaḥ 516 BCE. After this date, there is no record of Zerubbabel; the usual hypothesis is that he was removed from office after encouraging messianic hopes placed in him by Haggai (2.20ff.) and Zechariah (4.6, 6.12). However, the long genealogy (*1 Chr.* 3.19ff.) of his descendants, extending down to the time of the Chronicler (c.400–380 BCE) indicates that the family thrived. Furthermore, regarding his three children—Meshullam, Hananiah, and Shelomith—a horde of seals and bullae from the end of the sixth century BCE mention a governor by the name of Hanan(ia)h and another by the name of Elnathan the husband of a Shelomith. This suggests that the Persian policy continued to be one of appointmenting a descendant of King Jehoiachin, particularly from Zerubbabel's immediate family, as governor of the province of Yehud.

• Peter Ackroyd, *Exile and Restoration*, Old Testament Library (Philadelphia, 1968). Nahman Avigad, *Bullae and Seals from a Post-Exilic Judean Archive* (Jerusalem, 1976), pp. 5–6f., 11ff. Sara Japhet, "Sheshbazzar and Zerubbabel: Against the Background of the Historical and Religious Tendencies of Ezra–Nehemiah," *Zeitschrift für die alttestamentliche Wissenchaft* 94 (1982–1983): 66–98; pt. 2, 95 (1982–1983): 218–229.

—AARON DEMSKY

ZERUBBABEL, BOOK OF. See BOOK OF ZERUBBABEL.

ZEVAḤIM (זְבָחִים; Animal Sacrifices), tractate in Mishnah order Qodashim, with related material in Tosefta' and in the Talmud Bavli. It discusses the laws governing animal and bird sacrifices. A central theme of *Zevaḥim* is the requirement of proper sacrificial intent during the four central procedures of an animal or fowl offering: slaughtering, receiving blood in a sacred vessel, bringing the blood to the altar, and sprinkling of the blood on the altar. This emphasis on the importance of proper intent and on the capacity of improper intent to disqualify the sacrifice is typically rabbinic and is absent from the biblical discussion of sacrificial law (*Lv.* 1–7).

Zevaḥim further outlines the differences among kinds of sacrifices as regards sprinkling of the blood and the method of consumption of the sacrifice on the altar, by the priests, and by the owner of the sacrifice together with his fellows. The tractate closes with a survey of the places where the sanctuary was established, culminating with the Temple in Jerusalem.

An English translation by Harry Freedman is in the Soncino Talmud (London, 1948).

• Chanoch Albeck, ed., *Shishah Sidrei Mishnah, Seder Qodashim* (Jerusalem, 1956). Philip Blackman, ed. and trans., *Mishnayoth*, vol. 5, *Order Kodashim* (Gateshead, 1973). Pinhas Kehati, ed., *Mishnah: A New Translation with a Commentary, Seder Kodashim*, vol. 1, *Zevaḥim, Menaḥot, Ḥullin* (Jerusalem, 1994). Hermann Leberecht Strack and Günter Stemberger, *Introduction to the Talmud and Midrash*, rev. and updat. ed., translated by Markus Bockmuehl (Minneapolis, 1992).

—AVRAHAM WALFISH

ZIKHRONO LI-VERAKHAH (זִכְרוֹנוֹ לִבְרָכָה; "May his memory be for a blessing"), honorific phrase added to the mention of the name of a person held in fond and pious remembrance. It derives from the verse "The memory of the righteous is a blessing, but the name of the wicked shall rot" (*Prv.* 10.7). It is the custom when writing the name of the deceased in Hebrew to add the initial letters of the two words *zikhrono li-verakhah*. The phrase *zakhur la-tov*, "May he be remembered for good," is also used—this form is regularly used when speaking about *Elijah—and occurs several times in the Talmud.

ZIKHRONOT (זִכְרוֹנוֹת; Remembrances), the second of three sections of the additional service ʿAmidah on Roʾsh ha-Shanah, the other two being *Malkhuyyot and *Shofarot. Each consists of ten appropriate biblical verses, with an introductory paragraph and a concluding blessing. The ten verses in the Zikhronot refer to God as "remembering" (his mercies, his covenant, etc.). After their recital, the *shofar is sounded.

ZIMMUN. See BIRKAT HA-MAZON.

ZIMRA, DAVID BEN SHELOMOH IBN AVI. See DAVID BEN SHELOMOH IBN AVI ZIMRA.

ZION, originally a Jebusite hill fortress in southern *Jerusalem conquered by David (*2 Sm.* 5.6–9) and named the City of David. As the city expanded to the north, Zion also denoted the site of the Temple. The exact location of Zion is a matter of dispute. Already during the Second Temple period various views were held as to the exact location of the biblical Mount Zion. Josephus identified it with the western hill or upper city of Jerusalem. The hill sloping down to Gei Ben Hinnom (southwest of the present Old City wall) has been identified with Mount Zion for over one thousand years, though scholars agree that the original Zion is actually elsewhere. The identification of the present Mount Zion is of ancient Christian tradition (the site of the Last Supper; later also that of the "Dormition" of Mary); since the Crusader period, the Tomb of David (see DAVID, TOMB OF) has been located on the hill, and the tradition has been adopted by Jews. Mount Zion became a Jewish pilgrimage site, particularly for Jews from Muslim lands (notably between 1948 and 1967, when the Western Wall—then under Jordanian rule—was closed to Israelis). Modern scholarship favors the so-called Ophel—the hill of the Temple mount—as the true position.

In the language of the Prophets and *Psalms* (and in later rabbinic, homiletical, and liturgical usage), Zion was synonymous with Jerusalem. The Prophets speak of Zion to refer to the entire Jewish kingdom (*Is.* 1.27) or the people of Israel (*Zec.* 2.14). In the image of a forsaken spouse, Zion symbolized the fate of the Jewish people in distress (*Is.* 49.14), while in prophecies of redemption, Zion is depicted as the mother of a reborn Israel (*Is.* 66.8). By a further extension of meaning, Zion came to denote the messianic City of God (*Is.* 60.14). The concept of Zion became charged with an intense religious and eschatological current, fed by the prophetic vision of Zion as the divine seat from which the word of God was to issue forth for the salvation of all mankind (*Is.* 2.3) and as the source of justice and righteousness (*Is.* 33.5). Zion has been a symbol of Jewish restoration throughout the ages (see ZIONISM). It is frequently mentioned in the liturgy (where prayers are usually for a "return to Zion") and personified—both in poetry and Midrashic legend—as a virgin, mother, or widow in mourning (cf. *Lam.* 1.11). Yehudah ha-Levi's famous elegies addressed to Zion are known as Zionides.

• Elaine Follis, "The Holy City as Daughter," in *Directions in Biblical Hebrew Poetry*, edited by E. Follis (Sheffield, Eng., 1987), pp. 173–184. Jacob Neusner, ed., *Israel and Zion in American Judaism: The Zionist Fulfillment* (New York, 1993). John J. Schmitt, "Israel and Zion—Two Gendered Images: Biblical Speech Traditions and Their Contemporary Neglect," *Horizons* 18 (Spring 1991): 18–32. A. S. van der Woude, "Zion as Primeval Stone in Zechariah 3 and 4," in *Text and Context*, edited by J. W. Claassen (Sheffield, Eng., 1988).

ZIONISM. The return of the Jewish people to its own land (*shivat Tsiyyon*), poetically called *Zion, is deeply ingrained in Jewish religious thought. The dream of the exiles in Babylonia to return home, expressed in *Psalms* and the *Book of Ezekiel*, can be seen as an early manifestation of this idea, and after the destruction of the Second *Temple, it became imprinted in all forms of religious expression. Jews turned toward Jerusalem in prayer; their prayers contained appeals to God to return his people to their land (often associated with the rebuilding of the Temple); their festivals remained linked to the agricultural cycle of the Land of Israel; and their poems and art frequently turned to Zion. They developed folk customs, such as leaving a portion of a wall unpainted in memory of Zion or the breaking of a glass by the bridegroom at his wedding as a sign of mourning for the destruction of *Jerusalem. Messianism was inspired by the longing for the return to Zion, and the first action of the *Messiah was not to establish universal peace (that would come later) but to restore the Jews to their land. *Halakhah* ruled that a spouse who refused to accompany his or her partner to Israel deserved to be divorced (Maimonides, *Hilkhot Ishut* 13). The very air of the Land of Israel was said to make a person wise (*B. B.* 158b), and many *mitsvot* could be observed solely in Erets Yisra'el. Some Jews in the Diaspora asked to be interred in Israel after their death, while it was customary to be buried with a sack of earth from the Holy Land.

Modern Zionism emerged at the end of the nineteenth century as a political movement with mostly secular leadership, but its roots were religious and historical. The movement called for political, socioeconomic, demographic, and cultural normalization. Among religious Jews, only a small minority initially embraced Zionism. Most Orthodox Jews (some of whom organized themselves in the *Agudat Israel movement) believed that the Jews would return to their own land only under divine auspices and that human attempts to "hasten the end" were sinful. The ideological wickedness was compounded by the secular leadership of the movement. They therefore took an extreme stance against the Zionist movement, which they saw as a rebellion against the sovereignty of God, although they continued to maintain the hope for a return to Zion in messianic times. Those Orthodox Jews who supported Zionism established the Mizrachi party within the World Zionist Organization (see Religious Parties in Israel; Religious Zionism). Their outstanding ideologist was Avraham Yitsḥaq Kook (see Kook Family), who saw Zionism as a movement of redemption and of total Jewish renascence. In western Europe and North America, the Reform movement (see Reform Judaism) also opposed Zionism. Committed to a universalistic ideology, they held that the Jewish mission was to bring a moral message to the world at large, and the concept of a return to Zion was retrogressive. They excluded prayers for a return to Zion from their liturgy. *Conservative Judaism, and later *Reconstructionism, fully supported the Zionist movement.

The Holocaust virtually silenced opposition to Zionism. The Orthodox masses in eastern Europe had been killed, and their survivors had gone to the United States and Israel. They accepted de facto the establishment of the State of Israel in 1948, although they continued to refuse to participate in the World Zionist Organization. Certain groups, notably followers of the *Satmar *rebbi*, continue to refuse to recognize the State of Israel. The Reform movement began to abandon its anti-Zionism in the 1930s (see Columbus Platform) and eventually became an integral element of the World Zionist Organization. See also Emancipation; Israel, State of, Jewish Religious Life in; Israel, State of, Theological Aspects.

• Joseph Adler, "Religion and Herzl: Fact and Fable," in *Herzl Year Book*, edited by R. Patai, vol. 4 (New York, 1965), pp. 271–303. Aryei Fishman, *Ben Dat le-'Ideologyah: Yahadut u-Modernizatsyah ba-Qibbuts ha-Dati* (Jerusalem, 1990). Ben Halpern, *The Idea of the Jewish State* (Cambridge, Mass., 1969). Arthur Hertzberg, ed., *The Zionist Idea* (New York, 1960). Jacob Katz, *Le'umiyyut Yehudit* (Jerusalem, 1983). Ehud Luz, *Parallels Meet: Religion and Nationalism in the Early Zionist Movement, 1882–1904* (Philadelphia, 1988). Michael Z. Nehorai, "Rav Reines and Rav Kook: Two Approaches to Zionism," in *The World of Rav Kook's Thought* edited by Benjamin Ish Shalom and Shalom Rosenberg, translated by Shalom Carmy and Bernard Casper (Jerusalem, 1991). Aviezer Ravitzky, *Messianism, Zionism and Jewish Religious Radicalism* (Chicago, 1996). Gideon Shimoni, *The Zionist Ideology* (Hanover, N.H., 1995). Nachum Sokolow, *History of Zionism 1600–1918*, 2 vols. (London, 1919). David Vital, *The Origins of Zionism* (Oxford, 1975). David Vital, *Zionism: The Crucial Phase* (Oxford, 1987). David Vital, *Zionism: The Formative Years* (New York, 1982).

ZODIAC, an imaginary broad celestial belt within which ancient astronomers visualized the sun, moon, and planets as passing. It was divided into twelve equal parts, each of which was given a sign representing a zodiacal constellation. These were represented (both in the ancient Near East and in China) by mostly animal signs, hence the Greek term *zōdiakos kyklos* (circle of animals). The signs of the zodiac in Hebrew are Taleh (Aries), Shor (Taurus), Te'omim (Gemini), Sartan (Cancer), Aryeh (Leo), Betulah (Virgo), Mo'znayim (Libra), ʿAqrav (Scorpio), Qeshet (Sagittarius), Gedi (Capricorn), Deli (Aquarius), and Dagim (Pisces). The concept of the zodiac seems to have originated in Mesopotamia, from where it passed to Greek astronomy. It was the Greek Hellenistic version that influenced Jewish ideas and imagery on the subject. The signs are listed in the Hebrew calendar as corresponding to the twelve months of the year, beginning with Nisan. The first Jewish source to mention the twelve signs in their present form is **Sefer Yetsirah*, in which they also correspond to the twelve organs of the human body. The relationship of the twelve tribes to the zodiacal signs has also been noted (*Yalqut Shimʿoni, Nm.* 418). The origin of the signs is unknown; rabbis interpreted them symbolically, thus Mo'znayim (Libra) is the sign of Tishrei, the month of judgment.

The zodiac was a favorite theme in Jewish art and was prominent in the decoration of Palestinian synagogues from the fourth to the sixth century. The pattern includes not only the twelve signs but also Helios, the sun god, who is praised by name in the magical work *Sefer ha-Razim* (edited by Mordecai Margulies [Jerusalem, 1966], pp. 12–13) as an angel. The presence of the zodiac patterns on the floors of synagogues diminished their sanctity and prevented any tendency to regard them as objects of worship. Pictures of the zodiac are also to be found in medieval illuminated manuscripts, in prayer books, on marriage documents, and on kabbalistic scrolls of invocation. In more recent times, they reappeared in the decorations of Polish wooden synagogues. See also Astrology.

• Ida Huberman, *Living Symbols: Symbols in Jewish Art and Tradition* (Ramat Gan, 1988). Ernst Kitzinger, *Israeli Mosaics of the Byzantine Period* (New York, 1965). Erica Reiner, "The Uses of Astrology," *Journal of the American Oriental Society* 105 (1985): 589–595.

ZOGERQA (Yi.; זאָגערקע; female reciter), woman in eastern Europe who read the synagogue prayers in Yiddish to other women unable to follow the Hebrew text on their own.

ZOHAR, recognized by kabbalists since the fourteenth century as the most important work of mystical teaching; in some circles the book has achieved a sanctity only less than that of the Bible. The Zohar is composed of several literary units, not all by the same author. The largest section, the Zohar proper, consists of a mystical commentary on parts of the Bible, delivered in the form of discussions by a group of second-century rabbis and scholars in Palestine led by *Shim'on bar Yoḥ'ai. Most of their reflections and exchanges deal with the inner, esoteric meaning of scripture. Other sections of the Zohar, like the *Idra' Rabba'* and the *Idra' Zuta'* also depict scenes in the life of Shim'on bar Yoḥ'ai and his disciples. These sections are in Aramaic. Another section, the *Midrash ha-Ne'eman*, is written partly in Hebrew and attempts a more straightforward mystical interpretation of biblical passages. The *Ra'aya' Meheimana'* is a kabbalistic interpretation of the commandments and prohibitions in the Torah. The *Raza' de-Razin* contains material on physiognomy and chiromancy. These and other parts of the Zohar are characterized by an enthusiastic style, theosophical speculation, and mythological imagery. Traditional kabbalists ascribe all or most of these books to the authorship of Shim'on bar Yoḥ'ai and his contemporaries. Modern scholarship (notably by Gershom Gerhard *Scholem) has shown that the main part of the Zohar was written toward the end of the thirteenth century by *Mosheh de León, a Castilian kabbalist who died in 1305. Some parts of the Zohar were written shortly afterward and added to the main work.

The Zohar has been described as a mixture of theosophic theology, mystical psychology and anthropology, myth, and poetry. Old gnostic doctrines, mystical traditions, theurgies, popular superstitions, and mythological motifs dwell side by side with echoes of Neoplatonic and Aristotelian philosophic theories about the nature of the cosmos and about the relationship between a transcendent God and a finite world. The manner in which the inscrutable mystery of the Godhead, the *Ein Sof (literally the infinite, but actually signifying the hidden, mystical, divine nothingness), manifests itself in the divine creative process is one of the Zohar's major themes. The doctrine of the **sefirot* is the kabbalistic answer to this problem. The *sefirot* are the ten stages of the divine world through which God descends, from the innermost recesses of his concealment down to his manifestation in the *Shekhinah. The Shekhinah—the last of the *sefirot*—is also the heavenly archetype of the community of Israel. When the contrasting forces of the life divine (e.g., grace and stern judgment) are harmoniously balanced, the Shekhinah (conceived in female imagery) is united with the upper (male) *sefirot* and the abundance of divine life flows harmoniously into the world. There is a markedly erotic quality to the description of the holy union of the male and female aspects of the deity. When there is a defect in the proper conjunction of the upper *sefirot*, disorder, chaos, and evil result. The problem of evil occupies a large place in the Zohar. At times, evil is described as a negative but powerful and even demonic reality, resulting from the ascendancy of certain divine qualities (e.g., destructive judgment) over others (e.g., pure grace). The central doctrine of the Zohar is that the harmonious union of the divine life is brought about as well as rent by human action (i.e., by a religious life, good works, and mystical meditations; and by sins and improper thought, respectively). The Torah, for the Zohar, is an essential key to the mysteries of the divine processes. For the kabbalist, it is an actual manifestation of the divine. Hence, the author of the Zohar is less interested in the literal meaning of the historical events described in the Bible than in the theosophical mysteries that are their inner, and therefore more real, meaning. The basic premise of the Zohar is that there exists a complete correspondence between the lower and upper worlds. Consequently a quickening from below can arouse a quickening above. Hence, deeds and prayers have cosmic significance. The Zohar was first printed simultaneously in Cremona (1559–1560) and Mantua (1558–1560). The latter was the basis for later printings. It has been translated into several languages including English (by Harry Sperling and Maurice Simon, 5 vols. [London, 1931–1934]).

• Y. Lachower, Isaiah Tishby, and David Goldstein, *The Wisdom of the Zohar: An Anthology of Texts*, 3 vols. (London, 1991). Yehuda Liebes, *Studies in the Zohar* (Albany, 1993). Gershom Gerhard Scholem, *The Book of Splendor: Basic Readings from the Kabbalah* (New York, 1963).

ZOKHRENU LE-ḤAYYIM (זָכְרֵנוּ לְחַיִּים; "Remember us for life"), opening words of a sentence interpolated in the first benediction of the 'Amidah throughout the *'Aseret Yemei Teshuvah. Its plea for God to "inscribe us in the Book of Life" is based on the Talmudic concept of heavenly ledgers in which are recorded every person's fate at this season (*R. ha-Sh.* 16b). The theme recurs in other High Holy Days' supplications, notably *Avinu Malkenu and *U-Netanneh Toqef. —GABRIEL A. SIVAN

ZOROASTRIANISM. See DUALISM.

ZUGOT (זוגות; pairs), the term applied to the leading scholars of the five generations following the Men of the *Keneset ha-Gedolah and preceding the tanna'im (see TANNA'), spanning the period of approximately 200 BCE to 70 CE. They are listed in pairs in *Avot* 1, and, according to tradition, the first was president (*nasi'*) and the second head of the court (*av beit din*). The five pairs are *Yosei ben Yo'ezer and Yosei ben Yoḥanan; *Yehoshu'a ben Peraḥyah and Nitt'ai the Arbelite; *Yehudah ben Tabb'ai and *Shim'on ben Shetaḥ; *Shema'yah and *Avtalyon; and *Hillel and *Shamm'ai. There is a historiographic symmetry between the three early periods, that of the *zugot*, the tanna'im, and the amora'im (see AMORA'), each of which is divided into five generations (cf. *Sefer ha-*

Kabbalah, edited by Gerson Cohen [Philadelphia, 1967], pp. 172, 207 et seq.).

• R. Travers Herford, ed., *The Ethics of the Talmud: Sayings of the Fathers* (New York, 1975), annotated text and translation of *Avot*.

—DANIEL SPERBER

ZUNZ, LEOPOLD (1794–1886), German scholar; founder of the modern scientific study of Judaism, *Wissenschaft des Judentums. He studied at the University of Berlin and in 1819 was among the founders of the Verein für Kultur and Wissenschaft der Juden, a pioneer group that sought to place research into Hebrew literature on a scientific basis. In 1823 he became editor of the Society's *Zeitschrift für die Wissenschaft des Judentums*, in which he published some of his early works, including a biography of Rashi. Zunz was the first to employ consistently modern methods of historical and literary research in his study of Jewish works. His purpose was to elucidate the inner relations and mutual influences of various strands of Jewish thought with a wealth of historical and philosophical detail in order to demonstrate their continuity. From 1841 to 1850, he directed the newly opened Berlin Jewish Teachers' Seminary.

In his advocacy of Wissenschaft des Judentums, he criticized the state of Jewish studies and was the first to lay out a detailed program that covered the historical study of Hebrew literature and culture, including liturgy, law, ethics, and education. His stress on the need for Jewish statistics foreshadowed the sociological and demographic studies of the twentieth century. He also initiated the use of new types of sources such as community registers and inscriptions on tombstones. His goal was to have Jewish studies accepted in German academic circles.

On religious issues, he was guided by the conviction that true reform must preserve the essential vitality of historic Judaism, which is an original, growing force. His best-known work, *Gottesdienstlichen Vorträge der Juden* (1832), traced the historical evolution of the Jewish sermon and showed that preaching in the vernacular was not a modern innovation—which had been forbidden in Prussian law—but an ancient custom. A law forbidding Jews to use German first names moved him to write *Namen der Juden* (1837), a history of Jewish names, which showed that even in ancient times Jews commonly took first names from their surroundings. His trilogy *Die synagogale Poesie des Mittelalters* (1855), *Der Ritus des synagogalen Gottesdienstes* (1859), and *Literaturgeschichte der synagogalen Poesie* (1865) surveyed a thousand years of Jewish religious poetry, listing six thousand poems and over one thousand Jewish poets.

• Nahum Norbert Glatzer, *Leopold and Adelaide Zunz: An Account in Letters, 1815–1885* (London, 1958). Nahum Norbert Glatzer, *Leopold Zunz: Jude, Deutscher, Europaer* (Tübingen, 1964). Solomon Schechter, *Studies in Judaism: Third Series* (Philadelphia, 1924), pp. 84–142. Luitpold Wallach, *Liberty and Letters: The Thoughts of Leopold Zunz* (London, 1959).

ZUSYA OF HANIPOLI (died 1800), Hasidic master. He and his brother R. *Elimelekh of Lyzhansk were both members of the circle of R. *Dov Ber of Mezhirech. Hasidic legend depicts Zusya and his brother traveling the roads together in a voluntary state of exile, symbolizing the exile of the **shekhinah*. Zusya is often depicted as a holy fool, victimized and degraded in the eyes of others but cheerily carrying on his devoted service to God as though he had never known suffering at all. Unlike most of the Mezhirech circle, he did not write a book of his teachings. Legend has it that when the Maggid of Mezhirech began to speak, quoting a verse that opened with "The Lord spoke to Moses, saying," Zusya became so excited at the notion of God's speaking that he had to be ejected from the room. Thus, he knew no teachings. This may be a way of saying that his charismatic personality, rather than specific knowledge or teachings, was what made him a master. A collection of sayings attributed to him is called *Menorat Zahav* (Warsaw, 1902).

• *Torat ha-Rabbi: Rabbi Zusha* (Bene Beraq, 1994). —ARTHUR GREEN